2/08

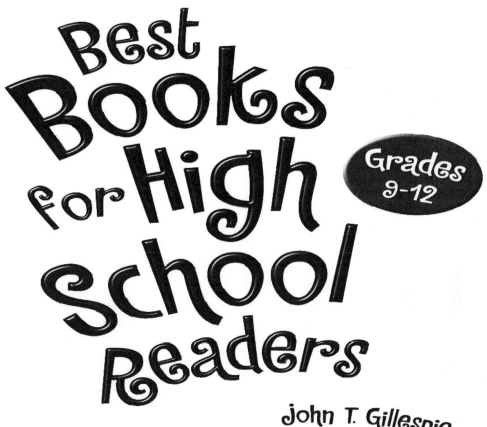

Best Books for High School Readers

Grades 9-12

John T. Gillespie
Catherine Barr

LIBRARIES
UNLIMITED
A Member of the Greenwood Publishing Group

Westport, Connecticut · London

British Library Cataloging in Publication Data is available.

ISBN: 1-59158-084-6

First published in 2004

Libraries Unlimited, 88 Post Road West, Westport, CT 06881
A Member of the Greenwood Publishing Group, Inc.
www.lu.com

Printed in the United States of America

∞™

The paper in this book complies with the
Permanent Paper Standard issued by the National
Information Standards Organization (Z39.48-1984).

10 9 8 7 6 5 4 3 2 1

Contents

Literary History and Criticism

Language and Communication

Biography, Memoirs, Etc.

The Arts and Entertainment

History and Geography

Philosophy and Religion

Society and the Individual

Guidance and Personal Development

Physical and Applied Sciences

Recreation and Sports

Major Subjects Arranged Alphabetically

Preface

At the present time, librarians and other specialists in children's literature have available, through both online and print sources, a large number of bibliographies that recommend books suitable for young people. Unfortunately, these sources vary widely in quality and usefulness. The Best Books series was created to furnish authoritative, reliable, and comprehensive bibliographies for use in libraries that collect materials for readers from preschool through grade 12. The series now consists of three volumes: *Best Books for Children, Best Books for Middle and Junior High School Readers*, and *Best Books for High School Readers*.

Best Books for High School Readers is a continuation of *Best Books for Middle and Junior High School Readers* (Libraries Unlimited, 2004), which covers books recommended for grades 6 though 9. The present volume, *Best Books for High School Readers*, supplies information on books recommended for readers in grades 9 through 12, or roughly ages 15 through 18.

As every librarian knows, reading levels are elastic. There is no such thing, for example, as a tenth-grade book. Instead there are only tenth-grade readers who, in their diversity, can represent a wide range of reading abilities and interests. This bibliography contains a liberal selection of entries that, one hopes, will accommodate readers in these four grades, and make allowance for their great range of tastes and reading competencies. By the ninth grade, a percentage of the books read should be at the adult level. Keeping this in mind, more than a third of the entries in this volume are adult books suitable for young adult readers (they are designated by a reading level usually of 10–12 within the entries and by S–Adult in the subject index). At the other end of the spectrum, there are also many titles that are suitable for younger readers (these are indicated by grade level designations such as 5–10, 6–10, 7–10, and so forth).

To be included in this bibliography, books must be suitable for at least two of the four grades (9–12) covered in this bibliography. There is, therefore, a slight duplication of titles in this book with those in *Best Books for Middle and Junior High School Readers*. For example, a book that is recommended for grades 7–10 would be found in both volumes. Librarians seeking a more comprehensive listing of books at the lower end of the reading level scale should also consult *Best Books for Middle and Junior High School Readers*.

In selecting books for inclusion, deciding on their arrangement, and collecting the information supplied on each, it was the editors' intention to reflect the current needs and interests of young readers while keeping in mind the latest trends and curricular emphases in today's schools.

General Scope and Criteria for Inclusion

Of the 14,198 titles listed in *Best Books for High School Readers*, 13,457 are individually numbered entries and 741 are cited within the annotations as additional recommended titles by the same author (often these are titles that are part of an extensive series — see "Additional Pointers for Users" later in the Preface). If these titles do not have separate entries elsewhere in the volume, publication dates are generally given. However, some popular titles may have been published in several editions (and some may be out of print); in these cases the year of publication is not given. It should also be noted that some series are so extensive that, because of space limitations, only representative titles are included.

Excluded from this bibliography are general reference works, such as dictionaries and encyclopedias, except for a few single-volume works that are so heavily illustrated and attractive that they can also be used in the general circulation collection. Also excluded are professional books for librarians and teachers and mass market series books.

For most fiction and nonfiction, a minimum of two recommendations were required from the current reviewing sources consulted for a title to be considered for listing. However, there were a number of necessary exceptions. For example, in some journals only a few representative titles from extensive nonfiction series are reviewed even though others in the series will also be recommended. In such cases a single favorable review was enough for inclusion. This also held true for some of the adult titles suitable for young adult readers where, it has been found, reviewing journals tend to be less inclusive than with juvenile titles. Depending on the strength of the review, a single positive one was sufficient for inclusion. As well as favorable reviews, additional criteria such as availability, up-to-dateness, accuracy, usefulness, and relevance were considered. All titles were in print as of the end of June 2004.

Sources Used

A number of current and retrospective sources were used in compiling this bibliography. Of the retrospective sources, two were used extensively. They were *Best Books for Young Adult Readers* (Bowker, 1997) and *Best Books for Young Teen Readers* (Bowker, 2000). After out-of-print titles were removed, remaining entries in these bibliographies were evaluated for content, suitability, and currency before inclusion was recommended. Other retrospective bibliographies consulted were *The Senior High School Catalog, 16th Edition* (H. W. Wilson, 2002), *Books for the Teen Age* (New York Public Library, 2004), and *A Core Collection for Young Adults* by Patrick Jones et al. (Neal-Schuman, 2003).

Book reviewing journals from 1998 on were also consulted to obtain current titles. These sources were *Booklist, Library Media Connection* (formerly *Book Report*), *School Library Journal*, and *VOYA (Voice of Youth Advocates)*. To a much lesser degree other sources used include *Bulletin of the Center for Children's Books, Horn Book*, and *Horn Book Guide*. Reviews in issues of these journals were read and evaluated from 1998 through June 2004, when this book's coverage ends.

Uses of This Book

Best Books for High School Readers was designed to help librarians and media specialists with four vital tasks: (1) evaluating the adequacy of existing collections; (2) building new collections or strengthening existing holdings; (3) providing reading guidance to young adults; and (4) preparing bibliographies and reading lists. To increase the book's usefulness, particularly in preparation of bibliographies or suggested reading lists, titles are arranged under broad areas of interest or, in the case of nonfiction works, by curriculum-oriented subjects rather than by the Dewey Decimal classification (suggested Dewey classification numbers are nevertheless provided within nonfiction entries). The subject arrangement corresponds roughly to the one used in *Best Books for Children* and *Best Books for Middle and Junior High School Readers*.

Arrangement

In the Table of Contents, subjects are arranged by the order in which they appear in the book. Following the Table of Contents is a listing of Major Subjects Arranged Alphabetically, which provides entry numbers as well as page numbers for easy access. Following the main body of the text, there are three indexes. The Author Index cites authors and editors, titles, and entry numbers (joint authors and editors are listed separately). The Title

Index gives the book's entry number. Works of fiction in both of these indexes are indicated by (F) following the entry number. Finally, an extensive Subject/Grade Level Index lists entry numbers under hundreds of subject headings with specific grade-level suitability given for each entry. The following codes are used to identify general grade levels:

JS   (Junior–Senior High) suitable for junior high and senior high grades (grades 7 and up)

S   (Senior High) suitable usually only for senior high grades (grades 10–12)

S–Adult   (Senior High–Adult) written for an adult audience but suitable for high school collections (usually grades 10–12)

In each case, the user should consult the grade levels indicated within the entry for specific grade recommendations.

Entries

A typical entry contains the following information where applicable: (1) author, joint author, or editor; (2) title and subtitle; (3) specific grade levels given in parentheses; (4) adapter or translator; (5) indication of illustrations; (6) publication date; (7) publisher and price of hardbound edition (LB = library binding); (8) International Standard Book Number (ISBN) of hardbound edition; (9) paperback publisher (paper) and price (if no publisher is listed it is the same as the hardbound edition); (10) ISBN of paperback edition; (11) annotation; (12) review citations; (13) Dewey Decimal classification number.

Review Citations

Review citations are given for books published and reviewed from 1985 through June 2004. These citations can be used to find more detailed information about each of the books listed. The periodical sources identified are:

Book Report (BR)
Booklist (BL)
Bulletin of the Center for Children's Books (BCCB)
Horn Book (HB)
Horn Book Guide (HBG)
Library Media Connection (LMC)
School Library Journal (SLJ)
VOYA (Voice of Youth Advocates) (VOYA)

Additional Pointers for Users

For series that contain an extensive number of titles that are too numerous to list and for very prolific authors of recommended books, only a representative number of books are listed. Examples of this would be the mysteries of Sue Grafton or Dick Francis, science fiction from writers such as Piers Anthony and Alan Dean Foster, and horror stories by Stephen King. In these cases, the entries of selected books will include a note such as "part of an extensive recommended series." For more complete listings of titles, it is suggested that the user consult Books in Print (Bowker, annual), book jobbers' catalogs (print or online), or the Web sites of such online booksellers as Amazon (amazon.com) and Barnes and Noble (bn.com).

Anthologies of short stories on a single subject are found under that subject (an anthology of science fiction short stories will be listed under "Science Fiction," for example), but general anthologies or collections by a singe author on diverse subjects are listed in the "Short Stories and General Anthologies" section.

Similarly, books of experiments and projects on a specific subject in science are placed under that subject, but general science project books are in the section "Physical and Applied Sciences — Experiments and Projects."

Books of criticism about individual authors, even though they contain some biographical information, are placed in the "Literary History and Criticism" section.

Books on World War II are found in the "World War II and Holocaust" section but books on internal conditions in the United States during this period are found in the United States history section under "World War II."

Books on the history of specific ethnic groups (for example, books that are historical accounts of African American slavery) are generally found in the "Ethnic Groups and Prejudice" section.

Books that contain material that might be objectionable to some readers (scenes of graphic sex, for example), usually include a note in the annotation indicating that the book is suitable for mature readers.

Acknowledgments

With this volume, I am happy to announce a new coauthor/editor, Catherine Barr. Ms. Barr has been involved in the production of previous editions of the Best Books series, including the 2003 supplement to *Best Books for Children* and *Best Books for Middle and Junior High School Readers* as well as many, many other publications. I welcome her expertise in the field, as well as her fine organizational and administrative talents. Many other people should be thanked for helping in the preparation of this bibliography. In particular, let me single out our computer genius Julie Miller and our editor-in-chief, Barbara Ittner. Thank you all.

John Gillespie

Literary Forms

Fiction

Adventure and Survival Stories

1 Aiken, Joan. *Midnight Is a Place* (7–10). Series: Wolves Chronicles. 1974, Scholastic paper $2.95 (0-590-45496-X). In Victorian England, two young waifs are cast adrift in a hostile town when their guardian's house burns.

2 Alexander, Lloyd. *Westmark* (7–10). 1981, Dell paper $4.50 (0-440-99731-3). In this first of three volumes, Theo, in the imaginary kingdom of Westmark, joins revolutionaries intent on establishing a democracy. Also in this series *The Beggar Queen* (1984). (Rev: BL 12/15/89)

3 Allende, Isabel. *City of the Beasts* (9–12). Trans. by Margaret Sayers Peden. 2002, HarperCollins $19.99 (0-06-050918-X). Fifteen-year-old Alex gets more than he bargained for when he accompanies his grandmother on a trip into the Amazon jungle on a search for a mysterious "beast." (Rev: BL 11/15/02; HB 1–2/03; HBG 3/03; SLJ 11/02; VOYA 2/03)

4 Allende, Isabel. *Kingdom of the Golden Dragon* (7–12). 2004, HarperCollins $19.99 (0-06-058942-6). Yetis, high in the Himalayas, help 16-year-old Alexander in his fight against American corporate villains in this sequel to *City of the Beasts*. (Rev: BL 2/15/04; SLJ 4/04)

5 Antal, John F. *Proud Legions: A Novel of America's Next War* (10–12). 1999, Presidio $24.95 (0-89141-667-6). An adventure thriller set in the near future about an American tank battalion that faces an invasion of South Korea by North Korean forces. (Rev: BL 2/1/99; SLJ 5/99)

6 Asai, Carrie. *The Book of the Sword* (6–12). Series: Samurai Girl. 2003, Simon & Schuster paper $6.99 (0-689-85948-1). Heaven abandons her adoptive family when her brother is murdered in the middle of her arranged wedding and devotes herself to studying to be a samurai and avenging her brother. (Rev: SLJ 8/03)

7 Bainbridge, Beryl. *The Birthday Boys* (9–12). 1994, Carroll & Graf $18.95 (0-7867-0071-8). A fictional account of an early 20th-century expedition to Antarctica, narrated by Captain Robert Scott and four fellow explorers who were doomed to die. (Rev: BL 4/1/94; SLJ 10/94)

8 Barr, Nevada. *Firestorm* (10–12). 1996, Putnam $22.95 (0-399-14126-X). Featuring a gallant female sleuth, this combination murder mystery and survival story takes place during a firestorm in Northern California. (Rev: BL 3/15/96; SLJ 9/96)

9 Bernardo, Anilu. *Jumping Off to Freedom* (7–10). 1996, Arte Publico paper $9.95 (1-55885-088-0). The story of four refugees, including teenage David, on a harrowing voyage from Cuba to Florida on a raft. (Rev: BL 5/1/96; BR 9–10/96; SLJ 7/96; VOYA 6/96)

10 Brand, Max. *Dan Barry's Daughter* (7–12). 1976, Amereon LB $25.95 (0-88411-516-X). Harry is an accused murderer who, though innocent, is forced to hide. One of many recommended westerns by this prolific author.

11 Brand, Max. *Way of the Lawless* (10–12). 1985, Warner paper $2.50 (0-446-32665-8). In this western by the prolific writer Brand, a basically decent young man finds himself on the wrong side of the law.

12 Bridal, Tessa. *The Tree of Red Stars* (10–12). 1997, Milkweed $21.95 (1-57131-013-4). In a series of flashbacks, Magdalena tells of her secret work with the Tupamaro rebels in Uruguay, her imprisonment and torture, and her subsequent life in Europe. (Rev: BL 6/1–15/97; SLJ 10/97)

13 Brockmann, Suzanne. *Flashpoint* (9–12). 2004, Ballantine $21.95 (0-345-46232-7). Field agents Tess and Jimmy Nash are assigned to Kazbekistan to find the computer of an al-Qaeda leader and both adventure and romance result. (Rev: BL 4/15/04)

14 Brown, Sam. *The Trail to Honk Ballard's Bones* (9–12). 1990, Walker $27.95 (0-8027-4101-0). In this western adventure, Honk Ballard discovers that his new trail buddy is really a bank robber. (Rev: BL 1/15/90)

15 Burroughs, Edgar Rice. *Tarzan of the Apes* (9–12). 1988, NAL paper $4.95 (0-451-52423-3). The beginning of the famous saga of the Ape Man, a series of more than 20 titles.

16 Burt, Guy. *The Hole* (10–12). 2001, Ballantine $21.00 (0-345-44654-2). A suspenseful novel about five teens who agree to spend three days in "the hole," an unused area in their English prep school, as a prank. Then things go amiss. (Rev: BL 7/01)

17 Butler, William. *The Butterfly Revolution* (7–12). 1961, Ballantine paper $6.50 (0-345-33182-6). A frightening story of problems in a boys' camp told in diary form by one of the campers.

18 Campbell, Eric. *The Shark Callers* (7–10). 1994, Harcourt $10.95 (0-15-200007-0); paper $4.95 (0-15-200010-0). Parallel stories of two boys' survival in Papua New Guinea during a volcanic eruption and tidal wave. (Rev: BL 11/15/94; SLJ 9/94; VOYA 10/94)

19 Castelli, Alfredo. *The Snowman* (9–12). Illus. 1990, Catalan Communications paper $9.95 (0-87416-124-X). A reporter on an Everest expedition encounters huge figures in the snow and later awakens in a lamasery, where, after terrifying dreams, he discovers the monks' secret. (Rev: BL 9/1/91)

20 Childress, Mark. *V for Victor* (9–12). 1990, Ballantine paper $5.99 (0-345-35427-3). In 1942, a 16-year-old boy living on the coast of Alabama gets involved in a spy plot. (Rev: BL 11/15/88; BR 9–10/89; SLJ 7/89; VOYA 2/90)

21 Clancy, Tom. *Clear and Present Danger* (9–12). 1989, Putnam $25.95 (0-399-13440-9). An intricate spy thriller that deals with the drug war in Colombia. (Rev: SLJ 1/90)

22 Clancy, Tom. *Patriot Games* (9–12). 1987, Putnam $25.95 (0-399-13241-4); Berkley paper $7.50 (0-425-10972-0). In this large adventure novel for better readers, hero Jack Ryan tries to prevent a terrorist plan to kidnap Princess Diana and Prince Charles. Also recommended by Clancy are *Red Storm Rising* (1986) and *The Hunt for Red October* (1984). (Rev: BL 6/1/87; SLJ 11/87)

23 Clavell, James. *Children's Story* (9–12). 1981, Delacorte $7.95 (0-385-28135-8); 1989, Dell paper $5.99 (0-440-20468-2). After a terrible war has been lost, thought control is introduced in the schools.

24 Clavell, James. *Noble House* (10–12). 1981, Dell paper $7.99 (0-440-16484-2). An action-filled story about a China trading firm in Hong Kong. Also use *Tai-Pan* (1983).

25 Cooney, Caroline B. *Flash Fire* (7–10). 1995, Scholastic paper $14.95 (0-590-25253-4). A girl's wish for a more exciting life comes true when a fire sweeps the wealthy Los Angeles neighborhood where she lives. (Rev: BL 11/1/95; SLJ 12/95; VOYA 12/95)

26 Cooney, Caroline B. *Flight No. 116 Is Down* (7–10). 1992, Scholastic paper $14.95 (0-590-44465-4). With a lightning pace, the author depicts the drama and human interest inherent in disaster. (Rev: BL 1/15/92; SLJ 2/92)

27 Cooney, Caroline B. *The Terrorist* (6–10). 1997, Scholastic paper $4.99 (0-590-22854-4). Teenage Laura devotes all her energies to finding the terrorist whose bomb was responsible for her young brother's death in London. (Rev: BL 7/97; BR 9–10/97; SLJ 9/97; VOYA 10/97)

28 Coonts, Stephen. *America* (10–12). 2001, St. Martin's $25.95 (0-312-25341-9). In this fast-moving tale of adventure and espionage, the U.S. Navy's most advanced submarine is hijacked by terrorists. (Rev: BL 7/01; SLJ 1/02)

29 Coonts, Stephen. *Fortunes of War* (10–12). 1998, St. Martin's $24.95 (0-312-18583-9); paper $7.99 (0-312-96941-4). A modern military thriller about two friends, one an American colonel in the Air Force and the other a Japanese fighter pilot, who find themselves on opposing sides when Japanese radicals attempt to take over Siberian oil fields. (Rev: BL 3/15/98; SLJ 9/98)

30 Cormier, Robert. *After the First Death* (7–12). 1979, Pantheon $14.99 (0-394-94122-5). A busload of schoolchildren become the victims of a terrorist plot.

31 Cussler, Clive. *Raise the Titanic* (9–12). 1990, Pocket paper $7.99 (0-671-72519-X). A thriller about trying to recover riches from the sunken *Titanic*.

32 Cussler, Clive. *Treasure* (9–12). 1989, Pocket paper $7.99 (0-671-70465-6). Adventurer Dirk Pitt combats terrorists to rescue hostages in a frozen wilderness in Greenland. (Rev: BL 3/15/88)

33 Cussler, Clive, and Paul Kemprecos. *Fire Ice* (10–12). 2002, Putnam $26.95 (0-399-14872-8). NUMA's Kurt Austin battles potential environmental devastation in an action-packed tale of suspense and political intrigue. (Rev: BL 4/1/02; SLJ 11/02)

34 Dickinson, Patti. *Hollywood the Hard Way: A Cowboy's Journey* (9–12). 1999, Univ. of Nebraska Pr. paper $13.95 (0-8032-6619-7). Cowboy Jerry Van Meter bravely undertakes a solo 1,500-mile horseback ride in this story — based on truth — set in 1945. (Rev: SLJ 2/00)

4

35 Doyon, Stephanie. *Leaving Home* (8–12). Series: On the Road. 1999, Simon & Schuster paper $4.50 (0-689-82107-7). High school graduate Miranda and friend Kirsten decide to postpone college for a year to travel cross-country. (Rev: BL 6/1–15/99; SLJ 9/99)

36 Ferris, Jean. *All That Glitters* (7–10). 1996, Farrar $16.00 (0-374-30204-9). In this adventure, Brian, 16, goes on a scuba-diving expedition with his father and an archaeologist investigating a shipwrecked Spanish galleon. (Rev: BL 2/15/96; SLJ 3/96; VOYA 6/96)

37 Follett, Ken. *Eye of the Needle* (9–12). 1979, NAL paper $4.95 (0-451-15524-6). A story of suspense and mounting horror involving a German spy and a family on a remote Scottish island.

38 Forester, C. S. *The African Queen* (9–12). 1935, Little, Brown paper $13.95 (0-316-28910-8). An English spinster and a cockney male friend decide, as an act of revenge, to blow up a German boat in this novel set in Africa.

39 Forsyth, Frederick. *The Day of the Jackal* (9–12). 1971, Bantam paper $7.50 (0-553-26630-6). A rousing thriller about an attempted assassination of Charles de Gaulle.

40 Forsyth, Frederick. *The Devil's Alternative* (9–12). 1980, Bantam paper $6.99 (0-553-26490-7). The rescue of a man from drowning in the Mediterranean Sea begins a series of events that almost leads to nuclear disaster in this thriller.

41 Forsyth, Frederick. *The Dogs of War* (9–12). 1982, Bantam paper $6.99 (0-553-26846-5). An adventure story about greed and an attempt to seize power in a small West African country.

42 Forsyth, Frederick. *The Fist of God* (9–12). 1994, Bantam paper $6.99 (0-553-57242-3). Two British brothers who are espionage experts organize an elaborate mission to find a secret weapon that's in Saddam Hussein's possession. (Rev: BL 3/1/94)

43 Forsyth, Frederick. *The Odessa File* (9–12). 1983, Bantam paper $6.99 (0-553-27198-9). A German reporter infiltrates an organization of former Nazis and is discovered.

44 Freedman, Benedict, and Nancy Freedman. *Mrs. Mike* (7–12). 1968, Berkley paper $4.99 (0-425-10328-5). Based on a true story, this tells of Kathy, her love for her Mountie husband Mike, and her hard life in the Canadian Northwest.

45 Gann, Ernest K. *Fate Is the Hunter* (9–12). 1986, Simon & Schuster paper $14.00 (0-671-63603-0). A thrilling adventure story that was the basis of a successful movie.

46 Glenn, Mel. *The Taking of Room 114* (8–12). 1997, Dutton $16.99 (0-525-67548-5). A story told in poetry form about a teacher, the villainous M. Wiedermayer, who held his history class hostage at

gunpoint, and the backgrounds of the young people in his class. (Rev: BL 3/1/97; BR 11–12/97; SLJ 4/97; VOYA 2/98)

47 Golding, William. *Lord of the Flies* (8–12). 1999, Viking paper $14.00 (0-14-028333-1). When they are marooned on a deserted island, a group of English schoolboys soon lose their civilized ways.

48 Goodman, Joan Elizabeth. *Paradise* (7–12). 2002, Houghton $16.00 (0-618-11450-5). The fictionalized story of Marguerite de la Rocque, who in 1536, after being left on Canada's Isle of Demons by her explorer uncle, struggled to survive along with her maid and the young man she loves. (Rev: BL 11/15/02; HBG 3/03; SLJ 12/02; VOYA 12/02)

49 Grimes, Martha. *Biting the Moon* (10–12). 1999, Holt $25.00 (0-8050-5621-1). This is a riveting, fast-moving story about a teenager with amnesia who names herself Andi, a girl who befriends her, and their quest to uncover Andi's past. (Rev: BL 1/1–15/99; SLJ 7/99)

50 Haggard, H. Rider. *King Solomon's Mines* (9–12). 1982, Amereon LB $20.95 (0-89190-703-3). First published in 1885, this is a story of old-fashioned adventure and romance and the search for the source of King Solomon's wealth in Africa.

51 Haldeman, Joe. *Tool of the Trade* (9–12). 1988, Avon paper $3.95 (0-380-70438-2). A thriller about a Russian spy being pursued by both the CIA and the KGB. (Rev: BL 4/15/87)

52 Harper, Jo. *Delfino's Journey* (6–12). 2001, Texas Tech Univ. Pr. $15.95 (0-89672-437-9). Delfino and Salvador travel from Mexico to the United States in search of a new life but face many difficult challenges in this novel that interweaves Aztec folklore and information on illegal immigration. (Rev: BL 4/15/01; HBG 10/01)

53 Heacox, Kim. *Caribou Crossing* (10–12). 2001, Winter Wren paper $24.95 (0-944197-70-1). In this fast-paced thriller, environmentalists are pitted against big oil interests to save a fragile landscape in Alaska. (Rev: BL 8/01)

54 Hemingway, Ernest. *The Old Man and the Sea* (9–12). 1977, Macmillan $30.00 (0-684-15363-7). A deceptively simple novel about an old Gulf fisherman and his encounter with a giant marlin.

55 Heneghan, James. *Torn Away* (7–10). 1994, Viking $14.99 (0-670-85180-9). A teenager, forced to leave his home in Northern Ireland where he wants to stay and fight with the IRA, must join his uncle's family in Canada. (Rev: BL 2/15/94; SLJ 9/94; VOYA 4/94)

56 Hernon, Peter. *8.4* (10–12). 1999, Putnam $24.95 (0-399-14400-5). A thriller about attempts to prevent a major earthquake in the Midwest by detonating an atomic bomb underground. (Rev: BL 2/15/99; SLJ 8/99)

57 Higgins, Jack. *Cold Harbour* (9–12). 1990, Pocket paper $6.50 (0-671-68426-4). A fast-paced thriller set during World War II about a submarine that takes agents to occupied France. (Rev: BL 1/1/90)

58 Higgins, Jack. *The Eagle Has Landed* (9–12). 1990, Pocket paper $6.99 (0-671-72773-7). In this thriller, a group of German paratroopers land in England during World War II to kidnap Churchill.

59 Higgins, Jack. *Flight of Eagles* (10–12). 1998, Putnam $24.95 (0-399-14376-9). Identical twins, separated as children, are on opposite sides during World War II in this action-packed novel filled with intrigue and danger. (Rev: SLJ 11/98)

60 Higgins, Jack. *Solo* (9–12). 1989, Pocket paper $6.99 (0-671-67617-2). A tough Welshman sets out to find out the identity of a terrorist who has murdered his child.

61 Higgins, Jack. *Touch the Devil* (10–12). 1983, NAL paper $6.99 (0-451-16677-9). A retired agent must stop a killer whose target is Margaret Thatcher.

62 Hill, David. *Take It Easy* (7–10). 1997, Dutton $14.99 (0-525-45763-1). After an argument with his father, Rob Kennedy joins a hiking trip to a remote part of New Zealand, an expedition that turns into a nightmare survival story. (Rev: BL 9/1/97; BR 1–2/98; SLJ 6/97; VOYA 10/97)

63 Hinton, S. E. *The Outsiders* (7–10). 1967, Viking $16.99 (0-670-53257-6). Two rival gangs — the "haves" and "have-nots" — fight it out on the streets of an Oklahoma city. (Rev: BL 11/15/97)

64 Hinton, S. E. *Rumble Fish* (7–10). 1975, Dell paper $5.99 (0-440-97534-4). Rusty-James loses everything he loves most including his brother.

65 Hinton, S. E. *Tex* (7–10). 1979, Dell paper $5.50 (0-440-97850-5). Tex and his 17-year-old older brother encounter problems with family, sex, and drugs.

66 Hinton, S. E. *That Was Then, This Is Now* (7–10). 1971, Viking $15.99 (0-670-69798-2). Bryon discovers that his "brother" Mark is a drug pusher.

67 Hobbs, Will. *The Big Wander* (7–10). 1992, Atheneum $17.00 (0-689-31767-0); Avon paper $5.95 (0-380-72140-6). Clay Lancaster, 14, and his brother Mike are on a "big wander," their last trip together before Mike goes away to college. (Rev: BL 10/15/92*; SLJ 11/92)

68 Hobbs, Will. *Downriver* (9–12). 1991, Atheneum $17.00 (0-689-31690-9). Jessie, 15, is one of eight problem teens in an outdoor survival program that almost ends in disaster. (Rev: BL 3/1/91; SLJ 3/91)

69 Hobbs, Will. *Far North* (7–12). 1996, Morrow $15.95 (0-688-14192-7). Fifteen-year old Gabe, his school roommate, and an elderly Native American are stranded in the Canadian wilderness. The boys survive even after the death of the wise old man. (Rev: BL 7/96; BR 9–10/96; SLJ 9/96; VOYA 2/97)

70 Hobbs, Will. *Leaving Protection* (7–12). 2004, HarperCollins $15.99 (0-688-17475-2). An exciting novel about a 16-year-old boy, his work on an Alaskan salmon trawler, and the secret plans of its skipper. (Rev: BL 3/1/04; SLJ 4/04)

71 Hobbs, Will. *The Maze* (6–12). 1998, Morrow $15.95 (0-688-15092-6). After living in a series of foster homes and detention centers, Rick escapes to Canyonlands National Park in Utah where he is befriended by a loner who helps him find himself. (Rev: BL 9/1/98; HBG 3/99; SLJ 10/98; VOYA 2/99)

72 Hobbs, Will. *River Thunder* (8–12). 1997, Delacorte $15.95 (0-385-32316-6). In this sequel to *Downriver* (1996), Troy and his troubled teenage friends undertake an adventure-filled rafting trip through the Grand Canyon. (Rev: BL 9/1/97; BR 3–4/98; HBG 3/98; SLJ 9/97; VOYA 10/97)

73 Hobbs, Will. *Wild Man Island* (7–10). 2002, HarperCollins LB $15.89 (0-06-029810-3); HarperTrophy paper $5.99 (0-380-73310-2). An adventure story in which 14-year-old Andy becomes stranded on a remote Alaska island, faces many dangers, and tests his dead archaeologist father's theories about the earliest prehistoric immigrants to America. (Rev: BL 4/15/02; HB 7–8/02; HBG 10/02; SLJ 5/02; VOYA 6/02)

74 Holt, Victoria. *The Time of the Hunter's Moon* (9–12). 1984, Fawcett paper $5.99 (0-449-45094-5). In 19th-century England a young schoolteacher is caught up in romance, adventure, and mystery.

75 Hubert, Cam. *Dreamspeaker* (9–12). 1981, Avon paper $3.50 (0-380-56622-2). A boy who escapes from an institution finds friendship in a British Columbia forest.

76 Innes, Hammond. *The Wreck of the Mary Deare* (9–12). 1985, Carroll & Graf paper $3.50 (0-88184-152-8). Gideon Patch boards what appears to be a ghost ship and his adventures begin. Also use *The Doomed Oasis* (1986).

77 Johnson, Wayne. *The Devil You Know* (10–12). 2004, Crown $23.00 (0-609-60964-5). With graphic sex and violence, this novel tells the story of a wilderness trip taken by a teenage boy and his estranged father and of their encounter with some fugitive meat packers. (Rev: BL 2/15/04*; SLJ 8/04)

78 Judson, William. *Cold River* (9–12). 1976, NAL paper $3.50 (0-451-16164-5). A survival story involving a brother and sister lost in the Adirondacks.

79 Kalpakian, Laura. *Caveat* (10–12). 1998, Blair $19.95 (0-89587-223-4). In this novel set in a small, drought-stricken California town in 1916, rainmaker Hank Beecham vows revenge when the city fathers refuse to pay him after his efforts result in life-destroying floods. (Rev: BL 6/1–15/98; SLJ 1/99)

80 Kehret, Peg. *Night of Fear* (6–10). 1994, Dutton $14.99 (0-525-65136-5). This suspense novel for reluctant readers concerns the escape attempts of a boy who is abducted and taken on the road by a man who fits the description of a bank robber. (Rev: BL 2/15/94; SLJ 4/94; VOYA 2/94)

81 Kerrigan, Philip. *Survival Game* (9–12). 1987, Avon paper $3.95 (0-380-70682-2). A simulated war game turns serious when a gunman begins picking off the participants. (Rev: SLJ 12/87)

82 King, Stephen. *The Girl Who Loved Tom Gordon* (9–12). 1999, Scribner $16.45 (0-684-86762-1). This is a vivid novel about the terrors experienced by a 9-year-girl who is lost in the Maine woods for nine days when she wanders away from her parents. (Rev: BL 4/1/99; SLJ 3/00; VOYA 8/99)

83 Kinsolving, William. *Mister Christian: The Further Adventures of Fletcher Christian, the Legendary Leader of the Bounty Mutiny* (10–12). 1996, Simon & Schuster $23.00 (0-684-81303-3). In this sequel to *Mutiny on the Bounty*, Fletcher Christian continues his worldwide wandering and reluctantly becomes involved in sea battles between France and England. (Rev: BL 3/15/96; SLJ 11/96)

84 Klaveness, Jan O'Donnell. *Ghost Island* (7–10). 1987, Dell paper $2.95 (0-440-93097-9). Delia, her mother, and new stepfather encounter both family trauma and a murder involving poachers when they vacation on a remote Canadian lake. (Rev: BL 5/15/85; BR 11–12/85; SLJ 9/85; VOYA 2/86)

85 Koontz, Dean. *Seize the Night* (9–12). 1998, Bantam $26.95 (0-553-10665-1). While investigating the kidnapping of a young boy, Chris Snow uncovers a plot to alter time and space in this enthralling adventure novel. (Rev: BL 12/1/98; VOYA 4/99)

86 Koontz, Dean. *Sole Survivor* (10–12). 1997, Knopf $25.95 (0-679-42526-8). When Joe Carpenter discovers that the airplane crash in which his wife and two daughters were killed was not an accident, he sets out on a dangerous mission to find the truth. (Rev: BL 1/1–15/97; SLJ 7/97)

87 L'Amour, Louis. *Bendigo Shafter* (9–12). 1983, Bantam paper $5.50 (0-553-26446-X). An old-fashioned western by a master of the genre. There are approximately 100 other westerns by this author available in paperback.

88 Lee, Stan, ed. *The Ultimate Spider-Man* (10–12). 1996, Berkley paper $5.99 (1-57297-103-7). Twelve short stories by different authors continue the adventures of the Amazing Spider-Man, the crime-fighting comic-book hero. (Rev: SLJ 5/96)

89 Leib, Franklin Allen. *The House of Pain* (10–12). 1999, Forge $23.95 (0-312-86616-X). In this legal thriller, a Vietnam veteran suffering from post-traumatic stress disorder rescues his goddaughter, 15-year-old Sally Collins, from kidnappers, and is then put on trial for his vigilante killings. (Rev: SLJ 5/99)

90 L'Engle, Madeleine. *The Arm of the Starfish* (7–10). 1965, Farrar $18.00 (0-374-30396-7); Dell paper $4.99 (0-440-90183-9). A young scientist becomes involved in intrigue and the disappearance of Polly O'Keefe in this tale of danger.

91 L'Engle, Madeleine. *The Young Unicorns* (7–10). 1968, Farrar $16.00 (0-374-38778-8); Dell paper $5.50 (0-440-99919-7). In this novel set in New York City and involving the Austin family, a young gang threatens the lives of an ex-member and a blind musician.

92 Leonard, Elmore. *Cuba Libre: A Novel* (10–12). 1998, Delacorte $23.95 (0-385-32383-2); Dell paper $7.50 (0-440-22559-0). An action-filled historical novel that includes a bank robbery, cattle rustling, suspense, and romance between an attractive hero and heroine, set at the time of the Spanish-American War and Cuba's fight for independence. (Rev: BL 11/15/97; SLJ 8/98)

93 Leonard, Elmore. *Out of Sight* (10–12). 1996, Delacorte $22.95 (0-385-30848-5). Deputy U. S. Marshal Karen Sisco is pitted against two convicts, one of whom is attracted to her. (Rev: SLJ 3/97)

94 Lester, Alison. *The Snow Pony* (6–12). 2003, Houghton $15.00 (0-618-25404-8). Fourteen-year-old Dusty's love for Snow Pony lightens the problems of her life in this novel set on an Australian cattle ranch. (Rev: BL 3/15/03; HBG 10/03; SLJ 4/03; VOYA 6/03)

95 Levin, Ira. *The Boys from Brazil* (9–12). 1976, Random $8.95 (0-394-40267-7). The story of a group of ex-Nazis and their diabolical plan to create a Fourth Reich.

96 London, Jack. *Best Short Stories of Jack London* (9–12). 1953, Amereon LB $15.50 (0-89190-656-8). These stories of action and adventure represent locales ranging from the South Seas to the Far North.

97 Lopez, Barry. *Winter Count* (9–12). 1982, Avon paper $4.95 (0-380-58107-8). This group of stories deals with survival in the wilds and man's battle with nature.

98 Ludlum, Robert. *The Bourne Identity* (9–12). 1984, Bantam paper $7.99 (0-553-26011-1). A man wakens to find that in spite of having no memory, he is the target of a killer's plot. Followed by *The Bourne Supremacy*.

99 MacInnes, Helen. *Above Suspicion* (9–12). 1954, Harcourt $24.95 (0-15-102707-2). This is one of the many novels of intrigue and suspense by this writer. Some others are *The Salzburg Connection*, *Snare of the Hunter*, *Decision at Delphi* (1984), *Agent in Place*, and *Assignment in Brittany*.

100 MacLean, Alistair. *Circus* (9–12). 1984, Amereon $24.95 (0-89190-672-X). In this spy thriller, an aerialist is sent on a secret mission by the CIA into Eastern Europe. Other recommended adventures by MacLean include *Secret Ways* and *South by Java Head*.

101 MacLean, Alistair. *H.M.S. Ulysses* (9–12). 1985, Fawcett paper $5.95 (0-449-12929-2). This is an exciting story of a British light cruiser's treacherous voyage to Murmansk during World War II. Other adventure stories by MacLean include *Athabasca* (1986) and *Way to Dusty Death* (1985).

102 MacLean, Norman. *A River Runs Through It and Other Stories* (10–12). 1979, Univ. of Chicago Pr. $20.00 (0-226-50055-1); paper $11.00 (0-226-50057-8). These stories convey the grandeur of our western mountain wilderness and the ways in which man has adjusted to this environment. (Rev: BL 3/87)

103 Mahy, Margaret. *24 Hours* (9–12). 2000, Simon & Schuster $17.00 (0-689-83884-0). An action-filled novel about 24 hours in 17-year-old Ellis's life that include dramatic rescues, a car chase, and more, with a happy ending that makes Ellis a hero. (Rev: BL 11/15/00; HB 9–10/00; HBG 3/01; SLJ 9/00; VOYA 12/00)

104 Marsden, John. *Burning for Revenge* (8–12). Series: Tomorrow. 2000, Houghton $16.00 (0-395-96054-1). Ellie and her four Australian friends attack an airfield held by the enemy in this continuing saga. (Rev: BL 10/1/00; HBG 3/01; SLJ 10/00)

105 Marsden, John. *Darkness, Be My Friend* (9–12). Series: Tomorrow. 1999, Houghton $15.00 (0-395-92274-7). In this sequel to *A Killing Frost*, Ellie, Fi, and other teenage combatants continue their struggle against the forces that have invaded Australia. (Rev: BL 6/1–15/99; HBG 9/99; SLJ 7/99; VOYA 10/99)

106 Marsden, John. *The Dead of Night* (6–10). Series: Tomorrow. 1997, Houghton $16.00 (0-395-83734-0). In this sequel to *Tomorrow, When the War Began* (1996), the teenage group continues its guerrilla activities against their enemy, a country that has invaded their homeland, Australia. (Rev: HBG 3/98; SLJ 11/97; VOYA 2/98)

107 Marsden, John. *A Killing Frost* (7–12). Series: Tomorrow. 1998, Houghton $16.00 (0-395-83735-9). In this third episode of an adventure series about a group of Australian teens who fight an enemy that has occupied their country, five young people carry out a plan to sink a containership. (Rev: BCCB 4/98; BL 5/15/98; HB 7–8/98; HBG 9/98; SLJ 6/98; VOYA 6/98)

108 Marsden, John. *The Night Is for Hunting* (8–12). Series: Tomorrow. 2001, Houghton $15.00 (0-618-07026-5). This sixth book in the Tomorrow series continues the action-packed story of a group of teenagers fighting to defend Australia against a band of invaders. (Rev: BCCB 2/02; BL 11/1/01; HBG 10/02; SLJ 10/01; VOYA 12/01)

109 Marsden, John. *The Other Side of Dawn* (8–12). Series: Tomorrow. 2002, Houghton $16.00 (0-618-07028-1). Ellie's exploits are at the center of this action-packed seventh and final installment in the Tomorrow series, which leaves Ellie back home after peace has been declared, trying to adjust to postwar life. (Rev: BCCB 10/02; BL 10/15/02; HB 11/02; HBG 3/03; SLJ 10/02; VOYA 2/03)

110 Marsden, John. *Tomorrow, When the War Began* (8–12). 1995, Houghton $15.00 (0-395-70673-4). A girl and her friends return from a camping trip in the bush to find that Australia has been invaded and their families taken prisoner. (Rev: BL 4/15/95; SLJ 6/95)

111 Martini, Steve. *Critical Mass* (10–12). 1998, Putnam $25.99 (0-399-14362-9). Jocelyn Cole, an attorney living on a remote island in Puget Sound, is taken prisoner by an arms-smuggling militia group that her client is involved with and which is assembling a nuclear device to destroy Washington, D.C. (Rev: SLJ 2/99)

112 Mazer, Harry. *The Island Keeper* (7–10). 1981, Dell paper $3.99 (0-440-94774-X). Feeling completely alone in this world, Cleo decides to run away to a desolate island that her father owns.

113 Mazer, Harry, and Norma Fox Mazer. *The Solid Gold Kid* (7–10). 1989, Bantam paper $4.50 (0-553-27851-7). A millionaire's son and four other teenagers are kidnapped.

114 Meltzer, Brad. *The Tenth Justice* (10–12). 1997, Morrow $23.00 (0-688-15089-6). Ben, a clerk for a Supreme Court justice, is being blackmailed and he thinks one of his friends is supplying information to the blackmailer in this thriller that also supplies lots of information about the Supreme Court. (Rev: BL 2/1/97; SLJ 11/97)

115 Mendelsohn, Jane. *I Was Amelia Earhart* (9–12). 1996, Knopf $18.00 (0-679-45054-8). A fictionalized account of what might have happened had Amelia Earhart's plane landed on an island rather than crashing into the ocean. (Rev: BL 4/15/96; SLJ 10/96)

116 Miklowitz, Gloria D. *After the Bomb* (7–12). 1987, Scholastic paper $2.50 (0-590-40568-3). This novel describes the experiences of a group of young people after an atomic bomb falls on Los Angeles. (Rev: BL 6/15/86; SLJ 9/85; VOYA 8/85)

117 Miklowitz, Gloria D. *Camouflage* (8–10). 1998, Harcourt $16.00 (0-15-201467-5). When 14-year-old Kyle visits northern Michigan to spend a summer with his father, he becomes involved in a government-hating militia movement in which his father is a general. (Rev: BCCB 5/98; HBG 9/98; SLJ 4/98; VOYA 10/98)

118 Miller, Frances A. *The Truth Trap* (7–10). 1986, Fawcett paper $4.50 (0-449-70247-2). When Matt's parents are killed in a car accident, he leaves town only to be accused of a murder.

119 Morey, Walt. *Death Walk* (6–10). 1991, Blue Heron $13.95 (0-936085-18-5). After being stranded in the Alaskan wilderness, a teenage boy must learn to survive in the harsh climate while on the run from killers. (Rev: BL 6/1/91; SLJ 6/91)

120 Nance, John J. *Blackout* (10–12). 2000, Putnam $23.95 (0-399-14594-X). An action-packed adult novel centered on an airborne chase from Hong Kong to Idaho. (Rev: BL 1/1–15/00; SLJ 7/00)

121 Nordhoff, Charles, and James N. Hall. *The Bounty Trilogy* (9–12). Illus. 1982, Little, Brown paper $21.95 (0-316-61166-2). An adventure story based on fact concerning a mutiny aboard the Bounty and its aftermath. The three individual books are *Mutiny on the Bounty, Men against the Sea,* and *Pitcairn's Island.* These books were originally published in 1932, 1934, and 1934, respectively.

122 Olshan, Matthew. *Finn* (8–12). 2001, Bancroft $19.95 (1-890862-13-4); paper $14.95 (1-890862-14-2). Teenage Chloe, who has suffered an abusive childhood, and a pregnant Hispanic girl set off to find new lives in a Huck Finn-like adventure full of insight and social commentary. (Rev: BL 4/1/01; SLJ 4/01; VOYA 4/01)

123 Paulsen, Gary. *Canyons* (7–10). 1991, Dell paper $5.99 (0-440-21023-2). Blennan becomes obsessed with the story of a young Indian boy murdered by white men 100 years before. (Rev: SLJ 9/90)

124 Paulsen, Gary. *Dogsong* (8–10). 1985, Bradbury LB $16.00 (0-02-770180-8). An Eskimo youth faces hardship and danger when he ventures alone by dogsled into the wilderness. (Rev: BL 4/1/85; SLJ 4/85; VOYA 12/85)

125 Paulsen, Gary. *The River* (5–10). 1991, Delacorte $15.95 (0-385-30388-2). In this sequel to *Hatchet,* Paulsen takes the wilderness adventure beyond self-preservation and makes teen Brian responsible for saving someone else. (Rev: BL 5/15/91)

126 Peck, Richard. *Secrets of the Shopping Mall* (7–10). 1979, Dell paper $3.99 (0-440-98099-2). Two 8th-graders find they are not alone when they take up residence in a shopping mall.

127 Petersen, P. J. *Rising Water* (6–12). 2002, Simon & Schuster $16.00 (0-689-84148-5). Three teens take on rising floodwater and dangerous villains in a suspenseful story told in alternating voices. (Rev: BCCB 2/02; BL 3/1/02; HBG 10/02; SLJ 2/02)

128 Preston, Douglas, and Lincoln Child. *Riptide* (10–12). 1998, Warner $25.00 (0-446-52336-4). A classic struggle between good and evil emerges in this adventure yarn after a group of treasure seekers tries to recover buried booty worth billions of dollars. (Rev: BL 5/15/98; SLJ 12/98; VOYA 12/98)

129 Pullman, Philip. *The Tiger in the Well* (8–12). 1996, Demco $11.04 (0-606-09969-7). This conclusion of the rich historical trilogy that began with *The Ruby in the Smoke* (1987) and *The Shadow in the North* (1988) completes the adventures of Victorian heroine Sally Lockhart who, in this novel, encounters a man who wants passionately to destroy her. (Rev: BL 10/15/90)

130 Puzo, Mario. *The Godfather* (10–12). 1969, Putnam $24.95 (0-399-10342-2); NAL paper $5.95 (0-451-15736-2). The story of a fictional crime family in New York led by Vito Corleone and then by his son Michael.

131 Rees, Celia. *Pirates!* (7–10). 2003, Bloomsbury $17.95 (1-58234-816-2). Horrified by the prospect of an arranged marriage to a plantation owner, teenage Nancy and a close slave friend run off and join a pirate crew in this swashbuckling adventure set in the 18th century. (Rev: BCCB 1/04; BL 12/15/03*; HBG 4/04; SLJ 10/03*)

132 Rochman, Hazel, and Darlene Z. McCampbell, eds. *Leaving Home* (7–12). 1997, HarperCollins LB $16.89 (0-06-024874-2). These 16 stories by well-known writers describe various forms of leaving home, from immigration to a new country to running away or taking a trip. (Rev: BL 1/1–15/97; SLJ 3/97*)

133 Rold, Marlys. *Heart of a Tiger* (9–12). 2004, Five Star $26.95 (1-5941-4113-4). There is a lot of fast action in this romance set in a dense jungle where Kelly and her helper Sam Tanner are looking for Kelly's brother. (Rev: BL 3/15/04)

134 Salisbury, Graham. *Shark Bait* (7–12). 1997, Bantam paper $4.50 (0-440-22803-4). Set in Hawaii, this novel deals with Eric Chock and his friends, one of whom is determined to kill a sailor like the one his mother ran away with. (Rev: BL 9/1/97; SLJ 9/97; VOYA 6/98)

135 Saul, John. *The Manhattan Hunt Club* (10–12). 2001, Ballantine $25.95 (0-345-43330-0). In this suspense novel, a college student is pursued for sport through abandoned tunnels beneath New York City streets by a wealthy and elite "hunt club." (Rev: BL 5/1/01)

136 Shusterman, Neal. *Dissidents* (7–10). 1989, Little, Brown $13.95 (0-316-78904-6). A teenage boy joins his mother, the American ambassador in Moscow, and becomes involved in a spy caper. (Rev: BL 8/89; BR 11–12/89; SLJ 10/89)

137 Smith, Cotton. *Dark Trail to Dodge* (7–10). 1997, Walker $20.95 (0-8027-4158-4). Eighteen-year-old Tyrel Bannon faces unusual problems on his first cattle drive when rustlers attack and plan on taking no prisoners. (Rev: BL 6/1–15/97; VOYA 8/97)

138 Smith, Diane. *Letters from Yellowstone* (10–12). Illus. 1999, Viking $24.95 (0-670-88631-9). A somewhat ragtag group of scientists explore Yellowstone National Park in 1899 in this novel, told entirely through letters, that reveals much about the issues of the time. (Rev: BL 6/99; SLJ 2/00)

139 Smith, Wilbur. *A Time to Die* (10–12). 1990, Random $19.95 (0-394-58475-9). An adventure novel set in Africa about a big-game hunter and an expedition into territory where two rival tribes are fighting. (Rev: SLJ 7/90)

140 Sullivan, Paul. *The Unforgiving Land* (7–10). 1996, Royal Fireworks paper $9.99 (0-88092-256-7). A white trader gives guns and bullets to a group of Inuit, causing a breakdown in the delicate harmony between nature and humankind and destruction of the Inuit way of life. (Rev: VOYA 8/96)

141 Svee, Gary. *Incident at Pishkin Creek* (9–12). 1989, Walker $28.95 (0-8027-4095-2). Max Bass exaggerated in his advertisement for a bride, as poor Catherine O'Dowd discovers when she arrives in Montana. (Rev: BL 7/89)

142 Swarthout, Glendon, and Kathryn Swarthout. *Whichaway* (7–10). 1997, Rising Moon paper $6.95 (0-87358-676-X). A reissue of an exciting story about a boy whose character is tested when he is trapped with two broken legs on top of a windmill in an isolated area of Texas. (Rev: BR 11–12/98; HBG 3/98; VOYA 2/98)

143 Sweeney, Joyce. *Free Fall* (9–12). 1996, Delacorte $15.95 (0-385-32211-9). Trapped in a cave in Ocala National Park, four boys plot their escape and in the process learn about themselves, their families, and personal tragedies. (Rev: BL 7/96; BR 9–10/96; SLJ 11/96; VOYA 6/96)

144 Taylor, Theodore. *Rogue Wave and Other Red-Blooded Sea Stories* (6–10). 1996, Harcourt $16.00 (0-15-201408-X). Eight compelling sea stories involve a range of characters and situations. (Rev: BL 11/1/96; BR 3–4/97; SLJ 4/97; VOYA 4/97)

145 Taylor, Theodore. *The Weirdo* (9–12). 1991, Harcourt $15.95 (0-15-294952-6). After his friend mysteriously disappears, Chip assumes leadership of the fight to protect bears living in the local swamp. (Rev: BL 12/15/91; SLJ 1/92)

146 Thompson, Julian. *A Band of Angels* (9–12). 1986, Scholastic $12.95 (0-590-33780-7). Jordan, his suitcase of money, and two friends hit the road to escape government agents who are searching for them. (Rev: BL 3/87; SLJ 8/86; VOYA 6/86)

147 Thompson, Julian. *Brothers* (7–12). 1998, Random $18.99 (0-679-99082-8). Chris trails his unstable brother to an eastern Montana militia camp, where there is a standoff between the zealots and local authorities. (Rev: BL 11/1/98; BR 5–6/99; HBG 3/99; SLJ 11/98; VOYA 10/98)

148 Thompson, Julian. *The Grounding of Group Six* (8–12). 1983, Avon paper $3.99 (0-380-83386-7). Five 16-year-olds think they are being sent to an exclusive school but actually they have been slated for murder.

149 Thompson, Julian. *The Taking of Mariasburg* (9–12). 1988, Scholastic paper $12.95 (0-590-41247-7). Maria buys a ghost town with her inheritance and populates it with teenagers. (Rev: BL 4/1/88; BR 9–10/88; SLJ 5/88; VOYA 4/88)

150 Thompson, Julian F. *Terry and the Pirates* (9–12). 2000, Simon & Schuster $17.00 (0-689-83076-9). Running away from her divorced parents, Terry finds herself among treasure-seeking pirates in this entertaining adventure. (Rev: BL 11/1/00; HBG 10/01; SLJ 10/00; VOYA 2/01)

151 Townsend, John Rowe. *The Islanders* (7–10). 1981, HarperCollins $11.95 (0-397-31940-1). Two strangers washed up on a remote island are regarded as enemies by the inhabitants.

152 Townsend, John Rowe. *Kate and the Revolution* (7–10). 1983, HarperCollins LB $12.89 (0-397-32016-7). A 17-year-old girl is attracted to a visiting prince and then the adventure begins.

153 Voigt, Cynthia. *On Fortune's Wheel* (7–12). 1990, Macmillan $17.00 (0-689-31636-4). In this historical adventure, a young runaway couple are captured by pirates and sold into slavery. (Rev: BL 2/15/90; SLJ 3/90; VOYA 4/90)

154 Wallace, Irving. *The Seventh Secret* (9–12). 1986, NAL paper $4.95 (0-451-14557-7). Emily Ashcroft is convinced that Hitler is still alive and sets out to find him. (Rev: BL 10/15/85)

155 Weaver, Will. *Memory Boy* (7–10). 2001, HarperCollins LB $15.89 (0-06-028812-4). In 2008, the global warming that follows a volcanic eruption forces Miles and his family to leave Minneapolis and seek refuge in their isolated vacation cabin. (Rev: BL 2/1/01; BR 11–12/01; HBG 10/01; SLJ 6/01; VOYA 8/01)

156 West, Cameron. *The Medici Dagger* (10–12). 2001, Pocket $25.00 (0-7434-2035-7). In this action-adventure, our hero is in a race with an evil billionaire arms manufacturer and several nefarious government agents to find a dagger created by Leonardo Da Vinci that is made of an unknown alloy both stronger and lighter than any metal ever developed. (Rev: BL 8/01; SLJ 2/02)

157 Williams, Michael. *The Genuine Half-Moon Kid* (7–10). 1994, Dutton $15.99 (0-525-67479-5). Like questing Jason in Greek mythology, 18-year-old South African Jay Watson sets out with some friends to find a yellow wood box left him by his grandfather. (Rev: BL 6/1–15/94)

158 Winkler, David. *The Return of Calico Bright* (9–12). 2003, Farrar $19.00 (0-374-38048-1). Callie hopes for a taste of her ancestor Calico Bright's life but encounters more danger than she bargained for in this adventure set in Oregon. (Rev: BL 9/15/03; HBG 4/04; SLJ 10/03; VOYA 4/04)

159 Yolen, Jane, and Bruce Coville. *Armageddon Summer* (7–12). 1998, Harcourt $17.00 (0-15-201767-4). When truckloads of artillery suddenly appear, events turn deadly for teenagers Marina and Jed, who are at a meeting of a millennial cult known as the Believers on a mountain in Massachusetts. (Rev: BCCB 9/98; BL 8/98; HBG 3/99; SLJ 10/98; VOYA 10/98)

160 Zindel, Paul. *Reef of Death* (7–12). 1998, HarperCollins $15.95 (0-06-024728-2). A tale of terror about two teens, a monster creature that lives on an Australian reef, and a mad geologist who has a torture chamber on her freighter. (Rev: BL 3/1/98; HBG 9/98; SLJ 3/98; VOYA 4/98)

Animal Stories

161 Benchley, Peter. *The Beast* (9–12). 1992, Fawcett paper $5.99 (0-449-22089-3). *Jaws* (1973) revisited, this time with a giant squid as villain. (Rev: BL 5/15/91; SLJ 11/91)

162 Benchley, Peter. *Jaws* (8–12). 1974, Doubleday paper $6.99 (0-449-21963-1). The best-selling novel about a small Long Island town and the creature that became a threat to its beaches.

163 Benchley, Peter. *White Shark* (9–12). 1995, St. Martin's paper $6.50 (0-312-95573-1). An evil Nazi scientist creates a water-breathing superkiller that is sunk in a U-boat at the end of World War II and gets loose 50 years later. (Rev: BL 1/15/94; SLJ 11/94)

164 Branford, Henrietta. *White Wolf* (7–12). 1999, Candlewick $16.99 (0-7636-0748-7). Kept as a pet, Snowy, a wolf cub, escapes, searches for a pack, and eventually has a family of its own in this tale set in the Pacific Northwest. (Rev: BL 8/99; HBG 9/99; SLJ 6/99; VOYA 10/99)

165 Campbell, Eric. *Papa Tembo* (7–12). 1998, Harcourt $16.00 (0-15-201727-5). This story set in Tanzania involves a fatal encounter between Papa Tembo, the father of elephants, and his arch enemy, Laurens Van Der Wel, the evil poacher. (Rev: BCCB 9/98; BL 8/98; HBG 9/99; SLJ 10/98; VOYA 10/98)

166 Caras, Roger A. *Roger Caras' Treasury of Great Cat Stories* (9–12). 1990, Galahad $10.98 (0-88365-763-5). A fine collection of short stories from internationally known writers, all about the mysterious creature, the cat. (Rev: BL 4/1/87)

167 Caras, Roger A. *Roger Caras' Treasury of Great Dog Stories* (9–12). 1987, Dutton paper $12.50 (0-525-48428-0). An anthology of dog stories written by great authors. (Rev: BL 4/1/87)

168 Curwood, James Oliver. *The Bear — A Novel* (8–12). 1989, Newmarket paper $6.95 (1-55704-053-2). A reissue of the 1916 novel about a grizzly bear and an orphaned black bear cub in the wilds of British Columbia. (Rev: VOYA 4/90)

169 Evans, Nicholas. *The Horse Whisperer* (9–12). 1995, Delacorte $24.95 (0-385-31523-6). After a teenager loses her leg in a riding accident, her mother moves them to Montana, where the "horse whisperer," a man of mystical powers, tries to rebuild their lives. (Rev: BL 8/95*)

170 Gallico, Paul. *The Snow Goose* (7–12). Illus. 1941, Knopf $15.00 (0-394-44593-7); Tundra paper $9.99 (0-7710-3250-1). A hunchbacked artist and a young child nurse a wounded snow goose back to health, and it later returns to protect them in this large, illustrated 50th anniversary edition of the classic tale. (Rev: BL 9/15/92)

171 Grey, Zane. *The Wolf Tracker and Other Animal Tales* (10–12). 1984, Santa Barbara paper $7.95 (0-915643-01-4). This collection of tales includes four stories about animals and the outdoors.

172 Herriot, James. *James Herriot's Favorite Dog Stories* (10–12). Illus. 1996, St. Martin's $17.95 (0-312-14841-0). A collection of 10 stories written by the famous veterinarian and author. (Rev: SLJ 5/97)

173 Hobbs, Will. *Beardance* (7–12). 1993, Atheneum $17.00 (0-689-31867-7). Prospector Cloyd Atcity stays the winter in the Colorado mountains to ensure the survival of the last two grizzly cubs in the state after their mother and sibling die. (Rev: BL 11/15/93; SLJ 12/93; VOYA 12/93)

174 Katz, Welwyn W. *Whalesinger* (7–10). 1991, Macmillan paper $14.95 (0-689-50511-6). Two Vancouver teens spending their summer on the California coast encounter a corrupt research scientist, endangered whales, and natural disasters. (Rev: BL 2/1/91; SLJ 5/91)

175 Klass, David. *California Blue* (7–10). 1994, Scholastic paper $13.95 (0-590-46688-7). A 17-year-old California boy who cares about track and butterflies finds a chrysalis that turns out to be an unknown species. (Rev: BL 3/1/94; SLJ 4/94*; VOYA 6/94)

176 Meyers, Kent. *The Work of Wolves* (10–12). 2004, Harcourt $24.00 (0-15-101057-9). Three misfits, including a German exchange student and a gifted Lakota high school student, conspire to rescue three abused horses. (Rev: BL 5/15/04*)

177 Michener, James A. *Creatures of the Kingdom: Stories of Animals and Nature* (9–12). 1995, Fawcett paper $6.99 (0-449-22092-3). Sections from Michener's novels that deal with animals and other aspects of nature, such as the volcanoes of Hawaii, the habits of the diplodocus dinosaur, and the life of the salmon. (Rev: BL 7/93; SLJ 5/94)

178 O'Hara, Mary. *My Friend Flicka* (7–12). 1988, HarperCollins paper $6.00 (0-06-080902-7). This story about Ken McLaughlin and the filly named Flicka is continued in *Thunderhead, Son of Flicka*.

179 Peck, Robert Newton. *The Horse Hunters* (7–10). 1988, Random $15.95 (0-394-56980-6). A 15-year-old boy reaches manhood through capturing a white stallion in this novel set in Florida of the 1930s. (Rev: BL 2/15/89; BR 5–6/89; VOYA 6/89)

180 Peyton, K. M. *Blind Beauty* (6–10). 2001, Dutton $17.99 (0-525-46652-5). Twelve-year-old Tessa is angry at the world until she meets Buffoon, an unlikely racehorse that she trains to win the Grand National. (Rev: BCCB 2/01; BR 9–10/01; HBG 10/01; SLJ 3/01; VOYA 4/01)

181 Peyton, K. M. *Darkling* (9–12). 1989, Doubleday $16.95 (0-385-26963-3). Jenny's unusual grandfather buys her a horse but it is her lover, Goddard, who gives her the help that this responsibility requires. (Rev: BL 5/1/90; SLJ 5/90; VOYA 6/90)

182 Schinto, Jeanne, ed. *The Literary Dog: Great Contemporary Dog Stories* (9–12). 1991, Grove Atlantic paper $15.00 (0-87113-504-3). Over 30 dog stories by such present-day writers as Doris Lessing and John Updike. (Rev: BL 9/1/90)

183 Steinbeck, John. *The Red Pony* (9–12). 1986, Viking paper $8.95 (0-14-018739-1). These stories about a young boy growing up on a farm in California involve such elements as a loving family, a colt, and an old hired hand.

184 Sullivan, Paul. *Legend of the North* (7–12). 1995, Royal Fireworks paper $9.99 (0-88092-308-3). Set in northern Canada, this novel contains two narratives, the first about a young wolf's struggle for dominance within the pack, and the second about an elderly Inuit and his survival in the harsh tundra regions. (Rev: BL 1/1–15/96; VOYA 4/96)

Classics

Europe

GENERAL AND MISCELLANEOUS

185 Camus, Albert. *The Plague* (10–12). 1948, Vintage paper $12.00 (0-67-972021-9). An allegory for mature readers that uses the bubonic plague as a symbol of the absurdity of life and each character as a different attitude towards it.

186 Davenport, Basil. *The Portable Roman Reader* (10–12). 1951, Viking paper $18.00 (0-14-015056-0). A cross-section of writings from ancient Roman times by such authors as Plautus, Virgil, Seneca, and Terence. [870.8]

187 Dumas, Alexandre. *The Count of Monte Cristo* (8–12). Illus. 1996, Random $25.95 (0-679-60199-6); NAL paper $6.95 (0-451-52195-1). The classic French novel about false imprisonment, escape, and revenge.

188 Dumas, Alexandre. *The Man in the Iron Mask* (9–12). 1976, Lightyear LB $35.95 (0-89968-146-8). This rousing French adventure story continues the exploits of the three Musketeers.

189 Dumas, Alexandre. *The Three Musketeers* (8–12). 1984, Dodd paper $5.95 (0-553-21337-7). A novel of daring and intrigue in France. Sequels are *The Man in the Iron Mask* and *Twenty Years After* (available in various editions).

190 Hudson, W. H. *Green Mansions: A Romance of the Tropical Forest* (10–12). 1982, Buccaneer LB $25.95 (0-89966-374-5). The haunting novel of a naturalist's encounter with the bird-girl, Rima, in a South American jungle.

191 Hugo, Victor. *The Hunchback of Notre Dame* (10–12). 1981, Buccaneer LB $31.95 (0-89966-382-6); NAL paper $5.95 (0-451-52222-2). The world of medieval Paris, from nobility to paupers, comes alive in this sprawling novel whose central characters are Quasimodo, a hunchback, and a gypsy named Esmeralda.

192 Hugo, Victor. *Les Miserables* (10–12). 1980, Random $16.95 (0-394-60489-X); Pocket paper $5.99 (0-671-50439-8). This lengthy novel describes the flight of Jean Valjean from the law in France during the first half of the 19th century. First published in 1862.

193 Kafka, Franz. *The Trial* (10–12). Trans. by Willa Muir and Edwin Muir. 1992, Knopf $17.00 (0-679-40994-7). A disturbing novel about a man who is arrested and fights charges about which he has no knowledge.

194 Kuper, Peter, and Franz Kafka. *The Metamorphosis* (10–12). Illus. 2003, Crown $18.00 (1-4000-4795-1). A graphic novel version of the classic horror story about a man who turns into an insect. (Rev: BL 7/03; SLJ 12/03)

195 Maupassant, Guy de. *The Best Short Stories of Guy de Maupassant* (7–12). 1968, Amereon $21.95 (0-88411-589-5). The French master is represented by 19 tales including "The Diamond Necklace."

196 Remarque, Erich Maria. *All Quiet on the Western Front* (10–12). 1929, Little, Brown $24.95 (0-316-73992-8); Fawcett paper $5.99 (0-449-21394-

3). The touching story of four young German boys and their army life during World War I. (Rev: BL 6/1/88)

197 Sienkiewicz, Henryk. *Quo Vadis* (10–12). 1981, Amereon LB $29.95 (0-89190-484-0). The contrast between the hedonistic pagans and the early Christians is highlighted in this novel set in ancient Rome.

198 Verne, Jules. *Around the World in Eighty Days* (7–12). 1996, Puffin paper $4.99 (0-14-036711-X). Phileas Fogg and servant Passepartout leave on a world trip in this 1873 classic adventure. (Rev: SLJ 7/96)

199 Verne, Jules. *A Journey to the Center of the Earth* (7–12). Illus. 1984, Penguin paper $4.95 (0-14-002265-1). A group of adventurers enter the earth through a volcano in Iceland. First published in French in 1864.

200 Verne, Jules. *Twenty Thousand Leagues Under the Sea* (7–12). 1990, Viking paper $3.99 (0-14-036721-7). Evil Captain Nemo captures a group of underwater explorers. First published in 1869. A sequel is *The Mysterious Island* (1988 Macmillan).

201 Voltaire, Francois M. *The Portable Voltaire* (10–12). Ed. by Ben Ray Redmen. 1949, Viking paper $17.00 (0-14-015041-2). A fine selection of Voltaire's works including the novel *Candide*. [848]

202 Wallace, Lew. *Ben Hur* (10–12). 1987, Buccaneer LB $35.95 (0-89966-289-7). The story of a Jewish slave who escapes a life on the galleys and later is converted to Christianity after an encounter with Christ's healing powers.

GREAT BRITAIN AND IRELAND

203 Austen, Jane. *Persuasion*. 1995 Modern Library ed (10–12). 1995, Modern Library $14.95 (0-679-60191-0). After eight years, Anne Elliott breaks off her engagement to Captain Wentworth in this classic Austen novel.

204 Austen, Jane. *Pride and Prejudice* (9–12). 1984, Putnam paper $2.25 (0-451-52226-5). Mrs. Bennet's fondest wish is to marry off her daughters but Elizabeth won't cooperate.

205 Brontë, Charlotte. *Jane Eyre* (6–12). Series: Illustrated Junior Library. 1983, Putnam $19.99 (0-448-06031-0); Bantam paper $4.95 (0-553-21140-4). The immortal love story of Jane and Mr. Rochester.

206 Brontë, Emily. *Wuthering Heights* (9–12). 1959, Signet paper $4.95 (0-451-52338-5). The love between Catherine and Heathcliff that even death cannot destroy.

207 Bryan, Francis. *The Curse of Treasure Island* (10–12). 2002, Viking $24.95 (0-670-03089-9). An adult Jim Hawkins returns to Treasure Island in a sequel full of action and adventure. (Rev: BL 5/15/02)

208 Carroll, Lewis. *Alice's Adventures in Wonderland* (5–12). 2003, Simply Read $29.95 (1-894965-00-0). Interesting illustrations by Ghiuselev that interpret incidents and characters in a different way highlight this new edition of an old classic. (Rev: BL 2/1/04; SLJ 6/04)

209 Collins, Wilkie. *The Moonstone* (9–12). 1984, Demco $12.30 (0-606-01905-7). Often called the first detective story in English, this mystery story revolves around the disappearance of a diamond named the Moonstone.

210 Collins, Wilkie. *The Woman in White* (10–12). 1998, Oxford paper $7.95 (0-19-283429-0). This mystery story first appeared in 1860 and tells of a plot to illegally obtain the inheritance of the heroine of the novel.

211 Defoe, Daniel. *Robinson Crusoe* (7–12). Illus. 1983, Macmillan $27.95 (0-684-17946-6); NAL paper $5.95 (0-451-52236-2). The classic survival story, with illustrations by N. C. Wyeth.

212 Dickens, Charles. *A Christmas Carol* (7–12). Illus. Series: Whole Story. 2000, Viking paper $17.99 (0-670-88879-6). This volume contains the full text of the classic, with new illustrations, reproductions of period pictures, a biography of Dickens, and material on social conditions of the time. (Rev: BL 9/1/00; HBG 3/01)

213 Dickens, Charles. *A Christmas Carol* (7–12). 1983, Pocket paper $3.99 (0-671-47369-7). Scrooge discovers the true meaning of Christmas after some trying experiences.

214 Dickens, Charles. *David Copperfield* (8–12). Illus. 1997, Viking paper $7.95 (0-14-043494-1). Includes some little-known episodes that Dickens excerpted from his book for public readings, information about dramatic performance, and illustrations. (Rev: BL 12/15/95)

215 Dickens, Charles. *Great Expectations* (8–12). 1998, NAL paper $4.95 (0-451-52671-6). The story of Pip and his slow journey to maturity and fortune.

216 Dickens, Charles. *Martin Chuzzlewit* (10–12). 1968, Viking paper $10.95 (0-14-043031-8). In order to placate his grandfather, Martin emigrates from England in this novel largely set in the United States. First published in 1844.

217 Dickens, Charles. *The Mystery of Edwin Drood* (9–12). Illus. 1987, Oxford $25.95 (0-19-254516-7). The last novel of Dickens, left unfinished at his death.

218 Dickens, Charles. *Oliver Twist* (7–12). 1961, NAL paper $4.95 (0-451-52351-2). In probably the most accessible of Dickens's works, readers meet such immortals as Fagin, Nancy, and Oliver himself.

219 Dickens, Charles. *A Tale of Two Cities* (7–12). 1960, NAL paper $3.95 (0-451-52441-1). The classic novel of sacrifice during the French Revolution.

220 Doyle, Arthur Conan. *The Adventures of Sherlock Holmes* (7–12). 1981, Avon paper $2.95 (0-380-78105-0). A collection of 12 of the most famous stories about this famous sleuth.

221 Doyle, Arthur Conan. *The Complete Sherlock Holmes: All 4 Novels and 56 Stories* (7–12). 1998, Bantam paper $13.90 (0-553-32825-5). In two volumes, all the stories and novels involving Holmes and his foil Watson.

222 Doyle, Arthur Conan. *The Hound of the Baskervilles* (9–12). 1983, Buccaneer LB $19.95 (0-89966-229-3). These are two of the many editions available of this Sherlock Holmes mystery about strange deaths on the moors close to the Baskerville estate.

223 Doyle, Arthur Conan. *Sherlock Holmes: The Complete Novels and Stories* (8–12). 1986, Bantam paper $6.95 each (Vol. 1: 0-553-21241-9; Vol. 2: 0-553-21242-7). A handy collection in two volumes of all the writings about Holmes and Watson. (Rev: BL 3/15/87)

224 Doyle, Arthur Conan. *The Sign of Four* (9–12). 1989, Buccaneer LB $15.95 (0-89966-230-7). This is one of the four full-length novels featuring Sherlock Holmes.

225 Doyle, Arthur Conan. *A Study in Scarlet* (9–12). 1982, Penguin paper $6.95 (0-14-005707-2). In this, Holmes's first appearance in a full-length novel, historical material involving the Mormons plays an important part.

226 Doyle, Arthur Conan. *Tales of Terror and Mystery* (9–12). 1982, Buccaneer LB $16.95 (0-89966-429-6). From the creator of Sherlock Holmes, 13 stories of mystery and the supernatural.

227 Eliot, George. *The Mill on the Floss* (10–12). 1965, NAL paper $3.95 (0-451-51922-1). The tragic story of Maggie, her brother, and the events that separate their love. First published in 1860.

228 Eliot, George. *Silas Marner* (8–12). 1960, NAL paper $3.95 (0-451-52427-6). The love of an old man for a young child brings redemption in this classic English novel.

229 Kipling, Rudyard. *Captains Courageous* (7–10). 1964, Amereon LB $20.95 (0-88411-818-5). The story of a spoiled teenager who learns about life from common fishermen who save him when he falls overboard from an ocean liner.

230 Kipling, Rudyard. *Kim* (10–12). 1997, Bantam paper $3.95 (0-553-21332-6). Beginning in Lahore, this novel follows a young street urchin through many adventures in British-controlled India.

231 Kipling, Rudyard. *The Portable Kipling* (9–12). Ed. by Irving Howe. 1982, Viking paper $16.95 (0-14-015097-8). This collection contains 28 short stories and a selection of 50 poems.

232 Stevenson, Robert Louis. *The Black Arrow* (7–12). 1998, Tor paper $3.99 (0-8125-6562-2). Set against the War of the Roses, this is an adventure story involving a young hero, Dick Shelton. First published in 1888.

233 Stevenson, Robert Louis. *Dr. Jekyll and Mr. Hyde* (7–12). 1990, Buccaneer LB $16.95 (0-89968-552-8). This 1886 horror classic involves a drug-induced change of personality. One of several editions.

234 Stevenson, Robert Louis. *The Strange Case of Dr. Jekyll and Mr. Hyde* (9–12). Illus. 1993, Oxford paper $11.95 (0-19-585429-2). An edition of this classic that includes comments by Joyce Carol Oates and engravings by Barry Moser. (Rev: BL 5/1/90)

235 Stevenson, Robert Louis. *Treasure Island* (6–10). Illus. Series: Whole Story. 1996, Viking $23.99 (0-670-86920-1). This edition contains the complete text of this novel along with illustrations that are used to explain details of life during this period, particularly life at sea. (Rev: SLJ 7/96)

236 Stoker, Bram. *Dracula* (10–12). 1985, Amereon LB $27.95 (0-88411-131-8). In epistolary form, this novel involves a baron who is a vampire and his mysterious castle in Transylvania.

237 Swift, Jonathan. *Gulliver's Travels* (7–12). 1947, Putnam $17.99 (0-448-06010-8); NAL paper $3.95 (0-451-52219-2). The four fantastic voyages of Lemuel Gulliver. First published in 1726.

238 Wilde, Oscar. *The Picture of Dorian Gray* (6–12). Illus. 2001, Viking $25.99 (0-670-89494-X); paper $17.99 (0-670-89495-8). Informative sidebars and bright illustrations amplify many of the more esoteric aspects of Wilde's classic story about the young man who never ages. (Rev: BL 5/15/01; HBG 10/01; SLJ 8/01; VOYA 8/01)

239 Woolf, Virginia. *A Room of One's Own* (10–12). 1991, Harcourt $15.95 (0-15-178733-6). This is a modern classic by the great English novelist and essayist.

240 Woolf, Virginia. *To the Lighthouse* (10–12). 1992, Random (0-679-40537-2). One of Woolf's most famous novels about the Ramsay family and their problems.

United States

241 Cather, Willa. *Death Comes for the Archbishop* (10–12). 1927, Knopf paper $14.95 (0-679-72889-9). The story of two clergymen who founded missions and pioneered missionary work in the West, chiefly in New Mexico.

14

242 Cather, Willa. *My Antonia* (10–12). 1973, Houghton $24.95 (0-395-07514-9); paper $5.95 (0-395-75514-X). A novel set in Nebraska about pioneering Bohemian farmers and the courageous heroine, Antonia. First published in 1918.

243 Cather, Willa. *Willa Cather: Early Novels and Stories* (10–12). 1987, Library of America $40.00 (0-940450-39-9). This collection of stories and novels includes the full text of four novels including *My Antonia, The Song of the Lark,* and *O Pioneers!*

244 Cather, Willa. *Willa Cather: Later Novels* (10–12). 1990, Library of America $35.00 (0-940450-52-6). This omnibus volume includes such novels as *Death Comes for the Archbishop, The Lost Lady,* and *Lucy Gayheart.*

245 Cather, Willa. *Willa Cather: Stories, Poems, and Other Writings* (9–12). 1992, Library of America $35.00 (0-940450-71-2). This collection includes novellas, stories, and poems. (Rev: SLJ 8/92)

246 Cooper, James Fenimore. *The Last of the Mohicans* (8–12). 1986, Macmillan $28.00 (0-684-18711-6); paper $4.95 (0-553-21329-6). This is the second of the classic Leatherstocking Tales. The others are *The Pioneers, The Prairie, The Pathfinder,* and *The Deerslayer* (all available in various editions). (Rev: BL 1/87)

247 Crane, Stephen. *The Red Badge of Courage* (8–12). 1991, Random $9.99 (0-517-66844-0); Airmont paper $2.50 (0-8049-0003-5). The classic novel of a young man who explored the meanings of courage during the Civil War.

248 Eisner, Will. *Moby Dick* (6–12). Illus. 2001, NBM $15.95 (1-56163-293-7). A faithful retelling of Melville's famous novel in full-color graphic-novel format. (Rev: BL 11/15/01; HBG 3/02; SLJ 1/02)

249 Faulkner, William. *Light in August* (10–12). 1967, Random paper $13.00 (0-679-73226-8). A classic novel by Faulkner that deals with Joe Christmas, a part-black, and his fate at the hands of bigots.

250 Hawthorne, Nathaniel. *The Scarlet Letter* (9–12). 1977, Cambridge Univ. Pr. paper $8.50 (0-521-56783-1). Set in New England during Colonial times, this is a novel of adultery and expiation.

251 Hawthorne, Nathaniel. *Tales and Sketches, Including Twice-Told Tales, Mosses from an Old Manse, and The Snow-Image; A Wonder Book for Girls and Boys; Tanglewood Tales for Girls and Boys, Being a Second Wonder Book* (10–12). 1982, Library of America $39.50 (0-940450-03-8). This volume contains all of Hawthorne's stories and sketches, arranged by publication date.

252 Henry, O. *The Gift of the Magi* (5–10). Illus. 1988, Simon & Schuster paper $14.00 (0-671-64706-7). A beautiful edition of this classic story of Christmas and true love, illustrated by Kevin King. (Rev: BL 12/15/88)

253 Irving, Washington. *The Legend of Sleepy Hollow and Other Selections* (7–12). 1963, Washington Square Pr. paper $3.99 (0-671-46211-3). The story of Ichabod Crane, the ill-fated schoolteacher, and his encounter with the headless horseman.

254 James, Henry. *Washington Square* (10–12). 1997, Modern Library $14.50 (0-679-60276-3). A short novel about a plain woman, her domineering father, and a young man who is courting her for her money.

255 Lewis, Sinclair. *Babbitt* (10–12). 1949, Harcourt $18.00 (0-15-110421-2); NAL paper $6.95 (0-451-52366-0). A satire on the shallow life led by members of the middle-class in an American city named Zenith.

256 Lewis, Sinclair. *Main Street* (10–12). 1950, NAL paper $4.50 (0-451-52147-1). A woman marries a small-town doctor and decides to change things in Gopher Prairie, Minnesota. First published in 1920.

257 London, Jack. *The Call of the Wild* (5–10). Illus. 1996, Viking $21.99 (0-670-86918-X). Along with the full text of this novel about the heroic dog Buck, this edition supplies background material on the Klondike, the gold rush, sled dogs, and the author. (Rev: SLJ 7/96)

258 London, Jack. *The Call of the Wild, White Fang, and Other Stories* (9–12). 1993, Viking paper $7.95 (0-14-018651-4). In addition to two complete novels, this collection contains two other stories with settings in the Arctic.

259 London, Jack. *The Sea-Wolf* (7–12). 1958, Macmillan $15.95 (0-02-574630-8). Wolf Larsen helps a ne'er-do-well and a female poet find their destinies in the classic that was originally published in 1904.

260 Lovecraft, H. P. *Graphic Classics: H. P. Lovecraft* (9–12). Illus. Series: Graphic Classics. 2002, Eureka paper $9.95 (0-9712464-4-0). Lovecraft's chilling stories are told in comic-book format. (Rev: BL 2/1/03)

261 Poe, Edgar Allan. *The Collected Tales and Poems of Edgar Allan Poe* (9–12). 1992, Modern Library $20.00 (0-679-60007-8). This collection of Edgar Allan Poe's writings includes such well-known works as "The Raven" and "The Murders in the Rue Morgue" plus other short stories, poems, essays, and literary criticism. [818]

262 Poe, Edgar Allan. *The Complete Tales and Poems of Edgar Allan Poe* (9–12). 1938, Modern Library $15.95 (0-394-60408-3); Random paper $16.00 (0-394-71678-7). In addition to 63 stories, this volume includes 53 poems and some nonfiction works.

263 Poe, Edgar Allan. *The Fall of the House of Usher and Other Tales* (9–12). 1960, NAL paper $2.95 (0-451-52174-9). A collection of 14 of the best known horror stories by Poe.

264 Poe, Edgar Allan. *Tales of Edgar Allan Poe* (7–12). 1991, Morrow $24.99 (0-688-07509-6). Eerie watercolor paintings illustrate 14 of Poe's most unsettling stories. (Rev: BL 8/91)

265 Stowe, Harriet Beecher. *Uncle Tom's Cabin* (10–12). Illus. 1982, Buccaneer LB $27.95 (0-89966-378-8); NAL paper $5.95 (0-451-52302-4). The American classic about slavery and racial violence in the old South.

266 Twain, Mark. *The Adventures of Huckleberry Finn* (7–12). 1993, Random $16.50 (0-679-42470-9). One of many editions of this classic.

267 Twain, Mark. *The Adventures of Tom Sawyer* (7–12). 1998, Oxford paper $5.95 (0-19-283389-8). The story of Tom, Aunt Polly, Becky Thatcher, and the villainous Injun Joe. First published in 1876.

268 Twain, Mark. *The Adventures of Tom Sawyer* (6–10). Illus. Series: Whole Story. 1996, Viking $23.99 (0-670-86984-8). In addition to the full text of Twain's novel, captioned illustrations are used to portray family life in the 1800s. One of many editions. (Rev: SLJ 1/97)

269 Twain, Mark. *The Complete Short Stories of Mark Twain* (9–12). 1957, Bantam paper $6.95 (0-553-21195-1). A total of 60 stories are included and arranged chronologically.

270 Twain, Mark. *A Connecticut Yankee in King Arthur's Court* (7–12). 1988, Morrow $24.99 (0-688-06346-2); Bantam paper $4.95 (0-553-21143-9). Through a time-travel fantasy, a swaggering Yankee is plummeted into the age of chivalry. First published in 1889. (Rev: BL 2/15/89)

271 Twain, Mark. *How Nancy Jackson Married Kate Wilson and Other Tales of Rebellious Girls and Daring Young Women* (10–12). Ed. by John Cooley. 2001, Univ. of Nebraska Pr. paper $16.95 (0-8032-9442-5). This is an unusual collection of Twain stories, all dealing with unconventional, bold, and resourceful heroines. (Rev: BL 8/01)

272 Twain, Mark. *A Murder, a Mystery, and a Marriage* (10–12). Ed. by Roy Blount Jr. 2001, Norton $16.95 (0-393-04376-2). This is a minor Twain work dealing with murder, greed, love, and a mysterious stranger in a small town called Deer Lick. (Rev: BL 8/01)

273 Twain, Mark. *The Prince and the Pauper* (7–12). 1996, Andre Deutsch $9.95 (0-233-99081-1); Airmont paper $2.50 (0-8049-0032-9). A king and a poor boy switch places in 16th-century England. First published in 1881.

274 Twain, Mark. *Pudd'nhead Wilson* (7–12). 1966, Airmont paper $2.50 (0-8049-0124-4). In the Mid-

west of over 100 years ago, a black servant switches her baby with a white couple's child to ensure that he gets a fair chance at life.

275 Twain, Mark. *Tom Sawyer Abroad [and] Tom Sawyer, Detective* (7–12). 1981, Univ. of California Pr. $45.00 (0-520-04560-2); paper $13.95 (0-520-04561-0). Two sequels to *The Adventures of Tom Sawyer*, both involving Tom and Huck.

276 Wharton, Edith. *Ethan Frome* (9–12). 1911, Macmillan $30.00 (0-684-15326-2). A love triangle involving Ethan, his wife Zeena, and her young cousin Mattie.

277 Wharton, Edith. *Novellas and Other Writings* (10–12). 1990, Library of America $45.00 (0-940450-53-4). This volume contains a memoir and eight novelettes, including *Summer* (1917) and *Ethan Frome* (1911).

278 Wolfe, Thomas. *Look Homeward, Angel* (10–12). 1997, Scribner $30.00 (0-684-84221-1). This classic American novel tells about the childhood and youth of a southern boy, Eugene Gant.

Contemporary Life and Problems

General and Miscellaneous

279 Abelove, Joan. *Saying It Out Loud* (8–12). 1999, Puffin paper $5.99 (0-14-131227-0). When Mindy's mother is dying of a brain tumor and her father provides little emotional support, Mindy turns to her friends. (Rev: BL 9/1/99; SLJ 9/99; VOYA 10/99)

280 Angell, Judie. *The Buffalo Nickel Blues Band* (7–10). 1991, Macmillan paper $3.95 (0-689-71448-3). Five youngsters form a band and are sent on the road.

281 Baird, Jon. *Songs from Nowhere Near the Heart* (10–12). Illus. 2001, St. Martin's paper $14.95 (0-312-27207-3). Life on the road with a struggling rock band is evoked through the stories of each of the main characters. (Rev: BL 4/15/01)

282 Barry, Lynda. *One Hundred Demons* (10–12). Illus. 2002, Sasquatch $24.95 (1-57061-537-0). In a combination of autobiography and fiction, comic-book creator Lynda Barry exorcises some of the demons that have haunted her personal life. (Rev: BL 8/02) [741.5]

283 Baxter, Charles. *Saul and Patsy* (10–12). 2003, Pantheon $24.00 (0-375-41029-5). Set in Michigan, this is a thoughtful and well-written story about a couple learning to cope with life in the Midwest and their struggles with one particularly difficult student. (Rev: BL 8/03*)

284 Binchy, Maeve. *Evening Class* (10–12). 1997, Delacorte $24.95 (0-385-31807-3). This novel set in Dublin brings together a diverse group of students who are attending a night school course in Italian taught by the intriguing Signora and supervised by an unhappy Latin teacher, Aidan Dunne. (Rev: SLJ 11/97)

285 Bird, Jessica. *Leaping Hearts* (11–12). 2002, Ballantine paper $6.99 (0-8041-1988-0). A former champion rider, still distraught over the accident that crippled him and left his horse dead, reluctantly agrees to help an attractive young lady with an unruly stallion; for mature teens. (Rev: BL 7/02)

286 Brashares, Ann. *The Second Summer of the Sisterhood* (8–12). 2003, Delacorte LB $17.99 (0-385-90852-0). Those traveling jeans continue to work their wonders for the four friends as they cope with romantic, family, and school challenges in this sequel that can be enjoyed without reading the earlier novel. (Rev: BL 4/15/03; HB 5–6/03; HBG 10/03; SLJ 5/03; VOYA 8/03)

287 Brooks, Bruce. *Dolores: Seven Stories About Her* (8–12). 2002, HarperCollins LB $15.89 (0-06-029473-6). Dolores is kidnapped, gossiped about, and fought over — but always manages to come out all right — in these stories that take her from age 7 to 16. (Rev: BCCB 5/02; BL 5/15/02; HBG 10/02; SLJ 4/02; VOYA 6/02)

288 Buckley, William F. *Elvis in the Morning* (10–12). 2001, Harcourt $25.00 (0-15-100643-1). An interesting story about Elvis Presley and his friendship with a Frenchman named Orson Killere, who follows him back to the United States after Elvis's Army days. (Rev: BL 5/1/01)

289 Cabot, Meg. *Boy Meets Girl* (9–12). 2004, Avon paper $13.95 (0-06-008545-2). Told in a series of e-mails, phone messages, and journal articles, this delightful novel reveals life behind the scenes of a New York newspaper. (Rev: BL 1/1–15/04)

290 Capote, Truman. *Other Voices, Other Rooms* (10–12). 1968, Random paper $12.00 (0-679-74564-5). Capote's first success as an novelist deals with a rundown Louisiana mansion peopled with eccentrics as seen through the eyes of a young boy.

291 Carroll, Jenny. *Sanctuary* (7–12). Series: 1-800-Where-R-You. 2002, Simon & Schuster paper $5.99 (0-7434-1142-0). Jessica uses her psychic ability in an effort to rescue a boy being held by a white supremacist group. (Rev: SLJ 1/03)

292 Carroll, Jenny. *When Lightning Strikes* (6–12). Series: 1-800-Where-R-You. 2001, Pocket paper $5.99 (0-7434-1139-0). When 16-year-old Jessica is struck by lightning, she acquires psychic powers. In the sequel *Code Name Cassandra*, she tries unsuccessfully to live the life of a normal teen. (Rev: BL 5/15/01)

293 Cheripko, Jan. *Rat* (7–12). 2002, Boyds Mills $15.95 (1-59078-034-5). Fifteen-year-old Jeremy faces difficult choices in this novel that looks at

moral questions against a backdrop of basketball. (Rev: HBG 10/03; SLJ 8/02)

294 Clark, Catherine. *Frozen Rodeo* (8–12). 2003, HarperCollins LB $16.89 (0-06-623008-5). What starts out as a dull summer has its high points for P.F. (Peggy Fleming) Farrell as she enjoys a teen romance, foils a robbery, and even finds time to help deliver her mother's baby. (Rev: BL 2/15/03; HBG 10/03; SLJ 3/03; VOYA 4/03)

295 Clinton, Cathryn. *The Calling* (6–10). 2001, Candlewick $15.99 (0-7636-1387-8). Twelve-year-old Esta Lea takes her healing powers on the road in this humorous story set in the South of the 1960s. (Rev: BCCB 12/01; BL 10/1/01; HBG 3/02; SLJ 8/01; VOYA 2/02)

296 Cobb, Katie. *Happenings* (6–10). 2002, Harper-Collins LB $15.89 (0-06-028928-7); paper $5.95 (0-06-447232-9). Kelsey and her classmates start a protest against their AP English teacher that spirals out of control, causing conflict between Kelsey and her guardian brother. (Rev: BL 3/1/02; HBG 10/02; SLJ 3/02; VOYA 2/02)

297 Coles, William E. *Compass in the Blood* (7–12). 2001, Simon & Schuster $16.00 (0-689-83181-1). A college student learns about betrayal while researching the story of a prison warden's wife who was accused of helping notorious villains to escape in 1902. (Rev: BL 5/1/01; HBG 10/01; SLJ 6/01; VOYA 8/01)

298 Coman, Carolyn. *Many Stones* (7–12). 2000, Front Street $15.95 (1-886910-55-3). A year after her sister was murdered there, Berry reluctantly travels with her father to South Africa to attend her memorial in this novel set during the proceedings of the Truth and Reconciliation Commission. (Rev: BL 11/1/00; BR 1–2/01; HB 1–2/01; HBG 3/01; SLJ 11/00*; VOYA 2/01)

299 Cooley, Beth. *Ostrich Eye* (7–10). 2004, Delacorte LB $17.99 (0-385-90132-1). Ginger decides that the photographer who is following her and her young sister is her long-lost father, with consequences that are nearly tragic. (Rev: BL 11/15/03; SLJ 1/04)

300 Craven, Margaret. *I Heard the Owl Call My Name* (7–12). 1973, Dell paper $6.99 (0-440-34369-0). A terminally ill Anglican priest and his assignment in a coastal Indian community in British Columbia. The nonfiction story behind this book is told in *Again Calls the Owl*.

301 Crew, Linda. *Brides of Eden: A True Story Imagined* (7–12). 2001, HarperCollins LB $15.89 (0-06-028751-9). Teenage Eva Mae Hurt describes the influence that magnetic preacher Joshua Crefield has on a group of women, who renounce their families and their everyday lives to follow his lead in this book based on fact, set in early 20th-century

Oregon. (Rev: BCCB 2/01; BL 12/15/00; HB 3–4/01; HBG 10/01; SLJ 2/01; VOYA 6/01)

302 Crutcher, Chris. *Whale Talk* (8–12). 2001, Greenwillow LB $15.89 (0-06-029369-1). T.J. Jones, a bright high school senior of mixed race who dislikes bullies and bigots, recounts his efforts to right some wrongs through recruiting unusual choices to his swim team. (Rev: BCCB 4/01; BL 4/1/01; HB 5–6/01; HBG 10/01; SLJ 5/01)

303 Deaver, Julie Reece. *Say Goodnight Gracie* (8–10). 1988, HarperCollins $15.00 (0-06-021418-X); paper $5.99 (0-06-447007-5). When her best friend Jimmy dies in an accident, Morgan struggles with her grief. (Rev: SLJ 2/88)

304 Doster, Stephen. *Lord Baltimore* (10–12). 2002, John F. Blair $22.95 (0-89587-264-1). A naive young man sets off on a maturing, adventure-filled journey through Georgia, collecting strange characters as he goes. (Rev: BL 5/15/02)

305 Doyon, Stephanie. *Taking Chances* (6–10). Series: On the Road. 1999, Simon & Schuster paper $4.50 (0-689-82109-3). Miranda and Kirsten compete for the same boy while on their way to California in this third book in the series. (Rev: SLJ 2/00)

306 Draper, Sharon M. *The Battle of Jericho* (7–10). 2003, Simon & Schuster $16.95 (0-689-84232-5). Sixteen-year-old Jericho is initially thrilled when he's asked to pledge for membership in the Warriors of Distinction club, but subsequent events turn chilling. (Rev: BL 6/1–15/03; HBG 4/04; SLJ 6/03; VOYA 8/03)

307 Draper, Sharon M. *Darkness Before Dawn* (8–12). Series: Hazelwood High. 2001, Simon & Schuster $16.95 (0-689-83080-7). Keisha Montgomery copes with many issues — the suicide of her ex-boyfriend, a new relationship, date rape, and more in this novel set at Hazelwood High. (Rev: BCCB 3/01; BL 1/1–15/01; HBG 10/01; SLJ 2/01; VOYA 8/01)

308 Draper, Sharon M. *Double Dutch* (7–10). 2002, Simon & Schuster $16.00 (0-689-84230-9). Eighth-graders Delia and Randy both have secrets — Delia can't read and Randy's father has disappeared, leaving him on his own. (Rev: BCCB 10/02; BL 9/1/02; HBG 10/02; SLJ 6/02; VOYA 8/02)

309 Elliot, Scott. *Coiled in the Heart* (11–12). 2003, Putnam $23.95 (0-399-15038-2). Young Tobias Caldwell has difficulty adapting when his father starts selling off parts of their southern plantation; and much as he likes his new neighbor Merritt, he truly dislikes her bullying twin brother Ben. (Rev: BL 8/03)

310 Ellis, Jamellah. *That Faith, That Trust, That Love* (10–12). 2003, Villard paper $12.95 (0-8129-6656-2). A young African American woman's new-found religious faith gives her strength to reassess

her engagement and to look after her ailing mother. (Rev: BL 2/1/03)

311 Finch, Susan. *The Intimacy of Indiana* (8–12). 2001, Tudor $15.95 (0-936389-79-6). Readers follow three teens through the trials of their senior year in high school in small-town Indiana — SATs, college finance, romance, drugs, and of course parents. (Rev: BL 7/01)

312 Fleischman, Paul. *Seek* (7–12). 2001, Cricket $16.95 (0-8126-4900-1). For a school autobiography project, 17-year-old Rob makes a recording of important sounds in his life, including the voice of the father he never knew. (Rev: BCCB 11/01; BL 12/15/01; HB 11–12/01; HBG 3/02; SLJ 9/01*; VOYA 12/01)

313 Frank, Hillary. *Better Than Running at Night* (10–12). 2002, Houghton $17.00 (0-618-10439-9); paper $10.00 (0-618-25073-5). An entertaining portrayal of a freshman college student's growth in confidence about her romantic and academic life. (Rev: BCCB 10/02; BL 10/02*; HBG 3/03; LMC 4–5/03; SLJ 1/03; VOYA 2/03)

314 Freymann-Weyr, Garret. *The Kings Are Already Here* (7–10). 2003, Houghton $15.00 (0-618-26363-2). Phebe's love of ballet dominates her life until she travels to Geneva to visit her father and meets Nikolai, a 16-year-old refugee who is obsessed with chess. (Rev: BL 2/15/03; HB 3–4/03; HBG 10/03; SLJ 4/03; VOYA 4/03)

315 Freymann-Weyr, Garret. *When I Was Older* (8–12). 2000, Houghton $15.00 (0-618-05545-2). The death of her younger brother precipitated the breakup of her parents' marriage, and Sophie has been careful to avoid new relationships until she meets Francis. (Rev: BL 11/1/00; HB 1–2/01; HBG 3/01; SLJ 10/00*)

316 Garcia, Cristina. *The Aguero Sisters: A Novel* (10–12). 1997, Knopf $24.00 (0-679-45090-4). Two half-sisters, one in the United States and the other in Cuba, try to forget their hatred of one another to find the truth about their parentage. (Rev: BL 5/1/97; SLJ 9/97)

317 Gilbert, Barbara Snow. *Paper Trail* (7–10). 2000, Front Street $15.95 (1-886910-44-8). A thought-provoking story of a boy torn between family loyalties and connections to a cult known as the Soldiers of God. (Rev: BL 7/00; HB 7–8/00; HBG 9/00; SLJ 8/00)

318 Glenn, Mel. *Foreign Exchange* (7–12). 1999, Morrow $16.99 (0-688-16472-2). Through free-verse reflections of teens and adults, the murder of a small-town girl is explored and, with it, the underlying prejudices, anger, and secrets of the town are revealed. (Rev: BL 4/15/99; SLJ 6/99; VOYA 12/99)

319 Glick, Susan. *One Shot* (6–12). 2003, Holt $16.95 (0-8050-6844-9). Lorrie reluctantly takes on a job helping a famous photographer to sort the contents of her house, but she soon becomes fascinated by the elderly woman's work and seeks her help with her own photography. (Rev: BCCB 6/03; HBG 10/03; SLJ 4/03; VOYA 6/03)

320 Goldsmith, Olivia. *Pen Pals* (10–12). 2002, Dutton $24.95 (0-525-94644-6). An inspiring story from the author of *The First Wives Club* (1992) about a Wall Street worker who agrees to be a point person to protect her mentor and finds herself in a women's prison. (Rev: BL 12/1/01*)

321 Goobie, Beth. *Before Wings* (7–10). 2001, Orca $16.95 (1-55143-161-0). An absorbing story that centers on the counselors at a summer camp and on 15-year-old Adrien's past illness and present mystical experiences. (Rev: BL 3/15/01; BR 11/01; HB 3–4/01; HBG 10/01; SLJ 4/01; VOYA 4/01)

322 Goobie, Beth. *The Lottery* (7–12). 2002, Orca $15.95 (1-55143-238-2). As the lottery winner, 15-year-old Sal must spend the year doing the bidding of a sinister student group, the Shadow Council. (Rev: BL 1/1–15/03; HBG 10/03; SLJ 3/03; VOYA 2/03)

323 Gowdy, Barbara. *The Romantic* (10–12). 2003, Holt $24.00 (0-8050-7190-3). Louise has loved Abel from a young age, but as she matures she discovers that he doesn't offer all the comfort she sought. (Rev: BL 5/15/03)

324 Guterson, David. *Our Lady of the Forest* (11–12). 2003, Knopf $25.95 (0-375-41211-5). A teenager becomes convinced that she has seen the Virgin Mary in the Pacific Northwest rain forest. (Rev: BL 8/03; SLJ 1/04)

325 Hay, Elizabeth. *Garbo Laughs* (11–12). 2003, Counterpoint $25.00 (1-58243-291-0). Obsession with movies is central to this compelling story full of characters who find celluloid essential to their lies. (Rev: BL 9/1/03*)

326 High, Linda Oatman. *Sister Slam and the Poetic Motormouth Road Trip* (8–12). 2004, Bloomsbury $16.95 (1-58234-948-7). Laura Rose Crapper, aka Sister Slam, and her friend Twig head for New York, where they meet a handsome boy named Jake. (Rev: BL 5/1/04; SLJ 5/04)

327 Hinton, Lynne. *The Things I Know Best* (10–12). 2001, HarperSF $20.00 (0-06-251727-9). An 18-year-old girl growing up in a small southern town shares her family's gift of foretelling the future. (Rev: BL 5/15/01)

328 Hirshberg, Glen. *The Snowman's Children* (10–12). 2002, Carroll & Graf $24.00 (0-7867-1082-9). A man is haunted by memories of his awkward childhood and the friends he had while a serial killer was stalking his neighborhood. (Rev: BL 10/1/02)

329 Hoffman, Alice. *Blue Diary* (10–12). 2001, Putnam $24.95 (0-399-14802-7). Kat sees that a photograph of a murderer shown on a "most-wanted" TV show is that of her apparently near-perfect next-door neighbor. (Rev: BL 5/15/01)

330 Holladay, Cary. *Mercury* (10–12). 2002, Harmony $22.00 (0-609-60814-2). This offbeat novel about the fatal sinking of a tourist boat intertwines stories of the survivors and of the girl who watched the accident while confined to her home. (Rev: BL 3/15/02)

331 Holtwijk, Ineke. *Asphalt Angels* (8–12). Trans. by Wanda Boeke. 1999, Front Street $15.95 (1-886910-24-3). When a homeless boy in the slums of Rio de Janeiro joins a street gang, the Asphalt Angels, for protection from corrupt police officers, pedophiles, and other homeless people, he finds himself being drawn into a life of crime. (Rev: BL 8/99; HBG 4/00; SLJ 9/99; VOYA 12/99)

332 Holubitsky, Katherine. *Last Summer in Agatha* (6–10). 2001, Orca $16.95 (1-55143-188-2); paper $9.95 (1-55143-190-4). Rachel enjoys her summer in a small Canadian town but is distressed by her new friend Michael's continuing grief over his brother's death. (Rev: HBG 3/02; SLJ 12/01)

333 Hruby, Andes. *The Trouble with Catherine* (10–12). 2002, Dutton $23.95 (0-525-94640-3). Catherine, a 29-year-old with a good deal of common sense, finds herself ambivalent about her upcoming marriage to Steve. (Rev: BL 1/1–15/02)

334 Ingold, Jeanette. *Airfield* (7–10). 1999, Harcourt $17.00 (0-15-202053-5); Puffin paper $5.99 (0-14-131216-5). In the early days of aviation, Beatty, 15, spends time at the airport, making a good friend and hoping to see her pilot father and learn more from him about her dead mother. (Rev: BCCB 1/00; HBG 4/00; SLJ 10/99; VOYA 2/00)

335 Jenkins, A. M. *Out of Order* (8–10). 2003, HarperCollins LB $16.89 (0-06-623969-9). Sophomore Colt relies on his good looks and athletic prowess to pull him through, but failing grades place him in the company of a brainy girl and his attitudes begin to change. (Rev: BL 9/1/03; HB 11–12/03; HBG 4/04; SLJ 9/03*; VOYA 10/03)

336 Jernigan, Brenda. *Every Good and Perfect Gift* (10–12). 2001, Crown $23.00 (0-609-60790-1). Ten-year-old Maggie has a vision of God — who is a woman — and a gift for healing, but runs afoul of the religious leaders in her small North Carolina town. (Rev: BL 5/15/01)

337 *Jump: Poetry and Prose by WritersCorps Youth* (6–12). Ed. by Valerie Chow Bush. 2001, WritersCorps $12.95 (1-888048-06-9). This collection of prose and poetry showcases the creativity of teenage members of the San Francisco-based WritersCorps youth writing program. (Rev: VOYA 6/02)

338 Karr, Kathleen. *Gilbert and Sullivan Set Me Free* (6–10). 2003, Hyperion $15.99 (0-7868-1916-2). A production of Gilbert and Sullivan's "Pirates of Penzance" brings together the inmates of a women's prison in this story based on a true 1914 event. (Rev: BCCB 9/03; BL 5/15/03; HB 7–8/03; HBG 10/03; SLJ 7/03; VOYA 6/03)

339 Kenney, Charles. *The Last Man* (10–12). 2001, Ballantine $23.95 (0-449-00588-7). A spellbinding novel about an elderly Polish woman, now living in Boston, who recognizes a Nazi officer from her death-camp days. (Rev: BL 4/15/01)

340 Kerr, M. E. *Deliver Us from Evie* (10–12). 1995, HarperTrophy paper $5.99 (0-06-447128-4). A multilayered story about the impact on the individual members of a Missouri farm family when 18-year-old Evie enters a lesbian relationship with the local banker's daughter. (Rev: BL 9/15/94; HB 1/95*)

341 Kowalski, William. *The Adventures of Flash Jackson* (11–12). 2003, HarperCollins $24.95 (0-06-621136-0). Seventeen-year-old Haley Bombauer (aka Flash Jackson), her wings clipped by a fall, spends a revealing time with her multitalented and eccentric grandmother. (Rev: BL 1/1–15/03; VOYA 8/03)

342 Krusoe, Jim. *Iceland* (11–12). 2002, Dalkey Archive paper $14.95 (1-56478-314-6). This offbeat novel follows typewriter repairman Paul through successive, strangely surreal medical and romantic encounters; for mature teens. (Rev: BL 5/15/02*)

343 Lamm, Drew. *Bittersweet* (8–11). 2003, Clarion $15.00 (0-618-16443-X). When Taylor's grandmother, who has essentially raised her, falls ill, artist Taylor suddenly finds she lacks creativity and is unsure of her other relationships. (Rev: BCCB 2/04; BL 11/15/03; HBG 4/04; SLJ 12/03; VOYA 12/03)

344 Lewis, Wendy. *Graveyard Girl* (7–10). 2000, Red Deer paper $7.95 (0-88995-202-7). While looking back at her high school yearbook, Ginger reminisces about her classmates and vignettes reveal their stories of marriage, achievement, and lost romance. (Rev: BL 1/1–15/01; SLJ 5/01; VOYA 6/01)

345 Lowry, Brigid. *Guitar Highway Rose* (8–12). 2003, Holiday $16.95 (0-8234-1790-5). Set in Australia, this story of two teens who run away from home presents the voices of various characters including teachers, family, and friends. (Rev: BL 2/15/04; HBG 4/04; SLJ 12/03; VOYA 4/04)

346 McCorkle, Jill. *Carolina Moon* (10–12). 1996, Algonquin $29.95 (1-56512-136-8). Quee opens a no-smoking clinic in Fulton, North Carolina, and finds that her staff and clients have a number of problems in addition to smoking in this novel that combines romance, mystery, and humor. (Rev: BL 5/1/98; SLJ 1/97)

347 MacCullough, Carolyn. *Falling Through Darkness* (7–12). 2003, Roaring Brook LB $22.90 (0-7613-2792-4). After her boyfriend is killed, Ginny retreats into herself, reliving their time together and avoiding contact with others. (Rev: BL 11/15/03; HB 11–12/03; HBG 4/04; SLJ 11/03; VOYA 4/04)

348 MacDonald, Ann-Marie. *The Way the Crow Flies* (11–12). 2003, HarperCollins $26.95 (0-06-057895-5). In the early 1960s, an innocently happy family finds that it must confront issues including former Nazis and sex abuse of an 8-year-old; for mature readers. (Rev: BL 9/1/03*)

349 McDonald, Janet. *Twists and Turns* (7–12). 2003, Farrar $16.00 (0-374-39955-7). Sisters Keeba and Teesha, who have successfully navigated their way through high school, open a hair salon in the projects of Brooklyn Heights and face new challenges. (Rev: BL 7/03*; HB 9–10/03; HBG 4/04; SLJ 9/03; VOYA 12/03)

350 McLaughlin, Emma, and Nicola Kraus. *The Nanny Diaries* (10–12). 2002, St. Martin's $24.95 (0-312-27858-6). Nanny (her real name) discovers the dark side of New York City's elite when she becomes a nanny for a wealthy family in this humorous novel based on the authors' experiences. (Rev: BL 2/1/02; VOYA 12/02)

351 Macomber, Debbie. *Thursdays at Eight* (10–12). 2001, MIRA $22.95 (1-55166-811-4). After meeting in a journal-writing class, four women get to know each other—and each other's problems—when they get together for a weekly breakfast. (Rev: BL 5/1/01)

352 Manning, Sarra. *Guitar Girl* (9–12). 2004, Dutton $15.99 (0-525-47234-7). Using a journal format, Molly Montgomery tells how she is being sued by her former record company in this British story about the music scene. (Rev: BL 5/1/04; SLJ 4/04; VOYA 6/04)

353 Mansbach, Adam. *Shackling Water* (11–12). 2002, Doubleday $22.95 (0-385-50205-2). In his quest to become a famous saxophone player, African American teenager Latif travels to New York City, where he becomes caught up with a fast and dangerous crowd; for mature teens. (Rev: BL 2/15/02*)

354 Marshall, Bev. *Walking Through Shadows* (11–12). 2002, MacAdam $25.00 (1-931561-05-2). In 1940s Mississippi, a girl with a humped back finds a generous employer and a young husband only to be murdered soon afterward; for mature readers. (Rev: BL 3/15/02; SLJ 8/02)

355 Mass, Wendy. *Leap Day* (8–12). 2004, Little, Brown $16.95 (0-316-53728-4). A leap year baby tells what she does on her fourth (actually sixteenth) birthday and some of the surprises she experiences. (Rev: BL 2/15/04; HB 5–6/04; SLJ 3/04; VOYA 2/04)

356 Minter, J. *The Insiders* (9–12). 2004, Blooms-bury paper $8.95 (1-58234-895-2). A novel about upper-class Manhattan teens, their social lives, and how they spend their parents' money. (Rev: BL 5/15/04; SLJ 6/04)

357 Moeyaert, Bart. *Hornet's Nest* (8–10). Trans. from Dutch by David Colmer. 2000, Front Street $15.95 (1-886910-48-0). Translated from Dutch, this is a fablelike story of Susanna's efforts to solve some of the problems in her life and her village. (Rev: BL 9/15/00; HB 11–12/00; HBG 3/01; SLJ 11/00)

358 Monroe, Mary Alice. *Skyward* (11–12). 2003, MIRA paper $6.99 (1-55166-700-2). Lonely Harris devotes his life to wounded birds of prey on the coast of South Carolina and learns to love Ella, the nurse who looks after his diabetic daughter. (Rev: BL 7/03*)

359 Moore, Terry. *Strangers in Paradise: High School* (10–12). Series: Strangers in Paradise. 1998, Abstract Studio paper $8.95 (1-892597-07-1). Francine and Katchoo become friends in high school, setting off the events chronicled in the adult Strangers in Paradise series. (Rev: BL 2/1/03)

360 Moriarty, Jaclyn. *Feeling Sorry for Celia: A Novel* (7–12). 2001, St. Martin's $16.95 (0-312-26923-4). The teenage uncertainties and complex family and peer relationships of a 15-year-old Australian girl are revealed through a series of notes and letters. (Rev: BL 11/15/00; BR 5/01; SLJ 5/01; VOYA 4/01)

361 Morris, Deborah. *Teens 911: Snowbound, Helicopter Crash and Other True Survival Stories* (7–12). 2002, Health Communications paper $12.95 (0-7573-0039-1). Five stories that portray teens facing emergencies (being stranded, in helicopter crashes, rescuing residents of burning houses, and so forth) are followed by postscripts and survival quizzes. (Rev: SLJ 2/03; VOYA 2/03)

362 Mukherjee, Bharati. *Desirable Daughters* (11–12). 2002, Hyperion $24.95 (0-7868-6598-9). A woman from a traditional Hindu family abandons her comfortable San Francisco life and faces some startling developments, including her son's declaration that he is gay; for mature teens. (Rev: BL 2/1/02)

363 Myers, Walter Dean. *Monster* (9–12). Illus. 1999, HarperCollins LB $14.89 (0-06-028078-6). Sixteen-year-old African American Steve, who is on trial for his role in a fatal robbery, uses film script and a journal to convey his anguish in this novel illustrated with black-and-white photographs. (Rev: BL 5/1/99; BR 9–10/99; HB 5–6/99; HBG 9/99; SLJ 7/99; VOYA 8/99)

364 Naylor, Phyllis Reynolds. *Blizzard's Wake* (7–12). 2002, Simon & Schuster $16.95 (0-689-85220-7). In a blizzard in 1941, 15-year-old Kate comes face to face with the man who caused her mother's death. (Rev: BCCB 1/03; BL 10/15/02; HBG 3/03; SLJ 12/02)

365 Newman, Nancy. *Disturbing the Peace* (11–12). 2002, Avon paper $13.95 (0-380-79839-5). Sarah, who teaches English as a second language to immigrants in New York City, becomes preoccupied with her search for her birth mother; for mature teens. (Rev: BL 1/1–15/02)

366 Nolan, Han. *When We Were Saints* (7–10). 2003, Harcourt $17.00 (0-15-216371-9). After his grandfather's death, Archie, 14, is overwhelmed by a need to find God and, with his religious friend Clare, sets off on a pilgrimage to the Cloisters in New York. (Rev: BL 10/1/03; HBG 4/04; SLJ 11/03; VOYA 12/03)

367 O'Brien, Judith. *Mary Jane* (7–10). 2003, Marvel $14.99 (0-7851-1308-8). Mary Jane has been fond of budding Spider-Man Peter Parker since they were both nine years old and now, in high school, she has a definite crush. (Rev: SLJ 12/03)

368 O'Dell, Tawni. *Coal Run* (10–12). 2004, Viking $24.95 (0-670-89995-X). Set in a run-down Pennsylvania mining town, this novel tells how the lives of two men intersect in an unusual way. (Rev: BL 5/1/04*)

369 O'Keefe, Matt. *You Think You Hear* (10–12). 2001, St. Martin's $23.95 (0-312-26903-X). In this novel, Lou Farren, 21, describes his life as a roadie for the Day Action Band, and how he fell in love with the female drummer. (Rev: BL 3/1/01)

370 O'Keefe, Susan Heyboer. *My Life and Death by Alexandra Canarsie* (7–10). 2002, Peachtree $14.95 (1-56145-264-5). Allie, a lonely teenager, finds a friend and a mystery when she starts going to strangers' funerals. (Rev: HBG 10/02; SLJ 9/02; VOYA 4/02)

371 O'Nan, Stewart. *The Night Country; or, The Darkness on the Edge of Town* (11–12). 2003, Farrar $23.00 (0-374-22215-0). Teens who died in a car crash the year before watch the various preparations for the anniversary of the tragedy. (Rev: BL 7/03)

372 Peck, Richard. *Amanda Miranda* (7–12). 1999, Dial $16.99 (0-8037-2489-6). An enthralling story of a servant and her look-alike mistress on board the *Titanic*, based on the 1979 adult novel. (Rev: BL 11/15/99; HBG 4/00)

373 Peck, Robert Newton. *Extra Innings* (7–12). 2001, HarperCollins LB $15.89 (0-06-028868-X). Aunt Vidalia reminisces about her early years and adventures with an African American baseball team during the Depression. (Rev: BCCB 3/01; BL 2/1/01; HBG 10/01; SLJ 3/01; VOYA 8/01)

374 Powell, Randy. *Three Clams and an Oyster* (7–10). 2002, Farrar $16.00 (0-374-37526-7). Three teens who have played flag football together for years struggle to decide who should be their fourth man in this humorous and realistic novel. (Rev: BCCB 7–8/02; HB 7–8/02; HBG 10/02; SLJ 3/02; VOYA 8/02)

375 Proulx, Annie. *That Old Ace in the Hole* (11–12). 2002, Scribner $26.00 (0-684-81307-6). History and environment play important roles in this story of a young man trying to make a living in the Texas/ Oklahoma panhandle; for mature readers. (Rev: BL 10/1/02)

376 Pruett, Lynn. *Ruby River* (11–12). 2002, Grove Atlantic $24.00 (0-87113-855-7). When Hattie's daughter's illicit affair becomes public, religious elements in their Alabama town boycott Hattie's truck stop; for mature teens. (Rev: BL 9/1/02)

377 Qualey, Marsha. *One Night* (8–12). 2002, Dial $16.99 (0-8037-2602-3). Kelly, 19 and a former drug addict, meets an attractive Balkan prince and plots to feature him on her aunt's talk-radio show. (Rev: BCCB 3/02; BL 4/1/02; HBG 10/02; SLJ 6/02; VOYA 6/02)

378 Raleigh, Michael. *The Blue Moon Circus* (10–12). 2003, Sourcebooks $22.00 (1-4022-0015-3). In the early 20th century, Lewis Tully puts together a circus — full of characterful animals, adults, and one young orphan — to tour the West. (Rev: BL 3/15/03)

379 Rand, Ayn. *The Fountainhead* (10–12). 1943, NAL paper $5.99 (0-451-15823-7). Individualism and independence are the themes explored in this novel about an architect and his struggle to pursue his own ideas.

380 Randle, Kristen D. *Slumming* (8–11). 2003, HarperTempest LB $16.89 (0-06-001023-1). Three Mormon high school seniors decide to befriend the friendless and invite them to the school prom. (Rev: BCCB 9/03; BL 8/03; HB 7–8/03; HBG 4/04; SLJ 8/03; VOYA 8/03)

381 Reynolds, Marilyn. *Love Rules: True-to-Life Stories from Hamilton High* (8–12). Series: True-to-Life. 2001, Morning Glory $18.95 (1-885356-75-7); paper $9.95 (1-885356-76-5). Lynn, a white high school senior, learns about prejudice as she dates an African American football player and supports her lesbian friend Kit. (Rev: BL 8/01; HBG 3/02; SLJ 9/01; VOYA 10/01)

382 Robbins, Kenneth. *City of Churches* (10–12). 2004, NewSouth $25.95 (1-58838-142-0). Cutting back and forth in time, this novel describes the return to their southern hometown of two men, one white and the other black, both of whom lost their fathers to racial violence. (Rev: BL 3/15/04)

383 Rosen, Roger, and Patra McSharry, eds. *Border Crossings: Emigration and Exile* (8–12). Series: Icarus World Issues. 1992, Rosen LB $16.95 (0-8239-1364-3); paper $8.95 (0-8239-1365-1). Twelve fiction and nonfiction selections that illus-

trate the lives of those affected by geopolitical change. (Rev: BL 11/1/92)

384 Rougeau, Remy. *All We Know of Heaven* (10–12). 2001, Houghton $23.00 (0-618-09499-7). An unusual novel about a man's adjustment to monastic life, his coming of age, and his struggles when he enters a Trappist monastery where the monks communicate only by sign language. (Rev: BL 5/1/01*)

385 Schreiber, Ellen. *Vampire Kisses* (7–10). 2003, HarperCollins LB $16.89 (0-06-009335-8). When a new family moves into the town's old mansion, Raven, 16, imaginative, and a self-styled Goth, decides the handsome son could be a vampire. (Rev: BCCB 10/03; BL 11/15/03; HBG 4/04; SLJ 8/03; VOYA 2/04)

386 Solwitz, Sharon. *Bloody Mary* (11–12). 2003, Sarabande paper $13.95 (1-889330-93-0). Hadley has to cope alone with her first period when her epileptic mother becomes absorbed in her new lover in this tense and absorbing story of crisis and change suitable for mature readers. (Rev: BL 7/03*)

387 Spitz, Marc. *How Soon Is Never?* (11–12). 2003, Crown paper $13.00 (0-609-81040-5). Joe Green is a rock journalist who pines for the sounds he heard in high school and sets off for England to find their creators. (Rev: BL 8/03)

388 Stark, Lynette. *Escape from Heart* (7–10). 2000, Harcourt $17.00 (0-15-202385-2). Sara Ruth's uncle is the autocratic and restrictive leader of the Mennonite community in which she lives. (Rev: BR 3–4/01; HBG 3/01; SLJ 10/00)

389 Steinbeck, John. *Cannery Row* (10–12). 1945, Viking paper $7.00 (0-14-018737-5). Like the author's earlier *Tortilla Flat* (1945), this novel deals with California workers, this time involving cannery employees and their friends.

390 Stoehr, Shelley. *Wannabe* (9–12). 1997, Delacorte $15.95 (0-385-32223-2). Streetwise 17-year-old Cat falls for a young mobster but tries to save her brother, a wannabe gangster, from going in that direction in this harsh portrayal of lives on the skids. (Rev: BR 5–6/97; SLJ 1/97; VOYA 4/97)

391 Stollman, Aryeh Lev. *The Illuminated Soul* (11–12). 2002, Riverhead $23.95 (1-57322-201-1). Joseph's family, trying to keep going after the death of his father, is strangely affected by the magical, mysterious Eva; for mature teens. (Rev: BL 1/1– 15/02)

392 *The Student Body: Short Stories About College Students and Professors* (10–12). Ed. by John McNally. 2001, Univ. of Wisconsin Pr. paper $16.95 (0-299-17404-2). These short stories about college life by writers including Richard Russo and Stephen King are divided into two groups, from the students' point of view and from the teachers'. (Rev: BL 9/15/01)

393 Tashjian, Janet. *The Gospel According to Larry* (7–10). 2001, Holt $16.95 (0-8050-6378-1). When Josh (a.k.a. "Larry") publishes his anticonsumerism worldview on the Web, he develops a cult following and discovers the dark side of fame. (Rev: BCCB 1/02; BL 11/1/01; HB 1–2/02*; HBG 3/02; SLJ 10/01; VOYA 12/01)

394 Tashjian, Janet. *Vote for Larry* (7–10). 2004, Holt $16.95 (0-8050-7201-2). In this sequel to *The Gospel According to Larry* (2001), our young hero decides to run for president of the United States. (Rev: BL 5/1/04; HB 7–8/04; SLJ 5/04; VOYA 6/04)

395 Thomas, Rob. *Doing Time: Notes from the Undergrad* (8–10). 1997, Simon & Schuster $16.00 (0-689-80958-1). The 10 short stories in this fine collection deal with various aspects of volunteerism, why people participate, and their rewards. (Rev: BL 10/1/97; SLJ 11/97*; VOYA 12/97)

396 Trujillo, Carla. *What Night Brings* (11–12). 2003, Curbstone paper $15.95 (1-880684-94-2). Marci is only 11, but she is smart, alert, amusing about her family's various secrets (including drugs, homosexuality, and infidelity), and already aware that she prefers girls. (Rev: BL 3/15/03*)

397 Velasquez, Gloria. *Ankiza* (7–12). Series: Roosevelt High School. 2000, Piñata $16.95 (1-55885-308-1); paper $9.95 (1-55885-309-X). African American Ankiza learns about prejudice when she starts dating a white boy. (Rev: SLJ 4/01; VOYA 8/01)

398 Von Ziegesar, Cecily. *Gossip Girl* (10–12). 2002, Little, Brown paper $8.95 (0-316-91033-3). *Gossip Girl* is full of tales about the teens of Manhattan's Upper East Side indulging in sex, drugs, high fashion, and high drama. (Rev: BL 6/1–15/02; SLJ 6/02; VOYA 6/02)

399 Wiesel, Elie. *Night, Dawn, The Accident: Three Tales* (10–12). 1972, Hill & Wang paper $12.00 (0-374-52140-9). In *Dawn* the protagonist is a young Jewish terrorist and in *Night* the central character is a survivor of Auschwitz.

400 Williams, Laura E. *Up a Creek* (7–10). 2001, Holt $15.95 (0-8050-6453-2). Thirteen-year-old Starshine Bott, daughter of a young, single-mother activist, wonders if her mother cares more for her social causes than she does for her. (Rev: BCCB 2/01; BL 1/1–15/01; HBG 10/01; SLJ 1/01; VOYA 4/01)

401 Witchel, Alex. *Me Times Three* (10–12). 2002, Knopf $22.00 (0-375-41179-8). When Sandra discovers that her fiance has been two-timing her, she breaks off the engagement and concentrates on dating, work, and friendships in this novel that succeeds in blending humor and tragedy. (Rev: BL 1/1–15/02)

402 Wittlinger, Ellen. *The Long Night of Leo and Bree* (9–12). 2002, Simon & Schuster $15.00 (0-689-83564-7). A troubled young kidnapper and his victim, a frustrated girl from a wealthy family, pour their hearts out as they spend a tense night together. (Rev: BL 1/1–15/02; HB 3–4/02; HBG 10/02; SLJ 3/02; VOYA 2/02)

403 Wittlinger, Ellen. *Razzle* (7–12). 2001, Simon & Schuster $17.00 (0-689-83565-5). New on Cape Cod, Kenyon becomes friends with an offbeat girl named Razzle — until he falls for beautiful Harley — in this mutilayered and appealing novel. (Rev: BCCB 10/01; BL 11/1/01; HB 11–12/01; HBG 3/02; SLJ 9/01; VOYA 10/01)

404 Wolff, Virginia E. *True Believer* (7–12). 2001, Simon & Schuster $17.00 (0-689-82827-6). Poverty and violence are continuing forces in this sequel to *Make Lemonade*, in which LaVaughn fosters her college ambitions and finds romance. (Rev: BL 6/1–15/02; HB 1–2/01; HBG 10/01; SLJ 1/01; VOYA 4/01)

405 Yandell, J. Belinda. *Small Change: The Secret Life of Penny Burford* (10–12). 2002, Cumberland House $14.95 (1-58182-304-5). A housewife secretly amasses a large amount of money for charity by collecting her husband's loose change. (Rev: BL 6/1–15/02)

Ethnic Groups and Problems

406 Alcala, Kathleen. *The Flower in the Skull* (10–12). 1998, Chronicle $22.95 (0-8118-1916-7). This adult novel set in the Southwest, told by three Latina women and spanning over 100 years, tells of the assimilation of Mexicans into Anglo culture and of their hardships, inner conflicts, survival, and loss. (Rev: BL 6/1–15/98; SLJ 1/99)

407 Allen, Paula Gunn, ed. *Song of the Turtle: American Indian Literature 1974–1994* (10–12). 1997, Ballantine $25.00 (0-345-37525-4). After a brief history of Native American literature, this volume anthologizes 33 stories, many by well-known writers, that tell about being a Native American in today's world. (Rev: BL 8/96; SLJ 6/97)

408 Allen, Paula Gunn. *Spider Woman's Granddaughters: Traditional Tales and Contemporary Writing by Native American Women* (10–12). 1989, Beacon paper $14 .00 (0-449-90508-X). This is an engrossing collection of 24 traditional and modern stories by Native American women.

409 Alvarez, Julia. *How the Garcia Girls Lost Their Accents* (10–12). 1991, Algonquin $18.95 (0-945575-57-2). This novel, told in reverse chronological order, tells how the four Garcia girls and their family became Americanized after leaving the Dominican Republic in the 1960s. (Rev: SLJ 9/91)

410 Alvarez, Julia. *Yo!* (10–12). 1997, Algonquin $29.95 (1-56512-157-0). The 16 stories in this collection feature the family and friends of Yolanda Garcia, whose roots are in the Dominican Republic. (Rev: BL 9/15/96; SLJ 4/97)

411 Anaya, Rudolfo. *Bless Me Ultima* (10–12). 1994, Warner paper $6.99 (0-446-60025-3). A novel about growing up Chicano in southeastern New Mexico during the 1940s.

412 Armstrong, William H. *Sounder* (6–10). Illus. 1969, HarperCollins LB $16.89 (0-06-020144-4); paper $5.99 (0-06-440020-4). The moving story of an African American sharecropper, his family, and his devoted coon dog, Sounder. Newbery Medal winner, 1970. A sequel is *Sour Land* (1971).

413 Augenbraum, Harold, and Ilan Stavans, eds. *Growing Up Latino: Memoirs and Stories* (9–12). 1993, Houghton paper $13.95 (0-395-66124-2). The "Hispanic journey from darkness to light, from rejection to assimilation, from silence to voice," in 25 diverse, eloquent voices. (Rev: BL 2/1/93)

414 Bailey-Williams, Nicole. *A Little Piece of Sky* (7–12). 2002, Broadway paper $9.95 (0-7679-1216-0). Song Byrd is an African American girl who rises above her very difficult circumstances in this realistic and compelling novel. (Rev: VOYA 4/03)

415 Baldwin, James. *Go Tell It on the Mountain* (10–12). 1953, Knopf $14.95 (0-679-60154-6). A novel about a black boy growing up and his relationships with his father and his church.

416 Baldwin, James. *If Beale Street Could Talk* (9–12). 1986, Dell paper $6.99 (0-440-34060-8). Fonny is sent to jail for a crime he didn't commit before he can marry his pregnant girlfriend, Tish.

417 Barrett, William E. *The Lilies of the Field* (8–12). Illus. 1988, Warner paper $5.99 (0-446-31500-1). A young black man, Homer Smith, helps a group of German nuns to achieve their dream.

418 Beake, Lesley. *Song of Be* (6–12). 1993, Penguin paper $3.99 (0-14-037498-1). The tragedy of Namibian natives who are caught in a changing world is told by the character Be, a 15-year-old girl working on a white man's ranch. (Rev: BL 12/1/93*; SLJ 3/94; VOYA 4/94)

419 Bedford, Simi. *Yoruba Girl Dancing* (9–12). 1994, Viking paper $10.95 (0-14-023293-1). A semiautobiographical novel about a Nigerian girl's adjustment to life at an English boarding school in the 1950s. (Rev: BL 10/1/92; SLJ 3/93*)

420 Bell, William. *Zack* (7–12). 1999, Simon & Schuster $16.95 (0-689-82248-0). Zack Lane, a biracial teenager growing up in Ontario, travels to rural Mississippi to find his African American grandfather in this disturbing novel that explores bigotry and prejudice. (Rev: BL 5/15/99; HBG 4/00; SLJ 7/99; VOYA 8/99)

421 Bennett, O. H. *The Colored Garden* (10–12). 2000, Laughing Owl paper $12.50 (0-9659701-9-1). Sarge, newly relocated to his grandparents' farm in Kentucky, tries to find out the story behind the grave marked "Kate" in an old slave cemetery. (Rev: BL 2/15/00)

422 Bertrand, Diane Gonzales. *Sweet Fifteen* (8–12). 1995, Arte Publico paper $9.95 (1-55885-133-X). While making a party dress for Stefanie Bonilla, age 14, Rita Navarro falls in love with her uncle and befriends her widowed mother, maturing in the process. (Rev: BL 6/1–15/95; SLJ 9/95)

423 Bolden, Tonya, ed. *Rites of Passage: Stories About Growing Up by Black Writers from Around the World* (7–12). 1994, Hyperion $16.95 (1-56282-688-3). A collection of 17 stories that focus on growing up black in the United States, Africa, Australia, Great Britain, the Caribbean, and Central America. (Rev: BL 3/1/94; SLJ 6/94)

424 Brown, John Gregory. *The Wrecked, Blessed Body of Shelton LaFleur* (10–12). 1996, Houghton $21.95 (0-395-72988-2). Life in the South during the 1930s Depression is presented in this novel about a poor black child who was deformed from a fall off a tree, and his search for his family. (Rev: BL 3/1/96; SLJ 8/96)

425 Brown, Linda Beatrice. *Crossing over Jordon* (9–12). 1996, One World paper $11.00 (0-345-40231-6). From the time of slavery to the early 21st century, the women of an African American family experience love, suffering, and the struggle to be free. (Rev: BL 2/15/95; SLJ 9/95)

426 Brown, Wesley, and Amy Ling, eds. *Imagining America: Stories from the Promised Land* (9–12). 1992, Persea paper $11.95 (0-89255-167-4). A multicultural anthology of 37 stories by distinguished writers about emigration to and migration within the United States during the 20th century. (Rev: BL 12/15/91*; SLJ 6/92)

427 Canales, Viola. *Orange Candy Slices and Other Secret Tales* (6–12). 2001, Arte Publico paper $9.95 (1-55885-332-4). Life on the Texas-Mexico border is the focus of this collection of coming-of-age short stories. (Rev: VOYA 6/02)

428 Carlson, Lori M., ed. *American Eyes: New Asian-American Short Stories for Young Adults* (8–12). 1994, Holt $15.95 (0-8050-3544-3). These stories present widely varied answers to the question, What does it mean to Asian American adolescents to grow up in a country that views them as aliens? (Rev: BL 1/1/95; SLJ 1/95; VOYA 5/95)

429 Childress, Alice. *A Hero Ain't Nothin' but a Sandwich* (7–10). 2000, Putnam paper $5.99 (0-698-11854-5). Benjie's life in Harlem, told from many viewpoints, involves drugs and rejection. (Rev: BL 10/15/88)

430 Childress, Alice. *Rainbow Jordan* (7–10). 1982, Avon paper $4.99 (0-380-58974-5). Rainbow is growing up alternately in a foster home and with a mother who is too preoccupied to care for her. (Rev: BL 10/15/88)

431 Cisneros, Sandra. *Caramelo* (10–12). 2002, Knopf $24.00 (0-679-43554-9). A rich saga of a Mexican American family, focusing on the coming of age of a girl named Celaya. (Rev: BL 8/02*; SLJ 5/03)

432 Cisneros, Sandra. *House on Mango Street* (10–12). 1994, Random $24.00 (0-679-43335-X); paper $9.95 (0-679-73477-5). The rich story of a young girl, Esperanza Cordero, growing up in a deprived Latino neighborhood in Chicago and aspiring to greater things.

433 Cofer, Judith O. *An Island Like You* (7–12). 1995, Orchard LB $16.99 (0-531-08747-6). A collection of stories about Puerto Rican immigrant children experiencing tensions between two cultures. (Rev: BL 2/15/95*; SLJ 7/95)

434 Cofer, Judith O. *The Latin Deli* (9–12). 1993, Univ. of Georgia Pr. $19.95 (0-8203-1556-7). At the heart of this collection of Ortiz Coffer's stories, essays, and poems is the conflict of her childhood as a first-generation immigrant. (Rev: BL 11/15/93*)

435 Coldsmith, Don. *The Long Journey Home* (10–12). 2001, Tor $24.95 (0-312-87617-3). Based indirectly on the career of Jim Thorpe, this novel tells the story of John Buffalo, a Native American athlete who strives for and receives recognition and fame. (Rev: BL 3/15/01)

436 Cooney, Caroline B. *Burning Up* (7–10). 1999, Delacorte $15.95 (0-385-32318-2). Macey uncovers shabby family secrets and learns about herself when she investigates the senseless murder of an African American teen and a long-ago incident in her town that nearly killed an African American teacher. (Rev: BL 12/1/98; BR 9–10/99; HBG 9/99; SLJ 2/99; VOYA 2/99)

437 Cruz, Angie. *Soledad* (10–12). 2001, Simon & Schuster $23.00 (0-7432-1201-0). This novel for mature readers tells the story of a Dominican family living as immigrants in New York City's Washington Heights. (Rev: BL 8/01)

438 Deberry, Virginia, and Donna Grant. *Tryin' to Sleep in the Bed You Made* (10–12). 1997, St. Martin's $24.95 (0-312-15233-7). This novel describes the friendship, from a childhood meeting to adulthood, of three African Americans, one who loses her rich husband and becomes homeless, another who finds her destiny in the corporate world, and the third a successful baseball player haunted by his brother's death. (Rev: BL 11/1/96; SLJ 8/97)

439 Divakaruni, Chitra Banerjee. *The Unknown Errors of Our Lives* (10–12). 2001, Doubleday $23.95 (0-385-49727-X). This collection of short stories set in India and the United States portrays two worlds of Indian people, native and immigrant. (Rev: BL 3/1/01*)

440 Dorris, Michael. *A Yellow Raft in Blue Water* (10–12). 1987, Holt $16.95 (0-8050-0045-3); Warner paper $14.00 (0-446-38787-8). A stirring novel dealing with three generations of females in a Native American family, beginning in the present and moving back in time. (Rev: BL 3/1/87; BR 11–12/87; SLJ 11/87; VOYA 8/87)

441 Dry, Richard. *Leaving* (11–12). 2002, St. Martin's $24.95 (0-312-28331-8). The saga of an African American family challenged by internal and external forces; for mature teens. (Rev: BL 2/15/02*)

442 Eagle, Kathleen. *You Never Can Tell* (9–12). 2001, Morrow $24.00 (0-06-620960-9). Kole Kills Crow, a civil rights leader who escapes from prison after being set up for a murder rap, falls in love with a writer who discovers his hideout. (Rev: BL 7/01)

443 Ellison, James W. *Finding Forrester* (7–12). 2000, Newmarket paper $9.95 (1-55704-479-1). This inspiring novel tells how a reclusive author helps a promising inner-city African American youth to develop his writing skills. (Rev: SLJ 9/01; VOYA 6/01)

444 Ellison, Ralph. *Flying Home and Other Stories* (10–12). Ed. by John F. Callahan. 1996, Random $23.00 (0-679-45704-6). A collection of 13 short stories written between the 1930s and 1950s by the African American writer best known for *Invisible Man*. (Rev: BL 10/15/96; SLJ 6/97)

445 Esquivel, Laura. *Like Water for Chocolate: A Novel in Monthly Installments, with Recipes, Romances, and Home Remedies* (10–12). 1992, Doubleday $23.00 (0-385-42016-1); paper $11.95 (0-385-42017-X). Recipes introduce each chapter of this novel about a traditional Mexican family, where much of the domestic drama takes place in the kitchen. (Rev: BL 9/15/92)

446 Even, Aaron Roy. *Bloodroot* (10–12). 2000, St. Martin's $22.95 (0-312-26561-1). Based on a true story, this novel set in Virginia during the 1930s chronicles the fate of an African American man and his sister when they defy townspeople who want their property for a turpentine factory. (Rev: BL 10/1/00)

447 Flake, Sharon. *Who Am I Without Him?* (6–12). 2004, Hyperion $15.99 (0-7868-0693-1). Funny, moving, and truthful, these 10 short stories deal with growing up black in today's society. (Rev: BL 4/15/04*; HB 7–8/04; SLJ 5/04; VOYA 6/04)

448 Foster, Sharon Ewell. *Riding Through Shadows* (9–12). 2001, Multnomah paper $11.99 (1-57673-807-8). A powerful novel about a troubled girl African American girl who is coming of age in East St. Louis and Alabama in the 1960s. (Rev: BL 10/1/01)

449 Gaines, Ernest J. *The Autobiography of Miss Jane Pittman* (9–12). 1971, Bantam paper $5.99 (0-553-26357-9). This novel, supposedly the memoirs of a 110-year-old ex-slave, is a stirring tribute to survival and courage.

450 Gaines, Ernest J. *A Gathering of Old Men* (10–12). 1983, Knopf $17.95 (0-394-51468-8). A group of old black men protect their own but assume collective guilt for a crime none of them committed.

451 Gallo, Donald, ed. *Join In: Multiethnic Short Stories by Outstanding Writers for Young Adults* (7–12). 1995, Bantam paper $5.99 (0-440-21957-4). Seventeen stories concerning the problems teenagers of various ethnic backgrounds have living in the United States. (Rev: BL 1/15/94; SLJ 11/93; VOYA 10/93)

452 Gardner, Mary. *Boat People* (9–12). 1995, Norton $21.00 (0-393-03738-X). A sympathetic fictional portrait of Vietnamese refugees in Galveston, Texas. (Rev: BL 2/15/95*)

453 Garland, Sherry. *Shadow of the Dragon* (6–12). 1993, Harcourt $10.95 (0-15-273530-5); paper $6.00 (0-15-273532-1). Danny Vo has grown up American since he emigrated from Vietnam as a child. Now traditional Vietnamese ways, the new American culture, and skinhead prejudice clash, resulting in his cousin's death. (Rev: BL 11/15/93*; SLJ 11/93; VOYA 12/93)

454 Gilmore, Rachna. *A Group of One* (7–10). 2001, Holt $16.95 (0-8050-6475-3). Fifteen-year-old Tara, a Canadian, learns to value her heritage when her grandmother arrives from India. (Rev: BCCB 9/01; BL 5/1/01; HB 9–10/01; HBG 3/02; SLJ 7/01; VOYA 8/01)

455 Gordon, Sheila. *Waiting for the Rain: A Novel of South Africa* (7–12). 1996, Bantam paper $5.50 (0-440-22698-8). The story of the friendship between a black boy and a white boy in apartheid-ridden South Africa. (Rev: BL 8/87; SLJ 8/87; VOYA 12/87)

456 Grimes, Nikki. *Jazmin's Notebook* (6–10). 1998, Dial $15.99 (0-8037-2224-9). The journal of 14-year-old Jazmin, who writes about her tough, tender, and angry life in Harlem in the 1960s, living with her sister after her mother is hospitalized with a breakdown and her father has died. (Rev: BL 9/15/98; BR 1–2/99; HBG 9/98; SLJ 7/98; VOYA 10/98)

457 Grooms, Anthony. *Bombingham* (10–12). 2001, Free Pr. $24.00 (0-7432-0558-8). An African American soldier during the Vietnam War recalls his life growing up in segregated Birmingham, Alabama, during the early years of the civil rights movement. (Rev: BL 8/01; SLJ 3/02)

458 *Growing Up Ethnic in America: Contemporary Fiction About Learning to Be American* (10–12). Ed. by Maria Mazziotti Gillan and Jennifer Gillan. 1999, Penguin paper $16.95 (0-14-028063-4). Thirty-five stories by such writers as Amy Tan, Toni Morrison, and E. L. Doctorow explore the ethnic experience. (Rev: BL 9/15/99)

459 *Growing Up Filipino: Stories for Young Adults* (9–12). Ed. by Cecilia Manguerra Brainard. 2003, PALH paper $18.95 (0-9719458-0-2). These stories by Filipino American writers will comfort and delight teenagers of Filipino descent. (Rev: BL 4/15/03; SLJ 6/03)

460 Gurley-Highgate, Hilda. *Sapphire's Grave* (11–12). 2002, Doubleday $24.95 (0-385-50323-7). Successive generations of black women display hope and tenacity in the face of incredible challenges; for mature teens. (Rev: BL 12/1/02)

461 Guy, Rosa. *The Music of Summer* (9–12). 1992, Doubleday $12.00 (0-385-30704-7). Sarah, age 17, weighs the pain of peer pressure against the excitement of first love during one summer on Cape Cod. (Rev: BL 4/15/92; SLJ 2/92)

462 Hale, Janet Campbell. *The Owl's Song* (10–12). 1976, Avon paper $2.50 (0-380-00605-7). A Native American boy faces new problems when he leaves the reservation to live with a half-sister in Los Angeles.

463 Haley, Alex, and David Stevens. *Mama Flora's Family* (10–12). 1998, Scribner $25.00 (0-684-83471-5). This novel traces an African American family from 1929 through 1968 and tells of the indomitable Flora and her struggle to keep her three children and their offspring intact through the troubled days of integration. (Rev: BL 8/98; SLJ 3/99)

464 Hamilton, Julia. *Other People's Rules* (10–12). 2000, St. Martin's $24.95 (0-312-26627-8). In this gripping novel for mature readers, 15-year-old Lucy enjoys the lifestyle of her aristocratic friend Sarah but later discovers ugly truths about Sarah's family. (Rev: BL 10/1/00)

465 Hamilton, Virginia. *A White Romance* (8–12). 1987, Scholastic paper $4.50 (0-590-13005-6). A formerly all-black high school becomes integrated and social values and relationships change. (Rev: SLJ 1/88; VOYA 2/88)

466 Hardrick, Jackie. *Imani in Never Say Goodbye* (9–12). 2004, Enlighten paper $15.00 (0-9706226-2-7). The life of 17-year-old Imani, a typical African American high school student, intersects with many others who have greater problems than she does. (Rev: BL 2/15/04; SLJ 4/04; VOYA 12/03)

467 Harris, Marilyn. *Hatter Fox* (9–12). 1986, Ballantine paper $5.99 (0-345-33157-5). A touching novel about a young Navaho girl and her many problems.

468 Hazelgrove, William Elliot. *Tobacco Sticks* (9–12). 1995, Pantonne Pr. $18.95 (0-9630052-8-6). Racial tensions come to a peak in 1945 Richmond, Virginia, when 13-year-old Lee Hartwell's lawyer father defends an African American maid in court. (Rev: BL 7/95; SLJ 9/95)

469 *Herencia: The Anthology of Hispanic Literature in the United States* (10–12). Ed. by Nicolas Kanellos et al. 2001, Oxford $30.00 (0-19-513824-4). This anthology traces the history of Hispanic writing in the U.S. from the chronicles of the early explorers to contemporary writers including Oscar Hijuelos and Reinaldo Arenas. (Rev: BL 10/15/01) [810.8]

470 Hernandez, Irene B. *Across the Great River* (7–10). 1989, Arte Publico paper $9.95 (0-934770-96-4). The harrowing story of a young Mexican girl and her family, who enter the United States illegally. (Rev: BL 8/89; SLJ 8/89)

471 Hernandez, Jo Ann Y. *White Bread Competition* (7–12). 1997, Arte Publico paper $9.95 (1-55885-210-7). The effects of winning a spelling bee on Luz Rios and her Hispanic American family in San Antonio are explored in a series of vignettes. (Rev: BL 1/1–15/98; BR 9–10/98; SLJ 8/98; VOYA 4/98)

472 Hewett, Lorri. *Dancer* (7–10). 1999, Dutton $15.99 (0-525-45968-5). A 16-year-old African American ballet student faces several obstacles, including hostile classmates and a father who doesn't approve of her career choice. (Rev: BL 8/99; HB 9–10/99; HBG 4/00)

473 Hewett, Lorri. *Soulfire* (7–12). Illus. 1996, Penguin paper $5.99 (0-14-038960-1). Todd Williams, 16, begins to take responsibility for his actions and seeks direction for his life in this coming-of-age novel set in the Denver projects. (Rev: BL 5/1/96; BR 9–10/96; SLJ 6/96*; VOYA 10/96)

474 Hidier, Tanuja Desai. *Born Confused* (9–12). 2002, Scholastic $16.95 (0-439-35762-4). Dimple Lala, a 17-year-old of Indian heritage who has been doing her best to fit in in America, is less than thrilled by her parents' choice of a suitor in this well-written novel. (Rev: BL 12/15/02; HBG 10/03; SLJ 12/02; VOYA 2/03)

475 Hobbs, Will. *Bearstone* (7–10). 1989, Macmillan $17.00 (0-689-31496-5). A hostile, resentful Indian teenager is sent to live with a rancher in Colorado. (Rev: BL 11/1/89; BR 3–4/90; SLJ 9/89; VOYA 12/89)

476 Hong, Maria, ed. *Growing Up Asian American* (9–12). 1995, Avon paper $12.50 (0-380-72418-9). This collection of stories and essays looks at the Asian American experience through such issues as education stratification, kinship, beauty standards, and intraethnic conflicts. (Rev: BL 12/15/93)

477 Hurston, Zora Neale. *Their Eyes Were Watching God* (10–12). 1990, Demco $18.85 (0-606-04401-

9). A novel about black Americans in Florida that centers on the life of Janie and her three marriages. First published in 1937.

478 Irwin, Hadley. *Kim / Kimi* (7–10). 1987, Macmillan $16.00 (0-689-50428-4); Penguin paper $5.99 (0-14-032593-X). A half-Japanese teenager brought up in an all-white small town sets out to explore her Asian roots. (Rev: BL 3/15/87; SLJ 5/87; VOYA 6/87)

479 Jackson, Brian Keith. *The View from Here* (10–12). 1998, Pocket paper $14.00 (0-671-56896-5). Set in rural Mississippi in the 1960s, this emotion-charged novel, told from various points of view, tells of a black family's struggle to succeed. (Rev: BL 2/15/97; SLJ 3/97)

480 Jimenez, Francisco. *The Circuit: Stories from the Life of a Migrant Child* (5–10). 1997, Univ. of New Mexico Pr. paper $10.95 (0-8263-1797-9). Eleven moving stories about the lives, fears, hopes, and problems of children in Mexican migrant worker families. (Rev: BL 12/1/97)

481 Johnson, Angela. *Toning the Sweep* (7–12). 1993, Scholastic paper $5.99 (0-590-48142-8). This novel captures the innocence, vulnerability, and love of human interaction, as well as the melancholy, self-discovery, and introspection of an African American adolescent. (Rev: BL 4/1/93*; SLJ 4/93*)

482 Johnson-Coleman, Lorraine. *Just Plain Folks* (10–12). 1998, Little, Brown $22.00 (0-316-46084-2). Rural blacks from the South are introduced in these short stories about ordinary people who lived during the periods of slavery, Reconstruction, the Depression, and the Civil Rights era, based on interviews conducted by the author as she traveled through her home state of North Carolina. (Rev: SLJ 5/99)

483 Kadohota, Cynthia. *Kira-Kira* (6–12). 2004, Simon & Schuster $15.95 (0-689-85639-3). The tale of two Japanese Americans who encounter prejudice in Georgia during the 1950s and how they help one another. (Rev: BL 5/15/04; HB 3–4/04; SLJ 3/04)

484 Kelley, William. *The Sweet Summer* (10–12). 2000, Westminster $19.95 (0-664-22224-2). A novel set in the 1940s about a white Army recruit who wins a position on an all-black boxing team. (Rev: BL 4/15/00)

485 Killens, John Oliver, and Jerry W. Ward, eds. *Black Southern Voices: An Anthology of Fiction, Poetry, Drama, Nonfiction, and Critical Essays* (9–12). 1992, NAL paper $15.00 (0-452-01096-9). Essays, poetry, drama, and fiction by such familiar names as Arna Bontemps, Alice Walker, and Nikki Giovanni, as well as less-well-known writers. (Rev: BL 10/15/92)

486 Kincaid, Jamaica. *The Autobiography of My Mother* (9–12). 1996, Farrar $20.00 (0-374-10731-9); NAL paper $10.95 (0-452-27466-4). Kincaid's essay *A Small Place* is expanded into this novel about a woman's search for identity as she searches for her mother. (Rev: BL 12/1/95*)

487 *Kori: The Beacon Anthology of Korean-American Fiction* (10–12). Ed. by Heinz Insu Fenkl and Walter K. Lew. 2001, Beacon $23.00 (0-8070-5916-1). These stories dealing with family and society all have Korean Americans as leading characters. (Rev: BL 6/1–15/01)

488 Lahiri, Jhumpa. *The Namesake* (11–12). 2003, Houghton $24.00 (0-395-92721-8). A young Bengali American struggles to escape his heritage and the strange name his father has given him: Gogol. (Rev: BL 6/1–15/03; SLJ 11/03)

489 Laird, Elizabeth. *Kiss the Dust* (6–10). 1992, Penguin $6.99 (0-14-036855-8). A docunovel about a refugee Kurdish teen caught up in the 1984 Iran-Iraq War. (Rev: BL 6/15/92)

490 Lansdale, Joe R. *The Bottoms* (10–12). 2000, Mysterious $24.95 (0-89296-704-8). Reminiscent of *To Kill a Mockingbird,* this novel set in East Texas in the early 1930s features two white youngsters and their father, caught up in the racially motivated murder of a young black woman. (Rev: BL 6/1–15/00; SLJ 1/01)

491 Lansens, Lori. *Rush Home Road* (11–12). 2002, Little, Brown $23.95 (0-316-06902-7). When an elderly Canadian black woman takes in an abandoned 5-year-old, she finds herself reviewing the many tragedies of her own life. (Rev: BL 5/1/02)

492 Lee, Gus. *China Boy* (9–12). 1994, NAL paper $11.95 (0-452-27158-4). Kai — or "China Boy," as he is called by the neighborhood bullies — turns his life around when he learns to stand his ground and fight back. (Rev: BL 3/1/91)

493 Lee, Gus. *Honor and Duty* (9–12). 1994, Knopf $24.00 (0-679-41258-1). A Chinese American cadet at West Point demonstrates honor and devotion to duty by implicating classmates and friends in a cheating incident. (Rev: BL 1/1/94*)

494 Lee, Harper. *To Kill a Mockingbird* (8–12). 1977, HarperCollins $23.00 (0-397-00151-7). A lawyer in a small Southern town defends an African American man wrongfully accused of rape.

495 Lee, Marie G. *Finding My Voice* (7–12). 1994, HarperCollins paper $5.99 (0-06-447245-0). Pressured by her strict Korean parents to get into Harvard, high-school senior Ellen Sung tries to find time for friendship, romance, and fun in her small Minnesota town. (Rev: BL 9/1/92; SLJ 10/92)

496 Lee, Marie G. *Necessary Roughness* (7–12). 1996, HarperCollins LB $14.89 (0-06-025130-1). Chan, a Korean American football enthusiast, and his twin sister, Young, encounter prejudice when their family moves to a small Minnesota community. (Rev: BL 1/1–15/97; BR 5–6/97; SLJ 1/97; VOYA 6/97)

497 Lester, Julius. *This Strange New Feeling* (9–12). 1985, Scholastic paper $4.50 (0-590-44047-0). Based on fact, this is a group of three short stories about slaves who react in different ways to gaining freedom.

498 Lewis, Beverly. *The Covenant* (10–12). Series: Abram's Daughters. 2002, Bethany paper $12.99 (0-7642-2330-5). Leah, a plain and practical Amish girl, is a contrast to her more flighty sister Sadie, whose romance with an outsider only brings trouble. (Rev: BL 8/02)

499 Lincoln, Christine. *Sap Rising* (10–12). 2001, Pantheon $20.00 (0-375-42140-8). This collection of 12 interconnected stories explores the lives of several African American people in a small Maryland town. (Rev: BL 8/01; SLJ 12/01)

500 Lipsyte, Robert. *The Brave* (8–12). 1991, HarperCollins paper $5.99 (0-06-447079-2). A Native American heavyweight boxer is rescued from drugs, pimps, and hookers by a tough but tender ex-boxer/New York City cop. (Rev: BL 10/15/91; SLJ 10/91*)

501 Lipsyte, Robert. *The Chief* (7–10). 1995, HarperCollins paper $5.99 (0-06-447097-0). Sonny Bear can't decide whether to go back to the reservation, continue boxing, or become Hollywood's new Native American darling. Sequel to *The Brave.* (Rev: BL 6/1–15/93; VOYA 12/93)

502 Lipsyte, Robert. *The Contender* (9–12). 1967, HarperCollins LB $14.89 (0-06-023920-4); paper $4.95 (0-06-447039-3). A black teenager hopes to get out of Harlem through a boxing career. (Rev: BL 3/1/90)

503 Lipsyte, Robert. *Warrior Angel* (7–12). 2003, HarperCollins LB $16.89 (0-06-000497-5). In this fourth book about the young boxer, Sonny — first seen in *The Contender* (1967) — is the heavyweight champion, yet he still struggles to find his identity. (Rev: BCCB 2/03; BL 1/1–15/03; HB 3–4/03; HBG 10/03; SLJ 3/03; VOYA 4/03)

504 Lopez, Lorraine. *Soy la Avon Lady and Other Stories* (11–12). 2002, Curbstone paper $15.95 (1-880684-86-1). Eleven short stories explore life for Hispanic Americans of all ages; for mature teens. (Rev: BL 8/02)

505 López, Tiffany Ana, ed. *Growing Up Chicana/o* (9–12). 1995, Avon paper $12.50 (0-380-72419-7). This anthology presents the writings of 20 current Chicano authors, including Rudolfo Anaya and Sandra Cisneros, on multicultural issues. (Rev: BL 12/1/93)

28

506 McFarland, Dennis. *Prince Edward* (9–12). 2004, Holt $25.00 (0-8050-6833-3). This emotionally charged story, seen through the eyes of 10-year-old Benjamin Rome, tells how the public schools in Prince Edward Country, Virginia, were closed in 1959 to prevent integration. (Rev: BL 5/1/04; SLJ 7/04)

507 McGahan, Jerry. *A Condor Brings the Sun* (10–12). 1996, Sierra Club $25.00 (0-87156-354-1). This is the story of Pilar, a Peruvian girl who is consumed with curiosity about her Inca heritage but leaves her homeland to live with an American zoologist in Montana, where she tries to free a bear and three cubs from captivity. (Rev: SLJ 2/97)

508 Major, Clarence, ed. *Calling the Wind: Twentieth-Century African-American Short Stories* (9–12). 1993, HarperCollins paper $17.00 (0-06-098201-2). Includes stories by Langston Hughes, Zora Neale Hurston, James Baldwin, Toni Morrison, and dozens more. (Rev: BL 12/1/92*)

509 Major, Devorah. *Brown Glass Windows* (10–12). 2002, Curbstone paper $15.95 (1-880684-87-X). An African American family in San Francisco faces competing demands from the Vietnam vet father and the graffiti artist son in a thoughtful, lyrical novel. (Rev: BL 5/1/02)

510 *Making Callaloo: 25 Years of Black Literature* (10–12). Ed. by Charles Henry Rowell. 2002, St. Martin's $34.95 (0-312-29021-7); paper $17.95 (0-312-28898-0). A collection of fiction and poetry from well-known and less-familiar black writers that represents the best in their output over the past 25 years. (Rev: BL 12/15/01) [820]

511 Malamud, Bernard. *The Assistant: A Novel* (10–12). 1957, Farrar paper $13.00 (0-06-095830-8). The Jewish owner of a failing grocery store tries to assimilate his assistant into Jewish ideas and religion.

512 Marino, Jan. *The Day That Elvis Came to Town* (7–10). 1993, Avon paper $3.50 (0-380-71672-0). In this tale of southern blacks, Wanda is thrilled when a room in her parents' boarding house is rented to Mercedes, who makes her feel pretty and smart — and who once went to school with Elvis Presley. (Rev: BL 12/15/90*; SLJ 1/91*)

513 Martin, Joe. *Fire in the Rock* (10–12). 2001, Novello Festival $21.95 (0-9708972-1-9). Racism and the role of religion in a person's life are the themes of this novel about the friendship between Bo, a white preacher's kid, and Poolo, an African American. (Rev: BL 10/15/01; SLJ 5/02)

514 Martinez, Victor. *Parrot in the Oven: Mi Vida* (7–10). 1996, HarperCollins LB $16.89 (0-06-026706-2). Through a series of vignettes, the story of Manuel, a teenage Mexican American, unfolds as he grows up in the city projects with an abusive

father and a loving mother. (Rev: BL 10/15/96; SLJ 11/96)

515 Menendez, Ana. *In Cuba I Was a German Shepherd* (10–12). 2001, Grove $23.00 (0-8021-1688-4). Six short stories explore the lives of Cuban refugees in Miami and the lives they left behind. (Rev: BL 4/15/01)

516 Meriwether, Louise. *Daddy Was a Numbers Runner* (7–12). 1986, Feminist Pr. paper $16.59 (1-5586-1442-7). The story of Frances, a black girl, growing up in Harlem during the Depression.

517 Miklowitz, Gloria D. *The War Between the Classes* (7–10). 1986, Dell paper $4.99 (0-440-99406-3). A Japanese American girl finds that hidden prejudices and bigotry emerge when students in school are divided into four socioeconomic groups. (Rev: BL 4/15/85; SLJ 8/85; VOYA 6/85)

518 Miller, Karen E. Quinones. *Satin Doll* (10–12). 2001, Simon & Schuster $23.00 (0-7432-1433-1). Romance, violence, and salvation are combined in this novel about an African American girl from Harlem who rises above a world of crime and drugs to find a better life. (Rev: BL 5/15/01)

519 Mitchell, Kathryn. *Proud and Angry Dust* (10–12). 2001, Univ. Press of Colorado $24.95 (0-87081-608-X). When oil is discovered in the African American section of a small Texas town in the 1920s, the result is a wave of lying, cheating, stealing, and even murder. The tale is told by Moose, an 11-year-old boy. (Rev: BL 6/1–15/01)

520 Mochizuki, Ken. *Beacon Hill Boys* (9–12). 2002, Scholastic $16.95 (0-439-26749-8). A Japanese American teenager searches for his ethnic identity in this novel set in 1970s Seattle. (Rev: BL 11/15/02; HBG 3/03; SLJ 1/03; VOYA 2/03)

521 Moore, Yvette. *Freedom Songs* (6–12). 1991, Penguin paper $5.99 (0-14-036017-4). In 1968, Sheryl, 14, witnesses and then experiences acts of prejudice while visiting relatives in North Carolina. (Rev: BL 4/15/91; SLJ 3/91)

522 Morrison, Toni. *The Bluest Eye* (10–12). 1993, Plume paper $12.95 (0-4522-8219-5). A form of racism is depicted in this moving novel about an African American adolescent girl's descent into madness because of her struggle to achieve personal beauty.

523 Mowry, Jess. *Way Past Cool* (9–12). 1992, Farrar $17.00 (0-374-28669-8). Kids struggle to survive in a violent California ghetto. (Rev: BL 3/15/92)

524 Mullane, Deirdre. *Crossing the Danger Water: Three Hundred Years of African-American Writing* (9–12). 1993, Doubleday paper $16.00 (0-385-42243-1). The history of African Americans is explored in their writings, narratives, letters, editorials, speeches, lyrics, and folktales, from U.S. colonial times to today. (Rev: BL 11/1/93) [810.8]

525 Murguia, Alejandro. *This War Called Love* (11–12). 2002, City Lights paper $11.95 (0-87286-394-8). A collection of poignant and often humorous stories about Hispanic Americans; for mature readers. (Rev: BL 8/02)

526 Myers, Walter Dean. *Fast Sam, Cool Clyde, and Stuff* (7–10). 1995, Peter Smith $20.25 (0-8446-6798-6); Puffin paper $5.99 (0-14-032613-8). Three male friends in Harlem join forces to found the 116th Street Good People.

527 Myers, Walter Dean. *The Glory Field* (7–10). 1994, Scholastic paper $14.95 (0-590-45897-3). This novel follows a family's 200-year history, from the capture of an African boy in the 1750s through the lives of his descendants on a small plot of South Carolina land called the Glory Field. (Rev: BL 10/1/94)

528 Myers, Walter Dean. *Slam!* (8–12). 1996, Scholastic paper $15.95 (0-590-48667-5). Although Slam is successful on the school's basketball court, his personal life has problems caused by difficulties fitting into an all-white school, a very sick grandmother, and a friend who is involved in drugs. (Rev: BL 11/15/96; BR 11–12/96; SLJ 11/96; VOYA 2/97)

529 Myers, Walter Dean. *The Young Landlords* (7–10). 1979, Penguin paper $5.99 (0-14-034244-3). A group of African American teenagers take over a slum building in Harlem.

530 Na, An. *A Step from Heaven* (9–12). 2001, Front Street $15.95 (1-886910-58-8). America has been portrayed as "heaven," but Young Ju finds life there difficult as she struggles to cope with the transition from life in Korea to life as an immigrant, and with the behavior of her unhappy and alcoholic father. (Rev: BCCB 7–8/01; BL 6/1–15/01*; HB 7–8/01*; HBG 10/01; SLJ 5/01*; VOYA 6/01)

531 Nailah, Anika. *Free and Other Stories* (10–12). 2002, Doubleday $21.95 (0-385-50293-1). Short stories explore the experience of being black in America. (Rev: BL 2/15/02*)

532 Namioka, Lensey. *April and the Dragon Lady* (7–12). 1994, Harcourt $10.95 (0-15-276644-8). A Chinese American high school junior must relinquish important activities to care for her ailing grandmother and struggles with the constraints of a traditional female role. (Rev: BL 3/1/94; SLJ 4/94; VOYA 6/94)

533 Naylor, Gloria, ed. *Children of the Night: The Best Short Stories by Black Writers, 1967 to the Present* (9–12). 1996, Little, Brown $24.95 (0-316-59926-3). A short-story collection, balanced thematically, from the editorial hands of one of the finest black female writers. (Rev: BL 12/1/95)

534 Ng, Fae Myenne. *Bone* (9–12). 1993, Hyperion $19.95 (1-56282-944-0). A look at the barriers and the love between generations in a Chinese American family. (Rev: BL 9/15/92*)

535 Okimoto, Jean D. *Talent Night* (6–10). 1995, Scholastic paper $14.95 (0-590-47809-5). In this story, Rodney Suyama, 17, wants to be the first Japanese American rapper and to date beautiful Ivy Ramos. (Rev: BL 6/1–15/95; SLJ 5/95)

536 Osa, Nancy. *Cuba 15* (6–10). 2003, Delacorte $15.95 (0-385-72021-7). Violet Paz, who considers herself totally American, is surprised when her grandmother insists that she celebrate a traditional coming-of-age ceremony. (Rev: BL 7/03*)

537 Oughton, Jerrie. *Music from a Place Called Half Moon* (6–10). 1995, Houghton $16.00 (0-395-70737-4). Small-town bigotry and personal transformation in the 1950s figure in this novel about Native Americans. (Rev: BL 5/1/95; SLJ 4/95)

538 Parker, Linda Busby. *Seven Laureis* (9–12). 2004, Southeast Missouri State Univ. $35.00 (0-9724304-8-2). Set in a small town in Alabama, this novel tells the story of one black family's struggle for civil rights from the 1950s on. (Rev: BL 2/15/04)

539 Parks, Gordon. *The Learning Tree* (10–12). 1987, Fawcett paper $5.99 (0-449-21504-0). The story of a black boy's coming of age in a small town in Kansas in the 1920s.

540 Placide, Jaira. *Fresh Girl* (8–10). 2002, Random LB $17.99 (0-385-90035-X). Mardi, an immigrant from Haiti, has some difficulties adjusting to life in New York. (Rev: BCCB 3/02; BL 11/15/01; HB 3–4/02; HBG 10/02; SLJ 1/02*; VOYA 8/02)

541 Potok, Chaim. *The Chosen*. 25th Anniversary Ed. (10–12). 1992, Knopf (0-679-40222-5). The story of Jewish youngsters coming of age in America.

542 Potok, Chaim. *The Promise* (10–12). 1969, Fawcett paper $6.99 (0-449-20910-5). The friendship between two Jewish boys in Brooklyn becomes strained because of family problems.

543 Power, Susan. *The Grass Dancer* (9–12). 1995, Berkley paper $6.99 (0-425-14962-5). Anna Thunder, a Sioux living in North Dakota, is the central character in this novel that tells the generational stories of Anna's family. (Rev: BL 8/94; SLJ 5/95; VOYA 12/94)

544 Power, Susan. *Roofwalker* (10–12). 2002, Milkweed $20.00 (1-57131-039-8). Power explores the Sioux heritage in short stories and autobiographical memoirs that include teen characters. (Rev: BL 9/1/02)

545 Price-Thompson, Tracy. *Chocolate Sangria* (10–12). 2003, Villard $21.95 (0-375-50651-9). A compelling, offbeat story of romance, homosexuality, and the racial and cultural problems faced by teens who do not fit into the mainstream mold. (Rev: BL 1/1–15/03)

546 Pullman, Philip. *The Broken Bridge* (8–12). 1992, Knopf $15.99 (0-679-91972-4). A biracial girl learns the truth about her heritage. (Rev: BL 2/15/92; SLJ 3/92*)

547 *The Pushcart Book of Short Stories: The Best Stories from a Quarter-Century of the Pushcart Prize* (10–12). Ed. by Bill Henderson. 2001, Pushcart $35.00 (1-888889-23-3). For better readers, this is an anthology of short stories from previous winners of the Pushcart Prize, including such writers as Tobias Wolff, Cynthia Ozick, and Richard Ford. (Rev: BL 10/15/01)

548 Qualey, Marsha. *Revolutions of the Heart* (7–12). 1993, Houghton $16.00 (0-395-64168-3). Cory lives in a small Wisconsin town that is torn by bigotry when Chippewa Indians reclaim their hunting and fishing rights. (Rev: BL 4/1/93; SLJ 5/93*)

549 Rana, Indi. *The Roller Birds of Rampur* (7–12). 1993, Ballantine paper $3.99 (0-449-70434-3). This coming-of-age story of a young woman caught between British and Indian cultures is a lively account of the immigration experience and of Indian culture. (Rev: BL 7/93; SLJ 5/93; VOYA 2/94)

550 Rebolledo, Tey Diana, and Eliana S. Rivero, eds. *Infinite Divisions: An Anthology of Chicana Literature* (9–12). 1993, Univ. of Arizona Pr. paper $22.50 (0-8165-1384-8). A collection that spans the history of prose and poetry by Mexican American women and the settlement of the "New World." (Rev: BL 6/1–15/93)

551 Ridley, John. *A Conversation with the Mann* (11–12). 2002, Warner $24.95 (0-446-52836-6). In the late 1950s, African American comedian Jackie Mann aspires to stardom and acceptance by whites; for mature teens. (Rev: BL 5/1/02)

552 Robinson, C. Kelly. *Between Brothers* (10–12). 2001, Villard paper $13.95 (0-375-75772-4). A story of the friendship of four African American college students: one a religious zealot, another from a wealthy family, a third who is financially strapped, and a fourth who wants to be a preacher. (Rev: BL 9/15/01)

553 Saldana, Rene, Jr. *The Jumping Tree: A Novel* (7–12). 2001, Delacorte $14.95 (0-385-32725-0). Rey, a Mexican American boy growing up in a poor family near the Mexican border, describes his life and his longing to become a man. (Rev: BL 5/15/01; HBG 10/01; SLJ 6/01)

554 Santiago, Danny. *Famous All over Town* (10–12). 1984, NAL paper $12.95 (0-452-25974-6). An honest, realistic novel about a young Mexican American growing up in a California barrio. (Rev: BL 12/15/89)

555 Savage, Deborah. *Kotuku* (7–12). 2002, Houghton $16.00 (0-618-07456-5). Struggling to recover from the death of her best friend, 17-year-old Wim throws herself into her job at a Cape Cod riding stable, but visitors from afar prompt her to delve into the mystery surrounding her Maori heritage. (Rev: BL 5/15/02; HBG 10/02; SLJ 3/02; VOYA 4/02)

556 Savage, Deborah. *A Stranger Calls Me Home* (9–12). 1992, Houghton $14.95 (0-395-59424-3). A mystical tale of three friends' search for cultural identity. (Rev: BL 3/15/92; SLJ 5/92)

557 Sebestyen, Ouida. *On Fire* (7–12). 1985, Little, Brown $12.95 (0-87113-010-6). Tater leaves home with his brother Sammy and takes a mining job where he confronts labor problems in this sequel to the author's powerful *Words by Heart*. (Rev: BL 5/15/85; SLJ 4/85; VOYA 8/85)

558 Senna, Danzy. *Caucasia* (10–12). 1998, Berkley paper $24.95 (1-57322-091-4). Two sisters, the products of a biracial marriage, are separated when their parents divorce, and the younger, named Birdie, is forced to go underground with her mother for political reasons and pass as white, all the while hoping to some day be reunited with her sister. (Rev: BL 2/15/98; SLJ 9/98)

559 Sherman, Eileen B. *The Violin Players* (6–10). 1998, Jewish Publication Soc. $14.95 (0-8276-0595-1). When Melissa leaves New York City to spend part of her junior year in a small Missouri town, she encounters the ugliness of anti-Semitism for the first time. (Rev: BL 12/1/98; HBG 3/99; SLJ 3/99)

560 Shtern, Ludmilla. *Leaving Leningrad* (10–12). 2001, Univ. Press of New England $19.95 (1-58465-100-8). This autobiographical novel follows Tatyana from her childhood in Soviet Russia to her marriage and resettlement in the United States. (Rev: BL 6/1–15/01)

561 Singer, Isaac Bashevis. *The Power of Light: Eight Stories for Hanukkah* (7–10). Illus. 1980, Avon paper $2.50 (0-380-60103-6). Eight stories of the Festival of Lights that span centuries of Jewish history.

562 Singleton, Elyse. *This Side of the Sky* (10–12). 2002, Putnam $24.95 (0-399-14920-1). Friends Myraleen and Lillian, African Americans born in the small Mississippi town of Nadir, grow up through the Depression and the war years, succeed in overcoming prejudice and poverty, and find love and fulfillment. (Rev: BL 9/15/02)

563 Skinner, Jose. *Flight and Other Stories* (10–12). 2001, Univ. of Nevada Pr. paper $15.00 (0-87417-359-0). These 14 lively coming-of-age stories deal with Latinos in the American Southwest. (Rev: BL 3/1/01)

564 Sneve, Virginia Driving Hawk. *Grandpa Was a Cowboy and an Indian and Other Stories* (10–12).

2000, Univ. of Nebraska Pr. $19.95 (0-8032-4274-3). History and folklore mix in this collection of stories that bring Native American traditions and values to life. (Rev: BL 10/15/00)

565 Soto, Gary. *Jesse* (10–12). 1994, Harcourt $14.95 (0-15-240239-X). Mexican American Jesse, 17, leaves high school in 1968, moves in with his poor older brother, takes college classes, worries about the draft, and faces racism. (Rev: BL 10/1/94; SLJ 12/94; VOYA 2/95)

566 Southgate, Martha. *The Fall of Rome* (10–12). 2002, Scribner $23.00 (0-684-86500-9). A black Latin teacher at a posh boarding school, a bright black scholarship student, and a new white teacher change each others' lives forever in this gripping story. (Rev: BL 9/15/01; SLJ 8/02)

567 Sprinkle, Patricia. *The Remember Box* (10–12). 2000, Zondervan paper $11.99 (0-310-22992-8). In this novel reminiscent of *To Kill a Mockingbird*, the setting is a small South Carolina town and 11-year-old Carly has an uncle, a minister, who is defending an innocent black man. (Rev: BL 10/1/00; SLJ 6/01)

568 Stepto, Michele, ed. *African-American Voices* (7–12). Series: Writers of America. 1995, Millbrook LB $23.90 (1-56294-474-6). Selections by W. E. B. Du Bois, Toni Morrison, Ralph Ellison, and others, plus traditional chants, speeches, and poetry. (Rev: BL 5/15/95; SLJ 3/95)

569 Stering, Shirley. *My Name Is Seepeetza* (5–10). 1997, Douglas & McIntyre paper $5.95 (0-88899-165-7). Told in diary form, this autobiographical novel about a 6th-grade Native American girl tells of her heartbreak at the terrible conditions at her school, where she is persecuted because of her race. (Rev: BL 3/1/97)

570 Stevens, Marcus. *Useful Girl* (10–12). 2004, Algonquin $24.95 (1-56512-366-2). In this novel involving Native Americans, two plots are developed: the first a contemporary story about young love, and the second, a historical story involving the death of a young Cheyenne girl. (Rev: BL 3/1/04; SLJ 6/04)

571 Straight, Susan. *Highwire Moon* (10–12). 2001, Houghton $24.00 (0-618-05614-9). The harsh world of the migrant worker is revealed in this story of a young girl, Elvia, and her mother, Serafina, and their struggle to be reunited after Serafina is arrested and deported. (Rev: BL 7/01*; SLJ 12/01)

572 Tan, Amy. *Joy Luck Club* (10–12). 1989, Putnam $24.95 (0-399-13420-4); paper $12.95 (0-679-72768-X). Through the stories of group of four Chinese women in San Francisco and their daughters, Tan looks immigrants' adjustment to their new lives and cultures.

573 Tan, Amy. *The Kitchen God's Wife* (9–12). 1992, Ivy Books paper $7.99 (0-8041-0753-X). The

mesmerizing story a Chinese emigré mother tells her daughter. (Rev: BL 4/15/91*; SLJ 12/91)

574 Taylor, Mildred D. *The Road to Memphis* (7–12). 1990, Dial $16.99 (0-8037-0340-6). Set in 1941, this is a continuation of the story of the Logans, a poor black southern family who were previously featured in *Roll of Thunder, Hear My Cry* and *Let the Circle Be Unbroken*. (Rev: BL 5/15/90; SLJ 1/90; VOYA 8/90)

575 Thomas, Joyce Carol. *House of Light* (10–12). 2001, Hyperion $22.95 (0-7868-6606-3). This novel about the African American residents of Ponca City, Oklahoma, presents a hopeful message and a sense of community. (Rev: BL 2/15/01)

576 Ujaama, E. James. *Coming Up* (10–12). 1996, Ujaama paper $12.95 (0-910303-66-5). The difficult realities of becoming successful as an African American male in white-dominated America are explored in this novel of two friends, Hakim and Andre, and their problems. (Rev: VOYA 8/96)

577 Velasquez, Gloria. *Maya's Divided World* (7–12). 1995, Arte Publico $12.95 (1-55885-126-7). A Chicana who seemingly leads a charmed life discovers that her parents are divorcing, and her world falls apart. (Rev: BL 3/1/95; SLJ 4/95)

578 Velie, Alan R., ed. *The Lightning Within: An Anthology of Contemporary American Indian Fiction* (9–12). 1991, Univ. of Nebraska Pr. $30.00 (0-8032-4659-5). A thoughtfully selected sampling of fiction by seven noted modern Native American writers, among them Momaday, Erdrich, Dorris, Silko, Vizenor, and Ortiz. (Rev: BL 5/15/91; SLJ 9/91)

579 Wartski, Maureen C. *Candle in the Wind* (9–12). 1995, Fawcett paper $4.50 (0-449-70442-4). Drawn from newspaper headlines, the shocking story of the murder of a Japanese American teen and the climate of racial hate that led to it. (Rev: BL 11/15/95; SLJ 3/96; VOYA 2/96)

580 Washington, Mary Helen, ed. *Memory of Kin: Stories About Family by Black Writers* (9–12). 1991, Doubleday paper $14.95 (0-385-24783-4). A wide-ranging collection of short stories and poetry dealing with the African American family experience. (Rev: BL 1/1/91; SLJ 7/91)

581 West, Dorothy. *The Wedding* (9–12). 1995, Doubleday $20.00 (0-385-47143-2). In an African American community on Martha's Vineyard, Massachusetts, Lute tries to win Shelby away from her white fiance. (Rev: BL 12/1/94; SLJ 7/95)

582 Williams-Garcia, Rita. *Blue Tights* (9–12). 1996, Viking paper $3.99 (0-14-038045-0). A talented black teenager has difficulty being accepted in her integrated high school. (Rev: BL 12/15/87)

583 Williams-Garcia, Rita. *Fast Talk on a Slow Track* (9–12). 1991, Dutton $15.00 (0-525-67334-2). After graduating from high school as valedictorian, Denzel attends Princeton's summer session for minority students and fails for the first time in his life. (Rev: BL 4/1/91; SLJ 4/91*)

584 Woodson, Jacqueline. *Behind You* (7–12). 2004, Putnam $15.99 (0-399-23988-X). In this sequel to *If You Come Softly* (1998), Jeremiah, though dead from a policeman's bullet, watches over the people he left behind. (Rev: BL 2/15/04; HB 5–6/04; SLJ 6/04; VOYA 6/04)

585 Woodson, Jacqueline. *From the Notebooks of Melanin Sun May* (6–10). 1995, Scholastic paper $5.99 (0-590-45881-7). A 13-year-old African American boy's mother announces that she loves a fellow student, a white woman. (Rev: BL 4/15/95; SLJ 8/95)

586 Wright, Richard. *Native Son* (10–12). 1998, HarperCollins paper $10.00 (0-06-092980-4). The tragic life of a black youth named Bigger Thomas who was raised in a Chicago slum.

587 Wright, Richard. *Rite of Passage* (7–12). 1994, HarperCollins paper $5.99 (0-06-447111-X). This newly discovered novella, written in the 1940s, concerns a gifted 15-year-old who runs away from his loving Harlem home and survives on the streets with a violent gang. (Rev: BL 1/1/94; SLJ 2/94; VOYA 4/94)

588 Wright, Richard. *Uncle Tom's Children: Five Long Stories* (9–12). 1938, Harper & Row paper $7.00 (0-06-081251-6). The five stories in this collection deal with racial conflicts in the South.

589 Yep, Laurence, ed. *American Dragons: Twenty-Five Asian American Voices* (7–12). 1995, HarperCollins paper $6.99 (0-06-440603-2). Autobiographical stories, poems, and essays about children whose parents come from China, Japan, Korea, and Tibet, struggling to find "an identity that isn't generic." (Rev: BL 5/15/93; SLJ 7/93; VOYA 10/93)

590 Yep, Laurence. *The Star Fisher* (6–10). 1991, Morrow $16.95 (0-688-09365-5). Drawing on his mother's childhood, Yep depicts a Chinese family's experiences when they arrive in West Virginia in 1927 to open a laundry. (Rev: BL 5/15/91; SLJ 5/91)

591 Zabytko, Irene. *When Luba Leaves Home* (9–12). 2003, Algonquin $22.95 (1-56512-332-8). Interconnected stories portray the life of Luba, a Ukrainian college student in Chicago in the 1960s who lives at home and is active in her own community while longing to be independent and become truly American. (Rev: BL 2/15/03; SLJ 6/03)

Family Life and Problems

592 Adler, C. S. *The Lump in the Middle* (6–10). 1991, Avon paper $3.50 (0-380-71176-1). Kelsey, the middle child, struggles for her identity after Dad loses his job. (Rev: BL 10/1/89; BR 1–2/90; SLJ 10/89; VOYA 2/90)

593 Allen, Charlotte Vale. *Parting Gifts* (10–12). 2001, MIRA $19.95 (1-55166-853-X). After her husband's accidental death, Kyra is approached by a woman who claims to be her daughter, long ago given up for adoption. She brings along a son she wants Kyra to adopt. (Rev: BL 5/1/01)

594 Allen, Nan Corbitt. *Asylum* (10–12). 2004, Moody paper $11.99 (0-8024-1117-7). Orphaned by a fire at the tender age of 10, Ian Lane is taken in by an aunt but flees and seeks refuge in a Florida church. (Rev: BL 10/1/03)

595 Allison, Dorothy. *Bastard Out of Carolina* (10–12). 1992, Dutton $20.00 (0-525-93425-1). Set in the rural South, this story for mature readers centers on the hard-drinking, womanizing Boatwright family.

596 Alphin, Elaine Marie. *Counterfeit Son* (8–12). 2000, Harcourt $17.00 (0-15-202645-2). Reeling from his life with his now-dead murderer father, Cameron adopts the identity of one of the victims, hoping to find a family of his own. (Rev: BL 9/15/00; HBG 3/01; SLJ 12/00)

597 Amsden, David. *Important Things That Don't Matter* (11–12). 2003, Morrow $24.95 (0-06-051388-8). In a moving narrative, a 20-year-old describes his youth and his difficult relationship with a troubled father. (Rev: BL 3/1/03; VOYA 10/03)

598 Anderson, Catherine. *Always in My Heart* (11–12). 2002, NAL paper $6.99 (0-451-20666-5). The death of their oldest son destroys Ellie and Tucker's marriage, but their younger sons have a plan to bring them back together; for mature teens. (Rev: BL 8/02)

599 Anfousse, Ginette. *A Terrible Secret* (7–12). Trans. from French by Jennifer Hutchison. 2001, Lorimer paper $4.99 (1-55028-704-4). A new neighbor, Ben, helps Maggie to recover from the death of her Down syndrome brother. (Rev: SLJ 9/01)

600 Anshaw, Carol. *Lucky in the Corner* (11–12). 2002, Houghton $23.00 (0-395-94040-0). Lucky the dog and cross-dressing uncle Harold are the constants in college student Fern's busy and complex life in this entertaining novel featuring a lesbian mother and a best friend who is an inept single mother. (Rev: BL 5/1/02*)

601 Banks, Kate. *Walk Softly, Rachel* (7–10). 2003, Farrar $16.00 (0-374-38230-1). When Rachel, 14, reads her dead brother's diary she discovers that his life was not the ideal she had thought. (Rev: BL 10/15/03; HBG 4/04; SLJ 9/03*; VOYA 2/04)

602 Barwin, Gary. *Seeing Stars* (6–12). 2002, Stoddart paper $7.95 (0-7737-6227-2). A quirky story about a boy who has been brought up in strange circumstances and who now wants the truth about his father and his family. (Rev: BL 7/02; SLJ 5/02)

603 Bauer, Cat. *Harley, Like a Person* (7–10). 2000, Winslow $16.95 (1-890817-48-1); paper $6.95 (1-890817-49-X). Unhappy with her distant mother and an alcoholic father, Harley Columba becomes convinced that she is an adopted child. (Rev: BL 6/1–15/00; HB 5–6/00; HBG 9/00; SLJ 5/00)

604 Bauer, Joan. *Backwater* (7–10). 1999, Putnam $16.99 (0-399-23141-2). When 16-year-old Ivy Breedlove begins working on her family history, the trail leads to the New York State Adirondacks and eccentric, talented Aunt Jo. (Rev: BL 5/15/99; HB 7–8/99; HBG 9/99; SLJ 6/99; VOYA 8/99)

605 Bauer, Joan. *Rules of the Road* (6–10). 1998, Putnam $16.99 (0-399-23140-4). Jenna Boller is the confident, smart, and moral heroine of this novel that deals with the effects of alcoholism on a family and a girl's growing friendship with a wealthy, elderly woman. (Rev: BL 2/1/98; BR 1–2/99; HB 5–6/98; HBG 9/98; SLJ 3/98*; VOYA 6/98)

606 Bedford, Deborah. *A Rose by the Door* (10–12). 2001, Warner paper $11.95 (0-446-67789-2). When Gemma appears on Bea's doorstep, claiming to be Bea's dead son's wife, Bea must make a choice. (Rev: BL 1/1–15/02)

607 Bellows, Nathaniel. *On This Day* (11–12). 2003, HarperCollins $24.95 (0-06-051211-3). Siblings Warren, 18, and Joan, 20, must find their own way in the world when their father dies of cancer and their mother commits suicide. (Rev: BL 2/15/03)

608 Berne, Suzanne. *A Crime in the Neighborhood* (10–12). 1997, Algonquin $28.95 (1-56512-165-1). A hurt and confused girl who can't accept her father's desertion begins to analyze her family and neighborhood using the same methods as Sherlock Holmes. (Rev: BL 4/15/97; SLJ 12/97)

609 Berry, James. *A Thief in the Village and Other Stories* (7–12). 1988, Penguin paper $5.99 (0-14-034357-1). Nine stories about a teenager in Jamaica and everyday life on the Caribbean island. (Rev: BL 4/15/88; BR 9–10/88)

610 Bledsoe, Jerry. *The Angel Doll* (10–12). 1997, St. Martin's $13.95 (0-312-17104-8). This novel tells how 10-year-old Whitey and his friends work together to grant the wish of Whitey's 4-year-old sister, a polio victim, to receive for Christmas a doll like the one in "The Littlest Angel." (Rev: BL 11/1/97; SLJ 2/98)

611 Block, Francesca L. *The Hanged Man* (10–12). 1994, HarperCollins LB $15.89 (0-06-024537-9). Against a backdrop of Hollywood excess, alienated Laura struggles to cope with her dead father's acts of incest while her mother lives in denial. (Rev: BL 9/15/94; SLJ 9/94; VOYA 12/94)

612 Block, Francesca L. *Witch Baby* (7–12). 1992, HarperCollins paper $5.99 (0-06-447065-2). This sequel to *Weetzie Bat* focuses on the foundling Witch Baby as she searches for her parents. (Rev: BL 8/91; SLJ 9/91*)

613 Bonosky, Phillip. *A Bird in Her Hair and Other Stories* (9–12). 1987, International Pubs. paper $5.95 (0-7178-0661-8). A collection of short stories about the struggles of working people in Pennsylvania from the 1930s into the 1950s. (Rev: BL 2/15/88)

614 Boswell, Robert. *Mystery Ride* (9–12). 1993, Knopf $22.00 (0-679-41292-1). Angela, unable to control her defiant daughter Dulcie, 15, drives her to Iowa, where Dulcie is expected to spend the summer with Dulcie's father, Angela's compassionate ex-husband. (Rev: BL 12/15/92*)

615 Boyd, Candy Dawson. *Chevrolet Saturdays* (5–10). 1993, Macmillan $16.00 (0-02-711765-0). After his parents divorce, Joey's mother marries Mr. Johnson, but Joey rejects and alienates his kindly stepfather. When Joey makes amends, new family ties are formed. (Rev: BL 5/15/93; SLJ 5/93)

616 Bradbury, Ray. *Dandelion Wine* (9–12). 1975, Knopf $24.95 (0-394-49605-1); Bantam paper $6.50 (0-553-27753-7). A tender novel about one summer in the life of a 12-year-old boy growing up in a small Illinois town during 1928. A reissue.

617 Bradford, Richard. *Red Sky at Morning: A Novel* (8–12). 1968, HarperCollins paper $13.00 (0-06-091361-4). A wonderful novel about a boy and his mother who move to a small town in New Mexico when the father joins the Navy in World War II.

618 Bridgers, Sue Ellen. *Home Before Dark* (7–10). 1998, Replica LB $29.95 (0-7351-0053-5). A migrant worker and his family settle down in a permanent home.

619 Bridgers, Sue Ellen. *Notes for Another Life* (7–12). 1981, Replica $24.95 (0-7351-0044-6). A brother and sister cope with a frequently absent mother and a mentally ill father. (Rev: BL 9/1/85; SLJ 10/85; VOYA 4/86)

620 Brooks, Bruce. *Midnight Hour Encores* (7–10). 1986, HarperCollins paper $6.99 (0-06-447021-0). Cello-playing Sib and her father Taxi take a transcontinental trip to meet Sib's mother, who left after her birth. (Rev: BL 9/15/86; SLJ 9/86; VOYA 12/86)

621 Brooks, Bruce. *What Hearts* (8–12). 1995, Demco $12.00 (0-606-08362-6). Four long stories about Asa, especially his relationship with his emotionally fragile mother and his hostile competition with his stepfather. (Rev: BL 9/1/92*; SLJ 11/92)

622 Brooks, Kevin. *Martyn Pig* (7–10). 2002, Scholastic $10.95 (0-439-29595-5). When Martyn's abusive father dies during a drunken argument, Martyn and a friend dispose of the body, setting off a complicated, suspenseful, and often amusing string of events. (Rev: BCCB 9/02; BL 5/1/02; HBG 10/02; SLJ 5/02*)

623 Brown, Rosellen. *Half a Heart* (10–12). 2000, Farrar $24.00 (0-374-29987-0). Comfortable Houston suburbanite Miriam Vener, troubled by a nagging secret from her past, seeks to reunite with the racially mixed daughter she gave up for adoption 18 years earlier. (Rev: BL 2/15/00; VOYA 4/01)

624 Bunting, Eve. *A Sudden Silence* (7–12). 1988, Fawcett paper $6.99 (0-449-70362-2). Jesse sets out to find the hit-and-run driver who killed his brother. (Rev: BL 4/15/88; SLJ 5/88)

625 Bunting, Eve. *Surrogate Sister* (7–10). 1984, HarperCollins LB $13.89 (0-397-32099-X). A 16-year-old girl copes with a pregnant mother who has offered to be a surrogate mother for a childless couple.

626 Bunting, Eve. *Will You Be My Posslq?* (9–12). 1987, Harcourt $12.95 (0-15-297399-0). Without her parents' approval freshman Kyle asks her friend Jamie to become her posslq (person of opposite sex sharing living quarters). (Rev: BL 10/1/87; SLJ 10/87; VOYA 4/88)

627 Cadnum, Michael. *Taking It* (9–12). 1995, Viking paper $15.99 (0-670-86130-8). Anna shoplifts as a way to test her limits amid her parents' divorce and her feelings of alienation from family and friends. But it eventually catches up to her. (Rev: BL 7/95*; SLJ 8/95; VOYA 2/96)

628 Cadnum, Michael. *Zero at the Bone* (8–12). 1996, Viking $15.99 (0-670-86725-X). Anita, Cray's independent older sister, mysteriously disappears and, then, several months later, a body is found that meets her general description. (Rev: BL 8/96*; BR 1–2/97; SLJ 7/96*; VOYA 2/97)

629 Caletti, Deb. *Honey, Baby, Sweetheart* (9–12). 2004, Simon & Schuster $15.95 (0-689-86765-4). Ann and Marie, a mother and daughter, get involved in a plan to reunite a friend with a lost love. (Rev: BL 5/15/04; SLJ 7/04)

630 Campbell, Bebe Moore. *Singing in the Comeback Choir* (10–12). 1998, Putnam $24.95 (0-399-14298-3); Berkley paper $7.50 (0-425-16662-7). This is the story of two strong black women, Maxine, a television producer with marital problems, and her grandmother, Lindy, a former blues singer, who has just suffered a minor stroke. (Rev: SLJ 4/99)

631 Cart, Michael, ed. *Necessary Noise: Stories About Our Families as They Really Are* (9–12). 2003, HarperCollins LB $16.89 (0-06-027500-6). YA authors familiar to young readers tell stories of families struggling to cope with contemporary problems. (Rev: BCCB 7–8/03; BL 5/15/03*; HB 7–8/03; HBG 10/03; SLJ 6/03; VOYA 6/03)

632 Caseley, Judith. *Losing Louisa* (8–12). 1999, Farrar $17.00 (0-374-34665-8). Lacey Levine, 16, who is living with her immature, profane mother, discovers that her older unmarried sister is pregnant. (Rev: BL 3/1/99; HBG 9/99; SLJ 3/99; VOYA 6/99)

633 Chambers, Veronica. *When Did You Stop Loving Me* (9–12). 2004, Doubleday $21.95 (0-385-50900-6). A heartfelt coming-of-age story about 11-year-old Angela, how her mother leaves her in late 1970s Brooklyn, and how her father copes with this situation. (Rev: BL 4/15/04)

634 Chorao, Ian. *Bruiser: A Novel* (10–12). 2003, Atria $24.00 (0-7434-3775-6). Nine-year-old Bruiser and 10-year-old Darla, both from troubled families in New York, take off on their own on a journey full of wonders, perils, and disappointments. (Rev: BL 2/15/03*)

635 Christiansen, C. B. *A Small Pleasure* (7–10). 1988, Macmillan $13.95 (0-689-31369-1). A young high school girl hides her grief over her father's fatal cancer by becoming the most popular girl in school. (Rev: BL 4/1/88; BR 9–10/88; SLJ 3/88; VOYA 6/88)

636 Cleaver, Vera, and Bill Cleaver. *Where the Lilies Bloom* (6–10). Illus. 1969, HarperCollins $15.95 (0-397-31111-7). When her father dies, Mary Call must take care of her two siblings and keep the family together. A sequel is *Trial Valley*. (Rev: BL 2/1/89)

637 Close, Jessie. *The Warping of Al* (9–12). 1990, HarperCollins $15.95 (0-06-021280-2). Al tries to cope with a domineering father and a subservient mother. (Rev: BL 1/1/91; SLJ 9/90)

638 Cochrane, Mick. *Sport* (10–12). 2001, St. Martin's $22.95 (0-312-26994-3). Twelve-year-old "Sport" Hawkins, growing up in St. Paul, Minnesota, during the 1960s, finds escape from his dysfunctional family life in his love of baseball; for mature teens. (Rev: VOYA 2/02)

639 Cohn, Rachel. *Gingerbread* (9–12). 2002, Simon & Schuster $15.95 (0-689-84337-2). Cyd, a rebellious 16-year-old, is sent to New York to spend the summer with her father in this hip and entertaining novel written in the first person. (Rev: BCCB 4/02; BL 4/15/02; HBG 10/02; SLJ 2/02*; VOYA 4/02)

640 Cole, Brock. *The Facts Speak for Themselves* (9–12). 1997, Front Street $15.95 (1-886910-14-6). A ground-breaking, sexually explicit story about

Linda and how the experiences in her life lead to murder. (Rev: BL 10/1/97; HBG 3/98; SLJ 10/97*; VOYA 12/97)

641 Coman, Carolyn. *Bee and Jacky* (9–12). 1998, Front Street $14.95 (1-886910-33-2). This is a controversial novel about the emotional consequences of an incestuous relationship between a 17-year-old boy and his younger sister. (Rev: BL 10/1/98; HB 11–12/98; HBG 3/99; SLJ 11/98; VOYA 12/98)

642 Connelly, Neil. *St. Michael's Scales* (6–10). 2002, Scholastic $16.95 (0-439-19445-8). Fifteen-year-old Keenan faces multiple problems — his mother is institutionalized, his older brother has run away, his father is distant, and Keenan is obsessed with the idea that his dead twin brother wants Keenan to kill himself. (Rev: BCCB 7–8/02; BL 3/15/02; HB 5–6/02; HBG 10/02; SLJ 6/02; VOYA 4/02)

643 Conroy, Pat. *The Great Santini* (10–12). 1987, Bantam paper $7.99 (0-553-26892-9). This novel about family dynamics centers on a Marine captain who treats his family as he does his troops. (Rev: BL 2/15/91)

644 Cook, Karin. *What Girls Learn: A Novel* (10–12). 1997, Pantheon $23.00 (0-679-44828-4). In this emotional novel, Tilden, an adolescent girl, and her slightly younger sister move with their mother to suburban Long Island, where Tilden has social problems and her mother discovers she is dying of cancer. (Rev: BL 2/15/97; BR 9–10/97; SLJ 7/97)

645 Cook, Lorna J. *Departures* (11–12). 2004, St. Martin's $22.95 (0-312-32128-7). An entertaining tale of a family whose eccentric members, including the two teens, seem to be constantly in motion; sexual discussion restricts this to mature teens. (Rev: BL 12/15/03)

646 Cooney, Caroline B. *Tune in Anytime* (7–10). 1999, Delacorte $8.95 (0-385-32649-1). When her father files for divorce to marry his older daughter's college roommate and her mother is too self-involved to do anything about it, Sophie's life seems to fly out of control. (Rev: HBG 4/00; SLJ 9/99; VOYA 12/99)

647 Cooney, Caroline B. *The Voice on the Radio* (7–10). 1996, Delacorte $15.95 (0-385-32213-5). In this sequel to *The Face on the Milk Carton* and *Whatever Happened to Janie?*, Janie realizes that her betrayer is actually her boyfriend, Reeve. (Rev: BL 10/1/96; BR 3–4/97; SLJ 9/96*; VOYA 12/96)

648 Cooney, Caroline B. *What Janie Found* (6–10). 2000, Delacorte $15.95 (0-385-32611-4). Janie, the heroine of previous books including *The Face on the Milk Carton,* finds closure for her family identity problems when she feels she must confront Hannah, her kidnapper and half-sister. (Rev: BL 2/15/00; HBG 3/01; SLJ 3/00; VOYA 4/00)

649 Cooney, Caroline B. *Whatever Happened to Janie?* (6–10). 1993, Delacorte $16.95 (0-385-31035-8); Dell paper $5.50 (0-440-21924-8). Janie, 15, after discovering she's a missing child on a milk carton, returns to her birth family, which has been searching for her since her kidnapping at age three. Sequel to *The Face on the Milk Carton.* (Rev: BL 6/1–15/93; SLJ 6/93; VOYA 8/93)

650 Darrow, Sharon. *The Painters of Lexieville* (7–10). 2003, Candlewick $16.99 (0-7636-1437-8). This story of poverty and violence features Pert, who yearns to go to Little Rock Beauty College and escape Lexieville and the unwelcome attentions of her Uncle Orris. (Rev: BCCB 1/04; BL 11/15/03; HBG 4/04; SLJ 3/04; VOYA 4/04)

651 Deaver, Julie Reece. *Chicago Blues* (6–10). 1995, HarperCollins $15.95 (0-06-024675-8). Two sisters are forced to make it on their own because of an alcoholic mother and experience struggle, success, and eventual forgiveness. (Rev: BL 9/1/95; SLJ 8/95; VOYA 12/95)

652 Deberry, Virginia, and Donna Grant. *Far from the Tree* (10–12). 2000, St. Martin's $24.95 (0-312-20291-1). Four generations of African American women converge at the family's property in Prosper, North Carolina, and discover decades-old secrets. (Rev: BL 7/00; SLJ 3/01)

653 Deedy, Carmen A. *The Last Dance* (7–10). Illus. 1995, Peachtree $16.95 (1-56145-109-6). A picture book for young adults that tells of the abiding love through the years of husband and wife Ninny and Bessie. (Rev: BL 1/1–15/96; SLJ 1/96)

654 Deem, James M. *3 NBs of Julian Drew* (7–12). 1994, Houghton $16.00 (0-395-69453-1). Julian, 15, is emotionally and physically abused by his father and his demented stepmother. He finds strength by writing to his deceased mother in coded notebooks. (Rev: BL 10/15/94; SLJ 10/94*; VOYA 12/94)

655 de la Garza, Beatriz. *Pillars of Gold and Silver* (9–12). 1997, Arte Publico paper $9.95 (1-55885-206-9). After her father is killed in the Korean War, young Blanca Estela and her mother move from California to Mexico in this story of a girl trying to fit into a new culture and make new friends. (Rev: BL 2/1/98; BR 5–6/98; SLJ 7/98)

656 Delinsky, Barbara. *Coast Road* (10–12). 1998, Simon & Schuster $24.00 (0-684-84576-8). When Jack McGill's ex-wife lies close to death after an auto accident, he and his two teenage daughters piece together the history of his failed marriage. (Rev: BL 5/1/98; SLJ 12/98)

657 Delinsky, Barbara. *The Vineyard* (10–12). 2000, Simon & Schuster $25.00 (0-684-86484-3). Seventy-six-year-old Natalie Seebring, a vineyard owner in Rhode Island, hires a younger woman to help her write her life story in this novel about nature, love, and survival. (Rev: BL 5/1/00)

658 Delinsky, Barbara. *The Woman Next Door* (10–12). 2001, Simon & Schuster $25.00 (0-7432-0469-7). When a young widow in their neighborhood becomes pregnant, several wives wonder if their husbands were involved with her. (Rev: BL 6/1–15/01)

659 Derby, Pat. *Grams, Her Boyfriend, My Family and Me* (7–10). 1994, Farrar paper $7.95 (0-374-42790-9). A laid-back teenager finds himself becoming involved in family politics when his mother returns to work and his grandmother comes to live in their tiny house. (Rev: BL 3/15/94; SLJ 11/94*; VOYA 4/94)

660 Doherty, Berlie. *Holly Starcross* (6–10). 2002, HarperCollins LB $17.89 (0-06-001342-7). Holly is forced to choose between her mother's new family and her long-lost father in this dramatic British novel. (Rev: BCCB 12/02; BL 11/1/02; HB 9–10/02; HBG 3/03; SLJ 8/02)

661 Doody, Margaret Anne, et al., ed. *The Annotated Anne of Green Gables* (7–12). 1997, Oxford $39.95 (0-19-510428-5). A biography of Lucy Maud Montgomery and notes and annotations explaining references to the places, people, and settings add to this edition of Montgomery's novel. (Rev: SLJ 3/98; VOYA 6/98)

662 Draper, Sharon M. *Forged by Fire* (7–10). 1997, Simon & Schuster $16.95 (0-689-80699-X). Nine-year-old African American Gerald Nickelby must leave the comfort of his aunt's home to live with a neglectful mother, her daughter Angel, and husband Jordan, who is secretly sexually abusing young Angel. A companion volume to *Tears of a Tiger*. (Rev: BL 2/15/97; SLJ 3/97; VOYA 6/97)

663 Dressen, Sarah. *The Truth About Forever* (9–12). 2004, Viking $16.99 (0-670-03639-0). Macy Queen hides her grief over her father's death and pretends that all is well. (Rev: BL 4/15/04; SLJ 6/04; VOYA 6/04)

664 Earle, Robert. *The Way Home* (11–12). 2004, DayBue $24.00 (0-9668940-6-5). After his beloved grandfather dies, Max is packed off to boarding school by his divorcing parents and must cope with many changes; for mature teens. (Rev: BL 12/15/03)

665 Enger, Leif. *Peace Like a River* (10–12). 2001, Atlantic Monthly $24.00 (0-87113-795-X). When his brother flees after killing two young men who were harassing his family, Reuben and his father and sister set out to find him. (Rev: BL 5/15/01*)

666 Eppes, Cindy. *South of Reason* (10–12). 2002, Pocket $24.00 (0-7434-3799-3). When 13-year-old Kayla's family moves back to Texas, she discovers that an intriguing neighbor is also a relative. (Rev: BL 2/1/02)

667 Eulo, Elena Yates. *Mixed-Up Doubles* (8–11). 2003, Holiday $16.95 (0-8234-1706-9). In this poignant yet funny story of a tennis-playing family hit by divorce, middle child Hank, 14, narrates the effects on the children. (Rev: BCCB 7–8/03; BL 5/15/03; HBG 4/04; SLJ 7/03; VOYA 6/03)

668 Fine, Anne. *Flour Babies* (9–12). 1995, Laurel Leaf paper $4.50 (0-440-21941-8). Three weeks looking after a flour "baby" allow Simon to explore his real feelings about his father and why he left home. (Rev: BL 4/1/94; BR 11/94; HB 9/94; SLJ 6/94)

669 Flake, Sharon G. *Begging for Change* (7–12). 2003, Hyperion $15.99 (0-7868-0601-X). Raspberry resorts to stealing from a friend when her mother is hospitalized after being hit in the head and her addicted father reappears on the scene in this sequel to *Money Hungry* (2001). (Rev: BL 8/03*; HBG 4/04; SLJ 7/03; VOYA 6/03)

670 Flake, Sharon G. *Money Hungry* (7–10). 2001, Hyperion $15.99 (0-7868-0548-X). Raspberry Hill, 13, struggles to amass a sum of money that will keep her mother and herself safe from a life on the streets. (Rev: BL 6/1–15/01; HBG 10/01; SLJ 7/01)

671 Fleischman, Paul. *Rear-View Mirrors* (7–10). 1986, HarperCollins $12.95 (0-06-021866-2). After her father's death, Olivia relives through memory a summer when she and her estranged father reconciled. (Rev: BL 3/1/86; BR 11–12/86; SLJ 5/86; VOYA 8/86)

672 Flinn, Alex. *Nothing to Lose* (7–12). 2004, HarperCollins $15.99 (0-06-051750-6). At age 17, Michael returns home after being a runaway for a year to find that his mother is on trial for the murder of his abusive father. (Rev: BL 3/15/04; HB 5–6/04; SLJ 3/04; VOYA 6/04)

673 Forbes, Kathryn. *Mama's Bank Account* (7–10). 1968, Harcourt paper $10.00 (0-15-656377-0). The story, told in vignettes, of a loving Norwegian family and of Mama's mythical bank account.

674 Fox, Paula. *The Eagle Kite* (6–10). 1995, Orchard LB $16.99 (0-531-08742-5). Liam goes through a tangle of denial, anger, shame, grief, and empathy after learning that his father is dying of AIDS. His mother says he got it from a blood transfusion, but Liam remembers seeing his father embrace a young man two years before. (Rev: BL 2/1/95*; SLJ 4/95*; VOYA 5/95)

675 Fox, Paula. *The Moonlight Man* (8–12). 1986, Bradbury LB $14.95 (0-02-735480-6). During a stay together in a house in Nova Scotia, teenager Catherine learns more about her adored alcoholic father than she wants to. (Rev: BL 4/15/86; SLJ 4/86; VOYA 8/86)

676 Fraustino, Lisa R., ed. *Dirty Laundry: Stories About Family Secrets* (9–12). 1998, Viking $16.99 (0-670-87911-8). A collection of 11 original stories by YA writers exploring various family relationships and secrets. (Rev: BL 5/15/98; HBG 9/98; SLJ 7/98; VOYA 12/98)

677 Fredriksson, Marianne. *Hanna's Daughters: A Novel of Three Generations* (10–12). Trans. from Swedish by Joan Tate. 1998, Ballantine $24.00 (0-345-42664-9). In this multigenerational novel set in Sweden, Anna recounts the difficult lives of her mother, Johanna, and grandmother, Hanna, and then tells about her own life. (Rev: BL 7/98; SLJ 3/99)

678 Freund, Diane. *Four Corners* (10–12). 2001, MacAdam $25.00 (0-9673701-8-3). When her mother has a nervous breakdown, 10-year-old Rainey and her four siblings are cared for by a flamboyant aunt who arrives with a wild daughter and a peculiar son. (Rev: BL 8/01)

679 Friesen, Gayle. *Losing Forever* (7–10). 2002, Kids Can $16.95 (1-55337-031-7). As her mother prepares to remarry, 9th-grader Jes is still coping with her parents' divorce, her changing relationships with her friends, and her beautiful soon-to-be stepsister. (Rev: BCCB 11/02; BL 1/1–15/03; HBG 3/03; SLJ 11/02; VOYA 2/03)

680 Fritz, April Young. *Waiting to Disappear* (7–10). 2002, Hyperion $15.99 (0-7868-0790-3). Buddy must deal with her mother's mental illness just as high school begins in this story set in the 1950s. (Rev: BL 11/15/02; HBG 3/03; SLJ 10/02; VOYA 2/03)

681 Fromm, Pete. *As Cool as I Am* (11–12). 2003, St. Martin's $23.00 (0-312-30775-6). Smart and funny, Lucy Diamond doesn't want to fall into the same trap as her parents but finds herself sexually attracted to her friend Kenny; for mature teens. (Rev: BL 9/1/03; VOYA 6/04)

682 Fuqua, Jonathon Scott. *The Reappearance of Sam Webber* (9–12). 1999, Bancroft $23.95 (1-890862-02-9). Confused and lonely, 11-year-old Sam can't adjust to the disappearance of his father and, when his mother is forced to move to a poor neighborhood in Baltimore, Sam faces new problems, including the school bully. (Rev: BL 3/1/99; SLJ 7/99)

683 Gaarder, Jostein. *The Solitaire Mystery* (10–12). Trans. from Norwegian by Sarah Jane Hails. Illus. 1996, Farrar $22.00 (0-374-26651-4). During a journey with his father to find his mother who disappeared years before, 12-year-old Hans Thomas is entertained by reading about the fantastic adventures of Baker Hans who traveled to a land where playing cards came to life. (Rev: BL 7/96; BR 3–4/97; SLJ 9/96; VOYA 12/96)

684 Gaffney, Patricia. *Circle of Three* (10–12). 2000, HarperCollins $24.00 (0-06-019375-1). This novel about growing up and growing old explores complex mother–daughter relationships in a small Virginia college town. (Rev: BL 5/15/00)

685 Goobie, Beth. *Who Owns Kelly Paddik?* (7–10). Series: Orca Soundings. 2003, Orca paper $7.95 (1-55143-239-0). Kelly, 15, slowly comes to realize

that she is not alone as she recovers from the sexual abuse inflicted by her father. (Rev: SLJ 11/03)

686 Gottlieb, Eli. *The Boy Who Went Away* (10–12). 1997, St. Martin's $21.95 (0-312-15070-9). An autobiographical novel set in New Jersey in 1967 about a teenage boy growing up in a family with a mentally ill older brother. (Rev: BL 12/15/96; SLJ 5/97)

687 Graham, Rosemary. *My Not-So-Terrible Time at the Hippie Hotel* (6–10). 2003, Viking $15.99 (0-670-03611-0). Fourteen-year-old Tracy has not dealt well with her parents' divorce but finds a new friend and new confidence during a "Together Time" retreat on Cape Cod. (Rev: BL 8/03; HBG 10/03; SLJ 7/03; VOYA 12/03)

688 Grant, Cynthia D. *Mary Wolf* (7–12). 1995, Atheneum $16.00 (0-689-80007-X). A tale of a homeless family in which the only person who is logical and reasonable is the 16-year-old daughter. (Rev: BL 10/1/95; SLJ 10/95; VOYA 12/95)

689 Gross, Gwendolen. *Getting Out* (10–12). 2002, Holt $24.00 (0-8050-6834-1). The lure of the outdoors and her Adventurers' Club competes with the needs of Hannah's boyfriend and various family members. (Rev: BL 6/1–15/02)

690 Gruen, Sara. *Riding Lessons* (10–12). 2004, HarperTorch paper $6.99 (0-06-058027-5). A mother returns with her rebellious 15-year-old daughter to her parents' riding school in New Hampshire where her father is dying of Lou Gehrig's disease. (Rev: BL 4/1/04*)

691 Grunwald, Lisa. *New Year's Eve* (10–12). 1997, Crown $24.00 (0-517-70491-9). Using observances of New Year's Eve from 1985 through 1991 as a focus, this novel tells of a family's adjustment to the death of a 4-year-old son and how the family members gradually build for the future. (Rev: BL 11/1/96; SLJ 7/97)

692 Guest, Judith. *Errands* (10–12). 1997, Ballantine $25.00 (0-345-40904-3). When her husband of 17 years dies of cancer, Annie Browner must find ways to support herself and her three children. (Rev: BL 10/15/96; SLJ 7/97; VOYA 8/97)

693 Guest, Judith. *Ordinary People* (10–12). 1982, Viking paper $8.95 (0-14-006517-2). The accidental death of one of two sons brings a family to crisis and disintegration. (Rev: BL 6/1/88)

694 Haddix, Margaret P. *Don't You Dare Read This, Mrs. Dunphrey* (7–10). 1996, Simon & Schuster $16.99 (0-689-80097-5). Tish keeps a journal for her sophomore English class in which she chronicles her many family problems culminating in her parents' abandonment of their children. (Rev: BL 10/15/96; SLJ 10/96; VOYA 12/96)

695 Haddix, Margaret P. *Takeoffs and Landings* (6–10). 2001, Simon & Schuster $16.00 (0-689-

83299-0). Popular 14-year-old Lori and her overweight older brother Chuck go on a lecture tour with their mother, and together the three finally start to talk about the guilt they feel over the death of the children's father. (Rev: BCCB 10/01; BL 11/15/01; HBG 3/02; SLJ 8/01; VOYA 10/01)

696 Haines, Lise. *In My Sister's Country* (11–12). 2002, Putnam $24.95 (0-399-14857-4). A dark story of rivalry between two sisters brought up by a difficult father; for mature teens. (Rev: BL 3/15/02)

697 Hall, Barbara. *Dixie Storms* (7–12). 1990, Harcourt $15.95 (0-15-223825-5). Dutch's troubled relationships within her family worsen when cousin Norma comes to stay. (Rev: BL 5/1/90; SLJ 9/90)

698 Hall, Lynn. *Flying Changes* (7–12). 1991, Harcourt $13.95 (0-15-228790-6). An awkward Kansas teenager must give up her romantic dreams after her father is paralyzed and her mother, who abandoned her years before, returns home. (Rev: BL 6/15/91*)

699 Hamilton, Jane. *Disobedience* (10–12). 2000, Doubleday $24.95 (0-385-50117-X). This novel of the Shaw family is narrated by teenage Henry, who discovers via the Internet that his mother is having an extramarital affair. (Rev: BL 8/00)

700 Hamilton, Virginia. *Junius over Far* (9–12). 1985, HarperCollins $12.95 (0-06-022194-1). Fearful that grandfather is lonely as he approaches death on a Caribbean island, 14-year-old Junius and his father go to visit him. (Rev: BL 5/15/85; BR 11–12/85; SLJ 8/85; VOYA 6/85)

701 Hamilton, Virginia. *M.C. Higgins, the Great* (6–10). 1974, Macmillan LB $17.00 (0-02-742480-4); paper $4.99 (0-02-043490-1). The Newbery Medal winner (1975) about a 13-year-old African American boy growing up in Appalachia as part of a loving family whose future is threatened by a possible mountain slide.

702 Hannah, Kristin. *Between Sisters* (11–12). 2003, Ballantine $23.95 (0-345-45073-6). As adults, Meghann and Claire tackle conflicts that separated them when they were children. (Rev: BL 3/15/03)

703 Hannah, Kristin. *Summer Island* (10–12). 2001, Crown $21.00 (0-609-60737-5). Ruby is hired to interview the mother who abandoned her family when Ruby was 16. (Rev: BL 1/1–15/01)

704 Harrison, Troon. *Goodbye to Atlantis* (7–10). 2002, Stoddart paper $7.95 (0-7737-6229-9). Stella, 14, whose mother died of cancer, initially resents being stuck with her father's girlfriend as a traveling companion. (Rev: BL 9/1/02; SLJ 4/02)

705 Hart, Lenore. *Waterwoman* (11–12). 2002, Berkley $21.95 (0-425-18471-4). In the early 20th century, a young woman — who has taken on the support of her fragile mother and envied younger sister — brings her lover home to meet her family; for mature teens. (Rev: BL 5/1/02)

706 Hartnett, Sonya. *What the Birds See* (7–12). 2003, Candlewick $15.99 (0-7636-2092-0). A beautifully written complex story featuring three missing children and a lonely and fearful boy who is fascinated by three children who move in next door. (Rev: BCCB 3/03; BL 4/15/03; HB 5–6/03; HBG 10/03; SLJ 5/03; VOYA 6/03)

707 Hassler, Jon. *Grand Opening* (9–12). 1987, Ballantine paper $6.99 (0-345-35016-2). The Foster family moves to a small, unfriendly town to open up a grocery store. (Rev: BR 11–12/87; SLJ 2/88)

708 Hathorn, Libby. *Thunderwith* (7–10). 1991, Little, Brown $15.95 (0-316-35034-6). This story of an unhappy 15-year-old girl and a beautiful dingolike dog she finds is set in the Australian rain forest. (Rev: BL 9/1/91; SLJ 5/91*)

709 Hay, Elizabeth. *A Student of Weather* (10–12). 2001, Counterpoint $24.00 (1-58243-123-X). Beginning in 1930 in the prairies of Saskatchewan, the sibling rivalry between two sisters continues throughout their lives. (Rev: BL 11/15/00)

710 Haynes, David. *Right by My Side* (9–12). 1993, New Rivers paper $12.95 (0-89823-147-7). African American teen Marshall Field Finney describes a year of his life — the year his mother left him and his father ran away to Las Vegas to find himself. (Rev: BL 2/15/93*; SLJ 12/93)

711 Hernandez, Irene B. *The Secret of Two Brothers* (7–10). 1995, Arte Publico paper $9.95 (1-55885-142-9). An action-packed story about two Mexican American boys who meet many challenges. Especially appealing to those whose first language is Spanish or for reluctant readers. (Rev: BL 10/1/95; SLJ 11/95)

712 Heuler, Karen. *The Soft Room* (10–12). 2004, Livingston $25.00 (1-931982-31-7). The story of twin girls, one of whom is unable to feel pain, and their mutual affection and care. (Rev: BL 3/15/04*)

713 Hill, Donna. *Rhythms* (10–12). 2001, St. Martin's $23.95 (0-312-27299-5). The gripping story of three generations of African American women and their different dreams of leaving the small town where they live. (Rev: BL 6/1–15/01)

714 Hill, Ernest. *Cry Me a River* (10–12). 2003, Kensington $24.00 (0-7582-0276-8). African American Tyrone Stokes, released from prison only to find out that his 17-year-old son is on death row, sets out to prove Marcus's innocence. (Rev: BL 2/15/03)

715 Hinton, S. E. *Taming the Star Runner* (7–12). 1989, Bantam paper $5.50 (0-440-20479-8). A tough delinquent is sent to his uncle's ranch to be straightened out and there he falls in love with Casey, who is trying to tame a wild horse named Star Runner. (Rev: BL 10/15/88; BR 11–12/88; SLJ 10/88; VOYA 12/88)

716 Hobbs, Valerie. *Tender* (8–12). 2001, Farrar $18.00 (0-374-37397-3). After her grandmother's death, Liv must adjust to a new life in California with a father she has never met. (Rev: BCCB 10/01; BL 8/01; HB 9–10/01; HBG 3/02; SLJ 9/01; VOYA 10/01)

717 Hoffman, Alice. *At Risk* (10–12). 1988, Putnam paper $7.99 (0-425-11738-3). The happy life of the Farrell family is shattered when they discover that their 11-year-old daughter has AIDS. (Rev: SLJ 12/88)

718 Hoffman, Alice. *Green Angel* (6–12). 2003, Scholastic $16.95 (0-439-44384-9). Fifteen-year-old Green, so-called for her gardening skills, is the only member of her family to survive a major disaster. (Rev: BL 4/15/03; HB 3–4/03; HBG 10/03; SLJ 3/03*; VOYA 4/03)

719 Holeman, Linda. *Raspberry House Blues* (6–10). 2000, Tundra paper $6.95 (0-88776-493-2). Poppy's search for her birth mother looks hopeful for a while when she spends a summer in Winnipeg. (Rev: SLJ 12/00; VOYA 2/01)

720 Holmes, Dee. *The Boy on the Porch,* (10–12). 2003, Berkley paper $6.99 (0-425-18815-9). A teenage boy claims to be the son of Annie's late husband in this deftly told tale. (Rev: BL 1/1–15/03)

721 Holt, Kimberley Willis. *Keeper of the Night* (6–10). 2003, Holt $16.95 (0-8050-6361-7). Isabel, a 13-year-old who lives on Guam, tells the story of her mother's suicide and the family's subsequent grief. (Rev: BL 4/15/03; HB 5–6/03; HBG 10/03; SLJ 5/03*; VOYA 6/03)

722 Horniman, Joanne. *Mahalia* (9–12). 2003, Knopf LB $17.99 (0-375-92325-X). Matt is only 17 but he succeeds in being a good parent to his baby daughter when her mother moves out. (Rev: BCCB 6/03; BL 7/03; HB 7–8/03; HBG 10/03; SLJ 4/03; VOYA 6/03)

723 Houston, Jeanne Wakatsuki. *The Legend of Fire Horse Woman* (10–12). 2003, Kensington $23.00 (0-7582-0455-8). This heartwarming multi-generational novel chronicles the lives of Sayo, a Japanese-born woman who emigrates to America after marriage and is interned during World War II; her daughter, Hana; and granddaughter, Terri. (Rev: BL 11/15/03)

724 Huddle, David. *La Tour Dreams of the Wolf Girl* (11–12). 2002, Houghton $24.00 (0-618-08173-9). Suzanne's rich fantasy life involving the paintings of Georges de La Tour helps her escape from her unsatisfying marriage to Jack; a thoughtful novel for mature teens. (Rev: BL 2/1/02*)

725 Iida, Deborah. *Middle Son* (10–12). 1996, Algonquin $29.95 (1-56512-119-8). The death of an older brother haunts Spencer in this novel about a Japanese American family in Hawaii. (Rev: BL 3/1/98; SLJ 1/97)

726 Inclan, Jessica Barclan. *When You Go Away* (11–12). 2003, NAL paper $12.95 (0-451-20787-4). The stresses of divorce, financial hardship, and caring for a disabled child are shown clearly in this moving novel that features two teenagers and is suitable for mature readers. (Rev: BL 3/15/03)

727 Irving, John. *The World According to Garp* (10–12). 1997, Ballantine paper $14.00 (0-345-41801-8). A satirical novel that spans four generations and two continents.

728 Jaffe, Sherril. *Ground Rules: What I Learned My Daughter's Fifteenth Year* (10–12). 1997, Kodansha $20.00 (1-56836-172-6). Told from a mother's point of view, this novel tells of the clash between the mother and her 15-year-old daughter, who becomes increasingly unhappy, uncooperative, and defiant. (Rev: SLJ 8/97)

729 Johnson, Angela. *Heaven* (6–10). 1998, Simon & Schuster $16.00 (0-689-82229-4). Marley, a 14-year-old African American girl, is devastated when she learns that she is adopted and that the couple she has regarded as her mother and father are really her aunt and uncle. (Rev: BCCB 12/98; BL 9/15/98; BR 5–6/99; HBG 3/99; SLJ 10/98; VOYA 2/99)

730 Johnson, R. M. *The Harris Men* (10–12). 1999, Simon & Schuster $22.50 (0-684-84470-2). This novel traces the fate of three African American boys after their father deserts them and the father's attempts to contact them after 20 years. (Rev: SLJ 9/99)

731 Johnston, Julie. *In Spite of Killer Bees* (7–10). 2001, Tundra $17.95 (0-88776-537-8). Aggie, 14, and her older sisters inherit a house from their grandfather and must endure suspicion on the part of their aunt and new neighbors before they succeed in forging new relationships. (Rev: BCCB 12/01; BL 1/1–15/02; HB 1–2/02; HBG 3/02; SLJ 12/01*; VOYA 12/01)

732 Johnston, Julie. *The Only Outcast* (6–10). 1998, Tundra $14.95 (0-88776-441-X). Based on fact, this is the story of the summer of 1904 when Fred Dickinson spent the summer with his grandparents in Ontario and found romance and a mystery. (Rev: BL 10/1/98; BR 1–2/99; HB 1–2/99; HBG 3/99; SLJ 1/99; VOYA 2/99)

733 Johnston, Tim. *Never So Green* (6–10). 2002, Farrar $18.00 (0-374-35509-6). Twelve-year-old Tex, who has a growing interest in sex, is horrified to find that his stepsister is being sexually abused in this novel full of realistic characters and subplots. (Rev: BCCB 12/02; BL 9/1/02; HBG 3/03; SLJ 10/02)

734 Kennedy, Kate. *End over End* (10–12). 2001, Soho Pr. $24.00 (1-56947-235-1). A mature novel about a rebellious 14-year-old girl who is doing drugs, drinking, and having sex, and about what happens to her family after she runs away from home. (Rev: BL 4/1/01)

735 Khashoggi, Soheir. *Mirage* (9–12). 1997, Forge paper $6.99 (0-614-20507-7). A novel with the plight of a Middle Eastern Islamic woman at its heart, from an author who is a product of a similar culture. (Rev: BL 12/1/95*)

736 Klein, Norma. *Breaking Up* (7–10). 1981, Avon paper $2.50 (0-380-55830-0). While visiting her divorced father in California, Alison falls in love with her best friend's brother.

737 Klein, Norma. *Going Backwards* (9–12). 1986, Scholastic paper $12.95 (0-590-40328-1). A wrenching story of a boy and his grandmother, who is suffering from Alzheimer's disease, that introduces the theme of mercy killing. (Rev: BL 10/15/86; SLJ 1/87; VOYA 2/87)

738 Klein, Norma. *It's OK If You Don't Love Me* (9–12). 1987, Fawcett paper $4.50 (0-449-70236-7). Young people must cope with their parents' marital crises.

739 Koller, Jackie F. *A Place to Call Home* (7–10). 1995, Atheneum $16.00 (0-689-80024-X). Biracial Anna, 15, is a strong character in search of love and roots following sexual abuse and rejection from her own family. (Rev: BL 10/15/95; SLJ 10/95; VOYA 2/96)

740 Kotker, Zane. *Try to Remember* (10–12). 1997, Random $23.00 (0-679-44042-9). Told from four different viewpoints (a father, mother, and their two grown daughters), this novel explores the turmoil caused when a therapist, who has her own agenda, persuades the oldest daughter to falsely accuse her father of sexual abuse. (Rev: SLJ 2/98)

741 Lamazares, Ivonne. *The Sugar Island* (10–12). 2000, Houghton $23.00 (0-395-86040-7). Beginning in Cuba in 1958, this novel about mother–daughter relationships becomes more complex when the two eventually make it to Miami. (Rev: BL 8/00; SLJ 3/01)

742 Lantz, Francess. *Someone to Love* (7–10). 1997, Avon $14.00 (0-380-97477-0). Sara's secure family life changes when her parents decide to adopt the yet-unborn child of Iris, an unmarried teen. (Rev: BL 4/15/97; BR 9–10/97)

743 Lattany, Kristin Hunter. *Kinfolks* (10–12). 1996, Ballantine $23.00 (0-345-40706-7). Two African American women, both single mothers, discover they have the same father and set out to find their kinfolk. (Rev: BL 10/15/96; SLJ 5/97)

744 Lawrence, Iain. *The Lightkeeper's Daughter* (10–12). 2002, Delacorte $16.95 (0-385-72925-1). When 17-year-old Squid returns to her childhood home after a long absence, her arrival forces Squid and her parents to confront secrets from the past and the painful loss of Alastair, Squid's brother. (Rev:

BCCB 11/02; BL 1/1–15/03; HB 11–12/02; HBG 3/03; SLJ 9/02; VOYA 12/02)

745 Lawson, Mary. *Crow Lake* (10–12). 2002, Dial $23.95 (0-385-33611-X). When Kate's parents died, her brother Luke had to forgo college in order to raise his siblings in their rural Canadian community. (Rev: BL 1/1–15/02; SLJ 9/02)

746 Lelchuk, Alan. *On Home Ground* (7–10). Illus. 1987, Harcourt $9.95 (0-15-200560-9). Aaron seems to have nothing in common with his father, a Russian immigrant. (Rev: BL 1/1/88; SLJ 12/87; VOYA 4/88)

747 L'Engle, Madeleine. *The Moon by Night* (7–10). 1963, Farrar $16.00 (0-374-35049-3); Dell paper $4.99 (0-440-95776-1). In this novel about the Austins, the family takes a cross-country camping trip and Vicki finds she is attracted to the wealthy, irresponsible Zachery Gray.

748 Lennon, J. Robert. *On the Night Plain* (10–12). 2001, Holt $23.00 (0-8050-6722-1). Grant hopes to rebuild the family ranch with the help of his brother, Max, but Max has other plans. (Rev: BL 7/01)

749 Lester, Julius. *When Dad Killed Mom* (8–12). 2001, Harcourt $17.00 (0-15-216305-0). In alternating chapters that include graphic language, a brother and sister relate their emotions and reactions as they struggle to understand why their father killed their mother. (Rev: BL 6/1–15/01; HB 5–6/01; HBG 10/01; SLJ 5/01; VOYA 10/01)

750 Levitin, Sonia. *The Singing Mountain* (7–12). 1998, Simon & Schuster $17.00 (0-689-80809-7). Family secrets are revealed when Carlie accompanies her aunt Vivian to Israel to convince Vivian's son to return to America. (Rev: BL 9/15/98; HB 11–12/98; HBG 3/99; SLJ 11/98; VOYA 2/99)

751 Levitin, Sonia. *Yesterday's Child* (7–10). 1997, Simon & Schuster $17.00 (0-689-80810-0). After her parent's death, Laura discovers some amazing family secrets when she goes through her mother's things. (Rev: BL 6/1–15/97; SLJ 6/97)

752 Lockhart, Zelda. *Fifth Born* (11–12). 2002, Pocket $24.00 (0-7434-1265-6). The fifth of eight children in a severely dysfunctional family, Odessa retreats within herself after being sexually abused by her father and witnessing the murder of her uncle; for mature readers. (Rev: BL 8/02)

753 Lowry, Lois. *Find a Stranger, Say Goodbye* (7–10). 1978, Houghton $17.00 (0-395-26459-6). A college-bound girl decides she wants to find her natural mother.

754 Lynch, Chris. *Gypsy Davey* (9–12). 1998, HarperCollins paper $11.00 (0064407306). The sad story of Davey, a boy growing up alone in the midst of a dysfunctional family. (Rev: BL 10/1/94; SLJ 10/94)

755 Lynch, Chris. *Shadow Boxer* (6–10). 1993, HarperCollins LB $14.89 (0-06-023028-2). Their father's death leaves 14-year-old George and his hyperactive younger brother in a conflict that can only be resolved by dispelling their father's shadow. (Rev: BL 12/15/93; SLJ 9/93*; VOYA 12/93)

756 Lynn, Tracy. *Snow* (7–10). 2003, Simon & Schuster paper $5.99 (0-689-85556-7). The story of Snow White gets a new twist in this exciting novel set in Victorian England, in which Snow's growing beauty inflames her stepmother with jealousy and Snow flees from her father's castle to the dangers of the London streets. (Rev: BCCB 5/03; SLJ 8/03; VOYA 8/03)

757 McCord, Patricia. *Pictures in the Dark* (7–10). 2004, Bloomsbury $16.95 (1-58234-848-0). Set in the 1950s, this is the story of two sisters, one 12 and the other 15, and how their mother gradually sank into insanity. (Rev: BL 5/15/04; HB 7–8/04; SLJ 5/04)

758 McDonald, Janet. *Spellbound* (7–12). 2001, Farrar $16.00 (0-374-37140-7). Despite enormous obstacles, 16-year-old African American mother Raven decides to enter a spelling bee in hopes of going to college. (Rev: BCCB 10/01; BL 11/1/01; HB 1–2/02; HBG 3/02; SLJ 9/01; VOYA 10/01)

759 McEwan, Ian. *Atonement* (10–12). 2002, Doubleday $26.00 (0-385-50395-4). Set on an English country estate at which there is a family reunion, this novel for mature readers tells how an imaginative young girl can cause events to spin out of control. (Rev: BL 11/15/01*; SLJ 6/02)

760 McFadden, Bernice L. *The Warmest December* (10–12). 2001, Dutton $22.95 (0-525-94564-4). Themes of abuse and alcoholism are explored in this touching novel for mature readers in which a young woman is compelled to visit her dying father. (Rev: BL 1/1–15/01)

761 McGhee, Alison. *Shadow Baby* (10–12). 2000, Crown $23.00 (0-609-60632-8). A strong, adult novel about a curious 11-year-old girl and her friendship with Georg, a man in his 70s without a family. (Rev: BL 4/1/00; SLJ 6/01)

762 McGovern, Cammie. *The Art of Seeing* (10–12). 2002, Scribner $24.00 (0-7432-2835-9). Sisters who have trouble communicating come together when the successful actress is hospitalized and her photographer sister can perhaps help. (Rev: BL 8/02)

763 Mack, Tracy. *Birdland* (7–10). 2003, Scholastic $16.95 (0-439-53590-5). Jed's family has not recovered from the death of his brother Zeke, and Jed finds some comfort in videotaping their neighborhood and finding links to Zeke through the poems and journal he left. (Rev: BL 10/15/03*; SLJ 10/03)

764 McKinney-Whetstone, Diane. *Tempest Rising* (10–12). 1998, Morrow $24.00 (0-688-14994-4); paper $12.00 (0-688-16640-7). After the death of

their father and the mental collapse of their mother, three African American adolescent sisters are placed in a foster-home, where new relationships are built. (Rev: BL 2/15/98; SLJ 10/98)

765 MacKinnon, Bernie. *Song for a Shadow* (8–12). 1991, Houghton $18.00 (0-395-55419-5). This novel concerns 18-year-old Aaron's attempts to sort out his relationships with his parents — his father has always seemed too wrapped up in his career, and his mother is emotionally troubled. (Rev: BL 3/15/91; SLJ 4/91)

766 MacLachlan, Patricia. *Baby* (5–10). 1993, Delacorte $15.95 (0-385-31133-8). In this moving, beautifully written story, "Baby" refers to two youngsters: Larkin's brother (who died before the story begins) and Sophie, who's left in a basket on the driveway of Larkin's home. (Rev: BL 9/1/93; SLJ 11/93; VOYA 10/93)

767 McMurtry, Larry. *Terms of Endearment* (10–12). 1989, Simon & Schuster paper $8.95 (0-671-68208-3). The complex relationship between mother and daughter, which involves adjustments to marriage, and a fatal illness form the basis of this novel.

768 McNamee, Graham. *Hate You* (9–12). 1999, Bantam $14.95 (0-385-32593-2). After Alice and her mother leave Alice's abusive father, Alice begins a new life and has a boyfriend, but then learns that her father is dying and wants to see her. (Rev: BL 2/1/99; HBG 9/99; SLJ 3/99; VOYA 4/99)

769 McPhee, Martha. *Bright Angel Time* (10–12). 1997, Random $23.00 (0-679-45008-4); Harcourt paper $12.00 (0-15-600586-7). A novel of loss and love as seen through the eyes of 8-year-old Kate who, after her father leaves the family, accompanies her mother, two older sisters, her mother's boyfriend, and his family as they travel through the Southwest in a camper. (Rev: BL 6/1–15/97; SLJ 6/98)

770 Manley, Frank. *The Cockfighter* (10–12). 1998, Coffee House $19.95 (1-56689-073-X). In this novel set in the rural South, the hatred that develops between a sensitive 13-year-boy and his crude, redneck father who raises cocks for illegal cockfighting erupts in a bloody climax. (Rev: BL 3/15/98; SLJ 10/98)

771 Marion, Stephen. *Hollow Ground* (10–12). 2002, Algonquin $23.95 (1-56512-323-9). Taft must deal with several problems including a long-absent father's sudden return to Zinctown, Tennessee. (Rev: BL 2/1/02)

772 Marsden, John. *Letters from the Inside* (8–12). 1994, Houghton $16.00 (0-395-68985-6). Two teenage girls begin a correspondence, with their initial letters describing ideal fictitious lives. With time, they reveal that one has a violent brother and the other feels trapped within her family. (Rev: BL 10/15/94*; SLJ 9/94*; VOYA 12/94)

773 Mazer, Harry. *Who Is Eddie Leonard?* (7–10). 1995, Demco $10.04 (0-606-08379-0). When his grandmother dies, Eddie sees a missing-child poster that convinces him he's really the kidnapped Jason Diaz. But the Diazes aren't the perfect family he imagined. (Rev: BL 11/15/93; SLJ 11/93; VOYA 4/94)

774 Mazer, Norma Fox. *After the Rain* (7–10). 1987, Morrow $17.99 (0-688-06867-7); Avon paper $5.99 (0-380-75025-2). Rachel gradually develops a warm relationship with her terminally ill grandfather who is noted for his bad temper. (Rev: BL 5/1/87; BR 5–6/87; SLJ 5/87; VOYA 6/87)

775 Mazer, Norma Fox. *Downtown* (7–10). 1984, Avon paper $4.95 (0-380-88534-4). Pete, 15, the son of anti-war demonstrators who are in hiding, faces problems when his mother reappears and wants to be part of his life.

776 Mazer, Norma Fox. *Missing Pieces* (7–10). 1995, Morrow $16.00 (0-688-13349-5). A 14-year-old seeks a missing part of her life by looking for a father who abandoned her. (Rev: BL 4/1/95; SLJ 4/95*; VOYA 5/95)

777 Mazer, Norma Fox. *Taking Terri Mueller* (7–10). 1983, Avon paper $5.99 (0-380-79004-1). Terri realizes that her beloved father has actually kidnapped her to keep her from her mother.

778 Mendelsohn, Jane. *Innocence* (10–12). 2000, Riverhead $21.95 (1-57322-164-3). For mature readers, this coming-of-age story of a privileged New York teenager includes violence, suicide, and some drug use. (Rev: BL 9/1/00)

779 Michaels, Fern. *Kentucky Heat* (11–12). 2002, Kensington $24.00 (1-57566-762-2). In this fast-paced sequel to *Kentucky Rich* (2001), Nealy handles family problems, finds romance, and trains a horse that might win the Triple Crown; one of many titles by this popular writer. (Rev: BL 3/1/02)

780 Mickle, Shelley Fraser. *Replacing Dad* (9–12). 1993, Algonquin $25.95 (1-56512-017-5). A teenage boy and his mother relate their experiences and the emotional upheaval that followed the mother's divorce, told in alternating chapters. (Rev: BL 5/15/93)

781 Mitchard, Jacquelyn. *The Most Wanted* (10–12). 1998, Viking $24.95 (0-6708-7884-7). Various aspects of motherhood are explored in this novel about a 14-year-old girl who falls in love with and bears the child of a prison inmate who later escapes. (Rev: BL 4/15/98*; SLJ 2/99)

782 Mitchard, Jacquelyn. *A Theory of Relativity* (10–12). 2001, HarperCollins $26.00 (0-06-621023-2). When a husband and wife die under mysterious

circumstances leaving a one-year-old daughter, a custody battle ensues. (Rev: BL 4/1/01)

783 Moore, Ishbel. *Daughter* (6–12). 1999, Kids Can $14.95 (1-55074-535-2). Sylvie struggles to cope with her parents' divorce and her mother's Alzheimer's disease in this moving story. (Rev: BCCB 12/99; BL 11/15/99; HBG 4/00; SLJ 11/99)

784 Morgan, Robert. *This Rock* (10–12). 2001, Algonquin $24.95 (1-56512-303-4). Set in the rural South in the early 1920s, this novel tells of the bitter and protracted rivalry between brothers Muir and Moody Powell. (Rev: BL 7/01; SLJ 4/02)

785 Mori, Kyoko. *One Bird* (8–12). 1996, Fawcett paper $6.50 (0-449-70453-X). A coming-of-age story set in Japan about 15-year-old girl Megumi, who loses her mother yet finds people who understand and love her. (Rev: BL 10/15/95; SLJ 11/95; VOYA 2/96)

786 Moring, Marcel. *The Dream Room* (10–12). 2002, Morrow $22.95 (0-06-621240-5). Twelve-year-old David, a happy boy with a love of cooking, believes his life in 1960s Holland is settled and comfortable despite a few challenges; but this peace will soon be shattered. (Rev: BL 2/1/02)

787 Morrell, David. *Fireflies* (9–12). 1999, Warner paper $12.99 (0-446-67590-3). A "nonfiction novel" about the death of the author's 15-year-old son from bone cancer. (Rev: BL 9/1/88)

788 Morris, Michael. *Slow Way Home* (11–12). 2003, HarperSF $22.95 (0-06-056898-4). An absorbing story of a neglected child who finds religion. (Rev: BL 8/03; SLJ 2/04)

789 Murray, Jaye. *Bottled Up* (7–12). 2003, Dial $16.99 (0-8037-2897-2). Pip, 17 and constantly in trouble, is coaxed by the school principal to clean up his act. (Rev: BCCB 7–8/03; HBG 4/04; LMC 2/03; SLJ 6/03; VOYA 8/03)

790 Myers, Walter Dean. *Somewhere in the Darkness* (7–12). 1992, Scholastic paper $14.95 (0-590-42411-4). A father and son get to know each other after the father is released from prison. (Rev: BL 2/1/92*; SLJ 4/92*)

791 Naylor, Phyllis Reynolds. *Walker's Crossing* (6–12). 1999, Simon & Schuster $16.00 (0-689-82939-6). Shy Ryan Walker is beset with family problems — a sick father, a depressed mother, an older sister who wants to become Rodeo Queen, and a brother who has joined a militia group. (Rev: BCCB 11/99; BL 9/15/99; HBG 4/00; SLJ 11/99; VOYA 2/00)

792 Nelson, Kent. *Land That Moves, Land That Stands Still* (11–12). 2003, Viking $24.95 (0-670-03226-3). Set in this West, this is the story of a widowed ranch owner and her daughter, who both work to keep the farm and their own lives going. (Rev: BL 7/03*)

793 Nissen, Thisbe. *The Good People of New York* (10–12). 2001, Knopf $23.00 (0-375-41145-3). Teenage Miranda is living with her father and loving mother, but she wants to grow up too fast and soon begins leading a wild life. (Rev: BL 4/15/01*)

794 Nolan, Han. *A Face in Every Window* (7–10). 1999, Harcourt $16.00 (0-15-201915-4). Fourteen-year-old JP's life is turned upside down when his grandmother dies and his flighty mother wins a house in a contest. (Rev: BCCB 12/99; BL 11/1/99; HBG 4/00; SLJ 9/99; VOYA 12/99)

795 Nye, Jody Lynn. *Don't Forget Your Spacesuit, Dear* (10–12). 1996, Baen paper $5.99 (0-671-87732-1). The various roles of mothers are explored in this imaginative collection of 18 stories, whose subjects include mothers who are computers, animals, or aliens. (Rev: SLJ 7/97)

796 Oates, Joyce Carol. *Freaky Green Eyes* (7–10). 2003, HarperCollins LB $17.89 (0-06-623757-2). Franky, 15, recounts the tensions between her artist mother and her abusive, controlling father and the buildup to her mother's eventual disappearance. (Rev: BL 12/1/03; HB 11–12/03; HBG 4/04; SLJ 10/03; VOYA 10/03)

797 Olsen, Sylvia. *The Girl with a Baby* (6–10). 2004, Sono Nis paper $7.95 (1-55039-142-9). A biracial girl of white and Indian parents wants to stay in school and raise her baby but finds it difficult. (Rev: BL 3/15/04; SLJ 7/04)

798 Oughton, Jerrie. *The War in Georgia* (7–12). 1997, Bantam paper $4.50 (0-440-22752-6). During the last days of World War II in Atlanta, 13-year-old Shanta befriends a girl and her brain-injured brother and, through them, enters the nightmare world of child abuse. (Rev: BL 4/1/97; BR 9–10/97; SLJ 5/97)

799 Owens, Janis. *The Schooling of Claybird Catts* (10–12). 2003, HarperCollins $24.95 (0-06-009062-6). Clay learns he is really his uncle's son in this third novel about the Catts family. (Rev: BL 3/1/03)

800 Parr, Delia. *Home to Trinity* (9–12). 2003, St. Martin's $24.95 (0-312-27098-4). Martha's daughter returns to Trinity and Martha must tackle building a new relationship with her while at the same time expanding her own horizons in this sequel to *A Place Called Trinity* (2002). (Rev: BL 3/1/03)

801 Pate, Alexs D. *West of Rehoboth* (10–12). 2001, Morrow $24.00 (0-380-97679-X). Twelve-year-old Edward, who is visiting his aunt for a summer in the 1960s, investigates the mystery surrounding Rufus, whom he believes is his uncle. (Rev: BL 9/1/01*)

802 Paterson, Katherine. *Come Sing, Jimmy Jo* (6–10). 1985, Avon paper $3.99 (0-380-70052-2). The family decides it's time to include James in their singing group. (Rev: BL 9/1/87; SLJ 4/85)

803 Paterson, Katherine. *Jacob Have I Loved* (6–10). 1980, HarperCollins LB $16.89 (0-690-04079-2); paper $6.50 (0-06-440368-8). A story set in the Chesapeake Bay region about the rivalry between two sisters. Newbery Medal winner, 1981.

804 Paulsen, Gary. *The Tent: A Parable in One Sitting* (6–10). 1995, Harcourt $15.00 (0-15-292879-0). A 14-year-old struggles to keep his values when his father fraudulently poses as an itinerant preacher. (Rev: BL 3/15/95; SLJ 5/95)

805 Peck, Richard. *Father Figure* (7–10). 1996, Puffin paper $5.99 (0-14-037969-X). Jim and his younger brother are sent to live in Florida with a father they scarcely know.

806 Pennebaker, Ruth. *Both Sides Now* (9–12). 2000, Holt $15.95 (0-8050-6105-3). Liza must deal with the reoccurrence of her mother's breast cancer and its effect on her family. (Rev: BL 6/1–15/00; HB 9–10/00; HBG 9/00; SLJ 7/00; VOYA 6/00)

807 Pfeffer, Susan Beth. *The Year Without Michael* (7–12). 1988, Demco $10.55 (0-606-03959-7). When Jody's brother Michael, a high school freshman, disappears, the solidarity of her family is shattered. (Rev: BL 10/1/87; BR 5–6/88; SLJ 11/87; VOYA 10/87)

808 Picoult, Jodi. *My Sister's Keeper* (10–12). 2004, Atria $25.00 (0-7434-5452-9). Thirteen-year-old Anna Fitzgerald decides not to donate a kidney to help her older sister, who has leukemia, and seeks legal assistance. (Rev: BL 1/1–15/04*)

809 Pilcher, Robin. *A Risk Worth Taking* (11–12). 2004, St. Martin's $24.95 (0-312-27002-X). In this charming tale of new beginnings, a former investment banker and father of two teenage daughters who was let go after the dot.com collapse searches for a new career and new meaning in his life; for mature teens. (Rev: BL 11/15/03)

810 Pilcher, Rosamunde. *Winter Solstice* (10–12). 2000, St. Martin's $27.95 (0-312-24426-6). A warm and thoughtful novel about a group, including a 14-year-old girl, gathered together in a small town in Scotland. (Rev: BL 6/1–15/00)

811 Pohl, Peter, and Kinna Gieth. *I Miss You, I Miss You!* (9–12). Trans. by Roger Greenwald. 1999, Farrar $17.00 (91-29-63935-2). After her twin sister is killed in an accident, young teen Tina, overwhelmed with grief, finds that her personality is becoming more like that of the sister she has lost. (Rev: BL 5/1/99; HBG 9/99; SLJ 3/99; VOYA 6/99)

812 Porte, Barbara Ann. *Something Terrible Happened* (6–10). 1994, Orchard LB $17.99 (0-531-08719-0); Troll paper $4.50 (0-8167-3868-8). Part white, part West Indian, Gillian, 12, must adjust to living with her deceased father's "plain white" relatives when her mother contracts AIDS. (Rev: BL 9/15/94; SLJ 10/94; VOYA 10/94)

813 Powell, Randy. *Run If You Dare* (7–10). 2001, Farrar $17.00 (0-374-39981-6). Gardner coasts through life until his father loses his job and then confides to Gardner that he is thinking about leaving home, causing Gardner to reassess both his father and himself. (Rev: BCCB 6/01; BL 8/01; HB 5–6/01*; HBG 10/01; SLJ 3/01*; VOYA 6/01)

814 Powell, Randy. *Tribute to Another Dead Rock Star* (7–12). 1999, Farrar $17.00 (0-374-37748-0). Fifteen-year-old Gary returns to Seattle to speak at a concert honoring his deceased rock-star mother, who abused drugs and behaved irresponsibly, and must confront his mother's ex-boyfriend, the ex-boyfriend's new wife, and his mentally disabled stepbrother. (Rev: BL 3/1/99; HB 5–6/99; HBG 9/99; SLJ 5/99; VOYA 6/99)

815 Powell, Sophie. *The Mushroom Man* (11–12). 2003, Putnam $23.95 (0-399-14963-5). Two very different sisters bring their children together for the first time, with unpredictable results, in this appealing story set in England and Wales. (Rev: BL 2/15/03)

816 Pressler, Mirjam. *Halinka* (7–10). Trans. by Elizabeth D. Crawford. Illus. 1998, Holt $16.95 (0-8050-5861-3). The disturbing story of a 12-year-old Gypsy girl who lives with six other girls in a welfare home in Germany and of her many problems and her hope for a stable homelife. (Rev: BL 10/15/98; HB 1–2/99; HBG 3/99; SLJ 1/99; VOYA 4/99)

817 Pringer, Nancy. *Toughing It* (7–10). 1994, Harcourt $10.95 (0-15-200008-9); paper $4.95 (0-15-200011-9). Tuff lives in a trailer with his alcoholic mother and her abusive boyfriend. When Tuff is murdered, Dillon, his younger brother, runs to the man who could be his father. (Rev: BL 9/1/94; SLJ 9/94; VOYA 8/94)

818 Quarles, Heather. *A Door Near Here* (7–10). 1998, Doubleday $13.95 (0-385-32595-9). When her mother loses her job and retreats into alcoholism, 15-year-old Katherine must take care of herself and three younger siblings. (Rev: BL 9/1/98; HBG 3/99; VOYA 10/98)

819 Quindlen, Anna. *Black and Blue* (10–12). 1998, Random $23.00 (0-375-50051-0). Love between parent and child, the importance of honesty in relationships, and self-knowledge as an essential part of healing are among the themes in this story of a battered wife who flees an abusive marriage with her 10-year-old son, but lives in fear that her husband will track her down. (Rev: SLJ 4/98)

820 Quindlen, Anna. *Object Lessons* (9–12). 1992, Ivy Books paper $6.99 (0-8041-0946-X). Maggie, 12, learns important lessons in life during the summer of 1960 in her home in the Bronx. (Rev: BL 1/15/91; SLJ 9/91)

821 Reynolds, April. *Knee-Deep in Wonder* (11–12). 2003, Holt $24.00 (0-8050-7346-9). Flashbacks during a day at a funeral reveal many secrets of four generations of Helene Strickland's complex African American family. (Rev: BL 9/1/03)

822 Reynolds, Marilyn. *Baby Help: True-to-Life Series from Hamilton High* (8–12). Series: Hamilton High. 1998, Morning Glory $15.95 (1-885356-26-9); paper $8.95 (1-885356-27-7). Partner-abuse is explored in this novel about a teenage mother who is living with a difficult boyfriend and his unsympathetic mother. (Rev: BL 2/1/98; HBG 9/98; SLJ 3/98; VOYA 6/98)

823 Reynolds, Marjorie. *The Starlite Drive-in* (10–12). 1997, Morrow $23.00 (0-688-15389-5). A 13-year-old girl growing up in rural Indiana during 1956 becomes alarmed when an attractive drifter begins paying attention to her emotionally unbalanced mother. (Rev: SLJ 3/98)

824 Rice, Ben. *Pobby and Dingan* (10–12). Illus. 2000, Knopf $16.00 (0-375-41127-5). When Kellyanne's imaginary playmates disappear, older brother Ashmol sets out to find them in this charming novel of childhood in a small Australian town. (Rev: BL 9/1/00)

825 Rice, Luanne. *The Perfect Summer* (11–12). 2003, Bantam paper $7.50 (0-553-58404-9). Life changes dramatically for Bay McCabe and her children when husband and father Sean McCabe is accused of theft. (Rev: BL 8/03)

826 Richler, Emma. *Sister Crazy* (10–12). 2001, Pantheon $22.00 (0-375-42108-4). The middle child of five siblings remembers her childhood as she faces trouble as an adult. (Rev: BL 4/15/01)

827 Riggs, Jack. *When the Finch Rises* (11–12). 2003, Ballantine $23.95 (0-345-46794-9). In this touching first novel, recommended only for mature teens, two 12-year-old boys in a North Carolina mill town find refuge from the dysfunction of their family lives in the bonds of friendship. (Rev: BL 9/1/03*)

828 Robinson, Elisabeth. *The True and Outstanding Adventures of the Hunt Sisters* (10–12). 2004, Little, Brown $23.95 (0-316-73502-7). Rising Hollywood producer Olivia Hunt faces some tough choices when her younger sister, who still lives in their Ohio hometown, is diagnosed with leukemia. (Rev: BL 11/1/03*)

829 Rosenfeld, Stephanie. *Massachusetts, California, Timbuktu* (11–12). 2003, Ballantine $23.95 (0-345-44825-1). Justine is only 12 but the plucky girl has learned to look after herself and her younger sister when their mother's wanderlust takes hold; for mature readers. (Rev: BL 5/15/03; SLJ 10/03)

830 Rottman, S. L. *Shadow of a Doubt* (7–10). Illus. 2003, Peachtree $14.95 (1-56145-291-2). Shadow is newly 15 and entering high school when his brother

Daniel, who has been missing for years, reappears on the scene, suspected of murder. (Rev: BCCB 1/04; BL 11/15/03; HBG 4/04; SLJ 1/04; VOYA 12/03)

831 Ryan, Mary. *The Song of the Tide* (10–12). 2000, St. Martin's $24.95 (0-312-26648-0). In this poignant novel for mature readers set in Ireland, young Aine falls in love with her American cousin. (Rev: BL 10/15/00; SLJ 3/01)

832 Sachs, Marilyn. *Baby Sister* (7–10). 1986, Avon paper $3.50 (0-380-70358-0). Penny is torn between her admiration for her older sister and the realization that she is really selfish. (Rev: BL 2/15/86; BR 5–6/86; SLJ 8/86; VOYA 8/86)

833 Salinger, J. D. *Franny and Zooey* (10–12). 1961, Little, Brown $24.95 (0-316-76954-1); paper $5.99 (0-316-76949-5). A Glass family story in which Zooey Glass tries to help his sister Franny out of her depression.

834 Samuel, Barbara. *A Piece of Heaven* (11–12). 2003, Ballantine $23.95 (0-345-44567-8). Sobriety, a new romance, and the arrival of her teenage daughter to live with her are some of Luna's preoccupations in this affecting novel; for mature teens. (Rev: BL 11/15/02)

835 Saroyan, William. *The Human Comedy* (7–12). 1973, Dell paper $6.50 (0-440-33933-2). Homer Macauley is growing up during World War II in America, part of the everyday life that is the human comedy.

836 Sarsfield, Mairuth. *No Crystal Stair* (10–12). 1997, Stoddart $14.95 (1-896867-02-2). Set in a black community in Quebec during the 1940s, this is a story of a widow with three children and her fight to keep her family fed and together. (Rev: SLJ 10/97)

837 Savage, Deborah. *Summer Hawk* (7–10). 1999, Houghton $16.00 (0-395-91163-X). In this coming-of-age story, 15-year-old Taylor has trouble relating to her mother and father, shuns the company of Rail Bogart, the other smart kid in her school, and showers her attention and affection on a young hawk she rescues. (Rev: BCCB 6/99; BL 3/1/99; HBG 9/99; SLJ 4/99; VOYA 4/99)

838 Scarbrough, George. *A Summer Ago* (10–12). 1986, St. Luke's $13.95 (0-918518-46-6). A gentle story about a teenage boy and summer spent in rural Tennessee in the early Depression years. (Rev: SLJ 2/87)

839 Schaffert, Timothy. *The Phantom Limbs of the Rollow Sisters* (10–12). 2002, Putnam $23.95 (0-399-14900-7). Although now in their late teens and early 20s, Mabel and Lily are still overwhelmed by their father's death years before and by their mother's disappearance soon after. (Rev: BL 5/1/02)

840 Schupack, Deborah. *The Boy on the Bus* (11–12). 2003, Free Pr. $23.00 (0-7432-4220-3). A compelling, tense novel about Meg, mother of teenage Katie and 8-year-old Charlie and somewhat discontented wife of Jeff, who suddenly becomes worried that Charlie is strangely not himself. (Rev: BL 2/15/03)

841 Schwartz, Steven. *Lives of the Fathers* (9–12). 1991, Univ. of Illinois Pr. $16.95 (0-252-01815-X). Ten short stories portray the powerful, often complicated relationships between fathers and sons. (Rev: BL 7/91*)

842 Searles, John. *Boy Still Missing* (10–12). 2001, Morrow $25.00 (0-688-17570-8). Because of family problems, adolescent Dominic sets out for New York City to find his long-lost half-brother and start a new life. (Rev: BL 1/1–15/01)

843 Sebestyen, Ouida. *Far from Home* (7–10). 1980, Little, Brown $15.95 (0-316-77932-6); Dell paper $2.50 (0-440-92640-8). An orphaned boy is taken in by a couple who run a boardinghouse and there he uncovers secrets about his family's past.

844 Sebold, Alice. *The Lovely Bones* (10–12). 2002, Little, Brown $21.95 (0-316-66634-3). Fourteen-year-old Susie Salmon, in heaven after being raped and murdered on her way home from school, watches over her grieving family with interest and humor and tracks the progress of the investigation into the crime. (Rev: BL 5/1/02; SLJ 10/02; VOYA 12/02)

845 Sedlack, Robert. *The African Safari Papers* (11–12). 2003, Overlook paper $13.95 (1-58567-300-5). On safari with his dysfunctional and feuding parents, Richard recounts in journal form the troubled family relationships and his own preoccupations (mainly sex and drugs); for mature teens. (Rev: BL 9/1/03)

846 Shepard, Karen. *An Empire of Women* (10–12). 2000, Putnam $24.95 (0-399-14667-9). United by a love of photography, three generations of women spend a week together in a Virginia cabin retreat. (Rev: BL 9/1/00)

847 Shimko, Bonnie. *Letters in the Attic* (7–12). 2002, Academy Chicago $23.50 (0-89733-511-2). Twelve-year-old Lizzie and her mother move to upstate New York after her father leaves home, and there Lizzie finds new attachments and a new understanding of her mother's behavior. (Rev: VOYA 4/03)

848 Shusterman, Neal. *What Daddy Did* (7–10). 1991, Little, Brown paper $15.95 (0-316-78906-2). A young boy recounts the story of how his father murdered his mother and how he ultimately comes to understand and forgive him. (Rev: BL 7/91; SLJ 6/91)

849 Simmons, Michael. *Pool Boy* (7–10). 2003, Millbrook LB $22.90 (0-7613-2924-2). Spoiled teen Brett finds his life upended when his father is jailed for insider trading in this realistic first-person novel full of humor. (Rev: BL 4/1/03; HBG 10/03; SLJ 4/03*)

850 Smith, Anne Warren. *Sister in the Shadow* (7–10). 1986, Avon paper $2.75 (0-380-70378-5). In competition with her successful younger sister, Sharon becomes a live-in baby-sitter, with unhappy results. (Rev: BL 5/1/86; SLJ 5/86; VOYA 8/86)

851 Smith, Danyel. *More Like Wrestling* (10–12). 2003, Crown $23.95 (1-4000-4644-0). After an abusive incident with their mother's alcoholic boyfriend, two young girls are allowed to live alone amid the drug culture of Oakland; for mature teens. (Rev: BL 11/15/02)

852 Snelling, Lauraine. *A Dream to Follow* (10–12). Series: Return to Red River. 2001, Bethany paper $11.99 (0-7642-2317-8). This first installment in a new Christian-based historical series about the Bjorklund family of North Dakota (first seen in the Red River of the North series) features Thorliff and his college aspirations. (Rev: BL 8/01; VOYA 4/02)

853 Sones, Sonya. *One of Those Hideous Books Where the Mother Dies* (7–12). 2004, Simon & Schuster $15.95 (0-689-85820-5). In this free-verse novel, a high schooler, after the death of her mother, is sent to live with her father, a famous movie actor whom she detests. (Rev: BL 5/1/04*; SLJ 8/04)

854 Stansbury, Nicole. *Places to Look for a Mother* (11–12). 2002, Carroll & Graf $22.00 (0-7867-0978-2). Lucy looks back on her childhood and her relationship with her irresponsible, flamboyant mother; for mature teens. (Rev: BL 2/15/02*)

855 Steinbeck, John. *The Pearl* (9–12). Illus. 1993, Viking paper $5.95 (0-14-017737-X). The lives of a poor Mexican pearl fisher and his family change dramatically after he uncovers a fabulous pearl.

856 Stern, Kathryn. *Another Song About the King* (10–12). 2000, Random $23.95 (0-375-50282-3). This first novel deals with the strained relationship between a daughter and her ailing mother who is fixated on Elvis. (Rev: BL 2/15/00)

857 Stokes, Penelope J. *The Amethyst Heart* (10–12). 2000, Word $21.99 (0-8499-3721-3); paper $12.00 (0-8499-4235-7). Amethyst Noble, 93, who lives in her ancestral Mississippi home, tells the story of her family from antebellum days to the present. (Rev: BL 6/1–15/00)

858 Sweeney, Joyce. *The Spirit Window* (7–12). 1998, Delacorte $15.95 (0-385-32510-X). When 15-year-old Miranda journeys to Florida with her father, she falls in love with an older, part-Cherokee boy and becomes involved in environmental causes, both of which bring her into conflict with her parent. (Rev: BL 2/15/98; BR 11–12/98; HBG 9/98; SLJ 3/98; VOYA 4/98)

859 Sweeney, Joyce. *The Tiger Orchard* (9–12). 1995, Dell paper $3.99 (0-440-21927-2). Zack leaves home to find his father, which is the key to understanding himself and shapes his maturation. (Rev: BL 4/1/93; SLJ 5/93)

860 Tanney, Katherine. *Carousel of Progress* (10–12). 2001, Villard $23.95 (0-375-50537-7). Set in the 1970s, this novel covers Meredith Herman's life from the ages of 14 to 17 as she watches her parents' marriage collapse. (Rev: BL 6/1–15/01)

861 Thesman, Jean. *The Last April Dancers* (7–10). 1987, Avon paper $2.75 (0-380-70614-8). Catherine tries to recover from the guilt caused by her father's suicide through friendship and love of a neighboring boy. (Rev: BL 9/15/87; SLJ 10/87; VOYA 10/87)

862 Thesman, Jean. *The Tree of Bells* (7–10). 1999, Houghton $15.00 (0-395-90510-9). In this sequel to *The Ornament Tree*, the strong Deveraux women and their boarding house in Seattle are again featured, with the focus on Claire, now 16 and anxious for independence. (Rev: BCCB 7–8/99; BL 6/1–15/99; HBG 9/99; SLJ 7/99; VOYA 10/99)

863 Torres, Laura. *Crossing Montana* (7–10). 2002, Holiday $15.95 (0-8234-1643-7). Callie sets off on a journey across Montana in search of her missing grandfather, and in the process finds out the truth about her father's death. (Rev: BCCB 10/02; BL 8/02; HBG 10/02; SLJ 7/02; VOYA 8/02)

864 Townsend, John Rowe. *Downstream* (9–12). 1987, HarperCollins LB $12.89 (0-397-32189-9). A teenage English boy finds himself in competition with his father for the affections of an attractive divorcée. (Rev: BL 7/87; SLJ 8/87; VOYA 6/87)

865 Treadway, Jessica. *And Give You Peace* (10–12). 2001, Graywolf paper $14.00 (1-55597-315-9). A young woman sets out to discover why her father shot her sister and then himself in this story of a family tragedy. (Rev: BL 11/15/00)

866 Trembath, Don. *The Popsicle Journal* (7–12). 2001, Orca paper $6.95 (1-55143-185-8). Fledgling journalist Harper Winslow finds himself torn between professional responsibility and family loyalty when his sister is involved in a DUI auto accident while his father is running for mayor. (Rev: SLJ 7/02; VOYA 4/02)

867 Trevor, Penelope. *Listening for Small Sounds* (9–12). 1997, Allen & Unwin paper $11.95 (1-86448-145-5). Raw language and brutal situations are featured in this Australian novel about a girl growing up in a family with an alcoholic father who physically abuses her and her mother. (Rev: BL 11/1/97; SLJ 1/98)

868 Trobaugh, Augusta. *Swan Place* (10–12). 2002, Dutton $22.95 (0-525-94688-8). Dove, 14, shoulders the responsibility for her younger siblings when her mother dies of cancer and her stepfather dies in a car crash. (Rev: BL 9/1/02)

869 Tyler, Anne. *Dinner at the Homesick Restaurant* (10–12). 1982, Knopf paper $14.00 (0-449-91159-4). This family story involves Pearl Tull, a woman deserted by her husband years before, and the lives of her three children.

870 Valgardson, W. D. *Frances* (6–10). 2000, Groundwood $15.95 (0-88899-386-2); paper $5.95 (0-88899-397-8). Growing up in Manitoba, young Frances probes into her Icelandic background and uncovers many family secrets, past and present. (Rev: BL 9/1/00; HBG 3/01; SLJ 9/00; VOYA 2/01)

871 Velasquez, Gloria. *Rina's Family Secret* (8–12). 1998, Arte Publico paper $9.95 (1-55885-233-6). Puerto Rican teenager Rina cannot endure life with her alcoholic stepfather, and so moves in with her grandmother. (Rev: BL 8/98; SLJ 10/98)

872 Voigt, Cynthia. *The Runner* (9–12). 1985, Macmillan LB $15.95 (0-689-31069-2). The story of Bullet Tillerman, a loner who escapes a terrible home situation through his love of running and later by enlisting and going to Vietnam. Other stories about the Tillermans include the trilogy of *Homecoming* (1981), *Dicey's Song* (1982), and *A Solitary Blue* (1983). (Rev: BL 3/15/85; SLJ 5/85)

873 Voigt, Cynthia. *Seventeen Against the Dealer* (7–12). 1989, Macmillan $18.00 (0-689-31497-3). In this, the last of the Tillerman cycle, Dicey, now 21, decides to earn her living building boats. (Rev: BL 3/15/89; BR 9–10/89; SLJ 2/89; VOYA 4/89)

874 Voigt, Cynthia. *Sons from Afar* (6–10). 1987, Macmillan LB $15.95 (0-689-31349-7); Fawcett paper $4.50 (0-449-70293-6). In this part of the Tillerman family story, sons James and Sammy set out to see a father they have never known. (Rev: BL 9/15/87; SLJ 9/87; VOYA 10/87)

875 Walsh, Jill Paton. *A Desert in Bohemia* (10–12). 2000, St. Martin's $23.95 (0-312-26263-9). The destinies of several families in Eastern Europe intersect in this novel of love, loss, and survival. (Rev: BL 12/15/00; SLJ 6/01)

876 Wartski, Maureen C. *Dark Silence* (7–10). 1994, Ballantine paper $5.50 (0-449-70418-1). Teenager Randy must deal with her mother's recent death and the abuse of her neighbor, Delia. (Rev: BL 4/1/94; SLJ 7/94; VOYA 6/94)

877 Waugh, Evelyn. *Brideshead Revisited* (10–12). 1993, Knopf $17.00 (0-679-42300-1). The famous novel for better readers about an English well-born family, their country house, Brideshead, and the army officer, Charles Ryder, who was billeted there. With an introduction by Frank Kermode.

878 Weaver, Will. *Claws* (7–10). 2003, Harper-Collins LB $16.89 (0-06-009474-5). An e-mailed photograph brings an end to Jed's perfect life in this tense and sometimes melodramatic novel about parental adultery. (Rev: BL 4/15/03; HBG 10/03; SLJ 3/03; VOYA 6/03)

879 Weber, Katherine. *The Little Women* (9–12). 2003, Farrar $22.00 (0-374-18959-5). Meg, Jo, and Amy — contemporary sisters — are so disillusioned when their father forgives their mother for an affair that they move from home into a seedy apartment. (Rev: BL 8/03)

880 Wenner, Kate. *Dancing with Einstein* (10–12). 2004, Scribner $24.00 (0-7432-5164-4). The story of the troubled inner life of Marea, who had an unusual childhood living with her Holocaust survivor father who helped develop the atomic bomb. (Rev: BL 3/1/04*)

881 White, Ellen E. *White House Autumn* (7–10). 1985, Avon paper $2.95 (0-380-89780-6). The daughter of the first female president of the United States feels her family is coming apart after an assassination attempt on her mother. (Rev: BL 11/1/85; SLJ 2/86; VOYA 4/86)

882 Whitney, Kim Ablon. *See You Down the Road* (9–12). 2004, Knopf $15.95 (0-375-82467-7). Bridget, a 16-year-old girl, and her family are known as Travelers, people who live in trailers and make their living dishonestly. (Rev: BL 3/15/04*; SLJ 2/04; VOYA 12/03)

883 Wilhelm, Kate. *The Good Children* (10–12). 1998, St. Martin's $22.95 (0-312-17914-6); Fawcett paper $6.99 (0-449-00455-4). When their only remaining parent dies, the four McNair children decide to hide the fact to prevent possible separation and institutionalization. (Rev: BL 2/1/98; SLJ 9/98; VOYA 10/98)

884 Wingate, Lisa. *Tending Roses* (10–12). 2001, NAL paper $12.95 (0-451-20307-0). Christmas is going to be difficult for Kate this year—it is the first family reunion since her mother's death, and she must make arrangements to put her grandmother in a nursing home. (Rev: BL 5/15/01)

885 Wolff, Virginia E. *Make Lemonade* (7–12). 1993, Holt $17.95 (0-8050-2228-7); Scholastic paper $5.99 (0-590-48141-X). Rooted in the community of poverty, this story offers a penetrating view of the conditions that foster ignorance, destroy self-esteem, and challenge strength. (Rev: BL 6/1–15/93*; SLJ 7/93*; VOYA 10/93)

886 Wong, Norman. *Cultural Revolution* (10–12). 1994, One World paper $10.00 (0-345-39648-0). In this story of two generations of a Chinese family, the first part focuses on Wei's childhood and family relationships in China; the second follows Wei's marriage and move to Hawaii, where he fathers two children, one of whom is gay and whose struggles are the focus of this part of the book. (Rev: VOYA 4/96)

887 Woodson, Jacqueline. *Miracle's Boys* (6–10). 2000, Putnam $15.99 (0-399-23113-7). Twelve-year-old African American LaFayette, growing up in a poor inner-city environment, is cared for by his oldest brother who is also responsible for the troubled middle brother, Charlie. (Rev: BL 2/15/00; HB 3–4/00; HBG 9/00; SLJ 5/00; VOYA 4/00)

888 Wynne-Jones, Tim. *Stephen Fair: A Novel* (7–10). 1998, HarperCollins paper $5.95 (0-06-447206-X). Long-hidden family secrets are revealed as 15-year-old Stephen Fair begins to experience nightmares that have deep meanings. (Rev: BL 6/1–15/98; BR 11–12/98; SLJ 5/98; VOYA 8/98)

889 Yansky, Brian. *My Road Trip to the Pretty Girl Capital of the World* (9–12). 2003, Cricket $16.95 (0-8126-2691-5). Simon's quest to find his birth parents introduces him to some offbeat characters and gives him a new appreciation of his adoptive home. (Rev: BL 11/15/03; HBG 4/04; SLJ 12/03)

890 Yorke, Christy. *Song of the Seals* (11–12). 2003, Berkley paper $14.00 (0-425-18824-8). Still grieving over the disappearance of her son many years before, Kate moves with her foster son and her father to a fishing village in northern California that turns out to be a strangely mystical community, reflecting Kate's own search for acceptance and hope. (Rev: BL 2/1/03)

Physical and Emotional Problems

891 Arrick, Fran. *Steffie Can't Come Out to Play* (7–10). 1978, Simon & Schuster $8.95 (0-87888-135-2). Steffie runs away to New York City and is dragged into the nightmare world of prostitution.

892 Atkins, Catherine. *Alt Ed* (8–10). 2003, Putnam $17.99 (0-399-23854-9). Susan, an unhappy sophomore, joins other outcast teens in an alternative education class designed to help them deal with differences. (Rev: BCCB 2/03; BL 1/1–15/03; HB 3–4/03; HBG 10/03; SLJ 3/03; VOYA 4/03)

893 Atkins, Catherine. *When Jeff Comes Home* (10–12). 1999, Putnam $17.99 (0-399-23366-0). Jeff must come to terms with his ordeal after being released by the man who held him captive for two years. (Rev: BL 10/15/99; HBG 4/00; SLJ 2/00)

894 Bennett, Cherie. *Searching for David's Heart: A Christmas Story* (10–12). 1988, Scholastic paper $4.50 (0-590-30673-1). Darcy's brother David dies after they have an argument and her guilt lessens only when she meets the boy who received David's heart.

895 Bradford, Barbara Taylor. *Her Own Rules* (10–12). 1996, HarperCollins $32.00 (0-06-017721-7). A successful businesswoman unravels the mystery of her past when she visits an ancient abbey in England and experiences feelings of sadness and loss. (Rev: SLJ 2/97)

896 Bryant, Sharon. *The Earth Kitchen* (6–12). 2002, HarperCollins $15.95 (0-06-029605-4). A lyrical story about a 12-year-old girl living in a ward for the mentally ill, and the comfort she finds in a world of fantasy. (Rev: HB 3–4/02; HBG 10/02; SLJ 3/02; VOYA 4/02)

897 Bunting, Eve. *Face at the Edge of the World* (9–12). 1985, Ticknor paper $6.95 (0-89919-800-7). Jed tries to find out the reasons behind the suicide of his friend Charlie, a gifted black student. (Rev: BL 8/85; BR 9–10/86; SLJ 12/85; VOYA 8/85)

898 Burgess, Melvin. *Smack* (10–12). 1998, Holt paper $16.95 (0-8050-5801-X). This novel, which won Britain's Carnegie Medal, is a harrowing, provocative story of teen heroin addiction in Bristol during the 1980s. (Rev: BCCB 4/98; BL 4/15/98; HB 5–6/98; HBG 9/98; SLJ 5/98)

899 Cadnum, Michael. *Edge* (8–12). 1997, Puffin paper $5.99 (0-14-038714-5). Zachary, a confused high school dropout from a broken home, seeks revenge when his father is shot in the spine during a street robbery. (Rev: BL 6/1–15/97; SLJ 7/97; VOYA 12/97)

900 Camus, Albert. *The Stranger* (10–12). 1988, Random $25.00 (0-394-53305-4); paper $9.95 (0-679-72020-0). For better readers, this novel describes how a convicted murderer at last finds some meaning in life.

901 Carlson, Melody. *Finding Alice* (10–12). 2003, WaterBrook paper $11.99 (1-57856-573-1). In this gripping novel, the title character struggles with the demons of paranoid schizophrenia. (Rev: BL 10/1/03*)

902 Clauser, Suzanne. *A Girl Named Sooner* (9–12). 1976, Avon paper $2.95 (0-380-00216-7). A neglected girl is given a home by a veterinarian and his wife.

903 Cole, Barbara. *Alex the Great* (8–12). 1989, Rosen LB $12.95 (0-8239-0941-7). The events leading up to Alex's drug overdose are told first by Alex and then by her friend, Deonna. (Rev: BR 9–10/89; VOYA 8/89)

904 Cormier, Robert. *The Bumblebee Flies Anyway* (7–12). 1983, Dell paper $4.99 (0-440-90871-X). A terminally ill boy and his gradual realization of his situation.

905 Cormier, Robert. *Heroes: A Novel* (7–12). 1998, Delacorte $15.95 (0-385-32590-8). In this powerful novel, Francis returns home disfigured after World War II to seek revenge and murder his childhood hero. (Rev: BL 6/1–15/98; HBG 3/99; SLJ 8/98; VOYA 8/98)

906 Covington, Dennis. *Lizard* (9–12). 1991, Dell paper $4.50 (0-440-21490-4). This work explores the themes of gaining worldly wisdom and resolving adolescent fears of being different — in this case, having a facial deformity and other birth defects. (Rev: BL 5/1/91*; SLJ 6/91)

907 Crutcher, Chris. *Chinese Handcuffs* (9–12). 1989, Greenwillow $14.00 (0-688-08345-5). A brutal novel about basketball, a young man trying to adjust to his brother's suicide, and a sexually abused girl. (Rev: BL 3/15/90; BR 9–10/89; SLJ 4/89; VOYA 6/89)

908 Crutcher, Chris. *Staying Fat for Sarah Byrnes* (7–12). 1993, Greenwillow $16.99 (0-688-11552-7). Overweight Eric's only friend is Sarah, whose face was severely burned as a child. Their attempt to escape her unbalanced father leads to an almost deadly climax. (Rev: BL 3/15/93; SLJ 3/93*; VOYA 8/93)

909 Davis, Amanda. *Wonder When You'll Miss Me* (11–12). 2003, Morrow $24.95 (0-688-16781-0). Faith, a troubled and lonely high school girl, loses weight after being sexually assaulted but finds that her inner "Fat Girl" won't leave her alone; suitable for mature readers. (Rev: BL 2/1/03; SLJ 8/03; VOYA 12/03)

910 Davis, Rebecca Fjelland. *Jake Riley: Irreparably Damaged* (7–10). 2003, HarperCollins LB $16.89 (0-06-051838-3). Lainey, a farm girl, struggles to cope with her friend Jake, a 15-year-old with frightening emotional problems. (Rev: BL 9/1/03; HBG 10/03; SLJ 7/03; VOYA 10/03)

911 Deaver, Julie Reece. *The Night I Disappeared* (9–12). 2002, Simon & Schuster paper $5.99 (0-7434-3979-1). Jamie's summer in Chicago includes institutionalization for mental illness and a realization that she was traumatized as a child. (Rev: BCCB 5/02; BL 5/1/02; SLJ 5/02)

912 Deford, Frank. *An American Summer* (10–12). 2002, Sourcebooks $24.00 (1-57071-992-6). A young woman in an iron lung becomes 14-year-old Christy's confidante and friend when he arrives in Baltimore during a summer in the 1950s. (Rev: BL 9/15/02; SLJ 11/02)

913 Dewey, Jennifer Owlings. *Borderlands* (7–12). 2002, Marshall Cavendish $14.95 (0-7614-5114-5). When Jamie, an unhappy 17-year-old, is hospitalized after a suicide attempt she finds new friends and slowly comes to terms with her difficult relationship with her parents. (Rev: BL 9/1/02; HBG 10/02; SLJ 7/02)

914 Diezeno, Patricia. *Why Me? The Story of Jenny* (7–10). 1976, Avon paper $3.50 (0-380-00563-8). A young rape victim doesn't know how to cope.

915 *Don't Cramp My Style: Stories About That Time of the Month* (8–12). Ed. by Lisa Rowe Fraustino. 2004, Simon & Schuster $15.95 (0-689-85882-5). This collection of stories about girls' menstrual periods includes fiction about different places, cultures, and times. (Rev: BL 3/1/04; HB 3–4/04; SLJ 4/04; VOYA 4/04)

916 Doyle, Malachy. *Georgie* (6–10). 2002, Bloomsbury $13.95 (1-58234-753-0). Georgie, 14, who has buried horrible memories under a cloak of isolation, slowly learns to trust his teacher and recovers his sanity. (Rev: BCCB 11/02; BL 9/1/02; SLJ 7/02; VOYA 12/03)

917 Draper, Sharon M. *Tears of a Tiger* (7–10). 1994, Atheneum $16.95 (0-689-31878-2). A star basketball player is killed in an accident after he and his friends drink and drive. The driver, who survives, is depressed and ultimately commits suicide. (Rev: BL 11/1/94; SLJ 2/95)

918 Egan, Jennifer. *Look at Me* (10–12). 2001, Doubleday $24.95 (0-385-50276-1). Facial injuries from a car crash cause a successful model to despair. (Rev: BL 7/01*)

919 Ellis, Ella Thorp. *The Year of My Indian Prince* (7–10). 2001, Delacorte $15.95 (0-385-32779-X). Sixteen-year-old April's battle with tuberculosis is eased by the attentions of a fellow patient, the son of an Indian maharajah, in this novel based on the author's own experiences. (Rev: BL 6/1–15/01; HBG 10/01; SLJ 6/01; VOYA 10/01)

920 Ethridge, Kenneth E. *Toothpick* (7–10). 1985, Troll paper $2.50 (0-8167-1316-2). A friendship between Jamie, an outsider who is unsure of himself, and Janice, a terminally ill girl, gives him the confidence he needs. (Rev: BL 11/15/85; SLJ 12/85; VOYA 4/86)

921 Eugenides, Jeffrey. *Middlesex* (11–12). 2002, Farrar $26.00 (0-374-19969-8). An absorbing story about the experiences of a young hermaphrodite and his incestuous ancestors; for mature teens. (Rev: BL 6/1–15/02; SLJ 3/03)

922 Ferris, Jean. *Invincible Summer* (9–12). 1987, Avon paper $3.50 (0-380-70619-9). The story of a friendship and later a love shared by two courageous teenagers, both suffering from leukemia. (Rev: SLJ 8/87)

923 Fields, Terri. *After the Death of Anna Gonzales* (7–12). 2002, Holt $16.95 (0-8050-7127-X). A collection of poems written by her friends reveal the terrible aftermath of a teenager's suicide. (Rev: BL 12/15/02; HBG 3/03; SLJ 11/02; VOYA 12/02)

924 Fischer, Jackie Moyer. *An Egg on Three Sticks* (9–12). 2004, St. Martin's paper $12.95 (0-312-31775-1). A deeply affecting novel about a 13-year-old girl who watches her mother sink into insanity and depression. (Rev: BL 5/1/04*; SLJ 7/04)

925 Fleischman, Paul. *Mind's Eye* (8–12). 1999, Holt $15.95 (0-8050-6314-5). The story of the relationship that develops among three people in a contemporary nursing home: Courtney, a 16-year-old girl paralyzed from an accident; May, who suffers from Alzheimer's disease; and Elva, a former high school English teacher, who tries to bring Courtney out of her bouts of sullenness and self-pity. (Rev:

BL 9/1/99; HB 11–12/99; HBG 4/00; SLJ 8/99; VOYA 12/99)

926 Frank, E. R. *America* (10–12). 2002, Simon & Schuster $18.00 (0-689-84729-7). While in a hospital after attempting suicide, America angrily describes his childhood full of sexual abuse and other agonies. (Rev: BL 2/15/02; HB 3–4/02; HBG 10/02; SLJ 3/02*; VOYA 2/02)

927 Fraustino, Lisa R. *Ash* (9–12). 1995, Orchard LB $17.99 (0-531-08739-5). A 15-year-old recalls, in diary form, his older brother's slide into schizophrenia. (Rev: BL 4/1/95; SLJ 4/95; VOYA 5/95)

928 Going, K. L. *Fat Kid Rules the World* (8–12). 2003, Putnam $17.99 (0-399-23990-1). An unlikely but beneficial friendship develops between suicidal, 300-pound Troy and dropout punk rock guitarist Curt. (Rev: BCCB 6/03*; BL 5/15/03*; HB 7–8/03; HBG 10/03; SLJ 5/03*; VOYA 6/03)

929 Grant, Cynthia D. *The White Horse* (9–12). 1998, Simon & Schuster $16.00 (0-689-82127-1). A brutally graphic story of a girl hooked on heroin, her life, emotional abuse, and decisions she must make when she discovers that she is pregnant. (Rev: BL 10/15/98; HBG 3/99; SLJ 12/98; VOYA 12/98)

930 Greenberg, Joanne. *I Never Promised You a Rose Garden* (10–12). 1989, NAL paper $5.99 (0-451-16031-2). A 16-year-old Jewish girl sinks into schizophrenia and receives help in an asylum.

931 Guy, Rosa. *My Love, My Love, or the Peasant Girl* (9–12). 1995, Holt paper $9.95 (0-8050-1659-7). This, a modern retelling of the Little Mermaid story, uses a Caribbean Island as its setting and tells of the tragic love of a poor peasant girl for a rich mulatto. (Rev: BL 9/15/85; SLJ 1/86; VOYA 4/86)

932 Hall, Rachel Howzell. *A Quiet Storm* (11–12). 2002, Scribner paper $13.00 (0-7432-2616-X). Stacey, younger than her sister Rikki by only 11 months, has been Rikki's protector since childhood, and as Rikki's mental imbalances worsen Stacey must balance her sister's needs with her own; for mature teens. (Rev: BL 9/1/02)

933 Halliday, John. *Shooting Monarchs* (6–12). 2003, Margaret K. McElderry $15.95 (0-689-84338-0). The lives of two very different teenage boys — lonely but gentle misfit Danny and abused and neglected serial killer Macy — intersect in this suspenseful novel. (Rev: BCCB 5/03; BL 3/15/03*; HBG 4/04; LMC 10/03; SLJ 6/03; VOYA 6/03)

934 Hallowell, Janis. *The Annunciation of Francesca Dunn* (10–12). 2004, Morrow $23.95 (0-06-055919-5). Told by different narrators, this novel describes how a 14-year-old girl is persuaded to believe that she is the embodiment of the Virgin Mary. (Rev: BL 2/15/04)

935 Harrar, George. *Not as Crazy as I Seem* (7–10). 2003, Houghton $15.00 (0-618-26365-9). Devon,

15, is frustrated by his obsessive-compulsive disorder and the different responses of his peers, his parents, and his doctor. (Rev: BL 2/15/03; HBG 10/03; SLJ 4/03; VOYA 6/03)

936 Harrison, Stuart. *The Snow Falcon* (10–12). 1999, St. Martin's $23.95 (0-312-20166-4). Michael Somers returns to his hometown from psychiatric treatment hoping to reshape his life and encounters a boy who has become mute because of trauma and a snow falcon that has been wounded by a hunter. (Rev: BL 1/1–15/99; SLJ 5/99)

937 Hautman, Pete. *Sweetblood* (8–12). 2003, Simon & Schuster $16.95 (0-689-85048-4). Sixteen-year-old Lucy, an insulin-dependent diabetic, links her condition with her interest in vampires. (Rev: BL 5/1/03*; HB 7–8/03; HBG 10/03; SLJ 7/03; VOYA 10/03)

938 Hesser, Terry S. *Kissing Doorknobs* (6–12). 1998, Delacorte $15.95 (0-385-32329-8). The funny, moving story of a girl afflicted with obsessive-compulsive disorder who even worries about her excessive worrying, and how she eventually gets help. (Rev: BL 6/1–15/98; BR 1–2/99; HBG 9/98; SLJ 6/98; VOYA 12/98)

939 Hoban, Julia. *Acting Normal* (9–12). 1998, HarperCollins $14.95 (0-06-023519-5). Stephanie confronts the memory of childhood abuse when she visits a therapist to determine the reasons for her recent nervous breakdown. (Rev: BL 4/15/98; HBG 9/98; SLJ 5/98; VOYA 12/98)

940 Hoekstra, Molly. *Upstream: A Novel* (7–12). 2001, Tudor paper $15.95 (0-936389-86-9). This story of a 16-year-old girl's struggle with anorexia gives a clear idea of the psychological problems associated with this illness. (Rev: SLJ 12/01)

941 Howe, James. *The Watcher* (8–12). 1997, Simon & Schuster $16.00 (0-689-80186-6). The lives of three troubled teens converge in a horrific climax in this novel of child abuse. (Rev: BL 6/1–15/97; BR 11–12/97; SLJ 5/97; VOYA 8/97)

942 Hughes, Monica. *Hunter in the Dark* (7–10). 1983, Avon paper $2.95 (0-380-67702-4). In spite of his leukemia, Mike goes on a secret hunting trip into a Canadian wilderness. (Rev: BL 11/1/88)

943 Hurwin, Davida Wills. *A Time for Dancing* (7–12). 1995, Puffin paper $5.99 (0-14-038618-1). A powerful story of two friends, one of whom is diagnosed with lymphoma. Their friendship becomes a story of saying good-bye and death. (Rev: BL 11/1/95*; SLJ 10/95; VOYA 12/95)

944 Jenkins, A. M. *Damage* (11–12). 2001, HarperCollins $15.95 (0-06-029099-4); paper $6.99 (0-06-447255-8). Football-playing high school senior Austin tries to escape his depression through sex with his girlfriend. (Rev: BL 9/15/01*; HB 9–10/01; HBG 3/02; SLJ 10/01; VOYA 10/01)

945 Johnson, Angela. *Humming Whispers* (8–12). 1995, Orchard LB $16.99 (0-531-08748-4). Sophy, 14, reveals the impact of her 24-year-old sister Nicole's schizophrenia on the lives of those who love her. (Rev: BL 2/15/95; SLJ 4/95; VOYA 5/95)

946 Kata, Elizabeth. *A Patch of Blue* (10–12). 1983, Amereon $18.95 (0-89190-119-1); Warner paper $5.99 (0-446-31485-4). A blind girl finds love with a man who also has a number of personal problems.

947 Keith, Lois. *A Different Life* (9–12). Series: Livewire. 1998, Women's Press paper $11.95 (0-7043-4946-9). In this moving novel, 15-year-old Libby adjusts to a crippling disease with the help of a handicapped social worker, a school chum named Jesse, and her own fortitude. (Rev: SLJ 7/98)

948 Kerouac, Jack. *On the Road* (10–12). 1997, Viking LB $24.95 (0-670-87478-7). This novel about a group of drifters expresses the ideas and attitudes of the Beat Generation of the 1960s.

949 Kesey, Ken. *One Flew over the Cuckoos Nest* (10–12). 1963, Signet paper $6.99 (0-451-16396-6). This novel deals with the power struggle between a sane inmate and the head nurse in a mental institution.

950 Keyes, Daniel. *Flowers for Algernon* (10–12). 1966, Harcourt $18.95 (0-15-131510-8). When the I.Q. of a mentally handicapped man is changed by an operation, he faces serious problems. (Rev: BL 10/15/88)

951 Klass, Sheila S. *Rhino* (7–10). 1993, Scholastic paper $13.95 (0-590-44250-3). Fourteen-year-old Annie suffers from a nose that is a family trait and looks too big for her face. (Rev: BL 1/15/94; SLJ 11/93; VOYA 12/93)

952 Klein, Norma. *Sunshine* (9–12). 1976, Avon paper $3.99 (0-380-00049-0). This is the moving account of a gallant woman who died of cancer at age 20.

953 Koertge, Ronald. *Stoner and Spaz* (8–12). 2002, Candlewick $15.99 (0-7636-1608-7). A fine young adult novel about a boy with cerebral palsy who gets help from a drug-addicted young woman. (Rev: BCCB 3/02; BL 5/1/02*; HB 7–8/02; HBG 10/02; SLJ 4/02)

954 Koller, Jackie F. *The Falcon* (7–12). 1998, Simon & Schuster $17.00 (0-689-81294-9). In fulfilling a school journalism assignment, Luke explores his inner feelings and finds an emotional demon that has haunted him for years. (Rev: BL 4/15/98; BR 1–2/99; HBG 9/98; SLJ 5/98; VOYA 2/99)

955 Lamb, Wally. *She's Come Undone* (10–12). 1998, Pocket paper $7.99 (0-671-02100-1). Delores Price is an observant youngster who faces many challenges and unfortunately tackles most of them

with a helping of Mallomars, and a dollop of humor. (Rev: BL 8/92)

956 Lawrence, Iain. *Ghost Boy* (7–10). 2000, Delacorte $15.95 (0-385-32739-0). Set in America shortly after World War II, this is the story of shy, neglected, albino Harold Kline, who finds a warm home when he runs away to join a circus. (Rev: BCCB 10/00; BL 11/1/00; HB 7–8/01; HBG 3/01; SLJ 9/00*; VOYA 12/00)

957 Levenkron, Steven. *The Best Little Girl in the World* (10–12). 1989, Warner paper $6.99 (0-446-35865-7). Francesca's desire to be perfect leads her into the world of anorexia.

958 Lewis, Catherine, and Jane Yeomans. *Postcards to Father Abraham* (6–10). 2000, Simon & Schuster $17.95 (0-689-82852-7). Teenage Megan finds it difficult to make adjustments when she loses a leg to cancer. (Rev: BL 1/1–15/00; HBG 9/00; SLJ 5/00; VOYA 2/00)

959 Lipsyte, Robert. *One Fat Summer* (7–12). 1991, HarperCollins paper $5.99 (0-06-447073-3). Bobby Marks is 14, fat, and unhappy in this first novel of three that traces Bobby's career through his first year of college. (Rev: BL 1/1–15/98)

960 McBay, Bruce, and James Heneghan. *Waiting for Sarah* (7–10). 2003, Orca paper $7.95 (1-55143-270-6). Crippled in a car accident, Mike suffers from depression and withdrawal until he gets to know 8th-grader Sarah. (Rev: BL 9/15/03; SLJ 10/03; VOYA 12/03)

961 McCormick, Patricia. *Cut* (7–10). 2000, Front Street $16.95 (1-886910-61-8). In a hospital that treats teens with serious issues, including drugs and anorexia, Callie participates in group therapy and tries to face her own self-mutilation. (Rev: BL 1/1–15/01; HB 11–12/00; HBG 3/01; SLJ 12/00; VOYA 2/01)

962 McCracken, Elizabeth. *The Giant's House* (10–12). 1996, Dial $19.95 (0-385-31433-7). This novel, set on Cape Cod, traces the friendship and love shared by Peggy Cort, a librarian, and a youngster, James Sweatt, who grows to over 8 feet by the age of 19. (Rev: BL 5/15/96; SLJ 11/96)

963 McDaniel, Lurlene. *How Do I Love Thee? Three Stories* (6–10). 2001, Bantam $9.95 (0-553-57154-0). Three dramatic stories combine young romance and critical illness with clever twists of plot. (Rev: BL 10/15/01; HBG 3/02; SLJ 11/01; VOYA 12/01)

964 McDaniel, Lurlene. *Saving Jessica* (7–10). 1996, Bantam paper $4.99 (0-553-56721-7). When Jessica is stricken with kidney failure, her boyfriend, Jeremy, volunteers to donate one of his but his parents, fearful that he will die, refuse permission. (Rev: VOYA 4/96)

965 Maclean, John. *Mac* (8–12). 1987, Avon paper $2.95 (0-380-70700-4). A high school sophomore's life falls apart after he is sexually assaulted by a doctor during a physical exam. (Rev: BL 10/1/87; SLJ 11/87)

966 Mahy, Margaret. *Memory* (9–12). 1999, Aladdin paper $8.00 (0-689-82911-6). Jonny befriends an old lady with Alzheimer's disease and from the relationship learns to accept his own past. (Rev: BL 4/15/88; BR 1-2/89; SLJ 3/88; VOYA 6/88)

967 Marsden, John. *Checkers* (7–12). 1998, Houghton $15.00 (0-395-85754-6). A harrowing story, set in Australia, about a teenager who suffers a nervous breakdown after her prominent father is accused of unethical business practices, and about the love she and her dog, Checkers, share. (Rev: BCCB 10/98; BL 10/15/98; BR 5–6/99; HBG 3/99; SLJ 9/98; VOYA 12/98)

968 Mass, Wendy. *A Mango-Shaped Space* (6–10). 2003, Little, Brown $16.95 (0-316-52388-7). Mia, 13, eventually seeks help when she can no longer cope with her synesthesia, a sensory condition that produces color visions. (Rev: BL 4/1/03; HB 7–8/03; HBG 10/03; SLJ 3/03; VOYA 4/03)

969 Mathis, Sharon. *Teacup Full of Roses* (7–12). 1987, Puffin paper $4.99 (0-14-032328-7). For mature teens, a novel about the devastating effects of drugs on an African American family.

970 Metzger, Lois. *Ellen's Case* (7–12). 1995, Atheneum $16.00 (0-689-31934-7). In this sequel to *Barry's Sister,* Ellen — now 16 and more understanding of her brother's cerebral palsy — is involved in an intense malpractice trial. (Rev: BL 8/95; SLJ 10/95; VOYA 12/95)

971 Miklowitz, Gloria D. *Past Forgiving* (8–10). 1995, Simon & Schuster $16.00 (0-671-88442-5). A teenage girl caught in an abusive relationship with her boyfriend. (Rev: BL 5/1/95; SLJ 6/95)

972 Miller, Karen E. Quinones. *I'm Telling* (11–12). 2002, Simon & Schuster $23.00 (0-7432-1435-8). Nearly 20 years after their stepfather abused Hope, she and her twin sister Faith are still suffering the consequences; for mature teens. (Rev: BL 7/02)

973 Miller, Mary Beth. *Aimee* (9–12). 2002, Dutton $16.99 (0-525-46894-3). Zoe, depressed and filled with guilt, turns to alcohol and sex following her best friend's suicide. (Rev: BL 5/1/02; HBG 10/02; SLJ 4/02; VOYA 6/02)

974 Minchin, Adele. *The Beat Goes On* (8–11). 2004, Simon & Schuster $15.95 (0-689-86611-9). In this British novel, 15-year-old Leyla is burdened with keeping secret the fact that her cousin Emma is HIV positive. (Rev: BL 2/15/04; SLJ 3/04; VOYA 4/04)

975 Moon, Elizabeth. *The Speed of Dark* (10–12). 2003, Ballantine $23.95 (0-345-44755-7). In a future world, a young autistic man named Lou falls

in love and must decide whether he wants to become "normal." (Rev: BL 2/1/03; VOYA 2/03)

976 Mowry, Jess. *Babylon Boyz* (9–12). 1997, Simon & Schuster paper $16.00 (0-689-80839-9). In this novel for mature readers, three alienated boys — one homosexual, another with a severe heart condition, and the third fat — try to escape their squalid inner-city neighborhood called Babylon in Oakland, California. (Rev: BL 2/15/97; SLJ 9/97*; VOYA 6/97)

977 Myers, Walter Dean. *Sweet Illusions* (10–12). 1987, Teachers & Writers paper $8.95 (0-915924-15-3). Stories about teenage pregnancy from both male and female points of view. (Rev: BL 6/15/87; VOYA 8/87)

978 Naylor, Phyllis Reynolds. *The Keeper* (6–10). 1986, Macmillan $16.00 (0-689-31204-0). Nick and his mother agonize over whether or not to have Nick's father institutionalized for mental illness. (Rev: BL 4/1/86; SLJ 5/86; VOYA 2/87)

979 Nolan, Han. *Born Blue* (10–12). 2001, Harcourt $17.00 (0-15-201916-2). Janie, a talented singer who has had a troubled childhood, changes her name to Leshaya and turns to sex, drugs, and the blues in this absorbing and thought-provoking novel. (Rev: BL 10/15/01; HB 1–2/02; HBG 3/02; SLJ 11/01*; VOYA 10/01)

980 Nolan, Han. *Dancing on the Edge* (7–10). 1997, Harcourt $16.00 (0-15-201648-1). Beset by a series of personal and family crises, Miracle slowly descends into madness. (Rev: BL 10/1/97; HBG 3/98; SLJ 9/97*; VOYA 2/98)

981 Oke, Janette, and Laurel Oke Logan. *Dana's Valley* (7–12). 2001, Bethany $15.99 (0-7642-2514-6); paper $11.95 (0-7642-2451-4). Erin, 10 years old and part of a happy Christian family, has her faith tested when her beloved older sister is diagnosed with leukemia. (Rev: VOYA 2/02)

982 Oneal, Zibby. *The Language of Goldfish* (7–10). 1990, Puffin paper $5.99 (0-14-034540-X). Carrie appears to be slowly sinking into mental illness and seems unable to help herself.

983 Orr, Wendy. *Peeling the Onion* (8–12). 1997, Holiday $16.95 (0-8234-1289-X); Bantam paper $4.99 (0-440-22773-9). An automobile accident leaves Anna with a broken back, debilitating pain, physical and mental handicaps, and questions about what to do with her life. (Rev: BL 4/1/97; SLJ 5/97*; VOYA 10/97)

984 Packer, Ann. *The Dive from Clausen's Pier: A Novel* (10–12). 2002, Knopf $24.00 (0-375-41282-4); paper $14.00 (0-375-72713-2). Mike's dive off Clausen's pier results in paralysis and also creates problems for his girlfriend, Carrie. (Rev: BL 3/15/02; SLJ 8/02)

985 Peck, Richard. *Remembering the Good Times* (7–10). 1986, Delacorte $12.95 (0-385-29396-8); Bantam paper $5.50 (0-440-97339-2). A strong friendship between two boys and a girl is destroyed when one of them commits suicide. (Rev: BL 3/1/85; BR 9–10/85)

986 Plath, Sylvia. *The Bell Jar* (10–12). 1971, Harper & Row $20.00 (0-06-013356-2); paper $13.00 (0-06-093018-7). This novel, based loosely on the author's own experiences, deals with a young girl who sinks into mental illness and attempts suicide.

987 Rapp, Adam. *Little Chicago* (10–12). 2002, Front Street $16.95 (1-886910-72-3). Blacky is sexually abused by his mother's boyfriend and ridiculed by his peers in this disturbing and sexually explicit novel. (Rev: BL 8/02; HB 9–10/02; HBG 3/03; SLJ 8/02; VOYA 8/02)

988 Reid, P. Carey. *Swimming in the Starry River* (9–12). 1994, Hyperion $19.95 (0-7868-6005-7). In this chronicle of courage, frustration, and compassion, a father forges a powerful bond with his young child who has a debilitating disease. (Rev: BL 5/15/94)

989 Ruckman, Ivy. *The Hunger Scream* (7–10). 1983, Walker $14.95 (0-8027-6514-9). Lily starves herself to become a popular member of the in-crowd.

990 Ruff, Matt. *Set This House in Order: A Romance of Souls* (11–12). 2003, HarperCollins $25.95 (0-06-019562-2). Best suited to mature teens, this sometimes disturbing novel tells the story of Andy Gage, a young man with multiple personality disorder who puts his own psyche in danger when he seeks to help a similarly troubled young woman. (Rev: BL 1/1–15/03)

991 Samuels, Gertrude. *Run, Shelley, Run!* (9–12). 1975, NAL paper $2.50 (0-451-13987-9). Shelley, a rebellious young girl, plans on escaping from the state training school where the courts have sent her.

992 Scott, Virginia M. *Belonging* (9–12). 1986, Kendall Green paper $2.95 (0-930323-33-5). A 15-year-old girl must adjust to deafness caused by an attack of meningitis. (Rev: VOYA 4/88)

993 Seago, Kate. *Matthew Unstrung* (7–12). 1998, Dial $16.99 (0-8037-2230-3). Set in 1910, this novel portrays the descent into madness of a sensitive, teenage seminarian and his institutionalization after a nervous breakdown. (Rev: BL 5/1/98; HBG 9/98; SLJ 3/98; VOYA 2/98)

994 Sirof, Harriet. *Because She's My Friend* (7–10). 1993, Atheneum $16.00 (0-689-31844-8). Two girls of opposite temperament become friends when strong-willed Valerie's right leg is paralyzed after an accident and she meets well-behaved Terri. (Rev: BL 9/15/93; SLJ 10/93; VOYA 12/93)

995 Stratton, Allan. *Leslie's Journal* (8–12). 2000, Annick $19.95 (1-55037-665-9); paper $8.95 (1-55037-664-0). A new teacher reads Leslie's journal and learns about her boyfriend's abusive behavior. (Rev: HBG 10/01; SLJ 4/01; VOYA 2/01)

996 Sultan, Faye, and Teresa Kennedy. *Over the Line* (10–12). 1997, Doubleday $21.95 (0-385-48525-5). Portia McTeague, a forensic psychologist, investigates the case of Jimmy the Weird, a mentally handicapped young man who has committed two murders, to make a decision concerning a plea of insanity. (Rev: BL 11/15/97; SLJ 8/98)

997 Synder, Anne. *Goodbye, Paper Doll* (10–12). 1980, NAL paper $2.95 (0-451-15943-8). Seventeen-year-old Rosemary must overcome anorexia nervosa as well as a multitude of other personal problems.

998 Tan, Shaun. *The Red Tree* (6–12). Illus. 2003, Simply Read $15.95 (0-9688767-3-8). This arresting picture book for older readers portrays a girl searching for meaning in a frightening world, with a glimmer of hope that grows as the book reaches its conclusion. (Rev: BL 5/1/03)

999 Tashjian, Janet. *Fault Line* (8–12). 2003, Holt $16.95 (0-8050-7200-4). Becky, 17, happy and enjoying doing comedy routines, finds her life changing when she falls for Kip, whose apparent self-confidence hides his abusive nature. (Rev: BL 9/1/03; HB 9–10/03; HBG 4/04; SLJ 10/03; VOYA 10/03)

1000 Tatlock, Ann. *All the Way Home* (10–12). 2002, Bethany paper $11.99 (0-7642-2663-0). As a lonely young girl, Augusta Schuler depended on her friendship with a Japanese American family and the heartache caused by their internment during World War II remains with her for many years, spurring her involvement in the civil rights movement. (Rev: BL 6/1–15/02*)

1001 Taylor, Michelle A. *The Angel of Barbican High* (7–12). 2002, Univ. of Queensland Pr. paper $15.95 (0-7022-3251-3). Jez feels responsible for the death of her boyfriend and pours out her guilt in her poems, which reveal that she is close to suicide. (Rev: SLJ 8/02)

1002 Terris, Susan. *Nell's Quilt* (9–12). 1996, Farrar paper $4.95 (0-374-45497-3). In turn-of-the-century Amherst, a young girl cracks under the strain of having to marry a man she does not like. (Rev: BL 11/1/87; SLJ 11/87)

1003 Thomas, Joyce C. *Marked by Fire* (8–12). 1982, Avon paper $4.50 (0-380-79327-X). After she is raped, a Southern black girl seems to lose her beautiful singing voice. A sequel is *Bright Shadow* (1984). (Rev: BL 7/88)

1004 Toten, Teresa. *The Game* (7–12). 2001, Red Deer paper $7.95 (0-88995-232-9). A dramatic story about Dani, a suicidal girl who finds friendship and succor at a clinic for troubled adolescents. (Rev: BL 2/15/02; VOYA 4/02)

1005 Trembath, Don. *Lefty Carmichael Has a Fit* (8–12). 2000, Orca paper $6.95 (1-55143-166-1). When 15-year-old Lefty discovers that he is an epileptic, he develops a fearful, cautious lifestyle that his friends and family try to change. (Rev: BL 1/1–15/00; SLJ 2/00; VOYA 4/00)

1006 Trueman, Terry. *Inside Out* (7–10). 2003, HarperCollins LB $16.89 (0-06-623963-X). An absorbing story about a schizophrenic teenager who is held hostage in a robbery attempt. (Rev: BL 9/1/03; HBG 4/04; SLJ 9/03; VOYA 10/03)

1007 Trueman, Terry. *Stuck in Neutral* (6–10). 2000, HarperCollins LB $16.89 (0-06-028518-4). Fourteen-year-old Shawn, whose severe cerebral palsy does not hamper his great intelligence, fears that his father may be planning to put him out of his misery. (Rev: BL 7/00* ; HB 5–6/00; HBG 10/00; SLJ 7/00; VOYA 12/00)

1008 Voigt, Cynthia. *Izzy, Willy-Nilly* (7–12). 1986, Macmillan $18.00 (0-689-31202-4). A 15-year-old girl's life changes dramatically when she has a leg amputated. (Rev: BL 5/1/86; SLJ 4/86; VOYA 12/86)

1009 Waite, Judy. *Shopaholic* (6–10). 2003, Simon & Schuster $16.95 (0-689-85138-3). Unhappy Taylor, a British 14-year-old, allows herself to fall in with glamorous Kat's plans despite her reservations. (Rev: BL 5/1/03; HBG 10/03; SLJ 7/03; VOYA 8/03)

1010 Walker, Alice. *The Color Purple* (10–12). 1992, Harcourt $24.00 (0-15-119154-9). For better readers, the candid memoirs of Celie, her abuse, and eventual triumph.

1011 Watt, Alan. *Diamond Dogs* (10–12). 2000, Little, Brown $23.95 (0-316-92581-0). Seventeen-year-old Neil Garvin becomes a bully, like his father, but the boy's aggression leads to the death of one of the boys he has bullied. (Rev: BL 7/00)

1012 Wersba, Barbara. *Fat: A Love Story* (8–12). 1987, HarperCollins $11.95 (0-06-026400-4). Rita Formica, fat and unhappy, falls for rich, attractive Robert. (Rev: BL 6/1/87; SLJ 8/87; VOYA 6/87)

1013 White, Ruth. *Memories of Summer* (7–12). 2000, Farrar $16.00 (0-374-34945-2). Lyric is devastated when her older sister, Summer, must be hospitalized for her schizophrenia in this novel set in 1955. (Rev: BL 9/1/00; HB 9–10/00; HBG 3/01; SLJ 8/00*; VOYA 12/00)

1014 White, Ruth. *Weeping Willow* (7–10). 1992, Farrar paper $5.95 (0-374-48280-2). This uplifting novel conveying hill country life is about a girl who overcomes abuse to make her own way. (Rev: BL 6/15/92; SLJ 7/92)

1015 Wilson, Dawn. *Saint Jude* (8–12). 2001, Tudor $15.95 (0-936389-68-0). Taylor, who is bipolar, makes friends and learns to cope with her illness while in an outpatient program at St. Jude Hospital. (Rev: BL 11/1/01; SLJ 11/01)

1016 Wolff, Virginia E. *Probably Still Nick Swansen* (7–12). 1988, Holt $14.95 (0-8050-0701-6). Nick, a 16-year-old victim of slight brain dysfunction, tells his story of rejection and separation. (Rev: BL 11/15/88; BR 5–6/89; SLJ 12/88; VOYA 6/89)

1017 Wooding, Chris. *Kerosene* (9–12). 2002, Scholastic paper $6.99 (0-439-09013-X). In despair over his hard life, Cal begins setting fires in this novel set in England. (Rev: BL 7/02; SLJ 7/02; VOYA 8/02)

1018 Woodruff, Joan L. *The Shiloh Renewal* (7–10). 1998, Black Heron $22.95 (0-930773-50-0). Sandy, who has been mentally and physically disabled since an automobile accident, tries to regain basic skills, recover from the brain trauma, and straighten out her life in this novel that takes place on a small farm near Shiloh National Park in Tennessee. (Rev: VOYA 12/98)

Personal Problems and Growing into Maturity

1019 Agee, James. *A Death in the Family* (10–12). 1957, McDowell, Obolensky paper $13.00 (0-375-70123-0). A poignant novel about a young boy and how he and his family adjust to the death of his father.

1020 Alphin, Elaine Marie. *Simon Says* (8–12). 2002, Harcourt $17.00 (0-15-216355-7). Charles, a brooding 16-year-old artist, is determined to remain nonconformist when he starts attending a boarding school for the arts in this thoughtful novel. (Rev: BCCB 6/02; BL 4/15/02; HBG 10/02; SLJ 6/02)

1021 Anderson, Laurie Halse. *Speak* (8–12). 1999, Farrar $16.00 (0-374-37152-0). A victim of rape, high school freshman Mellinda Sordino finds that her attacker is again threatening her. (Rev: BL 9/15/99; HB 9–10/99; HBG 4/00; SLJ 10/99; VOYA 12/99)

1022 *Annie's Baby: The Diary of Anonymous, a Pregnant Teenager* (6–10). 1998, Demco $11.04 (0-606-13145-0); Avon paper $5.99 (0-380-79141-2). In diary format, this is the story of 14-year-old Annie, her love for an abusive rich boyfriend, and her rape and subsequent pregnancy. (Rev: SLJ 7/98; VOYA 6/98)

1023 Antle, Nancy. *Lost in the War* (6–10). 1998, Dial $15.99 (0-8037-2299-0). Lisa's father was killed during the Vietnam War and her mother was a nurse during the conflict, so her family is haunted by memories of a war that many people in their lives opposed. (Rev: BCCB 9/98; BL 8/98; HBG 9/98; SLJ 8/98; VOYA 8/98)

1024 Ashley, Bernard. *Little Soldier* (8–12). 2002, Scholastic $16.95 (0-439-22424-1). Young Kaninda Bulumba is rescued from the incredible violence taking place in his native country only to find himself confronting gang violence in his new neighborhood in London. (Rev: BCCB 7–8/02; BL 5/1/02; HBG 10/02; SLJ 6/02*; VOYA 8/02)

1025 Atwood, Margaret. *Cat's Eye* (10–12). 1989, Doubleday paper $12.95 (0-385-49102-6). This is a novel about Elaine Risley who, at 50, has become a famous Canadian painter and who tells the reader the story of her life.

1026 Avi. *Nothing but the Truth: A Documentary Novel* (7–10). 1991, Orchard paper $17.99 (0-531-08559-7). A boy's expulsion from school is reported in a biased, inflammatory newspaper story and takes on patriotic and political overtones. (Rev: BL 9/15/91*; SLJ 9/91*)

1027 Bagdasarian, Adam. *First French Kiss and Other Traumas* (7–12). 2002, Farrar $16.00 (0-374-32338-0). A series of vignettes, based on the author's own experiences, relate comic, romantic, and sad "traumas" in Will's life from the ages of five to 20. (Rev: BL 8/02; HB 11–12/02; HBG 3/03; SLJ 10/02; VOYA 12/02)

1028 Baker, Jennifer. *Most Likely to Deceive* (6–10). Series: Class Secrets. 1995, Pocket paper $3.99 (0-671-51033-9). Newcomer Suzanne Willis discovers that even the most popular teens in the school have problems. (Rev: SLJ 2/96)

1029 Banks, Russell. *Rule of the Bone* (10–12). 1996, HarperTrade $13.00 (0-06-092724-0). The reader follows Chappie from his life in a trailer park to discovery of drugs, rejection by parents, petty crime, and decision to take on a new name, "Bone," and style of life; as a homeless teen he moves through a variety of experiences, including a trip to the mountains of Jamaica.

1030 Barnes, Kim. *Finding Caruso* (11–12). 2003, Putnam $23.95 (0-399-14967-8). Two orphaned brothers learn to make their way in the world in this coming-of-age novel full of frank sexual content, drama, and conflict. (Rev: BL 2/15/03*)

1031 Bathurst, Bella. *Special* (11–12). 2003, Houghton paper $12.00 (0-618-26327-6). Set in rural England, this is an eloquent portrayal of the aspirations, temptations, insecurities, and cruelties typical of 13-year-old girls. (Rev: BL 3/15/03)

1032 Bechard, Margaret. *Hanging on to Max* (8–12). 2002, Millbrook LB $22.90 (0-7613-2574-3). Sam, a 17-year-old single father, faces difficult decisions as he juggles his father's demands and his own wish to go to college. (Rev: BCCB 5/02; BL 5/1/02; HB 5–6/02; HBG 10/02; SLJ 5/02*; VOYA 4/02)

1033 Bechard, Margaret. *If It Doesn't Kill You* (9–12). 1999, Viking $15.99 (0-670-88547-9). Ben, a fine high school football player, is unhappy to be compared with his father, also a star athlete, because Ben has discovered his father is gay. (Rev: BL 7/99; HB 7–8/99; HBG 9/99; SLJ 7/99)

1034 Beddard, Michael. *Stained Glass* (7–12). 2001, Tundra $17.95 (0-88776-552-1). When a stained glass window breaks and injures a young girl, Charles accompanies her on her search for her identity and begins to come to terms with her father's death. (Rev: BL 12/15/01; HB 1–2/02*; HBG 3/02; SLJ 1/02*; VOYA 12/01)

1035 Bell, Madison Smartt. *Anything Goes* (11–12). 2002, Pantheon $24.00 (0-375-42125-4). A shy young musician with a real talent for songwriting makes connections with his long-absent father and with a young female singer; for mature teens. (Rev: BL 4/15/02*)

1036 Bell, William. *Death Wind* (7–12). 2002, Orca paper $7.95 (1-55143-215-3). After running away from her unhappy home when she thinks she may be pregnant, Allie returns to find that a tornado has devastated her town. (Rev: BR 11–12/02; SLJ 10/02; VOYA 12/02)

1037 Bellow, Saul. *The Adventures of Augie March* (10–12). 1995, Knopf $20.00 (0-679-44460-2). The much-loved novel about a poor Jewish boy from Chicago and his attempts to make sense of his world.

1038 Benduhn, Tea. *Gravel Queen* (9–12). 2003, Simon & Schuster $15.95 (0-689-84994-X). When Aurin feels a growing attraction to new-girl-in-town Nelia, she finds her relationships with her best friends also change. (Rev: BCCB 4/03; BL 6/1–15/03; HBG 10/03; LMC 10/03; SLJ 3/03; VOYA 4/03)

1039 Bennett, Cherie, and Jeff Gottesfeld. *Stranger in the Mirror* (6–10). Series: Mirror Image. 1999, Pocket paper $4.99 (0-671-03630-0). Callie wants the popularity and good looks that her sister has, so she starts working out, losing weight, and changing her wardrobe. (Rev: BL 2/15/00; SLJ 3/00)

1040 Bennett, James W. *Plunking Reggie Jackson* (8–12). 2001, Simon & Schuster $16.00 (0-689-83137-4). High school senior Coley initially seems to have a lot going for him, but he faces an increasing number of challenges as an injury retires him to the bench, his girlfriend says she's pregnant, he struggles with family problems, and his grades drop. (Rev: BCCB 2/01; BL 4/1/01; HBG 10/01; SLJ 2/01; VOYA 4/01)

1041 Benson, Angela. *Awakening Mercy* (10–12). 2000, Tyndale paper $9.99 (0-8423-1939-5). An African American unwed mother finds love and fulfillment when she works at Genesis House, a Christian charity in a depressed Atlanta neighborhood. (Rev: BL 1/1–15/01)

1042 Berg, Elizabeth. *Joy School* (9–12). 1997, Random $19.00 (0-679-44943-4); paper $11.95 (0-345-42309-7). Lonely 13-year-old Katie develops a crush on 23-year-old Jimmy and makes new friends after moving to Missouri. (Rev: BL 9/15/98)

1043 Berg, Elizabeth. *True to Form* (10–12). 2002, Pocket $24.00 (0-7434-1134-X). Katie faces babysitting, Girl Scouting, and a new school in this sequel to *Durable Goods* (1993) and prequel to *Joy School* (1997). (Rev: BL 3/1/02; VOYA 4/03)

1044 Berlin, Adam. *Headlock* (10–12). 2000, Algonquin $21.95 (1-56512-266-6). A tough, raw novel for mature readers that deals with a trip to Las Vegas by a young man with a violent temper and his cousin, a grossly obese professional gambler. (Rev: BL 4/1/00*)

1045 Bertrand, Diane Gonzales. *Trino's Time* (6–12). 2001, Arte Publico $14.95 (1-55885-316-2); paper $9.95 (1-55885-317-0). In this sequel to *Trino's Choice* (1999), things begin to look better for Trino's family as Trino gets a job and starts enjoying school. (Rev: BL 11/1/01; SLJ 7/01; VOYA 12/01)

1046 Black, Jonah. *The Black Book (Diary of a Teenage Stud): Vol. 1: Girls, Girls, Girls* (8–12). 2001, Avon paper $4.99 (0-06-440798-5). Jonah, who has been expelled from a private school and is repeating his junior year at home, reveals the comic but touching details of his life and family as well as his private fantasies. Sequels are *Vol. 2: Stop, Don't Stop*, *Vol. 3: Run, Jonah, Run*, and *Vol. 4: Faster, Faster, Faster*. (Rev: BL 10/15/01; SLJ 8/01)

1047 Block, Francesca L. *Baby Be-Bop* (8–12). 1995, HarperCollins LB $13.89 (0-06-024880-7). Dirk is gay and struggles with self-loathing, among a number of debilitating emotions and experiences, until his grandmother shares her wisdom about loving and living. (Rev: BL 10/1/95*; SLJ 9/95)

1048 Block, Francesca L. *Cherokee Bat and the Goat Guys* (9–12). 1993, HarperCollins paper $4.95 (0-06-447095-4). In Block's third punk fairy tale, the youths form a rock band, which finds success until corruption sets in, when wise Coyote puts them right and heals them. (Rev: BL 8/92; SLJ 9/92)

1049 Block, Francesca L. *Echo* (8–12). 2001, HarperCollins LB $14.89 (0-06-028128-6). A series of interconnected stories set in glamorous Los Angeles follows the maturing of an unhappy young girl called Echo, who feels neglected by her talented parents and seeks attention where she can find it. (Rev: BCCB 10/01; BL 8/01; HB 9–10/01; HBG 3/02; SLJ 8/01; VOYA 10/01)

1050 Block, Francesca L. *Girl Goddess #9* (10–12). 1996, HarperCollins $14.95 (0-06-027211-2); paper $4.99 (0-06-447187-X). Nine stories explore girl goddesses of all kinds — real young women growing up and learning about the world. (Rev: SLJ 9/96)

1051 Block, Francesca L. *Violet and Claire* (10–12). 1999, HarperCollins LB $14.89 (0-06-027750-5). The story of two talented and very different friends whose relationship goes awry when sex and drugs enter their lives. (Rev: BL 9/1/99; HBG 4/00; SLJ 9/99)

1052 Block, Francesca L. *Wasteland* (9–12). 2003, HarperCollins LB $16.89 (0-06-028645-8). Lex commits suicide after he and his sister have sex in this novel with a twist about two affectionate siblings. (Rev: BCCB 11/03; BL 7/03; HB 11–12/03; HBG 4/04; SLJ 10/03; VOYA 2/04)

1053 Block, Francesca L. *Weetzie Bat* (9–12). 1989, HarperCollins $14.95 (0-06-020534-2). Four teenagers into punk culture — two gay and a straight couple — set up housekeeping but the realities of life spoil their demi-Eden. A controversial book that received mixed reviews. (Rev: BL 3/15/89; BR 3–4/90; SLJ 4/89; VOYA 10/89)

1054 Bloor, Edward. *Tangerine* (7–10). 1997, Harcourt $17.00 (0-15-201246-X); Scholastic paper $4.99 (0-590-43277-X). Although he wears thick glasses, Paul is able to see clearly the people around him, their problems and their mistakes, as he adjusts to his new home in Tangerine County, Florida. (Rev: BL 5/15/97; SLJ 4/97; VOYA 8/97)

1055 Blume, Judy. *Forever . . .* (9–12). 1975, Bradbury LB $16.00 (0-02-711030-3). A girl's awakening sexuality is explored in this novel that contains frank language and explicit scenes. (Rev: BL 10/15/88)

1056 Blume, Judy. *Summer Sisters* (10–12). 1998, Delacorte $21.95 (0-385-32405-7). An entertaining adult novel about the friendship of two girls and their experiences, worries, and emotions as they grow into maturity during six summers together. (Rev: BL 3/15/98; SLJ 6/98)

1057 Blume, Judy. *Tiger Eyes* (7–10). 1981, Dell paper $5.99 (0-440-98469-6). A girl struggles to cope with her father's violent death. (Rev: BL 7/88)

1058 Bond, Nancy. *The Love of Friends* (9–12). 1997, Simon & Schuster paper $17.00 (0-689-81365-1). On a trip to remote parts of Scotland, Charlotte, Oliver, and an American friend discover a great deal about themselves, their families, and their friendship. (Rev: BL 11/15/97; BR 3–4/98; HBG 3/98; SLJ 10/97; VOYA 12/97)

1059 Boock, Paula. *Dare Truth or Promise* (8–12). 1999, Houghton $15.00 (0-395-97117-9). Two girls, Willa and Louise, attend a New Zealand high school and, though they are opposites in many ways, they fall in love. (Rev: BL 9/15/99; HB 9–10/99; HBG 4/00; SLJ 11/99; VOYA 10/99)

1060 Book, Rick. *Necking With Louise* (7–12). 1999, Red Deer paper $7.95 (0-88995-194-2). Set in Saskatchewan in 1965, this is a book of stories about Eric Anderson's 16th year, when he has his first date, plays in a championship hockey game, has a summer job, and reacts to his family and the land on which he lives. (Rev: BL 10/15/99* ; SLJ 3/00)

1061 Borntrager, Mary Christner. *Rebecca* (7–12). 1989, Herald Pr. paper $8.99 (0-8361-3500-8). A coming-of-age novel about an Amish girl and her attraction to a Mennonite young man. (Rev: SLJ 11/89)

1062 Bottner, Barbara. *Nothing in Common* (7–10). 1986, HarperCollins $12.95 (0-06-020604-7). When Mrs. Gregori dies, both her daughter and Melissa Warren, a teenager in the household where Mrs. Gregori worked, enter a period of grief. (Rev: VOYA 2/87)

1063 Boyle, T. C. *After the Plague and Other Stories* (10–12). 2001, Viking $25.95 (0-670-03005-8). A fine collection of short stories, each of which deals with a person in crisis. (Rev: BL 6/1–15/01*)

1064 Brancato, Robin F. *Facing Up* (9–12). 1984, Knopf LB $9.99 (0-394-95488-2). The friendship between Jep and Dave is strained by the attentions of Jep's girlfriend.

1065 Bridgers, Sue Ellen. *All We Know of Heaven* (10–12). 1996, Banks Channel $22.00 (0-9635967-4-8). For mature readers, this a shocking story, with finely drawn characters, about a love that eventually leads to betrayal, madness, and death. (Rev: BL 10/1/96; SLJ 1/97)

1066 Bridgers, Sue Ellen. *Keeping Christina* (7–10). 1998, Replica LB $29.95 (0-7351-0042-X). Annie takes sad newcomer Christina under her wing, but she turns out to be a liar and troublemaker, which creates conflicts with Annie's family, friends, and boyfriend. (Rev: BL 7/93; SLJ 7/93)

1067 Bridgers, Sue Ellen. *Permanent Connections* (8–12). 1998, Replica LB $29.95 (0-7351-0043-8). When Rob's behavior gets out of control, the teenager is sent to his uncle's farm to cool off. (Rev: BL 2/15/87; BR 9–10/87; SLJ 3/87; VOYA 4/87)

1068 Brockett, D. A. *Stained Glass Rose* (10–12). 2002, Western Reflections paper $14.95 (1-890437-61-1). An elderly woman revisits the murder of a great friend and at the same time seeks to rekindle her bereaved grandson's interest in life. (Rev: VOYA 4/03)

1069 Brooks, Kevin. *Kissing the Rain* (9–12). 2004, Scholastic $16.95 (0-439-57742-X). Moo, a fat, bullied British teen, witnesses a murder and finds himself torn between telling the truth and pleasing a cop who threatens to ruin Moo's father if he doesn't lie. (Rev: BL 2/15/04; SLJ 3/04; VOYA 4/04)

1070 Brooks, Martha. *Being with Henry* (7–12). 2000, DK paper $17.99 (0-7894-2588-2). This coming-of-age story is about 16-year-old Laker who has been kicked out of his home, and his friendship with Henry, a 83-year-old widower. (Rev: BL 4/1/00; HB 5–6/00; HBG 9/00; SLJ 5/00; VOYA 6/00)

1071 Brooks, Martha. *Bone Dance* (9–12). 1997, Orchard LB $17.99 (0-531-33021-4). When Alex drives out to see the property her dead father has left her, she meets and becomes involved with Lonnie, stepson of the land's former owner. (Rev: BL 10/1/97; HBG 3/98; SLJ 11/97; VOYA 12/97)

1072 Brooks, Martha. *Traveling On into the Light* (7–12). 1994, Orchard LB $16.99 (0-531-08713-1). Stories about runaways, suicide, and desertion, featuring romantic, sensitive, and smart teenage outsiders. (Rev: BL 8/94; SLJ 8/94*; VOYA 10/94)

1073 Brooks, Martha. *True Confessions of a Heartless Girl* (9–12). 2003, Farrar $16.00 (0-374-37806-1). A pregnant teenager wreaks havoc in Pembina Lake, Canada, in this gritty novel. (Rev: BL 4/1/03; HB 5–6/03; HBG 10/03; SLJ 2/03; VOYA 6/03)

1074 Brown, Larry. *Joe* (9–12). 1991, Algonquin $29.95 (0-945575-61-0). Hard-drinking Joe helps turn the life of a neglected teenager around. (Rev: BL 8/91*)

1075 Brugman, Alyssa. *Walking Naked* (7–12). 2002, Allen & Unwin $17.95 (1-86508-822-6). A tragic tale in which a member of a 10th-grade elite group finds peer pressure more important than her growing friendship for the class outcast. (Rev: BCCB 4/04; BL 2/1/04; HB 7–8/04; SLJ 7/04; VOYA 4/03)

1076 Bunin, Sherry. *Dear Great American Writers School* (9–12). 1995, Houghton $15.00 (0-395-71645-4). A sensitive, bittersweet story of a young aspiring writer who is drawn into a magazine's scheme to train young writers. (Rev: BL 11/15/95; SLJ 10/95; VOYA 12/95)

1077 Bunting, Eve. *Doll Baby* (5–10). 2000, Clarion $15.00 (0-395-93094-4). A simple, direct narrative in which 15-year-old Ellie explains how being pregnant and having a baby radically changed her life. (Rev: BL 11/1/00; HB 9–10/00; HBG 3/01; SLJ 10/00)

1078 Bunting, Eve. *If I Asked You, Would You Stay?* (8–10). 1984, HarperCollins LB $12.89 (0-397-32066-3). Two lonely people find comfort in love for each other.

1079 Bunting, Eve. *Jumping the Nail* (7–12). 1991, Harcourt $15.95 (0-15-241357-X). A dependent, unstable girl becomes unhinged when she is persuaded by her danger-seeking boyfriend to jump off a cliff with him. (Rev: BL 11/1/91; SLJ 12/91)

1080 Butler, Charles. *Timon's Tide* (6–12). 2000, Simon & Schuster $16.00 (0-689-82593-5). A surreal story about 17-year-old Daniel and how he gains control of his life through the intervention of his dead older brother. (Rev: BL 6/1–15/00; HBG 9/00; SLJ 6/00; VOYA 6/00)

1081 Cadnum, Michael. *Breaking the Fall* (8–12). 1992, Viking $15.00 (0-670-84687-2). To help him forget that his parents are separating and he isn't playing baseball anymore, Stanley and Jared start housebreaking, taking token items to mark their daring. (Rev: BL 11/15/92; SLJ 9/92)

1082 Cadnum, Michael. *Rundown* (9–12). 1999, Viking $15.99 (0-670-88377-8). In this fast-paced suspense novel, wealthy teenager Jennifer Thayer invents a rape in order to gain attention. (Rev: BL 6/1–15/99; HBG 9/99; SLJ 8/99; VOYA 10/99)

1083 Cadre, Adam. *Ready, Okay!* (10–12). 2000, HarperCollins $25.00 (0-06-019558-4). For mature readers, this is the saga of a 16-year-old boy and the sadness and violence that seem to touch everyone he knows. (Rev: BL 7/00)

1084 Caletti, Deb. *The Queen of Everything* (8–12). 2002, Simon & Schuster paper $5.99 (0-7434-3684-9). Jordan's life is turned upside-down by her grandmother's death, her father's new romance, and her own sexual experimentation. (Rev: BCCB 1/03; BL 11/15/02; SLJ 11/02; VOYA 2/03)

1085 Campbell, Bebe Moore. *What You Owe Me* (10–12). 2001, Putnam $26.95 (0-399-14784-5). Beginning in the 1940s, this novel combines betrayal and bitterness as it tells of the friendship between an African American woman from Texas and a Jewish woman who is a survivor of the Nazi death camps. (Rev: BL 7/01)

1086 Camus, Albert. *The Fall* (10–12). Trans. by Justin O'Brien. 1957, Knopf paper $10.00 (0-679-72022-7). A challenging novel about a man who is trying to avoid judging himself through a life of inaction and evaluating others.

1087 Cann, Kate. *Hard Cash* (10–12). 2003, Simon & Schuster paper $5.99 (0-689-85905-8). When Rich, a 17-year-old British aspiring artist, finds that others are interested in his art, he tries to use this to win his girlfriend, Portia. (Rev: BL 2/1/04; SLJ 11/03)

1088 Cannon, A. E. *The Shadow Brothers* (7–12). 1992, Dell paper $3.99 (0-440-21167-0). Two foster brothers, one an American Indian, gradually grow apart under the strain of outside pressures. (Rev: BL 5/1/90; BR 5–6/90; SLJ 6/90)

1089 Canty, Kevin. *Into the Great Wide Open* (11–12). 1997, Vintage Anchor paper $13.00 (0-679-77652-4). Kenny Kolodny, an unhappy, pot-smoking 17-year-old from a dysfunctional family finds comfort with Junie Williamson, a girl with her own troubles; for mature readers.

1090 Capote, Truman. *The Thanksgiving Visitor* (10–12). 1968, Random $27.71 (0-394-44824-3). In this tender reminiscence, a young boy learns the meaning of compassion from his spinster cousin. Also use *A Christmas Memory* (1966).

1091 Cart, Michael. *My Father's Scar* (7–12). 1996, Simon & Schuster paper $16.00 (0-689-80749-X). Andy Logan, a college freshman, is about to have his first gay relationship and recalls growing up a lonely boy in a homophobic community. (Rev: BL 4/1/96; BR 3–4/97; SLJ 5/96; VOYA 8/96)

1092 Carter, Alden R. *Dogwolf* (7–10). 1994, Scholastic paper $13.95 (0-590-46741-7). In this coming-of-age novel, Pete realizes that a dogwolf that he's set free must be found and killed before it harms a human. (Rev: BL 1/1/95; SLJ 4/95; VOYA 2/95)

1093 Chambers, Aidan. *NIK: Now I Know* (10–12). 1988, HarperCollins $13.95 (0-06-021208-X). Nik questions his religious beliefs but by a tortuous route recovers his faith. (Rev: BL 7/88; BR 5–6/89; SLJ 8/88; VOYA 10/88)

1094 Chambers, Aidan. *Postcards from No Man's Land* (9–12). 2002, Dutton $19.99 (0-525-46863-3). A multilayered novel in which Jacob, grandson of a World War II soldier, experiences bewildering emotions when he visits his grandfather's grave in Amsterdam. (Rev: BL 5/15/02; HB 7–8/02*; HBG 10/02; SLJ 7/02; VOYA 8/02)

1095 Chan, Gillian. *Glory Days and Other Stories* (7–10). 1997, Kids Can $16.95 (1-55074-381-3). Five stories about young people at Elmwood High School, each of whom faces problems because of decisions that have been made. (Rev: BL 1/1–15/98; SLJ 10/97)

1096 Chan, Gillian. *Golden Girl and Other Stories* (7–10). 1997, Kids Can $14.95 (1-55074-385-6). Short stories about students in a high school, with details of their pleasures, pains, and concerns. (Rev: BL 9/15/97; SLJ 11/97)

1097 Chbosky, Stephen. *The Perks of Being a Wallflower* (9–12). 1999, MTV paper $12.00 (0-671-02734-4). In letter format, outsider Charlie writes about his freshman year in high school, his new, insightful, bohemian friends, his defiance of conformity, and his evolution into a man of action. (Rev: BL 2/15/99; SLJ 6/99; VOYA 12/99)

1098 Chedid, Andree. *The Multiple Child* (10–12). 1995, Mercury House paper $12.95 (1-56279-079-X). In this novel, a lonely 10-year-old boy who has lost an arm in a car bombing in Lebanon is sent by his grandfather to live with relatives in Paris. (Rev: BL 9/1/95; SLJ 7/96)

1099 Childress, Alice. *Those Other People* (9–12). 1989, Putnam $14.95 (0-399-21510-7). A 17-year-old gay boy and an African American boy are blackmailed into silence over the attempted rape they have witnessed. (Rev: BL 1/1/89; SLJ 2/89; VOYA 4/89)

1100 Chin, Michael. *Free Throw* (7–12). 2001, PublishAmerica paper $19.95 (1-58851-166-9). Basketball and romance play major roles in the life of high school sophomore Mike Weaver. (Rev: VOYA 4/02)

1101 Choi, Sook N. *Gathering of Pearls* (7–10). 1994, Houghton $16.00 (0-395-67437-9). Sookan Bak leaves Korea in 1954 to attend a New York women's college, where she struggles to fit in. Second sequel to *The Year of Impossible Goodbyes*. (Rev: BL 9/1/94; SLJ 10/94; VOYA 10/94)

1102 Clark, Catherine. *Wurst Case Scenario* (10–12). 2001, HarperCollins LB $15.89 (0-06-029525-2); paper $6.95 (0-06-447287-6). The sequel to *Truth or Dairy* chronicles the adventures of vegan Courtney in her freshman year at a small college in Wisconsin. (Rev: BL 9/1/01; HBG 10/02; SLJ 10/01; VOYA 12/01)

1103 Clarke, Judith. *Night Train* (8–11). 2000, Holt $16.95 (0-8050-6151-7). Luke Leman, an Australian teenager, finds that he is cracking under scholastic and family pressures and thinks he might be going insane. (Rev: BCCB 5/00; BL 6/1–15/00; HBG 9/00; SLJ 5/00)

1104 Coady, Lynn. *Saints of Big Harbour* (11–12). 2002, Houghton $24.00 (0-618-11976-0). Rumors spread by a girl he liked make fatherless Guy Boucher's life even more miserable in this novel set in a small Nova Scotia community; for mature teens. (Rev: BL 10/1/02)

1105 Coburn, Jake. *Prep* (9–12). 2003, Dutton $15.99 (0-525-47135-9). This novel explores the dark side of privilege, looking at prep-school teens in New York and their violence and use of drugs, alcohol, and sex. (Rev: BCCB 1/04; BL 11/1/03; SLJ 10/03)

1106 Cohen, Leah H. *Heat Lightning* (10–12). 1997, Avon paper $22.00 (0-380-97468-1). Mole, 11, and her older sister, Tilly, become involved with a family that moves into their small Maine community for the summer, leading to unusual confrontations and sexual tensions. (Rev: BL 6/1–15/97; SLJ 6/98)

1107 Cole, Brock. *Celine* (8–10). 1989, Farrar paper $3.95 (0-374-41083-6). The story of a 16-year-old girl who is on a journey of self-discovery.

1108 Cole, Sheila. *What Kind of Love?* (8–10). 1995, Lothrop $15.00 (0-688-12848-3). A 15-year-old becomes pregnant and deals with hard decisions. (Rev: BL 3/15/95; SLJ 5/95)

1109 Collins, Pat L. *Signs and Wonders* (7–10). 1999, Houghton $15.00 (0-395-97119-5). Through letters to her grandmother, her father, and an imaginary guardian angel, a young girl in boarding school reveals her feelings of unhappiness, loneliness, and

betrayal — and her belief that she has been chosen to bear the prophet of the next millennium. (Rev: BCCB 11/99; BL 10/1/99; HBG 4/00; SLJ 10/99; VOYA 10/99)

1110 Conford, Ellen. *Crush* (7–12). 1998, HarperCollins $15.95 (0-06-025414-9). In this collection of interrelated short stories, high school students face problems such as peer pressure, low self-esteem, alienation, greed, and heartbreak. (Rev: BCCB 3/98; BL 1/1–15/98; HB 3–4/98; HBG 9/98; SLJ 1/98; VOYA 6/98)

1111 Conroy, Pat. *The Lords of Discipline* (10–12). 1980, Bantam paper $7.99 (0-553-27136-9). An engrossing novel set in a military academy during the Vietnam War and involving four roommates and the fate of the institution's first black cadet.

1112 Conroy, Pat. *The Prince of Tides* (10–12). 1986, Houghton $30.00 (0-395-35300-9). Tom, from the South Carolina tidewater areas, comes to New York to help his twin sister, a successful poet, who has attempted suicide. (Rev: SLJ 4/87)

1113 Cooney, Caroline B. *Driver's Ed* (7–12). 1994, Delacorte $16.95 (0-385-32087-6). Remy and Morgan are driving around town creating trouble when they accidentally cause the death of an innocent pedestrian. (Rev: BL 6/1–15/94*; SLJ 8/94; VOYA 10/94)

1114 Cooney, Caroline B. *Summer Nights* (7–12). 1992, Scholastic paper $3.25 (0-590-45786-1). At a farewell party, five high school girls look back on their school years and their friendship. (Rev: SLJ 1/89)

1115 Cooney, Caroline B. *What Child Is This? A Christmas Story* (6–10). 1997, Delacorte $14.95 (0-385-32317-4). In a New England community, three teenagers and a child try to find what Christmas is all about. (Rev: BL 9/1/97; HBG 3/98; SLJ 10/97; VOYA 12/97)

1116 Cormier, Robert. *Beyond the Chocolate War* (9–12). 1985, Dell paper $4.99 (0-440-90580-X). The misuse of power at Trinity High by Brother Leon and the secret society of Vigils is again explored in this sequel to *The Chocolate War* (1974). (Rev: BL 3/15/85; BR 9–10/85; SLJ 4/85)

1117 Cormier, Robert. *The Chocolate War* (7–12). 1993, Dell paper $3.99 (0-440-90032-8). A chocolate sale in a boys' private school creates power struggles. Followed by *Beyond the Chocolate War*.

1118 Cormier, Robert. *Eight Plus One* (9–12). 1980, Pantheon LB $7.99 (0-394-94595-6). These nine stories involve such problems of growing up as coping with one's first love experience and a boy trying to grow a mustache.

1119 Cormier, Robert. *Frenchtown Summer* (6–10). 1999, Delacorte $16.95 (0-385-32704-8). A verse novel about a boy growing up in a small town in

Massachusetts after World War I, the father he can't seem to reach, and the first pangs of adolescence. (Rev: BCCB 11/99; BL 9/15/99; HB 9–10/99; HBG 4/00; SLJ 9/99; VOYA 12/99)

1120 Cormier, Robert. *I Am the Cheese* (7–12). 1977, Pantheon $19.95 (0-394-83462-3). A multi-level novel about a boy's life after his parents are forced to go underground. (Rev: BL 6/1/88; HBG 3/98)

1121 Cormier, Robert. *The Rag and Bone Shop* (8–10). 2001, Delacorte $15.95 (0-385-72962-6). Shy, introverted 13-year-old Jason is a suspect in the murder of a 7-year-old girl in this dark and suspenseful story that features an ambitious and ruthless detective. (Rev: BCCB 12/01; BL 7/01; HB 11–12/01; HBG 3/02; SLJ 9/01; VOYA 10/01)

1122 Cormier, Robert. *Tunes for Bears to Dance To* (6–12). 1992, Dell paper $5.50 (0-440-21903-5). In a stark morality tale set in a Massachusetts town after World War II, Henry, 11, is tempted, corrupted, and redeemed. (Rev: BL 6/15/92; SLJ 9/92)

1123 Cormier, Robert. *We All Fall Down* (8–12). 1991, Dell paper $5.50 (0-440-21556-0). Random violence committed by four high school seniors is observed by the Avenger, who also witnesses the budding love affair of one of the victims of the attack. (Rev: BL 9/15/91*; SLJ 9/91*)

1124 Cottonwood, Joe. *Babcock* (7–10). 1996, Scholastic paper $15.95 (0-590-22221-X). A teenager named Babcock recounts with humor and insight several months of his life in a town in the California Bay area, including everyday school experiences, falling in love, playing softball, and coping with an unexpected visit by an unwanted uncle. (Rev: BR 11–12/96; VOYA 6/97)

1125 Cox, Elizabeth. *Night Talk* (10–12). 1997, Graywolf $23.95 (1-55597-267-5). This story tells of the 40-year friendship, beginning in 1949, between an African American woman and her white female employer in Georgia and of a similar bond between their two daughters. (Rev: BL 10/15/97; SLJ 2/98)

1126 Cronin, A. J. *The Citadel* (10–12). 1983, Little, Brown $16.95 (0-316-16158-6). An idealistic doctor finds he must battle with the establishment.

1127 Cronin, A. J. *The Keys of the Kingdom* (10–12). 1984, Little, Brown $16.45 (0-316-16189-6). An inspiring story about a young priest and his missionary work.

1128 Cross, Gillian. *Tightrope* (7–12). 1999, Holiday $16.95 (0-8234-1512-0). To take her mind off the hours she spends caring for her invalid mother, Ashley begins to hang out with a local street gang. (Rev: BCCB 12/99; BL 9/15/99; HBG 4/00; SLJ 10/99; VOYA 4/00)

1129 Crowe, Carole. *Waiting for Dolphins* (6–12). 2000, Boyds Mills $16.95 (1-56397-847-4). Still recovering from her father's death in a boating incident, Molly must also adjust to her mother's new love interest. (Rev: BL 3/1/00; HBG 9/00; SLJ 4/00; VOYA 6/00)

1130 Crutcher, Chris. *Athletic Shorts: 6 Short Stories* (8–12). 1991, Greenwillow $16.95 (0-688-10816-4). These short stories focus on themes important to teens, such as sports, father–son friction, insecurity, and friendship. (Rev: BL 10/15/91; SLJ 9/91*)

1131 Daoust, Jerry. *Waking Up Bees: Stories of Living Life's Questions* (7–12). 1999, Saint Mary's Press paper $6.95 (0-88489-527-0). In this collection of 10 short stories, young Christians find answers to life's dilemmas in their faith. (Rev: VOYA 4/00)

1132 Davis, Donald. *Thirteen Miles from Suncrest* (9–12). 1994, August House $22.95 (0-87483-379-5). The youngest child of a farm family comes of age in quaint Close Creek, North Carolina. This journal chronicles his life from 1910 to 1913. (Rev: BL 9/15/94; SLJ 1/95)

1133 Dean, Carolee. *Comfort* (7–10). 2002, Houghton $15.00 (0-618-13846-3). Fourteen-year-old Kenny persists in his dreams of making something of himself in spite of his mother's conflicting desires. (Rev: HBG 10/02; SLJ 3/02*; VOYA 4/02)

1134 Demsky, Andy. *Dark Refuge: A Story of Cults and Their Seductive Appeal* (9–12). 1995, Pacific paper $7.97 (0-8163-1241-9). A coming-of-age story in which young Anita is inadvertently abused by her mother and then falls into the hands of a "prophet" of a cult. (Rev: BL 11/1/95*)

1135 Dessen, Sarah. *Dreamland* (8–10). 2000, Viking $15.99 (0-670-89122-3). After her sister runs away, Caitlin's life comes apart and she descends into drugs and sex. (Rev: BL 11/1/00* ; HB 9–10/00; HBG 3/01; SLJ 9/00)

1136 Dessen, Sarah. *Keeping the Moon* (6–10). 1999, Viking $15.99 (0-670-88549-5). Colie, a 15-year-old girl with little self-esteem, spends a summer with an eccentric aunt and finds a kind of salvation in a friendship with two waitresses and the love of a shy teenage artist. (Rev: BL 9/1/99; HBG 4/00; SLJ 9/99; VOYA 12/99)

1137 Dessen, Sarah. *Someone Like You* (7–12). 1998, Viking $16.99 (0-670-87778-6). Young Halley discovers that her best friend Scarlett is pregnant and Scarlett's boyfriend has been killed in an accident. (Rev: BL 5/15/98; HB 7–8/98; HBG 9/98; SLJ 6/98; VOYA 8/98)

1138 Dessen, Sarah. *That Summer* (7–12). 1996, Orchard LB $17.99 (0-531-08888-X). Haven is 15 and 5 feet 11, and to make matters worse, she has to be bridesmaid at her picture-perfect sister's wedding. (Rev: BL 10/15/96*; BR 3–4/97; SLJ 10/96; VOYA 12/96)

1139 De Vries, Anke. *Bruises* (6–10). Trans. by Stacey Knecht. 1996, Front Street $15.95 (1-886910-03-0); Dell paper $4.50 (0-440-22694-5). This novel, set in Holland, tells of the friendship between a sympathetic boy, Michael, and Judith, a disturbed, abused young girl. (Rev: BL 4/1/96; SLJ 6/96; VOYA 6/96)

1140 Dines, Carol. *Talk to Me: Stories and a Novella* (8–12). 1997, Bantam $15.95 (0-385-32271-2). Teenage problems like romance, family relations, jobs, and school troubles are the subjects of these six stories and a novella. (Rev: BL 7/97; BR 9–10/97; SLJ 7/97; VOYA 8/97)

1141 Divakaruni, Chitra Banerjee. *The Vine of Desire* (10–12). 2002, Doubleday $23.95 (0-385-49729-6). Sudha in Calcutta accepts an invitation from her beloved cousin, Anju, in Berkeley to visit even though she knows Anju's husband is in love with her in this novel for mature readers. (Rev: BL 11/1/01)

1142 Doherty, Berlie. *Dear Nobody* (7–12). 1992, Morrow paper $5.95 (0-688-12764-9). This complex novel explores the consequences of a teenager's pregnancy and the resulting tensions with her boyfriend. (Rev: BL 10/1/92*; SLJ 10/92*)

1143 Dragonwagon, Crescent, and Paul Zindel. *To Take a Dare* (9–12). 1982, HarperCollins $12.95 (0-06-026858-1). After three years of wandering, Chrysta must find herself.

1144 Draper, Sharon M. *Romiette and Julio* (6–10). 1999, Simon & Schuster $16.00 (0-689-82180-8). An updated version of Romeo and Juliet set in contemporary Cincinnati involving a Hispanic American boy, an African American girl, street gangs, and, in this case, a happy ending. (Rev: BL 9/15/99; HBG 4/00; SLJ 9/99; VOYA 12/99)

1145 Ducornet, Rikki. *Gazelle* (11–12). 2003, Knopf $21.00 (0-375-41124-0). Elizabeth, 13 and living in Cairo, becomes interested in sex and seduction when her mother leaves home and her lonely father becomes more distant; suitable for mature teens. (Rev: BL 7/03)

1146 Duncan, Lois. *Trapped! Cages of the Mind and Body* (7–12). 1998, Simon & Schuster $16.00 (0-689-81335-X). Limitations caused by the mind and/or the body are explored in 13 stories, each by a different YA writer. (Rev: BL 7/98; HBG 3/99; SLJ 6/98; VOYA 8/98)

1147 Dybek, Stuart. *I Sailed with Magellan* (11–12). 2003, Farrar $24.00 (0-374-17407-5). This collection of interconnected short stories explores the wonders and angst of coming of age in inner city Chicago; for mature teens. (Rev: BL 10/15/03*)

1148 Eisen, Adrienne. *Making Scenes* (11–12). 2002, Alt-X paper $15.00 (0-9703517-0-4). In succeeding related chapters, a young college graduate describes her youth, her family, her bulimia, and her struggles with sex; for mature teens. (Rev: BL 3/1/02)

1149 Elderkin, Susan. *The Voices* (10–12). 2003, Grove $24.00 (0-8021-1757-0). In this gripping novel, the protagonist harks back to lessons he learned as a teen as he struggles to recover from a devastating and mysterious accident. (Rev: BL 9/15/03)

1150 Elliott, Stephen. *A Life Without Consequences* (10–12). 2001, MacAdam $25.00 (0-9673701-7-5). This is an explicit novel about Paul, a runaway from an abusive father, who lives in group homes beginning at age 14. (Rev: BL 8/01; SLJ 5/02)

1151 Evans, Elizabeth. *Rowing in Eden* (10–12). 2000, HarperCollins $25.00 (0-06-019550-9). In this novel for mature readers, set in the summer of 1965, Franny Wahl, 13, finds she is attracted to a college student who begins to return her attentions. (Rev: BL 9/15/00; VOYA 2/01)

1152 Eyerly, Jeannette. *Someone to Love Me* (7–10). 1987, HarperCollins LB $11.89 (0-397-32206-2). An unpopular high school girl is seduced by the school's glamour boy and decides, when she finds she is pregnant, to keep the child. (Rev: BL 2/1/87; BR 9–10/87; SLJ 4/87; VOYA 4/87)

1153 Farr, Judith. *I Never Came to You in White* (10–12). 1996, Houghton $21.95 (0-395-78840-4). Using imaginary letters from Emily Dickinson to and from friends, this novel probes the spirit, challenges, attitudes, pranks, and poems of the celebrated writer. (Rev: SLJ 1/97)

1154 Ferris, Jean. *Bad* (7–10). 1998, Farrar paper $4.95 (0-374-40475-5). Dallas gains self knowledge when she is sent to a women's correctional center for six months and meets gang members, drug dealers, a 14-year-old prostitute, and other unfortunates. (Rev: BL 10/1/98; SLJ 12/98; VOYA 2/99)

1155 Ferris, Jean. *Eight Seconds* (6–12). 2000, Harcourt $17.00 (0-15-202367-4). At rodeo camp, 18-year-old Ritchie discovers that his new rodeo friend is gay. (Rev: BL 10/1/00* ; HBG 3/01; SLJ 1/01)

1156 Ferry, Charles. *A Fresh Start* (7–10). 1996, Proctor paper $8.95 (1-882792-18-1). This novel explores the problems of troubled teens in a summer-school program for young alcoholics. (Rev: SLJ 5/96; VOYA 10/96)

1157 Fielding, Joy. *Grand Avenue* (10–12). 2001, Pocket $25.00 (0-7434-0707-5). Four young mothers meet at a local playground in 1970 and become fast friends. This novel traces their varied futures and the course of their friendship. (Rev: BL 8/01)

1158 Fienberg, Anna. *Borrowed Light* (8–10). 2000, Delacorte $14.95 (0-385-32758-7). Using many astrological images, the author of this novel tells about Callisto's pregnancy, her abortion, and her other family and personal problems. (Rev: BL 6/1–15/00; HB 7–8/00; HBG 9/00; SLJ 6/00)

1159 Filichia, Peter. *What's in a Name?* (7–12). 1988, Avon paper $2.75 (0-380-75536-X). Rose is so unhappy with her foreign-sounding last name that she decides to change it. (Rev: BL 3/1/89; VOYA 4/89)

1160 Fine, Africa. *Becoming Maren* (11–12). 2003, Five Star $26.95 (1-5941-4081-2). African American teens Maren and Ellison, who've lived a privileged life with little exposure to other blacks, find themselves thrust into an alien world alien when they must go to live with their father in North Carolina; for mature teens. (Rev: BL 12/15/03)

1161 Fleischman, Paul. *Breakout* (9–12). 2003, Cricket $16.95 (0-8126-2696-6). Present and future are interwoven in the narratives of Del, a 17-year-old foster child whose bid for freedom is hampered by a giant traffic jam, and of Elena (Del eight years in the future), whose one-woman show features observations about life and freeway traffic. (Rev: BCCB 10/03; BL 12/15/03; HB 11–12/03; HBG 4/04; SLJ 9/03; VOYA 12/03)

1162 Fleischman, Paul. *Whirligig* (7–10). 1998, Holt $16.95 (0-8050-5582-7). As penance for killing a teenager in an automobile accident, Brent must fashion four whirligigs and place them in the four corners of the United States. (Rev: BL 4/1/98; HB 7–8/98; HBG 9/98; SLJ 4/98; VOYA 6/98)

1163 Flinn, Alex. *Breaking Point* (7–10). 2002, HarperCollins LB $15.89 (0-06-623848-X). Paul is so desperate to be accepted at his new school that he allows himself to be lured into increasingly perilous situations. (Rev: BL 9/1/02; HBG 10/02; SLJ 5/02; VOYA 6/02)

1164 Flinn, Alex. *Breathing Underwater* (7–12). 2001, HarperCollins $15.95 (0-06-029198-2). In this harrowing account of domestic violence, the sins of the father are reflected in troubled teen Nick Andreas's savage treatment of his girlfriend, Caitlin. (Rev: BCCB 7–8/01; BL 8/01; BR 11–12/01; HBG 10/01; SLJ 5/01; VOYA 6/01)

1165 Foon, Dennis. *Double or Nothing* (6–12). 2000, Annick $17.95 (1-55037-627-6); paper $6.95 (1-55037-626-8). High school senior Kip feels secure that he has saved enough money for college until he meets King, a magician and con artist who takes advantage of Kip's love of gambling. (Rev: BL 8/00; HBG 9/00; SLJ 9/00)

1166 Fox, Laurie. *The Lost Girls* (11–12). 2004, Simon & Schuster $23.00 (0-7432-1790-X). Thirteen-year-old Wendy, great granddaughter of the now-elderly Wendy who years earlier inspired author J. M. Barrie to write *Peter Pan*, finds herself caught up in a latter-day version of the Peter Pan story; for mature teens. (Rev: BL 12/15/03)

1167 Frame, Ronald. *The Lantern Bearers* (10–12). 2001, Counterpoint $24.00 (1-58243-155-8). A young boy soprano falls in love with a composer and then fakes a molestation story when the composer rejects him. (Rev: BL 10/15/01)

1168 Franco, Betsy, ed. *Things I Have to Tell You: Poems and Writing by Teenage Girls* (7–12). Photos by Nina Nickles. 2001, Candlewick $15.99 (0-7636-0905-6); paper $8.99 (0-7636-1035-6). Teen girls reveal their aspirations, fears, and frustrations in this appealing collection of poems, stories, and essays. (Rev: BL 3/15/01; BR 11–12/01; HB 5–6/01; HBG 10/01; SLJ 5/01; VOYA 10/01)

1169 Frank, E. R. *Friction* (9–12). 2003, Simon & Schuster $16.95 (0-689-85384-X). A new student at Alex's school stirs up trouble by hinting at a sexual relationship between Alex and her teacher. (Rev: BCCB 6/03; BL 7/03*; HB 7–8/03; HBG 10/03; LMC 8–9/03; SLJ 6/03; VOYA 8/03)

1170 Frank, E. R. *Life Is Funny* (7–12). 2000, DK paper $19.99 (0-7894-2634-X). This novel of intersecting stories features the aspirations, problems, and everyday life of 11 teens growing up in Brooklyn. (Rev: BL 3/15/00* ; HB 5–6/00; HBG 9/00; SLJ 5/00; VOYA 6/00)

1171 Fredericks, Mariah. *The True Meaning of Cleavage* (7–10). 2003, Simon & Schuster $15.95 (0-689-85092-1). High school freshman Jess describes her friend Sari's obsession with an older student in this novel of sexuality, betrayal, and self-image. (Rev: BCCB 3/03; BL 3/15/03*; HB 7–8/03; HBG 10/03; SLJ 2/03; VOYA 4/03)

1172 Freymann-Weyr, Garret. *My Heartbeat* (8–12). 2002, Houghton $15.00 (0-618-14181-2). Fourteen-year-old Ellen is in love with James, but James and her older brother Link are also involved. (Rev: BCCB 5/02; BL 6/1–15/02; HB 5–6/02*; HBG 10/02; SLJ 4/02; VOYA 4/02)

1173 Friel, Maeve. *Charlie's Story* (8–10). 1997, Peachtree $14.95 (0-56145-167-3). Charlie, who was abandoned by her mother as a child, now lives with her father in Ireland and, at age 14, is facing a group of bullies at school who accuse her of a theft and cause a terrible field hockey incident. (Rev: BL 1/1–15/98; VOYA 2/98)

1174 Froese, Deborah. *Out of the Fire* (8–11). 2002, Sumach paper $7.95 (1-894549-09-0). Sixteen-year-old Dayle is badly burned at a riotous bonfire party and spends the painful months that follow reassessing her feelings about friends and family. (Rev: BL 7/02; SLJ 8/02)

1175 Fromm, Pete. *How All This Started* (10–12). 2000, Picador $23.00 (0-312-20933-9). Set in rural Texas, this novel focuses on the bond between a boy and his manic depressive sister and their love of baseball. (Rev: BL 9/15/00* ; VOYA 10/01)

1176 Frost, Helen. *Keesha's House* (6–10). 2003, Farrar $16.00 (0-374-34064-1). Keesha reaches out to other teens in trouble as they describe their problems in brief, poetic vignettes. (Rev: BL 3/1/03; HBG 10/03; SLJ 3/03*; VOYA 4/03)

1177 Fulton, John. *Retribution* (10–12). 2001, St. Martin's $23.00 (0-312-27680-X). These realistic short stories portray teenagers coping with situations and problems that required adult help. (Rev: BL 5/15/01)

1178 Gabriele, Lisa. *Tempting Faith DiNapoli* (11–12). 2002, Simon & Schuster $24.00 (0-7432-2522-8). Faith DiNapoli, a teen brought up to be a good Catholic, struggles with temptation and generally loses in this appealing novel of a dysfunctional Canadian family; for mature teens. (Rev: BL 6/1–15/02)

1179 Gallo, Donald, ed. *Destination Unexpected* (7–12). 2003, Candlewick $16.99 (0-7636-1764-4). This is a collection of 10 excellent short stories about teens who are undergoing changes in their lives. (Rev: BL 4/1/03*; HBG 10/03; SLJ 5/03; VOYA 6/03)

1180 Gallo, Donald, ed. *No Easy Answers: Short Stories About Teenagers Making Tough Choices* (6–12). 1997, Delacorte $16.95 (0-385-32290-9). A collection of short stories by some of today's best writers for young adults, including Ron Koertze and Gloria Miklowitz, about teenagers who face moral and ethical dilemmas. (Rev: BL 11/15/97; BR 5–6/98; SLJ 12/97; VOYA 10/97)

1181 Gallo, Donald, ed. *On the Fringe* (7–10). 2001, Dial $17.99 (0-8037-2656-2). Stories about outsiders — geeks, nerds, loners, and other "misfits" — are the focus of this anthology of fiction by well-known YA authors. (Rev: BCCB 6/01; BL 3/15/01; HBG 10/01; SLJ 5/01; VOYA 4/01)

1182 Gallo, Donald, ed. *Sixteen: Short Stories by Outstanding Writers for Young Adults* (9–12). 1984, Dell paper $5.50 (0-440-97757-6). This anthology of original short stories covers such subjects as friendship, love, and families.

1183 Garden, Nancy. *Good Moon Rising* (9–12). 1996, Farrar $16.00 (0-374-32746-7). While coaching a new junior in the school play, Jan, a senior, finds that she is falling in love, and soon gay baiting in the school begins. (Rev: BL 10/1/96; BR 3–4/97; SLJ 10/96; VOYA 12/96)

1184 Garden, Nancy. *The Year They Burned the Books* (7–12). 1999, Farrar $17.00 (0-374-38667-6). High school senior Jamie Crawford's problems as editor of the school newspaper under attack by a right-wing group are compounded when she realizes that she is a lesbian and falling in love with Tessa, a new girl in school. (Rev: BL 8/99; HBG 4/00; SLJ 9/99; VOYA 12/99)

1185 Garland, Sherry. *Letters from the Mountain* (6–10). 1996, Harcourt $12.00 (0-15-200661-3); paper $6.00 (0-15-200659-1). Tyler is unhappy spending the summer with elderly relatives and, through a series of letters to his mother and friends, he vents his anger and also tells of his gradual adjustment. (Rev: BL 10/1/96; BR 3–4/97; SLJ 11/96; VOYA 4/97)

1186 Gayle, Mike. *My Legendary Girlfriend* (10–12). 2001, Broadway $21.95 (0-7679-0973-9); paper $12.95 (0-7679-0655-1). Everything Will has hoped and dreamed for has gone sour, and then he meets Kate, the previous renter of his apartment. (Rev: BL 6/1–15/02; SLJ 1/03)

1187 Gearino, G. D. *Blue Hole* (10–12). 1999, Simon & Schuster $22.00 (0-684-83727-7). A compelling blend of mystery and coming of age, this is the story of 17-year-old high school drop-out Charley Selkirk who finds himself caught up in a search for a missing boy. (Rev: VOYA 2/00)

1188 Gelb, Alan. *Real Life: My Best Friend Died* (7–12). 1995, Pocket paper $3.50 (0-671-87273-7). A high school senior, living a happy, normal life, finds his world exploding when he feels responsible for his friend's death. (Rev: BL 4/1/95; SLJ 6/95; VOYA 5/95)

1189 Gifaldi, David. *Rearranging and Other Stories* (6–10). 1998, Simon & Schuster $16.00 (0-689-81750-9). In these nine short stories, young teens face problems related to adolescence and reaching maturity. (Rev: BL 4/15/98; BR 1–2/99; HBG 9/98; SLJ 6/98; VOYA 8/98)

1190 Gilbert, Barbara Snow. *Broken Chords* (8–12). 1998, Front Street $15.95 (1-886910-23-5). As she prepares for the piano competition that could lead to a place at Juilliard, Clara has doubts about the lifetime of sacrifice that a career in music would require. (Rev: BL 12/15/98; HB 11–12/98; HBG 3/99; SLJ 12/98; VOYA 2/99)

1191 Giles, Gail. *Shattering Glass* (8–10). 2002, Millbrook LB $22.90 (0-7613-2601-4). A suspenseful story of young people manipulating power and popularity that ends in stunning violence. (Rev: BCCB 5/02; BL 3/1/02; HBG 10/02; SLJ 4/02; VOYA 6/02)

1192 Godden, Rumer. *An Episode of Sparrows* (7–10). 1993, Pan paper $16.95 (0-330-32779-8). In postwar London two waifs try to grow a secret garden. (Rev: SLJ 6/89)

1193 Grant, Cynthia D. *The Cannibals: Starring Tiffany Spratt* (7–10). 2002, Millbrook LB $22.90 (0-7613-2759-2). Tiffany's senior year is definitely not what she had hoped for in this satirical tale of a pretty student with grand aspirations. (Rev: BL 10/1/02; HBG 3/03; SLJ 9/02; VOYA 12/02)

1194 Grattan-Dominguez, Alejandro. *Breaking Even* (9–12). 1997, Arte Publico paper $11.95 (1-55885-213-1). This coming-of-age story set in the 1950s tells how 18-year-old Valentin Cooper, a Mexican American, leaves his family and pregnant girlfriend in their small West Texas town on a quest to find his father. (Rev: SLJ 4/98)

1195 Gray, Keith. *Creepers* (7–10). 1997, Putnam $15.95 (0-399-23186-2). Creeping is the sport of running the length of a neighborhood through backyards, and two teenagers engage in a particularly difficult creep in this suspenseful British novel. (Rev: BL 2/1/98; HBG 3/98)

1196 Greene, Constance C. *Monday I Love You* (7–10). 1988, HarperCollins $11.95 (0-06-022183-6). An overdeveloped bust is just one of the problems 15-year-old Grace faces. (Rev: BL 7/88; VOYA 8/88)

1197 Grieve, James. *They're Only Human* (10–12). 2003, Allen & Unwin paper $7.95 (1-86508-438-7). Susie becomes sexually involved with her teacher, Mr. Laramour, and is caught up in his violent acts defending animal rights. (Rev: BL 5/1/03; VOYA 6/03)

1198 Grima, Tony, ed. *Not the Only One: Lesbian and Gay Fiction for Teens* (10–12). 1995, Alyson paper $7.95 (1-55583-275-X). This collection of lesbian/gay fiction deals with young adult characters and includes works by Leslea Newman, Laurel Winter, Emily Ormand, and Raymond Luczak. (Rev: BL 7/95; VOYA 4/96)

1199 Grimes, Martha. *Hotel Paradise* (10–12). 1996, Knopf $24.00 (0-679-44187-5). Set in a small town, this is the story of a lonely and disaffected 12-year-old girl who becomes obsessed first with the death of another ignored young girl in the past and then with a murder that has occurred in the present. (Rev: SLJ 10/96)

1200 Grimes, Nikki. *Bronx Masquerade* (7–12). 2002, Dial $16.99 (0-8037-2569-8). Eighteen high school English students enjoy the weekly open-mike opportunity to express themselves in poetry and prose, revealing much about their lives and their maturing selves. (Rev: BCCB 3/02; BL 2/15/02; HB 3–4/02; HBG 10/02; SLJ 1/02; VOYA 2/02)

1201 Grisham, John. *A Painted House* (10–12). 2001, Doubleday $27.95 (0-385-50120-X). More a family story than a mystery, this Grisham novel tells about the problems of a 7-year-old boy growing up in rural Arkansas who is fearful of many things, including admitting that he has witnessed two vicious killings. (Rev: BL 2/1/01)

1202 Haas, Jessie. *Skipping School* (7–10). 1992, Greenwillow $14.00 (0-688-10179-8). A realistic, ultimately upbeat portrait of a boy's reluctant coming-of-age and of a family's eventual acceptance of death. (Rev: BL 11/15/92; SLJ 11/92)

1203 Haddix, Margaret P. *Just Ella* (7–12). 1999, Simon & Schuster $17.00 (0-689-82186-7). The story of Cinderella after the ball, when she finds out that castle life with Prince Charming isn't all it's cut out to be, meets a social activist tutor, and rethinks her priorities in life. (Rev: BCCB 11/99; BL 9/1/99; HBG 4/00; SLJ 9/99; VOYA 12/99)

1204 Hall, Lynn. *Where Have All the Tigers Gone?* (7–12). 1989, Macmillan LB $13.95 (0-684-19003-6). A 50-year-old woman at her class reunion recalls her school years. (Rev: BL 4/15/89; BR 9–10/89; SLJ 5/89; VOYA 8/89)

1205 Halpern, Sue. *The Book of Hard Things* (11–12). 2003, Farrar $22.00 (0-374-11559-1). In this gripping debut novel, the unlikely alliance of 18-year-old Cuzzie, down on his luck in the New England mill town of his birth, and older sophisticate Tracy Edwards, newly arrived in town, moves inexorably toward a tragic confrontation; for mature teens. (Rev: BL 10/1/03)

1206 Hartinger, Brent. *Geography Club* (7–12). 2003, HarperTempest LB $16.89 (0-06-001222-6). A group of gay teens form a secret support group in this frank novel full of humor and romance. (Rev: BCCB 2/03; BL 4/1/03; HB 3–4/03; HBG 10/03; SLJ 2/03; VOYA 4/03)

1207 Hautman, Pete. *Stone Cold* (7–12). 1998, Simon & Schuster paper $16.00 (0-689-81759-2). In this entertaining first-person narrative, Fenn becomes adept at gambling and soon finds that he is a gambling addict. (Rev: BL 9/15/98; BR 5–6/99; HB 11–12/98; HBG 3/99; SLJ 9/98; VOYA 2/99)

1208 Hawes, Louise. *Waiting for Christopher* (7–10). 2002, Candlewick $15.99 (0-7636-1371-1). Two very different teenage girls form an unlikely friendship and work together to care for a small boy who was being abused by his mother. (Rev: BCCB 9/02; BL 7/02; HB 9–10/02; HBG 10/02; SLJ 6/02; VOYA 4/02)

1209 Hawks, Robert. *The Twenty-Six Minutes* (6–10). 1988, Square One paper $4.95 (0-938961-03-9). Two teenage misfits join an anti-nuclear protest group. (Rev: SLJ 11/88; VOYA 4/89)

1210 Hazelgrove, William Elliot. *Ripples* (9–12). 1992, Pantonne Pr. paper $6.95 (0-9630052-9-4). Brenton, age 18, feels betrayed when his best friend steals his summer love. (Rev: BL 3/15/92)

1211 Head, Ann. *Mr. and Mrs. Bo Jo Jones* (7–12). 1973, Signet paper $4.99 (0-451-16319-2). The perennial favorite of two teenagers madly in love but unprepared for the responsibilities of parenthood.

1212 Henson, Heather. *Making the Run* (9–12). 2002, HarperCollins LB $15.89 (0-06-029797-2). Unhappy with the restrictions of her small town, Lu turns to alcohol, drugs, and sex but is forced to confront her future when her best friend dies in a car crash. (Rev: BCCB 9/02; BL 4/15/02; HBG 10/02; SLJ 5/02; VOYA 8/02)

1213 Herrick, Steven. *Love, Ghosts, and Facial Hair* (9–12). 2004, Simon & Schuster paper $6.99 (0-689-86710-7). At age 16, Jack is an aspiring poet who falls in love with another soulful teenager, Annabel. Also use the sequel *A Place Like This* (2004). (Rev: BL 3/15/04*; SLJ 3/04; VOYA 6/04)

1214 Hesse, Hermann. *Steppenwolf* (10–12). 1990, Holt paper $13.00 (0-8050-1247-8). In this novel with fantastic overtones, a young man searches for self-discovery.

1215 Heynen, Jim. *Being Youngest* (7–12). 1997, Holt $15.95 (0-8050-5486-3). Two Iowa farm kids, Henry and Gretchen, become friends when they realize that being the youngest in their respective families brings a certain number of problems. (Rev: BL 10/15/97; BR 5–6/98; HBG 3/98; SLJ 11/97; VOYA 4/98)

1216 Hill, Ernest. *A Life for a Life* (10–12). 1998, Simon & Schuster $23.00 (0-684-82278-4). Young D-Ray flees after he kills a young clerk while robbing a convenience store to get money to rescue his brother from drug dealers, becomes involved in a life of crime, and eventually ends up in juvenile prison, where he must learn to forgive himself. (Rev: BL 6/1–15/98; SLJ 4/99)

1217 Hobbs, Valerie. *Get It While It's Hot; or Not* (9–12). 1996, Orchard LB $17.99 (0-531-08890-1). The pregnancy of her best friend forces Megan to rethink her relationships, particularly with boyfriend Joe, in a novel that also explores themes involving friendship, freedom of the press, and mother–daughter relations. (Rev: BL 10/15/96; SLJ 10/96; VOYA 12/96)

1218 Hobbs, Will. *Changes in Latitudes* (9–12). 1988, Macmillan $16.00 (0-689-31385-3). Teenager Travis supports his young brother's crusade to help endangered sea turtles. (Rev: BL 5/15/88; BR 9–10/88; SLJ 3/88; VOYA 6/88)

1219 Hoffman, Alice. *The River King* (10–12). 2000, Putnam $23.95 (0-399-14599-0). In this novel for mature readers, a misfit attending a posh prep school finds herself falling in love with a boy who is self-possessed and defiant of the system. (Rev: BL 4/15/00* ; SLJ 11/00)

1220 Holeman, Linda. *Mercy's Birds* (6–10). 1998, Tundra paper $5.95 (0-88776-463-0). Fifteen-year-old Mercy lives a life of loneliness and hurt as she cares for a depressed mother and an alcoholic aunt while working after school in a flower shop. (Rev: BL 12/15/98; SLJ 3/99; VOYA 12/98)

1221 Holland, Isabelle. *The Man Without a Face* (7–10). 1972, HarperCollins paper $5.99 (0-06-447028-8). Charles's close relations with his reclusive tutor lead to a physical experience.

1222 Hopkins, Cathy. *Mates, Dates, and Cosmic Kisses* (6–10). 2003, Simon & Schuster paper $5.99 (0-689-85545-1). Teen anxieties about dating, friendship, and making decisions fill this funny novel about Izzy's attraction to a boy — and how her friends help her cope. (Rev: BL 2/1/03; SLJ 4/03)

1223 Hopkins, Cathy. *Mates, Dates, and Inflatable Bras* (6–10). 2003, Simon & Schuster paper $4.99 (0-689-85544-3). Lucy, 14, is concerned about her lack of development but, with the help of her friends, she is able to accept herself and even attract a cute boy. Other titles in this series include *Mates, Dates, and Designer Divas* (2003). (Rev: BL 2/1/03; SLJ 4/03)

1224 Hornburg, Michael. *Downers Grove* (10–12). 1999, Morrow $23.00 (0-688-16528-1). Despite her dysfunctional family life, Chrissie Swanson is about to graduate from Downers Grove High School unless, of course, she falls victim to a longstanding curse that decrees one senior will die violently before getting a diploma. (Rev: BL 6/1–15/99; VOYA 2/00)

1225 Howe, Norma. *Blue Avenger and the Theory of Everything* (8–10). Series: Blue Avenger. 2002, Cricket $17.95 (0-8126-2654-0). David Schumacher (aka Blue Avenger) faces a dilemma as he seeks to save his girlfriend from eviction. (Rev: BCCB 7–8/02; BL 5/15/02; HBG 3/03; SLJ 7/02; VOYA 12/02)

1226 Howe, Norma. *God, the Universe, and Hot Fudge Sundaes* (7–10). 1986, Avon paper $2.50 (0-380-70074-3). A 16-year-old girl would like to share her mother's born-again faith but can't.

1227 Hrdlitschka, Shelley. *Dancing Naked* (7–12). 2001, Orca $6.95 (1-55143-210-2). Finding herself pregnant after her first sexual encounter, 16-year-old Kia walks away from an abortion at the last minute and must draw on her inner strength to deal with the consequences of that decision. (Rev: BL 3/15/02; SLJ 3/02*)

1228 Hrdlitschka, Shelley. *Disconnected* (7–12). 1999, Orca paper $6.95 (1-55143-105-X). The lives of Tanner, a hockey-playing teen who has recurring dreams of trying to escape an underwater attacker, and Alex, a boy escaping his father's abuse, connect in a most unusual way. (Rev: BL 4/1/99; SLJ 6/99; VOYA 6/99)

1229 Hurley, Valerie. *St. Ursula's Girls Against the Atomic Bomb* (11–12). 2003, MacAdam $19.00 (1-931561-55-9). In this offbeat novel, 18-year-old Raine, who is more interested in changing the world than in her studies, develops a close relationship with her guidance counselor; for mature teens. (Rev: BL 11/15/03; VOYA 6/04)

1230 Hurwin, Davida Wills. *The Farther You Run* (9–12). 2003, Viking $16.99 (0-670-03627-7). In this sequel to *A Time for Dancing* (1995), Samantha is still mourning Juliana's death from cancer, which affects her relationships with friends and family. (Rev: BL 8/03; SLJ 8/03; VOYA 8/03)

1231 Huser, Glen. *Stitches* (7–10). 2003, Groundwood $18.95 (0-88899-553-9); paper $9.95 (0-88899-578-4). Disfigured Chantelle and much-bullied Travis support each other through the difficult years of junior high school. (Rev: BCCB 2/04; HB 11–12/03*; HBG 4/04; SLJ 12/03; VOYA 4/04)

1232 Huser, Glen. *Touch of the Clown* (7–10). 1999, Groundwood $15.95 (0-88899-343-9). Neglected sisters Barbara and Livvy get a new lease on life when they meet the eccentric Cosmo, who runs a teen clown workshop. (Rev: SLJ 11/99; VOYA 10/99)

1233 Inclan, Jessica Barksdale. *Her Daughter's Eyes* (10–12). 2001, NAL paper $12.95 (0-451-20282-1). Seventeen-year-old Kate, with the help of her younger sister, struggles to keep her pregnancy a secret from the baby's father and her own father; for mature teens. (Rev: BL 4/01; VOYA 10/01)

1234 *Into the Widening World: International Coming-of-Age Stories* (9–12). 1995, Persea paper $12.95 (0-89255-204-2). The innocence and daring of youth are elegantly captured in this anthology of brilliant voices from 22 countries. (Rev: BL 1/1/95; SLJ 8/95; VOYA 5/95)

1235 Jackson, Jeremy. *In Summer* (10–12). 2004, St. Martin's $22.95 (0-312-32642-4). Leo, a new high school graduate, embarks on a journey of self-discovery after he learns that his mother has ovarian cancer. (Rev: BL 4/15/04)

1236 Jackson, Jeremy. *Life at These Speeds* (10–12). 2002, St. Martin's $24.95 (0-312-28808-5). In the wake of an accident that took the lives of his teammates and girlfriend, Kevin finds escape from his pain in running and in the process becomes a high school track star. (Rev: BL 7/02; VOYA 12/02)

1237 Jackson, Sheneska. *Caught Up in the Rapture* (10–12). 1996, Simon & Schuster $21.00 (0-634-81487-0). Street life in South Central Los Angeles is the subject of this novel about Jazmine Deems, who wants to be a singer, and her gangsta-rapper boyfriend known as the X-Man. (Rev: SLJ 8/96)

1238 Jenkins, A. M. *Breaking Boxes* (8–12). 1997, Delacorte $15.95 (0-385-32513-4). Charlie and Brandon form a friendship at high school, but when word gets out that Charlie's brother is gay, Brandon rejects both his friend and his family. (Rev: BL 9/1/97; BR 1–2/98; HBG 3/98; SLJ 10/97; VOYA 12/97)

1239 Jimenez, Francisco. *Breaking Through* (6–12). 2001, Houghton $15.00 (0-618-01173-0). In this sequel to *The Circuit: Stories from the Life of a Migrant Child* (2001), 14-year-old Francisco recounts his efforts to improve his lot in life and

describes his school and romantic experiences. (Rev: BCCB 1/02; BL 9/1/01; HB 11–12/01; HBG 3/02; SLJ 9/01; VOYA 12/01)

1240 Johnson, Angela. *The First Part Last* (6–12). 2003, Simon & Schuster $15.95 (0-689-84922-2). Sixteen-year-old single-parent Bobby is overwhelmed and exhausted, but he loves his baby daughter. (Rev: BL 9/1/03*; HB 7–8/03; HBG 10/03; SLJ 6/03*; VOYA 6/03)

1241 Johnson, Kathleen Jeffrie. *Parallel Universe of Liars* (10–12). 2002, Roaring Brook $15.95 (0-7316-1746-5). Lonely, overweight, and attuned to all the sex going on around her, 15-year-old Robin allows encounters with an adult neighbor and is drawn to a biracial boy called Tri. (Rev: BCCB 12/02; BL 9/15/02; HBG 3/03; LMC 1/03; SLJ 12/02; VOYA 12/02)

1242 Johnson, Lissa Halls. *Fast Forward to Normal* (6–10). Series: Brio Girls. 2001, Bethany paper $5.99 (1-56179-952-1). Becca, one of a quartet of high school juniors who call themselves the Brio Girls, isn't happy with her parents' idea of adopting the Guatemalan boy they have been fostering. Also in this series is *Stuck in the Sky* (2001). (Rev: BL 10/15/01)

1243 Johnston, Norma. *The Time of the Cranes* (7–10). 1990, Macmillan LB $14.95 (0-02-747713-4). A girl filled with self-doubt about her abilities receives an unexpected inheritance. (Rev: BL 4/1/90; SLJ 5/90; VOYA 6/88)

1244 Jones, Patrick. *Things Change* (8–11). 2004, Walker $16.95 (0-8027-8901-3). Johanna, age 16, has her first boyfriend, Paul, a disturbed boy, in this novel about dating, violence, and the problems of falling in love. (Rev: BL 5/1/04; SLJ 5/04; VOYA 6/04)

1245 Juby, Susan. *Alice, I Think* (8–12). 2003, HarperTempest LB $16.89 (0-06-051544-9). Alice, a quirky 15-year-old who has been homeschooled, enters public school and narrates in her diary all her new experiences. (Rev: BCCB 9/03; BL 8/03; HB 7–8/03; HBG 10/03; SLJ 7/03; VOYA 8/03)

1246 Kantner, Seth. *Ordinary Wolves* (10–12). 2004, Milkweed $22.00 (1-57131-044-4). This is a coming-of-age novel about Cutuk's rocky road to adulthood growing up in an Alaskan wilderness with a back-to-the-land father and siblings. (Rev: BL 5/1/04*)

1247 Kaplow, Robert. *Alessandra in Between* (8–12). 1992, HarperCollins LB $13.89 (0-06-023298-6). A young heroine has a lot on her mind, including her grandfather's deteriorating health, her friendships, and an unrequited love. (Rev: BL 9/15/92; SLJ 9/92)

1248 Kaplow, Robert. *Me and Orson Welles* (10–12). 2003, MacAdam $18.50 (1-931561-49-4). Set in the late 1930s, this is the entertaining story of a 17-

year-old who manages to land a role in an Orson Welles play and learns a lot about life during the experience. (Rev: BL 9/1/03; SLJ 12/03; VOYA 4/04)

1249 Keillor, Garrison. *Lake Wobegon Summer 1956* (9–12). 2001, Viking $24.95 (0-670-03003-1). This coming-of-age story set in Lake Wobegon tells about introspective 14-year-old Gary and his problems growing up. (Rev: BL 7/01)

1250 Kellogg, Marjorie. *Tell Me That You Love Me, Junie Moon*. 2nd ed. (10–12). 1993, Farrar paper $3.95 (0-374-47510-5). After they have been released from the hospital, three misfits decide to live together.

1251 Kennedy, Pagan. *The Exes* (10–12). 1998, Simon & Schuster $23.00 (0-684-83481-2). Four bright, creative young people — three men and one woman — form a band called the Exes because they were all romantically involved with each other at one time and set out in a broken-down van in search of success. (Rev: BL 7/98; SLJ 3/99)

1252 Kerr, M. E. *Gentlehands* (7–12). 1990, HarperCollins paper $5.99 (0-06-447067-9). Buddy Boyle wonders if the grandfather he has recently grown to love is really a Nazi war criminal in this novel set on the eastern tip of Long Island.

1253 Kerr, M. E. *"Hello," I Lied* (9–12). 1997, HarperCollins LB $15.89 (0-06-027530-8). Lang is gay and has a loving relationship with Alex, but he is torn about coming out to his friends and about feelings he has for a young woman. (Rev: BL 4/15/97; BR 11–12/97; SLJ 6/97; VOYA 6/97)

1254 Kerr, M. E. *I Stay Near You* (7–10). 1997, Harcourt paper $6.00 (0-15-201420-9). These three stories of love and self-acceptance span three generations in a small town. (Rev: BL 4/15/85; BR 1–2/86; SLJ 4/85; VOYA 6/85)

1255 Kerr, M. E. *Linger* (7–12). 1995, HarperCollins paper $4.95 (0-06-447102-0). In a story filled with wit and sadness, Kerr tells of kids entangled in love, war, and work. (Rev: BL 6/1–15/93; SLJ 7/93; VOYA 8/93)

1256 Kerr, M. E. *Night Kites* (9–12). 1987, HarperTrophy paper $5.99 (0-06-447035-0). Erick's life seems to be falling apart when he discovers that his older brother has AIDS and he unwillingly has an affair with his best friend's girlfriend. (Rev: BL 4/1/86; BR 1-2/87; SLJ 5/86; VOYA 6/86)

1257 Kerr, M. E. *The Son of Someone Famous* (7–10). 1991, HarperCollins paper $3.95 (0-06-447069-5). In chapters alternately written by each, two teenagers in rural Vermont write about their friendship and their problems.

1258 Kerr, M. E. *What I Really Think of You* (7–10). 1982, HarperCollins $13.00 (0-06-023188-2); paper $3.50 (0-06-447062-8). The meeting of two teen-agers who represent two kinds of religion — the evangelical mission and the TV pulpit. (Rev: BL 9/1/95)

1259 Ketchum, Liza. *Blue Coyote* (7–12). 1997, Simon & Schuster $16.00 (0-689-80790-2). High school junior Alex Beekman denies that he is gay, but, in time, he realizes the truth about himself. (Rev: BL 6/1–15/97; BR 9–10/97; SLJ 5/97; VOYA 8/97)

1260 Kidd, Chip. *The Cheese Monkeys: A Novel in Two Semesters* (10–12). 2001, Scribner $24.00 (0-7432-1492-7). This is an excellent novel about the first year of college during which the hero discovers the world of graphic design. (Rev: BL 9/1/01*)

1261 Kimmel, Haven. *Something Rising (Light and Swift)* (10–12). 2004, Free Pr. $24.00 (0-7432-4775-2). In this gritty novel, young Cassie finds redemption in playing — and winning at — pool, the game her absent father loved more than his family. (Rev: BL 10/15/03)

1262 Kincaid, Jamaica. *Annie John* (9–12). 1985, NAL paper $6.95 (0-452-26016-7). A beautifully detailed novel about a girl's childhood and adolescence on the Caribbean island of Antigua. (Rev: BL 4/1/85; SLJ 9/85)

1263 Kindl, Patrice. *The Woman in the Wall* (7–10). 1997, Houghton $16.00 (0-395-83014-1). A dreamlike story about a girl who emerges into the world after living alone for most of her 14 years in secret rooms in the family house. (Rev: BL 3/15/97; BR 9–10/97; SLJ 4/97; VOYA 8/97)

1264 Kingsolver, Barbara. *The Bean Trees*. 10th Anniversary Ed. (10–12). 1997, HarperFlamingo $18.00 (0-06-017579-6); paper $6.99 (0-06-109731-4). A poor young woman, heading west from her home, adopts a 2-year-old Cherokee girl and makes friends with an unusual widow.

1265 Kirshenbaum, Binnie. *An Almost Perfect Moment* (11–12). 2004, Ecco $23.95 (0-06-052086-8). In this humorous and edgy novel, teenage Valentine, growing up in a Brooklyn Jewish neighborhood in the 1970s, bears an eerie resemblance to the Virgin Mary; for mature teens. (Rev: BL 12/15/03*)

1266 Klass, David. *Home of the Braves* (8–12). 2002, Farrar $18.00 (0-374-39963-8). Joe's plans for his senior year in high school are changed by the arrival of a Brazilian student who threatens Joe's position as soccer star and steals his would-be girlfriend too. (Rev: BCCB 12/02; BL 9/1/02; HB 1–2/03; HBG 3/03; SLJ 9/02)

1267 Klass, Sheila S. *Next Stop: Nowhere* (6–10). 1995, Scholastic paper $14.95 (0-590-46686-0). Exiled to Vermont to live with her eccentric father, Beth must deal with separation from her close friend and from her new romantic interest, Josef, who's moved to Israel. (Rev: BL 1/15/95; SLJ 4/95; VOYA 2/95)

1268 Klein, Norma. *Family Secrets* (10–12). 1987, Fawcett paper $3.99 (0-449-70195-6). Two seniors in high school become lovers and then discover that the mother of one is going to marry the father of the other. (Rev: BL 10/1/85; BR 5–6/86; SLJ 12/85)

1269 Knowles, John. *Peace Breaks Out* (10–12). 1997, Bantam paper $5.99 (0-553-27574-7). During the 1945–46 school year a former student who is suffering from wartime trauma returns to his private prep school as a teacher. A sequel to *A Separate Peace*.

1270 Knowles, John. *A Separate Peace* (10–12). 1987, Macmillan $40.00 (0-02-564850-0); Bantam paper $5.99 (0-553-28041-4). Life during a World War II year in a private boys' school and a student rivalry that ends in tragedy.

1271 Koertge, Ron. *The Arizona Kid* (8–12). 1989, Avon paper $3.99 (0-380-70776-4). Teenage Billy discovers that his uncle Wes is gay and learns about rodeos as well as the nature of love when he meets an outspoken girl named Cara. (Rev: BL 5/1/88; BR 9–10/88; SLJ 6/88; VOYA 10/88)

1272 Koja, Kathe. *Buddha Boy* (6–10). 2003, Farrar $16.00 (0-374-30998-1). Justin is intrigued by "Buddha Boy," a new student whose appearance and beliefs make him the target of bullies. (Rev: BL 2/15/03; HB 5–6/03; HBG 10/03; SLJ 2/03; VOYA 4/03)

1273 Koja, Kathe. *Straydog* (7–10). 2002, Farrar $16.00 (0-374-37278-0). Rachel, a lonely teenager who enjoys writing, is devastated when her favorite dog at the animal shelter is put to sleep, and her anger affects the people closest to her. (Rev: BL 4/15/02; HB 5–6/02; HBG 10/02; SLJ 4/02; VOYA 6/02)

1274 Konigsburg, E. L. *Throwing Shadows* (7–10). 1988, Macmillan paper $4.50 (0-02-044140-1). Five short stories about teenagers learning about themselves and their emotions.

1275 Korman, Gordon. *Jake, Reinvented* (9–12). 2003, Hyperion $15.99 (0-7868-1957-X). The story line of *The Great Gatsby* is relocated to a contemporary high school and features amazing parties given by the cool and mysterious Jake. (Rev: BCCB 11/03; BL 12/1/03; HBG 4/04; SLJ 2/04; VOYA 6/04)

1276 Kowalski, William. *Somewhere South of Here* (10–12). 2001, HarperCollins $25.00 (0-06-019356-5). In this sequel to *Eddie's Bastard* (1999), Billy sets out on a trip that takes him from New York State to Santa Fe to find the mother who abandoned him. (Rev: BL 4/15/01)

1277 Kurland, Morton L. *Our Sacred Honor* (7–12). 1987, Rosen LB $12.95 (0-8239-0692-2). A story from two points of view about a pregnant teenage girl, her boyfriend, and their decision for abortion. (Rev: SLJ 6/87)

1278 Lamott, Anne. *Crooked Little Heart* (10–12). 1997, Pantheon $24.00 (0-679-43521-2). Using the world of tennis as a backdrop, this is the story of two adolescent friends and doubles partners, one of whom has problems adjusting to puberty. (Rev: BL 4/1/97; SLJ 7/97)

1279 Larimer, Tamela. *Buck* (7–10). 1986, Avon paper $2.50 (0-380-75172-0). The friendship between runaway Buck and Rich is threatened when Buck becomes friendly with Rich's girlfriend. (Rev: BL 4/87; SLJ 6/87; VOYA 4/87)

1280 Larson, Rodger. *What I Know Now* (9–12). 1997, Holt $15.95 (0-8050-4869-3). At 14, Dave becomes deeply attached to Gene Tole, the family gardener, because he represents all the virtues and integrity that Dave admires — then, suddenly, Dave discovers that Gene is gay. (Rev: BL 5/1/97; SLJ 5/97; VOYA 6/97)

1281 Leavitt, Caroline. *Girls in Trouble* (11–12). 2004, St. Martin's $24.95 (0-312-27122-0). Sixteen-year-old Sara must give up her infant daughter for adoption, a situation that haunts her for the next 10 years; for mature teens. (Rev: BL 12/15/03)

1282 LeClaire, Anne D. *Leaving Eden* (11–12). 2002, Ballantine $23.95 (0-345-44574-0). Tallie longs for high school to end so that she can follow her late mother's dreams to Hollywood; for mature teens. (Rev: BL 9/1/02; SLJ 2/03)

1283 Lehrman, Robert. *Juggling* (10–12). 1982, HarperCollins $11.50 (0-06-023818-6). An explicit novel about a teenager and his love for soccer and his first sexual encounters. (Rev: BL 3/87)

1284 Lemieux, Anne E. *All the Answers* (7–10). 2000, Avon $15.99 (0-380-97771-0). Unable to face the criticism of family and friends, 8th-grader Jason cheats on a math test to improve his grades but gets caught. (Rev: BL 1/1–15/00; HBG 9/00; SLJ 2/00; VOYA 4/00)

1285 L'Engle, Madeleine. *A House Like a Lotus* (7–12). 1984, Farrar $17.00 (0-374-33385-8); Dell paper $4.99 (0-440-93685-3). Polly O'Keefe, of previous L'Engle novels, is now 17 and encounters both lesbianism and a heterosexual romance in this probing novel.

1286 L'Engle, Madeleine. *A Ring of Endless Light* (7–10). 1980, Dell paper $5.99 (0-440-97232-9). The Austin family are again central characters in this novel in which Vicky must adjust to her grandfather's death while exploring her telepathic powers with dolphins. Newbery Honor Book, 1981.

1287 Leon, Peggy. *Mother Country* (10–12). 2003, Permanent Press $26.00 (1-57962-095-7). After the death of her grandmother, 13-year-old orphan Mala falls under the care of her Serbian American extended family in the small copper mining town of Taylor, Nevada, circa 1950. (Rev: BL 11/15/03)

1288 Leslie, Diane. *Fleur de Leigh in Exile: A Novel* (10–12). 2003, Simon & Schuster $23.00 (0-7432-2608-9). In this entertaining sequel to *Life of Crime* (1999), 15-year-old Fleur de Leigh is sent from her 1950s Hollywood home to a Tucson boarding school where neither the school nor the students meet her expectations. (Rev: BL 2/15/03)

1289 Lester, Jim. *Fallout* (7–10). 1996, Dell paper $3.99 (0-440-22683-X). A fast-paced novel told in a confessional format about the problems faced by Kenny Francis, self-styled "terminal goofball," when he transfers to a fancy prep school. (Rev: BL 1/1–15/96; BR 5–6/96; SLJ 2/96; VOYA 2/96)

1290 Letts, Billie. *The Honk and Holler Opening Soon* (10–12). 1998, Warner $22.00 (0-446-52158-2). A story of love, hope, and humanity revolving around Caney Paxton, a crippled Vietnam veteran, and a cast of memorable characters he attracts at his restaurant in rural Oklahoma. (Rev: BL 5/1/98; SLJ 1/99)

1291 Levy, Marilyn. *Is That Really Me in the Mirror?* (7–10). 1991, Ballantine paper $4.99 (0-449-70343-6). Joanne is envious of her beautiful, popular older sister until an automobile accident and plastic surgery transform Joanne into a very pretty stranger. (Rev: BL 11/1/91)

1292 Lin, Ed. *Waylaid* (11–12). 2002, Kaya paper $12.95 (1-885030-32-0). Brought up in a seedy New Jersey motel, the son of Taiwanese immigrants observes life and plans for sexual experiences; for mature teens. (Rev: BL 8/02*)

1293 Lissner, Caren. *Carrie Pilby* (10–12). 2003, Harlequin paper $12.95 (0-373-25029-0). Nineteen-year-old Carrie's efforts to blend into a social scene — any social scene — will entertain teen readers. (Rev: BL 6/1–15/03)

1294 Littke, Lael. *Loydene in Love* (8–10). 1986, Harcourt $13.95 (0-15-249888-5). A high school junior from a small town gets a different view of life when she visits Los Angeles for the summer. (Rev: BL 2/15/87; SLJ 3/87)

1295 Loughery, John, ed. *First Sightings: Stories of American Youth* (9–12). 1993, Persea $29.95 (0-89255-186-0); paper $11.95 (0-89255-187-9). An anthology of 20 dramatic stories about children and teens by John Updike, Philip Roth, Alice Walker, Joyce Carol Oates, and others. (Rev: BL 4/15/93)

1296 Lowry, Lois. *A Summer to Die* (7–10). Illus. 1977, Houghton $16.00 (0-395-25338-1). Meg is confused and dismayed by her older sister's death. (Rev: BL 7/88)

1297 Lubar, David. *Dunk* (8–12). 2002, Clarion $15.00 (0-618-19455-X). Over the course of a summer, troubled young Chad learns a lot about himself and his anger. (Rev: BCCB 12/02; BL 9/1/02; HB 11–12/02; HBG 3/03; SLJ 8/02*)

1298 Luna, Louisa. *Brave New Girl* (10–12). 2001, MTV paper $11.95 (0-7434-0786-5). Doreen, a 14-year-old who hides her vulnerability under a facade of toughness, is raped by her sister's 21-year-old boyfriend, a crime that goes unpunished; for mature teens. (Rev: BL 4/15/01; VOYA 2/02)

1299 Lynch, Chris. *Blood Relations* (8–12). 1996, HarperCollins LB $13.89 (0-06-025399-1); paper $4.50 (0-06-447122-5). The beginning of a violent, disturbing trilogy about 15-year-old Mick, his working-class Irish family, his drug-ridden neighborhood, and the Latino classmates to whom he turns for help. Followed by *Dog Eat Dog* (1996) and *Mick* (1996). (Rev: BL 4/1/96; SLJ 3/96; VOYA 8/96)

1300 Lynch, Chris. *Extreme Elvin* (8–10). 1999, HarperCollins LB $15.89 (0-06-028210-X). Elvin of *Slot Machine* is back, and this time he has discovered girls and a whole new set of relationships. (Rev: BL 2/1/99; HBG 9/99; SLJ 2/99; VOYA 10/99)

1301 Lynch, Chris. *Slot Machine* (8–10). 1995, HarperCollins LB $14.89 (0-06-023585-3). Elvin is a 13-year-old boy, overweight, and expected to perform with exuberance everything forced upon him. (Rev: BL 9/1/95*; SLJ 10/95; VOYA 12/95)

1302 Lyon, George. *Sonny's House of Spies* (6–10). 2004, Simon & Schuster $16.95 (0-689-85168-5). Both humorous and heartbreaking, this is the story of a 13-year-old coming of age in Alabama in the 1950s and the family secrets he uncovers. (Rev: BL 5/15/04; SLJ 8/04)

1303 Lyon, George E. *With a Hammer for My Heart* (10–12). 1997, DK $21.95 (0-7894-2460-6). The story of 15-year-old Lawanda, her life and family in Pine Mountain, and the friendship she develops with an older alcoholic veteran and its tragic consequences. (Rev: BL 9/1/97; BR 3–4/98; SLJ 10/97)

1304 McCafferty, Megan. *Sloppy Firsts* (10–12). 2001, Crown paper $10.95 (0-609-80790-0). All the angst of the teen years is beautifully captured in this story of 16-year-old Jess, who struggles to find meaning in her life after her brother dies of a drug overdose and her best friend moves away; for mature teens. (Rev: VOYA 4/02)

1305 McCants, William D. *Much Ado About Prom Night* (9–12). 1995, Harcourt $11.00 (0-15-200083-6); paper $5.00 (0-15-200081-X). Becca's ordeals form the basis for a witty novel joining the angst of high school with sly points about love and sex, politics, and peer pressure. (Rev: BL 7/95; SLJ 6/95)

1306 McColley, Kevin. *Sun Dance* (9–12). 1995, Simon & Schuster $16.00 (0-689-80008-8). Randy, his older brother, Mike, and two friends travel across the country in an old Firebird intent on carrying out a harebrained plan to blow up a nuclear reactor. (Rev: BL 1/1–15/96*; BR 5–6/96; SLJ 11/95; VOYA 12/95)

1307 McCullers, Carson. *The Heart Is a Lonely Hunter* (10–12). 1993, Modern Library $17.95 (0-679-42474-1). A deaf-mute is the central character in this challenging novel about several lonely individuals who seek companionship.

1308 McCullers, Carson. *The Member of the Wedding* (9–12). 1946, Houghton paper $5.99 (0-553-25051-5). A short but penetrating novel about 12-year-old Frankie and her need to find attachments and identity.

1309 McDaniel, Lurlene. *Starry, Starry Night* (6–10). 1998, Bantam $8.95 (0-553-57130-3). Three Christmas season stories about different heroines, each with a problem. One finally adjusts to her mother's pregnancy and then is devastated when the baby is born with severe brain damage; another discovers that a cancer patient has a crush on her; the third has difficulty with her boyfriend and must regain her perspective. (Rev: HBG 3/99; SLJ 10/98; VOYA 12/98)

1310 McDaniel, Lurlene. *Telling Christina Goodbye* (6–10). 2002, Bantam paper $4.99 (0-533-57087-0). Tucker, who had been driving recklessly, is the only person uninjured in the accident that kills Christina. (Rev: BL 3/15/02; SLJ 7/02)

1311 McDermott, Alice. *Child of My Heart* (11–12). 2002, Farrar $22.00 (0-374-12123-0). A happy summer of pet- and babysitting is marred when Theresa, a beautiful 15-year-old who is beginning to attract men, realizes that her cousin Daisy is ill; for mature teens. (Rev: BL 9/15/02; SLJ 2/03)

1312 MacDonald, Caroline. *Speaking to Miranda* (7–10). 1992, HarperCollins LB $13.89 (0-06-021103-2). Set in Australia and New Zealand, Ruby, 18, leaves her boyfriend, travels with her father, and gradually decides to explore the mysteries of her life: Who was her mother? Who is her family? Who is she? (Rev: BL 12/15/92*; SLJ 10/92)

1313 McDonald, Joyce. *Devil on My Heels* (7–10). 2004, Delacorte LB $17.99 (0-385-90133-X). When 15-year-old Dove discovers that her father's migrant pickers are working under terrible conditions on the Florida farm, she is forced to choose between family loyalties and her sense of justice. (Rev: BL 5/15/04; SLJ 7/04)

1314 McDonald, Joyce. *Shadow People* (9–12). 2000, Delacorte $15.95 (0-385-32662-9); Laurel Leaf paper $5.50 (0-440-22807-7). A tense story of violence created by four angry and frustrated teens. (Rev: BL 11/15/00; BR 5–6/01; HBG 3/01; SLJ 11/00)

1315 McDonald, Joyce. *Swallowing Stones* (7–10). 1997, Bantam paper $4.99 (0-440-22672-4). When Michael accidentally kills a man with his rifle, he

and his friend decide to hide the gun and feign ignorance. (Rev: BL 10/15/97; BR 11–12/97; SLJ 9/97; VOYA 12/97)

1316 McDonell, Nick. *Twelve* (11–12). 2002, Grove $23.00 (0-8021-1717-1). Drugs, sex, and violence feature prominently in this tale about wealthy prep-school kids written by a 17-year-old; for mature teens. (Rev: BL 6/1–15/02; VOYA 12/02)

1317 McFarland, Dennis. *Singing Boy* (10–12). 2001, Holt $25.00 (0-8050-6608-X). This is a moving novel about a mother and son who must adjust to the senseless murder of the father and how their grief and despair gradually turn to acceptance. (Rev: BL 2/1/01)

1318 McGowan, Heather. *Schooling* (10–12). 2001, Doubleday $24.95 (0-385-50138-2). A challenging first novel about a young American girl who, after the death of her mother, attends an English boarding school where she becomes infatuated with her chemistry teacher. (Rev: BL 5/15/01*)

1319 McInerney, Jay. *The Last of the Savages* (10–12). 1996, Knopf $24.00 (0-679-42845-3). The story of the lasting friendship between Patrick, who becomes a successful New York lawyer, and Will, who is involved in rock and soul music and a lifestyle that includes drink and drugs. (Rev: SLJ 9/96)

1320 McKenna, Colleen O'Shaughnessy. *The Brightest Light* (6–10). 1992, Scholastic paper $13.95 (0-590-45347-5). A young girl discovers the secret behind her hometown's strange behavior during one long, hot summer. (Rev: BL 9/15/92; SLJ 12/92)

1321 Mackler, Carolyn. *The Earth, My Butt, and Other Big Round Things* (7–10). 2003, Candlewick $15.99 (0-7636-1958-2). Virginia, a privileged New York 15-year-old, struggles with her weight, her lack of self confidence, her family, the absence of her best friend, and her aspiring boyfriend. (Rev: BL 9/1/03; HB 9–10/03; HBG 4/04; SLJ 9/03)

1322 McNaughton, Janet. *To Dance at the Palais Royale* (7–10). 1999, Stoddart paper $5.95 (0-7736-7473-X). The story of the loneliness and growing maturity of Aggie Maxwell who leaves her home in Scotland at age 17 to become a domestic servant with her sister in Toronto. (Rev: SLJ 5/99; VOYA 10/99)

1323 McNeal, Laura, and Tom McNeal. *Crooked* (7–12). 1999, Knopf LB $18.99 (0-679-99300-2). Ninth-graders Clara and Amos find they are falling in love and face the menace of the bullying Tripp brothers. (Rev: BL 10/15/99; HB 11–12/99; HBG 4/00; SLJ 11/99; VOYA 4/00)

1324 McNeal, Laura, and Tom McNeal. *Zipped* (6–12). 2003, Knopf $15.95 (0-375-81491-4). The problems facing Mick, 15, include a lost history paper, a budding romance, a new job, and the discovery that his attractive stepmother is having an affair. (Rev: BCCB 3/03; HBG 10/03; SLJ 2/03; VOYA 4/03)

1325 McVeity, Jen. *On Different Shores* (6–10). 1998, Orchard LB $17.99 (0-531-33115-6). The problems of a teenage Australian girl surface when the guerrilla environmental group to which she belongs is caught and a crisis develops over a beached whale. (Rev: BCCB 11/98; BL 11/15/98; BR 5–6/99; HBG 3/99; SLJ 3/99; VOYA 10/98)

1326 Maguire, Gregory. *Oasis* (7–10). 1996, Clarion $14.95 (0-395-67019-5). This story of grief and guilt involves 13-year-old Hand, his adjustment to his father's sudden death, and his mother's efforts to save the motel her husband had managed. (Rev: BL 9/15/96; BR 3–4/97; SLJ 11/96; VOYA 2/97)

1327 Mahon, K. L. *Just One Tear* (5–10). 1994, Lothrop $14.00 (0-688-13519-6). The diary of a 14-year-old girl tells the story of a 13-year-old boy whose father is shot in front of him and tells how the boy deals with his grief. (Rev: BL 5/15/94; SLJ 5/94; VOYA 10/94)

1328 Mahy, Margaret. *The Catalogue of the Universe* (8–12). 1987, Scholastic paper $2.75 (0-590-42318-5). Through their friendship, Angela, who longs to meet her absent father, and Tycho, who believes he is physically ugly, find tenderness and compassion. (Rev: BL 3/15/86; SLJ 4/86; VOYA 12/86)

1329 Mahy, Margaret. *The Other Side of Silence* (7–10). 1995, Viking $14.99 (0-670-86455-2). A gothic story with a menacing tone about a young woman's quest for individuality and personal power. (Rev: BL 10/1/95*; SLJ 10/95; VOYA 4/96)

1330 Major, Marcus. *A Family Affair* (11–12). 2004, Dutton $24.95 (0-525-94768-X). In this sequel to *Good Peoples* (2000), the close-knit African American family deals with a willful teenager, Jasmine, plus the shock of a parent caught cheating; for mature readers. (Rev: BL 11/1/03)

1331 Makris, Kathryn. *A Different Way* (7–10). 1989, Avon paper $2.95 (0-380-75728-1). A newcomer in a Texas high school wonders if acceptance by the in-crowd is worth the effort. (Rev: BL 10/15/89)

1332 Malloy, Brian. *The Year of Ice* (11–12). 2002, St. Martin's $22.95 (0-312-28948-0). Kevin's last year in high school proves difficult as he deals with his homosexuality, his mother's death, and his resentments toward his father; for mature teens. (Rev: BL 6/1–15/02*)

1333 Many, Paul. *My Life, Take Two* (9–12). 2000, Walker $16.95 (0-8027-8708-8). The summer before his senior year in high school, Neal discovers a hidden talent for filmmaking that dramatically changes his life. (Rev: BL 5/1/00; HB 9–10/00; HBG 9/00; SLJ 7/00)

1334 Many, Paul. *Walk Away Home* (8–10). 2002, Walker $16.95 (0-8027-8828-9). Nick leaves home in search of more welcoming surroundings, and finds himself on an interesting journey of growth involving romance and alternative lifestyles. (Rev: HB 1–2/03; HBG 3/03; SLJ 9/02; VOYA 12/02)

1335 Marineau, Michele. *Lean Mean Machines* (7–12). 2001, Red Deer paper $7.95 (0-88995-230-2). Canadian teen Jeremy Martucci befriends Laure, the new girl at his high school, but senses she's keeping a painful secret. (Rev: SLJ 11/01; VOYA 8/01)

1336 Marino, Jan. *Searching for Atticus* (7–10). 1997, Simon & Schuster $16.00 (0-689-80066-5). During a stay at an aunt's home with her exhausted father, a Vietnam War veteran, 15-year-old Tessa falls in love with handsome but dangerous Caleb. (Rev: BL 11/15/97; BR 3–4/98; HBG 3/98; SLJ 10/97; VOYA 12/97)

1337 Mason, Bobbie Ann. *In Country* (9–12). 1986, HarperCollins paper $13.00 (0-06-091350-9). This understated novel deals with a teenage girl and her gradual acceptance of the death of her father in the Vietnam War. (Rev: BL 8/85; SLJ 2/86)

1338 Matlock, Curtiss Ann. *Recipes for Easy Living* (10–12). 2003, MIRA paper $12.95 (1-55166-753-3). In the small Oklahoma town of Valentine, the arrival of the Christmas season teaches 13-year-old Corrine some important lessons about her family, town, and herself. (Rev: BL 10/15/03)

1339 Matthews, Andrew. *The Flip Side* (7–12). 2003, Delacorte $15.95 (0-385-73096-9). His role as Rosalind in "As You Like It" and the fact that he enjoys dressing as a woman cause Rob to explore his own sexuality. (Rev: BCCB 10/03; HBG 4/04; SLJ 10/03; VOYA 6/03)

1340 Matthews, Phoebe. *Switchstance* (7–10). 1989, Avon paper $2.95 (0-380-75729-X). After her parents' divorce, Elvy moves in with her grandmother and forms friendships with two very different boys. (Rev: VOYA 2/90)

1341 Maugham, W. Somerset. *The Razor's Edge* (10–12). 1944, Doubleday paper $12.95 (0-14-018523-2). In this novel, Larry Darrell's search for the meaning of life takes him to many locales and meetings with groups of different types.

1342 Maxwell, Katie. *The Year My Life Went down the Loo* (10–12). 2003, Dorchester paper $5.99 (0-8439-5251-2). Emily, 16 and spending a year in England, sends entertaining emails to her best friend in Seattle detailing the ups and downs of her school, family, and social life; for mature teens. (Rev: BL 11/1/03)

1343 Mayfield, Sue. *Drowning Anna* (8–12). 2002, Hyperion $15.99 (0-7868-0870-5). Anna is pretty and talented, but shy and an easy mark for master manipulator Hayley, whose bullying drives Anna to a suicide attempt. (Rev: BCCB 12/02; BL 10/15/02; HB 1–2/03; HBG 3/03; SLJ 12/02; VOYA 2/03)

1344 Maynard, Meredy. *Blue True Dream of Sky* (7–10). 1997, Polestar paper $7.95 (1-89609-523-2). Nickie, a 14-year-old albino girl, faces new problems when her brother sinks into a coma after a car crash, and she begins a crusade to save a stand of trees near her Pacific Northwest home. (Rev: BR 1–2/98; VOYA 10/97)

1345 Mazer, Anne, ed. *Working Days: Stories About Teenagers and Work* (6–12). 1997, Persea paper $9.95 (0-89255-224-7). An anthology of 15 varied, multicultural short stories about teenagers at their jobs. (Rev: BL 7/97; HBG 3/98; SLJ 9/97; VOYA 12/97)

1346 Mazer, Harry. *The Girl of His Dreams* (9–12). 1987, Avon paper $2.95 (0-380-70599-0). Willis Pierce is now 18 and into running while also being intent on his new girlfriend Sophie. Pierce was first introduced in Mazer's *The War on Villa Street*. (Rev: BL 9/15/87; BR 3–4/88; SLJ 1/88; VOYA 12/87)

1347 Mazer, Harry. *Hey, Kid! Does She Love Me?* (7–12). 1986, Avon paper $2.95 (0-380-70025-5). Stage-struck Jeff falls in love with a woman who was once an aspiring actress in this romance that contains some sexually explicit language.

1348 Mazer, Harry. *I Love You, Stupid!* (9–12). 1983, Avon paper $3.50 (0-380-61432-4). In this sequel to *The Dollar Man*, 17-year-old Marcus and friend Wendy experiment with sex and find love. (Rev: BL 6/87)

1349 Mazer, Norma Fox. *Out of Control* (7–12). 1993, Avon paper $5.99 (0-380-71347-0). This novel deals directly and realistically with the complexities of sexual harassment. (Rev: BL 6/1–15/93; VOYA 8/93)

1350 Mazer, Norma Fox. *Someone to Love* (7–12). 1985, Dell paper $3.25 (0-440-98062-3). A lonely college student moves in with her boyfriend, a dropout.

1351 Mazer, Norma Fox. *When She Was Good* (10–12). 1997, Scholastic $21.99 (0-590-13506-6). When her sister dies unexpectedly, Em feels a complicated mixture of liberation and loss. (Rev: BL 9/1/97; BR 1–2/98; HBG 3/98; SLJ 9/97*; VOYA 10/97)

1352 Meallet, Sandro. *Edgewater Angels* (10–12). 2001, Doubleday $21.95 (0-385-50151-X). This coming-of-age novel deals with adolescent Toomer and his pals growing up in a housing project in San Pedro, California, and their many scrapes with the law. (Rev: BL 6/1–15/01)

1353 Meno, Joe. *How the Hula Girl Sings* (10–12). 2001, HarperCollins $25.00 (0-06-039433-1). In this novel for mature readers, an ex-convict returns to his hometown in rural Illinois on parole and finds that he is inexorably drawn into a world of violence. (Rev: BL 8/01)

1354 Michaels, Fern. *Late Bloomer* (10–12). 2003, Atria $24.00 (0-7434-5778-1). A loving grandmother supports her 20-something granddaughter in her efforts to reexamine a childhood tragedy and to create a richer life. (Rev: BL 1/1–15/03)

1355 Miller-Lachmann, Lyn. *Hiding Places* (8–12). 1987, Square One paper $4.95 (0-938961-00-4). Mark runs away from his suburban home and ends up in a shelter in New York City. (Rev: SLJ 5/87)

1356 Moeyaert, Bart. *Bare Hands* (9–12). Trans. by Davi Colmer. 1998, Front Street $14.95 (1-886910-32-4). A provocative novel about a boy's confused feelings when his actions provoke a neighboring farmer, who is courting the boy's single mother, into killing the boy's dog. (Rev: BL 12/15/98; HBG 9/99; SLJ 2/99; VOYA 6/99)

1357 Moore, Peter. *Blind Sighted* (9–12). 2002, Viking $16.99 (0-670-03543-2). Kirk's mother runs off to California, leaving him to rely on his girlfriend and the blind woman whom he has befriended. (Rev: BL 9/1/02; HBG 3/03; SLJ 9/02*)

1358 Morgenstern, Susie. *Three Days Off* (7–12). Trans. by Gill Rosner. 2001, Viking $14.99 (0-670-03511-4). William, suspended from school after making a suggestive remark to a teacher, spends three days aimlessly wandering through his small French town in this brief novel translated from the French. (Rev: BL 12/15/01; HB 11–12/01; HBG 3/02; SLJ 12/01; VOYA 10/01)

1359 Mori, Kyoko. *Shizuko's Daughter* (9–12). 1993, Holt $15.95 (0-8050-2557-X). After an adolescence in protective, self-imposed isolation, Yuki leaves home in Kobe, Japan, to study art in Nagasaki. (Rev: BL 2/1/93; SLJ 6/93; VOYA 10/93)

1360 Moriarty, Laura. *The Center of Everything* (10–12). 2003, Hyperion $22.95 (1-4013-0031-6). Readers share the maturing of Evelyn Bucknow, a girl learning to cope with her young mother, with a new and retarded baby sister, and with new relationships outside her family. (Rev: BL 7/03; SLJ 12/03; VOYA 12/03)

1361 Morris, Willie. *Taps* (10–12). 2001, Houghton $26.00 (0-618-09859-3). For mature readers, this is a sensitive novel, rich in characterization, about the childhood and youth of a youngster growing up in Mississippi during the Korean War. (Rev: BL 2/15/01)

1362 Morris, Winifred. *Liar* (7–10). 1996, Walker $15.95 (0-8027-8461-5). Fourteen-year-old Alex starts life over on his grandparents' farm in Oregon, but there are many obstacles, including school bullies, a hostile principal, and an unloving grandfather. (Rev: BL 12/1/96; SLJ 1/97; VOYA 12/96)

1363 Mosier, Elizabeth. *My Life as a Girl* (8–12). 1999, Random $18.99 (0-679-99035-6). Jamie wants to become a new person when she enters Bryn Mawr as a freshman, but her precollege summer boyfriend reminds her that she must come to terms with persistent family problems, including a father who has driven the family into financial ruin. (Rev: BL 4/1/99; HBG 9/99; SLJ 6/99)

1364 Moynahan, Molly. *Stone Garden* (10–12). 2003, Morrow $23.95 (0-06-054426-0). High school student Alice is overwhelmed by the death of her best friend Matthew but finds some relief when she becomes involved in a teaching class at a local prison. (Rev: BL 9/1/03)

1365 Murphy, Claire Rudolf. *Free Radical* (7–10). 2002, Clarion $15.00 (0-618-11134-4). Luke, a baseball star in Fairbanks, Alaska, is stunned when his mother turns herself in for her role in a fatal bombing more than 30 years before. (Rev: BCCB 6/02; BL 3/15/02; HBG 10/02; SLJ 3/02; VOYA 6/02)

1366 Myers, Anna. *Ethan Between Us* (7–10). 1998, Walker $15.95 (0-8027-8670-7). The lives of two close friends growing up in a small Oklahoma town are changed and their friendship shattered when they become involved with a handsome, troubled young man to whom both are attracted. (Rev: BL 8/98; BR 1–2/99; HBG 9/99; SLJ 10/98)

1367 Myers, Walter Dean. *The Beast* (9–12). 2003, Scholastic $16.95 (0-439-36841-3). When Anthony goes off to a prep school in Connecticut, the girlfriend he left behind in Harlem begins to use heroin. (Rev: BL 10/1/03; HB 11–12/03; HBG 4/04; SLJ 12/03; VOYA 10/03)

1368 Myers, Walter Dean. *Crystal* (9–12). 1990, Bantam paper $5.95 (0-440-80157-5). A beautiful young black model finds success hard to handle. (Rev: BL 6/1/87; BR 9–10/87; SLJ 6/87; VOYA 4/88)

1369 Myers, Walter Dean. *Handbook for Boys: A Novel* (8–12). 2002, HarperCollins LB $15.89 (0-06-029147-8). Jimmy, 16, is the recipient of a lot of unsought advice when he starts work in a Harlem barbershop as part of a mentoring program. (Rev: HBG 10/02; SLJ 5/02; VOYA 8/02)

1370 Myers, Walter Dean. *Shooter* (7–12). 2004, HarperCollins $15.99 (0-06-029519-8). Told from many viewpoints, this is the story of a high school senior who commits suicide after shooting a star football player and injuring several others. (Rev: BL 2/15/04*; HB 5–6/04; SLJ 5/04; VOYA 6/04)

1371 Myers, Walter Dean. *Won't Know Till I Get There* (7–10). 1982, Penguin paper $5.99 (0-14-032612-X). A young subway graffiti artist is sentenced to help out in a senior citizens' home.

1372 Myracle, Lauren. *Kissing Kate* (7–10). 2003, Dutton $16.99 (0-525-46917-6). Lissa, 16, and best friend Kate have very different reactions after they share a passionate kiss. (Rev: BCCB 5/03; BL 8/03; HBG 10/03; SLJ 4/03; VOYA 4/03)

1373 Myracle, Lauren. *ttyl* (6–10). 2004, Abrams $15.95 (0-8109-4821-4). This story of three 10th-graders and their lives is told through instant messages. (Rev: BL 5/15/04; SLJ 4/04; VOYA 6/04)

1374 Namioka, Lensey. *Ties That Bind, Ties That Break* (7–10). 1999, Delacorte $15.95 (0-385-32666-1). In this novel set in early 20th-century China, a period of dramatic and political changes, Ailin rebels against traditions that repress women, and after a lonely and difficult journey to America, eventually achieves self-fulfillment. (Rev: BCCB 5/99; BL 5/15/99; HBG 9/99; SLJ 7/99)

1375 Neenan, Colin. *In Your Dreams* (9–12). 1995, Harcourt $11.00 (0-15-200885-3). In this humorous, first-person narrative, 15-year-old Hale O'Reilly reveals several problems, including adjusting to his parents' divorce, his secret love for his older brother's girlfriend, to whom he has been writing Cyrano de Bergerac-type letters for his brother, and the fact that his younger sister's punk girlfriend likes him. (Rev: SLJ 5/95; VOYA 2/96)

1376 Neenan, Colin. *Live a Little* (8–12). 1996, Harcourt $12.00 (0-15-201242-7); paper $6.00 (0-15-202143-5). Hale's last days in high school are plagued with disappointments and he experiences bouts of self-pity when he discovers that good friend Zoe is pregnant. (Rev: BL 9/1/96; BR 3–4/97; SLJ 3/97; VOYA 12/96)

1377 Nelson, Blake. *The New Rules of High School* (9–12). 2003, Viking $16.99 (0-670-03644-7). Max's final year in high school is full of ups and downs as he tries to concentrate on his job as editor-in-chief of the school newspaper and deal with romantic entanglements. (Rev: BL 8/03; HBG 10/03; SLJ 6/03; VOYA 6/03)

1378 Newbery, Linda. *The Shell House* (9–12). 2002, Knopf $15.95 (0-385-75011-0). Teenage photographer Greg finds himself questioning his religion and his sexuality in this effective story. (Rev: BCCB 11/02; BL 8/02; HBG 3/03; LMC 2/03; VOYA 8/02)

1379 Newbery, Linda. *Sisterland* (8–12). 2004, Random $15.95 (0-385-75026-9). This powerful story of love, anger, and guilt includes many generations and countries and revolves around Hilly, a contemporary British teen who is love with a Palestinian. (Rev: BL 3/1/04; HB 3–4/04; SLJ 4/04; VOYA 4/04)

1380 Niemi, Mikael. *Popular Music from Vittula* (10–12). Trans. by Laurie Thompson. 2003, Seven Stories $21.95 (1-58322-523-4). In a remote village in 1960s Sweden, 11-year-old Matti discovers the Beatles and the charms and angst of adolescence. (Rev: BL 10/15/03)

74

1381 Nixon, Joan Lowery. *Nobody's There* (7–12). 2000, Delacorte $15.95 (0-385-32567-3). Because of an act of vandalism, Abbie is sentenced to community service helping the cantankerous elderly Mrs. Merkel. (Rev: BCCB 7–8/00; BL 6/1–15/00; HBG 9/00; SLJ 7/00)

1382 Oates, Joyce Carol. *Big Mouth and Ugly Girl* (8–12). 2002, HarperCollins LB $16.89 (0-06-623758-0). Ursula ("Ugly Girl") stands up for Matt ("Big Mouth") when he is accused of plotting to blow up the high school. (Rev: BL 5/15/02; HB 7–8/02; HBG 10/02; SLJ 5/02*; VOYA 8/02)

1383 Oates, Joyce Carol. *Broke Heart Blues* (10–12). 1999, Dutton $24.95 (0-525-94451-6). A novel about a young man who commits a crime, does time in prison, then tries to resume a normal life. (Rev: BL 5/1/99; SLJ 12/99)

1384 O'Connell, Rebecca. *Myrtle of Willendorf* (10–12). 2000, Front Street $15.95 (1-886910-52-9). In this humorous but poignant novel, Myrtle, an overweight and lonely college student rooming with a sexually active beauty, finds solace in art. (Rev: BL 10/15/00; HB 9–10/00; HBG 3/01; SLJ 10/00; VOYA 12/00)

1385 Okimoto, Jean D. *The Eclipse of Moonbeam Dawson* (7–10). 1997, Tor $17.95 (0-312-86244-X). Fifteen-year-old Moonbeam Dawson rebels against his mother's unconventional ways and takes a job and an apartment at posh Stere Island Lodge, where he changes his name and tries to change his values. (Rev: HBG 9/98; SLJ 11/97; VOYA 4/98)

1386 Okimoto, Jean D. *To JayKae: Life Stinx* (8–12). 1999, Tor $18.95 (0-312-86732-8). In this sequel to *Jason's Women* (Tor, 1986), teenager Jason woos a girl over the Internet by pretending to be his handsome, very-popular stepbrother. (Rev: BL 12/15/99; HBG 4/00; SLJ 1/00; VOYA 2/00)

1387 O'Leary, Patsy Baker. *With Wings as Eagles* (7–10). 1997, Houghton $15.00 (0-395-70557-6). Set in rural North Carolina in 1938, this novel tells about young Bubba's becoming reacquainted with a father newly released from prison, his family's struggle with poverty, and Bubba's friendship with a black boy. (Rev: BL 10/15/97; BR 5–6/98; HBG 3/98; SLJ 12/97*)

1388 Orringer, Julie. *How to Breathe Underwater* (11–12). 2003, Knopf $21.00 (1-4000-4111-2). Young people struggle to deal with their own coming of age and sexual awakening amid accidents, family problems, fatal illness, and other challenges in these nine stories. (Rev: BL 9/1/03*)

1389 Paddock, Jennifer. *A Secret Word* (10–12). 2004, Simon & Schuster paper $13.00 (0-7432-4707-8). The story of three girlfriends, their coming of age, and their different destinies. (Rev: BL 4/1/04)

1390 Paulsen, Gary. *Alida's Song* (6–10). 1999, Delacorte $15.95 (0-385-32586-X). A 14-year-old boy discovers a new life away from his alcoholic parents when he accepts an invitation from his grandmother to spend time on her quiet northern Minnesota farm. (Rev: BL 6/1–15/99; BR 9–10/99; HBG 10/99; SLJ 7/99)

1391 Paulsen, Gary. *The Beet Fields: Memories of a Sixteenth Summer* (9–12). 2000, Delacorte $15.95 (0-385-32647-5). A young man leaves home to escape an alcoholic mother and learns about work, sex, injustice, love, and loneliness. (Rev: BL 7/00; HBG 3/01; SLJ 9/00; VOYA 12/00)

1392 Paulsen, Gary. *The Crossing* (8–10). 1987, Dell paper $5.99 (0-440-20582-4). An alcoholic American soldier and a homeless street waif become friends in a Mexican border town. (Rev: BL 10/15/87; BR 1–2/88; SLJ 11/87; VOYA 10/87)

1393 Paulsen, Gary. *The Island* (7–10). 1988, Orchard paper $17.95 (0-531-05749-6). A 15-year-old boy finds peace and a meaning to life when he explores his own private island. (Rev: BL 3/15/88; BR 9–10/88; SLJ 5/88; VOYA 6/88)

1394 Paulsen, Gary. *Popcorn Days and Buttermilk Nights* (8–12). 1989, Penguin paper $4.99 (0-14-034204-4). Carley finds adventure after he is sent to his Uncle David's farm in Minnesota to sort himself out.

1395 Paulsen, Gary. *Sisters / Hermanas* (8–10). Trans. by Gloria de Aragón Andújar. 1993, Harcourt $10.95 (0-15-275323-0); paper $6.00 (0-15-275324-9). The bilingual story of two girls, age 14, in a Texas town, one an illegal Mexican immigrant prostitute, the other a superficial blond cheerleader. (Rev: BL 1/1/94; SLJ 1/94; VOYA 12/93)

1396 Pearson, Michael. *Shohola Falls* (10–12). 2003, Syracuse Univ. Pr. $24.95 (0-8156-0785-7). Finding himself suddenly on his own, young Tommy Blanks finds love in the unlikely setting of a Catholic-run juvenile facility to which he's committed after a minor theft. (Rev: BL 9/15/03)

1397 Peck, Richard. *Are You in the House Alone?* (7–10). 1977, Bantam paper $4.99 (0-440-90227-4). Gail is raped by a classmate while she is on a baby-sitting assignment. (Rev: BL 2/15/88)

1398 Peck, Richard. *Bed and Breakfast* (10–12). 1998, Viking paper $23.95 (0-670-87368-3). A novel about the lasting friendship between Lesley, Julia, and Margo that culminates in a reunion where the three are dramatically changed after a stay at an elegant bed-and-breakfast in London run by the mysterious Mrs. Smith-Porter. (Rev: BL 6/1–15/98; SLJ 8/98)

1399 Pedersen, Laura. *Beginner's Luck* (11–12). 2003, Ballantine paper $13.95 (0-345-45830-3). Discontented Hallie Palmer is only 16 but she's determined to take charge of her own life, runs away, and soon finds a home with the eccentric Stockton family; for mature teens. (Rev: BL 12/15/02; VOYA 6/03)

1400 Pennebaker, Ruth. *Conditions of Love* (8–10). 1999, Holt $16.95 (0-8050-6104-5). In this first-person narrative, 14-year-old Sarah tells of her problems adjusting to her father's death and getting along with her mother, plus difficulties at her school where she is considered an outsider. (Rev: BL 5/15/99; HBG 9/99; SLJ 5/99; VOYA 6/99)

1401 Pennebaker, Ruth. *Don't Think Twice* (9–12). 1996, Holt $15.95 (0-8050-4407-8). Anne, an intelligent, caustic 18-year-old girl "in trouble," narrates this story about a group of girls in a home for pregnant teens in rural Texas. (Rev: BL 5/1/96; BR 1–2/97; SLJ 5/96*; VOYA 8/96)

1402 Perrotta, Tom. *Joe College* (10–12). 2000, St. Martin's $23.95 (0-312-26184-5). This novel about Danny, a junior at Yale in 1980, tells about his school, hometown, friends, girlfriends, and his job at semester breaks working in his father's lunch wagon. (Rev: BL 9/1/00)

1403 Peters, Julie Anne. *Keeping You a Secret* (8–12). 2003, Little, Brown $16.95 (0-316-70275-7). Senior class president Holland Jaeger, a girl who thought she had her life in control, falls in love with a lesbian. (Rev: BL 6/1–15/03; HBG 10/03; SLJ 5/03; VOYA 6/03)

1404 Peterson, Brian. *Move over, Girl* (10–12). 2000, Villard $19.95 (0-375-50402-8). This adult novel, which contains rough language and some sex, tells about a journey of self-discovery taken by a young African American man while he is a college junior. (Rev: BL 2/15/00)

1405 Philbrick, Rodman. *Freak the Mighty* (7–10). 1993, Scholastic paper $15.95 (0-590-47412-X). When Maxwell Kane, the son of Killer Kane, becomes friends with Kevin, a new boy with a birth defect, he gains a new interest in school and learning. (Rev: BL 12/15/93; SLJ 12/93*; VOYA 4/94)

1406 Piercy, Marge. *The Third Child* (11–12). 2003, Morrow $24.95 (0-06-621116-6). The third of four children and a misfit in a successful and ambitious family, Melissa rebels through an unsuitable love affair; suitable for mature readers. (Rev: BL 9/1/03)

1407 Pinkney, Andrea D. *Raven in a Dove House* (6–10). 1998, Harcourt $16.00 (0-15-201461-6). Twelve-year-old Nell, who is spending the summer with an aunt in upstate New York, is terrified when her male cousin, Foley, takes up with a smooth-talking boy who hides a gun in her dollhouse. (Rev: BCCB 5/98; BL 2/15/98; HBG 10/98; SLJ 5/98; VOYA 10/98)

1408 Platt, Kin. *Crocker* (7–10). 1983, Harper-Collins $11.95 (0-397-32025-6). Dorothy is attracted to a new boy in school.

1409 Platt, Randall B. *The Cornerstone* (8–12). 1998, Catbird $21.95 (0-945774-40-0). Using flashbacks, this novel tells about the growth of a tough 15-year-old charity case at summer camp on a scholarship in 1944, where he meets a Navy man on medical leave who changes his life. (Rev: VOYA 2/99)

1410 Platt, Randall Beth. *The Likes of Me* (9–12). 2000, Delacorte $15.95 (0-385-32692-0). Cordelia, a girl of mixed race, lives in a strange world featuring giants, transvestites, and gamblers in this offbeat novel set in 1918 Washington state. (Rev: BL 3/1/00; HBG 9/00; SLJ 2/00)

1411 Plum-Ucci, Carol. *What Happened to Lani Garver* (8–12). 2002, Harcourt $17.00 (0-15-216813-3). Claire, a popular 16-year-old who is battling private demons, finds support and a cause in a newly arrived, curiously androgynous student who disturbs her friends. (Rev: BCCB 11/02; BL 8/02; HBG 10/03; SLJ 10/02*; VOYA 12/02)

1412 Pope, Dan. *In the Cherry Tree* (11–12). 2003, St. Martin's paper $14.00 (0-312-42236-9). Timmy tells the story of the summer he was 12, a time of growing sexual awareness, family friction, and adolescent tensions painted against a backdrop of 1970s culture; suitable for mature teens. (Rev: BL 9/1/03)

1413 Porter, David. *Vienna Passage* (9–12). 1995, Crossway paper $10.99 (0-89107-824-X). A deeply religious young Englishman matures to an understanding of the evils of anti-Semitism and the fulfillment of a life with the love of a woman, art, and music. (Rev: BL 9/1/95*)

1414 Potok, Chaim. *My Name Is Asher Lev* (9–12). 1972, Knopf $25.00 (0-394-46137-1); Fawcett paper $6.99 (0-449-20714-5). This novel traces the conflict that a sensitive Jewish boy experiences with his strict Orthodox beliefs.

1415 Potok, Chaim. *Zebra and Other Stories* (7–12). Illus. 1998, Random $19.99 (0-679-95440-6); paper $4.99 (0-375-80686-5). An anthology of six stories about experiences that youngsters have that help them along the road to maturity. (Rev: BL 7/98; HBG 3/99; SLJ 9/98; VOYA 10/98)

1416 Rambach, Peggy. *Fighting Gravity* (10–12). 2001, Steerforth $19.00 (1-58642-023-2). For mature readers, this is the story of a 19-year-old Jewish college student and her love for a twice-married Catholic professor who has four children. (Rev: BL 4/1/01)

1417 Rapp, Adam. *The Buffalo Tree* (9–12). 1997, Front Street $15.95 (1-886910-19-7). Sura, who has adjusted to his confined world in a juvenile detention center, learns about himself through sessions with a counselor. (Rev: BL 9/1/97; SLJ 6/97*; VOYA 8/97)

1418 Rapp, Adam. *Missing the Piano* (9–12). 1994, Viking $14.99 (0-670-95340-2). In his new military academy, Mike discovers racism and intimidation in this story about values, basketball, and friendship. (Rev: BL 6/1–15/94; SLJ 6/94)

1419 Rapp, Adam. *33 Snowfish* (10–12). 2003, Candlewick $15.99 (0-7636-1874-8). A stark story about a preteen boy who bands together with a young man, his drug-addicted former-prostitute girlfriend, and a baby on an aimless journey to nowhere. (Rev: BCCB 5/03; HBG 4/04; SLJ 4/03; VOYA 4/03)

1420 Reed, Don C. *The Kraken* (6–10). 1997, Boyds Mills paper $7.95 (1-56397-693-5). In Newfoundland in the late 1800s, a boy struggles to survive against the impersonal rich and the harsh environment. (Rev: BL 3/15/95; SLJ 2/95)

1421 Reynolds, Clay. *Monuments* (10–12). 2000, Texas Tech Univ. Pr. $29.95 (0-89672-433-6). The story of 14-year-old Hugh Rudd, life in his small Texas town, and his journey to manhood. (Rev: BL 7/00)

1422 Reynolds, Marilyn. *Beyond Dreams* (9–12). 1995, Morning Glory $15.95 (1-885356-01-3); paper $8.95 (1-885356-00-5). Using alternate male and female voices, Reynolds presents short stories of teens in crisis. (Rev: BL 11/15/95; SLJ 9/95; VOYA 2/96)

1423 Reynolds, Marilyn. *But What About Me?* (9–12). Series: True-to-Life. 1996, Morning Glory $15.95 (1-885356-11-0); paper $8.95 (1-885356-10-2). Eighteen-year-old Erica is trying to remain true to herself while her boyfriend is spiraling down a path to self-destruction in this story of the trials of true love. (Rev: BR 3–4/97; SLJ 10/96; VOYA 2/97)

1424 Reynolds, Marilyn. *Detour for Emmy* (8–12). 1993, Morning Glory paper $8.95 (0-930934-76-8). Emmy is a good student and a hunk's girlfriend, but her home life includes a deserter father and an alcoholic mother. Emmy's pregnancy causes more hardship when she keeps the baby. (Rev: BL 10/1/93; SLJ 7/93; VOYA 12/93)

1425 Reynolds, Marilyn. *If You Loved Me: True-to-Life Series from Hamilton High* (8–12). 1999, Morning Glory paper $8.95 (1-885356-55-2). Seventeen-year-old Lauren, born to a drug-addicted mother now deceased, vows to abstain from drugs and sex, but the latter is particularly difficult because of an insistent boyfriend. (Rev: BL 9/1/99; HBG 4/00; VOYA 2/00)

1426 Reynolds, Marilyn. *Telling: True-to-Life Series from Hamilton High* (7–10). 1996, Morning Glory paper $8.95 (1-885356-03-X). Twelve-year-old Cassie is confused and embarrassed when her adult neighbor makes sexual advances towards her. (Rev: BL 4/1/96; SLJ 5/96; VOYA 6/96)

1427 Reynolds, Marilyn. *Too Soon for Jeff* (8–12). 1994, Morning Glory $15.95 (0-930934-90-3);

paper $8.95 (0-930934-91-1). Jeff's hopes of going to college on a debate scholarship are put in jeopardy when his girlfriend happily announces she's pregnant. Jeff reluctantly prepares for fatherhood. (Rev: BL 9/15/94; SLJ 9/94; VOYA 12/94)

1428 Rhue, Morton. *The Wave* (7–10). 1981, Dell paper $5.50 (0-440-99371-7). A high school experiment to test social interaction backfires when an elitist group is formed.

1429 Roberts, Laura P. *Get a Life* (7–10). Series: Clearwater Crossing. 1998, Bantam paper $4.50 (0-553-57118-4). A group of teenagers, each with a problem or a family secret not to be shared, come together as volunteers planning a high school charity carnival. (Rev: BR 9–10/98; SLJ 11/98)

1430 Rodowsky, Colby. *Remembering Mog* (7–12). 1996, Avon paper $3.99 (0-380-72922-9). With the death of her older sister and mentor, Annie must face the future alone and make her own decisions. (Rev: BL 2/1/96; BR 9–10/96; SLJ 3/96*; VOYA 6/96)

1431 Roos, Stephen. *Confessions of a Wayward Preppie* (7–10). 1986, Dell paper $2.75 (0-440-91586-4). Through an unusual bequest, Cary is able to attend a classy prep school but there his troubles begin. (Rev: BL 6/1/86; BR 9–10/86; SLJ 5/86; VOYA 8/86)

1432 Rosen, Roger, and Patra M. Sevastiades, eds. *Coming of Age: The Art of Growing Up* (9–12). 1994, Rosen LB $16.95 (0-8239-1805-X); paper $8.95 (0-8239-1806-8). This multicultural anthology of short fiction and essays confronts traditional — and more complex — coming-of-age issues. (Rev: BL 1/1/95; SLJ 1/95)

1433 Rosenberg, Liz. *Heart and Soul* (8–12). 1996, Harcourt $11.00 (0-15-200942-6); paper $5.00 (0-15-201270-2). It is only when Willie helps a troubled Jewish classmate that she is able to straighten out her own problems. (Rev: BL 6/1–15/96; VOYA 8/96)

1434 Rosenberg, Liz. *17: A Novel in Prose Poems* (10–12). 2002, Cricket $16.95 (0-8126-4915-X). Readers follow Stephanie through the stages of first love, from initial excitement to final separation. (Rev: BCCB 2/03; BL 11/15/02; HBG 3/03; SLJ 11/02; VOYA 4/03)

1435 Rottman, S. L. *Rough Waters* (7–12). 1998, Peachtree $14.95 (1-56145-172-X). After the deaths of their parents, teenage brothers Gregg and Scott move to Colorado to live with an uncle who runs a white-water rafting business. (Rev: BL 5/1/98; BR 11–12/98; HBG 9/98; SLJ 8/98; VOYA 8/98)

1436 Rottman, S. L. *Stetson* (6–12). 2002, Viking $16.99 (0-670-03542-4). Prankster Stetson tries to get his life on track and graduate from high school despite a troubled past. (Rev: BCCB 3/02; BL 4/1/02; HBG 10/02; SLJ 4/02; VOYA 2/02)

1437 Ryan, Sarah. *Empress of the World* (9–12). 2001, Viking $15.99 (0-670-89688-8). Nic struggles with her feelings when she falls in love with another girl. (Rev: BCCB 9/01; BL 7/01; BR 1–2/02; HB 9–10/01; HBG 3/02; SLJ 7/01; VOYA 8/01)

1438 Salinger, J. D. *The Catcher in the Rye* (7–12). 1951, Little, Brown $25.95 (0-316-76953-3); Bantam paper $3.95 (0-553-25025-6). For mature readers, the saga of Holden Caulfield and his three days in New York City. (Rev: BL 10/1/88)

1439 Sanchez, Alex. *Rainbow Boys* (9–12). 2001, Simon & Schuster $17.00 (0-689-84100-0). The challenges facing gay teenagers are the focus of this novel about acceptance. (Rev: BL 11/15/01; HBG 3/02; SLJ 10/01; VOYA 12/01)

1440 Schaeffer, Frank. *Portofino* (9–12). 1992, Macmillan $15.00 (0-02-607051-0). An insecure adolescent remembers vacations during the 1960s with his eccentric "born-again" family. (Rev: BL 9/15/92)

1441 Schmitt, Richard. *The Aerialist* (10–12). 2000, Overlook $26.95 (1-58567-070-7). This first novel presents a gritty behind-the-scenes look at life in a traveling circus. (Rev: BL 11/15/00*)

1442 Seymour, Tres. *The Revelation of Saint Bruce* (7–12). 1998, Orchard paper $16.95 (0-531-30109-5). Because of his honesty, Bruce is responsible for the expulsion of several friends from school. (Rev: BL 10/15/98; BR 5–6/99; HBG 3/99; SLJ 9/98; VOYA 2/99)

1443 Shay, Kathryn. *Trust in Me* (10–12). 2003, Berkley paper $6.99 (0-425-18884-1). Members of a group of teen troublemakers find themselves all back in their hometown as adults, much changed from their younger selves and facing new challenges. (Rev: BL 2/1/03)

1444 Sheldon, Dyan. *Planet Janet* (6–10). 2003, Candlewick $14.99 (0-7636-2048-3). Janet pours out to her diary the frustrations she and her friend Disha face in their dealings with family and friends in this entertaining novel set in London. (Rev: BCCB 3/03; BL 3/15/03; HBG 4/04; SLJ 5/03)

1445 Shepard, Jim. *Project X* (10–12). 2004, Knopf $20.00 (1-4000-4071-X). This story deals with the alienation of some teenage boys, their problems at school, a desire for revenge, and the accessibility of guns in the house. (Rev: BL 1/1–15/04*; SLJ 5/04; VOYA 6/04)

1446 Sheppard, Mary C. *Seven for a Secret* (10–12). 2001, Groundwood $15.95 (0-88899-437-0); paper $12.95 (0-88899-438-9). Three girls living in a tiny town in Newfoundland in 1960 share an eventful summer that includes an unexpected pregnancy. (Rev: BL 11/1/01; HBG 3/02; SLJ 12/01; VOYA 12/01)

1447 Shoup, Barbara. *Stranded in Harmony* (7–10). 1997, Hyperion LB $18.49 (0-7868-2284-8). Lucas, an 18-year-old popular senior in high school, is discontented until he meets and becomes friendly with an older woman. (Rev: BL 7/97; BR 11–12/97; HBG 3/98; SLJ 6/97*)

1448 Silvey, Anita, ed. *Help Wanted: Short Stories About Young People Working* (6–12). 1997, Little, Brown $15.95 (0-316-79148-2). A collection of 12 short stories by such writers as Michael Dorris, Norma Fox Mazer, and Gary Soto that deal with teenagers at work. (Rev: BL 11/1/97; BR 3–4/98; HBG 3/98; SLJ 11/97; VOYA 12/97)

1449 Sinclair, April. *Coffee Will Make You Black* (9–12). 1994, Hyperion $19.95 (1-56282-796-0). Set in late 1960s Chicago, 11-year-old "Stevie" Stevenson's growth from child to woman parallels the growth of African American pride and equality. (Rev: BL 12/15/93)

1450 Singer, Marilyn. *The Course of True Love Never Did Run Smooth* (10–12). 1983, HarperCollins $12.95 (0-06-025753-9). A gay couple "come out" during a school production of *A Midsummer Night's Dream*. (Rev: BL 6/87)

1451 Singer, Marilyn, ed. *Stay True: Short Stories for Strong Girls* (7–12). 1998, Scholastic paper $16.95 (0-590-36031-0). There are 11 new short stories in this collection that explores the problems girls face growing up and how they discover inner strength. (Rev: BL 4/1/98; BR 11–12/98; HB 3–4/98; SLJ 5/98; VOYA 4/98)

1452 Slade, Arthur. *Tribes* (7–10). 2002, Random $15.95 (0-385-73003-9). Percy Montmount views his senior classmates through the eyes of an anthropologist, giving some interesting and humorous insights. (Rev: BL 10/15/02; HB 1–2/03; HBG 3/03; SLJ 10/02; VOYA 2/03)

1453 Smith, Betty. *Joy in the Morning* (9–12). 1963, HarperCollins paper $6.50 (0-06-080368-1). Two young people face a number of problems when their families disown them after finding out about their marriage.

1454 Smith, Sherri L. *Lucy the Giant* (6–10). 2002, Delacorte LB $17.99 (0-385-90031-7). Lucy's height — 6 feet at the age of 15 — is a handicap until it helps her find a new life posing as an adult aboard a crabbing boat in Alaska. (Rev: BCCB 4/02; BL 2/15/02; HB 3–4/02*; HBG 10/02; SLJ 1/02)

1455 Snoe, Eboni. *The Ties that Bind* (10–12). 2002, BET paper $6.99 (1-58314-338-6). Essence believes that Cedric Johnson is really her father in this final installment of the series about reunions started in Geri Guillaume's *Hearts of Steel* and Shirley Hailstock's *A Family Affair* (both 2002). (Rev: BL 9/1/02)

1456   Soehnlein, K. M. *The World of Normal Boys* (10–12). 2000, Kensington $22.00 (1-57566-595-6). Graphic sex and violence are included in this novel about a high school boy from a troubled family who finds he is sexually attracted to other boys. (Rev: BL 9/15/00)

1457   Sones, Sonya. *What My Mother Doesn't Know* (6–10). 2001, Simon & Schuster $17.00 (0-689-84114-0). Sophie, 14, expresses her feelings about falling in and out of love in a poetic narrative that is humorous and romantic. (Rev: BCCB 12/01; BL 11/1/01; HBG 10/02; SLJ 10/01; VOYA 10/01)

1458   Soto, Gary. *Buried Onions* (8–12). 1997, Harcourt $17.00 (0-15-201333-4). A junior college dropout, 19-year-old Eddie is trying to support himself in this story set in the barrio of Fresno, California. (Rev: BL 11/15/97; HBG 3/98; SLJ 1/98; VOYA 10/97)

1459   Spark, Muriel. *The Prime of Miss Jean Brodie* (9–12). 1984, NAL paper $6.95 (0-452-26179-1). The story of an unusual teacher in a private girls' school in Edinburgh and of the changes she detects in her students.

1460   Spinelli, Jerry. *Jason and Marceline* (7–10). 2000, Little, Brown paper $6.99 (0-316-80662-5). Jason, now in the 9th grade, sorts out his feelings toward girls in general and Marceline in particular. Preceded by *Space Station Seventh Grade*. (Rev: BL 1/1/87; SLJ 2/87)

1461   Springer, Nancy. *Secret Star* (7–10). 1997, Putnam $15.95 (0-399-23028-9). Fourteen-year-old Tess Mathis, strong but dirt-poor, can't remember anything before age 10, but when a scar-faced stranger comes to town, she must confront her past. (Rev: BL 4/1/97; BR 5–6/97; SLJ 5/97; VOYA 12/97)

1462   Staples, Suzanne F. *Dangerous Skies* (7–10). 1996, Farrar $16.00 (0-374-31694-5). An interracial friendship, sexual abuse, and family secrets are themes in this novel about a white boy and a black girl growing up in the eastern shore of Virginia. (Rev: BL 9/1/96*; BR 1–2/97; SLJ 10/96; VOYA 12/96)

1463   Stevens, Diane. *Liza's Star Wish* (6–10). 1997, Greenwillow $15.00 (0-688-15310-0). In this sequel to *Liza's Blue Moon*, Liza and her mother spend time in Rockport one summer, and Liza deals with vast changes in her life, including family relationships and friendships. (Rev: BL 9/15/97; HBG 3/98; SLJ 10/97)

1464   Stinson, Susan. *Fat Girl Dances with Rocks* (9–12). 1994, Spinsters Ink paper $10.95 (1-883523-02-8). Char, 17 and overweight, struggles with her identity, the meaning of beauty, and her confusion when her best friend, Felice, kisses her on the lips. (Rev: BL 9/1/94; VOYA 5/95)

1465   Stolz, Karen. *World of Pies* (10–12). 2000, Hyperion $18.95 (0-7868-6550-4). A group of independent stories about a girl named Roxanne growing up in a small town in Texas. There are recipes after each story for the treats mentioned in the text. (Rev: BL 5/1/00; SLJ 8/00)

1466   Strasser, Todd. *Can't Get There from Here* (7–12). 2004, Simon & Schuster $15.95 (0-689-84169-8). A teenage girl who has been thrown out by an abusive mother tries to survive on the streets of New York City. (Rev: BL 3/15/04; SLJ 3/04; VOYA 6/04)

1467   Strasser, Todd. *How I Changed My Life* (7–12). 1995, Simon & Schuster paper $16.00 (0-671-88415-8). Introverted Bo, the theater department stage manager, works on her self-image and weight problem when handsome football captain Kyle joins a production. (Rev: BL 5/1/95; SLJ 5/95)

1468   Sullivan, Mary. *Ship Sooner* (11–12). 2004, Morrow $23.95 (0-06-056240-4). In the search for a father she never knew, 13-year-old Ship uncovers other life-changing family secrets in this appealing twist on the classic coming-of-age story; for mature teens. (Rev: BL 12/15/03; SLJ 6/04)

1469   Sumner, Melanie. *The School of Beauty and Charm* (10–12). 2001, Algonquin $23.95 (1-56512-286-0). After the sudden death of her brother, teenage Louise runs away and joins a circus in this story for mature readers. (Rev: BL 8/01; SLJ 3/02)

1470   Swann, Maxine. *Serious Girls* (11–12). 2003, St. Martin's $23.00 (0-312-28802-6). Teen friends Maya and Roe search for meaning in their lives and fall into difficult sexual relationships in the process; for mature teens. (Rev: BL 10/1/03; VOYA 6/04)

1471   Swarthout, Glendon. *Bless the Beasts and Children* (7–12). 1995, Pocket paper $6.99 (0-671-52151-9). At summer camp a group of misfits prove they have the right stuff. (Rev: BL 9/1/97)

1472   Sweeney, Joyce. *Waiting for June* (8–11). 2003, Marshall Cavendish $15.95 (0-7614-5138-2). High school senior Sophie is pregnant, reluctant to disclose the identity of the father, and in danger in this complex, suspenseful novel. (Rev: BL 9/1/03; HBG 4/04; SLJ 10/03; VOYA 4/04)

1473   Tarbox, Katherine. *Katie.Com: My Story* (6–10). 2000, Dutton $19.95 (0-525-94543-1). Katie, a lonely 8th-grader, forms an e-mail relationship with a man who turns out to be a 41-year-old pedophile. (Rev: BL 7/00; SLJ 9/00)

1474   Taylor, William. *The Blue Lawn* (9–12). 1999, Alyson paper $9.95 (1-55583-493-0). In this novel set in New Zealand, two teenage boys, one quiet and introspective, the other wild and adventurous, are drawn together in a friendship that in time turns sexual. (Rev: BL 12/1/99; HB 5–6/99; SLJ 7/99; VOYA 2/00)

1475 Taylor, William. *Jerome* (9–12). 1999, Alyson paper $9.95 (1-55583-512-0). Marco is stunned to learn — through letters and e-mail — that his dead friend's girlfriend is actually a lesbian. (Rev: BL 1/1–15/00; SLJ 7/00; VOYA 2/00)

1476 Thesman, Jean. *Couldn't I Start Over?* (7–10). 1989, Avon paper $2.95 (0-380-75717-6). Growing up in a caring family situation, teenager Shiloh still faces many problems in her coming of age. (Rev: BL 11/15/89; VOYA 2/90)

1477 Thesman, Jean. *The Rain Catchers* (7–12). 1991, Houghton $15.00 (0-395-55333-4). Grayling learns the importance of storytelling in keeping the past alive, understanding others and herself, and surviving difficult times. (Rev: BL 4/15/91*; SLJ 3/91)

1478 Thesman, Jean. *Summerspell* (7–10). 1995, Simon & Schuster $15.00 (0-671-50130-5). A web of lies and secrets are behind a girl's escape from sexual harassment to a cabin where life had been safe and happy in the past. (Rev: BL 5/1/95; SLJ 6/95)

1479 Thomas, Joyce C. *Bright Shadow* (10–12). 1983, Avon paper $4.99 (0-380-84509-1). A 20-year-old black college student's encounter with love is marred when she becomes involved in a murder.

1480 Thomas, Rob. *Rats Saw God* (8–12). 1996, Simon & Schuster paper $4.99 (0-689-80777-5). At the suggestion of his counselor, high school senior Steve York explores his life, his problems, and how things went wrong when he moved from Texas to California. (Rev: BL 6/1–15/96; BR 1–2/97; SLJ 6/96*; VOYA 6/96)

1481 Thomas, Rob. *Satellite Down* (9–12). 1998, Simon & Schuster $16.00 (0-689-80957-3). Seventeen-year-old Patrick Sheridan faces adult situations and decisions when he is chosen to leave his small Texas town to become a student journalist for a satellite television station, first in Los Angeles and later in Belfast. (Rev: BL 5/15/98; HB 5–6/98; HBG 9/98; SLJ 6/98; VOYA 6/98)

1482 Thompson, Julian. *Philo Fortune's Awesome Journey to His Comfort Zone* (8–12). 1995, Hyperion $16.95 (0-7868-0067-4). A story of a youth who discovers the possibilities of the man he might become. (Rev: BL 5/1/95; SLJ 5/95; VOYA 2/96)

1483 Tolan, Stephanie S. *Plague Year* (8–12). 1991, Fawcett paper $6.50 (0-449-70403-3). Nonconformist Bran, whose father is a mass murderer, faces problems of acceptance at his new high school. (Rev: BL 4/1/90; SLJ 6/90)

1484 Tomey, Ingrid. *Nobody Else Has to Know* (8–10). 1999, Delacorte $15.95 (0-385-32624-6). Fifteen-year-old Webb, a high school track star, feels increasing guilt after he hits a young girl while driving without a license and his grandfather takes

the blame. (Rev: BL 12/15/99; HBG 4/00; SLJ 9/99; VOYA 4/00)

1485 Torres, Laura. *November Ever After* (8–12). 1999, Holiday $16.95 (0-8234-1464-7). Still recovering from her mother's death, 16-yer-old Amy discovers that her best friend, Sara, is a lesbian and in love with a girl in her class. (Rev: BL 12/1/99; HBG 4/00; SLJ 1/00)

1486 Tullson, Diane. *Edge* (7–10). 2003, Fitzhenry & Whiteside paper $6.95 (0-7737-6230-2). Tired of being bullied, Marlie Peters, 14, joins a group of other outcast students only to realize that they are involved in a dangerous plot. (Rev: BL 3/1/03; SLJ 10/03; VOYA 6/03)

1487 Uppal, Priscila. *The Divine Economy of Salvation* (11–12). 2002, Algonquin $24.95 (1-56512-365-4). As Sister Angela looks back at her childhood in a Catholic girls' school and the cliques and jealousies that existed, she reassesses her role in a violent incident; for mature teens. (Rev: BL 8/02)

1488 Vande Velde, Vivian. *Curses, Inc.: And Other Stories* (6–10). 1997, Harcourt $16.00 (0-15-201452-7). In the title story in this collection of tales with surprise endings, Bill Essler thinks he has found the perfect way to get even with his girlfriend, who humiliated him, by utilizing a web site, Curses, Inc. (Rev: SLJ 6/97*; VOYA 6/97)

1489 Vega Yunque, Edgardo. *No Matter How Much You Promise to Cook or Pay the Rent You Blew It Cauze Bill Bailey Ain't Never Coming Home Again* (11–12). 2003, Farrar $25.00 (0-374-22311-4). Vidamia Farrell, who is half Puerto Rican and half Irish, sets off on a search for her father and in the process makes important discoveries about racism, love, and music in this rich and complex story; for mature teens. (Rev: BL 10/15/03)

1490 Velasquez, Gloria. *Tommy Stands Alone* (7–10). 1995, Arte Publico $14.95 (1-55885-146-1); paper $9.95 (1-55885-147-X). An engaging story about a Latino gay teen who is humiliated and rejected but finds understanding from a Chicano therapist. (Rev: BL 10/15/95; SLJ 11/95; VOYA 12/95)

1491 Verdelle, A. J. *The Good Negress* (9–12). 1995, Algonquin $29.95 (1-56512-085-X). Neesey, 13, returns to Detroit from her grandmother's in the South and rages internally over family obligations and a desire for white people's education. (Rev: BL 2/15/95; SLJ 10/95)

1492 Vida, Vendela. *And Now You Can Go* (11–12). 2003, Knopf $19.95 (1-4000-4027-2). A compelling first-person novel about a 21-year-old New York girl and her take on life after she is confronted by a young man intent on murder and suicide; suitable for older teens. (Rev: BL 7/03)

1493 Voigt, Cynthia. *Tell Me If the Lovers Are Losers* (7–10). 1982, Macmillan LB $17.00 (0-689-

30911-2). Three college roommates clash until they find a common interest in volleyball. (Rev: BL 3/87)

1494 Walker, Paul R. *The Method* (8–12). 1990, Harcourt $14.95 (0-15-200528-5). A candid novel about a 15-year-old boy, his acting aspirations, and his sexual problems. (Rev: BL 8/90; SLJ 6/90)

1495 Wallace, Rich. *Losing Is Not an Option* (6–10). 2003, Knopf $15.95 (0-375-81351-9). Nine stories follow Ron, a high school athlete, through coming-of-age experiences including family problems, budding sexual attractions, and competition with his peers. (Rev: BL 8/03; HB 9–10/03; HBG 4/04; SLJ 9/03; VOYA 10/03)

1496 Waltman, Kevin. *Nowhere Fast* (8–12). 2002, Scholastic paper $6.99 (0-439-41424-5). After stealing a car for joyriding, teenagers Gary and Wilson become entrapped in the activities of a former teacher with a dangerous agenda. (Rev: BL 2/1/03; SLJ 4/03; VOYA 4/03)

1497 Warlick, Ashley. *The Distance from the Heart of Things* (10–12). 1996, Houghton $21.95 (0-395-74177-7). Mavis Black returns to her small town in South Carolina after college and sees life from a different perspective. (Rev: BL 3/1/96; SLJ 8/96)

1498 Wartski, Maureen C. *My Name Is Nobody* (7–10). 1988, Walker $15.95 (0-8027-6770-2). A victim of child abuse survives a suicide attempt and is given a second chance by a tough ex-cop. (Rev: BL 2/1/88; BR 9–10/88; SLJ 3/88; VOYA 4/88)

1499 Watson, Sterling. *Sweet Dream Baby* (11–12). 2002, Sourcebooks $22.00 (1-4022-0017-X). In 1950s Florida, young Travis's obsession with his beautiful and wild 16-year-old Aunt Delia has shocking results; for mature teens. (Rev: BL 10/1/02)

1500 Watts, Julia. *Finding H.F* (7–12). 2001, Alyson paper $12.95 (1-55583-622-4). A humorous 16-year-old heroine named H.F. and her friend Bo, both gay, set off on a trip to that teaches them a lot about life outside their small Kentucky town. (Rev: BCCB 1/02; SLJ 2/02; VOYA 2/02)

1501 Weaver, Beth Nixon. *Rooster* (7–12). 2001, Winslow $15.95 (1-58837-001-1). In the 1960s, 15-year-old Kady is growing up in a confusing mix of poverty at home on a struggling orange grove, a devoted but disabled neighboring child, and a wealthy boyfriend who introduces her to marijuana. (Rev: BL 7/01; HB 7–8/01; HBG 10/01; SLJ 6/01; VOYA 2/02)

1502 Weisberg, Joseph. *10th Grade* (11–12). 2002, Random $23.95 (0-375-50584-9). Jeremy Reskin chronicles the events of his 10th-grade year — including school, soccer, crushes, and drugs — in his journal; for mature teens. (Rev: BL 1/1–15/02)

1503 Weiss, M. Jerry, and Helen S. Weiss, eds. *From One Experience to Another: Stories About Turning Points* (6–12). 1997, Tor $18.95 (0-312-86253-9). In 15 original stories, well-known young adult writers tell about incidents that were important turning points in their lives. (Rev: BL 2/1/98; BR 5–6/98; HBG 3/98; SLJ 11/97; VOYA 12/97)

1504 Wells, Ken. *Meely LaBauve* (10–12). 2000, Random $19.95 (0-375-50311-0). An engrossing novel for mature readers about 15-year-old Meely growing up on his own in the Louisiana bayou. Sequels are *Junior's Leg* and *Logan's Storm* (both 2002). (Rev: BL 1/1–15/00; SLJ 9/00)

1505 Wennick, Elizabeth. *Changing Jareth* (8–11). 2000, Polestar paper $6.95 (1-896095-97-6). Seventeen-year-old, street-smart Jareth is involved with two deaths, one of his younger brother and the other of a man who died of a heart attack while Jareth was robbing him. (Rev: BL 4/1/00; SLJ 5/00; VOYA 6/00)

1506 Wersba, Barbara. *Beautiful Losers* (9–12). 1988, HarperCollins $11.95 (0-06-026363-6). The concluding volume in the trilogy about teenaged Rita Formica and her love for Arnold, who is twice her age. Also use *Love Is the Crooked Thing* (1987). (Rev: BL 3/15/88; SLJ 3/88)

1507 Wersba, Barbara. *Whistle Me Home* (9–12). 1997, Holt $14.95 (0-8050-4850-2). The story of 17-year-old Noli, her former boyfriend, TJ, their relationship, and how it ended when she discovered he was gay. (Rev: BL 4/1/97; SLJ 6/97; VOYA 8/97)

1508 Wersba, Barbara. *Wonderful Me* (9–12). 1989, HarperCollins $12.95 (0-06-026361-X). Seventeen-year-old Heidi Rosenbloom spends the summer making money dog walking and coping with the worshipful attention of a mentally unstable English teacher. A sequel to *Just Be Gorgeous* (1988). (Rev: BL 5/1/89; BR 11–12/89; SLJ 4/89; VOYA 6/89)

1509 West, Nathanael. *Miss Lonelyhearts* (10–12). 1933, Liveright paper $8.95 (0-8112-0215-1). Loneliness is the main theme in this novel about a man who writes a lonelyhearts column for a newspaper.

1510 Whack, Rita Coburn. *Meant to Be* (11–12). 2002, Villard paper $11.95 (0-375-75809-7). Set in late 1970s Chicago, this is the story of a young African American woman with high career and romantic ambitions who must resolve family tensions. (Rev: BL 2/15/02)

1511 White, Edmund. *A Boy's Own Story* (10–12). 1982, Dutton paper $12.00 (0-375-70740-9). This is a coming-of-age story about a boy growing up gay and filled with conflicting emotions.

1512 Whitney, P. L. *This Is Graceanne's Book* (10–12). 1999, St. Martin's $22.95 (0-312-20597-X). Nine-year-old Charlie narrates this story about his older sister, 11-year-old Graceanne, the beatings she gets from her abusive mother, and the black girl next door who becomes her friend. (Rev: BL 5/99; SLJ 9/99)

1513 Wieler, Diana. *Drive* (10–12). 1999, Douglas & McIntyre $15.95 (0-88899-347-1). Jens Friesen and his younger brother Daniel, both talented musicians, set out on a road trip in Canada, playing gigs in small towns to raise much-needed money, in this mature novel for older teens. (Rev: BL 5/1/99; SLJ 4/99; VOYA 8/99)

1514 Wieler, Diana. *RanVan: A Worthy Opponent* (7–10). 1998, Douglas & McIntyre $16.95 (0-88899-271-8); paper $5.95 (0-88899-219-X). Nerdy 15-year-old RanVan finds his video game personality can spill over into real life. Preceded by *RanVan: The Defender* and followed by *RanVan: Magic Nation* (1998). (Rev: BL 11/15/98; SLJ 3/98)

1515 Wieler, Diana. *RanVan: The Defender* (7–12). 1997, Douglas & McIntyre $16.95 (0-88899-270-X). Orphaned Rhan Van, who lives with his grandmother in a city apartment, begins hanging out in bad company and soon finds he is vandalizing school and private property. (Rev: BL 2/1/98; SLJ 3/98)

1516 Wild, Margaret. *Jinx* (10–12). 2002, Walker $16.95 (0-8027-8830-0). In this novel told in verse, Jen's happy teenage life is transformed into a nightmare when two boyfriends die in rapid succession and she becomes "Jinx." (Rev: BL 9/15/02*; HB 11–12/02; HBG 3/03; LMC 1/03; SLJ 11/02; VOYA 12/02)

1517 Wild, Margaret. *One Night* (9–12). 2004, Knopf LB $17.99 (0-375-92920-7). After their one-night stand, Helen discovers she is pregnant by her boyfriend Gabe. (Rev: BL 5/15/04; SLJ 5/04)

1518 Williams, Carol Lynch. *Carolina Autumn* (7–10). 2000, Delacorte $14.95 (0-385-32716-1). Slowly Caroline begins the healing process adjusting to the deaths of her father and sister and the distant behavior of her mother. (Rev: BL 9/1/00; HBG 10/01; SLJ 9/00)

1519 Williams, Julie. *Escaping Tornado Season: A Story in Poems* (7–10). 2004, HarperCollins $15.99 (0-06-008639-4). After relocating with her mother to live with her grandparents, 14-year-old Allie becomes a friend of an Ojibwe classmate who is raped by a white teacher. (Rev: BL 3/1/04; SLJ 4/04; VOYA 4/04)

1520 Williams, Lori Aurelia. *Shayla's Double Brown Baby Blues* (7–12). 2003, Pulse $17.00 (0-689-85670-9). In this sequel to *When Kambia Elaine Flew in from Neptune* (2000), 13-year-old Shayla must cope with problems including the arrival of a new half-sister, her friend Kambia's traumatic and abusive past, and her friend Lemm's alcoholism. (Rev: BL 7/01; BR 3–4/02; HB 9–10/01; SLJ 8/01)

1521 Williams, Lori Aurelia. *When Kambia Elaine Flew in from Neptune* (7–12). 2001, Pulse paper $17.00 (0-689-84593-6). In this first-person narrative, 12-year-old Shayla adjusts to the unhappy departure from the family of her older sister and finds escape in her friendship with an imaginative girl named Kambia. (Rev: BL 2/15/00)

1522 Williams, Margaret. *Haverstraw* (10–12). 2004, Avocet paper $12.95 (0-9725078-1-7). Set in the early 20th century, this is a quiet story of a girl who leaves her comfortable home in Quebec City to live with her brutish father on a poor farm in upper New York State. (Rev: BL 4/15/04)

1523 Williams-Garcia, Rita. *Like Sisters on the Homefront* (8–10). 1995, Lodestar $15.99 (0-525-67465-9). After 14-year-old Gayle Ann has an abortion to end her second pregnancy, her mother sends her down South to be rehabilitated by her God-fearing brother, a minister, whose family leads a very structured life and where Gayle Ann must follow rules and help care for her aged but strong-minded grandmother. (Rev: BL 9/1/95*; BR 1–2/96; SLJ 10/95; VOYA 4/96)

1524 Willis, Sarah. *Some Things That Stay* (7–12). 2000, Farrar $24.00 (0-374-10580-4). Tamara is brave and strong but filled with guilt when her mother contracts tuberculosis, thus granting the teenager's wish that her family's nomadic lifestyle will end. (Rev: BL 12/1/99; VOYA 12/00)

1525 Wilson, Budge. *Sharla* (7–10). 1998, Stoddart paper $6.95 (0-7736-7467-5). A run-in with a polar bear, adjusting to a new school, trying to make friends, and getting used to severe weather are some of the problems 15-year-old Sharla faces when she moves with her family from Ottawa to Churchill, a small community in northern Manitoba. (Rev: SLJ 8/98)

1526 Wilson, Jacqueline. *Girls in Love* (7–10). Series: British Girls. 2002, Delacorte LB $11.99 (0-385-90040-6). The romantic ups and downs of 13-year-od schoolmates Ellie, Magda, and Nadine are the focus of this first book in a trilogy set in Britain. (Rev: BCCB 2/02; BL 5/15/02; HBG 10/02; SLJ 1/02)

1527 Wilson, Jacqueline. *Girls Under Pressure* (7–10). Series: British Girls. 2002, Delacorte LB $11.99 (0-385-90041-4). The second volume in this trilogy finds the girls striving — sometimes excessively — to be thin, beautiful, and popular. The third book is titled *Girls Out Late* (2002). (Rev: BCCB 10/02; BL 5/15/02; HBG 10/02; SLJ 12/02; VOYA 12/02)

1528 Wimsley, Jim. *Dream Boy* (10–12). 1995, Algonquin $29.95 (1-56512-106-6). Nathan — bookish and slight and sexually abused by his father — moves to a farm, where he meets and falls in love with Roy, the outgoing, popular boy next door. (Rev: BL 9/15/95; SLJ 3/96; VOYA 2/96)

1529 Wittlinger, Ellen. *Hard Love* (8–12). 1999, Simon & Schuster $16.95 (0-689-82134-4); paper $8.00 (0-689-84154-X). Two outsiders, John, a high school junior and fan of "zines," and Marisol, a self-proclaimed virgin lesbian, form an unusual relationship in this well-crafted novel that explores many teenage problems. (Rev: BL 10/1/99*; HB 7–8/99; HBG 9/99; SLJ 7/99; VOYA 8/99)

1530 Wittlinger, Ellen. *What's in a Name* (7–10). 2000, Simon & Schuster $16.00 (0-689-82551-X). Identity problems involving class, race, family, and sex are explored in these short stories about 10 different students at suburban Scrub Harbor High School. (Rev: BL 1/1–15/00; HB 3–4/00; HBG 9/00; SLJ 2/00; VOYA 4/00)

1531 Wittlinger, Ellen. *Zigzag* (8–12). 2003, Simon & Schuster $16.95 (0-689-84996-6). A summer cross-country car trip with her recently widowed aunt and two cousins poses many challenges for 17-year-old Robin. (Rev: BL 9/1/03; HB 7–8/03; HBG 4/04; SLJ 8/03; VOYA 10/03)

1532 Wolff, Tobias. *Old School* (10–12). 2003, Knopf $22.00 (0-375-40146-6). A fascinating and insightful story set in 1960 of a talented youth from a deprived background who is struggling to fit in and succeed at a private school known for its literary excellence. (Rev: BL 9/1/03*; SLJ 4/04)

1533 Wolff, Virginia E. *The Mozart Season* (9–12). 1991, Holt $15.95 (0-8050-1571-X). Violinist and softball player Allegra Shapiro learns about life through sports analogies when she becomes a finalist in a large youth music contest. (Rev: BL 6/1/91; SLJ 7/91)

1534 Woodhouse, Sarah. *My Summer with Julia* (10–12). 2001, St. Martin's $23.95 (0-312-26622-7). Annie reconstructs the life of her dead friend Julia from a box of letters, photographs, and trinkets that Julia has left her. (Rev: BL 2/15/01)

1535 Woodruff, Nancy. *Someone Else's Child* (10–12). 2000, Simon & Schuster $23.00 (0-684-86507-6). After he is involved in a deadly automobile accident, Matt struggles with his guilt while spending a summer working for his girlfriend's mother. (Rev: BL 6/1–15/00)

1536 Woods, Ron. *The Hero* (6–10). 2002, Knopf LB $17.99 (0-375-90612-6). When hapless young Dennis dies in a rafting incident in 1957, 14-year-old Jamie tells a lie intended to show the dead boy as a hero. (Rev: BCCB 3/02; BL 2/1/02; HB 3–4/02; HBG 10/02; SLJ 1/02; VOYA 8/02)

1537 Wright, Bil. *Sunday You Learn How to Box* (10–12). 2000, Scribner paper $12.00 (0-684-85795-2). This first novel, set in an inner-city housing project in Connecticut, is about a 14-year-old African American boy, Louis Bowman—his feelings, his past, his family, and his budding homosexuality. (Rev: BL 2/15/00; SLJ 9/00)

1538 Wright, Randall. *A Hundred Days from Home* (6–10). 2002, Holt $15.95 (0-8050-6885-6). Elam, 12, grief-stricken by the death of his best friend, slowly learns to trust a new friend when his family moves to the Arizona desert in the early 1960s. (Rev: BL 11/15/02; HBG 3/03; SLJ 9/02)

1539 Yates, Bart. *Leave Myself Behind* (11–12). 2003, Kensington $23.00 (0-7582-0348-9). Mystery and gay romance are interwoven in this compelling story of a gay teenager who moves with his difficult mother to a house full of secrets. (Rev: BL 2/15/03)

1540 Young, Karen Romano. *Video* (6–12). 1999, Greenwillow $16.00 (0-688-16517-6). A multilayered story in which Janine confronts a flasher and gains the support of classmates who have been shunning her. (Rev: BL 10/1/99; HBG 4/00; SLJ 10/99)

1541 Young, Ronder Thomas. *Objects in Mirror* (7–10). 2002, Millbrook LB $22.90 (0-7613-2600-6). Grace, 16, feels uncertain of her own image as she juggles the demands of a difficult family and high school friends. (Rev: BL 5/1/02; HBG 10/02; VOYA 6/02)

1542 Yumoto, Kazumi. *The Letters* (8–12). 2002, Farrar $16.00 (0-374-34383-7). Attending the funeral of her former landlady proves cathartic for Chaiki, a troubled young adult looking back at her childhood. (Rev: BCCB 7–8/02; BL 4/1/02; HB 9–10/02; HBG 10/02; SLJ 5/02)

1543 Zach, Cheryl. *Dear Diary: Runaway* (7–12). 1995, Berkley paper $4.50 (0-425-15047-X). In diary form, young, pregnant Cassie tells how she and her lover, Seth, become runaways seeking a place that will give them shelter and security. (Rev: BL 1/1–15/96)

1544 Zalben, Jane Breskin. *Water from the Moon* (8–10). 1987, Random paper $4.99 (0-440-22855-7). Nicky Berstein, a high school sophomore, tries too hard to make friends and is hurt in the process. (Rev: BL 5/15/87; SLJ 5/87; VOYA 8/87)

1545 Zeises, Lara M. *Bringing Up the Bones* (7–12). 2002, Delacorte $12.95 (0-385-73001-2). Eighteen-year-old Bridget cannot cope with her grief when her best friend/boyfriend Benji dies in a car crash. (Rev: BL 11/15/02; HBG 3/03; SLJ 11/02; VOYA 12/02)

1546 Zindel, Bonnie, and Paul Zindel. *A Star for the Latecomer* (7–10). 1980, HarperCollins $12.95 (0-06-026847-6). When her mother dies, Brooke is freed of the need to pursue a dancing career.

1547 Zindel, Paul. *The Amazing and Death-Defying Diary of Eugene Dingman* (9–12). 1987, Harper-Collins LB $14.89 (0-06-026863-8); Bantam paper $4.50 (0-553-27768-5). An unhappy teenager is sent to a resort hotel to work as a busboy. (Rev: BL 10/15/87; BR 3–4/88; SLJ 10/87; VOYA 10/87)

1548 Zindel, Paul. *A Begonia for Miss Applebaum* (7–12). 1990, Bantam paper $4.99 (0-553-28765-6). Two unconventional teens take under their wings a favorite teacher who is dying of cancer. (Rev: BL 3/15/89; BR 11–12/89; SLJ 4/89)

1549 Zindel, Paul. *David and Della* (7–12). 1995, Bantam paper $4.50 (0-553-56727-6). High school playwright David hires Della — who pretends to be blind and to have studied under Lee Strasberg — to be his coach until he overcomes writer's block. (Rev: BL 12/1/93; SLJ 12/93; VOYA 2/94)

1550 Zindel, Paul. *I Never Loved Your Mind* (8–12). 1970, Bantam paper $4.50 (0-553-27323-X). Two dropouts working in a hospital together suffer the pangs of love and loss.

1551 Zindel, Paul. *My Darling, My Hamburger* (8–12). 1969, Bantam paper $4.99 (0-553-27324-8). Two young couples in love face life's complications including one girl's abortion.

1552 Zindel, Paul. *Pardon Me, You're Stepping on My Eyeball* (10–12). 1983, Bantam paper $4.50 (0-553-26690-X). Marsh Mallow and Edna Shinglebox form a friendship to help solve problems caused by the adults around them. Also use: *Harry and Hortense at Hormone High* (1984).

1553 Zindel, Paul. *The Pigman* (10–12). 1984, Bantam paper $5.50 (0-553-26599-7). Two teenagers must face the responsibility for causing the death of an old man they befriend. A sequel is *The Pigman's Legacy* (1984). (Rev: BL 10/15/88)

1554 Zolotow, Charlotte, ed. *Early Sorrow: Ten Stories of Youth* (8–12). 1986, HarperCollins $12.95 (0-06-026936-7). This excellent collection of 12 adult stories about growing up is a companion piece to *An Overpraised Season* (o.p.), another anthology about adolescence. (Rev: BL 10/1/86; BR 3–4/87; SLJ 1/87; VOYA 2/87)

1555 Zusak, Markus. *Getting the Girl* (9–12). 2003, Scholastic $16.95 (0-439-38949-6). Cameron is torn between an unattainable girl and his brother's girlfriend in this story of the dynamics of teenage attraction, a sequel to *Fighting Ruben Wolfe*. (Rev: BCCB 7–8/03; BL 5/15/03; HB 5–6/03; HBG 10/03; SLJ 4/03; VOYA 8/03)

World Affairs and Contemporary Problems

1556 Abelove, Joan. *Go and Come Back* (8–10). 1998, Puffin paper $5.99 (0-14-130694-7). The story of two female anthropologists studying a primitive Peruvian Indian village, written from the perspective of Alicia, one of the village teenagers. (Rev: BL 3/1/98; BR 1–2/99; SLJ 3/98*; VOYA 10/98)

1557 Anderson, Mary. *The Unsinkable Molly Malone* (7–10). 1991, Harcourt $16.95 (0-15-213801-3). Molly, 16, sells her collages outside New York's Metropolitan Museum, starts an art class for kids on welfare, and learns that her boyfriend is rich. (Rev: BL 11/15/91; SLJ 12/91)

1558 Bandele, Asha. *Daughter* (10–12). 2003, Scribner $23.00 (0-7432-1184-7). An African American mother grieves over the shooting of her college student daughter and remembers the similar fate of the girl's father. (Rev: BL 9/1/03)

1559 Barfoot, Joan. *Critical Injuries* (11–12). 2002, Counterpoint $25.00 (1-58243-208-2). A grievously injured women and her jailed teen assailant look back at their lives and at the impact of the incident; for mature teens. (Rev: BL 7/02)

1560 Beale, Fleur. *I Am Not Esther* (7–10). 2002, Hyperion $15.99 (0-7868-0845-4). The insidious nature of cults is clearly shown in this novel about a spirited New Zealand girl sent to live with her fanatical Uncle Caleb. (Rev: BCCB 12/02; BL 10/15/02; HB 1–2/03; HBG 3/03; SLJ 11/02; VOYA 2/03)

1561 Bloor, Edward. *Crusader* (9–12). 1999, Harcourt $17.00 (0-15-201944-8). A teenager discovers that the truth about her mother's death is connected to a violent video game called Crusader in this challenging and thought-provoking novel featuring troubled teens. (Rev: BL 11/15/99; HB 1–2/00; HBG 4/00; SLJ 12/99)

1562 Carbone, Elisa. *The Pack* (8–11). 2003, Viking $15.99 (0-670-03619-6). Teen outcasts Becky and Omar take an interest in an unusual new student, Akhil, and the three of them struggle to deal with another student's plan for a violent attack at their school. (Rev: BCCB 3/03; BL 2/15/03; HBG 4/04; SLJ 3/03; VOYA 4/03)

1563 Carvell, Marlene. *Who Will Tell My Brother?* (7–10). 2002, Hyperion $15.99 (0-7868-0827-6). In free-verse poetry, part-Mohawk high school senior Evan relates his efforts to rid his school of its Indian mascot. (Rev: BCCB 10/02; BL 7/02; HBG 3/03; SLJ 7/02; VOYA 6/02)

1564 Castaneda, Omar S. *Among the Volcanoes* (7–10). 1996, Bantam paper $4.50 (0-440-91118-4). Set in a remote Guatemalan village, this story is about a Mayan woodcutter's daughter, Isabel, who is caught between her respect for the old ways and her yearning for something more. (Rev: BL 5/15/91; SLJ 3/91)

1565 Clinton, Cathryn. *A Stone in My Hand* (6–12). 2002, Candlewick $15.99 (0-7636-1388-6). Eleven-year-old Maalak's father is killed in the violence of 1988 Gaza, and she must worry about her brother's future. (Rev: BL 9/15/02; HBG 3/03; SLJ 11/02*; VOYA 2/03)

1566 Coleman, Evelyn. *Born in Sin* (7–12). 2001, Simon & Schuster $16.00 (0-689-83833-6). Keisha

Wright, 14, has strong ambitions and is determined to escape the poverty, racism, and dangers of her life in the all-black projects. (Rev: BCCB 2/01; BL 2/15/01; HBG 10/01; SLJ 3/01; VOYA 4/01)

1567 Collins, Pat Lowery. *The Fattening Hut* (8–12). 2003, Houghton $16.00 (0-618-30955-1). Fourteen-year-old Helen sets off on a dangerous journey, running away from the tropical tribe that requires her to undergo female circumcision before her impending marriage. (Rev: BL 11/1/03; HBG 4/04; SLJ 11/03; VOYA 2/04)

1568 Covington, Dennis. *Lasso the Moon* (7–10). 1996, Bantam $20.95 (0-385-30991-0). After April and her divorced doctor father move to Saint Simons Island, April takes a liking to Fernando, an illegal alien from El Salvador being treated by her father. (Rev: BL 1/15/95; SLJ 3/95; VOYA 4/95)

1569 Eskilsen, Erik E. *The Last Mall Rat* (7–10). 2003, Houghton $15.00 (0-618-23417-9). Bored and penniless, 15-year-old Mitch agrees to harass rude shoppers. (Rev: BL 4/1/03; HBG 4/04; SLJ 6/03; VOYA 6/03)

1570 Flegg, Aubrey. *The Cinnamon Tree* (7–10). 2002, O'Brien paper $7.95 (0-86278-657-6). The horror of the injuries inflicted by landmines is brought to life in this story of a girl who loses a leg and goes on to teach others about the dangers of these weapons. (Rev: BL 8/02; SLJ 8/02)

1571 Gauthier, Gail. *Saving the Planet and Stuff* (8–10). 2003, Putnam $17.99 (0-399-23761-5). Office politics turn out to be an unexpected pleasure for 16-year-old Michael when he spends the summer working for an environmental magazine. (Rev: BCCB 9/03; BL 5/15/03; HB 7–8/03; HBG 10/03; SLJ 6/03; VOYA 6/03)

1572 Gillison, Samantha. *The Undiscovered Country* (10–12). 1998, Grove Atlantic $23.00 (0-8021-1627-2). An American couple and their daughter journey into the rain forests of New Guinea to do medical research and find that their lives, values, and relationships change. (Rev: BL 6/1–15/98; SLJ 3/99)

1573 Gordimer, Nadine. *My Son's Story* (10–12). 1990, Farrar $19.95 (0-374-21751-3). The story of the love between a dedicated black teacher and Hannah, a white activist, set in South Africa. (Rev: BL 9/15/90)

1574 Gordimer, Nadine. *Selected Stories* (10–12). 1983, Penguin paper $14.95 (0-14-006737-X). The men of the stories in this collection reflect the racial situation in South Africa.

1575 Halaby, Laila. *West of the Jordan* (10–12). 2003, Beacon paper $13.00 (0-8070-8359-3). Four Arab cousins — all young women — have been brought up in very different circumstances and have very different aspirations. (Rev: BL 6/1–15/03; SLJ 10/03)

1576 Hall, Lynn. *If Winter Comes* (7–10). 1986, Macmillan LB $17.00 (0-684-18575-X). Two teenagers spend what they believe to be their last weekend on earth because of the imminent threat of a nuclear war. (Rev: BL 6/1/86; SLJ 9/86; VOYA 8/86)

1577 Hecht, Julie. *The Unprofessionals* (11–12). 2003, Random $23.95 (1-4000-6174-1). In Julie Hecht's first novel, a world-weary photographer, nearing 50, finds solace in her friendship with a 19-year-old who, tragically, is addicted to heroin. This book is recommended for mature teens only. (Rev: BL 9/1/03*)

1578 Hentoff, Nat. *The Day They Came to Arrest the Book* (7–10). 1983, Dell paper $5.50 (0-440-91814-6). Some students at George Mason High think *Huckleberry Finn* is a racist book.

1579 Ho, Minfong. *Rice Without Rain* (7–12). 1990, Lothrop $16.99 (0-688-06355-1). Jinda, a 17-year-old girl, experiences personal tragedy and the awakening of love in this novel set during revolutionary times in Thailand during the 1970s. (Rev: BL 7/90; SLJ 9/90)

1580 Hobbet, Anastasia. *Pleasure of Believing* (10–12). 1997, Soho Pr. $24.00 (1-56947-085-5). When Muirie retreats to her aunt and uncle's ranch in Wyoming, she finds that her aunt is in conflict with her neighbors because she has converted the ranch into a bird hospital. (Rev: BL 2/15/97; SLJ 7/97)

1581 Hoffman, Nancy, and Florence Howe, eds. *Women Working: An Anthology of Stories and Poems* (10–12). Illus. 1979, Feminist Pr. paper $13.95 (0-912670-57-6). This collection of stories and poems explores the world of work as experienced by women.

1582 Hower, Edward. *A Garden of Demons* (10–12). 2003, Ontario Review $22.95 (0-86538-106-2). An evocative novel set in Sri Lanka that juxtaposes terrorist threats and environmental aspirations. (Rev: BL 1/1–15/03)

1583 James, Brian. *Tomorrow, Maybe* (7–12). 2003, Scholastic paper $6.99 (0-439-49035-9). Living a hard life on the streets of New York, 15-year-old Gretchen, aka Chan, finds a purpose when she takes charge of an 11-year-old in the same predicament. (Rev: LMC 10/03; SLJ 6/03; VOYA 8/03)

1584 Jicai, Feng. *Let One Hundred Flowers Bloom* (7–10). Trans. by Christopher Smith. 1996, Viking $13.99 (0-670-85805-6). A bleak story about a talented artisan in contemporary China whose life is destroyed when he is accused of counterrevolutionary behavior. (Rev: BL 4/15/96; SLJ 6/96)

1585 Keizer, Garret. *God of Beer* (8–12). 2002, HarperCollins LB $15.89 (0-06-029457-4). A group of high schoolers form an association, Students Undermining a Drunk Society, in an effort to change their community's attitudes toward alcohol. (Rev: BCCB 5/02; HB 5–6/02; HBG 10/02; SLJ 2/02; VOYA 4/02)

1586 Kemal, Yasher. *Memed, My Hawk* (10–12). 1993, HarperCollins paper $12.00 (0-00-217112-0). This tragic story, set in southern Turkey, takes place in an area where feudal conditions still exist.

1587 Koestler, Arthur. *Darkness at Noon* (10–12). Trans. by Daphne Hardy. 1984, Bantam paper $6.99 (0-553-26595-4). In this 1940 novel, life in a Soviet political prison is depicted as seen through the experiences of one inmate.

1588 Levitin, Sonia. *The Return* (6–10). 1987, Macmillan $16.00 (0-689-31309-8); Fawcett paper $5.99 (0-449-70280-4). Seen from the viewpoint of a teenage girl, this is the story of a group of African Jews who journey from Ethiopia to the Sudan to escape persecution. (Rev: BL 4/15/87; BR 11–12/87; SLJ 5/87; VOYA 6/87)

1589 Ludington, Max. *Tiger in a Trance* (11–12). 2003, Doubleday $24.00 (0-385-50704-6). An absorbing story of life, love, community, and drug use among fans of the Grateful Dead. (Rev: BL 8/03; SLJ 4/04)

1590 McDaniel, Lurlene. *Baby Alicia Is Dying* (8–10). 1993, Bantam paper $4.99 (0-553-29605-1). In an attempt to feel needed, Desi volunteers to care for HIV-positive babies and discovers a deep commitment in herself. (Rev: BL 10/1/93; SLJ 7/93; VOYA 8/93)

1591 McDonald, Janet. *Chill Wind* (7–12). 2002, Farrar $16.00 (0-374-39958-1). Nineteen-year-old Aisha is inventive and determined in her efforts to avoid workfare and still support herself and her two children. (Rev: BCCB 1/03; BL 9/1/02; HB 9–10/02; HBG 3/03; SLJ 11/02)

1592 Martin, Nora. *Perfect Snow* (8–12). 2002, Bloomsbury $16.95 (1-58234-788-3). Ben feels strong and confident when he participates in the violent intolerance of the local white supremacists until he meets Eden, a new — and Jewish — girl at school, in this novel set in a small Montana community. (Rev: BL 8/02; SLJ 9/02)

1593 Maynard, Joyce. *The Usual Rules* (10–12). 2003, St. Martin's $24.95 (0-312-24261-1). A teenage girl struggling to make sense of her mother's death on September 11 finds new hope when she goes to live with her father in California. (Rev: BL 1/1–15/03; SLJ 7/03; VOYA 6/03)

1594 Mazer, Norma Fox, and Harry Mazer. *Bright Days, Stupid Nights* (7–10). 1993, Bantam paper $3.50 (0-553-56253-3). Charts the course of four youths who are brought together for a summer newspaper internship. (Rev: BL 6/15/92; SLJ 7/92)

1595 Michener, James A. *Legacy* (10–12). 1987, Fawcett paper $6.99 (0-449-21641-1). A contemporary novel about an army officer involved with the Contras in Nicaragua. (Rev: BL 8/87)

1596 Neufeld, John. *A Small Civil War* (7–10). 1996, Simon & Schuster $16.00 (0-689-80770-8). A revised edition of the 1981 novel about 13-year-old Georgia and her fight against censorship when *The Grapes of Wrath* is challenged in her high school. (Rev: BL 10/15/96; BR 5–6/97; SLJ 11/96; VOYA 2/97)

1597 Oates, Joyce Carol. *Rape: A Love Story* (11–12). 2004, Carroll & Graf $16.00 (0-7867-1294-5). In this unflinching portrait of a brutal gang rape and its aftermath, Oates focuses on the traumatic effects of the assault on the victim's 12-year-old daughter, who was a witness; for mature teens. (Rev: BL 11/1/03)

1598 O'Connor, Edwin. *The Last Hurrah* (10–12). 1956, Little, Brown paper $14.00 (0-316-62659-7). An old-style politician who has been mayor of a large American city for about 40 years finds that his power is being challenged.

1599 Orenstein, Denise Gosliner. *Unseen Companion* (10–12). 2003, HarperCollins LB $16.89 (0-06-052057-4). Four Alaskan teenagers explore in first-person narratives the impact on their lives of the imprisonment of a boy of mixed race who hit a white teacher. (Rev: BCCB 11/03; BL 10/15/03*; SLJ 1/04; VOYA 12/03)

1600 Ozeki, Ruth. *All over Creation* (11–12). 2003, Viking $24.95 (0-670-03091-0). Family problems, fragile health, and environmental activism are major themes of this compelling novel that brings a renegade daughter — now mother of three — back to her Idaho hometown and the parents she fled from at the age of 14. (Rev: BL 2/1/03*)

1601 Paton, Alan. *Cry, the Beloved Country* (10–12). 1948, Macmillan $35.00 (0-684-15559-1). A black minister tries to save his son, accused of murder, in this touching novel set in South Africa.

1602 Paulsen, Gary. *Sentries* (8–12). 1986, Bradbury LB $17.00 (0-02-770100-X); Penguin paper $3.95 (0-317-62279-X). The stories of four different young people are left unresolved when they are all wiped out by a superbomb. (Rev: BL 5/1/86; SLJ 8/86; VOYA 8/86)

1603 Peck, Richard. *The Last Safe Place on Earth* (7–10). 1996, Bantam paper $5.50 (0-440-22007-6). Todd has a crush on Laura, who baby-sits for his sister, but he discovers that she's a fundamentalist Christian who brainwashes and terrifies the child by telling her about witches and devils. (Rev: BL 1/15/95; SLJ 4/95; VOYA 2/95)

1604 Pierre, DBC. *Vernon God Little* (11–12). 2003, Canongate $23.00 (1-84195-460-8). Vernon God Little is falsely accused of a shooting spree in this entertaining novel full of digs at America's culture and criminal system; for mature teens. (Rev: BL 9/1/03)

1605 Prose, Francine. *After* (8–10). 2003, Harper-Collins LB $16.89 (0-06-008082-5). A school district hires an over-the-top crisis counselor to impose order in the name of safety after a massacre at a nearby high school. (Rev: HB 5–6/03; HBG 10/03; SLJ 5/03; VOYA 6/03)

1606 Rand, Ayn. *Anthem* (10–12). 1999, Plume paper $13.95 (0-452-28125-3). A short novel set in the future about an individual fighting a powerful collective state.

1607 Rand, Ayn. *Atlas Shrugged* (10–12). 1957, Random $35.00 (0-394-41576-0); NAL paper $6.95 (0-451-15748-6). In an age where everyone looks to the state for guidance and protection, one man wants to go it alone.

1608 Rochman, Hazel, ed. *Somehow Tenderness Survives: Stories of Southern Africa* (8–12). 1988, HarperCollins $12.95 (0-06-025022-4); paper $5.99 (0-06-447063-6). Ten stories by such writers as Nadine Gordimer about growing up in South Africa. (Rev: BL 8/88; BR 5–6/89; SLJ 12/88; VOYA 12/88)

1609 Ruby, Lois. *Skin Deep* (8–12). 1994, Scholastic paper $14.95 (0-590-47699-8). Dan, the frustrated new kid in town, falls in love with popular senior Laurel, but he destroys their relationship when he joins a neo-Nazi skinhead group. (Rev: BL 11/15/94*; SLJ 3/95; VOYA 12/94)

1610 Scott, Jefferson. *Operation Firebrand* (10–12). 2002, Barbour paper $11.99 (1-58660-586-0). Although it sometimes strains credulity, this is an absorbing tale of a born-again SEAL sniper who leaves the U.S. Navy to fight the enemy with non-lethal weapons. (Rev: BL 1/1–15/03)

1611 Scott, Paul. *Staying On* (10–12). 1979, Avon paper $3.50 (0-380-46045-9). Mr. and Mrs. Smalley decide to stay on in India after the country gains independence.

1612 Shamsie, Kamila. *Kartography* (11–12). 2003, Harcourt $24.00 (0-15-101010-2). For mature teen readers, this is a story of young love against a background of violence in war-torn Karachi. (Rev: BL 8/03)

1613 Silvey, Diane. *Raven's Flight* (7–12). 2001, Raincoast paper $6.95 (1-55192-344-0). When her sister's letters home suddenly stop, 15-year-old Raven sets off in pursuit, only to confront the horrors of drug addiction. (Rev: SLJ 12/01)

1614 Solzhenitsyn, Alexander. *One Day in the Life of Ivan Denisovich* (10–12). 1984, Bantam paper $4.99 (0-553-24777-8). A harrowing short novel about life in a Stalinist labor camp in Siberia.

1615 Staples, Suzanne F. *Shabanu: Daughter of the Wind* (7–10). 1989, Knopf LB $18.99 (0-394-94815-7). The story of a young girl coming-of-age in a family living in a desert region of Pakistan. (Rev: BL 10/1/89; SLJ 11/89; VOYA 4/90)

1616 Steinbeck, John. *Tortilla Flat* (10–12). 1962, Penguin paper $6.95 (0-14-004240-7). The life of some poor but carefree friends in Monterey, California, during the 1930s.

1617 Strasser, Todd. *Give a Boy a Gun* (6–12). 2000, Simon & Schuster $16.00 (0-689-81112-8). The story of Gary and Brendan, who go on a shooting spree at their school, is revealed through the voices of those who knew them — parents, friends, teachers, and classmates. (Rev: BL 10/1/00; HBG 3/01; SLJ 9/00)

1618 Styron, William. *Sophie's Choice* (10–12). 1979, Random $29.95 (0-394-46109-6). In a Jewish boarding house in Brooklyn, Sophie, a survivor of Auschwitz, meets two men who will change her life.

1619 Taylor, Theodore. *The Bomb* (7–10). 1995, Harcourt $15.00 (0-15-200867-5). In this tale — based on Taylor's memory of a visit to Bikini Atoll as it was being prepared for testing of the atomic bomb — a 14-year-old boy suspects that the Americans are less than honest about their plans. (Rev: BL 10/1/95*; SLJ 12/95; VOYA 4/96)

1620 Temple, Frances. *Grab Hands and Run* (6–12). 1993, Orchard LB $16.99 (0-531-08630-5). Jacinto opposes the oppressive government of El Salvador. When he disappears, his wife, Paloma, and their son, 12-year-old Felipe, try to escape to freedom in Canada. (Rev: BL 5/1/93*; SLJ 4/93*)

1621 Temple, Frances. *Tonight, by Sea* (6–10). 1995, Orchard LB $16.99 (0-531-08749-2). A docunovel about Haitian boat people who struggle for social justice and attempt harrowing escapes to freedom. (Rev: BL 3/15/95; SLJ 4/95)

1622 Trice, Dawn Turner. *Only Twice I've Wished for Heaven* (10–12). 1996, Crown $23.00 (0-517-70428-5). Prejudice, child abuse, friendship, pride, and poverty are some of the themes in this powerful novel about a wealthy African American community pitted against the poor, slum-infested community next door. (Rev: BL 11/15/96; SLJ 6/97)

1623 Trumbo, Dalton. *Johnny Got his Gun* (10–12). 1970, Bantam paper $6.99 (0-553-27432-5). This anti-war novel is also a moving tribute to the human instinct to survive.

1624 Williams-Garcia, Rita. *Every Time a Rainbow Dies* (9–12). 2001, HarperCollins LB $15.89 (0-06-029202-4). Thulani, a 16-year-old boy, becomes obsessed with fellow immigrant Ysa after seeing her being raped in this story set in Brooklyn. (Rev: BCCB 2/01; BL 12/15/00; HB 3–4/01*; HBG 10/01; SLJ 2/01; VOYA 6/01)

1625 Zephaniah, Benjamin. *Refugee Boy* (8–12). 2002, Bloomsbury $15.95 (1-58234-763-8). Abandoned in England by a father who believes he will be safer there, Alem — the son of an Eritrean mother and an Ethiopian father — struggles to cope with the judicial and social system as he seeks a new home. (Rev: BCCB 10/02; BL 9/1/02; SLJ 10/02)

Fantasy

1626 Aamodt, Donald. *A Name to Conjure With* (9–12). 1989, Avon paper $3.50 (0-380-75137-2). A reluctant participant embarks on a quest with a bumbling sorcerer. (Rev: BL 8/89; VOYA 10/89)

1627 Abbey, Lynn. *Behind Time* (10–12). 2001, Berkley paper $6.50 (0-441-00831-3). Emma Merrigan, who has received magical powers from her mother, must now rescue her from a hellish captivity. (Rev: BL 6/1–15/01; VOYA 12/01)

1628 Abbey, Lynn. *Sanctuary: An Epic Novel of Thieves' World* (11–12). Series: Thieves' World. 2002, Tor $27.95 (0-312-87517-7). A rich saga full of intrigue about the city of Sanctuary and efforts to guard its secrets; for mature teens. (Rev: BL 4/15/02)

1629 Abbey, Lynn, ed. *Turning Points* (10–12). Series: Thieves' World. 2002, Tor $25.95 (0-312-87491-X). The city featured in *Sanctuary* (2002) and its people are the focus of this stand-alone volume of short stories. (Rev: BL 11/15/02)

1630 Abbey, Lynn. *Unicorn and Dragon* (10–12). Illus. 1988, Avon paper $3.50 (0-380-75567-X). A fantasy set in 11th-century England that pits Druid magic against Norman sorcery. (Rev: SLJ 6/87)

1631 Adams, Richard. *The Plague Dogs* (10–12). 1986, Fawcett paper $5.95 (0-449-21182-7). For better readers, this is a novel about two dogs that flee from a research center.

1632 Adams, Richard. *Tales from Watership Down* (9–12). 1996, Knopf $23.00 (0-679-45125-0). Familiar animal characters from the author's *Watership Down* reappear in these delightful stories for animal fantasy fans. (Rev: BR 5–6/97; SLJ 1/97)

1633 Adams, Richard. *Watership Down* (7–12). Illus. 1974, Macmillan $40.00 (0-02-700030-3); Avon paper $12.00 (0-380-00428-3). Rabbits, frightened by the coming destruction of their warren, journey across the English downs in search of a new home.

1634 Aidinoff, Elsie V. *The Garden* (9–12). 2004, HarperTempest $15.99 (0-06-055606-4). This is a fine reworking of the Garden of Eden story complete with the Serpent and conversations with God. (Rev: BL 3/1/04; HB 7–8/04; SLJ 8/04)

1635 Almond, David. *Secret Heart* (6–10). 2002, Delacorte LB $17.99 (0-385-90065-1). An unhappy stutterer's dreams about a tiger coincide with the arrival of a seedy circus that has strange appeal for him, especially the girl who sees in the boy a heart of courage, in this gripping blend of fantasy and realism. (Rev: BCCB 12/02; BL 10/1/02; HB 11–12/02; HBG 3/03; SLJ 10/02; VOYA 12/02)

1636 Anderson, K. J. *Captain Nemo: The Fantastic History of a Dark Genius* (10–12). 2002, Pocket $23.00 (0-7434-4406-X). In this tribute to Jules Verne, Anderson takes the reader on action-packed adventures that he attributes to one Andre Nemo. (Rev: BL 1/1–15/02)

1637 Anthony, Mark. *Beyond the Pale* (9–12). 1998, Bantam paper $14.95 (0-553-37955-0). Two strangers find themselves in the land of Eldh, a medieval-like fantasy world, where they each discover their hidden magical powers. (Rev: VOYA 4/99)

1638 Anthony, Mark. *The Dark Remains* (10–12). Series: Last Rune. 2001, Bantam paper $14.95 (0-553-38101-6). People from Earth are being transported to a magical otherworld in this well-written fantasy. (Rev: BL 3/1/01; VOYA 10/01)

1639 Anthony, Piers. *Being a Green Mother* (10–12). 1987, Ballantine paper $5.95 (0-345-32223-1). In this concluding part of the five-book series Incarnations of Immortality, Orb falls in love with a man who might be Satan. (Rev: BL 10/15/87; VOYA 6/88)

1640 Anthony, Piers. *The Dastard* (10–12). Series: Xanth. 2000, Tor $24.95 (0-312-86900-2). In this Xanth story for better readers, Anomy sells his soul for the ability to "unhappen" events. (Rev: BL 10/15/00; VOYA 2/01)

1641 Anthony, Piers. *Demons Don't Dream* (9–12). Series: Xanth Saga. 1994, Tor paper $5.99 (0-8125-3483-2). An interactive video game transports a 16-year-old boy to the infamous land of Xanth. (Rev: BL 12/15/92; VOYA 8/93)

1642 Anthony, Piers. *DoOon Mode* (10–12). Series: Mode. 2001, Tor $27.95 (0-312-87463-4). A troubled youngster named Colleen lives her life in a series of alternate realities in this installment of the Mode series. (Rev: BL 3/1/01)

1643 Anthony, Piers. *Faun and Games* (9–12). 1997, St. Martin's $23.95 (0-312-86162-1). In this Xanth novel, Forrest Faun consults Good Magician Humfrey to find a suitable creature to adopt his neighboring tree. (Rev: BL 9/1/97; VOYA 4/98)

1644 Anthony, Piers. *For Love of Evil* (10–12). 1990, Avon paper $6.99 (0-380-75285-9). The penultimate volume (number 6) of the Incarnations of Immortality series. In this episode Satan is the protagonist. (Rev: BL 9/1/88)

1645 Anthony, Piers. *Geis of the Gargoyle* (9–12). Series: Xanth Saga. 1995, Tor $22.95 (0-312-85391-2). An environmentally conscious gargoyle searches for a spell to purify a polluted river. (Rev: BL 1/1/95)

1646 Anthony, Piers. *Golem in the Gears* (10–12). 1986, Ballantine paper $6.99 (0-345-31886-2). In this ninth Xanth novel, Grundy the Golem sets out to find the lost dragon of Princess Ivy. (Rev: BL 2/15/86; SLJ 5/86; VOYA 6/86)

1647 Anthony, Piers. *Man from Mundania* (9–12). 1989, Avon paper $5.99 (0-380-75289-1). A Xanth novel that completes the trilogy begun with *Vale of the Vole* and continued in *Heaven Cent*. (Rev: BL 9/89; VOYA 12/89)

1648 Anthony, Piers. *Roc and a Hard Place* (9–12). Series: Xanth Saga. 1995, Tor $23.95 (0-312-85392-0). Demoness Metria must find a jury to acquit Roxanne Roc of bizarre crimes. (Rev: BL 9/1/95; VOYA 4/96)

1649 Anthony, Piers. *A Spell for Chameleon* (10–12). 1987, Ballantine paper $6.99 (0-345-34753-6). This is the introductory Xanth novel where the reader first meets the young hero Bink and his quest to find magical powers. Two others in this extensive series are: *Castle Roogna* and *The Source of Magic* (both 1987).

1650 Anthony, Piers. *Swell Foop* (10–12). Series: Xanth. 2001, Tor $24.95 (0-312-86906-1). In this, the 25th book in the recommended Xanth series, Demon Earth has disappeared, which means that gravity will disappear from Earth and Xanth. The 26th installment is *Up in a Heaval* (2002). (Rev: BL 10/1/01; SLJ 5/02)

1651 Anthony, Piers. *Wielding a Red Sword* (10–12). 1987, Ballantine paper $6.99 (0-345-32221-5). In the fourth book of the Incarnations of Immortality series, Mym is forced to do Satan's work and finds it impossible to stop. For better readers. (Rev: BL 9/1/86)

1652 Anthony, Piers. *With a Tangled Skein* (10–12). 1985, Ballantine paper $6.99 (0-345-31885-4). In this volume in the Incarnations of Immortality series, Niobe sets out to avenge her lover's death. An earlier volume was *On a Pale Horse* (1986).

1653 Anthony, Piers. *Zombie Lover* (9–12). 1998, Tor $23.95 (0-312-86690-9). In this Xanth novel, 15-year-old Breanna doesn't want to marry the Zombie Xeth and sets out with friends to find another bride for him, learning valuable lessons about prejudice, love, and growing up along the way. (Rev: BL 9/15/98; VOYA 4/99)

1654 Anthony, Piers, and Mercedes Lackey. *If I Pay Thee Not in Gold* (9–12). 1993, Simon & Schuster $20.00 (0-671-72175-5). Xylina must retrieve a powerful shard of crystal from a distant, dangerous land. (Rev: BL 4/15/93; VOYA 12/93)

1655 Ashley, Mike, ed. *The Chronicles of the Holy Grail* (10–12). 1996, Carroll & Graf paper $12.95 (0-7867-0363-6). A collection of 12 stories that deal with the quest for the Holy Grail. (Rev: VOYA 4/97)

1656 Ashley, Mike, ed. *The Mammoth Book of Fantasy* (9–12). Series: Mammoth. 2001, Carroll & Graf paper $11.95 (0-7867-0917-0). From Victorian authors like George Macdonald to present-day masters, this is an excellent collection of thrilling fantasies and a fine overview of the genre. (Rev: BL 10/1/01)

1657 Ashley, Mike, ed. *The Merlin Chronicles* (10–12). 1995, Carroll & Graf paper $12.95 (0-7867-0275-3). A collection of Arthurian stories by fantasy authors like Jane Yolan, Marion Zimmer Bradley, and Tanith Lee. (Rev: VOYA 6/96)

1658 Asprin, Robert. *Myth Conception* (10–12). 1986, Ace paper $5.99 (0-441-55521-7). An apprentice magician and his friends are pitted against an army of invaders.

1659 Asprin, Robert, and Jody Lynn Nye. *Myth Alliances* (10–12). Series: Myth Adventures. 2003, Meisha Merlin $25.00 (1-59222-008-8); paper $14.00 (1-59222-009-6). Skeev the Wizard and his sidekicks help the Wuhses get rid of a band of female Pervects in a rollicking spoof of fashion and marketing. (Rev: BL 9/1/03)

1660 Atwater-Rhodes, Amelia. *Hawksong* (7–10). 2003, Delacorte $9.95 (0-385-73071-3). A gripping fantasy about two young leaders who seek to end the long war between their peoples — avian shapeshifters and serpent shapeshifters — and are prepared to consider marriage for the sake of peace. (Rev: HBG 4/04; SLJ 8/03*; VOYA 6/03)

1661 Atwater-Rhodes, Amelia. *Shattered Mirror* (6–10). 2001, Delacorte $9.95 (0-385-32793-5). A story full of suspense about a young vampire hunter, Sarah Tigress Vida, who finds there are two vampires in her high school class, one of whom is very attractive. (Rev: BCCB 10/01; BL 9/1/01; HBG 3/02; SLJ 9/01; VOYA 12/01)

1662 Audley, Anselm. *Heresy* (10–12). 2001, Pocket $25.00 (0-7434-2738-6). Young Cathan's life becomes complicated by the discovery of enough iron in the country of Lepidor to provide prosperity for all. (Rev: BL 9/1/01)

1663 Avi. *The Man Who Was Poe* (7–10). 1991, Avon paper $5.99 (0-380-71192-3). When Edmund goes out to search for his missing mother and sister, he encounters Edgar Allan Poe in disguise as detective Auguste Dupin. (Rev: BL 10/1/89; BR 5–6/90; SLJ 9/89; VOYA 2/90)

1664 Bach, Richard. *Jonathan Livingston Seagull* (10–12). 1970, Macmillan $20.00 (0-02-504540-7); Avon paper $5.99 (0-380-01286-3). Because of his unusual love of flying, Jonathan is treated as an outsider.

1665 Baker, Kage. *Mendoza in Hollywood* (10–12). 2000, Harcourt $23.00 (0-15-100448-X). The immortal Mendoza, heroine of other fantastic epics, finds herself in frontier Los Angeles surrounded by such types as a 1,000-year-old Norseman, a teen-aged rare-bird enthusiastic, and a tall and handsome Englishman. (Rev: BL 2/1/00)

1666 Ball, Margaret. *No Earthly Sunne* (9–12). 1994, Baen paper $5.99 (0-671-87633-3). A new version of the classic fantasy concerning the rescue of a mortal from the land of faerie. (Rev: BL 12/15/94; VOYA 5/95)

1667 Ball, Margaret. *The Shadow Gate* (9–12). 1991, Baen paper $5.99 (0-671-72032-5). A young secretary is drawn into a magical world where she is hailed as a long-exiled queen. (Rev: BL 1/1/91; SLJ 9/91)

1668 Banks, Lynne Reid. *Melusine* (8–12). 1997, Avon paper $4.99 (0-380-79135-8). While staying with his family in an old French chateau, Roger discovers Melusine, a supernatural creature that is half woman and half snake. (Rev: BL 10/1/89; SLJ 11/89; VOYA 2/90)

1669 Barker, Clive. *Abarat* (7–12). Illus. 2002, HarperCollins $24.99 (0-06-028092-1). Bored teen Candy Quackenbush is carried away to a strange and magical world called Abarat and finds herself at the center of a struggle between good and evil in this novel enhanced by full-color art. (Rev: BCCB 3/03; BL 9/1/02; HBG 10/03; SLJ 10/02)

1670 Barnes, Steven. *Lion's Blood* (11–12). 2002, Warner $24.95 (0-446-52668-1). A boy is sold into slavery in an alternate 19th-century world in which Africa is the colonial power; for mature teens. (Rev: BL 1/1–15/02)

1671 Barrett, Neal. *The Treachery of Kings* (10–12). 2001, Bantam paper $6.50 (0-553-58196-1). Among the strange characters in this fantasy are the Newlies, animals who have become humans, and a king who must imitate the sleep of the dead for months at a time. (Rev: BL 7/01; VOYA 6/02)

1672 Barron, T. A. *The Fires of Merlin* (7–10). Illus. Series: Lost Years of Merlin. 1998, Putnam $19.99 (0-399-23020-3). A complex sequel to *The Seven Songs of Merlin,* in which young Merlin once again faces the threat of the dragon Valdearg, who is preparing to conquer the land of Fincayra. (Rev: BL 9/1/98; BR 5–6/99; HBG 3/99; SLJ 3/99; VOYA 2/99)

1673 Barron, T. A. *The Lost Years of Merlin* (7–10). Series: Lost Years of Merlin. 1996, Putnam $19.99 (0-399-23018-1). The author has created a magical land populated by remarkable creatures in this first book of a trilogy about the early years of the magician Merlin. (Rev: BL 9/1/96; BR 3–4/97; SLJ 9/96; VOYA 10/96)

1674 Barron, T. A. *The Mirror of Merlin* (7–10). Series: Lost Years of Merlin. 1999, Putnam $19.99 (0-399-23455-1). Young Merlin faces a deadly disease and confronts his future self as he continues his dangerous search for his sword. (Rev: BL 10/1/99; HBG 4/00; SLJ 10/99; VOYA 2/00)

1675 Barron, T. A. *The Seven Songs of Merlin* (7–10). Series: Lost Years of Merlin. 1997, Putnam $19.99 (0-399-23019-X). In this sequel to *The Lost Years of Merlin,* Emrys, who will become Merlin, must travel to the Otherworld to save his mother who has been poisoned. (Rev: BL 9/1/97; HBG 3/98; SLJ 9/97)

1676 Barron, T. A. *The Wings of Merlin* (7–10). Series: Lost Years of Merlin. 2000, Philomel $19.99 (0-399-23456-X). In this, the concluding volume of the saga, Merlin faces his most difficult decision. (Rev: BL 10/1/00; HBG 3/01; SLJ 11/00; VOYA 12/00)

1677 Bass, L. G. *Sign of the Qin* (7–10). 2004, Hyperion $17.99 (0-7868-1918-9). This, the first volume of a proposed trilogy, draws on the myths and legends of China in this classic fantasy of good versus evil. (Rev: BL 4/15/04; HB 7–8/04; SLJ 4/04; VOYA 6/04)

1678 Beagle, Peter S. *A Dance for Emilia* (10–12). 2000, Penguin $14.95 (0-451-45800-1). An unusual story about how the spirit of a dead man returns through Millamant, his cat. (Rev: BL 8/00; VOYA 2/01)

1679 Beagle, Peter S. *A Fine and Private Place* (10–12). 1992, NAL paper $14.95 (0-451-45096-5). An unusual fantasy about an old man, a graveyard, and the ghosts he befriends there.

1680 Beagle, Peter S. *The Folk of the Air* (10–12). 1988, Ballantine paper $4.50 (0-345-34699-8). For better readers, a story of how role-playing at being medieval characters leads to unleashing a power involving black magic. (Rev: BL 11/1/86)

1681 Beagle, Peter S. *Giant Bones* (10–12). 1997, Roc paper $14.95 (0-451-45651-3). A fine collection of six novellas, including one in which a magician is forced by a wicked queen to teach her his secrets so she can take over the world. (Rev: BL 7/97; VOYA 10/97)

1682 Beagle, Peter S. *The Last Unicorn* (9–12). 1991, NAL paper $13.95 (0-451-45052-3). A beautiful unicorn sets off to find others of her species.

1683 Bell, Clare E. *Ratha's Challenge* (6–12). 1994, Macmillan paper $16.95 (0-689-50586-8). When a tribe of prehistoric cats faces challenges to survival, their leader, Ratha, hopes to domesticate the tusked face-tails to ensure a steady food supply. (Rev: BL 1/1/95; SLJ 1/95; VOYA 5/95)

1684 Bell, Hilari. *Flame* (6–10). Series: Book of Sorahb. 2003, Simon & Schuster $16.95 (0-689-

85413-7). Three young people — Jiaan, Soraya, and Kavi — play important roles in the country of Farsala's efforts to repel the Hrum in this first installment of a series that draws on Persian legends. (Rev: BL 9/1/03*; HB 9–10/03; HBG 4/04; SLJ 11/03*; VOYA 10/03)

1685 Bell, Hilari. *The Goblin Wood* (6–10). 2003, HarperCollins LB $17.89 (0-06-051372-1). A young hedgewitch befriends a band of goblins, and with them battles the evil Hierarchy in this novel that blends fantasy, intrigue, and romance. (Rev: BL 6/1–15/03; HB 5–6/03; HBG 10/03; SLJ 7/03; VOYA 8/03)

1686 Bell, Jadrien. A.D. *999* (10–12). 1999, Ace paper $5.99 (0-441-00673-6). Near the end of the first millennium, a one-armed monk and a pagan woman are joined in a battle against evil by real and mythic creatures. (Rev: VOYA 2/00)

1687 Bemmann, Hans. *The Stone and the Flute* (10–12). Trans. by Anthea Bell. 1987, Penguin paper $14.95 (0-14-007445-7). A lengthy book about young Listener and his quest for self-fulfillment. (Rev: BL 3/1/87)

1688 Benet, Stephen Vincent. *The Devil and Daniel Webster* (10–12). 1990, Creative Editions LB $13.95 (0-88682-295-5). This classic short novel is a variation on the Faust legend, this time set in New Hampshire.

1689 Benjamin, Curt. *The Prince of Dreams* (10–12). 2002, DAW $23.95 (0-7564-0089-0). Llesho, who is coming to grips with his powers, struggles to free his brothers and his land of Thebin in this sequel to *The Prince of Shadows* (2001). (Rev: BL 9/15/02)

1690 Bennett, Cherie. *Love Never Dies* (7–10). Series: Teen Angels. 1996, Avon paper $3.99 (0-380-78248-0). In this fantasy, a teen angel is sent back to earth to help a rock star bent on self-destruction. (Rev: VOYA 6/96)

1691 Benson, Ann. *The Plague Tales* (10–12). 1997, Delacorte $23.95 (0-385-31651-8). Two parallel tales are told, one about bubonic plague fighters in 14th-century England and the other concerning a deadly epidemic in 2005. (Rev: BL 4/15/97; SLJ 10/97)

1692 Berg, Carol. *Song of the Beast* (11–12). 2003, NAL paper $6.99 (0-451-45923-7). A musician emerges from a long jail sentence determined to discover the reason for his imprisonment in this appealing fantasy with a Celtic flair. (Rev: BL 5/15/03)

1693 Berry, Liz. *The China Garden* (8–12). 1996, HarperCollins paper $6.99 (0-380-73228-9). Mysterious occurrences involving villagers who appear to know Clare and a handsome young man on a motorcycle happen when she accompanies her mother to an estate named Ravensmere. (Rev: BL 3/15/96; BR 9–10/96; SLJ 5/96; VOYA 6/96)

1694 Bisson, Terry. *The Pickup Artist* (10–12). 2001, Tor $22.95 (0-312-87403-0). In this fantasy for mature readers, set in a time when art of all types is being seized by the authorities, Hank Shapiro must go underground to hear an old Hank Williams record. (Rev: BL 3/15/01*)

1695 Bisson, Terry. *Talking Man* (10–12). 1987, Avon paper $2.95 (0-380-75141-0). For better readers, this is a fantasy involving godlike creatures and their relations with humans. (Rev: BL 10/1/86)

1696 Black, Holly. *Tithe: A Modern Faerie Tale* (8–12). 2002, Simon & Schuster $16.95 (0-689-84924-9). Sixteen-year-old Kaye's adventures include rescuing a knight, Roiben, and being caught up in the battles between faerie kingdoms. (Rev: BL 2/15/03; HBG 3/03; SLJ 10/02)

1697 Block, Francesca L. *Dangerous Angels* (9–12). Series: Weetzie Bat. 1998, HarperCollins $12.00 (0-06-440697-0). A collection of five Weetzie Bat books: dark, modern fairy tales set in Los Angeles. (Rev: BL 10/1/98)

1698 Block, Francesca L. *I Was a Teenage Fairy* (8–12). 1998, HarperCollins LB $14.89 (0-06-027748-3). Barbie Marks, at 16 a successful model, sorts herself out with the help of a fairy named Mab, after her father leaves and she is molested by a photographer. (Rev: BL 10/15/98; HB 11–12/98; HBG 3/99; SLJ 12/98*; VOYA 10/98)

1699 Block, Francesca L. *Missing Angel Juan* (8–12). Series: Weetzie Bat. 1993, HarperCollins $14.89 (0-06-023007-X). Witch Baby, aided by her grandfather's ghost, roams New York City looking for Angel Juan, who's left her behind to play music on the city streets. (Rev: BL 10/15/93; SLJ 10/93*; VOYA 12/93)

1700 Botkin, Gleb. *Lost Tales: Stories for the Tsar's Children* (7–12). Trans. from Russian by Masha Tolstoya Sarandinaki. Illus. 1996, Random $12.99 (0-679-45142-0). This book contains three fantasies about a heroic bear who works to restore a monarch to his throne. They were written by the personal physician to Tsar Nicholas II and illustrated by his son to amuse the royal children held captive during the Russian Revolution. (Rev: SLJ 7/97)

1701 Bradbury, Ray. *A Graveyard for Lunatics* (10–12). 1990, Knopf $24.50 (0-394-57877-5). The real and the imaginary, the past and the present, all mingle in this fantasy set in a Hollywood back lot. (Rev: SLJ 12/90)

1702 Bradbury, Ray. *The Halloween Tree* (7–12). 1972, Knopf $19.95 (0-394-82409-1). Nine boys discover the true meaning — and horror — of Halloween.

1703 Bradbury, Ray. *The Illustrated Man* (7–12). 1990, Bantam paper $7.50 (0-553-27449-X). A tattooed man tells a story for each of his tattoos.

1704 Bradbury, Ray. *Something Wicked This Way Comes* (9–12). 1983, Bantam paper $5.50 (0-553-28032-5). This tale tells what happens after "The Pandemonium Shadow Show" plays in a small town.

1705 Bradbury, Ray. *The Toynbee Convector* (10–12). 1988, Knopf $17.95 (0-394-54703-9). A new collection of short stories that cover such areas as fantasy, horror, and science fiction. (Rev: BL 5/1/88; BR 1–2/89)

1706 Bradley, Marion Zimmer. *City of Sorcery* (10–12). 1984, DAW paper $6.99 (0-88677-332-6). This novel in the Darkover series traces the quest of Magdalen Lorne.

1707 Bradley, Marion Zimmer. *The Firebrand* (10–12). 1991, Pocket paper $6.99 (0-671-74406-2). A retelling of this fantasy of events concerned with the Trojan War by the author of *Mists of Avalon*. (Rev: BL 9/15/87)

1708 Bradley, Marion Zimmer. *Ghostlight* (10–12). 1995, Tor $22.95 (0-312-85881-7). In this contemporary fantasy, parapsychologist Truth Jourdemayne researches the life of her father, the leader of an occult group, and visits a 19th-century estate, Shadow's Gate, where she makes discoveries about her family, the death of her mother during an occult ritual, and ghosts of the past, while trying to elude evil spirits of the present. (Rev: BL 9/1/95; VOYA 4/96)

1709 Bradley, Marion Zimmer. *The Gratitude of Kings* (9–12). 1997, NAL paper $14.95 (0-451-45641-6). When magician/minstrel Lythande sees the bride-to-be of Lord Tashgan, she senses that magic is afoot. (Rev: VOYA 4/98)

1710 Bradley, Marion Zimmer. *Hawkmistress!* (10–12). 1982, DAW paper $5.99 (0-88677-239-7). A Darkover novel about Romilly, a girl who has special abilities to communicate with hawks and horses.

1711 Bradley, Marion Zimmer. *The Mists of Avalon* (9–12). 2000, Ballantine $30.00 (0-345-44118-4); paper $16.95 (0-345-35049-9). A popular retelling of the Arthurian legend with a focus on Morgan le Fay, also known as Morgaine.

1712 Bradley, Marion Zimmer. *Sword of Chaos* (10–12). 1982, DAW paper $3.50 (0-88677-172-2). This anthology of Darkover stories contains short fantasies by Zimmer and other writers using her locale.

1713 Bradley, Marion Zimmer, and Rachel E. Holmen, eds. *Sword and Sorceress XIV* (9–12). 1997, DAW paper $5.99 (0-88677-741-0). This edition of this annual collection of fantasy stories contains a variety of locales and mostly female-centered themes. (Rev: VOYA 2/98)

1714 Bradley, Marion Zimmer, and Diana L. Paxson. *Priestess of Avalon* (9–12). 2001, Viking $24.95 (0-670-91023-6). This prequel to *The Mists of Avalon* (1982) tells how Eilan, a priestess for the goddess at Avalon, later becomes the mother of Constantine, the first Christian emperor of Rome. (Rev: BL 4/15/01*; VOYA 2/02)

1715 Bradley, Marion Zimmer, and Deborah J. Ross. *The Fall of Neskaya* (10–12). Series: Darkover. 2001, DAW $24.95 (0-7564-0034-1). In this Darkover novel, many are aware that young Coryn might have the talent and power to bring down the reigning dynasty. (Rev: BL 7/01; VOYA 4/02)

1716 Bradshaw, Gillian. *Dangerous Notes* (11–12). 2002, Severn $26.99 (0-7278-5757-6). Val's talent as a musician is threatened when she is arrested and must undergo "risk-assessment testing" because of the brain regeneration treatment she received as a child; for mature teens. (Rev: BL 1/1–15/02)

1717 Brandon, Paul. *Swim the Moon* (10–12). 2001, Tor $25.95 (0-312-87794-3). Mystery, romance, and ghost fantasy mix in this tale, which begins when Richard meets the strange and beautiful Ailish on a beach one night. (Rev: BL 9/1/01)

1718 Bray, Libby. *A Great and Terrible Beauty* (8–12). 2003, Delacorte LB $17.99 (0-385-90161-5). Gemma, a troubled student in London, learns to control her visions and enter the Realms, a place of magic, in this multilayered novel that combines fantasy, mystery, and romance with a look at 19th-century manners. (Rev: BL 11/15/03; SLJ 2/04; VOYA 4/04)

1719 Bray, Patricia. *Devlin's Luck* (10–12). 2002, Bantam paper $5.99 (0-553-58475-8). Convinced he has nothing left to live for, Devlin Stonehand happily takes on the dangerous responsibilities of defending the kingdom as the Chosen One. (Rev: BL 5/1/02; VOYA 8/02)

1720 Brennan, Noel-Anne. *The Sword of the Land* (10–12). 2003, Berkley paper $6.99 (0-441-01031-8). Rilsin must decide whether to renege on a promise in order to save her people from the selfish rule of her cousin Sithli. (Rev: BL 2/15/03)

1721 Briggs, Patricia. *Dragon Blood* (10–12). 2003, Berkley paper $6.99 (0-441-01008-3). In this sequel to *Dragon Bones,* protagonist Ward of Hurog, aided and abetted by his companion Oreg, a dragon, struggles to foil the nefarious plans of King Jakoven. (Rev: BL 1/1–15/03; VOYA 6/03)

1722 Britain, Kristin. *Green Rider* (10–12). 1998, DAW $23.95 (0-88677-824-7). An adventure-filled fantasy about a young girl who must overcome incredible obstacles to deliver a message to the king. (Rev: VOYA 12/98)

1723 Broecker, Randy. *Fantasy of the 20th Century: An Illustrated History* (9–12). Illus. 2001, Collectors $60.00 (1-888054-52-2). This eye-catching collection showcases the very best in 20th-century fantasy writing and art. (Rev: BL 1/1–15/02) [809.3]

1724 Brooks, Terry. *The Druid of Shannara* (10–12). 1991, Ballantine $19.95 (0-345-36298-5). In this, the second of the Heritage of Shannara series, the evil Shadowen continue to control the Four Lands. (Rev: BL 12/1/90; SLJ 7/91)

1725 Brooks, Terry. *The Elf Queen of Shannara* (9–12). Series: Heritage of Shannara. 1993, Ballantine paper $6.99 (0-345-37558-0). Wren and her friend Garth must survive the perils of the jungle to find the Elves and then persuade them to return to the environmentally endangered Westlands. (Rev: BL 12/15/91)

1726 Brooks, Terry. *First King of Shannara* (9–12). 1996, Del Rey $23.50 (0-345-39652-9). The Druid Bremen seeks helps from followers who know the Druid Magic Arts to counter the threat of the evil Brona, the Warlock Lord, and his plans to conquer the Four Lands with his knowledge of Druid Magic. (Rev: VOYA 10/96)

1727 Brooks, Terry. *Jarka Ruus: High Druid of Shannara* (10–12). Series: High Druid of Shannara. 2003, Ballantine $27.95 (0-345-43573-7). Twenty years after the end of the Voyage of the Jerle Shannara trilogy, the disappearance of Grianne Ohmsford signals the start of a new quest full of new and familiar challenges. (Rev: BL 6/1–15/03; VOYA 2/04)

1728 Brooks, Terry. *A Knight of the Word* (10–12). 1998, Ballantine $25.95 (0-345-37963-2). Nest, of *Running with the Demon,* must warn her friend John Ross that the evil force known as the Void is after him in this novel set in contemporary Seattle. The final book in the trilogy is *Angel Fire East* (1999). (Rev: BL 5/15/98; VOYA 12/98)

1729 Brooks, Terry. *Morgawr* (7–12). Series: Voyage of the Jerle Shannara. 2002, Del Rey $27.95 (0-345-43572-9). In the concluding volume of the trilogy, Bek Ohsmford, a fledgling mage and brother of the Ilse Witch, enlists the help of others with magical powers to help protect his sister from the evil Morgawr. (Rev: BL 7/02; VOYA 12/02)

1730 Brooks, Terry. *Running with the Demon* (10–12). 1997, Ballantine $25.95 (0-345-37962-4). Nest, a 14-year-old girl who has a six-inch-tall friend and magical abilities, finds herself in the middle of a power struggle between Knight of the Word John Ross and the spirit of evil, who has taken the form of a human demon. (Rev: VOYA 4/98)

1731 Brooks, Terry. *The Scions of Shannara* (10–12). 1990, Ballantine $23.00 (0-345-35695-0). In this, the first of a new trilogy, The Heritage of Shannara, the forces of good battle a race using evil magic. (Rev: BL 1/1/90; SLJ 9/90)

1732 Brooks, Terry. *The Talismans of Shannara* (9–12). Series: Heritage of Shannara. 1993, Ballan-

tine paper $6.99 (0-345-38674-4). With their quests fulfilled, Par, Walker Bob, and Wren are drawn back together to face the Shadowen in the final book of the Shannara saga. (Rev: BL 1/1/93)

1733 Brooks, Terry. *The Tangle Box* (9–12). 1995, Ballantine paper $6.99 (0-345-38700-7). This humorous fantasy concerns Ben Holiday, sovereign of the magic kingdom of Landover, and some exiled sorcerers seeking revenge upon the fairy folk. (Rev: BL 3/15/94; VOYA 8/94)

1734 Brooks, Terry. *The Voyage of the Jerle Shannara: Antrax* (9–12). 2001, Del Rey $26.95 (0-345-39766-5). In this sequel to *The Voyage of the Jerle Shannara: Ilse Witch* (2000), druid Walker enters the mysterious structure known as Castledown. (Rev: BL 6/1–15/01)

1735 Brooks, Terry. *The Voyage of the Jerle Shannara: Ilse Witch* (10–12). 2000, Ballantine $26.95 (0-345-39654-5). This first installment in the trilogy (which is a continuation of the lengthy Shannara saga) tells how druid Walker Boh embarks on a voyage chronicled on a map found in the possession of a badly injured elf. (Rev: BL 6/1–15/00)

1736 Brooks, Terry. *The Wishsong of Shannara* (9–12). 1988, Ballantine paper $6.99 (0-345-35636-5). In the concluding volume of the Shannara saga, a young girl finds she holds the power of the wishsong, a weapon that the Four Lands can use against their enemies. Preceded by *The Sword of Shannara* and *The Elfstones of Shannara*. (Rev: BL 4/1/85; SLJ 8/85; VOYA 12/85)

1737 Brown, Mary. *Pigs Don't Fly* (9–12). 1994, Baen paper $6.99 (0-671-87601-5). With her unknown father's magic ring, the daughter of a village whore sets out to seek her fortune, accompanied by an assortment of animal characters and a blind, amnesiac knight. (Rev: BL 3/1/94; VOYA 10/94)

1738 Brown, Mary. *The Unlikely Ones* (10–12). 1986, Baen paper $4.99 (0-671-65361-X). Seven unlikely companions, including a hornless unicorn, are forced to go on a quest because of a witch's curse. (Rev: BL 10/1/86)

1739 Brown, Simon. *Inheritance* (10–12). Series: Keys of Power. 2003, DAW paper $6.99 (0-7564-0162-3). Sibling rivalry is at the heart of this fantasy saga in which the four children of the failing queen of Grenda Lear are entrusted with the four Keys of Power. (Rev: BL 9/15/03; VOYA 6/04)

1740 Browne, N. M. *Basilisk* (7–11). 2004, Bloomsbury $17.95 (1-58234-876-6). A fantasy about a city in which laborers under the control of a totalitarian ruler work above ground, and the so-called degenerates are confined to dank catacombs. (Rev: BL 4/15/04*; SLJ 6/04)

1741 Browne, N. M. *Warriors of Alavna* (7–10). 2002, Bloomsbury $16.95 (1-58234-775-1). This historical fantasy pits 15-year-olds Dan and Ursula against invaders in Roman Britain. A sequel is *Warriors of Camlann* (2003). (Rev: BCCB 10/02; SLJ 1/03; VOYA 2/03)

1742 Brust, Steven. *Issola* (10–12). 2001, Tor $22.95 (0-312-85927-9). In this sequel to *Orca* (1996), Vlad goes in search of his friends who have disappeared and neither sorcery nor telepathy can find them. (Rev: BL 6/1–15/01; VOYA 12/01)

1743 Brust, Steven. *Sethra Lavode* (10–12). Series: Khaavren. 2004, Tor $25.95 (0-312-85581-8). In this installment of the Khaavren series that follows *The Paths of the Dead* (2002) and *Lord of the Castle Black* (2003), the Phoenix Zerika has reclaimed the Imperial Orb and now hopes to reestablish the empire. (Rev: BL 4/15/04)

1744 Buffie, Margaret. *The Haunting of Frances Rain* (7–10). 1989, Scholastic paper $12.95 (0-590-42834-9). Through a pair of magic spectacles, Lizzie is able to see events that occurred more than 50 years ago. (Rev: BL 10/1/89; SLJ 9/89)

1745 Bujold, Lois M. *The Curse of Chalion* (10–12). 2001, HarperCollins $25.00 (0-380-97901-2). Cazaril, a crippled soldier, is a royal tutor at a court filled with magic and mayhem in this novel of intrigue, black magic, and nonstop action. (Rev: BL 5/1/01* ; SLJ 10/01)

1746 Bull, Emma. *Finder* (9–12). 1994, Tor $21.95 (0-312-85418-8). Set in Bordertown, just outside the Elflands, this is the story of a cop who exploits a finder's talents to track down a killer sorcerer. (Rev: BL 2/15/94; SLJ 6/95; VOYA 6/94)

1747 Bunch, Chris. *Knighthood of the Dragon* (10–12). 2003, Orbit paper $16.95 (1-84149-195-0). Teenage fans of the military fantasy genre will be captivated by this tale of dragonmaster Lord Hal Kailas' struggle to survive. A sequel to *Storm of Wings* (2002). (Rev: BL 9/15/03)

1748 Burgess, Melvin. *Lady: My Life as a Bitch* (9–12). 2002, Holt $16.95 (0-8050-7148-2). Sandra's life, veering out of control, changes dramatically — and in many ways for the better — when she is transformed into a dog and can roam the streets of Manchester, England. (Rev: BCCB 8/02; BL 6/1–15/02; HBG 10/02; SLJ 7/02; VOYA 8/02)

1749 Byers, Steven J. *The Life of Your Time* (9–12). 2001, Selah paper $10.95 (1-58930-008-4). In this humorous fantasy, sixth-grader Percival manipulates numbers to cause several coincidences involving characters in his small town. (Rev: BL 3/1/01*)

1750 Calhoun, Dia. *Firegold* (7–12). 1999, Winslow $15.95 (1-890817-10-4). A fantasy in which a 13-year-old boy is persecuted in his village because of his different looks and behavior and is forced to travel to the Red Mountains, home of fierce barbarians. (Rev: BL 5/15/99; BR 9–10/99; SLJ 6/99; VOYA 8/99)

1751 Calhoun, Dia. *White Midnight* (9–12). 2003, Farrar $18.00 (0-374-38389-8). Rose, a diffident 15-year-old bondgirl who loves her home in the Valley, agrees to marry a neighboring "monster" in this fantasy set in the world seen in *Firegold* (1999). (Rev: BCCB 3/04; BL 9/15/03; LMC 3/04; SLJ 3/04; VOYA 12/03)

1752 Callander, Don. *Geomancer* (9–12). 1994, Berkley paper $5.50 (0-441-28036-6). Captured apprentice Douglas Brightgale races to crack the spell of an ancient geomancer and to pass his firemaster examination in time for his wedding. (Rev: BL 1/1/94; VOYA 6/94)

1753 Card, Orson Scott. *Enchantment* (9–12). 1999, Ballantine $25.00 (0-345-41687-2); paper $6.99 (0-345-41688-0). A graduate student traveling in Russia finds a magical forest that takes him into a land of legend and fairy tales. (Rev: BL 3/1/99; SLJ 12/99)

1754 Card, Orson Scott. *Seventh Son* (10–12). 1993, Tor paper $5.99 (0-8125-3305-4). In this, the first volume of the Tales of Alvin Maker series, the author has created another world using early nineteenth-century America as a model. (Rev: BL 5/1/87; SLJ 12/87; VOYA 12/87)

1755 Carroll, Susan. *Midnight Bride* (10–12). 2001, Ballantine $22.00 (0-345-43397-1). In this fantasy that follows *The Bride Finder* (1998) and *The Night Drifter* (1998), Val, who possesses the ability to ease pain, is able to find a bride in spite of predictions that he can never marry. (Rev: BL 2/15/01)

1756 Chabon, Michael. *Summerland* (10–12). 2002, Hyperion $22.95 (0-7868-0877-2). Baseball is a central theme in this multilayered tale of alternate worlds, magic, and myth featuring a little leaguer named Ethan. (Rev: BL 8/02; HB 11–12/02; HBG 3/03; VOYA 2/03)

1757 Chalker, Jack L. *Midnight at the Well of Souls* (10–12). 1985, Ballantine paper $5.99 (0-345-32445-5). This story about Nathan Brazil is the first part of the Saga of the Well World. Other volumes are: *Exiles at the Well of Souls, Quest for the Well of Souls, The Return of Nathan Brazil,* and *Twilight at the Well of Souls.*

1758 Chamberlin, Ann. *The Merlin of the Oak Wood* (10–12). Series: Joan of Arc Tapestries. 2001, Tor $24.95 (0-312-87284-4). This blend of fantasy and history involves a complex plot and magic, as well as the appearance of Jeanne d'Arc whose "voices," in this novel, come from ancient powers. (Rev: BL 5/15/01*; VOYA 10/01)

1759 Charnas, Suzy McKee. *The Kingdom of Kevin Malone* (7–10). 1993, Harcourt $16.95 (0-15-200756-3). This novel melds the world of the teenage problem novel with that of fantasy in a story that pokes gentle fun at the conventions of fantasy fiction. (Rev: BL 6/1–15/93; SLJ 1/94; VOYA 8/93)

1760 Chernenko, Dan. *The Bastard King* (11–12). Series: Sceptre of Mercy. 2003, NAL paper $14.95 (0-451-45914-3). A missing sceptre plays a central role in this story of adventure and strife featuring a youthful king, the first installment in a new series. (Rev: BL 3/1/03)

1761 Chernenko, Dan. *The Chernagor Pirates* (10–12). 2004, NAL paper $14.95 (0-451-45956-3). In this sequel to *The Bastard King* (2003), King Grus and Lanius, the king he opposes, are engaged in an ethical as well as military conflict. (Rev: BL 3/1/04)

1762 Cherryh, C. J. *Exile's Gate* (10–12). 1988, NAL paper $5.50 (0-88677-254-0). In this fourth installment of the adventures of Morgaine, she and her liegeman continue their quest to close the disrupting Gates. The preceding volume was *Fires of Azeroth* (1979). (Rev: BL 11/1/87; VOYA 6/88)

1763 Cherryh, C. J. *Fortress of Dragons* (10–12). 2000, HarperCollins $24.00 (0-06-105055-5). In this, the fourth of the Fortress fantasy, the hero Cetwyn Marhanen continues his efforts to be recognized as king and regain his wife's inheritance. (Rev: BL 5/1/00)

1764 Cherryh, C. J. *Hammerfall* (10–12). Series: Gene Wars. 2001, HarperCollins $25.00 (0-06-105260-4). Marak, believed to be insane, saves his life by going into unknown territory to discover the secret of the tower that haunts his dreams. (Rev: BL 4/15/01*)

1765 Cherryh, C. J., and Mercedes Lackey. *Reap the Whirlwind* (9–12). 1989, Baen paper $4.99 (0-671-69846-X). In this fantasy, a horde of barbarians threaten the power of the Order of the Sword of Knowledge. (Rev: VOYA 4/90)

1766 Christensen, James C., and Renwick St. James. *Voyage of the Basset* (10–12). Illus. 1996, Workman $29.95 (1-885183-58-5). In 1850, a professor of myths and legends and his daughters are transported to the ancient land of myths, where they have a series of adventures and meet such mythical characters as a manticore, Oberon and Titania, harpies, a sphinx, minotaur, mermaids, trolls, gryphon, Medusa, unicorn, and a dragon. (Rev: SLJ 1/97)

1767 Clayton, Jo. *Drum Warning* (9–12). 1996, Tor $23.95 (0-312-86177-X). In this exciting fantasy two worlds touch magically, allowing magical energies and some inhabitants to cross over, and when the mages of each seek to conquer the other, two organizations and two youngsters from the two worlds band together to oppose these forces of chaos and save their worlds from destruction. (Rev: VOYA 4/97)

1768 Clement-Davies, David. *Fire Bringer* (6–12). 2000, Dutton $19.95 (0-525-46492-1). A fawn with a destiny readies himself to challenge the ruling stag in this absorbing and suspenseful novel set in medieval Scotland. (Rev: BL 9/1/00; BR 5–6/01; HB 1–2/01; HBG 3/01; SLJ 12/00)

1769 Clement-Davies, David. *The Sight* (7–12). 2002, Dutton $21.99 (0-525-46723-8). A wolf pack in Transylvania is the focus of this story of good and evil that entwines fantasy, history, mythology, and the supernatural. (Rev: BCCB 4/02; BL 3/1/02; HB 7–8/02; HBG 10/02; SLJ 6/02; VOYA 6/02)

1770 Cochran, Molly, and Warren Murphy. *The Broken Sword* (10–12). 1997, Tor $24.95 (0-312-86283-0). Merlin and King Arthur are reincarnated in the 20th century as an old man and a teenager whose mission is to rescue the Holy Grail from a gang of villains. (Rev: SLJ 8/97)

1771 Coe, David B. *Rules of Ascension* (11–12). 2002, Tor $27.95 (0-312-87807-9). Hundreds of years after the Qirsi War tore the Forelands apart, bad blood still remains between the Qirsi and the Eandi; and unrest and conflict are once more on the horizon. (Rev: BL 3/1/02)

1772 Coelho, Paulo. *The Alchemist* (9–12). 1993, HarperSF $18.00 (0-06-250217-4). Parable about a boy who must learn to listen to his heart before he can find his treasure. (Rev: BL 5/1/93; SLJ 7/93)

1773 Constable, Kate. *The Singer of All Songs* (7–10). Series: Chanters of Tremaris. 2004, Scholastic $16.95 (0-439-55478-0). In this impressive fantasy, Calwyn, a novice priestess, is able to control all things cold and uses this power to fight an evil sorcerer. (Rev: BL 2/1/04*; SLJ 4/04; VOYA 4/04)

1774 Constantine, Storm. *The Crown of Silence* (10–12). Series: Chronicle of Magravandias. 2001, Tor $27.95 (0-312-87329-8). This novel, the second of the series, tells how Shan, a peasant boy of 15, is taken to the local wizard to learn magic and manners. (Rev: BL 3/15/01)

1775 Constantine, Storm. *The Way of Light* (10–12). Series: Chronicle of Magravandias. 2002, Tor $27.95 (0-312-87328-X). When the emperor of Magravandias dies, his kingdom experiences a series of crises including determining a successor. (Rev: BL 12/1/01)

1776 Cook, Dawn. *First Truth* (10–12). 2002, Berkley paper $6.99 (0-441-00945-X). Alissa sets out to be trained as a Master at the Hold, unaware that the evil Bailic has other intentions. (Rev: BL 5/15/02)

1777 Cook, Dawn. *Forgotten Truth* (10–12). 2003, Berkley paper $6.99 (0-441-01117-9). In this highly readable fantasy, Alissa, an eager student of magic able to switch form readily from human to beast, finds herself transported 400 years into the past. (Rev: BL 12/1/03)

1778 Cooney, Caroline B. *For All Time* (6–10). Series: Time Travel. 2001, Delacorte $12.95 (0-385-32773-0). Annie and Strat's ill-timed romance continues in this stand-alone conclusion to the earlier trilogy as Annie tries to join Strat in 1899 and instead ends up in ancient Egypt. (Rev: BCCB 11/01; BL 9/15/01; HBG 3/02; SLJ 9/01; VOYA 12/01)

1779 Cooney, Caroline B. *Prisoner of Time* (6–10). Series: Time Travel. 1998, Laurel Leaf paper $5.50 (0-440-22019-X). In this conclusion to the trilogy, there is again a contrast between the lifestyles of today and those of 100 years ago as a girl is rescued from an unsuitable marriage. (Rev: BL 6/1–15/98; HBG 3/02; SLJ 5/98; VOYA 6/98)

1780 Cooper, Louise. *Inferno* (9–12). 1989, Tor paper $3.95 (0-8125-0246-9). In this sequel to *Nemesis* (1989), Indigo must kill the demon she freed from the Tower of Regrets. (Rev: VOYA 4/90)

1781 Coville, Bruce, ed. *Half-Human* (7–10). 2001, Scholastic $15.95 (0-590-95944-1). Ten stories by well-known YA authors feature beings that are half-human, half-animal, accompanied by striking illustrations. (Rev: BL 12/15/01; HBG 10/02; SLJ 12/01; VOYA 12/01)

1782 Craddock, Curtis. *Sparrow's Flight* (10–12). 2000, Write Way paper $18.99 (1-885173-85-7). In this fast-paced fantasy, Sparrow of Blackaker and a blind swordswoman fight the evil of the immortal Hezra-Thrall. (Rev: BL 7/00)

1783 Crichton, Michael. *Timeline* (9–12). 1999, Ballantine paper $17.99 (0-345-41762-3). In this fantasy novel, historians are sent back to France in 1357 and become involved in a war.

1784 Crispin, A. C. *The Paradise Snare* (9–12). 1997, Bantam paper $5.99 (0-553-57415-9). This is the first novel in a trilogy about the con man of *Star Wars* fame, Han Solo. The others are: *The Hunt Gambit* (1997) and *Rebel Dawn* (1997). (Rev: VOYA 12/98)

1785 Crispin, A. C. *Voices of Chaos* (8–12). 1998, Ace paper $5.99 (0-441-00516-0). In this story of romance, political intrigue, and coming of age, the students and teachers at Starbridge Academy are introduced to a race of feline beings — expressive, intelligent, ambitious, and skillful at deception and manipulation — when Prince Khyriz and Shiksara, a girl from the merchant class, come to study. (Rev: BL 3/1/98; VOYA 6/98)

1786 Crompton, Anne E. *Merlin's Harp* (9–12). 1995, Donald I. Fine paper $5.99 (0-451-45583-5). The Arthurian story is retold from the standpoint of a woman, Niviene, Merlin's apprentice and daughter of the Lady of the Lake. (Rev: VOYA 6/97)

1787 Cullum, J. A. *Lyskarion: The Song of the Wind* (9–12). 2001, EDGE paper $13.95 (1-894063-02-3).

Derwen, a wizard, has the task of finding the best of the children of Tamar and ensuring that the child becomes the greatest wizard ever. (Rev: BL 11/1/01; VOYA 8/02)

1788 Curley, Marianne. *The Dark* (7–12). 2003, Bloomsbury $16.95 (1-58234-853-7). Isabel, Ethan, and Matt must rescue their mentor, Akarian, from a frightening underworld in this sequel to *The Named* (2002). (Rev: BL 10/1/03; HBG 4/04; SLJ 1/04; VOYA 12/03)

1789 Curley, Marianne. *The Named* (7–11). 2002, Bloomsbury $16.95 (1-58234-779-4). Ethan and Isabel time-travel through history on a difficult quest in this first volume of a multilayered trilogy recounting the battle against the Order of Chaos. (Rev: BL 11/15/02; SLJ 1/03)

1790 Curry, Jane L. *Dark Shade* (6–10). 1998, Simon & Schuster $16.00 (0-689-81812-2). Maggie Gilmour and her silent, withdrawn friend, Kip, travel in time to 1758 and the time of the French and Indian Wars. (Rev: BL 4/1/98; BR 1–2/99; HB 5–6/98; HBG 9/98; SLJ 5/98; VOYA 8/98)

1791 Dahl, Roald. *Two Fables* (10–12). Illus. 1987, Farrar $12.95 (0-374-28018-5). Two parables for adults involving princesses and magic kingdoms. (Rev: BL 9/1/87)

1792 Dalkey, Kara. *Ascension* (7–10). Series: Water. 2002, Avon paper $4.99 (0-06-440808-6). Nia is an ambitious 16-year-old mermaid living in the city of Atlantis in this first installment in a richly detailed trilogy that blends fantasy, romance, and adventure. The sequels are *Reunion* and *Transformation*. (Rev: BCCB 4/02; BL 2/1/02; SLJ 3/02; VOYA 2/02)

1793 Dalkey, Kara. *The Heavenward Path* (7–12). 1998, Harcourt $17.00 (0-15-201652-X). In this sequel to *Little Sister*, 16-year-old Mitsuko escapes from an arranged marriage by flying away on the wings of her friend Goranu. (Rev: BL 6/1–15/98; HBG 9/98; SLJ 5/98; VOYA 6/98)

1794 Dalkey, Kara. *Little Sister* (7–10). 1996, Harcourt $17.00 (0-15-201392-X). In this historical fantasy, a Japanese girl from a noble family, who is a helper for her newly married oldest sister, travels into a hell-like land and back. (Rev: BL 10/1/96; BR 3–4/97; SLJ 12/96; VOYA 2/97)

1795 Danvers, Dennis. *The Watch* (9–12). 2002, HarperCollins $24.95 (0-380-97762-1). On his deathbed, a Russian prince accepts an offer from a man, who claims to come from the future, to restore his youth and deposit him in America in 1999. (Rev: BL 12/1/01*; SLJ 6/02)

1796 Dart-Thornton, Cecilia. *The Ill-Made Mute* (10–12). 2001, Warner $24.95 (0-446-52832-3). A mute child escapes from a tower where she is a servant to search for her origins and to find a way to recover the power of speech. (Rev: BL 4/15/01; VOYA 2/02)

1797 Datlow, Ellen, and Terri Windling, eds. *Black Thorn, White Rose* (9–12). 1994, Avon $22.00 (0-688-13713-X). Variations of famous European folktales involving dwarves, witches, elves, and trolls, including a retelling of "Rumpelstiltskin." (Rev: BL 8/94; VOYA 4/95)

1798 Datlow, Ellen, and Terri Windling, eds. *Swan Sister: Fairy Tales Retold* (5–10). 2003, Simon & Schuster $16.95 (0-689-84613-4). Retellings by well-known authors of traditional stories are inventive and entertaining. (Rev: BCCB 11/03; BL 9/15/03; HBG 4/04; SLJ 12/03)

1799 Datlow, Ellen, and Terri Windling, eds. *The Year's Best Fantasy and Horror: Thirteenth Annual Collection* (10–12). 2000, St. Martin's $29.95 (0-312-26274-4); paper $17.95 (0-312-26416-X). There are 49 fine poems and stories in this collection plus a rundown on the year's fantasy and horror publishing activities. (Rev: BL 9/1/00)

1800 Datlow, Ellen, and Terri Windling, eds. *The Year's Best Fantasy and Horror: Fourteenth Annual Collection* (10–12). 2001, St. Martin's $29.95 (0-312-27541-2); paper $18.95 (0-312-27544-7). Superior fantasy and horror short fiction by some of the best writers in these genres. (Rev: BL 7/01)

1801 Datlow, Ellen, and Terri Windling, eds. *The Year's Best Fantasy and Horror: Sixteenth Annual Collection* (11–12). 2003, St. Martin's $35.00 (0-312-31424-8); paper $19.95 (0-312-31425-6). A comprehensive and diverse collection of excellent fiction and poetry. (Rev: BL 8/03)

1802 David, Peter. *One Knight Only* (10–12). 2003, Berkley $23.95 (0-441-01057-1). Arthur Pendragon finds life as U.S. president quite acceptable despite Merlin's absence until ancient forces raise old and difficult choices. (Rev: BL 7/03; VOYA 2/04)

1803 Dean, J. David. *Ravennetus* (9–12). 1996, Pandea $21.95 (0-9646604-4-X). In this medieval fantasy, young Nelsyn is sent out into the world by two villains to find the secret power that will allow them to dominate the world. (Rev: BL 3/15/96)

1804 Deitz, Tom. *Fireshaper's Doom* (9–12). 1987, Avon paper $3.95 (0-380-75329-4). Because he accidentally caused the death of a faerie boy, Sullivan faces the wrath of the boy's mother in this sequel to *Windmaster's Bane.* (Rev: BL 11/15/87)

1805 Deitz, Tom. *Summerblood* (10–12). 2001, Bantam paper $13.95 (0-553-38070-2). In this continuation of the story begun in *Bloodwinter* (1999) and *Springwar* (2000), the war continues between the kingdoms of Eron and Ixti while internal problems also exist in each realm. (Rev: BL 3/1/01; VOYA 10/01)

1806 Deitz, Tom. *Windmaster's Bane* (10–12). 1986, Avon paper $4.99 (0-380-75029-5). A man with second sight finds himself back in the time of legendary struggles involving the Celts. (Rev: BL 11/15/86)

1807 Del Rey, Lester, and Risa Kessler, eds. *Once upon a Time: A Treasury of Modern Fairy Tales* (9–12). 1991, Ballantine $25.00 (0-345-36263-2). Ten original fairy tales for adults by Asimov, Cherryh, Hambly, McCaffrey, and others. (Rev: BL 11/15/91; SLJ 8/92)

1808 de Lint, Charles. *Forests of the Heart* (10–12). 2000, Tor $27.95 (0-312-86519-8). Quirky characters including the Gentry, a group of amoral Irish gods who have emigrated to the New World, inhabit this fantasy that combines myth and magic. (Rev: BL 5/1/00; VOYA 4/01)

1809 de Lint, Charles. *A Handful of Coppers* (10–12). 2003, Subterranean $40.00 (1-931081-73-5). The 15 early stories by de Lint included in this anthology display his usual writing skill and may be unfamiliar to his many fans. (Rev: BL 2/1/03)

1810 de Lint, Charles. *Medicine Road* (10–12). Illus. 2004, Subterranean $35.00 (1-931081-96-4). In this fantasy, a red dog and a jackalope are given human shapes and 100 years to find mates. (Rev: BL 4/15/04)

1811 de Lint, Charles. *The Onion Girl* (10–12). 2001, Tor $27.95 (0-312-87397-2). Creatures from the spirit world are involved in Jilly Coppercorn's recovery after being hit by a car and her attempts to fight the pain hidden in her past. (Rev: BL 10/1/01; VOYA 2/02)

1812 de Lint, Charles. *Seven Wild Sisters* (10–12). 2002, Subterranean $35.00 (1-931081-33-6). Contemporary life meets fairy life as the seven sisters become embroiled in Otherworldly intrigue. (Rev: BL 3/15/02)

1813 de Lint, Charles. *Spirits in the Wires* (10–12). 2003, Tor $27.95 (0-312-87398-0). In 21st-century Newford, a strange computer crash requires Christy and his friends to effect a rescue in another world. (Rev: BL 8/03; VOYA 12/03)

1814 de Lint, Charles. *Trader* (10–12). 1997, Tor $24.95 (0-312-85847-7). Max Trader awakens to find that he has inexplicably traded bodies with a womanizing loser named Johnny Devlin. (Rev: BL 1/1–15/97; VOYA 8/97)

1815 de Lint, Charles. *Triskell Tales: 22 Years of Chapbooks* (10–12). 2000, Subterranean $40.00 (1-892284-78-2). This collection of stories and poems is arranged chronologically over a period of 22 years and shows the development of this fantasy writer. (Rev: BL 11/15/00)

1816 de Lint, Charles. *Waifs and Strays* (7–12). 2002, Viking $17.99 (0-670-03584-X). A collection of 16 de Lint fantasies — the majority previously published — featuring urban teen characters. (Rev: BCCB 12/02; BL 10/1/02; HBG 3/03; SLJ 11/02; VOYA 12/02)

1817 DeVos, Elisabeth. *The Seraphim Rising* (10–12). 1997, Roc paper $5.99 (0-451-45655-6). An action-packed quest by two young men to prove or disprove the claim that a new messiah has arrived on earth. (Rev: VOYA 2/98)

1818 Dickinson, Peter. *The Ropemaker* (7–12). 2001, Delacorte $15.95 (0-385-72921-9). Two young people — Tilja and Tahl — and their grandparents set off on a perilous journey to find the magician who has protected their Valley from its enemies. (Rev: BCCB 1/02; BL 10/15/01; HB 11–12/01; HBG 3/02; SLJ 11/01*; VOYA 12/01)

1819 Dickson, Gordon R. *The Dragon and the Fair Maid of Kent* (10–12). 2000, Tor $26.95 (0-312-86160-5). This fantastic alternate history is set in the Middle Ages and features the black death, Prince Edward (known as the Black Prince), and an army of goblins. (Rev: BL 12/15/00; VOYA 8/01)

1820 Dickson, Gordon R. *The Dragon and the Gnarly King* (9–12). 1997, St. Martin's $24.95 (0-312-86157-5). Living in a time-warp medieval setting, Jim Ekert, a 20th-century college professor, matches wit and skills with the Gnarly King in a fight for the return of his kidnapped son. (Rev: BL 8/97; VOYA 4/98)

1821 Dickson, Gordon R. *The Dragon, the Earl, and the Troll* (9–12). 1994, Berkley paper $21.95 (0-441-00098-3). The latest in the series about Dragon Knight, a 20th-century American transported into an analogue of medieval England. (Rev: BL 12/1/94; VOYA 4/95)

1822 Doctorow, Cory. *Down and Out in the Magic Kingdom* (10–12). 2003, Tor $22.95 (0-765-30436-8). A highly readable fantasy romp in a futuristic Disneyland where the hero fights to protect the park and its attractions from mysterious forces that seek to take it over. (Rev: BL 1/1–15/03; VOYA 8/03)

1823 Doherty, Robert. *Area 51: Nosferatu* (10–12). Series: Area 51. 2003, Dell paper $6.99 (0-440-23724-6). Past and present are interwoven in this exciting tale of aliens and vampires that provides alternate histories of many world events. (Rev: BL 7/03)

1824 Donaldson, Stephen R. *Lord Foul's Bane* (10–12). 1987, Ballantine paper $6.99 (0-345-34865-6). Thomas Covenant, a leper, finds himself in a magical world in this first volume of the Chronicles of Thomas Covenant the Unbeliever series. Others are *The Illearth War* and *The Power That Preserves*.

1825 Donoghue, Emma. *Kissing the Witch: Old Tales in New Skins* (10–12). Series: Joanna Cotler Books. 1997, HarperCollins $14.89 (0-06-027576-

6). Such familiar tales as *Beauty and the Beast*, *Rumpelstiltskin*, and *Cinderella* are retold from a lesbian, feminist point of view. (Rev: BL 6/1–15/97; BR 1–2/98; HBG 3/98; SLJ 6/97; VOYA 8/97)

1826 Douglass, Sara. *Beyond the Hanging Wall* (10–12). 2003, Tor $24.95 (0-765-30449-X). Fourteen-year-old Garth, a talented healer, perceives that a prisoner he is tending is a long-missing prince and decides he must restore him to his birthright. (Rev: BL 7/03; VOYA 2/04)

1827 Douglass, Sara. *God's Concubine* (10–12). 2004, Tor $27.95 (0-765-30541-0). In this fantasy and alternative history that is a sequel to *Hades' Daughter* (2003), some of the characters are William the Conqueror and Edward the Confessor. (Rev: BL 2/1/04)

1828 Douglass, Sara. *Threshold* (11–12). 2003, Tor $25.95 (0-312-87687-4). As an Ashod pyramid finally nears the end of construction, a slave glassworker named Tirzah becomes aware that it poses a grave threat. (Rev: BL 9/1/03)

1829 Douglass, Sara. *The Wayfarer Redemption* (10–12). 2000, Tor $24.95 (0-312-87717-X). Lady Faraday accompanies the man she loves on a perilous journey that leads to a battle with the demonic Forbidden Ones. Sequels are *Enchanter* (2001) and *Starman* (2002). (Rev: BL 9/1/00)

1830 Drake, David. *Mistress of the Catacombs* (10–12). Series: Lord of the Isles. 2001, Tor $26.95 (0-312-87387-5). In this installment in the saga, Prince Garric of Haft tries to rule his kingdom fairly in spite of rogue wizards, some non-human, who harass him. (Rev: BL 10/15/01)

1831 Duane, Diane. *The Book of Night with Moon* (9–12). 1997, Warner paper $12.99 (0-446-67302-1). An Evil has invaded the underground culture of the magical world beneath Grand Central Station, and four cats are dispatched to send the Evil back to the Darkness. (Rev: VOYA 4/98)

1832 Duane, Diane. *A Wizard Alone* (6–10). Series: Young Wizards. 2002, Harcourt $17.00 (0-15-204562-7). The sixth book in the series of Nita and Kit's adventures in magic finds wizard Kit working on his own while Nita mourns the death of her mother. (Rev: BL 11/15/02; HBG 3/03; SLJ 2/03; VOYA 4/03)

1833 Duncan, Dave. *Impossible Odds* (10–12). Series: Chronicles of the King's Blades. 2003, HarperCollins $24.95 (0-380-81834-5). Grand Duke Rubin, who is actually a duchess in disguise, seeks to recruit Blades who can help her reclaim her duchy from an evil sorcerer. A sequel to the fourth installment, *Paragon Lost* (2002). (Rev: BL 11/15/03; VOYA 6/04)

1834 Duncan, Dave. *Sky of Swords* (10–12). Series: Tale of the King's Blades. 2000, HarperCollins $24.00 (0-380-97462-2). In this prequel to *The*

Gilded Chain (1998), Malinda, first a princess then a queen, struggles to ensure that her baby brother will succeed to the throne. (Rev: BL 9/15/00; SLJ 12/00; VOYA 4/01)

1835 Duncan, David. *The Stricken Field* (9–12). Series: Handful of Men. 1993, Ballantine $19.00 (0-345-37898-9). In the third book of the series, the magic-wielding King Rap and his comrades must fight the evil dwarf Zinixo and his legions of sorcerers. (Rev: BL 8/93; VOYA 2/94)

1836 Eddings, David. *The Belgariad*, Vol. I (10–12). 2000, Del Ray paper $16.95 (0-345-45632-7). This volume contains the first three books about a magical world full of sorcery: *Pawn of Prophecy* (1982), *Queen of Sorcery* (1983), and *Magician's Gambit* (1983). Vol. II contains *Castle of Wizardry* (1983) and *Enchanters' End Game* (1984). (Rev: BL 4/15/00)

1837 Eddings, David. *Guardians of the West* (10–12). 1987, Ballantine paper $6.99 (0-345-35266-1). The beginning volume of a saga about King Garion. In this installment he sets out to save his son from an evil force. (Rev: BL 3/1/87)

1838 Edgerton, Teresa. *The Queen's Necklace* (10–12). 2001, HarperCollins paper $15.00 (0-380-78911-6). For romantic fantasy fans, this is a thriller in which the goblins plan an attack on the divided and weak human kingdoms. (Rev: BL 5/1/01; VOYA 12/01)

1839 Ende, Michael. *The Neverending Story* (7–12). Trans. by Ralph Manheim. 1984, Penguin paper $11.95 (0-14-007431-7). An overweight boy with many problems enters the magic world of Fantastica in this charming fantasy.

1840 Ewing, Lynne. *Into the Cold Fire* (7–12). Series: Daughters of the Moon. 2000, Hyperion LB $9.99 (0-7868-0654-0). In this latest light-hearted tale about four Los Angeles girls with extraordinary powers, Serena is faced with a difficult choice: to succumb to the dark and seductive power of the Atrox or to remain loyal to her sister goddesses. (Rev: HBG 3/01; VOYA 6/01)

1841 *The Faery Reel: Tales for the Twilight Realm* (9–12). 2004, Viking $19.99 (0-670-05914-5). This is a fine collections of 17 original stories, many by well-known writers, and three poems on the theme of fairies and other spirits. (Rev: BL 4/15/04; SLJ 7/04)

1842 Farland, David. *The Lair of Bones* (11–12). Series: Runelords. 2003, Tor $27.95 (0-765-30176-8). This adventure fantasy brings a violent confrontation between immortal Raj Athen; Prince Gaborn, the Earth King; and the Queen of the Reavers; violent content makes this only suitable for mature teens. (Rev: BL 11/15/03)

1843 Farland, David. *Wizardborn* (10–12). 2001, Tor $27.95 (0-312-86741-7). In this sequel to *The*

Runelords (1998), the earth king, Gaborn, wages war against the Reavers, who are destroying his land. (Rev: BL 3/1/01)

1844 Farrell, S. L. *Mage of Clouds* (9–12). 2004, DAW $23.95 (0-7564-0169-0). A young girl seeks peace for her land but is caught up in a deadly struggle between her mother and her uncle. (Rev: BL 1/1–15/04; VOYA 6/04)

1845 Feist, Raymond E. *King of Foxes* (9–12). 2004, HarperCollins $24.95 (0-380-97709-5). This sequel to *Talon of the Silver Hawk* (2003) tells of Tal and his revenge against the duke of Olasko, the man who destroyed Tal's family and people. (Rev: BL 1/1–15/04)

1846 Fisher, Jude. *Wild Magic* (11–12). 2003, DAW $23.95 (0-7564-0145-3). This intricate sequel to *Sorcery Rising* (2002) features absorbing characters with important roles in the future of the land of Eldi. (Rev: BL 7/03; VOYA 2/04)

1847 Fisk, Pauline. *The Secret of Sabrina Fludde* (6–10). 2002, Bloomsbury $15.95 (1-58234-754-9). A young girl with no memory floats into the Welsh town of Pengwern, where she takes the name Abren and eventually discovers the secret of her past. (Rev: BL 9/1/02; SLJ 7/02)

1848 Fitch, Marina. *The Seventh Heart* (9–12). 1997, Ace paper $5.99 (0-441-00451-2). The four elements of the universe, Earth, Wind, Fresh Water, and Sea Water, rebel against humanity's abuses in this exciting fantasy. (Rev: VOYA 12/97)

1849 Fletcher, Susan. *Sign of the Dove* (6–10). 1996, Atheneum $17.00 (0-689-80460-1). Lyf, her foster sister, Kaeldra, and Kaeldra's husband are dedicated to saving dragon hatchlings from the Krags in this allegory in which Lyf finds herself alone in a world of wild dragons. A sequel to *Dragon's Milk* (1989). (Rev: BL 5/1/96; BR 1–2/97; HB 9–10/96; SLJ 5/96; VOYA 8/96)

1850 Flewelling, Lynn. *The Bone Doll's Twin* (10–12). 2001, Bantam paper $6.99 (0-553-57723-9). An fine epic in which Tobin, a female, is living in a time when highborn women are being murdered to ensure a male will mount the throne. (Rev: BL 10/1/01; VOYA 12/01)

1851 Flewelling, Lynn. *Hidden Warrior* (11–12). 2003, Bantam paper $6.99 (0-553-58342-5). A rich, multilayered story of a future queen whose guardian wizards decide to bring her up as a boy in an effort to ensure her safety. (Rev: BL 7/03)

1852 Flieger, Verlyn. *Pig Tale* (7–10). 2002, Hyperion $16.99 (0-7868-0792-X). Mokie, an orphan pig-tender, finds her life changed by a mysterious trio of gypsies after she is raped in this story that draws on Celtic mysticism. (Rev: BCCB 1/03; BL 11/15/02; HBG 3/03; SLJ 12/02; VOYA 2/03)

1853 Flint, Eric. *1632* (10–12). 2000, Baen $24.00 (0-671-57849-9). In this mature time-travel fantasy, a small patch of West Virginia and its inhabitants are sent to Germany in 1632 during the Thirty Years War. (Rev: BL 1/1–15/00)

1854 Flint, Eric, and Andrew Dennis. *1634: The Galileo Affair* (9–12). 2004, Baen $23.00 (0-7434-8815-6). In this alternate-history saga, a group of contemporaries travel to the rescue of Galileo. (Rev: BL 3/1/04; SLJ 7/04)

1855 Flint, Eric, and David Drake. *Fortune's Stroke* (10–12). 2000, Baen $24.00 (0-671-57871-5). Mixing times, cultures, and peoples, this is an action-filled alternate-world saga centered in 6th-century Byzantium. (Rev: BL 5/15/00; VOYA 2/01)

1856 Forbes, Tracy. *My Enchanted Enemy* (11–12). 2002, Pocket paper $6.99 (0-7434-1279-6). A half-dolphin, half-human woman hopes to seduce a man to break a family curse, and ends up falling in love. (Rev: BL 2/1/02)

1857 Foster, Alan Dean. *Kingdoms of Light* (7–12). 2001, Warner $24.95 (0-446-52667-3). When goblin-warlocks invade the peaceful country of Gowdlands and kill wizard Susnam Evyndd, the fallen mage's pets are transformed into human form and tasked to bring color back to the world. (Rev: VOYA 4/01)

1858 Foster, Alan Dean. *Spellsinger* (10–12). 1983, Warner paper $5.50 (0-446-35647-6). A young graduate student named Jonathan Meriweather is summoned to another world to lead a struggle for freedom. Others in this series are: *The Day of the Dissonance* (Phantasia, 1984), and *The Moment of the Magician* (Phantasia, 1986).

1859 Foster, Alan Dean. *A Triumph of Souls* (10–12). Series: Journeys of the Catechist. 2000, WarnerAspect $24.95 (0-446-52218-X). This, the last volume of the trilogy, combines fairy tale elements, monsters, and an evil wizard in the story of the simple herdsman Etjole Ehomba. (Rev: BL 2/1/00; VOYA 6/00)

1860 Frankowski, Leo. *The Fata Morgana* (10–12). 1999, Baen $21.00 (0-671-57822-7). When their yacht founders, two engineers are rescued by inhabitants of the floating island country of Westria, a population out of touch with the rest of the world for centuries. (Rev: VOYA 2/00)

1861 Friedman, C. S. *Crown of Shadows* (9–12). 1995, NAL paper $21.95 (0-88677-664-3). Racing against time to prevent the enslavement of their world, warrior priest Damien Vryce and immortal sorcerer Gerald Tarrant find themselves trapped between justice and retribution. (Rev: BL 9/15/95; VOYA 2/96)

1862 Fry, Stephen. *Making History* (10–12). 1998, Random $24.00 (0-679-45955-3). In this humorous yet thought-provoking fantasy written by a British comedian, a graduate student at Cambridge is able to stop the birth of Hitler through time travel, creating a contemporary world that is entirely different and unexpected. (Rev: BL 2/1/98; SLJ 8/98)

1863 Funke, Cornelia. *Inkheart* (6–12). 2003, Scholastic $19.95 (0-439-53164-0). Twelve-year-old Meggie, the key character in this complex novel, is the daughter of a bookbinder who can release fictional characters from their books. (Rev: BL 9/1/03; HBG 4/04; SLJ 10/03; VOYA 12/03)

1864 Furey, Maggie. *Heart of Myrial* (7–12). Series: Shadowleague. 2000, Bantam paper $6.99 (0-553-57938-X). As catastrophic events threaten Myrial, a firedrake, a telepathic dragon, and a woman warrior seek to avert destruction. (Rev: VOYA 6/00)

1865 Furlong, Monica. *Juniper* (7–12). 1992, Demco $11.04 (0-606-01569-8). A rich coming-of-age novel about Ninnoc, the only child of King Mark of Cornwall, as Christianity is beginning to overcome the ancient Celtic religion of the Mother Goddess. (Rev: BL 2/15/91; SLJ 5/91)

1866 Gaiman, Neil. *Stardust* (10–12). 1999, Avon paper $22.00 (0-380-97728-1). A fantasy fairy tale about a young man, an evil witch, and the sons of a lord, all seeking the star, a young woman living in the land of Faerie. (Rev: BL 11/1/98; SLJ 2/99)

1867 Gansky, Alton. *The Prodigy* (9–12). 2001, Zondervan paper $12.99 (0-310-23556-1). The story of a boy who has the power to heal, and how this gift is exploited by others. (Rev: BL 6/1–15/01*)

1868 Garcia Marquez, Gabriel. *One Hundred Years of Solitude* (10–12). Trans. by Gregory Rabassa. 1995, Knopf $20.00 (0-679-44465-3). This novel of magic realism looks at the adventures and aspirations of generations of the Buendia family, of the town of Macondo.

1869 Garcia y Robertson, R. *Knight Errant* (9–12). 2001, Tor $27.95 (0-312-86996-7). A contemporary American woman meets a 14th-century knight in England and is transported back to his time. (Rev: BL 10/1/01; VOYA 6/02)

1870 Gardner, John. *Grendel* (10–12). 1971, Knopf $15.95 (0-394-47143-1). A retelling of the Beowulf legend, from the standpoint of the monster Grendel.

1871 Garfield, Henry. *Tartabull's Throw* (7–10). 2001, Simon & Schuster $15.00 (0-689-83840-9). A 19-year-old baseball player and a mysterious young woman called Cassandra are the principal characters in this multifaceted story set in 1967 that entwines baseball, werewolves, romance, and suspense. (Rev: BL 5/15/01; HBG 10/01; SLJ 6/01; VOYA 8/01)

1872 Gemmell, David. *The Swords of Night and Day* (9–12). 2004, Del Rey $24.95 (0-345-45833-8). In this sequel to *White Wolf* (2002), the half-human, half-animal creations known as Joinings stalk the earth. (Rev: BL 3/15/04)

1873 Gemmell, David. *White Wolf* (11–12). Series: Drenai. 2003, Del Rey $24.95 (0-345-45831-1). Druss the Legend and Skilgannon battle werebeasts in this fantasy full of violent action. (Rev: BL 3/1/03; SLJ 9/03)

1874 Gilligan, Elizabeth. *The Silken Shroud* (10–12). 2004, DAW paper $6.99 (0-7564-0179-8). This sequel to *Magic's Silken Snare* (2003) continues the story of the quest for the body of Alessandra, murdered princess of the Rom. (Rev: BL 4/15/04)

1875 Gilman, Laura Anne, and Keith R. A. DeCandido, eds. *Otherwere: Stories of Transformation* (9–12). 1996, Ace paper $5.99 (0-441-00363-X). Fifteen stories whose plots focus on some sort of transformation — animals, creatures, or people. (Rev: VOYA 4/97)

1876 Glass, Isabel. *Daughter of Exile* (9–12). 2004, Tor $24.95 (0-765-30745-6). When her father, who was exiled from the royal court, is assassinated, his young daughter is determined to go to court to seek justice. (Rev: BL 3/15/04)

1877 Golden, Christopher. *The Boys Are Back in Town* (10–12). 2004, Bantam paper $12.00 (0-553-38207-1). Will James gets news from a friend whom he thought died 10 years before in this fantasy in which a teenage boy living in Will's house holds the key to these strange happenings. (Rev: BL 2/15/04*)

1878 Golden, Christopher. *Spike and Dru: "Pretty Maids All in a Row"* (9–12). 2000, Pocket $22.95 (0-7434-0046-1). Spike and Drusilla, the villains of "Buffy the Vampire Slayer," are featured in this fantasy that occurs about 50 years before the TV show's story. (Rev: BL 9/15/00)

1879 Goldman, William. *The Princess Bride: S. Morgenstern's Classic Tale of True Love and High Adventure* (9–12). 1982, Ballantine paper $6.99 (0-345-34803-6). A hilarious fast-paced fantasy with a hero named Westley and a heroine named Buttercup.

1880 Gonzalez, Ray. *The Ghost of John Wayne and Other Stories* (10–12). 2001, Univ. of Arizona Pr. $29.95 (0-8165-2065-8); paper $16.95 (0-8165-2066-6). These stories set in the U.S.-Mexican borderlands are filled with magic, ghosts, and visions. (Rev: BL 10/15/01)

1881 Goodkind, Terry. *Faith of the Fallen* (10–12). Series: Sword of Truth. 2000, Tor $27.95 (0-312-86786-7). In this sequel to *Soul of the Fire* (1999), our hero Richard is kidnapped by the Dark Sister Nicci, the emperor's mistress. (Rev: BL 8/00)

1882 Goodkind, Terry. *Wizard's First Rule* (9–12). 1994, Tor $27.95 (0-312-85705-5). With the sword of Truth, young Richard Cypher goes on a quest, encountering wizards, dragons, and other evils with a modern touch of ambiguity. (Rev: BL 9/1/94; VOYA 2/95)

1883 Gordon, Lawrence. *User Friendly* (7–10). Series: Ghost Chronicles. 1999, Karmichael paper $11.95 (0-9653966-0-6). Frank, a teenage ghost in limbo, contacts Eddie through the computer to get help to free himself and his friend, a runaway slave, from the purgatory in which they are living. (Rev: BL 1/1–15/99; SLJ 1/99)

1884 Grant, Alan. *Dragon* (10–12). Series: Smallville. 2002, Warner paper $5.99 (0-446-61214-6). A released murderer gains new, dragonlike strength and evil purpose just as Clark Kent loses his own powers. (Rev: BL 11/1/02)

1885 Grant, Charles. *Riders in the Sky* (10–12). Series: Millennium Quartet. 2000, Tor $25.95 (0-312-86279-2). The last volume of the quartet that involves the Four Horsemen of the Apocalypse and how humans unite to fight them. (Rev: BL 2/1/00)

1886 Greenberg, Martin H., ed. *Elf Fantastic* (8–12). 1997, DAW paper $5.99 (0-88677-736-4). Each of the 19 short stories about elves in this collection offers a fresh insight into humankind. (Rev: VOYA 10/97)

1887 Greenberg, Martin H., ed. *Wizard Fantastic* (9–12). 1997, DAW paper $5.99 (0-88677-756-9). This is a collection of 21 original stories about wizards, many of them by well-known writers. (Rev: VOYA 10/98)

1888 Greenberg, Martin H., and Russell Davis, eds. *Faerie Tales* (9–12). 2004, DAW paper $6.99 (0-7564-0182-8). This is an anthology of stories by numerous well-known authors based on British and Irish fairy lore. (Rev: BL 5/1/04)

1889 Greenberg, Martin H., and John Heifers, eds. *Knight Fantastic* (10–12). 2002, DAW paper $6.99 (0-7564-0052-X). A collection of 15 stories starring diverse knights. (Rev: BL 3/15/02; VOYA 12/02)

1890 Greenwood, Ed. *A Dragon's Ascension* (10–12). Series: Band of Four. 2002, Tor $25.95 (0-765-30222-5). The Band of Four (a warrior, a thief, a healer, and a sorceress) take on the Serpent and decide the fate of Aglirta in the third book in the series. (Rev: BL 2/15/02)

1891 Greenwood, Ed. *The Kingless Land: A Tale of the Band of Four* (10–12). Series: Tales of the Band of Four. 2000, Tor $24.95 (0-312-86721-2). In this, the first of a fantasy series, four unlikely friends set out to find the Dwaerindim stones to bring peace to their country. (Rev: BL 2/15/00)

1892 Grimsley, Jim. *The Ordinary* (10–12). 2004, Tor $24.95 (0-765-30528-2). For better readers, this is a fantasy about two different cultures separated by a huge gate and the girl who travels in time to find the secret past of these kingdoms. (Rev: BL 4/15/04*)

1893 Grove, Vicki. *Rimwalkers* (6–10). 1993, Putnam $14.95 (0-399-22430-0). On an Illinois farm for the summer, Tory develops self-esteem as she unravels a mystery involving the apparition of a small boy. (Rev: BL 10/15/93; SLJ 10/93; VOYA 12/93)

1894 Hambly, Barbara. *Knight of the Demon Queen* (10–12). 2000, Ballantine $24.00 (0-345-42189-2). In this very dark sequel to *Dragonshadow* (1999), Lord John Aversin must capture a renegade demon to save his family and people from a plague. (Rev: BL 2/1/00)

1895 Hambly, Barbara. *The Time of the Dark* (10–12). 1984, Ballantine paper $5.99 (0-345-31965-6). In this the first part of the Darweth trilogy, a wizard and a prince flee the powers of the Dark. Followed by *The Walls of Air* and *The Armies of Daylight* (both 1983).

1896 Hamilton, Virginia. *Justice and Her Brothers* (7–10). 1998, Scholastic paper $4.99 (0-590-36214-3). Four children with supernatural powers move in time in this complex novel. Sequels are *Dustland* and *The Gathering*.

1897 Hancock, Karen. *The Light of Eidon* (10–12). Series: Legends of the Guardian King. 2003, Bethany paper $12.99 (0-7642-2794-7). In this artful blend of Christian allegory and fantasy, protagonist Abramm Kalladorne overcomes countless challenges in his search for spiritual truths. (Rev: BL 10/1/03*; VOYA 2/04)

1898 Hanley, Victoria. *The Healer's Keep* (7–12). 2002, Holiday $17.95 (0-8234-1760-3). A princess, a former slave girl, and their companions battle evil in a land full of magic. (Rev: BCCB 1/03; HBG 3/03; SLJ 12/02; VOYA 2/03)

1899 Hanley, Victoria. *The Seer and the Sword* (6–10). 2000, Holiday $17.95 (0-8234-1532-5). Romance, court politics, battles, and suspense all are essential parts of this fantasy featuring Princess Torina and Prince Landen. (Rev: BCCB 2/01; BL 12/15/00; HBG 10/01; SLJ 3/01; VOYA 4/01)

1900 Hantman, Clea. *Heaven Sent: Goddesses #1* (7–10). 2002, Avon paper $4.99 (0-06-440875-2). Zeus sends three teenage daughters to Earth — Athens, Georgia, to be precise — to learn some manners in this amusing and hip novel that combines mythology and teen culture. (Rev: BCCB 3/02; BL 2/15/02; SLJ 3/02; VOYA 2/02)

1901 Harlan, Thomas. *The Gate of Fire* (10–12). 2000, Tor $27.95 (0-312-86544-9). This complex sequel to *The Shadow of Ararat* (1999), is set in an alternate Rome populated by sorcerers, queens, prophets, and such historical figures as Julius Caesar and Alexander the Great. (Rev: BL 5/1/00)

1902 Harlan, Thomas. *The Storm of Heaven* (10–12). 2001, Tor $27.95 (0-312-86559-7). In this historical fantasy with a 6th-century setting, the powers of Mohammed, Persia, and the allied eastern and west-ern Roman empires are in a three-way conflict. (Rev: BL 6/1–15/01)

1903 Harness, Charles L. *Cybele, with Bluebonnets* (10–12). 2002, NESFA $21.00 (1-887668-41-8). Joseph falls in love with his chemistry teacher, Cybele, in high school, later comes to appreciate her mystical strength, and even after she has died feels her guidance in his life and work. (Rev: BL 11/1/02)

1904 Harper, Steven. *Dreamer* (10–12). 2001, NAL paper $5.99 (0-451-45843-5). An unknown boy has the power to possess others' bodies against their will, and the mystical group known as the Children of Irfan are searching for him. (Rev: BL 8/01; SLJ 4/02)

1905 Harris, Anne. *Inventing Memory* (10–12). 2004, Tor $25.95 (0-312-86539-2). The lives of a female slave in ancient Sumeria and Wendy, a contemporary anthropology student, intersect in this experiment in virtual reality. (Rev: BL 3/1/04)

1906 Harris, Charlaine. *Dead to the World* (9–12). 2004, Berkley $19.95 (0-441-01167-5). Sookie Stackhouse discovers that a man she has just met has been robbed of his memory by a witch. (Rev: BL 4/15/04)

1907 Hartwell, David G. *Visions of Wonder* (9–12). 1996, St. Martin's $35.00 (0-312-86224-5); paper $24.95 (0-312-85287-8). An interesting anthology of 1990s science fiction and fantasy, plus several essays on various aspects of the genre. (Rev: VOYA 6/97)

1908 Hautman, Pete. *Mr. Was* (8–12). 1996, Simon & Schuster $16.00 (0-689-81068-7). In this complex fantasy, Jack escapes his father's drunken rage by entering a door in his grandfather's house that takes him back to 1941. (Rev: BL 9/15/96; SLJ 10/96; VOYA 12/96)

1909 Haydon, Elizabeth. *Destiny: Child of the Sky* (10–12). 2001, Tor $27.95 (0-312-86750-6). In this third volume in the trilogy that contained *Rhapsody: Child of Blood* (1999) and *Prophecy: Child of Earth* (2000), the author concludes the story as the three of the Prophecy continue to carry out their roles as saviors of the land. (Rev: BL 8/01)

1910 Haydon, Elizabeth. *Prophecy: Child of Earth* (10–12). 2000, Tor $27.95 (0-312-86751-4). In this sequel to *Rhapsody* (1999), the three heroes (including Rhapsody, who possesses a magic sword) attempt to defeat the demon that threatens life on Earth. (Rev: BL 5/15/00)

1911 Hearn, Lian. *Brilliance of the Moon: Tales of the Otori, Book Three* (9–12). Series: Tales of the Otori. 2004, Riverhead $24.95 (1-57322-270-4). In this continuation of *Grass for His Pillow* (2003), Takeo sets out to win back his bride's ancestral lands and those of his own adoptive father. (Rev: BL 5/1/04)

1912 Heinlein, Robert A. *The Fantasies of Robert A. Heinlein* (10–12). 1999, Tor $27.95 (0-312-87245-3). The fantasies included in this collection combine a magical element with scientific realism. (Rev: BL 11/1/99; VOYA 4/00)

1913 Heneghan, James. *The Grave* (7–10). 2000, Farrar $17.00 (0-374-32765-3). Fantasy and historical fiction blend as orphan Tom, 13, travels from 1974 Liverpool back to 19th-century Ireland and experiences both family life and the potato famine. (Rev: BCCB 3/01; BL 10/15/00; BR 3–4/01; HB 11–12/00; HBG 3/01; SLJ 11/00; VOYA 12/00)

1914 Herter, David. *Evening's Empire* (11–12). 2002, Tor $24.95 (0-312-87034-5). A bereaved husband finds a terrifying underground world in the town where his wife died; for mature teens. (Rev: BL 5/15/02)

1915 Hetley, James A. *The Summer Country* (11–12). 2002, Berkley paper $14.00 (0-441-00972-7). A handsome stranger claims that Maureen is a carrier of powerful old blood in this dark fantasy that includes contemporary tough language. (Rev: BL 10/1/02*)

1916 Hill, Pamela Smith. *The Last Grail Keeper* (7–10). 2001, Holiday $17.95 (0-8234-1574-0). While visiting England with her mother, 16-year-old Felicity discovers she is an Arthurian "grail keeper" with magical powers. (Rev: BCCB 2/02; BL 11/15/01; HBG 3/02; SLJ 12/01; VOYA 6/02)

1917 Hilton, James. *Lost Horizon* (9–12). 1983, Buccaneer LB $28.95 (0-89966-450-4). This fantasy is about Shangri-la, a land where time stands still.

1918 Hindle, Lee J. *Dragon Fall* (9–12). 1984, Avon paper $2.95 (0-380-88468-2). The monsters Gabe creates for a toy company come alive and try to kill him.

1919 Hite, Sid. *Answer My Prayer* (7–10). 1995, Holt $15.95 (0-8050-3406-4). A girl meets a fortune-teller who forecasts a strange future that includes a sleeping stranger. (Rev: BL 5/1/95*)

1920 Hite, Sid. *Dither Farm* (6–10). 1992, Holt $15.95 (0-8050-1871-9). An 11-year-old orphan is taken in by a farm family and discovers joys and miracles. (Rev: BL 5/15/92*; SLJ 5/92)

1921 Hobb, Robin. *Fool's Errand* (10–12). 2002, Bantam $24.95 (0-553-80148-1). FitzChivalry the Wit is persuaded to end his retirement and go questing again to help an errant prince. (Rev: BL 12/15/01; VOYA 2/02)

1922 Hobb, Robin. *Fool's Fate* (9–12). 2004, Bantam $24.95 (0-553-80154-6). In the last of the trilogy that began with *Fool's Errand* (2001) and *Golden Fool* (2002), FitzChivalry Farseer continues his quest that takes him to every part of the Six Duchies. (Rev: BL 1/1–15/04)

1923 Hoffman, Alice. *Blackbird House* (10–12). 2004, Doubleday $19.95 (0-385-50761-5). In these stories, interconnected by the setting of a humble abode on Cape Cod, 200 years of life are covered in a group of mystical tales. (Rev: BL 5/15/04)

1924 Hoffman, Alice. *The Probable Future* (11–12). 2003, Doubleday $24.95 (0-385-50760-7). Three generations of Sparrow women have unusual powers that both enrich and complicate their lives in this multilayered novel that blends realism and fantasy. (Rev: BL 3/1/03; SLJ 7/03)

1925 Hoffman, Mary. *Stravaganza: City of Masks* (7–12). Series: Stravaganza. 2002, Bloomsbury $16.95 (1-58234-791-3). Cancer-stricken Lucien time-travels from the 21st century to a 16th-century city much like Venice, where he meets the lovely Arianna and has many adventures. (Rev: BL 10/15/02; SLJ 11/02; VOYA 12/02)

1926 Hoffman, Mary. *Stravaganza: City of Stars* (6–10). Series: Stravaganza. 2003, Bloomsbury $17.95 (1-58234-839-1). In this sequel to *Stravaganza: City of Masks* (2002), horse-loving Georgia is transported to 16th-century Remora (Sienna), where she finds romance and intrigue. (Rev: BL 9/15/03*; HBG 4/04; SLJ 1/04; VOYA 12/03)

1927 Hoffman, Nina Kiriki. *A Fistful of Sky* (10–12). 2002, Berkley $23.95 (0-441-00975-1). Born into a family blessed with special powers, Gypsum causes much consternation when her magic fails to appear on time. (Rev: BL 10/1/02; VOYA 4/03)

1928 Hoffman, Nina Kiriki. *Past the Size of Dreaming* (10–12). 2001, Berkley $21.95 (0-441-00802-X). In this sequel to *Red Heart of Memories* (1999), gifted teen musician Julio must learn to manage the second personality that lives within him. (Rev: BL 3/15/01; VOYA 8/01)

1929 Hoffman, Nina Kiriki. *A Red Heart of Memories* (6–12). 1999, Ace $21.95 (0-441-00651-5). Matilda, who can communicate with inanimate objects, befriends troubled teen Edmund, who has special powers of his own, and together they seek the key to Edmund's woes. (Rev: VOYA 2/00)

1930 Holdstock, Robert. *Celtika* (11–12). 2003, Tor $25.95 (0-765-30692-1). Greek mythology and Merlin legend are intertwined in this fantasy full of adventure. (Rev: BL 3/15/03; VOYA 6/03)

1931 Holdstock, Robert. *The Iron Grail* (9–12). Series: Merlin Codex. 2004, Tor $24.95 (0-765-30726-X). In this installment of the saga, Merlin seeks the Hill of the White Bull currently in the possession of supernatural warriors. (Rev: BL 2/1/04; VOYA 4/04)

1932 Holman, Felice. *Real* (8–12). 1997, Simon & Schuster $16.00 (0-689-80772-4). While still trying to accept the death of his mother, young Colly, who is spending time in the desert with his father, is befriended by some Native Americans and meets

Sparrow, a Cahuilla Indian who, with his grandmother, is trapped in time. (Rev: BL 10/1/97; HBG 3/98; SLJ 11/97; VOYA 2/98)

1933 Holt, Tom. *Who's Afraid of Beowulf?* (9–12). 1991, Ace paper $5.50 (0-441-88591-8). In this time-warp story, a present-day archaeologist and some ancient Vikings combat an evil wizard. (Rev: BL 1/15/89; VOYA 6/89)

1934 Hoobler, Dorothy, and Thomas Hoobler. *The Ghost in the Tokaido Inn* (6–12). 1999, Putnam $17.99 (0-399-23330-X). Set in 18th-century Japan, this is the story of 14-year-old Seikei, his dreams of becoming a samurai, and what happened after he saw a legendary ghost stealing a valuable jewel. (Rev: BL 6/1–15/99; HBG 4/00; SLJ 6/99; VOYA 10/99)

1935 Hood, Daniel. *King's Cure* (7–12). 2000, Ace paper $5.99 (0-441-00789-9). While scouting out trade routes, Liam Rhenford, accompanied by his dragon familiar, discovers his true and dangerous mission is to deliver a potion to the king. (Rev: VOYA 6/01)

1936 Hood, David. *Wizard's Heir* (8–12). 1995, Ace paper $4.99 (0-441-00231-5). In this humorous fantasy, Liam insists he is not a wizard, but things keep happening that convince his neighbors otherwise. (Rev: VOYA 2/96)

1937 Houghton, Gordon. *Damned If You Do* (10–12). 2000, St. Martin's paper $13.00 (0-312-26288-4). Death in all its forms is observed in this black comedy about a recently deceased young man who has been chosen to be Death's assistant for a week. (Rev: BL 4/1/00)

1938 Hoyt, Sarah A. *Ill Met by Moonlight* (10–12). 2001, Berkley $21.95 (0-425-00860-7). Shakespeare must contend with treachery, deceit, murder, and an affair with an elf, after his wife and infant daughter are spirited away by elves. (Rev: BL 10/1/01)

1939 Huff, Tanya. *The Second Summoning: The Keeper's Chronicles #2* (7–12). 2001, DAW paper $6.99 (0-88677-975-8). Claire, a Keeper entrusted with protecting Canada, allows an angel and a demon to enter with humorous results. (Rev: VOYA 12/01)

1940 Huff, Tanya. *Summon the Keeper* (9–12). 1998, DAW paper $5.99 (0-88677-784-4). When she takes over the management of the Elysian Fields guesthouse, Claire discovers the Keeper upstairs asleep, which suggests there is a hole in the fabric of the universe. (Rev: VOYA 10/98)

1941 Hughes, Matthew. *Fools Errant: A Fantasy Picaresque* (10–12). 2001, Warner paper $6.99 (0-446-60923-4). Filidor Vesh, carefree nephew of the Archon of Old Earth, is dispatched on an ostensibly simple errand by his uncle and successfully tackles a series of challenges. (Rev: VOYA 4/01)

1942 Hughes, Monica, sel. *What If? Amazing Stories* (5–10). 1998, Tundra paper $6.95 (0-88776-458-4). Fourteen fantasy and science fiction short stories by noted Canadian writers are included in this anthology, plus a few related poems. (Rev: BL 2/15/99; SLJ 6/99; VOYA 6/99)

1943 Ingold, Jeanette. *The Window* (7–10). 1996, Harcourt $13.00 (0-15-201265-6); paper $6.00 (0-15-201264-8). While staying with relatives in Texas, a newly blinded girl time-travels to discover secrets about her family. (Rev: BL 11/1/96; BR 3–4/97; SLJ 12/96; VOYA 12/96)

1944 Jones, Diana Wynne. *Cart and Cwidder* (8–10). 1995, Greenwillow $16.95 (0-688-13360-6); paper $6.95 (0-688-13399-1). When his father dies, 11-year-old Moril becomes heir to the family's cwidder, a musical instrument that has magical powers.

1945 Jones, Diana Wynne. *Dark Lord of Derkholm* (7–10). 1998, Greenwillow $16.95 (0-688-16004-2). A humorous, scary fantasy about the efforts of a band of inhabitants to stop the incursions of Mr. Chesney's Pilgrim Parties, who have been wreaking havoc on their lands for 40 years. (Rev: BL 9/1/98; BR 5–6/99; HB 11–12/98; HBG 3/99; SLJ 10/98; VOYA 2/99)

1946 Jones, Diana Wynne. *Dogsbody* (7–10). 1990, Random $3.50 (0-394-82031-2). The Dogstar, Sirius, is sent to Earth in the form of a dog to fulfill a dangerous mission. (Rev: BR 11–12/88; VOYA 2/89)

1947 Jones, Diana Wynne. *Howl's Moving Castle* (7–12). 1986, Greenwillow $16.95 (0-688-06233-4). A fearful young girl is changed into an old woman and in that disguise moves into the castle of Wizard Howl. (Rev: BL 6/1/86; SLJ 8/86; VOYA 8/86)

1948 Jones, Diana Wynne. *The Merlin Conspiracy* (6–10). 2003, HarperCollins LB $17.89 (0-06-052319-0). Three teenagers blessed with magical powers collaborate to save the islands of Blest, an alternate England, from attack by wizards in this complex novel full of humor. (Rev: BL 4/15/03; HB 5–6/03; HBG 10/03; SLJ 5/03; VOYA 8/03)

1949 Jones, Diana Wynne. *Unexpected Magic: Collected Stories* (5–10). 2004, Greenwillow $16.99 (0-06-055533-5). An exciting anthology of 16 tales of mystery and magic by a master of fantasy. (Rev: BL 4/15/04)

1950 Jones, Diana Wynne. *Year of the Griffin* (7–10). 2000, Greenwillow LB $15.89 (0-06-029158-3). Pirates, assassins, and plain old magic are among the challenges faced by students at Wizard's University — including Elda, griffin daughter of the wizard Derk — in this sequel to the humorous *Dark Lord of Derkholm* (1998). (Rev: BL 11/1/00; HB 11–12/00; HBG 3/01; SLJ 10/00; VOYA 12/00)

1951 Jordan, Robert. *Crossroads of Twilight* (10–12). Series: Wheel of Time. 2003, Tor $29.95 (0-312-

86459-0). The 10th novel in this series follows the activities of a vast cast of characters as they move closer to a final, cataclysmic battle between good and evil. (Rev: BL 1/1–15/03)

1952 Jordan, Robert. *A Crown of Swords* (8–12). Series: Wheel of Time. 1996, Tor $29.95 (0-312-85767-5). In this seventh book of this series, Rand and his army of Aiel warriors prepare to do battle with the Dark One. (Rev: VOYA 2/97)

1953 Jordan, Robert. *Eye of the World* (10–12). 1990, Tor paper $6.99 (0-8125-1181-6). In this novel, the first of a series, a group of ordinary people flee from evil magic. (Rev: BL 10/1/89; VOYA 6/90)

1954 Jordan, Robert. *Lord of Chaos* (9–12). Series: Wheel of Time. 1994, Tor $25.95 (0-312-85428-5). Rand al'Thor teaches magic to men while being pursued by the hostile Aes Sedai. Mat Cauthon is advised by dead generals and Nynaeve learns to restore magic. (Rev: BL 10/15/94; VOYA 5/95)

1955 Jordan, Robert. *The Shadow Rising* (9–12). Series: Wheel of Time. 1992, Tor $27.95 (0-312-85431-5). The fourth volume in the saga is ambitious, rich, and detailed. (Rev: BL 10/1/92*)

1956 Jordan, Robert. *Winter's Heart* (10–12). Series: Wheel of Time. 2000, Tor $29.95 (0-312-86425-6). This ninth book in the Wheel of Time series (the eighth was *The Path of Daggers* in 1998), continues the struggle of good vs. evil in an epic fantasy format. (Rev: BL 11/1/00)

1957 Jordan, Sherryl. *The Hunting of the Last Dragon* (6–10). 2002, HarperCollins LB $15.89 (0-06-028903-1). In 14th-century England a monk records young peasant Jude's story of his quest, accompanied by a young Chinese woman, to kill a dragon. (Rev: BCCB 9/02; BL 4/15/02; HBG 10/02; SLJ 7/02)

1958 Jordan, Sherryl. *Secret Sacrament* (8–12). 2001, HarperCollins LB $15.89 (0-06-028905-8). In an ancient time, Gabriel trains at the Citadel to become a healer, hoping to intervene in the violence that surrounds him. (Rev: BCCB 3/01; BL 2/15/01; HBG 10/01; SLJ 2/01; VOYA 6/01)

1959 Kashina, Anna. *The Princess of Dhagabad* (10–12). 2000, Herodias $25.00 (1-928746-07-1). In this first volume of a trilogy, when a young princess opens a gift from her grandmother on her 12th birthday, her own personal djinn appears. (Rev: BL 6/1–15/00)

1960 Kay, Guy Gavriel. *The Last Light of the Sun* (9–12). 2004, NAL $24.95 (0-451-45965-2). An alternate history saga in which a king modeled on Britain's Alfred the Great wages war against the raiders from the north. (Rev: BL 3/1/04)

1961 Kaye, Marvin, ed. *The Dragon Quintet* (9–12). 2004, Tor $24.95 (0-765-31035-X). Written by five well-known writers including Orson Scott Card, these five new stories are about dragons and their world. (Rev: BL 4/15/04)

1962 Kellogg, Marjorie. *The Book of Water* (9–12). 1997, DAW paper $5.99 (0-88677-688-0). In this book set in 2013 in a land facing ecological disaster, Erde, the heroine from the first book in this series, and D'Nock, an egocentric, foul-mouthed adventurer, act as human guides for their dragons, Earth and Water, and the four of them face many challenges. (Rev: VOYA 6/98)

1963 Kemp, Kenny. *I Hated Heaven: A Novel of Life After Death* (10–12). 1998, Alta Films $12.00 (1-8924-4210-8). After his death, Tom Waring finds that Heaven will not allow him to fulfill his dying wish to return to earth once to tell his wife that heaven really exists. (Rev: BL 8/98; SLJ 12/98)

1964 Kerner, Charlotte. *Blueprint* (9–12). Trans. by Elizabeth D. Crawford. 2000, Lerner LB $16.95 (0-8225-0080-9). Siri is a clone — or, as she prefers, "blueprint" — of her famous musician mother in this novel translated from German. (Rev: BL 9/15/00; HBG 3/01; SLJ 10/00; VOYA 12/00)

1965 Kerner, Elizabeth. *Song in the Silence: The Tale of Lanen Kaelar* (9–12). 1996, Tor $23.95 (0-312-85780-2). After her father's death, Lanen gets her wish to travel to the Dragon Isle to speak to the Greater Kindred, the Dragons. (Rev: BL 2/15/97; VOYA 6/97)

1966 Kerr, Katharine. *The Fire Dragon* (10–12). Series: Deverry. 2001, Bantam paper $6.99 (0-553-58247-X). This volume in the Deverry saga follows *The Black Raven* (1999) and tells of the adventures of many souls who are reborn two centuries after their deaths. (Rev: BL 11/15/00)

1967 Kerr, Katherine. *Darkspell* (10–12). 1994, Bantam paper $6.99 (0-553-56888-4). Three companions combat a group of evil sorcerers in this sequel to *Daggerspell*. (Rev: BL 9/1/87)

1968 Kerr, Peg. *Emerald House Rising* (10–12). 1997, Warner paper $5.99 (0-446-60393-7). While struggling to master the skills of wizardry, Jena finds herself drawn to a mysterious nobleman named Morgan. (Rev: VOYA 8/97)

1969 Keyes, Greg. *The Briar King* (11–12). 2003, Del Rey $23.95 (0-345-44066-8). As the Briar King awakens from a long sleep, the Sefyr flee in terror and the end of the world is predicted; for mature teens. (Rev: BL 12/1/02; SLJ 8/03; VOYA 4/03)

1970 Keyes, J. Gregory. *The Shadows of God* (10–12). Series: Age of Unreason. 2001, Del Rey paper $15.00 (0-345-43904-X). An alternate history yarn in which the New World is trapped between Russia, which is ruled by a warlock, and Britain, which is determined to regain its colonies. (Rev: BL 4/15/01; VOYA 4/02)

1971 King, Gabriel. *The Golden Cat* (10–12). 1999, Del Rey $24.50 (0-345-42304-6). In this sequel to *The Wild Road,* a group of talking cats seek allies in the animal kingdom to counter renewed threats from the evil scientist known as the Alchemist. (Rev: BL 5/15/99; SLJ 8/99)

1972 King, Gabriel. *The Wild Road* (10–12). 1998, Ballantine $24.95 (0-345-42302-X). In this fantasy, an evil sorcerer tortures cats who can talk in order to harness the power of the Wild Road, a dimension that contains the memories of all animals that have gone before. (Rev: SLJ 2/99; VOYA 6/98)

1973 King, Stephen. *The Drawing of the Three* (10–12). Illus. Series: Dark Tower. 1989, NAL paper $16.95 (0-452-26214-3). Roland lives out the predictions of tarot cards dealt him by the man in black in the first volume in the series, *The Gunslinger* (1988). (Rev: BL 12/15/88)

1974 King, Stephen. *The Eyes of the Dragon* (9–12). 1987, NAL paper $7.99 (0-451-16658-2). In this tale of potions and evil magic, a king dies mysteriously and his older son is unjustly accused. (Rev: BL 11/1/86; BR 9–10/87; SLJ 6/87; VOYA 8/87)

1975 King, Stephen. *The Gunslinger* (10–12). Illus. Series: Dark Tower. 1988, NAL paper $10.95 (0-452-26134-1). A young marksman and a boy stalk a man in black in this first volume of the series. (Rev: BL 7/88)

1976 King, Stephen. *Song of Susannah* (10–12). Series: Dark Tower. 2004, Scribner $30.00 (1-880418-59-2). This epic novel follows *The Wolves of Calla* (2003) in the Dark Tower series, and continues the story of the gunslingers that is concluded in *The Dark Tower* (2004). (Rev: BL 5/1/04)

1977 King, Stephen. *The Waste Lands* (9–12). Series: Dark Tower. 1992, NAL paper $17.95 (0-452-26740-4). This third installment tells of Roland of Mid-World and three New Yorkers who proceed ever nearer the Dark Tower, where the source of the planet's cultural degradation lies. (Rev: BL 10/15/91*; SLJ 8/92)

1978 King-Smith, Richard. *Godhanger* (7–10). 1999, Crown $18.99 (0-517-80036-5). Skymaster, a Christlike bird, comes to Godhanger Wood to help save the animals from a merciless gamekeeper. (Rev: BL 3/1/99; HB 7–8/99; HBG 9/99; SLJ 2/99)

1979 Kipling, Rudyard. *Kipling's Fantasy* (9–12). Ed. by John Brunner. 1992, Tor $17.95 (0-312-85354-8). Atmospheric tales of myth and horror, with rich language and image. (Rev: BL 10/15/92; SLJ 6/93)

1980 Klasky, Mindy. *The Glasswright's Progress* (7–12). 2001, Roc paper $6.99 (0-451-45835-4). Rani Trader, living in the court of King Halaravilli of Morenia, seeks to resurrect the disbanded glasswrights' guild even as a formidable enemy sets his sights on the kingdom; a sequel to *The Glasswrights' Apprentice* (2000). (Rev: VOYA 4/02)

1981 Klasky, Mindy L. *The Glasswrights' Test* (10–12). 2003, NAL paper $6.99 (0-451-45931-8). Glass artist Ranita is right to be suspicious when she is sought out by the Glasswrights' Guild, and soon finds herself embroiled in political intrigue and adventure. (Rev: BL 6/1–15/03; VOYA 12/03)

1982 Kotzwinkle, William. *The Bear Went over the Mountain* (10–12). 1996, Doubleday $22.50 (0-385-48428-3). A satirical fantasy in which a humanlike bear named Hal Jam finds a manuscript under a tree and heads to New York to have it published. (Rev: SLJ 12/96)

1983 Krinard, Susan. *The Forest Lord* (10–12). 2002, Berkley paper $6.99 (0-425-18686-5). The Forest Lord needs a human mate to stop the extinction of the fairy people. (Rev: BL 10/1/02)

1984 Kritzer, Naomi. *Fires of the Faithful* (10–12). 2002, Bantam paper $6.99 (0-553-58517-7). Eliana's music studies are set aside when she decides to lead a defense of the Old Way religion against the goddess worshippers who are terrorizing her people. (Rev: BL 9/1/02; VOYA 2/03)

1985 Kurland, Lynn. *My Heart Stood Still* (9–12). 2001, Berkley paper $6.99 (0-425-18197-9). A ghost who has haunted her castle for 600 years falls in love with the American businessman who buys and begins to restore it. (Rev: BL 9/15/01)

1986 Kurtz, Katherine. *Camber of Culdi* (10–12). 1987, Ballantine paper $4.95 (0-345-34767-6). In this first volume of the Legends of Camber of Culdi series the Deryni, a race with unusual mental powers, revolt against their cruel masters. Others in the series are *Saint Camber* and *Camber the Heretic* (both 1987).

1987 Kurtz, Katherine. *In the King's Service* (10–12). Series: Deryni. 2003, Berkley $23.95 (0-441-01060-1). In this installment in her popular Deryni series, Kurtz goes back in time to lay out the history of the Kingdom of Gwynned and introduce the forebears of many characters. (Rev: BL 10/15/03; VOYA 4/04)

1988 Kurtz, Katherine. *King Kelson's Bride* (10–12). 2000, Berkley $22.95 (0-441-00732-5). Part of the highly praised and recommended Deryni saga, this novel deals with King Kelson and his choice of a bride. (Rev: BL 5/15/00)

1989 Kurtz, Katherine. *St. Patrick's Gargoyle* (10–12). 2001, Berkley $21.95 (0-441-00725-2). An amusing fantasy about Paddy, a gargoyle on Dublin's St. Patrick's Cathedral, who investigates some thefts from the church. (Rev: BL 2/1/01*)

1990 Kurtz, Katherine, and Deborah T. Harris. *The Adept* (9–12). 1991, Berkley paper $5.99 (0-441-00343-5). Strange events in museums, ruined abbeys, and Loch Ness lead Adam Sinclair, a Scottish psychiatrist, to the discovery that evil magic is being revived. (Rev: BL 3/1/91; SLJ 9/91)

1991 Kurtz, Katherine, and Deborah T. Harris. *The Adept, No. 3: The Templar Treasure* (9–12). 1993, Berkley paper $6.50 (0-441-00345-1). Psychiatrist Adam Sinclair and companions call upon the powers of King Solomon and the Knights Templar to prevent a crazed academic from freeing the powers of evil. (Rev: BL 6/1–15/93; VOYA 10/93)

1992 Kurtz, Katherine, and Deborah Turner Harris. *The Temple and the Crown* (10–12). 2001, Warner paper $6.99 (0-446-60854-8). The saga begun with *The Temple and the Stone* (1998) continues the story of the Templars, two members of the secret Cercle, and such historical characters as Robert the Bruce of Scotland and Philip the Fair of France. (Rev: BL 4/15/01; VOYA 8/01)

1993 Lackey, Mercedes. *Alta* (9–12). 2004, DAW $24.95 (0-7564-0216-6). In this sequel to *Joust* (2003), young Vetch becomes indispensable in his land because he knows how to tame newly hatched dragons. (Rev: BL 3/15/04)

1994 Lackey, Mercedes. *The Eagle and the Nightingales* (9–12). Series: Bardic Voices. 1995, Baen $22.00 (0-671-87636-8). One of the nightingales is a gypsy bard, who is up to her eyebrows in intrigues both mundane and magical at the Kingsford Faire. (Rev: BL 12/15/94; VOYA 5/95)

1995 Lackey, Mercedes. *Fiddler Fair* (9–12). 1998, Simon & Schuster paper $5.99 (0-671-87866-2). A collection of 12 fantastic stories that deal with such topics as televangelists, animals rights zealots, and old-fashioned men. (Rev: VOYA 10/98)

1996 Lackey, Mercedes. *The Fire Rose* (10–12). 1995, Baen $22.00 (0-671-87687-2). A fantasy retelling of *Beauty and the Beast*, set in San Francisco in 1905 at the time of the earthquake, in which a rich man who was partially transformed into a wolf by a magical spell is helped by an orphaned young woman. (Rev: VOYA 4/96)

1997 Lackey, Mercedes. *Firebird* (10–12). 1996, Tor $24.95 (0-312-85812-4). A retelling of the medieval Russian folktale in which an unhappy young son of a boyar makes contact with a magical bird, gains the power to speak with animals, and overcomes the evil Katschei. (Rev: BL 1/1–15/97; SLJ 5/97; VOYA 6/97)

1998 Lackey, Mercedes. *Joust* (10–12). 2003, DAW $24.95 (0-7564-0122-4). Young Vetch hopes to hatch a dragon and challenge the evil Tian, who have overrun and ruined his homeland. (Rev: BL 3/15/03*)

1999 Lackey, Mercedes. *The Serpent's Shadow* (10–12). 2001, DAW $24.95 (0-88677-915-4). Set in an alternative Victorian London touched with magic and romance, this novel features Maya, who

must seek aid to prevent the destruction of London by the forces of Kali. (Rev: BL 2/15/01; VOYA 10/01)

2000 Lackey, Mercedes. *Take a Thief* (6–12). 2001, DAW $24.95 (0-7564-0008-2). Skif, a young orphan who's adopted into a Valdemar band of thieves, seeks revenge when his newfound family perishes in a mysterious fire. (Rev: VOYA 2/02)

2001 Lackey, Mercedes. *Winds of Fate* (9–12). Series: Mage Winds. 1991, NAL $18.95 (0-88677-489-6). Princess Elspeth, heir to Valdemar's throne, rides in search of a mage to save the realm from the magical machinations of Ancar of Hardom. A long-running series that includes *Exile's Honor* (2002). (Rev: BL 8/91; SLJ 5/92)

2002 Lackey, Mercedes, and Larry Dixon. *The Silver Gryphon* (10–12). Series: The Mage Wars. 1996, DAW $21.95 (0-88677-684-8). In this third book of the series, Silverblade, a human, and Tadrith, a gryphon, are sent on a danger-filled mission to guard a remote outpost far from their peaceful city, White Gryphon. (Rev: SLJ 8/96; VOYA 8/96)

2003 Lackey, Mercedes, and Rosemary Edghill. *Mad Maudlin* (10–12). 2003, Baen $25.00 (0-7434-7143-1). Eric Banyon, hero of five previous tales, faces exciting action and adventure in a plot that includes a newly discovered brother, a royal elf, and rumors of a monster on the loose in New York. (Rev: BL 8/03; VOYA 12/03)

2004 Lackey, Mercedes, et al. *The Shadow of the Lion* (11–12). 2002, Baen $27.00 (0-7434-3523-0). Romance, political intrigue, and suspense are intermingled in a complex and richly detailed alternate version of 16th-century Venice; for mature teens. (Rev: BL 3/15/02; VOYA 8/02)

2005 Lackey, Mercedes, and Roberta Gellis. *This Scepter'd Isle* (10–12). 2004, Baen $25.00 (0-7434-7156-3). At the court of Henry VIII, there is evidence of elvish intervention in royal affairs. (Rev: BL 2/15/04)

2006 Lackey, Mercedes, and James Mallory. *The Outstretched Shadow* (10–12). 2003, Tor $25.95 (0-765-30219-5). Jaded with life as a young mage with high expectations, young Kellen is fascinated to find three books about forbidden magic, information that puts his life at risk. (Rev: BL 9/15/03; VOYA 12/03)

2007 Lally, Soinbhe. *A Hive for the Honeybee* (8–12). Illus. 1999, Scholastic paper $16.95 (0-590-51038-X). An allegory about life and work that takes place in a beehive with such characters as Alfred, the bee poet, and Mo, a radical drone. (Rev: BL 2/1/99; HB 3–4/99; HBG 10/99; SLJ 5/99*; VOYA 4/99)

2008 Larson, Gary. *There's a Hair in My Dirt! A Worm's Story* (10–12). Illus. 1998, HarperCollins

$15.95 (0-06-019104-X). An offbeat, macabre fantasy told by an earthworm to his son who is disgusted when he finds a human hair in his dirt and with his position in life as "the lowest of the low." (Rev: SLJ 12/98)

2009 Laumer, Keith, ed. *Dangerous Vegetables* (9–12). 1998, Baen paper $5.99 (0-671-57781-6). A collection of fantastic stories, all dealing with plant life, by such well-known authors as Bradbury, Saberhagen, and John Christopher. (Rev: VOYA 6/99)

2010 Lawhead, Stephen R. *Merlin* (10–12). 1990, Avon paper $6.99 (0-380-70889-2). The story of how Merlin prepared the world for the arrival of Arthur. (Rev: VOYA 4/89)

2011 Lee, Tanith. *Black Unicorn* (7–10). Illus. 1993, Tor paper $3.99 (0-8125-2459-4). The 16-year-old daughter of a sorceress reconstructs a unicorn from a cache of golden bones that impels her to run away from her desert home to a seaside city. (Rev: BL 10/15/91; SLJ 11/91)

2012 Lee, Tanith. *Gold Unicorn* (7–10). 1994, Atheneum $15.95 (0-689-31814-6). This sequel to *Black Unicorn* continues the adventures of Tanaquil, 16, runaway daughter of an odd sorceress, after she is captured by Empress Veriam, who turns out to be her half-sister. (Rev: BL 1/15/95; SLJ 2/95; VOYA 4/95)

2013 Lee, Tanith. *Mortal Suns* (10–12). 2003, Overlook $26.95 (1-58567-207-6). In the kingdom of Akhemony — a land reminiscent of ancient Greece — a queen gives birth to a beautiful daughter who has no feet. (Rev: BL 9/1/03)

2014 Lee, Tanith. *Red Unicorn* (7–10). 1997, St. Martin's paper $5.99 (0-7653-4568-4). This continuation of the fantasies *Black Unicorn* and *Gold Unicorn* tells of Tanaquil's encounters with her double, Princess Tanakil, who lives in an alternate world. (Rev: BL 6/1–15/97; VOYA 12/97)

2015 Le Guin, Ursula K. *The Other Wind* (10–12). 2001, Harcourt $25.00 (0-15-100684-9). The sorcerer Alder travels to the remote island of Gont to seek relief from his strange nightmares. (Rev: BL 6/1–15/01; SLJ 6/01)

2016 Le Guin, Ursula K. *Tales from Earthsea* (9–12). 2001, Harcourt $24.00 (0-15-100561-3). The author again uses her magical land and its inhabitants as the setting for these five tales. (Rev: BL 3/1/01)

2017 Le Guin, Ursula K. *Tehanu: The Last Book of Earthsea* (7–10). Series: Earthsea. 1990, Macmillan $21.00 (0-689-31595-3). In the fourth and last of the Earthsea books, Tenar is summoned by a dying mage, or wise one, to teach a child the spells and magic that give the power to lead. (Rev: BL 3/1/90; SLJ 4/90; VOYA 6/90)

2018 Le Guin, Ursula K. *The Wind's Twelve Quarters* (10–12). 1995, HarperCollins paper $4.99 (0-06-105605-7). This collection includes 17 stories by Le Guin, the winner of both Hugo and Nebula awards.

2019 Le Guin, Ursula K. *A Wizard of Earthsea* (8–12). Illus. Series: Earthsea. 1968, Bantam paper $7.50 (0-553-26250-5). An apprentice wizard accidentally unleashes an evil power onto the land of Earthsea. Followed by *The Tombs of Atuan* and *The Farthest Shore.*

2020 Leith, Valery. *The Riddled Night* (10–12). 2000, Bantam paper $13.95 (0-553-37939-9). This, the second Everien book, tells how Tash, the conqueror of Everien, wants to strengthen the Fire Houses to make weapons to fight the Clans. (Rev: BL 8/00)

2021 L'Engle, Madeleine. *An Acceptable Time* (8–12). 1989, Farrar $18.00 (0-374-30027-5). Polly O'Keefe time-travels (as her parents did years before in the Time trilogy) but this time to visit a civilization of Druids that lived 3,000 years ago. (Rev: BL 1/1/90; BR 5–6/90; SLJ 1/90; VOYA 4/90)

2022 Lewis, C. S. *Out of the Silent Planet* (10–12). 1996, Scribner $22.00 (0-684-83364-6). This volume contains a trilogy of fantasy novels about a classic battle between good and evil.

2023 Lickiss, Rebecca. *Eccentric Circles* (10–12). 2001, Berkley paper $5.99 (0-441-00828-3). Piper finds that her grandmother's backyard is an entrance to the land of Faerie. (Rev: BL 6/1–15/01; VOYA 12/01)

2024 Lindskold, Jane. *Through Wolf's Eyes* (10–12). 2001, Tor $27.95 (0-312-87427-8). Raised by wolves since infancy, 15-year-old Firekeeper, possible heir to the throne of a kingdom, finds herself at the center of political intrigue when she is returned to human society. (Rev: BL 6/1–15/01; VOYA 12/01)

2025 Lindskold, Jane. *Wolf's Head, Wolf's Heart* (10–12). 2002, Tor $27.95 (0-312-87426-X). Firekeeper, a woman raised by intelligent wolves, must recover three magical talismans that have been stolen from the royal castle in this sequel to *Through Wolf's Eyes* (2001). (Rev: BL 10/15/02; VOYA 12/02)

2026 Lipsyte, Robert. *The Chemo Kid* (9–12). 1992, HarperCollins $14.00 (0-06-020284-X). A high school junior gains superhuman strength after undergoing cancer treatments. (Rev: BL 3/1/92; SLJ 3/92)

2027 Lisle, Holly. *Courage of Falcons* (10–12). Series: The Secret Texts. 2000, Warner paper $12.95 (0-446-67397-8). Wizards Kait and Ry have the power to save their world from domination by the dragon Luercas, but its use could open them up to even greater peril; the third volume in the series that began with *Diplomacy of Wolves* (1998). (Rev: VOYA 12/00)

2028 Lisle, Holly. *In the Rift: Glenraven II* (9–12). Series: Glenraven. 1998, Simon & Schuster $21.00 (0-671-87870-0). Kate focuses her magical powers to help a group of wanderers return home to their parallel world of Glenraven. (Rev: VOYA 10/98)

2029 Little, Denise, ed. *Familiars* (10–12). 2002, DAW paper $6.99 (0-7564-0081-3). A collection of 15 original stories about human and animal magical companions. (Rev: BL 6/1–15/02)

2030 Little, Denise, ed. *The Magic Shop* (10–12). 2004, DAW paper $6.99 (0-7564-0173-9). The 17 stories in this anthology by different writers deal with magic and where one can buy it. (Rev: BL 2/15/04)

2031 Littlefield, Bill. *The Circus in the Woods* (6–10). 2001, Houghton $15.00 (0-618-06642-X). Mystery and fantasy are combined in this quiet, reflective story about a 13-year-old girl who finds a strange circus in the Vermont woods where she spends her summers. (Rev: BCCB 12/01; HBG 10/02; SLJ 11/01; VOYA 12/01)

2032 Livesey, Margot. *Eva Moves the Furniture* (10–12). 2001, Holt $23.00 (0-8050-6801-5). Eva seems to be an average woman, but no one knows about her "companions," the specters who are an important part of her life. (Rev: BL 7/01)

2033 Logue, Mary. *Dancing with an Alien* (8–10). 2000, HarperCollins LB $14.89 (0-06-028319-X). Tonia faces a tough decision when she falls in love with a boy from another planet who was sent to Earth to find a mate. (Rev: HBG 9/00; SLJ 7/00)

2034 Lowry, Lois. *Messenger* (6–10). 2004, Houghton $16.00 (0-618-40441-4). The residents of the Village where teenage Matty is a caregiver decide to build a wall to keep out undesirables in this fantasy filled with truth and symbolism. (Rev: BL 2/15/04*; HB 5–6/04; SLJ 4/04; VOYA 6/04)

2035 Macaulay, David. *Baaa* (6–10). Illus. 1985, Houghton LB $13.95 (0-395-38948-8); paper $5.95 (0-395-39588-7). An allegory about the world after humans have left and intelligent sheep take control. (Rev: BL 9/1/85; BR 3–4/86; SLJ 10/85)

2036 McCaffrey, Anne. *Acorna's Quest* (9–12). 1998, HarperCollins $23.00 (0-06-105297-3). In this sequel to *Acorna: The Unicorn Girl* (1997), the humanoid Acorna leaves with her friend Calum to search for the survival pod she came from and her home world. (Rev: VOYA 10/98)

2037 McCaffrey, Anne. *All the Weyrs of Pern* (9–12). Series: Pern. 1992, Tor paper $6.99 (0-345-36893-2). In this sequel to *Dragonsdawn*, human settlers of Pern rediscover their original landing site

and revitalize a long-lost artificial intelligence system. (Rev: BL 10/1/91*)

2038 McCaffrey, Anne. *Damia's Children* (9–12). 1993, 1994, Berkley paper $6.99 (0-441-00007-X). The saga of a telepathic/telekinetic family and alien contact, with teenage main characters. (Rev: BL 12/1/92; SLJ 11/93)

2039 McCaffrey, Anne. *Dragonflight* (6–12). Adapted by Brynne Stephens. Illus. Series: Dragonriders of Pern. 1991, Eclipse $4.95 (1-56060-074-8). Book one of a three-part graphic novel based on *Dragonflight* from the Dragonriders of Pern series. (Rev: BL 9/1/91)

2040 McCaffrey, Anne. *Dragonseye* (10–12). Series: Dragonriders of Pern. 1997, Ballantine $24.00 (0-345-38821-6). In this Dragonriders of Pern story, most of the riders want to prepare for the approach of the Red Star and the dreaded Thread, but Lord Holder, their abusive leader, refuses to take any action. (Rev: BL 12/15/96; SLJ 7/97)

2041 McCaffrey, Anne. *The Girl Who Heard Dragons* (9–12). 1995, Tor $3.99 (0-8125-1099-2). Fifteen short fiction pieces that demonstrate the range and scope of the author's work. (Rev: BL 3/15/94; VOYA 10/94)

2042 McCaffrey, Anne. *If Wishes Were Horses* (7–12). 1998, NAL $14.95 (0-451-45642-4). When Tirza turns 16 and earns her own magic crystal, she wishes for a horse for her twin brother — with unexpected results. (Rev: VOYA 2/99)

2043 McCaffrey, Anne. *The MasterHarper of Pern* (10–12). 1998, Ballantine $25.00 (0-345-38823-2). In this Pern novel (set prior to *Dragonflight*), the reader is told the story of the beloved harper Robinton — of rejection by his father during his childhood, the loss of his wife and best friend, and his career before he becomes Masterharper of Pern. (Rev: BL 10/15/97; SLJ 8/98; VOYA 8/98)

2044 McCaffrey, Anne. *Nerilka's Story: A Pern Adventure* (9–12). 1986, Ballantine paper $5.99 (0-345-33949-5). A young girl leaves her Hold to help nurse the sick stricken with a terrible plague. (Rev: BL 3/1/86; SLJ 5/86)

2045 McCaffrey, Anne. *The Renegades of Pern* (9–12). 1989, Ballantine paper $19.95 (0-345-34096-5). The adult Dragonriders series and the juvenile Harper Hall books are brought together by mixing their characters in this fantasy that takes place in the southern part of Pern. (Rev: BL 9/15/89; VOYA 4/90)

2046 McCaffrey, Anne, and Todd McCaffrey. *Dragon's Kin* (10–12). Series: Pern. 2003, Del Rey $24.95 (0-345-46198-3). Kindin and Nuella, two young people involved in the mines, learn the secrets of the watch-whers and how they communicate with the dragons. (Rev: BL 9/15/03; VOYA 4/04)

2047 McCaffrey, Anne, and Elizabeth Ann Scarborough. *Acorna's Search* (10–12). Series: Acorna. 2001, HarperCollins $25.00 (0-380-97898-9). In this installment of the recommended series, Acorna helps her people, the Linyaari, to try to restore their beloved home. (Rev: BL 10/1/01; VOYA 6/02)

2048 McCaffrey, Anne, and Elizabeth Ann Scarborough. *Acorna's World* (10–12). 2000, HarperCollins $24.00 (0-06-105095-4). In this fourth book about the unicorn girl Acorna, our young heroine has difficulties adjusting to her native culture because of her upbringing by humans. (Rev: BL 6/1–15/00)

2049 McGarry, Terry. *Illumination* (10–12). 2001, Tor $25.95 (0-312-87389-1). Young Liath, who has passed her examinations to become a mage, finds that her talent fails on the night of her triumph. (Rev: BL 8/01)

2050 McKiernan, Dennis L. *Caverns of Socrates* (9–12). 1995, Penguin $24.95 (0-451-45455-3); paper $14.95 (0-451-45476-6). Role-playing meets virtual reality, and both meet a mad computer. (Rev: BL 12/15/95; VOYA 4/96)

2051 McKiernan, Dennis L. *Once upon a Winter's Night* (9–12). 2001, Penguin $23.95 (0-451-45840-0). In spite of warnings, Camille decides to see the face of the prince she loves. As predicted, a curse is placed on her household in this charming retelling of East o' the Sun and West o' the Moon. (Rev: BL 5/15/01; VOYA 12/01)

2052 McKiernan, Dennis L. *Red Slippers* (9–12). Series: Mithgar. 2004, NAL $23.95 (0-451-45976-8). This collection of 12 stories contains characters found in many fantasies such as elves, giants, and dwarves. (Rev: BL 5/1/04)

2053 McKiernan, Dennis L. *Silver Wolf, Black Falcon* (10–12). 2000, Penguin $23.95 (0-451-45786-2). Bair, who can change into a silver wolf, and his elf mentor, who can become a black falcon, fight the forces of the Golden Horde in this Mithgar novel. (Rev: BL 4/15/00)

2054 McKillip, Patricia A. *Alphabet of Thorn* (9–12). 2004, Berkley $22.95 (0-441-01130-6). Nepenthe, a scribe and translator in the royal library, is given a mysterious book that no one can read and she is determined to discover its secret. (Rev: BL 1/1–15/04)

2055 McKillip, Patricia A. *The Cygnet and the Firebird* (9–12). 1993, Berkley paper $17.95 (0-441-12628-6). *The Sorceress and the Cygnet*'s (1991) sequel shows cousins Nyx Ro and Meguet Vervaine encountering a sorcerer in search of an ancient key, a firebird with amnesia, and a city of dragons. (Rev: BL 9/15/93; SLJ 5/94; VOYA 12/93)

2056 McKillip, Patricia A. *In the Forests of Serre* (10–12). 2003, Berkley $22.95 (0-441-01011-3). A bereaved prince eager to escape a forced marriage is lured into a magical realm in this adventure-packed fantasy. (Rev: BL 5/15/03; VOYA 12/03)

2057 McKillip, Patricia A. *Ombria in Shadow* (10–12). 2002, Ace $22.95 (0-441-00895-X). After the death of its prince, competing forces battle for control of the city-state of Ombria in this rich Gothic fantasy. (Rev: VOYA 6/02)

2058 McKillip, Patricia A. *The Tower at Stony Wood* (10–12). 2000, Berkley $22.95 (0-441-00733-3). Cyan Dag, a brave knight, sets out to rescue a queen who is imprisoned in a distant tower. (Rev: BL 4/15/00)

2059 McKillip, Patricia A. *Winter Rose* (10–12). 1996, Ace paper $19.95 (0-441-00334-6). Rois must cross the threshold between worlds to save her sister and rescue Corbet, whom both she and her sister love, from a curse that is keeping him a prisoner of winter. (Rev: BL 7/96; VOYA 2/97)

2060 McKinley, Robin. *Beauty: A Retelling of the Story of Beauty and the Beast* (9–12). 1978, HarperCollins $15.95 (0-06-024149-7). From the standpoint of Beauty, this is the story of her quest in the forest where she encounters Beast. (Rev: BL 6/1/88)

2061 McKinley, Robin. *The Blue Sword* (7–10). 1982, Greenwillow $16.99 (0-688-00938-7). The king of Damar kidnaps a girl to help in his war against the Northerners. A prequel to *The Hero and the Crown*. Newbery Medal 1985. (Rev: BL 12/15/89)

2062 McKinley, Robin. *A Knot in the Grain and Other Stories* (9–12). 1994, Greenwillow $14.00 (0-688-09201-2). Four love stories set in Damar, a world mixing the real and the magical, featuring magicians, witches, and healers. (Rev: BL 8/94; SLJ 5/94; VOYA 10/94)

2063 McKinley, Robin. *Rose Daughter* (6–12). Illus. 1997, Greenwillow $16.95 (0-688-15439-5). As in her award-winning *Beauty,* (1955) the author returns to the Beauty and the Beast fairy tale in this outstanding reworking of the traditional story. (Rev: BL 8/97; BR 11–12/97; HBG 3/98; SLJ 9/97; VOYA 2/98) [398.2]

2064 McKinley, Robin. *Spindle's End* (7–12). 2000, Putnam $19.99 (0-399-23466-7). An engrossing expansion of the Sleeping Beauty story told with humor, wit, and spellbinding magic. (Rev: BL 4/15/00* ; HB 5–6/00; HBG 9/00; SLJ 6/00; VOYA 4/00)

2065 McKinley, Robin. *The Stone Fey* (6–10). Illus. 1998, Harcourt $17.00 (0-15-200017-8). A fantasy in which young Maddy temporarily falls in love with a stone fey while her fiance is away earning money for their future together. (Rev: BL 11/1/98; HBG 9/99; SLJ 1/99)

2066 McMahon, Donna. *Dance of Knives* (10–12). 2001, Tor $25.95 (0-312-87431-6). In this story set in Vancouver in 2108, bartender Toni and Mary, the owner of the KlonDyke bar, find they must protect the city they love by enlisting the help of a new friend. (Rev: BL 7/01)

2067 McMullen, Sean. *Glass Dragons* (9–12). Series: Moonworlds. 2004, Tor $27.95 (0-765-30797-9). Using many of the characters from *The Voyage of the Shadowman* (2002), the author of this Moonworlds novel tells how Wallas, a royal musician, is falsely accused of regicide. (Rev: BL 3/1/04)

2068 McMullen, Sean. *Voyage of the Shadowmoon* (10–12). 2002, Tor $27.95 (0-312-87740-4). A motley and complex crew, passengers on the vessel *Silvermoon*, seek to disable a weapon known as Silverdeath. (Rev: BL 12/1/02; VOYA 6/03)

2069 McNaughton, Janet. *An Earthly Knight* (7–10). 2004, HarperCollins $15.99 (0-06-008992-X). In this romantic fantasy set in Scotland, 16-year-old Jennie falls in love with an enchanted lord and their love is so strong that it shatters a powerful curse. (Rev: BL 2/15/04; SLJ 3/04)

2070 Mahy, Margaret. *Alchemy* (7–10). 2003, Simon & Schuster $16.95 (0-689-85053-0). Sinister twists and horrifying thrills abound in this story of 17-year-old Roland, who has frightening dreams and finds the divide between dream and reality is beginning to blur. (Rev: BL 3/15/03; HB 5–6/03; HBG 10/03; SLJ 5/03; VOYA 6/03)

2071 Mahy, Margaret. *The Changeover: A Supernatural Romance* (8–12). 1984, Macmillan $16.00 (0-689-50303-2). To save her brother from an evil force, Laura must use the powers of witchcraft.

2072 Marcellas, Diana. *Mother Ocean, Daughter Sea* (10–12). 2001, Tor $27.95 (0-312-87484-7). When Brierley the witch is summoned to heal Melfallen's sick wife, she falls in love with him. (Rev: BL 9/1/01)

2073 Marco, John. *The Saints of the Sword* (10–12). Series: Tyrants and Kings. 2001, Bantam paper $14.95 (0-553-38023-0). In this, the third volume of a series, young Alazrian comes of age, develops his magical powers, and participates in a gigantic battle against his own grandfather. (Rev: BL 2/1/01; VOYA 2/02)

2074 Marillier, Juliet. *Child of the Prophecy* (10–12). Series: Sevenwaters Trilogy. 2002, Tor $26.95 (0-312-84881-1). In the final volume of a trilogy that blends fantasy, romance, and magic, 15-year-old Fainne, granddaughter of the Druid sorceress Oonagh, moves to claim her heritage, falls in love, and must choose between good and evil. (Rev: BL 2/15/02*; VOYA 8/02)

2075 Marillier, Juliet. *Daughter of the Forest* (9–12). 2000, Tor $25.95 (0-312-84879-X). In this first book of a trilogy, young Sorcha must weave magical shirts to free her brothers, who have been turned into swans by a wicked stepmother. (Rev: BL 4/15/00* ; VOYA 12/00)

2076 Marillier, Juliet. *Son of the Shadows* (10–12). 2001, Tor $25.95 (0-312-84880-3). In this sequel to *Daughter of the Forest* (2000), evil again stalks the land of Sevenwaters in the shape of a tattooed outlaw. (Rev: BL 5/15/01; VOYA 12/01)

2077 Marillier, Juliet. *Wolfskin* (10–12). 2003, Tor $25.95 (0-765-30672-7). Young Eyvind aims to serve Thor as a Viking warrior, but the fates intervene with even more challenging options. (Rev: BL 5/15/03)

2078 Marks, Laurie J. *Earth Logic* (10–12). 2003, Tor $25.95 (0-765-30952-1). A strong fantasy for better readers that deals with Karis and her determination to establish peace and leadership in her war-torn land. (Rev: BL 2/1/04*)

2079 Marks, Laurie J. *Fire Logic* (10–12). 2002, Tor $25.95 (0-312-87887-7). When its Earth witch ruler dies, the land of Shaftai is vulnerable to attack by the Sainnites and only three people hold the power to save it. (Rev: BL 6/1–15/02*)

2080 Marston, Ann. *Kingmaker's Sword* (10–12). 1996, HarperCollins paper $5.99 (0-06-105629-4). In this first book of the Rune Blade trilogy, a boy raised as a slave realizes that he is destined to be the bearer of one of the Ceale Rune Blades and form a ruling dynasty. Followed by *The Western King* and *Broken Blade*. (Rev: VOYA 8/97)

2081 Martin, George R. R. *Quartet: Four Tales from the Crossroads* (10–12). Ed. by Christine Carpenito. 2001, NESFA $25.00 (1-886778-31-0). These four stories are excellent examples of Martin's mastery of the fantasy genre. (Rev: BL 4/15/01)

2082 Melling, Orla. *The Druid's Tune* (6–10). 1993, O'Brien paper $9.95 (0-86278-285-6). Peter, a Druid lost in the 20th century, involves two teenagers in a time-travel spell that sends them back to Ireland's Iron Age. (Rev: BL 2/15/93)

2083 Michaels, Melisa C. *Far Harbor* (9–12). 1989, Tor paper $2.99 (0-8125-4581-8). A fantasy romance in which a clumsy, lanky girl meets the prince of her dreams. (Rev: VOYA 12/89)

2084 Mieville, China. *Perdido Street Station* (10–12). 2001, Ballantine paper $18.00 (0-345-44302-0). In an alternate version of Dickens's London, this novel for mature readers tells how a young scientist is trying to discover the secret of flight and instead raises the larva of a deadly snakemoth. (Rev: BL 2/15/01)

2085 Miller, Keith. *The Book of Flying* (10–12). 2004, Riverhead $23.95 (1-57322-249-6). In order to win Sisi, a beautiful, winged girl, Pico sets out to find his own wings. (Rev: BL 2/1/04)

2086 Modesitt, L. E. *Legacies* (10–12). 2002, Tor $27.95 (0-765-30561-5). In a world that has survived catastrophe and seen the development of new species, Alucius uses his secret Talents to influence the outcome of a war; the first installment in a new series. (Rev: BL 10/15/02; VOYA 4/03)

2087 Modesitt, L. E. *Magi'i of Cyador* (10–12). 2000, Tor $27.95 (0-312-87226-7). In this first novel of a new series, readers are introduced to the land of Cyador, the hero Lorn, and his mission to fight barbarians on the frontier. (Rev: BL 4/1/00)

2088 Modesitt, L. E. *Scion of Cyador* (10–12). 2000, Tor $27.95 (0-312-87379-4). In this sequel to *Magi'i of Cyador* (2000), Lorn, our hero and amateur mage, has a number of narrow escapes before becoming emperor. (Rev: BL 9/1/00; VOYA 2/01)

2089 Modesitt, L. E. *The Shadow Sorceress* (10–12). Series: Spellsong Cycle. 2001, Tor $27.95 (0-312-87877-X). Secca, a sorceress, must build up an alliance to fight both internal enemies and the invading Sea Priests in this Spellsong Cycle book that is preceded by *Darksong Rising* (1999). (Rev: BL 5/1/01; SLJ 9/01; VOYA 10/01)

2090 Modesitt, L. E. *Wellspring of Chaos* (10–12). 2004, Tor $27.95 (0-765-30907-6). The corrupt son of the local lord is responsible for the downfall of Kharl, the honest cooper of Brysta. (Rev: BL 3/1/04; VOYA 6/04)

2091 Modesitt, L. E., Jr. *The Soprano Sorceress* (9–12). 1997, Tor $25.95 (0-312-86022-6). Anna is transported in time to the land of Erde, where she can use her beautiful voice to create magic. (Rev: BL 2/1/97; VOYA 10/97)

2092 Moon, Elizabeth. *Against the Odds* (10–12). Series: Familias Regnant. 2000, Baen $24.00 (0-671-31961-2). In this, the last of the Familias Regnant saga, Esmay and Barin defeat a mutiny by followers of their late Nazi-like leader. (Rev: BL 12/1/00)

2093 Moorcock, Michael. *The Dreamthief's Daughter: A Tale of the Albino* (10–12). 2001, Warner $24.95 (0-446-52618-5). An alternate world fantasy in which Elric of Melnibone and Oona, the dreamkeeper's daughter, ally themselves with others to fight Gaynor the Damned. (Rev: BL 3/15/01)

2094 Moore, Alan, et al. *Promethea: Book 3* (10–12). Illus. 2002, DC Comics $24.95 (1-56389-900-0). The focus is more thoughtful than the usual superhero derring-do in this tale of teenage heroine Sophie Bangs and her encounters with famous figures from the occult. (Rev: BL 2/1/03)

2095 Murphy, Pat. *Wild Angel* (10–12). 2000, Tor $23.95 (0-312-86626-7). Susan, who has been raised by a wolf pack in mid-19th-century California, is stalked by her parents' murderer. (Rev: BL 6/1–15/00)

2096 Murphy, Rita. *Harmony* (6–10). 2002, Delacorte LB $17.99 (0-385-90069-4). Harmony — who apparently fell from a star to land in a chicken coop in the mountains of Tennessee — has strange telekinetic powers that she tries to keep secret. (Rev: BL 9/15/02; HB 1/03; HBG 3/03; SLJ 10/02; VOYA 12/02)

2097 Murphy, Rita. *Night Flying* (8–12). 2000, Delacorte $14.95 (0-385-32748-X). Everyone in the Hansen family, including 15-year-old Georgia, can fly, and the rules are obeyed by all, but family relationships change when an outspoken aunt arrives from California. (Rev: BL 12/15/00; HB 9–10/00; HBG 3/01; SLJ 11/00)

2098 Murphy, Shirley Rousseau. *Cat Fear No Evil* (9–12). 2004, HarperCollins $24.95 (0-06-620949-8). In this cat fantasy, Azrae, a sinister tomcat with burning yellow eyes, and his human cohorts plan a crime spree. (Rev: BL 1/1–15/04)

2099 Murphy, Shirley Rousseau. *Cat Raise the Dead* (9–12). 1997, HarperCollins paper $5.99 (0-06-105602-2). Two intrepid cats, Joe Grey and Dulcie, investigate some burglaries and several disappearances at an old folks home in their seaside village in California. (Rev: VOYA 2/98)

2100 Murphy, Shirley Rousseau. *The Catswold Portal* (9–12). 1993, NAL paper $6.99 (0-451-45275-5). Feline fantasy set on 1957 Earth, as well as in the Netherworld, ties an evil queen and a human artist together. (Rev: BL 4/15/92*; SLJ 8/92)

2101 Myers, John Myers. *Silverlock and the Silverlock Companion* (10–12). 2004, NESFA $26.00 (1-886778-52-3). Silverlock voyages in the Commonwealth of Letters where he meets Orpheus, visits hell, and hears about the Alamo. (Rev: BL 3/15/04)

2102 Nance, Kathleen. *Spellbound* (11–12). 2003, Love Spell paper $6.99 (0-505-52486-4). In a romantic fantasy set in New Orleans, Madeline meets a seductive minstrel from the land of Kaf; suitable for mature readers. (Rev: BL 6/1–15/03)

2103 Napoli, Donna Jo. *Beast* (7–10). 2000, Simon & Schuster $17.00 (0-689-83589-2). Beast's life is the focus of this retelling of Beauty and the Beast, in which a Persian prince is turned into a lion and travels to live in a lonely castle in France. (Rev: BL 9/15/00; HB 9–10/00; HBG 3/01; SLJ 10/00)

2104 Napoli, Donna Jo. *Zel* (7–12). 1996, Dutton $15.99 (0-525-45612-0). Set in 15th-century Switzerland, this is a brilliant reworking of the Rapunzel fairy tale told from three different points of view. (Rev: BL 9/1/96; BR 9–10/97; SLJ 9/96; VOYA 4/97)

2105 Napoli, Donna Jo, and Richard Tchen. *Spinners* (8–12). 1999, Dutton $15.99 (0-525-46065-9). Fifteen-year-old Saskia is saved by the mysterious spinner Rumpelstiltskin, whose secret is that he is the girl's father. (Rev: BL 9/1/99; HBG 4/00; SLJ 9/99; VOYA 12/99)

2106 Neason, Rebecca. *The Thirteenth Scroll* (9–12). 2001, Warner paper $6.99 (0-446-60953-6). The forces of evil led by Baron Geraldis are trying to prevent Selia, the rightful heir to the throne of Aghamore, from gaining power. (Rev: BL 5/1/01; VOYA 8/01)

2107 Nicholson, William. *Firesong* (7–12). Series: The Wind on Fire. 2002, Hyperion LB $18.49 (0-7868-2496-4). Twins Bowman and Kestrel have succeeded in their goal of rescuing the Manth people from slavery and travel to what they believe is the promised land. (Rev: HBG 3/03; SLJ 1/03; VOYA 12/02)

2108 Nicholson, William. *Slaves of the Mastery* (7–12). Series: The Wind on Fire. 2001, Hyperion $17.99 (0-7868-0570-6). In this sequel to *The Wind Singer* (2000), 15-year-old twins Bowman and Kestrel must use magic and mettle to combat the Master who has enslaved their people. (Rev: BL 10/15/01; HBG 3/02; SLJ 12/01; VOYA 12/01)

2109 Niffenegger, Audrey. *The Time Traveler's Wife* (11–12). 2003, MacAdam $25.00 (1-931561-46-X). An offbeat romance featuring a time-traveling husband and a normal wife who often find they are out of chronological order; for mature readers. (Rev: BL 9/1/03)

2110 Niles, Douglas. *A Breach in the Watershed* (10–12). 1995, Ace paper $13.00 (0-441-00208-0). The beginning of a fantasy series in which the land of Watershed is threatened by the power of the Sleepstealer and his minions. Followed by *Darkenheight* (1996). (Rev: VOYA 6/97)

2111 Niven, Larry, ed. *The Magic Goes Away* (10–12). 1985, Ace paper $4.99 (0-441-51554-1). The first novel in a trilogy about a land where magic is used for both good and evil. It is followed by *The Magic May Return*.

2112 Niven, Larry, and Jerry Pournelle. *The Burning City* (10–12). 2000, Pocket $24.95 (0-671-03660-2). This fantasy for better readers, set on Earth 12,000 years ago, deals with Yangin-Atep and his return home to Burning City (later Los Angeles) to fight his childhood enemies. (Rev: BL 2/15/00)

2113 Nix, Garth. *Abhorsen* (7–12). 2003, HarperCollins LB $18.89 (0-06-027826-9). Two previous books, *Sabriel* (1996) and *Lirael* (2001), set the stage for the confrontation between Lirael and the evil Hedge, who now controls the dead and is seeking to release the Destroyer. (Rev: BCCB 3/03; BL 1/1–15/03; HB 3–4/03; HBG 10/03; SLJ 2/03; VOYA 2/03)

2114 Nix, Garth. *Lirael: Daughter of the Clayr* (7–12). 2001, HarperCollins LB $16.89 (0-06-027824-2). In this sequel to *Sabriel* (1996), Lirael and Prince Sameth battle against a new evil that threatens the Old Kingdom. (Rev: BCCB 5/01; BL

4/15/01; HB 7–8/01; HBG 10/01; SLJ 5/01; VOYA 8/01)

2115 Norton, Andre. *Gryphon's Eyrie* (10–12). Illus. 1992, Tor paper $3.99 (0-8125-3169-8). In this installment of the Witch World series, two young lovers tell, in alternating chapters, of their war against the Dark.

2116 Norton, Andre. *The Monster's Legacy* (7–10). 1996, Simon & Schuster $17.00 (0-689-80731-7). In this novel, part of the *Dragonflight* series, a young apprentice embroiderer and her two friends flee invaders and escape to a land inhabited by Loden, a monster who preys on humans. (Rev: BL 4/1/96; SLJ 6/96; VOYA 8/96)

2117 Norton, Andre. *Moon Mirror* (10–12). 1989, Tor paper $4.99 (0-8125-0303-1). Nine short fantasies about such subjects as ESP, witches, magic, and quests. (Rev: BL 1/1/89; VOYA 6/89)

2118 Norton, Andre, and Martin H. Greenberg, eds. *Catfantastic IV* (9–12). 1996, DAW paper $5.99 (0-88677-711-9). This is the fourth collection of original stories about cats in fantastic situations. (Rev: VOYA 12/96)

2119 Norton, Andre, and Lyn McConchie. *Beast Master's Ark* (10–12). Series: Beast Master. 2002, Tor $23.95 (0-765-30041-9). On the planet Arzor, Storm hopes to find mates for three beasts he brought from Earth on the Ark; a sequel to *Beast Master* (1959). (Rev: BL 5/15/02)

2120 Norton, Andre, and Lyn McConchie. *Ciara's Song: A Chronicle of Witch World* (9–12). 1998, Warner paper $6.50 (0-446-60644-8). After her family, which has a witch ancestry, is murdered by a mob, Ciara is raised by the powerful Tarnoor, and under his protection she discovers her magical healing powers and dangers that they hold for her. (Rev: BL 6/1–15/98; VOYA 12/98)

2121 Norton, Andre, and Lyn McConchie. *The Key of the Keplian* (9–12). 1995, Warner paper $5.50 (0-446-60220-5). A part-Native American, part-Celtic girl passes into Witch World, where she must develop her own magic to survive in the realm. (Rev: BL 7/95; VOYA 2/96)

2122 Odom, Mel. *The Rover* (10–12). 2001, Tor $25.95 (0-312-87882-6). A rip-roaring adventure fantasy featuring a timid young librarian, Wick, and his aptitude for getting into trouble. (Rev: BL 7/01*; SLJ 1/02; VOYA 12/01)

2123 O'Donohoe, Nick. *Under the Healing Sign* (9–12). 1995, Berkley paper $4.99 (0-441-00180-7). In this sequel to *The Magic and the Healing* (o.p.), the community fights an amoral villain, which brings back veterinarian B. J. Vaugh. (Rev: BL 3/15/95; VOYA 5/95)

2124 Orgel, Doris. *The Princess and the God* (7–10). 1996, Orchard LB $16.99 (0-531-08866-9);

Bantam paper $4.50 (0-440-22691-0). A handsome retelling of the Cupid and Psyche myth in novel format, in which the power of pure love is shown conquering overwhelming obstacles. (Rev: BL 2/1/96; BR 9–10/96; SLJ 4/96)

2125 Orwell, George. *Animal Farm* (9–12). Illus. 1983, NAL paper $5.95 (0-451-52634-1). A fantasy of world politics in which farm animals revolt to form a society in which everyone is meant to be equal.

2126 Osborne-McKnight, Juilene. *Bright Sword of Ireland* (9–12). 2004, Tor $24.95 (0-765-30698-0). A reworking of an Irish legend in which Finnabair, a mousy princess, struggles to reclaim her destiny from her dangerous mother. (Rev: BL 1/1–15/04)

2127 Paolini, Christopher. *Eragon* (7–12). Series: Inheritance. 2003, Knopf LB $20.99 (0-375-92668-2). A 15-year-old boy called Eragon finds a stone that hatches a magnificent blue dragon, drawing him into a series of dangerous adventures as the two hunt killers and in turn are hunted. (Rev: BL 8/03*; HBG 4/04; SLJ 9/03; VOYA 8/03)

2128 Patton, Fiona. *The Golden Sword* (10–12). 2001, DAW paper $6.99 (0-88677-921-9). Four cousins organize a conspiracy that threatens to bring down the kingdom's ruling family in this well-told fantasy. (Rev: BL 8/01; VOYA 12/01)

2129 Pattou, Edith. *East* (6–10). 2003, Harcourt $18.00 (0-15-204563-5). A great white bear carries Rose away from home to her destiny in this romantic novelization of the East o' the Sun and West o' the Moon fairy tale. (Rev: BL 9/1/03*; HBG 4/04; SLJ 12/03; VOYA 12/03)

2130 Pattou, Edith. *Fire Arrow* (7–10). 1998, Harcourt $18.00 (0-15-201635-X); paper $6.00 (0-15-202264-3). In this sequel to *Hero's Song*, Brie sets out to avenge the death of her father by confronting his torturer. (Rev: BL 5/15/98; HBG 9/98; SLJ 7/98; VOYA 10/98)

2131 Pattou, Edith. *Hero's Song* (7–10). 1991, Harcourt $16.95 (0-15-233807-1). This fantasy-quest novel, infused with Irish myth and folklore, concerns a youth's search for his beloved sister, a wicked queen, and a clash between good and evil. (Rev: BL 10/15/91; SLJ 1/92)

2132 Paxson, Diana. *The Book of the Spear* (10–12). 1999, Avon paper $10.00 (0-380-80546-4). In this, the second part of a reworking of the Arthurian legend, Oesc, a Saxon warrior, uses his magic spear to combat the powers of Arthur's sword. (Rev: SLJ 8/99)

2133 Pierce, Meredith Ann. *Treasure at the Heart of the Tanglewood* (6–10). 2001, Viking $16.99 (0-670-89247-5). Hannah, a young healer who lives in a forest with her animal companions, embarks on a fantastic journey of self-discovery after she falls in love with a handsome young knight. (Rev: BCCB

7–8/01; BL 4/15/01; HB 7–8/01; HBG 10/01; SLJ 6/01*; VOYA 6/01)

2134 Pierce, Meredith Ann. *Waters Luminous and Deep: Shorter Fictions* (7–12). 2004, Viking $16.99 (0-670-03687-0). A stirring collection of fictional stories, long and short, that have water as a connecting link. (Rev: BL 4/15/04; SLJ 4/04)

2135 Pierce, Tamora. *Cold Fire* (6–10). Series: The Circle Opens. 2002, Scholastic $16.95 (0-590-39655-2). Daja is studying in the chilly northern city of Kugisko, where her ability to handle fire comes in handy but also draws her into a relationship with an arsonist. (Rev: BL 9/1/02; HB 7–8/02; HBG 10/02; SLJ 8/02; VOYA 6/02)

2136 Pierce, Tamora. *The Realms of the Gods* (6–10). Series: The Immortals. 1996, Simon & Schuster $17.00 (0-689-31990-8). In this fourth volume of the series, Daine and the mage Numair triumph over evil Stormwing and Uusoae, the Queen of Chaos. (Rev: BL 10/15/96; SLJ 11/96; VOYA 4/97)

2137 Pierce, Tamora. *Trickster's Choice* (7–12). Series: Daughter of the Lioness. 2003, Random LB $19.99 (0-375-91466-8). Aly, the 16-year-old daughter of Alanna the Lioness, uses her intelligence and magical powers to escape the trickster god Kyprioth's clutches. (Rev: BL 12/1/03; HBG 4/04; SLJ 12/03; VOYA 10/03)

2138 Pierce, Tamora. *Wild Magic* (6–10). Series: The Immortals. 1992, Atheneum $17.00 (0-689-31761-1). An exciting tale in which teenager Daine gradually accepts the fact that she possesses wild magic. (Rev: BL 10/15/92; SLJ 11/92)

2139 Pope, Elizabeth Marie. *The Perilous Gard* (9–12). 1992, Puffin paper $5.99 (0-14-034912-X). Kate wants to save Christopher who has given himself as a sacrifice to the Fairy folk. Also use *The Sherwood Ring* (Peter Smith, 1990).

2140 Porte, Barbara Ann. *Beauty and the Serpent: Thirteen Tales of Unnatural Animals* (6–10). 2001, Simon & Schuster $17.00 (0-689-84147-7). An eccentric school librarian introduces an exchange of offbeat stories about animals with strange, often dark, abilities and tendencies. (Rev: HBG 10/02; SLJ 11/01; VOYA 2/02)

2141 Pratchett, Terry. *The Fifth Elephant* (10–12). 2000, HarperCollins $24.00 (0-06-105157-8). For teens who are fans of the adult fantasies involving Discworld, this novel tells how Chief Constable Vimes tries to prevent a civil war in Ankh-Morporkh involving dwarfs, werewolves, and vampires. (Rev: BL 1/1–15/00; SLJ 7/00)

2142 Pratchett, Terry. *A Hat Full of Sky* (6–10). 2004, HarperCollins $17.89 (0-06-058661-3). In this sequel to *The Wee Free Men* (2003), Tiffany Aching is taken on as an apprentice to Miss Level, who is one person with two bodies. (Rev: BL 4/15/04; HB 7–8/04; SLJ 7/04; VOYA 6/04)

2143 Pratchett, Terry. *Jingo: A Novel of Discworld* (10–12). 1998, HarperCollins $24.00 (0-06-105047-4). In this clever, unpredictable Discworld novel, the cities of Ankh-Morpork and Al-Khali quarrel over which has the right to annex the newly found island of Leshp. (Rev: BL 6/1–15/98; SLJ 8/98; VOYA 12/98)

2144 Pratchett, Terry. *Monstrous Regiment* (11–12). Series: Discworld. 2003, HarperCollins $24.95 (0-06-001315-X). Humor and surprising twists make this a satisfying Discworld tale about war and patriotism. (Rev: BL 8/03; VOYA 2/04)

2145 Pratchett, Terry. *Thief of Time* (10–12). Series: Discworld. 2001, HarperCollins $25.00 (0-06-019956-3). In this Discworld novel, two young boys are closing in on immortality and only meet when time stops. (Rev: BL 4/15/01; SLJ 8/01; VOYA 10/01)

2146 Pratchett, Terry. *The Truth* (10–12). Series: Discworld. 2000, HarperCollins $24.00 (0-380-97895-4). Fans of the recommended Discworld series will enjoy this 25th installment about dwarfs who can turn lead into gold in the city of Ankh-Morpork. (Rev: BL 8/00; VOYA 6/01)

2147 Pratchett, Terry. *The Wee Free Men* (6–10). Series: Discworld. 2003, HarperCollins LB $17.89 (0-06-001237-4). Nine-year-old Tiffany, an aspiring witch, teams up with some feisty characters to rescue her younger brother from Fairyland in a novel that offers both humor and suspense. (Rev: BL 4/15/03; HB 5–6/03*; HBG 10/03; SLJ 5/03*; VOYA 8/03)

2148 Prince, Maggie. *The House on Hound Hill* (6–10). 1998, Houghton $16.00 (0-395-90702-0). When Emily and her family move to a historic house in London, she is gradually drawn into time-traveling to the 17th century and a London devastated by the bubonic plague. (Rev: BCCB 10/98; BL 11/15/98; HB 11–12/98; HBG 3/99; SLJ 9/98; VOYA 2/99)

2149 Prue, Sally. *The Devil's Toenail* (7–10). 2004, Scholastic $16.95 (0-439-48634-3). Stevie, who is disfigured, invests in the powers of a shell-like fossil known as the devil's toenail. (Rev: BL 4/15/04; SLJ 8/04)

2150 Pullman, Philip. *The Amber Spyglass* (7–12). Series: His Dark Materials. 2000, Knopf $19.95 (0-679-87926-9). Lyra and Will are key figures in the battle between good and evil in this final volume in the prize-winning trilogy. (Rev: BL 10/1/00; BR 1–2/01; HB 11–12/00; HBG 3/01; SLJ 10/00)

2151 Pullman, Philip. *The Golden Compass* (7–12). Series: His Dark Materials. 1996, Knopf $20.00 (0-679-87924-2); Ballantine paper $6.99 (0-345-41335-0). In this first book of a fantasy trilogy,

young Lyra and her alter ego, a protective animal named Pantalaimon, escape from the child-stealing Gobblers and join a group heading north to rescue a band of missing children. (Rev: BL 3/1/96*; BR 9–10/96; SLJ 4/96)

2152 Pullman, Philip. *The Subtle Knife* (7–12). Series: His Dark Materials. 1997, Random $20.00 (0-679-87925-0); Ballantine paper $6.99 (0-345-41336-9). In this second volume of a trilogy, Will and Lyra travel from world to world searching for the mysterious Dust and Will's long-lost father. (Rev: BL 7/97; HBG 3/98; SLJ 10/97)

2153 Pullman, Philip. *The Tin Princess* (9–12). 1994, Knopf $16.00 (0-679-84757-X). In the tiny Germanic kingdom of Razkavia, Adelaide, the unlikely Cockney queen, and her companion/translator, Becky Winter, are involved in political intrigue and romance. (Rev: BL 2/15/94; SLJ 4/94; VOYA 8/94)

2154 Quinn, Daniel. *After Dachau* (10–12). 2001, Context $21.95 (1-893956-13-X). A quirky novel about a young man interested in reincarnation and a girl who wakes from a coma with a second person housed in her body. (Rev: BL 2/15/01)

2155 Rabkin, Eric S., ed. *Fantastic Worlds: Myths, Tales and Stories* (10–12). 1979, Oxford paper $16.95 (0-19-502541-5). A classic collection of fantasy and some science fiction from the ancient Greeks to the present.

2156 Rapp, Adam. *The Copper Elephant* (9–12). 1999, Front Street $16.95 (1-886910-42-1). In this fantasy set in a future world of chaos, Whensday Bluehouse manages to avoid dying in the mines where children work as slaves, but life on the run is dangerous and difficult. (Rev: BL 11/15/99; HB 1–2/00; HBG 4/00; SLJ 12/99; VOYA 4/00)

2157 Rawn, Melanie. *The Mageborn Traitor* (10–12). 1997, DAW paper $23.95 (0-88677-730-5). On Lenfell, Cailet who dreams of creating her own mage academy, finds her plans thwarted by her sister, who is allied with the evil Malerrisi. (Rev: VOYA 10/97)

2158 Rawn, Melanie, et al. *The Golden Key* (10–12). 1996, DAW paper $24.95 (0-88677-691-0). A tour-de-force in which three authors have each written a third of this saga about the Limners, master painters whose masterpieces come to life. (Rev: VOYA 2/97)

2159 Reichert, Mickey Zucker. *The Beasts of Barakhai* (10–12). Series: Books of Barahkai. 2001, DAW $23.95 (0-7564-0013-9). In this first book of a series, we are introduced to the people of Barakhai who are involuntary shapeshifters, forced to spend half of their lives in animal form. (Rev: BL 7/01; VOYA 12/01)

2160 Reichert, Mickey Zucker, and Jennifer Wingert. *Spirit Fox* (9–12). 1998, DAW $23.95 (0-88677-

806–9). Kiarda is born at the moment that an orphaned fox is killed, and in later life, the animal's spirit gradually turns her into a fox. (Rev: VOYA 6/99)

2161 Reisert, Rebecca. *The Third Witch* (10–12). 2001, Pocket $25.00 (0-7434-1771-2). Because her life was ruined as a child by Macbeth, Gilly swears revenge and, disguised as a boy, finds work in the kitchen of his castle where she encounters Fleance, Macduff, and other characters we know from Shakespeare's play. (Rev: BL 9/15/01)

2162 Reiss, Kathryn. *Pale Phoenix* (7–10). 1994, Harcourt $10.95 (0-15-200030-5); paper $3.95 (0-15-200031-3). Miranda Browne's parents take in an orphan girl who can disappear at will and who was the victim of a tragedy in a past life in Puritan Massachusetts. (Rev: BL 3/15/94; SLJ 5/94; VOYA 6/94)

2163 Roberson, Jennifer. *Sword-Born: A Novel of Tiger and Del* (10–12). Series: Sword Dancer Saga. 1998, DAW $24.95 (0-88677-776-3). Two homeless wanderers, Tiger, a former slave of unknown origin, and his companion, Delila, travel to Skandi seeking Tiger's heritage and are captured by pirates in this novel that explores relationships and various types of power and control. (Rev: SLJ 8/98; VOYA 8/98)

2164 Roberts, Nora. *Key of Valor* (11–12). 2004, Penguin paper $7.99 (0-515-13653-0). In the final book of a recommended trilogy that mixes romance and fantasy, plucky hairdresser Zoe McCourt seeks the final key needed to unlock the mystical box holding the souls of three Celtic demigoddesses; for mature teens. (Rev: BL 11/15/03; SLJ 3/04)

2165 Roberts, Nora, et al. *Once Upon a Rose* (10–12). 2001, Jove paper $7.99 (0-515-13166-0). An evil sorceress, a princess, a mute girl in war-torn Scotland, and a kingdom imprisoned in ice figure in the four novellas collected here by four different authors. (Rev: BL 10/1/01)

2166 Robinson, Spider. *The Free Lunch* (10–12). 2001, Tor $22.95 (0-312-86524-4). In the near future, a 12-year-old boy decides he wants to stow away in a theme park called Dreamworld and is helped by a longtime resident. (Rev: BL 7/01)

2167 Rochelle, Warren. *The Wild Boy* (10–12). 2001, Golden Gryphon $22.95 (1-930846-04-5). When the space-faring Lindauzi lose their companion race to the plague, the Crown Prince sets out to find a replacement species. (Rev: BL 8/01)

2168 Rogers, Mark E. *Samurai Cat Goes to the Movies* (9–12). 1994, Tor paper $10.95 (0-312-85744-6). Japanese feline Miowara and his nephew, Shiro, take on Hollywood and satirize assorted film classics. (Rev: BL 9/15/94; VOYA 4/95)

2169 Rosenberg, Joel. *Not Quite Scaramouche* (9–12). 2001, Tor $23.95 (0-312-86897-9). This sequel to *Not Exactly the Three Musketeers* (1999) continues the adventures of Pirojil and Kethol who, with wizard Erenor, share many adventures including encounters with the dragon Ellegon. (Rev: BL 12/15/00; VOYA 6/01)

2170 Rosenberg, Joel. *Not Really the Prisoner of Zenda* (10–12). Series: Guardians of the Flame. 2003, Tor $24.95 (0-765-30046-X). This addition to the series that started with *Not Exactly the Three Musketeers* (1999) offers more breezy and satisfying adventures. (Rev: BL 5/15/03)

2171 Rowling, J. K. *Harry Potter and the Order of the Phoenix* (4–12). 2003, Scholastic LB $34.99 (0-439-56761-0). Adolescence, adult hypocrisy, and the deadly threat of Voldemort and his evil supporters combine to make Harry's fifth year at Hogwarts as eventful as ever. (Rev: BL 7/03; HB 9–10/03; HBG 10/03; SLJ 8/03; VOYA 8/03)

2172 Russell, Barbara T. *The Taker's Stone* (7–12). 1999, DK $16.95 (1-7894-2568-8). When 14-year-old Fischer steals some glowing red gemstones from a man at a campsite, he unleashes the terrible evil of Belial, some catastrophic weather, and the beginning of the end of the world. (Rev: VOYA 10/99)

2173 Saberhagen, Fred. *Ariadne's Web* (10–12). Series: Books of the Gods. 2000, Tor $25.95 (0-312-86629-1). Characters including Theseus, Ariadne, and Daedalus come to life in this action-filled fantasy that mixes myth and magic for better readers. (Rev: BL 1/1–15/00)

2174 Saberhagen, Fred. *The Arms of Hercules* (10–12). Series: Books of the Gods. 2000, Tor $25.95 (0-312-86774-3); paper $14.95 (0-312-87776-5). Number three in the series culminates in the gigantic battle between Hercules and the Titans. (Rev: BL 11/15/00)

2175 Saberhagen, Fred. *God of the Golden Fleece* (10–12). Series: Books of the Gods. 2001, Tor $24.95 (0-312-87037-X). In this fourth in the Books of the Gods series, Greek mythology is again reworked, this time with the story of Proteus who acquires the face of Triton, the sea god. (Rev: BL 5/15/01; VOYA 2/02)

2176 Saberhagen, Fred. *Gods of Fire and Thunder* (10–12). Series: Books of the Gods. 2002, Tor $24.95 (0-765-30201-2). Saberhagen revisits Norse myths involving Valhalla in this installment in the series. (Rev: BL 8/02)

2177 Sabin, E. Rose. *A Perilous Power* (9–12). 2004, Tor $19.95 (0-765-30859-2). Trevor wants to develop his magical powers by traveling to Port-of-Lords to study with gifted magicians, in this prequel to *A School for Sorcery* (2002). (Rev: BL 2/15/04; VOYA 6/04)

2178 Sabin, E. Rose. *A School for Sorcery* (6–12). 2002, Tor $17.95 (0-765-30289-6). Sixteen-year-old Tria Tesserell is accepted into the Lesley Simonton

School for the Magically Gifted, but finds she spends most of her time combating threats from a fellow student. (Rev: BL 9/15/02; VOYA 12/02)

2179 Saint-Exupery, Antoine de. *The Little Prince* (5–12). Trans. by Katherine Woods. 1943, Harcourt paper $10.00 (0-15-646511-6). An airplane pilot crashes in a desert and encounters a little prince who seeks harmony for his planet.

2180 Salvatore, R. A. *Ascendance* (10–12). Series: Second DemonWars. 2001, Del Rey $25.95 (0-345-43040-9). Queen Jilseponie confronts her son, Aydrian, whom she thought dead, in this book that combines a coming-of-age story with court/church intrigue. The second book in the series is *Transcendence* (2002). (Rev: BL 4/15/01; VOYA 12/01)

2181 Salvatore, R. A. *The Dragon's Dagger* (9–12). 1994, Berkley paper $6.50 (0-441-00078-9). Gary Leger, the reluctant hero of Faerie, must return to battle Robert the Dragon and the wicked witch with his magic talking lance. (Rev: BL 8/94; VOYA 12/94)

2182 Salvatore, R. A. *Highwayman* (9–12). 2004, CDS $25.95 (1-59315-016-4). A fast-paced tale about Corona, who has special powers and who has devoted his life to helping the oppressed. (Rev: BL 3/15/04)

2183 Salvatore, R. A. *Mortalis* (10–12). 2000, Ballantine $29.95 (0-345-43039-5). This spinoff from the recommended Demon Wars trilogy continues the story of Jilseponie (Pony), who tries to find healing magic to counter a plague that is destroying the population. (Rev: BL 5/15/00*)

2184 Salvatore, R. A. *The Woods Out Back* (9–12). 1993, Berkley paper $6.50 (0-441-90872-1). A young factory worker's imaginative daydreams become reality when a leprechaun transports him to the fairy realm to take part in a quest. (Rev: BL 10/15/93; VOYA 2/94)

2185 Sanders, William. *Are We Having Fun Yet?* (10–12). 2002, Wildside paper $15.95 (1-58715-709-8). A collection of diverse fantasy stories that are imbued with Native American culture. (Rev: BL 11/1/02)

2186 Sargent, Pamela. *Climb the Wind: A Novel of Another America* (9–12). 1998, HarperCollins $25.00 (0-06-105029-6). An alternate history that poses the question, What would have happened if Native American tribes in the West had united and used modern warfare methods to stop white expansionism in the years following the Civil War? (Rev: VOYA 4/99)

2187 Scarborough, Elizabeth Ann. *The Godmother's Apprentice* (9–12). 1995, Ace paper $19.95 (0-441-00252-8). In this fantasy, 14-year-old Sno Quantrill faces unexpected adventures and meets fantastic creatures when she flies to Ireland to become the apprentice of Dame Felicity Fortune. (Rev: BL 12/15/95; VOYA 6/96)

2188 Schimel, Lawrence. *Camelot Fantastic* (8–12). 1998, DAW paper $5.99 (0-88677-790-9). A collection of original novelettes — written by well-known authors of fantasy, science fiction, and mystery — that present different perspectives on characters and incidents associated with King Arthur's Camelot. (Rev: VOYA 12/98)

2189 Schultz, Mark. *Dinosaur Shaman: Nine Tales from the Xenozoic Age* (9–12). 1990, Kitchen Sink $29.95 (0-87816-117-1). These stories are set in the Xenozoic Age — a future time when humans and prehistoric beasts coexist — and describe the further adventures of Jack Tennrec and Hannah Dundee. (Rev: BL 9/1/91)

2190 Scott, Melissa, and Lisa A. Barnett. *Point of Dreams* (10–12). 2001, Tor $25.95 (0-312-86782-4). In the third novel about the city of Astreiant, a faux Middle Ages locale where magic prevails, a policeman discovers a dead body in a theater and must solve this mystery. (Rev: BL 2/15/01)

2191 Sheffield, Charles. *The Ganymede Club* (9–12). 1995, Tor $23.95 (0-312-85662-8). Two teenagers foil the fiendish plots of the Ganymede Club, a small group of people who have discovered the means to immortality. (Rev: VOYA 6/96)

2192 Sher, Ira. *Gentlemen of Space* (10–12). 2003, Free Pr. $23.00 (0-7432-4218-1). An offbeat and appealing novel of an astronaut so taken with the Moon that he's reluctant to return to family and friends on Earth. (Rev: BL 3/15/03)

2193 Sherman, Josepha. *Windleaf* (7–12). 1993, Walker $14.95 (0-8027-8259-0). Count Thierry falls in love with half-faerie Glinfinial, only to have her father, the Faerie Lord, steal her away. (Rev: BL 11/1/93*; SLJ 12/93; VOYA 2/94)

2194 Shetterly, Will. *Elsewhere* (8–12). 1991, Harcourt $16.95 (0-15-200731-8). Set in Bordertown, between the real world and Faerie world, home to runaway elves and humans, this is a fantasy of integration, survival, and coming of age. (Rev: BL 10/15/91; SLJ 11/91)

2195 Shetterly, Will. *Nevernever* (8–12). 1993, Harcourt $16.95 (0-15-257022-5); Tor paper $4.99 (0-8125-5151-6). This sequel to *Elsewhere* (1991) shows Wolfboy trying to protect Florida, the heir of Faerie, from gangs of Elves out to get her, while one of his friends is framed for murder. (Rev: BL 9/15/93; SLJ 10/93; VOYA 12/93)

2196 Shinn, Sharon. *Angelica* (11–12). 2003, Berkley $23.95 (0-441-01013-X). In the peaceful land of Samaria, Susannah's heretofore happy life is threatened by betrayal. (Rev: BL 3/1/03; VOYA 8/03)

2197 Shinn, Sharon. *The Safe-Keeper's Secret* (7–12). 2004, Viking $16.99 (0-670-05910-2).

Truth and justice are themes in this fantasy about Fiona, a girl whose family has many secrets, and Reed, a boy without an identity, who was left as a baby with Fiona's mother. (Rev: BL 4/15/04; SLJ 6/04; VOYA 6/04)

2198 Shinn, Sharon. *The Shape-Changer's Wife* (9–12). 1995, Ace paper $4.99 (0-441-00261-7). Apprentice wizard Aubrey falls in love with his master's wife but wonders if she is really only one of his master's shape changes. (Rev: VOYA 2/96)

2199 Shinn, Sharon. *Summers at Castle Auburn* (10–12). 2001, Berkley paper $14.00 (0-441-00803-8). Corie, age 17, who has been staying at Castle Auburn and learning the healer's craft, finds herself in a hotbed of court intrigue and must choose sides. (Rev: BL 4/15/01; VOYA 8/01)

2200 Shusterman, Neal. *Downsiders* (8–12). 1999, Simon & Schuster $16.95 (0-689-80375-3). A fantasy about the people who live in the Downside, the subterranean world beneath New York City, and a teenage boy who ventures Topside to get medicine for his sick sister, leading to a dangerous chain of events. (Rev: HBG 9/99; SLJ 7/99; VOYA 8/99)

2201 Shwartz, Susan. *Suppose They Gave a Peace and Other Stories* (10–12). 2002, Five Star $23.95 (0-7862-4166-7). Ten diverse short stories merge genres in an intriguing blend. (Rev: BL 6/1–15/02)

2202 Siegel, Jan. *The Dragon Charmer* (10–12). 2001, Del Rey $24.00 (0-345-43902-3). Following events in *Prospero's Children* (2000), heroine Fern finds that ancient evil forces have awakened and want to control her because she has "the gift." (Rev: BL 6/1–15/01)

2203 Silverberg, Robert, ed. *Legends: New Short Novels* (9–12). 1998, Tor $27.95 (0-312-86787-5). A collection of 11 fantasy novellas by such writers as Anne McCaffrey, Robert Silverberg, Tad Williams, and Ursula Le Guin. (Rev: BL 8/98; VOYA 4/99)

2204 Silverberg, Robert, ed. *Legends II* (9–12). 2004, Ballantine $28.95 (0-345-45644-0). A collection of short stories that are set in the worlds that authors have created for their successful series. (Rev: BL 1/1–15/04)

2205 Silverberg, Robert, ed. *SFFWA Fantasy Hall of Fame* (10–12). 1998, HarperCollins paper $14.00 (0-06-105215-9). This is a collection of short fantasy fiction written between 1939 and 1990 by such authors as James Blish, Poul Anderson, and Anthony Boucher. (Rev: VOYA 8/98)

2206 Smith, Sherwood. *Augur's Teacher* (10–12). 2001, Tor paper $13.95 (0-312-87799-4). Fourth-grade teacher Cece Robin and her friend Augur flee across the country to stop a dastardly plot by the notorious Zo'or. (Rev: BL 9/15/01; VOYA 12/01)

2207 Spencer, William Browning. *Zod Wallop* (9–12). 1995, St. Martin's $21.95 (0-312-13629-3).

In this thought-provoking, paradoxical fantasy, Raymond suspects that the dark, disturbing events in a children's book written by a friend are becoming part of his real life. (Rev: BL 10/15/95; VOYA 2/96)

2208 Stackpole, Michael A. *Fortress Draconis* (10–12). Series: DragonCrown War Cycle. 2001, Bantam paper $14.95 (0-553-37919-4). In a classic battle between the forces of good and evil, Will, an orphaned thief in training, joins forces with a warrior elf and a solider with a mysterious past to face off against the evil sorceress Chytrine. (Rev: BL 11/1/01; VOYA 4/02)

2209 Stackpole, Michael A. *The Grand Crusade* (11–12). Series: DragonCrown War Cycle. 2003, Bantam paper $14.95 (0-553-37921-6). In a state of disarray after Will Norrington's reported death, the fractured nations of the Southlands seem easy picking for evil sorceress Chytrine, but Will's friends and allies band together for a fight-to-the-finish confrontation with the forces of evil; for mature teens. (Rev: BL 12/15/03)

2210 Stearns, Michael, ed. *A Wizard's Dozen: Stories of the Fantastic* (7–12). 1993, Harcourt $16.95 (0-15-200965-5). This collection of 13 strange and magical tales includes works by Vivian Vande Velde, Patricia Wrede, and Bruce Coville. (Rev: BL 12/15/93; SLJ 12/93; VOYA 4/94)

2211 Stevermer, Caroline. *River Rats* (7–10). 1992, Harcourt $17.00 (0-15-200895-0). This action-packed story begins in the years following a nuclear disaster when six orphans, living on an old paddle wheeler, are threatened by a fugitive with a menacing past. (Rev: BL 4/1/92; SLJ 8/92)

2212 Stevermer, Caroline. *A Scholar of Magics* (9–12). 2004, Tor $19.95 (0-765-30308-6). This sequel to *A College of Magics* (2002) is a fantasy involving spies, strange assailants, and suspense as well as a tale about Samuel Lambert, sharpshooter, and his involvement with the Agincourt Project. (Rev: BL 4/1/04)

2213 Stewart, Mary. *Mary Stewart's Merlin Trilogy* (9–12). Illus. 1980, Morrow $19.95 (0-688-00347-8). This fictionalized account of the story of King Arthur consists of three novels: *The Crystal Cave*, *The Hollow Hills*, and *The Last Enchantment*. On the same subject use the author's *The Wicked Day* (1984).

2214 Stewart, Sean. *Galveston* (10–12). 2000, Berkley $23.95 (0-441-00686-8). Magic, adventure, and likable young characters are found in this novel about the world after an overdose of magic in 2004 destroys the infrastructure of cities. (Rev: BL 3/15/00)

2215 Stirling, S. M. *On the Oceans of Eternity* (10–12). 2000, Penguin paper $6.99 (0-451-45780-3). In this last of a time-travel trilogy that started with *Island in the Sea of Time* (1998) and *Against the Tide of Years* (1999), the story of Nantucket being dragged back in time continues. (Rev: BL 4/1/00)

2216 Strauss, Victoria. *Guardian of the Hills* (7–10). 1995, Morrow $15.00 (0-688-06998-3). Pamela, who is part Quapaw Indian, experiences cultural conflict when her grandfather organizes an excavation of sacred burial grounds to learn more of their spiritual heritage. (Rev: BL 10/15/95*; SLJ 10/95)

2217 Strieber, Whitley. *The Wild* (9–12). 1991, Tor paper $5.95 (0-8125-1277-4). Bob Duke stares at a wolf one day at a zoo, and its gaze seems to invade his soul. Soon Bob is transformed into a wolf and must flee the police. (Rev: BL 5/1/91*)

2218 Stroud, Jonathan. *The Amulet of Samarkand* (6–12). 2003, Hyperion $17.95 (0-7868-1859-X). Nathaniel, an apprentice magician, plots to steal an amulet and sets powerful forces in motion in this fantasy set in London. (Rev: BL 9/1/03*; HB 11–12/03; HBG 4/04; SLJ 1/04; VOYA 12/03)

2219 Sweeney, Joyce. *Shadow* (7–10). 1995, Bantam $20.95 (0-385-30988-0). Sarah's cat, Shadow, has mysteriously returned from the dead. Sarah and Cissy, the psychic housemaid, try to figure out why. (Rev: BL 7/94; SLJ 9/94; VOYA 10/94)

2220 Tarr, Judith. *Kingdom of the Grail* (10–12). 2000, Penguin paper $14.95 (0-451-45797-8). Roland, a young shape-changer, visits Merlin, who is imprisoned in an enchanted forest, and vows to free him. (Rev: BL 8/00; VOYA 2/01)

2221 Tarr, Judith. *Lady of Horses* (10–12). 2000, Tor $25.95 (0-312-86114-1). For mature readers, this novel set in prehistoric times blends mythology and fantasy in the tale of Sparrow, a girl who can foretell the future, and a cult that worships the Horse Goddess. (Rev: BL 6/1–15/00)

2222 Tarr, Judith. *Pride of Kings* (10–12). 2001, Roc paper $14.95 (0-451-45847-8). In this historical fantasy, Prince John seizes the thrones of England and of the fairy folk while his older brother, Richard the Lionhearted, is away on a crusade. (Rev: BL 8/01; VOYA 2/02)

2223 Thompson, Julian. *Herb Seasoning* (9–12). 1990, Scholastic paper $12.95 (0-590-43023-8). Herbie, a teenager at loose ends, uses a counseling service to travel through time to find his destiny. (Rev: BL 5/15/90; SLJ 3/90)

2224 Thompson, Julian F. *Hard Time* (7–11). 2003, Simon & Schuster $16.95 (0-689-85424-2). A leprechaun that lives in Annie's Life Skills doll coaxes Annie to write an inventive essay that prompts punishments including a jail sentence for Annie and her best friend in this irreverent fantasy. (Rev: BCCB 1/04; BL 12/15/03; HBG 4/04; SLJ 1/04; VOYA 12/03)

2225 Thomsen, Brian M., ed. *The American Fantasy Tradition* (7–12). 2002, Tor $27.95 (0-765-30152-0). A collection of fantasy short stories ranging from folk and tall tales to historical fantasy and fantasy adventures. (Rev: VOYA 4/03)

2226 Tolkien, J. R. R. *The Hobbit: Or, There and Back Again* (7–12). Illus. 1938, Houghton $16.00 (0-395-07122-4); Ballantine paper $7.99 (0-345-33968-1). In this prelude to *The Lord of the Rings*, the reader meets Bilbo Baggins, a hobbit, in a land filled with dwarfs, elves, goblins, and dragons.

2227 Tolkien, J. R. R. *The Lord of the Rings* (9–12). 1967, Houghton $14.95 each (Vol. 1: 0-395-08254-4; Vol. 2: 0-395-08255-2; Vol. 3: 0-395-08256-0); Ballantine paper $6.99 each (Vol. 1: 0-345-33970-3; Vol. 2: 0-345-33971-1; Vol. 3: 0-345-33973-8). This combined volume includes all three books of the trilogy first published in 1954 and 1955. They are: *The Fellowship of the Ring, The Two Towers,* and *The Return of the King.*

2228 Tolkien, J. R. R. *The Silmarillion* (9–12). 1977, Ballantine paper $5.95 (0-345-32581-8). These modern legends deal with such subjects as the creation of the world.

2229 Tolkien, J. R. R. *Unfinished Tales of Numenor and Middle-Earth* (8–12). Ed. by Christopher Tolkien. 2001, Houghton $26.00 (0-618-15404-3); paper $14.00 (0-618-15405-1). A collection of previously unpublished fantasy writings by this English master.

2230 Tower, S. D. *The Assassins of Tamurin* (10–12). 2003, HarperCollins $25.95 (0-380-97803-2). In this fantasy with a romantic twist, a young orphan girl is trained as an assassin but ends up falling in love with the man she's been sent to kill. (Rev: BL 1/1–15/03; VOYA 6/03)

2231 Townsend, John Rowe. *The Fortunate Isles* (7–12). 1989, HarperCollins LB $13.89 (0-397-32366-2). Eleni and her friend Andreas seek the living god in this novel set in a mythical land. (Rev: BL 10/15/89; SLJ 10/89)

2232 Trondheim, Lewis. *Harum Scarum* (10–12). Trans. from French by Kim Thompson. Illus. 1998, Fantagraphics paper $10.95 (1-56097-288-2). A graphic novel about McConey, who looks like a well-dressed pink rabbit, his friends, and magic powers that can turn a city's population (all animals) into self-destructing monsters. Also use for the same audience: *The Hoodoodad* (1998). (Rev: SLJ 2/99)

2233 Troop, Alan F. *The Dragon DelaSangre* (11–12). 2002, NAL paper $5.99 (0-451-45871-0). Peter and his father, dragons who can take human shape and are successful Florida entrepreneurs, are threatened with discovery; for mature teens. (Rev: BL 3/1/02*)

119

2234 Turtledove, Harry. *Blood and Iron* (10–12). 2001, Del Rey $27.95 (0-345-40565-X). This fascinating alternative reality novel mixes characters and situations from various periods in world history. (Rev: BL 4/15/01)

2235 Turtledove, Harry. *Marching Through Peachtree* (10–12). 2001, Baen $21.00 (0-671-31843-8). This alternate reality fantasy reworks Sherman's campaign against Atlanta in 1864 with renamed characters and lots of wordplay. (Rev: BL 10/15/01)

2236 Turtledove, Harry. *Out of the Darkness* (10–12). 2004, Tor $27.95 (0-765-30438-4). This is the last volume in the series of alternate history novels that supply a different look at World War II. (Rev: BL 2/1/04)

2237 Turtledove, Harry. *Sentry Peak* (10–12). 2000, Baen $24.00 (0-671-57887-1). This clever alternate history takes place during the Chickamauga campaign of the U.S. Civil War. (Rev: BL 9/1/00; VOYA 4/01)

2238 Turtledove, Harry. *Through the Darkness* (10–12). 2001, Tor $27.95 (0-312-87825-7). A continuation of a fantasy version of World War II in which characters use magic and other unearthly powers in fighting their battles. (Rev: BL 2/15/01)

2239 Vande Velde, Vivian. *Conjurer Princess* (9–12). 1997, HarperCollins paper $4.99 (0-06-105704-5). Sixteen-year-old Lylene sets out to rescue her older sister, who has been abducted by a warlord on her wedding day. (Rev: VOYA 2/98)

2240 Vande Velde, Vivian. *Dragon's Bait* (7–10). 1992, Harcourt $16.95 (0-15-200726-1). A young girl accused of being a witch and sentenced to be killed by a dragon becomes friends with a shapechanger who promises to help her take revenge. (Rev: BL 9/15/92; SLJ 9/92)

2241 Vande Velde, Vivian. *Magic Can Be Murder* (7–11). 2000, Harcourt $17.00 (0-15-202665-7). Teenage witch Nola finds romance while working to reveal the identity of a murderer. (Rev: BL 12/15/00; HBG 3/01; SLJ 11/00; VOYA 12/00)

2242 Velde, Vivan V. *Changeling Prince* (9–12). 1997, HarperCollins paper $5.99 (0-06-105705-3). Weiland, who was changed from a cub to a human child, is never sure when the capricious sorceress Daria will change him back again. (Rev: VOYA 6/98)

2243 Vick, Helen H. *Walker's Journey Home* (7–10). 1995, Harbinger $14.95 (1-57140-000-1); paper $9.95 (1-57140-001-X). Walker leads the Sinagua Indians through treacherous challenges from both old enemies and new, and learns that greed and jealousy have been destructive forces throughout history. Sequel to *Walker of Time* (1993). (Rev: BL 8/95)

2244 Vinge, Joan D. *The Snow Queen* (10–12). 1989, Warner paper $6.99 (0-445-20529-6). When spring comes, the Snow Queen does not want to give up her throne.

2245 Voigt, Cynthia. *Building Blocks* (7–10). 1985, Fawcett paper $3.99 (0-449-70130-1). A boy travels back in time to witness his father's childhood.

2246 Voigt, Cynthia. *Elske* (7–12). Series: The Kingdom. 1999, Simon & Schuster $18.00 (0-689-82472-6). In the fourth and final volume of this fantasy series, 12-year-old Elske accompanies Beriel, an exiled noblewoman, on her quest to recover her kingdom's throne. (Rev: BCCB 12/99; BL 9/1/99; HBG 4/00; SLJ 10/99; VOYA 10/99)

2247 Voigt, Cynthia. *The Wings of a Falcon* (7–12). 1993, Scholastic $15.95 (0-590-46712-3). Two boys escape from a remote island and face danger and adventure in this multilayered tale that includes themes of friendship, romance, and heroism. (Rev: SLJ 10/93*; VOYA 12/93)

2248 Volsky, Paula. *The Grand Ellipse* (10–12). 2000, Bantam $23.95 (0-553-10804-2). This fantasy about a race in which contestants travel through many lands and through harsh terrain combines adventure, humor, and romance. (Rev: BL 9/1/00; VOYA 4/01)

2249 Vonnegut, Kurt. *Slaughterhouse-Five: Or, The Children's Crusade, a Duty Dance with Death* (10–12). 1994, Bantam $23.95 (0-385-31208-3); paper $7.50 (0-440-18029-5). This is the surreal story of Billy Pilgrim who, after surviving the bombing of Dresden in World War II, spends time on the planet Trafalmador.

2250 Walton, Jo. *The King's Name* (9–12). 2001, Tor $26.95 (0-312-87653-X). In this sequel to *The King's Peace* (2000), the story of King Arthur and his knights continues with the role of Lancelot played by a female warrior. (Rev: BL 10/15/01; VOYA 6/02)

2251 Walton, Jo. *The King's Peace* (10–12). 2000, Tor $26.95 (0-312-87229-1). A fast-paced fantasy about a young female warrior and her allegiance to King Urdo, who is fighting invaders within his kingdom. (Rev: BL 10/1/00; VOYA 4/01)

2252 Wangerin, Walter, Jr. *The Book of the Dun Cow* (7–10). 1978, HarperCollins $12.95 (0-06-026346-6). A farmyard fable with talking animals that retells the story of Chanticleer the Rooster.

2253 Warner, Marina. *The Leto Bundle* (11–12). 2002, Farrar $26.00 (0-374-18548-4). Leto, the mother of divine twins in Greek mythology, plays a central role in this rich novel that takes the reader through history as she searches for her lost son; for mature teens. (Rev: BL 4/1/02*)

2254 Watt-Evans, Lawrence. *The Dragon Society* (10–12). Series: Obsidian Chronicles. 2001, Tor $27.95 (0-765-30007-9). With newfound knowledge of dragons' vulnerabilities, Dragonheart Arlian plans a final war to rid his people of this menace. (Rev: VOYA 4/02)

2255 Watt-Evans, Lawrence. *Dragon Weather* (10–12). Series: Obsidian Chronicles. 1999, Tor $25.95 (0-312-86978-9). Arlian, whose family was killed by dragons when he was only 11 years old, spends years plotting his revenge only to discover that he is part dragon himself. (Rev: VOYA 4/00)

2256 Watt-Evans, Lawrence. *Night of Madness* (10–12). Series: Ethshar. 2000, Tor $24.95 (0-312-87368-9). From the Ethshar series comes this novel about Lord Hanmer and how he becomes first chairman of the council of warlocks. Also recommended is *Ithanalin's Restoration* (2002). (Rev: BL 11/1/00; VOYA 4/01)

2257 Watt-Evans, Lawrence. *With a Single Spell* (9–12). 1987, Ballantine paper $4.95 (0-345-32616-4). In this humorous fantasy a wizard's apprentice decides to make it on his own. (Rev: BL 3/1/87)

2258 Weis, Margaret, ed. *A Quest-Lover's Treasury of the Fantastic* (10–12). 2002, Warner paper $13.95 (0-446-67927-5). Quests form the core of this collection of excellent and varied short stories. (Rev: BL 5/15/02)

2259 Weis, Margaret, and Tracey Hickman. *Well of Darkness* (10–12). 2000, HarperCollins $25.00 (0-06-105180-2). In this first volume of the Sovereign Stone trilogy, Gareth, who is studying the forbidden Void magic, helps Prince Dagnarus, who wants to succeed his father on the throne. (Rev: BL 9/15/00; VOYA 4/01)

2260 Weis, Margaret, and Tracy Hickman, eds. *Treasures of Fantasy* (10–12). 1997, HarperCollins paper $14.00 (0-06-105327-9). A collection of fantasy short stories by some of the best contemporary writers in the field. (Rev: VOYA 12/97)

2261 Westall, Robert. *The Promise* (6–10). 1991, Scholastic $13.95 (0-590-43760-7). Bob's friendship with beautiful, sickly Valerie becomes romantic; when she dies, only Bob knows that her spirit still lingers among the living. (Rev: BL 3/1/91; SLJ 3/91)

2262 White, T. H. *The Book of Merlyn: The Unpublished Conclusion to "The Once and Future King"* (9–12). 1988, Univ. of Texas Pr. paper $13.95 (0-292-70769-X). An antiwar postscript to White's retelling of the Arthurian legend.

2263 White, T. H. *The Once and Future King* (10–12). 1958, Putnam $25.95 (0-399-10597-2). Beginning with *The Sword in the Stone* (1939), this omnibus includes all four of T. H. White's novels about the life and career of King Arthur. It was this version that became the basis for the musical Camelot.

2264 White, T. H. *The Sword in the Stone* (7–12). 1993, Putnam $24.99 (0-399-22502-1); Dell paper $5.99 (0-440-98445-9). In this, the first part of *The Once and Future King,* the career of Wart is traced until he becomes King Arthur.

2265 Wilde, Oscar. *The Canterville Ghost* (7–12). Illus. 1996, North-South paper $6.95 (1-55858-611-3). An American family buys an English manor house and causes problems for the resident ghost in this classic fantasy. (Rev: BL 12/15/96; SLJ 1/97)

2266 Williams, Tad. *To Green Angel Tower* (9–12). 1993, NAL $25.00 (0-88677-521-3). The concluding volume of the epic Memory, Sorrow and Thorn trilogy about the exploits of Simon, the scullery boy turned knight. (Rev: BL 2/1/93; SLJ 11/93)

2267 Willingham, Bill, et al. *Taller Tales* (11–12). Illus. 2003, DC Comics paper $19.95 (1-4012-0100-8). Featuring characters that first appeared in Neil Gaiman's Sandman comic series, Willingham spins a series of captivating tales that, because of their violence and sexual content, should be recommended to mature teens. (Rev: BL 12/1/03) [741.5]

2268 Willis, Connie. *Passage* (10–12). 2001, Bantam $23.95 (0-553-11124-8). Near-death experiences and a visit, through a psychoactive drug, to the *Titanic* before its sinking are elements of this fantasy for better readers. (Rev: BL 3/15/01* ; SLJ 8/01)

2269 Windling, Terri. *The Wood Wife* (10–12). 1996, Tor $22.95 (0-312-85988-0). After Maggie moves to a cabin in the Arizona desert, she encounters spirits, both human and animal, that inhabited the area. (Rev: SLJ 7/97; VOYA 2/97)

2270 Wollheim, Elizabeth R., and Sheila E. Gilbert, eds. *30th Anniversary DAW Fantasy* (10–12). 2002, DAW $24.95 (0-7564-0070-8). A collection of short stories by well-known fantasy writers. (Rev: BL 5/1/02)

2271 Wrede, Patricia C. *Magician's Ward* (9–12). 1997, Tor $22.95 (0-312-85369-6). Teenager Kim, who is living with magician Mairelon in his London townhouse as his ward and apprentice, discovers that some wizards have disappeared and Mairelon's powers are mysteriously stolen. (Rev: BL 11/1/97; VOYA 4/98)

2272 Wrede, Patricia C. *Searching for Dragons* (6–10). Series: Enchanted Forest Chronicles. 1991, Harcourt $16.95 (0-15-200898-5). Cimorene goes on a quest with Mendanbar, king of the forest, to find the dragon king Kazul by borrowing a faulty magic carpet from a giant. (Rev: BL 10/1/91; SLJ 12/91)

2273 Wrede, Patricia C. *Talking to Dragons* (6–10). Series: Enchanted Forest Chronicles. 1993, Harcourt $16.95 (0-15-284247-0). The fourth book in the series opens 16 years after *Calling on Dragons* with King Menenbar still imprisoned in his castle by a wizard's spells. (Rev: BL 8/93; VOYA 12/93)

2274 Wrede, Patricia C., and Caroline Stevermer. *Sorcery and Cecelia or the Enchanted Chocolate Pot* (10–12). 2003, Harcourt $17.00 (0-15-204615-1). In 19th-century England, Kate and Cecelia conduct a lively correspondence that describes their adventures, which often include magical aspects. (Rev: HBG 10/03; VOYA 6/03)

2275 Wurts, Janny. *Peril's Gate* (10–12). Series: Alliance of the Light. 2002, HarperCollins $27.95 (0-06-105220-5). The future of the land of Athera rests on the shoulders of Arithon, Master of Shadow. (Rev: BL 12/15/01; VOYA 2/03)

2276 Yarbro, Chelsea Quinn. *Beyond the Waterlilies* (6–10). Illus. 1997, Simon & Schuster $17.00 (0-689-80732-5). Geena Howe has a unique talent — blending into paintings — and has an amazing adventure when she enters a huge Monet painting of water lilies in a castle moat. (Rev: BL 6/1–15/97; SLJ 6/97; VOYA 8/97)

2277 Yarbro, Chelsea Quinn. *Come Twilight* (10–12). 2000, Tor $27.95 (0-312-87330-1). This story about the vampire Saint-Germain spans five centuries of history and involves his loves, tragedies, and adventures. (Rev: BL 10/15/00; SLJ 3/01; VOYA 2/01)

2278 Yep, Laurence. *Dragon Cauldron* (6–10). 1991, HarperCollins paper $7.99 (0-06-440398-X). Monkey narrates this sequel to *Dragon Steel*, continuing the quest of a band of humans and wizards and Shimmer, a dragon princess, to fulfill Shimmer's task of repairing the damaged cauldron. (Rev: BL 5/15/91; SLJ 6/91)

2279 Yep, Laurence. *Dragon Steel* (6–10). 1985, HarperCollins $12.95 (0-06-026748-8). The dragon princess Shimmer tries to save her people who are forced to work in an undersea volcano in this sequel to *Dragon of the Lost Sea*. (Rev: BL 5/15/85; SLJ 9/85; VOYA 8/85)

2280 Yep, Laurence. *Dragon War* (6–10). 1992, HarperCollins paper $6.99 (0-06-440525-7). In this sequel to *Dragon Cauldron,* the heroes use shape-changing magic and the help of a Dragon King to save the day. (Rev: BL 4/15/92; SLJ 6/92)

2281 Yolen, Jane. *Briar Rose* (9–12). 1992, Tor $17.95 (0-312-85135-9). A young girl seeks to carry out a promise to her dying grandmother and discovers her roots in Poland and the Holocaust. (Rev: BL 9/15/92; SLJ 4/93*)

2282 Yolen, Jane. *The One-Armed Queen* (8–10). 1998, Tor $23.95 (0-312-85243-6). Scillia, the adopted daughter of Queen Jenna, is being groomed to rule when her younger brother decides that he should become king. (Rev: BL 10/1/98; VOYA 4/99)

2283 Yolen, Jane. *A Sending of Dragons* (7–12). Series: Pit Dragon. 1987, Harcourt paper $6.00 (0-15-200864-0). In this concluding volume of the trilogy, hero and heroine Jakkin and Akki are captured by primitive people who live underground. Previous volumes are *Dragon's Blood* and *Heart's Blood*. (Rev: BL 11/1/87; BR 11–12/87; SLJ 1/88)

2284 Yolen, Jane. *Sister Emily's Lightship and Other Stories* (10–12). 2000, Tor $22.95 (0-312-87378-6). This is a collection of 28 short stories, both fantasy and science fiction, by the 1998 Nebula Award winner. (Rev: BL 8/00)

2285 Yolen, Jane. *Sister Light, Sister Dark* (10–12). 1995, Tor $3.95 (0-8125-0249-3). The first of a series about an orphaned girl brought up by the Sisterhood. (Rev: BL 10/1/88; SLJ 12/88; VOYA 4/89)

2286 Yolen, Jane. *The Wild Hunt* (6–12). 1995, Harcourt $17.00 (0-15-200211-1). The myth of the Wild Hunt is combined with other European legends when Jerold and Gerund become pawns in a game between the Horned King Winter and his wife. (Rev: BL 6/1–15/95; SLJ 6/95; VOYA 12/95)

2287 Yolen, Jane, et al., eds. *Dragons and Dreams* (6–10). 1986, HarperCollins $12.95 (0-06-026792-5). A collection of 10 fantasy and some science fiction stories that can be a fine introduction to these genres. (Rev: BR 11–12/86; SLJ 5/86; VOYA 6/86)

2288 Zafon, Carlos Ruiz. *The Shadow of the Wind* (10–12). Trans. by Lucia Graves. 2004, Penguin $24.95 (1-59420-010-6). This challenging novel set in Franco's Spain combines adventure, horror, and fantasy as young Daniel travels to the Cemetery of Forgotten Books to choose one he will save. (Rev: BL 3/1/04)

2289 Zelazny, Roger. *Blood of Amber* (9–12). 1986, Avon paper $4.99 (0-380-89636-2). Merle Corey, hero of *Trumps of Doom* (1985), escapes from prison with the help of a woman who has many shapes. This is the seventh Amber novel. (Rev: BL 9/15/86; VOYA 2/87)

2290 Zelazny, Roger. *Trumps of Doom* (9–12). 1986, Avon paper $5.99 (0-380-89635-4). In this sixth Amber book, Merlin fights against mysterious foes from the worlds of Amber and Chaos. (Rev: BL 5/15/85)

2291 Zettel, Sarah. *A Sorcerer's Treason* (7–12). 2002, Tor $27.95 (0-312-87441-3). Unhappy with her life as a lighthouse keeper, Bridget Lederle takes a chance and accompanies a mysterious stranger to the snowbound world of Isavalta. (Rev: BL 4/1/02)

2292 Zuroy, Michael. *Second Death* (9–12). 1992, Walker $30.95 (0-8027-1181-2). A Special Intelligence Squad must track down the creator of a violent, zombielike killer. (Rev: BL 2/15/92; SLJ 11/92)

Graphic Novels

2293 Allie, Scott, et al. *The Devil's Footprints* (10–12). Illus. 2003, Dark Horse paper $14.95 (1-56971-933-0). A graphic novel about a young man who must exorcise the demon that stalks his father's spirit. Also use *The Dark Horse Book of Hauntings* (2003), edited by Scott Allie. (Rev: BL 2/1/04)

2294 Anderson, Kevin J., et al. *Veiled Alliances* (9–12). Illus. 2004, DC Comics $24.95 (1-56389-902-7). This graphic novel tells the story of some refugees from Earth and their life in the advanced civilization, the Ildaran Empire. (Rev: BL 2/1/04)

2295 Asamiya, Kia. *Batman: Child of Dreams* (7–12). Ed. by Max Allan Collins. Illus. 2003, DC Comics $24.95 (1-563-89906-X). In this Japanese spin-off from the Batman legend, rendered in the unique *manga* style, the Dark Knight fights a Japanese enemy who is pushing a drug that supposedly grants the realization of all dreams. (Rev: BL 2/1/04)

2296 Asamiya, Kia. *Dark Angel: The Path to Destiny* (8–12). Illus. Series: Dark Angel. 2000, CPM Comics paper $15.95 (1-56219-827-7). In this first volume of a series of graphic novels, a young swordsman named Dark travels through time and different worlds to complete his moral journey. (Rev: BL 12/1/00)

2297 Azzarello, Brian, et al. *Batman/Deathblow: After the Fire* (10–12). Illus. 2003, DC Comics paper $12.95 (1-4012-0034-6). This entry in the growing mountain of Batman tales teams the superhero with the mysterious Deathblow in the search for the murder of Batman's friend. (Rev: BL 5/15/03)

2298 Beatty, Scott. *Catwoman: The Visual Guide to the Feline Fatale* (6–12). Illus. 2004, DK $19.99 (0-7566-0383-8). This oversize, richly illustrated book tells all about Catwoman, including where she comes from and the equipment she uses. (Rev: BL 5/15/04)

2299 Beck, C. C., et al. *The Shazam! Archives.* v.4 (8–12). Illus. 2004, DC Comics $49.95 (1-4012-0160-1). This is a collection of Captain Marvel comic strips, most dating back to 1941–1942. (Rev: BL 5/1/04)

2300 Bishop, Debbie. *Black Tide: Awakening of the Key* (6–10). 2004, Angel Gate paper $19.99 (1-93243-100-4). This book collects the first eight issues of a comic series about Justin Braddock, who is learning secrets about his past. (Rev: BL 4/15/04)

2301 Bradbury, Ray. *The Best of Ray Bradbury: The Graphic Novel* (6–12). Illus. 2003, iBooks paper $18.95 (0-7434-7476-7). Some of the best artists working in the graphic novels field have adapted Bradbury's works. (Rev: BL 2/1/04)

2302 Brubaker, Ed, et al. *Crooked Little Town* (9–12). Illus. 2003, DC Comics paper $14.95 (1-4012-0008-7). Catwoman protects Gotham City's downtrodden in this collection of stories. (Rev: BL 2/1/04)

2303 Casey, Joe, and Charlie Adlard. *Codeflesh* (9–12). Illus. 2003, AiT paper $12.95 (1-932051-15-5). In this masked crime-fighter saga, bail bondsman Cameron Dalty dons a full-head mask to help catch the criminals. (Rev: BL 2/1/04)

2304 Clamp. *Wish* (9–12). 2002, TokyoPop paper $9.99 (1-59182-034-0). A graphic novel about a young surgeon and the angel he rescues. (Rev: BL 2/1/04)

2305 Deitch, Kim, and Simon Deitch. *The Boulevard of Broken Dreams* (11–12). Illus. 2002, Pantheon $21.00 (0-375-42191-2). An engrossing story of life at the pioneering Fontaine Talking Fables animation studio in New York in 1933; suited to mature teens. (Rev: BL 11/1/02; SLJ 8/03)

2306 DeMatteis, J. M., and Glenn Barr. *Brooklyn Dreams* (11–12). Illus. 2003, DC Comics paper $12.95 (1-4012-0051-6). An eminently readable graphic novel, best suited for mature teens, in which a 40-something narrator looks back on his final year in high school. (Rev: BL 7/03*)

2307 Dini, Paul. *The Batman Adventures: Dangerous Dames and Demons* (6–12). Illus. 2003, DC Comics paper $14.95 (1-56389-973-6). A collection of Batman stories originally published as single magazines. (Rev: BL 9/1/03)

2308 Dixon, Chuck. *Way of the Rat: The Walls of Zhumar* (7–12). Illus. 2003, CrossGeneration paper $15.95 (1-931484-51-1). Boon has stolen a scholar's magic ring and the Book of Hell and is now being chased by villains in this fantasy set in Asia and enhanced by dynamic illustrations. (Rev: BL 2/1/03)

2309 Doran, Colleen. *A Distant Soil: The Gathering* (9–12). 2001, Image Comics paper $18.95 (1-887279-51-2). This is a classic graphic novel about siblings from another world. (Rev: BL 2/1/04)

2310 Drechsler, Debbie. *Summer of Love* (10–12). Illus. 2002, Drawn & Quarterly $24.95 (1-896597-37-8). This poignant graphic novel about a 9th-grader coping with a new community and school explores themes that will resonate with teens everywhere. (Rev: BL 8/02)

2311 Eisner, Will. *Will Eisner's The Spirit Archives v. 12* (8–12). Illus. 2003, DC Comics $49.95 (1-4012-0006-0). This collection of comic strips covers the full 12-year career of the Spirit, a masked crime fighter. (Rev: BL 2/1/04)

2312 Ennis, Garth, and John Higgins. *Pride and Joy* (10–12). Illus. 2004, DC Comics paper $14.95 (1-4012-0190-3). Jimmy Kavanaugh learns that the criminal he helped send to prison is out and seeking revenge. (Rev: BL 3/15/04)

2313 Furman, Simon. *Transformers: The Ultimate Guide* (6–12). Illus. 2004, DK $24.99 (0-7566-0314-5). This book gives all sorts of information about the robots that have been so popular with young readers. (Rev: BL 5/15/04)

2314 Gaiman, Neil, et al. *Endless Nights* (10–12). Illus. Series: Sandman. 2003, DC Comics $24.95 (1-4012-0089-3). Gaiman's Sandman comic-book family returns in separate stories that focus on each of the series' main characters, including Death, Desire, Despair, Delirium, Destruction, and Destiny; for mature teens. (Rev: BL 9/1/03) [741.45]

2315 Gaiman, Neil, and P. Craig Russell. *Murder Mysteries* (11–12). Illus. 2002, Dark Horse $13.95 (1-56971-634-X). A graphic novel adaptation of Gaiman's short story about two mysterious murders; for mature teens. (Rev: BL 9/1/02)

2316 Gallagher, Fred, and Rodney Caston. *Megatokyo*, Vol. 2 (11–12). Illus. 2004, Dark Horse paper $9.95 (1-59307-118-3). This graphic novel tells about two young geeks, Piro and Largo, and their pilgrimage to Japan. (Rev: BL 5/1/04; SLJ 8/04)

2317 *Hellboy: Weird Tales, v.1* (10–12). Ed. by Scott Allie and Matt Dryer. Illus. 2003, Dark Horse paper $17.95 (1-56971-622-6). Hellboy, a humanoid demon, is an agent who investigates such paranormal phenomena as ghosts, poltergeists, and other supernatural creatures. (Rev: BL 2/1/04) [741.5]

2318 Hornschemeier, Paul. *Mother, Come Home* (10–12). Illus. 2003, Dark Horse paper $14.95 (1-59307-037-3). The wrenching story of a 17-year-boy who must cope with the deaths of his mother and then his father. (Rev: BL 2/1/04*; SLJ 6/04)

2319 Inzana, Ryan. *Johnny Jihad* (10–12). Illus. 2003, NBM paper $9.95 (1-56163-353-4). A gripping and well-illustrated tale of a young American recruited into Islamic radicalism. (Rev: BL 8/03)

2320 Irwin, Jane, and Jeff Berndt. *Vogelein: Clockwork Faerie* (5–12). Illus. 2003, Fiery Studios paper $12.95 (0-9743110-0-6). A beautiful 17th-century mechanical fairy who is immortal but depends on others to wind her up stars in this graphic novel. (Rev: BL 11/1/03)

2321 Johns, Geoff. *The Flash: Crossfire* (9–12). Illus. 2004, DC Comics paper $17.95 (1-4012-0195-4). From an old comic book series, here is a collection of the scripts that highlight the superhero known as The Flash. (Rev: BL 5/15/04)

2322 Jolley, Dan, and Tony Harris. *The Liberty Files* (9–12). Illus. 2004, DC Comics paper $19.95 (1-4012-0203-9). Batman is called in to help apprehend Jack the Grin, also known as the Joker. (Rev: BL 5/15/04)

2323 Kanan, Nabiel. *The Birthday Riots* (10–12). Illus. 2002, NBM $14.95 (1-56163-299-6). The midlife crisis of a British political adviser and his sometimes-fractious relationship with his teenage daughter, Natalie, are the focus of this offbeat graphic novel. (Rev: BL 2/15/02)

2324 Kane, Bob, et al. *Batman in the Forties* (9–12). Illus. 2004, DC Comics paper $19.95 (1-4012-0206-3). This is a collection of early Batman strips from his beginnings in May 1939 to the introduction of Robin. (Rev: BL 5/15/04)

2325 Kesel, Barbara. *Meridian: Flying Solo* (7–12). Illus. Series: Meridian. 2003, CrossGeneration paper $9.95 (1-931484-54-6). Sephie inherits her father's position as first minister of Meridian, a floating city, and must use her magical powers to battle an evil uncle. (Rev: BL 4/1/03)

2326 Kikuchi, Hideyuki, and Yuho Ashibe. *Darkside Blues* (9–12). Trans. by Tomoe Spencer. Illus. 2004, ADV Manga paper $14.98 (1-4139-0002-X). This *manga* takes place in a fictitious area of Toyko called the Darkside, which is owned by the evil Persona Century Corporation. (Rev: BL 5/1/04)

2327 Kim, Ho Sik. *My Sassy Girl* (11–12). 2003, ComicsOne paper $13.95 (1-58899-342-6). Beautiful artwork highlights this Korean graphic novel about the romantic misadventures of a college-age boy infatuated with a difficult young woman. (Rev: BL 12/1/03) [741.5]

2328 Kubert, Joe. *Yossel: April 19, 1943: A Story of the Warsaw Ghetto Uprising* (8–12). Illus. 2003, iBooks $24.95 (0-7434-7516-X). In this graphic novel, Yossel and his friends fight to the death against their Nazi oppressors. (Rev: BL 2/1/04; SLJ 7/04)

2329 Lash, Batton. *Mr. Negativity and Other Tales of Supernatural Law* (10–12). Illus. 2004, Exhibit A paper $15.95 (0-9633954-8-3). Two men who practice supernatural law take on the case of the man who is so pessimistic that he radiates negative energy. (Rev: BL 3/15/04)

2330 Lash, Batton. *The Vampire Brat and Other Tales of Supernatural Law* (10–12). 2001, Exhibit A paper $14.95 (0-9633954-7-5). This lighthearted romp features attorneys Alanna Wolff and Jeff Byrd and their unusual clients, who include a vampire, time-traveler, and a boy with a dual identity. (Rev: BL 2/1/02)

2331 Little, Jason. *Shutterbug Follies* (10–12). 2002, Doubleday Graphic Novels $24.95 (0-385-50346-6). In this graphic novel, 18-year-old Bea, who works in a New York City photo lab, sees a photograph of a naked female corpse and has some scary experiences. (Rev: SLJ 1/03)

2332 Loeb, Jeph, et al. *Batman: Hush.* v.2 (8–12). Illus. 2004, DC Comics $19.95 (1-4012-0084-2). This is a collection of recent Batman adventures that include appearances by Joker, Riddler, and Catwoman. (Rev: BL 4/1/04)

2333 Ma, Wing Shing. *Black Leopard* (9–12). Trans. by Ken Li and Wayne Moyung. Illus. 2003, ComicsOne paper $14.95 (1-58899-333-7). In this action adventure, Black Leopard, a top-notch agent, must regain his sword and rescue his girlfriend. (Rev: BL 2/1/04)

2334 Ma, Wing Shing. *Storm Riders: Invading Sun: Vol. 1* (8–12). Illus. 2003, ComicsOne paper $9.95 (1-58899-359-0). Martial arts and an alternate China are featured in this graphic novel about two expert fighters who set out to find their former master named Conquer. (Rev: BL 2/1/04)

2335 McCloud, Scott. *The New Adventures of Abraham Lincoln* (7–10). 1998, Homage Comics paper $19.00 (1-887-27987-3). Time travel, an encounter with Abraham Lincoln, and an alien attempt to rule America are some of the adventures faced by a middle-school student when he is sent to detention. (Rev: BL 2/1/03)

2336 Marz, Ron. *Crisis of Faith* (9–12). Series: The Path. 2003, CrossGeneration Comics paper $9.95 (1-59314-016-9). The illustrations are a major draw of this sometimes hard-to-follow graphic novel about a monk whose crisis of faith causes him to seek revenge against the gods and pits him against a boyhood friend. (Rev: BL 8/03) [741.5]

2337 Miller, Frank, et al. *Batman: The Dark Knight Strikes Again* (10–12). Illus. 2002, DC Comics $29.95 (1-56389-844-6). This long-awaited sequel to Frank Miller's *Dark Knight Returns* recounts an epic struggle against an authoritarian and repressive government. (Rev: BL 1/1–15/03)

2338 Mizuno, Ryo. *Record of Lodoss War: The Grey Witch — Birth of a New Knight* (7–12). Series: Grey Witch Trilogy. 2000, CPM Comics $15.95 (1-56219-928-S). This graphic novel is the second volume of the Grey Witch Trilogy and tells how Pam struggles to learn the identity of his father in a universe where gods, goddesses, and goblins exist. (Rev: BL 12/1/00)

2339 Moeller, Christopher. *Faith Conquers* (9–12). Illus. 2004, Dark Horse paper $17.95 (1-59307-015-2). Seasoned warrior Trevor Faith arrives on the planet Hotok to command the armed forces of the orthodox national church. Also use in this series *Sheva's War* (2004). (Rev: BL 5/15/04)

2340 Moore, Alan, et al. *Alan Moore's America's Best Comics. 2004* (8–12). Illus. 2004, DC Comics paper $17.95 (1-4012-0147-4). The author and illustrator who created imaginative comics in the 1990s is honored in this reprint of all 10 of his America's Best Comics group. (Rev: BL 3/1/04)

2341 Moore, Richard. *Boneyard, v.2* (11–12). 2004, NBM paper $9.95 (1-50163-369-0). In this comic-book romp, cemetery owner Richard Paris, faced with a tax bill of more than half a million dollars, enlists the help of his monstrous tenants in raising the funds he'll need to pay the bill; for mature teens. (Rev: BL 12/1/03) [741.5]

2342 Morvan, Jean David. *Wake: Fire and Ash* (9–12). 2001, NBM paper $9.95 (1-56163-267-8). The age-old struggle between good and evil takes center stage in this imaginatively illustrated story that pits Navee, a human girl, against an alien force from a world where mind control has replaced individual reason. (Rev: BL 4/15/01)

2343 Muth, Jon. *Swamp Thing: Roots* (8–12). 1998, DC Comics paper $7.95 (1-56389-377-0). Visual images enhance this story of the supernatural elements that influence life in a small community. (Rev: BL 2/1/03)

2344 Nishiyama, Yuriko. *Harlem Beat* (8–12). 1999, TokyoPop paper $9.95 (1-892-21304-4). Created and produced in Japan, this graphic novel follows the adventures of an urban, teenage boy who loves basketball. (Rev: BL 2/1/03)

2345 Palmiotti, Jimmy, et al. *The Conduit* (10–12). Illus. 2003, DC Comics paper $19.95 (1-4012-0120-2). This is a collection of the first seven issues of 21 Down, in which the hero has the gift of seeing the last thing that a murder victim has seen before his or her death. (Rev: BL 2/1/04)

2346 Pfeifer, Will. *H-E-R-O: Powers and Abilities* (8–12). 2003, DC Comics paper $9.95 (1-4012-0168-7). The three stories in this volume deal with a mysterious device that gives its user the powers and abilities of a super being. (Rev: BL 2/1/04)

2347 Pini, Wendy, and Richard Pini. *ElfQuest: Archives: Volume 1* (9–12). Illus. 2003, DC Comics $49.95 (1-4012-0128-8). These fantastic tales are reprinted from the comic books published in the late 1970s known as Elfquest. (Rev: BL 2/1/04)

2348 Pope, Paul. *Heavy Liquid* (9–12). 2001, DC Comics paper $29.95 (1-56389-635-4). A graphic novel depicting a future world in which a substance called "heavy liquid" is much sought-after. (Rev: BL 2/1/03; SLJ 1/02)

2349 Porcellino, John. *Perfect Example* (10–12). Illus. 2001, Highwater $11.95 (0-9665363-5-5). All the wildly varied emotions of the passage from high school to college are captured in this account of one teenaged boy's experiences in 1980s suburbia. (Rev: BL 4/15/01; VOYA 8/01)

2350 Powell, Eric. *My Murderous Childhood (and Other Grievous Yarns)* (10–12). Illus. 2004, Dark Horse paper $13.95 (1-59307-194-9). Gross humor and sexy scenes are found in this graphic novel that deals with the muscular hero known as the Goon.

Another in this series is *Rough Stuff* (2004). (Rev: BL 5/15/04)

2351 Rabagliati, Michel. *Paul Has a Summer Job* (9–12). 2003, Drawn & Quarterly $16.95 (1-896597-54-8). Paul, a discontented teen, takes a job as a camp counselor and finds romance and a new love of life in this graphic novel. (Rev: BL 2/1/03; SLJ 12/03; VOYA 10/03)

2352 Rodi, Rob. *Crossovers* (5–12). Illus. 2003, CrossGeneration paper $15.95 (1-931484-85-6). This graphic novel is an entertaining look at a suburban family whose members possess a unique power. (Rev: BL 2/1/04)

2353 Rodionoff, Hans, et al. *Lovecraft* (10–12). Illus. 2004, DC Comics $24.95 (1-4012-0110-5). This graphic novel for mature readers re-creates the harried life of H. P. Lovecraft, the author of many horror classics. (Rev: BL 2/1/04)

2354 Sacco, Joe. *Safe Area Gorazde* (11–12). 2000, Fantagraphics paper $19.95 (1-56097-470-2). A graphic novel depicting the conditions in a "safe area" during the recent unrest in Bosnia. (Rev: BL 2/1/03)

2355 Schuiten, Francois, and Benoit Peeters. *The Invisible Frontier. v. 1* (10–12). Trans. by Joe Johnson. Illus. Series: Cities of the Fantastic. 2003, NBM $15.95 (1-56163-333-X). Suitable for mature teens, this comic fantasy recounts the adventures of novice mapmaker Roland in the state of Sodrovno's giant cartographic facility. (Rev: BL 12/15/02)

2356 Seto, Andy. *Crouching Tiger, Hidden Dragon* (7–12). Illus. 2002, ComicsOne paper $13.95 (1-58899-999-8). A comic book version of the first installment of the martial arts story that was made into a successful movie. (Rev: BL 4/1/03)

2357 Shanower, Eric. *A Thousand Ships, Volume 1: The Story of the Trojan War* (9–12). Illus. Series: Age of Bronze. 2001, Hungry Tiger $29.95 (1-58240-221-3); paper $19.95 (1-58240-200-0). Drawing on the legend and mythology of ancient Greece, Eric Shanower weaves a fast-paced graphic novel tale of the Trojan War, which is supplemented by such useful features as a glossary, bibliography, and genealogy charts. (Rev: BL 9/15/01) [937]

2358 Smith, Jeff. *Rose* (9–12). 2002, Cartoon Books paper $19.95 (1-888963-10-7). A fairy tale told in a graphic novel format about two princesses, one of whom will become queen. (Rev: BL 2/1/04)

2359 Stoker, Bram. *Graphic Classics: Bram Stoker* (9–12). Illus. Series: Graphic Classics. 2003, Eureka paper $9.95 (0-9712464-7-5). This graphic rendition of some of Bram Stoker's works includes some vampire material as well as versions of lesser-known works. (Rev: BL 2/1/04)

2360 Sturm, James. *The Golem's Mighty Swing* (10–12). Illus. 2001, Drawn & Quarterly paper $12.95 (1-896597-45-9). This graphic novel takes place in the 1920s and involves a barnstorming Jewish baseball team, the Stars of David, and their sole black player who poses as a golem. (Rev: BL 10/15/01) [741.5]

2361 Talbot, Bryan. *The Tale of One Bad Rat* (9–12). 1995, Dark Horse Comics $14.95 (1-56971-077-5). A classic graphic novel about a teenage runaway girl who is escaping an abusive father. (Rev: BL 2/1/04)

2362 Templeton, Ty. *Batman Gotham Adventures* (5–10). 2000, DC Comics paper $9.95 (1-56389-616-8). This graphic novel offers six short stories about Batman, Catwoman, Robin, and the usual villains, drawn by Rick Burkett and others. (Rev: BL 12/1/00)

2363 Templeton, Ty. *Bigg Time: A Farcical Fable of Fleeting Fame* (11–12). Illus. 2002, DC Comics paper $14.95 (1-56389-905-1). Templeton's satiric graphic novel chronicles homeless Lester Bigg's ill-fated struggle to attain stardom; for mature teens. (Rev: BL 11/1/02) [741.5]

2364 Thomas, John Ira, and Carter Allen. *Man Is Vox: Barracudae* (9–12). Illus. 2003, Candle Light paper $9.95 (0-9743147-2-2). Our hero in a patched union suit and a store clerk join forces to further their various purposes in this graphic novel. (Rev: BL 2/1/04)

2365 Thomas, Roy, et al. *The Monster of the Monoliths and Other Stories* (9–12). Illus. 2004, Dark Horse paper $15.95 (1-59307-024-1). Conan the barbarian faces wizards, witches, demons, and pirates in this collection of stories. (Rev: BL 3/15/04)

2366 Thomas, Roy, et al. *The Song of Red Sonja and Other Stories* (9–12). Illus. 2004, Dark Horse paper $15.95 (1-59307-025-X). This reprint from Marvel Comics continues the early adventures of Conan the Barbarian. (Rev: BL 5/15/04)

2367 Thompson, Craig. *Blankets* (11–12). Illus. 2003, Top Shelf paper $29.95 (1-891830-43-0). First love and loss are central to this coming-of-age story, a sequel to *Good-bye Chunky Rice* (1999); suitable for mature teens. (Rev: BL 6/1–15/03*; SLJ 4/04)

2368 Thompson, Craig. *Good-bye Chunky Rice* (9–12). 1999, Top Shelf $14.95 (1-891830-09-0). A graphic novel telling of the story of anthropomorphic turtle Chunky Rice and the trip he takes, leaving his mouse girlfriend to long for his return. (Rev: BL 2/1/03; SLJ 4/00)

2369 Tinsley, Kevin, and Phil Singer. *Milk Cartons and Dog Biscuits* (7–12). Illus. 2004, Stickman Graphics paper $19.95 (0-9675423-4-0). People and elf-like creatures mingle in this adventure mystery about a state ranger who is searching for a runaway daughter. (Rev: BL 2/1/04)

2370 Tolkien, J. R. R. *The Hobbit; or, There and Back Again* (5–10). Adapted by Charles Dixon and Sean Deming. Illus. 1990, Eclipse paper $12.95 (0-345-36858-4). The classic story of Bilbo Baggins and his companions is introduced to reluctant readers in this full-color graphic novel. (Rev: BL 9/1/91)

2371 Ueda, Miwa. *Peach Girl* (9–12). 2000, TokyoPop paper $9.99 (1-59182-498-2). In this Japanese graphic novel, a young girl is shunned and maligned because she has dark skin. (Rev: BL 2/1/04)

2372 Uslan, Michael, and Peter Snejbjerg. *Detective No. 27* (7–12). Illus. 2003, DC Comics $19.95 (1-4012-0185-7). This story about the beginnings of Batman takes place at various times in our history including 1865, 1929, and 1939. (Rev: BL 2/1/04)

2373 Vaughan, Brian K., et al. *Cycles* (10–12). Illus. 2003, DC Comics paper $12.95 (1-4012-0076-1). Investigations continue into protagonist Yorick Brown's mysterious survival of a plague as he again confronts the Daughters of the Amazon and a new Israeli group; for mature teens. (Rev: BL 11/15/03; SLJ 2/04) [741.5]

2374 Veitch, Rick, et al. *Greyshirt: Indigo Sunset* (10–12). Illus. 2002, DC Comics paper $19.95 (1-56389-909-4). The title character, a masked hero first introduced in the *Tomorrow Stories* anthology, returns for six episodes in this collection of comic-strip derring-do that pits Greyshirt against the Lure and other criminal types in Indigo City. (Rev: BL 2/1/03)

2375 Von Sholly, Pete. *Pete Von Sholly's Morbid* (10–12). Illus. 2003, Dark Horse paper $14.95 (1-59307-028-4). For mature readers, this is a graphic novel dealing with huge creatures, star-trekking, the living dead, and mad doctors and is illustrated with processed photographs. (Rev: BL 2/1/04*)

2376 Waid, Mark. *Ruse: Inferno of Blue* (7–12). 2002, CrossGeneration paper $15.95 (1-931484-19-8). Mystery, action, and magical powers abound in this graphic novel set in an alternate universe and starring detective Simon Archard and sidekick Emma Bishop. (Rev: BL 8/02)

2377 Warner, Allen. *Ninja Boy: Faded Dreams* (8–12). 2003, DC Comics paper $14.95 (1-4012-0102-4). The first six issues of *Ninja Boy* are collected in this Japanese *anime* tale of Nakio, who is seeking to avenge his family, which has suffered at the hands of the evil Mikaboshi. (Rev: BL 11/1/03)

2378 Weissman, Steven. *White Flower Day* (9–12). Illus. 2003, Fantagraphics paper $14.95 (1-560-97514-8). Several weird young creatures who create mayhem are the stars of three different stories in this graphic novel. (Rev: BL 2/1/04)

2379 Willingham, Bill, et al. *Fables: Legends in Exile* (11–12). Illus. 2003, DC Comics paper $9.95 (1-56389-942-6). This humorous graphic novel suitable for mature teens is peopled with refugees from fairy tales — including Jack of beanstalk fame, Snow White, Prince Charming, and Bigby (formerly Big Bad) Wolf — who suddenly find themselves faced with a perplexing mystery. (Rev: BL 2/1/03) [741.5]

2380 Winick, Judd. *Pedro and Me: Friendship, Loss, and What I Learned* (8–12). Illus. 2000, Holt paper $16.00 (0-8050-6403-6). A graphic novel tribute to Pedro Zamora, an AIDS educator and actor who died of HIV complications at the age of 22. (Rev: BL 9/15/00; HB 11–12/00; HBG 3/01; SLJ 10/00)

2381 Won, Kim Kang. *I.N.U.V* (9–12). 2002, TokyoPop paper $9.99 (1-59182-001-4). In this graphic novel with Chinese characters, Sey discovers that the surly son of the family with whom she is staying is actually a girl. (Rev: BL 2/1/04)

2382 Woo, Park Sung. *Now.* Volume 1 (6–12). Illus. 2003, ComicsOne paper $9.95 (1-58899-327-2). Kung fu and humor are found in this fantasy about young descendants of warriors who are masters of the lost martial art of Sashinmu. (Rev: BL 2/1/04) [741.5]

2383 Wood, Brian, and Rob G. *Dirtbike Manifesto* (9–12). Illus. 2004, AiT paper $12.95 (1-932051-18-X). The Couriers, a young man and woman, deliver goods including drugs and weapons that no other bike messengers can. (Rev: BL 5/1/04)

2384 Yoshizaki, Mine. *Sgt. Frog.* v.1 (8–11). Illus. 2004, TokyoPop paper $9.99 (1-59182-703-5). In this *manga* work, a young brother and sister are dealing with an uninvited guest, an invader from another planet. (Rev: BL 3/15/04)

2385 Yune, Tommy. *From the Stars* (7–12). Illus. 2003, DC Comics paper $9.95 (1-4012-0144-X). When an alien ship crashes on earth, Roy Fokker signs up to be a test pilot and then learns a great deal about alien technology. (Rev: BL 2/1/04)

Historical Fiction and Foreign Lands

Prehistory

2386 Auel, Jean M. *The Mammoth Hunters* (10–12). 1985, Crown $19.95 (0-517-55627-8). This is the third story set in prehistoric times about the amazing woman Ayla and her ability to survive endless hardships. The first two were *The Clan of the Cave Bear* (1980) and *The Valley of Horses* (1982). (Rev: BL 11/1/85)

2387 Auel, Jean M. *The Plains of Passage* (10–12). 1990, Crown $24.95 (0-517-58049-7). A sexually explicit novel for mature readers that is part of the Earth's Children series. This installment tells of Ayla and her mate Jondalar and their journey back to Jondalar's people. In *The Shelters of Stone*

(2002), Ayla is pregnant with Jondalar's child and seeking friendship from his people. (Rev: BL 9/1/90; SLJ 4/91)

2388 Cornwell, Bernard. *Stonehenge: 2000 B.C.* (10–12). 2000, HarperCollins $26.00 (0-06-019700-5). Set in prehistoric Britain, this novel for older teens tells of the exploits of Hengall, the chief of his people, and his three sons. (Rev: BL 3/15/00)

2389 Dann, John R. *Song of the Axe* (10–12). 2001, Tor $25.95 (0-312-86984-3). In this prehistoric epic set during the Ice Age, Agon is in love with Eena, who is raped by Ka, the foul Snake Man. (Rev: BL 4/15/01)

2390 Dickinson, Peter. *A Bone from a Dry Sea* (7–10). 1993, Dell paper $4.99 (0-440-21928-0). The protagonists are Li, a girl in a tribe of "sea apes" living four million years ago, and Vinny, the teenage daughter of a modern-day paleontologist. (Rev: BL 2/1/93; SLJ 4/93*)

2391 Dickinson, Peter. *Po's Story* (7–10). Series: The Kin. 1998, Grosset $14.99 (0-399-23349-0); paper $3.99 (0-448-41711-1). In prehistoric times, Po sets out to find water for his people and instead finds a different tribe. (Rev: VOYA 10/99)

2392 Harrison, Sue. *Call Down the Stars* (10–12). Series: Storyteller. 2001, Morrow $25.00 (0-380-97372-3). Concluding the trilogy that included *Song of the River* (1997) and *Cry of the Wind* (1998), this novel is also set in prehistoric Alaska and features two narrators, one male and the other female. (Rev: BL 10/1/01)

2393 Holland, Cecelia. *Pillar of the Sky* (10–12). 2000, Forge paper $14.95 (0-312-86887-1). The story of one outcast boy is linked to the people of Salisbury Plain and the building of Stonehenge. (Rev: VOYA 12/00)

Ancient and Medieval History

GENERAL AND MISCELLANEOUS

2394 Assiniwi, Bernard. *The Beothuk Saga* (10–12). Trans. by Wayne Grady. Illus. 2002, St. Martin's $25.95 (0-312-28390-3). This story of the Beothuk people, a now-extinct tribe that once lived in Newfoundland, conveys much history about the eastern coast of Canada. (Rev: BL 1/1–15/02)

2395 Branford, Henrietta. *The Fated Sky* (8–12). 1999, Candlewick $16.99 (0-7636-0775-4). Set in Viking times, this novel tells of 16-year-old Ran and how she is saved from becoming a human sacrifice by a blind musician, Toki, with whom she later falls in love. (Rev: BL 12/1/99* ; HB 11–12/99; HBG 4/00; SLJ 11/99)

2396 Cadnum, Michael. *Daughter of the Wind* (7–10). 2003, Scholastic $17.95 (0-439-35224-X). Norse culture and atmosphere are strong in this

action-packed and violent story of three young people facing danger in the time of the Vikings. (Rev: BL 11/15/03; HBG 4/04; SLJ 12/03; VOYA 12/03)

2397 Cadnum, Michael. *Raven of the Waves* (7–10). 2001, Scholastic $17.95 (0-531-30334-9). In this gory tale set in the 8th century, 17-year-old Viking Lidsmod takes part in a bloodthirsty raid on an English community but later helps a boy who is taken captive. (Rev: BL 4/1/01; HB 9–10/01; HBG 3/02; SLJ 7/01; VOYA 8/01)

2398 Chen, Da. *Wandering Warrior* (8–12). 2003, Delacorte $15.95 (0-385-73020-9). Luka, 12, must survive on his own when he is separated from his teacher, Atami, in this adventure set in ancient China featuring monsters, kung fu, violent confrontations, and magic. (Rev: BL 2/15/03; HBG 4/04; SLJ 2/03; VOYA 6/03)

2399 Edghill, India. *Queenmaker: A Novel of King David's Queen* (10–12). 2002, St. Martin's $24.95 (0-312-28918-9). Saul's young daughter Michal meets and falls in love with David in this novel based on biblical characters. (Rev: BL 12/1/01)

2400 Fletcher, Susan. *Shadow Spinner* (7–10). 1998, Simon & Schuster $17.00 (0-689-81852-1). The story of Shahrazad and how she collected the tales that kept her and her harem companions alive for 1,001 nights. (Rev: BCCB 7–8/98; BL 6/1–15/98; BR 1–2/99; HB 7–8/98; HBG 10/98; SLJ 6/98; VOYA 4/99)

2401 Holland, Cecelia. *The Soul Thief* (10–12). 2002, Tor $24.95 (0-312-84885-4). A young Viking braves danger to rescue his twin sister in this multi-layered historical adventure; for mature teens. (Rev: BL 3/15/02)

2402 Hunt, Angela E. *Brothers* (10–12). 1997, Bethany paper $10.99 (1-55661-608-2). An exciting retelling of the Bible story of Joseph, a leader in Egypt, who is visited by his 10 brothers when they come to buy grain for the starving in Israel. (Rev: SLJ 1/98)

2403 Hunt, Angela E. *Dreamers* (10–12). 1996, Bethany paper $10.99 (1-55661-607-4). This retelling of the Bible story about Joseph, who is able to interpret dreams, tells how a capricious Joseph, sold by his jealous brothers into slavery in Egypt, went from being a servant to becoming an administrator favored by the pharaoh in a royal court permeated by intrigue. (Rev: SLJ 8/96; VOYA 8/96)

2404 Jacq, Christian. *The Stone of Light* (10–12). 2000, Pocket paper $16.00 (0-7434-0346-0). This novel, the beginning of a four-volume set, takes place in Egypt during the reign of Ramses the Great and is filled with intrigue, passion, and suspense. (Rev: BL 5/15/00)

2405 Levitin, Sonia. *Escape from Egypt* (8–10). 1996, Puffin paper $5.99 (0-14-037537-6). Historical fiction related to the biblical tale of the Exodus told from the point of view of two teens. (Rev: BL 5/1/94*; SLJ 4/94; VOYA 4/94)

2406 Mahfouz, Naguib. *Akhenaten: Dweller in Truth* (10–12). Trans. by Tagreid Abu-Hassabo. 2000, Doubleday paper $12.00 (0-385-49909-4). Mahfouz, the great contemporary Egyptian writer, has written a novel that takes place in ancient Egypt and tells how a young boy tries to uncover the truth about the dead pharaoh Akhenaten. (Rev: BL 3/15/00)

2407 Miklowitz, Gloria D. *Masada: The Last Fortress* (7–10). 1998, Eerdmans $16.00 (0-8028-5165-7). The siege of Masada comes alive through the eyes of a young Jewish man and a Roman commander. (Rev: BCCB 10/98; BL 10/1/98; HBG 3/99; SLJ 12/98; VOYA 2/99)

2408 Morris, Gilbert. *Heart of a Lion* (10–12). Series: Lions of Judah. 2002, Bethany paper $11.99 (0-7642-2681-9). In the first volume of a biblical history series, the author recounts the story of Noah and his struggle to follow God's wishes and resist the siren call of worldly pleasures. (Rev: BL 1/1–15/03*)

2409 Napoli, Donna Jo. *Song of the Magdalene* (9–12). 1996, Scholastic $21.99 (0-590-93705-7). In biblical times Miriam, who suffers from seizures, is helped by a crippled young man who becomes her lover. After experiencing many difficulties, Miriam makes sense of her life when she meets the healer Joshua. (Rev: BL 10/1/96; BR 1–2/97; SLJ 11/96; VOYA 2/97)

2410 Osborne-McKnight, Juilene. *Daughter of Ireland* (10–12). 2002, Tor $24.95 (0-765-30127-X). Young Druid Aislinn ni Sorar, while searching for a missing orphan, finds that her quest takes on greater import, involving the future of the Celtic people, in this tale of ancient Irish history. (Rev: BL 2/15/02)

2411 Pfitsch, Patricia C. *The Deeper Song* (8–10). 1998, Simon & Schuster $16.00 (0-689-81183-7). In this story, set at the time of King Solomon, a high-spirited girl named Judith decides to write down the oral traditions of the Jewish people, thus creating a book that will become a cornerstone of Judaism. (Rev: BL 10/1/98; HBG 3/99; SLJ 11/98; VOYA 8/99)

2412 Robinson, Lynda S. *Slayer of Gods* (10–12). 2001, Warner $23.95 (0-89296-705-6). In this mystery, part of a series set in Ancient Egypt, Lord Meren, adviser to King Tut, investigates the death of Queen Nefertiti, whom he believes was poisoned. (Rev: BL 5/1/01*; SLJ 9/01)

2413 Speare, Elizabeth G. *The Bronze Bow* (7–10). 1961, Houghton paper $6.95 (0-395-13719-5). A Jewish boy seeks revenge against the Romans who killed his parents, but finally his hatred abates when he hears the messages and teachings of Jesus. Newbery Medal winner, 1962. (Rev: BL 9/1/95)

2414 Tarr, Judith. *Lord of the Two Lands* (9–12). 1994, Tor paper $4.99 (0-8125-2078-5). Unveils the destiny of Alexander the Great, who is supported and guided by the Egyptian priestess Meriamon, daughter of a pharaoh. (Rev: BL 2/15/93; VOYA 8/93)

2415 Zelitch, Simone. *Moses in Sinai* (10–12). 2001, Black Heron $23.95 (0-930773-59-4). An graceful retelling of the biblical story of Moses and the journey he led to Sinai. (Rev: BL 12/1/01)

GREECE AND ROME

2416 Beye, Charles Rowan. *Odysseus: A Life* (10–12). 2004, Hyperion $23.95 (1-4013-0024-3). This is a modern novel that retells the life of Odysseus based on a variety of sources. (Rev: BL 2/15/04)

2417 Borchardt, Alice. *The Silver Wolf* (10–12). 1998, Ballantine $24.95 (0-345-42360-7). The splendor and decadence of ancient Rome are explored in this novel about a teenage female werewolf, Regeane, who must hide her natural wolfish instincts to save her life. (Rev: VOYA 12/98)

2418 Bradshaw, Gillian. *The Beacon at Alexandria* (9–12). 1986, Houghton $17.95 (0-395-41159-9). In the Roman Empire in the 4th century, a young girl disguises herself as a man to enter the medical school at Alexandria. (Rev: BL 9/1/86)

2419 Bradshaw, Gillian. *Island of Ghosts* (10–12). 1998, St. Martin's $22.95 (0-312-86439-6). In a tale of adventure, treachery, and romance, this novel traces the career of Ariantes, a Sarmatian mercenary, who leads an army of 8,000 against the forces that are threatening Roman authority in the far reaches of the empire. (Rev: BL 8/98; SLJ 3/99)

2420 Bradshaw, Gillian. *The Sand-Reckoner* (9–12). 2000, Forge $23.95 (0-312-87340-9); paper $14.95 (0-312-87581-9). This exciting historical novel deals with Archimedes' return to Syracuse after three years in Alexandria. (Rev: BL 4/1/00)

2421 Cooney, Caroline B. *Goddess of Yesterday* (7–12). 2002, Delacorte $15.95 (0-385-72945-6). Young Anaxandra adopts a false identity and is given a home by King Menelaus of Sparta despite the suspicions of the king's wife, Helen, in this exciting novel set in the build-up to the Trojan War. (Rev: BCCB 7–8/02; BL 6/1–15/02; HBG 10/02; SLJ 6/02; VOYA 8/02)

2422 Davis, Lindsey. *Three Hands in the Fountain* (10–12). 1999, Mysterious $23.00 (0-892-96691-2). In this mystery set in 1st-century Rome, Marcus Didius Falco investigates the appearance of body parts in the water supply. (Rev: BL 4/15/99; SLJ 9/99)

2423 Ford, Michael Curtis. *The Last King: Rome's Greatest Enemy* (10–12). 2004, St. Martin's $24.95

(0-312-27539-0). A well-crafted novel with lots of action about King Mithradates, the ruler of a small kingdom on the edge of the Black Sea and his hatred for Rome. (Rev: BL 1/1–15/04)

2424 Galloway, Priscilla. *The Courtesan's Daughter* (10–12). 2002, Delacorte LB $18.99 (0-385-90052-X). This romance set in ancient Greece is packed with historically accurate details. (Rev: BL 9/15/02; HBG 10/03; SLJ 9/02; VOYA 12/02)

2425 Geras, Adele. *Troy* (10–12). 2001, Harcourt $17.00 (0-15-216492-8). The saga of the *Iliad*, told from the point of view of the women involved. (Rev: BL 4/1/01; HB 7–8/01*; HBG 10/01; SLJ 7/01; VOYA 6/01)

2426 Graves, Robert. *I, Claudius: From the Autobiography of Tiberius Claudius, Born B.C. 10, Murdered and Deified A.D. 54* (10–12). 1983, Modern Library paper $14.00 (0-679-72477-X). Born lame and with a stammer, Claudius surprised everyone by becoming an outstanding Roman emperor.

2427 Iggulden, Conn. *Emperor: The Gates of Rome* (10–12). 2003, Delacorte $24.95 (0-385-33660-8). Caesar's youth, military training, and growing political acumen are the focus of this novel about the acquisition and use of power. (Rev: BL 11/15/02)

2428 McCullough, Colleen. *The Song of Troy* (10–12). 2001, Orion $27.50 (0-75281-413-3). This is a fast-paced, thrilling retelling of the Trojan War story and the 10-year siege that ended with the fall of Troy. (Rev: BL 5/15/01)

2429 McLaren, Clemence. *Aphrodite's Blessings: Love Stories from the Greek Myths* (7–12). 2002, Simon & Schuster $16.00 (0-689-84377-1). The lot of women in ancient Greece comes to life in three stories, based on mythology, about Atalanta, Andromeda, and Psyche. (Rev: BL 3/1/02; HBG 10/02; SLJ 1/02; VOYA 4/02)

2430 McLaren, Clemence. *Inside the Walls of Troy* (7–10). 1996, Simon & Schuster $17.00 (0-689-31820-0). The story of the Trojan War and the fall of Troy as told by Helen, the lover of Paris, and by Cassandra, who foresees the tragedy to come. (Rev: BL 10/15/96; BR 5–6/97; SLJ 10/96; VOYA 2/97)

2431 Napoli, Donna Jo. *The Great God Pan* (7–10). 2003, Random $15.95 (0-385-32777-2). A beautifully written novel about the life and aspirations of Pan, who was half man and half goat. (Rev: BL 4/15/03)

2432 Napoli, Donna Jo. *Sirena* (7–12). 1998, Scholastic $15.95 (0-590-38388-4); paper $4.99 (0-590-38389-2). This romantic expansion of the Greek myth of the Sirens describes the dilemma of an immortal mermaid who loves a mortal. (Rev: BL 1/1–15/03; BR 11–12/98; HBG 3/99; SLJ 10/98; VOYA 12/98)

2433 Renault, Mary. *The King Must Die* (10–12). 1958, Random paper $11.00 (0-394-75104-3). A historical adventure story based on the legend of Theseus. Followed by *The Bull from the Sea* (1962). Also use: *The Mask of Apollo* (1988).

2434 Saylor, Steven. *The Judgment of Caesar* (10–12). Series: Roma Sub Rosa. 2004, St. Martin's $24.95 (0-312-27119-0). Set at the time of Caesar and Pompey, this suspenseful mystery features Gordianus the Finder, a Roman citizen who has a gift for finding people and solving mysteries. Another title in this recommended series is *A Mist of Prophecies* (2002). (Rev: BL 5/1/04*)

2435 Sutcliff, Rosemary. *The Eagle of the Ninth* (7–12). 1993, Farrar paper $5.95 (0-374-41930-2). A reissue of the historical novel about the Roman legion that went to battle and disappeared. (Rev: BR 1–2/87)

2436 Tarr, Judith. *Throne of Isis* (9–12). 1995, Tor $5.99 (0-8125-2079-3). A carefully researched story about Antony and Cleopatra. (Rev: BL 4/15/94; VOYA 8/94)

MIDDLE AGES

2437 Alder, Elizabeth. *The King's Shadow* (7–12). 1995, Bantam paper $5.50 (0-440-22011-4). In medieval Britain, mute Evyn is sold into slavery, but as Earl Harold of Wessex's squire and eventual foster son, he chronicles the king's life and becomes a storyteller. (Rev: BL 7/95; SLJ 7/95)

2438 Cadnum, Michael. *The Book of the Lion* (7–12). 2000, Viking $15.99 (0-670-88386-7). Edmund, a young apprentice, is pressed into service as squire to a knight going to the Holy Land to fight in the Crusades. (Rev: BL 2/1/00; HB 3–4/00; HBG 9/00; SLJ 3/00; VOYA 4/00)

2439 Cadnum, Michael. *Forbidden Forest* (7–10). 2002, Scholastic $17.99 (0-439-31774-6). The story of Little John's entry into Robin Hood's band of merry men is told from John's point of view and combines realistic descriptions of medieval life with adventure and romance. (Rev: BL 4/15/02; HB 7–8/02; HBG 10/02; SLJ 6/02; VOYA 4/02)

2440 Cadnum, Michael. *In a Dark Wood* (7–10). 1998, Orchard LB $18.99 (0-531-33071-0). The story of Robin Hood as seen through the eyes of the sheriff of Nottingham and his young squire, Hugh. (Rev: BL 3/1/98; BR 11–12/98; HB 3–4/98; HBG 9/98; SLJ 4/98; VOYA 8/98)

2441 Cadnum, Michael. *The Leopard Sword* (7–10). 2002, Viking $15.99 (0-670-89908-9). Cadnum weaves realistic detail into this fictional story of crusaders returning to England after a long and dangerous journey only to meet new challenges. A sequel to *The Book of the Lion* (2000). (Rev: BCCB

1/03; BL 8/02; HBG 3/03; SLJ 10/02; VOYA 12/02)

2442 Calmann, Marianne. *Avignon* (10–12). 2000, Allison & Busby paper $14.95 (0-7490-0446-0). The plague, a case of amnesia, and Jewish-Christian relations are three elements in this adult romance set in the city of Avignon during 1346. (Rev: BL 2/1/00)

2443 Chaikin, Linda. *Swords and Scimitars* (9–12). Series: Golden Pavilions. 1996, Bethany paper $9.99 (1-55661-881-6). This historical adventure with Christian undertones tells the exciting story of two young people and events involving the First Crusade at the end of the 11th century. Followed by *Golden Palaces* (1996). (Rev: VOYA 10/97)

2444 Coulter, Catherine. *Lord of Falcon Ridge* (9–12). 1995, Berkley paper $6.99 (0-515-11584-3). In this conclusion to the trilogy, set in Britain in A.D. 922, Cleve and Chessa meet and fall in love as he transports her to her intended husband and she's pursued by a kidnapper. (Rev: BL 1/15/95; SLJ 9/95)

2445 Cushman, Karen. *The Midwife's Apprentice* (7–12). 1995, Clarion $12.00 (0-395-69229-6). A homeless young woman in medieval England becomes strong as she picks herself up and learns from a midwife to be brave. (Rev: BL 3/15/95*; SLJ 5/95)

2446 Dana, Barbara. *Young Joan* (6–10). 1991, HarperCollins $17.95 (0-06-021422-8); paper $6.99 (0-06-440661-X). A fictional account of Joan of Arc that questions how a simple French farm girl hears, assimilates, and acts upon a message from God. (Rev: BL 5/15/91*; SLJ 5/91)

2447 Doyle, Arthur Conan. *The White Company* (9–12). 1988, Morrow $22.00 (0-688-07817-6). This rich historical novel set in the dying days of the age of chivalry tells how lowly Alleyne achieved knighthood. (Rev: SLJ 2/88)

2448 Goodman, Joan Elizabeth. *Peregrine* (7–10). 2000, Houghton $15.00 (0-395-97729-0). Fifteen-year-old Lady Edith, who has lost her husband and baby, escapes her problems by going on a pilgrimage from England to the Holy Land. (Rev: BL 4/1/00; HBG 9/00; SLJ 5/00; VOYA 6/00)

2449 Holland, Cecelia. *The Angel and the Sword* (10–12). 2000, Tor $23.95 (0-312-86890-1). In this adventure set in the Middle Ages, Princess Ragny assumes the identity of a fearless knight, Roderick, to escape a brutal father. (Rev: BL 12/15/00)

2450 Jinks, Catherine. *Pagan in Exile* (9–12). 2004, Candlewick $15.99 (0-7636-2020-3). Squire Pagan accompanies Lord Roland to his castle in France in this sequel to *Pagan's Crusade* (2003), and describes the political and religious turmoil he finds there. (Rev: BCCB 2/04; BL 1/1–15/04; HB 5–6/04; VOYA 4/04)

2451 Jordan, Sherryl. *The Raging Quiet* (8–12). 1999, Simon & Schuster $17.00 (0-689-82140-9). In this novel set in the Middle Ages, 16-year-old Marnie is shunned when she befriends the local madman, whom she discovers is only deaf, not mad. (Rev: BL 5/1/99; HBG 9/99; SLJ 5/99; VOYA 8/99)

2452 McKenzie, Nancy. *Grail Prince* (10–12). 2003, Del Rey paper $14.95 (0-345-45648-3). After the death of Arthur, young Galahad sets out on a quest to locate the Holy Grail; a multilayered sequel to *Queen of Camelot* (2002). (Rev: BL 12/1/02; VOYA 6/03)

2453 Medeiros, Teresa. *Fairest of Them All* (10–12). 1995, Bantam paper $5.99 (0-553-56333-5). When the fair Holly de Chaste discovers that her father has offered her as the prize in a tournament of knights, she decides to disguise her beauty to foil the wedding plans. (Rev: SLJ 3/96)

2454 Morressy, John. *The Juggler* (7–10). 1996, Holt $16.95 (0-8050-4217-2); paper $5.95 (0-06-447174-8). In this adventure story set in the Middle Ages, a young man regrets the bargain he has made with the devil to become the world's greatest juggler in exchange for his soul. (Rev: BR 11–12/96; SLJ 6/96; VOYA 8/96)

2455 Newman, Sharan. *The Outcast Dove* (11–12). 2003, Tor $25.95 (0-765-30377-9). In this tale of medieval France, Solomon, the young Jewish protagonist, and his estranged father, who has converted to Christianity, find common cause when murder threatens; for mature teens. (Rev: BL 10/1/03)

2456 O'Dell, Scott. *The Road to Damietta* (7–10). 1987, Fawcett paper $6.50 (0-449-70233-2). A novel set in 13th-century Italy and involving St. Francis of Assisi. (Rev: SLJ 12/85; VOYA 2/86)

2457 Pargeter, Edith. *The Heaven Tree Trilogy* (9–12). 1993, Warner $24.95 (0-446-51708-9). *The Heaven Tree* (1960), *The Green Branch* (1962), and *The Scarlet Seed* (1963) make up this trilogy about a medieval British family of artisans and their power-hungry benefactors. (Rev: BL 10/1/93*)

2458 Patterson, James, and Andrew Gross. *The Jester* (10–12). 2003, Little, Brown $27.95 (0-316-60205-1). A weary Hugh De Luc returns from the Crusades only to discover that his home has been destroyed, his wife abducted, and he must confront an old enemy to rescue her. (Rev: BL 2/1/03)

2459 Penman, Sharon Kay. *Cruel as the Grave: A Medieval Mystery* (10–12). 1998, Holt $22.00 (0-8050-5608-4). Justin de Quincy, a medieval private eye, investigates the murder of the daughter of a poor peddler and negotiates with Prince John, who is plotting to gain the English throne while his brother, Richard Lionheart, is held hostage in Austria. (Rev: BL 10/15/98; SLJ 3/99)

2460 Penman, Sharon Kay. *The Reckoning* (9–12). 1991, Holt $24.95 (0-8050-1014-9). A battle over the Welsh throne in the 13th century leads to vows of revenge and acts of heroism. (Rev: BL 8/91; SLJ 7/92)

2461 Penman, Sharon Kay. *Time and Chance* (10–12). 2002, Putnam $27.95 (0-399-14785-3). King Henry II is on the throne and his subjects are full of plots, ambition, and passion in this sequel to *When Christ and His Saints Slept* (1994). (Rev: BL 2/15/02)

2462 Sauerwein, Leigh. *Song for Eloise* (8–10). 2003, Front Street $15.95 (1-886910-90-1). In the Middle Ages, an unhappy wife falls for a passing troubadour in a rich text full of historical detail. (Rev: BL 12/1/03; HBG 4/04; SLJ 12/03; VOYA 4/04)

2463 Sedley, Kate. *The Brothers of Glastonbury* (10–12). 2001, St. Martin's $23.95 (0-312-27282-0). In this medieval mystery, Roger the Chapman and bride-to-be Cicely Armstrong find that the girl's betrothed has disappeared. (Rev: BL 1/1–15/01)

2464 Sedley, Kate. *The Goldsmith's Daughter* (10–12). 2001, Severn $25.99 (0-7278-5732-0). Roger Chapman, an itinerant peddler, untangles a web of murder and deceit in this excellent medieval whodunit. (Rev: BL 12/1/01)

2465 Skurzynski, Gloria. *Spider's Voice* (8–12). 1999, Simon & Schuster $16.95 (0-689-82149-2). A retelling of the classic love story — set in 12th-century France — between the young teacher Abelard and his pupil, the beautiful Eloise. (Rev: BL 2/15/99; HBG 9/99; SLJ 3/99; VOYA 4/99)

2466 Springer, Nancy. *I Am Mordred: A Tale from Camelot* (7–12). 1998, Putnam $16.99 (0-399-23143-9). Told in the first person, this is the story of Mordred, bastard son of King Arthur, who is destined to kill his father. (Rev: BL 4/15/98; BR 1–2/99; HB 3–4/98; HBG 10/98; SLJ 5/98; VOYA 4/98)

2467 Springer, Nancy. *I Am Morgan le Fay: A Tale from Camelot* (6–10). 2001, Putnam $17.99 (0-399-23451-9). The legend of Morgan le Fay is expanded and enriched in this retelling, in which Morgan expresses her resentment of her older sister, Morgause, and her destructive love for Thomas. (Rev: BL 2/1/01; HB 1–2/01; HBG 10/01; SLJ 3/01; VOYA 2/01)

2468 Temple, Frances. *The Beduins' Gazelle* (7–10). 1996, Orchard LB $16.99 (0-531-08869-3). In this 14th-century adventure, a companion piece to *The Ramsey Scallop*, young scholar Etienne becomes involved in the lives of two lovers when he goes to Fez to study at the university. (Rev: BL 2/15/96; BR 9–10/96; SLJ 4/96*; VOYA 12/96)

2469 Temple, Frances. *The Ramsay Scallop* (7–10). 1994, Orchard LB $19.99 (0-531-08686-0). In 1299, 14-year-old Elenor and her betrothed nobleman are sent on a chaste pilgrimage to Spain and hear the stories of their fellow travelers. (Rev: BL 3/15/94*; SLJ 5/94; VOYA 4/94)

2470 Thomson, Sarah L. *The Dragon's Son* (7–12). 2001, Scholastic $17.95 (0-531-30333-0). This historical novel, based on Welsh legends about King Arthur, tells the stories of family members and others who were involved in Arthur's life. (Rev: BCCB 7–8/01; BL 5/1/01; HBG 10/01; SLJ 7/01; VOYA 6/01)

2471 Tingle, Rebecca. *The Edge on the Sword* (7–10). 2001, Putnam $19.99 (0-399-23580-9). This fascinating novel set in Britain in the late 800s describes the exploits of 15-year-old Aethelflaed, daughter of King Alfred of West Saxony, who is engaged to an older man she doesn't know and is allowed the freedom to learn many skills. (Rev: BCCB 10/01; BL 4/15/01; HBG 10/01; SLJ 7/01*; VOYA 8/01)

2472 Tomlinson, Theresa. *The Forestwife* (8–12). 1995, Orchard LB $17.99 (0-531-08750-6). A Robin Hood legend with Marian as the benevolent Green Lady of the forest. (Rev: BL 3/1/95*; SLJ 3/95; VOYA 5/95)

2473 Voigt, Cynthia. *Jackaroo* (8–10). 1985, Macmillan $20.00 (0-689-31123-0). In this novel set in the Middle Ages, a 16-year-old girl assumes the identity of a Robin Hood-like character named Jackaroo. (Rev: BL 9/15/85; SLJ 12/85)

2474 Watson, Elsa. *Maid Marian* (9–12). 2004, Crown $23.95 (1-4000-5041-3). A reworking of the Robin Hood story as narrated by Maid Marian who has traveled to Sherwood Forest to seek Robin's aid. (Rev: BL 2/15/04)

2475 Wein, Elizabeth E. *A Coalition of Lions* (7–12). Series: The Winter Prince. 2003, Viking $16.99 (0-370-03618-8). In the 6th century, a princess named Goewin travels from Britain to Africa on her way to an arranged marriage, in this absorbing sequel to *The Winter Prince* (1993). (Rev: BCCB 4/03; BL 2/15/03; SLJ 4/03)

Africa

2476 Abani, Chris. *Graceland* (11–12). 2004, Farrar $24.00 (0-374-16589-0). In dreams of an America that no longer exists, teenager Elvis Oke finds strength to endure the pain of his daily existence in Nigeria; for mature teens. (Rev: BL 11/15/03)

2477 Achebe, Chinua. *Things Fall Apart* (10–12). 1992, Knopf $14.50 (0-679-41714-1); paper $9.95 (0-385-47454-7). A proud Ibo leader, Okonkwo, sees his fortunes rise and fall and watches the disintegration of his village.

2478 Adichie, Chimamanda Ngozi. *Purple Hibiscus* (11–12). 2003, Algonquin $23.95 (1-56512-387-5). In Nigeria, Kambili, 15, and her older brother Jaja experience a new way of life when they visit their aunt's home and escape their father's brutally repressive influence; suitable for mature teens. (Rev: BL 9/15/03; SLJ 12/03)

2479 Dickinson, Peter. *AK* (7–10). 1992, Dell paper $3.99 (0-440-21897-7). A young soldier survives a bloody civil war in an African country but must use his gun again after his father is kidnapped during a military coup. (Rev: BL 4/15/92; SLJ 7/92)

2480 Dow, Unity. *Far and Beyon'* (9–12). 2002, Aunt Lute paper $11.95 (1-879960-64-8). A young girl growing up in Botswana must battle a culture filled with AIDS and sexual abuse. (Rev: BL 5/1/02)

2481 Drew, Eileen. *The Ivory Crocodile* (10–12). 1996, Coffee House $21.95 (1-56689-042-X). A novel about a young American woman who grew up in Africa and later returns to teach English in an isolated bush post, but finds she cannot escape her white skin and her Western heritage. (Rev: BL 5/1/96; SLJ 3/97)

2482 Essex, Karen. *Kleopatra* (10–12). 2001, Warner $24.95 (0-446-52740-8). This is a fascinating novel about the childhood of Cleopatra and her youthful initiation into politics and prominence in Egypt. (Rev: BL 9/1/01)

2483 Farmer, Nancy. *A Girl Named Disaster* (6–10). 1996, Orchard paper $19.95 (0-531-09539-8). Set in modern-day Africa, this is the story, with fantasy undertones, of Nhamo, who flees from her home in Mozambique to escape a planned marriage and settles with her father's family in Zimbabwe. (Rev: BL 9/1/96; SLJ 10/96*; VOYA 12/96)

2484 Gordimer, Nadine. *Crimes of Conscience* (9–12). Series: African Writers. 1991, Heinemann paper $8.95 (0-435-90668-2). The themes of these dark, beautiful stories by the great South African writer are betrayal and its opposite: the unexpected good people find in themselves. (Rev: BL 5/1/91)

2485 Habila, Helon. *Waiting for an Angel* (11–12). 2003, Norton $23.95 (0-393-05193-5). A compelling novel, suitable for mature teens, that paints a chilling picture of one man's struggle against oppression in 1990s Nigeria. (Rev: BL 1/1–15/03)

2486 Kessler, Cristina. *No Condition Is Permanent* (8–12). 2000, Putnam $17.99 (0-399-23486-1). Fourteen-year-old Jodie, who has moved to Sierra Leone with her mother, tries to prevent the female circumcision of her new friend, Khadi. (Rev: BL 12/1/99; HBG 9/00; SLJ 2/00; VOYA 4/00)

2487 Kingsolver, Barbara. *The Poisonwood Bible* (10–12). 1998, HarperFlamingo $26.00 (0-06-017540-0); paper $15.00 (0-06-093053-5). A challenging novel about preacher Nathan Price and his family, including four daughters, who move from America to the Belgian Congo in 1959. (Rev: BL 8/98)

2488 McDaniel, Lurlene. *Angel of Hope* (7–10). 2000, Bantam paper $8.95 (0-553-57148-6). In this sequel to *Angel of Mercy*, Heather returns from missionary work in Uganda and, in her place, her younger, spoiled sister, Amber, continues the work in Africa. (Rev: BL 5/1/00; HBG 9/00)

2489 McDaniel, Lurlene. *Angel of Mercy* (7–10). 1999, Bantam $8.95 (0-553-57145-1). Heather is not prepared for the misery she finds in Uganda where she is a volunteer, but falling in love with handsome Ian, another volunteer, helps takes her mind off her problems. (Rev: BL 1/1–15/00; HBG 4/00; SLJ 1/00)

2490 Matthee, Dalene. *Fiela's Child* (9–12). 1992, Univ. of Chicago Pr. paper $13.95 (0-226-51083-2). A white boy in South Africa, who has been raised by a black family, is suddenly at age 12 claimed by a white family as its own. (Rev: BL 5/1/86)

2491 Quintana, Anton. *The Baboon King* (8–12). Trans. by John Nieuwenhuizen. 1999, Walker $16.95 (0-8027-8711-8). After being exiled by his East African tribe after accidentally killing a tribesman, arrogant Morengru joins a troop of baboons, becomes their leader, and develops a sense of humanity. (Rev: HBG 9/99; SLJ 6/99; VOYA 10/99)

2492 Slovo, Gillian. *Red Dust* (10–12). 2002, Norton $25.95 (0-393-04148-4). Set in South Africa during the Truth and Reconciliation Commission hearings, this courtroom thriller involves the case of an apartheid killer. (Rev: BL 12/15/01)

2493 Zemser, Amy B. *Beyond the Mango Tree* (6–12). 1998, Greenwillow $14.95 (0-688-16005-0). Trapped in her home by a domineering mother, Sarina, a 12-year-old white American girl living in Liberia, befriends a gentle African boy named Boima. (Rev: BL 11/1/98; HB 11–12/98; HBG 3/99; SLJ 10/98; VOYA 4/99)

Asia and the Pacific

2494 Ali, Thalassa. *A Singular Hostage* (10–12). 2002, Bantam paper $13.95 (0-553-38176-8). An Englishwoman becomes the savior of a young orphan in this novel full of historical detail of 19th-century India. (Rev: BL 10/1/02; SLJ 4/03)

2495 Balasubramanyam, Rajeev. *In Beautiful Disguises* (10–12). 2001, Bloomsbury paper $14.95 (1-58234-127-3). A coming-of-age novel about a teenage girl in southern India who runs away from an abusive father and an arranged marriage to find a new life in Delhi. (Rev: BL 2/15/01)

133

2496 Ballard, J. G. *Empire of the Sun: A Novel* (9–12). 1984, Bucanneer $24.95 (1-568-49663-X). After the Japanese capture Shanghai in World War II, 11-year-old Jim is separated from his parents and spends time in an internment camp.

2497 Ballard, John H. *SoulMates: A Novel to End World Hunger, with an Introduction by Mother Theresa and The Gandhi Foundation* (9–12). Illus. 1998, World Citizens $16.95 (0-932279-06-6); paper $14.95 (0-932279-05-8). Teenager MacBurnie King discovers a whole new world when she and her father begin working in a mission in India and encounter disease, hunger, caste injustice, and monsoon rains. (Rev: HBG 9/98; SLJ 6/98; VOYA 8/98)

2498 Binstock, R. C. *Tree of Heaven* (9–12). 1995, Soho Pr. $22.00 (1-56947-038-3). Two lovers try to escape doom during the Japanese invasion of China in the 1930s. (Rev: BL 8/95; SLJ 10/95)

2499 Bosse, Malcolm. *Deep Dream of the Rain Forest* (6–10). 1993, Farrar paper $5.95 (0-374-41702-4). Orphaned Harry Windsor goes to Borneo to be with his uncle, where he's forced to join a native warrior's dreamquest. (Rev: BL 10/1/93; SLJ 10/93*; VOYA 12/93)

2500 Bosse, Malcolm. *The Examination* (8–12). 1994, Farrar $18.00 (0-374-32234-1). During the Ming Dynasty, two very different Chinese brothers try to understand each other as they travel to Beijing, where one brother hopes to pass a government examination. (Rev: BL 11/1/94*; SLJ 12/94; VOYA 12/94)

2501 Bosse, Malcolm. *Tusk and Stone* (6–10). 1995, Front Street $15.95 (1-886910-01-4). Set in 7th-century India, this story tells about a young Brahman who is separated from his sister and sold to the military as a slave, goes on to gain recognition and fame for his skills and bravery as a warrior, and ultimately discovers his true talents and nature as a sculptor and stonecarver. (Rev: BL 12/1/95; VOYA 2/96)

2502 Chen, Ran. *A Private Life* (10–12). Trans. by John Howard-Gibbon. 2004, Columbia Univ. Pr. $24.50 (0-231-13196-8). A coming-of-age story about a sensitive, gawky Chinese girl living through childhood and first love during the Cultural Revolution and the demonstrations in Tiananmen Square. (Rev: BL 4/15/04)

2503 Choi, Sook N. *Year of Impossible Goodbyes* (6–10). 1991, Houghton $16.00 (0-395-57419-6). An autobiographical novel of two children in North Korea following World War II who become separated from their mother while attempting to cross the border into South Korea. (Rev: BL 9/15/91; SLJ 10/91*)

2504 Clavell, James. *Shogun: A Novel of Japan* (10–12). 1983, Delacorte paper $7.99 (0-440-

17800-2). The story of an English sea captain in his adventures in feudal seventeenth-century Japan.

2505 Deb, Siddhartha. *The Point of Return* (10–12). 2003, Ecco $24.95 (0-06-050151-0). This moving coming-of-age novel is set in the India of Indira Gandhi and conveys the turbulence of the time as well as a difficult relationship between father and son. (Rev: BL 3/15/03)

2506 Fermine, Maxence. *Snow* (10–12). Trans. by Chris Mulhern. 2003, Atria $15.00 (0-7434-5684-X). In the late 19th century, a young Japanese poet enamored of white is encouraged to consult an artist who will give him an appreciation of color. (Rev: BL 12/15/02)

2507 Ganesan, Indira. *Inheritance* (10–12). 1998, Knopf $22.00 (0-679-43442-9). During a summer on an island off the coast of India at the home of her grandmother, 15-year-old Sonil meets her mother, who sent her to live with aunts when she was a baby, and tries to unravel family secrets while engaging in a passionate relationship with an American man twice her age. (Rev: BL 1/1–15/98; SLJ 7/98)

2508 Gardner, Katy. *Losing Gemma* (10–12). 2002, Riverhead paper $13.00 (1-57322-933-4). Two British young women's trip to India becomes tense when Gemma becomes involved with hippies and then disappears; for mature readers. (Rev: BL 4/1/02)

2509 Garland, Sherry. *Song of the Buffalo Boy* (7–10). 1992, Harcourt $16.00 (0-15-277107-7); paper $6.00 (0-15-200098-4). An Amerasian teenager wants to escape the prejudice of a Vietnam village and tries to find her father. (Rev: BL 4/1/92; SLJ 6/92)

2510 Gee, Maurice. *The Champion* (6–10). 1993, Simon & Schuster paper $16.00 (0-671-86561-7). Rex, 12, must overcome his own racism and recognize a true hero when an African American war veteran is sent to recuperate in Rex's New Zealand home. (Rev: BL 10/1/93*; SLJ 10/93; VOYA 2/94)

2511 Gillison, Samantha. *The King of America* (10–12). 2004, Random $21.95 (0-375-50819-8). Based loosely on the story of the life and death of Michael Rockefeller, this novel tells of a rich boy's search for art and himself in New Guinea. (Rev: BL 2/1/04)

2512 Golden, Arthur. *Memoirs of a Geisha* (10–12). 1997, Knopf $26.95 (0-375-40011-7); paper $14.00 (0-679-78158-7). This novel, set in Japan during the 1930s and 1940s, is about a young girl who is sold into slavery by her father and becomes an accomplished geisha. (Rev: BL 9/1/97)

2513 Gordon, Katharine. *The Palace Garden* (10–12). 2000, Severn House $26.00 (0-7278-5600-6). In Madore, India, in 1898, Zeena, who is betrothed to an evil older man, falls in love with a young Scottish officer. (Rev: BL 10/15/00)

2514 Gunesekera, Romesh. *Reef* (9–12). 1995, New Pr. $20.00 (1-56584-219-7). This coming-of-age story tells of defiance and growth during the Marxist rebellion in Sri Lanka in 1962. (Rev: BL 1/15/95; SLJ 4/95)

2515 Halam, Ann. *Taylor Five* (8–10). 2004, Random $15.95 (0-385-73094-2). When rebels attack 14-year-old Taylor's home in Borneo, she must flee through the jungle with her wounded younger brother. (Rev: BL 2/15/04; SLJ 4/04)

2516 Hartnett, Sonya. *Thursday's Child* (8–12). 2002, Candlewick $15.99 (0-7636-1620-6). An optimistic young girl tells the story of her Australian family's hapless struggles to weather the Great Depression, and of her brother's obsessive tunneling that results in the collapse of their shanty home. (Rev: BCCB 5/02; BL 7/02; HB 7–8/02; HBG 10/02; SLJ 5/02*; VOYA 6/02)

2517 Haugaard, Erik C. *The Revenge of the Forty-Seven Samurai* (7–12). 1995, Houghton $16.00 (0-395-70809-5). In a true story set in feudal Japan, a young servant is a witness to destiny when his master meets an unjust death. (Rev: BL 5/15/95; SLJ 4/95)

2518 Hausman, Gerald, and Loretta Hausman. *Escape from Botany Bay: The True Story of Mary Bryant* (6–10). 2003, Scholastic $16.95 (0-439-40327-8). This is an absorbing fictionalized account of 18th-century Englishwoman Mary Bryant's early life of crime, her sentence to the prison colony of Botany Bay in Australia, and her daring escape. (Rev: BL 3/1/03; HBG 4/04; SLJ 4/03; VOYA 6/03)

2519 Hesse, Hermann. *Siddhartha* (10–12). 1982, Bantam paper $5.99 (0-553-20884-5). An inspiring story set in India about a young man's journey to a state of peace and holiness. First published in 1923.

2520 Hoobler, Dorothy, and Thomas Hoobler. *In Darkness, Death* (7–10). 2004, Putnam $16.99 (0-399-23767-4). Set in 18th-century Japan like the authors' previous *The Ghost in the Tokaido Inn* (1999), this novel tells how 14-year-old Seikei and his adopted father set out to discover who murdered a powerful warlord. (Rev: BL 5/1/04; SLJ 3/04; VOYA 4/04)

2521 Hosseini, Khaled. *The Kite Runner* (11–12). 2003, Riverhead $24.95 (1-57322-245-3). The relationship between two Afghani boys — one wealthy, one a servant — is the central focus of this compelling novel covering events in the last quarter of the 20th century. (Rev: BL 7/03; SLJ 11/03)

2522 Ihimaera, Witi. *The Whale Rider* (7–12). 2003, Harcourt $17.00 (0-15-205017-5). Legend and contemporary Maori life are interwoven in this story of Kahu, a girl with a spiritual bent whose grandfather

would have preferred a grandson to name as his successor. (Rev: BL 7/03; HBG 4/04; SLJ 9/03; VOYA 10/03)

2523 Jin, Ha. *The Crazed* (11–12). 2002, Pantheon $24.00 (0-375-42181-5). Advanced readers will enjoy this story, set against the backdrop of the Cultural Revolution and the Tiananmen Square uprising, of a graduate student who must set aside his academic ambitions when his mentor (and future father-in-law) falls ill. (Rev: BL 9/1/02)

2524 Keating, H. R. F. *Breaking and Entering* (10–12). 2001, St. Martin's $23.95 (0-312-26952-8). Filled with mystery and cultural details, this is a whodunit about Inspector Ghote of the Mumbai (Bombay) Police and his friend, the Swede Axel Svensson. (Rev: BL 10/15/01*)

2525 Kim, Helen. *The Long Season of Rain* (10–12). 1996, Holt $15.95 (0-8050-4758-1). Set in Seoul, Korea, in 1969, this novel tells of the inequalities that women suffer in marriage and of one girl's struggle to help her mother. (Rev: BL 11/1/96; BR 9–10/97; SLJ 12/96*; VOYA 2/97)

2526 Lord, Bette Bao. *The Middle Heart* (9–12). 1996, Knopf $25.00 (0-394-53432-8). A tale of the horrible realities of modern China in which three youth forge an unlikely alliance that survives five decades, with China's cultural revolution and the Tiananmen Square uprising as the background. (Rev: BL 12/15/95*; SLJ 7/96)

2527 McConnochie, Mardi. *Coldwater* (9–12). 2001, Doubleday $24.95 (0-385-50260-5). This "reimagining" of the lives of the Brontë sisters is about Charlotte, Emily, and Anne Wolf, who live with their father, Captain Wolf, a prison warden, on the barren island of Coldwater off the Australian coast. (Rev: BL 7/01; SLJ 12/01)

2528 McCullough, Colleen. *The Thorn Birds* (10–12). 1998, Random $10.99 (0-517-20165-8); Avon paper $6.99 (0-380-01817-9). A family saga covering 1915 through 1969 in the lives of the Clearys of Australia.

2529 McCullough, Colleen. *The Touch* (11–12). 2003, Simon & Schuster $25.95 (0-684-85330-2). Sixteen-year-old Elizabeth is sent from Scotland to Australia to marry her successful cousin Alexander Kinross in this broad-ranging saga set in 19th-century Australia; for mature teens. (Rev: BL 10/15/03)

2530 McFerrin, Linda Watanabe. *Namako: Sea Cucumber* (10–12). 1998, Coffee House paper $14.95 (1-56689-075-6). Ellen, who is part Scottish and part Japanese, suffers culture shock when her parents uproot her from her comfortable American suburban existence and move to a Japanese countryside. (Rev: BL 7/98; SLJ 1/99)

2531 Manicka, Rani. *The Rice Mother* (11–12). 2003, Viking $24.95 (0-670-03192-5). A multilayered story about a Malaysian girl who is married to a much older man and struggles to protect her children from perils including World War II. (Rev: BL 8/03)

2532 Marchetta, Melina. *Looking for Alibrandi* (8–10). 1999, Orchard LB $17.99 (0-531-33142-3). In this novel set in Sydney, Australia, teenage Josie Alibrandi is torn between her family's cultural ties to Italy and her Australian environment. (Rev: BL 2/15/99; BR 9–10/99; HB 5–6/99; HBG 9/99; SLJ 7/99; VOYA 6/99)

2533 Min, Anchee. *Empress Orchid* (11–12). 2004, Houghton $24.00 (0-618-06887-2). This fictionalized life of China's last empress — Tzu Hsi, or Orchid — sympathetically and evocatively describes her impoverished childhood and ascent to a position of power; for mature teens. (Rev: BL 11/15/03*)

2534 Min, Anchee. *Wild Ginger* (11–12). 2002, Houghton $23.00 (0-618-06886-4). Fourteen-year-old Maple watches in despair as her friend Wild Ginger is won over by the Communists in this story set during China's Cultural Revolution; for mature teens. (Rev: BL 2/15/02; VOYA 2/03)

2535 Namioka, Lensey. *Den of the White Fox* (6–10). 1997, Harcourt $14.00 (0-15-201282-6); paper $6.00 (0-15-201283-4). Set in medieval Japan, this sequel to *The Coming of the Bear* (1992) continues the adventures of two ronin (unemployed samurai). In this tale, they try to solve the mystery of an elusive white fox. (Rev: BL 6/1–15/97; SLJ 6/97; VOYA 8/97)

2536 Namioka, Lensey. *An Ocean Apart, a World Away* (7–10). 2002, Delacorte LB $17.99 (0-385-90053-8). Yanyan, an independent teenager in the 1920s who rejects traditions such as the binding of feet, travels from her native China to study at Cornell, where she finds new challenges. (Rev: BCCB 10/02; BL 6/1–15/02; HBG 10/02; SLJ 7/02; VOYA 6/02)

2537 Nguyen, Kien. *The Tapestries* (10–12). 2002, Little, Brown $24.95 (0-316-28441-6). To save her young husband from his enemies, a Vietnamese woman sells him as a servant in this novel set in the early 20th century; for mature teens. (Rev: BL 10/1/02)

2538 Nothomb, Amelie. *Fear and Trembling* (10–12). Trans. by Adriana Hunter. 2001, St. Martin's $19.95 (0-312-27218-9). A Western girl gets a job with a Japanese corporation and finds that she is increasingly being given meaningless jobs and bypassed for promotion. (Rev: BL 2/15/01)

2539 Robson, Lucia St. Clair. *The Tokaido Road: A Novel of Feudal Japan* (9–12). 1992, Ballantine paper $5.99 (0-345-35639-X). This picaresque romance is based on an actual feud and steeped in the customs and culture of 18th-century Japan. (Rev: BL 4/1/91*)

2540 Schaffner, M. A. *War Boys* (11–12). 2002, Welcome Rain $25.00 (1-56649-244-0). A coming-of-age story set in the Philippines in the Vietnam era and featuring a 14-year-old boy living on a naval base and enjoying Explorer Scouts exercises in the jungle; for mature teens who are good readers. (Rev: BL 6/1–15/02)

2541 Scott, Joanna C. *The Lucky Gourd Shop* (10–12). 2000, MacMurray & Beck $27.00 (1-878448-01-3). Set in Korea, this is a moving novel about an orphan girl who marries a man with a terrible secret past. (Rev: BL 7/00*)

2542 Sijie, Dai. *Balzac and the Little Chinese Seamstress* (10–12). Trans. by Ina Rilke. 2001, Knopf $18.00 (0-375-41309-X). Two delightful young men are ordered into the Chinese countryside during the Cultural Revolution and find conditions are as bad as expected. (Rev: BL 9/15/01; SLJ 11/01)

2543 Staples, Suzanne F. *Haveli: A Young Woman's Courageous Struggle for Freedom in Present-Day Pakistan* (9–12). 1993, Knopf $18.00 (0-679-84157-1); 1995, Random paper $4.99 (0-679-86569-1). This novel, a sequel to *Shabanu*, presents the issue of a woman's role in traditional Pakistani society, intrigue, tough women characters, and fluid writing. (Rev: BL 6/1–15/93*; VOYA 12/93)

2544 Staples, Suzanne Fisher. *Shiva's Fire* (8–12). 2000, Farrar $18.00 (0-374-36824-4). The inspiring story of a mystical Indian girl who devotes her life to the dance. (Rev: BL 3/15/00* ; HBG 9/00; SLJ 4/00; VOYA 6/00)

2545 Tharoor, Shashi. *Riot: A Love Story* (10–12). 2001, Arcade $24.95 (1-55970-605-8). This novel for better readers describes how the parents of Priscilla Hart travel in India to investigate the death of their daughter and discover the depth of Hindu-Muslim conflicts. (Rev: BL 8/01)

2546 Toer, Pramoedya Ananta. *All That Is Gone* (9–12). Trans. by Willem Samuels. 2004, Hyperion $23.95 (1-4013-6663-5). Eight interconnected stories, many narrated by the same man, chronicle life in the little city of Brora in Java. (Rev: BL 2/1/04*)

2547 Toer, Pramoedya Ananta. *The Girl from the Coast* (11–12). Trans. by Willem Samuels. 2002, Hyperion $22.95 (0-7868-6820-1). A poor but beautiful girl from a Javanese fishing village marries a Muslim aristocrat only to find her husband never intended for her to be a wife; for mature teens. (Rev: BL 8/02*)

2548 Tremain, Rose. *The Colour* (10–12). 2003, Farrar $25.00 (0-374-12605-4). Newlyweds Joseph and Harriet Blackstone seek their fortunes in 19th-century New Zealand in this absorbing, meticulously presented novel. (Rev: BL 5/15/03*)

2549 Upadhyay, Samrat. *The Guru of Love* (11–12). 2003, Houghton $23.00 (0-618-24727-0). Ramchandra, a struggling math teacher with a wife and two teen children, becomes obsessed with a beautiful student in this story set in Nepal; for mature teens. (Rev: BL 11/1/02)

2550 Wang, Annie. *Lili: A Novel of Tiananmen* (10–12). 2001, Pantheon $24.00 (0-375-42085-1). This novel takes place during the Cultural Revolution in China and involves Lili, who runs away to Beijing and joins a gang of misplaced adolescents before finding love. (Rev: BL 5/1/01)

2551 Watkins, Yoko K. *My Brother, My Sister, and I* (6–10). 1994, Bradbury paper $17.00 (0-02-792526-9). Tells of a once-secure middle-class child who is now homeless, hungry, and in danger in post-World War II Japan. A sequel to the fictionalized autobiography *So Far from the Bamboo Grove* (1986). (Rev: BL 5/1/94; SLJ 9/94; VOYA 8/94)

2552 Wilson, Diane Lee. *I Rode a Horse of Milk White Jade* (6–10). 1998, Orchard paper $18.95 (0-531-30024-2). This adventure story set in medieval China tells the story of Oyuna and her adventures delivering a package to the court of the great Kublai Khan. (Rev: BL 4/1/98; BR 1–2/99; HBG 9/98; SLJ 6/98; VOYA 8/98)

2553 Yep, Laurence. *Mountain Light* (8–12). 1997, HarperCollins paper $6.95 (0-06-440667-9). Yep continues to explore life in 19th-century China through the experience of a girl, Cassia, her father and friends, and their struggle against the Manchus in this sequel to *The Serpent's Children* (1984). (Rev: BL 9/15/85; SLJ 1/87; VOYA 12/85)

Europe and the Middle East

2554 Aiken, Joan. *Lady Catherine's Necklace* (10–12). 2000, St. Martin's $21.95 (0-312-24406-1). The noted British novelist has written a charming sequel to Jane Austen's *Pride and Prejudice* that deals with Lady Catherine de Bourgh, her necklace, and a kidnapping. (Rev: BL 4/1/00)

2555 Alexander, Robert. *The Kitchen Boy: A Novel of the Last Tsar* (10–12). 2003, Viking $23.95 (0-670-03178-X). This fictionalized account of the final days of the Romanov dynasty is told from the point of view of Leonka, a boy who works in the kitchens of Tsar Nicholas II. (Rev: BL 1/1–15/03)

2556 Austen-Leigh, Joan. *Later Days at Highbury* (10–12). 1996, St. Martin's $19.95 (0-312-14642-6). Written by a descendent of Jane Austen, this novel uses the same locale and similar characters in this epistolary novel of manners. (Rev: SLJ 3/97)

2557 Bagdasarian, Adam. *Forgotten Fire* (8–12). 2000, DK paper $19.99 (0-7894-2627-7). The heartbreaking story of a young boy, Vahan Kenderian, and his harrowing experiences during the Turkish genocide of the Armenians. (Rev: BL 7/00; BR 3–4/01; HB 11–12/00; HBG 3/01; SLJ 12/00; VOYA 12/00)

2558 Banks, Lynne Reid. *Broken Bridge* (7–12). 1995, Morrow $16.00 (0-688-13595-1). In this sequel to *One More River* (1992), a woman's daughter sees her cousin killed by an Arab terrorist while living on a kibbutz, posing some tough moral questions. (Rev: BL 3/15/95; SLJ 4/95; VOYA 5/95)

2559 Berdoll, Linda. *Mr. Darcy Takes a Wife* (10–12). 2004, Sourcebooks paper $16.95 (1-4022-0273-3). For mature readers, this is a bawdy, enjoyable sequel to Jane Austen's *Pride and Prejudice*. (Rev: BL 4/15/04)

2560 Blackwell, Lawana. *The Maiden of Mayfair* (9–12). Series: Victorian Tales of London. 2001, Bethany paper $11.99 (0-7642-2258-9). In this Victorian romance, Sarah Matthews, a ward in a foundling home, is rescued by a rich widow who thinks Sarah may be her granddaughter. (Rev: BL 3/1/01; VOYA 8/01)

2561 Bowler, Tim. *Firmament* (6–10). 2004, Simon & Schuster $16.95 (0-689-86161-3). Reality and fantasy mix in this story of a 14-year-old English boy, a brilliant musician, who, because of his father's untimely death, finds his life falling apart. (Rev: BL 3/1/04; SLJ 4/04; VOYA 4/04)

2562 Bowler, Tim. *River Boy* (6–10). 2000, Simon & Schuster $16.00 (0-689-82908-6). Jess helps her sick grandfather by returning with him to his remote boyhood home to complete the painting he has begun called *River Boy*. (Rev: BL 5/1/00; HBG 3/01; SLJ 8/00)

2563 Bradshaw, Gillian. *The Wolf Hunt* (10–12). 2001, Tor $24.95 (0-312-87332-8). In this richly historical novel, Lady Marie becomes a pawn in the ongoing quarrel between the Normans and the Bretons. (Rev: BL 8/01; VOYA 6/02)

2564 Brontë, Charlotte, and Clare Boylan. *Emma Brown* (10–12). 2004, Viking $25.95 (0-670-03297-2). This is a completion of the two chapters of an incomplete novel left by Charlotte Brontë about a girl's search for identity. (Rev: BL 3/15/04)

2565 Brown, Molly. *Invitation to a Funeral* (10–12). 1998, St. Martin's $22.95 (0-312-18598-7). Set in London during 1676 and the reign of King Charles II, this adventure-mystery involves Aphra Behn, a young playwright, who becomes involved in the deaths of two brothers who helped her many years before. (Rev: BL 5/15/98; SLJ 11/98)

2566 Buckley, Fiona. *Queen of Ambition* (10–12). 2002, Scribner $23.00 (0-7432-0264-3). This historical mystery takes place at the court of Elizabeth I and involves a trusted lady-in-waiting who appears to be a spy and secret agent. (Rev: BL 11/1/01*)

2567 Cheaney, J. B. *The Playmaker* (7–10). 2000, Knopf LB $17.99 (0-375-90577-4). A well-written historical adventure story steeped in Elizabethan England and its theater and featuring a teenage boy caught up in dangerous political plots as he searches for his father. (Rev: BL 11/1/00; HB 1–2/01; HBG 3/01; SLJ 12/00; VOYA 4/01)

2568 Cheaney, J. B. *The True Prince* (7–10). 2002, Knopf $15.95 (0-375-81433-7). Richard Malory, a performer in Elizabethan England, becomes involved in mysterious and dangerous events. (Rev: BCCB 12/02; BL 1/1–15/03; HB 1–2/03; HBG 3/03; SLJ 11/02)

2569 Chevalier, Tracy. *Falling Angels* (10–12). 2001, Dutton $23.95 (0-525-94581-4). Friends since they met as 5-year-olds in 1901, Maude and Lavinia grow up together in Edwardian London and their friendship remains constant even though their destinies take them in different directions. (Rev: BL 8/01; SLJ 4/02; VOYA 8/02)

2570 Chevalier, Tracy. *Girl with a Pearl Earring* (9–12). 2000, Dutton $21.95 (0-525-94527-X). A moving novel about a young Dutch girl who becomes a servant in the house of the great artist Johannes Vermeer. (Rev: BL 12/1/99; SLJ 6/00)

2571 Chevalier, Tracy. *The Lady and the Unicorn* (10–12). 2004, Dutton $23.95 (0-525-94767-1). This historical novel set in France tells how the famous unicorn tapestries were commissioned and woven. (Rev: BL 11/1/03; SLJ 4/04)

2572 Chisholm, P. F. *A Surfeit of Guns* (10–12). 1997, Walker $31.95 (0-8027-3304-2). An adventure yarn set in 1592, based on real-life Englishman Sir Robert Carey, whose efforts to trace stolen arms leads him to the court of James VI at Dumfries, Scotland. (Rev: BL 5/1/97; SLJ 1/98)

2573 Clare, Alys. *Ashes of the Elements* (10–12). 2001, St. Martin's $23.95 (0-312-26124-1). Set in the time of Richard the Lionheart, this mystery involves an abbess, her friend who is a French knight, and the body of a murdered man found close to the abbey. (Rev: BL 4/1/01)

2574 Conlon-McKenna, Marita. *Fields of Home* (6–10). Illus. 1997, Holiday paper $15.95 (0-8234-1295-4). In this sequel to *Under the Hawthorn Tree* (1990) and *Wildflower Girl* (1992), the Irish O'Driscoll family saga continues as Michael and Eily try to make progress in spite of the hard times in Ireland. (Rev: BCCB 7–8/97; BL 4/15/97; BR 9–10/97; SLJ 6/97)

2575 Connery, Tom. *Honour Redeemed* (10–12). Series: Markam of the Marines. 2000, Regnery $21.95 (0-89526-255-X). Swashbuckling adventure during the wars of the French Revolution and Napoleon, starring Lieutenant George Markam, the hero of the first installment in this series, *A Shred of Honour* (1999), and the third, *Honour Be Damned* (2000). (Rev: BL 3/15/00)

2576 Cook, Gloria. *Touch the Silence* (10–12). 2003, Severn $26.99 (0-7278-5894-7). A British

family faces a time of hardship and change during World War I. (Rev: BL 6/1–15/03)

2577 Cornwell, Bernard. *The Archer's Tale* (10–12). 2001, HarperCollins $26.00 (0-06-621084-4). The author of the Richard Sharpe series spins an exciting story of honor and revenge involving the French and the Normans on the eve of the Hundred Years War. (Rev: BL 8/01)

2578 Cowell, Stephanie. *Marrying Mozart* (10–12). 2004, Viking $24.95 (0-670-03268-9). A lively novel about Mozart and his relations with the four Weber sisters. (Rev: BL 1/1–15/04)

2579 Crichton, Michael. *The Great Train Robbery* (10–12). 1975, Knopf $25.00 (0-394-49401-6); Ballantine paper $7.99 (0-345-39092-X). This is an entertaining re-creation of a robbery that shocked Victorian England.

2580 Crompton, Anne E. *Gawain and Lady Green: A Novel* (10–12). 1997, Penguin paper $20.95 (1-55611-507-5). Using both Sir Gawain and Lady Green as narrators, the Camelot of King Arthur is re-created with its code of honor and ideals of chivalry. (Rev: SLJ 9/97)

2581 Deane, Seamus. *Reading in the Dark* (10–12). 1997, Knopf $23.00 (0-394-57440-0). This fictional memoir of a boy growing up after World War II in Donegal is filled with pathos, hardship, mystery, and humor. (Rev: BL 4/1/97; BR 11–12/97; SLJ 7/97)

2582 Dickinson, Peter. *Shadow of a Hero* (7–12). 1995, Doubleday $20.95 (0-385-30976-7). Letta's grandfather fights for the freedom of Varina, her family's Eastern European homeland. Living in England, she becomes interested in Varina's struggle. (Rev: BL 9/15/94*; SLJ 11/94; VOYA 10/94)

2583 Dietrich, William. *Hadrian's Wall* (10–12). 2004, HarperCollins $24.95 (0-06-056371-0). An action-packed novel set in the 2nd century and dealing with the building of the 80-mile-long Hadrian's Wall in Roman Britain and its effects on the lives of several people. (Rev: BL 2/1/04)

2584 Donnelly, Jennifer. *The Tea Rose* (10–12). 2002, St. Martin's $24.95 (0-312-28835-2). At the turn of the 20th century, a now-wealthy Fiona Finnegan returns from America to London to take revenge on the man who murdered her father. (Rev: BL 8/02)

2585 Doughty, Anne. *The Woman from Kerry* (10–12). 2003, Severn $26.99 (0-7278-5975-7). The moving story of a girl who grows up to become a loving wife and mother during difficult times in 19th-century Ireland. (Rev: BL 8/03)

2586 Dukthas, Ann. *In the Time of the Poisoned Queen* (10–12). 1998, St. Martin's $22.95 (0-312-18030-6). With lots of action and a fast-moving plot, this historical novel investigates the poisoning of Queen Mary, the Bloody Mary of history, in 1558, weaving in historic facts, figures, and occurrences. (Rev: BL 4/15/98; SLJ 10/98)

2587 Du Maurier, Daphne. *Jamaica Inn* (9–12). 1977, Avon paper $4.95 (0-380-00072-5). A suspenseful yarn set on the coast of England during the days of pirates. Also use *Frenchman's Creek* (1971) and *Mary Anne* (1971).

2588 Du Maurier, Daphne. *My Cousin Rachel* (9–12). 1952, Bentley LB $20.00 (0-8376-0413-3). A rich historical novel about a young man who is beginning to believe his new wife is a murderer.

2589 Eisner, Michael Alexander. *The Crusader* (10–12). 2001, Doubleday $24.95 (0-385-50281-8). When Francisco returns from the Crusades, he appears to be possessed by a demon, and it is Brother Lucas who must determine the truth. (Rev: BL 8/01; SLJ 6/01)

2590 Emerson, Kathy Lynn. *Face Down Beneath the Eleanor Cross* (10–12). 2000, St. Martin's $23.95 (0-312-20544-9). Set in Elizabethan times, this murder mystery for better readers features Lady Susanna Appleton, who is accused of murdering her husband. (Rev: BL 1/1–15/00)

2591 Fenoglio, Beppe. *The Twenty-Three Days of the City of Alba* (11–12). 2002, Steerforth paper $14.00 (1-58642-040-2). Short stories relate terrible events that took place in northern Italy when partisans and fascists fought for control of the city of Alba; for mature teens. (Rev: BL 5/15/02)

2592 *For the Love of Ireland: A Literary Companion for Readers and Travelers* (10–12). Ed. by Susan Cahill. 2001, Ballantine paper $14.95 (0-345-43419-6). A collection of short stories by established authors including Joyce and Swift, plus many by today's writers, all of which describe a particular region in Ireland. (Rev: BL 3/1/01)

2593 Forester, C. S. *Mr. Midshipman Hornblower* (10–12). 1984, Little, Brown paper $13.00 (0-316-28912-4). This is one of a series of adventure stories about a courageous British seaman as he climbs the ranks. Some others are: *Admiral Hornblower in the West Indies*, *Lieutenant Hornblower*, and *Lord Hornblower*.

2594 Forster, E. M. *A Room with a View* (10–12). 1911, Kessenger $24.95 (1-419-10311-3). On a visit to Italy, Lucy Honeychurch gets involved in a conflict of the classes when she meets and is attracted to lower-class George Emerson.

2595 Garcia y Robertson, R. *Lady Robyn* (10–12). 2003, Tor $26.95 (0-312-86995-9). In this entertaining historical romance, Robyn — who was magically transported to 1460 England in *Knight Errant* (2001) — brings her contemporary values to the complex politics of the Wars of the Roses. (Rev: BL 2/1/03; VOYA 8/03)

2596 Garden, Nancy. *Dove and Sword* (10–12). 1995, Farrar $17.00 (0-374-34476-0). The story of Gabrielle, a French peasant girl who disguises herself as a boy and follows Joan of Arc into battle. (Rev: BL 12/15/95; BR 3–4/96; SLJ 11/95; VOYA 2/96)

2597 Giardino, Vittorio. *A Jew in Communist Prague: Rebellion* (10–12). Trans. from French by Joe Johnson. Illus. 1998, NBM paper $11.95 (1-56163-209-0). A novel in which the story and emotions are conveyed through text and drawings. This is the third in a series of novels about the hardships suffered by Jonas in Russian-occupied Prague. The others are *Loss of Innocence* and *Adolescence*. (Rev: BL 7/98; SLJ 2/99)

2598 Gooden, Philip. *Mask of Night* (10–12). 2004, Carroll & Graf $24.00 (0-7867-1312-7). Shakespeare's acting company, the Chamberlain's Men, are in Oxford when one of his friends is found dead backstage in this historical mystery. (Rev: BL 2/15/04*)

2599 Gooden, Philip. *The Pale Companion: A Shakespearean Murder Mystery* (11–12). 2002, Carroll & Graf $24.00 (0-7867-1008-X). In 1601, actor-detective Nick Revill investigates strange and murderous goings-on on a great estate; for mature teens. (Rev: BL 5/1/02)

2600 Grayson, Emily. *Night Train to Lisbon* (9–12). 2004, Morrow $21.95 (0-06-054264-0). In pre–World War II Europe, 18-year-old Carson meets and falls in love with a graduate student named Alex who is accused of being a spy for the Nazis. (Rev: BL 4/15/04)

2601 Harper, Karen. *The Twylight Tower* (10–12). 2001, Delacorte $23.95 (0-385-33477-X). Some mysterious deaths occur at the court of Elizabeth I, beginning with the fall of a lutenist from a parapet. (Rev: BL 2/15/01)

2602 Hassinger, Peter W. *Shakespeare's Daughter* (7–12). 2004, HarperCollins $15.99 (0-06-028467-6). An assortment of historical figures make appearances, including papa, in this story about the 14-year-old daughter of William Shakespeare. (Rev: BL 3/1/04; SLJ 4/04)

2603 Hawks, Kate. *Watch by Moonlight* (10–12). 2001, Morrow $24.00 (0-380-81465-X). Based on Alfred Noyes' poem "The Highwayman," this is the story of a beautiful daughter of an English innkeeper and her romance with a mysterious stranger. (Rev: BL 7/01; SLJ 12/01)

2604 Hemingway, Ernest. *For Whom the Bell Tolls* (10–12). 1996, Scribner $27.50 (0-684-83048-5); paper $14.00 (0-684-80335-6). A tale of romance and adventure set in the Spanish Civil War.

2605 Heuston, Kimberley. *Dante's Daughter* (10–12). 2003, Front Street $16.95 (1-886910-97-9). Historical fact and fiction are interwoven in this richly detailed story, narrated by the daughter of Dante, that traces her life from childhood in an unhappy family through her bid to become an artist in her own right. (Rev: BCCB 3/04; BL 1/1–15/04; HBG 4/04; LMC 3/04; SLJ 2/04*; VOYA 4/04)

2606 Hilton, James. *Good-bye Mr. Chips* (9–12). 1962, Little, Brown $17.95 (0-316-36420-7). A loving tribute, in novel form, to a tough but excellent teacher in an English private school. First published in 1934.

2607 Holeman, Linda. *Search of the Moon King's Daughter* (8–11). 2002, Tundra $17.95 (0-88776-592-0). Fifteen-year-old Emmaline goes to London to search for her deaf brother, who has been sold into service by their laudanum-addicted mother in this story set in Victorian England. (Rev: BL 12/15/02; HBG 3/03; SLJ 3/03*; VOYA 2/03)

2608 Holt, Victoria. *The Demon Lover* (9–12). 1983, Fawcett paper $3.50 (0-449-20098-1). This gothic novel is set in England of the mid-1800s. Some others by this author are *Lord of the Far Islands* (1986), *The Judas Kiss, Menfreya in the Morning*, and *King of the Castle* (all 1982).

2609 Holt, Victoria. *The Road to Paradise Island* (9–12). 1985, Fawcett paper $5.99 (0-449-20888-5). While investigating her ancestral home in England, Annalice finds a map of a Utopia-like island and a diary that reveals a murder. (Rev: BL 8/85)

2610 Holt, Victoria. *Shivering Sands* (9–12). 1986, Fawcett paper $5.99 (0-449-21361-7). An exciting gothic romance full of historical flavor. Also recommended are *The Devil on Horseback* (1987) and *House of a Thousand Lanterns* (1974).

2611 Housden, Roger. *Chasing Rumi: A Fable About Finding the Heart's True Desire* (10–12). 2002, HarperSF $17.95 (0-06-008445-6). A Greek icon painter in search of love journeys to Turkey, to the tomb of 13th-century Sufi poet Jelaluddin Rumi, a mystic he much admires. (Rev: BL 10/15/02)

2612 Hunter, Mollie. *The King's Swift Rider* (7–12). 1998, HarperCollins $16.95 (0-06-027186-8). A fast-paced historical novel about a young Scot, Martin Crawford, who became Robert the Bruce's page, confidante, and spy. (Rev: BL 9/15/98; HB 1–2/99; HBG 3/99; SLJ 12/98)

2613 Hunter, Mollie. *You Never Knew Her as I Did!* (7–10). Illus. 1981, HarperCollins $13.95 (0-06-022678-1). A historical novel about a plan to help the imprisoned Mary, Queen of Scots, to escape from prison.

2614 Jaffe, Michele. *The Water Nymph* (10–12). 2000, Pocket $22.95 (0-671-02741-7). A passionate, suspenseful novel set in Elizabethan England that deals with an aristocrat who tries to escape charges of treason. (Rev: BL 6/1–15/00)

2615 King, Susan. *The Sword Maiden* (10–12). 2001, Signet paper $6.99 (0-451-20433-6). This is the love story of Eva, the keeper of the Sword of Light, and Lachiann MacKerron, who returns home to Scotland a broken man after being unable to stop the execution of Joan of Arc. (Rev: BL 9/15/01)

2616 Knox, Elizabeth. *Billie's Kiss* (10–12). 2002, Ballantine $24.00 (0-345-45052-3). Billie and her brother-in-law are taken in by Lord Hallowhulme after a bomb destroys the ship on which they were passengers in this story set in 1903 Scotland. (Rev: BL 1/1–15/02*)

2617 Kurland, Michael. *The Great Game* (9–12). 2001, St. Martin's $23.95 (0-312-20891-X). Professor Moriarty (of Sherlock Holmes fame) works with Holmes to prevent the assassination of Queen Victoria and Emperor Franz Joseph. (Rev: BL 7/01)

2618 Lake, Deryn. *Death at St. James Palace* (10–12). 2003, Allison & Busby $24.95 (0-7490-0583-1). In 1761, apothecary-cum-detective John Rawlings investigates a death that took place in the presence of the queen. (Rev: BL 10/15/02)

2619 Lawhead, Stephen R. *The Black Rood* (10–12). Series: Celtic Crusades. 2000, HarperCollins $24.00 (0-06-105034-2). In this sequel to *The Iron Lance* (1998), Murdo returns to the Holy Land at the time of the Crusades to retrieve the Black Rood, a piece of the ancient cross on which Christ died, from the hands of the Saracens. (Rev: BL 6/1–15/00*)

2620 Lisson, Deborah. *Red Hugh* (6–12). 2001, O'Brien paper $7.95 (0-86278-604-5). A exciting tale of 16th-century Ireland's Hugh Roe O'Donnell, a teen whose life is endangered when he is caught up in clan violence. (Rev: BL 12/1/01; SLJ 12/01)

2621 Llewellyn, Richard. *How Green Was My Valley* (9–12). 1983, Amereon LB $30.95 (0-88411-936-X). The enduring saga of a Welsh mining town and of the Morgan family who live and work there.

2622 Llywelyn, Morgan. *1916* (10–12). 1998, St. Martin's $24.95 (0-312-86101-X). Fifteen-year-old Llwelyn becomes a courier for the rebels in this epic novel set in Ireland at the time of the Easter Rebellion in 1916. (Rev: BL 4/15/98; SLJ 8/98)

2623 Llywelyn, Morgan. *Pride of Lions* (10–12). 1996, Tor paper $6.99 (0-8125-3650-9). Love and war occupy Prince Donough in this book, set in 11th-century Ireland. A sequel to *Lion of Ireland* (1980). (Rev: BL 9/15/98)

2624 Lowe, Keith. *Tunnel Vision* (10–12). 2001, Pocket paper $12.95 (0-7434-2352-6). To win a bet, Andy travels the entire London Underground system with his pal Brian within a 24-hour period in this suspenseful, engaging novel. (Rev: BL 9/15/01)

2625 McCaughrean, Geraldine. *The Pirate's Son* (7–10). 1998, Scholastic $16.95 (0-590-20344-4). In 1717 England, Nathan and his little sister, Maud, are taken aboard a pirate ship and sail to Madagascar in this terrific adventure story. (Rev: BL 8/98; BR 11–12/98; HB 11–12/98; HBG 3/99; SLJ 11/98; VOYA 2/99)

2626 MacLaverty, Bernard. *The Anatomy School* (10–12). 2002, Norton $25.95 (0-393-05052-1). A thoughtful teenager in 1960s Belfast, shy Martin struggles to deal with his bossy mother, his school-friends, and the influence of the Catholic church. (Rev: BL 4/1/02)

2627 Makiya, Kanan. *The Rock: A Tale of Seventh-Century Jerusalem* (10–12). Illus. 2001, Pantheon $26.00 (0-375-40087-7). A stirring novel about K'ab, a 7th-century Jewish convert to Islam, and his son, who designed the mosque that became the Dome of the Rock on Mount Zion. (Rev: BL 11/1/01*)

2628 Malamud, Bernard. *The Fixer* (10–12). 1966, Farrar paper $14.00 (0-14-018515-1). Based on a true story, this novel tells of Yakov Bok who, in Czarist Russia, is accused of a crime he didn't commit.

2629 Matas, Carol. *The Garden* (8–12). 1997, Simon & Schuster paper $15.00 (0-689-80349-4). This novel, a continuation of *After the War,* follows Ruth Mendelson to a kibbutz in Palestine and describes the tensions she and other kibbutzniks face as the United Nations prepares to vote on a plan to partition Palestine into Jewish and Arab lands. (Rev: BL 4/1/97; BR 11–12/97; SLJ 5/97)

2630 Matas, Carol. *Sworn Enemies* (7–10). 1994, Dell paper $3.99 (0-440-21900-0). In czarist Russia, the enemies are Aaron, a young Jewish scholar, and Zev, hired to kidnap fellow Jews to fulfill military quotas. (Rev: BL 2/1/93; SLJ 2/93)

2631 Mayhew, Margaret. *The Little Ship* (10–12). 2004, Severn $27.99 (0-7278-6026-7). The lives of three teenage English boys change dramatically when they meet Anna Stein, a young Jewish refugee, in this novel set in pre-World War II England. (Rev: BL 3/1/04)

2632 Mead, Alice. *Girl of Kosovo* (5–10). 2001, Farrar $16.00 (0-374-32620-7). A moving novel about the ethnic wars in Kosovo as seen through the eyes of an 11-year-old Albanian girl who has witnessed the death of her father and two brothers and whose foot is smashed during the fighting. (Rev: BCCB 6/01; BL 3/15/01*; HBG 10/01; SLJ 3/01; VOYA 6/01)

2633 Miles, Rosalind. *Child of the Holy Grail* (10–12). 2001, Crown $22.00 (0-609-60624-7). In this third volume of the Guenevere trilogy, Guenevere aids the search for the Holy Grail but, at the end, must sacrifice her tottering kingdom. (Rev: BL 7/01; VOYA 4/02)

2634 Miles, Rosalind. *Isolde, Queen of the Western Isle* (10–12). 2002, Crown $22.95 (0-609-60960-2).

Isolde, princess of the Western Isle, and the wounded Tristan fall in love in this first volume of a new trilogy. (Rev: BL 7/02)

2635 Miles, Rosalind. *The Knight of the Sacred Lake* (10–12). 2000, Crown $24.00 (0-609-60623-9). Guenevere is torn between loyalty to husband Arthur and passion for Lancelot in this sequel to *Queen of the Summer Country* (1999) that explores the importance of Christianity. (Rev: VOYA 2/01)

2636 Napoli, Donna Jo. *Breath* (8–12). 2003, Simon & Schuster $16.95 (0-689-86174-5). Salz, a sickly youth, seems to be immune to the sufferings of the people of Hameln in this reinterpretation of the Pied Piper story that conveys much of the atmosphere of 13th-century Europe. (Rev: BL 9/15/03; HBG 4/04; SLJ 11/03; VOYA 12/03)

2637 Napoli, Donna Jo. *Daughter of Venice* (6–10). 2002, Random LB $18.99 (0-385-90036-8). In 1592 Venice, 14-year-old Donata rejects the limits placed on her life as daughter of a nobleman and, disguised as a boy, sets out to discover the world outside her palazzo. (Rev: BCCB 7–8/02; BL 3/1/02; HB 3–4/02; HBG 10/02; SLJ 3/02*; VOYA 8/02)

2638 Newth, Mette. *The Dark Light* (8–12). Trans. by Faith Ingwersen. 1998, Farrar $18.00 (0-374-31701-1). Set in early-19th-century Norway, this novel tells of Tora, afflicted with leprosy, and her harrowing stay at a hospital surrounded by the horror of the disease. (Rev: BCCB 5/98; BL 6/1–15/98; HB 7–8/98*; HBG 9/98; SLJ 6/98; VOYA 2/99)

2639 Newth, Mette. *The Transformation* (8–12). Trans. by Faith Ingwersen. 2000, Farrar $16.00 (0-374-37752-9). In 15th-century Greenland, the lives of Navarana, an Inuit girl, and Brendan, a monk from the mainland, intersect and together they form an unusual relationship. (Rev: BL 11/15/00* ; HB 1–2/01; HBG 3/01)

2640 Orczy, Emmuska. *The Scarlet Pimpernel* (10–12). 1984, Buccaneer LB $21.95 (0-89966-508-X). An English fop is actually a leader of a group that helps aristocrats flee the French Revolution in this novel first published in 1905. Others in the series are *The Triumph of the Scarlet Pimpernel, The Way of the Scarlet Pimpernel,* and *The Adventures of the Scarlet Pimpernel.*

2641 Orlev, Uri. *The Lady with the Hat* (7–10). Trans. by Hillel Halkin. 1995, Houghton $16.00 (0-395-69957-6). Yulek, a concentration camp survivor, encounters anti-Semitism on her return to Poland, while another Jewish girl, hidden from the Nazis, wants to be a nun. (Rev: BL 3/15/95; SLJ 5/95)

2642 Pasternak, Boris Leonidovich, et al. *Doctor Zhivago* (10–12). Trans. by Manya Harari and Max Hayward. 1991, Knopf $20.00 (0-679-40759-6). Using the Russian Revolution as a backdrop, this celebrated novel is about the life of a Russian doctor, poet, and intellectual during the first three decades of the 20th century.

2643 Perry, Anne. *The Whitechapel Conspiracy* (10–12). 2001, Ballantine $25.00 (0-345-43328-9). In 1892 London, while police superintendent Thomas Pitt is fighting to preserve his reputation, his wife Charlotte investigates the murder that has endangered her husband's career. One of more than 20 recommended historical mysteries starring this husband-and-wife team. (Rev: BL 10/15/00)

2644 Peyton, K. M. *Snowfall* (8–12). 1998, Houghton $16.00 (0-395-89598-7). Set in Victorian times, this novel tells of a young girl brought up in a vicarage and her escape into a world where she falls in love with three exciting men. (Rev: BL 9/15/98; HBG 3/99; SLJ 9/98; VOYA 4/99)

2645 Pressler, Mirjam. *Shylock's Daughter* (8–12). Trans. by Brian Murdoch. 2001, Penguin $17.99 (0-8037-2667-8). This novel based on *The Merchant of Venice* focuses on 16-year-old Jessica's love and aspirations, and gives readers insight into life in 16th-century Venice and into the motivations of Shakespeare's characters. (Rev: BCCB 7–8/01; BL 4/1/01; HBG 10/01; SLJ 6/01; VOYA 10/01)

2646 Pullman, Philip. *The Ruby in the Smoke* (8–10). 1987, Knopf paper $5.50 (0-394-89589-4). Sally Lockhart, alone in Dickensian London, encounters murder, opium dens, and romance in her search for her inheritance. Continued in *Shadow in the North* (1988) and *The Tiger in the Well*. (Rev: BL 3/1/87; BR 11–12/87; SLJ 4/87; VOYA 10/87)

2647 Ravel, Edeet. *Ten Thousand Lovers* (11–12). 2003, HarperPerennial paper $12.95 (0-06-056562-4). A young couple struggles to cling to love despite their opposing political stances in this moving novel set in Israel in the 1970s; for mature readers. (Rev: BL 9/15/03)

2648 Richardson, V. A. *The House of Windjammer* (7–10). 2003, Bloomsbury $16.95 (1-58234-811-1). Seventeenth-century Amsterdam in the midst of the tulip craze is the setting of the multilayered, suspenseful story of the Windjammer family, whose business and social standing are in jeopardy. (Rev: BCCB 9/03; BL 5/15/03*; HBG 4/04; SLJ 9/03; VOYA 10/03)

2649 Richler, Nancy. *Your Mouth Is Lovely* (10–12). 2002, Ecco $25.95 (0-06-009677-2). In Russia in the early 20th century, a young Jewish woman imprisoned for revolutionary activities writes a letter to the daughter she gave up at birth. (Rev: BL 11/1/02)

2650 Roiphe, Katie. *Still She Haunts Me* (10–12). 2001, Dial $23.95 (0-385-33527-X). For mature readers, this is a novel about a high-strung Oxford professor, Charles Dodgson, and his relationship with a young girl, Alice Liddell. The result: Alice in Wonderland. (Rev: BL 9/1/01*)

2651 Royal, Lauren. *Amber* (10–12). 2001, Signet paper $6.50 (0-451-20391-7). Passion and romance mingle in this story involving Kendra and her reluctant marriage to a mysterious highwayman. (Rev: BL 6/1–15/01)

2652 Rutherford, Edward. *London* (10–12). 1997, Crown $25.95 (0-517-59181-2). A lengthy novel that traces London's history from trading post to the hub of an empire, told through the everyday lives of families that lived through these ages. (Rev: BL 5/15/97; SLJ 12/97)

2653 Scarrow, Simon. *Under the Eagle* (10–12). 2001, St. Martin's $23.95 (0-312-27870-5). A pampered slave earns his freedom and respect of his commander when he foils a rebellious plot in Roman Britain. (Rev: BL 8/01)

2654 Schur, Maxine R. *The Circlemaker* (6–10). 1994, Dial $14.99 (0-8037-1354-1). A 12-year-old Jewish boy in a Ukrainian shtetl escapes 25 years of forced conscription in the czar's army in 1852. (Rev: BL 1/15/94; SLJ 2/94)

2655 Scott, Amanda. *Dreaming the Eagle* (10–12). 2003, Delacorte $23.95 (0-385-33670-5). Fantasy, romance, and history are interwoven in this story of a youthful Boudica in 1st-century Britain. (Rev: BL 4/1/03)

2656 Scott, Amanda. *The Secret Clan: Abducted Heiress* (10–12). 2001, Warner paper $5.99 (0-446-61026-7). A vivid Scottish setting, a strong-willed heroine, a dashing hero, a touch of fantasy, and the interesting times of King James all add to this historical romance. (Rev: BL 9/15/01)

2657 Scott, Joanna Catherine. *Cassandra, Lost* (10–12). 2004, St. Martin's $24.95 (0-312-31942-8). In this spirited love story, Cassandra must decide between her devoted husband and the dashing pirate she wants. (Rev: BL 2/15/04)

2658 Shimony, Abner. *Tibaldo and the Hole in the Calendar* (10–12). Illus. 1997, Springer-Verlag $21.00 (0-387-94935-6). Using both real and fictitious characters, this novel describes events in 1582 when the Gregorian calendar was adopted and the problem this causes for 11-year-old Tibaldo, who will lose his birthday as a result. (Rev: SLJ 3/98)

2659 Simoen, Jan. *What About Anna?* (9–12). Trans. by John Nieuwenhuizen. 2002, Walker $16.95 (0-8027-8808-4). Anna's life in Eastern Europe is haunted by the ethnic violence that claimed the life of her half-brother Michael. (Rev: BL 5/1/02; BR 11–12/02; HB 7–8/02; HBG 10/02; SLJ 6/02; VOYA 6/02)

2660 Singer, Isaac Bashevis. *The Certificate* (9–12). Trans. by Leonard Wolf. 1992, Farrar $22.00 (0-374-12029-3). A shy, 19-year-old aspiring writer seeking to migrate from Poland to Palestine in the 1920s enters into a "fictive marriage" with an aristocratic woman who loves another man. (Rev: BL 10/15/92)

2661 Smith, D. L. *The Miracles of Santo Fico* (10–12). 2003, Warner $22.95 (0-446-53103-0). Leo Pizzola comes up with some miraculous ways to attract tourists to a small Italian town that boasts a beautiful fresco in this entertaining and atmospheric novel. (Rev: BL 11/15/02)

2662 Smith, Dodie. *I Capture the Castle* (9–12). 1998, St. Martin's $23.95 (0312181108); paper $13.95 (0312201656). A classic, witty story of coming of age featuring 17-year-old Cassandra and the rest of her zany family who live in a rundown English castle. Originally published in 1948.

2663 Sole, Linda. *Kathy* (9–12). 2004, Severn $26.99 (0-7278-5869-6). In London during World War I, a nurse-trainee falls in love with a doctor. (Rev: BL 2/1/04)

2664 Sole, Linda. *The Rose Arch* (10–12). 2001, Severn $25.99 (0-7278-5651-0). An old-fashioned romance set in late-19th-century France about a convent-raised girl and her love for the son of her guardian. (Rev: BL 9/15/01)

2665 Stirling, Jessica. *The Piper's Tune* (11–12). 2002, St. Martin's $26.95 (0-312-28870-0). The shipbuilding industry in Edwardian Scotland is the backdrop for a story of love and betrayal featuring a young woman who marries a handsome cousin; for mature teens. (Rev: BL 3/15/02)

2666 Stockwin, Julian. *Kydd* (10–12). 2001, Scribner $24.00 (0-7432-1458-7). In this swashbuckling adventure, young Tom Kydd is impressed into the Royal Navy, where he finds friends, hardships, and plenty of action. (Rev: BL 4/1/01)

2667 Stone, Irving. *Lust for Life: The Novel of Vincent van Gogh* (10–12). Illus. 1954, NAL paper $14.95 (0-452-26249-6). A lengthy fictionalized biography of the Dutch painter, Vincent van Gogh.

2668 Stranger, Joyce. *A Cherished Freedom* (9–12). 2001, Severn $26.00 (0-7278-5682-0). Louise, who is trying to manage a farm in Wales during her husband's absence, takes in a vagrant teenager and some boarders in this lovely story that also describes the animal life on the farm. (Rev: BL 4/15/01)

2669 Sutcliff, Rosemary. *Bonnie Dundee* (10–12). 1990, Peter Smith $21.50 (0-8446-6363-8). An adventure story set in Scotland during the war between King James and William and featuring a 17-year-old hero.

2670 Sutcliff, Rosemary. *The Shining Company* (7–12). 1990, Farrar $14.95 (0-374-36807-4); paper $6.95 (0-374-46616-5). A novel set in early Britain about a young man who with his friends confronts the enemy Saxons. (Rev: BL 6/15/90; SLJ 7/90)

2671 Sutcliff, Rosemary. *Sword Song* (9–12). 1998, Farrar $18.00 (0-374-37363-9). A posthumously published novel about a Viking swordsman who, after being banished from his homeland as a boy, becomes a mercenary on a ship sailing from Dublin along the coast of Scotland. (Rev: BL 11/1/98; BR 5–6/99; HB 11–12/98; HBG 3/99; SLJ 9/98; VOYA 2/99)

2672 Tanner, Janet. *Tucker's Inn* (9–12). 2004, Severn $26.99 (0-7278-6022-4). In this gothic romance set in England during the French Revolution, Flora become involved with a mysterious stranger, known as the Lynx, who saves French aristocrats from the guillotine. (Rev: BL 2/1/04)

2673 Tel, Jonathan. *Arafat's Elephant* (10–12). 2002, Counterpoint paper $14.00 (1-58243-183-3). A rich collection of short stories about the Jews and Arabs who are fighting over Jerusalem. (Rev: BL 12/15/01)

2674 Tiffany, Grace. *Will* (10–12). 2004, Berkley $21.95 (0-425-19596-1). This is a fictionalized biography of Shakespeare from his boyhood in Stratford to his successes in London. (Rev: BL 5/15/04)

2675 Town, Florida Ann. *With a Silent Companion* (7–12). 2000, Red Deer paper $7.95 (0-88995-211-6). Beginning in 1806, this novel based on fact tells how a young Irish girl hides her identity and becomes a "man" to pursue a medical career. (Rev: BL 4/15/00; VOYA 6/00)

2676 Updike, John. *Gertrude and Claudius* (10–12). 2000, Knopf $23.00 (0-375-40908-4). A fascinating novel that presents the personalities and the events that occurred before the opening of Shakespeare's *Hamlet*. (Rev: BL 1/1–15/00; SLJ 8/00)

2677 Uris, Leon. *Exodus* (9–12). 1958, Bantam paper $7.99 (0-553-25847-8). A moving novel about Jewish immigration to Israel after World War II. Also use *The Haj* (1984).

2678 Veryan, Patricia. *The Riddle of the Shipwrecked Spinster* (10–12). 2001, St. Martin's $24.95 (0-312-26942-0). This suspenseful Georgian romance involves Cordelia and her quest for a man. (Rev: BL 3/1/01)

2679 Waldo, Anna Lee. *Circle of Stars* (10–12). Series: Druid Circle. 2001, St. Martin's $25.95 (0-312-20380-2). In this second volume of a series of historical novels, Madoc, a Welshman, embarks on a dangerous voyage across the seas with a group of Druids. (Rev: BL 7/01)

2680 Walsh, Jill Paton. *Grace* (9–12). 1992, Farrar $16.00 (0-374-32758-0); paper $5.95 (0-374-42792-5). A novel based on the life of Grace Darling, the young English woman who became a hero when she rowed out from a lighthouse in 1838 to save shipwreck survivors. (Rev: BL 6/15/92; SLJ 7/92*)

2681 Ward, Patricia Sarrafian. *The Bullet Collection* (11–12). 2003, Graywolf $25.00 (1-55597-376-0). Two sisters are differently affected by the stresses of growing up in war-torn Beirut. (Rev: BL 3/1/03*)

2682 Whelan, Gerard. *The Guns of Easter* (6–10). 2000, O'Brien paper $7.95 (0-86278-449-2). Twelve-year-old Jimmy Conway grapples with the reasons for, and impact of, the violence erupting in Ireland in the early 20th century. (Rev: BL 3/1/01)

2683 Whelan, Gerard. *A Winter of Spies* (6–10). 2002, O'Brien paper $6.95 (0-86278-566-9). The story of the Conway family, begun in *The Guns of Easter* (2001), continues in this novel as 11-year-old Sarah sees spies and counterspies all around her in 1920 Dublin. (Rev: BL 6/1–15/02)

2684 Whelan, Gloria. *Angel on the Square* (5–10). Illus. 2001, HarperCollins LB $15.89 (0-06-029031-5). The Russian Revolution, World War, and social upheaval totally change life for privileged young Katya, who learns to adapt in this story that starts in 1913. (Rev: BL 9/15/01; HBG 3/02; SLJ 10/01; VOYA 10/01)

2685 Whyte, Jack. *Saxon Shore* (10–12). 1998, St. Martin's $26.95 (0-312-86596-1). In this book, the third of a series about King Arthur, Merlin adopts Arthur to assure his safety until Arthur becomes king, and in a series of adventures rallies forces to support him. (Rev: BL 6/1–15/98; SLJ 4/99)

2686 Wilentz, Amy. *Martyrs' Crossing* (10–12). 2001, Simon & Schuster $24.00 (0-684-85436-8). The Israeli-Palestinian conflict comes to life in human terms in this novel when a Palestinian woman is denied access to a hospital in Israel where her son is a patient. (Rev: BL 1/1–15/01; SLJ 10/01)

2687 Williams, Gerard. *Dr. Mortimer and the Aldgate Mystery* (10–12). 2001, St. Martin's $22.95 (0-312-26920-X). Dr. Mortimer (who appears in *The Hound of the Baskervilles*) discovers that one of his patients is being kept a prisoner by the use of laudanum in this Victorian mystery. (Rev: BL 7/01)

2688 Willis, Jeanne. *The Truth or Something* (9–12). 2002, Holt $16.95 (0-8050-7079-6). Growing up in poverty in grim post-World War II England, Mick learns unpleasant truths about his family as he struggles with adolescence. (Rev: BL 6/1–15/02; HB 7–8/02; HBG 10/02; SLJ 5/02; VOYA 6/02)

2689 Woolley, Persia. *Queen of the Summer Stars* (10–12). 1991, Pocket paper $6.50 (0-671-62202-1). In this part of the retelling of the Arthurian legend, Arthur marries Guinevere, who now begins to have strong feelings for Lancelot. (Rev: BL 5/1/90; SLJ 9/90)

2690 Yolen, Jane, and Robert Harris. *Girl in a Cage* (6–10). 2002, Putnam $19.99 (0-399-23627-9). In 1306, the 11-year-old daughter of the Scottish king describes her plight when she is captured by the

English. (Rev: BCCB 2/03; BL 9/15/02; HB 1–2/03; HBG 3/03; SLJ 10/02*)

2691 Yolen, Jane, and Robert J. Harris. *The Queen's Own Fool: A Novel of Mary, Queen of Scots* (10–12). 2000, Philomel paper $7.99 (0-698-11918-5). Fiction and fact are interwoven in this novel about a 12-year-old girl who becomes a court fool for Mary, Queen of Scots. (Rev: BL 4/1/00; HB 5–6/00; HBG 9/00; SLJ 6/00; VOYA 6/00)

Latin America and Canada

2692 Alvarez, Julia. *Before We Were Free* (7–10). 2002, Knopf LB $17.99 (0-375-91544-3). Twelve-year-old Anita describes growing up in the repressive Dominican Republic of 1960 and her increasing understanding and personal experience of the political crisis taking place. (Rev: BCCB 11/02; BL 8/02; HB 9–10/02*; HBG 3/03; SLJ 8/02; VOYA 8/02)

2693 Alvarez, Julia. *In the Time of the Butterflies* (9–12). 1994, Algonquin $29.95 (1-56512-038-8). Follows the real-life struggles of the Mirabel sisters from girlhood to womanhood as they struggle under, and ultimately resist, the Trujillo dictatorship in the Dominican Republic. (Rev: BL 7/94)

2694 Atwood, Margaret. *Alias Grace* (10–12). 1996, Doubleday $24.95 (0-385-47571-3). Set in Canada, this complex novel, based on a true case, is about Grace Marks, who in 1843, at the age of 16, was convicted of being an accomplice in the murder of her employer and his housekeeper. (Rev: BL 9/15/96; SLJ 6/97)

2695 Berry, James. *Ajeemah and His Son* (10–12). 1994, HarperTrophy paper $4.99 (0-06-440523-0). Ajeemah and his 18-year-old son Atu are captured in Nigeria at the beginning of the 19th century and taken as slaves to Jamaica, where their experiences are very different.

2696 Danticat, Edwidge. *The Farming of Bones* (10–12). 1998, Soho Pr. $23.00 (1-56947-126-6). An emotion-charged historical novel about the people of Haiti and the Dominican Republic in which Amabelle, an aging Haitian woman, recalls the terrible massacre of 1937 and what happened to her and the man she loved. (Rev: BL 8/98; SLJ 11/98)

2697 de la Caridad Doval, Teresa. *A Girl Like Che Guevara* (10–12). 2004, Soho Pr. $24.00 (1-56947-358-7). The story of a 16-year-old's coming of age while living under Cuba's communist government is told in this explicit story for mature readers. (Rev: BL 2/1/04)

2698 Falconer, Colin. *Feathered Serpent: A Novel of the Mexican Conquest* (11–12). 2002, Crown $22.95 (0-609-61029-5). Falconer tells the story of Malinali, the Aztec princess who was Cortes's translator and lover; for mature teens. (Rev: BL 11/1/02)

2699 Gershten, Donna M. *Kissing the Virgin's Mouth* (10–12). 2001, HarperCollins $23.00 (0-06-018567-8). For mature readers, this is the saga of a Mexican woman known as Magda, her childhood, marriages, adventures, and her eventual return to her small town in her old age. (Rev: BL 2/1/01)

2700 Houston, James. *Running West* (10–12). Illus. 1992, Kensington paper $4.99 (0-8217-3505-5). Both a love story and an adventure novel, this is the story of a man indentured to the Hudson Bay Company, a Dene Indian woman, and a journey into the wilderness for furs and gold. (Rev: SLJ 11/90)

2701 Jenkins, Lyll Becerra de. *So Loud a Silence* (7–10). 1996, Dutton $16.99 (0-525-67538-8). In contemporary Colombia, 17-year-old Juan leaves the city slums to find peace at his grandmother's mountain home, but instead becomes involved in the civil war conflict and the violence of the army and the guerrillas. (Rev: BL 9/15/96; BR 3–4/97; SLJ 12/96; VOYA 2/97)

2702 Jocelyn, Marthe. *Mable Riley: A Reliable Record of Humdrum, Peril, and Romance* (5–10). Illus. 2004, Candlewick $15.99 (0-7636-2120-X). This is a charming, humorous diary set in 1901 by a 14-year-old girl who accompanies her sister when she becomes a teacher in Stratford, Ontario. (Rev: BL 3/1/04; HB 5–6/04; SLJ 3/04; VOYA 6/04)

2703 Limón, Graciela. *Song of the Hummingbird* (6–10). 1996, Arte Publico paper $12.95 (1-55885-091-0). The conquest of the Aztec Empire by Cortes is told through the experiences of Huizitzilin (Hummingbird), a descendent of Mexican kings. (Rev: VOYA 8/97)

2704 McCarthy, Cormac. *All the Pretty Horses* (10–12). 1992, Knopf $27.50 (0-394-57474-5); paper $13.00 (0-679-74439-8). The story of two young boys who venture into Mexico in 1950 and take jobs on a ranch working with horses.

2705 Mikaelsen, Ben. *Tree Girl* (7–12). 2004, HarperTempest $16.99 (0-06-009004-9). Through the first-person narrative of Mayan teenager Gabriela Flores, the reader experiences the civil war in Guatemala. (Rev: BL 2/15/04; SLJ 4/04; VOYA 6/04)

2706 Morrissey, Donna. *Kit's Law* (10–12). 2001, Houghton paper $13.00 (0-618-10927-7). Fourteen-year-old Kit is living in a remote Newfoundland village with her mother and grandmother in the 1950s when her life suddenly falls apart because of love, hidden secrets, and family intrigue. (Rev: BL 4/1/01)

2707 Newcomb, Kerry. *Mad Morgan* (10–12). 2000, St. Martin's $24.95 (0-312-26197-7). An old-fashioned adventure story filled with danger and suspense that tells of the exploits of the 17th-century buccaneer Captain Henry Morgan. (Rev: BL 8/00)

2708 O'Dell, Scott. *The King's Fifth* (7–10). 1966, Houghton $17.00 (0-395-06963-7). In a story told in flashbacks, Esteban explains why he is in jail in the Mexico of the Conquistadors. Also use *The Hawk That Dare Not Hunt by Day* (1975).

2709 Reuter, Bjarne. *The Ring of the Slave Prince* (7–12). Trans. by Tiina Nunnally. 2004, Dutton $21.99 (0-525-47146-4). Thrilling action scenes abound in this historical adventure set on 17th-century Caribbean plantations and also on the high seas with bloodthirsty pirates. (Rev: BL 2/1/04; SLJ 4/04; VOYA 2/04)

2710 Slade, Arthur. *Dust* (8–12). 2003, Random LB $17.99 (0-385-90093-7). Eleven-year-old Robert wonders why people are so accepting of the recent disappearance of a number of children and so willing to listen to the mysterious Harsich, who promises to bring rain to his drought-stricken Saskatchewan town in the 1930s. (Rev: BCCB 3/03; BL 2/15/03; HB 3–4/03; HBG 10/03; SLJ 3/03*; VOYA 2/03)

2711 Talbert, Marc. *Heart of a Jaguar* (7–10). 1995, Simon & Schuster $16.00 (0-689-80282-X). A death-inducing drought takes its toll in the heart of a Mayan village. (Rev: BL 9/15/95; SLJ 11/95; VOYA 12/95)

2712 Temple, Frances. *Taste of Salt: A Story of Modern Haiti* (7–12). 1992, Orchard LB $17.99 (0-531-08609-7). A first novel simply told in the voices of two Haitian teenagers who find political commitment and love. (Rev: BL 8/92; SLJ 9/92*)

2713 Wheeler, Kate. *When Mountains Walked* (10–12). 2000, Houghton $23.00 (0-395-85991-3). In this powerful adult novel, Maggie — who runs a medical center in rural Peru — discovers, with her husband, that a mining operation is polluting a river and causing a health crisis. (Rev: BL 2/1/00*)

2714 Wilder, Thornton. *The Bridge of San Luis Rey* (10–12). 1967, Perennial paper $11.00 (0-06-092986-3). This is the story of the five people who were killed when Peru's San Luis Rey bridge collapsed on July 14, 1714.

United States

NATIVE AMERICANS

2715 Borland, Hal. *When the Legends Die* (9–12). 1963, Bantam paper $5.99 (0-553-25738-2). At the death of his parents, a young Native American boy must enter the world of the white man. (Rev: BL 11/1/87)

2716 Bruchac, Joseph. *Turtle Meat and Other Stories* (9–12). 1992, Holy Cow! paper $12.95 (0-930100-49-2). Abenaki writer Bruchac presents mythic, historical, and contemporary stories with wit and a fine sense of character. (Rev: BL 11/15/92; SLJ 12/92)

2717 Chibbaro, Julie. *Redemption* (9–12). 2004, Simon & Schuster $16.95 (0-689-85736-5). Set in the early 16th century, this is the story of 12-year-old Lily from England and how she found a home and family with an Indian tribe in the northeast forests. (Rev: BL 5/15/04; HB 7–8/04; SLJ 8/04)

2718 Conley, Robert. *War Woman: A Novel of the Real People* (10–12). 1997, St. Martin's $25.95 (0-312-17058-0). This fast-moving novel tells about first encounters between Cherokees and Europeans from the viewpoint of War Woman, a Native American woman of extraordinary skills and abilities. (Rev: SLJ 5/98)

2719 Conley, Robert J. *The Cherokee Dragon* (10–12). 2000, St. Martin's $23.95 (0-312-20884-7). Written by a well-known Cherokee writer, this novel tells an exciting tale of his forebears when their land was being threatened by the arrival of Europeans. (Rev: BL 2/15/00)

2720 Gall, Grant. *Apache: The Long Ride Home* (7–10). 1988, Sunstone paper $9.95 (0-86534-105-2). Pedro was only nine when Apache raiders kidnapped him and renamed him Cuchillo. (Rev: BL 9/15/87; BR 9–10/88)

2721 Hausman, Gerald. *The Coyote Bead* (7–12). 1999, Hampton Roads paper $11.95 (1-57174-145-3). With the help of his grandfather and Indian magic, a young Navajo boy evades the American soldiers who killed his parents. (Rev: SLJ 1/00; VOYA 4/00)

2722 Highwater, Jamake. *Legend Days* (7–10). Series: Ghost Horse. 1984, HarperCollins $12.95 (0-06-022303-0). This story about a young Indian girl begins a moving trilogy about three generations of Native Americans and their fate in a white man's world. Followed by *The Ceremony of Innocence* and *I Wear the Morning Star.*

2723 Homstad, Daniel W. *Horse Dreamer* (7–12). 2001, PublishAmerica paper $24.95 (1-58851-042-5). A historical adventure in which 16-year-old Zakarias, son of a white father and a Dakota mother, serves as a scout for the army in the early 1860s until he is captured by renegade Dakotas and decides to join their cause. (Rev: VOYA 4/02)

2724 La Farge, Oliver. *Laughing Boy* (9–12). 1981, Buccaneer LB $24.95 (0-89966-367-2); NAL paper $3.50 (0-451-52244-3). A touching novel first published in 1929 about two young Navahos and the love they feel for each other.

2725 Lederer, Paul Joseph. *Cheyenne Dreams* (9–12). 1985, NAL paper $3.50 (0-451-13651-9). The story of a young Indian orphan and her adoption by a tribe of Cheyenne. Part of the Indian Heritage series. (Rev: VOYA 2/86)

2726 Medawar, Mardi O. *Witch of the Palo Duro: A Tay-Bodal Mystery* (10–12). 1997, St. Martin's $21.95 (0-312-17065-3). Set in the Wild West of 1866, this murder mystery involves Kiowa Indians, the ghosts of their forefathers, and the sudden death of the wife of their chief. (Rev: BL 9/15/97; SLJ 4/98)

2727 Oke, Janette. *Drums of Change* (9–12). 1996, Bethany paper $8.99 (1-55661-812-3). Two Blackfoot youngsters are taken from the tribe to attend a boarding school where the chief's son, Silver Fox, adopts the white man's religion, but the girl, Running Fawn, longs for the old ways of her tribe. (Rev: VOYA 10/96)

2728 Rees, Celia. *Sorceress* (7–11). 2002, Candlewick $15.99 (0-7636-1847-0). Agnes, a Native American who is beginning college, researches Mary Newbury, first seen in *Witch Child* (2001), and discovers a connection that results in a vision quest. (Rev: BL 1/1–15/03; HB 1–2/03; HBG 3/03; SLJ 12/02; VOYA 4/03)

2729 Thorn, James Alexander, and Dark Rain Thorn. *Warrior Woman: The Exceptional Life Story of Nonhelema, Shawnee Indian Woman Chief* (10–12). 2003, Ballantine $25.95 (0-345-44554-6). This prequel to *Panther in the Sky* (1989) tells the little-known story of female Shawnee chief, Nonhelema, a convert to Christianity who finds herself at odds with her people. (Rev: BL 11/15/03)

2730 Wood, Nancy. *Thunderwoman* (9–12). Illus. 1998, Viking $19.95 (0-525-45498-5). Enhanced by beautiful illustrations by Richard Erdoes, and weaving in legend, mysticism, and myth, this novel traces the tragic history of the Pueblos and other Indian peoples in the Western Hemisphere after 10,000 years of peace, beginning with Spanish conquests in the 1500s and up to atom bomb testing in New Mexico. (Rev: BL 2/15/99; HBG 9/99; SLJ 5/99)

DISCOVERY AND EXPLORATION

2731 Ambrose, Stephen. *This Vast Land: A Young Man's Journal of the Lewis and Clark Expedition* (9–12). 2003, Simon & Schuster $17.95 (0-689-86448-5). In a fictional diary, 19-year-old George describes events on the trail and his own aspirations and romantic adventures. (Rev: BCCB 1/04; BL 9/1/03; HB 1–2/04; HBG 4/04; SLJ 9/03; VOYA 12/03)

2732 Bruchac, Joseph. *Sacajawea: The Story of Bird Woman and the Lewis and Clark Expedition* (7–10). 2000, Harcourt $17.00 (0-15-202234-1). Told in alternating chapters by Sacajawea and William Clark, this novel re-creates the famous cross-country journey of Lewis and Clark. (Rev: BL 4/1/00; HBG 9/00; SLJ 5/00)

146

2733 Garland, Sherry. *Indio* (7–10). 1995, Harcourt $11.00 (0-15-238631-9); paper $6.00 (0-15-200021-6). Ipa-ta-chi's life is destroyed when Spanish conquistadors enslave her. When her brother is injured and her sister raped in the silver mines, Ipa attempts to escape but is charged with murder. (Rev: BL 6/1–15/95; SLJ 6/95)

2734 Glancy, Diane. *Stone Heart* (10–12). 2003, Overlook $21.95 (1-58567-365-X). Native American heroine Sacajawea comes alive as she narrates this fictionalized account of the Lewis and Clark expedition. (Rev: BL 1/1–15/03)

2735 Smith, Roland. *The Captain's Dog: My Journey with the Lewis and Clark Tribe* (9–12). 1999, Harcourt $17.00 (0-15-201989-8). The story of the Lewis and Clark expedition according to Lewis's dog, Seaman. (Rev: BL 10/15/99; HBG 4/00; SLJ 11/99; VOYA 4/00)

2736 Thom, James Alexander. *Sign-Talker: The Adventure of George Drouillard on the Lewis and Clark Expedition* (10–12). Illus. 2000, Ballantine $25.95 (0-345-39003-2). A fictional account of the Lewis and Clark expedition as narrated by George Drouillard, who was hired as a guide and interpreter for the journey. (Rev: BL 7/00; SLJ 6/00)

COLONIAL PERIOD AND FRENCH AND INDIAN WARS

2737 Bittner, Rosanne. *Into the Wilderness: The Long Hunters* (11–12). Series: Westward America! 2002, Tor $23.95 (0-7653-0066-4). Sixteen-year-old Jessica falls in love with the hunter/spy who rescues her from an Indian attack in 1753 Pennsylvania; for mature teens. (Rev: BL 3/1/02)

2738 Bruchac, Joseph. *Pocahontas* (6–12). 2003, Harcourt $17.00 (0-15-216737-4). Pocahontas and John Smith take turns describing the relationship between the Jamestown colonists and the Powhatan Indians. (Rev: BL 9/15/03; HBG 4/04; SLJ 5/04; VOYA 4/04)

2739 Bruchac, Joseph. *The Winter People* (6–10). 2002, Dial $16.99 (0-8037-2694-5). A 14-year-old Abenaki boy searches for his mother and sisters after they are kidnapped by English soldiers in the French and Indian War. (Rev: BL 10/1/02*; HBG 3/03; SLJ 11/02*)

2740 Collier, James L., and Christopher Collier. *The Bloody Country* (7–10). 1985, Macmillan $12.95 (0-590-07411-3); Scholastic paper $4.50 (0-590-43126-9). A pioneer story about a family that settles in the 1750s in what is now Wilkes-Barre, Pennsylvania. Also use another fine historical novel by these authors, *The Winter Hero* (1985).

2741 Coombs, Karen M. *Sarah on Her Own* (6–10). 1996, Avon paper $3.99 (0-380-78275-8). Through the eyes of a sensitive English teenager who voyaged to America in 1620, the reader relives the harsh realities and joys of life in an early Virginia settlement. (Rev: SLJ 9/96)

2742 Cooney, Caroline B. *The Ransom of Mercy Carter* (6–10). 2001, Delacorte $15.95 (0-385-32615-7). Eleven-year-old Mercy Carter is adopted by Mohawk Indians after her settlement in Massachusetts is raided in this historically accurate and detailed story based on a real event in 1704. (Rev: BL 4/1/01; HBG 10/01; SLJ 8/01; VOYA 4/01)

2743 Hudson, Joyce Rockwood. *Apalachee* (10–12). 2000, Univ. of Georgia Pr. $27.95 (0-8203-2190-7). A historical novel that deals with the Apalachee Indians of Florida, who were caught between two conflicting colonial powers, the Spanish conquistadors and the English settlers. (Rev: BL 4/1/00)

2744 Johnston, Mary. *To Have and to Hold* (9–12). 1976, Lightyear LB $18.95 (0-89968-149-2). In this historical novel first published in 1900, a young girl escapes an intolerable situation by fleeing to Virginia with a cargo of brides.

2745 Kilian, Michael. *Major Washington* (10–12). 1998, St. Martin's $25.95 (0-312-18131-0). A novel that fictionalizes the life of George Washington during the period from 1753–1755, when he made three journeys into the Allegheny wilderness to spy on the French. (Rev: BL 1/1–15/98; SLJ 1/99)

2746 Koller, Jackie F. *The Primrose Way* (7–10). 1992, Harcourt $15.95 (0-15-256745-3). A historical romance in which Rebekah, 16, falls in love with Mishannock, a Pawtucket holy man. (Rev: BL 10/15/92; SLJ 9/92)

2747 Larsen, Deborah. *The White* (11–12). 2002, Knopf $22.00 (0-375-41359-6). A young woman captured by the Shawnee in pre-Revolutionary America chooses to stay with the Indians despite opportunities to flee to her own people; for mature teens. (Rev: BL 6/1–15/02)

2748 Lasky, Kathryn. *Beyond the Burning Time* (7–12). 1994, Scholastic paper $14.95 (0-590-47331-X). In this docunovel that captures the ignorance, violence, and hysteria of the Salem witch trials, Mary, 12, tries to save her mother, accused of witchcraft. (Rev: BL 10/15/94; SLJ 1/95; VOYA 12/94)

2749 Moore, Robin. *The Man with the Silver Oar* (6–12). 2002, HarperCollins LB $15.89 (0-06-000048-1). Daniel, a Quaker 15-year-old, stows away on a ship hunting pirates in this fine adventure story set in 1718. (Rev: BL 6/1–15/02; HBG 10/02; SLJ 7/02; VOYA 8/02)

2750 Rees, Celia. *Witch Child* (8–12). 2001, Candlewick $15.99 (0-7636-1421-1). Young Mary Newbury, a witch, keeps a journal of her voyage to the New World and describes how the Puritan community views her with suspicion. (Rev: BCCB

7–8/01; BL 10/15/01; HB 9–10/01; HBG 3/02; SLJ 8/01; VOYA 10/01)

2751 Rinaldi, Ann. *A Break with Charity: A Story About the Salem Witch Trials* (7–10). 1992, Harcourt $17.00 (0-15-200353-3). This blend of history and fiction brings to life the dark period in American history of the Salem witch trials. (Rev: BL 10/1/92; SLJ 9/92)

2752 Rinaldi, Ann. *Hang a Thousand Trees with Ribbons* (7–12). 1996, Harcourt $14.00 (0-15-200876-4); paper $6.00 (0-15-200877-2). A well-researched novel about the life of Phillis Wheatley, who was bought by the Wheatleys in 1761 and who later became America's first black poet. (Rev: BL 9/1/96; BR 3–4/97; SLJ 11/96; VOYA 12/96)

2753 Rinaldi, Ann. *A Stitch in Time* (7–10). Series: Quilt Trilogy. 1994, Scholastic paper $13.95 (0-590-46055-2). This historical novel set in 18th-century Salem, Massachusetts, concerns the tribulations of a 16-year-old girl and her family. (Rev: BL 3/1/94; SLJ 5/94; VOYA 4/94)

2754 Wyeth, Sharon D. *Once on This River* (6–10). 1997, Knopf $16.00 (0-679-88350-9); paper $4.99 (0-679-89446-2). In this historical novel set in 1760, 11-year-old Monday de Groot travels from Madagascar to New York to save a man from slavery, only to find the shocking truth of her own birth. (Rev: BCCB 4/98; BL 12/15/97; BR 5–6/98; HBG 9/98; SLJ 4/98)

2755 Youmans, Marly. *Catherwood* (10–12). 1996, Farrar $20.00 (0-374-11972-4). While returning home from visiting friends in a neighboring community in 17th-century New York Colony, Catherwood and her infant daughter become lost and spend seven months in the wilderness in this gripping survival story. (Rev: BL 5/15/96; SLJ 11/96)

REVOLUTIONARY PERIOD AND THE YOUNG NATION (1775–1809)

2756 Anderson, Joan. *1787* (7–10). 1987, Harcourt $14.95 (0-15-200582-X). The story of a teenager who became James Madison's aide during the 1787 Constitutional Convention in Philadelphia. (Rev: BL 5/87; VOYA 12/87)

2757 Anderson, Laurie Halse. *Fever 1793* (6–10). 2000, Simon & Schuster $16.00 (0-689-83858-1). Matilda must find the strength to go on when her family is killed by yellow fever in a 1793 outbreak in Philadelphia. (Rev: BCCB 10/00; BL 10/1/00; HB 9–10/00; HBG 3/01; SLJ 8/00*)

2758 Ernst, Kathleen. *Betrayal at Cross Creek* (5–10). 2004, Pleasant $10.95 (1-58485-879-6). During the Revolutionary War, a young Scottish refugee and her grandparents are torn by conflicting loyalties. (Rev: BL 3/1/04; SLJ 5/04)

2759 Fast, Howard. *April Morning* (9–12). 1961, Bantam paper $5.99 (0-553-27322-1). A short novel about the first days of the American Revolution as experienced by a 15-year-old boy.

2760 Fast, Howard. *The Immigrants* (7–12). 1998, Harcourt paper $12.00 (0-15-600512-3). During the early stages of the Revolutionary War, 15-year-old Adam Cooper becomes a man.

2761 Morgan, Robert. *Brave Enemies* (11–12). 2003, Algonquin $24.95 (1-56512-365-5). In the Revolutionary War, 16-year-old Josie, who has been traveling as a man, meets and marries a preacher but must continue her disguise; suitable for mature teens. (Rev: BL 8/03)

2762 Rinaldi, Ann. *The Fifth of March: A Story of the Boston Massacre* (7–12). 1993, Harcourt $13.00 (0-15-200343-6); paper $6.00 (0-15-227517-7). In 1770, 14-year-old Rachel, an indentured servant in the household of John Adams, becomes caught up in political turmoil when she befriends a young British soldier. (Rev: BL 1/15/94*; SLJ 1/94; VOYA 2/94)

2763 Rinaldi, Ann. *Finishing Becca: The Story of Peggy Shippen and Benedict Arnold* (7–10). 1994, Harcourt $12.00 (0-15-200880-2). Historical fiction based on the author's contention that it was Peggy Shippen Arnold, wife of Benedict, who was responsible for her husband's betrayal of the American Revolution. (Rev: BL 11/15/94; SLJ 12/94; VOYA 2/95)

2764 Rinaldi, Ann. *A Ride into Morning: The Story of Temple Wick* (7–10). 1991, Harcourt $15.95 (0-15-200573-0). The story of a woman who hid her horse in her house to keep it from rebellious soldiers during the Revolutionary War. (Rev: BL 8/91; SLJ 5/91)

2765 Rinaldi, Ann. *The Secret of Sarah Revere* (7–10). 1995, Harcourt $13.00 (0-15-200393-2); paper $6.00 (0-15-200392-4). The daughter of Paul Revere recalls the events of the past two years against a background of historically significant events. (Rev: BL 11/15/95; SLJ 11/95; VOYA 12/95)

2766 Rinaldi, Ann. *Taking Liberty: The Story of Oney Judge, George Washington's Runaway Slave* (7–12). 2002, Simon & Schuster $16.95 (0-689-85187-1). An elderly Oney looks back on her life as Martha's personal slave, her initial acceptance of her lot, and her final decision to trade comfort for freedom. (Rev: HBG 3/03; SLJ 1/03; VOYA 2/03)

2767 Rinaldi, Ann. *Wolf by the Ears* (8–12). 1991, Scholastic $13.95 (0-590-43413-6). Harriet Hemings — the alleged daughter of Thomas Jefferson and his slave mistress — faces moral dilemmas in regard to freedom, equal rights, and her future. (Rev: BL 2/1/91; SLJ 4/91)

2768 Rosenburg, John. *First in War: George Washington in the American Revolution* (7–10). Illus. 1998, Millbrook LB $25.90 (0-7613-0311-1). This second part of the fictionalized biography of George Washington covers his career from 1775, when he was elected commander-in-chief, to the end of 1783, when he resigned from his military duties. (Rev: HBG 9/98; SLJ 7/98; VOYA 4/99)

2769 Walter, Mildred P. *Second Daughter: The Story of a Slave Girl* (6–10). 1996, Scholastic paper $15.95 (0-590-48282-3). A fictional account of the dramatic incident in Massachusetts during 1781 when a slave woman, Mum Bett, took her owner to court and won her freedom. (Rev: BL 2/15/96; BR 5–6/96; SLJ 2/96; VOYA 8/96)

NINETEENTH CENTURY TO THE CIVIL WAR (1809–1861)

2770 Avi. *Beyond the Western Sea: The Escape from Home* (6–10). 1996, Orchard LB $19.99 (0-531-08863-4). Three immigrant youngsters — two poor Irish peasants and the third, an English stowaway — face dangers and hardships on their journey to America in this suspenseful adventure novel set in the 1850s. (Rev: BL 2/1/96*; BR 9–10/96; SLJ 6/96; VOYA 6/96)

2771 Ayres, Katherine. *North by Night: A Story of the Underground Railroad* (6–10). 1998, Delacorte $15.95 (0-385-32564-9). Told in diary form, this is the story of 16-year-old Lucinda and her role in helping slaves escape via the Underground Railroad. (Rev: BL 10/1/98; HBG 3/99; SLJ 10/98; VOYA 2/99)

2772 Cadnum, Michael. *Blood Gold* (7–12). 2004, Viking $16.99 (0-670-05884-X). Eighteen-year-old William encounters greed, murder, and revenge in this exciting novel set during the 1849 California gold rush. (Rev: BL 5/15/04*; HB 7–8/04; SLJ 6/04)

2773 Carbone, Elisa. *Stealing Freedom* (7–10). 1998, Knopf $17.00 (0-679-89307-5). Based on fact, this historical novel tells of a young teenage slave in Maryland and her escape to Canada via the Underground Railway in the 1850s. (Rev: BL 1/1–15/99; HBG 3/99; SLJ 2/99)

2774 Chance, Megan. *Susanna Morrow* (10–12). 2002, Warner $24.95 (0-446-52953-2). Susannah arrives in Salem at the height of the morality crusade and her finery only enhances suspicions when she is accused of witchcraft. (Rev: BL 8/02)

2775 Charbonneau, Eileen. *Honor to the Hills* (8–10). 1996, Tor $18.95 (0-312-86094-3). Returning to her home in the Catskill Mountains in 1851, 15-year-old Lily Woods finds that her family is involved in the Underground Railroad. (Rev: VOYA 6/96)

2776 Chase-Riboud, Barbara. *The President's Daughter* (9–12). 1995, Ballantine paper $12.00 (0-345-38970-0). Harriet — daughter of Thomas Jefferson and his mistress and slave, Sally Hemings — passes as white and starts a new life as a free woman. Sequel to *Sally Hemings*. (Rev: BL 9/1/94)

2777 Cooper, J. California. *Family* (9–12). 1991, Doubleday $21.00 (0-385-41171-5). An African American slave commits suicide but returns as a spirit to watch her children mature and experience freedom after the Civil War. (Rev: BL 1/15/91; SLJ 8/91)

2778 Ferris, Jean. *Into the Wind* (9–12). Series: American Dreams. 1996, Avon paper $3.99 (0-380-78198-0). In this romantic historical novel set in 1814, 17-year-old Rosie sets sail on a ship engaged to fight the British Navy. (Rev: SLJ 9/96)

2779 Harrigan, Stephen. *The Gates of the Alamo* (10–12). 2000, Knopf $25.00 (0-679-44717-2). A long and detailed novel filled with action and intrigue about Texas in the early 19th century and the Battle of the Alamo. (Rev: BL 1/1–15/00; SLJ 7/00)

2780 Hurmence, Belinda. *My Folks Don't Want Me to Talk About Slavery: Twenty-One Oral Histories of Former North Carolina Slaves* (9–12). 1984, Blair paper $6.95 (0-89587-039-8). A unique view of slavery as provided by 21 narratives supplied by former slaves. [973]

2781 Jakes, John. *Charleston* (11–12). 2002, Dutton $26.95 (0-525-94650-0). This saga chronicles a southern family's ups and downs from the colonial days through the end of the Civil War, placing their personal stories against the backdrop of political events and social change; for mature teens. (Rev: BL 7/02)

2782 Jensen, Lisa. *The Witch from the Sea* (10–12). 2001, Beagle Bay paper $16.95 (0-9679591-5-2). A Boston girl who is part Native American disguises herself as a boy to live the life of a sailor in this romantic adventure set in 1823. (Rev: BL 8/01)

2783 Joslyn, Mauriel Phillips. *Shenandoah Autumn: Courage Under Fire* (6–10). 1999, White Mane paper $8.95 (1-57249-137-X). During the Civil War, young Mattie and her mother, though afraid of the Union troops around their Virginia home, save a wounded Confederate soldier and return him to his companions. (Rev: BL 5/1/99)

2784 Krisher, Trudy. *Uncommon Faith* (7–10). 2003, Holiday $17.95 (0-8234-1791-3). The year 1837–1838 is a time of change in Millbrook, Massachusetts, and 10 of the residents narrate their experiences in a collage that connects the reader to the townspeople and to the history. (Rev: BL 10/15/03; HBG 4/04; SLJ 10/03*; VOYA 10/03)

2785 LaFoy, Leslie. *Jackson's Way* (10–12). 2001, Bantam paper $5.99 (0-553-58313-1). In this historical romance, Jackson Stennett, with the help of his company's beautiful manager, investigates the family business and finds skullduggery and love in New York City in 1838. (Rev: BL 9/15/01)

2786 Landis, Jill Marie. *Just Once* (10–12). 1997, Jove paper $6.50 (0-515-12062-6). This romance set in the Louisiana woods of 1816 deals with adventurous Jemma and her woodsman guide, Hunter. (Rev: SLJ 4/98)

2787 Lyons, Mary E. *Letters from a Slave Girl: The Story of Harriet Jacobs* (7–12). 1992, Scribner $16.00 (0-684-19446-5). Based on Jacobs's autobiography, these "letters," written to lost relatives and friends, provide a look at what slavery meant for a young female in the mid-1800s. (Rev: BL 10/1/92; SLJ 12/92*)

2788 Martin, Valerie. *Property* (11–12). 2003, Doubleday $23.95 (0-385-50408-X). This novel recounting the troubled relationship between a well-to-do white woman and her slave in early-19th-century Louisiana is suitable for mature readers. (Rev: BL 1/1–15/03)

2789 Monfredo, Miriam G. *The Stalking Horse* (10–12). 1997, Berkley paper $21.95 (0-425-15783-0). In this fifth in a series of historical novels, Bronwyn Llyr and her friend try to foil a plan to assassinate President Lincoln. (Rev: BL 3/15/98; SLJ 8/98)

2790 Nevin, David. *Treason* (10–12). Series: American Story. 2001, Tor $27.95 (0-312-85512-5). This is a suspenseful fictional account of the unresolved Burr conspiracy to steal the Louisiana Purchase. (Rev: BL 9/15/01*)

2791 Oates, Stephen B. *The Fires of Jubilee: Nat Turner's Fierce Rebellion* (10–12). 1982, NAL paper $3.95 (0-451-62308-8). A fictionalized account of the slave rebellion led by Nat Turner in 1831 in Southampton County, Virginia.

2792 Paterson, Katherine. *Lyddie* (9–12). 1991, Dutton $15.99 (0-525-67338-5). The life and hard times of a young girl growing up in the mid-19th century. (Rev: BL 1/1/91*; SLJ 2/91*)

2793 Paulsen, Gary. *Nightjohn* (6–12). 1993, Delacorte $15.95 (0-385-30838-8). Told in the voice of Sarny, 12, Paulsen exposes the myths that African American slaves were content, well cared for, ignorant, and childlike, and that brave, resourceful slaves easily escaped. (Rev: BL 12/15/92)

2794 Pella, Judith, and Tracie Peterson. *Distant Dreams* (10–12). 1997, Bethany paper $10.99 (1-55661-862-X). This novel set in 1830 during Andrew Jackson's presidency tells of a 15-year-old girl who becomes fascinated with locomotives and railroads in spite of the scorn of her mother and sister. (Rev: SLJ 9/97)

2795 Pesci, David. *Amistad* (10–12). 1997, Marlowe $22.95 (1-56924-748-X). The author of this fine historical novel fills in gaps and creates fascinating characters in this retelling of the slave revolt aboard the Spanish ship *Amistad,* led by Singbe-Pleh, later known as Joseph Cinque. (Rev: BL 5/15/97; SLJ 2/98)

2796 Prince, Bryan. *I Came as a Stranger: The Underground Railroad* (7–12). 2004, Tundra paper $15.95 (0-88776-667-6). This account tells what happened after the runaway slaves reached Canada and contains material both about famous leaders and about ordinary people involved in the Underground Railroad. (Rev: BL 5/1/04; SLJ 6/04) [971.1]

2797 Rinaldi, Ann. *Broken Days* (6–10). Series: Quilt. 1995, Scholastic $14.95 (0-590-46053-6). When her cousin steals the piece of quilt that will establish her identity, Walking Breeze, who has come to live with her white family in Massachusetts at the age of 14 after being raised by Shawnees, is demoted to servant status in this story that takes place during the War of 1812. The second part of the Quilt trilogy. (Rev: VOYA 4/96)

2798 Rinaldi, Ann. *Mine Eyes Have Seen* (8–12). 1998, Scholastic paper $16.95 (0-590-54318-0). The story of the raid at Harper's Ferry is retold through the eyes of John Brown's daughter Annie. (Rev: BL 2/15/98; BR 11–12/98; HBG 9/98; SLJ 2/98; VOYA 4/98)

2799 Rossner, Judith. *Emmeline* (10–12). 1998, Doubleday paper $14.95 (0-385-33344-7). Based on fact, this is the story of a girl who was a mill girl in Lowell, Massachusetts, during the 1830s.

2800 Schwartz, Virginia Frances. *If I Just Had Two Wings* (6–10). 2001, Stoddart $15.95 (0-7737-3302-7). Accompanied by a friend and her two children, a young slave named Phoebe makes a daring escape to Canada and freedom via the Underground Railroad. (Rev: BL 12/1/01; SLJ 12/01; VOYA 12/01)

2801 Silvis, Randall. *On Night's Shore* (10–12). 2001, St. Martin's $24.95 (0-312-26201-9). In this mystery set in New York in 1849, the body of a young woman is found under a pier and Edgar Allan Poe is assigned to cover the story. (Rev: BL 12/1/00*)

2802 Stolz, Mary. *Cezanne Pinto: A Memoir* (6–10). 1994, Knopf $16.00 (0-679-84917-3). This fictionalized memoir of a runaway slave who became a soldier, cowboy, and teacher includes quotations and stories of the great figures of the time. (Rev: BL 1/15/94; SLJ 12/93; VOYA 6/94)

2803 Stone, Irving. *The President's Lady* (10–12). 1996, Rutledge Hill paper $14.95 (1-55853-431-8). The story of the great love between Andrew Jackson and his wife, Rachel.

2804 Styron, William. *The Confessions of Nat Turner* (10–12). 1994, Modern Library $18.95 (0-679-

60101-5); paper $14.00 (0-679-73663-8). Based on fact, this powerful novel tells of the life of the black slave who led a rebellion at age 31.

2805 Watts, Leander. *Stonecutter* (7–10). 2002, Houghton $15.00 (0-618-16474-X). In rural New York State in 1835, a gifted 14-year-old stonecutter rescues a beautiful girl who is being kept a prisoner by her wealthy and powerful father. (Rev: BCCB 11/02; BL 9/15/02; HB 11–12/02; HBG 3/03; SLJ 12/02; VOYA 12/02)

2806 Watts, Leander. *Wild Ride to Heaven* (9–12). 2003, Houghton $16.00 (0-618-26805-7). Hannah's father sells her to two men, but the plucky protagonist with the two strangely unmatched eyes manages to escape in this story set in 1800s New York state. (Rev: BL 11/1/03; HBG 4/04; SLJ 11/03; VOYA 4/04)

2807 Wood, Frances M. *Daughter of Madrugada* (7–10). 2002, Delacorte $15.95 (0-385-32719-6). Thirteen-year-old Cesa describes her privileged life in 1840s California, even as the social landscape is changing with the arrival of gold miners and as she herself faces pressures to abandon her tomboy freedom. (Rev: BCCB 6/02; BL 5/15/02; HBG 10/02; SLJ 5/02; VOYA 8/02)

THE CIVIL WAR (1861–1865)

2808 Armstrong, Jennifer. *The Dreams of Mairhe Mehan* (7–12). 1996, Knopf $18.00 (0-679-88152-2). A grim, challenging novel that takes place in Civil War Washington and involves a poor immigrant Irish serving maid and her family. (Rev: BL 1/1–15/97; BR 1–2/97; SLJ 10/96)

2809 Ballard, Allen B. *Where I'm Bound* (10–12). 2000, Simon & Schuster $24.00 (0-684-87031-2). This is an action-packed Civil War novel, that tells, in personal terms, of the contributions and heroics of African American soldiers in that war. (Rev: BL 10/15/00; SLJ 3/01)

2810 Bass, Cynthia. *Sherman's March* (9–12). 1994, Villard $21.00 (0-679-43033-4). A fast-paced fictionalized account of Sherman's infamous march to the sea. (Rev: SLJ 12/94)

2811 *The Blue and the Gray Undercover: All New Civil War Spy Adventures* (10–12). Ed. by Ed Gorman. 2001, Forge $24.95 (0-312-87487-1). This collection of 18 original short stories focuses on the exploits of spies for both the Union and Confederacy during the Civil War. (Rev: BL 1/1–15/02; VOYA 4/02)

2812 Brown, Dee Alexander. *The Way to Bright Star* (10–12). 1998, Forge $24.95 (0-312-86612-7). An adventure story, set in the American frontier during the Civil War, about Ben Butterfield, his friends, and the dangers they confront on a wagon train traveling through war-torn territory. (Rev: BL 5/1/98; SLJ 3/99)

2813 Clapp, Patricia. *The Tamarack Tree: A Novel of the Siege of Vicksburg* (7–10). 1986, Lothrop $15.99 (0-688-02852-7). The siege of Vicksburg as seen through the eyes of a 17-year-old English girl who is trapped inside the city. (Rev: BL 11/15/86; BR 1–2/87; SLJ 10/86; VOYA 2/87)

2814 Collier, James L., and Christopher Collier. *With Every Drop of Blood: A Novel of the Civil War* (6–10). 1994, Dell paper $5.99 (0-440-21983-3). A Civil War docunovel about Johnny, a young Confederate soldier, and Cush, a black Union soldier who captures him. Together, the two experience the horrors of war and bigotry. (Rev: BL 7/94; SLJ 8/94; VOYA 12/94)

2815 Coyle, Harold. *Look Away* (10–12). 1995, Simon & Schuster $24.00 (0-684-80392-5). An unscrupulous, politically ambitious father takes advantage of his two sons in such a way that they find themselves on opposite sides in this suspenseful Civil War novel. (Rev: BL 4/15/95; SLJ 5/96)

2816 Dallas, Sandra. *Alice's Tulips* (10–12). 2000, St. Martin's $22.95 (0-312-20359-4). In this charming homespun narrative, Alice Bullock moves in with her mother-in-law after Alice's husband enlists in the Union army during the Civil War. (Rev: BL 9/15/00; SLJ 1/01)

2817 Ernst, Kathleen. *Ghosts of Vicksburg* (6–10). 2003, White Mane paper $8.95 (1-57249-322-4). Jamie and Elisha, 15-year-old Union Army soldiers from Wisconsin, experience the horrors of war as their forces march to Mississippi. (Rev: SLJ 12/03)

2818 Fleischman, Paul. *Bull Run* (6–12). 1993, HarperCollins LB $16.89 (0-06-021447-3). Spotlights the diary entries of 16 fictional characters, eight each from the South and the North, throughout the battle. (Rev: BCCB 3/93; BL 1/15/93*; SLJ 3/93*)

2819 Fleming, Thomas. *When This Cruel War Is Over* (10–12). 2001, Tor $24.95 (0-312-87204-6). A headstrong southern girl tries to enlist support for the Confederacy in the northwestern Union states and hopes to win over a disillusioned Union officer with whom she falls in love. (Rev: BL 2/15/01)

2820 Forstchen, William R. *We Look Like Men of War* (10–12). 2001, Tor $21.95 (0-765-30114-8). This novel, set during the Civil War, tells how Sam Washburn, a former slave, returns south to fight for freedom. (Rev: BL 11/15/01; HBG 10/02; VOYA 2/02)

2821 Frazier, Charles. *Cold Mountain* (10–12). 1997, Atlantic Monthly $24.00 (0-87113-679-1). In this best-selling novel set during Civil War times, a soldier deserts and treks through the wilderness to Cold Mountain, where two women, Ruby and Ada, are trying to eke out a living. (Rev: BL 6/1–15/97; SLJ 11/97)

2822 Gibbons, Kaye. *On the Occasion of My Last Afternoon* (10–12). 1998, Putnam $22.95 (0-399-14299-1); Avon paper $12.50 (0-380-73214-9). This novel, set before and during the Civil War, tells of the childhood of a Southern belle, her marriage to a Northern doctor, and her transformation from a self-absorbed child to a loving, mature wife and mother. (Rev: BL 5/15/98; SLJ 9/98)

2823 Gindlesperger, James. *Escape from Libby Prison* (10–12). 1996, Burd Street $24.95 (0-942597-97-5). Fictional characters and figures from history are interwoven in this novel about the escape of 109 Union officers from the gruesome hell known as Libby Prison during the Civil War. (Rev: SLJ 2/97)

2824 Greenberg, Martin H., and Charles G. Waugh, eds. *Civil War Women II: Stories by Women About Women* (7–10). 1997, August House paper $9.95 (0-87483-487-2). A collection of short stories by such female writers as Louisa May Alcott and Edith Wharton that deal with women's lives during the Civil War. (Rev: SLJ 8/97)

2825 Hague, Nora. *Letters from an Age of Reason* (10–12). 2001, Morrow $28.00 (0-06-018491-4). Set in the Civil War era and told in dual-journal form, this is the story of slave Aubrey Paxton and upstate New York beauty Arabella Leeds and how they fall in love. (Rev: BL 7/01)

2826 Hughes, Pat. *Guerrilla Season* (7–12). 2003, Farrar $18.00 (0-374-32811-0). This multilayered novel clearly conveys the confusion that Matt, 15, feels in the face of the approaching violence of the Civil War. (Rev: BL 8/03; HBG 4/04; SLJ 11/03; VOYA 12/03)

2827 Hummel, Maria. *Wilderness Run* (10–12). 2002, St. Martin's $24.95 (0-312-28757-7). Slavery and the horrors of the Civil War form the backdrop of this story of a romantic triangle. (Rev: BL 8/02)

2828 Jiles, Paulette. *Enemy Women* (10–12). 2002, Morrow $24.95 (0-06-621444-0). Adair's home is burned and she is put in jail by Union soldiers in this story of the Civil War set in Missouri. (Rev: BL 1/1–15/02; SLJ 11/02)

2829 Johnson, Charles. *Soulcatcher and Other Stories* (10–12). 2001, Harvest paper $12.00 (0-15-601112-3). Based on solid research, these 12 short stories dramatize various aspects of slavery and its cruelty. (Rev: BL 3/1/01)

2830 Johnson, Nancy. *My Brother's Keeper: A Civil War Story* (6–10). 1997, Down East $14.95 (0-89272-414-5). Two orphaned brothers from upstate New York, ages 15 and 13, join the Union Army, one as a soldier, the other as a drummer boy, and soon find themselves surrounded by the blood and tragedy of battle in this story based on the experi-

ences of the author's great-great-uncles. (Rev: BR 5–6/98; HBG 9/98; SLJ 1/98)

2831 Jones, Madison. *Nashville 1864: The Dying of the Light* (10–12). 1997, Sanders $17.95 (1-879941-35-X). This novel, set during the Civil War, tells of 12-year-old Steven who, with his slave, Dink, sets out to locate his father who is fighting on the Confederate side. (Rev: SLJ 1/98)

2832 Kantor, MacKinlay. *Andersonville* (10–12). 1955, World Pub. paper $17.95 (0-452-26956-3). A realistic, harrowing novel about the prisoners and guards in the notorious southern prison during the Civil War.

2833 Maples, Jack. *Reconstructed Yankee* (10–12). 2002, Corinthian $19.95 (1-929175-29-9); paper $16.95 (1-929175-48-5). Two North Carolina friends, one white, the other black, join the Union militia but switch allegiances and join the Confederate army. (Rev: BL 12/1/01)

2834 Meriwether, Louise. *Fragments of the Ark* (9–12). 1995, Pocket paper $10.00 (0-671-79948-7). Based on a true account, this historical novel is about a group of slaves who escaped to join Union forces and the bigotry they faced from their "rescuers." (Rev: BL 2/15/94; SLJ 11/94)

2835 Mitchell, Margaret. *Gone with the Wind* (9–12). 1936, Avon paper $6.50 (0-380-00109-8). The magnificent Civil War novel about Scarlett O'Hara and her family at Tara.

2836 Monfredo, Miriam Grace. *Sisters of Cain* (10–12). 2000, Berkley $21.95 (0-425-17672-X). Former Pinkerton detective Bronwen Llyr is sent to spy behind Confederate lines while her sister Kathryn hopes to become a nurse to Union soldiers in a mystery full of suspense and historical detail. (Rev: VOYA 8/01)

2837 Moreau, C. X. *Promise of Glory* (10–12). 2000, Tor $24.95 (0-312-87272-0). Authentic historical characters are re-created in this novel about the battle at Antietam Creek in Maryland, the bloodiest battle of the Civil War. (Rev: BL 9/15/00)

2838 Mrazek, Robert. *Unholy Fire* (10–12). 2003, St. Martin's $24.95 (0-312-30673-3). A young man survives the Civil War only to be left with an opium addiction that deeply affects his life. (Rev: BL 3/1/03)

2839 Mrazek, Robert J. *Stonewall's Gold* (10–12). 1999, St. Martin's $22.95 (0-312-20024-2). During the last year of the Civil War, 15-year-old Jamie kills a man who attempts to rape his mother and comes into possession of a treasure map that will lead him into adventure and danger. (Rev: BL 12/15/98; SLJ 4/99)

2840 Murphy, Jim. *The Journal of James Edmond Pease: A Civil War Union Soldier* (7–12). Series: My Name Is America. 1998, Scholastic paper

$10.95 (0-590-43814-X). This novel takes the form of a journal kept by a misfit 16-year-old private in the New York Volunteers, describing his experiences, including the time he gets lost behind enemy lines. (Rev: BCCB 11/98; BL 11/15/98; HBG 3/99; SLJ 7/99)

2841 Paulsen, Gary. *Sarny: A Life Remembered* (6–12). 1997, Delacorte $15.95 (0-385-32195-3). In this sequel to *Nightjohn,* the slave Sarny sets out during the Civil War to find her son and daughter, who were sold and are now impossible to locate. (Rev: BL 10/1/97; BR 11–12/97; HBG 3/98; SLJ 9/97; VOYA 2/98)

2842 Peck, Richard. *The River Between Us* (7–12). 2003, Dial $16.99 (0-8037-2735-6). In 1861 Illinois, Tilly's family makes room for two young women of different complexions from the South. (Rev: BL 9/15/03*; HB 9–10/03; HBG 4/04; SLJ 9/03; VOYA 10/03)

2843 Poyer, David. *Fire on the Waters: A Novel of the Civil War at Sea* (10–12). Series: Civil War at Sea. 2001, Simon & Schuster $25.00 (0-684-87133-5). In this rousing sea adventure, the first of a trilogy, pampered Elisha Eaker joins the Navy and is assigned with Captain Parker Bucyrus Tresevant, a southerner torn between allegiances, to protect Union forces at Fort Sumter. (Rev: BL 7/01)

2844 Reasoner, James. *Antietam* (10–12). Series: Civil War Battle. 2000, Cumberland House $22.95 (1-58182-084-4). This novel, part three of the eight-volume Civil War Battle series, uses the background of the Battle of Antietam to tell the story of the six young Brannon brothers and sisters. (Rev: BL 5/15/00; VOYA 12/00)

2845 Rinaldi, Ann. *In My Father's House* (7–10). 1993, Scholastic paper $14.95 (0-590-44730-0). A coming-of-age novel set during the Civil War about 7-year-old Oscie. (Rev: BL 2/15/93)

2846 Rinaldi, Ann. *Numbering All the Bones* (7–10). 2002, Hyperion $15.99 (0-7868-0533-1). During the Civil War, young slave Eulinda braves the horrors of Andersonville Prison to search for her brother. (Rev: BCCB 6/02; BL 5/15/02; HBG 10/02; SLJ 6/02; VOYA 8/02)

2847 Sappey, Maureen Stack. *Letters from Vinnie* (7–10). 1999, Front Street $16.95 (1-886910-31-6). A novel that mixes fact and fiction to tell the story of the tiny woman who sculpted the large statue of Abraham Lincoln found in the Capitol Building in Washington. (Rev: BL 9/15/99; HBG 4/00; SLJ 11/99; VOYA 2/00)

2848 Severance, John B. *Braving the Fire* (7–12). 2002, Clarion $15.00 (0-618-22999-X). Jem finds war is far from the "glory" described by others in this coming-of-age story set in the realistic horrors of the Civil War. (Rev: BL 10/1/02; HBG 10/03; SLJ 11/02)

2849 Shaara, Jeff. *Gods and Generals* (10–12). 1996, Ballantine $25.00 (0-345-40492-0). This clever novel of the Civil War is told from the viewpoint of four important generals, Lee, Jackson, Hancock, and Chamberlain. (Rev: SLJ 8/97)

2850 Shaara, Michael. *The Killer Angels* (10–12). 1993, Random $24.00 (0-679-42541-1). A vivid, fast-moving adult novel that takes place during the Battle of Gettysburg in July 1863.

2851 Siegelson, Kim. *Trembling Earth* (7–12). 2004, Putnam $17.99 (0-399-24021-7). This Civil War novel is told from the point of view of 12-year-old Hamp, who tracks down a runaway slave in the Okefenokee Swamp. (Rev: BL 5/15/04*; SLJ 6/04)

2852 Stone, Irving. *Love Is Eternal* (10–12). 1994, Buccaneer LB $27.95 (1-56849-556-0). A lengthy, rewarding novel about Lincoln's marriage to Mary Todd.

2853 Vidal, Gore. *Lincoln: A Novel* (10–12). 1984, Random $19.95 (0-394-52895-6). A compelling novel based on the life of Lincoln. One of several historical novels by Gore Vidal that re-create various periods in American history.

2854 Walker, Margaret. *Jubilee* (9–12). 1983, Bantam paper $6.99 (0-553-27383-3). A novel often compared with *Gone with the Wind,* about blacks and poor whites living in the South before, during, and after the Civil War. (Rev: BL 2/15/98)

2855 West, Jessamyn. *The Friendly Persuasion* (9–12). 1982, Buccaneer LB $27.95 (0-89966-395-8). The pacifist views of the Quaker Birdwell family cause problems during the Civil War.

2856 Wisler, G. Clifton. *Thunder on the Tennessee* (7–10). 1995, Puffin paper $5.99 (0-14-037612-7). A 16-year-old Southern boy learns the value of courage and honor during the Civil War.

WESTWARD EXPANSION AND PIONEER LIFE

2857 Aldrich, Bess Streeter. *A Lantern in Her Hand* (9–12). 1983, Amereon LB $21.95 (0-88411-260-8). This novel, originally published in 1928, tells about a young bride and her husband who are homesteaders in Nebraska in 1865. A sequel is *A White Bird Flying.*

2858 Allende, Isabel. *Daughter of Fortune: A Novel* (10–12). Trans. by Margaret Sayers Peden. 1999, HarperCollins $26.00 (0-06-019491-X); paper $14.00 (0-06-093275-9). Set during the 1849 California Gold Rush, this novel combines elements from four cultures: English, Chilean, Chinese, and American. (Rev: BL 8/99)

2859 Altsheler, Joseph A. *Kentucky Frontiersman: The Adventures of Henry Ware, Hunter and Border Fighter* (6–10). Illus. 1988, Voyageur $16.95 (0-929146-01-8). A reissue of a fine frontier adventure story featuring young Henry Ware who is captured by an Indian hunting party. (Rev: BR 3–4/89; SLJ 3/89)

2860 Ammerman, Mark. *Longshot* (10–12). Series: The Cross and the Tomahawk. 2000, Horizon paper $11.99 (1-889651-65-5). Part of a series of novels about the Narragansett Indians, this one deals with an explorer-missionary and his Narragansett friend, who travel into the West in the mid-18th century to establish a settlement. (Rev: BL 6/1–15/00*)

2861 Arlington, Frances. *Prairie Whispers* (7–12). 2003, Putnam $17.99 (0-399-23975-8). During their covered wagon trip westward, Colleen switches her mother's stillborn child and gives her mother the newborn of a dying mother in a nearby wagon. (Rev: BL 5/15/04; HB 7–8/03; HBG 10/03; SLJ 5/03; VOYA 6/03)

2862 Arnold, Elliott. *Blood Brother* (10–12). 1979, Univ. of Nebraska Pr. paper $13.95 (0-8032-5901-8). This novel depicts the struggle between white settlers and the Apaches, led by Cochise.

2863 Berger, Thomas. *Little Big Man* (10–12). 1979, Dial paper $14.95 (0-385-29829-3). The amazing historical novel about Jack Crabb, who was a survivor of Custer's last stand.

2864 Blair, Clifford. *The Guns of Sacred Heart* (9–12). 1991, Walker $28.95 (0-8027-4123-1). Outlaws trying to free their leader, who is a prisoner at a remote mission school, are fought off by a marshal, a cowboy, and the school's staff and students. (Rev: BL 11/1/91; SLJ 5/92)

2865 Blake, Michael. *The Holy Road* (10–12). 2001, Villard $24.95 (0-679-44866-7). In this sequel to *Dances with Wolves* (1988), Lieutenant Dunbar is living in Comanche territory with his wife, Stands with a Fist, and their three children when white men encroach on their lives and habitat. (Rev: BL 7/01; VOYA 12/01)

2866 Bonner, Cindy. *Lily* (9–12). 1992, Algonquin $26.95 (0-945575-95-5). An old-fashioned Western romance in which an innocent girl falls in love with a worldly guy from an outlaw family. (Rev: BL 9/1/92*; SLJ 12/92)

2867 Bowers, Terrell L. *Ride Against the Wind* (7–10). 1996, Walker $21.95 (0-8027-4156-8). Set in Eden, Kansas, in the late 1800s, this sequel to *The Secret of Snake Canyon* (1993) involves Jerrod Danmyer and his attachment to Marion Gates, daughter of his family's sworn enemies. (Rev: BL 12/15/96; VOYA 8/97)

2868 Brewer, James D. *No Justice* (10–12). 1996, Walker $21.95 (0-8057-3283-6). Set along the Mississippi River during Reconstruction, this adult novel features an unlikely trio — a woman who makes a living entertaining gentlemen on riverboats, a former Union soldier, and a wounded Southern

soldier — who join forces to solve a murder mystery. (Rev: SLJ 12/96)

2869 Brouwer, Sigmund. *Evening Star* (10–12). 2000, Bethany paper $8.99 (0-7642-2366-6). Gunfighter Sam Keaton, jailed in 1870s Laramie for shooting a man in self-defense, manages to escape from jail but must draw on inner resources to stay one step ahead of the posse pursuing him. *Silver Moon* (2000) is a sequel. (Rev: VOYA 2/01)

2870 Brown, Irene Bennett. *The Long Road Turning* (10–12). Series: The Women of Paragon Springs. 2000, Macmillan $25.95 (0-7862-2813-X). In this engaging tale of pioneer life, Meg Brennon and a group of friends and relatives of various ages and abilities try to eke out a living on land in eastern Kansas. (Rev: BL 10/1/00)

2871 Brown, Irene Bennett. *Reap the South Wind* (10–12). Series: Five Star First Edition Romance. 2003, Five Star $26.95 (0-7862-2817-2). Widow Lucy Ann flouts convention when she supports her neighbor's passion for airplanes in this fourth installment in a series about women settlers in Kansas. (Rev: BL 2/1/03)

2872 Charbonneau, Eileen. *Rachel LeMoyne* (10–12). Series: Women of the West. 1998, Forge $22.95 (0-312-86448-5). An adventure story, based on fact, about a mixed-blood Choctaw student who goes to Ireland to help famine victims, marries, and returns to America with her Irish husband to cross the frontier to settle in Oregon. (Rev: BL 5/15/98; SLJ 2/99; VOYA 12/98)

2873 Clark, Walter Van Tilburg. *The Ox-Bow Incident* (10–12). 1989, NAL paper $5.95 (0-451-52525-6). Mob vengeance and a lynching are the focus of this novel about justice in the Old West.

2874 Conley, Robert J. *Spanish Jack* (10–12). 2001, St. Martin's $22.95 (0-312-26231-0). This is a fictionalized life of Spanish Jack, a Cherokee who was a fighter, card player, horse thief, and gentleman on the American frontier in the 1800s. (Rev: BL 7/01)

2875 Curtis, Jack. *Pepper Tree Rider* (9–12). 1994, Walker $30.95 (0-8027-4137-1). A subtle Western where a fast gun isn't always the answer; from the pen of the screenplay writer of *Gunsmoke*. (Rev: BL 5/1/94; SLJ 10/94)

2876 DeAndrea, William L. *Written in Fire* (9–12). 1995, Walker $28.95 (0-8027-3270-4). A mystery story set in the Wyoming Territory in the 1800s featuring Quinn Booker, a pulp fiction novelist who investigates the near-fatal shooting of his friend Lobo Blacke. (Rev: BL 1/1–15/96; VOYA 2/96)

2877 Eickhoff, Randy Lee, and Leonard Lewis. *Bowie* (10–12). 1998, Forge $23.95 (0-312-86619-4). A fictionalized biography of the adventurer James Bowie, gambler, slave runner, land speculator, and brawler, who died at the Alamo, told from various perspectives by a variety of "witnesses" to the events of his life. (Rev: SLJ 4/99)

2878 Estleman, Loren D. *Billy Gashade* (10–12). 1997, Forge $23.95 (0-312-85997-X). An exciting historical novel about a young boy who is an accomplished pianist and his adventures in the Wild West of "Wild Bill" Hickok and Billy the Kid. (Rev: BL 5/1/97; SLJ 3/98)

2879 Estleman, Loren D. *Journey of the Dead* (10–12). 1998, St. Martin's $21.95 (0-312-85999-6). A western for mature readers about Pat Garrett, Billy the Kid's killer, and how he is haunted by the ghost of the dead outlaw. (Rev: SLJ 10/98)

2880 Ferber, Edna. *Cimarron* (9–12). 1998, Amereon $28.95 (0-88411-548-8). The story of the fortunes of Yancey Cravat and his wife Sabra set against the days of the land rush of 1889 in Oklahoma. Also use: *Saratoga Trunk* (1986).

2881 Gloss, Molly. *The Jump-Off Creek* (9–12). 1989, Houghton $16.45 (0-395-51086-4). A realistic portrait of the struggles of a lone homesteader and her problems. (Rev: BL 9/1/89)

2882 Grey, Zane. *The Last Trail* (10–12). Illus. 1996, Univ. of Nebraska Pr. paper $12.00 (0-8032-7063-1). Originally published in 1909, this western tells of Helen Sheppard who, with her father, relocates to the Ohio Valley, where she encounters dangers from hostile Indians and romance with a borderman. (Rev: SLJ 8/96)

2883 Grey, Zane. *Riders of the Purple Sage* (9–12). 1990, Viking paper $9.95 (0-14-018440-6). This is probably the best known of Grey's westerns, a number of which are available in paperback. This one takes place in the wilderness of Utah in 1871.

2884 Heitzmann, Kristen. *Honor's Pledge* (8–12). 1997, Bethany paper $11.99 (0-7642-2031-4). Set in frontier America after the Civil War, this romance is about how, after a terrible storm, a kidnapping, encounters with local Comanches, and several deaths, Abbie finally gets the man she loves. (Rev: BL 5/1/98; VOYA 12/98)

2885 Holland, Cecelia. *The Bear Flag* (9–12). 1992, Kensington paper $5.99 (1-55817-635-7). A widow survives life on the American frontier in this novel about the race for settlement of California. (Rev: SLJ 8/90)

2886 Houston, James D. *Snow Mountain Passage* (10–12). 2001, Knopf $24.00 (0-375-41103-8). A gripping novel that reconstructs the drama and tragedy of the Donner party and its ill-fated trek west. (Rev: BL 4/1/01; SLJ 11/01)

2887 Kirkpatrick, Jane. *All Together in One Place* (10–12). 2000, WaterBrook paper $11.95 (1-57856-232-5). Faith and courage are key elements in this novel about pioneers on the Oregon Trail heading west in 1850. (Rev: BL 6/1–15/00*)

2888 Lawson, Julie. *Destination Gold!* (6–12). 2001, Orca $16.95 (1-55143-155-6). Ned, Catherine, and Sarah are all on their way to the Klondike in 1897, spurred by different motivations, but their stories all come together in an exciting climax, made more realistic by the background information and maps provided. (Rev: BCCB 4/01; BL 2/15/01; HBG 10/01; SLJ 7/01; VOYA 4/01)

2889 Laxalt, Robert. *Dust Devils* (6–10). 1997, Univ. of Nevada Pr. paper $16.00 (0-87417-300-0). A Native American teenager named Ira sets out to retrieve his prize-winning horse that has been stolen by a rustler named Hawkeye. (Rev: BL 10/15/97; VOYA 12/98)

2890 McClain, Margaret S. *Bellboy: A Mule Train Journey* (6–10). Illus. 1989, New Mexico $17.95 (0-9622468-1-6). Set in California in the 1870s, this is the story of a 12-year-old boy and his first job on a mule train. (Rev: BL 3/1/90; SLJ 3/90)

2891 McDonald, Brix. *Riding on the Wind* (5–10). 1998, Avenue paper $5.95 (0-9661306-0-X). In frontier Wyoming during the early 1860s, 15-year-old Carrie Sutton is determined to become a rider in the Pony Express after her family's ranch has been chosen as a relay station. (Rev: SLJ 1/99)

2892 McMurtry, Larry. *Boone's Lick* (10–12). 2000, Simon & Schuster $24.00 (0-684-86886-5). An excellent historical novel that takes place in the Old West during the second half of the 19th century and focuses on the fortunes and people of the Cecil family. (Rev: BL 9/15/00)

2893 McMurtry, Larry. *Lonesome Dove: A Novel* (9–12). 1985, Simon & Schuster $30.00 (0-671-50420-7); paper $7.99 (0-671-68390-X). Two former Texas Rangers head north from the Mexican border to find fame and fortune in this fine western novel.

2894 McMurtry, Larry. *Sin Killer* (10–12). 2002, Simon & Schuster $25.00 (0-7432-3302-6). A British family called the Berrybenders become involved with a frontier man of religion in this novel set on the Missouri River in 1832. (Rev: BL 4/1/02)

2895 Meyer, Carolyn. *Where the Broken Heart Still Beats: The Story of Cynthia Ann Parker* (7–12). 1992, Harcourt $16.95 (0-15-200639-7); paper $7.00 (0-15-295602-6). A fictional retelling of the abduction of Cynthia Parker, who was stolen by Comanches as a child and lived with them for 24 years, first as a slave, then as a chief's wife. (Rev: BL 12/1/92; SLJ 9/92)

2896 Moore, Robin. *The Bread Sister of Sinking Creek* (7–10). 1990, HarperCollins LB $14.89 (0-397-32419-7). An orphaned 14-year-old girl becomes a servant in Pennsylvania during pioneer days. (Rev: BL 7/90; SLJ 4/90; VOYA 8/90)

2897 Mosher, Howard Frank. *The True Account* (10–12). 2003, Houghton $24.00 (0-618-19721-4). The trials of exploration are exposed in comic manner in this story of an eccentric pair trying to beat Lewis and Clark to the Pacific, written in 19th-century style and featuring historical facts and characters. (Rev: BL 5/15/03; SLJ 9/03)

2898 Nesbitt, John D. *Twin Rivers* (9–12). 1995, Walker $28.95 (0-8027-4152-5). This western, set in the Wyoming countryside, involves Clay Westbrook, a wrangler who must fight a challenge to the claim he has filed for 160 acres of land, and the Mexican girl he loves. (Rev: BL 1/1–15/96; VOYA 6/96)

2899 Paine, Lauran. *Riders of the Trojan Horse* (9–12). 1991, Walker $30.95 (0-8027-4116-9). A brave stagecoach driver pursues thieves who have stolen his stagecoach and kidnapped the sheriff. (Rev: BL 7/91; SLJ 10/91)

2900 Portis, Charles. *True Grit* (7–12). 1995, NAL paper $5.50 (0-451-18545-5). A 14-year-old girl in the old West sets out to avenge her father's death.

2901 Riefe, Barbara. *Westward Hearts: The Amelia Dale Archer Story* (10–12). 1998, Forge $22.95 (0-312-86077-3). In the 1850s, Dr. Amelia Archer and her four granddaughters face hardships and danger as they travel by wagon trail west to Los Angeles, where she believes women have a chance to be recognized on their own merit. (Rev: SLJ 2/99)

2902 Rochlin, Harriet. *On Her Way Home* (10–12). Series: Desert Dwellers. 2001, Fithian $21.95 (1-56474-666-6). In this third volume of a trilogy set on the Arizona frontier in the 1880s, Frieda must care for her traumatized sister who has been made pregnant by a murderer. (Rev: BL 3/1/01)

2903 Schaefer, Jack. *Shane* (9–12). Illus. 1954, Houghton $18.00 (0-395-07090-2). A stranger enters the Starret household and helps them fight an oppressive land baron.

2904 Snelling, Lauraine. *An Untamed Land* (9–12). Series: Red River of the North. 1996, Bethany paper $9.99 (1-55661-576-0). This novel re-creates the experiences of the two Bjorklund brothers of Norway as they struggle to farm in the Dakota prairies, as told by the wife of the elder brother. (Rev: VOYA 8/96)

2905 Turner, Nancy E. *These Is My Words: The Diary of Sarah Agnes Prine, 1881–1902* (10–12). 1998, HarperCollins $23.00 (0-06-039225-8). A heartwarming and heartbreaking story, based on the author's family memoirs, about Sarah, who settles on a ranch in Tucson in the 1880s as an illiterate 17-year-old with her family and develops into an educated, determined, devoted wife and mother as she and her family encounter many hardships. (Rev: BL 2/15/98; SLJ 6/98)

2906 Watson, Jude. *Impetuous: Mattie's Story* (9–12). Series: Brides of Wildcat County. 1996, Simon & Schuster paper $3.99 (0-614-15784-6). In this title in the Brides of Wildcat County series, tomboy Mattie comes to Last Chance, a California mining town, as a mail-order bride but decides she wants to be independent upon discovering that she can do anything a man can do. (Rev: VOYA 6/96)

2907 Wheeler, Richard S. *Second Lives: A Novel of the Gilded Age* (10–12). 1997, Forge $24.95 (0-312-86330-0). A novel about ordinary people, their aspirations, failures, and fulfillments, in Denver during the late 1880s. (Rev: SLJ 4/98)

2908 Wister, Owen. *The Virginian* (10–12). 1988, Viking paper $10.95 (0-14-039065-0). The classic novel of the American West first published in 1902 and containing the phrase "When you call me that, smile."

RECONSTRUCTION TO WORLD WAR I (1865–1914)

2909 Alcott, Louisa May. *The Inheritance* (10–12). 1997, Dutton $18.00 (0-525-45756-9). This recently discovered novel was written by Alcott when she was only 17 and tells a rags-to-riches story of an orphan named Edith Adelon. (Rev: BL 2/15/97; SLJ 4/97)

2910 Armstrong, Jennifer. *Mary Mehan Awake* (6–10). 1997, Knopf $18.00 (0-679-88276-6). After the Civil War, Mary escapes the trauma the war caused by moving from Washington, D.C., to upstate New York, where she meets a deaf war veteran, Henry Till. A sequel to *The Dreams of Mairhe Mehan.* (Rev: BL 12/1/97; BR 3–4/98; SLJ 1/98)

2911 Auch, Mary Jane. *Ashes of Roses* (7–12). 2002, Holt $16.95 (0-8050-6686-1). Rose, a young immigrant from Ireland, suffers hardships that culminate in the Triangle Shirtwaist Factory fire in this fact-filled historical novel. (Rev: BCCB 7–8/02; BL 4/1/02; HBG 10/02; SLJ 5/02; VOYA 8/02)

2912 Bahr, Howard. *The Year of Jubilo* (10–12). 2000, Holt $25.00 (0-8050-5972-5). A former teacher returns to his Mississippi home after the Civil War and finds that he must right a terrible wrong that occurred in his absence. (Rev: BL 4/1/00)

2913 Burns, Olive Ann. *Cold Sassy Tree* (9–12). 1984, Ticknor $26.00 (0-89919-309-9). Fourteen-year-old Will has a crush on his grandfather's young bride in this novel set in turn-of-the-century Georgia. (Rev: BL 6/87)

2914 Carroll, Lenore. *One Hundred Girls' Mother* (10–12). 1998, Forge $24.95 (0-312-85994-5). An inspiring story, based on fact, about a mission director in San Francisco's Chinatown at the turn of the century and her efforts to save Chinese girls sold into slavery or prostitution. (Rev: BL 8/98; SLJ 11/98)

2915 Cohen, Paula. *Gramercy Park* (11–12). 2002, St. Martin's $24.95 (0-312-27552-8). Opera singer Mario Alfieri falls in love with frail, mysterious Clara in this romance set in 1890s New York City; for mature teens. (Rev: BL 1/1–15/02)

2916 Doctorow, E. L. *Ragtime* (10–12). 1994, Modern Library $16.95 (0-679-60088-4). Set in the early 20th century, this novel combines real people including Houdini and J. P. Morgan with fictional characters.

2917 Donnelly, Jennifer. *A Northern Light* (10–12). 2003, Harcourt $17.00 (0-15-216705-6). Set in upstate New York in 1906 against the backdrop of a murder that also inspired Dreiser's *An American Tragedy*, this story is about 16-year-old Mattie and the choice she must make between continuing her education and getting married. (Rev: BCCB 7–8/03; BL 5/15/04; HB 5–6/03; HBG 10/03; LMC 10/03; SLJ 5/03; VOYA 4/03)

2918 Durbin, William. *The Journal of Otto Peltonen: A Finnish Immigrant* (6–12). Illus. Series: My Name Is America. 2000, Scholastic paper $10.95 (0-439-09254-X). In a journal format, young Otto Peltonen describes his journey to America at the turn of the last century and his life in a Minnesota mining town. (Rev: BL 10/1/00; HBG 10/01; VOYA 12/00)

2919 Eidson, Tom. *All God's Children* (10–12). 1997, Dutton $23.95 (0-525-94235-1). A story of uplifting courage about a widowed Quaker woman raising four young sons in 1891 Kansas who faces the wrath of local rednecks when she takes a black fugitive and a family of poor Japanese immigrants into her home. (Rev: SLJ 1/98)

2920 Faulkner, William. *The Reivers: A Reminiscence* (10–12). 1962, Random paper $12.00 (0-679-74192-5). One of Faulkner's gentler novels, about an 11-year-old boy in small-town Mississippi in 1905.

2921 Ferber, Edna. *Show Boat* (9–12). 1994, NAL paper $5.95 (0-451-52600-7). The favorite novel about life on a Mississippi show boat and the romance between Magnolia and Gaylord Ravenal. Also use *So Big* and *Ice Palace*.

2922 Fitzgerald, F. Scott. *The Great Gatsby* (10–12). 1996, Simon & Schuster $25.00 (0-684-83042-6); paper $12.00 (0-684-80152-3). The emptiness of the Jazz Age is conveyed in this novel about the mysterious Jay Gatsby and his love for Daisy.

2923 Fitzwater, Marlin. *Esther's Pillow* (10–12). 2001, PublicAffairs $25.00 (1-58648-035-9). Set in Kansas in 1911, this is a story of how rumor and gossip change a young teacher's life. (Rev: BL 7/01; SLJ 10/01)

2924 Fletcher, Susan. *Walk Across the Sea* (6–10). 2001, Simon & Schuster $16.00 (0-689-84133-7). In spite of her father's dislike of immigrants, 15-year-old Eliza Jane helps a Chinese boy who rescued her and her goat in this story set in California in the late 19th century. (Rev: BCCB 12/01; BL 11/1/01; HBG 3/02; SLJ 11/01; VOYA 6/02)

2925 Forrester, Sandra. *My Home Is over Jordan* (7–10). 1997, Dutton $15.99 (0-525-67568-X). In this sequel to *Sound the Jubilee* (1995), the Civil War is over and Maddie and her family try to start life over in North Carolina, but some whites resent their intrusion. (Rev: BL 10/1/97; HBG 3/98; SLJ 12/97)

2926 Fuller, Jamie. *The Diary of Emily Dickinson* (9–12). 1993, Mercury House $18.00 (1-56279-048-X). This fictionalized diary combines Dickinson's poetry with made-up entries about her life, unrequited loves, relationship with her father, faith, and love of writing. (Rev: BL 9/15/93*)

2927 Gibbons, Kaye. *Charms for the Easy Life* (9–12). 1993, Putnam $19.95 (0-399-13791-2). Appealing characters and carefully selected period details make this intergenerational novel a delight. (Rev: BL 1/15/93; SLJ 9/93*)

2928 Goodger, Jane. *Gifts from the Sea* (9–12). 2001, Signet paper $5.99 (0-451-20478-6). In this historical romance, Rachel Best awaits her long-lost sailor husband at her home on Cape Cod but when she falls in love with a whaling captain, her feelings of loyalty to her husband are tested. (Rev: BL 12/1/01)

2929 Hale, Deborah. *Carpetbagger's Wife* (9–12). 2002, Silhouette paper $4.99 (0-373-29195-7). After the Civil War, Caddie Marsh returns to the family plantation where she receives some unexpected help from a Yankee stranger. (Rev: BL 11/15/01)

2930 Joinson, Carla. *A Diamond in the Dust* (6–10). 2001, Dial $17.99 (0-8037-2511-6). Sixteen-year-old Katy yearns to leave the confines of her Illinois mining town and make a life for herself in the big city in this novel set in the early 1900s. (Rev: HBG 10/01; SLJ 6/01; VOYA 8/01)

2931 Kline, Lisa Williams. *Eleanor Hill* (7–10). 1999, Front Street $15.95 (0-8126-2715-6). Set in the early 1900s, this is a story of 12-year-old Eleanor who is determined to escape from her small North Carolina town and see the world. (Rev: BCCB 1/00; BL 2/15/00; HBG 4/00; SLJ 2/00)

2932 Lafaye, Alexandria. *Edith Shay* (6–10). 1998, Viking $15.99 (0-670-87598-8). The story of a girl who decides to leave her 1860s Wisconsin settlement and find a new life for herself in Chicago. (Rev: BCCB 12/98; BL 10/15/98; BR 5–6/99; HBG 3/99; SLJ 10/98; VOYA 4/99)

2933 Lewin, Michael Z. *Cutting Loose* (9–12). 1999, Holt $23.95 (0-8050-6225-4). A complex, mature, historical novel about the early days of baseball, a girl who disguises herself as a man to play ball, and a murder that takes her to England. (Rev: BL 9/15/99; HB 9–10/99; HBG 4/00; SLJ 11/99)

2934 Lovelace, Merline. *The Captain's Woman* (11–12). 2003, MIRA paper $6.50 (1-55166-649-9). Set during the Spanish American War and featuring some key historical figures, this romance stars an intrepid young reporter, Victoria Parker, who follows her Rough Rider beau to Cuba and is inspired by the work of nurses there. (Rev: BL 2/1/03)

2935 Lowry, Lois. *The Silent Boy* (6–10). 2003, Houghton $15.00 (0-618-28231-9). Young Katy, who has a comfortable existence as a doctor's daughter in early-20th-century New England, makes friends with a mentally backward boy and learns that there are tragedies in life. (Rev: BL 4/15/03; HB 5–6/03; HBG 10/03; SLJ 4/03)

2936 McEachin, James. *Tell Me a Tale* (10–12). 1996, Lyford $18.95 (0-89141-584-X). Set in a small town in North Carolina at the beginning of Reconstruction, a young slave named Moses tells of his family's past to four old-timers who have stopped to listen to the youngster's tale. (Rev: SLJ 9/96)

2937 Marshall, Catherine. *Christy* (8–12). 1976, Avon paper $6.99 (0-380-00141-1). This story set in Appalachia in 1912 tells about a spunky young girl who goes there to teach. (Rev: BL 5/1/89)

2938 Miller, Linda Lael. *Courting Susannah* (10–12). 2000, Pocket $7.99 (0-671-00400-X). In this variation on the Jane Eyre story, Susannah travels to Seattle in 1906 to care for her deceased friend's child at the home of Aubrey, her friend's husband. (Rev: BL 9/15/00)

2939 Millett, Larry. *Sherlock Holmes and the Secret Alliance* (10–12). 2001, Viking $24.95 (0-670-03015-5). The fourth of a recommended series, this mystery novel, set in Minnesota in 1899, tells how Holmes and Watson are called in after a union activist is murdered. (Rev: BL 10/1/01)

2940 Morris, Lynn, and Gilbert Morris. *Toward the Sunrising* (10–12). 1996, Bethany paper $10.99 (1-55661-425-X). A complex novel about a feisty Yankee woman doctor, Cheney Duvall, and her struggles in Charleston, South Carolina, during Reconstruction. (Rev: SLJ 8/96; VOYA 10/96)

2941 Morrison, Toni. *Beloved: A Novel* (10–12). 1987, Vintage paper $10.40 (1-40003-341-1). This powerful novel deals with a runaway slave, Sethe, and the terrible past she has experienced.

2942 Peale, Cynthia. *Murder at Bertram's Bower: A Beacon Hill Mystery* (10–12). 2001, Doubleday $22.95 (0-385-49637-0). Set in Victorian Boston and full of historical detail, this tale of suspense describes the search for the perpetrator of two murders at a local home for wayward women. (Rev: BL 2/15/01; VOYA 8/01)

2943 Peterson, Tracie, and James Scott Bell. *City of Angels* (9–12). Series: Shannon Saga. 2001, Bethany paper $11.99 (0-7642-2418-2). Kathleen Shannon travels to Los Angeles in 1903 and, in spite of many obstacles, begins law studies. (Rev: BL 3/1/01; VOYA 12/01)

2944 Rinaldi, Ann. *Acquaintance with Darkness* (7–10). 1997, Harcourt $16.00 (0-15-201294-X). A coming-of-age historical novel about a 14-year-old girl living in Washington, D.C., who becomes involved in political intrigue after the assassination of Lincoln. (Rev: BL 9/15/97; HBG 3/98; SLJ 10/97; VOYA 2/98)

2945 Rinaldi, Ann. *The Coffin Quilt: The Feud Between the Hatfields and the McCoys* (6–10). 1999, Harcourt $16.00 (0-15-202015-2). The infamous Hatfield-McCoy feud is flamed into violence when a McCoy daughter elopes with a Hatfield in this novel set in the late 1800s in West Virginia/Kentucky. (Rev: BL 9/1/99; HBG 4/00; SLJ 5/00; VOYA 10/99)

2946 Schechter, Harold. *The Hum Bug* (10–12). 2001, Pocket $25.00 (0-671-04115-0). It is 1844 in New York City and a murder involves both P. T. Barnum and Edgar Allan Poe. (Rev: BL 10/1/01)

2947 Schmidt, Gary D. *Lizzie Bright and the Buckminster Boy* (7–12). 2004, Clarion $15.00 (0-618-43929-3). When Turner, son of a rigid minister, moves with his family to a small town in Maine during 1912, he doesn't fit in. (Rev: BL 5/15/04*; SLJ 5/04)

2948 Shivers, Louise. *A Whistling Woman* (9–12). 1993, Longstreet $15.00 (1-56352-085-0). Set in North Carolina after the Civil War, this novel examines the relationship between a mother and daughter. (Rev: BL 8/93*)

2949 Sinclair, Upton. *The Jungle* (10–12). 1981, Bantam paper $5.95 (0-553-21245-1). This frequently brutal novel tells about working in the Chicago stockyards at the turn of the 20th century.

2950 Skurzynski, Gloria. *Rockbuster* (6–12). 2001, Simon & Schuster $16.00 (0-689-83991-X). Tommy, a young coal miner and guitarist, becomes entangled in the labor movement in the early 20th century. (Rev: BCCB 2/02; BL 12/1/01; HBG 3/02; SLJ 12/01; VOYA 12/01)

2951 Smith, Betty. *A Tree Grows in Brooklyn* (9–12). 1943, Buccaneer LB $41.95 (0-89966-303-6). The touching story of Francie Nolan growing up in a poor section of Williamsburg in Brooklyn during the early 1900s.

2952 Stephens, C. A. *Stories from Old Squire's Farm* (10–12). 1995, Rutledge Hill $18.95 (1-55853-334-6). Written over 100 years ago, these 36 stories revolve around six cousins orphaned by the Civil War and their everyday life on Old Squire's farm in Maine. (Rev: SLJ 4/96)

2953 Taylor, Ardell L. D. *Whistling Girl* (10–12). 2001, Five Star $25.95 (0-7862-2854-7). In the 1880s, Anita Aldon, who lives on the family ranch in California, meets wealthy young John Vanderburg and love blossoms. (Rev: BL 12/15/00)

2954 Taylor, Mildred D. *The Land* (7–12). 2001, Penguin $17.99 (0-8037-1950-7). In this prequel to *Roll of Thunder, Hear My Cry* (1976), Taylor weaves her own family history into a moving story of a young man of mixed parentage facing prejudice, cruelty, and betrayal during the time of Reconstruction. (Rev: BCCB 10/01; BL 8/01; HB 9–10/01; HBG 3/02; SLJ 8/01; VOYA 10/01)

2955 Walker, Jim. *The Rail Kings* (9–12). 1995, Bethany paper $8.99 (1-55661-430-6). Undercover Wells Fargo agent Zac Cobb finds himself drawn into the no-holds-barred rivalry between two big railroad companies in the late 1800s, and must deal with kidnap attempts, nonstop fighting, and the love of the daughter of the president of one of the companies. (Rev: VOYA 4/96)

BETWEEN THE WARS AND THE GREAT DEPRESSION (1919–1941)

2956 Brooke, Peggy. *Jake's Orphan* (7–10). 2000, DK paper $16.99 (0-7894-2628-5). In 1926, 12-year-old Tree leaves his younger brother behind in the orphanage for a trial adoption with the Gunderson family in North Dakota. (Rev: BCCB 4/00; BL 4/1/00; HB 7–8/00; HBG 9/00; SLJ 6/00; VOYA 6/00)

2957 Earley, Tony. *Jim the Boy* (9–12). 2000, Little, Brown $23.95 (0-316-19964-8). A gentle, nostalgic story set in a small town in North Carolina in 1934 about a 10-year-old boy, his mother, and the three uncles who are raising him. (Rev: BL 5/1/00; VOYA 12/00)

2958 Ellison, Ralph. *Invisible Man* (10–12). 1994, Modern Library $19.95 (0-679-60139-2); paper $12.00 (0-679-73276-4). This acclaimed novel depicts the experiences of a single black man during the Depression.

2959 Garlock, Dorothy. *The Edge of Town* (10–12). 2001, Warner $19.95 (0-446-52769-6). In a small town in Missouri in the 1920s, Julie looks after her five younger siblings and begins dating a decorated veteran of the Great War. (Rev: BL 4/15/01)

2960 Hesse, Karen. *Out of the Dust* (6–12). 1997, Scholastic $15.95 (0-590-36080-9). In free verse, 15-year-old Billie Jo describes the tragedies that befall her family during the Dust Bowl years in Oklahoma. Newbery Medal, 1998. (Rev: HBG 3/98)

2961 Hesse, Karen. *Witness* (7–12). 2001, Scholastic paper $16.95 (0-439-27199-1). Hesse uses fictional first-person accounts in free verse to describe Ku Klux Klan activity in a 1924 Vermont town. (Rev: BCCB 11/01; BL 9/1/01; HB 11–12/01; HBG 3/02; SLJ 9/01*; VOYA 10/01)

2962 Kennedy, William. *Ironweed* (10–12). 1983, Viking paper $12.95 (0-14-007020-6). This novel, part of the author's Albany (NY) cycle, is a tale of skid-row life during the Depression.

2963 Kessler, Brad. *Lick Creek* (10–12). 2001, Scribner $24.00 (0-7432-0160-4). In 1920s West Virginia, Emily — a bitter, brassy woman — finds love with a lineman who is working on her property. (Rev: BL 1/1–15/01; VOYA 10/01)

2964 Knight, Arthur Winfield. *Johnnie D* (10–12). 2000, Tor $22.95 (0-312-86759-X). A fast-paced historical novel that deals with the last year in the life of legendary bank robber John Dillinger and with the social conditions in America during the Great Depression. (Rev: BL 3/15/00)

2965 Laskas, Gretchen Moran. *The Midwife's Tale* (10–12). 2003, Dial $23.95 (0-385-33551-2). In 1930s West Virginia, young Elizabeth regrets the loss of her innocent childhood as she trains for life as a midwife and learns the secrets of her neighbors. (Rev: BL 3/1/03)

2966 Laxalt, Robert. *Time of the Rabies* (7–12). 2000, Univ. of Nevada Pr. $16.00 (0-87417-350-7). Set in 1920s Nevada, this novella recalls a harrowing fight against a rabies epidemic. (Rev: VOYA 4/01)

2967 Lewis, Sinclair. *Elmer Gantry* (10–12). 1927, Harcourt paper $7.95 (0-451-52251-6). The story of a brazen ex-footballer who becomes a successful evangelist.

2968 McNichols, Ann. *Falling from Grace* (6–10). 2000, Walker $16.95 (0-8027-8750-9). In Prohibition-era Arkansas, 13-year-old Cassie is preoccupied by her sister's disappearance, her father's affair with the preacher's wife, and her growing feelings for an immigrant boy. (Rev: BL 10/15/00; BR 1–2/01; HBG 10/01; SLJ 11/00; VOYA 2/01)

2969 Marshall, Catherine. *Julie* (9–12). 1985, Avon paper $6.99 (0-380-69891-9). During the Depression, Julie and her family move to a small town in Pennsylvania where she finds fulfillment working on her father's newspaper.

2970 Myers, Anna. *Tulsa Burning* (8–10). 2002, Walker $16.95 (0-8027-8829-7). In 1921 Oklahoma, a 15-year-old boy helps an African American man who is injured during race riots. (Rev: BCCB 12/02; BL 10/1/02*; HBG 3/03; SLJ 9/02; VOYA 12/02)

2971 O'Sullivan, Mark. *Wash-Basin Street Blues* (7–10). 1996, Wolfhound paper $6.95 (0-86327-

467-6). In 1920s New York City, 16-year-old Nora is reunited with her two younger brothers but the reunion causes unforeseen problems. A sequel to *Melody for Nora* (1994). (Rev: BL 6/1–15/96)

2972 Peck, Robert Newton. *Horse Thief* (7–12). 2002, HarperCollins LB $16.89 (0-06-623792-0). In 1938, Tullis Yoder is determined to save 13 doomed rodeo horses in this entertaining cowboy tale. (Rev: BL 5/15/02; HBG 10/02; SLJ 7/02*; VOYA 8/02)

2973 Poupeney, Mollie. *Her Father's Daughter* (7–12). 2000, Delacorte $15.95 (0-385-32760-9). This is the story of Maggie's childhood in poverty with an alcoholic father during the years immediately preceding World War II. (Rev: BL 6/1–15/00; HBG 9/00; SLJ 7/00)

2974 Pratt, James Michael. *Ticket Home* (10–12). 2001, St. Martin's $23.95 (0-312-26633-2). The love between twin brothers is tested when they fall in love with the same woman in this novel that begins in Depression days in Oklahoma and ends during World War II. (Rev: BL 2/15/01)

2975 Reeder, Carolyn. *Moonshiner's Son* (7–10). 1993, Macmillan LB $14.95 (0-02-775805-2). It's Prohibition, and Tom, 12, is learning the art of moonshining from his father — until he becomes friendly with the new preacher's daughter. (Rev: BL 6/1–15/93; SLJ 5/93; VOYA 8/93)

2976 Robinet, Harriette G. *Mississippi Chariot* (6–10). 1994, Atheneum $14.95 (0-689-31960-6). Life in the 1930s Mississippi Delta is vividly evoked in this story of Shortning Bread, 12, whose father has been wrongfully convicted of a crime and sentenced to a chain gang. (Rev: BL 11/15/94; SLJ 12/94; VOYA 5/95)

2977 Steinbeck, John. *The Grapes of Wrath* (10–12). 1992, Viking paper $13.00 (0-14-018640-9). This 1939 classic tells of the odyssey of the Joad family from windswept Oklahoma to California.

2978 Steinbeck, John. *Of Mice and Men* (10–12). 1992, Demco $12.30 (0-606-00200-6). The friendship between two migrant workers — one a schemer and the other mentally deficient — is the subject of this short novel set in the Depression years.

2979 Thesman, Jean. *The Ornament Tree* (7–10). 1996, Houghton $16.00 (0-395-74278-1). Fourteen-year-old Bonnie moves into a boardinghouse run by her female relatives in Seattle in 1914, and through the years she adjusts to these strong-willed ladies and meets several interesting guests. (Rev: BL 5/1/96; BR 1–2/97; SLJ 3/96; VOYA 8/96)

POST WORLD WAR II UNITED STATES (1945–)

2980 Campbell, Bebe Moore. *Your Blues Ain't Like Mine* (10–12). 1992, Putnam $23.95 (0-399-13746-7); paper $6.99 (0-345-40112-3). Todd Armstrong, a 15-year-old African American boy from Chicago, is murdered in 1950s Mississippi in this compelling story about segregation. (Rev: BL 1/15/93; SLJ 1/93)

2981 Choi, Susan. *American Woman* (10–12). 2003, HarperCollins $24.95 (0-06-054221-7). Based on the Patty Hearst story, this is a novel of radical action and fugitives in the 1970s from the point of view of a young Japanese American woman. (Rev: BL 9/15/03)

2982 Collier, Kristi. *Jericho Walls* (6–10). 2002, Holt $16.95 (0-8050-6521-0). Preacher's kid Jo makes friends with an African American boy after her family moves to South Carolina in this story of racial tensions in the 1950s. (Rev: BL 4/1/02; HB 7–8/02; HBG 10/02; SLJ 4/02; VOYA 6/02)

2983 Crowe, Chris. *Mississippi Trial, 1955* (7–12). 2002, Penguin $17.99 (0-8037-2745-3). The story of the racist murder in 1955 of a 14-year-old black boy called Emmett Till is told through the eyes of Hiram, a white teenager. (Rev: BCCB 4/02; BL 2/15/02; HBG 10/02; SLJ 5/02; VOYA 4/02)

2984 Epstein, Leslie. *San Remo Drive* (10–12). 2003, Other $26.00 (1-59051-066-6). This story of Hollywood in the 1950s portrays young people growing up in the rarefied environment of filmmakers. (Rev: BL 5/15/03*)

2985 Guterson, David. *Snow Falling on Cedars* (10–12). 1994, Harcourt $21.95 (0-15-100100-6); paper $14.00 (0-679-76402-X). The murder trial of a Japanese American brings back memories of World War II and of young love between a journalist covering the trial and the accused's wife.

2986 Jones, Tayari. *Leaving Atlanta* (10–12). 2002, Warner $23.95 (0-446-52830-7). A moving novel about the impact on local children of the 1979 abductions and murders of 23 African American children in Atlanta. (Rev: BL 8/02)

2987 Kidd, Sue Monk. *The Secret Life of Bees* (10–12). 2002, Viking $24.95 (0-670-89460-5). In 1964 Lily, a white teenager haunted by her mother's death, and Rosaleen, an African American servant close to Lily, flee from Lily's abusive father and find refuge at a black-operated honey business in South Carolina. (Rev: BL 12/1/01; SLJ 5/02; VOYA 8/02)

2988 Matthews, Kezi. *Scorpio's Child* (7–10). 2001, Cricket $15.95 (0-8126-2890-X). In South Carolina in 1947, 14-year-old Afton has difficulty welcoming a taciturn, previously unknown uncle into her home despite her mother's pleas for compassion. (Rev: BCCB 10/01; BL 9/15/01; HB 1–2/02; HBG 3/02; SLJ 10/01; VOYA 4/02)

2989 Qualey, Marsha. *Too Big a Storm* (10–12). 2004, Dial $16.99 (0-8037-2839-5). In the 1960s, 18-year-old Brady is introduced into hippy lifestyles when she becomes friendly with Sally and Paul

Cooper, two rebellious young people. (Rev: BL 5/15/04; SLJ 7/04)

2990 Winegardner, Mark. *Crooked River Burning* (10–12). 2001, Harcourt $27.00 (0-15-100294-0). This engaging epic-length novel set in Cleveland, Ohio, during the 1950s and 1960s tells of two youngsters from opposite sides of the tracks and their troubled love story. (Rev: BL 1/1–15/01)

2991 Young, Karen Romano. *Outside In* (6–10). 2002, HarperCollins LB $16.89 (0-06-029368-3). Cherie, 12, is almost overwhelmed by the headlines of the newspapers she delivers daily in 1968. (Rev: BL 4/1/02; HBG 10/02; SLJ 5/02)

Twentieth-Century Wars

WORLD WAR I

2992 Breslin, Theresa. *Remembrance* (7–12). 2002, Delacorte LB $18.99 (0-385-90067-8). Francis, Charlotte, Maggie, and their friends and family find their lives drastically changed by World War I in this story of class differences, romance, loss, and bravery. (Rev: BL 12/15/02; HBG 3/03; SLJ 10/02; VOYA 12/02)

2993 Dugain, Marc. *The Officer's Ward* (10–12). Trans. by Howard Curtis. 2001, Soho Pr. $21.00 (1-56947-265-3). This French novel, set in World War I, tells of Lieutenant Fournier who is seriously wounded. (Rev: BL 11/15/01*)

2994 Hemingway, Ernest. *A Farewell to Arms* (10–12). 1997, Scribner $35.00 (0-684-83788-9). This love story set against the turmoil of World War I is considered to be one of Hemingway's finest works.

2995 Myers, Anna. *Fire in the Hills* (6–10). 1996, Walker $15.95 (0-8027-8421-6). In rural Oklahoma during World War I, 16-year-old Hallie takes care of her younger siblings after her mother's death and also tries to help a German family fight the prejudice of their neighbors. (Rev: BL 4/15/96*; BR 9–10/96; SLJ 4/96; VOYA 6/96)

2996 Wilson, John. *And in the Morning* (8–12). 2003, Kids Can $16.95 (1-55337-400-2). This absorbing story of fighting in the trenches of World War I, told in diary form by a teenage boy, is enhanced by newspaper headlines and clippings. (Rev: BL 3/15/03; HBG 10/03; SLJ 6/03)

WORLD WAR II AND THE HOLOCAUST

2997 Atlan, Lilane. *The Passersby* (9–12). Trans. by Rochelle Owens. Illus. 1993, Holt $13.95 (0-8050-3054-9). This prose poem depicts No, an anorexic teenager, who is searching for an ideal, purpose, and friends while confronted with the reality of her adopted brother's experiences in Auschwitz. (Rev: BL 12/1/93; SLJ 12/93; VOYA 2/94)

2998 Atlema, Martha. *A Time to Choose* (8–12). 1995, Orca paper $7.95 (1-55143-045-2). While growing up in Holland under the Nazi occupation, 16-year-old Johannes tries to separate himself from his father, who is considered a collaborator. (Rev: VOYA 10/97)

2999 Basu, Jay. *The Stars Can Wait* (10–12). 2002, Holt $21.00 (0-8050-6887-2). This coming-of-age novel involves a 15-year-old boy growing up in German-occupied Poland during the 1940s. (Rev: BL 12/1/01)

3000 Boulle, Pierre. *The Bridge over the River Kwai* (9–12). Trans. by Xan Fielding. 1954, Amereon $23.75 (0-89190-571-5). The thoughtful story of life in a Japanese prisoner-of-war camp and the building of a bridge that pits a British officer against his captors.

3001 Bradley, Kimberly Brubaker. *For Freedom: The Story of a French Spy* (6–12). 2003, Delacorte LB $17.99 (0-385-90087-2). This fascinating first-person novel about a young French girl who becomes a spy for the Resistance is based on a true story. (Rev: BL 4/1/03*; HB 7–8/03; HBG 10/03; SLJ 6/03; VOYA 6/03)

3002 Cavanaugh, Jack. *While Mortals Sleep* (10–12). Series: Songs in the Night. 2001, Bethany paper $11.99 (0-7642-2307-0). When a Christian minister is arrested by Nazis during an attempt to save disabled children from extermination, his timid wife Mady risks everything to rescue her husband. (Rev: BL 10/1/01; VOYA 6/02)

3003 Chan, Gillian. *A Foreign Field* (7–10). 2002, Kids Can $16.95 (1-55337-349-9). Friendship develops into love for 14-year-old Ellen and a young British pilot who is training at an air base near her home in Canada. (Rev: BCCB 12/02; BL 9/15/02; HBG 3/03; SLJ 11/02; VOYA 2/03)

3004 Cheng, Andrea. *Marika* (7–12). 2002, Front Street $16.95 (1-886910-78-2). Marika's earlier preoccupations disappear when the arrival of Nazis in 1944 Budapest changes her life. (Rev: BL 11/15/02; HB 11–12/02; HBG 3/03; SLJ 12/02; VOYA 2/03)

3005 Cookson, Catherine. *A Ruthless Need* (9–12). 2001, Center Point $29.95 (1-58547-066-X). During World War II, Geoff Fulton has a girlfriend named Janis, and then he meets Lizzie Gillespie and a love triangle begins. (Rev: BL 12/1/01)

3006 Craven, Margaret. *Walk Gently This Good Earth* (9–12). 1995, Buccaneer LB $21.95 (1-56849-646-X). The saga of an American family surviving the Depression and World War II.

3007 de Moor, Margriet. *Duke of Egypt* (10–12). Trans. by Paul Vincent. 2002, Arcade $24.95 (1-55970-546-9). A tragic but inspiring novel for mature readers that focuses on the persecution of the Gypsies in World War II and its aftermath. (Rev: BL 11/15/01)

3008 Disher, Gary. *The Divine Wind: A Love Story* (9–12). 2002, Scholastic $15.95 (0-439-36915-0). Racial prejudice, family tensions, and World War II interfere with the romance between Australian Hart and his Japanese immigrant girlfriend. (Rev: BL 5/15/03; HBG 10/02; SLJ 8/02; VOYA 8/02)

3009 Doughty, Louise. *Fires in the Dark* (11–12). 2004, HarperCollins $24.95 (0-06-057122-5). A tragic tale of a Gypsy family's fate during the Holocaust; for mature teens. (Rev: BL 11/15/03)

3010 Drucker, Malka, and Michael Halperin. *Jacob's Rescue: A Holocaust Story* (6–10). 1993, Dell paper $4.99 (0-440-40965-9). The fictionalized true story of two Jewish children saved from the Holocaust in Poland by "righteous Gentiles." (Rev: BL 2/15/93; SLJ 5/93)

3011 Dubis, Michael. *The Hangman* (10–12). 1998, Erica House paper $10.95 (0-9659308-6-6). The disturbing story of the Holocaust as experienced by Erik Byrnes, an SS officer whose assignment was to liquidate a ghetto outside of Vienna. (Rev: BL 12/15/98)

3012 Ellis, Virginia. *The Photograph* (11–12). 2003, Ballantine $22.95 (0-345-44484-1). This is the absorbing story of Maddy's life after the attack on Pearl Harbor, the day of her 17th birthday; suitable for mature readers. (Rev: BL 5/15/03)

3013 Follett, Ken. *Hornet Flight* (10–12). 2002, Dutton $26.95 (0-525-94689-6). In this tense story of danger during World War II, a trio of young people investigate a threat to British warplanes. (Rev: BL 11/15/02)

3014 Frank, Anne. *Anne Frank's Tales from the Secret Annex* (8–12). 1994, Bantam paper $4.50 (0-553-56983-X). This is a collection of all of Anne Frank's writings (apart from the diary, that is): stories, sketches, and fairy tales. [839.3]

3015 Frayn, Michael. *Spies* (11–12). 2002, Holt $23.00 (0-8050-7058-3). Keith and Stephen, sure that Keith's mother is a German spy, set out to uncover her secret in this story set during World War II; for mature teens. (Rev: BL 2/15/02)

3016 Friedman, Carl. *Nightfather* (9–12). Trans. by Arnold J. Pomerans and Erica Pomerans. 1994, Persea $18.50 (0-89255-193-3); paper $7.95 (0-89255-210-7). The daughter of a Dutch Holocaust survivor describes how her father's constant reliving of his experiences affected the whole family in this moving autobiographical novel. (Rev: BL 6/1–15/98; SLJ 1/95)

3017 Gardam, Jane. *The Flight of the Maidens* (10–12). 2001, Carroll & Graf $25.00 (0-7867-0879-4). A novel about the bittersweet time between high school and college as experienced by three girls in an English village during World War II. (Rev: BL 7/01)

3018 Gille, Elizabeth. *Shadows of a Childhood: A Novel of War and Friendship* (9–12). Trans. by Linda Coverdale. 1998, New Pr. $23.00 (1-56584-388-6). Based on fact, this novel traces the complex story of a Jewish girl in France who survived World War II as a Gentile and her subsequent search for truth and her own identity. (Rev: BL 1/1–15/98; VOYA 12/98)

3019 Greene, Bette. *Summer of My German Soldier* (10–12). 1973, Puffin paper $6.99 (0-14-130636-X). In World War II, Patty's family is not pleased when the young Jewish girl becomes involved with a German soldier who has escaped from a nearby Arkansas prison camp.

3020 Harlow, Joan Hiatt. *Shadows on the Sea* (7–10). 2003, Simon & Schuster $16.95 (0-689-84926-5). Fourteen-year-old Jill, staying with her grandmother in Maine in 1942, finds a pigeon carrying a message in German and suspects U-boats may be close. (Rev: BL 9/15/03; HBG 4/04; SLJ 9/03)

3021 Harris, Joanne. *Five Quarters of the Orange* (10–12). 2001, Morrow $25.00 (0-06-019813-3). A 65-year-old French woman recalls the World War II years in France, the Resistance movement, and why her family name is still despised in this novel by the author of *Chocolat*. (Rev: BL 3/1/01* ; SLJ 2/02)

3022 Harrison, Barbara. *Theo* (6–12). 1999, Clarion $15.00 (0-899-19959-3). In World War II Greece, Theo learns the meaning of heroism when he tries to save some of his fellow Jews from the Nazis. (Rev: BL 1/1–15/00; HB 11–12/99; HBG 4/00; SLJ 9/99)

3023 Heggen, Thomas. *Mister Roberts* (10–12). 1983, Buccaneer LB $16.95 (0-89966-445-8). The waste of war is one of the themes of this richly comic but also touching story of life on a supply ship during World War II.

3024 Heller, Joseph. *Catch-22* (10–12). 1995, Knopf $20.00 (0-679-43722-3). The much-praised World War II novel about the hypocrisy and stupidities that exist in our society.

3025 Hersey, John. *The Wall* (10–12). 1950, Knopf paper $17.00 (0-394-75696-7). A novel in diary form of a Jewish resident of the Warsaw Ghetto in World War II.

3026 Hertenstein, Jane. *Beyond Paradise* (6–10). 1999, Morrow $16.00 (0-688-16381-5). This historical novel recounts the horrors of life in Japanese internment camps in the Pacific during World War II as seen through the eyes of a missionary's daughter. (Rev: BCCB 9/99; BL 8/99; HBG 4/00; SLJ 9/99)

3027 Hesse, Karen. *Aleutian Sparrow* (7–12). 2003, Simon & Schuster $16.95 (0-689-86189-3). The unhappy story of the relocation of the Aleutian islanders during World War II is told in prose poetry from the perspective of young Vera. (Rev: BL 10/15/03; HBG 4/04; SLJ 10/03; VOYA 12/03)

3028 Holthe, Tess Uriza. *When the Elephants Dance* (10–12). 2002, Crown $24.95 (0-609-60952-1). This novel depicts the plight of the people caught between the Japanese invaders and the American troops in the Philippines during World War II. (Rev: BL 11/15/01; SLJ 4/02)

3029 Howard, Ellen. *A Different Kind of Courage* (7–12). 1996, Simon & Schuster $15.00 (0-689-80774-0). A complex novel about two youngsters from different parts of France and their perilous journey in 1940 to reach safety in the United States. (Rev: BL 9/15/96; SLJ 11/96)

3030 Huth, Angela. *Land Girls* (10–12). 1996, St. Martin's $23.95 (0-312-14296-X). This story, set in England during World War II, tells of three girls who become friends when they meet as Land Girls — volunteer workers who took the place of farm hands fighting in the war — on a small farm owned by the Lawrences. (Rev: SLJ 10/96)

3031 Isaacs, Anne. *Torn Thread* (6–12). 2000, Scholastic paper $15.95 (0-590-60363-9). Based on the author's mother-in-law's wartime experiences in World War II, this tells of Eva and her sister Rachel and their years in a Nazi labor camp for Jews in Czechoslovakia. (Rev: BL 3/1/00; HBG 9/00; SLJ 4/00; VOYA 4/00)

3032 Jackson, Mick. *Five Boys* (10–12). 2002, Morrow $24.95 (0-06-001394-X). A homesick young evacuee from London during World War II tries to adapt to his new surroundings and deal with the gang of boys who initially terrorize him. (Rev: BL 6/1–15/02; SLJ 12/02)

3033 Keneally, Thomas. *Schindler's List* (10–12). 1993, Simon & Schuster paper $12.00 (0-671-88031-4). A mature novel that is a fictionalized treatment of the life of the German industrialist who saved the lives of many Jews during World War II.

3034 Kerr, M. E. *Slap Your Sides* (7–10). 2001, HarperCollins $15.89 (0-06-029481-7). Pacifism during time of war is at the center of this novel about a Quaker family living in a small Pennsylvania town in the early 1940s. (Rev: BCCB 11/01; BL 10/1/01; HB 11–12/01; HBG 3/02; SLJ 10/01; VOYA 10/01)

3035 Kertesz, Imre. *Fateless* (9–12). Trans. by Christopher C. Wilson. 1992, Northwestern Univ. Pr. $58.95 (0-8101-1024-5); paper $14.95 (0-8101-1049-0). A Holocaust survival tale told from the viewpoint of a Hungarian Jewish teenager. (Rev: BL 9/15/92)

3036 Laird, Christa. *But Can the Phoenix Sing?* (7–10). 1995, Greenwillow $16.00 (0-688-13612-5). A Holocaust survivor story in which a young boy learns that cruelty and tenderness can reside at the same time in one person. (Rev: BL 11/15/95; SLJ 10/95)

3037 Levitin, Sonia. *Annie's Promise* (6–10). 1993, Atheneum $15.00 (0-689-31752-2); paper $4.99 (0-689-80440-7). Set near the end of World War II, this sequel to *Silver Days* focuses on 13-year-old Annie's break from her overprotective Jewish immigrant parents. (Rev: BCCB 3/93; BL 2/1/93; SLJ 4/93*)

3038 Levitin, Sonia. *Room in the Heart* (7–10). 2003, Dutton $16.99 (0-525-46871-4). Alternating characters in a multilayered novel show the Danes' assistance to Jews and resistance to the Nazis during World War II. (Rev: BL 11/1/03; HBG 4/04; SLJ 12/03; VOYA 2/04)

3039 McBride, James. *Miracle at St. Anna* (11–12). 2002, Riverhead $24.95 (1-57322-212-7). In World War II, four African American soldiers protect a young Italian victim of an atrocity. (Rev: BL 2/15/02)

3040 Manley, Joan B. *She Flew No Flags* (7–10). 1995, Houghton $16.00 (0-395-71130-4). A strongly autobiographical World War II novel about a 10-year-old's voyage from India to her new home in the United States and the people she meets on the ship. (Rev: BL 3/15/95; SLJ 4/95; VOYA 5/95)

3041 Matas, Carol. *Greater Than Angels* (7–10). 1998, Simon & Schuster paper $16.00 (0-689-81353-8). Although told in a somewhat confused manner, this is a gripping account of one of the Jewish children hidden from the Nazis in the French village of Le Chambon. (Rev: BCCB 7–8/98; BL 4/15/98; BR 1–2/99; HB 5–6/98; HBG 9/98; SLJ 6/98; VOYA 10/98)

3042 Matas, Carol. *In My Enemy's House* (7–10). 1999, Simon & Schuster paper $16.00 (0-689-81354-6). Marisa, 15, Jewish but Aryan-looking, assumes a new identity during World War II after her family and friends are killed by the Nazis in Poland. (Rev: BL 2/1/99; HBG 9/99; SLJ 3/99; VOYA 4/99)

3043 Mazer, Harry. *The Last Mission* (7–10). 1981, Dell paper $5.50 (0-440-94797-9). An underage Jewish American boy joins the Air Corps and is taken prisoner by the Germans. (Rev: BL 5/1/88)

3044 Melnikoff, Pamela. *Prisoner in Time: A Child of the Holocaust* (6–10). 2001, Jewish Publication Soc. paper $9.95 (0-8276-0735-0). Melnikoff combines history, fantasy, and Jewish legend in this story of 12-year-old Jan, in hiding from the Nazis in 1942 Czechoslovakia. (Rev: BL 10/1/01; SLJ 12/01)

3045 Melnyk, Eugenie. *My Darling Elia* (10–12). 1999, St. Martin's $23.95 (0-312-20565-1). A harrowing story, narrated decades later, of a Holocaust survivor's efforts to find his long-lost wife. (Rev: BL 5/15/99; SLJ 2/00)

3046 Michaels, Anne. *Fugitive Pieces* (10–12). 1997, Knopf $25.00 (0-679-45439-X). A novel about a survivor of the Holocaust, his memories of a peaceful past, and his life after he was smuggled out of Poland to Greece. (Rev: BL 2/15/97; SLJ 6/97)

3047 Michener, James A. *Tales of the South Pacific* (9–12). 1986, Macmillan paper $6.99 (0-449-20652-1). This volume contains 18 short stories about the life of servicemen in the South Pacific during World War II. Several formed the basis of the popular musical.

3048 Monsarrat, Nicholas. *The Cruel Sea* (9–12). 1988, Naval Institute Pr. $32.95 (0-87021-055-6). A novel that explores in human terms the war at sea during World War II.

3049 Nagorski, Andrew. *Last Stop Vienna* (10–12). 2003, Simon & Schuster $25.00 (0-7432-3750-1). This suspenseful exploration of what might have been follows the actions of Karl Naumann, a Nazi storm trooper who falls for Hitler's niece. (Rev: BL 11/15/02)

3050 Nolan, Han. *If I Should Die Before I Wake* (7–10). 1994, Harcourt $18.00 (0-15-238040-X). Teenager Hilary, who hangs out with neo-Nazis, is in a hospital after an accident. Next to her is a Holocaust survivor, Chana, and before Hilary regains consciousness, she slips into Chana's memory and travels back in time to Auschwitz. (Rev: BL 4/1/94; SLJ 4/94; VOYA 6/94)

3051 Orgel, Doris. *The Devil in Vienna* (7–10). 1978, Penguin paper $5.99 (0-14-032500-X). Two friends, one Jewish and the other the daughter of a Nazi, growing up in German-occupied Austria.

3052 Orlev, Uri. *The Man from the Other Side* (6–10). Trans. by Hillel Halkin. 1991, Houghton $16.00 (0-395-53808-4). The story of a teenager in Nazi-occupied Warsaw who helps desperate Jews despite his dislike of them. (Rev: BL 6/15/91*; SLJ 9/91*)

3053 Orlev, Uri. *Run, Boy, Run* (7–12). 2003, Houghton $15.00 (0-618-16465-0). A Polish boy survives the Holocaust by pretending to be a Catholic in this harrowing book full of historical detail. (Rev: BCCB 12/03; BL 10/15/03*; HB 11–12/03; HBG 4/04; SLJ 11/03; VOYA 12/03)

3054 Pausewang, Gudrun. *The Final Journey* (8–12). Trans. by Patricia Crampton. 1996, Puffin paper $5.99 (0-14-130104-X). The story of an 11-year-old Jewish girl and her horrifying train ride in a crowded freight car to a Nazi death camp. (Rev: BL 10/1/96; BR 3–4/97; VOYA 4/97)

3055 Peterson, Tracie. *Tidings of Peace* (10–12). 2000, Bethany paper $9.99 (0-7642-2291-0). Four novellas set during World War II explore stories of Christian faith, including a Jewish war veteran's conversion and the reawakening of faith in a pregnant teenage girl. (Rev: VOYA 6/01)

3056 Potok, Chaim. *Old Men at Midnight* (10–12). 2001, Knopf $23.00 (0-375-41071-6). The three novellas in this collection have the same character, Ilana Davita Dinn, but each deals with how warfare changes people, with many references to World War II, the Holocaust, and life in Stalin's Russia. (Rev: BL 9/15/01; SLJ 6/01)

3057 Pressler, Mirjam. *Malka* (6–10). Trans. by Brian Murdoch. 2003, Putnam $18.99 (0-399-23984-7). Escaping from the Nazis in Poland, a mother is forced to leave one daughter behind in this story based on truth that alternates between the difficult experiences of the anguished mother and the abandoned child. (Rev: BL 4/1/03; HB 5–6/03*; HBG 10/03; SLJ 5/03; VOYA 10/03)

3058 Ray, Karen. *To Cross a Line* (7–10). 1994, Orchard LB $16.99 (0-531-08681-X). The story of a 17-year-old Jewish boy who is pursued by the Gestapo and encounters barriers in his desperate attempts to escape Nazi Germany. (Rev: BL 2/15/94; SLJ 6/94; VOYA 6/94)

3059 Reuter, Bjarne. *The Boys from St. Petri* (7–10). Trans. by Anthea Bell. 1994, Dutton $15.99 (0-525-45121-8). Danish teenager Lars and his friends fight the Nazi occupation of their hometown during World War II and plan to blow up a train. (Rev: BL 2/1/94; SLJ 2/94; VOYA 4/94)

3060 Rylant, Cynthia. *I Had Seen Castles* (6–12). 1993, Harcourt $10.95 (0-15-238003-5). A strong message about the physical and emotional costs of war — in this story, the toll of World War II on John, a Canadian adolescent. (Rev: BL 9/1/93; VOYA 2/94)

3061 Sasson, Jean. *Ester's Child* (10–12). 2001, Windsor-Brooke $24.95 (0-9676737-3-9). The paths of families cross in this rich historical novel that moves from the Warsaw ghetto during World War II to postwar Palestine and Lebanon. (Rev: BL 8/01*; SLJ 3/02)

3062 Spinelli, Jerry. *Milkweed* (6–10). 2003, Knopf LB $17.99 (0-375-91374-2). A boy who is uncertain of his ethnic background and adopts the name of Misha struggles to survive in the Warsaw ghetto and is befriended by a generous family. (Rev: BCCB 11/03; BL 10/15/03*; HB 11–12/03; HBG 4/04; SLJ 11/03)

3063 Tamar, Erika. *Good-bye, Glamour Girl* (7–10). 1984, HarperCollins LB $12.89 (0-397-32088-4). Liesl and her family flee from Hitler's Europe and Liesl must now become Americanized. (Rev: BL 1/1/85)

3064 Tunnell, Michael O. *Brothers in Valor: A Story of Resistance* (6–10). 2001, Holiday $16.95 (0-8234-1541-4). Tunnell interweaves history and fiction in this account of three young Germans, members of the Mormon Church, who protest

Hitler's actions and put their own lives at risk. (Rev: BL 5/1/01; HBG 3/02; SLJ 6/01; VOYA 8/01)

3065 Twomey, Cathleen. *Beachmont Letters* (8–12). 2003, Boyds Mills $16.95 (1-59078-050-7). During World War II, 17-year-old Eleanor reaches out to a soldier through the letters that she writes him although she holds back those that deal with her own pain and suffering. (Rev: BL 3/1/03; HBG 10/03; SLJ 3/03)

3066 Uris, Leon. *Mila 18* (10–12). 1961, Bantam paper $7.99 (0-553-24160-5). A dramatic story involving the Warsaw Ghetto freedom fighters during World War II.

3067 Van Dijk, Lutz. *Damned Strong Love: The True Story of Willi G. and Stefan K.* (8–12). Trans. by Elizabeth D. Crawford. 1995, Holt $15.95 (0-8050-3770-5). Nazi persecution of homosexuals, based on the life of Stefan K., a Polish teenager. (Rev: BL 5/15/95; SLJ 8/95)

3068 Voigt, Cynthia. *David and Jonathan* (8–12). 1992, Scholastic paper $14.95 (0-590-45165-0). A Holocaust survivor darkens the life of his American cousin with gruesome stories of the prison camps. (Rev: BL 3/1/92; SLJ 3/92)

3069 Winter, Kathryn. *Katarina* (7–12). 1998, Scholastic paper $4.99 (0-439-09904-8). A gripping autobiographical novel about a Jewish orphan in hiding in Slovakia during World War II. (Rev: BCCB 3/98; BL 3/1/98; BR 11–12/98; SLJ 7/98)

3070 Wiseman, Eva. *My Canary Yellow Star* (8–12). Illus. 2002, Tundra paper $7.95 (0-88776-533-5). Marta Weisz's privileged life as the daughter of a wealthy Jewish surgeon comes to an abrupt end when Hitler invades Hungary, but her life is spared through the efforts of Raoul Wallenberg. (Rev: BL 1/1–15/02; SLJ 6/02)

3071 Wouk, Herman. *The Caine Mutiny* (10–12). 1992, Little, Brown paper $14.00 (0-316-95510-8). The story of the conflict between the men and the possibly unstable captain who sailed aboard the minesweeper *Caine*.

3072 Wouk, Herman. *The Winds of War* (10–12). 1992, Little, Brown paper $6.99 (0-316-95516-7). This novel traces the effects of the beginning of World War II on the family of Commander Pug Henry. A sequel is *War and Remembrance*.

3073 Wulffson, Don. *Soldier X* (8–12). 2001, Viking $15.99 (0-670-88863-X). After a battle in World War II, a 16-year-old German boy switches uniforms with a dead Russian in a desperate effort to survive. (Rev: BCCB 3/01; BL 5/1/01; HB 7–8/01; HBG 10/01; SLJ 3/01; VOYA 4/01)

3074 Yolen, Jane. *The Devil's Arithmetic* (7–12). 1988, Viking $15.99 (0-670-81027-4); Puffin paper $5.99 (0-14-034535-3). This time-warp story transports a young Jewish girl back to Poland in the 1940s, conveying the horrors of the Holocaust. (Rev: BL 9/1/88; BR 1–2/89; SLJ 11/88)

3075 Zindel, Paul. *The Gadget* (6–12). 2001, HarperCollins LB $15.89 (0-06-028255-X). Stephen has left London to live with his father who is on a secret scientific assignment in New Mexico — the Manhattan Project. (Rev: BL 1/1–15/01; HBG 10/01; SLJ 2/01; VOYA 8/01)

KOREAN, VIETNAM, AND OTHER WARS

3076 Brown, Don. *Our Time on the River* (7–10). 2003, Houghton $15.00 (0-618-31116-5). Two brothers learn more about each other on a canoe trip that precedes the older brother's departure to fight in Vietnam. (Rev: BL 4/1/03; HBG 10/03; SLJ 4/03)

3077 Choi, Sook N. *Echoes of the White Giraffe* (6–10). 1993, Houghton $16.00 (0-395-64721-5). Sookan, 15, struggles for independence within the restrictions of life in a refugee camp during the Korean War in this sequel to *Year of Impossible Goodbyes* (1991). (Rev: BL 4/1/93; SLJ 5/93; VOYA 8/93)

3078 Crist-Evans, Craig. *Amaryllis* (7–12). 2003, Candlewick $15.99 (0-7636-1863-2). Frank enlists to fight in Vietnam mainly to escape his alcoholic father's rages, and his younger brother is heartbroken when Frank becomes a heroin addict and then is listed as missing. (Rev: BL 11/1/03; HBG 4/04; SLJ 11/03; VOYA 12/03)

3079 Easton, Kelly. *The Life History of a Star* (7–10). 2001, Simon & Schuster $16.00 (0-689-83134-X). In the early 1970s, 14-year-old Kristin uses her journal as an outlet for her worries about her maturing body, her friends, her parents, and — most of all — her older brother, who has been wounded in Vietnam. (Rev: BCCB 3/01; BL 4/15/01; HBG 10/01; SLJ 7/01; VOYA 4/01)

3080 Hillerman, Tony. *Finding Moon* (9–12). 1996, HarperCollins paper $6.99 (0-06-109261-4). In Vietnam in 1975, Moon Mathias, a newspaper editor, searches for the daughter of his younger brother, who died in the war. (Rev: BL 9/15/95*)

3081 Hobbs, Valerie. *Sonny's War* (6–10). 2002, Farrar $16.00 (0-374-37136-9). Cory's world is in turmoil when her father dies and her older brother goes off to fight in Vietnam. (Rev: BCCB 11/02; BL 11/1/02; HB 11–12/02; HBG 3/03; SLJ 11/02*; VOYA 12/02)

3082 Karlin, Wayne, and Le Minh Khue, eds. *The Other Side of Heaven: Post-War Fiction by Vietnamese and American Writers* (10–12). 1995, Curbstone paper $17.95 (1-880684-31-4). A collection of short stories, many about the effects of the Vietnam War, written by Vietnamese and American writers. (Rev: BL 9/1/95; BR 3–4/96; SLJ 4/96)

3083 Michener, James A. *The Bridges at Toko-Ri* (9–12). 1953, Random $16.95 (0-394-41780-1); Fawcett paper $5.95 (0-449-20651-3). The story of a young navy pilot and his bombing missions over Korea during the early 1950s. (Rev: BL 10/1/88)

3084 Myers, Walter Dean. *Fallen Angels* (9–12). 1988, Scholastic $14.95 (0-590-40942-5). A 17-year-old black boy and his brutal but enabling experiences in the Vietnam War. (Rev: BL 4/15/88; BR 9–10/88; SLJ 6/88; VOYA 8/88)

3085 O'Brien, Tim. *Going After Cacciato* (10–12). 1999, Broadway paper $13.00 (0-7679-0442-7). In this surreal novel, Private Cacciato's company follows him when he leaves the Vietnam War to walk to Paris. For better readers.

3086 Porcelli, Joe. *The Photograph* (10–12). 1996, Wyrick & Co. $22.95 (0-941711-30-7). This autobiographical novel traces Joe's early years in Korea, his school years and military training in Charleston, South Carolina, his second rotation in Vietnam, during which he commanded an elite company of volunteers, and his lifelong search for his older brother, who disappeared after their parents were killed in the early days of Korea's civil war. (Rev: SLJ 11/96)

3087 Potok, Chaim. *I Am the Clay* (9–12). 1994, Fawcett paper $5.99 (0-449-22138-5). An injured orphan boy touches the hearts of a crusty Korean refugee and his more compassionate wife. (Rev: BL 4/1/92; SLJ 12/92)

3088 Poyer, David. *Black Storm* (10–12). 2002, St. Martin's $25.95 (0-312-26969-2). Dan Lenson finds plenty of action as he seeks to deactivate a bio-weapons plant in Baghdad during Desert Storm. (Rev: BL 5/1/02)

3089 Qualey, Marsha. *Come in from the Cold* (9–12). 1994, Houghton $16.00 (0-395-68986-4). In 1969, Maud, whose sister is killed while protesting the Vietnam War, and Jeff, whose brother dies fighting in it, are drawn together by mutual grief and hope. (Rev: BL 9/15/94; SLJ 12/94; VOYA 10/94)

3090 Rostkowski, Margaret I. *The Best of Friends* (7–12). 1989, HarperCollins $12.95 (0-06-025104-2). Three Utah teenagers have a growing interest in the Vietnam War and how it affects each of them. (Rev: BL 9/1/89; SLJ 9/89; VOYA 12/89)

3091 White, Ellen Emerson. *The Road Home* (8–12). 1995, Scholastic paper $15.95 (0-590-46737-9). This story re-creates a Vietnam War medical base in claustrophobic and horrific detail, and features army nurse Rebecca Phillips, from the Echo Company book series. (Rev: BL 1/15/95; SLJ 4/95; VOYA 4/95)

3092 White, Ellen Emerson. *Where Have All the Flowers Gone? The Diary of Molly MacKenzie Flaherty, Boston, Massachusetts, 1968* (7–10). Series:

Dear America. 2002, Scholastic paper $10.95 (0-439-14889-8). Fifteen-year-old Molly's brother is fighting in Vietnam, and she wrestles with pride, anxiety, and the antiwar sentiment around her. (Rev: BL 8/02; HBG 10/02; SLJ 7/02)

Horror Stories and the Supernatural

3093 Aiken, Joan. *A Fit of Shivers: Tales for Late at Night* (7–10). 1995, Bantam paper $4.50 (0-440-41120-3). Vengeful ghosts, eerie dreams, and haunted houses abound in these 10 tales. (Rev: BL 9/1/92)

3094 *Alfred Hitchcock's Supernatural Tales of Terror and Suspense* (7–10). Illus. 1973, Random paper $4.99 (0-394-85622-8). Horrifying tales by such masters as Patricia Highsmith and Raymond Chandler.

3095 Ambrose, David. *Superstition* (10–12). 1998, Warner $24.00 (0-446-52344-5). In a deadly experiment, eight people create the ghost of a fictitious person that, in time, seems to be responsible for the deaths of some of the participants. (Rev: SLJ 1/99)

3096 Anderson, M. T. *Thirsty* (7–12). 1997, Candlewick paper $6.99 (0-7636-2014-9). In addition to all kinds of family problems, Chris discovers that he is turning into a vampire. (Rev: BR 9–10/97; SLJ 3/97)

3097 Andrews, V. C. *Flowers in the Attic* (10–12). 1990, Pocket paper $7.50 (0-671-72941-1). This horror story about youngsters being held prisoners in an attic is long on horror but short on quality. Continued in *Petals on the Wind; If There Be Thorns;* and *Seeds of Yesterday.*

3098 Anthony, Piers. *Shade of the Tree* (10–12). 1987, Tor paper $3.95 (0-8125-3103-5). The horror mounts slowly as a New York man and his two children move into a deserted estate in Florida. (Rev: BL 3/15/86; VOYA 8/86)

3099 Asimov, Isaac, et al., eds. *Devils* (9–12). 1987, NAL paper $3.50 (0-451-14867-3). A devilish collection of stories drawn from such sources as folklore and tales of horror.

3100 Asimov, Isaac, et al., eds. *Tales of the Occult* (9–12). 1989, Prometheus paper $21.95 (0-87975-531-8). A collection of 22 stories that explore such subjects as telepathy and reincarnation. (Rev: BL 4/1/89)

3101 Atwater-Rhodes, Amelia. *Demon in My View* (6–10). 2000, Delacorte $9.95 (0-385-32720-X). Seventeen-year-old Jessica, who writes fiction about vampires and witches, finds her imagined world coming to life. (Rev: BR 11–12/00; HBG 9/00; SLJ 5/00)

3102 Atwater-Rhodes, Amelia. *In the Forests of the Night* (7–12). 1999, Delacorte $8.95 (0-385-32674-2). In this story written by a 13-year-old author, Risika, a 300-year-old vampire, takes revenge against Aubrey, another vampire and her age-old enemy, when Aubrey threatens to harm Risika's only friend, Tora, a Bengal tiger in a zoo. (Rev: BL 6/1–15/99; HBG 9/99; SLJ 7/99; VOYA 8/99)

3215 Baldick, Chris, ed. *The Oxford Book of Gothic Tales* (9–12). 1992, Oxford paper $16.95 (0-19-286219-7). There are 37 stories by such masters as Poe, Hardy, Faulkner, and Hawthorne in this collection of gothic stories, many of which involve the supernatural.

3103 Barker, Clive. *The Thief of Always* (10–12). 1997, HarperCollins paper $4.50 (0-06-105769-X). Ten-year-old Harvey Swick is bored, but he soon learns that entertainment can come at a high price when a mysterious stranger offers a trip to the magical Holiday House.

3104 Bedard, Michael. *Painted Devil* (7–10). 1994, Atheneum $15.95 (0-689-31827-8). A girl helping to renovate an old puppet theater discovers that the vicious-looking devil puppet has evil powers. (Rev: BL 3/1/94; SLJ 4/94; VOYA 6/94)

3105 Belkom, Edo Van, ed. *Be Afraid! Tales of Horror* (8–12). 2000, Tundra $6.95 (0-88776-496-7). Fifteen horror stories for and about teens feature sinister twists, hauntings, and violence. (Rev: BL 2/1/01; SLJ 3/01; VOYA 2/01)

3106 Buffie, Margaret. *The Dark Garden* (6–10). 1997, Kids Can $16.95 (1-55074-288-4). Thea, who suffers from amnesia after an accident, begins hearing voices, one of which belongs to a young woman who died tragically years before. (Rev: BL 10/15/97; BR 1–2/98; HBG 3/98; SLJ 10/97)

3107 Bunting, Eve. *The Presence: A Ghost Story* (6–10). 2003, Clarion $15.00 (0-618-26919-3). Catherine, 17, who is still grieving over the death of a friend, finds solace in a handsome young man but at the same time senses that something isn't quite right. (Rev: BL 10/15/03; HBG 4/04; SLJ 10/03; VOYA 2/04)

3108 Butcher, Jim. *Death Masks* (11–12). 2003, NAL paper $6.99 (0-451-45940-7). Harry Dresden's diverse friends band together to help him in this exciting adventure involving flight from vampires and the theft of the Shroud of Turin. (Rev: BL 7/03)

3109 Cabot, Meg. *Haunted* (7–10). Series: The Mediator. 2003, HarperCollins LB $16.89 (0-06-029472-8). In this fifth installment in The Mediator series (earlier volumes were published under the pseudonym Jenny Carroll), Susannah falls for teen "mediator" Paul Slater, who has just joined her school. (Rev: BL 3/1/03; HBG 10/03; SLJ 1/03; VOYA 4/03)

3110 Campbell, Ramsey. *The Darkest Part of the Woods* (11–12). 2003, Tor $24.95 (0-765-30766-9). A forest that is home to hallucinogenic mushrooms and to a more ancient threat is at the center of this effective horror novel suitable for mature teens. (Rev: BL 9/1/03)

3111 Campbell, Ramsey. *Silent Children* (10–12). 2000, Tor $24.95 (0-312-87056-6). For horror fans, this novel tells of the disappearance of two young children and the suspicion that a maniac, supposedly dead, may be responsible. (Rev: BL 6/1–15/00; VOYA 12/00)

3112 Card, Orson Scott. *Homebody: A Novel* (10–12). 1998, HarperCollins $24.00 (0-06-017655-5). A supernatural novel about a man who unleashes spirits from the past when he begins restoring a faded Southern mansion. (Rev: SLJ 8/98; VOYA 8/98)

3113 Card, Orson Scott. *Lost Boys* (10–12). 1993, Morrow paper $6.99 (0-06-109131-6). After a Mormon family, the Fletchers, moves to North Carolina, son Stevie starts to develop imaginary friends whose names mysteriously match those of children who have disappeared from the community. (Rev: BL 8/92)

3114 Carroll, Jenny. *Darkest Hour* (7–10). Series: The Mediator. 2001, Simon & Schuster paper $4.99 (0-671-78847-7). Suze's ability to communicate with ghosts comes in handy as a skeleton turns up in her backyard and she falls for a phantom called Jesse. (Rev: SLJ 4/02)

3115 Cerf, Bennett, ed. *Famous Ghost Stories* (10–12). 1956, Amereon LB $24.95 (0-88411-146-6). This is a superior anthology of truly scary stories.

3117 Cooney, Caroline B. *Night School* (7–10). 1995, Scholastic paper $3.50 (0-590-47878-8). Four California teens enroll in a mysterious night school course and encounter an evil instructor and their own worst character defects. (Rev: BL 5/1/95)

3118 Cox, Michael, and R. A. Gilbert. *The Oxford Book of English Ghost Stories* (9–12). 1987, Oxford paper $14.95 (0-19-282666-2). Dated from the 1820s through the 1980s, this is a scary collection of 42 stories of the supernatural.

3119 Cray, Jordan. *Gemini 7* (6–10). 1997, Simon & Schuster paper $4.50 (0-689-81432-1). In this horror story, Jonah Lanier begins to realize that his new friend, Nicole, might be responsible for the mysterious disasters that are befalling his family and other friends. (Rev: SLJ 1/98)

3120 Cuddon, J. A., ed. *The Penguin Book of Ghost Stories* (9–12). 1985, Penguin paper $13.95 (0-14-006800-7). A collection of 33 spine-tinglers by English, American, and European authors. (Rev: BL 7/85)

3121 Cusick, Richie Tankersley. *The House Next Door* (6–12). 2002, Simon & Schuster paper $4.99 (0-7434-1838-7). Emma dares to spend a night in a haunted house and becomes caught up in a struggle to free a spirit from the past in this tale of supernatural suspense. (Rev: BL 1/1–15/02; SLJ 2/02; VOYA 6/02)

3122 Datlow, Ellen, ed. *The Year's Best Fantasy and Horror: Tenth Annual Collection* (9–12). 1997, St. Martin's paper $17.95 (0-312-15701-0). A collection of horror and fantasy stories, some gripping, others stomach churning. (Rev: BL 9/1/97; VOYA 6/98)

3123 Dimartino, Nick. *Seattle Ghost Story* (10–12). Illus. 1998, Rosebriar paper $12.95 (0-9653918-2-5). A horror story in which Billy Beck accidentally unleashes a deadly ghost that brings havoc to his quiet neighborhood. (Rev: SLJ 1/99)

3124 Doyle, Arthur Conan. *The Best Supernatural Tales of Arthur Conan Doyle* (10–12). 1979, Dover paper $8.95 (0-486-23725-7). A group of 15 ghost stories by this master of suspense.

3126 Du Maurier, Daphne. *Echoes from the Macabre: Selected Stories* (9–12). 1977, Aeonian $25.95 (0-88411-543-7). Nine stories of suspense including the classic "The Birds".

3127 Duncan, Lois. *Locked in Time* (7–10). 1985, Dell paper $4.99 (0-440-94942-4). Nore's father marries into a family that somehow never seems to age. (Rev: BL 7/85; BR 9–10/85; SLJ 11/85)

3128 Duncan, Lois, ed. *Night Terrors: Stories of Shadow and Substance* (6–12). 1996, Simon & Schuster paper $16.00 (0-689-80346-X). An anthology of 11 horror/supernatural stories by such popular writers as Joan Aiken, Chris Lynch, and Norma Fox Mazer. (Rev: BL 5/15/96; BR 1–2/97; SLJ 6/96; VOYA 8/96)

3129 Duncan, Lois. *Stranger with My Face* (7–10). 1984, Dell paper $5.50 (0-440-98356-8). A girl encounters her evil twin who wishes to take her place.

3130 Duncan, Lois. *Summer of Fear* (7–10). 1976, Dell paper $5.50 (0-440-98324-X). An orphaned cousin who comes to live with Rachel's family is really a witch.

3131 Durant, Alan, ed. *Vampire and Werewolf Stories* (5–10). Illus. Series: Kingfisher Story Library. 1998, Kingfisher paper $6.95 (0-7534-5152-2). Eighteen stories, many written originally for an adult audience, make up this classic Gothic horror anthology about vampires and werewolves. (Rev: BL 1/1–15/99)

3132 Edgerton, Leslie H., ed. *Monday's Meal* (10–12). 1997, Univ. of North Texas Pr. paper $14.95 (1-57441-026-1). A collection of 21 unique, often gruesome, horror stories, many of which are set in the French Quarter of New Orleans. (Rev: SLJ 1/98)

3133 Ellis, Sarah. *Back of Beyond Stories* (6–10). 1997, Simon & Schuster $15.00 (0-689-81484-4). Each of the 12 stories in this collection begins with real-world problems but soon slips into the realm of the supernatural. (Rev: BL 1/1–15/98; HBG 3/98; SLJ 11/97*; VOYA 12/97)

3125 Elrod, P. N., ed. *Dracula in London* (10–12). 2001, Berkley paper $14.95 (0-441-00858-5). This is a collection of stories that take place in the same era as the original Bram Stoker novel. (Rev: BL 11/15/01; VOYA 4/02)

3134 Etchemendy, Nancy. *Cat in Glass: And Other Tales of the Unnatural* (8–12). 2002, Cricket $15.95 (0-8126-2674-5). Eight spooky and suspenseful stories will captivate brave readers. (Rev: BL 11/15/02; HBG 3/03; SLJ 12/02; VOYA 4/03)

3138 Etchison, Dennis, et al., eds. *Gathering the Bones: Original Stories from the World's Masters of Horror* (11–12). 2003, Tor paper $15.95 (0-765-30179-2). This collection of widely diverse horror fiction from the United States, Britain, and Australia is suitable only for mature readers. (Rev: BL 8/03)

3135 Forrest, Elizabeth. *Killjoy* (10–12). 1996, DAW paper $5.99 (0-88677-695-3). A horror thriller about three outsiders who are being pursued because one of them has in his possession a mysterious power that can create zombies. (Rev: VOYA 8/96)

3136 Gabhart, Ann. *Wish Come True* (7–10). 1988, Avon paper $2.50 (0-380-75653-6). Lyssie receives as a gift a mirror that grants her wishes. (Rev: VOYA 6/89)

3137 Garretson, Jerri. *The Secret of Whispering Springs* (7–12). 2002, Ravenstone paper $6.99 (0-9659712-4-4). A ghost and a mysterious stranger alert Cassie to potential danger, and a potential fortune, in this suspenseful adventure. (Rev: BL 8/02; SLJ 8/02)

3139 Gifaldi, David. *Yours Till Forever* (7–10). 1989, HarperCollins LB $13.89 (0-397-32356-5). In this easily read novel, a high school senior sees disturbing similarities between his friends and his dead parents. (Rev: BL 10/1/89; SLJ 11/89; VOYA 2/90)

3140 Golden, Christopher. *The Ferryman* (11–12). 2002, NAL paper $6.99 (0-451-20581-2). Disdain for the ferryman Charon in a near-death experience seems to be the catalyst for a series of frightening supernatural events; for mature teens. (Rev: BL 5/15/02)

3141 Golden, Christopher. *The Gathering Dark* (11–12). Series: Shadow. 2003, Berkley paper $6.99 (0-441-01081-4). A hair-raising and violent fourth installment of this tense saga full of vampires and demons. (Rev: BL 7/03; VOYA 6/04)

3142 Goldstein, Lisa. *The Alchemist's Door* (10–12). 2002, Tor $23.95 (0-765-30150-4). A Prague rabbi and a British alchemist fleeing a demon join together in a battle against evil in this rich tale full of historical detail about the 1580s. (Rev: BL 6/1–15/02*; VOYA 6/03)

3143 Gorog, Judith. *Please Do Not Touch* (6–12). 1995, Scholastic paper $3.50 (0-590-46683-6). The reader enters a different fantasy for each of the 11 horror stories. (Rev: BL 9/1/93; VOYA 12/93)

3144 Gorog, Judith. *When Nobody's Home* (6–12). 1996, Scholastic paper $15.95 (0-590-46862-6). A collection of 15 terrifying (supposedly true) tales on the theme of baby-sitting. (Rev: BL 5/1/96; BR 9–10/96; SLJ 4/96; VOYA 12/96)

3145 Greenberg, Martin H. *Miskatonic University* (10–12). 1996, DAW paper $5.99 (0-88677-722-4). These horror stories, not for the faint of heart, involve a university where spell casting and prophesy are taught and strange events occur in its underground tunnels and cellars. (Rev: VOYA 6/97)

3146 Hahn, Mary D. *Look for Me by Moonlight* (7–10). 1995, Clarion $16.00 (0-395-69843-X). A 16-year-old girl seeking friendship meets a boy whose attention has dangerous strings attached. (Rev: BL 3/15/95; SLJ 5/95)

3147 Hambly, Barbara. *Traveling with the Dead* (9–12). 1995, Ballantine $22.00 (0-345-38102-5). In this sequel to *Those Who Hunt the Night* (1988), a retired British intelligence officer discovers an Austrian spymaster who can command the services of the undead as well as the living. (Rev: BL 9/15/95; SLJ 6/96; VOYA 4/96)

3148 Hambly, Barbara, and Martin H. Greenberg, eds. *Sisters of the Night* (9–12). 1995, Warner paper $17.99 (0-446-67143-6). Fourteen original stories by such masters as Jane Yolan, Tanith Lee, and Larry Niven explore the world of the female vampire. (Rev: VOYA 4/96)

3149 Hamilton, Virginia. *Sweet Whispers, Brother Rush* (7–10). 1982, Putnam $21.99 (0-399-20894-1). A 14-year-old girl who cares for her older retarded brother meets a charming ghost who reveals secrets of her past.

3150 Hartwell, David G., ed. *The Screaming Skull and Other Great American Ghost Stories* (10–12). 1995, Tor $4.99 (0-812-55178-8). A collection of 12 high-quality ghost stories by such writers as Edgar Allan Poe, F. Marion Crawford, Mark Twain, Nathaniel Hawthorne, Willa Cather, and Edith Wharton. (Rev: VOYA 4/96)

3151 Hawes, Louise. *Rosey in the Present Tense* (8–12). 1999, Walker $15.95 (0-8027-8685-5). After the death of his girlfriend, Rosey, 17-year-old Franklin can't stop living in the past until the ghost of Rosey and his family and friends help him accept his loss and begin to think of the present. (Rev: BL 4/1/99; BR 9–10/99; HBG 9/99; SLJ 5/99; VOYA 10/99)

3152 Hendee, Barb, and J. C. Hendee. *Dhampir,* (11–12). 2003, NAL paper $5.99 (0-451-45906-7). Suitable for mature teens only, this is the story of Magiere and her companion Leesil, who is half elf, and their initially fraudulent but later for-real battles against vampires. (Rev: BL 1/1–15/03)

3153 Hendee, Barb, and J. C. Hendee. *Thief of Lives* (9–12). 2004, NAL paper $6.99 (0-451-45953-9). Magiere, a half-human-half-vampire female, is pressured to hunt down a vampire who has killed a councilman's daughter. (Rev: BL 1/1–15/04)

3154 Hill, Mary, ed. *Creepy Classics: Hair-Raising Horror from the Masters of the Macabre* (6–10). 1994, Random paper $4.99 (0-679-86692-2). Gothic horror stories, poems, and novel excerpts by masters of the genre, including selections from Poe and an excerpt from Shelley's *Frankenstein*. (Rev: BL 10/15/94; SLJ 11/94)

3155 Holder, Nancy. *Buffy the Vampire Slayer: The Book of Fours* (9–12). 2001, Pocket $22.95 (0-7434-1240-0). Plenty of action and fun can be found in this supernatural romp based on the hit TV series. (Rev: BL 2/15/01; VOYA 10/01)

3157 Huntington, Geoffrey. *Sorcerers of the Nightwing* (7–10). Series: Ravenscliff. 2002, Regan $17.95 (0-06-001425-3). Magic and mystery abound in this horror story featuring a young teenager with superpowers who is a sorcerer in the Order of the Nightwing. (Rev: BL 8/02; SLJ 10/02; VOYA 2/03)

3158 Jackson, Shirley. *The Haunting of Hill House* (9–12). 1984, Penguin paper $11.95 (0-14-007108-3). Four people decide to stay in Hill House to see if it is really haunted.

3159 Jackson, Shirley. *The Lottery* (8–12). 1949, Farrar paper $14.00 (0-374-51681-2). Macabre stories by this master that include the classic about a village and its horrifying annual tradition. (Rev: BL 9/1/97)

3201 Jones, Stephen, ed. *The Mammoth Book of Best New Horror.* v. 14 (11–12). 2003, Carroll & Graf paper $11.95 (0-7867-1217-6). Chilling tales by Ramsey Campbell, Neil Gaiman, and Stephen Gallagher are among those in this year's selection; for mature teens. (Rev: BL 11/1/03)

3202 Jones, Stephen, ed. *The Mammoth Book of Vampire Stories by Women* (10–12). Series: Mammoth. 2001, Carroll & Graf paper $11.95 (0-7867-0918-9). This is an excellent collection of vampire tales written over the years by women. (Rev: BL 11/15/01)

3160 Kelleher, Victor. *Del-Del* (7–12). Illus. 1992, Walker $17.95 (0-8027-8154-3). A family believes its son is possessed by an evil alien. (Rev: BL 3/1/92; SLJ 6/92)

3161 Kiernan, Caitlin R. *Threshold* (10–12). 2001, Roc $14.00 (0-451-45858-3). Her life disintegrating before her eyes, paleontology student Chance Matthews joins a strange albino named Dancy in a mission to seek out and destroy monsters; for mature teens. (Rev: BL 10/1/01; VOYA 4/02)

3162 King, Stephen. *Carrie* (10–12). 1974, Doubleday $29.95 (0-385-08695-4); NAL paper $4.95 (0-451-15071-6). Carrie, a teenager with telekenetic powers, takes horrible revenge on her tormentors.

3163 King, Stephen. *Christine* (9–12). 1983, Viking $4.99 (0-670-22026-4); NAL paper $7.99 (0-451-16044-4). Arnie buys an old Plymouth that has mystical powers to possess and destroy.

3164 King, Stephen. *Cujo* (10–12). 1981, NAL paper $7.99 (0-451-16135-1). This is a horror story about a huge Saint Bernard that runs amok.

3165 King, Stephen. *The Dead Zone* (9–12). 1979, NAL paper $7.99 (0-451-15575-0). A number of men named John Smith find themselves in the strange area known as The Dead Zone.

3166 King, Stephen. *Different Seasons* (10–12). 1998, NAL paper $7.99 (0-451-19712-7). Four short stories by this master of suspense and mystery.

3167 King, Stephen. *Dreamcatcher* (10–12). 2001, Scribner $28.00 (0-7432-1138-3). An ailing stranger stumbles into a hunting camp and explodes, releasing a monster that may herald an alien invasion. (Rev: BL 3/1/01)

3168 King, Stephen. *Everything's Eventual: 14 Dark Tales* (9–12). 2002, Scribner $28.00 (0-7432-3515-0). Fourteen horror stories by King with an introduction about the genre from the author.

3169 King, Stephen. *Firestarter* (9–12). 1980, NAL paper $7.99 (0-451-16780-5). A child is born with the incredible power to start fires.

3170 King, Stephen. *Four Past Midnight* (10–12). 1990, Viking paper $7.99 (0-451-17038-5). This book contains four horror stories bound to please those who enjoy chills with their reading.

3171 King, Stephen. *Night Shift* (10–12). 1978, Doubleday $30.00 (0-385-12991-2); paper $5.95 (0-451-16045-2). Vampires and demons inhabit these horror stories by a master of the macabre. (Rev: BL 10/15/88)

3172 King, Stephen. *Nightmares and Dreamscapes* (9–12). 1993, Viking paper $27.50 (0-670-85108-6). A collection of short stories, including pastiches of Doyle and Chandler, a vampire story, and a sports story. (Rev: BL 7/93*)

3173 King, Stephen. *Pet Sematary* (10–12). 1983, Doubleday $30.00 (0-385-18244-9); NAL paper $4.95 (0-451-15775-3). The frightening horror story about a family that moves next to an ancient Indian burial ground.

3174 King, Stephen. *The Shining* (10–12). 1977, Doubleday $27.50 (0-385-12167-9); NAL paper $7.99 (0-451-16091-6). The Torrances take over a deserted hotel that is haunted by the spirits of the dead.

3175 King, Stephen. *Skeleton Crew* (9–12). 1985, Putnam paper $7.99 (0-451-16861-5). This is a collection of King's short fiction.

3176 King, Stephen. *The Stand* (10–12). Illus. 1990, Doubleday $45.00 (0-385-19957-0). This mammoth volume (over 1,100 pages) restores all the cuts made in the original 1978 edition. (Rev: BL 3/15/90)

3177 King, Stephen, and Peter Straub. *Black House* (10–12). 2001, Random $28.95 (0-375-50439-7). A horror story involving a serial killer from a parallel world who is murdering young children, dismembering them, and cannibalizing them. (Rev: BL 9/1/01)

3178 Klause, Annette Curtis. *Blood and Chocolate* (9–12). 1997, Delacorte $16.95 (0-385-32305-0); paper $4.99 (0-440-22668-6). Vivian, 16, is a lonely werewolf when she moves to a new school and she hopes that Aiden, a human boy, can learn to love her. (Rev: BL 6/1/97; BR 1/98; HB 7/97; HBG 3/98; SLJ 8/97*; VOYA 8/97)

3179 Klause, Annette Curtis. *The Silver Kiss* (8–12). 1992, Bantam paper $5.50 (0-440-21346-0). A teenage girl, beset with personal problems, meets a silver-haired boy who is a vampire in this suspenseful, sometimes gory, novel. (Rev: BL 10/15/90; SLJ 9/90)

3180 Klein, Robin. *Tearaways* (6–10). 1991, Viking $12.95 (0-670-83212-X). This short-story collection combines shivery horror with laughter. (Rev: BL 6/15/91; SLJ 6/91)

3181 Koontz, Dean. *Odd Thomas* (10–12). 2003, Bantam $26.95 (0-553-80249-6). Odd Thomas, a 20-year-old fry cook in a California desert town, sees dead people — and talks to them too, unique gifts he uses to help track down the killers. (Rev: BL 12/15/03; SLJ 5/04)

3182 Koontz, Dean. *Phantoms* (10–12). 1983, Berkley paper $7.99 (0-425-10145-2). A quiet town in California is gradually being consumed by a beast from the past in this horror story.

3183 Koontz, Dean. *Strangers* (10–12). 1986, Berkley paper $7.99 (0-425-11992-0). In this somewhat complex novel eight unrelated characters share the same terrible fears and anxieties. (Rev: BL 3/1/86; VOYA 8/86)

3184 Krinard, Susan. *To Catch a Wolf* (11–12). 2003, Berkley Sensation paper $6.99 (0-425-19208-3). A crippled Denver socialite and a circus freak have more in common than is apparent in this novel about werewolves and acceptable forms of behavior. (Rev: BL 9/15/03)

3185 Kupfer, Allen C. *The Journal of Professor Abraham Van Helsing* (9–12). Illus. 2004, Tor $19.95 (0-765-31011-2). Val Helsing travels back to his native Romania where he has an encounter with a deadly vampiress known as Malia. (Rev: BL 3/1/04)

3186 Kurtz, Katherine, and Deborah T. Harris. *The Lodge of the Lynx* (9–12). Series: Adept. 1992, Berkley paper $6.99 (0-441-00344-3). Black magic and the occult are investigated by a would-be detective and his assistant. (Rev: BL 5/15/92; SLJ 9/92)

3187 Lebbon, Tim. *Face* (11–12). 2002, Night Shade $25.00 (1-892389-19-3). After the Powell family picks up a hitchhiker, he begins to intrude on their lives in this tense and frightening story that includes sex and violence. (Rev: BL 1/1–15/02)

3188 Levin, Ira. *Rosemary's Baby* (10–12). 1997, NAL paper $6.99 (0-451-19400-4). Rosemary is pregnant and under the increased influence of witchcraft.

3189 Levy, Elizabeth. *The Drowned* (9–12). 1995, Hyperion $16.95 (0-7868-0135-2). A supernatural thriller with a demented mother who ritually drowns a teenager and a drowned victim who returns to life. (Rev: BL 12/1/95; SLJ 12/95)

3190 Littke, Lael. *Haunted Sister* (7–10). 1998, Holt $16.95 (0-8050-5729-3). After a near-death experience, Janine becomes involved with the ghost of her dead twin sister, who in time inhabits Janine's spirit and body. (Rev: BCCB 10/98; BL 10/1/98; HBG 9/99; SLJ 10/98; VOYA 2/99)

3191 Lovecraft, H. P. *The Case of Charles Dexter Ward* (10–12). 1987, Ballantine paper $0.05 (0-345-35490-7). Charles discovers he has inherited the powers of witchcraft. Also use: *At the Mountains of Madness and Other Tales of Terror* (1985).

3192 Lovecraft, H. P. *The Horror in the Museum* (9–12). 1996, Carroll & Graf paper $4.95 (0-7867-0387-3). A collection of Lovecraft's collaborations with other authors. (Rev: VOYA 6/97)

3193 Lumley, Brian. *The Source* (9–12). 1998, Tor $26.95 (0-312-86764-6); paper $6.99 (0-8125-2127-7). In this, the third volume of the Necroscope series, scientists find in the Ural mountains the entrance to a world where vampires and other horrible creatures live. (Rev: VOYA 2/90)

3194 Lumley, Brian. *The Whisperer and Other Voices* (10–12). 2001, Tor $24.95 (0-312-87695-5). This is a collection of creepy horror tales by one of the masters. (Rev: BL 12/15/00)

3195 Lutzen, Hanna. *Vlad the Undead* (9–12). 1998, Groundwood $15.95 (0-88899-341-2). A haunting novel, told in a series of manuscripts, letters, and diary entries, that deals with the Dracula legend and Lucia, a Danish medical student who becomes the Romanian Vlad Dracula. (Rev: SLJ 3/99)

3196 MacDonald, Caroline. *Hostilities: Nine Bizarre Stories* (7–10). 1994, Scholastic paper $13.95 (0-590-46063-3). A collection of nine tales with strange, unsettling themes and Australian locales. (Rev: BL 1/15/94; SLJ 3/94; VOYA 10/94)

3197 McKinley, Robin. *Sunshine* (10–12). 2003, Berkley $23.95 (0-425-19178-8). Captured by vampires, Rae "Sunshine" Seddon uses her own magic to save herself and an out-of-favor vampire. (Rev: BL 10/15/03; VOYA 12/03)

3198 McNally, Clare. *Stage Fright* (9–12). 1993, Tor paper $5.99 (0-812-54839-6). Years after her lover and best friend were murdered, Hayley Seagel discovers that their ghosts have returned to help her and her friends fight a malevolent ghost. (Rev: VOYA 2/96)

3199 McNeil, W. K., ed. *Ghost Stories from the American South* (9–12). Illus. 1985, August House paper $9.95 (0-935304-84-3). A collection of bloodcurdlers from locales ranging from Virginia to Texas. (Rev: SLJ 12/85)

3200 Mahy, Margaret, and Susan Cooper. *Don't Read This! And Other Tales of the Unnatural* (7–10). 1998, Front Street $15.95 (1-886910-22-7). Great stories of ghosts and the supernatural are included in this international collection that represents some of the top writers of scary fiction at work today. (Rev: BL 4/1/99; BR 9–10/99; HBG 9/99; SLJ 7/99; VOYA 6/99)

3203 Martin, Valerie. *Mary Reilly* (9–12). 1996, Pocket paper $5.99 (0-671-52113-6). A retelling of Stevenson's classic horror story from the standpoint of Dr. Jekyll's maid. (Rev: BL 12/1/89)

3204 Masterton, Graham. *Swimmer* (10–12). 2002, Severn $25.99 (0-7278-5697-9). A child's drowning moves teacher Jim Rook to discover that the culprit is in an evil spirit that takes its form in water. (Rev: BL 12/15/01)

3205 Matheson, Richard. *Nightmare at 20,000 Feet* (11–12). 2002, Tor $24.95 (0-765-30411-2); paper $14.95 (0-312-87827-3). Fourteen classic spine-chilling horror stories vary in theme; for mature teens. (Rev: BL 2/1/02)

3206 Mertz, Stephen. *Night Wind* (10–12). 2002, Five Star $26.95 (0-7862-4353-8). Robin and her son flee her abusive husband only to find themselves in an even worse situation in this gripping tale of horror and romance with a touch of the mystic. (Rev: BL 9/1/02)

3207 Michaels, Barbara. *Other Worlds* (10–12). 1999, HarperCollins $23.00 (0-06-019235-6). A group of experts on the occult, among them Sir Arthur Conan Doyle and Harry Houdini, listen to two famous folktales about poltergeists and hauntings and then venture their ideas concerning what really happened and why. (Rev: SLJ 7/99)

3208 Moon, Russell. *Witch Boy* (11–12). Series: Witch Boy Trilogy. 2002, HarperTempest paper $6.95 (0-06-440795-0). Marcus's suspicions that he has supernatural powers are encouraged by his new friends in this novel, which includes explicit sexual scenes; sequels are *Dark Prince* and *Blood War*. (Rev: BCCB 9/02; BL 4/15/02; SLJ 5/02; VOYA 6/02)

3209 Moore, Michael Scott. *Too Much of Nothing* (11–12). 2003, Carroll & Graf paper $13.00 (0-7867-1196-5). Eric, a ghost seeking a confrontation with his killer, reflects on his former life as a teenager. (Rev: BL 8/03)

3210 Moser, Barry, ed. *Great Ghost Stories* (7–12). Illus. 1998, Morrow $24.99 (0-688-14587-6). A collection of 13 effective and well-illustrated ghost stories by established and less-familiar authors. (Rev: BL 11/15/98; HBG 3/99; SLJ 10/98; VOYA 2/99)

3211 Mosiman, Billie Sue. *Malachi's Moon* (11–12). 2002, DAW paper $6.99 (0-7564-0048-1). Vampire worlds collide and half-vampire Malachi finds himself in danger in this thrilling sequel to *Red Moon Rising* (2000); for mature teens. (Rev: BL 1/1–15/02; VOYA 8/02)

3213 Nixon, Joan Lowery. *The Haunting* (6–10). 1998, Doubleday $15.95 (0-385-32247-X). Anne is determined to rid Graymoss, an old mansion, of ghosts so that her mother can convert it into a home for unwanted children. (Rev: BL 7/98; HB 11–12/98; HBG 3/99; SLJ 8/98; VOYA 12/98)

3214 Nixon, Joan Lowery. *Whispers from the Dead* (7–12). 1991, Bantam paper $4.99 (0-440-20809-2). After being saved from drowning, Sarah is able to communicate with dead spirits. (Rev: BL 9/15/89; BR 11–12/89; SLJ 9/89; VOYA 12/89)

3116 Pelan, John, and Benjamin Adams, eds. *The Children of Cthulhu: Chilling New Tales Inspired by H. P. Lovecraft* (10–12). 2002, Del Rey $23.95 (0-345-44926-6). A collection of horror stories, often dark and disgusting, that are not for the squeamish. (Rev: BL 12/15/01)

3216 Pepper, Dennis, ed. *The New Young Oxford Book of Ghost Stories* (6–12). Illus. 1999, Oxford $22.95 (0-19-278154-5). Many of the 23 stories in this scary collection are new to print. (Rev: BL 10/15/99; HBG 4/00)

3212 Phillips, Robert, ed. *Nightshade: 20th Century Ghost Stories* (9–12). 1999, Carroll & Graf $25.00 (0-7867-0614-7); paper $14.00 (0-7867-0808-5). Well-known authors including Isak Dinesen, Elizabeth Bowen, and Gabriel Garcia Marquez are represented in this collection of 27 tales of ghosts and the supernatural. (Rev: BL 5/15/99)

3217 Pierce, Meredith Ann. *The Darkangel* (10–12). 1998, Harcourt paper $6.00 (0-15-201768-2). In this vampire story, Airiel tries to rescue the fiend's brides.

3218 Pike, Christopher. *Bury Me Deep* (6–10). 1991, Pocket paper $4.50 (0-671-69057-4). A scuba-diving vacation in Hawaii turns into an adventure involving murder, ghosts, and underwater thrills. (Rev: BL 9/1/91)

3219 Pike, Christopher. *Last Vampire* (10–12). 1994, Archway paper $5.99 (0-671-87264-8). A 5,000-year-old vampire named Alisa, fleeing from a hunter, befriends a high school boy.

3220 Pike, Christopher. *Scavenger Hunt* (9–12). 1990, Pocket paper $3.99 (0-671-73686-8). Two groups of teenagers on a scavenger hunt encounter horror that leads to a terrifying climax. Also use: *Remember Me* (1989). (Rev: BL 9/1/89; VOYA 2/90)

3221 Pines, T., ed. *Thirteen: 13 Tales of Horror by 13 Masters of Horror* (8–12). 1991, Scholastic paper $4.99 (0-590-45256-8). Popular horror writers' stories of revenge, lust, and betrayal. (Rev: BL 3/1/92)

3222 Pockell, Leslie, ed. *The 13 Best Horror Stories of All Time* (10–12). 2002, Warner paper $13.95 (0-446-67950-X). Classic tales including Poe's "Tell-Tale Heart" and LeFanu's "Green Tea." (Rev: BL 8/02)

3223 Poe, Edgar Allan. *The Pit and the Pendulum and Other Stories* (6–12). Illus. Series: Whole Story. 1999, Viking $25.99 (0-670-88706-4). This handsome collection of Poe's mystery stories is enhanced with striking illustrations, historical notes, sidebars, and material about the author's life and times. (Rev: BL 12/1/99; HBG 4/00)

3224 Pratchett, Terry. *Carpe Jugulum* (10–12). Series: Discworld. 1999, HarperCollins $24.00 (0-06-105158-6). King Verence regrets his decision to invite the Magpyr family to Lancre to celebrate his daughter's birth. (Rev: SLJ 4/00; VOYA 2/00)

3225 Preussler, Otfried. *The Satanic Mill* (7–10). 1987, Peter Smith $26.50 (0-8446-6196-1). A young apprentice outwits a strange magician in this fantasy first published in 1972. (Rev: BL 6/1–15/98)

3226 Price, Susan, ed. *Horror Stories* (6–12). 1995, Kingfisher paper $7.95 (1-85697-592-4). Two dozen Halloween read-alouds from such writers as Joan Aiken, Stephen King, Edgar Allan Poe, and John Steinbeck. (Rev: BL 10/15/95)

3227 Prill, David. *Dating Secrets of the Dead* (11–12). 2002, Subterranean $35.00 (1-931081-60-3). Humor and horror meld in the three offerings in this slim volume; for mature teens. (Rev: BL 8/02)

3229 Rice, Anne. *Interview with the Vampire* (10–12). 1986, Ballantine paper $7.99 (0-345-33766-2). A

200-year-old vampire reveals every horrifying detail of his life. Rice has written other horror novels involving vampires.

3230 Roberts, Nora. *River's End* (10–12). 1999, Putnam $23.95 (0-399-14470-6). When she was only 4, Olivia saw a monster with her father's face kill her mother, and now, years later, the vision resurfaces when a young writer contacts her about the murder. (Rev: BL 1/1–15/99; SLJ 9/99)

3231 Ryan, Alan, ed. *Haunting Women* (9–12). 1988, Avon paper $3.95 (0-380-89881-0). Fourteen horror stories written by such women as Shirley Jackson and Ruth Rendell. (Rev: BL 11/15/88; VOYA 2/89)

3232 Saberhagen, Fred. *A Sharpness on the Neck* (10–12). 1996, Tor $23.95 (0-312-85799-3). In this novel that switches between the French Revolution and today, contemporary newlyweds in the western United States are kidnapped by Vlad Dracula to protect them from Vlad's evil brother, Radu Dracula. (Rev: BL 11/15/97; VOYA 4/97)

3233 Saul, John. *Black Creek Crossing* (10–12). 2004, Ballantine $25.95 (0-345-43332-7). Thirteen-year-old Angel and her family move into a haunted house but a witch's spirit shows Angel how she can defeat her foes. (Rev: BL 2/15/04)

3234 Saul, John. *Comes the Blind Fury* (9–12). 1990, Dell paper $6.99 (0-440-11475-6). An antique doll actually contains the evil spirit of a dead girl. Also use *Cry for the Strangers* (1986), *Suffer the Children,* and *When the Wind Blows.*

3235 Saul, John. *Midnight Voices* (11–12). 2002, Ballantine $25.95 (0-345-43331-9). Nail-biting suspense results when Caroline remarries and moves with her two children and new husband into an exclusive apartment building; are there unseen residents? (Rev: BL 5/1/02)

3236 Shepard, Leslie, ed. *The Dracula Book of Great Horror Stories* (10–12). 1977, Citadel $10.00 (0-8065-0565-6). Thirteen old-fashioned but still chilling horror stories.

3237 Shusterman, Neal. *Full Tilt* (6–10). 2003, Simon & Schuster $16.95 (0-689-80374-5). A suspenseful drama in which 16-year-old Blake must tackle frightening rides at a mysterious carnival and face his own worst fears in order to save his daredevil older brother Quinn. (Rev: BCCB 9/03; BL 5/15/03; HB 7–8/03; HBG 10/03; SLJ 6/03; VOYA 10/03)

3238 Shusterman, Neal. *Scorpion Shards* (8–12). 1996, Tor paper $5.99 (0-8125-2465-9). A horror story in which six misfits and outsiders must face and exorcise the monsters that dwell within them. (Rev: BL 2/1/96; SLJ 3/96; VOYA 4/96)

3156 Silver, Steven H., and Martin H. Greenberg, eds. *Horrible Beginnings* (11–12). 2003, DAW paper $6.99 (0-7564-0123-2). A collection of first-published horror stories by well-known writers in the genre; suitable for mature readers. (Rev: BL 2/1/03)

3239 Slott, Dan, et al. *Arkham Asylum: Living Hell* (10–12). Illus. 2004, DC Comics paper $12.95 (1-4012-0193-8). Horror and humor are combined in this story of a person who is caught in a stock fraud, and is committed to a nightmarish institution called Arkham Asylum. (Rev: BL 4/1/04*)

3240 Smith, L. J. *Night World: Secret Vampire* (9–12). 1996, Pocket paper $3.99 (0-671-55133-7). Faced with certain death from cancer, teenage Poppy accepts an invitation from a friend to become a vampire. (Rev: BL 8/96; VOYA 8/96)

3241 Soto, Gary. *The Afterlife* (7–10). 2003, Harcourt $16.00 (0-15-204774-3). After he is stabbed to death, 17-year-old Chuy lingers long enough to watch the reactions of family and friends while getting to know some other ghosts. (Rev: BL 8/03*; HB 11–12/03; HBG 4/04; SLJ 11/03; VOYA 2/04)

3242 Spruill, Steven. *Daughter of Darkness* (10–12). 1997, Doubleday $22.95 (0-385-48432-1). A haunting novel about hemophages, humans with a genetic defect that requires them to feed on human blood to survive. (Rev: BL 5/15/97; SLJ 12/97)

3243 Starkey, Dinah, ed. *Ghosts and Bogles* (5–10). Illus. 1987, David & Charles $17.95 (0-434-96440-9). A collection of 16 British ghost stories, each nicely presented with illustrations. (Rev: SLJ 9/87)

3244 Stevens, Brooke. *Tattoo Girl* (10–12). 2001, St. Martin's paper $12.95 (0-312-26910-2). This horror novel for older teens tells the story of a girl covered in tattooed fish scales and the people who murder to find her. (Rev: BL 3/15/01)

3228 Thomsen, Brian, and Martin H. Greenberg, eds. *The Repentant* (11–12). 2003, DAW paper $6.99 (0-7564-0163-1). The beneficent side of witches and vampires and their like is explored in the stories in this collection that nonetheless contains a fair amount of violence; for mature teens. (Rev: BL 10/15/03)

3245 Tiernan, Cate. *Sweep: Book of Shadows* (8–12). Series: Sweep. 2001, Penguin paper $4.99 (0-14-131046-4). Morgan isn't interested in witchcraft until she meets Cal, a high school senior who is a Wiccan and who draws Morgan into his world. (Rev: BL 2/15/01)

3246 Vande Velde, Vivian. *Being Dead* (7–10). 2001, Harcourt $17.00 (0-15-216320-4). A collection of seven chilling stories about death and the supernatural. (Rev: BCCB 9/01; BL 9/1/01; HB 11–12/01; HBG 3/02; SLJ 9/01; VOYA 12/01)

3247 Vande Velde, Vivian. *Companions of the Night* (7–10). 1995, Harcourt $17.00 (0-15-200221-9). A 16-year-old finds herself caught in a life-and-death chase after she helps an injured young man who may be a vampire. (Rev: BL 4/1/95; SLJ 5/95)

3248 Vande Velde, Vivian. *Never Trust a Dead Man* (7–12). 1999, Harcourt $17.00 (0-15-201899-9). A witch helps Selwyn escape the death penalty for a murder he didn't commit and, with the help of the ghost of the dead man, he solves the mystery. (Rev: BL 4/1/99; BR 9–10/99; HB 5–6/99; HBG 9/99; SLJ 5/99; VOYA 8/99)

3249 Wallace, Rich. *Restless: A Ghost's Story* (8–12). 2003, Viking $15.99 (0-670-03605-6). Sports and the supernatural take center stage in 17-year-old Herbie's life after he becomes aware of a ghostly being on a run through a graveyard. (Rev: BL 9/15/03; HBG 4/04; SLJ 11/03; VOYA 10/03)

3250 Westall, Robert. *Shades of Darkness: More of the Ghostly Best Stories of Robert Westall* (7–12). 1994, Macmillan paper $11.95 (0-330-35318-7). Eleven eerie tales, not the guts-and-gore variety of supernatural fiction but haunting and insightful stories. (Rev: BL 4/15/94; SLJ 5/94; VOYA 8/94)

3251 Westwood, Chris. *Calling All Monsters* (7–12). 1993, HarperCollins LB $14.89 (0-06-022462-2). Joanne is a huge fan of a horror writer, so when she starts seeing nightmare creatures from his books, she recognizes them. (Rev: BL 6/1–15/93; SLJ 7/93; VOYA 12/93)

3252 Wilson, F. Paul. *Midnight Mass* (10–12). 2004, Tor $25.95 (0-765-30705-7). Vampires are rapidly taking over the planet in this horror story with lots of violence; for mature readers. (Rev: BL 4/15/04*)

3253 Windsor, Patricia. *The Blooding* (9–12). 1996, Scholastic $15.95 (0-590-43309-1). A horror story that involves a young American girl in England, the death of a woman in whose house she is living, and the menace of werewolves. (Rev: BR 1–2/97; SLJ 12/96; VOYA 4/97)

3254 Yarbro, Chelsea Quinn. *In the Face of Death* (9–12). 2004, BenBella paper $14.95 (1-932100-29-6). In this novel that blends, fantasy, history, and romance, a vampire named Madelaine leaves her home in London to travel to the U.S. to write a book about Indians in the mid-1800s. (Rev: BL 4/15/04)

3255 Yashinsky, Dan, ed. *Ghostwise: A Book of Midnight Stories* (7–12). 1997, August House $11.95 (0-87483-499-6). A collection of 35 short but chilling stories of the supernatural and ghosts. (Rev: BCCB 3/98; VOYA 2/98)

3256 Young, Richard, and Judy Dockery Young. *Ozark Ghost Stories* (6–12). 1995, August House paper $12.95 (0-87483-410-4). Spooky Ozark stories are the focus of this horror anthology, including old favorites and less-well-known jokes and tales. (Rev: BL 6/1–15/95)

3257 Zindel, Paul. *The Doom Stone* (6–10). 1995, Hyperion paper $4.95 (0-7868-1157-9). A slimy,

truly evil creature stalks the moors and inhabits the mind of the protagonist's aunt. (Rev: BL 12/15/95; SLJ 12/95; VOYA 4/96)

3258 Zindel, Paul. *Loch* (7–10). 1994, Harper-Collins LB $15.89 (0-06-024543-3). Lovable, though human-eating, creatures trapped in a Vermont lake become prey for a ruthless man. (Rev: BL 11/15/94; SLJ 1/95; VOYA 4/95)

Humor

3259 Anderson, M. T. *Burger Wuss* (7–10). 1999, Candlewick paper $6.99 (0-7636-1567-6). In this funny novel, Anthony gets a job at a hamburger joint and battles his archrival and the fast-food franchise with the help of an activist co-worker. (Rev: BL 11/15/99)

3260 Boffa, Alessandro. *You're an Animal, Viskovitz* (10–12). Trans. by John Casey and Maria Sanminiatelli. 2002, Knopf $18.00 (0-375-40528-3). This satirical novel follows Viskovitz through a number of animal reincarnations, documenting his romantic failures in each. (Rev: BL 5/15/02)

3261 Burnham, Niki. *Royally Jacked* (8–10). 2004, Simon & Schuster paper $5.99 (0-689-86668-2). Valerie, a 15-year-old product of divorce accompanies her father to live in a castle in Europe in this lively, humorous story. (Rev: BL 3/1/04; SLJ 2/04)

3262 Cabot, Meg. *All-American Girl* (9–12). 2002, HarperCollins LB $17.89 (0-06-029470-1). Samantha is suddenly thrust into the spotlight when she thwarts a would-be assassin and saves the president, winning the love of the president's son. (Rev: BL 10/1/02; HBG 3/03; SLJ 10/02)

3263 Cabot, Meg. *The Princess Diaries* (7–10). Series: Princess Diaries. 2000, HarperCollins LB $15.89 (0-06-029210-5). Fourteen-year-old Mia's diary reveals a fairly interesting life even before she learns that she is actually a royal princess, heir to the throne of Genovia. (Rev: BCCB 12/00; BL 9/15/00; HBG 3/01; SLJ 10/00; VOYA 4/01)

3264 Cabot, Meg. *Princess in Pink* (7–10). Series: Princess Diaries. 2004, HarperCollins $15.99 (0-06-009610-1). In this, the fifth volume of the Princess Diaries series, Mia celebrates her 15th birthday and her pregnant mom is about to give birth. (Rev: BL 4/15/04; SLJ 8/04)

3265 Cabot, Meg. *Princess in the Spotlight: The Princess Diaries, Volume II* (7–10). Series: Princess Diaries. 2001, HarperCollins LB $15.89 (0-06-029466-3). In this sequel to *The Princess Diaries* (2000), readers find out how Mia is coping with being a princess and with more typical teen concerns such as a pregnant mother and a romance. (Rev: BCCB 9/01; BL 9/1/01; HBG 3/02; SLJ 8/01; VOYA 10/01)

3266 Capote, Truman. *Breakfast at Tiffany's: A Short Novel and Three Stories* (10–12). 1994, Modern Library $14.95 (0-679-60085-X); paper $11.00 (0-679-74565-3). In addition to this short novel about Holly Golightly, there are three short stories in this volume.

3267 Clark, Catherine. *Truth or Dairy* (7–12). 2000, HarperCollins paper $6.95 (0-380-81443-9). Told in diary form, this breezy narrative chronicles Courtney's senior year in her Colorado school. (Rev: BL 4/15/00; SLJ 7/00; VOYA 12/00)

3268 Clarke, J. *Al Capsella and the Watchdogs* (7–10). 1991, Holt $14.95 (0-8050-1598-1). Al Capsella, 15, and his Australian high school friends spend much of their time bemoaning the tactics their parents use to be involved in all phases of their lives. (Rev: BL 8/91; SLJ 8/91)

3269 Corbet, Robert. *Fifteen Love* (7–10). 2003, Walker $16.95 (0-8027-8851-3). A humorous story about a 15-year-old boy and girl whose romantic feelings seem to be doomed. (Rev: BL 4/15/03; HB 7–8/03; HBG 10/03; SLJ 5/03; VOYA 8/03)

3270 Dahl, Roald. *The Umbrella Man and Other Stories* (8–12). 1998, Viking $16.99 (0-670-87854-5). A collection of 13 stories originally written for adults that display Dahl's wit and penchant for irony. (Rev: BL 5/15/98; BR 5–6/99; HBG 9/98; SLJ 8/98; VOYA 8/98)

3271 David, Peter. *Knight Life* (10–12). 2002, Berkley $22.95 (0-441-00936-0). As promised, King Arthur returns when he is needed — to contemporary New York City — and his gallant knights and enemies are there too. (Rev: BL 6/1–15/02)

3272 Davis, Donald. *Barking at a Fox-Fur Coat* (9–12). 1991, August House $19.95 (0-87483-141-5); paper $12.95 (0-87483-140-7). Seventeen original tales based on the author's childhood and family experiences in rural North Carolina, each highlighting a set of human foibles and ending with an ironic twist. (Rev: BL 10/15/91; SLJ 4/92)

3273 Feherty, David. *A Nasty Bit of Rough* (10–12). 2002, Rugged Land $22.95 (1-59071-000-2). An irreverent tall tale of a golfing contest in deepest Scotland. (Rev: BL 3/15/02)

3274 Ferris, Jean. *Love Among the Walnuts* (7–10). 1998, Harcourt $16.00 (0-15-201590-6). A good-natured, hilarious spoof in which young Sandy and his rich family are forced to move to a loony bin to escape the schemes of relatives intent on stealing their money. (Rev: HB 1–2/99; HBG 3/99; SLJ 8/98; VOYA 2/99)

3275 Fleischman, Paul. *A Fate Totally Worse Than Death* (7–12). Illus. 1995, Candlewick $15.99 (1-

56402-627-2). An offbeat mix of horror story and satire about self-centered rich girls who want to teach a beautiful exchange student a lesson. (Rev: BL 10/15/95; SLJ 10/95; VOYA 4/96)

3276 Hardman, Ric L. *Sunshine Rider: The First Vegetarian Western* (9–12). 1998, Delacorte $15.95 (0-385-32543-6). This humorous adventure story about 17-year-old Wylie Jackson, who becomes a vegetarian after he is instructed to shoot a calf while on a cattle drive and then decides to become a doctor, is part western, part cookbook, and part picturesque novel. (Rev: BL 2/15/98; BR 9–10/98; HBG 9/98; SLJ 2/98; VOYA 4/98)

3277 Hayes, Daniel. *Flyers* (8–12). Illus. 1996, Simon & Schuster $16.00 (0-689-80372-9). A funny and clever novel that involves 15-year-old Gabe, the movie he and his friends are making, and a series of odd events that change their lives. (Rev: BL 9/15/96; SLJ 11/96; VOYA 2/97)

3278 Henry, Chad. *DogBreath Victorious* (6–10). 1999, Holiday $16.95 (0-8234-1458-2). Tim's rock band, DogBreath, ends up competing against his mom's group, the Angry Housewives, in this entertaining story. (Rev: HBG 9/00; SLJ 2/00; VOYA 6/00)

3279 Howe, Norma. *The Adventures of Blue Avenger* (8–10). 1999, Holt $16.95 (0-8050-6062-6). When David Schumacher, 16, changes his name to Blue Avenger, he finds he can tackle all sorts of problems. (Rev: BL 3/15/99; HBG 9/99; SLJ 4/99; VOYA 6/99)

3280 Howe, Norma. *Blue Avenger Cracks the Code* (7–12). 2000, Holt $17.00 (0-8050-6372-2). David (aka Blue Avenger) pursues several lines of interest, including romance and the question of the true authorship of Shakespeare's plays. (Rev: HBG 3/01; SLJ 9/00; VOYA 12/00)

3281 Juby, Susan. *Miss Smithers* (7–12). 2004, HarperCollins LB $16.89 (0-06-051547-3). Told through journal articles and a zine, this is the story of Alice of *Alice, I Think* (2003) and how she enters a beauty contest in spite of her mother's opposition. (Rev: BL 5/1/04; HB 7–8/04)

3282 Kaufman, Bel. *Up the Down Staircase* (10–12). 1991, Demco $18.85 (0-606-12559-0). A humorous, often poignant story of a young schoolteacher in a New York high school.

3283 Keller, Beverly. *The Amazon Papers* (7–10). 1996, Harcourt $12.00 (0-15-201345-8); paper $6.00 (0-15-201346-6). Iris's life is transformed, not necessarily for the better, when she falls for a handsome, pizza-delivering, high school dropout named Foster Prizer. (Rev: BL 1/1–15/97; BR 3–4/97; SLJ 10/96; VOYA 12/96)

3284 Kinsella, Sophie. *Shopaholic Ties the Knot* (10–12). 2003, Delta paper $10.95 (0-385-33617-9). Wedding bells are set to ring on the same day in two cities an ocean apart as Becky, of *Confessions of a Shopaholic* (2001) and *Shopaholic Takes Manhattan* (2002), tries to unravel another difficult situation. (Rev: BL 3/15/03)

3285 Koertge, Ron. *Where the Kissing Never Stops* (10–12). 1993, Avon paper $3.99 (0-380-71796-4). A candid, sometimes bawdy story about a 17-year-old boy, his love life, and his mother who is a stripper. (Rev: BL 11/1/86; SLJ 12/86; VOYA 12/86)

3286 Korman, Gordon. *Don't Care High* (7–10). 1986, Scholastic paper $2.50 (0-590-40251-X). A new student in a high school where apathy is so rife it's nicknamed Don't Care High decides to infuse some school spirit into the student body. (Rev: BL 10/15/85)

3287 Letts, Billie. *Where the Heart Is* (10–12). 1995, Warner $17.95 (0-446-51972-3). An unusual, humorous novel about a pregnant teenager who finds herself stranded outside a Wal-Mart in Sequoyah, Oklahoma, and is adopted and helped by an unlikely group of local inhabitants. (Rev: BL 9/1/95; SLJ 4/96)

3288 Lowry, Brigid. *Follow the Blue* (8–12). 2004, Holiday $16.95 (0-8234-1827-8). A delightful novel from Australia about 15-year-old Bec, who, with her two younger siblings, is left in the care of a dowdy housekeeper while her parents are away. (Rev: BL 5/1/04*; HB 7–8/04; SLJ 5/04)

3289 Lynch, Chris. *Political Timber* (7–10). 1996, HarperCollins LB $14.89 (0-06-027361-5). In this political satire, Mayor Foley, in prison on several counts of racketeering, coaches his 18-year-old grandson to win the mayoral election and become his successor. (Rev: BL 10/15/96; BR 3–4/97; SLJ 1/97; VOYA 2/97)

3290 McCandless, Sarah Grace. *Grosse Pointe Girl: Tales from a Suburban Adolescence* (10–12). Illus. 2004, Simon & Schuster paper $12.00 (0-7432-5612-3). This hilarious novel tells about adolescence along with its humiliations and victories as experienced by Emma Harris, a privileged teenager in Grosse Point, Michigan. (Rev: BL 5/1/04)

3291 McCauley, Stephen. *The Object of My Affection* (10–12). 1998, Pocket paper $6.99 (0-671-02066-8). In this sunny novel a gay teacher decides to help his roommate who is expecting a baby. (Rev: BL 3/1/87)

3292 McFann, Jane. *Deathtrap and Dinosaur* (7–12). 1989, Avon paper $2.75 (0-380-75624-2). An unlikely pair works to force the departure of a disliked history teacher. (Rev: SLJ 10/89; VOYA 10/89)

3293 Mackler, Carolyn. *Love and Other Four-Letter Words* (6–10). 2000, Delacorte $14.95 (0-385-32743-9). A humorous novel in which Sammie, an average 16-year-old, tries to make sense of family,

friendships, and romance. (Rev: BL 8/00; HBG 3/01; SLJ 9/00)

3294 Manes, Stephen. *Comedy High* (7–10). 1992, Scholastic paper $13.95 (0-590-44436-0). A comic story of a new high school designed to graduate jocks, performers, gambling experts, and hotel workers. (Rev: BL 12/1/92; SLJ 11/92)

3295 Many, Paul. *These Are the Rules* (7–10). 1997, Walker $15.95 (0-8027-8619-7); Knopf paper $4.99 (0-679-88978-7). In this hilarious first-person narrative, Colm tries to figure out the rules of dating, driving, girls, and getting some direction in his life. (Rev: BL 5/1/97; HBG 3/98; SLJ 5/97)

3296 Martin, Steve. *The Pleasure of My Company* (10–12). 2003, Hyperion $19.95 (0-7868-6921-6). Daniel Pecan Cambridge learns to put his phobias in second place in this entertaining novel. (Rev: BL 9/1/03*)

3297 Moore, Christopher. *Lamb: The Gospel According to Biff, Christ's Childhood Pal* (10–12). 2002, Morrow $25.95 (0-380-97840-7). A lighthearted and thoroughly irreverent view of Christ's youth; for mature teens. (Rev: BL 3/1/02; SLJ 12/02; VOYA 12/02)

3298 Naylor, Phyllis Reynolds. *Alice Alone* (6–10). 2001, Simon & Schuster $15.00 (0-689-82634-6). Alice's story continues as she starts high school and deals with the misery of breaking up with her boyfriend. (Rev: BCCB 5/01; BL 5/15/01; HB 7–8/01; HBG 10/01; SLJ 6/01; VOYA 8/01)

3299 Nicholls, David. *A Question of Attraction* (10–12). 2004, Villard $23.95 (1-4000-6181-4). A humorous coming-of-age story about a British university student who, wanting to live life to the fullest, lands a position on a TV quiz program and falls in love with a beautiful, wealthy girl. (Rev: BL 2/15/04*)

3300 Nodelman, Perry. *Behaving Bradley* (8–10). 1998, Simon & Schuster $16.00 (0-689-81466-6). In this screwball comedy, junior Bradley Gold represents student interests when his high school prepares a code of conduct. (Rev: BL 6/1–15/98; HBG 3/99; SLJ 6/98; VOYA 8/98)

3301 O'Brien, Gerry. *Planting Out: The Second Book of the Borough* (10–12). 2002, Colin Smythe $29.95 (0-86140-440-8). In the second entertaining book set in a fictional London borough, a vitally important microchip is lost and the corpse of the monastery's gardener hopes to rest in peace. (Rev: BL 1/1–15/02)

3302 Parks, Adele. *Larger Than Life* (11–12). 2003, Pocket paper $12.00 (0-7434-5760-9). An amusing British story of a steadfast love that begins to falter when Georgie finally gets to live with Hugh. (Rev: BL 8/03)

3303 Paulsen, Gary. *Harris and Me: A Summer Remembered* (6–10). 1993, Harcourt $16.00 (0-15-292877-4); paper $4.99 (0-440-40994-2). A humorous story in which the 11-year-old narrator often gets the blame for mischief caused by troublemaker Harris. (Rev: BL 12/1/93*; SLJ 2/00; VOYA 2/94)

3304 Payne, C. D. *Revolting Youth* (10–12). 2000, Aivia $14.95 (1-882647-15-7). Fourteen-year-old Nick Twisp, in spite of good intentions, continues to create havoc in this hilarious sequel to *Youth in Revolt* (1993) that contains some explicit sex. (Rev: BL 10/15/00)

3305 Peck, Richard. *A Long Way from Chicago* (6–10). 1998, Dial $15.99 (0-8037-2290-7). Seven stories are included in this book, each representing a different summer from 1929 to 1935 that Joey spent visiting in Illinois with his lying, cheating, conniving, and thoroughly charming grandmother. (Rev: BCCB 10/98; BL 9/1/98; HB 11–12/98; HBG 3/99; SLJ 10/98*; VOYA 12/98)

3306 Peck, Richard. *A Year Down Yonder* (6–10). 2000, Dial $16.99 (0-8037-2518-3). In this 2001 Newbery Medal winner, 15-year-old Mary Alice visits her feisty, independent, but lovable Grandma Dowdel in rural Illinois during the Great Depression. A sequel to *A Long Way from Chicago* (1998). (Rev: BCCB 1/01; BL 10/15/00* ; HB 11–12/00; HBG 3/01; SLJ 9/00; VOYA 12/00)

3307 Pinkwater, Daniel. *The Education of Robert Nifkin* (10–12). 1998, Farrar $16.00 (0-374-31969-3). In this humorous novel, a nerd growing up in 1950s Chicago becomes involved with some weird people and events. (Rev: BL 6/1–15/98; HB 7–8/98*; HBG 9/98; SLJ 7/98; VOYA 8/98)

3308 Rennison, Louise. *Knocked Out by My Nunga-Nungas* (7–10). 2002, HarperCollins LB $15.89 (0-06-623695-9). British teenager Georgia Nicolson is back with more saucy talk, recorded in the pages of her diary along with her latest troubles with her boyfriend, family, and schoolmates. (Rev: BL 4/15/02; HB 7–8/02; HBG 10/02; SLJ 5/02)

3309 Rennison, Louise. *On the Bright Side, I'm Now the Girlfriend of a Sex God: The Further Confessions of Georgia Nicolson* (7–10). 2001, HarperCollins LB $15.89 (0-06-028872-8). Georgia records in her diary the details of her daily life and of her crush on "Robbie the Sex God" and her hilarious machinations to snare him in this sequel to *Angus, Thongs, and Full-Frontal Snogging* (2000). (Rev: BL 5/15/01; HB 5–6/01; HBG 10/01; SLJ 5/01; VOYA 6/01)

3310 Riggs, Bob. *My Best Defense* (6–10). 1996, Ward Hill paper $5.95 (1-886747-01-6). Sarcasm is the best defense of the narrator in this humorous story of a family and the unusual characters they attract. (Rev: SLJ 8/96; VOYA 10/96)

3311 Rosenfeld, Lucinda. *What She Saw In . . .* (10–12). 2000, Random $23.95 (0-375-50375-7). A hilarious, sexually explicit novel about Phoebe Fine's search for Mr. Right. (Rev: BL 8/00; VOYA 2/01)

3312 Ross, Leonard Q. *The Education of H*Y*M*A*N K*A*P*L*A*N* (9–12). 1968, Harcourt paper $9.00 (0-15-627811-1). A series of hilarious stories about an immigrant Jew and his battle with the English language at night school.

3313 Ryan, Mary C. *Who Says I Can't?* (7–10). 1988, Little, Brown $12.95 (0-316-76374-8). Tessa decides to get revenge on a boy who shows too much ardor in his romancing. (Rev: SLJ 11/88)

3314 Samuels, Dorothy. *Filthy Rich* (10–12). 2001, Morrow $24.00 (0-06-621016-X). In this funny spoof on the reality TV craze, Marcy Mallowitz loses her fiance on national TV. (Rev: VOYA 2/02)

3315 Shaw, Tucker. *Flavor of the Week* (8–10). 2003, Hyperion $15.99 (0-7868-1890-5). Overweight, diffident, and in love, aspiring chef Cyril agrees to a culinary ruse that backfires, leaving a happy Cyril winning the girl. (Rev: BL 11/15/03; HBG 4/04; SLJ 12/03; VOYA 2/04)

3316 Sheldon, Dyan. *My Perfect Life* (7–10). 2002, Candlewick $16.99 (0-7636-1839-X). A hard-fought race for class president pits timid Ella against arrogant Carla in this humorous novel that reintroduces the characters from *Confessions of a Teenage Drama Queen* (1999). (Rev: BL 7/02; HBG 3/03; SLJ 8/02; VOYA 12/02)

3317 Sleator, William. *Oddballs* (8–12). 1995, Penguin paper $5.99 (0-14-037438-8). A collection of stories based on experiences from the author's youth and peopled with an unusual assortment of family and friends.

3318 Smith, Edwin R. *Blue Star Highway, Vol. 1: A Tale of Redemption from North Florida* (7–12). 1997, Mile Marker Twelve paper $9.95 (0-9659054-0-3). In this humorous novel, 14-year-old Marty Crane tells of the events in his life leading up to being sentenced to a detention home in 1962. (Rev: BL 2/15/99)

3319 Somtow, S. P. *The Vampire's Beautiful Daughter* (7–10). Illus. 1997, Simon & Schuster $17.00 (0-689-31968-1). Johnny meets Rebecca Teppish, a fascinating girl who is part vampire. (Rev: BL 9/1/97; HBG 3/98; SLJ 10/97)

3320 Strasser, Todd. *Girl Gives Birth to Own Prom Date* (7–10). 1996, Simon & Schuster LB $16.00 (0-689-80482-2). Telling their stories in alternating chapters, friends Nichole and Brad discuss the frantic high school social scene and the upcoming senior prom. (Rev: BL 10/1/96; SLJ 9/96; VOYA 4/97)

3321 Thomas, Rob. *Slave Day* (9–12). 1997, Simon & Schuster paper $16.00 (0-689-80206-4). A clever, funny school story for mature readers about African American students who object to a fund-raising event called Slave Day where student body leaders and several teachers allow themselves to be "slaves" for a good cause. (Rev: BR 3–4/98; SLJ 4/97*)

3322 Thompson, Julian. *Simon Pure* (10–12). 1987, Scholastic paper $3.50 (0-590-41823-8). Simon has some unusual but always hilarious adventures when he enters Riddle University. (Rev: BL 4/15/87; SLJ 3/87; VOYA 4/87)

3323 Townsend, Sue. *Adrian Mole: The Lost Years* (9–12). 1994, Soho Pr. $22.00 (1-56947-014-6). In this sequel to *The Secret Diary of Adrian Mole,* Adrian chronicles his struggle with the raging hormones of adolescence and his search for a suitable career. (Rev: BL 8/94; SLJ 1/95)

3324 Townsend, Sue. *The Secret Diary of Adrian Mole, Age Thirteen and Three Quarters* (9–12). 1984, Avon paper $4.99 (0-380-86876-8). The trials and tribulations of a young English boy as revealed through his hilarious diary entries. (Rev: BL 1/1–15/97)

3325 Trembath, Don. *A Fly Named Alfred* (7–10). 1997, Orca paper $6.95 (1-55143-083-5). In this sequel to *The Tuesday Cafe,* Harper Winslow gets into more trouble when he write an anonymous column in the school newspaper that enrages the school bully. (Rev: BL 8/97; SLJ 9/96)

3326 Welter, John. *I Want to Buy a Vowel: A Novel of Illegal Alienation* (10–12). 1996, Algonquin $29.95 (1-56512-118-X). A humorous novel about an illegal alien who speaks only lines from TV commercials, two young sisters, and the teenage son of the local preacher, and how their lives intersect in their small Texas town. (Rev: SLJ 5/97)

3327 Wersba, Barbara. *You'll Never Guess the End* (7–12). 1992, HarperCollins $14.00 (0-06-020448-6). A send-up of the New York City literary scene, rich dilettantes, and scientology. (Rev: BL 11/15/92; SLJ 9/92)

3328 Wibberley, Leonard. *The Mouse That Roared* (7–12). 1992, Buccaneer LB $27.95 (0-89966-887-9). To get foreign aid, the tiny Duchy of Grand Fenwick declares war on the United States.

Mysteries, Thrillers, and Spy Stories

3329 Abrahams, Peter. *The Tutor* (10–12). 2002, Ballantine $25.95 (0-345-43938-4). Parents obsessed with their son's forthcoming SATs come to regret their decision to hire a tutor in this novel full of suspense. (Rev: BL 5/1/02; SLJ 11/02)

3330 Adamson, Isaac. *Hokkaido Popsicle* (11–12). 2002, HarperPerennial paper $12.95 (0-380-81292-

4). Teen reporter Billy Chaka investigates two possibly related deaths in this entertaining sequel to *Tokyo Suckerpunch* (2000). (Rev: BL 4/1/02; SLJ 10/02)

3331 Adamson, Lydia. *A Cat on Stage Left: An Alice Nestleton Mystery* (10–12). 1998, NAL $19.95 (0-525-94419-2). Told with humor and lots of dialogue, this mystery involves Alice, professional cat sitter and amateur sleuth, and the murder of Mary, one of Alice's wealthy clients. (Rev: BL 4/15/98; SLJ 9/98)

3332 Albert, Susan Wittig. *Chile Death* (10–12). Series: China Bayles Mystery. 1998, Prime Crime $21.95 (0-425-16539-6). China Bayles and her fiance, Mike, a disabled former police officer, investigate the mysterious sudden death of a judge at a chili cook-off and the mistreatment of several older residents at Mike's nursing home, and the two investigations become linked. (Rev: BL 10/15/98; SLJ 1/99)

3333 Allen, Conrad. *Murder on the Mauretania* (10–12). 2000, St. Martin's $23.75 (0-312-24116-X). A humorous mystery that involves a murder during the maiden voyage of the *Mauretania*. (Rev: BL 12/1/00)

3334 Altman, John. *A Gathering of Spies* (10–12). 2000, Putnam $24.95 (0-399-14641-5). For spy-thriller fans, this novel, set in 1943, mixes espionage, secrets involving the atomic bomb, and a plot to kill Hitler. (Rev: BL 5/1/00)

3335 Amato, Angela, and Joe Sharkey. *Lady Gold* (10–12). 1998, St. Martin's $23.95 (0-312-18541-3). A tense, realistic tale of two undercover policemen, a man and a woman, and their efforts to arrest a top Mafia boss. (Rev: BL 5/15/98; SLJ 3/99)

3336 Apone, Claudio. *My Grandfather, Jack the Ripper* (6–12). 2000, Herodias $19.00 (1-928746-16-0). Thirteen-year-old Andy Dobson, a clairvoyant Londoner, travels back in time — with the help of hallucinogenic drugs — to discover the true identity of the legendary murderer. (Rev: HBG 10/01; SLJ 6/01; VOYA 6/01)

3337 Archer, Jeffrey. *A Matter of Honor* (10–12). 1993, HarperCollins paper $6.50 (0-06-100713-7). For better readers, a tense thriller about a chase across Europe to secure a priceless icon. (Rev: BL 6/15/86)

3338 Archer, Jeffrey. *Shall We Tell the President?* (10–12). 1987, Pocket paper $5.50 (0-671-63305-8). Someone is out to kill the president in this exciting tale told with a dash of humor.

3339 Ashford, Jeffrey. *A Fair Exchange Is Robbery* (10–12). 2003, Severn $26.99 (0-7278-5972-2). Gavin Penfold is accused of a crime he did not commit and sets out to expose the perpetrators in this thought-provoking novel. (Rev: BL 9/1/03)

3340 Asinof, Eliot. *Off-Season* (10–12). 2000, Southern Illinois Univ. Pr. $22.50 (0-8093-2297-8). In this murder mystery with a baseball setting, the hero, a major league pitcher, investigates the murder of his African American coach and uncovers a case of racism and corruption. (Rev: BL 4/1/00)

3341 Aubert, Rosemary. *Free Reign: A Suspense Novel* (10–12). 1997, Bridge Works. $21.95 (1-882593-18-9). A recluse rejoins society and experiences romance and extreme danger while investigating the meaning of a ringed hand placed in his garden. (Rev: BL 4/15/97; SLJ 10/97)

3342 Avi. *Wolf Rider: A Tale of Terror* (7–12). 1986, Macmillan paper $17.00 (0-02-707760-8). In this thrilling mystery, a 15-year-old boy tries to learn the identity of a telephone caller who claims he is a murderer. (Rev: BL 11/15/86; BR 5–6/87; SLJ 12/86)

3343 Babson, Marian. *To Catch a Cat* (10–12). 2000, St. Martin's $23.95 (0-312-20918-5). This mystery, part of an extensive and recommended English series, features 12-year-old hero Robin, the villain Nils Nordling, and a prize-winning cat, Leif Eriksson. (Rev: BL 12/1/00)

3344 Baldacci, David. *Split Second* (11–12). 2003, Warner $26.95 (0-446-53089-1). An exciting combination of romance between two independently minded characters and suspense involving the Secret Service. (Rev: BL 8/03)

3345 Ball, Pamela. *The Floating City* (11–12). 2002, Viking $23.95 (0-670-89472-9). Historical detail is interwoven into the suspenseful narrative of this mystery set in Hawaii at the end of the 19th century and featuring a clairvoyant; for mature teens. (Rev: BL 3/1/02)

3346 Barnard, Robert. *A Fatal Attachment* (9–12). 1992, Scribner $20.00 (0-684-19412-0). By taking control of her nephews' lives, Lydia alienated her sister and brother-in-law from their adolescent sons. Twenty years later, history seems to be repeating itself. (Rev: BL 8/92; SLJ 2/93)

3347 Barnard, Robert. *A Murder in Mayfair* (10–12). 2000, Scribner $23.00 (0-684-86445-2). An expertly plotted whodunit in which a newcomer to British political life tries to determine the history of his parentage. (Rev: BL 3/15/00; SLJ 11/00)

3348 Barr, Nevada. *Blind Descent* (10–12). 1998, Putnam $22.95 (0-399-14371-8). Anna Pigeon investigates dirty dealings and the murder of a fellow park ranger in the depths of Lechugilla Cavern, forcing herself to overcome claustrophobia and near terror as she works her way through the total blackness underground. (Rev: BL 2/15/98; SLJ 7/98)

3349 Barr, Nevada. *Deep South* (10–12). 2000, Putnam $23.95 (0-399-14586-9). In this Anna Pigeon adult mystery story, our heroine, a forest ranger, must solve a deadly crime in the Natchez Trace Parkway area of Mississippi and Tennessee. (Rev: BL 1/1–15/00; SLJ 7/00)

3350 Barr, Nevada. *Endangered Species* (10–12). 1997, Putnam $22.95 (0-399-14246-0). Ranger Anna Pigeon investigates the wreckage of an airplane on Cumberland Island, Georgia, and suspects foul play. (Rev: BL 2/15/97; SLJ 11/97)

3351 Barr, Nevada. *Hunting Season* (10–12). Series: National Park. 2002, Putnam $24.95 (0-399-14846-9). District Ranger Anna Pigeon investigates a murder at an old inn on Mississippi Natchez Trace Parkway. (Rev: BL 12/15/01*)

3352 Barron, Stephanie. *Jane and the Wandering Eye* (10–12). 1998, Bantam paper $5.99 (0-553-57817-0). Jane Austen turns sleuth when a theater manager is murdered in Bath and a portrait of an eye is found on the body. (Rev: SLJ 7/98)

3353 Barry, Max. *Jennifer Government* (10–12). 2003, Doubleday $21.95 (0-385-50759-3). In an entertaining and thought-provoking novel about a hyper-commercial near future, Jennifer Government investigates a Nike marketing scheme that involves assassinating teens. (Rev: BL 12/1/02; SLJ 8/03)

3354 Baum, Thomas. *Out of Body* (10–12). 1997, St. Martin's $22.95 (0-312-15620-0). A gripping mystery story about a man accused of murder who finds that he can have out-of-body experiences and witness events in other locations. (Rev: BL 4/15/97; SLJ 10/97)

3355 Beaton, M. C. *Death of a Perfect Wife* (9–12). 1990, Ivy Books paper $4.99 (0-8041-0593-6). A delightful mystery about some unusual characters who get involved in a murder in a quiet Scottish village. (Rev: BL 11/15/89)

3356 Beaton, M. C. *Death of an Addict* (10–12). 1999, Mysterious $22.00 (0-89296-675-0). Set in the highlands of Scotland, Constable Hamish Macbeth goes undercover and solves the mysterious death of a young man, supposedly from a drug overdose, and uncovers a drug ring. (Rev: BL 4/15/99; SLJ 9/99)

3357 Bebris, Carrie. *Pride and Prescience; or, A Truth Universally Acknowledged* (10–12). 2004, Tor $24.95 (0-765-30508-9). Picking up where Austen left off at the end of *Pride and Prejudice*, newlywed Elizabeth Bennett and Fitzwilliam Darcy turn sleuths to discover the truth behind savage injuries suffered by Caroline Bingley, Elizabeth's former rival. (Rev: BL 12/15/03)

3358 Beechey, Alan. *An Embarrassment of Corpses* (10–12). 1997, Thomas Dunne $22.95 (0-312-16936-1). A witty mystery set in London about serial murders investigated by a police detective and his nephew, a writer of children's books. (Rev: SLJ 5/98)

3359 Benjamin, Carol Lea. *The Dog Who Knew Too Much* (10–12). 1997, Walker $29.95 (0-8027-3312-3). With the help of her pit bull Dashiell, private investigator Rachel Alexander investigates the death of a young woman in Greenwich Village. (Rev: BL 9/1/97; VOYA 12/97)

3360 Benjamin, Carol Lea. *This Dog for Hire* (10–12). 1996, Walker $30.95 (0-8027-3292-5). Private investigator Rachel Alexander and her pit bull, Dashiell, are hired to track down a hit-and-run driver who killed a young New York artist. (Rev: SLJ 4/97; VOYA 2/97)

3361 Bennett, Jay. *Coverup* (8–10). 1992, Fawcett paper $5.99 (0-449-70409-2). Realizing his friend has killed a pedestrian on a deserted road after a party, Brad returns to the accident scene and meets a girl searching for her homeless father. (Rev: BL 11/1/91)

3362 Bennett, Jay. *The Dark Corridor* (7–12). 1990, Fawcett paper $4.50 (0-449-70337-1). Kerry believes that his girlfriend's death was not suicide but murder. (Rev: BR 3–4/89; SLJ 11/88; VOYA 2/89)

3363 Bennett, Jay. *The Haunted One* (7–12). 1987, Fawcett paper $3.99 (0-449-70314-2). Paul Barrett, an 18-year-old lifeguard, is haunted by the memory of the girl he loved, who drowned before his eyes. (Rev: BR 3–4/88; SLJ 11/87)

3364 Bennett, Jay. *Sing Me a Death Song* (7–12). 1991, Fawcett paper $6.50 (0-449-70369-X). Eighteen-year-old Jason wonders if his accused mother is really a murderer. (Rev: SLJ 4/90; VOYA 8/90)

3365 Bennett, Jay. *The Skeleton Man* (7–12). 1988, Fawcett paper $4.50 (0-449-70284-7). Ray receives money from his uncle just before his death — but the gambling syndicate claims it as theirs. (Rev: BL 11/1/86; BR 1–2/87; SLJ 10/86; VOYA 4/87)

3366 Benson, Raymond. *Never Dream of Dying* (10–12). 2001, Putnam $23.95 (0-399-14746-2). In this James Bond thriller, 007 encounters the mysterious leader of the Union, an international terrorist organization. Part of a recommended series for Bond fans. (Rev: BL 5/1/01)

3367 Berenson, Laurien. *Watchdog* (10–12). 1998, Kensington $20.00 (1-57566-350-3). Mel Travis puts her detective skills to work when her brother is wrongfully accused of murdering his financial backer. (Rev: BL 8/98; SLJ 3/99)

3368 Bernhardt, William. *Naked Justice* (10–12). 1997, Ballantine $22.00 (0-345-38685-X). The public believes that Tulsa's black mayor, Wallace Barrett, murdered his wife and daughters, but are they correct? (Rev: BL 1/1–15/97; SLJ 6/97)

3369 Black, Veronica. *A Vow of Adoration* (10–12). 1997, St. Martin's $20.95 (0-312-18205-8). An English adventure mystery involving Sister Joan, her convent, and a murder on the Cornish moors. (Rev: SLJ 6/98)

3370 Blakely, Mike. *Summer of Pearls* (7–12). 2000, Forge $22.95 (0-312-87516-9). Narrator Ben Crowell, now in his 80s, recounts a series of mysterious happenings he witnessed as a Texas 14-year-old during the summer of 1874. (Rev: SLJ 5/01; VOYA 12/00)

3371 Block, Barbara. *Blowing Smoke* (10–12). 2001, Kensington $22.00 (1-57566-670-7). In this mystery, part of the recommended series about Robin Light, the part-time private investigator goes to work to expose a woman who claims she can talk to animals. (Rev: BL 5/1/01)

3372 Bone, Ian. *The Song of an Innocent Bystander* (10–12). 2004, Dutton $16.99 (0-525-47282-7). Freda was only 9 years old when she was held captive by a madman; ten years later a stranger appears who knows details of the incident that no one else does. (Rev: BL 5/1/04; VOYA 6/04)

3373 Booth, Stephen. *Dancing with the Virgins* (10–12). 2001, Scribner $24.00 (0-7432-1690-3). A woman's corpse is found in a Bronze Age stone circle known as the Nine Virgins in England's Peak District. (Rev: BL 9/1/01)

3374 Borthwick, J. S. *Coup de Grace* (10–12). 2000, St. Martin's $24.95 (0-312-25313-3). Amateur sleuth Sarah Deane becomes involved in a murder mystery at a girls' boarding school in Massachusetts. (Rev: BL 2/15/00)

3375 Bowen, Peter. *Stick Game* (10–12). 2000, St. Martin's $23.95 (0-312-20297-0). An engrossing mystery about a Metais Indian cattle inspector, his wife, the disappearance of a cousin's son, and the poisoning of a reservation's water supply. (Rev: BL 2/15/00*)

3376 Bowen, Rhys, and J. Bowen. *Evans Above* (10–12). 1997, St. Martin's $21.95 (0-312-16828-4). A well-crafted mystery about a young constable in a Welsh village who sets out to solve the mystery of the murders of three alpine hikers. (Rev: SLJ 5/98)

3377 Bowler, Tim. *Storm Catchers* (6–10). 2003, Simon & Schuster $16.95 (0-689-84573-1). A multilayered, suspenseful story of the kidnapping of a 13-year-old girl on the Cornwall coast, her brother's agonized guilt, and the discovery of a dark family secret. (Rev: BL 9/1/03; HBG 4/04; SLJ 5/03; VOYA 8/03)

3378 Box, C. J. *Open Season* (10–12). 2001, Putnam $23.95 (0-399-14748-9). In this excellent mystery, rookie game warden Joe Pickett investigates the suspicious deaths of three hunters. Also recommended is *Savage Run* (2002). (Rev: BL 5/1/01*)

3379 Brandon, Jay. *Rules of Evidence* (9–12). 1992, Pocket paper $6.50 (0-671-79389-6). A loner cop accused of murder hires an African American lawyer to defend him. (Rev: BL 1/1/92*)

3380 Braun, Lilian Jackson. *The Cat Who Sang for the Birds* (10–12). 1998, Putnam $22.95 (0-399-14333-5); Jove paper $6.99 (0-515-12463-X). In this part of the mystery series involving the sleuthing team of Jim Qwilleran and his cats, Koko the cat uses his talents to predict future events and helps Jim solve the mystery of the death of his elderly neighbor and the disappearance of a young artist. (Rev: BL 11/1/97; SLJ 8/98)

3381 Brewer, James D. *No Escape* (9–12). 1998, Walker $32.95 (0-8027-3318-2). Luke Williamson, Masey Baldridge, and Salina Tyner of the Big River Detective Agency are hired by the mayor of Memphis, Tennessee, to investigate embezzlement and the murders of fever victims at the beginning of the 1873 Yellow Fever epidemic. (Rev: VOYA 10/98)

3382 Brewer, James D. *No Remorse: A Masey Baldridge/Luke Williamson Mystery* (10–12). 1997, Walker $32.95 (0-8027-3302-6). Set after the end of the Civil War, this novel features riverboat captain/detective Luke Williamson and detective agency partners Masey Baldridge and Salina Tyner, who take on a case in which the widow of Williamson's competitor engages him to clear her son of his father's murder. (Rev: BL 8/97; VOYA 4/98)

3383 Brockmann, Suzanne. *Gone Too Far* (11–12). Series: Troubleshooter. 2003, Ballantine $19.95 (0-345-46227-0). A sexy and suspenseful story in which U.S. Navy SEAL Sam Starrett and FBI agent Alyssa Locke find mystery and romance. (Rev: BL 5/15/03)

3384 Brooks, Kevin. *Lucas* (8–10). 2003, Scholastic $16.95 (0-439-45698-3). The arrival of an attractive young stranger on Cait's remote British island signals the start of a series of calamitous events. (Rev: BL 5/1/03*; HB 3–4/03; HBG 10/03; SLJ 5/03; VOYA 4/03)

3385 Brown, Rita Mae, and Sneaky Pie Brown. *Catch as Cat Can* (10–12). Illus. Series: Mrs. Murphy. 2002, Bantam $24.95 (0-553-10744-5). Mrs. Murphy the cat is at it again, on the trail of a murder with the help of her animal friends in this 10th book in the series. (Rev: BL 1/1–15/02)

3386 Brown, Rita Mae, and Sneaky Pie Brown. *Murder on the Prowl* (10–12). Illus. 1998, Bantam $23.95 (0-553-09970-1). When obituaries begin appearing before the deaths have occurred, Harry Haristeen and her talking pets begin an investigation. (Rev: BL 2/1/98; SLJ 12/98)

3387 Brown, Sandra. *Hello, Darkness* (11–12). 2003, Simon & Schuster $25.95 (0-7432-4552-0). A late-night radio personality and an attractive police psychologist reawaken old longings as they search for a young girl in danger; for mature teens. (Rev: BL 9/1/03)

3388 Bunkley, Anita. *Mirrored Life* (11–12). 2002, Kensington $24.00 (0-7582-0077-3). Sara Jane, an African American girl jailed at the age of 15, spends her time behind bars earning a cosmetology license; on her release she changes her name to Serena but her subsequent success brings her to the attention of someone from her past; for mature teens. (Rev: BL 10/15/02)

3389 Bunting, Eve. *The Haunting of Safe Keep* (7–10). 1985, HarperCollins LB $12.89 (0-397-32113-9). In this romantic mystery, two college friends work out their family problems while investigating strange occurrences where they work. (Rev: BL 4/15/85; BR 11–12/85; SLJ 5/85; VOYA 8/85)

3390 Burke, Jan. *Bones* (10–12). 1999, Simon & Schuster $23.00 (0-684-85551-8). Crime reporter Irene Kelly finds herself in a world of trouble when she joins a police team heading into the mountains to find a murder victim's burial site; for mature teens. (Rev: BL 8/99*; VOYA 12/00)

3391 Burke, Jan. *Hocus* (10–12). 1997, Simon & Schuster $22.00 (0-684-80344-5). When her police hero husband is kidnapped by a group out to avenge murders that occurred years ago, sleuth/reporter Irene Kelly must unravel the complicated, long-ago murder case and find the real killer in order to save him. (Rev: BL 5/1/97; SLJ 11/97)

3392 Burns, Rex, and Mary Rose Sullivan. *Crime Classics: The Mystery Story from Poe to the Present* (9–12). 1990, Viking paper $14.95 (0-14-013128-0). Some of the mystery story writers represented in this fine anthology are Poe, Doyle, and Hammett.

3393 Busch, Frederick. *Girls* (10–12). 1997, Harmony $23.00 (0-517-70455-2). Jack, a disturbed Vietnam veteran who feels grief and guilt over the accidental death of his baby daughter, sets out to find the murderer of an adolescent girl who has been killed in a neighboring town in western New York state. (Rev: BL 1/1–15/97; SLJ 7/97)

3394 Butcher, A. J. *Spy High: Mission One* (7–10). 2004, Little, Brown $15.95 (0-316-73759-3); paper $6.99 (0-316-73760-7). This thriller is set in the year 2060 and deals with a group of students at a school known as Spy High who are training to become secret agents. (Rev: BL 5/1/04; SLJ 7/04)

3395 Cappo, Nan Willard. *Cheating Lessons* (7–10). 2002, Simon & Schuster $16.00 (0-689-84378-X). Bernadette, star of the high school quiz team, faces a dilemma when she guesses that cheating may explain her team's success. (Rev: BCCB 4/02; BL 3/15/02; HB 3–4/02*; HBG 10/02; SLJ 3/02; VOYA 2/02)

3396 Cargill, Linda. *Pool Party* (7–10). 1996, Scholastic paper $3.99 (0-590-58111-2). Sharon's beach party at a resort with a reputation for being haunted ends in murder. (Rev: SLJ 1/97)

3397 Carlon, Patricia. *The Souvenir* (10–12). 1996, Soho Pr. $20.00 (1-56947-048-0). The story of two girls who are hitchhiking in Australia, a murder, and a conspiracy of lies. (Rev: BL 1/1–15/96; SLJ 4/96)

3398 Carroll, James. *Secret Father* (10–12). 2003, Houghton $25.00 (0-618-15284-9). Foolishly adventurous American teens add to the tension in this riveting novel set in Cold War Berlin. (Rev: BL 6/1–15/03)

3399 Case, John. *The Genesis Code* (10–12). 1997, Fawcett $24.95 (0-449-91101-2). In this suspense novel that shifts from Italy to the United States, Joe Lassiter sets out to find the murderer of his sister and her son, and finds that the leads take him to a fertility clinic in Italy that has links to similar murders. (Rev: SLJ 10/97)

3400 Castaldo, Meg. *The Foreigner* (10–12). 2001, Pocket paper $12.95 (0-7434-1264-8). Alex Orlando, who is spending a few weeks house-sitting in Manhattan, gets involved in a dangerous situation when her neighbor is murdered. (Rev: BL 5/15/01)

3401 Chamberlain, Diane. *The Courage Tree* (11–12). 2001, MIRA $22.95 (1-55166-799-1). Aided by her lover, Janine searches frantically for her critically ill 8-year-old child who has disappeared from the scene of a car accident. (Rev: BL 2/15/01)

3402 Chamberlain, Diane. *Kiss River* (11–12). 2003, MIRA $23.95 (1-55166-664-2). A World War II romance and contemporary mystery and romantic relationship are interwoven in alternating suspenseful chapters set in a small Outer Banks community. (Rev: BL 2/1/03)

3403 Chandler, Elizabeth. *Dark Secrets: Legacy of Lies* (6–12). Series: Dark Secrets. 2000, Pocket paper $4.99 (0-7434-0028-3). Megan, 16, has finally met her grandmother, but she still feels like an outsider and her frightening dreams become more and more intense. (Rev: BCCB 2/01; BL 2/1/01; SLJ 1/01; VOYA 12/00)

3404 Chazin, Suzanne. *Flashover* (10–12). 2002, Putnam $25.95 (0-399-14850-7). Georgia, a New York fire marshal and single parent, investigates two suspicious deaths in this realistic and suspenseful novel. (Rev: BL 5/1/02)

3405 Christie, Agatha. *Curtain* (9–12). 1975, Amereon $22.95 (0-88411-386-8). Hercule Poirot returns to the country manor of Styles, the site of his first case (The Mysterious Affair at Styles), to solve another murder. This is one of many suitable titles by Christie.

3406 Christie, Agatha. *Death on the Nile* (9–12). 1992, HarperCollins paper $5.99 (0-06-100369-7). Everyone on board the steamer sailing along the Nile envies Linnet Doyle — until she is murdered. One of many recommended mysteries involving Hercule Poirot.

3407 Christie, Agatha. *Evil Under the Sun* (9–12). 1991, Berkley paper $5.99 (0-425-12960-8). M. Poirot solves the mystery of the murder of beautiful Arlena Marshall. One of many suitable Poirot mysteries.

3408 Christie, Agatha. *The Harlequin Tea Set and Other Stories* (10–12). 1997, Putnam $21.95 (0-399-14287-8). A collection of nine mystery stories never before published in the United States. (Rev: BL 3/15/97; SLJ 11/97)

3409 Christie, Agatha. *Miss Marple: The Complete Short Stories* (9–12). 1985, Berkley paper $12.95 (0-425-09486-3). Miss Marple, the sleuth of St. Mary Mead, shines in this collection of 20 stories. (Rev: BL 12/15/85)

3410 Christie, Agatha. *The Murder at the Vicarage* (9–12). 1984, Berkley paper $5.99 (0-425-09453-7). The first Miss Marple mystery by this prolific author, who has about 100 mysteries in print.

3411 Christie, Agatha. *The Murder of Roger Ackroyd* (9–12). 1985, Pocket paper $3.50 (0-671-49856-8). One of the earlier Hercule Poirot mysteries (first published in 1926), this one involves the murder of a retired businessman.

3412 Christie, Agatha. *Murder on the Orient Express* (9–12). 1991, HarperCollins paper $5.99 (0-06-100274-7). M. Poirot in one of his most famous cases, where each of the suspects appears to have a valid motive for murder.

3413 Christie, Agatha. *Sleeping Murder* (9–12). 1992, Demco $11.34 (0-606-12521-3); HarperCollins paper $5.99 (0-06-100380-8). Christie's famous female sleuth, Miss Marple, solves the mystery of a murder that occurred 18 years earlier. One of many recommended titles involving this unusual sleuth.

3414 Christie, Agatha. *Ten Little Indians* (9–12). 1984, Samuel French paper $5.50 (0-573-61639-6). One of the earliest (1939) and best of this prolific writer's mysteries.

3415 Christie, Agatha. *Witness for the Prosecution* (10–12). 1987, Berkley paper $5.99 (0-425-06809-9). One of the most famous mystery tales by this very popular writer.

3416 Ciencin, Scott. *Faceless* (6–10). Series: The Lurker Files. 1996, Random paper $6.99 (0-679-88235-9). An online/offline complicated thriller involving university students, a chat room, cyberidentities, and e-mail threats from "Dethboy" who claims to be responsible for the disappearance and possible death of one of the students. (Rev: SLJ 4/97)

3417 Clancy, Tom. *Without Remorse* (10–12). 1993, Putnam $24.95 (0-399-13825-0). Vietnam vet John Kelly's revenge against the murderers of his 20-

year-old girlfriend is an integral part of this complex thriller. (Rev: BL 6/1–15/93; SLJ 11/93)

3418 Clark, Carol Higgins. *Fleeced* (9–12). 2001, Scribner $22.00 (0-7432-0581-2). Detective Regan Reilly investigates the deaths of two men who had planned to endow their social club with millions. (Rev: BL 9/1/01)

3419 Clark, Carol Higgins. *Iced* (9–12). 1996, Warner paper $5.99 (0-446-60198-5). Los Angeles PI Regan Reilly, vacationing in Colorado, stumbles across a series of art thefts. (Rev: BL 5/15/95; SLJ 1/96)

3420 Clark, Mary Higgins. *Before I Say Good-Bye* (9–12). 2000, Simon & Schuster $26.00 (0-684-83598-3). This is one of the many suspenseful recommended mysteries by Clark, a masterful weaver of plots and characters. (Rev: BL 4/15/00)

3421 Clark, Mary Higgins, ed. *The International Association of Crime Writers Presents Bad Behavior* (8–12). 1995, Harcourt $20.00 (0-15-200179-4). Features many stories with young characters and less overt violence than adult fare. Includes works by Sara Paretsky, P. D. James, Lawrence Block, and Liza Cody. (Rev: BL 7/95)

3422 Clark, Mary Higgins. *Let Me Call You Sweetheart* (9–12). 1995, Simon & Schuster $7.50 (0-684-80396-8). Prosecutor Kerry McGrath scours the world of gem thieves, child stalkers, the Irish Mafia, and more to solve the murder of the beautiful Suzanne Reardon. (Rev: BL 4/1/95; SLJ 9/95)

3423 Clark, Mary Higgins. *On the Street Where You Live* (9–12). 2001, Simon & Schuster $26.00 (0-7432-0602-9). A fast-paced thriller about a murderer who seems to be following the pattern established by an 1890s killer. (Rev: BL 4/15/01)

3424 Clark, Mary Higgins. *Silent Night* (9–12). 1995, Simon & Schuster $16.00 (0-684-81545-1). Following a thief who has stolen his mother's wallet, 7-year-old Brian is kidnapped by an escaped convict who needs a hostage. (Rev: SLJ 2/96)

3425 Clark, Mary Higgins. *Stillwatch* (9–12). 1997, Pocket paper $7.99 (0-671-52820-3). A TV documentary producer finds mystery and danger when she begins investigating a vice presidential candidate in Washington.

3426 Clark, Mary Higgins. *Weep No More, My Lady* (9–12). 1993, Dell paper $6.99 (0-440-20098-9). At a fashionable California spa, Elizabeth encounters the man she thinks murdered her sister in this taut mystery. (Rev: BL 5/1/87)

3427 Clark, Mary Higgins. *Where Are the Children?* (9–12). 1992, Pocket paper $7.99 (0-671-74118-7). The son and daughter of Nancy Eldredge, a Cape Cod housewife, disappear and the police believe that she has murdered them.

3428 Clark, Mary Higgins. *While My Pretty One Sleeps* (9–12). 1990, Pocket paper $7.99 (0-671-67368-8). While investigating a murder, our heroine becomes convinced that someone has been hired to kill her. (Rev: BL 4/1/89; VOYA 4/89)

3429 Clark, Mary Higgins, and Carol Higgins Clark. *Deck the Halls* (10–12). 2000, Simon & Schuster $18.00 (0-7432-1200-2). In this first mystery by the mother-daughter team, characters from other books reappear and a touch of humor is added to the proceedings. (Rev: BL 11/1/00)

3430 Clark, Robert. *Love Among the Ruins* (10–12). 2001, Norton $24.95 (0-393-02015-0). In the summer of 1968 in Minneapolis, two thoughtful teens fall in love, causing their parents to rethink their lives. (Rev: BL 6/1–15/01)

3431 Cobb, James H. *Target Lock* (10–12). 2002, Putnam $25.95 (0-399-14849-3). Sea Fighter commander Amanda becomes entangled with a pirate named Makara Harkonon in this action-packed fourth book in the series. (Rev: BL 1/1–15/02)

3432 Coel, Margaret. *The Eagle Catcher* (10–12). 1987, Univ. Press of Colorado $22.50 (0-870-81367-6); Berkley paper $6.50 (0-425-15483-7). When a tribal councilman is murdered, his young nephew is a prime suspect in this first book in a series of fine mysteries that feature Father John O'Malley and Arapaho lawyer Vicky Holden. (Rev: BL BL 5/1/00)

3433 Coel, Margaret. *The Story Teller* (10–12). 1998, Prime Crime $21.95 (0-425-16538-8). Native American lawyer Vicky Holden's quest for a historic Arapaho ledger book leads to a trail of murder and deception. (Rev: BL 9/15/98; SLJ 5/99)

3434 Cohen, Mark. *The Fractal Murders* (10–12). 2004, Mysterious $25.00 (0-89296-799-4). In this clever mystery, a detective is challenged by a murderer who is systematically killing off the top American mathematicians. (Rev: BL 3/15/04)

3435 Conant, Susan. *Animal Appetite* (10–12). 1997, Doubleday $21.95 (0-385-47725-2). Holly Winter, a writer challenged to write about something other than her usual topic, dogs, researches a local 17th-century heroine who turned out to have been a murderer and ends up investigating a murder that took place 18 years earlier — which involved a dog. (Rev: SLJ 12/97)

3436 Cook, Robin. *Coma* (10–12). 1977, NAL paper $7.99 (0-451-15953-5). A young medical student uncovers a plot to kill patients.

3437 Cook, Robin. *Sphinx* (9–12). 1983, NAL paper $7.99 (0-451-15949-7). Set in Egypt, this thriller involves a young art specialist from Boston and an antique statue in a tale of danger and romance.

3438 Cook, Robin. *Vital Signs* (10–12). 1992, Berkley paper $7.99 (0-425-13176-9). A medical thriller that combines murder and infertility therapy. (Rev: BL 11/15/90)

3439 Coonts, Stephen. *Hong Kong* (10–12). 2000, St. Martin's $25.95 (0-312-25339-7). In this novel of international intrigue, Admiral Jake Grafton defends his wife against a Hong Kong gangster. (Rev: BL 7/00)

3440 Cormier, Robert. *In the Middle of the Night* (10–12). 1995, Delacorte $15.95 (0-385-32158-9). In this exploration of the dark underside of human emotions, a 16-year-old is drawn into a telephone game that drags him close to disaster. (Rev: BL 4/1/95; SLJ 5/95; VOYA 5/95)

3441 Cormier, Robert. *Tenderness* (10–12). 1997, Delacorte $16.95 (0-385-32286-0). For mature high school readers, this is a glimpse into the mind of a teenage serial killer who is about to be released from a detention center for murdering his mother and stepfather. (Rev: BL 2/1/97; BR 9–10/97; SLJ 3/97*; VOYA 4/97)

3442 Cornwell, Patricia. *All That Remains* (10–12). 1992, Scribner $20.00 (0-684-19395-7). A whodunit about the baffling serial murders of five college-age couples. (Rev: BL 6/1/92; SLJ 12/92)

3443 Cornwell, Patricia. *Cruel and Unusual* (10–12). 1993, Scribner $21.00 (0-684-19530-5). An edge-of-your-seat thriller with plenty of action, a gripping plot, and a mind-boggling climax. (Rev: BL 4/15/93; SLJ 11/93)

3444 Cornwell, Patricia. *From Potter's Field* (10–12). 1995, Scribner $23.50 (0-684-19598-4); 1996, Berkley paper $7.99 (0-425-15409-2). The Central Park (New York) murder of a young, homeless woman on Christmas sends medical examiner Scarpetta, her friend Captain Marino, and her niece on a chase that ends in the subway. (Rev: BL 5/1/95*)

3445 Coulter, Catherine. *Hemlock Bay* (10–12). 2001, Putnam $24.95 (0-399-14738-1). Could someone be out to kill Lily because she has inherited paintings worth millions of dollars? (Rev: BL 6/1–15/01)

3446 Coulter, Catherine. *Riptide* (10–12). 2000, Putnam $23.95 (0-399-14616-4). A suspenseful, violent thriller about Becca Matlock, a political speech-writer, and the stalker who follows her to a small town in Maine called Riptide. (Rev: BL 5/15/00)

3447 Cresswell, Helen, ed. *Mystery Stories: An Intriguing Collection* (8–12). Illus. 1996, Kingfisher paper $7.95 (0-7534-5025-9). A collection of 19 mystery stories from such writers as Sir Arthur Conan Doyle, Agatha Christie, Ray Bradbury, and Emily Brontë. (Rev: SLJ 2/97)

3448 Crew, Gary. *Angel's Gate* (8–12). 1995, Simon & Schuster paper $16.00 (0-689-80166-1). A murder mystery/coming-of-age story about a dead man's children who have escaped to live in the wild

and a 13-year-old girl who draws them back to civilization. (Rev: BL 10/1/95; SLJ 10/95; VOYA 4/96)

3449 Crichton, Michael. *Airframe* (10–12). 1996, Knopf $26.00 (0-679-44648-6). Casey Singleton leads an investigation into a mysterious airplane disaster in which three people are killed. (Rev: BL 11/15/96; SLJ 3/97)

3450 Crichton, Michael. *Prey* (10–12). 2002, HarperCollins $26.95 (0-06-621412-2). An experiment using nanoparticles runs amok in this suspenseful thriller. (Rev: BL 12/1/02*; SLJ 5/03)

3451 Crider, Bill. *Murder Takes a Break* (9–12). 1997, Walker $29.95 (0-8027-3308-5). Tru Smith, a detective who hates to leave his home and computer, investigates the disappearance of a college student. (Rev: BL 10/15/97; VOYA 12/97)

3452 Crider, Bill. *A Romantic Way to Die* (10–12). 2001, St. Martin's $22.95 (0-312-20907-X). Sheriff Dan Rhodes gets involved in a conference of romance writers after there is a murder. (Rev: BL 9/15/01)

3453 Cross, Amanda. *The Collected Stories of Amanda Cross* (10–12). 1997, Ballantine $19.95 (0-345-40817-9). In this collection of mystery stories, the reader is invited to solve each case from a complete set of clues. (Rev: BL 12/15/96; SLJ 5/97)

3454 Cross, Amanda. *Honest Doubt* (10–12). 2000, Ballantine $22.00 (0-345-44011-0). One of a series of recommended mysteries that feature the sleuth Kate Fansler and some fascinating puzzles. (Rev: BL 9/1/00)

3455 Cross, Gillian. *Phoning a Dead Man* (6–10). 2002, Holiday $16.95 (0-8234-1685-2). This suspenseful novel set in Russia alternates between the story of John, an amnesiac who is fleeing danger, and that of his sister and wheelchair-bound fiancee who are searching for him. (Rev: BCCB 5/02; BL 5/1/02; HB 7–8/02; HBG 10/02; SLJ 5/02; VOYA 6/02)

3456 Cullen, Robert. *Dispatch from a Cold Country* (10–12). 1996, Fawcett $21.00 (0-449-91258-2). Deputy foreign news editor Colin Burke takes a leave from his job and goes to Russia to investigate the brutal murder there of Jennifer Morelli, a young reporter, who had discovered important information for a news story but was killed before she could reveal it. (Rev: SLJ 3/97)

3457 Cussler, Clive. *Cyclops* (9–12). 1986, Pocket paper $7.99 (0-671-70464-8). A thriller involving hero Dirk Pitt and such elements as a missing blimp and a secret mission to the moon. (Rev: BL 1/15/86)

3458 Cussler, Clive. *Flood Tide* (10–12). 1997, Simon & Schuster $26.00 (0-684-80298-8). A page-turner that involves the adventurer Dirk Pitt, who finds a lost treasure, destroys an evil villain, and saves a woman's life while protecting the country from possible economic collapse. (Rev: BL 8/97; SLJ 12/97)

3459 Dailey, Janet. *Shifting Calder Wind* (11–12). 2003, Kensington $24.00 (0-7582-0067-6). The romantic and suspenseful saga of the Calder family continues in this installment, which finds Chase Calder a victim of amnesia. (Rev: BL 6/1–15/03)

3460 Dain, Claudia. *A Kiss to Die For* (10–12). 2003, Leisure paper $6.99 (0-8439-5059-5). A tale of romance, adventure, and suspense featuring a hunt for a killer of young women in the Old West. (Rev: BL 3/15/03)

3461 D'Amato, Barbara. *Authorized Personnel Only* (10–12). 2000, Tor $24.95 (0-312-86564-3). Suze Figueroa and her partner Norm Bennis are the street cops assigned to catch a serial killer of homeless people in this thriller for older teens. (Rev: BL 11/1/00)

3462 D'Amato, Barbara. *Hard Road* (10–12). 2001, Scribner $24.00 (0-7432-0095-0). When journalist Cat Marsala takes her young nephew to the fictional Oz festival in Chicago, two murders occur within yards of the pair. (Rev: BL 7/01*; SLJ 2/02; VOYA 6/02)

3463 Dams, Jeanne M. *Green Grow the Victims* (10–12). 2001, Walker $23.95 (0-8027-3355-7). Hilda Johansson, a housekeeper and amateur sleuth in early-20th-century South Bend, Indiana, is asked by her boss to look into the mysterious disappearance of city council candidate Dan Malloy, who also happens to be the uncle of her boyfriend. (Rev: BL 5/1/01)

3464 Darnton, John. *Mind Catcher* (11–12). 2002, Dutton $25.95 (0-525-94662-4). Drama and science abound as 13-year-old Tyler is scheduled for experimental stem cell implantation; for mature teens. (Rev: BL 8/02)

3465 David, James F. *Before the Cradle Falls* (10–12). 2002, Tor $25.95 (0-765-30319-1). Time travel adds a fantasy element to this suspenseful tale of a serial killer called the Cradle Robber. (Rev: BL 5/15/02)

3466 Davidson, Diane Mott. *Sticks and Scones* (10–12). 2001, Bantam $23.95 (0-553-10724-0). Caterer Goldy Schultz is planning several Elizabethan meals in a castle transported from England to Colorado when a body is found on the castle grounds and her husband is wounded. (Rev: BL 3/15/01)

3467 Davidson, Nicole. *Dying to Dance* (8–12). 1996, Avon paper $3.99 (0-380-78152-2). Carrie, a competitor on the ballroom-dance circuit, is suspected of murdering her archrival. (Rev: SLJ 7/96)

3468 Davis, Lindsey. *The Iron Hand of Mars* (10–12). 1993, Ballantine paper $5.99 (0-345-38024-X). Roman history and the detective story meet: Marcus

Didius Falco, a private eye in 70 A.D., becomes involved with a rebel chief, a priestess, a legion, and a missing legate. (Rev: BL 9/15/93; SLJ 3/94)

3469 Davis, Linsey. *Silver Pigs* (9–12). 1989, Ballantine paper $5.99 (0-345-36907-6). In this first in a series of mysteries set in Rome in the first century A.D. involving private detective Marcus Didius Falco, he discovers a plan to overthrow the emperor, Vespasian. (Rev: BL 5/1/00)

3470 Dawson, Janet. *Nobody's Child* (10–12). 1995, Fawcett $21.00 (0-449-90976-X). In this baffling mystery, private investigator Jeri Howard is hired by a woman to find out if a recently discovered body is that of her missing teenage daughter. (Rev: BL 10/1/95; SLJ 4/96)

3471 Day, Dianne. *The Bohemian Murders: A Fremont Jones Mystery* (10–12). 1997, Doubleday $21.95 (0-385-47923-9). While working as a lighthouse keeper on the California coast in 1907, Fremont Jones discovers the body of a murdered woman and decides she must find the culprit. (Rev: BL 7/97; SLJ 12/97)

3472 Day, Marele. *The Disappearances of Madalena Grimaldi* (10–12). 1996, Walker $29.95 (0-8027-3277-1). Claudia, an Australian detective, is hired to find a missing teenage girl, while at the same time trying to solve the 30-year-old mystery of her own missing father. (Rev: SLJ 11/96)

3473 Deaver, Jeffery. *The Empty Chair* (10–12). 2000, Simon & Schuster $25.00 (0-684-85563-1). This Lincoln Rhyme mystery for better readers involves the quadriplegic criminalist and his associate, Amelia Sachs, in a case of kidnapping, murder, and forensic detail. (Rev: BL 3/1/00* ; SLJ 12/00; VOYA 12/00)

3474 Deaver, Jeffery. *Speaking in Tongues* (10–12). 2000, Simon & Schuster $25.00 (0-684-87126-2). The teenage daughter in a dysfunctional family is kidnapped by a madman in this suspenseful thriller. (Rev: BL 11/1/00)

3475 DeCure, John. *Reef Dance* (10–12). 2001, St. Martin's $24.95 (0-312-27297-9). A young lawyer who likes surfing gets a case involving parents who are accused of selling their newborn son. (Rev: BL 8/01)

3476 DeFelice, Cynthia. *Death at Devil's Bridge* (6–10). 2000, Farrar $16.00 (0-374-31723-2). On Martha's Vineyard, 13-year-old Ben Daggett and his friend Jeff become a little too involved with an older boy who is dealing in drugs. (Rev: BCCB 9/00; BL 8/00; HBG 3/01; SLJ 9/00; VOYA 12/00)

3477 Dekker, Ted. *Three* (10–12). 2003, W Publishing Group $19.99 (0-8499-4372-8). A seminary student struggles to figure out the riddles posed by a mysterious phone call. (Rev: BL 10/1/03)

3478 Delaney, Mark. *Of Heroes and Villains* (7–10). 1999, Peachtree paper $5.95 (1-56145-178-9). Using the world of comic books as a backdrop, this mystery features four teen sleuths known as the Misfits and the puzzle of a stolen film starring comic book hero Hyperman. (Rev: BL 7/99)

3479 Deveraux, Jude. *Forever: A Novel of Good and Evil, Love and Hope* (10–12). 2002, Pocket paper $7.99 (0-671-01420-X). Darci Monroe, a young woman with psychic powers, is hired to help wealthy Adam Montgomery find information about the deaths of his parents in this tale that blends mystery, fantasy, and romance. (Rev: BL 10/15/02)

3480 Diamond, Diana. *The Babysitter* (10–12). 2001, St. Martin's $23.95 (0-312-28047-5). In this suspenseful thriller, Ellie and Gordon realize that the 19-year-old babysitter they have hired for the summer is in a position to blackmail them and therefore must go. (Rev: BL 5/15/01)

3481 Diggs, Anita D. *A Meeting in the Ladies Room* (10–12). 2004, Dafina $24.00 (0-4582-0234-2). This mystery that involves the murder of a white publishing executive also explores the world of a group of black professionals in Manhattan's publishing world. (Rev: BL 3/1/04)

3482 Doss, James D. *Grandmother Spider* (10–12). 2001, Morrow $23.00 (0-380-97722-2). In this book, part of a recommended mystery series, Charlie Moon, a Ute police officer, and his aunt, a Ute shaman, join forces to investigate the disappearance of two men from the shores of a local lake. (Rev: BL 1/1–15/01; SLJ 8/01)

3483 Doss, James D. *White Shell Woman: A Charlie Moon Mystery* (10–12). 2002, Morrow $23.95 (0-06-019932-6). Ute Indian Charlie Moon tries to find who — or what — is responsible for two deaths at a sacred burial site. (Rev: BL 1/1–15/02)

3484 Doughty, Louise. *An English Murder* (10–12). 2000, Carroll & Graf $23.00 (0-7867-0757-7). A young reporter for a Cotswold village newspaper finds she is one of the investigators when a local couple is murdered. (Rev: BL 5/1/00)

3485 Ducker, Bruce. *Bloodlines* (10–12). 2000, Permanent Press $25.00 (1-57962-060-4). In this thriller for mature readers, a young man's desire to claim his inheritance and find out more about his family takes him on a romp through Europe. (Rev: BL 1/1–15/00)

3486 Du Maurier, Daphne. *Rebecca* (9–12). 1938, Doubleday $20.00 (0-385-04380-5); Avon paper $5.99 (0-380-00917-X). In this gothic romance, a timid girl marries a wealthy widower whose wife died mysteriously. Two other exciting novels by Du Maurier are *Hungry Hill* and *The Scapegoat*. (Rev: BL 6/1/88)

3487 Dunant, Sarah. *Fatlands* (9–12). 1994, Penzler paper $21.00 (1-883402-82-4). Investigator Hannah Wolfe baby-sits for a famous scientist's daughter. When a bomb kills the child, Hannah believes it was meant for the scientist so she hunts for the killers. (Rev: BL 11/1/94*)

3488 Duncan, Lois. *Daughters of Eve* (7–10). 1979, Dell paper $4.99 (0-440-91864-2). A group of girls comes under the evil influence of the faculty sponsor of their club.

3489 Duncan, Lois. *Don't Look Behind You* (7–12). 1990, Bantam paper $5.50 (0-440-20729-0). April and her family are on the run trying to escape from a hired hit man. (Rev: BL 5/15/89; SLJ 7/89; VOYA 8/89)

3490 Duncan, Lois. *Down a Dark Hall* (7–10). 1974, Little, Brown paper $5.50 (0-440-91805-7). From the moment of arrival, Kit feels uneasy at her new boarding school.

3491 Duncan, Lois. *I Know What You Did Last Summer* (7–10). 1990, Pocket paper $3.99 (0-671-73589-6). Four teenagers try to hide a hit-and-run accident in which they were involved.

3492 Duncan, Lois. *Killing Mr. Griffin* (7–10). 1978, Dell paper $5.50 (0-440-94515-1). A kidnapping plot involving a disliked English teacher leads to murder. (Rev: BL 10/15/88)

3493 Duncan, Lois. *The Third Eye* (7–10). 1984, Little, Brown $15.95 (0-316-19553-7); Dell paper $5.50 (0-440-98720-2). Karen learns that she has mental powers that enable her to locate missing children. (Rev: BL 7/87)

3494 Duncan, Lois. *The Twisted Window* (7–10). 1987, Dell paper $5.50 (0-440-20184-5). Tracy grows to regret the fact that she has helped a young man kidnap his 2-year-old half-sister. (Rev: BL 9/1/87; BR 1–2/88; SLJ 9/87; VOYA 11/87)

3495 Dunn, Hilda. *The Hanged Man: A Romance of 1947* (10–12). 2001, Creative Arts paper $13.95 (0-88739-324-1). On a ship bound for England in 1947, a woman is murdered and one of the passengers, Kate Clark, soon finds she is involved with a ring of Nazi thieves. (Rev: BL 4/15/01)

3496 Dunning, John. *The Bookman's Wake* (9–12). 1995, Scribner $21.00 (0-684-80003-9). Ex-cop-turned-book dealer Cliff Janeway tracks down a priceless edition of a book and encounters intrigue and murder. (Rev: BL 4/1/95*)

3497 Edwards, Grace. *If I Should Die* (10–12). 1977, Bantam paper $5.99 (0-533-57631-9). Former New York City cop Mali Anderson is drawn into a murder case that involves a crack cocaine operation and a journey through Harlem's rich cultural life. Part of a fine series. (Rev: BL 5/1/00)

3498 Edwards, Grace F. *A Toast Before Dying* (9–12). 1998, Doubleday $21.95 (0-385-48524-7). During a sizzling hot summer in Harlem, former cop Mali Anderson has to keep her wits about her in life-compromising situations as she races to clear the name of a murder suspect. (Rev: BL 4/15/98; VOYA 12/98)

3499 Elrod, P. N. *The Vampire Files: Lady Crymsyn* (10–12). 2000, Ace $22.95 (0-441-00724-4). Detective Jack Fleming, who is a sympathetic vampire with human friends, takes on the mob in post-Prohibition Chicago. (Rev: VOYA 4/01)

3500 Epstein, Carole. *Perilous Relations: A Barbara Simons Mystery* (9–12). 1997, Walker $29.95 (0-8027-3309-3). Barbara Simons, who loves poking her nose into other people's business, has her hands full when she tries to solve the mystery surrounding the death of her former boss. (Rev: VOYA 4/98)

3501 Erickson, K. J. *Third Person Singular* (10–12). 2001, St. Martin's $24.95 (0-312-26666-9). This mystery involving the murder of teenage girl is told from four different points of view. (Rev: BL 12/1/00)

3502 Evanovich, Janet. *One for the Money* (9–12). 1994, Scribner $20.00 (0-684-19639-5). An out-of-work discount-lingerie buyer becomes a bounty hunter to earn money and is hired to find a wanted cop from her past. (Rev: BL 9/1/94*)

3503 Feder, Harriet K. *Death on Sacred Ground* (6–10). Series: Vivi Hartman. 2001, Lerner $14.95 (0-8225-0741-2). Teen sleuth Vivi Hartman encounters a mystery at the funeral of an Orthodox Jewish girl who died on sacred Indian ground. (Rev: BCCB 3/01; BL 11/15/01; HBG 10/01; SLJ 3/01)

3504 *Felonious Felines* (10–12). Ed. by Carol Gorman and Ed Gorman. 2000, Five Star $22.95 (0-7862-2672-2). There are 12 mystery stories in this collection, all dealing with cats in a variety of situations and locales. (Rev: BL 7/00)

3505 Ferguson, Alane. *Overkill* (7–10). 1992, Bradbury LB $14.95 (0-02-734523-8); Avon paper $3.99 (0-380-72167-8). Lacey is seeing a therapist about nightmares in which she stabs her friend Celeste; when Celeste is found dead, Lacey is falsely arrested for the crime. (Rev: BL 1/1/93; SLJ 1/93)

3506 Ferguson, Alane. *Show Me the Evidence* (7–12). 1989, Avon paper $3.99 (0-380-70962-7). In this mystery story, a 17-year-old girl is fearful that her best friend might be involved in the mysterious deaths of several children. (Rev: BL 4/1/89; BR 1–2/90; SLJ 3/89; VOYA 6/89)

3507 Follett, Ken. *Code to Zero* (10–12). 2000, Dutton $26.95 (0-525-94563-6). As in his first big success, *Eye of the Needle* (1978), the author uses Cold War espionage as a subject with plenty of page-turning suspense. (Rev: BL 10/15/00*)

3508 Ford, G. M. *Cast in Stone* (10–12). 1996, Walker $32.95 (0-8027-3267-4). Marge contacts hard-boiled Leo Waterman, a former flame and now a private investigator, to examine the mysterious

circumstances surrounding the death of her son and his fiancee. (Rev: BL 4/1/96; SLJ 1/97)

3509 Forsyth, Frederick. *Avenger* (11–12). 2003, St. Martin's $26.95 (0-312-31951-7). A riveting story of international intrigue that ranges from World War II to the eve of September 11, 2001, and includes the underground tunnels of the Vietnam War and the horrors of the conflict in Bosnia. (Rev: BL 7/03*)

3510 Francis, Dick. *Bolt* (10–12). 1988, Fawcett paper $5.95 (0-449-21239-4). Steeplechase jockey Kit Fielding becomes involved in a plot to sell guns to terrorists. (Rev: BL 12/1/86)

3511 Francis, Dick. *Come to Grief* (9–12). 1999, Pocket paper $9.98 (0-671-04422-2). Ex-jockey-turned-sleuth Sid Halley searches for the culprit who has committed senseless acts of mutilation on prized race horses and discovers it is his old pal and rival. (Rev: BL 8/95*)

3512 Francis, Dick. *The Edge* (10–12). 1990, Fawcett paper $6.99 (0-449-21719-1). In a mixture of horse racing and railroads, this murder mystery takes place on a transcontinental train in Canada. (Rev: BL 11/15/88)

3513 Francis, Dick. *Shattered* (10–12). 2000, Putnam $25.95 (0-399-14660-1). This writer of more than 40 recommended mysteries again uses the racetrack as his setting in this story of the mysterious death of a jockey. (Rev: BL 8/00)

3514 Francis, Dick. *To the Hilt* (10–12). 1996, Putnam $24.95 (0-399-14185-5). A young painter living in Scotland returns to London and investigates the disappearance of his stepfather's financial advisor and a considerable amount of cash. (Rev: SLJ 1/97)

3515 Francis, Dick. *Whip Hand* (10–12). 1999, Penguin paper $6.99 (0-515-12504-0). An ex-jockey turned private investigator is hired to probe into the causes of several mysterious events at a racetrack. Also use *Proof* and *Risk*.

3516 Francis, Dick. *Wild Horses* (9–12). 1995, Jove paper $5.99 (0-515-11789-7). A filmmaker's latest movie is based upon a real-life horse-racing tragedy involving a hanging death ruled a suicide. As the film producer uncovers new secrets, he suspects murder. (Rev: BL 8/94; SLJ 1/95)

3517 Friedman, Kinky. *God Bless John Wayne* (10–12). 1995, Simon & Schuster $22.00 (0-684-81051-4). A fast-paced mystery about detective Kinky Friedman, who is hired to find the birth mother of his friend Ratso (a.k.a. Larry Sloman) and confronts a number of obstacles in solving the case, among them Ratso's failure to fill him in on everything (including the death of a previous investigator). (Rev: BL 9/1/95; SLJ 4/96)

3518 Funderburk, Robert. *Winter of Grace* (10–12). 1998, Bethany paper $8.99 (1-55661-616-3). Deputy Dylan St. John investigates a string of robberies and murders that lead him to a troubled Vietnam vet, his small daughter, and his younger brother. (Rev: SLJ 3/99)

3519 Gaines, Ernest J. *A Lesson Before Dying* (9–12). Series: Borzoi Reader. 1993, Knopf $25.00 (0-679-41477-0); Random paper $12.00 (0-679-74166-6). In the 1940s in rural Louisiana, an uneducated African American man is sentenced to die for a crime he was incapable of committing. (Rev: SLJ 7/93*; VOYA 10/93)

3520 Gansky, Alton. *Dark Moon* (10–12). 2002, Zondervan paper $12.99 (0-310-23558-8). A mysterious red cloud on the moon causes consternation. (Rev: BL 10/1/02)

3521 Garcia, Eric. *Anonymous Rex: A Detective Story* (10–12). 1999, Villard $23.00 (0-375-50326-9). A velociraptor-turned-detective investigates a fire at dinosaur club in this entertaining spoof set in a world in which dinosaurs coexist with humans through the use of elaborate disguises. (Rev: BL 7/99; SLJ 2/00; VOYA 4/00)

3522 Gardner, John. *Bottled Spider* (11–12). 2002, Severn $26.95 (0-7278-5829-7). In World War II London, a serial killer called Golly Goldfinch is eventually caught through the efforts of Detective Sergeant Suzie Mountford and her handsome supervisor "Dandy Tom" Livermore; for mature teens. (Rev: BL 9/15/02)

3523 Gardner, John. *Maestro* (9–12). 1993, Penzler $23.00 (1-883402-24-7). A multigenerational epic spanning 10 decades that focuses on a world-famous orchestra conductor who becomes a spy. (Rev: BL 9/1/93*)

3524 Garretson, James D. *The Deadwood Conspiracy* (10–12). 1996, DeHart $23.75 (0-9649706-0-0). Complete with a surprise ending, this thrilling adult novel combines international intrigue, murder, romance, and a conspiracy involving top-ranking government officials. (Rev: SLJ 9/96)

3525 Gaus, P. L. *Clouds Without Rain* (10–12). 2001, Ohio Univ. $24.95 (0-8214-1379-1); paper $12.95 (0-8214-1380-5). A fascinating mystery (part of a series) involving the Ohio Amish and a local college professor who helps solve crimes. (Rev: BL 5/1/01)

3526 Gavin, Thomas. *Breathing Water* (9–12). 1994, Arcade $21.95 (1-55970-232-X). The mystery of a young boy's identity confuses the citizens of Rising Sun and causes tragedy to the boy. (Rev: SLJ 7/94)

3527 Gear, Kathleen, and W. Michael Gear. *The Summoning God* (10–12). Illus. 2000, Tor $25.95 (0-312-86532-5). Part of the successful Anasazi series, this mystery tells how a white archaeologist and a Seneca university professor combine forces to solve murders that have taken place in both the past and the present. (Rev: BL 6/1–15/00)

3528 Gear, Kathleen O'Neal, and W. Michael Gear. *The Visitant* (10–12). 1999, Forge $19.95 (0-312-86531-7). Anasazi history and modern archaeological methods feature in this mystery story involving the discovery of women's remains at a site in New Mexico. (Rev: BL 7/99; VOYA 2/00)

3529 Gee, Maurice. *The Fat Man* (8–10). 1997, Simon & Schuster $16.00 (0-689-81182-9). At first, this small New Zealand town welcomes back Herbert, a mysterious fat man who supposedly made good in America, but soon everyone becomes suspicious of his motives. (Rev: BL 12/15/97; BR 5–6/98; HBG 3/98; SLJ 11/97*; VOYA 12/97)

3530 Gee, Maurice. *The Fire-Raiser* (6–12). 1992, Houghton $16.00 (0-395-62428-2). A thriller set in New Zealand during World War I dramatizes the secret fury of a pyromaniac and relates it to the mob violence let loose in the community by jingoism and war. (Rev: BL 10/15/92*; SLJ 9/92)

3531 Gerritsen, Tess. *Bloodstream* (10–12). 1998, Pocket $23.00 (0-671-01675-X). In this gory medical thriller, Dr. Claire Elliot becomes involved in a mysterious epidemic of teen violence at her son's high school in a small town. (Rev: BL 7/97; SLJ 1/99)

3532 Gibbs, Tony. *Shadow Queen* (9–12). 1992, Mysterious paper $4.99 (0-446-40108-0). The security of the House of Windsor is threatened by a girl possessed by the spirit of her ancestor, Mary, Queen of Scots, and her possession of letters supposedly written by her. (Rev: BL 12/15/91*)

3533 Giberga, Jane Sughure. *Friends to Die For* (9–12). 1997, Dial $15.99 (0-8037-2094-7). In the world of wealthy New York teens, Crissy does not realize that she has invited a murderer to her party. (Rev: BR 1–2/98; HBG 3/98; VOYA 12/97)

3534 Gilbert, Anna. *A Hint of Witchcraft* (10–12). 2000, St. Martin's $23.95 (0-312-19984-8). This mystery with a touch of witchcraft is set in the 1920s and deals with an enigmatic stranger in town, Linden Grey, and how people are strangely attracted to her. (Rev: BL 8/00)

3535 Gilder, Joshua. *Ghost Image* (11–12). 2002, Simon & Schuster $23.00 (0-7432-2312-8). A gripping story of a doctor suspected of crimes including a vicious attack on his girlfriend; for mature teens. (Rev: BL 10/15/02; SLJ 6/03)

3536 Gilman, Dorothy. *Mrs. Pollifax and the Hong Kong Buddha* (9–12). 1985, Fawcett paper $5.99 (0-449-20983-0). This unlikely CIA agent gets involved in a plan by terrorists to destroy Hong Kong. Another in this series is *Mrs. Pollifax on the China Station* (1983). (Rev: BL 11/1/85)

3537 Gilstrap, John. *Nathan's Run* (8–12). 1997, Warner paper $6.99 (0-446-60468-2). At the age of only 12, Nathan Bailey is on the run from the police and determined to tell his side of the story. (Rev: BL 12/15/95; SLJ 4/97)

3538 Goldberg, Leonard S. *Deadly Exposure* (10–12). 1998, NAL $23.95 (0-525-94427-3). Forensic pathologist Joanna Blalock joins a scientific expedition off the coast of Alaska and encounters murder, a deadly bacterium, a pending epidemic, an earthquake, a shipwreck, and icebergs. (Rev: BL 9/15/98; SLJ 4/99)

3539 Goulart, Ron. *Groucho Marx: Master Detective* (10–12). 1998, Thomas Dunne $22.95 (0-312-18106-X). Set in Hollywood during 1937, this murder mystery involving the death of a starlet features Groucho Marx and detective Frank Denby, who is hired by the comedian to solve the crime. (Rev: SLJ 7/98)

3540 Grace, C. L. *The Merchant of Death* (9–12). 1995, St. Martin's $19.95 (0-312-13124-0). In this mystery set in medieval Britain, healer Kathryn Swinbrooke and soldier Colum Murtagh must find a tax collector's murderer to recover the royal taxes stolen from him. (Rev: BL 6/1–15/95; SLJ 11/95)

3541 Grafton, Sue. *G Is for Gumshoe* (10–12). 1990, Holt $25.00 (0-8050-0461-0). In this installment of the alphabet murders, Kinsey Millhone is involved in a missing persons case and a hired killer is out to get her. (Rev: BL 3/15/90; SLJ 9/90)

3542 Grafton, Sue. *M Is for Malice* (10–12). 1996, Holt $25.00 (0-8050-3637-7). After detective Kinsey finds Guy Malek, missing heir to a huge fortune, the man is murdered in this part of Grafton's alphabet mystery series. (Rev: BL 9/15/96; SLJ 3/97)

3543 Grafton, Sue. *P Is for Peril* (10–12). 2001, Putnam $26.95 (0-399-14719-5). In this Kinsey Millhone mystery, part of a recommended series, a rich doctor is found dead and his ex-wife is among the suspects. (Rev: BL 3/15/01)

3544 Green, Chloe. *Fashion Victim: A Dallas O'Connor Mystery* (11–12). 2002, Kensington $22.00 (1-57566-715-0). All is not as perfect as it seems when stylist-sleuth Dallas arrives for a video shoot in the Caribbean; for mature teens. (Rev: BL 12/1/02)

3545 Green, Timothy. *Twilight Boy* (7–10). 1998, Northland LB $12.95 (0-873586-70-0); paper $6.95 (0-873586-40-9). Navajo folkways form the background of this gripping mystery about a boy who is haunted by the memory of his dead brother and an evil that is preying on his Navajo community. (Rev: BL 4/15/98; HBG 9/98; VOYA 8/98)

3546 Greene, Graham. *The Heart of the Matter* (10–12). 1948, Viking paper $13.00 (0-14-018496-

1). A thriller about a man caught in a web of adultery and blackmail from which he can't escape.

3547 Greene, Graham. *The Power and the Glory* (10–12). 1990, Viking paper $12.95 (0-14-018499-6). This thriller set in Mexico presents as its central character an alcoholic priest who has fathered a daughter.

3548 Grindle, Lucretia. *The Nightspinners* (10–12). 2003, Random $23.95 (0-375-50776-0). In this suspenseful tale, Susannah, whose identical twin Marina has been murdered, begins to fear for her own life after she experiences some of the same strange events that preceded her sister's death. (Rev: BL 1/1–15/03)

3549 Grisham, John. *The Client* (9–12). 1993, Doubleday $23.50 (0-385-42471-X). Mark Sway, 11, witnesses a Mafia lawyer's suicide, which puts him in danger from Barry the Blade and a politically ambitious U.S. attorney. (Rev: BL 2/1/93*; SLJ 7/93; VOYA 8/93)

3550 Grisham, John. *The Pelican Brief* (9–12). 1992, Doubleday $24.95 (0-385-42198-2). A law student runs for her life after discovering who murdered two supreme court justices. (Rev: BL 1/15/92)

3551 Grisham, John. *The Street Lawyer* (10–12). 1998, Doubleday $27.95 (0-385-49099-2); Dell paper $7.99 (0-440-22570-1). In this fast-moving plot, a successful young lawyer's investigations raise serious questions about his firm's role in evicting homeless people during a cold winter. (Rev: BL 2/15/98; SLJ 6/98)

3552 Guy, Rosa. *The Disappearance* (7–10). 1979, Delacorte paper $4.99 (0-440-92064-7). A 16-year-old African American boy is accused of a kidnapping. Followed by *New Guys Around the Block* and *And I Heard a Bird Sing*.

3553 Hall, Lynn. *A Killing Freeze* (6–10). 1990, Avon paper $2.95 (0-380-75491-6). A loner endangers her own life to find a murderer. (Rev: BL 8/88; BR 1–2/89; SLJ 9/88; VOYA 12/88)

3554 Hall, Lynn. *Ride a Dark Horse* (7–10). 1987, Avon paper $2.95 (0-380-75370-7). A teenage girl is fired from her job on a horse-breeding farm because she is getting too close to solving a mystery. (Rev: BL 9/15/87; BR 11–12/87; SLJ 12/87; VOYA 10/87)

3555 Hardwick, Michael. *The Revenge of the Hound: The New Sherlock Holmes Novel* (9–12). Illus. 1987, Windsor paper $3.95 (1-55817-166-5). A collection of short stories that faithfully re-create the characters and the suspense of the original Sherlock Holmes stories. (Rev: BR 5–6/88; SLJ 4/88; VOYA 6/88)

3556 Harris, Lee. *The Labor Day Murder* (9–12). 1998, Fawcett paper $5.99 (0-449-15017-8). A murder is committed on Fire Island over Labor Day, and vacationers Christine Bennett and husband Jack begin an investigation. (Rev: SLJ 12/98)

3557 Hathaway, Robin. *The Doctor Digs a Grave* (10–12). 1998, St. Martin's $22.95 (0-312-18568-5). This mystery involves a sleuth cardiologist, Dr. Andrew Fenimore, the forgotten customs of the Lenape Indians, and the death of a young girl, whose body is found buried in an upright position facing east. (Rev: SLJ 10/98)

3558 Haynes, Betsy. *Deadly Deception* (7–10). 1994, Dell paper $3.99 (0-440-21947-7). A 17-year-old gets involved in the murder of a favorite school counselor. (Rev: BL 5/15/94; SLJ 6/94)

3559 Heilbrun, Robert. *Offer of Proof* (10–12). 2003, Morrow $24.95 (0-06-053812-0). Arch Gold takes on the defense of a young African American man accused of murder in this compelling thriller. (Rev: BL 9/15/03; SLJ 3/04)

3560 Henry, April. *Learning to Fly* (11–12). 2002, St. Martin's $23.95 (0-312-29052-7). Free, a pregnant 19-year-old in search of a new life, adopts the identity of a hitchhiker who dies in a car accident in this suspenseful mystery; for mature teens. (Rev: BL 3/15/02*)

3561 Henry, April. *Square in the Face* (10–12). 2000, HarperCollins $24.00 (0-06-019205-4). An adult mystery that features a plucky young woman who investigates a shady adoption clinic. (Rev: BL 1/1–15/00)

3562 Henry, Sue. *Beneath the Ashes* (10–12). 2000, Morrow $23.00 (0-380-97662-5). In this novel set in Alaska and part of the Jessie Arnold series, our heroine, who is training a new pack of sled dogs, becomes part of a mystery that involves arson and perhaps murder. (Rev: BL 5/1/00)

3563 Henry, Sue. *Dead North* (10–12). 2001, Morrow $24.00 (0-380-97881-4). In this, the sixth Jessie Arnold story, dogsledder Jessie gets involved with a teenage runaway and the boy's shadowy pursuer. (Rev: BL 5/1/01)

3564 Henry, Sue. *Death Takes Passage* (10–12). 1997, Avon paper $22.00 (0-380-97469-X). An Alaska state trooper and his girlfriend investigate a series of grave crimes including murder aboard a ship during a reenactment of a historic moment during the Klondike Gold Rush. (Rev: BL 7/97; SLJ 12/97)

3565 Hess, Joan. *Dear Miss Demeanor* (10–12). 1987, St. Martin's paper $5.99 (0-312-97313-6). In this first of a recommended series, Claire Malloy investigates the sudden death of the principal of the school at which she is a substitute teacher. (Rev: BL 5/1/00)

3566 Hess, Joan. *The Maggody Militia* (10–12). 1997, Dutton paper $21.95 (0-525-94236-X). This humorous mystery set in a small Arkansas town

involves the murder of a visiting survivalist. (Rev: BL 2/15/97; SLJ 9/97)

3567 Heynen, Jim. *Cosmos Coyote and William the Nice* (9–12). 2000, Holt $16.95 (0-8050-6434-6). Cosmos is sent to a Christian school as a punishment and ends up falling in love with born-again Christian Cherlyn. (Rev: BL 6/1–15/00; HBG 3/01; SLJ 7/00)

3568 Higgins, Jack. *The Eagle Has Flown* (9–12). 1990, Pocket paper $6.99 (0-671-72737-7). The sequel to *The Eagle Has Landed,* in which Devlin is asked by the Germans to parachute into England to free the formerly believed-dead Steiner. (Rev: BL 3/1/91)

3569 Higgins, Jack. *The President's Daughter* (10–12). 1997, Putnam $23.95 (0-399-14239-8). Three dedicated sleuths try to locate the president's daughter, who has been kidnapped by a group of villains. (Rev: BL 3/15/97; SLJ 11/97)

3570 Hill, Reginald. *Killing the Lawyers* (10–12). 1997, St. Martin's $23.95 (0-312-16877-2). Joe Six-smith, a black English private investigator, tries to clear his own name as a murder suspect while solving the mystery of threats to the life of a popular young athlete. (Rev: SLJ 3/98)

3571 Hill, William. *The Vampire Hunters* (7–12). 1998, Otter Creek $19.95 (1-890611-05-0); paper $12.95 (1-890611-02-6). Members of a gang called the Graveyard Armadillos are convinced that Marcus Chandler is a vampire, and 15-year-old Scooter Keyshaw is determined to find the truth. (Rev: BL 10/15/98; SLJ 2/99)

3572 Hillerman, Tony. *The First Eagle* (10–12). 1998, HarperCollins $25.00 (0-06-017581-8). Jim Chee of the Navajo Tribal Police and Joe Leaphorn, now a private detective, join forces once again to investigate a murder and the disappearance of a noted biologist. (Rev: BL 7/97; SLJ 1/99)

3573 Hillerman, Tony. *The Joe Leaphorn Mysteries: Dance Hall of the Dead, Listening Woman* (9–12). 1994, Random $9.99 (0-517-12584-6). Three stories all feature the Navajo police lieutenant Joe Leaphorn in western settings. (Rev: BL 10/15/89)

3574 Hillerman, Tony, ed. *The Mysterious West* (9–12). 1995, HarperCollins paper $6.50 (0-06-109262-2). This collection of 20 mystery and suspense stories with western themes features humor, action, and murder. (Rev: BL 10/1/94; SLJ 3/95)

3575 Hillerman, Tony. *People of Darkness* (10–12). 1991, HarperCollins paper $6.50 (0-06-109915-5). Set in the Southwest, this mystery features Navajo police detective Jim Chee and gives rich background information about the culture of these Native Americans. Others in this series are *Listening Woman, The Blessing Way, Dance Hall of the Dead,* and *The Fly on the Wall.*

3576 Hillerman, Tony. *The Sinister Pig* (10–12). 2003, HarperCollins $25.95 (0-06-019443-X). Hillerman blends Native American concerns with a melange of mystery, romance, bureaucracy, and criminal activity in this novel populated with familiar characters. (Rev: BL 5/1/03; SLJ 12/03)

3577 Hillerman, Tony. *Talking God* (10–12). 1991, HarperCollins paper $6.99 (0-06-109918-X). The two Navajo police officers, Jim Chee and Joe Leaphorn, featured together in the author's earlier *A Thief of Time* and *Skinwalkers*, once more solve a puzzling, complex murder mystery set in New Mexico. (Rev: BL 5/1/89; SLJ 11/89; VOYA 10/89)

3578 Hoff, B. J. *Winds of Graystone Manor* (9–12). 1995, Bethany paper $9.99 (1-55661-435-7). In this gothic novel set in Staten Island after the Civil War, the first in a trilogy, Roman St. Clare, exhausted by his search for the murderer of his pregnant wife, is drawn unwillingly into involvement with murder, kidnapping, grave robberies, and mutilations by the guests and employees at Graystone Manor, the rooming house in which he is staying. (Rev: BL 9/1/95; VOYA 4/96)

3579 Hoffman, William. *Tidewater Blood* (10–12). 1998, Algonquin $31.95 (1-56512-187-2). Charley LeBlanc, the black sheep of a wealthy plantation family in Virginia, is wrongfully accused of killing his mother and father and sets out to find the real murderer. (Rev: BL 2/1/98; SLJ 10/98)

3580 Holt, Victoria. *The Captive* (9–12). 1990, Fawcett paper $3.50 (0-449-21817-1). A romantic mystery involving a young heroine trapped on a desert island with a murderer. (Rev: BL 8/89; VOYA 2/90)

3581 Hooper, Mary. *Amy* (9–12). 2002, Bloomsbury $14.95 (1-58234-793-X). Amy meets a man online and becomes the victim of a terrible crime when she finally meets him in person. (Rev: BL 9/15/02; SLJ 9/02; VOYA 12/02)

3582 Horowitz, Anthony. *Eagle Strike* (7–12). 2004, Putnam $17.99 (0-399-23979-0). Alex Rider, the hero of many adventures, recognizes a famous Russian assassin while Alex is vacationing in France, and a new thriller begins. (Rev: BL 5/1/04; SLJ 3/04; VOYA 4/04)

3583 Horowitz, Anthony. *Point Blank* (6–10). Series: Alex Rider Adventure. 2002, Putnam $16.99 (0-399-23621-X). Alex, the young British spy, infiltrates an exclusive Swiss boarding school in this action-filled adventure. (Rev: BL 4/1/02; HBG 10/02; SLJ 3/02; VOYA 2/02)

3584 Howard, Mary. *Discovering the Body* (10–12). 2000, Morrow $24.00 (0-688-17156-7). Both a mystery and a story of small-town life, this novel deals with a girl who has second thoughts about her identification of the murderer of a good friend. (Rev: BL 8/00)

3585 Hrdlitschka, Shelley. *Tangled Web* (6–12). 2000, Orca paper $6.95 (1-55143-178-5). Telepathic twins Alex and Tanner again tangle with their former kidnapper in this fast-paced sequel to *Disconnected* (1999). (Rev: BL 10/15/00; SLJ 10/00; VOYA 12/00)

3586 Jackson, Shirley. *We Have Always Lived in the Castle* (9–12). 1962, Amereon LB $22.95 (0-89190-623-1); Penguin paper $9.95 (0-14-007107-5). Two sisters have become recluses after the arsenic poisoning of four members of their family.

3587 James, Bill. *Take* (9–12). 1994, Countryman $20.00 (0-88150-294-4). A small-time crook gets involved in a plan to steal a payroll, but the caper turns out to be much more than expected. (Rev: BL 5/15/94*)

3588 James, P. D. *A Certain Justice* (10–12). 1997, Knopf $25.00 (0-375-40109-1). A challenging adult English mystery concerning detective Adam Dalgleish and his investigation of the murder of a brilliant barrister. (Rev: BL 10/15/97; SLJ 4/98)

3589 James, P. D. *Original Sin* (9–12). 1995, Knopf $24.00 (0-679-43889-0). Set in the modern publishing world, where traditions may crumble but such timeless emotions as grief, rage, love — and murder — prevail. (Rev: BL 1/1/95*)

3590 Johansen, Iris. *Body of Lies* (11–12). 2002, Bantam $24.95 (0-553-80097-3). Forensic sculptor Eve is lured to Louisiana to help solve a mystery and finds herself and her family in danger; for mature teens. (Rev: BL 2/1/02; SLJ 7/02)

3591 Johansen, Iris. *Dead Aim* (11–12). 2003, Bantam $25.95 (0-553-80246-1). Domestic terrorism is the focus of this exciting story about a photographer and a former government agent who are determined to find the perpetrators of a dam collapse and stop further tragedies. (Rev: BL 2/1/03)

3592 Johansen, Iris. *Fatal Tide* (11–12). 2003, Bantam $24.95 (0-553-80247-X). Melis abandons her work with dolphins to investigate the suspicious death of her foster father, who has been obsessed with the lost city of Marinth. (Rev: BL 7/03)

3593 Johnston, Norma. *The Dragon's Eye* (7–10). 1990, Four Winds LB $14.95 (0-02-747701-0). The life of high school junior Jenny begins to unravel when nasty, cryptic messages start appearing at school. (Rev: BL 1/15/91; SLJ 12/90)

3594 Johnston, Wayne. *The Navigator of New York* (10–12). 2002, Doubleday $27.95 (0-385-50767-4). A young man seeks the truth about his family against the backdrop of late-19th-century polar exploration. (Rev: BL 10/15/02*)

3595 Jorgensen, Christine T. *Curl Up and Die* (10–12). 1997, Walker $32.95 (0-8027-3288-7). Stella Stargazer, writer of an astrology lovelorn column, tries to help a friend with romantic problems and finds herself involved in a case of blackmail and murder. (Rev: BL 12/15/96; SLJ 6/97)

3596 Jorgensen, Christine T. *Death of a Dustbunny: A Stella the Stargazer Mystery* (8–12). 1998, Walker $22.95 (0-8027-3315-8). An uncomplicated mystery in which sleuth Stella the Stargazer, who writes a combination astrology and advice-to-the-lovelorn column for a local newspaper, investigates the disappearance of her friend Elena Ruiz, an employee of the Dustbunnies housekeeping and nanny agency. (Rev: BL 4/15/98; VOYA 8/98)

3597 Kaminsky, Stuart. *The Dog Who Bit a Policeman* (10–12). 1998, Mysterious $22.00 (0-89296-667-X). A story of murder, corruption, and mayhem in contemporary Moscow that features Inspector Porfiry Rostnikov and an investigation of an illegal dogfight ring. (Rev: BL 6/1–15/98; SLJ 3/99)

3598 Kaminsky, Stuart. *Lieberman's Day* (9–12). 1994, Holt $19.95 (0-8050-2575-8). Two Chicago police officers deal with murder, brutality, drugs, and difficult moral issues in this action-filled novel. (Rev: BL 2/15/94*)

3599 Kaminsky, Stuart M. *Fall of a Cosmonaut* (10–12). 2000, Mysterious $24.95 (0-89296-668-8). In the 13th novel in this recommended series set in contemporary Russia, Inspector Rostnikov must juggle three different mysteries. (Rev: BL 8/00)

3600 Kane, Andrea. *Scent of Danger* (11–12). 2003, Pocket paper $7.99 (0-7434-4613-5). Romance and suspense abound in this entertaining novel about a daughter who works to save her sperm-donor father's perfume empire. (Rev: BL 2/1/03)

3601 Karas, Phyllis. *The Hate Crime* (7–10). 1995, Avon paper $3.99 (0-380-78214-6). A docunovel/whodunit about a teen who scrawls the names of seven concentration camps on a Jewish temple. (Rev: BL 12/1/95; VOYA 2/96)

3602 Kellerman, Faye. *The Forgotten* (10–12). 2001, Morrow $25.00 (0-688-15614-2). In this thriller featuring detective Peter Decker, Peter's teenage stepson has a friend who is a delinquent, involved in drugs, and possibly responsible for destroying public property. (Rev: BL 7/01)

3603 Kellerman, Faye. *Stalker* (10–12). 2000, Morrow $25.00 (0-688-15613-4). In this installment of the recommended Peter Decker/Rina Lazarus mystery series, Peter's daughter, a police officer, is sure she is being stalked. (Rev: BL 5/1/00)

3604 Kelly, Mary Anne. *Foxglove* (9–12). 1994, St. Martin's paper $4.50 (0-312-95202-3). After moving to a new home with her son and police officer husband, a woman becomes involved in the mystery of the death of an old friend. (Rev: BL 12/1/92*)

3605 Kemelman, Harry. *The Day the Rabbi Resigned* (9–12). 1993, Fawcett paper $5.99 (0-449-21908-9). A rabbi joins forces with the police to discover the

truth behind the death of a prominent professor. (Rev: BL 3/1/92; SLJ 9/92)

3606 Kerr, M. E. *Fell* (8–12). 1987, HarperCollins paper $4.95 (0-06-447031-8). In a bizarre identity switch, a teenager from a middle-class background enters a posh prep school. Followed by *Fell Back* and *Fell Down*. (Rev: BL 6/1/87; SLJ 8/87; VOYA 10/87)

3607 Kerr, M. E. *Fell Down* (7–12). 1991, HarperCollins $15.00 (0-06-021763-4). Fell has dropped out of prep school but is haunted by the death of his best friend there, so he returns, to find kidnapping, murder, and obsession. (Rev: BL 9/15/91*; SLJ 10/91)

3608 Kerr, M. E. *What Became of Her* (7–10). 2000, HarperCollins LB $15.89 (0-06-028436-6). Sixteen-year-old E. C. Tobbit's life is forever changed when he meets eccentric Rosalind Slaymaster, her niece Julie, and her doll, Peale. (Rev: BL 7/00; HB 5–6/00; HBG 9/00; SLJ 7/00)

3609 King, Laurie R. *The Beekeeper's Apprentice* (9–12). 1994, St. Martin's $23.95 (0-312-10423-5). In this first of a recommended Mary Russell series, the young American-born girl joins forces with Sherlock Holmes to solve a particularly challenging mystery. (Rev: BL 2/1/94*; SLJ 7/94)

3610 King, Laurie R. *A Darker Place* (10–12). 1999, Bantam $23.95 (0-553-10711-9). Ann Waverly, a theology professor, occasional FBI agent, and former cult member, is called in to conduct an undercover investigation of a cult group with international ties and becomes unable to emotionally detach herself from the assignment, placing herself in danger. (Rev: BL 1/1–15/99; SLJ 7/99)

3611 King, Laurie R. *A Monstrous Regiment of Women* (10–12). 1995, St. Martin's $22.95 (0-312-13565-3). Sherlock Holmes's apprentice, Mary Russell, solves a case involving the strange deaths of several wealthy young women in Oxford. (Rev: BL 9/1/95; SLJ 2/96)

3612 King, Laurie R. *The Moor* (10–12). 1998, St. Martin's $23.95 (0-312-16934-5). Mr. and Mrs. Sherlock Holmes visit the site of *The Hound of the Baskervilles* to solve an eerie murder. (Rev: BL 1/1–15/98; SLJ 4/98; VOYA 10/98)

3613 King, Stephen. *The Green Mile* (10–12). 1996, Signet paper $18.94 (0-451-93302-8). This six-part series involves, among others, a sadistic prison guard, Percy Wetmore, a seemingly simple-minded criminal, John Coffey, and a mouse named Mr. Jingles. (Rev: VOYA 12/96)

3614 Koontz, Dean. *The Face* (11–12). 2003, Bantam $26.95 (0-533-80248-8). Ten-year-old Fric, son of a major movie star, is the target of a lunatic professor in this gripping thriller. (Rev: BL 5/15/03)

3615 Koontz, Dean. *Fear Nothing* (10–12). 1998, Bantam paper $7.99 (0-553-57975-4). A well-plotted thriller about a nocturnal person whose investigation of his father's death uncovers a sinister conspiracy involving experiments with animal intelligence. (Rev: SLJ 6/98; VOYA 6/98)

3616 Koontz, Dean. *From the Corner of His Eye* (10–12). 2000, Bantam $26.95 (0-553-80134-1). Three seemingly unrelated deaths occur on the same day in the mid-1960s, but it is more than coincidence that brings the people involved together. This is one of many recommended thrillers by this author. (Rev: BL 11/15/00; VOYA 6/01)

3617 Koontz, Dean. *One Door Away from Heaven* (10–12). 2001, Bantam $26.95 (0-553-80137-6). This novel consists of two interwoven stories, one involving a deformed girl and the other about a boy who is fleeing a killer. (Rev: BL 12/15/01)

3618 Koontz, Dean. *Watchers* (9–12). 1987, Putnam paper $7.99 (0-425-10746-9). Two creatures escape from a genetic research lab in California — one is a dog with a high IQ and the other is a vicious monster called the Outsider.

3619 Krentz, Jayne Ann. *Light in Shadow* (11–12). 2003, Putnam $24.95 (0-399-14938-4). Interior decorator Zoe Luce hires a private eye to look into the scary intuitions she is getting from a client's house; meanwhile, her past may be about to catch up with her; for mature teens. (Rev: BL 11/1/02)

3620 Krich, Rochelle M. *Fertile Ground: A Mystery* (10–12). 1998, Avon paper $22.00 (0-380-97378-2). Dr. Lisa Brockman uncovers a web of greed, fraud, and coverups following the murder of an egg donor at a renowned fertility clinic and the disappearance of its director, while at the same time struggling with her feelings about the religious practices of the Orthodox Jewish parents who adopted her. (Rev: BL 1/1–15/98; SLJ 6/98)

3621 Lachtman, Ofelia Dumas. *The Summer of El Pintor* (7–10). 2001, Arte Publico paper $9.95 (1-55885-327-8). Sixteen-year-old Monica's father loses his job and the two move from their wealthy neighborhood to the barrio house in which her dead mother grew up, where Monica searches for a missing neighbor and discovers the truth of her past. (Rev: BL 8/01; SLJ 7/01; VOYA 12/01)

3622 Langton, Jane. *The Face on the Wall* (10–12). 1998, Viking $21.95 (0-670-87674-7); Penguin paper $5.99 (0-140-28157-6). Part of the recommended Homer Kelly mystery series, this story tells how the retired police officer and his wife help a children's book illustrator falsely accused of murder. (Rev: BL 5/1/00; SLJ 9/98)

3623 Lanier, Virginia. *Blind Bloodhound Justice* (10–12). 1998, HarperCollins $24.00 (0-06-017547-8). A cleverly crafted mystery novel that involves Jo Beth Sidden and her trusty bloodhounds in an investigation of two kidnappings and murders that occurred 30 years apart. (Rev: SLJ 1/99)

3624 Lansdale, Joe R. *A Fine Dark Line* (11–12). 2003, Mysterious $24.95 (0-89296-729-3). Young Stanley discovers a cache of love letters and sets off an investigation into a double murder that took place 20 years before in this multilayered story for mature teens. (Rev: BL 12/1/02)

3625 Lardo, Vincent. *The Hampton Connection* (10–12). 2001, Putnam $24.95 (0-399-14631-8). For mature readers, this is the story of a handsome actor who returns home to East Hampton on Long Island and becomes involved in a murder. (Rev: BL 4/1/01)

3626 Laurie, Hugh. *The Gun Seller* (10–12). 1997, Soho Pr. $24.00 (1-56947-087-1). A British spoof of spy thrillers that moves at an exciting pace and involves not only Brits but CIA personnel, international arms dealers, and terrorists. (Rev: BL 4/15/97; SLJ 6/97)

3627 Lawrence, Martha C. *Ashes of Aries* (10–12). 2001, St. Martin's $23.95 (0-312-20299-7). Psychic detective Elizabeth Chase is brought in to locate a 4-year-old boy who has disappeared. (Rev: BL 8/01)

3628 Lawrence, Martha C. *Pisces Rising* (10–12). 2000, St. Martin's $23.95 (0-312-20298-9). A compelling mystery involving the psychic detective Elizabeth Chase and the murder of the owner of a casino on an Indian reservation. (Rev: BL 2/15/00)

3629 Le Carre, John. *The Spy Who Came in from the Cold* (10–12). 1964, Coward-McCann paper $14.00 (0-743-44253-9). One of the classic thrillers. This one is about Alec Leamus, a secret agent operating during the Cold War.

3630 Le Carre, John. *The Tailor of Panama* (10–12). 1996, Knopf $25.00 (0-679-45446-2). This humorous satire on spies features an unwilling espionage agent in Panama who invents news when he has nothing to report. (Rev: SLJ 2/97)

3631 Lehane, Dennis. *A Drink Before the War* (9–12). 1994, Harcourt $22.95 (0-15-100093-X). Patrick and Angelo are hired by two state senators to locate a black cleaning woman who filched several sensitive documents. (Rev: BL 11/15/94*)

3632 Lehane, Dennis. *Sacred* (10–12). 1997, Morrow $23.00 (0-688-14381-4). An intricate mystery story that involves detectives Patrick Kenzie and Angie Gennaro on the trail of a missing heiress. (Rev: BL 6/1–15/97; SLJ 1/98)

3633 Lehmann, Christian. *Ultimate Game* (9–12). Trans. by William Rodarmor. 1999, Godine $16.95 (1-56792-107-8). A dark, suspenseful story of a virtual reality game run amok that frightens two of its teen players but seduces the third into acts of violence; for mature teens. (Rev: BL 8/99; HB 7–8/99; HBG 9/99; SLJ 8/00)

3634 L'Engle, Madeleine. *Troubling a Star* (7–10). 1994, Farrar $19.00 (0-374-37783-9). Vicki Austin, 16, travels to Antarctica and meets a Baltic prince looking for romance, and the two try to solve a mystery involving nuclear waste. (Rev: BL 8/94; SLJ 10/94; VOYA 12/94)

3635 Levitin, Sonia. *Evil Encounter* (8–10). 1996, Simon & Schuster $17.00 (0-689-80216-1). Michelle must find the killer when her mother is wrongfully accused of murdering the charismatic leader of a therapy group to which they belong. (Rev: BL 5/1/96; BR 1–2/97; SLJ 5/96; VOYA 6/96)

3636 Levitin, Sonia. *Incident at Loring Groves* (7–12). 1988, Fawcett paper $5.50 (vol. 1); $2.95 (vol. 2) (0-449-70347-9). High school students find the body of a murdered classmate and decide to remain silent about it. (Rev: BL 9/1/88; BR 11–12/88; SLJ 6/88; VOYA 12/88)

3637 Levy, Harry. *Chain of Custody* (10–12). 1999, Fawcett paper $6.99 (0-449-00449-X). A cardiologist and now practicing attorney is wrongfully accused of his estranged wife's murder in this mystery that also features the hero's angry and confused teenage son. (Rev: SLJ 9/98)

3638 Lewin, Michael Z. *Underdog* (9–12). 1993, Mysterious $18.95 (0-89296-440-5). When homeless Jan Moro uncovers a police sting to catch thug Billy Cigar, his own entrepreneurial plan, which depends on Cigar's partnership, is endangered. (Rev: BL 10/1/93*)

3639 Lewin, Patricia. *Blind Run* (10–12). 2003, Ballantine $23.95 (0-345-44322-5). Ethan Decker, a former operative for a secret government agency, seeks to protect his ex-wife and others from assassination in this thriller best suited to mature teens. (Rev: BL 1/1–15/03)

3640 Lewin, Patricia. *Out of Reach* (9–12). 2004, Ballantine $23.95 (0-345-44320-9). CIA agent Erin Baker and FBI agent Alec Donovan join forces to break a kidnapping ring that preys on young children. (Rev: BL 1/1–15/04)

3641 Littke, Lael. *Lake of Secrets* (7–10). 2002, Holt $16.95 (0-8050-6730-2). Carlene experiences strong and puzzling feelings of deja vu when she and her mother go to the town where Carlene's younger brother died 18 years earlier, before Carlene's birth. (Rev: BCCB 4/02; BL 3/1/02; HB 5–6/02; HBG 10/02; SLJ 3/02; VOYA 6/02)

3642 Long, David Ryan. *Ezekiel's Shadow* (9–12). 2001, Bethany paper $10.99 (0-7642-2443-3). In this thriller, a famous horror writer is being stalked by someone who resembles one of the author's characters. (Rev: BL 1/1–15/01)

3643 Lott, Bret. *The Hunt Club: A Novel* (10–12). 1999, HarperCollins paper $5.99 (0-06-101390-0). In this murder mystery, 15-year-old Huger Dillard, his mother, and blind uncle are kidnapped and must fight for their lives. (Rev: SLJ 11/98)

3644 Lovelace, Merline. *After Midnight* (10–12). 2003, NAL paper $6.99 (0-451-41072-6). Jessica Blackwell, an army colonel, reluctantly agrees to an assignment that sends her to her hometown, and there becomes embroiled in a murder investigation and romance; suitable for mature readers. (Rev: BL 2/15/03*)

3645 Lovesey, Peter. *Goldengirl* (10–12). 2002, Severn $26.99 (0-7278-5835-1). The ability to excel at sports is taken to an extreme in this suspenseful novel about a child adopted by an ambitious doctor. (Rev: BL 9/15/02)

3646 Lovesey, Peter. *The Vault* (10–12). 2000, Soho Pr. $23.00 (1-56947-208-4). In this mystery set in Bath, England, Detective Peter Diamond is trying to solve an ugly crime while being pestered by an American professor who is searching for Mary Shelley's diary. (Rev: BL 8/00)

3647 Lowell, Elizabeth. *Die in Plain Sight* (11–12). 2003, Morrow $24.95 (0-06-050412-9). Lacey's interest in her grandfather's paintings — and in an art investigator — leads her into danger and into additional conflict with her parents. (Rev: BL 5/15/03)

3648 Lucashenko, Melissa. *Killing Darcy* (8–10). 1998, Univ. of Queensland Pr. paper $13.95 (0-7022-3041-3). In this complex supernatural murder mystery set in New South Wales, 16-year-old Filomena uncovers a family murder, discovers a camera that can take pictures of the past, and is helped by a gay Aboriginal boy to solve the mystery. (Rev: SLJ 2/99)

3649 Lynch, Chris. *Freewill* (10–12). 2001, HarperCollins $15.95 (0-06-028176-6). Reeling from the death of his father and stepmother, 17-year-old Will, who is enrolled in a special woodworking class, falls under suspicion when his wood sculptures mysteriously turn up at the scenes of several teen suicides. (Rev: BCCB 3/01; BL 5/15/01; BR 11–12/01; HB 7–8/01; HBG 10/01; SLJ 3/01; VOYA 8/01)

3650 McClure, Ken. *Tangled Web* (10–12). 2000, Simon & Schuster $25.00 (0-7432-0508-1). Genetic research and human cloning are subjects touched on in this novel about the murder of a 3-month-old girl. The setting is a small town in Wales. (Rev: BL 6/1–15/00)

3651 McCrumb, Sharyn. *The Hangman's Beautiful Daughter* (9–12). Series: Ballad. 1992, Scribner $19.00 (0-684-19407-4). A minister's wife unravels the mystery of a family's murder-suicide in Appalachia. (Rev: BL 3/15/92*)

3652 McCrumb, Sharyn. *She Walks These Hills* (9–12). Series: Ballad. 1994, Scribner $21.00 (0-684-19556-9). A radio talk show host, a graduate student, and a police dispatcher travel the haunted foothills of the Appalachian Trail, each searching for clues to troubled pasts. (Rev: BL 8/94; SLJ 3/95)

3653 McDermid, Val. *The Distant Echo* (11–12). 2003, St. Martin's $24.95 (0-312-30199-5). The 1978 murder of a teenage girl in St. Andrew's, Scotland, is reopened in 2003 with the idea that new DNA technology will bring resolution to this unsolved crime. (Rev: BL 8/03)

3654 MacDonald, Patricia. *Not Guilty* (10–12). 2002, Pocket $24.00 (0-7434-2355-0). Keely's teenaged son, who was scarred by his father's suicide years earlier, is accused of a terrible crime and Keely must fight to find the truth. (Rev: BL 2/15/02)

3655 McGarrity, Michael. *Tularosa* (10–12). 1996, Norton $25.00 (0-393-03922-6). A private eye named Kevin Kerney travels to Tularosa, New Mexico, to investigate the strange disappearance of his godson, a soldier at the White Sands Missile Range. (Rev: BL 3/15/96; SLJ 1/97)

3656 MacGregor, Rob. *Hawk Moon* (7–10). 1996, Simon & Schuster paper $16.00 (0-689-80171-8). Sixteen-year-old Will Lansa, having returned to Aspen, Colorado, to learn more about his Hopi heritage, finds himself at the center of an investigation of the murder of his girlfriend. (Rev: SLJ 11/96*; VOYA 2/97)

3657 McKevett, G. A. *Peaches and Screams* (9–12). 2002, Kensington $22.00 (1-57566-711-8). Private investigator Savannah Reid discovers that her little brother is in jail accused of murder in this mystery story with lots of family ties. (Rev: BL 11/15/01)

3658 McKinney, Meagan. *Still of the Night* (10–12). 2001, Kensington $23.00 (1-57566-615-4). When Stella takes a leave from her university position to tend to the family plantation outside New Orleans, she happens on what could be a smuggling operation. (Rev: BL 2/15/01)

3659 McNamee, Graham. *Acceleration* (9–12). 2003, Random LB $17.99 (0-385-90144-5). A teenager ends up on the trail of a murderer when he takes a summer job in the Toronto subway. (Rev: BL 5/1/04; HBG 4/04; SLJ 11/03; VOYA 12/03)

3660 MacPhail, Catherine. *Dark Waters* (7–10). 2003, Bloomsbury $15.95 (1-58234-846-4). This exciting story set in Scotland features Col McCann, who saves a boy from drowning only to realize that his own brother may have played a dangerous role in the mishap. (Rev: BCCB 3/03; BL 3/15/03; HBG 10/03; SLJ 6/03; VOYA 6/03)

3661 McQuillan, Karin. *The Cheetah Chase* (9–12). 1994, Ballantine $20.00 (0-345-38183-1). When safari specialist Jazz Jasper witnesses her friend Nick being stung to death by a scorpion, she teams up with Inspector Ormondi to investigate the suspicious death, and uncovers murder. (Rev: BL 8/94; SLJ 12/94)

3662 Malone, Michael. *Red Clay, Blue Cadillac: Twelve Southern Women* (10–12). 2002, Sourcebooks paper $15.00 (1-57071-824-5). A collection of 12 compelling short stories featuring mystery, murder, and suspense in the South. (Rev: BL 2/1/02)

3663 Margolin, Phillip. *Sleeping Beauty* (10–12). 2004, HarperCollins $25.95 (0-06-008326-3). Emotionally scarred, Ashely survives an intruder's attack that leaves her father dead and her friend raped only to find that the ordeal has not ended in this tightly knit thriller. (Rev: BL 2/15/04)

3664 Maron, Margaret. *High Country Fall* (10–12). 2004, Mysterious $24.00 (0-89296-808-1). Judge Deborah Knott gets involved in a murder case in which the accused is a friend of her relatives. Part of a recommended series with this character. (Rev: BL 5/1/04*)

3665 Maron, Margaret. *Storm Track* (10–12). 2000, Mysterious $22.95 (0-89296-656-4). Judge Deborah Knott is featured in this mystery set in rural North Carolina that deals with dual threats: a hurricane and the presence of a murderer in the community. (Rev: BL 2/15/00)

3666 Marsden, John. *Winter* (7–10). 2002, Scholastic $16.95 (0-439-36849-9). Winter, a 16-year-old Australian girl who believes that her parents died together in an accident, returns to her family home to find puzzling secrets. (Rev: BCCB 11/02; HBG 3/03; SLJ 8/02)

3667 Martini, Steve. *The Jury* (10–12). 2001, Putnam $25.95 (0-399-14672-5). In this legal suspense thriller, the head of a research lab is accused of murdering a brilliant female colleague who was about to take over his job. (Rev: BL 5/15/01)

3668 Massey, Sujata. *The Bride's Kimono* (10–12). 2001, HarperCollins $25.00 (0-06-019933-4). Tokyo antiques dealer Rei Shimura finds mystery and romance as she escorts historic kimonos to an exhibit in Washington, D.C. (Rev: BL 8/01; VOYA 2/02)

3669 Mazzio, Joann. *The One Who Came Back* (7–10). 1992, Houghton $17.00 (0-395-59506-1). A New Mexico teen must prove he didn't kill his best friend. (Rev: BL 4/1/92; SLJ 5/92)

3670 Michaels, Barbara. *Shattered Silk* (10–12). 1998, HarperCollins paper $6.50 (0-06-104473-3). When Karen sets up a boutique in Georgetown, she receives mysterious threats on her life. (Rev: BL 8/86; SLJ 2/87)

3671 Michaels, Barbara. *Stitches in Time* (9–12). 1998, HarperCollins paper $6.99 (0-06-104474-1).

This novel weaves an incredible mystery based on a haunted quilt. (Rev: BL 5/1/95; SLJ 11/95)

3672 Michaels, Fern. *Picture Perfect* (10–12). 2000, Severn House $26.00 (0-7278-5515-8). In this romantic thriller, the young hemophiliac nephew Lorrie Ryan is caring for disappears, and she is fearful that he will die without his daily injections. (Rev: BL 9/1/00)

3673 Michaels, Fern. *Plain Jane* (10–12). 2001, Kensington $24.00 (1-57566-673-5). In this romantic suspense story with a touch of the supernatural, psychotherapist Jane Lewis is hunting down a rapist. (Rev: BL 3/1/01)

3674 Michaels, Kasey. *Maggie Needs an Alibi* (10–12). 2002, Kensington $22.00 (1-57566-879-3). A humorous mystery in which the characters from a Regency novel emerge in contemporary New York and attempt to investigate incidents in their author's life. (Rev: BL 5/15/02)

3675 Miles, Keith. *Murder in Perspective: An Architectural Mystery* (10–12). 1997, Walker $29.95 (0-8027-3298-4). A solid mystery with a sympathetic hero who has been wrongfully accused of murder and a glimpse at the world of architecture through appearances by Frank Lloyd Wright. (Rev: BL 2/15/97; VOYA 6/97)

3676 Miller, Linda Lael. *The Last Chance Cafe* (10–12). 2002, Pocket $24.00 (0-671-04250-5). Hallie and her twin daughters flee Phoenix when she finds her ex-husband is implicated in a drug operation; she finds succor and more at the Last Chance Cafe. (Rev: BL 5/1/02)

3677 Mitchell, Sara. *Trial of the Innocent* (10–12). Series: Shadow Catchers. 1995, Bethany paper $9.99 (1-55661-497-7). In this romantic mystery set in Virginia in 1891, Eve suspects her new brother-in-law of crimes. (Rev: SLJ 5/96)

3678 Monfredo, Miriam Grace. *Must the Maiden Die: A Seneca Falls Historical Mystery* (6–12). 1999, Berkley $21.95 (0-425-16699-6). In the opening days of the Civil War, Glynis Tryon, a librarian who is also an amateur detective, is asked to join an investigation into the murder of a local businessman. (Rev: BL 8/99; VOYA 2/00)

3679 Moody, Bill. *The Sound of the Trumpet* (10–12). 1997, Walker $32.95 (0-8027-3291-7). A murder mystery with a jazz backdrop that involves the death of a secretive man who collects jazz tapes. (Rev: BL 2/15/97; VOYA 4/97)

3680 Mortman, Doris. *Before and Again* (11–12). 2003, St. Martin's $24.95 (0-312-27557-9). The intriguing possibility of inherited memory is at the center of this fast-paced thriller in which reporter Callie Jamieson and detective Ezra Chapin find mutual attraction. (Rev: BL 9/1/03)

3681 Mosley, Walter. *Bad Boy Brawly Brown: An Easy Rawlins Mystery* (10–12). 2002, Little, Brown $24.95 (0-316-07301-6). Mystery and detail of 1960s Los Angeles abound as Easy looks for a teenage boy who is involved with a radical political group. (Rev: BL 5/1/02; SLJ 11/02)

3682 Muller, Marcia. *Point Deception* (10–12). 2001, Warner $23.95 (0-89296-690-4). Rhoda, a deputy sheriff in a small California coastal town, investigates the disappearance of three women. (Rev: BL 5/1/01*)

3683 Muller, Marcia. *While Other People Sleep* (10–12). 1998, Mysterious $23.00 (0-892-96650-5); Little, Brown paper $6.99 (0-446-60721-5). In this compelling suspense novel, the first of a recommended series, private investigator Sharon McCone is being impersonated by someone who is also stalking her. (Rev: BL 5/1/00)

3684 *Murder in Baker Street: New Tales of Sherlock Holmes* (9–12). Ed. by Martin H. Greenberg, et al. 2001, Carroll & Graf $25.00 (0-7867-0898-0). A collection of 11 Sherlock Holmes mystery stories by 11 contemporary authors. (Rev: BL 9/15/01)

3685 Murphy, Shirley Rousseau. *Cat in the Dark* (10–12). 1999, HarperCollins $22.00 (0-06-105096-2). In this mystery-fantasy, Joe Grey and Dulcie, two cats who can speak, read, and detect, come across an investment scam and three deaths. (Rev: BL 12/15/98; SLJ 5/99)

3686 Murphy, Shirley Rousseau. *Cat Spitting Mad* (10–12). 2001, HarperCollins $23.00 (0-06-105098-9). This, the sixth mystery featuring the talking cats Joe Grey, Kit, and Dulcie, involves a murder in a small town in California and the framing of a sympathetic police chief. (Rev: BL 12/1/00; SLJ 5/01)

3687 Myers, Bill. *The Face of God* (11–12). 2002, Zondervan paper $12.99 (0-310-22755-0). A search for missing stones that will bring forth the presence of god has added suspense through a pending release of smallpox. (Rev: BL 8/02*)

3688 Nelscott, Kris. *A Dangerous Road* (10–12). 2000, St. Martin's $24.95 (0-312-26264-7). In Memphis of 1968, a black private detective named Smokey Dalton wants to find out why a rich white woman from Chicago has left him $10,000. (Rev: BL 7/00)

3689 Nelscott, Kris. *Smoke-Filled Rooms* (10–12). 2001, St. Martin's $24.95 (0-312-26265-5). African American private eye Smokey Dalton is on the lam in 1968 with a 10-year-old boy who claims to know who is behind the recent murder of Martin Luther King, Jr. (Rev: BL 7/01*)

3690 Nevins, Francis M., and Martin H. Greenberg, eds. *Hitchcock in Prime Time* (10–12). 1985, Avon paper $9.00 (0-380-89673-7). This is a collection of 20 stories that formed the basis of some of Hitchcock's best television shows.

3691 Nixon, Joan Lowery. *A Candidate for Murder* (6–12). 1991, Dell paper $4.99 (0-440-21212-X). While Cary's father enters the political limelight, his daughter becomes embroiled in a series of strange events. (Rev: BL 3/1/91)

3692 Nixon, Joan Lowery. *The Dark and Deadly Pool* (7–12). 1989, Bantam paper $4.99 (0-440-20348-1). Mary Elizabeth becomes aware of strange happenings at the health club where she works. (Rev: BL 11/1/87; BR 11–12/87; SLJ 2/88; VOYA 12/87)

3693 Nixon, Joan Lowery. *The Ghosts of Now* (7–10). 1984, Dell paper $4.99 (0-440-93115-0). Angie investigates a hit-and-run accident that has left her brother in a coma.

3694 Nixon, Joan Lowery. *The Island of Dangerous Dreams* (7–12). 1989, Dell paper $4.99 (0-440-20258-2). Seventeen-year-old Andrea helps in the investigation of the murder of a judge in the Bahamas. (Rev: VOYA 8/89)

3695 Nixon, Joan Lowery. *Nightmare* (6–10). 2003, Delacorte LB $17.99 (0-385-90151-8). This suspenseful mystery features 10th-grader Emily, who has suffered a recurring nightmare since childhood and now finds herself facing a killer at her summer camp. (Rev: BL 10/15/03; HBG 4/04; SLJ 10/03; VOYA 10/03)

3696 Nixon, Joan Lowery. *The Other Side of Dark* (7–10). 1986, Dell paper $4.99 (0-440-96638-8). After waking from a four-year coma, Stacy is now the target of the man who wounded her and killed her mother. (Rev: BL 9/15/86; BR 3–4/87; SLJ 9/86; VOYA 12/86)

3697 Nixon, Joan Lowery. *Playing for Keeps* (6–10). 2001, Delacorte $15.95 (0-385-32759-5). While on a cruise in the Caribbean, 16-year-old Rose falls for a Cuban refugee and becomes embroiled in suspenseful intrigue. (Rev: BCCB 7–8/01; BL 5/1/01; HBG 10/02; VOYA 8/01)

3698 Nixon, Joan Lowery. *The Seance* (7–10). 1981, Dell paper $4.99 (0-440-97937-4). An innocent seance leads to a double murder in this fast-paced mystery.

3699 Nixon, Joan Lowery. *The Specter* (7–10). 1993, Dell paper $4.99 (0-440-97740-1). Seventeen-year-old Dina protects a child who believes she is going to be murdered.

3700 Nixon, Joan Lowery. *The Stalker* (9–12). 1985, Dell paper $4.50 (0-440-97753-3). In Corpus Christi, Jennifer sets out to prove the innocence of her friend, who has been accused of murder. (Rev: BR 9–10/85; SLJ 5/85; VOYA 6/85)

3701 Nixon, Joan Lowery. *The Weekend Was Murder!* (6–10). 1992, Dell paper $4.99 (0-440-21901-9). A teen sleuth and her boyfriend attend a murder mystery enactment weekend and discover a real murder. (Rev: BL 2/15/92; SLJ 3/92)

3702 Nixon, Joan Lowery. *Who Are You?* (6–10). 1999, Bantam $15.95 (0-385-32566-5); Bantam paper $5.95 (0-440-22757-7). Teenager Kristi Evans sets out to solve the mystery of a murdered art collector and find out why he had been keeping a file on her. (Rev: BL 4/15/99; HBG 10/99; SLJ 6/99; VOYA 10/99)

3703 Norman, Hilary. *The Pact* (10–12). 1997, Dutton paper $24.95 (0-525-94256-4). Three friends who were orphaned as a result of a helicopter crash find that someone is trying to harm them in this mystery that involves flashbacks to the Holocaust. (Rev: BL 6/1–15/97; SLJ 12/97)

3704 North, Suzanne. *Seeing Is Deceiving* (10–12). 1996, McClelland & Stewart $25.99 (0-7710-6805-0). TV camerawoman Phoebe Fairfax gets involved in a murder when she is sent to cover a psychic fair. (Rev: SLJ 4/97)

3705 Osborn, Karen. *The River Road* (10–12). 2002, Morrow $23.95 (0-688-15899-4). Two families' lives are changed abruptly when one son jumps off a bridge after taking LSD and his brother accuses their friend Kay of involvement. (Rev: BL 10/15/02; SLJ 2/03)

3706 Osborne, Charles, adapt. *Black Coffee: A Hercule Poirot Novel* (10–12). 1998, St. Martin's $22.95 (0-312-19241-X). Before Hercule Poirot can fulfill his obligation to visit Sir Claud, the man is murdered in this clever adaptation of Christie's play *Black Coffee*. (Rev: BL 8/98; SLJ 12/98)

3707 Palmer, Michael. *Fatal* (10–12). 2002, Bantam $24.95 (0-553-80203-8). An action-packed search for the cause of skin and mental abnormalities in a West Virginia town. (Rev: BL 5/1/02; SLJ 12/02)

3708 Palmer, Michael. *The Patient* (10–12). 2000, Bantam $24.95 (0-553-10983-9). An adult thriller that pits spy-versus-spy and science-versus-disease in a tense, satisfying series of suspenseful situations. (Rev: BL 2/1/00)

3709 Palmer, William J. *The Dons and Mr. Dickens: The Strange Case of the Oxford Christmas Plot* (10–12). 2000, St. Martin's $23.95 (0-312-26576-X). In this thriller set in Victorian times, Inspector Field seeks the help of Charles Dickens in solving the mystery of a gentleman murdered in an opium den. (Rev: BL 11/1/00)

3710 Pappano, Marilyn. *Heaven on Earth* (11–12). Series: Bethlehem. 2002, Dell paper $6.50 (0-440-23714-9). Romance blossoms between Melina and Sebastian as they search for runaway children in this stand-alone installment in the series set in Bethlehem, New York, a town guarded by angels; for mature teens. (Rev: BL 1/1–15/02)

3711 Paretsky, Sara. *Guardian Angel* (9–12). 1993, Dell paper $6.99 (0-440-21399-1). Intrepid female private eye V. I. Warshawski is involved with greedy Yuppies offloading risky bonds on Chicago seniors. (Rev: BL 12/1/91; SLJ 9/92)

3712 Pascal, Francine. *Twisted* (7–10). Series: Fearless. 2000, Pocket paper $5.99 (0-671-03944-X). Fearless Gaia, alone after her mother's death and her father's disappearance, finds she is being stalked in this fourth book in the series. (Rev: BL 4/1/00)

3713 Pendergrass, Tess. *Dark of the Moon* (9–12). 2004, Five Star $26.95 (0-7862-5109-3). In this romantic, entertaining story, a librarian and a detective work on a case involving the murder of a politician's daughter. (Rev: BL 2/1/04)

3714 Penman, Sharon Kay. *The Queen's Man: A Medieval Mystery* (10–12). 1996, Holt $20.00 (0-8050-3885-X). An intriguing mystery set in England during the time of Eleanor of Aquitaine and Richard Lionheart. (Rev: BL 11/1/96; SLJ 3/97)

3715 Perry, Anne. *Brunswick Gardens* (10–12). 1998, Fawcett $25.00 (0-449-90845-3); paper $6.99 (0-449-00318-3). A murder mystery set in Victorian England in which Inspector Pitt investigates the death of a woman noted as an agitator for women's rights. (Rev: SLJ 11/98)

3716 Perutz, Leo. *Master of the Day of Judgment* (9–12). 1994, Arcade $19.95 (1-55970-171-4). In 1909 Vienna, Baron von Yosch is accused of killing an actor whose wife was once his lover and discovers a terrifying secret when he investigates. (Rev: BL 10/15/94*)

3717 Peters, Elizabeth. *The Ape Who Guards the Balance* (10–12). 1998, Avon paper $24.00 (0-380-97657-9). A complex murder mystery set in 1907 that involves grisly murder and archaeological sites in Egypt. (Rev: BL 6/1–15/98; SLJ 2/99)

3718 Peters, Elizabeth. *Crocodile on the Sandbank* (10–12). 1975, Warner paper $6.99 (0-445-40651-8). Amelia Peabody, a wealthy and independent woman who is traveling in Egypt, finds herself involved in archaeology, villains, and a mystery in this novel that is part of a recommended series. (Rev: BL 5/1/00)

3719 Peters, Elizabeth. *He Shall Thunder in the Sky* (10–12). 2000, Morrow $25.00 (0-380-97659-5). Amelia and family are on archaeological digs in 1915 Egypt and find themselves up to their necks in intrigue in this installment of the recommended Amelia Peabody series. (Rev: BL 5/1/00)

3720 Peters, Ellis. *The Holy Thief* (9–12). 1993, Mysterious $17.95 (0-89296-524-X). In this mystery set in medieval times, thievery and murder intrude upon Brother Cadfael's well-ordered monastery life. (Rev: BL 3/1/93; SLJ 7/93)

3721 Picoult, Jodi. *Plain Truth* (10–12). 2000, Pocket $24.95 (0-671-77612-6). Ellie Hathaway, a Philadelphia attorney, during a holiday in Amish country, becomes involved in the murder trial of an unmarried Amish teenager accused of killing her newborn. (Rev: BL 4/15/00; SLJ 11/00)

3722 Pike, Christopher. *Chain Letter* (9–12). 1986, Avon paper $3.99 (0-380-89968-X). Six teenagers must perform acts of repentance in connection with the hit-and-run death of a man. (Rev: VOYA 8/86)

3723 Pike, Christopher. *Gimme a Kiss* (7–12). 1991, Pocket paper $4.50 (0-671-63682-5). A girl fakes her own death in a wild plot to get revenge. (Rev: BL 10/15/88; VOYA 4/89)

3724 Pike, Christopher. *Last Act* (7–10). 1991, Pocket paper $3.99 (0-671-73683-3). The blanks in Melanie's stage pistol turn out to be real. Is she really guilty of murder? (Rev: BL 6/15/88; SLJ 11/88; VOYA 8/88)

3725 Pike, Christopher. *Slumber Party* (7–10). 1985, Scholastic paper $3.50 (0-590-43014-9). Six teenage girls stranded in a winter vacation home experience mysterious occurrences that bring terror into their lives. (Rev: SLJ 12/86)

3726 Pike, Christopher. *Spellbound* (10–12). 1990, Pocket paper $4.50 (0-671-73681-7). Cindy is determined to find out who murdered one of the cheerleaders at her high school. (Rev: VOYA 8/88)

3727 Plum-Ucci, Carol. *The Body of Christopher Creed* (8–12). 2000, Harcourt $17.00 (0-15-202388-7). Torey and his friends are implicated in the disappearance of his classmate Chris, causing Torey to examine his life while trying to find Chris. (Rev: HBG 9/00; SLJ 7/00)

3728 Plum-Ucci, Carol. *The She* (8–12). 2003, Harcourt $17.00 (0-15-216819-2). Evan, his brother, and a friend set out to find the truth behind the disappearance of Evan's parents years before. (Rev: BL 9/15/03*; SLJ 10/03; VOYA 12/03)

3729 Powers, Martha. *Sunflower* (10–12). 1998, Simon & Schuster $22.00 (0-684-83767-6). A gripping mystery story in which Sheila Brady, a police detective, investigates a series of murders in her small Wisconsin town of young girls who are killed and then raped. (Rev: SLJ 1/99)

3730 Preston, Douglas, and Lincoln Child. *The Ice Limit* (10–12). 2000, Warner $25.99 (0-446-52587-1). This absorbing, action-packed thriller involves a secret expedition to recover the world's largest meteorite from an island off the coast of Chile. (Rev: BL 5/15/00; SLJ 11/00; VOYA 12/00)

3731 Preston, Douglas, and Lincoln Child. *Reliquary* (10–12). 1997, Tom Doherty Assoc. $24.95 (0-312-86095-1). Margo Green of the Natural History Museum joins several investigators as their search for a brutal murderer leads them to investigate the mole people who live underground in New York City. (Rev: BL 3/15/97; SLJ 9/97)

3732 Preston, Richard. *The Cobra Event* (10–12). 1997, Random $25.95 (0-679-45714-3). A frightening thriller about a mad scientist who releases a deadly virus in New York City. (Rev: BL 11/15/97; SLJ 3/98)

3733 Priestley, Chris. *Death and the Arrow* (6–10). 2003, Knopf LB $17.99 (0-375-92466-3). In this historical mystery set in 1715 London, 15-year-old Tom Marlowe and Dr. Harker investigate a murder that has international implications. (Rev: BCCB 7–8/03; HBG 10/03; SLJ 7/03; VOYA 10/03)

3734 Pronzini, Bill. *A Wasteland of Strangers* (10–12). 1997, Walker $29.95 (0-8027-3301-8). A swiftly plotted mystery in which scar-faced John Faith is wrongfully accused of murder and is sheltered by three women during an escape attempt. (Rev: BL 6/1–15/97; VOYA 2/98)

3735 Prowell, Sandra West. *The Killing of Monday Brown* (9–12). 1994, Walker $19.95 (0-8027-3184-8). Private eye Phoebe Siegel investigates a missing dealer in Native American artifacts. (Rev: BL 5/15/94*)

3736 Prowell, Sandra West. *When Wallflowers Die* (10–12). 1996, Walker $32.95 (0-8027-3254-2). An exciting mystery in which Phoebe Siegal, a gutsy PI, finds her life is in danger when she begins an investigation of a murder that occurred years before. (Rev: BL 7/96; SLJ 2/97)

3737 Pullman, Philip, ed. *Detective Stories* (7–12). Illus. 1998, Larousse Kingfisher Chambers $14.95 (0-7534-5157-3); paper $6.95 (0-7534-5146-8). A collection of mystery and detective stories by such authors as Agatha Christie, Ellery Queen, Conan Doyle, Damon Runyan, and Dorothy Sayers. (Rev: BL 5/15/98; SLJ 9/98)

3738 Purser, Ann. *Murder on Monday* (11–12). 2002, Severn $25.99 (0-7278-5860-2). Lois Meade, British mother of two and feeling that there may be more to life than cleaning houses, tries her hand at sleuthing with scary results; for mature teens. (Rev: BL 9/15/02)

3739 Qualey, Marsha. *Close to a Killer* (9–12). 1999, Bantam $15.95 (0-385-32597-5). Barrie finds herself in the middle of a puzzling mystery when her mother's beauty salon is linked to two murders. (Rev: BL 2/1/99; HBG 9/99; SLJ 3/99; VOYA 4/99)

3740 Qualey, Marsha. *Thin Ice* (7–12). 1997, Delacorte $14.95 (0-385-32298-4). Arden Munro's brother appears to have been drowned after a snowmobile accident but no body has been found, and the girl believes he has simply escaped his dull life by running away. (Rev: BL 11/1/97; HBG 3/98; SLJ 11/97; VOYA 10/97)

3741 Quick, Amanda. *I Thee Wed* (10–12). 1999, Bantam $23.95 (0-553-10084-X). An amusing murder mystery and love story, set in Regency England, involving a young financier, Edison, and his new fiancee, Emma, originally hired by Edison to help him investigate a stolen ancient manuscript. (Rev: BL 2/1/99; SLJ 7/99)

3742 Rabb, M. E. *The Chocolate Lover* (7–10). Series: Missing Persons. 2004, Penguin paper $5.99 (0-14-250042-9). Teen orphans Samantha and Sophie Shattenberg are able to connect art stolen during the Holocaust with its missing owner. Another mystery adventure with these girls is *The Rose Queen* (2004). (Rev: BL 5/1/04; SLJ 5/04)

3743 Ramthun, Bonnie. *Earthquake Games* (10–12). 2000, Putnam $24.95 (0-399-14666-0). In this sequel to *Ground Zero* (1999), detective Eileen Reed and her partner Dave investigate the supposed suicide of an Army major and find themselves involved with UFOs and an earthquake machine. (Rev: BL 8/00)

3744 Rankin, Ian. *A Good Hanging* (10–12). 2002, St. Martin's $23.95 (0-312-28027-0). Twelve short stories feature the dazzling detective work of Inspector John Rebus, a member of the Edinburgh police force. (Rev: BL 1/1–15/02)

3745 Reaver, Chap. *A Little Bit Dead* (8–12). 1992, Delacorte $15.00 (0-385-30801-9); Dell paper $3.99 (0-440-21910-8). When Reece saves an Indian boy from lynching by U.S. marshals, lawmen claim that Reece murdered one of the marshals and he must clear himself. (Rev: BL 9/1/92; SLJ 9/92)

3746 Rendell, Ruth. *Heartstones* (10–12). Illus. 1987, Ballantine paper $4.95 (0-345-34800-1). In this short but powerful mystery an anorexic girl believes she is guilty of murder. (Rev: BL 6/1/87; SLJ 11/87)

3747 Rendell, Ruth. *The Keys to the Street* (10–12). 1996, Crown $24.00 (0-517-70685-7). A mystery story and a romance set in London about a mousy woman who falls in love and inherits a massive fortune, and a series of murders of homeless men. (Rev: SLJ 3/97)

3748 Riccio, Dolores Stewart. *Circle of Five* (11–12). 2003, Kensington paper $14.00 (0-7582-0300-4). A group of five Wiccan women have little success in their efforts to catch a murderer in this novel that mixes humor and suspense. (Rev: BL 3/1/03*)

3749 Rice, Christopher. *A Density of Souls* (10–12). 2000, Talk $23.95 (0-7868-6646-2). For mature readers, this first novel by Anne Rice's son is a gothic that deals with tangled relationships involving four friends. (Rev: BL 7/00)

3750 Richman, Phyllis. *Who's Afraid of Virginia Ham?* (10–12). 2001, HarperCollins $23.00 (0-06-018389-6). A slick young reporter on the *Washing-*

ton Examiner is murdered and everyone in the newsroom is baffled. (Rev: BL 4/1/01)

3751 Robards, Karen. *Beachcomber* (11–12). 2003, Atria $25.00 (0-7434-5348-4). Christy, who is trying to escape her Mafia background, finds that Luke, a neighbor and supposed surfer, keeps turning up just in time to save her from desperate situations; suitable for mature teens. (Rev: BL 8/03)

3752 Robards, Karen. *Whispers at Midnight* (11–12). 2003, Atria $25.00 (0-7434-5346-8). This highly readable mystery novel tells the story of divorcee Carly Linton's return to the small Georgia town in which she was raised and her reunion with her first love; frank sexual content makes this suitable only for mature teens. (Rev: BL 1/1–15/03)

3753 Robb, Candace. *The Riddle of St. Leonard's: An Owen Archer Mystery* (10–12). 1997, St. Martin's $21.95 (0-312-16983-3). In England during 1369, Owen Archer is pressed into service for Sir Richard to investigate murders at St. Leonard's Hospital during a resurgence of the plague. (Rev: BL 9/15/97; SLJ 12/97)

3754 Roberts, Les. *The Lake Effect* (9–12). 1994, St. Martin's $21.95 (0-312-11537-7). Private-eye Milan Jacovich returns a favor for a mobster and helps run Barbara Corn's mayoral campaign. When the competing candidate's wife is murdered, Jacovich investigates. (Rev: BL 11/1/94*)

3755 Roberts, Willo Davis. *Nightmare* (7–10). 1989, Macmillan $16.00 (0-689-31551-1). After a series of unusual occurrences, 17-year-old Nick finds he is being followed. (Rev: BL 9/15/89; BR 3–4/90; SLJ 9/89; VOYA 12/89)

3756 Roberts, Willo Davis. *Undercurrents* (7–10). 2002, Simon & Schuster $16.00 (0-689-81671-5). Fourteen-year-old Nikki is troubled when her father remarries only months after her mother's death and his new wife seems to be hiding facts about her unhappy past. (Rev: BCCB 4/02; BL 2/15/02; HBG 10/02; SLJ 2/02; VOYA 2/02)

3757 Robinson, Lynda S. *Eater of Souls* (10–12). 1997, Walker $29.95 (0-8027-3294-1). An engrossing mystery in which Lord Meren, King Tutankhamun's guru, tries to solve the mystery of Queen Nefertiti's death and becomes involved with a serial killer. (Rev: BL 4/15/97; SLJ 8/97; VOYA 4/98)

3758 Robinson, Lynda S. *Murder at the Feast of Rejoicing* (10–12). 1996, Walker $30.95 (0-8027-3274-7). An unusual murder mystery takes place on the Egyptian Nile at the time of Tutankhamun in this third book in the highly praised series featuring Lord Meren, confidant to the young pharaoh. (Rev: BL 1/1–15/96; SLJ 5/96)

3759 Robinson, Peter. *In a Dry Season* (10–12). 1999, Avon paper $24.00 (0-380-97581-5). Detective Chief Inspector Alan Banks is brought in to investigate the 50-year-old murder of a young woman during World War II discovered when a skeleton is found in the ruins of a deserted village in England. (Rev: BL 3/15/99*; SLJ 9/99)

3760 Robinson, Peter. *Playing with Fire* (11–12). 2004, Morrow $23.95 (0-06-019877-X). Yorkshire detectives Alan Banks and Annie Cabbot investigate two arson-related deaths; for mature teens. (Rev: BL 11/15/03*)

3761 Rollins, James. *Amazonia* (10–12). 2002, Morrow $24.95 (0-06-008906-7). Hoping to discover the fate of his missing father, Nathan travels deep into the Brazilian rain forest and encounters disease and other unseen forces in this fast-paced thriller. (Rev: BL 2/15/02)

3762 Rollins, James. *Ice Hunt* (10–12). 2003, Morrow $24.95 (0-06-052156-2). An Alaskan park ranger and his Inuit former wife become entangled in a deadly struggle for supremacy over a facility hidden under the Arctic ice. (Rev: BL 6/1–15/03)

3763 Roosevelt, Elliott. *Murder and the First Lady* (10–12). 1985, Avon paper $4.99 (0-380-69937-0). A mystery in which Eleanor Roosevelt serves as supersleuth.

3764 Roosevelt, Elliott. *Murder at the Palace* (10–12). 1989, Avon paper $4.99 (0-380-70405-6). Eleanor Roosevelt again stars in this, the fifth of this series. The locale is Buckingham Palace during World War II. (Rev: BL 2/15/88)

3765 Roosevelt, Elliott. *Murder in the Oval Office* (10–12). 1990, Avon paper $4.99 (0-380-70528-1). First Lady Eleanor Roosevelt solves the murder of a congressman. (Rev: BL 12/15/88)

3766 Roosevelt, Elliott. *The White House Pantry Murder* (10–12). 1987, Avon paper $4.50 (0-380-70404-8). This is the fourth mystery involving Eleanor Roosevelt as sleuth. In this one, a body is found in a large White House refrigerator. (Rev: BL 12/15/86)

3767 Rozan, S. J. *Concourse* (10–12). 1995, St. Martin's paper $5.99 (0-312-95924-3). In this book, which is part of a series, Bill Smith and Lydia Chin, a Chinese American living in New York City's Chinatown, form a detecting partnership to solve a retirement home murder mystery. (Rev: BL 5/1/00)

3768 Rozan, S. J. *Winter and Night* (10–12). 2002, St. Martin's $24.95 (0-312-24555-6). Bill Smith and Lydia Chin finds themselves entangled in a murder mystery when Bill's football player nephew calls from jail seeking help. (Rev: BL 1/1–15/02*)

3769 Rushford, Patricia H. *Betrayed* (6–10). Series: Jennie McGrady Mystery. 1996, Bethany paper $4.99 (1-55661-560-4). Jennie encounters a long list of suspects when she tries to find the murderer of her uncle on a dude ranch in Montana. (Rev: BL 6/1–15/96; SLJ 6/96; VOYA 12/96)

3770 Rushford, Patricia H. *Dying to Win* (6–10). Series: Jennie McGrady Mystery. 1995, Bethany paper $4.99 (1-55661-559-0). A suspenseful Jennie McGrady mystery about the disappearance of a rebellious schoolchum known as the "Rainbow Girl." (Rev: BL 1/1–15/96; SLJ 2/96; VOYA 6/96)

3771 Rushford, Patricia H. *Stranded* (6–12). 2001, Bethany paper $4.99 (0-7642-2122-1). Jennie McGrady seeks to learn the truth about a religious colony in remote Oregon after the plane in which she and her grandmother are flying crashes near the group's compound. (Rev: VOYA 10/01)

3772 Russell, Kirk. *Shell Games* (10–12). 2003, Chronicle $23.95 (0-8118-4186-3). Lieutenant Marquez finds his experience as a DEA agent is unexpectedly useful in his new job with the Department of Fish and Game. (Rev: BL 7/03)

3773 Ryan, Mary E. *Alias* (6–10). 1997, Simon & Schuster $16.00 (0-689-80789-9); paper $4.99 (0-689-82264-2). Teenager Toby discovers that his mother's constant moves and change of identity are because she is wanted by the FBI for terrorist activities during the Vietnam War. (Rev: BL 4/15/97; BR 11–12/97; SLJ 7/97*; VOYA 8/97)

3774 Sandford, John. *The Devil's Code* (10–12). 2000, Putnam $25.95 (0-399-14650-4). In this novel with computer overtones, a group of renegade hackers solve a mystery and bring a gang of murderers and blackmailers to justice. (Rev: BL 8/00)

3775 Sandford, John. *The Hanged Man's Song* (10–12). 2003, Putnam $25.95 (0-399-15139-7). A thriller for computer geeks in which a young hacker disappears under suspicious circumstances. (Rev: BL 9/1/03)

3776 Saul, John. *Black Lightning* (9–12). 1995, Ballantine $23.00 (0-449-90864-X). Two years after the execution of serial killer Richard Kraven, reporter Anne Jeffer finds her husband has changed and the murders have begun again. (Rev: BL 6/1–15/95; SLJ 12/95)

3777 Saul, John. *The Presence* (10–12). 1997, Fawcett $25.00 (0-449-91055-5). An action-packed thriller that involves an archaeologist, her 16-year-old son, and the discovery that deadly medical experiments are being performed in a seemingly harmless high-tech laboratory. (Rev: SLJ 4/98)

3778 Saulnier, Beth. *Ecstasy* (11–12). 2003, Warner $23.95 (0-89296-750-1). Alex Bernier, reporter and amateur detective, investigates the drug-induced deaths of teens attending a rock festival in this fifth installment in the entertaining series suitable for mature readers. (Rev: BL 2/1/03)

3779 Sayers, Dorothy L., and Jill Paton-Walsh. *Thrones, Dominations* (10–12). 1998, St. Martin's $23.95 (0-312-18196-5). This murder mystery featuring the famous Lord Peter Wimsey and his wife,

Harriet Vane, was completed after Sayers's death. (Rev: SLJ 7/98)

3780 Saylor, Steven. *Last Seen in Massilia* (10–12). Series: Roma Sub Rosa. 2000, St. Martin's $23.95 (0-312-20928-2). An intriguing mystery story set in Rome in 49 B.C. during the civil war fought between Pompey and Julius Caesar, this is part of a recommended series of historical mysteries by Saylor. (Rev: BL 9/1/00)

3781 Scott, Holden. *Skeptic* (10–12). 1999, St. Martin's $24.95 (0-312-19334-3). In this medical thriller, a graduate student in physician Mike Ballantine's lab discovers that ghosts exist and that the memories of dead people are incorporated into the brains of the living — and there are villains who will stop at nothing, including murder, to get hold of the research. (Rev: BL 3/15/99; SLJ 7/99)

3782 Scott, Willard. *Murder Under Blue Skies: A Stanley Waters Mystery* (10–12). 1998, NAL $23.95 (0-525-94324-2). When one of his guests at his bed-and-breakfast is murdered, Stanley Waters finds that the chief investigator is his high-school sweetheart. (Rev: BL 1/1–15/98; SLJ 9/98)

3783 Sebestyen, Ouida. *The Girl in the Box* (9–12). 1988, Little, Brown $12.95 (0-316-77935-0). A high school girl is kidnapped by a masked man and kept prisoner in a damp, dark room. (Rev: BL 11/1/88; BR 1–2/89; SLJ 10/88; VOYA 2/89)

3784 Sedley, Kate. *The Saint John's Fern* (10–12). 2002, St. Martin's $23.95 (0-312-27683-4). Roger Chapman, a medieval peddler, probes a murder and discovers a frame-up. (Rev: BL 8/02)

3785 Seil, William. *Sherlock Holmes and the Titanic Tragedy: A Case to Remember* (10–12). 1996, Breese Books paper $14.95 (0-947533-35-4). Holmes and Watson are aboard the *Titanic* guarding a young secret agent who is transporting important submarine plans for the U. S. Navy. (Rev: SLJ 4/97)

3786 Seranella, Barbara. *Unwilling Accomplice* (10–12). 2004, Scribner $24.00 (0-7432-4558-X). The heroine of this recommended series is a garage mechanic and limo driver and, in this installment, she is involved in the disappearance of a young cousin who is a Goth. (Rev: BL 3/15/04*)

3787 Sheffield, Charles. *The Amazing Dr. Darwin* (10–12). 2002, Baen $24.00 (0-7434-3529-X). Mystery and history are intertwined in these stories of Darwin's physician-cum-sleuth grandfather. (Rev: BL 6/1–15/02; VOYA 2/03)

3788 Sherbaniuk, Richard. *The Fifth Horseman* (10–12). 2001, Tor $25.95 (0-312-87435-9). This high-tech thriller involves the huge Ataturk Dam in Turkey and a group of unusual terrorists. (Rev: BL 2/1/01)

3789 Siciliano, Sam. *The Angel of the Opera: Sherlock Holmes Meets the Phantom of the Opera*

(9–12). 1994, Penzler $21.95 (1-883402-46-8). Sherlock Holmes's cousin is the narrator in this mystery that takes place at the Paris Opera house. (Rev: BL 5/15/94; SLJ 12/94)

3790 Silverberg, Robert. *The Longest Way Home* (10–12). 2002, Eos $25.95 (0-380-97858-X). On a planet similar to Earth, young Joseph finds himself in the middle of a rebellion far from home and must confront many dangers — and some pleasures — on his long journey south. (Rev: BL 4/15/02; SLJ 3/03; VOYA 2/03)

3791 Simpson, Marcia. *Sound Tracks* (10–12). 2001, Poisoned Pen $24.95 (1-890208-72-8). When Lisa Romero moves to Wrangell, Alaska, to manage a floating bookmobile, strange events occur, such as whales getting sick and the death of a marine biologist. (Rev: BL 6/1–15/01*)

3792 Singer, Nicky. *Feather Boy* (6–10). 2002, Delacorte LB $17.99 (0-385-90043-0). Robert, a timid and unpopular 12-year-old, spends a scary night in an abandoned house and makes some discoveries about himself. (Rev: BCCB 4/02; BL 5/1/02; HBG 3/03; SLJ 4/02)

3793 Slater, Susan. *Thunderbird* (10–12). 2002, Intrigue $23.95 (1-890768-41-3). Tommy Spottedhorse is confronted with a disturbing mystery involving mutilated animals, UFOs, and his own girlfriend in this Ben Pecos story. (Rev: BL 1/1–15/02)

3794 Smith, April. *North of Montana* (9–12). 1994, Knopf $23.00 (0-679-43197-7). FBI agent Ana, hungry for a career-making case, investigates movie star Jayne Mason's claim that her doctor has hooked her on painkillers. (Rev: BL 9/15/94*; SLJ 5/95)

3795 Smith, Taylor. *Deadly Grace* (10–12). 2001, MIRA $22.95 (1-55166-829-7). This first-rate political thriller is set in 1979 and involves the murder of a former World War II secret agent. (Rev: BL 11/15/01)

3796 Snyder, Keith. *Trouble Comes Back* (10–12). 1999, Walker $22.95 (0-8027-3338-7). Jason Keltner and his buddies Robert and Martin try to protect a drugged-out rock star's daughter. (Rev: BL 9/15/99; VOYA 2/00)

3797 Squires, Susan. *No More Lies* (11–12). 2003, Love Spell paper $6.99 (0-505-52566-6). Psychiatrist Holland Banks, plagued by voices in her head, discovers she has a telepathic link with the investigative reporter who is dogging her footsteps; for mature teens. (Rev: BL 10/15/03)

3798 Stabenow, Dana. *A Cold-Blooded Business* (9–12). 1994, Berkley paper $17.95 (0-425-14173-X). Aleut private eye Kate Shugak travels north of the Arctic Circle to investigate a rise in cocaine use among Alaskan oil field workers. Also use *Play with Fire* (1995). (Rev: BL 3/1/94*; SLJ 9/94)

3799 Stabenow, Dana. *A Fine and Bitter Snow* (10–12). 2002, St. Martin's $24.95 (0-312-20548-1). Environmental issues come to the fore as Kate Shugak investigates a murder and the firing of a forest ranger. (Rev: BL 5/1/02)

3800 Stabenow, Dana. *A Grave Denied* (11–12). 2003, St. Martin's $24.95 (0-312-30681-4). An 8th-grade field trip discovers a body in an Alaskan ice cave, leading to an investigation by PI Kate Shugak and a tentative romance between Shugak and trooper Jim Chopin. (Rev: BL 8/03)

3801 Steiner, Barbara. *Dreamstalker* (8–12). 1992, Avon paper $3.50 (0-380-76611-6). A girl wonders if she's psychic when her terrifying nightmares start coming true. (Rev: BL 3/15/92)

3802 Steiner, Barbara. *Spring Break* (7–10). 1996, Scholastic paper $3.99 (0-590-54419-5). Five high schoolers rent a haunted house where they contend with odd appearances and disappearances, arson, and a skeleton. (Rev: SLJ 12/96)

3803 Stewart, Mary. *Thornyhold* (9–12). 1989, Fawcett paper $6.99 (0-449-21712-4). Geillis discovers that a magic spell controls the people in her cousin's house. (Rev: BL 10/1/88)

3804 Stine, R. L. *The Overnight* (7–10). 1991, Pocket paper $3.99 (0-671-74650-2). While on an overnight camping trip, one of six campers accidentally kills a stranger she meets in the woods. Also use *The New Girl* (1991). (Rev: BL 12/15/89)

3805 Straub, Peter. *Lost Boy Lost Girl* (10–12). 2003, Random $24.95 (1-4000-6092-3). Novelist Tim Underhill and detective Tom Pasmore appear in this compelling and complex story of deaths and disappearances in an Illinois town. (Rev: BL 9/1/03*)

3806 Sumner, M. C. *Night Terrors* (7–10). 1997, Pocket paper $3.99 (0-671-00241-4). When her father disappears from his top-secret research facility and her friend begins having terrifying nightmares, Kathleen decides to investigate. (Rev: SLJ 8/97)

3807 Sykes, Shelley. *For Mike* (7–10). 1998, Delacorte $15.95 (0-385-32337-9). Mystery, suspense, and romance are combined in this novel in which Jeff and a girlfriend try to solve the mystery of the disappearance of Jeff's best friend, Mike. (Rev: BL 4/1/98; BR 9–10/98; HBG 9/98; SLJ 5/98; VOYA 4/98)

3808 Talton, Jon. *Concrete Desert* (10–12). 2001, St. Martin's $22.95 (0-312-26953-6). In this novel set in Phoenix, former sheriff's deputy David Mapstone finds unusual links between a 40-year-old mystery involving a serial killer and the disappearance of a friend. (Rev: BL 6/1–15/01*)

3809 Tanenbaum, Robert K. *Absolute Rage* (10–12). 2002, Pocket $25.00 (0-7434-0344-4). A murder investigation moves the Karp-Ciampi family to West Virginia, where they meet violence, tragedy, and moral challenges. (Rev: BL 5/1/02)

3810 Tanenbaum, Robert K. *True Justice* (10–12). 2000, Pocket $24.95 (0-7434-0589-7). Plots involving infanticides, one in Delaware and the other in New York City, intersect in this mystery book by the author of several other recommended mysteries. (Rev: BL 8/00; SLJ 1/01)

3811 Tanner, Janet. *Shadows of the Past* (11–12). 2003, Severn $26.99 (0-7278-5926-9). Cerys, a young widow in perilous 1860 Australia, must decide whom to trust as she struggles to keep her home and small family afloat. (Rev: BL 6/1–15/03)

3812 Tasker, Peter. *Samurai Boogie* (10–12). 2001, Orion paper $13.00 (0-75283-676-5). Tokyo-based detective N. Mori is hired by a beautiful woman to find her lover's killer. (Rev: BL 9/15/01*)

3813 Taylor, Theodore. *Lord of the Kill* (6–10). 2002, Scholastic $16.95 (0-439-33725-9). Ben Jepson, 16, is involved in a murder mystery in which the suspects include big game hunters, an organized crime ring, and other groups who dislike the animal-rights activities of Ben's family. (Rev: BCCB 1/03; BL 1/1–15/03; HBG 3/03; SLJ 1/03; VOYA 4/03)

3814 Tey, Josephine. *The Daughter of Time* (10–12). 1952, Macmillan paper $12.00 (0-684-80386-0). A classic mystery story that travels in time from the present to the reign of Richard III.

3815 Thomas, Donald. *Sherlock Holmes and the Voice from the Crypt* (10–12). 2002, Carroll & Graf $25.00 (0-7867-0973-1). Six more cases, some based on actual crimes, for Holmes and his sidekick Watson. (Rev: BL 2/1/02)

3816 Thurlo, Aimée, and David Thurlo. *Changing Woman* (10–12). 2002, Tor $24.95 (0-312-87059-0). Navajo investigator Ella must deal with crime on her reservation, as well as personal tragedy when her daughter disappears. (Rev: BL 2/15/02; SLJ 6/02)

3817 Thurlo, Aimée, and David Thurlo. *Death Walker* (10–12). 1996, Tom Doherty Assoc. $23.95 (0-312-85651-2). Ella Clah, a police investigator on the Navajo Reservation, sets out to find the killer of several of the tribal cultural leaders. (Rev: SLJ 3/97)

3818 Thurlo, Aimée, and David Thurlo. *Enemy Way* (10–12). 1998, Forge $23.95 (0-312-85520-6). The geography on the Southwest figures prominently in this mystery involving Ella Clah of the Navajo police force, gang warfare, a murder, and skinwalkers, or Navajo witches. (Rev: BL 9/15/98; SLJ 1/99)

3819 Thurlo, Aimée, and David Thurlo. *Tracking Bear* (9–12). 2002, Tor $24.95 (0-765-30476-7). Navajo Police Special Investigator Ella Clah looks into murders that are related to a proposed nuclear

power plant in this absorbing novel, the eighth in the series. (Rev: BL 2/15/03*; SLJ 8/03)

3820 Thurlo, David, and Aimée Thurlo. *The Spirit Line* (6–10). 2004, Viking $15.99 (0-670-03645-5). Fifteen-year-old Crystal Manyfeathers solves a theft and in so doing begins to question her Navajo beliefs. (Rev: BL 5/1/04; SLJ 6/04; VOYA 6/04)

3821 Todd, Charles. *A Fearsome Doubt* (11–12). 2002, Bantam $24.95 (0-553-80180-5). Ian Rutledge, a thoughtful Scotland Yard inspector who is assisted by a helpful ghost, is worried that he may be responsible for an innocent man's hanging; for mature teens. (Rev: BL 8/02)

3822 Tolkien, Simon. *Final Witness* (10–12). 2003, Random $24.95 (0-375-50882-1). A British teenager accuses his stepmother of involvement in his mother's murder. (Rev: BL 10/15/02*)

3823 Truman, Margaret. *Murder at the FBI* (10–12). 1986, Fawcett paper $5.99 (0-449-20618-1). In this, the sixth of her murder mysteries set in Washington, Truman poses the question, "Who murdered FBI special agent George L. Pritchard?" (Rev: BL 5/15/85)

3824 Truman, Margaret. *Murder at the Kennedy Center* (10–12). 1989, Random $17.95 (0-394-57602-0). A fund-raiser at Kennedy Center seems to be a success until the body of a murdered girl is found. (Rev: BL 6/1/89)

3825 Truman, Margaret. *Murder in Foggy Bottom* (10–12). Series: Capital Crimes. 2000, Random $24.95 (0-375-50069-3). This book is part of a recommended mystery series, each of which has as its locale a landmark spot in Washington, D.C., such as the National Gallery, the Watergate hotel, the Library of Congress, or, in this case, Foggy Bottom. (Rev: BL 6/1–15/00; SLJ 11/00)

3826 Truman, Margaret. *Murder in the White House* (10–12). 1988, Warner paper $5.99 (0-446-31488-9). In this thriller, the secretary of state is murdered in private quarters in the White House. This is one of many recommended mysteries set in Washington, D.C., that include *Murder in the Supreme Court* and *Murder in the Smithsonian*.

3827 Truman, Margaret. *Murder on Capitol Hill* (10–12). 1989, Warren paper $5.99 (0-446-31518-4). A prominent senator is murdered at his own testimonial dinner in this mystery which is part of a series that includes *Murder on Embassy Row*.

3828 Vance, Susanna. *Deep* (7–10). 2003, Delacorte $15.95 (0-385-73057-8). Two girls from very different backgrounds confront a psychopathic kidnapper in a taut story of suspense. (Rev: BL 4/15/03; HB 5–6/03; HBG 10/03; SLJ 6/03)

3829 Vanneman, Alan. *Sherlock Holmes and the Giant Rat of Sumatra* (9–12). 2002, Carroll & Graf $24.00 (0-7867-0956-1). A widow whose husband was murdered in Singapore and a depraved lord who is planning evil acts are the two elements that bring Sherlock Holmes and Watson onto the case. (Rev: BL 12/15/01)

3830 Van Thal, Herbert, ed. *The Mammoth Book of Great Detective Stories* (9–12). 1989, Carroll & Graf paper $9.95 (0-88184-530-2). A total of 26 classic stories by such writers as Sayers, Simenon, Chandler, and Chesterton. (Rev: BL 9/15/89)

3831 Van Tine, Stuart M. *A Fine and Private War* (10–12). 2002, Force paper $24.95 (0-9717394-0-4). A fast-paced, high-tech story about wealthy families seeking to recover their offspring from a terrorist named Jinnah. (Rev: BL 6/1–15/02)

3832 Veryan, Patricia. *The Riddle of Alabaster Royal* (10–12). 1997, St. Martin's $23.95 (0-312-17121-8). Set in Regency England, this witty mystery novel involves Captain Jack Vesper and lovely Consuela Jones, who believes that her father was murdered on Vesper's estate. (Rev: SLJ 4/98)

3833 Vine, Barbara. *No Night Is Too Long* (9–12). 1995, Crown $23.00 (0-517-79964-2). A man who thinks he has gotten away with murder begins receiving mysterious letters in this tale of psychological suspense. (Rev: BL 12/1/94*)

3834 Voigt, Cynthia. *The Callender Papers* (9–12). 1983, Fawcett paper $4.50 (0-449-70184-0). A part-time position sorting out some archival papers leads to uncovering unsolved family mysteries.

3835 Wager, Walter. *Kelly's People* (10–12). 2002, Tor $24.95 (0-312-30131-8). Five anti-terrorist agents track potential perpetrators in a tense and realistic story. (Rev: BL 4/15/02)

3836 Wallens, Scott. *Shattered: Week 1* (6–12). Series: Sevens Series. 2002, Puffin paper $1.77 (0-14-230098-5). This first installment in a new series of suspense introduces seven teens who over a period of seven weeks will confront the terrible experiences of their pasts. (Rev: SLJ 11/02)

3837 Werlin, Nancy. *Black Mirror* (7–12). 2001, Dial $16.99 (0-8037-2605-8). Lonely Frances, 16, struggles with her Jewish-Japanese heritage and with her guilt and puzzlement over her brother's suicide in this intriguing and suspenseful novel set in a private boarding school. (Rev: BCCB 10/01; BL 9/15/01; HB 9–10/01; HBG 3/02; SLJ 9/01*; VOYA 10/01)

3838 Werlin, Nancy. *Double Helix* (9–12). 2004, Dial $15.99 (0-8037-2606-6). A thoughtful, exciting story about an 18-year-old who takes a job involving genetic engineering and discovers truths about himself and his family. (Rev: BL 2/1/04*; HB 5–6/04; SLJ 3/04; VOYA 4/04)

3839 Werlin, Nancy. *The Killer's Cousin* (7–12). 1998, Bantam $15.95 (0-385-32560-6). A tautly plotted thriller about a boy who tries to escape the guilt related to the accidental death of his girlfriend by moving in with relatives, but instead uncovers some horrifying family secrets. (Rev: BL 9/1/98; BR 5–6/99; HB 1–2/99; HBG 3/99; SLJ 11/98; VOYA 10/98)

3840 Werlin, Nancy. *Locked Inside* (7–10). 2000, Delacorte $15.95 (0-385-32700-5). In this thriller, teenager Marnie is kidnapped and held prisoner by a demented teacher who thinks she is Marnie's half-sister. (Rev: BL 12/1/99; HBG 9/00; SLJ 3/00; VOYA 4/00)

3841 Wesley, Valerie W. *Easier to Kill* (10–12). 1998, Putnam $23.95 (0-399-14445-5). African American detective Tamara Hayle is hired by a radio personality to find the identity of the person sending her threatening letters and to solve the mystery of the stabbing death of her stylist. (Rev: SLJ 2/99)

3842 Wheat, Carolyn. *Tales out of School* (10–12). 2000, Crippen & Landru paper $16.00 (1-885941-48-X). Fascinating plots and memorable characters abound in this collection of 19 crime stories by this mystery story veteran. (Rev: BL 12/15/00)

3843 Whitlow, Robert. *The Sacrifice* (10–12). 2002, W Publishing Group paper $14.99 (0-8499-4318-3). A tense and well-plotted legal thriller featuring a high school boy accused of a hate crime. (Rev: BL 6/1–15/02*)

3844 Whitney, Phyllis A. *Daughter of the Stars* (9–12). 1994, Crown $20.00 (0-517-59929-5). Lacy discovers the family that has been her mother's secret for years. She ventures to Harper's Ferry to help them and learns of her father's unsolved murder. (Rev: BL 9/15/94; SLJ 3/95)

3845 Whitney, Phyllis A. *Dream of Orchids* (9–12). 1987, Fawcett paper $5.99 (0-449-20743-9). While visiting on the Florida Keys, Laurel becomes involved in murder. (Rev: SLJ 5/85)

3846 Whitney, Phyllis A. *Emerald* (9–12). 1983, Fawcett paper $5.99 (0-449-20099-X). When Carol and her son relocate to Palm Springs, she confronts a terrible mystery. This is one of many recommended romantic mysteries by this author that include *Golden Unicorns, Seven Tears for Apollo,* and *Stone Bull.*

3847 Whitney, Phyllis A. *Feather on the Moon* (9–12). 1989, Fawcett paper $5.99 (0-449-21625-X). Jennifer Blake travels to Victoria, British Columbia, in search of her daughter, kidnapped four years before. (Rev: BL 2/1/88)

3848 Whitney, Phyllis A. *Rainbow in the Mist* (9–12). 1990, Fawcett paper $5.95 (0-449-21742-6). Christy has the psychic gift of locating dead bodies — a talent that leads her to a murder mystery. (Rev: BL 11/15/88)

3849 Whitney, Phyllis A. *Rainsong* (9–12). 1984, Fawcett paper $5.99 (0-449-20510-X). Some question whether rock singer Ricky Sands's death was a suicide.

3850 Whitney, Phyllis A. *The Singing Stones* (9–12). 1991, Fawcett paper $5.95 (0-449-21897-X). A therapist is brought in to help the disturbed daughter of her first husband in this tale of mystery and romance. (Rev: BL 12/15/89; SLJ 8/90; VOYA 6/90)

3851 Williams, Billy Dee, and Rob MacGregor. *Justin/Time* (10–12). 2000, Tor $22.95 (0-312-87271-2). Trent Calloway, a former spy and hero of the novel *PSI/Net* (1999), uses his ESP powers in his investigation of a cult leader who may be responsible for releasing a deadly virus. (Rev: BL 8/00)

3852 Williams, Darren. *Angel Rock* (11–12). 2002, Knopf $23.00 (0-375-41451-7). A young boy disappears in the Australian outback in this novel of suspense; for mature teens. (Rev: BL 6/1–15/02)

3853 Winslow, Don. *California Fire and Life* (10–12). 1999, Knopf $23.00 (0-679-45431-4). A compelling story about an arson investigator probing the mystery surrounding a deadly fire in a wealthy couple's home. (Rev: SLJ 2/00)

3854 Woods, Paula L., ed. *Spooks, Spies, and Private Eyes: Black Mystery, Crime, and Suspense Fiction* (9–12). 1995, Doubleday $22.95 (0-385-48082-2). Short mysteries by such African American writers as Richard Wright (*The Man Who Killed a Shadow*) and George Schuyler (*The Shoemaker Murder*). (Rev: BL 11/15/95)

3855 Woods, Stuart. *Orchid Beach* (10–12). 1998, HarperCollins $25.00 (0-06-019181-3). Holly Barker, newly appointed assistant police chief in Orchid Beach, Florida, discovers her boss and his friend have been murdered. (Rev: BL 9/1/98; SLJ 3/99)

3856 Wootson, Alice. *Escape to Love* (10–12). 2003, BET paper $6.99 (1-58314-373-4). A young woman who accidentally witnesses a murder has an admiring protector in this novel of romance and high suspense. (Rev: BL 6/1–15/03*)

3857 *The World's Finest Mystery and Crime Stories* (10–12). Ed. by Ed Gorman and Martin H. Greenberg. 2001, Tor $29.95 (0-765-30029-X); paper $18.95 (0-765-30101-6). In addition to an excellent selection of mystery stories, this overview contains great introductory material including reports on mystery fiction in various countries and a section on current trends. Also use *The World's Finest Mystery and Crime Stories: Third Annual Collection* (2002). (Rev: BL 11/1/01)

3858 Wynne-Jones, Tim. *The Boy in the Burning House* (7–12). 2001, Farrar $16.00 (0-374-30930-2). Disturbed Ruth Rose and 14-year-old Jim investigate the mystery of his father's disappearance —

was he killed by Ruth Rose's pastor stepfather? (Rev: BCCB 11/01; BL 9/1/01; HB 11–12/01; HBG 3/02; SLJ 10/01; VOYA 10/01)

Romances

3859 Abu-Jaber, Diana. *Crescent* (11–12). 2003, Norton $24.95 (0-393-05747-X). Historical fantasy, contemporary fact, and passionate romance are combined in this rich story of a young couple living in America and sharing Iraqi roots. (Rev: BL 3/15/03)

3860 Alcott, Louisa May. *A Long Fatal Love Chase* (9–12). 1996, Dell paper $6.99 (0-440-22301-6). Written in 1866, this racy tale about Rosamond is melodramatic but intriguing, dramatizing the plight of women in oppressive times. (Rev: BL 9/15/95; SLJ 2/96)

3861 Allenbaugh, Kay, ed. *Chocolate for a Lover's Heart: Soul-Soothing Stories That Celebrate the Power of Love* (10–12). Series: Chocolate. 1999, Simon & Schuster paper $11.00 (0-684-86298-0). This collection of 49 stories tells how love conquers all and shines through in spite of misunderstandings, unfaithfulness, illness, or death. (Rev: SLJ 7/99)

3862 Anderson, Catherine. *Sweet Nothings* (10–12). 2002, NAL paper $6.99 (0-451-41015-7). Molly Sterling, her wounded horse, a ranch, and its handsome owner are all elements in this excellent romance. (Rev: BL 12/15/01)

3863 Anton, Shar. *The Ideal Husband* (11–12). 2003, Warner paper $5.99 (0-446-61228-6). In this engrossing blend of historical romance and deception, Leah of Pecham takes advantage of Geoffrey Hamelin's memory loss to pass him off to family and friends as her husband; for mature teens. (Rev: BL 10/1/03)

3864 Applegate, Katherine. *July's Promise* (7–10). 1995, Archway paper $3.99 (0-671-51031-2). Sixteen-year-old Summer finds romance and adventure when she visits her hostile cousin on Crab Claw Key in Florida. Preceded by *June Dreams* and followed by *August Magic*. (Rev: VOYA 2/96)

3865 Applegate, Katherine. *Sharing Sam* (7–10). 1995, Bantam paper $4.50 (0-553-56660-1). A sacrificial love story in which a girl's best friend is dying of a brain tumor and boyfriend Sam is shared. (Rev: BL 3/15/95; SLJ 2/95)

3866 Balogh, Mary. *Slightly Tempted* (11–12). 2004, Dell paper $5.99 (0-440-24106-5). In the fourth installment in the popular Bedwyn family saga, 18-year-old Morgan meets and eventually wins the heart of Gervase Ashford as together they search for Morgan's brother, Alleyne, who's gone missing after the Battle of Waterloo; for mature teens. (Rev: BL 12/15/03)

3867 Barclay, Tessa. *A Lovely Illusion* (10–12). 2001, Severn $25.99 (0-7278-5639-1). Erica falls in love with a handsome New Zealander who has just bought an expensive painting that Erica believes is a fake. (Rev: BL 7/01)

3868 Barton, Beverly. *What She Doesn't Know* (11–12). 2002, Zebra paper $6.50 (0-8217-7214-7). Twenty years after a shooting that took the lives of her mother and aunt, Jolie returns to the scene suspecting everyone, even her stepbrother; for mature readers. (Rev: BL 4/1/02)

3869 Bat-Ami, Miriam. *Two Suns in the Sky* (8–12). 1999, Front Street $15.95 (0-8126-2900-0). A docunovel set in upstate New York during 1944 about the love between a Catholic teenage girl and a Jewish Holocaust survivor from Yugoslavia who is living in a refugee camp. (Rev: BL 4/15/99; HB 7–8/99; HBG 9/99; SLJ 7/99; VOYA 10/99)

3870 Bauer, Joan. *Thwonk* (7–10). 1996, Bantam paper $4.50 (0-440-21980-9). "Thwonk" is the sound of Cupid's bow when A. J.'s wish that hunky Peter become hers alone comes true. Unfortunately, Peter's adoration is more than she bargained for. (Rev: BL 1/1/95; SLJ 1/95)

3871 Beard, Julie. *Very Truly Yours* (9–12). 2001, Jove paper $6.99 (0-515-13039-7). In this Regency romance, rake Jack Fairchild escapes creditors by moving to a small English town, and there he meets Liza Cranshaw, daughter of a wealthy merchant. (Rev: BL 4/15/01)

3872 Bedford, Martyn. *The Houdini Girl* (10–12). 1999, Pantheon $24.00 (0-375-40527-5). When the wife of professional magician Red Brandon dies after only one year of marriage, the young man travels across Europe to collect information about her past and the reasons for her death. (Rev: SLJ 7/99)

3873 Bennett, Jay. *I Never Said I Love You* (9–12). 1984, Avon paper $2.50 (0-380-86900-4). A boy must choose between fulfilling his father's wishes and the girl he loves.

3874 Bernardo, Anilu. *Loves Me, Loves Me Not* (7–10). 1998, Arte Publico $16.95 (1-55885-258-1). A teen romance that involves Cuban American Maggie, a basketball player named Zach, newcomer Justin, and Maggie's friend, Susie. (Rev: BL 1/1–15/99)

3875 Bertrand, Diane Gonzales. *Lessons of the Game* (7–10). 1998, Arte Publico paper $9.95 (1-55885-245-X). Student teacher Kaylene Morales is attracted to the freshman football coach but wonders if romance and her school assignments will mix. (Rev: BL 1/1–15/99; VOYA 10/99)

3876 Binchy, Maeve. *The Glass Lake* (9–12). 1995, Delacorte $23.95 (0-385-31354-3). Helen is pre-

sumed to have drowned in an Irish lake, but she's fled to London with her lover. Years later, she tries to reestablish contact with her teenage daughter, Kit. (Rev: BL 1/1/95; SLJ 8/95)

3877 Blake, Michael. *Airman Mortensen* (9–12). 1991, Seven Wolves $20.00 (0-9627387-7-8). The poignant summer romance between an 18-year-old airman awaiting court martial and the base commander's daughter is described in this story of the loss of innocence. (Rev: BL 10/1/91; SLJ 11/91)

3878 Bly, Stephen. *The Senator's Other Daughter* (9–12). Series: Belles of Lordsburg. 2001, Crossway paper $10.99 (1-58134-236-5). Grace Denison leaves her stuffy home and takes a job as a telegraph operator in a town in New Mexico in this romantic novel by the author of numerous Christian westerns. (Rev: BL 3/1/01)

3879 Bretton, Barbara. *At Last* (10–12). 2000, Berkley paper $6.99 (0-425-17737-8). Gracie Taylor and Noah Chase fell in love in kindergarten, but as they grew older fate and their families kept them apart. (Rev: BL 9/15/00)

3880 Brockway, Connie. *Bridal Favors* (11–12). 2002, Bantam paper $6.99 (0-440-23674-6). An handsome, undercover spy lends his British estate to a pretty young lady in return for her silence long ago; for mature teens. (Rev: BL 9/15/02*)

3881 Brooks, Martha. *Two Moons in August* (7–12). 1992, Little, Brown $15.95 (0-316-10979-7). A midsummer romance in the 1950s between a newcomer to a small Canadian community and a 16-year-old girl who is mourning her mother's death. (Rev: BL 11/15/91*; SLJ 3/92*)

3882 Brownrigg, Sylvia. *Pages for You* (10–12). 2001, Farrar $22.00 (0-374-22859-0). A 17-year-old college student is attracted to Anne, a teaching assistant who is 11 years her senior, and the two fall in love in this account with some explicit sex. (Rev: BL 3/1/01)

3883 Burrows, Geraldine. *Stranger in Paradise* (11–12). 2003, Five Star $26.95 (1-5941-4025-1). Kate Elliot is suspicious of the new guest at her aunt's Maui hotel but finds herself drawn to him nonetheless. (Rev: BL 9/15/03)

3884 Byrd, Nicole. *Lady in Waiting* (11–12). 2002, Penguin paper $6.99 (0-515-13292-6). Circe, an independent-minded artist, reluctantly agrees to a London Season and there comes across a man she had admired greatly as a teen; an entertaining romance full of intrigue and historical detail, for mature teens. (Rev: BL 5/1/02)

3885 Camp, Candace. *Mesmerized* (11–12). 2003, MIRA paper $6.99 (1-55166-729-0). Despite their disbelief in the supernatural, Olivia and Stephen find they are seeing ghosts — and experiencing a strong and growing connection to each other. (Rev: BL 9/15/03)

3886 Camp, Candace. *So Wild a Heart* (10–12). 2002, MIRA paper $6.50 (1-55166-877-7). Miranda and Devin, who married only to aid their families' social ambitions, find themselves drawn to each other in spite of themselves in this Regency romance tinged with mystery. (Rev: BL 2/1/02)

3887 Cann, Kate. *Grecian Holiday: Or, How I Turned Down the Best Possible Thing Only to Have the Time of My Life* (7–12). 2002, Avon paper $5.99 (0-06-447302-3). In addition to the beach, the food, and the drink, Kelly's vacation in Greece is a time of learning about herself, friendship, romance, and sex; for mature teens. (Rev: VOYA 2/03)

3888 Cann, Kate. *Ready? Love Trilogy #1* (8–12). 2001, HarperCollins LB $15.89 (0-06-028938-4); paper $6.95 (0-06-440869-8). In the first book of a British romantic trilogy, 16-year-old Collette falls for Art, who is both rich and handsome, but she is troubled by his unrelenting pressure for physical intimacy. The sequels are *Sex* (2001) and *Go!* (2001). (Rev: HBG 10/02; SLJ 8/01; VOYA 10/01)

3889 Carr, Philippa. *The Changeling* (9–12). 1990, Fawcett paper $4.95 (0-449-14697-9). A historical romance involving two babies being switched at birth. (Rev: BL 3/1/89)

3890 Claire, Edie. *Long Time Coming* (10–12). 2003, Warner paper $5.99 (0-446-61277-4). After almost two decades away, Joy Hudson, now a veterinarian, returns to her Kentucky hometown and must confront some ghosts from her high school past. (Rev: BL 11/15/03)

3891 Coleman, Jane Candia. *Desperate Acts* (10–12). 2001, Five Star $25.95 (0-7862-3210-2). Nan, an abused wife, and her daughter go on a vacation to a dude ranch where Nan falls in love with the ranch's sensitive owner. (Rev: BL 2/15/01)

3892 Cooney, Caroline B. *Both Sides of Time* (6–10). 1997, Delacorte paper $4.99 (0-440-21932-9). Annie Lockwood, who has been yearning for love, suddenly finds herself in the 1890s, in a much more appealing era; however, traveling through time can lack romance. (Rev: BL 9/15/95; HB 11/95; HBG 3/02; SLJ 7/95)

3893 Counts, Wilma. *Rules of Marriage* (11–12). 2002, Zebra paper $5.99 (0-8217-7043-8). An injured soldier falls in love with a married nurse against the detailed backdrop of war against Napoleon; for mature teens. (Rev: BL 4/15/02)

3894 Criswell, Millie. *Mad About Mia* (11–12). 2004, Ballantine paper $6.99 (0-8041-1994-5). FBI agent Nick Caruso, who's posing as a nerdy author to investigate the Baltimore mob, hires unlikely bodyguard Mia DeNero to get closer to his quarry but soon finds himself falling under her spell; for mature teens. (Rev: BL 12/15/03)

3895 Dailey, Janet. *A Capital Holiday* (9–12). 2001, Zebra paper $6.99 (0-8217-7224-4). Jocelyn, the daughter of a widowed American president, disguises herself to get away from unwanted press attention and, in her new identity, falls in love. (Rev: BL 9/15/01)

3896 Daly, Maureen. *First a Dream* (7–10). 1990, Scholastic paper $12.95 (0-590-40846-1). The love that Retta and Dallas feel for each other is tested during a summer when they are separated in this sequel to *Acts of Love* (1986). (Rev: BL 4/1/90; SLJ 4/90; VOYA 4/90)

3897 Danziger, Paula. *Thames Doesn't Rhyme with James* (7–10). 1994, Putnam $15.95 (0-399-22526-9). Kendra and her family take a joint vacation to London with the Lees and their son Frank, Kendra's boyfriend. (Rev: BL 12/1/94; SLJ 1/95; VOYA 4/95)

3898 Davis, Jill. *Girls' Poker Night: A Novel of High Stakes* (10–12). 2002, Random $23.95 (0-375-50514-8). Newspaper columnist Ruby and her friends try to make sense of their love lives in this entertaining novel set in New York City. (Rev: BL 1/1–15/02)

3899 Davis, Leila. *Lover Boy* (7–12). 1989, Avon paper $2.95 (0-380-75722-2). Ryan finds that his racy reputation is keeping him from the girl he really loves. (Rev: SLJ 10/89; VOYA 8/89)

3900 Delinsky, Barbara. *Three Wishes* (10–12). 1997, Simon & Schuster $23.00 (0-684-84507-5). A near-fatal accident brings Bree and Tom together in a love that transcends time and death. (Rev: SLJ 1/98)

3901 Dessen, Sarah. *This Lullaby* (8–12). 2002, Viking $16.99 (0-670-03530-0). Eighteen-year-old Remy's complex family life leads her to avoid deep romantic attachments until she meets Dexter. (Rev: BCCB 5/02; BL 4/1/02; HB 7–8/02; HBG 10/02; SLJ 4/02; VOYA 6/02)

3902 Deveraux, Jude. *The Summerhouse* (10–12). 2001, Pocket $24.95 (0-671-01418-8). Three discontented friends meet for a reunion and are granted a gift from mysterious Madame Zoya to relive any three weeks of their lives. (Rev: BL 4/1/01)

3903 Dokey, Cameron. *Hindenburg, 1937* (7–10). 1999, Archway paper $4.99 (0-671-03601-7). On board the *Hindenburg* on its last voyage to America in 1937, Anna, a German girl fleeing from her Nazi brother who is pressuring her to accept an arranged marriage, is torn between two suitors who each suspect the other of being a spy. (Rev: VOYA 10/99)

3904 Dufresne, John. *Deep in the Shade of Paradise* (10–12). 2002, Norton $26.95 (0-393-02020-7). Adlai falls in love with his cousin's fiancee only days before their wedding. (Rev: BL 1/1–15/02)

3905 Eagle, Kathleen. *Once Upon a Wedding* (11–12). 2002, Morrow $24.95 (0-06-621472-6). A Minnesota wedding brings new and old relationships to life in this intergenerational romance; for mature teens. (Rev: BL 6/1–15/02)

3906 Ephron, Amy. *A Cup of Tea* (10–12). 1997, Morrow $20.00 (0-688-14997-9). When Rosemary Fell invited a penniless young woman into her house, she did not anticipate that her fiance would fall in love with her. (Rev: BL 8/97; SLJ 11/97)

3907 Fairchild, Elisabeth. *A Game of Patience* (10–12). 2002, NAL paper $4.99 (0-451-20606-1). Ready for romance, Patience looks at two old friends; she first selects the handsome Pip but eventually sees the charms of the less dashing Richard. (Rev: BL 5/1/02)

3908 Feather, Jane. *Bachelor List* (11–12). 2004, Bantam paper $6.99 (0-553-58618-1). London suffragette Constance Duncan finds herself falling under the spell of Max Ensor, a member of Parliament and outspoken opponent of giving women the vote; for mature teens. (Rev: BL 12/15/03)

3909 Feather, Jane. *Kissed by Shadows* (10–12). Series: Kiss. 2003, Bantam paper $5.99 (0-533-58308-5). This final installment in a trilogy set in 16th-century England and featuring Lady Philippa Nielson abounds in political and sexual intrigue. (Rev: BL 2/15/03)

3910 Ferguson, Jo Ann. *His Lady Midnight* (10–12). 2001, Zebra paper $4.99 (0-8217-6863-8). A Regency romance that features Phoebe Brackenton, a secret protector of the oppressed, and the gallant Lord Galen Townsend, who helps her escape when she is nearly caught during one of her adventures. (Rev: BL 9/15/01)

3911 Fiedler, Lisa. *Dating Hamlet: Ophelia's Story* (9–12). 2002, Holt $16.95 (0-8050-7054-0). With help from her friend Anne, Ophelia comes to Hamlet's rescue following the death of his father. (Rev: BL 9/15/02; HB 1–2/03; HBG 3/03; SLJ 11/02; VOYA 2/03)

3912 Fiedler, Lisa. *Lucky Me* (6–10). 1998, Clarion $15.00 (0-395-89131-0). In this sequel to *Curtis Piperfield's Biggest Fan* (1995), Cecily Caruthers wants to be more adventurous sexually and this leads to a series of humorous situations. (Rev: BCCB 10/98; BL 11/15/98; BR 5–6/99; HB 11–12/98; HBG 3/99; SLJ 3/99; VOYA 6/99)

3913 Filichia, Peter. *Not Just Another Pretty Face* (7–10). 1988, Avon paper $2.50 (0-380-75244-1). A high school story in which the course of true love does not run smoothly for Bill Richards. (Rev: BL 3/1/88; SLJ 5/88)

3914 Foley, Gaelen. *Lord of Fire* (11–12). 2002, Ballantine paper $6.99 (0-449-00637-9). Lord Lucien Knight's reckless ways are tamed by young Alice despite his best intentions in this romance with a touch of spy story thrown in. (Rev: BL 1/1–15/02)

3915 Frank, Lucy. *Will You Be My Brussels Sprout?* (7–10). 1996, Holiday $15.95 (0-8234-1220-2). In this continuation of *I Am an Artichoke*, Emily, now 16, studies the cello at a New York music conservatory and falls in love for the first time. (Rev: BL 4/15/96; SLJ 4/96; VOYA 10/96)

3916 Garcia Marquez, Gabriel. *Love in the Time of Cholera* (10–12). Trans. by Edith Grossman. 1988, Knopf $30.00 (0-394-56161-9). The story of a love that lasts for more than 50 years but is unrequited as the two people involved go their separate ways.

3917 Garner, Tracee Lydia. *Come What May* (11–12). 2003, BET paper $5.99 (1-58314-392-0). A suspenseful romance featuring African Americans Tisha, a young teacher, and Chase, a single father. (Rev: BL 2/15/03)

3918 Geras, Adele. *Pictures of the Night* (7–12). 1993, Harcourt $16.95 (0-15-261588-1). A modern version of *Snow White,* with the heroine an 18-year-old singer in London and Paris. (Rev: BL 3/1/93; SLJ 6/93)

3919 Geras, Adele. *The Tower Room* (7–12). 1992, Harcourt $15.95 (0-15-289627-9). The fairy tale *Rapunzel* is updated and set in an English girls' boarding school in the 1960s. (Rev: BL 2/15/92; SLJ 5/92)

3920 Gerber, Merrill Joan. *Handsome as Anything* (8–12). 1990, Scholastic $13.95 (0-590-43019-X). Rachel is attracted to three different boys and in making her choice learns a lot about herself. (Rev: BL 9/15/90; SLJ 12/90)

3921 Gilson, Chris. *Crazy for Cornelia* (10–12). 2000, Warner $23.95 (0-446-52536-7). This is a humorous romantic novel involving a Fifth Avenue debutante and the new doorman in her building, struggling artist Kevin Doyle. (Rev: BL 2/15/00)

3922 Givens, Kathleen. *The Destiny* (11–12). 2003, Warner paper $5.99 (0-446-61053-4). Two young lovers struggle to make a life together despite overwhelming odds in this novel set during the reign of William and Mary. (Rev: BL 3/15/03)

3923 Gordon, Katharine. *The Long Love* (9–12). 2001, Severn $25.99 (0-7278-5601-4). Arina Begum travels back to India to marry a man she has not seen since she was 3 in this romance with adventure and a kidnapping. (Rev: BL 6/1–15/01)

3924 Gregory, Diana. *Two's a Crowd* (7–10). 1985, Bantam paper $3.50 (0-553-24992-4). Peggy finds that her business rival is a handsome young man. (Rev: BL 10/15/85; SLJ 9/85)

3925 Grey, Amelia. *A Dash of Scandal* (11–12). 2002, Berkley paper $5.99 (0-515-13401-5). Filling in for her society-column-writing aunt (who uses a male pseudonym), Millicent attracts the attention of an earl in this witty Regency romance; for mature teens. (Rev: BL 9/15/02)

3926 Griggs, Winnie. *Whatever It Takes* (10–12). 2002, Leisure paper $5.99 (0-8439-5138-9). Thrust together by Maddy's desire to adopt a child, Maddy and Clay find their courtship is more than make-believe; a warm romance set in the late 19th century. (Rev: BL 10/1/02)

3927 Grossman, David. *Someone to Run With* (10–12). Trans. by Vered Almog and Maya Gurantz. 2004, Farrar $25.00 (0-374-26657-3). In a skillful blend of romance and mystery, two middle-class teens, Tamar and Assaf, find themselves drawn into the perilous drug underworld of Jerusalem. (Rev: BL 12/1/03)

3928 Guillaume, Geri. *Hearts of Steel* (11–12). 2002, BET paper $6.99 (1-58314-364-5). On her way to a family reunion, Shiri falls hard for an attractive football player despite her disdain for the game; for mature teens. (Rev: BL 7/02)

3929 Gunn, Robin Jones. *I Promise* (6–12). Series: Christy and Todd, The College Years. 2001, Bethany $10.99 (0-7642-2274-0). Christy and Todd are finally engaged, but the complicated wedding plans and accompanying turmoil threaten to derail their happiness. (Rev: BL 1/1–15/02; VOYA 12/01)

3930 Gutcheon, Beth. *More than You Know* (10–12). 2000, Morrow $22.00 (0-688-17403-5). An enjoyable novel that weaves together two love stories, one contemporary and the other from the past, but both with touches of the supernatural. (Rev: BL 2/15/00; SLJ 8/00)

3931 Hahn, Mary D. *The Wind Blows Backward* (8–12). 1993, Clarion $16.00 (0-395-62975-6); Avon paper $4.95 (0-380-77530-1). Spencer's downward emotional spiral and Lauren's deep commitment evoke a fantasy love gone awry. (Rev: BL 5/1/93; SLJ 5/93)

3932 Hale, Gena. *Paradise Island* (10–12). 2001, NAL paper $5.99 (0-451-40982-5). A handsome marine archaeologist working on his private island on a secret State Department project is disturbed when a raft arrives carrying a scantily clad woman. (Rev: BL 3/15/01)

3933 Hart, Bruce, and Carole Hart. *Sooner or Later* (8–12). 1978, Avon paper $2.95 (0-380-42978-0). In order to fool her 17-year-old boyfriend into thinking she is older than 13, Jessie begins an intricate pattern of lies.

3934 Hart, Bruce, and Carole Hart. *Waiting Games* (7–10). 1981, Avon paper $3.50 (0-380-79012-2). Jessie and Michael are in love and must make difficult decisions about sex.

3935 Hayes, Hunter. *A Pair Like No Otha'* (10–12). 2002, Avon paper $13.95 (0-380-81485-4). Successful Shemone and released convict Darnell have been friends since childhood and are now romantically involved. (Rev: BL 11/15/02)

3936 Heath, Sandra. *False Steps* (10–12). 2003, NAL paper $4.99 (0-451-20770-X). This delightful regency romance involves English nobleman Cassian Stratford and Winifred "Freddie" Smith, who disguises her lowly heritage. (Rev: BL 1/1–15/03)

3937 Henderson, Dee. *True Valor* (10–12). Series: Uncommon Heroes. 2002, Multnomah paper $11.99 (1-57673-887-6). When Gracie, a pilot fighting in Iraq, is pulled from behind enemy lines by a former love, Bruce, sparks fly once more. (Rev: BL 1/1–15/02*)

3938 Henry, Patti Callahan. *Losing the Moon* (9–12). 2004, NAL paper $12.95 (0-451-21195-2). Amy finds that her son is romancing the daughter of the man who broke her heart many years before. (Rev: BL 5/1/04*)

3939 Hilton, James. *Random Harvest* (10–12). 1982, Buccaneer LB $29.95 (0-89966-414-8). A highly romantic novel set in World War I days about an amnesia victim who has forgotten his first true love.

3940 Hite, Sid. *Cecil in Space* (7–10). 1999, Holt $16.95 (0-8050-5055-8). At 17, Cecil begins to takes life seriously when he falls in love with the richest, sexiest girl in town. (Rev: BL 4/15/99; HBG 9/99; SLJ 5/99; VOYA 6/99)

3941 Hoh, Diane. *Titanic, the Long Night* (7–12). 1998, Scholastic paper $4.99 (0-590-33123-X). In this novel set on the ill-fated *Titanic* in 1912, wealthy first-class passenger Elizabeth Farr meets Max Whittaker, a wealthy but rebellious artist; in a parallel plot in third class, Irish rogue Paddy Kelleher and talented singer Katie Hanrahan fall in love. (Rev: BR 1–2/99; VOYA 2/99)

3942 Holt, Victoria. *Daughter of Deceit* (9–12). 1992, Fawcett paper $5.99 (0-449-22058-3). The daughter of a recently deceased London actress must call off her wedding when it is revealed that her fiance is probably her half-brother. (Rev: BL 9/1/91; SLJ 4/92)

3943 Holt, Victoria. *Secret for a Nightingale* (10–12). 1987, Fawcett paper $3.50 (0-449-21296-3). In this Gothic romance set in the 19th century, a young woman seeks revenge for the death of her son. (Rev: BL 8/86)

3944 Holt, Victoria. *The Silk Vendetta* (9–12). 1989, Fawcett paper $5.99 (0-449-21548-2). A suspenseful romance that uses the historic trade of silk weaving as its subject. (Rev: BL 8/87)

3945 Hood-Stewart, Fiona. *Silent Wishes* (11–12). 2003, MIRA paper $6.50 (1-55166-728-2). CEO Sylvia Hansen and colleague Jeremy Warmouth work together to find the identity of the traitor who is seeking to ruin both the company and Sylvia herself. (Rev: BL 9/15/03)

3946 Hough, John. *The Last Summer* (11–12). 2002, Simon & Schuster $25.00 (0-7432-2705-0). Against the backdrop of the turbulent events of 1968, a woman with a 15-year-old daughter who becomes involved with a much younger man and together become involved in a murder mystery; for mature teens. (Rev: BL 6/1–15/02)

3947 Hudson, Harriet. *To My Own Desire* (10–12). 2000, Severn $26.00 (0-7278-5589-1). While visiting Paris, Tara meets and falls in love with a street performer and learns that they are linked by a relationship that occurred many years before. (Rev: BL 11/15/00)

3948 Jaffe, Rona. *The Road Taken* (10–12). 2000, Dutton $24.95 (0-525-94474-5). This multigenerational melodrama follows the story of Rose Smith Carson and her family through the end of the 20th century. (Rev: BL 3/15/00)

3949 Jenkins, Beverly. *Belle and the Beau* (6–12). Series: Avon True Romance. 2002, Avon paper $4.99 (0-06-447342-2). Jenkins incorporates historical detail and atmosphere in this story of romance between an escaped slave and the son of an African American abolitionist family. (Rev: BL 9/15/02; SLJ 5/02)

3950 Jocks, Yvonne. *Say Goodnight, Gracie* (9–12). 2004, Zebra paper $5.99 (0-8217-7457-3). The third novel in the lighthearted trilogy that began with *Belle of the Ball* (2002) and *A Touch of Charm* (2003), about three sisters who are looking for romance. (Rev: BL 1/1–15/04)

3951 Johnson, Doris. *Midsummer Moon* (10–12). 2001, BET paper $5.99 (1-58314-213-4). Just when things look bleak for June Saxon, she is offered a job in Paris and she becomes attracted to the ex-husband of a former friend. (Rev: BL 10/1/01)

3952 Jones, Jill. *Emily's Secret* (10–12). 1995, St. Martin's paper $4.99 (0-312-95576-6). This historical novel combines a modern-day romance with the life of Emily Brontë as seen through the eyes of one of her descendants. (Rev: BL 8/95; SLJ 4/96)

3953 Jukes, Mavis. *Cinderella 2000* (6–10). 1999, Delacorte paper $8.95 (0-385-32711-0). Fourteen-year-old Ashley is desperate to go to the New Year's Eve party with the love of her life, but her stepmother wants her to babysit for her stepsisters. (Rev: BCCB 1/00; BL 10/1/99; HBG 4/00; SLJ 11/99)

3954 Kane, Andrea. *No Way Out* (10–12). 2001, Pocket paper $6.99 (0-7434-1275-3). In this romantic suspense novel, a second-grade teacher's concern over an emotionally abused child leads to political intrigue and involvement with the boy's uncle. (Rev: BL 9/15/01)

3955 Kane, Kathleen. *Catch a Fallen Angel* (10–12). 2000, St. Martin's paper $5.99 (0-312-97575-9). After his death outside Reno in 1880, Gabe makes a deal with the devil for two more months of life—

only to fall helplessly in love with Maggie Benson. For better readers. (Rev: BL 9/15/00)

3956 Kaplow, Robert. *Alessandra in Love* (8–10). 1989, HarperCollins LB $12.89 (0-397-32282-8). Alessandra's boyfriend turns out to be a self-centered disappointment. (Rev: BL 4/15/89; SLJ 4/89; VOYA 8/89)

3957 Kay, Susan. *Phantom* (9–12). 1992, Dell paper $6.99 (0-440-21169-7). Fans of *Phantom of the Opera* will recognize Erik, whose character is well drawn in his dual roles of adored hero and hated villain. (Rev: BL 2/15/91; SLJ 9/91)

3958 King, Tabitha. *One on One* (9–12). 1994, NAL paper $5.99 (0-451-17981-1). A coming-of-age story featuring a fierce, unexpected attraction between two mismatched high school basketball stars: Deannie, female, who's a pierced, tattooed skinhead, and Sam, a virgin who's an Adonis with a ponytail. (Rev: BL 2/1/93; SLJ 7/93)

3959 Kirkland, Martha. *An Inconvenient Heir* (10–12). 2003, NAL paper $4.99 (0-451-20771-8). In an effort to save her friend's son, Delia must pose as a gypsy in this Regency romance. (Rev: BL 12/15/02)

3960 Kirkland, Martha. *The Secret Diary* (10–12). 2003, NAL paper $4.99 (0-451-20907-9). Love poems and grateful orphaned sisters are central features of this entertaining Regency romance. (Rev: BL 6/1–15/03)

3961 Kirkwood, Gwen. *The Laird of Lochandee* (10–12). 2003, Severn $26.99 (0-7278-5877-7). Mature teens will enjoy this highly readable tale set in Scotland in which Rachel, an unwed mother, is reunited with Ross, her first love and the father of her child. Together they survive a series of misfortunes. (Rev: BL 1/1–15/03)

3962 Knudson, R. R. *Just Another Love Story* (7–10). 1983, Avon paper $2.50 (0-380-65532-2). Dusty takes up body building to help forget the girlfriend who has spurned him.

3963 Koja, Kathe. *The Blue Mirror* (9–12). 2004, Farrar $16.00 (0-374-30849-7). This story of first love that doesn't last tells of 17-year-old Maggy and her love for a beautiful but flawed boy named Cole. (Rev: BL 2/15/04; HB 5–6/04; SLJ 3/04; VOYA 4/04)

3964 Korbel, Kathleen. *Some Men's Dreams* (11–12). 2003, Harlequin paper $4.75 (0-373-27307-X). Gen is very attracted to her new boss, Jack, and is worried that his daughter suffers from an eating disorder. (Rev: BL 8/03)

3965 Krahn, Betina. *The Wife Test* (11–12). 2003, Berkley paper $6.99 (0-425-19092-7). Four potential noblemen's brides are sent from France to England in this amusing romance set in the Middle Ages. (Rev: BL 7/03)

3966 Krentz, Jayne Ann. *Truth or Dare* (11–12). 2004, Putnam $24.95 (0-399-15073-0). Interior designer Zoe and private detective Ethan struggle to make a go of their marriage while each seeks to dispel demons from the past; for mature teens. (Rev: BL 11/1/03)

3967 Krinard, Susan. *Secret of the Wolf* (10–12). 2001, Berkley paper $6.99 (0-425-18199-5). Psychiatrist Johanna Schell finds she is growing attracted to an alcoholic in her asylum despite his delusions of being a werewolf. (Rev: BL 9/15/01)

3968 Kurland, Lynn. *If I Had You* (10–12). 2000, Berkley $6.99 (0-425-17694-0). In this tender medieval romance, Anne of Fenwyck, a cripple, falls in love with Robin de Piaget, who appears to reject her. (Rev: BL 9/15/00)

3969 Lachtman, Ofelia Dumas. *The Girl from Playa Bianca* (7–12). 1995, Arte Publico paper $9.95 (1-55885-149-6). A gothic romance in which a Mexican teenager and her young brother travel to Los Angeles in search of their father. (Rev: BL 11/15/95; SLJ 10/95; VOYA 12/95)

3970 Landvik, Lorna. *Welcome to the Great Mysterious* (10–12). 2000, Ballantine $23.00 (0-449-43881-7). New Yorker Geneva Jordan finds unexpected romance when she goes home to Minnesota for a month to care for her 13-year-old nephew who has Down's syndrome. (Rev: BL 10/15/00)

3971 Lane, Connie. *Dirty Little Lies* (10–12). 2004, Dell paper $6.50 (0-440-23747-5). Lacie Jo Baxter survives a kidnapping and becomes attracted to one of the men sent to protect her in this hilarious romantic comedy. (Rev: BL 2/15/04*)

3972 Lansdowne, Judith A. *Shall We Dance?* (10–12). 2002, Zebra paper $5.99 (0-8217-7018-7). This lively and well-written novel offers an entertaining blend of humor, suspense, and historical romance. (Rev: BL 3/1/02)

3973 Lee, Rebecca Hagan. *Always a Lady* (10–12). Series: Marquess of Templeston's Heir. 2002, Penguin paper $6.99 (0-515-13347-7). When Kit Ramsey claims his inheritance in 1838, he finds he is also responsible for a beautiful young woman whom he must launch into society. (Rev: BL 10/15/02)

3974 L'Engle, Madeleine. *And Both Were Young* (9–12). 1983, Dell paper $4.99 (0-440-90229-0). Flip feels like a misfit at her Swiss school until she meets Paul.

3975 L'Engle, Madeleine. *Camilla* (10–12). 1982, Dell paper $4.50 (0-440-91171-0). A sensitive young girl experiences first love and the breakup of her family.

3976 Levithan, David. *Boy Meets Boy* (9–12). 2003, Knopf LB $17.99 (0-375-92400-0). The love story of Paul and Noah, who enjoy the approval of their friends and family. (Rev: BL 8/03; HBG 4/04; SLJ 9/03; VOYA 10/03)

3977 Lindsey, Johanna. *Home for the Holidays* (10–12). 2000, Morrow $18.00 (0-380-97856-3). In his mission to destroy the man he believes harmed his brother, Vincent Everett finds love instead. (Rev: BL 11/1/00)

3978 Lovelace, Merline. *A Savage Beauty* (11–12). 2003, MIRA paper $6.50 (1-55166-707-X). Romance and historical detail are combined in an absorbing story about an Osage woman in the early 19th century. (Rev: BL 9/1/03)

3979 Luntta, Karl. *Know It by Heart* (10–12). 2003, Curbstone paper $15.95 (1-880684-95-0). This teenage love story plays out in a tony Connecticut suburb torn apart by hatred and racism. (Rev: BL 9/1/03; VOYA 2/04)

3980 MacAlister, Katie. *Improper English* (11–12). 2003, Leisure paper $6.99 (0-8439-4985-1). Alix is determined to write a novel in this entertaining romance set in contemporary England. (Rev: BL 3/1/03)

3981 McCafferty, Jeanne. *Set to Music* (10–12). 2000, Severn $26.00 (0-7278-5557-3). Anne breaks into the music business through working with a young composer, and a friendship develops that overcomes a tragedy. (Rev: BL 11/15/00)

3982 McDaniel, Lurlene. *Angels Watching over Me* (8–10). 1996, Bantam paper $4.99 (0-553-56724-1). Romance, mystery, and personal problems mingle in this novel about a girl who has bone cancer, the boy she is attracted to in the hospital, and a mysterious nurse. (Rev: BR 11–12/96; SLJ 3/97)

3983 McDaniel, Lurlene. *Don't Die, My Love* (7–12). 1995, Bantam paper $4.99 (0-553-56715-2). A young couple, Julie and Luke, "engaged" since 6th grade, discover that Luke has Hodgkin's lymphoma. (Rev: BL 9/15/95; SLJ 10/95; VOYA 12/95)

3984 Macdonald, Malcolm. *Tamsin Harte* (10–12). 2000, St. Martin's $24.95 (0-312-20628-3). In this romantic novel set in Cornwall during 1907, Tamsin, the heroine, sets out to find a wealthy husband. (Rev: BL 2/15/00)

3985 McEachern, Shelagh. *Mr. Perfect* (9–12). 2004, Avalon $21.95 (0-8034-9644-3). When Verrick Grant moves to a new condo in Vancouver, she meets the impeccable and charming Lionel Parford and a gentle, sweet romance is the result. (Rev: BL 4/15/04)

3986 McGoldrick, May. *The Rebel* (10–12). 2002, NAL paper $6.99 (0-451-20654-1). On his way to claim a beautiful Irish bride, Englishman Sir Nicholas Spencer meets and is captivated by her wayward older sister. (Rev: BL 7/02)

3987 McNeill, Elizabeth. *A Bombay Affair* (10–12). 2000, Severn House $26.00 (0-7278-5514-X). Using intriguing characters and the setting of Bombay in 1959, this romance involves love affairs, betrayals, blackmail, and—finally—hope. (Rev: BL 5/1/00)

3988 Magorian, Michelle. *Not a Swan* (9–12). 1992, HarperCollins LB $17.89 (0-06-024215-9). During World War II, Rose, 17, and her two older sisters are evacuated to the English countryside, where Rose falls in love with a veteran who supports her efforts to become a writer. (Rev: BL 8/92)

3989 Mallory, Tess. *Highland Fling* (10–12). 2003, Dorchester paper $5.99 (0-505-52526-7). This romantic and humorous time-travel romp brings together in the Old West a handsome 7th-century Scotsman and a gutsy 21st-century woman scientist. (Rev: BL 2/15/03)

3990 Manning, Jo. *The Sicilian Amulet* (9–12). 2004, Five Star $26.95 (1-59414-181-9). Jane, who is in Sicily visiting her relatives, becomes involved with a handsome prince who brings her love and danger. (Rev: BL 4/1/04)

3991 Mason, Sarah. *Playing James* (10–12). 2004, Ballantine paper $12.95 (0-345-46955-0). Holly, a reporter, is assigned to detective sergeant James Sabine who dislikes her in spite of the fact that Holly thinks she is falling in love with him. (Rev: BL 5/1/04)

3992 Mauser, Pat Rhoads. *Love Is for the Dogs* (7–10). 1989, Avon paper $2.50 (0-380-75723-0). Janna realizes that Brian, the boy next door, can be very desirable. (Rev: BL 4/15/89; SLJ 4/89)

3993 Mayhew, Margaret. *The Pathfinder* (11–12). 2003, Severn $26.99 (0-7278-5879-3). In postwar Berlin, Michael Harrison feels no sympathy for the German people until he meets Lili and falls in love. (Rev: BL 3/1/03)

3994 Mekler, Eva. *Sunrise Shows Late* (10–12). 1997, Bridge Works. $21.95 (1-882593-17-0). Manya, living in a displaced-persons camp in Germany after World War II, is attracted to two very different men and must make a choice. (Rev: BL 3/15/97; SLJ 7/97)

3995 Metzger, Barbara. *Wedded Bliss* (9–12). 2004, NAL paper $6.99 (0-451-20859-5). Rockland, a snobbish British diplomat gets an unwanted makeover when his new wife and her children move into his London townhouse in this humorous Regency romance. (Rev: BL 3/1/04*)

3996 Michaels, Fern. *The Future Scrolls* (10–12). 2001, Severn $25.99 (0-7278-5721-5). A wholesome story about a daughter who is sent by her father to her unloving mother in order to prevent the mother from selling the family's collection of ancient religious scrolls. (Rev: BL 11/1/01)

3997 Michaels, Kasey. *The Kissing Game* (10–12). 2003, Warner paper $5.99 (0-446-61085-2). This amusing regency romance tells the story of Lady Allegra Nesbitt, the fiercely independent daughter of a newly minted nobleman, and how she finds love with her London neighbor, Armand Gauthier. (Rev: BL 1/1–15/03)

3998 Michaels, Kasey. *Love to Love You Baby* (10–12). 2001, Kensington paper $6.99 (0-8217-6844-1). A humorous romance about a former New York Yankees pitcher and the girl who comes to redecorate his 15-room house and stays to babysit his cousin's infant daughter. (Rev: BL 9/15/01)

3999 Michaels, Kasey. *Maggie by the Book* (10–12). 2003, Kensington $20.00 (1-57566-881-5). Humor, romance, and mystery are interwoven in this rollicking tale of a New York writer whose Regency characters have come to life; a sequel to *Maggie Needs an Alibi* (2002). (Rev: BL 7/03)

4000 Michaels, Kasey. *This Can't Be Love* (9–12). 2004, Zebra paper $6.99 (0-8217-7119-1). Molly Applegate, an extremely rich girl, trades places with a friend and takes a job babysitting for an attractive Broadway producer. (Rev: BL 3/15/04)

4001 Mitchell, Sharon. *Near Perfect* (10–12). 2001, Dutton $23.95 (0-525-94621-7). Four very different young women move on to new romances and relationships, but they remain close friends. (Rev: BL 9/1/01)

4002 Moon, Marliss. *By Starlight* (11–12). 2003, Berkley Sensation paper $5.99 (0-425-19103-6). Merry Duboise needs Luke le Noir's help to escape being burned as a witch in this sequel to *Danger's Promise* (2002) that realistically portrays life in the Middle Ages. (Rev: BL 7/03)

4003 Moore, Margaret. *Gwyneth and the Thief* (8–12). Series: Avon True Romance. 2002, Avon paper $4.99 (0-06-447337-6). In an effort to save her family estate from a predatory baron, Lady Gwyneth seeks the help of a young — and increasingly appealing — thief. (Rev: BL 9/15/02)

4004 Nathan, Melissa. *Pride, Prejudice, and Jasmin Field* (10–12). 2001, Avon paper $14.00 (0-06-018495-7). A modern and witty retelling of *Pride and Prejudice* with Jasmin Field playing the part of Elizabeth Bennet. (Rev: BL 5/1/01)

4005 Nelson, D-L. *Chickpea Lover: (Not a Cookbook)* (10–12). 2003, Five Star $26.95 (0-7862-4706-1). Nursing college professor Liz Adams must choose between the two men in her life when she discovers she's pregnant in this entertaining novel with subplots involving sexual harassment and campus power politics. (Rev: BL 2/15/03)

4006 Nilsson, Per. *Heart's Delight* (9–12). Trans. by Tara Chace. 2003, Front Street $16.95 (1-886910-92-8). Full of jealousy, a 16-year-old boy looks back at a failed romance. (Rev: BCCB 2/04; BL

11/1/03*; HB 1–2/04*; HBG 4/04; LMC 3/04; SLJ 12/03; VOYA 4/04)

4007 O'Brien, Judith. *Timeless Love* (7–10). 2002, Simon & Schuster paper $4.99 (0-7434-1921-9). A 16th birthday present transports Sam to Tudor England where she finds romance and intrigue in this novel that blends fantasy and history. (Rev: SLJ 3/02)

4008 Orcutt, Jane. *The Living Stone* (10–12). 2000, WaterBrook paper $10.95 (1-57856-292-9). In this contemporary romance, Leah Travers, who has lost her husband and son in a car crash, becomes involved with the brother-in-law of the man who was responsible for their deaths. (Rev: BL 8/00)

4009 Palmer, Catherine. *A Victorian Rose* (10–12). 2002, Tyndale $12.99 (0-8423-1957-3). In Victorian Yorkshire, Clementine, a lonely artist, falls for a doctor who has been vilified unfairly. (Rev: BL 10/1/02)

4010 Parra, Nancy J. *Loving Lana* (11–12). 2003, Avalon $19.95 (0-8034-9617-6). Bored with life in Wyoming, Lana sets out to win a $2,000 reward for capturing a wild horse and in the process finds love with Taggart; for mature teens. (Rev: BL 10/15/03)

4011 Parra, Nancy J. *A Wanted Man* (10–12). 2002, Avalon $19.95 (0-8034-3566-8). A feisty librarian sets off to rescue her younger brother Ethan, who was sent West on an orphan train, and finds romance in the process. (Rev: BL 9/15/02)

4012 Pascal, Francine. *Can't Stay Away* (7–10). Series: Sweet Valley High Senior Year. 1999, Bantam paper $4.50 (0-553-49234-9). A better-than-average Sweet Valley High novel about new friendships and rivalries that result when the students of El Carro High have to finish the year at Sweet Valley because of an earthquake. (Rev: SLJ 2/99)

4013 Patterson, James. *Suzanne's Diary for Nicholas* (10–12). 2001, Little, Brown $22.95 (0-316-96944-3). In this romance, Matt suddenly breaks off his affair with Katie but leaves behind a diary kept by his first wife that may explain his actions. (Rev: BL 5/15/01)

4014 Peterson, Tracie. *Controlling Interests* (10–12). 1998, Bethany paper $8.99 (0-7642-2064-0). A love story that involves a modern, adult orphan, Denali Deveraux, who, though brilliant and successful, longs for the security and comfort of a family. (Rev: SLJ 2/99)

4015 Phillips, Susan Elizabeth. *Breathing Room* (11–12). 2002, Morrow $24.95 (0-066-21122-0). This entertaining and sexy novel places two attractive Americans of opposing natures in close proximity in Tuscany; for mature teens. (Rev: BL 5/15/02)

4016 Pickens, Andrea. *The Banished Bride* (11–12). 2002, Signet paper $4.99 (0-451-20561-8). Adventure and romance are intertwined in this Regency featuring a strong heroine and the man who abandoned her years before; for mature teens. (Rev: BL 3/1/02)

4017 Plain, Belva. *Eden Burning* (10–12). 1987, Dell paper $7.50 (0-440-12135-3). This is one of several recommended family sagas by the author of the popular *Evergreen* (1982) and *Random Winds*.

4018 Plummer, Louise. *The Unlikely Romance of Kate Bjorkman* (7–10). 1997, Bantam paper $4.50 (0-440-22704-6). A brainy teen foils a beautiful, evil temptress and gets the man of her dreams. (Rev: SLJ 10/95; VOYA 12/95)

4019 Potter, Patricia. *Dancing with a Rogue* (11–12). 2003, Berkley Sensation paper $6.99 (0-425-19100-1). Unbeknownst to each other, Merry and Gabriel are both determined to seek vengeance on the same man in this historical romance. (Rev: BL 7/03)

4020 Powell, Randy. *Is Kissing a Girl Who Smokes Like Licking an Ashtray?* (7–12). 2003, Farrar paper $5.95 (0-374-43628-2). High school senior Biff has never had a girlfriend until he meets the wild, beautiful loner Heidi, who is as troubled and mouthy as he is shy and fumbling. (Rev: BL 6/1/92*; SLJ 6/92)

4021 Ramsay, Eileen. *Never Call It Loving* (10–12). 2001, Severn $25.99 (0-7278-5704-5). Fern Graham, a happily married writer, has an affair with opera star Pietro Petrungero, who is also married. (Rev: BL 7/01)

4022 Randle, Kristen D. *Breaking Rank* (7–12). 1999, Morrow $15.95 (0-688-16243-6). Told from alternating viewpoints, this is the story of 17-year-old Casey and her experiences after she has agreed to tutor the enigmatic rebel, Thomas, who belongs to a group of outsiders known as the Clan. (Rev: BL 5/1/99; HB 3–4/99; HBG 9/99; SLJ 5/99; VOYA 12/99)

4023 Reding, Jaclyn. *The Adventurer* (10–12). Series: Highland Heroes. 2002, NAL paper $6.50 (0-451-20740-8). Lady Isabella Drayton falls into the hands of a handsome Scottish adventurer with a base in a remote castle. (Rev: BL 10/15/02*)

4024 Reding, Jaclyn. *The Pretender* (11–12). Series: Highland Heroes. 2002, Signet paper $6.50 (0-451-20416-6). Against a backdrop of Jacobite rebellion, two independent-minded characters find romance despite themselves in a story laced with humor; for mature teens. (Rev: BL 3/1/02)

4025 Reding, Jaclyn. *White Mist* (9–12). 2000, Signet paper $5.99 (0-451-20157-4). In this Regency romance, Lady Eleanor Wycliffe becomes governess to the mute young daughter of Gabriel MacFeagh, who believes he is under a curse that will destroy anyone he loves. (Rev: BL 10/1/00)

213

4026 Rees, Elizabeth M. *Moving as One* (6–10). Series: Heart Beats. 1998, Aladdin paper $3.99 (0-689-81948-X). When teenage ballerina Sophy's dance school merges with a school of Latin dance run by attractive Carlos Vargas, everyone wonders if ballet and salsa will mix. (Rev: BL 8/98; SLJ 11/98)

4027 Reiken, Frederick. *The Lost Legends of New Jersey* (10–12). 2000, Harcourt $24.00 (0-15-100507-9). For better readers, this mixture of realism and fantasy is an update of the Lancelot and Guinevere story set in the present-day suburbs of New Jersey. (Rev: BL 5/1/00; VOYA 4/01)

4028 Rice, Luanne. *Dance with Me* (11–12). 2004, Bantam $22.95 (0-553-80227-5). Jane Porter, long estranged from the mother who pressured her to give up her infant daughter years earlier, returns to her Rhode Island hometown where she finds love with the uncle of her daughter; for mature teens. (Rev: BL 12/1/03)

4029 Rice, Luanne. *True Blue* (11–12). 2002, Bantam paper $7.50 (0-553-58398-0). Rumer is nervous when she hears that Zeb, the man she loved who married her sister instead, is returning to Safe Harbor; for mature teens. (Rev: BL 8/02)

4030 Riggs, Paula Detmer. *Never Walk Alone* (11–12). 2003, NAL paper $6.99 (0-451-41083-1). An accident that took place years before threatens to derail the budding romance between Rhys and Brina. (Rev: BL 6/1–15/03)

4031 Riley, Mildred. *Bad to the Bone* (11–12). 2003, BET paper $5.99 (1-583-14390-4). African Americans Sherissa, a reporter, and Peter, a detective, fall in love while he tries to protect her from danger. (Rev: BL 2/15/03)

4032 Ripslinger, Jon. *How I Fell in Love and Learned to Shoot Free Throws* (9–12). 2003, Millbrook LB $22.90 (0-7613-2747-9). Angel and Danny share a love of basketball, a reluctance to reveal sensitive information about their families, and a growing mutual attraction. (Rev: BL 4/15/03; HBG 10/03; SLJ 4/03; VOYA 6/03)

4033 Roberts, Nora. *Birthright* (10–12). 2003, Putnam $25.95 (0-399-14984-8); Berkley paper $7.99 (0-515-13711-1). An eminently readable suspenseful romance in which archaeologist Callie Dunbrook searches for the truth about her past; one of many recommended books by this prolific author, this is more suitable for mature teens. (Rev: BL 1/1–15/03)

4034 Roberts, Nora. *Born in Ice* (10–12). 1995, Jove paper $7.50 (0-515-11675-0). A readable romance about an Irish innkeeper and an American mystery writer. (Rev: SLJ 3/96)

4035 Roberts, Nora, and J. D. Robb. *Remember When* (11–12). 2003, Putnam $25.95 (0-399-15106-0). A suspenseful story of stolen diamonds and romance that stretches across decades. (Rev: BL 8/03)

4036 Robinson, C. Kelly. *No More Mr. Nice Guy* (11–12). 2002, Villard paper $13.95 (0-375-76047-4). Mitchell is tired of his dating ineptitude and seeks advice from his friends; explicit sex scenes make this suitable only for mature readers. (Rev: BL 9/1/02)

4037 Rodowsky, Colby. *Lucy Peale* (8–12). 1992, Farrar paper $3.95 (0-374-44659-8). Lucy, a rape victim, is pregnant, alone, and terrified when she meets Jake, and their friendship slowly evolves into love. (Rev: BL 7/92; SLJ 7/92)

4038 Rosenthal, Lucy, ed. *Great American Love Stories* (9–12). 1988, Little, Brown $24.95 (0-316-75734-9). A collection of 28 stories and short novels that show the varied and changing faces of love. (Rev: BL 7/88; BR 1–2/89)

4039 Rostkowski, Margaret I. *Moon Dancer* (7–10). 1995, Harcourt $11.00 (0-15-276638-3); paper $6.00 (0-15-200194-8). A 15-year-old on a trek to view ancient canyon rock art feels connections to the images and to an accompanying boy. (Rev: BL 5/1/95; SLJ 9/95)

4040 Royal, Lauren. *Violet* (11–12). 2002, NAL paper $6.99 (0-451-20688-6). Wealthy and intellectual, Violet Ashcroft has no interest in marriage but is pulled toward her attractive neighbor Ford Chase, who for his part has decided to concentrate on science in this humorous romance for mature teens set in the 17th century. (Rev: BL 9/1/02)

4041 Sachs, Marilyn. *Thunderbird* (7–10). Illus. 1985, Dutton $10.95 (0-525-44163-8). Two high school seniors meet and fall in love in the public library. (Rev: BL 4/15/85; SLJ 10/85)

4042 Schuster, Melanie. *Until the End of Time* (11–12). 2003, BET paper $5.99 (1-58314-363-7). Years after Andrew got a sneak peek of Renee coming out of the shower, the tables are turned and an older, more poised Renee catches a similar glimpse; the African American pair's formerly uneasy friendship soon becomes warmer. (Rev: BL 2/15/03)

4043 Schwartz, John Burnham. *Claire Marvel* (10–12). 2002, Doubleday $25.00 (0-385-50344-X). As graduate students, Julian and Claire share a complicated relationship, and Julian remains infatuated even after they both marry others. (Rev: BL 1/1–15/02*)

4044 Shay, Kathryn. *Promises to Keep* (11–12). 2002, Berkley paper $6.99 (0-425-18574-5). A student's fatal shooting brings an undercover Secret Service agent into a high school with an attractive principal; for mature teens. (Rev: BL 8/02)

4045 Shea, Suzanne Strempek. *Around Again* (10–12). 2001, Pocket $23.95 (0-7434-0375-4). Robyn Panek returns to her Massachusetts homestead and recalls the fateful summer there when she was 18 and was involved with Frankie and best friends with Lucy Dragon. (Rev: BL 6/1–15/01)

4046 Sheldon, Dyan. *The Boy of My Dreams* (6–10). 1997, Candlewick $16.99 (0-7636-0004-0). Mike (short for Michelle) falls head over heels in love with sophisticated Bill and begins to neglect her true friends. (Rev: BL 11/1/97; BR 1–2/98; HBG 3/98; SLJ 10/97; VOYA 2/98)

4047 Sierra, Patricia. *One-Way Romance* (7–10). 1986, Avon paper $2.50 (0-380-75107-0). A talented girl who does well with carpentry and track seems to be losing out with her boyfriend. (Rev: BL 8/86; SLJ 11/86; VOYA 12/86)

4048 Smith, Annie. *Home Again* (10–12). 2002, Zebra paper $5.99 (0-8217-7370-4). Sally turns to the local dog trainer when she suddenly becomes responsible for an injured orphaned boy and his dog. (Rev: BL 9/15/02)

4049 Smith-Brown, Fern. *Unforgettable* (9–12). 2000, GoldenIsle $21.95 (0-9666721-6-X). A romantic thriller about how a young woman vacationing in Maine becomes involved with an undercover agent tracking down arms smugglers. (Rev: BL 5/15/00)

4050 Sneed, Tamara. *When I Fall in Love* (10–12). 2002, BET paper $5.99 (1-58314-273-8). In this twist on the Cinderella story, an African American FBI agent named Sean agrees to a makeover before attending her stepsister's wedding, much to the surprised appreciation of Inspector Logan Riley. (Rev: BL 2/15/02)

4051 Sole, Linda. *Bridget* (11–12). 2003, Severn $26.99 (0-7278-5868-8). Sixteen-year-old Bridget finds time for romance while looking after her siblings and mother. (Rev: BL 3/1/03)

4052 Sparks, Nicholas. *A Bend in the Road* (9–12). 2001, Warner $23.95 (0-446-52778-5). Miles Ryan, a widower, meets his son's teacher, Sarah Andrews, and his life takes on a new meaning. (Rev: BL 9/1/01)

4053 Sparks, Nicholas. *The Guardian* (11–12). 2003, Warner $24.95 (0-446-52779-3). Recovering from her husband's untimely death, Julie is very aware of her dog's responses to new suitors in this thriller/romance. (Rev: BL 3/1/03)

4054 Sparks, Nicholas. *The Wedding* (10–12). 2003, Warner $23.95 (0-446-53245-2). Worried that he is losing his wife, Jane, through his thoughtlessness, Wilson seizes their daughter's wedding as a way to prove his love. (Rev: BL 9/1/03)

4055 Stanek, Lou W. *Katy Did* (8–12). 1992, Avon paper $2.99 (0-380-76170-X). A shy country girl and popular city boy fall in love, with tragic consequences. (Rev: BL 3/15/92)

4056 Steel, Danielle. *The House on Hope Street* (10–12). 2000, Delacorte $19.95 (0-385-33306-4). This standard Steel romantic novel involves a privileged woman, newly widowed, and her struggle to raise her family and still gain self-fulfillment. (Rev: BL 3/15/00)

4057 Steel, Danielle. *Leap of Faith* (10–12). 2001, Delacorte $19.95 (0-385-33296-3). Marie-Ange, a pampered orphan, is sent to Iowa to live with a wicked elderly aunt in this light romance. (Rev: BL 3/15/01; SLJ 11/01)

4058 Steel, Danielle. *The Promise* (10–12). 1978, Dell paper $6.99 (0-440-17079-6). A wealthy architect and a poor artist decide to marry in this romance. Other recommended titles by the author are *Once in a Lifetime*, *Now and Forever*, *Palomino*, *The Ring*, and *Season of Passion*.

4059 Steel, Danielle. *The Wedding* (10–12). 2000, Delacorte $26.95 (0-385-31437-X). In her 48th novel, the author combines a glamorous Hollywood setting with beautiful people and their amorous adventures and insecurities. (Rev: BL 2/1/00)

4060 Stewart, Sally. *Appointment in Venice* (10–12). 2003, Severn $26.99 (0-7278-6003-8). Sarah, a young Englishwoman, travels to Venice to work as a governess but rediscovers a lost love. (Rev: BL 10/15/03)

4061 Strasser, Todd. *How I Spent My Last Night on Earth* (7–10). Series: Time Zone High. 1998, Simon & Schuster $16.00 (0-689-81113-6). Rumors spread that a giant asteroid is heading for Earth, and "Legs" Hanover finds romance with a handsome surfer classmate after being jilted by her boyfriend. (Rev: BL 11/1/98; BR 5–6/99; HBG 9/99; SLJ 11/98; VOYA 8/99)

4062 Summers, Rowena. *September Morning* (10–12). Series: Cornish Clay. 2000, Severn House $26.00 (0-7278-5446-1). Part of the Cornish Clay series, this romance set in rural Cornwall in the late 1930s tells how two girls, fresh from a Swiss finishing school, fall in love. (Rev: BL 1/1–15/00)

4063 Thomas, Abigail. *An Actual Life* (10–12). 1996, Algonquin $28.95 (1-56512-133-3). This novel tells of a young couple who married because of a pregnancy and of their eventual attractions to other possible partners. (Rev: BL 4/1/96; SLJ 3/97)

4064 Thomas, Jodi. *The Texan's Dream* (10–12). 2001, Jove paper $6.99 (0-515-13176-8). Kara O'Riley's relations with the ranch owner for whom she works become close in this historical western romance. (Rev: BL 10/15/01)

4065 Thomas, Jodi. *When a Texan Gambles* (10–12). 2003, Penguin paper $6.99 (0-515-13629-8). In this charming western romance novel, plucky Sarah Andrews stands by her man — bounty hunter Sam Gatlin — when all others turn their backs on him. (Rev: BL 10/15/03*)

4066 Thompson, Julian. *Shepherd* (9–12). 1993, Holt $15.95 (0-8050-2106-X). When popular Mary Sutherland makes advances to Shep Catlett, he declares himself in love and tries to save her from her drinking. (Rev: BL 12/15/93; SLJ 11/93; VOYA 2/94)

4067 Thornton, Elizabeth. *The Perfect Princess* (9–12). 2001, Bantam paper $6.50 (0-553-58123-6). In this Regency romance, Lady Rosamunde Devere visits Newgate Prison and is carried off by a dashing escaping prisoner. (Rev: BL 9/15/01)

4068 Trembath, Don. *A Beautiful Place on Yonge Street* (8–10). 1999, Orca paper $6.95 (1-55143-121-1). Budding writer Harper Winslow falls in love with Sunny Taylor when he attends a summer writing camp, and experiences all the angst that goes with it. (Rev: BL 3/1/99; SLJ 7/99; VOYA 6/99)

4069 Veryan, Patricia. *Lanterns* (10–12). 1996, St. Martin's $23.95 (0-312-14640-X). This historical romance set in Sussex, England, in 1818, tells of Marietta Warrington's struggles to keep the family together after her father's gambling debts drive them into poverty, and involves kidnapping, ancient treasure, sinister dealings, and true love. (Rev: BL 10/15/96; SLJ 3/97)

4070 Victor, Cynthia. *The Secret* (10–12). 1997, Dutton $23.95 (0-525-94034-0). When her husband suddenly leaves her and her three children, Miranda takes over his secret identity as a writer of trashy best-sellers. (Rev: BL 6/1–15/97; SLJ 3/98)

4071 Voigt, Cynthia. *Glass Mountain* (9–12). 1991, Harcourt $19.95 (0-15-135825-7). A wealthy New Yorker posing as a butler falls in love with his employer's fiancee. (Rev: BL 11/1/91; SLJ 4/92)

4072 Ware, Ciji. *A Light on the Veranda* (10–12). 2001, Ballantine paper $6.99 (0-449-15029-1). In this sequel to *Midnight on Julia Street* (1999), Daphne Duvallon goes to Natchez for her brother's wedding and finds love there. (Rev: BL 5/1/01)

4073 Watson, Jude. *Dangerous: Savannah's Story* (7–10). Series: Brides of Wildcat County. 1995, Simon & Schuster paper $3.95 (0-689-80326-5). Savannah leaves the East and heads to a gold-mining town in California, where she finds romance in the arms of the son of a gold mine owner. (Rev: SLJ 2/96)

4074 Watson, Jude. *Scandalous: Eden's Story* (7–10). Series: Brides of Wildcat County. 1995, Simon & Schuster paper $3.95 (0-689-80327-3). Eden, who has a criminal background, arrives in Last Chance, a gold mining town in California, where her reputation as a cardshark threatens her love for rich Josiah Bullock. (Rev: SLJ 2/96; VOYA 4/96)

4075 Weinstock, Nicholas. *As Long as She Needs Me* (10–12). 2001, HarperCollins $22.00 (0-06-

019824-9). This is a romantic, humorous tale about Oscar, an assistant in a Manhattan publishing house, who falls in love with an attractive female writer. (Rev: BL 3/1/01; SLJ 12/01)

4076 Winfrey, Elizabeth. *More Than a Friend* (9–12). 1995, Bantam paper $4.50 (0-553-56666-0). Cain and Delia, two high school seniors who have been best friends for years, slowly realize that they love one another. (Rev: VOYA 6/96)

4077 Winfrey, Elizabeth. *My So-Called Boyfriend* (6–10). Series: Love Stories. 1996, Bantam paper $3.99 (0-553-56668-7). After a fall that causes snobbish Tashi Pendleton to lose her memory, a boy she once embarrassed concocts a scheme to get even in this light romance. (Rev: SLJ 8/96)

4078 Wingate, Lisa. *Texas Cooking* (11–12). 2003, NAL paper $6.99 (0-451-41102-1). A hotshot Washington reporter fallen on hard times is surprised to find friendship and romance in a small Texas town; soon she must make a difficult choice. (Rev: BL 9/15/03)

4079 Wittlinger, Ellen. *Lombardo's Law* (7–10). 1993, Houghton $16.00 (0-395-65969-8); Morrow paper $4.95 (0-688-05294-0). The conventions of romance are thrown aside when sophomore Justine and 8th-grader Mike find themselves attracted to each other, despite obstacles. (Rev: BL 9/15/93; VOYA 12/93)

4080 Woodson, Jacqueline. *If You Come Softly* (7–10). 1998, Putnam $15.99 (0-399-23112-9). The story of the love between a black boy and a white girl, their families, and the prejudice they encounter. (Rev: BL 10/1/98; HBG 9/99; SLJ 12/98; VOYA 12/98)

4081 Zalben, Jane Breskin. *Here's Looking at You, Kid* (9–12). 1984, Dell paper $2.50 (0-440-93573-3). A high school senior finds he is attracted to two girls.

Science Fiction

4082 Adams, Douglas. *The Hitchhiker's Guide to the Galaxy* (9–12). 1989, Crown $15.00 (0-517-54209-9); Pocket paper $5.99 (0-671-74606-5). An episodic science fiction novel that is made up of equal parts of adventure and humor. Others in the series are *The Restaurant at the End of the Universe*; *Life, the Universe, and Everything*; and *So Long, Thanks for the Fish*. (Rev: BL 6/87)

4083 Adams, Douglas. *The Long Dark Tea-Time of the Soul* (9–12). 1988, Demco $12.09 (0-606-01764-X); Pocket paper $6.99 (0-671-74251-5). Dirk Gently, private detective and slob first introduced in *Dirk Gently's Holistic Detective Agency*, returns in another hilarious series of misadventures. (Rev: BL 1/15/89)

4084 Adams, Douglas. *Mostly Harmless* (9–12). Series: Hitchhiker's Trilogy. 1992, Crown $20.00 (0-517-57740-2). The intergalactic adventures of Arthur Dent and Ford Prefect continue as the heroes are whipped between parallel universes that eventually collide. (Rev: BL 9/15/92)

4085 Adams, Douglas. *The Salmon of Doubt: Hitchhiking the Galaxy One Last Time* (9–12). Ed. by Christopher Cerf. 2002, Harmony $24.00 (1-4000-4508-8). A posthumous collection of Adams's diverse writings — essays, articles, and stories — including part of an unfinished Hitchhiker novel. (Rev: BL 4/15/02)

4086 Adler, Bill, ed. *Time Machines* (9–12). 1997, Carroll & Graf $24.00 (0-7867-0493-4). A fine collection of 22 time travel stories by such authors as Poe, Kipling, Asimov, Bradbury, and Serling. (Rev: SLJ 6/98)

4087 Allen, Roger MacBride. *David Brin's Out of Time: The Game of Worlds* (7–12). Series: David Brin's Out of Time. 1999, Avon paper $4.99 (0-380-79969-3). Adam O'Connor, a mischievous high school student in the late 20th century, finds himself facing a whole new set of problems when he's yanked 350 years into the future. (Rev: VOYA 4/00)

4088 Allen, Roger MacBride. *The Depths of Time* (10–12). 2000, Bantam paper $13.00 (0-553-37811-2). When Captain Koffield destroys the wormhole to the planet Solace, it brings him into conflict with its inhabitants. (Rev: BL 3/15/00)

4089 Allen, Roger MacBride. *Isaac Asimov's Inferno* (9–12). 1994, Berkley paper $12.00 (0-441-00023-1). In this sequel to *Caliban* (o.p.), the Three Laws of Robotics are further explored when a murder takes place on a planet of Earth Settlers and Spacers. (Rev: BL 9/15/94; VOYA 4/95)

4090 Anderson, Kevin J. *Dogged Persistence* (10–12). 2001, Golden Gryphon $25.95 (1-930846-03-7). Hard science and action subjects are combined in this collection of 18 stories for older teens by this well-known author. (Rev: BL 5/15/01)

4091 Anderson, Kevin J. *Hopscotch* (10–12). 2002, Bantam $24.95 (0-553-10474-8). The search for identity is one of the themes in this science fiction mystery about a future where people's personalities can hop from one body to another. (Rev: BL 12/15/01)

4092 Anderson, Kevin J., ed. *War of the Worlds: Global Dispatches* (7–12). 1996, Bantam $22.95 (0-553-10352-9). This tribute to H. G. Wells's *War of the Worlds* features stories of Martian invasions that are either take-offs on the writing styles of such famous authors as Conrad, London, Verne, and Kipling, or the experiences of famous individuals,

such as Teddy Roosevelt and Pablo Picasso, during a Martian invasion. (Rev: VOYA 10/96)

4093 Anderson, M. T. *Feed* (9–12). 2002, Candlewick $16.99 (0-7636-1726-1). In a future society where feeds supply information and other needs directly to each individual, Titus meets a rebellious girl named Violet. (Rev: BL 10/15/02; HB 9–10/02*; HBG 3/03; SLJ 9/02; VOYA 12/02)

4094 Anderson, Poul. *Cold Victory* (10–12). 1985, Tor paper $2.95 (0-8125-3057-8). Six stories about the Psychotechnic League. Some other books by this master are: *Conflict*, *Fire Time*, and *A Midsummer Tempest*.

4095 Anderson, Poul. *Genesis* (10–12). 2000, Tor $23.95 (0-312-86707-7). Christian Brannock, immortalized through computer imprinting, embarks on a billion-year exploration of the stars. (Rev: BL 2/15/00; VOYA 6/00)

4096 Anderson, Poul. *The Long Night* (10–12). 1999, Tor paper $3.95 (0-8125-1396-7). This is a collection of five novellas.

4097 Anthony, Piers. *Race Against Time* (7–12). 1986, Tor paper $5.99 (0-8125-3101-9). John Smith and an African girl named Ala are different from others because they are racially pure.

4098 Anthony, Piers. *Split Infinity* (10–12). 1987, Ballantine paper $6.99 (0-345-35491-5). In this first part of the Apprentice Adept series, someone is trying to kill Stile on the planet Proton. Other titles are *Blue Adept* and *Juxtaposition*.

4099 Anthony, Piers. *Total Recall* (9–12). 1990, Avon paper $4.50 (0-380-70874-4). A novelization of the movie about a secret agent on Mars searching for his past. Also use *But What of Earth?* (Tor, 1989). (Rev: BL 8/89)

4100 Armstrong, Jennifer, and Nancy Butcher. *The Keepers of the Flame* (7–10). Series: Fire-Us. 2002, HarperCollins LB $17.89 (0-06-029412-4). The plucky children who survived the deadly virus that hit in *The Kindling* (2002) meet a group of strange grownups. (Rev: BL 8/02*; HBG 3/03; SLJ 12/02)

4101 Armstrong, Jennifer, and Nancy Butcher. *The Kindling* (7–10). Series: Fire-Us. 2002, HarperCollins LB $15.89 (0-06-029411-6). In 2007, after a virus has killed the adults, a small band of children join together in a Florida town and try to carry on with life. (Rev: BCCB 6/02; BL 4/15/02; HBG 10/02; SLJ 10/02)

4102 Asaro, Catherine. *Ascendant Sun* (10–12). Series: Skolian Empire. 2000, Tor $24.95 (0-312-86824-3). In this, one of the Skolian Empire books, Kelric finds himself in Euban space ruled by the heartless Aristos. (Rev: BL 2/1/00)

4103 Asaro, Catherine. *The Phoenix Code* (10–12). 2000, Bantam paper $5.99 (0-553-58154-6). An expert in artificial intelligence works on developing a self-aware android in this thriller. Also recommended is *The Quantum Rose* (2000). (Rev: BL 12/1/00; VOYA 4/01)

4104 Ashley, Mike, ed. *The Mammoth Book of Science Fiction* (10–12). 2002, Carroll & Graf paper $11.95 (0-7867-1004-7). A diverse collection of stories from established and new writers. (Rev: BL 5/1/02)

4105 Asimov, Isaac. *The Best Science Fiction of Isaac Asimov* (9–12). 1988, NAL paper $4.95 (0-451-15196-8). A collection of 28 of the stories the author thinks are his best. (Rev: BL 8/86)

4106 Asimov, Isaac. *Caves of Steel* (7–12). 1955, Spectra paper $6.99 (0-553-29034-0). A human and a robot combine forces in this science fiction classic to work together to help mankind. Part of Asimov's well-written Robot series. (Rev: BL BL 5/1/00)

4107 Asimov, Isaac. *Fantastic Voyage: A Novel* (8–12). 1966, Houghton paper $6.99 (0-553-27572-0). Five people are miniaturized to enter the body of a sick man and save his life.

4108 Asimov, Isaac. *Forward the Foundation* (9–12). 1993, 1994, Bantam paper $6.99 (0-553-56507-9). The conclusion to Asimov's efforts to bind his various universes together into one vast future history. Part of the Foundation series. (Rev: BL 2/15/93; SLJ 3/94)

4109 Asimov, Isaac. *I, Robot* (10–12). 1991, Bantam paper $6.99 (0-553-29438-5). A collection about Dr. Susan Calvin and the robots she produces.

4110 Asimov, Isaac. *Nemesis* (9–12). 1990, Bantam paper $6.99 (0-553-28628-5). A space colony arrives at a planet only to find it is slated for destruction. (Rev: BL 8/89)

4111 Asimov, Isaac. *Prelude to Foundation* (10–12). 1989, Bantam paper $6.99 (0-553-27839-8). This novel links the Empire and Foundation series and supplies a chronology of novels in these two series as a guide to readers. (Rev: BL 4/1/88; VOYA 10/88)

4112 Asimov, Isaac. *Robots and Empire* (9–12). 1985, Ballantine paper $5.99 (0-345-32894-9). The heroine of the earlier *Robots at Dawn* travels through space with a friend and two robots to defeat a plot against Earth. (Rev: BL 8/85)

4113 Asimov, Isaac, and Roger MacBride Allen. *Utopia* (9–12). Series: Utopia. 1993, Berkley paper $9.95 (0-441-09079-6). A sheriff trails a rogue robot that has escaped from a lab. (Rev: BL 3/1/93; VOYA 8/93)

4114 Asimov, Isaac, et al., eds. *Computer Crimes and Capers* (9–12). 1983, Academy Chicago paper $10.00 (0-89733-087-0). A lively anthology of stories featuring computers as masters, servants, or — sometimes — arch criminals.

4115 Asprin, Robert. *Phule's Company* (10–12). 1990, Berkley paper $8.99 (0-441-66251-X). The beginning of a new series about the adventures of Captain Willard Phule, an officer in the Space Legion. (Rev: BL 6/15/90)

4116 Asprin, Robert, and Peter J. Heck. *No Phule Like an Old Phule* (9–12). 2004, Berkley paper $7.99 (0-441-01152-7). In this humorous science fiction novel, Willard Phule must put up with a series of misadventures including a bungled kidnapping attempt and a celebrity canine named Barky the Environmental Dog. (Rev: BL 4/1/04)

4117 Atwood, Margaret. *The Handmaid's Tale* (10–12). 1998, Houghton $16.95 (0-395-40425-8); Doubleday paper $12.95 (0-385-49081-X). A chilling look into the future where repression of women is rampant. For mature readers. (Rev: VOYA 12/86)

4118 Baker, Kage. *Black Projects, White Knights: The Company Dossiers* (10–12). 2002, Golden Gryphon $24.95 (1-930846-11-8). Fourteen short stories about the adventures of time-traveling cyberagents in search of treasures from the past. (Rev: BL 9/1/02)

4119 Ball, Margaret. *Lost in Translation* (8–12). 1995, Baen $5.99 (0-671-87638-0). American teenager Allie flies to France to attend a university but lands in a fantasy world filled with spells of every kind, where people communicate through voice-bubbles and a group of terrifying monsters controls an important subterranean substance called landvirtue. (Rev: VOYA 4/96)

4120 Banks, Iain M. *Inversions* (10–12). 2000, Pocket $23.95 (0-671-03668-8). Dr. Vosill, a female court physician, and Dewar, the potentate's bodyguard, join forces to fight numerous enemies in this adventure that has a romantic subplot. (Rev: BL 2/15/00)

4121 Banks, Iain M. *Look to Windward* (10–12). 2001, Pocket $23.95 (0-7434-2191-4). A suspenseful adventure involving continent-sized living entities and a culture with 31 trillion inhabitants. (Rev: BL 6/1–15/01)

4122 Barnes, John. *The Duke of Uranium* (10–12). 2002, Warner paper $6.99 (0-446-61081-X). Teen Jak Jinnaka learns that this generous Uncle Sib is actually a spy and that Jak's girlfriend, Sesh, is really a princess when Sesh is kidnapped. (Rev: BL 9/1/02)

4123 Barnes, John. *The Merchants of Souls* (9–12). 2001, Tor $25.95 (0-312-89076-1). In this sequel to *Earth Made of Glass* (1998), Giraut Leones is persuaded to leave his planet to find ways to defeat an ugly criminal conspiracy. (Rev: BL 12/15/01)

4124 Barnes, John. *A Princess of the Aerie* (10–12). 2003, Warner paper $6.99 (0-446-61082-8). Best suited for mature teens because of its sexual content, this sequel to *The Duke of Uranium* recounts the adventures of 36th-century teen spy Jak Jinnaka as he discovers the duplicity of an ex-girlfriend who's set herself up as the despotic ruler of Greenworld. (Rev: BL 1/1–15/03)

4125 Barnes, John. *The Sky So Big and Black* (10–12). 2002, Tor $24.95 (0-765-30303-5). At the age of 15, Teri is enjoying working as an eco-prospector on Mars and looking forward to taking her Full Adult test when a crisis erupts that challenges her skills and will. (Rev: BL 8/02; SLJ 12/02)

4126 Barnes, Steven. *Charisma* (11–12). 2002, Tor $24.95 (0-312-87004-3). An experiment in imprinting needy children with the personality of a successful self-made man appears carries an unexpected downside; for mature teens. (Rev: BL 6/1–15/02)

4127 Barrett, Neal. *Perpetuity Blues and Other Stories* (11–12). 2000, Golden Gryphon $21.95 (0-9655901-4-3). Science fiction stories with a southern flavor, for mature readers. (Rev: BL 5/15/00)

4128 Baxter, Stephen. *Manifold: Origin* (11–12). 2002, Del Rey $26.00 (0-345-43079-4). This sequel to *Manifold: Time* (1999) and *Manifold: Space* (2001) finds Reid Malenfant and his wife Emma on a red moon inhabited by hominids; for mature teens. (Rev: BL 1/1–15/02)

4129 Baxter, Stephen. *Manifold: Space* (10–12). 2001, Ballantine $24.00 (0-345-43077-8). In this sequel to *Manifold: Time* (1999) extraterrestrials and humanoids try to overcome barriers to the spreading of intelligent life. (Rev: BL 12/15/00; SLJ 7/01)

4130 Bear, Greg. *Darwin's Children* (10–12). Series: Darwin's Radio. 2003, Ballantine $24.95 (0-345-44835-9). This sequel to *Darwin's Radio* (1999) focuses on the government's efforts to isolate the genetically different "virus children" and these children's problems as they face antagonism and disease. (Rev: BL 2/15/03; SLJ 8/03)

4131 Bear, Greg. *Moving Mars* (9–12). 1994, Tor paper $6.99 (0-8125-2480-2). A physicist on Mars links up with an artificial intelligence and a revolutionary woman determined to give her world a future. (Rev: BL 9/15/93; VOYA 4/94)

4132 Bear, Greg, ed. *New Legends* (10–12). 1995, Tor $22.95 (0-312-85930-9). A collection of original hard science fiction stories by writers that include Poul Anderson, Gregory Benford, Ursula K. Le Guin, and Robert Silverberg. (Rev: VOYA 2/96)

4133 BeauSeigneur, James. *In His Image* (10–12). Series: Christ Clone. 2003, Warner $18.95 (0-446-53125-1). In the first volume of a trilogy, skillful writing and plotting make plausible the tale of an Antichrist — Christopher Goodman — cloned from blood found on the shroud of Turin. (Rev: BL 1/1–15/03*)

4134 Bell, Hilari. *A Matter of Profit* (6–10). 2001, HarperCollins LB $15.89 (0-06-029514-7). Eighteen-year-old Ahvren, who wants to give up his interplanetary military career, agrees to look into a threat against the leader of the T'Chin Empire in hopes of saving his sister from an unwanted marriage and winning his own independence. (Rev: BL 8/01; HB 1–2/02; HBG 3/02; SLJ 10/01; VOYA 10/01)

4135 Benford, Gregory. *Eater* (10–12). 2000, Avon Eos $24.00 (0-380-97436-3). In this suspenseful adventure, Benjamin Knowlton must divert a destructive black hole that is apparently headed for Earth. (Rev: BL 4/15/00; SLJ 9/00)

4136 Benford, Gregory, ed. *Nebula Awards Showcase 2000: The Year's Best SF and Fantasy Chosen by the Science Fiction and Fantasy Writers of America* (9–12). 2000, Harcourt $28.00 (0-15-100479-X); paper $14.00 (0-15-600705-3). Four prize-winning stories from 1998 are reprinted, with additional background material on science fiction publishing and authors. (Rev: BL 3/15/00)

4137 Benford, Gregory. *Worlds Vast and Various* (10–12). 2000, HarperCollins paper $13.50 (0-380-79054-8). This volume contains 12 thought-provoking short stories by one of the best science fiction writers. (Rev: BL 10/15/00)

4138 Benford, Gregory, and George Zebrowski, eds. *Skylife: Space Habitats in Story and Science* (10–12). Illus. 2000, Harcourt $28.00 (0-15-100292-4). Using the theme of life in space habitats, this anthology includes stories by Ray Bradbury, Arthur C. Clarke, and David Brin. (Rev: BL 3/1/00)

4139 Blisson, Terry. *Pirates of the Universe* (10–12). 1996, Tor $22.95 (0-312-85412-9). Science fiction and a page-turning adventure yarn combine in this story of Gunter Glenn and his search for justice in a world gone mad. (Rev: BL 4/15/96; SLJ 10/96; VOYA 8/96)

4140 Boulle, Pierre. *Planet of the Apes* (7–12). 2001, Random paper $6.99 (0-345-44798-0). Stranded on the planet Soror, Ulysse Merou discovers a civilization ruled by apes.

4141 Bova, Ben. *Jupiter* (10–12). 2001, Tor $24.95 (0-312-87217-8). Astrophysicist Grant Archer, dispatched by Earth's theocratic rulers to find out what's going on at a research station orbiting Jupiter, joins a manned mission to the planet's surface. (Rev: BL 1/1–15/01; VOYA 6/01)

4142 Bova, Ben. *Orion Among the Stars* (9–12). Series: Orion the Hunter. 1995, Tor $22.95 (0-312-85637-7). Orion the Hunter realizes that he and his human clone soldiers are pawns of the gods, whose fighting among themselves has placed the very survival of the Galaxy at risk, and learns that his love, the goddess Anya, is on the opposite side. (Rev: VOYA 2/96)

4143 Bova, Ben. *The Precipice* (10–12). 2001, Tor $25.95 (0-312-84876-5). Dan Randolph hopes to restore his lost fortune and humanity's fortune with an industry based among the asteroids. (Rev: BL 10/1/01)

4144 Bova, Ben. *The Silent War* (9–12). Series: Asteroid Wars. 2004, Tor $24.95 (0-312-84878-1). This, the concluding volume in this series, is filled with intrigues, suspense, and a fast-moving plot. (Rev: BL 5/1/04)

4145 Bova, Ben. *Tales of the Grand Tour* (9–12). 2004, Tor $24.95 (0-765-30722-7). A series of page-turning short stories that deal with space exploration. (Rev: BL 1/1–15/04)

4146 Bova, Ben. *Vengeance of Orion* (9–12). 1988, Tor paper $3.95 (0-8125-3161-2). In this novel, Orion travels to the time of Troy and ancient Egypt. This is a sequel to *Orion*. (Rev: VOYA 6/88)

4147 Bova, Ben. *Venus* (10–12). 2000, Tor $24.95 (0-312-87216-X). For hard science fiction fans, this novel tells how a sickly and despised second son of a wealthy family sets out to recover the body of his brother who was killed during the first attempt to land a man on Venus. (Rev: BL 4/1/00)

4148 Bradbury, Ray. *Bradbury Stories: 100 of His Most Celebrated Tales* (10–12). 2003, Morrow $29.95 (0-06-054242-X). Bradbury's selection of his own 100 best guarantees remarkable readability and many happy laughs. (Rev: BL 7/03)

4149 Bradbury, Ray. *Fahrenheit 451 .* 40th Anniversary Ed. (9–12). 1993, Simon & Schuster $22.00 (0-671-87036-X). This novel depicts book burning and thought control in a future fascist state. Included in this edition are two additional short stories.

4150 Bradbury, Ray. *Farenheit 451* (7–12). 1953, Ballantine paper $6.99 (0-345-34296-8). In this futuristic novel, book reading has become a crime.

4151 Bradbury, Ray. *The Martian Chronicles* (10–12). 1999, Simon & Schuster $24.95 (0-7838-8635-7). These interrelated short stories tell of the colonization of Mars.

4152 Bradbury, Ray. *The October Country* (7–12). 1999, Avon $16.00 (0-380-97387-1). Ordinary people are caught up in unreal situations in these 19 strange stories.

4153 Bradbury, Ray. *The Stories of Ray Bradbury* (8–12). 1980, Knopf $40.00 (0-394-51335-5). An imaginative group of stories that often bridge the gap between fantasy and science fiction.

4154 Bradley, Marion Zimmer. *Exile's Song: A Novel of Darkover* (10–12). 1996, DAW paper $21.95 (0-88677-705-4). After 20 years, Margaret returns to the planet of her childhood, Darkover, and confronts disturbing memories. (Rev: BL 6/1–15/96; VOYA 12/96)

4155 Braver, Gary. *Gray Matter* (11–12). 2002, Tor $25.95 (0-312-87613-0). Lucius Malenko, a neurologist who claims expertise in mental enhancement, sets out to exploit wealthy American parents who are ambitious for their children; for mature teens. (Rev: BL 9/1/02)

4156 Brin, David. *Otherness* (9–12). 1994, Bantam paper $6.99 (0-553-29528-4). Short fiction, essays, and commentaries that strive to define the term *otherness,* including stories about extraterrestrial contact and the limits of our perception of reality. (Rev: BL 8/94; VOYA 2/95)

4157 Brin, David. *The Postman* (9–12). 1985, Bantam paper $6.99 (0-553-27874-6). This novel deals with the aftermath of a nuclear war, when communication with survivors often depended on people like the Postman.

4158 Brin, David, and Kevin Lenagh. *Contacting Aliens: An Illustrated Guide to David Brin's Uplift Universe* (10–12). Illus. 2002, Bantam paper $14.95 (0-553-37796-5). The alien species of Brin's Uplift Universe are described and illustrated in this handy guide. (Rev: BL 5/15/02) [813]

4159 Broderick, Damien. *Transcension* (10–12). 2002, Tor $25.95 (0-765-30369-8). A tale of youthfully reckless behavior that may have cataclysmic results in a near-future technotopia bordered by an enclave called the Valley of the God of One's Choice. (Rev: BL 2/1/02; SLJ 8/02)

4160 Brooks, Terry. *Wizard at Large* (10–12). 1989, Ballantine paper $6.99 (0-345-36227-6). In this, the third book about the Magic Kingdom of Landover, High Lord Ben Holiday travels to Earth. Preceded by: *Magic Kingdom for Sale — Sold!* and *The Black Unicorn.* (Rev: BL 9/1/88; VOYA 4/89)

4161 Brotherton, Mike. *Star Dragon* (10–12). 2003, Tor $24.95 (0-765-30758-8). With strong underpinnings in real science, this is the story of a mission to investigate a mysterious life form on the star system Cygni. (Rev: BL 10/1/03*)

4162 Bujold, Lois M. *Cetaganda* (9–12). 1996, Baen $21.00 (0-671-87701-1). In this Vorkosigan saga (number 10), hero Miles and his handsome cousin Ivan encounter intrigue and romance when they are sent to the planet Cetaganda on a diplomatic mission. (Rev: BL 11/15/95; VOYA 6/96)

4163 Bujold, Lois M. *A Civil Campaign: A Comedy of Biology and Manners* (10–12). 1999, Baen $24.00 (0-671-57827-8). In this deftly crafted intergalactic romance, brilliant military strategist Miles Vorkosigan mounts a campaign to win the heart of Ekaterin. (Rev: BL 9/1/99; VOYA 4/00)

4164 Bujold, Lois M. *Komarr* (10–12). 1998, Pocket $22.00 (0-671-87877-8). Investigator Miles Vorkosigan's first case is to determine if the collision between a space freighter and a satellite was really an accident. (Rev: BL 5/15/98; VOYA 10/98)

4165 Burroughs, Edgar Rice. *At the Earth's Core* (7–12). 1990, Ballantine paper $3.95 (0-345-36668-9). David Innes travels 500 miles into the earth and finds a subterranean world. Sequels *Pellucidar* and *Tamar of Pellucidar* are also included in this volume.

4166 Burroughs, Edgar Rice. *A Princess of Mars* (9–12). 1985, Ballantine paper $4.99 (0-345-33138-9). This is the beginning of a series of "space operas" involving John Carter on Mars. Some others are: *Gods of Mars, Warlord of Mars*, and *The Chessmen of Mars.*

4167 Butler, Octavia E. *Parable of the Sower* (10–12). 1993, Four Walls Eight Windows $19.95 (1-8883-6325-8). In a 2025 California in which civilization has collapsed and violent drug-addicted "Paints" roam the land, a young African American woman sets out in hope of finding a better world. (Rev: BL 11/15/93)

4168 Butler, Octavia E. *Wild Seed* (11–12). 1980, Warner paper $6.50 (0-446-60672-3). Two very different immortal beings — Doro, who devours other beings, and Anyanwu, who prefers to love and heal — find their lives are intertwined throughout time.

4169 Cadigan, Pat. *Dervish Is Digital* (10–12). 2001, Tor $22.95 (0-312-85377-7). This is a high-tech mystery that involves a crime, a detective, and AR—alternative reality. (Rev: BL 8/01)

4170 Card, Orson Scott. *Alvin Journeyman* (10–12). Series: Tales of Alvin Maker. 1995, Tor $23.95 (0-312-85053-0). In this fourth installment of the series, Alvin Maker falls victim to the manipulations of The Unmaker, an ancient enemy. (Rev: SLJ 6/96; VOYA 4/96)

4171 Card, Orson Scott. *The Call of Earth* (9–12). Series: Homecoming Saga. 1994, Tor paper $6.99 (0-8125-3261-9). Teenagers are at the heart of this story featuring a sentient computer whose plans involve a return to Earth. (Rev: BL 11/15/92; VOYA 8/93)

4172 Card, Orson Scott. *Children of the Mind* (10–12). 1996, Tor $23.95 (0-312-85395-5). This novel is the last of the Ender saga and deals with the fate of humankind as well as the death of our hero. (Rev: SLJ 1/97; VOYA 2/97)

4173 Card, Orson Scott, ed. *Future on Ice* (9–12). 1998, Tor $24.95 (0-312-86694-1). A fine collection of 18 short stories by some of the most popular science fiction writers of the 1980s. (Rev: BL 9/15/98; SLJ 3/99; VOYA 4/99)

4174 Card, Orson Scott, ed. *Masterpieces: The Best Science Fiction of the Century* (9–12). 2001, Berkley $24.95 (0-441-00864-X). The 29 classic stories in this collection cover the years 1936 to 1995 and include such masters as Clarke, Heinlein, Bradbury, Pohl, and Le Guin. (Rev: BL 10/1/01; VOYA 4/02)

4175 Card, Orson Scott. *The Memory of Earth: Homecoming, Vol. 1* (9–12). Series: Homecoming Saga. 1993, Tor paper $5.99 (0-8125-3259-7). A science fiction saga set on the planet Harmony, where a computer rules the population. (Rev: BL 1/1/92)

4176 Card, Orson Scott. *Pastwatch: The Redemption of Christopher Columbus* (9–12). 1996, Tor $23.95 (0-312-85058-1). Time travelers from a ruined future Earth journey to the time of Columbus, hoping to reshape events. (Rev: BL 12/1/95; VOYA 4/96)

4177 Card, Orson Scott. *Shadow of the Hegemon* (9–12). 2000, Tor $25.95 (0-312-87651-3). In this sequel to *Ender's Shadow,* Bean is again the main character and he is faced with the mystery of who is kidnapping graduates of the Battle School. The next volume in the series is *Shadow Puppets* (2002). (Rev: BL 11/1/00; SLJ 6/01; VOYA 6/01)

4178 Card, Orson Scott. *Speaker for the Dead* (10–12). 1986, Tor $21.95 (0-312-93738-5). Ender tries to prevent a war with a nonhuman intelligent race in this sequel to *Ender's Game.* (Rev: BL 12/15/85; VOYA 8/86)

4179 Carr, Caleb. *Killing Time* (10–12). 2000, Random $25.95 (0-679-46332-1). In this thriller set in 2024, criminologist Gordon Wolfe investigates the murder of a video wizard who has been vaporized by an unknown weapon. (Rev: BL 10/1/00; VOYA 6/01)

4180 Cart, Michael, ed. *Tomorrowland: 10 Stories About the Future* (7–10). 1999, Scholastic paper $15.95 (0-590-37678-0). Ten writers, including Ron Koertge, Lois Lowry, and Katherine Paterson, have contributed original stories to this anthology that reflect their concepts of the future. (Rev: BCCB 12/99; BL 8/99; HBG 4/00; SLJ 9/99; VOYA 12/99)

4181 Carter, Raphael. *The Fortunate Fall* (9–12). 1996, Tor $21.95 (0-312-86034-X). In a future world where 20th century pop culture is viewed as "classical civilization," schoolchildren study the Brady Bunch the way students today study Shakespeare, and past horrors are hidden through manipulation of people's thoughts and memories, young Maya uncovers a genocide that was committed 100 years before and defies the authorities by trying to tell others about it. (Rev: BL 7/96; VOYA 4/97)

4182 Carver, Jeffrey A. *Eternity's End* (10–12). 2000, Tor $26.00 (0-312-85642-3). A space navigator doesn't realize that his captain has betrayed his ship and is in league with space pirates. (Rev: BL 12/1/00)

4183 Carver, Jeffrey A. *A Neptune Crossing* (9–12). 1995, Tor $5.99 (0-8125-3515-4). While doing survey work on Neptune's moon Triton, loner John Bandicut becomes a reluctant accomplice to aliens' efforts to save Earth. (Rev: BL 3/15/94; VOYA 12/94)

4184 Caselberg, Jay. *Wyrmhole* (11–12). 2003, NAL paper $5.99 (0-451-45949-0). Jack Stein, a psychic investigating the disappearance of miners working on a distant planet, is puzzled by the signals he receives in his dreams; suitable for mature teens. (Rev: BL 9/15/03)

4185 Castro, Adam-Troy. *Spider-Man: Secret of the Sinister Six* (7–12). 2002, BP $24.95 (0-7434-4464-7). Six supervillians attack New York City and Spider-Man comes to the rescue in this humorous and action-packed final installment in a trilogy. (Rev: SLJ 7/02)

4186 Cherryh, C. J. *The Collected Short Fiction of C. J. Cherryh* (9–12). 2004, DAW $23.95 (0-7564-0217-4). A massive collection of the short fiction of this great science fiction writer noted for her versatility. (Rev: BL 2/15/04)

4187 Cherryh, C. J. *Defender* (10–12). 2001, DAW $23.95 (0-88677-911-1). Bren Cameron is sent out to a space station to investigate unusual problems and discovers double and triple crosses and other skullduggery. (Rev: BL 11/15/01; VOYA 4/02)

4188 Cherryh, C. J. *Finity's End* (9–12). 1997, Warner paper $22.00 (0-446-57072-1). Fletcher, who has spent his first 17 years on Pell as a "stationer," is suddenly claimed by the crew of *Finity's End,* a space vehicle where his deceased mother once lived, and taken aboard to be a member of their community. (Rev: BL 8/97; VOYA 12/97)

4189 Cherryh, C. J. *Forge of Heaven* (10–12). 2004, HarperCollins $24.95 (0-380-97903-9). There is a tentative treaty between human and alien powers on a desert planet in this sequel to *Hammerfall* (2001). (Rev: BL 3/1/04*)

4190 Cherryh, C. J. *Inheritor* (10–12). 1996, DAW $21.95 (0-88677-689-9). In this third story about Bren, a human, and the alien culture of Atevi, Bren works to promote trust and understanding between the two very different cultures. (Rev: BL 4/15/96; VOYA 6/96)

4191 Cherryh, C. J. *The Pride of Chanur* (10–12). 1987, Phantasia $17.00 (0-932096-45-X); NAL paper $5.99 (0-88677-292-3). A human finds refuge on a spaceship operated by catlike beings. A sequel is *Chanur's Venture.*

4192 Christopher, John. *The White Mountains* (7–10). Series: Tripods. 1967, Simon & Schuster $17.95 (0-02-718360-2); Macmillan paper $4.99 (0-02-042711-5). The first of the Tripods trilogy, followed by *The City of Gold and Lead* and *The Pool of Fire.* (Rev: BL 9/15/98)

4193 Clancy, Tom, and Steve Pieczenik. *Virtual Vandals* (7–12). Series: Net Force. 1999, Berkley paper $4.99 (0-425-16173-0). In 2025, after Matt

Hunter and his computer friends attend an all-star virtual reality baseball game where terrorists shoot wildly at the stands, our hero and his pals set out to catch the culprits. Followed by *The Deadliest Game.* (Rev: BL 3/15/99)

4194 Clarke, Arthur C. *Childhood's End* (7–12). 1963, Harcourt $14.95 (0-15-117205-6); Ballantine paper $6.99 (0-345-34795-1). The overlords' arrival on Earth marks the beginning of the end for humankind.

4195 Clarke, Arthur C. *The City and the Stars* (10–12). 1957, NAL paper $3.50 (0-451-14822-3). This novel is now considered a science fiction classic. Also by the same author are *Reach for Tomorrow* (1975), *Island in the Sky* (1979), *The Deep Range* (1981), and *The Sentinel* (1986).

4196 Clarke, Arthur C. *The Collected Stories of Arthur C. Clarke* (10–12). 2001, Tor $29.95 (0-312-87821-4). This contains all the short fiction that the author wishes to preserve. Most of the stories date from 1946 through 1970. (Rev: BL 1/1–15/01)

4197 Clarke, Arthur C. *Expedition to Earth* (7–10). 1998, Ballantine paper $10.00 (0-345-43073-5). Eleven stories about space exploration.

4198 Clarke, Arthur C. *The Hammer of God* (9–12). 1994, Bantam paper $6.99 (0-553-56871-X). The struggle to avoid an asteroid on a collision course with Earth. (Rev: BL 4/15/93; VOYA 12/93)

4199 Clarke, Arthur C. *Rendezvous with Rama* (10–12). 1990, Bantam paper $6.99 (0-553-28789-3). Bill Norton and his crew set out to investigate a strange missile that has entered the earth's atmosphere.

4200 Clarke, Arthur C. *2001: A Space Odyssey* (9–12). 1968, NAL paper $3.95 (0-451-15580-7). This novel, an allegory about the history of the world based on the screenplay of the famous movie, introduces a most unusual computer named Hal.

4201 Clarke, Arthur C. *2010: Odyssey Two* (9–12). 1997, Ballantine paper $11.00 (0-345-41397-0). A team of scientists try to save the deserted spaceship Discovery.

4202 Clarke, Arthur C. *2061: Odyssey Three* (9–12). 1988, Ballantine paper $6.99 (0-345-35879-1). Heywood Floyd takes part in the space mission of landing on Halley's Comet. (Rev: BL 11/1/87; BR 9–10/88)

4203 Clarke, Arthur C. *The Wind from the Sun: Stories from the Space Age* (9–12). 1972, NAL paper $1.95 (0-451-11475-2). Eighteen science fiction stories, many with surprise endings.

4204 Clarke, Arthur C., and Stephen Baxter. *The Light of Other Days* (10–12). 2000, Tor $24.95 (0-312-87199-6). In the mid-2300s, wormhole technology is developed to allow manipulation of the past in this adult novel about human adaptation. (Rev: BL 2/1/00)

4205 Clarke, Arthur C., and Michael Kube-McDowell. *The Trigger* (10–12). 1999, Bantam $24.95 (0-553-10458-6). This thriller explores the broad-ranging reverberations set off by the invention of a device capable of neutralizing all the world's nitrate-based weaponry. (Rev: BL 9/15/99; VOYA 4/00)

4206 Clarke, Arthur C., and Gentry Lee. *Rama Revealed* (9–12). Series: Rama. 1995, Bantam paper $6.99 (0-553-56947-3). The fourth book of the series focuses on the New Eden colony, which is ruled by Nakamura, a dictator who overthrew the governess and wages war on the octospiders. (Rev: BL 12/1/93; VOYA 6/94)

4207 Clement, Hal. *The Essential Hal Clement, v.3: Variations on a Theme by Sir Isaac Newton* (10–12). 2000, NESFA $25.00 (1-886778-08-6). For advanced science fiction fans, this volume contains reprints of two of Clement's best novels, *Mission of Gravity* from 1954 and *Star Light,* first published in 1971. (Rev: BL 11/1/00)

4208 Clement, Hal. *Noise* (10–12). 2003, Tor $23.95 (0-765-30857-6). A researcher sets out to study the evolution of the languages of Kainui, a fascinating and dangerous world of floating cities populated by isolated seafarers. (Rev: BL 9/1/03)

4209 Clements, Andrew. *Things Not Seen* (7–10). 2002, Putnam $15.99 (0-399-23626-0). Bobby, 15, suddenly becomes invisible and must deal with all the problems his "disappearance" causes. (Rev: BCCB 6/02; BL 4/15/02; HB 3–4/02; HBG 10/02; SLJ 3/02; VOYA 2/02)

4210 Clute, John. *Appleseed* (10–12). 2002, Tor $25.95 (0-7653-0378-7). Nathaniel Freer, an interstellar trader, faces many obstacles to deliver a cargo of nanotechnology. (Rev: BL 12/15/01)

4211 Cormier, Robert. *Fade* (10–12). 1991, Bantam paper $4.99 (0-440-21091-7). A disturbing and sometimes terrifying novel about a 13-year-old who can make himself disappear. (Rev: BL 9/1/88; BR 11–12/88; SLJ 10/88; VOYA 12/88)

4212 Costikyan, Greg. *First Contract* (10–12). 2000, Tor $23.95 (0-312-87396-4). In this action-packed thriller, Johnson Mukherjii hatches a clever plot to make money selling aliens gadgets for their spaceships. (Rev: BL 6/1–15/00)

4213 Crichton, Michael. *The Andromeda Strain* (9–12). 1969, Knopf $25.00 (0-394-41525-6). A mysterious capsule from space brings a threat of a deadly epidemic in this fast-paced novel.

4214 Crichton, Michael. *Jurassic Park* (9–12). 1990, Knopf $25.00 (0-394-58816-9). This thriller takes place in an amusement park on an island off Costa Rica where genetically engineered dinosaurs live. (Rev: BL 10/1/90; SLJ 3/91)

4215 Crichton, Michael. *Sphere* (9–12). 1987, Knopf $27.50 (0-394-56110-4); Ballantine paper $7.99 (0-345-35314-5). A group of scientists journey to the bottom of the sea to explore a sunken spaceship in this thriller from the author of *The Andromeda Strain* (1969). (Rev: BL 5/15/87; SLJ 11/87)

4216 Crichton, Michael. *The Terminal Man* (9–12). 1972, Knopf $23.00 (0-394-44768-9); Ballantine paper $7.99 (0-345-35462-1). A man who is slipping into insanity has a computer implanted into his brain.

4217 Czerneda, Julie E. *In the Company of Others* (7–12). 2001, DAW paper $6.99 (0-88677-999-5). Biologist Gail Smith embarks on the space ship Seeker to track down Aaron Pardell, whose help she needs in her mission to find and destroy a deadly life form called the Quill. (Rev: VOYA 2/02)

4218 Daniel, Tony. *Metaplanetary* (10–12). 2001, HarperCollins $25.00 (0-06-105142-X). Centuries from now, both human and artificial intelligences have evolved—and are at war. (Rev: BL 3/15/01)

4219 Dann, Jack, and Gardner Dozois, eds. *Armageddons* (10–12). 1999, Ace paper $5.99 (0-441-00675-2). This collection of doomsday tales offers chilling visions of how the world as we know it might end. (Rev: VOYA 4/00)

4220 Danvers, Dennis. *The Fourth World* (10–12). 2000, Avon Eos $23.00 (0-380-97761-3). For better readers, this adventure involves computer technology, a massacre in Mexico, a coverup, and a worldwide plot. (Rev: BL 3/1/00* ; SLJ 9/00)

4221 David, Peter. *Babylon 5: In the Beginning* (7–10). 1998, Ballantine paper $6.99 (0-345-42452-2). This is a novelization of the first full-length movie in the TV science fiction series *Babylon 5.* (Rev: VOYA 8/98)

4222 Dayton, Arwen Elys. *Resurrection* (10–12). 2001, Roc paper $6.99 (0-451-45834-6). Two rival groups that inhabit neighboring planets independently send rival teams to Earth to recover technology lost on a previous flight. (Rev: BL 5/1/01)

4223 DeCandido, Keith R. A. *Destruction of Illusions* (9–12). 2003, Tor $24.95 (0-765-30483-X). This addition to the Gene Roddenberry TV show *Andromeda* brings together Captain Beka Valentine and Tyr Anasazi in an exciting adventure. (Rev: BL 2/15/03)

4224 Dedman, Stephen. *The Art of Arrow Cutting* (10–12). 1997, Tor $22.95 (0-312-86320-9). Mage, a young man who holds the power to perform miracles, is pursued by Tamenaga, a dead man who wants to possess this power. (Rev: VOYA 12/97)

4225 De Haven, Tom. *The Orphan's Tent* (7–10). 1996, Simon & Schuster $18.00 (0-689-31967-3). After Del, a young singer-songwriter, mysteriously disappears, her two friends, while trying to trace her, find themselves transported to another world. (Rev: SLJ 10/96; VOYA 12/96)

4226 Del Rey, Lester. *The Best of Lester del Rey* (7–10). 1978, Ballantine paper $5.99 (0-345-32933-3). Sixteen stories by this master of science fiction writing. Some full-length novels by del Rey are *Attack from Atlantis; Moon from Atlantis; Mysterious Planet;* and *Rocket Jockey* (all 1982).

4227 Dick, Philip K. *Do Androids Dream of Electric Sheep* (10–12). 1996, Ballantine paper $13.00 (0-345-40447-5). In the world of 2021, after a brutal war, androids have become so sophisticated that it is hard to distinguish them from humans. First published in 1968.

4228 Dickinson, Peter. *Eva* (8–12). 1990, Dell paper $5.50 (0-440-20766-5). When Eva wakes up after an accident she finds that she has retained her memory but been given the body of a chimpanzee. (Rev: HB 7/89; SLJ 4/89)

4229 Dietz, William C. *Death Day* (10–12). 2001, Berkley $21.95 (0-441-00857-7). This is a novel about an invasion by aliens who destroy everything and everybody they don't need. (Rev: BL 9/1/01)

4230 Dietz, William C. *Rebel Agent* (9–12). Series: Star Wars: Dark Forces. 1998, Putnam $24.95 (0-399-14396-3); Berkley paper $14.95 (0-425-16862-X). In this Star Wars novel, Kyle accepts the power of the Force, begins training as a Jedi Knight, falls in love, and completes a quest for secret information. (Rev: SLJ 10/98)

4231 Doctorow, Cory. *Eastern Standard Tribe* (9–12). 2004, Tor $23.95 (0-765-30759-6). A futuristic thriller about agents working in Greenwich Mean Time and the problems of instant global communication. (Rev: BL 2/15/04)

4232 Doohan, James, and S. M. Stirling. *The Independent Command* (10–12). 2000, Baen $25.00 (0-671-31951-5). In this, the third volume in the Flight Engineer saga, Peter Raeder faces new problems when the insectoid Fibians launch an attack on human-inhibited planets. (Rev: BL 11/1/00)

4233 Doyle, Debra, and James D. MacDonald. *Requiem for Boone* (10–12). 2000, Tor $24.95 (0-312-87460-X); paper $13.95 (0-312-87461-8). In this high-tech thriller, Will Boone serves as a double agent to investigate the mysterious Companions. (Rev: BL 8/00; VOYA 6/01)

4234 Dozois, Gardner, ed. *Explorers: SF Adventures to Far Horizons* (10–12). 2000, St. Martin's paper $17.95 (0-312-25462-8). A sterling collection of short stories about space exploration by such writers as Arthur C. Clarke, Poul Anderson, and Ursula LeGuin. (Rev: BL 3/1/00)

4235 Dozois, Gardner, ed. *The Furthest Horizon: SF Adventures to the Far Future* (10–12). 2000, St. Martin's paper $17.95 (0-312-26326-0). A fine anthology of stories that take place far in the future by 17 well-known writers. (Rev: BL 5/1/00)

4236 Dozois, Gardner, ed. *Supermen: Tales of the Posthuman Future* (9–12). 2002, St. Martin's paper $17.95 (0-312-27569-2). This book contains 29 stories published between 1955 and 2000, all dealing with the next stages of human evolution. (Rev: BL 11/15/01)

4237 Dozois, Gardner, ed. *The Year's Best Science Fiction: Eleventh Annual Collection* (9–12). 1994, St. Martin's paper $17.95 (0-312-11104-5). The annual collection of outstanding sci-fi short stories. (Rev: BL 7/94; VOYA 2/95)

4238 Dozois, Gardner, ed. *The Year's Best Science Fiction: Fifteenth Annual Collection* (9–12). 1998, St. Martin's paper $17.95 (0-312-19033-6). A worthwhile collection of 28 of the best science fiction stories. (Rev: BL 7/98; VOYA 12/98)

4239 Dozois, Gardner, ed. *The Year's Best Science Fiction: Seventeenth Annual Collection* (9–12). 2000, St. Martin's $29.95 (0-312-26275-2); paper $17.95 (0-312-26417-8). A fine collection of stories published in 1999, many by well-known authors such as Gene Wolfe and Robert Silverberg. (Rev: BL 5/15/00)

4240 Dozois, Gardner, ed. *The Year's Best Science Fiction: Eighteenth Annual Collection* (10–12). 2001, Tor $29.95 (0-312-27465-3); paper $18.95 (0-312-27478-5). Some of the finest science fiction writers are represented in this edition of the annual anthology. (Rev: BL 7/01)

4241 Dozois, Gardner, and Sheil Williams, eds. *Isaac Asimov's Moons* (9–12). 1997, Ace paper $5.99 (0-441-00453-9). This is a collection of seven well-crafted stories about lunar exploits with themes involving revenge, love, endurance, and survival. (Rev: VOYA 10/97)

4242 Drake, David. *Lt. Leary, Commanding* (10–12). 2000, Baen $24.00 (0-671-57875-8). In this sequel to *With the Lightnings* (1998), Lieutenant Daniel Leary and his sidekick become involved in a political crisis on a distant planet. (Rev: BL 7/00)

4243 Duane, Diane. *Doctor's Orders* (9–12). 1990, Pocket paper $5.50 (0-671-66189-2). In this Star Trek novel, Kirk disappears and Dr. McCoy must take over the *Enterprise*. (Rev: BL 6/15/90; SLJ 12/90)

4244 Dvorkin, David. *The Captain's Honor* (9–12). 1991, Pocket paper $5.50 (0-671-74140-3). In this Star Trek novel, the *Enterprise* tries to help the planet Tenara after it is attacked by the M'dok. (Rev: VOYA 2/90)

4245 Dvorkin, David. *Timetrap* (9–12). 1988, Pocket paper $4.95 (0-671-64870-5). Captain Kirk travels 100 years into the future in this Star Trek novel. (Rev: BL 6/15/88)

4246 Effinger, George Alec. *Budayeen Nights* (11–12). 2003, Golden Gryphon $24.95 (1-930846-19-3). The imagined Islamic city of Budayeen is the setting for a collection of stories featuring an offbeat cop and some equally questionable characters, many of them teens; for mature teens. (Rev: BL 9/1/03)

4247 Emshwiller, Carol. *The Mount* (10–12). 2002, Small Beer paper $16.00 (1-931520-03-8). Humans are the mounts for the alien hoots in this appealing novel about a young and ambitious mount named Charley. (Rev: BL 8/02; SLJ 6/03)

4248 Engdahl, Sylvia Louise. *The Far Side of Evil* (9–12). 2003, Walker $18.95 (0-8027-8848-3). Elana is sent to the planet Toris, a world poised on the brink of nuclear war. (Rev: HBG 10/03)

4249 Engdahl, Sylvia Louise, and Diane Dillon. *Enchantress from the Stars* (8–10). 2001, Walker $18.95 (0-8027-8764-9). This science fiction novel has become a classic and remains popular with readers of both sexes. (Rev: HBG 10/01)

4250 Enzensberger, Hans Magnus. *Lost in Time* (9–12). Trans. from German by Anthea Bell. 2000, Holt $18.00 (0-8050-6571-7). This time-travel novel transports Robert to seven different periods in history, finding himself embroiled in adventures that teach the reader, in entertaining fashion, about life in that era. (Rev: BL 11/15/00; HBG 3/01; SLJ 12/00; VOYA 2/01)

4251 Eskridge, Kelley. *Solitaire* (11–12). 2002, HarperCollins $24.95 (0-06-008857-5). At birth, Jackal was chosen as a future leader, but circumstances intervene and she instead faces 80 years of solitary confinement; for mature teens. (Rev: BL 8/02; SLJ 2/03)

4252 Farmer, Nancy. *The Ear, the Eye and the Arm* (7–10). 1994, Orchard LB $19.99 (0-531-08679-8). In Zimbabwe in 2194, the military ruler's son, 13, and his younger siblings leave their technologically overcontrolled home and embark on a series of perilous adventures. (Rev: BL 4/1/94; SLJ 6/94; VOYA 6/94)

4253 Farmer, Nancy. *House of the Scorpion* (7–10). 2002, Simon & Schuster $17.95 (0-689-85222-3). Young Matt, who has spent his childhood in cruel circumstances, discovers he is in fact a clone of the 142-year-old ruler of Opium, a land south of the U.S. border. (Rev: BL 9/15/02; HB 11–12/02; HBG 3/03; SLJ 9/02)

4254 Farmer, Philip Jose. *Dayworld Breakup* (10–12). 1991, Tor paper $4.95 (0-8125-0889-0). The third volume about Dayworld, the land where overcrowding is so acute that people must spend half of their lives in suspended animation. Preceded by *Day-world* (1984) and *Dayworld Rebel* (1987). (Rev: BL 5/1/90)

4255 Farmer, Philip Jose. *The Gods of Riverworld* (10–12). 1998, Ballantine paper $12.95 (0-345-41971-5). In this, the fifth and last of the recommended Riverworld series, people who lived on Earth in the past are resurrected.

4256 Farmer, Philip Jose. *The Magic Labyrinth* (10–12). 1998, Ballantine paper $12.95 (0-345-41970-7). This is a volume in one of the major science creations, the Riverworld saga. Some others are: *The Gods of Riverworld* (1985), *The Dark Design* (1984), and *To Your Scattered Bodies Go* (1985).

4257 Fawcett, Bill, ed. *The Warmasters* (10–12). 2002, Baen $24.00 (0-7434-3534-6). Three novellas — by David Weber, David Drake, and Eric Flint — featuring military science fiction. (Rev: BL 5/1/02)

4258 Feintuch, David. *Children of Hope* (10–12). 2001, Berkley $23.95 (0-441-00804-6). In this part of the recommended Nicholas Seafort series, young Randy Carr is adopted by Seafort and helps him in a struggle against vengeful theocrats. (Rev: BL 3/15/01)

4259 Feintuch, David. *Fisherman's Hope* (10–12). Series: Seafort Saga. 1996, Warner paper $6.50 (0-446-60099-7). In this science fiction novel, Seafort, in his mid-20s, is responsible for the training of 400 Navy cadets and stands up to inept authority. (Rev: VOYA 8/96)

4260 Feintuch, David. *Voices of Hope* (9–12). Series: Seafort Saga. 1996, Warner paper $6.50 (0-446-60333-3). Jared, the rebellious son of Seafort's close friend, runs away with plans to sell information about Seafort to a cyberspace news outlet, only to find himself in the middle of violent class conflict and a genocidal war. (Rev: BL 10/15/96; VOYA 10/96)

4261 Florman, Samuel C. *The Aftermath: A Novel of Survival* (10–12). 2001, St. Martin's $23.95 (0-312-26652-9). This speculative novel tells of the consequences of a comet hitting Earth leaving only small communities in South Africa and Madagascar intact. (Rev: BL 11/15/01)

4262 Flynn, Michael. *Falling Stars* (9–12). 2001, Tor $25.95 (0-312-87443-X). In this sequel to *Rogue Star* (1998), an asteroid sent by aliens is only months away from Earth and a solution must be found quickly. (Rev: BL 3/1/01)

4263 Flynn, Michael. *Lodestar* (10–12). 2000, Tor $24.95 (0-312-86137-0). In this sequel to *Firestar* (1996) and *Rogue Star* (1998), heroine Mariesa van Huyten must mount a defense against the possible destruction of the world by asteroids. (Rev: BL 3/15/00)

4264 Forstchen, William R. *Down to the Sea* (10–12). 2000, Penguin paper $6.99 (0-451-45806-0). Navy pilots Sean O'Donald and Richard Cromwell fly their aerosteamer into the dreaded area of the Kazars and are taken prisoner in this action-filled adventure. (Rev: BL 12/15/00)

4265 Forward, Robert L. *Dragon's Egg* (10–12). 1983, Ballantine paper $5.99 (0-345-31666-5). In this imaginative novel, life on a neutron star is depicted.

4266 Foster, Alan Dean. *The Deluge Drivers* (10–12). 1987, Ballantine paper $5.99 (0-345-33330-6). In this conclusion to the trilogy that began with *Icerigger* and *Mission to Moulokin* (both 1987), Ethan Fortune must foil a plot to disturb the ecological balance on his planet. (Rev: BL 5/15/87)

4267 Foster, Alan Dean. *Drowning World* (10–12). 2003, Del Rey $23.95 (0-345-45035-3). On the edge of the Commonwealth is a rain-drenched planet that is home to warring natives and immigrants and to an interesting jungle. (Rev: BL 12/1/02)

4268 Foster, Alan Dean. *The Hand of Dinotopia* (6–10). Series: Dinotopia. 1999, HarperCollins $22.99 (0-06-028005-0). In this adventure involving dinosaurs, our heroes journey through the Great Desert and Outer Island to find the key to a sea route that will link Dinotopia to the rest of the world. (Rev: BL 5/1/99; HBG 10/99; SLJ 4/99)

4269 Foster, Alan Dean. *Jed the Dead* (9–12). 1997, Ace paper $5.99 (0-441-00399-0). An unusual fantasy in which Ross Ed finds a dead alien in a cave and begins using it as a ventriloquist's dummy on a wild ride across the country. (Rev: VOYA 4/97)

4270 Foster, Alan Dean. *Quozl* (9–12). 1989, Berkley paper $5.99 (0-441-69454-3). An amusing science fiction novel about aliens who look like large rabbits and their visit to Earth. (Rev: BL 5/15/89; SLJ 8/89)

4271 Foster, Alan Dean. *Reunion* (10–12). 2001, Del Rey $24.00 (0-345-41867-0). A genetically altered human is determined to discover the secrets of this process and finds that he has broken into a sophisticated artificial intelligence. (Rev: BL 4/15/01; VOYA 10/01)

4272 Foster, Alan Dean. *Splinter of the Mind's Eye* (8–12). 1978, Ballantine paper $6.99 (0-345-32023-9). A novel about Luke Skywalker and Princess Leia of *Star Wars* fame and their battle against the Empire.

4273 Freer, Dave, and Eric Flint. *Rats, Bats and Vats* (10–12). 2000, Baen $23.00 (0-671-31940-X). Human "grunt" Chip and a group of rats help the planet Harmony and Reason when it is invaded by insectoid aliens. (Rev: BL 9/15/00)

4274 Fuller, Kimberly. *Home* (7–10). 1997, Tor $16.95 (0-312-86152-4). When an attractive alien lands on her planet, Maran Thopel is attracted to him and to his mission to regain the planet for the people from whom it was taken. (Rev: BR 9–10/97; SLJ 7/97; VOYA 8/97)

4275 Gerrold, David. *Blood and Fire* (8–12). 2004, BenBella paper $14.95 (1-932100-11-3). In this story that is a metaphor for the AIDS problem, a starship happens on another one, adrift in space, that contains blood worms, a deadly parasite. (Rev: BL 1/1–15/04)

4276 Gerrold, David. *Bouncing Off the Moon* (9–12). 2001, Tor $22.95 (0-312-87841-9). In this sequel to *Jumping Off the Planet* (2000), the three Dingillian brothers and a robot monkey sneak off to the moon. (Rev: BL 3/1/01)

4277 Gerrold, David. *Chess with a Dragon* (8–12). 1988, Avon paper $3.50 (0-380-70662-8). The entire human race becomes slaves of giant slugs and Yake must save them. (Rev: BL 6/15/87; BR 11–12/87; SLJ 9/87)

4278 Gerrold, David. *Jumping Off the Planet* (10–12). 2000, Tor $19.95 (0-312-89069-9). A humorous, outrageous caper, the first of the Starsiders Trilogy, involves a coming-of-age story and a trip to the moon by three very different brothers. (Rev: BL 3/1/00)

4279 Gerrold, David. *Leaping to the Stars* (10–12). 2002, Tor $24.95 (0-312-89067-2). Young Charlie Dingillian heads from the moon to a distant colony with his robot HARLIE in this last volume in the series that started with *Jumping Off the Planet* (2000) and *Bouncing Off the Moon* (2001). (Rev: BL 3/1/02)

4280 Gibson, William. *Neuromancer* (10–12). 1994, Ace $21.95 (0-441-00068-1); paper $6.99 (0-441-56959-5). In this variation on the Faust story, a computer expert sells his soul for money.

4281 Gier, Scott G. *Genellan: Planetfall* (10–12). 1995, Del Rey paper $5.99 (0-345-39509-3). Lieutenant Sharl Buccari faces problems when her spaceship lands in an unfamiliar world with winged natives hovering about. (Rev: VOYA 2/96)

4282 Goodman, Alison. *Singing the Dogstar Blues* (7–12). 2003, Viking $16.99 (0-670-03610-2). Science fiction, adventure, mystery, and humor are all combined in this story of a spunky time-travel student who shares a room with an alien. (Rev: BL 4/15/03; HBG 10/03; SLJ 4/03*; VOYA 2/03)

4283 Goonan, Kathleen Ann. *Crescent City Rhapsody* (10–12). Series: Nanotech Cycle. 2000, Avon Eos $23.00 (0-380-97711-7). This last book in the Nanotech Cycle tells how, in 2012, Earth is blanketed by an electromagnetic pulse known as The Silence. (Rev: BL 1/1–15/00)

4284 Gould, Steven. *Blind Waves* (10–12). 2000, Tor $23.95 (0-312-86445-0). For mature readers, this novel set in the 21st century tells of the consequences faced by Patricia Beenan, a salvage diver, after she finds a sunken freighter with a hold full of chained corpses. (Rev: BL 2/15/00)

4285 Gould, Steven. *Wild Side* (10–12). 1996, Tor $22.95 (0-312-85473-0). In this riveting science fiction novel, 18-year-old Charlie discovers a gateway to a parallel earth that is a pollution-free, human-free Eden, where animals extinct on earth still survive. (Rev: BL 3/15/96; VOYA 2/97)

4286 Green, Simon R. *Deathstalker Legacy* (10–12). 2003, NAL $23.95 (0-451-45907-5). Appropriate for mature teens only, this latest installment in the continuing saga of the Deathstalkers is loaded with action as hero Douglas Campbell lashes back after terrorists attack his wedding party. (Rev: BL 1/1–15/03)

4287 Greenberg, Martin H., ed. *Lord of the Fantastic: Stories in Honor of Roger Zelazny* (9–12). 1998, Avon paper $14.00 (0-380-78737-7). This collection of 20 original science fiction novels by well-known writers is a tribute to sci-fi great Roger Zelazny, who died at age 58 in 1995. (Rev: SLJ 3/99)

4288 Greenberg, Martin H., and John Helfers, eds. *Space Stations* (9–12). 2004, DAW paper $6.99 (0-7564-0176-3). A fine collection of short stories whose topic is space stations and life on them. (Rev: BL 3/1/04)

4289 Greenberg, Martin H., and Larry Segroff, eds. *Past Imperfect* (9–12). 2001, DAW paper $6.99 (0-7564-0012-0). Twelve excellent short stories that deal with time travel. (Rev: BL 9/1/01)

4290 Greeno, Gayle. *Mind Snare* (9–12). 1997, DAW paper $5.99 (0-88677-749-6). In this novel set in 2158, Rose, who wants revenge because of her husband's infidelity many years before, plots to kill both the woman he had an affair with and the teenage son who was the product of this union. (Rev: VOYA 12/97)

4291 Haddix, Margaret P. *Turnabout* (7–10). 2000, Simon & Schuster $17.00 (0-689-82187-5). Life is turned upside down as two centenarian nursing home residents opt at the start of the 21st century to grow younger rather than older, and by 2085, after complicated lives, realize they'll need care in their childhoods. (Rev: BL 10/15/00; HBG 3/01; SLJ 9/00)

4292 Halam, Ann. *Dr. Franklin's Island* (6–10). 2002, Random LB $14.99 (0-385-90056-2). Three British teens survive a plane crash on a remote island only to find they have fallen into the hands of a mad scientist. (Rev: BCCB 5/02; BL 7/02; HBG 10/02; SLJ 5/02)

4293 Haldeman, Joe. *Forever Peace* (10–12). 1997, Ace $21.95 (0-441-00406-7). In the world of 2043, Julian Class, a physicist and pacifist, must kill to prevent worldwide destruction. (Rev: BL 9/15/97; VOYA 2/98)

4294 Halperin, James L. *The First Immortal* (10–12). 1998, Del Rey $24.95 (0-345-42092-6). This family saga spans 200 years, from 1925 to 2125, with most of the same characters present throughout, or in different periods, because of cryogenics, the science of freezing people to be resurrected at a later time. (Rev: SLJ 12/98; VOYA 8/98)

4295 Hambly, Barbara. *Ishmael* (9–12). 1991, Pocket paper $5.50 (0-671-74355-4). In this Star Trek novel, Spock goes back in time to foil a plan to change history. (Rev: BL 7/85; VOYA 2/86)

4296 Hamilton, Peter F. *Pandora's Star* (10–12). 2004, Del Rey $25.95 (0-345-46162-2). In the 24th century, humanity has colonized the stars and through wormwood travel has established a successful commonwealth. (Rev: BL 3/1/04)

4297 Harper, Steven. *Nightmare* (11–12). 2002, NAL paper $6.99 (0-451-45898-2). In this sequel to *Dreamer* (2001), telepathic Weaver must enter the traumatizing dreams of victims of a serial killer who is loose on the planet Bellerophon; for mature teens. (Rev: BL 10/1/02)

4298 Harrison, Harry. *50 in 50: A Collection of Short Stories, One for Each of Fifty Years* (10–12). 2001, Tor $24.95 (0-312-87789-7). A collection of 50 stories that span the 50-year writing career of this prolific and admired writer. (Rev: BL 5/15/01)

4299 Hartwell, David G., ed. *Year's Best SF* (9–12). 1996, HarperCollins paper $6.50 (0-06-105641-3). In this edition of an annual collection, there are 14 well-constructed, thoughtful, and entertaining stories, many by well-known authors, representing a variety of SF subgenres including cyberpunk, time travel, alternative history, and hard science fiction. (Rev: VOYA 4/97)

4300 Hartwell, David G., ed. *Year's Best SF 5* (10–12). 2000, HarperCollins paper $6.99 (0-06-102054-0). A fine anthology of stories that appeared in 1999, representing a good cross section of science fiction topics and authors. (Rev: BL 5/15/00)

4301 Hartwell, David G., and Kathryn Cramer. *The Hard SF Renaissance* (9–12). 2002, Tor $29.95 (0-312-87635-1). This is a fine collection of 41 hard science fiction stories written since 1990. (Rev: BL 12/1/02)

4302 Hautman, Pete. *Hole in the Sky* (9–12). 2001, Simon & Schuster $16.00 (0-689-83118-8). In 2028, after a deadly flu has wiped out most of the world's population, a group of teens set out on a rescue mission that entails both adventure and the mystical promise of renewal. (Rev: BCCB 6/01; BL 4/15/01; HB 5–6/01; HBG 10/01; SLJ 6/01; VOYA 6/01)

4303 Heinlein, Robert A. *Between Planets* (7–10). 1984, Ballantine paper $6.99 (0-345-32099-9). A revolt on Venus against an interplanetary alliance causes painful decisions for Don.

4304 Heinlein, Robert A. *The Cat Who Walks Through Walls* (10–12). 1985, Ace paper $7.50 (0-441-09499-6). Colonel Colin Campbell and his wife travel through time to get help solving a murder mystery. (Rev: BL 8/85)

4305 Heinlein, Robert A. *The Door into Summer* (9–12). 1986, Ballantine paper $5.99 (0-345-33012-9). An inventor has an opportunity to look into the future in this science fiction novel.

4306 Heinlein, Robert A. *Farmer in the Sky* (7–10). 1985, Ballantine paper $6.99 (0-345-32438-2). A family decides to leave Earth to find better resources on another planet. A reissue.

4307 Heinlein, Robert A. *The Moon Is a Harsh Mistress* (10–12). 1996, St. Martin's $24.95 (0-312-86176-1); paper $14.95 (0-312-86355-1). For better readers, the story of a penal colony on the Earth's moon.

4308 Heinlein, Robert A. *Red Planet* (7–10). 1981, Ballantine paper $6.99 (0-345-34039-6). A novel about the first space exploration of the planet Mars.

4309 Heinlein, Robert A. *The Rolling Stones* (7–10). 1985, Ballantine paper $6.99 (0-345-32451-X). The Stone family takes on the universe in this unusual science fiction adventure. A reissue.

4310 Heinlein, Robert A. *Space Cadet* (7–10). 1984, Ballantine paper $5.99 (0-345-35311-0). In the year 2075, several members of the Solar Patrol have fantastic adventures.

4311 Heinlein, Robert A. *The Star Beast* (7–10). 1977, Macmillan $15.00 (0-684-15329-7). A pet smuggled to Earth never seems to stop growing.

4312 Heinlein, Robert A. *Starman Jones* (7–10). 1985, Ballantine paper $6.99 (0-345-32811-6). Eager for adventure, Max Jones stows away on an intergalactic spaceship. A reissue.

4313 Heinlein, Robert A. *Stranger in a Strange Land* (10–12). 1991, Ace paper $16.95 (0-441-78838-6). A young man from Mars comes to Earth and must learn our strange ways.

4314 Herbert, Brian, and Kevin J. Anderson. *Dune: House Atreides* (9–12). 1999, Bantam $27.50 (0-553-11061-6); paper $6.99 (0-553-58027-2). This prequel to the recommended Dune series describes the plots and schemes that lay the foundation of the saga. (Rev: BL 8/99; VOYA 4/00)

4315 Herbert, Brian, and Kevin J. Anderson. *Dune: House Harkonnen* (10–12). Series: Dune. 2000, Bantam $27.50 (0-553-11072-1). The eighth book in the recommended Dune series and the second in the House Trilogy (the first was *Dune: House Atrei-*

des published in 1999). Baron Harkonnen, fearing that death is coming soon, turns to his outcast brother's family to help his clan's future existence. (Rev: BL 8/00)

4316 Herbert, Frank. *Dune* (10–12). 1984, Putnam $26.95 (0-399-12896-4). In this, the first of a series, the Atreides family is banished to planet Dune where the ferocious Fremen live. Others in the series include *Children of Dune* (1985), *Dune Messiah* (1976), and *God Emperor of Dune* (1981).

4317 Hickman, Tracy. *The Immortals* (10–12). 1996, Roc $19.95 (0-451-45402-2). In this futuristic novel, a terrible plague is covering the United States and Michael Barris finds his son in an internment camp for infected, "pre-deceased" people and he becomes involved in the inmates' struggle for survival. (Rev: VOYA 10/96)

4318 Hillerman, Tony. *The Best American Mystery Stories of the Century* (9–12). 2000, Houghton $28.00 (0-618-01267-2). A 20th-century survey of the mystery story with contributions from such writers as Raymond Chandler, John Steinbeck, and Ellery Queen. (Rev: BL 4/1/00)

4319 Hoffman, Eva. *The Secret* (11–12). 2002, PublicAffairs $25.00 (1-58648-150-9). An adolescent clone named Iris is the heroine of this thought-provoking novel set in the near future; for mature teens. (Rev: BL 12/1/02)

4320 Hogan, James P. *Martian Knightlife* (10–12). 2001, Baen $22.00 (0-671-31844-6). While vacationing on Mars, Kieran Thane (also known as Knight) becomes involved in a devious plot. (Rev: BL 9/1/01)

4321 Hopkinson, Nalo. *Brown Girl in the Ring* (10–12). 1998, Warner paper $13.99 (0-446-67433-8). In this science fiction novel set in postmodern Toronto in the near future, Ti-Jeanne, living with her child and grandmother in urban squalor, must conquer her fears and find a way out of their dismal situation. (Rev: BL 5/15/98; SLJ 11/98; VOYA 8/98)

4322 Hughes, Monica. *Invitation to the Game* (7–10). 1991, Simon & Schuster paper $4.99 (0-671-86692-3). In 2154, a high school graduate and her friends face life on welfare in a highly robotic society and are invited to participate in a sinister government "game." (Rev: BL 9/15/91)

4323 Hunt, Walter H. *The Dark Path* (10–12). 2003, Tor $27.95 (0-765-30606-9). In this sequel to *The Dark Wing* (2001) full of zor mythology, the zor and human beings have joined forces to battle the shape-changing, mind-controlling vuhl. (Rev: BL 2/15/03)

4324 Hunt, Walter H. *The Dark Wing* (10–12). 2001, Tor $27.95 (0-7653-0113-X). Will Ivan Marais be able to save the Solar Empire from the deadly attacks of the birdlike zor? (Rev: BL 10/15/01; VOYA 6/02)

4325 Huxley, Aldous. *Brave New World* (10–12). 1998, HarperPerennial paper $11.95 (0-06-092987-1). A science fiction classic set in a future when science controls the life of mankind.

4326 Jablokov, Alexander. *The Breath of Suspension* (9–12). 1994, Arkham $20.95 (0-87054-167-6). Short stories with such themes as time-traveling detectives, a cyborg whale that explores Jupiter's atmosphere, and manmade alternate universes. (Rev: BL 8/94; VOYA 12/94)

4327 James, Roby. *Commencement* (9–12). 1996, Del Rey paper $5.99 (0-345-40038-0). Ronica finds herself on a low-technology planet and without the power to control her mind, and she consents to work with the Lord of one of the tribes in exchange for getting back her lost mental functions. (Rev: VOYA 8/96)

4328 Jeapes, Ben. *The Xenocide Mission* (7–10). 2002, Viking $15.95 (0-385-75007-2). A complex and exciting adventure set in the distant future in which humans and their quadruped companions must fight against ferocious aliens known as the Kin. (Rev: BCCB 6/02; BL 4/15/02; HBG 3/03; SLJ 6/02; VOYA 8/02)

4329 Jones, Diana Wynne. *Hexwood* (8–12). 1994, Greenwillow $16.00 (0-688-12488-7). A complex science fiction story about virtual realism, time manipulation, and a young girl who investigates the disappearance of guests at Hexwood Farm. (Rev: BL 6/1–15/94; SLJ 3/94; VOYA 10/94)

4330 Jones, Terry. *Douglas Adams' Starship Titanic* (10–12). 1997, Harmony $20.00 (0-609-60103-2). Inspired by an episode in one of Douglas Adams's novels, this is a comic science fiction novel loaded with absurdities about a group of inept characters who must bring a starship's computer brain back online while avoiding destruction by a bomb and an army of hostile shipbuilders. (Rev: BL 9/15/97; SLJ 5/98; VOYA 4/98)

4331 Kanaly, Michael. *Virus Clans: A Story of Evolution* (10–12). 1998, Ace paper $12.00 (0-441-00500-4). A science fiction thriller in which a young entomologist discovers that a group of viruses he has grown are communicating with each other. (Rev: BL 2/15/98; SLJ 9/98)

4332 Kaye, Marilyn. *Amy, Number Seven: How Many Are Out There?* (6–10). Series: Replica. 1998, Bantam paper $4.50 (0-553-49238-1). When Amy finds that her personality is mysteriously changing, her mother is acting strangely, and she is developing extraordinary new abilities, she sets out to find the truth about her past. (Rev: BL 10/15/98; SLJ 10/98)

4333 Kenyon, Kay. *Maximum Ice* (10–12). 2002, Bantam paper $5.99 (0-553-58376-X). An action-packed tale of a starship's return to Earth to find it nearly covered in a strange substance and the remaining population living under the surface. (Rev: BL 2/1/02; VOYA 4/02)

4334 Koontz, Dean. *The Taking* (10–12). 2004, Bantam $27.00 (0-553-80250-X). A glowing rain falls in the San Bernardino Mountains in California and soon appliances come on unexpectedly and the hands of clocks run wildly in the opposite direction. (Rev: BL 5/1/04*)

4335 Krane, Steven. *Stranger Inside* (10–12). 2003, DAW paper $6.99 (0-7564-0128-3). Alien powers and government secrecy feature in this sci-fi detective story about teens who suffer spontaneous combustion. (Rev: BL 2/1/03)

4336 Kress, Nancy. *Beggars and Choosers* (9–12). 1994, Tor $22.95 (0-312-85749-7). The future world is divided among three feuding groups: the superhuman Sleepless, the genetically altered ruling elite called "homo superior," and the poor masses. (Rev: BL 10/1/94; SLJ 5/95; VOYA 4/95)

4337 Kress, Nancy. *Beggars Ride* (10–12). 1996, Tor $23.95 (0-312-85817-5). The concluding volume in this thrilling science fiction trilogy about a genetically altered ruling elite that began with *Beggars in Spain* (1993) and *Beggars and Choosers*. (Rev: SLJ 7/97; VOYA 6/97)

4338 Kress, Nancy. *Probability Moon* (10–12). 2000, Tor $23.95 (0-312-87406-5). Set in the far future, this novel describes a war that breaks out between earth-born creatures and aliens. (Rev: BL 4/15/00; VOYA 12/00)

4339 Kress, Nancy. *Probability Sun* (10–12). 2001, Tor $24.95 (0-312-87407-3). In this sequel to *Probability Moon* (2000), humans are losing their war against the Fallers until their examination of a POW Faller gives them some fresh ideas. The last volume in the trilogy is *Probability Space* (2002). (Rev: BL 5/1/01)

4340 Kurtz, Katherine. *The Bishop's Heir* (10–12). 1987, Ballantine paper $5.99 (0-345-34761-7). This is the beginning of a trilogy in the Deryni series, The Histories of King Kelson.

4341 Lackey, Mercedes. *Brightly Burning* (9–12). Series: Heralds of Valdemar. 2000, DAW $24.95 (0-88677-889-1). Lan, who has the mental ability to create raging fires, finds that this gift is a mixed blessing in this novel, the concluding volume in The Last Herald-Mage trilogy and sequel to *Magic's Price* (1990). (Rev: BL 4/15/00*)

4342 Landis, Geoffrey A. *Impact Parameter and Other Quantum Realities* (10–12). 2001, Golden Gryphon $24.95 (1-930846-06-1). A fine, varied assortment of 16 stories by the award-winning hard-science sf writer. (Rev: BL 10/15/01)

4343 Landis, Geoffrey A. *Mars Crossing* (9–12). 2000, Tor $24.95 (0-312-87201-1). Set in 2028, this space adventure tells of a manned mission to Mars that hopes to be the first to return to Earth safely after two earlier missions failed. (Rev: BL 12/1/00)

4344 Lassiter, Rhiannon. *Hex* (7–10). 2001, Simon & Schuster paper $4.99 (0-7434-2211-2). An exciting, futuristic action story about 24th-century teens who use their computer savvy to combat an evil government agency. (Rev: BL 1/1–15/02)

4345 Lassiter, Rhiannon. *Shadows* (7–10). 2002, Simon & Schuster paper $4.99 (0-7434-2212-0). Raven, the superhacker introduced in *Hex*, faces new dangers as the government seeks to destroy her and her fellow mutants. The last volume in the trilogy is *Ghosts* (2002). (Rev: BL 4/15/02; SLJ 4/02)

4346 Lawrence, Louise. *Andra* (6–10). 1991, HarperCollins $14.95 (0-06-023685-X). This novel is set 2,000 years in the future, when humanity, having destroyed Earth's environment, lives in rigidly governed, sealed underground cities. (Rev: BL 5/1/91; SLJ 5/91)

4347 Lawrence, Louise. *Dream-Weaver* (7–12). 1996, Clarion $15.00 (0-395-71812-0). The horror of psychic manipulation is explored in this science fiction thriller about a girl who, in her dream body, joins a spaceship full of colonists bound for her planet. (Rev: BL 10/1/96*; SLJ 10/96; VOYA 2/97)

4348 Lawrence, Louise. *The Patchwork People* (7–10). 1994, Clarion $14.95 (0-395-67892-7). This brooding story takes place in a bleak Wales of the future, where natural resources are nearly depleted and jobs are scarce. (Rev: BL 12/15/94*; SLJ 11/94)

4349 Layne, Steven L. *This Side of Paradise* (7–10). 2001, North Star $15.99 (0-9712336-9-1). Jack, a junior in high school, soon questions his father's motives for moving the family into a town called Paradise, where things are definitely not what they seem. (Rev: BL 2/1/02; SLJ 1/02; VOYA 2/02)

4350 Le Guin, Ursula K. *The Lathe of Heaven* (10–12). 1982, Bentley $14.00 (0-8376-0464-8); Avon paper $5.50 (0-380-01320-7). In this novel set in the 21st century, a young man finds that his dreams are premonitions of events to come.

4351 Le Guin, Ursula K. *The Left Hand of Darkness* (7–12). 1969, Ace paper $7.99 (0-441-47812-3). An envoy is sent to the ice-covered planet Gethen where people can be either male or female at will.

4352 Le Guin, Ursula K. *The Telling* (10–12). 2000, Harcourt $24.00 (0-15-100567-2). Part of the recommended Hainish cycle that includes *The Left Hand of Darkness* (1997) and *The Dispossessed* (1999), this novel tells how Sutty, a linguist, finds herself on the planet Aka, which is ruled by a strongly controlling regime. (Rev: BL 6/1–15/00; VOYA 12/00)

4353 Le Guin, Ursula K., and Brian Attebery, eds. *The Norton Book of Science Fiction: North American Science Fiction, 1960–1990* (9–12). 1993, Norton paper $35.50 (0-393-97241-0). This excellent collection includes more than 60 vintage science fiction short stories.

4354 Le Guin, Ursula K., and Brian Attebery, eds. *The Norton Book of Science Fiction, 1960–1990* (9–12). 1993, Norton $29.95 (0-393-03546-8). The last three decades of North American science fiction are represented in 60 stories that focus on themes rather than on author reputation. (Rev: BL 10/1/93)

4355 Leiber, Fritz. *The Big Time* (10–12). 1976, Amereon LB $20.95 (0-88411-931-9). A young girl lives outside the confines of time on a space station.

4356 Leiber, Fritz. *The Dealings of Daniel Kesserich* (9–12). 1997, Tor $18.95 (0-312-85408-0). When George Kramer visits his friend John to comfort him after his wife's death, mysterious events begin to occur, including the disappearance of the wife's body. (Rev: BL 2/1/97; VOYA 8/97)

4357 Lem, Stanislaw. *Cyberiad: Fables for the Cybernetic Age* (10–12). 1985, Harcourt paper $11.00 (0-15-623550-1). Each of these 13 stories deals with computers. Also use: *Tales of Pirx the Pilot* (1990).

4358 L'Engle, Madeleine. *Many Waters* (7–10). 1986, Farrar $18.00 (0-374-34796-4); Dell paper $6.50 (0-440-40548-3). The Murry twins, from the author's Wrinkle in Time trilogy, time-travel to the Holy Land prior to the Great Flood. (Rev: BL 8/86; SLJ 11/86; VOYA 12/86)

4359 Lettow, Donna. *Highlander: Zealot* (9–12). 1997, Warner paper $5.99 (0-446-60457-7). In this tie-in to the television and movie series, Duncan MacLeod, an Immortal who was born in 1592 and who can die only if another Immortal beheads him, takes on the Israeli-Palestinian conflict. (Rev: VOYA 6/98)

4360 Levinson, Paul. *Borrowed Tides* (10–12). 2001, Tor $22.95 (0-312-84869-2). In this adventure tale it is decided in 2023 to send a mission to Alpha Centauri, but is it fated to be a one-way trip? (Rev: BL 3/15/01)

4361 London, Jack. *The Science Fiction Stories of Jack London* (9–12). Ed. by James Bankes. 1993, Carol paper $9.95 (0-8065-1407-8). This collection of 15 of London's science fiction explores such themes as rejuvenation.

4362 Lowachee, Karin. *Warchild* (10–12). 2002, Warner paper $6.99 (0-446-61077-1). Jos, an 8-year-old whose family is killed by pirates, escapes his initial captors only to wind up subject to the alien strint, enemies of humanity. (Rev: BL 3/15/02)

4363 Lucas, George, and Chris Claremont. *Shadow Moon: First in the Chronicles of the Shadow War*

(9–12). 1996, Bantam paper $5.99 (0-553-57285-7). Lucas of *Star Wars* fame and Claremont of Marvel Comics offer the first in a planned trilogy of sci-fi novels. (Rev: BL 10/1/95; VOYA 2/96)

4364 Luiken, Nicole. *Silver Eyes* (7–12). 2001, Simon & Schuster paper $5.99 (0-7434-0078-X). Romance and suspenseful mystery combine with science fiction in this story set in the future about a girl endangered by her memory losses. (Rev: SLJ 5/02)

4365 Lumley, Brian. *Necroscope: Defilers* (10–12). 2000, Tor $25.95 (0-312-87261-5). In this sequel to *Necroscope: Invaders* (1999), Jake Cutter continues to seek revenge on the vampire mafiosi who killed his beloved. (Rev: BL 4/15/00)

4366 McArthur, Maxine. *Time Future* (10–12). 2001, Warner paper $6.99 (0-446-60963-3). Commander Maria Halley is on a deep space station when suddenly a tiny ship appears bearing humans in suspended animation. (Rev: BL 4/15/01)

4367 McAuley, Paul. *The Secret of Life* (10–12). 2001, Tor $25.95 (0-765-30080-X). Biologist Mariella Anders goes to Mars to investigate the rumor that the Chinese have discovered life at the Red Planet's poles. (Rev: BL 5/15/01)

4368 McAuley, Paul. *White Devils* (11–12). 2004, Tor $25.95 (0-765-30761-8). In a disturbing vision of a world gone mad, this is the story of a man who investigates strange creatures he believes are the products of a failed genetic engineering experiment; violence makes this suitable only for mature teens. (Rev: BL 12/1/03)

4369 McCaffrey, Anne. *The Chronicles of Pern: First Fall* (9–12). 1994, Ballantine paper $5.99 (0-345-36899-1). Five original stories by the author of the popular Pern series offer a glimpse into the early history of the Dragonriders. (Rev: BL 9/1/93; VOYA 4/94)

4370 McCaffrey, Anne. *The Crystal Singer* (10–12). 1985, Ballantine paper $6.99 (0-345-32786-1). This novel involves a crystal singer from the Planet Ballybran and the young girl he influences. (Rev: BL 12/15/87)

4371 McCaffrey, Anne. *Dinosaur Planet Survivors* (9–12). 1984, Ballantine paper $5.99 (0-345-27246-3). After 43 years of suspended animation, the two central characters of the author's earlier *Dinosaur Planet* (1978) awake to find their beloved planet is again in danger. (Rev: BL 1/15/85)

4372 McCaffrey, Anne. *The Dolphins of Pern* (9–12). Series: Pern. 1995, Ballantine paper $6.99 (0-345-36895-9). Young Dragonrider T'lion rebuilds the world of Pern's ancient relationship with the "shipfish," dolphins that came to Pern with its early human settlers. (Rev: BL 9/15/94; VOYA 2/95)

4373 McCaffrey, Anne. *Dragonflight* (9–12). 1981, Ballantine $8.95 (0-345-27749-X); paper $6.99 (0-345-33546-5). This is the first volume of the author's popular Dragonriders of Pern series. It is followed by *Dragonquest* and *White Dragon* (both 1986).

4374 McCaffrey, Anne. *Dragonsdawn* (9–12). 1989, Ballantine paper $6.99 (0-345-36286-1). A novel that takes place before the Dragonriders of Pern series. This describes how the planet Pern was colonized and the origins of the deadly Threadfall. (Rev: BL 9/1/88; VOYA 4/89)

4375 McCaffrey, Anne. *Freedom's Landing* (9–12). 1995, Putnam paper $6.99 (0-441-00338-9). The first volume in a series about survival and cooperation on an uncharted planet. (Rev: BL 5/15/98; SLJ 8/95)

4376 McCaffrey, Anne. *A Gift of Dragons* (10–12). Illus. 2002, Del Rey $15.95 (0-345-45635-1). Four stories — one previously unpublished— set on the planet Pern are accompanied by eye-catching illustrations. (Rev: BL 10/15/02; VOYA 4/03)

4377 McCaffrey, Anne. *Killashandra* (9–12). 1985, Ultramarine $25.00 (0-89366-187-2); Ballantine paper $6.99 (0-345-31600-2). While visiting a neighboring planet, crystal singer Killashandra is kidnapped. (Rev: SLJ 2/86)

4378 McCaffrey, Anne. *Lyon's Pride* (9–12). 1995, Ace paper $6.99 (0-441-00141-6). An alliance between humans and aliens searches for creatures that destroy indigenous life forms on any planet they inhabit. (Rev: BL 1/1/94; SLJ 9/94; VOYA 10/94)

4379 McCaffrey, Anne. *Moreta: Dragonlady of Pern* (9–12). 1984, Ballantine paper $6.99 (0-345-29873-X). The dragonriders of Pern are in danger from a mutated strain of influenza. (Rev: BL 12/15/87)

4380 McCaffrey, Anne. *Pegasus in Space* (9–12). 2000, Ballantine $25.00 (0-345-43466-8). This, the third of the Pegasus novels that are prequels to the Rowan series features as its main character Peter Reidinger, a quadriplegic teenager who possesses unusual telekinetic talents. (Rev: BL 4/15/00; SLJ 8/00)

4381 McCaffrey, Anne. *The Skies of Pern* (9–12). 2001, Ballantine $25.00 (0-345-43468-4). Now that the fear of Thread has disappeared, the planet Pern faces another crisis when a massive comet crashes into the Eastern Ring Sea. Part of an excellent series. (Rev: BL 1/1–15/01)

4382 McCaffrey, Anne, and Elizabeth Ann Scarborough. *Acorna's Triumph* (9–12). 2004, HarperCollins $24.95 (0-380-97900-4). In this Acorna novel, gems used in terraforming are stolen and must be retrieved from the planet of sulfur beings. (Rev: BL 1/1–15/04)

4383 McCarthy, Wil, ed., et al. *Once Upon a Galaxy* (11–12). 2002, DAW paper $6.99 (0-7564-0091-0). Familiar fairy tales get a science fiction spin in this collection of varied stories suitable for mature teens. (Rev: BL 9/1/02)

4384 McDevitt, Jack. *Chindi* (10–12). 2002, Berkley $22.95 (0-441-00938-7). Captain Priscilla Hutchins, commanding a starship with a motley crew of amateurs, investigates alien signals. (Rev: BL 7/02)

4385 McDevitt, Jack. *Deepsix* (9–12). 2001, HarperCollins $25.00 (0-06-105124-1). While onlookers await the destruction of the planet Deepsix, Priscilla "Hutch" Hutchins leads a mission to prevent its demise. (Rev: BL 2/15/01; SLJ 8/01)

4386 McDevitt, Jack. *The Engines of God* (9–12). 1994, Berkley $21.95 (0-441-00077-0). An interstellar archeologist races to uncover the secrets of planet Quragua's alien artifacts before it is settled by humans fleeing an environmentally destroyed Earth. (Rev: BL 9/15/94; VOYA 12/94)

4387 McDevitt, Jack. *Infinity Beach* (10–12). 2000, HarperCollins $25.00 (0-06-105123-3). A mystery involving scientist Kay Brandywine on the distant planet Greenway and the disappearance of her clone-sister. (Rev: BL 2/15/00; SLJ 7/00)

4388 McDevitt, Jack. *Moonfall* (9–12). 1998, HarperCollins $24.00 (0-06-105036-9). An action-packed near-future story of disaster when a comet destroys the moon. (Rev: BL 5/15/98)

4389 Mackay, Scott. *Omnifix* (10–12). 2004, NAL paper $6.99 (0-451-45960-1). When Earth is threatened by a newly devised alien weapons platform (AWP), discredited scientist Alex Denver, who has successfully foiled AWPs in the past, is called back into service. (Rev: BL 12/1/03)

4390 Mackay, Scott. *Orbis* (10–12). 2002, NAL paper $6.99 (0-451-45874-5). The Benefactors, aliens from outer space, have been bending the truth on Earth in this alternate history that stretches back to the Roman empire. (Rev: BL 4/1/02)

4391 McKinney, Jack. *Invid Invasion* (9–12). 1987, Del Rey paper $5.99 (0-345-34143-0). Scott Bernard is battling the Invid Regis to regain Earth in this story continued in *Metamorphosis* and *Symphony of Light* (both 1987). (Rev: VOYA 4/88)

4392 MacLeod, Ken. *Dark Light* (10–12). 2002, Tor $24.95 (0-765-30302-7). This novel focuses on the humans on the planet Croatan and how they cope with other intelligent life forms. (Rev: BL 12/1/01)

4393 MacLeod, Ken. *The Sky Road* (10–12). 2000, Tor $24.95 (0-312-87335-2). There is plenty of action in this sf tale that tells two stories in alternating chapters. (Rev: BL 9/15/00)

4394 McMullen, Sean. *Eyes of the Calculor* (10–12). Series: Greenwinter. 2001, Tor $27.95 (0-312-87736-6). The chief librarian at Libris gets involved in fighting a fanatical religious movement that is becoming dangerous. (Rev: BL 9/15/01*)

4395 McMullen, Sean. *The Miocene Arrow* (10–12). 2000, Tor $27.95 (0-312-87054-X). In a futuristic United States where the people are controlled by the mysterious Call and orbiting satellites called the Sentinels, a new race suddenly appears. (Rev: BL 8/00*)

4396 Marley, Louise. *The Glass Harmonica* (7–12). 2000, Ace paper $13.95 (0-441-00729-5). In an appealing blend of science fiction, mystery, romance, and historical fiction, two related stories — one from the 18th century and the other from the not-so-distant future — feature young girls and a glass harmonica. (Rev: VOYA 2/01)

4397 Marley, Louise. *The Maquisarde* (10–12). 2002, Berkley $23.95 (0-441-00976-X). In a future Paris, Ebriel Serique and her family live happily on the "haves" sign of the Line of Partition until Ebriel's husband and daughter are killed for supposedly crossing the line. (Rev: BL 11/1/02)

4398 Marley, Louise. *Receive the Gift* (10–12). 1997, Ace paper $5.99 (0-441-00486-5). When Oho plots to take over the planet Nevya, it takes an alliance of several unlikely individuals to stop him. (Rev: VOYA 2/98)

4399 Miller, Walter M., Jr. *A Canticle for Leibowitz: A Novel* (9–12). 1960, HarperCollins paper $12.95 (0-553-37926-7). This sf classic deals with a monastery that survives an atomic war.

4400 Mixon, Laura J. *Burning the Ice* (11–12). 2002, Tor $25.95 (0-312-86903-7). An action-packed story of colonist clones in danger featuring an appealing young female character; for mature teens. (Rev: BL 8/02)

4401 Modesitt, L. E. *Chaos Balance* (10–12). 1997, St. Martin's $25.95 (0-312-86389-6); Tor paper $6.99 (0-8125-7130-4). A complex story, combining science fiction and fantasy, of the travels of Nylan and his companion, Ayrlyn, as they seek a new home and peace. This is eighth in a series of challenging novels. (Rev: BL 9/15/97; SLJ 7/98; VOYA 2/98)

4402 Modesitt, L. E. *The Octagonal Raven* (10–12). 2001, Tor $27.95 (0-312-87720-X). Because of genetic enhancement, a new class of wealthy and powerful people has emerged with its members all struggling for more power. (Rev: BL 1/1–15/01)

4403 Modesitt, L. E., Jr. *The Death of Chaos* (10–12). 1995, Tor $24.95 (0-312-85721-7). In this fifth and final volume of the Recluse series, Lerris, a woodworker and earth wizard, combats the technology-based empire of Hamor. (Rev: BL 9/1/95; VOYA 2/96)

4404 Mohan, Kim, ed. *Amazing Stories: The Anthology* (9–12). 1995, Tor paper $13.95 (0-312-89048-

6). Classic science fiction short stories. (Rev: BL 4/15/95)

4405 Moon, Elizabeth. *Remnant Population* (10–12). 1996, Baen $22.00 (0-671-87718-6). Ofelia hides when her people abandon their space colony in this novel about survival, self-esteem, and courage. (Rev: BL 4/15/96; SLJ 1/97; VOYA 10/96)

4406 Moore, James A. *Fireworks* (10–12). 2001, Meisha Merlin paper $16.00 (1-892065-40-1). When a UFO crash-lands in a town in Georgia, the nation is divided on what its fate should be. (Rev: BL 4/15/01)

4407 Morrow, James, ed. *Nebula Awards 26: SFWA's Choices for the Best Science Fiction and Fantasy of the Year* (9–12). 1992, Harcourt paper $12.95 (0-15-665472-5). The best science fiction and fantasy stories of 1990. (Rev: BL 3/15/92)

4408 Morrow, James, ed. *Nebula Awards 27: SFWA's Choices for the Best Science Fiction and Fantasy of the Year* (9–12). 1993, Harcourt $24.95 (0-15-164935-9). The best science fiction stories of 1991, including a series of tributes to Isaac Asimov. (Rev: BL 3/15/93; VOYA 10/93)

4409 Morwood, Peter. *Star Trek: Rules of Engagement* (9–12). 1990, Pocket paper $4.99 (0-671-66129-9). Kirk and the *Enterprise* are sent to evacuate personnel from a politically dangerous planet. (Rev: BL 2/15/90; VOYA 6/90)

4410 Nissenson, Hugh. *The Song of the Earth* (10–12). Illus. 2001, Algonquin $24.95 (1-56512-298-4). This book, which has been called a masterpiece, presents a mock documentary about John First Baker, one of three genetically engineered children. (Rev: BL 4/15/01*)

4411 Niven, Larry. *Ringworld* (10–12). 1981, Ballantine paper $5.99 (0-345-33392-6). In this prize-winning book, four unique characters are sent to explore a distant place called Ringworld. A sequel is *The Ringworld Engineers* (1985).

4412 Niven, Larry. *Scatterbrain* (10–12). 2003, Tor $24.95 (0-765-30137-7). Short stories, personal anecdotes, book excerpts, and commentary are just some of the features of this compelling volume. (Rev: BL 10/1/03) [823]

4413 Nix, Garth. *Shade's Children* (7–12). 1997, HarperCollins LB $15.89 (0-06-027325-9). In this science fiction novel, when a person reaches age 16, he or she is sent to the Meat Factory, where body parts are turned into hideous creatures. (Rev: BL 10/1/97; BR 3–4/98; SLJ 8/97; VOYA 6/98)

4414 Norton, Andre. *Key Out of Time* (7–12). 1978, Ultramarine $25.00 (0-89366-186-4). Two Time Agents re-create the conflict that destroyed life on the planet Hawaika.

4415 Norton, Andre. *Time Traders II* (8–12). Series: Time Traders. 2001, Baen $24.00 (0-671-31968-X).

This single volume contains two of Norton's Time Traders novellas: *Key Out of Time* and *The Defiant Agents.* (Rev: BL 2/1/01)

4416 Norton, Andre, and Martin H. Greenberg, eds. *Catfantastic* (9–12). 1989, NAL paper $6.99 (0-88677-355-5). A collection of 13 stories about cat-beings with unusual powers. (Rev: BL 7/89; VOYA 2/90)

4417 Nova, Craig. *Wetware* (10–12). 2001, Harmony $22.00 (0-609-60595-X). A lonely guy who designs wetware (not-quite-humans who are serfs) changes the genetic code and gives them intelligence and sexuality in this futuristic novel. (Rev: BL 12/1/01)

4418 Nylund, Eric. *Halo: The Fall of Reach* (10–12). 2001, Del Rey paper $6.99 (0-345-45132-5). Super-warriors, known as Spartans, face off against the forces of the Covenant in a battle that may hold the fate of humankind. (Rev: VOYA 4/02)

4419 O'Brien, Robert C. *Z for Zachariah* (7–10). 1975, Macmillan paper $4.99 (0-02-044650-0). After a nuclear holocaust, Ann believes she is the only surviving human — but is she? (Rev: BL 7/88)

4420 Oldham, June. *Found* (7–12). 1996, Orchard LB $17.99 (0-531-08893-6). In this novel set in the 21st century, Ren becomes lost in a bleak countryside, gets involved with three other misfits, and finds an abandoned baby. (Rev: BL 9/15/96; BR 3–4/97; SLJ 10/96; VOYA 2/97)

4421 Oltion, Jerry. *Abandon in Place* (10–12). 2000, Tor $24.95 (0-312-87264-X). Ghosts of the rockets that sent men to the moon are suddenly found back on the launchpad and travel into space again. (Rev: BL 11/15/00; SLJ 4/01)

4422 Oltion, Jerry. *The Getaway Special* (9–12). 2001, Tor $26.95 (0-312-87777-3). Allen and Judy, who are about to be arrested because of a misunderstanding, flee to Wyoming where friendly citizens help them build a spaceship out of a septic tank. (Rev: BL 11/1/01; SLJ 4/02)

4423 Orwell, George. *Nineteen Eighty Four* (10–12). 1950, Signet paper $6.95 (0-451-52493-4). This prophetic novel published in 1945 tells of a future world where complete mind control is practiced.

4424 Parker, Daniel. *April* (7–10). Series: Countdown. 1999, Simon & Schuster paper $3.99 (0-689-81822-X). In this fourth book in a complex series, teenagers find that they must take over the earth when a terrible plague kills everyone except those between 16 and 20 years of age. It is necessary to read all the books in sequence to follow the story. The others are *January, February,* and *March* (1999). (Rev: SLJ 6/99)

4425 Paulsen, Gary. *The Transall Saga* (7–12). 1998, Delacorte $15.95 (0-385-32196-1). While on a hiking trip, young Mark is transported to a primitive world in this science fiction novel with a strong survival theme. (Rev: BCCB 7–8/98; BL 5/15/98; BR 11–12/98; HBG 10/98; SLJ 5/98; VOYA 10/98)

4426 Peel, John. *The Zanti Misfits* (6–10). 1997, Tor paper $3.99 (0-8125-9063-5). This quick read, a product of *The Outer Limits* television show, tells how the planet Zanti sent to Earth a shipload of its worst criminals and how three teenagers wander into the landing area. Also use *The Choice* and *The Time Shifter* (both 1997). (Rev: VOYA 4/98)

4427 Pohl, Frederik. *Midas World* (10–12). 1984, Tor paper $2.95 (0-8125-4925-2). In this novel, the world's energy crisis is solved by using robots.

4428 Pohl, Frederik, ed. *The SFWA Grand Masters, v.2* (9–12). 2000, Tor $25.95 (0-312-86879-0). This second anthology of short works by Grand Master Nebula Award winners includes stories by Andre Norton, Arthur C. Clarke, and Ray Bradbury. (Rev: BL 3/1/00)

4429 Pohl, Frederik, and Jack Williamson. *Land's End* (9–12). 1989, Tor paper $4.95 (0-8125-0024-5). A meteor shower wakens an alien asleep on the ocean bottom. (Rev: BL 8/88; VOYA 2/89)

4430 Pratchett, Terry. *The Last Hero* (9–12). Illus. Series: Discworld. 2001, HarperCollins $35.00 (0-06-104096-7). With 90 color illustrations, this is another science fiction adventure involving the possible end of the world. (Rev: BL 9/15/01)

4431 Price, Susan. *The Sterkarm Handshake* (7–10). 2000, HarperCollins LB $17.89 (0-06-029392-6). Violent confrontations result when a 21st-century corporation makes inroads into the 16th-century Scottish Borders. (Rev: BL 10/1/00; BR 3–4/01; HBG 3/01; SLJ 12/00)

4432 Randle, Kevin D. *Operation Roswell* (10–12). 2002, Tor $25.95 (0-312-86710-7). A novelized account of the strange goings-on in Roswell in the late 1940s. (Rev: BL 9/15/02)

4433 Reed, Robert. *Marrow* (10–12). 2000, Tor $25.95 (0-312-86801-4). The Ship, on a journey of eons through the universe, is now in the Milky Way and a team must leave it to explore the surface of a dangerous planet. (Rev: BL 9/1/00)

4434 Reeve, Philip. *Mortal Engines* (7–10). 2003, HarperCollins LB $17.89 (0-06-008208-9). An imaginative story of cities on the rampage — London is seeking to devour smaller towns to fuel its ability to move about — and the brave youngsters who resist. (Rev: BL 11/1/03; HB 11–12/03; HBG 4/04; SLJ 12/03*)

4435 Resnick, Mike. *Kirinyaga: A Fable of Utopia* (10–12). 1998, Del Rey $25.00 (0-345-41701-1). Set in the 22nd century, Koriba, a well-educated man, tries to save his utopian planetoid society by reinstating the ancient customs and strict laws of his Kikuyu ancestors of Kenya, but in spite of the best

intentions, it appears his efforts will fail. (Rev: BL 2/15/98; SLJ 3/99; VOYA 10/98)

4436 Ringo, John. *Gust Front* (10–12). 2001, Baen $24.00 (0-671-31976-0). From the author of *A Hymn Before Battle* (2000) comes this novel about the attack on an unprepared Earth by the reptilian Posleen. (Rev: BL 3/15/01)

4437 Ringo, John. *A Hymn Before Battle* (10–12). 2000, Baen $24.00 (0-671-31941-8). For the sake of Earth's allies, Michael O'Shea leads an infantry troop against the deadly Posleen in this violent, exciting novel. (Rev: BL 10/15/00)

4438 Roberts, Adam. *Salt* (11–12). 2002, Gollancz paper $14.95 (0-57506-897-3). Two tribes of Earth colonists battle over intermarriage on their new planet, a land of salty deserts; for mature teens. (Rev: BL 2/15/02)

4439 Robinson, Spider. *God Is an Iron and Other Stories* (10–12). 2002, Five Star $24.95 (0-7862-4162-4). A collection of short stories including the award-winning "Stardance," cowritten by Robinson's wife. (Rev: BL 5/1/02)

4440 Rubenstein, Gillian. *Galax-Arena* (7–10). 1995, Simon & Schuster paper $15.00 (0-689-80136-X). A 13-year-old girl and 20 other children from Earth are removed to another planet and trained to perform dangerous acrobatic tricks. (Rev: BL 10/15/95*; SLJ 10/95)

4441 Rucker, Rudy. *Frek and the Elixir* (9–12). 2004, Tor $27.95 (0-765-31058-9). Frek, an average kid, is taken on a tour of the galaxy when the alien starship Anvil takes him aboard. (Rev: BL 4/1/04)

4442 Rusch, Kristine Kathryn. *Stories for an Enchanted Afternoon* (9–12). 2001, Golden Gryphon $24.95 (1-930846-02-9). These 11 stories exploring alternate worlds and other eerie situations give readers an opportunity to sample this fine young writer's work. (Rev: BL 4/15/01)

4443 Russell, Eric Frank. *Entities: The Selected Novels of Eric Frank Russell* (10–12). Ed. by Rick Katze. 2001, NESFA $29.00 (1-886778-33-7). This anthology contains five novels by one of the great pioneers of science fiction. (Rev: BL 11/15/01)

4444 Saberhagen, Fred. *Berserker Prime* (9–12). 2004, Tor $25.95 (0-765-30625-5). The people of the Twin Worlds meet the challenge of the Berserkers, who kidnap humans and reprogram them into collaborators. (Rev: BL 1/1–15/04)

4445 Sagan, Nick. *Idlewild* (10–12). 2003, Putnam $23.95 (0-399-15097-8). Murder, virtual reality, computer hacking, and a deadly plague are just some of the facets of this multilayered story featuring a youthful protagonist named Halloween. (Rev: BL 6/1–15/03)

4446 Sargent, Pamela. *Alien Child* (8–12). 1988, HarperCollins $13.95 (0-06-025202-2). A teenage girl raised in an alien world discovers there is another human living in her complex. (Rev: BL 2/1/88; BR 9–10/88; SLJ 4/88; VOYA 8/88)

4447 Sargent, Pamela, ed. *Nebula Awards 29: SFWA's Choices for the Best Science Fiction and Fantasy of the Year* (9–12). 1995, Harcourt paper $17.00 (0-15-600119-5). A collection of prize-winning science fiction and fantasy stories for the year 1993. (Rev: BL 4/15/95; SLJ 10/95)

4448 Sargent, Pamela, ed. *Women of Wonder: The Classic Years: Science Fiction by Women from the 1940s to the 1970s* (9–12). 1995, Harcourt paper $15.00 (0-15-600031-8). The first of two volumes updating the previous three out-of-print *Women of Wonder* titles. Includes 21 stories and a perceptive introductory overview of women in science fiction. (Rev: BL 8/95)

4449 Sargent, Pamela, ed. *Women of Wonder: The Contemporary Years: Science Fiction by Women from the 1970s to the 1990s* (9–12). 1995, Harcourt paper $15.00 (0-15-600033-4). The second of two volumes updating the out-of-print *Women of Wonder* titles includes 21 stories published between 1978 and 1993, with suggestions for further reading. (Rev: BL 8/95)

4450 Sarrantonio, Al, ed. *Redshift: Extreme Visions of Speculative Fiction* (10–12). 2001, NAL $24.95 (0-451-45859-1). For mature readers (some stories contain sex and violence), this is an excellent collection of speculative fiction by such writers as Joyce Carol Oates, Larry Niven, and Ursula Le Guin. (Rev: BL 11/1/01*)

4451 Sawyer, Robert I. *Hybrids* (11–12). Series: Neanderthal Parallax. 2003, Tor $24.95 (0-312-87690-4). The challenge of conceiving a human-Neanderthal child is surrounded by technological and ethical questions in this thought-provoking finale to the trilogy that began with *Hominids* (2002). (Rev: BL 9/1/03*)

4452 Sawyer, Robert J. *Calculating God* (10–12). 2000, Tor $23.95 (0-312-86713-1). Ethical and spiritual questions are presented in this adventure about aliens who arrive on Earth from a planet whose history is amazingly like ours. (Rev: BL 4/15/00)

4453 Sawyer, Robert J. *Humans* (10–12). 2003, Tor $24.95 (0-312-87691-2). Best suited for mature teens because of its sexual content, this sequel to *Hominids* reunites Neanderthal physicist Ponter Boddit with his human friend, Mary Vaughn, who pays him a visit in his Neanderthal universe. (Rev: BL 1/1–15/03)

4454 Sawyer, Robert J. *Illegal Alien* (10–12). 1997, Ace paper $21.95 (0-441-00476-8). Science fiction and a legal thriller are combined in this novel in which a popular astronomer and TV personality is found horribly murdered after a disabled alien

spacecraft lands on an aircraft carrier he's on in the middle of the ocean. (Rev: VOYA 8/98)

4455 Scarborough, Elizabeth Ann. *Scarborough Faire and Other Stories* (11–12). 2003, Five Star $25.95 (0-7862-5053-4). A collection of science fiction stories by this Nebula award winner, some lighthearted and others more serious, several of which feature cats. (Rev: BL 2/15/03)

4456 Schroeder, Karl. *Permanence* (10–12). 2002, Tor $27.95 (0-765-30371-X). Young Rue's discovery of an unclaimed starship places her in the center of interstellar intrigue. (Rev: BL 4/15/02; SLJ 9/02)

4457 Schroeder, Karl. *Ventus* (9–12). 2000, Tor $27.95 (0-312-87197-X). A stoneworker who lives on the planet Ventus discovers that he is seeing life through another man's eyes in this absorbing fantasy. (Rev: BL 12/15/00*)

4458 Scott, Melissa. *The Jazz* (10–12). 2000, Tor $23.95 (0-312-86802-2). Tin Lizzy decides she will help Keyz, a teen hacker, fight a paranoid film executive in this sf novel set in various cyberconnected locales. (Rev: BL 5/15/00)

4459 Shatner, William. *Beyond the Stars* (10–12). 2000, HarperCollins $24.00 (0-06-105118-7). This novel, the fourth in the author's adult science fiction series, tells of Jim Endicott's adventures aboard the intergalactic colony ship *Outward Bound*. (Rev: BL 1/1–15/00)

4460 Sheffield, Charles. *Cold As Ice* (9–12). 1993, Tor paper $4.99 (0-8125-1163-8). Nine sleeping infants nestled in pods and ejected from a doomed ship grow up to become the key to an extraordinary race. (Rev: BL 6/15/92*)

4461 Sheffield, Charles. *Godspeed* (9–12). 1994, Tor $4.99 (0-8125-1992-2). Teenager Jay Hara falls into a space voyage to find the Godspeed Drive, which would make interstellar travel possible and bring Jay's home planet out of isolation. (Rev: BL 11/15/93; VOYA 4/94)

4462 Sheffield, Charles. *The Lady Vanishes and Other Oddities of Nature* (10–12). 2002, Five Star $24.95 (0-7862-4169-1). A collection of recent short stories drawing on physics. (Rev: BL 5/1/02)

4463 Sheffield, Charles. *Putting Up Roots: A Jupiter Novel* (9–12). 1997, Tor $21.95 (0-312-86241-5). Fourteen-year-old Josh and an autistic girl his age, Dawn, are sold into service to a company that has a farming franchise on the planet Solferino. (Rev: BL 8/97; VOYA 2/98)

4464 Sheffield, Charles. *Resurgence* (10–12). 2002, Baen $24.00 (0-7434-3567-2). A motley crew of investigators set off through a wormhole to investigate mysterious galactic events that seem to be related to vanished race of Builders. (Rev: BL 11/1/02)

4465 Sheffield, Charles. *The Spheres of Heaven* (10–12). 2001, Baen $24.00 (0-671-31969-8). Set 20 years after *The Mind Pool* (1993), this novel finds humanity still quarantined by the nonhuman Stellar Authority because of the deaths of other intelligent life forms. (Rev: BL 2/15/01)

4466 Shelley, Mary. *Frankenstein* (8–12). Illus. Series: Whole Story. 1998, Viking $25.99 (0-670-87800-6). Illustrations plus period prints and maps enhance this complete version of the early science fiction thriller. (Rev: BL 9/1/98; HBG 9/99; SLJ 10/98)

4467 Shetterly, Will. *Chimera* (10–12). 2000, Tor $23.95 (0-312-86630-5). This cyberthriller deals with gene-splicing procedures that have produced human-shaped beings called Chimeras with enormous strength. (Rev: BL 8/00; VOYA 2/01)

4468 Shinn, Sharon. *Jenna Starborn* (7–12). 2002, Ace paper $14.95 (0-441-00900-X). A far-future retelling of *Jane Eyre* in which Jenna Starborn, the unwanted product of a gen-tank, falls in love with the master of Thorrastone Park. (Rev: BL 4/1/02; VOYA 8/02)

4469 Shusterman, Neal. *Shattered Sky* (10–12). Series: Star Shards Chronicles. 2002, Tor $25.95 (0-312-85508-7). In the concluding volume of the series, the six Star Shards — two of whom are dead, must reunite to combat an alien force; for mature teens. (Rev: BL 5/15/02*; VOYA 12/02)

4470 Shwartz, Susan. *Second Chances* (10–12). 2001, Tor $24.95 (0-312-87342-5). This military science fiction saga borrows both characters and themes from the writings of Joseph Conrad in its account of a young war veteran's efforts to redeem himself after abandoning his space ship. (Rev: BL 7/01; VOYA 10/01)

4471 Silver, Steven H., and Martin H. Greenberg, eds. *Wondrous Beginnings* (10–12). 2003, DAW paper $6.99 (0-7564-0098-8). A collection of 22 of the first published stories of well-known writers, including Hall Clement, Murray Leinster, Orson Scott Card, Jack McDevitt, and Stephen Baxter. (Rev: BL 1/1–15/03)

4472 Silverberg, Robert. *Lord Valentine's Castle* (10–12). 1995, HarperCollins paper $6.50 (0-06-105487-9). A young amnesiac slowly realizes that he is the real Lord Valentine, ruler of his planet. Sequels in this series are *Majipoor Chronicles* and *Valentine Pontifex* (both 1983).

4473 Silverberg, Robert, ed. *Nebula Awards Showcase, 2001* (10–12). 2001, Harcourt $28.00 (0-15-100581-8); paper $14.00 (0-15-601335-5). Several short stories, and excerpts from other winning works, are presented in this tribute to the 2001 winners of this coveted science fiction award. (Rev: BL 3/15/01)

4474 Silverberg, Robert. *Phases of the Moon: Stories of Six Decades* (9–12). 2004, Subterranean $40.00 (1-931081-99-9). Covering the author's short fiction output for almost 50 years, this a fine collection that can serve as an introduction to the many talents of this sf writer. (Rev: BL 5/15/04)

4475 Silverberg, Robert, ed. *Robert Silverberg's Worlds of Wonder: Exploring the Craft of Science Fiction* (9–12). 1987, Warner $12.95 (0-446-39012-7). A collection of short science fiction plus a guide to science fiction writing. (Rev: BL 10/1/87; VOYA 2/88)

4476 Simmons, Dan. *Worlds Enough and Time* (10–12). 2002, Subterranean $40.00 (1-931081-54-9). Four stories and a screen treatment are accompanied by insightful introductions by the author. (Rev: BL 5/1/02)

4477 Sleator, William. *The Boy Who Reversed Himself* (8–12). 1998, Puffin paper $5.99 (0-14-038965-2). Laura travels into the fourth dimension with her gifted neighbor and literally everything in her life becomes upside-down. (Rev: BL 10/15/86; BR 5–6/87; SLJ 11/86; VOYA 6/87)

4478 Sleator, William. *The Duplicate* (7–10). 1990, Bantam paper $3.99 (0-553-28634-X). A teenager discovers a machine that allows him the power to duplicate himself. (Rev: BL 5/15/88; SLJ 4/88; VOYA 12/88)

4479 Sleator, William. *House of Stairs* (7–10). 1991, Puffin paper $5.99 (0-14-034580-9). Five teenage orphans are kidnapped to become part of an experiment on aggression.

4480 Sleator, William. *Interstellar Pig* (7–10). 1996, Peter Smith $20.75 (0-8446-6898-2); Puffin paper $6.99 (0-14-037595-3). Barney plays an odd board game with strangers who are actually aliens from space.

4481 Sleator, William. *Parasite Pig* (7–10). 2002, Dutton $15.99 (0-525-46918-4). Barney and Katie continue playing the board game they began in *Interstellar Pig* and wind up on a planet called J'koot, threatened by crablike aliens with cannibal tendencies. (Rev: BCCB 2/03; BL 11/15/02; HB 11–12/02*; HBG 3/03; SLJ 10/02; VOYA 12/02)

4482 Sleator, William. *Singularity* (7–12). 1995, Puffin paper $5.99 (0-14-037598-8). Twin boys discover a playhouse on the property they have inherited that contains a mystery involving monsters from space and a new dimension in time. (Rev: BL 4/1/85; SLJ 8/85)

4483 Smith, Mitchell. *Kingdom River* (11–12). 2003, Tor $25.95 (0-765-30008-7). This post-apocalyptic tale features violence and political intrigue in a North America that has suffered a new ice age. (Rev: BL 5/15/03*)

4484 Smith, Mitchell. *Moonrise* (9–12). 2004, Tor $25.95 (0-765-30009-5). Finishing the trilogy begun in *Snowfall* (2002) and *Kingdom River* (2003), this novel describes a future ice age when Earth's population is divided into tribes and ruled by a feudal nobility. (Rev: BL 4/1/04)

4485 Stabenow, Dana. *Red Planet Run* (9–12). 1995, Berkley paper $5.50 (0-441-00135-1). The feisty heroine, Star Svensdottir, and her twins experience a series of fast-paced adventures, beginning with trouble over the design of an asteroid being turned into a space habitat. (Rev: BL 1/1/95; VOYA 5/95)

4486 Stableford, Brian. *Dark Ararat* (10–12). 2002, Tor $25.95 (0-765-30168-7). Colonists on a distant planet must solve a murder and decide whether their new home is truly habitable in this fifth volume in Stableford's future history. (Rev: BL 3/1/02)

4487 Stackpole, Michael A. *I, Jedi* (8–12). 1998, Random paper $6.99 (0-553-57873-1). In order to find his wife, Corran must take a quick course at the Jedi Academy founded by Luke Skywalker and learn to use his hidden powers. (Rev: VOYA 12/98)

4488 Stasheff, Christopher. *A Wizard and a Warlord* (10–12). 2000, Tor $22.95 (0-312-86649-6). Another adventure novel about the interstellar traveler Magnus d'Armand. This time he and his friend Alea journey to a utopian universe. (Rev: BL 2/1/00; VOYA 6/00)

4489 Stasheff, Christopher. *A Wizard in a Feud* (10–12). 2001, Tor $22.95 (0-312-86674-7). Heroes Gar Pike and Alea travel to help a planet where basically decent people can't stop feuding. (Rev: BL 6/1–15/01; VOYA 12/01)

4490 Stasheff, Christopher. *A Wizard in the Way* (10–12). 2000, Tor $22.95 (0-312-86648-8). In this installment of a popular series, troubleshooter Magnus d'Armand and his companion Alea go to the distant planet Oldeira. (Rev: BL 9/1/00; VOYA 4/01)

4491 Steele, Allen. *ChronoSpace* (10–12). 2001, Berkley $22.95 (0-441-00832-1). In the year 2314, a group of scientists who have learned to travel into the past via wormholes crash-land in 1998. (Rev: BL 4/15/01)

4492 Steele, Allen. *Coyote: A Novel of Interstellar Exploration* (10–12). 2002, Berkley $23.95 (0-441-00974-3). The planet Coyote becomes home to colonists, led by Captain Robert E. Lee, who have abandoned planet Earth. (Rev: BL 10/15/02)

4493 Steele, Allen. *The Jericho Iteration* (9–12). 1994, Berkley paper $19.95 (0-441-00097-5). In 2012, a reporter uncovers the militaristic Emergency Relief Agency's scheme to use an antimissile satellite to stop civilian unrest and implement martial law. (Rev: BL 10/1/94; VOYA 12/94)

4494 Steele, Allen. *Oceanspace* (10–12). 2000, Berkley $21.95 (0-441-00685-X). This dramatic, suspenseful plot deals with the launching of an inhabited underwater research facility and the enemies who plot to prevent its use. (Rev: BL 2/15/00)

4495 Stemp, Jane. *Waterbound* (6–10). 1996, Dial $15.99 (0-8037-1994-9). Gem, who lives in a tightly controlled culture of the future, discovers another world where the misfits are kept. (Rev: BL 8/96; BR 3–4/97; SLJ 9/96; VOYA 8/97)

4496 Stewart, George R. *Earth Abides* (10–12). 1993, Buccaneer LB $29.95 (0-89969-370-3); Fawcett paper $6.99 (0-449-21301-3). A classic about a group of people who survive a catastrophe that almost destroys the Earth.

4497 Tenn, William. *Here Comes Civilization: The Complete Science Fiction of William Tenn.* v.2 (10–12). Ed. by James A. Mann and Mary C. Tabasko. 2001, NESFA $29.00 (1-886778-28-0). As well as a collection of classic sf by this master, there are tributes to him in this volume by such writers as Robert Silverberg and George Zebrowski. (Rev: BL 10/15/01)

4498 Tenn, William. *Immodest Proposals: The Complete Science Fiction of William Tenn.* v.1 (10–12). Ed. by James A. Mann and Mary C. Tabasko. 2001, NESFA $29.00 (1-886778-19-1). For older readers, this is a collection of 33 ingenious, entertaining science fiction pieces by one of the masters. (Rev: BL 4/15/01)

4499 Tepper, Sheri S. *The Visitor* (10–12). 2002, HarperCollins $25.95 (0-380-97905-5). A chilling tale about an asteroid strike on earth in the 21st century and how this event changes a woman's life a thousand years later. (Rev: BL 12/1/01; SLJ 6/02)

4500 Thompson, Julian. *Goofbang Value Daze* (9–12). 1989, Scholastic paper $12.95 (0-590-41946-3). In a high school of the future, the students are being unfairly dictated to by the administrators. (Rev: BL 3/1/89; SLJ 2/89; VOYA 6/89)

4501 Thomsen, Brian M., and Martin H. Greenberg, eds. *Oceans of Space* (10–12). 2002, DAW paper $6.99 (0-7564-0063-5). Space pirates and intrepid explorers are the focus of many of this lighthearted collection of short stories. (Rev: BL 3/1/02)

4502 Thomson, Amy. *The Color of Distance* (10–12). 1995, Ace paper $13.00 (0-441-00244-7). Biologist/space explorer Juna, the lone human survivor on a strange, rain forest planet inhabited by the Tendu — intelligent, tree-dwelling amphibian creatures — must almost totally transform herself and assimilate into Tendu society. (Rev: VOYA 4/96)

4503 Tolan, Stephanie S. *Welcome to the Ark* (7–10). 1996, Morrow $15.00 (0-688-13724-5). Science fiction and adventure combine in the story of four young people who are able to act for good or evil through telecommunications. (Rev: BL 10/15/96; BR 11–12/96; SLJ 10/96; VOYA 4/97)

4504 Townsend, John Rowe. *The Creatures* (7–10). 1980, HarperCollins $12.95 (0-397-31864-2). Earth is dominated by creatures from another planet who believe in mind over emotion.

4505 Turtledove, Harry. *Colonization: Aftershocks* (10–12). 2001, Ballantine $26.00 (0-345-43021-2). This is the last installment of the author's recommended, highly entertaining Worldwar alternate-history saga. (Rev: BL 11/15/00)

4506 Turtledove, Harry. *Colonization: Down to Earth* (10–12). 2000, Ballantine $26.00 (0-345-43020-4). In this exciting slice of alternate history, Earth is invaded during World War II by colonizing aliens known as Lizards. (Rev: BL 1/1–15/00)

4507 Turtledove, Harry. *The Great War: American Front* (10–12). Series: The Great War. 1998, Del Rey $25.00 (0-345-40615-X). An alternate history set during the early 20th century, at the outbreak of World War I, in which Teddy Roosevelt allies his supporters with Germany and Woodrow Wilson joins with France and Great Britain, bringing a divided nation into trench warfare on U.S. soil. (Rev: BL 4/15/98*; SLJ 3/99; VOYA 12/98)

4508 Turtledove, Harry, and Martin H. Greenberg, eds. *The Best Alternate History Stories of the 20th Century* (10–12). 2001, Del Rey paper $18.00 (0-345-43990-2). This is a superb collection of 14 stories that make a fine introduction to the alternate history genre. (Rev: BL 9/15/01; SLJ 3/02; VOYA 2/02)

4509 Turtledove, Harry, and Martin H. Greenberg, eds. *The Best Military Science Fiction of the 20th Century* (10–12). 2001, Del Rey paper $18.00 (0-345-43989-9). Thirteen science fiction stories with military themes by such writers as Orson Scott Card and Anne McCaffrey are included in this anthology. (Rev: BL 3/15/01)

4510 Ure, Jean. *Plague* (7–12). 1991, Harcourt $16.95 (0-15-262429-5); Puffin paper $4.99 (0-14-036283-5). Three teenagers must band together to survive in a hostile, nearly deserted London after a catastrophe has killed almost everyone. (Rev: BL 11/15/91*; SLJ 10/91)

4511 Van Lustbader, Eric. *Mistress of the Pearl* (10–12). Series: Pearl. 2004, Tor $27.95 (0-312-87237-2). *The Ring of the Five Dragons* (2001) and *The Veil of a Thousand Tears* (2002) precede this Pearl novel about two races in conflict: the invading V'ornn and the peaceful Kundalan. (Rev: BL 3/1/04*)

4512 Van Pelt, James. *Strangers and Beggars* (10–12). 2002, Fairwood paper $17.99 (0-9668184-5-8). The appealing and diverse stories in this collection offer science fiction combined with fantasy, mystery, and horror. (Rev: BL 7/02; VOYA 6/03)

4513 Verne, Jules. *Master of the World* (9–12). 1979, Amereon $20.95 (0-89190-518-9). A scientist who has invented an amazing machine claims he is the master of the world. Originally published in 1904. Also use other Verne novels including *Round the Moon* and *From the Earth to the Moon*.

4514 Vinge, Joan D. *Psion* (9–12). 1996, Warner paper $5.99 (0-446-60354-6). A 16-year-old boy named Cat finds the gift of telepathy a mixed blessing.

4515 Vinge, Vernor. *The Collected Stories of Vernor Vinge* (10–12). 2002, Tor $27.95 (0-312-87373-5). This is an excellent collection of stories written mostly in the 60s and 70s by one of the masters. (Rev: BL 12/15/01*)

4516 Vonnegut, Kurt. *Cat's Cradle* (10–12). 1987, Delta paper $12.95 (0-385-33348-X). A mordantly humorous novel about a mythical island and the discovery of a weapon more powerful than the nuclear bomb.

4517 Waugh, Charles G., and Martin H. Greenberg, eds. *Sci-Fi Private Eye* (9–12). 1997, Roc paper $5.99 (0-451-45582-4). Most of the nine stories in this collection, by such writers as Donald Westlake, Robert Silverberg, and Philip K. Dick, are mysteries with a science fiction twist. (Rev: VOYA 10/97)

4518 Weber, David. *Ashes of Victory* (10–12). 2000, Baen $24.00 (0-671-57854-5). This Honor Harrington novel continues the war between the Star Kingdom and the People's Republic of Haven. (Rev: BL 3/1/00)

4519 Weber, David. *The Excalibur Alternative* (10–12). 2002, Baen $21.00 (0-671-31860-8). Sir George Wincester with his company and family are transported from 1346 to the future, where they become slaves on primitive planets. (Rev: BL 12/1/01)

4520 Weber, David. *Honor Among Enemies* (9–12). 1996, Baen $21.00 (0-671-87723-2). Captain Honor Harrington is brought out of retirement by the Royal Manticoran Navy to lead a task force of interstellar vessels against pirates who are plundering merchant ships and ravaging their crews. (Rev: BL 6/1–15/96; VOYA 12/96)

4521 Weber, David, and John Ringo. *March to the Sea* (10–12). 2001, Baen $24.00 (0-671-31826-8). In this sequel to *March Upcountry* (2001), Prince Roger and his marines must blast their way across alien landscapes to the planet's only spaceport. (Rev: BL 7/01)

4522 Weber, David, and John Ringo. *March to the Stars* (10–12). 2003, Baen $26.00 (0-7434-3562-1). Prince Roger McClintock stars in another epic battle of good against evil that will appeal to military science fiction fans. (Rev: BL 1/1–15/03)

4523 Weber, David, and John Ringo. *March Upcountry* (9–12). 2001, Baen $24.00 (0-671-31985-X). Prince Roger is sent on a war mission, but his ship is sabotaged and he makes a landing on a disputed planet. (Rev: BL 4/15/01*)

4524 Weis, Margaret, ed. *A Magic-Lover's Treasury of the Fantastic* (9–12). 1998, Warner paper $13.99 (0-446-67284-X). Twenty stories of science fiction and fantasy by such well-known writers as Katherine Kurtz, Orson Scott Card, and Robert Silverberg. (Rev: VOYA 10/98)

4525 Wells, H. G. *First Men in the Moon* (7–12). 1993, Tuttle paper $7.95 (0-460-87304-0). The first men on the moon discover strange creatures living there.

4526 Wells, H. G. *The Food of the Gods* (10–12). 1978, Pendulum paper $2.95 (0-88301-314-2). This novel is set in a land where people do not stop growing.

4527 Wells, H. G. *In the Days of the Comet* (10–12). 1999, Troll paper $2.95 (0-89375-704-7). The world changes as a result of gases emitted by an approaching comet.

4528 Wells, H. G. *The Invisible Man* (8–12). 1987, Buccaneer LB $21.95 (0-89966-377-X); Bantam paper $4.95 (0-553-21353-9). Two editions of many available of the story of a scientist who finds a way to make himself invisible.

4529 Wells, H. G. *Island of Doctor Moreau* (9–12). 1983, Buccaneer LB $16.95 (0-89966-470-9); NAL paper $4.95 (0-451-52191-9). A shipwrecked sailor arrives at an island where strange experiments are taking place.

4530 Wells, H. G. *Time Machine* (7–12). 1984, Bantam paper $4.95 (0-553-21351-2). This is one of the earliest novels to use traveling through time as its subject.

4531 Wells, H. G. *The War of the Worlds* (7–12). 1988, Bantam paper $4.95 (0-553-21338-5). In this early science fiction novel, first published in 1898, strange creatures from Mars invade England.

4532 Westerfeld, Scott. *The Killing of Worlds* (10–12). 2003, Tor $25.95 (0-765-30850-9). In this sequel to *The Risen Empire,* Westerfeld recounts the climactic conflict between cyborg forces and humans, led by Captain Laurent Zia. (Rev: BL 9/15/03)

4533 White, James. *The First Protector* (10–12). 2000, Tor $23.95 (0-312-84890-0). This science fiction epic combines Irish folklore, aliens known as Taelons, some romance, and a great deal of hearty adventure. (Rev: BL 1/1–15/00)

4534 Williams, Liz. *The Ghost Sister* (10–12). 2001, Bantam paper $5.99 (0-553-58374-3). Ethical questions are presented in this story about genetic engineering and a girl who is to be killed because she is different. (Rev: BL 5/15/01; VOYA 12/01)

4535 Williams, Walter Jon. *Star Wars: The New Jedi Order: Destiny's Way* (10–12). 2002, Del Rey $25.95 (0-345-42850-1). A complex story featuring familiar characters, political intrigue, and tough ethical choices. (Rev: VOYA 4/03)

4536 Williamson, Jack. *The Black Sun* (9–12). 1997, Tor $23.95 (0-312-85937-6). Carlos Mondragon, who always dreamed of space travel, stows away on the last of the quantum-wave starships. (Rev: VOYA 8/97)

4537 Williamson, Jack. *Terraforming Earth* (9–12). 2001, Tor $24.95 (0-312-87200-3). A sf adventure in which an asteroid has wiped out nearly all life on Earth except for a few survivors who are in a Moon colony. (Rev: BL 5/15/01)

4538 Willis, Connie. *Impossible Things* (9–12). 1994, Bantam paper $6.50 (0-553-56436-6). In this second collection of her science fiction short stories, Willis presents 11 works, including award-winning "The Last of the Winnebagos," "Even the Queen," and "At the Rialto." (Rev: BL 12/15/93*; SLJ 3/95; VOYA 6/94)

4539 Willis, Connie, and Sheila Williams, eds. *A Woman's Liberation: A Choice of Futures by and About Women* (10–12). 2001, Warner paper $12.95 (0-446-67742-6). A recommended collection of speculative fiction by such women writers as Anne McCaffrey and Ursula Le Guin. (Rev: BL 8/01; VOYA 12/01)

4540 Wilson, F. Paul, and Matthew J. Costello. *Masque* (9–12). 1998, Warner $23.00 (0-446-51977-4). A high-tech adventure set in 2058 in which Kaze Glom secret agent Tristan, who is a mime — a cloned human being who can be transformed into a genetic copy of any human or creature — is tricked into bringing back a virus that destroys the Kaze Glom's entire mime population. (Rev: VOYA 8/98)

4541 Wilson, Robert Charles. *Blind Lake* (10–12). 2003, Tor $24.95 (0-765-30262-4). A riveting story of cutting-edge technology and suspenseful adventure in a research facility studying aliens on a far-off planet. (Rev: BL 8/03)

4542 Wolfe, Gene. *In Green's Jungles* (10–12). 2000, Tor $24.95 (0-312-87315-8). In this sequel to *On Blue's Waters* (1999), Horn is taken into the household of Duko and becomes the military adviser in their fight against the blood-drinking Fava. (Rev: BL 8/00; VOYA 2/01)

4543 Wolfe, Gene. *On Blue's Waters* (10–12). Series: Book of the Short Sun. 1999, Tor $24.95 (0-312-86614-3). Papermaker Horn abandons his job and embarks on a voyage in search of legendary leader Patera Silk. (Rev: BL 10/15/99; VOYA 6/00)

4544 Wolfe, Gene. *Return to the Whorl* (10–12). Series: Book of the Short Sun. 2001, Tor $25.95 (0-312-87314-X). Intriguing characters and humorous situations are found in this volume about Horn, the narrator, who is searching for the venerated Patera Silk. (Rev: BL 2/15/01)

4545 Wollheim, Elizabeth R., and Sheila E. Gilbert, eds. *30th Anniversary DAW Science Fiction* (10–12). 2002, DAW $24.95 (0-7564-0064-3). A collection of short stories by well-known science fiction writers. (Rev: BL 5/1/02)

4546 Wyndham, John. *The Day of the Triffids* (10–12). 1985, Ballantine paper $5.99 (0-345-32817-5). A combined science fiction and horror story about flesh-eating plants that cause havoc on Earth.

4547 Yolen, Jane, ed. *Xanadu* (9–12). 1994, Tor paper $4.99 (0-8125-2082-3). An anthology of sci-fi tales and poems, many with youthful protagonists and situations. Also use *Xanadu 2* and *Xanadu 3*. (Rev: BL 1/15/93; VOYA 8/93)

4548 Zahn, Timothy. *Angelmass* (10–12). 2001, Tor $27.95 (0-312-87828-1). A young academic gets involved in espionage and an aggressive empire that has an impressive flagship. (Rev: BL 9/15/01)

4549 Zahn, Timothy. *Dragon and Thief* (9–12). Series: Dragonback. 2003, Tor paper $24.95 (0-765-30124-5). In this fast-paced first volume in a series, 14-year-old orphan Jack and a dragonlike warrior band together to clear Jack of a crime he did not commit. (Rev: BL 2/15/03; VOYA 8/03)

4550 Zelazny, Roger. *A Dark Traveling* (9–12). 1987, Avon paper $3.50 (0-380-70567-2). A fast-moving plot about parallel worlds highlights this Hugo Award-winning novella. (Rev: BL 4/1/87; SLJ 8/87; VOYA 8/87)

4551 Zelazny, Roger. *Knight of Shadows* (10–12). 1990, Avon paper $5.99 (0-380-75501-7). This is the ninth book in the Amber series about a modern Merlin. (Rev: BL 10/15/89)

4552 Zettel, Sarah. *Kingdom of Cages* (10–12). 2001, Warner $24.95 (0-446-52491-3). When Pandora is the only Earth-colonized world to survive a deadly plague, genetic wizards come to find its secrets. (Rev: BL 7/01)

4553 Zettel, Sarah. *Quiet Invasion* (10–12). 2000, Warner $24.00 (0-446-52489-1). A colony of Venus and a conflict between humans and aliens are the subjects of this tension-filled adult yarn featuring scientist Helen Failia. (Rev: BL 1/1–15/00; VOYA 4/00)

4554 Zicree, Marc Scott, and Barbara Hambly. *Magic Time* (10–12). 2001, HarperCollins $25.00 (0-06-105068-7). When the Source is opened, all modern technology, including electricity, fails and New York lawyer Cal Griffin works to find the source of the chaos. (Rev: BL 10/15/01; VOYA 12/02)

Sports

4555 Altman, Millys N. *Racing in Her Blood* (7–12). 1980, HarperCollins LB $12.89 (0-397-31895-2). A junior novel about a young girl who wants to succeed in the world of automobile racing.

4556 Bennett, James. *Blue Star Rapture* (7–12). 1998, Simon & Schuster $16.00 (0-689-81580-8). T. J., a basketball hopeful, goes to a basketball camp where he meets a girl from a religious cult in this novel about sports, politicking, religion, and loyalty. (Rev: BL 4/15/98; BR 1–2/99; HBG 9/98; SLJ 6/98; VOYA 12/98)

4557 Bo, Ben. *Skullcrack* (7–12). 2000, Lerner LB $14.95 (0-8225-3308-1). Jonah, an avid surfer, travels with his father to Florida to be united with his twin sister who was put up for adoption at birth. (Rev: BL 6/1–15/00; HBG 9/00; SLJ 6/00)

4558 Cadnum, Michael. *Redhanded* (8–10). 2000, Viking $15.99 (0-670-88775-7). In this gripping novel, teenager Steven tries to further his boxing career by getting involved with streetwise Chad and planning a robbery to raise money for tournament fees. (Rev: BL 9/1/00; HBG 3/01; SLJ 11/00)

4559 Carter, Alden R. *Bull Catcher* (7–10). 1997, Scholastic paper $15.95 (0-590-50958-6). High school friends Bull and Jeff seem to live for baseball and plan their futures around the sport, but one of them begins to move in a different direction. (Rev: BL 4/15/97; BR 5–6/97; SLJ 5/97; VOYA 10/97)

4560 Cochran, Thomas. *Roughnecks* (8–12). 1997, Harcourt $15.00 (0-15-201433-0). Senior Travis Cody, the narrator, wonders if he will be able to redeem himself with his football teammates after being responsible for a crucial loss because of a missed block. (Rev: BL 9/15/97; HBG 3/98; SLJ 10/97; VOYA 12/97)

4561 Coyne, Tom. *A Gentleman's Game* (10–12). 2001, Atlantic Monthly $24.00 (0-87113-791-7). This is the story of Timmy Price, a young star golfer whose father makes him become a caddy to learn humility. (Rev: BL 2/15/01)

4562 Crutcher, Chris. *The Crazy Horse Electric Game* (7–12). 1987, Greenwillow $16.99 (0-688-06683-6); Dell paper $5.50 (0-440-20094-6). A motorboat accident ends the comfortable life and budding baseball career of a teenage boy. (Rev: BL 4/15/87; BR 9–10/87; SLJ 5/87; VOYA 6/87)

4563 Crutcher, Chris. *Ironman* (8–12). 1995, Greenwillow $16.99 (0-688-13503-X). A psychological sports novel in which a 17-year-old carries an attitude that fuels the plot. (Rev: BL 3/1/95*; SLJ 3/95; VOYA 5/95)

4564 Crutcher, Chris. *Running Loose* (7–10). 1983, Greenwillow $18.99 (0-688-02002-X); Bantam paper $5.50 (0-440-97570-0). A senior in high school faces problems when he opposes the decisions of a football coach. (Rev: BL 3/87)

4565 Crutcher, Chris. *Stotan* (9–12). 1986, Greenwillow $16.95 (0-688-05715-2); paper $4.99 (0-440-20080-6). Stotan Week tests the mettle of the swim team — four high school boys who face personal as well as physical challenges.

4566 Deuker, Carl. *Heart of a Champion* (8–10). 1993, Avon paper $5.99 (0-380-72269-0). Explores the ups and downs of the five-year friendship between Seth and Jimmy, from their first meeting on a baseball field at age 12. (Rev: BL 6/1–15/93; SLJ 6/93)

4567 Deuker, Carl. *Night Hoops* (7–11). 2000, Houghton $15.00 (0-395-97936-6). When older brother Scott gives up basketball for music, Nick develops his own presence on the court. (Rev: BL 5/1/00; HB 5–6/00; HBG 9/00; SLJ 5/00)

4568 Deuker, Carl. *On the Devil's Court* (8–12). 1991, Avon paper $4.99 (0-380-70879-5). In this variation on the Faust legend, a senior high basketball star believes he has sold his soul to have a perfect season. (Rev: BL 12/15/88; BR 9–10/89; SLJ 1/89; VOYA 4/89)

4569 Deuker, Carl. *Painting the Black* (8–12). 1997, Houghton $14.95 (0-395-82848-1). Ryan's spot on the baseball team hinges on catching the pitches of Josh Daniels, a sharp new player who is adept in both baseball and football. (Rev: BL 6/1–15/97; BR 11–12/97; SLJ 5/97; VOYA 8/97)

4570 Dygard, Thomas J. *Backfield Package* (6–10). 1992, Morrow $15.99 (0-688-11471-7). Two high school football stars want to play together in college, but only one of them is offered a scholarship. (Rev: BL 9/15/92; SLJ 9/92)

4571 Dygard, Thomas J. *The Rebounder* (7–10). 1994, Morrow $16.00 (0-688-12821-1). Chris quits playing basketball after accidentally injuring an opponent. When he transfers to a new school, he is guided back to the sport by a sensitive coach. (Rev: BL 9/1/94; SLJ 10/94)

4572 Dygard, Thomas J. *The Rookie Arrives* (7–12). 1989, Puffin paper $5.99 (0-14-034112-9). Ted Bell comes of age when he becomes a major-leaguer fresh from high school. (Rev: BL 3/1/88; BR 5–6/88; SLJ 3/88)

4573 Dygard, Thomas J. *Running Wild* (7–10). 1996, Morrow $15.00 (0-688-14853-0). When Pete is forced to attend football practices, he discovers that he really enjoys the game. (Rev: BL 8/96; SLJ 9/96)

4574 Dygard, Thomas J. *Second Stringer* (6–12). 1998, Morrow $15.99 (0-688-15981-8). A star quarterback's knee injury gives second-stringer Kevin Taylor the opportunity of a lifetime during his senior year in high school. (Rev: BL 9/1/98; HBG 3/99; SLJ 12/98; VOYA 2/99)

4575 *Fishing for Chickens: Short Stories About Rural Youth* (9–12). Ed. by Jim Heynen. 2001, Persea $19.95 (0-89255-264-6); paper $8.95 (0-89255-265-4). Stories from 16 authors describe the realities of growing up in the country. (Rev: BL 9/15/01; HBG 3/02; SLJ 10/01; VOYA 10/01)

4576 Flynn, Pat. *Alex Jackson: SWA* (6–10). 2002, Univ. of Queensland Pr. paper $13.50 (0-7022-3307-2). Alex flirts with physical danger and trouble with the police when he joins up with Skateboarders with Attitude. (Rev: SLJ 1/03)

4577 Galloway, Stephen. *Finnie Walsh* (10–12). 2001, Raincoast $16.95 (1-55192-372-6). Paul's friendship with Finnie, which centers around hockey, is forever changed when Paul's father is injured. (Rev: BL 5/1/01)

4578 Godfrey, Martyn. *Ice Hawk* (7–12). Illus. 1986, EMC paper $13.50 (0-8219-0235-0). An easy-to-read story about a young minor league hockey player who balks at unnecessary use of violence. (Rev: BL 2/1/87)

4579 Guy, David. *Football Dreams* (9–12). 1982, NAL paper $5.95 (0-451-15868-7). A story about the thoughts and actions of a freshman at Arnold Academy who wants to make the football team.

4580 Hoffius, Stephen. *Winners and Losers* (7–10). 1993, Simon & Schuster paper $16.00 (0-671-79194-X). When star runner Daryl collapses during a meet, the coach — his father — starts to ignore him and push Daryl's friend Curt to train harder. (Rev: BL 7/93; VOYA 2/94)

4581 Jenkins, Jerry B. *Hometown Legend* (10–12). 2001, Warner $24.95 (0-446-52902-8). Readers of Christian fiction will enjoy this novel about small-town life, football, and the positive thinking that brings people together. (Rev: BL 7/01)

4582 Kinsella, W. P. *Shoeless Joe* (10–12). 1982, Houghton paper $12.00 (0-345-41007-6). This baseball fantasy about an Iowa farmer, Ray Kinsella, and his field of dreams was made into an inspiring motion picture.

4583 Klass, David. *Danger Zone* (7–12). 1996, Scholastic paper $16.95 (0-590-48590-3). Jimmy Doyle, a young basketball star, tries to prove to himself as well as to his mostly African American teammates that he deserves a place on the American High School Dream Team. (Rev: BL 4/1/96; BR 5–6/96; SLJ 3/96; VOYA 4/96)

4584 Lynch, Chris. *Iceman* (8–12). 1994, Harper-Collins $15.00 (0-06-023340-0). An emotionally fragile teenager expresses his anger in violent hockey games and spends time at the local mortuary with a disturbed recluse who works there. (Rev: BL 2/1/94; SLJ 3/94; VOYA 4/94)

4585 Myers, Walter Dean. *Hoops* (7–10). 1981, Dell paper $5.50 (0-440-93884-8). Lonnie plays basketball in spite of his coach, a has-been named Cal. Followed by *The Outside Shot* (1987).

4586 Norman, Rick. *Cross Body Block* (8–10). 1996, Colonial Pr. paper $9.95 (1-56883-060-2). An anguished story about a middle-aged football coach and his personal family tragedies, including the brutal death of a son. (Rev: BR 9–10/96; VOYA 8/96)

4587 Powell, Randy. *Dean Duffy* (8–12). 1995, Farrar paper $5.95 (0-374-41698-2). A Little League baseball great has problems with his pitching arm and sees his career collapse. (Rev: BL 4/15/95; SLJ 5/95)

4588 Powell, Randy. *The Whistling Toilets* (7–10). 1996, Farrar paper $5.95 (0-374-48369-8). When Stan tries to help his friend Ginny with her tennis game, he finds that something strange is troubling the rising young tennis star. (Rev: BL 9/15/96; BR 3–4/97; SLJ 10/96; VOYA 12/96)

4589 Revoyr, Nina. *The Necessary Hunger* (10–12). 1997, Simon & Schuster $22.50 (0-684-83234-8). Nancy Takahiro, a senior in high school and a gifted basketball player, is attracted to another player, Raina Webber, in this novel that also explores the many layers of racial prejudice. (Rev: SLJ 12/97; VOYA 12/97)

4590 Ritter, John H. *Over the Wall* (6–10). 2000, Putnam $17.99 (0-399-23489-6). Fleeing a family tragedy, 14-year-old Tyler goes to live with relatives in New York City and plays on a baseball league in Central Park. (Rev: BCCB 5/00; BL 4/1/00; HBG 9/00; SLJ 6/00; VOYA 6/00)

4591 Romain, Joseph. *The Mystery of the Wagner Whacker* (7–12). 1997, Warwick paper $8.95 (1-895629-94-2). Matt, a baseball enthusiast, is upset at moving to a small Canadian town where the sport is all but unknown, but an accidental travel in time to 1928 changes the situation. (Rev: BL 7/98; SLJ 7/98)

4592 Smiley, Jane. *Horse Heaven* (10–12). Illus. 2000, Knopf $26.00 (0-375-40600-X). The world of horse racing is created in this adult novel that features a cast of characters including owners, jockeys, trainers, and fans. (Rev: BL 2/15/00*)

4593 Staudohar, Paul D., ed. *Baseball's Best Short Stories* (9–12). 1997, Chicago Review paper $16.95 (1-55652-319-X). Baseball stories from such renowned authors as Zane Grey, Robert Penn Warren, and James Thurber. (Rev: BL 11/15/95)

4594 Sweeney, Joyce. *Players* (6–12). 2000, Winslow $16.95 (1-890817-54-6). Corey, leader of the basketball team, is determined to find out who is sabotaging its chances of success. (Rev: BL 10/1/00; HBG 10/01; SLJ 9/00; VOYA 12/00)

4595 Wallace, Rich. *Playing Without the Ball: A Novel in Four Quarters* (7–11). 2000, Knopf LB $17.99 (0-679-98672-3). Senior Jay McLeod is obsessed with basketball in a life that also includes his job as a short-order cook, family problems, a lonely existence, and fleeting attachments to girls. (Rev: BCCB 3–4/01; BL 9/1/00; HB 11–12/00; HBG 3/01; SLJ 10/00)

4596 Wallace, Rich. *Shots on Goal* (7–10). 1997, Knopf $18.99 (0-679-98670-7). Set against the exciting world of high school soccer, this novel also deals with the friendship of two of the team's players and how trouble with girls is dividing them. (Rev: BL 9/15/97; BR 1–2/98; HBG 3/98; SLJ 11/97)

4597 Wallace, Rich. *Wrestling Sturbridge* (9–12). 1996, Knopf $17.00 (0-679-87803-3). Ben, a high school senior, faces a bleak future in his Pennsylvania hometown and decides to turn things around by trying out for a state wrestling title. (Rev: BL 9/1/96*; BR 11–12/96; SLJ 10/96; VOYA 6/97)

4598 Weaver, Will. *Farm Team* (7–12). 1995, HarperCollins LB $15.89 (0-06-023589-6). Shy Billy Baggs, with many responsibilities for his age, finds success playing baseball. A sequel to *Striking Out*. (Rev: BL 9/1/95)

4599 Weaver, Will. *Hard Ball* (7–12). 1998, Harper-Collins LB $15.89 (0-06-027122-1). Billy Baggs discovers that his rival for the star position on the freshman baseball team is also his rival for the attention of the girl he is attracted to. (Rev: BL 1/1–15/98; HBG 9/98; SLJ 4/98; VOYA 6/98)

4600 Weaver, Will. *Striking Out* (8–12). 1993, HarperCollins paper $6.99 (0-06-447113-6). When Minnesota farmboy Billy Baggs picks up a stray baseball and fires it back to the pitcher, his baseball career begins, but his family isn't enthusiastic. (Rev: BL 11/1/93; SLJ 10/93; VOYA 12/93)

4601 Wells, Rosemary. *When No One Was Looking* (8–12). 1987, Fawcett paper $2.95 (0-449-70251-0). This story about tennis is also a mystery involving the death of the heroine's arch rival.

4602 Zusak, Markus. *Fighting Ruben Wolfe* (8–12). 2001, Scholastic $15.95 (0-439-24188-X). Two brothers, Ruben and Cameron, try to assist their struggling family by boxing under the direction of an unethical promoter. (Rev: BL 2/15/01; HB 3–4/01; HBG 10/01; SLJ 3/01; VOYA 4/01)

Short Stories and General Anthologies

4603 *The African American West: A Century of Short Stories* (10–12). Ed. by Bruce A. Glasrud and Laurie Champion. 2000, Univ. Press of Colorado $29.95 (0-87081-559-8). Set in the American West, these 46 short stories are told from the standpoint of African Americans at various times and settings. (Rev: BL 2/15/00)

4604 Aleichem, Sholem. *Tevye the Dairyman and The Railroad Stories* (9–12). Trans. by Hillel Halkin. 1987, Schocken paper $15.00 (0-8052-1069-5). Several of the 30 stories in this collection feature Tevye, the Russian Jew of "Fiddler on the Roof" fame.

4605 Anderson, Poul. *Going for Infinity: A Literary Journey* (10–12). 2002, Tor $25.95 (0-765-30359-0). With introduction by the late author, this is a collection of richly layered science fiction and fantasy stories. (Rev: BL 5/15/02)

4606 Armstrong, Jennifer, ed. *Shattered: Stories of Children and War* (5–12). 2002, Knopf LB $17.99 (0-375-91112-X). A collection of thought-provoking short stories by well-known writers about war and its impact. (Rev: BL 12/15/01; HB 5–6/02; HBG 10/02; SLJ 1/02)

4607 Arvin, Nick. *In the Electric Eden* (11–12). 2003, Penguin paper $14.00 (0-14-200256-9). The power of technology to enhance and to endanger is explored in a collection of absorbing short stories. (Rev: BL 1/1–15/03*)

4608 Bass, Rick. *The Hermit's Story* (11–12). 2002, Houghton $23.00 (0-618-13932-X). An excellent collection of evocative and tender short stories; for mature teens. (Rev: BL 5/1/02)

4609 Bauer, Marion Dane, ed. *Am I Blue?* (8–12). 1995, HarperCollins paper $6.99 (0-06-440587-7). Sixteen short stories from well-known YA writers who have something meaningful to share about gay awareness and want to present positive, credible gay role models. (Rev: BL 5/1/94*; SLJ 6/94; VOYA 8/94)

4610 *Best-Loved Stories Told at the National Storytelling Festival* (9–12). 1991, National Storytelling Pr. paper $11.95 (1-879991-00-4). The 37 traditional stories collected here cover a wide range of ethnic backgrounds, genres, and colloquial voices. (Rev: BL 10/15/91)

4611 Bloom, Harold. *Black American Prose Writers of the Harlem Renaissance* (10–12). Series: Writers of English: Lives and Works. 1994, Chelsea $34.95 (0-7910-2203-X). Thirteen writers of the Harlem Renaissance, including Langston Hughes and Countee Cullen, are represented in this fine anthology.

4612 Blume, Judy, ed. *Places I Never Meant to Be: Original Stories by Censored Writers* (7–12). 1999, Simon & Schuster $16.95 (0-689-82034-8). A collection of original stories by 12 authors who have been both honored and censored, among them Walter Dean Myers, Norma Fox Mazer, Julius Lester, Katherine Paterson, Harry Mazer, David Klass, Chris Lynch, and Paul Zindel. Royalties from this book go to the National Coalition Against Censorship. (Rev: BL 6/1–15/99; HBG 4/00; SLJ 8/99; VOYA 12/99)

4613 Brooks, Bruce. *All That Remains* (7–12). 2001, Simon & Schuster $16.00 (0-689-83351-2). Three darkly entertaining novellas tackle the topic of death and how young people cope with it. (Rev: BCCB 6/01; BL 5/1/01; HB 7–8/01; HBG 10/01; SLJ 5/01; VOYA 6/01)

4614 Busby, Margaret. *Daughters of Africa: An International Anthology of Words and Writings by Women of African Descent: From the Ancient Egyptian to the Present* (9–12). 1992, Pantheon $35.00 (0-679-41634-X). A compelling collection of writings — short stories, poetry, memoirs, songs, and oral histories — by women of African descent, arranged chronologically. (Rev: SLJ 2/93) [808.8]

4615 *The Campfire Collection: Spine-Tingling Tales to Tell in the Dark* (9–12). Ed. by Eric B. Martin. 2000, Chronicle paper $15.95 (0-8118-2454-3). A collection of 17 thrillers by such writers as Jack London, Edgar Allan Poe, and Tobias Wolff. (Rev: SLJ 1/01)

4616 Capote, Truman. *A Christmas Memory, One Christmas, and The Thanksgiving Visitor* (10–12). 1996, Modern Library $13.95 (0-679-60237-2). Three short stories present Capote's memories of holidays of his youth. [818]

4617 Carter, Anne Laurel. *No Missing Parts and Other Stories About Real Princesses* (7–12). 2003, Red Deer paper $9.95 (0-88995-253-1). Ten thoughtful stories from Canada portray young women who rely on their own resources in difficult situations. (Rev: BL 5/1/03; SLJ 5/03; VOYA 10/03)

4618 Carver, Raymond, and Tom Jenks. *American Short Story Masterpieces* (10–12). 1987, Delacorte paper $7.50 (0-440-20423-2). The 36 stories reprinted here by such authors as Updike, O'Connor, Baldwin, and Malamud emphasize the realistic genre of writing.

4619 Chekhov, Anton Pavlovich. *The Russian Master and Other Stories* (10–12). Trans. by Ronald Hingley. Series: World's Classics. 1999, Oxford paper $7.95 (0-19-283687-0). A collection of 11 short stories written by Chekhov between 1892 and 1899.

4620 Chopin, Kate. *The Awakening and Selected Stories* (10–12). 1981, Modern Library paper $7.95 (0-14-039022-7). As well as the novel *The Awakening,* this collection contains 12 short stories.

4621 Christensen, Bonnie, ed. *In My Grandmother's House: Award-Winning Authors Tell Stories About Their Grandmothers* (6–12). Illus. 2003, Harper-Collins LB $19.89 (0-06-029110-9). A collection of stories by well-known authors including Beverly Cleary, Jean Craighead George, and Alma Flor Ada. (Rev: BL 6/1–15/03; HBG 10/03; SLJ 5/03; VOYA 10/03) [306.87]

4622 Clarke, Judith. *Wolf on the Fold* (9–12). 2002, Front Street $16.95 (1-886910-79-0). Fear, death, aging, war, divorce, and other hard topics are the focus of six short stories set in Australia. Winner of the Australian Children's Book of the Year award. (Rev: BL 9/1/02; HBG 10/02; SLJ 9/02)

4623 Crane, Milton, ed. *50 Great American Short Stories* (10–12). 1984, Bantam paper $5.99 (0-553-27294-2). This excellent anthology spans the entire history of American literature and represents the best work of many authors.

4624 Dahl, Roald. *Skin and Other Stories* (7–12). 2000, Viking $15.99 (0-670-89184-3). Selected from the author's short stories for adults, these 13 bizarre tales will also delight younger readers. (Rev: BL 10/1/00; HBG 3/01; VOYA 12/00)

4625 Dann, Jack. *Jubilee* (10–12). 2003, Tor $27.95 (0-765-30676-X). An absorbing retrospective collection of short stories that include fantasy, horror, and magic realism, as well as science fiction. (Rev: BL 1/1–15/03)

4626 Datlow, Ellen, and Terri Windling, eds. *The Green Man: Tales from the Mythic Forest* (7–12). 2002, Viking $18.99 (0-670-03526-2). Mythical beings with special relevance to the natural world are portrayed in a collection of stories and poems. (Rev: BL 4/15/02; HBG 10/02; SLJ 7/02; VOYA 6/02)

4627 Delany, Samuel R. *Aye, and Gomorrah* (10–12). 2003, Vintage paper $14.00 (0-375-70671-2). This collection of short stories, some featuring graphic sexual content, includes examples of the science fiction, fantasy, and horror genres. (Rev: BL 2/15/03)

4628 Edghill, Rosemary. *Paying the Piper at the Gates of Dawn* (10–12). 2003, Five Star $25.95 (0-7862-5345-2). A collection of appealing and varied fantasy and science fiction short stories. (Rev: BL 6/1–15/03)

4629 *Eighth Grade: Stories of Friendship, Passage and Discovery by Eighth Grade Writers* (6–12). Ed. by Christine Lord. Series: American Teen Writer. 1996, Merlyn's Pen paper $9.95 (1-886427-08-9).

This is a group of short stories collected by *Merlyn's Pen* magazine that were written by 8th-graders. Also in this series are *Freshman: Fiction, Fantasy, and Humor by Ninth Grade Writers* and *Sophomores: Tales of Reality, Conflict, and the Road,* plus eight other volumes (all 1996). Each is accompanied by an audiotape. (Rev: VOYA 6/98)

4630 Engstrom, Elizabeth. *Suspicions* (11–12). 2002, Triple Tree paper $16.95 (0-9666272-9-6). A collection of short stories that entertain, provoke, and disturb; for mature teens. (Rev: BL 1/1–15/02)

4631 Faulkner, William. *Collected Stories of William Faulkner* (10–12). 1950, Random paper $19.00 (0-679-76403-8). There are 42 short stories in this collection, many of which take place in Yoknapatawpha County, Mississippi.

4632 Fitzgerald, F. Scott. *The Short Stories of F. Scott Fitzgerald: A New Collection* (10–12). Ed. by Matthew J. Bruccoli. 1989, Scribner $37.50 (0-684-19160-1); paper $18.00 (0-684-80445-X). This is the definitive collection of Fitzgerald's stories.

4633 Fox, Carol, et al. *In Times of War: An Anthology of War and Peace in Children's Literature* (6–12). Illus. 2001, Pavilion $24.95 (1-86205-446-0). Educators in the United Kingdom, Belgium, and Portugal worked together on this anthology of fiction, memoirs, and poetry — most of which deals with World Wars I and II in Europe — that is presented in thematic groupings. (Rev: BL 4/15/01; SLJ 6/01)

4634 Fraustino, Lisa R., ed. *Soul Searching: Thirteen Stories About Faith and Belief* (6–10). 2002, Simon & Schuster $17.95 (0-689-83484-5). Young people's beliefs and faith form the center of this collection of thought-provoking stories. (Rev: BL 10/1/02; HB 1–2/03; HBG 3/03; SLJ 12/02; VOYA 2/03)

4635 Furst, Joshua. *Short People* (11–12). 2003, Knopf $23.00 (0-375-41431-2). This collection of strong, often disturbing, stories written in compelling prose is suitable for mature and able teen readers. (Rev: BL 6/1–15/03*)

4636 Gilchrist, Ellen. *I, Rhoda Manning, Go Hunting with My Daddy* (11–12). 2002, Little, Brown $25.95 (0-316-17358-4). Rhoda is just one of the many characters — both adult and teen — who will be familiar to Gilchrist readers in this collection of stories; for mature teens. (Rev: BL 5/15/02)

4637 Giovanni, Nikki, ed. *Grand Fathers: Reminiscences, Poems, Recipes, and Photos of the Keepers of Our Traditions* (6–12). Illus. 1999, Holt $18.95 (0-8050-5484-7). A collection of family stories and memoirs, some by famous writers but most by ordinary people, with memories about fathers that range from the inspirational to the sad and angry. (Rev: BL 6/1–15/99; SLJ 7/99; VOYA 10/99)

4638 Golden, Lilly, ed. *A Literary Christmas: Great Contemporary Christmas Stories* (9–12). 1994, Grove Atlantic paper $15.00 (0-87113-583-3). Twenty-seven stories and novel excerpts from such authors as Annie Dillard, Raymond Carver, Leo Rosten, Tobias Wolf, and Ntozake Shange. (Rev: BL 10/15/92)

4639 Grant, Douglas. *Classic American Short Stories* (9–12). 1989, Oxford paper $13.95 (0-19-282685-9). A collection of 14 classic short stories by authors including Hawthorne, Twain, and Hemingway, arranged chronologically.

4640 Greene, Graham. *The Portable Graham Greene.* Rev. ed. (10–12). Ed. by Philip Stratford. 1994, Penguin paper $16.95 (0-14-023359-8). As well as excerpts from novels and short stories, this volume contains the full text of *The Heart of the Matter* and *The Third Man.*

4641 Harfenist, Jean. *A Brief History of the Flood* (11–12). 2002, Knopf $23.00 (0-375-41393-6). Growing up in 1960s Minnesota, Lillian longs for independence and struggles with her family and the usual teen woes in a series of interrelated short stories; for mature teens. (Rev: BL 5/15/02)

4642 Haynes, David, and Julie Landsman, eds. *Welcome to Your Life: Writings for the Heart of Young America* (7–12). 1999, Milkweed paper $15.95 (1-57131-017-7). Nearly 50 award-winning contributors each tell of a pivotal childhood experience, most with a focus on race and ethnicity, that affected the rest of his or her life. Subjects include gangs, bigotry, enemies, parents, and friends. (Rev: BL 5/1/99)

4643 Hemingway, Ernest. *The Complete Short Stories of Ernest Hemingway: The Finca Vigia Edition* (10–12). 1987, Scribner paper $20.00 (0-684-84332-3). This definitive collection of Hemingway's short stories numbers 49, including 7 that were never published before.

4644 Henry, O. *The Best Short Stories of O. Henry* (9–12). Ed. by Bennett A. Cerf and Van H. Cartmell. 1994, Modern Library $21.95 (0-679-60122-8). An excellent collection of short stories by this master of the surprise ending.

4645 Henry, O. *Forty-One Stories* (9–12). 1986, NAL paper $5.95 (0-451-52254-0). A collection that includes all of the favorites such as "Gift of the Magi."

4646 Hillerman, Tony. *The Best of the West: An Anthology of Classic Writing from the American West* (9–12). 1991, HarperCollins paper $18.00 (0-06-092352-0). This collection of short fiction and nonfiction showcases classic and contemporary portrayals of the American West. [818]

4647 Hopkinson, Nalo. *Skin Folk* (10–12). 2001, Warner paper $12.95 (0-446-67803-1). Drawing inspiration from Caribbean folklore, Hopkinson

blends science fiction and realism in this collection of short stories. (Rev: BL 11/1/01; VOYA 2/02)

4648 Howe, James, ed. *The Color of Absence: 12 Stories About Loss and Hope* (6–10). 2001, Simon & Schuster $16.00 (0-689-82862-4). Well-known YA authors including Walter Dean Myers, Norma Fox Mazer, and Naomi Shihab Nye have contributed widely varied stories to this volume dealing with loss and hope. (Rev: BL 7/01; HB 9–10/01; HBG 3/02; SLJ 9/01; VOYA 8/01)

4649 Hudson, Wade, and Cheryl W. Hudson, eds. *In Praise of Our Fathers and Our Mothers* (6–12). Illus. 1997, Just Us $29.95 (0-940975-59-9); paper $17.95 (0-940975-60-2). Nearly 50 well-known African American writers, among them Walter Dean Myers, Virginia Hamilton, and Brian Pinkney, recall their family life in this anthology of poetry, essays, paintings, and interviews. (Rev: BL 4/1/97; HB 3–4/97; SLJ 6/97) [920]

4650 Hughes, Langston. *The Return of Simple* (9–12). Ed. by Akiba Sullivan Harper. 1994, Hill & Wang paper $11.00 (0-8090-1582-X). A collection of stories about Jesse B. Semple that first appeared in newspapers and contain acute social commentaries.

4651 Hurston, Zora Neale. *The Complete Stories* (10–12). 1995, HarperCollins paper $14.00 (0-06-092171-4). There are 26 short stories in this collection, arranged in the order that they were published.

4652 Hurston, Zora Neale. *Novels and Stories* (10–12). 1995, Library of America $35.00 (0-940450-83-6). Four novels including *Their Eyes Were Watching God* are included, plus nine short stories. (Rev: BL 1/1/95)

4653 *Irreconcilable Differences* (10–12). Ed. by Lia Matera. 1999, HarperCollins $24.00 (0-06-019225-9); paper $6.50 (0-06-109733-0). A collection of 20 original short stories by some of the best contemporary writers. (Rev: BL 12/1/99)

4654 Jones, Diana Wynne. *Believing Is Seeing* (6–12). 1999, Greenwillow $16.00 (0-688-16843-4). Seven stories of fantasy, horror, and the supernatural that vary dramatically in tone and content. (Rev: BL 11/15/99; HBG 4/00)

4655 Kafka, Franz. *The Metamorphosis and Other Stories* (10–12). Trans. by Joachim Neugroschel. 1993, Scribner paper $13.00 (0-684-80070-5). This is a collection of 30 macabre, highly original stories by the great European writer.

4656 Kerouac, Jack, and Ann Charters. *The Portable Jack Kerouac* (10–12). 1995, Viking paper $15.95 (0-14-017819-8). This compilation consists of excerpts from each of Kerouac's 14 novels plus some essays and poetry. [818]

4657 Ketchin, Susan, and Neil Giordano, eds. *25 and Under: Fiction* (10–12). 1997, Norton $25.00

(0-393-04120-4). This is a collection of 15 stories that deal with such themes as sexuality, friendship, families, loneliness, addiction, and death, all written by authors age 25 or younger. (Rev: VOYA 6/98)

4658 Kulpa, Kathryn, ed. *Something Like a Hero* (6–10). 1995, Merlyn's Pen paper $9.95 (1-886427-03-8). A collection of 11 short stories from different genres, reprinted from the national magazine of student writing *Merlyn's Pen*. (Rev: VOYA 2/96)

4659 Lardner, Ring. *The Best Short Stories of Ring Lardner* (9–12). 1976, Scribner $40.00 (0-684-14743-2). A selection of 25 stories by one of the most original figures in American literature.

4660 Le Clezio, J. M. G. *The Round and Other Cold Hard Facts* (11–12). Trans. by C. Dickson. 2003, Univ. of Nebraska Pr. $60.00 (0-8032-2946-1); paper $19.95 (0-8032-8007-6). Challenging short stories by this French writer feature teens seeking to escape depressing boundaries and finding danger instead. (Rev: BL 1/1–15/03)

4661 Lewis, David Levering. *The Portable Harlem Renaissance Reader* (10–12). 1994, Viking paper $17.00 (0-14-017036-7). All kinds of writing genres, including fiction, memoir, poetry, and drama, are included in this overview of the great flowering of writing talent known as the Harlem Renaissance. [810.8]

4662 London, Jack. *The Portable Jack London* (8–12). Ed. by Earle Labor. 1994, Penguin paper $15.95 (0-14-017969-0). As well as several short stories and the full text of *The Call of the Wild,* this anthology contains some letters and general nonfiction. [818]

4663 *Love and Sex: 10 Stories of Truth* (9–12). Ed. by Michael Cart. 2001, Simon & Schuster $18.00 (0-689-83203-6). Laurie Halse Anderson, Joan Bauer, Chris Lynch, and Garth Nix are among the authors of these 10 stories about the impact of love and sex on teen lives. (Rev: BL 6/1–15/02; HB 7–8/01; HBG 10/01; SLJ 6/01; VOYA 6/01)

4664 Lupoff, Richard A. *Claremont Tales II* (11–12). Series: Claremont Tales. 2002, Golden Gryphon $23.95 (1-930846-07-X). A varied short story collection for fans of fantasy, science fiction, mysteries, thrillers, and horror stories; for mature teens. (Rev: BL 2/15/02)

4665 Lynch, Chris. *All the Old Haunts* (8–12). 2001, HarperCollins LB $15.89 (0-06-028179-0). This collection of 10 dark short stories frankly explores such "old haunts" as young love, unwanted pregnancy, and difficult family relationships. (Rev: BCCB 10/01; BR 3–4/02; HB 9–10/01; HBG 3/02; SLJ 11/01; VOYA 10/01)

4666 McCullers, Carson. *The Ballad of the Sad Cafe: The Novels and Stories of Carson McCullers* (10–12). 1951, Houghton paper $5.99 (0-553-27254-3). An omnibus volume of the works of this famous southern writer who explored loneliness and alienation.

4667 McEwen, Christian, ed. *Jo's Girls: Tomboy Tales of High Adventure, True Grit and Real Life* (10–12). 1997, Beacon paper $30.50 (0-8070-6211-1). A well-edited collection of fiction and memoirs about girls who assume the role of tomboy by such writers as Annie Dillard, Ursula Le Guin, Toni Morrison, Colette, and Willa Cather. (Rev: BL 6/1–15/97; SLJ 3/98)

4668 McKinley, Robin, and Peter Dickinson. *Water: Tales of Elemental Spirits* (7–12). 2002, Putnam $18.99 (0-399-23796-8). Six captivating and imaginative stories feature magical sea-beings and the humans who love or fight them. (Rev: BL 4/15/02; HB 7–8/02; HBG 10/02; SLJ 6/02*; VOYA 6/02)

4669 Matheson, Richard. *Duel* (10–12). 2003, Tor $27.95 (0-765-30695-6); paper $15.95 (0-312-87826-5). A varied collection of stories with elements of humor, fantasy, horror, and science fiction. (Rev: BL 12/15/02; VOYA 10/03)

4670 Mazer, Anne, ed. *A Walk in My World: International Short Stories About Youth* (9–12). 1998, Persea $17.95 (0-89255-237-9). Sixteen stories about young people from the pens of distinguished writers from around the world afford a powerful and lasting reading experience. (Rev: BL 1/1–15/99; BR 5–6/99; HBG 3/99; SLJ 6/99; VOYA 4/99)

4671 Mee, Susie, ed. *Downhome: An Anthology of Southern Women Writers* (10–12). 1995, Harcourt paper $17.00 (0-15-600121-7). Southern life is reflected in this collection of short stories spanning several decades by women authors ranging from Eudora Welty and Zora Neale Hurston to Ellen Gilchrist and Dorothy Allison. (Rev: BL 10/15/95; SLJ 2/96)

4672 *More Best-Loved Stories Told at the National Storytelling Festival* (9–12). 1992, National Storytelling Pr. $19.95 (1-879991-09-8); paper $11.95 (1-879991-08-X). Stories featuring familiar folklore, family anecdotes, and tales from many cultures, with a brief note on each storyteller. (Rev: BL 11/15/92)

4673 Murphy, Mark. *House of Java* (10–12). Illus. 1998, NBM paper $8.95 (1-56163-202-3). A collection of short stories about the frequenters of a Seattle coffee shop and its neighborhood. (Rev: SLJ 8/98)

4674 Myers, Walter Dean. *A Time to Love: Stories from the Old Testament* (7–10). 2003, Scholastic $19.95 (0-439-22000-9). Six well-known Old Testament stories are told from unusual first-person perspectives and accompanied by colorful illustrations. (Rev: BCCB 9/03; BL 5/15/03; HBG 10/03; SLJ 5/03; VOYA 8/03)

4675 Naidoo, Beverley. *Out of Bounds: Seven Stories of Conflict and Hope* (6–10). 2003, Harper-

Collins LB $17.89 (0-06-050800-0). The seven stories in this book, with a foreword by Archbishop Desmond Tutu, look at the racism, apartheid, discrimination, and progress in South Africa from the 1950s to the present. (Rev: BL 2/15/03; HB 3–4/03*; HBG 10/03; SLJ 1/03; VOYA 6/03)

4676 *Night Is Gone, Day Is Still Coming: Stories and Poems by American Indian Teens and Young Adults* (10–12). Ed. by Annette Pina Ochoa et al. 2003, Candlewick $16.99 (0-7636-1518-8). Native American teens and young adults explore their experiences and aspirations in this highly readable collection of short stories and poems. (Rev: BL 10/1/03; HBG 4/04; SLJ 8/03; VOYA 10/03) [819]

4677 *Noche Buena: Hispanic American Christmas Stories* (10–12). Ed. by Nicholas Kanellos. Illus. 2000, Oxford $32.50 (0-19-513527-X). The stories, poems, and songs included in this Christmas anthology represent Hispanic Americans from a variety of countries and cultures. (Rev: BL 11/15/00) [810.8]

4678 November, Sharyn, ed. *Firebirds* (7–12). 2003, Putnam $19.99 (0-14-250142-5). An excellent collection of stories by authors who publish with the Firebird imprint, including Michael Cadnum, Garth Nix, and Meredith Ann Pierce. (Rev: BL 10/15/03; HBG 4/04; VOYA 12/03)

4679 Oates, Joyce Carol. *Small Avalanches and Other Stories* (9–12). 2003, HarperCollins LB $17.89 (0-06-001218-8). Stories of complicated young women, often making bad choices, make up this collection. (Rev: BL 3/15/03*; HBG 10/03; SLJ 7/03; VOYA 6/03)

4680 O'Connor, Flannery. *Collected Works* (10–12). 1988, Library of America $35.00 (0-940450-37-2). As well as the novels *Wise Blood* and *The Violent Carry It Away,* this collection includes many short stories. (Rev: SLJ 1/89)

4681 O'Connor, Flannery. *The Complete Stories* (10–12). 1971, Farrar paper $15.00 (0-374-51536-0). This collection of short stories by one of the South's most famous writers is arranged chronologically.

4682 *On Glorious Wings: The Best Flying Stories of the Centuries* (10–12). Ed. by Stephen Coonts. 2003, Tor $27.95 (0-312-87724-2). Short stories and novel excerpts about flying including offerings from such notable authors as James Michener, Rudyard Kipling, Jules Verne, Louis L'Amour, and Joseph Heller. (Rev: BL 10/15/03)

4683 *The Oxford Book of American Short Stories* (10–12). Ed. by Joyce Carol Oates. 1992, Oxford $40.00 (0-19-507065-8); paper $18.95 (0-19-509262-7). An excellent collection of 56 stories by such authors as Poe, Hemingway, and Sandra Cisneros.

4684 *The Oxford Book of English Short Stories* (10–12). Ed. by A. S. Byatt. 1998, Oxford $40.00

(0-19-214238-0); paper $18.95 (0-19-288111-6). Short stories by both well-known and obscure English writers are represented in this fine anthology. (Rev: BL 4/1/98)

4685 Packer, ZZ. *Drinking Coffee Elsewhere* (11–12). 2003, Riverhead $24.95 (1-57322-234-8). A collection of short stories, mostly featuring African American characters, about young people facing varied challenges; suitable for mature readers. (Rev: BL 2/15/03; SLJ 9/03)

4686 *Past Lives, Present Tense* (7–12). Ed. by Elizabeth Ann Scarborough. 1999, Ace paper $13.00 (0-441-00649-3). A thoughtful and entertaining collection of stories that incorporate the use of DNA from historical figures. (Rev: BL 11/1/99; VOYA 4/00)

4687 Paterson, Katherine. *A Midnight Clear: Stories for the Christmas Season* (5–10). 1995, Dutton $16.00 (0-525-67529-9). Stories that reveal the spirit of Christmas in contemporary life and provide hope and light in a dark, uncertain world. (Rev: BL 9/15/95)

4688 Pawlak, Mark, et al., eds. *Bullseye: Stories and Poems by Outstanding High School Writers* (9–12). 1995, Hanging Loose paper $15.00 (1-882413-12-1). A collection of poems and short narratives written by 68 teenagers, taken from the pages of the literary magazine *Hanging Loose.* (Rev: BL 2/1/96; SLJ 12/95)

4689 *Politically Inspired: An Anthology of Fiction for Our Time* (11–12). Ed. by Stephen Elliott. 2003, MacAdam $21.00 (1-931561-58-3); paper $13.00 (1-931561-45-1). A broad range of modern-day concerns, from suburban malaise and the oppression of women to rising crime and terrorism, are reflected in the contemporary fiction collected here; for mature teens. (Rev: BL 10/15/03)

4690 *The Portable Sixties Reader* (10–12). Ed. by Ann Charters. 2003, Penguin paper $16.00 (0-14-200194-5). The many voices of the turbulent 1960s have been beautifully captured in this collection of writings by such diverse literary icons as James Baldwin, Rachel Carson, Thomas Merton, Alan Ginsburg, Susan Sontag, and Kate Millett. (Rev: BL 1/1–15/03) [810.8]

4691 Porter, Katherine Anne. *The Collected Stories of Katherine Anne Porter* (10–12). 1965, Harcourt paper $16.00 (0-15-618876-7). This collection includes all the stories published previously in other books plus the addition of several others.

4692 Prescott, Peter S. *The Norton Book of American Short Stories* (10–12). 1988, Norton $29.95 (0-393-02619-1). An excellent survey of the American short story, with 70 examples beginning with Poe and Hawthorne and ending with some modern masters.

4693 Pritchett, V. S. *The Oxford Book of Short Stories* (10–12). 1981, Oxford $35.00 (0-19-214116-3); paper $16.95 (0-19-282113-X). A collection of 41 short stories by such writers in English as Lawrence, Faulkner, and Welty.

4694 Rice, David. *Crazy Loco* (7–12). 2001, Dial $16.99 (0-8037-2598-1). A collection of nine stories about Mexican American youngsters growing up in South Texas. (Rev: BCCB 9/01; BL 5/15/01; HB 9–10/01; HBG 3/02; SLJ 6/01; VOYA 6/01)

4695 Robison, Mary. *Tell Me* (11–12). 2002, Counterpoint paper $16.00 (1-58243-258-9). Family relationships are the focus of many of the 30 short stories in this collection; for mature teens. (Rev: BL 11/15/02)

4696 Rodriguez, Luis. *The Republic of East L.A* (11–12). 2002, HarperCollins $23.95 (0-06-621263-4). Life for the multicultural residents of East Los Angeles is the focus of this collection of short stories; for mature teens. (Rev: BL 4/15/02)

4697 Rosen, Roger, and Patra McSharry, eds. *Teenage Soldiers, Adult Wars* (9–12). Series: Icarus World Issues. 1991, Rosen LB $16.95 (0-8239-1304-X); paper $8.95 (0-8239-1305-8). Short stories and essays by teenage soldiers in troubled areas around the world — from Northern Ireland to the Middle East — who express their frontline views of military conflict. (Rev: BL 6/15/91; SLJ 4/91)

4698 Rosen, Roger, and Patra M. Sevastiades, eds. *On Heroes and the Heroic: In Search of Good Deeds* (7–12). Series: Icarus World Issues. 1993, Rosen LB $16.95 (0-8239-1384-8); paper $8.95 (0-8239-1385-6). Nine fiction and nonfiction pieces explore the concepts of heroes and antiheroes. (Rev: BL 9/15/93; SLJ 1/94; VOYA 12/93)

4699 Roth, Philip. *Goodbye, Columbus, and Five Short Stories* (10–12). 1995, Modern Library $17.95 (0-679-60159-7); paper $13.00 (0-679-74826-1). As well as the title story about young love, there are five other short stories in this collection.

4700 *Rush Hour: A Journal of Contemporary Voices. v.1: Sin* (9–12). Ed. by Michael Cart. 2004, Delacorte LB $12.99 (0-385-90166-6). This is volume one of a literary journal designed for teens. The first issue contains 18 entries (stories, poems, essays) loosely held together by the general theme of sin. (Rev: BL 5/1/04; VOYA 4/04)

4701 Saldana, Rene. *Finding Our Way* (7–12). 2003, Random $15.95 (0-385-73051-9). Featuring several Hispanic characters, these short stories focus on critical decisions in the lives of young adults. (Rev: BL 2/15/03; HB 3–4/03; HBG 10/03; SLJ 3/03; VOYA 8/03)

4702 Salinger, J. D. *Nine Stories* (10–12). 1953, Little, Brown $24.95 (0-316-76956-8); paper $5.99 (0-316-76950-9). A collection of Salinger's short fiction, mostly dealing with troubled youngsters.

4703 Salisbury, Graham. *Blue Skin of the Sea* (8–12). 1992, Delacorte $15.95 (0-385-30596-6). These 11 stories contain a strong sense of time and place, fully realized characters, stylish prose, and universal themes. (Rev: BL 6/15/92*; SLJ 6/92*)

4704 Salisbury, Graham. *Island Boyz: Short Stories* (7–12). 2002, Random LB $18.99 (0-385-90037-6). Hawaii is the setting for this collection of varied stories about teenage boys growing into maturity. (Rev: BL 4/15/02*; HB 3–4/02; HBG 10/02; SLJ 3/02*)

4705 *Second Sight: Stories for a New Millennium* (7–12). 1999, Putnam $14.99 (0-399-23458-6). A collection of eight stories that focus on the millennium by such writers as Avi, Natalie Babbitt, and Richard Peck. (Rev: BL 9/15/99; HBG 4/00; VOYA 2/00)

4706 *Shadows over Baker Street: New Tales of Terror* (10–12). Ed. by Michael Reaves and Joan Pelan. 2003, Ballantine $23.95 (0-345-45528-2). A blend of horror and detection is the backbone of this collection of 20 original stories laced with touches of Sherlock Holmes and H. P. Lovecraft. (Rev: BL 9/1/03)

4707 *Shaking the Tree: A Collection of New Fiction and Memoir by Black Women* (10–12). Ed. by Meri Nana-Ama Danquah. Illus. 2003, Norton $23.95 (0-393-05067-X). This collection of recent writings by African American women displays their varied talents and concerns. (Rev: BL 8/03) [818]

4708 Shepard, Sam. *Great Dream of Heaven* (11–12). 2002, Knopf $20.00 (0-375-40505-4). Compelling short stories delve into the psychologies of the characters; for mature readers. (Rev: BL 9/1/02*)

4709 Sherman, Josepha, ed. *Orphans of the Night* (6–10). 1995, Walker $16.95 (0-8027-8368-6). Brings together 11 short stories and two poems about creatures from folklore, most with teen protagonists. (Rev: BL 6/1–15/95; SLJ 6/95; VOYA 12/95)

4710 *Short Stories by Latin American Women: The Magic and the Real* (11–12). Ed. by Celia Correas de Zapata. 2003, Modern Library paper $12.95 (0-8129-6707-0). A collection of stories full of realism, surrealism, and the unreal; for mature teens. (Rev: BL 12/1/02)

4711 Simonds, Merilyn. *The Lion in the Room Next Door* (10–12). 2000, Putnam $23.95 (0-399-14591-5). Excellent adult short stories from this Canadian writer for literary readers who enjoy the melancholy and dark in their stories. (Rev: BL 1/1–15/00*)

4712 Singer, Isaac Bashevis. *The Collected Stories of Isaac Bashevis Singer* (10–12). 1982, Farrar paper $18.00 (0-374-51788-6). This collection contains 47 short stories chosen by the author for inclusion.

4713 Singer, Marilyn, comp. *I Believe in Water: Twelve Brushes with Religion* (7–10). 2000, Harper-Collins LB $15.89 (0-06-028398-X). Short stories by writers including Virginia Euwer Wolff and M. E. Kerr look at religion from varied viewpoints. (Rev: BL 10/1/00; HBG 3/01; SLJ 11/00; VOYA 4/01)

4714 Snell, Gordon, ed. *Thicker than Water: Coming-of-Age Stories by Irish and Irish American Writers* (7–12). 2001, Delacorte $17.95 (0-385-32571-1). Twelve stories dealing with such topics as abortion, eating disorders, and hazing will resonate with American teens. (Rev: BCCB 3/01; BL 1/1–15/01; HB 3–4/01*; HBG 10/01; SLJ 5/01)

4715 Stolar, Daniel. *The Middle of the Night* (10–12). 2003, St. Martin's $23.00 (0-312-30409-9). Familiar situations and concerns are central to this collection of eight absorbing stories. (Rev: BL 5/15/03)

4716 Thomas, Roy E. *Come Go with Me* (9–12). 1994, Farrar $16.00 (0-374-37089-3). Ninety-four stories taken from interviews in the Appalachians, Ozarks, and Ouachita mountain regions. (Rev: BL 5/1/94; SLJ 7/94)

4717 *Time Capsule: Short Stories About Teenagers Throughout the Twentieth Century* (9–12). Ed. by Donald R. Gallo. 1999, Delacorte $16.95 (0-385-32675-0). A selection of 10 stories, one for each decade of the century, that entertain while informing about the issues of the times. (Rev: BL 9/15/99; HBG 4/00; SLJ 11/99; VOYA 2/00)

4718 Tolstoy, Leo. *Great Short Works of Leo Tolstoy* (10–12). 1967, Harper & Row paper $7.50 (0-06-083071-9). This is a collection of the major short works by Tolstoy including *The Death of Ivan Ilych* and *The Kreutzer Sonata.*

4719 Tolstoy, Leo, and John Bayley. *The Portable Tolstoy* (10–12). 1978, Viking paper $17.95 (0-14-015091-9). This volume contains a cross section of this Russian writer's output, including a play, a novelette, short stories, and a sampling of his nonfiction writing. [891.7]

4720 Trelease, Jim. *Read All About It! Great Read-Aloud Stories, Poems, and Newspaper Pieces for Preteens and Teens* (9–12). 1993, Penguin paper $11.95 (0-14-014655-5). This anthology of good read-alouds comes from 52 authors and consists of fiction, poetry, and some nonfiction. [808.8]

4721 Vapnyar, Lara. *There Are Jews in My House* (11–12). 2003, Pantheon $19.95 (0-375-42250-1). In this collection of six deftly drawn short stories, Vapnyar explores various aspects of Russian and Russian American life. (Rev: BL 11/15/03)

4722 Villasenor, Victor. *Walking Stars: Stories of Magic and Power* (7–12). 1994, Arte Publico $16.95 (1-55885-118-6). Short stories, based on fact, describing the everyday magic and family love found in the author's Mexican and Native American

heritage. (Rev: BL 10/15/94; SLJ 11/94; VOYA 4/95)

4723 Warren, Robert Penn, and Albert Erskine, eds. *Short Story Masterpieces* (10–12). 1954, Dell paper $7.50 (0-440-37864-8). An international collection of 36 masterpieces of short fiction.

4724 Weiss, M. Jerry, and Helen S. Weiss, eds. *Big City Cool: Short Stories About Urban Youth* (7–12). 2002, Persea paper $8.95 (0-89255-278-6). A variety of urban settings and cultural and racial experiences are portrayed in these 14 stories, half of which have previously appeared in print. (Rev: BL 10/15/02; SLJ 11/02; VOYA 12/02)

4725 Weiss, M. Jerry, and Helen S. Weiss, eds. *Lost and Found: Award-Winning Authors Sharing Real-Life Experiences Through Fiction* (8–12). 2000, Forge $19.95 (0-312-87048-5). Thirteen well-known YA authors' stories are prefaced by explanations of the real-life origins of each story. (Rev: BL 11/1/00; SLJ 11/00)

4726 Welty, Eudora. *The Collected Stories of Eudora Welty* (10–12). 1980, Harcourt $35.00 (0-15-118994-3); paper $16.00 (0-15-618921-6). This omnibus volume contains stories from four previously published collections by one of America's great masters of the genre.

4727 Wharton, Edith. *The Selected Short Stories of Edith Wharton* (10–12). 1991, Scribner $24.95 (0-684-19304-3). An introduction that includes material on Wharton's life and works is followed by a collection of 21 of her best stories.

4728 White, Trudy. *Table of Everything* (7–12). Illus. 2001, Allen & Unwin paper $16.95 (1-86508-135-3). Australian writer White captivates readers with this collection of offbeat short stories. (Rev: VOYA 8/02)

4729 Wilde, Oscar. *The Portable Oscar Wilde.* Rev. ed. (10–12). Ed. by Richard Aldington and Stanley Weintraub. 1981, Viking paper $15.95 (0-14-015093-5). The collection contains plays including *The Importance of Being Earnest,* the novel *The Picture of Dorian Gray,* poems, letters, and quotations. [828]

4730 Wolfe, Thomas. *The Complete Short Stories of Thomas Wolfe* (10–12). Ed. by Francis E. Skipp. 1987, Scribner paper $15 .00 (0-02-040891-9). All of Wolfe's 55 short stories are reprinted in this volume.

4731 Wynne-Jones, Tim. *Lord of the Fries* (6–10). 1999, DK paper $17.95 (0-7894-2623-4). A collection of short stories by the author about young people and the decisions they make. (Rev: BCCB 3/99; BL 2/15/99; HB 7–8/99; HBG 10/99; SLJ 4/99; VOYA 10/99)

4732 Yee, Paul. *Dead Man's Gold and Other Stories* (6–12). 2002, Groundwood $16.95 (0-88899-

475-3). A collection of disturbing ghost stories featuring Chinese immigrants to America and Canada. (Rev: BL 11/1/02; HB 1–2/03*; HBG 3/03; SLJ 1/03)

4733 Young, Cathy, ed. *One Hot Second: Stories About Desire* (7–12). 2002, Knopf LB $17.99 (0-375-91203-7). A collection of stories, some witty and some moving, by YA writers about teen yearnings — for romance, for a first kiss, even for a dream car. (Rev: BL 6/1–15/02; HBG 10/02; SLJ 6/02; VOYA 6/02)

4734 *A Yuletide Universe: Sixteen Fantastical Tales* (11–12). Ed. by Brian M. Thomsen. 2003, Warner paper $12.95 (0-446-69187-9). Christmas-themed short stories represent many genres, among them fantasy, mystery, science fiction, and westerns; recommended for mature teens because of violence. (Rev: BL 10/15/03*)

Plays

General and Miscellaneous Collections

4735 Beard, Jocelyn A., ed. *The Best Men's Stage Monologues of 1993* (9–12). 1994, Smith & Kraus paper $8.95 (1-880399-43-1). Includes 52 monologues from 1993 plays. (Rev: BL 4/1/94; VOYA 8/94) [808.82]

4736 Beard, Jocelyn A., ed. *The Best Men's Stage Monologues of 1992* (9–12). 1993, Smith & Kraus paper $8.95 (1-880399-11-3). Monologues for men from outstanding 1992 theatrical works. (Rev: BL 6/1–15/93) [808.82]

4737 Beard, Jocelyn A., ed. *The Best Women's Stage Monologues of 1993* (9–12). 1994, Smith & Kraus paper $8.95 (1-880399-42-3). Includes 58 monologues from 1993 plays. (Rev: BL 4/1/94; VOYA 8/94) [808.82]

4738 Beard, Jocelyn A., ed. *The Best Women's Stage Monologues of 1992* (9–12). 1993, Smith & Kraus paper $8.95 (1-880399-10-5). Monologues for women from outstanding 1992 theatrical works. (Rev: BL 6/1–15/93) [808.82]

4339 Beard, Jocelyn A., ed. *Monologues from Classic Plays 468 B.C. to 1960 A.D.* (9–12). 1993, Smith & Kraus paper $11.95 (1-880399-09-1). Monologues from early Greek, Roman, medieval, and Restoration plays and the modern works of Williams, Pinter, and Beckett. (Rev: BL 6/1–15/93) [808.82]

4740 Beard, Jocelyn A. *Scenes from Classic Plays, 468 B.C. to 1970 A.D.* (10–12). 1993, Smith & Kraus paper $11.95 (1-880399-36-9). These scenes, averaging three pages in length, are taken from the world's greatest plays, and each is introduced by a brief synopsis. (Rev: BL 6/1–15/94) [808.82]

4741 Cerf, Bennett, and Van H. Cartmell, eds. *Thirty Famous One-Act Plays* (10–12). 1949, Modern Library $16.00 (0-394-60473-3). The playwrights range from Strindberg to Coward and Saroyan in an anthology that also includes biographical sketches. [808.82]

4742 Cerf, Bennett, and Van H. Cartmell, eds. *24 Favorite One-Act Plays* (10–12). 1958, Doubleday paper $14.95 (0-385-06617-1). An international collection of short plays — both comedies and tragedies — by such masters as Inge, Coward, and O'Neill. [808.82]

4743 Ellis, Roger, ed. *Audition Monologs for Student Actors: Selections from Contemporary Plays* (9–12). 1999, Meriwether paper $15.95 (1-56608-055-X). One-person scenes for girls and boys offer many diverse roles, plus suggestions for the actor. (Rev: BL 2/1/00) [812]

4744 Ellis, Roger, ed. *Audition Monologs for Student Actors II: Selections from Contemporary Plays* (8–12). 2001, Meriwether paper $15.95 (1-56608-073-8). Fifty monologues for both sexes from ages 10 to mid-20s are accompanied by scene-setting notes and acting tips. (Rev: SLJ 4/02)

4745 Ellis, Roger, ed. *International Plays for Young Audiences: Contemporary Works from Leading Playwrights* (7–12). 2000, Meriwether paper $16.95 (1-56608-065-7). The 12 short plays in this collection come from varied cultures and deal with situations of interest to young people. (Rev: SLJ 2/01)

4746 Horvath, John, et al., eds. *Duo! The Best Scenes for the 90's* (9–12). 1995, Applause Theatre paper $14.95 (1-55783-030-4). Some 130 scenes for two actors from productions by established playwrights of the 1980s and 1990s. (Rev: BL 4/15/95) [808.82]

4747 Houghton, Norris, ed. *Romeo and Juliet and West Side Story* (10–12). 1965, Dell paper $5.99 (0-

440-97483-6). This combined edition affords an interesting comparison between the two versions of the same story. [808.1]

4748 Kamerman, Sylvia, ed. *The Big Book of Large-Cast Plays: 27 One-Act Plays for Young Actors* (5–10). 1994, Plays $12.95 (0-8238-0302-3). Thirty short plays on varied subjects, arranged according to audience appeal. (Rev: BL 3/15/95) [812]

4749 Kamerman, Sylvia, ed. *Christmas Play Favorites for Young People* (6–10). 1983, Plays paper $13.95 (0-8238-0257-4). Eighteen one-act plays that can be used in elementary, middle, and high schools. [812.08]

4750 Kehret, Peg. *Encore! More Winning Monologs for Young Actors* (9–12). 1988, Meriwether paper $14.95 (0-916260-54-2). A collection of 63 short pieces suitable for recitations or auditions. (Rev: SLJ 8/88) [808.85]

4751 Kraus, Eric, ed. *Monologues from Contemporary Literature, Vol. 1* (9–12). 1993, Smith & Kraus paper $8.95 (1-880399-04-0). Monologues from such literary sources as Paul Theroux's *Chicago Loop*. (Rev: BL 6/1–15/93) [808.82]

4752 Lamedman, Debbie. *The Ultimate Audition Book for Teens: 111 One-Minute Monologues*, vol. 4 (7–12). Series: Young Actors. 2003, Smith & Kraus paper $11.95 (1-57525-353-4). Monologues for both girls and boys give young actors ample opportunity to display their talent in a range of selections. (Rev: SLJ 4/03) [812]

4753 Latrobe, Kathy Howard, and Mildred Knight Laughlin. *Readers Theatre for Young Adults: Scripts and Script Development* (7–12). 1989, Libraries Unlimited paper $22.00 (0-87287-743-4). A collection of short scripts based on literary classics, plus tips on how to do one's own adaptations. (Rev: BL 1/1/90) [808.5]

4754 Nolan, Paul T. *Folk Tale Plays Round the World* (9–12). 1982, Plays paper $13.95 (0-8238-0253-1). This collection contains short plays based on folktales from both the western and eastern worlds. [808.2]

4755 Ratliff, Gerald L., ed. *Millennium Monologs: 95 Contemporary Characterizations for Young Actors* (8–12). 2002, Meriwether paper $15.95 (1-56608-082-7). High school thespians will appreciate this collection of monologues, which are arranged by theme, as well as the advice on auditions. (Rev: BL 3/15/03; SLJ 5/03) [792]

4756 Ratliff, Gerald L., and Theodore O. Zapel, eds. *Playing Contemporary Scenes: 31 Famous Scenes and How to Play Them* (8–12). 1996, Meriwether paper $16.95 (1-56608-025-8). A selection of scenes by contemporary playwrights, arranged according to age and gender. (Rev: VOYA 6/97) [812]

4757 Shengold, Nina, ed. *The Actor's Book of Contemporary Stage Monologues* (9–12). Illus. 1987, Penguin paper $12.95 (0-14-009649-3). A splendid collection of monologues from both well-known and obscure scripts. (Rev: SLJ 1/88; VOYA 4/88) [659.1]

4758 Slaight, Craig, and Jack Sharrar, eds. *Great Monologues for Young Actors* (9–12). 1999, Smith & Kraus paper $14.95 (1-57525-106-X). Taken from the writing of contemporary playwrights as well as classical sources, this is a fine collection of monologues for older students. (Rev: SLJ 10/99; VOYA 10/99) [808.82]

4759 Slaight, Craig, and Jack Sharrar, eds. *Great Scenes for Young Actors from the Stage* (9–12). 1991, Smith & Kraus paper $11.95 (0-9622722-6-4). A collection of 45 scenes from contemporary and classic theater, graded according to ability level and including a brief synopsis of each play. (Rev: BL 11/1/91) [808.82]

4760 Slaight, Craig, and Jack Sharrar, eds. *Multicultural Monologues for Young Actors* (9–12). 1995, Smith & Kraus paper $11.95 (1-880399-47-4). Includes 20 poems, plays, and other fiction, arranged by gender. Monologues represent various cultures and dramatic literatures, both contemporary and classic. Some strong language and mature themes. (Rev: BL 8/95; SLJ 9/95) [808.82]

4761 Slaight, Craig, and Jack Sharrar, eds. *Multicultural Scenes for Young Actors* (9–12). 1995, Smith & Kraus paper $11.95 (1-880399-48-2). Contemporary and classic materials for groups and pairs from a variety of cultural and dramatic literatures. Some strong language and mature themes. (Rev: BL 8/95) [808.82]

4762 Slaight, Craig, and Jack Sharrar, eds. *Short Plays for Young Actors* (8–12). 1996, Smith & Kraus paper $16.95 (1-880399-74-1). An impressive collection of short plays in a variety of genres, plus material on how to approach acting as a serious pursuit. (Rev: BL 9/15/96; BR 1–2/97) [812]

4763 Smith, Marissa, ed. *Showtime's Act One Festival: The One-Act Plays 1994* (10–12). 1995, Smith & Kraus paper $16.95 (1-800399-96-2). This is a collection of 13 prize-winning one-act plays, some of which deal with teen situations. (Rev: BL 11/15/95; VOYA 6/96) [812]

4764 Steffensen, James L., Jr., ed. *Great Scenes from the World Theater* (10–12). 1972, Avon paper $5.95 (0-380-00793-2). A collection of 180 scenes ranging from Euripides to Albee. [808.82]

4765 Swortzell, Lowell, ed. *Theatre for Young Audiences: Around the World in Twenty-One Plays* (6–12). 1996, Applause Theatre $35.00 (1-55783-263-3). A collection of 21 plays, with background information, including eight traditional and 13 contemporary works by such authors as Langston

Hughes, Ossie Davis, Gertrude Stein, and August Strindberg. (Rev: BL 6/1–15/97; SLJ 6/97) [808.82]

4766 Winther, Barbara. *Plays from Hispanic Tales: One-Act, Royalty-Free Dramatizations for Young People, from Hispanic Stories and Folktales* (6–10). 1998, Plays paper $14.95 (0-8238-0307-4). A nicely balanced collection of 11 short plays based on folktales and legends from Spain, South and Central America, and the Caribbean. (Rev: BL 11/15/98; SLJ 9/98) [812]

Geographical Regions

Europe

GREAT BRITAIN AND IRELAND

4767 Bolt, Robert. *A Man for All Seasons* (9–12). 1990, Vintage paper $9.00 (0-679-72822-8). The story in play form of the conflict between Sir Thomas More and Henry VIII. [822]

4768 Christie, Agatha. *The Mousetrap and Other Plays* (10–12). 1993, HarperCollins paper $7.50 (0-06-100374-3). Eight mystery thrillers, including *Witness for the Prosecution.* [822]

4769 Dominic, Catherine C. *Shakespeare's Characters for Students* (9–12). 1997, Gale $85.00 (0-7876-1300-2). A useful tool for students of Shakespeare, this volume contains profiles of the characters appearing in the 38 plays, summaries of the plots, and connections to modern situations and feelings. (Rev: BL 9/15/97; SLJ 1/98) [822.3]

4770 Lipson, Greta Barclay, and Susan Solomon. *Romeo and Juliet: Plainspoken* (10–12). Illus. 1985, Good Apple paper $17.99 (0-86653-283-8). A modern-language version of *Romeo and Juliet* is given on one page and the Shakespeare version opposite. (Rev: SLJ 8/86) [822.3]

4771 Miles, Bernard. *Favorite Tales from Shakespeare* (7–10). Illus. 1993, Checkerboard $14.95 (1-56288-257-0). Shakespeare's most famous plays in a modern retelling. [822.3]

4772 Rosen, Michael. *Shakespeare's Romeo and Juliet* (7–10). 2004, Candlewick $17.99 (0-7636-2258-3). Vivid, evocative illustrations and a conversational narrative accompany passages of Shakespeare in an appealing retelling of the popular story that includes references and glossaries. (Rev: BL 12/1/03; SLJ 2/04) [823]

4773 Shakespeare, William. *The Complete Works of William Shakespeare* (9–12). Illus. 1990, Random $18.99 (0-517-05361-6). One of many editions available of the complete works of Shakespeare. [822.3]

4774 Shakespeare, William. *A Midsummer Night's Dream* (10–12). 1980, Oxford paper $8.95 (0-19-

831926-6). One of many editions of this comedy about two pairs of lovers lost in an enchanted forest. [822.3]

4775 Shakespeare, William. *Romeo and Juliet* (10–12). 1989, NAL paper $2.75 (0-451-52136-6). One of many editions of this play currently available. [822.3]

4776 Stoppard, Tom. *Rosencrantz and Guildenstern Are Dead* (10–12). 1967, Grove paper $12.00 (0-8021-3275-8). In this play, there is a reworking of some of the situations found in *Hamlet* using two of Hamlet's friends as the central characters. [822]

4777 Thomas, Dylan. *Under Milk Wood: A Play for Voices* (10–12). 1954, New Directions paper $8.95 (0-8112-0209-7). This radio play about the people of a small Welsh village is also performed as a theater piece. [822]

4778 Wilde, Oscar. *The Importance of Being Earnest* (9–12). 1976, Avon paper $4.50 (0-380-01277-4). Mistaken identities is one of the dramatic ploys used in this comedy of manners. [822]

OTHER COUNTRIES

4779 Beckett, Samuel. *Waiting for Godot: Tragicomedy in 2 Acts* (10–12). 1954, Grove paper $12.00 (0-8021-3034-8). A difficult but rewarding play by the Irish playwright who lived in Paris. [842]

4780 Brecht, Bertolt, and Charles Laughton. *Galileo* (9–12). 1991, Grove Weidenfeld paper $6.95 (0-8021-3059-3). Brecht's play chronicles the clash between Italian scientist Galileo and the Roman Catholic Church over Galileo's theories about the solar system. [832]

4781 Chekhov, Anton Pavlovich. *The Plays of Anton Chekhov* (9–12). Trans. by Paul Schmidt. 1997, HarperCollins paper $14.95 (0-06-092875-1). These new translations capture the humor of Chekhov's plays. [891.7]

4782 Fugard, Athol. *"Master Harold" — and the Boys* (10–12). 1982, Knopf paper $10.00 (0-14-048187-7). A moving play set in South Africa that deals with relations between a white boy and his family's servants. [822]

4783 Genet, Jean. *The Maids and Deathwatch: Two Plays* (10–12). Trans. by Bernard Frechtman. 1954, Grove paper $13.00 (0-8021-5056-X). This volume consists of two of Genet's most popular plays. [842]

4784 Goldoni, Carlo. *Villeggiatura: A Trilogy Condensed* (9–12). Trans. by Robert Cornthwaite. Series: Young Actors. 1995, Smith & Kraus paper $14.95 (1-880399-72-5). A three-act comedy of manners in 18th-century Italian court life, perfect for drama classes or theater groups. (Rev: BL 2/1/95; SLJ 4/95) [852]

4785 Oates, Whitney J., and Eugene O'Neill, Jr. *Seven Famous Greek Plays* (10–12). 1950, Modern Library paper $9.00 (0-394-70125-9). A collection of the most famous plays from ancient Greece. [882.008]

United States

4786 Bert, Norman A., and Deb Bert. *Play it Again! More One-Act Plays for Acting Students* (8–12). 1993, Meriwether paper $14.95 (0-916260-97-6). This is a collection of 21 one-act plays and monologues for young actors. [812.008]

4787 Blinn, William. *Brian's Song* (9–12). 1983, Bantam paper $4.99 (0-553-26618-7). This edition is the screenplay of the television movie about the doomed football player Brian Piccolo. [808.1]

4788 Cassady, Marsh, ed. *Great Scenes from Minority Playwrights: Seventy-four Scenes of Cultural Diversity* (9–12). 1997, Meriwether paper $15.95 (1-56608-029-0). This work contains condensations of nine modern plays representing five minority groups and exploring insights into the various cultures and aspects of prejudice. (Rev: BL 10/1/97; SLJ 11/97) [812]

4789 Dove, Rita. *The Darker Face of the Earth* (9–12). 1994, Story Line paper $10.95 (0-934257-74-4). This verse play, based on the story of Oedipus and placed within the context of slavery, is set on a plantation in antebellum South Carolina. (Rev: BL 2/15/94*) [812.54]

4790 Fairbanks, Stephanie S. *Spotlight: Solo Scenes for Student Actors* (7–12). 1996, Meriwether paper $14.95 (1-56608-020-7). This book contains 55 excellent one- to three-page monologues, some specifically for girls, others for boys, and others nonspecific. (Rev: BL 12/1/96; SLJ 5/97) [812]

4791 Gallo, Donald, ed. *Center Stage: One-Act Plays for Teenage Readers and Actors* (7–12). 1990, HarperCollins $17.00 (0-06-022170-4); paper $8.99 (0-06-447078-4). A collection of 10 one-act plays especially written for this collection by such authors as Walter Dean Myers and Ouida Sebestyen. (Rev: BL 12/1/90; SLJ 9/90) [812]

4792 Gardner, Herb. *The Collected Plays* (9–12). Illus. 2000, Applause Theatre $27.95 (1-55783-394-X). Five plays include *A Thousand Clowns, I'm Not Rappaport,* and *Conversations with My Father,* and one screenplay. (Rev: BL 5/15/00) [812]

4793 Gardner, Herb. *Conversations with My Father* (9–12). 1994, Pantheon $20.00 (0-679-42405-9); paper $11.00 (0-679-74766-4). This play — set in a New York City bar spanning the 1930s and 1940s — depicts the relationship between a Jewish immigrant and his two sons. (Rev: BL 1/1/94) [812]

4794 Garner, Joan. *Stagings* (6–12). 1995, Teacher Ideas paper $27.00 (1-56308-343-4). A collection of royalty-free short plays suitable for teens, also including character and costume descriptions, set suggestions, staging options, and lesson plans. (Rev: BL 2/1/96; BR 3–4/96; VOYA 4/96) [812]

4795 Gibson, William. *The Miracle Worker: A Play for Television* (7–12). 1957, Knopf $20.00 (0-394-40630-3); Bantam paper $5.99 (0-553-24778-6). An expanded version of the TV play about Annie Sullivan and Helen Keller. [812]

4796 Goldman, James. *A Lion in Winter* (10–12). 1983, Penguin paper $8.95 (0-14-048174-5). A rich historical play about Henry II, his wife Eleanor of Aquitaine, and their three sons. [812]

4797 Goodrich, Frances. *The Diary of Anne Frank* (7–12). Illus. 1958, Dramatists Play Service paper $6.50 (0-8222-0307-3). This is the prize-winning play based on the diary. [812]

4798 Graham, Kristen, ed. *The Great Monologues from the Women's Project* (9–12). 1995, Smith & Kraus paper $7.95 (1-880399-35-0). Fifty-three monologues provide dramatic, funny, angry, and sexy performance opportunities. (Rev: BL 2/15/95) [808.82]

4799 *Great Scenes for Young Actors* (7–12). Series: Young Actors. 1997, Smith & Kraus paper $14.95 (1-57525-107-8). A variety of scenes representing different forms of drama are reprinted from such playwrights as Arthur Miller, George S. Kaufman, Horton Foote, and Paul Zindel. (Rev: BL 3/1/99; SLJ 6/99) [808.82]

4800 Halline, Allan G., ed. *Six Modern American Plays* (10–12). 1966, McGraw-Hill paper $7.75 (0-07-553660-9). The six plays in this collection are *The Glass Menagerie, Mister Roberts, The Emperor Jones, The Man Who Came to Dinner, The Little Foxes,* and *Winterset.* [812]

4801 Hamlett, Christina. *Humorous Plays for Teen-Agers* (7–10). 1987, Plays paper $12.95 (0-8238-0276-0). Easily read one-act plays for beginners in acting. (Rev: BL 5/1/87; BR 5–6/87; SLJ 11/87) [812]

4802 Handman, Wynn, ed. *Modern American Scenes for Student Actors* (9–12). 1978, Bantam paper $4.95 (0-553-25844-3). A total of 50 scenes are included, plus information on the plot of each play and its playwright. [812.08]

4803 Hansberry, Lorraine. *A Raisin in the Sun: A Drama in Three Acts* (7–12). Illus. 1987, NAL paper $8.95 (0-452-25942-8). The drama that involves a middle-class African American family in Chicago. [812]

4804 Hellman, Lillian. *Six Plays by Lillian Hellman* (9–12). 1979, Random paper $15.00 (0-394-74112-

9). This collection includes *Watch on the Rhine, The Little Foxes,* and *The Children's Hour.* [812]

4805 Henderson, Heather H. *The Flip Side: 64 Point-of-View Monologs for Teens* (10–12). 1998, Meriwether paper $12.95 (1-56608-045-2). This is a collection of original, short monologues written for this anthology. (Rev: VOYA 10/99) [808.82]

4806 Jones, Tom, and Harvey Schmidt. *The Fantasticks: The Thirtieth Anniversary Edition* (9–12). 1990, Applause Theatre $19.95 (1-55783-074-6). The text and lyrics of the long-running musical about young love and meddling fathers. [812]

4807 Kamerman, Sylvia, ed. *Plays of Black Americans: The Black Experience in America, Dramatized for Young People* (7–12). 1994, Plays paper $13.95 (0-8238-0301-5). Eleven dramas focus on the history of African Americans. (Rev: BL 5/15/95; SLJ 2/95) [812]

4808 Krell-Oishi, Mary. *Perspectives: Relevant Scenes for Teens* (9–12). 1997, Meriwether paper $12.95 (1-56608-030-4). Problems in such areas as dating, teen pregnancy, family relationships, abortion, and homosexuality are explored in 23 original scenes for high school and college actors. (Rev: BL 10/1/97; SLJ 11/97) [812]

4809 Laurents, Arthur. *West Side Story: A Musical* (7–12). Illus. 1958, Random $13.95 (0-394-40788-1). This contemporary variation on the Romeo and Juliet story contains the script and lyrics by Stephen Sondheim. (Rev: BL 10/1/88) [812]

4810 Lawrence, Jerome, and Robert E. Lee. *Inherit the Wind* (9–12). 1969, Bantam paper $5.50 (0-553-26915-1). A dramatic re-creation of the evolution trial that pitted Darrow against Bryan. [812]

4811 Lawrence, Jerome, and Robert E. Lee. *The Night Thoreau Spent in Jail* (9–12). 1983, Bantam paper $5.99 (0-553-27838-X). A play based on the incident when Thoreau refused to pay taxes. [812]

4812 Lerner, Alan Jay. *Camelot* (7–12). 1961, Random $13.95 (0-394-40521-8). This musical tells of the tragic love of King Arthur and Guinevere. [812]

4813 Levin, Ira. *Deathtrap* (9–12). 1979, Random $9.95 (0-394-50727-4). A suspenseful mystery with interesting plot twists that keep the reader guessing. [812]

4814 Luce, William. *The Belle of Amherst: A Play Based on the Life of Emily Dickinson* (9–12). 1978, Houghton paper $7.95 (0-395-26253-4). A one-woman play based on the life of the famous poet. [812]

4815 McCullers, Carson. *The Member of the Wedding: A Play* (9–12). 1951, New Directions paper $9.95 (0-8112-0093-0). This play, based on the author's novel, tells of a young girl growing up in a southern town and searching for identity. [812]

4816 McCullough, L. E. *Plays of America from American Folklore for Young Actors* (7–12). Series: Young Actors. 1996, Smith & Kraus paper $14.95 (1-57525-040-3). Ten original short plays based on folk traditions are included, along with suggestions for staging and costumes. (Rev: BL 8/96; SLJ 8/96) [812]

4817 Miller, Arthur. *The Crucible* (10–12). 1987, Penguin paper $8.95 (0-14-048138-9). A powerful play that deals with the Salem witch trials of 1692. [812]

4818 Miller, Arthur. *Death of a Salesman* (10–12). 1949, Viking paper $7.95 (0-14-048134-6). The powerful drama of Willy Loman and his tragic end. (Rev: BL 2/15/91) [812]

4819 Miller, Arthur. *The Portable Arthur Miller.* Rev. ed. (9–12). 1995, Penguin paper $16.95 (0-14-024709-2). As well as some autobiographical material, this book supplies full texts for several plays including *Death of a Salesman, The Crucible,* and *After the Fall.* [812]

4820 Nelson, Anne. *The Guys* (10–12). 2002, Random paper $12.95 (0-8129-6729-1). This moving two-person play re-creates the horrors of September 11, 2001, as seen through the eyes of a journalist and a fire captain. (Rev: BL 8/02) [812]

4821 Nemiroff, Robert, ed. *Lorraine Hansberry: The Collected Last Plays* (10–12). 1983, NAL paper $8.95 (0-452-25414-0). This collection of three plays includes *Les Blancs, The Drinking Gourd,* and *What Use Are Flowers?* [812]

4822 O'Neill, Eugene. *Long Day's Journey into Night* (10–12). 1956, Yale Univ. Pr. $20.00 (0-300-00807-4); paper $10.95 (0-300-00176-2). A harrowing play about a night in lives of a theatrical family in their New England home in 1912. [812]

4823 Richards, Stanley, ed. *The Most Popular Plays of the American Theatre: Ten of Broadway's Longest-Running Plays* (9–12). Illus. 1979, Scarborough House $24.95 (0-8128-2682-5). The 10 hits include *Life with Father, Tobacco Road, Abie's Irish Rose,* and more recent plays like *Same Time, Next Year* and *Barefoot in the Park.* [812.08]

4824 Shaffer, Peter. *Amadeus* (9–12). 1981, Harper-Collins paper $11.00 (0-06-090783-5). A highly subjective view in dramatic format of the relationship between Mozart and Salieri. [822]

4825 Simon, Neil. *Barefoot in the Park* (9–12). Illus. 1984, Random $11.95 (0-394-40515-3). A witty play about a young married couple coping in a New York apartment. [812]

4826 Simon, Neil. *Brighton Beach Memoirs* (7–12). 1984, Random $14.95 (0-394-53739-4). The first of three semiautobiographical plays about the growing pains of Brooklyn-born Eugene Jerome. The other

255

two are *Biloxi Blues* (1986) and *Broadway Bound* (1988). (Rev: BL 6/87) [812]

4827 Simon, Neil. *Broadway Bound* (9–12). 1987, Random $13.95 (0-394-56395-6). The concluding semiautobiographical play in the humorous but touching trilogy that included the also-recommended *Brighton Beach Memoirs* (1984) and *Biloxi Blues* (1986). (Rev: BL 3/1/88; SLJ 5/88) [812]

4828 Simon, Neil. *The Collected Plays of Neil Simon* (9–12). 1979, Random $29.95 (0-394-50770-3); NAL paper $12.95 (0-452-25871-5). This volume includes such plays as *The Sunshine Boys* and *California Suite*. Earlier plays are found in volume one, published by NAL. [812]

4829 Simon, Neil. *Lost in Yonkers* (9–12). 1992, Random $16.50 (0-679-40890-8). Prize-winning play about two brothers forced to live with their strict grandmother and ditzy aunt after their mother dies. (Rev: BL 3/15/92; SLJ 6/92) [812]

4830 Slaight, Craig, ed. *New Plays from A.C.T.'s Young Conservatory* (9–12). 1993, Smith & Kraus paper $14.95 (1-880399-25-3). Five contemporary plays written from the viewpoints of the young actors ages 13 to 22, who perform them. (Rev: BL 8/93; VOYA 8/93) [812]

4831 Slaight, Craig, ed. *New Plays from A.C.T.'s Young Conservatory, vol. II* (10–12). 1996, Smith & Kraus paper $14.95 (1-880399-73-3). Mature in subject matter and language, this is a collection of four thought-provoking new plays (including a heart-breaker by Paul Zindel) for today's teens. (Rev: SLJ 7/96; VOYA 12/96) [812]

4832 Smith, Marisa, ed. *Seattle Children's Theatre: Six Plays for Young Audiences* (9–12). 1996, Smith & Kraus $14.95 (1-57525-008-X). A collection of six plays commissioned and performed by the Seattle Children's Theatre that explore adolescence, its problems and concerns. (Rev: BL 6/1–15/97; BR 11–12/97; SLJ 6/97) [812]

4833 Smith, Ronn. *Nothing but the Truth* (7–10). 1997, Avon paper $4.99 (0-380-78715-6). This is a play version of Avi's novel about a 9th-grader whose suspension from school becomes a national issue. (Rev: VOYA 8/97) [812]

4834 Soto, Gary. *Nerdlandia: A Play* (8–12). 1999, Penguin paper $55.99 (0-698-11784-0). Young love causes transformations in nerdy Martin and cool Ceci in this hip play full of Spanish dialogue. (Rev: BL 10/1/99) [812.4]

4835 Stein, Joseph, and Sheldon Harnick. *Fiddler on the Roof: Based on Sholem Aleichem's Stories* (9–12). 1990, Limelight paper $8.95 (0-87910-136-9). The script and lyrics of this musical set in pre-revolutionary Russia. [812]

4836 Thoms, Annie, ed. *With Their Eyes: September 11th: The View from a High School at Ground Zero* (7–12). Photos by Ethan Moses. 2002, HarperCollins paper $6.99 (0-06-051718-2). A collection of moving and dramatic monologues created after students at a high school near Ground Zero interviewed fellow students, faculty, and others about their experiences that day. (Rev: BL 9/1/02; SLJ 1/03) [812]

4837 Wasserman, Dale. *Man of La Mancha* (7–12). Illus. 1966, Random paper $9.95 (0-394-40619-2). Based loosely on Cervantes's novel, this is a musical play of the adventures of Don Quixote and his servant Sancho Panza. [812]

4838 Wasserstein, Wendy. *The Heidi Chronicles, and Other Plays* (10–12). 1990, Harcourt paper $13.00 (0-679-73499-6). A collection of plays from one of America's current playwrights noted for her good humor and depth of feeling. [812]

4839 Wilder, Thornton. *Our Town* (10–12). 1998, HarperCollins paper $8.00 (0-06-092984-7). Life in the town of Grover's Corners in New Hampshire as portrayed in the prize-winning play. [812]

4840 Wilder, Thornton. *Three Plays: Our Town, The Skin of Our Teeth, The Matchmaker: With a Preface* (10–12). 1957, Harper & Row paper $15.00 (0-06-092985-5). Three of Wilder's best-known plays. [812]

4841 Williams, Tennessee. *The Glass Menagerie* (9–12). 1999, New Directions paper $7.95 (0-8112-1404-4). A touching play in which a domineering mother persuades her son to help find a suitor for her crippled daughter. [812]

4842 Williams, Tennessee. *A Streetcar Named Desire* (10–12). 1980, New Directions paper $9.95 (0-8112-0765-X). This is a full text of the great play set in New Orleans about a faded beauty clinging to sanity. Also use *Cat on a Hot Tin Roof* (1975). [812]

4843 Wilson, August. *Fences* (10–12). 1986, NAL paper $6.95 (0-452-26048-5). The prize-winning play about a black family living in Pittsburgh in 1957 and ruled by a domineering father. (Rev: BL 9/1/86) [812]

4844 Wilson, August. *Jitney* (10–12). 2001, Overlook paper $14.95 (1-58567-370-6). The adventure and misadventures of a group of African Americans involved in running a gypsy cab service are told in this engrossing play. [812]

4845 Wilson, August. *Joe Turner's Come and Gone: A Play in Two Acts* (10–12). 1988, New Am. Lib. paper $11.00 (0-452-26009-4). This is a fine addition to the cycle of plays by Wilson that explores black America during different decade intervals. [812]

4846 Wilson, August. *The Piano Lesson* (9–12). 1990, 1990, NAL paper $9.95 (0-452-26534-7). The Pulitzer Prize-winning play about an African American family in Pittsburgh in the 1930s. (Rev: BL 1/1/91) [812.54]

4847 Zindel, Paul. *The Effect of Gamma Rays on Man-in-the-Moon Marigolds* (9–12). Illus. 1971, HarperCollins $18.00 (0-06-026829-8); Bantam paper $5.99 (0-553-28028-7). This play deals with a widow and her two daughters, one of whom finds fulfillment in a science project. (Rev: BL 10/15/88) [812]

Other Regions

4848 Perry, Mark. *A Dress for Mona* (7–12). 2002, Fifth Epoch $10.00 (1-931492-02-6). Iranian persecution of people of the Baha'i faith is illustrated in this moving play that features Mona, a 16-year-old who will die for her beliefs; staging advice and a pronunciation guide are among the aids provided. (Rev: VOYA 6/03)

Poetry

General and Miscellaneous Collections

4849 *Americans' Favorite Poems: The Favorite Poem Project Anthology* (9–12). Ed. by Robert Pinsky and Maggie Dietz. 1999, Norton $27.50 (0-393-04820-9). From John Keats to Lucille Clifton, this is a collection of poetry chosen by Americans of all ages. (Rev: BL 11/1/99) [808.81]

4850 Appelt, Kathi. *Poems from Homeroom: A Writer's Place to Start* (7–12). 2002, Holt $16.95 (0-8050-6978-X). Poems that speak to the adolescent experience are accompanied by encouraging writing tips from the poet. (Rev: BL 11/15/02; SLJ 9/02) [811]

4851 Baker, Russell, ed. *The Norton Book of Light Verse* (10–12). 1986, Norton $29.95 (0-393-02366-4). An amusing collection that spans centuries and a large number of past and present writers. (Rev: BL 1/1/87) [821]

4852 Barnstone, Aliki, and Willis Barnstone. *A Book of Women Poets from Antiquity to Now*. Rev. ed. (9–12). 1992, Schocken paper $22.00 (0-8052-0997-2). This revised edition of the anthology first published in 1980 still offers representative writings by women of many cultures, but has broadened its selection of American poetry. [808.81]

4853 *The Best Poems in the English Language: From Chaucer Through Robert Frost* (9–12). Ed. by Harold Bloom. 2004, HarperCollins $34.95 (0-06-054041-9). This is a massive anthology of the best of British and American poets writing in English. (Rev: BL 2/1/04; SLJ 8/04) [821]

4854 Bloom, Harold, ed. *Poets of World War I: Wilfred Owen and Isaac Rosenberg* (7–12). Series: Bloom's Major Poets. 2002, Chelsea LB $21.95 (0-7910-5932-4). This introduction to the work of these two poets includes four poems by each, with analysis. (Rev: BR 11–12/02; SLJ 7/02) [821]

4855 Bowman, Catherine. *Word of Mouth* (10–12). 2003, Vintage paper $12.00 (0-375-71315-8). A stunning collection of contemporary poetry, including representative writings by Elizabeth Spires, Czeslaw Milosz, Lucille Clifton, Kevin Young, and Marilyn Chin. (Rev: BL 3/15/03) [811]

4856 Brenner, Barbara, ed. *Voices: Poetry and Art from Around the World* (6–12). Illus. 2000, National Geographic $18.95 (0-7922-7071-1). A fine collection of world poetry and art, arranged geographically in a handsome oversized book. (Rev: BL 12/1/00; HBG 3/01; SLJ 3/01; VOYA 4/02) [808.81]

4857 Ciardi, John, and Miller Williams. *How Does a Poem Mean?* (10–12). 1975, Houghton paper $27.16 (0-395-18605-6). By analyzing several poems, the authors explain the value and nature of poetry. [821.08]

4858 Dore, Anita, ed. *The Premier Book of Major Poets* (10–12). 1996, Fawcett paper $11.00 (0-449-91186-1). This is a collection of English and American poetry from the Middle Ages to the present. [808.1]

4859 Duffy, Carol Ann, ed. *Stopping for Death: Poems of Death and Loss* (7–10). Illus. 1996, Holt $14.95 (0-8050-4717-4). An anthology of poems from around the world, including many contemporary poets, that deal with dying, death, and loss. (Rev: BL 8/96; SLJ 8/96; VOYA 10/96) [808.81]

4860 Felleman, Hazel, ed. *Poems That Live Forever* (9–12). 1965, Doubleday $18.95 (0-385-00358-7). A collection of familiar poems arranged under subjects like love, friendship, and home. [821.08]

4861 Foster, John, ed. *Let's Celebrate: Festival Poems* (8–12). Illus. 1997, Oxford paper $11.95 (0-19-276085-8). With many illustrations, this handsome volume includes poems on many of the world's holidays by 41 English-speaking poets. (Rev: VOYA 8/90) [808.81]

4862 Gilbert, Sandra M., et al., eds. *Mother Songs: Poems for, by, and About Mothers* (9–12). 1995, Norton $22.50 (0-393-03771-1). Poems by men and women for and about mothers. (Rev: BL 5/1/95) [811.008]

4863 Glenn, Mel. *Split Image: A Story in Poems* (9–12). 2000, HarperCollins $15.95 (0-688-16249-5). A troubled Chinese American girl records her thoughts in verse in this disturbing book that ends with the girl's suicide. (Rev: BL 4/1/00; HBG 3/01; SLJ 6/00) [811.54]

4864 *Gods and Mortals: Modern Poems on Classical Myths* (10–12). Ed. by Nina Kossman. 2000, Oxford $27.50 (0-19-513341-2). There are more than 300 20th-century poems in this anthology, all of which deal with the gods and goddesses of ancient Greece. (Rev: BL 10/1/00) [808.81]

4865 *Good Poems* (10–12). Ed. by Garrison Keillor. 2002, Viking $25.95 (0-670-03126-7). A cross section of outstanding English-language poems that Keillor originally selected to be read on air. (Rev: BL 8/02*; SLJ 3/03) [811]

4866 Gordon, Ruth, ed. *Peeling the Onion* (8–12). 1993, HarperCollins $15.89 (0-06-021728-6). A collection of 66 poems with multilayered meanings by world-famous contemporary poets. (Rev: BL 6/1–15/93*; SLJ 7/93; VOYA 8/93) [808.81]

4867 Gordon, Ruth, ed. *Pierced by a Ray of Sun* (7–12). 1995, HarperCollins LB $16.89 (0-06-023614-0). A compilation of poems from across cultures and eras on topics from the timely to the timeless and emotions from hope to despair. (Rev: BL 5/1/95*; SLJ 6/95) [808.81]

4868 Gordon, Ruth, sel. *Under All Silences: Shades of Love* (8–12). 1987, HarperCollins $13.00 (0-06-022154-2). Sixty-six love poems, dating from ancient Egypt to modern days. (Rev: BL 9/15/87; BR 3–4/88; SLJ 10/87; VOYA 4/88) [808.1]

4869 Greenberg, Jan, ed. *Heart to Heart: New Poems Inspired by Twentieth-Century American Art* (5–10). Illus. 2001, Abrams $19.95 (0-8109-4386-7). This book contains specially commissioned poems from well-known writers to accompany some of the finest artworks of the 20th century. (Rev: BL 3/15/01*; HBG 10/01; SLJ 4/01*; VOYA 8/01) [811]

4870 Hall, Linda, ed. *An Anthology of Poetry by Women: Tracing the Tradition* (9–12). 1995, Cassell paper $15.95 (0-304-32434-5). Women's poetry from early times, organized by themes. (Rev: BL 3/1/95) [811]

4871 Harmon, William. *The Top 500 Poems* (9–12). 1992, Columbia Univ. Pr. $36.95 (0-231-08028-X).

A compilation of the 500 poems that appear most frequently in anthologies. (Rev: BL 4/1/93; SLJ 2/93) [821.008]

4872 Harrison, Michael, and Christopher Stuart-Clark, eds. *The Oxford Book of Christmas Poems* (7–12). Illus. 1999, Oxford paper $12.95 (0-19-276214-1). A total of 120 British and American poems are included. [808.81]

4873 Herrera, Juan Felipe. *CrashBoomLove* (9–12). 1999, Univ. of New Mexico Pr. $18.95 (0-8263-2113-5); paper $10.95 (0-8263-2114-3). A powerful narrative poem describes the alienation and anger felt by 16-year-old Cesar Garcia. (Rev: BL 2/1/00; SLJ 3/00) [811]

4874 Hill, Selma. *Bunny* (10–12). 2002, Bloodaxe paper $17.95 (1-85224-507-7). These poems take readers inside the mind of a troubled teenage girl flirting with depression and increasingly obsessed by morbid thoughts; recommended for mature teens. (Rev: BL 3/15/02) [821]

4875 Hirsch, Edward. *Lay Back the Darkness* (11–12). 2003, Knopf $23.00 (0-375-41521-1). Hirsch draws on a wide variety of themes — from the mythology of ancient Greece to the all-too-real horrors of the Holocaust — for the poems in this sixth collection of his poetry. (Rev: BL 2/1/03*) [811]

4876 Hollis, Jill, ed. *Love's Witness: Five Centuries of Love Poetry by Women* (9–12). 1993, Carroll & Graf paper $11.95 (0-7867-0030-0). This anthology of five centuries of love poetry by women reflects the similarities and differences of love through the ages. (Rev: BL 11/15/93) [821]

4877 Homer. *The Iliad* (10–12). 1989, Doubleday paper $8.95 (0-385-05941-8). One of many recommended editions of this great Greek epic about the Trojan War. [883]

4878 Homer. *The Odyssey* (10–12). 1996, Viking $49.95 (0-14-086430-X); Farrar paper $10.00 (0-374-52574-9). These two editions represent the many available of this epic poem about the wanderings of Odysseus on his way home from the Trojan War. [883]

4879 Janeczko, Paul B., ed. *Looking for Your Name: A Collection of Contemporary Poems* (9–12). 1993, Orchard LB $17.99 (0-531-08625-9). A wide variety of poems by men and women about soldiers' war memories, family violence, gay/lesbian lives, sports, love, AIDS, suicide, and other aspects of life. (Rev: BL 1/15/93*) [811]

4880 Janeczko, Paul B., ed. *Stone Bench in an Empty Park* (5–12). Illus. 2000, Orchard LB $16.99 (0-531-33259-4). An inspired collection of haiku from a variety of poets, illustrated with stunning black-and-white photographs. (Rev: BCCB 6/00; BL 3/15/00*; HB 3–4/00; HBG 10/00; SLJ 3/00) [811]

4881 Janeczko, Paul B., ed. *Wherever Home Begins: 100 Contemporary Poems* (8–12). 1995, Orchard LB $17.99 (0-531-08781-6). One hundred poems that express various approaches to a sense of place. (Rev: BL 10/1/95; SLJ 11/95; VOYA 12/95) [811]

4882 Koertge, Ron. *Shakespeare Bats Cleanup* (7–10). 2003, Candlewick $15.99 (0-7636-2116-1). Recuperating from an illness, 14-year-old Kevin amuses himself writing poetry and recounts the triumphs and problems of his life in verse. (Rev: BL 4/1/03*; HB 7–8/03; HBG 10/03; SLJ 5/03*; VOYA 8/03) [811]

4883 Livingston, Myra Cohn, ed. *Call Down the Moon: Poems of Music* (6–12). 1995, Macmillan $16.00 (0-689-80416-4). A collection of poems by Tennyson, Whitman, and others, who use words to express how we create and listen to music. (Rev: BL 10/1/95; SLJ 11/95; VOYA 2/96) [821.008]

4884 Livingston, Myra Cohn, ed. *A Time to Talk: Poems of Friendship* (7–12). 1992, Macmillan paper $14.00 (0-689-50558-2). Poems from many times and places express how friends bring us joy and support, how they betray and leave us, how we miss them when they're gone, and other aspects of friendship. (Rev: BL 10/15/92; SLJ 11/92) [808.81]

4885 *Love Poems* (9–12). 1993, Knopf $12.50 (0-679-42906-9). Represented in this collection of classic love poems are such well-known poets as Robert Browning, W. B. Yeats, Robert Graves, Christina Rossetti, William Carlos Williams, and Pablo Neruda. [808.81]

4886 McCullough, Frances, ed. *Earth, Air, Fire, and Water.* Rev. ed. (9–12). 1989, HarperCollins $13.95 (0-06-024207-8). A collection of poems from many cultures that have been chosen for their specific appeal to young adults. (Rev: BL 5/15/89; SLJ 6/89; VOYA 8/89) [808.81]

4887 McCullough, Frances, ed. *Love Is Like a Lion's Tooth: An Anthology of Love Poems* (7–12). 1984, HarperCollins $12.95 (0-06-024138-1). A collection of love poems that span time from ancient days to the 20th century. [808.81]

4888 Merrell, Billy. *Talking in the Dark* (9–12). 2003, Scholastic paper $6.99 (0-439-49036-7). This free-verse memoir, written at the age of 22, touches on a wide array of painful experiences, including parental divorce and remarriage, coming to terms with homosexuality, and a series of failed and new relationships, yet retains at its core a tone of hopefulness. (Rev: BL 12/1/03; SLJ 1/04; VOYA 4/04) [811]

4889 Nye, Naomi S. *19 Varieties of Gazelle: Poems of the Middle East* (5–10). 2002, Greenwillow LB $16.89 (0-06-009766-3). Poems by Palestinian American Nye confide details of her life and the impact of war and terrorism on the peoples of Mid-

dle Eastern heritage. (Rev: BL 4/1/02; HB 9–10/02*; HBG 10/02; SLJ 5/02*; VOYA 6/02) [811]

4890 Nye, Naomi S., ed. *This Same Sky: A Collection of Poems from Around the World* (7–12). 1992, Four Winds $20.00 (0-02-768440-7). An extraordinary collection of 129 poems by contemporary poets from 68 countries, with an index by country. (Rev: BL 10/15/92*; SLJ 12/92) [808.81]

4891 Nye, Naomi S. *What Have You Lost?* (6–12). Illus. 1999, Greenwillow $18.95 (0-688-16184-7). A collection of 140 poems about loss — some losses that are trivial, others that are serious. (Rev: BL 4/1/99; BR 9–10/99; HB 3–4/99; SLJ 4/99; VOYA 10/99) [811.008]

4892 Nye, Naomi S., and Paul B. Janeczko, eds. *I Feel a Little Jumpy Around You: A Book of Her Poems and His Poems Collected in Pairs* (8–12). 1996, Simon & Schuster paper $18.00 (0-689-80518-7). This anthology of some 200 poems explores how the genders sometimes view things differently and sometimes the same. (Rev: BL 4/1/96; BR 3–4/97; SLJ 5/96*; VOYA 8/96) [808.81]

4893 Okutoro, Lydia Omolola, ed. *Quiet Storm: Voices of Young Black Poets* (8–12). 1999, Hyperion $16.99 (0-7868-0461-0). This anthology features poems written by black youths ages 13 to 21 from the United States, Canada, England, the West Indies, and several African countries. (Rev: BL 6/1–15/99; SLJ 7/99; VOYA 12/99) [811.008]

4894 Oliver, Mary. *A Poetry Handbook* (9–12). 1994, Harcourt paper $12.00 (0-15-672400-6). A handbook on the formal aspects and structure of poetry from a Pulitzer Prize-winning poet. (Rev: BL 7/94) [808.1]

4895 Philip, Neil, ed. *It's a Woman's World: A Century of Women's Voices in Poetry* (7–12). Illus. 2000, Dutton $17.99 (0-525-46328-3). An international collection of poetry that celebrates woman's many roles in society. (Rev: BL 3/15/00; HBG 9/00; SLJ 5/00) [808.81]

4896 Philip, Neil, ed. *War and the Pity of War* (6–12). 1998, Clarion $20.00 (0-395-84982-9). An outstanding collection of poetry from different times and cultures that explores the cruelty, bravery, and tragedy of war. (Rev: BL 9/15/98; BR 5–6/99; HBG 10/99; SLJ 9/98; VOYA 2/99) [808.81]

4897 *Poems Then and Now: Poetry Collection 3* (9–12). Ed. by Fiona Waters. Illus. Series: Poems Then and Now. 2001, Evans $22.95 (0-237-52127-X). This anthology of poetry, although somewhat confusingly organized, offers a broad selection of poems from both well-known poets and those whose writings have not yet been widely read. (Rev: BL 8/01) [809.1]

4898 *Poems to Read: A New Favorite Poems Project Anthology* (10–12). Ed. by Robert Pinsky and Maggie Dietz. 2002, Norton $27.95 (0-393-01074-

0). A wide-ranging collection of poems selected by poetry lovers. (Rev: BL 6/1–15/02) [811]

4899 *Poetically Correct* (10–12). Ed. by Kristine Wright. 2000, Be-Mused paper $17.99 (0-9704868-1-2). Twelve teens give voice to their innermost thoughts about such universal issues as love, alienation, friendship, and loneliness. (Rev: VOYA 12/01) [811]

4900 *The Poetry Anthology, 1912–2002: Ninety Years of America's Most Distinguished Verse Magazine* (10–12). Ed. by Joseph Parisi and Stephen Young. 2002, Ivan R. Dee $29.95 (1-56663-468-7). This anthology, published to mark the 90th anniversary of *Poetry* magazine, offers a retrospective sampling of the best poems to appear in its pages. (Rev: BL 10/15/02*) [811]

4901 *Poetry Speaks: Hear Great Poets Read Their Work from Tennyson to Plath* (10–12). Ed. by Elise Paschen and Rebekah Presson Mosby. 2001, Sourcebooks $49.95 (1-57071-720-6). Along with essays on each great poet discussed, written by another poet, this book comes with three CDs of poetry readings. (Rev: SLJ 2/02) [808.81]

4902 *Revenge and Forgiveness: An Anthology of Poems* (8–12). Ed. by Patrice Vecchione. 2004, Holt $16.95 (0-8050-7376-0). This anthology on war, violence, and the search for peace contains poems from many lands and times. (Rev: BL 3/15/04; HB 3–4/04; SLJ 7/04; VOYA 6/04) [808.81]

4903 Rosenberg, Liz, ed. *Earth-Shattering Poems* (7–12). 1997, Holt $17.00 (0-8050-4821-9). An anthology of poems from more than 40 poets that deal with life's serious moments and intense experiences. (Rev: BL 12/15/97; BR 9–10/98; SLJ 2/98; VOYA 2/98) [808.81]

4904 Rosenberg, Liz, ed. *Light-Gathering Poems* (6–12). 2000, Holt $15.95 (0-8050-6223-8). An excellent anthology of high-quality poems, mainly from classic writers such as Byron and Frost but also from some newer voices. (Rev: BL 3/15/00; HB 5–6/00; HBG 9/00; SLJ 6/00; VOYA 6/00) [808.81]

4905 Rosenberg, Liz, ed. *Roots and Flowers: Poets and Poems on Family* (9–12). 2001, Holt $21.95 (0-8050-6433-8). An enticing collection of poems about family, with photographs of the poets and personal notes about their own families. (Rev: BL 3/15/01; HBG 10/01; SLJ 5/01*; VOYA 8/01) [811]

4906 Rothenberg, Jerome, and Pierre Joris, eds. *Poems for the Millennium: The University of California Book of Modern and Postmodern Poetry, vol. 2* (10–12). 1998, Univ. of California Pr. $70.00 (0-520-20863-3); paper $24.95 (0-520-20864-1). An excellent international collection of poetry from post-World War II through the Cold War and its aftermath, representing a wide range of well-known poets and movements. (Rev: SLJ 12/98) [808.8]

4907 Rubin, Robert Alden. *Poetry Out Loud* (9–12). 1993, Algonquin paper $9.95 (1-56512-122-8). This is a selection of 100 poems specifically chosen for reading aloud. [821.008]

4908 Schiff, Hilda, ed. *Holocaust Poetry* (9–12). 1995, St. Martin's $20.00 (0-312-13086-4). An anthology of 85 poems provides a stark memoir of the Holocaust. (Rev: BL 5/15/95*) [808.81]

4909 *Shooting the Rat: Outstanding Poems and Stories by High School Writers* (10–12). Ed. by Mark Pawlak et al. 2003, Hanging Loose $26.00 (1-931236-24-0); paper $16.00 (1-931236-23-2). This third anthology of poems by high school students that have appeared in the pages of *Hanging Loose* magazine covers a broad spectrum of issues and includes frank sexual content. (Rev: BL 9/1/03; HBG 4/04; SLJ 10/03; VOYA 10/03) [810.8]

4910 Sidman, Joyce. *The World According to Dog: Poems and Teen Voices* (6–12). Illus. 2003, Houghton $15.00 (0-618-17497-4). Poems by the author and essays by teens celebrate dogs and the companionship they offer. (Rev: BL 4/1/03; HBG 10/03; SLJ 5/03; VOYA 4/03) [810.8]

4911 Siegen-Smith, Nikki, comp. *Welcome to the World: A Celebration of Birth and Babies from Many Cultures* (10–12). 1996, Orchard $17.95 (0-531-36006-7). A collection of 20 international poems, each with a full-page photograph, that describe the pain and joy of childbirth and raising babies. (Rev: SLJ 10/96) [811]

4912 *The Spoken Word Revolution: Slam, Hip Hop and the Poetry of a New Generation* (10–12). Ed. by Marc Smith and Mark Eleveld. 2003, Sourcebooks $24.95 (1-4022-0037-4). A lively, teen-friendly collection of representative poems from cutting-edge performance poets. (Rev: BL 4/1/03) [811]

4913 Stallworthy, Jon, ed. *The Oxford Book of War Poetry* (10–12). 1984, Oxford $30.00 (0-19-214125-2). This anthology covers war poetry from ancient times to Vietnam and contemporary Northern Ireland. [808.81]

4914 Sullivan, Charles, ed. *Imaginary Animals* (6–10). 1996, Abrams $22.95 (0-8109-3470-1). A collection of works by such writers as D. H. Lawrence, Ogden Nash, and William Butler Yeats, and by artists from Andy Warhol to Winslow Homer, featuring all kinds of delightful animals, imaginary and real, among them the Jabberwock, prancing centaurs, rearing dragons, the Loch Ness monster and Salvador Dali's lobster telephone. (Rev: SLJ 2/97) [811]

4915 Thomas, Joyce Carol. *A Mother's Heart, A Daughter's Love* (6–12). 2001, HarperCollins LB $14.89 (0-06-029650-X). Two poetic voices — a mother's and a daughter's — describe their life together from the birth of the daughter through the death of the mother. (Rev: BL 3/15/01; HBG 10/01; SLJ 9/01) [811]

4916 Tom, Karen, ed. *Angst! Teen Verses from the Edge* (8–12). 2001, Workman paper $8.95 (0-7611-2383-0). A compilation of poems of varied literary standard, and some containing strong language, culled from PlanetKiki.com. (Rev: SLJ 11/01; VOYA 2/02) [811]

4917 Vecchione, Patrice, ed. *Truth and Lies: An Anthology of Poems* (6–12). 2001, Holt $17.00 (0-8050-6479-6). A collection of poems from around the world, from a variety of eras, and from well-known and obscure authors, with biographical notes. (Rev: BL 12/15/00; BR 9–10/01; HBG 10/01; SLJ 2/01*; VOYA 2/01) [808]

4918 Virgil. *The Aeneid of Virgil* (10–12). 1981, Bantam paper $4.95 (0-553-21041-6). One of several fine editions of the epic poem about the journey of Aeneas from Troy to Italy. [873]

4919 Waters, Fiona. *Poems from Many Cultures: Poetry Collection 4* (9–12). Illus. 2002, Evans $19.95 (0-237-52104-0). A diverse collection that reveals a wide range of cultures and experiences. (Rev: BL 3/15/02; SLJ 5/02) [808.81]

4920 Watson, Esther Pearl, and Mark Todd, sels. *The Pain Tree: And Other Teenage Angst-Ridden Poetry* (7–12). 2000, Houghton $16.00 (0-618-01558-2); paper $6.95 (0-618-04758-1). Poems collected from teen Web sites and magazines and illustrated with paintings express a wide range of emotions. (Rev: BR 11–12/00; HBG 9/00; SLJ 9/00; VOYA 6/00) [811]

4921 Willard, Nancy, ed. *Step Lightly: Poems for the Journey* (7–12). 1998, Harcourt paper $12.00 (0-15-202052-7). These works from the pens of about 40 poets represent the poems that the editor particularly loves. (Rev: BL 10/1/98; BR 5–6/99; HBG 3/99; SLJ 11/98; VOYA 4/99) [811:008]

Geographical Regions

Europe

GREAT BRITAIN AND IRELAND

4922 Auden, W. H. *Auden: Poems* (10–12). Ed. by Edward Mendelson. Series: Everyman's Library Pocket Poets. 1995, Knopf $12.50 (0-679-44367-3). This is a representative collection of Auden's poems that spans his entire career. [821]

4923 Barron, W. R., ed. *Sir Gawain and the Green Knight* (10–12). 1972, Viking paper $7.95 (0-14-044902-5). A fine edition of the medieval poem dealing with the testing of Gawain's courage. [821]

4924 *Beowulf: A New Verse Translation* (10–12). Trans. by Seamus Heaney. 2000, Farrar $25.00 (0-

374-11119-7). The contemporary poet supplies a beautiful, lucid translation of the most famous and longest-surviving epic poem in Old English. (Rev: BL 2/15/00) [829]

4925 Coleridge, Samuel Taylor. *The Rime of the Ancient Mariner* (7–12). Illus. 1994, Random $8.99 (0-517-11849-1). A haunting interpretation of a 200-year-old poem that tells the story of a sailor locked in a living nightmare after he shoots an innocent albatross and watches all his shipmates die. (Rev: BL 3/15/92; SLJ 4/92) [821]

4926 Coleridge, Samuel Taylor. *Samuel Taylor Coleridge* (6–10). Ed. by James Engell. Series: Poetry for Young People. 2003, Sterling $14.95 (0-8069-6951-2). Biographical information introduces a sampling of Coleridge's most famous poems, which are accompanied by editorial notes and full-color illustrations. Also use *William Wordsworth* and *William Butler Yeats* (both 2003). (Rev: BL 4/1/03; HBG 4/04; SLJ 9/03) [821]

4927 *The Columbia Anthology of British Poetry* (10–12). Ed. by Carl Woodring and James Shapiro. 1995, Columbia Univ. Pr. $34.00 (0-231-10180-5). A collection of major British poetry from Beowulf to the present. (Rev: SLJ 5/96) [821]

4928 Dahl, Roald. *Rhyme Stew* (7–10). Illus. 1999, Viking paper $3.99 (0-14-034365-2). Lots of silly poems and parodies charmingly illustrated by Quentin Blake. (Rev: BL 5/15/90; SLJ 9/90) [821]

4929 Eliot, T. S. *The Complete Poems and Plays, 1909–1950* (10–12). 1952, Harcourt $35.00 (0-15-121185-X). An omnibus volume of poetry and plays by the American-born writer who lived most of his life in England. [818]

4930 Eliot, T. S. *Old Possum's Book of Practical Cats* (9–12). 1982, Harcourt $15.00 (0-15-168656-4); paper $7.00 (0-15-668570-1). Many of the poems in this delightful collection were used in the musical *Cats*. [821]

4931 Gardner, Helen, ed. *The New Oxford Book of English Verse, 1250–1950* (10–12). 1972, Oxford $52.50 (0-19-812136-9). The first edition of this anthology appeared in 1900, and it has continued to maintain its high standards in all subsequent editions. [821.08]

4932 Gillooly, Eileen, ed. *Robert Browning* (7–12). Series: Poetry for Young People. 2001, Sterling $14.95 (0-8069-5543-0). A fine, well-illustrated introduction to the works of the English poet that gives historical context, references, and explanations of terms. (Rev: HBG 10/01; SLJ 10/01) [811]

4933 Heaney, Seamus. *The Spirit Level* (10–12). 1996, Farrar $18.00 (0-374-26779-0). A collection of poems by the Nobel Prize-winning Irish poet that deal with balances in life and the middle ground one often must settle for. (Rev: BL 5/1/96; SLJ 11/96) [821]

4934 Hughes, Ted. *Birthday Letters* (10–12). 1998, Farrar paper $12 .00 (0-374-52581-1). Published shortly after his death, this collection of poems chronicles Hughes's sometimes tortured relationship with fellow poet Sylvia Plath. [821]

4935 *John Keats: The Major Works* (10–12). Ed. by Elizabeth Cook. 2001, Oxford paper $16.95 (0-19-284063-0). This collection includes the poems published during Keats's lifetime, some published after his death, some unpublished ones, and some letters. [821]

4936 Keats, John. *Poems* (10–12). Series: Everyman's Library Pocket Poets. 1994, Knopf $12.50 (0-679-43319-8). This volume contains a good selection of the poetry of this English genius. [821]

4937 Kipling, Rudyard. *Gunga Din* (7–12). Illus. 1987, Harcourt $12.95 (0-15-200456-4). A splendid edition of this poem dealing with the Indian Mutiny of 1857 and the heroics of an abused water carrier. (Rev: BCCB 10/87; BL 11/1/87; SLJ 12/87) [821]

4938 Opie, Iona, and Peter Opie. *I Saw Esau: The Schoolchild's Pocket Book* (7–12). Illus. 1992, Candlewick $19.99 (1-56402-046-0). Traces schoolyard folk rhymes to their roots. (Rev: BL 4/15/92*; SLJ 6/92) [821]

4939 *The Poems of Dylan Thomas*. Rev. ed. (10–12). Ed. by Daniel Jones. 2003, New Directions $34.95 (0-8112-1541-5). There are approximately 200 poems in this collection, arranged chronologically. [821]

4940 Shakespeare, William. *The Essential Shakespeare* (9–12). Ed. by Ted Hughes. Series: Essential Poets. 1991, Ecco paper $8.00 (0-88001-314-1). Editor Ted Hughes has chosen representative selections of Shakespeare's poetry and other writings that illustrate his great versatility. [822.3]

4941 *Sir Gawain and the Green Knight* (10–12). Trans. by W. S. Merwin. 2002, Knopf $22.00 (0-375-41476-2). This translation of the 14th-century Middle English poem about Gawain's encounters with the Green Knight offers a fresh look at a horror classic. (Rev: BL 8/02) [821]

4942 Thomas, Dylan. *A Child's Christmas in Wales* (10–12). Illus. 1997, New Directions $10.95 (0-8112-1308-0); paper $6.00 (0-8112-1309-9). A poem that deals with the celebration of Christmas in a small Welsh town. [828]

4943 Wordsworth, William. *Poems* (10–12). Series: Everyman's Library Pocket Poets. 1995, Knopf $12.50 (0-679-44369-X). This is a representative collection of Wordworth's poems spanning his writing career. [821]

4944 *The Yeats Reader: A Portable Compendium of His Best Poetry, Drama, and Prose* (9–12). Ed. by Richard J. Finneran. 1997, Scribner $23.80 (0-684-83188-0). A rich sampling of the Irish author's plays, poetry, prose, memoirs, and writings on mysticism. [828]

OTHER COUNTRIES

4945 Poole, Adrian, and Jeremy Maule, eds. *The Oxford Book of Classical Verse in Translation* (10–12). 1995, Oxford (0-19-214209-7). This is a collection of Greek and Latin verses beginning with Homer and translated by some of the great names in English literature. (Rev: SLJ 5/96) [881.008]

United States

4946 Adoff, Arnold, ed. *I Am the Darker Brother: An Anthology of Modern Poems by Black Americans* (9–12). Illus. 1997, Simon & Schuster paper $4.99 (0-689-80869-0). This anthology of 64 poems by 29 African American poets of the 20th century explores the black person's role in American life. (Rev: BL 2/15/97; SLJ 5/97) [811.08]

4947 Adoff, Arnold. *Slow Dance Heartbreak Blues* (7–10). 1995, Lothrop $15.95 (0-688-10569-6). Gritty hip-hop poetry for modern urban teens. (Rev: BL 12/15/95; SLJ 9/95; VOYA 6/96) [811]

4948 Angelou, Maya. *And Still I Rise* (10–12). 1978, Random $13.00 (0-394-50252-3). A highly personalized volume of poetry by the author of such companion books of poetry as *Just Give Me a Cool Drink of Water 'fore I Die* (1971), *Oh Pray My Wings Are Gonna Fit Me Well* (1975), and *Shaker, Why Don't You Sing?* (1983). [811]

4949 Angelou, Maya. *Complete Collected Poems of Maya Angelou* (10–12). 1994, Random $24.00 (0-679-42895-X). Love, travel, and age are among the topics discussed in this anthology. [811]

4950 Angelou, Maya. *I Shall Not Be Moved* (10–12). 1990, Random $16.00 (0-394-58618-2). This slim volume is the author's fifth book of poetry and like the others conveys the richness, joy, and pain of being African American. (Rev: BL 5/15/90; SLJ 9/90) [811]

4951 Baker, Paul. *Joker, Joker, Deuce* (9–12). 1994, Penguin paper $14.95 (0-14-058723-3). This hip-hop poetry expresses the emotions of inner city youth. (Rev: BL 2/15/94) [811]

4952 Begay, Shonto. *Navajo: Visions and Voices Across the Mesa* (7–12). 1995, Scholastic paper $17.95 (0-590-46153-2). Poetry that speaks to the ongoing struggle of living in a "dual society" and paintings firmly rooted in Navajo culture. (Rev: BL 4/1/95; SLJ 3/95) [811]

4953 Blum, Joshua, et al. *The United States of Poetry* (10–12). 1996, Abrams $29.95 (0-8109-3927-4). A collection of 80 poems from a variety of sources including famous poets, rappers, rockers, beats, and cowboys, all reflecting a fresh view of America in this handsomely illustrated book. (Rev: BL 5/15/96; SLJ 9/96) [811]

4954 Brooks, Gwendolyn. *In Montgomery* (10–12). 2003, Third World $22.95 (0-88378-232-4). In this posthumously published collection, Brooks delivers a message of hope from bleak settings. (Rev: BL 8/03) [811]

4955 Carlson, Lori M., ed. *Cool Salsa: Bilingual Poems on Growing Up Latino in the United States* (7–12). 1994, Holt $16.95 (0-8050-3135-9). An anthology of poetry that describes the experience of growing up with a dual heritage. (Rev: BL 11/1/94; SLJ 8/94*; VOYA 2/95) [811]

4956 Clinton, Catherine, ed. *I, Too, Sing America: Three Centuries of African American Poetry* (6–10). Illus. 1998, Houghton $21.00 (0-395-89599-5). This heavily illustrated volume of 36 poems by 25 authors traces the history of African American poetry, from Phillis Wheatley to Rita Dove. (Rev: BL 11/15/98; BR 5–6/99; HBG 3/99; SLJ 11/98; VOYA 8/99) [712.2]

4957 *The Collected Poems of Langston Hughes* (9–12). Ed. by Arnold Rampersad, et al. 1994, Knopf $35.50 (0-679-42631-0). A large collection of the African American poet's work. Hughes speaks in jazzlike rhythms of the pain of everyday life, Harlem street life, prejudice, Southern violence, and love. (Rev: BL 10/1/94*) [811]

4958 Collins, Billy. *Nine Horses* (10–12). 2002, Random $21.95 (0-375-50381-1). In this collection, poet laureate Collins muses on such diverse subjects as the serenity of home and the adventure of travel. (Rev: BL 12/1/02) [811]

4959 cummings, e. e. *100 Selected Poems by e. e. cummings* (9–12). 1959, Grove paper $11.00 (0-8021-3072-0). Many of cummings's best-known works appear in this slim volume. [811]

4960 Daniels, Jim, ed. *Letters to America: Contemporary American Poetry on Race* (9–12). 1995, Wayne State Univ. Pr. paper $21.95 (0-8143-2542-4). Accessible, readable poems that speak to race and racism. (Rev: BL 11/15/95) [811]

4961 Dickinson, Emily. *The Complete Poems of Emily Dickinson* (10–12). 1960, Little, Brown $32.50 (0-316-18414-4); paper $18.00 (0-316-18413-6). This definitive edition contains 1,775 poems and fragments. [811]

4962 Dickinson, Emily. *New Poems of Emily Dickinson* (9–12). Ed. by William H. Shurr. 1993, Univ. of North Carolina Pr. $27.50 (0-8078-2115-2); paper $13.95 (0-8078-4416-0). This collection of poetry comes from writings such as letters that had been hidden for years. (Rev: BL 9/15/93; SLJ 5/94) [811]

4963 Dickinson, Emily. *The Selected Poems of Emily Dickinson* (10–12). 1996, Modern Library

$14.50 (0-679-60201-1). This stunning collection of Emily Dickinson's poetry contains more than 400 poems that were first published between the poet's death in 1886 and 1900. [811]

4964 Dove, Rita. *Mother Love* (9–12). 1995, Norton $17.95 (0-393-03808-4). Sonnets on the timeless tragedy of Demeter and Persephone. (Rev: BL 5/1/95*) [811]

4965 Dove, Rita. *Selected Poems* (9–12). 1993, Random paper $12.00 (0-679-75080-0). Three collections of poetry by the U.S. poet laureate are gathered here into one volume: *The Yellow House on the Corner; Museum;* and the Pulitzer Prize-winning *Thomas and Beulah.* Dove's images draw on African American history and family experiences to illuminate today's world. (Rev: BL 10/15/93) [811]

4966 Dunbar, Paul Laurence. *The Complete Poems of Paul Laurence Dunbar* (7–12). 1980, Dodd paper $10.95 (0-396-07895-8). The definitive collection, first published in 1913, of this African American poet's work. [811]

4967 Dunbar, Paul Laurence. *In His Own Voice: The Dramatic and Other Uncollected Works of Paul Laurence Dunbar* (10–12). Ed. by Herbert Woodward Martin and Ronald Primeau. Illus. 2002, Ohio Univ. $49.95 (0-8214-1421-6); paper $22.95 (0-8214-1422-4). Essays, plays, poems, and short stories form the backbone of this collection of works by Dunbar. (Rev: BL 2/15/02) [811]

4968 Eliot, T. S. *Eliot: Poems and Prose* (10–12). Series: Everyman's Library Pocket Poets. 1998, Knopf $12.50 (0-375-40185-7). A representative selection of the Nobel Prize winner's works. [818]

4969 Fletcher, Ralph. *Room Enough for Love: The Complete Poems of I Am Wings and Buried Alive* (7–12). 1998, Simon & Schuster paper $4.99 (0-689-81976-5). A collection of simple, gentle poems about various aspects of romantic love, taken from Fletcher's earlier books. (Rev: VOYA 8/98) [811]

4970 Franco, Betsy, ed. *You Hear Me? Poems and Writings by Teenage Boys* (7–12). 2000, Candlewick $14.99 (0-7636-1158-1). A fine collection of poems about boys coming of age that covers such topics as sex, jealousy, drugs, rejection, bullying, and being gay. (Rev: BL 10/1/00; HBG 3/01; SLJ 10/00; VOYA 12/00) [810.8]

4971 Frost, Robert. *Collected Poems, Prose, and Plays* (9–12). 1995, Library of America $35.00 (1-883011-06-X). There are several previously unpublished poems in this collection as well as plays and some prose selections. [818]

4972 Gardner, Joann, ed. *Runaway with Words: Poems from Florida's Youth Shelters* (6–12). 1996, Anhinga paper $14.95 (0-938078-47-X). Joy, anger, confusion, and fear are some of the emotions expressed in this collection of poems culled from writing workshops for teens in Florida's shelters. (Rev: BL 6/1–15/97) [811]

4973 Gibran, Kahlil. *The Prophet* (10–12). 1923, Knopf $15.00 (0-394-40428-9). A group of poems that deal with such subjects as love, good and evil, friendship, freedom, and death. [811]

4974 Gillan, Maria M., and Jennifer Gillan, eds. *Unsettling America: An Anthology of Contemporary Multicultural Poetry* (9–12). 1994, Penguin paper $15.95 (0-14-023778-X). Features poets from various cultures and backgrounds, including Native American Joy Harjo, Hawaiian Garrett Hongo, and African American Rita Dove. (Rev: BL 10/1/94; SLJ 5/95) [811]

4975 Giovanni, Nikki. *The Collected Poetry of Nikki Giovanni, 1968–1998* (10–12). 2003, Morrow $24.95 (0-06-054133-4). This magnificent collection showcases three decades of Giovanni's poems plus notes, a biographical timeline, and an afterword by the author. (Rev: BL 12/15/03) [811]

4976 Giovanni, Nikki. *Ego-Tripping and Other Poems for Young People* (9–12). Illus. 1994, Chicago Review $14.95 (1-55652-188-X). Ten poems have been added to Giovanni's 1973 collection for a total of 23 poems celebrating ordinary people and their struggles for liberation. (Rev: BL 4/15/94) [811]

4977 Giovanni, Nikki, ed. *Grand Mothers: Poems, Reminiscences, and Short Stories About the Keepers of Our Traditions* (7–12). 1994, Holt $17.95 (0-8050-2766-1). An anthology of 27 poems, memories, and stories about grandmothers, written in diverse styles and expressing a wide range of sentiments and experiences. (Rev: BL 9/15/94; SLJ 10/94; VOYA 12/94) [811]

4978 Giovanni, Nikki. *Quilting the Black-Eyed Pea* (10–12). 2002, Morrow $16.95 (0-06-009952-6). In this collection, Giovanni celebrates the lives of both her grandmother and fellow poet Gwendolyn Brooks, while also musing on topics that range widely (from Harry Potter to George W. Bush). (Rev: BL 12/15/02; VOYA 6/03) [811]

4979 Giovanni, Nikki. *The Selected Poems of Nikki Giovanni (1968–1995)* (9–12). 1996, Morrow $22.00 (0-688-14047-5). A rich synthesis of Giovanni's work that reveals the evolution of her poetic voice. (Rev: BL 12/15/95) [811]

4980 Giovanni, Nikki, ed. *Shimmy Shimmy Shimmy Like My Sister Kate: Looking at the Harlem Renaissance Through Poems* (9–12). 1996, Holt $17.95 (0-8050-3494-3). A collection of African American poetry that covers both the Harlem Renaissance with writers such as Langston Hughes as well as contemporaries including Ntozake Shange and LeRoi Jones. (Rev: BL 3/15/96; BR 11–12/96; SLJ 5/96*; VOYA 10/96) [811]

4981 Giovanni, Nikki. *Those Who Ride the Night Winds* (10–12). 1984, Morrow paper $9.00 (0-688-02653-2). Poems about love and about people who are special to the poet, among them Rosa Parks and John Lennon. [811]

4982 Glenn, Mel. *Jump Ball: A Basketball Season in Poems* (6–12). 1997, Dutton $15.99 (0-525-67554-X). In a series of poems, people involved in an inner-city high school are introduced, including basketball players, parents, teachers, and friends. (Rev: BL 10/15/97; SLJ 11/97*; VOYA 12/97) [811]

4983 Glenn, Mel. *Who Killed Mr. Chippendale? A Mystery in Poems* (7–12). 1996, Dutton $14.99 (0-525-67530-2). Using free verse, the author explores the shooting death of a high school teacher from the point of view of several characters, including students in his class and investigating police officers. (Rev: BL 6/1–15/96; SLJ 7/96*; VOYA 12/96) [811]

4984 Harmon, William, ed. *The Oxford Book of American Light Verse* (7–12). 1979, Oxford $63.95 (0-19-502509-1). In addition to such poems as "A Visit from St. Nicholas," this anthology covers lyrics by Cole Porter and Stephen Sondheim. [811.08]

4985 Harris, Jana. *We Never Speak of It: Idaho-Wyoming Poems, 1889–90* (10–12). Illus. 2003, Ontario Review paper $14.95 (0-86538-109-7). These dramatic verse monologues in the voices of a schoolteacher and a handful of her pupils paint a revealing picture of pioneer life on the Idaho-Wyoming border in the late 19th century. (Rev: BL 3/1/03) [811]

4986 Hearne, Betsy. *Polaroid and Other Poems of View* (7–12). Illus. 1991, Macmillan $13.95 (0-689-50530-2). A collection of short poems using the camera as a metaphor, drawing connections between word pictures created by the poet and pictures taken by a photographer. (Rev: BL 8/91) [811]

4987 Hernandez Cruz, Victor, et al. *Paper Dance: 55 Latino Poets* (10–12). 1995, Persea $14.00 (0-89255-201-8). A collection of the work of 55 Hispanic American poets. [811.008]

4988 Herrera, Juan F. *Laughing Out Loud, I Fly (A Caracajadas Yo Vuelo): Poems in English and Spanish* (6–10). Illus. 1998, HarperCollins $15.99 (0-06-027604-5). In this series of poems in both languages, the poet celebrates incidents in his childhood. (Rev: SLJ 5/98; VOYA 6/99) [811]

4989 Holbrook, Sara. *Walking on the Boundaries of Change: Poems of Transition* (8–12). 1998, Boyds Mills paper $8.95 (1-56397-737-0). In this collection of 53 poems, the author explores the problems of being a teen with amazing insight into concerns and decisions. (Rev: VOYA 2/99) [811]

4990 Hughes, Langston. *The Dream Keeper and Other Poems* (6–12). Illus. 1994, Knopf LB $14.99

(0-679-94421-4). A classic collection by the renowned African American poet, originally published in 1932, is presented in an updated, illustrated edition. (Rev: BL 3/15/94; VOYA 6/94) [811]

4991 Hughes, Langston. *Vintage Hughes* (10–12). 2004, Vintage paper $9.95 (1-4000-3402-7). Three short stories are included with a selection of poems in this Vintage Reader edition. (Rev: BL 12/15/03) [811]

4992 Janeczko, Paul B., ed. *Poetspeak: In Their Work, About Their Work* (7–12). Illus. 1991, Simon & Schuster paper $9.95 (0-02-043850-8). The works of 60 modern American poets are included, with comments by the poets themselves on their work. [811.08]

4993 Johnson, Angela. *The Other Side: Shorter Poems* (6–12). 1998, Orchard LB $16.99 (0-531-33114-8). This African American poet gives us glimpses of her childhood in Alabama, her family life, and her views on such issues as the Vietnam War, racism, and the Black Panthers. (Rev: BL 11/15/98; BR 5–6/99; HB 11–12/98; HBG 3/99; SLJ 9/98; VOYA 2/99) [811]

4994 Johnson, Dave, ed. *Movin': Teen Poets Take Voice* (5–10). 2000, Orchard $15.95 (0-531-30258-X); paper $6.95 (0-531-07171-5). An anthology of poems by teens who participated in New York Public Library workshops or submitted their work via the Web. (Rev: BL 3/15/00; HBG 10/00; SLJ 5/00; VOYA 6/00) [811]

4995 Knudson, R. R., and May Swenson, eds. *American Sports Poems* (7–12). 1988, Watts LB $19.99 (0-531-08353-5). An excellent collection that concentrates on such popular sports as baseball, football, and swimming. (Rev: BL 8/88; BR 3–4/89; SLJ 11/88; VOYA 10/88) [811]

4996 Koertge, Ron. *The Brimstone Journals* (7–12). 2001, Candlewick $15.99 (0-7636-1302-9). Fifteen students at Brimstone High describe in poetry the issues that trouble them, such as overambitious parents, sexual abuse, dating, bullies, racism, and violence. (Rev: BCCB 4/01; BL 4/15/01; HBG 10/01; SLJ 3/01; VOYA 8/01) [811]

4997 Lawrence, Jacob. *Harriet and the Promised Land* (6–12). 1993, Simon & Schuster $18.95 (0-671-86673-7). The efforts of Harriet Tubman's to lead slaves to freedom in the North is retold in rhythmic text and narrative paintings. (Rev: BL 10/1/93*) [811]

4998 Le Guin, Ursula K. *Sixty Odd: New Poems* (9–12). 1999, Shambhala paper $14.00 (1-57062-388-0). A collection of poems by the popular science fiction author. (Rev: SLJ 2/00) [811]

4999 Lewis, J. Patrick. *Freedom Like Sunlight: Praisesongs for Black Americans* (5–12). Illus. 2000, Creative Co. $17.95 (1-56846-163-1). This collection of original poems pays tribute to such important African Americans as Sojourner Truth, Arthur Ashe, Rosa Parks, Marian Anderson, Malcolm X, and Langston Hughes. (Rev: BL 9/15/00*; HBG 3/01; SLJ 12/00) [811]

5000 *Like Thunder: Poets Respond to Violence in America* (10–12). Ed. by Virgil Suarez and Ryan G. Van Cleave. 2002, Univ. of Iowa Pr. $44.95 (0-87745-791-3); paper $19.95 (0-87745-792-1). More than 100 poets from diverse backgrounds speak out about such disturbing topics as child abuse, rape, gang shootings, and school violence. (Rev: BL 3/1/02*) [811]

5001 Livingston, Myra Cohn, ed. *I Am Writing a Poem About . . . A Game of Poetry* (9–12). 1997, Simon & Schuster $16.00 (0-689-81156-X). These are the poems that resulted when students in the author's poetry-writing classes were asked to write poems using randomly selected words as inspirations. (Rev: BL 9/1/97; HBG 3/98; SLJ 10/97; VOYA 2/98) [811]

5002 Loewen, Nancy, ed. *Walt Whitman* (7–12). 1994, Creative Editions LB $23.95 (0-88682-608-X). A dozen selections from *Leaves of Grass* are juxtaposed with biographical vignettes and sepia photographs. (Rev: SLJ 7/94*) [811]

5003 Longfellow, Henry Wadsworth. *Poems and Other Writings* (9–12). 2000, Library of America $35.00 (1-88301-185-X). Included in this anthology of Longfellow's poems are "Hiawatha," "Evangeline," and "The Courtship of Miles Standish." [811]

5004 Major, Clarence, ed. *The Garden Thrives: Twentieth Century African-American Poetry* (10–12). 1996, HarperPerennial paper $20.00 (0-06-095121-4). An impressive anthology arranged chronologically that includes the work of Paul Lawrence Dunbar, Langston Hughes, Lucille Clifton, Nikki Giovanni, and Rita Dove. (Rev: SLJ 5/97) [811]

5005 Marius, Richard, and Keith Frome, eds. *The Columbia Book of Civil War Poetry* (9–12). 1994, Columbia Univ. Pr. $31.50 (0-231-10002-7). An anthology of Civil War poetry, including famous songs and verses that appeared in newspapers by unknown writers. (Rev: BL 9/15/94; SLJ 11/94) [811.008]

5006 Marquis, Don. *Archyology: The Long Lost Tales of Archy and Mehitabel* (10–12). Illus. 1996, Univ. Press of New England $14.95 (0-874-51745-1). Light, humorous verse about Archy the cockroach and Mehitabel the cat. (Rev: BL 4/1/96; SLJ 2/97) [811]

5007 Meltzer, Milton, ed. *Hour of Freedom: American History in Poetry* (6–12). 2003, Boyds Mills $16.95 (1-59078-021-3). Brief histories introduce many classic and some less-familiar poems — plus lyrics and speeches — that are grouped in chronological chapters, ranging from the colonial period to the 20th century. (Rev: BL 9/1/03; HBG 4/04; SLJ 7/03; VOYA 2/04) [811.54]

5008 Merriam, Eve. *The Inner City Mother Goose* (9–12). Illus. 1996, Simon & Schuster $16.00 (0-689-80677-9). A new edition (with a few additional poems) of this unflinchingly sour parody of Mother Goose that deals straightforwardly with topics like city violence, racism, and corruption. (Rev: BL 4/15/96; BR 1–2/97; SLJ 5/96*) [811]

5009 Millay, Edna St. Vincent. *Edna St. Vincent Millay's Poems Selected for Young People* (7–10). Illus. 1979, HarperCollins $14.00 (0-06-024218-3). A fine selection of the poet's work, illustrated with woodcuts. [811]

5010 Miller, E. Ethelbert. *In Search of Color Everywhere: A Collection of African-American Poetry* (9–12). 1994, Stewart, Tabori & Chang $24.95 (1-55670-339-2); paper $17.95 (1-55670-451-8). This is a brilliant collection of African American poetry by writers both well-known and unfamiliar. [811.008]

5011 Mora, Pat. *My Own True Name: New and Selected Poems for Young Adults, 1984–1999* (6–12). Illus. 2000, Arte Publico paper $11.95 (1-55885-292-1). The Mexican American poet looks at her bilingual heritage, the beauty of the desert country in which she was raised, her love of language, and racial discrimination. (Rev: SLJ 7/00; VOYA 12/00) [811]

5012 Nash, Ogden. *I Wouldn't Have Missed It: Selected Poems of Ogden Nash* (9–12). Illus. 1975, Little, Brown $33.00 (0-316-59830-5). A selection of over 400 poems chosen by the poet's daughter after his death. [811]

5013 Nash, Ogden. *The Pocket Book of Ogden Nash* (9–12). 1991, Buccaneer LB $18.95 (0-89966-867-4). A fine collection of this writer's wittiest and most endearing poems. [811]

5014 *Off the Cuffs: Poetry by and About the Police* (10–12). Ed. by Jackie Sheeler. 2003, Soft Skull paper $15.00 (1-887128-81-6). This anthology interlaces poems protesting brutality and excessive force with paeans of praise for the important work done by the police. (Rev: BL 3/15/03) [811]

5015 Ortiz, Simon J. *Out There Somewhere* (10–12). 2002, Univ. of Arizona Pr. $35.00 (0-8165-2208-1); paper $16.95 (0-8165-2210-3). Ortiz's poetry gives voice to the disaffection among many Native Americans at the obstacles they face in carving out a place for themselves in mainstream society. (Rev: BL 3/15/02) [811]

5016 Paley, Grace. *Begin Again: Collected Poems* (10–12). 2000, Farrar $23.00 (0-374-12642-9). This is a collection of direct poems by the well-known fiction writer that deal with such subjects as family, friends, war, New York City, and Vermont. (Rev: BL 2/1/00) [811]

5017 Parini, Jay. *The Columbia Anthology of American Poetry* (10–12). 1995, Columbia Univ. Pr. $40.95 (0-231-08122-7). This anthology gives a good representation of various schools of American poetry writing and a good sampling from women and minority groups. [811.008]

5018 Plath, Sylvia. *The Collected Poems* (10–12). 1992, HarperCollins paper $17.50 (0-06-090900-5). This collection contains 224 poems, including a selection of her very earliest work. Also use *Crossing the River* (1971), a volume that contains the poet's last works. [811]

5019 Poe, Edgar Allan. *Complete Poems* (8–12). Ed. by Thomas Ollive Mabbott. 2000, Univ. of Illinois Pr. paper $25.00 (0-252-06921-8). This is an exhaustive collection of Poe's poems, totaling 101 works. [811]

5020 Rosenberg, Liz, ed. *The Invisible Ladder: An Anthology of Contemporary American Poems for Young Readers* (6–10). 1996, Holt $19.95 (0-8050-3836-1). As well as an excellent anthology of modern American poetry, this volume provides commentary by the poets, photographs of them, and suggestions for using each of the poems. (Rev: BL 9/15/96; BR 9–10/97; SLJ 2/97; VOYA 2/97) [811]

5021 Rylant, Cynthia. *Soda Jerk* (7–12). Illus. 1990, Watts LB $16.99 (0-531-08464-7). A group of poems about the inhabitants of a small town, written from the viewpoint of a teenage soda jerk. (Rev: BL 2/15/90; SLJ 4/90; VOYA 6/90) [811]

5022 Rylant, Cynthia. *Something Permanent* (7–12). Illus. 1994, Harcourt $18.00 (0-15-277090-9). Combines Rylant's poetry with Walker Evans's photographs to evoke strong emotions of southern life during the Depression. (Rev: BL 7/94*; SLJ 8/94; VOYA 12/94) [811]

5023 Sandburg, Carl. *The Complete Poems of Carl Sandburg*. Rev. ed. (9–12). 1970, Harcourt $40.00 (0-15-100996-1). A collection of seven of the author's books of poetry, including *Chicago Poems* and *The People, Yes*. [811]

5024 Sandburg, Carl. *Selected Poems* (9–12). Ed. by George Hendrick and Willene Hendrick. 1996, Harcourt (0-15-600396-1). This collection of Sandburg's poetry contains a number of poems not previously collected or published. [811]

5025 Soto, Gary. *A Fire in My Hands: A Book of Poems* (6–10). Illus. 1992, Scholastic paper $4.50 (0-590-44579-0). An illustrated collection of 23 poems, accompanied by advice to young poets. (Rev: BL 4/1/92; SLJ 3/92) [811]

5026 Soto, Gary. *A Natural Man* (10–12). 1999, Chronicle paper $13.95 (0-8118-2518-3). These poems about the sometimes harsh reality of being a young Chicano in California will resonate with all teens. (Rev: SLJ 2/00) [811]

5027 Soto, Gary. *New and Selected Poems* (9–12). 1995, Chronicle paper $14.95 (0-8118-0758-4). This is a collection of the work of the Mexican American poet in which he expresses his innermost feelings and emotions. [811]

5028 Stafford, William. *Learning to Live in the World: Earth Poems* (8–12). 1994, Harcourt $17.00 (0-15-200208-1). Fifty nature poems that will appeal to teens. (Rev: BL 1/1/95; SLJ 12/94) [811]

5029 Stepanek, Mattie J. T. *Hope Through Heartsongs* (6–12). Illus. 2002, Hyperion $14.95 (0-7868-6944-5). Hope and courage are central to this third collection of poems by Mattie Stepanek, who died of muscular dystrophy in June 2004, less than a month before his 14th birthday. (Rev: SLJ 8/02; VOYA 8/02) [811]

5030 Stern, Gerald. *What I Can't Bear Losing: Notes from a Life* (10–12). 2003, Norton $24.95 (0-393-05818-2). Stern revisits pivotal periods in his life, including his rough-and-tumble childhood in Pittsburgh, encounters with anti-Semitism, love affairs, and experiences in the military; for mature teens. (Rev: BL 11/1/03) [811]

5031 Stowe, Harriet Beecher. *The Oxford Harriet Beecher Stowe Reader* (10–12). Ed. by Joan D. Hedrick. 1999, Oxford paper $34.95 (0-19-509117-5). A fine cross-section of the writings (both fiction and nonfiction) of Harriet Beecher Stowe, including the entire text of *Uncle Tom's Cabin*. [818]

5032 Strickland, Michael R., ed. *My Own Song: And Other Poems to Groove To* (6–12). Illus. 1997, Boyds Mills $14.95 (1-56397-686-2). A collection of poems about music and its relationship to such subjects as love, cities, and birds. (Rev: BL 10/15/97; HBG 3/98; SLJ 12/97) [811]

5033 Sullivan, Charles, ed. *Imaginary Gardens: American Poetry and Art for Young People* (6–10). Illus. 1989, Abrams $19.95 (0-8109-1130-2). A collection of well-known poems, from such poets as Ogden Nash and Walt Whitman, with accompanying illustrations that also represent a wide range of artists and styles. (Rev: BL 12/1/89; SLJ 2/89) [700]

5034 Trethewey, Natasha. *Bellocq's Ophelia* (10–12). 2002, Graywolf paper $14.00 (1-55597-359-0). This collection of poems breathes life into the subject of an E. J. Bellocq photograph: a light-skinned African American prostitute in early-20th-century New Orleans. (Rev: BL 3/1/02) [811]

5035 Turner, Ann. *Grass Songs: Poems* (7–12). Illus. 1993, Harcourt $16.95 (0-15-136788-4). Dramatic monologues in poetic form that express courage and despair, passion and loneliness, and the struggle to find a home in the wilderness. (Rev: BL 6/1–15/93; VOYA 8/93) [811]

5036 Turner, Ann. *Learning to Swim: A Memoir* (6–12). 2000, Scholastic paper $14.95 (0-439-15309-3). In this memoir told in free verse, the author looks back at the summer she learned to swim and was sexually abused by an older boy. (Rev: BL 10/1/00; BR 1–2/01; HBG 3/01; SLJ 11/00; VOYA 12/00) [811.54]

5037 Turner, Ann W. *A Lion's Hunger: Poems of First Love* (8–12). Illus. 1999, Marshall Cavendish $15.95 (0-7614-5035-1). Written from a young woman's point of view, this is a collection of poems by the author chronicling the joys and sorrows of first love. (Rev: BL 3/1/99; BR 5–6/99; HBG 3/99; SLJ 1/99; VOYA 2/99) [811]

5038 *The Vintage Book of African American Poetry* (10–12). Ed. by Michael S. Harper and Anthony Walton. 2000, Random paper $14.00 (0-375-70300-4). A comprehensive collection of representative poems by 52 African American poets spanning more than two centuries. (Rev: BL 2/15/00) [811]

5039 Wayland, April Halprin. *Girl Coming in for a Landing* (6–12). 2002, Knopf paper $14.95 (0-375-80158-8). A teenage girl expresses in appealing poetry the social and academic trials and tribulations of a year of high school. (Rev: BL 10/15/02; HB 9–10/02; HBG 3/03; SLJ 8/02) [811.54]

5040 Weatherford, Carole Boston. *Remember the Bridge: Poems of a People* (7–12). Illus. 2002, Putnam $17.99 (0-399-23726-7). This collection of poems celebrates African Americans from the era of slavery through today, with accompanying archival images. (Rev: BL 2/15/02; HBG 10/02; SLJ 1/02; VOYA 8/02) [811]

5041 *When the Rain Sings: Poems by Young Native Americans* (5–10). Illus. 1999, Simon & Schuster $16.00 (0-689-82283-9). A collection of 37 poems from Native Americans ranging in age from seven to 17. (Rev: BL 12/1/99; HBG 3/00; SLJ 11/99) [811]

5042 Whipple, Laura, ed. *Celebrating America: A Collection of Poems and Images of the American Spirit* (5–10). 1994, Putnam $19.95 (0-399-22036-4). An anthology of poetry and art that reflects the wide range of American cultures, styles, and periods. (Rev: BL 9/1/94*; SLJ 9/94) [811.008]

5043 Whitman, Walt. *Complete Poetry and Collected Prose* (10–12). 1982, Library of America $35.00 (0-940450-02-X); paper $17.95 (1-883011-35-3). This collection contains *Leaves of Grass*, plus all of Whitman's prose works. [818]

5044 Whitman, Walt. *Voyages: Poems by Walt Whitman* (7–12). Illus. 1988, Harcourt $15.95 (0-15-294495-8). An introductory biographical sketch is followed by 53 representative poems selected by Lee Bennett Hopkins. (Rev: BL 11/15/88; BR 3–4/89; SLJ 12/88; VOYA 1/89) [811.3]

5045 Wong, Janet S. *Behind the Wheel* (7–12). 1999, Simon & Schuster $15.00 (0-689-82531-5). In a series of free-verse poems, the author explores individuals and their relationships within families.

(Rev: BL 1/1–15/00* ; HB 11–12/99; HBG 4/00; VOYA 2/00) [811]

Other Regions

5046 Berry, James R. *Everywhere Faces Everywhere* (6–10). Illus. 1997, Simon & Schuster $16.00 (0-689-80996-4). A collection of 46 of the author's poems that describe his childhood in Jamaica and his adult life in the United Kingdom. (Rev: BL 5/1/97; BR 11–12/97; SLJ 6/97; VOYA 10/97) [821]

5047 *Brother Enemy: Poems of the Korean War* (10–12). Ed. and trans. by Suh Ji-Moon and James A. Perkins. 2002, White Pine paper $16.00 (1-893996-20-4). This collection of moving poems revisits the horrors of Korea's mid-20th-century civil war that pitted brother against brother. (Rev: BL 9/1/02) [895.7]

5048 Chipasula, Stella, and Frank Chipasula, eds. *Heinemann Book of African Women's Poetry* (9–12). 1995, Heinemann paper $10.95 (0-435-90680-1). A wide range of poetic voices celebrating Africa's racial and cultural diversity. (Rev: BL 2/15/95*) [821]

5049 Liu, Siyu, and Orel Protopopescu. *A Thousand Peaks: Poems from China* (6–10). 2002, Pacific View $19.95 (1-881896-24-2). Thirty-five transla-

tions of Chinese poems are accompanied by information giving historical and cultural context, the original in Chinese characters and pinyin transliteration, a literal translation, and black-and-white drawings. (Rev: BL 3/15/02; SLJ 2/02*) [895.1]

5050 Mado, Michio. *The Animals: Selected Poems* (5–10). Trans. by the Empress Michiko of Japan. Illus. 1992, Simon & Schuster LB $16.95 (0-689-50574-4). Twenty Japanese poems about animals, with English versions on facing pages. (Rev: BL 12/1/92; SLJ 2/93) [895.6]

5051 Neruda, Pablo. *The Poetry of Pablo Neruda* (10–12). Ed. by Ilan Stavans. 2003, Farrar $40.00 (0-374-29995-1). This definitive collection contains some 600 of Neruda's poems, plus analysis by literary critic Ilan Stavans. (Rev: BL 7/03*) [861]

5052 Nye, Naomi S., ed. *The Space Between Our Footsteps: Poems and Paintings from the Middle East* (8–12). Illus. 1998, Simon & Schuster $21.95 (0-689-81233-7). More than 100 poets and artists from 19 countries in the Middle East are featured in this handsome volume of verse about families, friends, and everyday events. (Rev: BCCB 5/98; BL 3/1/98; HB 3–4/98; SLJ 5/98; VOYA 10/98) [808.81]

5053 Service, Robert W. *The Best of Robert Service* (9–12). 1989, Putnam $12.95 (0-399-55008-9). The poet of the Yukon is presented well in this collection of his most popular poems. [811]

Folklore and Fairy Tales

General and Miscellaneous

5054 Ausubel, Nathan, ed. *A Treasury of Jewish Folklore, Stories, Traditions, Legends, Humor, Wisdom and Folk Songs of the Jewish People* (9–12). 1989, Crown $22.00 (0-517-50293-3). A treasury of Jewish wit and wisdom through the ages that also reveals a great deal about Jewish history and religion. (Rev: SLJ 6/90) [296]

5055 Bettelheim, Bruno. *The Uses of Enchantment: The Meaning and Importance of Fairy Tales* (10–12). 1989, Vintage paper $14.00 (0-679-72393-5). An insightful explanation of the hidden meanings of fairy tales. Originally published in 1976. [398]

5056 Block, Francesca L. *The Rose and the Beast: Fairy Tales Retold* (9–12). 2000, HarperCollins LB $14.89 (0-06-028130-8). Familiar fairy tales are retold as modern and sometimes disturbing fables. (Rev: BL 8/00; HBG 3/01; SLJ 9/00; VOYA 2/01) [398.2]

5057 Cole, Joanna, ed. *Best-Loved Folktales of the World* (7–12). Illus. 1982, Doubleday paper $17.00 (0-385-18949-4). A collection of 200 tales from around the globe, arranged geographically. [398.2]

5058 Creeden, Sharon. *Fair Is Fair: World Folktales of Justice* (9–12). 1995, August House $19.95 (0-87483-400-7). Thirty folktales, adapted from different times and places, relating to law and justice. (Rev: BL 5/15/95; SLJ 10/95) [398.2]

5059 Datlow, Ellen, and Terri Windling, eds. *A Wolf at the Door and Other Retold Fairy Tales* (6–10). 2000, Simon & Schuster $16.00 (0-689-82138-7). This collection of variations on standard fairy tales by prominent authors includes such titles as "The Seven Stage Comeback" (Snow White) and "Cinder

Elephant" about a lovely but very large girl. (Rev: BL 9/1/00; HBG 3/01; SLJ 8/00; VOYA 6/00)

5060 De Caro, Frank, ed. *The Folktale Cat* (9–12). 1993, August House paper $14.95 (0-87483-303-5). An international collection of 51 classic and lesser-known feline folktales, with a discussion of the domestic cat's role in folklore. (Rev: BL 4/15/93; SLJ 11/93) [398.2]

5061 Dorson, Richard M., ed. *Folktales Told Around the World* (10–12). Illus. 1987, Univ. of Chicago Pr. paper $30.00 (0-226-15874-8). An international selection of folktales in authentic retellings and translations. [398.2]

5062 Ferguson, Gary. *Spirits of the Wild: The World's Great Nature Myths* (10–12). 1996, Clarkson Potter $21.00 (0-517-70369-6). A collection of 60 short myths and legends from around the world explaining how a variety of natural phenomena came to be. (Rev: BR 3–4/97; SLJ 1/97) [398.2]

5063 Forest, Heather. *Wisdom Tales from Around the World: Fifty Gems of Story and Wisdom from Such Diverse Traditions as Sufi, Zen, Taoist, Christian, Jewish, Buddhist, African, and Native American* (10–12). 1996, August House $27.95 (0-87483-478-3); paper $17.95 (0-87483-479-1). Gems of wisdom on the conduct of life are contained in this collection of folktales, proverbs, and parables from around the world. (Rev: BL 3/1/97; SLJ 4/97; VOYA 6/97) [398.2]

5064 Hale, Shannon. *The Goose Girl* (6–10). 2003, Bloomsbury $17.95 (1-58234-843-X). Crown Princess Ani, who can talk to the animals, is betrayed by her guards and disguises herself as a goose girl until she can reclaim her crown. (Rev: BL 8/03; HBG 4/04; SLJ 8/03*; VOYA 10/03)

5065 Hamilton, Martha, and Mitch Weiss. *How and Why Stories: World Tales Kids Can Read and Tell* (5–10). Illus. 1999, August House $21.95 (0-87483-

562-3); paper $12.95 (0-87483-561-5). This excellent collection of 25 pourquoi (how and why) stories from around the world also contains a useful introduction on folklore, plus tips on delivering each of the tales. (Rev: BL 5/15/00; HBG 3/00; SLJ 1/00) [398.2]

5066 Opie, Iona, and Peter Opie, eds. *The Classic Fairy Tales* (9–12). Illus. 1987, Oxford paper $23.95 (0-19-520219-8). The definitive retelling of 24 of the most popular fairy tales of all time. [398.2]

5067 Sadeh, Pinhas, ed. *Jewish Folktales* (9–12). Illus. 1989, Doubleday paper $16.00 (0-385-19574-5). This collection is distinguished by the worldwide coverage represented. (Rev: BL 11/1/89) [398.2]

5068 Saunders, George. *The Very Persistent Gappers of Frip* (6–12). 2000, Villard $23.95 (0-375-50383-8). A delightful, beautifully illustrated fable about community featuring the improbable gapper, a baseball-sized sea creature with an uncommon passion for goats. (Rev: SLJ 1/01; VOYA 2/01)

5069 Yolen, Jane, ed. *Favorite Folktales from Around the World* (9–12). 1988, Pantheon paper $18.00 (0-394-75188-4). This collection of 160 tales represents such diverse stories as American Indian legends and tales from the Brothers Grimm. (Rev: SLJ 12/86) [398]

5070 Yolen, Jane, and Shulamith Oppenheim. *The Fish Prince and Other Stories* (7–12). 2001, Interlink $29.95 (1-56656-389-5); paper $15.00 (1-56656-390-9). An absorbing and informative collection of stories of mermaids and mermen from around the world, accompanied by black-and-white illustrations. (Rev: BL 11/15/01) [398.21]

5071 Yolen, Jane, and Heidi E. Y. Stemple. *Mirror, Mirror: Forty Folktales for Mothers and Daughters to Share* (10–12). 2000, Viking $24.95 (0-670-88907-5). This mother-daughter team has selected a global mixture of folktales, such as variations on Cinderella and Rapunzel, that explore themes involving mother-daughter relationships. (Rev: BL 5/1/00; SLJ 5/01) [306.874]

5072 Zeitlin, Steve. *The Four Corners of the Sky: Creation Stories and Cosmologies from Around the World* (7–12). Illus. 2000, Holt $17.00 (0-8050-4816-2). This is a thoughtful collection of folktales about the beginning of the universe from 16 diverse cultures and religions. (Rev: BL 11/15/00; HB 1–2/01; HBG 3/01; SLJ 12/00) [291.2]

Geographical Regions

Africa

5073 Abrahams, Roger D., ed. *African Folktales: Traditional Stories of the Black World* (7–12). Illus. 1983, Pantheon paper $18.00 (0-394-72117-9). A collection of about 100 tales from south of the Sahara. [398.2]

5074 Berry, Jack. *West African Folktales* (9–12). Ed. by Richard Spears. 1991, Northwestern Univ. Pr. $29.00 (0-8101-0979-4); paper $14.95 (0-8101-0993-X). Vivid folktales imparting basic life lessons collected over 35 years by a linguist who specialized in the spoken art of Sierra Leone, Ghana, and Nigeria. (Rev: BL 10/15/91) [398.2]

5075 Courlander, Harold, ed. *Treasury of African Folklore* (10–12). Illus. 1995, Marlowe paper $15.95 (1-56924-816-8). A wide and varied selection of myths from various African tribes south of the Sahara. [398.2]

5076 Giles, Bridget. *Myths of West Africa* (6–10). Series: Mythic World. 2002, Gale LB $17.98 (0-7398-4976-X). A general introduction to this area of Africa through text and pictures is followed by retellings of important myths and relevant background information. (Rev: BL 7/02; HBG 10/02; SLJ 5/02) [398.2]

5077 *Nelson Mandela's Favorite African Folktales* (6–12). Illus. 2002, Norton $24.95 (0-393-05212-5). Thirty-two folktales from the African continent are complemented by artwork as diverse as the stories. (Rev: BL 12/1/02; HBG 10/03; SLJ 2/03) [398.2]

5078 Offodile, Buchi. *The Orphan Girl and Other Stories: West African Folk Tales* (9–12). Illus. 2001, Interlink paper $15.00 (1-56656-375-5). From trickster tales to creation stories, this is a fine collection of folktales from West Africa, mainly from Nigeria. (Rev: BL 9/15/01) [398.2]

Asia and the Middle East

5079 *The Arabian Nights* (9–12). 1991, NAL paper $5.95 (0-451-52542-6). Sinbad and Aladdin are only two of the famous characters that come alive in these ancient tales. [398]

5080 Atangan, Patrick. *The Yellow Jar: Two Tales from Japanese Tradition*, Vol. 1 (10–12). 2003, NBM $12.95 (1-56163-331-3). "The Yellow Jar" and "Two Chrysanthemum Maidens" are told in beautiful graphic-novel form. (Rev: BL 12/02; SLJ 4/03) [398.2]

5081 Beck, Brenda E. F., et al., eds. *Folktales of India* (9–12). 1989, Univ. of Chicago Pr. paper $22.50 (0-226-04082-8). There are 99 tales in this collection representing a number of cultures and districts. (Rev: BL 5/1/87) [398.2]

5082 Dokey, Cameron. *The Storyteller's Daughter* (6–10). 2002, Simon & Schuster paper $5.99 (0-7434-2220-1). A retelling of the story of Shahrazad that interweaves fantasy, court intrigue, and romance. (Rev: SLJ 12/02)

5083 Faurot, Jeannette L. *Asian-Pacific Folktales and Legends* (9–12). 1995, Simon & Schuster paper $12.00 (0-684-81197-9). This is a collection of 65 myths and folktales from eight East and South Asian countries, including China. [398.2]

5084 Krishnaswami, Uma, retel. *Shower of Gold: Girls and Women in the Stories of India* (6–10). 1999, Linnet LB $21.50 (0-208-02484-0). All of the enchanting tales in this fine collection of Indian folklore feature wise and powerful women. (Rev: BCCB 5/99; BL 3/15/99; HBG 3/00; SLJ 8/99) [891]

5085 Livo, Norma J., and Dia Cha, eds. *Folk Stories of the Hmong: Peoples of Laos, Thailand, and Vietnam* (9–12). 1991, Libraries Unlimited LB $22.00 (0-87287-854-6). The unique culture and heritage of the Hmong people are celebrated in this collection of folktales. Includes an introduction to Hmong history. (Rev: BL 10/1/91) [398.2]

5086 Nuweihed, Jamal Sleem. *Abu Jmeel's Daughter and Other Stories: Arab Folk Tales from Palestine and Lebanon* (10–12). 2002, Interlink paper $16.95 (1-56656-418-2). Twenty-seven fairly lengthy traditional folktales in which women play a prominent role are presented in a lively and enticing format. (Rev: BL 5/15/02) [398.2]

5087 Roberts, Moss. *Chinese Fairy Tales and Fantasies* (10–12). 1980, Pantheon paper $16.00 (0-394-73994-9). Culled from 25 centuries of folklore, this is a collection of 100 tales. [398]

5088 Tyler, Royall, ed. *Japanese Tales* (9–12). 1989, Pantheon paper $18.00 (0-394-75656-8). Arranged by themes, this is a mammoth collection of folktales that concentrates on those originating in the 12th through the 14th centuries. (Rev: BL 5/1/87) [398.2]

5089 Yep, Laurence. *The Rainbow People* (7–10). Illus. 1989, HarperCollins $16.00 (0-06-026760-7); paper $5.99 (0-06-440441-2). The retelling of 20 Chinese folktales with illustrations by David Wiesner. (Rev: BL 4/1/89; BR 11–12/90; SLJ 5/89) [398.2]

Australia and the Pacific Islands

5090 Flood, Bo, and Beret E. Strong. *Pacific Island Legends: Tales from Micronesia, Melanesia, Polynesia, and Australia* (6–12). 1999, Bess $22.95 (1-57306-084-4); paper $14.95 (1-57306-078-X). The ocean's impact on island life is a theme that runs through many of these tales, which are organized in geographical groupings with introductions on each area's culture and history. (Rev: HBG 4/00; SLJ 10/99) [398.2]

5091 Oodgeroo. *Dreamtime: Aboriginal Stories* (6–10). Illus. 1994, Lothrop $16.00 (0-688-13296-0). Traditional and autobiographical stories of abo-

riginal culture and its roots. Also examines current aboriginal life alongside white civilization. (Rev: BCCB 1/99; BL 10/1/94; SLJ 10/94) [398.2]

5092 Te Kanawa, Kiri. *Land of the Long White Cloud: Maori Myths, Tales and Legends* (7–12). Illus. 1997, Pavilion paper $17.95 (1-86205-075-9). A group of magical Maori folktales about sea gods, fairies, monsters, and fantastic voyages, retold by the famous opera singer from New Zealand. (Rev: BL 9/1/97) [398.2]

Europe

5093 Afanasév, Aleksandr. *Russian Folk Tales* (9–12). 1976, Pantheon paper $18.00 (0-394-73090-9). This is a standard collection of these traditional Russian tales. [398]

5094 Altom, Laura Marie. *Kissing Frogs* (11–12). 2004, Love Spell paper $5.99 (0-505-52568-2). In this humorous retelling of the Frog Prince fable, modern-day biologist Lucy Gordon faces tough choices when the frog she kisses is transformed into a prince. (Rev: BL 12/1/03*)

5095 Andersen, Hans Christian. *Tales and Stories* (9–12). Illus. 1980, Univ. of Washington Pr. paper $18.95 (0-295-95936-3). These 27 stories are retold for an adult audience. [398.2]

5096 *The Annotated Classic Fairy Tales* (10–12). Ed. and trans. by Maria Tatar. Illus. 2002, Norton $35.00 (0-393-05163-3). A highly readable and well illustrated collection of 26 classic fairy tales retold in contemporary language and with notes on their original context, variations, and so forth. (Rev: BL 10/1/02; SLJ 2/03) [398.2]

5097 Asbjörnsen, Peter Christen, and Jörgen Moe. *Norwegian Folk Tales* (9–12). Trans. by Pat Shaw and Carl Norman. Illus. 1982, Pantheon paper $14.00 (0-394-71054-1). About 25 Norwegian folktales are reprinted from an authoritative collection that first appeared in 1845. [398]

5098 Bell, Anthea. *Jack and the Beanstalk: An English Fairy Tale Retold* (8–12). Illus. 2000, North-South LB $15.88 (0-7358-1375-2). This picture book for older readers offers unusual illustrations and a modernized text. (Rev: BL 9/15/00; HBG 3/01; SLJ 12/00)

5099 Calvino, Italo, retel. *Italian Folktales* (9–12). Trans. by George Martin. 1956, Harcourt $27.95 (0-15-145770-0); paper $24.00 (0-15-645489-0). A lively retelling of Italian folktales that include variations on such stories as Snow White and Cinderella. (Rev: BL 12/15/89) [398]

5100 Colum, Padraic, ed. *A Treasury of Irish Folklore.* 2nd rev. ed. (9–12). 1985, Random $12.99 (0-517-42046-5). In addition to folktales, this anthology includes jokes, anecdotes, and songs. [398.2]

5101 D'Aulnoy, Madame. *Beauty and the Beast* (9–12). Illus. 2000, Creative Editions $17.95 (1-56846-129-1). Most remarkable for its stunning artwork, this retelling of the Beauty and the Beast legend will probably be of greatest interest to design students. (Rev: BL 11/15/00; HBG 10/01) [398.2]

5102 Day, David. *The Search for King Arthur* (10–12). 1995, Facts on File $24.95 (0-8160-3370-6). Complemented by 170 stunning color illustrations, this work traces the evolution of the King Arthur legend from the earliest records to the present. (Rev: BL 11/15/95; BR 5–6/96; SLJ 2/96) [942]

5103 Dean, Pamela. *Tam Lin* (10–12). 1992, Tor paper $4.99 (0-8125-4450-1). The classic Scottish love story is transported to a 1970s Midwestern college campus. (Rev: BL 4/15/91)

5104 Delamare, David. *Cinderella* (7–12). 1993, Simon & Schuster paper $15.00 (0-671-76944-8). The familiar story is set in a locale much like Venice and enhanced by Delamare's paintings, both realistic and surreal. (Rev: BCCB 11/00; BL 9/15/93; SLJ 12/93) [398.2]

5105 Grimm Brothers. *The Complete Grimms' Fairy Tales* (10–12). 1974, Pantheon $17.00 (0-394-49415-6). This early collection of folktales by the Grimm brothers is still considered the authoritative one. [398]

5106 Jacobs, Joseph, ed. *Celtic Fairy Tales* (10–12). 1968, Dover paper $6.95 (0-486-21826-0). One of the great collectors of folktales presents these from Ireland. Also use: *More Celtic Fairy Tales* (1968), *Indian Fairy Tales* (1969), and *English Fairy Tales* (Penguin, 1990). [398]

5107 McKinley, Robin. *The Outlaws of Sherwood* (9–12). 1988, Greenwillow $17.00 (0-688-07178-3). A reworking of the Robin Hood story in which our hero becomes a moody, self-doubting, somewhat ordinary man. (Rev: BL 12/15/88; BR 5–6/89; SLJ 1/89; VOYA 4/89) [398.2]

5108 Markale, Jean. *King of the Celts: Arthurian Legends and Celtic Tradition* (9–12). Trans. by Christine Hauch. 1994, Inner Traditions paper $14.95 (0-89281-452-7). A survey of Arthurian lore in Celtic history that illustrates how the legends were misappropriated by propagandists of the courtly nobility. (Rev: BL 3/1/94) [942.01]

5109 Napoli, Donna Jo. *The Magic Circle* (6–12). 1993, Dutton $15.99 (0-525-45127-7). A "history" of the witch in *Hansel and Gretel*. (Rev: BL 7/93; VOYA 8/93) [398.2]

5110 *Out of Avalon: An Anthology of Old Magic and New Myths* (7–12). Ed. by Jennifer Roberson. 2001, Roc paper $5.99 (0-451-45831-1). This anthology of fantasy stories based on Arthurian legend includes contributions by such well-known writers as Marion Zimmer Bradley and Judith Tarr. (Rev: VOYA 10/01)

5111 Perrault, Charles. *Cinderella* (9–12). Illus. 2000, Creative Editions $17.95 (1-56846-130-5). The high quality of the illustrations are the main attraction of this retelling set in the Roaring '20s. (Rev: BL 11/15/00; HBG 10/01) [398.2]

5112 Phillips, Graham, and Martin Keatman. *King Arthur: The True Story* (9–12). 1994, Arrow paper $9.95 (0-09-929681-0). A scholarly examination of the Arthurian legend that attempts to document its roots and determine whether the king really existed. (Rev: BL 1/15/94) [942.01]

5113 Pyle, Howard. *Merry Adventures of Robin Hood* (10–12). 1986, NAL paper $4.95 (0-451-52284-2). One of many retellings of the stories about Robin Hood and his merry men. [398]

5114 Pyle, Howard. *The Story of King Arthur and His Knights* (8–12). Illus. 1973, Peter Smith $25.75 (0-8446-2766-6); Dover paper $9.95 (0-486-21445-1). A retelling that has been in print since its first publication in 1903. [398.2]

5115 Pyle, Howard. *The Story of Sir Launcelot and His Companions* (7–12). Illus. 1991, Dover paper $12.95 (0-486-26701-6). This book of episodes in the Arthurian legend is noteworthy because of the illustrations of Howard Pyle. [398.2]

5116 Spariosu, Mihai I., and Dezso Benedek. *Ghosts, Vampires, and Werewolves: Eerie Tales from Transylvania* (6–10). 1994, Orchard LB $19.99 (0-531-08710-7). An anthology of horror tales by two authors who heard the stories as children living in the Transylvanian Alps. (Rev: BL 10/15/94; SLJ 10/94) [398.2]

5117 Tolkien, J. R. R. *Sir Gawain and the Green Knight* (10–12). 1979, Ballantine paper $5.99 (0-345-27760-0). A retelling of three tales from the age of chivalry. [398]

5118 Weinreich, Beatrice Silverman. *Yiddish Folktales* (9–12). Trans. by Leonard Wolf. Series: Pantheon Fairy Tale and Folklore Library. 1988, Pantheon paper $18.00 (0-8052-1090-3). There are more than 200 selections in this volume from the world of Eastern European Jewry. [398.2]

5119 Wyly, Michael. *King Arthur* (7–10). Series: Mystery Library. 2001, Lucent LB $19.96 (1-56006-771-3). An engrossing account that explores the fact and fiction surrounding this legendary king and his knights. (Rev: BL 9/15/01) [942]

North America

GENERAL AND MISCELLANEOUS

5120 Abrahams, Roger D., ed. *Afro-American Folktales: Stories from Black Traditions in the New World* (9–12). 1985, Pantheon paper $17.00 (0-394-72885-8). A rich collection of African American folktales from South and Central America, the

Caribbean, and southern United States. (Rev: BL 2/1/85; BR 11–12/85) [398.2]

5121 Pohl, John M. D. *The Legend of Lord Eight Deer: An Epic of Ancient Mexico* (6–12). Illus. 2001, Oxford LB $19.95 (0-19-514019-2). A retelling of the complex story of Eight Deer, a Mixtec leader, with a final chapter that explains how Pohl interpreted the historical codices that contributed to this tale. (Rev: BL 1/1–15/02; HBG 3/02; SLJ 1/02) [398.2]

5122 West, John O., ed. *Mexican-American Folklore* (9–12). Illus. 1988, August House paper $17.95 (0-87483-059-1). A collection of stories, proverbs, legends, and other forms of folklore reflecting the Mexican American culture. (Rev: BL 11/15/88) [398]

NATIVE AMERICANS

5123 Bierhorst, John. *The Mythology of North America* (8–12). Illus. 1986, Morrow paper $13.00 (0-688-06666-6). A region-by-region examination of the folklore and mythology of the North American Indian. (Rev: BL 6/15/85; SLJ 8/85) [291.1]

5124 Bierhorst, John. *Native American Stories* (6–12). Illus. 1998, Morrow $16.00 (0-688-14837-9). A collection of 22 tales about "little people" from 14 Native American groups, including the Inuits, Aztecs, and Mayans. (Rev: BCCB 7–8/98; BL 5/15/98; HBG 9/98; SLJ 9/98) [398.208997]

5125 Bierhorst, John. *The Way of the Earth: Native America and the Environment* (7–12). 1994, Morrow $15.00 (0-688-11560-8). Explores the mythologic and folkloric patterns of Native American belief systems. (Rev: BL 5/15/94; SLJ 5/94; VOYA 10/94) [179]

5126 Bierhorst, John. *The White Deer and Other Stories Told by the Lenape* (8–12). 1995, Morrow $15.00 (0-688-12900-5). This collection of Lenape/Delaware tribal stories is organized by type and includes a history of the tribe. (Rev: BL 6/1–15/95; SLJ 9/95) [398.2]

5127 Bruchac, Joseph. *Our Stories Remember: American Indian History, Culture, and Values Through Storytelling* (10–12). 2003, Fulcrum paper $16.95 (1-55591-129-3). Bruchac draws on the traditional folklore of many tribal groups to emphasize the importance of the storytelling tradition and the themes common to most Native American folk tales. (Rev: BL 4/15/03; SLJ 7/03; VOYA 10/03) [973.04]

5128 Bruchac, Joseph, and Gayle Ross. *The Girl Who Married the Moon: Tales from Native North America* (9–12). 1994, Troll paper $5.95 (0-8167-3481-X). Sixteen stories from various North American native peoples that explore the roles of women

in their cultures. (Rev: BL 10/1/94; SLJ 11/94) [398.2]

5129 Erdoes, Richard, and Alfonso Ortiz, eds. *American Indian Myths and Legends* (10–12). Illus. 1984, Pantheon paper $18.00 (0-394-74018-1). From the entire North American continent, here is a collection of 160 tales from Native American folklore. [398.2]

5130 Ferguson, Diana. *Native American Myths* (10–12). Illus. 2001, Collins & Brown $24.95 (1-85585-824-X). From the Arctic north to the southwestern desert, here are the most important myths of Native Americans collected in a handsome volume. (Rev: BL 11/15/01) [398 2097]

5131 Philip, Neil, ed. *The Great Mystery: Myths of Native America* (8–12). Illus. 2001, Clarion $25.00 (0-395-98405-X). A collection of creation and other stories from many Native American tribes, organized by region. (Rev: BL 11/15/01; HBG 10/02; SLJ 11/01) [398.2]

5132 Pijoan, Teresa. *White Wolf Woman: Native American Transformation Myths* (7–12). 1992, August House paper $11.95 (0-87483-200-4). Drawn from a wide range of Indian tribes, a collection of 37 stories about animal and human transformations and connections. (Rev: BL 10/1/92) [398.2]

5133 Tingle, Tim. *Walking the Choctaw Road* (6–12). 2003, Cinco Puntos $16.95 (0-938317-74-1). A collection of stories that convey Choctaw traditions and culture, including experiences on the Trail of Tears. (Rev: BL 6/1–15/03; HBG 4/04; VOYA 2/04) [398.2]

5134 Van Etten, Teresa. *Ways of Indian Magic* (7–12). Illus. 1985, Sunstone paper $8.95 (0-86534-061-7). A fine retelling of six legends of the Pueblo Indians. (Rev: BR 3–4/86) [398.2]

5135 Van Etten, Teresa. *Ways of Indian Wisdom* (7–10). 1987, Sunstone paper $10.95 (0-86534-090-0). A collection of 20 Pueblo tales that reflect the Southeastern Indians' culture and customs. (Rev: BR 1–2/88) [398.2]

5136 Zitkala-Sa. *American Indian Stories, Legends, and Other Writings* (10–12). Ed. by Cathy N. Davidson and Ada Norris. 2003, Penguin paper $13.00 (0-14-243709-3). Published 65 years after her death, this collection of the writings of the late Sioux writer/activist Zitkala-Sa paints a poignant portrait of Native American life and lore. (Rev: BL 3/15/03) [398.2]

UNITED STATES

5137 Blair, Walter. *Tall Tale America: A Legendary History of Our Humorous Heroes* (10–12). Illus. 1987, Univ. of Chicago Pr. paper $17.95 (0-226-05596-5). Mike Fink, Davy Crockett, Johnny Appleseed, and Pecos Bill are only four of the many tall-tale heroes the reader meets in this collection of folktales. [398.2]

5138 Botkin, B. A., ed. *A Treasury of American Folklore* (9–12). 1989, Crown $14.99 (0-517-67978-7). This collection, first published in 1944, cuts across racial and ethnic lines and represents various parts of the country. [398.2]

5139 Cohen, Daniel. *Southern Fried Rat and Other Gruesome Tales* (6–10). Illus. 1989, Avon paper $3.50 (0-380-70655-5). A collection of stories — some funny, some grisly — about people living in urban areas today. [398.2]

5140 *From My People: 400 Years of African American Folklore* (10–12). Ed. by Daryl Cumber Dance. Illus. 2002, Norton $35.00 (0-393-04798-9). The cultural evolution of black America is beautifully documented in this collection of folktales, speeches, work songs, proverbs, sermons, and other representative examples of African American culture. (Rev: BL 1/1–15/02) [398.2]

5141 Hurston, Zora Neale. *Every Tongue Got to Confess: Negro Folk-tales from the Gulf States* (9–12). 2001, HarperCollins $25.00 (0-06-018893-6). Published here for the first time are some of the folktales collected by Hurston and transcribed with great care to preserve the original sound and sense of these tales. (Rev: BL 10/1/01) [398.2]

5142 Lester, Julius. *Black Folktales* (9–12). Illus. 1991, Grove Atlantic paper $11.00 (0-8021-3242-1). A modern retelling with contemporary references to 12 African and African American folktales. [398.2]

5143 MacDonald, Margaret Read. *Ghost Stories from the Pacific Northwest* (10–12). Series: American Folklore. 1995, August House $24.95 (0-87483-436-8). A collection of folktales and ghost stories from Oregon, Washington, and British Columbia that are ideal for telling around a campfire. (Rev: SLJ 3/96) [398.2]

5144 Shepherd, Esther. *Paul Bunyan* (7–10). Illus. 1941, Harcourt $12.95 (0-15-259749-2); paper $6.95 (0-15-259755-7). The tall-tale lumberjack is brought to life by the text and the stunning illustrations by Rockwell Kent. [398.2]

5145 Smith, Jimmy Neil. *Homespun* (9–12). Illus. 1988, Crown $19.95 (0-517-56936-1). A wonderful collection of 22 favorite folktales from top storytellers. (Rev: SLJ 3/89) [398.2]

South and Central America

5146 Kimmel, Eric A. *The Witch's Face: A Mexican Tale* (7–12). Illus. 1993, Holiday $15.95 (0-8234-1038-2). Kimmel uses a picture book format for this Mexican tale of a man who rescues his love from becoming a witch, only to lose her to his own doubt. (Rev: BL 11/15/93; SLJ 2/94) [398.22]

5147 *Latin American Folktales: Stories from Hispanic and Indian Traditions* (10–12). Ed. by John Bierhorst. 2001, Pantheon $26.00 (0-375-42066-5). A collection of more than 100 folktales from the Spanish oral tradition. (Rev: BL 12/15/01; SLJ 5/02) [398.2]

Mythology

General and Miscellaneous

5148 Echlin, Kim. *Inanna: From the Myths of Ancient Sumer* (7–12). 2003, Groundwood $19.95 (0-88899-496-6). The stories of the powerful goddess Inanna and her adventures in love and war, based on 4,000-year-old sources. (Rev: BL 3/1/04; HBG 4/04; SLJ 3/04; VOYA 12/03) [398.2]

5149 Evslin, Bernard. *Pig's Ploughman* (7–12). Illus. 1990, Chelsea LB $19.95 (1-55546-256-1). In Celtic mythology, Pig's Ploughman is the huge hog who fights Finn McCool. (Rev: BL 8/90; SLJ 3/91) [398.2]

5150 Frazer, James George. *The Golden Bough: A Study in Magic and Religion*. Abridged ed. (10–12). 1958, Macmillan paper $16.95 (0-02-095570-7). In one volume, this classic traces the origins of religions to the world of mythology, superstition, and fables. [291]

5151 Gifford, Douglas. *Warriors, Gods and Spirits from Central and South American Mythology* (7–12). Illus. 1993, NTC paper $14.95 (0-87226-915-9). Latin American mythology from Aztec tales to those reflecting Western influences. [299]

5152 Hamilton, Dorothy. *Mythology* (8–12). Illus. 1942, Little, Brown $27.95 (0-316-34114-2). An introduction to the mythology of Greece and Scandinavia, plus a retelling of the principal myths. [292]

5153 Nardo, Don. *Monsters* (7–12). Illus. Series: Discovering Mythology. 2001, Gale LB $27.45 (1-56006-853-1). Monsters of yore from mythologies around the world are presented, with accounts of their exploits. (Rev: SLJ 1/02) [001.9]

5154 Ross, Anne. *Druids, Gods and Heroes of Celtic Mythology* (6–10). Illus. 1994, Bedrick LB $24.95 (0-87226-918-3); paper $14.95 (0-87226-

919-1). An oversized book that gives detailed information on Irish and Welsh Celtic mythology as well as material on King Arthur. (Rev: SLJ 2/87) [291.1]

5155 Van Over, Raymond, ed. *Sun Songs: Creation Myths from Around the World* (10–12). 1980, NAL paper $4.95 (0-452-00730-5). This work of general mythology discusses creation myths from all regions of the world. [291.1]

Classical

5156 Aesop. *Aesop's Fables* (7–12). 1988, Scholastic paper $4.50 (0-590-43880-8). This is one of many editions of the short moral tales from ancient Greece. (Rev: BCCB 12/00) [398.2]

5157 Aesop. *The Fables of Aesop* (9–12). Trans. by Patrick Gregory and Justina Gregory. Illus. 1975, Gambit $13.95 (0-87645-074-5); paper $8.95 (0-87645-116-4). This book, one of many available editions, covers 100 of the fables and deletes the moralizing conclusions. [398.2]

5158 Claybourne, Anna, and Kamini Khanduri, retellers. *Greek Myths: Ulysses and the Trojan War* (5–10). Illus. 1999, EDC $24.95 (0-7460-3361-3). A chatty retelling of the adventures of Ulysses on his way home from Troy, with illustrations that resemble comic-book drawings. (Rev: HBG 3/00; SLJ 6/99) [398.2]

5159 Evslin, Bernard. *The Adventures of Ulysses: The Odyssey of Homer* (8–12). 1989, Scholastic paper $4.50 (0-590-42599-4). A modern retelling of the adventures of Ulysses during the 10 years he wandered after the Trojan War. [292]

5160 Evslin, Bernard. *Cerberus* (6–12). Illus. 1987, Chelsea LB $19.95 (1-55546-243-X). The story of the three-headed dog in Greek mythology that guards the gates of Hell. Also in this series are *The*

Dragons of Boeotia and *Geryon* (both 1987). (Rev: BL 11/15/87; SLJ 1/88) [398.2]

5161 Evslin, Bernard. *The Chimaera* (6–10). Illus. 1987, Chelsea LB $19.95 (1-55546-244-8). This ugly, dangerous creature is composed of equal parts lion, goat, and reptile. Another in the series is *The Sirens* (1987). (Rev: BL 3/1/88) [398.2]

5162 Evslin, Bernard. *The Cyclopes* (6–12). Illus. 1987, Chelsea LB $19.95 (1-55546-236-7). The story of the ferocious one-eyed monster and how he was blinded by Ulysses. Others in this series about mythical monsters are *Medusa, The Minotaur,* and *Procrustes* (all 1987). (Rev: BL 6/15/87; SLJ 8/87) [398.2]

5163 Evslin, Bernard. *The Furies* (7–12). Illus. 1989, Chelsea LB $19.95 (1-55546-249-9). In Greek mythology the Furies were three witches. This retelling also includes the story of Circe, the famous sorceress. (Rev: BL 12/15/89; SLJ 4/90) [398.21]

5164 Evslin, Bernard. *Heroes, Gods and Monsters of Greek Myths* (8–12). Illus. 1984, Bantam paper $5.99 (0-553-25920-2). The most popular Greek myths are retold in modern language. [292]

5165 Evslin, Bernard. *Ladon* (7–12). Illus. 1990, Chelsea LB $19.95 (1-55546-254-5). A splendid retelling of the Greek myth about the sea serpent called up by Hera to fight Hercules. (Rev: BL 8/90) [398.24]

5166 Evslin, Bernard. *The Trojan War: The Iliad of Homer* (8–12). 1988, Scholastic paper $2.95 (0-590-41626-X). The story of the 10-year war between the Greeks and the Trojans is retold for the modern reader. [292]

5167 Evslin, Bernard, et al. *Heroes and Monsters of Greek Myth* (7–12). 1984, Scholastic paper $3.99 (0-590-43440-3). A simple retelling of the most famous Greek myths. Also use *The Greek Gods* (1988). [292]

5168 Grant, Michael. *Myths of the Greeks and Romans* (9–12). 1989, NAL paper $5.95 (0-317-02799-9). This collection of stories bridges the gap between these two similar mythologies. [292]

5169 Kindl, Patrice. *Lost in the Labyrinth* (6–10). 2002, Houghton $16.00 (0-618-16684-X). Told by Xenodice, a 14-year-old princess and the younger sister of Ariadne, this is an expanded version of the legend of Theseus and the Minotaur. (Rev: BCCB 11/02; BL 1/1–15/03; HB 11–12/02; HBG 3/03; SLJ 11/02; VOYA 2/03)

5170 McBride-Smith, Barbara. *Greek Myths, Western Style: Toga Tales with an Attitude* (9–12). 1999, August House $14.95 (0-87483-524-0). These 16 Greek myths take on a new life when their locale is changed to wild and woolly Texas and their characters become contemporaries, e.g., Bacchus is a drunken womanizer. (Rev: HBG 3/99; SLJ 8/99) [398.2]

5171 McLaren, Clemence. *Waiting for Odysseus* (9–12). 2000, Simon & Schuster $16.00 (0-689-82875-6). The story of *The Odyssey* is told from the point of view of the women in Odysseus's life. (Rev: BL 3/1/00; HBG 9/00; SLJ 3/00; VOYA 4/00)

5172 Messner-Loebs, William, and Sam Kieth. *Epicurus the Sage* (10–12). Illus. 2003, DC Comics paper $19.95 (1-4012-0028-1). Starring in this comic collection of stories is Greek philosopher Epicurus, who unaccountably finds himself teamed with Plato and a younger Alexander the Great in an exploration of some classic Greek myths. (Rev: BL 12/1/03*) [741.5]

5173 Mikolaycak, Charles. *Orpheus* (9–12). 1992, Harcourt $19.95 (0-15-258804-3). A picture book version of the Orpheus myth that combines classical and romantic images that celebrate the human body. (Rev: BL 10/15/92; SLJ 9/92) [398.21]

5174 Nardo, Don. *Egyptian Mythology* (6–12). Illus. Series: Mythology. 2001, Enslow $20.95 (0-7660-1407-X). Eight Egyptian myths are related here, with background historical and cultural information, question-and-answer sections, and commentary from scholars. (Rev: BL 5/15/01; SLJ 5/01) [299]

5175 Spinner, Stephanie. *Quiver* (7–12). 2002, Knopf LB $17.99 (0-375-91489-7). A deft retelling of the Greek myth of Atalanta, who will marry only a man who can outrun her. (Rev: BCCB 2/03; BL 1/1–15/03*; HB 1–2/03; HBG 3/03; SLJ 10/02; VOYA 12/02)

5176 Steig, Jeanne. *A Gift from Zeus: Sixteen Favorite Myths* (10–12). Illus. 2001, HarperCollins LB $17.89 (0-06-028406-4). Despite illustrations by William Steig that are likely to appeal to a younger audience, this bawdy collection of classical myths from ancient Greece and Rome touches on such mature topics as incest, sexual violence, brutality, and bestiality. (Rev: BL 7/01; HB 5–6/01*; HBG 10/01; SLJ 6/01) [398.2]

5177 Sutcliff, Rosemary. *Black Ships Before Troy: The Story of the Iliad* (6–12). Illus. 1993, Delacorte $24.95 (0-385-31069-2). A re-creation of the classic epic, with a compelling vision and sensitivity to language, history, and heroics. (Rev: BCCB 1/94; BL 10/15/93) [883]

5178 Switzer, Ellen. *Greek Myths: Gods, Heroes, and Monsters — Their Sources, Their Stories and Their Meanings* (7–12). Illus. 1988, Macmillan $18.00 (0-689-31253-9). A collection of myths that includes 13 stories about such characters as Perseus, Odysseus, and Medusa. (Rev: BL 4/1/88; BR 1–2/89; SLJ 4/88) [292]

5179 Usher, Kerry. *Heroes, Gods and Emperors from Roman Mythology* (8–12). Illus. 1992, NTC LB $24.95 (0-87226-909-4). The origins of Roman mythology are given, accompanying retellings of famous myths. [292]

Humor and Satire

5180 Allen, Woody. *Without Feathers* (9–12). 1987, Ballantine paper $5.99 (0-345-33697-6). Sixteen humorous pieces plus two one-act plays are included in this collection. Also use: *Getting Even* (1971). [817]

5181 Ayres, Alex, ed. *The Wit and Wisdom of Mark Twain* (9–12). 1987, NAL paper $7.95 (0-452-00982-0). An alphabetically arranged collection of mostly humorous quotations by Mark Twain. (Rev: BL 8/87) [818]

5182 Barry, Dave. *Boogers Are My Beat: More Lies, but Some Actual Journalism* (10–12). 2003, Crown $23.95 (1-4000-4757-9). Barry waxes hilarious on such diverse subjects as the Winter Olympics in Salt Lake City, North Dakota politics, and cell phones. (Rev: BL 7/03) [814]

5183 Barry, Dave. *Dave Barry in Cyberspace* (10–12). 1996, Crown $22.00 (0-517-59575-3). These short, amusing pieces are particularly suited to those who are not impressed with computers, enjoy a few laughs, and can absorb some sexual innuendos. (Rev: SLJ 2/97) [808.84]

5184 Black, Baxter. *Horseshoes, Cowsocks and Duckfeet: More Commentary by NPR's Cowboy Poet and Former Large Animal Veterinarian* (10–12). 2002, Crown $23.95 (0-609-61090-2). In his humorously dry style, the Cowboy Poet brings to life the past and present of the American West. (Rev: BL 8/02) [814]

5185 Bombeck, Erma. *At Wit's End* (9–12). 1986, Fawcett paper $5.99 (0-449-21184-3). A fine collection of pieces by one of America's favorite humorists. Also use: *Just Wait Till You Have Children of Your Own, If Life Is a Bowl of Cherries, What Am I Doing in the Pits?, The Grass Is Always Greener over the Septic Tank*, and *I Lost Everything in the Post-Natal Depression* (1986). [808.7]

5186 Bombeck, Erma. *Family: The Ties That Bind . . . and Gag!* (9–12). 1987, Fawcett paper $5.95 (0-449-21529-6). Bombeck writes humorously about family life and being a mother, as she did in *Motherhood: The Second Oldest Profession* (1983). (Rev: BL 8/87) [306.85]

5187 Cosby, Bill. *Love and Marriage* (9–12). 1990, Bantam paper $6.50 (0-553-28467-3). The comedian remembers his first attempts at love affairs and his experiences in marriage. (Rev: BL 4/15/89) [306.7]

5188 Keillor, Garrison. *Leaving Home: A Collection of Lake Woebegon Stories* (9–12). 1990, Penguin paper $12.95 (0-14-013160-4). A collection of stories and anecdotes about Lake Woebegon culled from monologues given on radio's "Prairie Home Companion." (Rev: BR 1–2/88; SLJ 2/88; VOYA 4/88) [808.7]

5189 Kerr, Jean. *Please Don't Eat the Daisies* (9–12). 1994, Buccaneer LB $28.95 (0-56849-298-7). This is a humorous look at bringing up a family in suburbia. [808.7]

5190 Kostman, Joel. *Keys to the City: Tales of a New York City Locksmith* (10–12). 1997, DK $19.95 (0-7894-2461-4). This is a collection of 14 mostly humorous true stories about the author's experiences as a professional locksmith in New York. (Rev: BL 9/1/97; SLJ 9/97; VOYA 4/98) [808.84]

5191 Macaulay, David. *Motel of the Mysteries* (10–12). Illus. 1979, Houghton paper $13.00 (0-395-28425-2). A satire on archaeology and civilization that involves unearthing a motel in the year 4022. (Rev: BL 6/87) [817]

5192 Macsai, Gwen. *Lipshtick: Life as a Girl* (10–12). 2000, HarperCollins $23.00 (0-06-019101-5). For mature high school girls, this collection of witty essays is about the bumpy road from girlhood to womanhood. (Rev: BL 2/15/00) [814]

5193 *Mirth of a Nation: The Best Contemporary Humor* (10–12). Ed. by Michael J. Rosen. 2000, HarperPerennial paper $15.00 (0-06-095321-7). More than 50 top contemporary humorists including Dave Barry and David Sedaris have contributed short pieces that demonstrate the new wave in American humor. A second volume, *More Mirth of a Nation,* was published in 2002. (Rev: BL 2/15/00) [817]

5194 Rooney, Andrew A. *A Few Minutes with Andy Rooney* (9–12). 1982, Warner paper $4.95 (0-446-34766-3). This is a collection of short humorous pieces by the writer who gained prominence on television's "60 Minutes." Also use *And More by Andy Rooney* (1983). [808.7]

5195 Rooney, Andrew A. *Not That You Asked . . .* (9–12). 1989, Random $15.95 (0-394-57837-6). A collection of short pieces on such topics as women's underwear and real estate deals. (Rev: BL 2/15/89) [814.54]

5196 Sherrin, Ned, ed. *The Oxford Dictionary of Humorous Quotations* (10–12). 1995, Oxford $45.00 (0-19-214244-5). This volume includes more than 5,000 quotations that represent a wide selection of puns, insults, one-liners, and other types of witty and humorous quotations. (Rev: SLJ 6/96) [808.87]

5197 Twain, Mark. *The Innocents Abroad and Roughing It* (9–12). 1984, Library of America $35.00 (0-940450-25-9). This volume of Twain's works includes two travel books, *The Innocents Abroad* and *Roughing It.* [818]

5198 Twain, Mark. *Life on the Mississippi* (10–12). 1983, Buccaneer LB $25.95 (0-89966-469-5). A nonfiction account of life on the Mississippi, with many humorous passages. First published in 1874. [817]

5199 Twain, Mark. *Roughing It* (10–12). 1986, Buccaneer LB $25.95 (0-89966-524-1); Penguin paper $11.95 (0-14-039010-3). A humorous account first published in 1872 of a trip to California and Hawaii. [817]

Speeches, Essays, and General Literary Works

5200 Angelou, Maya. *Wouldn't Take Nothing for My Journey Now* (10–12). 1993, Random $17.00 (0-679-42743-0); paper $12.00 (0-553-38017-6). In this collection of inspiring essays, author/poet Maya Angelou muses on a wide variety of subjects, including domestic violence, respect, jealousy, and death. (Rev: BL 9/1/93; SLJ 5/94) [814]

5201 Baker, Russell, ed. *Russell Baker's Book of American Humor* (9–12). 1993, Norton $30.00 (0-393-03592-1). More than 100 humorous pieces divided into 12 categories, such as "Shameless Frivolity" and "This Sex Problem." (Rev: BL 11/1/93) [818.02]

5202 Baldwin, James. *Nobody Knows My Name: More Notes of a Native Son* (10–12). 1961, Dial paper $12.00 (0-679-74473-8). A collection of essays about race relations and the relationship between a writer and society. [305.8]

5203 *The Best American Essays* (10–12). Ed. by Stephen J. Gould and Robert Atwan. 2002, Houghton $27.50 (0-618-21388-0); paper $13.00 (0-618-04932-0). Terrorism and illness are among the themes of this anthology. (Rev: BL 10/15/02) [808]

5204 *The Best American Essays of the Century* (10–12). Ed. by Joyce Carol Oates and Robert Atwan. 2000, Houghton $30.00 (0-618-04370-5). The 55 essays in this landmark collection cover a variety of topics from war and nature to families and race, and are by such writers as H. L. Mencken, Rachel Carson, Joan Didion, and James Baldwin. (Rev: BL 8/00) [814]

5205 *The Best American Essays, 2000* (10–12). Ed. by Alan Lightman and Robert Atwan. 2000, Houghton $27.50 (0-618-03578-8); paper $13.00 (0-618-03580-X). An excellent collection of 21 fine essays that deal with a variety of topics and ideas. (Rev: BL 10/1/00) [808]

5206 *The Best American Essays, 2003* (10–12). Ed. by Anne Fadiman and Robert Atwan. 2003, Houghton $27.50 (0-618-34160-9); paper $13.00 (0-618-34161-7). Essays in this edition cover such diverse topics as a 3-year-old girl's imaginary friend, the fall of France through the eyes of a child, and the plight of industrially farmed animals. (Rev: BL 10/15/03) [808]

5207 *The Best American Nonrequired Reading, 2002* (10–12). Ed. by Dave Eggers and Michael Cart. Illus. 2002, Houghton $27.50 (0-618-24693-2); paper $13.00 (0-618-24694-0). This wide-ranging collection of fiction, satire, and reportage explores the humor and angst of growing up. (Rev: BL 10/15/02) [818]

5208 *The Best Spiritual Writing, 2002* (10–12). Ed. by Philip Zaleski. 2002, HarperSF paper $15.95 (0-06-050603-2). For his 2002 anthology of the best in spiritual writing, editor Philip Zaleski has gathered together such diverse pieces as a tale of how a predominantly white Ohio community embraced its first black basketball coach and a portrait of Muslim pacifist Abdul Ghaffar Khan. (Rev: BL 9/15/02) [810.8]

5209 Brown, Larry. *Billy Ray's Farm* (10–12). 2001, Algonquin $22.95 (1-56512-167-8). The prize-winning southern author presents a number of outspoken, interesting essays on many topics. (Rev: BL 3/1/01) [813]

5210 Emerson, Ralph Waldo. *The Portable Emerson.* Rev. ed. (10–12). 1981, Penguin paper $16.95 (0-14-015094-3). This volume contains a generous sampling of Emerson's essays, plus 22 poems. [818]

5211 Fiffer, Sharon S., and Steve Fiffer, eds. *Home: American Writers Remember Rooms of Their Own* (10–12). Illus. 1995, Pantheon $22.00 (0-679-44206-5). In this collection of essays, 18 contemporary American writers remember rooms that were important to them in the past. For example, Jane Smiley sought peace and solitude in bathrooms. (Rev: BL 11/1/95; SLJ 6/96) [808.84]

5212 *Giant Steps: The New Generation of African American Writers* (10–12). Ed. by Kevin Young. 2000, HarperCollins paper $15.00 (0-688-16876-0). This is a collection of poems, essays, and fiction by 35 African Americans, the oldest of whom was born in 1960. (Rev: BL 2/15/00) [810]

5213 *The Greatest Escape Stories Ever Told: Twenty-Five Unforgettable Tales* (10–12). Ed. by Darren Brown. Series: Greatest Stories. 2002, Lyons Pr. $22.95 (1-58574-454-9). These memorable escape stories — all but three of them true — are set in such diverse locales as 18th-century London and a Comanche Indian encampment. (Rev: BL 10/15/02) [818]

5214 Halliburton, Warren J., ed. *Historic Speeches of African Americans* (7–12). Series: African American Experience. 1993, Watts LB $23.00 (0-531-11034-6). Chronologically organized speeches by such leaders as Sojourner Truth, Frederick Douglass, Marcus Garvey, James Baldwin, Angela Davis, and Jesse Jackson. (Rev: BL 4/15/93; SLJ 7/93) [815]

5215 *The Harlem Reader: A Celebration of New York's Most Famous Neighborhood, from the Renaissance Years to the 21st Century* (10–12). Ed. by Herb Boyd. 2003, Crown paper $15.00 (1-4000-4681-5). The many faces of Harlem emerge in this collection of essays and fiction by both well-established and lesser-known writers. (Rev: BL 4/15/03) [974.7]

5216 Hurley, Jennifer A., ed. *Women's Rights* (7–12). Series: Great Speeches in History. 2001, Greenhaven LB $31.20 (0-7377-0773-9); paper $19.95 (0-7377-0772-0). This anthology of speeches by noted women including Elizabeth Cady Stanton, Susan B. Anthony, Gloria Steinem, and Phyllis Schlafly also offers historical context, analytical headnotes, and biographical details. (Rev: BL 10/15/01) [305.42]

5217 Huxley, Aldous. *Brave New World Revisited* (10–12). 1958, Harper & Row paper $10.00 (0-06-095551-1). A series of essays about the prophecies made in the author's novel *Brave New World* and how some have come to pass. [303.3]

5218 *I Like Being American: Treasured Traditions, Symbols, and Stories* (10–12). Ed. by Michael Leach. 2003, Doubleday $19.95 (0-385-50743-7). The editor has selected essays, quotations, speeches, and anecdotes from both celebrated and ordinary citizens to paint a luminous portrait of what it means to be an American. (Rev: BL 3/15/03) [973]

5219 *I Thought My Father Was God and Other True Tales from NPR's National Story Project* (10–12). Ed. by Paul Auster. 2001, Holt $25.00 (0-8050-

6714-0). Collected by Auster for a National Public Radio program, these 179 true stories are arranged in 10 categories, among them animals, families, war, love, and death. (Rev: BL 9/15/01*; SLJ 7/02) [973.9]

5220 Kingsolver, Barbara. *High Tide in Tucson* (10–12). 1995, HarperCollins $22.00 (0-06-017291-6). A collection of general essays about such diverse subjects as hermit crabs, weddings in Benin, and an obsolete Titan missile site, weaving in such themes as the joys of parenting; respect for all creatures, religions, and points of view; and the importance of the natural world in our lives. (Rev: SLJ 2/96) [808]

5221 *Lend Me Your Ears: Great Speeches in History*. Rev. ed. (9–12). Ed. by William Safire. 1997, Norton $39.95 (0-393-04005-4). Memorable speeches from across history and around the world are accompanied by Safire's own tips on making a great speech. [808.85]

5222 *Lines in the Sand: New Writing on War and Peace* (6–10). 2003, Disinformation paper $7.95 (0-9729529-1-8). More than 150 children from around the world have written essays, stories, and memoirs or drawn pictures calling for peace. (Rev: BL 2/1/04) [808.803]

5223 McIntire, Suzanne, ed. *The American Heritage Book of Great American Speeches for Young People* (7–12). 2001, Wiley paper $14.95 (0-471-38942-0). More than 100 key speeches by individuals ranging from politicians to athletes are provided in this single volume. (Rev: SLJ 12/01) [815.008]

5224 *Merlyn's Pen: Fiction, Essays, and Poems by American Teens* (6–12). Illus. 2001, Merlyn's Pen paper $15.95 (1-886427-50-X). This annual anthology of teen writings offers selected poetry, fiction, and essays written by students in middle school and high school. (Rev: VOYA 8/01)

5225 Meyer, Stephanie H., and John Meyer, eds. *Teen Ink: Friends and Family* (6–12). 2001, Health Communications paper $12.95 (1-55874-931-4). This collection of fiction, poetry, and essays written by young people that appeared in *Teen Ink* magazine is organized by themes such as "Snapshots: Friends and Family" and "Out of Focus: Facing Challenges." (Rev: BL 1/1–15/02; SLJ 12/01) [810.8]

5226 *Open Your Eyes: Extraordinary Experiences in Faraway Places* (8–12). Ed. by Jill Davis. 2003, Viking $16.99 (0-670-03616-1). Ten writers, among them Lois Lowry and Harry Mazer, tell stories about how travel changed their lives. (Rev: HBG 4/04; SLJ 1/04; VOYA 4/04) [910.4]

5227 Paine, Thomas. *Rights of Man and Common Sense* (10–12). 1994, Knopf $17.00 (0-679-43314-7). This volume contains the basic writing of Thomas Paine including *Rights of Man*. [320]

5228 *Planet on the Table: Poets on the Reading Life* (10–12). Ed. by Sharon Bryan and William Olsen. 2003, Sarabande paper $16.95 (1-889330-91-4). In this collection of essays, poets write about their reading habits and the importance of reading to their own art. (Rev: BL 2/15/03) [809.1]

5229 Roberts, Cokie. *We Are Our Mothers' Daughters* (10–12). 1998, Morrow $19.95 (0-688-15198-1). This noted TV and radio news correspondent has written a series of personal essays on her relationship to her mother and family and the place of women and mothers in the world today. (Rev: SLJ 8/98) [808]

5230 Rosen, Roger, and Patra McSharry, eds. *East-West: The Landscape Within* (7–12). Series: World Issues. 1992, Rosen LB $16.95 (0-8239-1375-9); paper $8.95 (0-8239-1376-7). Short stories and non-fiction selections by diverse authors of varied nationalities on their cultures' beliefs and values, among them the Dalai Lama, Joseph Campbell, Lydia Minatoya, and Aung Aung Taik. (Rev: BL 12/15/92; SLJ 2/93) [909]

5231 Sanders, Scott R. *Writing from the Center* (10–12). 1995, Indiana Univ. Pr. $25.00 (0-253-32941-8). In this collection of 12 inspiring and penetrating essays, the author examines technology, community, love and strife within families, and the search for spiritual ground as seen through the eyes of a midwesterner. (Rev: SLJ 2/96) [808]

5232 Soto, Gary. *The Effects of Knut Hamsun on a Fresno Boy: Recollections and Short Essays* (10–12). 2000, Persea paper $12.95 (0-89255-254-9). This is a collection of 48 short autobiographical essays by this renowned Chicano writer, who muses on his childhood, his vocation, and his racial heritage. (Rev: BL 11/1/00) [811]

5233 Stone, Miriam. *At the End of Words: A Daughter's Memoir* (6–12). 2003, Candlewick $14.00 (0-7636-1854-3). Moving poetry and narrative describe the author's grief and emotional upheaval over her

mother's death from cancer. (Rev: BL 4/15/03; HBG 10/03; SLJ 5/03; VOYA 12/03) [362.1]

5234 *Teen Ink: Love and Relationships* (6–12). Ed. by Stephanie H. Meyer and Joh Meyer. 2002, Health Communications paper $12.95 (1-55874-969-1). In this collection of poems, essays, and photographs, teens give voice to their thoughts about love in all its many forms. (Rev: SLJ 8/02; VOYA 8/02) [810.8]

5235 *Teen Ink 2: More Voices, More Visions* (6–12). Ed. by Stephanie H. Meyer and Joh Meyer. 2001, Health Communications paper $12.95 (1-55874-913-6). This collection of teen creativity includes poems, essays, short stories, and photographs that reflect their views on such themes as Family, Love, Friends, Challenges, Imagination, Fitting In, Memories, and School Days. (Rev: SLJ 8/01; VOYA 12/01)

5236 Thoreau, Henry David. *A Week on the Concord and Merrimack Rivers; Walden, or, Life in the Woods; The Maine Woods; Cape Cod* (10–12). 1985, Library of America $35.00 (0-940450-27-5). This volume contains the most important of Thoreau's writing, including *Walden*. [818]

5237 Thurber, James. *The Thurber Carnival* (10–12). 1994, Modern Library $15.50 (0-679-60089-2). A collection of witty essays, complete with the author's equally witty illustrations. [817]

5238 Woolf, Virginia. *The Virginia Woolf Reader* (10–12). Ed. by Mitchell A. Leaska. 1984, Harcourt paper $16.00 (0-15-693590-2). A generous selection from the works of Woolf including excerpts from novels, essays, short stories, letters, and diary entries. [828]

5239 WritersCorps Youth. *Smart Mouth: Poetry and Prose by WritersCorps Youth* (7–12). 2000, San Francisco WritersCorps paper $12.95 (1-888048-05-0). This anthology offers multiple selections of both prose and poetry written by students who participated in the WritersCorps program. (Rev: VOYA 6/01)

Literary History and Criticism

General and Miscellaneous

5240 *Anton Chekhov* (10–12). Ed. by Harold Bloom. Series: Bloom's Biocritiques. 2002, Chelsea LB $25.95 (0-7910-6381-X). A biography of Chekhov is followed by a series of critical essays on his plays and fiction. [891.7]

5241 *Autobiography* (9–12). Ed. by Lawrence Kappel. Series: Literary Movements and Genres. 2001, Greenhaven LB $32.45 (0-7377-0673-2); paper $19.95 (0-7377-0672-4). This collection of essays explores various forms of personal narratives, with material on different aspects of this genre and how some authors blend fact and fiction. (Rev: BL 8/01; SLJ 10/01) [808.4]

5242 Bloom, Harold. *How to Read and Why* (10–12). 2000, Scribner $25.00 (0-684-85906-8). While exploring the hows and whys of reading for pleasure, the author looks at some of the great writers of all time, including Shakespeare, Austen, Melville, and Proust, in this book for mature readers.. (Rev: BL 5/15/00) [809]

5243 Cain, William E. *A Historical Guide to Henry David Thoreau* (10–12). Series: Historical Guides to American Authors. 2000, Oxford $39.95 (0-19-513862-7); paper $16.95 (0-19-513863-5). After a biographical essay on Thoreau, this collection of essays assesses his writing and his social and scientific importance. [818]

5244 Kanigel, Robert. *Vintage Reading: From Plato to Bradbury, a Personal Tour of Some of the World's Best Books* (10–12). 1998, Bancroft paper $16.95 (0-9631246-7-6). In a series of essays, the author presents his personal choices of the world's best books, among them *Pride and Prejudice* and *Native Son.* (Rev: BL 2/15/98; BR 9–10/98; SLJ 9/98) [807]

5245 Knox, Bernard, ed. *The Norton Book of Classical Literature* (9–12). 1993, Norton $29.95 (0-393-03426-7). More than 300 pieces of classical literature, primarily Greek but also some Roman. (Rev: BL 2/15/93) [880]

5246 *Slave Narratives* (9–12). Ed. by James Tackach. Series: Literary Movements and Genres. 2001, Greenhaven LB $32.45 (0-7377-0550-7); paper $19.95 (0-7377-0549-3). Critical essays discuss the origins and development of slave narratives, with material on important works in this genre and information on gender issues. (Rev: BL 8/01; SLJ 6/01) [808.4]

5247 *W. E. B. Du Bois* (10–12). Ed. by Harold Bloom. Series: Modern Critical Views. 2001, Chelsea $36.95 (0-7910-5915-4). As well as some biographical information, this book supplies a critical look at Du Bois's creative writing and literary achievements. (Rev: SLJ 12/01) [305.8]

Fiction

General and Miscellaneous

5248 Barlowe, Wayne Douglas. *Barlowe's Guide to Extraterrestrials.* 2nd ed. (9–12). Illus. 1987, Workman $13.95 (0-89480-324-7). From the world of science fiction, Barlowe has pictured in words and illustrations 50 aliens and has identified the books in which they were introduced. (Rev: VOYA 4/88) [808.83]

5249 Barlowe, Wayne Douglas, and Neil Duskis. *Barlowe's Guide to Fantasy* (7–12). Illus. 1996, HarperCollins $35.00 (0-06-105238-8); paper $19.95 (0-06-100817-6). Using double-page spreads, this handsome book covers the history of fantasy literature from ancient times to the present by highlighting 50 examples, among them *Beowulf, Wind in the Willows,* and *Mists of Avalon.* (Rev: VOYA 10/97)

5250 *Children's Literature* (9–12). Ed. by Wendy Mass. Series: Literary Movements and Genres. 2001, Greenhaven LB $32.45 (0-7477-0568-X); paper $19.95 (0-7377-0567-1). A series of essays covers a wide range of genres, including classics, picture books, easy-to-read titles, fairy tales, and fables. (Rev: BL 8/01) [808.3]

5251 Clute, John. *The Illustrated Encyclopedia* (10–12). 1995, DK $39.95 (0-7894-0185-1). Arranged chiefly by decade in each chapter, this history of science fiction covers visions of the future, themes in history, influential magazines, nonprint media, and other subjects, with sketches of more than 100 writers, photographs, signatures, and chronological bibliographies of major works. (Rev: BL 5/15/98; BR 5–6/96; SLJ 1/96; VOYA 6/96) [813]

5252 Clute, John, and John Grant, eds. *The Encyclopedia of Fantasy* (10–12). 1997, St. Martin's $75.00 (0-312-15897-1). This comprehensive research on fantasy literature and media includes material on authors, awards, movies, TV shows, themes, and articles on the fantasy literature of various countries. (Rev: BL 9/1/97; SLJ 8/97) [813]

5253 *Fantasy* (9–12). Ed. by Wendy Mass and Stuart P. Levine. Series: Literary Movements and Genres. 2002, Gale LB $32.45 (0-7377-1086-1); paper $19.95 (0-7377-1085-3). This anthology contains several critical articles that explore aspects of fantasy writing, past and present, with coverage of important authors and their works. (Rev: BL 4/15/02) [808.1]

5254 Miller, Ron. *The History of Science Fiction* (6–10). Illus. 2001, Watts LB $28.00 (0-531-11866-5). An enticing overview of the genre, its development, recurring themes, primary authors, TV and movie presentations, and most important awards. (Rev: BL 7/01; SLJ 7/01; VOYA 6/02) [809.3]

5255 *Postmodernism* (9–12). Ed. by Derek Maus. Series: Literary Movements and Genres. 2001, Greenhaven LB $32.45 (0-7377-0640-6); paper $19.95 (0-7377-0641-4). The manipulation of the elements of fiction known as postmoderism is explored in this series of challenging critical essays. (Rev: BL 8/01) [808.3]

5256 Rainey, Richard. *The Monster Factory* (6–12). 1993, Macmillan LB $19.00 (0-02-775663-7). A discussion of seven famous monster-story writers and their most-loved works. (Rev: BL 8/93; VOYA 10/93) [809.3]

5257 Reid, Suzanne Elizabeth. *Presenting Young Adult Science Fiction* (7–12). Series: Twayne's United States Authors. 1998, Twayne $29.00 (0-8057-1653-X). This comprehensive introduction to science fiction describes the history of the genre, profiles such classical masters as Asimov, Bradbury, Heinlein, and Le Guin, and presents members of the new generation, among them Orson Scott Card, Pamela Service, Piers Anthony, and Douglas Adams. (Rev: SLJ 6/99) [808.3]

5258 Rovin, Jeff. *Aliens, Robots, and Spaceships* (7–12). Illus. 1995, Facts on File $38.50 (0-8160-3107-X). Alphabetically arranged entries on characters, creatures, and places in the world of science fiction, with more than 100 black-and-white illustrations. (Rev: BR 1–2/96; SLJ 12/95; VOYA 4/96) [813]

5259 *Science Fiction* (9–12). Ed. by Jesse Cunningham. Series: Literary Movements and Genres. 2002, Gale LB $32.45 (0-7377-0571-X); paper $19.95 (0-7377-0572-8). Explores the history and contemporary status of science fiction writing, with an emphasis on landmark writers and their creations. (Rev: BL 4/15/02) [808.3]

5260 Smith, Lucinda I. *Women Who Write*, Vol. 2 (8–12). 1994, Messner $15.00 (0-671-87253-2). Interviews and short biographies of contemporary women writers, including Margaret Atwood and Sue Grafton. Addresses the desire to write and provides tips for aspiring authors. (Rev: BL 10/15/94; SLJ 11/94; VOYA 12/94) [809.8]

5261 Stuprich, Michael, ed. *Horror* (8–12). Series: Literary Movements and Genres. 2001, Greenhaven $32.45 (0-7377-0667-8); paper $19.95 (0-7377-0666-X). A thorough introduction to the horror genre, with essays by writers including Stephen King and Joyce Carol Oates. (Rev: BL 8/01; SLJ 11/01) [823]

5262 Yolen, Jane. *Touch Magic: Fantasy, Faerie, and Folklore in the Literature of Childhood.* 2nd ed. (10–12). 2000, August House paper $11.95 (0-87483-591-7). This celebrated author has written a series of critical essays on the nature of fantasy and folklore and their lasting importance in literature for young people. (Rev: BL 5/15/00) [398]

Europe

Great Britain and Ireland

5263 Beetz, Kirk H. *Exploring C. S. Lewis' The Chronicles of Narnia* (10–12). 2001, Beacham paper $16.95 (0-933833-58-X). This is a critical examination of *The Chronicles of Narnia*, with material on characters, mythology, backgrounds, and literary importance. (Rev: SLJ 8/01) [823.009]

5264 Blom, Margaret Howard. *Charlotte Brontë* (10–12). 1977, Twayne $21.95 (0-8057-6673-1). A critical study of the life and works of the creator of *Jane Eyre.* [823.09]

5265 Bloom, Harold, ed. *Charlotte Brontë's Jane Eyre* (8–12). Series: Bloom's Notes. 1996, Chelsea LB $21.95 (0-7910-4063-1). In addition to a collection of critical essays on *Jane Eyre,* there is a biography of the author, a plot summary, and character sketches. (Rev: BL 1/1–15/97; SLJ 4/97) [823]

5266 Bloom, Harold, ed. *Jane Austen* (10–12). Series: Bloom's Modern Critical Views. 2004, Chelsea (0-7910-7656-3). Various themes found in Jane Austen's novels are explored in these critical essays. plus material on plots, characters, and settings. (Rev: SLJ 6/04) [823.009]

5267 Bloom, Harold, ed. *Jane Austen* (10–12). Series: Bloom's Biocritiques. 2002, Chelsea LB $25.95 (0-7910-6184-1). Several important critics write about Austen, her life, plots, characters, style, and influence. [823.009]

5268 Bloom, Harold, ed. *Lord of the Flies* (10–12). Series: Modern Critical Interpretations. 1998, Chelsea LB $34.95 (0-7910-4777-6). Sixteen critical essays written between 1961 and 1993 examine various aspects of this modern classic. (Rev: SLJ 2/99) [823]

5269 Bloom, Harold, ed. *Thomas Hardy* (10–12). Series: Bloom's Major Novelists. 2003, Chelsea LB $22.95 (0-7910-6348-8). This book covers the life of Hardy with an emphasis on his novels, their plots, construction, characters, and critical interpretations. [823.009]

5270 Bloom, Harold, ed. *The Victorian Novel* (10–12). Series: Bloom's Period Studies. 2004, Chelsea $37.95 (0-7910-7678-4). The works of such authors as Dickens, the Brontës, Trollope, Thackeray, and Hardy are examined in this history of the Victorian novel. (Rev: SLJ 3/04) [820.9]

5271 Brontë, Charlotte. *Jane Eyre* (8–12). Series: Case Studies in Contemporary Criticism. 1964, Airmont paper $4.95 (0-8049-0017-5). An author biography is accompanied by brief critical comments, plot and theme analysis, and a list of characters.

5272 Brunsdale, Mitzi. *Student Companion to George Orwell* (9–12). Series: Student Companions to Classic Writers. 2000, Greenwood $35.00 (0-313-30637-0). With particular emphasis on *Animal Farm* and *1984*, this is a critical survey of the works of George Orwell. (Rev: VOYA 12/00) [828]

5273 Colbert, David. *The Magical Worlds of Harry Potter: A Treasury of Myths, Legends, and Fascinating Facts* (6–12). Illus. 2002, Berkley $13.00 (0-425-18701-2). A useful alphabetical guide to the origins of the magic and mythology of Hogwarts; illustrations and sidebar features aid comprehension. (Rev: VOYA 12/02) [823]

5274 Foster, Robert. *The Complete Guide to Middle-Earth: From The Hobbit to The Silmarillion* (10–12). 1985, Ballantine paper $6.99 (0-345-32436-6). An alphabetically arranged concordance to the writing of Tolkien. [808.3]

5275 Goodman, Barbara A., ed. *Readings on Silas Marner* (9–12). Series: Literary Companions. 2000, Greenhaven LB $21.96 (0-7377-0358-X); paper $13.96 (0-7377-0357-1). Eliot's epic novel is analyzed in a series of essays that includes a chapter on the author's life. (Rev: BL 8/00) [823]

5276 Haber, Karen, ed. *Meditations on Middle-Earth* (9–12). Illus. 2001, St. Martin's $24.95 (0-312-27536-6). All but two of the contributors are fantasy writers in this tribute to Tolkien and exploration of the meanings of Middle Earth. (Rev: BL 11/1/01) [823]

5277 Hallissy, Margaret. *A Companion to Chaucer's Canterbury Tales* (10–12). 1995, Greenwood $49.95 (0-313-29189-6). After an introduction to Chaucer's world and language, this companion supplies a guide to each of the tales and to the many colorful characters in them. (Rev: SLJ 6/96; VOYA 4/96) [823]

5278 Hornback, Bert G. *Great Expectations: A Novel of Friendship* (9–12). Illus. 1987, Twayne $23.95 (0-8057-7956-6). A critical analysis of this novel often studied in high school. (Rev: BL 5/15/87; SLJ 9/87) [823]

5279 Kappel, Lawrence, ed. *Readings on Great Expectations* (10–12). Series: Literary Companions. 1998, Greenhaven paper $17.45 (1-56510-820-5). This volume includes analysis and criticism of *Great Expectations,* as well as essays on Dickens's social criticism, characters, and use of humor and tragedy. (Rev: BL 9/15/98; BR 5–6/99) [823]

5280 Karson, Jill, ed. *Readings on A Christmas Carol* (9–12). Series: Literary Companions. 2000, Greenhaven LB $21.96 (0-7377-0340-7); paper $13.96 (0-7377-0339-3). After a biography of Charles Dickens, this collection of essays explores the plot, characters, and themes found in *A Christmas Carol.* (Rev: BL 8/00) [823]

5281 Karson, Jill, ed. *Readings on Jane Eyre* (10–12). Series: Literary Companions. 2000, Greenhaven LB $21.96 (0-7377-0177-3); paper $13.95 (0-7377-0176-5). Provides a thorough analysis of many aspects of this important English novel and covers the life of the author. (Rev: BL 1/1–15/00) [823]

5282 Kelly, Richard. *Lewis Carroll* (9–12). 1990, Twayne $32.00 (0-8057-6988-9). A critical survey of Carroll's writings concentrating on the Alice books and *The Hunting of the Snark.* [828]

5283 Koster, Katie de, ed. *Readings on Brave New World* (9–12). Series: Literary Companion. 1999, Greenhaven LB $20.96 (1-56510-835-3); paper $12.96 (1-56510-834-5). A collection of essays on this masterpiece of science fiction by Aldous Huxley with material on the author and his times. (Rev: BL 9/15/99) [823]

5284 Koster, Katie de, ed. *Readings on J. R. R. Tolkien* (10–12). Series: Literary Companions. 2000, Greenhaven LB $21.96 (0-7377-0245-1); paper $13.95 (0-7377-0244-3). The life and works of this great English fantasy writer are covered in this collection of essays that concentrate on *Lord of the Rings.* (Rev: BL 1/1–15/00; SLJ 5/00) [808.3]

5285 Mitchell, Hayley R., ed. *Readings on Wuthering Heights* (10–12). Series: Literary Companions. 1998, Greenhaven LB $20.96 (1-56510-833-7); paper $17.45 (1-56510-832-9). The essays in this book guide readers through the tempestuous love of Cathy and Heathcliff, with material on the complex structure and themes of Emily Brontë's only novel. (Rev: BL 1/1–15/99) [823]

5286 Nardo, Don, ed. *Readings on Frankenstein* (10–12). Series: Literary Companions. 1999, Greenhaven LB $21.96 (0-7377-0183-8); paper $13.96 (0-7377-0182-X). Mary Shelley's masterpiece is covered in a series of essays that explore the novel's importance, themes, plot, and characters as well as the author's life. (Rev: BL 12/15/99) [823]

5287 Nardo, Don, ed. *Readings on The Canterbury Tales* (10–12). Series: Literary Companion. 1997, Greenhaven LB $21.96 (1-56510-586-9); paper $16.20 (1-56510-585-0). Incisive essays by Chaucer scholars analyze the themes, stories, and characters in *The Canterbury Tales.* (Rev: BL 12/15/96; SLJ 2/97) [821]

5288 Nardo, Don, ed. *A Tale of Two Cities* (10–12). Series: Literary Companions. 1997, Greenhaven LB $21.96 (1-56510-649-0); paper $22.00 (1-56510-648-2). This collection of critical essays on Dickens's novel of the French Revolution covers major themes, characters, and the social and historical background. (Rev: BL 6/1–15/97; SLJ 8/97; VOYA 12/97) [823]

5289 Nelson, Harland S. *Charles Dickens* (10–12). 1981, Twayne $32.00 (0-8057-6805-X). This account focuses on five novels, including *David Copperfield, Oliver Twist,* and *Great Expectations.* [823.09]

5290 O'Neill, Jane. *The World of the Brontës* (8–12). Illus. 1999, Carlton $24.95 (1-85868-341-6). This book describes the lives and works of Emily, Charlotte, and Anne Brontë and gives a good picture of 19th-century English society, quoting frequently from the Brontës' diaries and letters as well as their novels. (Rev: BL 9/1/99; SLJ 2/00) [823.809]

5291 O'Neill, Terry, ed. *Readings on Animal Farm* (10–12). Series: Literary Companions. 1998, Greenhaven LB $20.96 (1-56510-651-2). The plot, symbolism, characters, and structure of this highly respected fable are approached from different perspectives. (Rev: BL 3/15/98; SLJ 6/98) [823]

5292 Prose, Francine, ed. *The Mrs. Dalloway Reader* (10–12). 2003, Harcourt $24.00 (0-15-101044-7).

Critical essays and analysis accompany the text of Virginia Woolf's classic novel plus *Mrs. Dalloway's Party* and letters by Woolf about the writing of this masterpiece. (Rev: BL 11/15/03) [823]

5293 Riley, Dick, and Pam McAllister. *The Bedside, Bathtub and Armchair Companion to Sherlock Holmes* (10–12). 1999, Continuum $29.95 (0-8264-1140-1). Everything one would like to know about Sherlock Holmes, including a synopsis of all his adventures and a brief biography of his creator. (Rev: BL 1/1–15/99; SLJ 7/99) [823]

5294 Riley, Dick, and Pam McAllister, eds. *The New Bedside, Bathtub and Armchair Companion to Agatha Christie* (10–12). Illus. 1986, Ungar paper $15.95 (0-8044-6725-0). Many enthusiasts of Christie have contributed articles on her novels, their plots, and characters. [823.09]

5295 Saposnik, Irving S. *Robert Louis Stevenson* (10–12). 1974, Twayne $22.95 (0-8057-1517-7). Biographical information accompanies an analysis of Stevenson's works in several genres. [828]

5296 Severin, Tim. *In Search of Robinson Crusoe* (10–12). Illus. 2002, Basic $25.00 (0-465-07698-X). The absorbing and informative story of Severin's search for the roots of Defoe's classic novel. (Rev: BL 6/1–15/02) [910.4]

5297 Shippey, T. A. *J. R. R. Tolkien: Author of the Century* (10–12). 2001, Houghton $26.00 (0-618-12764-X). A thorough, critical analysis of Tolkien's books with particular emphasis on "the greatest book of the 20th century," *The Lord of the Rings.* (Rev: BL 5/15/01*) [823]

5298 Smyer, Richard I. *Animal Farm: Pastoralism and Politics* (9–12). 1988, Twayne $25.95 (0-8057-7980-9); paper $14.95 (0-8057-8030-0). A detailed analysis of this allegory that explains its structure and layers of meaning. (Rev: SLJ 8/88) [823.09]

5299 Swisher, Clarice, ed. *Lord of the Flies* (10–12). Series: Literary Companion. 1997, Greenhaven LB $21.96 (1-56510-629-6); paper $16.20 (1-56510-628-8). This dark novel of evil and human nature is examined in essays that explore its themes, symbolism, characters, and continued popularity. (Rev: BL 6/1–15/97; SLJ 7/97) [823]

5300 Swisher, Clarice, ed. *Readings on A Portrait of the Artist as a Young Man* (9–12). Series: Literary Companions. 2000, Greenhaven LB $21.96 (0-7377-0360-1); paper $13.96 (0-7377-0359-8). The autobiographical novel by James Joyce is analyzed in a series of scholarly essays preceded by a short biography of the author. (Rev: BL 8/00) [823]

5301 Swisher, Clarice, ed. *Readings on Charles Dickens* (10–12). Series: Literary Companions. 1997, Greenhaven LB $21.96 (1-56510-590-7). Includes essays on Dickens's many literary talents, such as character creation, plus articles on individ-

ual works like *A Christmas Carol* and *Oliver Twist.* (Rev: BL 12/15/97; SLJ 4/98) [823]

5302 Swisher, Clarice, ed. *Readings on Heart of Darkness* (9–12). 1999, Greenhaven LB $34.95 (1-56510-823-X); paper $23.70 (1-56510-822-1). Critical essays discuss the structure and interpretation of Conrad's masterpiece. (Rev: BL 9/15/99) [825.9]

5303 Swisher, Clarice, ed. *Readings on Jane Austen* (10–12). Series: Literary Companions. 1997, Greenhaven paper $16.20 (1-56510-577-X). In this anthology, essays on such specific works as *Pride and Prejudice* are complemented by general overviews of themes in Austen's novels and biographical material. (Rev: BL 1/1–15/97; SLJ 5/97) [823]

5304 Swisher, Clarice, ed. *Readings on Joseph Conrad* (10–12). Series: Literary Companions. 1998, Greenhaven LB $20.96 (1-56510-637-7). Themes, characters, and literary style are the subjects of some of the essays in this anthology on Conrad that also contains writings on individual works such as *Lord Jim.* (Rev: BL 2/15/98; SLJ 3/98) [823]

5305 Swisher, Clarice, ed. *Readings on Pride and Prejudice* (10–12). Series: Literary Companions. 1998, Greenhaven LB $20.96 (1-56510-861-2); paper $17.45 (1-56510-860-4). This collection of essays delves into the themes, characters, writing style, gentle satire, and lifestyles found in *Pride and Prejudice,* Jane Austen's most popular novel. (Rev: BL 12/15/98) [823]

5306 Swisher, Clarice, ed. *Victorian Literature* (9–12). Series: Literary Movements and Genres. 1999, Greenhaven LB $21.96 (0-7377-0209-5); paper $13.96 (0-7377-0208-7). Essays discuss how Victorian life influenced the literature of the time. (Rev: BL 3/15/00; SLJ 5/00) [820.9]

5307 Szumski, Bonnie, ed. *Readings on Tess of the d'Urbervilles* (9–12). Series: Literary Companions. 2000, Greenhaven LB $21.96 (0-7377-0197-8); paper $13.96 (0-7377-0196-X). Representing a wide range of sources, this collection of essays about Hardy's masterpiece also includes a life of the author and extensive bibliographies. (Rev: BL 3/15/00) [823]

5308 Teachman, Debra. *Understanding Pride and Prejudice: A Student Casebook to Issues, Sources, and Historical Documents* (9–12). Series: Literature in Context. 1997, Greenwood $39.95 (0-313-30126-3). An engaging introduction to this classic novel, with material on characters, plot, themes, and information on the history, customs, attitudes, and culture of 18th-century England. (Rev: SLJ 9/98) [823]

5309 Thompson, Stephen P., ed. *Readings on Beowulf* (10–12). Series: Literary Companions. 1998, Greenhaven LB $21.96 (1-56510-813-2); paper $17.45 (1-56510-812-4). The 18 essays reprinted in this book provide the historical and cultural background of this epic and an analysis of themes, characters, and style. (Rev: BL 7/98; SLJ 11/98) [829]

5310 Tolkien, J. R. R. *The Shaping of Middle-Earth* (9–12). Illus. 1986, Houghton $24.95 (0-395-42501-8). Background notes and information on the famous fantasy written by Tolkien and edited by his son. (Rev: BL 11/86; SLJ 3/87) [808.3]

5311 Wagoner, Mary S. *Agatha Christie* (9–12). 1986, Twayne $22.95 (0-8057-6936-6). An analysis of this mystery story writer's works with an accompanying brief biography. (Rev: BL 2/1/87) [823]

5312 Wiener, Gary, ed. *Readings on Gulliver's Travels* (9–12). Series: Literary Companions. 2000, Greenhaven LB $21.96 (0-7377-0342-3); paper $13.96 (0-7377-0341-5). Swift's satirical masterpiece is analyzed in a series of essays that cover a variety of topics relating to the author and his work. (Rev: BL 8/00) [823]

Other Countries

5313 Bloom, Harold, ed. *Fyodor Dostoevsky's Crime and Punishment* (10–12). Series: Bloom's Notes. 1996, Chelsea LB $17.95 (0-7910-4056-9). This introduction to Dostoyevsky's novel contains excerpts and scholarly essays about the work, discusses the author's life, summarizes the themes and the plot, and describes the characters. (Rev: SLJ 4/97) [891.7]

5314 Bloom, Harold, ed. *Hermann Hesse* (10–12). Series: Modern Critical Views. 2002, Chelsea $37.95 (0-7910-7398-X). Besides biographical information on Hesse, this group of essays discusses his writing style, themes, characters, philosophy, and influences. (Rev: SLJ 9/03) [838]

5315 Cunningham, Jesse G., ed. *Readings on The Plague* (8–12). Series: Literary Companion to World Literature. 2001, Greenhaven LB $28.70 (0-7377-0691-0); paper $18.70 (0-7377-0690-2). Discussions of the structure, meaning, and historical context of Camus's novel provide a variety of viewpoints and interpretations. (Rev: SLJ 11/01) [843]

5316 Immell, Myra H., ed. *Readings on The Diary of a Young Girl* (10–12). Series: Literary Companions. 1998, Greenhaven LB $20.96 (1-56510-661-X). A collection of essays about the themes and historical background of Anne Frank's *Diary*. (Rev: BL 2/15/98; SLJ 4/98) [839.3]

5317 Johnson, Tamara, ed. *Readings on Fyodor Dostoyevsky* (10–12). Series: Literary Companions. 1997, Greenhaven paper $12.96 (1-56510-587-7). Essays explore Dostoyevsky's themes, characters, plots, and settings, and others that deal with individual major works. (Rev: BL 3/15/98; SLJ 7/98) [891.7]

5318 Mass, Wendy, ed. *Readings on Night* (9–12). Series: Literary Companions. 2000, Greenhaven LB $21.96 (0-7377-0370-9); paper $13.96 (0-7377-0369-5). The structure, themes, and significance of Elie Wiesel's harrowing Holocaust autobiography are some of the topics covered in this literary guide. (Rev: BL 8/00; SLJ 1/01) [833]

5319 Maus, Derek C., ed. *Readings on Crime and Punishment* (9–12). Series: Literary Companions. 2000, Greenhaven LB $21.96 (0-7377-0235-4); paper $13.96 (0-7377-0234-6). Essays offer insight into the classic novel's construction and layers of meaning. (Rev: BL 2/15/00) [891.73]

5320 Nardo, Don, ed. *Readings on Homer* (10–12). Series: Literary Companions. 1997, Greenhaven LB $21.96 (1-56510-639-3); paper $17.45 (1-56510-638-5). Essays in this collection discuss the *Iliad* and *Odyssey,* their themes, characters, structure, and continuing popularity. (Rev: BL 10/15/97; SLJ 4/98) [883]

5321 O'Neill, Terry, ed. *Readings on All Quiet On the Western Front* (10–12). Series: Literary Companions. 1998, Greenhaven LB $20.96 (1-56510-825-6); paper $17.45 (1-56510-824-8). Essays in this anthology discuss this amazing novel that captures the terror, bitterness, and boredom experienced by a young German soldier during World War I. (Rev: BL 12/15/98) [833]

5322 *A Scholarly Look at Anne Frank* (10–12). Series: Modern Critical Interpretations. 1999, Chelsea LB $34.95 (0-7910-5192-7). A mature look at the Anne Frank legacy, including the various adaptations and versions of the diary. (Rev: VOYA 10/99) [839.3]

5323 Walsh, Thomas, ed. *Readings on Candide* (9–12). Series: Literary Companion. 2000, Greenhaven LB $22.96 (0-7377-0362-8); paper $14.96 (0-7377-0361-X). As well as a biography of Voltaire, this anthology contains many essays that provide a literary analysis and criticism of this masterpiece. (Rev: BL 3/1/01) [891.7]

United States

5324 Bail, Paul. *John Saul: A Critical Companion* (10–12). Series: Critical Companions to Popular Contemporary Writers. 1996, Greenwood $29.95 (0-313-29575-1). An extensive analysis of the works of John Saul, a famous writer of horror stories whose works include *Suffer the Children* and *Black Lightning.* (Rev: SLJ 10/96) [813]

5325 Barbour, Scott, ed. *American Modernism* (9–12). Series: Literary Movements and Genres. 1999, Greenhaven LB $21.96 (0-7377-0200-1); paper $13.96 (0-7377-0201-X). Explores American literature during the early decades of the 20th century and focuses on the New Poetry of 1910 and the fiction of the Lost Generation. (Rev: BL 4/15/00; SLJ 4/00) [813]

5326 Baughman, Judith, and Matthew Joseph Bruccoli. *Literary Masters: F. Scott Fitzgerald* (10–12). Series: Literary Masters. 2000, Gale $49.95 (0-7876-3958-3). After a brief biography of Fitzgerald, essays discuss both his novels and his short stories. [813.009]

5327 Baym, Nina. *The Scarlet Letter: A Reading* (10–12). 1986, Twayne $29.00 (0-8057-7957-4); paper $13.95 (0-8057-8001-7). An analysis of this novel, often studied in high school, plus an introduction to the life of its author, Nathaniel Hawthorne. (Rev: BL 7/86; SLJ 5/87) [813]

5328 Bishop, Rudine Sims. *Presenting Walter Dean Myers* (9–12). 1990, Twayne $28.00 (0-8057-8214-1). A profile of the life and work of this African American writer with an analysis of each of his most important books. (Rev: BL 10/15/90) [813]

5329 Bloom, Harold, ed. *Alice Walker* (9–12). Series: Major Novelists. 1999, Chelsea $19.95 (0-7910-5250-8). Readings on Walker's *Meridian* and *The Color Purple* are accompanied by biographical information about the author. (Rev: BL 2/15/00; SLJ 3/00) [813]

5330 Bloom, Harold. *Carson McCullers* (10–12). Series: Modern Critical Views. 1986, Chelsea $36.95 (0-87754-630-4). This is a collection of critical essays that evaluate McCullers's four major novels, including *The Ballad of the Sad Cafe, The Heart Is a Lonely Hunter,* and *The Member of the Wedding.* [813.009]

5331 Bloom, Harold, ed. *Ernest Hemingway's The Sun Also Rises* (10–12). Series: Bloom's Notes. 1996, Chelsea LB $17.95 (0-7910-4075-5). After a short biographical sketch and a thorough description of the novel, a number of critical essays discuss various aspects of this classic. (Rev: SLJ 3/97) [813]

5332 Bloom, Harold, ed. *Eudora Welty* (9–12). 1999, Chelsea LB $18.95 (0-7910-5126-9). This study of four of Welty's most popular stories also contains some biographical material and an index to themes and ideas in her work. (Rev: SLJ 7/99) [8113]

5333 Bloom, Harold, ed. *F. Scott Fitzgerald* (9–12). Series: Major Novelists. 1999, Chelsea $18.95 (0-7910-5254-0). Readings on *The Great Gatsby* and *Tender Is the Night* offer biographical information, plot summaries, and analysis. (Rev: BL 3/15/00; SLJ 4/00) [813]

5334 Bloom, Harold, ed. *Harper Lee's To Kill a Mockingbird* (9–12). Series: Modern Critical Interpretations. 1998, Chelsea LB $34.95 (0-7910-4779-2). An outstanding collection about *To Kill a Mockingbird,* including critical essays, initial

reviews from the *Saturday Review* and *New York Herald Tribune Book Review,* a catalog of attempts in Hanover County, Virginia, to censor the book in 1966, an exploration of the novel and the law, and an analysis of Horton Foote's screenplay for the 1962 film based on the novel. (Rev: VOYA 10/99) [813]

5335 Bloom, Harold, ed. *Invisible Man* (10–12). Series: Modern Critical Interpretations. 1998, Chelsea LB $34.95 (0-7910-4776-8). Reprints of 12 highly intellectual articles that deal with various aspects of Ralph Ellison's novel in a somewhat esoteric manner. (Rev: SLJ 3/99) [813]

5336 Bloom, Harold. *Maya Angelou* (9–12). Series: Modern Critical Views. 1998, Chelsea $36.95 (0-7910-4782-2). In addition to a brief biography, critical essays explore the themes found in Angelou's prose and poetry. [818]

5337 Bloom, Harold, ed. *Maya Angelou's I Know Why the Caged Bird Sings* (8–12). Series: Bloom's Notes. 1996, Chelsea LB $21.95 (0-7910-3666-9). A collection of critical essays on this work by Maya Angelou, plus a detailed analysis of the book and its characters, accompanied by material on the author's life. (Rev: BL 1/1–15/97; SLJ 3/97) [818]

5338 Bloom, Harold, ed. *William Faulkner* (9–12). Series: Major Novelists. 1999, Chelsea $18.95 (0-7910-5255-9). Readings on *Light in August, The Sound and the Fury,* and *Absalom, Absalom!* offer biographical information, plot summaries, and analysis. (Rev: BL 3/15/00) [813]

5339 Buranelli, Vincent. *Edgar Allan Poe* (10–12). 1977, Twayne $28.95 (0-8057-7189-1); paper $4.95 (0-672-61502-9). This book analyzes the fiction as well as the poetry and nonfiction by Poe. [818]

5340 Burkhead, Cynthia. *Student Companion to John Steinbeck* (10–12). Series: Student Companions to Classic Writers. 2002, Greenwood LB $35.95 (0-313-31457-8). This collection examines Steinbeck's life, career, and works, with material on themes, characters, symbolism, and plots. [813.009]

5341 Burns, Landon C. *Pat Conroy: A Critical Companion* (10–12). Series: Critical Companions to Popular Contemporary Writers. 1996, Greenwood $29.95 (0-313-29419-4). Biographical material is combined with critical comments on the themes, plots, character development, and writing style in the works of Pat Conroy. (Rev: SLJ 10/96) [813]

5342 Cady, Edwin H. *Stephen Crane* (10–12). 1980, Twayne $32.00 (0-8057-7299-5). An analysis of the short-lived author's work and career. [813.09]

5343 Campbell, Patricia J. *Presenting Robert Cormier.* 2nd ed. (9–12). Illus. 1989, Twayne $20.95 (0-8057-8212-5). A profile of this author and his work through the novel *Fade.* (Rev: BL 9/15/89; BR 5–6/90; SLJ 12/89) [813.54]

5344 Carmean, Karen. *Ernest J. Gaines: A Critical Companion* (10–12). Series: Critical Companions to Popular Contemporary Writers. 1998, Greenwood $29.95 (0-313-30286-3). The author provides biographical information about Gaines followed by a literary analysis of several of his novels, including *The Autobiography of Miss Jane Pittman,* and a collection of short stories. Other books in this series cover Tom Clancy, James Herriot, Anne McCaffrey, Toni Morrison, Anne Tyler, and Leon Uris. (Rev: BR 1–2/99; VOYA 6/99) [813]

5345 Cart, Michael. *Presenting Robert Lipsyte* (8–12). 1995, Twayne $29.00 (0-8057-4151-8). A probing look at Lipsyte's life and work. (Rev: BL 6/1–15/95; BR 3–4/96; VOYA 6/96) [813]

5346 Cassedy, Patrice. *Understanding Flowers for Algernon* (7–12). Illus. Series: Understanding Great Literature. 2001, Lucent LB $19.96 (1-56006-784-5). Clear and thoughtful analysis of *Flowers for Algernon*, a science fiction YA novel by Daniel Keyes, is accompanied by biographical information, historical context, a timeline, and sources. (Rev: BL 3/1/01) [813]

5347 Clareson, Thomas D. *Frederik Pohl* (10–12). 1987, Starmont House LB $31.00 (0-930261-34-8); paper $21.00 (0-930261-33-X). An analysis of the works and life of one of sci-fi's greatest writers. (Rev: BL 1/15/88) [813]

5348 Crowe, Chris. *Presenting Mildred D. Taylor* (6–12). Illus. Series: United States Authors. 1999, Twayne $33.00 (0-8057-1687-4). As well as some biographical material, this book gives an analysis of Taylor's works, their historical context, and a history of racism and the civil rights movement in Mississippi. (Rev: BL 2/15/00; VOYA 6/00) [813]

5349 Daly, Jay. *Presenting S. E. Hinton.* 2nd ed. (9–12). Illus. 1989, Twayne $20.95 (0-8057-8211-7). A biography of this popular author plus an analysis of her work, including *Taming the Star Runner.* (Rev: BL 9/15/89; SLJ 3/90) [813.54]

5350 De Koster, Katie, ed. *Readings on Ernest Hemingway* (10–12). Series: Literary Companions. 1997, Greenhaven LB $19.95 (1-56510-463-5); paper $17.45 (1-56510-462-5). General essays about Hemingway and his work, along with essays on *The Sun Also Rises* and several other Hemingway novels. (Rev: BL 1/1–15/97; SLJ 4/97) [813]

5351 De Koster, Katie, ed. *Readings on F. Scott Fitzgerald* (10–12). Series: Literary Companions. 1997, Greenhaven LB $21.96 (1-56510-461-7); paper $20.25 (1-56510-460-9). Essays in this volume explore Fitzgerald's major novels, themes, characters, and the lifestyle of the 1920s that he depicted in his works. (Rev: BL 10/15/97; SLJ 12/97) [813]

5352 De Koster, Katie. *Readings on Mark Twain* (9–12). Series: Literary Companion to American

Authors. 1996, Greenhaven LB $21.96 (1-56510-471-4). After a brief biography, there are 24 critical essays on Twain's writings, some general, others on specific works including *Huckleberry Finn.* (Rev: BL 5/15/96; SLJ 8/96) [818]

5353 De Koster, Katie, ed. *Readings on The Adventures of Huckleberry Finn* (10–12). Series: Literary Companions. 1998, Greenhaven LB $20.96 (1-56510-819-1); paper $20.96 (1-56510-818-3). This landmark work in the history of American literature is discussed in 15 essays on background material, characters, themes, plot, and the controversies surrounding it. (Rev: BL 7/98; SLJ 12/98) [813]

5354 De Koster, Katie, ed. *Readings on The Adventures of Tom Sawyer* (10–12). Series: Literary Companions. 1998, Greenhaven LB $20.96 (1-56510-845-0); paper $17.45 (1-56510-844-2). Explores facets of Twain's masterpiece based partly on his Missouri childhood. (Rev: BL 11/15/98; BR 5–6/99) [813]

5355 De Koster, Katie, ed. *Readings on The Call of the Wild* (9–12). Series: Literary Companions. 1999, Greenhaven LB $20.96 (1-56510-831-0). A collection of articles that examine the allegorical elements in this adventure story as well as exploring its main themes and London's personal and political beliefs. (Rev: BL 9/15/99) [813]

5356 De Koster, Katie, ed. *Readings on The Great Gatsby* (10–12). Series: Literary Companions. 1997, Greenhaven paper $16.20 (1-56510-644-X). The novel that epitomizes the "lost generation" is discussed in this collection of essays that comment on its themes, symbols, structure, and characters. (Rev: BL 12/15/97; SLJ 1/98) [813]

5357 De Koster, Katie, ed. *Readings on Thornton Wilder* (10–12). Series: Literary Companions. 1998, Greenhaven LB $20.96 (1-56510-815-9); paper $17.45 (1-56510-814-0). General essays in this anthology discuss Wilder's style, themes, and characters, and others deal with specific works like *Our Town.* (Rev: BL 7/98; SLJ 8/98) [812]

5358 Doyle, Paul A. *Pearl S. Buck* (10–12). 1980, Twayne $22.95 (0-8057-7325-8). A critical study of this writer that covers such topics as plots, themes, and writing style. [813.09]

5359 Engle, Steven. *Readings on The Catcher in the Rye* (7–12). Series: Literary Companions. 1998, Greenhaven LB $33.70 (1-56510-817-5); paper $22.45 (1-56510-816-7). A helpful collection about this coming-of-age classic that explores the novel's themes, imagery, issues, and the narrator, Holden Caulfield. (Rev: BL 8/98) [813.54]

5360 Fargnoli, A. Nicholas, and Michael Golay. *William Faulkner A to Z: The Essential Reference to His Life and Work* (10–12). Series: Literary A to Z. 2001, Facts on File $65.00 (0-8160-3860-0); paper $17.95 (0-8160-4159-8). The authors of these readings provide information on Faulkner, his life, his work, and family and friends. (Rev: BL 6/1–15/02; VOYA 6/02) [813.009]

5361 Felgar, Robert. *Understanding Richard Wright's Black Boy: A Student Casebook to Issues, Sources, and Historical Documents* (8–12). Series: Literature in Context. 1998, Greenwood $45.00 (0-313-30221-9). Analyzes *Black Boy* from various standpoints, including structure and themes, its position in relation to other important autobiographies, and its place in the cultural and social conditions of the time. (Rev: BR 1–2/99; SLJ 9/98) [818]

5362 Gallo, Donald. *Presenting Richard Peck* (9–12). 1989, Twayne $20.95 (0-8057-8209-5). Part biography but chiefly an examination of Peck's works, including those intended for an adult audience. (Rev: BL 11/1/89; BR 3–4/90; SLJ 12/89; VOYA 12/89) [818]

5363 Gates, Henry Louis, Jr., and K. A. Appiah. *Langston Hughes: Critical Perspectives Past and Present* (10–12). 1993, Amistad paper $14.95 (1-56743-029-5). The poetry and prose of Langston Hughes are critically appraised in this collection of reviews and essays by such leading literary lights as Carl Van Vechten, Richard Wright, James Baldwin, and Countee Cullen. [818]

5364 Gates, Henry Louis, Jr., and K. A. Appiah. *Richard Wright: Critical Perspectives Past and Present* (10–12). 1993, Amistad paper $14.95 (1-56743-027-9). The writings of Richard Wright are critically appraised in this collection of present-day essays and of reviews by leading literary lights of his time (including Sinclair Lewis, Zora Neale Hurston, and Ralph Ellison). [813.009]

5365 Gates, Henry Louis, Jr., and K. A. Appiah. *Zora Neale Hurston: Critical Perspectives Past and Present* (10–12). Series: Amistad Literary. 1993, Amistad $24.95 (1-56743-015-5); paper $14.95 (1-56743-028-7). A selection of critical writing about Hurston, including book reviews and critical essays. [813.009]

5366 Gibson, Donald B. *The Red Badge of Courage* (10–12). 1988, Twayne $25.95 (0-8057-7961-2); paper $18.00 (0-8057-8014-9). Part of an extensive series from Twayne that provides in-depth analysis of the great works of literature. (Rev: SLJ 8/88) [813.09]

5367 Hipple, Ted. *Presenting Sue Ellen Bridgers* (9–12). 1990, Twayne $20.95 (0-8057-8213-3). A biography and analysis of the work of one of the major writers of young adult novels. (Rev: BL 6/1/90) [813]

5368 Howard, Todd. *The Outsiders* (7–12). Series: Understanding Great Literature. 2001, Lucent $24.95 (1-56006-702-0). This classic in young adult literature is examined with material on its structure,

characters, themes, concepts, importance, and the life of the author. (Rev: BL 8/01; SLJ 7/01) [813]

5369 Huntley, E. D. *Amy Tan: A Critical Companion* (10–12). 1998, Greenwood $29.95 (0-313-30207-3). The life and works of Amy Tan, including discussion of the Asian American literary tradition, concerns about biculturalism that Tan shares with other Asian American writers, and the universality of Tan's work, plus a literary analysis of *The Joy Luck Club, The Kitchen God's Wife,* and *The Hundred Secret Senses.* (Rev: BR 1–2/99; VOYA 6/99) [813]

5370 Hurley, Jennifer A., ed. *American Romanticism* (9–12). Series: Literary Movements and Genres. 1999, Greenhaven LB $21.96 (0-7377-0203-6); paper $13.96 (0-7377-0202-8). This work focuses on writing from the mid-19th century, including works by Emerson, Hawthorne, Melville, Poe, and Thoreau. (Rev: BL 10/15/99; SLJ 4/00) [813]

5371 Johnson, Claudia Durst. *Understanding Adventures of Huckleberry Finn: A Student Casebook to Issues, Sources, and Historic Documents* (10–12). Series: Literature in Context. 1996, Greenwood $35.00 (0-313-29327-9). This work not only analyzes the novel, but also discusses censorship, racism, the life of Mark Twain, and the complex social and political issues of the time. (Rev: SLJ 12/96) [813]

5372 Johnson, Claudia Durst. *Understanding The Red Badge of Courage* (9–12). Series: Literature in Context. 1998, Greenwood $39.95 (0-313-30122-0). Describes the novel's Civil War setting and everyday life in the war camps and in the battlefield, analyzes the novel, with a chapter-by-chapter breakdown of the novel's plot and discussion of symbols and characters, and examines the concepts of desertion and cowardice and the antiwar novel. (Rev: VOYA 4/99) [813]

5373 Johnson, Claudia Durst. *Understanding The Scarlet Letter* (10–12). 1995, Greenwood $35.00 (0-313-29328-7). In addition to a literary analysis of the novel, the author uses both historical and contemporary documents to provide a deeper understanding of the themes, including records on Hawthorne's family history, the transcript of Anne Hutchinson's trial, and articles on such contemporary issues as single motherhood, corrupt ministries, child custody, separation of church and state, and corporal punishment. (Rev: VOYA 2/96) [813]

5374 Johnson-Feelings, Dianne. *Presenting Laurence Yep* (8–12). 1995, Twayne $29.00 (0-8057-8201-X). A biocritical study that uses material from the Chinese American's autobiography, *The Lost Garden.* (Rev: BL 12/15/95) [813]

5375 Jones, Patrick. *What's So Scary About R. L. Stine?* (9–12). Series: Scarecrow Studies in Young Adult Literature. 1998, Scarecrow $32.50 (0-8108-

3468-5). An appreciation and critique of R. L. Stine's popular horror stories for young people. (Rev: SLJ 7/99) [813]

5376 Jordan, Shirley M., ed. *Broken Silences: Interviews with Black and White Women Writers* (9–12). 1993, Rutgers Univ. Pr. $35.00 (0-8135-1932-2). Focuses on how African American and white women writers have depicted each other in their stories, with specific inquiries into each author's handling of race in her work. (Rev: BL 5/1/93) [810.9]

5377 Kappe, Lawrence, ed. *Readings on One Flew over the Cuckoo's Nest* (9–12). Series: Literary Companions. 1999, Greenhaven paper $13.96 (0-7377-0184-6). After material on the author, Ken Kesey, this anthology covers various aspects of the novel, with material on characters, plot, structure, themes, and so forth. (Rev: BL 10/15/99) [813]

5378 Karson, Jill, ed. *Readings on A Separate Peace* (10–12). Series: Literary Companions. 1998, Greenhaven LB $20.96 (1-56510-827-2); paper $17.45 (1-56510-826-4). First published in 1960, this novel has remained a favorite of young adults. This collection of essays examines the themes, structure, characters, and locale of the novel. (Rev: BL 2/15/98) [813]

5379 Karson, Jill, ed. *Readings on Of Mice and Men* (10–12). Series: Literary Companions. 1997, Greenhaven paper $16.20 (1-56510-652-0). Essays analyze the story of the tragic relationship between George and Lennie, as well as the novel's themes, structure, symbols, and its adaptation to stage and screen. (Rev: BL 12/15/97; SLJ 2/98; VOYA 6/99) [813]

5380 Karson, Jill, ed. *Readings on The Pearl* (10–12). Series: Literary Companions. 1998, Greenhaven LB $26.20 (1-56510-855-8); paper $17.45 (1-56510-854-X). This anthology of writings on the novel about a poor peasant who finds a valuable pearl discusses its structure, symbolism, language, and characters. (Rev: BL 10/15/98; BR 5–6/99) [813]

5381 Keeley, Jennifer. *Understanding I Am the Cheese* (7–12). Series: Understanding Great Literature. 2000, Lucent LB $19.96 (1-56006-678-4). An introduction to Robert Cormier's book, discussing the plot and characters as well as the author's life and other works. (Rev: BL 3/1/01; SLJ 4/01) [813]

5382 Keeley, Jennifer. *The Yearling* (7–12). Series: Understanding Great Literature. 2001, Lucent $24.95 (1-56006-811-6). Explores the famous tale published in 1938 about a boy and his pet fawn as well as material on the eccentric author who wrote it. (Rev: BL 8/01) [813]

5383 Kennedy, J. Gerald. *A Historical Guide to Edgar Allan Poe* (9–12). Series: Historical Guides to American Authors. 2001, Oxford $39.95 (0-19-512149-X); paper $15.95 (0-19-512150-3). After a short biography of Poe, this account covers topics relating to his works and his influence. [818]

5384 Koster, Katie de, ed. *Readings on Fahrenheit 451* (10–12). Series: Literary Companions. 2000, Greenhaven LB $21.96 (1-565-10857-4); paper $13.95 (1-565-10856-6). The plot, characters, themes, and importance of this science fiction classic are explored in a rich collection of essays. (Rev: BL 1/1–15/00) [813]

5385 Kotzen, Kip, and Thomas Beller, eds. *With Love and Squalor: 14 Writers Respond to the Work of J. D. Salinger* (10–12). 2001, Broadway paper $12.95 (0-7679-0799-X). To celebrate the 50th anniversary of the publication of *The Catcher in the Rye,* here is a collection of thoughtful essays about Salinger and his work by other writers. (Rev: BL 10/1/01) [813]

5386 MacDonald, Gina. *James Clavell: A Critical Companion* (10–12). Series: Critical Companions to Popular Contemporary Writers. 1996, Greenwood $29.95 (0-313-29494-1). In addition to biographical information and general material on Clavell's writing, this book contains chapters on *King Rat, Shogun,* and other individual works. (Rev: SLJ 10/96) [813]

5387 MacRae, Cathi Dunn. *Presenting Young Adult Fantasy Fiction* (7–12). 1998, Twayne $29.00 (0-8057-8220-6). An excellent survey of current writers of fantasy plus in-depth interviews with Terry Brooks, Barbara Hambly, Jane Yolen, and Meredith Ann Pierce. (Rev: BL 1/1–15/99; VOYA 8/98) [813]

5388 Magistrale, Tony. *Student Companion to Edgar Allan Poe* (9–12). Series: Student Companions to Classic Writers. 2001, Greenwood $35.00 (0-313-30992-2). As well as material on Poe's life and times, this book gives a critical introduction to his major works. [818]

5389 Megna-Wallace, Joanne. *Understanding I Know Why the Caged Bird Sings: A Student Casebook to Issues, Sources, and Historical Documents* (9–12). Series: Literature in Context. 1998, Greenwood $39.95 (0-313-30229-4). Along with literary criticism, this book places *Caged Bird* in its historical context with material and original documents on race relations in the South, sexual abuse, the African American family, the African American church, and censorship. (Rev: SLJ 1/99; VOYA 8/99) [808.4]

5390 Mitchell, Hayley, ed. *Readings on Black Boy* (10–12). Series: Literary Companions. 1999, Greenhaven LB $21.96 (0-7377-0243-5); paper $13.96 (0-7377-0242-7). As well as a biography of Richard Wright and evaluations of his literary importance, this collection of essays covers the plot, characters, and themes of this important novel. (Rev: BL 12/15/99) [813]

5391 Mitchell, Hayley R., ed. *Readings on Native Son* (9–12). Series: Literary Companions. 2000, Greenhaven LB $21.96 (0-7377-0320-2); paper $13.96 (0-7377-0319-9). Richard Wright's life and his brilliant novel are the focus of this series of essays that explore the plot, characters, themes, and significance of this work. (Rev: BL 8/00) [813]

5392 Morey, Eileen, ed. *Readings on The Scarlet Letter* (10–12). Series: Literary Companions. 1997, Greenhaven paper $16.20 (1-56510-756-X). This anthology of critical essays about Hester Prynne's scarlet "A" includes contributors such as Henry James and Carl van Doren. (Rev: BL 12/15/97; SLJ 5/98) [813]

5393 Nolan, Michael, ed. *American Humor* (9–12). Series: Literary Movements and Genres. 2001, Greenhaven LB $32.45 (0-7377-0415-2); paper $19.95 (0-7377-0414-4). In a series of critical essays, the characteristics of humor in American literature are discussed, with material on regional variations and the transformation of humor in the 20th century. (Rev: BL 8/01; SLJ 7/01) [808.7]

5394 O'Keefe, Deborah. *Good Girl Messages: How Young Women Were Misled by Their Favorite Books* (9–12). 2000, Continuum $26.95 (0-8264-1236-X). An examination of the good-girl stereotypes found in literature for young people with a final chapter on how this has changed in recent times. (Rev: BL 3/15/00) [810.9]

5395 O'Neill, Terry, ed. *Readings on To Kill a Mockingbird* (10–12). Series: Literary Companions. 1999, Greenhaven LB $21.96 (1-56510-576-1); paper $13.96 (1-56510-575-3). Harper Lee's life is covered briefly in a collection of many essays on her masterpiece and its importance in contemporary American literature. (Rev: BL 12/15/99) [813]

5396 Pelzer, Linda. *Mary Higgins Clark: A Critical Companion* (9–12). 1995, Greenwood $29.95 (0-313-29413-5). A guide to the life and work of this best-selling author of popular mysteries. (Rev: VOYA 6/96) [813]

5397 Perret, Patti. *The Faces of Fantasy* (9–12). 1996, St. Martin's paper $22.95 (0-312-86216-4). A handsome, oversize book of revealing black-and-white photographic portraits of fantasy authors, accompanied by brief reflections by the authors. (Rev: VOYA 6/97) [813]

5398 Perret, Patti. *The Faces of Science Fiction* (9–12). Illus. 1984, St. Martin's $35.00 (0-698-10348-X); paper $11.95 (0-685-10347-1). Photographs of 80 major science fiction and fantasy writers are given as well as comments on their work. (Rev: BL 2/15/85) [813]

5399 Pinsker, Sanford, and Ann Pinsker. *Understanding The Catcher in the Rye: A Student Casebook to Issues, Sources, and Historical Documents* (7–12). Series: Literature in Context. 1999, Green-wood $39.95 (0-313-30200-6). Excerpts from primary materials are used to convey a historical context to young readers of Holden Caulfield's story. (Rev: SLJ 6/00) [813]

5400 Reed, Arthea J. S. *Norma Fox Mazer: A Writer's World* (9–12). Illus. Series: Scarecrow Studies in Young Adult Literature. 2001, Scarecrow LB $29.50 (0-8108-3814-1). The central themes and writing techniques of YA author Mazer are explored in this objective overview of her novels and short stories, which draws on interviews with the author as well as other sources. (Rev: BL 6/1–15/01; SLJ 6/01) [813]

5401 Reid, Suzanne. *Presenting Cynthia Voigt* (9–12). 1995, Twayne $28.00 (0-8057-8219-2). A biographical sketch of this popular author, followed by literary criticism in thematic chapters of 20 of Voigt's young adult novels. (Rev: BL 1/1/95; BR 3–4/96; VOYA 4/96) [813]

5402 Reino, Joseph. *Stephen King: The First Decade, Carrie to Pet Sematary* (9–12). Illus. 1988, Twayne $32.00 (0-8057-7512-9). An analysis of King's most important works published from 1973 to 1983. (Rev: BL 2/15/88) [813]

5403 Reynolds, Larry J., ed. *A Historical Guide to Nathaniel Hawthorne* (10–12). Series: Historical Guides to American Authors. 2001, Oxford $34.95 (0-19-512413-8); paper $15.95 (0-19-512414-6). A collection of sources both old and new that supply a critical introduction to Hawthorne's works. [813.009]

5404 Roiphe, Anne. *To Rabbit, with Love and Squalor: An American Read* (10–12). 2000, Free Pr. $23.00 (0-7432-0505-7). For the serious student of literature, Roiphe reflects on the impact of various fictional characters on her life, including Salinger's Holden Caulfield, Hemingway's Robert Jordan, Fitzgerald's Dick Diver, and Updike's Rabbit Angstrom. (Rev: BL 11/1/00) [813]

5405 Russell, Sharon A. *Revisiting Stephen King: A Critical Companion* (9–12). Series: Critical Companions to Popular Contemporary Writers. 2002, Greenwood $34.95 (0-313-31788-7). Plots, characters, themes, and literary techniques in eight of King's novels are discussed. [813.009]

5406 Russell, Sharon A. *Stephen King: A Critical Companion* (9–12). 1996, Greenwood $29.95 (0-313-29417-8). Following biographical information about Stephen King and background on the horror genre, the author examines the plots, character development, and themes of King's most important, most popular, and most recent works, in chronological order. (Rev: VOYA 6/97) [813]

5407 Salvner, Gary M. *Presenting Gary Paulsen* (9–12). Series: Young Adult Authors. 1996, Macmillan $28.00 (0-8057-4150-X). After two chapters on the eventful life of Gary Paulsen, the author of more than 100 books for people of all ages, this book analyzes the major themes and subjects of his young adult novels. (Rev: VOYA 8/98) [813]

5408 Sloane, David E. *The Adventures of Huckleberry Finn: American Comic Vision* (9–12). 1988, Twayne $29.00 (0-8057-7963-9); paper $18.00 (0-8057-8016-5). A detailed analysis of this novel — its structure, themes, and characters. (Rev: BR 9–10/88; SLJ 8/88; VOYA 2/89) [813.09]

5409 Smith, Christopher. *American Realism* (9–12). Series: Literary Movements and Genres. 2000, Greenhaven LB $21.96 (0-7377-0324-4); paper $13.96 (0-7377-0323-7). A variety of literary articles explore the realists in American literature with coverage on such notables as Sinclair Lewis and Theodore Dreiser. (Rev: BL 6/1–15/00) [813]

5410 Smith, Christopher, ed. *Readings on Ethan Frome* (10–12). Series: Literary Companions. 2000, Greenhaven LB $21.96 (0-7377-0199-4); paper $13.95 (0-7377-0198-6). This collection of essays analyzes many aspects of this important novel as well as supplying biographical and background information about Edith Wharton. (Rev: BL 1/1–15/00) [813]

5411 Smith, Henry Nash, ed. *Mark Twain: A Collection of Critical Essays* (10–12). 1963, Prentice Hall $12.95 (0-13-933317-7). Many prominent writers and critics have contributed to this collection of essays, many of which deal with individual works by Twain. [813.09]

5412 Stover, Leon. *Robert A. Heinlein* (9–12). 1987, Twayne $21.00 (0-8057-7509-9). An in-depth study of the science fiction of this acclaimed American writer. (Rev: BL 11/15/87) [813]

5413 Stover, Lois T. *Presenting Phyllis Reynolds Naylor* (9–12). 1997, Twayne $28.00 (0-8057-7805-5). In this scholarly work, the author presents a brief biography and an analysis of the Alice series, several novels, and other writings, showing how Naylor's life experiences are reflected in her major themes: how characters cope with family instability, how they develop a sense of self apart from family, and how they solve moral dilemmas. (Rev: SLJ 4/98; VOYA 10/98) [813]

5414 Swisher, Clarice, ed. *Readings on John Steinbeck* (9–12). Series: Literary Companion to American Authors. 1996, Greenhaven LB $21.96 (1-56510-469-2); paper $20.25 (1-56510-468-4). The 21 critical essays about Steinbeck and his work contained in this volume focus on his short novels and *The Grapes of Wrath*. (Rev: BL 5/15/96; SLJ 8/96) [813]

5415 Swisher, Clarice, ed. *Readings on Nathaniel Hawthorne* (9–12). Series: Literary Companion to American Authors. 1996, Greenhaven LB $21.96 (1-56510-459-5); paper $16.20 (1-56510-458-7). The 22 critical readings in this volume cover Hawthorne's principal stories and novels including

four examinations of *The Scarlet Letter*. (Rev: BL 5/15/96; SLJ 8/96) [813]

5416 Swisher, Clarice, ed. *Readings on The Red Pony* (9–12). Series: Literary Companions. 2000, Greenhaven LB $22.96 (0-7377-0193-5); paper $14.96 (0-7377-0192-7). John Steinbeck's short novel is examined in a series of articles that discuss plot, structure, characters, themes, and the life of the author. (Rev: BL 9/15/00) [813]

5417 Swisher, Clarice, ed. *Readings on William Faulkner* (10–12). Series: Literary Companions. 1997, Greenhaven paper $17.45 (1-56510-640-7). Includes general essays on Faulkner's literary style, sense of structure, and characters as well as on individual works like *The Sound and the Fury* and such important short stories as *The Bear*. (Rev: BL 12/15/97; SLJ 2/98) [813]

5418 Szumski, Bonnie, ed. *Readings on Edgar Allan Poe* (10–12). Series: Literary Companions. 1997, Greenhaven LB $26.20 (0-56510-589-3). The first essays explore Poe's many accomplishments, among them the perfection of the short story form and creation of the detective story, followed by critiques of his most popular works. (Rev: BL 12/15/97) [813.09]

5419 Szumski, Bonnie, ed. *Readings on Herman Melville* (10–12). Series: Literary Companions. 1997, Greenhaven paper $32.75 (1-56510-583-4). Some essays in this anthology analyze themes in Melville's works, such as ancient mythology, the Civil War, and religion, while others discuss specific works like *Billy Budd* and *Moby Dick*. (Rev: BL 1/1–15/97; SLJ 3/97) [813]

5420 Szumski, Bonnie, ed. *Readings on Stephen Crane* (9–12). Series: Literary Companion to American Authors. 1997, Greenhaven LB $20.96 (1-56510-643-1); paper $17.45 (1-56510-642-3). After a short biography of Crane, this collection of essays focuses on his themes, style, and major works, including *The Red Badge of Courage* and *The Open Boat*. (Rev: SLJ 4/98; VOYA 4/99) [813]

5421 Szumski, Bonnie, ed. *Readings on The Old Man and the Sea* (10–12). Series: Literary Companions. 1998, Greenhaven LB $20.96 (1-56510-843-4); paper $17.45 (1-56510-842-6). A collection of critical essays on the last of Ernest Hemingway's books published during his lifetime. (Rev: BL 10/15/98; BR 5–6/99) [813]

5422 Trembley, Elizabeth A. *Michael Crichton: A Critical Companion* (10–12). 1996, Greenwood LB $29.95 (0-313-29414-4). A carefully researched book that gives a biography of Crichton plus an analysis of 10 of his most popular books, beginning with *The Andromeda Strain*. (Rev: BR 9–10/96; VOYA 10/96) [813]

5423 Underwood, Tim, and Chuck Miller, eds. *Kingdom of Fear: The World of Stephen King*

(10–12). 1987, NAL paper $3.95 (0-451-14962-9). For all Stephen King enthusiasts, here is a collection of essays about his writing and the films they inspired. (Rev: SLJ 1/87; VOYA 2/87) [809.3]

5424 Vollstadt, Elizabeth Weiss. *Understanding Johnny Tremain* (6–12). Series: Understanding Great Literature. 2001, Lucent LB $24.95 (1-56006-849-3). As well as an analysis of the plot and characters of *Johnny Tremain*, Vollstadt provides insight into the life and viewpoint of the author. (Rev: SLJ 9/01) [813]

5425 Wagner-Martin, Linda. *A Historical Guide to Ernest Hemingway* (10–12). Series: Historical Guides to American Authors. 1999, Oxford $45.00 (0-19-512151-1); paper $16.95 (0-19-512152-X). After a brief biography, this work discusses such themes in Hemingway's work as gender, war, wilderness, and machismo. [813.009]

5426 Weidt, Maryann N. *Presenting Judy Blume* (9–12). Illus. 1989, Twayne $20.95 (0-8057-8208-7). A biography and a thorough analysis of Judy Blume's work with asides from both critics and Ms. Blume. (Rev: BL 11/1/89; VOYA 12/89) [813]

5427 Wiener, Gary, ed. *Readings on A Farewell to Arms* (10–12). Series: Literary Companions. 2000, Greenhaven LB $21.96 (0-7377-0233-8); paper $13.95 (0-7377-0232-X). A biography of Hemingway and numerous bibliographies are included in this collection of essays, which explore various facets of this classic novel about World War I. (Rev: BL 1/1–15/00) [813]

5428 Wiener, Gary, ed. *Readings on The Grapes of Wrath* (10–12). Series: Literary Companions. 1998, Greenhaven LB $220.96 (0-56510-955-4); paper $17.45 (1-56510-954-6). The saga of the Joad family is covered in this anthology that includes writings on the novel's creation, characters, themes, and structure, and an evaluation of its merits and flaws. (Rev: BL 9/15/98; BR 5–6/99) [813]

5429 Winter, Douglas E. *Stephen King: The Art of Darkness* (10–12). Illus. 1986, NAL paper $5.95 (0-451-14612-3). A study of the novels and novellas by this master of horror fiction. [813.09]

Plays and Poetry

General and Miscellaneous

5430 *Ancient Egyptian Literature* (10–12). Trans. by John L. Foster. 2001, Univ. of Texas Pr. $45.00 (0-292-72526-4); paper $19.95 (0-292-72527-2). An amazing collection of poems, some of the first ever written and many translated from ancient Egyptian hieroglyphics. (Rev: BL 6/1–15/01) [893]

5431 Auslander, Joseph, and Frank Ernest Hill. *The Winged Horse: The Story of Poets and Their Poetry* (10–12). 1969, Haskell House LB $75.00 (0-8383-0328-5). This book, first published in 1928, gives a history of world poetry from its beginning to the early 20th century. [809.1]

5432 Bloom, Harold, ed. *Anton Chekhov* (10–12). Series: Modern Critical Views. 1998, Chelsea LB $34.95 (0-7910-4783-0). A collection of literary criticism that discusses both the plays and short stories of Chekhov, with additional material on his life and personality. (Rev: SLJ 2/99) [891.7]

5433 Bloom, Harold, ed. *Dante Alighieri* (10–12). Series: Bloom's Biocritiques. 2002, Chelsea LB $25.95 (0-7910-6366-6). The life and work of Dante are examined and evaluated. [851]

5434 Bloom, Harold, ed. *Sophocles' Oedipus Plays* (10–12). Series: Bloom's Notes. 1996, Chelsea LB $17.95 (0-7910-4070-4). A comprehensive collection of essays on Sophocles and his works are included plus notes on the plots, themes, and characters. (Rev: SLJ 4/97) [882]

5435 Boland, Eavan, and Mark Strand, eds. *The Making of a Poem: A Norton Anthology of Poetic Forms* (9–12). 2000, Norton $27.50 (0-393-04916-7). This is not only a fine anthology of classic poems but also a text that demonstrates various poetic forms, metres, moods, and purposes. (Rev: BL 4/15/00) [821.008]

5436 Bugeja, Michael J. *The Art and Craft of Poetry* (9–12). 1994, Writer's Digest $19.99 (0-89879-633-4). Describes various genres, elements, styles, and forms of poetry, and includes exercises and examples from master poets. (Rev: BL 3/15/94) [808.1]

5437 Chaucer, Geoffrey. *The Portable Chaucer.* Rev. ed. (10–12). Trans. by Theodore Morrison. 1975, Viking paper $15.95 (0-14-015081-1). An excellent collection of the works of Chaucer including selections from *The Canterbury Tales* and *Troilus and Cressida.* [821]

5438 Chekhov, Anton Pavlovich. *Anton Chekhov's Plays — Backgrounds, Criticism* (10–12). Ed. and trans. by Eugene K. Bristow. 1978, Norton paper $14.95 (0-393-09163-5). A fine collection of critical essays about Chekhov, his plays, and theatrical techniques. [891.7]

5439 Chweh, Crystal R., ed. *Readings on Cyrano de Bergerac* (9–12). Series: Literary Companion. 2000, Greenhaven LB $22.96 (0-7377-0434-9); paper $14.96 (0-7377-0433-0). Through a series of critical essays, various aspects of this enduring play are examined and the author's life and times covered. (Rev: BL 3/1/01) [840]

5440 Dante, Alighieri, and Mark Musa. *The Portable Dante* (10–12). 1995, Penguin paper $17.00 (0-14-243754-9). Contains complete verse translations of both the *Divine Comedy* and *La Vita Nuova.* [851]

5441 Deutsch, Babette. *Poetry Handbook: A Dictionary of Terms.* 4th ed. (7–12). 1981, Barnes & Noble paper $14.00 (0-06-463548-1). The standard introduction to the technical aspects of poetry through definitions of terms with examples. [808.1]

5442 Egendorf, Laura K., ed. *Elizabethan Drama* (9–12). Series: Literary Movements and Genres. 2000, Greenhaven LB $21.96 (0-7377-0205-2); paper $13.96 (0-7377-0204-4). This collection of scholarly essays discusses the rise of Elizabethan drama and the works of such playwrights as William Shakespeare, Christopher Marlowe, and Ben Jonson. (Rev: BL 4/15/00) [822]

5443 Fuller, John, ed. *The Oxford Book of Sonnets* (10–12). 2001, Oxford $22.00 (0-19-214267-4). After an excellent introduction, this volume gives a generous sampling of these 14-line poems as found in English literature. (Rev: BL 12/15/00) [821]

5444 Gransden, K. W. *Virgil, the Aeneid* (10–12). Series: Landmarks of World Literature. 1990, Cambridge Univ. Pr. $34.95 (0-521-32329-0); paper $12.95 (0-521-31157-8). A critical evaluation of Virgil's masterpiece with material on its lasting influences. [873]

5445 Heaney, Seamus. *Opened Ground: Selected Poems, 1966–1996* (10–12). 1998, Farrar paper $16.00 (0-374-52678-8). The Nobel Prize winner's most important works are collected in this volume. [821]

5446 Housman, A. E. *The Collected Poems of A. E. Housman* (10–12). 1965, Holt paper $16.00 (0-8050-0547-1). The authorized edition of the poems of this great English writer. [821]

5447 Ibsen, Henrik. *The Complete Major Prose Plays* (10–12). Trans. by Rolf Fjelde. 1978, Farrar paper $28.00 (0-452-26205-4). This is a fine collection of Ibsen's plays, including *Ghosts, A Doll's House,* and *The Master Builder.* [839.8]

5448 Ionesco, Eugene. *Four Plays* (10–12). Trans. by Donald M. Allen. 1958, Grove paper $13.00 (0-8021-3079-8). A collection of four of the most popular plays by this modern playwright. [842]

5449 Ionesco, Eugene. *Rhinoceros, and Other Plays* (10–12). Trans. by Derek Prouse. 1960, Grove paper $10.00 (0-8021-3098-4). Three plays, including *Rhinoceros,* by one of the leaders of the movement known as "theater of the absurd." [842]

5450 Jerome, Judson. *The Poet's Handbook* (10–12). 1980, Writer's Digest paper $14.99 (0-89879-219-3). A handbook that covers such topics as meter, rhyme, rhythm, and the history of poetry. [808.1]

5451 Milstein, Janet. *The Ultimate Audition Book for Teens: 111 One-Minute Monologues* (10–12). 2000, Smith & Kraus $11.95 (1-57525-236-8). An excellent resource for would-be actors who are looking for age-appropriate audition material, this collection of one-minute monologues is divided into comic and dramatic scenarios. (Rev: BL 1/1–15/01; SLJ 3/01) [812]

5452 Milton, John. *The Portable Milton* (10–12). Ed. by Douglas Bush. 1949, Viking paper $15.95 (0-14-015044-7). A fine selection of Milton's prose and poetry, including such lengthy poems as *Paradise Lost* and *Paradise Regained.* [828]

5453 Mitchell, Hayley R., ed. *Readings on a Doll's House* (10–12). Series: Literary Companions. 1998,

Greenhaven LB $16.20 (0-7377-0048-3). This drama by Ibsen is discussed in essays on its structure, characters, and the sociological implications of Nora's leaving. (Rev: BL 1/1–15/99) [839.8]

5454 Nardo, Don, ed. *Greek Drama* (9–12). Series: Literary Movements and Genres. 1999, Greenhaven LB $21.96 (0-7377-0207-9); paper $13.96 (0-7377-0206-0). Topics in Greek drama are featured in a series of essays. (Rev: BL 4/1/00) [882]

5455 Nardo, Don, ed. *Readings on Antigone* (9–12). Series: Literary Companion. 1999, Greenhaven LB $20.96 (1-56510-968-6); paper $12.96 (1-56510-969-4). This collection of essays on the great tragedy by Sophocles contains great background material on the writer, his times, and Greek theater. (Rev: BL 9/15/99; SLJ 9/99) [882]

5456 Nardo, Don, ed. *Readings on Medea* (9–12). Series: Literary Companion. 2000, Greenhaven LB $22.96 (0-7377-0403-9); paper $14.96 (0-7377-0402-0). The history of the famous Greek play is included in this collection, as well as material on its plot, characters, and themes. (Rev: BL 11/15/00) [882]

5457 Nardo, Don, ed. *Readings on Sophocles* (10–12). Series: Literary Companion. 1997, Greenhaven paper $16.20 (1-56510-581-8). Though Sophocles wrote more than 100 plays, only 7 survive. This collection of critical essays discusses these plays, with emphasis on the Oedipus trilogy, and the ancient Greek theater in general. (Rev: BL 12/15/96; SLJ 2/97) [882]

5458 Pomerance, Bernard. *The Elephant Man: A Play* (10–12). 1979, Grove paper $11.00 (0-8021-3041-0). The full text of the play that later became a successful motion picture based on a true story about the British medical phenomenon. [822]

5459 Vecchione, Patrice, ed. *The Body Eclectic: An Anthology of Poems* (8–12). 2002, Holt $16.95 (0-8050-6935-6). A collection of poems, both contemporary and classic, that look at parts of the body from serious, comic, tragic, reflective, and romantic points of view. (Rev: BL 7/02; HB 7–8/02; HBG 10/02; SLJ 8/02; VOYA 8/02) [808.81]

Shakespeare

5460 Allison, Amy. *Shakespeare's Globe* (7–10). Series: Building History. 1999, Lucent LB $18.96 (1-56006-526-5). The story of the theater built on the south bank of the Thames in London by Shakespeare and his partners and how this building became a landmark in theatrical history. (Rev: BL 10/15/99; HBG 9/00; SLJ 2/00) [822.3]

5461 Bloom, Harold. *Hamlet: Poem Unlimited* (10–12). 2003, Riverhead $19.95 (1-57322-233-X).

A clear-cut and accessible analysis of the play *Hamlet* and of the character himself. (Rev: BL 3/15/03) [822]

5462 Bloom, Harold. *Shakespeare: The Invention of the Human* (10–12). 1998, Riverhead paper $18 .00 (1-57322-751-X). In this thought-provoking study of Shakespeare's plays, Bloom underlines Shakespeare's contribution to our understanding of human personality. (Rev: BL 10/1/98) [822.3]

5463 Bloom, Harold, ed. *Shakespeare's Histories* (10–12). Illus. Series: Major Dramatists. 1999, Chelsea $19.95 (0-7910-5241-9). Readings on *Richard III*, *Henry IV* (parts 1 and 2), and *Henry V*, for the advanced student of Shakespeare. (Rev: BL 4/1/00; SLJ 3/00) [822.3]

5464 Bloom, Harold, ed. *William Shakespeare* (10–12). Series: Bloom's Biocritiques. 2002, Chelsea LB $25.95 (0-7910-6171-X). After a biographical profile, such renowned authors as Emerson and Samuel Johnson voice their opinions about Shakespeare and his work. [822.3]

5465 Bloom, Harold, ed. *William Shakespeare's A Midsummer Night's Dream* (10–12). Series: Bloom's Notes. 1996, Chelsea LB $17.95 (0-7910-4066-6). After a selection of critical excerpts, this book gives a biography of Shakespeare, a summary of the play, analysis of themes and characters, and a bibliography. (Rev: SLJ 4/97) [822.3]

5466 Cahn, Victor L. *The Plays of Shakespeare: A Thematic Guide* (10–12). 2001, Greenwood $49.95 (0-313-30981-7). This book presents 19 thematic essays on Shakespeare's plays that treat such subjects as fate, honor, justice, love, money, and power. [822.3]

5467 Coursen, Herbert R. *Macbeth: A Guide to the Play* (9–12). Series: Greenwood Guides to Shakespeare. 1997, Greenwood $60.00 (0-313-30047-X). This critical analysis dissects the play's structure, examines major themes, and offers reviews of memorable past productions. [822.3]

5468 Derrick, Thomas. *Understanding Shakespeare's Julius Caesar* (8–12). Illus. Series: Literature in Context. 1998, Greenwood $45.00 (0-313-29638-3). An entertaining approach to *Julius Caesar* that brings to life the diverse worlds of history, theater, language, metaphor, plot, and source material, and even includes a chapter on pop culture treatments of the play. (Rev: VOYA 10/99) [822.3]

5469 Fallon, Robert Thomas. *A Theatergoer's Guide to Shakespeare* (10–12). 2001, Ivan R. Dee $29.95 (1-56663-342-7). The author gives a detailed plot summary of each of Shakespeare's plays with accompanying background material. (Rev: BL 4/15/01) [822]

5470 Garfield, Leon. *Shakespeare Stories II* (6–10). Illus. 1995, Houghton $26.00 (0-395-70893-1). Plot synopses of *Julius Caesar* and eight less familiar plays. (Rev: BL 4/1/95; SLJ 6/95) [823]

5471 Gurr, Andrew, and John Orrell. *Rebuilding Shakespeare's Globe* (9–12). 1989, Routledge $25.00 (0-685-26528-5). A history of the project in London to rebuild the Globe as it was originally. (Rev: BR 3–4/90) [822.3]

5472 Kermode, Frank. *The Age of Shakespeare* (10–12). 2004, Modern Library $19.95 (0-679-64244-7). As well as coverage on Shakespeare, this scholarly account covers such subjects as his contemporaries, the theater world and facilities of the time, and technical and financial aspects of play production. (Rev: BL 2/1/04; SLJ 4/04) [792]

5473 Marvel, Laura, ed. *Readings on The Taming of the Shrew* (9–12). Series: Literary Companions. 2000, Greenhaven LB $21.96 (0-7377-0237-0); paper $13.96 (0-7377-0236-2). Shakespeare's play on the battle of the sexes is analyzed in a series of essays that also cover the Bard's life. (Rev: BL 8/00) [822.3]

5474 Nardo, Don. *Hamlet* (7–12). Series: Understanding Great Literature. 2001, Lucent $24.95 (1-56006-830-2). As well as a discussion of this play's themes, characters, and plot, this work covers Shakespeare's life, work, and times. (Rev: BL 8/01; SLJ 4/01) [822.3]

5475 Nardo, Don, ed. *Readings on Hamlet* (10–12). Series: Literary Companions. 1998, Greenhaven LB $21.96 (1-56510-837-X); paper $17.45 (1-56510-836-1). This collection of readings on *Hamlet* will help students understand the play's structure, themes, plot, and characters. (Rev: BL 11/15/98; VOYA 4/99) [822]

5476 Nardo, Don, ed. *Readings on Julius Caesar* (10–12). Series: Literary Companions. 1998, Greenhaven LB $20.96 (1-56510-853-1); paper $17.45 (1-56510-852-3). Contributors to this anthology on Shakespeare's tragedy examine major themes of the play, its characters, historical background, and Shakespeare's use of language. (Rev: BL 2/15/98) [822.3]

5477 Nardo, Don. *Readings on Othello* (9–12). Series: Literary Companions. 1999, Greenhaven LB $21.96 (0-7377-0187-0); paper $13.96 (0-7377-0186-2). A collection of readings that explore the background, characters, plot, themes, and setting of Shakespeare's *Othello*. (Rev: BL 10/15/99) [822.3]

5478 Nardo, Don, ed. *Readings on Romeo and Juliet* (10–12). Series: Literary Companions. 1997, Greenhaven LB $21.96 (1-56510-647-4); paper $16.20 (1-56510-646-6). A collection of essays on Shakespeare's famous tragedy that discuss structure, characters, themes, staging considerations, plot, and ways of interpreting the play. (Rev: SLJ 12/97; VOYA 4/99) [822.3]

5479 Nostbakken, Faith. *Understanding Macbeth: A Student Casebook to Issues, Sources, and Historical Documents* (9–12). Series: Greenwood Press Literature in Context. 1997, Greenwood $39.95 (0-313-29630-8). This guide provides a critical analysis of the play, examines how some of its themes have been reflected in contemporary history, and also includes reviews of film adaptations. (Rev: BL 6/1–15/97; SLJ 9/97) [822.3]

5480 Olster, Fredi, and Rick Hamilton. *A Midsummer Night's Dream: A Workbook for Students* (8–12). Series: Discovering Shakespeare. 1996, Smith & Kraus paper $19.95 (1-57525-042-X). The text of the play is presented in a double-page, four-column format that provides stage directions, scene description, and the original text, plus a version in the vernacular. Supplemental background material is also appended. (Rev: BL 1/1–15/97; SLJ 12/96; VOYA 2/97) [822.3]

5481 Olster, Fredi, and Rick Hamilton. *Romeo and Juliet: A Workbook for Students* (8–12). Series: Discovering Shakespeare. 1996, Smith & Kraus paper $19.95 (1-57525-044-6). This Shakespearean tragedy is presented in a four-column format that gives the original text, stage directions, scene descriptions, and a reworking into modern English. (Rev: BL 1/1–15/97; VOYA 2/97) [822.3]

5482 Olster, Fredi, and Rick Hamilton. *The Taming of the Shrew* (7–12). Series: Discovering Shakespeare. 1997, Smith & Kraus paper $19.95 (1-57525-046-2). This guide to Shakespeare's comedy uses a paraphrased text opposite the original script with details on stage directions. (Rev: BL 2/15/97; BR 11–12/97; SLJ 6/97; VOYA 2/97) [822.3]

5483 Riley, Dick, and Pam McAllister. *The Bedside, Bathtub and Armchair Companion to Shakespeare* (9–12). Illus. 2001, Continuum $39.95 (0-8264-1249-1); paper $22.95 (0-8264-1250-5). In an appealing format, the authors clearly introduce Shakespeare, his times, and each of his works. (Rev: BL 7/01) [822.33]

5484 Rosenblum, Joseph. *Shakespeare* (10–12). Series: Magill's Choice. 1998, Salem Press $68.00 (0-89356-966-6). Following a brief biography, this volume gives summaries and critical analysis of Shakespeare's plays and poetry. [822.3]

5485 Shakespeare, William. *Poems* (10–12). Series: Everyman's Library Pocket Poets. 1994, Knopf $12.50 (0-679-43320-1). This is a representative collection of Shakespeare's poetry. [821]

5486 Shakespeare, William. *The Sonnets* (9–12). Ed. by Rex Gibson. 1997, Cambridge Univ. Pr. paper $12.50 (0-521-55947-2). Each of Shakespeare's 154 sonnets is accompanied by a brief critical discussion of its theme and possible meanings. [821]

5487 Swisher, Clarice, ed. *Readings on Macbeth* (10–12). Series: Literary Companions. 1998, Greenhaven LB $20.96 (1-56510-851-5); paper $17.45 (1-56510-850-7). Topics covered in this anthology include the motivations of Macbeth and his wife, the use of the themes of guilt, fear, and ambition, the production and directing of the drama, and its structure and language. (Rev: BL 11/15/98; BR 5–6/99; VOYA 4/99) [822]

5488 Swisher, Clarice, ed. *Readings on Shakespeare: The Comedies* (10–12). Series: Literary Companion. 1997, Greenhaven LB $19.95 (1-56510-574-7); paper $17.45 (1-56510-573-7). Well known writers and famous Shakespearian scholars are represented in this collection of critical essays on the Bard's lighter works. (Rev: BL 12/15/96; SLJ 4/97) [822.3]

5489 Swisher, Clarice, ed. *Readings on The Merchant of Venice* (9–12). Series: Literary Companions. 2000, Greenhaven LB $21.96 (0-7377-0179-X); paper $13.96 (0-7377-0178-1). Various aspects of this classic play are explored in this fine anthology of essays, which includes a life of Shakespeare. (Rev: BL 3/15/00) [822]

5490 Swisher, Clarice, ed. *Readings on The Sonnets of William Shakespeare* (10–12). 1997, Greenhaven LB $20.96 (1-56510-572-9); paper $17.45 (1-56510-571-0). In this collection of critical essays, the form and content of Shakespeare's sonnets, as well as individual poems, are analyzed. (Rev: BL 12/15/96; SLJ 1/97) [821]

5491 Swisher, Clarice, ed. *Readings on the Tragedies of William Shakespeare* (10–12). Series: Literary Companion. 1996, Greenhaven LB $20.96 (1-56510-467-6); paper $17.45 (1-56510-466-8). A collection of critical essays on six of Shakespeare's popular tragedies, including *Romeo and Juliet* and *Macbeth*. (Rev: BL 11/15/96; SLJ 8/96) [822.3]

5492 Swisher, Clarice, ed. *Readings on William Shakespeare: The Histories* (10–12). Series: Literary Companions. 1998, Greenhaven LB $20.96 (1-56510-556-7); paper $17.45 (1-56510-555-9). Critical essays examine the historical background of these plays, with material on their language, characters, and structure. There are also companion volumes on Shakespeare's comedies, tragedies, and sonnets. (Rev: BL 7/98; SLJ 8/98) [822.3]

5493 Thompson, Stephen P., ed. *Readings on A Midsummer Night's Dream* (9–12). Series: Literary Companion. 2000, Greenhaven LB $22.96 (1-56510-691-1); paper $14.96 (1-56510-690-3). Shakespeare's complex comedy is examined in a series of critical essays that also comment on the playwright's life. (Rev: BL 3/1/01) [822.3]

5494 Thrasher, Thomas. *Romeo and Juliet* (7–12). Series: Understanding Great Literature. 2001, Lucent $24.95 (1-56006-787-X). After introducing the life and times of Shakespeare, this work discusses, in depth, the background, plot, characters, and themes of this classic play. (Rev: BL 8/01; SLJ 6/01) [822.3]

5495 Whalen, Richard F. *Shakespeare: Who Was He? The Oxford Challenge to the Bard of Avon* (9–12). 1994, Praeger $19.95 (0-275-94850-1). Probes the authorship of the works of Shakespeare and presents evidence suggesting the plays were written by others. (Rev: BL 11/1/94) [822.3]

United States

5496 Abbotson, Susan C. W. *Student Companion to Arthur Miller* (9–12). Series: Student Companions to Classic Writers. 2000, Greenwood LB $35.00 (0-313-30949-3). Following a biographical section, there is a critical examination of each of Miller's plays. (Rev: SLJ 11/00) [812]

5497 *African-American Poets: Phillis Wheatley Through Melvin B. Tolson* (10–12). Ed. by Harold Bloom. Series: Modern Critical Views. 2002, Chelsea LB $37.95 (0-7910-6332-1). A collection of critical essays about African American poets. (Rev: SLJ 3/03) [811.009]

5498 Albee, Edward. *Who's Afraid of Virginia Woolf? A Play* (10–12). 1962, Atheneum paper $5.99 (0-451-15871-7). The searing play about a marriage on the rocks by one of America's finest contemporary playwrights. [812]

5499 Angelou, Maya, and Tom Feelings. *Now Sheba Sings the Song* (9–12). Illus. 1987, Dutton paper $9.95 (0-525-48374-8). Drawings of 25 African American women from various backgrounds by Tom Feelings are accompanied by short poems by Maya Angelou. (Rev: BL 3/15/87; BR 11–12/87; SLJ 10/87; VOYA 10/87) [811]

5500 *August Wilson* (10–12). Ed. by Harold Bloom. Series: Bloom's Major Dramatists. 2002, Chelsea LB $21.95 (0-7910-6362-3). The life and works of this major African American playwright are the subjects of this collection of critical essays. [812]

5501 Bloom, Harold, ed. *The Crucible* (10–12). Series: Modern Critical Interpretations. 1998, Chelsea LB $34.95 (0-7910-4775-X). A collection of 13 critical essays on various aspects of *The Crucible,* including language, characters, feminist perspectives, and structure. (Rev: SLJ 2/99) [812]

5502 Bloom, Harold. *Gwendolyn Brooks* (10–12). Series: Modern Critical Views. 2000, Chelsea $36.95 (0-7910-5656-2). Critical essays analyze the life and work of this important African American poet. [811]

5503 Bush, Valerie Chow, ed. *Believe Me, I Know: Poetry and Photographs by WritersCorps Youth* (6–12). Illus. 2002, WritersCorps paper $14.95 (1-888048-08-5). These poems and photographs dealing with a wide range of subjects were created during a WritersCorps workshop attended by a multicultural group of students. (Rev: BL 8/02; SLJ 11/02*; VOYA 12/02) [811]

5504 Crane, Stephen. *The Complete Poems of Stephen Crane* (10–12). Ed. by Joseph Katz. 1972, Cornell Univ. Pr. paper $16.95 (0-8014-9130-4). This is a fine edition of the poetry of the American author best known for his fiction. [811]

5505 DeFusco, Andrea, ed. *Readings on Robert Frost* (9–12). Series: Literary Companion. 1999, Greenhaven $34.95 (1-56510-999-6); paper $23.70 (1-56510-998-8). A collection of essays that explores the life of the "people's poet" and examines individual poems as well as his major themes and imagery. (Rev: BL 9/15/99) [811]

5506 Dickinson, Emily. *Final Harvest: Emily Dickinson's Poems* (9–12). 1961, Back Bay paper $14.95 (0-316-18415-2). A collection of poems by one of the most widely read American poets. [811]

5507 Ellmann, Richard. *The New Oxford Book of American Verse* (9–12). 1976, Oxford $49.95 (0-19-502058-8). A classic anthology of American verse that begins with colonial times and ends in the late 20th century. [811.008]

5508 Ferlazzo, Paul J. *Emily Dickinson* (10–12). 1976, Twayne $32.00 (0-8057-7180-8); Macmillan paper $4.95 (0-672-61511-8). Analyzes such subjects in Dickinson's poetry as love, death, and nature. [811.09]

5509 Gerber, Philip. *Robert Frost* (10–12). 1982, Twayne $32.00 (0-8057-7348-7). This book concentrates on an analysis of Frost's work but also covers his life and career. [811.09]

5510 Giovanni, Nikki. *Blues: For All the Changes* (10–12). 1999, Morrow $15.00 (0-688-15698-3). A collection of poems by Nikki Giovanni, a writer popular with young adults. (Rev: BL 3/15/99) [811]

5511 Haas, Jessie. *Hoofprints: Horse Poems* (8–12). 2004, Greenwillow $15.99 (0-06-053406-0). In these sophisticated poems, the author writes about different aspects of the horse, including its prehistoric origins and the first pairing of a horse and rider. (Rev: BL 3/15/04; SLJ 3/04; VOYA 4/04) [811]

5512 Hughes, Langston. *Poems* (10–12). Ed. by David Roessel. 1999, Knopf $12.50 (0-375-40551-8). This is a selection of poems by this important African American writer. [811]

5513 Inge, William. *4 Plays* (10–12). 1979, Grove $13.50 (0-8021-3209-X). Four of Inge's best plays: *Picnic, Bus Stop, The Dark at the Top of the Stairs,* and *Come Back, Little Sheba.* [812]

5514 *J. D. Salinger* (10–12). Ed. by Harold Bloom. Series: Bloom's Biocritiques. 2002, Chelsea LB $25.95 (0-7910-6175-2). These essays cover Salinger's style, themes, and influence as well as his life. [813.009]

5515 Johnson, Tamara, ed. *Emily Dickinson* (10–12). Series: Literary Companions. 1997, Greenhaven LB $21.96 (1-56510-635-0); paper $18.75 (1-56510-634-2). A collection of commentaries, many by well-known poets, on Emily Dickinson's life, her poetic themes, and her reclusive nature and how it affected her poetry, plus a line-by-line analysis of several poems. (Rev: BL 6/1–15/97; SLJ 8/97) [811]

5516 Kappel, Lawrence, ed. *Readings on A Raisin in the Sun* (7–12). Series: Literary Companions. 2000, Greenhaven LB $22.96 (0-7377-0368-7); paper $14.96 (0-7377-0367-9). The essays in this collection look at the play from the African American and female points of view as well as discussing its important themes and its relevance. (Rev: BL 11/15/00; SLJ 2/01) [823]

5517 Kaufman, Moises, et al. *The Laramie Project* (10–12). 2001, Vintage paper $11.00 (0-375-72719-1). This docudrama script tells about the homophobia in Laramie, Wyoming, that resulted in the torture and murder of Matthew Shepard. (Rev: BL 9/1/01; SLJ 11/01) [812]

5518 *Langston Hughes* (10–12). Ed. by Harold Bloom. Series: Bloom's Biocritiques. 2002, Chelsea LB $25.95 (0-7910-6186-8). The work of this African American poet and essayist is examined. A short biography is also included. [818]

5519 Lansana, Quraysh Ali. *They Shall Run: Harriet Tubman Poems* (10–12). 2004, Third World $20.00 (088-378-257-X). These poems pay tribute to famous African Americans, chiefly Harriet Tubman. (Rev: BL 2/15/04) [811]

5520 Moss, Leonard. *Arthur Miller* (10–12). 1980, Twayne $21.95 (0-8057-7311-8). A thorough review of the components of each of Miller's plays, their themes, and structure. [812.09]

5521 Mueller, Melinda. *What the Ice Gets: Shackleton's Antarctic Expedition, 1914–1916* (10–12). 2000, Van West paper $14.00 (0-9677021-1-9). The second expedition of Sir Ernest Shackleton is recounted in this unusual book-length poem. (Rev: BL 10/15/00) [811]

5522 *Poetry for Young People: William Carlos Williams* (6–12). Ed. by Christopher MacGowan. 2004, Sterling $14.95 (1-4027-0006-7). Thirty-one poems by Williams plus biographical and critical material are included in this excellent collection. (Rev: BL 3/1/04) [811]

5523 *Readings on Our Town* (9–12). Ed. by Thomas Siebold. Series: Literary Companions. 1999, Greenhaven LB $21.96 (0-7377-0188-9); paper $13.96 (0-7377-0189-7). Thornton Wilder and his play are examined in this collection of critical essays. (Rev: BL 10/15/99) [812]

5524 *Readings on Twelve Angry Men* (9–12). Ed. by Russ Munyan. Series: Literary Companions. 2000, Greenhaven LB $21.96 (0-7377-0314-8); paper $13.96 (0-7377-0313-X). Both Reginald Rose's play and the movie version of 1957 are covered in this collection of essays, which includes several reviews. (Rev: BL 8/00; SLJ 11/00) [812]

5525 Reynolds, David S. *A Historical Guide to Walt Whitman* (10–12). Series: Historical Guides to American Authors. 2000, Oxford $39.95 (0-19-512081-7); paper $19.95 (0-19-512082-5). After a brief biography, a series of critical essays examines and assesses Whitman's writing. [811]

5526 Shange, Ntozake. *For Colored Girls Who Have Considered Suicide/When The Rainbow Is Enuf: A Choreopoem* (9–12). 1977, Macmillan paper $9.00 (0-684-84326-9). The joys and sorrows of being a black woman are celebrated in this prize-winning play. [812]

5527 Siebold, Thomas, ed. *Readings on Arthur Miller* (10–12). Series: Literary Companions. 1996, Greenhaven LB $20.96 (1-56510-580-X); paper $22.00 (1-56510-579-6). This collection of critical essays covers general topics relating to the playwright's work as well as individual plays including *Death of a Salesman.* (Rev: BL 2/15/97; SLJ 4/97) [812]

5528 Siebold, Thomas, ed. *Readings on Death of a Salesman* (10–12). Series: Literary Companions. 1998, Greenhaven LB $20.96 (1-56510-839-6); paper $17.45 (1-56510-838-8). This drama about Willy Loman's descent into insanity and suicide is covered in a series of essays that also discuss American materialism, the business world, and the meaning of success. (Rev: BL 1/1–15/99) [812]

5529 Siebold, Thomas, ed. *Readings on Eugene O'Neill* (10–12). Series: Literary Companions. 1997, Greenhaven paper $17.45 (1-56510-654-7). Essays look at the major plays of O'Neill, including *Long Day's Journey into Night,* as well as material on major themes and characters. (Rev: BL 12/15/97; SLJ 4/98) [813]

5530 Siebold, Thomas, ed. *Readings on The Crucible* (10–12). Series: Literary Companions. 1998, Greenhaven LB $20.96 (1-56510-849-3); paper $20.25 (1-56510-848-5). This collection of readings shows how Arthur Miller used historical events to explore themes such as evil, power, freedom, fear,

303

hysteria, and guilt. (Rev: BL 10/15/98; BR 5–6/99; SLJ 3/99) [812]

5531 Siebold, Thomas, ed. *Readings on The Glass Menagerie* (10–12). Series: Literary Companions. 1998, Greenhaven LB $20.96 (1-56510-829-9); paper $16.20 (1-56510-828-0). More than 15 essays explore the play's themes, characters, structure, philosophy, and impact on the American theater. (Rev: BL 7/98; SLJ 8/98) [812]

5532 *Tennessee Williams* (10–12). Ed. by Harold Bloom. Series: Bloom's Biocritiques. 2002, Chelsea LB $25.95 (0-7910-6185-X). The works of this southern dramatist are analyzed after an introductory biography. [812]

5533 *Walt Whitman* (10–12). Ed. by Harold Bloom. Series: Bloom's Biocritiques. 2002, Chelsea LB $25.95 (0-7910-6377-1). Critical essays from important critics plus a short biography are included in this work on one of America's most important poets. [811]

5534 Wiener, Gary, ed. *Readings on Walt Whitman* (9–12). Series: Literary Companion. 1999, Greenhaven LB $27.46 (0-7377-0077-7). The articles in this collection explore Whitman's output as a poet, essayist, and journalist, and discuss such topics as why he was not popular with his contemporaries. (Rev: BL 9/15/99) [811]

5535 Williams, Mary E., ed. *Maya Angelou* (10–12). Series: Literary Companions. 1997, Greenhaven LB $21.96 (1-56510-631-8); paper $16.20 (1-56510-630-X). A collection of critical essays that analyze the works of this noted poet, essayist, and writer of her autobiography. (Rev: BL 6/1–15/97; SLJ 9/97; VOYA 12/97) [818]

Language and Communication

Signs and Symbols

5536 Grayson, Gabriel. *Talking with Your Hands, Listening with Your Eyes: A Complete Photographic Guide to American Sign Language* (9–12). Illus. 2003, Square One paper $26.95 (0-7570-0007-X). This excellent guide to American Sign Language makes extensive use of photographs to show readers not only how to begin and end each sign but also to illustrate the appropriate facial expression for each. (Rev: BL 1/1–15/03*; SLJ 8/03) [419]

5537 Lewis, Karen B., and Roxanne Henderson. *Sign Language Made Simple* (9–12). 1997, Doubleday (0-385-48857-2). This book explains the development of sign language and gives a short course on how to master it. [419]

5538 Modley, Rudolf. *Handbook of Pictorial Symbols: 3,250 Examples from International Sources* (9–12). Illus. 1976, Dover paper $10.95 (0-486-23357-X). All sorts of symbols are presented and explained in this source organized by subjects. [001.56]

5539 Singh, Simon. *The Code Book: How to Make It, Break It, Hack It, Crack It* (7–12). Illus. 2002, Random LB $18.99 (0-385-90032-5). This abridged version of an adult book provides an absorbing introduction to codes and cryptography, giving historical examples and discussing contemporary Internet issues. (Rev: BL 1/1–15/02; HB 3–4/02; HBG 10/02; SLJ 5/02; VOYA 8/02) [652.8]

Words and Languages

5540 Agee, Jon. *Who Ordered the Jumbo Shrimp? And Other Oxymorons* (5–10). Illus. 1998, Harper-Collins $15.95 (0-06-205159-8). An amusing collection of oxymorons such as "permanent temp" and "Great Depression," cleverly illustrated with black-and-white cartoons. (Rev: BCCB 12/98; HBG 3/99; SLJ 11/98) [412]

5541 Ammer, Christine. *Cool Cats, Top Dogs, and Other Beastly Expressions* (9–12). Illus. 1999, Houghton paper $14.00 (0-395-95730-3). This entertaining book gives the meanings and origins of 1,200 English expressions involving animals, such as scapegoat and hot dog. (Rev: SLJ 8/99) [410]

5542 Cox, Brenda S. *Who Talks Funny? A Book About Languages for Kids* (7–12). 1995, Linnet LB $25.00 (0-208-02378-X). Explores the importance of learning other languages, describes the development of languages and common elements, and provides interesting information, such as how to say the days of the week in 27 languages. (Rev: BL 7/95; SLJ 4/95) [400]

5543 Ehrlich, Eugene, comp. *Les Bons Mots* (10–12). 1997, Holt $24.00 (0-8050-4711-5). A delightful collection of French phrases and aphorisms, with their pronunciations and both literal and colloquial meanings. (Rev: BR 1–2/98; SLJ 1/98) [440]

5544 Fakih, Kimberly O. *Off the Clock: A Lexicon of Time Words and Expressions* (6–10). 1995, Ticknor $16.00 (0-395-66374-1). A look at how we talk about time in folklore, anthropology, mythology, history, semantics, and physics. (Rev: BL 1/1/95; SLJ 3/95) [428.1]

5545 Flexner, Stuart, and Anne H. Soukhanov. *Speaking Freely: A Guided Tour of American English from Plymouth Rock to Silicon Valley* (10–12). 1997, Oxford $63.95 (0-19-510692-X). An informal look at the development of American English that includes a general history plus material on specific

words and phrases. (Rev: BL 10/1/97; SLJ 2/98) [422]

5546 Gay, Kathlyn. *Getting Your Message Across* (6–12). 1993, Macmillan LB $22.00 (0-02-735815-1). Factors in communication are examined, such as body language, facial expression, ability to listen, and clothing. Also covers advertising. (Rev: BL 10/1/93; SLJ 11/93; VOYA 2/94) [302.2]

5547 *In Few Words / En Pocas Palabras: A Compendium of Latino Folk Wit and Wisdom* (6–12). Trans. by Jose A. Burciaga. 1996, Mercury House paper $14.95 (1-56279-093-5). This bilingual collection features popular sayings, proverbs, maxims, and adages that permeate Hispanic culture. (Rev: VOYA 6/97) [468.1]

5548 Jean, Georges. *Writing: The Story of Alphabets and Scripts* (7–12). Series: Discoveries. 1992, Abrams paper $12.95 (0-8109-2893-0). Traces the beginnings of writing from the development of alphabets to printing and bookmaking, emphasizing the technological rather than intellectual aspects of the process. (Rev: BL 7/92) [652.1]

5549 Kelly, Martin. *Parents Book of Baby Names* (9–12). 1985, Ballantine paper $5.99 (0-345-31428-X). This handbook consists of lists of boys' and girls' names and their derivations. (Rev: BL 10/1/85) [929.44]

5550 Kennedy, John. *Word Stems: A Dictionary* (10–12). 1996, Soho Pr. paper $12.00 (1-56947-051-0). Supplies the word stems for common words used in English and gives definitions and language roots for each. (Rev: SLJ 5/97) [420]

5551 Muschell, David. *What in the Word? Origins of Words Dealing with People and Places* (9–12). 1996, McGuinn & McGuire paper $14.95 (1-881117-14-6). Explains the origins of real and imaginary person and place names. (Rev: BL 1/1/91) [422]

5552 Ogg, Oscar. *The 26 Letters*. Rev. ed. (10–12). Illus. 1971, HarperCollins $13.95 (0-690-84115-9). Traces the history of writing from the caveman on. [411]

5553 Singh, Simon. *The Code Book: The Evolution of Secrecy from Mary, Queen of Scots, to Quantum Cryptography* (10–12). 1999, Doubleday $24.95 (0-385-49531-5); paper $15.00 (0-385-49532-3). The history and nature of codes and cryptology are discussed with material on Mary, Queen of Scots, inventor and mathematician Charles Babbage, and the Navajo code-talkers of World War II. (Rev: BL 9/1/99) [652]

5554 *The Skin That We Speak: Thoughts on Language* (10–12). Ed. by Lisa Delpit and Joanne Kilgour Dowdy. 2002, New Pr. $24.95 (1-56584-544-7). This collection of essays by linguists and educators explores how attitudes about speech and speech patterns color our perceptions of the speaker. (Rev: BL 2/15/02) [370.117]

5555 Soukhanov, Anne H. *Watch Word: The Stories Behind the Words of Our Lives* (9–12). 1995, Holt $25.00 (0-8050-3564-8). The editor of *The American Heritage Dictionary* discusses definitions, usage, and history of common words and looks at new words in our vernacular. (Rev: BL 6/1–15/95) [422]

5556 Strunk, William, and E. B. White. *The Elements of Style*. 4th ed. (10–12). 1999, Allyn & Bacon $14.95 (0-205-31342-6); paper $7.95 (0-205-30902-X). A simple, direct guide to proper usage and composition. [808]

5557 vos Savant, Marilyn. *The Art of Spelling: The Madness and the Method* (10–12). Illus. 2000, Norton $22.95 (0-393-04903-5); paper $12.95 (0-393-32208-4). As well as analyzing why some people cannot spell, the author describes spelling rules, gives tips on spelling methods and 500 problem words, and discusses changes in pronunciation and usage. (Rev: BL 8/00) [421]

5558 Wade, Nicholas. *The Science Times Book of Language and Linguistics* (10–12). Illus. 2000, Lyons Pr. $25.00 (1-55821-934-X). The current state of research on language — its purposes, origins, and uses — is explored in this collection of interesting columns from the *New York Times*. (Rev: BL 2/15/00) [400]

5559 Winchester, Simon. *The Professor and the Madman: A Tale of Murder, Insanity, and the Making of the Oxford English Dictionary* (10–12). 1998, HarperCollins $22.00 (0-06-017596-6). The story of the writing of the famous *Oxford English Dictionary* and the relationship between its editor, James Murray, and Dr. William Chester Minor, a major contributor and former Civil War doctor who was a patient in England's most famous insane asylum during their entire collaboration. (Rev: BL 8/98; SLJ 3/99) [410]

Writing and the Media

General and Miscellaneous

5560 Bauer, Marion Dane. *Our Stories: A Fiction Workshop for Young Authors* (6–10). 1996, Clarion $16.00 (0-395-81598-3); paper $6.95 (0-395-81599-1). Using critiques of 30 selections by students, the author explores such writing techniques as character development, dialogue, and point of view. (Rev: BL 10/15/96; BR 3–4/97; SLJ 12/96; VOYA 12/96) [808.3]

5561 Mirriam-Goldberg, Caryn, and Elizabeth Verdick. *Write Where You Are: How to Use Writing to Make Sense of Your Life: A Guide for Teens* (9–12). 1999, Free Spirit $14.95 (1-57542-060-0). This book contains information for teens on how to get to know themselves and how to learn the craft of writing at the same time. (Rev: SLJ 2/00; VOYA 4/00) [808]

5562 *Passing the Word: Writers on Their Mentors* (10–12). Ed. by Jeffrey Skinner and Lee Martin. Illus. 2001, Sarabande paper $16.95 (1-889330-59-0). This collection of tributes by writers to the writers who inspired them should interest aspiring young authors. (Rev: BL 6/1–15/01) [810.9]

5563 Senn, Joyce. *The Young People's Book of Quotations* (5–10). 1999, Millbrook LB $39.90 (0-7613-0267-0). Beginning with "accomplishment" and ending with "zoos," this is a collection of 2,000 quotations of special interest to young people, arranged by topic. (Rev: BL 3/1/99*; SLJ 4/99) [082]

Books and Publishing

5564 *The Art of the Book: From Medieval Manuscript to Graphic Novel* (10–12). Ed. by James Bettley. Illus. 2001, Abrams $49.50 (0-8109-6572-0). From the collection of books at London's Victoria and Albert Museum comes this handsome book with each chapter focusing on a different aspect of bookmaking, including illustrations, typography, poetry, and children's books. (Rev: BL 8/01; SLJ 9/01) [741.64]

5565 *The Book That Changed My Life: Interviews with National Book Award Winners and Finalists* (10–12). Ed. by Diane Osen. Illus. 2002, Modern Library paper $13.95 (0-679-78351-2). Fifteen authors talk about the books that most deeply affected their lives and helped to lay the groundwork for their own writings. (Rev: BL 9/1/02) [810.9]

5566 Harvey, Robert C. *The Art of the Comic Book: An Aesthetic History* (10–12). Series: Studies in Popular Culture. 1996, Univ. Press of Mississippi paper $22.00 (0-87805-758-7). An overview of the first century of comic books and the evolution of the art therein. (Rev: BL 1/1–15/96) [741.5]

5567 Madama, John. *Desktop Publishing: The Art of Communication* (7–12). Series: Media Workshop. 1993, Lerner LB $21.27 (0-8225-2303-5). Introduces desktop publishing elements and terminology, with advice on writing, editing, layout, type, illustration, and printing. (Rev: BL 5/15/93; SLJ 6/93) [686.2]

5568 Olmert, Michael. *The Smithsonian Book of Books* (9–12). 1992, Smithsonian $49.95 (0-89599-030-X). Celebrates the powerful link between readers and the printed page as it follows books from the days of scribes to moveable type to children's book illustration. (Rev: BL 9/1/92; SLJ 1/93*) [002]

5569 Rhodes, Jewell Parker. *The African American Guide to Writing and Publishing Nonfiction* (10–12). 2001, Broadway paper $14.00 (0-7679-0578-4). Though specifically written to help blacks become authors and get published, there are many tips here for any aspiring writer. (Rev: BL 12/15/01) [808]

5570 Robbins, Trina. *From Girls to Grrrlz: A History of Women's Comics from Teens to Zines* (7–12). Illus. 1999, Chronicle paper $17.95 (0-8118-2199-4). Focusing in particular on how comic books have reflected the changes in women's lives, this is a look back at the authors, artists, and characters of 60 years of the genre. (Rev: BL 6/1–15/99; VOYA 2/00) [741.5]

5571 Toussaint, Pamela. *Great Books for African American Children* (6–12). 1999, NAL paper $12.95 (0-452-28044-3). This book lists 250 recommended books for African American children from preschool to young adults, each with a lengthy, informative annotation. (Rev: BL 2/15/99; SLJ 9/99) [810]

5572 *Writing Creative Nonfiction* (10–12). Ed. by Carolyn Forcheand Philip Gerard. 2001, F & W paper $18.99 (1-884910-50-5). From the book proposal to the finished product, this is a guide to writing in various formats and genres — journals, essays, biography, nature writing, and plotted narrative. (Rev: BL 4/1/01) [808]

Print and Other Media

5573 Beatty, Scott. *Superman: The Ultimate Guide to the Man of Steel* (6–12). Illus. 2002, DK $19.99 (0-7894-8853-1). This comprehensive guide to Superman's life, powers, and friends and foes juxtaposes illustrations from different eras. (Rev: BL 8/02; SLJ 9/02) [741.5]

5574 *The Best of Emerge Magazine* (11–12). Ed. by George E. Curry and William Sandifer. Illus. 2003, Ballantine paper $19.95 (0-345-46228-9). For mature teens, this collection spotlights a wide array of topics of interest to African Americans and others, including affirmative action, mandatory sentencing for drug-related crimes, Malcolm X, the murder of Emmett Till, and racism on the Internet. (Rev: BL 7/03) [305.896]

5575 *Blue Jean: What Young Women Are Thinking, Saying, and Doing* (9–12). Ed. by Sherry S. Handel. 2001, Blue Jean paper $14.95 (0-9706609-1-X). Taken from the pages of *blue jean* magazine, the articles in this anthology were written and edited by teenage girls and cover a broad range of subjects, including racial discrimination, sexual violence, homelessness, and the creation of e-zines. (Rev: BL 6/1–15/01; SLJ 8/01; VOYA 4/02) [305.235]

5576 *Clive Barker's Hellraiser: Collected Best II* (11–12). Ed. by Clive Barker et al. Illus. 2003, Checker paper $21.95 (0-9710249-7-9). In this second collection of the best of the Clive Barker-inspired *Hellraiser* comic series, best suited for mature teens, the focus is on the visual narratives of Bill Koeb, John Van Fleet, Steven Johnson, John Bolton, and others. (Rev: BL 6/1–15/03) [741.5]

5577 Cohen, Daniel. *Yellow Journalism: Scandal, Sensationalism, and Gossip in the Media* (6–12). Illus. 2000, Twenty-First Century LB $22.90 (0-7613-1502-0). The history of tabloid journalism and sensation-driven media is the focus of this fascinating book that uses many modern cases as examples. (Rev: BL 5/15/00; SLJ 8/00) [302.23]

5578 Daniels, Les. *Marvel: Five Fabulous Decades of the World's Greatest Comics* (9–12). 1991, Abrams $49.50 (0-8109-3821-9). The story of the development of Marvel Comics is told through artwork, biographies, and profiles of the publishers' foremost heroes and villains. (Rev: BL 11/1/91) [741.5]

5579 Day, Nancy. *Sensational TV: Trash or Journalism?* (7–10). Illus. Series: Issues in Focus. 1996, Enslow LB $20.95 (0-89490-733-6). A history of tabloid journalism both in print and on TV, plus a discussion of present-day controversies surrounding it. (Rev: BL 4/1/96; SLJ 4/96; VOYA 6/96) [791.45]

5580 DeFalco, Tom. *Hulk: The Incredible Guide* (6–12). Illus. 2003, DK $24.99 (0-7894-9771-9). Full-color illustrations spanning 40 years of comics portray the Hulk's life and escapades in this oversize volume. Also use *X-Men: The Ultimate Guide* (2003). (Rev: BL 5/1/03) [741.5]

5581 Evanier, Mark. *Mad Art: A Visual Celebration of the Art of Mad Magazine and the Idiots Who Create It* (10–12). Illus. 2003, Watson-Guptill paper $24.95 (0-8230-3080-6). The artists responsible for a half century of *Mad* magazine's offbeat cartoons and comic strips are celebrated in this retrospective on their work. (Rev: BL 2/1/03) [741.6]

5582 Fleming, Thomas. *Behind the Headlines: The Story of American Newspapers* (6–10). 1989, Walker LB $15.85 (0-8027-6891-1). A lively history of American newspapers from the Revolution on and an indication of their continued importance today. (Rev: BL 1/1/90; BR 5–6/90; SLJ 1/90; VOYA 12/90) [071.3]

5583 *Frank Miller* (10–12). Ed. by Milo George. Illus. Series: Comics Journal Library. 2003, Fantagraphics paper $18.95 (1-56097-528-8). New insights into the life and work of Frank Miller, one of the leading forces in the modern era of comics, can be found in this collection of six in-depth interviews. (Rev: BL 10/1/03) [741.5]

5584 Garcia, John. *The Success of Hispanic Magazine* (7–10). Illus. Series: Success. 1996, Walker LB $16.85 (0-8027-8310-4). A behind-the-scenes look at the magazine business, from starting out to marketing research, staffing, sales, circulation, and distribution. Traces an article from initial conception to final version and publication. (Rev: BL 5/15/96; SLJ 4/96) [051]

5585 Goulart, Ron. *Comic Book Culture: An Illustrated History* (9–12). Illus. 2000, Collectors $49.95 (1-888054-38-7). This lavishly illustrated volume traces the history of the comic book from the mid-1930s through the late 1940s, with 400 examples including such staples as *Batman.* (Rev: BL 9/1/00; VOYA 12/00) [741.5]

5586 Herriman, George. *Krazy and Ignatz: "Love Letters in Ancient Brick."* (11–12). Ed. by Bill Blackbeard. Illus. 2002, Fantagraphics paper $14.95 (1-56097-507-5). Comic characters Krazy Kat, Ignatz, and Offissa Pupp are brought to life once again in a volume of black-and-white strips that first ran in 1927 and 1928; for mature teens. (Rev: BL 2/1/03)

5587 Howe, Peter. *Shooting Under Fire: The World of the War Photographer* (10–12). Illus. 2002, Artisan $35.00 (1-57965-215-8). Ten well-known war photographers discuss the obstacles they must overcome, which include danger and censorship. (Rev: BL 10/15/02; SLJ 8/03) [070.4]

5588 Katovsky, Bill, and Timothy Carlson. *Embedded: The Media at War in Iraq* (10–12). 2003, Lyons Pr. $23.95 (1-59228-265-2). Stories from embedded reporters offer insights into battlefront journalism and the very practice of embedding. (Rev: BL 10/15/03) [956.70443]

5589 Kieth, Sam, and William Messner-Loebs. *The Maxx* (11–12). Illus. 2003, DC Comics paper $17.95 (1-4012-0124-5). This collection packages the late 1980s-early 1990s comic book series that chronicles the adventures of The Maxx, illustrator Sam Kieth's parody of a superhero; best suited for mature teens. (Rev: BL 12/1/03) [741.5]

5590 Kurtzman, Harvey, et al. *The Mad Archives: Vol. 1, Issues 1–6* (10–12). Illus. 2002, DC Comics $49.95 (1-56389-816-0). The early days of *Mad* magazine are revisited in this collection of its first six issues, which hit American newsstands in the early 1950s in comic-book format. (Rev: BL 2/1/03) [741.5]

5591 *Live from the Trenches: The Changing Role of the Television News Correspondent* (10–12). Ed. by Joe S. Foote. Illus. 1998, Southern Illinois Univ. Pr. $22.95 (0-8093-2232-3). The evolution of television journalism — including technological advances and changes in staffing — is analyzed in this collection of essays. (Rev: BL 12/1/98) [070]

5592 *Mad: Cover to Cover: 48 Years, 6 Months, and 3 Days of Mad Magazine Covers* (10–12). Illus. 2000, Watson-Guptill paper $24.95 (0-8230-1684-6). The first 400 covers of *Mad* magazine are showcased in this all-color album. (Rev: BL 11/15/00) [741.6]

5593 Mindich, David T. Z. *Just the Facts: How "Objectivity" Came to Define American Journalism* (11–12). Illus. 1998, New York Univ. $27.95 (0-8147-5613-1). Advanced students of journalism and its role in history will be interested in this overview of the news media and the elusive goal of objectivity. (Rev: BL 11/15/98) [071]

5594 Morrison, Grant, et al. *Deus ex Machina* (11–12). Illus. 2003, DC Comics paper $19.95 (1-56389-968-X). The final issues of Morrison's Animal Man series, collected here, feature a protagonist who is able to assume the abilities of assorted creatures in his ongoing battle for animal rights; for mature teens. (Rev: BL 12/1/03) [741.5]

5595 Pavlik, John V. *Journalism and New Media* (10–12). Illus. 2001, Columbia Univ. Pr. $49.50 (0-231-11482-6); paper $17.50 (0-231-11483-4). This account looks at how telecommunications, computing, and traditional media are coming together and how this combination is changing journalism. (Rev: BL 7/01; SLJ 2/02) [070.4]

5596 Phillips, Peter, et al. *Censored 2003: The Top 25 Censored Stories* (10–12). Illus. 2002, Seven Stories paper $17.95 (1-58322-515-3). The authors spotlight 25 specific cases where corporate interests have persuaded major news organizations to overlook important stories. (Rev: BL 11/15/02) [909.83]

5597 Reeves, Richard. *What the People Know: Freedom and the Press* (11–12). 1998, Harvard $19.95 (0-674-61622-7). Syndicated columnist Reeves examines what he sees as the major influences on — and threats to — journalism, including technological advances, the concentration of media control in the hands of conglomerates, and the ill-defined line between news and entertainment. (Rev: BL 11/15/98) [070.1]

5598 *Reporting America at War* (10–12). Ed. by Michelle Ferrari and Iames Tobin. Illus. 2003,

Hyperion $25.95 (1-4013-0072-3). A collection of reminiscences from 11 war correspondents of past and present, including Edward R. Murrow, Walter Cronkite, and Peter Arnett. (Rev: BL 10/15/03) [070.4]

5599 Ritchie, Donald A. *American Journalists: Getting the Story* (8–12). Illus. 1998, Oxford $50.00 (0-19-509907-9). Fifty-six biographical sketches of journalists, supplemented by photographs, illustrations, and brief items about other news media notables, provide a glimpse into the journalism profession from Benjamin Franklin's time to today. (Rev: BL 2/15/98; BR 5–6/98; SLJ 7/98; VOYA 10/98) [070]

5600 Schulz, Charles M. *The Complete Peanuts: 1950 to 1952* (7–12). Ed. by Gary Groth. Illus. 2004, Fantagraphics paper $28.95 (1-56097-589-X). The first volume of a series that will eventually include the entire 50 years of this classic comic strip. (Rev: BL 4/1/04)

5601 Schulz, Charles M., and David Larkin. *Peanuts: A Golden Celebration: the Art and the Story of the World's Best-Loved Comic Strip* (8–12). 1999, HarperCollins $45.00 (0-06-270244-0). A selection of 1,000 strips that chronicle the lives of Charlie Brown and his friends. (Rev: BL 12/15/99) [741.5]

5602 Seib, Philip. *Going Live: Getting the News Right in a Real-Time, Online World* (10–12). 2001, Rowman & Littlefield $24.95 (0-7425-0900-1). This book observes the news-gathering styles of various media and finds that slick presentations may be becoming more important than accuracy. (Rev: BL 2/15/01) [070.1]

5603 Senna, Carl. *The Black Press and the Struggle for Civil Rights* (7–12). Series: African American Experience. 1993, Watts LB $24.00 (0-531-11036-2). The history of African American publications and their role in the fight for freedom and civil rights is traced from *Freedom's Journal* in 1827 to today. (Rev: BL 1/1/94; SLJ 1/94; VOYA 2/94) [071]

5604 Serrin, Judith, and William Serrin. *Muckraking! The Journalism That Changed America* (10–12). 2002, New Pr. paper $25.00 (1-56584-681-8). Positive newspaper stories that addressed societal ills and helped individuals and causes are the focus of this collection. (Rev: BL 7/02) [306]

5605 *Shaking the Foundations: 200 Years of American Investigative Journalism* (10–12). Ed. by Bruce Shapiro. 2003, Thunder's Mouth paper $15.95 (1-56025-433-5). Two centuries of investigative journalism are celebrated in this imposing collection of articles, book excerpts, essays, and memoirs from such diverse reporters as Nellie Bly, Ida B. Wells, Upton Sinclair, Jack Anderson, Ralph Nader, Bob Woodward, and Carl Bernstein. (Rev: BL 9/15/03) [070.4]

5606 Shepard, Richard. *The Paper's Papers: A Reporter's Journey Through the Archives of the New York Times* (10–12). 1996, Times Books $30.00 (0-8129-2453-3). An entertaining, anecdotal history of *The New York Times* that relies heavily on archival memos, letters, excerpts from articles, and cartoons. (Rev: SLJ 4/97) [070]

5607 Stay, Byron L., ed. *Mass Media* (8–12). 1999, Greenhaven LB $32.45 (0-7377-0055-6); paper $21.20 (0-7377-0054-8). How does television affect society? Is advertising harmful? How do the media influence politics? Should pornography on the Internet be regulated? Do TV content labels benefit children? These are some of the questions explored in this collection of writings about the mass media. (Rev: BL 4/15/99) [303.6]

5608 Streitmatter, Rodger. *Voices of Revolution: The Dissident Press in America* (10–12). Illus. 2001, Columbia Univ. Pr. $49.50 (0-231-12248-9); paper $18.50 (0-231-12249-7). From different periods in American history, here are 14 different case studies in which the press has played a vital role in bringing about social change. (Rev: BL 8/01) [071]

5609 Vaughan, Brian K., et al. *Y: The Last Man* (11–12). Illus. 2003, DC Comics paper $12.95 (1-56389-980-3). This volume contains the first five adventure-filled issues of *The Last Man* comic book series featuring Yorick Brown, son of a U.S. congresswoman and sole survivor of a bizarre plague that has killed the rest of the world's men. (Rev: BL 2/1/03) [741.5]

5610 Wakin, Edward. *How TV Changed America's Mind* (7–12). 1996, Lothrop $15.00 (0-688-13482-3). This book chronicles the impact of television journalism on U.S. history over the past 50 years by analyzing how the major news stories of the time were reported. (Rev: SLJ 7/96) [070.1]

5611 Woodward, Fred. *Rolling Stone: The Complete Covers, 1967–1997* (9–12). Illus. 1998, Harry N. Abrams $39.95 (0-8109-3797-2). A collection of the 773 covers of *Rolling Stone* magazine from November 1967 (the first issue) through November 1997 (Mick Jagger holds the record with 19 covers), supplemented by magazine headlines and features reflecting the political and social issues of that period and commentary about how the magazine developed into a major publication of popular culture. (Rev: BL 5/15/98; SLJ 8/98) [050]

5612 Wright, Bradford W. *Comic Book Nation: Transforming American Culture* (10–12). Illus. 2001, Johns Hopkins Univ. Pr. $34.95 (0-8018-6514-X). With references to politics, social trends, and pop culture, this account traces the history of comic books in the United States over the past 60 years. (Rev: BL 4/1/01) [741.5]

313

Biography, Memoirs, Etc.

General and Miscellaneous

5613 Felder, Deborah G. *The 100 Most Influential Women of All Time: A Ranking Past and Present* (9–12). 1995, Citadel $24.95 (0-8065-1726-3). Part of the series that includes *The Black 100* and *The Jewish 100*. (Rev: BL 12/1/95) [920]

5614 Salisbury, Harrison E. *Heroes of My Time* (9–12). 1993, Walker $30.95 (0-8027-1217-7). The *New York Times* journalist emeritus profiles both famous and unknown people who strove to reform the world through deeds, not words. (Rev: BL 4/15/93; VOYA 12/93) [920]

Adventurers and Explorers

Collective

5615 *As Told at the Explorers Club: More than Fifty Gripping Tales of Adventure* (10–12). Ed. by George Plimpton. 2003, Lyons Pr. $24.95 (1-59228-035-8). Diverse tales of adventure and misadventure make for great browsing. (Rev: BL 11/15/03) [910.4]

5616 Doherty, Kieran. *Ranchers, Homesteaders, and Traders: Frontiersmen of the South-Central States* (6–10). Illus. 2001, Oliver LB $21.95 (1-881508-53-6). Seven important settlers — including Sam Houston, Daniel Boone, and Eli Thayer — are introduced with plenty of historical and geographical background material. (Rev: BL 5/1/02; HBG 10/02; SLJ 1/02) [976]

5617 Druett, Joan. *She Captains: Heroines and Hellions of the Sea* (10–12). Illus. 2000, Simon & Schuster $26.00 (0-684-85690-5). A collection of biographies of famous women seafarers from the days of ancient Greece and Egypt to Cheng I Sao, who ruled the South China Sea. (Rev: BL 2/15/00) [920]

5618 Foss, Joe, and Matthew Brennan. *Top Guns: America's Fighter Aces Tell Their Stories* (9–12). 1992, Pocket paper $5.99 (0-671-68318-7). Twenty-seven aviators who served in various conflicts from World War II to Vietnam give stirring accounts of combat. (Rev: BL 5/15/91) [920]

5619 Holden, Henry M. *American Women of Flight: Pilots and Pioneers* (7–12). Series: Collective Biographies. 2003, Enslow LB $20.95 (0-7660-2005-3). This collection of profiles includes sketches on Harriet Quimby, Bessie Coleman, Amelia Earhart, Anne Morrow Lindbergh, and Jacqueline Cochran. (Rev: BL 6/1–15/03; HBG 10/03) [920]

5620 Murphy, Claire R., and Jane G. Haigh. *Gold Rush Women* (7–12). Illus. 1997, Alaska Northwest paper $16.95 (0-88240-484-9). A collective biography of several women in the late 19th century who went to the Yukon and Alaska, where they panned for gold, ran boarding houses, and worked as dance hall girls and prostitutes. (Rev: BL 8/97; BR 1–2/98; SLJ 11/97*) [920]

5621 Norton, Trevor. *Stars Beneath the Sea: The Pioneers of Diving* (10–12). Illus. 2000, Carroll & Graf $25.00 (0-7867-0750-X). There are 13 prose portraits in this biographical approach to the history of underwater exploration that includes material on William Beebe, J. B. S. Haldane, Frederic Dumas, and the founder of underwater archaeology, Peter Throckmorton. (Rev: BL 5/1/00) [920]

5622 Richie, Jason. *Spectacular Space Travelers* (6–10). Series: Profiles. 2001, Oliver LB $19.95 (1-881508-71-4). Three Soviet cosmonauts and four American astronauts are profiled in this volume that provides a brief history of the space race. (Rev: HBG 10/02; SLJ 4/02) [629.45]

5623 Wren, Laura Lee. *Pirates and Privateers of the High Seas* (6–10). Series: Collective Biographies. 2003, Enslow LB $20.95 (0-7660-1542-4). The piratical exploits of seafarers including Sir Francis Drake, Jean Laffite, Anne Bonny, and Mary Read are related in a lively narrative. (Rev: BL 6/1–15/03; HBG 10/03; SLJ 9/03) [910.4]

Individual

ARMSTRONG, NEIL

5624 Wagener, Leon. *One Giant Leap: Neil Armstrong's Stellar American Journey* (10–12). Illus. 2004, Tor $25.95 (0-312-87343-3). Based on interviews and detailed research this is a biography of Armstrong, the first human to walk on the moon. (Rev: BL 4/1/04) [921]

BLIGH CAPTAIN WILLIAM

5625 Toohey, John. *Captain Bligh's Portable Nightmare* (10–12). Illus. 2000, HarperCollins $24.00 (0-06-019532-0). A riveting account of the voyage in an open boat by Captain Bligh and his men after the famous mutiny on the *Bounty,* plus a detailed examination of this controversial man. (Rev: BL 3/1/00) [921]

BROWN, TOM, JR.

5626 Brown, Tom, Jr. *The Way of the Scout* (10–12). 1995, Berkley paper $12.95 (0-425-14779-7). This autobiographical account of the adolescence and young adulthood of a forest scout who now runs a wilderness survival school combines a message of spirituality, love of beauty, and environmentalism with breathtaking adventures. (Rev: SLJ 7/96) [921]

CAHILL, TIM

5627 Cahill, Tim. *A Wolverine Is Eating My Leg* (9–12). 1989, Random paper $13.00 (0-679-72026-X). A fascinating travel writer tells about his adventures around the world in this continuation of *Jaguars Ripped My Flesh* (1987). (Rev: BL 2/15/89) [921]

CARTER, JENNIFER

5628 Carter, Jennifer, and Joel Hirschhorn. *Titanic Adventure* (9–12). 1999, New Horizon $26.95 (0-88282-170-9). The autobiography of this courageous woman who was a skydiver, balloonist, river rafter, hang glider and, eventually, a deep sea diver who became the leader of a French American expedition to film a documentary on salvaging artifacts from the *Titanic.* (Rev: BL 9/1/98; SLJ 7/99) [921]

COLUMBUS, CHRISTOPHER

5629 Jones, Mary Ellen, ed. *Christopher Columbus and His Legacy* (9–12). Series: Opposing Viewpoints. 1992, Greenhaven paper $16.20 (0-89908-171-1). Offers differing perspectives from writers of various ethnic and national backgrounds on Columbus and his impact on the New World. (Rev: BL 1/15/93) [921]

5630 Meltzer, Milton. *Columbus and the World Around Him* (7–10). 1990, Watts LB $20.00 (0-531-10899-6). A handsome addition to the literature about Columbus that also deals with the culture and attitudes of the Spanish at the time. (Rev: BL 4/15/90; SLJ 7/90) [970.01]

5631 Sundel, Al. *Christopher Columbus and the Age of Exploration in World History* (8–12). Illus. Series: In World History. 2001, Enslow LB $20.95 (0-7660-1820-2). A detailed biography of Columbus that looks at the political climate of the time and discusses the atrocities inflicted on native peoples. (Rev: BL 3/1/02; HBG 10/02) [970.01]

COOK, CAPTAIN JAMES

5632 Dugard, Martin. *Farther than Any Man: The Rise and Fall of Captain James Cook* (10–12). 2001, Pocket $25.95 (0-7434-0068-2). A biography of the famous explorer, navigator, scientist, and cartographer who commanded amazing naval expeditions in the latter half of the 18th century. (Rev: BL 6/1–15/01) [921]

5633 Gaines, Ann Graham. *Captain Cook Explores the Pacific* (8–12). Series: In World History. 2002, Enslow LB $20.95 (0-7660-1823-7). A mature account of the life and exploits of the famous British explorer known principally for his voyages in the Pacific Ocean. (Rev: BL 4/1/02; HBG 10/02; SLJ 8/02) [921]

5634 Lawlor, Laurie. *Magnificent Voyage: An American Adventurer on Captain James Cook's Final Expedition* (7–12). Illus. 2002, Holiday $22.95 (0-8234-1575-9). This absorbing account of Captain Cook's ill-fated efforts to locate the Northwest Passage gives details of the various difficulties encountered and of Cook's violent death. (Rev: BL 1/1–15/03; HBG 10/03; SLJ 2/03; VOYA 4/03) [910]

COOPER, GORDON

5635 Cooper, Gordon, and Bruce Henderson. *Leap of Faith: An Astronaut's Journey into the Unknown* (10–12). Illus. 2000, HarperCollins $25.00 (0-06-019416-2). The autobiography of the astronaut involved in such flights as Gemini 5, with material on his abiding belief in UFOs. (Rev: BL 5/15/00) [921]

CORTES, HERNANDO

5636 Marks, Richard. *Cortés: The Great Adventurer and the Fate of Aztec Mexico* (9–12). 1993, Knopf $27.50 (0-679-40609-3). A presentation of the life of Cortes and his conquest of the Aztecs in which Cortes is portrayed as neither a hero nor a murderer. (Rev: BL 9/15/93*) [921]

CREAN, TOM

5637 Smith, Michael. *Tom Crean: Unsung Hero of the Scott and Shackleton Antarctic Expedition* (10–12). 2002, Mountaineers $24.95 (0-89886-870-X). This compelling biography of a man who explored with Scott and Shackleton includes excerpts from such primary sources as diaries, ships' logs, letters, and journals. (Rev: BL 2/15/02) [919.8]

D'ABOVILLE, GERARD

5638 D'Aboville, Gerard. *Alone: The Man Who Braved the Vast Pacific — and Won* (9–12). 1993, Arcade $21.95 (1-55970-218-4). Journal entries describe d'Aboville's solo crossing of the Pacific in a 26-foot rowboat. (Rev: BL 7/93) [920]

DE SOTO, HERNANDO

5639 Duncan, David Ewing. *Hernando de Soto: A Savage Quest in the Americas* (9–12). 1996, Crown $40.00 (0-517-58222-8). A carefully researched and documented text on a controversial conquistador. (Rev: BL 12/15/95) [921]

5640 Gaines, Ann Graham. *Hernando de Soto and the Search for Gold* (8–12). Series: In World History. 2002, Enslow LB $20.95 (0-7660-1821-0). The story of the famous Spanish conquistador who explored the southeastern United States in his search for gold. (Rev: BL 4/1/02; HBG 10/02; SLJ 8/02) [921]

DRAKE, SIR FRANCIS

5641 Kelsey, Harry. *Sir Francis Drake: The Queen's Pirate* (10–12). 1998, Yale Univ. Pr. $40.00 (0-300-07182-5); paper $18.95 (0-300-08963-3). Much about Drake's character is revealed in this well-researched volume. (Rev: BL 9/15/98) [921]

5642 Marrin, Albert. *The Sea King: Sir Francis Drake and His Times* (6–10). 1995, Atheneum $20.00 (0-689-31887-1). This biography includes Drake's trip around the world, his life as a privateer, and his role in defeating the Spanish Armada. (Rev: BL 7/95; SLJ 9/95) [921]

EARHART, AMELIA

5643 Earhart, Amelia. *The Fun of It: Random Records of My Own Flying and of Women in Aviation* (7–12). 1990, Omnigraphics $42.00 (1-55888-980-9). Autobiographical in part, this account is also a tribute to other women aviation pioneers. First published in 1932. [921]

5644 Goldstein, Donald M., and Katherine V. Dillon. *Amelia* (10–12). 1997, Brassey's $24.95 (1-57488-134-5). A well-written adult biography of Amelia Earhart that depicts a woman interested in both aviation and women's rights. (Rev: SLJ 3/98) [921]

5645 Rich, Doris L. *Amelia Earhart: A Biography* (10–12). 1989, Smithsonian paper $16.95 (1-56098-725-1). This scholarly account of Earhart's life emphasizes her flying career and the personalities behind her fame. [921]

5646 Ware, Susan. *Still Missing: Amelia Earhart and the Search for Modern Feminism* (9–12). 1993, Norton $22.00 (0-393-03551-4). Portrays Earhart as an inspiration to the women's movement of the 1920s and 1930s. (Rev: BL 11/15/93) [629.13]

FLIPPER, HENRY O.

5647 Harris, Theodore, ed. *Black Frontiersman: The Memoirs of Henry O. Flipper* (10–12). 1997, Texas Christian Univ. Pr. $22.95 (0-87565-171-2). A biography of Henry Flipper, the first African American West Point graduate, who was court-martialed and dismissed from the army on trumped-up charges; he left detailed accounts of his life as an army officer, mining engineer, surveyor, and Senate aide in the post-Civil War American Southwest and the Depression Era. (Rev: SLJ 2/98; VOYA 6/98) [921]

GRAHAM, ROBIN LEE

5648 Graham, Robin Lee, and Derek Gill. *Dove* (7–12). Illus. 1991, HarperCollins paper $13.00 (0-06-092047-5). A five-year solo voyage around the world and a tender romance with a girl the author met in Fiji. [921]

HENSON, MATTHEW

5649 Gilman, Michael. *Matthew Henson* (6–10). Illus. 1988, Chelsea LB $21.95 (1-55546-590-0). The life story of the African American explorer who accompanied Peary on expeditions in search of the North Pole. (Rev: BL 6/15/88; SLJ 4/88) [921]

JEMISON, MAE

5650 Jemison, Mae. *Find Where the Wind Goes* (7–12). 2001, Scholastic $16.95 (0-439-13195-2). The fascinating autobiography of the first African American woman in space. (Rev: BL 11/1/01; HBG 10/01; SLJ 4/01; VOYA 8/01) [629.45]

KILEY, DEBORAH SCALING

5651 Kiley, Deborah Scaling, and Meg Noonan. *Albatross: The True Story of a Woman's Survival at Sea* (9–12). 1994, Houghton $19.95 (0-395-65573-0). What happened when Kiley and four companion sailors were shipwrecked off the coast of North Carolina. (Rev: BL 4/1/94) [921]

LEWIS AND CLARK

5652 Ambrose, Stephen. *Undaunted Courage: Meriwether Lewis, Thomas Jefferson, and the Opening of the American West* (10–12). 1996, Simon & Schuster $27.50 (0-684-81107-3). Though primarily a biography of Meriwether Lewis, this book also provides fascinating sketches of Thomas Jefferson, William Clark, Sacagawea, and other contemporaries. (Rev: BL 1/1–15/96; SLJ 6/96) [921]

5653 Edwards, Judith. *Lewis and Clark's Journey of Discovery* (6–10). Series: In American History. 1998, Enslow LB $20.95 (0-7660-1127-5). This story of the overland expedition to find the Pacific Ocean begins with Lewis and Clark getting their commission from Jefferson and ends with their return home two years later. (Rev: BL 2/15/99; HBG 9/99) [921]

5654 Lavender, David Sievert. *The Way to the Western Sea: Lewis and Clark Cross the Continent* (10–12). 2001, Univ. of Nebraska Pr. paper (0-8032-8003-3). An exciting account of the cross-continental expedition of Lewis and Clark two centuries ago. [973.4]

5655 National Geographic Society, eds. *Lewis and Clark* (10–12). 1998, National Geographic $35.00 (0-7922-7084-3). The author and his family retraced the route taken by Lewis and Clark that opened up the American West. The book is equally about the explorers' expedition and the author's thoughts about their impact on the land and the people. This volume is superbly illustrated with full-color photographs and reproductions of paintings by the two explorers. (Rev: BL 9/15/98; SLJ 4/99) [917.3]

LINDBERGH, CHARLES

5656 Davies, R. E. *Charles Lindbergh: An Airman, His Aircraft, and His Great Flights* (9–12). Illus. 1997, Paladwr Pr. $30.00 (1-888962-04-6). Using many illustrations, including full paintings of his aircraft, this biography of Lindbergh is a gripping, human document. (Rev: VOYA 6/98) [921]

5657 Denenberg, Barry. *An American Hero: The True Story of Charles A. Lindbergh* (8–12). Illus. 1996, Scholastic paper $16.95 (0-590-46923-1). Beginning with Lindbergh's transatlantic flight, this fascinating biography then recounts the story of his early years followed by details about his multifaceted life. (Rev: BL 3/15/96*; BR 9–10/96; SLJ 7/96; VOYA 6/96) [921]

5658 Giblin, James Cross. *Charles A. Lindbergh: A Human Hero* (6–12). Illus. 1997, Clarion $21.00 (0-395-63389-3). A book about the public and private life of one of America's heroes that deals with his pro-Nazi sympathies and anti-Semitism, the adoration he received for his transatlantic flight, and pity the public felt for the kidnapping and murder of his child. (Rev: BL 9/15/97; HBG 3/98; SLJ 11/97*; VOYA 6/98) [921]

5659 Hardesty, Von. *Lindbergh: Flight's Enigmatic Hero* (10–12). Illus. 2002, Harcourt $40.00 (0-15-100973-2). The reasons underlying Lindbergh's immense popularity are a major focus of this appealing biography full of photographs. (Rev: BL 11/15/02) [921]

5660 Kent, Zachary. *Charles Lindbergh and the Spirit of St. Louis* (6–10). Series: In American History. 2001, Enslow LB $20.95 (0-7660-1683-8). Lindbergh's life and accomplishments are re-created, including the first solo trip by airplane across the Atlantic Ocean, made when he was only 25 years old. (Rev: BL 8/01; HBG 10/01) [921]

5661 Koopman, Andy. *Charles Lindbergh* (7–12). Series: The Importance Of. 2003, Gale LB $27.45 (1-59018-245-6). Using many original sources, this is a lively biography of the aviation hero who captured the hearts of Americans. (Rev: BL 6/1–15/03; SLJ 8/03) [921]

5662 Meachum, Virginia. *Charles Lindbergh: American Hero of Flight* (6–10). Series: People to Know. 2002, Enslow LB $20.95 (0-7660-1535-1). A well-illustrated, appealing biography of the American hero of aviation with insights into his personal life. (Rev: BL 9/15/02; HBG 10/02; SLJ 9/02) [921]

5663 Pisano, Dominic A., and F. Robert van der Linden. *Charles Lindbergh and the Spirit of St. Louis* (9–12). Illus. 2002, Abrams $22.95 (0-8109-0552-3). This richly illustrated overview of Lindbergh's life and history-making flight also discusses his opposition to American participation in World War II and his environmental concerns. (Rev: BL 5/15/02) [629.13]

LIVINGSTONE, DAVID

5664 Wellman, Sam. *David Livingstone: Missionary and Explorer* (9–12). Series: Heroes of the Faith. 1998, Chelsea LB $17.95 (0-7910-5038-6). A detailed biography of David Livingstone, a Scottish missionary and doctor who explored central Africa while attempting to spread Christianity. (Rev: BL 10/1/98) [921]

MACKENZIE, ALEXANDER

5665 Hayes, Derek. *First Crossing: Alexander Mackenzie, His Expedition Across North America, and the Opening of the Continent* (10–12). Illus. 2001, Sasquatch $40.00 (1-57061-308-7). This biography of Alexander Mackenzie focuses on his exploration of the Canadian river named after him in 1789 and his expedition by boat and land to the Pacific Ocean in 1793. (Rev: BL 9/1/01) [921]

MAGELLAN, FERDINAND

5666 Joyner, Tim. *Magellan* (9–12). 1992, International Marine paper $16.95 (0-87742-263-X). Details the adventures of the 16th-century explorer best known for being the first to sail around the world. (Rev: BL 3/1/92) [921]

5667 Stefoff, Rebecca. *Ferdinand Magellan and the Discovery of the World Ocean* (7–12). Illus. 1990, Chelsea LB $21.95 (0-7910-1291-3). Using many quotations from original sources, this is an engrossing account of the explorer and his voyage. (Rev: BL 6/15/90) [921]

MARKHAM, BERYL

5668 Gourley, Catherine. *Beryl Markham: Never Turn Back* (6–10). Series: Bernard Biography. 1997, Conari paper $6.95 (1-57324-073-7). An exciting biography of the unconventional Englishwoman who was the first person to fly the Atlantic from east to west. (Rev: BL 3/15/97; SLJ 5/97; VOYA 12/97) [921]

5669 Trzebinski, Errol. *The Lives of Beryl Markham* (10–12). 1995, Norton paper $12.00 (0-393-31252-6). A deft and intimate portrait of the aviator who made a pioneering transatlantic flight. (Rev: BL 3/15/97; BR 9–10/97) [921]

MARTIN, JESSE

5670 Martin, Jesse. *Lionheart: A Journey of the Human Spirit* (8–12). 2002, Allen & Unwin paper $14.95 (1-86508-347-X). Martin details the exciting events and extreme isolation of his inspiring round-the-world solo voyage at the age of 17. (Rev: SLJ 5/02; VOYA 6/02) [910.4]

MIKKELSEN, EINAR

5671 Mikkelsen, Einar. *Two Against the Ice: A Classic Arctic Survival Story and a Remarkable Account of Companionship in the Face of Adversity* (10–12). Trans. by Maurice Michael. Illus. 2003, Steerforth paper $14.95 (1-58642-057-7). An exciting, simply told story of the author's harrowing trip by dogsled, accompanied by Iver Iversen, to retrieve the diaries of earlier Greenland explorers. (Rev: BL 1/1–15/03) [919.8]

MORGAN, SIR HENRY

5672 Marrin, Albert. *Terror of the Spanish Main: Sir Henry Morgan and His Buccaneers* (7–12). 1999, Dutton $21.99 (0-525-45942-1). The story of Henry Morgan, a murderous cutthroat who, in the name of the English flag, wreaked havoc on Spanish colonies, using Jamaica as his home base. (Rev: BL 1/1–15/99; HB 3–4/99; HBG 9/99; SLJ 1/99*; VOYA 8/99) [921]

PFETZER, MARK

5673 Pfetzer, Mark, and Jack Galvin. *Within Reach: My Everest Story* (7–12). 1998, Dutton $16.95 (0-525-46089-6). The autobiography of the youngest person to climb Mount Everest, with material on how he became interested in mountain climbing. (Rev: BL 11/15/98; SLJ 11/98; VOYA 2/99) [921]

POLO, MARCO

5674 Polo, Marco. *The Travels of Marco Polo* (10–12). 1958, Penguin paper $13.95 (0-14-044057-7). One of many editions of this account kept by Marco Polo of his travels in Asia in the 13th century. [915]

RALEIGH, SIR WALTER

5675 Aronson, Marc. *Sir Walter Ralegh and the Quest for El Dorado* (7–10). 2000, Clarion $20.00 (0-395-84827-X). The fascinating life and times of the colorful Elizabethan explorer, with illustrations, maps, and quotations from Sir Walter himself. (Rev: BL 8/00; HB 9–10/00; HBG 9/00; SLJ 7/00*) [942.05]

RIDE, SALLY

5676 Camp, Carole Ann. *Sally Ride: First American Woman in Space* (6–10). Illus. Series: People to Know. 1997, Enslow LB $20.95 (0-89490-829-4). A lively account of Sally Ride's work as an astronaut and astrophysicist, with material on her training, shuttle flight, and life in microgravity. (Rev: BL 1/1–15/98; HBG 3/98; SLJ 12/97) [921]

SACAGAWEA

5677 Waldo, Donna Lee. *Sacajawea* (10–12). 1979, Avon paper $8.50 (0-380-84293-9). A lengthy account of the Indian girl who accompanied the Lewis and Clark Expedition. [921]

SELKIRK, ALEXANDER

5678 Souhami, Diana. *Selkirk's Island: The True and Strange Adventures of the Real Robinson Crusoe* (9–12). 2002, Harcourt $24.00 (0-15-100526-5); paper $13.00 (0-15-602717-8). This is the biography of the man on whom Daniel Defoe based his character Robinson Crusoe. (Rev: BL 1/1–15/02) [921]

SHACKLETON, SIR ERNEST

5679 Johnson, Rebecca. *Ernest Shackleton: Gripped by the Antarctic* (6–10). Illus. Series: Trailblazer Biographies. 2003, Carolrhoda LB $25.26 (0-87614-920-4). Photographs, anecdotes, and quotations are sprinkled throughout this exciting account of Shackleton's youth and famous expeditions. (Rev: BL 6/1–15/03; HBG 10/03; SLJ 8/03; VOYA 8/03) [919.8]

5680 Plimpton, George. *Ernest Shackleton* (10–12). Illus. 2003, DK $23.00 (0-7894-9318-7). Beautifully illustrated, this biography focuses on Shackleton's life and four voyages to Antarctica. (Rev: BL 5/15/03; SLJ 8/03) [919.8]

WEBB, MATTHEW

5681 Watson, Kathy. *The Crossing: The Glorious Tragedy of the First Man to Swim the English Channel* (10–12). 2001, Putnam $22.95 (1-58542-109-X). The story of the first man to swim the English Channel (in 1875) and how he became a victim of his own success. (Rev: BL 7/01) [921]

WEIHENMAYER, ERIK

5682 Weihenmayer, Erik. *Touch the Top of the World: A Blind Man's Journey to Climb Farther than the Eye Can See* (10–12). Illus. 2001, Dutton $23.95 (0-525-94578-4). This true adventure story of a man who, although blind, has accomplished amazing physical feats including climbing Mount McKinley in Alaska. (Rev: BL 2/1/01) [796.52]

Artists, Authors, Composers, and Entertainers

Collective

5683 Bearden, Romare, and Harry Henderson. *A History of African-American Artists: From 1792 to the Present* (9–12). 1993, Pantheon $65.00 (0-394-57016-2). The lives and careers of 36 African American artists born before 1925 are part of this comprehensive history of African American art. Includes more than 300 black-and-white and color prints. (Rev: BL 10/15/93*) [920]

5684 Bloom, Harold, ed. *American Women Fiction Writers 1900–1960*, vol. 2 (9–12). Series: Women Writers of English and Their Works. 1997, Chelsea LB $29.95 (0-7910-4481-5); paper $16.95 (0-7910-4497-1). This volume, the second in a set of three, gives biographies and criticism for 11 women authors, including Zora Neale Hurston, Shirley Jackson, and Carson McCullers. (Rev: BR 3–4/98; SLJ 1/98) [920]

5685 Bloom, Harold. *Black American Poets and Dramatists of the Harlem Renaissance* (10–12). Series: Writers of English: Lives and Works. 1995, Chelsea LB $34.95 (0-7910-2207-2); paper $18.65 (0-7910-2232-3). Profiles writers including Langston Hughes, Countee Cullen, Jean Toomer, and Claude McKay. [920]

5686 Bloom, Harold. *Black American Women Fiction Writers* (10–12). Series: Writers of English: Lives and Works. 1995, Chelsea $34.95 (0-7910-2208-0). This volume supplies biographical and critical information on such authors as Toni Morrison, Maya Angelou, Zora Neale Hurston, and Gloria Naylor. [920]

5687 Bloom, Harold. *Black American Women Poets and Dramatists* (10–12). Series: Writers of English: Lives and Works. 1995, Chelsea LB $34.95 (0-7910-2209-9); paper $18.65 (0-7910-2234-X). Pro-

files 17 African American poets and playwrights from Phillis Wheatley to June Jordan and Rita Dove. [920]

5688 Bloom, Harold. *Major Modern Black American Writers* (10–12). Series: Writers of English: Lives and Works. 1995, Chelsea $34.95 (0-7910-2219-6); paper $18.65 (0-7910-2244-7). Some of the authors covered in this collective bio-bibliography are Maya Angelou, Gwendolyn Brooks, Alice Walker, and James Baldwin. [920]

5689 Bloom, Harold, ed. *Native American Women Writers* (10–12). Illus. 1998, Chelsea LB $29.95 (0-7910-4479-3); paper $16.95 (0-7910-4495-5). This collective biography contains biographical material and literary criticism on such Native American poets and novelists as Paula Gunn Allen, Louise Erdrich, Joy Harjo, E. Pauline Johnson, and Mourning Dove. (Rev: SLJ 9/98) [920]

5690 Blum, David. *Quintet: Five Journeys Toward Musical Fulfillment* (10–12). Illus. 2000, Cornell $25.00 (0-8014-3731-8). This adult work profiles five individuals who have devoted their lives to classical music, including cellist Yo-Yo Ma, conductor Jeffrey Tate, pianist Richard Goode, and singer Birgit Nilsson. (Rev: BL 1/1–15/00) [920]

5691 Cahill, Susan, ed. *Writing Women's Lives: An Anthology of Autobiographical Narratives by Twentieth-Century American Women Writers* (9–12). 1994, HarperPerennial paper $18.00 (0-06-096998-9). A collection of autobiographical narratives by 20th-century women writers, including Jane Addams and Edith Wharton. (Rev: BL 4/15/94) [920]

5692 Chiu, Christina. *Lives of Notable Asian Americans: Literature and Education* (6–10). Illus. Series: Asian American Experience. 1995, Chelsea LB $19.95 (0-7910-2182-3). Brief biographies of important Asian American writers and educators. (Rev: BL 1/1–15/96; BR 9–10/96) [920]

5693 Cumming, Robert. *Great Artists* (9–12). Illus. 1998, DK $24.95 (0-7894-2391-X). Arranged in chronological order, this volume gives facts on 50 great artists plus reproductions of their most famous works and a discussion of their techniques and impact. (Rev: SLJ 7/98; VOYA 12/98) [920]

5694 Davidson, Sue. *Getting the Real Story: Nellie Bly and Ida B. Wells* (6–10). 1992, Seal paper $8.95 (1-878067-16-8). A dual biography of two women who broke down barriers in journalism and how their different races shaped their individual stories. (Rev: BL 3/1/92; SLJ 7/92) [920]

5695 *Dream Me Home Safely* (10–12). Ed. by Susan Richards Shreve. 2003, Houghton paper $13.00 (0-618-37902-9). Thirty-four American writers reveal details of their adolescence in this valuable collection of memoirs. (Rev: BL 10/15/03) [921]

5696 Earls, Irene. *Young Musicians in World History* (7–12). 2002, Greenwood $44.95 (0-313-31442-X). Thirteen musicians whose skills were recognized before the age of 25 are profiled, ranging from Bach and Beethoven to Louis Armstrong, Bob Dylan, and John Lennon. (Rev: LMC 2/03; SLJ 1/03) [780]

5697 Glossbrenner, Alfred, and Emily Glossbrenner. *About the Author: The Passionate Reader's Guide to the Authors You Love, Including Things You Never Knew, Juicy Bits You'll Want to Know, and Hundreds of Ideas for What to Read Next* (9–12). Illus. 2000, Harcourt paper $16.00 (0-15-601302-9). This work contains two-page profiles of 125 important writers, including a section on the best books of each and a column of gossipy details. (Rev: BL 5/1/00; SLJ 10/00) [920]

5698 Gourse, Leslie. *Fancy Fretwork: The Great Jazz Guitarists* (8–12). Illus. Series: Art of Jazz. 1999, Watts LB $25.00 (0-531-11565-8). Gourse profiles some of the genre's best guitarists, providing quotations from the artists and a brief history of the art form. Also use *Timekeepers: The Great Jazz Drummers* (1999). (Rev: BL 11/15/99) [787.87]

5699 Gourse, Leslie. *Swingers and Crooners: The Art of Jazz Singing* (6–10). 1997, Watts LB $23.00 (0-531-11321-3). Through the biographies of such great singers as Ella Fitzgerald, Louis Armstrong, Bing Crosby, and Harry Connick, Jr., the history of jazz is covered, from its roots in gospel and blues through the big band and bebop eras to the singers of today. (Rev: SLJ 6/97) [920]

5700 Gowing, Lawrence. *Biographical Dictionary of Artists* (9–12). 1995, Facts on File $50.00 (0-8160-3252-1). Biographical sketches summarize the individual styles and important works of 1,340 artists. (Rev: BL 1/1–15/96; SLJ 1/96) [920]

5701 Hill, Anne E. *Ten American Movie Directors: The Men Behind the Camera* (7–12). Series: Collective Biographies. 2003, Enslow LB $20.95 (0-7660-1836-9). This collective biography features profiles of 10 famous movie directors, including Alfred Hitchcock, Frank Capra, Woody Allen, Martin Scorsese, George Lucas, Spike Lee, and Steven Spielberg. (Rev: BL 6/1–15/03; HBG 10/03) [920]

5702 Hill, Christine M. *Ten Hispanic American Authors* (6–12). Illus. Series: Collective Biographies. 2002, Enslow LB $20.95 (0-7660-1541-6). Ten Hispanic Americans — including Sandra Cisneros, Gary Soto, and Piri Thomas — are introduced here, with information on how they became successful writers. (Rev: BL 5/1/02; HBG 10/02; SLJ 6/02) [810.9]

5703 Hipple, Ted. *Writers for Young Adults* (7–12). 1997, Macmillan $310.00 (0-684-80474-3). This resource presents biographical and critical essays on 129 classic and contemporary writers for young adults, from Joan Aiken to Paul Zindel. (Rev: BL 10/15/97; SLJ 8/98) [920]

5704 Hirschfelder, Arlene B. *Artists and Craftspeople* (8–12). Illus. Series: American Indian Lives. 1994, Facts on File $25.00 (0-8160-2960-1). Profiles 18 historical and contemporary Native Americans including Nampeyo, Maria Martinez, and Oscar Howe, who are famous for their contributions to craftwork and art. (Rev: BL 11/15/94; SLJ 11/94; VOYA 4/95) [920]

5705 Horitz, Margot F. *A Female Focus: Great Women Photographers* (7–12). Illus. Series: Women Then — Women Now. 1996, Watts LB $25.00 (0-531-11302-7). This collective biography highlights the lives of several dozen female photographers, from early women who helped their photographer-husbands to photographers including Margaret Bourke-White, Dorothea Lange, and Annie Leibovitz. (Rev: BL 3/15/97; SLJ 2/97; VOYA 8/97) [920]

5706 Jackson, Nancy. *Photographers: History and Culture Through the Camera* (7–12). Illus. Series: American Profiles. 1997, Facts on File $25.00 (0-8160-3358-7). The life stories of eight famous photographers, including Mathew Brady, Alfred Stieglitz, Edward Steichen, Dorothea Lange, and Gordon Parks. (Rev: BL 5/1/97; SLJ 7/97) [920]

5707 Koolish, Lynda. *African American Writers: Portraits and Visions* (9–12). Illus. 2001, Univ. Press of Mississippi $40.00 (1-57806-258-6). This stylish collection features black-and-white photographs and brief accompanying profiles of influential African American writers including August Wilson, Lucille Clifton, Edwidge Danticat, and Sonia Sanchez. (Rev: BL 2/15/02) [810.9]

5708 McKenna, Kristine. *Book of Changes: A Collection of Interviews* (10–12). Illus. 2001, Fantagraphics paper $14.95 (1-56097-417-6). More than 40 interviews with such pop icons as Ray Charles,

James Brown, and Bo Diddley are included in this unusual collection. (Rev: BL 1/1–15/01) [920]

5709 Madison, Bob. *American Horror Writers* (7–12). Series: Collective Biographies. 2001, Enslow LB $20.95 (0-7660-1379-0). Edgar Allan Poe, H. P. Lovecraft, Dean Koontz, R. L. Stine, Anne Rice, and Stephen King are among the 10 writers profiled here. (Rev: HBG 10/01; SLJ 4/01) [813]

5710 Mandell, Sherri Lederman. *Writers of the Holocaust* (9–12). Illus. Series: Global Profiles. 1999, Facts on File LB $19.95 (0-8160-3729-9). This collective biography profiles the lives and work of 10 writers who experienced the Holocaust and in some cases fell victim to its horrors, including such well-known names as Anne Frank, Elie Wiesel, Primo Levi, and Jerzy Kosinski. (Rev: BL 2/1/99; SLJ 7/99) [940.53]

5711 Mass, Wendy. *Great Authors of Children's Literature* (6–10). Series: History Makers. 2000, Lucent LB $18.96 (1-56006-589-3). From early children's books to the present, this is a collection of brief biographies of trailblazers in the field of children's literature including Milne, Dahl, Dr. Seuss, Sendak, and Judy Blume. (Rev: BL 3/15/00; HBG 9/00; SLJ 6/00) [920]

5712 Mazer, Anne, ed. *Going Where I'm Coming From: Memoirs of American Youth* (8–12). 1995, Persea paper $7.95 (0-89255-206-9). Writers from different cultures talk about growing up and the incidents in their lives that helped to establish their identities. (Rev: BL 1/15/95; VOYA 5/95) [818]

5713 Otfinoski, Steven. *African Americans in the Performing Arts* (8–12). Illus. Series: A to Z of African Americans. 2003, Facts on File $44.00 (0-8160-4807-X). Profiles of African American actors, dancers, choreographers, composers, musicians, and singers, mostly from the 20th century, give personal and career information. (Rev: BL 8/03; SLJ 6/03) [791]

5714 *Playwrights at Work* (10–12). Ed. by George Plimpton. Illus. 2000, Random paper $14.95 (0-679-64021-5). This collection of 16 interviews with authors from the pages of the *Paris Review* includes material on Thornton Wilder, Arthur Miller, Tennessee Williams, David Mamet, and Edward Albee. (Rev: BL 5/1/00) [920]

5715 Price-Groff, Claire. *Extraordinary Women Journalists* (7–10). Series: Extraordinary People. 1997, Children's LB $39.00 (0-516-20474-2). More than 50 well-known and lesser-known female reporters, publishers, humorists, columnists, photographers, and television journalists from colonial times to the present are profiled, including Nellie Bly, Hedda Hopper, Ann Landers, Abigail Van Buren, and Barbara Walters. (Rev: BR 5–6/98; SLJ 3/98; VOYA 4/98) [920]

5716 Shirley, Lynn M. *Latin American Writers* (8–12). Illus. Series: Global Profiles. 1996, Facts on File $25.00 (0-8160-3202-5). This work profiles the life and works of eight prominent contemporary Latin American authors including Borges, Marquez, Amado, Fuentes, Vargas Llosa, and Isabel Allende. (Rev: BL 3/15/97) [920]

5717 Sills, Leslie. *In Real Life: Six Women Photographers* (6–12). Illus. 2000, Holiday $19.95 (0-8234-1498-1). This broad-ranging collective biography not only looks at the lives and works of artists including Dorothea Lange and Carrie Mae Weems but also gives the reader guidance on appreciating the women's technique and artistry. (Rev: BL 12/1/00; BR 3–4/01; HB 1–2/01; HBG 3/01; SLJ 2/01; VOYA 2/01) [770]

5718 *Streetwise: Autobiographical Stories* (10–12). Ed. by Jon Cooke and John Morrow. 2000, TwoMorrows $19.95 (1-893905-04-7). The lives of many famous comic-book artists, told in graphic form. (Rev: BL 2/1/03)

5719 Strickland, Michael R. *African-American Poets* (5–10). Illus. Series: Collective Biographies. 1996, Enslow LB $20.95 (0-89490-774-3). The lives and works of 10 prominent African American poets from Phillis Wheatley to Rita Dove are covered, with quotations from their works and a single full-length poem from each. (Rev: BL 2/15/97; SLJ 1/97) [920]

5720 Stux, Erica. *Eight Who Made a Difference: Pioneer Women in the Arts* (7–10). 1999, Avisson LB $19.95 (1-888105-37-2). Profiles eight famous women in the arts: Marian Anderson, Mary Cassatt, Nadia Boulanger, Margaret Bourke-White, Julia Morgan, Louise Nevelson, Beverly Sills, and Maria Tallchief. (Rev: BL 2/15/99; SLJ 5/99; VOYA 10/99) [920]

5721 Terkel, Studs, and Milly Hawk Daniel. *Giants of Jazz.* 2nd ed. (7–10). 1992, HarperCollins LB $16.89 (0-690-04917-X). Thirteen subjects are highlighted, including Benny Goodman, Louis Armstrong, Bessie Smith, and Dizzy Gillespie. [920]

5722 Verde, Tom. *Twentieth-Century Writers, 1950–1990* (9–12). Illus. Series: American Profiles. 1996, Facts on File $19.95 (0-8160-2967-9). Presents biographies and critical analyses of the works of Eudora Welty, Saul Bellow, J. D. Salinger, Jack Kerouac, Kurt Vonnegut, James Baldwin, Flannery O'Connor, and James Updike. (Rev: BL 5/1/96; BR 11–12/96; VOYA 4/96) [920]

5723 Weitzman, David. *Great Lives: Theater* (8–12). Illus. 1996, Simon & Schuster $24.00 (0-689-80579-9). This collective biography gives thumbnail sketches of 26 people (mostly dead) who have contributed to the theater as actors, producers, or playwrights, including Edwin Booth, Sarah Bernhardt, and P. T. Barnum. (Rev: BL 2/1/97; BR 5–6/97; SLJ 11/96; VOYA 12/96) [920]

5724 Whitelaw, Nancy. *They Wrote Their Own Headlines: American Women Journalists* (6–10). 1994, Morgan Reynolds LB $21.95 (1-883846-06-4). Biographies of seven women journalists such as advice columnist Ann Landers and war correspondent Marguerite Higgins, examining the drive that brought success in a male-dominated field. (Rev: BL 7/94; SLJ 6/94; VOYA 8/94) [920]

5725 Woog, Adam. *Magicians and Illusionists* (6–10). Series: History Makers. 1999, Lucent LB $18.96 (1-56006-573-7). Eight illusionists — including Houdini and David Copperfield — are profiled, with discussion of their performances and many quotations from original sources. (Rev: BL 10/15/99; HBG 9/00; SLJ 3/00) [793.8]

5726 Zucker, Carole. *In the Company of Actors: Reflections on the Craft of Acting* (10–12). Illus. 2000, Routledge $25.00 (0-415-92545-2). For mature theater fans, here are interviews with 16 Irish and British actors including Judi Dench, Alan Bates, Simon Callow, Nigel Hawthorne, Janet McTeer, and Eileen Atkins. (Rev: BL 1/1–15/00) [920]

Artists and Architects

ADAMS, ANSEL

5727 Gherman, Beverly. *Ansel Adams: America's Photographer* (6–10). Illus. 2002, Little, Brown $19.95 (0-316-82445-3). This splendid introduction to Adams's photography includes high-quality reproductions of his work and a lively account of his life and love of the natural world. (Rev: BL 6/1–15/03*; HBG 10/03) [770.92]

BANTOCK, NICK

5728 Bantock, Nick. *The Artful Dodger: Images and Reflections* (10–12). Illus. 2000, Chronicle $40.00 (0-8118-2752-6). This is the inspiring story of the creator of several important graphic novels and of his life in art, chiefly as a book cover illustrator. (Rev: BL 7/00) [921]

BEARDEN, ROMARE

5729 Brown, Kevin. *Romare Bearden* (7–10). Series: Black Americans of Achievement. 1995, Chelsea LB $19.95 (0-7910-1119-4). The story of the Harlem-raised African American painter who tries to portray the everyday experiences of African Americans. (Rev: BL 3/15/95; SLJ 3/95) [921]

5730 Schwartzman, Myron. *Romare Bearden: Celebrating the Victory* (9–12). Illus. 1999, Watts LB

$26.00 (0-531-11387-6). A biography of the African American painter, with a focus on his work, enhanced by color plates. (Rev: BL 1/1–15/00; SLJ 4/00) [709]

BLAKE, WILLIAM

5731 Hamlyn, Robin, et al. *William Blake* (10–12). Illus. 2001, Abrams $75.00 (0-8109-5710-8). A superbly illustrated volume in which contributors discuss various facets of this artistic and literary genius. (Rev: BL 6/1–15/01) [921]

BOSCH, HIERONYMUS

5732 Schwartz, Gary. *Hieronymus Bosch* (9–12). Illus. Series: First Impressions. 1997, Abrams $19.95 (0-8109-3138-9). An introduction to the life and paintings of the 15th-century Dutch painter Hieronymus Bosch, with many full-color reproductions of his bizarre, surreal paintings. (Rev: BL 12/15/97; BR 5–6/98) [921]

BOURGEOIS, LOUISE

5733 Greenberg, Jan, and Sandra Jordan. *Runaway Girl: The Artist Louise Bourgeois* (8–12). Illus. 2003, Abrams $19.95 (0-8109-4237-2). The life of the famous sculptor, with details of her youth and her difficult relations with her parents, is accompanied by many black-and-white and color photographs. (Rev: BL 4/15/03*; HB 7–8/03; HBG 10/03; SLJ 5/03*; VOYA 8/03) [730]

BOURKE-WHITE, MARGARET

5734 Ayer, Eleanor. *Margaret Bourke-White: Photographing the World* (6–10). Series: People in Focus. 1992, Dillon LB $13.95 (0-87518-513-4). A lively account of the photographer's craft and technique, her long association with *Life* magazine, and the subjects she recorded, from the Depression and Buchenwald concentration camp to Gandhi. (Rev: BL 12/1/92; SLJ 11/92) [921]

5735 Daffron, Carolyn. *Margaret Bourke-White* (7–12). Illus. 1988, Chelsea LB $19.95 (1-55546-644-3). The life story of this famous photographer in an account well illustrated with the artist's work. (Rev: BL 5/1/88; BR 5–6/88; SLJ 8/88) [921]

5736 Rubin, Susan Goldman. *Margaret Bourke-White: Her Pictures Were Her Life* (6–12). Illus. 1999, Abrams $19.95 (0-8109-4381-6). An excellent biography of a courageous, highly disciplined photographer whose work remains a hallmark of quality in the field. (Rev: BL 11/1/99* ; HBG 4/00) [770]

5737 Wooten, Sara McIntosh. *Margaret Bourke-White: Daring Photographer* (6–10). Series: People to Know. 2002, Enslow LB $20.95 (0-7660-1534-

3). An accessible biography of the adventurous photographer with many examples of her work. (Rev: BL 9/15/02; HBG 3/03; SLJ 11/02; VOYA 6/03) [921]

BRADY, MATHEW

5738 Sullivan, George. *Mathew Brady: His Life and Photographs* (6–10). 1994, Dutton $15.99 (0-525-65186-1). A biography of the photographer known for capturing the Civil War on film; includes reproductions of Brady's photographs. (Rev: BL 7/94; SLJ 12/94; VOYA 12/94) [921]

BRAQUE, GEORGES

5739 Wilkin, Karen. *Georges Braque* (9–12). Series: Modern Masters. 1992, Abbeville $35.00 (0-89659-944-2); paper $22.50 (0-89659-947-7). Examines the life, works, and style of the co-creator of Cubism. (Rev: BL 3/15/92) [921]

CALDER, ALEXANDER

5740 Lemaire, Gerard-Georges, ed. *Calder* (10–12). Trans. by Sophie Hawkes. Illus. 1998, Harry N. Abrams $11.98 (0-8109-4668-8). A colorful book that presents an overview of Calder's life and work, supplemented by full-color plates that introduce his major periods and styles. (Rev: SLJ 11/98) [921]

CASSATT, MARY

5741 Mathews, Nancy Mowll. *Mary Cassatt: A Life* (9–12). Series: Rizzoli Art. 1994, Villard $28.00 (0-394-58497-X); 1993, Rizzoli paper $7.95 (0-8478-1611-7). This biography of the renowned American Impressionist painter details her life as a single woman in the Parisian artistic community. (Rev: BL 3/1/94*) [921]

CEZANNE, PAUL

5742 Rewald, John. *Cezanne: A Biography* (10–12). 1986, Abrams (0-8109-0775-5). This handsome book tells the life story of the artist Paul Cezanne and reproduces many of his works. [921]

CHAGALL, MARC

5743 Kagan, Andrew. *Marc Chagall* (9–12). Illus. 1989, Abbeville $32.95 (0-89659-932-9); paper $14.95 (0-89659-935-3). The life and work of this Russian Jewish painter whose faith and fantastic imagination dominated his work. (Rev: BL 12/15/89) [921]

5744 Pozzi, Gianni. *Chagall* (6–12). Illus. Series: Masters of Art. 1998, Bedrick $22.50 (0-87226-527-7). The life and times of Chagall, along with his painting techniques, methods, and materials, are covered in text and full-color illustrations in this oversize book. (Rev: BL 3/1/98; SLJ 12/97) [709]

CHONG, GORDON H.

5745 *The Success of Gordon H. Chong and Associates: An Architecture Success Story* (7–10). Illus. Series: Success. 1996, Walker $15.95 (0-8027-8307-4). The amazing rise of the contemporary American architect, with examples of his work. (Rev: BL 5/15/96; SLJ 9/96) [921]

CLAUDEL, CAMILLE

5746 Ayral-Clause, Odile. *Camille Claudel* (10–12). Illus. 2002, Abrams $29.95 (0-8109-4077-9). French sculptor Claudel's tragic life is revealed in this moving biography that discusses her youth, career, her tortured relationship with Rodin, and her failing mental health. (Rev: BL 4/1/02*) [921]

CLOSE, CHUCK

5747 Greenberg, Jan, and Sandra Jordan. *Chuck Close, Up Close* (7–12). 1998, DK paper $19.95 (0-7894-2486-X). This is the inspiring story of the artist Chuck Close, who, in spite of a spinal collapse that left him paralyzed and in a wheelchair, continued to paint with a brush strapped to his hand. (Rev: BCCB 5/98; BL 3/15/98; HB 5–6/98*; HBG 9/98; SLJ 3/98; VOYA 8/98) [921]

CURTIS, EDWARD S.

5748 Lawlor, Laurie. *Shadow Catcher: The Life and Work of Edward S. Curtis* (6–12). 1994, Walker LB $20.85 (0-8027-8289-2). The personal and professional highlights of the life of this little-known, largely unappreciated photojournalist who was determined to preserve the lore of Native Americans. (Rev: BL 12/1/94; SLJ 2/95; VOYA 12/94) [921]

DALI, SALVADOR

5749 Ross, Michael Elsohn. *Salvador Dali and the Surrealists: Their Lives and Ideas* (9–12). Illus. 2003, Chicago Review paper $17.95 (1-55652-479-X). This profile of the life and work of the Spanish-born painter and his fellow Surrealists is supplemented by period photographs and representative examples of their works. (Rev: BL 11/1/03; HBG 4/04; SLJ 12/03) [759.6]

DA VINCI, LEONARDO

5750 Kallen, Stuart A., and P. M. Boekkhoff. *Leonardo da Vinci* (7–12). Series: The Importance Of. 2000, Lucent LB $18.96 (1-56006-604-0). The life, accomplishments, and significance of this multi-talented genius are covered in this fine biography. (Rev: BL 8/00; HBG 9/00) [921]

5751 McLanathan, Richard. *Leonardo da Vinci* (7–12). 1990, Abrams $22.95 (0-8109-1256-2). A readable, inviting introduction to the master painter, inventor, and scientist. (Rev: BL 12/15/90; SLJ 2/91*) [921]

5752 Romei, Francesca. *Leonardo da Vinci: Artist, Inventor and Scientist of the Renaissance* (6–12). Illus. Series: Masters of Art. 1995, Bedrick $22.50 (0-87226-313-4). A historical and artistic overview of Leonardo, his life, art, inventions, and other accomplishments. (Rev: BL 4/1/95; SLJ 2/95) [921]

5753 White, Michael. *Leonardo: The First Scientist* (10–12). Illus. 2000, St. Martin's $27.95 (0-312-20333-0). For better readers, this is a fine portrayal of the personal and public lives of the famous painter, sculptor, writer, scientist, and philosopher. (Rev: BL 6/1–15/00) [921]

DEGAS, EDGAR

5754 Meyer, Susan E. *Edgar Degas* (7–12). 1994, Abrams $19.95 (0-8109-3220-2). The life and work of this French artist are examined in this well-illustrated volume that contains reproductions of both his paintings and sculpture. (Rev: BL 1/1/95; SLJ 10/94) [921]

FABERGÉ, CARL

5755 von Habsburg-Lothringen, Geza. *Carl Fabergé* (6–10). 1994, Abrams $19.95 (0-8109-3324-1). The history of the creations of the Russian artisan known for the priceless eggs, with color photographs. (Rev: BL 7/94; SLJ 6/94) [921]

GAUGUIN, PAUL

5756 Greenfeld, Howard. *Paul Gauguin* (7–12). Series: First Impressions. 1993, Abrams $19.95 (0-8109-3376-4). An examination of the life and work of this sometime-friend of van Gogh who journeyed to the South Seas in search of artistic inspiration and freedom. (Rev: BL 12/1/93; SLJ 1/94) [921]

HUNTER, CLEMENTINE

5757 Lyons, Mary E. *Talking with Tebe: Clementine Hunter, Memory Artist* (7–12). 1998, Houghton $17.00 (0-395-72031-1). This richly illustrated book, which quotes extensively from taped interviews and is as much about social history as about painting, tells the story of the first illiterate, self-taught African American folk artist to receive national attention for her work. (Rev: BCCB 1/99; BL 8/98; BR 5–6/99; HB 9–10/98; HBG 3/99; SLJ 9/98) [921]

KANE, BOB

5758 Kane, Bob, and Tom Andrae. *Batman and Me* (9–12). Illus. 1989, Eclipse $39.95 (1-56060-016-0); paper $14.95 (1-56060-017-9). An autobiography of the creator of Batman, Robin, and other characters in the comics plus lots of illustrations. (Rev: BL 4/15/90) [921]

LANGE, DOROTHEA

5759 Acker, Kerry. *Dorothea Lange* (9–12). Series: Women in the Arts. 2004, Chelsea LB $22.95 (0-7910-7460-9). The story of the great photographer of the Depression and the New Deal. (Rev: BL 3/15/04) [921]

5760 Lange, Dorothea, and Elizabeth Partridge. *Dorothea Lange — a Visual Life* (9–12). 1994, Smithsonian $55.00 (1-56098-350-7). As well as a biography of this important photographer, this volume includes examples of her work. (Rev: SLJ 7/95) [921]

5761 Partridge, Elizabeth. *Restless Spirit: The Life and Work of Dorothea Lange* (6–12). 1998, Viking $22.99 (0-670-87888-X). Using over 60 photographs, this photoessay tells of the personal and professional life of photographer Lange, her many problems, and her artistic accomplishments, particularly during the Depression and World War II. (Rev: BCCB 12/98; BL 10/15/98; HB 3–4/99; HBG 3/99; SLJ 10/98; VOYA 8/99) [921]

LEWIN, TED

5762 Lewin, Ted. *I Was a Teenage Professional Wrestler* (7–12). 1993, Hyperion paper $6.95 (0-7868-1009-2). Memoir of a children's book author/illustrator about his wrestling career in the 1950s, showing the human side of the sport. (Rev: BL 6/1–15/93*; SLJ 7/93*; VOYA 10/93) [921]

LEWIS, EDMONIA

5763 Wolfe, Rinna. *Edmonia Lewis: Wildfire in Marble* (6–10). Illus. Series: People in Focus. 1998, Silver Burdett LB $18.95 (0-382-39713-4); paper $7.95 (0-382-39714-2). An excellent documentary about the life and work of a woman of African/Chippewa Indian heritage who overcame racism to win a college education, went to Europe to develop her talent, and achieved international acclaim as a sculptor. (Rev: SLJ 8/98; VOYA 8/98) [921]

MANET, EDOUARD

5764 Wright, Patricia. *Manet* (10–12). Series: Eyewitness Art. 1993, DK $16.95 (1-56458-172-1). An excellent introduction to the life and work of this French painter with many reproductions of his paintings. [921]

MARSHALL, KERRY JAMES

5765 Marshall, Kerry James, et al. *Kerry James Marshall* (10–12). Illus. 2000, Abrams $29.95 (0-8109-3527-9). A beautifully illustrated volume on this great African American artist with essays by a number of people on his life and art. (Rev: BL 12/15/00) [921]

MATISSE, HENRI

5766 Kostenevich, Albert, and Lory Frankel. *Henri Matisse* (9–12). Illus. Series: First Impressions Introductions to Art. 1997, Abrams $19.95 (0-8109-4296-8). A handsome introduction to the life and work of Matisse, with material on his artistic experimentation and evolving techniques. (Rev: BL 2/1/98; BR 5–6/98) [921]

MICHELANGELO

5767 Di Cagno, Gabriella. *Michelangelo* (6–12). Illus. Series: Masters of Art. 1996, Bedrick $22.50 (0-87226-319-3). The life, times, and accomplishments of Michelangelo are covered through outstanding reproductions, brief text, and many illustrations. (Rev: BL 11/15/96; SLJ 12/96; VOYA 4/97) [921]

5768 McLanathan, Richard. *Michelangelo* (7–12). Series: First Impressions. 1993, Abrams $19.95 (0-8109-3634-8). A handsomely illustrated volume that surveys the life, times, and art of this Italian master. (Rev: BL 6/1–15/93) [700921]

5769 Murray, Linda. *Michelangelo: His Life, Work and Times* (10–12). 1984, Thames & Hudson paper $14.95 (0-500-20174-9). A short, accurate biography that also introduces Michelangelo's art and architecture. [921]

MIRÓ, JOAN

5770 Higdon, Elizabeth. *Joan Miró* (7–12). Series: Rizzoli Art. 1993, Rizzoli paper $7.95 (0-8478-1667-2). A lavishly illustrated biography of this influential, innovative 20th-century Spanish painter. (Rev: BL 1/15/94) [921]

MONET, CLAUDE

5771 Waldron, Ann. *Claude Monet* (7–12). Series: First Impressions. 1991, Abrams $19.95 (0-8109-3620-8). This illustrated biographical study of the pioneering Impressionist painter explores his fascination with nature and his experimentation with the effects of light. (Rev: BL 11/15/91; SLJ 1/92) [921]

MORGAN, JULIA

5772 James, Cary. *Julia Morgan: Architect* (7–10). Illus. 1990, Chelsea LB $19.95 (1-55546-669-9).

The story of the outstanding female architect who now has more than 700 projects to her credit. (Rev: SLJ 8/90) [921]

MOSES, GRANDMA

5773 Biracree, Tom. *Grandma Moses* (7–10). Illus. 1989, Chelsea LB $19.95 (1-55546-670-2). This primitive artist's life and works are discussed, and insets are provided of some of her paintings. (Rev: BL 12/1/89; BR 3–4/90; SLJ 1/90; VOYA 2/90) [921]

O'KEEFFE, GEORGIA

5774 Berry, Michael. *Georgia O'Keeffe: Painter* (7–12). Illus. 1988, Chelsea LB $19.95 (1-55546-673-7). Illustrated chiefly in black and white, this is the story of the artist who reached maturity painting subjects in the southwestern states. (Rev: BL 9/15/88; BR 5–6/89; SLJ 9/88; VOYA 2/89) [921]

OROZCO, JOSE

5775 Cruz, Barbara C. *Jose Clemente Orozco: Mexican Artist* (7–12). Series: Hispanic Biographies. 1998, Enslow LB $20.95 (0-7660-1041-4). The story of the great artist Orozco, as well as an introduction to the mural painters of Mexico and how they used designs from Aztec and Mayan art. (Rev: BL 1/1–15/99; HBG 3/99; SLJ 3/99) [921]

PARKS, GORDON

5776 Parks, Gordon. *Half Past Autumn: A Retrospective* (7–12). 1997, Bulfinch $65.00 (0-8212-2298-8); paper $40.00 (0-8212-2503-0). Using nearly 300 photographs, this great photographer recounts and reflects on his life and struggles. (Rev: BL 8/97; VOYA 12/98) [921]

PICASSO, PABLO

5777 Beardsley, John. *Pablo Picasso* (7–12). Series: First Impressions. 1991, Abrams $19.95 (0-8109-3713-1). Succinctly describes Picasso's bohemian lifestyle and analyzes his ever-changing styles, methods, and subjects. (Rev: BL 11/15/91; SLJ 1/92) [921]

5778 Leal, Brigitte, et al. *The Ultimate Picasso* (10–12). Trans. by Molly Stevens and Marjolijn de Jager. Illus. 2000, Abrams $95.00 (0-8109-3940-1). This expensive but definitive volume on the life and work of Picasso contains thought-provoking articles and 1,235 illustrations. (Rev: BL 12/15/00; SLJ 6/01) [921]

5779 Loria, Stefano. *Picasso* (6–12). Illus. Series: Masters of Art. 1996, Bedrick $22.50 (0-87226-318-5). A stunning combination of text and excellent reproductions brings this Spanish artist's life and work into focus. (Rev: BL 5/15/96) [921]

5780 MacDonald, Patricia A. *Pablo Picasso: Greatest Artist of the 20th Century* (7–10). Illus. Series: Giants of Art and Culture. 2001, Blackbirch LB $21.95 (1-56711-504-7). Picasso's life and career are placed in historical context, with photographs, a timeline, a glossary, and lists of resources. (Rev: BL 8/01; HBG 3/02) [709]

REMBRANDT VAN RIJN

5781 Pescio, Claudio. *Rembrandt and Seventeenth-Century Holland* (6–12). Illus. Series: Masters of Art. 1996, Bedrick $22.50 (0-87226-317-7). This excellent art book traces the flowering of Dutch art through text and reproductions by focusing on Rembrandt, his work, and his followers. (Rev: BL 5/15/96; SLJ 3/96*; VOYA 6/96) [921]

5782 Schwartz, Gary. *Rembrandt* (7–12). Series: First Impressions. 1992, Abrams $19.95 (0-8109-3760-3). This jargon-free, accessible biography presents Rembrandt with all his flaws and quirks. (Rev: BL 5/1/92; SLJ 6/92*) [921]

5783 Silver, Larry. *Rembrandt* (9–12). Series: Rizzoli Art. 1993, Rizzoli paper $7.95 (0-8478-1519-6). This handsome, oversize book consists mainly of reproductions but also provides material on the artist's life and times. (Rev: BL 4/1/93; SLJ 1/93) [921]

RENOIR, PIERRE AUGUSTE

5784 Rayfield, Susan. *Pierre-Auguste Renoir* (7–12). Series: First Impressions. 1998, Abrams $19.95 (0-8109-3795-6). A stunning book that focuses on Renoir's development as an Impressionist painter, with detailed discussions about individual pictures, full-color, full-page reproductions, and two double-page foldouts. (Rev: BL 12/1/98; HBG 3/99) [921]

RIVERA, DIEGO

5785 Goldstein, Ernest. *The Journey of Diego Rivera* (7–10). Illus. 1996, Lerner LB $23.93 (0-8225-2066-4). Though short on biographical material, this profusely illustrated volume is a fine introduction to Rivera's art and its connections to the history of Mexico. (Rev: BL 4/15/96; SLJ 1/96; VOYA 10/96) [921]

SCHULKE, FLIP

5786 Schulke, Flip. *Witness to Our Times: My Life as a Photojournalist* (6–12). Illus. 2003, Cricket $19.95 (0-8126-2682-6). In this volume full of examples of his work, Schulke describes his early life and his career covering events of the 20th century including the space program and the civil rights

movement. (Rev: BL 4/15/03; HBG 10/03; SLJ 6/03; VOYA 2/04) [070.4]

SCHULZ, CHARLES M.

5787 *Schulz: Conversations* (9–12). Ed. by M. Thomas Inge. Illus. 2000, Univ. Press of Mississippi $48.00 (1-57806-304-3); paper $20.00 (1-57806-305-1). This collection of 16 interviews with the modest creator of Peanuts covers his biography, work, attitudes, and his philosophy of life. (Rev: BL 10/1/00) [921]

5788 Schuman, Michael A. *Charles M. Schulz: Cartoonist and Creator of Peanuts* (6–10). Series: People to Know. 2002, Enslow LB $20.95 (0-7660-1846-6). A fine biography of the creator of Peanuts, complete with many illustrations and cartoons. (Rev: BL 9/15/02; HBG 10/02) [921]

ULMANN, DORIS

5789 Jacobs, Philip Walker. *The Life and Photography of Doris Ulmann* (9–12). Illus. 2001, Univ. Press of Kentucky $40.00 (0-8131-2175-2). The people of Appalachia and rural African Americans were the main subjects of the pioneering American photographer whose life and work are chronicled in this handsome volume. (Rev: BL 2/15/01) [921]

UNGERER, TOMI

5790 Ungerer, Tomi. *Tomi: A Childhood Under the Nazis* (6–10). 1998, Roberts Rinehart $29.95 (1-57098-163-9). Using many memorabilia of the time, this is the illustrator's story of his life during World War II after the Germans entered his Alsace town in 1940 when he was 8 years old. (Rev: BL 12/15/98; SLJ 3/99) [921]

VAN GOGH, VINCENT

5791 Bonafoux, Pascal. *Van Gogh: The Passionate Eye* (7–12). Series: Discoveries. 1992, Abrams paper $12.95 (0-8109-2828-0). An overview of the life and work of this disturbed Dutch painter. (Rev: BL 7/92) [021]

5792 Crispino, Enrica. *Van Gogh* (6–12). Illus. Series: Masters of Art. 1996, Bedrick $22.50 (0-87226-525-0). The story of van Gogh's life and art is covered in a concise text, excellent reproductions, and engrossing diagrams. (Rev: BL 11/15/96; SLJ 12/96; VOYA 4/97) [921]

5793 Greenberg, Jan, and Sandra Jordan. *Vincent van Gogh: Portrait of an Artist* (7–12). Illus. 2001, Delacorte $14.95 (0-385-32806-0). This absorbing biography gives details of van Gogh's life and work, but also presents his complex personality, attributing his erratic behavior not to madness but to

331

epilepsy. (Rev: BL 8/01*; HB 11–12/01; HBG 3/02; SLJ 9/01*) [759.9492]

5794 Schapiro, Meyer. *Vincent van Gogh* (10–12). 2000, Abradale $19.98 (0-8109-8117-3). The life of van Gogh is detailed, with a generous use of quotations from his letters. [921]

5795 Tyson, Peter. *Vincent van Gogh: Artist* (8–12). Illus. Series: Great Achievers: Lives of the Physically Challenged. 1996, Chelsea LB $21.95 (0-7910-2422-9). This mature biography discusses van Gogh's life and work and his contributions to Impressionism, achieved despite the deterioration of his mental health. (Rev: BL 5/1/96; SLJ 8/96) [921]

VERMEER, JOHANNES

5796 Bailey, Anthony. *Vermeer: A View of Delft* (10–12). 2001, Holt paper $16.00 (0-8050-6930-5). The story of the personal and professional life of this great Dutch painter and of his life in Delft. (Rev: BL 4/15/01) [921]

WARHOL, ANDY

5797 Faerna, Jose M., ed. *Warhol* (10–12). Illus. 1997, Harry N. Abrams $11.98 (0-8109-4655-6). This tribute to the artist Andy Warhol contains an essay about the times in which he lived, a biography, and a section of full-color reproductions of his work. (Rev: BL 11/15/97; SLJ 5/98) [921]

WHISTLER, JAMES MCNEILL

5798 Berman, Avis. *James McNeill Whistler* (7–12). Series: First Impressions. 1993, Abrams $19.95 (0-8109-3968-1). A failure at West Point and in the Coast Guard, Whistler later pursued a career in art in Paris, where he gained worldwide renown. This well-illustrated account traces his life and work. (Rev: BL 12/1/93) [921]

WRIGHT, FRANK LLOYD

5799 Boulton, Alexander O. *Frank Lloyd Wright, Architect: An Illustrated Biography* (8–12). 1993, Rizzoli $24.95 (0-8478-1683-4). Examines both Wright's architecture and his private life in detail. (Rev: BL 12/15/93; SLJ 11/93) [921]

5800 Rubin, Susan G. *Frank Lloyd Wright* (9–12). Series: First Impressions. 1994, Abrams $19.95 (0-8109-3974-6). A handsomely illustrated look at the architect's life and work. (Rev: BL 1/1/95; SLJ 1/95) [921]

WYETH, ANDREW

5801 Meryman, Richard. *Andrew Wyeth* (6–12). Series: First Impressions. 1991, Abrams $19.95 (0-8109-3956-8). Insights into the artist's childhood

show how various events influenced his life in this introduction to the work of this contemporary American master. (Rev: BL 8/91) [921]

5802 Wyeth, Andrew. *Andrew Wyeth, Autobiography* (10–12). 1995, Little, Brown $50.00 (0-8212-2159-0); paper $29.95 (0-8212-2569-3). This autobiography contains reproductions of 137 of Wyeth's paintings. (Rev: BL 11/15/95) [921]

Authors

ALCOTT, LOUISA MAY

5803 Anderson, William T. *The World of Louisa May Alcott: A First-Time Glimpse into the Life and Times of Louisa May Alcott, Author of "Little Women"* (10–12). 1995, HarperPerennial paper $25.00 (0-06-095156-7). A heavily illustrated look at the life, times, and important contemporaries of Louisa May Alcott. [921]

ALLENDE, ISABEL

5804 Allende, Isabel. *My Invented Country: A Nostalgic Journey Through Chile* (10–12). Trans. by Margaret Sayers Peden. 2003, HarperCollins $23.95 (0-06-054564-X). Along with the tale of her exile from her native Chile and her growing affection for the United States, Allende shares stories of her family and youth and of her career as a writer. (Rev: BL 4/1/03) [863]

ALVAREZ, JULIA

5805 Alvarez, Julia. *Something to Declare* (10–12). 1998, Algonquin $32.95 (1-56512-193-7). In 24 autobiographical essays, the author presents her Dominican childhood, her family's immigration to the United States, her college years, writing, marriages, and return trips to her homeland. (Rev: BL 8/98; SLJ 4/99) [921]

ANGELOU, MAYA

5806 Angelou, Maya. *All God's Children Need Traveling Shoes* (10–12). 1986, Random $19.95 (0-394-52143-9). In this fifth volume of Angelou's autobiography she tells of her four years in Ghana and a visit from Malcolm X. In order of publication and coverage the first four volumes are: *I Know Why the Caged Bird Sings* (1970), *Gather Together in My Name* (1974), *Singin' and Swingin' and Gettin' Merry Like Christmas* (1976), and *The Heart of a Woman* (1981). (Rev: BL 2/1/86; SLJ 8/86; VOYA 8/86) [921]

5807 Lisandrelli, Elaine S. *Maya Angelou: More than a Poet* (7–12). Illus. Series: African-American Biographies. 1996, Enslow LB $20.95 (0-89490-

684-4). A biography of the famous African American writer that includes her work as a dancer, singer, actress, and spokesperson for African American causes. (Rev: BL 9/1/96; BR 9–10/96; SLJ 6/96; VOYA 10/96) [921]

5808 Shapiro, Miles. *Maya Angelou* (7–10). Illus. Series: Black Americans of Achievement. 1994, Chelsea LB $21.95 (0-7910-1862-8). A chronological narrative of the life of this amazing African American writer that describes her hardships and triumphs. (Rev: BL 6/1–15/94; SLJ 6/94) [921]

AUSTEN, JANE

5809 Le Faye, Deirdre. *Jane Austen* (9–12). Series: British Library Writers' Lives. 1999, Oxford $36.95 (0-19-521440-4). An entertaining biography of this writer who lived a short, quiet life. The work is illustrated with plenty of photographs and sketches of places and people. (Rev: BL 3/15/99; BR 9–10/99; VOYA 6/99) [921]

5810 Shields, Carol. *Jane Austen* (10–12). Series: Penguin Lives. 2001, Viking $19.95 (0-670-89488-5). A concise biography of Austen with material on her influences, works, and impact on world literature. (Rev: BL 1/1–15/01) [921]

AVI

5811 Mercier, Cathryn M., and Susan P. Bloom. *Presenting Avi* (6–10). Series: Twayne's United States Authors. 1997, Macmillan $29.00 (0-8057-4569-6). This biography of the noted writer of books for children and young adults is divided into chapters based on roles he has assumed as a writer, including storyteller, stylist, magician, and historian, and explores his many beliefs about the significance of literature. (Rev: SLJ 6/98) [921]

BALDWIN, JAMES

5812 Gottfried, Ted. *James Baldwin: Voice from Harlem* (7–12). Series: Impact Biographies. 1997, Watts LB $20.00 (0-531-11318-3). This biography, enlivened with many photographs, discusses Baldwin's childhood, beliefs, gay identity, and principal works. (Rev: BL 5/15/97; SLJ 7/97; VOYA 10/97) [921]

5813 Kenan, Randall. *James Baldwin* (9–12). Series: Lives of Notable Gay Men and Lesbians. 1994, Chelsea LB $19.95 (0-7910-2301-X). Chronicles the pain and poverty of Baldwin's early adult years in Paris and gives a sense of his life as a black homosexual in a white world. (Rev: BL 3/1/94; SLJ 6/94; VOYA 6/94) [921]

BAWDEN, NINA

5814 Bawden, Nina. *In My Own Time: Almost an Autobiography* (8–12). 1995, Clarion $25.95 (0-395-74429-6). Bawden, the British author of numerous well-loved children's stories, writes of her own life. (Rev: BL 12/1/95) [921]

BIRSTEIN, ANN

5815 Birstein, Ann. *What I Saw at the Fair* (10–12). 2003, Welcome Rain $26.95 (1-56649-267-X). In this insightful, often-humorous memoir, novelist/critic Birstein recounts her childhood in New York City and looks back in anger at her 30-year marriage and the toll it took on her creativity. (Rev: BL 3/1/03) [810.9]

BRAGG, RICK

5816 Bragg, Rick. *All Over but the Shoutin'* (10–12). 1997, Pantheon $25.00 (0-679-44258-8). A memoir of the Pulitzer Prize-winning journalist who grew up in poverty in Alabama. (Rev: BL 9/15/97; SLJ 4/98) [921]

BRAY, ROSEMARY

5817 Bray, Rosemary L. *Unafraid of the Dark: A Memoir* (10–12). 1998, Random $24.00 (0-679-42555-1); Doubleday paper $14.00 (0-385-49475-0). The author recounts growing up in Chicago on welfare, developing an interest in the civil rights movement while in high school, winning a scholarship to Yale, and becoming an editor at the *New York Times Book Review*. She concludes with a strong statement, based on her childhood, against the 1996 welfare-reform bill. (Rev: BL 1/1–15/98; SLJ 6/98) [921]

BRESLIN, ROSEMARY

5818 Breslin, Rosemary. *Not Exactly What I Had in Mind: An Incurable Love Story* (10–12). 1997, Villard $23.00 (0-679-45217-6). This painful yet humorous and heartwarming autobiography of the daughter of writer Jimmy Breslin tells of her rebellious teens and early 20s, her incurable blood disease, and the great love who came into her life and later became her husband. (Rev: BL 12/1/96; SLJ 9/97) [921]

BRONTË, CHARLOTTE

5819 Gordon, Lyndall. *Charlotte Brontë: A Passionate Life* (10–12). 1995, Norton paper $17.00 (0-393-31448-0). A skilled biography of the English writer who was also a courageous survivor and a woman of great emotion. [921]

BRONTË FAMILY

5820 Bentley, Phyllis. *The Brontës and Their World* (9–12). Illus. 1986, Thames & Hudson paper $12.95 (0-500-26016-8). A richly illustrated biography of the three Brontë sisters and their wayward brother. [921]

BROOKS, GWENDOLYN

5821 Rhynes, Martha E. *Gwendolyn Brooks: Poet from Chicago* (6–10). Illus. Series: World Writers. 2003, Morgan Reynolds LB $21.95 (1-931798-05-2). The chronological presentation in this biography provides readers with an understanding of Brooks's changing views and themes. (Rev: BL 2/15/03; HBG 10/03; SLJ 4/03; VOYA 6/03) [811]

BROWN, CLAUDE

5822 Brown, Claude. *Manchild in the Promised Land* (9–12). 1965, NAL paper $4.95 (0-451-15741-9). A realistic picture of growing up in Harlem in the 1950s. [921]

BRUCHAC, JOSEPH

5823 Bruchac, Joseph. *Bowman's Store: A Journey to Myself* (9–12). Illus. 1997, Dial $17.99 (0-8037-1997-3). The prolific Native American author writes about his childhood, his racial heritage, and his maternal grandfather, who raised him and gave him support and encouragement. (Rev: BL 9/1/97; SLJ 12/97; VOYA 2/98) [921]

BUCK, PEARL S.

5824 La Farge, Ann. *Pearl Buck* (7–10). Illus. 1988, Chelsea LB $19.95 (1-55546-645-1). The life of the writer who introduced pre-Revolutionary China to millions of American readers. (Rev: BL 8/88) [921]

BYRON, LORD

5825 Garrett, Martin. *George Gordon, Lord Byron* (9–12). Series: British Library Writers' Lives. 2000, Oxford LB $22.95 (0-19-521677-6). This biography of the dashing poet and adventurer Lord Byron uses many quotations from his works and his other writings. (Rev: BL 3/1/01; HBG 10/01; SLJ 2/01) [921]

CAMUS, ALBERT

5826 Bronner, Stephen Eric. *Albert Camus: The Thinker, the Artist, the Man* (9–12). Series: Impact Biographies. 1996, Watts LB $24.00 (0-531-11305-1). A clear examination of the Nobel Prize winner's personal life, thoughts, and writing. (Rev: SLJ 2/97) [921]

CARROLL, LEWIS

5827 Cohen, Morton Norton. *Lewis Carroll: A Biography* (10–12). 1995, Knopf paper $14.36 (0-679-74562-9). Illustrated with many drawings by Carroll, this is a fine biography of the author-mathematician. [921]

CATHER, WILLA

5828 Keene, Ann T. *Willa Cather* (7–12). 1994, Messner LB $15.00 (0-671-86760-1). A biography examining the writer's childhood, college years, jobs as editor and teacher, travels, and friends, as well as her reputed lesbianism. (Rev: BL 10/1/94; SLJ 11/94; VOYA 4/95) [813]

5829 O'Brien, Sharon. *Willa Cather* (7–12). Series: Lives of Notable Gay Men and Lesbians. 1994, Chelsea LB $19.95 (0-7910-2302-8); paper $9.95 (0-7910-2877-1). Focuses on the author's reputed lesbianism and shows how Cather created a nurturing network of women friends and lovers. (Rev: BL 11/1/94; SLJ 11/94; VOYA 2/95) [921]

CHESNUTT, CHARLES

5830 Thompson, Cliff. *Charles Chesnutt* (7–10). Series: Black Americans of Achievement. 1992, Chelsea LB $19.95 (1-55546-578-1). The life of this pioneering African American writer who explored themes relating to slavery and the Reconstruction period in his fiction. (Rev: BL 12/1/92) [921]

CHRISTIE, AGATHA

5831 Gill, Gillian. *Agatha Christie: The Woman and Her Mysteries* (9–12). 1990, Free Pr. (0-02-911702-X). This is a fine biography of the English mystery story writer and of the multitude of thrillers she produced. (Rev: SLJ 2/91) [92]

CLARK, MARY HIGGINS

5832 Clark, Mary Higgins. *Kitchen Privileges* (10–12). 2002, Simon & Schuster $24.00 (0-7432-0605-3). The mystery writer describes her childhood and her struggles as an adult to get her writings published. (Rev: BL 11/15/02) [921]

CLEARY, BEVERLY

5833 Cleary, Beverly. *A Girl from Yamhill: A Memoir* (6–12). Illus. 1988, Morrow $21.99 (0-688-07800-1). Details the early life in the Northwest of one of the greats of children's literature. (Rev: BL 6/1/88; BR 5–6/88; SLJ 5/88; VOYA 6/88) [921]

5834 Cleary, Beverly. *My Own Two Feet* (7–12). 1995, Morrow $15.00 (0-688-14267-2). In the second part of Cleary's candid autobiography, she departs for college. Although most appreciated by adults who grew up with her books, it also has a place on youth shelves. (Rev: BL 8/95*; SLJ 9/95) [921]

CONROY, PAT

5835 Conroy, Pat. *My Losing Season* (10–12). 2002, Doubleday $26.00 (0-385-48912-9). Conroy describes his lifelong love of basketball and the lessons the game has taught him. (Rev: BL 8/02) [796.323]

COURLANDER, HAROLD

5836 Jaffe, Nina. *A Voice for the People: The Life and Work of Harold Courlander* (7–10). Illus. 1997, Holt $16.95 (0-8050-3444-7). A biography of the famous collector of folk tales from minority groups who was also a noted writer and storyteller. (Rev: BL 11/1/97; HBG 3/98; SLJ 12/97) [921]

CRANE, STEPHEN

5837 Davis, Linda H. *Badge of Courage: The Life of Stephen Crane* (10–12). 1998, Houghton $35.00 (0-89919-934-8). A look at Crane's short life and his literary accomplishments. (Rev: BL 7/98) [921]

CRUTCHER, CHRIS

5838 Crutcher, Chris. *King of the Mild Frontier: An Ill-Advised Autobiography* (8–12). 2003, Greenwillow LB $17.89 (0-06-050250-9). With humor and honesty, Crutcher describes his youth and his tense relationship with his family. (Rev: BL 4/15/03*; HB 5–6/03; HBG 10/03; SLJ 4/03; VOYA 6/03) [813]

5839 Davis, Terry. *Presenting Chris Crutcher* (6–10). 1997, Macmillan $29.00 (0-8057-8223-0). A warm biography of this important young adult author who combines sports stories with important themes such as tolerance and the meaning of friendship. (Rev: SLJ 6/98; VOYA 6/98) [921]

DAHL, ROALD

5840 Dahl, Roald. *Boy: Tales of Childhood* (7–12). Illus. 1984, Farrar $17.00 (0-374-37374-4). The famous author's autobiography — sometimes humorous, sometimes touching — of growing up in Wales and spending summers in Norway. (Rev: BL 6/87) [921]

5841 Dahl, Roald. *Going Solo* (9–12). Illus. 1986, Farrar $14.95 (0-374-16503-3); Penguin paper $9.95 (0-14-010306-6). This book recounts the author's World War II activities in Africa and the Royal Air Force. For an older audience than his earlier autobiographical *Boy* (1985). (Rev: BL 9/1/86; VOYA 2/87) [921]

D'ANGELO, PASCAL

5842 Murphy, Jim. *Pick and Shovel Poet: The Journeys of Pascal D'Angelo* (6–12). Illus. 2000, Clarion $20.00 (0-395-77610-4). The story of the short, hard life of the Italian American poet who wrote an important autobiography about coming to the New World. (Rev: BCCB 12/00; BL 3/1/01; HB 1–2/01; HBG 3/01; SLJ 1/01; VOYA 2/02) [973.04]

DANZIGER, PAULA

5843 Krull, Kathleen. *Presenting Paula Danziger* (6–12). Series: United States Authors. 1995, Twayne $29.00 (0-8057-4153-4). Examines writer Danziger's personal problems, humorous teaching experiences, and group discussions of her books in six thematic chapters. (Rev: BL 9/1/95; VOYA 2/96) [921]

DICKENS, CHARLES

5844 Kaplan, Fred. *Dickens: A Biography* (10–12). 1998, Johns Hopkins Univ. Pr. $19.95 (0-8018-6018-0). A portrait of Dickens's life from youth with details of his various adult roles. [921]

5845 Smiley, Jane. *Charles Dickens* (10–12). 2002, Viking $19.95 (0-670-03077-5). In her insightful biography, Smiley traces Dickens's life through his work, beginning with essays he wrote for a monthly magazine. (Rev: BL 4/1/02) [921]

DICKINSON, EMILY

5846 Longsworth, Polly. *The World of Emily Dickinson* (9–12). 1990, Norton paper $19.95 (0-393-31656-4). This volume uses maps, drawings, and photographs to re-create the home, friends, and life of Emily Dickinson. [921]

5847 Olsen, Victoria. *Emily Dickinson* (7–12). Illus. 1990, Chelsea LB $19.95 (1-55546-649-4). An illustrated biography that describes the life of Emily Dickinson as well as her work. (Rev: BL 7/90) [921]

DINESEN, ISAK

5848 Dinesen, Isak. *Out of Africa and Shadows on the Grass* (10–12). 1989, Vintage paper $13.95 (0-679-72475-3). These two books, reprinted in one volume, tell of the author's experiences in Africa and her recollections of her servants. [921]

DOYLE, SIR ARTHUR CONAN

5849 Pascal, Janet B. *Arthur Conan Doyle: Beyond Baker Street* (7–12). Illus. 2000, Oxford $28.00 (0-19-512262-3). This biography of the creator of Sherlock Holmes tells how he was also a defender of those unjustly accused of crimes, a spiritualist, and a prolific author in various genres. (Rev: BL 2/15/00; HBG 9/00; SLJ 6/00) [921]

5850 Symons, Julian. *Conan Doyle: Portrait of an Artist* (9–12). Illus. 1987, Mysterious $9.95 (0-89296-926-1). A biography that points out the similarities between Doyle and his creation, Sherlock Holmes. (Rev: BL 11/1/87) [921]

DUNBAR, PAUL LAURENCE

5851 Gentry, Tony. *Paul Laurence Dunbar* (7–12). Illus. 1988, Chelsea LB $21.95 (1-55546-583-8). A richly illustrated biography of one of the chief poets of the Harlem Renaissance of the 1920s. (Rev: BL 2/15/89; BR 1–289; SLJ 3/89; VOYA 2/89) [921]

EDMONDS, WALTER D.

5852 Edmonds, Walter D. *Tales My Father Never Told* (9–12). 1995, Syracuse Univ. Pr. $29.95 (0-8156-0307-X). An author's memoir of his privileged New York upbringing by a demanding father and loving mother. (Rev: BL 3/15/95) [921]

EGGERS, DAVE

5853 Eggers, Dave. *A Heartbreaking Work of Staggering Genius* (10–12). 2000, Simon & Schuster $26.00 (0-684-86347-2). Part truth and part fiction, this adult humorous memoir tells how the author, just out of college, relocates to Berkeley, California, to found a satirical magazine and care for his 8-year-old brother. (Rev: BL 1/1–15/00*) [921]

ELLISON, RALPH

5854 Bishop, Jack. *Ralph Ellison* (9–12). Illus. 1987, Chelsea LB $19.95 (1-55546-585-4). A biography of the writer of the acclaimed novel *Invisible Man* and his struggle for acceptance in both black and white cultures. (Rev: BL 2/15/88; SLJ 6/88) [921]

FEIG, PAUL

5855 Feig, Paul. *Kick Me: Adventures in Adolescence* (10–12). 2002, Crown paper $12.95 (0-609-80943-1). In this collection of humorous essays about his youth, Feig, creator of the television show *Freaks and Geeks*, covers everything from his lack of success with the opposite sex to a disastrous secret excursion into the world of cross-dressing. (Rev: BL 9/15/02; SLJ 2/03) [305.235]

FISHER, ANTWONE QUENTON

5856 Fisher, Antwone Quenton. *Finding Fish: A Memoir* (10–12). 2001, HarperCollins $25.00 (0-688-17699-2). Antwone Quenton Fisher, now a screenwriter and movie producer, relates his diffi-

cult childhood — born to a single teen mother in a prison hospital — and adolescence. (Rev: VOYA 10/01) [921]

FITZGERALD, F. SCOTT

5857 Prigozy, Ruth. *F. Scott Fitzgerald* (10–12). Illus. Series: Overlook Illustrated Lives. 2002, Overlook $19.95 (1-58567-265-3). This brief, well-illustrated, and accessible biography focuses mainly on the author's life. (Rev: BL 7/02) [921]

5858 Tessitore, John. *F. Scott Fitzgerald: The American Dreamer* (7–12). Illus. 2001, Watts LB $24.00 (0-531-13955-7). An absorbing biography that recounts the author's complicated and ultimately tragic life. (Rev: BL 11/1/01; SLJ 11/01) [813]

FLEISCHMAN, SID

5859 Fleischman, Sid. *The Abracadabra Kid: A Writer's Life* (6–12). Illus. 1996, Greenwillow $16.99 (0-688-14859-X). The exciting autobiography of the famous author who was also a magician, gold miner, and World War II sailor. (Rev: BL 9/1/96*; BR 9–10/96; SLJ 8/96*; VOYA 4/97) [921]

FOX, PAULA

5860 Fox, Paula. *Borrowed Finery* (10–12). 2001, Holt $23.00 (0-8050-6815-5). The prize-winning author tells of her childhood in a family where her mother rejected her and her father was an alcoholic. (Rev: BL 9/1/01) [921]

FRITZ, JEAN

5861 Fritz, Jean. *China Homecoming* (8–12). Illus. 1985, Putnam $19.99 (0-399-21182-9). This autobiographical account describes the author's return to China, where she spent her childhood. (Rev: SLJ 8/85) [921]

5862 Fritz, Jean. *Homesick, My Own Story* (9–12). 1982, Putnam $15.99 (0-399-20933-6); Dell paper $4.99 (0-440-43683-4). This popular author writes about her early life in China. (Rev: BL 2/1/89) [921]

FROST, ROBERT

5863 Meyers, Jeffrey. *Robert Frost: A Biography* (10–12). 1996, Houghton $30.00 (0-395-72809-6). A detailed biography of this beloved American poet, focusing on his development as a poet and including explanations of many of his literary allusions. (Rev: BL 4/1/96; SLJ 9/96) [921]

GANTOS, JACK

5864 Gantos, Jack. *Hole in My Life* (8–12). 2002, Farrar $16.00 (0-374-39988-3). The gritty story of

336

the author's experiences in prison after being convicted for drug smuggling — and his successful efforts to live a better life. (Rev: BCCB 5/02; BL 4/1/02; HB 5–6/02*; HBG 10/02; SLJ 5/02*; VOYA 6/02) [813.54]

GARCIA MARQUEZ, GABRIEL

5865 Garcia Marquez, Gabriel. *Living to Tell the Tale* (11–12). Trans. by Edith Grossman. 2003, Knopf $26.95 (1-4000-4134-1). In this first installment of what will be a three-volume memoir, recommended for mature teens only, author Gabriel Garcia Marquez interweaves recollections of his youth in Colombia with the contemporaneous history of his homeland. (Rev: BL 10/15/03*) [808]

GIOVANNI, NIKKI

5866 Josephson, Judith Pinkerton. *Nikki Giovanni: Poet of the People* (7–12). Series: African-American Biographies. 2000, Enslow LB $20.95 (0-7660-1238-7). The life and work of one of the most popular living poets, who has written both for adults and children, is covered in prose and pictures. (Rev: BL 9/15/00; HBG 3/01; SLJ 1/01) [921]

GORE, ARIEL

5867 Gore, Ariel. *Atlas of the Human Heart* (10–12). 2003, Seal paper $14.95 (1-58005-088-3). In this fascinating memoir, Ariel Gore, founder of *Hip Mama* magazine, describes her adventures on a three-year odyssey, starting at the age of 16, to the Far East and Europe. (Rev: BL 4/1/03) [305.235]

GUY, ROSA

5868 Norris, Jerrie. *Presenting Rosa Guy* (9–12). 1988, Twayne $20.95 (0-8057-8207-9). A critical biography of the West Indian-born writer who has re-created Harlem life so vividly in her books for young adults. (Rev: BR 5–6/89; SLJ 12/88; VOYA 12/88) [921]

HALEY, ALEX

5869 Shirley, David. *Alex Haley* (7–10). Series: Black Americans of Achievement. 1993, Chelsea LB $21.95 (0-7910-1979-9); paper $8.95 (0-7910-1980-2). The story of the African American writer who gave us the family saga *Roots*. (Rev: BL 2/15/94) [921]

HANSBERRY, LORRAINE

5870 Hansberry, Lorraine. *To Be Young, Gifted and Black* (9–12). 1970, NAL paper $6.99 (0-451-15952-7). An autobiographical collection of reminiscences, letters, and quotations from Hansberry's plays. [921]

5871 McKissack, Patricia, and Fredrick McKissack. *Young, Black, and Determined: A Biography of Lorraine Hansberry* (8–12). Illus. 1997, Holiday $18.95 (0-8234-1300-4). The story of the late African American playwright who skyrocketed to fame in 1959 when she was only 28 for the play *A Raisin in the Sun*, which opened on Broadway and won the Drama Critics Award. (Rev: BCCB 5/98; BL 2/15/98; SLJ 4/98; VOYA 8/98) [921]

5872 Scheader, Catherine. *Lorraine Hansberry: Playright and Voice of Justice* (7–10). Illus. Series: African-American Biographies. 1998, Enslow LB $20.95 (0-89490-945-2). Raised on Chicago's South Side, Lorraine Hansberry, writer and civil rights activist, used this setting for her prize-winning play *A Raisin in the Sun*. (Rev: BL 9/1/98; HBG 3/99; SLJ 11/98) [921]

5873 Sinnott, Susan. *Lorraine Hansberry: Award-Winning Playwright and Civil Rights Activist* (7–12). 1998, Conari paper $6.95 (1-57324-093-1). This story of the great African American playwright who grew up with a passion for theater and politics conveys a sense of the politics from the 1930s to the 1960s and the pressures of fame on an artist. (Rev: BL 2/15/99) [921]

HARRISON, JIM

5874 Harrison, Jim. *Off to the Side* (10–12). 2002, Grove Atlantic $25.00 (0-87113-860-3). Novelist Harrison looks at his career in writing and the circumstances of his early life that led to this choice. (Rev: BL 10/15/02) [921]

HARRISON, KATHRYN

5875 Harrison, Kathryn. *Seeking Rapture: Scenes from a Life* (11–12). 2003, Random $23.95 (0-375-50558-X). In her first collection of essays, the author describes her difficult childhood and her complex relationships with her mother and maternal grandparents. (Rev: BL 2/1/03) [921]

HAWTHORNE, NATHANIEL

5876 Miller, Edwin Haviland. *Salem Is My Dwelling Place: A Life of Nathaniel Hawthorne* (9–12). 1991, Univ. of Iowa Pr. $39.95 (0-87745-332-2); paper $24.95 (0-87745-381-0). Miller examines how the painfully shy 19th-century American writer gave voice to his inner torment through his writings, which include such classic novels as *The House of Seven Gables* and *The Scarlet Letter*. [921]

HEMINGWAY, ERNEST

5877 McDaniel, Melissa. *Ernest Hemingway: The Writer Who Suffered from Depression* (8–12). Series: Great Achievers: Lives of the Physically Challenged. 1996, Chelsea LB $19.95 (0-7910-

2420-2). This personal and literary biography emphasizes the way Hemingway contributed to and changed American literature, using many excerpts from his works as well as quotations from reviewers and critics, while also discussing his alcoholism and the emotional problems that eventually led to his suicide. (Rev: BR 5–6/97; SLJ 3/97) [921]

5878 Sandison, David. *Ernest Hemingway: An Illustrated Biography* (9–12). 1999, Chicago Review $24.95 (1-55652-399-4). A visually attractive, insightful biography organized into eight chronological chapters, combining biography, history, literature, and photography to show an amazingly talented yet tormented man. (Rev: SLJ 8/99) [921]

5879 Tessitore, John. *The Hunt and the Feast: A Life of Ernest Hemingway* (7–12). Illus. Series: Impact Biographies. 1996, Watts LB $24.00 (0-531-11289-6). An excellent introduction to the life and works of the writer considered to be one of America's great 20th-century masters. (Rev: BL 1/1–15/97; BR 3–4/97; SLJ 1/97) [921]

5880 Yannuzzi, Della A. *Ernest Hemingway: Writer and Adventurer* (6–10). Series: People to Know. 1998, Enslow LB $20.95 (0-89490-979-7). An engrossing biography of the tempestuous writer whose life and loves were as exciting as his novels. (Rev: BL 11/15/98; HBG 3/99; SLJ 4/99) [921]

HENRY, MARGUERITE

5881 Collins, David R. *Write a Book for Me: The Story of Marguerite Henry* (7–10). Illus. Series: World Writers. 1999, Morgan Reynolds LB $21.95 (1-883846-39-0). A short, simple biography of the writer of such memorable books for young people as *King of the Wind.* (Rev: BL 3/15/99; SLJ 9/99; VOYA 10/99) [921]

HERBERT, FRANK

5882 Herbert, Brian. *Dreamer of Dune: The Biography of Frank Herbert* (10–12). Illus. 2003, Tor $27.95 (0-765-30646-8). A loving but frank biography of the science fiction author by his son. (Rev: BL 2/15/03) [813]

HOOKS, BELL

5883 Hooks, Bell. *Bone Black, Memories of Girlhood* (10–12). 1996, Holt $20.00 (0-8050-4145-1). Using 61 short vignettes, the author describes growing up in a southern town as an African American rebel in a large family, and how she became the writer she is today. (Rev: BL 9/15/96; SLJ 3/97) [921]

HUGHES, LANGSTON

5884 Hill, Christine M. *Langston Hughes: Poet of the Harlem Renaissance* (6–10). Series: African-American Biographies. 1997, Enslow LB $20.95 (0-89490-815-4). An easy-to-read, accurate look at the poet's life and times, with good-quality black-and-white photographs. (Rev: BR 3–4/98; SLJ 1/98) [921]

5885 Meltzer, Milton. *Langston Hughes: An Illustrated Edition* (6–12). Illus. 1997, Millbrook paper $20.95 (0-7613-0327-8). A new, large, well-illustrated edition of the highly respected 1968 biography of Langston Hughes. (Rev: BL 8/97; BR 3–4/98; SLJ 11/97; VOYA 2/98) [920]

5886 Osofsky, Audrey. *Free to Dream: The Making of a Poet, Langston Hughes* (6–10). Illus. 1996, Lothrop $16.00 (0-688-10605-6). An attractive biography that covers the writer's life and works as well as providing general information on the Harlem Renaissance. (Rev: BL 4/1/96; BR 9–10/96; SLJ 7/96) [921]

5887 Rummel, Jack. *Langston Hughes* (8–10). Illus. Series: Black Americans of Achievement. 1988, Chelsea LB $21.95 (1-55546-595-1). A highly readable biography of the African American poet and fiction writer that is well illustrated and contains excerpts from his writings. (Rev: BL 12/1/87; BR 1–2/89; VOYA 10/88) [921]

HURSTON, ZORA NEALE

5888 Boyd, Valerie. *Wrapped in Rainbows: The Life of Zora Neale Hurston* (10–12). Illus. 2003, Scribner $30.00 (0-684-84230-0). The extraordinary life of African American anthropologist/writer Zora Neale Hurston is chronicled in detail in this beautifully realized biography suitable for mature teens. (Rev: BL 12/15/02*) [921]

5889 Hemenway, Robert E. *Zora Neale Hurston: A Literary Biography* (10–12). 1977, Univ. of Illinois Pr. paper $16.95 (0-252-00807-3). As well as a fine biography, this volume includes an analysis of all of Hurston's works. [921]

5890 Hurston, Zora Neale. *Folklore, Memoirs, and Other Writings* (10–12). 1995, Library of America $35.00 (0-940450-84-4). In addition to Hurston's autobiography, *Dust Tracks on the Road,* and other personal writing, this volume includes a generous sampling of the African American folktales she collected. (Rev: BL 2/15/95) [818]

5891 Lyons, Mary E. *Sorrow's Kitchen: The Life and Folklore of Zora Neale Hurston* (7–12). 1990, Scribner $15.00 (0-684-19198-9). A brief biography of the African American novelist whose use of dialect sometimes brought criticism from other writers and who until recently was largely forgotten. (Rev: BL 12/15/90; SLJ 1/91*) [921]

5892 Porter, A. P. *Jump at de Sun: The Story of Zora Neale Hurston* (7–12). 1992, Carolrhoda paper $12.75 (0-87614-546-2). A brief, easy-to-read biography that places Hurston within the context of the racism of her era. (Rev: BL 12/15/92; SLJ 1/93*) [921]

5893 Witcover, Paul. *Zora Neale Hurston* (9–12). Illus. 1990, Chelsea LB $19.95 (0-7910-1129-1). A biography of this African American who was a folklorist, author, and anthropologist during the Harlem renaissance. (Rev: BL 12/15/90; SLJ 3/91) [921]

5894 Yannuzzi, Della A. *Zora Neale Hurston: Southern Storyteller* (7–12). Illus. Series: African-American Biographies. 1996, Enslow LB $20.95 (0-89490-685-2). The story of the Harlem Renaissance author who died penniless but left a priceless legacy in her writings. (Rev: BL 9/1/96; BR 9–10/96; SLJ 6/96) [921]

JEWETT, SARAH ORNE

5895 Silverthorne, Elizabeth. *Sarah Orne Jewett: A Writer's Life* (9–12). 1993, Overlook $22.95 (0-87951-484-1). A sympathetic biography of the American realist/regionalist author that draws on unpublished letters and diaries. (Rev: BL 3/15/93) [921]

JOHNSON, JAMES WELDON

5896 Tolbert-Rouchaleau, Jane. *James Weldon Johnson* (9–12). Illus. 1988, Chelsea LB $19.95 (1-55546-596-X). The biography of the African American writer who was also involved with the NAACP and the struggle for equality. (Rev: BL 6/1/88) [921]

KAFKA, FRANZ

5897 Adler, Jeremy. *Franz Kafka* (10–12). Illus. Series: Overlook Illustrated Lives. 2002, Overlook $19.95 (1-58567-267-X). This brief, well-illustrated, and accessible biography focuses mainly on the author's life. (Rev: BL 7/02) [921]

KERR, M. E.

5898 Nilsen, Alleen P. *Presenting M. E. Kerr.* Rev. ed. (8–12). Series: Twayne's United States Authors. 1997, Twayne $29.00 (0-8057-9248-1). A biography of this popular young adult writer that also discusses her works, with a detailed analysis of her five most popular books. (Rev: SLJ 4/98; VOYA 4/98) [810]

KING-SMITH, DICK

5899 King-Smith, Dick. *Chewing the Cud* (8–12). Illus. 2002, Knopf LB $18.99 (0-375-91459-5). King-Smith's humor and love of animals shine in this interesting and informative memoir of his career as a children's book writer and his various preceding jobs. (Rev: BCCB 1/03; BL 10/15/02; HB 1–2/03; HBG 3/03; SLJ 11/02) [823]

KING, STEPHEN

5900 Keyishian, Amy, and Marjorie Keyishian. *Stephen King* (7–12). Series: Pop Culture Legends. 1995, Chelsea LB $21.95 (0-7910-2340-0). Gives insight into the life of one of the world's most successful writers, covering King's childhood poverty and abandonment by his father, support by his mother, and influences on his work by such giants as C. S. Lewis, H. G. Wells, and Bram Stoker. (Rev: BL 12/15/95; BR 11–12/96; SLJ 1/96) [921]

5901 King, Stephen. *On Writing: A Memoir of the Craft* (10–12). 2000, Scribner $25.00 (0-684-85352-3). As well as recounting his life story, King gives good advice to would-be writers in this interesting memoir. (Rev: BL 7/00; SLJ 3/01) [921]

5902 Wukovits, John F. *Stephen King* (6–10). Illus. Series: People in the News. 1999, Lucent LB $17.96 (1-56006-562-1). A biography of the rags-to-riches prize-winning author whose mysteries and supernatural stories have thrilled millions. (Rev: BL 12/15/99; HBG 4/00; SLJ 11/99) [921]

KLEIN, NORMA

5903 Phy, Allene Stuart. *Presenting Norma Klein* (9–12). Illus. 1988, Twayne $20.95 (0-8057-8205-2). A biography and critical analysis of the writer who broke many taboos regarding young adult literature. (Rev: BL 7/88; SLJ 10/88) [921]

KOONTZ, DEAN

5904 Greenberg, Martin H., ed. *The Dean Koontz Companion* (9–12). 1994, Berkley paper $13.00 (0-425-14135-7). An interview with the prolific author of horror fiction, commentary on his works, and short tongue-in-cheek pieces by Koontz himself. (Rev: BL 1/1/94; SLJ 5/94; VOYA 8/94) [814.54]

LASKY, KATHRYN

5905 Brown, Joanne. *Presenting Kathryn Lasky* (9–12). Series: Twayne's United States Authors. 1998, Twayne $28.00 (0-8057-1677-7). An objective, lively biography of this popular young adult author that illuminates how her experiences have influenced her writing, plus a critical analysis of her books. (Rev: SLJ 6/99) [921]

LONDON, JACK

5906 Dyer, Daniel. *Jack London: A Biography* (7–10). Illus. 1997, Scholastic paper $17.95 (0-590-22216-3). The hard life and early death of author

Jack London, an adventurous, passionate lover of life. (Rev: BL 9/15/97; BR 3–4/98; SLJ 9/97; VOYA 10/98) [921]

5907 Stefoff, Rebecca. *Jack London: An American Original* (7–10). Series: Oxford Portraits. 2002, Oxford LB $24.00 (0-19-512223-2). A profile of this American original, his life, his work, and his lasting importance. (Rev: BL 7/02; HBG 10/02; SLJ 8/02) [921]

MCCAFFREY, ANNE

5908 Trachtenberg, Martha P. *Anne McCaffrey: Science Fiction Storyteller* (6–10). Illus. Series: People to Know. 2001, Enslow LB $20.95 (0-7660-1151-8). Trachtenberg introduces readers to McCaffrey's life and writing career, detailing the setbacks the author faced before winning the Hugo Award in 1968. (Rev: BL 7/01; HBG 3/02; SLJ 9/01) [813]

MCCALL, BRUCE

5909 McCall, Bruce. *Thin Ice: Coming of Age in Canada* (10–12). 1997, Random $24.00 (0-679-44847-0). A memoir by a Canadian humorist about his life growing up with an abusive father, an alcoholic mother, and four brothers, who, like him, sought escape in the arts. (Rev: BL 6/1–15/97; BR 1–2/98; SLJ 10/97) [921]

MELVILLE, HERMAN

5910 Hardwick, Elizabeth. *Herman Melville* (10–12). Series: Penguin Lives. 2000, Viking $19.95 (0-670-89158-4). A highly interpretive, concise biography of this enigmatic genius, with a fine analysis of his works. (Rev: BL 6/1–15/00) [921]

MILLAY, EDNA ST. VINCENT

5911 Daffron, Carolyn. *Edna St. Vincent Millay* (7–12). Illus. 1989, Chelsea LB $19.95 (1-55546-668-0). The life and career of this noted poet with examples of her work. (Rev: BL 12/1/89; BR 3–4/90; SLJ 3/90) [921]

MORRISON, TONI

5912 Century, Douglas. *Toni Morrison* (8–12). Series: Black Americans of Achievement. 1994, Chelsea LB $21.95 (0-7910-1877-6). A biography of the Nobel Prize–winning African American author, examining her life and the major themes of her novels. (Rev: BL 9/1/94; SLJ 7/94; VOYA 8/94) [921]

5913 Haskins, Jim. *Toni Morrison: Telling a Tale Untold* (7–12). Illus. 2002, Millbrook LB $26.90 (0-7613-1852-6). Haskins adds discussion of each of Morrison's books to this account of her life and lit-

erary career. (Rev: BL 10/1/02; HBG 3/03; VOYA 12/02) [813]

5914 Kramer, Barbara. *Toni Morrison: Nobel Prize–Winning Author* (7–12). Series: African-American Biographies. 1996, Enslow LB $20.95 (0-89490-688-7). Using many quotations and first-person comments, this biography re-creates the life and important works of this African American Nobel Prize winner. (Rev: BL 9/15/96; BR 1–2/97; SLJ 11/96; VOYA 6/97) [921]

MYERS, WALTER DEAN

5915 Jordan, Denise M. *Walter Dean Myers: Writer for Real Teens* (7–10). Series: African-American Biographies. 1999, Enslow LB $19.95 (0-7660-1206-9). Jordan tells the story of the prolific African American writer who continues a storytelling tradition. (Rev: BL 11/15/99; HBG 4/00; SLJ 1/00) [921]

5916 Myers, Walter Dean. *Bad Boy: A Memoir* (7–12). 2001, HarperCollins LB $15.89 (0-06-029524-4). Myers describes his turbulent youth in Harlem in the 1940s, his difficulties in school, and his lifelong love of books. (Rev: BL 5/1/01; HB 7–8/01; HBG 10/01; SLJ 5/01; VOYA 6/01) [921]

NERUDA, PABLO

5917 Goodnough, David. *Pablo Neruda: Nobel Prize–Winning Poet* (6–12). Illus. Series: Hispanic Biographies. 1998, Enslow LB $20.95 (0-7660-1042-2). A brief, interesting biography of the great Chilean poet that includes good background material on the rise and fall of the dictator Allende. (Rev: BL 8/98; HBG 3/99; SLJ 9/98; VOYA 10/98) [921]

ORR, GREGORY

5918 Orr, Gregory. *The Blessing* (10–12). 2002, Council Oak $24.95 (1-57178-111-0). In this memoir of his troubled childhood, which included the accidental fatal shooting of his brother on a hunting trip, poet Orr searches for the factors that led him to a career in writing. (Rev: BL 10/15/02*) [921]

ORWELL, GEORGE

5919 Agathocleous, Tanya. *George Orwell: Battling Big Brother* (8–12). Illus. Series: Oxford Portraits. 2000, Oxford $28.00 (0-19-512185-6). A concise, well-written life of this fascinating English writer and his contributions to world literature. (Rev: BL 10/1/00; HBG 10/01) [921]

PAULSEN, GARY

5920 Paulsen, Gary. *Eastern Sun, Winter Moon: An Autobiographical Odyssey* (9–12). 1993, Harcourt $22.95 (0-15-127260-3). The vivid, sometimes horrifying, story of Paulsen's incredible childhood, and his journey to and stay in the Philippines. (Rev: BL 1/15/93) [921]

5921 Paulsen, Gary. *Guts: The True Stories Behind Hatchet and the Brian Books* (5–10). 2001, Delacorte $16.95 (0-385-32650-5). These six exciting stories re-create childhood experiences of the author, who was born to alcoholic parents in 1939 and who developed a love of hunting and fishing in the woods of Minnesota. (Rev: BL 2/15/01; HB 3–4/01; HBG 10/01; SLJ 2/01; VOYA 6/01) [813]

POE, EDGAR ALLAN

5922 Meltzer, Milton. *Edgar Allan Poe* (6–12). Illus. 2003, Millbrook LB $31.90 (0-7613-2910-2). Poe's difficult life and literary accomplishments are described within the larger context of early 19th-century society in this well-illustrated and well-documented biography. (Rev: BL 11/15/03; HBG 4/04; VOYA 2/04) [818]

RAWLINGS, MARJORIE KINNAN

5923 Silverthorne, Elizabeth. *Marjorie Kinnan Rawlings: Sojourner at Cross Creek* (10–12). 1988, Overlook $24.95 (0-87951-308-X). This is the biography of the acclaimed author of such moving novels as *Cross Creek* and *The Yearling*. [921]

REID, JAN

5924 Reid, Jan. *The Bullet Meant for Me* (10–12). 2002, Broadway $24.95 (0-7679-0595-4). Reid recounts his brush with death at the hands of Mexican *pistoleros* and uses this experience as a backdrop for reflection on his own nature and the importance of machismo. (Rev: BL 2/15/02) [362.4]

ROWLING, J. K.

5925 Chippendale, Lisa A. *Triumph of the Imagination: The Story of Writer J. K. Rowling* (7–10). Illus. Series: Overcoming Adversity. 2001, Chelsea LB $21.95 (0-7910-6312-7). Rowling's period on public assistance and the legal challenges to the Harry Potter books are among the topics touched on in this biography. (Rev: BL 3/15/02; HBG 10/02; SLJ 5/02) [823]

SANDBURG, CARL

5926 Meltzer, Milton. *Carl Sandburg: A Biography* (5–10). Illus. 1999, Millbrook LB $31.90 (0-7613-1364-8). The story of a literary giant who, in addition to his poetry, is noted for nonfiction works including a biography of Abraham Lincoln. (Rev: BL 12/15/99; HBG 10/00; VOYA 6/00) [921]

SEBESTYEN, OUIDA

5927 Monseau, Virginia R. *Presenting Ouida Sebestyen* (6–12). Series: United States Authors. 1995, Twayne $28.00 (0-8057-8224-9). Sebestyen's unorthodox writing habits enliven this text, with biographical information and detailed analysis of six novels. (Rev: BL 9/1/95) [921]

SEUSS, DR.

5928 Cohen, Charles D. *The Seuss, the Whole Seuss, and Nothing but the Seuss* (8–12). Illus. 2004, Random $35.00 (0-375-82248-8). This oversize, abundantly illustrated book gives a profile of the great author/illustrator and an analysis of his ideas and work. (Rev: BL 3/15/04; SLJ 6/04) [921]

SHAKESPEARE, WILLIAM

5929 Holden, Anthony. *William Shakespeare: The Man Behind the Genius: A Biography* (10–12). 2000, Little, Brown $29.95 (0-316-51849-2). An exhaustive biography that uses a number of primary sources as evidence. (Rev: BL 6/1–15/00) [921]

5930 Rowse, A. L. *Shakespeare the Man*. Rev. ed. (10–12). 1989, St. Martin's paper $15.95 (0-312-03425-3). An readable account that traces the life of Shakespeare and covers his works and times. [921]

5931 Wood, Michael. *Shakespeare* (10–12). Illus. 2003, Basic $29.95 (0-465-09264-0). A highly accessible and well-illustrated biography that places Shakespeare in geographical and social context. (Rev: BL 10/1/03) [822.3]

SHELLEY, MARY WOLLSTONECRAFT

5932 Miller, Calvin C. *Spirit Like a Storm: The Story of Mary Shelley* (7–10). Illus. 1996, Morgan Reynolds LB $21.95 (1-883846-13-7). The life story of the fascinating, talented creator of *Frankenstein,* who was also the wife of poet Percy Bysshe Shelley. (Rev: BL 2/15/96; BR 1–2/97; SLJ 3/96; VOYA 6/96) [921]

5933 Nichols, Joan Kane. *Mary Shelley: Frankenstein's Creator, First Science Fiction Writer* (10–12). Series: Barnard Biography. 1998, Conari paper $6.95 (1-57324-087-7). A compelling biography of the spirited rebel and talented author who was the creator of *Frankenstein* and the wife of the poet Shelley. (Rev: SLJ 2/99) [921]

STEINBECK, JOHN

5934 Parini, Jay. *John Steinbeck* (10–12). 1995, Holt $30.00 (0-8050-1673-2). A finely wrought portrait of Steinbeck's youth, friendships, marriages, travels, and the creation of each book, play, and film. (Rev: BL 1/15/95*) [921]

341

5935 Reef, Catherine. *John Steinbeck* (7–12). Illus. 1996, Clarion $17.95 (0-395-71278-5). A handsome photobiography that not only covers salient aspects of Steinbeck's life but also explores the themes and locales of his work. (Rev: BL 5/1/96; BR 9–10/96; SLJ 3/96; VOYA 8/96) [921]

5936 Tessitore, John. *John Steinbeck: A Writer's Life* (8–10). 2001, Watts LB $25.00 (0-531-11707-3). This readable biography focuses on Steinbeck's career, giving excerpts from his work at the beginning of each chapter. (Rev: SLJ 7/01) [813]

STOKER, BRAM

5937 Whitelaw, Nancy. *Bram Stoker: Author of Dracula* (6–10). Illus. 1998, Morgan Reynolds LB $21.95 (1-883846-30-7). A well-documented biography of the writer who was fascinated with horror even as a child and eventually wrote the classic vampire tale *Dracula*. (Rev: BL 10/1/98; SLJ 6/98; VOYA 10/99) [921]

STOWE, HARRIET BEECHER

5938 Coil, Suzanne M. *Harriet Beecher Stowe* (7–12). 1993, Watts LB $20.00 (0-531-13006-1). An admiring biography of the celebrated author that documents the writing of *Uncle Tom's Cabin* and includes excerpts from her letters and works. (Rev: BL 1/15/94; SLJ 1/94; VOYA 4/94) [921]

5939 Hedrick, Joan D. *Harriet Beecher Stowe: A Life* (9–12). 1994, Oxford $56.00 (0-19-506639-1). This biography of the influential author of *Uncle Tom's Cabin* relates her complex personal story while capturing the spirit of the antebellum United States. (Rev: BL 1/15/94*) [921]

TAN, AMY

5940 Kramer, Barbara. *Amy Tan: Author of the Joy Luck Club* (6–12). Illus. 1996, Enslow LB $20.95 (0-89490-699-2). The story of the Chinese American writer who at first denied her immigrant background and later grew to accept and celebrate it in her fiction. (Rev: BL 6/1–15/96; SLJ 10/96; VOYA 10/96) [921]

5941 Shields, Charles J. *Amy Tan* (7–10). Illus. Series: Women of Achievement. 2001, Chelsea LB $21.95 (0-7910-5889-1); paper $9.95 (0-7910-5890-5). An appealing biography of Amy Tan that explores Tan's relationship with her mother and interest in her Chinese heritage. (Rev: BL 3/1/02; HBG 10/02; SLJ 6/02) [813]

5942 Tan, Amy. *The Opposite of Fate: A Book of Musings* (10–12). Illus. 2003, Putnam $24.95 (0-399-15074-9). Tan's autobiographical essays are as rich and entertaining as her fiction, covering her family, her much-traveled youth, and her career as a writer. (Rev: BL 9/15/03) [813]

THOREAU, HENRY DAVID

5943 Miller, Douglas T. *Henry David Thoreau: A Man for all Seasons* (9–12). Series: Makers of America. 1991, Replica $26.00 (0-7351-0220-1). This slim but insightful biography covers Thoreau's life and beliefs on civil liberty and nature. [921]

TOLKIEN, J. R. R.

5944 Hammond, Wayne G., and Christina Scull. *J.R.R. Tolkien: Artist and Illustrator* (10–12). 1996, Houghton $40.00 (0-395-74816-X). In addition to covering the life, ideas, and writings of this imaginative author, this book includes reproductions of more than 200 of Tolkien's paintings, drawings, and sketches. (Rev: BL 1/1–15/96; SLJ 7/96) [921]

TWAIN, MARK

5945 Howard, Todd, ed. *Mark Twain* (7–12). Series: People Who Made History. 2002, Gale LB $31.20 (0-7377-0896-4); paper $19.95 (0-7377-0897-2). Detailed essays that explore various aspects of Twain's life and writing are preceded by a general introductory that gives an overview of his life and times. (Rev: BL 4/1/02) [921]

5946 Lyttle, Richard B. *Mark Twain: The Man and His Adventures* (7–12). 1994, Atheneum $15.95 (0-689-31712-3). A sturdy biography that concentrates on the adventurous life Twain led during his formative years. (Rev: BL 12/1/94; SLJ 1/95; VOYA 2/95) [921]

5947 Neider, Charles, ed. *The Autobiography of Mark Twain* (10–12). Illus. 1990, HarperCollins paper $14.00 (0-06-092025-4). This is a well-edited version of the mass of material left by Twain to serve as his autobiography. [921]

5948 Rasmussen, R. Kent. *Mark Twain from A to Z: The Essential Reference to His Life and Writings* (9–12). Series: Literary A to Z. 1995, Facts on File $45.00 (0-8160-2845-1). This award-winning, comprehensive study of Twain's life and times contains nearly 1,300 entries that cover all important aspects of his life and works. (Rev: BR 3–4/96; SLJ 3/96) [921]

5949 Ward, Geoffrey C., et al. *Mark Twain* (8–12). Illus. 2001, Knopf $40.00 (0-375-40561-5). As well as a good text, this biography contains a treasure trove of photographs and other illustrations that depict the life and times of Mark Twain. (Rev: BL 10/15/01; SLJ 6/02) [921]

UCHIDA, YOSHIKO

5950 Uchida, Yoshiko. *The Invisible Thread* (9–12). 1991, Messner paper $4.95 (0-688-13703-2). In this moving memoir, Yoshiko Uchida, best known as an author of children's books, tells of her childhood in

California and her family's internment with other Japanese Americans during World War II. [921]

VONNEGUT, KURT

5951 Vonnegut, Kurt. *Conversations with Kurt Vonnegut* (10–12). Ed. by William Rodney Allen. Series: Literary Conversations. 1988, Univ. Press of Mississippi paper $15.95 (0-87805-358-1). A collection of interviews from various sources that reveal many facets of the life, character, and work of this amazing author. [921]

WALKER, ALICE

5952 Lazo, Caroline Evensen. *Alice Walker: Freedom Writer* (6–12). Illus. Series: Lerner Biographies. 2000, Lerner LB $25.26 (0-8225-4960-3). The personal life and literary career of the woman who won the Pulitzer Prize for *The Color Purple* is enhanced by the frequent use of quotations. (Rev: BL 8/00; HBG 9/00; SLJ 8/00; VOYA 2/01) [921]

WALTON, JENNY

5953 Walton, Jenny. *Jenny Walton's Packing for a Woman's Journey* (10–12). 1998, Crown $20.00 (0-517-70662-8). This work consists of a series of upbeat stories about families and friends involved with the author during her years growing up in the Midwest. (Rev: SLJ 7/98) [921]

WERSBA, BARBARA

5954 Poe, Elizabeth Ann. *Presenting Barbara Wersba* (8–12). Series: United States Authors. 1998, Macmillan $29.00 (0-8057-4154-2). An excellent introduction to the life and works of this groundbreaking YA novelist. (Rev: BL 9/1/98; SLJ 9/98; VOYA 12/98) [921]

WHARTON, EDITH

5955 Worth, Richard. *Edith Wharton* (10–12). 1994, Messner $15.00 (0-671-86615-X). A discussion of Wharton's life and an examination of her works. (Rev: BL 5/15/94; SLJ 11/94; VOYA 4/95) [921]

WHEATLEY, PHILLIS

5956 Gates, Henry Louis, Jr. *The Trials of Phillis Wheatley: America's First Black Poet and Her Encounters with the Founding Fathers* (10–12). 2003, Basic $18.95 (0-465-02729-6). A fascinating analysis of Wheatley's poetry and her lasting fame despite some initial public skepticism. (Rev: BL 6/1–15/03) [921]

5957 Jensen, Marilyn. *Phillis Wheatley: Negro Slave of Mr. John Wheatley of Boston* (9–12). 1987, Sayre LB $21.95 (0-87460-326-9). The story of a slave in Boston who became the first black poet in colonial America and gained sufficient fame to be invited to England to meet the king. (Rev: BR 11–12/87; SLJ 12/87) [921]

5958 Richmond, Merle. *Phillis Wheatley* (7–10). Illus. 1988, Chelsea LB $19.95 (1-55546-683-4). A heavily illustrated account of this poet who triumphed over slavery. (Rev: BL 2/15/88; SLJ 4/88) [921]

WHEDON, JOSS

5959 Havens, Candace. *Joss Whedon: The Genius Behind Buffy* (10–12). Illus. 2003, BenBella paper $15.95 (1-932100-00-8). Teen fans of TV's *Buffy the Vampire Slayer* will enjoy this entertaining profile of its creator. (Rev: BL 5/15/03) [921]

WHITE, E. B.

5960 Tingum, Janice. *E. B. White: The Elements of a Writer* (7–10). 1995, Lerner LB $30.35 (0-8225-4922-0). This quiet biography of the author of the much-beloved *Charlotte's Web* and other books discusses the underside of White's success: his shyness and depression. (Rev: BL 11/1/95) [921]

WHITMAN, WALT

5961 Meltzer, Milton. *Walt Whitman: A Biography* (6–12). Illus. 2002, Millbrook LB $31.40 (0-7613-2272-8). This life story of the American poet emphasizes his place in the country's history. (Rev: BL 4/1/02; HB 9–10/02; HBG 3/03; SLJ 3/02; VOYA 6/03) [921]

5962 Reef, Catherine. *Walt Whitman* (7–12). 1995, Clarion $16.95 (0-395-68705-5). A biography of the 19th-century poet who sang of America and the self. (Rev: BL 5/1/95; SLJ 5/95) [921]

WILDE, OSCAR

5963 Nunokawa, Jeff. *Oscar Wilde* (10–12). Series: Notable Biographies. 1994, Chelsea LB $19.95 (0-7910-2311-7); paper $9.95 (0-7910-2884-4). A well-researched biography of the witty English playwright and author who was imprisoned under Dickensian conditions because of a homosexual scandal and died three years after his release at the age of 46. (Rev: BL 11/15/94; SLJ 11/94; VOYA 2/95) [921]

WILDER, LAURA INGALLS

5964 Zochert, Donald. *Laura: The Life of Laura Ingalls Wilder* (9–12). 1976, Avon paper $5.99 (0-380-01636-2). An honest, sympathetic biography of and tribute to the author of the Little House books. [921]

WINNEMUCCA, SARAH

5965 Scordato, Ellen. *Sarah Winnemucca: Northern Paiute Writer and Diplomat* (9–12). Series: North American Indians of Achievement. 1992, Chelsea LB $19.95 (0-7910-1710-9). The story of this extraordinary Native American woman and her diverse achievements. (Rev: BL 11/1/92; SLJ 1/93) [921]

WOLFF, TOBIAS

5966 Wolff, Tobias. *This Boy's Life: A Memoir* (10–12). 1989, Atlantic Monthly paper $13.00 (0-8021-3668-0). This nonfiction work is an engrossing, entertaining look at the author's youth and adolescence. [921]

WOODSON, CARTER G.

5967 Durden, Robert F. *Carter G. Woodson: Father of African-American History* (6–10). Series: African-American Biographies. 1998, Enslow LB $20.95 (0-89490-946-0). This balanced, documented account focuses on the successes and failures of this historian, pioneering writer, and publisher, who devoted his life to the study of African American history and culture. (Rev: BR 11–12/98; SLJ 1/99) [921]

WOOLF, VIRGINIA

5968 Caws, Mary Ann. *Virginia Woolf* (10–12). Illus. Series: Overlook Illustrated Lives. 2002, Overlook $19.95 (1-58567-264-5). This brief, well-illustrated, and accessible biography focuses mainly on Woolf's life. (Rev: BL 7/02) [921]

5969 Mills, Cliff. *Virginia Woolf* (9–12). Illus. 2004, Chelsea LB $22.95 (0-7910-7459-5). The personal and professional lives of this great English writer are covered with many quotations from a number of original sources. (Rev: BL 3/1/04) [921]

WORDSWORTH, WILLIAM

5970 Hebron, Stephen. *William Wordsworth* (9–12). Illus. Series: British Writers' Lives. 2000, Oxford $22.95 (0-19-521560-5). The life, writings, and times of William Wordsworth are explored in this succinct but quite detailed profile that includes excerpts from letters and diaries. (Rev: BL 11/1/00; HBG 3/01; SLJ 12/00; VOYA 12/00) [921]

WRIGHT, RICHARD

5971 Hart, Joyce. *Native Son: The Story of Richard Wright* (6–10). Illus. Series: World Writers. 2002, Morgan Reynolds LB $21.95 (1-931798-06-0). This biography describes best-selling African American author Richard Wright's controversial works and his

development as a writer. (Rev: BL 2/15/03; HBG 3/03; SLJ 4/03) [921]

5972 Rowley, Hazel. *Richard Wright: The Life and Times* (10–12). Illus. 2001, Holt $35.00 (0-8050-4776-X). The story of African American author Richard Wright, his unusual childhood, his complicated life, and his outstanding writings. (Rev: BL 7/01*) [921]

5973 Urban, Joan. *Richard Wright* (7–10). Illus. 1989, Chelsea LB $19.95 (1-55546-618-4). A well-illustrated biography that also tells a little about the author's work. (Rev: BL 6/15/89; BR 9–10/89; SLJ 8/89) [921]

5974 Westen, Robin. *Richard Wright: Author of Native Son and Black Boy* (7–10). Series: African-American Biographies. 2002, Enslow LB $20.95 (0-7660-1769-9). The life and achievements of the African American novelist known for opposition to racial discrimination. (Rev: HBG 3/03; SLJ 1/03) [921]

5975 Wright, Richard. *Black Boy: A Record of Childhood and Youth* (8–12). 1998, HarperCollins paper $13.00 (0-06-092978-2). The tortured boyhood of the great black writer growing up in the South. This autobiography is continued in *American Hunger* (1977). [921]

YEATS, WILLIAM BUTLER

5976 Allison, Jonathan, ed. *William Butler Yeats* (6–12). Series: Poetry for Young People. 2003, Sterling $14.95 (0-8069-6615-7). A handsomely illustrated collection of Yeats's poems, each introduced with commentary and followed by explanations of any challenging vocabulary. (Rev: BL 4/1/03; HBG 10/03; SLJ 2/03) [921]

ZINDEL, PAUL

5977 Forman, Jack Jacob. *Presenting Paul Zindel* (9–12). Illus. 1988, Twayne $20.95 (0-8057-8206-0). An analysis of both the life and works of this popular author whose trailblazing books have influenced the course of young adult literature. (Rev: BL 7/88; SLJ 9/88; VOYA 10/88) [921]

Composers

BACH, JOHANN SEBASTIAN

5978 Bettmann, Otto L. *Johann Sebastian Bach As His World Knew Him* (9–12). 1995, Birch Lane $22.50 (1-55972-279-7). A biography of the great musician and personal essays on Bach's life. (Rev: BL 3/15/95) [921]

BERNSTEIN, LEONARD

5979 Lazo, Caroline Evensen. *Leonard Bernstein: In Love with Music* (7–12). Illus. 2002, Lerner LB $25.26 (0-8225-0072-8). This detailed portrait of Bernstein's life and musical accomplishments includes many black-and-white photographs. (Rev: BL 10/15/02; HBG 3/03; VOYA 12/02) [780]

DVORAK, ANTONIN

5980 Horowitz, Joseph. *Dvorak in America* (6–12). Illus. 2003, Cricket $17.95 (0-8126-2481-8). Dvorak's life in the United States (he arrived from Prague in the 1890s) is the focus of this narrative, which also covers the composition of the New World symphony. (Rev: BL 6/1–15/03) [780]

GUTHRIE, WOODY

5981 Guthrie, Woody. *Bound for Glory* (10–12). Illus. 1943, Peter Smith $23.50 (0-8446-6178-3); NAL paper $13.95 (0-452-26445-6). The saga of the man who grew up in poverty in the Oklahoma Dust Bowl and in time became one of America's most famous troubadours. [921]

5982 Neimark, Anne E. *There Ain't Nobody That Can Sing Like Me: The Life of Woody Guthrie* (6–12). Illus. 2002, Simon & Schuster $17.95 (0-689-83369-5). This biography of the famous folk singer draws on Guthrie's own words to tell the story of his life. (Rev: BL 12/15/02; HB 9–10/02; HBG 3/03; SLJ 10/02; VOYA 2/03) [782.42162]

5983 Partridge, Elizabeth. *This Land Was Made for You and Me: The Life and Songs of Woodie Guthrie* (6–12). Illus. 2002, Viking $21.99 (0-670-03535-1). The life, work, and times of the folk singer, from his childhood in the Dust Bowl to his death from Huntington's Disease. (Rev: BL 4/1/02; HB 3–4/02*; HBG 10/02; SLJ 4/02; VOYA 8/02) [782.42162]

5984 Yates, Janelle. *Woody Guthrie: American Balladeer* (6–10). 1995, Ward Hill LB $14.95 (0-9623380-0-1); paper $10.95 (0-9623380-5-2). Describes Guthrie's creative life and provides important historical information, including the many tragedies suffered by his family and his friendly relationship with labor, members of the Communist Party, and other musicians. (Rev: BL 2/1/95; SLJ 3/95) [921]

JOPLIN, SCOTT

5985 Curtis, Susan. *Dancing to a Black Man's Tune: A Life of Scott Joplin* (9–12). 1994, Univ. of Missouri Pr. $29.95 (0-8262-0949-1). Curtis traces the life of Joplin, best known for his piano rag "The Entertainer," from his Texas origins through his success as a performer and composer to his troubled stay in Harlem and the failure of his opera, *Treemonisha*. (Rev: BL 5/1/94) [780]

5986 Otfinoski, Steven. *Scott Joplin: A Life in Ragtime* (8–10). Series: Impact Biographies. 1995, Watts LB $18.95 (0-531-11244-6). A biography of the great ragtime musician and composer. [921]

5987 Preston, Katherine. *Scott Joplin: Composer* (7–10). Illus. 1988, Chelsea LB $21.95 (1-55546-598-6). The story of the talented musician, composer, and performer and the legacy of ragtime music he has left us. (Rev: BL 2/1/88; SLJ 5/88) [921]

VIVALDI, ANTONIO

5988 Getzinger, Donna, and Daniel Felsenfeld. *Antonio Vivaldi and the Baroque Tradition* (6–10). Series: Classical Composers. 2004, Morgan Reynolds LB $23.95 (1-931798-20-6). The story of the rise and fall of this prolific composer as well as of his music world and the importance of Venice in this sphere. (Rev: BL 4/15/04; SLJ 6/04) [921]

WEBBER, ANDREW LLOYD

5989 Walsh, Michael. *Andrew Lloyd Webber* (9–12). Illus. 1989, Abrams $49.50 (0-8109-1275-9). An oversized volume that deals with the British musical phenomenon and composer of the music for such hits as *Cats* and *Phantom of the Opera*. (Rev: BL 1/1/90) [921]

Performers and Media Personalities (Actors, Musicians, Directors, etc.)

AEROSMITH (ROCK GROUP)

5990 Huxley, Martin. *Aerosmith: The Fall and the Rise of Rock's Greatest Band* (9–12). 1995, St. Martin's paper $12.95 (0-312-11737-X). Picks up the Aerosmith story after their youth and looks at the elements of the rock group's rise to fame and fortune. (Rev: BL 3/1/95) [921]

ALLEN, WOODY

5991 Brode, Douglas. *Woody Allen* (9–12). Illus. 1987, Carol paper $14.95 (0-8065-1067-6). Biographical details on this writer and comedian, plus critical comment on his films through the mid-1980s. [921]

ALONSO, ALICIA

5992 Arnold, Sandra M. *Alicia Alonso: First Lady of the Ballet* (6–10). 1993, Walker LB $15.85 (0-8027-8243-4). Overcoming the lack of dance schools in her native Cuba and going blind in her 20s, Alicia Alonso became a prima ballerina and went on to teach, study, and perform in Cuba. (Rev: BL 12/15/93; SLJ 11/93; VOYA 2/94) [921]

ANDERSON, MARIAN

5993 Broadwater, Andrea. *Marian Anderson: Singer and Humanitarian* (7–12). Series: African-American Biographies. 2000, Enslow LB $19.95 (0-7660-1211-5). The story of the great African American singer who broke many color barriers in the world of music. (Rev: BL 4/15/00; HBG 9/00) [921]

5994 Keiler, Allan. *Marian Anderson: A Singer's Journey* (9–12). 2000, Scribner paper $21.95 (0-252-07067-4). A moving biography of the quiet, modest, African American concert singer who nevertheless contributed significantly to breaking the barriers of segregation. (Rev: BL 2/1/00) [921]

5995 Tedards, Anne. *Marian Anderson* (6–10). Illus. 1987, Chelsea LB $19.95 (1-55546-638-9). The life story of the great singer-artist who helped tear down many color barriers. (Rev: BL 2/1/88; SLJ 4/88) [921]

ARMSTRONG, LOUIS

5996 Bergreen, Laurence. *Louis Armstrong: An Extravagant Life* (9–12). 1997, Broadway $24.95 (0-553-06768-0). Bergreen chronicles the musician's rise from poverty in New Orleans to international stardom and examines the impact of racism on his life and career. (Rev: BL 6/1–15/97) [921]

5997 Bradbury, David. *Armstrong* (10–12). Illus. 2004, Haus $22.95 (1-904341-47-0). This concise biography of Louis Armstrong deals with his life and legacy and, through sidebars, tells of his times and associates. (Rev: BL 2/15/04) [921]

5998 Collier, James L. *Louis Armstrong: An American Genius* (10–12). Illus. 1983, Oxford paper $22.50 (0-19-503727-8). A thoroughly researched biography of this jazz great who was also a popular entertainer. [921]

5999 Tanenhaus, Sam. *Louis Armstrong* (7–10). Illus. 1989, Chelsea LB $21.95 (1-55546-571-4). The story of the African American musician who rose from poverty in New Orleans to the heights of the jazz world. (Rev: BL 3/15/89) [921]

BALANCHINE, GEORGE

6000 Taper, Bernard. *Balanchine: A Biography* (9–12). 1984, Times Books paper $18.95 (0-520-20639-8). A thrilling biography of the great choreographer who was also an amazing person and teacher. [921]

BASIE, COUNT

6001 Kliment, Bud. *Count Basie* (7–10). Series: Black Americans of Achievement. 1992, Chelsea LB $21.95 (0-7910-1118-6). The story of this trail-

blazing band leader and his contributions to jazz and popular music. (Rev: BL 9/15/92) [921]

BEATLES (MUSICAL GROUP)

6002 *The Beatles Anthology* (9–12). Illus. 2000, Chronicle $60.00 (0-8118-2684-8). Based on extensive interviews with Paul, George, and Ringo, this massive tribute to the Beatles contains 1,300 photographs plus many original documents and letters. (Rev: BL 9/15/00) [921]

6003 DeWitt, Howard A. *The Beatles: Untold Tales* (9–12). Illus. 1985, Horizon paper $14.95 (0-938840-03-7). This is a fine behind-the-scenes look at the lads from Liverpool, based on more than 50 interviews. (Rev: SLJ 1/86) [921]

6004 Norman, Philip. *Shout! The Beatles in Their Generation* (9–12). 1983, Warner paper $4.95 (0-446-32255-5). A candid, honest portrayal of the rock group from Liverpool and of each of its four members. [921]

BEIDERBECKE, BIX

6005 Berton, Ralph. *Remembering Bix: A Memoir of the Jazz Age* (9–12). 2000 Da Capo Press, pap. $12.60 (0-306-80937-0). A lively account of the legendary cornetist's brief career by a respected jazz writer and professor of jazz history.

6006 Collins, David R. *Bix Beiderbecke: Jazz Age Genius* (7–12). Illus. Series: Notable Americans. 1998, Morgan Reynolds LB $21.95 (1-883846-36-6). This biography chronicles the rise and fall of the amazing jazz cornet player Bix Beiderbecke, who died of alcoholism at age 28. (Rev: BL 7/98; SLJ 1/99) [921]

BROKAW, TOM

6007 Brokaw, Tom. *A Long Way from Home: Growing Up in the American Heartland* (10–12). Illus. 2002, Random $24.95 (0-375-50763-9). In this candid memoir, the NBC news anchor remembers his youth in South Dakota. (Rev: BL 10/15/02) [921]

BROOKS, GARTH

6008 Wren, Laura Lee. *Garth Brooks: Country Music Superstar* (6–10). Series: People to Know. 2002, Enslow LB $20.95 (0-7660-1672-2). The story of the country music star and his incredible rise to fame is told in text and pictures. (Rev: BL 9/15/02; HBG 3/03; SLJ 1/03) [921]

BURNETT, CAROL

6009 Burnett, Carol. *One More Time* (9–12). Illus. 1987, Avon paper $4.95 (0-380-70449-8). Using the form of letters to her daughters, the famous performer talks about her life and rise to fame. (Rev: BR 3–4/87; SLJ 2/87) [921]

CAREY, MARIAH

6010 Cole, Melanie. *Mariah Carey* (5–10). Series: A Real-Life Reader Biography. 1997, Mitchell Lane LB $15.95 (1-883845-51-3). For high-low collections, this biography of the popular singer tells of her difficulties in reaching the top and of her career since then. (Rev: BL 6/1–15/98; HBG 3/98; SLJ 2/98) [921]

6011 Nickson, Chris. *Mariah Carey: Her Story* (8–10). 1995, St. Martin's paper $9.95 (0-312-13121-6). Traces Carey's fairy-tale rise to stardom. (Rev: BL 6/1–15/95) [921]

CASH, JOHNNY

6012 Fine, Jason, ed. *Cash* (9–12). Illus. 2004, Crown $29.95 (1-4000-5480-X). A stunning biography of the country music star. (Rev: BL 5/15/04) [921]

CHAPLIN, CHARLIE

6013 Schroeder, Alan. *Charlie Chaplin: The Beauty of Silence* (7–12). Series: Impact Biographies. 1997, Watts LB $20.00 (0-531-11317-5). This biography re-creates a history of Hollywood in its golden days while capturing the life and work of this comic artist who was able, through his art and technique, to explore the relationship between tragedy and humor in his films. (Rev: BL 6/1–15/97; SLJ 6/97) [921]

CHARLES, RAY

6014 Ritz, David. *Ray Charles: Voice of Soul* (6–10). 1994, Chelsea LB $21.95 (0-7910-2080-0); paper $8.95 (0-7910-2093-2). The story of Ray Charles Robinson, who overcame the hardships of poverty, racism, drug addiction, and blindness to become one of America's most influential musicians. (Rev: BL 11/15/94) [921]

CHO, MARGARET

6015 Cho, Margaret. *I'm the One That I Want* (10–12). 2001, Ballantine $22.95 (0-345-44013-7). This often hilarious autobiographical tale is about the Asian American comedian's childhood and adolescence, alcoholism, self-hatred, acceptance, and rise to fame. (Rev: BL 5/1/01) [921]

CLAPTON, ERIC

6016 Coleman, Ray. *Clapton!* (9–12). 1988, Warner paper $14.95 (0-446-38630-8). A biography of the famous rock guitarist from late adolescence to the mid-1980s. (Rev: SLJ 1/87) [921]

6017 Schumacher, Michael. *Crossroads: The Life and Music of Eric Clapton* (9–12). 1995, Hyperion $24.95 (0-7868-6074-X). A biography of British rock star Eric Clapton. (Rev: BL 4/1/95) [921]

COBAIN, KURT

6018 Cross, Charles R. *Heavier than Heaven: A Biography of Kurt Cobain* (10–12). Illus. 2001, Hyperion $24.95 (0-7868-6505-9). The life and legacy of Kurt Cobain, singer and songwriter of the rock band Nirvana, who committed suicide. (Rev: BL 7/01) [921]

COLTRANE, JOHN

6019 Barron, Rachel Stiffler. *John Coltrane: Jazz Revolutionary* (6–10). 2001, Morgan Reynolds LB $20.95 (1-883846-57-9). Coltrane's love of music and jazz innovations are the main focus of this biography. (Rev: HBG 3/02; SLJ 1/02; VOYA 10/03) [921]

6020 Selfridge, John. *John Coltrane: A Sound Supreme* (7–12). 1999, Watts LB $24.00 (0-531-11542-9). An appealing biography that discusses jazz in general as well as profiling Coltrane and his contributions to the genre. (Rev: SLJ 11/99) [921]

COSBY, BILL

6021 Schuman, Michael A. *Bill Cosby: Actor and Comedian* (6–12). Series: People to Know. 1995, Enslow LB $20.95 (0-89490-548-1). Describes the life and career of one of the most successful comedians in modern times. (Rev: BL 9/15/95; SLJ 2/96; VOYA 2/96) [921]

6022 Smith, Ronald L. *Cosby: The Life of a Comedy Legend*. Rev. ed. (10–12). 1997, Prometheus $25.95 (1-57392-126-2). A serious, adult look at Cosby's life, from his early childhood through his climb to fame. The book ends with the tragic death of his son, Ennis. (Rev: BL 2/1/97; SLJ 11/97) [921]

CRONKITE, WALTER

6023 Cronkite, Walter. *A Reporter's Life* (10–12). 1996, Knopf $26.95 (0-394-57879-1). A memoir by one of America's most respected journalists, with material on the important stories he covered, including World War II, the Vietnam War, and the Apollo space program. (Rev: BL 11/1/96; SLJ 7/97) [921]

DAMON, MATT

6024 Busch, Kristen. *Golden Boy* (6–12). 1998, Ballantine paper $5.99 (0-345-42816-1). This is a well-researched, entertaining read about Matt Damon, the young star who was co-author and star of *Good Will Hunting* and star of *Saving Private Ryan*. (Rev: VOYA 12/98) [921]

6025 Diamond, Maxine, with Harriet Hemmings. *Matt Damon: A Biography* (6–12). 1998, Pocket paper $4.50 (0-671-02649-6). A fast read that gives a well-researched look at this likable, multitalented young movie star, with plenty of off-screen gossip. (Rev: VOYA 12/98) [921]

DAVIS, MILES

6026 Crisp, George. *Miles Davis* (9–12). Series: Impact Biographies. 1997, Watts LB $24.00 (0-531-11319-1). The amazing life of this jazz great who was a trumpeter, bandleader, and composer, as well as a great influence on the course of jazz history. (Rev: BL 5/15/97; SLJ 7/97) [921]

6027 Frankl, Ron. *Miles Davis* (7–10). Series: Black Americans of Achievement. 1995, Chelsea LB $21.95 (0-7910-2156-4). The story of the famous African American trumpeter and his contributions to jazz. (Rev: BL 11/15/95) [921]

6028 Szwed, John. *So What: The Life of Miles Davis* (10–12). 2002, Simon & Schuster $27.00 (0-684-85982-3). Szwed draws on a variety of sources for this detailed biography of eccentric jazz trumpeter Miles Davis; suitable for mature teens. (Rev: BL 11/15/02; SLJ 4/03) [921]

6029 Tingen, Paul. *Miles Beyond: The Electric Explorations of Miles Davis, 1967–1991* (9–12). 2001, Billboard $24.95 (0-8230-8346-2). A true fans will enjoy this biography of jazzman Miles Davis and his crusade to restore jazz to its rightful place in the African American heritage. (Rev: BL 4/15/01) [921]

DEAN, JAMES

6030 Oleksy, Walter. *The Importance of James Dean* (7–12). Series: The Importance Of. 2000, Lucent LB $19.96 (1-56006-698-9). Using a number of firsthand quotations, this book traces the life of James Dean, his tragic death, and his impact on motion pictures. (Rev: BL 3/1/01) [921]

DE MILLE, AGNES

6031 Hasday, Judy L. *Agnes de Mille* (9–12). Series: Women in the Arts. 2004, Chelsea LB $22.95 (0-7910-7457-9). The story of the great female choreographer, who was active both in ballet and the Broadway stage. (Rev: BL 3/15/04) [921]

DICAPRIO, LEONARDO

6032 Thompson, Douglas. *Leonardo DiCaprio* (6–12). 1998, Berkley paper $11.95 (0-425-16752-6). Sixty color photographs highlight this tribute to the young actor's life through *Titanic* and *Man in the Iron Mask*. (Rev: BR 11–12/98; VOYA 10/98) [921]

DISNEY, WALT

6033 Schickel, Richard. *The Disney Version: The Life, Times, Art, and Commerce of Walt Disney*. 3rd ed (9–12). 1997, Ivan R. Dee paper $14.95 (1-56663-158-0). Chronicles the animator's rise from a job as a draftsman in Kansas City to control of an entertainment empire with a profound influence on America's popular culture. [921]

DIXIE CHICKS

6034 Dickerson, James L. *Dixie Chicks: Down-Home and Backstage* (9–12). Illus. 2000, Taylor paper $16.95 (0-87833-189-1). The story of the popular country music stars and how they rose to stardom after years of obscurity. (Rev: BL 9/1/00) [921]

DYLAN, BOB

6035 Heylin, Clinton. *Bob Dylan: Behind the Shades: The Biography Revisited* (9–12). Illus. 2000, Morrow $30.00 (0-688-16593-1). This is an update of the excellent biography of Bob Dylan published earlier. (Rev: BL 10/15/00) [921]

6036 Richardson, Susan. *Bob Dylan* (7–12). Series: Pop Culture Legends. 1995, Chelsea paper $8.95 (0-7910-2360-5). The life of this creative icon who influenced both country and pop music. (Rev: BL 8/95) [921]

EDWARDS, HONEYBOY

6037 Edwards, David H. *The World Don't Owe Me Nothing: The Life and Times of Delta Bluesman Honeyboy Edwards* (10–12). Illus. 1997, Chicago Review $24.00 (1-55652-275-4). The biography of a black traveling country-blues musician that chronicles the brutality he suffered because of his class and color and recounts his experiences with gambling, romance, and classic blues artists over 65-plus years. (Rev: SLJ 5/98) [921]

ELLINGTON, DUKE

6038 Brown, Gene. *Duke Ellington: Jazz Master* (7–10). Illus. Series: Giants of Art and Culture. 2001, Blackbirch LB $21.95 (1-56711-505-5). Ellington's life and career are placed in historical context, with photographs, a timeline, a glossary, and lists of resources. (Rev: BL 8/01; HBG 3/02) [921]

6039 Dance, Stanley. *The World of Duke Ellington* (10–12). Illus. 1970, Da Capo paper $12.95 (0-306-80136-1). Based on a series of interviews, this is a portrait of Duke Ellington, the people around him, and the world of jazz. [921]

6040 Frankl, Ron. *Duke Ellington: Bandleader and Composer* (6–10). Illus. 1988, Chelsea LB $21.95

(1-55546-584-6). The story of the evolution of a great composer and of his life in music. (Rev: BR 1–2/89; SLJ 8/88) [921]

6041 Old, Wendie C. *Duke Ellington: Giant of Jazz* (7–12). Series: African-American Biographies. 1996, Enslow LB $20.95 (0-89490-691-7). An attractive biography of this giant of jazz who was a brilliant composer and arranger as well as an outstanding performer. (Rev: BL 9/15/96) [921]

EMINEM

6042 Bozza, Anthony. *Whatever You Say I Am: The Life and Times of Eminem* (11–12). Illus. 2003, Crown $22.00 (1-4000-5059-6). This laudatory profile of white rapper Eminem analyzes his popularity and contribution to the genre; for mature teens. (Rev: BL 9/15/03) [782.4]

ETHERIDGE, MELISSA

6043 Etheridge, Melissa, and Laura Morton. *The Truth Is —: My Life in Love and Music* (10–12). 2001, Villard $24.95 (0-375-50599-7). The life of this openly "out" rock guitarist is told from her childhood in Kansas to achieving stardom. (Rev: BL 8/01) [921]

FRANKLIN, ARETHA

6044 Gourse, Leslie. *Aretha Franklin, Lady Soul* (7–10). 1995, Watts LB $20.00 (0-531-13037-1). A biography of the now-legendary singer that recalls the problems in her life, including the disappearance of her mother when she was 6 years old, as well as her many concert triumphs. (Rev: SLJ 10/95; VOYA 2/96) [921]

6045 Sheafer, Silvia A. *Aretha Franklin: Motown Superstar* (6–10). Series: African-American Biographies. 1996, Enslow LB $20.95 (0-89490-686-0). The life story of one of America's most popular singers is accompanied by a discography, chronology, and index. (Rev: BL 12/15/96; SLJ 9/96) [921]

FREEMAN, MORGAN

6046 De Angelis, Gina. *Morgan Freeman* (7–12). Series: Black Americans of Achievement. 1999, Chelsea LB $19.95 (0-7910-4963-9). The life and career of the African American actor who has starred on Broadway, on television, and in movies. (Rev: HBG 4/00; SLJ 1/00) [791.43]

GILLESPIE, DIZZY

6047 Gourse, Leslie. *Dizzy Gillespie and the Birth of Bebop* (6–10). 1994, Atheneum $14.95 (0-689-31869-3). Bebop became a national music trend due in part to the influence of this trumpet-playing jazz legend. (Rev: BL 1/1/95; SLJ 3/95) [921]

GOH, CHAN HON

6048 Goh, Chan Hon, and Cary Fagan. *Beyond the Dance: A Ballerina's Life* (6–12). 2002, Tundra LB $15.95 (0-88776-596-3). A readable account of Goh's childhood in Vancouver and rapid rise as a ballet dancer to become a prima ballerina with the National Ballet of Canada. (Rev: HBG 10/03; SLJ 4/03; VOYA 4/03) [921]

GOLDBERG, WHOOPI

6049 Blue, Rose, and Corinne J. Naden. *Whoopi Goldberg* (7–10). Series: Black Americans of Achievement. 1995, Chelsea LB $21.95 (0-7910-2152-1); paper $8.95 (0-7910-2153-X). A biography that tells how, in spite of great odds, this unusual comedian and actress rose to the top. (Rev: BL 3/15/95) [921]

GRAHAM, MARTHA

6050 Probosz, Kathilyn S. *Martha Graham* (6–10). Series: People in Focus. 1995, Silver Burdett paper $7.95 (0-382-24961-5). With high-quality photographs, the author describes the dancer's many accomplishments and gives details on her youth and the influences on her work. (Rev: BL 8/95; SLJ 10/95) [921]

HARRISON, GEORGE

6051 *Harrison* (10–12). Ed. by the editors of Rolling Stone. Illus. 2002, Simon & Schuster $29.95 (0-7432-3581-9). The late Beatle's life is celebrated in a well-illustrated blend of original content and interviews and articles that originally appeared in *Rolling Stone*. (Rev: BL 6/1–15/02) [921]

HELFGOTT, DAVID

6052 Helfgott, Gillian, and Alissa Tanskaya. *Love You to Bits and Pieces: Life with David Helfgott* (10–12). 1997, Penguin paper $11.95 (0-14-026644-5). The story, by his wife, of the brilliant Australian pianist David Helfgott, who was institutionalized for 12 years after suffering a complete mental breakdown and whose life inspired the movie *Shine*. (Rev: SLJ 6/97) [921]

HENDRIX, JIMI

6053 Black, Johnny. *Jimi Hendrix: The Ultimate Experience* (10–12). Illus. 2000, Thunder's Mouth paper $21.95 (1-56025-240-5). A well-illustrated biography of the innovative guitarist with details garnered from a number of sources. (Rev: BL 2/1/00) [921]

6054 Markel, Rita J. *Jimi Hendrix* (7–10). Illus. Series: A&E Biography. 2001, Lerner LB $25.26 (0-8225-4990-5); paper $7.95 (0-8225-9697-0). The unhappy life and drug-related death of rock guitarist Jimi Hendrix are related with evocative descriptions of his music, a bibliography, Web sites, and discography. (Rev: BL 2/15/01; HBG 10/01; SLJ 3/01) [921]

HENSON, JIM

6055 Finch, Christopher. *Jim Henson: The Works* (9–12). 1993, Random $40.00 (0-679-41203-4). Traces the career of the creator of the Muppets from local television in the 1950s through the triumph of *Sesame Street* and his experimental work. (Rev: BL 1/15/94) [921]

HITCHCOCK, ALFRED

6056 Adair, Gene. *Alfred Hitchcock: Filming Our Fears* (7–10). Series: Oxford Portraits. 2002, Oxford LB $24.00 (0-19-511967-3). Hitchcock's youth in England is covered in addition to chronological details of his career from the silent movies through his classic creations. (Rev: HBG 3/03; SLJ 11/02) [921]

HOLIDAY, BILLIE

6057 Griffin, Farah Jasmine. *If You Can't Be Free, Be a Mystery* (10–12). 2001, Free Pr. $25.00 (0-684-86808-3). For better readers, this is a biography of talented but tragic jazz singer Billie Holiday and her deadly addiction to drugs. (Rev: BL 5/1/01) [921]

6058 Holiday, Billie, and William Dufty. *Lady Sings the Blues* (10–12). 1956, Doubleday paper $12.95 (0-14-006762-0). A brutally frank autobiography by the famous singer describing her problems being a black artist in America. [921]

6059 Kliment, Bud. *Billie Holiday* (8–12). Illus. 1990, Chelsea LB $19.95 (1-55546-592-7). A stirring biography of one of the great ladies of song whose life ended tragically. (Rev: BL 2/15/90; SLJ 5/90; VOYA 5/90) [921]

6060 Nicholson, Stuart. *Billie Holiday* (9–12). 1995, Northeastern Univ. Pr. $42.50 (1-55553-248-9). A careful, factual account of the singer's tumultuous life. (Rev: BL 10/15/95) [921]

HOUDINI, HARRY

6061 Brandon, Ruth. *The Life and Many Deaths of Harry Houdini* (9–12). 1994, Random $25.00 (0-679-42437-7). A biography of the escape artist, revealing his perfectionism, his obsession with death, and many of the secrets to his daring feats. (Rev: BL 9/15/94*; SLJ 5/95) [912]

HOWARD, RON

6062 Kramer, Barbara. *Ron Howard: Child Star and Hollywood Director* (7–10). Series: People to Know. 1998, Enslow LB $20.95 (0-89490-981-9). Using many photographs of Howard at work, this book traces his career from sitcoms such as *Happy Days* to becoming the director of fine films including *Apollo 13*. (Rev: BL 2/15/99; HBG 3/99; SLJ 3/99) [921]

IRWIN, STEVE (THE CROCODILE HUNTER)

6063 Irwin, Steve, and Terri Irwin. *The Crocodile Hunter: The Incredible Life and Adventures of Steve and Terri Irwin* (8–12). Illus. 2001, Dutton $23.95 (0-525-94635-7). The biography of the wildlife maven who grew up surrounded by animals and has become a TV personality using his talent, skills, and daring working with dangerous beasts. (Rev: BL 10/15/01; SLJ 2/02) [921]

JACKSON, MAHALIA

6064 Gourse, Leslie. *Mahalia Jackson: Queen of Gospel Song* (6–10). Illus. Series: Impact Biographies. 1996, Watts LB $24.00 (0-531-11228-4). Although she could have been a famous blues singer, Mahalia Jackson devoted her life to religious music and became the "Queen of Gospel Soul." (Rev: BL 8/96; BR 11–12/96; SLJ 8/96) [921]

6065 Kramer, Barbara. *Mahalia Jackson: The Voice of Gospel and Civil Rights* (6–10). Illus. Series: African-American Biographies. 2004, Enslow LB $20.95 (0-7660-2115-7). This biography traces the life of the singer and civil rights activist from her childhood in New Orleans to her great successes as a gospel singer. (Rev: BL 2/15/04; HBG 4/04) [921]

JACKSON, MICHAEL

6066 Taraborelli, J. Randy. *Michael Jackson: The Magic and the Madness* (9–12). 1991, Birch Lane $21.95 (1-55972-064-6). An adult biography that probes into the public and personal life of this talented, controversial entertainer. (Rev: BL 4/15/91) [921]

JEWEL (SINGER)

6067 Kemp, Kristen. *Jewel: Pieces of a Dream* (6–10). 1998, Simon & Schuster paper $4.99 (0-671-02455-8). A somewhat sanitized version of the life of the phenomenal Jewel, musician and songwriter, that tells about her rugged childhood in Alaska; overcoming dyslexia; yodeling in bars with her folk-singing parents; a year in an exclusive boarding school; living out of a VW van while singing in coffee shops; and the release of her first successful CD. (Rev: SLJ 4/99) [921]

JOHN, ELTON

6068 Crimp, Susan, and Patricia Burstein. *The Many Lives of Elton John* (10–12). 1992, Birch Lane $19.95 (1-55972-111-1). An intimate glimpse into the singer's life, for mature readers. (Rev: BL 4/15/92) [921]

6069 Norman, Philip. *Elton John* (9–12). 1992, Crown $22.50 (0-517-58762-9). An exhaustive biography of the legendary pop/rock musician by a celebrated rock journalist. (Rev: BL 12/15/91) [921]

JOHNSON, ROBERT

6070 Wald, Elijah. *Escaping the Delta: Robert Johnson and the Invention of the Blues* (10–12). 2004, HarperCollins $24.95 (0-06-052423-5). The blues pioneer's brief life is placed in social and cultural context. (Rev: BL 12/15/03*) [921]

JONES, JAMES EARL

6071 Hasday, Judy. *James Earl Jones: Actor* (7–10). Illus. Series: Overcoming Adversity. 1999, Chelsea LB $21.95 (0-7910-4702-4). A story of the great African American actor, noted for his deep, resonant voice, who conquered stuttering and muteness as a child. (Rev: HBG 9/98; SLJ 8/98; VOYA 8/98) [921]

6072 Jones, James Earl, and Penelope Niven. *James Earl Jones: Voices and Silences* (10–12). 1993, Scribner paper $14.00 (0-671-89945-7). In this highly readable autobiography, Jones recounts how he overcame a childhood problem with stammering and went on to establish a distinguished career in acting. [921]

LANG, K. D.

6073 Martinac, Paula. *k.d. lang* (9–12). Series: Lives of Notable Gay Men and Lesbians. 1996, Chelsea LB $19.95 (0-7910-2872-0); paper $9.95 (0-7910-2899-2). A highly readable biography of this successful Canadian country/jazz/rock singer that traces her rise to stardom, with emphasis on her creative genius, her down-to-earth personality, and her many facets as an individual, rather than her sexuality. (Rev: SLJ 11/96; VOYA 4/97) [921]

LATIFAH, QUEEN

6074 Latifah, Queen, and Karen Hunter. *Ladies First: Revelations of a Strong Woman* (10–12). 1999, Morrow $22.00 (0-688-15623-1). An honest, candid book by this actress and rapper who tells about her life, strength, faith in God, and problems as well as giving advice about drugs, sex, and men. (Rev: BL 1/1–15/99; SLJ 5/99) [921]

LEE, BRUCE

6075 *Bruce Lee: The Celebrated Life of the Golden Dragon* (6–12). Ed. by John Little. 2000, Charles E. Tuttle $24.95 (0-804-83230-7). Stunning photographs and excerpts from Lee's own writings paint an absorbing portrait of the late martial arts film star. (Rev: VOYA 8/01) [921]

6076 Tagliaferro, Linda. *Bruce Lee* (5–10). Series: A&E Biography. 2000, Lerner LB $25.26 (0-8225-4948-4); paper $7.95 (0-8225-9688-1). This colorful biography of the famous action star is filled with information about him, his films, and his family. (Rev: HBG 10/00; SLJ 5/00) [921]

LEE, SPIKE

6077 Hardy, James Earl. *Spike Lee* (7–10). Series: Black Americans of Achievement. 1995, Chelsea LB $21.95 (0-7910-1875-X); paper $9.95 (0-7910-1904-7). The story of the African American film producer and director who has fought for the right to express his ideas in a tough motion picture world. (Rev: BL 11/15/95; SLJ 12/95) [921]

6078 Haskins, Jim. *Spike Lee: By Any Means Necessary* (6–10). Illus. 1997, Walker LB $16.85 (0-8027-8496-8). Compiling previously published biographical material, the author has produced an interesting profile of this important African American filmmaker, including a behind-the-cameras view of each of Lee's 10 films. (Rev: BL 5/1/97; SLJ 6/97; VOYA 10/97) [921]

LENNON, JOHN

6079 Conord, Bruce W. *John Lennon* (7–12). Series: Pop Culture Legends. 1993, Chelsea LB $21.95 (0-7910-1739-7); paper $8.95 (0-7910-1740-0). Looks at Lennon's childhood in Liverpool, his career with the Beatles, and his life after their breakup. (Rev: BL 12/15/93; SLJ 11/93) [921]

6080 Wiener, Jon. *Come Together: John Lennon in His Time* (9–12). 1990, Univ. of Illinois Pr. $18.95 (0-252-06131-4). This biography gives many insights into the 1960s and the important issues of that time. [921]

6081 Wright, David K. *John Lennon: The Beatles and Beyond* (6–10). Series: People to Know. 1996, Enslow LB $20.95 (0-89490-702-6). This biography of the legendary founder of one of the most popular music groups of all time explores Lennon's background and his development as a songwriter and as a political activist, as well as recounting the history of the Beatles. (Rev: BL 10/15/96; SLJ 12/96; VOYA 2/97) [921]

MCCARTNEY, PAUL

6082 Gracen, Jorie B. *Paul McCartney: I Saw Him Standing There* (9–12). 2000, Billboard $35.00 (0-8230-8372-1). A biography of the musician that focuses on his post-Beatles career. (Rev: BL 9/1/00) [921]

MCKAY, JIM

6083 McPhee, Jim. *The Real McKay: My Wide World of Sports* (10–12). 1998, NAL $24.95 (0-525-94418-4). The autobiography of the famous sportscaster, in which he shares his personal views and memories of the many notable events and people he covered. (Rev: SLJ 9/98) [921]

MCKOY, MILLIE AND CHRISTINE

6084 Martell, Joanne. *Millie-Christine: Fearfully and Wonderfully Made* (10–12). Illus. 2000, John F. Blair $17.95 (0-89587-194-7); paper $12.95 (0-89587-188-2). The story of conjoined African American twins Millie and Christine McKoy who were born slaves in 1851 and became entertainers who traveled with circus entrepreneur P. T. Barnum's shows and met Queen Victoria. (Rev: BL 1/1–15/00; SLJ 10/00) [921]

MADONNA

6085 Claro, Nicole. *Madonna* (7–10). Series: Pop Culture Legends. 1994, Chelsea LB $21.95 (0-7910-2330-3); paper $8.95 (0-7910-2355-9). Examines the pop diva's childhood, the early death of her mother, her rise to stardom, her love affairs, and her controversial personality. (Rev: BL 10/15/94; SLJ 11/94; VOYA 12/94) [021]

MARLEY, BOB

6086 Booker, Cedella Marley, and Anthony Winkler. *Bob Marley, My Son* (10–12). Illus. 2003, Taylor $22.95 (0-87833-298-7). In this biography of reggae pioneer Bob Marley, the mother of the late Jamaican artist offers new insights about Marley's white father and her son's personal life. (Rev: BL 5/1/03) [781.66]

6087 Boot, Adrian, and Chris Salewicz. *Bob Marley: Songs of Freedom* (9–12). 1995, Viking paper $34.95 (0-670-85784-X). A review of the life and career of Jamaican Bob Marley. (Rev: BL 4/15/95) [921]

6088 Taylor, Don. *Marley and Me: The Real Bob Marley* (9–12). 1995, Barricade paper $14.95 (1-56980-044-8). Marley's business manager sheds light on the complexities of this charismatic reggae musician's life. (Rev: BL 9/1/95) [921]

MARSALIS, WYNTON

6089 Marsalis, Wynton. *Sweet Swing Blues on the Road* (9–12). 1994, Norton $29.95 (0-393-03514-X). Jazz musician and composer Marsalis takes the reader with him and his band on their travels around the world. (Rev: BL 12/15/94) [921]

MARTIN, RICKY

6090 Zymet, Cathy Alter. *Ricky Martin* (7–10). Series: Latinos in the Limelight. 2001, Chelsea LB $25.00 (0-7910-6100-0). From his debut in the Menudo group to the year 2000, this is the story of the famous Puerto Rican singer. (Rev: HBG 10/01) [921]

MARX, GROUCHO

6091 Tyson, Peter. *Groucho Marx* (7–12). Illus. Series: Pop Culture Legends. 1995, Chelsea $18.95 (0-7910-2341-9). The story of Groucho Marx, from his childhood on the Lower East Side of Manhattan to stardom with his brothers and, lastly, to fame as a quiz show host. (Rev: BL 7/95) [921]

MATHIS, GREG

6092 Mathis, Greg. *Inner City Miracle* (10–12). 2002, Ballantine $23.95 (0-345-44642-9). TV courtroom Judge Mathis relates how he managed to escape the grip of inner city crime and violence and make something of his life. (Rev: BL 9/1/02; VOYA 4/03) [347.73]

MONROE, MARILYN

6093 Lefkowitz, Frances. *Marilyn Monroe* (7–12). Series: Pop Culture Legends. 1995, Chelsea LB $21.95 (0-7910-2342-7); paper $8.95 (0-7910-2367-2). The story of the Hollywood star who, despite immense popularity, had a tragic life. (Rev: BL 8/95) [921]

6094 Woog, Adam. *Marilyn Monroe* (6–10). Series: Mysterious Deaths. 1996, Lucent LB $22.45 (1-56006-265-7). After a brief overview of the star's life and career, this account describes her last night alive and the many theories surrounding her death. (Rev: SLJ 3/97; VOYA 8/97) [921]

MONTAGUE, MAGNIFICENT

6095 Montague, Magnificent, and Bob Baker. *Burn, Baby! Burn! The Autobiography of Magnificent Montague* (10–12). 2003, Univ. of Illinois Pr. $24.95 (0-252-02873-2). A popular black disc jockey from the mid-1950s to the mid-1960s, the Magnificent Montague offers not only the story of his life but valuable insights into the cultural integration of the United States. (Rev: BL 10/15/03) [921]

MURPHY, EDDIE

6096 Wilburn, Deborah A. *Eddie Murphy* (7–10). Series: Black Americans of Achievement. 1993, Chelsea LB $21.95 (0-7910-1879-2); paper $9.95 (0-7910-1908-X). A nicely illustrated introduction to the life of this talented actor/comedian. (Rev: BL 1/1/94; SLJ 1/94) [921]

NIMOY, LEONARD

6097 Nimoy, Leonard. *I Am Spock* (9–12). 1995, Hyperion $24.95 (0-7868-6182-7). This entertaining memoir of Nimoy's years with *Star Trek* comes 20 years after his earlier book, *I Am Not Spock*. (Rev: BL 9/15/95) [921]

OAKLEY, ANNIE

6098 Riley, Glenda. *The Life and Legacy of Annie Oakley* (9–12). 1994, Univ. of Oklahoma Pr. $24.95 (0-8061-2656-6). A biography of the sharpshooter of Buffalo Bill Cody's Wild West Show, describing her personal and professional accomplishments in historical, cultural, and sociological contexts. (Rev: BL 10/1/94) [921]

6099 Sayers, Isabelle S. *Annie Oakley and Buffalo Bill's Wild West* (9–12). Illus. 1981, Dover paper $6.95 (0-486-24120-3). Through a number of old photographs, the life of this sharp-shooter is re-created. [921]

PARKER, CHARLIE

6100 Frankl, Ron. *Charlie Parker* (7–10). Series: Black Americans of Achievement. 1992, Chelsea LB $21.95 (0-7910-1134-8). The story of the "Bird," his alto sax, and his contributions to jazz, particularly bebop. (Rev: BL 2/1/93) [921]

PAVAROTTI, LUCIANO

6101 Pavarotti, Luciano, and William Wright. *Pavarotti: My World* (9–12). 1995, Crown $25.00 (0-517-70027-1). The great tenor Pavarotti writes of his career and life, including his happiest and saddest moments. (Rev: BL 9/1/95) [921]

PREMICE, JOSEPHINE

6102 Fales-Hill, Susan. *Always Wear Joy: My Mother Bold and Beautiful* (10–12). Illus. 2003, HarperCollins $24.95 (0-06-052356-5). Television producer Fales-Hill paints an unforgettable portrait of her mother, the late actress Josephine Premice, who was born in Brooklyn of Haitian parents. (Rev: BL 5/1/03) [974.7]

PRESLEY, ELVIS

6103 Gentry, Tony. *Elvis Presley* (7–12). Series: Pop Culture Legends. 1994, Chelsea LB $21.95 (0-7910-2329-X); paper $8.95 (0-7910-2354-0). The life of the "King" is re-created in this nicely illustrated biography. (Rev: BL 9/15/94) [921]

6104 Guralnick, Peter. *Careless Love: The Unmaking of Elvis Presley* (10–12). 1999, Little, Brown $27.95 (0-316-33222-4); paper $17.95 (0-316-33297-6). This is the second, concluding volume of this definitive biography of the King, Elvis Presley. (Rev: BL 11/1/98*) [921]

6105 Guralnick, Peter. *Last Train to Memphis: The Rise of Elvis Presley* (9–12). 1994, Little, Brown $27.95 (0-316-33220-8); paper $17.95 (0-316-33225-9). This is the first part of the highly acclaimed biography of Elvis Presley. (Rev: BL 7/94) [921]

6106 Kricun, Morrie E., and Virginia M. Kricun. *Elvis 1956 Reflections* (9–12). 1992, Morgin Pr. $49.95 (0-9630976-0-1). Follows Presley through 1956, an important year in his life and career. (Rev: BL 9/15/92) [782.42166]

6107 Mason, Bobbie Ann. *Elvis Presley* (10–12). Series: Penguin Lives. 2003, Viking $19.95 (0-670-03174-7). A sympathetic look at the life, career, and untimely death of the rock star. (Rev: BL 12/1/02; VOYA 8/03) [921]

6108 Torr, James D., ed. *Elvis Presley* (7–12). Series: People Who Made History. 2001, Greenhaven LB $31.20 (0-7377-0644-9); paper $19.95 (0-7377-0643-0). This volume contains a selection of serious essays that assess the life, contributions, and place in entertainment history of Elvis Presley. (Rev: BL 9/15/01; SLJ 9/01) [921]

REEVE, CHRISTOPHER

6109 Finn, Margaret L. *Christopher Reeve: Actor and Activist* (6–10). 1997, Chelsea LB $21.95 (0-7910-4446-7); paper $8.95 (0-7910-4447-5). The story of the gallant film actor, his tragic accident, and the causes he champions. (Rev: BR 5–6/98; HBG 3/98; VOYA 2/98) [921]

6110 Reeve, Christopher. *Still Me* (9–12). 1998, Random paper $7.99 (0-345-43241-X). Reeve looks at his life and work today and at his life before his injury in 1995. [921]

ROBESON, PAUL

6111 Ehrlich, Scott. *Paul Robeson: Singer and Actor* (7–10). Illus. 1988, Chelsea LB $21.95 (1-55546-608-7). A biography of this talented actor, singer, and athlete, whose career suffered because of his civil rights activities and Communist affiliations. (Rev: BL 2/1/88; SLJ 5/88) [921]

6112 Robeson, Susan. *The Whole World in His Hands* (9–12). Illus. 1981, Citadel $17.95 (0-8065-0754-3); paper $14.95 (0-8065-0977-5). An album of photographs with captions from Paul Robeson's own words that describe his life, career, and persecutions. (Rev: BL 10/15/88) [921]

6113 Stewart, Jeffrey C., ed. *Paul Robeson: Artist and Citizen* (10–12). 1998, Rutgers Univ. Pr. $40.00 (0-8135-2510-1); paper $22.00 (0-8135-2511-X). A well-organized, skillfully designed collection of essays that offers an in-depth look at the famous African American performing artist, film actor, college athlete, political and civil rights activist, and government target, bringing out the complexity of Robeson's life and his many contributions. (Rev: BL 2/15/98; SLJ 2/99) [921]

RODRIGUEZ, ROBERT

6114 Marvis, Barbara. *Robert Rodriguez* (5–10). Series: A Real-Life Reader Biography. 1997, Mitchell Lane LB $15.95 (1-883845-48-3). This simple, attractive biography of the successful movie maker focuses on his problems growing up in a large family and clinging to his career dreams. (Rev: BL 6/1–15/98; HBG 3/98; SLJ 2/98) [921]

ROGERS, WILL

6115 Sonneborn, Liz. *Will Rogers: Cherokee Entertainer* (9–12). Series: North American Indians of Achievement. 1993, Chelsea LB $19.95 (0-7910-1719-2). A simple biography of the famous vaudeville star who later became popular in Hollywood and died tragically in an airplane crash. (Rev: BL 12/1/93; SLJ 1/94) [921]

SANTANA, CARLOS

6116 Leng, Simon. *Soul Sacrifice: The Santana Story* (10–12). Illus. 2000, SAF-Helter Skelter paper $18.95 (0-946719-29-2). A story of influential guitarist Carlos Santana and of the music he and his group produced. (Rev: BL 5/1/00) [921]

SAVION

6117 Glover, Savion, and Bruce Weber. *Savion! My Life in Tap* (5–10). 2000, Morrow $19.95 (0-688-15629-0). A fascinating autobiography of the young dancer and choreographer whose tap dancing includes rap and hip-hop in a wonderful combination that has entranced audiences. (Rev: BCCB 2/00; BL 1/1–15/00; HBG 10/00; SLJ 3/00) [921]

SCHWARZENEGGER, ARNOLD

6118 Doherty, Craig A., and Katherine M. Doherty. *Arnold Schwarzenegger: Larger Than Life* (6–10).

1993, Walker LB $15.85 (0-8027-8238-8). This biography portrays Schwarzenegger as an "American hero," outlining his life and applauding his physical fitness and business sense. (Rev: BL 12/1/93; SLJ 2/94; VOYA 4/94) [921]

SELENA

6119 Marvis, Barbara. *Selena* (5–10). Series: A Real-Life Reader Biography. 1997, Mitchell Lane LB $15.95 (1-883845-47-5). A simple, attractive biography of the singer, her supportive family, and her tragic death. (Rev: BL 6/1–15/98; HBG 3/98; SLJ 2/98) [921]

SHAKUR, TUPAC

6120 Dyson, Michael Eric. *Holler if You Hear Me: Searching for Tupac Shakur* (11–12). Illus. 2001, Basic $24.00 (0-465-01755-X). A fascinating biography of the murdered rapper Tupac Shakur that provides insights into the artist's complexities and continuing popularity in death; for mature teens. (Rev: BL 8/01; VOYA 4/02) [921]

SIMON AND GARFUNKEL (MUSICAL GROUP)

6121 Morella, Joseph, and Patricia Barey. *Simon and Garfunkel: Old Friends* (9–12). 1991, Birch Lane $19.95 (1-55972-089-1). A dual biography of the famous folk-rock singer/songwriter pair, covering their Queens boyhoods, rise to fame in the 1960s, breakup at the decade's end, and subsequent separate careers. (Rev: BL 10/1/91) [921]

SIMONE, NINA

6122 Acker, Kerry. *Nina Simone* (9–12). Illus. Series: Women in the Arts. 2004, Chelsea LB $22.95 (0-7910-7456-0). This account covers both the personal and professional lives of this great entertainer and singer. (Rev: BL 3/1/04) [921]

SMITH, WILL

6123 Anderson, Marilyn D. *Will Smith* (6–10). Series: People in the News. 2003, Gale LB $21.96 (1-59018-140-9). The story of Will Smith's youth, life as a rapper, and stardom in movies including *Men in Black* will appeal to his many fans. (Rev: SLJ 3/03) [921]

6124 Rodriguez, K. S. *Will Smith: From Fresh Prince to King of Cool* (6–10). 1998, HarperCollins paper $3.99 (0-06-107319-9). An appealing, easily read biography of this impressive TV/movie star and rap artist. (Rev: VOYA 4/99) [921]

6125 Stauffer, Stacey. *Will Smith* (6–10). Series: Black Americans of Achievement. 1998, Chelsea

$21.95 (0-7910-4914-0); paper $9.95 (0-7910-4915-9). A serious biography of this popular star, beginning with *Independence Day* then moving back to Smith's childhood. (Rev: HBG 3/99; VOYA 8/99) [921]

6126 Stern, Dave. *Will Smith* (6–10). Illus. 1999, Aladdin paper $6.99 (0-689-82407-6). An oversize paperback with many color photographs that give a fan-magazine treatment to this star's life and career. (Rev: VOYA 8/99) [921]

SPIELBERG, STEVEN

6127 Ferber, Elizabeth. *Steven Spielberg* (7–12). Illus. Series: Pop Culture Legends. 1996, Chelsea LB $21.95 (0-7910-3256-6); paper $9.95 (0-7910-3257-4). An account of America's popular filmmaker that includes material on *Jaws*, *E.T.*, and *Jurassic Park*, and ends with *Schindler's List*. (Rev: BL 11/15/96; SLJ 1/97) [921]

SPRINGSTEEN, BRUCE

6128 Frankl, Ron. *Bruce Springsteen* (7–10). Illus. Series: Pop Culture Legends. 1994, Chelsea paper $9.95 (0-7910-2352-4). The compelling story of the famous rocker who has never forgotten his working-class roots. (Rev: BL 6/1–15/94) [921]

STEWART, SHELLEY

6129 Stewart, Shelley, and Nathan Hale Turner. *The Road South* (11–12). 2002, Warner $23.95 (0-446-53027-1). African American radio personality Shelley Stewart tells how he struggled to overcome a childhood of violence, abuse, and poverty; for mature teens. (Rev: BL 7/02) [921]

STONE, OLIVER

6130 Riordan, James. *Stone: The Controversies, Excesses and Exploits of a Radical Filmmaker* (9–12). 1995, Hyperion $24.95 (0-7868-6026-X). The first biography written about Oliver Stone shows a complex personality who takes risks in his own life as well as presenting them on screen. (Rev: BL 10/15/95) [9212]

SUMMER, DONNA

6131 Haskins, Jim, and J. M. Stifle. *Donna Summer: An Unauthorized Biography* (7–12). Illus. 1983, Little, Brown $14.95 (0-316-35003-6). Covers Summer's life and rise from a bit part in *Hair* to full stardom. [921]

TEMPTATIONS (MUSICAL GROUP)

6132 Cox, Ted. *The Temptations* (6–10). Series: African-American Achievers. 1997, Chelsea LB $21.95 (0-7910-2587-X); paper $9.95 (0-7910-2588-8). A chronicle of the rise and fall of this musical group, with profiles of each of the members and insights into the influence of Motown records on the careers of many African American musicians in the 1960s. (Rev: HBG 3/98; SLJ 1/98) [921]

THREE STOOGES

6133 Scordato, Mark, and Ellen Scordato. *The Three Stooges* (7–12). Series: Pop Culture Legends. 1995, Chelsea LB $19.95 (0-7910-2344-3); paper $9.95 (0-7910-2369-9). A look at the six men who composed the Three Stooges at various times. Includes black-and-white photographs, a filmography, and a chronology. (Rev: BL 6/1–15/95) [921]

VALENS, RITCHIE

6134 Mendheim, Beverly. *Ritchie Valens: The First Latino Rocker* (8–12). Illus. 1987, Bilingual paper $15.00 (0-916950-79-4). The story of the popular Latino rocker who died in a plane crash in 1959. (Rev: BL 12/15/87) [921]

VON TRAPP FAMILY

6135 Von Trapp, Maria. *Story of the Von Trapp Family Singers* (9–12). 1987, Doubleday paper $11.95 (0-385-02896-2). The story of the Von Trapp family, their stepmother Maria, and their escape from the Nazis. [921]

WALLENDA, DELILAH

6136 Wallenda, Delilah, and Nan De Vicentis-Hayes. *The Last of the Wallendas* (9–12). 1993, New Horizon $22.95 (0-88282-116-4). Master high-wire artist Karl Wallenda's granddaughter describes the fading charisma and finances of the circus in the United States from a personal perspective and presents her version of family squabbles. (Rev: BL 4/15/93) [921]

WASHINGTON, DENZEL

6137 Hill, Anne E. *Denzel Washington* (7–10). Series: Black Americans of Achievement. 1998, Chelsea $21.95 (0-7910-4692-3); paper $9.95 (0-7910-4693-1). A complimentary biography of this versatile, attractive actor who quickly rose to the top of the acting profession. (Rev: HBG 3/99; SLJ 3/99) [921]

WATERS, MUDDY

6138 Gordon, Robert. *Can't Be Satisfied: The Life and Times of Muddy Waters* (10–12). Illus. 2002, Little, Brown $25.95 (0-316-32849-9). Legendary blues musician Muddy Waters comes to life in this vivid portrait packed with atmosphere, facts, and references. (Rev: BL 4/1/02*) [921]

WILLIAMS, HANK

6139 Escott, Colin, and Kira Florita. *Hank Williams: Snapshots from the Lost Highway* (10–12). Illus. 2001, Da Capo $35.00 (0-306-81052-2). This life, which includes lyrics never set to music, is really an oral biography assembled from interviews with associates and material that he wrote. (Rev: BL 9/15/01) [921]

WINFREY, OPRAH

6140 Wooten, Sara McIntosh. *Oprah Winfrey: Talk Show Legend* (6–10). Illus. Series: African-American Biographies. 1999, Enslow LB $20.95 (0-7660-1207-7). The story of the amazing television personality who rose from a background of poverty, loneliness, and sexual abuse to become world-famous. (Rev: BL 9/15/99; HBG 4/00; VOYA 12/99) [921]

WONDER, STEVIE

6141 Williams, Tenley. *Stevie Wonder* (7–10). Illus. Series: Overcoming Adversity. 2001, Chelsea LB $21.95 (0-7910-5903-0). This look at the musician's life and career puts an emphasis on the difficulties

he has had to overcome. (Rev: BL 3/15/02; HBG 10/02) [782.421644]

YOUNG, NEIL

6142 Heatley, Michael. *Neil Young: His Life and Music* (9–12). 1995, Hamlyn $29.95 (0-600-58541-7). A pictorial tribute to the godfather of grunge. (Rev: BL 2/15/95) [921]

6143 Rolling Stone, eds. *Neil Young: The Rolling Stone Files* (9–12). 1994, Hyperion paper $12.95 (0-7868-8043-0). Traces Young's musical career from his stint with Crosby, Stills, and Nash to the present. (Rev: BL 8/94) [921]

Miscellaneous Artists

BARNUM, P. T.

6144 Barnum, P. T. *Barnum's Own Story* (7–12). Illus. 1962, Peter Smith $33.00 (0-8446-4001-8). The autobiography of the showman who could fool people like no one else. [921]

6145 Barnum, P. T. *Struggles and Triumphs* (10–12). 1971, Ayer $53.95 (0-405-01651-4). An abridgment of the autobiography of one of America's first and greatest showmen. [921]

6146 Kunhardt, Philip B., et al. *P. T. Barnum: America's Greatest Showman* (9–12). 1995, Knopf $45.00 (0-679-43574-3). The story of the master of showmanship and the greatest purveyor of freaks and wonders under the big top. (Rev: BL 9/1/95) [921]

Contemporary and Historical Americans

Collective

6147 Abdul-Jabbar, Kareem, and Alan Steinberg. *Black Profiles in Courage: A Legacy of African American Achievement* (10–12). 1996, HarperPerennial paper $13.00 (0-308-81341-6). An inspiring collection of profiles of 11 courageous African Americans, including Rosa Parks, Crispus Attucks, Frederick Douglass, and Harriet Tubman. (Rev: BL 10/15/96) [920]

6148 Alter, Judith. *Extraordinary Women of the American West* (6–10). 1999, Children's LB $39.00 (0-516-20974-4). Profiles of 50 women, from the 18th century to modern times, representing a variety of races, careers, and contributions. (Rev: BL 8/99; SLJ 9/99) [920]

6149 *American Rebels* (9–12). Ed. by Jack Newfield. 2004, Thunder's Mouth paper $16.95 (1-56025-543-9). From Margaret Sanger to Bob Dylan and from Norman Mailer to Noam Chomsky, here is a series of miniature biographies of unconventional Americans whose contributions have changed our world in many fields of endeavor. (Rev: BL 1/1–15/04) [920]

6150 Angelo, Bonnie. *First Mothers: The Women Who Shaped the Presidents* (10–12). 2000, Morrow paper $15.95 (0-06-093711-4). The story of 11 women who raised sons who became presidents of the United States. (Rev: BL 10/15/00) [920]

6151 Anthony, Carl Sferrazza. *America's First Families: An Inside View of 200 Years of Private Life in the White House* (9–12). 2000, Touchstone paper $18.00 (0-684-86442-8). This work gives a behind-the-scenes look at the home life of each of the presidents and their families. (Rev: BL 11/1/00) [920]

6152 Archer, Jules. *They Had a Dream* (10–12). 1996, Puffin paper $6.99 (0-14-034954-5). Biogra-phies of Frederick Douglass, Marcus Garvey, Martin Luther King, Jr. and Malcolm X are accompanied by discussion of the history of the civil rights. [323]

6153 Bontemps, Arna, ed. *Great Slave Narratives* (10–12). 1969, Beacon paper $31.50 (0-8070-5473-9). This is a collection of autobiographical writings by slaves. [920]

6154 *The Devil May Care: Fifty Intrepid Americans and Their Quest for the Unknown* (10–12). Ed. by Tony Horowitz. Illus. 2003, Oxford $26.00 (0-19-516922-0). Biographical essays introduce readers to lesser known adventurers and heroes such as Kentucky frontiersman Simon Kenton and Hannah Duston, famous for escaping her Indian captors in 1697. (Rev: BL 10/15/03) [917.304]

6155 Diamonstein, Barbaralee. *Singular Voices: Conversations with Americans Who Make a Difference* (10–12). 1997, Abrams $19.95 (0-8109-2698-9). This volume consists of 17 interviews with noted contemporary contributors to American life, among them writers Edward Albee and William Styron and public figures Jimmy Carter and Gloria Steinem. (Rev: SLJ 12/97) [920]

6156 Franklin, John Hope, and August Meier, eds. *Black Leaders of the Twentieth Century* (7–12). Illus. 1982, Univ. of Illinois Pr. $34.95 (0-252-00870-7); paper $18.95 (0-252-00939-8). A total of 15 African Americans, including W. E. B. Du Bois, Marcus Garvey, and Whitney Young, Jr., are highlighted. A companion volume is *Black Leaders of the Nineteenth Century*. [920]

6157 Gilbreth, Frank B., and Ernestine Gilbreth Carey. *Cheaper by the Dozen*. Updated ed (8–12). 1963, Crowell paper $9.95 (0-06-008460-X). A biographical account of the Gilbreth family, whose 12 children were reared by a father who believed in time and efficiency applications even in the home. [920]

6158 Gould, Lewis L. *American First Ladies: Their Lives and Their Legacy*. 2nd ed. (9–12). 2001, Routledge $125.00 (0-415-93021-9). This, the definitive work on the subject, give excellent biographical information on each of the first ladies through 2000. (Rev: BL 3/1/02; BR 1–2/97; SLJ 8/96; VOYA 12/96) [920]

6159 Hancock, Sibyl. *Famous Firsts of Black Americans* (7–12). Illus. 1983, Pelican $12.95 (0-88289-240-1). Biographies of 20 famous African Americans who have contributed in a unique way to our culture. [920]

6160 Hansen, Joyce. *Women of Hope: African Americans Who Made a Difference* (6–12). 1998, Scholastic paper $16.95 (0-590-93973-4). A large-size volume that celebrates the lives and accomplishments of 13 female African American leaders from various walks of life, including civil rights activists such as Fannie Lou Hamer and writers such as Maya Angelou. (Rev: BL 12/1/98; HBG 3/99; SLJ 10/98; VOYA 4/99) [920]

6161 Haskins, Jim. *African American Military Heroes* (7–12). Series: Black Stars. 1998, Wiley $24.95 (0-471-14577-7). Profiles of 33 African American servicemen and servicewomen and their contributions, from the 1760s to the 1990s, are given in this book that stresses the struggle for equality. (Rev: BL 9/1/98; HBG 3/99; SLJ 11/98) [920]

6162 Helmer, Diana Star. *Women Suffragists* (7–10). Series: American Profiles. 1998, Facts on File $25.00 (0-8160-3579-2). This is a fine introduction to 10 outspoken women in the struggle for women's rights, including Sojourner Truth, Elizabeth Cady Stanton, Victoria Woodhull, Carrie Chapman Catt, and Alice Paul. (Rev: BL 8/98; BR 11–12/98; SLJ 12/98) [920]

6163 *Invisible Giants: Fifty Americans Who Shaped the Nation but Missed the History Books* (9–12). Ed. by Mark Carnes. Illus. 2002, Oxford $26.00 (0-19-515417-7). Profiles highlight the varied contributions of 50 influential but relatively obscure Americans. (Rev: BL 5/1/02) [920]

6164 Kallen, Stuart A. *Native American Chiefs and Warriors* (6–10). Illus. Series: History Makers. 1999, Lucent LB $17.96 (1-56006-364-5). This collective biography gives basic information on some historically important Native American leaders. (Rev: BL 1/1–15/00; HBG 4/00; SLJ 1/00) [920]

6165 Kennedy, Caroline. *Profiles in Courage for our Time* (10–12). 2002, Hyperion $23.95 (0-7868-6793-0). There are 14 chapters in this book, each focusing on a different recipient of the Profiles in Courage Award. Among them are Bob Woodward,

Anna Quindlen, and Pete Hamill. (Rev: BL 3/15/02) [920]

6166 Kennedy, John F. *Profiles in Courage*. Memorial Ed. (7–12). 1964, Perennial paper $7.00 (0-06-080698-2). Sketches of several famous Americans who took unpopular stands during their lives. (Rev: BL 4/87) [920]

6167 Ketchum, Liza. *Into a New Country: Eight Remarkable Women of the West* (6–12). Illus. 2000, Little, Brown $18.95 (0-316-49597-2). The women featured in this book were pioneers, activists, and philanthropists who faced both the dangers of settling the West and prejudice toward women. (Rev: BCCB 10/00; BL 1/1–15/01; HBG 10/01; SLJ 12/00) [978]

6168 Kranz, Rachel, and Philip Koslow. *The Biographical Dictionary of African Americans* (6–12). 1999, Facts on File $44.00 (0-8160-3903-8); paper $18.95 (0-8160-3904-6). Arranged chronologically, this volume contains brief profiles of 230 African Americans ranging from colonial days to contemporary entries for Queen Latifah and Tupac Shakur. (Rev: BL 4/15/99; SLJ 8/99) [973]

6169 Lamb, Brian, comp. *Booknotes: Life Stories: Notable Biographies on the People Who Shaped America* (10–12). 1999, Times Books $27.50 (0-8129-3081-9). A collection of light, conversational interviews with biographers for C-SPAN's *Booknotes,* who provide insightful, colorful, and well-rounded portraits of their famous subjects, from George Washington and Abraham Lincoln to Newt Gingrich and Bill Clinton. (Rev: BL 3/1/99; SLJ 7/99) [920]

6170 Lilley, Stephen R. *Fighters Against American Slavery* (9–12). Illus. Series: History Makers. 1998, Lucent LB $17.96 (1-56006-036-0). Moral convictions and personal experience were the motivating forces that inspired abolitionists to act. This book highlights such heroes as Nat Turner, William Lloyd Garrison, Frederick Douglass, and Harriet Tubman. (Rev: BL 2/15/99; SLJ 6/99) [920]

6171 Lindop, Laurie. *Champions of Equality* (7–10). Illus. Series: Dynamic Modern Women. 1997, Twenty-First Century LB $24.90 (0-8050-4165-6). A look at 10 women activists for human and equal rights, among them Margarethe Cammermeyer, Marian Wright Edelman, Wilma Mankiller, and Eleanor Holmes Norton. (Rev: BL 9/1/97; BR 1–2/98; SLJ 9/97) [303.48]

6172 Lindop, Laurie. *Political Leaders* (6–12). Illus. Series: Dynamic Modern Women. 1996, Twenty-First Century LB $24.90 (0-8050-4164-8). Elizabeth Dole, Dianne Feinstein, Geraldine Ferraro, Ruth Bader Ginsburg, and Barbara Jordan are five of the 10 prominent women in politics profiled in this book, with details on the childhood, influences, education, and political career of each. (Rev: BL 1/1–15/97; SLJ 1/97; VOYA 2/97) [320]

6173 Litwack, Leon F., and August Meier, eds. *Black Leaders of the Nineteenth Century* (10–12). Illus. 1988, Univ. of Illinois Pr. $29.95 (0-252-01506-1). Seventeen biographical sketches about such famous African Americans as Nat Turner and Harriet Tubman. (Rev: BL 4/1/88) [920]

6174 McElroy, Richard L. *American Presidents* (9–12). 1984, Daring paper $5.95 (0-938936-18-2). A pleasant collection of trivia and facts about American presidents. [920]

6175 McPherson, James M., ed. *"To the Best of My Ability": The American Presidents* (9–12). Illus. 2000, DK $29.95 (0-7894-5073-9). This lavishly illustrated overview contains a series of essays by noted academics on each of the presidents. (Rev: BL 8/00) [920]

6176 Mayo, Edith P., ed. *The Smithsonian Book of the First Ladies: Their Lives, Times, and Issues* (6–10). Illus. 1996, Holt $29.95 (0-8050-1751-8). From Martha Washington to Hillary Rodham Clinton, this book examines the lives and accomplishments of each First Lady with a three- to four-page biography and pictures. (Rev: BL 6/1–15/96; BR 1–2/97; SLJ 6/96; VOYA 8/96) [920]

6177 Morey, Janet Nomura, and Wendy Dunn. *Famous Hispanic Americans* (7–10). Illus. 1996, Dutton $16.99 (0-525-65190-X). Fourteen men and women of Hispanic heritage from science, sports, the arts, and other professions are featured in this collective biography. (Rev: BL 2/15/96; BR 9–10/96; SLJ 2/96; VOYA 8/96) [920]

6178 Morin, Isobel V. *Women of the U.S. Congress* (6–10). 1994, Oliver LB $19.95 (1-881508-12-9). Lists all the women who have served in Congress as of 1994 and provides political biographies of seven of them, citing their accomplishments and their different backgrounds and views. (Rev: BL 7/94; SLJ 5/94; VOYA 6/94) [920]

6179 Morin, Isobel V. *Women Who Reformed Politics* (7–12). 1994, Oliver LB $19.95 (1-881508-16-1). Describes the political activism of eight American women, including Abby Foster's abolition fight, Carrie Catt's suffrage battle, and Gloria Steinem's feminist crusade. (Rev: BL 10/15/94; SLJ 11/94; VOYA 2/95) [920]

6180 Peters, Margaret. *The Ebony Book of Black Achievement* (10–12). Illus. 1974, JIST $10.95 (0-87485-040-1). This volume contains brief biographies of 26 African American men and women who have achieved in a number of fields. [920]

6181 *The Reader's Companion to the American Presidency* (10–12). Ed. by Alan Brinkley and Davis Dyer. Illus. 2000, Houghton $40.00 (0-395-78889-7). A collection of scholarly essays written

by specialists, each of which deals with the life and accomplishments of a different United States president. (Rev: BL 2/1/00; SLJ 10/00) [920]

6182 Roberts, Cokie. *Founding Mothers: The Women Who Raised Our Nation* (10–12). 2004, Morrow $23.95 (0-06-009025-1). This collective biography that uses many original documents introduces heroines of the revolutionary period including Deborah Franklin (wife of Benjamin), Abigail Adams, Martha Washington, and Phillis Wheatley. (Rev: BL 3/15/04) [920]

6183 Satter, James. *Journalists Who Made History* (7–12). Illus. Series: Profiles. 1998, Oliver LB $19.95 (1-881508-39-0). Ten journalists famous for their fearless reporting are profiled, including Horace Greeley, Ida Tarbell, Carl Bernstein and Bob Woodward, William Randolph Hearst, and Edward R. Murrow. (Rev: BL 10/15/98; SLJ 11/98) [920]

6184 Smith, Gene. *Lee and Grant: A Dual Biography* (9–12). 1984, NAL paper $10.95 (0-452-00773-9). A double biography of the two opposing generals and their fateful clash. [921]

6185 Steele, Phillip W., and Marie Barrow Scoma. *The Family Story of Bonnie and Clyde* (10–12). Illus. 2000, Pelican paper $7.95 (1-56554-756-X). Heavily illustrated with photographs, this is the story of the two outlaws, their exploits, and their personal lives. (Rev: BL 3/15/00) [920]

6186 Straub, Deborah G., ed. *Hispanic American Voices* (6–12). 1997, Gale $52.00 (0-8103-9827-3). Profiles of 16 Hispanic Americans, most of whom are civil and human rights leaders, politicians, attorneys, or civil rights activists. (Rev: BR 9–10/97; SLJ 11/97) [920]

6187 Streissguth, Thomas. *Legendary Labor Leaders* (7–12). Illus. Series: Profiles. 1998, Oliver LB $19.95 (1-881508-44-7). The eight labor leaders profiled in this collective biography are Samuel Gompers, Cesar Chavez, A. Philip Randolph, Jimmy Hoffa, Eugene Debs, William Haywood, Mother Jones, and John L. Lewis. (Rev: BL 10/15/98; SLJ 1/99) [920]

6188 Taylor, Kimberly H. *Black Abolitionists and Freedom Fighters* (6–10). 1996, Oliver LB $19.95 (1-881508-30-7). Profiles are given for eight African Americans who fought to end slavery, some well-known (including Nat Turner and Harriet Tubman) and others less familiar, such as Richard Allen and Mary Terrell. (Rev: BR 1–2/97; SLJ 10/96) [920]

6189 Taylor, Kimberly H. *Black Civil Rights Champions* (6–12). Illus. 1995, Oliver LB $19.95 (1-881508-22-6). In separate chapters, seven civil rights leaders, including W. E. B. Du Bois, James Farmer, Ella Baker, and Malcolm X, are profiled, with a final chapter that gives thumbnail sketches of many more. (Rev: BL 1/1–15/96; BR 1–2/97; SLJ 3/96; VOYA 6/96) [920]

6190 Thro, Ellen. *Twentieth-Century Women Politicians* (7–12). Series: American Profiles. 1998, Facts on File $25.00 (0-8160-3758-2). Beginning in the mid-20th century, this work features 10 women who were elected to important public offices, including Margaret Chase Smith, Geraldine Ferraro, Dianne Feinstein, Christine Todd Whitman, and Ann Richards. (Rev: BL 12/15/98) [920]

6191 Unger, Harlow G. *Teachers and Educators* (7–10). Illus. Series: American Profiles. 1994, Facts on File $25.00 (0-8160-2990-3). This book profiles eight great American educators of the past, including John Dewey, Horace Mann, Emma Willard, Booker T. Washington, and Henry Barnard. (Rev: BL 7/95; VOYA 5/95) [920]

6192 Uschan, Michael V. *America's Founders* (6–10). Series: History Makers. 1999, Lucent LB $18.96 (1-56006-571-0). These brief biographies of Washington, Franklin, Jefferson, John Adams, and Alexander Hamilton focus on their lasting contributions to this country. (Rev: BL 10/15/99; HBG 9/00) [920]

6193 Vernell, Marjorie. *Leaders of Black Civil Rights* (6–10). Illus. Series: History Makers. 1999, Lucent LB $18.96 (1-56006-670-9). After a review of the civil rights movements of the 1950s and 1960s, this collective biography features seven short sketches of such subjects as A. Philip Randolph, Malcolm X, Fannie Lou Hamer, and Jesse Jackson. (Rev: BL 2/15/00; HBG 9/00) [920]

6194 Waldrup, Carole Chandler. *The Vice Presidents: Biographies of the 45 Men Who Have Held the Second Highest Office in the United States* (9–12). 1996, McFarland $45.00 (0-7864-0179-6). Brief biographies cover every man to hold the office from John Adams to Al Gore. (Rev: BL 12/1/96) [920.003]

6195 Weatherford, Carole Boston. *Great African-American Lawyers: Raising the Bar of Freedom* (7–12). Illus. Series: Collective Biographies. 2003, Enslow $20.95 (0-7660-1837-7). From Macon Allen, the first black lawyer in America, through more familiar names such as Thurgood Marshall and Marian Wright Edelman, this is an overview of the accomplishments of African American lawyers. (Rev: BL 2/15/03; HBG 10/03) [340.09]

Civil and Human Rights Leaders

ABERNATHY, RALPH

6196 Reef, Catherine. *Ralph David Abernathy* (6–10). Series: People in Focus. 1995, Silver Bur-

dett $13.95 (0-87518-653-X); paper $7.95 (0-382-24965-8). A straightforward biography that describes this civil rights leader's youth and many accomplishments. (Rev: BL 8/95; SLJ 10/95) [921]

ANTHONY, SUSAN B.

6197 Sherr, Lynn. *Failure Is Impossible: Susan B. Anthony in Her Own Words* (9–12). 1995, Times Books $23.00 (0-8129-2430-4). One woman's passionate belief in equal rights for all people, as expressed in her own speeches, correspondence, and diary entries. (Rev: BL 2/1/95; SLJ 3/96) [921]

6198 Stalcup, Brenda, ed. *Susan B. Anthony* (7–12). Series: People Who Made History. 2001, Gale LB $31.20 (0-7377-0890-5); paper $19.95 (0-7377-0891-3). The story of the American reformer and leader of the woman-suffrage movement is covered in this anthology of mature essays. (Rev: BL 4/1/02) [921]

6199 Weisberg, Barbara. *Susan B. Anthony* (6–10). Illus. 1988, Chelsea LB $19.95 (1-55546-639-7). The biography of the woman who led the early suffragette movement. (Rev: BL 12/1/88) [921]

BATES, DAISY

6200 Polakow, Amy. *Daisy Bates: Civil Rights Crusader* (6–12). Illus. 2003, Linnet $25.00 (0-208-02513-8). In 1957, Bates supported the Little Rock Nine students who were the first African Americans to take advantage of school integration. (Rev: BL 6/1–15/03; HBG 10/03; SLJ 8/03; VOYA 6/04) [921]

BETHUNE, MARY MCLEOD

6201 Halasa, Malu. *Mary McLeod Bethune* (6–10). Illus. 1988, Chelsea LB $21.95 (1-55546-574-9). A stirring biography of the African American woman who fought for the right to a quality education for her people. (Rev: BL 3/15/89) [921]

BROWN, JOHN

6202 Cox, Clinton. *Fiery Vision: The Life and Death of John Brown* (7–10). Illus. 1997, Scholastic paper $15.95 (0-590-47574-6). A well-researched, detailed account of the life of the abolitionist who was hanged for the raid at Harper's Ferry. (Rev: BL 2/15/97; HBG 3/98; SLJ 6/97; VOYA 10/98) [921]

BURNS, ANTHONY

6203 Hamilton, Virginia. *Anthony Burns: The Defeat and Triumph of a Fugitive Slave* (7–12). 1988, Knopf $14.99 (0-394-98185-5). Burns, who lived only 28 years, rebelled against his slave status with repercussions felt around the country. (Rev:

BL 6/1/88; BR 11–12/88; SLJ 6/88; VOYA 10/88) [921]

CHAVEZ, CESAR

6204 Gonzales, Doreen. *Cesar Chavez: Leader for Migrant Farm Workers* (6–10). Illus. Series: Hispanic Biographies. 1996, Enslow LB $20.95 (0-89490-760-3). This biography concentrates on Chavez's struggle to organize California farmworkers, his belief in nonviolence, and his inspirational leadership. (Rev: BL 10/1/96; SLJ 6/96) [921]

6205 Houle, Michelle E., ed. *Cesar Chavez* (7–12). Series: People Who Made History. 2003, Gale LB $33.70 (0-7377-1298-8); paper $22.45 (0-7377-1299-6). A compilation of essays about the champion of migrant workers that show his achievements from various points of view. (Rev: SLJ 10/03) [921]

CHILD, LYDIA MARIA

6206 Kenschaft, Lori. *Lydia Maria Child: The Quest for Racial Justice* (6–10). Illus. Series: Oxford Portraits. 2002, Oxford LB $24.00 (0-19-513257-2). Lydia Maria Child, an activist for civil rights in the early and middle 1800s, is also known for her literary career. (Rev: BL 3/1/03; HBG 3/03; SLJ 1/03) [303.48]

DATCHER, MICHAEL

6207 Datcher, Michael. *Raising Fences: A Black Man's Love Story* (10–12). 2001, Riverhead $23.95 (1-57322-171-6). Though raised in an environment of poverty and squalor, Michael Datcher rose above his painful childhood, went to college, and became a responsible parent who was aware, as an African American, of the oppression of his people. (Rev: BL 2/1/01) [921]

DE LA CRUZ, JESSIE

6208 Soto, Gary. *Jessie de la Cruz: A Profile of a United Farm Worker* (7–12). 2000, Persea $17.95 (0-89255-253-0). De la Cruz grew up working in the fields of California with her migrant family and later became an organizer for the United Farm Workers. (Rev: BCCB 2/01; BL 11/15/00; BR 3–4/01; HBG 3/01; SLJ 1/01) [921]

DOUGLASS, FREDERICK

6209 Burchard, Peter. *Frederick Douglass: For the Great Family of Man* (7–12). Illus. 2003, Simon & Schuster $18.95 (0-689-83240-0). This absorbing biography includes information about the impact of events in Douglass's early life on his development as an important human rights advocate. (Rev: BL 2/15/03; HB 3–4/03; HBG 10/03; SLJ 1/03; VOYA 2/03) [921]

6210 Douglass, Frederick. *Autobiographies* (10–12). 1994, Library of America $35.00 (0-940450-79-8); paper $13.95 (1-883011-30-2). This single volume contains all of the autobiographical writings of Frederick Douglass. [921]

6211 Douglass, Frederick. *Escape from Slavery: The Boyhood of Frederick Douglass in His Own Words* (5–10). Illus. 1994, Knopf $15.00 (0-679-84652-2); paper $6.99 (0-679-84651-4). This shortened version of the famous abolitionist's 1845 autobiography dramatizes the abomination of slavery and the struggle of a man to break free. (Rev: BL 2/15/94*; SLJ 2/94) [921]

6212 Douglass, Frederick. *The Life and Times of Frederick Douglass* (10–12). 1962, Macmillan paper $14.95 (0-02-002350-2). The autobiography of the former slave who became an adviser to presidents. (Rev: BL 1/15/90) [921]

6213 Douglass, Frederick. *Narrative of the Life of Frederick Douglass, an American Slave* (10–12). 1982, Penguin paper $8.95 (0-14-039012-X). An autobiography that tells of the life of this former slave and abolitionist. [921]

6214 McKivigan, John R., ed. *Frederick Douglass* (10–12). Illus. Series: People Who Made History. 2004, Gale LB $33.70 (0-7377-1522-7). A collection of 17 scholarly essays that begin with a biography and continue to explore Douglass's ideas and contributions. (Rev: BL 2/15/04) [921]

6215 Meltzer, Milton, ed. *Frederick Douglass: In His Own Words* (8–12). Illus. 1995, Harcourt $22.00 (0-15-229492-9). An introduction to the articles and speeches of the great 19th-century abolitionist leader, arranged chronologically. (Rev: BL 12/15/94; SLJ 2/95) [305.8]

6216 Miller, Douglas T. *Frederick Douglass and the Fight for Freedom* (7–12). Illus. 1988, Facts on File $19.95 (0-8160-1617-8). An engrossing biography of the self-taught former slave who led the abolitionist movement. (Rev: BL 11/1/88; BR 1–2/89; SLJ 10/88; VOYA 2/89) [921]

DU BOIS, W. E. B.

6217 Du Bois, W. E. B. *The Autobiography of W. E. B. Du Bois* (10–12). Illus. 1976, Kraus $20.00 (0-527-25262-X). Written when he was over 90, this is both an autobiography of a distinguished African American and a history of the civil rights movement. [921]

6218 Marable, Manning. *W. E. B. Du Bois: Black Radical Democrat* (10–12). Illus. 1986, Twayne $28.95 (0-8057-7750-4). A compact biography of the great African American intellectual, humanitarian, and civil rights leader. (Rev: BL 11/1/86) [921]

6219 Rowh, Mark. *W. E. B. DuBois: Champion of Civil Rights* (7–12). Series: African-American

Biographies. 1999, Enslow LB $19.95 (0-7660-1209-3). The inspiring biography of the African American educator and writer who helped found the NAACP. (Rev: BL 11/15/99; HBG 4/00) [921]

FARRAKHAN, LOUIS

6220 Haskins, Jim. *Louis Farrakhan and the Nation of Islam* (7–12). Illus. 1996, Walker LB $16.85 (0-8027-8423-2). Beginning with a history of African American nationalism and the Nation of Islam, this biography places the life of Farrakhan within the movement for black solidarity. (Rev: BL 10/1/96; BR 1–2/97; SLJ 1/97) [921]

FREEMAN, ELIZABETH

6221 Wilds, Mary. *MumBet: The Life and Times of Elizabeth Freeman: The True Story of a Slave Who Won Her Freedom* (7–12). Illus. 1999, Avisson LB $19.95 (1-888105-40-2). The story of MumBet (Elizabeth Freeman), a slave who sued for her freedom in Massachusetts in 1781 after hearing a reading of the Declaration of Independence and won, helping to set the legal precedents that ended slavery in New England. (Rev: BL 6/1–15/99; SLJ 6/99; VOYA 2/00) [921]

GARVEY, MARCUS

6222 Caravantes, Peggy. *Marcus Garvey: Black Nationalist* (6–10). Series: Twentieth Century Leaders. 2004, Morgan Reynolds LB $21.95 (1-931798-14-1). A biography of this black nationalist, Pan-Africanist, and exponent of black civil rights. (Rev: BL 2/15/04; HBG 4/04; SLJ 11/03; VOYA 6/04) [921]

6223 Cronon, E. David. *Black Moses: The Story of Marcus Garvey and the Universal Negro Improvement Association* (10–12). 1955, Univ. of Wisconsin Pr. paper $15.95 (0-299-01214-X). This vivid, detailed account traces the life of the Jamaica-born black leader. [921]

6224 Lawler, Mary. *Marcus Garvey* (7–10). Illus. Series: Black Americans of Achievement. 1987, Chelsea LB $21.95 (1-55546-587-0). The story of the black leader who preached black separation and founded the Universal Negro Improvement Association. (Rev: BL 12/1/87; BR 1–2/89; VOYA 10/88) [921]

6225 Schraff, Anne. *Marcus Garvey: Controversial Champion of Black Pride* (6–10). Illus. Series: African-American Biographies. 2004, Enslow LB $20.95 (0-7660-2168-8). This is a fine biography of the controversial leader of the early 20th-century Pan-African movement with discussion of his opinions, including his separatist views on race. (Rev: BL 2/15/04) [921]

GRIMKE, ANGELINA

6226 Todras, Ellen H. *Angelina Grimke: Voice of Abolition* (9–12). Illus. 1999, Linnet LB $25.00 (0-208-02485-9). A handsome biography of the woman, born in Charleston in 1805, who became an outspoken foe of slavery and left the South for New England to work for the abolition of slavery and for women's rights. (Rev: BL 6/1–15/99; SLJ 5/99; VOYA 12/99) [921]

HAYDEN, LEWIS

6227 Strangis, Joel. *Lewis Hayden and the War Against Slavery* (7–12). 1998, Shoe String LB $25.00 (0-208-02430-1). The dramatic story of the former slave who became an active abolitionist and a stationmaster on the Underground Railroad. (Rev: BL 2/15/99; BR 9–10/99; HBG 9/99; SLJ 5/99; VOYA 10/99) [921]

HEIGHT, DOROTHY

6228 Height, Dorothy. *Open Wide the Freedom* (10–12). 2003, PublicAffairs $26.00 (1-58648-157-6). In her memoir of a lifetime spent in the struggle for equality, the African American author paints a vivid portrait of the 20th-century civil rights movement. (Rev: BL 7/03) [921]

JACKSON, JESSE

6229 Haskins, James. *Jesse Jackson: Civil Rights Activist* (6–10). Series: African-American Biographies. 2000, Enslow LB $19.95 (0-7660-1390-1). A biography of the man who has been a defender of the poor, minorities, and underprivileged. (Rev: BL 9/15/00; HBG 3/01; SLJ 11/00) [921]

JONES, MOTHER

6230 Gorn, Elliott J. *Mother Jones: The Most Dangerous Woman in America* (10–12). Illus. 2001, Hill & Wang $27.00 (0-8090-7093-6). An entertaining study of the life and accomplishments of Mary Harris "Mother" Jones and her activities as a labor organizer and fighter against child labor. (Rev: BL 3/15/01; SLJ 11/01) [921]

6231 Josephson, Judith P. *Mother Jones: Fierce Fighter for Workers' Rights* (6–10). Illus. 1997, Lerner LB $30.35 (0-8225-4924-7). The story of this early labor leader in coal country is also a history of the struggle against long work hours, unsafe working conditions, poor wages, and child labor. (Rev: BL 2/1/97; SLJ 4/97*) [921]

JORDAN, VERNON E.

6232 Jordan, Vernon E., and Annette Gordon-Reed. *Vernon Can Read!* (10–12). Illus. 2001, PublicAffairs $26.00 (1-891620-69-X). Jordan, the great civil rights leader, writes his autobiography and tells how he went from the law to working with the NAACP, the United Negro College Fund, and the Urban League. (Rev: BL 10/15/01) [921]

KING, CORETTA SCOTT

6233 King, Coretta Scott. *My Life with Martin Luther King, Jr.* Rev. ed. (9–12). 1993, Holt $17.95 (0-8050-2445-X). A revised, shortened edition of King's memoir of her life with her husband, Martin Luther King, Jr., with black-and-white photographs. (Rev: BL 2/15/93; SLJ 2/93) [323]

6234 Schraff, Anne. *Coretta Scott King: Striving for Civil Rights* (7–12). Series: African-American Biographies. 1997, Enslow LB $20.95 (0-89490-811-1). The life story of the gallant woman who has, with her family, continued the struggle for civil rights begun by her husband. (Rev: BL 6/1–15/97) [921]

KING, DEXTER

6235 King, Dexter Scott, and Ralph Wiley. *Growing Up King: An Intimate Memoir* (10–12). 2003, Warner $24.95 (0-446-52942-7). Only 7 years old when his father was assassinated, Dexter King tells what it was like to grow up in the shadow of Martin Luther King, Jr. (Rev: BL 1/1–15/03) [921]

KING, MARTIN LUTHER, JR.

6236 Anderson, Ho Che. *King Volume 2* (10–12). Illus. 2002, Fantagraphics paper $11.95 (1-56097-496-6). Martin Luther King, Jr.'s life from 1958 through the historic March on Washington in August 1963 is the focus of this second volume of a comic-book biography. The third volume, *King Volume 3*, covers the years from 1963 to 1968. (Rev: BL 5/15/02; SLJ 1/03) [921]

6237 Dyson, Michael Eric. *I May Not Get There with You: The True Martin Luther King Jr.* (10–12). 2000, Free Pr. $25.00 (0-684-86776-1). In this adult assessment of King's impact on American society, the author outlines King's philosophy, legacy, and personal failings. (Rev: BL 1/1–15/00*) [921]

6238 Frady, Marshall. *Martin Luther King, Jr.* (10–12). 2002, Viking $19.95 (0-670-88231-3). This slim volume, for better readers, examines the life and accomplishments of Martin Luther King, Jr. with material on the times in which he lived. (Rev: BL 12/15/01) [921]

6239 Haskins, Jim. *I Have a Dream: The Life and Words of Martin Luther King, Jr.* (6–12). 1993, Millbrook LB $29.90 (1-56294-087-2). Describes King's early life, family, and education, and the impact of the civil rights movement and beliefs that he espoused. (Rev: BL 2/15/93; SLJ 6/93*) [921]

6240 Johnson, Charles, and Bob Adelman. *King: A Photobiography of Martin Luther King, Jr.* (9–12). Illus. 2000, Viking Studio $40.00 (0-670-89216-5). This impressive album contains more than 300 photographs and a running narrative that covers King's life and accomplishments. (Rev: BL 11/1/00; SLJ 4/01) [921]

6241 King, Martin Luther, Jr. *The Autobiography of Martin Luther King, Jr.* (10–12). Ed. by Clayborne Carson. 1998, Warner $25.00 (0-446-52412-3). King comes alive in this collection of his writings and speeches that reveals much about the national and international issues of the time. (Rev: BL 11/15/98*) [921]

6242 Oates, Stephen B. *Let the Trumpet Sound: The Life of Martin Luther King, Jr.* (9–12). 1982, Harper & Row $19.95 (0-06-014993-0). A highly regarded biography of the great civil rights leader and his legacy. [921]

6243 Patterson, Lillie. *Martin Luther King, Jr. and the Freedom Movement* (7–12). Illus. 1989, Facts on File $19.95 (0-8160-1605-4). A biography of the civil rights leader and the movement he led. (Rev: BL 7/89; BR 11–12/89; SLJ 9/89; VOYA 12/89) [921]

6244 Schloredt, Valerie, and Pam Brown. *Martin Luther King Jr.* (5–10). Illus. Series: World Peacemakers. 2004, Gale LB $27.44 (1-56711-977-8). A readable account of this civil rights leader and the times in which he lived. (Rev: BL 2/15/04) [921]

6245 Schulke, Flip. *He Had a Dream: Martin Luther King, Jr., and the Civil Rights Movement* (9–12). 1995, Norton $39.95 (0-393-03729-0); paper $19.95 (0-393-31264-X). A photoessay documenting the life of Dr. Martin Luther King, Jr. (Rev: BL 3/1/95) [921]

6246 Schulke, Flip, and Penelope McPhee. *King Remembered* (9–12). Illus. 1986, Norton $22.95 (0-393-02256-0); paper $12.00 (0-671-62018-5). A heavily illustrated biography that stresses King's work in civil rights. (Rev: BL 1/1/86) [921]

6247 Siebold, Thomas, ed. *Martin Luther King, Jr.* (7–12). 2000, Greenhaven LB $21.96 (0-7377-0227-3); paper $13.96 (0-7377-0226-5). This collection of primary source documents concentrates on Dr. King's life, mission, and his effects on African Americans and the nation. (Rev: BL 4/15/00; SLJ 9/00) [921]

LEWIS, JOHN

6248 Lewis, John. *Walking with the Wind: A Memoir of the Movement* (10–12). 1998, Simon & Schuster $25.50 (0-684-81065-4). The autobiography of the pioneer civil rights leader who was active in the movement almost from the beginning, including the lunch-counter sit-ins in 1960 and the march on Washington in 1963. (Rev: BL 4/15/98*; SLJ 12/98) [921]

MALCOLM X

6249 Diamond, Arthur. *Malcolm X: A Voice for Black America* (6–12). Illus. Series: People to Know. 1994, Enslow $18.95 (0-89490-453-3). A sympathetic but unbiased account of the man, once a convict, who became an important African American leader. (Rev: BL 6/1–15/94) [921]

6250 Gallen, David. *Malcolm X: As They Knew Him* (9–12). 1992, Carroll & Graf $21.95 (0-88184-851-4); paper $11.95 (0-88184-850-6). Interviews with and about Malcolm X, essays analyzing his political role, and personal reminiscences from individuals including Maya Angelou, Alex Haley, and James Baldwin. (Rev: BL 5/15/92) [921]

6251 Malcolm X, and Alex Haley. *The Autobiography of Malcolm X* (7–12). 1999, Ballantine $20.00 (0-345-91536-4); paper $12.00 (0-345-91503-8). The story of the man who turned from Harlem drug pusher into a charismatic leader of his people. [921]

6252 Myers, Walter Dean. *Malcolm X: By Any Means Necessary* (6–12). 1993, Scholastic paper $13.95 (0-590-46484-1). An eloquent tribute to the brilliant, radical African American leader, quoting extensively from *The Autobiography of Malcolm X*. (Rev: BCCB 3/93; BL 11/15/92; SLJ 2/93) [921]

6253 Perry, Bruce. *Malcolm: A Life of the Man Who Changed Black America* (9–12). 1991, Station Hill $24.95 (0-88268-103-6). This biography shows various sides of the African American leader. (Rev: BL 6/15/91; SLJ 3/92) [921]

PANTOJA, ANTONIA

6254 Pantoja, Antonia. *Memoir of a Visionary: Antonia Pantoja* (10–12). 2002, Arte Publico $26.95 (1-55885-365-0). Pantoja, winner of the Medal of Freedom, describes the childhood of deprivation that motivated her work in helping Puerto Rican youth. (Rev: BL 2/15/02) [972.95]

PARKER, JOHN P.

6255 Sprague, Stuart Seely, ed. *His Promised Land: The Autobiography of John P. Parker, Former Slave and Conductor on the Underground Railroad* (10–12). 1997, Norton $20.00 (0-393-03941-2). The recently discovered action-packed autobiography of John Parker begins with his life as a slave in chains when he was 8 years old and continues to his amazing work with the Underground Railroad in Ripley, Ohio. (Rev: BL 10/15/96; SLJ 5/97) [921]

PARKS, ROSA

6256 Brinkley, Douglas. *Rosa Parks* (10–12). Series: Penguin Lives. 2000, Viking $19.95 (0-670-89160-6). A fine biography of the woman whom the author calls "a symbol of the triumph of steadfastness in the name of justice" for her role in the struggle for civil rights. (Rev: BL 7/00) [921]

6257 Hull, Mary. *Rosa Parks* (7–10). Illus. Series: Black Americans of Achievement. 1994, Chelsea LB $21.95 (0-7910-1881-4). The story of the seemingly ordinary African American woman who had the courage to fight bus segregation in Montgomery, Alabama. (Rev: BL 6/1–15/94; SLJ 8/94; VOYA 8/94) [921]

6258 Parks, Rosa, and Jim Haskins. *Rosa Parks: My Story* (6–10). 1992, Dial $17.99 (0-8037-0673-1). This autobiography of the civil rights hero becomes an oral history of the movement, including her recollections of Martin Luther King, Jr., Roy Wilkins, and others. (Rev: BL 12/15/91; SLJ 2/92) [921]

SHABAZZ, BETTY

6259 Jeffrey, Laura S. *Betty Shabazz: Sharing the Vision of Malcolm X* (6–10). Series: African-American Biographies. 2000, Enslow LB $20.95 (0-7660-1210-7). The wife of Malcolm X was only 31 years old when her husband was assassinated and she was left to raise six children and continue his fight for civil rights. (Rev: BL 9/15/00; HBG 3/01; SLJ 1/01) [921]

6260 Rickford, Russell J. *Betty Shabazz: A Life Before and After Malcolm X* (10–12). Illus. 2003, Sourcebooks $35.00 (1-4022-0171-0). A lengthy but readable biography that traces the life of Malcolm X's widow from childhood through her marriage and on to her own triumphs as a civil rights leader. (Rev: BL 11/15/03) [921]

STANTON, ELIZABETH CADY

6261 Bohannon, Lisa Frederiksen. *Women's Rights and Nothing Less: The Story of Elizabeth Cady Stanton* (6–12). Illus. 2000, Morgan Reynolds LB $21.95 (1-883846-66-8). An engrossing biography of this great fighter for human rights and her relations with such people as Susan B. Anthony and Frederick Douglass. (Rev: BL 12/15/00; HBG 3/01; SLJ 12/00) [921]

6262 Cullen-DuPont, Kathryn. *Elizabeth Cady Stanton and Women's Liberty* (6–10). 1992, Facts on File $25.00 (0-8160-2413-8). Presents a humanistic picture of one of the founders of the women's rights movement and provides an intimate portrait of Stanton as wife, mother, and activist. (Rev: BL 10/1/92; SLJ 7/92) [921]

6263 Sigerman, Harriet. *Elizabeth Cady Stanton: The Right Is Ours* (6–10). Illus. Series: Oxford Portraits. 2001, Oxford $24.00 (0-19-511969-X). The life of the pioneering suffragist, accompanied by photographs and historic documents such as newspaper articles and cartoons. (Rev: BL 12/15/01; HBG 3/02; SLJ 11/01; VOYA 2/02) [921]

STEINEM, GLORIA

6264 Daffron, Carolyn. *Gloria Steinem* (7–12). Illus. 1988, Chelsea LB $19.95 (1-55546-679-6). The story of the influential feminist leader who founded *Ms.* magazine. (Rev: BL 11/1/87; BR 11–12/88; VOYA 2/89) [921]

6265 Hoff, Mark. *Gloria Steinem: The Women's Movement* (6–12). Series: New Directions. 1991, Millbrook LB $21.90 (1-878841-19-X). A biography of the famous feminist. (Rev: BL 2/1/91) [921]

TOUSSAINT, PIERRE

6266 Jones, Arthur. *Pierre Toussaint* (10–12). 2003, Doubleday $24.95 (0-385-49994-9). This inspiring biography tracks Toussaint's life from birth as a slave in Saint-Domingue (now Haiti) to his selfless support of the Catholic Church, former slaves, and the impoverished in New York. (Rev: BL 8/03) [921]

TRUTH, SOJOURNER

6267 Krass, Peter. *Sojourner Truth* (7–12). Illus. 1988, Chelsea LB $21.95 (1-55546-611-7). The life of a woman who began as a slave and ended as a respected abolitionist and feminist. (Rev: BL 10/1/88) [921]

6268 Sheehan, Jacqueline. *Truth* (11–12). 2003, Free Pr. $24.00 (0-7432-4444-3). A gritty, fictionalized biography of Sojourner Truth's experiences as a slave and abolitionist. (Rev: BL 8/03)

6269 Whalin, Terry. *Sojourner Truth: American Abolitionist* (9–12). Series: Heroes of the Faith. 1998, Chelsea $21.95 (0-7910-5034-3). Truth's life and work as an abolitionist are placed in historical context. (Rev: HBG 3/99) [921]

TUBMAN, HARRIET

6270 Bradford, Sarah. *Harriet Tubman, the Moses of Her People* (7–12). Illus. 1961, Peter Smith $18.75 (0-8446-1717-2). A biography first published in 1869 of this former slave who brought hundreds of slaves north to freedom. [921]

6271 Clinton, Catherine. *Harriet Tubman: The Road to Freedom* (10–12). Illus. 2004, Little, Brown $25.95 (0-316-14492-4). Harvard history professor Clinton places Tubman's life and contributions to the Underground Railroad in historical context and introduces details of her contemporaries. (Rev: BL 12/15/03) [921]

6272 Larson, Kate Clifford. *Bound for the Promised Land: Harriet Tubman, Portrait of an American Hero* (10–12). 2004, Ballantine $24.95 (0-345-45627-0). This well-researched biography delves into Tubman's background and covers her post-Civil War life to give a well-rounded portrait. (Rev: BL 12/15/03) [973.7]

TURNER, NAT

6273 Bisson, Terry. *Nat Turner: Slave Revolt Leader* (7–10). Illus. 1988, Chelsea LB $21.95 (1-55546-613-3). A biography of the courageous black man who led one of the nation's most important slave revolts. (Rev: BL 8/88; BR 1–2/89; SLJ 2/89; VOYA 2/89) [921]

6274 Edwards, Judith. *Nat Turner's Slave Rebellion* (7–12). Illus. Series: In American History. 2000, Enslow LB $19.95 (0-7660-1302-2). After some general material on slavery and other slave rebellions, this account stresses the life of Nat Turner and the consequences of his belief that he was sent by God to free the slaves. (Rev: BL 2/15/00; HBG 9/00; SLJ 7/00) [921]

WASHINGTON, BOOKER T.

6275 Washington, Booker T. *Up from Slavery: An Autobiography by Booker T. Washington* (7–12). Illus. 1963, Airmont paper $3.95 (0-8049-0157-0). The story of the slave who later organized the Tuskegee Institute. [921]

WELLS, IDA B.

6276 Fradin, Dennis B., and Judith B. Fradin. *Ida B. Wells: Mother of the Civil Rights Movement* (5–10). 2000, Clarion $18.00 (0-395-89898-6). An inspiring biography of the African American who was born a slave and went on to become a school teacher, journalist, and an activist who fought for black women's right to vote and helped found the NAACP. (Rev: BL 2/15/00; HB 5–6/00; HBG 10/00; SLJ 4/00*) [921]

WILLIAMS, ROGER

6277 Gaustad, Edwin S. *Roger Williams: Prophet of Liberty* (9–12). Series: Oxford Portraits. 2001, Oxford $24.00 (0-19-513000-6). An in-depth look at the life and accomplishments of Roger Williams, founder of Rhode Island and advocate of religious freedom. (Rev: BL 9/15/01; HBG 10/01; SLJ 7/01) [921]

ZITKALA-SA (RED BIRD)

6278 Rappaport, Doreen. *The Flight of Red Bird: The Life of Zitkala-Sa* (7–10). 1997, NewStar Media $15.99 (0-8037-1438-6). The remarkable story of Zitkala-Sa (Red Bird), who was born to a Sioux mother and a white father in 1876 and devoted her life to advocating the rights of Native Americans. (Rev: BL 7/97; SLJ 7/97; VOYA 10/98) [921]

Presidents and Their Families

ADAMS, ABIGAIL

6279 Bober, Natalie S. *Abigail Adams: Witness to a Revolution* (6–12). 1995, Atheneum $18.00 (0-689-31760-3). A portrait of a woman and the age she lived in. (Rev: BL 4/15/95*; SLJ 6/95) [921]

6280 Osborne, Angela. *Abigail Adams* (6–10). Illus. 1988, Chelsea LB $19.95 (1-55546-635-4). The biography of the early feminist who was a strong influence on husband John and a fine recorder of American history. (Rev: BL 12/1/88; BR 5–6/89; SLJ 1/89) [921]

ADAMS, JOHN

6281 Lukes, Bonnie L. *John Adams: Public Servant* (8–12). Illus. Series: Notable Americans. 2000, Morgan Reynolds LB $21.95 (1-883846-80-3). An excellent biography of the second president of the United States that reveals both his virtues and his flaws. (Rev: BL 12/1/00; HBG 3/01; SLJ 2/01) [921]

6282 McCullough, David. *John Adams* (10–12). 2001, Simon & Schuster $35.00 (0-684-81363-7). In this prize-winning biography, the author sees the second president of the United States as a blunt, thin-skinned, compassionate, intelligent man. (Rev: BL 3/1/01*) [921]

ADAMS, JOHN QUINCY

6283 Remini, Robert. *John Quincy Adams* (11–12). Series: American Presidents. 2002, Holt $20.00 (0-8050-6939-9). This frank and engaging biography of America's sixth president paints a portrait of a well-meaning son who was unable to live up to the legacy of his illustrious father. (Rev: BL 7/02) [921]

ARTHUR, CHESTER A.

6284 Karabell, Zachary. *Chester Alan Arthur* (10–12). Series: American Presidents. 2004, Holt $20.00 (0-8050-6951-8). Arthur became the nation's leader after the assassination of Garfield in 1881. (Rev: BL 5/15/04) [921]

BUSH, GEORGE H. W.

6285 Anderson, Ken. *George Bush: A Lifetime of Service* (6–12). Illus. 2003, Eakin $17.95 (1-57168-663-0); paper $12.95 (1-57168-600-2). George Herbert Walker Bush, the 41st president, is profiled in this biography that gives insights into his relationship with his son, George W. Bush. (Rev: BL 1/1–15/03; HBG 10/03; SLJ 2/03) [921]

6286 Pemberton, William E. *George Bush* (6–12). Series: World Leaders. 1993, Rourke LB $25.27 (0-86625-478-1). A biography of the former president and an assessment of his accomplishments in office. (Rev: BL 12/1/93) [921]

6287 Schuman, Michael A. *George H. W. Bush* (6–12). Illus. Series: United States Presidents. 2002, Enslow LB $20.95 (0-7660-1702-8). Bush's youth, family, education, career, and presidency are all covered here, as is his role raising children with strong political agendas. (Rev: BL 3/1/03; HBG 10/03) [921]

BUSH, GEORGE W.

6288 Bruni, Frank. *Ambling into History: The Unlikely Odyssey of George W. Bush* (10–12). 2002, HarperCollins $23.95 (0-06-621371-1). A generally positive overview of the 43rd president George W. Bush that focuses on his character and intelligence. (Rev: BL 2/15/02) [921]

6289 McNeese, Tim. *George W. Bush: First President of the New Century* (6–10). Series: Notable Americans. 2001, Morgan Reynolds LB $20.95 (1-883846-85-4). This biography of the former Texas governor covers his life from childhood and gives details of the controversial 2000 presidential election. (Rev: HBG 3/02; SLJ 4/02) [921]

CARTER, JIMMY

6290 Carter, Jimmy. *An Hour Before Daylight: Memoirs of a Rural Boyhood* (10–12). Illus. 2001, Simon & Schuster $26.00 (0-7432-1193-6). In this touching memoir, the former president discusses his Georgia childhood and all the people who cared for him on the farm and in Plains. (Rev: BL 11/1/00) [921]

6291 Carter, Jimmy. *Living Faith* (10–12). 1996, Times Books $23.00 (0-8129-2736-2). In this first-person account, the former president tells about his beliefs and how he tries to practice them in everyday life. (Rev: BL 9/15/96; SLJ 4/97) [921]

6292 Whitelaw, Nancy. *Jimmy Carter: President and Peacemaker* (7–10). Illus. 2003, Morgan Reynolds LB $21.95 (1-931798-18-4). From childhood in rural Georgia to his current work for charities and international peace, this is the story of the 39th president. (Rev: BL 12/15/03; HBG 4/04; VOYA 12/03) [921]

CLEVELAND, GROVER

6293 Graff, Henry. *Grover Cleveland* (10–12). 2002, Holt $20.00 (0-8050-6923-2). A concise overview of the life and political career of the only American president elected to two non-consecutive terms in office. (Rev: BL 8/02) [921]

CLINTON, BILL

6294 Gallen, David. *Bill Clinton: As They Know Him: An Oral Biography* (9–12). 1994, Richard Gallen $21.95 (0-9636477-2-5). Interviews with people who have known the president provide anecdotes and observations about his childhood, governorship, and candidacy. (Rev: BL 3/15/94; SLJ 8/94) [921]

6295 Kelly, Michael. *Bill Clinton* (6–10). Series: Overcoming Adversity. 1998, Chelsea LB $21.95 (0-7910-4700-8). This book describes Bill Clinton's difficult childhood but focuses on his political career, emphasizing the important role Hillary Rodham Clinton has played in his success, with a good balance between coverage of Clinton's achievements and problems. (Rev: HBG 3/99; SLJ 2/99) [921]

6296 Maraniss, David. *First in His Class: The Biography of Bill Clinton* (9–12). 1995, Simon & Schuster $25.00 (0-671-87109-9). An adult biography of Bill Clinton that ends before the scandals of his second term. (Rev: BL 1/15/95) [921]

6297 *William J. Clinton* (9–12). Ed. by Todd Howard. Illus. Series: Presidents and Their Decisions. 2000, Greenhaven LB $22.96 (0-7377-0498-5); paper $14.96 (0-7377-0497-7). After an introduction that tracks Clinton's climb from an impoverished childhood in Arkansas to the highest office in the land, issue-specific essays look at his handling of the key challenges facing his presidency. (Rev: BL 2/15/01; SLJ 4/01) [921]

COOLIDGE, CALVIN

6298 Allen, Michael Geoffrey. *Calvin Coolidge* (6–12). Illus. Series: United States Presidents. 2002, Enslow LB $20.95 (0-7660-1703-6). Coolidge's youth, family, education, career, and presidency are all covered here, as are his character and his legacy. (Rev: BL 3/1/03; HBG 3/03; SLJ 2/03) [921]

EISENHOWER, DWIGHT D.

6299 Ambrose, Stephen. *Eisenhower: Soldier and President* (10–12). 1990, Simon & Schuster paper $18.00 (0-671-74758-4). An excellent one-volume biography of Eisenhower that includes his failures as well as his triumphs. [921]

6300 Sandberg, Peter Lars. *Dwight D. Eisenhower* (7–12). Illus. 1986, Chelsea LB $19.95 (0-87754-

521-9). A brief biography of the president and war leader that emphasizes his human side. (Rev: SLJ 11/86) [921]

6301 Wicker, Tom. *Dwight D. Eisenhower* (10–12). Series: American Presidents. 2002, Holt $20.00 (0-8050-6907-0). A concise appraisal of the life and presidency of Dwight D. Eisenhower; useful for report writers. (Rev: BL 10/15/02) [921]

6302 Young, Jeff C. *Dwight D. Eisenhower: Soldier and President* (6–12). Illus. 2001, Morgan Reynolds LB $20.95 (1-883846-76-5). This well-written and interesting biography of the 34th president covers his life from boyhood, his career, and his personality. (Rev: BL 11/15/01; HBG 3/02; SLJ 2/02) [921]

GRANT, ULYSSES S.

6303 Marrin, Albert. *Unconditional Surrender: U. S. Grant and the Civil War* (6–12). 1994, Atheneum LB $21.00 (0-689-31837-5). Part history, part biography, this is a fine study of Grant and his pivotal role in the Civil War. (Rev: BL 4/1/94*; SLJ 7/94*; VOYA 6/94) [921]

6304 Smith, Jean Edward. *Grant* (10–12). 2001, Simon & Schuster $35.00 (0-684-84926-7); paper $20.00 (0-684-84927-5). An outstanding biography of Ulysses S. Grant from his youth and career at West Point to his presidency and after. (Rev: BL 4/1/01) [921]

HARDING, WARREN G.

6305 Dean, John W. *Warren G. Harding* (10–12). Series: American Presidents. 2004, Holt $20.00 (0-8050-6956-9). A useful biography of this often-overlooked president that depicts him as an innovative, intelligent, and conscientious man. (Rev: BL 1/1–15/04; SLJ 6/04) [921]

HAYES, RUTHERFORD B.

6306 Trefousse, Hans L. *Rutherford B. Hayes* (10–12). Series: American Presidents. 2002, Holt $20.00 (0-8050-6908-9). A concise profile of America's 19th and often-overlooked president; useful for report writers. (Rev: BL 10/15/02) [921]

JACKSON, ANDREW

6307 Meltzer, Milton. *Andrew Jackson and His America* (8–12). 1993, Watts LB $20.00 (0-531-11157-1). Presents a multifaceted picture of Jackson and his role in such historic operations as the Indian removal and the abolitionist movement. (Rev: BL 1/15/94*; SLJ 1/94; VOYA 2/94) [921]

6308 Whitelaw, Nancy. *Andrew Jackson: Frontier President* (7–10). Illus. Series: Notable Americans. 2000, Morgan Reynolds LB $19.95 (1-883846-67-6). A fine biography of an interesting, multifaceted man who overcame many obstacles to achieve prominence. (Rev: BL 11/1/00; HBG 3/01; SLJ 2/01) [921]

JEFFERSON, THOMAS

6309 Appleby, Joyce. *Thomas Jefferson* (10–12). Series: American Presidents. 2003, Holt $20.00 (0-8050-6924-0). An appreciative look at Jefferson's life and presidency that offers insight into his political and social philosophies. (Rev: BL 1/1–15/03) [921]

6310 Ellis, Joseph J. *American Sphinx: The Character of Thomas Jefferson* (10–12). 1997, Knopf $29.95 (0-679-44490-4). This well-written study of Jefferson shows the human side of this great historical figure — a man who made mistakes, a man with debts, a man with family problems. (Rev: BL 1/1–15/97; SLJ 9/97) [921]

6311 Meltzer, Milton. *Thomas Jefferson: The Revolutionary Aristocrat* (6–10). 1991, Watts LB $18.95 (0-531-11069-9). A presentation of the major events of Jefferson's life and a discussion of some troubling inconsistencies, such as his ownership of slaves. (Rev: BL 12/15/91*; SLJ 12/91*) [921]

6312 Miller, Douglas T. *Thomas Jefferson and the Creation of America* (8–12). Series: Makers of America. 1997, Facts on File $25.00 (0-8160-3393-5). This biography presents Jefferson as a complex character who personified ideals of equality and liberty yet lived a life of many contradictions and conflicts. (Rev: BL 11/15/97; BR 3–4/98) [921]

6313 Severance, John B. *Thomas Jefferson; Architect of Democracy* (7–12). 1998, Clarion $18.00 (0-395-84513-0). A thoughtful, well-rounded biography that focuses on Jefferson's accomplishments and his beliefs, with many quotations from his writings. (Rev: BL 9/1/98; BR 5–6/99; HBG 3/99; SLJ 12/98; VOYA 4/99) [921]

6314 Whitelaw, Nancy. *Thomas Jefferson: Philosopher and President* (7–10). 2001, Morgan Reynolds LB $20.95 (1-883846-81-1). This concise and thorough biography, which covers Jefferson's strengths and weaknesses, will be useful for report writers. (Rev: HBG 3/02; SLJ 3/02) [921]

JOHNSON, LYNDON B.

6315 Eskow, Dennis. *Lyndon Baines Johnson* (8–12). Series: Impact Biographies. 1993, Watts paper $24.00 (0-531-13019-3). Well-chosen episodes and anecdotes illustrate the life of this Texas-born president. (Rev: BL 9/1/93; VOYA 10/93) [921]

6316 Goodwin, Doris Kearns. *Lyndon Johnson and the American Dream* (10–12). 1976, Harper & Row paper $17.95 (0-312-06027-0). For better readers, this is a biography of Johnson that reveals the real man behind the power. [921]

6317 Kaye, Tony. *Lyndon B. Johnson* (6–10). Illus. 1987, Chelsea LB $19.95 (0-87754-536-7). A biography of the president associated with Great Society legislation and the Vietnam War. (Rev: BL 1/15/88; SLJ 4/88) [921]

6318 *Lyndon B. Johnson* (9–12). Ed. by Scott Barbour. Series: Presidents and Their Decisions. 2001, Greenhaven LB $22.96 (0-7377-0500-0); paper $14.96 (0-7377-0499-3). This collection of essays covers highlights of LBJ's presidency, including his Great Society legislation and his inability to end the war in Vietnam. (Rev: BL 3/1/01) [921]

6319 Schuman, Michael A. *Lyndon B. Johnson* (6–10). Series: United States Presidents. 1998, Enslow LB $20.95 (0-89490-938-X). Johnson's public career, presidential administration, and legacy are the focus of this biography. (Rev: HBG 3/99; SLJ 3/99) [921]

KENNEDY FAMILY

6320 Uschan, Michael V. *The Kennedys* (7–12). 2001, Gale LB $27.45 (1-56006-875-2). The Kennedys presented here — with their achievements and their failings — are Joseph P.; his sons John, Robert, and Ted; and John's wife Jacqueline and son John Jr. (Rev: SLJ 1/02) [920]

KENNEDY, JOHN F.

6321 Cooper, Ilene. *Jack: The Early Years of John F. Kennedy* (7–12). 2003, Dutton $22.99 (0-525-46923-0). Jack's youth and school years — in particular his rivalry with his older brother — are described in a narrative peppered with anecdotes and quotations from family and friends. (Rev: BCCB 2/03; BL 1/1–15/03; HB 3–4/03; HBG 10/03; SLJ 2/03; VOYA 4/03) [921]

6322 Lowe, Jacques. *JFK Remembered* (9–12). 1993, Random $37.50 (0-679-42399-0). The photographs Lowe took as Kennedy's personal photographer are presented as full-page black-and-white spreads with identifying text. (Rev: BL 12/1/93) [921]

6323 Manchester, William. *One Brief Shining Moment: Remembering Kennedy* (9–12). Illus. 1988, Little, Brown paper $16.95 (0-316-54511-2). A remembrance of Kennedy in 200 photographs and quotations from friends and associates. [921]

6324 Netzley, Patricia. *The Assassination of President John F. Kennedy* (7–12). Series: American Events. 1994, Macmillan LB $18.95 (0-02-768127-0). An account of the events leading up to the assassination, the event itself, and the consequences. (Rev: BL 7/94) [921]

6325 Randall, Marta. *John F. Kennedy* (6–10). Illus. 1987, Chelsea LB $19.95 (0-87754-586-3). A biography of this beloved president that includes coverage of domestic and international crises. (Rev: BL 1/15/88; BR 9–10/88; VOYA 10/88) [921]

6326 Spencer, Lauren. *The Assassination of John F. Kennedy* (6–10). Series: Library of Political Assassinations. 2001, Rosen LB $26.50 (0-8239-3541-8). This is a highly readable account of the assassination, its political buildup, and the social fallout. (Rev: BL 3/15/02; SLJ 6/02) [921]

6327 Swisher, Clarice, ed. *John F. Kennedy* (8–12). Illus. Series: People Who Made History. 1999, Greenhaven LB $21.96 (0-7377-0225-7); paper $13.96 (0-7377-0224-9). This collection of essays covers such topics as major influences on JFK, the presidential debates, the new frontier, foreign policy, and assessments of his presidency. (Rev: BL 2/1/00) [921]

6328 Uschan, Michael V. *John F. Kennedy* (6–10). Illus. 1998, Lucent LB $27.45 (1-56006-482-X). An objective account that uses quotations from many original sources, chronicling fairly and honestly Kennedy's rise to power, his triumphs, and his faults. (Rev: SLJ 4/99; VOYA 8/99) [921]

KENNEDY, JOHN F., JR.

6329 Blow, Richard. *American Son: A Portrait of John F Kennedy, Jr.* (10–12). 2002, Holt $25.00 (0-8050-7051-6). This profile of the late John F. Kennedy Jr. focuses primarily on his involvement with *George,* the political magazine he founded. (Rev: BL 3/15/02) [921]

KENNEDY, ROBERT F.

6330 Mills, Judie. *Robert Kennedy* (8–12). Illus. 1998, Millbrook LB $36.90 (1-56294-250-6). A useful, informative biography that tells of Robert Kennedy's life and career and places them in the context of other historical events. (Rev: BL 8/98; SLJ 9/98) [921]

6331 Steel, Ronald. *In Love with the Night: The American Romance with Robert Kennedy* (10–12). 2000, Simon & Schuster $23.00 (0-684-80829-3). A candid assessment of the life and career of this famous member of the Kennedy family. (Rev: BL 1/1–15/00) [921]

6332 Thomas, Evan. *Robert Kennedy* (10–12). 2000, Simon & Schuster $27.50 (0-684-83480-4). A biography of the Kennedy who changed dramatically during his 42 years, and of the impact his brother's assassination had on him. (Rev: BL 8/00) [921]

LINCOLN, ABRAHAM

6333 *Abraham Lincoln* (9–12). Ed. by Helen Cothran. Series: Presidents and Their Decisions. 2001, Gale $19.95 (0-7377-0917-0). This collection of essays about Lincoln covers such topics as his

involvement in the outbreak of the Civil War, his efforts to free the slaves, and his plans for reconstruction of the Confederacy. (Rev: BL 1/1–15/02; SLJ 2/02) [921]

6334 Barter, James. *Abraham Lincoln* (7–12). Series: The Importance Of. 2003, Gale LB $21.96 (1-56006-965-1). This biography of Lincoln uses ample quotations from important sources and tries to evaluate Lincoln's importance by present-day standards. (Rev: BL 3/15/03) [921]

6335 Donald, David Herbert. *Lincoln* (9–12). 1995, Simon & Schuster $35.00 (0-684-80846-3). A psychological portrait of the man from humble roots who slowly but determinedly found his niche as an attorney, then as a politician, and finally as president. (Rev: BL 8/95*) [921]

6336 Gienapp, William E. *Abraham Lincoln and Civil War America* (10–12). Illus. 2002, Oxford $25.00 (0-19-515099-6). Students researching Lincoln's political career will find useful material in this biography that draws heavily on the president's writings. (Rev: BL 2/1/02) [921]

6337 Holzer, Harold. *Abraham Lincoln: The Writer* (6–10). Illus. 2000, Boyds Mills $15.95 (1-56397-772-9). Following a brief biography, this resource contains letters, excerpts from speeches, notes, debates, and inaugural addresses, each with explanatory introductions that connect the snippet to his life. (Rev: BL 5/1/00; HBG 9/00; SLJ 6/00) [921]

6338 Keneally, Thomas. *Abraham Lincoln* (10–12). 2003, Viking $19.95 (0-670-03175-5). In this accessible and detailed biography, Keneally looks at the president's character and his many anxieties. (Rev: BL 12/1/02) [921]

6339 Kunhardt, Philip B., et al. *Lincoln* (9–12). 1992, Knopf $50.00 (0-679-40862-2). With many rare photographs, this illustrated biography of Lincoln deserves a spot in high school collections. (Rev: BL 9/1/92; SLJ 7/93; VOYA 8/93) [921]

6340 Lincoln, Abraham. *The Portable Abraham Lincoln* (9–12). Ed. by Andrew Delbanco. 1992, Viking paper $13.95 (0-14-017031-6). Lincoln comes to life in this collection of his writings, speeches, correspondence, and notes. [921]

6341 Marrin, Albert. *Commander in Chief Abraham Lincoln and the Civil War* (7–12). Illus. 1997, Dutton $25.00 (0-525-45822-0). This is not only a stirring biography of Lincoln but also a history of the Civil War, with profiles of people involved in the fight against slavery, such as John Brown. (Rev: BL 12/15/97; BR 5–6/98; SLJ 2/98*; VOYA 4/98) [921]

6342 Morris, Jan. *Lincoln: A Foreigner's Quest* (10–12). 2000, Simon & Schuster $23.00 (0-684-85515-1). In this bold, intimate, mature look at the life and works of Abraham Lincoln, the famed English writer and historian explores her own attitudes and feelings toward this great American. (Rev: BL 1/1–15/00; SLJ 11/00) [921]

6343 Oates, Stephen B. *With Malice Toward None: The Life of Abraham Lincoln* (10–12). 1978, NAL paper $4.95 (0-451-62314-2). This account probes into the personal life of Lincoln as well as his public career. [921]

6344 O'Neal, Michael. *The Assassination of Abraham Lincoln* (6–10). Series: Great Mysteries. 1991, Greenhaven LB $18.96 (0-89908-092-8). Outlines known facts about Lincoln's assassination and poses questions about the mysteries that remain unsolved. (Rev: BL 3/1/92; SLJ 4/92) [921]

6345 Reck, W. Emerson. *A. Lincoln: His Last 24 Hours* (9–12). Illus. 1987, McFarland LB $27.50 (0-89950-216-4). A vivid hour-by-hour recreation of the last day of Lincoln's life. (Rev: BL 8/87; BR 11–12/87; SLJ 11/87; VOYA 12/87) [921]

6346 Sandburg, Carl. *Abraham Lincoln: The Prairie Years and the War Years.* illustrated ed (10–12). 1970, Harcourt paper $26.00 (0-15-602752-6). This one-volume work condenses Sandburg's esteemed longer work on the life of Lincoln. [921]

MCKINLEY, WILLIAM

6347 Phillips, Kevin. *William McKinley* (10–12). Series: American Presidents. 2003, Holt $20.00 (0-8050-6953-4). High school report writers will appreciate this detailed biography of McKinley that makes a convincing case for reevaluating the widely held perception that the 25th president made few worthwhile contributions. (Rev: BL 7/03) [921]

MADISON, JAMES

6348 Wills, Garry. *James Madison* (10–12). 2002, Holt $20.00 (0-8050-6905-4). Wills paints a portrait of America's fourth president as a well-meaning intellectual who was ill-equipped to lead his nation in war. (Rev: BL 3/1/02*) [921]

MONROE, JAMES

6349 Wetzel, Charles. *James Monroe* (6–10). Illus. 1989, Chelsea LB $19.95 (1-55546-817-9). The life of the Revolutionary War hero and details of his presidency and the foreign policy named after him. (Rev: BL 7/89; BR 9–10/89) [921]

NIXON, RICHARD M.

6350 Barron, Rachel. *Richard Nixon: American Politician* (7–12). Illus. Series: Notable Americans. 1998, Morgan Reynolds LB $21.95 (1-883846-33-1). An objective biography of this contradictory figure who became the century's most controversial president. (Rev: BL 8/98; HBG 3/99; SLJ 12/98; VOYA 10/98) [921]

6351 Nixon, Richard M. *RN: The Memoirs of Richard Nixon* (10–12). 1990, Simon & Schuster paper $35.00 (0-671-70741-8). This autobiography discusses such topics as Nixon's negotiations with the Soviets and Chinese and the conduct of the Vietnam War. [921]

6352 *Richard M. Nixon* (9–12). Ed. by Jeff Hay. Series: Presidents and Their Decisions. 2000, Greenhaven LB $22.96 (0-7377-0405-5); paper $14.96 (0-7377-0404-7). This collection of essays about Richard Nixon discusses his environmental reforms, improved relations with China, the slow ending of the Vietnam War, and the Watergate scandal. (Rev: BL 3/1/01; SLJ 3/01) [921]

6353 Ripley, C. Peter. *Richard Nixon* (6–10). Illus. 1987, Chelsea LB $19.95 (0-87754-585-5). Beginning with his 1974 resignation, Nixon's life is retraced and an assessment of his career is given. (Rev: BL 12/1/87; BR 5–6/88; SLJ 12/87) [921]

ONASSIS, JACQUELINE KENNEDY

6354 Spoto, Donald. *Jacqueline Bouvier Kennedy Onassis: A Life* (10–12). 2000, St. Martin's $24.95 (0-312-24650-1). Drawn from interviews and published material, this is a biography of an intelligent and complex person and her role both before and during her husband's presidency. (Rev: BL 12/1/99) [921]

POLK, JAMES K.

6355 Seigenthaler, John. *James K. Polk* (10–12). Series: American Presidents. 2004, Holt $20.00 (0-8050-6942-9). An accessible biography of the honest, hard-working president whom most people consider a near-great. (Rev: BL 1/1–15/04) [921]

REAGAN, RONALD

6356 Torr, James D., ed. *Ronald Reagan* (9–12). Illus. Series: Presidents and Their Decisions. 2000, Greenhaven LB $22.96 (0-7377-0502-7); paper $14.96 (0-7377-0501-9). An overview of Reagan's life and presidency precedes essays examining the central issues of his eight-year administration. (Rev: BL 2/15/01) [921]

6357 Young, Jeff C. *Great Communicator: The Story of Ronald Reagan* (6–10). Illus. Series: Twentieth-Century Leaders. 2003, Morgan Reynolds LB $21.95 (1-931798-10-9). Reagan's career is the main focus of this biography that includes many quotations and black-and-white photographs and deals objectively with the former president's strengths and weaknesses. (Rev: BL 6/1–15/03; HBG 10/03; SLJ 10/03; VOYA 12/03) [921]

ROOSEVELT, ELEANOR

6358 Spangenburg, Ray, and Diane Moser. *Eleanor Roosevelt: A Passion to Improve* (8–12). Series: Makers of America. 1996, Facts on File $25.00 (0-8160-3371-4). A superior introduction to the life and significant achievements of Eleanor Roosevelt and her lifetime struggle for social equality for all people. (Rev: BL 1/1–15/97) [921]

6359 Toor, Rachel. *Eleanor Roosevelt* (6–10). Illus. 1989, Chelsea LB $19.95 (1-55546-674-5). An affectionate portrait of a first lady who was also a great humanitarian and internationalist. (Rev: BL 4/1/89; BR 5–6/89; SLJ 5/89; VOYA 8/89) [921]

ROOSEVELT, FRANKLIN D.

6360 Devaney, John. *Franklin Delano Roosevelt, President* (6–10). Illus. 1987, Walker $12.95 (0-8027-6713-3). A detailed account of Roosevelt's personality and career. (Rev: SLJ 1/88; VOYA 12/87) [921]

6361 Grapes, Bryan J., ed. *Franklin D. Roosevelt* (9–12). Series: Presidents and Their Decisions. 2000, Greenhaven LB $22.96 (0-7377-0504-3); paper $14.96 (0-7377-0503-5). These essays cover the 12 years of FDR's presidency and how he guided America through two major crises, the Great Depression and World War II. (Rev: BL 3/1/01) [921]

6362 Jenkins, Roy. *Franklin Delano Roosevelt* (10–12). Series: American Presidents. 2003, Holt $20.00 (0-8050-6959-3). A very readable and insightful biography that concentrates on Roosevelt's political career. (Rev: BL 10/15/03; SLJ 5/04) [921]

6363 Nardo, Don. *Franklin D. Roosevelt: U.S. President* (7–10). Series: Great Achievers: Lives of the Physically Challenged. 1995, Chelsea LB $21.95 (0-7910-2406-7). This biography stresses the physical challenges Roosevelt faced and the strong personality that allowed him to achieve great success. (Rev: BR 3–4/96; SLJ 1/96) [921]

ROOSEVELT, THEODORE

6364 Auchincloss, Louis. *Theodore Roosevelt* (10–12). 2002, Times Books $20.00 (0-8050-6906-2). A sparkling short biography that catches the major events in Roosevelt's life and their significance. (Rev: BL 11/15/01) [921]

TRUMAN, HARRY S

6365 Feinberg, Barbara S. *Harry S Truman* (7–12). 1994, Watts paper $24.00 (0-531-13036-3). Examines Truman's life and presidential administration, analyzing the events of his two terms and his struggles and triumphs. (Rev: BL 9/1/94; SLJ 9/94) [921]

6366 Fleming, Thomas. *Harry S Truman, President* (6–12). 1993, Walker LB $15.85 (0-8027-8269-8). The author of this uncritical biography of the former president had access to family photographs and documents. (Rev: BL 1/1/94; SLJ 12/93; VOYA 2/94) [921]

6367 *Harry S Truman* (9–12). Ed. by Laura K. Egendorf. Series: Presidents and Their Decisions. 2001, Gale $19.95 (0-7377-0919-7). Some of the presidential decisions dealt with in this biographical study include the use of the atomic bomb against Japan, entering the Cold War, and expanding civil rights. (Rev: BL 1/1–15/02; SLJ 3/02) [921]

6368 McCullough, David. *Truman* (9–12). 1992, Simon & Schuster $32.00 (0-671-45654-7). A landmark biography of the 33rd president and his times. (Rev: BL 4/15/92*) [921]

WASHINGTON, GEORGE

6369 Bruns, Roger. *George Washington* (6–10). Illus. 1986, Chelsea LB $19.95 (0-87754-584-7). A solid, readable biography of the first president. (Rev: BL 3/1/87; SLJ 5/87) [921]

6370 Burns, James MacGregor, and Susan Dunn. *George Washington* (10–12). Series: American Presidents. 2004, Holt $20.00 (0-8050-6936-4). A concise biography of the first president that concentrates on his political life and contributions. (Rev: BL 1/1–15/04) [921]

6371 Flexner, James Thomas. *Washington, the Indispensable Man* (10–12). 1974, Little, Brown paper $17.95 (0-316-28616-8). Noted historian Flexner has written one of the best biographies of the first U.S. president. [921]

6372 *George Washington: A Biographical Companion* (9–12). Ed. by Frank E. Grizzard, Jr. Series: ABC-CLIO Biographical Companion. 2002, ABC-CLIO $55.00 (1-57607-082-4). In the 200 articles reprinted in this collection, the reader learns about life in Colonial and Revolutionary America as well as about the first president. [921]

6373 Marrin, Albert. *George Washington and the Founding of a Nation* (7–12). Illus. 2001, Dutton $30.00 (0-525-46481-6). A detailed account of this complex leader that examines the facts and the myths. (Rev: BCCB 2/01; BL 1/1–15/01; HB 5–6/01; HBG 10/01; SLJ 1/01) [921]

6374 Rosenburg, John. *First in Peace: George Washington, the Constitution, and the Presidency* (7–10). 1998, Millbrook LB $25.90 (0-7613-0422-3). The last of a trilogy about Washington, this installment describes the emergence of the new nation and the role played by the first president. (Rev: HBG 3/99; SLJ 1/99) [921]

6375 Smith, Richard Norton. *Patriarch: George Washington and the New American Nation* (9–12).

1993, Houghton $24.95 (0-395-52442-3). A detailed account of Washington's presidency, leavened with quotations and anecdotes. (Rev: BL 12/1/92) [921]

6376 Yoder, Carolyn P., ed. *George Washington: The Writer: A Treasury of Letters, Diaries, and Public Documents* (7–10). Illus. 2003, Boyds Mills $16.95 (1-56397-199-2). Washington's speeches, letters, will, and other documents — many excerpted — reveal much about his life and career. (Rev: BL 3/15/03; HBG 10/03; SLJ 2/03; VOYA 12/03) [921]

WILSON, WOODROW

6377 Auchincloss, Louis. *Woodrow Wilson* (10–12). Series: Penguin Lives. 2000, Viking $19.95 (0-670-88904-0). For better readers, this is a concise, subjective biography of an often-misunderstood president. (Rev: BL 4/15/00) [921]

6378 Rogers, James T. *Woodrow Wilson: Visionary for Peace* (7–10). Illus. Series: Makers of America. 1997, Facts on File $25.00 (0-8160-3396-X). A thoughtful, in-depth biography of the idealistic American president who overcame obstacles throughout his life and whose dream of an international League of Nations was shattered when the United States declined to join. (Rev: BL 5/15/97) [921]

Other Government and Public Figures

ADAMS, SAMUEL

6379 Irvin, Benjamin H. *Samuel Adams: Son of Liberty, Father of Revolution* (9–12). Illus. Series: Oxford Portraits. 2002, Oxford LB $24.00 (0-19-513225-4). This well-researched profile of Samuel Adams, who worked feverishly for American independence and later served as governor of Massachusetts, sheds light on the life of a very private man. (Rev: BL 2/1/03; HBG 10/03; SLJ 2/03; VOYA 8/03) [921]

ALBRIGHT, MADELEINE

6380 Burgan, Michael. *Madeleine Albright* (8–10). 1998, Millbrook LB $24.90 (0-7613-0367-7). This life of the first woman U.S. secretary of state describes her European childhood, her arrival as a refugee in this country, and her experiences as a student, journalist, activist, teacher, mother, ambassador, and, finally, cabinet member. (Rev: SLJ 6/99) [921]

6381 Hasday, Judy. *Madeleine Albright* (8–12). Series: Women of Achievement. 1998, Chelsea $21.95 (0-7910-4708-3); paper $8.95 (0-7910-4709-

1). A well-rounded biography of Madeleine Albright, covering her career in American public service and her childhood in Eastern Europe. (Rev: HBG 3/99; SLJ 3/99) [921]

BARTON, CLARA

6382 Hamilton, Leni. *Clara Barton* (5–10). Illus. 1987, Chelsea LB $19.95 (1-55546-641-9). The story of the Civil War nurse and how she prepared for the founding of the American Red Cross. (Rev: BL 11/1/87) [921]

6383 Oates, Stephen B. *A Woman of Valor: Clara Barton and the Civil War* (10–12). 1994, Free Pr. paper $16.95 (0-02-874012-2). Known as the angel of the battlefield, this is the story of Clara Barton, her part in the Civil War, and the founding of the Red Cross. [921]

BLACK HAWK

6384 Bonvillain, Nancy. *Black Hawk: Sac Rebel* (9–12). Series: North American Indians of Achievement. 1994, Chelsea LB $19.95 (0-7910-1711-7). The story of the Sac Indian leader who fought on the side of the British in the War of 1812 and led his people in the Black Hawk War of 1832 in an unsuccessful attempt to protect their land. (Rev: BL 7/94) [921]

BOONE, DANIEL

6385 Faragher, John Mack. *Daniel Boone: The Life and Legend of an American Pioneer* (7–12). 1992, Holt paper $18.00 (0-8050-3007-7). A biography of the complex frontier pioneer/politician/maverick. (Rev: BL 11/1/92*; SLJ 5/93*) [921]

6386 Green, Carl R. *Blazing the Wilderness Road with Daniel Boone* (6–10). Series: In American History. 2000, Enslow LB $20.95 (0-7660-1346-4). The story of Daniel Boone, his contributions to opening up the West, and his role in the American Revolution. (Rev: BL 12/15/00; HBG 3/01) [921]

BRADLEY, BILL

6387 Bradley, Bill. *Time Present, Time Past* (9–12). 1996, Knopf $26.00 (0-679-44488-2). An impressive job of writing his memoirs. (Rev: BL 12/15/95*) [921]

6388 Jaspersohn, William. *Senator: A Profile of Bill Bradley in the U.S. Senate* (6–10). 1992, Harcourt $19.95 (0-15-272880-5). An in-depth photoessay about Congress in general and Senator Bradley of New Jersey in particular, showing how his sports career led to the Senate. (Rev: BL 7/92; SLJ 10/92) [921]

BUNCHE, RALPH

6389 Henry, Charles P. *Ralph Bunche: Model Negro or American Other?* (10–12). Illus. 1999, New York Univ. $34.95 (0-8147-3582-7). Bunche's lasting contributions in the diverse realms of statesmanship and civil rights are covered in detail. (Rev: BL 12/15/98) [921]

6390 Schraff, Anne. *Ralph Bunche: Winner of the Nobel Peace Prize* (7–12). Series: African-American Biographies. 1999, Enslow LB $20.95 (0-7660-1203-4). The story of the great American diplomat who helped mediate several international disputes and won the Nobel peace prize in 1950. (Rev: BL 11/15/99; SLJ 8/99) [921]

6391 Urquhart, Brian E. *Ralph Bunche — An American Life* (10–12). 1993, Norton $27.50 (0-393-03527-1). The story of the African American diplomat who was awarded the Nobel Peace Prize for his work on the United Nations Palestine Commission. [921]

CHIEF JOSEPH

6392 Yates, Diana. *Chief Joseph: Thunder Rolling from the Mountains* (7–12). 1992, Ward Hill LB $14.95 (0-9623380-9-5); paper $10.95 (0-9623380-8-7). A sensitive distillation of the life and times of Chief Joseph of the Nez Perce. (Rev: BL 12/15/92; SLJ 12/92) [921]

COCHISE

6393 Schwarz, Melissa. *Cochise: Apache Chief* (9–12). Series: North American Indians of Achievement. 1992, Chelsea LB $19.95 (0-7910-1706-0). The story of the Apache chief who became involved in the struggle against the attempts of white Americans to subdue the Indian peoples of the Southwest during the 1860s. (Rev: BL 10/1/92; SLJ 12/92) [921]

CODY, BUFFALO BILL

6394 Carter, Robert A. *Buffalo Bill Cody: The Man Behind the Legend* (10–12). 2000, Wiley $30.00 (0-471-31996-1); paper $18.95 (0-471-07780-1). The many facets of Buffalo Bill Cody's talents as a scout, marksman, buffalo hunter, and showman are chronicled in this biography. (Rev: BL 10/15/00) [92i]

CRAZY HORSE (SIOUX CHIEF)

6395 Freedman, Russell. *The Life and Death of Crazy Horse* (6–12). Illus. 1996, Holiday $21.95 (0-8234-1219-9). This biography of Crazy Horse tells an uncompromising story of bloody wars, terrible grief, tragedy, and the Sioux's losing battle to preserve their independence and their land. (Rev: BL 6/1–15/96*; BR 11–12/96; SLJ 6/96*; VOYA 10/96) [921]

6396 Goldman, Martin S. *Crazy Horse: War Chief of the Oglala Sioux* (6–12). Series: American Indian Experience. 1996, Watts paper $24.00 (0-531-11258-6). This carefully researched biography recounts the life of this fascinating leader and of the decline of the Sioux. (Rev: SLJ 9/96) [921]

6397 McMurtry, Larry. *Crazy Horse* (10–12). Series: Penguin Lives. 1999, Viking $19.95 (0-670-88234-8). A portrait of both the man and the myth is accomplished in this biography of the Sioux chief who was a fine military tactician. (Rev: BL 1/1–15/99) [921]

6398 St. George, Judith. *Crazy Horse* (7–10). 1994, Putnam $17.95 (0-399-22667-2). An account of the legendary Lakota leader who struggled to save his people's culture and way of life from destruction by white soldiers and settlers. (Rev: BL 10/1/94; SLJ 11/94; VOYA 2/95) [921]

CUSTER, GEORGE ARMSTRONG

6399 Langellier, John Phillip. *Custer: The Man, the Myth, the Movies* (10–12). Illus. 2000, Stackpole paper $29.95 (0-8117-3201-0). As well as a biography of General Custer, this multidimensional book describes how his image has changed through the years and how he has been portrayed in the media, particularly the movies. (Rev: BL 7/00) [921]

DAVIS, JEFFERSON

6400 King, Perry Scott. *Jefferson Davis* (7–10). Illus. 1990, Chelsea LB $21.95 (1-55546-806-3). With many illustrations, King re-creates the life and times of the president of the Confederacy. (Rev: BL 8/90; SLJ 8/90) [921]

DAY, DOROTHY

6401 Kent, Deborah. *Dorothy Day: Friend to the Forgotten* (7–12). Illus. 1996, Eerdmans $15.00 (0-8028-5117-7). A profile of the great friend of the poor and helpless whose own life's drama involved an abortion, a short-lived marriage, imprisonment, political involvement, and questioning of her deep religious beliefs. (Rev: BL 6/1–15/96; BR 1–2/97; SLJ 8/96) [921]

FRANKLIN, BENJAMIN

6402 Brands, H. W. *The First American: The Life and Times of Benjamin Franklin* (10–12). 2000, Doubleday paper $17 .00 (0-385-49540-4). A highly readable biography about this multitalented American who amassed an amazing list of achievements. [921]

6403 Franklin, Benjamin. *The Autobiography of Benjamin Franklin* (10–12). 1986, Norton paper $14.75 (0-393-95294-0). Written between 1771 and 1788, this is more than an account of Revolutionary times; it is also an exploration of the mind of a man of varied and deep interests. [921]

6404 Lee, Tanja, ed. *Benjamin Franklin* (7–12). Series: People Who Made History. 2002, Gale LB $31.20 (0-7377-0898-0); paper $19.95 (0-7377-0899-9). After a general introduction to Franklin, his life, and his times, essays explore his talents, contributions, accomplishments, and his place in world history. (Rev: BL 4/1/02) [921]

6405 Looby, Chris. *Benjamin Franklin* (6–10). Illus. 1990, Chelsea LB $21.95 (1-55546-808-X). A well-illustrated account of the life of this complex man that also introduces many of his contemporaries. (Rev: BL 8/90; SLJ 7/90; VOYA 8/90) [921]

6406 Morgan, Edmund S. *Benjamin Franklin* (10–12). Illus. 2002, Yale $24.95 (0-300-09532-5). An absorbing and insightful biography that will also be useful for reports. (Rev: BL 8/02; SLJ 4/03) [921]

GERONIMO

6407 Barrett, S. M., ed. *Geronimo: His Own Story* (10–12). 1983, Irvington paper $15.95 (0-8290-0658-3). The memoirs of the Apache warrior Geronimo with valuable background information about his people and their culture. [921]

GOODE, W. WILSON

6408 Goode, W. Wilson, and Joann Stevens. *In Goode Faith: Philadelphia's First Black Mayor Tells His Story* (9–12). 1992, Judson $15.00 (0-8170-1186-2). Philadelphia's first African American mayor recounts his early life and candidly describes his turbulent political career. (Rev: BL 10/1/92) [921]

JACKSON, STONEWALL

6409 Fritz, Jean. *Stonewall* (7–10). Illus. 1979, Putnam $16.99 (0-399-20698-1). The great Confederate general is portrayed realistically as the complex man he was. [921]

JARAMILLO, MARI-LUCI

6410 Jaramillo, Mari-Luci. *Madame Ambassador: The Shoemaker's Daughter* (10–12). 2002, Bilingual paper $15.00 (1-931010-04-8). In this inspiring autobiography, the former U.S. ambassador to Honduras chronicles her rise from a childhood of poverty to prominence as a civil rights advocate and diplomat. (Rev: BL 3/15/02) [921]

JORDAN, BARBARA

6411 Blue, Rose, and Corinne J. Naden. *Barbara Jordan* (7–10). Series: Black Americans of Achievement. 1992, Chelsea LB $21.95 (0-7910-1131-3). The colorful life of this former congresswoman and educator is re-created in this illustrated biography. (Rev: BL 9/15/92; SLJ 11/92) [921]

6412 Jeffrey, Laura S. *Barbara Jordan: Congresswoman, Lawyer, Educator* (7–12). Illus. Series: African-American Biographies. 1997, Enslow LB $20.95 (0-89490-692-5). This biography covers both the personal and professional life of this amazing woman who overcame great obstacles to fulfill a multi-faceted career. (Rev: BL 5/15/97; SLJ 3/97) [921]

6413 Mendelsohn, James. *Barbara Jordan: Getting Things Done* (9–12). Illus. 2000, Twenty-First Century $23.90 (0-7613-1467-9). The congresswoman's career is the main focus of this interesting and well-researched biography. (Rev: BL 2/15/01; HBG 10/01; VOYA 6/01) [921]

JOSEPH (NEZ PERCE CHIEF)

6414 Scott, Robert Alan. *Chief Joseph and the Nez Perces* (10–12). Series: Makers of America. 1993, Facts on File LB $25.00 (0-8160-2475-8). A stirring biography of the Nez Perce chief who fought for peace and equality for his people. [921]

6415 Taylor, Marian W. *Chief Joseph: Nez Perce Leader* (9–12). Illus. Series: North American Indians of Achievement. 1993, Chelsea LB $19.95 (0-7910-1708-7). The biography of the Nez Perce Indian leader who led a skillful but ultimately unsuccessful retreat from U.S. forces in 1877. (Rev: BL 10/15/93; SLJ 10/93) [921]

LEE, ROBERT E.

6416 Blount, Roy. *Robert E. Lee* (10–12). Series: Penguin Lives. 2003, Holt $19.95 (0-670-03220-4). This well-written biography explores Lee's life, covering his much-vaunted reputation as a military leader and his personal political philosophy. (Rev: BL 4/1/03; SLJ 9/03) [921]

6417 Brown, Warren. *Robert E. Lee* (6–10). Series: World Leaders — Past and Present. 1991, Chelsea LB $19.95 (1-55546-814-4). Using many illustrations and maps, this volume re-creates the life of the Confederate Civil War general. (Rev: BL 11/15/91) [921]

6418 Fellman, Michael. *The Making of Robert E. Lee* (10–12). 2000, Random $29.95 (0-679-45650-3). A biography of the great Civil War leader that gives material on his religious and political beliefs and his attitudes toward slavery and racism. (Rev: BL 10/1/00) [921]

6419 Thomas, Emory M. *Robert E. Lee* (9–12). 1995, Norton $30.00 (0-393-03730-4). A large, well-researched biography of Civil War general Robert E. Lee. (Rev: BL 4/1/95*) [921]

LONG, HUEY

6420 La Vert, Suzanne. *Huey Long: The Kingfish of Louisiana* (8–12). Series: Makers of America. 1995, Facts on File $25.00 (0-8160-2880-X). Looks at the motivations and political life of Huey Long, including his assassination. (Rev: BL 6/1–15/95) [921]

MACARTHUR, DOUGLAS

6421 Scott, Robert A. *Douglas MacArthur and the Century of War* (7–12). Series: Makers of America. 1997, Facts on File $25.00 (0-8160-3098-7). From the battlefields of World War I to his opposition to the Vietnam War, this biography follows the life of one of the most famous generals in American history. (Rev: BL 11/15/97; BR 3–4/98) [921]

MCCAIN, JOHN

6422 Kozar, Richard. *John McCain* (8–12). Series: Overcoming Adversity. 2002, Chelsea LB $21.95 (0-7910-6299-6). The story of the prominent U.S. politician and how he survived the ordeal of a POW camp in Vietnam. (Rev: BL 4/15/02; HBG 10/02) [921]

MCCARTHY, JOSEPH

6423 Cohen, Daniel. *Joseph McCarthy: The Misuse of Political Power* (7–12). Illus. 1996, Millbrook LB $23.90 (1-56294-917-9). The dramatic story of the U.S. senator who used the threat of communism to gain power and ruin innocent lives. (Rev: BL 10/1/96; BR 1–2/97; SLJ 10/96) [921]

MANKILLER, WILMA

6424 Schwarz, Melissa. *Wilma Mankiller: Principal Chief of the Cherokees* (9–12). Series: North American Indians of Achievement. 1994, Chelsea LB $19.95 (0-7910-1715-X). The biography of this Cherokee leader, born in 1945, who became an activist in the 1960s and participated in the symbolic occupation of Alcatraz Island by Native Americans in 1969. (Rev: BL 10/15/94; VOYA 2/95) [921]

MARSHALL, GEORGE C.

6425 Saunders, Alan. *George C. Marshall* (10–12). Series: Makers of America. 1995, Facts on File $19.95 (0-8160-2666-1). This work examines the colorful career of the man who was an army general, secretary of state, and secretary of defense. (Rev: BL 11/15/95; BR 9–10/96; SLJ 2/96) [921]

MARSHALL, THURGOOD

6426 Davis, Michael D., and Hunter R. Clark. *Thurgood Marshall: Warrior at the Bar, Rebel on the Bench* (9–12). 1992, Birch Lane $22.00 (1-55972-133-2). Reviews the career of the first African American Supreme Court justice, who spearheaded great legal victories for desegregation and civil rights. (Rev: BL 11/1/92) [921]

6427 Herda, D. J. *Thurgood Marshall: Civil Rights Champion* (6–10). Illus. Series: Justices of the Supreme Court. 1995, Enslow LB $20.95 (0-89490-557-0). The story of the first African American Supreme Court justice and his lifelong fight to champion the rights of the oppressed. (Rev: BL 3/15/96) [921]

6428 Williams, Juan. *Thurgood Marshall: American Revolutionary* (10–12). 1998, Times Books paper $16 .00 (0-8129-3299-4). A thorough biography of the African American lawyer who won *Brown* v. *Board of Education* and was named to the Supreme Court. (Rev: BL 8/98) [921]

NADER, RALPH

6429 Bowen, Nancy. *Ralph Nader: Man with a Mission* (6–10). Illus. 2002, Millbrook LB $24.90 (0-7613-2365-1). An absorbing biography of the consumer advocate, environmentalist, and politician, with photographs. (Rev: BL 4/1/02; HBG 10/02; SLJ 4/02) [921]

6430 Celsi, Teresa. *Ralph Nader: The Consumer Revolution* (6–12). Series: New Directions. 1991, Millbrook LB $21.90 (1-56294-044-9). The story of the consumer advocate who has taken on some of the largest corporations in America and won. (Rev: BL 10/1/91; SLJ 10/91) [921]

6431 Graham, Kevin. *Ralph Nader: Battling for Democracy* (6–12). 2000, Windom paper $9.95 (0-9700323-0-7). A readable biography of the man who has devoted his life to fighting for liberty and justice for all. (Rev: BL 12/1/00; SLJ 11/00) [921]

NATION, CARRY

6432 Grace, Fran. *Carry A. Nation: Retelling the Life* (10–12). Series: Religion in North America. 2001, Indiana Univ. Pr. $35.00 (0-253-33846-8). A sympathetic portrayal of the 19th-century prohibitionist. [92]

NAVA, JULIAN

6433 Nava, Julian. *Julian Nava: My Mexican-American Journey* (7–12). 2002, Arte Publico $16.95 (1-55885-364-2); paper $9.95 (1-55885-351-0). Nava tells the story of his life and his journey from the barrio to become the first Mexican American ambassador to Mexico. (Rev: BL 10/15/02) [921]

O'CONNOR, SANDRA DAY

6434 Herda, D. J. *Sandra Day O'Connor: Independent Thinker* (6–10). Illus. Series: Justices of the Supreme Court. 1995, Enslow LB $17.95 (0-89480-558-9). The story of the first female Supreme Court justice, including her personal life and some key decisions since becoming a Supreme Court member in 1981. (Rev: BL 2/15/96) [921]

PAINE, THOMAS

6435 Kaye, Harvey J. *Thomas Paine: Firebrand of the Revolution* (6–10). Illus. 2000, Oxford LB $22.00 (0-19-511627-5). A readable, well-illustrated biography on the career, accomplishments, and lasting importance of this Revolutionary War personality, with material on the social and political conditions of the period. (Rev: BL 3/1/00; HBG 9/00; SLJ 4/00) [921]

6436 Meltzer, Milton. *Tom Paine: Voice of Revolution* (9–12). Illus. 1996, Watts LB $29.00 (0-531-11291-8). A well-researched biography of this English-born American patriot known best for his influential revolutionary writings, notably *Common Sense* and *The Rights of Man*. (Rev: BL 12/15/96; BR 3–4/97; SLJ 12/96; VOYA 2/97) [921]

6437 Vail, John. *Thomas Paine* (6–10). Illus. 1990, Chelsea LB $19.95 (1-55546-819-5). The story of the outspoken radical whose writings influenced the development of the American Revolution. (Rev: BL 8/90; SLJ 6/90; VOYA 8/90) [921]

PARKER, QUANAH

6438 Wilson, Claire. *Quanah Parker: Comanche Chief* (9–12). Series: North American Indians of Achievement. 1991, Chelsea LB $19.95 (0-7910-1702-8). Biography of the Comanche leader who fought white confiscation and settlement of his lands. (Rev: BL 3/1/92; SLJ 3/92) [921]

PERKINS, FRANCES

6439 Pasachoff, Naomi. *Frances Perkins: Champion of the New Deal* (6–12). Series: Oxford Portraits. 1999, Oxford LB $22.00 (0-19-512222-4). A biography of the first woman to become a cabinet member in the United States, including both her achievements and her flaws. (Rev: BR 11–12/99; HBG 4/00; SLJ 1/00) [921]

PHILIP, KING (WAMPANOAG CHIEF)

6440 Roman, Joseph. *King Philip: Wampanoag Rebel* (9–12). Series: North American Indians of Achievement. 1991, Chelsea LB $19.95 (0-7910-1704-4). The story of the Wampanoag chief known as King Philip, New England's devastating war with the Indians, and King Philip's eventual death at the hands of an angry dissident. (Rev: BL 3/1/92) [921]

PICKETT, GEORGE EDWARD

6441 Gordon, Lesley J. *General George E. Pickett in Life and Legend* (10–12). Illus. 1998, Univ. of North Carolina Pr. $29.95 (0-8078-2450-X). The third wife of this Confederate general is a principal figure in this biography that will appeal to teens who enjoy the genre or who are interested in the Civil War. (Rev: BL 12/1/98) [921]

POCAHONTAS

6442 Holler, Anne. *Pocahontas: Powhatan Peacemaker* (9–12). Series: North American Indians of Achievement. 1992, Chelsea $19.95 (0-7910-1705-2). A colorful re-creation of the life of this legendary Native American woman, how she saved Captain John Smith's life, and her death in England before she could return home. (Rev: BL 2/1/93) [921]

6443 Woodward, Grace Steele. *Pocahontas* (10–12). Series: Civilization of the American Indian. 1969, Univ. of Oklahoma Pr. paper $17.95 (0-8061-1642-0). A vivid adult recreation of the life of the daughter of Chief Powhatan and her role in the history of the Jamestown settlement. [921]

POWELL, COLIN

6444 Brown, Warren. *Colin Powell* (7–10). Series: Black Americans of Achievement. 1992, Chelsea LB $21.95 (0-7910-1647-1). A nicely illustrated account of the African American general who distinguished himself during the Persian Gulf War. (Rev: BL 8/92) [921]

6445 Powell, Colin. *My American Journey* (10–12). 1995, Random $25.95 (0-679-43296-5). The autobiography of the American hero who grew up in the South Bronx and later became chairman of the Joint Chiefs of Staff. (Rev: BR 5–6/96; SLJ 2/96) [921]

6446 Schraff, Anne. *Colin Powell: Soldier and Patriot* (7–12). Illus. Series: African-American Biographies. 1997, Enslow LB $20.95 (0-89490-810-3). A profile of the career soldier who led U.S. forces in war and peace. (Rev: BL 5/15/97; SLJ 3/97; VOYA 6/97) [921]

REVERE, PAUL

6447 Forbes, Esther. *Paul Revere and the World He Lived In* (10–12). 1942, Houghton paper $16.00 (0-395-08370-2). This excellent biography not only covers the life of Paul Revere but also tells about revolutionary Boston. [921]

RICE, CONDOLEEZZA

6448 Felix, Antonia. *Condi: The Condoleezza Rice Story* (7–12). 2002, Newmarket $19.95 (1-55704-539-9). Rice's childhood, education, and career are all covered in this well-written biography, as are her wide-ranging interests. (Rev: VOYA 4/03) [921]

SCHWARZKOPF, NORMAN

6449 Hughes, Libby. *Norman Schwarzkopf: Hero with a Heart* (6–10). Series: People in Focus. 1992, Dillon LB $13.95 (0-87518-521-5). The story of the leader of the Persian Gulf War's Operation Desert Storm in 1991 and how he emerged a popular hero. (Rev: BL 1/15/93; SLJ 2/93) [921]

SEQUOYAH

6450 Shumate, Jane. *Sequoyah: Inventor of the Cherokee Alphabet* (9–12). Series: North American Indians of Achievement. 1994, Chelsea LB $19.95 (0-7910-1720-6). Using characters from the Greek and Roman alphabets, Sequoyah devised a Cherokee syllabary so that his language could be written and set in type. (Rev: BL 1/1/94) [921]

SEWARD, WILLIAM

6451 Kent, Zachary. *William Seward: The Mastermind of the Alaska Purchase* (6–10). Series: Historical American Biographies. 2001, Enslow LB $20.95 (0-7660-1391-X). The story of the man who was appointed secretary of state by Lincoln and who engineered the purchase of Alaska is the focus of this biography full of period illustrations, maps, and cartoons. (Rev: BL 3/1/01; HBG 10/01; SLJ 5/01) [921]

SITTING BULL

6452 Bernotas, Bob. *Sitting Bull: Chief of the Sioux* (9–12). Series: North American Indians of Achievement. 1991, Chelsea LB $19.95 (0-7910-1703-6). Chronicles the life of the Native American leader. (Rev: BL 3/1/92; SLJ 6/92) [921]

6453 Marrin, Albert. *Sitting Bull and His World* (6–12). Illus. 2000, Dutton $27.50 (0-525-45944-8). A well-illustrated, carefully researched biography of this misunderstood Sioux leader. (Rev: BL 5/1/00* ; HB 7–8/00; HBG 9/00; SLJ 7/00) [921]

6454 Utley, Robert M. *The Lance and the Shield: The Life and Times of Sitting Bull* (9–12). 1993, Holt $25.00 (0-8050-1274-5). Presents a realistic picture of the culture of Sitting Bull's people and re-creates the actions he took that earned him the deep respect and loyalty of his people. (Rev: BL 4/15/93) [921]

6455 Vestal, Stanley. *Sitting Bull, Champion of the Sioux: A Biography*. new ed (10–12). Series: Civi-lization of the American Indian. 1969, Univ. of Oklahoma Pr. paper $16.57 (0-8061-2219-6). An excellent and well-documented biography of the great Sioux chief who died in 1890. [921]

SNYDER, LESLIE CROCKER

6456 Snyder, Leslie Crocker, and Tom Shachtman. *25 to Life: The Truth, the Whole Truth, and Nothing but the Truth* (10–12). 2002, Warner $26.95 (0-446-53020-4). A woman judge describes the challenges she faced as she rose from an entry-level position at a Manhattan law firm to appointment as a New York Supreme Court justice. (Rev: BL 9/15/02) [921]

TECUMSEH

6457 Cwiklik, Robert. *Tecumseh: Shawnee Rebel* (9–12). Series: North American Indians of Achievement. 1993, Chelsea LB $19.95 (0-7910-1721-4). The story of the Shawnee chief and military leader who tried to form a pan-tribal confederacy to resist white American expansion onto Indian lands in the early 1800s. (Rev: BL 4/1/93; SLJ 7/93) [921]

6458 Stefoff, Rebecca. *Tecumseh and the Shawnee Confederacy* (6–10). Illus. Series: Library of American Indian History. 1998, Facts on File $25.00 (0-8160-3648-9). Through an examination of the life of Tecumseh, the charismatic leader of the Shawnee Confederation, this volume presents the Shawnee culture and an illuminating history of the Indian wars in the Ohio River Valley. (Rev: SLJ 7/98) [921]

THURMOND, STROM

6459 Cohodas, Nadine. *Strom Thurmond and the Politics of Southern Change* (9–12). 1993, Simon & Schuster $27.50 (0-671-68935-5). A detailed profile of a pivotal figure in the emergence of the new South. (Rev: BL 12/1/92) [921]

WARREN, EARL

6460 Compston, Christine L. *Earl Warren: Justice for All* (7–10). Illus. Series: Oxford Portraits. 2002, Oxford $24.00 (0-19-513001-4). In addition to Warren's family life and career, this portrait presents his belief in the rule of law and his dealings with successive presidents. (Rev: BL 4/15/02; HBG 10/02; SLJ 6/02) [921]

6461 Herda, D. J. *Earl Warren: Chief Justice for Social Change* (6–10). Illus. Series: Justices of the Supreme Court. 1995, Enslow LB $20.95 (0-89490-556-2). The story of the chief justice who led the Supreme Court during a period of great change and who headed the commission that investigated President Kennedy's death. (Rev: BL 3/15/96; SLJ 3/96) [921]

WOODHULL, VICTORIA

6462 Gabriel, Mary. *Notorious Victoria: The Life of Victoria Woodhull Uncensored* (10–12). 1998, Algonquin $39.95 (1-56512-132-5). The biography of the amazing 19th-century suffragette who at one time earned her keep as a clairvoyant and later established a brokerage firm and a newspaper, ran for president of the United States, espoused the ideals of both communism and free love, and was finally hounded out of the country. (Rev: BL 1/1–15/98; BR 3–4/98; SLJ 3/98; VOYA 6/98) [921]

6463 McLean, Jacqueline. *Victoria Woodhull: First Woman Presidential Candidate* (7–12). 1999, Morgan Reynolds LB $21.95 (1-883846-47-1). The fascinating story of Victoria Woodhull, an ardent suffragist and feminist who was nominated by the Equal Rights Party in 1872 as its presidential candidate. (Rev: BL 8/99; HBG 4/00; SLJ 10/99; VOYA 12/99) [921]

Miscellaneous Persons

ADDAMS, JANE

6464 Hovde, Jane. *Jane Addams* (8–12). Illus. 1989, Facts on File $19.95 (0-8160-1547-3). The life and work of this early feminist and social worker. (Rev: BL 9/15/89; BR 11–12/89; VOYA 12/89) [921]

6465 Kittredge, Mary. *Jane Addams* (6–10). Illus. 1988, Chelsea LB $19.95 (1-55546-636-2). Jane Addams helped immigrants by founding the first settlement house, Hull House, in Chicago. (Rev: BL 6/15/88; BR 11–12/88; SLJ 1/89) [921]

ALEXANDER, SALLY HOBART

6466 Alexander, Sally H. *Taking Hold: My Journey into Blindness* (6–12). 1994, Macmillan paper $14.95 (0-02-700402-3). A true story of a 3rd-grade teacher who lost her sight but found independence. (Rev: BL 1/15/95; SLJ 4/95; VOYA 4/95) [921]

BAILEY, ANNE

6467 Furbee, Mary R. *Anne Bailey: Frontier Scout* (6–12). Illus. 2001, Morgan Reynolds $20.95 (1-883846-70-6). This is the absorbing story of a courageous woman who became a scout in the Revolutionary War. (Rev: BL 12/1/01; HBG 3/02; SLJ 3/02) [921]

BLACK ELK (NATIVE AMERICAN)

6468 Black Elk, and John Gneisenau Neihardt. *Black Elk Speaks: Being the Life Story of a Holy Man of the Oglala Sioux* (10–12). 1979, Univ. of Nebraska Pr. $50.00 (0-8032-1309-3); paper $14.95 (0-8032-6170-5). The biography of the famous Native American warrior and hunter who was born in 1863 and became a famous medicine man later in life. [921]

BLY, NELLIE

6469 Kroeger, Brooke. *Nellie Bly: Daredevil, Reporter, Feminist* (9–12). 1994, Times Books $27.50 (0-8129-1973-4). A comprehensive biography of the pioneering 19th-century investigative reporter that highlights her fearlessness and instinct for drama. (Rev: BL 2/1/94*) [921]

6470 Marks, Jason. *Around the World in 72 Days: The Race Between Pulitzer's Nellie Bly and Cosmopolitan's Elizabeth Bisland* (9–12). 1993, Gemittarius paper $12.95 (0-9633696-2-8). An account of the 1889 publicity stunt by rival publishers sending two female reporters on a race to beat the fictional record of Jules Verne's Phileas Fogg. (Rev: BL 4/15/93) [921]

BONNEY, WILLIAM

6471 Cline, Don. *Alias Billy the Kid, the Man Behind the Legend* (8–12). Illus. 1986, Sunstone paper $12.95 (0-86534-080-3). The real story of Billy the Kid, clearing up many misconceptions. (Rev: BR 11–12/86) [921]

BRADLEY, GUY

6472 McIver, Stuart B. *Death in the Everglades: The Murder of Guy Bradley, America's First Martyr to Environmentalism* (10–12). Illus. 2003, Univ. Press of Florida $24.95 (0-8130-2671-7). The life of pioneering environmentalist Guy Bradley and his death for his cause (protecting egrets, herons, and other birds) are recounted in gripping detail. (Rev: BL 6/1–15/03) [333.95]

BRAGG, JANET HARMON

6473 Bragg, Janet Harmon. *Soaring Above Setbacks: Autobiography of Janet Harmon Bragg as Told to Marjorie M. Kriz* (10–12). 1996, Smithsonian $19.95 (1-56098-458-9). An inspiring autobiography of the African American woman who excelled in the health field, became the first black woman to earn a commercial pilot's license, and then as a social worker was so helpful to Ethiopian students in the United States that she was invited to visit Ethiopia as a guest of the king. (Rev: SLJ 9/96) [921]

BRAZILE, DONNA L.

6474 Brazile, Donna L. *Cooking with Grease: Stirring the Pots in American Politics* (10–12). Illus.

2004, Simon & Schuster $23.00 (0-7432-5398-1). The personal and public lives of the black woman who led the Gore-Lieberman campaign in 2000 and who remains a champion of the poor and minorities. (Rev: BL 5/15/04*) [921]

BRIDGMAN, LAURA

6475 Freeberg, Ernest. *The Education of Laura Bridgman: First Deaf and Blind Person to Learn Language* (9–12). 2001, Harvard Univ. Pr. $27.95 (0-674-00589-9). This is the story of a blind-deaf girl named Laura Bridgman and of her relationship with her teacher, Samuel Howe. [921]

BROWN, JESSE LEROY

6476 Taylor, Theodore. *The Flight of Jesse Leroy Brown* (10–12). 1998, Avon paper $23.00 (0-380-97689-7). This is the inspiring story of Jesse Brown, born to poor Southern sharecroppers, who went on to become the first black man to fly a navy fighter. Killed during the Korean War, he continues to be a symbol of courage and dignity. (Rev: BL 10/15/98; SLJ 4/99) [921]

CAPONE, AL

6477 Bergreen, Laurence. *Capone: The Man and the Era* (9–12). 1994, Simon & Schuster $30.00 (0-671-74456-9). Examines the career of Chicago gangster Al Capone, recounting his actions during the 1920s as well as his boyhood poverty and final years in prison. (Rev: BL 10/15/94) [921]

CARSON, KIT

6478 Dunlay, Thomas W. *Kit Carson and the Indians* (10–12). 2000, Univ. of Nebraska Pr. $45.00 (0-8032-1715-3). A well-researched biography of Carson, who was an Indian guide, scout, agent, and later soldier and frontier peacemaker. (Rev: BL 10/15/00) [921]

6479 Quaife, Milo Milton, ed. *Kit Carson's Autobiography* (10–12). 1966, Univ. of Nebraska Pr. paper $9.00 (0-8032-5031-2). This autobiography dictated in the years 1856–57 gives fascinating details of the life of this famous hunter, trapper, and Indian fighter. [921]

CARTER, EDDIE

6480 Carter, Allene G., and Robert L. Allen. *Honoring Sergeant Carter: Redeeming a Black World War II Hero's Legacy* (10–12). Illus. 2003, HarperCollins $24.95 (0-06-621236-7). More than just a profile of an African American hero in World War II, this book recounts the decades-long struggle to win for Sergeant Eddie Carter the honors and recog-

nition he so richly deserved but didn't live to receive. (Rev: BL 1/1–15/03) [940.54]

DAVIS, DONALD

6481 Davis, Donald. *See Rock City* (10–12). 1996, August House $22.95 (0-87483-448-1); paper $12.95 (0-87483-456-2). From his first day in kindergarten in 1948 through his sophomore year in college, this is the gentle, family-oriented autobiography of Donald Davis and his life in rural North Carolina. (Rev: BR 11–12/96; SLJ 9/96) [921]

ESCALANTE, JAIME

6482 Byers, Ann. *Jaime Escalante: Sensational Teacher* (6–10). Illus. Series: Hispanic Biographies. 1996, Enslow LB $20.95 (0-89490-763-8). A profile of the unique, inspiring teacher whose career became the basis of the film *Stand and Deliver*. (Rev: BL 10/1/96; SLJ 9/96; VOYA 12/96) [921]

FLEMING, EDWARD

6483 Fleming, Edward. *Heart of the Storm: My Adventures as a Helicopter Rescue Pilot and Commander* (9–12). Illus. 2004, Wiley $24.95 (0-471-26436-9). This is an adventure-filled memoir of a veteran U.S. Air Force and Air National Guard rescue helicopter pilot. (Rev: BL 5/15/04) [921]

GALLAGHER, HUGH

6484 Gallagher, Hugh Gregory. *Black Bird Fly Away: Disabled in an Able-Bodied World* (10–12). 1998, Vandamere $21.95 (0-918339-44-8). The autobiography of Hugh Gallagher, who, after becoming crippled by polio in college, became a disabled rights activist, lobbied for the Architectural Barriers Act of 1968, and became known as the grandfather of the Americans with Disabilities Act. The work weaves in his reaction to his paralysis and the evolution of his own feelings about himself as a paraplegic and as a human being. (Rev: BL 5/15/98; SLJ 1/99) [921]

GRAHAM, BILLY

6485 Wooten, Sara McIntosh. *Billy Graham: World-Famous Evangelist* (6–10). Illus. Series: People to Know. 2001, Enslow LB $20.95 (0-7660-1533-5). A well-rounded and interesting account of Graham's life, education, and career, with coverage of his boisterous youth. (Rev: BL 10/1/01; HBG 3/02) [921]

HUNTER-GAULT, CHARLAYNE

6486 Hunter-Gault, Charlayne. *In My Place* (9–12). 1992, Farrar $19.00 (0-374-17563-2). The renowned journalist writes about her experiences as one of the first two African American students at the University of Georgia. (Rev: BL 11/1/92; SLJ 5/93) [921]

JONES, DR. BOBBY

6487 Jones, Bobby, and Lesley Sussman. *Make a Joyful Noise: My 25 Years in Gospel Music* (10–12). Illus. 2000, St. Martin's $22.95 (0-312-25258-7). This is the autobiography of Dr. Bobby Jones, host of a popular TV gospel show, who writes about his life and friends and gives a behind the scenes look at BET, the Black Entertainment Network. (Rev: BL 10/1/00) [921]

KELLER, HELEN

6488 Herrmann, Dorothy. *Helen Keller: A Life* (10–12). 1998, Knopf paper $20 .00 (0-226-32763-9). Herrmann captures Keller's successful struggle to overcome her physical disabilities and develop into a truly multidimensional adult and looks at the important role of her teacher, Annie Sullivan. (Rev: BL 7/98) [921]

6489 Keller, Helen. *The Story of My Life: The Restored Classic, Complete and Unabridged, Centennial Edition* (8–12). 2003, Norton $21.95 (0393057445). The autobiography of the blind and deaf women who overcame her handicaps through the help of a devoted teacher, Anne Sullivan. Originally published in 1903. [921]

6490 Nicholson, Lois. *Helen Keller: Humanitarian* (7–10). Series: Great Achievers: Lives of the Physically Challenged. 1995, Chelsea LB $21.95 (0-7910-2086-X). The strong personality traits that allowed Keller to rise above her physical handicaps are stressed in this biography of a remarkable woman. (Rev: BR 3–4/96; SLJ 1/96) [921]

6491 Wepman, Dennis. *Helen Keller* (6–10). Illus. 1987, Chelsea LB $19.95 (1-55546-662-1). The inspiring story of this handicapped woman and her struggle to help people like herself. (Rev: BL 8/87; SLJ 9/87) [921]

KINGSLEY, ANNA MADGIGINE JAI

6492 Schafer, Daniel. *Anna Madgigine Jai Kingsley: African Princess, Florida Slave, Plantation Slaveowner* (10–12). Illus. 2003, Univ. Press of Florida $24.95 (0-8130-2616-4). This absorbing biography chronicles the incredible life of a Senegalese woman who was thrust into slavery in the early 19th century at the age of 13, married her American owner, and became manager of his plantation. (Rev: BL 5/15/03) [975.9]

KLECKLEY, ELIZABETH

6493 Rutberg, Becky. *Mary Lincoln's Dressmaker: Elizabeth Kleckley's Remarkable Rise from Slave to White House Confidante* (6–10). 1995, Walker $15.95 (0-8027-8224-8). The story of a slave, a fine seamstress, who was freed and became Mary Todd Lincoln's dressmaker. (Rev: BL 10/15/95; SLJ 12/95; VOYA 12/95) [921]

KOVIC, RON

6494 Moss, Nathaniel. *Ron Kovic: Antiwar Activist* (7–12). Series: Great Achievers: Lives of the Physically Challenged. 1994, Chelsea LB $19.95 (0-7910-2076-2). A biography of the disabled Vietnam veteran, antiwar activist, and author. (Rev: BL 1/15/94) [921]

KUUSISTO, STEPHEN

6495 Kuusisto, Stephen. *Planet of the Blind* (10–12). 1997, Doubleday $22.95 (0-385-31615-1); Dell paper $11.95 (0-385-33327-7). The biography of a young man who coped with legal blindness and bouts of obesity and anorexia before he reached out for help, accepted his disability, and learned to trust a seeing eye dog. (Rev: BL 11/15/97; SLJ 5/98) [921]

LINDBERGH, REEVE

6496 Lindbergh, Reeve. *Under a Wing: A Memoir* (10–12). 1998, Simon & Schuster $23.00 (0-684-80770-X). The story of the Lindbergh family from the standpoint of daughter Reeve, whose vivid descriptions of events range from taking flying lessons with her father to the effects of her brother's kidnapping on her parents and the rest of the family. (Rev: SLJ 3/99) [921]

LONG LANCE, CHIEF BUFFALO CHILD

6497 Smith, Donald B. *Chief Buffalo Child Long Lance: The Glorious Impostor* (10–12). Illus. 2000, Red Deer paper $14.95 (0-88995-197-7). The incredible biography of a man who posed as a Native American hero and became famous—until he was found out. (Rev: BL 5/15/00*) [921]

LOZEN

6498 Aleshire, Peter. *Warrior Woman: The Story of Lozen, Apache Warrior and Shaman* (10–12). 2001, St. Martin's $24.95 (0-312-24408-8). This is a biography of Lozen, a remarkable Apache woman who became a warrior and a shaman during the 19th century. (Rev: BL 3/1/01) [921]

MCNEILL, ROBERT

6499 Pekar, Harvey, and David Collier. *Unsung Hero: The Story of Robert McNeill* (10–12). Illus. 2003, Dark Horse paper $11.95 (1-59307-040-3). This nonfiction graphic account tells the story of Robert McNeil a 17-year-old who joined the marines, went through boot camp, and fought in the Vietnam War. (Rev: BL 2/1/04*) [921]

OSBORN, SHANE

6500 Osborn, Shane, with Malcolm McConnell. *Born to Fly: The Heroic Story of Downed U.S. Navy Pilot Lt. Shane Osborn* (7–12). 2001, Delacorte $15.95 (0-385-72999-5). Osborn, commander of a U.S. Navy reconnaissance flight forced to make an emergency landing on China's Hainan Island in 2001, describes his fascination with flight from early childhood and how it led him into the center of an international political crisis. (Rev: HBG 3/02; SLJ 1/02; VOYA 4/02)

PAYNE, LUCILLE M. W.

6501 Rice, Dorothy M., and Lucille Payne. *The Seventeenth Child* (7–12). 1998, Linnet LB $18.50 (0-208-02414-X). The story of an African American woman growing up in rural Virginia during the 1930s and 40s, as recorded and edited by her daughter. (Rev: HBG 3/99; SLJ 1/99; VOYA 6/99) [921]

RAY, JAMES EARL

6502 Posner, Gerald. *Killing the Dream: James Earl Ray and the Assassination of Martin Luther King,* *Jr.* (10–12). 1998, Random $25.00 (0-375-50082-0). The author examines in detail all of the conflicting stories about the killing of Martin Luther King Jr., with a particular focus on the life of James Earl Ray. (Rev: BL 5/1/98; SLJ 3/99) [921]

SANTIAGO, ESMERALDA

6503 Santiago, Esmeralda. *When I Was Puerto Rican* (9–12). 1993, Addison-Wesley $20.00 (0-201-58117-5). The author recalls the hardships and joys of her life with humor and poignancy, from her childhood in Puerto Rico to her move to a very different life in Brooklyn, and, finally, her admission to the High School of Performing Arts. (Rev: BL 10/1/93; SLJ 2/94) [921]

SIEGEL, BUGSY

6504 Otfinoski, Steve. *Bugsy Siegel and the Postwar Boom* (7–10). Illus. Series: Notorious Americans and Their Times. 2000, Blackbirch LB $27.44 (1-56711-224-2). The story of the gangster and the times in which he and his fellow mobsters were active. (Rev: BL 12/1/00; HBG 3/01; SLJ 1/01) [921]

SMITH, JOSEPH

6505 Remini, Robert V. *Joseph Smith* (10–12). 2002, Viking $19.95 (0-670-03083-X). A balanced account of Smith's formative years and religious beliefs, placed in the context of the social environment of the time. (Rev: BL 9/1/02) [921]

Science, Medicine, Industry, and Business Figures

Collective

6506 Aaseng, Nathan. *Black Inventors* (6–12). Illus. Series: American Profiles. 1997, Facts on File $25.00 (0-8160-3407-9). This work profiles 10 African American inventors, including Lewis Temple, Elijah McCoy, and Sarah Breedlove Walker, and tells how they overcame social and economic obstacles to achieve success but were denied recognition for their achievements. (Rev: BL 2/15/98; BR 1–2/98) [920]

6507 Bussing-Burks, Marie. *Influential Economists* (7–12). Illus. 2003, Oliver $19.95 (1-881508-72-2). The historical perspective of this book provides insights into economic theories and introduces some of the key people — including John Maynard Keynes and Milton Friedman — who have shaped the world's economy. (Rev: BL 3/1/03; HBG 10/03; SLJ 12/03) [920]

6508 Byrnes, Patricia. *Environmental Pioneers* (6–10). 1998, Oliver LB $19.95 (1-881508-45-5). This collective biography of early environmentalists includes profiles of John Muir, David Brower, Rachel Carson, Jay Darling, Rosalie Edge, Aldo Leopold, and Gaylord Nelson. (Rev: BL 9/15/98; BR 1–2/99; SLJ 11/98) [920]

6509 Camp, Carole Ann. *American Women Inventors* (5–10). Illus. Series: Collective Biographies. 2004, Enslow LB $20.95 (0-7660-1913-6). A collective biography of 10 important American female inventors, their lives, and their discoveries. (Rev: BL 3/1/04) [920]

6510 Cooney, Miriam P. *Celebrating Women in Mathematics and Science* (6–10). 1996, National Council of Teachers of Math paper $26.95 (0-87353-425-5). Covering ancient times to the present, this collective biography highlights the struggles and triumphs of women in the fields of mathematics and sciences. (Rev: SLJ 10/96) [920]

6511 Cropper, William H. *Great Physicists: The Life and Times of Leading Physicists from Galileo to Hawking* (10–12). Illus. 2001, Oxford $35.00 (0-19-513748-5). This readable collective biography profiles 30 scientists who made significant contributions to physics. (Rev: BL 12/1/01) [920]

6512 Dash, Joan. *The Triumph of Discovery: Four Nobel Women* (7–12). 1991, Messner paper $8.95 (0-671-69333-6). Highlights the work of four women who won the Nobel Prize in science, including Rita Levi-Montalcini and Barbara McClintock. (Rev: BL 3/15/91) [920]

6513 Fox, Karen. *The Chain Reaction: Pioneers of Nuclear Science* (6–12). Series: Lives of Science. 1998, Watts LB $20.00 (0-531-11425-2). The world of nuclear science is introduced through profiles of seven men and women who have studied the atom: Curie, Rutherford, Fermi, Lawrence, Oppenheimer, Goeppert-Mayer, and Sakharov. (Rev: BL 1/1–15/99; HBG 3/99; SLJ 2/99) [920]

6514 Fridell, Ron. *Solving Crimes: Pioneers of Forensic Science* (7–12). Illus. Series: Lives in Science. 2000, Watts LB $25.00 (0-531-11721-9). Six key figures in forensic science are profiled in an absorbing narrative that explains the science behind the evolving techniques. (Rev: BL 8/00; SLJ 6/00) [920]

6515 Haskins, Jim. *African American Entrepreneurs* (6–12). Illus. Series: Black Stars. 1998, Wiley $24.95 (0-471-14576-9). A collective biography of more than 30 African Americans who have made their mark on the business community. (Rev: BL 2/15/98; BR 11–12/98; SLJ 7/98) [920]

6516 Haskins, Jim. *Outward Dreams: Black Inventors and Their Inventions* (7–12). 1991, Walker LB $14.85 (0-8027-6994-2). Examines the lives and inventions of African American men and women who did not receive recognition for their contributions until after the Civil War. (Rev: BL 5/15/91) [920]

6517 Henderson, Harry. *Modern Mathematicians* (7–12). Illus. 1995, Facts on File LB $25.00 (0-8160-3235-1). Profiles of the lives and accomplishments of nine men and four women, among them George Boole, Alan Turing, and Sophia Kovalevsky, who have contributed to the development of modern mathematics. (Rev: BL 1/1–15/96; BR 5–6/96; SLJ 2/96; VOYA 2/96) [920]

6518 Leuzzi, Linda. *To the Young Environmentalist: Lives Dedicated to Preserving the Natural World* (6–10). Illus. Series: To the Young. 1997, Watts LB $23.00 (0-531-11359-0). Eight environmentalists describe the circumstances that motivated them to choose a career in this field. (Rev: BL 12/1/97; VOYA 6/98) [920]

6519 Lindop, Laurie. *Scientists and Doctors* (6–10). Series: Dynamic Women. 1997, Twenty-First Century LB $24.90 (0-8050-4166-4). Biographies of women who have excelled in such areas as archaeology, physics, astronautics, and genetics feature Mae Jemison, Susan Love, and Rosalyn Yalow, among others. (Rev: SLJ 9/97) [920]

6520 Malone, John Williams. *It Doesn't Take a Rocket Scientist: Great Amateurs of Science* (9–12). 2002, Wiley (0-471-41431-X). The lives of 10 amateur scientists — among them Gregor Mendel, Joseph Priestley, Michael Faraday, and Arthur C. Clarke — are examined in this collective biography. [920]

6521 Meadows, A. J. *The Great Scientists* (9–12). 1987, Oxford $45.00 (0-19-520620-7); paper $25.00 (0-19-520815-3). Including Aristotle, Galileo, Freud, and Einstein, this is a collective biography of 12 important world scientists. [920]

6522 Northrup, Mary. *American Computer Pioneers* (6–12). Illus. Series: Collective Biographies. 1998, Enslow LB $20.95 (0-7660-1053-8). Profiles individuals who revolutionized modern technology and gives a concise history of the evolution of computers and their capabilities. (Rev: BL 10/15/98; BR 11–12/98; HBG 3/99; SLJ 8/98) [920]

6523 Oleksy, Walter. *Hispanic-American Scientists* (7–10). Illus. Series: American Profiles. 1998, Facts on File $25.00 (0-8160-3704-3). Ten Hispanic American scientists are profiled, including Pedro Sanchez, Henry Diaz, Adriana Ocampo, and Francisco Dallmeier. (Rev: BL 3/1/99; BR 5–6/99; SLJ 2/99) [920]

6524 Pais, Abraham. *The Genius of Science: A Portrait Gallery of 20th-Century Physicists* (10–12). Illus. 2000, Oxford $30.00 (0-19-850614-7). This volume contains profiles of 16 contemporary physicists, many of whom, like Albert Einstein and Niels Bohr, were acquaintances of the author. (Rev: BL 4/15/00) [920]

6525 Pile, Robert B. *Top Entrepreneurs and Their Business* (6–12). 1993, Oliver LB $19.95 (1-881508-04-8). The rags-to-riches stories of nine entrepreneurs, among them L. L. Bean, Walt Disney, and Sam Walton. With photographs. (Rev: BL 11/15/93; SLJ 1/94) [920]

6526 Pile, Robert B. *Women Business Leaders* (6–12). Illus. Series: Profiles. 1995, Oliver LB $19.95 (1-881508-24-2). Profiles of eight women, most of them not well known (except for Mary Kay Ash of the cosmetics firm), who have the "creativity, strength, and determination to run thriving businesses." (Rev: BL 1/1–15/96; SLJ 5/96; VOYA 4/96) [920]

6527 Ragaza, Angelo. *Lives of Notable Asian Americans: Business, Politics, Science* (6–10). Series: Asian American Experience. 1995, Chelsea LB $18.95 (0-7910-2189-0). Asian Americans who have contributed in the business, political, and scientific arenas. (Rev: BL 8/95; VOYA 12/95) [973]

6528 Sullivan, Otha Richard. *African American Women Scientists and Inventors* (7–10). Series: Black Stars. 2001, Wiley $22.95 (0-471-38707-X). Twenty-six African American women born between 1849 and 1967 are profiled in this accessible book, with details of their lives and accomplishments. (Rev: SLJ 4/02) [920]

6529 Veglahn, Nancy. *Women Scientists* (7–10). Series: American Profiles. 1991, Facts on File LB $25.00 (0-8160-2482-0). Profiles 11 women scientists of the 19th and 20th centuries, including Alice Eastwood, Alice Hamilton, Margaret Mead, Barbara McClintock, and Rachel Carson. (Rev: BL 11/15/91; SLJ 3/92) [920]

6530 Yount, Lisa. *Asian-American Scientists* (6–10). Series: American Profiles. 1998, Facts on File $25.00 (0-8160-3756-6). This work features 12 Asian American scientists who have contributed to major scientific advances in the past century, among them Flossie Wong-Staal, Subrahmanyan Chandrasekhar, Tsutomu Shimomura, and David Da-i Ho. (Rev: BL 12/15/98; BR 5–6/99; SLJ 7/99) [920]

6531 Yount, Lisa. *Black Scientists* (7–12). Series: American Profiles. 1991, Facts on File LB $25.00 (0-8160-2549-5). Descriptions of the professional achievements of eight African American scientists and what led each to his/her particular field. (Rev: BL 11/15/91; SLJ 1/92) [920]

6532 Yount, Lisa. *Twentieth-Century Women Scientists* (7–12). Illus. 1995, Facts on File $25.00 (0-8160-3173-8). Provides details of the obstacles these 11 women faced, as well as information on their contributions and diverse backgrounds. (Rev: BL 4/15/96; SLJ 2/96; VOYA 4/96) [920]

6533 Zach, Kim K. *Hidden from History: The Lives of Eight American Women Scientists* (6–12). Illus. 2002, Avisson paper $19.95 (1-888105-54-2). The important achievements of eight women who made often unacknowledged contributions to the sciences are accompanied by some personal details. (Rev: BL 12/1/02; SLJ 4/03; VOYA 12/03) [920]

Science and Medicine

BABBAGE, CHARLES

6534 Swade, Doron. *The Difference Engine: Charles Babbage and the Quest to Build the First Computer* (10–12). 2001, Viking $24.95 (0-670-91020-1). A biography of Charles Babbage, a pioneer in the development of computers, with discussion of his lasting contributions to the field. (Rev: BL 8/01) [921]

BANNEKER, BENJAMIN

6535 Litwin, Laura Baskes. *Benjamin Banneker: Astronomer and Mathematician* (6–10). Illus. Series: African-American Biographies. 1999, Enslow LB $20.95 (0-7660-1208-5). The story of the self-taught African American scientist who lived during the days of slavery and was responsible for some brilliant scientific inventions. (Rev: BL 9/15/99; HBG 4/00) [921]

BELL, ALEXANDER GRAHAM

6536 Grosvenor, Edwin S., and Morgan Wesson. *Alexander Graham Bell: The Life and Times of the Man Who Invented the Telephone* (9–12). 1997, Abrams (0-8109-4005-1). Richly illustrated, this biography of Alexander Graham Bell chronicles the life and accomplishments of the Scottish-born inventor. [921]

6537 Weaver, Robyn M. *Alexander Graham Bell* (7–12). Series: The Importance Of. 2000, Lucent LB $18.96 (1-56006-603-2). The life and accomplishments of this scientific genius are covered, with emphasis on Bell's lasting importance. (Rev: BL 8/00; HBG 9/00) [921]

BLACKWELL, ELIZABETH

6538 Brown, Jordan. *Elizabeth Blackwell* (7–10). Illus. 1989, Chelsea LB $19.95 (1-55546-642-7). The life story of the first woman doctor; she also organized a nursing service during the Civil War and helped provide educational opportunities for other young women. (Rev: BL 5/15/89) [921]

BOHR, NIELS

6539 Pasachoff, Naomi. *Niels Bohr: Physicist and Humanitarian* (7–10). Illus. Series: Great Minds of Science. 2003, Enslow $20.95 (0-7660-1997-7). An appealing biography that explains Bohr's scientific achievements in clear, understandable terms and covers his protests against the Nazis and against the use of nuclear weapons. (Rev: BL 6/1–15/03; HBG 10/03; VOYA 6/04) [530]

BONNER, JOHN TYLER

6540 Bonner, John Tyler. *Lives of a Biologist: Adventures in a Century of Extraordinary Science* (10–12). 2002, Harvard $24.95 (0-674-00763-8). Bonner's eminently readable autobiography recounts how he was drawn to a career in science, chronicles the impressive advances made in biology during his lifetime, and conveys good information about the scientific process. (Rev: BL 3/15/02) [921]

CARSON, RACHEL

6541 Wheeler, Leslie A. *Rachel Carson* (7–12). Series: Pioneers in Change. 1991, Silver Burdett LB $13.95 (0-382-24167-3); paper $6.95 (0-382-24174-6). A portrait of the pioneer conservationist whose exposé on the lasting damage caused by widespread use of pesticides had a major impact. (Rev: BL 2/1/92) [921]

CARVER, GEORGE WASHINGTON

6542 Nelson, Marilyn. *Carver: A Life in Poems* (10–12). Illus. 2001, Front Street $16.00 (1-886910-53-7). This is a fine biography of botanist and teacher George Washington Carver, told in easy-to-read free verse that is also moving. (Rev: BL 5/1/01; BR 11–12/01; HB 9–10/01*; HBG 3/02; SLJ 7/01; VOYA 8/01) [921]

CRANE, KATHLEEN

6543 Crane, Kathleen. *Sea Legs: Tales of a Woman Oceanographer* (10–12). Illus. 2003, Westview $27.50 (0-8133-4004-7). The noted oceanographer describes the difficulties she faced establishing herself in a profession dominated by men. (Rev: BL 3/1/03*) [921]

CURIE, MARIE

6544 Pasachoff, Naomi. *Marie Curie and the Science of Radioactivity* (7–12). Illus. Series: Portraits in Science. 1996, Oxford $28.00 (0-19-509214-7). Combining details of her scientific research with information on her personal life, this is a fascinating biography of Madame Curie. (Rev: BL 9/1/96; SLJ 8/96) [921]

6545 Quinn, Susan. *Marie Curie: A Life* (10–12). 1995, Simon & Schuster paper $20.00 (0-201-88794-0). A biography of the Polish-born scientist who won the Nobel Prize twice for her work with radium. [921]

CURTISS, GLENN

6546 Shulman, Seth. *Unlocking the Sky: Glenn Hammond Curtiss and the Race to Invent the Airplane* (10–12). Illus. 2002, HarperCollins $25.95 (0-06-019633-5). Told in present tense, this appealing biography covers the life and accomplishments of American aviation pioneer and inventor Glenn Curtiss. (Rev: BL 8/02) [629.13]

DARWIN, CHARLES

6547 Bowlby, John. *Charles Darwin: A Biography* (9–12). 1991, Norton paper $14.95 (0-393-30930-4). The story of the dedicated scientist, his many voyages to gather data, and the development of his theory of evolution. (Rev: BL 3/1/91) [921]

6548 *Charles Darwin* (10–12). Ed. by Don Nardo. Illus. 1999, Greenhaven LB $21.96 (0-7377-0081-5); paper $13.96 (0-7377-0080-7). Readings on the naturalist explore his life and how his ideas have affected modern thought. (Rev: BL 3/1/00) [921]

6549 Milner, Richard. *Charles Darwin: Evolution of a Naturalist* (10–12). Series: Makers of Modern Science. 1994, Facts on File $25.00 (0-8160-2557-6). This biography explores Darwin's accomplishments as a naturalist, philosopher, and evolutionist. [921]

6550 Patent, Dorothy Hinshaw. *Charles Darwin: The Life of a Revolutionary Thinker* (7–12). Illus. 2001, Holiday $22.95 (0-8234-1494-9). An absorbing portrait of the man who came late to the career that made him famous, with information on his youth, education, family life, and interests in science and literature. (Rev: BL 8/01; HB 9–10/01; HBG 3/02; SLJ 8/01) [921]

DREW, CHARLES

6551 Mahone-Lonesome, Robyn. *Charles Drew* (6–10). Illus. 1990, Chelsea LB $21.95 (1-55546-581-1). The biography of the African American scientist who did pioneer work in blood preservation and the establishment of blood banks. (Rev: BL 2/15/90; BR 5–6/90) [921]

EDISON, THOMAS ALVA

6552 Adair, Gene. *Thomas Alva Edison: Inventing the Electric Age* (7–10). Illus. 1996, Oxford $28.00 (0-19-508799-2). A biography of this astounding genius who not only invented the light bulb, but also was involved with improving the telegraph, inventing the phonograph, and developing early motion pictures. (Rev: BL 6/1–15/96; SLJ 6/96; VOYA 8/96) [921]

6553 Baldwin, Neil. *Edison: Inventing the Century* (9–12). 1995, Hyperion $27.95 (0-7868-6041-3). A biography of the great inventor known as the "wizard of Menlo Park," the New Jersey city where he lived. (Rev: BL 2/15/95) [921]

6554 Cramer, Carol, ed. *Thomas Edison* (7–12). Series: People Who Made History. 2001, Greenhaven LB $22.96 (0-7377-0428-4); paper $14.96 (0-7377-0427-6). An introductory overview of Edison's life and times is followed by a series of detailed chapters that explore various facets of his accomplishments and lasting contributions to society. (Rev: BL 4/15/01) [921]

6555 Israel, Paul. *Edison: A Life of Invention* (10–12). 1998, Wiley $50.00 (0-471-52942-7); paper $18.95 (0-471-36270-0). Edison's inventions and commercial enterprises are at the center of this biography that includes many reproductions of his drawings. (Rev: BL 10/1/98) [921]

EINSTEIN, ALBERT

6556 Bernstein, Jeremy. *Albert Einstein and the Frontiers of Physics* (9–12). Series: Oxford Portraits in Science. 1996, Oxford LB $24.00 (0-19-509275-9); paper $12.95 (0-19-512029-9). This illuminating biography looks beyond the facts and figures of Einstein's life and into the physicist's personality; many scientific concepts are explained in depth. (Rev: BL 9/1/96; SLJ 12/96; VOYA 10/96) [921]

6557 Brian, Denis. *Einstein: A Life* (10–12). 1996, Wiley paper $19.95 (0-471-19362-3). A well-researched profile that looks both at Einstein's life and personality. (Rev: BL 5/1/96) [921]

6558 Kaku, Michio. *Einstein's Cosmos: How Albert Einstein's Vision Transformed Our Understanding of Space and Time* (10–12). 2004, Norton $22.95 (0-393-05165-X). The works of the great physicist are the focus of this volume, with material of on all of his theories including special relativity and general relativity. (Rev: BL 3/15/04) [921]

6559 Severance, John B. *Einstein: Visionary Scientist* (7–12). Illus. 1999, Clarion $16.00 (0-395-93100-2). This book covers Einstein's academic theories as well as his private life and his celebrity. (Rev: BCCB 9/99; BL 9/1/99; HB 9–10/99; HBG 4/00; SLJ 9/99) [921]

6560 Strathern, Paul. *Einstein and Relativity* (10–12). 1999, Anchor Bks. paper $9.95 (0-385-49244-8). As well as an account of Einstein's life, this book explains the theory of relativity and how it changed scientific thinking. (Rev: BL 5/1/99) [921]

6561 Swisher, Clarice, ed. *Albert Einstein* (7–12). Series: People Who Made History. 2002, Gale LB $31.20 (0-7377-0892-1); paper $19.95 (0-7377-

0893-X). After an introductory overview chapter, the remaining 19 essays explore different facets of the life and accomplishments of this great scientist and mathematician. (Rev: BL 4/1/02; SLJ 5/02) [921]

FARADAY, MICHAEL

6562 Ludwig, Charles. *Michael Faraday: Father of Electronics* (9–12). 1988, Herald Pr. $9.99 (0-8361-3479-6). The life of the scientist who worked on such inventions as the dynamo, the generator, and the transformer. [921]

6563 Russell, Colin A. *Michael Faraday: Physics and Faith* (8–12). Illus. Series: Oxford Portraits in Science. 2001, Oxford LB $22.00 (0-19-511763-8). The story of the inventor of the electric transformer and the dynamo is placed in interesting historical context. (Rev: HBG 10/01; SLJ 3/01) [921]

FERMI, ENRICO

6564 Cooper, Dan. *Enrico Fermi: And the Revolutions of Modern Physics* (8–12). Series: Oxford Portraits in Science. 1999, Oxford $28.00 (0-19-511762-X). A readable biography of the Italian scientist who immigrated to the United States in 1939 and worked on the first atomic bomb. Some of the coverage of quantum and nuclear physics is challenging. (Rev: SLJ 6/99) [921]

FLEMING, ALEXANDER

6565 Gottfried, Ted. *Alexander Fleming: Discoverer of Penicillin* (6–10). Illus. Series: Book Report Biographies. 1997, Watts LB $22.00 (0-531-11370-1). In 1928, bacteriologist Alexander Fleming discovered a blue mold growing on a culture dish in his lab in London. This discovery led to the development of the first antibiotic, penicillin, and a Nobel Prize. (Rev: BL 12/1/97; HBG 3/98; SLJ 2/98) [921]

FOSSEY, DIAN

6566 Mowat, Farley. *Woman in the Mists: The Story of Dian Fossey and the Mountain Gorillas of Africa* (10–12). Illus. 1987, Warner paper $19.99 (0-446-38720-7). A naturalist writer has created a stirring life of the zoologist whose study of gorillas was trailblazing. (Rev: BL 9/1/87; SLJ 2/88; VOYA 4/88) [921]

6567 Nicholson, Lois P. *Dian Fossey: Primatologist* (7–12). Series: Women in Science. 2003, Chelsea LB $22.95 (0-7910-6907-9). An absorbing portrait of the woman who overcame obstacles to study and protect mountain gorillas in central Africa. (Rev: LMC 11–12/03; SLJ 7/03) [599.884]

FRANKLIN, ROSALIND

6568 Maddox, Brenda. *Rosalind Franklin: The Dark Lady of DNA* (10–12). Illus. 2002, HarperCollins $29.95 (0-06-018407-8). Maddox profiles the life and lasting scientific contributions of Rosalind Franklin, the chemist who played a vital — but generally overlooked — role in the unraveling of DNA's structure. (Rev: BL 10/15/02) [921]

FREUD, SIGMUND

6569 Muckenhoupt, Margaret. *Sigmund Freud: Explorer of the Unconscious* (10–12). Illus. Series: Oxford Portraits in Science. 1997, Oxford $32.00 (0-19-509933-8). A detailed biography of the father of psychoanalysis that contains material on Freud's theories concerning dreams, the Oedipus complex, sexuality, and the unconscious. (Rev: BL 12/1/97; SLJ 1/98) [921]

6570 Reef, Catherine. *Sigmund Freud: Pioneer of the Mind* (7–12). Illus. 2001, Clarion $19.00 (0-618-01762-3). Reef looks at Freud's life and career, showing the ways in which his ideas evolved over time and the initial rejection of many of his revolutionary thoughts. (Rev: BL 7/01; HB 7–8/01*; HBG 10/01; SLJ 8/01; VOYA 10/01) [921]

GALILEO

6571 Boerst, William J. *Galileo Galilei and the Science of Motion* (6–10). Illus. Series: Great Scientists. 2003, Morgan Reynolds LB $23.95 (1-931798-00-1). Galileo's early insistence on adherence to scientific verification is emphasized in this detailed yet accessible biography that includes color period reproductions and a timeline. (Rev: BL 11/1/03; HBG 4/04; SLJ 12/03) [921]

6572 MacLachlan, James. *Galileo Galilei: First Physicist* (6–10). Series: Oxford Portraits in Science. 1997, Oxford $28.00 (0-19-509342-9). A fine portrait of this mathematician/physicist and his accomplishments, and a good introduction to the Renaissance world. (Rev: SLJ 3/98) [921]

6573 Reston, James, Jr. *Galileo: A Life* (10–12). 1994, Beard paper $19.95 (1-893-12262-X). The story of this great scientist and his many conflicts with the Church. (Rev: BL 4/15/94) [921]

6574 Swisher, Clarice, ed. *Galileo* (7–12). Series: People Who Made History. 2001, Greenhaven LB $31.20 (0-7377-0671-6); paper $19.95 (0-7377-0670-8). This series of essays explores the life of Galileo, his problems with the Inquisition, and his many contributions to mathematics, astronomy, and physics. (Rev: BL 9/15/01) [921]

GOODALL, JANE

6575 Kozleski, Lisa. *Jane Goodall: Primatologist/ Naturalist* (7–12). Series: Women in Science. 2003, Chelsea LB $22.95 (0-7910-6905-2). An absorbing biography that discusses the primatologist's personal life as well as her dedicated work with chimpanzees in Tanzania. (Rev: LMC 11–12/03; SLJ 7/03) [921]

6576 Meachum, Virginia. *Jane Goodall: Protector of Chimpanzees* (6–10). Illus. Series: People to Know. 1997, Enslow LB $20.95 (0-89490-827-8). The story of the great naturalist who fulfilled her childhood dream and made groundbreaking observations of chimpanzee behavior. (Rev: BL 1/1–15/98; HBG 3/98) [921]

HARRIOT, THOMAS

6577 Staiger, Ralph C. *Thomas Harriot: Science Pioneer* (6–10). 1998, Clarion $19.00 (0-395-67296-1). The biography of the Elizabethan scientist who made contributions to navigation, optics, and astronomy and who accompanied Sir Walter Raleigh to Roanoke Island in 1585, where he studied the flora, fauna, and the native people. (Rev: BL 12/1/98; BR 5–6/99; HBG 3/99; SLJ 5/99; VOYA 2/99) [921]

HARRISON, JOHN

6578 Dash, Joan. *The Longitude Prize* (10–12). Illus. 2000, Farrar $16.00 (0-374-34636-4). This colorful — but quite technical — biography tells how 18th-century English clockmaker John Harrison developed instruments to help sailors determine their relative east-west position as they sailed the seas, sharply reducing the number of ships that foundered when their crews became disoriented. (Rev: BL 1/1–15/01; HB 11–12/00; HBG 3/01; SLJ 11/00; VOYA 2/01) [921]

HAWKING, STEPHEN

6579 Boslough, John. *Stephen Hawking's Universe* (10–12). 1985, Morrow paper $5.99 (0-380-70763-2). This biography of Hawking focuses on his contributions to physics and cosmology. [921]

6580 Ferguson, Kitty. *Stephen Hawking: Quest for a Theory of the Universe* (9–12). 1991, Watts LB $24.00 (0-531-11067-2). This biography of the physicist, in addition to recounting his life story, uses everyday examples to help make his complex cosmological concepts more understandable. (Rev: BL 9/1/91*; SLJ 4/92) [921]

6581 McDaniel, Melissa. *Stephen Hawking: Revolutionary Physicist* (8–10). Series: Great Achievers: Lives of the Physically Challenged. 1994, Chelsea LB $21.95 (0-7910-2078-9). The life and work of

this great scientific theorist are explored in this fascinating biography. [921]

HUBBLE, EDWIN

6582 Christianson, Gale E. *Edwin Hubble: Mariner of the Nebulae* (9–12). 1995, Farrar $27.50 (0-374-14660-8). An exploration of Hubble's contributions, his personal successes, and the activities and views that sometimes annoyed others inside and outside the scientific community. (Rev: BL 8/95*) [921]

KRAFT, CHRIS

6583 Kraft, Chris. *Flight: My Life in Mission Control* (10–12). Illus. 2001, Dutton $25.95 (0-525-94571-7). A pioneer in space flight tells of his many exploits, including the flight control operation of the Mercury, Gemini, and Apollo flights. (Rev: BL 12/15/00) [921]

LEAKEY, LOUIS AND MARY

6584 Morell, Virginia. *Ancestral Passions: The Leakey Family and the Quest for Humankind's Beginnings* (9–12). 1995, Simon & Schuster $30.00 (0-684-80192-2). The story of the Leakey family — Louis, Mary, and their son, Richard — and their paleoanthropologic work in the field of human evolution. (Rev: BL 7/95*) [921]

MCCLINTOCK, BARBARA

6585 Cullen, J. Heather. *Barbara McClintock: Geneticist* (6–12). Illus. Series: Women in Science. 2003, Chelsea LB $22.95 (0-7910-7248-7). Cullen explores the life and achievements of McClintock, who won a Nobel Prize in 1983 for research in genetics that she conducted decades earlier. (Rev: HBG 10/03; SLJ 10/03) [921]

MAYER, MARIA GOEPPERT

6586 Ferry, Joseph P. *Maria Goeppert Mayer: Physicist* (6–12). Series: Women in Science. 2003, Chelsea LB $22.95 (0-7910-7247-9). Ferry explores the life and achievements of Mayer, who won a Nobel Prize in 1963 for research into the atomic nucleus. (Rev: HBG 10/03; SLJ 10/03) [921]

MEAD, MARGARET

6587 Mark, Joan. *Margaret Mead: Coming of Age in America* (6–10). Ed. by Owen Gingerich. Illus. Series: Oxford Portraits in Science. 1999, Oxford $28.00 (0-19-511679-8). An introduction to the life and work of the pioneering anthropologist and her research with the peoples of the South Seas, particularly in Samoa. (Rev: BL 4/1/99; SLJ 3/99) [921]

MEITNER, LISE

6588 Barron, Rachel Stiffler. *Lise Meitner: Discoverer of Nuclear Fission* (7–12). Series: Great Scientists. 2000, Morgan Reynolds LB $21.95 (1-883846-52-8). The story of the Jewish scientist who fled Nazi Germany to the U.S., where her findings concerning nuclear fission led to the first atomic bomb. (Rev: BL 3/15/00; HBG 4/00; SLJ 6/00) [921]

6589 Hamilton, Janet. *Lise Meitner: Pioneer of Nuclear Fission* (6–10). Illus. Series: Great Minds of Science. 2002, Enslow LB $20.95 (0-7660-1756-7). This readable biography of the nuclear physicist who fled Nazi Germany before the outbreak of World War II, and who subsequently refused to work on developing nuclear weapons, is notable for placing her life and work in historical context. (Rev: HBG 10/02; SLJ 10/02) [921]

MENDEL, GREGOR

6590 Edelson, Edward. *Gregor Mendel: And the Roots of Genetics* (7–10). Series: Oxford Portraits in Science. 1999, Oxford $28.00 (0-19-512226-7). Describes Mendel's life and his work on plant heredity and the study of genetics in the context of the social, scientific, and political events of his time. (Rev: SLJ 7/99) [921]

6591 Henig, Robin Marantz. *The Monk in the Garden: The Lost and Found Genius of Gregor Mendel, the Father of Genetics* (10–12). Illus. 2000, Houghton $24.00 (0-395-97765-7). For advanced science students, this is a biography of the monk Gregor Mendel, with information on his experiments with pea plants, and the laws he formulated about genetics. (Rev: BL 6/1–15/00) [921]

MORSE, SAMUEL F. B.

6592 Silverman, Kenneth. *Lightning Man: The Accursed Life of Samuel F. B. Morse* (10–12). 2003, Knopf $35.00 (0-375-40128-8). A comprehensive biography that reveals Morse's complex character and his sense that he was a failure. (Rev: BL 9/15/03) [921]

MUIR, JOHN

6593 Ehrlich, Gretel. *John Muir: Nature's Visionary* (10–12). Illus. 2000, National Geographic $35.00 (0-7922-7954-9). The story of the early conservationist and how he loved nature, fought to preserve it, and cofounded the Sierra Club. (Rev: BL 1/1–15/01) [921]

6594 Wadsworth, Ginger. *John Muir: Wilderness Protector* (6–12). 1992, Lerner LB $30.35 (0-8225-4912-3). Original photographs and Muir's letters, journals, and writings provide an overview of the conservationist's personal life, achievements, and

contributions to the environmental movement. (Rev: BL 8/92) [921]

6595 Wilkins, Thurman. *John Muir: Apostle of Nature* (10–12). Series: Oklahoma Western Biographies. 1995, Univ. of Oklahoma Pr. paper $19.95 (0-8061-2797-X). An excellent biography of an American folk hero who loved the wilderness and fought to preserve it. (Rev: BL 10/15/95) [921]

NEWTON, ISAAC

6596 Boerst, William J. *Isaac Newton: Organizing the Universe* (6–10). Illus. Series: Renaissance Scientists. 2004, Morgan Reynolds LB $23.95 (1-931798-01-X). A fine biography of Newton that includes good explanations of the laws of motion and excellent color reproductions of period paintings. (Rev: BL 2/1/04; SLJ 4/04) [921]

6597 Christianson, Gale E. *Isaac Newton and the Scientific Revolution* (8–12). Illus. Series: Oxford Portraits in Science. 1996, Oxford $28.00 (0-19-509224-4). A challenging biography that gives the scientist's life history plus detailed explanations of theories of gravity, relativity, and calculus. (Rev: BL 12/1/96; SLJ 1/97; VOYA 2/97) [921]

6598 Gleick, James. *Isaac Newton* (10–12). Illus. 2003, Pantheon $22.95 (0-375-42233-1). This profile of the English mathematician/physicist offers an intriguing introduction to his thought processes. (Rev: BL 5/1/03) [921]

OFRI, DANIELLE

6599 Ofri, Danielle. *Singular Intimacies: Becoming a Doctor at Bellevue* (10–12). 2003, Beacon $24.00 (0-8070-7252-4). In this collection of essays, the author chronicles the decade she spent as a medical student, intern, and resident, focusing in particular on her interactions with colleagues and patients. (Rev: BL 3/1/03*) [610]

OPPENHEIMER, ROBERT

6600 Rummel, Jack. *Robert Oppenheimer: Dark Prince* (7–12). 1992, Facts on File LB $19.95 (0-8160-2598-3). A straightforward biography of the physicist credited with developing the atomic bomb. (Rev: BL 9/15/92; SLJ 9/92) [921]

PASTEUR, LOUIS

6601 Ackerman, Jane. *Louis Pasteur and the Founding of Microbiology* (7–12). Illus. Series: Great Scientists. 2004, Morgan Reynolds $23.95 (1-931798-13-3). Using his microscope, Pasteur developed the fields of immunology and microbiology and invented the pasteurization of milk. (Rev: BL 2/1/04; SLJ 4/04) [921]

6602 Robbins, Louise E. *Louis Pasteur and the Hidden World of Microbes* (8–12). Series: Oxford Portraits in Science. 2001, Oxford $24.00 (0-19-512227-5). A look at the life of the famous scientist, with glimpses of his personality as well as his research and discoveries. (Rev: BL 12/1/01; HBG 3/02; SLJ 12/01) [921]

PAULING, LINUS

6603 Hager, Tom. *Linus Pauling and the Chemistry of Life* (9–12). Illus. Series: Portraits in Science. 1998, Oxford $33.95 (0-19-510853-1). A profile of the multitalented giant who won the Nobel Prize in chemistry as well as the Nobel Peace Prize for his participation in the antiwar and disarmament movements. (Rev: BL 5/15/98; SLJ 8/98) [921]

SACKS, OLIVER

6604 Sacks, Oliver. *Uncle Tungsten: Memories of a Chemical Boyhood* (10–12). Illus. 2001, Knopf $25.00 (0-375-40448-1). The renowned neurologist has written an engaging memoir about his childhood in England before, during, and after World War II. (Rev: BL 9/1/01*; SLJ 6/01) [921]

SALK, JONAS

6605 Sherrow, Victoria. *Jonas Salk* (7–12). 1993, Facts on File $25.00 (0-8160-2805-2). Begins with a history of polio, moves on to Salk's education, research, and development of the polio vaccine, and ends with the Salk Institute's work on cancer and AIDS. (Rev: BL 9/15/93) [921]

WRIGHT, WILBUR AND ORVILLE

6606 Freedman, Russell. *The Wright Brothers: How They Invented the Airplane* (6–10). 1991, Holiday $22.95 (0-8234-0875-2). Chronicles the achievements of two brothers who built the first flying machine in an Ohio bicycle shop and ultimately saw their dream come true. (Rev: BL 6/15/91*; SLJ 6/91*) [921]

6607 Martin, Michael J. *The Wright Brothers* (7–12). Series: The Importance Of. 2003, Gale LB $27.45 (1-56006-847-7). With lengthy quotations from primary and secondary sources, this is a lively biography of Wilbur and Orville Wright and how they changed history at Kitty Hawk. (Rev: BL 6/1–15/03) [921]

Industry and Business

ARDEN, ELIZABETH

6608 Shuker, Nancy. *Elizabeth Arden: Beauty Empire Builder* (7–10). Illus. Series: Giants of American Industry. 2001, Blackbirch LB $21.95 (1-56711-510-1). A farmer's daughter, Elizabeth

Arden was an assistant to a beauty specialist before opening her first salon. (Rev: BL 10/15/01; HBG 3/02) [921]

CARNEGIE, ANDREW

6609 Meltzer, Milton. *The Many Lives of Andrew Carnegie* (7–10). Illus. 1997, Watts LB $20.00 (0-531-11427-9). The amazing life of this complex, successful businessman and philanthropist who sought to project himself as a generous industrial leader but used unscrupulous business tactics and treated his workers ruthlessly. (Rev: BL 10/1/97; BR 5–6/98; HBG 3/98; SLJ 10/97; VOYA 10/98) [921]

6610 Wall, Joseph Frazier. *Andrew Carnegie* (10–12). 1989, Univ. of Pittsburgh Pr. paper $22.50 (0-8229-5904-6). The story of the immigrant boy from Scotland and his rise to fame and fortune in various industries including iron and steel. [921]

EASTMAN, GEORGE

6611 Holmes, Burnham. *George Eastman* (7–12). Series: Pioneers in Change. 1992, Silver Burdett LB $13.95 (0-382-24170-3); paper $6.95 (0-382-24176-2). The story of the great inventor of photographic equipment, founder of Eastman Kodak Company, and renowned philanthropist. (Rev: BL 9/15/92) [921]

6612 Pflueger, Lynda. *George Eastman: Bringing Photography to the People* (7–10). Series: Historical American Biographies. 2002, Enslow LB $20.95 (0-7660-1617-X). Eastman's success in bringing photography to the masses is described, as are his philanthropy and personal life. (Rev: HBG 3/03; SLJ 11/02) [921]

FARNSWORTH, PHILO

6613 Schatzkin, Paul. *The Boy Who Invented Television: A Story of Inspiration, Persistence and Quiet Passion* (10–12). 2002, TeamCom paper $16.95 (1-928791-30-1). A candid and absorbing portrait of Farnsworth and his technical genius from a young age. (Rev: BL 9/1/02) [921]

6614 Stashower, Daniel. *The Boy Genius and the Mogul: The Untold Story of Television* (9–12). Illus. 2002, Broadway $24.95 (0-7679-0759-0). Stashower celebrates the contributions of Idaho teenager Philo Farnsworth, who came up with the idea for a television-like "image dissector" but lacked the finances to turn his dream into a reality. (Rev: BL 3/15/02) [921]

FORD, HENRY

6615 Tilton, Rafael. *Henry Ford* (7–12). Series: The Importance Of. 2003, Gale LB $27.45 (1-56006-846-9). The designer of an efficient gasoline engine and developer of the assembly line is profiled in this biography that uses many quotations from original sources. (Rev: BL 6/1–15/03) [921]

GATES, BILL

6616 Boyd, Aaron. *Smart Money: The Story of Bill Gates* (6–10). 1995, Morgan Reynolds LB $21.95 (1-883846-09-9). A biography of Microsoft's billionaire mogul. (Rev: BL 4/1/95; SLJ 4/95; VOYA 2/96) [921]

GETTY, JOHN PAUL

6617 Glassman, Bruce S. *John Paul Getty: Billionaire Oilman* (7–10). Illus. Series: Giants of American Industry. 2001, Blackbirch LB $21.95 (1-56711-513-6). Glassman covers Getty's life from childhood, describing how he became a millionaire in his 20s and later was known for his philanthropy and art collection. (Rev: BL 10/15/01; HBG 3/02) [921]

GOODYEAR, CHARLES

6618 Slack, Charles. *Noble Obsession: Charles Goodyear, Thomas Hancock, and the Race to Unlock the Greatest Industrial Secret of the Nineteenth Century* (10–12). 2002, Hyperion $24.95 (0-7868-6789-2). Goodyear's struggles to perfect his vulcanization process — making use of natural rubber practical — are chronicled in this excellent portrait full of accessible history and technological information. (Rev: BL 7/02) [921]

GRAHAM, KATHARINE

6619 Asirvatham, Sandy. *Katharine Graham* (7–10). Illus. Series: Women of Achievement. 2001, Chelsea LB $21.95 (0-7910-6310-0); paper $9.95 (0-7910-6311-9). A concise and readable account of Graham's life and her success in taking over the *Washington Post* after her husband's suicide. (Rev: BL 3/1/02; HBG 10/02; SLJ 6/02) [921]

6620 Whitelaw, Nancy. *Let's Go! Let's Publish! Katharine Graham and the Washington Post* (7–10). 1998, Morgan Reynolds LB $21.95 (1-883846-37-4). The life story of the famous woman editor of the *Washington Post,* who led it through such turbulent times as the Pentagon Papers and Watergate. (Rev: BL 1/1–15/99; HBG 3/99; SLJ 5/99; VOYA 6/00) [921]

GROVE, ANDREW

6621 Byman, Jeremy. *Andrew Grove and the Intel Corporation* (6–12). 1999, Morgan Reynolds LB $21.95 (1-883846-38-2). From hiding with his mother in Nazi-occupied Budapest to the founding of Intel, the company that changed computer history, this is the story of Andrew Grove. (Rev: BL 3/15/99; SLJ 5/99) [921]

6622 Grove, Andrew S. *Swimming Across* (10–12). 2001, Warner $26.95 (0-446-52859-5). The autobiography of the young Hungarian Jewish boy who escaped the Nazis, came to this country, and became cofounder of Intel, the world's largest semiconductor manufacturer. (Rev: BL 10/1/01) [921]

HANKINS, ANTHONY M.

6623 Hankins, Anthony M., and Debbie Markley. *Fabric of Dreams: Designing My Own Success* (10–12). 1998, NAL $27.95 (0-525-94329-3). An easy-to-read, inspiring autobiography of the enterprising African American fashion designer, the obstacles he overcame, and the founding of his multimillion-dollar business while he was still in his 20s. (Rev: BL 2/15/98; SLJ 10/98) [921]

HARPER, MARTHA MATILDA

6624 Plitt, Jane R. *Martha Matilda Harper and the American Dream: How One Woman Changed the Face of Modern Business* (10–12). Illus. 2000, Syracuse Univ. Pr. $26.95 (0-8156-0638-9). This inspirational biography tells how Harper became a successful businesswoman in the early 20th century through a chain of beauty salons and America's first franchise network. (Rev: BL 6/1–15/00) [921]

HEARST, WILLIAM RANDOLPH

6625 Whitelaw, Nancy. *William Randolph Hearst and the American Century* (6–12). Illus. 1999, Morgan Reynolds $19.95 (1-883846-46-3). Hearst's eccentricities and lively, thrusting approach to life are well portrayed in this vivid biography. (Rev: BL 10/1/99; HBG 4/00; VOYA 6/00) [921]

JONES, CAROLINE

6626 Fleming, Robert. *The Success of Caroline Jones Advertising, Inc.* (7–10). Illus. Series: Success. 1996, Walker LB $16.85 (0-8027-8354-6). The story of Jones's rapid rise in the world of advertising. (Rev: BL 1/1–15/96; SLJ 4/96) [921]

LATIMER, LEWIS

6627 Norman, Winifred Latimer, and Lily Patterson. *Lewis Latimer* (7–10). Series: Black Americans of Achievement. 1993, Chelsea LB $21.95 (0-7910-1977-2). Follows Latimer's career from Civil War veteran to executive at the Edison Company, where he helped Thomas Edison improve the light bulb and supervised the installation of electrical systems in several cities. (Rev: BL 11/15/93) [921]

MORGAN, J. P.

6628 Byman, Jeremy. *J. P. Morgan: Banker to a Growing Nation* (6–10). Series: American Business Leaders. 2001, Morgan Reynolds LB $20.95 (1-883846-60-9). An easily read introduction to Morgan's importance that places his contributions in political and social context. (Rev: BR 9–10/01; HBG 10/01; SLJ 7/01) [021]

OCHS, ADOLPH S.

6629 Faber, Doris. *Printer's Devil to Publisher: Adolph S. Ochs of The New York Times* (10–12). 1996, Black Dome paper $8.95 (1-883789-09-5). A rags-to-riches story about the trailblazing journalist and how he ran *The New York Times,* with a behind-the-scenes look at the newspaper's role in covering such stories as the sinking of the *Titanic.* (Rev: SLJ 10/96) [921]

PULITZER, JOSEPH

6630 Whitelaw, Nancy. *Joseph Pulitzer and the New York World* (7–10). Illus. Series: Makers of the Media. 1999, Morgan Reynolds LB $21.95 (1-883846-44-7). The life story of the founder of "tabloid journalism," who revolutionized the newspaper industry by combining sensational news, visuals, and reports on political corruption to both attract readers and encourage social change, and for whom the Pulitzer Prize is named. (Rev: BL 6/1–15/99; SLJ 9/99) [921]

PULITZER, JOSEPH, II

6631 Pfaff, Daniel W. *Joseph Pulitzer II and the Post-Dispatch: A Newspaperman's Life* (9–12). 1991, Pennsylvania State Univ. Pr. $45.00 (0-271-00748-6). This biography of the son of the newspaper empire's founder shows him to be an astute, principled journalist who helped establish the reputation of the St. Louis newspaper. (Rev: BL 9/15/91) [921]

ROCKEFELLER, JOHN D.

6632 Segall, Grant. *John D. Rockefeller: Anointed with Oil* (9–12). Illus. Series: Oxford Portraits. 2001, Oxford $22.00 (0-19-512147-3). One of America's giants of industry, John D. Rockefeller comes alive in this well-researched biography that chronicles his life from childhood and provides an excellent resource for students writing reports or simply curious about the man and his times. (Rev: BL 1/1–15/01; HBG 10/01; SLJ 3/01) [921]

STEWART, MARTHA

6633 Meachum, Virginia. *Martha Stewart: Successful Businesswoman* (6–10). Series: People to Know. 1998, Enslow LB $20.95 (0-89490-984-3). A well-documented biography of Martha Kostyra Stewart, the human dynamo who has achieved fame as a model, master chef, expert homemaker, entertainer, author, and TV celebrity. (Rev: HBG 3/99; SLJ 1/99) [921]

TURNER, TED

6634 Byman, Jeremy. *Ted Turner: Cable Television Tycoon* (7–10). Illus. 1998, Morgan Reynolds LB $21.95 (1-883846-25-0). Known as the "mouth of the south," media mogul Ted Turner, a born rebel, introduced CNN in 1980. (Rev: BL 4/1/98; BR 1–2/99; HBG 9/98; SLJ 8/98) [921]

WALKER, MADAM C. J.

6635 Bundles, A'Lelia. *Madam C. J. Walker* (5–10). Series: Black Americans of Achievement. 1993, Chelsea LB $21.95 (1-55546-615-X); paper $9.95 (0-7910-0251-9). Written by Walker's great-great-granddaughter, this volume describes the developer of a line of hair-care products whose entrepreneurial ability made her into the "foremost colored businesswoman in America." (Rev: BL 3/1/94) [921]

6636 Bundles, A'Lelia. *On Her Own Ground: The Life and Times of Madam C. J. Walker* (10–12). Illus. 2001, Scribner $30.00 (0-684-82582-1). A portrait of the fascinating African American businesswoman and how she made a fortune in the hair-care business. (Rev: BL 1/1–15/01) [921]

6637 Lowry, Beverly. *Her Dream of Dreams: The Rise and Triumph of Madam C. J. Walker* (10–12). Illus. 2003, Knopf $27.50 (0-679-44642-7). The transformation of impoverished Sarah Breedlove into millionaire black businesswoman Madam C. J. Walker is captured beautifully in this skillfully written biography that draws on historical accounts, interviews, and speeches. (Rev: BL 4/1/03) [921]

Sports Figures

Collective

6638 Aaseng, Nathan. *African-American Athletes* (8–12). Series: A to Z of African Americans. 2003, Facts on File $44.00 (0-8160-4805-3). Profiles of more than 150 African American athletes, past and present and representing all kinds of sports, give personal and career information. (Rev: SLJ 6/03) [920]

6639 Aaseng, Nathan. *Athletes* (7–12). Series: American Indian Lives. 1995, Facts on File $25.00 (0-8160-3019-7). A collective biography that highlights the lives of 11 Native American athletes, including Jim Thorpe, Kitty O'Neil, Sonny Sixkiller, Billy Mills, and Henry Boucha. (Rev: BL 4/1/95) [920]

6640 Breton, Marcos. *Home Is Everything: The Latino Baseball Story* (7–12). Trans. by Daniel Santacruz. Photos by Jos Luis Villegas. 2003, Cinco Puntos paper $25.95 (0-938317-70-9). The story of Miguel Tejada is spotlighted in this photoessay that also profiles other Latino baseball players including Jose Santana, Orlando Cepeda, and Roberto Clemente. (Rev: SLJ 12/03; VOYA 12/03) [920]

6641 Gutman, Bill. *Teammates: Michael Jordan and Scottie Pippen* (7–10). 1998, Millbrook LB $23.90 (0-7613-0420-7). A look at the life stories of these two NBA stars with emphasis on their personal and professional development and their dedication to basketball and team spirit. (Rev: HBG 3/99; SLJ 1/99; VOYA 4/99) [920]

6642 Halberstam, David. *The Teammates* (8–12). 2003, Hyperion $22.95 (1-401-30057-X). The story of the lives and friendships of four Boston Red Sox players: Ted Williams, Dominic DiMaggio, Johnny Pesky, and Bobby Doerr. [920]

6643 Hasday, Judy L. *Extraordinary Women Athletes* (6–12). Illus. Series: Extraordinary People. 2000, Children's LB $37.00 (0-516-27039-7); paper $16.95 (0-516-21608-2). A collective biography of 45 women who have gained recognition in a wide variety of sports. (Rev: BL 10/1/00; VOYA 2/01) [920]

6644 Hurley, Bob, and Phil Pepe. *Divided Loyalties: The Diary of a Basketball Father* (9–12). 1993, Zebra $19.95 (0-8217-4391-0). Bob Hurley's diary is the basis of this look at his work as basketball coach at an inner-city Catholic school and as father to two basketball stars. (Rev: BL 12/1/93) [920]

6645 Kaufman, Alan S., and James C. Kaufman. *The Worst Baseball Pitchers of All Time: Bad Luck, Bad Arms, Bad Teams, and Just Plain Bad* (9–12). 1993, McFarland paper $23.95 (0-89950-824-3). Honors pitchers since 1876 who "made a habit of losing." Includes statistics, anecdotes, and player profiles. (Rev: BL 4/1/93; VOYA 8/93) [920]

6646 Mattern, Joanne. *Basketball Greats* (6–10). Series: History Makers. 2003, Gale LB $27.45 (1-59018-228-6). Some of the basketball heroes featured in this collection are Wilt Chamberlain, Kareem Abdul-Jabbar, Magic Johnson, John Stockton, and Michael Jordan. (Rev: BL 6/1–15/03) [920]

6647 Pare, Michael A. *Sports Stars: Series 2* (6–10). 1996, Gale LB $158.40 (0-7876-0867-X). This second installment in the series is in two volumes and contains biographical sketches of 60 leading professional and amateur figures from many different sports. (Rev: BL 9/1/97; BR 1–2/97; SLJ 2/97) [920]

6648 Pare, Michael A. *Sports Stars: Series 3* (6–10). 1997, Gale LB $55.00 (0-7876-1749-0). Like the others in this series, this volume introduces biographical material on athletes from a variety of sports. (Rev: BL 9/1/97; SLJ 2/98) [920]

6649 Pare, Michael A. *Sports Stars: Series 4* (6–10). 1998, Visible Ink LB $55.00 (0-7876-2784-4). Thirty minibiographies introduce some of today's important athletes, including Mark McGwire, Marion Jones, Dominik Hasek, and Martina Hingis. (Rev: BL 9/15/98; VOYA 2/99) [920]

6650 Patrick, Dan. *Outtakes* (9–12). Illus. 2000, Hyperion paper $12.95 (0-7868-8539-4). A collection of 25 interviews with such sports greats as Mike Piazza, Charles Barkley, Mark McGwire, Dennis Rodman, and Wayne Gretzky. (Rev: BL 5/1/00) [920]

6651 Porter, David L., ed. *African-American Sports Greats: A Biographical Dictionary* (8–12). 1995, Greenwood $67.95 (0-313-28987-5). This reference book contains realistic, readable profiles of all the African American sports greats, both well known and less familiar, with information about their lives, who influenced them, and the challenges they faced on the road to success. (Rev: BR 9–10/96; VOYA 4/96) [920]

6652 Schulman, Arlene. *The Prizefighters: An Intimate Look at Champions and Contenders* (9–12). 1994, Lyons Pr. $27.95 (1-55821-309-0). Interviews with various figures in the world of boxing, including cornermen, trainers, and fighters, with photographs. (Rev: BL 10/1/94) [920]

6653 Sullivan, George. *Quarterbacks! 18 of Football's Greatest* (5–10). 1998, Simon & Schuster $18.00 (0-689-81334-1). In two- to four-page entries, the author profiles 18 quarterbacks (including Brett Favre, Troy Aikman, Sammy Baugh, and Sid Luckman), explains why he chose them, and highlights their contributions to the game. (Rev: HBG 3/99; SLJ 9/98) [920]

6654 Teitelbaum, Michael. *Grand Slam Stars: Martina Hingis and Venus Williams* (6–10). 1998, HarperCollins paper $4.50 (0-06-107100-5). An easy read that contains biographies of two teen sensations in the tennis world, Martina Hingis and Venus Williams. (Rev: VOYA 4/99) [920]

6655 Uschan, Michael V. *Male Olympic Champions* (6–12). Illus. Series: History Makers. 1999, Lucent LB $18.96 (1-56006-614-8). This collective biography introduces the Olympic Games and seven champions including Jim Thorpe, Jesse Owens, Mark Spitz, and Jean-Claude Killy. (Rev: BL 1/1–15/00; HBG 9/00; SLJ 5/00) [921]

Automobile Racing

EARNHARDT, DALE

6656 Montville, Leigh. *At the Altar of Speed: The Fast Life and Tragic Death of Dale Earnhardt* (9–12). Illus. 2001, Doubleday $24.95 (0-385-50363-6). This biography of NASCAR driver Dale Earnhardt, who was killed in a race in 2001, explores his vast appeal to racing fans. (Rev: BL 9/1/01; SLJ 6/01) [921]

STEWART, TONY

6657 Stewart, Tony, and Bones Bourcier. *True Speed: My Racing Life* (9–12). Illus. 2002, Harper-Entertainment $24.95 (0-06-018817-0). Stewart tells the story of his long ascent to the top ranks of NASCAR racing, interweaving comments from family, friends, and the media and many black-and-white photographs. (Rev: BL 4/15/02) [796.72]

Baseball

AARON, HANK

6658 Rennert, Richard. *Henry Aaron* (7–10). Series: Black Americans of Achievement. 1993, Chelsea LB $19.95 (0-7910-1859-8). The story of the African American baseball great who broke Babe Ruth's batting record in 1974. (Rev: BL 5/1/93) [921]

6659 Stanton, Tom. *Hank Aaron and the Home Run That Changed America* (9–12). Illus. 2004, Morrow $23.95 (0-06-057976-5). Combining baseball and black history, this is the story of Hank Aaron's career in baseball from the death of Jackie Robinson to his 715th home run. (Rev: BL 4/1/04) [921]

6660 Tolan, Sandy. *Me and Hank: A Boy and His Hero, Twenty-five Years Later* (9–12). 2000, Free Pr. $24.00 (0-684-97130-0); paper $14.00 (0-684-87131-9). This is a biography of baseball legend Hank Aaron by a man who grew up admiring him. [921]

ALOMAR, ROBERTO

6661 Macht, Norman L. *Roberto Alomar* (6–10). Series: Latinos in Baseball. 1999, Mitchell Lane LB $18.95 (1-883845-84-X). Using extensive interviews with Alomar, his family, friends, and colleagues, this profile of the famous Puerto Rican baseball player shows his strong self-discipline, work ethic, and close family ties. (Rev: BL 4/15/99; HBG 10/99; SLJ 5/99) [921]

ALOU, MOISES

6662 Muskat, Carrie. *Moises Alou* (6–10). Illus. Series: Latinos in Baseball. 1999, Mitchell Lane LB $18.95 (1-883845-86-6). This is the story of the baseball giant who came from a sports-minded family, and who faced a number of personal tragedies on his way to the top. (Rev: BL 4/15/99; HBG 9/99) [921]

BERRA, YOGI

6663 Berra, Yogi, and Tom Horton. *Yogi: It Ain't Over . . .* (9–12). Illus. 1990, HarperCollins paper $5.99 (0-06-100012-4). A somewhat confusing memoir by this baseball great, plus tributes from his friends. (Rev: BL 4/15/89) [921]

DIMAGGIO, JOE

6664 Cramer, Richard Ben. *Joe DiMaggio: The Hero's Life* (10–12). 2000, Simon & Schuster $28.00 (0-684-85391-4); paper $16.00 (0-684-86547-5). For mature readers, this biography of baseball great Joe DiMaggio includes both his virtues and his faults. (Rev: BL 11/15/00) [92i]

6665 Johnson, Dick, and Glenn Stout. *DiMaggio: An Illustrated Life* (10–12). 1995, Walker $39.95 (0-8027-1311-4). Written before his death, this is a stirring biography of a baseball giant, with material on his life off the field and his impact on the game. (Rev: SLJ 6/96) [921]

DOBY, LARRY

6666 Moore, Joseph Thomas. *Pride Against Prejudice: The Biography of Larry Doby* (9–12). 1988, Greenwood $55.00 (0-313-25995-X). The story of the first black player in the American League following Jackie Robinson's debut in the National League. (Rev: BL 3/15/88) [921]

GEHRIG, LOU

6667 Robinson, Ray. *Iron Horse: Lou Gehrig in His Time* (9–12). Illus. 1990, Norton $22.50 (0-393-02857-7). A stirring life story of the quiet, dignified baseball great who inspired millions with his courage. (Rev: BL 7/90; SLJ 1/91) [921]

GIBSON, JOSH

6668 Holway, John B. *Josh Gibson* (7–10). Series: Black Americans of Achievement. 1995, Chelsea LB $19.95 (0-7910-1872-5). The inspiring story of this African American baseball hero. (Rev: BL 8/95) [921]

HERNANDEZ, ORLANDO "EL DUQUE"

6669 Fainaru, Steve, and Ray Sanchez. *The Duke of Havana: Baseball, Cuba, and the Search for the American Dream* (9–12). Illus. 2001, Villard $24.00 (0-375-50345-5). This is a biography of Orlando "El Duque" Hernandez, looking at his life in Cuba and his spectacular career in American baseball. (Rev: BL 3/1/01) [921]

KOUFAX, SANDY

6670 Gruver, Edward. *Koufax* (9–12). Illus. 2000, Taylor $24.95 (0-87833-157-3). An enlightening biography of Sandy Koufax, a humble, gracious baseball pitcher who became a Hall of Famer. (Rev: BL 5/15/00) [921]

LEACH, TERRY

6671 Leach, Terry, and Tom Clark. *Things Happen for a Reason: The True Story of an Itinerant Life in Baseball* (9–12). Illus. 2000, Frog $14.95 (1-58394-050-2). The ups and downs of life in the minor and major leagues are revealed through the experiences of Terry Leach, a pitcher who never became a star. (Rev: BL 5/15/00) [921]

MCGWIRE, MARK

6672 Hall, Jonathan. *Mark McGwire: A Biography* (6–10). 1998, Archway paper $4.99 (0-671-03273-9). Covers the batter's childhood, his progress through minor leagues, early major league experiences, and the sensational 1998 season. (Rev: VOYA 4/99) [921]

MANTLE, MICKEY

6673 Berger, Phil. *Mickey Mantle* (10–12). Series: Biography. 1998, Park Lane $20.00 (0-517-20099-6). This comprehensive profile traces Mantle's rise to stardom and his struggle with alcoholism. [921]

6674 Falkner, David. *The Last Hero: The Life of Mickey Mantle* (9–12). 1996, Simon & Schuster $24.00 (0-684-81424-2). Focuses on Mantle's influence as a ballplayer and as a person. (Rev: BL 12/15/95) [921]

MARTINEZ, PEDRO

6675 Gallagher, Jim. *Pedro Martinez* (6–10). Series: Latinos in Baseball. 1999, Mitchell Lane LB $18.95 (1-883845-85-8). The life history and career highlights of Pedro Martinez, one of the many Hispanic Americans to become baseball stars. (Rev: BL 4/15/99; HBG 9/99) [921]

MATHEWS, EDDIE

6676 Mathews, Eddie, and Bob Buege. *Eddie Mathews and the National Pastime* (9–12). 1994, Douglas American Sports $22.95 (1-882134-41-9). Hall of Famer Mathews chronicles his life and baseball career, including anecdotes about Hank Aaron and Bob Uecker. (Rev: BL 9/15/94) [921]

MATHEWSON, CHRISTY

6677 Robinson, Ray. *Matty: American Hero: The Life and Career of Christy Mathewson* (9–12).

1994, Oxford paper $12.95 (0-19-509263-5). Tracks the pitching feats of the New York Giants' pitching hero of 1900–1916. (Rev: BL 7/93) [921]

MATSUI, HIDEKI

6678 Beach, Jerry. *Godzilla Takes the Bronx: The Inside Story of Hideki Matsui* (8–12). 2004, Taylor $24.95 (1-58979-113-4). A biography of the Japanese baseball player who recently joined the Yankees. (Rev: BL 3/15/04) [921]

MORRIS, JIM

6679 Morris, Jim, and Joel Engel. *The Oldest Rookie: Big-League Dreams from a Small-Town Guy* (9–12). 2001, Little, Brown $22.95 (0-316-59156-4). The amazing story of the ups and downs of Jim Morris, a boy in love with baseball, and how he finally made it to the majors. (Rev: BL 4/1/01*) [921]

MUSIAL, STAN

6680 Lansche, Jerry. *Stan the Man Musial: Born to Be a Ballplayer* (9–12). 1994, Taylor $19.95 (0-87833-846-2). A biography that sticks to baseball and avoids the fluffy, swell-guy approach. (Rev: BL 5/15/94) [921]

PAIGE, SATCHEL

6681 Shirley, David. *Satchel Paige* (7–10). Series: Black Americans of Achievement. 1993, Chelsea LB $19.95 (0-7910-1880-6). The story of the baseball Hall of Famer who was the first African American to pitch in the American League. (Rev: BL 5/1/93) [921]

ROBINSON, JACKIE

6682 Robinson, Jackie, and Alfred A. Duckett. *I Never Had It Made: An Autobiography* (8–12). 1995, Ecco paper $14.00 (0-88001-544-6). An autobiography of the baseball great with material on breaking the color barrier in baseball and on his activities after retirement. [921]

6683 Scott, Richard. *Jackie Robinson* (5–10). Illus. 1987, Chelsea LB $21.95 (1-55546-609-5). A well-researched biography giving good material on Robinson's life outside baseball. (Rev: BL 9/1/87; SLJ 9/87) [921]

6684 Weidhorn, Manfred. *Jackie Robinson* (6–12). 1993, Atheneum LB $15.95 (0-689-31644-5). This biography of the African American legend who integrated baseball in 1947 focuses on the personal qualities of the boy, the man, and the athlete. (Rev: BL 3/15/94; SLJ 2/94; VOYA 4/94) [921]

RUTH, BABE

6685 Creamer, Robert W. *Babe: The Legend Comes to Life* (9–12). 1974, Simon & Schuster paper $14.00 (0-671-76070-X). A biography of Babe Ruth that covers both his professional baseball career and his private life. [921]

6686 Gilbert, Brother. *Young Babe Ruth: His Early Life and Baseball Career, from the Memoirs of a Xaverian Brother* (9–12). Illus. 1999, McFarland paper $24.95 (0-7864-0652-6). A former teacher of the boy who grew up to be Babe Ruth recounts memories of the baseball star's formative years. (Rev: BL 4/1/00) [921]

SOSA, SAMMY

6687 Gutman, Bill. *Sammy Sosa: A Biography* (6–10). 1998, Archway paper $4.99 (0-671-03274-7). The life story of this sensational slugger, in both English and Spanish, with about half the book devoted to the exciting 1998 season. (Rev: VOYA 4/99) [921]

6688 Muskat, Carrie. *Sammy Sosa* (6–10). Illus. Series: Latinos in Baseball. 1999, Mitchell Lane LB $18.95 (1-883845-92-0). This account of Sosa's life tells of his beginning as a poor shoeshine boy in the Dominican Republic and his rise in baseball to his record-setting home run at age 29. (Rev: BL 4/15/99; HBG 10/99; SLJ 5/99) [921]

WELLS, DAVID

6689 Wells, David, and Chris Kreski. *Perfect I'm Not! Boomer on Beer, Brawls, Backaches and Baseball* (10–12). Illus. 2003, Morrow $25.95 (0-06-050824-8). Teens will enjoy pitcher David Wells's candid — and controversial — autobiography that touches, among other things, on the widespread use of painkillers and stimulants by major league players. (Rev: BL 4/1/03) [921]

WILLIAMS, TED

6690 Linn, Ed. *Hitter: The Life and Turmoil of Ted Williams* (9–12). 1993, Harcourt $23.95 (0-15-193100-3). Examines the baseball career of the legendary Boston Red Sox slugger, considered by many to be the greatest of all time. (Rev: BL 4/15/93) [921]

Basketball

ABDUL-JABBAR, KAREEM

6691 Abdul-Jabbar, Kareem. *A Season on the Reservation: My Sojourn with the White Mountain Apaches* (10–12). 2000, Morrow $24.00 (0-688-

17077-3). This adult memoir by the famous basketball player tells of his experiences as an assistant coach of a basketball team on the Whiteriver Reservation in Arizona and of his encounters with Native American culture. (Rev: BL 1/1–15/00; SLJ 12/00) [921]

6692 Abdul-Jabbar, Kareem, and Mignon McCarthy. *Kareem* (9–12). Illus. 1990, Random $18.95 (0-394-55927-4). A memoir of the great basketball player in the form of a diary of his last playing year. This forms a complementary volume to the player's earlier autobiography, *Giant Steps* (1985). (Rev: BL 2/1/90; SLJ 8/90) [921]

BOGUES, TYRONE "MUGGSY"

6693 Bogues, Tyrone "Muggsy," and David Levine. *In the Land of the Giants* (9–12). 1994, Little, Brown $19.95 (0-316-10173-7). The autobiography of the Charlotte Hornets' "Muggsy" Bogues, the shortest basketball player in the NBA, tells of his poverty-stricken youth and convict father. (Rev: 11/1/94; SLJ 5/95) [921]

BROWN, DALE

6694 Brown, Dale, and Don Yaeger. *Tiger in a Lion's Den: Adventures in LSU Basketball* (9–12). 1994, Hyperion $22.95 (0-7868-6044-8). Autobiography of the controversial Louisiana coach Brown, who once coached Shaquille O'Neal. (Rev: BL 10/15/94) [921]

COOPER, CYNTHIA

6695 Cooper, Cynthia. *She Got Game: A Personal Odyssey* (9–12). 1999, Warner paper $6.99 (0-446-60839-4). This is an autobiography of the woman who became Most Valuable Player twice in the Women's National Basketball Association. [921]

HILL, GRANT

6696 Gutman, Bill. *Grant Hill: A Biography* (6–10). 1997, Archway paper $3.99 (0-671-88738-6). Covers the life and career of the Detroit Pistons basketball star who is outstanding not only as an athlete but also as a modest, well-liked man. (Rev: VOYA 8/97) [921]

HOLDSCLAW, CHAMIQUE

6697 Holdsclaw, Chamique, and Jennifer Frey. *Chamique Holdsclaw: My Story* (6–12). Illus. 2001, Simon & Schuster paper $4.99 (0-689-83592-2). Holdsclaw tells readers how her athletic ability at first hindered but later helped her, and attributes much of her success to the grandmother who raised her. (Rev: BL 9/1/01) [796.323]

JOHNSON, MAGIC

6698 Dolan, Sean. *Magic Johnson* (7–10). 1993, Chelsea LB $21.95 (0-7910-1975-6). The story to 1992 of the Los Angeles Lakers star and his battle after testing HIV-positive. (Rev: BL 9/15/93) [921]

JORDAN, MICHAEL

6699 Dolan, Sean. *Michael Jordan* (7–10). Series: Black Americans of Achievement. 1993, Chelsea paper $9.95 (0-7910-2151-3). The life of this basketball legend to 1992 and how his determination and family support helped him rise to the top. (Rev: BL 3/1/94; VOYA 6/94) [921]

6700 Lovitt, Chip. *Michael Jordan* (6–10). 1998, Scholastic paper $4.50 (0-590-59644-6). This quick read, an update of the 1993 edition, traces Jordan's remarkable career from a young age to the end of the Chicago Bulls' 1998 season. (Rev: VOYA 4/99) [921]

6701 Williams, Pat, and Michael Weinreb. *How to Be Like Mike: Life Lessons About Basketball's Best* (10–12). 2001, Health Communications paper $10.95 (1-55874-955-1). Interviews with more than 1,400 people bring to life basketball great Michael Jordan, who has become a role model for many. (Rev: BL 9/1/01; SLJ 1/02) [921]

KNIGHT, BOBBY

6702 Knight, Bob, and Bob Hammel. *Knight: My Story* (9–12). Illus. 2002, St. Martin's $24.95 (0-312-28257-5). The undisputed "bad boy" among college basketball coaches, Bobby Knight reveals himself as a man of many parts, not all of them violent, in this absorbing autobiography. (Rev: BL 1/1–15/02) [796.323]

LEBRON, JAMES

6703 Morgan, David Lee. *LeBron James* (7–12). Illus. 2003, Gray & Co. paper $14.95 (1-886228-74-4). The biography of the African American basketball superstar who came from a culture of poverty and drugs to reach the peak of the sports world. (Rev: BL 2/15/04; SLJ 6/04) [921]

NUNEZ, TOMMY

6704 Marvis, Barbara. *Tommy Nunez, NBA Referee: Taking My Best Shot* (6–10). Illus. 1996, Mitchell Lane paper $12.95 (1-883845-28-9). The story of the youngster who grew up in the poverty of Phoenix's barrio to become the first Mexican American referee in the NBA. (Rev: BL 5/15/96; SLJ 3/96; VOYA 6/96) [921]

O'NEAL, SHAQUILLE

6705 O'Neal, Shaquille. *Shaq Talks Back* (9–12). Illus. 2001, St. Martin's $23.95 (0-312-27845-4). An autobiography by the great NBA player and star of the Los Angeles Lakers. (Rev: BL 3/15/01) [921]

Boxing

ALI, MUHAMMAD

6706 Hauser, Thomas. *Muhammad Ali: His Life and Times* (9–12). 1992, Simon & Schuster paper $16.00 (0-671-77971-0). This biography traces Ali's contributions to boxing and to the betterment of his people through 1990. (Rev: BL 5/15/91) [921]

6707 Myers, Walter Dean. *The Greatest: Muhammad Ali* (6–10). Illus. 2001, Scholastic paper $16.95 (0-590-54342-3). This engaging biography explores Ali's life from childhood, his careers as boxer and political activist, and his impact on generations of African Americans. (Rev: BL 1/1–15/01; HB 1–2/01; HBG 10/01; SLJ 1/01; VOYA 2/01) [921]

6708 Random House, eds. *Muhammad Ali* (6–10). 1997, Random $20.00 (0-517-20080-5). Using plenty of sidebars, quotations from his poetry, and photographs, this excellent biography, based on A&E cable TV's *Biography* show, traces the boxer's life from his days as a scrawny kid named Cassius Clay, Jr. to his becoming "the greatest," ending with the 1996 lighting of the Olympic torch in Atlanta. (Rev: VOYA 8/98) [921]

6709 Remnick, David. *King of the World: Muhammad Ali and the Rise of an American Hero* (10–12). Illus. 1998, Random $25.00 (0-375-50065-0). This balanced portrait of the heavyweight boxing champion captures his transformation from Cassius Clay to a worldwide sports hero and potent political symbol of the turbulent late 1960s. (Rev: BL 9/15/98*) [921]

6710 Rummel, Jack. *Muhammad Ali* (6–10). Illus. 1988, Chelsea LB $21.95 (1-55546-569-2). A biography that emphasizes the boxer's professional career rather than his personal life. (Rev: BL 6/15/88) [921]

6711 Tessitore, John. *Muhammad Ali: The World's Champion* (7–12). Series: Impact Biographies. 1998, Watts LB $20.00 (0-531-11437-6). Crowned heavyweight champion of the world three times, Muhammad Ali also stands out as a courageous humanitarian, a champion of peace and civil rights, and a role model for all. (Rev: BL 11/15/98; HBG 3/99; SLJ 12/98) [921]

CARTER, RUBIN "HURRICANE"

6712 Hirsch, James S. *Hurricane: The Miraculous Journey of Rubin Carter* (10–12). 2000, Houghton $25.00 (0-395-97985-4); paper $14.00 (0-618-08728-1). The story of the African American boxing champion and of his ordeal and fight for justice after being wrongly convicted of murdering three people. (Rev: BL 12/1/99) [921]

HAWKINS, DWIGHT

6713 Hawkins, Dwight, and Morrie Greenberg. *Survival in the Square* (7–10). Illus. 1989, Brooke-Richards paper $5.95 (0-9622652-0-9). The story of an African American who overcame a physical handicap and became a boxing champion. (Rev: BL 11/15/89; VOYA 12/89) [921]

Football

PICCOLO, BRIAN

6714 Morris, Jeannie. *Brian Piccolo: A Short Season*. Special 25th anniversary ed (10–12). 1995, Bonus paper $12.95 (1-56625-024-2). The biography of Brian Piccolo, a running back for the Chicago Bears, who died of cancer at 28. [921]

PRIETO, JORGE

6715 Prieto, Jorge. *The Quarterback Who Almost Wasn't* (7–10). 1994, Arte Publico paper $9.95 (1-55885-109-7). The autobiography of a Mexican physician who struggled with poverty, racism, and political exile before he received a scholarship to play football at Notre Dame. (Rev: BL 8/94) [921]

WILLIAMS, AENEAS

6716 Williams, Aeneas. *It Takes Respect* (9–12). 1998, Multnomah paper $11.99 (1-57673-453-6). This autobiography of the top defensive player of the Phoenix Cardinals tells of his professional career and devotion to Christ and his teachings. (Rev: VOYA 4/99) [921]

Gymnastics

MILLER, SHANNON

6717 Miller, Claudia. *Shannon Miller: My Child, My Hero* (9–12). 1999, Oklahoma Univ. Pr. $19.95 (0-8061-3110-1). Told by her mother, this is the story of Shannon Miller, who overcame enormous odds, including painful injuries, to become a world champion gymnast and gold medal winner. (Rev: VOYA 10/99) [921]

Ice Skating and Hockey

HALL, GLENN

6718 Adrahtas, Tom. *Glenn Hall: The Man They Call Mr. Goalie* (10–12). Illus. 2003, Moyer Bell paper $16.95 (0-9709170-1-5). Glenn Hall, one of the most successful goalies in National Hockey League history and master of the "butterfly" style of goal tending, is candidly profiled in this absorbing biography. (Rev: BL 4/1/03) [921]

KWAN, MICHELLE

6719 Epstein, Edward Z. *Born to Skate* (6–12). 1997, Ballantine paper $5.99 (0-345-42136-1). Describes the career of figure skater Michelle Kwan from her first steps on ice at age 5 to her world championship in 1996 and disappointments in 1997. (This book was written before her 1998 Olympic triumphs.) (Rev: VOYA 4/98) [921]

LEMIEUX, MARIO

6720 O'Shei, Tim. *Mario Lemieux* (8–12). Series: Overcoming Adversity. 2002, Chelsea LB $21.95 (0-7910-6305-4). This biography of the renowned hockey legend tells how he made an amazing comeback from Hodgkin's Disease. (Rev: BL 4/15/02; HBG 10/02) [921]

OHNO, APOLO ANTON

6721 Ohno, Apolo Anton, and Nancy Ann Richardson. *A Journey: The Autobiography of Apolo Anton Ohno* (7–12). Illus. 2002, Simon & Schuster $16.95 (0-689-85608-3). The story of the difficult childhood and rigorous preparation endured by Ohno, the winner of two medals for ice skating in the 2002 Olympics. (Rev: BL 12/1/02; HBG 3/03; SLJ 2/03; VOYA 2/03) [796.91]

Tennis

ASHE, ARTHUR

6722 Martin, Marvin. *Arthur Ashe: Of Tennis and the Human Spirit* (6–12). 1999, Watts LB $18.95 (0-531-11432-5). In spite of incredible obstacles, Arthur Ashe achieved great heights in the tennis world, including becoming the first African American world champion, and was admired as much for his humanitarian efforts and his dignified struggle

against racism as for his tennis achievements. (Rev: BL 7/99; SLJ 6/99) [921]

6723 Wright, David K. *Arthur Ashe: Breaking the Color Barrier in Tennis* (7–12). Illus. Series: African-American Biographies. 1996, Enslow LB $20.95 (0-89490-689-5). A look at the life of this revered tennis star, his professional career, and his valiant struggle against AIDS. (Rev: BL 12/15/96; SLJ 10/96) [921]

GIBSON, ALTHEA

6724 Biracree, Tom. *Althea Gibson* (7–12). Illus. 1989, Chelsea LB $19.95 (1-55546-654-0). The rags-to-riches story of the African American athlete who was once the best woman tennis player in the world. (Rev: BL 2/15/90; BR 3–4/90; SLJ 2/90; VOYA 2/90) [921]

NAVRATILOVA, MARTINA

6725 Blue, Adrianne. *Martina: The Lives and Times of Martina Navratilova* (9–12). 1995, Birch Lane $19.95 (1-55972-300-9). This volume focuses on her career and touches on aspects of her personal life. (Rev: BL 9/15/95) [921]

SAMPRAS, PETE

6726 Miller, Calvin C. *Pete Sampras* (6–10). Illus. 1998, Morgan Reynolds LB $18.95 (1-883846-26-9). A candid biography of this usually quiet and staid tennis professional, with details on his phenomenal career. (Rev: BL 4/1/98; BR 1–2/99; HBG 9/98) [921]

SELES, MONICA

6727 Blue, Rose, and Corinne J. Naden. *Monica Seles* (8–12). Series: Overcoming Adversity. 2002, Chelsea LB $21.95 (0-7910-5899-9). The biography of the courageous tennis star who returned to competition after being stabbed during a match. (Rev: BL 4/15/02; HBG 10/02) [921]

Track and Field

DEVERS, GAIL

6728 Worth, Richard. *Gail Devers* (8–12). Series: Overcoming Adversity. 2002, Chelsea LB $21.95 (0-7910-6307-0). While battling Bright's Disease, a serious thyroid disorder, Gail Devers won a gold medal in the 100-meter sprint at the 1992 Olympics. (Rev: BL 4/15/02; HBG 10/02) [921]

JOYNER-KERSEE, JACKIE

6729 Harrington, Geri. *Jackie Joyner-Kersee: Champion Athlete* (6–10). 1995, Chelsea LB $21.95 (0-7910-2085-1). Describes Joyner-Kersee's four Olympic championships, despite asthma attacks. (Rev: BL 10/1/95) [921]

LEWIS, CARL

6730 Klots, Steve. *Carl Lewis* (7–10). Series: Black Americans of Achievement. 1994, Chelsea LB $21.75 (0-7910-2164-5). Describes the childhood, college career, and Olympic performances of this athlete, including his attempts at the long-jump record. (Rev: BL 3/15/95) [921]

LONGBOAT, TOM

6731 Batten, Jack. *The Man Who Ran Faster Than Everyone: The Story of Tom Longboat* (7–12). Illus. 2002, Tundra paper $12.95 (0-88776-507-6). A straightforward biography of the Onondaga Indian distance runner who won fame in the early 20th century. (Rev: BL 4/1/02; SLJ 6/02) [796.42]

OWENS, JESSE

6732 Baker, William J. *Jesse Owens: An American Life* (10–12). Illus. 1986, Free Pr. paper $18.95 (0-02-901760-2). The story of the black track star whose career involved triumph at Hitler's Olympics. [921]

6733 Josephson, Judith P. *Jesse Owens: Track and Field Legend* (6–10). Series: African-American Biographies. 1997, Enslow LB $20.95 (0-89490-812-X). The life of this track star is retold with details about the prejudice he faced throughout his personal and professional life and his performance at the 1936 Berlin Olympics, where he won four gold medals, defying Adolf Hitler's view of Aryans as the "Master Race." (Rev: SLJ 1/98) [921]

6734 Nuwer, Hank. *The Legend of Jesse Owens* (7–12). Series: Impact Biographies. 1998, Watts LB $20.00 (0-531-11356-6). The inspiring life of the track-and-field star who won a gold medal in the 1936 Olympics despite pervasive racism and a frail constitution. (Rev: BL 1/1–15/99; HBG 3/99; SLJ 1/99) [921]

RUDOLPH, WILMA

6735 Biracree, Tom. *Wilma Rudolph* (7–12). Illus. 1987, Chelsea LB $19.95 (1-55546-675-3). The inspiring story of the African American athlete who conquered polio and won three Olympic gold medals in track in a single year. (Rev: BL 8/88) [921]

THORPE, JIM

6736 Bernotas, Bob. *Jim Thorpe: Sac and Fox Athlete* (9–12). Series: North American Indians of Achievement. 1992, Chelsea LB $19.95 (0-7910-1722-2). The story of this great all-around athlete who was stripped of his Olympic medals. (Rev: BL 11/1/92) [921]

6737 Wheeler, Robert W. *Jim Thorpe: World's Greatest Athlete* (9–12). 1981, Univ. of Oklahoma Pr. paper $14.95 (0-8061-1745-1). This biography traces the amazing career of the Native American athlete who won both the decathlon and the pentathlon at the 1912 Olympics. [921]

Miscellaneous Sports

ARMSTRONG, LANCE

6738 Armstrong, Lance, and Sally Jenkins. *Every Second Counts* (10–12). 2003, Broadway $24.95 (0-385-50871-9). In this second memoir, the seemingly invincible cyclist talks about his successes since 1999 and his enjoyment of life. (Rev: BL 9/1/03; SLJ 1/04) [796.6]

6739 Armstrong, Lance, and Sally Jenkins. *It's Not About the Bike: My Journey Back to Life* (9–12). 2000, Putnam $24.95 (0-399-14611-3). The inspiring autobiography of the courageous bicycle racer who conquered cancer and came back to win the Tour de France. (Rev: BL 5/15/00; SLJ 1/01) [921]

6740 Stewart, Mark. *Sweet Victory: Lance Armstrong's Incredible Journey* (6–10). Illus. Series: Inspiring People. 2000, Millbrook LB $24.90 (0-7613-1861-5). The inspiring story of Lance Armstrong who became an American hero when he fought and won a battle with cancer and triumphed at the Tour de France in 1999. (Rev: BL 8/00; HBG 10/00; SLJ 8/00) [921]

6741 Thompson, John. *Lance Armstrong* (6–12). Series: Overcoming Adversity. 2001, Chelsea LB $21.95 (0-7910-5879-4). An inspiring account of Armstrong's triumph over multiple challenges — including testicular cancer — to climb to the top ranks of cycling. (Rev: HBG 3/02; SLJ 12/01; VOYA 4/02) [921]

EDWARDS, BRUCE

6742 Feinstein, John. *Caddy for Life: The Bruce Edwards Story* (9–12). Illus. 2004, Little, Brown $25.95 (0-316-77788-9). The story of the caddy who, from his first employment in 1973 to his death from Lou Gehrig's disease, was employed by Tom Watson, top name in golf. (Rev: BL 4/15/04) [921]

FOLEY, MICK

6743 Foley, Mick. *Foley Is Good: And the Real World Is Faker than Wrestling* (10–12). 2001, Regan $26.95 (0-06-039300-9). In this sequel to his best-selling *Have a Nice Day,* pro wrestler Mick Foley concludes the story of his active career in the World Wrestling Federation (WWF) and tells about his relationship with Vince McMahon, the brains behind the WWF; for mature teens. (Rev: VOYA 10/01)

HARGREAVES, ALISON

6744 Rose, David, and Ed Douglas. *Regions of the Heart: The Triumph and Tragedy of Alison Hargreaves* (10–12). Illus. 2000, National Geographic $25.00 (0-7922-7696-5). A moving, harrowing biography of the female mountaineer who climbed Everest but lost her life on K2. (Rev: BL 6/1–15/00*) [921]

MACDONALD, ANDY

6745 MacDonald, Andy, and Theresa Foy Digeronimo. *Dropping In with Andy Mac: The Life of a Pro Skateboarder* (6–12). Illus. 2003, Simon & Schuster paper $9.99 (0-689-85784-5). Andy Mac describes his life from early childhood, telling readers about his family, his teen years, and his love of sports. (Rev: BL 6/1–15/03; SLJ 1/04; VOYA 8/03) [921]

MCGRATH, JEREMY

6746 McGrath, Jeremy, and Chris Palmer. *Wide Open: A Life in Supercross* (10–12). Illus. 2004, HarperEntertainment $23.95 (0-06-053727-2). McGrath, the superstar of supercross — supercharged motocross racing — describes his climb to the pinnacle of his sport. (Rev: BL 12/1/03) [921]

REECE, GABRIELLE

6747 Reece, Gabrielle, and Karen Karbo. *Big Girl in the Middle* (9–12). 1997, Crown $24.00 (0-517-70835-3). In this autobiography, Reece, a professional volleyball player as well as a television personality and fashion model, discusses how her contrasting careers reflect the different aspects of her personality and outlines her personal philosophies of Christian spirituality and self-esteem as well as her work ethic as an athlete and a model. (Rev: VOYA 4/98) [921]

SCOTT, TONY

6748 Hawk, Tony, and Sean Mortimer. *Hawk: Occupation, Skateboarder* (8–12). 2000, Regan $23.00 (0-06-019860-5); paper $15.00 (0-06-095831-6). The biography of a man who, during a rebellious youth, discovered skateboarding and was determined to excel at it. [921]

STARK, PETER

6749 Stark, Peter. *Driving to Greenland* (9–12). 1994, Lyons Pr. $22.95 (1-55821-320-1). The author describes his adventures on skis, dogsled, and luge on mountains in Greenland and Iceland. (Rev: BL 9/1/94) [796.93]

VENTURA, JESSE

6750 Cohen, Daniel. *Jesse Ventura: The Body, the Mouth, the Mind* (6–10). Illus. 2001, Millbrook LB $25.90 (0-7613-1905-0). A comprehensive profile of Ventura's private life and his stints as Navy Seal, talk-show host, actor, wrestler, and politician. (Rev: BL 10/1/01; HBG 3/02; SLJ 12/01; VOYA 12/01) [977.6]

WOODS, TIGER

6751 Boyd, Aaron. *Tiger Woods* (9–12). 1997, Morgan Reynolds LB $17.95 (1-883846-19-6). This introduction to the life and golf training of this superstar contains many interesting anecdotes and includes his first Masters triumph. (Rev: BL 5/1/97; HBG 3/98; SLJ 8/97; VOYA 10/97) [921]

6752 Rosaforte, Tim. *Raising the Bar: The Championship Years of Tiger Woods* (9–12). 2001, Thomas Dunne (0-312-27212-X). A fine biography of championship golfer Tiger Woods that takes his story through early 2001. [921]

6753 Rosaforte, Tim. *Tiger Woods: The Makings of a Champion* (10–12). 1997, St. Martin's $21.95 (0-312-15672-3). This book tells of Tiger Woods's childhood and teen years and his rapid rise to the top of the golf world, ending prior to his winning the 1997 Masters tournament. (Rev: SLJ 9/97; VOYA 10/97) [921]

6754 Teague, Allison L. *Prince of the Fairway: The Tiger Woods Story* (8–12). 1997, Avisson LB $18.50 (1-888105-22-4). Written for young adults, this biography probes into Woods's childhood and the cultural values of his family as well as describing his golf training and career. (Rev: SLJ 10/97; VOYA 10/97) [921]

ZAHARIAS, BABE DIDRIKSON

6755 Cayleff, Susan E. *Babe: The Life and Legend of Babe Didrikson Zaharias* (9–12). 1996, Univ. of Illinois Pr. $14.95 (0-252-06593-X). Looks at Babe Didrikson Zaharias, pro golfer and Olympic gold medalist, examining how she lived her life, her public persona, and her lesbianism. (Rev: BL 6/1–15/95) [921]

6756 Cayleff, Susan E. *Babe Didrikson: The Greatest All-Sport Athlete of All Time* (7–12). Illus. 2000, Conari paper $8.95 (1-57324-194-6). A candid, honest look at the life of this difficult, brash, competitive golf legend. (Rev: BL 10/1/00; VOYA 8/01) [921]

6757 Freedman, Russell. *Babe Didrikson Zaharias: The Making of a Champion* (6–12). 1999, Clarion $18.00 (0-395-63367-2). Although she was known to most for her golf career, this entertaining biography points out that Babe Didrikson Zaharias was also an Olympic athlete, a track star, leader of a women's amateur basketball team, and an entrepreneur. (Rev: BCCB 10/99; BL 7/99; HB 9–10/99; HBG 3/00; SLJ 7/99; VOYA 12/00) [921]

6758 Lynn, Elizabeth A. *Babe Didrikson Zaharias* (6–10). Illus. 1988, Chelsea LB $19.95 (1-55546-684-2). The story of the all-around athlete best known for her accomplishments in golf. (Rev: BL 12/1/88; BR 5–6/89) [921]

World Figures

Collective

6759 Axelrod-Contrada, Joan. *Women Who Led Nations* (7–10). Series: Profiles. 1999, Oliver LB $18.95 (1-881508-48-X). Corazon Aquino, Benazir Bhutto, and Golda Meir are among the seven women profiled in detail in this collective biography. (Rev: HBG 4/00; SLJ 10/99) [920]

6760 Baker, Rosalie, and Charles Baker. *Ancient Egyptians: People of the Pyramids* (6–12). Illus. Series: Oxford Profiles. 2001, Oxford $40.00 (0-19-512221-6). Detailed biographies of key figures such as Nefertiti, Hatshepsut, Tutankhamen, and Ramses give plenty of background social and cultural information and are accompanied by sidebar features and black-and-white photographs. (Rev: BL 9/15/01; HBG 10/02; SLJ 11/01) [920.032]

6761 Benson, Sonia G. *Korean War: Biographies* (6–10). 2001, Gale LB $52.00 (0-7876-5692-5). A collection of 25 biographies of individuals — Koreans, Americans, and other nationalities — who participated in or affected the course of the Korean War. (Rev: BL 3/15/02; SLJ 5/02) [920]

6762 Bowers, Barbara, et al. *1,000 Years, 1,000 People: The Men and Women Who Charted the Course of History for the Last Millennium* (10–12). 1998, Kodansha $25.00 (1-56836-273-0); paper $16.00 (1-56836-253-6). A fascinating but not particularly objective master list with brief biographical data on the 1,000 men and women who have had great influence on history and culture over the past millennium. (Rev: BL 12/15/98) [920.02]

6763 Glick, Susan. *Heroes of the Holocaust* (6–10). Series: History Makers. 2003, Gale LB $27.45 (1-59018-063-1). This work contains brief biographies of such heroes as Oskar Schindler, Raul Wallenberg, Vladka Reed, Hannah Senech, and Jan Karski. (Rev: BL 6/1–15/03; SLJ 7/03) [920]

6764 James, Lesley. *Women in Government: Politicians, Lawmakers, Law Enforcers* (6–10). Illus. Series: Remarkable Women. 2000, Raintree Steck-Vaughn LB $28.54 (0-8172-5730-6). A collection of illustrated, alphabetically arranged biographies of famous queens, presidents, activists, and empresses. (Rev: BL 6/1–15/00) [920]

6765 Kjelle, Marylou Morano. *Hitler's Henchmen* (6–10). Series: History Makers. 2003, Gale LB $27.45 (1-59018-229-4). Hitler's assistants are profiled in this collective biography that includes Goebbels and Himmler. (Rev: BL 6/1–15/03; SLJ 7/03) [920]

6766 Lace, William W. *Leaders and Generals* (5–10). Series: American War. 2000, Lucent LB $27.45 (1-56006-664-4). The following World War II leaders are profiled: Erwin Rommel, Georgi Zhukov, Erich von Manstein, Yamamoto Isoroku, Douglas MacArthur, Chester Nimitz, Dwight Eisenhower, and Bernard Law Montgomery. (Rev: BL 4/15/00; HBG 10/00; SLJ 6/00) [920]

6767 Nardo, Don. *Women Leaders of Nations* (6–10). Illus. Series: History Makers. 1999, Lucent LB $17.96 (1-56006-397-1). An overview of women in government, followed by chapters on several female leaders of nations, among them Cleopatra and Margaret Thatcher, and a chapter on other women leaders, including Amazon warriors and Queen Boudicca. (Rev: BL 6/1–15/99) [920]

6768 Pasachoff, Naomi. *Links in the Chain: Shapers of the Jewish Tradition* (9–12). Series: Oxford Profiles. 1998, Oxford $56.00 (0-19-509939-7). From Maimonides to Yitzhak Rabin, this collective biography supplies material on 40 shapers of Judaism and the Jewish state of Israel. (Rev: BL 1/1–15/98; BR 5–6/98; SLJ 4/98) [920]

6769 Price-Groff, Claire. *Great Conquerors* (6–10). Series: History Makers. 2000, Lucent LB $18.96 (1-56006-612-5). This work profiles seven world conquerors, including Alexander the Great and Napoleon, each representing a different time period and a different culture. (Rev: BL 3/15/00) [920]

6770 Price-Groff, Claire. *Twentieth-Century Women Political Leaders* (7–10). Series: Global Profiles. 1998, Facts on File LB $25.00 (0-8160-3672-1). A look at 12 women political leaders in the second half of the 20th century: Golda Meir, Indira Gandhi, Eva Peron, Margaret Thatcher, Corazon Aquino, Winnie Mandela, Barbara Jordan, Violeta Chamorro, Wilma Mankiller, Gro Harlem Brundtland, Aung San Suu Kyi, and Benazir Bhutto. (Rev: BR 1–2/99; SLJ 1/99) [920]

6771 Rasmussen, R. Kent. *Modern African Political Leaders* (7–12). Illus. Series: Global Profiles. 1998, Facts on File $25.00 (0-8160-3277-7). Focuses on how personal incidents inspired the political actions of eight African leaders of the 20th century who played major roles in political changes throughout the continent, including Haile Selassie, Gamal Abdel Nasser, Kwame Nkrumah, Robert Mugabe, and Nelson Mandela. (Rev: BL 8/98; BR 11–12/98; SLJ 9/98) [920]

6772 Salsitz, Norman, and Amalie Petranker Salsitz. *Against All Odds: A Tale of Two Survivors* (9–12). 1991, Holocaust Publns. $24.95 (0-89604-148-4); paper $12.95 (0-89604-149-2). In these recollections of the Holocaust by two Polish Jews who married after the war, similar tales of Nazi brutality, false identities, close escapes, and great endurance are told. (Rev: BL 9/15/91) [920]

6773 Traub, Carol G. *Philanthropists and Their Legacies* (7–12). Illus. Series: Profiles. 1997, Oliver LB $19.95 (1-881508-42-0). Profiles — warts and all — of nine of the world's greatest benefactors, including Alfred Nobel, Andrew Carnegie, Cecil Rhodes, George Eastman, and Will Kellogg. (Rev: BL 2/15/98; BR 1–2/98; SLJ 2/98) [920]

6774 Wakin, Edward. *Contemporary Political Leaders of the Middle East* (6–12). Illus. Series: Global Profiles. 1996, Facts on File $25.00 (0-8160-3154-1). Profiles of eight Israeli and Arab leaders who have shaped events in the Middle East, including Saddam Hussein, Mubarak, Qadafi, Rabin, and Peres. (Rev: BL 4/15/96; SLJ 3/96; VOYA 4/96) [920]

Africa

ADAMSON, JOY

6775 Neimark, Anne E. *Wild Heart: The Story of Joy Adamson, Author of Born Free* (6–10). 1999, Harcourt $17.00 (0-15-201368-7). Discusses Adamson's childhood in Austria, her later work with wild animals in Kenya (including raising the lion cub Elsa), and her pioneer work in conservation. (Rev: BL 3/15/99; SLJ 6/99; VOYA 10/99) [921]

CLEOPATRA

6776 Brooks, Polly Schoyer. *Cleopatra: Goddess of Egypt, Enemy of Rome* (7–10). 1995, HarperCollins LB $16.89 (0-06-023608-6). As much an account of the Roman struggle for power as a biography of the Egyptian queen, an intelligent and capable leader. (Rev: BL 11/1/95; SLJ 12/95; VOYA 4/96) [921]

6777 *Cleopatra of Egypt: From History to Myth* (9–12). Ed. by Susan Walker and Peter Higgs. Illus. 2001, Princeton Univ. Pr. $60.00 (0-691-08835-7). A wonderfully illustrated book with essays that describe Cleopatra's family lineage, her beauty, her life, and her impact on Egypt, Rome, and history. (Rev: BL 8/01) [921]

6778 Hoobler, Dorothy, and Thomas Hoobler. *Cleopatra* (6–10). Illus. 1986, Chelsea LB $21.95 (0-87754-589-8). Through recounting the story of this amazing queen, the author tells about life in ancient Egypt. (Rev: BL 2/1/87; SLJ 2/87) [921]

6779 Nardo, Don, ed. *Cleopatra* (7–12). Series: People Who Made History. 2000, Greenhaven LB $22.96 (0-7377-0322-9); paper $14.96 (0-7377-0321-0). This collection of essays focuses on the life of Cleopatra, her contributions, and her place in history. (Rev: BL 3/1/01; SLJ 3/01) [921]

MANDELA, NELSON

6780 Gaines, Ann. *Nelson Mandela and Apartheid in World History* (10–12). Series: In World History. 2001, Enslow $20.95 (0-7660-1463-0). This biography integrates personal stories about Nelson Mandela with a history of modern South Africa and the battle against apartheid. (Rev: BL 6/1–15/01; HBG 10/01) [921]

6781 Hoobler, Dorothy, and Thomas Hoobler. *Mandela: The Man, the Struggle, the Triumph* (6–12). 1992, Watts paper $24.00 (0-531-11141-5). A review of the struggle against apartheid in South Africa from 1987 to 1992, which encompassed the repeal of the apartheid laws and the release of Nelson Mandela and other political prisoners from prison. (Rev: BL 5/15/92; SLJ 12/92) [921]

6782 Hughes, Libby. *Nelson Mandela: Voice of Freedom* (6–10). Series: People in Focus. 1992, Dillon LB $18.95 (0-87518-484-7). Integrates Mandela's political struggle against apartheid with his personal story. Extensive bibliography, photographs. (Rev: BL 12/1/92; SLJ 1/93) [921]

6783 Kramer, Ann. *Nelson Mandela* (6–10). Illus. Series: Twentieth Century History. 2003, Raintree

Steck-Vaughn LB $32.85 (0-7398-5258-2). An attractive and absorbing account of Mandela's life and efforts to bring equality to his country. (Rev: BL 6/1–15/03; SLJ 7/03) [968.06]

6784 Mandela, Nelson. *Mandela: An Illustrated Autobiography* (10–12). 1996, Little, Brown $29.95 (0-316-55038-8). In this beautifully illustrated autobiography, Nelson Mandela describes his lifelong battle against South Africa's system of racial oppression, including his 27 years as a political prisoner and his election as president in his country's first multiracial balloting. (Rev: BL 11/15/96) [921]

6785 Pogrund, Benjamin. *Nelson Mandela* (5–10). Illus. Series: World Peacemakers. 2004, Gale LB $27.44 (1-56711-978-6). As well as a fine biography of Mandela, this book gives a concise history of apartheid in South Africa. (Rev: BL 2/15/04; SLJ 5/04) [921]

TUTANKHAMEN

6786 El Mahdy, Christine. *Tutankhamen: The Life and Death of a Boy-King* (10–12). Illus. 2000, St. Martin's $24.95 (0-312-26241-8). A portrait of the ancient Egyptian ruler who died mysteriously at age 16 or 17. (Rev: BL 8/00) [921]

Asia and the Middle East

ARAFAT, YASIR

6787 Ferber, Elizabeth. *Yasir Arafat: The Battle for Peace in Palestine* (7–12). 1995, Millbrook $23.90 (1-56294-585-8). A balanced presentation of Arafat's political career. (Rev: BL 10/1/95; SLJ 12/95) [921]

6788 Rubinstein, Danny. *The Mystery of Arafat* (9–12). 1995, Steerforth $18.00 (1-883642-10-8). An Israeli journalist looks at the life of the PLO leader and considers his place in history. (Rev: BL 5/15/95) [921]

BIN LADEN, OSAMA

6789 Landau, Elaine. *Osama bin Laden: A War Against the West* (6–10). Illus. 2002, Millbrook LB $23.90 (0-7613-1709-0). Landau combines what is known of Bin Laden's youth, fundamentalist beliefs, and terrorist organization with a look at his assumed involvement in the September 11, 2001, and other attacks. (Rev: BL 1/1–15/02; HBG 10/02; SLJ 3/02) [921]

BUDDHA

6790 Armstrong, Karen. *Buddha* (10–12). 2001, Viking $19.95 (0-670-89193-2). As well as a con-

cise biography of the Buddha, this account gives material on his revelations, principles, and influence. (Rev: BL 1/1–15/01) [921]

DALAI LAMA

6791 Perez, Louis G. *The Dalai Lama* (6–12). Series: World Leaders. 1993, Rourke LB $25.27 (0-86625-480-3). Tells of the Dalai Lama's lonely childhood, nonviolent struggle for his people, years in exile, his impact and life through 1992. (Rev: BL 12/1/93) [921]

FARMAN FARMAIAN, SATTAREH

6792 Farman Farmaian, Sattareh, and Dona Munker. *Daughter of Persia: A Woman's Journey from Her Father's Harem Through the Islamic Revolution* (9–12). 1992, Crown $22.00 (0-517-58697-5). The daughter of a prominent Iranian recalls her privileged life in Tehran, her U.S. education, and her social reform work, which outraged Khomeini. (Rev: BL 1/1/92*) [921]

GANDHI, INDIRA

6793 Dommermuth-Costa, Carol. *Indira Gandhi: Daughter of India* (7–12). Series: Lerner Biographies. 2001, Lerner LB $25.26 (0-8225-4963-8). A thorough profile that places Gandhi's life in historical context and provides a good history of modern India. (Rev: HBG 3/02; SLJ 3/02) [921]

GANDHI, MAHATMA

6794 Fischer, Louis. *Gandhi* (10–12). 1982, NAL paper $5.99 (0-451-62742-3). An admiring biography of the man who led India through nonviolent revolt to freedom. [921]

6795 Furbee, Mary, and Mike Furbee. *Mohandas Gandhi* (7–12). Series: The Importance Of. 2000, Lucent LB $18.96 (1-56006-674-1). Using a number of quotations from original sources, this account traces the life, importance, and world significance of the Indian leader. (Rev: BL 8/00; HBG 3/01) [921]

6796 Gandhi, Mahatma. *All Men Are Brothers: Life and Thoughts of Mahatma Gandhi as Told in His Own Words* (10–12). 1958, Unesco paper $12.95 (0-8264-0003-5). A partial autobiography of Mahatma Gandhi, garnered from his writings and speeches. [92I]

6797 Shields, Charles J. *Mohandas K. Gandhi* (8–12). Illus. Series: Overcoming Adversity. 2001, Chelsea LB $21.95 (0-7910-6301-1). This thorough account of Gandhi's beliefs and work also discusses his influence on other leaders and opposition to his ideas. (Rev: BL 2/15/02; HBG 10/02) [921]

GENGHIS KHAN

6798 Humphrey, Judy. *Genghis Khan* (6–10). Illus. 1987, Chelsea LB $21.95 (0-87754-527-8). The story of the fierce warrior who shaped the Mongolian empire in the 12th century. (Rev: BL 11/15/87; SLJ 12/87) [921]

HERZL, THEODOR

6799 Finkelstein, Norman H. *Theodor Herzl: Architect of a Nation* (7–12). 1991, Lerner LB $30.35 (0-8225-4913-1). The story of the respected playwright/journalist who dedicated himself to helping the Jewish people obtain their own country. (Rev: BL 4/15/92; SLJ 7/92) [921]

HIROHITO (EMPEROR OF JAPAN)

6800 Hoyt, Edwin. *Hirohito: The Emperor and the Man* (9–12). 1992, Praeger $49.95 (0-275-94069-1). This biography presents the Japanese leader as a man of peace and goodwill. (Rev: BL 3/15/92) [921]

HO CHI MINH

6801 Duiker, William J. *Ho Chi Minh* (10–12). 2000, Hyperion $35.00 (0-7868-6387-0); paper $16.95 (0-7868-8701-X). A biography of the public and personal life of this Vietnamese leader. (Rev: BL 8/00) [921]

HUSSEIN, SADDAM

6802 Claypool, Jane. *Saddam Hussein* (6–12). Series: World Leaders. 1993, Rourke LB $25.27 (0-86625-477-3). Describes Hussein's violent childhood, his rise to power, his impact, and his life to 1992. (Rev: BL 12/1/93; SLJ 1/94) [921]

JIANG, JI-LI

6803 Jiang, Ji-li. *Red Scarf Girl: A Memoir of the Cultural Revolution* (6–10). 1997, HarperCollins $16.99 (0-06-027585-5). An engrossing memoir of a Chinese girl, her family, and how their lives became a nightmare during Chairman Mao's Cultural Revolution of the late 1960s. (Rev: BL 10/1/97; BR 3–4/98; SLJ 12/97; VOYA 6/98) [921]

KORDI, GOHAR

6804 Kordi, Gohar. *An Iranian Odyssey* (9–12). 1993, Serpent's Tail paper $13.95 (1-85242-213-0). A memoir of a blind Iranian-born woman, who, without financial or emotional support from her parents, graduated from Teheran University in 1970. (Rev: BL 1/15/93) [921]

MASIH, IQBAL

6805 Kuklin, Susan. *Iqbal Masih and the Crusaders Against Child Slavery* (6–12). Illus. 1998, Holt $17.95 (0-8050-5459-6). The story of the Pakistani boy who, after escaping slavery, devoted his young life to a crusade against child labor abuse until he was murdered at age 12. (Rev: BCCB 11/98; BL 11/1/98; HB 1–2/99; HBG 3/99; SLJ 11/98; VOYA 4/99) [921]

MIN, ANCHEE

6806 Min, Anchee. *Red Azalea* (9–12). 1999, Berkley paper $13.00 (0-425-16687-2). The hardships of Min's youth in Shanghai as a child of Mao's Cultural Revolution — a harsh portrait of China in the 1960s and 1970s. (Rev: BL 2/1/94) [921]

MUHAMMAD

6807 Oliver, Marilyn Tower. *Muhammad* (6–10). 2003, Gale LB $27.45 (1-59018-232-4). A thorough and balanced account of Muhammad's life and legacy as the founder of Islam. (Rev: SLJ 6/03) [921]

RABIN, YITZHAK

6808 Kort, Michael G. *Yitzhak Rabin: Israel's Soldier Statesman* (9–12). Illus. 1996, Millbrook LB $23.90 (0-7613-0100-3); paper $8.95 (0-7613-0135-6). The story of the slain Israeli leader and his struggle for peace are told against the backdrop of Middle East conflicts. (Rev: BL 1/1–15/97; BR 3–4/97; SLJ 2/97; VOYA 6/97) [956.9405]

SASAKI, SADAKO

6809 Nasu, Masamoto. *Children of the Paper Crane: The Story of Sadako Sasaki and Her Struggle with the A-Bomb Disease* (9–12). Trans. by Elizabeth W. Baldwin and others. 1991, M.E. Sharpe $50.95 (0-87332-715-2). A personal account of the legacy of the Hiroshima bombing that describes the devastating decline of one child and the effects on her family and all Japan. (Rev: BL 12/15/91) [921]

TAJ AL-SALTANA

6810 al-Saltana, Taj. *Crowning Anguish: Memoirs of a Persian Princess from the Harem to Modernity, 1884-1914* (9–12). Ed. by Abbas Amanat. Trans. by Anna Vanzan and Amin Neshati. 1993, Mage $29.95 (0-934211-35-3); paper $14.95 (0-934211-36-1). An Iranian princess's memoirs of her life in a sheik's palace. (Rev: BL 9/15/93) [921]

TAMERLANE

6811 Wepman, Dennis. *Tamerlane* (6–10). Illus. 1987, Chelsea LB $19.95 (0-87754-442-5). The story of the barbaric Mongol chieftain who lived in the 14th century and was responsible for the deaths of millions. (Rev: BL 7/87; SLJ 8/87) [921]

TERESA, MOTHER

6812 Schaefer, Linda. *Come and See: A Photojournalist's Journey into the World of Mother Teresa* (10–12). Illus. 2003, DC $29.95 (1-932021-08-6). Moving text and beautiful photographs document Schaefer's time with Mother Teresa in India. (Rev: BL 10/1/03) [921]

6813 Spink, Kathryn. *Mother Teresa: A Complete Authorized Biography* (9–12). 1997, HarperSF paper $15.95 (0-06-251553-5). This authorized biography, written by a woman who for several years worked with Mother Teresa's Missionaries of Charity, chronicles the nun's life story from her birth in the Balkans to her death in Calcutta in 1997. (Rev: BL 11/1/97) [921]

ZEDONG, MAO

6814 Hatt, Christine. *Mao Zedong* (8–11). Illus. Series: Judge for Yourself. 2003, World Almanac LB $29.26 (0-8368-5536-1). Mao's life is presented, followed by two essays that give different viewpoints of his importance and accomplishments. (Rev: BL 2/1/04; SLJ 3/04) [921]

6815 Stefoff, Rebecca. *Mao Zedong: Founder of the People's Republic of China* (7–12). Illus. 1996, Millbrook LB $22.40 (1-56294-531-9). A well-documented biography of this important Chinese politician that covers childhood influences, contributions to the development of his nation, and his lasting impact on world history. (Rev: BL 5/1/96; BR 9–10/96; SLJ 6/96) [921]

Australia and the Pacific Islands

CONWAY, JILL KER

6816 Conway, Jill Ker. *The Road from Coorain* (10–12). 1990, Vintage paper $12.00 (0-679-72436-2). The youth and adolescence in Australia of the woman who would later be the president of Smith College. (Rev: VOYA 4/90) [921]

Europe

ATATURK, KEMAL

6817 Tachau, Frank. *Kemal Ataturk* (6–10). Illus. 1987, Chelsea LB $19.95 (0-87754-507-3). A biography of the man who transformed Turkey and

brought it into the 20th century. (Rev: BL 1/1/88; SLJ 3/88) [921]

CAESAR, JULIUS

6818 Barter, James. *Julius Caesar and Ancient Rome in World History* (8–12). Illus. Series: In World History. 2001, Enslow LB $20.95 (0-7660-1461-4). A detailed look at Caesar's life and accomplishments, along with information about the empire he ruled and the political and social climate of the time; with quotations from primary sources. (Rev: BL 3/1/02; HBG 3/02; SLJ 1/02) [921]

6819 Bruns, Roger. *Julius Caesar* (6–10). Illus. 1987, Chelsea LB $21.95 (0-87754-514-6). Using many sources, the author creates an accurate picture of the rise and fall of this Roman leader. (Rev: BL 11/15/87; BR 9–10/88; SLJ 12/87; VOYA 10/88) [921]

CALVIN, JOHN

6820 Stepanek, Sally. *John Calvin* (6–10). Illus. 1986, Chelsea LB $21.95 (0-87754-515-4). A well-researched biography of the 16th-century leader of the Protestant Reformation. (Rev: BL 3/1/87; SLJ 3/87) [921]

CARY, ELIZABETH

6821 Brackett, Ginger Roberts. *Elizabeth Cary: Writer of Conscience* (7–10). Illus. 1996, Morgan Reynolds LB $21.95 (1-883846-15-3). The story of the 17th-century Englishwoman and brilliant writer who defied society by becoming a Roman Catholic in heavily Protestant England. (Rev: BL 10/1/96; SLJ 10/96; VOYA 6/97) [921]

CATHERINE THE GREAT

6822 Alexander, John T. *Catherine the Great: Life and Legend* (10–12). 1989, Oxford paper $21.50 (0-19-506162-4). In a compelling narrative, the author traces the life of this amazing Russian leader who was born an obscure German princess. [921]

6823 Hatt, Christine. *Catherine the Great* (8–11). Illus. Series: Judge for Yourself. 2003, World Almanac LB $29.26 (0-8368-5535-3). After an interesting illustrated biography of Catherine the Great, two essays present differing views on her importance. (Rev: BL 2/1/04; SLJ 4/04) [921]

CHARLEMAGNE

6824 Greenblatt, Miriam. *Charlemagne and the Early Middle Ages* (8–12). Series: Rulers and Their Times. 2002, Marshall Cavendish LB $19.95 (0-7614-1487-8). The story of the King of the Franks and the founder of the Holy Roman Empire, who ruled at the beginning of the Middle Ages. (Rev: BL 1/1–15/03; HBG 3/03; SLJ 3/03) [921]

CHURCHILL, WINSTON

6825 Rose, Norman. *Churchill: The Unruly Giant* (9–12). 1995, Free Pr. $26.00 (0-02-874009-2). Charts Churchill's career and paints an image of the ambition, determination, and pugnacity that won him both respect and resentment. (Rev: BL 7/95) [921]

CICERO

6826 Everitt, Anthony. *Cicero: The Life and Times of Rome's Greatest Politician* (10–12). Illus. 2002, Random $25.95 (0-375-50746-9). This well-researched profile of Roman orator Cicero draws heavily on letters he wrote to his close friend Atticus. (Rev: BL 5/15/02*) [921]

CLEMENCEAU, GEORGES

6827 Gottfried, Ted. *Georges Clemenceau* (6–10). Illus. 1987, Chelsea LB $21.95 (0-87754-518-9). A biography of the French political leader who served his country with distinction during World War I. (Rev: BL 11/15/87; SLJ 3/88) [921]

EICHENGREEN, LUCILLE

6828 Eichengreen, Lucille. *From Ashes to Life: My Memories of the Holocaust* (9–12). 1994, Mercury House paper $17.95 (1-56279-052-8). A young girl's harrowing experiences in the Nazi death camps end with liberation, followed by survivor guilt and search for meaning. (Rev: SLJ 10/94) [921]

ELEANOR OF AQUITAINE

6829 Weir, Alison. *Eleanor of Aquitaine: A Life* (10–12). 2000, Ballantine $28.00 (0-345-40540-4); paper $15.95 (0-345-43487-0). The biography of the 12th-century French queen who later became Queen of England and mother of Richard the Lionhearted. (Rev: BL 1/1–15/00) [921]

ELIZABETH I

6830 Price-Groff, Claire. *The Importance of Queen Elizabeth I* (7–12). Series: The Importance Of. 2000, Lucent LB $19.96 (1-56006-700-4). As well as tracing the life of this famous monarch, this account comments on her lasting importance in world history. (Rev: BL 3/1/01; SLJ 2/01) [921]

6831 Somerset, Anne. *Elizabeth I* (9–12). 1991, Knopf paper $15.95 (0-312-08183-9). A well-researched biography of the 16th-century monarch that draws heavily on primary sources. [921]

6832 Weir, Alison. *The Life of Elizabeth I* (9–12). 1998, Ballantine $27.50 (0-345-40533-1). A fully rounded portrait of the complex queen who surmounted intrigues, jealousies, plots, disease, and the betrayal of a loved one to lead her kingdom in its transformation from a debt-ridden country of little influence into a major European power. She gave her name to an age and influenced the course of British and European history for centuries. (Rev: BL 7/98; SLJ 4/99) [921]

ELIZABETH II

6833 Auerbach, Susan. *Queen Elizabeth II* (6–12). Series: World Leaders. 1993, Rourke LB $25.27 (0-86625-481-1). Queen Elizabeth's childhood during World War II, how she came to the throne, and the major events in her reign up to 1993. (Rev: BL 12/1/93) [921]

6834 Bradford, Sarah. *Elizabeth: A Biography of Britain's Queen* (10–12). 1996, Farrar $30.00 (0-374-14749-3). This well-researched biography focuses on the life and times of Elizabeth II, including coverage of tensions between her career and her family. (Rev: BL 3/1/96) [921]

6835 Lacey, Robert. *Monarch: The Life and Reign of Elizabeth II* (10–12). Illus. 2002, Free Pr. $27.50 (0-7432-3559-2). In addition to a fairly comprehensive overview of Queen Elizabeth II's private and public life, this volume provides a behind-the-scenes look at the royal family's reaction to Princess Diana's death. (Rev: BL 3/15/02) [921]

6836 Shawcross, William. *Queen and Country: The Fifty-Year Reign of Elizabeth II* (8–12). 2002, Simon & Schuster $35.00 (0-7432-2676-3). The queen's concern with the commonwealth and her relationships with consecutive British governments are among the interesting aspects of this frank and balanced biography that includes family details. (Rev: BL 3/1/02) [921]

FILIPOVIC, ZLATA

6837 Filipovic, Zlata. *Zlata's Diary* (9–12). 1995, Demco $14.30 (0-606-08416-9). The personal journal of a talented 11-year-old Sarajevan girl whose world was shattered by the chaos and terror of war. (Rev: BL 3/1/94; SLJ 7/94; VOYA 8/94) [921]

FRANCIS OF ASSISI, SAINT

6838 Martin, Valerie. *Salvation: Scenes from the Life of St. Francis* (10–12). 2001, Knopf $24.00 (0-375-40983-1). The life of St. Francis of Assisi is recreated through a series of biographical sketches, beginning with his death in 1226 and working backward. (Rev: BL 3/1/01) [921]

6839 Spoto, Donald. *Reluctant Saint: The Life of Francis of Assisi* (10–12). 2002, Viking $24.95 (0-670-03128-3). An insightful biography of the 13th-century saint. (Rev: BL 9/1/02) [921]

FRANK, ANNE

6840 Anne Frank House, comp. *Anne Frank in the World: 1929–1945* (7–12). 2001, Knopf LB $20.99 (0-375-91177-4). This photoessay, based on the Frank family's experiences, clearly shows the Nazis' impact on the lives of Jewish families and includes many photographs that will be new to readers. (Rev: BCCB 3/02; BL 9/1/01; HBG 3/02; SLJ 10/01; VOYA 12/01) [921]

6841 Frank, Anne. *The Diary of a Young Girl* (7–12). Trans. by B. M. Mooyaart. Illus. 1967, Doubleday $25.95 (0-385-04019-9). The world-famous diary the young Jewish girl kept while she was being hidden with her family from the Nazis. (Rev: BL 2/15/88) [921]

6842 Frank, Anne. *The Diary of a Young Girl: The Definitive Edition* (7–12). Trans. by Susan Massotty. 1995, Doubleday $27.50 (0-385-47378-8). This edition contains all of the writings of Anne Frank, including some short passages in the diary that had been formerly suppressed. (Rev: BL 4/15/95) [921]

6843 Frank, Anne. *The Diary of Anne Frank: The Critical Edition* (7–12). Illus. 1989, Doubleday $60.00 (0-385-24023-6). The most complete version of the diary to appear in English plus a history of the volume. (Rev: BL 5/15/89) [921]

6844 Lindwer, Willy. *The Last Seven Months of Anne Frank* (8–12). 1992, Doubleday paper $12.95 (0-385-42360-8). Moving testimony from six women interned in a concentration camp with Anne Frank tells of the tragic conclusion of the young diarist's life. (Rev: BL 3/15/91) [921]

6845 Muller, Melissa. *Anne Frank: A Biography* (9–12). Trans. by Robert Kimber. 1998, Holt $23.00 (0-8050-5996-2); paper $14.00 (0-8050-5997-0). In this supplement to Anne Frank's diary, the author includes new information about the Frank family and about possible betrayers of their hiding place, as well as insights into the character, personality, and quality of life of Anne's parents, relatives, and friends. (Rev: SLJ 4/99) [921]

6846 Wukovits, John F. *Anne Frank* (6–10). Series: The Importance Of. 1998, Lucent LB $27.45 (1-56006-353-X). This biographical account also supplies good background material on Nazism, the death camps, the writing of the diary, and the controversy surrounding it. (Rev: BL 1/1–15/99; VOYA 8/99) [921]

FRANK, OTTO

6847 Lee, Carol Ann. *The Hidden Life of Otto Frank* (10–12). Illus. 2003, Morrow $26.95 (0-06-052082-5). Lee looks at the life of Anne Frank's father and seeks to answer the question of who alerted the Nazis to the Franks' hiding place. (Rev: BL 2/15/03) [940.53]

GARIBALDI, GIUSEPPI

6848 Viola, Herman J., and Susan P. Viola. *Giuseppi Garibaldi* (6–10). Illus. 1987, Chelsea LB $21.95 (0-87754-526-X). Garibaldi was a hero, patriot, and the man who led the movement to unify his country, Italy. (Rev: BL 11/15/87; SLJ 3/88) [921]

HAMMARSKJOLD, DAG

6849 Sheldon, Richard N. *Dag Hammarskjold* (6–10). Illus. 1987, Chelsea LB $19.95 (0-87754-529-4). The life story of the Swedish man who served as the secretary general of the United Nations for eight years. (Rev: BL 9/1/87; SLJ 10/87) [921]

HENRY VIII, KING OF ENGLAND

6850 Dwyer, Frank. *Henry VIII* (7–12). Illus. 1988, Chelsea LB $21.95 (0-87754-530-8). A fact-filled biography with a great deal of English history given for background. (Rev: BL 1/15/88; SLJ 3/88) [921]

HINDENBURG, PAUL VON

6851 Berman, Russell A. *Paul von Hindenburg* (6–10). Illus. 1987, Chelsea LB $19.95 (0-87754-532-4). The story of the German military and political leader who became famous during World War I. (Rev: BL 8/87; SLJ 11/87) [921]

HITLER, ADOLF

6852 Fuchs, Thomas. *The Hitler Fact Book* (10–12). Illus. 1990, Fountain paper $14.95 (0-9623202-9-3). All sorts of trivia about the dictator and the high German officials around him. (Rev: BL 3/1/90; SLJ 6/90) [921]

6853 Harris, Nathaniel. *Hitler* (8–12). Illus. 1989, David & Charles $19.95 (0-7134-5961-1). This biography surveys the life and times of Hitler and his impact on history. (Rev: SLJ 12/89) [921]

6854 Hitler, Adolf. *Mein Kampf* (11–12). Trans. by Ralph Manheim. 1998, Houghton $35.00 (0-395-95105-4); paper $20.00 (0-395-92503-7). Hitler's blueprint for the Third Reich includes autobiographical reflections. [921]

6855 Kershaw, Ian. *Hitler, 1889–1936: Hubris* (10–12). 1999, Norton $35.00 (0-393-04671-0);

paper $21.95 (0-393-32035-9). As well as a biography, this account stresses historical issues, events, and circumstances surrounding Hitler's rise to power. (Rev: BL 1/1–15/99*) [92i]

6856 Stalcup, Brenda, ed. *Adolf Hitler* (7–12). Series: People Who Made History. 2000, Greenhaven LB $21.96 (0-7377-0223-0); paper $13.96 (0-7377-0222-2). The dictator's life is depicted through a collection of documents that give special emphasis to his role in World War II and the Holocaust and the impact on the German people. (Rev: BL 4/15/00; SLJ 11/00) [921]

6857 Toland, John. *Adolf Hitler* (10–12). 1976, Doubleday paper $23.00 (0-385-42053-6). A detailed biography of Hitler that is based on many documents and interviews with more than 250 people. [921]

JAMES I, KING OF ENGLAND

6858 Dwyer, Frank. *James I* (6–10). Illus. 1988, Chelsea LB $19.95 (1-55546-811-X). The story of the first Stuart king of both England and Scotland. (Rev: BL 6/15/88) [921]

JOAN OF ARC

6859 Gordon, Mary. *Joan of Arc* (10–12). 2000, Viking $19.95 (0-670-88537-1). For sophisticated readers, this is a concise, introspective view of this controversial figure in French history. (Rev: BL 4/15/00; SLJ 1/01) [921]

JOHN PAUL II, POPE

6860 Accattoli, Luigi, et al. *John Paul II: A Pope for the People* (9–12). Trans. by Russell Stockman. Illus. 2004, Abrams $40.00 (0-8109-4984-9). Using about 250 photographs and an accessible text, this biography of John Paul II focuses on his 25 years as pope. (Rev: BL 4/15/04) [921]

6861 Flynn, Raymond. *John Paul II: A Personal Portrait of the Pope and the Man* (10–12). 2001, St. Martin's paper $14.95 (0-312-28328-8). A profile of Pope John Paul II by a former U.S. ambassador to the Vatican. (Rev: BL 4/15/01) [921]

LENIN, VLADIMIR ILICH

6862 Haney, John. *Vladimir Ilich Lenin* (6–10). Illus. 1988, Chelsea LB $19.95 (0-87754-570-7). A biography of the man who led the Russian Revolution and established the U.S.S.R. (Rev: BL 4/1/88) [921]

6863 Rawcliffe, Michael. *Lenin* (7–10). Illus. 1989, David & Charles $19.95 (0-7134-5611-6). Besides supplying a biography of this Russian leader, this

book evaluates Lenin's significance in history. (Rev: SLJ 5/89) [921]

LLOYD GEORGE, DAVID

6864 Shearman, Deidre. *David Lloyd George* (7–12). Illus. 1987, Chelsea LB $21.95 (0-87754-581-2). The life of the Welsh statesman who was British prime minister during World War I. (Rev: BL 1/15/88) [921]

MARIE ANTOINETTE

6865 Fraser, Antonia. *Marie Antoinette: The Journey* (10–12). Illus. 2001, Doubleday $35.00 (0-385-48948-X). A vivid, well-rounded biography of the young queen of France who never actually said "Let them eat cake." (Rev: BL 8/01) [921]

6866 Lever, Evelyne. *Marie Antoinette: The Last Queen of France* (10–12). Trans. by Catherine Temerson. 2000, Farrar paper $16.95 (0-312-28333-4). Using memoirs and other primary documents, the author has written a fine biography of Marie Antoinette and an accurate picture of court life at Versailles. [921]

MARY, QUEEN OF SCOTS

6867 Random House, eds. *Mary Stuart's Scotland* (9–12). Illus. 1995, Random $18.99 (0-517-14205-8). An accurate account of this tragic queen's life with beautiful photographs of her Scottish homeland. (Rev: SLJ 4/88) [921]

6868 Stepanek, Sally. *Mary, Queen of Scots* (6–10). Illus. 1987, Chelsea LB $21.95 (0-87754-540-5). The tragic story of this ill-fated queen, in prose and many pictures. (Rev: BL 6/1/87; SLJ 12/87) [921]

MEDICI, LORENZO DE

6869 Greenblatt, Miriam. *Lorenzo de' Medici* (8–12). Series: Rulers and Their Times. 2002, Marshall Cavendish LB $19.95 (0-7614-1490-8). This towering figure of the Renaissance was known as the Magnificent because he was a great politician, patron, poet, and scholar. (Rev: BL 1/1–15/03; HBG 3/03) [921]

MUSSOLINI, BENITO

6870 Bosworth, R. J. B. *Mussolini* (10–12). 2002, Oxford $35.00 (0-340-73144-3); paper $14.95 (0-340-80988-4). A fascinating biography of the Italian dictator who used his power for selfish ends. (Rev: BL 6/1–15/02) [921]

6871 Hartenian, Larry. *Benito Mussolini* (6–10). Illus. 1988, Chelsea LB $19.95 (0-87754-572-3). A fascinating biography of the Italian Fascist leader who brought his country to defeat in World War II. (Rev: BL 6/1/88) [921]

6872 Hoyt, Edwin. *Mussolini's Empire: The Rise and Fall of the Fascist Vision* (9–12). 1994, Wiley $24.95 (0-471-59151-3). Examines the career and personal life of Mussolini and provides psychological insight into the Italian dictator's character. (Rev: BL 2/15/94) [921]

6873 Ridley, Jasper Godwin. *Mussolini* (11–12). 1998, St. Martin's $27.50 (0-312-19303-3). A comprehensive and even-handed portrait of Il Duce's socialist formation, rise to power, and 21-year fascist dictatorship. (Rev: BL 11/1/98) [921]

NAPOLEON I

6874 Johnson, Paul. *Napoleon* (10–12). Series: Penguin Lives. 2002, Viking $19.95 (0-670-03078-3). Napoleon's failings are clearly presented in this introduction to the diminutive French leader's life and career. (Rev: BL 4/1/02) [921]

6875 Obstfeld, Raymond, and Loretta Obstfeld, eds. *Napoleon Bonaparte* (7–12). Series: People Who Made History. 2001, Greenhaven LB $22.96 (0-7377-0423-3); paper $14.96 (0-7377-0422-5). After an introductory overview chapter covering Napoleon's career, there are a number of specialized essays that focus on his contributions and place in history. (Rev: BL 4/15/01) [921]

PETER THE GREAT, CZAR OF RUSSIA

6876 Massie, Robert K. *Peter the Great: His Life and World* (10–12). 1980, Knopf paper $16.00 (0-345-29806-3). A lengthy but readable biography of the great Russian czar who founded the city that for centuries was the country's capital. [921]

PUTIN, VLADIMIR

6877 Putin, Vladimir, et al. *First Person: An Astonishingly Frank Self-Portrait by Russia's President* (10–12). Trans. by Catherine A. Fitzpatrick. Illus. 2000, PublicAffairs paper $15.00 (1-58648-018-9). Although now out of date (coverage ends in early 2000), this biographical sketch assembled from a number of interviews gives valuable background information on this leader of the Russian state. (Rev: BL 5/1/00) [921]

RASPUTIN

6878 Moynahan, Brian. *Rasputin: The Saint Who Sinned* (10–12). 1997, Random (0-679-41930-6). The biography of the Russian monk who influenced the course of history because of his relations with the family of the last czar. (Rev: BL 9/15/97) [921]

ROMANOV, ANASTASIA

6879 Lovell, James Blair. *Anastasia: The Lost Princess* (9–12). 1991, Regnery $24.95 (0-89526-536-2). The story of the woman who claims to be the only surviving daughter of the last czar of Russia. (Rev: BL 8/91) [921]

SCHINDLER, OSKAR

6880 Fensch, Thomas, ed. *Oskar Schindler and His List: The Man, the Book, the Film, the Holocaust and Its Survivors* (9–12). 1995, Paul S. Eriksson $24.95 (0-8397-6472-3). Articles, essays, and interviews relating to the development of the book and the film *Schindler's List.* (Rev: BL 9/15/95) [921]

6881 Thompson, Bruce, ed. *Oskar Schindler* (7–12). Series: People Who Made History. 2002, Gale LB $31.20 (0-7377-0894-8); paper $19.95 (0-7377-0895-6). The life and times of a hero of the Jewish Holocaust are explored in a series of essays that deal with different aspects of his career and contributions. (Rev: BL 4/1/02; SLJ 7/02) [921]

SCHOLL, HANS AND SOPHIE

6882 Axelrod, Toby. *Hans and Sophie Scholl: German Resisters of the White Rose* (7–12). Series: Holocaust Biographies. 2001, Rosen LB $19.95 (0-8239-3316-4). The Scholls, brother and sister, were arrested and executed for their role in organizing the group known as the White Rose, which worked to expose the Nazis' atrocities. (Rev: SLJ 6/01) [921]

STALIN, JOSEPH

6883 Radzinsky, Edvard. *Stalin: The First In-depth Biography Based on Explosive New Documents from Russia's Secret Archives* (10–12). Trans. by H. T. Willetts. 1996, Doubleday paper $16.95 (0-385-47954-9). Radzinsky's access to previously unavailable archival information makes this a vivid portrait of the iron-fist dictator. [921]

SUGIHARA, CHIUNE

6884 Gold, Alison L. *A Special Fate: Chiune Sugihara: Hero of the Holocaust* (5–10). 2000, Scholastic paper $15.95 (0-590-39525-4). The life story of the Japanese diplomat who saved thousands of Jewish lives during the Holocaust while he was stationed in Lithuania. (Rev: BCCB 5/00; BL 4/1/00; HB 5–6/00; HBG 10/00; SLJ 5/00; VOYA 6/00) [921]

SULEIMAN THE MAGNIFICENT

6885 Greenblatt, Miriam. *Süleyman the Magnificent and the Ottoman Empire* (8–12). Series: Rulers and Their Times. 2002, Marshall Cavendish LB $19.95 (0-7614-1489-4). The story of the great sultan who ruled during the 16th century and brought the Ottoman Empire to its height of power. (Rev: BL 1/1–15/03; HBG 3/03) [921]

TITO, JOSIP BROZ

6886 Schiffman, Ruth. *Josip Broz Tito* (6–10). Illus. 1987, Chelsea LB $19.95 (0-87754-443-3). The story of this unusual Yugoslavian leader and of the unique Communist regime he founded. (Rev: BL 6/15/87; SLJ 8/87) [921]

VAN BEEK, CATO BONTJES

6887 Friedman, Ina R. *Flying Against the Wind: The Story of a Young Woman Who Defied the Nazis* (6–10). 1995, Lodgepole paper $11.95 (1-886721-00-9). The story of Cato Bontjes van Beek, who grew up in a progressive German household and was executed by the Nazis with her boyfriend for joining an underground movement. (Rev: BL 7/95; VOYA 4/96) [921]

VICTORIA, QUEEN

6888 Chiflet, Jean-Loup, and Alain Beaulet. *Victoria and Her Times* (6–10). Trans. from French by George Wen. Series: W5. 1996, Holt $19.95 (0-8050-5084-1). This oversized volume contains double-page spreads that describe various aspects of the life and times of Queen Victoria. (Rev: SLJ 3/97) [921]

6889 Erickson, Carolly. *Her Little Majesty: The Life of Queen Victoria* (10–12). 1997, Simon & Schuster $22.50 (0-684-80765-3). An entertaining biography of the stubborn, hot-tempered, but romantic queen who gave her name to an age, describing her unhappy childhood and difficult teen years, and the amazing inner resources that saw her through crisis after crisis during the major changes of the 19th century. (Rev: SLJ 8/97) [921]

6890 Hibbert, Christopher. *Queen Victoria: A Personal History* (10–12). 2000, Basic paper $21 .00 (0-306-81085-9). Using many original sources, including Victoria's letters and journals, the author has produced an intimate look at the life and reign of this long-serving British monarch. [921]

6891 Price-Groff, Claire. *Queen Victoria and Nineteenth-Century England* (8–12). Series: Rulers and Their Times. 2002, Marshall Cavendish LB $19.95 (0-7614-1488-6). The story of the great British monarch who gave her name to the age she dominated. (Rev: BL 1/1–15/03; HBG 3/03) [921]

6892 Strachey, Lytton. *Queen Victoria* (10–12). 1921, Harcourt paper $16.00 (0-15-602756-9). A matter-of-fact biography of Queen Victoria and the statesmen who surrounded her. [921]

WALLENBERG, RAOUL

6893 Smith, Danny. *Lost Hero: Raoul Wallenberg's Dramatic Quest to Save the Jews of Hungary* (9–12). 2002, Trafalgar paper $12.00 (0-00-711117-7). This readable biography details Wallenberg's efforts to help thousands of Jews escape from the Nazis; a revised and updated edition. (Rev: BL 1/1–15/02) [921]

6894 Streissguth, Thomas. *Raoul Wallenberg: Swedish Diplomat and Humanitarian* (7–12). Series: Holocaust Biographies. 2001, Rosen LB $19.95 (0-8239-3318-0). Wallenberg's efforts to save Hungarian Jews during World War II and his subsequent disappearance are described here. (Rev: SLJ 6/01) [921]

WIESENTHAL, SIMON

6895 Altman, Linda J. *Simon Wiesenthal* (7–12). Series: The Importance Of. 2000, Lucent LB $18.96 (1-56006-490-0). A frank and compelling biography of the Holocaust survivor and his efforts to bring Nazis to justice. (Rev: BL 7/00; HBG 9/00; SLJ 8/00) [921]

WOLLSTONECRAFT, MARY

6896 Miller, Calvin C. *Mary Wollstonecraft and the Rights of Women* (7–12). Illus. 1999, Morgan Reynolds LB $21.95 (1-883846-41-2). This is a biography of the passionate English fighter for women's rights who was motivated by the grinding poverty, discrimination, and lack of opportunity suffered by women in the late 18th and early 19th centuries. (Rev: BL 5/1/99; BR 9–10/99; SLJ 5/99; VOYA 12/99) [921]

South and Central America, Canada, and Mexico

BOLIVAR, SIMON

6897 Goodnough, David. *Simon Bolivar: South American Liberator* (7–12). Series: Hispanic Biographies. 1998, Enslow LB $20.95 (0-7660-1044-9). The inspiring story of the young military leader who led the fight to free several South American countries from the oppression of the Spaniards. (Rev: BL 1/1–15/99; HBG 3/99; VOYA 10/99) [921]

CARLOS THE JACKAL

6898 Follain, John. *Jackal: The Complete Story of the Legendary Terrorist, Carlos the Jackal* (11–12). Illus. 1998, Arcade $25.95 (1-55970-466-7). The life and times of Ilich Ramirez Sanchez, better known as international terrorist Carlos the Jackal, are explored in detail. (Rev: BL 11/15/98) [921]

CASTRO, FIDEL

6899 Bentley, Judith. *Fidel Castro of Cuba* (7–12). Series: In Focus Biographies. 1991, Messner LB $13.95 (0-671-70198-3); paper $7.95 (0-671-70199-1). Relates the Cuban leader's personal story to a detailed history of his country, its problems and achievements, and the changing international scene up to 1991. (Rev: BL 11/1/91) [921]

6900 Castro, Fidel. *My Early Years* (10–12). Ed. by Deborah Shnookal and Pedro Alvarez Tabio. Illus. 1998, Ocean paper $14.95 (1-876175-07-9). An appealing account of Castro's early life and decision to enter politics that draws on his writings, interviews, and speeches and shows the excitement of his achievements. (Rev: BL 12/1/98) [972.9106]

6901 Foss, Clive. *Fidel Castro* (10–12). Illus. 2000, Sutton paper $9.95 (0-7509-2384-9). A short, readable introduction to Cuba and the ruler who has withstood America's opposition for nearly 50 years. (Rev: BL 8/00) [921]

6902 Geyer, Georgie Anne. *Guerrilla Prince: The Untold Story of Fidel Castro*. 3rd rev. ed. (10–12). 2001, Andrews & McMeel paper $16.95 (0-7407-2064-3). This biography focuses on Castro's personality and pictures him as a paranoid megalomaniac. [921]

GUEVARA, CHE

6903 Neimark, Anne E. *Ch'e! Latin America's Legendary Guerrilla Leader* (7–10). Illus. 1989, HarperCollins LB $13.89 (0-397-32309-3). A portrait of the Latin American revolutionary who tried to help the oppressed and poor of the nations in Spanish America. (Rev: BL 5/15/89; SLJ 5/89) [921]

MARTI, JOSE

6904 Goodnough, David. *Jose Marti: Cuban Patriot and Poet* (6–10). Illus. Series: Hispanic Biographies. 1996, Enslow LB $20.95 (0-89490-761-1). This biography of the Cuban revolutionary who fought against Spanish rule also contains samples of his poetry in both Spanish and English. (Rev: BL 9/1/96; BR 9–10/96; SLJ 6/96) [921]

TUM, RIGOBERTA MENCHU

6905 Schulze, Julie. *Rigoberta Menchú Túm: Champion of Human Rights* (8–12). Illus. Series: Contemporary Profile and Policy. 1998, John Gordon Burke $20.00 (0-934272-42-5); paper $12.95 (0-934272-43-3). This biography combines the life story of Nobel Peace Prize-winner Rigoberta Menchu Tum with the story of the struggle of the Mayan people for equality in Guatemala and throughout Central America. (Rev: BL 4/1/98) [921]

Miscellaneous Interesting Lives

Collective

6906 Berson, Robin Kadison. *Young Heroes in World History* (7–12). 1999, Greenwood $45.00 (0-313-30257-X). Real people — of both sexes and many nationalities — who achieved amazing things before the age of 25 are profiled, with quotations and black-and-white illustrations. (Rev: SLJ 1/00; VOYA 4/00) [920.02]

6907 Gifford, Clive, et al. *1000 Years of Famous People* (6–10). Illus. 2002, Kingfisher $24.95 (0-7534-5540-4). Brief descriptions of famous men and women in sports, medicine, politics, the arts, and other fields are included in this large-format book that is organized by subject and provides historical overviews of each discipline. (Rev: BL 12/1/02; HBG 3/03; SLJ 2/03; VOYA 6/03) [920.02]

6908 Gonzales, Doreen. *AIDS: Ten Stories of Courage* (6–10). Illus. Series: Collective Biographies. 1996, Enslow LB $20.95 (0-89490-766-2). A collection of 10 biographies of individuals, including Ryan White and Magic Johnson, who have helped people understand AIDS and its effects. (Rev: BL 4/15/96; SLJ 5/96; VOYA 6/96) [920]

6909 Kamen, Gloria, ed. *Heading Out: The Start of Some Splendid Careers* (6–12). 2003, Bloomsbury $15.95 (1-58234-787-5). Twenty-four famous figures — including artists, athletes, politicians — tell in their own words how they became what they are today. (Rev: BL 12/1/02; HBG 10/03; SLJ 2/03; VOYA 4/03) [331.7]

6910 Rose, Phyllis, ed. *The Norton Book of Women's Lives* (9–12). 1993, Norton $30.00 (0-393-03532-8). This culturally and socially diverse anthology presents biographies of 61 20th-century women, among them Virginia Woolf, Anais Nin, and Kate Simon. (Rev: BL 9/15/93) [920.72]

Individual

ALBANY, A. J.

6911 Albany, A. J. *Low Down: Junk, Jazz, and Other Fairy Tales from Childhood* (10–12). Illus. 2003, Bloomsbury $23.95 (1-58234-333-0). A. J. Albany, daughter of jazz pianist Joe Albany, exposes the seamy side of Hollywood in this memoir of a childhood peopled by celebrities, junkies, hookers, and transvestites; suitable for mature teens only. (Rev: BL 3/15/03) [786.2]

ALEXANDER, DONNELL

6912 Alexander, Donnell. *Ghetto Celebrity: Searching for the Delbert in Me* (11–12). Illus. 2003, Crown $22.95 (1-4000-4602-5). In this eminently readable memoir suitable for mature teens, the author contrasts the story of his own successes and failures with the unhappiness and addictions of his father. (Rev: BL 5/1/03) [977.1]

ANSARY, TAMIM

6913 Ansary, Tamim. *West of Kabul, East of New York: An Afghan American Story* (10–12). 2002, Farra $18.00 (0-374-28757-0). Valuable insights into Afghanistan and its people — and into Islam — are offered in this powerful autobiography by the son of an Afghan father and an American mother. (Rev: BL 3/15/02*; SLJ 9/02) [958.104]

BAIEV, KHASSAN

6914 Baiev, Khassan, et al. *The Oath: A Surgeon Under Fire* (10–12). Illus. 2003, Walker $26.00 (0-8027-1404-8). A Chechnya doctor explains his support for his country in the face of great danger and offers insights into the republic's reasons for seeking independence from Russia. (Rev: BL 8/03) [947.5]

BELL, MARGARET

6915 Bell, Margaret. *When Montana and I Were Young: A Frontier Childhood* (10–12). 2002, Univ. of Nebraska Pr. $24.95 (0-8032-1325-5). In this compelling memoir of a childhood on America's Great Plains frontier, Bell tells how she managed to hold on to both dignity and hope despite a series of daunting hardships. (Rev: BL 2/15/02) [978.6]

BENJAMIN, DAVID

6916 Benjamin, David. *The Life and Times of the Last Kid Picked* (10–12). 2002, Random $23.95 (0-375-50728-0). In this often-poignant memoir of his 1950s Wisconsin childhood, Benjamin paints a picture of a different time and looks back with wry humor at his scrapes with bullies and wild animals. (Rev: BL 1/1–15/02) [977.5]

BITTON-JACKSON, LIVIA

6917 Bitton-Jackson, Livia. *My Bridges of Hope: Searching for Life and Love After Auschwitz* (8–12). 1999, Simon & Schuster $17.00 (0-689-82026-7). The true story of the author's life after her Holocaust experiences until she and her mother manage to migrate to the U.S. in 1951. (Rev: BL 5/1/99; SLJ 5/99; VOYA 6/99) [921]

BLAIR, ANEITA JEAN

6918 Glock, Allison. *Beauty Before Comfort* (10–12). Illus. 2003, Knopf $20.00 (0-375-40121-0). Aneita Jean Blair, a West Virginia grandmother justly proud of her looks and exciting romantic past, comes to life in this loving profile by her granddaughter. (Rev: BL 5/1/03) [975.4]

BLANCO, JODEE

6919 Blanco, Jodee. *Please Stop Laughing at Me . . . One Woman's Inspirational Journey* (10–12). 2003, Adams paper $12.95 (1-58062-836-2). In this memoir of her school years, Blanco recounts the years of relentless bullying and torment she endured before corrective surgery for a physical deformity changed her appearance and outlook. (Rev: BL 3/15/03; SLJ 5/03) [305.235]

BONO, CHASTITY

6920 Bono, Chastity, and Michele Kort. *The End of Innocence* (10–12). 2002, Alyson $22.95 (1-55583-620-8). Chastity Bono, daughter of Sonny and Cher, recounts in painful detail her relationship and final days with lover Joan Stephens, who died of non-

Hodgkin's lymphoma; suitable for mature teens. (Rev: BL 4/15/02) [792.7]

BOYLE, FATHER GREG

6921 Fremon, Celeste. *Father Greg and the Homeboys: The Extraordinary Journey of Father Greg Boyle and His Work with the Latino Gangs of East L.A.* (9–12). 1995, Hyperion $24.95 (0-7868-6089-8). This look at the intervention work of Father Greg Boyle with inner-city gangbangers features 10 of their autobiographies. (Rev: BL 6/1–15/95) [921]

BRAITHWAITE, E. R.

6922 Braithwaite, E. R. *To Sir, with Love* (9–12). 1990, Jove paper $4.99 (0-515-10519-8). The inspiring story of a young black teacher from British Guiana and his class in a school in London's slums. [921]

BROOKS, GERALDINE

6923 Brooks, Geraldine. *Foreign Correspondence: A Pen Pal's Journey from Down Under to All Over* (10–12). Illus. 1997, Doubleday $22.95 (0-385-48269-8). As a youngster growing up in Australia, Geraldine Brooks had many pen pals from around the world; as an adult, she rediscovered their letters and set out to find out what happened to them. (Rev: BL 11/1/97; SLJ 6/98) [921]

BRUCK, EDITH

6924 Bruck, Edith. *Who Loves You Like This* (10–12). Trans. by Thoma Kelso. 2000, Paul Dry paper $14.95 (0-9664913-7-8). In this haunting memoir, Bruck recounts her tumultuous life after surviving the Holocaust. (Rev: VOYA 4/01) [853]

BURCH, JENNINGS MICHAEL

6925 Burch, Jennings Michael. *They Cage the Animals at Night* (9–12). 1984, NAL paper $5.99 (0-451-15941-1). The story of a youth from a broken home and of the many shelters and foster homes where he spent his childhood while his mother tried to cope with her mounting responsibilities. [921]

CANTWELL, MARY

6926 Cantwell, Mary. *Manhattan, When I Was Young* (10–12). 1995, Houghton $21.95 (0-395-74441-5). An interesting autobiography of a fashion-magazine writer who came to New York in the 1950s fresh from college, lived in Greenwich Village, and found a new, exciting life. (Rev: BL 8/95; SLJ 1/96) [921]

CARROLL, JIM

6927 Carroll, Jim. *Basketball Diaries* (11–12). 1995, Penguin paper $13.00 (0-14-024999-0). For mature teens, these autobiographical journal entries describe adolescence on the streets of New York and a descent into drug addiction and prostitution. [921]

CARY, LORENE

6928 Cary, Lorene. *Black Ice* (9–12). 1991, Knopf $25.00 (0-394-57465-6). A 15-year-old black student from Philadelphia who won a scholarship to an elite prep school in New England describes her transition to an unfamiliar life and the racism over which she triumphed. (Rev: BL 2/15/91*; SLJ 8/91) [921]

CHE, SUNNY

6929 Che, Sunny. *Forever Alien: A Korean Memoir, 1930–51* (10–12). Illus. 2000, McFarland $37.50 (0-7864-0685-2). This coming-of-age memoir tells of Che, a Korean, who felt like an alien when she lived in pre-World War II Japan and also when she later returned to her native land. (Rev: BL 4/1/00) [921]

CHOQUETTE, SONIA

6930 Choquette, Sonia. *Diary of a Psychic: Shattering the Myths* (10–12). 2003, Hay $14.95 (1-4019-0192-1). In this memoir of her childhood and teenage years, spiritual teacher Sonia Choquette tells how she first discovered and developed her psychic abilities. (Rev: BL 8/03) [133.8]

CHOY, WAYSON

6931 Choy, Wayson. *Paper Shadows: A Memoir of a Past Lost and Found* (10–12). Illus. 2000, Picador $24.00 (0-312-26218-3). While discovering the identity of his real mother, the author relives his childhood growing up in Vancouver's Chinatown as a member of an isolated minority. (Rev: BL 10/15/00*; SLJ 6/01) [921]

CONWAY, EUSTACE

6932 Gilbert, Elizabeth. *The Last American Man* (10–12). 2002, Viking $24.95 (0-670-03086-4). A fascinating portrait of Eustace Conway, who believes passionately that Americans must reconnect with nature in order to save their society. (Rev: BL 4/1/02*) [813]

CURTISS, HURSTON

6933 Curtiss, Hurston. *Sins of the 7th Sister: A Memoir of the Gothic South* (11–12). 2003, Harmony $24.95 (1-4000-4538-X). In relating the story of his own childhood, the author has created an indelible portrait of his extraordinary mother; sex and violence make this best suited for mature teens. (Rev: BL 2/15/03) [975.4]

DA CHEN

6934 Da Chen. *Sounds of the River* (10–12). 2002, HarperCollins $25.95 (0-06-019925-3). Chen describes his arrival in Beijing and the years he spends there studying English in this appealing second volume of memoirs, following *Colors of the Mountain* (2000). (Rev: VOYA 2/03) [951.05]

DE FERRARI, GABRIELLA

6935 De Ferrari, Gabriella. *Gringa Latina: A Woman of Two Worlds* (10–12). 1995, Houghton $19.95 (0-395-70934-2). An autobiographical account told in short vignettes of the American art curator's youth in a village in Peru, where her father was a successful businessman. (Rev: SLJ 1/96) [921]

DONOFRIO, BEVERLY

6936 Donofrio, Beverly. *Riding in Cars with Boys: Confessions of a Bad Girl Who Makes Good* (10–12). 1992, Penguin paper $13.00 (0-14-015629-1). Donofrio describes her rebellious teens and her experiences as a single young mother. [921]

DUMAS, FIROOZEH

6937 Dumas, Firoozeh. *Funny in Farsi: A Memoir of Growing Up Iranian in America* (10–12). 2003, Villard $21.95 (1-4000-6040-0). This engaging memoir recounts the story — sometimes hilarious, sometimes sad — of the Iranian-born author's adjustment to America after moving here with her family in the early 1970s. (Rev: BL 6/1–15/03; SLJ 11/03; VOYA 4/04) [979.4]

EIRE, CARLOS

6938 Eire, Carlos. *Waiting for Snow in Havana: Confessions of a Cuban Boy* (10–12). Illus. 2003, Free Pr. $25.00 (0-7432-1965-1). In this portrait of the Cuban revolution from the viewpoint of a child of privilege, Carlos Eire tells of the profound changes in his life after Fidel Castro came to power. (Rev: BL 2/15/03) [972.91]

EVANS, DALE

6939 Rogers, Dale Evans. *Angel Unaware* (10–12). 1991, Buccaneer LB $10.95 (0-89966-811-9); Revell paper $8.99 (0-8007-5434-4). Dale Evans tells about herself and her daughter's brief life in this moving autobiography. [921]

FELLOWS, WARREN

6940 Fellows, Warren. *4,000 Days: My Life and Survival in a Bangkok Prison* (9–12). 1998, St. Martin's $20.95 (0-312-18296-1). In taut, compelling prose, Fellows relates his horrifying experiences after being convicted of heroin trafficking. (Rev: BL 11/15/98) [365]

FOUNTAIN, JOHN W.

6941 Fountain, John W. *True Vine: A Young Black Man's Journey of Faith, Hope, and Clarity* (11–12). 2003, PublicAffairs $26.00 (1-58648-084-7). A powerful memoir of an African American youth's experiences growing up on Chicago's west side amid rampant drug use and street crime; recommended for mature teens. (Rev: BL 6/1–15/03) [277.3]

FRY, VARIAN

6942 Isenberg, Sheila. *A Hero of Our Own: The Story of Varian Fry* (10–12). Illus. 2001, Random $26.95 (0-375-50221-1). This readable biography tells how Varian Fry helped more than 1,000 refugees, including Marc Chagall and Hannah Arendt, escape the Nazis. (Rev: BL 9/1/01) [921]

GAO, ANHUA

6943 Gao, Anhua. *To the Edge of the Sky: A Story of Love, Betrayal, Suffering and the Strength of Human Courage* (10–12). Illus. 2003, Overlook $27.95 (1-58567-362-5). Gao tells the courageous story of her struggle to survive and carve out a meaningful life for herself amid the political volatility of Maoist China. (Rev: BL 1/1–15/03) [951.05]

GARNER, ELEANOR

6944 Garner, Eleanor Ramrath. *Eleanor's Story: An American Girl in Hitler's Germany* (7–12). 1999, Peachtree $14.95 (1-56145-193-2). The author recounts her family's struggle to survive in Germany during World War II. (Rev: BL 10/1/99*; BR 1/00; HBG 4/00; SLJ 3/00) [940.54]

GLASBERG, RUTH

6945 Gold, Ruth G. *Ruth's Journey: A Survivor's Memoir* (10–12). 1996, Univ. of Florida Pr. $34.95 (0-8130-1400-X). When World War II came to Europe, Ruth Glasberg was 11 years old. This is the story of how she survived the concentration camp of Transnistria and finally found freedom in Palestine as the sole survivor of her family. (Rev: SLJ 8/96) [921]

GODIN, ISABELA

6946 Smith, Anthony. *The Lost Lady of the Amazon: The Story of Isabela Godin and Her Epic Journey* (10–12). 2003, Carroll & Graf $25.00 (0-7867-1048-9). Adventure-loving teens will devour this tale of Godin's epic 18th-century journey across the mountains and rain forests of South America. (Rev: BL 3/15/03) [980.013]

GRAY, AMY

6947 Gray, Amy. *Spygirl: True Adventures from My Life as a Private Eye* (10–12). 2003, Villard paper $12.95 (0-8129-7152-3). Gray blends the story of her experiences as a fledgling private investigator with humorous and poignant anecdotes from her personal life; for mature teens. (Rev: BL 9/15/03) [921]

GREENBERG, ALVIN

6948 Greenberg, Alvin. *The Dog of Memory: A Family Album of Secrets and Silences* (10–12). Illus. 2002, Univ. of Utah Pr. $19.95 (0-87480-727-1). In this beautifully written memoir, Greenberg relates his discovery at the age of 19 that his mother had died giving birth to him. (Rev: BL 7/02) [818]

GUNTHER, JOHN

6949 Gunther, John. *Death Be Not Proud: A Memoir* (7–12). 1989, HarperCollins paper $11.95 (0-06-092989-8). The moving tribute to the author's son who died at age 17 of a brain tumor. [921]

HAIZLIP, SHIRLEY TAYLOR

6950 Haizlip, Shirley Taylor. *The Sweeter the Juice: A Family Memoir in Black and White* (9–12). 1994, Simon & Schuster $21.50 (0-671-79235-0). The author, a woman of African American, white, and Native American heritage, tells how race shattered the lives of her relatives and how she's tried to pick up the pieces. (Rev: BL 12/1/93*) [929.2]

HALO, THEA

6951 Halo, Thea. *Not Even My Name: From a Death March in Turkey to a New Home in America, a Young Girl's True Story of Genocide and Survival* (10–12). Illus. 2000, St. Martin's $24.00 (0-312-26211-6). The unforgettable saga of a Greek woman who, as a young girl of 10 in 1920, was driven from her home at gunpoint by the Turkish army and sent on a death march. (Rev: BL 4/15/00*) [921]

HANNAM, CHARLES

6952 Hannam, Charles. *A Boy in That Situation: An Autobiography* (9–12). 1978, HarperCollins $12.95

(0-06-022218-2). The story of an unattractive Jewish boy growing up as the Nazis come to power. [921]

HAUTZIG, ESTHER

6953 Hautzig, Esther. *The Endless Steppe: Growing Up in Siberia* (7–12). 1968, HarperCollins paper $5.99 (0-06-447027-X). The autobiography of a Polish girl who, with her family, was exiled to Siberia during World War II. [921]

HERRIOT, JAMES

6954 Herriot, James. *All Creatures Great and Small* (8–12). 1972, Bantam paper $7.50 (0-553-26812-0). The first volume of Herriot's memories of being a veterinarian in Yorkshire, England, during the 1930s. Continued in *All Things Bright and Beautiful* (1974), *All Things Wise and Wonderful* (1977), and *The Lord God Made Them All* (1981). [921]

6955 Herriot, James. *Every Living Thing* (9–12). 1992, St. Martin's $22.95 (0-312-08188-X). Veterinarian Herriot continues his delightful recollections of his work among the animals and people of the Yorkshire Dales in the 1950s. (Rev: BL 8/92; SLJ 12/92) [921]

HICKAM, HOMER

6956 Hickam, Homer. *The Coalwood Way* (10–12). 2000, Delacorte $23.95 (0-385-33516-4). In this sequel to *Rocket Boys* (1998), the author tells of his senior year in high school in 1959 and growing up with teenage problems in the West Virginia mining town of Coalwood. (Rev: BL 8/00; VOYA 4/01) [921]

6957 Hickam, Homer. *Sky of Stone* (10–12). 2001, Delacorte $24.95 (0-385-33522-9). In this memoir of growing up in Coalwood, West Virginia, the author finds himself in the summer of 1961 working underground in the mines and facing some family problems. (Rev: BL 8/01; SLJ 1/02) [921]

HIGA, TOMIKO

6958 Higa, Tomiko. *Girl with White Flag* (9–12). 1995, Kondansha paper $9.95 (4-77001-946-7). As a 7-year-old in 1945, Higa wandered alone for weeks amid the battles on Okinawa. (Rev: SLJ 9/91) [950]

HOBBES, ANNE

6959 Specht, Robert. *Tisha: The Story of a Young Teacher in the Alaska Wilderness* (9–12). 1984, Bantam paper $5.99 (0-553-26596-2). The heartwarming biography of a young schoolteacher who at age 19 began working in the tiny Alaska town of Chicken. [921]

HUNTLEY, PAULA

6960 Huntley, Paula. *The Hemingway Book Club of Kosovo* (11–12). 2003, Putnam $22.95 (1-58542-211-8). This touching memoir recounts the author's experiences teaching English to a group of Albanian-speaking children in war-torn Kosovo; graphic descriptions of violence, including rape, make this suitable for mature teens only. (Rev: BL 2/1/03) [949.71]

HURD, BARBARA

6961 Hurd, Barbara. *Entering the Stone: On Caves and Feeling Through the Dark* (10–12). 2003, Houghton $23.00 (0-618-19138-0). This engaging memoir examines the author's innermost thoughts through the prism of her love — and fear — of caving. (Rev: BL 7/03) [796.52]

HYNES, SAMUEL

6962 Hynes, Samuel. *The Growing Seasons: An American Boyhood Before the War* (10–12). Illus. 2003, Viking $24.95 (0-670-03193-3). Hynes, a Princeton professor, revisits his Depression-era childhood in this moving memoir that places his experiences against the backdrop of world events. (Rev: BL 2/15/03) [973.9]

JENNINGS, CEDRIC

6963 Suskind, Ron. *A Hope in the Unseen: An American Odyssey from the Inner City to the Ivy League* (9–12). 1998, Broadway $25.00 (0-7679-0125-8). The true story of a poor inner-city African American boy and the determination, fortitude, and courage that allowed him to finish high school and gain admission to Brown University. (Rev: BL 3/1/98; SLJ 10/98) [921]

KASHNER, SAM

6964 Kashner, Sam. *When I Was Cool: My Life at the Jack Kerouac School* (11–12). Illus. 2003, HarperCollins $25.95 (0-06-000566-1). In this often amusing memoir, Kashner recalls his experiences as a student at the Jack Kerouac School of Disembodied Poetics and paints a sensitive portrait of his own and his mentors' perceptions and flaws; for mature teens. (Rev: BL 12/1/03) [921]

KINGSLAND, ROSEMARY

6965 Kingsland, Rosemary. *The Secret Life of a Schoolgirl* (10–12). 2003, Crown $24.95 (1-4000-4782-X). An appealing memoir of Kingsland's dysfunctional family, early childhood in India, move to a grim postwar England, and affair (at the age of 14) with actor Richard Burton. (Rev: BL 7/03; SLJ 11/03) [823]

LABORIT, EMMANUELLE

6966 Laborit, Emmanuelle. *The Cry of the Gull* (10–12). Trans. by Constantina Mitchell and Paul Raymond Cote. Illus. 1998, Gallaudet Univ. $29.95 (1-56368-072-6). The noted deaf actress recounts her experiences growing up in a hearing household and how learning sign language profoundly changed her life. (Rev: BL 12/1/98) [792]

LEDERER, KATY

6967 Lederer, Katy. *Poker Face: A Girlhood Among Gamblers* (10–12). 2003, Crown $23.95 (0-609-60898-3). Lederer's offbeat memoir tells of her childhood in a dysfunctional family and how she herself eventually took up gambling. (Rev: BL 7/03) [921]

LEKUTON, JOSEPH LEMASOLAI

6968 Lekuton, Joseph Lemasolai. *Facing the Lion: Growing Up Maasai on the African Savanna* (5–12). 2003, National Geographic $15.95 (0-7922-5125-3). Lekuton, a member of a nomadic Masai tribe and now a teacher in Virginia, remembers his youth in Kenya. (Rev: BL 9/15/03; HBG 4/04; SLJ 10/03*) [967.62]

LEONOWENS, ANNA

6969 Landon, Margaret. *Anna and the King of Siam* (7–12). Illus. 1944, HarperCollins $16.95 (0-381-98136-3). The career of the indomitable schoolteacher whose life became the basis of a play, a musical, and two movies. [921]

LERNER, BETSY

6970 Lerner, Betsy. *Food and Loathing: A Lament* (10–12). 2003, Simon & Schuster $23.00 (0-7432-2183-4). A candid account of the author's lifelong battle with weight problems and the accompanying blows to her self-esteem. (Rev: BL 1/1–15/03) [362.2]

LERNER, GERDA

6971 Lerner, Gerda. *Fireweed: A Political Autobiography* (10–12). Illus. 2002, Temple Univ. $34.50 (1-56639-889-4). Lerner, an expert in women's history, looks back on her earlier life, including her youth in Austria, escape from fascism, immigration to the United States, membership in the Communist Party, and brushes with Hollywood blacklisting. (Rev: BL 4/15/02) [921]

LUND, ERIC

6972 Lund, Doris. *Eric* (9–12). 1974, HarperCollins $16.95 (0-397-01046-X). The tragic story of a gifted young man and his fatal bout with leukemia, as told by his mother. [921]

MACE, NANCY

6973 Mace, Nancy, and Mary Jane Ross. *In the Company of Men: A Woman at the Citadel* (7–12). 2001, Simon & Schuster $18.00 (0-689-84002-0). Nancy Mace, the first woman graduate of the Citadel, describes the humiliations and harassment she endured in this previously all-male military college. (Rev: BL 10/1/01; HB 1–2/02; HBG 3/02; SLJ 12/01; VOYA 12/01) [355]

MCLAIN, PAULA

6974 McLain, Paula. *Like Family: Growing Up in Other People's Houses* (10–12). 2003, Little, Brown $23.95 (0-316-59742-2). McLain tells how she and her sisters were abandoned by their mother and shuttled between a series of homes, leaving them with a feeling of disconnection that was hard to overcome. (Rev: BL 2/1/03) [362.73]

MAH, ADELINE YEN

6975 Mah, Adeline Yen. *Chinese Cinderella: The True Story of an Unwanted Daughter* (6–12). 1999, Delacorte $16.95 (0-385-32707-2). The author recounts her sad childhood in China in the 1940s and 1950s and her struggle to succeed in spite of her father's disdain and her stepmother's neglect. (Rev: BCCB 11/99; BL 10/1/99; HBG 4/00; SLJ 10/99) [979.4]

MINIK

6976 Harper, Kenn. *Give Me My Father's Body: The Life of Minik, the New York Eskimo* (7–12). 2001, Archway paper $5.99 (0-7434-1257-5). The sad story of the Inuit boy brought to New York in the late 19th century as an example of the Eskimo race. (Rev: VOYA 8/01) [921]

MOODY, ANNE

6977 Moody, Anne. *Coming of Age in Mississippi* (10–12). 1970, Dell paper $6.99 (0-440-31488-7). The story of a black girl growing up in the desperate poverty of rural Mississippi. [921]

NAMU, YANG ERCHE

6978 Namu, Yang Erche, and Christine Mathieu. *Leaving Mother Lake: A Girlhood at the Edge of the World* (10–12). Illus. 2003, Little, Brown $23.95 (0-316-12471-0). This memoir recounts the author's childhood among the Moso people in a remote corner of southern China, her travels among the Han majority, and her personal struggle to find a place for herself between the two clashing cultures. (Rev: BL 2/15/03; SLJ 6/03) [782.42]

NASDIJJ

6979 Nasdijj. *The Boy and the Dog Are Sleeping* (10–12). 2003, Ballantine $22.95 (0-345-45389-1). The author, who himself is part Navajo, celebrates the life and courage of Awee, an HIV-positive Navajo boy whom he adopted and cared for through the ravages of AIDS. (Rev: BL 1/1–15/03*) [979.1004]

NORLING, DONNA SCOTT

6980 Norling, Donna Scott. *Patty's Journey* (10–12). 1996, Univ. of Minnesota Pr. $17.95 (0-8166-2866-1). A thought-provoking true story of a girl growing up during the Depression who at the age of four was taken from her family by the state after her father was imprisoned for robbing a store, of her unhappy experiences in foster homes, eventual adoption, marriage, and search for her lost sister and brother. (Rev: SLJ 3/97) [921]

NYE, NAOMI SHIHAB

6981 Nye, Naomi S. *Never in a Hurry: Essays on People and Places* (10–12). 1996, Univ. of South Carolina Pr. paper $16.95 (1-57003-082-0). This collection of autobiographical essays on a variety of subjects reflects the people and places encountered by the author, a Palestinian American married to a Swedish American who has lived most of her life in San Antonio, Texas. (Rev: BL 8/96; SLJ 11/96) [921]

O'CONNOR, LARRY

6982 O'Connor, Larry. *Tip of the Iceberg* (10–12). 2002, Univ. of Georgia Pr. $24.95 (0-8203-2356-X). O'Connor describes his childhood in central Canada, in a place of long, hard winters and with a father of a wintry disposition that turns out to hide a secret. (Rev: BL 5/1/02) [971.064]

ORTLIP, CAROL A.

6983 Ortlip, Carol A. *We Became Like a Hand: A Story of Five Sisters* (10–12). Illus. 2002, Ballantine $23.00 (0-345-44342-X). Ortlip recalls the close bond that developed between her and her four younger sisters as they grew up with minimal supervision from a mother sidelined by depression and a father with pressing responsibilities outside the home. (Rev: BL 3/1/02) [306.875]

OTOTAKE, HIROTADA

6984 Ototake, Hirotada. *No One's Perfect* (10–12). Trans. by Gerry Harcourt. 2000, Kodansha $19.95 (4-7700-2500-9). The story of a Japanese man who

was born without arms or legs and how he has tried to lead a normal life, including playing basketball and football. (Rev: BL 9/1/00) [921]

PACHEN, ANI

6985 Pachen, Ani, and Adelaide Donnelly. *Sorrow Mountain: The Journey of a Tibetan Warrior Nun* (10–12). 2000, Kodansha $24.00 (1-56836-294-3). The autobiography of a brave Tibetan woman who suffered imprisonment and torture by the Chinese because she opposed their occupation of her country. (Rev: BL 1/1–15/00) [921]

PATTON, LARRY

6986 Kastner, Janet. *More Than an Average Guy* (9–12). Illus. 1989, Life Enrichment paper $8.95 (0-938736-25-6). An inspiring story of a boy who was born with cerebral palsy and of the family that loved him. (Rev: BL 5/15/89) [921]

PETROSKI, HENRY

6987 Petroski, Henry. *Paperboy* (10–12). Illus. 2002, Knopf $25.00 (0-375-41353-7). In this engaging memoir of his childhood in Queens, Petroski tells how a bicycle he received for his 12th birthday opened up a new world full of opportunities. (Rev: BL 3/1/02) [974.7]

PRICE, MICHELLE

6988 Phillips, Carolyn E. *Michelle* (9–12). Illus. 1989, NAL paper $2.50 (0-451-14929-7). The inspiring story of a young girl's fight against bone cancer and how she never gave up, even after her leg was amputated. [921]

RAMOS, JORGE

6989 Ramos, Jorge. *No Borders: A Journalist's Search for Home* (10–12). Trans. by Patricia J. Duncan. Illus. 2002, HarperCollins $24.95 (0-06-621414-9). Television journalist Jorge Ramos, who emigrated to the United States more than two decades ago, recalls his youth in Mexico and tells how his personal history gives him a unique perspective on the news. (Rev: BL 10/15/02) [921]

REICHL, RUTH

6990 Reichl, Ruth. *Tender at the Bone: Growing Up at the Table* (10–12). 1997, Random $23.00 (0-679-44987-6); Broadway paper $13.00 (0-7679-0338-2). This entertaining autobiography by a woman who reviewed restaurants for *The New York Times* for many years tells how she became interested in food, describes some of her kitchen disasters, and gives a few mouth-watering recipes. (Rev: BL 2/15/98; SLJ 6/98) [921]

REISS, JOHANNA

6991 Reiss, Johanna. *The Upstairs Room* (7–10). 1972, HarperCollins $16.99 (0-690-85127-8); paper $5.99 (0-06-447043-1). The author's story of her years spent hiding from the Nazis in occupied Holland. Followed by *The Journey Back* (1976). (Rev: BL 3/1/88) [921]

REZENDES, PAUL

6992 Rezendes, Paul. *The Wild Within: Adventures in Nature and Animal Teachings* (10–12). Illus. 1999, Putnam $24.95 (0-87477-931-6). Longtime animal tracker Paul Rezendes, who describes his vocation as a form of meditation, offers an insightful account of animal behavior and how and why he chose tracking for his life's work. (Rev: BL 12/1/98*) [508]

ROWLAND, MARY CANAGA

6993 Rowland, Mary Canaga. *As Long As Life: The Memoirs of a Frontier Woman Doctor* (9–12). 1994, Storm Peak paper $11.95 (0-9641357-0-1). The memoirs of an early 19th-century doctor who braved the wilderness to treat wounds, pull teeth, and deliver babies. (Rev: BL 11/1/94) [610]

SATRAPI, MARJANE

6994 Satrapi, Marjane. *Persepolis: The Story of a Childhood* (10–12). Illus. 2003, Pantheon paper $17.95 (0-375-42230-7). In simple black-and-white drawings, the author chronicles her childhood in Iran between the ages of 10 and 14, during a time of revolution and turmoil. (Rev: BL 5/1/03; SLJ 8/03) [741.5]

SAWYER, ANH VU

6995 Sawyer, Anh Vu, and Pam Proctor. *Song of Saigon: One Woman's Journey to Freedom* (10–12). 2003, Warner $17.95 (0-446-52908-7). Sawyer tells the story of her childhood in a Vietnam full of strife and describes her family's escape on one of the last American helicopters to leave Saigon and their subsequent adjustment to life in America. (Rev: BL 2/15/03)

SCHOEN, ALLEN M.

6996 Schoen, Allen M., and Pam Proctor. *Love, Miracles, and Animal Healing: A Veterinarian's Journey from Physical Medicine to Spiritual Understanding* (9–12). 1995, Simon & Schuster $21.50 (0-684-80207-4). A memoir of a veterinarian who gained new understanding and insights as he treated injured, ill, and abused animals over the years. (Rev: BL 4/15/95) [921]

SHABAZZ, ILYASAH

6997 Shabazz, Ilyasah, and Kim McLarin. *Growing Up X* (10–12). 2002, Ballantine $25.00 (0-345-44495-7). In this coming-of-age memoir, Ilyasah Shabazz, daughter of Malcolm X and Betty Shabazz, describes the difficulties she encountered finding her own identity in the shadow of her parents' fame. (Rev: BL 3/15/02; SLJ 8/02; VOYA 4/03) [320.5]

SIEGAL, ARANKA

6998 Siegal, Aranka. *Upon the Head of the Goat: A Childhood in Hungary* (7–10). 1981, Farrar $16.00 (0-374-38059-7). A childhood in Hungary during Hitler's rise to power. (Rev: BL 12/15/89) [921]

SLAUGHTER, CAROLYN

6999 Slaughter, Carolyn. *Before the Knife: Memoirs of an African Childhood* (11–12). 2002, Knopf $23.00 (0-375-41397-9). In this painfully candid memoir, Carolyn Slaughter describes her troubled childhood in Africa during the waning years of colonialism; the rapes by her father make this suitable for mature teens. (Rev: BL 5/1/02; SLJ 11/02) [823]

SOFFEE, ANNE THOMAS

7000 Soffee, Anne Thomas. *Snake Hips: Belly Dancing and How I Found True Love* (10–12). 2002, Chicago Review $22.95 (1-55652-458-7). A passion for belly dancing taught the author, who is half Lebanese, important lessons about herself and her romantic life; for mature teens. (Rev: BL 8/02) [793.3]

SONE, MONICA

7001 Sone, Monica. *Nisei Daughter* (9–12). 1987, Univ. of Washington Pr. paper $14.95 (0-295-95688-7). From a happy childhood in Seattle to a World War II relocation center as seen through the eyes of a Japanese American girl. [921]

STEWART, BRIDGETT

7002 Stewart, Bridgett, and Franklin White. *No Matter What* (7–12). 2002, Blue/Black $14.99 (0-965-28271-6). In diary form, Stewart relates the hardships of growing up poor in a shack in Georgia and the uphill battle she faced in her effort to get a full education. (Rev: BL 7/02) [921]

STILL, PETER

7003 Fradin, Dennis B. *My Family Shall Be Free! The Life of Peter Still* (6–12). Illus. 2001, HarperCollins LB $16.89 (0-06-029328-4). Along with his brother, Peter Still was taken and sold into slavery;

this compelling story of his struggle to win freedom and reunite with his family incorporates historical documents, interviews, and maps. (Rev: BCCB 5/01; BL 2/15/01; HBG 10/01; SLJ 4/01; VOYA 8/01) [921]

SUBERMAN, STELLA

7004 Suberman, Stella. *When It Was Our War: A Soldier's Wife in World War II* (10–12). 2003, Algonquin $23.95 (1-56512-403-0). In this continuation of her autobiography, begun in *The Jew Store,* Suberman recounts her emotional experiences as a military wife during World War II. (Rev: BL 9/1/03; SLJ 5/04) [921]

SUMMER, LAURALEE

7005 Summer, Lauralee. *Learning Joy from Dogs Without Collars* (10–12). 2003, Simon & Schuster $24.00 (0-7432-0102-7). A moving story of a girl who despite a childhood of homelessness and poverty succeeds in winning a wrestling scholarship to Harvard. (Rev: BL 5/1/03; SLJ 11/03) [305.23]

SWEENEY, KEVIN

7006 Sweeney, Kevin. *Father Figures: A Boy Goes Searching* (10–12). 2003, Regan $21.95 (0-06-051192-3). At the age of 8, the fatherless author secretly selected three men close to his family as models for his own passage into manhood. (Rev: BL 5/15/03) [305.8]

THOMAS-EL, SALOME

7007 Thomas-EL, Salome, and Cecil Murphey. *I Choose to Stay: A Black Teacher Refuses to Desert the Inner City* (10–12). 2003, Kensington $23.00 (0-7582-0186-9). The author, who grew up in Philadelphia's projects, tells of returning to the same neighborhood to teach in an effort to bring hope and inspiration to other disadvantaged children. (Rev: BL 2/15/03) [371.93]

VIZZINI, NED

7008 Vizzini, Ned. *Teen Angst? Naaah . . . A Quasi-Autobiography* (9–12). 2000, Free Spirit paper $12.95 (1-57542-084-8). In a funny, breezy style, both humorous and poignant, 19-year-old Vizzini recounts his high school experiences as a self-acknowledged nerd. (Rev: BL 10/15/00; SLJ 11/00) [305.235]

VLAD III, PRINCE OF WALLACHIA

7009 Florescu, Radu R. N., and Raymond T. McNally. *Dracula: Prince of Many Faces, His Life and His Times* (9–12). 1989, Little, Brown paper $16.95 (0-316-28656-7). The biography of the 15th-century Romanian prince who is the real man behind the vampire stories. [921]

WATSON, PAUL

7010 Watson, Paul. *Seal Wars: Twenty-Five Years on the Front Lines with the Harp Seals* (10–12). Illus. 2003, Firefly paper $16.95 (1-55297-751-X). Watson describes the quarter century he's spent fighting to end the wholesale slaughter of harp seal pups in the northern reaches of Canada. (Rev: BL 5/15/03) [639.9]

WHITESTONE, HEATHER

7011 Whitestone, Heather, and Angela E. Hunt. *Listening with My Heart* (10–12). 1997, Doubleday $19.95 (0-385-48675-8). The life story of the first Miss America with a disability (she has been deaf since the age of 18 months), with details on her year as the reigning Miss America. (Rev: BL 6/1–15/97; SLJ 11/97) [921]

WILLIAMS, PHILIP LEE

7012 Williams, Philip Lee. *The Silent Stars Go By* (11–12). 1998, Hill Street $14.95 (1-892514-07-9). This memoir draws on recollections of family members to paint a poignant portrait of family life in small-town Georgia during the late 1950s. (Rev: BL 11/15/98) [818]

WILLIS, JAN

7013 Willis, Jan. *Dreaming Me: An African American Woman's Spiritual Journey* (10–12). 2001, Riverhead $23.95 (1-57322-173-2). This is the autobiography of an African American girl and her journey from a life of poverty to a life of fulfillment teaching and writing about Buddhism. (Rev: BL 3/15/01) [921]

YING, HONG

7014 Ying, Hong. *Daughter of the River* (11–12). Trans. by Howard Goldblatt. 1999, Grove $24.00 (0-8021-1637-X). An inspiring account of one Chinese woman's successful struggle to leave behind her impoverished childhood and tawdry youth; suitable only for mature teens because of candid sexual content. (Rev: BL 12/15/98) [895.6]

ZOYA

7015 Zoya. *Zoya's Story: An Afghan Woman's Struggle for Freedom* (9–12). 2002, Morrow $24.95 (0-06-009782-5). Zoya describes her life in Afghanistan under Taliban rule. (Rev: BL 3/1/03; SLJ 8/02; VOYA 2/03)

The Arts and Entertainment

General and Miscellaneous

7016 Aronson, Marc. *Art Attack: A Short Cultural History of the Avant-Garde* (11–12). Illus. 1998, Clarion $20.00 (0-395-79729-2). Eminently readable, this overview traces the avant-garde movement from its mid-19th-century origins in Paris to today's post-avant-garde age and examines the interrelationships among culture, the arts, history, and politics. (Rev: BL 7/98) [700]

7017 Craven, Wayne. *American Art: History and Culture* (9–12). 1994, Abrams $65.00 (0-8109-1942-7). Places architecture, decorative arts, painting, photography, and sculpture within a cultural and historical context. (Rev: BL 3/15/94) [709.73]

7018 Heide, Robert, and John Gilman. *Popular Art Deco: Depression Era Style and Design* (9–12). 1991, Abbeville $39.95 (1-55859-030-7). Explores art deco's origins and illustrates its influence on the futuristic, streamlined appearance of everything from toasters to skyscrapers. (Rev: BL 9/1/91) [709]

Architecture and Building

General and Miscellaneous

7019 *Architecture: The Critics' Choice* (10–12). Ed. by Dan Cruickshank. Illus. 2000, Watson-Guptill $50.00 (0-8230-0289-6). In this beautifully illustrated volume, 10 prominent architecture experts highlight 150 structures from ancient Greece to modern times that illustrate major movements in the development of world architecture. (Rev: BL 10/15/00) [720.9]

7020 Rybczynski, Witold. *The Look of Architecture* (10–12). Illus. 2001, Oxford $25.00 (0-19-513443-5). The author discusses various forms of architecture and architectural styles with examples from world history, ending with Frank Gehry's Guggenheim Museum in Bilbao, Spain. (Rev: BL 6/1–15/01) [721]

7021 Young, Michael. *Architectural and Building Design: An Introduction* (9–12). Illus. 1987, David & Charles paper $29.95 (0-434-92448-2). An interesting introduction to all sorts of building styles, external factors in planning structures, and special problems designers face. (Rev: BL 4/15/88) [721]

History of Architecture

7022 Glancey, Jonathan. *The Story of Architecture* (9–12). 2000, DK $30.00 (0-7894-5965-5); paper $25.00 (0-7894-9334-9). With special attention to the modern era, this is a colorful history of architecture. [720.9]

7023 Hocker, Christoph. *Architecture* (10–12).

Trans. by Sally Schreiber. Series: Crash Course. 2000, Barron's paper $12.95 (0-7641-0908-1). Using 240 illustrations, this is a well-organized history of architecture. [720]

7024 Lace, William W. *The Medieval Cathedral* (7–10). Series: Building History. 2000, Lucent LB $19.96 (1-56006-720-9). The whys and hows of cathedral building in the Middle Ages are explained with many color illustrations, diagrams, and examples of existing structures. (Rev: BL 4/15/01) [726]

7025 Nardo, Don. *The Medieval Castle* (6–10). Illus. Series: Building History. 1997, Lucent LB $27.45 (1-56006-430-7). This study presents a history of the medieval European castle, including its structure, design, usage, and construction. (Rev: SLJ 5/98) [940.1]

7026 Watkin, David. *A History of Western Architecture*. 3rd ed. (10–12). 2000, Watson-Guptill $50.00 (0-8230-2273-0); paper $40.00 (0-8230-2274-9). Beginning with ancient architecture like that of Egypt and Mesopotamia and continuing to he present, this history of the architecture of Europe and the United Sates is well illustrated and easily read. [720.9]

Various Types of Buildings

7027 Glanz, James, and Eric Lipton. *City in the Sky: The Rise and Fall of the World Trade Center* (10–12). Illus. 2003, Holt $26.00 (0-8050-7428-7). This story of the World Trade Center — from initial conception to horrific destruction — blends themes of both inspiration and despair. (Rev: BL 11/1/03*) [720]

Painting, Sculpture, and Photography

General and Miscellaneous

7028 Bateman, Robert. *Birds* (10–12). Illus. 2002, Pantheon $40.00 (0-375-42182-3). This collection of artist Bateman's breathtaking bird paintings includes commentary about each subject and about the artwork. (Rev: BL 1/1–15/03) [598]

7029 Beckett, Sister Wendy. *My Favorite Things: 75 Works of Art from Around the World* (9–12). Illus. 1999, Abrams $29.95 (0-8109-4387-5). A joyful introduction to great works of art from various periods and artists selected by Sister Wendy and explained in her usual enthusiastic style. (Rev: BL 1/1–15/00; SLJ 6/00) [709]

7030 Belloli, Andrea. *Exploring World Art* (7–12). Illus. 1999, J. Paul Getty Museum $24.95 (0-89236-510-2). Using examples from world art and artifacts, this work introduces a variety of media and images under such chapter headings as "Daily Life" and "History and Myth." (Rev: BL 1/1–15/00; HBG 4/00; SLJ 4/00) [709]

7031 Berkey, John. *Painted Space* (9–12). 1991, Friedlander paper $19.95 (0-9627154-1-7). A collection of a science fiction artist's creations, including historical works and movie posters. (Rev: BL 1/15/92) [759.13]

7032 Billout, Guy. *Something's Not Quite Right* (6–12). Illus. 2002, Godine $18.95 (1-56792-230-9). The detailed illustrations in this book, reminiscent of Dali and Escher, offer intriguing perspectives on the world and will encourage creative writing. (Rev: BL 2/15/03; HB 1–2/03; HBG 3/03; SLJ 1/03) [741.6]

7033 Clarke, Michael. *Watercolor* (8–12). Series: DK Eyewitness Books. 2000, DK $15.95 (0-7894-5584-6). This is a quick overview of this medium, with photographic reproductions of some of the world's finest watercolor paintings. [751.42]

7034 Cumming, Robert. *Annotated Art* (9–12). 1995, DK $24.95 (1-56458-848-3). Forty-five art masterpieces from the gothic, Renaissance, neoclassic, baroque, and romantic periods are reproduced in two-page spreads, with history and technique notes on each. (Rev: BL 6/1–15/95; SLJ 8/95) [750]

7035 Frankel, David. *Masterpieces: The Best-Loved Paintings from America's Museums* (9–12). 1995, Simon & Schuster $35.00 (0-684-80197-3). Directors of 33 American art museums each chose their most popular painting and these are reproduced with background material. [750]

7036 Govignon, Brigitte, ed. *The Beginner's Guide to Art* (8–12). Trans. from French by John Goodman. 1998, Abrams $24.95 (0-8109-4002-7). Using a broad subject approach (architecture, sculpture, painting), this is a comprehensive guide to world art and artists, with generous use of color illustrations. (Rev: SLJ 3/99) [709]

7037 Greenway, Shirley. *Art: An A–Z Guide* (6–12). 2000, Watts LB $32.50 (0-531-11729-4). An alphabetical introduction to art history and techniques, with full-color photographs. (Rev: SLJ 4/01)

7038 Hildebrandt, Gregory. *Greg and Tim Hildebrandt: The Tolkien Years* (10–12). Illus. 2001, Watson-Guptill paper $24.95 (0-8230-5124-2). This is a collection of art works by the Hildebrandts that illustrated Tolkien's *The Lord of the Rings,* with photographs of the sketches and drawings that preceded the final work. (Rev: BL 7/01; SLJ 4/02; VOYA 4/02) [741.6]

7039 Livingstone, Margaret. *Vision and Art: The Biology of Seeing* (10–12). Illus. 2002, Abrams $45.00 (0-8109-0406-3). A challenging but rewarding exploration of the relationship between our visual and artistic abilities. (Rev: BL 8/02) [750.1]

7040 Opie, Mary-Jane. *Sculpture* (7–12). Series: Eyewitness Art. 1994, DK $16.95 (1-56458-613-8). A handsome book filled with color illustrations introducing the world of sculpture, its history, and its various forms and materials. (Rev: BL 12/1/94; SLJ 6/95; VOYA 5/95) [730]

7041 Sturgis, Alexander. *Understanding Paintings: Themes in Art Explored and Explained* (9–12). 2000, Watson-Guptill $45.00 (0-8230-5579-5). Using such topics as religious painting, mythology, and the nude, this is a well-illustrated history of painting. [759]

7042 Yenawine, Philip. *Key Art Terms for Beginners* (9–12). 1995, Abrams $24.95 (0-8109-1225-2). This is an introduction to terms used in the art world, with more than 140 reproductions as examples. (Rev: BL 6/1–15/95) [703]

History of Art

7043 Arnason, H. H., and Marla F. Prather. *History of Modern Art: Painting, Sculpture, Architecture, Photography.* 4th ed. (10–12). Illus. 1998, Abrams $75.00 (0-8109-3439-6). A revised edition of the landmark historical survey that is both attractive and informative. (Rev: BL 11/15/98) [709]

7044 *Art: A World History* (10–12). Illus. 1998, DK $59.95 (0-7894-2382-0). This richly illustrated historical survey chronicles the evolution of art from prehistoric times through the present. (Rev: BL 11/15/98) [709]

7045 Ball, Philip. *Bright Earth: Art and the Invention of Color* (10–12). Illus. 2002, Farrar $27.00 (0-374-11679-2). In this unique approach to art history, Ball traces the science and history of paint making and in the process shows how the art of various periods was significantly influenced by the materials available. (Rev: BL 1/1–15/02) [701]

7046 Beckett, Wendy. *Sister Wendy's 1,000 Masterpieces* (9–12). 1999, DK $40.00 (0-7894-4603-0). Arranged by artist, this book introduces 1,000 great works of art by 500 artists. [759]

7047 Beckett, Wendy, and Patricia Wright. *The Story of Painting* (9–12). 1994, DK $39.95 (1-56458-615-4). A look at artists, historical periods, styles, movements, aesthetics, and spirituality. (Rev: BL 11/1/94*; SLJ 5/95; VOYA 4/95) [759]

7048 Cole, Alison. *Renaissance* (9–12). Series: DK Eyewitness Books. 2000, DK $15.95 (0-7894-5582-X). A guide to the art of Northern Europe and Italy from the 14th century to the 16th. [709.02]

7049 Cole, Bruce, and Adelheid M. Gealt. *Art of the Western World: From Ancient Greece to Post-Modernism* (9–12). 1989, Summit paper $22.00 (0-671-74728-2). Along with many full-color reproductions, this is a excellent compact survey of the history of Western art. [709]

7050 Gombrich, E. H. *The Story of Art.* Rev. ed. (9–12). 1995, Chronicle $49.95 (0-7148-3355-X); paper $29.95 (0-7148-3247-2). A revision of a comprehensive standard art book, with 443 color illustrations. (Rev: BL 10/1/95) [709]

7051 Guerrilla Girls Staff. *The Guerrilla Girls' Bedside Companion to the History of Western Art* (10–12). Illus. 1998, Viking paper $18.95 (0-14-025997-X). An introductory overview of traditional art history is followed by chapters highlighting the work of female artists during each time period, with reproductions of "mistresspieces" that have been overlooked by traditional male critics. The Guerrilla Girls are a group of anonymous artists and art professionals who seek to expose racism, sexism, and homophobia in the art world. (Rev: SLJ 9/98) [709]

7052 Homer, William Innes. *Stieglitz and the Photo-Secession, 1902* (10–12). Ed. by Catherine Johnson. Illus. 2002, Viking $29.95 (0-670-03038-4). The original catalog for the important 1902 New York exhibition of photography is accompanied by an introductory essay and many photographs and illustrations. (Rev: BL 10/15/02) [770.92]

7053 *Icons of Photography: The 19th Century* (10–12). Ed. by Freddy Langer. Trans. by John W. Gabriel. Illus. 2002, Prestel $29.95 (3-7913-2771-2). This stunning album celebrates the very best in 19th-century photography and provides biographical information on the artists. (Rev: BL 12/1/02) [779]

7054 Janson, H. W., and Anthony F. Janson. *History of Art.* 6th ed. (9–12). Illus. 2001, Abrams $95.00 (0-8109-3446-9). This is a basic, well-respected (but expensive) history of art that is particularly strong on coverage of 20th-century art. (Rev: BL 5/1/01) [709]

7055 Janson, H. W., and Anthony F. Janson. *History of Art for Young People.* 5th ed. (7–12). Illus. 1997, Abrams $49.50 (0-8109-4150-3). A much-expanded, thoroughly revised edition of the standard history of art for young people that now includes the 1990s. (Rev: BL 2/1/97; BR 9–10/97) [709]

7056 Johnson, Paul. *Art: A New History* (10–12). Illus. 2003, HarperCollins $39.95 (0-06-053075-8). In a fresh, new look at the history of art, Johnson traces the cultural backdrop of artistic vision from the cave paintings of prehistory to the modern era. (Rev: BL 10/1/03*) [709]

7057 Kampen O'Riley, Michael. *Art Beyond the West: The Arts of Africa, India and Southeast Asia, China, Japan and Korea, the Pacific, and the Americas* (10–12). Illus. 2002, Abrams $75.00 (0-8109-1433-6). This beautifully illustrated introduction to the aesthetic traditions of many cultures offers readable text and helpful charts and sidebars. (Rev: BL 4/1/02) [709]

7058 *Louvre* (10–12). Trans. from French by Susan Mackervoy, Anthony Roberts and Simon Dalgleish. 1995, Knopf paper $25.00 (0-679-76452-6). This small volume provides a quick tour of the art and architecture of the world-famous museum and art gallery. (Rev: SLJ 1/96) [708]

7059 Newhall, Beaumont. *The History of Photography: From 1839 to the Present Day*. Rev. ed. (10–12). Illus. 1982, Bulfinch paper $32.95 (0-87070-381-1). A history of photography that gives many prints representing the best from the past and present. [770.9]

7060 Powell, Jillian. *Ancient Art* (6–10). Series: Art and Artists. 1994, Thomson Learning LB $24.26 (1-56847-216-1). This book covers the ancient civilizations and their contributions to the history of art. (Rev: BL 11/15/94; SLJ 10/94) [709]

7061 Romei, Francesca. *The Story of Sculpture* (6–12). Series: Masters of Art. 1995, Bedrick $22.50 (0-87226-316-9). Using outstanding illustrations, this book covers a world history of sculpture with many examples of various styles and materials. (Rev: BL 11/15/95) [730]

7062 Roukes, Nicholas. *Humor in Art: A Celebration of Visual Wit* (10–12). 1997, Davis $32.50 (0-87912-304-1). With numerous black-and-white and color illustrations and a lively text, this book explores humor in art, with examples from artists both past and present. (Rev: SLJ 12/97) [701]

7063 Sandler, Martin W. *Photography: An Illustrated History* (6–12). Illus. 2002, Oxford $29.95 (0-19-512608-4). An overview of photography's major figures and developments, from its invention to new technologies, featuring many photographs. (Rev: BL 4/15/02; HBG 3/03; SLJ 6/02; VOYA 4/02) [770.9]

7064 Steffens, Bradley. *Photography: Preserving the Past* (6–10). Series: Encyclopedia of Discovery and Invention. 1991, Lucent LB $52.44 (1-56006-212-6). A history of photography that describes its impact on the modern world and profiles men and women involved in it. (Rev: BL 4/15/92) [770]

7065 *Treasures from the Art Institute of Chicago* (9–12). Illus. 2000, Art Institute of Chicago $75.00 (0-86559-182-2). More than 400 reproductions are the glory of this volume, which traces the history of world art through the holdings of the Art Institute of Chicago. (Rev: BL 12/15/00) [709]

7066 Welton, Jude. *Impressionism* (9–12). Series: Eyewitness Art. 1993, DK $16.95 (1-56458-173-X). Brief text copiously illustrated with reproductions of artworks, details of paintings, photographs of artists' materials, equipment, maps, and artist portraits. (Rev: BL 5/1/93) [759.09]

Regions

Africa

7067 Coulson, David, and Alec Campbell. *African Rock Art: Paintings and Engravings on Stone* (9–12). Illus. 2001, Abrams $60.00 (0-8109-4363-8). This book surveys Africa's prehistoric art with material on all regions and times plus information on dating methods and artistic techniques. (Rev: BL 8/01) [709]

7068 Thompson, Robert Farris. *Face of the Gods: Art and Altars of Africa and the African Americas* (9–12). 1994, Prestel $85.00 (3-7913-1281-2). A survey of the sacred art of Africa and its influence on the art and worship practices of African Americans. (Rev: BL 2/15/94) [726.5]

Europe

7069 Adams, Laurie Schneider. *Italian Renaissance Art* (9–12). Illus. 2001, Westview $85.00 (0-8133-3690-2); paper $60.00 (0-8133-3691-0). This is an exquisite introduction to the people, places, and events associated with the art of the Italian Renaissance, with a focus on paintings but additional coverage of architecture and sculpture. (Rev: BL 5/15/01) [709.02]

7070 Barter, James. *Artists of the Renaissance* (6–10). Illus. Series: History Makers. 1999, Lucent LB $27.45 (1-56006-439-0). Following an overview of the Renaissance, including explanations of humanism and classicism, this book focuses on several great artists, among them Giotto, Leonardo da Vinci, and Michelangelo. (Rev: BL 6/1–15/99; SLJ 7/99) [709]

7071 Brettell, Richard R. *Impression: Painting Quickly in France, 1860–1890* (10–12). Illus. 2001, Yale $35.00 (0-300-08446-3). Impressionism is explored in this beautiful book, with special material that shows the techniques employed by such artists as Manet, Monet, and van Gogh. (Rev: BL 3/15/01) [759.054]

7072 Corrain, Lucia. *The Art of the Renaissance* (6–12). Illus. Series: Masters of Art. 1998, Bedrick $22.50 (0-87226-526-9). An oversize volume full of small, full-color pictures and information-packed text introducing Renaissance artists and their times. (Rev: BL 3/1/98; SLJ 2/98) [709]

7073 Corrain, Lucia. *Giotto and Medieval Art* (6–12). Series: Masters of Art. 1995, Bedrick $22.50 (0-87226-315-0). A beautifully illustrated book that explores the art of Giotto and other masters of the Middle Ages. (Rev: BL 11/15/95) [759.5]

7074 Escher, M. C. *The Magic of M. C. Escher* (10–12). Illus. 2000, Abrams $39.95 (0-8109-6720-0). This volume contains 380 well-reproduced illustrations plus excerpts from the writings of the visionary Dutch graphic artist. (Rev: BL 12/15/00; SLJ 3/01) [769.92]

7075 Harris, Nathaniel. *Renaissance Art* (6–10). Series: Art and Artists. 1994, Thomson Learning LB $24.26 (1-56847-217-X). A general overview of this rich period in art history, with illustrations of paintings, sculpture, and architecture. (Rev: BL 11/15/94; SLJ 10/94) [709]

7076 Marani, Pietro C. *Leonardo da Vinci: The Complete Paintings* (9–12). Illus. 2000, Abrams $85.00 (0-8109-3581-3). This enormous tome tracks only 31 paintings in all media, with exhaustive material on each work and a total of 295 illustrations, most of them colorplates. (Rev: BL 12/15/00) [759.5]

7077 Mason, Antony. *In the Time of Michelangelo: The Renaissance Period* (7–10). Series: Art Around the World. 2001, Millbrook LB $23.90 (0-7613-2455-0). Full of full-color reproductions, this volume not only looks at the work of major artists of the Renaissance but also profiles artists in other parts of the world during the 15th and 16th centuries. Also use *In the Time of Renoir: The Impressionist Era* (2001). (Rev: HBG 10/02; SLJ 3/02) [709]

7078 Muhlberger, Richard. *What Makes a Raphael a Raphael?* (5–10). Series: What Makes A . . . 1993, Viking $9.95 (0-670-85204-X). An in-depth look at the paintings of Raphael and distinguishing features. (Rev: BL 1/15/94; SLJ 12/93) [759.5]

7079 Muhlberger, Richard. *What Makes a Rembrandt a Rembrandt?* (5–10). Series: What Makes A . . . 1993, Viking $9.95 (0-670-85199-X). The basic characteristics of this great Dutch master's work are pinpointed through a series of reproductions. (Rev: BL 1/15/94) [759.9492]

7080 Rebman, Renee C. *The Sistine Chapel* (7–10). Series: Building History. 2000, Lucent LB $19.96 (1-56006-640-7). This account includes material on Michelangelo's original creation, his conflicts with the Pope, and the recent restorations of the ceiling. (Rev: BL 9/15/00; HBG 3/01) [945]

7081 Salvi, Francesco. *The Impressionists: The Origins of Modern Painting* (6–12). Series: Masters of Art. 1995, Bedrick $22.50 (0-87226-314-2). An overview of Paris during the Impressionist period that includes many large, handsome reproductions. (Rev: BL 4/1/95; VOYA 5/95) [759.05]

North America

7082 *Celebrating Inuit Art, 1948–1970* (10–12). Ed. by Maria von Finckenstein. Illus. 2000, Key Porter $40.00 (1-55263-104-4). An exquisite book with fabulous photographs on the current bone and stone sculptures being produced in the art collectives of northern Canada, with addition material on anthropology, culture, and commerce. (Rev: BL 5/15/00*) [730]

UNITED STATES

7083 Adams, Ansel. *Ansel Adams: Our National Parks* (9–12). 1992, Little, Brown paper $19.95 (0-8212-1910-3). A collection of photographs, essays, and letters. (Rev: BL 5/15/92) [770]

7084 Adams, Ansel. *The Portfolios of Ansel Adams* (9–12). Illus. 1977, Bulfinch $45.00 (0-8212-0723-7). A collection of 85 examples of this master photographer's work in black and white. [779]

7085 *The American Art Book* (10–12). Ed. by Editors of Phaidon Press . 1999, Phaidon Press $45.00 (0-7148-3845-4). A handsome volume that surveys the history of American art from colonial times to the present as represented by about 500 artists. (Rev: BL 8/99) [709.73]

7086 Becker, Heather. *Art for the People: The Rediscovery and Preservation of Progressive- and WPA-Era Murals in Chicago Public Schools, 1904-1943* (10–12). Illus. 2003, Chronicle $45.00 (0-8118-3640-1); paper $29.95 (0-8118-3579-0). The discovery of hundreds of government-sponsored, Depression-Era murals in the public schools of Chicago is chronicled in this fascinating volume full of reproductions. (Rev: BL 1/1–15/03) [751.7]

7087 Bolden, Tonya. *Wake Up Our Souls: A Celebration of Black American Artists* (6–12). Illus. 2004, Abrams $24.95 (0-8109-4809-5). Beginning with the 19th century and ending with the present, this is a beautifully illustrated history of a selection of African American artists along with short biographies and material on the social conditions under which they worked. (Rev: BL 2/15/04*) [704.03]

7088 Callahan, Sean. *Margaret Bourke-White: Photographer* (9–12). Illus. 1998, Little, Brown $65.00 (0-8212-2490-5). This retrospective of the American's life work includes 138 photographs representing every stage in her three-decade-long career, including industrial, wartime, and architectural photography. (Rev: BL 12/15/98) [779]

7089 Cockcroft, James D., and Jane Canning. *Latino Visions: Contemporary Chicano, Puerto Rican, and Cuban American Artists* (7–12). 2000, Watts LB $26.00 (0-531-11312-4). The central themes of modern Latino art and the interests of individual artists are explored in this comprehensive survey that includes sections of full-color plates and many black-and-white illustrations and photographs. (Rev: SLJ 2/01; VOYA 6/01) [704.03]

7090 Finch, Christopher. *The Art of Walt Disney: From Mickey Mouse to the Magic Kingdoms* (7–12). Illus. 1973, Crown $4.99 (0-517-66474-7). The life and career of Walt Disney are covered, but the main attraction in this book is a collection of almost 800 illustrations from his work. [791.43]

7091 Glaser, Milton. *Art Is Work: Graphic Design, Interiors, Objects, and Illustration* (10–12). Illus. 2000, Overlook $85.00 (1-58567-069-3). The author uses his own work on book jackets, record covers, ad posters, and soup cans to illustrate the many sides of graphic, commercial art. (Rev: BL 12/15/00) [741.6]

7092 Goldstein, Bobbye S., ed. *Mother Goose on the Loose: Cartoons from the New Yorker* (6–12). Illus. 2003, Abrams $18.95 (0-8109-4239-9). Eighty cartoons that appeared in the *New Yorker* are accompanied by original nursery rhymes written by the editor. (Rev: BL 4/15/03; SLJ 5/03) [398.8]

7093 Gordon, Robert. *Deborah Butterfield* (10–12). Illus. 2003, Abrams $50.00 (0-8109-4629-7). A beautiful volume on sculptor Deborah Butterfield and her depictions of horses in such unlikely media as twigs, mud, and junk metal, with an introduction by Jane Smiley. (Rev: BL 11/1/03*) [730]

7094 Grant, John, and Elizabeth Humphrey. *The Chesley Awards for Science Fiction and Fantasy Art: A Retrospective* (10–12). Illus. 2003, AAPL $45.00 (1-904332-10-2). This stunning collection showcases winners of the Association of Science Fiction and Fantasy Artists' annual awards. (Rev: BL 12/1/03*) [700.415]

7095 Greenberg, Jan, and Sandra Jordon. *The American Eye: Eleven Artists of the Twentieth Century* (6–12). 1995, Delacorte $22.50 (0-385-32173-2). The art of these 11 artists is analyzed without jargon or pretension. A list of museums displaying their artwork is included. (Rev: BL 9/1/95*; SLJ 11/95) [709]

7096 Hainey, Michael. *Blue* (5–10). Illus. 1997, Addison-Wesley paper $12.99 (0-201-87396-6). Collages, cartoons, and funky art are used with a clever text to illustrate uses of the color blue in American culture. (Rev: BL 2/1/98) [535.6]

7097 Henkes, Robert. *World War II in American Art* (9–12). Illus. 2001, McFarland paper $39.95 (0-7864-0985-1). Paintings, woodcuts, and other art forms are represented in this collection of over 100 art works that depict World War II both at the front and at home. (Rev: BL 11/15/01) [758]

7098 Inches, Alison. *Jim Henson's Designs and Doodles: A Muppet Sketchbook* (9–12). Illus. 2001, Abrams $24.95 (0-8109-3240-7). The art of the creator of Big Bird and Cookie Monster, among others,

is chronicled in this survey of his achievements. (Rev: BL 5/1/01) [791.5]

7099 Kanfer, Stefan. *Serious Business: Cartoons and America, from Betty Boop to Toy Story* (8–12). 1997, Scribner (0-684-80079-9). This history of cartoons and animation in America gives details on the creators and their creations, with many illustrations. (Rev: BL 4/1/97) [741.5]

7100 Kloss, William. *Treasures from the National Museum of American Art* (9–12). Illus. 1986, Smithsonian $45.00 (0-87474-594-2). This book highlights 81 color paintings (and others in black and white) and gives a good introduction to the most important artists in the history of American art. (Rev: BL 6/1/86) [709]

7101 Leibovitz, Annie, and Susan Sontag. *Women* (10–12). Photos by Annie Leibovitz. 1999, Random $75.00 (0-375-50020-0). Leibovitz's captivating photographs of women from all walks of life are accompanied by Sontag's reflections on feminism. (Rev: BL 11/1/99; SLJ 2/00)

7102 Nesbitt, Peter T., and Michelle DuBois. *The Complete Jacob Lawrence* (10–12). Illus. 2000, Univ. of Washington Pr. $125.00 (0-295-97963-1). Though very expensive, this two-volume set is a magnificent tribute to one of the great African American artists. (Rev: BL 11/15/00) [759.13]

7103 Ross, Alex. *Mythology: The DC Comics Art of Alan Ross* (10–12). Illus. 2003, Pantheon $35.00 (0-375-42240-4). The comic book art of Alan Ross is magnificently showcased in this large-format retrospective of his work. (Rev: BL 11/1/03*; SLJ 5/04) [741.5]

7104 Salinger, Margaretta. *Masterpieces of American Painting in the Metropolitan Museum of Art* (9–12). Illus. 1986, Random $50.00 (0-394-55491-4). Historical and descriptive notes are given for reproductions of 100 paintings from the Met's collection that effectively trace a history of American art. (Rev: BL 2/1/87) [759.13]

7105 Sandler, Martin W. *America! A Celebration* (9–12). 2000, DK $50.00 (0-7894-6806-9). A lavish, oversized volume that contains more than 1,000 photographs and covers American life since the invention of the camera. (Rev: BL 12/15/00) [779]

7106 Sneden, Robert Knox. *Images from the Storm: 300 Civil War Images by the Author of Eye of the Storm* (10–12). Illus. 2001, Free Pr. $50.00 (0-7432-2360-8). This is an outstanding collection of the paintings Robert Knox Sneden began while he was a Union soldier and reworked after the war. (Rev: BL 8/01*; SLJ 2/02) [973.7]

7107 Steichen, Joanna. *Steichen's Legacy: Photographs, 1895–1973* (10–12). Illus. 2000, Knopf $100.00 (0-679-45076-9). More than 300 photographs are reproduced in this tribute to the great photographer Edward Steichen, with a text written by his wife. (Rev: BL 10/15/00) [770.92]

7108 Storr, Robert, et al. *Art 21: Art in the Twenty-first Century* (10–12). Illus. 2001, Abrams $65.00 (0-8109-1397-6). Twenty-one living artists of different generations, backgrounds, and artistic metiers are introduced in this overview of contemporary American visual artists. (Rev: BL 12/15/01) [709]

7109 Troccoli, Joan Carpenter, et al. *Painters and the American West: The Anschutz Collection* (9–12). Illus. 2000, Yale and the Denver Art Museum $45.00 (0-300-08722-5). With 188 excellent colorplates and an engrossing text, this is a history of the painting of the people and the landscapes of the American West. (Rev: BL 12/15/00; SLJ 7/01) [758.9978]

7110 *Visions of Adventure: N. C. Wyeth and the Brandywine Artists* (9–12). Ed. by John Edward Dell and Walt Reed. Illus. 2000, Watson-Guptill $35.00 (0-8230-5608-2). The works of such great American book illustrators as N. C. Wyeth, Howard Pyle, and four others are outlined in text and full-color prints in this attractive book for larger collections. (Rev: BL 8/00) [759.13]

7111 Wagner, Margaret E. *Maxfield Parrish and the Illustrators of the Golden Age* (10–12). Illus. 2000, Pomegranate $30.00 (0-7649-1257-7). As well as the work of Maxfield Parrish, illustrations by Howard Pyle, N. C. Wyeth, and others of the period are featured in this attractive volume. (Rev: BL 8/00) [741.6]

Music

General and Miscellaneous

7112 Evans, Roger. *How to Read Music: For Singing, Guitar, Piano, Organ, and Most Instruments* (8–12). 1979, Crown paper $10.00 (0-517-88438-0). An easily understood introduction to music notation and score reading for the beginner. [781.4]

7113 Leikin, Molly-Ann. *How to Write a Hit Song* (10–12). Illus. 1995, Hal Leonard paper $9.95 (0-88188-881-8). Practical advice on writing lyrics, composing, collaborating, and publishing songs. (Rev: VOYA 2/96) [784]

7114 Liggett, Mark, and Cathy Liggett. *The Complete Handbook of Songwriting: An Insider's Guide to Making It in the Music Industry* (9–12). 1985, NAL paper $9.95 (0-452-25687-9). This manual not only outlines the techniques of songwriting but also covers such areas as royalties, contracts, and even setting up one's own music publishing firm. (Rev: BL 8/85) [784]

7115 Turnbull, Walter. *Lift Every Voice: Expecting the Most and Getting the Best from All God's Children* (9–12). 1995, Hyperion $19.95 (0-7868-6164-9). The director of the Boys Choir of Harlem describes his beliefs and successes in sharing the joys of music with African American children. (Rev: BL 12/1/95) [780.7]

History of Music

7116 *American Mavericks* (10–12). Ed. by Susan Key and Larry Rothe. Illus. 2001, Univ. of California Pr. $45.00 (0-520-23304-2); paper $24.95 (0-520-23305-0). This handsome volume (packaged with a companion audio CD) blends program notes and supplementary text to paint a vivid portrait of the diversity of modern American music and its creators. (Rev: BL 4/1/02) [780.97]

7117 Davis, Francis. *The History of the Blues: The Roots, the Music, the People — From Charley Patton to Robert Cray* (9–12). 1995, Hyperion $24.95 (0-7868-6052-9). Using a first-person perspective, Davis explores the history, evolution, and marketing of contemporary blues artists and their music. (Rev: BL 1/15/95*) [781.643]

7118 Floyd, Samuel A. *The Power of Black Music* (9–12). 1995, Oxford $56.00 (0-19-508235-4). Traces African American music from Africa to the United States and explores the influence and contribution of African American musicians. (Rev: BL 4/1/95) [780]

7119 Gaar, Gillian. *She's a Rebel: The History of Women in Rock and Roll* (9–12). 1992, Seal paper $16.95 (1-878067-08-7). The contributions of female songwriters, singers, and other female musicians are traced through four decades of popular music. (Rev: BL 10/1/92) [781.66]

7120 Kallen, Stuart A. *The History of Classical Music* (6–10). Illus. Series: Music Library. 2002, Gale LB $21.96 (1-59018-123-9). This overview covers classical music and composers starting with the Middle Ages, providing interesting excerpts from primary documents. Also use *The History of Jazz* (2002). (Rev: BL 11/1/02) [781.6]

7121 Reagon, Bernice Johnson. *If You Don't Go, Don't Hinder Me: The African American Sacred Song Traditions* (9–12). 2001, Univ. of Nebraska Pr. $30.00 (0-8032-3913-0); paper $15.00 (0-8032-8983-9). A history of African American gospel music and the migrations that helped nurture and spread this form of sacred music around the United States. (Rev: BL 2/15/01) [782.25]

7122 Rushton, Julian. *Classical Music: A Concise History from Gluck to Beethoven* (10–12). Series: World of Art. 1986, Thames & Hudson paper $14.95 (0-500-20210-9). A brief history of music and of the development of the orchestra beginning with Gluck and ending with the start of the romantic period. [781.6]

7123 Southern, Eileen. *The Music of Black Americans: A History*. 3rd ed (9–12). 1997, Norton $37.95 (0-393-03843-2). Traces African American music's evolution and its impact on music in America generally. [780.89]

7124 Swafford, Jan. *The Vintage Guide to Classical Music* (9–12). 1992, Vintage paper $17.00 (0-679-72805-8). Chronological essays cover the lives and compositions of nearly 100 of the world's greatest composers. [781.6]

Jazz and Popular Music (Country, Rap, Rock, etc.)

7125 *American Roots Music* (10–12). Ed. by Robert Santelli et al. Illus. 2001, Abrams $49.50 (0-8109-1432-8). Such musical forms as early country, pre-World-War-II blues, black gospel, and Native American music are discussed in this volume that covers the origins of communal noncommercial music in America. (Rev: BL 11/1/01) [781.62]

7126 Andriote, John-Manuel. *Hot Stuff: A Brief History of Disco* (10–12). Illus. 2001, HarperEntertainment paper $13.00 (0-380-80907-9). Here is a lively history of the disco craze of the 1970s and of the people involved. (Rev: BL 3/1/01; VOYA 10/01) [781.64]

7127 Aquila, Richard. *That Old Time Rock and Roll: A Chronicle of an Era, 1954–1963* (8–12). 1989, Schirmer $25.00 (0-02-870082-1). A history complete with important biographies from the first decade of rock. (Rev: BL 9/15/89) [784.5]

7128 Asirvatham, Sandy. *The History of Jazz* (7–12). Series: American Mosaic. 2003, Chelsea LB $22.95 (0-7910-7265-7). Jazz, a unique American musical form shaped largely by African Americans, is covered from its beginnings in New Orleans to the present. (Rev: BL 10/15/03; HBG 10/03; SLJ 8/03) [781.61]

7129 Asirvatham, Sandy. *The History of the Blues* (6–10). Series: American Mosaic. 2003, Chelsea LB $22.95 (0-7910-7266-5). The origin, style, and technique of blues, along with its evolution and key figures, are presented with drawings and photographs. Also use *The History of Jazz* (2003). (Rev: BL 10/15/03; HBG 10/03; SLJ 8/03) [781.643]

7130 Bradley, Lloyd. *This Is Reggae Music: The Story of Jamaica's Music* (10–12). 2001, Grove Atlantic paper $18.00 (0-8021-3828-4). An overview that identifies and covers the origins and history of reggae, the personalities involved, and how it came to the U.S. and became commercialized. (Rev: BL 10/15/01) [782.4]

7131 *Bubblegum Music Is the Naked Truth: The Dark History of Prepubescent Pop, from the Banana Splits to Britney Spears* (10–12). Ed. by Kim Cooper and David Smay. Illus. 2001, Feral House paper $19.95 (0-922915-69-5). This book explores the music that is merchandised to preteens and young teens with articles on individual bands, record labels, and spinoffs to other media. (Rev: BL 9/15/01) [782.42166]

7132 Carlin, Richard. *Jazz* (9–12). Series: World of Music. 1991, Facts on File $19.95 (0-8160-2229-1). A history of this distinctly American music form, highlighting jazz greats and others who contributed to its development. (Rev: BL 9/15/91; SLJ 6/91) [781.65]

7133 Carr, Ian Digby Fairweather, and Brian Priestly, ed. *Jazz: The Rough Guide* (10–12). 1995, Penguin paper $24.95 (1-85828-137-7). There are profiles of nearly 2,000 jazz musicians and groups from the 20th century, plus a list of recommended recordings and a glossary of terms. (Rev: SLJ 8/96) [781]

7134 Christgau, Robert. *Christgau's Record Guide: Rock Albums of the '80's* (9–12). 1990, Pantheon paper $17.95 (0-679-73015-X). This is a guide to the rock albums of the 1980s with quotations from over 3,000 reviews. (Rev: BL 10/1/90; SLJ 6/91) [016.78]

7135 Christgau, Robert. *Grown Up All Wrong: 75 Great Rock and Pop Artists from Vaudeville to Techno* (11–12). 1998, Harvard $29.95 (0-674-44318-7). This collection of 75 articles and reviews by veteran music critic Christgau provides an excellent overview of pop music's evolution over the last several decades, for sophisticated teen readers. (Rev: BL 11/15/98) [781]

7136 Christie, Jan. *Sound of the Beast: The Complete Headbanging History of Heavy Metal* (10–12). Illus. 2003, HarperEntertainment $25.95 (0-06-052362-X). This nostalgic look at the heyday of heavy metal ranges from Black Sabbath to less well-known groups and includes a list of the 25 best albums. (Rev: BL 3/1/03; SLJ 9/03) [781.66]

7137 Clemente, John. *Girl Groups: Fabulous Females that Rocked the World* (9–12). 2000, Krause paper $19.95 (0-87341-816-6). This book identifies and describes 60 women's rock groups popular from the 1950s through the 1980s. [781.66]

7138 Collier, James L. *Jazz: An American Saga* (7–10). 1997, Holt $18.00 (0-8050-4121-4). A concise history of this uniquely American art form, from its African and European roots to the present day, and including the influences of various musicians on its development. (Rev: SLJ 1/98; VOYA 4/98) [781.65]

7139 Dawidoff, Nicholas. *In the Country of Country: People and Places in American Music* (10–12). 1997, Pantheon $25.00 (0-679-41567-X). Using a geographical approach, this work consists of a series of biographical essays about country and western music stars, among them Buck Owens, Patsy Cline, Chet Atkins, and Johnny Cash. (Rev: BL 2/15/97; SLJ 2/98) [780]

7140 Delancey, Morgan. *Dave Matthews Band: Step Into the Light.* Rev. 2nd ed. (7–12). 2001, ECW Press paper $16.95 (1-55022-443-3). In addition to a detailed history of the band, this revised edition includes interviews with band members. (Rev: VOYA 8/02) [782.42]

7141 Ellison, Curtis W. *Country Music Culture: From Hard Times to Heaven* (9–12). 1995, Univ. Press of Mississippi $40.00 (0-87805-721-8); paper $14.95 (0-87805-722-6). An account of the country music industry and its performers. (Rev: BL 2/15/95) [781.642]

7142 Fast, Susan. *In the Houses of the Holy: Led Zeppelin and the Power of Rock Music* (10–12). Illus. 2001, Oxford $55.00 (0-19-511756-5); paper $19.95 (0-19-514723-5). Using many primary sources including interviews, this is an interesting portrait of Led Zeppelin and the band's place in the history of rock. (Rev: BL 9/1/01) [782.42166]

7143 Furia, Philip. *The Poets of Tin Pan Alley: A History of America's Great Lyricists* (10–12). 1990, Oxford $27.50 (0-19-506408-9). This is the story of such great lyric writers as Lorenz Hart, Oscar Hammerstein, Cole Porter, and Irving Berlin. [782.42]

7144 Fyfe, Andy. *When the Levee Breaks: The Making of Led Zeppelin IV* (10–12). Illus. 2003, Chicago Review paper $14.95 (1-55652-508-7). A behind-the-scenes look at the making of the influential rockers' best-selling album. (Rev: BL 10/1/03) [781.42166]

7145 Gibbon, Sean. *Run Like an Antelope: On the Road with Phish* (10–12). Illus. 2001, St. Martin's paper $12.95 (0-312-26330-9). The author of this account accompanied the band Phish for the entire summer tour of 1999 and reports in detail on many interesting and entertaining experiences. Some strong language and drug use. (Rev: BL 1/1–15/01; SLJ 9/01) [782.4]

7146 Gioia, Ted. *The History of Jazz* (9–12). 1997, Oxford $37.50 (0-19-509081-0); paper $16.95 (0-19-512653-X). The evolution of jazz and its key figures are covered in this well-researched volume. (Rev: BL 11/15/97) [781.65]

7147 Gourse, Leslie. *Blowing on the Changes: The Art of the Jazz Horn Players* (8–12). Series: Art of Jazz. 1997, Watts LB $23.00 (0-531-11357-4). This book explores the influence on jazz of great artists of the trumpet, saxophone, trombone, clarinet, and other wind instruments. (Rev: BR 5–6/98; HBG 3/98; SLJ 11/97) [784]

7148 Gourse, Leslie. *Deep Down in Music: The Art of the Great Jazz Bassists* (7–10). Series: Art of Jazz. 1998, Watts LB $23.00 (0-531-11410-4). By tracing the work of the great innovators on the bass fiddle, this book explores the development of jazz bass techniques and how these low sounds supply the foundation of the music. (Rev: BR 11–12/98; SLJ 7/98; VOYA 10/99) [781.65]

7149 Gourse, Leslie. *Striders to Beboppers and Beyond: The Art of Jazz Piano* (7–10). 1997, Watts LB $23.00 (0-531-11320-5). In this history of jazz pianists, the author profiles 23 great performers, including Jelly Roll Morton, Mary Lou Williams, Thelonius Monk, and Bud Powell. (Rev: SLJ 7/97) [786.4]

7150 Greenwald, Andy. *Nothing Feels Good: Punk Rock, Teenagers, and Emo* (10–12). 2003, St. Martin's paper $14.95 (0-312-30863-9). In this thoughtful analysis, a music historian profiles the rise of emo, an increasingly popular musical genre that some have described as emotionally charged punk rock. (Rev: BL 11/1/03) [782.42166]

7151 Gregory, Hugh. *A Century of Pop: A Hundred Years of Music That Changed the World* (9–12). 1998, A Capella paper $29.95 (1-55652-338-6). Using a magazine format with plenty of illustrations, this book gives a decade-by-decade history of popular music in the United States during the 20th century. (Rev: SLJ 3/99) [781]

7152 Guterman, Jimmy, and Owen O'Donnell. *The Worst Rock and Roll Records of All Time: A Fan's Guide to the Stuff You Love to Hate* (9–12). 1991, Citadel paper $14.95 (0-8065-1231-8). An opinionated guide to 50 "atrocious" rock-and-roll songs. (Rev: BL 6/1/91) [781.66]

7153 Haskins, James. *One Love, One Heart: A History of Reggae* (7–12). Illus. 2002, Hyperion $15.99 (0-7868-0479-3). The story of the birth and growth of this musical genre, including its roots in Jamaica and the Rastafarian religion. (Rev: BL 4/15/02; HBG 10/02; SLJ 5/02; VOYA 12/02) [781.646]

7154 Haskins, James. *One Nation Under a Groove: Rap Music and Its Roots* (9–12). Illus. 2000, Hyperion LB $16.49 (0-7868-2414-X). This story of rap music traces its development from the griot storytelling traditions of West Africa to its current place in American popular music. (Rev: BL 2/15/01; HBG 10/01; SLJ 4/01; VOYA 6/01) [782.421]

7155 *Hip Hop Divas* (10–12). Illus. 2001, Crown paper $17.95 (0-609-80836-2). This collection of profiles from Vibe magazine covers such hip hop women as Lil' Kim, Erykah Badu, and Lauryn Hill. (Rev: BL 10/15/01) [782.4]

7156 Jackson, Blair, et al. *Grateful Dead: The Illustrated Trip* (10–12). Illus. 2003, DK $50.00 (0-7894-9963-0). A highly visual history that traces the band from its earlier incarnation as the Warlocks through two attempts to regroup after the death of Jerry Garcia. (Rev: BL 11/15/03) [782.42166]

7157 James, Billy. *Necessity Is . . . . The Early Years of Frank Zappa and the Mothers of Invention* (9–12). Illus. 2001, SAF paper $18.95 (0-946719-14-4). With many great details and photographs, this is a fine history of Frank Zappa and his years with the innovative band. (Rev: BL 4/15/01*) [782.42166]

7158 Jancik, Wayne, and Ted Lathrop. *Cult Rockers* (10–12). 1995, Fireside paper $14.00 (0-684-81112-X). Profiles are given of 150 of the most popular, outrageous, and intriguing rock musicians around. (Rev: SLJ 7/96) [782]

7159 *Jazz: The First Century* (10–12). Ed. by John Edward Hasse. Illus. 2000, Morrow $37.00 (0-688-17074-9). An excellent overview that traces the history of jazz from its origins in New Orleans to the present day. (Rev: BL 2/15/00) [781.65]

7160 Kallen, Stuart A. *The History of Rock and Roll* (6–10). Series: Music Library. 2002, Gale LB $21.96 (1-59018-126-3). Beginning in the early 1950s, this account traces the history of rock and roll, profiles many musicians involved, and describes the unique characteristics of this form of music. (Rev: BL 3/15/03) [781.66]

7161 Keely, Jennifer. *Rap Music* (6–12). Series: Overview. 2001, Lucent LB $27.45 (1-56006-504-4). This richly illustrated book gives an in-depth overview of rap music and profiles of many celebrities connected with it. (Rev: BL 9/15/01; SLJ 10/01) [782.42]

7162 Leaf, David, and Ken Sharp. *Kiss: Behind the Mask* (10–12). Illus. 2003, Warner $27.95 (0-446-53073-5). A nicely designed and readable profile of the eye-catching heavy metal band Kiss. (Rev: BL 10/1/03) [782.42166]

7163 Lommel, Cookie. *The History of Rap Music* (8–12). Series: African-American Achievers. 2001, Chelsea $21.95 (0-7910-5820-4). The history of rap music from its origins in the hip hop of the 1970s through its growing popularity through the 1990s to 2000. (Rev: HBG 10/01) [782.42]

7164 Marsalis, Wynton. *Marsalis on Music* (9–12). 1995, Norton $29.95 (0-393-03881-5). A manual that uses examples from jazz greats to teach the fundamentals of jazz and the elements of improvisation. Includes a CD. (Rev: BL 10/1/95) [780]

7165 Marsalis, Wynton, and Carl Vigeland. *Jazz in the Bittersweet Blues of Life* (10–12). 2001, Da Capo $25.00 (0-306-81033-6). This is an account of five years spent on the road with Wynton Marsalis and his jazz band. (Rev: BL 6/1–15/01) [788.9]

7166 Morse, Tim. *Classic Rock Stories: The Stories Behind the Greatest Songs of All Time* (10–12). 1998, Griffin paper $12.95 (0-312-18067-5). A history of rock during the 1960s and 1970s, with insights into hit songs and the artists who recorded them, among them Paul McCartney, Mick Jagger, Rod Stewart, Elton John, and Alice Cooper, plus an update on where they are today. (Rev: SLJ 1/99) [781.66]

7167 Nisenson, Eric. *The Making of Kind of Blue: Miles Davis and His Masterpiece* (10–12). Illus. 2000, St. Martin's $22.95 (0-312-26617-0). Combining memoir, biography, history, and musicology, this is the story of Miles Davis's great 1959 recording, "Kind of Blue." (Rev: BL 11/15/00) [781.65]

7168 O'Dair, Barbara. *The Rolling Stone Book of Women in Rock: Trouble Girls* (10–12). 1997, Random paper $25.00 (0-679-76874-2). Fifty-six well-written essays by 44 women discuss the role of women in popular music, including rock and roll, jazz, gospel, rhythm and blues, and country; solo artists and girl groups of the 1950s and 1960s; rock in the 1960s and 1970s; pop singers and punksters of the 1970s; and more. (Rev: SLJ 6/98) [780]

7169 Oermann, Robert K. *A Century of Country: An Illustrated History of Country Music* (9–12). 1999, TV Books $39.95 (1-57500-083-0). A history of country music in America with material on many of the artists involved. (Rev: BL 11/1/99) [781.642]

7170 Robertson, Brian. *Little Blues Book* (10–12). Illus. 1996, Algonquin paper $15.95 (1-56512-137-6). A history of the blues and blues singers covering the past 70 years, with numerous quotations from the artists and their songs. (Rev: SLJ 6/97) [782]

7171 *Rock and Roll Is Here to Stay: An Anthology* (9–12). Ed. by William McKeen. Illus. 2000, Norton $35.00 (0-393-04700-8). This collection of short articles covers such subjects as a history of rock and roll, key performers, and audience reactions. (Rev: BL 10/15/00) [781.66]

7172 Rose, Tricia. *Black Noise: Rap Music and Black Culture in Contemporary America* (9–12). 1994, Wesleyan Univ. Pr. paper $16.95 (0-8195-6275-0). An analysis of various facets of rap, including a discussion of hip-hop and the neglected recognition of women's role in rap. (Rev: BL 4/15/94) [782.42]

7173 Russell, Tony. *The Blues: From Robert Johnson to Robert Cray* (10–12). 1998, Schirmer paper $18.00 (0-028-64886-2). More than 400 blues musicians are profiled — 24 in depth — and lists highlight important recordings and festivals in the United States and Europe. [781.643]

7174 Scherman, Tony, and Mark Rowland, eds. *The Jazz Musician* (9–12). 1994, St. Martin's paper $12.95 (0-312-09500-7). Profiles of jazz greats in which the legendary musicians recall important points in their lives. (Rev: BL 2/1/94) [781.65]

7175 Shipton, Alyn. *A New History of Jazz* (9–12). Illus. 2001, Continuum $35.00 (0-8264-4754-6). The true history of jazz is revealed in this excellent account that offers several theories on the origins of jazz. (Rev: BL 9/1/01) [781.65]

7176 Soocher, Stan. *They Fought the Law: Rock Music Goes to Court* (11–12). 1998, Schirmer $25.00 (0-02-864731-9). Collisions of pop music and litigation — most of them relating to questions of copyright and liability — are explored in this survey of court cases, for teens with a serious interest in the subject. (Rev: BL 11/15/98) [781.66]

7177 Stroff, Stephen M. *Discovering Great Jazz: A New Listener's Guide to the Sounds and Styles of the Top Musicians and Their Recordings on CDs, LPs, and Cassettes* (9–12). 1991, Newmarket $19.95 (1-55704-103-2). A description of the stylistic developments in the history of jazz, with recommendations for the best recorded performances from each period up to the 1990s. (Rev: BL 10/1/91) [781.65]

7178 Sullivan, Caroline. *Bye Bye Baby: My Tragic Love Affair with the Bay City Rollers* (10–12). 2001, Bloomsbury paper $14.95 (0-7475-4703-3). This is a memoir by a rabid fan of the Bay City Rollers and an account of the band's popularity during the 1970s. (Rev: BL 2/15/01) [782.421]

7179 Szwed, John F. *Jazz 101: A Complete Guide to Learning and Loving Jazz* (10–12). 2000, Hyperion paper $14.95 (0-7876-8496-7). This comprehensive introduction to jazz is arranged chronologically and covers the trends in jazz and the key players. (Rev: BL 8/00) [781.65]

7180 Talevski, Nick. *The Unofficial Encyclopedia of the Rock and Roll Hall of Fame* (8–12). 1998, Greenwood $65.95 (0-313-30032-1). This book provides background on the Rock and Roll Hall of Fame in Cleveland and covers, in alphabetical order, the first 150 inductees, with interesting personal as well as professional information, anecdotes, comments, and insights. (Rev: VOYA 2/99) [781.66]

7181 Ward, Geoffrey C., and Ken Burns. *Jazz: A History of America's Music* (10–12). Illus. 2000, Knopf $65.00 (0-679-44551-X). This history of jazz (based on the PBS television series) focuses on such greats as Louis Armstrong, Duke Ellington, Charlie Parker, and Miles Davis. (Rev: BL 9/15/00; SLJ 6/01) [781.65]

7182 Williams, Robbie, and Mark McCrum. *Robbie Williams: Somebody Someday* (10–12). Illus. 2002, Ebury $24.95 (0-09-188119-6). Popular British rock star Robbie Williams tells of his struggles with alcohol and drugs and offers an inside look at life on a concert tour; for mature teens. (Rev: BL 2/15/02) [782.4]

7183 Wyman, Bill, and Richard Havers. *Bill Wyman's Blues Odyssey* (10–12). Illus. 2001, DK $40.00 (0-7894-8046-8). A lavishly illustrated, chronologically arranged book about the blues and its most important performers. (Rev: BL 11/1/01) [781.643]

7184 Wyman, Bill, and Richard Havers. *Rolling With the Stones* (9–12). 2002, DK (0-7894-8967-8). This inside look at the Rolling Stones and the music they have produced also contains a discography. (Rev: BL 11/15/02) [782.42]

Opera and Musicals

7185 Brener, Milton. *Opera Offstage: Passion and Politics Behind the Great Operas* (10–12). 1996, Walker $38.95 (0-8027-1313-0). For each of the 26 operas discussed, a full plot summary is provided, along with material on musical forms used in the opera and its sources, which may include history, mythology, literature, politics, even the everyday experiences of the composer. (Rev: SLJ 7/97) [782.1]

7186 Englander, Roger. *Opera: What's All the Screaming About?* (7–12). Illus. 1983, Walker $12.95 (0-8027-6491-6). After a general introduction to the history and conventions of opera, 50 popular operas are introduced. (Rev: BL 9/1/87) [782.1]

7187 Freeman, John W. *The Metropolitan Opera Stories of the Great Operas* (9–12). Illus. 1984, Norton $29.95 (0-393-01888-1). Plots are given for 150 great operas with accompanying biographical material on their composers. [782.1]

7188 Lerner, Alan Jay. *The Musical Theatre: A Celebration* (9–12). Illus. 1989, Da Capo paper $16.95 (0-306-80364-X). An anecdotal history of the American musical from its beginning to its maturity after World War II. (Rev: BL 11/15/86) [782.81]

7189 Novak, Elaine A., and Deborah Novak. *Staging Musical Theatre: A Complete Guide for Directors, Choreographers and Producers* (10–12). 1996, Betterway paper $19.99 (1-55870-407-8). A practical, readable guide to staging musicals, from auditions to printing the programs. (Rev: SLJ 2/97) [792]

7190 Perry, George. *The Complete Phantom of the Opera* (9–12). Illus. 1987, Holt $35.00 (0-8050-0657-5). A lavish volume that includes the original novel, the history of the musical, and the complete script. (Rev: BL 1/15/88; BR 5–6/88; SLJ 3/88; VOYA 6/88) [782.81]

7191 Raeburn, Michael. *The Chronicle of the Opera* (11–12). Illus. 1998, Thames & Hudson $45.00 (0-500-01867-7). A detailed chronological survey of the history of opera that will appeal to teens with some knowledge of this form of music. (Rev: BL 11/15/98) [782.1]

7192 Sondheim, Stephen, and James Lapine. *Into the Woods* (9–12). 1989, Theatre Communications paper $10.95 (0-930452-93-3). The text and lyrics of the prize-winning musical about fairy tale characters and what happens to their "happily ever after." (Rev: BL 9/1/89) [782.81]

7193 Townshend, Pete, and Des McAnuff. *The Who's Tommy: The Musical* (9–12). 1993, Pantheon $40.00 (0-679-43066-0). This behind-the-scenes look at the rock opera by The Who includes production stills, anecdotes by cast and production members, and a CD. (Rev: BL 12/15/93) [782.1]

Orchestra and Musical Instruments

7194 Bacon, Tony, and Paul Day. *The Ultimate Guitar Book* (9–12). 1991, Knopf paper $27.50 (0-375-70090-0). Richly illustrated, this overview traces the guitar's evolution from its origins in 16th-century Spain through today's electronically enhanced instruments. [787.87]

7195 Dearling, Robert, ed. *The Illustrated Encyclopedia of Musical Instruments* (8–12). 1996, Schirmer $90.00 (0-02-864667-3). In addition to material on the history, development, and characteristics of each musical instrument, this oversize, well-illustrated book gives a history of music-making, plus coverage of composers and performers. (Rev: BL 1/1–15/97; SLJ 5/97) [784.19]

7196 Evans, Roger. *How to Play Guitar: A New Book for Everyone Interested in Guitar* (8–12). Illus. 1980, St. Martin's paper $9.95 (0-312-36609-0). An easily followed basic guidebook on how to play the guitar with information on such topics as buying equipment and reading music. [787.6]

7197 Gruhn, George, and Walter Carter. *Acoustic Guitars and Other Fretted Instruments: A Photographic History* (9–12). 1993, Miller Freeman $49.95 (0-87930-240-2). Presents a history of U.S. fretted instruments from their beginnings to the present day, including photographs of celebrity guitars. (Rev: BL 6/1–15/93) [787.87]

7198 Monath, Norman. *How to Play Popular Piano in Ten Easy Lessons* (10–12). 1984, Simon & Schuster paper $12.00 (0-671-53067-4). A useful guide that requires a great deal of work on the part of the reader. [786.2]

7199 Roth, Arlen. *Arlen Roth's Complete Acoustic Guitar* (9–12). Illus. 1985, Schirmer paper $18.95 (0-02-872150-0). Various styles of music such as folk and rock are discussed and essential information on how to play each is given. (Rev: BL 4/1/86) [787.6]

7200 Steinberg, Michael. *The Symphony: A Concert Guide* (9–12). 1995, Oxford $30.00 (0-19-506177-2). Essays based on program notes Steinberg wrote for the Boston and San Francisco orchestras spanning 20 years. (Rev: BL 11/1/95) [784.2]

7201 Wollitz, Kenneth. *The Recorder Book* (9–12). 1982, Knopf paper $17.00 (0-394-74999-5). From beginning player to expert, this book covers all levels of recorder playing. [781.91]

Songs and Folk Songs

7202 Blood-Patterson, Peter, ed. *Rise Up Singing* (8–12). Illus. 1988, Sing Out LB $39.95 (0-9626704-8-0); paper $17.95 (0-9626704-9-9). Words, chords, and some background material on 1,200 songs, some folk, others pop. (Rev: BL 12/15/88; BR 3–4/89) [784.5]

7203 Collins, Ace. *Stories Behind the Best-Loved Songs of Christmas* (9–12). 2001, Zondervan $14.99 (0-310-23926-5). These are the stories behind such pop Christmas songs as "Silver Bells" and "Have Yourself a Merry Little Christmas." (Rev: BL 10/1/01) [264]

7204 Downes, Belinda. *Silent Night: A Christmas Carol Sampler* (7–12). 1995, Knopf $18.00 (0-679-86959-X). This 32-page collection of Christmas carols is illustrated with a full-page embroidered tapestry facing each carol. Words and piano music are provided. (Rev: BL 9/15/95*) [782.281]

7205 Hart, Mickey, and K. M. Kostyal. *Songcatchers: In Search of the World's Music* (10–12). Illus. 2003, National Geographic $30.00 (0-7922-4107-X). Period photographs enhance this clearly written overview of the "songcatchers," men and women who track down and record traditional music. (Rev: BL 6/1–15/03) [780]

7206 McNeil, Keith, and Rusty McNeil, eds. *California Songbook with Historical Commentary* (6–10). Illus. 2001, WEM Records $15.95 (1-878360-27-2). Music, chords, lyrics, and background information are given for a large selection of songs that originated in California. (Rev: BL 8/01) [782.42]

7207 McNeil, Keith, and Rusty McNeil. *Moving West Songbook: With Historical Commentary* (7–10). Illus. 2003, WEM Records $15.95 (1-878360-30-2). Historical information, anecdotes, illustrations, and guitar chords accompany this large-format selection of about 50 songs of the early to mid-19th century. (Rev: BL 7/03; SLJ 11/03) [782.42]

7208 Sandburg, Carl. *The American Songbag* (7–12). Illus. 1970, Harcourt paper $24.00 (0-15-605650-X). A fine collection of all kinds of American folk songs with music and background notes from Mr. Sandburg. [784.7]

7209 Seeger, Pete. *The Incompleat Folksinger* (9–12). 1992, Univ. of Nebraska Pr. paper $16.95 (0-8032-9216-3). This is a handbook on folksongs and folk music in the United States. Also use *American Favorite Ballads* (1981). [781.7]

7210 Turner, Steve. *Amazing Grace: The Story of America's Most Beloved Song* (10–12). Illus. 2002, HarperCollins $23.95 (0-06-000218-2). Turner, a music historian, traces the song's evolution from the hymn written by an 18th-century English minister. (Rev: BL 11/1/02) [264]

Theater, Dance, and Other Performing Arts

Dance (Ballet, Modern, etc.)

7211 Balanchine, George, and Francis Mason. *101 Stories of the Great Ballets* (7–12). 1975, Doubleday paper $16.00 (0-385-03398-2). Both the classics and newer ballets are introduced plus general background material such as a brief history of ballet. [792.8]

7212 Haskins, Jim. *Black Dance in America: A History Through Its People* (7–12). 1990, HarperCollins LB $14.89 (0-690-04659-6). Beginning with the dances brought from Africa by the slaves, this history moves to the present with the contributions of such people as Gregory Hines and Alvin Ailey. (Rev: BL 8/90; SLJ 6/90; VOYA 6/90) [792.8]

7213 Heth, Charlotte, ed. *Native American Dance: Ceremonies and Social Traditions* (9–12). 1993, Starwood paper $29.95 (1-56373-021-9). Celebrates Indian dance ceremonies and social traditions, past and present, throughout the Americas. Color photographs. (Rev: BL 4/1/93*) [394.3]

7214 Horosko, Marian, ed. *Martha Graham: The Evolution of Her Dance Theory and Training, 1926–1991* (9–12). 1992, Chicago Review $29.95 (1-55652-142-1). Recollections by dancers and actors that provide insight into the development of Graham's training theories and methods. (Rev: BL 12/15/91) [792.8]

7215 Pilobolus. *Twisted Yoga* (8–12). Photos by John Kane. 2002, North-South $9.95 (1-58717-136-8). Members of the Pilobolus Dance Theatre pose in eye-catching, contortionist positions. (Rev: SLJ 8/02) [792.8]

7216 Roseman, Janet Lynn. *Dance Masters: Interviews with Legends of Dance* (10–12). Illus. 2001, Routledge $65.00 (0-415-92951-2); paper $20.95 (0-415-92952-0). Fans of contemporary dance will

be interested in these seven conversations with such dancers and choreographers as Mark Morris, Merce Cunningham, and Edward Villella. (Rev: BL 5/1/01) [792.8]

7217 Sonnenfeld, Sandi. *This Is How I Speak: The Diary of a Young Woman* (10–12). 2002, Impassio paper $15.00 (0-9711583-1-2). A year in the life of a graduate dance student at the University of Washington; includes social and academic issues, plus an attack by a friend's boyfriend. (Rev: BL 6/1–15/02) [818]

Motion Pictures

7218 Adamson, Joe. *The Bugs Bunny Golden Jubilee: 50 Years of America's Favorite Rabbit* (9–12). Illus. 1990, Holt $35.00 (0-8050-1190-0). An oversize book that is a profusely illustrated tribute to the life and times of this fabulous rabbit. (Rev: BL 2/15/90; SLJ 12/90) [741.5]

7219 *Amistad: "Give us Free": A Celebration of the Film by Steven Spielberg* (9–12). Illus. 1998, Newmarket paper $27.50 (1-55704-351-5). After reviewing the *Amistad* insurrection, this book focuses on the casting, producing, and shooting of the film. (Rev: SLJ 12/98) [791.43]

7220 Beck, Jerry. *"I Tawt I Taw a Puddy Tat": Fifty Years of Sylvester and Tweety* (9–12). 1991, Holt $35.00 (0-8050-1644-9). A tribute to Sylvester and Tweety on their 50th birthdays. Includes over 300 color-frame enlargements, cels, storyboards, and animation drawings. (Rev: BL 1/1/92) [741.5]

7221 Bergan, Ronald. *The Coen Brothers* (10–12). 2000, Thunder's Mouth $14.95 (1-56025-254-5). This is an in-depth look at the offbeat Coen brothers, Joel and Ethan, and a probing analysis of their films made prior to 2000, including *Fargo.* (Rev: BL 11/15/00) [791.43]

7222 Brackett, Leigh, and Lawrence Kasdan. *The Empire Strikes Back: The Illustrated Screenplay* (8–12). 1998, Ballantine paper $12.00 (0-345-42070-5). The shooting script for the second of the original *Star Wars* trilogy, with action direction and drawings of action scenes, preceded by an introduction that includes background and thoughts about the movie trilogy from the perspectives of people who were involved with the first release of the films. (Rev: SLJ 12/98) [791.43]

7223 Burtt, Ben. *Star Wars Galactic Phrase Book and Travel Guide: Beeps, Bleats, and Other Common Intergalactic Verbiage* (7–12). Illus. 2001, Ballantine $8.00 (0-345-44074-9). A small-format, travel guide/phrase book that will fascinate devotees of Star Wars. (Rev: SLJ 12/01; VOYA 6/02) [791.43]

7224 Cavelos, Jeanne. *The Science of Star Wars* (9–12). 1999, St. Martin's $22.95 (0-312-20958-4). An astrophysicist and mathematician examines the actual science in the *Star Wars* films and finds that in the two decades since the debut of *Star Wars: A New Hope,* George Lucas's fictional universe has come much closer to reality. (Rev: SLJ 7/99) [791.43]

7225 Cowie, Peter, ed. *World Cinema: Diary of a Day* (9–12). 1995, Overlook $29.95 (0-87951-573-2). An overview of filmmaking, with input from directors, producers, technicians, and performers. (Rev: BL 3/15/95) [791.43]

7226 Ebert, Roger, and Gene Siskel. *The Future of the Movies* (9–12). 1991, Andrews & McMeel paper $9.95 (0-8362-6216-6). Interviews and discussions of cinema craft with three influential American filmmakers: Martin Scorsese, Steven Spielberg, and George Lucas. (Rev: BL 9/1/91) [791.43]

7227 Finch, Christopher. *The Art of the Lion King* (9–12). 1994, Hyperion $50.00 (0-7868-6028-6). Describes the making of the Disney film, including hundreds of production stills, sketches, animation drawings, and background paintings. (Rev: BL 9/1/94) [741.5]

7228 Flynn, John L. *The Films of Arnold Schwarzenegger* (9–12). 1993, Citadel paper $17.95 (0-8065-1423-X). Schwarzenegger's films, from *Hercules in New York* to his most recent, are given a critical look, with behind-the-scenes glimpses of the actor. (Rev: BL 11/1/93) [791.43]

7229 Hemming, Roy. *The Melody Lingers On: The Great Songwriters and Their Movie Musicals* (9–12). 1999, Newmarket paper $24.95 (1-55704-380-9). A look at the great Hollywood musicals that featured songs and lyrics of 10 great writers, including Berlin, Gershwin, Kern, Porter, and Rogers. (Rev: SLJ 8/99) [791.43]

7230 Holden, Anthony. *Behind the Oscar: The Secret History of the Academy Awards* (9–12). 1994, NAL paper $16.95 (0-452-27131-2). Facts and statistics about the Oscar and the Academy Awards show, as well as backstage gossip. (Rev: BL 3/15/93; SLJ 2/94) [791.43]

7231 *James Cameron's Titanic* (6–12). Illus. 1997, HarperCollins $50.00 (0-06-757516-1); paper $20.00 (0-00-649060-3). A behind-the-scenes look at the creation of this blockbuster movie, with material and pictures on subjects including set design, costuming, and digital imaging. (Rev: VOYA 8/98) [791.43]

7232 Jenkins, Robert. *Life Signs: The Biology of Star Trek* (9–12). 1998, HarperCollins $22.00 (0-06-019154-6). The authors, both medical researchers, use incidents and characters from *Star Trek* to speculate on such possible fascinating science developments as interspecies mating, gene manipulation, and increased use of the senses. (Rev: BL 5/15/98; VOYA 10/98) [791.43]

7233 Johnson, Shane. *Technical Star Wars Journal* (7–12). Illus. 1995, Del Rey $35.00 (0-345-40182-4). An intriguing look at the ships, droids, armor, and appliances that were developed for and featured in the original *Star Wars* trilogy. (Rev: VOYA 4/96) [791.43]

7234 Jones, Sarah. *Film* (7–10). Illus. Series: MediaWise. 2003, Smart Apple LB $28.50 (1-58340-256-X). The world of film making is clearly explained, with information on everything from initial concept to financing to the mechanics of production. (Rev: BL 10/15/03; SLJ 11/03) [791.43]

7235 Kasdan, Lawrence, and George Lucas. *Return of the Jedi: The Illustrated Screenplay* (8–12). 1998, Ballantine paper $12.00 (0-345-42079-9). The third of the original *Star Wars* trilogy is featured, with the screenplay, background information, and drawings of action scenes from the film. (Rev: SLJ 12/98) [791.43]

7236 Kerr, Walter. *The Silent Clowns* (10–12). Illus. 1975, Da Capo paper $19.95 (0-306-80387-9). A series of sketches about the great comedians who flourished during the days of silent film. [791.43]

7237 King, Emily. *A Century of Movie Posters: From Silent to Art House* (10–12). Illus. 2003, Barron's $39.95 (0-7641-5599-7). Hundreds of posters, in chronological and style groupings, are introduced by commentary. (Rev: BL 11/15/03) [791.43]

7238 Koenig, David. *Mouse Under Glass: Secrets of Disney Animation and Theme Parks* (10–12). 1997, Bonaventure $23.95 (0-9640605-0-7). This is a chronological overview of Disney's 30 films, from "Snow White" through "The Hunchback of Notre Dame," giving background information (but no pictures) about each. (Rev: BL 1/1–15/97; SLJ 11/97) [791.43]

7239 Laverty, Paul. *Sweet Sixteen* (9–12). 2003, ScreenPress paper $9.95 (1-901680-67-3). This prize-winning screenplay relates the struggles of a Scottish teenager to escape a dysfunctional family environment and to create for his mother, sister, and nephew an idyllic life, safe from abuse. (Rev: BL 7/03) [302.7]

7240 Margulies, Edward, and Stephen Rebello. *Bad Movies We Love* (9–12). 1993, NAL paper $12.00 (0-452-27005-7). A compendium of movies so bad that they are entertaining. (Rev: BL 7/93) [791.43]

7241 Mast, Gerald. *A Short History of the Movies.* 6th ed. (8–12). Illus. 1992, Macmillan $35.00 (0-02-580510-X). A lavishly illustrated history that deals with both the creative and technical aspects of movie history. (Rev: BL 1/15/87) [791.43]

7242 Merritt, Russell, and J. B. Kaufman. *Walt in Wonderland: The Silent Films of Walt Disney* (9–12). 1994, Johns Hopkins Univ. Pr. $39.95 (0-8018-4907-1). Profiles Disney films of the 1920s, showing how they laid the foundation for later animation techniques and conventions. (Rev: BL 9/1/94) [791.43]

7243 Morgan, David. *Knowing the Score: Film Composers Talk About the Art, Craft, Blood, Sweat, and Tears of Writing for Cinema* (10–12). Illus. 2001, HarperCollins paper $14.00 (0-380-80482-4). Sixteen composers of movie scores, including Philip Glass, Elmer Bernstein, and Bernard Herrmann, talk about their art, its problems, and its satisfactions. (Rev: BL 1/1–15/01) [781.5]

7244 Nowell-Smith, Geoffrey, ed. *The Oxford History of World Cinema* (10–12). 1996, Oxford $79.95 (0-19-811257-2). This is a fine resource on world cinema that highlights major figures and their contributions. (Rev: SLJ 4/97) [791.43]

7245 Osborne, Robert A. *75 Years of the Oscar: The Official History of the Academy Awards* (8–12). 2003, Abbeville $75.00 (0-7892-0787-7). A history of the Oscars through 2003, with asides about the ceremonies, winners, nominees, and the Academy of Motion Picture Arts and Sciences. [791.43]

7246 Plympton, Bill. *Hair High* (10–12). Illus. 2003, NBM paper $10.95 (1-56163-354-2). Mature teens will enjoy this sneak peek at animated filmmaker Plympton's film of the same name, told here in storyboard form. (Rev: BL 6/1–15/03) [741.5]

7247 Richards, Andrea. *Girl Director: A How-to Guide for the First-Time Flat-Broke Film Maker (and Video Maker)* (7–12). 2001, Alloy $17.95 (1-9314-9700-1). Technical tips, inspiration, and instruction for would-be directors, with plenty of illustrations and other graphic elements. (Rev: BL 11/1/01; VOYA 6/01) [791.43]

7248 Salisbury, Mark. *Planet of the Apes: Re-Imagined by Tim Burton* (6–12). Illus. 2001, Newmarket $32.95 (1-55704-487-2); paper $22.95 (1-55704-

486-4). A richly illustrated look behind the scenes at film director Tim Burton's recent remake of *The Planet of the Apes.* (Rev: VOYA 2/02)

7249 Sanello, Frank. *Reel v. Real: How Hollywood Turns Fact into Fiction* (10–12). Illus. 2003, Taylor paper $19.95 (0-87833-268-5). Sanello takes filmmakers to task for the ways in which they distort historical reality in the processing of transferring it to the screen. (Rev: BL 12/15/02) [791.43]

7250 Sansweet, Stephen J. *Star Wars Encyclopedia* (9–12). 1998, Ballantine $49.95 (0-345-40227-8). Made for browsing, this is an exhaustive, alphabetically arranged collection of data about *Star Wars* — characters, memorabilia, weapons, movies, books, toys, and planets. (Rev: SLJ 12/98) [791.43]

7251 Sauter, Michael. *The Worst Movies of All Time; or, What Were They Thinking?* (9–12). 1995, Citadel paper $14.95 (0-8065-1577-5). A delight in chronicling bad movies motivates this book, with a look at some behind-the-scenes craziness. (Rev: BL 11/15/95) [791.43]

7252 Shipman, David. *A Pictorial History of Science Fiction Films* (8–12). Illus. 1986, Salem House $17.95 (0-600-38520-5). From the French 19th-century efforts to today's works by Lucas and Spielberg, this is a heavily illustrated account of science fiction and fantasy movies. (Rev: BL 2/15/86) [791.435]

7253 Sklar, Robert. *A World History of Film.* Rev. ed. (8–12). 2002, Abrams $75.00 (0-8109-0606-6). An excellent history of movies from the magic lantern to today's blockbusters is found in this well-illustrated volume. (Rev: BL 2/1/02) [791.43]

7254 Smith, Marisa, and Amy Schewel, eds. *The Actor's Book of Movie Monologues* (9–12). 1986, Penguin paper $12.95 (0-14-009475-X). A collection of 80 monologues starting with *M* and ending with *The Breakfast Club.* (Rev: BL 11/1/86) [791.43]

7255 Solomon, Charles. *The Disney That Never Was: The Stories and Art from Five Decades of Unproduced Animation* (9–12). 1995, Hyperion $40.00 (0-7868-6037-5). The Disney projects that were abandoned, accompanied by many illustrations, concept art, and animation drawings. (Rev: BL 12/1/95) [741.5]

7256 Thomas, Bob. *Disney's Art of Animation: From Mickey Mouse to Beauty and the Beast* (9–12). 1991, Hyperion $39.95 (1-56282-997-1). An update of the 1958 book, written with the cooperation of the Disney studio, chronicling the history of Disney animation using art from studio archives. (Rev: BL 11/1/91; SLJ 3/92) [741.5]

7257 Wallace, Daniel. *Star Wars: The Essential Guide to Planets and Moons* (6–12). Illus. 1998, Del Rey paper $19.95 (0-345-42068-3). This volume provides fascinating information on 110 different planets and moons in the *Star Wars* universe, arranged alphabetically from Abregado-rae, a popular stop for smugglers, to Zhar, a gas-filled giant, covering each world's inhabitants, climate, language, points of interest, and history. (Rev: VOYA 6/99) [791.45]

7258 Winfrey, Oprah. *Journey to Beloved* (10–12). 1998, Hyperion $40.00 (0-7868-6458-3). This is the diary Oprah Winfrey kept during the filming of Toni Morrison's *Beloved,* in which she writes about her fears and insecurities as an actress, the emotions she felt in dealing with the subject matter, and the pull of outside events. (Rev: SLJ 2/99) [791.43]

7259 Wright, Bruce Lanier. *Yesterday's Tomorrows: The Golden Age of Science Fiction Movie Posters, 1950–1964* (9–12). 1993, Taylor $29.95 (0-87833-818-7); paper $19.95 (0-87833-824-1). Nearly 100 color posters for vintage sci-fi movies, accompanied by mini-essays on each film and a guide for collectors. (Rev: BL 5/1/93) [791.43]

Radio, Television, and Video

7260 Borgenicht, David. *Sesame Street Unpaved: Scripts, Stories, Secrets, and Songs* (9–12). 1998, Hyperion $24.95 (0-7868-6460-5). The author reveals the behind-the-scenes secrets of the successful 30-year-old public television program in this book, which includes many illustrations and stories about the characters and activities that have made *Sesame Street* a cultural icon. (Rev: SLJ 3/99) [791.45]

7261 Cader, Michael, ed. *Saturday Night Live: The First Twenty Years* (9–12). 1994, Houghton $25.00 (0-395-70895-8). Celebrates the 20th anniversary of the TV show *Saturday Night Live,* with photographs and descriptions of many sketches. (Rev: BL 9/1/94; SLJ 3/95) [791.4572]

7262 Cartwright, Nancy. *My Life as a 10-Year-Old Boy* (9–12). Illus. 2000, Hyperion $19.95 (0-7868-6696-9). The author, who is the voice of Bart Simpson of "The Simpsons," presents a candid insider's look at this popular television program. (Rev: BL 9/15/00) [791.45]

7263 Catalano, Grace. *Meet the Stars of Dawson's Creek* (6–10). 1998, Bantam paper $4.99 (0-440-22821-2). This book describes how the *Dawson's Creek* television show was developed, profiles its stars and creator/producer, and summarizes the first six episodes. (Rev: VOYA 12/98) [791.45]

7264 Cavelos, Jeanne. *The Science of The X-Files* (8–12). 1998, Berkley paper $12.95 (0-425-16711-9). Combining pop culture and hard science, this book analyzes specific episodes of the *X-Files* from a scientific perspective. (Rev: VOYA 4/99) [791.45]

7265 Johnson, Hillary, and Nancy Rommelmann. *The Real Real World* (9–12). Illus. 1995, Pocket paper $16.00 (0-671-54525-6). This book chronicles the first four seasons of MTV's popular *Real World* program, with lots of pictures and an episode-by-episode synopsis. (Rev: VOYA 6/96) [791.45]

7266 Kerbel, Matthew R. *If It Bleeds, It Leads: An Anatomy of Television News* (10–12). 2000, Westview $25.00 (0-8133-6836-7). A frank explanation of how television talk and news shows—from Jerry Springer and Ricky Lane to Dan Rather and Tom Brokaw—are produced. (Rev: BL 2/15/00; SLJ 5/01) [070.1]

7267 Killick, Jane. *Babylon 5: The Coming of Shadows* (7–12). 1998, Ballantine paper $11.00 (0-345-42448-4). This is the second of a five-volume guide to this popular television series. (Rev: VOYA 12/98) [791.45]

7268 Kraus, Lawrence M. *The Physics of Star Trek* (7–12). Illus. 1996, HarperPerennial paper $13.00 (0-06-097710-8). Warp, transporter beams, antimatter, and other scientific concepts popularized in the TV series are examined, with speculations on their possible application in the future. (Rev: VOYA 8/97) [791.45]

7269 Lackman, Ron. *Same Time . . . Same Station: An A to Z Guide to Radio from Jack Benny to Howard Stern* (10–12). 1996, Facts on File $45.00 (0-8160-2862-1). A history of radio as a source of both news and entertainment, covering hundreds of old radio shows and their stars. (Rev: SLJ 4/96) [791.44]

7270 Lommel, Cookie. *African Americans in Film and Television* (7–12). Series: American Mosaic. 2003, Chelsea LB $22.95 (0-7910-7268-1). The history of the struggle of African Americans to be accepted in films and television and their position in these media today. (Rev: BL 10/15/03; HBG 10/03) [791.45]

7271 Okuda, Michael, and Denise Okuda. *Star Trek Chronology: The History of the Future* (10–12). 1996, Pocket paper $25.00 (0-671-53610-9). Using over 1,000 color photographs and exhaustive coverage, this is a guide to all four of the *Star Trek* TV series as well as the motion pictures. (Rev: SLJ 5/97) [384.55]

7272 Owen, Rob. *Gen X TV: The Brady Bunch to Melrose Place* (10–12). 1997, Syracuse Univ. Pr. $29.95 (0-8156-0443-2). A history of popular television programs that shows not only how Gen Xers influenced network programming, but also how television affected their lives. (Rev: SLJ 2/98) [384.55]

7273 Perry, George. *Life of Python* (10–12). 1984, Little, Brown paper $12.95 (0-316-70015-0). A thorough rundown on the Monty Python gang and their television programs. [384.55]

7274 *Reality TV* (6–12). Ed. by Karen F. Balkin. Series: At Issue. 2004, Gale LB $27.45 (0-7377-2254-1). The pros and cons of reality television shows are the focus of this collection of writings. (Rev: BL 2/15/04; SLJ 7/04) [791.45]

7275 Riess, Jana. *What Would Buffy Do? The Vampire Slayer as Spiritual Guide* (7–12). 2004, Jossey-Bass paper $14.00 (0-7879-6922-2). For fans of the TV series, this is a guide to the first seven seasons with material on the show's values and characters. (Rev: BL 5/1/04) [791.45]

7276 Ritchie, Michael. *Please Stand By: A Prehistory of Television* (9–12). 1994, Overlook $23.95 (0-87951-546-5). The story of television before 1948, chronicling the technological struggles and advances during the medium's infancy. (Rev: BL 9/15/94; SLJ 5/95) [791.45]

7277 Shales, Tom, and James Andrew Miller. *Live from New York: An Uncensored History of Saturday Night Live* (10–12). Illus. 2002, Little, Brown $25.95 (0-316-78146-0). A collection of revealing behind-the-scenes memories from the show's stars, producers, writers, guest hosts, and staffers. (Rev: BL 10/1/02) [791.45]

7278 Solow, Herbert F., and Robert H. Justman. *Inside Star Trek: The Real Story* (10–12). 1996, Pocket $30.00 (0-671-89628-8). A behind-the-scenes look at the phenomenal original *Star Trek* TV series that reveals how it was conceived, the obstacles to production such as personality conflicts, production difficulties, battles with NBC executives, etc., and reasons for its success. (Rev: SLJ 6/97) [791.45]

7279 Stone, Brad. *Gearheads: The Turbulent Rise of Robotic Sports* (10–12). 2003, Simon & Schuster $23.00 (0-7432-2951-7). An insider's look at the phenomenon of robotic combat and its popularity with American television viewers. (Rev: BL 2/15/03) [796.15]

7280 Wallner, Rosemary. *Fresh Prince of Bel-Air: The History of the Future* (7–10). 1992, ABDO LB $18.48 (1-56239-140-2). The story behind the TV series, now in reruns, that made a star of Will Smith. (Rev: BL 3/1/93; SLJ 11/93) [791.45]

Recordings

7281 Early, Gerald. *One Nation Under a Groove: Motown and American Culture* (9–12). 1995, Ecco $17.00 (0-88001-379-6). The history of the African American record company Motown and how it brought rhythm and blues into the mainstream. (Rev: BL 6/1–15/95) [306.4]

Theater and Other Dramatic Forms

7282 Alberts, David. *Talking About Mime: An Illustrated Guide* (9–12). 1994, Heinemann paper $14.95 (0-435-08641-3). Instructions for learning mime fundamentals and performance, including specific exercises and a short history of the art. (Rev: BL 11/1/94) [792.3]

7283 Bone, Howard, and Daniel Waldron. *Side Show: My Life with Geeks, Freaks and Vagabonds in the Carny Trade* (9–12). Illus. 2001, Sun Dog paper $12.95 (0-941543-28-5). This is the sometimes sordid, sometimes hilarious story of a traveling carnival, with its freaks, frauds, and tricks. (Rev: BL 5/15/01) [791.3]

7284 Brown, John Russell, ed. *The Oxford Illustrated History of Theatre* (9–12). 1995, Oxford $35.00 (0-19-212997-X). A well-written general history of the theater, in the form of connected essays, that avoids the usual Eurocentric approach. (Rev: BL 11/1/95; SLJ 3/96) [792]

7285 Caruso, Sandra, and Susan Kosoff. *The Young Actor's Book of Improvisation: Dramatic Situations from Shakespeare to Spielberg: Ages 12–16* (6–12). 1998, Heinemann paper $22.95 (0-325-00049-2). This work supplies hundreds of situations suitable for improvisation culled from all forms of literature, plays, and movie scripts, arranged by themes such as confrontation and relationships. (Rev: BL 9/15/98; SLJ 1/99) [793]

7286 Cassady, Marsh. *The Theatre and You: A Beginning* (9–12). 1992, Meriwether paper $15.95 (0-916260-83-6). A comprehensive introduction to theater as a performing art and craft, outlining five broad areas of study: theaters and stages, directing, design, acting, and theater history. (Rev: BL 11/1/92) [792]

7287 Currie, Stephen. *An Actor on the Elizabethan Stage* (7–10). Illus. 2003, Gale LB $27.45 (1-59018-174-3). An entertaining look at the Elizabethan theater and the skills that the all-male actors required. (Rev: SLJ 11/03) [792]

7288 Currie, Stephen. *Life in a Wild West Show* (6–10). Series: The Way People Live. 1998, Lucent LB $27.45 (1-56006-352-1). Personal struggles, individual jobs, and daily routines are stressed in this account of traveling shows that depicted life on the wild American frontier. (Rev: BL 11/15/98) [791.8]

7289 Curtis, Susan. *The First Black Actors on the Great White Way* (10–12). Illus. 1998, Univ. of Missouri Pr. paper $29.95 (0-8262-1195-X). A well-researched account of Broadway's first serious play starring African Americans, which opened to critical acclaim in 1917 but ultimately failed to open New York theater to blacks; of particular interest to high school history and drama students. (Rev: BL 12/1/98) [792]

7290 Cushman, Kathleen, and Montana Miller. *Circus Dreams* (6–12). Illus. 1990, Little, Brown $15.95 (0-316-16561-1). A look at the professional college for circus artists in France, following the experiences of one of its students. (Rev: BL 1/15/91; SLJ 1/91) [791.3]

7291 Frantz, Donald. *Beauty and the Beast: A Celebration of the Broadway Musical* (9–12). 1995, Hyperion $35.00 (0-7868-6179-7). Production photographs from the stage production, plus behind-the-scenes information. (Rev: BL 12/15/95) [782.1]

7292 Grote, David. *Staging the Musical: Planning, Rehearsing, and Marketing the Amateur Production* (10–12). 1986, Simon & Schuster $10.95 (0-13-840182-9). An excellent guide for anyone involved in amateur theatrics with tips on such topics as scenery, costumes, and sound. (Rev: BL 4/15/86) [782.81]

7293 Halpern, Charna, et al. *Truth in Comedy: The Manual for Improvisation* (9–12). 1994, Meriwether paper $16.95 (1-56608-003-7). A thorough manual of comedic improvisation by three improv gurus. (Rev: BL 4/15/94) [792]

7294 Haskins, Jim, and Kathleen Benson. *Conjure Times: Black Magicians in America* (6–12). Illus. 2001, Walker LB $17.85 (0-8027-8763-0). The authors explore the substantial contributions of black performers to the early theater in America. (Rev: BL 7/01; HBG 3/02; SLJ 11/01; VOYA 4/02) [793.8]

7295 Kipnis, Claude. *The Mime Book* (7–12). Illus. 1988, Meriwether paper $16.95 (0-916260-55-0). One of the world's greatest mimes explains what it is and how it is done. [792.3]

7296 Lee, Robert L. *Everything About Theatre! The Guidebook of Theatre Fundamentals* (7–12). Illus. 1996, Meriwether paper $19.95 (1-56608-019-3). This excellent introduction to the backstage world includes material ranging from theater history to stagecraft, acting, and play production. (Rev: BL 12/1/96; SLJ 2/97) [792]

7297 McCullough, L. E. *Anyone Can Produce Plays with Kids: The Absolute Basics of Staging Your Own At-Home, In-School, Round-the-Neighborhood Plays* (9–12). Illus. Series: Young Actors. 1998, Smith & Kraus $14.95 (1-57525-151-1). McCullough offers solid advice on all aspects of staging plays — choosing the script, set construction, publicity, and so forth. (Rev: BL 2/1/99) [792]

7298 Nevraumont, Edward J., et al. *The Ultimate Improv: A Complete Guide to Comedy Improvisation* (9–12). Illus. 2001, Meriwether paper $16.95 (1-56608-075-4). This guide explores the arena of comedic improvisation and offers step-by-step advice to help interested students create well-rounded skits. (Rev: BL 2/15/02) [792.7]

7299 Patinkin, Sheldon, et al. *The Second City: Backstage at the World's Greatest Comedy Theater* (10–12). Illus. 2000, Sourcebooks $45.00 (1-57071-561-0). This is a history of Chicago's great improvisational theater group that included many "Saturday Night Live" cast members. (Rev: BL 10/15/00) [792.7]

7300 Schindler, George. *Ventriloquism: Magic with Your Voice* (8–12). Illus. 1986, McKay paper $6.95 (0-679-14127-8). This book not only explains how to throw one's voice but also gives material on stage techniques, kinds of puppet figures, and writing routines. [793.8]

7301 Stevens, Chambers. *Sensational Scenes for Teens: The Scene Studyguide for Teen Actors!* (7–10). Illus. Series: Hollywood 101. 2001, Sandcastle paper $14.95 (1-883995-10-8). Acting coach Stevens includes more than 30 scenes — both comedy and drama — suitable for two teen actors, with choices for boy-girl, boy-boy, and girl-girl combinations. (Rev: BL 5/15/01; SLJ 4/01) [812.6]

7302 Stolzenberg, Mark. *Be a Clown!* (7–12). Illus. 1989, Sterling paper $10.95 (0-8069-5804-9). A how-to manual that describes how to create a clown character and supplies a number of routines. (Rev: BL 1/1/90) [791.3]

7303 Straub, Cindie, and Matthew Straub. *Mime: Basics for Beginners* (7–12). Illus. 1984, Plays paper $13.95 (0-8238-0263-9). The fundamentals of traditional mime are explained in text, line drawings, and photographs. (Rev: BL 2/1/85) [792.3]

7304 Trussler, Simon. *The Cambridge Illustrated History of British Theatre* (9–12). 1994, Cambridge Univ. Pr. $39.95 (0-521-41913-1). A historical overview of British theater. (Rev: BL 3/1/95) [792]

History and Geography

General History and Geography

Atlases, Maps, and Mapmaking

7305 Jouris, David. *All over the Map: An Extraordinary Atlas of the United States* (8–10). 1994, Ten Speed paper $11.95 (0-89815-649-1). A U.S. atlas that explores the history of the names of towns and cities, including such places as Peculiar, Ding Dong, Vendor, and Joy. (Rev: BL 7/94) [910]

7306 Pratt, Paula B. *Maps: Plotting Places on the Globe* (6–10). Series: Encyclopedia of Discovery and Invention. 1995, Lucent LB $52.44 (1-56006-255-X). Traces the evolution of mapmaking/cartography from ancient times to the present. (Rev: BL 4/15/95; SLJ 3/95) [912]

7307 Ross, Val. *The Road to There: Mapmakers and Their Stories* (7–10). Illus. 2003, Tundra $19.95 (0-88776-621-8). Mapmakers of different eras and nationalities, well-known figures such as Henry the Navigator and less familiar individuals, and the charts they created are featured in this interesting volume with period illustrations and many maps. (Rev: BCCB 1/04; BL 12/15/03; HBG 4/04; SLJ 12/03*) [912]

7308 Whitfield, Peter. *The Image of the World: 20 Centuries of World Maps* (9–12). 1994, Pomegranate $35.00 (0-87654-080-9). Covers the important names in the history of world cartography. Includes 70 maps from the Middle Ages, the age of discovery, and modern times. (Rev: BL 11/15/94*) [912]

7309 Young, Karen Romano. *Small Worlds: Maps and Mapmaking* (7–12). 2002, Scholastic $17.95 (0-439-09545-X). Maps of all kinds — from airport diagrams and neighborhood plans to a full globe and a chart of the universe — are introduced with many illustrations and historical and scientific explanations. (Rev: SLJ 6/03) [912]

Paleontology

7310 Arduini, Paolo, and Giorgio Teruzzi. *Simon and Schuster's Guide to Fossils* (9–12). Illus. 1987, Simon & Schuster paper $14.00 (0-671-63132-2). In addition to a detailed description of the science of paleontology, this account, through photographs and text, identifies particular fossils and gives hints on how to collect them. (Rev: BL 5/1/87) [560.9]

7311 Barrett, Paul. *National Geographic Dinosaurs* (6–10). Illus. 2001, National Geographic $29.95 (0-7922-8224-8). This comprehensive and attractive guide provides a wealth of information about dinosaurs, their timeframe and evolution, individual species, and eventual extinction, with maps, fact boxes, and graphics. (Rev: BL 7/01; SLJ 10/01) [567.9]

7312 Cadbury, Deborah. *Terrible Lizard: The First Dinosaur Hunters and the Birth of a New Science* (10–12). 2001, Holt $27.50 (0-8050-6772-8). For dinosaur enthusiasts, this is the story of the first fossil-hunters and their troubles, including being challenged by religious authorities. (Rev: BL 5/15/01) [560]

7313 Chiappe, Luis M., and Lowell Dingus. *Walking on Eggs: The Astonishing Discovery of Thousands of Dinosaur Eggs in the Badlands of Patagonia* (10–12). Illus. 2001, Scribner $25.00 (0-7432-1211-8). For advanced students, this is an account of the discovery of dinosaur eggs in Argentina's Patagonia region and of the significance of this discovery. (Rev: BL 6/1–15/01) [567.9]

7314 Clark, Neil, and William Lindsay. *1001 Facts About Dinosaurs* (7–12). Series: Backpack Books. 2002, DK paper $8.95 (0-7894-8448-X). Lively prose and more than 500 colorful illustrations present basic facts about various kinds of dinosaurs. (Rev: BL 3/15/02) [567.9]

7315 Clinton, Susan. *Reading Between the Bones: The Pioneers of Dinosaur Paleontology* (6–10).

Series: Lives in Science. 1997, Watts LB $25.00 (0-531-11324-8). The lives and work of eight major scientists involved in dinosaur paleontology are profiled in this carefully documented book. (Rev: BL 5/1/97; SLJ 6/97; VOYA 12/97) [560]

7316 Cohen, Claudine. *The Fate of the Mammoth: Fossils, Myth, and History* (10–12). Trans. by William Rodarmor. Illus. 2002, Univ. of Chicago Pr. $30.00 (0-226-11292-6). Drawing on what has been learned from cave drawings, fossils, and frozen remains, paleontologist Stephen Jay Gould provides a comprehensive and well-illustrated overview of the mammoth. (Rev: BL 4/15/02) [569]

7317 Currie, Philip, and Kevin Padian, eds. *Encyclopedia of Dinosaurs* (8–12). Illus. 1997, Academic $116.95 (0-12-226810-5). An adult reference book, written by scientists, with interesting, alphabetically arranged articles on dinosaurs, digs, and sites. (Rev: BL 11/1/97; SLJ 5/98) [567.9]

7318 Debus, Allen A., and Diane E. Debus. *Paleoimagery: The Evolution of Dinosaurs in Art* (10–12). Illus. 2003, McFarland $49.95 (0-7864-1222-4). Plentiful black-and-white illustrations add to the interest of this study of the blend of scientific speculation and creative artistry that goes into artists' renderings of dinosaurs. (Rev: BL 12/1/02) [567.9]

7319 DeCourten, Frank. *Dinosaurs of Utah* (10–12). Illus. 1998, Univ. of Utah Pr. $45.00 (0-87480-556-2). Beautifully illustrated, this is nevertheless a serious, information-packed volume suitable for classroom use. (Rev: BL 12/1/98) [567.9]

7320 Fiffer, Steve. *Tyrannosaurus Sue: The Extraordinary Saga of the Largest, Most Fought over T. Rex Ever Found* (10–12). 2000, W. H. Freeman paper $14.95 (0-7167-9462-4). This is the story of the discovery in 1990 of the largest Tyrannosaurus rex ever excavated and of the struggles and intrigues it produced. [567.9]

7321 Fortey, Richard. *Trilobite! Eyewitness to Evolution* (10–12). Illus. 2000, Knopf $26.00 (0-375-40625-5). An engrossing history of the study of trilobite fossils, which has helped to clarify evolution and supply details on continental drift. (Rev: BL 10/15/00) [565.39]

7322 Gee, Henry. *A Field Guide to Dinosaurs: The Essential Handbook for Travelers in the Mesozoic* (6–12). Illus. 2003, Barron's $24.95 (0-7641-5511-3). Fact and speculation are interwoven in this guide to dinosaur species that follows the format of a field guide to birds. (Rev: BL 8/03; HBG 10/03; SLJ 9/03) [567.9]

7323 Haines, Tim. *Walking with Dinosaurs: A Natural History* (9–12). Illus. 2000, BBC Books $30.00 (0-563-38449-2). This heavily illustrated book, part of a spinoff from a TV series, tells of the life cycle of an individual dinosaur living in its prehistoric environment. (Rev: BL 3/15/00) [567.9]

7324 Haines, Tim. *Walking with Prehistoric Beasts* (9–12). Illus. 2001, DK $29.95 (0-7894-7829-3). Published as a companion to the BBC TV series of the same name, this beautifully illustrated book traces the evolution of life on Earth over the course of millions of years, looking closely at such prehistoric creatures as the mammoth, saber-toothed tiger, and early whale species. (Rev: BL 12/15/01; VOYA 6/02) [567.9]

7325 Holmes, Thom, and Laurie Holmes. *Armored, Plated, and Bone-Headed Dinosaurs: The Ankylosaurs, Stegosaurs, and Pachycephalosaurs* (6–10). Series: Dinosaur Library. 2002, Enslow LB $20.95 (0-7660-1453-3). A well-organized introduction to these dinosaurs and their adaptation of anatomical defenses, with illustrations, graphic elements, a timeline of scientific discoveries, and a glossary. (Rev: BL 8/02; HBG 10/02; SLJ 10/02) [567.915]

7326 Holmes, Thom, and Laurie Holmes. *Feathered Dinosaurs: The Origin of Birds* (6–10). Series: Dinosaur Library. 2002, Enslow LB $20.95 (0-7660-1454-1). A well-organized introduction to these dinosaurs and their relationship to today's birds, with illustrations, graphic elements, a timeline of scientific discoveries, and a glossary. (Rev: BL 8/02; HBG 10/02; SLJ 10/02) [567.9]

7327 Holmes, Thom, and Laurie Holmes. *Horned Dinosaurs: The Ceratopsians* (6–10). Series: Dinosaur Library. 2001, Enslow LB $20.95 (0-7660-1451-7). A detailed survey of psittacosaurs, protoceratopsids, and ceratopsids. Other recommended titles in this series are *Meat-Eating Dinosaurs: The Theropods* and *Peaceful Plant-Eating Dinosaurs: The Iguanodonts, Duckbills, and Other Ornithopods* (2001). (Rev: HBG 3/02; SLJ 11/01) [567.915]

7328 Lambert, David. *A Field Guide to Dinosaurs* (7–12). Illus. 1983, Avon paper $9.95 (0-380-83519-3). A well-illustrated guide to more than 340 different dinosaurs arranged by family groups. [567.9]

7329 Lambert, David. *The Ultimate Dinosaur Book* (9–12). 1993, DK $29.95 (1-56458-304-X). A handsomely illustrated survey of dinosaur anatomy and behavior, excavation and museum restoration techniques, and 55 types of dinosaur. (Rev: BL 10/15/93; SLJ 3/94) [567.9]

7330 Lanzendorf, John, et al. *Dinosaur Imagery: The Lanzendorf Collection* (9–12). Illus. 2000, Academic $49.95 (0-12-436590-6). This beautiful album contains information about and illustrations of dinosaurs from the famous collection of a great dinophile. (Rev: BL 9/15/00) [567.9]

7331 McGowan, Christopher. *T-Rex to Go* (7–12). Illus. 1999, HarperPerennial paper $14.00 (0-06-095281-4). Along with a great deal of information about dinosaurs, particularly Tyrannosaurus Rex, this fascinating book explains in great detail how to make a model of the dinosaur using chicken bones and simple tools. (Rev: VOYA 10/99) [567.9]

7332 Mitchell, W. I. T. *The Last Dinosaur Book* (9–12). Illus. 1998, Univ. of Chicago Pr. $35.00 (0-226-53204-6). In this well-researched study, Mitchell looks at our abiding interest in dinosaurs and the ways in which they appear in movies, comic strips, and earlier cultural media. (Rev: BL 11/15/98)

7333 Nardo, Don. *Dinosaurs: Unearthing the Secrets of Ancient Beasts* (6–10). Series: Encyclopedia of Discovery and Invention. 1995, Lucent LB $52.44 (1-56006-253-3). Describes dinosaurs and their habitats and highlights the dedicated men and women who have made significant discoveries about them. (Rev: BL 4/15/95) [567.9]

7334 Norell, Mark, et al. *Discovering Dinosaurs: Evolution, Extinction, and the Lessons of Prehistory.* Rev. ed. (9–12). 2000, Univ. of California Pr. paper $24.95 (0-520-22501-5). Using fine illustrations and an interesting text, this account introduces dinosaurs and explains their evolution and extinction. [567.9]

7335 Palmer, Douglas. *Fossils* (6–10). Series: Pockets. 1996, DK paper $6.95 (0-7894-0606-3). A beautifully illustrated introduction to the forces that created fossils, where they are most likely to be found, and what can be learned from them. [560]

7336 Parker, Steve. *The Practical Paleontologist* (9–12). 1991, Simon & Schuster paper $15.00 (0-671-69307-7). An overview of paleontology and how these specialists do their jobs. (Rev: BL 6/15/91) [560]

451

7337 Psihoyos, Louie, and John Knoebber. *Hunting Dinosaurs* (10–12). 1995, Random paper $23.00 (0-679-76420-8). Important figures in modern paleontology and their findings are introduced, featuring spectacular color photography. (Rev: SLJ 4/96; VOYA 4/96) [567.9]

7338 Rea, Tom. *Bone Wars: The Excavation and Celebrity of Andrew Carnegie's Dinosaur* (9–12). Illus. 2001, Univ. of Pittsburgh Pr. $25.00 (0-8229-4173-2). The discovery of dinosaur bones in Wyoming in the late 1880s began a carnival-like stampede involving museums, universities, and assorted opportunists. (Rev: BL 12/1/01) [560]

7339 Stein, Wendy. *Dinosaurs* (6–10). Series: Great Mysteries. 1994, Greenhaven $18.96 (1-56510-096-4). An introduction to dinosaurs and an examination of the various theories about their extinction. (Rev: BL 4/15/94) [567.9]

7340 Stone, Richard. *Mammoth: The Resurrection of an Ice Age Giant* (9–12). 2001, Perseus Bks. $26.00 (0-7382-0281-9). The story of a scientific team in Siberia, its discoveries of mammoths frozen since the Ice Age, and what we know about the life and death of this hairy monster. (Rev: BL 8/01) [560]

7341 Thompson, Ida. *The Audubon Society Field Guide to North American Fossils* (7–12). Illus. 1982, Knopf $19.95 (0-394-52412-8). An illustrated guide to the identification of North American fossils plus some background information on their formation. [560]

7342 Wilford, John Noble. *The Riddle of the Dinosaur* (10–12). 1986, Random paper $13.00 (0-394-74392-X). This fascinating account traces a history of paleontology in relation to dinosaurs and discusses current theories concerning their extinction. (Rev: BL 1/15/86; BR 9–10/86; SLJ 8/86; VOYA 6/86) [567.9]

Anthropology and Evolution

7343 Angela, Alberto, and Piero Angela. *The Extraordinary Story of Human Origins* (9–12). Trans. by Gabriele Tonne. 1993, Prometheus $29.95 (0-87975-803-1). A comprehensive presentation of the still-growing body of knowledge of human evolution, including interesting speculations and conflicting claims. (Rev: BL 6/1–15/93) [573.2]

7344 Berger, Lee. *In the Footsteps of Eve: The Mystery of Human Origins* (10–12). Illus. 2000, National Geographic $26.00 (0-7922-7682-5). A readable account by the paleoanthropologist who has probed human fossil bones found in South African caves. (Rev: BL 6/1–15/00) [599.93]

7345 Chatters, James C. *Ancient Encounters: Kennewick Man and the First Americans* (10–12). 2001, Simon & Schuster $26.00 (0-684-85936-X). The first part of this book is about the discovery by two college students of a 9,500-year-old skull in Kennewick, Washington, and its aftermath, and the second is a review of what physical remains we have from this period and what we can surmise about life at this time. (Rev: BL 5/15/01*) [569.9]

7346 Crump, Donald J., ed. *Giants from the Past: The Age of Mammals* (7–10). Illus. 1983, National Geographic LB $12.50 (0-87044-429-8). A description of early animals, such as the mastodon, and how they evolved during the Ice Age. [569]

7347 Darwin, Charles. *The Darwin Reader.* 2nd ed. (10–12). Ed. by Mark Ridley. 1996, Norton paper $21.30 (0-393-96967-3). The many faces of Charles Darwin are revealed in this collection of excerpts from the scientist's greatest works, including *Origin of Species.* [576.8]

7348 Davis, Wade. *Light at the Edge of the World: A Journey Through the Realm of Vanishing Cultures* (10–12). Illus. 2002, National Geographic $35.00 (0-7922-6474-6). The author, an ethnobotanist/anthropologist, recounts in evocative text and images his experiences living among indigenous peoples, describes their connections with nature, and decries the destructive behavior of the so-called civilized world. (Rev: BL 2/1/02*) [306]

7349 Gallant, Roy A. *The Origins of Life* (6–10). Series: Story of Science. 2000, Marshall Cavendish LB $19.95 (0-7614-1151-8). This prize-winning author presents a clear, attractive introduction to the beginning of life on this earth. (Rev: BL 12/15/00; HBG 10/01) [575]

7350 Gardner, Robert. *Human Evolution* (10–12). 1999, Watts $24.00 (0-531-11528-3). This work traces the past and present theories of human evolution and stages of development. (Rev: SLJ 2/00; VOYA 2/00) [599.93]

7351 Hooper, Judith. *Of Moths and Men: The Untold Story of Science and the Peppered Moth* (10–12). Illus. 2002, Norton $26.95 (0-393-05121-8). Hooper relates the story of the peppered moth and its questionable importance as a proof of evolutionary theories. (Rev: BL 8/02) [576.8]

7352 Johanson, Donald C., and Maitland Armstrong Edey. *Lucy: The Beginnings of Humankind* (10–12). 1981, Simon & Schuster paper $15.00 (0-671-72499-1). The story of the great anthropological find of bones of a hominid named Lucy who lived 3.5 million years ago. [599.93]

7353 Jones, Steve. *Darwin's Ghost: The Origin of Species Updated* (10–12). 2000, Random $25.95 (0-375-50103-7). The author explains and supports Darwin's theory of evolution and supplies contemporary examples to prove his point. (Rev: BL 4/1/00) [576.8]

7354 Lauber, Patricia. *Who Came First? New Clues to Prehistoric Americans* (5–10). Illus. 2003, National Geographic $18.95 (0-7922-8228-0). An attractive, oversized volume that encompasses anthropology, archaeology, genetics, and linguistics in its discussion of the provenance of the peoples of the Americas. (Rev: BL 7/03*; HB 7–8/03; HBG 10/03; SLJ 8/03*) [970.01]

7355 Leakey, Richard E. *The Origin of Humankind* (10–12). Series: Science Masters. 1994, Basic paper $14.95 (0-465-05313-0). This is a summary of various theories involving evolution and their similarities and differences. (Rev: BL 10/1/94) [599.93]

7356 Leakey, Richard E., and Roger Lewin. *Origins Reconsidered: In Search of What Makes Us Human* (10–12). 1992, Doubleday paper $16.95 (0-385-46792-3). Leakey and Lewin look back at what has been learned about human origins and reflect on the characteristics that distinguish humans from other, closely related primates. (Rev: SLJ 6/93) [599.93]

7357 Lewin, Roger. *Thread of Life: The Smithsonian Looks at Evolution* (9–12). Illus. 1982, Smithsonian $35.00 (0-89599-010-5). A panoramic look at evolution with more than 300 color plates on animals, plants, and fossils. [575]

7358 Mayr, Ernst. *What Evolution Is* (10–12). Illus. 2001, Basic $24.00 (0-465-04425-5). The entire evolutionary structure and its ramifications are discussed and the author concludes that Darwin's original theory has stood the test of time. (Rev: BL 12/1/01*) [576.8]

7359 National Geographic Society, eds. *Primitive Worlds: People Lost in Time* (9–12). Illus. 1973, National Geographic $8.95 (0-87044-127-2). The societies of several primitive peoples in Africa, New Guinea, and Central America are described. [306]

7360 Netzley, Patricia. *The Stone Age* (6–10). Illus. 1997, Lucent LB $27.45 (1-56006-316-5). This book describes the major epochs in the evolution of humans and the development of stone-tool technology. (Rev: BL 5/15/98; SLJ 6/98) [930.12]

7361 Schilthuizen, Menno. *Frogs, Flies, and Dandelions: The Making of Species* (10–12). Illus. 2001, Oxford $25.00 (0-19-850393-8). The author explores the world of evolution to determine if new species are appearing today and uses such species as the apple maggots of the Hudson River and the cave beetles of France to prove his theories. (Rev: BL 5/15/01) [576.8]

7362 Sloan, Christopher. *The Human Story: Our Evolution from Prehistoric Ancestors to Today* (8–12). Illus. 2004, National Geographic $19.95 (0-7922-6325-1). Using evidence from fossils and

DNA, this is the history of human evolution for a period of more than 6 million years, with recent findings on the subject. (Rev: BL 3/1/04; SLJ 3/04) [599.93]

7363 Sonder, Ben. *Evolutionism and Creationism* (8–12). Illus. 1999, Watts LB $24.00 (0-531-11416-3). A well-researched, unbiased look at the history and present status of the conflict between evolutionists and creationists. (Rev: BL 12/1/99; SLJ 1/00; VOYA 2/00) [231.7]

7364 Stefoff, Rebecca. *Charles Darwin and the Evolution Revolution* (9–12). Illus. 1996, Oxford $33.95 (0-19-508996-0). A well-illustrated account that describes Darwin's theories and their scientific, social, and political effects, with sidebars that give related information. (Rev: BL 7/96; SLJ 9/96) [575]

7365 Tattersall, Ian. *The Monkey in the Mirror: Essays on the Science of What Makes Us Human* (10–12). Illus. 2001, Harcourt $25.00 (0-15-100520-6). The eight engaging essays in this book discuss evolution and the origins of human life. (Rev: BL 9/1/01) [599.93]

7366 Thorndike, Jonathan L. *Epperson v. Arkansas: The Evolution–Creationism Debate* (6–10). Series: Landmark Supreme Court Cases. 1999, Enslow LB $20.95 (0-7660-1084-8). This book examines the issues involved in this case of evolution versus creationism, traces the case from lower courts to the Supreme Court, and discusses the present-day impact of the court's decision. (Rev: BL 3/15/99) [116]

7367 Ward, Peter. *Future Evolution* (10–12). Illus. 2001, W. H. Freeman $30.00 (0-7167-3496-6). After examining two earlier periods of mass extinction in the earth's history, the author discusses the present period and what will evolve from it. (Rev: BL 12/1/01) [576.8]

7368 Whitfield, Philip J. *Evolution* (10–12). Series: Living Universe. 2000, Gale $95.00 (0-02-865593-1). From Darwin's theory to modern generic research, this is a history of the study of evolution. (Rev: SLJ 8/01) [576.8]

7369 Zimmer, Carl. *Evolution: The Triumph of an Idea* (10–12). Illus. 2001, HarperCollins $40.00 (0-06-019906-7). Based on a PBS series, this is a fine introduction to the theory of evolution, how it was formulated, and how it explains the history of life. (Rev: BL 9/1/01) [576.8]

Archaeology

7370 Ceram, C. W. *Gods, Graves, and Scholars: The Story of Archaeology.* 2nd rev. ed. (10–12). Trans. by E. B. Garside and Sophie Wilkins. 1967, Knopf paper $14.00 (0-394-74319-9). A classic history of archaeology that tells of the Rosetta Stone, the excavations at Ur, and more. [930.1]

7371 Clapp, Nicholas. *The Road to Ubar: Finding the Atlantis of the Sands* (9–12). 1998, Houghton $24.00 (0-395-87596-X). An engrossing book about how cultural myths, historical chronicles and maps, and scientific analysis of satellite images were all applied in the recent discovery of the fabled lost city of Ubar in Oman that was supposedly destroyed by God because of its sin of greed. (Rev: BL 2/1/98; SLJ 12/98) [930]

7372 Echo-Hawk, Roger C., and Walter R. Echo-Hawk. *Battlefields and Burial Grounds: The Indian Struggle to Protect Ancestral Graves in the United States* (7–10). 1994, Lerner LB $22.60 (0-8225-2663-8); paper $8.95 (0-8225-9722-5). A solid discussion of the conflict over Indian graves that have been plundered in the name of scientific research. (Rev: BL 5/15/94; SLJ 7/94*) [393]

7373 Forte, Maurizio, and Alberto Siliotti. *Virtual Archaeology: Re-Creating Ancient Worlds* (10–12). Trans. from Italian by Judith Toms and Robin Skeates. 1997, Abrams $49.50 (0-8109-3943-6). A beautiful book that covers archaeological sites in Africa, the Near East, Europe, Asia, and the Americas. (Rev: BL 4/15/97; SLJ 1/98) [930]

7374 Hawass, Zahi. *Valley of the Golden Mummies* (10–12). Illus. 2000, Abrams $49.50 (0-8109-3942-8). This is the story of the discovery and ongoing excavation of the site at the Bahariya Oasis in Egypt where hundreds of mummies, many with golden masks, have been found. (Rev: BL 9/1/00) [932]

7375 McIntosh, Jane. *The Practical Archaeologist* (8–12). 1986, Facts on File $26.95 (0-8160-1400-0);

paper $15.95 (0-8160-1814-6). A discussion of how an archaeologist operates with particular emphasis on how sites are found and excavated. (Rev: BR 1–2/89; VOYA 10/88) [930.1]

7376 Malone, Caroline, and Nancy Stone Bernard. *Stonehenge* (7–10). Illus. Series: Digging for the Past. 2002, Oxford $19.95 (0-19-514314-0). This fascinating look at Stonehenge's history and at the work of archaeologists there over the years will attract report writers and browsers. (Rev: BL 10/15/02; HBG 10/03; SLJ 12/02) [936.2]

7377 National Geographic Society, eds. *Splendors of the Past: Lost Cities of the Ancient World* (9–12). Illus. 1981, National Geographic $19.00 (0-87044-358-5). A lavishly illustrated volume that deals with such historical sites as Pompeii, Angkor Wat, and those associated with the Hittite Empire. [930]

7378 Perring, Stefania, and Dominic Perring. *Then and Now* (9–12). 1991, Macmillan $29.95 (0-02-599461-1). Two archaeologists fabricate reconstructions of 20 famous ruins using illustrated transparent overlays and photographs, accompanied by text describing the civilizations that produced the ruins. (Rev: BL 12/15/91) [930]

7379 Pringle, Heather. *The Mummy Congress: Science, Obsession, and the Everlasting Dead* (10–12). Illus. 2001, Hyperion $23.95 (0-7868-6551-2). This is a collection of reports based on the experiences of some of the world's foremost mummy experts and their findings. (Rev: BL 6/1–15/01*) [393]

7380 Robbins, Lawrence H. *Stones, Bones, and Ancient Cities: The Greatest Archaeological Discoveries of All Time* (10–12). 1990, St. Martin's paper $10.95 (0-312-07848-X). A fascinating history of archaeology that includes stories of burial practices, lost cities, and links to human ancestors. [930.1]

7381 Scarre, Chris, and Rebecca Stefoff. *Palace of Minos at Knossos* (7–10). Series: Digging for the Past. 2002, Oxford $19.95 (0-19-514272-1). After a map and timeline, this account describes various archaeological digs at Knossos, tells how the palace was built, and gives material on the original structure. (Rev: BL 10/15/02; HBG 4/04; SLJ 2/04) [930]

7382 Scheller, William. *Amazing Archaeologists and Their Finds* (6–10). 1994, Oliver LB $19.95 (1-881508-17-X). This work presents eight archaeologists' discoveries, including the walls of Troy, the tomb of King Tut, Jericho, and Incan ruins. (Rev: BL 11/1/94; SLJ 2/95; VOYA 2/95) [930.1]

7383 Stefoff, Rebecca. *Finding the Lost Cities* (7–12). Illus. 1997, Oxford $48.00 (0-19-509249-X); paper $15.95 (0-19-572541-X). Archaeological finds from around the world are introduced in text and more than 100 photographs. (Rev: BL 3/1/97; BR 1–2/98; SLJ 7/97*) [930.1]

7384 Stiebing, William H. *Uncovering the Past: A History of Archaeology* (9–12). 1993, Prometheus $29.95 (0-87975-764-7). Surveys the history of archaeology and documents the discoveries of numerous explorers. (Rev: BL 3/1/93) [930.1]

7385 Vivian, R. Gwinn, and Margaret Anderson. *Chaco Canyon* (7–10). Illus. Series: Digging for the Past. 2002, Oxford $19.95 (0-19-514280-2). An interesting overview of Chaco Canyon's history and the work of archaeologists there over the years. (Rev: BL 10/15/02; HBG 10/02; SLJ 10/02) [973]

7386 Wood, Barbara. *Sacred Ground* (9–12). 2001, St. Martin's $24.95 (0-312-27537-4). An archaeologist becomes obsessed with a mysterious cave in California and through her interest comes the story of Marimi, a female of the Topaa Indians who lived 2,000 years ago. (Rev: BL 9/1/01)

World History and Geography

7387 Aczel, Amir D. *The Riddle of the Compass: The Invention That Changed the World* (10–12). Illus. 2001, Harcourt $23.00 (0-15-100506-0). This is a history of the invention of the compass and how it changed world history; for instance, it allowed the Venetians to navigate the Mediterranean in winter. (Rev: BL 7/01; SLJ 1/02) [912]

7388 Amery, Colin, and Brian Curran. *Vanishing Histories: 100 Endangered Sites from the World Monuments Watch* (10–12). Illus. 2001, Abrams $60.00 (0-8109-1435-2). Using lovely photographs, this book present the histories and present status of 100 monuments around the world that are in need of preservation. (Rev: BL 11/15/01) [363.6]

7389 Aron, Paul. *Unsolved Mysteries of History* (9–12). Illus. 2000, Wiley $24.95 (0-471-35190-3). This book explores a number of unanswered questions in history, such as "Who was King Arthur?" "Did Jesus die on the cross?" and "Did Hitler murder his niece?" (Rev: BL 9/15/00) [902]

7390 Asimov, Isaac. *Asimov's Chronology of the World* (9–12). 1991, HarperCollins $40.00 (0-06-270036-7). This is a broadly based log of events in world history, concentrating on dates, leaders, generals, and wars. (Rev: BL 9/1/91) [902]

7391 Beyer, Rick. *The Greatest Stories Never Told: 100 Tales from History to Astonish, Bewilder, and Stupefy* (6–12). Illus. 2003, HarperCollins $17.95 (0-06-001401-6). Browsers will enjoy this well-illustrated and well-researched chronological overview of historical tidbits. (Rev: VOYA 10/03)

7392 Blainey, Geoffrey. *A Short History of the World* (10–12). Illus. 2002, Ivan R. Dee $27.50 (1-56663-421-0). This satisfying, well-written overview of world history contains some provocative conclusions about the most important development in human history and other key events. (Rev: BL 2/15/02) [909]

7393 Boren, Mark Edelman. *Student Resistance: A History of the Unruly Subject* (10–12). 2001, Routledge $75.00 (0-415-92623-8); paper $19.95 (0-415-92624-6). This is a history of student resistance from the Renaissance to the present, with emphasis on the 1960s and the decades that follow. (Rev: BL 7/01) [378.1]

7394 Clifford, Barry, and Paul Perry. *The Return to Treasure Island and the Search for Captain Kidd* (10–12). Illus. 2003, Morrow $24.95 (0-06-018509-0). The history of the notorious pirate is interwoven into this account of Clifford's modern-day search for the wreckage of Kidd's ship in the waters off Madagascar. (Rev: BL 10/15/03) [910]

7395 Cowley, Robert, and Geoffrey Parker, eds. *The Reader's Companion to Military History* (10–12). 1996, Houghton $45.00 (0-395-66969-3). This well-illustrated, solidly researched book contains writings by military historians on many aspects of world military history, including wars and major battles, military philosophers and their theories, combat leaders, military technological advances, and strategies. (Rev: BL 2/1/97; SLJ 4/97) [355.1]

7396 Currie, Stephen. *Pirates* (6–10). Series: World History. 2001, Lucent LB $19.96 (1-56006-807-8). Although pirates of all eras are mentioned, the "Golden Age of Piracy" in the 17th and 18th centuries is the focus of this detailed overview. (Rev: SLJ 7/01) [910.4]

7397 Davis, Lee Allyn. *Man-Made Catastrophes*. Rev. ed. (9–12). 2002, Facts on File $60.00 (0-8160-4418-X). All kinds of man-made disasters — including the September 11, 2001, attack on the World Trade Center — are included under such headings as terrorism, airplane crashes, explosions, maritime disasters, and railway disasters. (Rev: BL 11/1/02) [904]

7398 Davis, Lee Allyn. *Natural Disasters*. Rev. ed. (9–12). 2002, Checkmark $60.00 (0-8160-4338-8); paper $21.95 (0-8160-4339-6). In alphabetical order, this book covers 500 of the worst natural disasters to occur in world history. [904]

7399 Davis, Paul K. *100 Decisive Battles: From Ancient Times to the Present* (9–12). 1999, ABC-CLIO paper $18.95 (0-19-514366-3). From the Battle of Megiddo in 1469 to Operation Desert Storm in 1991, this volume highlights 100 great battles. [904]

7400 Demko, George J., et al. *Why in the World: Geography for Everyone* (9–12). 1992, Doubleday paper $14.95 (0-385-26629-4). A study of the influences geography has had on physical, political, human, and historical matters. (Rev: BL 4/15/92) [910]

7401 Durschmied, Erik. *Blood of Revolution: From the Reign of Terror to the Rise of Khomeini* (10–12). Illus. 2002, Arcade $25.95 (1-55970-607-4). This absorbing overview focuses on the key personalities and interesting events of two centuries of political revolution. (Rev: BL 2/1/02) [303.6]

7402 Evans, Colin. *Great Feuds in History: Ten of the Liveliest Disputes Ever* (10–12). 2001, Wiley $24.95 (0-471-38038-5); paper $15.95 (0-471-22588-6). Ten famous feuds, starting with Elizabeth I vs. Mary and ending with Johnson vs. Kennedy and Hoover vs. King, are described with good background information. [909]

7403 *Explore: Stories of Survival from off the Map* (10–12). Ed. by Jennifer Schwamm Willis and Clint Willis. Illus. 2000, Thunder's Mouth paper $16.95 (1-56025-278-2). This volume contains 19 excellent adventure tales that span five centuries of exploration from Cabeza de Vaca's journeys in Mexico to Harold Brodkey's AIDS journal. (Rev: BL 11/1/00) [910.4]

7404 Feldman, Burton. *The Nobel Prize: A History of Genius, Controversy, and Prestige* (9–12). 2000, Arcade $29.95 (1-55970-537-X); paper $15.95 (1-55970-592-2). This is a comprehensive history of all of the Nobel Prizes — science, literature, social sciences, and so forth. (Rev: BL 12/1/00) [001.4]

7405 Fernandez-Armesto, Felipe. *Ideas That Changed the World* (10–12). Illus. 2003, DK $30.00 (0-7894-9609-7). The power of innovation is a central theme in this well-illustrated discussion of civilization's forward progress. (Rev: BL 10/15/03) [900]

7406 Findling, John E., and Frank W. Thackeray, eds. *Events that Changed America in the Twentieth Century* (9–12). Series: Events That Changed America. 1996, Greenwood $39.95 (0-313-29080-6). This book covers important events in the 20th century, from World War I to the collapse of the

Soviet Union, among them the Russian Revolution, the Great Depression, the rise of fascism, World War II, the Cold War, the Civil Rights Movement, and the Chinese Revolution. (Rev: SLJ 2/97; VOYA 12/96) [909.82]

7407 Foner, Eric. *Who Owns History? Rethinking the Past in a Changing World* (10–12). 2002, Hill & Wang $24.00 (0-8090-9704-4). In this collection of essays and addresses, Columbia University history professor Foner examines the diverse ways in which the public — and historians — perceive the story of our past. (Rev: BL 3/15/02) [973.01]

7408 Gardner, Robert. *Where on Earth Am I?* (8–12). Illus. 1996, Watts LB $20.00 (0-531-11297-7). Topics relating to geography and geology, such as the earth's shape and motion, maps, and distance and direction, are explored in 45 projects and activities. (Rev: BL 2/15/97; SLJ 2/97) [526]

7409 Gilbert, Martin. *The Jews in the Twentieth Century* (10–12). Illus. 2001, Pantheon $50.00 (0-8052-4190-6). Using an interesting text and over 450 photographs, this book traces the history of the Jews in the 20th century, with the last three chapters covering the years 1945 through 2000. (Rev: BL 10/1/01) [909]

7410 Gonick, Larry. *The Cartoon History of the Universe III: From the Rise of Arabia to the Renaissance* (10–12). Illus. 2002, Norton $35.00 (0-393-05184-6); paper $21.95 (0-393-32403-6). Comic book artist Larry Gonick chronicles world history from the rise of Islam to the Renaissance. (Rev: BL 9/15/02; SLJ 1/03) [909.07]

7411 Hinds, Kathryn. *The Celts of Northern Europe* (7–10). Series: Cultures of the Past. 1996, Benchmark LB $28.50 (0-7614-0092-3). This book gives a history of the Celts, their religion, social structure, art, folklore, and how they helped keep Christianity alive in Ireland. (Rev: SLJ 3/97) [940.1]

7412 Holland, Barbara. *They Went Whistling: Women Wayfarers, Warriors, Runaways, and Renegades* (9–12). 2001, Pantheon $23.00 (0-375-42055-X). This is a rundown on important women in history arranged by such themes as warriors, wayfarers, outlaws, and radicals. (Rev: BL 2/1/01; SLJ 8/01) [920.72]

7413 Hoopes, James. *Oral History: An Introduction for Students* (10–12). 1979, Univ. of North Carolina Pr. paper $12.95 (0-8078-1344-3). This work explains the methodologies used in oral history collections and gives tips on how to put them into practice. [907]

7414 James, Naomi. *Courage at Sea: Tales of Heroic Voyages* (10–12). 1988, Salem House $24.95 (0-88162-320-2). Beginning with Magellan's trip, 15 harrowing sea voyages are reported in this book. (Rev: VOYA 12/88) [910]

7415 Kallen, Stuart A. *Life Among the Pirates* (6–10). Series: The Way People Live. 1998, Lucent LB $27.45 (1-56006-393-9). A fascinating history of world piracy with an emphasis on the "Golden Age" from 1519 until the 1720s. (Rev: BL 11/15/98; SLJ 3/99) [910.45]

7416 Kurlansky, Mark. *Salt: A World History* (10–12). Illus. 2002, Walker $28.00 (0-8027-1373-4). An interesting chronicle of the age-old commerce in salt, its uses, and its importance to a variety of communities. (Rev: BL 1/1–15/02*) [553.63]

7417 Leon, Vicki. *Uppity Women of the New World* (10–12). Illus. Series: Uppity Women. 2001, Conari paper $15.95 (1-57324-187-3). In this book there are profiles of 220 women—from explorers, spies, and religious leaders to criminals and pirates—who contributed to the establishment of colonies in the Americas, New Zealand, and Australia. (Rev: BL 3/1/01) [305.4]

7418 Lindop, Edmund. *Great Britain and the United States: Rivals and Partners* (9–12). Illus. 1999, Twenty-First Century $24.40 (0-7613-1471-7). A contemporary look at the events that have influenced the relationship between the two countries, from colonial times to the present. (Rev: BL 12/15/99; HBG 4/00; SLJ 1/00) [327.4]

7419 *Lonely Planet . . . on the Edge: Adventurous Escapades from Around the World* (10–12). Ed. by Cecil Kuhne. Illus. 2000, Lonely Planet paper $12.99 (1-86450-222-3). This is an anthology of travel pieces by 33 contributors who describe sights in each of the continents and—in a piece by astronaut Buzz Aldrin—on the moon. (Rev: BL 10/15/00) [910.4]

7420 MacDonald, John. *Great Battlefields of the World* (9–12). Illus. 1985, Macmillan paper $25.95 (0-02-044464-8). This account describes 30 significant battles in world history. [904]

7421 McLynn, Frank. *Famous Trials: Cases That Made History* (10–12). 1995, Reader's Digest $27.95 (0-89577-655-1). Using many attractive illustrations, this work includes descriptions and the long-range ramifications of the trials of Socrates, Jesus, Thomas More, Danton, Dreyfus, Galileo, John Brown, Tojo, Scopes, and Nelson Mandela, and other famous people throughout history. (Rev: SLJ 5/96) [909]

7422 Marley, David F. *Wars of the Americas: A Chronology of Armed Conflict in the New World, 1492 to the Present* (9–12). 1998, ABC-CLIO LB $99.00 (0-87436-837-5). This annotated chronology covers every major war and most minor ones fought in North, South, and Central America from the arrival of Columbus to March 1998. (Rev: BL 1/1–15/99; BR 5–6/99; SLJ 2/99; VOYA 4/99) [909]

7423 *National Geographic Expeditions Atlas* (9–12). Illus. 2000, National Geographic $40.00 (0-7922-7616-7). Using maps and photographs, this volume chronicles the many scientific expeditions, including some underwater ones, that have been financed by National Geographic. (Rev: BL 9/1/00) [910.4]

7424 *National Geographic's Last Wild Places* (10–12). 1996, National Geographic $35.00 (0-7922-3500-2). With more than 200 full-color photographs, this photoessay celebrates more than 30 areas around the world that remain relatively untouched by civilization. [508]

7425 Noland, David. *Travels Along the Edge* (10–12). 1997, Vintage paper $14.00 (0-679-76344-9). A world traveler describes 40 different adventure trips around the world with tips and detailed advice. (Rev: BL 9/1/97; SLJ 2/98) [910.2]

7426 Obregon, Mauricio. *Beyond the Edge of the Sea: Sailing with Jason and the Argonauts, Ulysses, the Vikings, and Other Explorers of the Ancient World* (10–12). Illus. 2001, Random $21.95 (0-679-46326-7). In this heavily illustrated volume the author re-creates the epic maritime adventures of such explorers as Jason, Ulysses, and the Vikings, treating both the mythical and factual. (Rev: BL 1/1–15/01) [930]

7427 Perry, James M. *Arrogant Armies: Great Military Disasters and the Generals Behind Them* (10–12). 1996, Wiley $27.95 (0-471-11976-8). This collection of failed military missions over the past two and a half centuries, such as Braddock's campaign during the French and Indian Wars and Gordon's loss of Khartoum in the Sudan, underlines the waste and horror of war. (Rev: SLJ 11/96) [900]

7428 *Photographs: Then and Now* (10–12). 1998, National Geographic $50.00 (0-7922-7202-1). The world's peoples, places, and cultures are presented in this collection of outstanding photographs from the *National Geographic* that span the period from 1888 to the present. (Rev: SLJ 3/99) [910]

7429 Poole, Robert M., ed. *Nature's Wonderlands: National Parks of the World* (9–12). Illus. 1990, National Geographic $29.95 (0-87044-766-1). A photo-text tour of the national parks of the world with fuller coverage of those that are most important. (Rev: BL 5/1/90) [363.7]

7430 Reid, Howard. *In Search of the Immortals: Mummies, Death, and the Afterlife* (9–12). 2001, St. Martin's $27.50 (0-312-28006-8). An anthropologist shares his views on death and burials with a sharp focus on mummification as it has been practiced around the world at various times. (Rev: BL 8/01) [393]

7431 Rushby, Kevin. *Hunting Pirate Heaven: In Search of the Lost Pirate Utopias of the Indian Ocean* (10–12). 2003, Walker $25.00 (0-8027-1423-4). Exciting, entertaining and informative, this is an account of the author's search for the Indian Ocean haunts of early privateers. (Rev: BL 10/15/03) [910]

7432 Russell, Jeffrey B. *A History of Witchcraft: Sorcerers, Heretics and Pagans* (9–12). Illus. 1983, Peter Smith $23.50 (0-8446-6052-3). A history of witchcraft that concentrates on Western Europe, Africa, and the United States. [133.4]

7433 Scharfstein, Sol, and Dorcas Gelabert. *Chronicle of Jewish History: From the Patriarchs to the 21st Century* (10–12). 1997, KTAV paper $36.88 (0-81125-606-4). Richly illustrated with more than 400 photographs and maps, this volume traces the story of the Jewish people from biblical times to the 1993 Oslo Agreement between Israel and the Palestine Liberation Organization. [909]

7434 Smith, Bonnie G. *Imperialism: A History in Documents* (6–12). Series: Pages from History. 2000, Oxford $36.95 (0-19-510801-9). This detailed account of how powerful nations spread their influence around the globe draws on many primary sources and includes eye-catching photographs and a useful timeline. (Rev: BL 11/15/00; HBG 10/01; SLJ 4/01) [325]

7435 Sobel, Dava. *Longitude: The True Story of a Lone Genius Who Solved the Greatest Scientific Problem of His Time* (10–12). 1995, Walker $27.95 (0-8027-1312-2). The story of mariners' centuries-long search for ways of determining longitude that tells not only of the scientific advances but also of the perseverance, pettiness, politics, and interesting anecdotes involved. (Rev: BL 9/1/95; SLJ 2/96) [527]

7436 Stewart, Robert, et al. *Mysteries of History* (7–12). Illus. 2003, National Geographic $29.95 (0-7922-6232-8). Such controversial topics as Stonehenge, Napoleon's death, and Custer's Last Stand are presented with 16 others in this well-illustrated book. (Rev: BL 2/1/04; HBG 4/04) [902]

7437 Strouthes, Daniel P. *Law and Politics: A Cross-Cultural Encyclopedia* (10–12). Series: Encyclopedia of the Human Experience. 1995, ABC-CLIO LB $49.50 (0-87436-777-8). Using an alphabetical arrangement, this title explores how law and politics exist and function in different cultures. (Rev: BR 9–10/96; SLJ 6/96) [341]

7438 Thackeray, Frank W., and John E. Findling. *Events that Changed the World in the Seventeenth Century* (10–12). 1999, Greenwood $39.95 (0-313-29078-4). Some of the events of the 1600s covered here are the Thirty Years War, the Scientific Revolution, and the Manchu conquest of China. (Rev: BL 4/1/00) [909]

7439 *Western Civilization: From the Origins of Civilization to the Age of Absolutism* (11–12). Ed. by Benjamin C. Sax. Illus. 2001, Greenhaven $33.96 (1-56510-989-9); paper $18.96 (1-56510-988-0). This first volume of a two-volume overview of Western civilization chronicles the forward march from the days of ancient Mesopotamia and Egypt through the Protestant Reformation in Europe. The second volume is *Western Civilization: From the Scientific Revolution to the Present*. (Rev: BL 5/15/01) [909]

7440 Wilson, Ian. *Past Lives: Unlocking the Secrets of Our Ancestors* (10–12). Illus. 2001, Cassell $29.95 (0-304-35474-0). This profusely illustrated volume shows how historians, scientists, and artists work together to re-create the faces of such long-dead individuals as Scotland's Robert the Bruce, a Minoan princess dead for 3,600 years, and many others. (Rev: BL 9/15/01) [930.10285]

7441 *A Woman Alone: Travel Tales from Around the Clock* (10–12). Ed. by Faith Conlon et al. 2001, Seal paper $15.95 (1-58005-059-X). This is collection of 29 essays by women travels whose journeys involve six continents. (Rev: BL 11/15/01) [910.4]

7442 Wren, Christopher S. *The Cat Who Covered the World: The Adventures of Henrietta and Her Foreign Correspondent* (10–12). Illus. 2000, Simon & Schuster $21.00 (0-684-87100-9). The author, a foreign correspondent for the *New York Times,* tells of his travels around the world with his cat. (Rev: BL 10/15/00; SLJ 5/01) [910.4]

Ancient History

General and Miscellaneous

7443 *Ancient Civilizations* (8–12). Ed. by Don Nardo. Series: World History by Era. 2002, Greenhaven LB $43.70 (0-7377-0646-5); paper $27.45 (0-7377-0645-7). Primary and secondary sources are reprinted in this collection of documents that deals with such ancient empires as the Sumerians, Babylonians, Egyptians, Jews, Celts, and others. [930]

7444 Brewer, Paul. *Warfare in the Ancient World* (7–10). Series: History of Warfare. 1999, Raintree Steck-Vaughn LB $29.97 (0-8172-5442-0). This account describes important wars and battles in the ancient world, from Egypt through the Roman Empire. (Rev: HBG 3/99; SLJ 3/99) [930]

7445 *Classical Greece and Rome* (8–12). Ed. by Don Nardo. Series: World History by Era. 2002, Greenhaven LB $43.70 (0-7377-0578-7); paper $27.45 (0-7377-0577-9). Carefully selected primary and secondary sources explore the classical world of the Greeks and Romans and the joint civilization that lasted for about 1,000 years. [938]

7446 Connolly, Peter, and Hazel Dodge. *The Ancient City: Life in Classical Athens and Rome* (9–12). Illus. 1998, Oxford LB $52.95 (0-19-521409-9). The daily life, history, and architecture of Athens and Rome are extensively covered, with extraordinary full-page color drawings detailing the design, construction, and use of such landmark constructions as the Parthenon and the Roman Colosseum. (Rev: BL 5/1/98; BR 1–2/99; SLJ 7/98; VOYA 2/99) [930]

7447 Finlay, Victoria. *Color: A Natural History of the Palette* (10–12). Illus. 2003, Ballantine $24.95 (0-345-44430-2). Personal anecdotes are interwoven with cultural and technical information as Finley describes her search for ancient civilizations' sources of colors. (Rev: BL 12/1/02) [667]

7448 Hall, Eleanor J. *Ancient Chinese Dynasties* (7–10). Series: World History. 2000, Lucent LB $18.96 (1-56006-624-5). This well-illustrated account describes the dynasties that laid the foundations of Chinese culture and highlights their unsurpassed works of art, architecture, and philosophy. (Rev: BL 6/1–15/00; HBG 9/00; SLJ 6/00) [951]

7449 Haywood, John. *The Encyclopedia of Ancient Civilizations of the Near East and the Mediterranean* (8–12). Illus. 1997, M.E. Sharpe $95.00 (1-56324-799-2). Divided into three parts — ancient Near East and Egypt, the Greek world, and the Roman world — this adult narrative presents basic history and, through the use of sidebars, provides material on important places, cultural advances, scientific progress, religious practices, and military advances. (Rev: SLJ 8/98) [909]

7450 Jenkins, Earnestine. *A Glorious Past: Ancient Egypt, Ethiopia and Nubia* (7–10). Series: Milestones in Black History. 1995, Chelsea LB $21.95 (0-7910-2258-7); paper $8.95 (0-7910-2684-1). A social and political survey of ancient Egypt, Nubia, the civilization to the south, and Ethiopia. (Rev: BL 4/15/95; SLJ 4/95) [932]

7451 Nardo, Don. *Greek and Roman Sport* (5–10). Series: World History. 1999, Lucent LB $27.45 (1-56006-436-6). A very detailed account, using many quotations from classical sources, that gives a realistic picture of the place of sports in both ancient Greece and Rome, the different events, and the rewards and hardships of participants. (Rev: BL 7/99; SLJ 8/99) [930]

7452 Starr, Chester G. *A History of the Ancient World*. 4th (9–12). 1991, Oxford $49.95 (0-19-506629-4). This comprehensive overview focuses primarily on the Greeks and Romans but also covers early civilizations in Mesopotamia, China, Egypt, and India. [930]

7453 *Vanished Civilizations: The Hidden Secrets of Lost Cities and Forgotten Peoples* (10–12). Illus. 2002, Reader's Digest $29.95 (0-276-42658-4). A stunning and informative pictorial tour of ruins of such man-made wonders as Angkor Wat, Pompeii, and Mycenae. (Rev: BL 11/15/02) [930]

Egypt and Mesopotamia

7454 *Ancient Egypt* (9–12). 1997, Oxford $39.95 (0-19-521270-3). Maps, charts, and color photographs complement essays on the culture, economy, geography, architecture, and other key aspects of ancient Egypt. [932]

7455 Brier, Bob. *The Murder of Tutankhamen: A True Story* (10–12). 1998, Berkley paper $24.95 (0-399-14383-1). Reading like a contemporary whodunit, this is a reconstruction of Tutankhamen's life and death, arguing plausibly that he was murdered by his grand vizier. (Rev: BL 4/1/98*; SLJ 10/98) [932]

7456 David, Rosalie. *Handbook to Life in Ancient Egypt* (10–12). 1998, Facts on File $45.00 (0-8160-3312-9). Using topically arranged chapters, this overview presents a rounded picture of civilization of Egypt from its earliest times through the Roman period. (Rev: SLJ 1/99) [932]

7457 Doherty, Paul. *The Mysterious Death of Tutankhamun* (10–12). 2002, Carroll & Graf $26.00 (0-7867-1075-6). Doherty offers a number of possible explanations for the 18-year-old pharaoh's untimely death. (Rev: BL 11/15/02) [932.014]

7458 Jackson, Kevin, and Jonathan Stamp. *Building the Great Pyramid* (10–12). Illus. 2003, Firefly $29.95 (1-55297-721-8); paper $19.95 (1-55297-719-6). Designed as a companion to the BBC/Discovery Channel documentary of the same name, this richly illustrated book outlines the authors' controversial theories about the building of Egypt's Great Pyramid. (Rev: BL 3/1/03) [932]

7459 James, T. G. H. *Tutankhamun* (9–12). Illus. 2000, Friedman $60.00 (1-56799-032-6). This lavish book tells, in great photographs and an interesting text, about the discovery in 1922 of the famous tomb of the king buried 3,000 years ago. (Rev: BL 12/15/00) [932]

7460 Kallen, Stuart A. *Pyramids* (7–10). Series: Mystery Library. 2002, Gale LB $27.45 (1-56006-773-X). This work explores the mysterious and intriguing aspects of the purposes behind and construction of the Egyptian pyramids. (Rev: BL 7/02; SLJ 7/02) [932]

7461 King, Michael R., et al. *Who Killed King Tut? Using Modern Forensics to Solve a 3,300-Year-Old Mystery* (9–12). Illus. 2004, Prometheus $25.00 (1-59102-183-9). This fascinating piece of historical detection investigates the death of King Tutankhamen, and points the finger of guilt at one of his most trusted advisers. (Rev: BL 4/15/04) [932]

7462 Meltzer, Milton. *In the Days of the Pharaohs: A Look at Ancient Egypt* (6–12). Illus. 2001, Watts LB $33.50 (0-531-11791-X). A series of color plates add to the visual appeal of this look at ancient

Egypt and how archaeological discoveries have contributed to our knowledge of this intriguing society. (Rev: BL 12/1/01; SLJ 12/01) [932]

7463 Mertz, Barbara. *Temples, Tombs, and Hieroglyphs: A Popular History of Ancient Egypt.* Rev. ed. (10–12). 1990, Bedrick paper $16.95 (0-87226-223-5). This book about ancient Egypt not only describes its history but also explains how archaeology has helped us gain knowledge about this civilization. [932]

7464 Nardo, Don. *Ancient Alexandria* (6–10). Illus. Series: A Travel Guide To. 2003, Gale LB $21.96 (1-59018-142-5). Readers are treated to a guidebook-style survey of ancient Alexandria's attractions, with a focus on weather, transport, hotels, shopping, festivals and sporting events, institutions, and people. (Rev: SLJ 6/03) [962]

7465 Nardo, Don. *Ancient Egypt* (7–12). Illus. Series: History of Weapons and Warfare. 2003, Gale LB $21.96 (1-59018-066-6). The Battle of Kadesh is a central part of this account that discusses the ancient Egyptians' military weapons and techniques. (Rev: SLJ 2/03) [355]

7466 Roberts, Russell. *Rulers of Ancient Egypt* (7–10). Series: History Makers. 1999, Lucent LB $27.45 (1-56006-438-2). The author uses both primary and secondary sources to describe the contributions and personalities of Hatshepsut, Akhenaten, Tutankhamon, Ramses II, and Cleopatra and to provide further insight into this period's culture and power structure. (Rev: SLJ 8/99) [932]

7467 Shuter, Jane. *Egypt* (5–10). Series: Ancient World. 1998, Raintree Steck-Vaughn LB $27.12 (0-8172-5058-1). Ancient Egypt's mysterious hieroglyphics, treasure-filled tombs, puzzling pyramid construction, and embalming techniques, as well as its history, politics, ideas, religion, art, architecture, science, and everyday life are covered in this introductory volume. (Rev: BL 1/1–15/99; HBG 3/99; SLJ 3/99) [932]

7468 Smith, Stuart Tyson, and Nancy Stone Bernard. *Valley of the Kings* (7–10). Series: Digging for the Past. 2002, Oxford $19.95 (0-19-514770-7). After a map, timeline, and some historical background material, this account describes the tombs in the Valley of the Kings, how they were built, and what they contained. (Rev: BL 10/15/02; HBG 10/03; SLJ 2/03) [932]

7469 Stalcup, Brenda, ed. *Ancient Egyptian Civilization* (7–12). Series: Turning Points in World History. 2001, Greenhaven LB $22.96 (0-7377-0480-2); paper $14.96 (0-7377-0479-9). Following an introductory overview, this anthology of essays presents various aspects of the history of ancient Egypt, its culture, and its contributions to world civilization. (Rev: BL 6/1–15/01; SLJ 7/01) [932]

7470 Stetter, Cornelius. *The Secret Medicine of the Pharaohs: Ancient Egyptian Healing* (9–12). 1993, Quintessence paper $19.95 (0-86715-265-6). Uses Egyptian papyri to reconstruct ancient Egyptian medicine and explain it in a modern scientific context. Many color illustrations. (Rev: BL 9/15/93) [610]

7471 Streissguth, Thomas. *Life in Ancient Egypt* (6–10). Series: The Way People Live. 2000, Lucent LB $19.96 (1-56006-643-1). Everyday life within the different social classes that existed in ancient Egypt is covered in this account that contains many black-and-white illustrations. (Rev: BL 3/1/01) [932]

7472 Tiano, Oliver. *Ramses II and Egypt* (6–10). Series: W5. 1996, Holt $19.95 (0-8050-4659-3). Using all sorts of gimmicky illustrations and diagrams, this work presents basic facts about ancient Egypt, its culture, and its people. (Rev: SLJ 12/96) [932]

7473 Weeks, John. *The Pyramids* (7–12). Illus. 1977, Cambridge Univ. Pr. paper $12.95 (0-521-07240-9). An introduction to the construction of the pyramids of ancient Egypt. [726]

7474 *What Life Was Like on the Banks of the Nile, Egypt 3050–30 BC* (8–12). Illus. 1996, Time-Life $34.95 (0-8094-9378-0). An illustrated account that concentrates on everyday life in ancient Egypt, with information on several important kings. (Rev: BL 11/1/96; BR 1–2/97; SLJ 12/96) [932]

Greece

7475 Adkins, Larry. *Handbook to Life in Ancient Greece* (10–12). 1997, Facts on File $45.00 (0-8160-3111-8). This excellent resource covers, in broad subject areas, 3,000 years of Greek history, from the Minoan civilization of Crete to the defeat of the Greeks by the Romans in 30 B.C. (Rev: BL 8/97; BR 1–2/98; SLJ 1/98) [938]

7476 Archibald, Zofia. *Discovering the World of the Ancient Greeks* (9–12). 1991, Facts on File $29.95 (0-8160-2614-9). A recounting of classical Greek history (from 6500–2900 B.C. to A.D. 550), through archaeological discoveries. (Rev: BL 1/1/92; SLJ 3/92) [938]

7477 *At the Dawn of Democracy: Classical Athens, 525–332 BC* (7–12). Illus. 1997, Time-Life $34.95 (0-7835-5453-2). Using lavish color illustrations, this book re-creates the world of ancient Athens with coverage of daily life, sports, laws, politics, art, and religion. (Rev: BL 2/1/98; SLJ 5/98) [938]

7478 Baker, Rosalie, and Charles F. Baker. *Ancient Greeks* (9–12). Illus. 1997, Oxford $51.95 (0-19-509940-0). Using the timespan of 700 to 200 B.C., this work profiles the lives and accomplishments of

37 prominent men and women of ancient Greece. (Rev: BL 8/97; BR 3–4/98; SLJ 9/97) [938]

7479 Green, Peter. *Ancient Greece* (10–12). Illus. 1979, Thames & Hudson paper $16.95 (0-500-27161-5). In 200 illustrations and ample text, the history of Greece is traced to the death of Alexander the Great in 323 B.C. [938]

7480 Hamilton, Edith. *The Greek Way* (10–12). 1943, Norton paper $12.95 (0-393-31077-9). A discussion of the great works and writers of the golden age of Greece, including Pindar, Aristophanes, and Aeschylus. [880.9]

7481 Hull, Robert. *Greece* (5–10). Series: Ancient World. 1998, Raintree Steck-Vaughn LB $27.12 (0-8172-5055-7). This brief introduction to ancient Greece touches on its religion and mythology, its great philosophers, important historical events, and its contributions to world culture. (Rev: BL 1/1–15/99; HBG 3/99) [938]

7482 Kirby, John T. *Classical Greek Civilization, 800–323 B.C.E.* (9–12). Series: World Eras. 2001, Gale $99.00 (0-7876-1707-5). This work covers the classical Greek period under such topics as the arts, class system, the family and social trends, and religion and philosophy. (Rev: BL 5/15/01) [938]

7483 Levi, Peter. *Atlas of the Greek World* (10–12). Illus. 1981, Facts on File $45.00 (0-87196-448-1). Through maps and other kinds of illustrations, the history of ancient Greece is traced along with discussion of its lasting influence. [938]

7484 Nardo, Don. *Ancient Greece* (7–10). Series: History of Weapons and Warfare. 2003, Gale LB $21.96 (1-59018-004-6). A look at weapons, techniques, and strategies of the ancient Greeks — both on land and at sea — with quotations from a variety of sources and maps, diagrams, and other illustrations. (Rev: SLJ 1/03) [355]

7485 Nardo, Don, ed. *Ancient Greece* (6–12). Illus. Series: Complete History Of. 2001, Greenhaven LB $99.00 (0-7377-0425-X). This anthology provides a well-organized and balanced look at Ancient Greece with more than 90 selections on a wide variety of topics. (Rev: BL 11/1/01; SLJ 7/01) [938]

7486 Nardo, Don. *The Battle of Marathon* (6–10). Illus. 1996, Lucent LB $26.20 (1-56006-412-9). A colorful, well-illustrated account that describes the causes, events, and aftermath of the battle in which the ancient Greeks repelled the Persian invasion. (Rev: BL 4/15/96; BR 9–10/96; SLJ 1/96) [938]

7487 Nardo, Don, ed. *The Decline and Fall of Ancient Greece* (8–12). Series: Turning Points in World History. 2000, Greenhaven LB $21.96 (0-7377-0241-9); paper $13.96 (0-7377-0240-0). This anthology discusses the leaders and military campaigns of the various Greek states and the events that led to their complete overthrow by the Romans. (Rev: BL 5/15/00; SLJ 11/00) [938]

7488 Nardo, Don. *Life in Ancient Athens* (6–10). Series: The Way People Live. 1999, Lucent LB $18.96 (1-56006-494-3). This account describes how people lived in ancient Athens with material on how they dressed, worked, ate, socialized, played, and went to school. (Rev: BL 10/15/99; HBG 9/00) [938]

7489 Nardo, Don. *The Parthenon of Ancient Greece* (6–10). 1998, Lucent LB $27.45 (1-56006-431-5). The how and why of the construction of the Parthenon, its legacy as a symbol of classical Greek society and artistry, and its influence on Roman, American, and European architecture. (Rev: BL 12/15/98; BR 5–6/99; SLJ 3/99) [726]

7490 Nardo, Don. *Philip II and Alexander the Great Unify Greece in World History* (6–10). Illus. Series: In World History. 2000, Enslow LB $19.95 (0-7660-1399-5). Primary and secondary sources are used in this survey of relations between the city-states of Greece in the 4th century B.C. (Rev: HBG 9/00; SLJ 6/00) [938]

7491 Nardo, Don. *Scientists of Ancient Greece* (7–12). Illus. 1998, Lucent LB $18.96 (1-56006-362-9). An introduction to the development of scientific thought in ancient Greece precedes chapters on the scientific theories and work of Democritus, Plato, Aristotle, Theophrastus, Archimedes, Ptolemy, and Galen. (Rev: BR 5–6/99; SLJ 4/99) [938]

7492 Nardo, Don. *The Trial of Socrates* (9–12). Illus. Series: Famous Trials. 1996, Lucent LB $17.96 (1-56006-267-3). This book describes the legal and ethical issues involved in the trial of Socrates and introduces the Greek city-state and the teachings of this great philosopher. (Rev: BL 6/1–15/97; BR 11–12/97; SLJ 6/97) [940.54]

7493 Nardo, Don. *Women of Ancient Greece* (7–10). Series: World History. 2000, Lucent LB $18.96 (1-56006-646-6). The story of the place of women in ancient Greek society, how they lacked political rights and lived sheltered lives yet performed many important duties. (Rev: BL 6/1–15/00; HBG 3/01) [938]

7494 Robinson, C. E. *Everyday Life in Ancient Greece* (7–12). Illus. 1933, AMS $45.00 (0-404-14592-2). The classic account, first published in 1933, of how people lived during various periods in ancient Greek history. [938]

7495 Sacks, David. *Encyclopedia of the Ancient Greek World* (10–12). 1995, Facts on File $45.00 (0-8160-2323-9). An alphabetically arranged, browsable compendium of ancient Greek history, warfare, society, the arts, literature, mythology, science, clothing, religion, and geography. (Rev: BR 3–4/96; SLJ 4/96; VOYA 4/96) [938]

7496 Tournikiotis, Panayotis, ed. *The Parthenon and Its Impact in Modern Times* (10–12). 1996, Abrams $75.00 (0-8109-6314-0). The Parthenon's construction, its impact on Western democracy, architecture, and philosophy, and other perspectives on this structure are discussed in 11 original essays by noted Greek scholars and writers, enhanced by pictures. (Rev: SLJ 7/97) [938]

7497 Wilde, Lyn Webster. *On the Trail of the Women Warriors: The Amazons in Myth and Mystery* (10–12). Illus. 2000, St. Martin's $24.95 (0-312-26213-2). An enjoyable, intriguing account that traces the mythological ancient tribe of the Amazons in order to separate fact from fiction. (Rev: BL 6/1–15/00) [939]

7498 Wood, Michael. *In the Footsteps of Alexander the Great: A Journey from Greece to Asia* (9–12). 1997, Univ. of California Pr. paper $18.95 (0-520-23192-9). Published as a companion to the BBC series of the same name, this richly illustrated volume retraces the epic travels of the king of Macedonia. (Rev: BL 11/15/97) [938]

7499 Woodford, Susan. *The Parthenon* (6–10). Illus. 1983, Cambridge Univ. Pr. paper $16.00 (0-521-22629-5). A history of the famous temple in Athens and of the religion of ancient Greece. [938]

Middle East

7500 Palmer, Alan. *The Decline and Fall of the Ottoman Empire* (9–12). 1994, M. Evans $22.50 (0-87131-754-0). Traces the long decline of the Ottoman Empire from 1683 to 1922 and explores the impact of its legacy on contemporary Middle Eastern society. (Rev: BL 2/1/94) [958.1]

7501 Zeinert, Karen. *The Persian Empire* (7–10). Series: Cultures of the Past. 1996, Benchmark LB $28.50 (0-7614-0089-3). A brief history of the Persian Empire, with material on the kings Cyrus, Darius, and Xerxes, is followed by chapters on daily life, culture, religion, and lasting contributions the empire made to human achievement. (Rev: SLJ 3/97) [935]

Rome

7502 Baker, Alan. *The Gladiator: The Secret History of Rome's Warrior Slaves* (9–12). Illus. 2001, St. Martin's $22.95 (0-312-28403-9). This work traces the history of Roman gladiatorial combats for a period of about a thousand years, from their origins as human sacrifices to their gradual suppression by Christian regimes. (Rev: BL 9/1/01; SLJ 5/02) [937]

7503 Baker, Rosalie, and Charles F. Baker. *Ancient Romans: Expanding the Classical Tradition* (9–12). Illus. Series: Oxford Profiles. 1998, Oxford $56.00 (0-19-510884-1). Divided into five time periods spanning 400 B.C. to 350 A.D., this work recounts the history of Rome's rise to power through profiles of 39 notable Romans, including Virgil, Ovid, Julius Caesar, Constantine, Livia, and Spartacus. (Rev: BL 5/1/98; SLJ 8/98) [937]

7504 Cornell, Tim, and John Matthews. *Atlas of the Roman World* (10–12). Illus. 1982, Facts on File $45.00 (0-87196-652-2). In addition to many maps, an extensive text traces the history of the Roman Empire to A.D. 565. [937]

7505 Davis, William Stearns. *A Day in Old Rome: A Picture of Roman Life* (9–12). Illus. 1959, Biblo & Tannen paper $10.00 (0-8196-0106-3). This account of the daily life, habits, and customs of ancient Romans first appeared in 1925. A companion volume is *A Day in Old Athens* (1959). [937]

7506 Hamilton, Edith. *The Roman Way* (10–12). 1932, Norton paper $11.95 (0-393-31078-7). By examining the great writers and thinkers of ancient Rome, this book gives an interpretation of the life of the period. [870.9]

7507 Hinds, Kathryn. *The Ancient Romans* (7–10). Series: Cultures of the Past. 1996, Benchmark LB $28.50 (0-7614-0090-7). A well-illustrated volume that tells about the Roman Empire, the architectural feats of the Romans, their religion and entertainment, and their lasting contributions to world civilization. (Rev: SLJ 3/97) [937]

7508 Laing, Jennifer, and Lloyd Laing. *Warriors of the Dark Ages* (10–12). Illus. Series: Warriors of Europe. 2000, Sutton $34.95 (0-7509-1920-5). Beginning in the 4th century, this account traces the history of raiding tribes such as the Visigoths and Huns and their contributions to the destruction of the Roman Empire. (Rev: BL 3/15/00) [940.12]

7509 Langguth, A. J. *A Noise of War: Caesar, Pompey, Octavian and the Struggle for Rome* (9–12). 1994, Simon & Schuster $25.00 (0-671-70829-5). A history of the Roman Empire during its glory days that focuses on Caesar and Cicero and their political intrigues and alliances. (Rev: BL 3/15/94) [937]

7510 Macaulay, David. *City: A Story of Roman Planning and Construction* (6–10). Illus. 1974, Houghton $18.00 (0-395-19492-X); paper $8.95 (0-395-34922-2). In text and detailed drawing, the artist explores an imaginary Roman city over approximately 125 years. [711]

7511 Nardo, Don. *The Battle of Zama* (6–10). Illus. 1996, Lucent LB $26.20 (1-56006-420-X). An exciting account of the 202 B.C. battle in North Africa in which Hannibal's forces were defeated by the Romans during the second Punic War. (Rev: BL 4/15/96; BR 9–10/96; SLJ 4/96) [937]

7512 Nardo, Don. *Caesar's Conquest of Gaul* (7–10). Series: World History. 1996, Lucent LB $27.45 (1-56006-301-7). This is the story of how Caesar's conquest of Gaul destroyed one culture and created a new one that was to influence the development of modern Europe. (Rev: BL 2/15/96; SLJ 2/96) [937]

7513 Nardo, Don, ed. *The End of Ancient Rome* (7–12). Series: Turning Points in World History. 2000, Greenhaven LB $22.96 (0-7377-0372-5); paper $14.96 (0-7377-0371-7). This collection of essays from recognized historians traces the decline and fall of the Roman Empire and the reasons for failure. (Rev: BL 12/15/00; SLJ 1/01) [937]

7514 Nardo, Don. *The Fall of the Roman Empire* (7–12). Illus. Series: Opposing Viewpoints Digests. 1997, Greenhaven LB $27.45 (1-56510-739-X); paper $17.45 (1-56510-738-1). Theories about why Rome fell are presented in a pro and con format. (Rev: BL 3/1/98) [937]

7515 Nardo, Don. *Games of Ancient Rome* (6–10). Series: The Way People Live. 2000, Lucent LB $18.96 (1-56006-655-5). Nardo gives an interesting overview of popular sports in ancient Rome (gladiators, wild animal shows, and chariot races, for example), their importance in daily life, and the reasons for their decline. (Rev: BL 1/1–15/00; HBG 9/00; SLJ 5/00) [937]

7516 Nardo, Don. *The Punic Wars* (8–12). Illus. Series: World History. 1996, Lucent LB $27.45 (1-56006-417-X). A description of the three wars between Rome and Carthage, Hannibal and other leaders, and the significance of Rome's victory. (Rev: BL 2/15/96; SLJ 2/96) [937]

7517 Nardo, Don, ed. *The Rise of the Roman Empire* (7–12). Series: Turning Points in World History. 2001, Greenhaven LB $31.20 (0-7377-0756-9); paper $19.95 (0-7377-0757-7). After an introductory overview, this anthology of essays explores various facets of the growth of the Roman Empire and its social and cultural effects on life in the ancient world. (Rev: BL 3/15/02; SLJ 4/02) [937]

7518 Nardo, Don. *Women of Ancient Rome* (6–10). Illus. Series: Women in History. 2002, Gale LB $21.96 (1-59018-169-7). The daily lives of Roman women, from slaves to aristocrats, are portrayed here, with details of social status, work, attire, religion, and even sexuality. (Rev: BL 10/15/02; SLJ 1/03) [305.4]

7519 Scarre, Chris. *Chronicle of the Roman Emperors: The Reign-by-Reign Record of the Rulers of Imperial Rome* (9–12). 1995, Thames & Hudson $29.95 (0-500-05077-5). The story of emperors from Augustus to Romulus Augustulus is told through surviving annals of classical historians, with photographs of ruins from their reigns. (Rev: BL 10/15/95) [937]

7520 Sheehan, Sean, and Pat Levy. *Rome* (5–10). Series: Ancient World. 1998, Raintree Steck-Vaughn LB $27.12 (0-8172-5057-3). A brief history of Rome and the Roman Empire, including its culture, buildings, amusements, and emperors. (Rev: BL 1/1–15/99; HBG 3/99; SLJ 3/99) [937]

7521 Time-Life Books, eds. *When Rome Ruled the World: The Roman Empire, 100 B.C.–A.D. 200* (8–12). Series: What Life Was Like. 1997, Time-Life $34.95 (0-7835-5452-4). A wordy introduction to everyday life during the Roman Empire that is noteworthy for its excellent illustrations of art and artifacts. (Rev: SLJ 3/98) [937]

Middle Ages Through the Renaissance (500–1700)

7522 Aston, Margaret. *Panorama of the Renaissance* (10–12). 1996, Abrams $45.00 (0-8109-3704-2). An illustrated tour for better readers through the Renaissance, including the period's art, architecture, religion, rulers, finances, philosophy, literature, and social life. (Rev: BL 11/1/96; SLJ 2/97) [940.2]

7523 Baker, Alan. *The Knight: A Portrait of Europe's Warrior Elite* (10–12). 2003, Wiley $22.95 (0-471-25135-6). This well-researched study touches on virtually every aspect of the life of medieval knights, including weaponry, jousting, castle sieges, and crusades. (Rev: BL 2/1/03) [940.1]

7524 Bishop, Morris. *The Middle Ages* (10–12). Series: American Heritage Library. 2001, American Heritage paper $16.00 (0-618-05703-X). This volume covers the period from Constantine's conversion in 312 A.D. to the end of the Hundred Years War in 1461. [940.1]

7525 Blackwood, Gary L. *Life in a Medieval Castle* (6–10). Series: The Way People Live. 1999, Lucent LB $18.96 (1-56006-582-6). The daily life and personal problems involved in living in a castle during the Middle Ages are two of the topics discussed in this book that uses quotations from original sources. (Rev: BL 11/15/99) [940.1]

7526 Brewer, Paul. *Warfare in the Renaissance World* (7–10). Series: History of Warfare. 1999, Raintree Steck-Vaughn LB $29.97 (0-8172-5444-7). Using diagrams and other illustrations, this is an account of the wars and battles fought during the Renaissance. (Rev: HBG 3/99; SLJ 3/99) [940.2]

7527 Cantor, Norman F. *In the Wake of the Plague: The Black Death and the World It Made* (10–12). Illus. 2001, Free Pr. $25.50 (0-684-85735-9). This work describes the plague of 1347–1350 that destroyed half of Europe's population and its lasting effects. (Rev: BL 3/1/01) [614.5]

7528 Cooper, Tracy E. *Renaissance* (10–12). Series: Abbeville Stylebooks. 1995, Abbeville $12.95 (0-7892-0023-6). A handy, well-illustrated overview of the Age of Exploration and Renaissance architecture and design, with material on various kinds of buildings and furnishings. (Rev: SLJ 4/96) [940.2]

7529 Corrick, James A. *The Early Middle Ages* (8–12). Illus. Series: World History. 1995, Lucent LB $27.45 (1-56006-246-0). This account tells how Europe recovered and regrouped its power structure into a feudal economy after the barbarian invasions destroyed the Roman Empire. (Rev: BL 2/15/95) [940.1]

7530 Corrick, James A. *Life of a Medieval Knight* (6–10). Series: The Way People Live. 2001, Lucent LB $19.96 (1-56006-817-5). With generous quotations from primary and secondary sources, the daily life and routines of knights are chronicled plus coverage of sensational exploits and struggles. (Rev: BL 6/1–15/01) [941]

7531 Doherty, Katherine M., and Craig A. Doherty. *King Richard the Lionhearted and the Crusades* (8–12). Series: In World History. 2002, Enslow LB $20.95 (0-7660-1459-2). Combining both biography and history, this account re-creates the life of Richard the Lionhearted and his contributions to freeing the Holy Land during the Crusades. (Rev: BL 4/1/02; HBG 10/02; SLJ 6/02) [921]

7532 Durant, William James. *The Age of Faith* (10–12). Series: Story of Civilization. 1950, Simon & Schuster $40.00 (0-671-01200-2). A history of medieval civilization from Constantine to Dante — A.D. 325–1300. [940.1]

7533 Durant, William James. *The Reformation* (10–12). Series: Story of Civilization. 1957, Simon & Schuster $40.00 (0-671-61050-3). Among the personalities introduced in this account of the breakup of the Catholic church are Luther, Knox, Wolsey, Rabelais, and Chaucer. [940.2]

7534 Durant, William James. *The Renaissance* (10–12). Series: Story of Civilization. 1953, Simon & Schuster $35.00 (0-671-61600-5). A detailed and rewarding picture of the Italian Renaissance, and of the events and people involved. [945]

7535 *The 1100s* (10–12). Ed. by Helen Cothran. Series: Headlines in History. 2001, Greenhaven LB $43.70 (0-7377-0530-2); paper $27.45 (0-7377-0529-9). The century that saw many crusades in the Holy Land and the signing of the Magna Carta is covered in a series of serious essays that explore various facets of life. (Rev: BL 10/15/01) [909.2]

7536 Emerson, Kathy Lynn. *The Writer's Guide to Everyday Life in Renaissance England, from 1485–1649* (10–12). 1996, Writer's Digest $18.99 (0-89879-752-7). This complete guide to the Renaissance covers everyday life, government and war, and society, with subtopics such as food and drink, clothing, crime, witchcraft, entertainment, and marriage. (Rev: SLJ 2/97) [940.2]

7537 *The 1500s* (10–12). Ed. by Stephen Currie. Series: Headlines in History. 2001, Greenhaven LB $43.70 (0-7377-0538-8); paper $27.45 (0-7377-0537-X). The century that included Shakespeare, the Spanish Armada, and Copernicus is covered in a series of thematic essays that examine various events and cultural aspects. (Rev: BL 10/15/01) [909.5]

7538 *The 1400s* (10–12). Ed. by Stuart A. Kallen. Series: Headlines in History. 2001, Greenhaven LB $43.70 (0-7377-0536-1); paper $27.45 (0-7377-0535-3). In a series of concise essays, important events in history, culture, and science are covered for the century that included the discovery of America. (Rev: BL 10/15/01; SLJ 9/01) [909.4]

7539 Gies, Frances. *The Knight in History* (10–12). Illus. 1987, Harper & Row paper $14.00 (0-06-091413-0). The story of the beginnings, flowering, and decline of the institution of knighthood. [940.1]

7540 Gies, Joseph, and Frances Gies. *Life in a Medieval Castle* (10–12). Illus. 1979, HarperCollins paper $13.50 (0-06-090674-X). A Welsh castle is used as a model in this exploration of the feudal system and description of everyday life. [940.1]

7541 Gravett, Christopher. *The World of the Medieval Knight* (5–10). Illus. 1997, Bedrick $19.95 (0-87226-277-4). Various aspects of knighthood — from armor and jousting to castle life and the Crusades — are presented in this richly illustrated book. (Rev: BL 1/1–15/97; SLJ 3/97) [940.1]

7542 Hanawalt, Barbara. *Growing Up in Medieval London: The Experience of Childhood in History* (9–12). 1993, Oxford $56.00 (0-19-508405-5). Court records lend immediacy to the lives of London's children in the Middle Ages. (Rev: SLJ 12/94) [940]

7543 Hanawalt, Barbara. *The Middle Ages: An Illustrated History* (8–12). Illus. 1999, Oxford $29.95 (0-19-510359-9). A carefully researched account of the Roman Empire and its gradual fall, the rise of the church, its use of power, and feudal society, including such topics as castles, the Crusades, the Black Death, the rise of guilds and universities, and the growth of the middle class. (Rev: BL 3/1/99; HBG 3/99; SLJ 4/99) [909.07]

7544 Harpur, James. *Revelations: The Medieval World* (10–12). 1995, Holt $35.00 (0-8050-4140-0). With extensive use of illustrations, this is a handsome description of life in the Middle Ages, divided into four sections: knights, nobles and castles; urban decline and the prosperity that resulted from increased commerce in the 11th century; the building of many cathedrals and churches; and the endemic warfare. (Rev: BR 5–6/96; SLJ 2/96) [940.1]

7545 Hay, Jeff, ed. *The Early Middle Ages* (7–12). Series: Turning Points in World History. 2001, Greenhaven LB $22.96 (0-7377-0482-9); paper $14.96 (0-7377-0481-0). After a general introduction to this period in western history, several detailed essays present various aspects of the culture and social conditions of the time. (Rev: BL 6/1–15/01) [940.1]

7546 Hindley, Geoffrey. *The Crusades: A History* (10–12). 2003, Carroll & Graf $25.00 (0-7867-1105-1). This historical survey of the Crusades focuses particular attention on the key leaders and battles. (Rev: BL 4/15/03) [909.07]

7547 Jordan, William Chester. *Great Famine* (10–12). 1996, Princeton Univ. Pr. $42.50 (0-691-01134-6). From 1315 through 1322, Europe was in the grip of a terrible famine caused by heavy rains, harsh winters, animal disease, class warfare, and other factors. (Rev: SLJ 2/97) [940.1]

7548 Knight, Judson. *Middle Ages: Almanac* (6–10). Series: UXL Middle Ages Reference Library. 2000, Gale LB $45.00 (0-7876-4856-6). A comprehensive review of events around the world during the Middle Ages, with material on Africa and Asia as well as on Europe and the Middle East. Also use *Middle Ages: Biographies* and *Middle Ages: Primary Sources* (both 2000). (Rev: BL 4/1/01; SLJ 5/01) [940.1]

7549 Knight, Judson. *Middle Ages: Primary Sources* (8–12). 2000, UXL $52.00 (0-7876-4860-4). This book includes 19 entire or excerpted documents from the Middle Ages by such authors as Dante and Marco Polo. (Rev: BL 4/1/01; SLJ 5/01) [909.07]

7550 Lace, William W. *Defeat of the Spanish Armada* (6–10). Series: Battles. 1996, Lucent LB $26.20 (1-56006-458-7). The story of the war between England and Spain during the time of Elizabeth I, and how the defeat of Spain established England as a major sea power. (Rev: BL 4/15/97; BR 11–12/97; SLJ 6/97) [947]

7551 Man, John. *Atlas of the Year 1000* (10–12). Illus. 1999, Harvard $26.00 (0-674-54187-1). This beautifully illustrated book uses maps and photographs of artifacts to produce an engaging view of the world in the year 1000. (Rev: BL 1/1–15/00) [909.1]

7552 Marshall, Chris. *Warfare in the Medieval World* (7–10). Series: History of Warfare. 1999, Raintree Steck-Vaughn LB $29.97 (0-8172-5443-9). The Hundred Years' War is one of the wars highlighted in this book that focuses on individual battles and is illustrated with many full-color maps and reproductions. (Rev: HBG 3/99; SLJ 3/99; VOYA 2/00) [940.1]

7553 Matthew, Donald. *Atlas of Medieval Europe* (10–12). Illus. 1983, Facts on File $45.00 (0-87196-133-4). This collection of maps and pictures illustrates the political, social, and cultural history of Europe from the decline of the Roman Empire to the discovery of the New World. [911]

7554 *The Middle Ages* (10–12). Ed. by Bruno Leone. Series: History Firsthand. 2002, Gale LB $31.20 (0-7377-1073-X); paper $19.95 (0-7377-

1074-8). Vivid eyewitness accounts re-create the history, social life, and culture of the Middle Ages. (Rev: BL 8/02) [940.1]

7555 Norwich, Julius J. *A Short History of Byzantium* (10–12). 1997, Knopf $40.00 (0-679-45088-2). An exciting, detailed history of the intrigues, betrayals, rulers, and conquests that made up the 1,000-year history of the Byzantine Empire. (Rev: SLJ 2/98) [949.5]

7556 Orme, Nicholas. *Medieval Children* (10–12). Illus. 2001, Yale $39.95 (0-300-08541-9). A scholarly but fascinating account of the daily lives of medieval children from diverse classes and backgrounds. (Rev: BL 11/1/01; SLJ 5/02) [305.23]

7557 *The Renaissance* (10–12). Ed. by Raymond Obstfeld and Loretta Obstfeld. Series: History Firsthand. 2002, Gale LB $25.96 (0-7377-1080-2); paper $16.96 (0-7377-1079-9). Firsthand accounts are used to re-create the life, culture, history, and famous personalities of the Renaissance. (Rev: BL 12/15/02) [940.2]

7558 *The Renaissance* (10–12). Ed. by Stephen P. Thompson. Series: Turning Points in World History. 2000, Greenhaven LB $21.96 (0-7377-0219-2); paper $13.96 (0-7377-0218-4). This book of essays helps the advanced student explore the importance of the Renaissance. (Rev: BL 3/15/00) [940.1]

7559 *The Renaissance* (8–12). Ed. by Jeff Hay. Series: World History by Era. 2002, Greenhaven LB $41.20 (0-7377-0765-8); paper $24.95 (0-7377-0764-X). This collection of primary and secondary documents covers the European Renaissance as well as the Ottoman Empire and the Mughal Empire in India. (Rev: SLJ 3/02) [940.2]

7560 Rice, Earle, Jr. *Life During the Crusades* (8–10). Illus. Series: The Way People Live. 1998, Lucent LB $27.45 (1-56006-379-3). The period of the Crusades (1096–1272) is introduced, with material on feudal life, knighthood, reasons for the Crusades, Muslim culture, and key events of each of the Crusades. (Rev: BL 3/15/98; SLJ 5/98) [909.07]

7561 Rice, Earle, Jr. *Life During the Middle Ages* (6–10). Series: The Way People Live. 1998, Lucent LB $27.45 (1-56006-386-6). An account of how serfs, lords, and clergy lived under feudalism in the Middle Ages, enduring warfare, famine, and disease. (Rev: BL 7/98; SLJ 8/98) [941]

7562 Riley-Smith, Jonathan, ed. *The Oxford Illustrated History of the Crusades* (9–12). 1995, Oxford $72.50 (0-19-820435-3). A history of the Crusades and their odd blend of conquest and compassion. (Rev: BL 11/1/95) [909.7]

7563 *The 1600s* (10–12). Ed. by Louise I. Gerdes. Series: Headlines in History. 2001, Greenhaven LB $43.70 (0-7377-0635-X); paper $27.45 (0-7377-0634-1). This anthology of eyewitness accounts explores various aspects of social, political, and cultural history relating to the 17th century. (Rev: BL 10/15/01) [909.6]

7564 Stalcup, Brenda. *The Crusades* (9–12). Series: Turning Points in World History. 2000, Greenhaven LB $32.45 (1-565-10993-7); paper $21.20 (1-565-10992-9). The history of the Crusades is covered, along with a look at their effect on world history and culture. [909.07]

7565 Stalcup, Brenda, ed. *The Inquisition* (7–12). Series: Turning Points in World History. 2001, Greenhaven LB $22.96 (0-7377-0486-1); paper $14.96 (0-7377-0485-3). The history of this form of religious intolerance and persecution in Western Europe is traced in a series of essays that cover its beginnings in the 13th century and its eventual abolition. (Rev: BL 6/1–15/01; SLJ 7/01) [940]

7566 Sypeck, Jeff. *The Holy Roman Empire and Charlemagne in World History* (8–12). Series: In World History. 2002, Enslow LB $20.95 (0-7660-1901-2). This combination of biography and history tells the story of the life and reign of Charlemagne and the foundation of the Holy Roman Empire, which lasted for more than 700 years. (Rev: BL 3/15/03; HBG 3/03) [940.1]

7567 Taylor, Robert. *Life in Genghis Khan's Mongolia* (6–10). Series: The Way People Live. 2001, Lucent LB $19.96 (1-56006-348-3). As well as a life of this 13th-century Mongol conqueror and his empire, this account, which uses many original sources, describes the daily life of his subjects. (Rev: BL 6/1–15/01; SLJ 6/01) [951]

7568 Thackeray, Frank W., and John E. Findling. *Events that Changed the World Through the Sixteenth Century* (9–12). 2001, Greenwood $39.50 (0-313-29079-2). This book highlights 10 important events of the 15th and 16th centuries, ending with a description of the defeat of the Spanish Armada. (Rev: BL 11/1/01) [909]

7569 *The 1300s* (10–12). Ed. by Stephen Currie. Series: Headlines in History. 2001, Greenhaven LB $43.70 (0-7377-0534-5); paper $27.45 (0-7377-0533-7). For the serious student, this anthology of scholarly essays explores various faces of life in the 1300s, during which the Hundred Years War began and the Black Death struck Europe. (Rev: BL 10/15/01) [909.3]

7570 Thompson, Stephen P., ed. *The Reformation* (9–12). Series: Turning Points in World History. 1998, Greenhaven LB $21.96 (1-56510-961-9); paper $17.45 (1-56510-960-0). Beginning in the early 1500s, this book recounts the history of the movement to reform the Catholic Church, with emphasis on the work of Luther, Zwingli, and Calvin. (Rev: BL 5/15/99) [909.5]

7571 *The 1000s* (10–12). Ed. by Brenda Stalcup. Series: Headlines in History. 2001, Greenhaven LB $43.70 (0-7377-0528-0); paper $27.45 (0-7377-

0527-2). A series of scholarly essays and eyewitness accounts look at social, cultural, and political topics such as the Norman invasion of England and the First Crusade. (Rev: BL 10/15/01; SLJ 9/01) [909.2]

7572 Time-Life Books, eds. *What Life Was Like in the Age of Chivalry: Medieval Europe A.D. 800–1500* (10–12). Series: What Life Was Like. 1997, Time-Life $34.95 (0-7835-5451-6). Divided into four main sections — on the clergy, knights, peasants and rural landowners, and town dwellers — this handsome volume describes life in the Middle Ages through descriptions of important figures including Charlemagne, Heloise and Abelard, Joan of Arc, and Thomas Becket. (Rev: SLJ 1/98) [940]

7573 Tuchman, Barbara Wertheim. *A Distant Mirror: The Calamitous 14th Century* (10–12). 1978, Knopf paper $17.95 (0-345-34957-1). A scholarly but accessible account of the political, social, and cultural life of the 14th century as experienced by a French feudal lord. [944]

7574 *The 1200s* (10–12). Ed. by Thomas Siebold. Series: Headlines in History. 2001, Greenhaven LB $43.70 (0-7377-0532-9); paper $27.45 (0-7377-0531-0). Using firsthand accounts from the period as well as articles and commentary by contemporary historians, this scholarly volume provides readers with information on world cultures and important events of the 13th century. (Rev: BL 10/15/01) [909.2]

Eighteenth Through Nineteenth Centuries (1700–1900)

7575 Bachrach, Deborah. *The Charge of the Light Brigade* (6–10). Illus. Series: Battles. 1996, Lucent LB $26.20 (1-56006-455-2). An account of the "death charge of the 600" at Balaclava on Sept. 20, 1854, during the Crimean War. (Rev: BL 4/15/97; BR 11–12/97; SLJ 6/97) [947]

7576 Bachrach, Deborah. *The Crimean War* (8–12). Illus. Series: World History. 1997, Lucent LB $27.45 (1-56006-315-7). An easy-to-read account of the causes, main events, and consequences of the Crimean War, the first war to be extensively covered by the press, fought from 1853 to 1856 and involving Great Britain, France, Russia, and Turkey. (Rev: SLJ 6/98) [947]

7577 Corrick, James A. *The Industrial Revolution* (7–10). Illus. Series: World History. 1998, Lucent LB $27.45 (1-56006-318-1). Using more than 20 original documents, this work examines the changes in technology and working conditions brought about by the Industrial Revolution in England, Europe, and America, and explores its far-reaching social impact spanning the 18th, 19th, and 20th centuries. (Rev: BL 9/1/98) [909.81]

7578 *The 1800s* (10–12). Ed. by James Miller. Series: Headlines in History. 2001, Greenhaven LB $43.70 (0-7377-0543-3); paper $27.45 (0-7377-0544-2). The American Civil War and the Victorian Age in Britain are two of the important landmarks explored in this collection of original sources and commentaries relating to various aspects of life in the 1800s. (Rev: BL 10/15/01) [909.8]

7579 Killingray, David. *The Transatlantic Slave Trade* (7–12). Illus. 1987, Batsford $19.95 (0-7134-5469-5). This book gives detailed coverage of the causes, history, and end of the international slave trade and how it has affected demographics today. (Rev: SLJ 1/88) [380.1]

7580 Monaghan, Tom. *The Slave Trade* (6–10). Series: Events and Outcomes. 2002, Raintree Steck-Vaughn LB $28.54 (0-7398-5802-5). An interesting overview of the supply of slaves to the New World from its early days through its abolition, with information on key abolitionists and discussion of the economic reasons for this trade. (Rev: HBG 3/03; SLJ 4/03) [306.3]

7581 Phillips, Caryl. *The Atlantic Sound* (10–12). 2000, Knopf $26.00 (0-375-40110-5). This scholarly look at the triangular Atlantic slave trade combines history, sociology, and profound thoughts about race. (Rev: BL 9/1/00) [380.1]

7582 Pietrusza, David. *The Battle of Waterloo* (6–10). Illus. Series: Great Battles in History. 1996, Lucent LB $26.20 (1-56006-423-4). The story of the last battle of the Napoleonic Wars is told with generous use of graphics, including a timeline and maps. (Rev: BL 4/15/96; BR 9–10/96; SLJ 4/96) [940.2]

7583 Postma, Johannes. *The Atlantic Slave Trade* (9–12). 2003, Greenwood (0-313-31862-X). From the 1400s to the final abolition of slavery in the New World in 1888, this is the history of the Atlantic slave trade and its influence on economic development. (Rev: SLJ 12/03) [326]

7584 *The 1700s* (10–12). Ed. by Stuart A. Kallen. Series: Headlines in History. 2001, Greenhaven LB $43.70 (0-7377-0542-6); paper $27.45 (0-7377-0541-8). This collection of eyewitness accounts and general essays explores various aspects of world history during the 18th century. (Rev: BL 10/15/01) [909.7]

7585 Sommerville, Donald. *Revolutionary and Napoleonic Wars* (8–10). Series: History of Warfare. 1998, Raintree Steck-Vaughn LB $29.97 (0-8172-5446-3). This well-illustrated book looks at the wars fought from the late-18th through mid-19th centuries, focusing primarily on the Americans and the French and their wars of independence and sub-

sequent battles with other enemies. (Rev: HBG 3/99; SLJ 1/99) [909]

7586 Spencer, Lloyd. *Introducing the Enlightenment* (10–12). Illus. 1997, Totem paper $10.95 (1-874166-56-0). A serious but interesting introduction to 18th-century Europe that discusses individuals, events, accomplishments, and concepts of the Age of Enlightenment. (Rev: SLJ 1/98) [909]

7587 Stevens, Peter. *The Voyage of the Catalpa: A Perilous Journey and Six Irish Rebels' Flight to Freedom* (10–12). Illus. 2002, Carroll & Graf $26.00 (0-7867-0974-X). In 1875, the whaler *Catalpa* set sail from Massachusetts on a dangerous mission to rescue six Irish political prisoners being held by British forces in Fremantle, Australia. (Rev: BL 2/15/02) [910.4]

7588 Thackeray, Frank W., and John E. Findling, eds. *Events that Changed the World in the Eighteenth Century* (9–12). 1998, Greenwood $39.95 (0-313-29077-6). Topics included in this resource include the reforms of Peter the Great, the War of the Spanish Succession, the Seven Years' War, the Enlightenment, the Agricultural Revolution, the American Revolution, the Atlantic slave trade, the French Revolution, and the Industrial Revolution. (Rev: BR 9–10/98; SLJ 2/99) [909.7]

7589 Thackeray, Frank W., and John E. Findling. *Events that Changed the World in the Nineteenth Century* (10–12). 1996, Greenwood $39.95 (0-313-29076-8). Provides profiles of 10 pivotal 19th-century events, providing brief histories and interpretive essays by scholars specializing in the period. (Rev: BL 10/15/96) [909.81]

7590 Westwell, Ian. *Warfare in the 18th Century* (8–10). Series: History of Warfare. 1998, Raintree Steck-Vaughn LB $29.97 (0-8172-5445-5). A look at wars fought from the Great Northern War in 1700 to the death of Catherine the Great in 1796, including wars fought with Native Americans and over the fate of India. (Rev: HBG 3/99; SLJ 1/99) [909]

Twentieth Century

General and Miscellaneous

7591 Clare, John D. *Growing Up in the People's Century* (6–12). 1998, BBC Books $20.00 (0-563-40410-8). Wonderful for browsers, this book uses double-page spreads with pictures and quotations to present a quick view of events of historical or cultural significance in the 20th century. (Rev: BL 1/1–15/99) [909.82]

7592 *Developing Nations* (9–12). Ed. by Berna Miller and James D. Torr. Series: Current Controversies. 2003, Gale LB $32.45 (0-7377-1180-9); paper $21.20 (0-7377-1179-5). The many challenges facing the world's developing countries are explored in a collection of essays written mainly by Westerners. (Rev: BL 4/15/03; SLJ 12/03) [330.9172]

7593 *Events that Shaped the Century* (7–12). 1998, Time-Life $29.95 (0-7835-5502-4). Using outstanding photographs, this volume describes 125 events since 1900 that transformed America and affected all aspects of American life. (Rev: BR 11–12/98; SLJ 9/98) [909.82]

7594 Fralon, Jose-Alain. *A Good Man in Evil Times: The Heroic Story of Aristides de Sousa Mendes — The Man Who Saved the Lives of Countless Refugees in World War II* (10–12). Trans. by Peter Graham. Illus. 2001, Carroll & Graf $22.00 (0-7867-0848-4). The heroic story of the Portuguese consul in Bordeaux during 1940 and how he wrote visas that saved the lives of about 10,000 refugees, mostly Jews. (Rev: BL 3/1/01) [940.533]

7595 Garner, Joe. *We Interrupt This Broadcast: Relive the Events That Stopped Our Lives . . . from the Hindenburg to the Death of Princess Diana* (11–12). Illus. 1998, Sourcebooks $45.00 (1-57071-328-6). This book and its companion CD capture some of the landmark moments in 20th-century history through audio clips of the breaking news such as the 1937 Hindenberg disaster and Neil Armstrong's first step on the moon. (Rev: BL 11/15/98) [070.1]

7596 Hodgson, Godfrey. *People's Century: The Ordinary Men and Women Who Made the Twentieth Century* (9–12). 1998, Times Books $60.00 (0-8129-2843-1). An English publication that presents a broad chronological view of the 20th century, with many sidebars, quotations from individuals who lived through particular events, and thousands of photographs. (Rev: SLJ 9/98) [909.82]

7597 Howard, Michael, and Wm. Roger Louis. *The Oxford History of the Twentieth Century* (10–12). 1998, Oxford paper $22.50 (0-19-285370-8). Leading historians look at the important developments of the 20th century. (Rev: BL 11/1/98) [909.82]

7598 Jennings, Peter, and Todd Brewster. *The Century for Young People* (7–10). Illus. 1999, Doubleday $29.95 (0-385-32708-0). An attractive presentation of the major events of 1900–1998, with photographs and first-person accounts. (Rev: BL 11/15/99; HBG 4/00; SLJ 11/99*; VOYA 2/00) [909.82]

7599 *National Geographic Eyewitness to the 20th Century* (9–12). 1998, National Geographic $40.00 (0-7922-7049-5). A record of the 20th century as recorded in *National Geographic* magazine, arranged by decades, each with a six-page introduction followed by outstanding illustrations. (Rev: SLJ 3/99) [909]

7600 *The 1900s* (10–12). Ed. by James Miller. Series: Headlines in History. 2001, Greenhaven LB

$43.70 (0-7377-0546-9); paper $27.45 (0-7377-0545-0). This collection of 33 readings, including firsthand accounts as well as commentary from historians, provides a fairly complete — if somewhat challenging — overview of 20th-century history. (Rev: BL 10/15/01) [909.82]

7601 Stolley, Richard B., ed. *Life: Our Century in Pictures for Young People* (5–12). Illus. 2000, Little, Brown $25.45 (0-316-81577-2). Adapted from an adult coffee-table book, this survey of the last century is divided into nine chronological, heavily illustrated chapters with contributions from many children's writers including Lois Lowry and Robert Cormier. (Rev: BL 12/15/00) [909.82]

7602 Thackeray, Frank W., and John E. Findling. *Events that Changed the World in the Twentieth Century* (9–12). 1995, Greenwood $39.95 (0-313-29075-X). This book contains descriptions of major news events in the 20th century from World War I to the collapse of the Soviet Union. [909.82]

7603 Tuchman, Barbara Wertheim. *The Proud Tower: A Portrait of the World Before the War, 1890–1914* (10–12). 1966, Macmillan paper $15.95 (0-345-40501-3). This nonfiction work describes conditions in Europe and the events that led up to World War I. [909.82]

World War I

7604 Adams, Simon. *World War I* (6–12). Illus. 2001, DK $15.95 (0-7894-7939-7). This attractive large-format book is full of information and graphics relating to the war. (Rev: BL 12/15/01) [940.3]

7605 Bosco, Peter. *World War I* (7–12). Series: America at War. 1991, Facts on File $25.00 (0-8160-2460-X). Highlights the major battles and personalities of World War I and discusses events leading to a declaration of war and the changes following the peace. (Rev: BL 10/15/91; SLJ 8/91) [940.3]

7606 Coetzee, Frans, and Marilyn Shevin-Coetzee. *World War I: A History in Documents* (7–12). Series: Pages from History. 2002, Oxford LB $32.95 (0-19-513746-9). Letters, poems, posters, quotations, and other documents are accompanied by advice on evaluating their content. (Rev: SLJ 8/02) [940.3]

7607 Currie, Stephen. *Life in the Trenches* (6–12). Series: American War Library: World War I. 2002, Gale LB $27.45 (1-56006-838-8). This volume describes daily life for American servicemen in European battlefields and behind the scenes during World War I. (Rev: BL 6/1–15/02) [940.3]

7608 Dudley, William, ed. *World War I* (6–12). Illus. Series: Opposing Viewpoints: American History. 1997, Greenhaven LB $32.45 (1-56510-703-9); paper $21.20 (1-56510-702-0). The disagreements, debates, and international problems relating to the First World War, including U.S. war preparedness, neutrality, and the League of Nations, are covered in this collection of viewpoints. (Rev: BL 5/15/98) [940.3]

7609 Farwell, Byron. *Over There: The United States in the Great War, 1917–1918* (10–12). 1999, Norton $27.95 (0-393-04698-2); paper $15.95 (0-393-32028-6). The focus of this account is the military aspects of the war after America's entrance, but there is also material on the previous two years of the conflict and on its social and economic impact. [940.4]

7610 Gilbert, Martin. *The First World War: A Complete History* (10–12). 1994, Holt paper $21.95 (0-8050-4734-4). This rewarding, stimulating book views World War I from many standpoints and traces causes, events, domestic issues, and results. (Rev: BL 11/1/94) [940.3]

7611 Howard, Michael. *The First World War* (10–12). Illus. 2002, Oxford $23.00 (0-19-285362-7). A concise overview of the causes and major events of World War I. (Rev: BL 9/15/02) [940.3]

7612 *Intimate Voices from the First World War* (10–12). Ed. by Sarah Wallis and Svetlana Palmer. Illus. 2004, HarperCollins $25.95 (0-06-058259-6). Using previously unpublished memoirs, diaries, and other original documents, this is a collection of records representing points of view from all sides of World War I. (Rev: BL 1/1–15/04) [940.4]

7613 Jantzen, Steven. *Hooray for Peace, Hurrah for War: The United States During World War I* (9–12). 1990, Facts on File $19.95 (0-8160-2453-7). A brief, accessible account of American policy during the war and rejection of the League of Nations. (Rev: SLJ 5/91) [940.3]

7614 Keegan, John. *An Illustrated History of the First World War* (9–12). 2001, Knopf $50.00 (0-375-41259-X). Complete with 500 illustrations, this is a clear, interesting account of the events, people, and causes of World War I. (Rev: BL 10/15/01) [940.3]

7615 Lawrence, T. E. *Seven Pillars of Wisdom: A Triumph* (10–12). 1935, Doubleday paper $19.95 (0-385-41895-7). From Lawrence of Arabia comes this account of the Arab revolt during World War I and of the national character of the countries involved. [940.4]

7616 Murphy, Donald J., ed. *World War I* (7–12). Series: Turning Points in World History. 2002, Gale LB $31.20 (0-7377-0932-4); paper $19.95 (0-7377-0933-2). The causes, campaigns, battles, effects, and personal aspects of World War I are explored in this anthology of important essays for the serious student. (Rev: BL 6/1–15/02) [940.3]

7617 Rice, Earle, Jr. *The Battle of Belleau Wood* (6–10). Illus. Series: Great Battles in History. 1996,

Lucent LB $19.95 (1-56006-424-2). The story of the victory over the Germans in June 1918 by chiefly American troops is told with generous use of illustrations, maps, and a timeline. (Rev: BL 4/15/96; BR 9–10/96) [940.4]

7618 Ross, Stewart. *Causes and Consequences of World War I* (7–10). Series: Causes and Consequences. 1998, Raintree Steck-Vaughn LB $29.97 (0-8172-4057-8). This volume analyzes the factors that led to World War I and the conflict's short-term and long-term effects, with illustrations. (Rev: BL 8/98; SLJ 6/98) [940.311]

7619 Stokesbury, James L. *A Short History of World War I* (9–12). 1981, Morrow paper $14.00 (0-688-00129-7). A brief but penetrating history of World War I that gives both political and military perspectives. [940.3]

7620 Tuchman, Barbara Wertheim. *The Guns of August* (10–12). 1988, Macmillan paper $14.95 (0-345-38623-X). The story of the negotiations that preceded World War I, how and why they failed, and the events of the first weeks of the war. [940.3]

7621 Tuchman, Barbara Wertheim. *The Zimmermann Telegram.* New ed (10–12). 1966, Macmillan paper $14.00 (0-345-32425-0). This work describes the attempts made by Germany to persuade Mexico to attack the United States during World War I. [940.3]

7622 Tucker, Spencer C. *The Great War, 1914–18* (10–12). 1998, Indiana Univ. Pr. $44.95 (0-253-33372-5); paper $17.95 (0-253-21171-9). A concise introduction to the key events of the war, with discussion of economic and social aspects. [940.3]

World War II and the Holocaust

7623 Aaseng, Nathan. *Paris* (6–12). Series: Cities at War. 1992, Macmillan LB $18.00 (0-02-700010-9). Remembrances from people who experienced World War II in Paris. (Rev: BL 10/15/92) [944]

7624 Adelson, Alan, ed. *The Diary of Dawid Sierakowiak* (10–12). Trans. from Polish by Kamil Turowski. 1996, Oxford $56.00 (0-19-510450-1). These are the journals kept by a young Jewish boy in the Lodz ghetto from 1939 when he was 15 until his death from tuberculosis in 1943. (Rev: BL 8/96; SLJ 6/97) [940.54]

7625 Altman, Linda J. *Crimes and Criminals of the Holocaust* (5–10). Illus. Series: Holocaust in History. 2004, Enslow LB $20.95 (0-7660-1995-0). This book focuses on the end of World War II and the war crimes trials in Nuremberg as well as other cases such as that of Adolf Eichmann. (Rev: BL 5/1/04) [940.53]

7626 Altman, Linda J. *Forever Outsiders: Jews and History from Ancient Times to August 1935* (6–12).

Illus. Series: Holocaust. 1997, Blackbirch LB $27.44 (1-56711-200-5). An authoritative look at anti-Semitism throughout history, ending with Hitler's rise to power and the beginnings of his Final Solution. (Rev: BL 10/15/97; BR 1–2/98; HBG 3/98; SLJ 2/98) [940.53]

7627 Altman, Linda J. *The Forgotten Victims of the Holocaust* (5–10). Illus. Series: Holocaust in History. 2003, Enslow LB $20.95 (0-7660-1993-4). Altman looks at populations victimized by the Nazis that are often overlooked: Poles, Russians, gypsies, homosexuals, and the disabled. Also use *The Jewish Victims of the Holocaust* (2003), which describes Hitler's genocide of the Jews. (Rev: BL 7/03; HBG 4/04; SLJ 10/03) [940.53]

7628 Altman, Linda J. *The Holocaust Ghettos* (8–12). Series: Holocaust Remembered. 1998, Enslow LB $20.95 (0-89490-994-0). This volume explains the role that ghettos played in the Nazis' scheme to isolate and control the Jews in preparation for relocation to death camps. (Rev: BR 9–10/98; SLJ 7/98; VOYA 8/98) [940.54]

7629 Altman, Linda J. *The Holocaust, Hitler, and Nazi Germany* (6–12). Illus. Series: Holocaust Remembered. 1999, Enslow LB $19.95 (0-7660-1230-1). This book explores the many causes and forces that produced the Holocaust. (Rev: BL 4/1/00; HBG 4/00; SLJ 5/00) [943.08]

7630 Altman, Linda J. *Impact of the Holocaust* (5–10). Illus. Series: Holocaust in History. 2004, Enslow LB $20.95 (0-7660-1996-9). This book discusses the Holocaust's influence in the creation of a homeland for the Jews, and a Universal Declaration of Human Rights. (Rev: BL 5/1/04) [940.53]

7631 Altshuler, David A. *Hitler's War Against the Jews: A Young Reader's Version of The War Against the Jews, 1933–1945, by Lucy S. Dawidowicz* (7–10). Illus. 1995, Behrman paper $14.95 (0-87441-298-6). The tragic story of Hitler's Final Solution and its aftermath. [940.54]

7632 Ambrose, Stephen. *Citizen Soldiers: The U.S. Army from the Normandy Beaches to the Bulge to the Surrender of Germany, June 7, 1944–May 7, 1945* (9–12). 1997, Simon & Schuster paper $17 .00 (0-684-84801-5). Beginning the day after the landing on the beaches of Normandy, this highly readable narrative traces the advance of U.S. armed forces toward the Rhineland. (Rev: BL 9/15/97) [940.54]

7633 Ambrose, Stephen. *D-Day: June 6, 1944: The Climactic Battle of World War II* (9–12). 1994, Simon & Schuster $29.50 (0-671-67334-3). Long, detailed, immediate, and readable, this history is for teens who can't get enough of World War II drama. (Rev: BL 4/1/94) [940.54]

7634 Ambrose, Stephen. *The Good Fight: How World War II Was Won* (7–12). Illus. 2001, Simon & Schuster $19.95 (0-689-84361-5). Historian Ambrose presents an appealing and well-written overview of World War II, from its origins through the Marshall Plan, with many photographs, fact boxes, and maps. (Rev: BL 7/01; HBG 10/01; SLJ 5/01; VOYA 6/01) [940.53]

7635 Ambrose, Stephen. *The Victors: Eisenhower and His Boys: The Men of World War II* (10–12). 1998, Simon & Schuster $28.00 (0-684-85628-X). Through hundreds of interviews and the examination of countless documents, the author has created a rounded portrait of Eisenhower in World War II, his relationship with his "boys," and a chronicle of American participation in the European theater. (Rev: BL 10/1/98; SLJ 5/99) [940.54]

7636 Anthony, Nathan, and Robert Gardner. *The Bombing of Pearl Harbor in American History* (6–10). Series: In American History. 2001, Enslow LB $20.95 (0-7660-1126-7). This is a well-researched account that covers the bombing of Pearl Harbor by the Japanese in 1941 and the consequences. (Rev: BL 3/1/01; HBG 10/01) [940.54]

7637 Ayer, Eleanor. *Berlin* (6–12). Series: Cities at War. 1992, Macmillan LB $18.00 (0-02-707800-0). A photoessay on the lives of ordinary people in Berlin during World War II, with eyewitness quotations. (Rev: BL 6/15/92; SLJ 9/92) [940.53]

7638 Ayer, Eleanor. *A Firestorm Unleashed: January 1942 to June 1943* (6–12). Illus. Series: Holocaust. 1997, Blackbirch LB $27.44 (1-56711-204-8). Historical narratives and personal accounts are blended in this story of the Holocaust that covers the first year and a half of American participation in the war. (Rev: BL 10/15/97; BR 1–2/98; HBG 3/98; SLJ 2/98) [940.53]

7639 Ayer, Eleanor. *Inferno: June 1943 to May 1945* (6–12). Illus. Series: Holocaust. 1997, Blackbirch LB $27.44 (1-56711-205-6). During the two-year period covered in this part of the series, Hitler and the Nazis fully implement their plans to destroy European Jews and the death camps reach their peak of activity. (Rev: BL 10/15/97; BR 1–2/98; HBG 3/98; SLJ 2/98) [940.53]

7640 Ayer, Eleanor. *The Survivors* (10–12). Series: Holocaust Library. 1997, Lucent LB $17.96 (1-56006-096-4). This is the story of the hundreds of thousands of Jews who survived the death camps, and of those who created a new homeland in the state of Israel. (Rev: BL 3/15/98; SLJ 7/98; VOYA 12/98) [940.54]

7641 Ayer, Eleanor, and Stephen D. Chicoine. *From the Ashes: May 1945 and After* (6–12). Illus. Series: Holocaust. 1997, Blackbirch LB $27.44 (1-56711-206-4). This account of the Holocaust covers the end of the war, its aftermath, the war crimes trials, and the stories of death camp survivors. (Rev: BL 10/15/97; BR 1–2/98; HBG 3/98; SLJ 2/98) [940.53]

7642 Ayer, Eleanor, et al. *Parallel Journeys* (7–12). 1995, Atheneum $16.00 (0-689-31830-8). Personal narratives in alternating chapters contrast the experiences of a Jewish woman and of a former ardent member of the Hitler Youth, who grew up a few miles from each other. (Rev: BL 5/15/95*; SLJ 6/95) [943.086]

7643 Bachrach, Deborah. *The Resistance* (10–12). Series: Holocaust Library. 1997, Lucent LB $17.96 (1-56006-092-1). This account traces the history of the rare individuals and groups that opposed the Nazi tyranny to try to save lives and end Hitler's reign. (Rev: BL 12/15/97; HBG 3/99; SLJ 2/98) [940.54]

7644 Bar-on, Dan. *Legacy of Silence: Encounters with Children of the Third Reich* (9–12). 1989, Harvard Univ. Pr. $37.00 (0-674-52185-4). Interviews with 13 German men and women who were children during World War II reveal the roles their parents played in the Holocaust. (Rev: BL 9/15/89) [940.531]

7645 Bard, Mitchell G., ed. *The Holocaust* (6–12). Illus. Series: Complete History Of. 2001, Greenhaven LB $99.00 (0-7377-0373-3). A well-organized and balanced look at the Holocaust comprising more than 90 entries. (Rev: BL 11/1/01; SLJ 8/01) [940.53]

7646 Bard, Mitchell G., ed. *The Holocaust* (7–12). Series: Turning Points in World History. 2001, Greenhaven LB $22.96 (0-7377-0576-0); paper $14.96 (0-7377-0575-2). The Jewish genocide in Nazi Germany is explored in an anthology of essays, each of which examines a different aspect of this terrible period in history. (Rev: BL 6/1–15/01) [940.54]

7647 Bastable, Jonathan. *Voices from D-Day* (10–12). Illus. 2004, David & Charles $24.99 (0-7153-1790-3). A series of eyewitness accounts, including some from elite combat soldiers, that describe D-Day and the invasion of France. (Rev: BL 4/15/04) [940.54]

7648 Bauer, Yehuda. *Rethinking the Holocaust* (10–12). 2001, Yale $29.95 (0-300-08256-8). The book raises critical issues relating to the Holocaust and includes material on its origins, other attempts at genocide, and Jewish reactions during the Holocaust. (Rev: BL 12/1/00) [940.53]

7649 Berenbaum, Michael. *The World Must Know: A History of the Holocaust as Told in the United States Holocaust Memorial Museum* (9–12). 1993, Little, Brown paper $23.00 (0-316-09134-0). Includes moving photographs of the Warsaw ghetto selected from the Holocaust Memorial Museum in Washington, D.C. (Rev: BL 3/1/93) [940.53]

7650 Berland-Hyatt, Felicia. *Close Calls: Memoirs of a Survivor* (9–12). 1991, Holocaust Publns. paper $13.95 (0-89604-138-7). A survivor's account of the Holocaust. (Rev: BL 1/15/92) [921]

7651 Bitton-Jackson, Livia. *I Have Lived a Thousand Years: Growing Up in the Holocaust* (7–12). 1997, Simon & Schuster $17.00 (0-689-81022-9). Abridged from the author's adult book, this is the story of a 13-year-old Hungarian Jewish girl and how she survived Auschwitz. (Rev: BL 3/15/97; BR 9–10/97; SLJ 5/97; VOYA 6/97) [940.54]

7652 Bles, Mark. *Child at War: The True Story of a Young Belgian Resistance Fighter* (9–12). 1991, Mercury House $20.95 (1-56279-004-8). An exciting behind-the-front story of a teenager's fight for freedom in Belgium during World War II. (Rev: BL 3/1/91; SLJ 2/92) [921]

7653 Block, Gay, and Malka Drucker. *Rescuers: Portraits of Moral Courage in the Holocaust* (9–12). 1992, Holmes & Meier $49.95 (0-8419-1322-6); paper $29.95 (0-8419-1323-4). Profiles of 49 people who risked their lives to hide and protect Jews during the Holocaust. (Rev: BL 3/15/92) [940.53]

7654 Boas, Jacob. *We Are Witnesses: The Diaries of Five Teenagers Who Died in the Holocaust* (7–12). 1995, Holt $17.95 (0-8050-3702-0). Boas, born in 1943 in a Nazi camp, talks about being a Holocaust survivor and the deaths of five other young inmates. (Rev: BL 5/15/95*) [940.53]

7655 Boisclaire, Yvonne. *In the Shadow of the Rising Sun* (10–12). 1997, Clearwood paper $14.95 (0-9649997-3-0). The horrifying, true story of U.S. Army Sergeant Robert Davis and how he and some colleagues survived inhuman treatment in Japanese prison camps in the Pacific. (Rev: VOYA 12/97) [940.54]

7656 Boraks-Nemetz, Lillian, and Irene N. Watts, eds. *Tapestry of Hope: Holocaust Writing for Young People* (6–12). 2003, Tundra $24.99 (0-88776-638-2). Two Holocaust survivors have collected fiction, poetry, drama, and nonfiction excerpts that detail the experiences of those who went into hiding, were sent to the camps, joined the resistance movement, and made their way to other countries. (Rev: BL 6/1–15/03; HBG 10/03; SLJ 8/03; VOYA 10/03) [810.8]

7657 Boyington, Gregory. *Baa Baa Black Sheep* (10–12). 1989, TAB $22.95 (0-8306-4008-8). This book deals with the men and exploits of the daring Flying Tigers during World War II. [940.54]

7658 Bradley, James, and Ron Powers. *Flags of Our Fathers: Heroes of Iwo Jima* (7–10). Adapted by Michael French. 2001, Delacorte $15.95 (0-385-72932-4). The son of one of the Marines who raised the flag at Iwo Jima tells the story behind the event in this adaptation of an adult bestseller. (Rev: BL 4/1/01; BR 11/01; HBG 10/01; SLJ 5/01*; VOYA 10/01) [940.54]

7659 Brager, Bruce L. *The Trial of Adolf Eichmann: The Holocaust on Trial* (8–12). Series: Famous Trials. 1999, Lucent LB $27.45 (1-56006-469-2). The story of the search for the infamous war criminal and of his trial in Israel in 1961, during which the horror of the Holocaust was relived. (Rev: BL 5/1/99; SLJ 8/99) [364.15]

7660 Brash, Sarah, ed. *World War II* (7–12). Illus. Series: American Story. 1997, Time-Life $19.95 (0-7835-6253-5). The causes, events, and outcomes of World War II are covered in this well-illustrated account that emphasizes American participation. (Rev: BL 5/15/97) [940.53]

7661 Brickhill, Paul. *The Great Escape* (9–12). Illus. 1986, Fawcett paper $5.99 (0-449-21068-5). The exciting story of the digging of three tunnels in a German prisoner-of-war camp during World War II that allowed 100 men to escape. [940.54]

7662 Byers, Ann. *The Holocaust Camps* (8–12). Series: Holocaust Remembered. 1998, Enslow LB $18.95 (0-89490-955-9). This work traces the evolution of political prison camps to labor camps and eventually to death camps during the Nazi regime. (Rev: BR 9–10/98; VOYA 8/98) [940.54]

7663 Churchill, Winston. *The Gathering Storm* (10–12). Series: Second World War. 1948, Houghton paper $19.00 (0-395-41055-X). The first volume of Churchill's history of World War II traces the causes of war and Hitler's victories prior to Dunkirk. [940.53]

7664 Churchill, Winston. *The Grand Alliance* (10–12). Series: Second World War. 1950, Houghton paper $18.00 (0-395-41057-6). This volume in Churchill's history of World War II deals with the entrance into the war of Russia and later the United States. [940.53]

7665 Churchill, Winston. *The Great Battles and Leaders of the Second World War: An Illustrated History* (9–12). 1995, Houghton $40.00 (0-395-75516-6). A picture album with text excerpted from Churchill's classic six-volume work *The Second World War.* (Rev: BL 12/1/95) [940.53]

7666 Churchill, Winston. *The Hinge of Fate* (10–12). Series: Second World War. 1950, Houghton paper $18.00 (0-395-41058-4). This volume in Churchill's history covers January 1942 through May 1943 and involves the war in Africa and the planned invasion of Sicily. [940.53]

7667 Churchill, Winston. *Their Finest Hour* (10–12). Series: Second World War. 1949, Houghton paper $19.00 (0-395-41056-8). The Battle of Britain and the evacuations at Dunkirk are covered in this volume of Churchill's history that focuses on the events of 1940. [940.53]

7668 Churchill, Winston. *Triumph and Tragedy* (9–12). Series: Second World War. 1953, Houghton paper $18.00 (0-395-41060-6). This, the last volume of Churchill's history of World War Ii, deals with

the closing days of the war and the defeat of Germany and Japan. [940.53]

7669 Cohn, Marthe, and Wendy Holden. *Behind Enemy Lines: The True Story of a Jewish Spy in Nazi Germany* (10–12). Illus. 2002, Harmony $24.00 (0-609-61054-6). An exciting account of the author's experiences in the French Resistance, including her dangerous trips into Germany. (Rev: BL 10/1/02) [940.54]

7670 Crane, Cynthia A. *Divided Lives: The Untold Stories of Jewish-Christian Women in Nazi Germany* (10–12). Illus. 2000, St. Martin's $26.95 (0-312-21953-9). Ten women who survived the Holocaust and were "mischling"—the children of Jewish-Christian marriages—tell their stories. (Rev: BL 12/15/00) [940.53]

7671 David, Kati. *A Child's War: Fifteen Children Tell Their Story* (9–12). 1989, Four Walls Eight Windows $17.95 (0-941423-24-7). Fifteen people representing a wide range of perspectives tell of their childhoods when they were between the ages of 5 and 10 during World War II. (Rev: BL 5/1/89) [940.53]

7672 de Clercq Zubli, Rita la Fontaine. *Disguised: A Teenage Girl's Survival in World War II Japanese Prison Camps* (10–12). 2001, Southfarm $30.00 (0-913337-41-2). In this unique, moving memoir, the author describes how she survived by being disguised as a boy. (Rev: BL 6/1–15/01) [940.54]

7673 Del Calzo, Rick. *The Triumphant Spirit: Portraits and Stories of Holocaust Survivors, Their Messages of Hope and Compassion* (10–12). 1997, Triumphant Spirit $45.00 (0-9655260-0-3); paper $29.95 (0-9655260-1-1). Black-and-white photographs are intertwined with narratives of more than 90 Holocaust survivors. (Rev: BL 3/15/97; SLJ 10/97) [940.54]

7674 Devaney, John. *America Fights the Tide: 1942* (6–10). 1991, Walker $17.95 (0-8027-6997-7). Using a diary format and anecdotal accounts, this volume focuses on the United States' entry into World War II in both the European and the Pacific theaters. (Rev: BL 10/15/91; SLJ 10/91) [940.54]

7675 Devaney, John. *America on the Attack: 1943* (6–10). Series: Walker's World War II. 1992, Walker LB $18.85 (0-8027-8195-0). This well-illustrated account describes America's active participation in World War II once the war effort got under way. (Rev: BL 12/1/92) [940.53]

7676 Devaney, John. *America Storms the Beaches: 1944* (6–10). Series: World War II. 1993, Walker LB $18.85 (0-8027-8245-0). The story of D Day and the other invasions that spelled the beginning of the end of Nazi Germany. (Rev: BL 12/15/93; SLJ 12/93; VOYA 2/94) [940.54]

7677 Drez, Ronald J. *Twenty-Five Yards of War: The Extraordinary Courage of Ordinary Men in*

World War II (10–12). 2001, Hyperion $23.95 (0-7868-6783-3). Personal World War II experiences of 12 Americans include coverage of the Doolittle attack and the battles of Midway and Iwo Jima. (Rev: BL 11/15/01) [940.53]

7678 Dudley, William, ed. *World War II* (7–12). Series: Opposing Viewpoints: American History. 1996, Greenhaven LB $32.45 (1-56510-528-1); paper $16.20 (1-56510-527-3). A thought-provoking anthology of different viewpoints on various aspects of World War II, representative of that time, including whether the United States should enter the war, the use of the atomic bomb, women's roles, and the internment of Japanese Americans but not German Americans or Italian Americans. (Rev: SLJ 3/97) [940.54]

7679 Dunnigan, James F., and Albert A. Nofi. *Victory at Sea: World War II in the Pacific* (9–12). 1995, Morrow paper $17.00 (0-688-14947-2). A thorough overview of the war in the Pacific, looking at such topics as campaigns, ships, and aircraft, with brief biographies and a chronology. (Rev: BL 5/1/95) [940.54]

7680 Durrett, Deanne. *Unsung Heroes of World War II: The Story of the Navajo Code Talkers* (7–12). Illus. Series: Library of American Indian History. 1998, Facts on File $25.00 (0-8160-3603-9). The story of the gallant Native American servicemen who developed a unique, unbreakable code based on the Navajo's complex, inflection-sensitive language, and transmitted and translated more than 800 messages in 48 hours without error during the battle of Iwo Jima. (Rev: BL 11/1/98; SLJ 1/99) [940.548673]

7681 Edvardson, Cordelia. *Burned Child Seeks the Fire: A Memoir* (10–12). Trans. from German by Joel Agee. 1997, Beacon $28.95 (0-8070-7094-7). The memoir of a girl who was raised as a Catholic but, because she is discovered to be part Jewish, is sent to Auschwitz, where she miraculously survived. (Rev: BL 7/97; SLJ 12/97) [940.54]

7682 Fantlova, Zdenka. *My Lucky Star* (10–12). 2001, Herodias $24.00 (1-928746-20-9). A Holocaust memoir in which a Czech Jewish woman tells of her survival of the Nazi death camps. (Rev: BL 4/15/01) [940.54]

7683 Fest, Joachim. *Inside Hitler's Bunker: The Last Days of the Third Reich* (9–12). Trans. by Margot Bettauer Dembo. Illus. 2004, Farrar $21.00 (0-374-13577-0). Besides presenting details of life in Hitler's bunker, this account describes the fate of Berlin and its people during the last days of World War II. (Rev: BL 2/15/04) [943.086]

7684 Filar, Marian, and Charles Patterson. *From Buchenwald to Carnegie Hall* (10–12). 2002, Univ. Press of Mississippi $29.00 (1-57806-419-8). In this touching memoir of Holocaust survival, Polish-born concert pianist Filar recounts his experiences as a

young man in the Warsaw Ghetto and a series of Nazi concentration camps. (Rev: BL 1/1–15/02) [786.2]

7685 Fisch, Robert O. *Light from the Yellow Star: A Lesson of Love from the Holocaust* (7–12). Illus. 1996, Univ. of Minnesota Pr. $14.95 (1-885116-00-4); paper $9.95 (0-9644896-0-0). A biographical account that uses the author's abstract paintings to tell about his childhood in Budapest and his death camp experiences. (Rev: BL 4/15/96) [940.53]

7686 *Flares of Memory: Stories of Childhood During the Holocaust* (10–12). Ed. by Anita Brostoff and Sheila Chamovitz. 2001, Oxford $27.50 (0-19-513871-6). This volume contains 41 stories of Holocaust survivors who were youngsters when their horror began, plus the recollections of six American liberators of the death camps. (Rev: BL 5/15/01) [940.53]

7687 *Flight and Rescue* (10–12). Illus. 2001, United States Holocaust Memorial Museum $45.00 (0-89604-704-0). This is the story of the Jews who were saved by the Japanese consul and the Dutch acting consul in Lithuania in 1940. (Rev: BL 7/01) [362.87]

7688 Fountain, Nigel. *WWII: The People's Story* (8–12). 2003, Reader's Digest $39.95 (0-7621-0376-0). Letters, speeches, diaries, and interviews give a first-person quality to this book that, through print and an accompanying CD, re-creates the human side of World War II. (Rev: SLJ 4/04) [940.53]

7689 Freeman, Charles. *The Rise of the Nazis* (7–12). Series: New Perspectives. 1998, Raintree Steck-Vaughn $28.54 (0-8172-5015-8). Presents differing views on Hitler and the Nazi Party as expressed by German politicians, leaders, and ordinary citizens. (Rev: BL 3/15/98; BR 1–2/99; HBG 9/98; SLJ 7/98) [940.54]

7690 Freeman, Joseph. *Job: The Story of a Holocaust Survivor* (9–12). 1995, Paragon House paper $9.95 (1-55778-738-7). A survivor tells what he witnessed in the Polish ghetto and at Auschwitz. (Rev: BL 9/15/95) [921]

7691 Fremon, David K. *The Holocaust Heroes* (6–10). Series: Holocaust Remembered. 1998, Enslow LB $20.95 (0-7660-1046-5). This account of the Holocaust focuses on Resistance fighters, such as the people of the Warsaw Ghetto, and on individuals including Raoul Wallenberg and the Danish nation who took risks to help Jews escape. (Rev: BL 9/15/98; BR 1–2/99; HBG 3/99; SLJ 12/98) [940.5318]

7692 Galloway, Priscilla, ed. *Too Young to Fight: Memories from Our Youth During World War II* (6–12). 2000, Stoddart $22.95 (0-7737-3190-3). Eleven Canadian authors of books for young people describe what it was like growing up on the home front during World War II. (Rev: BL 5/1/00; SLJ 7/00) [940.53]

7693 Geier, Arnold. *Heroes of the Holocaust: Extra-ordinary Accounts of Triumph* (10–12). 1998, Berkley paper $14.00 (0-425-16029-7). A moving collection of accounts by 28 survivors of the Holo-caust who owe their lives to the unselfish acts of others. (Rev: SLJ 7/98) [940.54]

7694 Gies, Miep, and Alison L. Gold. *Anne Frank Remembered: The Story of Miep Gies, Who Helped to Hide the Frank Family* (8–12). Illus. 1987, Simon & Schuster paper $14.00 (0-671-66234-1). The story of the woman who helped the Frank family during World War II and of the Resistance move-ment in the Netherlands. (Rev: BL 4/1/87; SLJ 11/87; VOYA 12/87) [940.53]

7695 Gilbert, Martin. *The Day the War Ended: May 8, 1945 — Victory in Europe* (9–12). 1995, Holt $30.00 (0-8050-3926-0). In commemoration of the 50th anniversary of the end of World War II. Chron-icles events surrounding the end of the war in Europe. (Rev: BL 4/15/95) [940.54]

7696 Gilbert, Martin. *The Holocaust: A History of the Jews of Europe During the Second World War* (10–12). 1986, Holt paper $24 .00 (0-8050-0348-7). Drawing on many original sources and interviews, this is a forceful chronicle of Hitler's rise to power, the final solution, and the liberation of the death camps. [940.53]

7697 Gilbert, Martin. *Never Again: A History of the Holocaust* (10–12). Illus. 2000, Universe $29.95 (0-7893-0409-0). A well-organized, well-illustrated overview of the Holocaust and its aftermath. (Rev: BL 7/00) [940.53]

7698 Gimpel, Erich. *Agent 146: The True Story of a Nazi Spy in America* (10–12). 2003, St. Martin's $24.95 (0-312-30797-7). Gimpel tells the suspense-ful story of his espionage efforts and his betrayal by a one-time colleague. (Rev: BL 12/1/02) [940.54]

7699 Gold, Alison Leslie. *Fiet's Vase and Other Stories of Survival, Europe 1939–1945* (10–12). Illus. 2003, Putnam $24.95 (1-58542-259-2). This collection of 20 survival stories from World War II, most of which are related to young people in the Holocaust, is dominated by themes of courage and sacrifice. (Rev: BL 9/1/03) [940.53]

7700 Goldstein, Donald M., and Katherine V. Dil-lon. *Rain of Ruin: A Photographic History of Hiroshima and Nagasaki* (9–12). 1995, Brassey's $31.95 (1-57488-033-0). More than 400 black-and-white photographs are accompanied by text that generally supports the bombing of Hiroshima and Nagasaki. (Rev: BL 8/95) [940.54]

7701 Gonzales, Doreen. *The Manhattan Project and the Atomic Bomb in American History* (6–12). Illus. Series: American History. 2000, Enslow LB $19.95 (0-89490-879-0). This work traces the events that

produced the atomic bomb, introduces the people involved, and gives details on the impact of its use during World War II. (Rev: BL 1/1–15/00; HBG 9/00; SLJ 9/00) [355.8]

7702 Gottfried, Ted. *Children of the Slaughter: Young People of the Holocaust* (7–12). Illus. Series: Holocaust. 2001, Twenty-First Century LB $28.90 (0-7613-1716-3). Gottfried provides a clear and thought-provoking account of the suffering of chil-dren at the hands of the Nazis, looking not only at the genocide of Jewish children but also at the expe-riences of German youngsters forced into Hitler Youth, spying on their families, and dying in battle. Also use *Heroes of the Holocaust* (2001), which tells the stories of heroic rescuers. (Rev: BL 5/15/01; HBG 10/01; SLJ 6/01) [940.53]

7703 Gottfried, Ted. *Displaced Persons: The Liber-ation and Abuse of Holocaust Survivors* (6–12). Illus. 2001, Twenty-First Century LB $28.90 (0-7613-1924-7). Survivors of the Holocaust went on to suffer many indignities and rejections, as Gott-fried shows in this account of continued racism, dis-placed persons camps, and denial of shelter by countries including the United States. (Rev: BL 9/1/01; HBG 3/02) [940]

7704 Gottfried, Ted. *Martyrs to Madness: The Vic-tims of the Holocaust* (8–12). Illus. Series: Holo-caust. 2000, Twenty-First Century LB $21.68 (0-7613-1715-5). After a brief overview of the Holocaust, the author devotes separate chapters to each group of victims including Jews, Slavs, gyp-sies, homosexuals, and POWs. (Rev: BL 7/00; HBG 10/01; SLJ 12/00; VOYA 6/01) [940.53]

7705 Gottfried, Ted. *Nazi Germany: The Face of Tyranny* (8–12). Illus. Series: Holocaust. 2000, Twenty-First Century LB $21.68 (0-7613-1714-7). Gottfried describes the Nazis' rise to power, their expansion through Europe, and the systematic attacks against Jews and other groups. (Rev: BL 7/00; HBG 10/01; SLJ 12/00; VOYA 6/01) [940.53]

7706 Grant, R. G. *Hiroshima and Nagasaki* (7–12). Illus. Series: New Perspectives. 1998, Raintree Steck-Vaughn $28.54 (0-8172-5013-1). This account of the dropping of atomic bombs on Japan examines the different viewpoints of the scientists, politicians, and air crews involved, and the people who survived it. (Rev: BL 3/15/98; BR 1–2/99; HBG 9/98) [940.54]

7707 Grant, R. G. *The Holocaust* (7–12). Series: New Perspectives. 1998, Raintree Steck-Vaughn $19.98 (0-8172-5016-6). The story of the Holo-caust, one of history's darkest moments, as shaped by the German perpetrators, witnessed by onlook-ers, and recalled by survivors. (Rev: BL 3/15/98; BR 1–2/99; HBG 9/98; SLJ 7/98) [940.54]

7708 Greenfeld, Howard. *After the Holocaust* (6–12). Illus. 2001, Greenwillow LB $15.89 (0-06-

029420-5). Greenfeld tells the stories of eight Jewish survivors of the Holocaust, describing the conditions in the camps for displaced persons, the search for a new home, and the very different ways in which people react to adversity. (Rev: BCCB 1/02; BL 10/1/01*; HB 11–12/01; HBG 3/02; SLJ 11/01*; VOYA 12/01) [804.48]

7709 Greenfeld, Howard. *The Hidden Children* (5–10). 1993, Ticknor $18.00 (0-395-66074-2). This account of what it was like to be a Jewish child hiding from the Nazis in World War II includes painful personal narratives of survivors. (Rev: BL 1/1/94*; SLJ 5/94*; VOYA 6/94) [940.53]

7710 Grohs-Martin, Silvia. *Silvie* (10–12). 2000, Welcome Rain $24.95 (1-56649-150-9). A moving remembrance by a Jewish girl who survived the Nazi death camps with her spirit still intact. (Rev: BL 7/00) [940.53]

7711 Gruhzit-Hoyt, Olga. *They Also Served: American Women in World War II* (9–12). 1995, Birch Lane $19.95 (1-55972-280-0). Short profiles of women who served in World War II. (Rev: BL 5/1/95) [940.54]

7712 Handler, Andrew, and Susan V. Meschel, eds. *Young People Speak: Surviving the Holocaust in Hungary* (7–12). 1993, Watts paper $24.00 (0-531-11044-3). Memoirs of 11 Holocaust survivors who were children in Hungary during the Nazi occupation at the end of World War II. (Rev: BL 6/1–15/93; SLJ 7/93; VOYA 10/93) [940.53]

7713 Hanmer, Trudy J. *Leningrad* (6–12). Series: Cities at War. 1992, Macmillan $18.00 (0-02-742615-7). The story of the city of Leningrad during World War II and the terrible siege that destroyed a large percentage of the city and its inhabitants. (Rev: BL 10/15/92) [947]

7714 Hargrove, Hondon. *Buffalo Soldiers in Italy: Black Americans in World War II* (8–12). 1985, McFarland LB $39.95 (0-89950-116-8). A history of the last all-black U.S. army division and its record during World War II. (Rev: BR 9–10/85) [940.53]

7715 Hastings, Max. *Overlord: D-Day and the Battle for Normandy* (10–12). 1985, Simon & Schuster paper $13.00 (0-671-55435-2). A history of the events surrounding the Allied landings in Normandy during World War II. [940.53]

7716 Hastings, Max. *Victory in Europe: D-Day to V-E Day* (9–12). Illus. 1985, Little, Brown $25.00 (0-316-81334-6). Stills from a film by George Stevens are used to illustrate this account of the war in Europe after the Normandy invasions. (Rev: BL 6/15/85) [940.542]

7717 Hecht, Thomas T. *Life Death Memories* (9–12). Illus. 2002, Leopolis paper $14.95 (0-9679960-1-5). This powerful memoir recounts the story of a Jewish teenager who, with his mother, survives the

Nazis' arrival in their Polish *shtetl*. (Rev: BL 5/1/02) [940.53]

7718 Herbst, Jurgen. *Requiem for a German Past: A Boyhood Among the Nazis* (10–12). 1999, Univ. of Wisconsin Pr. $34.95 (0-299-16410-1). The key to survival is silence in this frank memoir of boyhood in Nazi Germany. (Rev: VOYA 6/00) [940.54]

7719 Hersey, John. *Hiroshima: A New Edition with a Final Chapter Written Forty Years After the Explosion* (10–12). 1985, Knopf $26.00 (0-394-54844-2); paper $6.50 (0-679-72103-7). Using the stories of six survivors, this is a devastating account of the atomic bombing of Hiroshima during World War II. [940.54]

7720 Heyes, Eileen. *Children of the Swastika: The Hitler Youth* (7–12). 1993, Millbrook LB $22.40 (1-56294-237-9). A study of the Hitler Youth's structure, purpose, impact on the war effort, and effects on the youth. (Rev: BL 2/15/93) [324.243]

7721 Hillesum, Etty. *Etty Hillesum: An Interrupted Life and Letters from Westerbork* (10–12). Trans. from Dutch by Arnold J. Pomerans. 1996, Holt $27.50 (0-8050-4894-4). This inspiring book contains the diaries and letters of a Jewish woman who died in her mid-20s in the Holocaust. (Rev: SLJ 4/97) [940.54]

7722 Hills, C. A. R. *The Second World War* (7–12). Illus. 1986, David & Charles $19.95 (0-7134-4531-9). A brief but comprehensive history of World War II as seen through the eyes of its leaders. (Rev: SLJ 11/86) [940.53]

7723 Holliday, Laurel. *Children in the Holocaust and World War II* (9–12). 1995, Pocket $20.00 (0-671-52054-7). Excerpts from 23 World War II diaries provide glimpses into the lives and thoughts of teenagers. (Rev: SLJ 9/95) [940.53]

7724 Holmes, Richard. *World War II in Photographs* (9–12). Illus. 2000, Carlton $50.00 (1-84222-073-X). This exceptional visual history includes about 500 well-captioned photographs that cover the history of World War II. (Rev: BL 12/1/00) [940.54]

7725 *The Holocaust: Death Camps* (10–12). Ed. by Tamara L. Roleff. Series: History Firsthand. 2002, Gale LB $31.20 (0-7377-0883-2); paper $19.95 (0-7377-0882-4). Life in the Holocaust death camps is re-created in a series of contemporary narratives and reminiscences from various viewpoints. (Rev: BL 4/15/02; SLJ 3/02) [940.54]

7726 Hoyt, Edwin. *McCampbell's Heroes* (9–12). 1984, Avon paper $3.95 (0-380-68841-7). The story of the U.S. Navy's carrier fighters and their role in the Pacific area during World War II. Also use *Blue Skies and Blood: The Battle of the Coral Sea* (1989). [940.53]

477

7727 Immell, Myra H., ed. *World War II* (7–12). Series: Turning Points in World History. 2001, Greenhaven LB $31.20 (0-7377-0699-6); paper $19.95 (0-7377-0698-8). This collection of scholarly documents and essays explores various aspects of the Second World War. (Rev: BL 3/15/02) [940.54]

7728 Ippisch, Hanneke. *Sky: A True Story of Resistance During World War II* (6–10). Illus. 1996, Simon & Schuster $18.00 (0-689-80508-X). An autobiographical account by the author who, as a teenage girl in 1943, joined the Dutch underground resistance movement and, after participating in many dangerous missions against the Nazis, was caught by the Germans and sent to prison. (Rev: BL 4/15/96; BR 1–2/97; SLJ 6/96; VOYA 8/96) [940.53]

7729 Irwin, John P. *Another River, Another Town: A Teenage Tank Gunner Comes of Age in Combat — 1945* (10–12). 2002, Random $21.95 (0-375-50775-2). Irwin recounts both the horrors and exhilaration of combat in this gripping memoir of his experiences as an 18-year-old tank gunner. (Rev: BL 5/1/02) [940.54]

7730 Isserman, Maurice. *World War II* (7–12). Series: America at War. 1991, Facts on File $25.00 (0-8160-2374-3). The major battles and personalities of World War II, events leading to war, and discussion of changes following the conflict. (Rev: BL 10/15/91; SLJ 8/92) [940.53]

7731 Jacobsen, Ruth. *Rescued Images: Memories of a Childhood in Hiding* (6–12). 2001, Mikaya $19.95 (1-931414-00-9). The author, who was 8 years old when her family fled the Nazis and went into hiding in the Netherlands, relates memories evoked by family photographs, which are also included. (Rev: BCCB 2/02; BL 1/1–15/02; HBG 3/02; SLJ 1/02; VOYA 2/02) [921]

7732 Jones, Catherine. *Navajo Code Talkers: Native American Heroes* (6–10). 1998, Tudor $12.95 (0-936389-51-6); paper $7.95 (0-936389-52-4). This is the story of the Navajo Code Talkers of the Marine Corps who, during World War II in the Pacific, communicated in a code that neither the Japanese nor the Americans could decipher. (Rev: SLJ 4/98) [940.54]

7733 Keegan, John. *The Second World War* (10–12). 1990, Viking paper $20.95 (0-14-011341-X). This fine history of World War II covers both the western and eastern fronts in Europe and the war in the Pacific. [940.53]

7734 Keeley, Jennifer. *Life in the Hitler Youth* (7–12). Illus. Series: The Way People Live. 1999, Lucent LB $18.96 (1-56006-613-X). A compelling narrative, using many eyewitness accounts, of the training and indoctrination of Hitler's Youth and the part its members played in World War II. (Rev: BL 1/1–15/00; HBG 9/00; SLJ 3/00) [943.086]

7735 Kelly, Clara Olink. *The Flamboya Tree: Memories of a Mother's Wartime Courage* (10–12). Illus. 2002, Random $21.95 (0-375-50621-7). In this harrowing memoir of childhood internment in a Japanese prison camp during World War II, the author paints a loving portrait of her mother, whose sacrifices helped to ensure her family's survival. (Rev: BL 2/15/02) [940.53]

7736 Kimmett, Larry, and Margaret Regis. *The Attack on Pearl Harbor: An Illustrated History* (9–12). 1991, Navigator Publg. paper $15.95 (1-879932-00-8). An overview of the infamous attack, with numerous photographs and maps of various targets. (Rev: BL 1/15/92) [940.54]

7737 Klein, Gerda Weissmann, and Kurt Klein. *The Hours After: Letters of Love and Longing in the War's Aftermath* (10–12). Illus. 2000, St. Martin's $23.95 (0-312-24258-1). A tender, true love story about a Polish Jew who survived the Holocaust and her love for the American soldier who liberated her. (Rev: BL 3/1/00) [940.53]

7738 Kopf, Hedda Rosner. *Understanding Anne Frank's The Diary of a Young Girl: A Student Casebook to Issues, Sources, and Historical Documents* (7–12). 1997, Greenwood $45.00 (0-313-29607-3). In addition to examining Anne Frank's diary as literature, this collection of materials supplies great amounts of background information on the Holocaust, anti-Semitism, the Frank family, and World War II. (Rev: SLJ 3/98) [940.54]

7739 Kronenwetter, Michael. *London* (6–12). Series: Cities at War. 1992, Macmillan $18.00 (0-02-751050-6). A photoessay on the lives of ordinary people in London during World War II, with eyewitness quotations. (Rev: BL 6/15/92; SLJ 9/92) [942.1084]

7740 Lace, William W. *The Death Camps* (10–12). Series: Holocaust Library. 1997, Lucent LB $17.96 (1-56006-094-8). The story of the concentration camps that were specifically designed to murder Jews and other "undesirables." (Rev: BL 3/15/98; HBG 3/99; SLJ 5/98) [940.54]

7741 Lace, William W. *Hitler and the Nazis* (6–12). Series: American War Library. 2000, Lucent LB $18.96 (1-56006-372-6). The story of the rise of Adolf Hitler and the emergence of the Nazi Party. (Rev: BL 4/15/00; HBG 9/00) [940.54]

7742 Lace, William W. *The Nazis* (10–12). Illus. Series: Holocaust Library. 1997, Lucent LB $17.96 (1-56006-091-3). One of a planned seven-volume Holocaust Library series, this volume traces the Nazi movement and its relationship to the Holocaust and the killings based solely on racial hatred. (Rev: BL 10/1/97; HBG 3/99; SLJ 2/98) [943.086]

7743 Landau, Elaine. *The Warsaw Ghetto Uprising* (7–10). 1992, Macmillan LB $19.00 (0-02-751392-0). Recounts the horrors of the month-long battles between Nazis and Jews in 1943 Poland. (Rev: BL 2/15/93) [940.53]

7744 Landau, Elaine. *We Survived the Holocaust* (7–10). 1991, Watts paper $24.00 (0-531-11115-6). A series of personal accounts of survivors who were children during World War II, presenting a picture of ethnic and religious persecution and courageous endurance. (Rev: BL 9/15/91; SLJ 10/91) [940.53]

7745 Laqueur, Walter. *Generation Exodus: The Fate of Young Jewish Refugees from Nazi Germany* (10–12). 2001, Brandeis $29.95 (1-58465-106-7). The author traces the fates of the approximately 80,000 young Jews from Germany and Austria who emigrated after the Nazis took power. (Rev: BL 3/1/01) [943]

7746 Lawton, Clive A. *Auschwitz* (9–12). Illus. 2002, Candlewick LB $17.99 (0-7636-1595-1). This large-format photoessay starkly documents the atrocities that took place in the Nazi concentration camp and includes facts, quotations, a timeline, and a glossary. (Rev: BL 8/02; HBG 3/03; SLJ 9/02*; VOYA 12/02) [940.53]

7747 Leapman, Michael. *Witnesses to War: Eight True-Life Stories of Nazi Persecution* (8–12). Illus. 1998, Viking $16.99 (0-670-87386-1). Eight case histories of children who suffered at the hands of the Nazis, some by being selected for "Germanization" and others who survived death camps and Nazi massacres. (Rev: BL 10/1/98; HBG 3/99; SLJ 11/98; VOYA 12/98) [940.53]

7748 Leckie, Robert. *Okinawa: The Last Battle of World War II* (9–12). 1995, Viking paper $13.95 (0-14-017389-7). A history of the Battle of Okinawa with good background material on the war in the Pacific. (Rev: BL 4/15/95) [940.54]

7749 Lee, Loyd E. *World War II* (9–12). Series: Guides to Historic Events of the Twentieth Century. 1999, Greenwood $39.95 (0-313-29998-6). This information-packed book covers the war from the rise of Hitler to its end in 1945, with additional material on its continuing significance and influence on international relations plus a section containing 17 primary source documents. (Rev: BL 5/99; SLJ 7/99; VOYA 10/99) [940.54]

7750 Levi, Primo. *Survival in Auschwitz* (10–12). Trans. by Stuart Woolf. 1995, Touchstone paper $14.00 (0-684-82680-1). A moving memoir of the author's 10 months in a concentration camp. Also use *The Reawakening*, the story of his journey home to Italy via the Soviet Union. [940.53]

7751 Levine, Ellen. *Darkness over Denmark: The Danish Resistance and the Rescue of the Jews* (6–12). Illus. 2000, Holiday $19.95 (0-8234-1447-7). This is a straightforward history that uses many first-person accounts to relate the Danish people's remarkable efforts to save their Jewish citizens during

World War II. (Rev: BL 7/00* ; HB 9–10/00; HBG 10/00; SLJ 8/00; VOYA 2/01) [940.531809489]

7752 Lewin, Rhoda G., ed. *Witness to the Holocaust: An Oral History* (9–12). 1990, Twayne $20.95 (0-8057-9100-0). More than 50 interviews present the stories of survivors of death camps, of survivors who did not go to death camps, and of American liberators. (Rev: BR 5–6/90; SLJ 8/90; VOYA 6/90) [940.53]

7753 *LIFE: World War 2: History's Greatest Conflict in Pictures* (8–12). Ed. by Richard B. Stolley. Illus. 2001, Little, Brown $60.00 (0-8212-2771-8). The years leading up to the war and major events of the war itself are chronicled in this collection of 665 photographs. (Rev: BL 1/1–15/02) [779.994]

7754 Lifton, Betty Jean. *A Place Called Hiroshima* (9–12). Illus. 1985, Kodansha $24.95 (0-87011-649-5). In this album of text and photographs, the author tells what has happened to Hiroshima and the survivors of the atomic attack 40 years after. (Rev: BL 10/1/85; SLJ 11/85) [940.54]

7755 Lobel, Anita. *No Pretty Pictures: A Child of War* (6–12). 1998, Greenwillow $17.99 (0-688-15935-4). The author, today a successful illustrator, tells the gripping story of her childhood during World War II in Poland — five years in hiding beginning at the age of 5, then her capture and transport, with her younger brother disguised as a girl, to a concentration camp. (Rev: BCCB 10/98; BL 8/98; HB 11–12/98; HBG 3/99; SLJ 9/98; VOYA 2/99) [940.5318092]

7756 Lord, Walter. *Day of Infamy* (8–12). Illus. 1998, NTC paper $12.99 (1-85326-670-1). An hour-by-hour re-creation of the attack on Pearl Harbor with extensive background information. [940.54]

7757 Loy, Rosetta. *First Words* (10–12). Trans. by Gregory Conti. 2000, Holt $23.00 (0-8050-6258-0). A memoir by an Italian writer that covers the years 1936 through 1943 and deals with the fate of Italian Jews under Mussolini and the role of the Roman Catholic Church. (Rev: BL 7/00) [940.53]

7758 McKain, Mark, ed. *Making and Using the Atomic Bomb* (8–12). Series: History Firsthand. 2003, Gale LB $25.96 (0-7377-1412-3); paper $16.96 (0-7377-1413-1). A collection of documents relating to the discovery of fission, the Manhattan Project, the decision to use the bomb and the choice of targets, and stories of survivors of Hiroshima and Nagasaki. (Rev: SLJ 7/03) [355.8]

7759 Maddox, Robert James. *Weapons for Victory: The Hiroshima Decision Fifty Years Later* (9–12). 1995, Univ. of Missouri Pr. $19.95 (0-8262-1037-6). The author argues that President Truman dropped the bomb to end the war, contrary to arguments made by revisionist historians. (Rev: BL 8/95) [940.54]

479

7760 Manz, Bruno. *A Mind in Prison: The Memoir of a Son and a Soldier of the Third Reich* (10–12). Illus. 2000, Brassey's $24.95 (1-57488-242-2). A German World War II veteran talks about his experiences on the arctic front and his disillusionment with Hitler. (Rev: BL 6/1–15/00) [943.086]

7761 Maruki, Toshi. *Hiroshima No Pika* (7–10). Illus. 1982, Lothrop $17.99 (0-688-01297-3). One family's experiences during the day the bomb dropped on Hiroshima, told in text and moving illustrations by the author. (Rev: BL 3/87) [940.54]

7762 Maynard, Mary McKay. *My Faraway Home: An American Family's WWII Tale of Adventure and Survival in the Philippines* (10–12). 2001, Lyons Pr. $22.95 (1-58574-261-9). The horror of war is conveyed in this account of a family in the Philippines who were forced to live in the jungle during the Japanese occupation of their island. (Rev: BL 6/1–15/01) [959.9]

7763 Meltzer, Milton. *Never to Forget: The Jews of the Holocaust* (8–12). 1976, HarperCollins LB $15.89 (0-06-024175-6). A history of the murder of 6 million Jews and of anti-Semitism. [940.54]

7764 Meyers, Odette. *Doors to Madame Marie* (10–12). 1997, Univ. of Washington Pr. $24.95 (0-295-97576-8). A deeply moving memoir of a Jewish girl in wartime France who was sent to live in the countryside, pretending to be Catholic for safety's sake, and who returns to visit years later. (Rev: SLJ 12/97) [940.54]

7765 Miller, Nathan. *War at Sea: A Naval History of World War II* (9–12). 1995, Scribner $32.50 (0-684-80380-1). Miller, the author of four previous volumes of popular naval history, presents this overview in an informal style. (Rev: BL 9/1/95) [940.54]

7766 Mitcham, Samuel W., Jr. *Rommel's Greatest Victory: The Desert Fox and the Fall of Tobruk, Spring 1942* (10–12). 1998, Presidio $27.95 (0-89141-656-0). A readable narrative, combined with firsthand accounts, about the amazing successes of General Erwin Rommel's efforts in World War II to drive the British out of the Sahara and back to Egypt, allowing the Germans to keep their toehold in Africa for another year and preventing the Allies from using the troops on another front. (Rev: SLJ 2/99) [940.54]

7767 Nardo, Don. *World War II in the Pacific* (7–10). Series: World History. 2002, Gale LB $27.45 (1-59018-015-1). From Pearl Harbor to Japan's surrender, this is a history of the battles, decisions, and important people involved in the war in the Pacific. (Rev: BL 8/02) [940.54]

7768 Nelson, Pete. *Left for Dead: A Young Man's Search for Justice for the U.S.S. Indianapolis* (6–12). Illus. 2002, Delacorte LB $17.99 (0-385-90033-3). The gripping story of young Hunter Scott's efforts to clear the name of the captain of the

U.S.S. *Indianapolis*, which was sunk by the Japanese during World War II. (Rev: BL 5/1/02; HB 7–8/02; HBG 10/02; SLJ 4/02; VOYA 8/02) [940.54]

7769 Newman, Amy. *The Nuremberg Laws* (7–12). Illus. Series: Words That Changed History. 1998, Lucent LB $27.45 (1-56006-354-8). An overview of the Holocaust, including the roots and growth of Nazism and the war against the Jews, and a discussion of contemporary ethnic violence, laws that promote bigotry, and the power of words. (Rev: BL 4/15/99; SLJ 9/99) [342.43]

7770 Newman, Richard, and Karen Kirtley. *Alma Rose: Vienna to Auschwitz* (10–12). Illus. 2000, Timber $29.95 (1-57467-051-4). This compelling book about the Holocaust tells the story of Alma Rose, a Viennese violinist who became the conductor of the Auschwitz-Birkenau Women's Orchestra. (Rev: BL 3/15/00) [921]

7771 Newton, David E. *Tokyo* (6–12). Series: Cities at War. 1992, Macmillan LB $18.00 (0-02-768235-8). Remembrances from people who experienced World War II in Tokyo. (Rev: BL 10/15/92; SLJ 1/93) [952]

7772 Nieuwsma, Milton J., ed. *Kinderlager: An Oral History of Young Holocaust Survivors* (9–12). Illus. 1998, Holiday $18.95 (0-8234-1358-6). This book contains the memoirs of three Jewish American women who, as children growing up in Poland, were sent to the children's section of the Auschwitz death camp. (Rev: BL 11/1/98; HB 1–2/99; HBG 3/99; SLJ 12/98; VOYA 12/98) [940.53180922438]

7773 Nir, Yehuda. *The Lost Childhood* (9–12). 1989, Harcourt $19.95 (0-15-158862-7). How three Polish Jews — a mother and two children — used their wits to elude their Nazi pursuers. (Rev: BL 4/1/02; HB 3–4/02; HBG 10/02; SLJ 7/02; VOYA 4/02) [940.53]

7774 *No End Save Victory: Perspectives on World War II* (10–12). Ed. by Robert Cowley. Illus. 2001, Putnam $30.00 (0-399-14711-X). These articles, written by top military historians, examine various episodes and aspects of World War II, many of which have not been written about before. (Rev: BL 2/15/01) [940.54]

7775 *The Nuremberg Trial* (10–12). Ed. by Mitchell Bard. Series: History Firsthand. 2002, Gale LB $31.20 (0-7377-1075-6); paper $19.95 (0-7377-1076-4). The trials in which several Nazi war criminals were brought to justice are presented from various points of view through original documents, narratives, and reminiscences. (Rev: BL 8/02; SLJ 7/02) [940.54]

7776 Oertelt, Henry A., and Stephanie Oertelt Samuels. *An Unbroken Chain: My Journey Through the Nazi Holocaust* (9–12). 2000, Lerner paper $16.95 (0-8225-2952-1). Oertelt ascribes his survival of the Holocaust, including time in several

480

concentration camps, to a mix of fortunate circumstances. (Rev: BL 8/00; SLJ 1/01; VOYA 2/01) [943.1]

7777 Oleksy, Walter. *Military Leaders of World War II* (7–10). Series: American Profiles. 1994, Facts on File $25.00 (0-8160-3008-1). Profiles of 10 American World War II leaders, including Claire Lee Chennault, Douglas MacArthur, Chester Nimitz, Jacqueline Cochran, Curtis LeMay, and George Patton. (Rev: BL 1/1/95; SLJ 3/95; VOYA 5/95) [940.54]

7778 O'Neill, William L. *World War II: A Student Companion* (9–12). Series: Oxford Student Companions to American History. 1999, Oxford $64.00 (0-19-510800-0). An alphabetically arranged series of articles covering all aspects of World War II, illustrated with photographs, maps, and reproductions. (Rev: BL 7/99; BR 9–10/99; SLJ 7/99) [940.54]

7779 Opdyke, Irene Gut, and Jennifer Armstrong. *In My Hands: Memories of a Holocaust Rescuer* (9–12). 1999, Knopf LB $19.99 (0-679-99181-6). A first-person narrative of a Polish teenager recounting her experiences during the war, including rape by Russian soldiers, and her involvement in rescuing Jews. (Rev: BL 6/1–15/99; HB 7–8/99; HBG 4/00; SLJ 6/99; VOYA 10/99) [940.53]

7780 Paldiel, Mordecai. *Saving the Jews: Amazing Stories of Men and Women Who Defied the 'Final Solution.'* (10–12). Illus. 2000, Schreiber $24.95 (1-887563-55-5). This contains 47 accounts of Gentiles from different parts of Europe who saved Jews during the Holocaust. (Rev: BL 11/15/00) [940.53]

7781 Popescu, Petru. *The Oasis: A Memoir of Love and Survival in a Concentration Camp* (10–12). 2001, St. Martin's $24.95 (0-312-27869-1). The inspiring story of two Holocaust survivors who met in a Nazi death camp, fell in love, were separated, and then found each other after the war. (Rev: BL 9/15/01) [940.53]

7782 Prange, Gordon W., et al. *December 7, 1941: The Day the Japanese Attacked Pearl Harbor* (9–12). 1987, Warner paper $21.99 (0-446-38997-8). A re-creation of the attack on Pearl Harbor with much material from eyewitness sources. (Rev: BL 10/15/87) [940.54]

7783 Prefer, Lathan N. *Patton's Ghost Corps: Cracking the Siegfried Line* (10–12). Illus. 1998, Presidio $24.95 (0-89141-646-3). This is the account of a little-known 1945 campaign in which General George S. Patton led an attack on the German Siegfried Line through blinding snow. (Rev: SLJ 7/98) [940.54]

7784 Rabinovici, Schoschana. *Thanks to My Mother* (8–12). Trans. from German by James Skofield. 1998, Dial $17.99 (0-8037-2235-4). A harrowing memoir of how the Holocaust destroyed this

Lithuanian author's large, extended Jewish family, and how she and her mother were able to survive. (Rev: BR 11–12/98; SLJ 4/98; VOYA 4/98) [940.54]

7785 Read, Anthony, and David Fisher. *The Fall of Berlin* (9–12). 1993, Norton paper $18.50 (0-306-80619-3). Life in Berlin during World War II is described, often with reference to diaries of residents. [940.54]

7786 Reader's Digest, eds. *The World at Arms: The Reader's Digest Illustrated History of World War II* (9–12). Illus. 1989, Reader's Digest $29.95 (0-89577-333-3). An attractively organized and well-illustrated history of World War II. (Rev: BL 9/1/89; BR 1–2/90) [940.53]

7787 Rice, Earle. *Strategic Battles in the Pacific* (6–12). Series: American War Library. 2000, Lucent LB $18.96 (1-56006-537-0). Beginning with the rise of Japanese power in the Pacific, this account traces the war in this area from Pearl Harbor through such crucial battles as Midway. (Rev: BL 4/15/00; HBG 9/00) [940.54]

7788 Rice, Earle, Jr. *The Battle of Britain* (6–10). Illus. Series: Great Battles in History. 1996, Lucent LB $19.95 (1-56006-414-3). This account of the air battle in the skies over Britain during 1940 quotes many primary sources and uses extensive illustrations. (Rev: BL 4/15/96; BR 9–10/96) [940.54]

7789 Rice, Earle, Jr. *The Bombing of Pearl Harbor* (7–10). Series: World History. 2000, Lucent LB $19.96 (1-56006-652-0). This account covers the causes, effects, and significance in world history of the attack on Pearl Harbor by the Japanese. (Rev: BL 12/15/00; SLJ 2/01) [940.54]

7790 Rice, Earle, Jr. *The Final Solution* (10–12). Illus. Series: Holocaust Library. 1997, Lucent LB $18.96 (1-56006-095-6). This volume tells of Hitler's plan to annihilate the Jews of Europe and how it was devised and implemented. (Rev: BL 10/1/97; SLJ 9/97) [940.53]

7791 Rice, Earle, Jr. *Nazi War Criminals* (10–12). Illus. Series: Holocaust Library. 1997, Lucent LB $18.96 (1-56006-097-2). Six of the most vicious perpetrators of the Holocaust are profiled: Heinrich Himmler, Julius Streicher, Reinhard Heydrich, Adolf Eichmann, Rudolf Hess, and Josef Mengele. (Rev: BL 10/1/97; SLJ 2/98) [341.6]

7792 Rice, Earle, Jr. *The Nuremberg Trials* (6–10). Illus. Series: Famous Trials. 1996, Lucent LB $27.45 (1-56006-269-X). Beginning with an account of the Nazi atrocities during World War II, this book describes the trials of the war criminals during 1945–1946, the background of the accused, and their fate. (Rev: BL 3/15/97; BR 11–12/97; SLJ 3/97) [341.6]

7793 Rice, Earle, Jr. *Strategic Battles in Europe: World War II* (6–12). Series: American War Library. 2000, Lucent LB $18.96 (1-56006-536-2). This gripping account that includes many firsthand narratives chronicles major battles. (Rev: BL 9/15/00; HBG 9/00) [940.54]

7794 Rice, Earle, Jr. *The Third Reich: Demise of the Nazi Dream* (8–12). Series: History's Great Defeats. 2000, Lucent $27.45 (1-56006-630-X). Rice explores the factors that led to the Nazis' defeat, pointing at Hitler's overconfidence and strategic errors and detailing key battles. (Rev: BL 10/15/00; BR 3–4/01; HBG 3/01; SLJ 9/00) [943.086]

7795 Richman, Sophia. *A Wolf in the Attic: The Legacy of a Hidden Child of the Holocaust* (9–12). 2002, Haworth $49.95 (0-7890-1549-8); paper $24.95 (0-7890-1550-1). The author and her mother, both Jews, spent much of World War II in hiding in Poland. This is the daughter's story and tells what happened when they came to the United States in 1951. (Rev: BL 12/15/01) [940.53]

7796 Rochman, Hazel, and Darlene Z. McCampbell, eds. *Bearing Witness: Stories of the Holocaust* (7–12). 1995, Orchard LB $16.99 (0-531-08788-3). This anthology of 24 works revolving around the Holocaust includes memoirs, poetry, short stories, a film script, a letter, and a comic strip. (Rev: BL 6/1–15/95; SLJ 9/95; VOYA 12/95) [808]

7797 Rogasky, Barbara. *Smoke and Ashes: The Story of the Holocaust.* Rev. ed. (6–12). 2002, Holiday $27.50 (0-8234-1612-7); paper $14.95 (0-8234-1677-1). In this new edition, Rogasky updates information where new facts have come to light and expands the details of resistance efforts. (Rev: BL 10/15/02; HBG 3/03; SLJ 10/02) [940.53]

7798 Rogers, James T. *The Secret War* (8–12). Series: World Espionage. 1991, Facts on File LB $16.95 (0-8160-2395-6). A well-supported thesis stating that the British and Americans were more successful at espionage, counterespionage, and detection than either the Germans or the Japanese. (Rev: BL 3/1/92; SLJ 5/92) [940.54]

7799 Roleff, Tamara L., ed. *The Atom Bomb* (8–12). Series: Turning Points in World History. 2000, Greenhaven LB $21.96 (0-7377-0215-X); paper $13.96 (0-7377-0214-1). This anthology of thoughtful essays covers the development of the bomb, the scientists who worked on it, and its impact and legacy. (Rev: BL 5/15/00) [940.54]

7800 Ross, Bill D. *Iwo Jima: Legacy of Valor* (9–12). Illus. 1985, Random paper $15.00 (0-394-74288-5). A day-by-day account of the 1945 battle against the Japanese. [940.54]

7801 Ross, Stewart. *World War II* (7–12). Series: Causes and Consequences. 1995, Raintree Steck-Vaughn LB $29.97 (0-8172-4050-0). This book identifies the factors that led to the outbreak of World War II and discusses its outcome, using eyewitness accounts. (Rev: BL 12/15/95) [940.53]

7802 Roubickova, Eva M. *We're Alive and Life Goes On: A Theresienstadt Diary* (8–12). Trans. by Zaia Alexander. 1997, Holt $16.95 (0-8050-5352-2). A translation of a diary kept by a young Jewish woman during her four years in a Nazi concentration camp. (Rev: BL 11/1/97; BR 5–6/98; SLJ 2/98) [940.53]

7803 Rubin, Susan G. *Fireflies in the Dark: The Story of Friedl Dicker-Brandeis and the Children of Terezin* (5–10). Illus. 2000, Holiday $18.95 (0-8234-1461-2). A heartbreaking picture book that reproduces some of the artwork and writings of the children imprisoned at the Terezin concentration camp, where only 100 of 15,000 children survived. (Rev: BCCB 11/00; BL 7/00*; HB 9–10/00; HBG 10/00; SLJ 8/00) [940.53]

7804 Rubin, Susan Goldman. *Searching for Anne Frank: Letters from Amsterdam to Iowa* (5–12). 2003, Abrams $19.95 (0-8109-4514-2). A brief pen-pal exchange between two sisters in Iowa and Anne Frank and her sister serves as the basis for a comparison between life in America and life for Jews in Europe. (Rev: BL 11/1/03; HB 11–12/03; HBG 4/04; SLJ 11/03; VOYA 10/03) [940.5]

7805 Ryan, Cornelius. *The Last Battle* (10–12). 1966, Simon & Schuster paper $16.00 (0-684-80329-1). The story of the last three weeks in Berlin before its fall during World War II. [940.54]

7806 Saldinger, Anne Green. *Life in a Nazi Concentration Camp* (6–10). Series: The Way People Live. 2000, Lucent LB $19.96 (1-56006-485-4). Daily life and death in Nazi death camps is covered in this shocking chronicle of inhumanity during World War II. (Rev: BL 3/1/01) [940.54]

7807 Salisbury, Harrison Evans. *The 900 Days: The Siege of Leningrad* (10–12). 1969, Harper & Row paper $20.00 (0-306-80253-8). This is a vivid account of the siege of Leningrad, the suffering of its people, and Stalin's role. [940.54]

7808 *Salvaged Pages: Young Writers' Diaries of the Holocaust* (10–12). Ed. by Alexandra Zapruder. 2002, Yale $35.00 (0-300-09243-1). A collection of 14 Holocaust diaries from throughout Europe, all written by young people and introduced with historical and biographical notes. (Rev: BL 4/1/02) [940.531]

7809 Samuel, Wolfgang W. E. *The War of Our Childhood: Memories of World War II* (10–12). Illus. 2002, Univ. Press of Mississippi $30.00 (1-57806-482-1). German World War II survivors share their wartime experiences as children. (Rev: BL 9/1/02) [940.53]

7810 Schneider, Carl J., and Dorothy Schneider. *World War II* (8–12). Series: Eyewitness History. 2003, Facts on File $75.00 (0-8160-4484-8); paper $21.95 (0-8160-4485-6). Letters, speeches, articles, and excerpts from other documents are used to re-create the events and personalities of World War II. (Rev: SLJ 2/04) [940.53]

7811 Sendyk, Helen. *New Dawn: A Triumph of Life After the Holocaust* (10–12). Illus. 2002, Syracuse Univ. Pr. $29.95 (0-8156-0735-0). In this sequel to *The End of Days,* author Helen Sendyk tells how she, her older sister, and her cousin created new lives for themselves in Israel after surviving the horrors of World War II in Poland. (Rev: BL 9/1/02) [940.53]

7812 Sherrow, Victoria. *Amsterdam* (6–12). Series: Cities at War. 1992, Macmillan LB $18.00 (0-02-782465-9). A photoessay on the lives of ordinary people in Amsterdam during World War II, with quotations by eyewitnesses. (Rev: BL 6/15/92; SLJ 9/92) [940.53]

7813 Sherrow, Victoria. *The Blaze Engulfs: January 1939 to December 1941* (6–12). Illus. Series: Holocaust. 1997, Blackbirch LB $27.44 (1-56711-202-1). This account describes the first two years of World War II, when Hitler's racial programs were being put into place. (Rev: BL 10/15/97; BR 1–2/98; HBG 3/98; SLJ 2/98) [940.53]

7814 Sherrow, Victoria. *Hiroshima* (6–12). 1994, Silver Burdett LB $14.95 (0-02-782467-5). Chronicles the birth of the atomic age, concluding with graphic descriptions of the World War II bombing of Hiroshima. (Rev: BL 10/1/94; SLJ 11/94) [940.54]

7815 Sherrow, Victoria. *The Righteous Gentiles* (10–12). Series: Holocaust Library. 1997, Lucent LB $17.96 (1-56006-093-X). The uplifting story of gentiles who braved death to help the Jews and others escape the Holocaust. (Rev: BL 3/15/98; HBG 3/99; SLJ 7/98) [940.54]

7816 Sherrow, Victoria. *Smoke to Flame: September 1935 to December 1938* (6–12). Illus. Series: Holocaust. 1997, Blackbirch LB $27.44 (1-56711-201-3). This volume covers the growing anti-Semitism of Hitler's first years in power. (Rev: BL 10/15/97; HBG 3/98; SLJ 2/98) [940.53]

7817 Shirer, William L. *The Rise and Fall of the Third Reich: A History of Nazi Germany* (9–12). 1990, Simon & Schuster paper $25.00 (0-671-72868-7). This is the standard history of the rise of Adolf Hitler, World War II, and the defeat of Germany. [943.086]

7818 Shohei, Ooka. *Taken Captive* (10–12). Trans. by Wayne P. Lammers. 1996, Wiley $27.95 (0-471-14285-9). The story of a Japanese soldier who was drafted into the army in 1944 and spent most of the remaining part of the war as a prisoner of the Americans. (Rev: BL 5/15/96; SLJ 2/97) [940.54]

7819 Shulman, William L., ed. *Resource Guide: A Comprehensive Listing of Media for Further Study* (6–12). Illus. Series: Holocaust. 1997, Blackbirch LB $27.44 (1-56711-208-0). This eighth and last volume of the Holocaust series is a guide to other sources on the subject including CD-ROMS, books, videos, museums, and other resource centers. (Rev: BL 10/15/97; BR 1–2/98; SLJ 2/98) [940.53]

7820 Shulman, William L., ed. *Voices and Visions: A Collection of Primary Sources* (6–12). Illus. Series: Holocaust. 1997, Blackbirch LB $27.44 (1-56711-207-2). A collection of primary sources, including eyewitness accounts, of the Holocaust and its many targets. (Rev: BL 10/15/97; BR 1–2/98; HBG 3/98; SLJ 2/98) [940.53]

7821 Shuter, Jane. *The Camp System* (7–12). Illus. Series: Holocaust. 2003, Heinemann LB $28.50 (1-4034-0809-2). This book explores the horrors of life in the concentration camps of the Holocaust. (Rev: BL 3/1/03; SLJ 4/03) [940.53]

7822 Shuter, Jane. *Resistance to the Nazis* (7–12). Illus. Series: Holocaust. 2003, Heinemann LB $28.50 (1-4034-0814-9). An account of the acts of heroism by the many people who risked and lost their lives resisting the Nazis and their Holocaust agenda. (Rev: BL 3/1/03; SLJ 4/03) [943.086]

7823 Sides, Hampton. *Ghost Soldiers: The Forgotten Epic Story of World War II's Most Dramatic Mission* (10–12). 2001, Doubleday $24.95 (0-385-49564-1). This is an exciting account of the daring raid on Luzon in January 1945 to rescue the survivors of the infamous Bataan Death March. (Rev: BL 4/1/01) [940.54]

7824 Smith, Carl. *Pearl Harbor, 1941: The Day of Infamy* (9–12). 2004, Praeger $35.00 (1-84176-390-X). This work is a visually attractive, informative overview of the attack in December 1941. (Rev: BL 3/15/04) [940.54]

7825 Spiegelman, Art. *Maus: A Survivor's Tale II: And Here My Troubles Began* (9–12). 1991, Pantheon $23.00 (0-394-55655-0). Using a unique comic-strip-as-graphic-art format, the story of Vladek Spiegelman's passage through the Nazi Holocaust is told in his own words. (Rev: BL 10/15/91) [940.53]

7826 Spinelli, Angelo M., and Lewis H. Carlson. *Life Behind Barbed Wire: The Secret World War II Photographs of Prisoner of War Angelo M. Spinelli* (9–12). Illus. 2004, Fordham Univ. $35.00 (0-8232-2305-1). A collection of about 400 photographs that were taken secretly by the author while he was a prisoner in a German camp. (Rev: BL 3/15/04*) [940.54]

7827 Stalcup, Ann. *On the Home Front: Growing up in Wartime England* (6–10). Illus. 1998, Shoe String LB $19.50 (0-208-02482-4). A vivid first-person account about growing up in a small town in Shropshire during World War II. (Rev: BCCB 9/98; BL 10/15/98; BR 11–12/98; HBG 9/98; SLJ 7/98) [940.54]

7828 Stanton, Doug. *In Harm's Way: The Sinking of the USS Indianapolis and the Extraordinary Story of Its Survivors* (10–12). Illus. 2001, Holt $25.00 (0-8050-6632-2). This story of the *USS Indianapolis* and its sinking by a Japanese submarine on July 16, 1945, with the loss of about 900 lives, draws on the memories of survivors. (Rev: BL 3/15/01; SLJ 11/01) [940.54]

7829 Steidl, Franz. *Lost Battalions: Going for Broke in the Vosges Autumn 1944* (10–12). 1997, Presidio $21.95 (0-89141-622-6). The story of the famous battle in which Japanese American soldiers distinguished themselves. (Rev: SLJ 9/97) [940.54]

7830 Stillman, Larry. *A Match Made in Hell: The Jewish Boy and the Polish Outlaw Who Defied the Nazis* (10–12). 2003, Univ. of Wisconsin Pr. $29.95 (0-299-19390-X). In this gripping story of Holocaust survival, a Jewish teenager escapes the horrors of genocide by joining forces with a notorious Polish criminal. (Rev: BL 11/1/03) [940.53]

7831 Stokesbury, James L. *A Short History of World War II* (9–12). 1980, Morrow paper $13.50 (0-688-08587-3). A concise history of the war with coverage of its causes and immediate aftermath. [940.53]

7832 Strahinich, Helen. *The Holocaust: Understanding and Remembering* (6–10). Illus. Series: Issues in Focus. 1996, Enslow LB $20.95 (0-89490-725-5). A fully documented account that covers such topics as the roots of anti-Semitism, the rise of Nazism, ghetto life, the roundups, death camps, liberation, and the Nuremberg trials. (Rev: BL 9/15/96; SLJ 10/96; VOYA 10/96) [940.53]

7833 Sullivan, George. *Strange but True Stories of World War II* (7–12). Illus. 1983, Walker $14.95 (0-8027-6489-4). Eleven true stories of bizarre incidents during World War II. [940.53]

7834 Taylor, Theodore. *Battle in the English Channel* (7–10). Illus. 1983, Avon paper $3.50 (0-380-85225-X). A retelling of the exciting World War II incident when Hitler tried to free three of his battleships from French waters. [940.54]

7835 Taylor, Theodore. *The Battle of Midway Island* (7–10). Illus. 1981, Avon paper $3.95 (0-380-78790-3). The story of the brilliant victory of U.S. forces at Midway is excitingly retold. [940.54]

7836 Taylor, Theodore. *H.M.S. Hood vs. Bismarck: The Battleship Battle* (7–10). Illus. 1982, Avon paper $3.95 (0-380-81174-X). The subject of this book is the sinking of the battleship *Bismarck* by the Royal Navy. [940.54]

7837 Ten Boom, Corrie, and John Sherrill. *The Hiding Place* (9–12). 1984, Bantam paper $6.99 (0-553-25669-6). An account of a Dutch girl growing up in Nazi-occupied Holland and her family's help hiding Jewish people. [940.54]

7838 *To Life: 36 Stories of Memory and Hope* (10–12). Ed. by David G. Marwell. Illus. 2002, Little, Brown $40.00 (0-8212-2773-4). A richly illustrated collection of personal stories from survivors, liberators, partisans, and Zionists that paints a chilling picture of the Holocaust. (Rev: BL 1/1–15/03) [973]

7839 Travers, Susan, and Wendy Holden. *Tomorrow to Be Brave: A Memoir of the Only Woman Ever to Serve in the French Foreign Legion* (10–12). Illus. 2001, Free Pr. $25.00 (0-7432-0001-2). The incredible story of an Englishwoman who was raised in France and her service as a nurse and driver in the French Foreign Legion during World War II. (Rev: BL 6/1–15/01) [940.54]

7840 van der Vat, Dan. *D-Day: The Greatest Invasion — a People's History* (10–12). Illus. 2003, Bloomsbury $40.00 (1-58234-314-4). Personal anecdotes add to the well-illustrated coverage of the 1944 invasion of Nazi-occupied Europe. (Rev: BL 10/1/03) [940.54]

7841 Velmans, Loet. *Long Way Back to the River Kwai: Memories of World War II* (10–12). Illus. 2003, Arcade $24.95 (1-55970-706-2). The Dutch-born author recounts his World War II experiences, including his family's escape from the Netherlands, military service in the Dutch East Indies, and life as a Japanese prisoner of war. (Rev: BL 11/1/03) [940.34]

7842 Verhoeven, Rian, and Ruud van der Rol. *Anne Frank: Beyond the Diary: A Photographic Remembrance* (6–12). Trans. by Tony Langham and Plym Peters. 1993, Viking $18.99 (0-670-84932-4). Includes photographs of people who knew Anne and of the places she lived and hid in, with excerpts from her diary. (Rev: BL 10/1/93*; SLJ 12/93*) [940.53]

7843 Warren, Andrea. *Surviving Hitler: A Boy in the Nazi Death Camps* (5–10). Illus. 2001, HarperCollins LB $17.89 (0-06-029218-0). The true story of Jack Mandelbaum, who as a teenager survived three years in Nazi death camps through a combination of luck, courage, and friendship. (Rev: BCCB 3/01; BL 1/1–15/01; HB 3–4/01; HBG 10/01; SLJ 3/01) [940.53]

7844 Wassiljewa, Tatjana. *Hostage to War: A True Story* (6–10). 1997, Scholastic paper $15.95 (0-590-13446-9). The World War II diary of a young Russian girl who endured hunger, cold, disease, and brutality during the German occupation of Leningrad and then spent years in forced labor camps and factories in Germany. (Rev: BL 4/15/97; SLJ 6/97; VOYA 12/98) [940.54]

7845 *Weapons of War: World War II* (6–10). Series: American War Library. 2000, Lucent LB $27.45 (1-56006-584-2). The weapons used by the American Army, Navy, and Air Force during World War II are covered in both text and pictures. (Rev: BL 9/15/00; HBG 10/00; SLJ 7/00) [940.54]

7846 Whitaker, Denis, et al. *Normandy: The Real Story* (10–12). Illus. 2004, Presidio paper $15.95 (0-345-45907-5). This is a gripping account of the great 1944 invasion campaign with material on problems, mistakes, and heroism. (Rev: BL 5/1/04) [940.54]

7847 Wiesel, Elie. *Night* (10–12). 1992, Bantam paper $5.99 (0-553-27253-5). For mature readers, this is the story of the famous writer's experiences as a boy living through the horrors of Auschwitz and Buchenwald. [940.53]

7848 Wieviorka, Annette. *Auschwitz Explained to My Daughter* (10–12). Trans. by Leah Brumer. 2002, Marlowe $14.95 (1-56924-516-9); paper $7.95 (1-56924-552-5). A Holocaust scholar tries to answer her daughter's questions about the motivations and events of the Holocaust. (Rev: BL 10/15/02) [940.53]

7849 Winston, Keith. *Letters from a World War II G.I.* (8–12). Ed. by Judith E. Greenberg and Helen Carey McKeever. 1995, Watts LB $23.00 (0-531-11212-8). A collection of letters home speaking of the hardships of life as a soldier. (Rev: BL 9/15/95; SLJ 9/95; VOYA 12/95) [940.54]

7850 Wistrich, Robert S. *Hitler and the Holocaust* (10–12). 2001, Modern Library $19.95 (0-679-64222-6). This is a well-organized overview that explains the background of the Holocaust as well as its history and aftermath. (Rev: BL 9/1/01) [940.53]

7851 *Witness: Voices from the Holocaust* (10–12). Ed. by Joshua M. Greene, et al. Illus. 2000, Free Pr. $26.00 (0-684-86525-4). This important book offers first-person accounts of survivors and witnesses of the Holocaust. (Rev: BL 4/15/00) [940.53]

7852 *Words to Outlive Us: Voices from the Warsaw Ghetto* (10–12). Ed. by Michal Grynberg. Trans. by Philip Boehm. Illus. 2002, Holt $35.00 (0-8050-5833-8). This collection of eyewitness accounts captures the horrors of the Warsaw Ghetto from its establishment by Nazi occupiers in 1940 through liberation in 1945. (Rev: BL 9/1/02) [940.53]

7853 *World War II: The Axis Assault, 1939–1942* (10–12). Ed. by David Rubel and Douglas Brinkley. Illus. 2003, Holt $30.00 (0-8050-7246-2). This ambitious survey of World War II history interweaves contemporaneous newspaper accounts with primary source documents to paint a comprehensive picture of the Axis's progress in the early years of the war. (Rev: BL 10/1/03) [940.53]

7854 *World War II Letters: A Glimpse into the Heart of the Second World War Through Those Who Were Fighting It* (10–12). Ed. by Bill Adler and Tracy Quinn McLennan. Illus. 2002, St. Martin's $27.95 (0-312-30432-3). Letters from both Allied and Axis soldiers to loved ones at home clearly convey the men's fears and hopes. (Rev: BL 11/15/02) [940.548]

7855 Wright, Mike. *What They Didn't Teach You About World War II* (9–12). Illus. 1998, Presidio $24.95 (0-89141-649-8). Little-known facts about World War II are presented on such topics as submarines, the home front, prisoners of war, spying, rationing, unusual weapons, and actors, comedians, and professional athletes who served. (Rev: SLJ 7/98) [940.54]

7856 Wukovits, John F. *Life as a POW: World War II* (6–12). Series: American War Library. 2000, Lucent LB $27.45 (1-56006-665-2). Using archival photographs and many firsthand accounts, this work explores the treatment of World War II prisoners of war by the Germans and Japanese, the emotional upheavals the prisoners suffered, and the transition to freedom after release. (Rev: BL 9/15/00; HBG 10/00; SLJ 7/00) [940.54]

7857 Wukovits, John F. *Life of an American Soldier in Europe* (6–10). Series: American War Library. 2000, Lucent LB $27.45 (1-56006-666-0). As well as giving a history of World War II and the major battles involving Americans in Europe, this account describes the soldiers' training, daily life, and living conditions. (Rev: BL 4/15/00; HBG 10/00; SLJ 6/00) [940.54]

7858 Yamazaki, James N., and Louis B. Fleming. *Children of the Atomic Bomb: An American Physician's Memoir of Nagasaki, Hiroshima, and the Marshall Islands* (9–12). 1995, Duke Univ. Pr. $18.95 (0-8223-1658-7). Yamazaki, a pediatrician and a Nisei, writes this poignant memoir of his journey to Japan to gather firsthand accounts of the attack on Nagasaki. (Rev: BL 8/95) [618.92]

7859 Zargani, Aldo. *For Solo Violin: A Jewish Childhood in Fascist Italy* (10–12). Trans. by Marina Harss. Illus. 2002, Paul Dry paper $15.95 (0-9679675-3-8). In this poignant memoir, Aldo Zargani, an Italian Jew, tells how he and his family managed to survive Fascist persecution during World War II. (Rev: BL 5/1/02) [858]

Modern World History (1945–)

7860 Anderson, Jon Lee. *The Lion's Grave: Dispatches from Afghanistan* (10–12). 2002, Grove $23.00 (0-8021-1723-6). Budding journalists and students debating the war on terror will be interested in Anderson's account of reporting from post-9/11 Afghanistan. (Rev: BL 11/15/02) [958.104]

7861 Benson, Sonia G. *Korean War: Almanac and Primary Sources* (6–10). 2001, Gale LB $52.00 (0-7876-5691-7). After an almanac section that traces the progress of the war, a selection of primary materials — speeches, memoirs, government documents, and so forth — are presented with introductions that place them in historical context. (Rev: SLJ 5/02) [951.904]

7862 Bizot, Francois. *The Gate* (10–12). Trans. by Euan Cameron. Illus. 2003, Knoof $24.95 (0-375-41293-X). The horrors of the Khmer Rouge's bloody rise to power in Cambodia come alive in this chilling account by the only Western captive ever to be released alive by the Khmer Rouge. (Rev: BL 2/15/03*) [959.604]

7863 Bjornlund, Britta. *The Cold War* (7–10). Series: World History. 2002, Gale LB $27.45 (1-59018-003-8). With ample quotations from original sources and a timeline, Bjornlund looks at the origins and development of the Cold War, and details the crises and periods of reduced tension that marked the length of the conflict. (Rev: BL 8/02; SLJ 10/02) [909.83]

7864 Brubaker, Paul. *The Cuban Missile Crisis in American History* (6–10). Series: In American History. 2001, Enslow LB $20.95 (0-7660-1414-2). This is a gripping account of how diplomacy and quick-thinking averted a war when the Soviets brought missiles to Cuba in 1962. (Rev: BL 8/01; HBG 10/01; SLJ 7/01) [973.992]

7865 Burnett, John S. *Dangerous Waters: Modern Piracy and Terror on the High Seas* (10–12). 2002, Dutton $24.95 (0-525-94679-9). An eye-opening look at modern piracy and the modern techniques employed by both perpetrators and potential targets. (Rev: BL 10/1/02) [910.4]

7866 Denenberg, Barry. *Voices from Vietnam* (7–12). 1995, Scholastic paper $16.95 (0-590-44267-8). Personal narratives of the Vietnam War from the late 1940s to 1975. (Rev: BL 2/15/95*; SLJ 3/95) [959.704]

7867 Dolan, Edward. *America in the Korean War* (7–12). 1998, Millbrook LB $30.90 (0-7613-0361-8). This study of the Korean War focuses on the battles, strategies, technological limitations, and personalities involved. (Rev: BL 1/1–15/99; HBG 3/99; SLJ 3/99) [951.904]

7868 Fisher, Trevor. *The 1960s* (8–12). Illus. 1989, David & Charles $19.95 (0-7134-5603-5). Under a broad subject arrangement, the major news stories and trends of the 1960s are chronicled. (Rev: SLJ 5/89) [973.92]

7869 Gerdes, Louise I., ed. *The Cold War* (6–12). Series: Great Speeches in History. 2003, Gale LB $32.45 (0-7377-0869-7); paper $21.20 (0-7377-0868-9). Winston Churchill and Che Guevara are among the world leaders whose words are given in this collection that examines the confrontation between East and West. (Rev: BL 5/1/03; SLJ 9/03) [909.82]

7870 Harrison, A. Cleveland. *Unsung Valor: A GI's Story of World War II* (10–12). 2000, Univ. Press of Mississippi $28.00 (1-57806-214-4). This is a com-

ing-of-age memoir about a young soldier in World War II and his participation in the Battle of the Bulge, in which he was seriously wounded. (Rev: BL 3/1/00) [940.54]

7871 Hillstrom, Kevin, and Laurie Collier Hillstrom. *Vietnam War: Almanac* (7–12). Series: UXL Vietnam War Reference Library. 2000, Gale LB $45.00 (0-7876-4883-3). An absorbing and comprehensive overview of the causes, conduct, and aftermath of the war that includes interesting sidebars and black-and-white photographs. Also use *Vietnam War: Biographies* and *Vietnam War: Primary Sources* (both 2000). (Rev: BL 3/15/01; SLJ 5/01) [959.704]

7872 Isaacs, Jeremy, and Taylor Downing. *Cold War: An Illustrated History, 1945–1989* (10–12). 1998, Little, Brown $39.95 (0-316-43953-3). A handsome companion to a CNN series, this volume traces the events of the Cold War from the end of World War II to the fall of the Berlin Wall. (Rev: BL 9/1/98) [909.82]

7873 Isserman, Maurice. *The Korean War* (7–12). Series: America at War. 1992, Facts on File $25.00 (0-8160-2688-2). A thorough re-creation of the Korean War, the first armed conflict of the Cold War. (Rev: BL 11/1/92) [951.904]

7874 Isserman, Maurice. *The Vietnam War: America at War* (7–12). Series: America at War. 1992, Facts on File $25.00 (0-8160-2375-1). A riveting account of the Vietnam War from its roots after World War II to U.S. withdrawal in 1975, and a review of the lessons learned. (Rev: BL 3/1/92) [959.7]

7875 Jordan, June. *Affirmative Acts* (11–12). 1998, Doubleday paper $12.95 (0-385-49225-1). Through the 40 poems and essays collected here, Jordan, a poet and professor of African American studies, paints a fascinating portrait of events of the 1990s from the vantage point of a black activist intellectual. (Rev: BL 11/15/98) [305.896]

7876 King, John. *The Gulf War* (7–10). 1991, Dillon $13.95 (0-87518-514-2). A factual account of the Iraqi invasion of Kuwait, wartime operations, and the aftermath. (Rev: BL 3/1/92; SLJ 4/92) [956.704]

7877 Nardo, Don. *The War Against Iraq* (6–12). Series: American War Library: The Persian Gulf War. 2000, Lucent LB $35.15 (1-56006-715-2). This vividly written and nonjudgmental account of the Gulf War of 1991 includes a good final chapter on the results of the war. (Rev: BL 3/1/01; SLJ 3/01) [956.7]

7878 Parker, Thomas. *Day by Day: The Sixties* (9–12). Illus. 1983, Facts on File $125.00 (0-87196-648-4). Using a day-by-day chronology, this book, like others in the series, traces the events of a decade, in this case the 1960s. [909.82]

7879 Rice, Earle. *Point of No Return: Tonkin Gulf and the Vietnam War* (7–12). Illus. 2003, Morgan

Reynolds LB $21.95 (1-931798-16-8). Rice presents the events that led up to the passage in 1964 of the Tonkin Gulf Resolution, which gave Lyndon Johnson authority to take action against North Vietnam. (Rev: BL 9/1/03; HBG 4/04; SLJ 11/03) [959.704]

7880 Rice, Earle, Jr. *The Inchon Invasion* (6–10). Illus. Series: Great Battles in History. 1996, Lucent LB $26.20 (1-56006-418-8). The invasion of this Korean city on Sept. 15, 1950, during the Korean War is highlighted in this well-illustrated account that contains many quotations from primary and secondary sources. (Rev: BL 4/15/96) [951.904]

7881 Rice, Earle, Jr. *The Tet Offensive* (6–10). Illus. Series: Battles. 1996, Lucent LB $26.20 (1-56006-422-6). The story of the bloody Vietnam War battle and its consequences, with some general background coverage of the war. (Rev: BL 1/1–15/97; BR 11–12/97; SLJ 8/97) [959.704]

7882 Roberts, Russell. *Leaders and Generals* (6–12). Series: American War Library: The Vietnam War. 2001, Lucent LB $19.96 (1-56006-717-9). Ho Chi Minh, Lyndon Johnson, Richard Nixon, and Henry Kissinger are among the leaders whose roles in the Vietnam War are examined here. (Rev: BL 3/15/01; SLJ 6/01) [957.704]

7883 Saenger, Diana, and Bradley Steffens. *Life as a POW* (6–12). Series: American War Library: The Vietnam War. 2001, Lucent LB $19.96 (1-56006-716-0). The treatment and morale of prisoners of war during the Vietnam War is covered with many references to actual case histories. (Rev: BL 3/15/01) [959.704]

7884 Uschan, Michael V. *The Korean War* (6–10). Series: World History. 2001, Lucent LB $19.96 (1-56006-704-7). This book traces the causes and course of the war, starting in 1946 with the beginning of the Cold War, and includes maps, archival photographs, sidebar features, and quotations. (Rev: SLJ 9/01) [951.904]

7885 Winkler, Allan M. *The Cold War: A History in Documents* (10–12). Illus. 2000, Oxford $30.00 (0-19-512356-5). This excellent collection of primary

sources covers the Cold War and attempts to trace the course of U. S. policy through these documents. (Rev: BL 12/15/00; HBG 10/01) [909.8]

7886 Wright, David K. *War in Vietnam* (5–10). 1998, Children's paper $20.60 (0-516-02287-3). This is the first volume of an excellent four-volume set. The other volumes are *War in Vietnam, Book II: A Wider War; War in Vietnam, Book III: Vietnamization;* and *War in Vietnam, Book IV: Fall of Vietnam* (all 1989, available only as a set). (Rev: BL 6/1/89; SLJ 6/89) [959.704]

7887 Wukovits, John F. *Leaders and Generals* (6–12). Series: American War Library: The Persian Gulf War. 2001, Lucent LB $19.96 (1-56006-714-4). Key personnel who led the army during the Persian Gulf War of 1991 are profiled in this work that comments on the contributions of each. (Rev: BL 3/15/01) [956.7044]

7888 Yancey, Diane, ed. *The Vietnam War* (7–12). Series: Turning Points in World History. 2001, Greenhaven LB $22.96 (0-7377-0614-7); paper $14.96 (0-7377-0613-9). In a series of separate essays, some from scholarly works, various aspects of the Vietnam War are covered and different points of view expressed. (Rev: BL 6/1–15/01) [959.704]

7889 Yeatts, Tabatha. *The Holocaust Survivors* (6–10). Series: Holocaust Remembered. 1998, Enslow LB $20.95 (0-89490-993-2). This work concentrates on the liberation of the Nazi death camps, the capture of war criminals, the Nuremberg trials, the founding of Israel, and the lives of individual survivors. (Rev: BL 9/15/98; BR 1–2/99; HBG 3/99; SLJ 12/98) [940.5318]

7890 Young, Marilyn B., and John J. Fitzgerald. *The Vietnam War: A History in Documents* (6–12). Series: Pages from History. 2002, Oxford $32.95 (0-19-512278-X). Primary sources cover the conflict in Vietnam from French involvement through the U.S. withdrawal and include everything from official documents, speeches, and transcripts of White House tapes to North Vietnamese political cartoons and U.S. anti-war posters. (Rev: BCCB 9/02; BL 6/1–15/02; HBG 10/02; SLJ 9/02) [959.704]

Geographical Regions

Africa

General and Miscellaneous

7891 *Africa* (9–12). Ed. by William Dudley. Illus. Series: Opposing Viewpoints. 1999, Greenhaven LB $27.45 (0-7377-0119-6); paper $17.45 (0-7377-0118-8). This book examines human rights, economic conditions, environmental concerns, and other issues important to this continent. (Rev: BL 10/15/99) [960.3]

7892 Baroin, Catherine. *Tubu: The Teda and the Daza* (7–12). Illus. Series: Heritage Library of African Peoples. 1997, Rosen LB $28.75 (0-8239-2000-3). The history and contemporary life of these peoples of Chad, Libya, Niger, and the Sudan are presented in easy-reading text. (Rev: BL 4/15/97) [967.43]

7893 Coppard, Kit. *Africa's Animal Kingdom: A Visual Celebration* (9–12). Illus. 2001, PRC paper $24.95 (1-85648-590-0). This handsome book covers the basic ecology of Africa, its climate, natural vegetation, and, in its largest section, its wildlife. (Rev: BL 4/1/01) [591.96]

7894 Davidson, Basil. *The African Slave Trade.* Rev. ed. (10–12). Illus. 1988, Little, Brown paper $15.95 (0-316-17438-6). This account gives details on the four centuries of the African slave trade, during which millions of people were cruelly forced to leave their homes. (Rev: BL 9/86) [967]

7895 Davidson, Basil. *The Lost Cities of Africa.* Rev. ed. (10–12). Illus. 1988, Little, Brown paper $16.95 (0-316-17431-9). This volume attempts to reconstruct the history and culture of Africa below the Sahara before the arrival of Europeans. [960]

7896 Davidson, Basil. *The Search for Africa: History, Culture, Politics* (9–12). 1993, Times Books $25.00 (0-8129-2278-6). Twenty wide-ranging essays that introduce major issues of African history, culture, politics, and economics. (Rev: BL 2/15/94) [967]

7897 *A Day in the Life of Africa* (9–12). Series: Day in the Life. 2002, Tides Foundation $50.00 (0-9718021-0-6). Stunning photographs capture the diverse peoples, cultures, and landscapes of Africa. (Rev: BL 10/1/02) [916]

7898 de Villiers, Marq, and Sheila Hirtle. *Sahara: A Natural History* (10–12). Illus. 2002, Walker $26.00 (0-8027-1372-6). A fascinating survey of the world's largest desert and the people who have lived there. (Rev: BL 9/1/02) [508.66]

7899 Fage, J. D., and William Tordoff. *A History of Africa.* 4th ed. (10–12). 2002, Routledge $95.00 (0-415-25247-4); paper $28.95 (0-415-25248-2). From prehistoric times to the beginning of this century, this is a readable, comprehensive history of Africa. [960]

7900 French, Howard W. *A Continent for the Taking: The Tragedy and Hope of Africa* (10–12). Illus. 2004, Knopf $25.00 (0-375-41461-4). Blaming both corrupt African leaders and Western powers, this account concentrates on the tragedy that is modern Africa. (Rev: BL 3/15/04) [967.03]

7901 Harrison, Peter, ed. *African Nations and Leaders* (7–12). Illus. Series: History of Africa. 2003, Facts on File $30.00 (0-8160-5066-X). Double-page spreads provide a wealth of information on the nations of Africa, their leaders, and important historical events. (Rev: BL 9/15/03) [900]

7902 Jones, Constance. *A Short History of Africa: 1500–1900* (8–12). 1993, Facts on File $19.95 (0-8160-2774-9). Jones describes the Islamic cultures of North Africa, the city-states and kingdoms of East Africa, the rich traditions of West Africa, and the roots of apartheid in South Africa. (Rev: BL 3/1/93; SLJ 10/93) [960]

7903 Laine, Daniel. *African Kings* (10–12). Illus. 2000, Ten Speed $40.00 (1-58008-224-6). This book features pictures and text about 70 contemporary African monarchs with background material on the history, rituals, and culture of the various tribes. (Rev: BL 11/1/00) [960]

7904 Macintosh, Donald. *Travels in the White Man's Grave: Memoirs from West and Central Africa* (10–12). 2002, Abacus paper $13.95 (0-349-11435-8). In this collection of tales from three decades spent in Africa, Scottish-born Macintosh relates various exciting encounters with an assortment of unforgettable humans and deadly wildlife. (Rev: BL 4/15/02) [966.032092]

7905 Morrell, Virginia. *Blue Nile: Ethiopia's River of Magic and Mystery* (10–12). Illus. 2001, National Geographic $26.00 (0-7922-7951-4). As well as a history of the exploration of the Blue Nile, this is an engrossing account of the author's journey through these treacherous waters. (Rev: BL 7/01) [962.6]

7906 Murray, Jocelyn, ed. *Cultural Atlas of Africa* (9–12). Illus. 1981, Facts on File $45.00 (0-87196-558-5). With hundreds of maps and illustrations plus text, such topics as language, religion, culture, and education are covered for each country. (Rev: BL 9/86) [960]

7907 Pavitt, Nigel. *Africa's Great Rift Valley* (10–12). Illus. 2001, Abrams $49.50 (0-8109-0602-3). This book describes the history, geography, people, and wildlife of this valley that stretches south from Ethiopia. (Rev: BL 10/15/01) [967.6]

7908 Reader, John. *Africa* (8–12). 2001, National Geographic $50.00 (0-7922-7681-7). A lavishly illustrated overview of Africa with sections on each of the many ecological divisions, such as savanna, desert, mountains, and coast. (Rev: BL 8/01) [960]

7909 Reader, John. *Africa: A Biography of the Continent* (10–12). 1998, Knopf $45.00 (0-679-40979-3). A massive survey of the history of Africa and its people, from its earliest inhabitants to the present day, with extensive notes and lists of sources. (Rev: SLJ 1/99) [960]

7910 Rowell, Trevor. *The Scramble for Africa* (9–12). Illus. 1987, David & Charles $19.95 (0-7134-5200-5). The breakup of the continent of Africa by imperialists is documented by the key people involved. (Rev: SLJ 2/88) [960]

7911 Segal, Ronald. *The Black Diaspora* (9–12). 1995, Farrar $27.50 (0-374-11396-3). The first white South African to join the African National Congress, Segal brings a rich personal background to this history of the black experience outside Africa over five centuries. (Rev: BL 8/95*) [970.004]

7912 Segal, Ronald. *Islam's Black Slaves: The Other Black Diaspora* (10–12). 2001, Farrar $30.00 (0-374-22774-8). This account traces the history of the black slave trade as practiced in northern Africa

by Islamic nations, a trade that involved about 12 million captives over a period of 1,000 years. (Rev: BL 2/15/01) [306.3]

7913 Sheehan, Sean. *Great African Kingdoms* (5–10). Series: Ancient World. 1998, Raintree Steck-Vaughn LB $27.12 (0-8172-5124-3). Coverage of the great African kingdoms includes the spectacular palace of Great Zimbabwe, the majestic sculptures of Benin, and the Zulu empire's struggle for survival. (Rev: BL 1/1–15/99; HBG 3/99) [960]

7914 Wekesser, Carol, and Christina Pierce. *Africa* (7–12). Series: Opposing Viewpoints. 1992, Greenhaven paper $16.20 (0-89908-161-4). The history and present conditions of Africa, from politics to social issues, are discussed in essays offering varying perspectives. (Rev: BL 5/15/92; SLJ 7/92) [960]

7915 Wepman, Dennis. *Africa: The Struggle for Independence* (7–10). 1993, Facts on File $25.00 (0-8160-2820-6). Focuses on the arbitrary division of the African continent by European countries and the struggles in different regions against colonial rule. (Rev: BL 2/15/94; VOYA 6/94) [960]

7916 Wolfe, Art, and Michelle A. Gliders. *Africa* (8–12). Illus. 2001, Wildlands $75.00 (0-9675918-1-3). Magnificent photographs are the highlight of this expensive book that introduces Africa by five separate ecosystems: savanna, woodland, rain forest, wetland, and desert. (Rev: BL 9/15/01) [960]

Central and Eastern Africa

7917 Barnes, Virginia Lee, and Janice Boddy, retels. *Aman* (10–12). 1995, Vintage paper $14.00 (0-679-76209-4). The candid story of a young Somali woman and the sexual and social taboos of tribal society in her country. (Rev: BR 3–4/96; SLJ 2/96) [967]

7918 Bodnarchuk, Kari. *Rwanda: Country Torn Apart* (7–10). Illus. Series: World in Conflict. 1999, Lerner LB $25.26 (0-8225-3557-2). This history of Rwanda concentrates on the Tutsi/Hutu civil war in 1994 that left over a million people dead. (Rev: BL 1/1–15/00; HBG 4/00) [967.571]

7919 Bowden, Rob. *Kenya* (6–10). Illus. Series: Countries of the World. 2003, Facts on File $30.00 (0-8160-5384-7). This profile of an impoverished nation gives material on physical geography, resources, population, tourism, commerce, and geography. (Rev: BL 2/1/04) [967.62]

7920 Broberg, Catherine. *Kenya in Pictures* (6–10). Series: Visual Geography. 2002, Lerner LB $27.93 (0-8225-1957-7). Information on all aspects of life in this African country, including extensive coverage of its history, is accompanied by plenty of photographs and a Web site that offers up-to-date links. (Rev: BL 10/15/02; HBG 3/03; SLJ 12/02) [967]

7921 Burnham, Philip. *Gbaya* (7–12). Illus. Series: Heritage Library of African Peoples. 1997, Rosen LB $17.95 (0-8239-1995-1). These African people who live in Cameroon, Central African Republic, Congo, and Zaire, are introduced through illustrations and simple text. (Rev: BL 4/15/97) [967]

7922 Creed, Alexander. *Uganda* (6–12). Series: Major World Nations. 1998, Chelsea LB $21.95 (0-7910-4770-9). This book presents background material on the history and geography of Uganda and good current information on the country's economic, cultural, and social conditions. (Rev: BL 9/15/98; BR 1–2/99) [967.61]

7923 Dugard, Martin. *Into Africa: The Epic Adventures of Stanley and Livingstone* (10–12). 2003, Doubleday $24.95 (0-385-50451-9). Alternating chapters full of rich detail drawn from primary sources chronicle the lives of these men and the dangers they faced in their explorations. (Rev: BL 6/1–15/03; SLJ 11/03) [967.04]

7924 Edgerton, Robert B. *The Troubled Heart of Africa: A History of the Congo* (10–12). Illus. 2002, St. Martin's $25.95 (0-312-30486-2). Edgerton chronicles the turbulent history of the Congo from the first European exploration of its interior in the 15th century to the present. (Rev: BL 12/15/02) [967.24]

7925 Freeman, Charles. *Crisis in Rwanda* (7–12). Series: New Perspectives. 1998, Raintree Steck-Vaughn LB $28.54 (0-8172-5020-4). This book tells of the genocide of the Tutsi, the movements of Hutu refugees, and the actions of the international community from the viewpoints of survivors, aid workers, politicians, historians, and journalists. (Rev: BL 12/15/98; HBG 3/99; SLJ 2/99) [967.57]

7926 Gaertner, Ursula. *Elmolo* (7–10). Series: Heritage Library of African Peoples. 1995, Rosen LB $17.95 (0-8239-1764-9). Looks at the customs, daily life, and values of the Elmolo tribe in Kenya. (Rev: BL 7/95; SLJ 5/95) [967.62]

7927 Holtzman, Jon. *Samburu* (7–10). Series: Heritage Library of African Peoples. 1995, Rosen LB $17.95 (0-8239-1759-2). Discusses in detailed but simple text the culture and lifestyle of the Samburu people of Kenya. (Rev: BL 7/95; SLJ 5/95) [967]

7928 Hussein, Ikram. *Teenage Refugees from Somalia Speak Out* (7–12). Series: Teenage Refugees Speak Out. 1997, Rosen LB $16.95 (0-8239-2444-0). Teenage refugees from Somalia recount the violent anarchy and acute famine in their country and their journey from Africa to the United States. (Rev: BL 12/15/97; SLJ 12/97) [967]

7929 Ifemesia, Chieka. *Turkana* (7–10). Illus. Series: Heritage Library of African Peoples. 1996, Rosen LB $17.95 (0-8239-1761-4). Using a simple text and color photographs, this account describes the past and present of the Turkana people, who now live in Ethiopia, Kenya, Sudan, and Uganda. (Rev: BL 2/15/95) [960]

7930 Kabira, Wanjiku M. *Agikuyu* (7–10). Series: Heritage Library of African Peoples. 1995, Rosen LB $17.95 (0-8239-1762-2). Presents social and cultural aspects of the Agikuyu community of Kenya in ways that make them accessible to Western readers. (Rev: BL 7/95; SLJ 6/95) [967]

7931 Leakey, Richard, and Virginia Morell. *Wildlife Wars: My Fight to Save Africa's Natural Treasures* (10–12). Illus. 2001, St. Martin's $25.95 (0-312-20626-7). The politics of wildlife protection in Kenya is the subject of this book written by the anthropologist who was appointed to reform the corrupt Kenyan Wildlife Department. (Rev: BL 8/01) [967.6]

7932 Nwaezeigwe, Nwankwo T. *Ngoni* (7–12). Illus. Series: Heritage Library of African Peoples. 1997, Rosen LB $17.95 (0-8239-2006-2). The history, traditions, and struggle for freedom of this African group in Malawi are laid out in accessible text. (Rev: BL 4/15/97) [968.97]

7933 Ojo, Onukaba A. *Mbuti* (7–10). Illus. Series: Heritage Library of African Peoples. 1996, Rosen LB $17.95 (0-8239-1998-6). The Mbuti people of Zaire are introduced with details on their environment, history, customs, and present situation. (Rev: BL 2/15/96; SLJ 7/96) [305.896]

7934 Okeke, Chika. *Kongo* (7–12). Illus. Series: Heritage Library of African Peoples. 1997, Rosen LB $17.95 (0-8239-2001-1). The Kongo people of Angola, Congo, and Zaire in Central Africa are featured in easy-reading text with material on their land, kingdoms, political life, and culture. (Rev: BL 4/15/97) [967]

7935 *Peoples of Central Africa* (8–12). Series: Peoples of Africa. 1997, Facts on File $28.00 (0-8160-3486-9). A description of the history, culture, and present status of 17 African peoples who live in and around the present-day countries of Angola, Congo, and Zaire. (Rev: BR 11–12/97; SLJ 2/98) [967]

7936 *Peoples of East Africa* (6–12). Series: Peoples of Africa. 1997, Facts on File $28.00 (0-8160-3484-2). This book gives a concise overview of 15 ethnic groups of eastern Africa, with details on history, language, way of life, society, religion, and culture. Included are Falasha, Ganda, Hutus and Tutsis, Masai, Nyoro, Somalis, and Swahili. (Rev: BR 11–12/97; SLJ 10/97) [967]

7937 Roberts, Mary N., and Allen F. Roberts. *Luba* (6–10). Series: Heritage Library of African Peoples. 1997, Rosen LB $17.95 (0-8239-2002-X). The Luba people of Zaire are introduced with material on their history, present conditions, and cultural resources. (Rev: BL 9/15/97) [967]

7938 Ross, Mark C. *Dangerous Beauty: Life and Death in Africa: True Stories from a Safari Guide*

(10–12). 2001, Hyperion $24.95 (0-7868-6672-1). The story of a safari guide in Africa whose life changed when, in 1999, he lived through days of horror after he was kidnapped by Rwandan rebels and many of his party were murdered. (Rev: BL 7/01) [599]

7939 Schnapper, LaDena. *Teenage Refugees from Ethiopia Speak Out* (5–10). Series: Teenage Refugees Speak Out. 1997, Rosen LB $16.95 (0-8239-2438-6). Ethiopian teens now living in America tell of the violence, famine, and civil war that drove them from their country and of their reception in America. (Rev: SLJ 2/98) [963]

7940 Scott, Jonathan, and Angela Scott. *Mara-Serengeti: A Photographer's Paradise* (9–12). Illus. 2001, Voyageur $39.95 (0-86343-398-7). This account contains a superb collection of photographs and drawings plus a running text, all dealing with the complex grassland area known as the Mara-Serengeti ecosystem of Kenya and Tanzania. (Rev: BL 4/1/01) [591.967]

7941 Twagilimana, Aimable. *Teenage Refugees from Rwanda Speak Out* (5–10). Series: Teenage Refugees Speak Out. 1997, Rosen LB $16.95 (0-8239-2443-2). Teenage refugees from Rwanda describe the warfare between Tutsi and Hutu peoples, the terrible living conditions that forced them to leave their country, and the challenges and difficulties they have experienced in the United States. (Rev: SLJ 2/98) [967]

7942 Wa Wamwere, Koigi. *I Refuse to Die: My Journey for Freedom* (10–12). Illus. 2002, Seven Stories $24.95 (1-58322-521-8). In this inspiring autobiography, Kenyan human rights activist Koigi wa Wamwere recounts his courageous resistance to the repressive regimes of Jomo Kenyatta and Daniel Arap Moi. (Rev: BL 9/1/02) [967.6227]

7943 Wangari, Esther. *Ameru* (7–10). Illus. Series: Heritage Library of African Peoples. 1995, Rosen LB $17.95 (0-8239-1766-5). An introduction to the history, traditions, and culture of the Ameru people of Kenya in easy-reading text. (Rev: BL 9/15/95; SLJ 11/95) [967.6]

7944 Zeleza, Tiyambe. *Akamba* (7–10). Illus. Series: Heritage Library of African Peoples. 1995, Rosen LB $17.95 (0-8239-1768-1). The history, traditions, and fight for freedom of the Akamba people of Kenya are covered in this book with many color illustrations. (Rev: BL 7/95; SLJ 6/95) [960]

7945 Zeleza, Tiyambe. *Mijikenda* (7–10). Series: Heritage Library of African Peoples. 1995, Rosen LB $17.95 (0-8239-1767-3). Combines history and anthropology to provide an easy-to-read portrait of the Mijikenda people. (Rev: BL 9/15/95; SLJ 11/95) [967]

North Africa

7946 Azuonye, Chukwuma. *Dogon* (7–10). Illus. Series: Heritage Library of African Peoples. 1995, Rosen LB $28.75 (0-8239-1976-5). Provides information on the history, culture, and lifestyles of the Dogon people of Mali. (Rev: BL 2/15/96) [966.23]

7947 Genini, Izza, et al. *Splendours of Morocco* (10–12). Illus. 2000, Tauris Parke $45.00 (1-86064-482-1). A large, handsome volume that reproduces the colors and sights of Morocco in text, photographs, and even through some recipes. (Rev: BL 10/15/00) [916.4]

7948 Hollyman, Stephenie, and Walter E. A. van Beek. *Dogon: Africa's People of the Cliffs* (10–12). Illus. 2001, Abrams $49.50 (0-8109-4373-5). This account describes the culture, history, and lifestyles of the Dogon people who live in a remote part of Mali in western Africa. (Rev: BL 5/15/01) [966.23]

7949 Oufkir, Malika, and Michele Fitoussi. *Stolen Lives: Twenty Years in a Desert Jail* (10–12). Illus. 2001, Hyperion $23.95 (0-7868-6732-9). Because a man was involved in a plot to kill the king of Morocco, his wife and children spent 20 years in jail. A harrowing account of maltreatment and faith. (Rev: BL 4/1/01*) [365]

7950 *Peoples of North Africa* (8–12). Series: Peoples of Africa. 1997, Facts on File $28.00 (0-8160-3483-4). This book describes the history and cultures of North African peoples, including Arabs, Baggara, Beja, Berbers, Copts, Dinka, Muba, Nuer, Shilluk, and Tuareg. (Rev: BR 11–12/97; SLJ 2/98) [961]

7951 Schlesinger, Arthur M., Jr., and Fred L. Israel, eds. *Mysteries of the Sahara: Chronicles from National Geographic* (9–12). Series: Cultural and Geographical Exploration. 1999, Chelsea LB $19.95 (0-7910-5097-1). This article and its photographs originally appeared in a 1914 issue of *National Geographic* magazine and describes the then-current conditions in Morocco, Algeria, Tunisia, and Libya. (Rev: SLJ 6/99) [961]

Southern Africa

7952 Beck, Roger. *The History of South Africa* (10–12). 2000, Greenwood $39.95 (0-313-30730-X). From prehistory through the European invasions and ending with the Mandela years, this is a readable basic guide to South African history. [968]

7953 Biesele, Megan, and Kxao Royal. *San* (7–10). Series: Heritage Library of African Peoples. 1997, Rosen LB $17.95 (0-8239-1997-8). The San people of Botswana, Namibia, and South Africa are featured in this accessible account that describes their rich tradition and struggle for freedom. (Rev: BL 9/15/97) [960]

7954 Blauer, Ettagale, and Jason Lauré. *South Africa* (5–10). Series: Enchantment of the World. 1998, Children's LB $34.50 (0-516-20606-0). An introduction to South Africa that gives good coverage of the struggle of black Africans for freedom and the problems facing the population today. (Rev: HBG 3/99; SLJ 11/98) [968]

7955 Bolaane, Maitseo, and Part T. Mgadla. *Batswana* (6–10). Series: Heritage Library of African Peoples. 1997, Rosen LB $17.95 (0-8239-2008-9). This work discusses the history, culture, and present status of the Batswana people of southern Africa. (Rev: BL 1/1–15/98) [968]

7956 Canesso, Claudia. *South Africa* (6–10). Series: Major World Nations. 1998, Chelsea LB $21.95 (0-7910-4766-0). An accurate, informative, and unbiased account of the social, political, and economic conditions in South Africa today, supplemented by illustrations and maps. (Rev: BL 9/15/98; BR 1–2/99; HBG 3/99; SLJ 6/99) [968.06]

7957 Carter, Jason. *Power Lines: Two Years on South Africa's Borders* (10–12). Illus. 2002, National Geographic $26.00 (0-7922-8012-1). The grandson of President Jimmy Carter describes his daily life and the friends he made during a two-year Peace Corps stint in a South African village. (Rev: BL 5/15/02) [968.06]

7958 Cunningham, Carol, and Joel Berger. *Horn of Darkness* (10–12). 1997, Oxford $36.95 (0-19-511113-3). Black rhinos and life in the Namibian desert are featured in this account of how the authors, field biologists, tried to help in the crusade to save the black rhino from extinction. (Rev: SLJ 8/97) [968]

7959 Fish, Bruce, and Becky Durost Fish. *South Africa: 1880 to the Present: Imperialism, Nationalism, and Apartheid* (6–12). 2000, Chelsea LB $29.95 (0-7910-5676-7). This survey of South African history is careful to highlight changes and achievements that did not involve European influence; it includes many Royal Geographic Society black-and-white photographs. (Rev: BR 9–10/01; HBG 3/01; SLJ 2/01) [968]

7960 Fuller, Alexandra. *Don't Let's Go to the Dogs Tonight: An African Childhood* (10–12). Illus. 2001, Random $24.95 (0-375-50750-7). As told by a young daughter, this is the story of a white family in Rhodesia (now Zimbabwe) before and during the civil war and their flight to Zambia where they finally settled. (Rev: BL 11/1/01*; SLJ 7/02) [968.91]

7961 Fuller, Alexandra. *Scribbling the Cat: Travels with an African Soldier* (10–12). Illus. 2004, Penguin $24.95 (1-59420-016-5). This is the story of K., a white farmer who fought in the Rhodesian war, its battles, and its outcome. (Rev: BL 4/15/04*) [968.9]

7962 Gobodo-Madikizela, Pumla. *A Human Being Died That Night: A South African Story of Forgiveness* (10–12). 2003, Houghton $24.00 (0-618-21189-6). Gobodo-Madikizela, who served on South Africa's Truth and Reconciliation Commission, assesses what the commission learned and addresses the usual questions about the motivations and excuses of perpetrators of violence. (Rev: BL 12/15/02) [363.2]

7963 Green, Rebecca L. *Merina* (7–12). Illus. Series: Heritage Library of African Peoples. 1997, Rosen LB $17.95 (0-8239-1991-9). The history and culture of the Merina people of Madagascar are covered in simple text and many illustrations. (Rev: BL 4/15/97; VOYA 6/97) [969.1]

7964 Harrison, Peter, ed. *History of Southern Africa* (7–12). Illus. Series: History of Africa. 2003, Facts on File $30.00 (0-8160-5065-1). From prehistory to today, this volume covers in detail the history of southern Africa, detailing in particular European settlement, independence, and apartheid. (Rev: BL 9/15/03; SLJ 5/04) [968]

7965 Hays, David, and Daniel Hays. *My Old Man and the Sea* (10–12). 1995, Algonquin $19.95 (1-56512-102-3). An exciting account of a father and grown son (plus their cat, Tiger), and their perilous voyage around Cape Horn in a 25-foot boat. (Rev: BL 6/1/95; SLJ 2/96) [968]

7966 Joubert, Dereck, and Beverly Joubert. *The Africa Diaries: An Illustrated Memoir of Life in the Bush* (10–12). Illus. 2000, National Geographic $30.00 (0-7922-7962-X). This is a beautifully illustrated book with a text that includes excerpts from field journals and tells about the hardships and splendor of living for 20 years in the bush of Botswana. (Rev: BL 1/1–15/01) [591.9]

7967 Kaschula, Russel. *Xhosa* (7–12). Series: Heritage Library of African Peoples. 1997, Rosen LB $17.95 (0-8239-2013-5). The Xhosa people of South Africa are introduced with stunning photographs and simple text describing their past and present culture and lifestyles. (Rev: BL 1/1–15/98) [968]

7968 Kruger, Kobie. *The Wilderness Family: At Home with Africa's Wildlife* (9–12). Illus. 2001, Ballantine $26.95 (0-345-44426-4). The wife of a game ranger in a national park in South Africa reports on the family's experiences there and tells about adopting an abandoned lion cub whom they named Leo. (Rev: BL 5/1/01) [639.9]

7969 Mann, Kenny. *Monomotapa, Zulu, Basuto: Southern Africa* (8–12). Series: African Kingdoms of the Past. 1996, Silver Burdett LB $15.95 (0-87518-659-9); paper $7.95 (0-382-39300-7). The history of three southern African kingdoms, using striking layouts, plenty of color, and clear writing. (Rev: SLJ 2/97; VOYA 2/97) [968]

7970 Mendes, Pedro. *Bay of Tigers: An Odyssey Through War-Torn Angola* (10–12). Trans. by Clifford Landers. 2003, Harcourt $25.00 (0-15-100655-5). Suitable for mature teens only, Mendes's portrait of war-torn Angola unflinchingly documents the grisly toll taken by decades of conflict. (Rev: BL 5/15/03) [910.7304]

7971 Nagle, Garrett. *South Africa* (6–12). Series: Country Studies. 1999, Heinemann LB $27.07 (1-57572-896-6). An excellent overview of South Africa, with particularly good coverage of current conditions and problems. (Rev: BL 8/99) [968]

7972 Ngwane, Zolani. *Zulu* (7–12). Series: Heritage Library of African Peoples. 1997, Rosen LB $17.95 (0-8239-2014-3). This readable work introduces the history and culture of the Zulus of South Africa. (Rev: BL 9/15/97; VOYA 12/97) [968]

7973 Njoku, Onwuka N. *Mbundu* (7–12). Illus. Series: Heritage Library of African Peoples. 1997, Rosen LB $28.75 (0-8239-2004-6). An easy-to-read introduction to the history and contemporary culture of this people of Angola. (Rev: BL 4/15/97) [967.3]

7974 Oluikpe, Benson O. *Swazi* (7–12). Illus. Series: Heritage Library of African Peoples. 1997, Rosen LB $28.75 (0-8239-2012-7). This accessible book describes the history, traditions, and struggles for freedom of the Swazi people of Swaziland and South Africa. (Rev: BL 4/15/97; SLJ 12/97) [968]

7975 *Peoples of Southern Africa* (6–12). Series: Peoples of Africa. 1997, Facts on File $28.00 (0-8160-3487-7). The history, geography, culture, religion, and social life of 17 different South African peoples are highlighted, including Afrikaners, Cape Coloreds, Cape Malays, Indian South Africans, Ndebele, Swazi, Tswana, Venda, and Zulu. (Rev: BR 11–12/97; SLJ 10/97) [968]

7976 Schneider, Elizabeth Ann. *Ndebele* (7–12). Illus. Series: Heritage Library of African Peoples. 1997, Rosen LB $17.95 (0-8239-2009-7). Topics covered about the Ndebele people of South Africa include environment, history, religion, social organization, politics, and customs. (Rev: BL 4/15/97) [968]

7977 Smith, Chris. *Conflict in Southern Africa* (6–12). Series: Conflicts. 1993, Macmillan LB $22.00 (0-02-785956-8). An overview of the politics of southern Africa: Angola, Mozambique, Zambia, Namibia, and South Africa. (Rev: BL 7/93; SLJ 12/93) [968]

7978 Thompson, Leonard Monteath. *A History of South Africa.* 3rd ed. (10–12). 2001, Yale Univ. Pr. paper $17.95 (0-300-08776-4). An account of South African history that focuses more on the nation's black inhabitants than on the white. [968]

7979 Udechukwu, Ada. *Herero* (7–10). Series: Heritage Library of African Peoples. 1996, Rosen LB $17.95 (0-8239-2003-8). In simple text, this book introduces the three Herero subgroups that share a similar language and culture in today's Botswana, Angola, and Namibia, with an emphasis on their political history. (Rev: BL 3/15/96; SLJ 6/96) [968]

7980 *Women Writing Africa: The Southern Region* (10–12). Ed. by M. J. Daymond et al. 2002, Feminist Pr. $75.00 (1-55861-406-0). A collection of varied writings — letters, memoirs, work songs, prison diaries, and poetry — by women from six countries in southern Africa. (Rev: BL 11/1/02) [808.8]

West Africa

7981 Alonso, Alfanso, and Carlton Ward. *The Edge of Africa: All Life Is Here* (8–12). 2003, Hylas $39.95 (1-59258-040-8). The natural history of Gabon is detailed in a series of stunning photographs of wildlife and plants, some familiar, others not. (Rev: BL 2/15/04) [590.9]

7982 Anda, Michael O. *Yoruba* (7–10). Series: Heritage Library of African Peoples. 1996, Rosen LB $17.95 (0-8239-1988-9). This work describes one of the largest sub-Saharan ethnic groups, whose influence, because of the slave trade, spread to the New World, especially Brazil. (Rev: BL 3/15/96; SLJ 6/96) [966.9]

7983 Azuonye, Chukwuma. *Edo: The Bini People of the Benin Kingdom* (7–10). Illus. Series: Heritage Library of African Peoples. 1996, Rosen LB $28.75 (0-8239-1985-4). A review of the history, culture, society, and the struggle for freedom of the Bini people, whose empire was part of present-day Nigeria. (Rev: BL 3/15/96) [966.9]

7984 Campbell, Greg. *Blood Diamonds: Tracing the Deadly Path of the World's Most Precious Stones* (10–12). Illus. 2002, Westview $26.00 (0-8133-3939-1). A fascinating overview of the trade in Sierra Leone diamonds and its sinister links to violence and conflicts elsewhere in the world. (Rev: BL 8/02) [966.404]

7985 Falola, Toyin. *History of Nigeria* (10–12). Series: Histories of Modern Nations. 1999, Greenwood $35.00 (0-313-30682-6). Falola traces the country's development from prehistoric times to the late 20th century, focusing in particular on the country's interaction with Europeans, most notably the British. (Rev: VOYA 12/00) [966.9]

7986 Harmon, Daniel E. *Nigeria: 1880 to the Present: The Struggle, the Tragedy, the Promise* (6–12). 2000, Chelsea LB $29.95 (0-7910-5452-7). This survey of Nigerian history is careful to highlight changes and achievements that did not involve European influence; it includes many Royal Geographic Society black-and-white photographs. (Rev: BR 9–10/01; HBG 3/01; SLJ 2/01) [966.9]

493

7987 Koslow, Philip. *Lords of the Savanna: The Bambara, Fulani, Igbo, Mossi, and Nupe* (7–10). Series: Kingdoms of Africa. 1997, Chelsea paper $8.95 (0-7910-3142-X). A strong narrative style and attractive illustrations are used to present the history and culture of these West African peoples of present-day Nigeria, Cameroon, and Burkina Faso. (Rev: SLJ 1/98) [966]

7988 Mack-Williams, Kibibi V. *Mossi* (7–10). Illus. Series: Heritage Library of African Peoples. 1996, Rosen LB $28.75 (0-8239-1984-6). The history, social organization, and culture of the Mossi people of West Africa are described. (Rev: BL 3/15/96) [966.25]

7989 Mann, Kenny. *Kongo Ndongo: West Central Africa* (8–12). Series: African Kingdoms of the Past. 1996, Silver Burdett $15.95 (0-87518-658-0); paper $7.95 (0-382-39298-1). A visually attractive book that outlines the history of this West African kingdom and utilizes many excellent sources. (Rev: SLJ 2/97; VOYA 2/97) [966]

7990 Mann, Kenny. *Oyo, Benin, Ashanti: The Guinea Coast* (6–10). Series: African Kingdoms of the Past. 1996, Silver Burdett $15.95 (0-87518-657-2); paper $7.95 (0-382-39177-2). Through legends and history, the author re-creates the story of these three West Africa kingdoms and their culture. (Rev: SLJ 6/96) [960]

7991 Ndukwe, Pat I. *Fulani* (7–10). Illus. Series: Heritage Library of African Peoples. 1995, Rosen LB $28.75 (0-8239-1982-X). A description of the history, surroundings, politics, customs, and current conditions of the Fulani people, who live in Cameroon, Mali, and Nigeria. (Rev: BL 2/15/96; SLJ 7/96) [966]

7992 Nnoromele, Salome C. *Life Among the Ibo Women of Nigeria* (9–12). Illus. Series: The Way People Live. 1997, Lucent LB $17.96 (1-56006-344-0). Before European contact, Ibo women were equal in power with men in the economy, politics, and the family, but English influences changed this. Today these women are caught between two cultures. (Rev: BL 9/1/98; SLJ 10/98) [966.9]

7993 Ogbaa, Kalu. *Igbo* (7–10). Series: Heritage Library of African Peoples. 1995, Rosen LB $17.95 (0-8239-1977-3). An introduction to the Igbo people, one of the three most important ethnic groups in Nigeria. (Rev: BL 9/15/95; SLJ 11/95) [966.9]

7994 *Peoples of West Africa* (6–12). Series: Peoples of Africa. 1997, Facts on File $28.00 (0-8160-3485-0). Extensive background material is provided on the history, geography, languages, art, music, religion, and society of 13 West African peoples, including the Asante, Bambara, Dogon, Fon, Hausa, Moors, Mossi, and Yoruba. (Rev: BL 8/97; BR 11–12/97; SLJ 10/97) [966]

7995 Reef, Catherine. *This Our Dark Country: The American Settlers of Liberia* (7–12). 2002, Clarion $17.00 (0-618-14785-3). This chronological account of Liberia's history makes good use of excerpts from letters and diaries. (Rev: BL 11/15/02; HBG 3/03; SLJ 12/02; VOYA 6/03) [966.62]

7996 Sallah, Tijan M. *Wolof* (7–12). Series: Heritage Library of African Peoples. 1996, Rosen LB $17.95 (0-8239-1987-0). Using maps, many color illustrations, and simple text, this book introduces the Wolof people of Senegal and their history, social and political life, customs, religious beliefs, and relations with other peoples in their region. (Rev: BL 3/15/96; SLJ 7/96) [966.3]

Asia

General and Miscellaneous

7997 Angus, Colin. *Lost in Mongolia: Rafting the World's Last Unchallenged River* (10–12). Illus. 2003, Broadway paper $12.95 (0-7679-1280-2). Angus details the first successful navigation of Asia's 3,250-mile-long Yenisey River, a thrilling journey that took the author and two companions by raft and kayak from the heart of Mongolia to the Arctic Ocean. (Rev: BL 9/1/03) [796.1]

7998 Franck, Irene M., and David M. Brownstone. *Across Asia by Land* (6–10). Series: Travel and Trade Routes. 1991, Facts on File $17.95 (0-8160-1874-X). Trade and travel routes tell tales from ancient times to the present. (Rev: BL 1/15/91; SLJ 6/91) [380.1]

7999 Pascoe, Elaine. *The Pacific Rim: East Asia at the Dawn of a New Century* (7–12). 1999, Twenty-First Century LB $25.90 (0-7613-3015-1). Brief historical information and current economic figures are given for Japan, China, Taiwan, the Koreas, Indonesia, Singapore, Malaysia, and the Philippines. (Rev: BL 7/99; SLJ 9/99) [950.4]

8000 Schmidt, Jeremy. *Himalayan Passage: Seven Months in the High Country of Tibet, Nepal, China, India and Pakistan* (9–12). 1991, Mountaineers $22.95 (0-89886-262-0). The adventure-filled travels of four experienced mountaineers — on foot, by mountain bike, and in overcrowded buses and trucks — from Tibet to Sikkim. (Rev: BL 9/15/91) [915.49]

China

8001 Allison, Amy. *Life in Ancient China* (6–10). Series: The Way People Live. 2000, Lucent LB $19.96 (1-56006-694-6). After a general history of ancient China, this account focuses on the daily life of the people, their struggles, and their accomplishments. (Rev: BL 3/1/01) [951]

8002 Becker, Jasper. *The Chinese* (10–12). 2000, Free Pr. $26.00 (0-684-84412-5). From the author's 20 years of traveling in China comes this book about its people and their social, ethnic, cultural, and economic lives. (Rev: BL 11/1/00) [951]

8003 Behnke, Alison. *China in Pictures.* Rev. ed. (6–10). Illus. Series: Visual Geography. 2002, Lerner LB $27.93 (0-8225-0370-0). An excellent introduction to China that includes material on geography, history, people, economy, and culture with maps, photographs, and illustrations. (Rev: BL 10/15/02; HBG 3/03; SLJ 3/03) [951]

8004 *China* (9–12). Ed. by James Torr. Series: Opposing Viewpoints. 2001, Greenhaven LB $31.20 (0-7377-0650-3); paper $19.95 (0-7377-0649-X). China's economy, social conditions, and foreign relations come under scrutiny in this collection of essays that present differing views. [951]

8005 *China: Fifty Years Inside the People's Republic* (9–12). Illus. 1999, Aperture $50.00 (0-89381-862-3). Using the work of 20 renowned photographers and an explanatory introductory essay, this work explores 50 years of Chinese cultural, political, and social life under the communists. (Rev: BL 1/1–15/00) [951]

8006 Cozic, Charles P., ed. *U.S. Policy Toward China* (8–12). Series: At Issue. 1996, Greenhaven LB $35.15 (1-56510-389-0); paper $17.45 (1-56510-388-2). Differences between China and the U.S. on such issues as human rights and copyright policies are explored from various points of view in this collection of articles. (Rev: BL 1/1–15/96; SLJ 5/96) [327.73]

8007 Ebrey, Patricia Buckley. *The Cambridge Illustrated History of China* (10–12). 1996, Cambridge Univ. Pr. $39.95 (0-521-43519-0). More than 5,000 years of Chinese civilization are covered, with a focus on cultural and social issues. (Rev: SLJ 5/97) [951]

8008 Fairbank, John King. *The Great Chinese Revolution: 1800–1985* (10–12). 1986, HarperCollins $15.00 (0-06-039076-X). This account covers 185 years of Chinese history from the late imperial period to the mid-1980s. [951]

8009 Green, Robert. *China* (6–10). Series: Modern Nations of the World. 1999, Lucent LB $27.45 (1-56006-440-4). A well-organized overview of China and its emergence as a major political and economic power. (Rev: SLJ 8/99) [051]

8010 Immell, Myra. *The Han Dynasty* (6–10). Illus. Series: Lost Civilizations. 2003, Gale LB $21.96 (1-59018-096-8). An informative and readable overview of the long Han dynasty and the social and agricultural systems of the time. (Rev: SLJ 5/03) [931]

8011 Israel, Fred L., and Arthur M. Schlesinger, Jr., eds. *Peking* (6–10). Illus. Series: The World 100

Years Ago. 1999, Chelsea LB $29.95 (0-7910-4666-4). This is an edited version of travel essays by Burton Holmes, a popular traveler-lecturer during the first half of the 20th century, about the sights he saw in Peking. (Rev: SLJ 7/98) [951]

8012 *Journey into China* (9–12). Illus. 1982, National Geographic LB $23.00 (0-87044-461-1). A region-by-region description by several travelers of their journeys in China. [915.1]

8013 Ko, Dorothy. *Every Step a Lotus: Shoes for Bound Feet* (10–12). Illus. 2002, Univ. of California Pr. $45.00 (0-520-23283-6); paper $24.95 (0-520-23284-4). An interesting look at the ancient Chinese custom of foot binding, defending the practice as a cultural phenomenon with roots in Chinese history and philosophy. (Rev: BL 3/1/02) [391]

8014 Kort, Michael G. *China Under Communism* (9–12). 1995, Millbrook LB $26.40 (1-56294-450-9). This detailed history of the Communist movement in China offers opportunities for discussion from both historical and cultural perspectives. (Rev: BL 1/1/95; SLJ 3/95) [951.05]

8015 Kwan, Michael David. *Things That Must Not Be Forgotten: A Childhood in Wartime China* (10–12). 2001, Soho Pr. $26.00 (1-56947-248-3). Growing up in China of a Caucasian mother and a Chinese father is the theme of this memoir that tells how the author's father was arrested when the communists came to power. (Rev: BL 5/1/01) [951.04]

8016 Lord, Bette Bao. *Legacies: A Chinese Mosaic* (9–12). 1990, Knopf $19.95 (0-394-58325-6). Through interviews with members of Chinese families, the author re-creates Chinese social history from 1949 to 1989. (Rev: SLJ 7/90) [951]

8017 Murowchick, Robert E. *China: Ancient Culture, Modern Land* (9–12). Series: Cradles of Civilization. 1994, Univ. of Oklahoma Pr. $34.95 (0-8061-2683-3). Follows the development of Chinese cultural history from ancient times to the present, tracing the evolution of religion, philosophy, government, land, and language. (Rev: BL 10/1/94) [951]

8018 Nanchu. *Red Sorrow* (10–12). Illus. 2001, Arcade $24.95 (1-55970-569-8). The engrossing story of a Chinese family and how they suffered during Chairman Mao's Cultural Revolution. (Rev: BL 7/01) [951.05]

8019 Salisbury, Harrison E. *Tiananmen Diary: Thirteen Days in June* (9–12). 1989, Little, Brown $18.95 (0-316-80904-7); paper $10.95 (0-316-80905-5). An eyewitness account by a master correspondent of the crackdown on student protests in China. (Rev: BL 9/15/89) [951.058]

8020 Starr, John B. *Understanding China: A Guide to China's Economy, History, and Political Structure* (10–12). 1997, Hill & Wang $25.00 (0-8090-9488-6). A series of articles that provide a fine introduction to China by covering such topics as culture, the Communist Party, urban and rural problems, population control, foreign relations, human rights, and background history. (Rev: BL 9/1/97; SLJ 4/98) [951]

8021 Xinran. *The Good Women of China: Hidden Voices* (10–12). Trans. by Ether Tyldesley. 2002, Pantheon $24.00 (0-375-42201-3). Xinran, who hosted a radio show in China, explores women's issues in that nation and recounts tragic stories of women living on the edge of society. (Rev: BL 10/1/02) [305.48]

8022 Zurlo, Tony. *Life in Hong Kong* (6–10). Series: The Way People Live. 2002, Gale LB $27.45 (1-56006-384-X). Contemporary life in Hong Kong at many levels of wealth and position is the topic of this fascinating narrative that includes many illustrations and some historical coverage. (Rev: BL 7/02; SLJ 6/02) [951]

India and Pakistan

8023 Brace, Steve. *India* (7–10). Series: Country Studies. 1999, Heinemann LB $27.07 (1-57572-893-1). An excellent introduction to India that gives current information on such subjects as population, environment, problems, and economy. (Rev: BL 8/99) [954]

8024 Collins, Larry, and Dominique Lapierre. *Freedom at Midnight* (10–12). Illus. 1976, Avon paper $5.95 (0-380-00693-6). This covers the fateful final days of the British regime in India and the bloody riots during partition, and ends with the assassination of Gandhi in January 1948. [954.04]

8025 Crompton, Samuel Willard. *Pakistan* (7–12). Series: Modern World Nations. 2002, Chelsea LB $24.95 (0-7910-7098-0). An overview of the history, geography, people, politics, and religion of Pakistan, with discussion of current difficulties such as ethnic strife, population problems, and disputes with India. (Rev: SLJ 2/03) [954.91]

8026 Goodwin, William. *Pakistan* (6–12). Illus. Series: Modern Nations of the World. 2002, Gale LB $21.96 (1-59018-218-9). An overview of Pakistan's geography, history, culture, and society, with biographical information on key individuals. (Rev: BL 11/15/02; SLJ 1/03) [954.91]

8027 Keay, John. *The Great Arc: The Dramatic Tale of How India Was Mapped and Everest Was Named* (10–12). Illus. 2000, HarperCollins $24.00 (0-06-019518-5). The great survey of India that began in 1800 is the subject of this gripping piece of historical writing. (Rev: BL 7/00*) [526]

8028 Keay, John. *India: A History* (10–12). 2000, Atlantic Monthly paper $19.95 (0-8021-3797-0). From prehistoric cities such as Harappa through the period of British administration to modern times,

this is a compact history of India and its many cultures. [954]

8029 Koul, Sudha. *The Tiger Ladies: A Memoir of Kashmir* (10–12). 2002, Beacon $23.00 (0-8070-5918-8). In this poignant memoir, Sudha Koul fondly recalls her childhood in Kashmir, a paradise that in recent decades has become the subject of strife between India and Pakistan. (Rev: BL 4/15/02) [954]

8030 MacDonald, Sarah. *Holy Cow: An Indian Adventure* (10–12). 2004, Broadway paper $12.95 (0-7679-1574-7). A lively journey around India in an account that looks at the country's cultures and religions. (Rev: BL 3/15/04) [954]

8031 Mehta, Gita. *Snakes and Ladders: Glimpses of Modern India* (10–12). 1997, Nan A. Talese $22.95 (0-385-47495-4). In these 35 essays, the author discusses the paths of endeavor and conflict that India has experienced since gaining independence 50 years ago. (Rev: BL 5/1/97; SLJ 10/97) [954]

8032 Rothfarb, Ed. *In the Land of Taj Mahal: The World of the Fabulous Mughals* (9–12). 1998, Holt $21.95 (0-8050-5299-2). This is the story of the great Mughal Empire of the 16th and 17th centuries and its many contributions to art, architecture, and literature. (Rev: BL 5/1/98; SLJ 6/98) [954.025]

8033 Viswanath, R. *Teenage Refugees and Immigrants from India Speak Out* (7–12). Series: Teenage Refugees Speak Out. 1997, Rosen LB $16.95 (0-8239-2440-8). A description of the ethnic and religious conflicts and economic conditions that have caused the displacement of tens of thousands of Indians, plus the stories of those who came to the United States, told in first-person teenage accounts. (Rev: BL 12/15/97; SLJ 4/98) [954]

8034 Wagner, Heather Lehr. *India and Pakistan* (6–12). Illus. Series: People at Odds. 2002, Chelsea LB $21.95 (0-7910-6709-2). An easy-to-understand, chronological summary of the ongoing conflict between the two nations, with photographs and maps. (Rev: BL 11/1/02; HBG 3/03; SLJ 12/02) [954.03]

Japan

8035 Behnke, Alison. *Japan in Pictures* (6–10). Series: Visual Geography. 2002, Lerner LB $27.93 (0-8225-1956-9). This revised edition of an old title contains all new material on Japan's history, government, people, customs, economy, and culture. (Rev: BL 10/15/02; HBG 3/03) [952]

8036 Case, Robert. *Japan* (6–10). Series: Countries of the World. 2003, Facts on File $30.00 (0-8160-5381-2). An attractive introduction to Japan that includes material on history, geography, economy, people, and culture. (Rev: BL 1/1–15/04) [952]

8037 Dunn, Charles. *Everyday Life in Traditional Japan* (10–12). Illus. 1977, Tuttle paper $12.95 (0-8048-1384-1). A description of Japanese life during the reign of the Tokugawa shoguns, a period roughly from 1600 to 1850. [952]

8038 Hall, Eleanor J. *Life Among the Samurai* (6–10). Series: The Way People Live. 1998, Lucent LB $27.45 (1-56006-390-4). A history of the feudal period in Japanese history that focuses on the warrior class and their exploits. (Rev: BL 11/15/98) [952]

8039 Kallen, Stuart A. *Life in Tokyo* (6–10). Series: The Way People Live. 2001, Lucent LB $19.96 (1-56006-797-7). After a brief historical introduction, life in present-day Tokyo is featured with material on such topics as daily life, education, entertainment, jobs, food, and culture. (Rev: BL 6/1–15/01; SLJ 6/01) [952]

8040 Roberson, John R. *Japan Meets the World: The Birth of a Super Power* (7–12). 1998, Millbrook LB $24.90 (0-7613-0407-X). Beginning with the shoguns of the 16th century, this book traces Japanese history through various stages of progress, its development into an economic superpower, and its current economic crisis and social stresses. (Rev: BL 1/1–15/99; HBG 3/99; SLJ 2/99) [952]

8041 Ross, Stewart. *The Rise of Japan and the Pacific Rim* (7–12). Series: Causes and Consequences. 1995, Raintree Steck-Vaughn LB $29.97 (0-8172-4054-3). A thorough, unbiased account of the remarkable history of Japan since World War II, with well-documented details on the political, social, and economic conditions that made it possible, and also including material on the economic rise of other Pacific Rim nations. (Rev: BL 12/15/95; BR 3–4/96; SLJ 2/96) [952]

8042 Stefoff, Rebecca. *Japan* (6–10). Series: Major World Nations. 1998, Chelsea LB $21.95 (0-7910-4761-X). With emphasis on social, economic, and cultural conditions, this is a readable, informative introduction to Japan. (Rev: BL 9/15/98; BR 1–2/99) [952.04]

Other Asian Countries

8043 Balf, Todd. *The Last River: The Tragic Race for Shangri-La* (10–12). 2000, Crown $24.00 (0-609-60625-5). The thrilling story of eight kayakers and their tragic expedition to conquer the dangerous gorge on the Tsangpo River in Tibet where the walls are gigantic and the waterfalls deadly. (Rev: BL 8/00) [915.49]

8044 Benard, Cheryl. *Veiled Courage: Inside the Afghan Women's Resistance* (10–12). 2002, Broadway $23.95 (0-7679-1301-9). Personal stories contribute to this account of the courageous efforts by the Revolutionary Association of the Women of

Afghanistan (RAWA) to fight oppression and improve education and women's rights. (Rev: BL 4/15/02; SLJ 11/02) [958.104]

8045 Cole, Wendy M. *Vietnam* (6–10). Illus. Series: Major World Nations. 1999, Chelsea LB $21.95 (0-7910-4751-2). A revised edition of the author's 1989 introduction to Vietnam, with chapters on history, geography, people, culture, cities and villages, government and social services, resources and economy, and transportation and communications. (Rev: SLJ 5/98) [959.7]

8046 Corona, Laurel. *Afghanistan* (6–12). Illus. Series: Modern Nations of the World. 2002, Gale LB $21.96 (1-59018-217-0). This book covers cultural, geographical, religious, and other aspects of Afghanistan, with discussion of the Taliban and the role of women. (Rev: BL 11/15/02; SLJ 12/02) [958.1]

8047 FitzGerald, Frances. *Vietnam: Spirits of the Earth* (9–12). Photos by Mary Cross. Photos by Mary Cross. 2002, Little, Brown $50.00 (0-8212-2742-4). Narrative and photographs document Vietnam today, exploring the geography, people, and culture. (Rev: BL 2/15/02) [959.7]

8048 Gritzner, Jeffrey A. *Afghanistan* (7–12). Series: Modern World Nations. 2002, Chelsea LB $24.95 (0-7910-6774-2). An overview of the history, geography, people, politics, and religion of Afghanistan, with discussion of the current antiterrorist and rebuilding efforts. (Rev: SLJ 2/03) [958.1]

8049 Kamm, Henry. *Dragon Ascending: Vietnam and the Vietnamese* (10–12). 1996, Arcade $24.95 (1-55970-306-7). This is a detailed, accurate, personal account of Vietnam, written by a Pulitzer Prize-winning journalist. (Rev: BL 1/1–15/96; SLJ 10/96) [959.7]

8050 Karnow, Stanley. *Vietnam: A History.* 2nd rev. and updated ed. (9–12). 1997, Penguin paper $17.95 (0-14-026547-3). Stanley Karnow's insightful history focuses on the Vietnam War and the historical developments that led to the bloody conflict. [959.704]

8051 Kaufman, Murray S. *Reefs and Rain Forests: The Natural Heritage of Malaysian Borneo* (10–12). Illus. 2002, Reefs and Rain Forests $49.95 (0-9710655-0-0). The natural beauty of Borneo — home of ancient rain forests and reefs — is captured in this collection of photographs accompanied by informative essays. (Rev: BL 2/1/03) [577.7]

8052 Kizilos, Peter. *Tibet: Disputed Land* (7–10). Series: World in Conflict. 2000, Lerner LB $25.26 (0-8225-3563-7). The history of Tibet and its present political divisions are covered in this well-illustrated account. (Rev: BL 10/15/2000; HBG 3/01) [951.1]

8053 Lamb, Christina. *The Sewing Circles of Herat: A Personal Voyage Through Afghanistan* (11–12). 2002, HarperCollins $24.95 (0-06-050526-5). An award-winning journalist describes the horrors the people of Afghanistan endured during the years of Taliban rule. (Rev: BL 12/15/02; VOYA 6/03) [958.1046]

8054 Latifah, Queen, and Chekeba Hachemi. *My Forbidden Face: Growing Up Under the Taliban: A Young Woman's Story* (10–12). Trans. by Linda Coverdale. 2002, Hyperion $21.95 (0-7868-6901-1). In this riveting memoir, a young Afghani woman writing under the pseudonym of Latifa paints a chilling portrait of life under the Taliban. (Rev: BL 3/15/02) [958.1]

8055 Marsden, Peter. *The Taliban: War and Religion in Afghanistan.* New expanded ed, (10–12). 2002, Zed Bks. $55.00 (1-8427-7166-3); paper $19.95 (1-8427-7167-1). This book introduces the radical Islamic sect, its work in Afghanistan, and how it has been influenced by Osama bin Laden. [958.1]

8056 Ridgeway, Rick. *Below Another Sky: A Mountain Adventure in Search of a Lost Father* (10–12). 2001, Holt $25.00 (0-8050-6284-X). Twenty years after his friend was killed in an avalanche in Tibet, the author returns to the site accompanied by his friend's daughter. (Rev: BL 11/15/00) [915.1]

8057 Salter, Christopher. *North Korea* (6–12). Illus. 2003, Chelsea LB $24.95 (0-7910-7233-9). A thorough and concise overview of North Korea's geography, history, government, politics, economics, language, peoples, and religion, with maps, photographs, and a look at the future. (Rev: BL 9/15/03; HBG 10/03) [951.93]

8058 Seierstad, Asne. *The Bookseller of Kabul* (10–12). Trans. by Ingrid Christophersen. 2003, Little, Brown $19.95 (0-316-73450-0). A Swedish journalist offers a look at life in Afghanistan with this account of time she spent living with the extended family of a Kabul merchant. (Rev: BL 11/1/03; SLJ 6/04) [958.1]

8059 Shah, Saira. *The Storyteller's Daughter* (10–12). 2003, Knopf $24.00 (0-375-41531-9). In this story of the search for her identity, the author, born in Afghanistan but raised in England, describes her disillusionment upon learning that the glorious tales her father spun about their homeland bore little resemblance to reality. (Rev: BL 9/1/03) [958.1046]

8060 Sis, Peter. *Tibet: Through the Red Box* (7–12). Illus. 1998, Farrar $25.00 (0-374-37552-6). Using a journal kept by the author's filmmaker father when he journeyed to Tibet long ago, old tales, and pictures of landscapes and intriguing illustrations inspired by the Tibetan wheel of life, the author writes about the past and present of this land, its culture, and its religion. (Rev: BCCB 12/98; BL

9/15/98; BR 5–6/99; HB 11–12/98; HBG 3/99; SLJ 10/98) [954.96]

8061 Skaine, Rosemarie. *The Women of Afghanistan Under the Taliban* (10–12). Illus. 2002, McFarland paper $29.95 (0-7864-1090-6). Sociologist Skaine explains in detail how the Taliban's rise to power profoundly altered life for women in Afghanistan. (Rev: BL 3/15/02; VOYA 6/02) [305.4]

8062 Zwier, Lawrence J. *Sri Lanka: War Torn Island* (8–12). Illus. Series: World in Conflict. 1998, Lerner LB $25.26 (0-8225-3550-5). The author describes the long political struggle in Sri Lanka. (Rev: BL 4/15/98) [305.8]

Australia and the Pacific Islands

8063 Ansell, Rod, and Rachel Percy. *To Fight the Wild* (9–12). Illus. 1986, Harcourt $12.95 (0-15-289068-8). An amazing survival story about a 22-year-old man isolated in a remote part of the Australian bush country. (Rev: BL 6/15/86; SLJ 9/86) [613.6]

8064 Bligh, William. *Mutiny on Board HMS Bounty* (10–12). 1989, NAL paper $3.50 (0-451-52293-1). The story of the famous mutiny is told from the standpoint of Captain Bligh. [904]

8065 Flannery, Tim. *Throwim Way Leg: Tree-Kangaroos, Possums and Penis Gourds: On the Track of Unknown Mammals in Wildest New Guinea* (9–12). 1999, Atlantic Monthly $25.00 (0-87113-731-3). The adventures of an explorer and scientist during his many trips to the outreaches of New Guinea. (Rev: BL 12/15/98; SLJ 9/99) [996]

8066 Francia, Luis H. *Eye of the Fish: A Personal Archipelago* (10–12). 2001, Kaya paper $15.95 (1-885030-31-2). From his own experiences, background history, and stories collected from others, the author has produced an honest portrait of his country, the Philippines, a nation of more than 7,000 islands. (Rev: BL 3/15/01) [915.9]

8067 Heyerdahl, Thor. *Easter Island: The Mystery Solved* (10–12). Illus. 1989, Random $24.95 (0-394-57906-2). The engrossing story of the explorer and his attempt to explain the existence of the huge monuments on Easter Island. (Rev: VOYA 6/90) [996]

8068 Heyerdahl, Thor. *Kon-Tiki: Across the Pacific by Raft* (9–12). Trans. by F. H. Lyon. 1950, Rand McNally paper $5.99 (0-671-72652-8). The landmark adventure story about crossing the Pacific in a primitive raft such as the Peruvian natives of the fifth century used. [910.4]

8069 Jones, Phillip. *Boomerang* (10–12). Illus. 1997, Ten Speed paper $14.95 (0-89815-943-1). A history of the development and use of the boomerang, which has been part of many cultures for more than 10,000 years, focusing on the aboriginal culture of Australia. (Rev: SLJ 6/98) [994]

8070 Lightner, Sam. *All Elevations Unknown: An Adventure in the Heart of Borneo* (10–12). Illus. 2001, Broadway $24.95 (0-7679-0756-6). In this book about Borneo, two stories are interwoven: the first about the author's recent rock-climbing expedition there and the second about the small Allied force that landed on the island during World War II. (Rev: BL 5/15/01) [915.98]

8071 McGuinn, Taro. *East Timor: Island in Turmoil* (7–10). Series: World in Conflict. 1998, Lerner LB $25.26 (0-8225-3555-6). The country of East Timor, an island east of Indonesia, is introduced, with material on its internal ethnic and political conflicts. (Rev: BL 10/15/98; BR 1–2/99; HBG 3/99; SLJ 10/98) [959.86]

8072 Morris, Rod, and Alison Ballance. *South Sea Islands: A Natural History* (10–12). Illus. 2003, Firefly $35.00 (1-55297-609-2). This lushly illustrated book explores the unique natural environments of 14 South Sea islands, including Fiji, Madagascar, Sulawesi, and Hawaii. (Rev: BL 12/1/03) [508.95]

8073 Smith, Roff. *Cold Beer and Crocodiles: A Bicycle Journey into Australia* (9–12). Illus. 2000, National Geographic $26.00 (0-7922-7952-2). This is the adventure-filled story of an amazing bicycle trek that took the author through cities, mountains, deserts, and remote outback villages. (Rev: BL 9/1/00) [919.4]

Europe

General and Miscellaneous

8074 Blanning, T. C. W. *The Oxford Illustrated History of Modern Europe* (10–12). 1996, Oxford paper $24.95 (0-19-285426-7). Eleven chronologically arranged essays examine European culture, economics, industrialization, and politics from the mid-18th century to the closing years of the 20th century. (Rev: BL 4/1/96; SLJ 8/96) [940.2]

8075 Davies, Norman. *Europe: A History* (10–12). 1996, Oxford $45.00 (0-19-520912-5). This massive survey of European history traces human development on the continent from prehistoric times until the closing years of the 20th century. [940]

8076 Dornberg, John. *Central and Eastern Europe* (10–12). Series: International Government and Politics. 1995, Oryx paper $45.00 (0-89774-942-1). A look at the people, ethnic groups, economics, and internal affairs of the 12 countries of Central and Eastern Europe, beginning with the end of the Cold War. (Rev: SLJ 5/96) [914]

8077 Dornberg, John. *Western Europe* (9–12). Series: International Government and Politics. 1996, Oryx paper $45.00 (0-89774-943-X). After a general introduction of Western Europe and the formation of the European Union, the author discusses controversial issues such as nationalism, the economy, crime, pollution, and immigration, followed by profiles of the individual countries involved. (Rev: SLJ 9/96) [940]

Eastern Europe and the Balkans

8078 Balakian, Peter. *Black Dog of Fate* (10–12). 1997, Basic $24.00 (0-465-00704-X). A memoir of growing up in comfort in suburban New Jersey and slowly coming to understand the atrocities that his family had experienced during the Armenian genocide in 1915. (Rev: SLJ 11/97) [961]

8079 Black, Eric. *Bosnia: Fractured Region* (9–12). Series: World in Conflict. 1999, Lerner LB $25.26 (0-8225-3553-X). In this book about the war in Bosnia, the author presents a clear, detailed, history of Yugoslavia and its neighbors; a careful account of the armed conflicts among Serbs, Croats, and Muslims; and a measured assessment of the future of the region. (Rev: BL 8/99*; SLJ 5/99) [949.6]

8080 Fleming, Thomas. *Montenegro: The Divided Land* (10–12). Illus. 2002, Chronicle paper $16.95 (0-9619364-9-5). An introduction to the little-known but eventful history of tiny Montenegro. (Rev: BL 7/02) [949.745]

8081 Glenny, Misha. *The Balkans: Nationalism, War, and the Great Powers, 1804–1999* (10–12). 2000, Viking paper $20 .00 (0-14-023377-6). A thoroughly researched account that explores the history of the Balkan countries during the 19th and 20th centuries. (Rev: BL 5/15/00) [949.6]

8082 Harbor, Bernard. *Conflict in Eastern Europe* (6–12). Series: Conflicts. 1993, Macmillan LB $13.95 (0-02-742626-2). An overview of events that led to the demise of the Soviet empire in Eastern Europe and the aftermath. (Rev: BL 10/1/93; SLJ 12/93) [947]

8083 Harris, Nathaniel. *The War in Former Yugoslavia* (7–12). Illus. Series: New Perspectives. 1998, Raintree Steck-Vaughn LB $28.54 (0-8172-5014-X). Different perspectives on this war are expressed through the viewpoints of political leaders, ordinary citizens, soldiers, militiamen, foreign diplomats, rescue workers, and news reporters. (Rev: BL 3/15/98; BR 1–2/99; HBG 9/98) [940.54]

8084 Kort, Michael G. *The Handbook of the New Eastern Europe* (9–12). Illus. 2001, Twenty-First Century LB $39.90 (0-7613-1362-1). The history and current affairs of Eastern Europe are explored in considerable detail in this volume that includes photographs and biographies of key individuals. (Rev: BL 4/1/01; HBG 10/01; VOYA 8/01) [943]

8085 Mazower, Mark. *The Balkans: A Short History* (10–12). 2000, Random $19.95 (0-679-64087-8). A short, interesting account that tells about the history, cultures, and countries of this troubled area. (Rev: BL 11/15/00; SLJ 5/01) [949.6]

8086 Otfinoski, Steven. *Bulgaria* (6–10). Series: Nations in Transition. 1998, Facts on File $25.00 (0-8160-3705-1). This book reviews the history, politics, people, and culture of Bulgaria, including material on relationships with Gypsies and other minorities. (Rev: BL 3/1/99; BR 5–6/99; SLJ 6/99) [949.903]

8087 Otfinoski, Steven. *Poland* (6–10). Series: Nations in Transition. 1995, Facts on File $25.00 (0-8160-3063-4). This work explains Poland's past and explores its religion, economy, culture, and daily life. (Rev: BR 9–10/96; VOYA 8/96) [943]

8088 Rollyson, Carl S. *Teenage Refugees from Eastern Europe Speak Out* (7–12). Series: Teenage Refugees Speak Out. 1997, Rosen LB $16.95 (0-8239-2437-8). Young refugees from Slovakia, Bulgaria, Hungary, Romania, Poland, Yugoslavia, and the former East Germany tell about conditions in their homelands and their receptions in the United States. (Rev: BL 12/15/97) [947]

8089 Sanborne, Mark. *Romania* (9–12). 1996, Facts on File $19.95 (0-8160-3089-8). The first half of this book describes the history of Romania, and the second deals with current political and economic conditions and problems. (Rev: VOYA 10/96) [949.8]

8090 Sioras, Efstathia. *Czech Republic* (7–10). Series: Cultures of the World. 1998, Marshall Cavendish LB $35.64 (0-7614-0870-3). An attractive volume that covers the standard topics: geography, history, government, economy, leisure, festivals, and food, and includes full-color photographs, colorful sidebars, maps, charts, and recipes. (Rev: HBG 9/99; SLJ 6/99) [943.7]

France

8091 Banfield, Susan. *The Rights of Man, the Reign of Terror: The Story of the French Revolution* (9–12). 1989, HarperCollins LB $14.00 (0-397-32354-9). A dramatically told account of the causes, events, and aftermath of the French Revolution. (Rev: BL 1/1/89; SLJ 4/90; VOYA 12/89) [944]

8092 Barter, James. *The Palace of Versailles* (6–10). Series: Building History. 1998, Lucent LB $27.45 (1-56006-433-1). An informative account of the building of the palace for King Louis XIV of France, which took 40 years and represents a pinna-

cle of opulence and grandeur. (Rev: BL 12/15/98; BR 5–6/99; SLJ 2/99) [944]

8093 Cobb, Richard, and Colin Jones, eds. *Voices of the French Revolution* (10–12). Illus. 1988, Salem House $29.95 (0-88162-338-5). Using eyewitness accounts plus additional material, this is an introduction to the major events and people involved in the French Revolution. (Rev: BL 10/15/88; VOYA 4/89) [944.04219]

8094 Durant, William James, and Ariel Durant. *The Age of Louis XIV* (10–12). Series: Story of Civilization. 1963, Simon & Schuster $40.00 (0-671-01215-0). A readable account of France, Louis XIV, and how this age changed world history. [940.2]

8095 *France in Mind* (10–12). Ed. by Alice Leccese Powers. 2003, Vintage paper $14.00 (0-375-71425-9). Both francophiles and literati will delight in this anthology of fiction and nonfiction by English-language writers who spent time in France, among them Charles Dickens, Ernest Hemingway, and Mary McCarthy. (Rev: BL 1/1–15/03) [820.8]

8096 *The French Revolution* (7–12). Ed. by Laura K. Egendorf. Series: Opposing Viewpoints: World History. 2004, Gale LB $33.70 (0-7377-1815-3). Questions about the French Revolution, such as the justification for the many executions, are explored in this collection of different points of view about this turning point in French history. (Rev: BL 2/15/04; SLJ 5/04) [944]

8097 Greene, Meg. *The Eiffel Tower* (7–10). Series: Building History. 2000, Lucent LB $19.96 (1-56006-826-4). This account describes the building of this Paris landmark with coverage of the social and technical obstacles that confronted its builders. (Rev: BL 4/15/01; SLJ 6/01) [944]

8098 Libby, Megan M. *Postcards from France* (8–12). 1998, HarperCollins paper $5.99 (0-06-101170-3). Megan Libby, a high school student from Connecticut, describes her junior year in France. (Rev: BL 4/15/97) [944]

8099 Nardo, Don, ed. *The French Revolution* (9–12). Series: Turning Points in World History. 1998, Greenhaven LB $21.96 (1-56510-934-1); paper $17.45 (1-56510-933-3). The 19 essays in this anthology explore the historical background leading up to the French Revolution, the social upheaval it created, and its lasting impact on France and the world. (Rev: SLJ 11/98) [944]

8100 Nardo, Don. *The Trial of Joan of Arc* (7–10). Series: Famous Trials. 1997, Lucent LB $27.45 (1-56006-466-8). A scholarly discussion and analysis of Joan of Arc's trial and execution, with a brief introductory biography. (Rev: SLJ 10/97) [944]

8101 Prosser, Robert. *France* (6–10). Series: Countries of the World. 2003, Facts on File $30.00 (0-8160-5380-4). This basic introduction to the land and people of France includes material on economy, culture, and present-day problems. (Rev: BL 1/1–15/04) [944]

8102 Schama, Simon. *Citizens: A Chronicle of the French Revolution* (9–12). 1989, Knopf paper $28.00 (0-679-72601-1). A popular, intelligent look at the French Revolution and the key people involved. [944.04]

8103 Schom, Alan. *One Hundred Days: Napoleon's Road to Waterloo* (9–12). 1992, Atheneum paper $21.50 (0-19-508177-3). An absorbing account of Napoleon's escape from Elba and final military campaign. [944.05]

Germany, Austria, and Switzerland

8104 Bornstein, Jerry. *The Wall Came Tumbling Down: The Berlin Wall and the Fall of Communism* (10–12). Illus. 1990, Arch Cape $12.99 (0-517-03306-2). A concise history with photographs of the events that led to the opening of the Berlin Wall on November 9, 1989. (Rev: BL 7/90) [335.43]

8105 Cartlidge, Cherese, and Charles Clark. *Life of a Nazi Soldier* (6–10). Series: The Way People Live. 2000, Lucent LB $19.96 (1-56006-484-6). The living conditions and military requirements of German soldiers during World War II are the primary focus of this volume, which condemns the atrocities that took place while attempting to explain why they were allowed to happen. (Rev: BL 3/1/01; SLJ 7/01) [940.54]

8106 Fulbrook, Mary. *A Concise History of Germany* (9–12). 1991, Cambridge Univ. Pr. $54.95 (0-521-36283-0); paper $18.95 (0-521-36836-7). Covers Germany from the medieval period and examines the political, social, and cultural circumstances that led to reunification. (Rev: BL 2/15/91) [943]

8107 Grant, R. G. *The Berlin Wall* (7–12). Series: New Perspectives. 1998, Raintree Steck-Vaughn LB $28.54 (0-8172-5017-4). This presentation of various perspectives on the Berlin Wall, its uses, and its destruction in 1989, is also an overview of the Cold War in Europe and the collapse of communism there. (Rev: BL 1/1–15/99; HBG 3/99) [943.1]

8108 Kitchen, Martin. *The Cambridge Illustrated History of Germany* (10–12). 1996, Cambridge Univ. Pr. $39.95 (0-521-45341-0). A lavishly illustrated history of Germany that covers 2,000 years of history, from the days of Julius Caesar to reunification in the 1990s. (Rev: BL 10/1/96; SLJ 3/97) [943]

8109 McGowen, Tom. *Frederick the Great, Bismarck, and the Building of the German Empire in World History* (8–12). Series: In World History. 2002, Enslow LB $20.95 (0-7660-1822-9). From Frederick, ruler of Prussia, through the careers of Otto von Bismarck and William I, this is the story of the uni-

fication of Germany. (Rev: BL 3/15/03; HBG 3/03; SLJ 12/02) [943]

8110 Nardo, Don, ed. *The Rise of Nazi Germany* (7–12). Series: Turning Points in World History. 1999, Greenhaven LB $32.45 (1-56510-965-1); paper $21.20 (1-56510-964-3). This anthology of writings examines the emergence of fascism and National Socialism in Germany, the personality of Hitler, his use of propaganda, and his political maneuvering to seize control in 1933. (Rev: BL 6/1–15/99; SLJ 5/99) [943.086]

8111 Tames, Richard. *Nazi Germany* (9–12). Illus. 1986, Batsford $19.95 (0-7134-3538-0). This is a history of the Nazi period in Germany as seen through a series of portraits of people who lived through it. (Rev: SLJ 4/86) [943.08]

Great Britain and Ireland

8112 Atkins, Sinclair. *From Stone Age to Conquest* (7–10). Illus. 1986, Hulton paper $14.95 (0-7175-1305-X). A well-illustrated account of British history from prehistoric times to the Norman Conquest. (Rev: SLJ 4/86) [941.01]

8113 Bartoletti, Susan Campbell. *Black Potatoes: The Story of the Great Irish Famine, 1845–1850* (6–12). Illus. 2001, Houghton $18.00 (0-618-00271-5). First-person narratives and a chronological account of events interspersed with illustrations, letters, and news reports clearly portray the sufferings of the Irish people during the famine of the late 1840s. (Rev: BL 10/15/01; HB 1–2/02; HBG 3/02; SLJ 11/01*; VOYA 12/01) [941.5081]

8114 Bernard, Catherine. *The British Empire and Queen Victoria in World History* (8–12). Series: In World History. 2002, Enslow LB $20.95 (0-7660-1824-5). Combining both biography and history, this account describes Victoria's 63-year reign and how, during it, the British Empire flourished. (Rev: BL 3/15/03; HBG 10/03; SLJ 7/03) [941]

8115 Black, Eric. *Northern Ireland: Troubled Land* (8–12). Illus. Series: World in Conflict. 1998, Lerner LB $25.26 (0-8225-3552-1). An information-packed, illustrated account of the conflict in Northern Ireland. (Rev: BL 4/15/98; HBG 9/98) [941.6]

8116 Bowden, Rob. *United Kingdom* (6–10). Series: Countries of the World. 2003, Facts on File $30.00 (0-8160-5383-9). An attractive volume that presents basic material about Great Britain including history, geography, and present social conditions. (Rev: BL 1/1–15/04) [941]

8117 Childress, Diana. *Chaucer's England* (7–12). Illus. 2000, Linnet LB $25.00 (0-208-02489-1). A fascinating glimpse into the social life, community structure, landscape, and economy of 14th-century

England. (Rev: BL 9/15/00; BR 5–6/01; HBG 10/01; SLJ 10/00; VOYA 4/01) [942.03]

8118 Corey, Melinda, and George Ochoa, eds. *The Encyclopedia of the Victorian World: A Reader's Companion to the People, Places, Events, and Everyday Life of the Victorian Era* (9–12). 1996, Holt $50.00 (0-8050-2622-3). A readable, fun reference tool that brings Victorian times to life with details on people, books, terms, discoveries, clothing, events, and slang. (Rev: BL 9/15/96; SLJ 5/96) [942]

8119 Dahl, Roald. *The Mildenhall Treasure* (7–12). 2000, Knopf $22.95 (0-375-81035-8). A British farmer's discovery of ancient Roman artifacts in 1942 leads to intrigue and greed in this fascinating nonfiction account. (Rev: BL 2/1/01; HBG 3/01; SLJ 12/00) [642]

8120 Eagleton, Terry. *The Truth About the Irish* (10–12). Illus. 2000, St. Martin's $18.95 (0-312-25488-1). Using an A-to-Z approach, the author, a renowned literary critic, supplies odd facts about Ireland's geography and people. (Rev: BL 3/1/00* ; SLJ 10/00) [941.7]

8121 English, Richard. *Armed Struggle: The History of the IRA* (10–12). 2003, Oxford $30.00 (0-19-516605-1). A balanced look at the Irish Republican Army and its often-violent campaign to expel the British and reunify Ireland. (Rev: BL 8/03) [941.60824]

8122 Hallam, Elizabeth, and Andrew Prescott. *The British Inheritance: A Treasury of Historic Documents* (10–12). 1999, Univ. of California Pr. $39.95 (0-520-22470-1). This is a collection of original documents that are of great importance in the history of Britain. [941]

8123 Hodges, Michael. *Ireland* (9–12). 1988, David & Charles $20.75 (0-7134-5542-X). A history of Ireland that concentrates on the gaining of freedom and Irish-English relationships. (Rev: BR 9–10/89) [941.7]

8124 Holliday, Laurel, ed. *Children of "The Troubles": Our Lives in the Crossfire of Northern Ireland* (10–12). Series: Children in Conflict. 1997, Pocket $22.00 (0-671-53736-9). Children of Northern Ireland tell their stories of the internal conflict in their country through prose pieces, remembrances, and some poetry. (Rev: SLJ 7/97; VOYA 10/97) [941]

8125 Howarth, David Armine. *1066: The Year of the Conquest* (10–12). 1978, Viking paper $12.95 (0-14-005850-8). This readable history re-creates the Norman invasion of England in 1066 and the victory of William the Conqueror at the Battle of Hastings. [942.02]

8126 James, Lawrence. *The Rise and Fall of the British Empire* (10–12). 1995, St. Martin's paper $19.95 (0-312-16985-X). This is an excellent overview of Britain's rise and decline as a colonial power with particularly good biographical material on key personalities. [909]

8127 Lace, William W. *The British Empire* (6–12). Illus. Series: History's Great Defeats. 2000, Lucent LB $23.70 (1-56006-683-0). Subtitled "The End of Colonialism," this account traces the rise and growth of the British Empire, its accomplishments and failures, and its decline and fall. (Rev: BL 11/1/00; HBG 3/01; SLJ 10/00) [909]

8128 Lace, William W. *Elizabeth I and Her Court* (6–10). Series: Lucent Library of Historical Eras: Elizabethan England. 2002, Gale LB $27.45 (1-59018-098-4). A well-written account of life at court during Elizabeth I's reign, with black-and-white reproductions and photographs. Also recommended in this series are *Life in Elizabethan London* and *Primary Sources* (both 2002). (Rev: LMC 11–12/03; SLJ 9/03)

8129 Lace, William W. *England* (7–10). Series: Modern Nations of the World. 1997, Lucent LB $27.45 (1-56006-194-4). A compact introduction to the past and present of England, arranged in six theme-based chapters, with good illustrations and interesting sidebars. (Rev: SLJ 9/97) [941]

8130 Lace, William W. *Oliver Cromwell and the English Civil War in World History* (8–12). Series: In World History. 2002, Enslow LB $20.95 (0-7660-1937-3). The story of the English Civil War leader who defeated both Charles I and Charles II and became, for a time, Lord Protector of England. (Rev: BL 3/15/03; HBG 10/03; VOYA 8/03) [941]

8131 McCourt, Frank. *Angela's Ashes* (10–12). 1996, Scribner $23.00 (0-684-87435-0). The harrowing, true story of growing up in extreme poverty in Limerick, Ireland, by a writer whose humor and humanity outshine the terrible conditions he describes. (Rev: SLJ 6/97) [941.5]

8132 McMurtry, Jo. *Understanding Shakespeare's England: A Companion for the American Reader* (9–12). 1989, Archon. LB $37.50 (0-208-02248-1). This account covers all aspects of Elizabethan life including such topics as marriage customs, women's roles, city and country life, and witches and criminals. [942.05]

8133 Marvel, Laura, ed. *Elizabethan England* (7–12). Series: Turning Points in World History. 2001, Greenhaven LB $31.20 (0-7377-0483-7); paper $19.95 (0-7377-0484-5). Well-written essays by well-known historians, and a collection of original documents, are featured in this account that explores various aspects of the Elizabethan age including cultural and social topics. (Rev: BL 3/15/02; SLJ 4/02)

8134 Morgan, Kenneth O. *The Oxford Illustrated History of Britain* (10–12). 1984, Oxford $49.95 (0-19-822684-5); paper $25.00 (0-19-285174-8). Ten leading historians have contributed essays to this well-illustrated overview of British history. [941]

8135 Morrill, John, ed. *The Oxford Illustrated History of Tudor and Stuart Britain* (10–12). 1996, Oxford $72.50 (0-19-820325-X). Essays on various aspects of life in 16th- and 17th-century Great Britain — arranged by such topics as education, theater, and religion — are followed by a detailed survey of the major events of the two centuries that adds historical context. (Rev: BL 11/1/96; SLJ 7/97) [941]

8136 Sancha, Sheila. *The Luttrell Village: Country Life in the Middle Ages* (7–10). Illus. 1983, HarperCollins LB $13.89 (0-690-04324-4). Life and activities in an English village of 1328 are revealed in words and excellent drawings by the author. [942.03]

8137 Swisher, Clarice. *Victorian England* (7–10). Series: World History. 2000, Lucent LB $19.96 (1-56006-323-8). Quotations and period reproductions enhance this interesting survey of the long and eventful reign of Queen Victoria, a time of technological and social innovation and of growing power for Great Britain. (Rev: BL 12/15/00; SLJ 3/01) [942]

8138 Tabraham, Chris, and Colin Baxter. *The Illustrated History of Scotland* (9–12). Illus. 2004, Voyageur $35.00 (1-932573-01-1). A fine introduction to the history of Scotland illustrated with old paintings, period photographs, and other drawings. (Rev: BL 3/15/04) [941.1]

8139 *Victorian England* (10–12). Ed. by Clarice Swisher. Series: Turning Points in World History. 2000, Greenhaven LB $21.96 (0-7377-0221-4); paper $13.96 (0-7377-0220-6). This book of essays helps the more advanced student explore this time period. (Rev: BL 3/15/00; SLJ 5/00) [941.081]

8140 Viney, Michael. *Ireland* (10–12). Illus. Series: Smithsonian Natural History. 2003, Smithsonian $34.95 (1-58834-057-0). This beautifully written volume explores the largely neglected natural history of Ireland. (Rev: BL 3/15/03) [508.415]

8141 Weir, Alison. *The Wars of the Roses* (10–12). 1995, Ballantine paper $14.95 (0-345-40433-5). This book covers the civil wars fought in England, mainly between the houses of Lancaster and York, from 1399 through 1471. (Rev: BL 8/95; SLJ 5/96) [942.04]

8142 Yancey, Diane. *Life in Charles Dickens's England* (6–10). Series: The Way People Live. 1998, Lucent LB $27.45 (1-56006-098-0). From terrible squalor and grinding poverty to great wealth and comfort, the spectrum of British society, rural and urban, is explored during the days of Charles Dickens. (Rev: BL 10/15/98; SLJ 1/99; VOYA 12/99) [942]

8143 Yancey, Diane. *Life in the Elizabethan Theater* (6–10). Illus. Series: The Way People Live. 1997, Lucent LB $18.96 (1-56006-343-2). An explanation of the design of the Elizabethan theater and of the roles of various people connected with it, such as actors, playwrights, and the audience. (Rev: BL 3/15/97; SLJ 4/97) [792]

Italy

8144 Barter, James. *The Tower of Pisa* (7–10). Series: Building History. 2001, Lucent $24.95 (1-56006-874-4). The story of the construction and history of the famous landmark that was begun in 1173, unfortunately on sandy subsoil. (Rev: BL 8/01) [945]

8145 Hibbert, Christopher. *Rome: The Biography of a City* (10–12). Illus. 1985, Penguin paper $26.95 (0-14-007078-8). An illustrated history of the Eternal City from pre-Roman Etruscan times to World War II. (Rev: BL 6/15/85) [945]

8146 *Italy* (10–12). Series: Eyewitness Travel. 1996, DK paper $29.95 (0-7894-0425-7). A guide to Italy that includes much helpful information found in standard travel guides, but with extensive use of photographs, pictures, cutaway drawings, and maps. This book is part of an extensive recommended series. (Rev: SLJ 9/96) [945]

8147 Nardo, Don. *Roman Roads and Aqueducts* (7–10). Series: Building History. 2000, Lucent LB $19.96 (1-56006-721-7). This look at the highways, roads, and aqueducts of the ancient Roman Empire combines history and scientific and technological principles. (Rev: BL 4/15/01; SLJ 3/01) [930]

8148 Paolicelli, Paul. *Dances with Luigi: A Grandson's Determined Quest to Comprehend Italy and the Italians* (10–12). 2000, St. Martin's $24.95 (0-312-25188-2). A deeply felt narrative about an Italian American's search for his roots, which involved spending his savings to live in Italy and discover its present and past. (Rev: BL 3/15/00*) [945.092]

Russia and Other Former Soviet Republics

8149 Batalden, Stephen K., and Sandra L. Batalden. *The Newly Independent States of Eurasia: Handbook of Former Soviet Republics.* 2nd ed. (7–12). 1997, Oryx paper $45.00 (0-89774-940-5). Arranged by geographical region, this volume examines each of the newly formed republics created from the former USSR, with details on their past, their culture, and key problems facing each today. (Rev: SLJ 11/97) [947]

8150 Cartlidge, Cherese. *The Central Asian States* (6–12). Illus. Series: Modern Nations of the World: Former Soviet Republics. 2001, Lucent LB $19.96 (1-56006-735-7). This well-illustrated introduction to the former Soviet republics of Kazakhstan, Turkmenistan, Uzbekistan, Kyrgyzstan, and Tajikistan presents material on physical features, people, culture, economy, history, and efforts to enter the global market. (Rev: BL 8/01; SLJ 9/01) [958]

8151 Corona, Laurel. *Life in Moscow* (6–10). Series: The Way People Live. 2000, Lucent LB $19.96 (1-56006-795-0). After background historical information, this account introduces modern Moscow and the daily lives of its citizens. (Rev: BL 3/1/01; SLJ 3/01) [947]

8152 Corona, Laurel. *The Russian Federation* (6–12). Illus. Series: Former Soviet Republics. 2001, Lucent LB $19.96 (1-56006-675-X). Corona introduces readers to the dramatic changes that took place in Russia during the 20th century and looks at the economic and political challenges facing the country today. (Rev: BL 7/01; SLJ 9/01) [958]

8153 Duffy, James P., and Vincent L. Ricci. *Czars: Russia's Rulers for over One Thousand Years* (10–12). 1995, Facts on File $35.00 (0-8160-2873-7). The history of the rulers of the Russian Empire from the Viking Rurik to the death of Nicholas II in 1918, 1,000 years later. (Rev: SLJ 6/96) [947.07]

8154 Fader, Kim B. *Russia* (9–12). Illus. Series: Modern Nations of the World. 1997, Lucent LB $17.96 (1-56006-521-4). This history of Russia, with good use of maps and sidebars, covers the period from the Scythians in 800–200 B.C., to the collapse of the Soviet Union and the creation of the Russian Federation in 1997. (Rev: SLJ 5/98) [947]

8155 Gottfried, Ted. *The Road to Communism* (8–12). 2002, Millbrook LB $28.90 (0-7613-2557-3). This first volume on the rise and fall of the Soviet Union traces in depth the developments that led to the establishment of a communist state. The second volume is titled *Stalinist Empire*. (Rev: BL 10/15/02; HBG 3/03; SLJ 11/02) [957]

8156 Harbor, Bernard. *The Breakup of the Soviet Union* (6–12). Series: Conflicts. 1993, Macmillan LB $22.00 (0-02-742625-4). An overview of the conflicts and changes in the region. (Rev: BL 7/93; SLJ 12/93) [947.08]

8157 Israel, Fred L., and Arthur M. Schlesinger, Jr., eds. *Moscow* (6–10). Illus. Series: The World 100 Years Ago. 1999, Chelsea $29.95 (0-7910-4658-3). This book describes what Burton Holmes, a traveler-lecturer during the first half of the 20th century, saw when he visited Moscow around the beginning of the century, including a trip to the Kremlin, a visit to the public baths, and a breakfast with Leo Tolstoy. (Rev: SLJ 7/98) [947]

8158 Kort, Michael G. *The Handbook of the Former Soviet Union* (7–12). Illus. 1997, Millbrook LB $39.90 (0-7613-0016-3). An expert in Russian history gives an overview of the former Soviet Union, the problems each state faces today and the impor-

tant personalities involved. (Rev: BL 2/1/98; BR 5–6/98; SLJ 1/98; VOYA 6/98) [947]

8159 Kort, Michael G. *Russia*. Rev. ed. (7–12). Series: Nations in Transition. 1998, Facts on File $25.00 (0-8160-3776-0). This book explains the rapid changes in Russia's economy, politics, social conditions, and daily life in recent years and reviews the country's complex history and importance today. (Rev: BL 3/15/99; SLJ 4/99) [947.085]

8160 Loory, Stuart H., and Ann Imse. *CNN Reports: Seven Days That Shook the World: The Collapse of Soviet Communism* (9–12). 1992, Turner $29.95 (1-878685-11-2); paper $19.95 (1-878685-12-0). The fall of communism is told largely through photographs. (Rev: BL 1/1/92) [947.085]

8161 Lustig, Michael M. *Ukraine* (7–12). Series: Nations in Transition. 1999, Facts on File $25.00 (0-8160-3757-4). A slim volume that traces the history of Ukraine and its people, with emphasis on today — its faltering economy, corruption in government, Crimean independence, and other problems. (Rev: BL 4/15/99; SLJ 6/99) [947.7]

8162 Massie, Robert K. *The Romanovs: The Final Chapter* (9–12). 1995, Random paper $14.95 (0-345-40640-0). This book covers the last days of the Romanov family with material on how their remains were identified and on how some relatives survived. [947.08]

8163 Medvedev, Roy Aleksandrovich. *Let History Judge: The Origins and Consequences of Stalinism*. Rev. and expanded ed (10–12). 1989, Columbia Univ. Pr. $104.00 (0-231-06350-4); paper $35.00 (0-231-06351-2). This is a forceful, well-documented account of the crimes committed by Stalin during his years in power. [947.084]

8164 Moore, Robert. *A Time to Die: The Untold Story of the Kursk Tragedy* (10–12). Illus. 2003, Crown $25.00 (0-609-61000-7). A gripping account of the Russian navy's attempt to cover up the sinking of the submarine *Kursk* in the Barents Sea in 2000. (Rev: BL 1/1–15/03) [910]

8165 Pavlenkov, Victor, and Peter Pappas, eds. *Russia: Yesterday, Today, Tomorrow: Voice of the Young Generation* (8–12). Illus. 1997, FC-Izdat paper $12.95 (0-9637035-5-2). This is a collection of essays written by Russian high school students who reflect on the past, present, and future of their country. (Rev: BL 2/15/97) [947.08]

8166 Pipes, Richard. *A Concise History of the Russian Revolution* (9–12). 1995, Knopf $30.00 (0-679-42277-3). A skillfully researched history and analysis of Russia's revolution and the events that preceded and followed it. (Rev: BL 10/1/95*) [947.084]

8167 Rice, Earle. *The Cold War: Collapse of Communism* (8–12). Illus. Series: History's Great Defeats. 2000, Lucent LB $23.70 (1-56006-634-2).

A detailed account that traces the events and trends that caused the collapse of communism in the USSR from World War II through Gorbachev's reforms. (Rev: BL 11/1/00; HBG 3/01; SLJ 12/00) [372.47]

8168 *Russia* (9–12). Ed. by William Dudley. Series: Opposing Viewpoints. 2000, Greenhaven LB $22.96 (0-7377-0522-1); paper $14.96 (0-7377-0521-3). This collection of essays presents material on the past, present, and possible future of Russia from a variety of conflicting viewpoints. (Rev: BL 3/1/01; SLJ 12/00) [947]

8169 Spilling, Michael. *Estonia* (7–10). Series: Cultures of the World. 1999, Marshall Cavendish LB $35.64 (0-7614-0951-3). An overview of this Baltic land that covers basic information and contemporary life and culture. (Rev: HBG 9/99; SLJ 7/99) [947]

8170 Spilling, Michael. *Georgia* (6–10). Series: Cultures of the World. 1997, Marshall Cavendish LB $35.64 (0-7614-0691-3). A detailed introduction to the former Soviet republic of Georgia, its geography, history, government, and culture. (Rev: HBG 3/98; SLJ 2/98) [947]

8171 Streissguth, Thomas. *Life in Communist Russia* (6–10). Series: The Way People Live. 2001, Lucent LB $19.96 (1-56006-378-5). From the 1917 revolution through the collapse of the regime in the 1980s, the history of Communist Russia is told with emphasis on social and economic conditions and everyday life. (Rev: BL 6/1–15/01; SLJ 7/01) [947]

8172 Streissguth, Thomas, ed. *The Rise of the Soviet Union* (7–12). Series: Turning Points in World History. 2002, Gale LB $31.20 (0-7377-0928-6); paper $19.95 (0-7377-0929-4). Following an overview of Russian and Soviet history, each of the essays in this anthology explores a different aspect of the rise of Communism and the creation of the Soviet Union. (Rev: BL 6/1–15/02; SLJ 6/02) [947]

8173 Strickler, Jim. *Russia of the Tsars* (6–12). Series: World History. 1997, Lucent LB $22.45 (1-56006-295-9). This history of Russia's ruling dynasty gives special material on Peter the Great and Catherine as well as the events and czars immediately preceding the Russian Revolution. (Rev: BL 12/15/97; SLJ 11/97) [947]

8174 Vadrot, Claude-Maria, and Victoria Ivleva. *Russia Today: From Holy Russia to Perestroika* (9–12). Trans. by Harry Swalef. 1991, Atomium $31.95 (1-56182-004-0). A French photographer and Soviet photographer capture the essence of Russian life just before the fall of socialism. (Rev: BL 7/91) [947.08]

8175 Vail, John. *"Peace, Land, Bread?": A History of the Russian Revolution* (7–12). Illus. Series: World History Library. 1996, Facts on File $25.00 (0-8160-2818-4). This volume, illustrated with photographs and maps, covers the period in Russian

history from the revolt against the czar to the rise of Joseph Stalin. (Rev: BL 2/15/96; BR 9–10/96; SLJ 2/96; VOYA 4/96) [947.084]

8176 Wade, Rex A. *The Bolshevik Revolution and Russian Civil War* (10–12). 2001, Greenwood $45.00 (0-313-29974-9). This is a well-researched account that traces the history of the Russian Revolution and its international consequences. (Rev: SLJ 4/01) [947.084]

8177 Walton, C. S. *Little Tenement on the Volga* (10–12). 2001, Garrett County paper $12.95 (1-891053-78-7). This engaging, sometimes amusing account describes typical life in a cramped apartment in a small town in contemporary Russia. (Rev: BL 2/15/01) [947]

8178 Warnes, David. *Chronicle of the Russian Tsars: The Reign by Reign Record of the Rulers of Imperial Russia* (9–12). Illus. Series: Chronicle. 1999, Thames & Hudson $29.95 (0-500-05093-7). An in-depth look at the czars of Russia and the times in which they ruled, with excerpts from primary sources, extensive maps, and other aids. (Rev: BL 8/99; SLJ 2/00) [947.0099]

8179 Winters, Paul A., ed. *The Collapse of the Soviet Union* (10–12). 1998, Greenhaven LB $20.96 (1-56510-997-X); paper $20.25 (1-56510-996-1). A collection of 21 brief essays, most by U.S. writers, chronicles the disintegration of the Soviet empire from the reforms of the 1980s to the dramatic events of 1991, with projections for the future of the newly independent states. (Rev: BL 11/15/98; BR 5–6/99; SLJ 12/98) [947.085]

Scandinavia, Iceland, and Greenland

8180 Schaffer, David. *Viking Conquests* (7–10). Series: World History. 2002, Gale LB $27.45 (1-56006-322-X). Though the Vikings were known mainly for their raids and pillaging, this account also gives details of their lasting contributions to the world. (Rev: BL 8/02) [948]

8181 Streissguth, Thomas. *Life Among the Vikings* (7–10). Series: The Way People Live. 1998, Lucent LB $27.45 (1-56006-392-0). Using a topical approach, this book covers the Vikings' everyday life, warfare, ships, farming, language, art, and poetry. (Rev: SLJ 6/99) [948]

8182 *Vikings: The North Atlantic Saga* (10–12). Ed. by William W. Fitzhugh and Elisabeth I. Ward. Illus. 2000, Smithsonian and National Museum of Natural History $60.00 (1-56098-970-X); paper $34.95 (1-56098-995-5). A handsomely illustrated resource that traces the history of the old Norse people, their culture, and their expansion across the North Atlantic to Newfoundland. (Rev: BL 6/1–15/00) [970.01]

Spain and Portugal

8183 McDowall, David. *The Spanish Armada* (8–12). Illus. 1988, David & Charles $19.95 (0-7134-5671-X). A British import that tells about the events surrounding this Spanish fleet and also supplies many short biographies of the people involved. (Rev: BR 11–12/88; SLJ 3/89) [946]

8184 Paris, Erna. *The End of Days: A Story of Tolerance, Tyranny, and the Expulsion of the Jews from Spain* (10–12). 1995, Prometheus $29.95 (1-57392-017-7). Spanish history from 1300 through 1500, including the early harmonious relationships and flourishing culture, the development of divisions within the Catholic Church, the forced conversions of Jews, and the Inquisition and eventual expulsion of the Jews and the Moors from Spain by the Catholic Church. (Rev: SLJ 11/96) [946]

8185 Worth, Richard. *The Spanish Inquisition in World History* (8–12). Series: In World History. 2002, Enslow LB $20.95 (0-7660-1825-3). This account describes the formation of the Spanish Inquisition, the work of Torquemada, and how the Catholic Church tried to punish those who went against the teachings of Christianity. (Rev: BL 3/15/03; HBG 10/03; SLJ 4/03) [946]

Middle East

General and Miscellaneous

8186 Dudley, William, ed. *The Middle East* (7–10). Series: Opposing Viewpoints. 1992, Greenhaven paper $16.20 (0-89908-160-6). Articles and essays examine the background causes of the Middle East conflicts. (Rev: BL 6/15/92; SLJ 7/92) [320.956]

8187 Harik, Ramsay M., and Elsa Marston. *Women in the Middle East*. Rev. ed. (7–12). Illus. 2003, Watts LB $29.50 (0-531-12222-0). A chapter on the women of Afghanistan has been added to this revised and updated edition that looks at topics including health, education, and family and public life. (Rev: BL 4/15/03; SLJ 5/03; VOYA 8/03) [305.42]

8188 King, John. *Conflict in the Middle East* (6–12). Series: Conflicts. 1993, Macmillan LB $13.95 (0-02-785955-X). This book gives good background information and history on the origins of the current problems in the Middle East. (Rev: BL 10/1/93; SLJ 12/93) [956.04]

8189 Kort, Michael G. *The Handbook of the Middle East* (7–12). Illus. 2002, Twenty-First Century LB $39.90 (0-7613-1611-6). History, geography, culture, politics (current and future), and religion are all covered in this overview of the region that includes maps, flags, a timeline, and material on key figures. (Rev: HBG 10/02; SLJ 3/02; VOYA 6/02) [956]

8190 Leeming, David. *Jealous Gods and Chosen People: The Mythology of the Middle East* (10–12). Illus. 2004, Oxford $20.00 (0-19-514789-8). This book covers early Middle East history with particular focus on the mythologies of Mesopotamia, Egypt, Anatolia, and Arabia. (Rev: BL 2/1/04) [291.1]

8191 *The Middle East* (9–12). Ed. by Mary E. Williams. Illus. Series: Opposing Viewpoints. 1999, Greenhaven LB $27.45 (0-7377-0133-1); paper $17.45 (0-7377-0132-3). A varied group of essays examine the ongoing conflicts in this part of the world. (Rev: BL 10/15/99; SLJ 1/00) [956.04]

8192 Wagner, Heather Lehr. *Israel and the Arab World* (6–12). Illus. Series: People at Odds. 2002, Chelsea LB $21.95 (0-7910-6705-X). An easy-to-understand summary of the conflict between the two groups, with illustrative photographs. (Rev: BL 11/1/02; HBG 3/03) [956.9405]

Egypt

8193 Stewart, Gail. *The Suez Canal* (7–10). Series: Building History. 2001, Lucent $24.95 (1-56006-842-6). This is the dramatic story of the construction and utilization of the Suez Canal, one of the great engineering marvels of the 19th century. (Rev: BL 8/01) [962]

8194 *Valley of the Kings* (8–12). Ed. by Ken R. Weeks. Illus. 2001, Friedman $65.00 (1-58663-295-7). This profusely illustrated, oversize book covers the Thebian necropolis where archaeologists have uncovered thousands of tombs, temples, houses, villages, shrines, and work stations. (Rev: BL 12/1/01) [932]

Israel and Palestine

8195 Blumberg, Arnold. *The History of Israel* (9–12). Series: Histories of Modern Nations. 1998, Greenwood $35.00 (0-313-30224-3). Following a brief survey of Israel's early history, the author stresses events of the latter years of the 20th century. (Rev: BR 5–6/99; VOYA 6/99) [956.94]

8196 Bucaille, Laetitia. *Growing Up Palestinian: Israeli Occupation and the Intifada Generation* (10–12). Trans. by Anthony Roberts. Series: Studies in Muslim Politics. 2004, Princeton Univ. Pr. paper $19.95 (0-691-11670-9). This contemporary account profiles the Palestinian people, their politics, and their differences. (Rev: BL 3/15/04) [956.95]

8197 Chacham, Remit. *Breaking Ranks: Refusing to Serve in the West Bank and Gaza Strip* (10–12). 2003, Other Press $25.00 (1-59051-043-7). The fascinating story of 52 Israeli army reservists who refused to serve in the occupied Palestinian territories of Gaza and the West Bank and encouraged others to join their action. (Rev: BL 5/15/03) [355.2]

8198 Corzine, Phyllis. *The Palestinian-Israeli Accord* (6–10). Series: Overview. 1996, Lucent LB $27.45 (1-56006-181-2). This work explores the historical roots of the Israeli-Palestinian conflict, discusses the foundation of Israel and its need for land, and traces the rise of Yasir Arafat. (Rev: BR 11–12/97; SLJ 5/97) [956.94]

8199 Finkelstein, Norman H. *Friends Indeed: The Special Relationship of Israel and the United States* (7–12). 1998, Millbrook LB $24.90 (0-7613-0114-3). This book explores the close, often rocky, relationship between Israel and the U.S. through 10 administrations and several wars. (Rev: BL 8/98; BR 9–10/98; SLJ 6/98) [327.73]

8200 Gorkin, Michael, and Rafiqa Othman. *Three Mothers, Three Daughters* (10–12). 1996, Univ. of California Pr. $24.95 (0-520-20329-1). Interviews with three Palestinian Muslim women from three different environments — one from East Jerusalem, one from a small village, and the other from a refugee camp on the West Bank. (Rev: SLJ 12/96) [956]

8201 Grossman, David. *Death as a Way of Life: Israel Ten Years After Oslo* (10–12). Trans. by Haim Watzman. 2003, Farrar $21.00 (0-374-10211-2). In this collection of 33 essays, the author, a peace activist, vents his frustration with the agonizingly slow progress toward an end to the Israeli-Palestinian conflict. (Rev: BL 4/15/03) [956.9405]

8202 Katz, Samuel M. *Jerusalem or Death: Palestinian Terrorism* (7–12). Illus. Series: Terrorist Dossiers. 2003, Lerner LB $26.60 (0-8225-4033-9). This book focuses on the terrorist groups that have been active in Israel and the West Bank. (Rev: BL 3/15/04; HBG 4/04; SLJ 3/04; VOYA 4/04) [956.9]

8203 La Guardia, Anton. *War Without End: Israelis, Palestinians, and the Struggle for a Promised Land* (10–12). Illus. 2002, St. Martin's $25.95 (0-312-27669-9). The intransigence of both Israelis and Palestinians comes under fire in this objective analysis of the conflict in the Middle East. (Rev: BL 5/15/02) [956.04]

8204 Marshood, Nabil. *Palestinian Teenage Refugees and Immigrants Speak Out* (7–12). Series: Teenage Refugees Speak Out. 1997, Rosen LB $17.95 (0-8239-2442-4). The exodus of Palestinians, many to the United States, and their reasons for leaving their homes are shown through the stories of several teenage immigrants. (Rev: BL 12/15/97) [956.04]

8205 Mozeson, I. E., and Lois Stavsky. *Jerusalem Mosaic: Young Voices from the Holy City* (6–12). 1994, Four Winds paper $15.95 (0-02-767651-X). Thirty-six lively monologues based on interviews

with teenagers living in Jerusalem in the early 1990s — Jew and Arab, Muslim and Christian. (Rev: BL 12/1/94; SLJ 1/95) [305.23]

8206 Ross, Stewart. *The Arab-Israeli Conflict* (7–12). Series: Causes and Consequences. 1995, Raintree Steck-Vaughn LB $29.97 (0-8172-4051-9). This conflict is presented in a historical context, using a magazine format, maps, and photographs, laying the basis for understanding the continuing hostility. (Rev: BL 12/15/95; BR 3–4/96; SLJ 2/96) [956.94]

8207 Schroeter, Daniel J. *Israel: An Illustrated History* (10–12). 1998, Oxford $40.00 (0-19-510885-X). From prebiblical times to the present, this is a history of Israel that uses historic photographs, archival documents, and many art reproductions. (Rev: BL 1/1–15/99; VOYA 6/99) [956.94]

8208 Shehadeh, Raja. *When the Birds Stopped Singing: Life in Ramallah Under Siege* (10–12). 2003, Steerforth paper $12.95 (1-58642-069-0). The plight of the Palestinians in the West Bank is clearly illustrated in this account covering the events of a single month in Ramallah. (Rev: BL 9/1/03) [956.9405]

8209 Souad, and Marie-Therese Cuny. *Burned Alive* (10–12). 2004, Warner $24.00 (0-446-53346-7). This horrifying coming-of-age memoir tells of an 18-year-old Palestinian girl who was almost burned alive by her brother because she was pregnant and unmarried. (Rev: BL 4/1/04) [362.82]

8210 Stefoff, Rebecca. *West Bank / Gaza Strip* (7–12). Series: Major World Nations. 1999, Chelsea LB $21.95 (0-7910-4771-7). This work describes the long, confrontational history of this area, with information on its people, economics, geography, and the outlook for the future. (Rev: HBG 3/99; SLJ 6/99) [956.94]

8211 Victor, Barbara. *Army of Roses: Inside the World of Palestinian Women Suicide Bombers* (11–12). 2003, Rodale $25.95 (1-57954-830-X). This compelling book examines the psyche and motivation of Palestinian women prepared to martyr themselves for their cause. (Rev: BL 9/15/03) [956.9405]

Other Middle East Countries

8212 Asayesh, Gelareh. *Saffron Sky: A Life Between Iran and America* (10–12). 1999, Beacon $24.00 (0-8070-7210-9); paper $15.00 (0-8070-7211-7). Iran's recent history is covered in this personal account about the author's many trips to and from Iran as a child and young woman. (Rev: BL 10/1/99) [955]

8213 Bird, Christiane. *Neither East Nor West: One Woman's Journey Through the Islamic Republic of Iran* (10–12). Illus. 2001, Pocket $26.95 (0-671-02755-7). This is an absorbing account of a three-month journey through Iran by a woman who observed many sights and had many experiences unknown to most travelers. (Rev: BL 2/1/01) [955.05]

8214 Bodnarchuk, Karl J. *Kurdistan: Region Under Siege* (7–10). Series: World in Conflict. 2000, Lerner LB $25.26 (0-8225-3556-4). This work gives an unbiased historical picture of this mountainous region of the Middle East and tells of the frequent upheavals that mark its past and present. (Rev: BL 6/1–15/00; HBG 3/01; SLJ 12/00) [955]

8215 Broberg, Catherine. *Saudi Arabia in Pictures* (6–10). Illus. Series: Visual Geography. 2002, Lerner LB $27.93 (0-8225-1958-5). Full-color photographs complement information on the country's geography, history, government, economy, people, and culture. (Rev: BL 10/15/02; HBG 3/03) [953.8]

8216 Clark, Charles. *Iran* (7–12). Series: Nations in Transition. 2002, Gale LB $21.96 (0-7377-1096-9). Iran's internal political upheavals and difficult relationship with the rest of the world are the focus of this thorough and concise volume that includes biographical and cultural features. (Rev: SLJ 1/03) [955]

8217 Foster, Leila M. *Kuwait* (5–10). Series: Enchantment of the World. 1998, Children's LB $34.50 (0-516-20604-4). An introduction to Kuwait for older readers, with extensive coverage of the Gulf War. (Rev: SLJ 11/98) [956]

8218 Hiro, Dilip. *The Longest War: The Iran-Iraq Military Conflict* (9–12). 1991, Routledge paper $20.99 (0-415-90407-2). A detailed account of the 1980–1988 war between Iran and Iraq. (Rev: BL 2/1/91) [955.05]

8219 Isiorho, Solomon A. *Kuwait* (7–12). Series: Modern World Nations. 2002, Chelsea LB $24.95 (0-7910-6781-5). An overview of the history, geography, people, politics, and religion of Kuwait, with discussion of the importance of Islam. Also use *Bahrain* (2002). (Rev: SLJ 2/03) [953.67]

8220 Kheirabadi, Masoud. *Iran* (6–12). Illus. Series: Modern World Nations. 2003, Chelsea LB $24.95 (0-7910-7234-7). A thorough and concise overview of Iran's geography, history, government, politics, economics, language, peoples, and religion, with maps, photographs, and a look at the future. (Rev: BL 9/15/03; HBG 10/03) [955]

8221 Khouri, Norma. *Honor Lost: Love and Death in Modern-Day Jordan* (11–12). 2003, Atria $25.00 (0-7434-4878-2). Recommended for mature teens, this is a heart-rending account of a young Muslim woman who was murdered by her father for falling in love with a Christian. (Rev: BL 2/15/03) [956.9504]

8222 Mackintosh-Smith, Tim. *Yemen: Travels in Dictionary Land* (10–12). Illus. 2000, Overlook $35.00 (1-58567-001-4). This adult account is a fascinating introduction to the history and geography of Yemen by a renowned traveler and observer. (Rev: BL 1/1–15/00) [915.330453]

8223 Marcovitz, Hal. *Jordan* (7–12). Series: Creation of the Modern Middle East. 2002, Chelsea LB $30.95 (0-7910-6507-3). This volume on the history of Jordan, its importance in the Middle East, and its relations with the United States will be useful for report writers. Also use *Syria*, *Oman*, and *The Kurds* (all 2002). (Rev: LMC 4–5/03; SLJ 2/03) [956.9504]

8224 Meiselas, Susan, and A. Whitley. *Kurdistan: In the Shadow of History* (10–12). Illus. 1997, Random $100.00 (0-679-42389-3). This photodocumentary presents the long, agonizing history of the Kurdish people and their refugee status since the Gulf War, serving as both a personal testimony of survivors and a historical record. (Rev: SLJ 5/98) [955]

8225 Sheehan, Sean. *Lebanon* (5–10). Series: Cultures of the World. 1996, Marshall Cavendish LB $35.64 (0-7614-0283-7). A lively, well-written introduction to this war-ravaged country with details on history, economy, culture, religion and foods, including a recipe for a typical dish. (Rev: SLJ 6/97) [569.2]

8226 South, Coleman. *Jordan* (5–10). Series: Cultures of the World. 1996, Marshall Cavendish LB $35.64 (0-7614-0287-X). Everyday life in Jordan is the focus of this book that also covers history, religion, culture, geography, festivals, and foods; a single recipe is included. (Rev: SLJ 6/97) [569.5]

8227 Spencer, William. *Iraq: Old Land, New Nation in Conflict* (7–12). Illus. 2000, Twenty-First Century LB $23.90 (0-7613-1356-7). This account traces the history of Iraq from its Mesopotamian origins to Saddam Hussein's rule prior to the American invasion. (Rev: BL 11/15/00; HBG 3/01; SLJ 12/00) [956.7]

8228 Spencer, William. *The United States and Iran* (7–12). Illus. 2000, Twenty-First Century LB $23.90 (0-7613-1554-3). After covering Iranian culture and history, this account explores Iran's rocky relations with the U.S. to the beginning of 2000, with material on the hostage crisis of 1979. (Rev: BL 4/15/00; HBG 9/00; SLJ 7/00; VOYA 6/01) [327.73055]

8229 Wright, Robin. *The Last Great Revolution: Turmoil and Transformation in Iran* (10–12). Illus. 2000, Knopf $27.50 (0-375-40639-5). An adult account of the Iranian revolution and the changes the country has experienced in the 20 years since the Shah's deposition. (Rev: BL 1/1–15/00) [955.05]

North and South America

General and Miscellaneous

8230 Flannery, Tim. *The Eternal Frontier: An Ecological History of North America and Its Peoples* (10–12). Illus. 2001, Grove Atlantic $27.50 (0-87113-789-5). This ecological history of North America begins with the asteroid that crashed into the Yucatan 65 million yeas ago and charts the land's gradual development, tracing its animal and plant life through the arrival of humans about 13,000 years ago. (Rev: BL 5/1/01*) [508.7]

8231 Long, Catheryn J. *Ancient America* (7–10). Series: World History. 2002, Gale LB $27.45 (1-56006-889-2). The story of the hunter-gatherers, agriculturalists, and city dwellers of North and South America from the arrival of the first humans in America to Columbus. (Rev: BL 8/02) [970]

8232 Morgan, Ted. *Wilderness at Dawn: The Settling of the North American Continent* (9–12). 1993, Simon & Schuster paper $20.00 (0-671-88237-6). A historical overview of migration to North America that spans more than 15,000 years — from the arrival of the first human settlers who crossed the Bering landbridge to 18th-century arrivals. [970]

8233 Murphy, Jim. *Gone a-Whaling: The Lure of the Sea and the Hunt for the Great Whale* (7–12). Illus. 1998, Clarion $18.00 (0-395-69847-2). Diary entries are used to describe American whale hunting and life aboard whaling vessels from the 19th century to the present. (Rev: BCCB 4/98; BL 3/15/98; BR 11–12/98; HB 5–6/98; SLJ 5/98; VOYA 12/98) [306.3]

8234 O'Neill, Thomas. *Lakes, Peaks, and Prairies: Discovering the United States-Canadian Border* (7–12). Illus. 1984, National Geographic LB $12.95 (0-87044-483-2). A trip across the continent that reveals much about the diversity of these regions. [973]

8235 Patent, Dorothy Hinshaw. *Treasures of the Spanish Main* (6–10). Series: Frozen in Time. 1999, Marshall Cavendish LB $27.07 (0-7614-0786-3). This lavishly illustrated book describes the sinking of Spanish galleons near the Florida Keys in the 1600s and how their excavation has brought us amazing information about life and culture in the New World at that time. (Rev: BL 2/15/00; HBG 10/00; SLJ 3/00) [930]

8236 Slatta, Richard W. *Cowboys of the Americas* (9–12). Series: Yale Western Americana. 1990, Yale Univ. Pr. paper $19.95 (0-300-05671-0). This book describes the history and lifestyles of a variety of mounted herders including those of Mexico, Argentina, Chile, Venezuela, and, of course, the cowboy of the United States and Canada. [978]

North America

CANADA

8237 Campbell, Marjorie Wilkins. *The Nor'westers: The Fight for the Fur Trade* (6–12). Illus. 2003, Fitzhenry & Whiteside paper $12.95 (1-894004-97-3). An absorbing account of the Canadian fur trade in the 19th century, with details of company politics and relations between traders and Native Americans. (Rev: BL 4/1/03) [380.1]

8238 Greene, Melissa Fay. *Last Man Out: The Story of the Springhill Mine Disaster* (10–12). Illus. 2003, Harcourt $25.00 (0-15-100559-1). First-person accounts from survivors enliven this story of the 1958 mine collapse in Nova Scotia and the extraordinary efforts to rescue miners who were trapped far below ground for more than a week. (Rev: BL 4/15/03) [363.11]

8239 Kizilos, Peter. *Quebec: Province Divided* (7–10). Series: World in Conflict. 2000, Lerner LB $25.26 (0-8225-3562-9). The history of the French Canadian province and the separatist movement there. (Rev: BL 10/15/2000; HBG 4/00; VOYA 8/01) [971]

8240 Krajick, Kevin. *Barren Lands: An Epic Search for Diamonds in the North American Arctic* (9–12). 2001, W. H. Freeman $24.95 (0-7167-4026-5). The true-life adventure story of Charles Fipke and Stewart Blusson and their search for diamonds in Canada's Northwest Territories. (Rev: BL 7/01) [338.4]

8241 Powell-Williams, Clive. *Cold Burial: A True Story of Endurance and Disaster* (9–12). Illus. 2002, St. Martin's $24.95 (0-312-28854-9). The author draws on a diary, letters, and the recollections of others to reconstruct the ill-fated journey of three young men to Canada's far north. (Rev: BL 1/1–15/02) [971.9]

8242 Riendeau, Roger E. *A Brief History of Canada* (9–12). 2000, Facts on File $45.00 (0-8160-3157-6). From the Norse discovery to the present day, this history of Canada is enriched with photographs and maps. (Rev: VOYA 4/00) [971]

CENTRAL AMERICA

8243 Belli, Gioconda. *The Country Under My Skin: A Memoir of Love and War* (10–12). Trans. by Kristina Cordero. Illus. 2002, Knopf $25.00 (0-375-40370-1). In this thought-provoking memoir, Nicaraguan author and poet Gioconda Belli describes her personal liberation from the strictures of domesticity against the backdrop of her country's struggle to free itself. (Rev: BL 11/1/02*) [972.8505]

8244 Foster, Lynn V. *A Brief History of Central America* (9–12). 2000, Facts on File $35.00 (0-8160-3962-3). The political, economic, and social history of all the countries in Central America is given, with material on present conditions. [972.8]

8245 Gold, Susan D. *The Panama Canal Transfer: Controversy at the Crossroads* (7–10). 1999, Raintree Steck-Vaughn $19.98 (0-8172-5762-4). The first half of this book describes the building of the canal and the second half traces the process of returning the Canal Zone to Panama, including the 1978 treaty providing for the return and the ill will and controversy that developed. (Rev: SLJ 8/99) [972.8]

8246 Hadden, Gerry. *Teenage Refugees from Guatemala Speak Out* (7–12). Series: Teenage Refugees Speak Out. 1997, Rosen LB $16.95 (0-8239-2439-4). Teens from Guatemala who now live in the U.S. describe the violent military campaigns that destroyed villages and lives in their homeland. (Rev: BL 10/15/97; SLJ 1/98) [972.8]

8247 Kallen, Stuart A. *The Mayans* (7–12). Illus. Series: Lost Civilizations. 2001, Lucent LB $19.96 (1-56006-757-8). Kallen covers all aspects of Mayan civilization and emphasizes the ongoing archaeological discoveries that add to our knowledge. (Rev: SLJ 5/01) [972.81]

8248 McCullough, David G. *The Path Between the Seas: The Creation of the Panama Canal, 1870–1914* (10–12). 1977, Simon & Schuster paper $18.00 (0-671-24409-4). A well-told history of the building of the Panama Canal from early attempts to the American completion in 1914. [972.87]

8249 *Route of the Mayas* (9–12). Illus. 1995, Knopf paper $25.00 (0-679-75569-1). Though designed as a travel guide, with standard information on history and food, this book is a valuable reference source on Mayan culture, with recipes and explanations of the symbolism of Mayan clothing. (Rev: VOYA 4/96) [972.81]

8250 Schlesinger, Arthur M., Jr., and Fred L. Israel, eds. *Building the Panama Canal: Chronicles from National Geographic* (9–12). Series: Cultural and Geographical Exploration. 1999, Chelsea LB $19.95 (0-7910-5102-1). In this reprint of four articles and pictures from *National Geographic* magazine originally published between 1904 and 1914, the reader gets an insider's look at the construction of the Panama Canal. Two of the articles were written by George Goethals, the project's chief engineer. (Rev: SLJ 8/99) [972.8]

8251 Sharer, Robert J. *Daily Life in Maya Civilization* (8–12). Series: Daily Life Through History. 1996, Greenwood $49.95 (0-313-29342-2). The latest research is included in this thorough study of Mayan civilization from its beginnings to the Spanish conquest. (Rev: BR 5–6/97; SLJ 2/97) [972.81]

8252 Sheehan, Sean. *Guatemala* (6–10). Series: Cultures of the World. 1998, Marshall Cavendish LB $35.64 (0-7614-0812-6). A solid introduction to Guatemala's geography, politics, and culture. (Rev: HBG 9/98; SLJ 2/99) [972.8]

MEXICO

8253 Barghusen, Joan D. *The Aztecs: End of a Civilization* (6–10). Series: History's Great Defeats. 2000, Lucent LB $19.96 (1-56006-620-2). The defeat of the large Aztec population by a small number of Spanish invaders is detailed using primary and secondary sources. (Rev: BR 3–4/01; HBG 3/01; SLJ 12/00) [972]

8254 Castillo, Ana. *My Daughter, My Son, the Eagle, the Dove* (7–12). Illus. 2000, Dutton $12.99 (0-525-45856-5). In this series of short poems that originated with the Aztecs, each of which is illustrated by traditional figures, the cultural life of the Aztecs comes alive. (Rev: BL 6/1–15/00; HBG 9/00; SLJ 6/00; VOYA 6/00) [398.2]

8255 Diaz del Castillo, Bernal. *Cortez and the Conquest of Mexico by the Spaniards in 1521* (9–12). Illus. 1988, Linnet LB $22.50 (0-208-02221-X). In abridged form, this is the actual diary of a man who accompanied Cortes on his conquest of Mexico. (Rev: VOYA 2/89) [972]

8256 Flowers, Charles. *Cortés and the Conquest of the Aztec Empire in World History* (6–10). Illus. Series: In World History. 2001, Enslow LB $20.95 (0-7660-1395-2). This accessible and interesting account describes Cortes's incursion into the Aztec empire and explains how the Aztecs' beliefs contributed to the ease of this conquest. (Rev: HBG 10/01; SLJ 8/01) [972]

8257 Foster, Lynn V. *A Brief History of Mexico* (9–12). 1997, Facts on File $29.95 (0-8160-3165-7). Traces the country's development from pre-Columbian times to the present and offers insights into the people, language, art, religion, economy, and politics. [972]

8258 Hadden, Gerry. *Teenage Refugees from Mexico Speak Out* (7–12). Series: Teenage Refugees Speak Out. 1997, Rosen LB $16.95 (0-8239-2441-6). Teens who have left Mexico and come to the U.S. to escape economic conditions and political instability tell about their experiences. (Rev: BL 10/15/97; SLJ 1/98) [972]

8259 Helly, Mathilde, and Rémi Courgeon. *Montezuma and the Aztecs* (7–10). 1996, Holt $19.95 (0-8050-5060-4). Although the presentation is somewhat disorganized, this account describes the Aztecs, their culture, political structure, everyday life, and human sacrifices, as well as European invaders and the ruler Montezuma. (Rev: BR 1–2/98; SLJ 3/97) [972]

8260 Hull, Robert. *The Aztecs* (5–10). Series: Ancient World. 1998, Raintree Steck-Vaughn LB $27.12 (0-8172-5056-5). This history of the Aztecs and their culture describes their great pyramids, feathered headdresses, gods, human sacrifices, and the coming of the Spanish. (Rev: BL 1/1–15/99; HBG 3/99) [972]

8261 Kirkwood, Burton. *The History of Mexico* (10–12). Series: Greenwood Histories of the Modern Nations. 2000, Greenwood $45.00 (0-313-30351-7). A fine basic history of Mexico with material on its cultural past and present problems. [972]

8262 Marrin, Albert. *Aztecs and Spaniards: Cortes and the Conquest of Mexico* (7–10). Illus. 1986, Macmillan $15.95 (0-689-31176-1). The story of the decline and fall of the Aztec civilization and the Spanish conquistadors who caused it. (Rev: BL 4/15/86; SLJ 8/86; VOYA 2/87) [972.01]

8263 Pascoe, Elaine. *Mexico and the United States: Cooperation and Conflict* (7–12). Illus. 1996, Twenty-First Century LB $24.90 (0-8050-4180-X). After a history of the stormy relations between Mexico and the U.S., the author discusses current problems, such as drug trafficking, oil, the peso, and immigration. (Rev: BL 12/1/96; BR 3–4/97; SLJ 1/97) [303.48]

8264 Rummel, Jack. *Mexico* (6–10). Series: Major World Nations. 1998, Chelsea LB $19.95 (0-7910-4763-6). A well-illustrated account that emphasizes current economic, political, and cultural conditions, supplemented by good background information. (Rev: BL 9/15/98; BR 1–2/99; HBG 3/99; SLJ 12/98) [917.2]

8265 Schlesinger, Arthur M., Jr., and Fred L. Israel, eds. *Ancient Civilizations of the Aztecs and Maya: Chronicles from National Geographic* (9–12). 1999, Chelsea LB $19.95 (0-7910-5103-X). A collection of *National Geographic* magazine articles written by scholars, adventurers, and explorers in the early 20th century on the then-latest findings about the ancient Aztec and Mayan cultures, with an introduction that makes corrections and updates information. (Rev: SLJ 8/99) [972]

8266 Stefoff, Rebecca. *Independence and Revolution in Mexico, 1810–1940* (7–12). 1993, Facts on File $19.95 (0-8160-2841-9). The history of Mexico's 130-year struggle for independence is explored, highlighting notable events and people. (Rev: BL 12/1/93) [972]

8267 Taylor, Lawrence, and Maeve Hickey. *Tunnel Kids* (10–12). Illus. 2001, Univ. of Arizona Pr. $45.00 (0-8165-1925-0); paper $17.95 (0-8165-1926-9). The poignant story of the children who live and work in the mile-long drainage tunnels connecting Mexico and the U.S. at the Arizona border. (Rev: BL 4/1/01) [305.235]

8268 Townsend, Richard F. *The Aztecs* (10–12). 1992, Thames & Hudson (0-500-02113-9). The story of the Aztec empire, how it grew, its culture, and how it was destroyed by the Spanish conquistadores. [972]

8269 Wood, Michael. *Conquistadors* (10–12). Illus. 2001, Univ. of California Pr. $27.50 (0-520-23064-7). A well-illustrated volume that traces the paths of the such legendary conquistadors as Cortes, Pizarro, Orellana, and de Vaca, and the roles they played in the destruction of the Aztec and Mayan empires. (Rev: BL 5/15/01) [970.16]

PUERTO RICO, CUBA, AND OTHER CARIBBEAN ISLANDS

8270 Anthony, Suzanne. *West Indies* (6–12). Series: Major World Nations. 1998, Chelsea LB $19.95 (0-7910-4772-5). An introduction to the people, geography, history, and economy of the West Indies, with a focus on current conditions. (Rev: BL 9/15/98; BR 1–2/99) [975.9]

8271 Baker, Christopher P. *Mi Moto Fidel: Motorcycling Through Castro's Cuba* (10–12). Illus. 2001, National Geographic $26.00 (0-7922-7961-1). This is a vivid portrait of all kinds of life and situations in Cuba, from a writer who traveled more than 7,000 miles around the island by motorcycle. (Rev: BL 2/1/01) [917.29]

8272 Fernandez, Ronald M., et al. *Puerto Rico Past and Present: An Encyclopedia* (8–12). 1998, Greenwood $67.95 (0-313-29822-X). A browsable book that contains biographies of famous Puerto Ricans as well as political terms and groups, buildings, important court decisions, and other information on the island's cultural and historical developments. (Rev: BL 7/97; VOYA 10/98) [972.95]

8273 Harlan, Judith. *Puerto Rico: Deciding Its Future* (7–10). Illus. 1996, Twenty-First Century LB $23.40 (0-8050-4372-1). The statehood-commonwealth-independence question is presented with clarity, simplicity, and objectivity. (Rev: BL 1/1–15/97; SLJ 7/97) [972.95]

8274 Harvey, David Alan, and Elizabeth Newhouse. *Cuba* (10–12). Illus. 1999, National Geographic $50.00 (0-7922-7501-2). Stunning photographs and a brief text introduce the land and people of Cuba. (Rev: BL 1/1–15/00) [972.91]

8275 Regler, Margaret, and Rhoda Hoff. *Uneasy Neighbors: Cuba and the United States* (9–12). Series: International Affairs. 1997, Watts LB $24.00 (0-531-11326-4). A compilation of primary source materials documenting Cuban-American relations from 1492 to the present. (Rev: BL 6/1–15/97; SLJ 7/97) [327.729]

8276 Salas, Osvaldo, and Roberto Salas. *Fidel's Cuba: A Revolution in Pictures* (10–12). Illus. 1998,

Thunder's Mouth $34.95 (1-56025-192-1). The Cuban Revolution is documented by this father-and-son team, who served for years as photographers for the Castro government's official newspaper, *Revolucion*. (Rev: BL 12/1/98*) [927.9106]

8277 Sherrow, Victoria. *Cuba* (7–12). Illus. 2001, Twenty-First Century LB $24.40 (0-7613-1404-0). Fidel Castro is a key figure in this overview of Cuba's internal affairs and relations with the outside world that will be useful for report writers. (Rev: BL 9/15/01; HBG 3/02; SLJ 12/01; VOYA 12/01) [973.91]

8278 Turck, Mary C. *Haiti: Land of Inequality* (8–12). Series: World in Conflict. 1999, Lerner $25.26 (0-8225-3554-8). Though now out of date, this well-illustrated book gives good background information on this troubled land and its history. (Rev: BL 10/15/99; HBG 4/00; SLJ 2/00) [975.9]

South America

8279 Barter, James. *The Galapagos Islands* (7–10). Series: Endangered Animals and Habitats. 2002, Gale LB $27.45 (1-56006-920-1). In text and many color illustrations, this endangered habitat and its history are described with material on the methods employed to save these unique islands from destruction. (Rev: BL 5/15/02) [508.866]

8280 Bender, Evelyn. *Brazil* (6–12). Series: Major World Nations. 1998, Chelsea LB $21.95 (0-7910-4758-X). Current economic and social conditions in Brazil are emphasized, supplemented by background material on history and geography. (Rev: BL 9/15/98; BR 1–2/99; HBG 3/99) [981]

8281 Cameron, Sara. *Out of War: True Stories from the Front Lines of the Children's Movement for Peace in Colombia* (7–12). 2001, Scholastic $15.95 (0-439-29721-4). Nine teen members of the Colombian peace movement describe their lives in this war-torn country and express their desire for peace rather than retribution. (Rev: BL 9/1/01; HBG 3/02; SLJ 8/01; VOYA 10/01) [305.23]

8282 Castner, James L. *Native Peoples* (6–12). Illus. Series: Deep in the Amazon. 2001, Marshall Cavendish LB $18.95 (0-7614-1128-3). This volume looks at the people of the Amazon, their way of life, and the encroachment of outsiders. Also use *Rainforest Researchers* (2001). (Rev: BL 12/15/01; HBG 3/02) [981]

8283 Chasteen, John Charles. *Born in Blood and Fire: A Concise History of Latin America* (10–12). Illus. 2001, Norton $26.95 (0-393-05048-3). This brief but insightful history begins with the European invasions and continues through the colonial period to eventual political and economic independence. (Rev: BL 1/1–15/01) [980]

8284 Dicks, Brian. *Brazil* (6–10). Illus. Series: Countries of the World. 2003, Facts on File $30.00 (0-8160-5382-0). A well-illustrated account that covers all important topics including present-day racial friction and economic inequality. (Rev: BL 2/1/04) [949.12]

8285 Hemming, John. *The Conquest of the Incas* (10–12). Illus. 1973, Harcourt paper $22.00 (0-15-622300-7). The story of the Spanish conquest and the fall of the Inca Empire. [985]

8286 Jermyn, Leslie. *Uruguay* (7–10). Series: Cultures of the World. 1998, Marshall Cavendish LB $35.64 (0-7614-0873-8). An attractive book that covers all the basic topics relating to Uruguay, plus material on leisure activities, festivals, and food. (Rev: HBG 9/99; SLJ 6/99) [980]

8287 Kane, Joe. *Running the Amazon* (9–12). Illus. 1989, Knopf $19.95 (0-394-55331-4). The story of the expedition that tried to be the first to traverse the Amazon from its source to its mouth. (Rev: BR 11–12/90; SLJ 2/90; VOYA 2/90) [981]

8288 Kane, Joe. *Savages* (9–12). 1995, Knopf $25.00 (0-679-41191-7). An environmentalist recounts recent journeys to Amazonia, where he investigated the issues and parties involved in the destruction of the rain forest. (Rev: BL 9/15/95*) [333.3]

8289 Litteral, Linda L. *Boobies, Iguanas, and Other Critters: Nature's Story in the Galapagos* (6–10). 1994, American Kestrel $23.00 (1-883966-01-9). After a historical overview of the Galapagos Islands, this richly illustrated book covers the islands' animals, plants, and geology. (Rev: BL 6/1–15/94; SLJ 9/94) [508.866]

8290 McIntyre, Loren. *Exploring South America* (9–12). Illus. 1990, Crown $40.00 (0-517-56134-4). A photographic journey exploring the wonders of the vast, varied continent of South America. (Rev: BL 7/90) [918]

8291 McIntyre, Loren. *The Incredible Incas and Their Timeless Land* (10–12). Illus. 1975, National Geographic LB $12.00 (0-87044-182-5). An examination of the Incas, their history and culture, and the destruction of their empire by the Spaniards. [985]

8292 Moseley, Michael Edward. *The Incas and Their Ancestors: The Archaeology of Peru* (10–12). 1992, Thames & Hudson $35.00 (0-500-05063-5). This is a fascinating account that explores the history, people, and culture of the Incas of Peru as revealed by archaeological findings. [985]

8293 Muller, Karin. *Along the Inca Road: A Woman's Journey into an Ancient Empire* (10–12). Illus. 2000, National Geographic $26.00 (0-7922-7685-X). The intriguing story of a six-month trek that took the author through parts of Ecuador, Peru, Bolivia, and Chile. (Rev: BL 9/1/00) [918]

8294 Murphy, Dallas. *Rounding the Horn: Being the Story of Williwaws and Windjammers, Drake, Darwin, Murdered Missionaries and Naked Natives, a Deck's Eye View of Cape Horn* (9–12). 2004, Basic $25.00 (0-465-04759-9). As well as his own trip around the tip of South America, the author describes in detail the voyages of Drake, Darwin, and others. (Rev: BL 4/15/04) [918.3]

8295 Nishi, Dennis. *The Inca Empire* (7–10). Series: World History. 2000, Lucent LB $18.96 (1-56006-538-9). This book discusses the mightiest of the Andean civilizations and how it spread over a great part of South America and created an intricate social structure. (Rev: BL 6/1–15/00; HBG 9/00; SLJ 7/00) [985]

8296 Peck, Robert McCracken. *Headhunters and Hummingbirds: An Expedition into Ecuador* (7–10). Illus. 1987, Walker LB $14.85 (0-8027-6646-3). An account of an ill-fated scientific expedition into the land of the Jívaro Indians in Ecuador. (Rev: SLJ 6/87; VOYA 8/87) [986]

8297 Read, Piers Paul. *Alive: The Story of the Andes Survivors* (9–12). 1979, Avon paper $6.99 (0-380-00321-X). The harrowing story of a group of men and women who survive a plane crash in the Andes. [910.4]

8298 Sayer, Chloe. *The Incas* (5–10). Series: Ancient World. 1998, Raintree Steck-Vaughn LB $27.12 (0-8172-5125-1). An in-depth look at Inca life, from their beautiful gold ornaments to their unique form of record keeping and impressive citadels and forts. (Rev: BL 1/1–15/99; HBG 3/99) [985]

Polar Regions

8299 Alexander, Caroline. *The Endurance: Shackleton's Legendary Antarctic Expedition* (10–12). 1998, Knopf $29.95 (0-375-40403-1). Drawing on first-person accounts, some previously unpublished, Alexander brings to life Shackleton's ill-fated trans-Antarctic expedition. (Rev: BL 10/15/98) [998]

8300 Armstrong, Jennifer. *Shipwreck at the Bottom of the World: The True Story of the Endurance Expedition* (7–12). 1999, Crown LB $19.99 (0-517-80014-4). A gripping account of Sir Ernest Shackleton's trans-Antarctic expedition, during which he and his team were trapped for 19 months in the frozen Antarctic wasteland, enduring extreme cold, dangerous ice, and a perilous 800-mile open-boat journey — all without losing a single man. (Rev: BL 12/1/98; HBG 9/99; SLJ 4/99) [919.8]

8301 Arnesen, Liv, et al. *No Horizon Is So Far: Two Women and Their Extraordinary Journey Across Antarctica* (10–12). Illus. 2003, Da Capo $26.00 (0-7382-0794-2). The compelling story of the first women to cross Antarctica on foot is accompanied by interesting details of their preparations, their equipment, and their high-tech contacts with the outside world. (Rev: BL 9/15/03; SLJ 4/04) [919]

8302 Burch, Ernest S., and Werner Forman. *The Eskimos* (9–12). Illus. 1988, Univ. of Oklahoma Pr. $29.95 (0-8061-2126-2). Color photographs highlight this account of the history, livelihood, and culture of the Eskimo. (Rev: BL 9/1/88) [306]

8303 Cookman, Scott. *Iceblink: The Tragic Fate of Sir John Franklin's Lost Polar Expedition* (10–12). Illus. 2000, Wiley $24.95 (0-471-37790-2). An absorbing adult account of the ill-fated 1845 Franklin expedition in search of the Northwest Passage across the Arctic. (Rev: BL 1/1–15/00) [919.804]

8304 Edinger, Ray. *Fury Beach: The Four-Year Odyssey of Captain John Ross and the Victory* (10–12). Illus. 2003, Berkley $22.95 (0-425-18845-0). In this fascinating book, the author chronicles a privately financed 1829–1833 expedition in search of the Northwest Passage. (Rev: BL 3/15/03) [910]

8305 Fuchs, Arved. *In Shackleton's Wake* (10–12). Trans. by Martin Sokolinsky. Illus. 2001, Sheridan House $24.95 (1-57409-138-7). In this true sea adventure, the author reenacts the boat journey of Shackleton's 1915–16 Antarctic expedition. (Rev: BL 10/15/01) [919.8]

8306 Guttridge, Leonard. *Ghosts of Cape Sabine: The Harrowing True Story of the Greely Expedition* (10–12). 2000, Putnam $26.95 (0-399-14589-3). A grim story of survival and tragedy in the Arctic in 1881–1884. (Rev: BL 2/1/00; SLJ 12/00) [919.804]

8307 Heacox, Kim. *Shackleton: The Antarctic Challenge* (9–12). 1999, National Geographic $35.00 (0-7922-7536-5). Text and illustrations trace the fate of the 1914 Antarctic expedition of Sir Ernest Shackleton. [998]

8308 Henderson, Bruce. *Fatal North: Adventure and Survival Aboard U.S.S. Polaris, the First U.S. Expedition to the North Pole* (10–12). 2001, NAL $22.95 (0-451-40935-3). An account of the ill-fated 1871 expedition of the steamer *Polaris* to find the North Pole. (Rev: BL 2/1/01) [919.804]

8309 Jago, Lucy. *The Northern Lights* (10–12). Illus. 2001, Pure Sciences Knopf $24.00 (0-375-40980-7). Norwegian Kristian Birkeland set off in 1899 to explore the Arctic and the northern lights. (Rev: BL 9/1/01*) [538]

8310 Kobalenko, Jerry. *The Horizontal Everest: Extreme Journeys on Ellesmere Island* (10–12). Illus. 2002, Soho Pr. $30.00 (1-56947-266-1). This beautifully illustrated introduction to the Arctic island of Ellesmere includes details of its history and wildlife. (Rev: BL 2/15/02) [917.19]

8311 Landis, Marilyn J. *Antarctica: Exploring the Extreme: 400 Years of Adventure* (10–12). Illus. 2001, Chicago Review $26.95 (1-55652-428-5). The author used various data including those collected on site to reconstruct the feats of Antarctic explorers including Magellan, Drake, Cook, Scott, and Shackleton. (Rev: BL 10/1/01) [919.8]

8312 Lynch, Wayne. *A Is for Arctic: Natural Wonders of a Polar World* (10–12). 1996, Firefly paper $24.95 (1-55209-048-5). Using an alphabetical arrangement, the author presents one or two fascinating facts about a variety of phenomenon and creatures found in the Arctic, including the aurora borealis, blizzards, ducks, lemmings, mosquitoes, spiders, and wolves. (Rev: BR 3–4/97; SLJ 6/97) [979.8]

8313 Niven, Jennifer. *Ada Blackjack: A True Story of Survival in the Arctic:* (10–12). Illus. 2003, Hyperion $24.95 (0-7868-6863-5). An ill-fated expedition to the Arctic ends with a sole survivor in this exciting true-life tale. (Rev: BL 10/15/03*) [915.7]

8314 Niven, Jennifer. *The Ice Master: The Doomed 1913 Voyage of the Karluk* (10–12). 2000, Hyperion $24.95 (0-7868-6529-6). Drawn from diaries and first-person accounts, this is a riveting account of an ill-fated expedition to the Arctic in which the ship *Karluk* became trapped in a giant ice floe. (Rev: BL 10/1/00*) [919.804]

8315 Officer, Charles B., and Jake Page. *A Fabulous Kingdom: The Exploration of the Arctic* (10–12). 2001, Oxford $25.00 (0-19-512382-4). A fascinating history of the various attempts to explore the Arctic. [998]

8316 Parry, Richard. *Trial by Ice: The True Story of Murder and Survival on the 1871 Polaris Expedition* (10–12). Illus. 2001, Ballantine $23.95 (0-345-43925-2). This is an excellent retelling of the misadventures that occurred during the *Polaris* expedition of 1871 to reach the North Pole. (Rev: BL 1/1–15/01) [919.804]

8317 Schlesinger, Arthur M., Jr., and Fred L. Israel, eds. *Race for the South Pole: The Antarctic Challenge: Chronicles from National Geographic* (9–12). 1999, Chelsea LB $19.95 (0-7910-5100-5). This is a collection of 27 articles and original archival photographs that appeared in *National Geographic* magazine in 1899–1912 covering the race to the South Pole, including the expeditions led by Robert Scott, Ernest Shackleton, and the eventual winner, Roald Amundsen. (Rev: SLJ 7/99) [979.8]

8318 Schlesinger, Arthur M., Jr., and Fred L. Israel. *Robert E. Peary and the Rush to the North Pole: Chronicles from National Geographic* (9–12). 1999, Chelsea LB $19.95 (0-7910-5099-8). Twenty-three original articles and archival photographs published by *National Geographic* magazine in 1899–1920 highlight the Peary expeditions in the Arctic and include a report by one of his competitors. (Rev: SLJ 7/99) [979.8]

8319 Senungetuk, Vivian, and Paul Tiulana. *A Place for Winter: Paul Tiulana's Story* (7–12). Illus. 1988, CIRI Foundation $17.95 (0-938227-02-5). The story of a King Island Eskimo boy, his childhood, and his people. (Rev: BL 5/15/88) [917.98]

8320 Solomon, Susan. *The Coldest March: Scott's Fatal Antarctic Expedition* (9–12). Illus. 2001, Yale $29.95 (0-300-08967-8). A well-researched book that describes Captain Scott's trip to the South Pole in 1921 and the return trip, during which he and his companions perished. (Rev: BL 8/01) [919.8]

8321 Vaughan, Norman D., and Cecil Murphey. *With Byrd at the Bottom of the World* (10–12). 1990, Stackpole $22.95 (0-8117-1904-9). A re-creation of the Byrd expedition to the South Pole by the man who tended the dogs during this stressful trek. (Rev: BL 10/1/90) [919]

8322 Warrick, Karen Clemens. *The Race for the North Pole in World History* (8–12). Series: In World History. 2002, Enslow LB $20.95 (0-7660-1933-0). Various explorers of the Arctic are introduced with emphasis on Robert Peary and Frederick Cook, both of whom claimed to be the first to reach the North Pole. (Rev: BL 3/15/03; HBG 10/03; VOYA 8/03) [979.8]

8323 Waterman, Jonathan. *Arctic Crossing: A Journey Through the Northwest Passage and Inuit Culture* (10–12). Illus. 2001, Knopf $29.95 (0-375-40409-0). One man's journey over more than 2,000 miles by foot, kayak, skis, and dogsled. (Rev: BL 3/15/01) [910]

United States

General History and Geography

8324 Adams, John Winthrop, ed. *Stars and Stripes Forever: The History of Our Flag* (9–12). 1992, Smithmark $9.98 (0-8317-6658-1). A general history of the U.S. flag with a focus on colonial times. (Rev: BL 9/15/92) [929.9]

8325 Agel, Jerome. *Words That Make America Great* (10–12). 1996, Random $30.00 (0-679-44959-0). This useful anthology contains 130 documents that are vital to American history, divided into 15 sections and spanning the years 1570 to 1996. (Rev: BL 3/15/97; BR 5–6/97; SLJ 7/97; VOYA 6/97) [973]

8326 Allen, Henry. *What It Felt Like: Living in the American Century* (9–12). Illus. 2000, Pantheon $20.00 (0-375-42063-0). In a series of detailed chapters arranged by decades, the author explores the social and political life of the American people during the 20th century. (Rev: BL 10/1/00) [973.9]

8327 Allen, Thomas B. *America from Space* (11–12). Illus. 1998, Firefly $29.95 (1-55209-280-1). An impressive collection of aerial views of the American landscape stretching from Hawaii to the busy Northeast, showing wilderness and urban areas, geological phenomena and human activity. (Rev: BL 11/15/98) [917]

8328 Ambrose, Stephen, and Douglas Brinkley. *Witness to America: An Illustrated Documentary History of the United States from the Revolution to Today* (8–12). 1999, HarperCollins $39.95 (0-06-271611-5). This collection of primary sources on key moments in American history also includes a CD with dramatizations. (Rev: BL 10/15/99) [973]

8329 *American History: Original and Secondary Source Readings* (9–12). Ed. by Michael S. Mayer. Series: Perspectives on History. 2002, Greenhaven LB $36.96 (0-7377-0708-9); paper $20.96 (0-7377-0707-0). This analysis of early American history (from the colonial era to the Civil War) draws on primary and secondary source materials to give students a more complete understanding of events and what caused them. (Rev: BL 1/1–15/03; VOYA 10/03) [973]

8330 *The Appalachians: America's First and Last Frontier* (9–12). Ed. by Mari-Lynn Evans et al. Illus. 2004, Random $29.95 (1-4000-5186-5). This collection of photographs, essays, and oral histories describes the Appalachian region, which covers thousands of square miles in 13 states. (Rev: BL 3/1/04) [974]

8331 Baker, Patricia. *Fashions of a Decade: The 1940s* (7–12). Illus. Series: Fashions of a Decade. 1992, Facts on File $25.00 (0-8160-2467-7). Each book in this series that covers the 1920s through the 1990s connects political and social history with particular modes of dress. (Rev: BL 4/1/92) [391]

8332 Baxandall, Rosalyn, and Linda Gordon, eds. *America's Working Women: A Documentary History 1600 to the Present* (9–12). 1995, Norton paper $14.95 (0-393-31262-3). A chronologically arranged overview of the changing roles and contributions of women. (Rev: BL 3/15/95*) [331.4]

8333 Boorstin, Daniel J., ed. *An American Primer* (7–12). 1968, NAL paper $19.95 (0-452-00922-7). Eighty-three documents vital to our history are reproduced plus accompanying background articles. [973]

8334 Boorstin, Daniel J. *The Americans: The Democratic Experience* (10–12). 1973, Random paper $19.00 (0-394-71011-8). This work chronicles the growth of the democratic spirit in America in the past 100 years. [973]

8335 Bowman, John S. *Facts About the American Wars* (10–12). 1998, H.W. Wilson $110.00 (0-8242-0929-X). Military conflicts from the mid-16th-century to the Persian Gulf War of 1991 are covered in detail, with illustrations and maps. [355]

8336 Brinkley, Douglas. *The American Heritage History of the United States* (11–12). Illus. 1998, Viking $50.00 (0-670-86966-X). An excellent overview, suitable for students of American history, that focuses on the economic dynamism of the United States and looks at Americans' efforts to earn money and improve their standard of living in every era. (Rev: BL 11/15/98) [973.2]

8337 Brokaw, Tom. *An Album of Memories: Personal Histories from the Greatest Generation* (10–12). Illus. 2001, Random $29.95 (0-375-50581-4). This is a collection of letters sent to Tom Brokaw by Americans who lived through the Depression and World War II. (Rev: BL 4/1/01) [940.54]

8338 Brokaw, Tom. *The Greatest Generation* (10–12). 1998, Random $24.95 (0-375-50202-5); paper $24.95 (0-375-70569-4). The TV anchorman describes the Americans who came of age during the Great Depression and World War II and created today's America, with stories told by a cross-section of men and woman around the country and divided into eight topics: Ordinary People; Homefront; Heroes; Women in Uniform and Out; Shame; Love, Marriage, and Commitment; Famous People; and the Arena. (Rev: BL 1/1–15/99; SLJ 4/99) [973.9]

8339 Bruun, Erik, and Jay Crosby. *Our National Archive: Key Documents, Opinions, Speeches, Letters, and Songs that Shaped Our Nation* (9–12). 1999, Black Dog & Leventhal $29.98 (1-57912-067-9). A chronologically arranged collection of 1,000 original sources covering 300 years of American history. (Rev: SLJ 4/00) [973]

8340 Colbert, David, ed. *Eyewitness to America: 500 Years of America in the Words of Those Who Saw It Happen* (10–12). 1997, Random $30.00 (0-679-44224-3). Using diaries, letters, interviews, memoirs, and other primary sources chronologically arranged, this book contains 300 firsthand observations of events, developments, and innovations that have changed America. (Rev: SLJ 8/97) [973]

8341 Collins, Gail. *America's Women: 400 Years of Dolls, Drudges, Helpmates, and Heroines* (10–12). Illus. 2003, Morrow $27.95 (0-06-018510-4). This ambitious survey of women's role in American history looks at the challenges faced and contributions made. (Rev: BL 9/1/03) [305.4]

8342 Coppens, Linda Miles. *What American Women Did, 1789–1920* (9–12). 2001, McFarland $38.50 (0-7864-0899-5). Coppens provides a thorough, chronological overview of women's achievements, looking specifically at accomplishments in the areas of domesticity, employment, education, religion, the arts, law and politics, and civil rights. (Rev: BL 6/01; SLJ 8/01) [305.4]

8343 Cordingly, David. *Women Sailors and Sailors' Women* (10–12). Illus. 2001, Random $24.95 (0-375-50041-3). This book for mature readers covers the lives of women who went to sea (some disguised as men) during the 17th, 18th, and 19th centuries. (Rev: BL 3/1/01) [910.4]

8344 Crump, Donald J., ed. *Exploring America's Scenic Highways* (9–12). Illus. 1985, National Geographic $12.95 (0-87044-479-4). A celebration of America's colorful highways in words and pictures. [917.3]

8345 Davis, Kenneth C. *Don't Know Much About History: Everything You Need to Know About American History but Never Learned* (9–12). 1990, Crown $24.95 (0-517-57706-2). Basic facts about American history are given and myths and misconceptions exposed. (Rev: BL 6/15/90; SLJ 10/90) [973]

8346 Druckman, Nancy. *American Flags: Designs for a Young Nation* (8–12). Illus. 2003, Abrams $16.95 (0-8109-4506-1). Photographs of more than 60 flags form the basis of this guide to the evolution of the national symbol. (Rev: BL 11/1/03; HBG 4/04; SLJ 10/03) [929.9]

8347 Dudley, William, ed. *The Industrial Revolution* (9–12). Series: Opposing Viewpoints: American History. 1998, Greenhaven LB $21.96 (1-56510-707-1); paper $16.20 (1-56510-706-3). The views of industrialists, labor organizers, and social critics are represented in this anthology that traces the evolution of the United States from agricultural colonies to industrial giant. (Rev: BL 7/98) [973]

8348 Dudley, William, ed. *The 1960s* (6–12). Series: America's Decades. 2000, Greenhaven LB $29.96 (0-7377-0306-7); paper $17.96 (0-7377-0305-9). The Vietnam War, the moon landing, assassinations, Woodstock, and the civil rights movement are some of the topics covered in this collection of articles on the 1960s. (Rev: BL 7/00) [073.9]

8349 Dudley, William, ed. *Opposing Viewpoints in American History, Vol. 1: From Colonial Times to Reconstruction* (8–12). Illus. Series: Opposing Viewpoints. 1996, Greenhaven LB $37.44 (1-56510-348-3); paper $27.45 (1-56510-347-5). Alternative primary source opinions are given for such issues in early American history as Native American rights, acceptance of the Bill of Rights, and slavery. (Rev: BL 3/15/96) [973]

8350 Dudley, William, ed. *Opposing Viewpoints in American History, Vol. 2: From Reconstruction to the Present* (8–12). Illus. Series: Opposing Viewpoints. 1996, Greenhaven LB $37.44 (1-56510-350-5); paper $36.75 (1-56510-349-1). Conflicting opinions from primary sources are presented on such topics as women's rights, U.S. participation in

World War I, the New Deal, the dropping of the atomic bomb, and the Cold War. (Rev: BL 3/15/96) [973]

8351 Ehlert, Willis J. *America's Heritage: Capitols of the United States* (6–12). 1993, State House Publg. paper $10.95 (0-9634908-3-4). Provides data on state capitals and capitol buildings, descriptions of architectural details, brief state histories, state symbols, and an extensive bibliography. (Rev: BL 4/15/93) [725]

8352 Evans, Harold. *The American Century* (10–12). 1998, Knopf $50.00 (0-679-41070-8). Using more than 1,000 excellent illustrations, this lively narrative traces the political history of the United States from 1889 to 1989, with the author's main thesis being that the United States dominated the world scene during these years because of its founding ideals of political and economic freedom. (Rev: BL 8/98; SLJ 2/99) [973]

8353 Faragher, John Mack, ed. *The American Heritage Encyclopedia of American History* (9–12). 1998, Holt $45.00 (0-8050-4438-8). With more than 2,750 alphabetically arranged articles and numerous maps, pictures, drawings, and cartoons, this is a browsable, appealing overview of American history. (Rev: BL 11/15/98; SLJ 5/99) [973]

8354 Findling, John E., and Frank W. Thackeray, eds. *Events that Changed America in the Eighteenth Century* (7–12). 1998, Greenwood $45.00 (0-313-29082-2). Using an essay format, this overview of the 18th century covers the French and Indian War, the Stamp Act, the Boston Tea Party, the American Revolution, and the Constitutional Convention. (Rev: BR 1–2/99; SLJ 5/99) [973.3]

8355 Fodor's Travel Publications Staff. *The Complete Guide to America's National Parks, 1998–99* (9–12). 1998, Fodor's paper $18.00 (0-679-03515-X). This is the official guide to America's national parks, prepared by the National Park Foundation. [719]

8356 Garrington, Sally. *The United States* (6–10). Series: Countries of the World. 2003, Facts on File $30.00 (0-8160-5385-5). This basic work supplies an overview of information on the United States with emphasis on present conditions. (Rev: BL 1/1–15/04) [973]

8357 Gay, Kathlyn, and Martin Gay. *After the Shooting Stops: The Aftermath of War* (7–12). 1998, Millbrook LB $24.90 (0-7613-3006-2). A look at the political, economic, and social changes that have followed U.S. involvement in various wars. (Rev: BL 8/98; HBG 3/99; SLJ 9/98) [355.00973]

8358 Gerdes, Louise I., ed. *The 1940s* (6–12). Series: America's Decades. 2000, Greenhaven LB $29.96 (0-7377-0302-4); paper $17.96 (0-7377-0301-6). This anthology of articles and essays deals with the beginning of the atomic age, the growth of motion pictures, and World War II: its causes, effects, home front activities, and the battles. (Rev: BL 7/00) [973.9]

8359 Giblin, James Cross, ed. *The Century That Was: Reflections on the Last One Hundred Years* (6–12). Illus. 2000, Simon & Schuster $20.00 (0-689-82281-2). Eleven well-known writers for young people, including Katherine Paterson, Walter Dean Myers, and Laurence Pringle, write about the last century in America and cover such topics as civil rights, religion, conservation, and sports. (Rev: BL 3/1/00; HB 3–4/00; HBG 9/00; SLJ 7/00) [973.91]

8360 Glackens, Ira. *Did Molly Pitcher Say That? The Men and Women Who Made American History* (9–12). Illus. 1989, Writers & Readers $18.95 (0-86316-097-2); paper $12.95 (0-86316-094-8). An informal view of American history with several amusing and fascinating sidebar features. (Rev: BL 9/15/89) [973]

8361 Gross, Ernie. *The American Years: A Chronology of United States History* (6–12). 1998, Scribner $130.00 (0-684-80590-1). A chronology of events, developments, and trends from 1776 to 1997, in the following categories: international, national, transportation, religion, entertainment, education, arts/music, sports, business/industry/inventions, science/medicine, and literature/journalism. (Rev: BL 7/99; BR 9–10/99; SLJ 8/99) [973]

8362 Hakim, Joy. *Freedom: A History of US* (10–12). Illus. 2002, Oxford $40.00 (0-19-515711-7). In this ambitious, well-illustrated survey of American history, tracing the country's story from independence to the present, Hakim focuses on Americans' quest for freedom. (Rev: BL 10/15/02; SLJ 5/03) [973]

8363 Head, Judith. *America's Daughters: 400 Years of American Women* (6–12). Illus. 1999, Perspectives paper $16.95 (0-9622036-8-8). This overview of the part played by women in American history highlights the work of many who have been unjustly ignored. (Rev: BL 1/1–15/00; SLJ 3/00) [305.4]

8364 Heffner, Richard D. *A Documentary History of the United States* (9–12). 1952, NAL paper $7.99 (0-451-62413-0). A basic collection of documents relating to important events in American history. [973]

8365 Heinemann, Sue. *The New York Public Library Amazing Women in History* (6–10). Illus. 1998, Wiley paper $12.95 (0-471-19216-3). Using a question-and-answer format, this work supplies hundreds of facts about women in American history, arranged by topics that include activism, sports, recreation, and racial and ethnic groups. (Rev: BL 4/15/98; BR 11–12/98; SLJ 8/98) [973]

8366 *Historic Places* (8–12). Series: Explore America. 1993, Reader's Digest LB $19.95 (0-89577-506-9). This handsome book features material on 10 historical sites in America including Saint Augus-tine in Florida and Williamsburg in Virginia and explains their importance and present condition. [917.3]

8367 Holsinger, M. Paul, ed. *War and American Popular Culture: A Historical Encyclopedia* (9–12). 1999, Greenwood LB $89.50 (0-313-29908-0). Arranged by war periods from colonial days to the present, articles examine how wars have changed U.S. popular culture in the areas of songs, poetry, novels, television, movies, toys, and controversial war memorials. (Rev: BL 4/15/99; SLJ 8/99) [973]

8368 Howarth, W., et al. *America's Wild Woodlands* (9–12). Illus. 1985, National Geographic LB $12.95 (0-87044-547-2). From the flowering trees of the East to the West's sequoias, this is a description of the wonders of America's forests. [917.3]

8369 *Images of America: A Panorama of History in Photographs* (9–12). Illus. 1989, Smithsonian $47.50 (0-89599-023-7). A history of the United States as seen through the eyes of our great photographers. (Rev: BL 9/15/89) [973]

8370 Jacoby, Susan. *Freethinkers: A History of American Secularism* (10–12). Illus. 2004, Holt $27.50 (0-8050-7442-2). This is a history of American freethinkers such as Thomas Jefferson, Walt Whitman, and John F. Kennedy and how they changed American thinking and history. (Rev: BL 4/1/04*) [211]

8371 Jaffe, Steven H. *Who Were the Founding Fathers? Two Hundred Years of Reinventing American History* (7–12). Illus. 1996, Holt $18.95 (0-8050-3102-2). An exploration of the nation's founding fathers and how their ideas have been interpreted and reinterpreted by groups as diverse as suffragettes, the Ku Klux Klan, McCarthyites, and the yippies to promote their programs and theories. An excellent source for material on the Revolution, the Constitution, and issues associated with civil rights, immigration, citizenship, and slavery. (Rev: BL 12/1/96*; BR 3–4/97; SLJ 1/97*; VOYA 4/97) [973.3]

8372 Jennings, Peter, and Todd Brewster. *The Century* (10–12). Illus. 1998, Doubleday $60.00 (0-385-48327-9). A profusely illustrated, easy-to-read survey of the 20th century that focuses on how events affected American life. (Rev: BL 10/1/98; SLJ 4/99) [973.9]

8373 Jennings, Peter, and Todd Brewster. *In Search of America* (10–12). Illus. 2002, Hyperion $50.00 (0-7868-6708-6). Six tales of modern America offer contemporary insights into the ideals of the country's Founding Fathers. (Rev: BL 8/02) [973]

8374 Katz, William L. *Exploration to the War of 1812, 1492–1814* (7–10). Series: History of Multicultural America. 1993, Raintree Steck-Vaughn LB $27.11 (0-8114-6275-7). Discusses America from before European colonization through the formation of the new nation, exploration of new territory, and the War of 1812. Includes the role and treatment of Native Americans, women, slaves, and free blacks. (Rev: BL 6/1–15/93) [973]

8375 Langdon, William Chauncey. *Everyday Things in American Life, 1776–1876* (7–12). Illus. 1941, Macmillan $45.00 (0-684-17416-2). This illustrated account covers such topics as clothing, machinery, canals, bridges, and turnpikes. [973]

8376 Levy, Peter B. *100 Key Documents in American Democracy* (8–12). 1994, Greenwood $59.95 (0-313-28424-5). Arranged chronologically, these documents are reprinted in full with commentary and notes on historical context. (Rev: BL 2/15/94) [973]

8377 Lucey, Donna M. *I Dwell in Possibility: Women Build a Nation, 1600–1920* (10–12). Illus. 2001, National Geographic $40.00 (0-7922-6360-X). Through photographs and lucid prose, the contributions of women to the United States and its culture are outlined and celebrated. (Rev: BL 12/15/01) [305.4]

8378 Lunardini, Christine. *What Every American Should Know About Women's History* (9–12). Series: What Every American Should Know. 1994, Bob Adams $16.00 (1-55850-417-6). Deals with significant contributions made by U.S. women from the early 17th century to the present. (Rev: BL 12/1/94) [973]

8379 Mee, Sue. *1900–20: Linen and Lace* (5–10). Series: 20th Century Fashion. 2000, Gareth Stevens LB $25.26 (0-8368-2598-5). The fashion and design of the first two decades of the last century are pictured and described in this book that also contains a great deal of social history. (Rev: HBG 10/00; SLJ 6/00) [973.9]

8380 Mills, Kay. *From Pocahontas to Power Suits: Everything You Need to Know About Women's History in America* (9–12). 1995, NAL paper $11.95 (0-452-27152-5). A celebration of women in America's history, from civil rights and women in the workplace to education, arts, and sports. (Rev: BL 3/15/95) [305.4]

8381 *Monuments and Historic Places of America* (9–12). Series: Macmillan Profiles. 2000, Macmillan $100.00 (0-02-865374-2). Battlefields, churches, homes, forts, and cemeteries are some of the 90 monuments and memorials highlighted in this guide to famous places in the United States. (Rev: BL 5/1/00) [973]

8382 Morris, Richard B. *Basic Documents in American History* (9–12). 1980, Krieger paper $13.50 (0-89874-202-1). This collection of important documents in American history covers the years 1620 through the 1960s. [973]

8383 Moser, Diane, and Ray Spangenburg. *Political and Social Movements* (7–12). Illus. Series: Ameri-

can Historic Places. 1998, Facts on File $25.00 (0-8160-3404-4). Important political, philosophical, and social movements that changed America are traced using as a backdrop the places where they originated or took place, such as Valley Forge, Ellis Island, Ford's Theater, Clara Barton's house, and Wounded Knee, from the Revolution through the civil rights era. (Rev: BL 5/15/98; SLJ 8/98) [973]

8384 National Geographic Society, eds. *Preserving America's Past* (9–12). Illus. 1983, National Geographic LB $12.95 (0-87044-420-4). This volume highlights attempts to preserve America's past by restoring buildings, relearning crafts, and similar activities. [973]

8385 *No Small Courage: A History of Women in the United States* (10–12). Ed. by Nancy F. Cott. Illus. 2000, Oxford $35.00 (0-19-513946-1). This collection of writings about women in American history starts with Native American women during the colonial period and ends with a chapter that covers the last four decades of the 20th century. (Rev: BL 11/1/00) [305.4]

8386 Packard, Jerrold M. *American Nightmare: The History of Jim Crow* (10–12). 2002, St. Martin's $24.95 (0-312-26122-5). An excellent overview of Jim Crowism from Reconstruction through the passage of the Voting Rights Act in 1965. (Rev: BL 12/15/01) [973]

8387 *A Patriot's Handbook: Songs, Poems, Stories, and Speeches Celebrating the Land We Love* (9–12). Ed. by Caroline Kennedy. Illus. 2003, Hyperion $24.95 (0-7868-6918-6). Compiled by Caroline Kennedy, this anthology of patriotic stories, poems, speeches, and other documents ranges from the lyrics of "The Star-Spangled Banner" to the text of the Supreme Court's decision in Brown *v.* the Board of Education. (Rev: BL 3/1/03) [810]

8388 Reader's Digest, eds. *America's Historic Places: An Illustrated Guide to Our Country's Past* (9–12). Illus. 1988, Reader's Digest $29.95 (0-89577-265-5). A guided tour in words and pictures of 500 important sites. (Rev: BL 5/15/88) [917.3]

8389 Reader's Digest, eds. *Reader's Digest Strange Stories, Amazing Facts of America's Past* (9–12). Illus. 1989, Reader's Digest $32.95 (0-89577-307-4). A collection of unusual facts and anecdotes about the famous and infamous in American history with a chronological index by month and year. (Rev: BL 11/1/89) [973]

8390 Reeves, Thomas C. *Twentieth-Century America: A Brief History* (10–12). 2000, Oxford paper $28.95 (0-19-504484-3). A concise history of the United States in the 20th century. [973.9]

8391 Ruth, Maria Mudd. *The Mississippi River* (7–12). Illus. Series: Ecosystems of North America. 2000, Benchmark LB $18.95 (0-7614-0934-3). A detailed look at the largest river in North America, its flora and fauna, and the effects of human development on the ecosystem. (Rev: HBG 3/01; SLJ 4/01) [577.6]

8392 Rydell, Robert W., et al. *Fair America: World's Fairs in the United States* (8–12). 2000, Smithsonian $29.95 (1-56098-968-8); paper $15.95 (1-56098-384-1). This book examines world's fairs held in the United States from 1853 to 1984. [907]

8393 Schneider, Richard H. *Stars and Stripes Forever: The History, Stories, and Memories of Our American Flag* (10–12). Illus. 2003, Morrow $14.95 (0-06-052537-1). This celebration of the flag provides a history of its development, assorted flag trivia, and a number of moving flag-related anecdotes from military personnel, celebrities, and ordinary citizens. (Rev: BL 6/1–15/03) [929.9]

8394 Sedeen, Margaret. *Star-Spangled Banner: Our Nation and Its Flag* (9–12). 1993, National Geographic $37.50 (0-87044-944-3). Legends — such as the tale of Betsy Ross — are sorted from fact in this history of the U.S. flag, from Francis Scott Key to the modern controversy about flag desecration. Color photographs. (Rev: BL 10/15/93) [929.9]

8395 Sheafer, Silvia A. *Women in America's Wars* (6–12). Illus. 1996, Enslow LB $20.95 (0-89490-553-8). From the American Revolution to the Persian Gulf War, this account profiles 10 women and the amazingly diversified roles they played in U.S. wars. (Rev: BL 4/15/96; BR 9–10/96; SLJ 5/96; VOYA 6/96) [355]

8396 Sinclair, Andrew. *A Concise History of the United States* (9–12). Illus. 2000, Sutton paper $19.95 (0-7509-2351-2). This brief overview of important events, personalities, achievements, and ideals relating to American history contains many useful illustrations. (Rev: BL 4/15/00) [973]

8397 *Slavery* (7–12). Ed. by James D. Torr. Series: Opposing Viewpoints: World History. 2004, Gale LB $33.70 (0-7377-1705-X). Various perspectives of slavery are presented through carefully selected primary documents; includes coverage of events leading to the Civil War. (Rev: BL 2/15/04) [306.3]

8398 Smith, Martin J., and Patrick J. Kiger. *Poplorica: A Popular History of the Fads, Mavericks, Inventors, and Lore that Shaped America* (10–12). 2004, HarperResource $22.95 (0-06-053531-8). A fascinating look at the unexpected influence on American culture of items such as air conditioning, panty hose, and lawn care. (Rev: BL 3/1/04) [306]

8399 Sonneborn, Liz. *The American West: An Illustrated History* (6–12). Illus. 2002, Scholastic $19.95 (0-439-21970-1). An inviting introduction to the settlement of the American West, beginning with the first Native Americans and ending in the present day. (Rev: BL 12/15/02; HBG 3/03; SLJ 2/03) [978]

8400 Stone, Nathaniel. *On the Water: Discovering America in a Rowboat* (10–12). 2002, Broadway $21.95 (0-7679-0841-4). In this engaging memoir/travel book, the author describes his 6,000-mile journey in and around America and the many fascinating people and places he encountered along the way. (Rev: BL 7/02*) [917.304]

8401 Streissguth, Thomas. *Utopian Visionaries* (7–12). Illus. 1999, Oliver LB $19.95 (1-881508-47-1). This account presents material on attempts to build utopian communities in the U.S. during the 18th and 19th centuries by such visionaries as Ann Lee, a Shaker, and John Humphrey Noyes, who created the Oneida community. (Rev: BL 12/15/99; HBG 4/00; SLJ 11/99) [321]

8402 Sullivan, Mark, and Dan Rather, ed. *Our Times* (10–12). 1996, Scribner $40.00 (0-684-81573-7). This is a history of the United States from the 1890s to the late 1920s that conveys what the average person of the day thought of such topics as flight, automobiles, Teddy Roosevelt, World War I, jazz, unions, and Woodrow Wilson, using primary source documents. (Rev: BL 12/15/95; SLJ 8/96) [973.9]

8403 Thompson, Kathleen, and Hilary Mac Austin. *America's Children: Picturing Childhood from Early America to the Present* (10–12). Illus. 2002, Norton $39.95 (0-393-05182-X). Children's lives at home, at school, and at work are portrayed in narrative, photographs, and extracts from primary sources. (Rev: BL 10/1/02) [305.23]

8404 Torricelli, Robert G., and Andrew Carroll. *In Our Own Words: Extraordinary Speeches of the American Century* (10–12). 1999, Kodansha $28.00 (1-56836-291-9). A collection of texts that includes sermons, "fireside chats," eulogies, and other forms of speeches that were delivered throughout the 20th century. (Rev: BL 10/15/99; SLJ 4/00) [815.008]

8405 Uschan, Michael V. *The 1910s* (7–10). Illus. 1998, Lucent LB $27.45 (1-56006-551-6). This volume presents an overview of the 1910s, highlighting social and technical developments as well as the U.S. role in world affairs and World War I. (Rev: SLJ 4/99) [973.9]

8406 Uschan, Michael V. *The 1940s* (5–10). Series: Cultural History of the United States. 1998, Lucent LB $18.96 (1-56510-554-0). Life at home and abroad during World War II dominate this book, which also discusses the Great Depression, the New Deal, events leading up to U.S. participation in the war, the beginnings of the Cold War, the growth of suburban living, and the rise of television, with sidebars on such topics as the Holocaust, the influences of radio, movies, and comics, 1940s slang, and the first computers. (Rev: SLJ 1/99) [973.9]

8407 Vesilind, Priit. *National Geographic on Assignment U.S.A.* (10–12). 1997, National Geographic $50.00 (0-7922-7010-X). This masterpiece of photojournalism chronicles life in the United States as it explores both the geography of the country and the diversity of its people and their activities. (Rev: SLJ 5/98) [917.3]

8408 Watson, Robert P. *The Presidents' Wives: Reassessing the Office of the First Lady* (10–12). 2000, Lynne Rienner $55.00 (1-55587-860-1). A history of the evolution of the office of the First Lady, with a chapter that ranks the first ladies by a variety of criteria. (Rev: BL 1/1–15/00) [973]

8409 *We Americans: Celebrating a Nation, Its People, Its Past* (9–12). Ed. by Thomas B. Allen and Charles O. Hyman. Illus. 1999, National Geographic $40.00 (0-7922-7005-3). Using excellent illustrations and commentary by eminent historians and writers, this is a fine book for browsing America's past and present. (Rev: BL 3/1/00) [973]

8410 Weinstein, Allen, and David Rubel. *The Story of America: Freedom and Crisis from Settlement to Superpower* (10–12). Illus. 2002, DK $35.00 (0-7894-8903-1). A concise and visual survey that uses 26 narratives recounting pivotal moments in U.S. history. (Rev: BL 11/15/02) [973]

8411 Wormser, Richard. *American Childhoods: Three Centuries of Youth at Risk* (7–12). Illus. 1996, Walker LB $17.85 (0-8027-8427-5). A graphic, realistic picture of childhood and growing up in America from the repressive Puritans to the present day with chapters on work, crime, disease, education, sex, and related topics. (Rev: BL 9/15/96; BR 11–12/96; SLJ 9/96; VOYA 12/96) [305.23]

8412 Wormser, Richard. *Hoboes: Wandering in America, 1870–1940* (6–12). Illus. 1994, Walker $17.95 (0-8027-8279-5). This account covers the history, rules, literature, songs, and customs of those who rode the rails from the end of the Civil War to the outbreak of World War II. (Rev: BL 6/1–15/94; SLJ 7/94) [305.5]

8413 Wukovits, John F., ed. *The 1910s* (6–12). Series: America's Decades. 2000, Greenhaven LB $29.96 (0-7377-0296-6); paper $17.96 (0-7377-0295-8). Articles in this anthology cover important events of the decade, including World War I, and introduce such personalities as Charlie Chaplin, Woodrow Wilson, and Henry Ford. (Rev: BL 7/00) [973.9]

8414 Wukovits, John F., ed. *The 1920s* (6–12). Series: America's Decades. 2000, Greenhaven LB $29.96 (0-7377-0298-2); paper $17.96 (0-7377-0297-4). This anthology of articles about the 20s covers such topics as prohibition, the stock market crash of 1929, and the rising importance of radio. (Rev: BL 7/00; SLJ 9/00) [973.9]

8415 Young, Dwight, and Ira Block. *Saving America's Treasures: National Trust for Historic Preservation* (9–12). 2000, National Geographic $35.00 (0-7922-7942-5). This splendid book highlights in text and pictures 43 places, artifacts, and documents

that the National Trust has restored and preserved. (Rev: BL 11/1/00) [973]

Historical Periods

NATIVE AMERICANS

8416 Acatoz, Sylvio. *Pueblos: Prehistoric Indian Cultures of the Southwest* (9–12). Trans. by Barbara Fritzemeier. 1990, Facts on File $45.00 (0-8160-2437-5). An illustrated study of early Indian culture in the American Southwest. (Rev: BL 4/15/91) [979]

8417 Ake, Anne. *The Apache* (7–10). Series: Indigenous Peoples of North America. 2000, Lucent LB $19.96 (1-56006-616-4). The fierce warriors of the American Southwest are featured with material on their history, religion, culture, and present affairs. One of several recommended titles in this series. (Rev: BL 9/15/00) [973]

8418 Baillargeon, Morgan, and Leslie Tepper. *Legends of Our Times: Native Cowboy Life* (10–12). Illus. 1998, Univ. of Washington Pr. $38.95 (0-295-97728-0). Richly illustrated, this well-researched book shows how native peoples in North America's Great Plains region were able to retain their cultural heritage while adopting a cowboy way of life. (Rev: BL 12/1/98) [971.2]

8419 Barth, Kelly. *Native Americans of the Northwest Plateau* (7–10). Series: Indigenous Peoples of North America. 2002, Gale LB $27.45 (1-56006-877-9). This work explores the social, cultural, and political history and contemporary life of these groups of Native Americans found in the central Northwest. (Rev: BL 4/15/02) [970.004]

8420 Baughman, Michael. *Mohawk Blood* (9–12). 1995, Lyons Pr. $19.95 (1-55821-376-7). Past and present struggles with Indian tradition and nonnative ways, from the grandson of the great Mohawk war chief Joseph Brant. (Rev: BL 3/1/95) [973]

8421 Bjornlund, Lydia. *The Iroquois* (7–10). Series: Indigenous Peoples of North America. 2000, Lucent LB $19.96 (1-56006-618-0). This volume gives material on the history, culture, and present condition of the Indian nation that was the most powerful Native American group in the 17th century. (Rev: BL 9/15/00) [973]

8422 Bond, Fred G. *Flatboating on the Yellowstone, 1877* (7–12). 1998, Ward Hill $19.95 (1-886747-03-2). A first-person account of the relocation in 1877 of Chief Joseph and other Nez Perce Indians from Oregon to Oklahoma by raft down the Yellowstone and Missouri Rivers, written by their pilot, who documented the trip for the New York Public Library in 1925. (Rev: BL 12/15/98) [973]

8423 Bonvillain, Nancy. *Native American Religion* (6–10). Series: Indians of North America. 1995, Chelsea LB $21.95 (0-7910-2652-3); paper $9.95

(0-7910-3479-8). Explanations of native spiritual life, emphasizing the natural world and the earth. Also discusses holistic approaches toward illness and well-being. (Rev: BL 3/1/96; SLJ 2/96) [973]

8424 Brown, Dee. *Bury My Heart at Wounded Knee: An Indian History of the American West* (10–12). 1971, Holt $27.50 (0-8050-1045-9). The story of the white man's conquest of the Old West told from the Indians' point of view. [970.004]

8425 Bruchac, Joseph. *Lasting Echoes: An Oral History of Native American People* (7–12). Illus. 1997, Harcourt $16.00 (0-15-201327-X). Beginning with the welcoming speeches that Indian leaders delivered to the first Europeans, this work traces the history of Native Americans through their own words. (Rev: BCCB 3/98; BL 12/15/97; HBG 3/98; SLJ 3/98; VOYA 10/98) [973]

8426 Bruchac, Joseph. *The Native American Sweat Lodge: History and Legends* (9–12). 1993, Crossing paper $12.95 (0-89594-636-X). Bruchac celebrates the importance of the sweat lodge (lodges or huts heated by steam from water poured on hot stones) in this overview of its history, meaning, and use. Includes 25 traditional Native American poems and stories. (Rev: BL 10/15/93) [391]

8427 Calloway, Colin G. *Indians of the Northeast* (6–10). Series: First Americans. 1991, Facts on File LB $26.35 (0-8160-2389-1). Focuses on the major tribes of the region. Coverage includes the French and Indian Wars and the government's policy toward Native Americans today. (Rev: BL 1/15/92) [974]

8428 Calvert, Patricia. *Standoff at Standing Rock: The Story of Sitting Bull and James McLaughlin* (6–12). Illus. 2001, Twenty-First Century LB $24.90 (0-7613-1360-5). The confrontation between these two determined men serves as the central focus of an examination of the treatment of Native Americans, the Indian Wars, boarding schools, and the efforts to impose new beliefs. (Rev: BL 2/15/01; HBG 10/01; VOYA 12/01) [978.004]

8429 Child, Brenda J. *Boarding School Seasons: American Indian Families, 1900–1940* (10–12). Illus. 1998, Univ. of Nebraska Pr. $35.00 (0-8032-1480-4). The Native American author draws on her own experiences and those of others to paint a moving portrait of early-20th-century boarding schools for Native Americans. (Rev: BL 12/1/98) [970.004]

8430 Coe, Michael D., et al. *Atlas of Ancient America* (10–12). Illus. 1986, Facts on File $45.00 (0-8160-1199-0). A colorful collection of maps and other illustrations plus a comprehensive text explore the various Indian groups and their homelands. (Rev: BL 1/1/87; SLJ 3/87) [970]

8431 Cooper, Michael L. *Indian School: Teaching the White Man's Way* (5–10). Illus. 1999, Clarion $16.00 (0-395-92084-1). A moving photoessay

about Native American children and how they were removed from their homes and uprooted from their culture to attend Indian boarding schools in an effort to "civilize" them. (Rev: BL 12/1/99; HBG 3/00; SLJ 2/00; VOYA 4/00) [370]

8432 Curtis, Edward S. *Native Nations: First Americans as Seen by Edward S. Curtis* (9–12). 1993, Little, Brown $75.00 (0-8212-2052-7). One hundred plates and excerpts of Curtis's work illustrate this smaller version of the original book. (Rev: BL 11/15/93) [306]

8433 Curtis, Edward S. *The Plains Indian Photography of Edward S. Curtis* (10–12). Illus. 2001, Univ. of Nebraska Pr. $50.00 (0-8032-1512-6). For more than 20 years, Curtis photographed the North American Indian. This is a compilation of 91 of his greatest photographs, with essays by four scholars and commentary by Curtis himself. (Rev: BL 7/01) [779]

8434 Debo, Angie. *A History of the Indians of the United States* (10–12). Series: Civilization of the American Indian. 1970, Univ. of Oklahoma Pr. paper $24.95 (0-8061-1888-1). This is a historical survey of the Indians of North America with material on the Eskimos and Aleuts of Alaska. [970.004]

8435 Deloria, Vine, Jr. *Custer Died for Your Sins: An Indian Manifesto* (10–12). 1969, Macmillan paper $19.95 (0-8061-2129-7). The author tellingly and, at times, shockingly, reconstructs the history of the Native American. [970.004]

8436 Dramer, Kim. *Native Americans and Black Americans* (7–10). Illus. Series: Indians of North America. 1997, Chelsea LB $19.95 (0-7910-2653-1). This work gives a historic overview of the relationship between these two groups through slavery, the Civil War, land battles, segregation, and various political movements, as well as a basic history of each group's struggle for civil rights. (Rev: BL 8/97; SLJ 9/97) [303.48]

8437 Dudley, William, ed. *Native Americans* (9–12). Illus. Series: Opposing Viewpoints: American History. 1998, Greenhaven LB $21.96 (1-56510-705-5); paper $16.20 (1-56510-704-7). The complex relationship between Native Americans and European settlers is discussed in this collection of documents, beginning with Powhatan's dealings with John Smith and ending with the recent American Indian Movement. (Rev: BL 4/1/98) [973]

8438 Durrett, Deanne. *Healers* (8–12). Series: American Indian Lives. 1997, Facts on File $17.95 (0-8160-3460-0). This work profiles 12 Native American healers, ranging from the traditional medicine man to modern physicians and nurses. (Rev: VOYA 8/97) [973]

8439 Engels, Mary Tate, ed. *Tales from Wide Ruins: Jean and Bill Cousins, Traders* (10–12). 1996, Texas Tech Univ. Pr. $29.95 (0-89672-368-2). The

Cousines were traders with Native Americans during the 1930s and 1940s. This book presents the stories they heard and experiences they had involving the past life of Native Americans and other ethnic groups living in the desert of the Southwest. (Rev: SLJ 12/96) [979]

8440 Fronval, George, and Daniel Dubois. *Indian Signs and Signals* (9–12). Trans. by E. W. Egan. Illus. 1985, Crown $12.99 (0-517-46612-0). In thorough text and many illustrations, this book describes the sign language of the Plains Indian. [001.56]

8441 Gilbert, Joan. *The Trail of Tears Across Missouri* (10–12). 1996, Univ. of Missouri Pr. paper $9.95 (0-8262-1063-5). A simple retelling of the forced exodus of the Cherokee people. [970.004]

8442 Girod, Christina M. *Native Americans of the Southeast* (7–10). Series: Indigenous Peoples of North America. 2000, Lucent LB $19.96 (1-56006-610-5). The native peoples of the Southeast are featured with material on systems of government, lifestyles, struggle for survival, and attempts to preserve their unique heritage and culture. (Rev: BL 9/15/00) [973]

8443 Goetzmann, William H. *The First Americans: Photographs from the Library of Congress* (9–12). 1991, Starwood $34.95 (0-912347-96-1). This collection of turn-of-the-century commercial photographs of Native Americans illustrates the "sentimental notions about the vanishing American" popular at the time. (Rev: BL 11/15/91) [973.0497]

8444 Hirschfelder, Arlene B. *Native Americans: A History in Pictures* (9–12). Illus. 2000, DK $24.95 (0-7894-5162-X). A large, mainly pictorial book that traces the history of Native Americans and their cultures from ancestral times to the present, in part through excerpts from Indian autobiographies. (Rev: BL 6/1–15/00) [970.004]

8445 Hoig, Stan. *Night of the Cruel Moon: Cherokee Removal and the Trail of Tears* (7–10). Illus. Series: Library of American Indian History. 1996, Facts on File $25.00 (0-8160-3307-2). Using original sources and first-person narratives, this well-documented account describes the tragic Cherokee Trail of Tears and the complexities of the situation. (Rev: BL 7/96) [976.6]

8446 Johansen, Bruce E., and Donald A. Grinde, Jr. *Encyclopedia of Native American Biography: Six Hundred Life Stories of Important People from Powhatan to Wilma Mankiller* (9–12). 1997, Holt $50.00 (0-8050-3270-3). Though intended for an adult audience, this is an easily read collective biographical work listing hundreds of Native and non-Native Americans who played significant roles in Native American history and culture. (Rev: BL 5/1/97; BR 9–10/97; SLJ 2/98) [973]

8447 Jones, Constance. *The European Conquest of North America* (7–12). 1995, Facts on File $25.00 (0-8160-3041-3). A detailed account of Native American cultures and the methods used by European conquerors to subdue them. (Rev: BL 5/1/95) [970.01]

8448 Jones, Veda Boyd. *Native Americans of the Northwest Coast* (7–10). Series: Indigenous Peoples of North America. 2000, Lucent LB $19.96 (1-56006-691-1). This account features the native peoples of the Pacific coast from Alaska south to Washington and how they created a unique culture and art including totem poles. (Rev: BL 9/15/00) [973]

8449 Josephy, Alvin M. *500 Nations: An Illustrated History of North American Indians* (9–12). 1994, Knopf $50.00 (0-679-42930-1). This companion to the television documentary gives a chronological overview of the history of North American Indians from ancient legends to the present. (Rev: BL 10/15/94; SLJ 6/95) [970.004]

8450 Josephy, Alvin M. *The Indian Heritage of America* (10–12). Illus. 1991, Houghton paper $15.00 (0-395-57320-3). This is a fine survey of the cultures and history of the Native Americans of North, Central, and South America. [970.004]

8451 Kallen, Stuart A. *Native Americans of the Great Lakes* (7–10). Illus. Series: Indigenous Peoples of North America. 1999, Lucent LB $18.96 (1-56006-568-0). This book covers the history, culture, and famous people connected with the Six Nations of the Iroquois in the east around the Great Lakes and the Algonquins in the west. (Rev: BL 3/1/00; HBG 9/00) [977.004]

8452 Kallen, Stuart A. *Native Americans of the Northeast* (7–10). Series: Indigenous Peoples of North America. 2000, Lucent LB $18.96 (1-56006-629-6). Kallen looks at the history, culture, religion, and conflicts of these Indians, with material on their daily lives in the past and today. (Rev: BL 3/15/00; BR 11–12/00; HBG 9/00; SLJ 5/00) [973]

8453 Kallen, Stuart A. *Native Americans of the Southwest* (7–10). Series: Indigenous Peoples of North America. 2000, Lucent LB $18.96 (1-56006-681-4). This account covers the daily lives, past and present, and culture of tribes including the Hopi, Navajo, and Zuni. (Rev: BL 8/00; HBG 3/01; SLJ 9/00) [973]

8454 Kallen, Stuart A. *The Pawnee* (7–10). Series: Indigenous Peoples of North America. 2002, Gale LB $27.45 (1-56006-825-6). The history and contributions of this Native American group who lived in the Midwest and were the enemies of their neighbors, the Cheyenne. (Rev: BL 4/15/02) [970.004]

8455 Katz, Jane B., ed. *We Rode the Wind: Recollections of Native American Life*. Rev. ed. (6–10). 1995, Lerner LB $22.60 (0-8225-3154-2). A collection of the autobiographical writings of eight notable Native Americans, among them Charles

Eastman and Black Elk, who grew up on the Great Plains. (Rev: BL 2/1/96; SLJ 12/95) [978]

8456 Klots, Steve. *Native Americans and Christianity* (7–10). Illus. Series: Indians of North America. 1997, Chelsea paper $9.95 (0-7910-4463-7). The story of how early explorers and settlers tried to convert Native Americans to Christianity, the forms that this religion took, and the many ways Native Americans practice their religion today. (Rev: BL 8/97; SLJ 9/97) [277]

8457 Lassieur, Allison. *Before the Storm: American Indians Before the Europeans* (7–12). Series: Library of American Indian History. 1998, Facts on File $25.00 (0-8160-3651-9). This unique study reports on the flourishing civilizations of seven "precontact Native American" peoples before contact with the European invaders. (Rev: BL 11/15/98; BR 1–2/99; SLJ 9/98) [970]

8458 Liptak, Karen. *Indians of the Southwest* (6–10). Series: First Americans. 1991, Facts on File $26.35 (0-8160-2385-9). Describes the first Indian inhabitants of the area and highlights their social, political, and religious life before and after contact with Europeans. (Rev: BL 1/15/92) [979]

8459 Long, Cathryn J. *The Cherokee* (7–10). Series: Indigenous Peoples of North America. 2000, Lucent LB $18.96 (1-56006-617-2). The story of the Cherokee from their origins in the southern Appalachian mountains, through the Trail of Tears to Oklahoma, to their present status. (Rev: BL 3/15/00; HBG 9/00; VOYA 6/01) [973]

8460 McCormick, Anita Louise. *Native Americans and the Reservation in American History* (7–10). Illus. Series: American History. 1996, Enslow LB $20.95 (0-89490-769-7). An overview of the relationship between whites and Native Americans that covers hundreds of years of history and discusses the cruelty of forced marches and life on the reservations. (Rev: BL 1/1–15/97; BR 3–4/97; SLJ 2/97) [973]

8461 McCutchen, David. *The Red Record: The Wallam Olum of the Lenni Lenape* (9–12). 1993, Avery paper $14.95 (0-89529-525-3). A translation/interpretation of the Wallam Olum, an ancient history of the Lenni Lenape (Delaware) Indians. (Rev: BL 2/15/93*; VOYA 10/93) [973]

8462 Marrin, Albert. *Plains Warrior: Chief Quanah Parker and the Comanches* (6–10). Illus. 1996, Simon & Schuster $18.00 (0-689-80081-9). The story of the great Comanche leader and his clashes with U.S. policy toward Native Americans makes for fine historical writing enlivened with many photographs. (Rev: BL 6/1–15/96*; BR 3–4/97; SLJ 6/96; VOYA 8/96) [973]

8463 Miller, Lee, ed. *From the Heart: Voices of the American Indian* (9–12). 1995, Knopf $24.00 (0-679-43549-2). An anthology of four centuries of

Northern Hemisphere Native American speeches, excerpts, and quotations. (Rev: BL 5/15/95) [973]

8464 Nichols, Roger L. *American Indians in U.S. History* (10–12). Illus. 2003, Univ. of Oklahoma Pr. $29.95 (0-8061-3557-3). Interactions between Native Americans and early European settlers are a central focus in this ambitious and effective survey. (Rev: BL 11/15/03) [973.04]

8465 Nies, Judith. *Native American History: A Chronology of a Culture's Vast Achievements and Their Links to World Events* (6–12). 1997, Ballantine paper $15.00 (0-345-39350-3). This chronology of Native North American history and culture from 28,000 B.C. through 1996, using a split-page format to juxtapose simultaneous political, social, religious, and military developments occurring in North America and in other parts of the world. (Rev: SLJ 5/97) [970.003]

8466 *North American Indian Wars* (9–12). Ed. by Don Nardo. Series: Turning Points in World History. 1999, Greenhaven LB $32.45 (1-56510-959-7); paper $22.45 (1-56510-958-9). Seventeen essays discuss the wars between Native American tribes and the United States, focusing on the effect the wars had on the Native American population and culture. (Rev: BL 9/1/99; SLJ 11/99) [973]

8467 Page, Jake. *In the Hands of the Great Spirit: The 20,000-Year History of American Indians* (10–12). Illus. 2003, Free Pr. $30.00 (0-684-85576-3). In this sweeping survey of Native American history, Page covers key events, personalities, characteristics and beliefs, and interactions between Indians and European settlers. (Rev: BL 4/15/03) [973.04]

8468 Red Shirt, Delphine. *Bead on an Anthill: A Lakota Childhood* (10–12). 1998, Univ. of Nebraska Pr. $25.00 (0-8032-3908-4); paper $9.95 (0-8032-8976-6). The story of a Lakota Indian woman, her childhood on a reservation in South Dakota in the 1960s and 1970s, and her memories of the culture and traditions of her people. (Rev: SLJ 11/98) [909]

8469 Remington, Gwen. *The Cheyenne* (7–10). Series: Indigenous Peoples of North America. 2000, Lucent LB $19.96 (1-56006-750-0). The story of the past and present of the nomadic rulers of the High Plains who were considered to be the most civilized of the Great Plains Indians. (Rev: BL 9/15/00) [973]

8470 Richter, Daniel. *Facing East from Indian Country: A Native History History of Early America* (10–12). Illus. 2001, Harvard $26.00 (0-674-00638-0). Scholarly but readable, this is the story of Native Americans and their culture before and during the arrival of white men. (Rev: BL 11/15/01*) [970]

8471 Roberts, David. *In Search of the Old Ones: Exploring the Anasazi World of the Southwest* (10–12). 1996, Simon & Schuster $24.00 (0-684-

81078-6). This account takes the reader back 1,000 years to explore the life and culture of the "ancient ones," the Anasazi, the people of the Southwest who disappeared. (Rev: BL 3/1/96; SLJ 7/96) [973]

8472 Robinson, Charles M. *A Good Year to Die: The Story of the Great Sioux War* (9–12). 1995, Random $27.50 (0-679-43025-3). A balanced narrative about the Great Sioux War (1876), in which Custer, Crazy Horse, and George Crook were major figures. (Rev: BL 9/1/95) [973.8]

8473 Rozema, Vicki. *Voices from the Trail of Tears* (10–12). 2003, John F. Blair paper $11.95 (0-89587-271-4). Primary sources, including many first-person accounts, make this an affecting portrait of the government-mandated relocation of the Cherokees. (Rev: BL 4/15/03) [973.04]

8474 Sandoz, Mari. *The Battle of the Little Bighorn* (10–12). 1966, Amereon $20.95 (0-89190-879-X). The story of this battle in the war against the Sioux and of the ambitions of General Custer. [973.8]

8475 Sandoz, Mari. *Cheyenne Autumn* (10–12). Illus. 1976, Avon paper $4.95 (0-380-01094-1). The heartbreaking saga of the Cheyenne Indian trek in 1878 back to their home in Yellowstone. [970.004]

8476 Sherrow, Victoria. *Cherokee Nation v. Georgia: Native American Rights* (6–10). Series: Landmark Supreme Court Cases. 1997, Enslow LB $20.95 (0-89490-856-1). This book re-creates vividly the important case of 1831 when the Supreme Court ruled that the Cherokee tribe was a "domestic, dependent nation" and not liable to regulation by the state of Georgia. (Rev: BL 10/15/97; HBG 3/98) [973]

8477 *The Story of the Blackfoot People: Nitsitapiisinni* (7–12). Illus. 2001, Firefly paper $15.95 (1-55297-583-5). Blackfoot leaders reveal details of their people's history, beliefs, social structure, traditions, and culture, with numerous photographs and a glossary of Blackfoot terms. (Rev: BL 2/15/02; SLJ 3/02) [970.004]

8478 Streissguth, Thomas. *The Comanche* (7–10). Series: Indigenous Peoples of North America. 2000, Lucent LB $18.96 (1-56006-633-4). The history of these fierce raiders and expert horsemen who became the "Masters of the South," and one of the most feared of all Native American tribes. (Rev: BL 8/00; HBG 3/01) [973]

8479 Streissguth, Thomas. *Wounded Knee, 1890: The End of the Plains Indian Wars* (7–12). Illus. Series: Library of American Indian History. 1998, Facts on File $25.00 (0-8160-3600-4). Using primary sources from soldiers, pioneers, missionaries, reporters, and Lakota Indians, this is the story of the events of 1890 that led to the devastation of an entire race. (Rev: BL 10/1/98; BR 1–2/99) [973.8]

8480 Swisher, Karen Gayton, and AnCita Benally. *Native North American Firsts* (9–12). 1997, Gale $70.00 (0-7876-0518-2). Notable accomplishments of Native Americans over a timespan of nearly ten millennia are organized in categories such as arts and crafts, language and law, and Indian rights and activism. (Rev: BL 2/15/98) [970.004]

8481 Tehanetorens. *Roots of the Iroquois* (7–10). Illus. 2000, Native Voices paper $9.95 (1-57067-097-8). A lively, detailed look at the history of the Iroquois Confederation before and after the arrival of European settlers. (Rev: BL 11/15/00) [974.004]

8482 Thompson, William N. *Native American Issues: A Reference Handbook* (9–12). 1996, ABC-CLIO $39.50 (0-87436-828-6). This is a fascinating reference book that provides an overview of major issues concerning Native Americans in the United States and Canada, summaries of such critical issues as land claims and sacred sites, religious freedom, gaming on reservations, political jurisdiction, and water rights, and discussions of Native sovereignty and court cases and legislation. (Rev: BR 5–6/97; SLJ 8/97) [909]

8483 Waldman, Carl. *Atlas of the North American Indian* (9–12). Illus. 1985, Facts on File $35.00 (0-87196-850-9). Maps and accompanying essays give an excellent introduction to the history, culture, and present-day status of the American Indian. (Rev: BL 1/15/86) [970]

8484 Wallace, Anthony F. C. *The Long, Bitter Trail: Andrew Jackson and the Indians* (9–12). 1993, Hill & Wang paper $8.00 (0-8090-1552-8). The story of the forced removal of the Cherokees over the Trail of Tears to the Oklahoma Territory in the 1830s. (Rev: BL 7/93; SLJ 12/93) [323.1]

8485 Welch, James, and Paul Stekler. *Killing Custer: The Battle of the Little Big Horn and the Fate of the Plains Indians* (9–12). 1994, Norton $25.00 (0-393-03657-X). Examines Custer's death at Little Bighorn and the Great Sioux War from a Native American perspective. (Rev: BL 11/1/94) [973.8]

8486 Williams, Jeanne. *Trails of Tears: American Indians Driven from Their Lands* (9–12). 1992, Hendrick-Long $15.95 (0-937460-76-1). Details the U.S. government's forced removal of Comanche, Cheyenne, Apache, Navajo, and Cherokee Indians from their native lands. (Rev: BL 6/1/92) [973]

8487 Wood, Nancy. *Sacred Fire* (7–12). Illus. 1998, Bantam $25.00 (0-385-32515-0). This meditation on the world of the Pueblo Indians, their beliefs about nature, and the drastic change in their lives after the Spanish invasion in 1540, is illustrated with breathtakingly beautiful paintings by Frank Howell. (Rev: BL 7/98; HBG 3/99; SLJ 10/98) [973]

8488 Woodhead, Edward, ed. *The Woman's Way* (9–12). 1995, Time-Life $19.95 (0-8094-9729-8). Explains the traditional duties and customs of North American Indian women throughout history, with biographical sketches of several well-known Native American women. (Rev: BL 9/1/95; SLJ 11/95) [305.48]

DISCOVERY AND EXPLORATION

8489 Clark, William, and Meriwether Lewis. *The Essential Lewis and Clark* (10–12). Ed. by Landon Y. Jones. 2000, HarperCollins $24.00 (0-06-019600-9). This is a collection of the most exciting and beautiful passages from the journal of these explorers, chronicling the highlights of their incredible journey. (Rev: BL 2/15/00) [917.8]

8490 Duncan, Dayton, and Ken Burns. *Lewis and Clark: The Journey of the Corps of Discovery* (9–12). 1997, Knopf paper $25.00 (0-375-70652-6). A beautifully illustrated companion to a PBS special of the same name, this book chronicles the epic journey from St. Louis through uncharted territory to the Pacific Ocean. (Rev: BL 8/97) [978]

8491 Faber, Harold. *The Discoverers of America* (6–12). 1992, Scribner $17.95 (0-684-19217-9). Discusses the exploration of North and South America, focusing on the period from Columbus to Lewis and Clark. (Rev: BL 5/15/92; SLJ 6/92) [970.01]

8492 Findling, John E., and Frank W. Thackeray. *Events that Changed America Through the Seventeenth Century* (10–12). 2000, Greenwood $39.95 (0-313-29083-0). Ten important events from the 17th century, such as Coronado's expedition and the founding of St. Augustine, are detailed in this book. [973.2]

8493 Lepore, Jill. *Encounters in the New World: A History in Documents* (7–12). Series: Pages from History. 1999, Oxford LB $32.95 (0-19-510513-3). Documents including letters, journals, and advertisements make relations between Native Americans and European arrivals more real to readers. (Rev: BR 3–4/00; HBG 9/00; SLJ 3/00) [970]

8494 MacGregor, Greg. *Lewis and Clark Revisited: A Photographer's Trail* (8–12). Ed. by Iris Tillman Hill. Illus. 2004, Univ. of Washington Pr. $50.00 (0-295-98342-6). This book, which contains many eye-catching photographs, traces the route of the Lewis and Clark expedition in 1804-06 and shows the route as it looks today. (Rev: BL 2/15/04) [917.804]

8495 McLaughlin, Castle, et al. *Arts of Diplomacy: Lewis and Clark's Indian Collection* (9–12). Illus. 2004, Univ. of Washington Pr. $60.00 (0-295-98360-4). Amazing photography is used to show the collection now in Harvard's Peabody Museum of artifacts that Lewis and Clark gathered on their expedition. (Rev: BL 2/15/04) [978.004]

COLONIAL PERIOD AND FRENCH AND INDIAN WARS

8496 Aronson, Marc. *Witch-Hunt: Mysteries of the Salem Witch Trials* (9–12). Illus. 2003, Simon & Schuster $18.95 (0-689-84864-1). This scholarly yet absorbing study thoughtfully examines the factors that led to the infamous witch trials in late-17th-century Massachusetts. (Rev: BL 11/1/03; HBG 4/04; SLJ 12/03; VOYA 12/03) [133.4]

8497 Boorstin, Daniel J. *The Americans: The Colonial Experience* (10–12). 1958, Random paper $15.00 (0-394-70513-0). This scholarly work about our colonial period traces its history and shows how it gave birth to a distinctive culture. [973.2]

8498 Copeland, David A. *Debating the Issues in Colonial Newspapers: Primary Documents on Events of the Period* (9–12). 2000, Greenwood $59.95 (0-313-30982-5). This is a collection of original documents from the colonial period that express differing views on such topics as women's rights, censorship, and separation from Britain. (Rev: BL 1/1–15/01; SLJ 2/01) [973.2]

8499 Edwards, Judith. *Jamestown: John Smith and Pocahontas in American History* (6–10). Series: In American History. 2002, Enslow LB $20.95 (0-7660-1842-3). This is a well-documented account that describes this crucial period in American colonial history and the key people involved. (Rev: BL 5/15/02; HBG 10/02) [973.2]

8500 Gray, Edward G. *Colonial America: A History in Documents* (9–12). Ed. by Edward G. Gray. Illus. Series: Pages from History. 2002, Oxford LB $32.95 (0-19-513747-7). Excerpts from primary sources — accompanied by reproductions of documents, maps, and works of art — shed light on the lifestyles and important issues of the colonial period. (Rev: BL 2/15/03; SLJ 3/03) [973.2]

8501 Hansen, Chadwick. *Witchcraft at Salem* (9–12). Illus. 1969, Braziller $12.95 (0-8076-0492-5); paper $11.95 (0-8076-1137-9). A readable, well-researched account of the Salem witch hunt and of colonial life in New England. [133.4]

8502 Hawke, David Freeman. *Everyday Life in Early America* (9–12). Illus. 1988, HarperCollins paper $13.00 (0-06-091251-0). A detailed account of what life was like for the average colonists in America. (Rev: BL 12/1/87; SLJ 12/88) [973.2]

8503 Hill, Frances. *A Delusion of Satan: The Full Story of the Salem Witch Trials* (9–12). 1995, Doubleday $23.95 (0-385-47255-2). A careful, analytical examination of the Salem witch hunts, in which a group of young girls accused innocent women of practicing witchcraft. (Rev: BL 11/1/95*) [133.4]

8504 Hofstadter, Richard. *America at 1750: A Social Portrait* (10–12). 1971, Knopf paper $11.00 (0-394-71795-3). Using a number of sources, this noted historian re-creates life in the colonies in 1750 with material on the slave trade, middle-class life, and the colonists' religious life. [973.2]

8505 Kent, Zachary. *The Mysterious Disappearance of Roanoke Colony in American History* (7–10). Illus. Series: American History. 2004, Enslow LB $20.95 (0-7660-2147-5). A detailed account of the settlement on Roanoke Island with recent research material on the fate of the colony. (Rev: BL 3/1/04; SLJ 6/04) [975.6]

8506 Lukes, Bonnie L. *Colonial America* (7–10). Illus. 1999, Lucent LB $18.96 (1-56006-321-1). Using extensive quotations from many sources, this book traces the basic history of colonial America, and gives good material on the obstacles settlers faced and their relations with Native Americans. (Rev: BL 2/15/00; HBG 9/00; SLJ 3/00) [940.2]

8507 Miller, Lee. *Roanoke: Solving the Mystery of the Lost Colony* (10–12). 2001, Arcade $25.95 (1-55970-584-1). This interesting book attempts to explain the disappearance of the ill-fated Roanoke colony. [975.6]

8508 Nardo, Don. *Braving the New World, 1619–1784: From the Arrival of the Enslaved Africans to the End of the American Revolution* (7–10). Series: Milestones in Black History. 1995, Chelsea LB $21.95 (0-7910-2259-5); paper $9.95 (0-7910-2685-X). How and why the slave trade became established in North America and the legacy of the slave culture. (Rev: BL 4/15/95) [973.2]

8509 Purvis, Thomas L. *Colonial America to 1763* (9–12). Illus. Series: Almanacs of American Life. 1999, Facts on File $75.00 (0-8160-2527-4). This volume covers the big picture and the small details of life in colonial America in chapters on topics that include diet, health, crime, and recreation. (Rev: BL 10/15/99; SLJ 2/00) [973.2]

8510 Rice, Earle, Jr. *The Salem Witch Trials* (7–10). Series: Famous Trials. 1996, Lucent LB $27.45 (1-56006-272-X). This account of the Salem trials discusses dozens of the people involved in the proceedings and provides a social, political, and legal context. (Rev: BR 11–12/97; SLJ 6/97; VOYA 8/97) [973.2]

8511 Schouweiler, Thomas. *The Lost Colony of Roanoke* (6–10). Series: Great Mysteries. 1991, Greenhaven LB $22.45 (0-89908-093-6). Outlines what is known about the colony that disappeared and poses questions about its unsolved mysteries. (Rev: BL 3/1/92) [975.6]

8512 Stiles, T. J. *In Their Own Words: The Colonizers* (10–12). Series: In Their Own Words. 1998, Putnam $16.00 (0-399-52390-1). A collection of fascinating narratives by ordinary people as well as more prominent figures in French and British colonies from Canada to South Carolina, starting with Champlain's views on Quebec in 1608 and

ending in 1760, with Bougainville's account of the French surrender to the British. (Rev: BL 3/1/98; SLJ 11/98) [973.2]

8513 Washington, George. *George-isms* (5–10). 2000, Atheneum $7.95 (0-689-84082-9). This is a collection of the rules of behavior copied out by George Washington as a teenager and includes dos and don'ts in such areas as dress, table manners, and polite conversation. (Rev: BL 10/15/00; HBG 3/01; SLJ 8/00) [973.4]

8514 Wilson, Lori L. *The Salem Witch Trials: How History Is Invented* (6–12). Illus. Series: How History Is Invented. 1997, Lerner LB $23.93 (0-8225-4889-5). The story of the famous trial of 100 people in Massachusetts during 1692, and the hysteria and falsehoods that led to 20 people being put to death. (Rev: BL 9/1/97; HBG 3/98; SLJ 8/97*) [133.4]

8515 Wood, Peter H. *Strange New Land: African Americans 1617–1776* (7–12). Illus. Series: Young Oxford History of African Americans. 1996, Oxford $24.00 (0-19-508700-3). A well-organized description of slavery during the colonial period and early Revolution. A chronology and illustrations add to the book's usefulness. (Rev: BL 2/15/96; SLJ 3/96) [973]

REVOLUTIONARY PERIOD AND THE YOUNG NATION (1775–1809)

8516 Allison, Robert J., ed. *American Eras: The Revolutionary Era (1754–1783)* (7–12). 1998, Gale $115.00 (0-7876-1480-7). A good reference source that opens with an overview of world events during the Revolutionary period, followed by chapters on specific topics such as the arts; business and the economy; law and justice; lifestyles, social trends, and fashions; religion; and sports and recreation. (Rev: BL 3/15/99; SLJ 2/99) [973.3]

8517 *The American Revolution* (9–12). Ed. by Kirk D. Werner. Series: Turning Points in World History. 2000, Greenhaven LB $31.20 (0-7377-0239-7); paper $19.95 (0-7377-0238-9). The 16 essays in this volume by noted historians center on various aspects of the Revolution, including causes and effects. (Rev: SLJ 3/00) [973.3]

8518 Bennett, William J., ed. *The Country's Founders: A Book of Advice for Young People* (7–12). 1998, Simon & Schuster $17.00 (0-689-82106-9). The guiding principles of the founders of the U.S. are revealed in this collection of writings by Washington, Jefferson, Adams, and others. (Rev: BL 8/98; HBG 3/99; SLJ 10/98) [973.099]

8519 Bober, Natalie S. *Countdown to Independence: A Revolution of Ideas in England and Her American Colonies, 1760–1776* (7–12). Illus. 2001, Simon & Schuster $26.95 (0-689-81329-5). Bober offers a concise, scholarly, and readable overview of the events, influences, and personalities that spurred the

American Revolution. (Rev: BCCB 3/01; BL 5/15/01; HB 3–4/01; HBG 10/01; SLJ 6/01*; VOYA 4/01) [973.3]

8520 Bowen, Catherine Drinker. *Miracle at Philadelphia: The Story of the Constitutional Convention, May to September, 1787* (10–12). 1986, Little, Brown $18.95 (0-316-10388-8); paper $8.95 (0-316-10398-5). This is considered one of the best accounts of the Constitutional Convention and the people involved. [973.3]

8521 Corrick, James A. *The Louisiana Purchase* (7–10). Series: World History. 2000, Lucent LB $19.96 (1-56006-637-7). The story of the transaction of 1803 that doubled the size of the United States, assured expansion westward, and changed the destinies of France, Spain, and the United States. (Rev: BL 10/15/2000; SLJ 1/01) [973.6]

8522 De Pauw, Linda Grant. *Founding Mothers: Women in America in the Revolutionary Era* (7–10). Illus. 1975, Houghton $18.00 (0-395-21896-9). The role of women during the Revolutionary War period. [305.4]

8523 Diouf, Sylviane A. *Growing Up in Slavery* (6–12). 2001, Millbrook LB $25.90 (0-7613-1763-5). A compelling account that dispels any myths about happy slave children and describes the hard life on the plantation as well as the atrocious conditions on slave ships. (Rev: BL 3/1/01; HBG 10/01; SLJ 6/01) [380.1]

8524 Dudley, William, ed. *The American Revolution* (10–12). Series: Opposing Viewpoints: American History. 1992, Greenhaven LB $17.95 (1-56510-011-5); paper $15.00 (1-56510-010-7). Provides scholarly material representing a wide range of viewpoints, with a long annotated bibliography. (Rev: BL 4/15/93) [973.3]

8525 Ellis, Joseph J. *Founding Brothers: The Revolutionary Generation* (10–12). 2000, Knopf $26.00 (0-375-40544-5). Using events in the lives of Founding Fathers including Washington, Hamilton, and Franklin, the author presents six episodes that highlight the character and convictions of each. (Rev: BL 9/15/00) [973.4]

8526 Gaines, Ann Graham. *The Louisiana Purchase in American History* (7–10). Series: In American History. 2000, Enslow LB $19.95 (0-7660-1301-4). A well-documented and illustrated account of the 1803 purchase of southern land from the French government. (Rev: BL 1/1–15/00; HBG 9/00) [973.5]

8527 Greenberg, Judith E., and Helen C. McKeever. *Journal of a Revolutionary War Woman* (6–10). Illus. Series: In Their Own Words. 1996, Watts LB $23.00 (0-531-11259-4). An intimate view of the American Revolution through the eyes of the wife of an officer in the Continental Army. (Rev: BL 9/1/96; BR 11–12/96; SLJ 8/96; VOYA 2/97) [973.3]

8528 Hibbert, Christopher. *Redcoats and Rebels: The American Revolution Through British Eyes* (10–12). 1990, Norton paper $16.95 (0-393-32293-9). Beginning with the Stamp Act of 1765, this account presents the American Revolution from the standpoint of the British. [973.3]

8529 Hull, Mary. *The Boston Tea Party in American History* (6–10). Series: In American History. 1999, Enslow LB $20.95 (0-7660-1139-9). A look at the events leading up to this act of defiance that sparked the American Revolution. (Rev: BL 2/15/99; HBG 9/99) [973.3115]

8530 Hull, Mary. *Shays' Rebellion and the Constitution in American History* (6–10). Series: In American History. 2000, Enslow LB $20.95 (0-7660-1418-5). The story of the economic depression of the 1780s and the resulting violent protests and government reforms. (Rev: BL 2/15/00; HBG 10/00; SLJ 6/00) [973.4]

8531 Kallen, Stuart A. *Life During the American Revolution* (6–10). Series: The Way People Live. 2002, Gale LB $27.45 (1-59018-007-0). Everyday life on the home front during the American Revolution is re-created in this account that uses primary and secondary source quotations extensively. (Rev: BL 7/02) [973.3]

8532 Karapalides, Harry J. *Dates of the American Revolution: Who, What, and Where in the War for Independence* (7–12). 1998, Burd Street paper $19.95 (1-57249-106-X). A chronological record tracing the American Revolution from 1760, when King George II inherited the British throne, to George Washington's death in 1799, with an emphasis on military action and commanders. (Rev: SLJ 2/99) [973.3]

8533 Lancaster, Bruce, and J. H. Plumb. *The American Heritage Book of the Revolution* (9–12). 1985, Dell paper $15.00 (0-8281-0281-3). A concise, readable account of the causes, events, and consequences of the American Revolution. [973.3]

8534 Leckie, Robert. *George Washington's War: The Saga of the American Revolution* (9–12). 1992, HarperCollins paper $18.00 (0-06-092215-X). A valuable historical overview of the American Revolution from the initial split between Britain and its American colonies to the British surrender at Yorktown, Virginia, on October 19, 1781. [973.3]

8535 McGowen, Tom. *The Revolutionary War and George Washington's Army in American History* (7–10). Illus. Series: American History. 2004, Enslow LB $20.95 (0-7660-2143-2). This is a readable account of all the battles in the Revolution plus a great assessment of George Washington's strengths and weaknesses. (Rev: BL 3/1/04; SLJ 3/04) [973.3]

8536 Maltz, Leora, ed. *The Founding of America* (7–12). Series: Great Speeches in History. 2002, Gale LB $31.20 (0-7377-0871-9); paper $19.95 (0-7377-0870-0). After introductory essays, this anthology of about 20 important speeches (each with its own introduction) re-creates the important events and issues involved in the creation of the United States. (Rev: BL 4/15/02) [973.2]

8537 Minks, Louise, and Benton Minks. *The Revolutionary War* (7–12). Series: America at War. 1992, Facts on File $25.00 (0-8160-2508-8). A colorful account of the causes, main battles, and outcomes of the Revolutionary War. (Rev: BL 2/1/93) [973.3]

8538 Mitchell, Joseph B. *Decisive Battles of the American Revolution* (9–12). 1985, Fawcett paper $5.99 (0-449-30031-5). A re-creation of all the important battles in the Revolution from Lexington to Yorktown. [973.3]

8539 Murphy, Jim. *An American Plague: The True and Terrifying Story of the Yellow Fever Epidemic of 1793* (6–12). Illus. 2003, Clarion $17.00 (0-395-77608-2). Narrative, newspaper articles, and archival prints and photographs combine to tell the dramatic story of the epidemic that hit Philadelphia in the late 18th century. (Rev: BL 6/1–15/03; HB 7–8/03; HBG 10/03; SLJ 6/03*; VOYA 12/03) [614.5]

8540 Nardo, Don. *The American Revolution* (7–12). Series: Opposing Viewpoints Digests. 1998, Greenhaven LB $27.45 (1-56510-755-1); paper $17.45 (1-56510-754-3). Quoting from dozens of primary and secondary sources, this book explores issues relating to the Revolution, such as prewar disputes, patriotic vs. loyalist views, wartime concerns, and modern attitudes. (Rev: BL 5/15/98; SLJ 6/98) [973.3]

8541 Nardo, Don. *The Declaration of Independence: A Model for Individual Rights* (9–12). Series: Words That Changed History. 1998, Lucent LB $18.96 (1-56006-368-8). Using many primary and secondary source quotations, this is the history of the document that continues to serve America 200 years after its signing. (Rev: BL 1/1–15/99; BR 5–6/99) [973.3]

8542 Purvis, Thomas L. *Revolutionary America, 1763–1800* (9–12). Series: Almanacs of American Life. 1995, Facts on File $95.00 (0-8160-2528-2). Life during revolutionary times in various parts of the country is described under such headings as education, population, health, and religion. (Rev: BL 10/1/95; SLJ 2/96) [973.3]

8543 Raphael, Ray. *A People's History of the American Revolution: How Common People Shaped the Fight for Independence* (10–12). 2001, New Pr. $25.95 (1-56584-653-2). The experiences of ordinary people—farmers, townspeople, Native Ameri-

cans, African Americans, and women—during the Revolution are told in this readable account. (Rev: BL 3/1/01) [973.3]

8544 *The Revolutionaries* (7–12). Illus. Series: American Story. 1996, Time-Life $19.95 (0-7835-6250-0). Illustrations and personal narratives enhance this detailed chronological account of the drive for independence and the military high points of the American Revolution. (Rev: BL 12/15/96; BR 3–4/97; SLJ 1/97) [973.3]

8545 Slavicek, Louise Chipley. *The Women of the American Revolution* (6–10). Illus. Series: Women in History. 2002, Gale LB $21.96 (1-59018-172-7). An absorbing, well-illustrated account of the roles women played during the Revolutionary War — on the battlefield and on the home front. (Rev: BL 10/15/02) [973.3]

8546 Stewart, Gail B. *Weapons of War* (6–12). Series: American War Library. 2000, Lucent LB $18.96 (1-56006-616-1). This book discusses weapons used during the American Revolution including muskets, swords, rifles, warships, and even intelligence and espionage. (Rev: BL 2/15/00) [973.3]

8547 Stokesbury, James L. *A Short History of the American Revolution* (10–12). 1991, Morrow paper $15.00 (0-688-12304-X). A concise examination of the factors that led to the American Revolution as well as the war for independence itself. [973.3]

8548 Wilkins, Roger. *Jefferson's Pillow: The Founding Fathers and the Dilemma of Black Patriotism* (10–12). 2001, Beacon $23.00 (0-8070-0956-3). This book explores questions of slavery and patriotism among African Americans during the founding of the nation and the opinions and actions of such men as Madison, Washington, and Jefferson. (Rev: BL 6/1–15/01) [973]

8549 Wood, Gordon S. *The American Revolution* (10–12). Illus. 2002, Random $19.95 (0-679-64057-6). An absorbing and easily understood summary of the causes and key events of the struggle against British rule. (Rev: BL 1/1–15/02) [973.3]

8550 Wood, W. J. *Battles of the Revolutionary War, 1775–1781* (9–12). Series: Major Battles and Campaigns. 1990, Algonquin paper $17 .00 (0-306-80617-7). This book describes in illustrations and text 10 of the major battles of the Revolutionary War. [973.3]

8551 Zall, P. M. *Becoming American: Young People in the American Revolution* (8–12). 1993, Linnet LB $25.00 (0-208-02355-0). Letters, journal entries, and testimony by young people describing their lives, events, and social conditions in the years immediately before, during, and immediately after the Revolution. (Rev: BL 5/1/93; VOYA 8/93) [973.3]

NINETEENTH CENTURY TO THE CIVIL WAR
(1809–1861)

8552 Baker, Lindsay, and Julie P. Baker, eds. *Till Freedom Cried Out: Memories of Texas Slave Life* (10–12). Illus. 1997, Texas A & M Univ. Pr. $29.95 (0-89096-736-9). Part of the Oklahoma Slave Narrative Project established as part of the WPA, this is a collection of narratives by 32 slaves who were born in Texas and relocated to Oklahoma. (Rev: SLJ 12/97) [973.6]

8553 Berlin, Ira, and Marc Favreau, eds. *Remembering Slavery: African Americans Talk About Their Personal Experiences of Slavery and Emancipation* (10–12). Illus. 1998, New Pr. $49.95 (1-56584-425-4). This book and cassette set recaptures the narratives of former slaves as they were first recorded in the 1930s as part of the Federal Writers' Project. These personal recollections convey the harshness, sadism, and brutality of slavery as well as the resilience, survival skills, sense of family, and community among the slaves. (Rev: BL 8/98; SLJ 4/99) [973]

8554 Boorstin, Daniel J. *The Americans: The National Experience* (10–12). 1965, Random paper $16.00 (0-394-70358-8). This work focuses on the years between the Revolution and the Civil War and how this period shaped modern America. [973]

8555 Chalfant, William Y. *Dangerous Passage: The Santa Fe Trail and the Mexican War* (9–12). 1994, Univ. of Oklahoma Pr. $32.95 (0-8061-2613-2). A detailed account of the Santa Fe Trail during the Mexican War. (Rev: BL 2/1/94) [978]

8556 Coffin, Levi, and William Still. *Fleeing for Freedom: Stories of the Underground Railroad as Told by Levi Coffin and William Still* (10–12). Ed. by George Hendrick and Willene Hendrick. Illus. 2004, Ivan R. Dee $24.95 (1-56663-545-4); paper $14.95 (1-56663-546-2). This inside look at the workings of the Underground Railroad is built around the firsthand accounts of two abolitionists who took part. (Rev: BL 12/15/03) [973.7]

8557 Currie, Stephanie. *Life of a Slave on a Southern Plantation* (6–10). Series: The Way People Live. 1999, Lucent LB $18.96 (1-56006-539-7). Using many quotations from original sources, this book about everyday life on a southern slave plantation covers family life, food and housing, work, play, and methods of escape. (Rev: BL 10/15/99; HBG 9/00; SLJ 1/00) [975]

8558 DeVillers, David. *The John Brown Slavery Revolt Trial: A Headline Court Case* (8–12). 2000, Enslow $20.95 (0-7660-1385-5). An account of the trial of the abolitionist who was hanged for treason and murder. (Rev: HBG 3/01; SLJ 9/00) [306.3]

8559 Dudley, William, ed. *American Slavery* (8–12). Series: Turning Points in World History. 2000, Greenhaven LB $21.96 (0-7377-0223-3); paper $13.96 (0-7377-0212-5). This anthology of essays covers the rise of slavery in America and how this issue led to the Civil War at a time when there were more than 4 million African American slaves in the South. (Rev: BL 5/15/00; SLJ 10/00) [973.7]

8560 Fradin, Dennis B. *Bound for the North Star: True Stories of Fugitive Slaves* (8–12). Illus. 2000, Clarion $20.00 (0-395-97017-2). Personal experiences form the basis of these moving profiles that spare no details of the horrors suffered by escaping slaves and the courage of their helpers. (Rev: BL 1/1–15/01*; BR 1–2/01; HB 1–2/01; HBG 3/01; SLJ 11/00*; VOYA 10/01) [973.7]

8561 Geary, Rick. *The Mystery of Mary Rogers* (10–12). Illus. Series: Treasury of Victorian Murder. 2001, NBM $15.95 (1-56163-274-0). In comic-book format, Geary tells of the 1841 murder of cigar girl Mary Rogers in New York City, a crime that was never solved and was used as the basis for Edgar Allan Poe's story. (Rev: BL 4/15/01; SLJ 8/01; VOYA 8/01) [364.1]

8562 Gorrell, Gena K. *North Star to Freedom: The Story of the Underground Railroad* (5–10). Illus. 1997, Delacorte $17.95 (0-385-32319-0). A handsome, readable account that captures the danger and excitement connected to the Underground Railroad and the heroism and dedication of abolitionists in Canada as well as in the United States who helped slaves escape from the South. (Rev: BL 2/15/97; BR 9–10/97; SLJ 1/97*) [973.7]

8563 Greenblatt, Miriam. *The War of 1812* (7–12). Illus. Series: America at War. 1994, Facts on File $25.00 (0-8160-2879-6). A lively account of how the young nation tried to rid itself of foreign influences, tracing the causes of the war and describing the battles fought on land and sea. (Rev: BL 11/15/94; SLJ 12/94) [973.5]

8564 Griffler, Keith P. *Front Line of Freedom: African Americans and the Forging of the Underground Railroad in the Ohio Valley* (10–12). Illus. Series: Ohio River Valley. 2004, Univ. Press of Kentucky $35.00 (0-8131-2298-8). Using many first-person narratives, this book details the roles played by African Americans in the operation of the Underground Railroad. (Rev: BL 2/15/04) [973.7]

8565 Hagedorn, Ann. *Beyond the River: The Untold Story of the Heroes of the Underground Railroad* (10–12). 2003, Simon & Schuster $25.00 (0-684-87065-7). In this study of the U.S. abolitionist movement, Hagedorn focuses on the small town of Ripley, Ohio, and the activities of Rev. John Rankin and others to help slaves escape to the safety of the North in the early 1820s. (Rev: BL 2/15/03) [973.7]

8566 Heidler, David S., and Jeanne T. Heidler. *The War of 1812* (8–12). Series: Greenwood Guides to Historic Events, 1500–1900. 2002, Greenwood $44.95 (0-313-31687-2). This thorough and detailed description of the causes, events, and key figures of the War of 1812 will be useful for report writers. (Rev: BL 10/15/02; SLJ 10/02) [973.5]

8567 Hendrick, George, and Willene Hendrick. *The Creole Mutiny: A Tale of Revolt Aboard a Slave Ship* (10–12). 2003, Ivan R. Dee $24.95 (1-56663-493-8). The authors recount how slaves being transported aboard the slave ship *Creole* in the early 1840s revolted, took control of the vessel, and sailed to freedom in the Bahamas. (Rev: BL 2/15/03) [326]

8568 Herda, D. J. *The Dred Scott Case: Slavery and Citizenship* (6–10). Illus. Series: Landmark Supreme Court Cases. 1994, Enslow LB $20.95 (0-89490-460-4). An examination of the pre-Civil War case in which a slave was denied his freedom, and its consequences. (Rev: BL 6/1–15/94) [342.73]

8569 Hickey, Donald R. *The War of 1812: A Forgotten Conflict* (10–12). 1989, Univ. of Illinois Pr. paper $18.95 (0-252-06059-8). A well-researched account of the causes, campaigns, and consequences of the War of 1812. [973.5]

8570 Kallen, Stuart A. *Life on the Underground Railroad* (6–10). Series: The Way People Live. 2000, Lucent LB $27.45 (1-56006-667-9). After a brief history of slavery in America, this account covers the organization of and people involved in the Underground Railroad, the journeys made on it, and its impact on the future. (Rev: BL 2/15/00; HBG 10/00; SLJ 5/00) [973.6]

8571 Katz, William L. *Breaking the Chains: African-American Slave Resistance* (9–12). Illus. 1990, Simon & Schuster $16.00 (0-689-31493-0). A revealing account of American slavery that focuses on the many uprisings and rebellions. (Rev: BL 12/1/90; SLJ 11/90) [305.6]

8572 Lord, Walter. *A Time to Stand* (9–12). 1978, Univ. of Nebraska Pr. paper $10.95 (0-8032-7902-7). A gripping account of the siege and fall of the Alamo. [973.6]

8573 Lukes, Bonnie L. *The Dred Scott Decision* (9–12). Illus. Series: Famous Trials. 1996, Lucent LB $17.96 (1-56006-270-3). The story of the slave Dred Scott and the historic 1857 court case against his owner, John Sanford. (Rev: BL 6/1–15/97; BR 11–12/97; SLJ 4/97) [342.73]

8574 Molotsky, Irvin. *The Flag, the Poet and the Song: The Story of the Star Spangled Banner* (10–12). Illus. 2001, Dutton $22.95 (0-525-94600-4). An investigation of the creation of the flag that flew over Fort McHenry, an account of the poet who wrote the words to the national anthem, and a general discussion of the War of 1812 are to be found in this interesting history book. (Rev: BL 6/1–15/01) [973.5]

8575 Nardo, Don. *The War of 1812* (8–12). Series: World History. 1999, Lucent LB $18.96 (1-56006-

581-8). A well-organized account of "Mr. Madison's War" that includes primary-source material, a timeline, maps, and other interesting elements. (Rev: BL 11/15/99; HBG 9/00; SLJ 2/00) [973.5]

8576 Philbrick, Nathaniel. *The Heart of the Sea: The Tragedy of the Whaleship Essex* (10–12). Illus. 2000, Viking $24.95 (0-670-89157-6). A fascinating telling of the tragic whaling voyage of the *Essex* from Nantucket in the 1820s that was the inspiration for *Moby Dick*. (Rev: BL 3/1/00* ; SLJ 11/00) [910]

8577 Philbrick, Nathaniel. *Sea of Glory: America's Voyage of Discovery, the U.S. Exploring Expedition, 1838–1842* (10–12). 2003, Viking $27.95 (0-670-03231-X). In this real-life adventure tale, Philbrick recounts the story of a team that set out in 1838 to search the Southern Hemisphere for new lands. (Rev: BL 9/15/03; SLJ 5/04) [910]

8578 Remini, Robert V. *The Battle of New Orleans: Andrew Jackson and America's First Military Victory* (9–12). Illus. 1999, Viking $24.95 (0-670-88551-7). An absorbing account of how the United States won this important battle, with an emphasis on Jackson's leadership. (Rev: BL 8/99; SLJ 2/00)

8579 Roberts, Randy, and James N. Olson. *A Line in the Sand: The Alamo in Blood and Memory* (10–12). 2001, Free Pr. $26.00 (0-684-83544-4). This book traces the events prior to and during the Texas Revolution of 1835–1836 and then moves on to a detailed account of the Battle of the Alamo and its aftermath. (Rev: BL 12/15/00) [976.4]

8580 Rose, Joel. *New York Sawed in Half* (10–12). 2001, Bloomsbury $19.95 (1-58234-098-6). The story of an amazing hoax perpetrated in early 19th-century New York during which people believed that half of Manhattan was sinking because of the weight of its buildings. (Rev: BL 4/15/01) [974.7]

8581 Sawyer, Kem K. *The Underground Railroad in American History* (7–10). Illus. Series: In American History. 1997, Enslow LB $20.95 (0-89490-885-5). A description of the formation of the Underground Railroad, its functions, key people connected with it, and its importance in American history. (Rev: BL 7/97; BR 9–10/97) [973.7]

8582 Sigerman, Harriet. *An Unfinished Battle: American Women 1848–1865* (8–12). Illus. Series: Young Oxford History of Women in the United States. 1994, Oxford $24.00 (0-19-508110-2). This volume explores the social and political conditions of women during the years prior to the Civil War and their contributions to and participation in the war. (Rev: BL 12/15/94; SLJ 1/95) [305.4]

8583 Sisson, Mary Barr. *The Gathering Storm: From the Framing of the Constitution to Walker's Appeal, 1787–1829* (7–10). Illus. Series: Milestones in Black American History. 1996, Chelsea LB $21.95 (0-7910-2252-8); paper $9.95 (0-7910-2678-7). The story of slavery in the early days of the

Republic with emphasis on civil disobedience, militant action, and important figures of the period. (Rev: BL 10/15/96; BR 1–2/97; SLJ 2/97) [973]

8584 *Slave Narratives* (9–12). Ed. by William L. Andrews and Henry Louis Gates, Jr. 2000, Library of America $40.00 (1-88301-176-0). These 10 narratives — including those by Nat Turner, Frederick Douglass, and Sojourner Truth — paint a vivid picture of the cruelties and injustices of slavery. (Rev: BL 2/15/00) [326]

8585 Stein, R. Conrad. *John Brown's Raid on Harpers Ferry* (7–10). Series: In American History. 1999, Enslow LB $20.95 (0-7660-1123-2). This account gives an in-depth look at this important moment in American history and its effects on the events to come. (Rev: BL 9/15/99; HBG 4/00) [973.6]

8586 White, Deborah Gray. *Let My People Go: African Americans, 1804–1860* (7–12). Illus. Series: Young Oxford History of African Americans. 1996, Oxford $24.00 (0-19-508769-0). The story of slavery in the United States during the 19th century, attempts to end it, efforts to rescue slaves, and events leading up to the Civil War. (Rev: BL 5/15/96; SLJ 6/96; VOYA 8/96) [973]

8587 Young, Mary, and Gerald Horne. *Testaments of Courage: Selections from Men's Slave Narratives* (7–12). Series: African-American Slave Narratives. 1995, Watts LB $25.00 (0-531-11205-5). Chilling and illuminating excerpts from the writings of slaves, beginning with one from 1831. (Rev: BR 1–2/96; SLJ 2/96) [973.6]

8588 Zeinert, Karen. *The Amistad Slave Revolt and American Abolition* (7–10). Illus. 1997, Shoe String LB $21.50 (0-208-02438-7); paper $12.95 (0-208-02439-5). The dramatic story of Cinque and 52 other slaves onboard the Spanish ship *Amistad* in 1839 and of their historic mutiny and subsequent trial. (Rev: BL 7/97; SLJ 6/97) [326]

8589 Zeinert, Karen. *Tragic Prelude: Bleeding Kansas* (6–10). Illus. 2001, Linnet $25.00 (0-208-02446-8). An accessible account of the conflict that erupted in Kansas over the question of slavery, with information on individuals including John Brown and Hannah Ropes, a timeline, extracts from primary documents, photographs, and references. (Rev: BL 6/1–15/01; HBG 10/01; SLJ 6/01; VOYA 2/02) [978.1]

CIVIL WAR (1861–1865)

8590 Allen, Thomas B., and Sam Abell. *The Blue and the Gray* (9–12). 1992, National Geographic $40.00 (0-87044-876-5). This lavishly illustrated overview of the Civil War blends period images with modern-day photographs of Civil War battlefields, memorials, and related historic sites; also

included is a map of Civil War battlefield sites. [973.7]

8591 Anders, Curt. *Hearts in Conflict: A One-Volume History of the Civil War* (9–12). 1994, Birch Lane $29.95 (1-55972-184-7). A quick-reading journey through the battles and leaders of the Civil War. (Rev: BL 4/15/94) [973.7]

8592 Bailey, Ronald H. *Battle for Atlanta: Sherman Moves East* (9–12). Illus. 1985, Time-Life $29.95 (0-8094-4773-8). In pictures and text, this account tells of the Atlanta Campaign of 1864. Others in this Time-Life series on the Civil War include *The Assassination* (1987), *The Coastal War,* and *Confederate Ordeal* (both 1984). [973.7]

8593 Bailey, Ronald H. *The Bloodiest Day: The Battle of Antietam* (7–12). Illus. 1984, Silver Burdett LB $25.93 (0-8094-4741-X). The story of Lee's defeat in the battle that caused terrible losses on both sides. [973.7]

8594 Bailey, Ronald H. *Forward to Richmond* (9–12). Illus. 1983, Silver Burdett LB $25.93 (0-8094-4721-5). A lavishly illustrated volume that deals with the Peninsula campaign of 1862. Some others in the Time-Life series on the Civil War are *Decoying the Yanks* (1984), *The Fight for Chattanooga* (1985), and *Pursuit to Appomattox* (1989). [973.7]

8595 Barney, William L. *The Civil War and Reconstruction: A Student Companion* (7–12). Series: Oxford Student Companions to American History. 2001, Oxford LB $45.00 (0-19-511559-7). An alphabetically arranged series of articles covering all aspects of the Civil War and Reconstruction, illustrated with photographs, maps, and reproductions. (Rev: BL 9/15/01; SLJ 6/01) [973.7]

8596 Batty, Peter, and Peter Parish. *The Divided Union: The Story of the Great American War 1861–1865* (9–12). Illus. 1987, Salem House $24.95 (0-88162-234-6). A fine popular history of the Civil War notable both for its clarity and excellent illustrations. (Rev: SLJ 3/88) [973.7]

8597 Beller, Susan P. *To Hold This Ground: A Desperate Battle at Gettysburg* (8–12). 1995, Simon & Schuster $15.00 (0-689-50621-X). After a brief history of the Civil War to July 2, 1863, the author combines narrative and primary sources to recount the Battle of Gettysburg, with alternate chapters focusing on each regiment involved, telling their histories, giving brief biographies of their commanders, and describing the battle as opportunities were taken and lost. (Rev: BR 3–4/96; SLJ 12/95; VOYA 4/96) [973.7]

8598 Biel, Timothy L. *Life in the North During the Civil War* (6–10). Illus. Series: The Way People Live. 1997, Lucent LB $27.45 (1-56006-334-3). This book tells how civilians in the North lived during the Civil War, far from the battles but nevertheless deeply affected by the war's terrible toll. (Rev: BL 3/15/97; SLJ 5/97) [973.7]

8599 *The Blockade: Runners and Raiders* (9–12). Illus. 1983, Silver Burdett LB $25.93 (0-8094-4709-6). With many authentic illustrations, this volume tells of the naval events of the Civil War. Some others in this Time-Life series on the Civil War are *War on the Mississippi* (1985), *War on the Frontier* (1986), and *The Shenandoah in Flames* (1987). [973.7]

8600 *Blood: Stories of Life and Death from the Civil War* (10–12). Ed. by Peter Kadzis. Illus. 2000, Thunder's Mouth paper $16.95 (1-56025-259-6). For serious history students, this is a collection of material, including some fiction, that reproduces the history, glory, and horror of the Civil War. (Rev: BL 7/00) [973.7]

8601 Bobrick, Benson. *Testament: A Soldier's Story of the Civil War* (10–12). 2003, Simon & Schuster $23.00 (0-7432-5091-5). Bobrick blends well-researched narrative with excerpts from his great-grandfather's letters describing his experiences serving in the Union Army. (Rev: BL 9/15/03) [973.7]

8602 Boritt, Gabor S., ed. *Why the Civil War Came* (9–12). 1995, Oxford $48.00 (0-19-507941-8). A breakdown of political developments in the 1850s on either side of the Mason-Dixon Line. (Rev: BL 10/15/95) [973.7]

8603 Bowman, John S., ed. *The Civil War Almanac* (9–12). Illus. 1986, Newspaper Enterprise Assn. paper $14.95 (0-345-35434-6). This book consists chiefly of a detailed chronology of the war plus 133 biographical sketches of key figures. [973.7]

8604 Buell, Thomas B. *The Warrior Generals: Combat Leadership in the Civil War* (10–12). 1997, Crown $35.00 (0-517-59571-0). An insightful examination of the successes and failures of three Union generals — Grant, Thomas, and Barlow — and three Confederate generals — Lee, Hood, and Gordon. (Rev: SLJ 7/97) [973.7]

8605 Burchard, Peter. *Lincoln and Slavery* (6–10). 1999, Simon & Schuster $17.00 (0-689-81570-0). This book discusses the predominance of slavery as a political and moral issue in 19th-century America and traces the evolution of Lincoln's ideas on slavery and how he put his beliefs into practice. (Rev: HB 7–8/99; SLJ 7/99; VOYA 8/99) [973.7]

8606 Burgess, Lauren Cook, ed. *An Uncommon Soldier* (9–12). 1994, Minerva Center $25.00 (0-9634895-1-8). Letters of a New York farmer's daughter who disguised herself as a man to enlist in the Union Army in 1862 — only the second such published account. (Rev: BL 5/15/94) [973.7]

8607 Catton, Bruce. *The Civil War* (7–12). Illus. 1985, Houghton paper $16.00 (0-8281-0305-4). A

well-illustrated book that deals with the major events and personalities of the war. [973.7]

8608 Catton, Bruce. *Reflections on the Civil War* (10–12). Illus. 1984, Berkley paper $6.99 (0-425-10495-8). The well-known Civil War historian reflects on the causes and consequences of this war. [973.7]

8609 Catton, Bruce. *A Stillness at Appomattox* (10–12). 1953, Doubleday paper $14.95 (0-385-04451-8). One of the best accounts of the Civil War by a leading American historian. [973.7]

8610 Catton, Bruce. *This Hallowed Ground: The Story of the Union Side of the Civil War* (10–12). Series: Mainstream of America. 1956, Doubleday paper $12.99 (1-85326-696-5). The entire Civil War as experienced by the Union side. [973.7]

8611 *Chancellorsville* (7–12). Illus. Series: Voices of the Civil War. 1996, Time-Life $24.95 (0-7853-4708-0). A handsome description of this key Civil War battle, featuring regimental histories, letters, diaries, and memoirs. (Rev: BL 1/1–15/97) [973.7]

8612 *Charleston* (7–12). Series: Voices of the Civil War. 1997, Time-Life $29.95 (0-7835-4709-9). The story of the siege of Charleston and its fall to Union forces in February 1865, with quotations from original sources. (Rev: BL 5/15/97) [973.7]

8613 *Chickamauga* (7–12). Series: Voices of the Civil War. 1997, Time-Life $29.95 (0-7835-4710-2). Using many original sources, this is the story of the 1863 battle in northern Georgia after which the Union Army fell back to Chattanooga. (Rev: BL 7/97) [973.7]

8614 *The Civil War* (9–12). Ed. by David M. Haugen and Lori Shein. Series: Opposing Viewpoints Digests. 1999, Greenhaven LB $21.45 (1-56510-887-6); paper $17.45 (1-56510-886-8). Different viewpoints are included on such aspects of the Civil War as slavery, the Emancipation Proclamation, and secession. [973.7]

8615 *The Civil War: The North* (10–12). Ed. by Thomas Streissguth. Series: History Firsthand. 2000, Greenhaven LB $22.96 (0-7377-0364-4); paper $14.96 (0-7377-0363-6). The Civil War from the point of view of various participants in the North is explored in this collection of original sources. (Rev: BL 3/1/01) [973.7]

8616 *The Civil War: The South* (10–12). Ed. by Thomas Streissguth. Illus. Series: History Firsthand. 2001, Greenhaven LB $22.96 (0-7377-0409-8); paper $14.96 (0-7377-0408-X). Drawing on period documents such as journals and letters, this volume provides a fairly comprehensive overview of the U.S. Civil War from the vantage point of the South. (Rev: BL 2/15/01) [973.7]

8617 Clark, Champ. *Gettysburg: The Confederate High Tide* (9–12). Illus. 1985, Silver Burdett LB

$25.93 (0-8094-4757-6). This volume in the Time-Life series vividly re-creates in words and pictures the horror and glory of this important battle. The final volume in this series is *The Nation Reunited* (1987). [973.7]

8618 Colbert, Nancy. *The Firing on Fort Sumter: A Splintered Nation Goes to War* (6–12). Illus. 2000, Morgan Reynolds LB $19.95 (1-883846-51-X). An intriguing, detailed account, told in lively prose and many photographs, of the incident that began the Civil War. (Rev: BL 10/1/00; HBG 3/01; VOYA 6/01) [973.7]

8619 Corrick, James A. *The Battle of Gettysburg* (6–10). Illus. Series: Great Battles in History. 1996, Lucent LB $26.20 (1-56006-451-X). This account of the decisive battle of the Civil War contains useful maps and timelines plus many excerpts from primary sources. (Rev: BL 4/15/96; SLJ 7/96) [973.7]

8620 Corrick, James A. *Life Among the Soldiers and Cavalry* (6–12). Illus. Series: American War Library. 1999, Lucent LB $18.96 (1-56006-491-9). This concise account examines soldiers' everyday life during the Civil War with material on topics including enlistment, clothing, weapons, training, and recreation. (Rev: BL 1/1–15/00; HBG 9/00; SLJ 3/00) [973]

8621 Davis, Burke. *The Civil War: Strange and Fascinating Facts* (9–12). Illus. 1982, Crown $7.99 (0-517-37151-0). An unusual compendium of little-known facts about the Civil War. [973.7]

8622 Davis, Burke. *Sherman's March* (9–12). Illus. 1980, Random $21.95 (0-394-50739-8); paper $14.00 (0-394-75763-7). This volume deals with the destructive march of Sherman and his men through Georgia and the Carolinas. [973.7]

8623 Davis, William C. *Brother Against Brother: The War Begins* (9–12). Illus. 1983, Silver Burdett LB $25.93 (0-8094-4701-0). This is the first volume in the Time-Life series on the Civil War (see other entries in this section). It traces the events leading up to the outbreak of war. [973.7]

8624 Davis, William C. *Death in the Trenches: Grant at Petersburg* (9–12). Illus. 1986, Silver Burdett LB $25.93 (0-8094-4777-0). This volume of the Time-Life series deals with the Union Army's siege of Petersburg, Virginia. [973.7]

8625 Davis, William C. *First Blood: Fort Sumter to Bull Run* (9–12). Illus. 1983, Silver Burdett LB $25.93 (0-8094-4705-3). A survey in pictures and text of such early battles of the Civil War as Bull Run and Fort Sumter. Part of the Time-Life series. [973.7]

8626 *Faith in God and Generals: An Anthology of Faith, Hope, and Love in the American Civil War* (10–12). Ed. by Ted Baehr and Susan Wales. Illus. 2003, Broadman & Holman $24.99 (0-8054-2728-7). Published as a companion piece to the film *Gods*

and Generals, this richly illustrated book's examination of the role of religion during the Civil War era stands on its own. (Rev: BL 1/1–15/03) [241]

8627 Farwell, Byron. *Ball's Bluff* (9–12). Illus. 1990, EPM paper $12.95 (0-939009-36-6). A gripping account of the small Civil War battle of Ball's Bluff and its aftermath. (Rev: SLJ 9/90) [973.7]

8628 Faust, Drew Gilpin. *Mothers of Invention: Women of the Slaveholding South in the American Civil War* (10–12). 1996, Univ. of North Carolina Pr. $34.95 (0-8078-2255-8). Using letters, journals, and other original sources, this account tells how upper-class Southern women coped during the Civil War, "reinventing" themselves and assuming new roles while their fathers, husbands, brothers, and sons were off fighting. (Rev: BL 3/1/96; SLJ 11/96) [973.7]

8629 Feinberg, Barbara Silberdick. *Abraham Lincoln's Gettysburg Address: Four Score and More* (7–12). 2000, 21st Century Books $24.40 (0-7613-1610-8). A readable account that contains material on the events leading up to the speech, the text itself, and period photographs and facsimiles. (Rev: BL 11/15/00; HBG 3/01; SLJ 1/01) [973.7]

8630 *First Manassas* (7–12). Series: Voices of the Civil War. 1997, Time-Life $29.95 (0-7835-4712-9). The story of the first Battle of Bull Run, fought close to the town of Manassas in north Virginia, is told with extensive use of personal narratives. (Rev: BL 10/15/97) [973.7]

8631 Freehling, William W. *The South vs. the South: How Anti-Confederate Southerners Shaped the Course of the Civil War* (10–12). Illus. 2001, Oxford $25.00 (0-19-513027-8). This is the story of the southern anti-Confederates. (Rev: BL 3/1/01) [973.7]

8632 Furgurson, Ernest B. *Ashes of Glory: Richmond at War* (10–12). 1996, Knopf $30.00 (0-679-42232-3). A unique work that looks at the Civil War as experienced by the people of Richmond, Virginia, including politicians, soldiers, workers, women, slaves, and Union prisoners of war. (Rev: SLJ 5/97) [973.7]

8633 Furgurson, Ernest B. *Chancellorsville 1863: The Souls of the Brave* (9–12). 1992, Knopf $25.00 (0-394-58301-9). A recounting of the many legendary episodes in the Chancellorsville campaign during the Civil War, supplemented by 15 maps. (Rev: BL 11/1/92*) [973.7]

8634 Gaines, Ann Graham. *The Battle of Gettysburg in American History* (6–10). Series: In American History. 2001, Enslow LB $20.95 (0-7660-1455-X). The causes and events relating to this, the most momentous battle of the Civil War, are retold with a fine interweaving of personal stories. (Rev: BL 8/01; HBG 10/01) [973.7]

8635 Gallagher, Gary, ed. *The Wilderness Campaign* (10–12). 1997, Univ. of North Carolina Pr. $29.95 (0-8078-2334-1). Eight essays by noted Civil War scholars examine various aspects of this 1864 battle. (Rev: SLJ 3/98) [973.7]

8636 Gallman, J. Matthew. *The North Fights the Civil War: The Home Front* (9–12). 1994, Ivan R. Dee $22.50 (1-56663-049-5). The effects of the Civil War on the home front in the North, including its impact on women, African Americans, and immigrants. (Rev: BL 4/1/94) [973.7]

8637 Garrison, Webb. *A Treasury of Civil War Tales* (9–12). Illus. 1988, Rutledge Hill $14.95 (0-934395-95-0). A collection of 57 stories dealing with the Civil War from the first outcries against slavery to Reconstruction. (Rev: BL 10/15/88) [973.7]

8638 Garrison, Webb B. *Brady's Civil War* (9–12). 2000, Lyons Pr. $40.00 (1-58574-122-1). This pictorial history of the Civil War uses the photographs of Matthew Brady and his assistants. (Rev: BL 10/15/00) [973.7]

8639 *Gettysburg* (8–12). Series: Voices of the Civil War. 1995, Time-Life $29.95 (0-7835-4700-5). The Battle of Gettysburg, with illustrations showing the human dimension of the battle. (Rev: BL 5/15/95) [973.7]

8640 Golay, Michael. *The Civil War* (7–12). Series: America at War. 1992, Facts on File $25.00 (0-8160-2514-2). A comprehensive chronicle of the war, from the issues that gave rise to it to Lee's surrender at Appomattox. (Rev: BL 10/15/92) [973.7]

8641 Goolrick, William K. *Rebels Resurgent: Fredericksburg to Chancellorsville* (9–12). Illus. 1985, Silver Burdett LB $25.93 (0-8094-4749-5). In this volume in the Time-Life series, the early southern victories of 1862 and 1863 are reconstructed. [973.7]

8642 Gragg, Rod. *The Civil War Quiz and Fact Book* (9–12). 1985, HarperCollins paper $14.00 (0-06-091226-X). Fascinating questions and answers involving little-known facts about the Civil War. (Rev: BL 4/15/85) [973.7]

8643 Guelzo, Allen C. *Lincoln's Emancipation Proclamation: The End of Slavery in America* (10–12). 2004, Simon & Schuster $26.00 (0-7432-2182-6). Discussion of Abraham Lincoln's true feelings about slavery will be of interest to advanced history students. (Rev: BL 12/15/03) [973.7]

8644 Guernsey, Alfred H., and Henry M. Alden. *Harper's Pictorial History of the Civil War* (10–12). 1996, Random $39.99 (0-517-18334-X). This is a facsimile edition of the original work published in 1869, with thorough discussion of military, political, and social issues, accompanied by many maps, portraits, and black-and-white illustrations. (Rev: SLJ 12/96) [973.7]

8645 Haythornthwaite, Philip. *Uniforms of the American Civil War in Color* (9–12). Illus. 1990, Sterling paper $14.95 (0-8069-5846-4). In vivid color, this book presents more than 150 Confederate and Union army uniforms. (Rev: SLJ 11/85) [973.7]

8646 Hoehling, A. A. *Damn the Torpedoes! Naval Incidents of the Civil War* (10–12). Illus. 1989, John F. Blair $12.95 (0-89587-073-8). The author re-creates the ships and the naval battles of the Civil War from a variety of sources. (Rev: BL 12/15/89) [973.7]

8647 Horwitz, Tony. *Confederates in the Attic: Dispatches from the Unfinished Civil War* (10–12). 1998, Pantheon $27.50 (0-679-43978-1); Knopf paper $14.00 (0-679-75833-X). This is an exploration by a Pulitzer Prize-winning reporter of why the Civil War continues to fascinate Americans. The author gathered material for a year throughout the Old South, where he visited battlefields and interviewed hundreds of people. (Rev: BL 2/1/98; SLJ 7/98) [973.7]

8648 Hull, Mary E. *The Union and the Civil War in American History* (6–10). Series: In American History. 2000, Enslow LB $19.95 (0-7660-1416-9). This account explains how the North tried to keep the nation together through the Civil War and highlights how different groups — from nurses and soldiers to people on the home front — helped the war effort. (Rev: BL 7/00; HBG 3/01) [973.7]

8649 Jackson, Donald Dale. *Twenty Million Yankees: The Northern Home Front* (9–12). Illus. 1985, Silver Burdett LB $25.93 (0-8094-4753-3). This volume in the Time-Life series deals with life in the North during the Civil War. [973.7]

8650 Jaynes, Gregory. *The Killing Ground: Wilderness to Cold Harbor* (9–12). Illus. 1986, Silver Burdett LB $25.93 (0-8094-4769-X). The story of the bloody battles in Virginia early in 1864 are retold in this volume in the Time-Life series. [973.7]

8651 Katcher, Philip. *The Civil War Source Book* (9–12). 1992, Facts on File $35.00 (0-8160-2823-0). This resource that can be read from cover to cover provides comprehensive coverage of events, issues, and details of the Civil War. (Rev: SLJ 1/93*) [973.7]

8652 Kelly, Orr, and Mary D. Kelly. *Dream's End: Two Iowa Brothers in the Civil War* (10–12). 1998, Kodansha $25.00 (1-56836-226-9). A genealogist uses creative historical research to re-create the world and events experienced by two young Iowa brothers who died in the Civil War. (Rev: BL 9/15/98; SLJ 4/99) [973.7]

8653 Korn, Jerry. *The Fight for Chattanooga: Chickamauga to Missionary Ridge* (9–12). Illus. 1985, Silver Burdett LB $25.93 (0-8094-4817-3). In this volume in the Time-Life Civil War series, four battles — Chickamauga, Chattanooga, Lookout

Mountain, and Missionary Ridge — are highlighted. [973.7]

8654 Lawliss, Chuck. *The Civil War: A Traveler's Guide and Sourcebook* (9–12). 1991, Crown paper $20.00 (0-517-57767-4). A comprehensive guide to places, events, and personages of the Civil War. (Rev: BL 4/15/91; SLJ 4/92) [917.304]

8655 *Lee Takes Command: From Seven Days to Second Bull Run* (7–12). Illus. 1984, Silver Burdett LB $25.93 (0-8094-4805-X). A graphic account complemented with many illustrations of Lee's campaign during 1862. [973.7]

8656 Leonard, Elizabeth D. *All the Daring of the Soldier: Women of the Civil War Armies* (9–12). 1999, Norton paper $15 .00 (0-14-029858-4). The story of female soldiers in the Civil War, some of whom were spies, others who were women disguised as male soldiers. [973.7]

8657 Logue, Larry M. *To Appomattox and Beyond: The Civil War Soldier in War and Peace* (9–12). 1995, Ivan R. Dee $22.50 (1-56663-093-2). Traces Civil War soldiers from the time they enlisted to their discharge and their lives after the war. (Rev: BL 10/15/95) [973.7]

8658 McPherson, James M. *For Cause and Comrades: Why Men Fought in the Civil War* (10–12). 1997, Oxford $40.00 (0-19-509023-3). To show what motivated the soldiers on both sides in the Civil War, the famed historian uses quotations from more than 25,000 letters and 249 diaries. (Rev: BL 2/1/97; SLJ 10/97) [973.7]

8659 McPherson, James M. *Hallowed Ground: A Walk at Gettysburg* (10–12). 2003, Crown $16.00 (0-609-61023-6). The Battle of Gettysburg is beautifully chronicled in three chapters, each covering a single day of the three-day conflict. (Rev: BL 3/1/03*; SLJ 8/03) [973.7]

8660 McPherson, James M. *Images of the Civil War: The Paintings of Mort Kunstler* (9–12). 1992, Gramercy $24.99 (0-517-07356-0). An album of 70 full-color paintings covering a wide range of Civil War subjects, accompanied by a brief description of the war by McPherson, a renowned historian. (Rev: BL 11/1/92; SLJ 5/93) [973.7]

8661 Malone, John. *The Civil War Quiz Book* (9–12). 1992, Morrow paper $10.00 (0-688-11269-2). A year-by-year roundup of Civil War facts. (Rev: BL 2/15/92) [973.7]

8662 Marten, James A. *Children for the Union: The War Spirit on the Northern Home Front* (9–12). Illus. Series: American Childhoods. 2004, Ivan R. Dee $26.00 (1-56663-563-2). This volume surveys the lives and living conditions of children growing up in the North during the Civil War. (Rev: BL 4/1/04) [974]

8663 *The Most Fearful Ordeal: Original Coverage of the Civil War* (9–12). Ed. by James M. McPherson. Illus. 2004, St. Martin's $35.00 (0-312-33123-1). This is a collection of *New York Times* articles that cover the Civil War from John Brown at Harper's Ferry to Lincoln at Ford's Theater. (Rev: BL 5/15/04) [973.7]

8664 Murphy, Jim. *The Boys' War: Confederate and Union Soldiers Talk About the Civil War* (6–12). Series: Icarus World Issues. 1990, Clarion $18.00 (0-89919-893-7). Diaries, journals, and letters of young soldiers on both sides of the Civil War are used to describe their military role, early impressions of the war, life in the camps and field, and return home. (Rev: BL 12/1/90; SLJ 1/91*) [973.7]

8665 Nevin, David. *The Road to Shiloh: Early Battles in the West* (9–12). Illus. 1983, Silver Burdett LB $25.93 (0-8094-4717-7). This volume of the Time-Life series deals with the early battles in Kentucky and the Battle of Shiloh in 1862. [973.7]

8666 Nevin, David. *Sherman's March: Atlanta to the Sea* (9–12). Illus. 1986, Silver Burdett LB $25.93 (0-8094-4813-0). A reconstruction of the destructive march through Georgia and the Carolinas by Sherman. Part of the Time-Life Civil War series. [973.7]

8667 Ray, Delia. *Behind the Blue and Gray: The Soldier's Life in the Civil War* (5–10). Series: Young Readers' History of the Civil War. 1991, Dutton $17.99 (0-525-67333-4). This sequel to *A Nation Torn* uses personal accounts to describe the life of the common soldier on both sides of the Civil War. (Rev: BL 9/1/91; SLJ 8/91*) [973.7]

8668 Reger, James P. *The Battle of Antietam* (6–10). Illus. Series: Battles. 1996, Lucent LB $26.20 (1-56006-454-4). The story of the bloody 1862 Civil War battle that cost both sides dearly but stopped the northern invasion of General Lee. (Rev: BL 1/1–15/97; SLJ 7/97) [973.7]

8669 Reger, James P. *Life in the South During the Civil War* (6–10). Illus. Series: The Way People Live. 1997, Lucent LB $27.45 (1-56006-333-5). A behind-the-battlefront look at life in the cities and on the plantations of the South during the Civil War and how the war affected everyday activities. (Rev: BL 3/15/97; SLJ 3/97) [975]

8670 Ripple, Ezra Hoyt. *Dancing Along the Deadline: The Andersonville Memoir of a Prisoner of the Confederacy* (10–12). Ed. by Mark A. Snell. Illus. 1996, Presidio $19.95 (0-89141-577-7). This slim volume contains the memoirs of a Union soldier who was captured in July 1864 and spent time in Confederate prisons, including the infamous Andersonville. (Rev: SLJ 5/97) [973.7]

8671 Roberts, Russell. *Lincoln and the Abolition of Slavery* (5–12). Series: American War. 1999, Lucent LB $27.45 (1-56006-580-X). This gripping, fully documented account describes the events leading to the Civil War and Lincoln's role in these events. (Rev: BL 1/1–15/00; HBG 10/00) [973.7]

8672 Robertson, James I., Jr. *Civil War! America Becomes One Nation* (6–10). 1992, Knopf $16.99 (0-394-92996-9). A basic history of the Civil War, with each chapter devoted to one calendar year of the conflict. (Rev: BL 4/1/92; SLJ 5/92) [973.7]

8673 Schultz, Duane. *The Most Glorious Fourth: Vicksburg and Gettysburg, July 4th, 1863* (10–12). Illus. 2001, Norton $27.95 (0-393-04870-5). Using many original sources, the author re-creates July 4, 1863, the day that Vicksburg was surrendered by Confederate troops and Lee's army retreated from Gettysburg. (Rev: BL 9/15/01) [973.7]

8674 Sears, Stephen W. *Chancellorsville* (10–12). 1996, Houghton paper $17 .00 (0-395-87744-X). A thorough examination of the course and importance of this Confederate victory. (Rev: BL 10/15/96) [973.7]

8675 *Second Manassas* (8–12). Illus. Series: Voices of the Civil War. 1995, Time-Life $29.95 (0-7835-4701-3). The gripping story of the important Second Battle of Bull Run, in 1862, is re-created with extensive use of original documents. (Rev: BL 7/95) [973.7]

8676 Seidman, Rachel Filene. *The Civil War: A History in Documents* (9–12). Illus. 2000, Oxford $30.00 (0-19-511558-9). These documents, many of which are about the experiences of ordinary people, cover the causes and aftermath of the Civil War as well as the war itself. (Rev: BL 12/15/00; HBG 10/01; SLJ 3/01) [973.7]

8677 Shea, William L., and Earl J. Hess. *Pea Ridge: Civil War Campaign in the West* (9–12). 1992, Univ. of North Carolina Pr. $34.95 (0-8078-2042-3). A comprehensive study of the 1862 Arkansas conflict that was the largest Civil War battle fought west of the Mississippi. (Rev: BL 11/1/92) [973.7]

8678 *Shiloh* (7–12). Illus. Series: Voices of the Civil War. 1996, Time-Life $29.95 (0-7835-4707-2). The horror and gallantry associated with the Battle of Shiloh come alive through this account rich in excerpts from military histories, letters, diary entries, and memoirs. (Rev: BL 1/1–15/97; BR 3–4/97) [973.7]

8679 Sneden, Robert Knox. *Eye of the Storm: A Civil War Odyssey* (10–12). Illus. 2000, Free Pr. $37.50 (0-684-86365-0). This unusual first-person account of a Union soldier in the Civil War, which includes time in the infamous Andersonville prison, presents the human side of this war. (Rev: BL 8/00) [973.7]

8680 *South Carolina in the Civil War: The Confederate Experience in Letters and Diaries* (10–12). Ed. by J. Edward Lee and Ron Chepesiuk. Illus. 2001, McFarland $28.50 (0-7864-0794-8). Though limited geographically, this book supplies details of the hardships of war both at home and on the battlefield by using excerpts from the diaries and letters of 17 Confederate citizens. (Rev: BL 1/1–15/01) [973.7]

8681 Spaulding, Lily May, and John Spaulding, eds. *Civil War Recipes: Recipes from the Pages of Godey's Lady's Book* (9–12). 1999, Univ. Press of Kentucky $19.95 (0-8131-2082-9). Recipes for common, everyday meals drawn from 19th-century women's magazines, to which the authors have added interesting historical information such as Confederate and Union army rations, cooking utensils, and food substitutions frequently used by southern cooks. (Rev: SLJ 7/99) [973.7]

8682 *Spies, Scouts, and Raiders: Irregular Operations* (9–12). Illus. 1985, Silver Burdett LB $25.93 (0-8094-4713-4). This pictorial volume, part of the Time-Life series, presents some of the unusual military operations of the Civil War. [973.7]

8683 Stiles, T. J., ed. *In Their Own Words: Civil War Commanders* (9–12). 1995, Putnam paper $15.00 (0-399-51909-2). Writings by Civil War commanders from both the North and South. (Rev: BL 3/15/95; SLJ 8/95) [973.7]

8684 Stokesbury, James L. *A Short History of the Civil War* (9–12). 1995, Morrow $25.00 (0-688-11523-3). This fine history of the Civil War focuses on the military aspects of the war. (Rev: BL 10/15/95; SLJ 8/96) [973.7]

8685 Street, James, Jr. *The Struggle for Tennessee: Tupelo to Stones River* (9–12). Illus. 1985, Silver Burdett LB $25.93 (0-8094-4761-4). This part of the Time-Life series deals with the important areas of Tennessee and Kentucky during the Civil War. [973.7]

8686 Symonds, Craig L. *The American Heritage History of the Battle of Gettysburg* (10–12). Illus. 2001, HarperCollins $50.00 (0-06-019474-X). A richly illustrated overview that draws on letters, diaries, and memoirs. (Rev: BL 1/1–15/02) [973.7]

8687 Tackach, James, ed. *The Battle of Gettysburg* (8–12). Illus. Series: At Issue in History. 2002, Greenhaven paper $18.70 (0-7377-0826-6). Excerpts from historical documents and contemporary writings portray events at Gettysburg from both Union and Confederate points of view, with maps, photographs, and other illustrations. (Rev: BL 5/1/02) [973.7]

8688 Tackach, James. *The Emancipation Proclamation: Abolishing Slavery in the South* (8–12). Illus. Series: Words That Changed History. 1999, Lucent LB $27.45 (1-56006-370-X). This is the story of the short proclamation that changed U.S. history, with material on slavery, Abraham Lincoln, the Civil War, and the document's historical legacy. (Rev: BL 6/1–15/99; HBG 4/00; SLJ 8/99) [973.7]

8689 *Vicksburg* (7–12). Illus. Series: Voices of the Civil War. 1997, Time-Life $29.95 (0-7835-4713-7). The story of the siege of Vicksburg in 1863 and the Union victory that cut the Confederacy in two. (Rev: BL 1/1–15/97) [973.7]

8690 *War Between Brothers* (7–12). Illus. 1996, Time-Life $19.95 (0-7835-6251-9). A discussion of the Civil War, including secession of the Confederate states, key Civil War battles, and the assassination of Abraham Lincoln, using vivid text, first-person narratives, and numerous illustrations. (Rev: BL 12/15/96; BR 3–4/97) [973.7]

8691 Ward, Geoffrey, et al. *The Civil War: An Illustrated History* (9–12). Illus. 1990, Knopf $75.00 (0-394-56285-2). A handsome, readable account that was prepared for the television series on the Civil War that aired in 1990. (Rev: BL 8/90; SLJ 3/91) [973.7]

8692 Woodhead, Henry, et al. *Atlanta* (10–12). Series: Voices of the Civil War. 1996, Time-Life $29.95 (0-7835-4702-1). The history of Atlanta during the Civil War is retold with extensive use of diaries, memoirs, and letters, as well as outstanding illustrations. (Rev: BR 1–2/97; SLJ 3/97) [973.7]

8693 Woodhead, Henry, et al. *Soldier Life* (10–12). 1996, Time-Life $29.95 (0-7835-4703-X). The human side of being a soldier on both the Confederate and Union sides during the Civil War is explored in this account that uses primary sources extensively plus many illustrations and maps. (Rev: BR 1–2/97; SLJ 3/97) [973.3]

8694 Woodworth, Steven E. *Cultures in Conflict: The American Civil War* (10–12). 2000, Greenwood $45.00 (0-313-30651-6). Documents including memoirs, diaries, letters, and photographs illustrate the cultural differences between North and South. (Rev: VOYA 2/01) [973.7]

8695 Yancey, Diane. *Strategic Battles* (5–12). Series: American War. 1999, Lucent LB $27.45 (1-56006-496-X). The key battles of the Civil War are covered in chronological order with maps and other illustrations. (Rev: BL 1/1–15/00; HBG 10/00) [973.7]

8696 Zeinert, Karen. *The Lincoln Murder Plot* (6–12). 1999, Shoe String LB $22.50 (0-208-02451-4). A detailed, well-documented retelling of the first assassination of a U.S. president and its world-shaking results. (Rev: BL 3/1/99; BR 9–10/99; HB 7–8/99; SLJ 5/99; VOYA 4/99) [973.7]

WESTWARD EXPANSION AND PIONEER LIFE

8697 Brown, Dee. *The American West* (9–12). 1994, Scribner $25.00 (0-02-517421-5). Diaries, letters, and newspaper articles are used to describe conflicts and culture in the American West, including Indian wars, settlers' town life, and the gold rush. (Rev: BL 10/15/94*) [978]

8698 Brown, Dee. *Wondrous Times on the Frontier* (9–12). 1991, August House $23.95 (0-87483-137-7). A series of humorous stories from the American West, including bawdy and outrageous tales of American Indian and Mexican confrontations with pioneer settlers. (Rev: BL 10/15/91) [978]

8699 Bryan, Howard. *Robbers, Rogues and Ruffians: True Tales of the Wild West* (9–12). 1991, Clear Light $22.95 (0-940666-04-9). Includes accounts about lesser-known New Mexico Territory desperadoes and pioneers based on period newspaper stories and interviews. (Rev: BL 12/1/91) [978.9]

8700 Dary, David. *Cowboy Culture* (10–12). 1989, Avon paper $14.95 (0-7006-0390-5). A 500-year history of the American cowboy. [973]

8701 Dary, David. *The Santa Fe Trail: Its History, Legends, and Lore* (10–12). Illus. 2000, Knopf $30.00 (0-375-40361-2). From Zebulon Pike's trek to Santa Fe in 1807 to the building of a network of trading posts and towns, this is the story of the Santa Fe Trail. (Rev: BL 9/1/00) [978]

8702 Dary, David. *Seeking Pleasure in the Old West* (10–12). 1995, Knopf $30.00 (0-394-56178-3). Using diaries, recollections, and period newspapers, the author re-creates everyday life in the old West and tells of the interesting and creative ways ordinary people entertained themselves, shattering the stereotypical portrayals of cowboys, gun fights, and bawdy houses. (Rev: BL 12/1/95; SLJ 7/96) [978]

8703 Dolan, Edward F. *Beyond the Frontier: The Story of the Trails West* (6–10). Series: Great Journeys. 1999, Benchmark LB $31.36 (0-7614-0969-6). As well as describing life on the Santa Fe, Oregon, and California trails, and the sea routes taken west, this account covers such specific topics as the Donner Party and life in western settlements. (Rev: BL 1/1–15/00; HBG 3/00; SLJ 2/00) [978]

8704 Duncan, Dayton. *People of the West* (5–10). Illus. 1996, Little, Brown $19.95 (0-316-19627-4). Individual people — both famous and less well known — describe in their own words the opening up of the West. Based on the PBS series. (Rev: BL 8/96; SLJ 10/96) [978]

8705 Flood, Elizabeth Clair, and William Mannis. *Cowgirls: Women of the Wild West* (10–12). Illus. 2000, Zon International $45.00 (0-939549-18-2). Covering the years 1880 to 1950, this is a lively pictorial history of a rare breed of woman, the American cowgirl. (Rev: BL 6/1–15/00) [978]

8706 Freedman, Russell. *Buffalo Hunt* (7–10). 1988, Holiday $21.95 (0-8234-0702-0). A history of how the buffalo were hunted from the times of the Indians to the slaughter by whites that brought on the near extinction of this animal. (Rev: BL 10/1/88; SLJ 10/88) [973]

8707 Green, Carl R. *The California Trail to Gold in American History* (6–10). Series: In American History. 2000, Enslow LB $20.95 (0-7660-1347-2). Searchers for gold in California first used the Oregon Trail to go west, then they made their own separate, more direct trail. This is the history of that trail. (Rev: BL 10/15/2000; HBG 3/01) [978]

8708 Herb, Angela. *Beyond the Mississippi: Early Westward Expansion of the United States* (7–12). Illus. Series: Young Readers' History of the West. 1996, Dutton $16.99 (0-525-67503-5). This large-size, heavily illustrated history of westward expansion covers such subjects as traders and trappers, missionaries, the treatment of Native Americans, homesteaders, the Mexican War, the gold rush, and the Oregon Trail. (Rev: BL 10/15/96; SLJ 11/96; VOYA 2/97) [978]

8709 Hirschfelder, Arlene B. *Photo Odyssey: Solomon Cavalho's Remarkable Western Adventure, 1853–54* (6–10). Illus. 2000, Clarion $18.00 (0-395-89123-X). The story of the last westward journey of John C. Fremont as seen through the eyes of a painter/photographer who was a member of the expedition. (Rev: BCCB 9/00; BL 7/00; HBG 9/00; SLJ 8/00*; VOYA 12/00) [917.8]

8710 Holt, Marilyn Irvin. *Children of the Western Plains: The Nineteenth-Century Experience* (10–12). Illus. Series: American Childhoods. 2003, Ivan R. Dee $26.00 (1-56663-540-3). Life on the prairie is portrayed through well-researched narrative and the use of period correspondence, diaries, and memoirs. (Rev: BL 10/15/03) [978]

8711 Kallen, Stuart A. *Life on the American Frontier* (6–10). Series: The Way People Live. 1998, Lucent LB $27.45 (1-56006-366-1). Thematically arranged chapters offer material on everyday life on the American frontier and on such groups as the trailblazers, the mountain men, the miners, the railroad men, the sodbusters, and the cattlemen. (Rev: BL 10/15/98; SLJ 1/99; VOYA 12/99) [978]

8712 Katz, William L. *Black Pioneers: An Untold Story* (7–12). 1999, Simon & Schuster $17.00 (0-689-81410-0). The stories of the many determined African Americans who defied prejudice, slavery, and severe legal restrictions such as the Northwest Territory's "Black Laws" to make a new life for themselves in the frontier of pre-Civil War days. (Rev: BL 7/99; HB 7–8/99; HBG 9/99; SLJ 9/99; VOYA 8/99) [977]

8713 Lavender, David. *The Great West* (9–12). Illus. 1985, Houghton paper $8.95 (0-8281-0481-6). This richly illustrated volume covers the history of the West and its development from 1763 through the beginning of the 20th century. [978]

8714 Lavender, David. *Snowbound: The Tragic Story of the Donner Party* (6–10). Illus. 1996, Holiday $18.95 (0-8234-1231-8). With extensive use of primary documents and excellent illustrations, this account vividly reconstructs the hardships and horror of the Donner Party's attempt to cross the Rockies. (Rev: BL 6/1–15/96; SLJ 7/96; VOYA 8/96) [978]

8715 Luchetti, Cathy. *Children of the West: Frontier Family Life* (10–12). Illus. 2001, Norton $39.95 (0-393-04913-2). Using more than 100 photographs plus excerpts from letters, diaries, and other sources, the author re-creates child bearing, child rearing, and childhood in frontier America. (Rev: BL 6/1–15/01) [978]

8716 Luchetti, Cathy. *Home on the Range: A Culinary History of the American West* (9–12). 1993, Random paper $25.00 (0-679-74484-3). A complete picture of the role food preparation and meals played in 19th-century daily life on the frontier, with photographs, diary extracts, and recipes. (Rev: BL 7/93; SLJ 12/93) [394.1]

8717 Luchetti, Cathy. *Men of the West: Life on the American Frontier* (9–12). Illus. 2004, Norton $39.95 (0-393-05905-7). Using many photographs and excerpts from original sources, this is a fine history of the roles played by men in opening up, settling, and farming the American West. (Rev: BL 2/1/04) [978]

8718 McCormick, Anita Louise. *The Pony Express in American History* (6–10). Series: In American History. 2001, Enslow LB $20.95 (0-7660-1296-4). This account traces the development and the short life of this phenomenon that linked the East to the West and created an American legend. (Rev: BL 8/01; HBG 10/01) [383]

8719 Mancall, Peter C., ed. *American Eras: Westward Expansion (1800–1860)* (8–12). 1999, Gale $115.00 (0-7876-1483-1). The period of growth and change in America from the early 19th century up to the Civil War is examined. (Rev: BL 3/15/99; SLJ 8/99) [973.6]

8720 Marrin, Albert. *Cowboys, Indians, and Gunfighters: The Story of the Cattle Kingdom* (6–10). 1993, Atheneum $22.95 (0-689-31774-3). An exciting account of the Old West, including Comanche vengeance, buffalo hunts, and frontier lawlessness. (Rev: BL 8/93; VOYA 10/93) [978]

8721 Murphy, Virginia R. *Across the Plains in the Donner Party* (6–10). Ed. by Karen Zeinert. 1996, Linnet LB $21.50 (0-208-02404-2). As well as being a condensation of the memoirs of a teenage survivor of the Donner Party, this account gives good background information and excerpts from other original sources. (Rev: BL 6/1–15/96; BR 1–2/97; SLJ 8/96; VOYA 8/96) [979.4]

8722 Parkman, Francis. *The Oregon Trail* (10–12). Illus. 1950, NAL paper $4.95 (0-451-52513-2). Parkman describes his adventures traveling west as a young man in 1846. First published in 1849. [978]

8723 Peavy, Linda, and Ursula Smith. *Frontier Children* (6–12). 1999, Univ. of Oklahoma Pr. $24.95 (0-8061-3161-6). This richly illustrated volume full of excerpts from primary sources looks at the lives of children on America's frontier during the 19th century. (Rev: BL 10/1/99; VOYA 12/00) [978]

8724 Peavy, Linda Sellers, and Ursula Smith. *Pioneer Women: The Lives of Women on the Frontier* (9–12). 1996, Smithmark paper $16.05 (0-8061-3054-7). Firsthand accounts and stark black-and-white photographs bring to life the social and physical challenges facing women pioneers in the American West. [305.4]

8725 Peters, Arthur K. *Seven Trails West* (10–12). 1996, Abbeville $39.95 (1-55859-782-4). This well-researched work traces the expansion of the American continent from 1804 to 1869 through the development of seven important trails, including the Santa Fe Trail, the Oregon-California Trail, the Pony Express, the Transcontinental Telegraph, and the Transcontinental Railroad, and the trail taken by Lewis and Clark's expedition. (Rev: BL 6/1–15/96; SLJ 12/96) [978]

8726 *Pioneers* (10–12). Ed. by Mark McKain. Series: History Firsthand. 2002, Gale LB $25.96 (0-7377-1078-0); paper $16.96 (0-7377-1077-2). Original documents cover topics ranging from journey preparations to claiming land to battling nature to create homes and farms in the West. (Rev: BL 12/15/02) [978]

8727 Rau, Margaret. *The Wells Fargo Book of the Gold Rush* (6–10). 2001, Simon & Schuster $18.00 (0-689-83019-X). This comprehensive account of the California Gold Rush, which includes many period photographs and illustrations from the Wells Fargo archives, looks at the miners themselves, their techniques, daily life, the impact on the environment, and the relations among various ethnic groups. (Rev: BCCB 6/01; BL 7/01; HBG 10/01; SLJ 6/01; VOYA 10/01) [979.4]

8728 Reinfeld, Fred. *Pony Express* (7–12). Illus. 1973, Univ. of Nebraska Pr. paper $10.95 (0-8032-5786-4). A history of the communication system that linked the East and West and the courageous riders who manned it. [383]

8729 Richards, Colin. *Sheriff Pat Garrett's Last Days* (8–12). Illus. 1986, Sunstone paper $8.95 (0-86534-079-X). A history of the Wild West drawn into focus by the death of the man who shot Billy the Kid. (Rev: BR 11–12/86) [978]

8730 Rothschild, Mary Logan, and Pamela Claire Hronek. *Doing What the Day Brought: An Oral History of Arizona Women* (9–12). 1992, Univ. of Arizona Pr. $43.50 (0-8165-1032-6); paper $18.95 (0-8165-1276-0). The role and lives of pioneer women in Arizona. (Rev: BL 2/1/92) [305.4]

8731 Sanford, William R. *The Chisholm Trail* (6–10). Series: In American History. 2000, Enslow LB $20.95 (0-7660-1345-6). A look at this important trail that stretched from Texas to Kansas, and became the main route for driving longhorn cattle to the North. (Rev: BL 7/00; HBG 3/01; SLJ 12/00) [978]

8732 Sanford, William R. *The Santa Fe Trail in American History* (6–10). Series: In American History. 2000, Enslow LB $20.95 (0-7660-1348-0). The story of the trail from Missouri to New Mexico that opened in 1821 and became an important continental trade route. (Rev: BL 10/15/2000; HBG 3/01) [978]

8733 Savage, William W. *The Cowboy Hero: His Image in American History and Culture* (10–12). Illus. 1987, Univ. of Oklahoma Pr. paper $15.95 (0-8061-1920-9). A history of the American cowboy with material on how he has been portrayed in the media. [973]

8734 Schlissel, Lillian, et al. *Far from Home: Families of the Westward Journey* (9–12). Illus. 1989, Schocken $19.95 (0-8052-4052-7). From a number of different sources, the authors have pieced together the stories of four families, their journeys west, and their lives as pioneers. (Rev: BL 4/1/89) [978]

8735 Sigerman, Harriet. *Land of Many Hands: Women in the American West* (7–12). 1998, Oxford $24.95 (0-19-509942-7). A well-researched account that uses many original documents to tell the story of women's role in the opening up of the West, their struggles and triumphs, and how different ethnic groups were treated. (Rev: BL 2/15/98; BR 5–6/98; HBG 3/99; SLJ 4/98; VOYA 4/98) [978]

8736 Stanley, Jerry. *Cowboys and Longhorns: A Portrait of the Long Drive* (5–12). Illus. 2003, Crown $18.95 (0-375-81565-1). Stanley debunks the popular view of cowboys, using the long cattle drives from Texas to Kansas to illustrate the dangers and discomforts of an unglamorous life on horseback. (Rev: BL 7/03*; HBG 4/04; SLJ 8/03) [636.2]

8737 Stanley, Jerry. *Frontier Merchants: Lionel and Barron Jacobs and the Jewish Pioneers Who Settled the West* (5–10). 1998, Crown $20.99 (0-517-80020-9). This fascinating biography of the Jacobs brothers, who set up a successful business venture in Tucson in 1867, illustrates business development in pioneer communities and the role of Jewish immigrants in building the economic foundation of the West. (Rev: BR 5–6/99; HBG 3/99; SLJ 3/99) [973.8]

8738 Stefoff, Rebecca. *The Oregon Trail in American History* (6–10). Illus. Series: In American History. 1997, Enslow LB $20.95 (0-89490-771-9). The story of the Oregon Trail and the everyday life of the settlers who traveled it are re-created, with a guide to the trail as it exists today. (Rev: BL 2/1/98; HBG 3/98; SLJ 2/98) [978]

8739 Stefoff, Rebecca. *Women Pioneers* (6–12). Series: American Profiles. 1995, Facts on File $25.00 (0-8160-3134-7). Nine profiles of pioneer women noted for their courage, ingenuity, and triumphs are presented in this readable account that gives details of life on the American frontier. (Rev: BL 1/1–15/96; SLJ 2/96; VOYA 4/96) [973.8]

8740 Stovall, TaRessa. *The Buffalo Soldiers* (6–10). Illus. Series: African-American Achievers. 1997, Chelsea LB $21.95 (0-7910-2595-0); paper $9.95 (0-7910-2596-9). The story of the stirring achievements of the black U.S. Army regiments that distinguished themselves during numerous campaigns and played a vital role in the settlement of the American West. (Rev: BL 12/1/97; HBG 3/98) [978]

8741 Stratton, Joanne L. *Pioneer Women: Voices from the Kansas Frontier* (10–12). Illus. 1981, Simon & Schuster paper $12.95 (0-671-44748-3). This book is based on first-person accounts of almost 800 pioneer women who lived in Kansas between 1854 and 1890. [978.1]

8742 Torr, James D., ed. *The American Frontier* (7–12). Series: Turning Points in World History. 2001, Greenhaven LB $31.20 (0-7377-0785-2); paper $19.95 (0-7377-0786-0). A collection of essays that explores the opening up of the West, the nature of the pioneer spirit, and the changes this development brought to our history. (Rev: BL 3/15/02) [973.7]

8743 Torr, James D., ed. *Westward Expansion* (7–12). Series: Interpreting Primary Documents. 2003, Gale LB $16.96 (0-7377-1134-5); paper $21.20 (0-7377-1133-7). A broad selection of primary sources present different perspectives on issues relating to the United States' westward expansion (the Indian Wars, building the transcontinental railroad, the gold rush, and so forth). (Rev: BL 1/1–15/03; SLJ 2/03) [978]

8744 Tunis, Edwin. *Frontier Living* (7–12). 1976, Crowell paper $18.95 (1-58574-137-X). Using more than 200 original drawings and a fine text, the author portrays the life, artifacts, and customs of the American frontier. [978]

8745 Uscham, Michael V. *Westward Expansion* (7–10). Series: World History. 2000, Lucent LB $19.96 (1-56006-690-3). The story of how the quest for economic opportunities, land, and personal freedom stretched the boundaries of the United States to the Pacific Ocean. (Rev: BL 10/15/2000; SLJ 1/01) [978]

8746 Viola, Herman J. *Little Big Horn Remembered: The Untold Story of Custer's Last Stand* (10–12). 1999, Times Books (0-8129-3256-0). The story of the Battle of Little Big Horn in 1876 and the death of General Custer at the hands of Sioux and Cheyenne warriors. [973.8]

8747 Walker, Paul R. *Great Figures of the Wild West* (7–10). Series: American Profiles. 1992, Facts on File LB $25.00 (0-8160-2576-2). A vivid picture of the American West, with profiles of such people as Jesse James, Sitting Bull, Wyatt Earp, Geronimo, Judge Roy Bean, and Belle Starr. (Rev: BL 9/1/92; SLJ 8/92) [978]

8748 Walker, Paul R. *Trail of the Wild West* (10–12). 1997, National Geographic $30.00 (0-79227-021-5). An easily read introduction to the history of the American West, including the California gold rush, cattle drives, the Oregon Trail, and notorious outlaws, in National Geographic format with wonderful photographs. (Rev: SLJ 2/98) [973.8]

8749 Wexler, Sanford. *Westward Expansion* (9–12). Series: Facts on File's Eyewitness History. 1991, Facts on File $50.00 (0-8160-2407-3). The territorial growth of the United States from 1754 to 1897 is described through diaries, letters, and official documents. (Rev: BL 7/91; SLJ 12/91) [973]

8750 Worth, Richard. *Westward Expansion and Manifest Destiny in American History* (6–10). Series: In American History. 2001, Enslow LB $20.95 (0-7660-1457-6). This account chronicles events after the Revolution when Americans believed that westward expansion was their destiny and acted on this impulse. (Rev: BL 8/01; HBG 10/01; SLJ 7/01) [978]

8751 Yancey, Diane. *Life in the Pony Express* (6–10). Series: The Way People Live. 2001, Lucent LB $19.96 (1-56006-793-4). Though only in existence for 18 months, this transcontinental mail service, presented well in both text and pictures, made a great impact on American history. (Rev: BL 6/1–15/01; SLJ 8/01) [383]

RECONSTRUCTION TO WORLD WAR I (1865–1914)

8752 Currie, Stephen. *We Have Marched Together: The Working Children's Crusade* (7–12). Series: People's History. 1996, Lerner LB $30.35 (0-8225-1733-7). The focus of this book is on child labor in the United States and the protest march from Philadelphia to New York led by Mother Jones in 1903. (Rev: BL 5/1/97; SLJ 7/97) [331.3]

8753 De Angelis, Gina. *The Triangle Shirtwaist Company Fire of 1911* (7–12). Illus. Series: Great Disasters: Reforms and Ramifications. 2000, Chelsea $19.95 (0-7910-5267-2). This is a dramatic and detailed account of the fire, the conditions that made such a disaster possible, and the union protests that followed. (Rev: BL 10/15/00; HBG 3/01; SLJ 2/01; VOYA 2/01) [974.7]

8754 Fireside, Bryna J. *The Haymarket Square Riot Trial* (6–10). Series: Headline Court Cases. 2002, Enslow LB $20.95 (0-7660-1761-3). This is an account of the trial that resulted from the arrest of several people after a bomb-throwing incident during a labor protest rally in Chicago on May 4, 1886. (Rev: BL 3/15/03; HBG 3/03) [973.8]

8755 Fremon, David K. *The Alaska Purchase in American History* (7–10). Series: In American History. 1999, Enslow LB $20.95 (0-7660-1138-0). This account covers both the purchase of Alaska in 1867 and an early history of the Native Americans who lived there. (Rev: BL 11/15/99; HBG 3/00; SLJ 3/00) [979.8]

8756 Fry, Annette R. *The Orphan Trains* (7–12). Series: American Events. 1994, Macmillan LB $14.95 (0-02-735721-X). Interviews, letters, and photographs chronicle how slum children were sent on "orphan trains" to live in the West and how the move affected them. (Rev: BL 7/94; SLJ 1/95) [362.7]

8757 Golay, Michael. *The Spanish-American War* (10–12). Series: America at War. 1995, Facts on File LB $25.00 (0-8160-3174-6). With many illustrations and quotations from original sources, this is a fine history of the Spanish-American War. [973.8]

8758 Gourley, Catherine. *Good Girl Work: Factories, Sweatshops, and How Women Changed Their Role in the American Workforce* (7–10). 1999, Millbrook LB $26.90 (0-7613-0951-9). This history of the exploitation of female children around the turn of the 20th century includes dramatic, in-depth personal testimonies and first-person accounts from letters, diaries, memoirs, and newspaper interviews. (Rev: BL 5/1/99; BR 9–10/99; SLJ 8/99) [331.3]

8759 Greenwood, Janette Thomas. *The Gilded Age: A History in Documents* (6–12). Illus. 2000, Oxford LB $36.95 (0-19-510523-0). Documents of all kinds are used to show readers the many changes that took place in American society in the last years of the 19th century. (Rev: BL 10/1/00; HBG 3/01; SLJ 10/00) [973.8]

8760 Hansen, Joyce. *"Bury Me Not in a Land of Slaves": African-Americans in the Time of Reconstruction* (6–10). Illus. 2000, Watts LB $25.00 (0-531-11539-9). An excellent overview of the complex era that followed the Civil War and how compromises were reached on giving civil rights to African Americans. (Rev: BL 6/1–15/00; SLJ 6/00) [973]

8761 Haskins, Jim. *Geography of Hope: Black Exodus from the South After Reconstruction* (7–12). Illus. 1999, Twenty-First Century LB $31.90 (0-7613-0323-5). After information on slavery and the Reconstruction, the author describes the migrations of African Americans to the North, their leaders,

and the politics that made life in the South intolerable. (Rev: BL 10/15/99; HBG 4/00; SLJ 11/99; VOYA 6/00) [973]

8762 Immell, Myra H., ed. *The 1900s* (6–12). Series: America's Decades. 2000, Greenhaven LB $29.96 (0-7377-0294-X); paper $17.96 (0-7377-0293-1). After an overview chapter, the articles in this anthology cover the important events of this decade and highlight cultural and technological trends. (Rev: BL 7/00; SLJ 9/00) [973.9]

8763 Isserman, Maurice. *Journey to Freedom* (7–12). Illus. Series: Library of African American History. 1997, Facts on File $25.00 (0-8160-3413-3). An account of the African American men and women who traveled north at the beginning of the 20th century filled with hope and looking for freedom, dignity, and economic opportunity, and of the impact on the nation's politics and culture. (Rev: BL 2/15/98; BR 3–4/98) [975]

8764 McNeese, Tim. *Remember the Maine: The Spanish-American War Begins* (6–12). Illus. Series: First Battles. 2001, Morgan Reynolds LB $20.95 (1-883846-79-X). The story of the sinking of the battleship *Maine*, an event that led to the Spanish-American War in 1898. (Rev: BL 11/1/01; HBG 3/02; SLJ 4/02) [973.8]

8765 Roosevelt, Theodore. *The Rough Riders* (10–12). 1990, Da Capo paper $16.00 (0-306-80405-0). This is a history of the cavalry that fought under the command of Theodore Roosevelt during the Spanish-American War. [973.8]

8766 Smith, John David. *Black Voices from Reconstruction, 1865–1877* (10–12). 1996, Millbrook LB $28.40 (1-56294-583-1). The experiences of former slaves in the 12 years following the end of the Civil War are vividly presented in this overview that blends deftly written narrative with firsthand accounts. (Rev: BL 11/1/96; SLJ 2/97) [305.8]

8767 Smith, Karen M. *New Paths to Power: American Women 1890–1920* (8–12). Series: Young Oxford History of Women in the United States. 1994, Oxford $24.00 (0-19-508111-0). A history of American women from the end of the 19th century to 1920, the year they finally won the right to vote. (Rev: BL 12/15/94; SLJ 1/95) [305.4]

8768 Somerlott, Robert. *The Spanish-American War: "Remember the Maine!"* (6–12). Illus. Series: American War. 2002, Enslow LB $20.95 (0-7660-1855-5). This overview of the Spanish-American War's key events and individuals includes information on President William McKinley, Teddy Roosevelt and his Rough Riders, and Clara Barton. (Rev: BL 3/1/03; HBG 3/03; SLJ 6/03) [973.8]

8769 Stalcup, Brenda, ed. *Reconstruction* (8–12). Illus. Series: Opposing Viewpoints: American History. 1995, Greenhaven LB $32.45 (1-56510-227-4). An anthology of writings that present various points of view on the period of social transformation and controversy from 1865 through 1877 that is known as Reconstruction. (Rev: BL 3/15/95; SLJ 5/95) [973.8]

8770 Stein, R. Conrad. *The Transcontinental Railroad in American History* (6–10). Illus. Series: In American History. 1997, Enslow LB $20.95 (0-89490-882-0). This is a lively account of the building of the transcontinental railroad and the people involved, including the essential role of Chinese Americans. (Rev: BL 2/1/98; HBG 3/98; SLJ 1/98) [385]

8771 Tintori, Karen. *Trapped: The 1909 Cherry Mine Disaster* (10–12). Illus. 2002, Atria $25.00 (0-7434-2194-9). The author draws on primary sources to chronicle the story of a disastrous coal mine fire in Cherry, Illinois. (Rev: BL 9/1/02) [973.9]

8772 Woog, Adam. *The 1900's* (7–10). Illus. 1998, Lucent LB $27.45 (1-56006-550-8). This overview of the 1900s includes material on the economy, working and living conditions, politics, important events and personalities, and the growing influences of advertising, movies, and mass transportation. (Rev: SLJ 4/99) [973.9]

8773 Wukovits, John F. *The Spanish-American War* (7–10). Series: World History. 2002, Gale LB $27.45 (1-56006-682-2). The story of the 1898 war that freed Cuba and ceded Puerto Rico and Guam to the U.S. (Rev: BL 4/15/02; SLJ 1/02) [973.8]

8774 Ziff, Marsha. *Reconstruction Following the Civil War in American History* (7–10). Series: In American History. 1999, Enslow LB $19.95 (0-7660-1140-2). A look at the events, personalities, and movements associated with the period from 1865 to 1877. (Rev: BL 11/15/99; HBG 4/00; SLJ 3/00) [973.8]

WORLD WAR I

8775 Torr, James D., ed. *Primary Sources* (6–12). Series: American War Library: World War I. 2002, Gale LB $27.45 (1-59018-008-9). This is a collection of documents, letters, and memorabilia that describe key events and America's participation in World War I. (Rev: BL 6/1–15/02) [940.1]

8776 Wukovits, John F. *Flying Aces* (6–12). Series: American War Library: World War I. 2002, Gale LB $27.45 (1-56006-810-8). With an emphasis on American airmen, this account describes the war in the air and the people involved during World War I. (Rev: BL 6/1–15/02) [940.3]

8777 Wukovits, John F. *Strategic Battles* (6–12). Series: American War Library: World War I. 2002, Gale LB $27.45 (1-56006-836-1). The important battles of World War I are described with an emphasis on those involving Americans, with first-

hand accounts, maps, and archival photographs. (Rev: BL 6/1–15/02) [940.3]

BETWEEN THE WARS AND THE GREAT DEPRESSION (1918–1941)

8778 Agee, James, and Walker Evans. *Let Us Now Praise Famous Men* (10–12). Illus. 1989, Houghton paper $16.95 (0-395-48897-4). Through photographs and thoughtful text, this volume looks at the Depression and some of the families it affected. [973.9]

8779 Allen, Frederick L. *Only Yesterday* (10–12). 1957, HarperCollins paper $8.00 (0-06-080004-6). An informal history of American life and politics in the decade before the Crash. [973.91]

8780 Allen, Frederick L. *Since Yesterday: The 1930s in America* (10–12). 1986, HarperCollins paper $14.00 (0-06-091322-3). From the stock market crash to the outbreak of war in Europe, this is a social history of America in the 30s. [973.91]

8781 Altman, Linda J. *The Decade That Roared: America During Prohibition* (7–10). 1997, Twenty-First Century $21.40 (0-8050-4133-8). The excitement and significance of the roaring 20s are conveyed, with vivid depictions of bootleggers, flagpole sitters, mobsters, revivalist preachers, and speakeasy queens, as well as laborers, blues and jazz musicians, participants in the "Scopes monkey trial," and even conservative rural dwellers. (Rev: BR 3–4/98; SLJ 1/98) [973.9]

8782 Barry, John M. *The Great Influenza: The Epic Story of the Deadliest Plague in History* (10–12). 2004, Viking $29.95 (0-670-89473-7). This account of the deadly flu of 1918 tells how it started in Kansas and spread around the world and describes the reactions of the medical profession and politicians. (Rev: BL 2/15/04*) [614.5]

8783 Blackman, Cally. *The 20s and 30s: Flappers and Vamps* (5–10). Series: 20th Century Fashion. 2000, Gareth Stevens LB $25.26 (0-8368-2599-3). Social history is combined with fashion and design in this account of the 1920s and 1930s that is illustrated with period photographs and magazine covers. (Rev: HBG 10/00; SLJ 6/00) [973.9]

8784 Blumenthal, Karen. *Six Days in October: The Stock Market Crash of 1929* (7–12). Illus. 2002, Simon & Schuster $17.95 (0-689-84276-7). An absorbing look at the factors that led to the infamous crash and the fortunes that were lost, with clear definitions of economic concepts and interesting illustrations. (Rev: BL 11/1/02; HB 1–2/03; HBG 3/03; SLJ 10/02; VOYA 12/02) [332.64]

8785 Bragg, Rick. *Ava's Man* (7–12). 2001, Knopf $25.00 (0-375-41062-7). Bragg paints a loving portrait of his maternal grandfather, Charlie Bundrum, a simple backwoods man who, with his wife Ava, struggled to raise seven children to adulthood during the lean years of the Great Depression. (Rev: BL 6/1–15/01*; VOYA 4/02) [975]

8786 Burg, David F. *The Great Depression: An Eyewitness History* (9–12). 1996, Facts on File $50.00 (0-8160-3095-2). Primary sources help the reader understand what it was like to live during the Great Depression. (Rev: BL 12/15/95; VOYA 4/96) [973.91]

8787 Candaele, Kerry. *Bound for Glory: From the Great Migration to the Harlem Renaissance, 1910–1930* (7–10). Illus. Series: Milestones in Black American History. 1996, Chelsea LB $21.95 (0-7910-2261-7); paper $9.95 (0-7910-2687-6). This account covers the mass movement of African Americans from the rural South to the northern cities in the early 20th century and their achievements in the arts, politics, business, and sports, with emphasis on the origins of the Harlem Renaissance. (Rev: BL 10/15/96; BR 1–2/97; SLJ 2/97) [973]

8788 Caudill, Edward, et al. *The Scopes Trial: A Photographic History* (9–12). Illus. 2000, Univ. of Tennessee Pr. $45.00 (1-57233-080-5); paper $18.95 (1-57233-081-3). Well-annotated photographs are used to re-create the famous "monkey trial" of 1925. An introduction and afterword give useful background material. (Rev: BL 6/1–15/00) [345.73]

8789 Chambers, Veronica. *The Harlem Renaissance* (7–12). Illus. Series: African-American Achievers. 1997, Chelsea LB $21.95 (0-7910-2597-7); paper $9.95 (0-7910-2598-5). This history discusses the emergence of Harlem as a cultural center in the 1920s in the context of the social and political forces of the time, weaving in accounts of such greats as Langston Hughes, Countee Cullen, Zora Neale Hurston, and others who were part of this artistic and intellectual movement. (Rev: BL 2/15/98; BR 3–4/98; HBG 3/98; SLJ 4/98) [700]

8790 Davies, Nancy M. *The Stock Market Crash of 1929* (7–12). Series: American Events. 1994, Macmillan LB $14.95 (0-02-726221-9). The causes and effects of the devastating stock market crash of 1929 are traced, with a discussion of safeguards that were put in place. (Rev: BL 7/94) [338.5]

8791 *Dear Mrs. Roosevelt: Letters from Children of the Great Depression* (9–12). Ed. by Robert Cohen. Illus. 2002, Univ. of North Carolina Pr. $29.95 (0-8078-2747-9); paper $16.95 (0-8078-5413-1). Letters written during the Depression reveal the wide-ranging needs of children living in poverty and fear. (Rev: BL 10/15/02) [973.917]

8792 Dudley, William, ed. *The Great Depression: Opposing Viewpoints* (7–12). Illus. Series: Opposing Viewpoints Digests. 1994, Greenhaven LB $17.95 (1-56510-084-0). This account uses dozens of quotations from primary and secondary sources

to explore various facets of the Great Depression, including its causes, its effects, and the New Deal. (Rev: BL 2/1/94) [973.9]

8793 Edwards, Judith. *The Lindbergh Baby Kidnapping* (7–10). Series: In American History. 2000, Enslow LB $19.95 (0-7660-1299-9). The 1932 kidnapping and subsequent trial are covered in detail, followed by a discussion of capital punishment and the pressures involved in this celebrity case. (Rev: BL 1/1–15/00; HBG 9/00; SLJ 4/00) [973.9]

8794 Fremon, David K. *The Great Depression* (7–10). Series: In American History. 1997, Enslow LB $20.95 (0-89490-881-2). The Great Depression, its causes, its effects, and how it was ended, are covered in a lively text and many black-and-white photographs. (Rev: BL 5/15/97; BR 9–10/97) [338.5]

8795 Galbraith, John Kenneth. *The Great Crash, 1929* (10–12). 1988, Houghton paper $14.00 (0-395-85999-9). The economist traces the causes of the stock market crash of 1929 and speculates about the possibility of another one. [338.5]

8796 Gerdes, Louise I., ed. *The Great Depression* (7–12). Series: Great Speeches in History. 2002, Gale LB $31.20 (0-7377-0873-5); paper $19.95 (0-7377-0872-7). Various viewpoints on internal U.S. history from 1928 through 1939 are expressed in this collection of 21 speeches by such notables as Franklin Roosevelt, Huey Long, and Will Rogers. (Rev: BL 4/15/02; SLJ 4/02) [973.91]

8797 Gerdes, Louise I., ed. *The 1930s* (6–12). Series: America's Decades. 2000, Greenhaven LB $29.96 (0-7377-0030-8); paper $17.96 (0-7377-0299-0). After an overview chapter, this collection of essays covers such topics as the Great Depression, the New Deal, the Lindbergh kidnapping, labor disputes, and the importance of radio. (Rev: BL 7/00; SLJ 9/00) [973.9]

8798 Grant, R. G. *The Great Depression* (6–12). Illus. Series: Lives in Crisis. 2003, Barron's $14.95 (0-7641-5601-2). Period photographs and excerpts from letters, articles, and speeches add to the narrative about the economic collapse in the 1920s and 1930s, both in the United States and abroad. (Rev: BL 10/15/03*; HBG 4/04; SLJ 9/03) [303.9]

8799 *The Harlem Renaissance* (9–12). Ed. by Harold Bloom. Series: Bloom's Period Studies. 2003, Chelsea $37.95 (0-7910-7679-2). This is a fine history of the Harlem Renaissance, the literary themes explored, and how the phenomenon changed modern African American literature. [810.9]

8800 Harris, Nathaniel. *The Great Depression* (7–12). Illus. 1988, David & Charles $19.95 (0-7134-5658-2). This account describes the 1930s in the United States and in Britain and Europe. (Rev: SLJ 1/89) [973.91]

8801 Haskins, Jim. *The Harlem Renaissance* (6–10). Illus. 1996, Millbrook LB $30.90 (1-56294-565-3). This book offers a guided tour of the Harlem Renaissance from 1916 through 1940 and an introduction to the artists and writers involved. (Rev: BL 9/1/96; BR 11–12/96; SLJ 9/96; VOYA 12/96) [700]

8802 Herald, Jacqueline. *Fashions of a Decade: The 1920s* (7–12). Series: Fashions of a Decade. 1991, Facts on File $25.00 (0-8160-2465-0). An illustrated overview of fashions and trends of the 1920s as they reflected the development of modern life after World War I. (Rev: BL 12/15/91; SLJ 2/92) [391]

8803 Hill, Laban Carrick. *Harlem Stomp! A Cultural History of the Harlem Renaissance* (7–12). Illus. 2004, Little, Brown $18.95 (0-316-81411-3). This illustrated history covers developments during the roaring 1920s and the great creations and creators of the Harlem Renaissance. (Rev: BL 2/15/04*; SLJ 1/04; VOYA 2/04) [810.9]

8804 Hintz, Martin. *Farewell, John Barleycorn: Prohibition in the United States* (6–10). Illus. Series: People's History. 1996, Lerner LB $25.26 (0-8225-1734-5). A well-organized, readable account that traces the history of alcohol use in the United States, covers the 18th Amendment and its effects, and ends with repeal of Prohibition. (Rev: BL 8/96; SLJ 10/96) [363.4]

8805 Jacques, Geoffrey. *Free Within Ourselves: The Harlem Renaissance* (7–10). Illus. Series: African-American Experience. 1996, Watts LB $22.00 (0-531-11272-1). The important African American artists of the late 1920s, including writers, painters, musicians, actors, and sculptors, are profiled in this history of the Harlem Renaissance. (Rev: BL 2/15/97; SLJ 1/97) [700]

8806 McArthur, Debra. *The Dust Bowl and the Depression* (6–10). Series: In American History. 2002, Enslow LB $20.95 (0-7660-1838-5). A well-researched and well-documented account of the Great Depression in the Midwest, the plight of the farmers, and the lasting effects. (Rev: BL 5/15/02; HBG 10/02; SLJ 7/02) [973.91]

8807 McElvaine, Robert S. *The Depression and the New Deal: A History in Documents* (10–12). Illus. Series: Pages from History. 2000, Oxford $30.00 (0-19-510493-5). An adult documentary account of the 1930s in America that uses such primary sources as government papers, diaries, songs, poetry, art, cartoons, photographs, and newspaper articles to re-create life during the Great Depression and the New Deal. (Rev: BL 1/1–15/00; HBG 9/00; SLJ 4/00) [973.91]

8808 McElvaine, Robert S. *The Great Depression: America, 1929–1941* (10–12). 1984, Times Books paper $16.00 (0-8129-2327-8). This account begins with the presidency of Herbert Hoover and ends with the coming of World War II. [973.91]

8809 Meltzer, Milton. *Brother, Can You Spare a Dime? The Great Depression, 1929–1933* (7–12). Series: Library of American History. 1991, Facts on File $19.95 (0-8160-2372-7). Through firsthand accounts of workers, farmers, sharecroppers, veterans, and professionals, the author re-creates how this economic catastrophe affected millions of ordinary people. (Rev: BL 5/15/91; SLJ 10/91) [330.973]

8810 Nardo, Don, ed. *The Great Depression* (7–12). Series: Turning Points in World History. 2000, Greenhaven LB $21.96 (0-7377-0231-1); paper $13.96 (0-7377-0230-3). After a general overview of the Great Depression, this collection of informative essays and eyewitness accounts explores various aspects of this bleak period. (Rev: BL 5/15/00; SLJ 3/00) [338]

8811 Nardo, Don. *The Great Depression* (7–12). Illus. Series: Opposing Viewpoints Digests. 1997, Greenhaven paper $17.45 (1-56510-742-X). This volume presents various viewpoints on why the Depression occurred, the role of the government, and the pros and cons surrounding the New Deal as they were argued at the time, followed by modern historians' assessments. (Rev: BL 3/1/98; SLJ 4/98; VOYA 2/99) [973.917]

8812 Nardo, Don. *The Scopes Trial* (6–10). Illus. Series: Famous Trials. 1996, Lucent LB $27.45 (1-56006-268-1). The story of the "Great Monkey Trial" of 1925 that revolved around a schoolteacher named Scopes and the teaching of evolution in schools, and involved a confrontation between two great orators, attorneys Clarence Darrow and William Jennings Bryan. (Rev: BL 5/1/97; BR 11–12/97; SLJ 4/97) [345.73]

8813 Nishi, Dennis, ed. *The Great Depression* (6–12). Illus. Series: History Firsthand. 2001, Greenhaven LB $22.96 (0-7377-0411-X); paper $14.96 (0-7377-0410-1). More than 20 first-person accounts introduce readers to life during the Depression — on Wall Street, among the unemployed and the homeless, and the New Deal efforts of President Roosevelt. (Rev: BL 5/15/01) [338.5]

8814 Pietrusza, David. *The Roaring '20s* (7–10). Illus. Series: World History. 1997, Lucent LB $27.45 (1-56006-309-2). Prohibition, the Teapot Dome scandal, jazz, the economy and the stock market, the automobile, the speakeasy, and the Scopes Trial are among the topics covered in this history of the prosperous 1920s, when America became an urban society and headed for the Great Depression. (Rev: SLJ 7/98) [973.9]

8815 *The Roaring Twenties* (10–12). Ed. by Stuart A. Kallen. Series: History Firsthand. 2002, Gale LB $31.20 (0-7377-0885-9); paper $19.95 (0-7377-0884-0). This is a compilation of contemporary narratives and reminiscences that explore many points of view of the 1920s, particularly in the United States. (Rev: BL 4/15/02; SLJ 4/02) [973.9]

8816 *The Roaring Twenties: An Eyewitness History* (10–12). Ed. by Thomas Streissguth. 2001, Facts on File $75.00 (0-8160-4023-0). A collection of eyewitness accounts that covers the 1920s under such topics as Prohibition, scandals, women's suffrage, prosperity, and the stock market crash of 1929. (Rev: VOYA 2/02) [973.91]

8817 Ross, Stewart. *Causes and Consequences of the Great Depression* (7–10). Series: Causes and Consequences. 1998, Raintree Steck-Vaughn LB $29.97 (0-8172-4059-4). A thorough analysis that uses illustrations including cartoons, posters, photographs, and statistical charts as well as quotations from historians and world leaders. (Rev: BL 8/98; SLJ 6/98; VOYA 2/99) [338.542]

8818 Shannon, David, ed. *The Great Depression* (10–12). 1977, Peter Smith $20.00 (0-8446-2925-1). A look at how the Great Depression changed the lives of individuals. [330-973]

8819 Sonnenfeld, Kelly. *Memories of Clason Point* (6–12). 1998, Dutton $16.99 (0-525-45961-8). This candid memoir written by a daughter in a Jewish immigrant family living in the Bronx during the Great Depression recalls the material and emotional hardships. (Rev: BL 2/1/98; SLJ 3/98; VOYA 4/98) [974.7]

8820 Stimpson, Eddie, Jr. *My Remembers: A Black Sharecropper's Recollections of the Depression* (10–12). 1996, Univ. of North Texas Pr. $19.95 (0-929398-98-X). The story of an African American family and their life of poverty and hardship in rural Texas during and after the Great Depression. (Rev: SLJ 8/96) [973.9]

8821 Terkel, Studs. *Hard Times: An Oral History of the Great Depression* (9–12). 1970, Pantheon paper $15.00 (0-394-74691-0). This collection of first-person accounts graphically re-creates the ordeal of America during the 1930s. [973.91]

8822 Watkins, T. H. *The Great Depression: America in the 1930s* (9–12). 1993, Little, Brown $24.95 (0-316-92453-9). Explores the impact of the Great Depression in the 1930s and its continuing effect today, with more than 100 black-and-white photographs. (Rev: BL 11/15/93; SLJ 6/94) [973.917]

8823 Watkins, T. H. *The Hungry Years: A Narrative History of the Great Depression in America* (10–12). 1999, Holt paper $17 .00 (0-8050-6506-7). This book explores the Great Depression through a series of firsthand reports. (Rev: BL 9/15/99) [973.91]

8824 Woog, Adam. *Roosevelt and the New Deal* (7–10). Illus. Series: World History. 1997, Lucent LB $27.45 (1-56006-324-6). With double-page spreads, sidebars, political cartoons, photographs, reproductions, and first-person accounts, this book discusses Roosevelt's efforts to end the Great Depression through the New Deal and looks at its impact on the nation. (Rev: SLJ 8/98) [973.9]

8825 Wormser, Richard. *Growing Up in the Great Depression* (6–12). 1994, Atheneum $15.95 (0-689-31711-5). Letters, photographs, and interviews examine children's lives during the Great Depression. Includes accounts of job loss, child labor, and the struggles of African Americans. (Rev: BL 10/15/94; SLJ 12/94; VOYA 2/95) [973.91]

8826 Worster, Donald. *Dust Bowl: The Southern Plains in the 1930s* (10–12). 1979, Oxford paper $15.95 (0-19-503212-8). This story of one of the country's worst ecological disasters focuses on two counties, one in Oklahoma and one in Kansas, and how the Depression and New Deal changed them. [978]

WORLD WAR II

8827 Alonso, Karen. *Korematsu v. United States: Japanese-American Internment Camps* (7–12). Illus. Series: Landmark Supreme Court Cases. 1998, Enslow LB $20.95 (0-89490-966-5). This book discusses the Japanese American internments during World War II and focuses on Fred Korematsu's case challenging the government's right to remove him from his home and imprison him simply because he was a Japanese American. (Rev: BL 5/1/98; BR 9–10/98; SLJ 8/98; VOYA 2/99) [323.1]

8828 Armor, John, and Peter Wright. *Manzanar* (10–12). Illus. 1988, Times Books $27.00 (0-8129-1727-8). A description of the internment camp used to house Japanese Americans during World War II, illustrated with touching photographs by Ansel Adams. (Rev: BL 11/1/88; BR 5–6/89; SLJ 5/89; VOYA 6/89) [940.5472]

8829 Bernstein, Mark, and Alex Lubertozzi. *World War II on the Air: Hear Edward R. Murrow and the Voices That Carried the War Home* (8–12). 2003, Sourcebooks $29.95 (1-4022-0026-9). Murrow and other radio greats of the war are featured in this book-and-audio-CD set. (Rev: BL 5/1/03; SLJ 6/03)

8830 Brimner, Larry Dane. *Voices from the Camps: Internment of Japanese Americans During World War II* (7–12). Illus. 1994, Watts LB $17.70 (0-531-11179-2). The shameful treatment of Japanese Americans in California during the Second World War is re-created through interviews with survivors and their children. (Rev: BL 6/1–15/94) [940.53]

8831 Colman, Penny. *Rosie the Riveter* (6–12). 1995, Crown $20.99 (0-517-59791-8). An overview of the new role women played in the wartime workplace. (Rev: BL 4/15/95; SLJ 5/95) [331.4]

8832 Cooper, Michael L. *Fighting for Honor: Japanese Americans and World War II* (6–12). Illus. 2000, Clarion $16.00 (0-395-91375-6). The experiences of Japanese Americans who were sent to internment camps or faced anti-Asian attacks in their communities are well-documented here. (Rev: BCCB 2/01; BL 1/1–15/01; HB 3–4/01; HBG 10/01; SLJ 3/01) [940.53]

8833 Daniels, Roger. *Prisoners Without Trial: Japanese Americans in World War II* (9–12). 1993, Hill & Wang paper $9.00 (0-8090-1553-6). A history of the racist internment of Japanese Americans in World War II. (Rev: BL 7/93; SLJ 6/94) [940.53]

8834 Dobbs, Michael. *Saboteurs: The Nazi Raid on America* (10–12). Illus. 2004, Knopf $25.00 (0-375-41470-3). The gripping account of the landing of eight German saboteurs on the U.S. East Coast in 1942. (Rev: BL 2/1/04*) [940.54]

8835 Dudley, William, ed. *Japanese American Internment Camps* (7–12). Series: At Issue in History. 2002, Gale LB $27.45 (0-7377-0821-2); paper $18.70 (0-7377-0820-4). Primary texts revealing different attitudes toward the internment of Japanese Americans are introduced by statements explaining the historical context. (Rev: SLJ 3/02) [940.53]

8836 Fremon, David K. *Japanese-American Internment in American History* (7–10). Illus. Series: In American History. 1996, Enslow LB $20.95 (0-89490-767-0). Drawing on a wide range of personal narratives, the author re-creates the shameful period during World War II when Japanese Americans were forcibly evacuated to internment camps. (Rev: BL 1/1–15/97; BR 3–4/97; SLJ 6/97; VOYA 12/96) [940.53]

8837 Goodwin, Doris Kearns. *No Ordinary Time: Franklin and Eleanor Roosevelt: The Homefront in World War II* (9–12). 1994, Simon & Schuster $29.50 (0-671-64240-5). Details the inner workings of the White House during World War II, including FDR's and Eleanor's home-front activities. (Rev: BL 8/94*) [973.917]

8838 Grapes, Bryan J., ed. *Japanese American Internment Camps* (6–12). Series: History Firsthand. 2000, Greenhaven LB $22.96 (0-7377-0413-6); paper $14.96 (0-7377-0412-8). Essays, speeches, and firsthand accounts tell the story of the relocation of Japanese Americans during World War II. (Rev: BL 3/1/01; SLJ 4/01) [940.53]

8839 Hasday, Judy L. *The Tuskegee Airmen* (7–12). Series: American Mosaic. 2003, Chelsea LB $22.95 (0-7910-7267-3). During World War II, few could match the obstacles and accomplishments of the Tuskegee Airmen, a group of African American pilots. (Rev: BL 10/15/03; HBG 10/03) [940.54]

8840 Homan, Lynn M., and Thomas Reilly. *Black Knights: The Story of the Tuskegee Airmen* (10–12). Illus. 2001, Pelican $23.00 (1-56554-828-0). This is the story of the social experiment that happened between 1941 and 1948 involving the African

American unit known as the Tuskegee Airmen, eventually leading to the desegregation of the armed services. (Rev: BL 2/15/01) [940.5]

8841 Houston, Jeanne W., and James D. Houston. *Farewell to Manzanar* (9–12). 1983, Bantam paper $5.99 (0-553-27258-6). The story of the three years that Jeanne Houston, a Japanese American, and her family spent at the Manzanar internment camp during World War II. [940.54]

8842 Humes, James C. *Eisenhower and Churchill: The Partnership That Saved the World* (10–12). 2001, Prima $24.95 (0-7615-2561-0). As well as including brief biographies, this work examines how, in spite of dissimilar backgrounds, these two world leaders worked well together. (Rev: BL 9/1/01) [941.08]

8843 Kallen, Stuart A. *The War at Home* (6–12). Illus. 1999, Lucent LB $18.96 (1-56006-531-1). This book describes conditions within the United States during World War II and covers such topics as daily life, the changing workplace and workforce, civil defense, and racial discrimination. (Rev: BL 1/1–15/00; HBG 9/00; SLJ 2/00) [940.53]

8844 Levine, Ellen. *A Fence Away from Freedom: Japanese Americans and World War II* (7–12). 1995, Putnam $18.99 (0-399-22638-9). Many voices tell of their bitter experiences as Japanese Americans were forced into internment camps during World War II. (Rev: BL 10/1/95; SLJ 12/95; VOYA 2/96) [940.53]

8845 Okihiro, Gary Y. *Whispered Silences: Japanese Americans and World War II* (10–12). 1996, Univ. of Washington Pr. $60.00 (0-295-97497-4); paper $29.95 (0-295-97498-2). A brief history of Japanese immigration to the United States precedes this account of the relocation of 110,000 Japanese Americans to 10 concentration camps in California, Washington, Oregon, and Arizona during World War II, and the racial enmity experienced by Japanese Americans. (Rev: SLJ 11/96) [973.9]

8846 Stanley, Jerry. *I Am an American: A True Story of Japanese Internment* (5–10). 1994, Crown LB $17.99 (0-517-59787-X). A photoessay detailing the experiences of Japanese Americans during World War II. Focuses on war hysteria and the unjust use of internment camps. (Rev: BL 10/15/94*; SLJ 11/94*) [940.53]

8847 Stein, R. Conrad. *The World War II D-Day Invasion* (7–10). Series: In American History. 2004, Enslow LB $20.95 (0-7660-2136-X). This great landing in Normandy is re-created in pictures and text. (Rev: BL 3/15/04; SLJ 3/04) [940.54]

8848 Streissguth, Thomas, ed. *The Attack on Pearl Harbor* (7–10). Series: At Issue in History. 2002, Gale LB $27.45 (0-7377-0752-6); paper $18.70 (0-7377-0751-8). Primary sources present opposing views on the attack and on who was responsible for the lack of preparation for such a possibility. (Rev: SLJ 7/02) [940.54]

8849 Takaki, Ronald. *Double Victory: A Multicultural History of America in World War II* (10–12). Illus. 2000, Little, Brown $29.95 (0-316-83155-7). The book examines the roles played during World War II by such minorities as African Americans, Asian Americans, Hispanic Americans, and Native Americans, as well as Italian, German, and Jewish Americans. (Rev: BL 5/15/00) [940.53]

8850 Terkel, Studs. *"The Good War": An Oral History of World War Two* (10–12). 1984, Pantheon paper $7.99 (0-345-32568-0). Through the use of interviews, the author has collected material on how World War II affected the lives of average Americans. [940.53]

8851 Tunnell, Michael O., and George W. Chilcoat. *The Children of Topaz: The Story of a Japanese-American Internment Camp Based on a Classroom Diary* (6–10). Illus. 1996, Holiday $18.95 (0-8234-1239-3). This book consists of 20 excerpts from a classroom diary kept by a 3rd-grade Japanese American schoolteacher during her confinement in a desert relocation camp during 1943. (Rev: BL 7/96; SLJ 8/96*; VOYA 12/96) [769.8]

8852 Weatherford, Doris. *American Women and World War II* (10–12). Illus. 1990, Facts on File $29.95 (0-8160-2038-8). A detailed social history of the contributions made by American women during World War II. (Rev: BL 9/1/90) [940.54]

8853 Yancey, Diane. *The Internment of the Japanese* (7–10). Series: World History. 2002, Gale LB $27.45 (1-59018-013-5). An accessible account of the causes of the internment of many Japanese Americans during World War II, the conditions they endured, and the aftermath. (Rev: BL 8/02; SLJ 8/02) [940.54]

8854 Yancey, Diane. *Life in a Japanese American Internment Camp* (6–12). Illus. Series: The Way People Live. 1997, Lucent LB $27.45 (1-56006-345-9). Black-and-white photographs and excerpts from personal narratives are used to describe the upheaval in the lives of Japanese Americans during World War II. (Rev: BL 1/1–15/98) [940.53]

8855 Zamperini, Louis, and David Rensin. *Devil at My Heels: The Incredible Saga of a World War 11 Hero Who Spent Forty-Seven Days Adrift and More Than Two Years as a POW* (10–12). Illus. 2003, Morrow $24.95 (0-06-018860-X). In this inspirational and exciting autobiography, Olympic runner and World War II hero Zamperini tells how a spiritual awakening turned him away from a life of self - destruction. (Rev: BL 12/15/02) [940.54]

POST WORLD WAR II UNITED STATES (1945–)

8856 Alonso, Karen. *The Chicago Seven Political Protest Trial* (6–10). Series: Headline Court Cases. 2002, Enslow LB $20.95 (0-7660-1764-8). This is an account of the trial of the Chicago Seven, a group that was arrested during a demonstration at the Democratic National Convention in Chicago. (Rev: BL 3/15/03; HBG 10/03) [973.92]

8857 Archer, Jules. *The Incredible Sixties: The Stormy Years That Changed America* (7–12). 1986, Harcourt $17.95 (0-15-238298-4). A topically arranged overview of the events, trends, and significance of the 1960s and how they have shaped our future. (Rev: BL 5/15/86; SLJ 9/86; VOYA 4/87) [973.922]

8858 Baker, Patricia. *Fashions of a Decade: The 1950s* (7–12). Series: Fashions of a Decade. 1991, Facts on File $25.00 (0-8160-2468-5). An illustrated overview of fashions of the 1950s and the political, economic, and social developments of the time. (Rev: BL 12/15/91; SLJ 2/92) [391]

8859 Beals, Melba Pattillo. *Warriors Don't Cry: A Searing Memoir of the Battle to Integrate Little Rock's Central High* (10–12). 1995, Washington Square Pr. $14.00 (0-671-86639-7). The author was one of nine African American teenagers chosen to integrate the Little Rock high school in 1957. [323]

8860 Bernstein, Carl, and Bob Woodward. *All the President's Men* (10–12). 1999, Simon & Schuster $26.00 (0-684-86355-3); paper $14.00 (0-671-89441-2). The story behind the Watergate scandal that led to Richard Nixon's resignation. [973.924]

8861 Ching, Jacqueline. *The Assassination of Martin Luther King Jr.* (6–10). Series: The Library of Political Assassinations. 2002, Rosen LB $26.50 (0-8239-3543-4). A look at the life and death of Martin Luther King, Jr., and his legacy. (Rev: BL 8/02; SLJ 8/02) [976]

8862 Ching, Juliet. *The Assassination of Robert F. Kennedy* (6–10). Series: The Library of Political Assassinations. 2002, Rosen LB $26.50 (0-8239-3545-0). In addition to discussing the assassination and the events preceding it, the author looks at the rumors of a conspiracy and allegations of incompetence on the part of the Los Angeles police force. (Rev: BL 8/02; SLJ 8/02) [976]

8863 Cunningham, Jesse G., ed. *The McCarthy Hearings* (8–12). Series: At Issue in History. 2003, Gale LB $21.96 (0-7377-1346-1); paper $14.96 (0-7377-1347-X). An objective look at the activities of the senator from Wisconsin that gives clear historical context. (Rev: SLJ 4/03) [973.921]

8864 Daniel, Pete. *Lost Revolutions: The South in the 1950s* (10–12). Illus. 2000, Univ. of North Carolina Pr. $45.00 (0-8078-2537-9); paper $19.95 (0-

8078-4848-4). This portrait of the southern states after World War II contains material on their changing culture, the resistance to integration, the growth of religious fundamentalism, and the evolution of popular music. (Rev: BL 4/1/00) [975.043]

8865 Dolan, Sean. *Pursuing the Dream: From the Selma-Montgomery March to the Formation of PUSH (1965–1971)* (7–10). Illus. Series: Milestones in Black American History. 1995, Chelsea LB $19.95 (0-7910-2254-4); paper $8.95 (0-7910-2680-9). This chronicle of the civil rights movement of the 1960s describes the demonstrations and confrontations and gives background information on participation of African Americans in sports and the arts. (Rev: BL 7/95) [323.1]

8866 Draper, Allison Stark. *The Assassination of Malcolm X* (6–10). Series: The Library of Political Assassinations. 2002, Rosen LB $31.95 (0-8239-3542-6). A description of the assassination and its aftermath is followed by information on Malcolm X's life and beliefs. (Rev: BL 2/15/02; SLJ 7/02) [976.2]

8867 Dudley, William, ed. *The 1960s* (9–12). Illus. Series: Opposing Viewpoints. 1996, Greenhaven LB $21.96 (1-56510-526-5); paper $16.20 (1-56510-525-7). A collection of opinions ranging from conservative to liberal to radical about issues of the 1960s, including the Vietnam War, minority rights, and the counterculture. (Rev: BL 4/15/97; SLJ 7/97) [973.923]

8868 Dudley, William, and Bonnie Szumski, eds. *America's Future* (9–12). Illus. Series: Opposing Viewpoints. 1990, Greenhaven LB $26.20 (0-89908-448-6); paper $16.20 (0-89908-423-0). A collection of different points of views on America's direction. (Rev: BL 7/90; SLJ 8/90) [324.2]

8869 Epstein, Dan. *The 80s: The Decade of Plenty* (7–10). Series: 20th Century Pop Culture. 2000, Chelsea LB $17.95 (0-7910-6088-8). A mix of popular entertainment and fashion with key news events, all arranged chronologically and accompanied by lots of color photographs. Other books in the series include *The 50s: America Tunes In* and *The 60s: A Decade of Change: The Flintstones to Woodstock.* (Rev: SLJ 6/01) [973.9]

8870 Farber, David, et al. *The Columbia Guide to America in the 1960s* (10–12). 2001, Columbia Univ. Pr. $50.00 (0-231-11372-2). After an excellent overview of the 1960s, this book contains a section on key political, social, and cultural issues and an A-to-Z glossary of people and organizations. (Rev: BL 8/01) [973.923]

8871 Finkelstein, Norman H. *Thirteen Days / Ninety Miles: The Cuban Missile Crisis* (8–12). 1994, Messner LB $18.95 (0-671-86622-2). Declassified materials, letters, and memoirs describe the tension-filled Cuban missile crisis, documenting the actions and ideologies of Kennedy and Khrushchev and revealing how narrowly nuclear war was averted. (Rev: BL 7/94*; SLJ 6/94) [973.992]

8872 Fremon, David K. *The Watergate Scandal in American History* (7–10). Series: In American History. 1997, Enslow LB $20.95 (0-89490-883-9). A clear, logically arranged, and objective account of the famous political scandal that ended the Nixon presidency. (Rev: BL 4/15/98; SLJ 5/98) [973.9]

8873 Genovese, Michael A. *The Watergate Crisis* (10–12). 1999, Greenwood (0-313-29878-5). A good overview of the Watergate crisis that brought down the Nixon presidency, why it occurred, and its consequences. (Rev: BL 4/1/00; SLJ 3/00) [973.924]

8874 Harding, Vincent, et al. *We Changed the World: African Americans, 1945–1970* (7–12). Illus. Series: Young Oxford History of African Americans. 1997, Oxford $24.00 (0-19-508796-8). This volume covers African American history immediately after World War II and traces the beginnings of the modern civil rights movement. (Rev: BL 9/1/97; BR 11–12/97) [973]

8875 Haskins, Jim. *Power to the People: The Rise and Fall of the Black Panther Party* (7–12). Illus. 1997, Simon & Schuster paper $16.00 (0-689-80085-1). A somewhat plodding account of this radical 1960s political organization whose leaders included Huey Newton and Bobby Seale. (Rev: BL 3/15/97; SLJ 3/97; VOYA 8/97) [322.4]

8876 Heineman, Kenneth J. *Put Your Bodies Upon the Wheels: Student Revolt in the 1960s* (10–12). Series: American Way. 2001, Ivan R. Dee $26.00 (1-56663-351-6). This is a detailed history of the campus-based counterculture of the 1960s and the young people who participated. (Rev: BL 3/1/01) [378.1]

8877 Hendler, Herb. *Year by Year in the Rock Era* (7–12). 1983, Greenwood $62.95 (0-313-23456-6). A year-by-year chronicle of social events matched with information about artists, hits, and so on, of the rock era from 1954 through 1981. [973.92]

8878 Herda, D. J. *United States v. Nixon: Watergate and the President* (6–10). Illus. Series: Landmark Supreme Court Cases. 1996, Enslow LB $20.95 (0-89490-753-0). The Watergate scandal is reviewed with special emphasis on the legal aspects of this case that brought down the presidency of Richard Nixon. (Rev: BL 8/96; SLJ 7/96) [342.73]

8879 Hull, Mary. *Struggle and Love, 1972–1997* (7–10). Illus. Series: Milestones in Black American History. 1996, Chelsea LB $21.95 (0-7910-2262-5); paper $9.95 (0-7910-2688-4). This book covers the past quarter of a century in African American history, highlighting the lives and careers of prominent individuals including Jesse Jackson, Colin Powell, and Michael Jordan. (Rev: BL 3/15/97; SLJ 6/97) [973]

8880 Hunt, Conover. *JFK for a New Generation* (10–12). 1996, Southern Methodist Univ. Pr. $34.95 (0-87074-415-1); paper $19.95 (0-87074-395-3). This book is not a biography, but rather a commentary on how the myth of JFK was created and developed, with a minute-by-minute re-creation of his assassination and an assessment of subsequent theories about it. (Rev: SLJ 1/97) [973.9]

8881 Hurley, Jennifer A. *The 1960s* (7–12). Series: Opposing Viewpoints Digests. 1999, Greenhaven LB $21.96 (0-7377-0211-7); paper $13.96 (0-7377-0210-9). The Vietnam War and the many social changes of the 1960s are discussed from different perspectives; an appendix of original documents includes excerpts from news articles, speeches, government papers, and other primary materials of interest. (Rev: SLJ 4/00) [306]

8882 Javna, John, and Gordon Javna. *60s!* (9–12). Illus. 1983, St. Martin's paper $17.95 (0-312-01725-1). A portfolio of pictures with text about the popular culture of the 1960s. [973.92]

8883 Johnson, Darv. *The Reagan Years* (7–10). Series: World History. 2000, Lucent LB $18.96 (1-56006-592-3). This account of the two-term president focuses on conservatism, his economic agenda, and relations with the Soviet Union, the Middle East, and Central America. (Rev: BL 6/1–15/00; HBG 9/00; SLJ 9/00) [973.9]

8884 Kallen, Stuart A., ed. *The Baby Boom* (7–12). Series: Turning Points in World History. 2001, Greenhaven LB $31.20 (0-7377-0924-3); paper $19.95 (0-7377-0925-1). This collection of essays and documents arranged in chronological order explores the social, economic, and cultural effects of the large generation born in the United States after World War II. (Rev: BL 3/15/02; SLJ 7/02) [973.9]

8885 Kallen, Stuart A. *Life in America During the 1960s* (6–10). Series: The Way People Live. 2001, Lucent LB $19.96 (1-56006-790-X). Using as a backdrop the presidencies of Kennedy and Johnson, the civil rights movement and the Vietnam War, this work focuses in pictures and text on the daily life of Americans in this difficult period. (Rev: BL 6/1–15/01) [973.9]

8886 Kallen, Stuart A., ed. *The 1950s* (6–12). Series: America's Decades. 2000, Greenhaven LB $29.96 (0-7377-0304-0); paper $17.96 (0-7377-0303-2). This history of the 1950s in America covers such topics as fear about a nuclear war, the growth of suburbia, racial tensions, and the importance of television and rock and roll. (Rev: BL 7/00; SLJ 9/00) [973.9]

8887 Kallen, Stuart A., ed. *The 1990s* (6–12). Illus. Series: American Decades. 2000, Greenhaven LB $29.96 (0-7377-0312-1); paper $17.96 (0-7377-0311-3). Major events of the 1990s are discussed and arranged under six headings: politics, war, violence, race and gender, pop culture, and technology. (Rev: BL 6/1–15/00) [973.929]

8888 Lindop, Edmund. *America in the 1950s* (6–10). Illus. 2002, Millbrook LB $25.90 (0-7613-2551-4). Lindop looks at the lighter sides of life in the 1950s — including the influence of TV on popular culture, the move to the suburbs, and sports — as well as the political and social upheavals of the Korean War, the Cold War, McCarthyism, and desegregation. (Rev: BL 9/1/02; HBG 3/03; SLJ 10/02) [973.921]

8889 Lomas, Clare. *The 80s and 90s: Power Dressing to Sportswear* (5–10). Series: 20th Century Fashion. 2000, Gareth Stevens LB $25.26 (0-8368-2603-5). Power dressing, androgyny, sportswear, and grunge characterize the world of fashion during the 1980s and 1990s in this book that covers both design and social history. (Rev: HBG 10/00; SLJ 6/00) [973.9]

8890 McNeely, Robert. *The Clinton Years: The Photographs of Robert McNeely* (9–12). Illus. 2000, Callaway $40.00 (0-935112-61-8). A photographic album with brief captions that chronicles events associated with the presidency of Bill Clinton. (Rev: BL 9/1/00; SLJ 5/01) [973.9]

8891 Meltzer, Milton, ed. *The American Promise: Voices of a Changing Nation* (8–12). Illus. 1990, Bantam $15.95 (0-553-07020-7). In a series of excerpts from books, speeches, and interviews, the major movements affecting American life since World War II are outlined. (Rev: BL 12/15/90; SLJ 2/91) [973.92]

8892 O'Neil, Doris C., ed. *Life: The '60s* (9–12). Illus. 1989, Little, Brown $35.00 (0-8212-1752-6). An illustrated introduction to the 1960s through 250 photographs and connecting text. (Rev: BL 12/15/89) [973.92]

8893 Powe-Temperley, Kitty. *The 60s: Mods and Hippies* (5–10). Series: 20th Century Fashion. 2000, Gareth Stevens LB $25.26 (0-8368-2601-9). Mods, hippies, miniskirts, Eastern influences, and art as fashion are covered in this overview of clothing fads of the 1960s, along with background information. (Rev: HBG 10/00; SLJ 6/00) [973.9]

8894 Rather, Dan. *The American Dream: Stories from the Heart of Our Nation* (10–12). 2001, Morrow $25.00 (0-688-17892-8). This is a collection of reports on people who found fulfillment in such areas as family, fame, education, innovation, and liberty. (Rev: BL 4/1/01) [973.92]

8895 Reynolds, Helen. *The 40s and 50s: Utility to New Look* (5–10). Series: 20th Century Fashion. 2000, Gareth Stevens LB $25.26 (0-8368-2600-0). Using a lively style and many period illustrations, this book highlights the world of fashion and design during and after World War II and gives some background social history. (Rev: HBG 10/00; SLJ 6/00) [973.9]

8896 Ribeiro, Myra. *The Assassination of Medgar Evers* (6–10). Series: The Library of Political Assassinations. 2002, Rosen LB $26.50 (0-8239-3544-2). A description of the assassination and its aftermath is followed by information on Evers's life and beliefs. (Rev: BL 2/15/02; SLJ 7/02) [976]

8897 *The Rock and Roll Generation: Teen Life in the '50s* (7–12). Illus. Series: Our American Century. 1998, Time-Life $29.95 (0-7835-5501-6). Outstanding photographs and short, simple text document important developments in the 1950s, including the birth of rock music, the beat generation, television, the Cold War and Korean War, McCarthyism, and the beginnings of the civil rights movement, with insights into teen life. (Rev: BR 9–10/98; SLJ 9/98) [973.9]

8898 Scheibach, Michael. *Atomic Narratives and American Youth: Coming of Age with the Atom, 1945–1955* (10–12). Illus. 2003, McFarland paper $35.00 (0-7864-1566-5). The varied ways in which government, media, educators, and parents informed young people about the advent and implications of the atom bomb are the focus of this intriguing study. (Rev: BL 9/15/03) [305.235]

8899 Schmidt, Mark Ray, ed. *The 1970s* (6–12). Series: America's Decades. 2000, Greenhaven LB $29.96 (0-7377-0308-3); paper $17.96 (0-7377-0307-5). This anthology contains articles on topics including environmental and energy issues, racial integration, the Watergate scandal, and interracial conflicts. (Rev: BL 7/00; SLJ 7/00) [973.9]

8900 Schwartz, Richard A. *Cold War Culture: Media and the Arts, 1945–1990* (10–12). 1997, Facts on File $40.00 (0-8160-3104-5). This reference book is also a browsable history of American culture during the years 1945 to 1990, with chapters on art, cartoons, consumer goods, dance, film, games, television, and theater. (Rev: BL 3/1/98; BR 5–6/98; SLJ 6/98) [973.9]

8901 Schwartz, Richard Alan. *The 1950s* (9–12). Series: Eyewitness History. 2003, Facts on File $75.00 (0-8160-4597-6). Each year of the 1950s is described, with coverage of important social, cultural, and political developments. [973.921]

8902 Sitkoff, Harvard. *Postwar America: A Student Companion* (7–12). 2000, Oxford $45.00 (0-19-510300-9). Alphabetically arranged articles cover the major events, people, legal cases, movements, and documents relating to life in the United States since World War II. (Rev: BL 5/1/00; SLJ 5/00) [973.92]

8903 Torr, James D., ed. *The 1980s* (6–12). Series: America's Decades. 2000, Greenhaven LB $29.96 (0-7377-0310-5); paper $17.96 (0-7377-0309-2). The election of Reagan, the appearance of AIDS,

the rise of personal computers, and the fall of the Berlin Wall are some of the topics covered in this anthology of articles. (Rev: BL 7/00; SLJ 7/00) [973.9]

8904 *Turbulent Years: The 60s* (9–12). Series: Our American Century. 1998, Time-Life $19.99 (0-7835-5503-2). Using photographs from *Time* and *Life* magazines, this is a chronicle of the 1960s, including coverage of the Vietnam War, the civil rights movement, the space race, the counterculture, music, sports, and the arts. (Rev: BR 1–2/99; SLJ 5/99) [973.9]

8905 Warren, James A. *Cold War: The American Crusade Against World Communism, 1945–1991* (7–12). Illus. 1996, Lothrop $16.00 (0-688-10596-3). A meticulously researched account that covers the events, strategies, and personalities involved in the nation's 50-year effort to contain and subvert communism around the world. (Rev: BL 1/1–15/97; BR 11–12/96; SLJ 10/96*; VOYA 4/97) [327.73047]

8906 Woodward, Bob, and Carl Bernstein. *The Final Days* (10–12). 1994, Simon & Schuster paper $14.00 (0-671-89440-4). This book chronicles the last two months of the Nixon presidency from the dismissal of John Dean to the resignation of Nixon. [973.924]

8907 Wright, Mike. *What They Didn't Teach You About the 60s* (10–12). Illus. 2001, Presidio $24.95 (0-89141-724-9). This is a topically arranged overview of the 60s that includes material on Nixon, civil rights, Vietnam War, the Cold War, music and drugs, and the deaths of famous personalities. (Rev: BL 11/1/01) [973.923]

8908 Zeinert, Karen. *McCarthy and the Fear of Communism* (7–10). Series: In American History. 1998, Enslow LB $20.95 (0-89490-987-8). The story of the reign of terror inflicted on America during the 1950s by the senator from Wisconsin. (Rev: BL 8/98; HBG 9/99; SLJ 12/98) [973.9]

KOREAN, VIETNAM, AND OTHER WARS

8909 Al-Windawi, Thura. *Thura's Diary: My Life in Wartime Iraq* (6–12). 2004, Viking $15.99 (0-670-05886-6). This diary was kept by a 19-year-old girl in Baghdad from the first bombings to the first days of the occupation by American forces. (Rev: BL 5/15/04; HB 7–8/04; SLJ 7/04) [956]

8910 Atkinson, Rick. *In the Company of Soldiers: A Chronicle of Combat* (10–12). 2004, Holt $25.00 (0-8050-7561-5). This account covers two months in the spring of 2003 when the author accompanied U.S. combat units in Iraq. (Rev: SLJ 6/04) [956.7]

8911 Barr, Roger. *The Vietnam War* (9–12). Series: America's Wars. 1991, Lucent LB $20.96 (1-56006-410-2). A view of U.S. military involvement in Southeast Asia. (Rev: BL 5/15/92; SLJ 6/92) [959.704]

8912 Bartimus, Tad, et al. *War Torn: Stories of War from the Women Reporters Who Covered Vietnam* (10–12). Illus. 2002, Random $24.95 (0-375-50628-4). Nine women journalists recount their experiences covering the Vietnam War, which range from death and loss to the blossoming of romance. (Rev: BL 7/02) [959.704]

8913 Berry, F. Clifton, and Dennis Steele. *United States Army at War: 9/11 Through Iraq* (10–12). Illus. 2003, Naval Institute Pr. $34.95 (1-59114-063-3). From the immediate aftermath of 9/11 through the downfall of the Taliban in Afghanistan and the beginning of the occupation of Iraq, this is the story of the part played by the U.S. Army. (Rev: BL 2/1/04) [973.931]

8914 Boettcher, Thomas D. *Vietnam: The Valor and the Sorrow* (9–12). Illus. 1985, Little, Brown paper $21.95 (0-316-10081-1). An excellent popular history of the Vietnam War with many black-and-white photographs. (Rev: BL 7/85) [959.73]

8915 Burrows, Larry. *Vietnam* (10–12). Illus. 2002, Knopf $50.00 (0-375-41102-X). The many faces of the Vietnam War are revisited in this collection of *Life* photographer Burrows's stunning work between 1962 and 1971, when the helicopter on which he was traveling disappeared. (Rev: BL 10/15/02) [959.704]

8916 Capps, Walter, ed. *The Vietnam Reader* (9–12). 1991, Routledge $45.00 (0-415-90126-X); paper $22.99 (0-415-90127-8). Essays by 36 writers, many of them veterans, on war experiences and the continuing effects of the Vietnam War. (Rev: BL 10/1/91) [959.704]

8917 Caraccilo, Dominic J. *The Ready Brigade of the 82nd Airborne in Desert Storm: A Combat Memoir by the Headquarters Company Commander* (9–12). 1993, McFarland paper $19.95 (0-89950-829-4). A memoir describing the company's eight months in the desert during the Persian Gulf War, spent moving, supplying, and setting up troops and equipment. (Rev: BL 6/1–15/93; VOYA 10/93) [956.704]

8918 Clark, Eugene Franklin. *The Secrets of Inchon: The Untold Story of the Most Daring Covert Mission of the Korean War* (10–12). Illus. 2002, Putnam $26.95 (0-399-14871-X). In this absorbing memoir, published nearly half a century after it was written, Clark describes his role in the intelligence-gathering mission that paved the way for the successful amphibious landing at Inchon. (Rev: BL 4/15/02) [940.55]

8919 Dudley, William, ed. *The Vietnam War* (9–12). Series: Opposing Viewpoints: American History. 1997, Greenhaven LB $21.96 (1-56510-701-2); paper $16.20 (1-56510-700-4). Presidents, antiwar

activists, and soldiers are among those who debate the causes and consequences of America's involvement in Vietnam in this collection of documents. (Rev: BL 10/15/97; SLJ 11/97) [959.704]

8920 Dudley, William, and Stacey L. Tipp, eds. *Iraq* (9–12). Series: Current Controversies. 1991, Greenhaven LB $26.20 (0-89908-575-X); paper $16.20 (0-89908-581-4). A study of the Persian Gulf War that examines military lessons of the war, media coverage, and other controversial aspects. (Rev: BL 6/15/92; SLJ 5/92) [956.704]

8921 Dunnigan, James, and Albert A. Nofi. *Dirty Little Secrets of the Vietnam War: Military Information You're Not Supposed to Know* (10–12). 1999, St. Martin's $27.50 (0-312-19857-4). This well-researched overview of the Vietnam War chronicles America's still-controversial involvement in the Southeast Asia country from the days of the French defeat through the war's lasting impact on those suffering from post-traumatic stress disorder. (Rev: BL 12/15/98) [959.704]

8922 Esper, George. *The Eyewitness History of the Vietnam War: 1961–1975* (9–12). Illus. 1986, Ballantine paper $20.00 (0-345-34294-1). This book contains a simple text and hundreds of photographs, which present a basic history of the war. [959.704]

8923 FitzGerald, Frances. *Fire in the Lake: The Vietnamese and the Americans in Vietnam* (10–12). 1972, Little, Brown paper $16.95 (0-316-15919-0). This work deals with the effects that the American intervention had on Vietnamese social and cultural life. [959.704]

8924 Freedman, Suzanne. *Clay v. United States: Muhammad Ali Objects to War* (6–10). Series: Landmark Supreme Court Cases. 1997, Enslow LB $20.95 (0-89490-855-3). A thorough examination of Muhammad Ali's court case involving the Vietnam War. (Rev: BL 10/15/97; HBG 3/98; SLJ 12/97) [959.704]

8925 Friedman, Norman. *Desert Victory: The War for Kuwait* (9–12). 1991, Naval Institute Pr. $42.50 (1-55750-254-4). This book published by the Naval Institute concludes that U.S. strategy in the Persian Gulf War was largely successful but that U.S. intelligence failed to accurately gauge the strength and morale of Iraqi forces. (Rev: BL 10/15/91) [956.704]

8926 Galt, Margot Fortunato. *Stop This War! American Protest of the Conflict in Vietnam* (8–12). Series: People's History. 2000, Lerner LB $30.35 (0-8225-1740-X). The author cites her husband, a conscientious objector, among those who protested the war from the early 1960s until its end, and details key events and student and other groups. (Rev: BL 7/00; HBG 9/00; SLJ 8/00) [959.704]

8927 Garrels, Anne. *Naked in Baghdad: The Iraq War as Seen by NPR's Correspondent* (10–12). 2003, Farrar $22.00 (0-374-52903-5). Garrels interweaves information on the fighting in Baghdad with details of a war correspondent's duties. (Rev: BL 9/15/03) [956.7044]

8928 Granfield, Linda. *I Remember Korea: Veterans Tell Their Stories of the Korean War, 1950–53* (6–12). Illus. 2003, Clarion $16.00 (0-618-17740-X). First-person accounts by American combatants that reveal a wide variety of experiences are accompanied by brief introductory notes, photographs, and a short account of the war itself. (Rev: BCCB 2/04; BL 12/15/03; HBG 4/04; SLJ 2/04) [951.904]

8929 Hastings, Max. *The Korean War* (9–12). Illus. 1988, Simon & Schuster paper $15.00 (0-671-66834-X). A readable, objective account of the war both in Korea and on the home front. (Rev: BL 10/15/87) [951.8]

8930 Hodgins, Michael C. *Reluctant Warrior* (10–12). 1996, Ballantine $24.00 (0-449-91059-8). This account of the final days of the Vietnam War tells what life was like for the common American soldier in the jungles and rice fields of Vietnam. (Rev: BL 1/1–15/97; SLJ 8/97) [959.704]

8931 Kallen, Stuart A. *The Home Front: Americans Protest the War* (6–12). Series: American War Library: The Vietnam War. 2000, Lucent LB $19.96 (1-56006-718-7). Campus protests against the war, peace marches, the burning of draft cards, and Woodstock are among the topics covered in this informative volume. (Rev: BL 3/1/01; SLJ 4/01) [959.704]

8932 Kovic, Ron. *Born on the Fourth of July* (10–12). 1990, Pocket paper $6.99 (0-671-73914-X). The biography of a young marine who was physically and emotionally ruined by the Vietnam War. [959.704]

8933 Kutler, Stanley I. *Encyclopedia of the Vietnam War* (10–12). 1996, Scribner $125.00 (0-13-276932-8); paper $39.95 (0-684-80522-7). This exhaustive examination of the Vietnam War contains more than 550 original articles about the country's history and every aspect of the war. [959.704]

8934 *Letters from Vietnam* (11–12). Ed. by Bill Adler. 2003, Ballantine $21.95 (0-89141-831-8). Letters written by soldiers, medical personnel, and volunteers who served in the war zone provide a candid portrayal of the writers' experiences and attitudes. (Rev: BL 11/15/03) [959.704]

8935 McCloud, Bill. *What Should We Tell Our Children About Vietnam?* (7–12). 1989, Univ. of Oklahoma Pr. paper $14.95 (0-8061-3240-X). More than 120 individuals, including the first President Bush and Gary Trudeau, tell what they think young people should know about the war. (Rev: BL 9/15/89) [959.704]

8936 McCormick, Anita Louise. *The Vietnam Antiwar Movement* (6–12). Illus. Series: In American History. 2000, Enslow LB $19.95 (0-7660-1295-6).

Historical photographs and clear prose are used in this account of the many anti-Vietnam War protests in the United States and their effect on the course of history. (Rev: BL 1/1–15/00; HBG 9/00; SLJ 4/00) [959.704]

8937 McDonald, Cherokee Paul. *Into the Green: A Reconnaissance by Fire* (10–12). 2001, Plume paper $14.00 (0-452-28252-7). In a book not for the squeamish, the author reveals, through a series of vignettes, battlefield realities of the war in Vietnam. (Rev: BL 5/15/01) [959.704]

8938 MacLear, Michael. *The Ten Thousand Day War: Vietnam 1945–1975* (10–12). 1982, Avon paper $10.95 (0-380-60970-3). This account integrates four points of view on the conflict — French and American as well as those of North and South Vietnam. [959.704]

8939 Marrin, Albert. *America and Vietnam: The Elephant and the Tiger* (9–12). 1992, Viking paper $16.00 (0-670-84063-7). A historical review of Vietnam's fight for independence and the repercussions of U.S. involvement. (Rev: BL 3/1/92; SLJ 6/92*) [959.704]

8940 Mills, Randy, and Roxanne Mills. *Unexpected Journey: A Marine Corps Reserve Company in the Korean War* (10–12). Illus. 2000, Naval Institute Pr. $29.95 (1-55750-546-2). This is the story of 240 men, a reserve company of U.S. Marines from Evansville, Indiana, and their fighting record during the Korean War in 1951. (Rev: BL 10/1/00) [951.904]

8941 Noble, Dennis L. *Forgotten Warriors: Combat Art from Vietnam* (9–12). 1992, Praeger $37.95 (0-275-93868-9). Reproductions of drawings and paintings by combat artists illustrate letters, oral and official military histories, and excerpts from novels about the U.S. role in the Vietnam War. (Rev: BL 10/1/92) [959.704]

8942 Paschall, Rod. *Witness to War: Korea* (9–12). 1995, Putnam paper $12.00 (0-399-51934-3). First-hand accounts from soldiers and strategists who fought in the Korean War. (Rev: BL 5/1/95) [951.904]

8943 Prochnau, William. *Once Upon a Distant War: Young War Correspondents and the Early Vietnam Battles* (10–12). 1995, Times Books $27.50 (0-8129-2633-1). This is the story of a group of young U.S. journalists who were sent to cover the beginnings of what would become the lengthy Vietnam War, how they reported on what they saw, and the development of the "credibility gap" between what was reported and what the government said. (Rev: BL 11/1/95; SLJ 8/96) [959.704]

8944 Reich, Dale. *Rockets Like Rain: A Year in Vietnam* (10–12). 2001, Oasis paper $15.95 (1-55571-615-6). A readable, profoundly personal account of a native of a tiny Wisconsin town who spent a harrowing year in the army in Vietnam. (Rev: BL 11/15/01) [959.704]

8945 Richie, Jason. *Iraq and the Fall of Saddam Hussein.* Rev. ed. (8–10). Illus. 2004, Oliver LB $24.95 (1-881508-63-3). This account traces the story of the invasion of Iraq and ends with the capture of Saddam Hussein in December 2003. (Rev: BL 5/1/04; HBG 4/04; SLJ 1/04) [956.7]

8946 Santoli, Al. *Everything We Had* (10–12). 1982, Ballantine paper $6.99 (0-345-32279-7). Interviews with 33 veterans of the Vietnam War on the war and its impact on their lives. (Rev: BL 9/15/89) [959.704]

8947 Sifry, Micah L., and Christopher Cerf, eds. *The Gulf War Reader: History, Documents, Opinions* (9–12). 1991, Times Books paper $17.00 (0-8129-1947-5). Writings by columnists, politicians, and political advisers on the 1990 events in Kuwait and Iraq. (Rev: BL 9/1/91) [956.704]

8948 *Sixties Counterculture* (10–12). Ed. by Stuart A. Kallen. Illus. Series: History Firsthand. 2001, Greenhaven LB $22.96 (0-7377-0407-1); paper $14.96 (0-7377-0406-3). The rise of the so-called counterculture is documented in the writings of some of the period's most prominent figures, including Abbie Hoffman, John Lennon, Malcolm X, and Betty Friedan. (Rev: BL 2/15/01; SLJ 4/01) [973.923]

8949 Stokesbury, James L. *A Short History of the Korean War* (10–12). 1988, Morrow paper $11.00 (0-688-09513-5). Solid scholarship and clear writing characterize this fine history of the Korean War and its aftermath. [951.9]

8950 Taylor, Thomas. *Lightning in the Storm: The 101st Air Assault Division in the Gulf War* (9–12). 1994, Hippocrene $29.50 (0-7818-0268-7). A mix of anecdotal and analytical descriptions of the division's contributions in the Persian Gulf War. (Rev: BL 4/15/94) [956.704]

8951 Terry, Wallace, ed. *Bloods: An Oral History of the Vietnam War by Black Veterans* (10–12). Illus. 1985, Ballantine paper $6.99 (0-345-31197-3). This volume consists of 20 narratives that reveal the experiences and contributions of African American servicemen in the Vietnam War. [959.704]

8952 Van Devanter, Lynda, and Joan A. Furey, eds. *Visions of War, Dreams of Peace: Writings of Women in the Vietnam War* (9–12). 1991, Warner paper $9.95 (0-446-39251-0). Recollections of women who served in the Vietnam War. (Rev: BL 5/15/91) [811]

8953 *The Vietnam War* (10–12). Ed. by Tamara L. Roleff. Series: History Firsthand. 2002, Gale LB $31.20 (0-7377-0887-5); paper $19.95 (0-7377-0886-7). First-person accounts, narratives, and remembrances are used to explore various aspects of the Vietnam War. (Rev: BL 4/15/02) [959.704]

8954 *A War Remembered* (9–12). Illus. 1986, Silver Burdett $16.95 (0-939526-20-4). This is one volume in an extensive 25-volume set from Time-Life Books that chronicles in text and many pictures the Vietnam War. [959.704]

8955 Willenson, Kim, et al. *The Bad War: An Oral History of the Vietnam War* (10–12). 1988, NAL paper $8.95 (0-452-26063-9). This book is the result of a series of interviews conducted by *Newsweek* reporters with both Vietnamese and Americans involved in this war. (Rev: SLJ 12/87) [959.704]

8956 Williams, William Appleman, et al. *America in Vietnam: A Documentary History* (10–12). 1985, Anchor Press paper $14.95 (0-393-30555-4). Original essays and other sources trace America's involvement in Asia and the progress of the Vietnam War from 1963 through 1975. [959.704]

8957 Wormser, Richard. *Three Faces of Vietnam* (9–12). 1993, Watts LB $23.60 (0-531-11142-3). Examines the tragedy of the Vietnam War from a human perspective, narrating personal histories of those who fought, those who protested, and Vietnamese civilians. (Rev: BL 2/15/94; SLJ 1/94; VOYA 2/94) [959.704]

8958 Yancey, Diane. *Life of an American Soldier* (6–12). Series: American War Library: The Vietnam War. 2001, Lucent LB $19.96 (1-56006-676-8). A candid, well-illustrated look at the problems faced by American soldiers during their service in Vietnam and after their return to the United States, with many firsthand accounts. (Rev: BL 3/15/01; SLJ 6/01) [957.704]

8959 Yetiv, Steve A. *The Persian Gulf Crisis* (10–12). Series: Guides to Historic Events of the Twentieth Century. 1997, Greenwood $39.95 (0-313-29943-9). This thorough examination of the Gulf War describes causes, personalities, events, and consequences. (Rev: BL 1/1–15/98; BR 3–4/98; SLJ 3/98) [956.7]

Regions

MIDWEST

8960 Dennis, Jerry. *The Living Great Lakes: Exploring North America's Inland Seas* (10–12). Illus. 2003, St. Martin's $25.95 (0-312-25193-9). In a riveting account that will appeal to ecology-minded teens as well as outdoors lovers, the author talks about his explorations of the Great Lakes and looks at their history. (Rev: BL 2/15/03) [977]

8961 Gess, Denise, and William Lutz. *Firestorm at Peshtigo: A Town, Its People, and the Deadliest Fire in American History* (10–12). Illus. 2002, Holt $26.00 (0-8050-6780-9). This is the grisly story of the worst forest fire in American history. (Rev: BL 7/02) [977.5]

8962 Larner, Jesse. *Mount Rushmore: An Icon Reconsidered* (10–12). 2002, Thunder's Mouth $24.95 (1-56025-346-0). This behind-the-scenes story of the making of the Mount Rushmore National Memorial reveals some unsavory truths about its architect and his vision of what the finished work was to represent. (Rev: BL 3/1/02) [978.3]

8963 Presnall, Judith Janda. *Mount Rushmore* (7–10). Series: Building History. 1999, Lucent LB $18.96 (1-56006-529-X). Conceived by Doune Robinson and sculpted by Gutzon Borglum, this mountainside monument has become a national landmark. (Rev: BL 10/15/99; HBG 9/00) [978.3]

8964 Rydjord, John. *Indian Place-Names* (9–12). 1982, Univ. of Oklahoma Pr. paper $19.95 (0-8061-1763-X). This book, organized by tribes and linguistic families, tells the stories behind Kansas place names originated by American Indians. [910]

MOUNTAIN AND PLAINS STATES

8965 Bass, Rick. *The Lost Grizzlies: A Search for Survivors in the Wilderness of Colorado* (10–12). Illus. 1995, Houghton $22.95 (0-395-71759-0). This is the story of the adventures of a small group of men who set out on several expeditions in the early 1990s to see if grizzly bears lived in the San Juan Mountains of southern Colorado. (Rev: BL 11/1/95; SLJ 7/96) [978.8]

8966 Bauer, Erwin A. *Yellowstone* (9–12). 1993, Voyageur $29.95 (0-89658-177-2). Accessible text and beautiful color photographs present the flora and fauna of the nation's first national park. (Rev: BL 3/15/93) [917.87]

8967 Dolnick, Edward. *Down the Great Unknown: John Wesley Powell's 1869 Journey of Discovery and Tragedy Through the Grand Canyon* (10–12). Illus. 2001, HarperCollins $27.50 (0-06-019619-X). The author dramatically reproduces John Wesley Powell's exploration of the Colorado River through the explorer's journals, documents from others on the journey, and his own experiences duplicating the trip. (Rev: BL 9/15/01) [917.91]

8968 Melford, Michael. *Big Sky Country: A View of Paradise* (10–12). 1996, Rizzoli $50.00 (0-8478-1964-7). This is a stunning pictorial survey of the natural beauty of Montana, North Dakota, Wyoming, and Idaho. (Rev: SLJ 5/97) [978.8]

NORTHEASTERN AND MID-ATLANTIC STATES

8969 Aaseng, Nathan. *The White House* (7–10). Series: Building History. 2000, Lucent LB $19.96 (1-56006-708-X). The history of this Washington landmark is given plus material on the presidents and architects who shaped this building through the years. (Rev: BL 9/15/00) [975.3]

8970 Allen, Thomas B. *The Washington Monument: It Stands for All* (8–12). Illus. 2000, Discovery $29.95 (1-56331-921-7). Full of photographs and drawings plus an interesting text that supplies good background material, this is a handsome guide to one of the capital's most famous landmarks. (Rev: BL 6/1–15/00) [975.3]

8971 Arnosky, Jim. *Nearer Nature* (6–12). Illus. 1996, Lothrop $18.00 (0-688-12213-2). In 26 short chapters and using his own pencil sketches, the author introduces the animals and the beauty of life on a wooded sheep farm in rural Vermont. (Rev: BL 8/96; SLJ 11/96; VOYA 4/97) [508.743]

8972 Attie, Alice. *Harlem on the Verge* (8–12). Illus. 2003, Quantuck Lane $35.00 (0-9714548-7-6). After an introductory essay, this book consists of unforgettable color photographs that depict life in Manhattan's Harlem and Spanish Harlem. (Rev: BL 2/15/04*) [974.7]

8973 Bigler, Philip. *Washington in Focus: The Photo History of the Nation's Capital* (9–12). Illus. 1988, Vandamere paper $8.95 (0-918339-07-3). A history in pictures and text of Washington, D.C., from its beginnings to the building of the Metro and the Vietnam Memorial. (Rev: BL 12/15/88) [975.3]

8974 Bourdain, Anthony. *Typhoid Mary* (10–12). Series: Urban Historicals. 2001, Bloomsbury $19.95 (1-58234-133-8). The story of "Typhoid Mary" Mallon, a cook who unwittingly caused epidemics of typhoid fever on Long Island and in New York City in the early 1900s. (Rev: BL 4/15/01) [974.7]

8975 Conaway, James. *The Smithsonian: 150 Years of Adventure, Discovery, and Wonder* (9–12). 1995, Knopf $60.00 (0-679-44175-1). Provides historical background and a multitude of photographs, with sidebars about many of the museum's scientific expeditions. (Rev: BL 11/1/95) [069]

8976 Durham, Michael S., and Donald Young. *The Mid-Atlantic States*. Rev. ed. (9–12). Series: Smithsonian Guide to Historic America. 1998, Stewart, Tabori & Chang paper $9.95 (1-55670-634-0). A directory of historical sites of interest in New Jersey, New York, and Pennsylvania, with visitor information. [917.4]

8977 Garrett, Wendell, ed. *Our Changing White House* (9–12). 1995, Northeastern Univ. Pr. $45.00 (1-55553-222-5). Ten authoritative essays chart the White House's evolution, physically and politically, through the last two centuries, with photographs, facts, and anecdotes. (Rev: BL 7/95*) [975.3]

8978 Greenlaw, Linda. *The Lobster Chronicles: Life on a Very Small Island* (10–12). 2002, Hyperion $22.95 (0-7868-6677-2). Personal anecdotes are interwoven throughout this entertaining snapshot of the Maine lobstering business. (Rev: BL 6/1–15/02) [818]

8979 Katz, William L. *Black Legacy: A History of New York's African Americans* (6–10). Illus. 1997, Simon & Schuster $19.00 (0-689-31913-4). A history of New York City's African American community, beginning with New Amsterdam, continuing through the Revolution and Civil War to the Harlem Renaissance, and ending with the mayoralty of David Dinkins in the early 1990s. (Rev: BL 2/15/97; BR 1–2/98; SLJ 10/97*; VOYA 6/97) [974.7]

8980 Korman, Marvin. *In My Father's Bakery: A Bronx Memoir* (10–12). 2003, Red Rock $22.00 (0-9714372-4-6). The Bronx of the 1930s and 1940s is brought to life through Korman's memories of growing up in a Jewish family there. (Rev: BL 10/15/03) [974.7]

8981 Locker, Thomas. *In Blue Mountains: An Artist's Return to America's First Wilderness* (6–12). Illus. 2000, Bell Pond $18.00 (0-88010-471-6). This picture book is a tribute to nature, chronicling the author-artist's return to Kaaterskill Cove in New York State to find inspiration. (Rev: BL 7/00; SLJ 11/00) [974.7]

8982 McNeese, Tim. *The New York Subway System* (6–10). Illus. Series: Building History. 1997, Lucent LB $27.45 (1-56006-427-7). The story of the building of the 722 miles of tunnels that compose the subway system of New York City, the longest underground system in the world. (Rev: BL 12/1/97; BR 1–2/98; HBG 3/98; SLJ 11/97) [388.4]

8983 Marberry, Craig, and Michael Cunningham. *The Spirit of Harlem: A Portrait of America's Most Exciting Neighborhood* (10–12). Illus. 2003, Doubleday $27.50 (0-385-50406-3). Photographs and interviews with current residents of Harlem offer fascinating insights into the past, present, and future of America's most famous African American community. (Rev: BL 10/15/03) [974.7]

8984 Myers, Walter Dean. *Harlem* (6–12). Illus. 1997, Scholastic paper $16.95 (0-590-54340-7). This book is an impressionistic appreciation of Harlem and its culture as seen through the eyes of author Walter Dean Myers and his artist son, Christopher. (Rev: BL 2/15/97; SLJ 2/97; VOYA 10/97) [811]

8985 Rock, Howard B., and Deborah Moore. *Cityscapes: A History of New York in Images* (8–12). Illus. 2001, Columbia Univ. Pr. $60.00 (0-231-10624-6). Using fine prints and photographs, this account traces the evolution of Manhattan from a Dutch settlement to the great modern city of massive towers that it is today. (Rev: BL 12/1/01) [974.7]

8986 Truman, Margaret. *The President's House: A First Daughter Shares the History and Secrets of the World's Most Famous Home* (9–12). Illus. 2003, Ballantine $27.95 (0-345-44452-3). Truman provides a friendly and chatty introduction to her for-mer home, with tidbits of history about the structure and the people who've lived there. (Rev: BL 10/1/03; SLJ 7/04) [973]

8987 *Washington, D.C.: A Smithsonian Book of the Nation's Capital* (9–12). 1992, Smithsonian $39.95 (0-89599-032-6). Photoessays by historians, journalists, and scholars on the city's history, its artworks and documents, and its buildings, parks, and streets. (Rev: BL 11/1/92) [975.3]

8988 Weinberg, Jeshajahu, and Rina Elieli Weinberg. *The Holocaust Museum in Washington* (9–12). 1995, Rizzoli $45.00 (0-8478-1906-X). Insights are given into the design, plan, and construction of the museum and its exhibits. (Rev: BL 1/1–15/96; SLJ 3/96) [975.3]

PACIFIC STATES

8989 *Alaska: Tales of Adventure from the Last Frontier* (10–12). Ed. by Spike Walker. 2002, St. Martin's paper $14.95 (0-312-27562-5). This collection of 31 stories from such well-known writers as Jack London, John Muir, Washington Irving, and Gary Paulsen paints a colorful portrait of life in Alaska, past and present. (Rev: BL 1/1–15/02) [979.8]

8990 Barter, James. *Alcatraz* (7–10). Series: Building History. 2000, Lucent LB $18.96 (1-56006-596-6). The story of how and why buildings were placed on Alcatraz Island and how it functions today as a popular park. (Rev: BL 1/1–15/00; HBG 9/00) [979.4]

8991 Barter, James. *The Golden Gate Bridge* (7–10). Series: Building History. 2001, Lucent $24.95 (1-56006-856-6). Using many quotations from first-hand sources, this account presents both the human and technological aspects of the construction and use of San Francisco's landmark bridge. (Rev: BL 8/01) [979.4]

8992 Behler, Deborah A. *The Rain Forests of the Pacific Northwest* (7–12). Illus. Series: Ecosystems of North America. 2000, Benchmark LB $18.95 (0-7614-0926-2). A detailed look at the flora and fauna of this ecosystem that covers each layer of the forest from top to bottom as well as the impact of human activities. (Rev: HBG 3/01; SLJ 4/01) [577.34]

8993 Bowermaster, John. *Aleutian Adventure* (6–12). Illus. 2001, National Geographic $17.95 (0-7922-7999-9). Beautifully illustrated, this book chronicles a harrowing but ultimately successful kayak expedition among the rugged islands of the Aleutian chain. (Rev: VOYA 8/01) [797.1]

8994 Bowermaster, Jon. *Birthplace of the Winds: Storming Alaska's Islands of Fire and Ice* (10–12). Illus. 2001, National Geographic $26.00 (0-7922-7506-3). This is an account of a thrilling journey to a group of uninhabited, foggy, rarely visited islands in the Aleutian archipelago, where survival is a struggle. (Rev: BL 2/1/01) [917.98]

8995 Bruder, Gerry. *Heroes of the Horizon: Flying Adventures of Alaska's Legendary Bush Pilots* (9–12). 1991, Alaska Northwest paper $14.95 (0-88240-363-X). Reveals the feats of the last generation of frontier pilots to fly open planes to uncharted Alaskan settlements. (Rev: BL 10/1/91) [629.13]

8996 Chippendale, Lisa A. *The San Francisco Earthquake of 1906* (7–12). Series: Great Disasters: Reforms and Ramifications. 2001, Chelsea $21.95 (0-7910-5270-2). An interesting account full of photographs, eyewitness accounts, and good background information on earthquakes and California history that focuses on the appropriateness of the responses to the disaster by the various authorities and the lessons learned. (Rev: BL 4/15/01; HBG 10/01; SLJ 6/01) [979.4]

8997 Fradkin, Philip L. *Wildest Alaska: Journeys of Great Peril in Lituya Bay* (10–12). Illus. 2001, Univ. of California Pr. $24.95 (0-520-22467-1). Enormous waves, shipwrecks, and murder are featured in this book about the history of Lituya Bay, an extremely dangerous inlet in Alaska. (Rev: BL 6/1–15/01) [979.8]

8998 Green, Carl R. *The Mission Trails* (6–10). Series: In American History. 2001, Enslow LB $20.95 (0-7660-1349-9). A well-researched and well-documented history of the southwestern Spanish missions and the trails that were built to connect them. (Rev: BL 12/15/01; HBG 3/02; SLJ 3/02) [979.4]

8999 Jenkins, Peter. *Looking for Alaska* (9–12). Illus. 2001, St. Martin's $25.95 (0-312-26178-0). The author describes a 1999 trip to Alaska, using kayaks, fishing boats, dogsleds, and conventional methods in an effort to get to know the people and the places of this state. (Rev: BL 10/1/01) [917.3]

9000 Krakauer, Jon. *Into the Wild* (9–12). 1996, Villard $22.00 (0-679-42850-X). A true story expanded from Krakauer's article about a young man who starved to death in Denali National Park in Alaska. (Rev: BL 12/1/95*) [917.9]

9001 Kurzman, Dan. *Disaster! The Great San Francisco Earthquake and Fire of 1906* (9–12). Illus. 2001, Morrow $25.00 (0-06-105174-8). A riveting narrative of the San Francisco earthquake of 1906 and the resulting fires that almost destroyed the city. (Rev: BL 4/1/01) [979.4]

9002 McConnaughey, Bayard, and Evelyn McConnaughey. *Pacific Coast* (9–12). Illus. 1985, Knopf paper $19.95 (0-394-73130-1). A nature guide to the ecology of the Pacific states with emphasis on the bird life. (Rev: SLJ 9/85) [979]

9003 Maharidge, Dale. *Yosemite: A Landscape of Life* (9–12). 1990, Yosemite paper $14.95 (0-

939666-56-1). An insightful look at the inner workings of the national park. (Rev: BL 1/15/91) [979.4]

9004 *A Road of Her Own: Women's Journeys in the West* (10–12). Ed. by Marlene Blessing. 2002, Fulcrum $24.95 (1-55591-307-5). Women's experiences — both physical and spiritual — exploring the American West are the focus of this collection of essays celebrating freedom. (Rev: BL 11/1/02) [917.804]

9005 Ruth, Maria Mudd. *The Pacific Coast* (7–12). Illus. Series: Ecosystems of North America. 2000, Benchmark LB $18.95 (0-7614-0935-1). A detailed look at the tides, plants, animals, and ecosystems found along the Pacific Coast from Alaska south to Mexico. (Rev: HBG 3/01; SLJ 4/01) [577.5]

9006 Ryan, Alan, ed. *The Reader's Companion to Alaska* (10–12). 1997, Harcourt paper $16.00 (0-15-600368-6). A compilation of writings, many of them first-person accounts, about impressions of Alaska, arranged geographically. (Rev: SLJ 1/98) [979.8]

9007 Salisbury, Gay, and Laney Salisbury. *The Cruelest Miles: The Heroic Story of Dogs and Men in a Race Against an Epidemic* (10–12). Illus. 2003, Norton $24.95 (0-393-01962-4). A detailed and compelling account of the challenges facing the dogs and humans who undertook the 700-mile expedition to deliver serum to Nome in 1925. (Rev: BL 5/1/03; SLJ 12/03) [614.5]

9008 Takaki, Ronald. *Raising Cane: The World of Plantation Hawaii* (6–10). Adapted by Rebecca Stefoff. Illus. Series: Asian American Experience. 1994, Chelsea LB $19.95 (0-7910-2178-5). A fascinating look at the part that Asian immigrants played in the development of the economy of Hawaii. (Rev: BL 6/1–15/94; SLJ 7/94) [996.9]

9009 Ward, Kennan. *Denali: Reflections of a Naturalist* (9–12). Illus. 2000, Creative Publishing $24.95 (1-55971-716-5). Using stunning photographs and an interesting text, the author has created an outstanding introduction to Denali National Park, home of Mount McKinley, in Alaska. (Rev: BL 5/1/00) [508.798]

9010 *Writing Los Angeles: A Literary Anthology* (10–12). Ed. by David L. Ulin. Illus. 2002, Library of America $40.00 (1-931082-27-8). The many faces of Los Angeles are brought to life in this anthology of fiction and nonfiction by such diverse writers as F. Scott Fitzgerald, H. L. Mencken, Tom Wolfe, Helen Hunt Jackson, and Truman Capote. (Rev: BL 9/15/02) [810.8]

SOUTH

9011 Ayers, Harvard, and Jenny Hager, eds. *An Appalachian Tragedy: Air Pollution and Tree Death in the Eastern Forests of North America* (10–12).

1998, Sierra Club $45.00 (0-87156-976-0). Forest ecology is highlighted in this beautifully illustrated account of the effects of 40 years of pollution on the Appalachian Mountains. (Rev: SLJ 12/98) [976.1]

9012 *The Book of the Everglades* (10–12). Ed. by Susan Cerulean. 2002, Milkweed paper $18.95 (1-57131-260-9). Experts assess the threats to the Everglades' biodiversity. (Rev: BL 8/02) [508.75]

9013 Bresee, Clyde. *How Grand a Flame: A Chronicle of a Plantation Family, 1813–1947* (9–12). 1991, Algonquin $33.95 (0-945575-55-6). An illustrated reconstruction of family life on a South Carolina cotton plantation based on original documents and personal remembrances. (Rev: BL 10/1/91) [975.7]

9014 St. Antoine, Sara, ed. *Stories from Where We Live: The Gulf Coast* (7–12). Illus. 2002, Milkweed $19.95 (1-57131-636-1). A variety of literary forms including poetry, essays, and stories describe experiences on the Gulf Coast. (Rev: BL 1/1–15/03; HBG 10/03) [976]

SOUTHWEST

9015 Fishbein, Seymour L. *Yellowstone Country: The Enduring Wonder* (9–12). Illus. 1989, National Geographic LB $12.00 (0-87044-718-1). A profile of the world's oldest national park with particularly good coverage of its flora and fauna. (Rev: BL 11/1/89; SLJ 1/90) [917.87]

9016 Lavender, David. *The Southwest* (10–12). 1984, Univ. of New Mexico Pr. paper $17.95 (0-8263-0736-1). The history of the entire Southwest is given, with emphasis on New Mexico and Arizona. [979.1]

9017 McCarry, Charles. *The Great Southwest* (7–12). Illus. 1980, National Geographic LB $12.95 (0-87044-288-0). In pictures and text, descriptions are given of such states as New Mexico, Colorado, and Arizona. [979.1]

9018 Marrin, Albert. *Empires Lost and Won* (6–10). Illus. 1997, Simon & Schuster $19.00 (0-689-80414-8). Beginning with the destruction of Pueblo Indian cities and ending with the war between the U.S. and Mexico, this book provides a fascinating history of the 300-year struggle for control of the Southwest. (Rev: BL 7/97; BR 9–10/97; SLJ 6/97*; VOYA 6/97) [979]

9019 Melzer, Richard. *When We Were Young in the West: True Histories of Childhood* (10–12). 2003, Sunstone paper $19.95 (0-86534-338-1). This unique history of New Mexico from the viewpoint of children draws on first-person accounts and oral histories to bring alive such memorable events as pioneering wagon train travel and school desegregation. (Rev: BL 6/1–15/03) [978.9]

9020 Pyne, Stephen J. *How the Canyon Became Grand: A Short History* (10–12). 1998, Viking paper $12.95 (0-14-028056-1). The Grand Canyon languished in obscurity until the 19th century, when John Wesley Powell sang its praises, spurring its elevation to the national attraction it is today. (Rev: BL 8/98) [979.1]

Philosophy and Religion

Philosophy

9021 Adler, Mortimer J. *How to Think About the Great Ideas from the Great Books of Western Civilization* (10–12). 2000, Open Court paper $24.95 (0-8126-9412-0). Basic philosophical questions involving such subjects as evolution, art, law, government, good and evil, and war and peace are introduced in this book that is useful for beginning group discussions. (Rev: BL 5/1/00) [081]

9022 Bender, David L., ed. *Constructing a Life Philosophy* (9–12). Series: Opposing Viewpoints. 1993, Greenhaven LB $26.20 (0-89908-198-3); paper $21.81 (0-89908-173-8). Essays relating to developing a philosophy on the meaning of life by such diverse writers as Plato, Joseph Campbell, and Billy Graham. (Rev: BL 6/1–15/93) [140]

9023 Blackburn, Simon. *Think: A Compelling Introduction to Philosophy* (10–12). 1999, Oxford $25.00 (0-19-210024-6). This introduction to philosophy explores questions relating to knowledge, free will, mind, and goodness. (Rev: BL 10/1/99) [100]

9024 Boorstin, Daniel J. *The Seekers: The Story of Man's Continuing Quest to Understand His World* (10–12). 1998, Random paper $15.00 (0-375-70475-2). Historian Boorstin examines the ongoing human search for the meaning and purpose of existence, covering in detail some of the more widely accepted theories put forward by history's great thinkers in both the secular and religious worlds. (Rev: BL 8/98; SLJ 5/99) [909]

9025 Curry, Patrick, and Oscar Zarate. *Introducing Machiavelli* (10–12). Ed. by Richard Appignanesi. 1996, Totem paper $9.95 (1-874166-28-5). The life and political theories of this Italian philosopher are introduced through black-and-white comics and brief text. (Rev: SLJ 7/96) [100]

9026 Durant, William James. *The Story of Philosophy: The Lives and Opinions of the Great Philosophers.* 2nd ed. (10–12). 1933, Simon & Schuster paper $15.00 (0-671-20159-X). A basic history of philosophy and key thoughts from the ancient Greeks to Dewey. [109]

9027 Eichhoefer, Gerald W. *Enduring Issues in Philosophy* (10–12). Series: Enduring Issues. 1995, Greenhaven LB $27.45 (1-56510-252-5); paper $17.45 (1-56510-251-7). This book explores six controversies in philosophy such as "What is ultimately real?" "Does God exist?" and "What is morality?" (Rev: BL 7/95; SLJ 8/95) [100]

9028 Fulghum, Robert. *All I Really Need to Know I Learned in Kindergarten: Uncommon Thoughts on Common Things* (10–12). 1988, Random $18.95 (0-394-57102-9). A collection of essays extolling the simple things in life. (Rev: BL 10/15/88) [128]

9029 Law, Stephen. *Philosophy Rocks!* (7–12). 2002, Hyperion paper $12.99 (0-7868-1699-6). A lighthearted approach is used in tackling eight basic philosophical questions, including "What is real?" and "Does God exist?" (Rev: LMC 2/03; SLJ 10/02; VOYA 12/02) [100]

9030 Magee, Bryan. *The Story of Philosophy* (10–12). Illus. 1998, DK $29.95 (0-7894-3511-X). This handsome survey of Western philosophy covers more than 2,500 years, profiling the leading thinkers and providing brief listings of their writings; suitable for high school humanities classes. (Rev: BL 12/1/98; SLJ 3/99) [190]

9031 Morris, Richard. *The Big Questions: Probing the Promise and Limits of Science* (11–12). 2002, Holt $26.00 (0-8050-7092-3). Morris searches our scientific knowledge for answers to age-old philosophical questions (What is time? Does the future already exist?) and provides readable information about such topics as quantum mechanics, cosmology, and genetics in the process. (Rev: BL 4/1/02) [616.8]

9032 Morrow, Lance. *Evil: An Investigation* (10–12). 2003, Basic $26.00 (0-465-04754-8). Our changing perceptions of evil are examined in this fascinating study by *Time* columnist Morrow. (Rev: BL 8/03) [170]

9033 Phillips, Christopher. *Six Questions of Socrates: A Modern-Day Journey of Discovery Through World Philosophy* (10–12). 2004, Norton $23.95 (0-393-05157-9). Phillips visits countries around the world in search of answers to eternal questions: What is virtue?, for example. (Rev: BL 12/1/03; SLJ 7/04) [179]

9034 Pirsig, Robert M. *Zen and the Art of Motorcycle Maintenance: An Inquiry into Values* (10–12). 1974, HarperCollins $26.00 (0-688-00230-7). A number of philosophical musings are presented, all prompted by a motorcycle trip with Pirsig's young son. [191.092]

9035 Russell, Bertrand. *A History of Western Philosophy: And Its Connection with Political and Social Circumstances from the Earliest Times to the Present Day* (10–12). 1945, Simon & Schuster paper $24.00 (0-671-20158-1). The author of this overview has stated that his purpose is to show that philosophy is an integral part of everyone's social and political life. [109]

9036 Solomon, Robert C., and Kathleen Marie Higgins. *A Short History of Philosophy* (10–12). 1996, Oxford paper $23.95 (0-19-510196-0). This ambitious historical survey of philosophy examines the evolution of human thinking about life's central questions. [109]

9037 Spalding, John D. *A Pilgrim's Digress: My Perilous, Fumbling Quest for the Celestial City* (10–12). 2003, Harmony $23.00 (1-4000-4653-X). This 21st-century take on John Bunyan's *The Pilgrim's Progress* profiles a number of America's offbeat philosophies and belief systems. (Rev: BL 3/15/03) [291.4]

9038 Weate, Jeremy. *A Young Person's Guide to Philosophy* (6–12). 1998, DK paper $16.99 (0-7894-3074-6). After a discussion of what constitutes philosophy, this well-illustrated volume tells about the lives, times, and thoughts of 25 of the world's great thinkers. (Rev: BL 12/15/98; BR 5–6/99; HBG 3/99; SLJ 1/99) [100]

World Religions and Holidays

General and Miscellaneous

9039 Aaseng, Rolf E. *A Beginner's Guide to Study-ing the Bible* (9–12). 1991, Augsburg paper $10.99 (0-8066-2571-6). Outlines basic techniques and resources for enriching Bible study. (Rev: BL 4/1/92) [220.07]

9040 Andryszewski, Tricia. *Communities of the Faithful: American Religious Movements Outside the Mainstream* (6–10). 1997, Millbrook LB $24.90 (0-7613-0067-8). Seven religious orders — Old Order Amish, Shakers, Mormons, Catholic Work-ers, Nation of Islam, Lubavitcher Hasidim, and Quakers — are introduced, with material on their beliefs and contributions to American culture. (Rev: BR 5–6/98; SLJ 2/98) [200]

9041 Asimov, Isaac. *Asimov's Guide to the Bible* (7–12). 1981, Crown $19.99 (0-517-34582-X). This is a book-by-book guide to both the Old and New Testaments. [220.7]

9042 Asimov, Isaac. *Asimov's Guide to the Bible: The Old Testament* (10–12). 1976, Avon paper $10.95 (0-380-01032-1). A historical study of the Old Testament. Followed by *Asimov's Guide to the Bible: The New Testament* (1982). [220]

9043 Balmer, Randall. *Religion in Twentieth-Centu-ry America* (6–12). Illus. Series: Religion in Ameri-can Life. 2001, Oxford LB $22.00 (0-19-511295-4). Balmer looks at the evolution of religious move-ments across America, including the emergence of the Religious Right and televangelism, and at important events such as the Scopes Trial and the FBI attack on the Branch Davidians. (Rev: BL 8/01; HBG 10/01; SLJ 6/01) [200]

9044 Barr, Robert R. *What Is the Bible?* (9–12). 1984, HarperCollins $4.95 (0-86683-727-2). This is a popular introduction to the characters and stories in the Bible and their significance. [220]

9045 Berthrong, John H., and E. Nagai-Berthrong. *Confucianism: A Short Introduction* (10–12). 2000, Oneworld Publs. paper $15.95 (1-85168-236-8). This work describes the history of Confucianism, its principles, and its impact, particularly on Chinese life. [299]

9046 Bowker, John. *World Religions* (10–12). 1997, DK $34.95 (0-7894-1439-2). In this heavily illus-trated volume, two or three pages are devoted to each of the world's important religions, with materi-al on principles, symbols, events, people, buildings, works of art, and similarities to other religions. (Rev: BR 9–10/97; SLJ 12/97; VOYA 10/97) [200]

9047 Braude, Ann. *Women and American Religion* (8–12). Illus. Series: Religion in America. 2000, Oxford LB $22.00 (0-19-510676-8). Beginning with Native American and Puritan women and continu-ing to the present, this account traces the many con-tributions women have made to religion in America. (Rev: BL 3/15/00; HBG 3/01; SLJ 5/00) [200]

9048 Breuilly, Elizabeth, et al. *Religions of the World: The Illustrated Guide to Origins, Beliefs, Traditions and Festivals* (7–12). Illus. 1997, Facts on File $29.95 (0-8160-3723-X). This well-illustrat-ed work defines religion generally, discusses each of the world's major religions, points out similari-ties, and links each religion to current events and international politics. (Rev: BL 10/1/97; HBG 3/98; SLJ 2/98) [291]

9049 Carlson, Melody. *Piercing Proverbs: Wise Words for Today's Teens* (7–12). 2002, Multnomah paper $7.99 (1-57673-895-7). The author presents a selection of proverbs and asks readers to consider their relevance to circumstances today. (Rev: BL 7/02) [223]

9050 Cornuke, Robert, and David Halbrook. *In Search of the Lost Mountains of Noah: The Discovery of the Real Mt. Ararat* (9–12). 2001, Broadman & Holman $21.99 (0-8054-2054-1). Using scriptural evidence and detailed terrain maps, the author, through his expeditions, believes he has located the spot where Noah's Ark landed on what is now Mount Sabalon in Iran. (Rev: BL 9/1/01) [221.9]

9051 Cotner, June, ed. *Teen Sunshine Reflections: Words for the Heart and Soul* (6–12). 2002, HarperCollins $15.95 (0-06-000525-4); paper $9.95 (0-06-000527-0). This anthology of poems and quotations that celebrate spiritual beliefs and appreciation of the world about us includes the works of the well-known (such as Saint Francis, Gandhi, and Anne Frank) and the unknown. (Rev: BL 7/02; HBG 10/02; SLJ 8/02; VOYA 8/02) [082]

9052 Deloria, Vine. *Evolution, Creationism, and Other Modern Myths: A Critical Inquiry* (10–12). 2002, Fulcrum $24.95 (1-55591-159-5). Native American scholar Deloria examines the arguments on both sides of the ongoing debate between creationists and evolutionists and finds them wanting. (Rev: BL 12/1/02*) [291.1]

9053 Dhanjal, Beryl. *Sikhism* (7–10). Illus. 1987, David & Charles $19.95 (0-7134-5202-1). The major tenets, doctrines, and personages of this religion are discussed in alphabetical order. (Rev: SLJ 9/87) [294.6]

9054 Dudley, William, ed. *Religion in America* (7–12). Illus. Series: Opposing Viewpoints. 2001, Greenhaven LB $31.20 (1-56510-003-4); paper $19.95 (1-56510-002-6). Essays assess the importance of religion in America today, with debate of such questions as the proper role for religion in education, how to accommodate religious freedom, and whether religion can solve social problems. (Rev: BL 10/1/01) [200]

9055 *Eerdmans' Handbook to the World's Religions.* Rev. ed. (9–12). 1994, Eerdmans paper $26.00 (0-8028-0853-0). Divided by geographical region, this is a fine overview of the world's religions with coverage on history, beliefs, and practices. [291]

9056 Ellwood, Robert S., and Gregory D. Alles, eds. *The Encyclopedia of World Religions* (7–12). Illus. 1998, Facts on File $45.00 (0-8160-3504-0). Though basically intended as a reference book, this is an absorbing work that offers information on religions past and present and on general topics of interest, such as the sun, moon, music, and science. (Rev: BL 9/1/98; SLJ 11/98) [200]

9057 Fletcher, Richard. *The Cross and the Crescent: Christianity and Islam from Muhammad to the Reformation* (10–12). 2004, Viking $22.95 (0-670-03271-9). This is a thorough discussion for better students of 900 years of relations between the

realms of Christianity and Islam. (Rev: BL 1/1–15/04) [261.2]

9058 Ford, Michael Thomas. *Paths of Faith: Conversations About Religion and Spirituality* (8–12). 2000, Simon & Schuster $17.00 (0-689-82263-4). In a series of interviews, 12 young people discuss religion, what it means to them, and the nature of their spiritual journeys. (Rev: BL 10/1/00; HB 1–2/01; HBG 3/01; SLJ 1/01) [291]

9059 France, Peter. *An Encyclopedia of Bible Animals* (9–12). Illus. 1986, Salem House $26.95 (0-7099-3737-7). An alphabetically arranged treatment of all the animals mentioned in the Bible with references to specific passages and illustrations. (Rev: BL 11/1/86) [220]

9060 Fuller, Cheri, and Ron Luce. *When Teens Pray: Powerful Stories of How God Works* (9–12). 2002, Multnomah paper $9.99 (1-57673-970-8). The power of prayer in the lives of young people is explored in this collection of stories, most of which are related by the teens who lived them. (Rev: BL 7/02) [291.4]

9061 Hartz, Paula. *Baha'i Faith* (6–10). Series: World Religions. 2002, Facts on File $30.00 (0-8160-4729-4). A look at the history and beliefs of the Baha'i Faith and its spread from Persia to the rest of the world. (Rev: HBG 3/03; SLJ 12/02) [297.9]

9062 Hartz, Paula R. *Zoroastrianism* (8–12). Illus. Series: World Religions. 1999, Facts on File $26.95 (0-8160-3877-5). A thorough description of the beliefs and customs of followers of Zarathushtra. (Rev: BR 1–2/00; HBG 4/00; SLJ 1/00) [295]

9063 Harvey, Michael. *Miracles* (9–12). Series: Great Mysteries. 1990, Greenhaven LB $22.45 (0-89908-084-7). Explores mostly Christian miracles, including healings and the appearance of religious images. (Rev: BL 1/1/91) [231.7]

9064 Ikeda, Daisaku. *The Way of Youth* (6–12). 2000, Middleway paper $14.95 (0-9674697-0-8). The great questions of human behavior — such as the nature of love, friendship, and compassion — are discussed from a Buddhist perspective. (Rev: BL 12/1/00) [294.3]

9065 *The Illustrated Guide to World Religions* (10–12). 1998, Oxford $45.00 (0-19-521366-1). An accessible and highly visual survey of Buddhism, Christianity, Hinduism, Islam, and Judaism as well as Chinese and Japanese religious traditions. [291]

9066 Joselit, Jenna Weissman. *Immigration and American Religion* (6–12). Illus. Series: Religion in American Life. 2001, Oxford $22.00 (0-19-511083-8). Joselit looks at Protestant, Catholic, Jewish, and Asian immigrants to the United States and how their religious beliefs and practices have evolved to suit their new circumstances. (Rev: BL 5/15/01; HBG 10/01; SLJ 8/01) [200.86]

9067 Kingsbury, Karen. *A Treasury of Miracles for Teens: True Stories of God's Presence Today* (7–12). 2003, Warner $12.95 (0-446-52962-1). Kingsbury recounts stories in which teens seek God's help and are rewarded. (Rev: BL 7/03) [231.7]

9068 Levinson, David. *Religion: A Cross-Cultural Dictionary* (10–12). 1996, ABC-CLIO LB $49.50 (0-87436-865-0). A browsable reference book that gives information of 16 religions as well as 41 allied subjects like ritual, taboo, and supernatural beings. (Rev: BL 3/1/97; BR 9–10/97; SLJ 8/97) [200]

9069 Losch, Richard R. *The Many Faces of Faith* (9–12). 2001, Eerdmans $19.00 (0-8028-3910-X). This book contains profiles of the world's major religions as well as material on various Christian sects such as the Mormons and Jehovah's Witnesses. (Rev: BL 8/01) [200]

9070 Lugira, Aloysius. *African Religion* (7–10). Illus. Series: World Religions. 1999, Facts on File $30.00 (0-8160-3876-7). The author gives a fine overview of the major religious beliefs of the different ethnic groups in Africa plus material on organized religion, witchcraft, and the influence of Western religions on the area. (Rev: BL 1/1–15/00; HBG 4/00; SLJ 1/00) [299]

9071 Lyden, John, ed. *Enduring Issues in Religion* (10–12). Series: Enduring Issues. 1995, Greenhaven LB $27.45 (1-56510-260-6). Classic religious texts and the writings of modern theologians are used to explore topics involving the nature of religion, the meaning of life, and what lies beyond death. (Rev: BL 7/95) [200]

9072 McFarlane, Marilyn, retel. *Sacred Myths: Stories of World Religions* (6–10). 1996, Sibyl $26.95 (0-9638327-7-8). A collection of myths from a number of religions, including Judaism, Christianity, Islam, and Hinduism. (Rev: BL 10/1/96; SLJ 1/97) [200]

9073 Magida, Arthur J. *How to Be a Perfect Stranger: A Guide to Etiquette in Other People's Religious Ceremonies* (9–12). 1995, Jewish Lights $24.95 (1-879045-39-7). An excellent reference to the rites and rituals of North America's major religions and denominations, this guide offers valuable advice about how to dress and conduct oneself. [291.3]

9074 Mann, Gruinder Singh, et al. *Buddhists, Hindus, and Sikhs in America* (6–12). Illus. Series: Religion in American Life. 2002, Oxford $24.00 (0-19-512442-1). Photographs, anecdotes, and excerpts from primary sources add appeal to this survey of how three major religions have affected, and been affected by, life in America. (Rev: BL 1/1–15/02; HBG 10/02; SLJ 1/02; VOYA 4/02) [294]

9075 Martin, Joel W. *Native American Religion* (7–12). 1999, Oxford LB $22.00 (0-19-511035-8). An overview of historical and contemporary Native American religious beliefs and practices, their importance in daily life, and the conflicts introduced by the Europeans. (Rev: HBG 4/00; SLJ 9/99; VOYA 10/99) [299]

9076 Mayer, Marianna. *Remembering the Prophets of Sacred Scripture* (6–10). Illus. 2003, Penguin $16.99 (0-8034-2727-5). Old Testament prophets — from Daniel and Moses to Amos and Obadiah — are introduced in this handsome picture book for older readers. (Rev: BL 7/03; SLJ 8/03) [224]

9077 Melton, J. Gordon. *American Religions: An Illustrated History* (10–12). 2000, ABC-CLIO $99.00 (1-57607-222-3). From the early beliefs of Native Americans to the present, this account gives a brief but accurate glimpse at the history of religions in America. [200.9]

9078 Metcalf, Franz. *Buddha in Your Backpack: Everyday Buddhism for Teens* (7–12). 2002, Ulysses paper $12.95 (1-56975-321-0). This humorous and informative guide will satisfy young adults' interest in the spiritual world of Buddhism. (Rev: BL 1/1–15/03; SLJ 2/03; VOYA 2/04) [294.3]

9079 Morgan, Peggy. *Buddhism* (7–10). Illus. 1987, David & Charles $19.95 (0-7134-5203-X). In a dictionary format, the major points concerning this religion and its founder are described. (Rev: SLJ 9/87) [294.3]

9080 Murphy, Claire Rudolf, et al. *Daughters of the Desert: Stories of Remarkable Women from Christian, Jewish, and Muslim Traditions* (7–10). 2003, Skylight Paths $19.95 (1-893361-72-1). Five authors contributed to these 18 stories, based on the Bible and Koran, of the lives of women including Eve, Esther, Mary Magdalene, Sarah, and Khadiji, the wife of Mohammed. (Rev: BL 10/15/03) [220.9]

9081 Netzley, Patricia D. *Angels* (7–10). Series: Mystery Library. 2001, Lucent LB $19.96 (1-56006-768-3). A serious examination of sources and occurrences that have been used to prove or disprove the existence of angels. (Rev: BL 9/15/01) [291.2]

9082 *Nothing Sacred: Women Respond to Religious Fundamentalism and Terror* (10–12). Ed. by Betsy Reed. 2003, Thunder's Mouth paper $17.95 (1-56025-450-5). In this collection of brief, often scholarly essays, women explore the anti-feminist attitudes of religious fundamentalism in all its many guises. (Rev: BL 2/15/03) [200]

9083 Parrinder, Geoffrey, ed. *World Religions from Ancient History to the Present*. Rev. ed. (10–12). Illus. 1985, Facts on File paper $17.95 (0-8160-1289-X). The first 12 chapters describe ancient religions and the final nine chapters discuss the most important modern religions. (Rev: BR 9–10/86) [200]

9084 Potter, Charles Francis. *Is That in the Bible?* (9–12). 1985, Ballantine paper $4.99 (0-345-32109-

X). An amazing collection of facts and trivia culled from the Bible. [220]

9085 Ries, Julien. *The Many Faces of Buddhism* (7–10). Illus. Series: Religions of Humanity. 2002, Chelsea LB $17.55 (0-7910-6626-6). This brief overview covers the history, beliefs, and various forms of Buddhism, with information on the spread of this religion from India into neighboring countries and on how Buddhism has evolved. (Rev: SLJ 10/02; VOYA 12/02) [294.3]

9086 Rohr, Janelle, ed. *Science and Religion: Opposing Viewpoints* (9–12). Illus. Series: Opposing Viewpoints. 1988, Greenhaven paper $16.20 (0-89908-406-0). The conflicts and areas of agreement between scientific truth and religious beliefs are explored from various viewpoints. (Rev: BL 5/1/88) [215]

9087 *Sacred Voices: Essential Women's Wisdom Through the Ages* (10–12). Ed. by Mary Ford-Grabowsky. 2002, HarperSF $24.95 (0-06-251702-3). This impressive anthology documents women's spiritual thinking with selections from such diverse figures as ancient Egypt's Hashepsowe, 8th-century poet Rabia Al-Adawiyya, Sojourner Truth, Emily Dickinson, and Louise Erdrich. (Rev: BL 3/1/02) [200]

9088 Seeger, Elizabeth. *Eastern Religions* (7–12). Illus. 1973, HarperCollins $14.95 (0-690-25342-7). A fine overview of such religions as Hinduism, Buddhism, Confucianism, and Taoism. [291]

9089 Smith, Huston, and Philip Novak. *Buddhism: A Concise Introduction* (10–12). 2003, HarperSF $17.95 (0-06-050696-2). This history of Buddhism begins with the life of Buddha and ends with the growth of Buddhism in the West in recent times. (Rev: BL 4/1/03) [294.3]

9090 Stein, Stephen J. *Alternative American Religions* (8–12). Series: Religion in American Life. 2000, Oxford LB $22.00 (0-19-511196-6). From Puritan dissenters to cults like Heaven's Gate, this is a look at the alternative religions that have attracted followers in the America. (Rev: HBG 9/00; SLJ 4/00; VOYA 12/00) [291.9]

9091 Sweeney, Jon M., ed. *God Within: Our Spiritual Future — As Told by Today's New Adults* (8–12). 2001, Skylight Paths paper $14.95 (1-893361-15-2). Writers in their teens and 20s, who reflect a wide variety of beliefs, present very personal essays on their faiths and their paths to spirituality. (Rev: BL 1/1–15/02) [200]

9092 Tutu, Desmond, ed. *The African Prayer Book* (9–12). 1995, Doubleday $19.95 (0-385-47730-9). African prayers, poems, and litanies, both Christian and non-Christian. (Rev: BL 5/1/95) [242]

9093 Viswanathan, Ed. *Am I a Hindu?* (9–12). 1992, Halo paper $15.95 (1-879904-06-3). A comprehensive introduction to Hinduism written in "cate-chism" form, with questions and answers grouped according to topic. (Rev: BL 10/15/92) [294.5]

9094 Westwood, Jennifer. *Sacred Journeys: An Illustrated Guide to Pilgrimages Around the World* (10–12). 1997, Holt $35.00 (0-8050-4845-6). Representing all faiths, this heavily illustrated book describes various modern-day religious pilgrimages, including the sites, routes, rules, dates, etc. (Rev: BR 9–10/97; SLJ 7/97) [200]

9095 Wilson, Colin. *The Atlas of Holy Places and Sacred Sites* (10–12). 1996, DK $29.95 (0-7894-1051-6). After a series of double-page spreads on sites like Stonehenge and Easter Island, there is a gazetteer with 16 maps and a listing of more than 1,000 sacred places in this well-illustrated volume. (Rev: BL 10/15/96; BR 5–6/97; SLJ 7/97; VOYA 4/97) [200]

9096 Winston, Diana. *Wide Awake: A Buddhist Guide for Teens* (6–10). 2003, Putnam paper $13.95 (0-399-52897-0). In a conversational style, the author introduces the tenets of Buddhism, explains her own beliefs and how she arrived at them, and looks at ways teens can apply Buddhist teachings to their own experiences. (Rev: BL 10/1/03) [294]

Christianity

9097 Beckett, Wendy. *Sister Wendy's Book of Saints* (10–12). 1998, DK $19.95 (0-7894-2398-7). Using artwork from the Italian State Libraries, Sister Wendy introduces the lives and works of 35 saints. (Rev: BR 11–12/98; SLJ 6/98; VOYA 10/98) [200]

9098 Bushman, Claudia L., and Richard L. Bushman. *Mormons in America* (10–12). Series: Religion in American Life. 1998, Oxford $24.00 (0-19-510677-6). A historical survey of the Church of Jesus Christ of Latter-Day Saints, illustrated with black-and-white photographs. (Rev: BL 10/1/98; HBG 3/99) [289.3]

9099 Carroll, Vincent, and David Shiflett. *Christianity on Trial: The Arguments Against Anti-Religious Bigotry* (10–12). 2001, Encounter paper $14.95 (1-893554-15-5). The author looks at all the criticisms aimed at Christianity, such as encouraging slavery, inaction during the Holocaust, hindering science, etc., and tries to refute them. (Rev: BL 10/15/01) [239]

9100 Carter, Jimmy. *Christmas in Plains* (9–12). Illus. 2001, Simon & Schuster $20.00 (0-7432-2491-4). In this stirring memoir, the former president recalls Christmases spent in Plains, Georgia, from his boyhood through to the present. (Rev: BL 10/1/01) [973.92]

9101 *Christmas in Greece* (5–10). Illus. Series: Christmas Around the World. 2000, World Book

$19.00 (0-7166-0859-6). This account focuses on the religious practices of the Greek Orthodox Church at Christmastime, which begins with a long fasting period. (Rev: BL 9/1/00) [398.2]

9102 Corzine, Phyllis. *The King James Bible: Christianity's Definitive Text* (7–12). 2000, Lucent LB $18.96 (1-56006-673-3). The author traces the history of translations of the Bible into English and looks at the cultural and religious climate at the time of the King James version (1611), giving examples of differing translations of specific passages. (Rev: HBG 9/00; SLJ 8/00)

9103 Erickson, John H. *Orthodox Christians in America* (7–12). Illus. Series: Religion in American Life. 1999, Oxford LB $22.00 (0-19-510852-3). A detailed account of the growth of Eastern Orthodox churches —and of the various ethnic groups they serve — in the United States. (Rev: HBG 4/00; SLJ 1/00) [281.9]

9104 Fialka, John J. *Sisters: Catholic Nuns and the Making of America* (10–12). Illus. 2003, St. Martin's $27.95 (0-312-26229-9). Nuns' contributions to the Catholic Church in America, as well as to education and nursing, are documented here. (Rev: BL 12/15/02) [271]

9105 Garrett, Ruth Irene, and Rick Garrett. *Crossing Over: One Woman's Exodus from Amish Life* (10–12). 2001, Thomas More $18.95 (0-88347-472-7). This is the story of a women who ran afoul of her Amish religion, broke the strict Amish order, and suffered being shunned by her home community in Iowa. (Rev: BL 10/1/01) [299.7]

9106 Ghezzi, Bert. *Mystics and Miracles: True Stories of Lives Touched by God* (10–12). 2002, Loyola $19.95 (0-8294-1772-9). In this thought-provoking overview of mystics and the miracles attributed to them, author Bert Ghezzi concludes that "ordinary people can lead extraordinary lives." (Rev: BL 2/1/02) [282]

9107 Griffin, Justin. *The Holy Grail: The Legend, the History, the Evidence* (10–12). Illus. 2001, McFarland paper $29.95 (0-7864-0999-1). Approaching this material as a historian, the author explores theories on the identity of the grail. (Rev: BL 10/1/01) [398]

9108 Hofmann, Paul. *The Vatican's Women: Female Influence in the Holy See* (10–12). 2002, St. Martin's $23.95 (0-312-27490-4). An interesting look at the ways in which women — mistresses, relatives, royals, household staff members, even saints — have influenced Roman Catholic policy. (Rev: BL 10/1/02) [282]

9109 Kung, Hans. *The Catholic Church: A Short History* (10–12). Trans. by John Bowden. Series: Modern Library Chronicles. 2001, Random $19.95 (0-679-60492-4). As well as presenting an interesting history of the Roman Catholic Church, this

account views the church today and recommends democratic reforms. (Rev: BL 4/1/01) [282]

9110 MacArthur, John F., Jr. *God with Us: The Miracle of Christmas* (9–12). Illus. 1989, Zondervan $12.99 (0-310-28690-5). A splendidly illustrated account of the events surrounding the birth of Christ and their significance. (Rev: VOYA 4/90) [263]

9111 Mitchell, Stephen. *Jesus: What He Really Said and Did* (8–12). 2002, HarperCollins LB $15.89 (0-06-000707-9). This abridged version of *The Gospel According to Jesus* (1991) gives Mitchell's controversial interpretation of the Gospels, looking at topics such as resurrection and spiritual healing. (Rev: BL 3/15/02; HB 9–10/02; HBG 3/03; SLJ 8/02; VOYA 2/03) [232.9]

9112 Nardo, Don, ed. *The Rise of Christianity* (10–12). Series: Turning Points in World History. 1999, Lucent LB $19.96 (1-56006-808-6). This anthology of 19 essays by top scholars in the fields of religion and history provides an overview of the birth, growth, and spread of Christianity, the problems faced by the early church, and Christianity's emergence as a world religion. (Rev: BL 1/1–15/99; BR 5–6/99; SLJ 3/01) [270.1]

9113 Noll, Mark. *Protestants in America* (7–12). Illus. Series: Religion in America. 2000, Oxford $28.00 (0-19-511034-X). From the arrival of the Puritans to today, this is a well-organized overview of Protestantism and how it has evolved, changed, and splintered in America. (Rev: BL 10/1/00; HBG 3/01; SLJ 2/01) [280]

9114 Rollins, Charlemae Hill, ed. *Christmas Gif': An Anthology of Christmas Poems, Songs, and Stories* (5–10). Illus. 1993, Morrow $14.00 (0-688-11667-1). A reissue of this Christmas anthology of African American songs, stories, poems, spirituals, and recipes, newly illustrated by Ashley Bryan. (Rev: BL 7/93) [810.8]

9115 Sprigg, June. *Simple Gifts: A Memoir of a Shaker Village* (10–12). Illus. 1998, Knopf $22.00 (0-679-45504-3). This is an account of the author's summer with small Shaker groups in Canterbury, New Hampshire, with good background material on the history, beliefs, and spiritual rewards of this sect. (Rev: BL 6/1–15/98; SLJ 12/98) [246]

9116 Stein, Stephen J. *The Shaker Experience in America: A History of the United Society of Believers* (9–12). 1992, Yale Univ. Pr. $55.00 (0-300-05139-5). A history of these seemingly radical religious people from the classic 18th-century Shaker period to their modern resurgence. (Rev: BL 5/1/92) [289]

9117 Stewart, Martha. *Martha Stewart's Christmas* (9–12). Illus. 1989, Random $25.00 (0-517-57416-0). A how-to book on making Christmas decorations and gifts. (Rev: BR 3–4/90) [293]

9118 Stoltzfus, Louise. *Amish Women: Lives and Stories* (9–12). 1994, Good Books $14.95 (1-56148-129-7). Amish women reveal their unique place in their religion as well as their hopes and aspirations. (Rev: BL 12/1/94; SLJ 6/95) [305.48]

9119 Teresa, Mother. *Words to Love By* (7–12). 1983, Ave Maria paper $9.95 (0-87793-261-1). A collection of the writing and meditations of the Nobel Prize–winning nun. [242]

9120 Wagner, Katherine. *Life in an Amish Community* (6–10). Series: The Way People Live. 2001, Lucent $27.45 (1-56006-654-7). Wagner explains the traditions of the Amish, traces their history, and discusses some of the contemporary disagreements within the community and problems with outsiders. (Rev: BL 10/1/01; SLJ 1/02) [973]

9121 Wernecke, Herbert H. *Christmas Customs Around the World* (9–12). Illus. 1959, Westminster paper $13.95 (0-664-24258-8). Using a geographical arrangement, the author describes unusual Christmas traditions around the world. [394.2]

9122 Williams, Jean K. *The Christian Scientists* (7–12). Series: American Religious Experience. 1997, Watts LB $25.00 (0-531-11309-4). This serves as both a history and exploration of the Christian Science faith and a biography of founder Mary Baker Eddy, who believed that mind is spirit and that sin and disease should be conquered solely by prayer. (Rev: SLJ 8/97) [289.5]

9123 Williams, Jean K. *The Quakers* (6–12). Illus. Series: American Religious Experience. 1998, Watts LB $25.00 (0-531-11377-9). From the time they left England and came to this country in the 17th century, this is the story of the Quakers, their beliefs and doctrines, and the role they have played in American history. (Rev: BL 10/1/98; HBG 3/99; SLJ 1/99) [289.6]

9124 Williams, Jean K. *The Shakers* (6–10). Illus. Series: American Religious Experience. 1997, Watts LB $25.00 (0-531-11342-6). The story of this religious sect, its origins in England, how members came to America in the late 1700s, its history here, and the group's emphasis on hard work, celibacy, orderliness, and simplicity. (Rev: BL 12/1/97; SLJ 2/98) [289]

Islam

9125 Armstrong, Karen. *Islam: A Short History* (10–12). 2000, Random $19.95 (0-679-64040-1). In addition to presenting a gripping history of this important world religion, the author probes many of its beliefs, including attitudes toward politics. (Rev: BL 8/00*) [297]

9126 Ben Jelloun, Tahar. *Islam Explained* (10–12). Trans. by Franklin Philip. 2002, New Pr. $19.95 (1-56584-781-4). Using the format of a conversation with his young daughter, Ben Jelloun offers insights into Islam, its teachings, its evolution, and its attitudes about violence and terrorism. (Rev: BL 10/1/02) [297.1]

9127 Bloom, Jonathan, and Sheila Blair. *Islam: A Thousand Years of Faith and Power* (10–12). 2000, TV Books $28.00 (1-57500-092-X). A history of Islam from its origins to modern times. [297]

9128 *Extreme Islam: Anti-American Propaganda of Muslim Fundamentalism* (11–12). Ed. by Adam Parfrey. Illus. 2002, Feral House paper $16.00 (0-922915-78-4). Despite sloppy editing, this overview of the rise of anti-American rhetoric and violence offers valuable insights for mature teens. (Rev: BL 3/15/02) [297.09]

9129 Farah, Caesar E. *Islam: Beliefs and Observances.* 6th ed. (10–12). 2000, Barron's paper $13.95 (0-7641-1205-8). This work traces the history of Islam and examines the Koran and the wide spectrum of Islamic beliefs. [297]

9130 Gordon, Matthew. *Islam.* Rev. ed. (10–12). Series: World Religions. 2001, Facts on File $30.00 (0-8160-4401-5). The origins of Islam are covered, along with beliefs, ceremonies, structure, mosques, and the impact of this religion on the modern world. (Rev: HBG 3/02) [297]

9131 Gordon, Matthew. *Islam: Origins, Practices, Holy Texts, Sacred Persons, Sacred Places* (10–12). 2002, Oxford $17.95 (0-19-521885-X). Topics included in this introduction to Islam include the rise of Islam, the Koran, the importance of Muhammad, and the major events in the history of both Sunni and Shi'a Islam. (Rev: BL 5/15/02) [297]

9132 Hurley, Jennifer A., ed. *Islam* (8–12). Illus. Series: Opposing Viewpoints. 2000, Greenhaven LB $22.96 (0-7377-0514-0); paper $14.96 (0-7377-0513-2). Essays offer widely contrasting viewpoints on Islam, looking in particular at the religion's basic values, women's role in Muslim society, terrorism, and relations with the West. (Rev: SLJ 2/01) [297]

9133 Lippman, Thomas W. *Understanding Islam: An Introduction to the Moslem World* (10–12). 1982, NAL paper $3.95 (0-451-62666-4). The life and works of Mohammed are introduced as well as a discussion of the beliefs and practices of Islam. [297]

9134 Lunde, Paul. *Islam: Faith, Culture, History* (6–12). Illus. 2002, DK paper $17.95 (0-7894-8797-7). Full of illustrations, maps, and facts, this is an attractive and accessible guide to the faith, history, and traditions of Islam. (Rev: VOYA 12/02) [297]

9135 Manji, Irshad. *The Trouble with Islam: A Muslim's Call for Reform in Her Faith* (10–12). 2004, St. Martin's $22.95 (0-312-32699-8). A Canadian Muslim woman questions the positions of her religion on such topics as sexism, anti-Semitism, and anti-intellectualism. (Rev: BL 1/1–15/04) [297]

9136 Ojeda, Auriana, ed. *Islamic Fundamentalism* (6–12). Series: At Issue. 2002, Gale LB $20.96 (0-7377-1332-5); paper $13.96 (0-7377-1331-3). The essays in this collection describe the beliefs associated with Islam and those embraced by more extreme Islamic fundamentalists. (Rev: BL 3/15/03; SLJ 7/03) [297]

9137 *The Oxford History of Islam* (10–12). Ed. by John Esposito. 1999, Oxford $49.95 (0-19-510799-3). Leading scholars contribute material on the history of Islam, its laws, traditions, culture, differences, and contemporary thinking. [297]

9138 Rashid, Ahmed. *Taliban: Militant Islam, Oil, and Fundamentalism in Central Asia* (10–12). 2000, Yale Univ. Pr. $40.00 (0-300-08340-8); paper $14.95 (0-300-08902-3). Though now somewhat dated, this account describes the origin and rise of the Taliban and tells of its Islamic beliefs and practices. (Rev: BL 4/15/00) [958.1]

9139 Robinson, Francis, ed. *The Cambridge Illustrated History of the Islamic World* (10–12). 1996, Cambridge Univ. Pr. $39.95 (0-521-43510-2). With outstanding illustrations, this work explores the history and practices of Islam and its economic and social ramifications. (Rev: SLJ 3/97) [297]

9140 Spencer, William. *Islam Fundamentalism in the Modern World* (7–10). 1995, Millbrook LB $24.90 (1-56294-435-5). Explains the tenets of Islam and the general nature of religious fundamentalism. (Rev: BL 4/15/95; SLJ 5/95) [320.5]

9141 Swisher, Clarice, ed. *The Spread of Islam* (9–12). Series: Turning Points in World History. 1998, Greenhaven LB $20.96 (1-56510-967-8); paper $17.45 (1-56510-966-X). This anthology traces the growth of Islam from Mohammed's teachings in the 7th century to the present, with chapters on Islamic art and thought, sects, and modern Islamic fundamentalism. (Rev: BL 10/15/98) [297.09]

9142 Tames, Richard. *Islam* (8–10). Illus. 1985, David & Charles $18.95 (0-7134-3655-7). A topically arranged overview of Islam that covers such subjects as marriage, mosques, festivals, and beliefs. (Rev: BL 8/85; SLJ 1/86) [297]

9143 Wormser, Richard. *American Islam: Growing Up Muslim in America* (7–12). 1994, Walker $16.85 (0-8027-8344-9). A portrait of Muslim American youth and their faith. (Rev: BL 12/15/94; SLJ 3/95; VOYA 2/95) [297]

Judaism

9144 Canfield, Jack, et al. *Chicken Soup for the Jewish Soul: Stories to Open the Heart and Rekindle the Spirit* (9–12). Illus. 2001, Health Communications $24.00 (1-55874-899-7); paper $12.95 (1-55874-898-9). A charming book that collects 86 stories that deal with life, being a Jew, love, kindness, the Holocaust, and wisdom. (Rev: BL 10/15/01) [296.7]

9145 Cardozo, Arlene. *Jewish Family Celebrations: Shabbat, Festivals and Traditional Ceremonies* (9–12). Illus. 1982, St. Martin's paper $11.95 (0-312-44232-7). This account explores the year from the standpoint of Jewish religious holidays and observances. [296.4]

9146 Diner, Hasia, and Beryl Lieff Benderly. *Her Works Praise Her: A History of Jewish Women in America from Colonial Times to the Present* (10–12). Illus. 2002, Basic $35.00 (0-465-01711-8). This is an ambitious historical survey of Jewish women in America from colonial days until the present, chronicling their contributions and the ways in which their role has evolved across the years. (Rev: BL 3/1/02) [296.09]

9147 Isaacs, Ron. *Ask the Rabbi: The Who, What, Where, Why, and How of Being Jewish* (7–12). 2003, Jossey-Bass paper $22.95 (0-7879-6784-X). Questions and answers are divided into thematic chapters and provide information on practices in different denominations. (Rev: BL 10/15/03) [296]

9148 Jacobs, Louis. *The Jewish Religion: A Companion* (10–12). 1995, Oxford $72.50 (0-19-826463-1). Arranged alphabetically, this compendium of information covers a wide variety of topics about one of the world's oldest religions, Judaism. (Rev: SLJ 6/96) [296]

9149 Kushner, Lawrence. *Jewish Spirituality: A Brief Introduction for Christians* (10–12). 2001, Jewish Lights paper $12.95 (1-58023-150-0). The author explains the Jewish understanding of creation, the Torah, the commandments of God, and communion with God. (Rev: BL 10/1/01) [296]

9150 Mack, Stanley. *The Story of the Jews: A 4,000 Year Adventure* (10–12). 1998, Random $19.95 (0-375-50130-4). A presentation of the history and experiences of the Jewish people in relation to major social and political developments in world history. (Rev: SLJ 9/98; VOYA 6/99) [296]

9151 Robinson, George. *Essential Judaism: A Complete Guide to Beliefs, Customs and Rituals* (9–12). 2000, Pocket paper $18 .00 (0-671-03481-2). An introductory account that explains the essentials of Judaism, its beliefs, practices, and customs. (Rev: BL 1/1–15/00) [296]

9152 Trepp, Leo. *The Complete Book of Jewish Observance* (9–12). Illus. 1980, Simon & Schuster $25.50 (0-671-47197-5). Working from a weekly schedule of the important observances of a lifetime, Jewish rituals are explained. [296.4]

9153 Wood, Angela. *Being a Jew* (6–10). Illus. 1988, David & Charles $19.95 (0-7134-4668-4). This book deals with the history, religion, customs, and traditions of Jewish people around the world. (Rev: SLJ 8/88) [296]

Religious Cults

9154 Barghusen, Joan D. *Cults* (7–12). Illus. Series: Overview. 1997, Lucent LB $27.45 (1-56006-199-5). The author recounts the history of cults in America, attempts to demystify them through an examination of their beliefs, recruitment methods, funding, and various practices, and reviews the anticult movement, including the practice of de-programming. (Rev: BL 5/1/98; SLJ 8/98) [291.0460973]

9155 Cohen, Daniel. *Cults* (7–10). 1994, Millbrook LB $23.40 (1-56294-324-3). This work describes cults throughout American history, including Pilgrims, Quakers, Moonies, and Satanists, and examines their recruiting methods. (Rev: BL 11/1/94; SLJ 2/95; VOYA 2/95) [291.9]

9156 Gay, Kathlyn. *Communes and Cults* (7–12). 1997, Twenty-First Century LB $24.40 (0-8050-3803-5). After tracing the history of cults that rely on communal living, the author discusses contemporary cults, their similarities and differences, their appeal, and their problems. (Rev: BL 9/1/97; BR 11–12/97; SLJ 7/97; VOYA 10/97) [280]

9157 Karson, Jill. *Cults* (9–12). Series: Contemporary Issues Companion. 2000, Greenhaven LB $31.20 (0-7377-0163-3); paper $19.95 (0-7377-0162-5). Using many case studies, interviews, and personal papers, this book explores cults and their nature. [291.9]

9158 Roleff, Tamara L., ed. *Satanism* (6–12). Series: At Issue. 2002, Gale $24.95 (0-7377-0807-7); paper $16.20 (0-7377-0806-9). A series of essays examine Satanism and the beliefs and rituals of the Church of Satan. (Rev: BL 5/15/02; SLJ 7/02) [113.4]

9159 Singer, Margaret, and Janja Lalich. *Cults in Our Midst* (9–12). 1995, Jossey-Bass $25.00 (0-7879-0051-6). An analysis of the cult phenomenon. (Rev: BL 4/15/95) [291.9]

9160 Snow, Robert L. *Deadly Cults: The Crimes of the True Believers* (9–12). 2004, Praeger $49.95 (0-275-98052-9). Using sources such as magazines and newspapers, this is a fascinating look at cults and their leaders, including the charismatic Jim Jones and David Koresh. (Rev: BL 3/1/04) [209]

9161 Streissguth, Thomas. *Charismatic Cult Leaders* (7–12). 1995, Oliver LB $19.95 (1-881508-18-8). A balanced presentation of a potentially sensational topic. Includes biblical references where appropriate in the discussion of various cults and their leaders. (Rev: BL 8/95; SLJ 5/95) [291]

9162 Zeinert, Karen. *Cults* (7–12). Illus. Series: Issues in Focus. 1997, Enslow LB $20.95 (0-89490-900-2). Following a history of cults in America from the days of the Salem witches on, this book discusses all forms of present-day cults, from the more establishment (Jehovah's Witnesses and Mormonism) to the extremist (Branch Davidians and the Freemen of Montana). (Rev: BL 6/1–15/97; BR 11–12/97; VOYA 10/97) [291.9]

Society and the Individual

Government and Political Science

United Nations and Other International Organizations

9163 Fasulo, Linda. *An Insider's Guide to the UN* (10–12). 2004, Yale $27.00 (0-300-10155-4). This fascinating guide explores the organizational structure of the international body and offers insights into some of the problems caused by its size and the nature of its composition. (Rev: BL 12/1/03; SLJ 6/04) [341.23]

9164 Jacobs, William J. *Search for Peace: The Story of the United Nations* (7–10). 1994, Scribner paper $14.95 (0-684-19652-2). Describes the formation of the United Nations and discusses the difficulties the organization has faced in its efforts to maintain peace. (Rev: BL 7/94; SLJ 8/94) [341.23]

9165 Janello, Amy, and Brennon Jones, eds. *A Global Affair: An Inside Look at the United Nations* (9–12). 1995, Jones & Janello $35.00 (0-9646322-0-9). A celebration in essay form of the political and humanitarian work of the United Nations. (Rev: BL 9/15/95) [341.23]

9166 Meisler, Stanley. *United Nations: The First Fifty Years.* (10–12) 1997, Atlantic Monthly paper $15.00 (0-871-13656-2). A look at the successes and failures, the key players, and the organization of this international body, with particular emphasis on its humanitarian and peace-keeping efforts and its role in crises such as Suez and the Six-Day War. [341.23]

9167 Ross, Stewart. *The United Nations* (7–12). Illus. Series: 20th Century Perspectives. 2003, Heinemann LB $25.64 (1-4034-0152-7). An overview of the history, importance, abilities, and current activities of the United Nations, including efforts of UN agencies such as the World Health Organization. (Rev: BL 3/1/03; HBG 10/03; SLJ 5/03) [341.23]

9168 *The United Nations* (8–12). Series: At Issue. 1996, Greenhaven paper $17.45 (1-56510-547-8). This book traces the history, composition, and functions of the United Nations in such areas as population control, pollution, hunger, and economic development. (Rev: BL 5/15/97; SLJ 7/97) [341.23]

9169 *Your United Nations: The Official Guidebook* (9–12). 1985, U.N. Publns. $11.95 (92-1-100315-6). A guide to the United Nations buildings that also describes the UN's structure and routines. [341.23]

International Relations, Peace, and War

9170 Altman, Linda J. *Genocide: The Systematic Killing of a People* (7–12). Series: Issues in Focus. 1995, Enslow LB $20.95 (0-89490-664-X). Discusses the history of genocide and explores the Us-Them mentality and racist stereotypes that are still used today to execute genocidal policies. (Rev: BL 10/15/95; SLJ 11/95; VOYA 12/95) [364.15]

9171 *Americans' Views About War* (11–12). Ed. by James D. Torr. Series: Examining Pop Culture. 2001, Greenhaven LB $31.20 (0-7377-0754-2); paper $19.95 (0-7377-0753-4). This overview of U.S. attitudes uses excerpts from a wide array of periodicals and primary sources to document America's essential ambivalence on the issue of war. (Rev: BL 10/15/01; SLJ 2/02) [973.9]

9172 Barber, Benjamin, and Patrick Watson. *The Struggle for Democracy* (9–12). Illus. 1989, Little, Brown $29.95 (0-316-08058-6). An examination of the nature of democracy and its problems from the ancient Greeks to the present. (Rev: BL 10/1/89) [321.8]

9173 Carter, Jimmy. *Talking Peace: A Vision for the Next Generation* (8–12). 1995, Puffin paper $6.99 (0-14-037440-X). Carter encourages youth to work for world peace by improving human rights, civil liberties, environmental protection, and aid for the poor. The 1995 revised edition updates events in some of the wartorn areas Carter discussed previously and includes a chapter about his peace missions to Korea, Haiti, Bosnia, and Sudan. (Rev: BL 8/93; SLJ 10/93*) [327.1]

9174 Chalberg, John C., ed. *Isolationism* (9–12). Series: Opposing Viewpoints: American History. 1995, Greenhaven LB $26.20 (1-56510-223-1); paper $20.25 (1-56510-222-3). Excerpts from historical speeches, editorials, and essays espousing and opposing isolationist views. (Rev: BL 3/15/95; SLJ 5/95) [327.73]

9175 Cheney, Glenn. *Nuclear Proliferation: The Problems and Possibilities* (8–12). 1999, Watts LB $22.00 (0-531-11431-7). This account traces the history of nuclear weapons and radioactive materials, describes the treaties to control them, and discusses the current problems in controlling their use, the role of rogue nations, and illegal trade in radioactive materials. (Rev: BL 7/99; SLJ 6/99) [327.1]

9176 Chippendale, Neil. *Crimes Against Humanity* (7–10). Series: Crime, Justice, and Punishment. 2001, Chelsea LB $19.95 (0-7910-4254-5). A clearly written, informative account that explores such international crimes as genocide. (Rev: BL 6/1–15/01; HBG 3/01; SLJ 2/01) [341]

9177 Cozic, Charles P., ed. *Nationalism and Ethnic Conflict* (10–12). Series: Current Controversies. 1994, Greenhaven LB $26.20 (1-56510-080-8); paper $16.20 (1-56510-079-4). This collection of articles probes questions relating to nationalism involving ethnic violence, whether it is ever justified, the advisability of intervention, and how ethnic conflicts can be prevented. (Rev: BL 6/1–15/94; SLJ 3/94) [306.82]

9178 Dudley, William, ed. *Genocide* (8–12). Series: Opposing Viewpoints. 2001, Greenhaven LB $22.96 (0-7377-0681-3); paper $14.96 (0-7377-0680-5). This is an unflinching examination of genocides and "ethnic cleansings" in history. (Rev: BL 12/1/01) [304.6]

9179 Grant, R. G. *Genocide* (5–10). Illus. Series: Talking Points. 1999, Raintree Steck-Vaughn LB $27.12 (0-8172-5314-9). This book covers the Holocaust in World War II as well as more recent massacres in Cambodia, Rwanda, and Bosnia, and probes such controversies as who is guilty of genocide — the person who pulls the trigger or those

who plan and organize it, and what about the bystander? (Rev: BL 9/1/99; BR 9–10/99) [304.6]

9180 Holliday, Laurel, ed. *Why Do They Hate Me? Young Lives Caught in War and Conflict* (7–12). 1999, Pocket paper $4.99 (0-671-03454-5). Using diaries, letters, and other first-person accounts the editor has captured the turmoil of growing up during the Holocaust, World War II, and present-day Northern Ireland. (Rev: BL 11/1/99; SLJ 11/99) [920]

9181 Junger, Sebastian. *Fire* (10–12). 2001, Norton $23.95 (0-393-01046-5). A collection of 10 essays about people facing life-threatening situations, from war crimes in Kosovo to the hostage crisis in Kashmir. (Rev: BL 9/1/01) [363.378]

9182 Keegan, John. *War and Our World* (10–12). 2001, Vintage paper $10.00 (0-375-70520-1). A review of the wars of the 20th century and a look at the underlying causes and actual results of warfare. (Rev: BL 5/15/01) [303.6]

9183 Kronenwetter, Michael. *Covert Action* (9–12). 1991, Watts LB $24.00 (0-531-13018-5). An overview of the history and impact of covert activity by the U.S. government from Washington to Reagan, with material on modern-day operations in places like Afghanistan, Guatemala, and Iran. (Rev: BL 3/1/91; SLJ 5/91) [327.12]

9184 Landau, Elaine. *Big Brother Is Watching: Secret Police and Intelligence Services* (7–12). 1992, Walker LB $15.85 (0-8027-8161-6). Describes the activities and methods of intelligence and police services in several Western and former Eastern-bloc nations, including the KGB, the Mossad, the CIA, and Honduran death squads. (Rev: BL 6/1/92; SLJ 8/92) [363.2]

9185 Leone, Bruno, ed. *Internationalism: Opposing Viewpoints*. Rev. ed. (9–12). Illus. Series: Opposing Viewpoints. 1986, Greenhaven $26.20 (0-89908-383-8); paper $16.20 (0-89908-358-7). The original sources in this volume explore conflicting viewpoints on parochial versus global interests and how they can or cannot be reconciled. (Rev: BL 8/86; SLJ 10/86) [341.2]

9186 Leone, Bruno, ed. *Nationalism: Opposing Viewpoints*. Rev. ed. (9–12). Illus. 1986, Greenhaven LB $26.20 (0-89908-387-0); paper $16.20 (0-89908-362-5). A compendium of opinions on the beneficial and harmful aspects of nationalism. (Rev: BL 7/86; SLJ 10/86) [320]

9187 Loescher, Gil, and Ann D. Loescher. *The Global Refugee Crisis* (7–12). Series: Contemporary World Issues. 1995, ABC-CLIO LB $45.00 (0-87436-753-0). This volume introduces the problem of refugees and discusses how the United States and the international community have dealt with it. (Rev: BR 9–10/96; SLJ 1/96) [341.4]

9188 *The Mammoth Book of War Diaries and Letters* (9–12). Ed. by Jon E. Lewis. Series: Mammoth Book. 1999, Carroll & Graf paper $10.95 (0-7867-0589-2). Soldiers' letters and diaries, from the American Revolution through the Gulf War, provide a unique view of the horrors of war. (Rev: BL 12/15/98) [355.02]

9189 Naimark, Norman M. *Fires of Hatred: Ethnic Cleansing in Twentieth-Century Europe* (10–12). Illus. 2001, Harvard $24.95 (0-674-00313-6). From the Armenian genocide and the Holocaust to Bosnia and Kosovo, this history shows the ugliness of ethnic cleansing in the 20th century. (Rev: BL 1/1–15/01) [305.8]

9190 Ousseimi, Maria. *Caught in the Crossfire: Growing Up in a War Zone* (6–10). 1995, Walker LB $20.85 (0-8027-8364-3). Examines the effects of violence on children and how violence changes children's perception of the world. (Rev: BL 9/1/95; SLJ 9/95; VOYA 12/95) [305.23]

9191 Owen, David. *Hidden Secrets: A Complete History of Espionage and the Technology Used to Support It* (10–12). Illus. 2002, Firefly $35.00 (1-55297-565-7); paper $24.95 (1-55297-564-9). Case studies and a wealth of well-chosen illustrations add to this overview of spying and the tools of the trade. (Rev: BL 4/1/02) [327.12]

9192 Raymond, Alan, and Susan Raymond. *Children in War* (10–12). Illus. 2000, TV Books $24.00 (1-57500-098-9). Children who were victims of wars and civil unrest in Bosnia, Israel, Rwanda, and Northern Ireland were interviewed to determine the physical, emotional, and psychological effects of war on children. (Rev: BL 6/1–15/00; SLJ 4/01) [303.6]

9193 Roleff, Tamara L., ed. *War* (8–12). Series: Opposing Viewpoints. 1999, Greenhaven paper $21.20 (0-7377-0060-2). An anthology of varying viewpoints on topics relating to the causes and prevention of war, international intervention, and the role of the U.S. as a peace broker. (Rev: BL 3/15/99) [341.6]

9194 Roy, Arundhati. *War Talk* (10–12). 2003, South End $40.00 (0-89608-724-7); paper $12.00 (0-89608-723-9). In this collection of political observations, Indian novelist-turned-essayist Arundhati Roy addresses a broad range of timely topics, including the quest for peace in the Middle East, U.S. foreign policy, and the religious conflicts plaguing her homeland. (Rev: BL 4/15/03) [327.1]

9195 Shaw, Tucker. *Peace* (6–12). Illus. 2002, Alloy paper $9.99 (0-14-230221-X). Teens from around the globe voice their feelings about the events of September 11, 2001, and the prospects of world peace. (Rev: BL 9/1/02; VOYA 12/02)

9196 Spangenburg, Ray, and Kit Moser. *The Crime of Genocide: Terror Against Humanity* (8–12).

Series: Issues in Focus. 2000, Enslow LB $20.95 (0-7660-1249-2). Separate chapters address the mass killings of the 20th century — during the Holocaust and in Armenia, Bosnia and Kosovo, Cambodia, and Rwanda. (Rev: HBG 3/01; SLJ 3/01) [364.15]

9197 *War Crimes* (11–12). Ed. by Henny H. Kim. Series: Contemporary Issues Companion. 2000, Greenhaven LB $21.96 (0-7377-0171-4); paper $13.96 (0-7377-0170-6). Essays use examples from conflicts in Bosnia, Rwanda, Vietnam, and elsewhere in discussions of what constitutes a war crime and who is to blame. (Rev: BL 7/00; SLJ 7/00) [341.6]

9198 Winters, Paul A., ed. *Interventionism* (7–12). Series: Current Controversies. 1995, Greenhaven LB $32.45 (1-56510-233-9). Various kinds of international intervention — military, trade, economic sanctions, and humanitarian aid — are explored in this collection of documents. (Rev: BL 6/1–15/95) [341.5]

9199 *Women on War: An International Anthology of Writings from Antiquity to the Present* (10–12). Ed. by Daniela Gioseffi. 2003, Feminist Pr. paper $19.95 (1-55861-409-5). The poems, essays, and eyewitness accounts in this anthology make a passionate case for an end to global violence. (Rev: BL 3/15/03*) [303.6]

United States Government and Institutions

General and Miscellaneous

9200 Clucas, Richard A. *Encyclopedia of American Political Reform* (9–12). 1996, ABC-CLIO LB $60.00 (0-87436-855-3). From "Abscam" to "zero-based budgeting," this work identifies and gives background information on a variety of terms, places, and people connected with American political reform. (Rev: BR 5–6/97; SLJ 5/97) [336.73]

9201 Kronenwetter, Michael. *How Democratic Is the United States?* (7–12). Series: Democracy in Action. 1994, Watts paper $24.00 (0-531-11155-5). Presents the problems of politics and government in the United States and discusses proposals for change. (Rev: BL 11/15/94; SLJ 1/95) [324.6]

The Constitution

9202 Banfield, Susan. *The Fifteenth Amendment: African-American Men's Right to Vote* (7–12). Illus. Series: Constitution. 1998, Enslow LB $20.95 (0-7660-1033-3). This is the stormy history of the constitutional amendment passed during Reconstruction that barred states from denying voting rights to black males. (Rev: BL 9/1/98) [324.6]

9203 Bartholomew, Paul C., and Joseph F. Menez. *Summaries of Leading Cases on the Constitution* (10–12). 1991, Littlefield Adams paper $21.95 (0-8226-3008-7). This volume summarizes the cases involving constitutional law that have come before the Supreme Court. [342]

9204 Bjornlund, Lydia. *The U.S. Constitution* (8–12). Illus. Series: Words That Changed History. 1999, Lucent LB $27.45 (1-56006-486-2). Topics covered in this volume include the need for the Constitution, factors considered in deciding on the structure of the government, important figures in its history, controversies and compromises, amendments, and an evaluation of its success. (Rev: BL 6/1–15/99; SLJ 8/99) [342.73]

9205 Dudley, William, ed. *The Bill of Rights* (9–12). Series: Opposing Viewpoints. 1994, Greenhaven LB $21.96 (1-56510-088-3). Differing views on various civil rights issues arising from contemporary interpretations of constitutional intent. (Rev: BL 3/1/94) [342.73]

9206 Dudley, William, ed. *The Creation of the Constitution* (9–12). Series: Opposing Viewpoints: American History. 1995, Greenhaven paper $20.25 (1-56510-220-7). An in-depth look at the controversies surrounding the creation and ratification of the U.S. Constitution. (Rev: BL 7/95; SLJ 1/95) [342.73]

9207 Feinberg, Barbara Silberdick. *The Articles of Confederation: The First Constitution of the United States* (7–10). Illus. 2002, Twenty-First Century LB $24.90 (0-7613-2114-4). Feinberg presents the history and text of the constitution that was in force from 1776 to 1787, along with a list of the signers, a timeline, and source notes. (Rev: BL 2/1/02; HBG 10/02; SLJ 3/02) [342.73]

9208 Freedman, Russell. *In Defense of Liberty: The Story of America's Bill of Rights* (5–10). 2003, Holiday $24.95 (0-8234-1585-6). A succinct explanation of the history of the Bill of Rights, discussing each amendment in turn and its particular relevance to today's controversies, with many references to cases involving young people. (Rev: BCCB 10/03*; BL 10/1/03*; HB 9–10/03*; HBG 4/04; SLJ 10/03*; VOYA 4/04) [342.73]

9209 Gay, Kathlyn. *Church and State: Government and Religion in the United States* (9–12). 1992, Millbrook LB $23.90 (1-56294-063-5). Explores the legal, political, and social questions surrounding the doctrine of separation of church and state, using actual court cases. (Rev: BL 9/1/92; SLJ 10/92) [322]

9210 Gerberg, Mort. *The U.S. Constitution for Everyone* (8–12). Illus. 1987, Putnam paper $6.95 (0-399-51305-1). The text of the Constitution and amendments is analyzed with many interesting asides and background information. (Rev: BL 5/1/87) [342.73]

9211 Judson, Karen. *The Constitution of the United States* (7–10). Series: American Government in Action. 1996, Enslow LB $20.95 (0-89490-586-4). This book focuses on the historical background of the constitutional convention and the issues that were debated. (Rev: SLJ 5/96) [342.73]

9212 Leone, Bruno, ed. *Free Speech* (9–12). Series: Current Controversies. 1994, Greenhaven LB $17.95 (1-56510-078-6); paper $16.20 (1-56510-077-8). Places current censorship battles in a historical context. (Rev: BL 4/15/94; SLJ 6/94) [323.44]

9213 Lucas, Eileen. *The Eighteenth and Twenty-First Amendments: Alcohol, Prohibition, and Repeal* (7–12). Illus. Series: Constitution. 1998, Enslow LB $20.95 (0-89490-926-6). An account of the circumstances that led to the passage of Prohibition, its effects, and later repeal. (Rev: BL 9/1/98) [344.730541]

9214 Monk, Linda R. *The Words We Live By: Your Annotated Guide to the Constitution* (10–12). Illus. 2003, Hyperion $23.95 (0-7868-6720-5). In easy-to-understand language with plenty of photographs and interesting sidebar features, this is a comprehensive introduction to the U.S. Constitution. (Rev: BL 12/15/02) [342.73]

9215 Morin, Isobel V. *Our Changing Constitution: How and Why We Have Amended It* (9–12). Illus. 1998, Millbrook LB $22.90 (0-7613-0222-0). After historical background on the U.S. Constitution and the provisions for revising it, each of the amendments is discussed, including the historical events and constitutional and legal arguments surrounding each, how each was passed, and their impact. (Rev: BL 6/1–15/98; VOYA 8/98) [347]

9216 Padover, Saul Kussiel. *The Living U.S. Constitution*. 3rd rev. ed. (9–12). 1995, Penguin paper $14.95 (0-452-01147-7). This book gives a history of the U.S. Constitution and a description of the landmark Supreme Court cases interpreting it. [342]

9217 Palmer, Kris E. *Constitutional Amendments, 1789 to the Present* (10–12). 2000, Gale $105.00 (0-7876-0782-7). After a preface in which the amendment process is discussed, a chapter is devoted to each of the 27 amendments. (Rev: BL 2/15/00; SLJ 5/00) [342]

9218 Patrick, John J. *The Bill of Rights: A History in Documents* (9–12). Ed. by John J. Patrick. Illus. Series: Pages from History. 2002, Oxford LB $32.95 (0-19-510354-8). Excerpts from primary sources — accompanied by reproductions of documents, maps, and works of art — shed light on the first 10 amendments to the U.S. Constitution and their historical background and current relevance. (Rev: BL 2/15/03; HBG 10/03; SLJ 3/03) [342.73]

9219 Schleichert, Elizabeth. *The Thirteenth Amendment: Ending Slavery* (8–10). 1998, Enslow LB $20.95 (0-89490-923-1). The stormy history of this constitutional amendment that ended slavery and fundamentally changed American society. (Rev: BL 8/98; BR 11–12/98; HBG 3/99; SLJ 1/99) [342.73]

9220 Spitzer, Robert J. *The Right to Bear Arms: Rights and Liberties Under the Law* (10–12). Series: America's Freedoms. 2001, ABC-CLIO LB $55.00 (1-57607-347-5). This examination of the Second Amendment to the U.S. Constitution explores the history, laws, and controversies about the right to bear arms. (Rev: VOYA 6/02) [344]

9221 Vile, John R. *The United States Constitution: Questions and Answers* (10–12). 1998, Greenwood $39.95 (0-313-30643-5). This guide dissects the Constitution section by section and provides insights into the historical events that helped to shape it. [342]

9222 Wetterer, Charles M. *The Fourth Amendment: Search and Seizure* (8–10). 1998, Enslow LB $20.95 (0-89490-924-X). Though enacted early in this country's history, this amendment on privacy has continued to have an important impact throughout the years. (Rev: BL 8/98) [342.73]

The Presidency

9223 Aaseng, Nathan. *You Are the President* (7–10). 1994, Oliver LB $19.95 (1-881508-10-2). Devotes one chapter each to a crisis faced by eight presidents in the 20th century, among them Theodore Roosevelt, Eisenhower, and Nixon. (Rev: BL 4/1/94; SLJ 7/94; VOYA 8/94) [973.9]

9224 Aaseng, Nathan. *You Are the President II: 1800–1899* (7–10). Illus. Series: Great Decisions. 1994, Oliver LB $19.95 (1-881508-15-3). This work discusses the powers of the presidency during the 19th century and the major decisions made by presidents during that time. (Rev: BL 11/15/94; SLJ 12/94) [973.5]

9225 Bernstein, Richard B., and Jerome Agel. *The Presidency* (8–12). Illus. 1989, Walker LB $13.85 (0-8027-6831-8). A basic history of this institution with some biographical information and a final section that explores the advisability of concentrating such power in one office. (Rev: BL 5/1/89; BR 3–4/89; SLJ 1/89; VOYA 4/89) [353.03]

9226 Black, Christine M. *The Pursuit of the Presidency: '92 and Beyond* (7–12). 1993, Oryx paper $24.50 (0-89774-845-X). Using the presidential campaign of 1992, the author examines the inner workings of a political campaign and how campaigns relate to actual governing. (Rev: BL 4/15/94) [324.973]

9227 Boller, Paul F. *Presidential Inaugurations: Behind the Scenes — An Informal, Anecdotal Histo-*

ry from Washington's Election to the 2001 Gala (10–12). 2001, Harcourt $25.00 (0-15-100546-X). Covering such topics as the choosing of the date, weather problems, the addresses, receptions, and goofs, this is a history of U.S. presidential inaugurations. (Rev: BL 5/15/01) [973]

9228 Bunch, Lonnie G., et al. *The American Presidency: A Glorious Burden* (9–12). Illus. 2001, Smithsonian $50.00 (1-56098-992-0); paper $24.95 (1-56098-835-5). This overview of the presidency is organized thematically, with material on creating the presidency, campaigns and inaugurations, powers of the office, function of the White House, and so forth. (Rev: BL 1/1–15/01) [973]

9229 Cohen, Daniel. *The Impeachment of William Jefferson Clinton* (6–12). 2000, Twenty-First Century LB $23.90 (0-7613-1711-2). Extensive background information sets the stage for this account of the impeachment proceedings. (Rev: HBG 9/00; SLJ 6/00; VOYA 2/01) [973.929]

9230 Fernandez, Justin. *High Crimes and Misdemeanors: The Impeachment Process* (7–10). Illus. Series: Crime, Justice, and Punishment. 2000, Chelsea LB $19.95 (0-7910-5450-0). Attorney Fernandez explains this process, looking at the early history and at the impeachment of Bill Clinton. (Rev: BL 1/1–15/01; HBG 3/01; SLJ 12/00; VOYA 2/01) [342.73]

9231 Graff, Henry F., ed. *The Presidents: A Reference History*. 2nd. ed. (10–12). 1996, Scribner $173.75 (0-684-80471-9). Each president is introduced by a different presidential scholar and material is given on each administration. (Rev: SLJ 5/97) [353.03]

9232 Hardesty, Von. *Air Force One: The Aircraft That Shaped the Modern Presidency* (6–12). 2003, NorthWord $29.95 (1-55971-894-3). From FDR's first presidential flights through today's dependence on air travel, this highly visual book describes the interior redesigns and other evolutions in this symbol of prestige. (Rev: SLJ 11/03*) [387.7]

9233 Judson, Karen. *The Presidency of the United States* (7–10). Series: American Government in Action. 1996, Enslow LB $20.95 (0-89490-585-6). This introduction to the American presidency includes material on the roles of the president, the constitutional basis of the office, the operations of the White House, and the organization of the executive branch. (Rev: SLJ 5/96) [353.03]

9234 Morin, Isobel V. *Impeaching the President* (8–12). 1996, Millbrook LB $24.90 (1-56294-668-4). This book, written before the Clinton impeachment, explains what impeachment is, its processes, and its role in American history. (Rev: BR 9–10/96; SLJ 6/96; VOYA 10/96) [336.73]

9235 Nelson, W. Dale. *Who Speaks for the President? The White House Press Secretary from Cleve-*

land to Clinton (10–12). 1998, Syracuse Univ. Pr. $29.95 (0-8156-0514-5). In 1893, President Grover Cleveland appointed a confidential stenographer. This account traces the evolution of the White House press secretary to what is today, with information on the people, the powers, and the relationships connected with the position. (Rev: BL 6/1–15/98; SLJ 2/99) [324]

9236 Pious, Richard M. *The Presidency of the United States: A Student Companion.* 2nd ed. (10–12). 2001, Oxford LB $45.00 (0-19-515006-6). This work covers the political careers of all the presidents up to and including Bill Clinton. [353]

9237 *President Kennedy Has Been Shot* (10–12). Illus. 2003, Sourcebooks $29.95 (1-4022-0158-3). In minute-by-minute detail, this unique book and CD package chronicles the assassination and the events that followed, using print reports, photographs, and original broadcasts. (Rev: BL 11/15/03; SLJ 5/04) [364.15]

9238 Schlesinger, Arthur M., Jr., ed. *The Election of 2000 and the Administration of George W. Bush* (8–12). Series: Major Presidential Elections and the Administrations That Followed. 2003, Mason Crest LB $24.95 (1-59084-365-7). The circumstances of Bush's election and the major events of his administration through 2002 are presented with reference to many primary sources; brief biographical facts about the president and his cabinet are also included. (Rev: HBG 4/04; SLJ 10/03) [324.973]

9239 Shenkman, Richard. *Presidential Ambition: How the Presidents Gained Power, Kept Power, and Got Things Done* (9–12). 1999, HarperCollins $26.00 (0-06-018373-X). A historical survey of the forces — and political machinations — that have propelled America's presidents into office and of their questionable behavior once in power. (Rev: BL 12/15/98) [973]

9240 Waldman, Michael, comp. *My Fellow Americans: The Most Important Speeches of American Presidents from George Washington to George W. Bush* (7–12). 2003, Sourcebooks paper $45.00 (1-4022-0027-7). A collection of more than 40 speeches by 17 presidents, some of which are shown with early drafts; two accompanying CDs contain all the speeches, with the actual voices of presidents starting with Teddy Roosevelt. (Rev: BL 10/15/03; SLJ 10/03*) [352.23]

9241 Woronoff, Kristen. *American Inaugurals: The Speeches, the Presidents, and Their Times* (7–10). Illus. 2002, Gale $64.94 (1-56711-854-5). An attractive, well-illustrated, large-format presentation of all the inaugural speeches, with background information, fast-fact sidebars, and commentary. (Rev: BL 8/02; SLJ 11/02) [352.23]

Federal Government, Its Agencies, and Public Administration

9242 Aaseng, Nathan. *You Are the Senator* (7–10). Illus. Series: Great Decisions. 1997, Oliver LB $19.95 (1-881508-36-6). This book describes the duties and responsibilities of a U.S. senator and the nature of the decisions that senators make. (Rev: BL 4/15/97; BR 11–12/97; SLJ 8/97; VOYA 8/97) [328.73]

9243 Bernstein, Richard B., and Jerome Agel. *The Congress* (7–12). Illus. 1989, Walker LB $13.85 (0-8027-6833-4). An introduction to this branch of the government with material arranged chronologically and including some coverage of scandals and decline in prestige. (Rev: BL 5/1/89; SLJ 1/89; VOYA 4/89) [328.73]

9244 Cothran, Helen, ed. *The Central Intelligence Agency* (6–12). Series: At Issue. 2003, Gale LB $26.60 (0-7377-1725-4); paper $17.45 (0-7377-1726-2). This collection of essays examines the purpose and scope of operations of the CIA, especially in light of September 11, 2001. (Rev: BL 5/15/03) [327.127]

9245 Dolan, Edward F., and Margaret M. Scariano. *Shaping U.S. Foreign Policy: Profiles of Twelve Secretaries of State* (7–12). Illus. Series: Democracy in Action. 1996, Watts LB $22.00 (0-531-11264-0). A look at five secretaries of state who made major acquisitions of land, and seven who dealt with the search for peace or with the Cold War. (Rev: BL 6/1–15/96; SLJ 7/96) [327.73]

9246 Duvall, Jill D. *Congressional Committees* (10–12). 1997, Watts LB $24.00 (0-531-11343-4). This work presents a vast amount of information on congressional committees, their types, functions, and their changing roles. (Rev: BR 5–6/98; SLJ 2/98) [336.73]

9247 Greenberg, Ellen. *The House and Senate Explained* (10–12). 1996, Norton $19.95 (0-393-03984-6); paper $12.00 (0-393-31496-0). A clear, well-organized guide to the organization, powers, and composition of the legislative branch of our government. (Rev: SLJ 4/97) [328.73]

9248 Harmon, Daniel E. *The FBI* (7–10). Series: Crime, Justice, and Punishment. 2001, Chelsea LB $19.95 (0-7910-4289-8). The highest branch of criminal investigation in the United States is discussed with material on powers, methods, and personnel. (Rev: BL 6/1–15/01; HBG 10/01) [363.2]

9249 *Homeland Security* (6–12). Ed. by James D. Torr. Series: At Issue. 2004, Gale LB $27.45 (0-7377-2188-X). The creation of this department, its duties, and its possible impact on civil liberties are topics raised in this collection of writings expressing different viewpoints. (Rev: BL 2/15/04) [336]

9250 *How Congress Works*. 3rd ed. (9–12). 1998, Congressional Quarterly paper $35.50 (1-56802-391-X). The inner workings, rules, and procedures of Congress are laid out in a clear and concise manner. [328.73]

9251 Partner, Daniel. *The House of Representatives* (7–12). Series: Your Government — How It Works. 2000, Chelsea $17.95 (0-7910-5535-3). A discussion of the history, structure, functions, and importance of the U.S. House of Representatives. [328.73]

9252 Richie, Jason. *Secretaries of State: Making Foreign Policy* (7–10). Illus. Series: Cabinet. 2002, Oliver LB $22.95 (1-881508-65-X). Succinct profiles of eight secretaries of state, ranging chronologically from John Quincy Adams to James Baker, look at their beliefs and how they influenced the nation's foreign policy. Also recommended in this series is *Secretaries of War, Navy, and Defense: Ensuring National Security* (2002). (Rev: BL 10/15/02; HBG 3/03; SLJ 4/03) [327.73]

9253 Ritchie, Donald A. *The Congress of the United States: A Student Companion*. 2nd ed. (8–12). Series: Oxford Student Companions to American Government. 2002, Oxford LB $45.00 (0-19-515007-4). An alphabetically arranged series of articles covering all aspects of Congress, illustrated with photographs, maps, and reproductions. (Rev: SLJ 5/02) [328.73]

State and Municipal Governments and Agencies

9254 Conlon, Edward. *Blue Blood* (10–12). 2004, Riverhead $26.95 (1-57322-266-6). This is a collection of pieces by a New York City policemen and his life on the force told without sparing the author's true feelings and emotions. (Rev: BL 2/15/04*) [363.2]

9255 Conway, W. Fred. *Firefighting Lore: Strange but True Stories from Firefighting History* (9–12). 1993, Fire Buff House paper $9.95 (0-925165-14-X). Written by a former fire chief, this history of firefighting in the United States provides short accounts of famous and lesser-known major fires. (Rev: BL 1/1/94) [363.378]

9256 Gorrell, Gena K. *Catching Fire: The Story of Firefighting* (7–10). 1999, Tundra paper $16.95 (0-88776-430-4). This is a history of firefighting, from the bucket brigades of the past to the sophisticated equipment of today, with related information on how fires burn, important fires in history, equipment, firefighting tactics, forms of arson, wildfires, and more. (Rev: BCCB 5/99; BL 6/1–15/99; SLJ 6/99) [363.3]

9257 Levinson, Isabel Simone. *Gibbons v. Ogden: Controlling Trade Between States* (8–10). Series: Landmark Supreme Court Cases. 1999, Enslow LB $20.95 (0-7660-1086-4). States' rights and autonomy were the subject of this important Supreme Court case that focused on trade between the states. (Rev: BL 8/99) [353]

9258 Ryan, Bernard. *Serving with Police, Fire, and EMS* (7–12). Series: Community Service for Teens. 1998, Ferguson LB $15.95 (0-89434-232-0). This work explains how teens can play an active and productive role in police, fire, and allied community agencies. (Rev: BL 9/15/98; BR 11–12/98; SLJ 2/99) [361.8]

Libraries and Other Educational Institutions

9259 Lerner, Fred. *Libraries Through the Ages* (7–10). Illus. 1999, Continuum $15.95 (0-8264-1201-7). A history of libraries, the books they hold, and their readers, adapted from the adult title *The Story of Libraries*. (Rev: BL 11/15/99) [027]

9260 Thomson, Peggy, and Barbara Moore. *The Nine-Ton Cat: Behind the Scenes at an Art Museum* (5–10). 1997, Houghton paper $14.95 (0-395-82683-7). An inside look at the workings of the National Gallery in Washington, with descriptions in photographs and text of the contributions of workers including curators, conservators, and gardeners. (Rev: BCCB 4/97; BL 3/15/97*; HB 5–6/97; SLJ 4/97) [069]

The Law and the Courts

9261 Aaseng, Nathan. *You Are the Juror* (6–10). 1997, Oliver LB $19.95 (1-881508-40-4). The author re-creates eight famous criminal trials of the 20th century, including the Lindbergh kidnapping case, the Patty Hearst and O. J. Simpson trials, and the Ford Pinto case, and asks the reader to become a jury member and make a decision. (Rev: SLJ 1/98) [347.73]

9262 Aaseng, Nathan. *You Are the Supreme Court Justice* (7–10). Illus. Series: Great Decisions. 1994, Oliver LB $19.95 (1-881508-14-5). A description of how the Supreme Court works and the decisions and responsibilities involved in being a Justice. (Rev: BL 11/15/94; SLJ 12/94) [347.73]

9263 Alonso, Karen. *The Alger Hiss Communist Spy Trial* (6–10). Series: Headline Court Cases. 2001, Enslow LB $20.95 (0-7660-1481-9). Alonso provides a clear explanation of the political climate of the time and of the intricacies of this important trial, with a glossary, discussion questions, and excerpts from recently declassified documents. (Rev: BL 12/15/01; HBG 3/02; SLJ 11/01) [345]

9264 Alonso, Karen. *Loving v. Virginia: Interracial Marriage* (7–12). Series: Landmark Supreme Court Cases. 2000, Enslow LB $19.95 (0-7660-1338-3). A thorough examination of the case that overturned Virginia's law forbidding interracial marriage. (Rev: HBG 3/01; SLJ 10/00) [346.7301]

9265 Anderson, Kelly C. *Police Brutality* (6–10). Series: Overview. 1995, Lucent LB $27.45 (1-56006-164-2). A discussion of the reasons for police behavior, the stress and danger of the job and the possible misuse of power. (Rev: BL 4/15/95; SLJ 3/95) [363.2]

9266 Andryszewski, Tricia. *School Prayer: A History of the Debate* (8–12). Illus. Series: Issues in Focus. 1997, Enslow LB $20.95 (0-89490-904-5). A thorough, balanced account that explores all sides of the controversy concerning school prayer, with material on the separation of church and state. (Rev: BL 10/1/97; SLJ 3/98; VOYA 2/98) [344.73]

9267 Arnest, Lauren Krohn. *Children, Young Adults, and the Law: A Dictionary* (8–12). 1998, ABC-CLIO LB $55.00 (0-87436-879-0). Using a dictionary arrangement, this volume contains about 200 articles on legal issues involving children and young adults, with entries on important court cases and decisions. (Rev: BL 10/15/98; SLJ 2/99; VOYA 6/99) [346.73]

9268 Banner, Stuart. *The Death Penalty: An American History* (10–12). Illus. 2002, Harvard $29.95 (0-674-00751-4). Banner looks at the evolution of the public's ideas of justice and examines the death penalty's evolution from outdoor spectacle to antiseptic procedure carried out behind closed doors. (Rev: BL 2/15/02) [364.66]

9269 Berger, Leslie. *The Grand Jury* (7–12). Illus. Series: Crime, Justice, and Punishment. 2000, Chelsea $21.95 (0-7910-4290-1). This work traces the history of the grand jury system, outlines procedures at the local and national level, and cites famous grand jury hearings including the Monica Lewinsky case. (Rev: BL 8/00) [345.73]

9270 Bernstein, Richard B., and Jerome Agel. *The Supreme Court* (8–12). Illus. 1989, Walker LB $13.85 (0-8027-6835-0). An account that gives a history of the Supreme Court, details on landmark cases, and an outline of how it operates today. (Rev: BL 5/1/89; BR 3–4/89; SLJ 1/89; VOYA 4/89) [347]

9271 Billitteri, Thomas J. *The Gault Case: Legal Rights for Young People* (7–12). Series: Landmark Supreme Court Cases. 2000, Enslow LB $20.95 (0-7660-1340-5). Children's rights and due process were the focus of this 1960s case — involving a 15-year-old — that was eventually decided by the Supreme Court. (Rev: HBG 3/01; SLJ 2/01) [345.73]

9272 Biskup, Michael D., ed. *Criminal Justice* (9–12). Series: Opposing Viewpoints. 1993, Greenhaven LB $19.95 (0-89908-624-1); paper $16.20 (0-89908-623-3). A collection of articles that present

opposing viewpoints on the criminal justice system. (Rev: BL 6/1–15/93) [364.098]

9273 Brown, Elaine. *The Condemnation of Little B* (10–12). 2002, Beacon $24.00 (0-8070-0974-1). A thought-provoking analysis of the political and social questions raised by the murder trial of a 13-year-old black youth in Atlanta. (Rev: BL 2/15/02*) [364.15]

9274 Campbell, Andrew. *Rights of the Accused* (7–10). Series: Crime, Justice, and Punishment. 2001, Chelsea LB $19.95 (0-7910-4303-7). A cleverly written, informative exploration of how and why the judicial system tries to safeguard the rights of accused criminals. (Rev: BL 6/1–15/01; HBG 3/01; SLJ 2/01; VOYA 12/01) [345]

9275 *Capital Punishment* (9–12). Ed. by Mary E. Williams. Series: Current Controversies. 2000, Greenhaven LB $31.20 (0-7377-0141-2); paper $19.95 (0-7377-0140-4). In the 30 essays collected here, all by reputable authorities, various aspects of capital punishment are discussed. (Rev: SLJ 6/00) [364.66]

9276 *Capital Punishment*. Rev. ed. (9–12). Ed. by Harry Henderson and Stephen A. Flanders. Series: Library in a Book. 2000, Facts on File $45.00 (0-8160-4193-8). This series of readings looks at capital punishment from various viewpoints, including social, political, ethical, and religious perspectives. (Rev: BL 3/1/01) [364.66]

9277 Carrel, Annette. *It's the Law! A Young Person's Guide to Our Legal System* (8–12). 1994, Volcano paper $12.95 (1-884244-01-7). The book's goal is voter responsibility through understanding of the laws, how they developed, and how they can be changed. (Rev: BL 2/15/95; VOYA 12/95) [349.73]

9278 Cothran, Helen, ed. *Police Brutality* (7–12). Illus. Series: Opposing Viewpoints. 2001, Greenhaven LB $22.96 (0-7377-0516-7); paper $14.96 (0-7377-0515-9). Contributors address various aspects of police conduct and overview, with a special interest in the treatment of teen suspects and a focus on New York City and Los Angeles. (Rev: BL 5/15/01) [363.2]

9279 Day, Nancy. *The Death Penalty for Teens: A Pro/Con Issue* (6–10). Illus. Series: Hot Pro/Con Issues. 2000, Enslow LB $19.95 (0-7660-1370-7). Strong, opposing opinions on juvenile justice and the death penalty are accompanied by a historical overview and comparisons between the United States and other countries. (Rev: BL 2/15/01; HBG 3/01; SLJ 4/01; VOYA 6/01) [364.66]

9280 *The Death Penalty* (9–12). Ed. by Mary E. Williams. Series: Opposing Viewpoints. 2001, Greenhaven LB $31.20 (0-7377-0792-5); paper $19.95 (0-7377-0791-7). These essays and articles present differing viewpoints on capital punishment. [364.66]

9281 *Debating the Death Penalty: Should America Have Capital Punishment? The Experts from Both Sides Make Their Case* (9–12). Ed. by Hugo Bedau and Paul Cassell. 2004, Oxford $26.00 (0-19-516983-2). A collection of essays that presents a balanced discussion of different viewpoints relating to this issue. (Rev: BL 1/1–15/04) [364.66]

9282 DeVillers, David. *Marbury v. Madison: Powers of the Supreme Court* (6–10). Series: Landmark Supreme Court Cases. 1998, Enslow LB $20.95 (0-89490-967-3). A look at the steps, arguments, and personalities in this early court case that helped define the powers of the Supreme Court. (Rev: BL 2/15/98; SLJ 6/98) [343.7]

9283 Dudley, Mark E. *Gideon v. Wainwright (1963): Right to Counsel* (6–10). Series: Supreme Court Decisions. 1995, Twenty-First Century LB $25.90 (0-8050-3914-7). Reviews how the case was built, argued, and decided, and discusses its impact. (Rev: BL 6/1–15/95; SLJ 8/95) [347.3]

9284 Dudley, Mark E. *United States v. Nixon (1974)* (6–10). Illus. Series: Supreme Court Decisions. 1994, Twenty-First Century LB $25.90 (0-8050-3658-X). This landmark Supreme Court case concerning the definition of presidential powers is reported on in a step-by-step analysis of the arguments in the Watergate case. (Rev: BL 12/15/94; SLJ 2/95) [342.73]

9285 Dwyer, William L. *In the Hands of the People: The Trial Jury's Origins, Triumphs, Troubles and Future in American Democracy* (10–12). 2002, St. Martin's $24.95 (0-312-27812-8). This is an examination of the past and present of the jury system and the possible future development in this area. (Rev: BL 11/15/01) [347]

9286 Egendorf, Laura K., ed. *The Death Penalty* (7–12). Illus. Series: Examining Issues Through Political Cartoons. 2002, Gale $24.95 (0-7377-1102-7); paper $16.20 (0-7377-1101-9). Egendorf uses cartoons focusing on the death penalty as the basis for a discussion of the controversies surrounding this practice. Also recommended in this series is *Euthanasia* (2002). (Rev: BL 8/02) [364.44]

9287 Ehrenfeld, Norbert, and Lawrence Treat. *You're the Jury: Solve Twelve Real-Life Court Cases Along with the Juries Who Decided Them* (9–12). 1992, Holt paper $9.95 (0-8050-1951-0). Presents the testimony and evidence of 12 actual court cases, with analysis, pertinent questions, and the courtroom verdict. (Rev: BL 7/92; SLJ 9/92) [347.73]

9288 Feinman, Jay M. *Law 101: Everything You Need to Know About the American Legal System* (10–12). 2000, Oxford $27.50 (0-19-513265-3). Using a question-and-answer approach, this book supplies a good overview of the U.S. legal system. (Rev: BL 3/15/00) [340]

9289 Garza, Hedda. *Barred from the Bar: A History of Women and the Legal Profession* (10–12). Series: Women Then — Women Now. 1996, Watts LB $25.00 (0-531-11265-9). A well-researched history of how women won the right to practice law as well as rights in other fields, weaving in the stories of several remarkable women from the mid-19th century to the present whose determination has slowly rolled back legal and social obstacles to equality. An entire chapter highlights the double discrimination experienced by women of color. (Rev: BR 11–12/96; SLJ 7/96; VOYA 8/96) [346]

9290 Gold, Susan D. *Miranda v. Arizona (1966)* (6–10). Series: Supreme Court Decisions. 1995, Twenty-First Century LB $25.90 (0-8050-3915-5). This book describes the court case that defined the rights of suspects, with good historical background and a discussion of its impact through 1994. (Rev: BL 6/1–15/95; SLJ 8/95) [345.73]

9291 Gottfried, Ted. *Capital Punishment: The Death Penalty Debate* (6–12). Illus. Series: Issues in Focus. 1997, Enslow LB $20.95 (0-89490-899-5). The author presents strong arguments on all sides of the death penalty controversy, including material on its history, moral justification, purpose, legal procedures, and questions of race and geography. (Rev: BL 2/1/97; SLJ 7/97) [345.73]

9292 Gottfried, Ted. *The Death Penalty: Justice or Legalized Murder?* (7–12). Illus. 2002, Twenty-First Century LB $24.90 (0-7613-2155-1). Gottfried presents an absorbing and balanced examination of the arguments for and against the death penalty, with historical information and details of specific cases. (Rev: BL 3/15/02; HBG 10/02; SLJ 3/02) [364.66]

9293 Gottfried, Ted. *Police Under Fire* (7–12). Illus. 1999, Twenty-First Century LB $22.90 (0-7613-1313-3). A well-balanced account that gives a history of policing, police culture, pressures on police personnel, corruption, and cases of police brutality. (Rev: BL 12/15/99; HBG 4/00; SLJ 1/00) [363.2]

9294 Grant, Robert, and Joseph Katz. *The Great Trials of the Twenties: The Watershed Decade in America's Courtrooms* (10–12). Illus. 1998, Sarpedon $24.95 (1-885119-52-6). Ten history-making court cases of the 1920s — including the trial of Sacco and Vanzetti on charges of anarchy and the face-off between Clarence Darrow and William Jennings Bryan — are presented in an absorbing narrative. (Rev: BL 12/15/98) [347]

9295 Haas, Carol. *Engel v. Vitale: Separation of Church and State* (6–10). 1994, Enslow LB $20.95 (0-89490-461-2). A discussion of the arguments presented by both sides in this landmark Supreme Court case concerning the separation of church and state as it applies to religion in public schools. (Rev: BL 11/15/94; VOYA 12/94) [344.73]

9296 Hanson, Freya Ottem. *The Scopes Monkey Trial: A Headline Court Case* (6–10). Illus. Series: Headline Court Cases. 2000, Enslow LB $20.95 (0-7660-1388-X). The story of the famous trial of a Tennessee high school teacher for teaching evolution. (Rev: BL 10/1/00; HBG 3/01; SLJ 9/00) [345.73]

9297 Harmon, Daniel E. *Defense Lawyers* (7–10). Series: Crime, Justice, and Punishment. 2001, Chelsea LB $21.95 (0-7910-4284-7). This introduction to the roles of defense attorney and public defender provides brief profiles of figures including Clarence Darrow and Alan Dershowitz. (Rev: HBG 10/02; SLJ 4/02) [345.73]

9298 Harrington, Mon. *Women Lawyers: Rewriting the Rules* (9–12). 1994, Knopf $24.00 (0-394-58025-7). Through interviews with female graduates of Harvard Law School, the author paints a disturbing picture of sexism in the legal profession and offers practical solutions. (Rev: BL 1/15/94*) [349.73]

9299 Harris, David A. *Profiles in Injustice: Why Racial Profiling Cannot Work* (10–12). 2002, New Pr. $24.95 (1-56584-696-6). In addition to citing all the impressive arguments against racial profiling on moral, ethical, and constitutional grounds, Harris provides statistical evidence that the technique simply isn't very effective. (Rev: BL 1/1–15/02) [305.8]

9300 Harrison, Maureen, and Steve Gilbert, eds. *Landmark Decisions of the United States Supreme Court II* (9–12). 1992, Excellent Books paper $20.25 (0-9628014-2-9). Synopses of far-reaching Supreme Court rulings, including decisions on slavery, women's suffrage, Bible reading in public schools, book banning, and the death penalty. (Rev: BL 1/1/92) [347]

9301 Henson, Burt, and Ross R. Olney. *Furman v. Georgia: The Constitution and the Death Penalty* (7–10). Series: Historic Supreme Court Cases. 1996, Watts LB $25.00 (0-531-11285-3). In this 1972 case, the Supreme Court ruled that the imposition of the death penalty as then applied was unconstitutional. This account gives the legal background, a history of capital punishment, and pros and cons of the death penalty. (Rev: SLJ 4/97) [345]

9302 Herda, D. J. *Furman v. Georgia: The Death Penalty Case* (6–10). Series: Landmark Supreme Court Cases. 1994, Enslow LB $20.95 (0-89490-489-2). Summarizes the historical background of this case, the case itself, and its impact. (Rev: BL 11/15/94; SLJ 11/94) [345.73]

9303 Herda, D. J. *New York Times v. United States: National Security and Censorship* (6–10). Illus. Series: Landmark Supreme Court Cases. 1994, Enslow LB $20.95 (0-89490-490-6). This exciting, controversial Supreme Court case involved the Pen-

tagon Papers and helped define freedom of the press when it conflicts with what may be considered national security. (Rev: BL 11/15/94; SLJ 1/95) [342.73]

9304 Herda, D. J. *Roe v. Wade: The Abortion Question* (6–10). Illus. Series: Landmark Supreme Court Cases. 1994, Enslow LB $20.95 (0-89490-459-0). This book describes the arguments on both sides of the abortion debate, how the justices of the Supreme Court reacted, their decision, and its consequences. (Rev: BL 6/1–15/94; SLJ 7/94; VOYA 8/94) [344.73]

9305 Hogrogian, John. *Miranda v. Arizona: The Rights of the Accused* (9–12). Series: Famous Trials. 1999, Lucent $22.45 (1-56006-471-4). This groundbreaking Supreme Court case changed criminal justice in the United States by defining the rights of accused criminals. (Rev: BL 9/15/99; HBG 4/00) [347]

9306 Horne, Gerald. *Powell vs. Alabama: The Scottsboro Boys and American Justice* (9–12). Series: Historic Supreme Court Cases. 1997, Watts LB $25.00 (0-531-11314-0). The right to effective counsel in court cases was established by this Supreme Court decision that came after the tragic miscarriage of justice involving the Scottsboro boys. (Rev: BL 4/15/97; SLJ 6/97) [345.73]

9307 Hull, N. E. H., and Peter Charles Hoffer. *Roe v. Wade: The Abortion Rights Controversy in American History* (10–12). Series: Landmark Law Cases. 2001, Univ. Press of Kansas $35.00 (0-7006-1142-8); paper $15.95 (0-7006-1143-6). After a history of U.S. abortion law, this account describes this landmark court case, and the continuing battles of the years since. (Rev: BL 10/1/01) [344.73]

9308 Irons, Peter H. *A People's History of the Supreme Court* (10–12). 1999, Viking $32.95 (0-670-87006-4); paper $15.95 (0-14-029201-2). This history of the Supreme Court focuses on major decisions and how they have changed the United States. (Rev: BL 8/99) [347]

9309 Jacobs, Thomas A. *Teens on Trial: Young People Who Challenged the Law — and Changed Your Life* (8–12). 2000, Free Spirit paper $14.95 (1-57542-081-3). Student rights and responsibilities are explored through this examination of 21 cases in which teens participated in the legal process. (Rev: BL 1/1–15/01; SLJ 1/01; VOYA 4/01) [346.7301]

9310 Jacobs, Thomas A. *They Broke the Law, You Be the Judge: True Cases of Teen Crime* (7–12). 2003, Free Spirit paper $15.95 (1-57542-134-8). A former juvenile court judge presents 21 real-life cases involving juveniles, gives the reader the sentencing options, and reveals the actual outcome of each case. (Rev: BL 2/1/04; SLJ 1/04) [345.73]

9311 Jones-Brown, Delores D. *Race, Crime, and Punishment* (7–12). Illus. Series: Crime, Justice, and

Punishment. 2000, Chelsea $19.95 (0-7910-4273-1). This book explores the double standard often applied to black and white offenders and also discusses police brutality as related to race. (Rev: BL 8/00; HBG 9/00) [364]

9312 Knappman, Edward W. *Great World Trials* (9–12). 1997, Visible Ink $70.00 (0-7876-0805-X); paper $21.95 (1-57859-001-9). Profiles of 100 important trials include information on such notable defendants as Socrates, Jesus Christ, Joan of Arc, Galileo, Oscar Wilde, Mata Hari, and Nelson Mandela. (Rev: BL 6/1–15/97; SLJ 8/97) [347]

9313 Kraft, Betsy H. *Sensational Trials of the 20th Century* (6–10). Illus. 1998, Scholastic paper $16.95 (0-590-37205-X). This book profiles eight important American trials including Sacco and Vanzetti, the Rosenbergs, Scopes, Watergate, O. J. Simpson, and John Hinckley. (Rev: BL 3/1/99; HBG 3/99; SLJ 11/98; VOYA 6/99) [347.73]

9314 Kronenwetter, Michael. *The Supreme Court of the United States* (7–10). Series: American Government in Action. 1996, Enslow LB $20.95 (0-89490-536-8). After presenting an example of the power of the Supreme Court, the author describes the judicial system and a brief history of the court, discusses how it operates and the increasingly political nature of appointments and decisions, and details some of its most significant decisions. (Rev: SLJ 5/96) [347]

9315 Kuklin, Susan. *Trial: The Inside Story* (8–12). Illus. 2001, Holt $17.95 (0-8050-6457-5). The story of a kidnapping of illegal Chinese immigrants and the subsequent trial is used to illustrate legal concepts, the trial process, and the roles of attorneys, police, and witnesses. (Rev: BL 12/15/00; HBG 10/01; SLJ 1/01; VOYA 2/01) [345.73]

9316 Manaugh, Sara. *Judges and Sentencing* (7–10). Series: Crime, Justice, and Punishment. 2001, Chelsea LB $21.95 (0-7910-4296-0). An introduction to the role of judges and to the sentencing process, with material on sentencing reform. (Rev: HBG 10/02; SLJ 4/02) [345.73]

9317 Mitchell, Hayley R., ed. *The Death Penalty* (6–12). Illus. Series: Complete History Of. 2001, Greenhaven LB $123.75 (0-7377-0426-8). This anthology provides a well-organized and balanced look at the death penalty, with selections that offer differing viewpoints. (Rev: BL 11/1/01; SLJ 8/01) [364.6]

9318 Mitchell, Hayley R., ed. *The Death Penalty* (7–12). Series: Contemporary Issues Companion. 2001, Greenhaven LB $17.96 (0-7377-0458-6); paper $11.96 (0-7377-0457-8). Diverse viewpoints on the death penalty are presented in this well-organized text, which includes historical, legal, and personal insights. (Rev: BL 3/1/01; SLJ 4/01) [364.66]

9319 Moats, David. *Civil Wars: A Battle for Gay Marriage* (10–12). 2004, Harcourt $25.00 (0-15-101017-X). A behind-the-scenes account of how the Vermont Supreme Court decided that gays could marry and the consequences of that ruling. (Rev: BL 2/15/04) [306.84]

9320 Monroe, Judy. *The Sacco and Vanzetti Controversial Murder Trial: A Headline Court Case* (6–10). Illus. Series: Headline Court Cases. 2000, Enslow $19.95 (0-7660-1387-1). The story of the murder trials of two Italian immigrants in 1921, the long-questioned conviction, and the abuse and protection of suspects' rights then and today. (Rev: BL 10/1/00; BR 1–2/01; HBG 9/00; SLJ 1/01) [345.73]

9321 Moran, Richard. *Executioner's Current: Thomas Edison, George Westinghouse, and the Invention of the Electric Chair* (10–12). Illus. 2002, Knopf $25.00 (0-375-41059-7). Discussions of the death penalty and the early uses of electricity are intertwined in this absorbing account. (Rev: BL 9/1/02) [364.66]

9322 Netzley, Patricia D. *Issues in Crime* (7–10). Illus. Series: Contemporary Issues. 2000, Lucent LB $18.96 (1-56006-480-3). A general presentation of issues that pit the rights of individuals against the rights of society, such as gun control, mandatory sentencing, and juvenile justice rules. (Rev: HBG 9/00; SLJ 8/00) [364.973]

9323 Paddock, Lisa. *Facts About the Supreme Court of the United States* (8–12). 1996, H.W. Wilson $105.00 (0-8242-0896-X). A one-stop reference source for information about the Supreme Court, from individual justices to the court's history and important cases. (Rev: VOYA 12/96) [347]

9324 Peacock, Nancy. *Great Prosecutions* (8–12). Illus. Series: Crime, Justice, and Punishment. 2001, Chelsea LB $21.95 (0-7910-4292-8). Accounts of five famous trials — including those of the Manson "family" and Al Capone — show readers how prosecutors work to prove guilt. (Rev: BL 1/1–15/02) [345]

9325 Pellowski, Michael J. *The O. J. Simpson Murder Trial: A Headline Court Case* (7–12). Series: Headline Court Cases. 2001, Enslow LB $20.95 (0-7660-1480-0). An objective summary of the murder investigation, the murder trial and the civil trial, and the personalities involved. (Rev: HBG 3/02; SLJ 12/01) [345.73]

9326 Persico, Deborah A. *Mapp vs. Ohio: Evidence and Search Warrants* (6–10). Illus. Series: Landmark Supreme Court Cases. 1997, Enslow LB $20.95 (0-89490-857-X). A step-by-step account of the Supreme Court decision that established a citizen's rights concerning search warrants and the collection of evidence. (Rev: BL 4/15/97; SLJ 6/97) [345.73]

583

9327 Persico, Deborah A. *New Jersey v. T.L.O.: Drug Searches in Schools* (7–12). Illus. Series: Landmark Supreme Court Cases. 1998, Enslow LB $20.95 (0-89490-969-X). This Supreme Court case lasted five years and explored the rights of a student, identified as T.L.O., whose handbag was searched by a school administrator who found marijuana and articles that indicated the student was selling drugs. (Rev: BL 8/98; HBG 9/98; SLJ 8/98; VOYA 2/99) [345.73]

9328 Persico, Deborah A. *Vernonia School District v. Acton: Drug Testing in Schools* (7–12). Series: Landmark Supreme Court Cases. 1999, Enslow LB $19.95 (0-7660-1087-2). An examination of an Oregon court case involving random drug testing introduces the reader to important legal concepts. (Rev: HBG 4/00; SLJ 1/00) [344.73]

9329 *Police Brutality* (10–12). Ed. by Jill Nelson. 2000, Norton $24.95 (0-393-04883-7). This collection of critical essays explores the history and politics of police brutality as it exists in U.S. society, particularly against minorities. (Rev: BL 5/15/00) [363.2]

9330 Ramen, Fred. *The Rights of the Accused* (7–12). Series: Individual Rights and Civic Responsibility. 2001, Rosen LB $26.50 (0-8239-3238-9). Real cases illustrate how constitutional provisions play a significant role in protecting the rights of the accused. (Rev: SLJ 8/01; VOYA 12/01) [345.73]

9331 Riley, Gail B. *Miranda v. Arizona: Rights of the Accused* (6–10). Illus. 1994, Enslow LB $18.95 (0-89490-404-X). This account analyzes the Supreme Court case that defined the rights of an accused person based on what became known as Miranda rights. (Rev: BL 11/15/94) [345.73]

9332 Roleff, Tamara L., ed. *The Legal System* (8–12). Series: Opposing Viewpoints. 1996, Greenhaven LB $26.20 (1-56510-405-6); paper $16.20 (1-56510-404-8). This collection of original sources tackles such questions as: Does the legal system work? Does it need reforms? Is there too much litigation in this country? Is the criminal justice system fair? and How do the media affect the legal system? (Rev: BL 7/96) [347.73]

9333 Roleff, Tamara L., ed. *Police Brutality* (9–12). Series: Current Controversies. 1998, Greenhaven LB $21.96 (0-7377-0013-0); paper $20.25 (0-7377-0012-2). Topics debated in this anthology include the extent of police brutality, its causes, its effects on society, and how it can be reduced. (Rev: BL 2/1/99) [363.232]

9334 Schonebaum, Steve, ed. *Does Capital Punishment Deter Crime?* (8–12). Series: At Issue. 1998, Greenhaven LB $26.20 (1-56510-791-8); paper $17.45 (1-56510-091-3). This anthology presents arguments by those who maintain the death penalty deters crime and by others with statistics, studies, and other evidence that point to the opposite conclusion. (Rev: BL 6/1–15/98) [364.6]

9335 *Selected Readings in Criminal Justice* (11–12). Ed. by Philip L. Reichel. Series: Contemporary Perspectives. 1998, Greenhaven LB $29.96 (1-56510-901-5); paper $16.96 (1-56510-900-7). This scholarly but readable survey of the American criminal justice system, including victims' rights and causes of crime, offers thoughtful essays by law enforcement officials, judges, sociologists, and legal scholars. (Rev: BL 7/98) [364]

9336 Stevens, Leonard A. *The Case of Roe v. Wade* (8–12). 1996, Putnam $16.99 (0-399-22812-8). Complete with fascinating details and numerous quotations, this book gives an objective account of this landmark court case and its ramifications. (Rev: BL 10/1/96*; BR 11–12/96; SLJ 1/97; VOYA 12/96) [344.73]

9337 Swisher, Carl Brent. *Historic Decisions of the Supreme Court*. 2nd ed. (10–12). 1979, Krieger paper $11.50 (0-88275-813-6). In chronological order, the decisions of the Supreme Court are introduced with appropriate background material. [342]

9338 Tompkins, Nancy. *Roe v. Wade: The Fight over Life and Liberty* (7–12). Illus. Series: Supreme Court Cases. 1996, Watts LB $25.00 (0-531-11286-1). This account of the landmark Supreme Court case focuses on the case itself and the controversy that the decision has caused. (Rev: BL 2/1/97; SLJ 2/97) [344.73]

9339 Trespacz, Karen L. *Ferrell v. Dallas I. S. D.* (6–10). Series: Landmark Supreme Court Cases. 1998, Enslow LB $20.95 (0-7660-1054-6). The dramatic story of the school district case that was adjudicated by the Supreme Court. (Rev: BL 8/98; BR 11–12/98; HBG 3/99; SLJ 1/99; VOYA 2/99) [347]

9340 Truly, Traci. *Teen Rights: A Legal Guide for Teens and the Adults in Their Lives* (7–12). 2002, Sphinx paper $22.95 (1-57248-221-4). This book examines issues and outcomes of legal actions of specific interest to young adults. (Rev: BL 1/1–15/03; SLJ 11/02) [346.7301]

9341 Tushnet, Mark V. *Brown v. Board of Education: The Battle for Integration* (10–12). Series: Historic Supreme Court Cases. 1995, Watts LB $25.00 (0-531-11230-6). The full story of the landmark court case and its repercussions. [344]

9342 Wice, Paul B. *Miranda v. Arizona* (7–12). Series: Historic Supreme Court Cases. 1996, Watts LB $25.00 (0-531-11250-0). A reconstruction of the important Supreme Court case in which a confession was judged invalid because the suspect had not been informed of his rights. (Rev: SLJ 9/96) [347]

9343 Wormser, Richard. *Defending the Accused: Stories from the Courtroom* (9–12). Illus. 2001, Watts $24.00 (0-531-11378-7). This thought-provoking examination of the role of the defense attorney uses a number of actual court cases to help illuminate the sometimes controversial and always challenging responsibilities involved. (Rev: BL 7/01; SLJ 8/01; VOYA 12/01) [345.73]

9344 Worth, Richard. *The Insanity Defense* (7–10). Series: Crime, Justice, and Punishment. 2001, Chelsea LB $19.95 (0-7910-4294-4). After some historical background material, this account uses specific examples to explore facets of the question of how far mental illness goes in excusing criminal behavior. (Rev: BL 6/1–15/01; HBG 10/01; SLJ 7/01; VOYA 6/02) [345]

Politics

GENERAL AND MISCELLANEOUS

9345 Archer, Jules. *Special Interests: How Lobbyists Influence Legislation* (7–12). Illus. 1997, Millbrook LB $24.90 (0-7613-0060-0). This timely account looks at special interest groups, why lobbyists have so much power, how lobbies were created, and the role they play in influencing policy. (Rev: BL 12/15/97; BR 3–4/98; SLJ 1/98; VOYA 2/98) [324]

9346 Boyers, Sara Jane. *Teen Power Politics: Make Yourself Heard* (7–12). 2000, Twenty-First Century LB $25.90 (0-7613-1307-9); paper $9.95 (0-7613-1391-5). An in-depth and inspiring look at the ways in which teens too young to vote can nonetheless exert their influence. (Rev: BL 11/15/00; BR 3–4/01; HBG 3/01; SLJ 1/01; VOYA 4/01) [323]

9347 *Campaign Finance Reform* (10–12). Ed. by Christopher Luna. Series: Reference Shelf. 2001, H.W. Wilson paper $45.00 (0-8242-0998-2). The essays in this collection cover such topics as corporate influence, soft money, fund-raising, and political action committees, plus other topics relating to money and political campaigns. [324.7]

9348 Cozic, Charles P., ed. *Politicians and Ethics* (7–12). Series: Current Controversies. 1996, Greenhaven LB $32.45 (1-56510-407-2). This collection of original sources covers various points of view concerning the behavior and ethics of politicians, the problems of scrutiny, and the degree to which legal measures should be used. (Rev: BL 6/1–15/96) [172]

9349 Gay, Kathlyn. *Who's Running the Nation? How Corporate Power Threatens Democracy* (7–12). Series: Impact. 1998, Watts LB $23.00 (0-531-11489-9). In this analysis of business's influence on government, the author explains in a fairly objective tone exactly how corporations use campaign contributions and lobbying to influence policies, and demonstrates how this disenfranchises ordinary citizens. (Rev: HBG 3/99; SLJ 3/99) [324.2]

9350 Morin, Isobel V. *Politics, American Style: Political Parties in American History* (6–12). Illus. 1999, Twenty-First Century $24.90 (0-7613-1267-6). An engaging account of the history of American political parties, accompanied by political cartoons. (Rev: BL 11/15/99; HBG 4/00; SLJ 1/00) [324.273]

9351 *Political Scandals* (8–12). Ed. by William Dudley. Series: Opposing Viewpoints. 2000, Greenhaven LB $31.20 (0-7377-0518-3); paper $19.95 (0-7377-0517-5). A number of political scandals, including campaign financing and the Clinton impeachment, are discussed in these essays that express different viewpoints. (Rev: SLJ 3/01) [324.7]

9352 *The Radical Reader: A Documentary History of the American Radical Tradition* (10–12). Ed. by Timothy Patrick McCarthy and John McMillan. 2003, New Pr. $65.00 (1-56584-827-6); paper $21.95 (1-56584-682-6). This comprehensive overview of American radicalism includes more than 200 essays, editorials, and other statements by such notable historic figures as Henry David Thoreau, Frederick Douglass, Sarah Grimke, Emma Goldman, Betty Friedan, Angela Davis, and Cesar Chavez. (Rev: BL 7/03) [303.484]

9353 White, John Kenneth, and Daniel M. Shea. *New Party Politics: From Jefferson and Hamilton to the Information Age* (10–12). Illus. 2000, St. Martin's $35.00 (0-312-23225-1). This account traces the evolution of political parties and describes how they function at various levels of government. (Rev: BL 7/00) [324.273]

9354 Winters, Paul A., ed. *The Media and Politics* (8–12). 1996, Greenhaven LB $11.95 (1-56510-383-6); paper $17.45 (1-56510-382-3). A collection of articles about the relationship between the media and politics and how messages can be influenced by the agendas of journalists, politicians, and special interest groups. (Rev: BL 3/15/96; SLJ 4/96; VOYA 8/96) [302.23]

ELECTIONS

9355 Cornog, Evan, and Richard Whelan. *Hats in the Ring: An Illustrated History of American Presidential Campaigns* (9–12). 2000, Random (0-679-45730-5). This is a pictorial guide to American presidential elections from their origins up to the election of 2000. (Rev: BL 9/1/00; SLJ 3/01) [324]

9356 Cunningham, Liz. *Talking Politics: Choosing the President in the Television Age* (9–12). 1995, Praeger $19.95 (0-275-94187-6). Ten well-known media and political personalities discuss the relationship between presidential candidates and television broadcasters. (Rev: BL 4/15/95) [791.45]

9357 Greenfield, Jeff. *"Oh, Waiter! One Order of Crow!": Inside the Strangest Presidential Election Finish in American History* (10–12). 2001, Putnam

$24.95 (0-399-14776-4). A well-known political commentator takes a cynical look at the 2000 election and its intrigues. (Rev: BL 5/1/01*) [324.973]

9358 Israel, Fred L. *Student's Atlas of American Presidential Elections 1789 to 1996* (7–12). 1997, Congressional Quarterly $45.00 (1-56802-377-4). Each of the 53 presidential elections in U.S. history is described on a page or two, accompanied by maps to illustrate election results. (Rev: BL 11/15/97; SLJ 11/97) [973]

9359 Kaplan, David A. *The Accidental President: How 413 Lawyers, 9 Supreme Court Justices, and 5,963,110 Floridians (Give or Take a Few) Landed George W. Bush in the White House* (10–12). 2001, Morrow $26.00 (0-06-621283-9). An entertaining look at the curious string of events that led to George W. Bush's election as America's first "accidental" president. (Rev: BL 11/1/01; VOYA 6/02) [324.973]

9360 Kowalski, Kathiann M. *Campaign Politics: What's Fair? What's Foul?* (8–12). Series: Pro/Con. 2000, Lerner LB $25.26 (0-8225-2630-1). Elections are examined along with the practices, both fair and unfair, that are often used to win them. (Rev: HBG 10/01; SLJ 3/01) [324.7]

9361 Melder, Keith. *Hail to the Candidate: Presidential Campaigns from Banners to Broadcasts* (9–12). 1992, Smithsonian paper $24.95 (1-56098-178-4). A look at the many components of a presidential campaign and how they help determine the course of history. (Rev: BL 5/1/92; SLJ 6/92) [324.973]

9362 Nader, Ralph. *Crashing the Party: How to Tell the Truth and Still Run for President* (10–12). 2002, St. Martin's $24.95 (0-312-28433-0). In this report on his 2000 presidential campaign, reformer Nader maintains that the two major political parties are ignoring the poor and concentrating exclusively on the corporations that bankroll elections. (Rev: BL 12/15/01) [973.9]

9363 Reische, Diana. *Electing a U.S. President* (7–12). 1992, Watts paper $24.00 (0-531-11043-5). A straightforward look at the presidential campaign process and the people involved in it. (Rev: BL 4/15/92; SLJ 8/92) [324.0973]

9364 Winters, Paul A., ed. *Voting Behavior* (8–12). Series: At Issue. 1996, Greenhaven LB $26.20 (1-56510-413-7); paper $23.95 (1-56510-412-9). Various opinions are represented on such topics as citizen participation in a democracy, the role of public opinion polls and the media, and the significance of campaign politics. (Rev: BL 8/96; SLJ 8/96; VOYA 12/96) [324.973]

The Armed Forces

9365 Aaseng, Nathan. *You Are the General* (7–12). Illus. Series: Great Decisions. 1994, Oliver $14.95 (1-881-50811-0). This book deals with decisions that have to be made by members of the military, with many examples. (Rev: BL 6/1–15/94) [355]

9366 da Cruz, Daniel. *Boot: The Inside Story of How a Few Good Men Became Today's Marines* (10–12). Illus. 1987, St. Martin's paper $6.99 (0-312-90060-0). The story of a Marine boot camp platoon from induction to graduation. (Rev: BL 2/15/87) [359.9]

9367 Fine, Jil. *Life Inside the Naval Academy* (7–12). Series: Insider's Look. 2002, Children's LB $20.00 (0-516-23922-8); paper $6.95 (0-516-24005-6). The story of the Naval Academy at Annapolis, Maryland, and of its history, traditions, and programs. (Rev: BL 10/15/02) [359]

9368 Haney, Eric L. *Inside Delta Force: The Story of America's Elite Counterterrorist Unit* (10–12). 2002, Delacorte $25.95 (0-385-33603-9). This absorbing profile of Delta Force offers an insider's view of its operations and the rigorous testing volunteers must undergo to join its ranks. (Rev: BL 3/15/02) [356]

9369 Kohlhagen, Gale Gibson, and Ellen Heinbach. *The United States Naval Academy: A Pictorial Celebration of 150 Years* (9–12). 1995, Abrams $49.95 (0-8109-3932-0). A pictorial retrospective of the United States Naval Academy. (Rev: BL 3/15/95) [359]

9370 McNab, Chris. *Protecting the Nation with the U.S. Army* (6–10). Series: Rescue and Prevention: Defending Our Nation. 2003, Mason Crest LB $22.95 (1-59084-414-9). This series about the specific roles the various services play in defending U.S. interests at home and abroad also discusses each service's history, structure, equipment, and recent operations. Also use *Protecting the Nation with the U.S. Air Force* and *Protecting the Nation with the U.S. Navy* (2003). (Rev: HBG 4/04; SLJ 7/03) [355]

9371 *Semper Fi: Stories of the United States Marines from Boot Camp to Battle* (11–12). Ed. by Clint Willis. 2003, Thunder's Mouth paper $17.95 (1-56025-504-8). Peacetime and wartime experiences of U.S. Marines have been culled from a variety of well-written sources; the violence in these stories limits the book's use to mature teens. (Rev: BL 10/1/03) [359.9]

9372 Stewart, Robert. *The Brigade in Review: A Year at the U.S. Naval Academy* (9–12). 1993,

Naval Institute Pr. $41.95 (1-55750-776-7). This illustrated volume covers the Annapolis year, from the introduction of the academy plebes to the senior midshipmen's graduation. (Rev: BL 2/1/94) [359]

9373 Stillwell, Paul, ed. *The Golden Thirteen: Recollections of the First Black Naval Officers* (9–12). 1993, Naval Institute Pr. $34.95 (1-55750-779-1). Oral histories of African Americans who faced prejudice and overcame limitations to become the first commissioned officers of their race in the U.S. Navy. (Rev: BL 1/15/93) [359]

9374 Stremlow, Mary V. *Coping with Sexism in the Military* (7–12). 1990, Rosen LB $17.95 (0-8239-1025-3). An analysis of the military from the perspective of the female recruit that reflects conditions in the late 1980s. (Rev: BL 2/15/91) [355]

9375 Waller, Douglas C. *The Commandos: The Inside Story of America's Secret Soldiers* (9–12). 1994, Simon & Schuster $22.50 (0-671-78717-9). This history of U.S. military special operations gives an account of the training of special forces and the SEALs and describes their activities in Panama and the Persian Gulf. (Rev: BL 1/1/94) [356]

9376 Wekesser, Carol, and Matthew Polesetsky, eds. *Women in the Military* (9–12). Series: Current Controversies. 1991, Greenhaven LB $26.20 (0-89908-579-2); paper $16.20 (0-89908-585-7). A look at the pros and cons of women serving in the armed forces. (Rev: BL 6/15/92; SLJ 3/92) [355.4]

9377 Worth, Richard. *Women in Combat: The Battle for Equality* (7–12). Series: Issues in Focus. 1999, Enslow LB $20.95 (0-7660-1103-8). A study of the changing role of women in the armed forces from the First World War to the Gulf War. (Rev: BL 5/1/99) [355]

Citizenship and Civil Rights

General and Miscellaneous

9378 Bickman, Connie. *Tribe of Women: A Photojournalist Chronicles the Lives of Her Sisters Around the Globe* (6–12). 2001, New World Library $24.95 (1-57731-130-2). A stunning collection of photographs and writings that offer an intimate look at the lives of women around the world. (Rev: VOYA 12/01) [779]

9379 D'Souza, Dinesh. *What's So Great About America* (10–12). 2002, Regnery $27.95 (0-89526-153-7). D'Souza, a neo-conservative and immigrant from India, discusses some of the accusations leveled at the West and enumerates America's political blessings. (Rev: BL 4/15/02) [973]

9380 Vowell, Sarah. *The Partly Cloudy Patriot* (10–12). 2002, Simon & Schuster $22.95 (0-7432-2352-7). In this collection of thought-provoking, often humorous essays, radio personality Vowell offers her unique views of what is — and isn't — true patriotism. (Rev: BL 8/02; SLJ 4/03) [973]

Civil and Human Rights

9381 Alderman, Ellen, and Caroline Kennedy. *The Right to Privacy* (10–12). 1995, Knopf $26.95 (0-679-41986-1). This adult look at the right to privacy features a rundown of court cases on such subjects as strip searches, right-to-die decisions, ownership of frozen embryos, televised death, searches in schools, and videotaping of sex acts without the subject's approval. (Rev: BL 10/1/95; BR 5–6/96; SLJ 5/96) [323.44]

9382 Alonso, Karen. *Schenck v. United States: Restrictions on Free Speech* (7–10). Series: Landmark Supreme Court Cases. 1999, Enslow LB $20.95 (0-7660-1089-9). A re-creation of this landmark Supreme Court case that explored the limitations of free speech, including a follow-up on its consequences. (Rev: BL 8/99) [323.44]

9383 Altman, Linda J. *Human Rights: Issues for a New Millennium* (7–10). 2002, Enslow LB $20.95 (0-7660-1689-7). A general introduction to the topic of human rights, with historical information and a survey of international organizations working in this area today. (Rev: HBG 10/03; SLJ 5/03; VOYA 8/03) [323]

9384 Altman, Linda J. *Slavery and Abolition in American History* (7–10). Series: In American History. 1999, Enslow LB $19.95 (0-7660-1124-0). A well-researched and well-documented account of slavery and the abolitionist movement in the United States. (Rev: BL 11/15/99; HBG 4/00; SLJ 3/00) [973.7]

9385 *American Civil Rights: Primary Sources* (7–12). Ed. by Phillis Englebert and Beth Des Chenes. 1999, UXL $52.00 (0-7876-3170-1). This is a collection of 15 documents relating to the civil rights movement in America, such as speeches, proclamations, and autobiographical texts. (Rev: BL 1/1–15/00; SLJ 5/00; VOYA 4/00) [323.1]

9386 Anderson, Henry Clay, and Clifton L. Taulbert. *Separate, but Equal: The Mississippi Photographs of Henry Clay Anderson* (10–12). Illus. 2002, PublicAffairs $35.00 (1-58648-092-8). Anderson's photographs bring to life the Jim Crow era with depictions of families and communities in the segregated South. (Rev: BL 11/15/02) [305.896]

9387 Andryszewski, Tricia. *Gay Rights* (6–12). Illus. 2000, Twenty-First Century LB $23.90 (0-7613-1568-3). The author presents many viewpoints in this book that discusses gay rights in relation to the law, the military, the church, marriage, the family, government, and politics. (Rev: BL 10/15/00; HBG 10/01; SLJ 10/00; VOYA 12/00) [305.9]

9388 Asante, Molefi K. *Erasing Racism: The Survival of the American Nation* (11–12). 2003, Prometheus $27.00 (1-59102-069-7). The legacy of racism is explored in detail in this scholarly study by writer/educator Asante, who offers abundant evidence of the lingering damage caused by racial discrimination. (Rev: BL 2/15/03*) [973]

9389 Baldwin, James. *James Baldwin: Collected Essays* (10–12). 1998, Library of America $35.00 (1-88301-152-3). A collection of essays that demonstrate the novelist's support of civil rights. [814]

9390 Bender, David, and Bruno Leone, eds. *Feminism* (7–12). Series: Opposing Viewpoints. 1995, Greenhaven paper $16.20 (1-56510-179-0). Essays supporting different viewpoints are presented. Topics include feminism's effects on women and society and its future and goals. (Rev: BL 7/95; SLJ 2/95) [305.42]

9391 Blake, John. *Children of the Movement* (10–12). Illus. 2004, Lawrence Hill $24.95 (1-55652-537-0). This work looks at the children of civil rights activists such as those of Martin Luther King, Jr., Malcolm X, and Julian Bond, and how the movement affected them. (Rev: BL 5/1/04) [323]

9392 Booker, Christopher C. *African-Americans and the Presidency: A History of Broken Promises* (6–12). Illus. 2000, Watts $25.00 (0-531-11882-7). A chronological survey of U.S. presidents' promises and actions regarding equal rights for African Americans. (Rev: BL 2/15/01; SLJ 3/01; VOYA 6/01) [973]

9393 Bradley, David, and Shelley Fisher Fishkin, eds. *The Encyclopedia of Civil Rights in America* (5–10). 1997, Sharpe Reference $299.00 (0-7656-8000-9). This three-volume set contains 683 alphabetically arranged articles that explore the history, meaning, and application of civil rights issues in the United States. (Rev: BL 2/15/98; SLJ 5/98) [323]

9394 Brill, Marlene T. *Women for Peace* (6–10). Series: Women Then — Women Now. 1997, Watts LB $23.00 (0-531-11328-0). A chronicle of the involvement of women in peace movements from ancient Greece to the Vietnam War. (Rev: BL 5/15/97; SLJ 4/97; VOYA 12/97) [327.1]

9395 Bullard, Sara. *Free at Last: A History of the Civil Rights Movement and Those Who Died in the Struggle* (6–10). 1993, Oxford $28.00 (0-19-508381-4). Following an overview of the history of African Americans, an in-depth look at the civil rights movement is presented, with 40 biographies of civil rights martyrs. (Rev: BL 11/1/93; VOYA 8/93) [323.1]

9396 Carson, Clayborne, et al., eds. *The Eyes on the Prize Civil Rights Reader: Documents, Speeches, and Firsthand Accounts from the Black Freedom Struggle, 1954–1990* (9–12). 1991, Penguin paper $16.95 (0-14-015403-5). Contains much of the material that is basic to the U.S. civil rights movement, including speeches by Martin Luther King, Jr. and writings by Malcolm X. (Rev: BL 9/15/91) [973]

9397 Cary, Eve. *The Rights of Students* (6–12). Series: ACLU Handbooks for Young Americans. 1997, Penguin paper $8.99 (0-14-037784-0). Published with the cooperation of the American Civil Liberties Union, this book outlines the rights of young people at home, at school, and in the workplace. (Rev: BL 1/1–15/98) [344.73]

9398 *Civil Rights in America: 1500 to the Present* (9–12). 1998, Gale $125.35 (0-7876-0612-X). A well-researched book that explores historical and contemporary issues involved in civil rights, including the experiences of various ethnic, racial, cultural, and religious groups; rights that all Americans enjoy (voting and education); and major court decisions that have had an impact on civil rights. (Rev: BL 11/15/98; VOYA 2/99) [323.4]

9399 Connerly, Ward. *Creating Equal: My Fight Against Race Preferences* (10–12). Illus. 2000, Encounter $24.95 (1-893554-04-X). A successful African American businessman and University of California regent explains why he has taken a stand against affirmative action in a book that contains additional coverage on what should take its place. (Rev: BL 2/15/00) [305.8]

9400 Currie, Stephen. *Slavery* (7–12). Series: Opposing Viewpoints Digests. 1998, Greenhaven LB $27.45 (1-56510-881-7); paper $17.45 (1-56510-880-9). Diverse opinions are presented in this anthology on issues relating to slavery and human rights, morality, justice, abolition, and resistance. (Rev: BL 4/15/99) [177]

9401 Dolan, Edward F. *Your Privacy: Protecting It in a Nosy World* (7–12). 1995, Dutton $14.99 (0-525-65187-X). A historical and practical look at one of our most important rights. (Rev: BL 1/1/95; SLJ 2/95) [323.44]

9402 Du Bois, W. E. B. *The Oxford W. E. B. Du Bois Reader* (10–12). Ed. by Eric J. Sundquist. 1996, Oxford paper $34.95 (0-19-509178-7). This broad-ranging collection of Du Bois's writings offers insights into his thinking about African American leadership, colonialism, communism in America, women's rights, black art and music, and politics. [305.8]

9403 Dudley, William, ed. *The Civil Rights Movement* (9–12). Series: Opposing Viewpoints. 1996, Greenhaven LB $21.96 (1-56510-369-6); paper $20.25 (1-56510-368-8). A collection of primary source documents that express a variety of views on the civil rights movement, including those of demonstrators, segregationists, movement leaders,

Supreme Court justices, and journalists. (Rev: BL 6/1–15/96; SLJ 8/96) [323.1]

9404 Egendorf, Laura K., ed. *Human Rights* (8–12). Series: Opposing Viewpoints. 2003, Gale LB $33.70 (0-7377-1689-4); paper $22.45 (0-7377-1690-8). This collection of essays covers a definition of human rights, the state of these rights today, and ways in which the United States and the world can respond to human rights abuse. (Rev: BL 1/1–15/04) [323.4]

9405 Eubanks, W. Ralph. *Ever Is a Long Time: A Journey into Mississippi's Dark Past* (10–12). Illus. 2003, Basic $26.00 (0-7382-0570-2). In this memoir of his childhood in 1960s Mississippi, the African American author contrasts the idyllic life he enjoyed on the isolated farm with the reality of the racism from which he was protected. (Rev: BL 9/15/03) [305.8]

9406 Evans, Sara M. *Tidal Wave: How Women Changed America at Century's End* (10–12). 2003, Free Pr. $26.00 (0-02-909912-9). A detailed overview of American women's advances during the latter half of the 20th century. (Rev: BL 2/1/03) [305.42]

9407 Faherty, Sara. *Victims and Victims' Rights* (7–12). Series: Justice and Punishment. 1998, Chelsea LB $21.95 (0-7910-4308-8). A multifaceted overview of the victims' rights movement in the United States and its development over the past 25 years. (Rev: BL 3/15/99) [362.88]

9408 Fairclough, Adam. *Better Day Coming: Blacks and Equality, 1890–2000* (10–12). 2001, Viking $25.95 (0-670-87592-9). From post-Reconstruction days to the present, this is an overview of the events and people who built the modern civil rights movement in the United States. (Rev: BL 7/01) [323.1]

9409 Farish, Leah. *Tinker vs. Des Moines: Student Protest* (6–10). Illus. Series: Landmark Supreme Court Cases. 1997, Enslow LB $20.95 (0-89490-859-6). This book traces step-by-step this case that was argued in the Supreme Court and that determined the rights of students in schools and campuses. (Rev: BL 4/15/97; SLJ 5/97) [341.4]

9410 Feagin, Joe, and Eileen O'Brien. *White Men on Race: Power, Privilege, and the Shaping of Cultural Consciousness* (10–12). 2003, Beacon $26.00 (0-8070-0980-6). Drawing on their interviews with "elite white men," the authors explore the nature of today's subtler forms of racism. (Rev: BL 8/03) [305.896]

9411 *Feminism: Opposing Viewpoints* (9–12). Ed. by Jennifer A. Hurley. 2000, Greenhaven LB $31.20 (0-7377-0508-6); paper $19.95 (0-7377-0507-8). These 25 essays express varying opinions toward feminism in America, women's rights, and the status and goals of the feminist movement. (Rev: SLJ 5/01) [305.4]

9412 *The Feminist Movement* (10–12). Ed. by Nick Treanor. Series: New American Social Movements. 2002, Gale LB $32.45 (0-7377-1050-0); paper $21.20 (0-7377-1049-7). This anthology of essays, speeches, and interviews chronicles the strides made by the women's movement from the mid-19th-century suffrage campaigns of Elizabeth Cady Stanton through the present. (Rev: BL 8/02) [305.42]

9413 Finlayson, Reggie. *We Shall Overcome: The History of the American Civil Rights Movement* (6–10). Illus. Series: People's History. 2003, Lerner $25.26 (0-8225-0647-5). In chronological order, this book explores important civil rights events of the 1950s and 1960s — including demonstrations, marches, lynchings, assassinations, and violent protests — and provides historical context and key quotations. (Rev: BL 2/15/03; HBG 3/03; SLJ 1/03; VOYA 12/03) [323.1]

9414 Fireside, Harvey. *The "Mississippi Burning" Civil Rights Murder Conspiracy Trial* (6–10). Series: Headline Court Cases. 2002, Enslow LB $20.95 (0-7660-1762-1). This account describes the vicious murder of three young civil rights workers in Mississippi in 1964 and how their killers were brought to justice. (Rev: BL 3/15/03; HBG 3/03; SLJ 3/03) [973.9]

9415 Fireside, Harvey. *New York Times v. Sullivan: Affirming Freedom of the Press* (6–10). Series: Landmark Supreme Court Cases. 1999, Enslow LB $20.95 (0-7660-1085-6). The limits to freedom of the press was the subject of this Supreme Court case that had far-reaching results in the world of journalism. (Rev: BL 8/99) [347.3]

9416 Fireside, Harvey. *Plessy vs. Ferguson: Separate but Equal?* (6–10). Illus. Series: Landmark Supreme Court Cases. 1997, Enslow LB $20.95 (0-89490-860-X). This book gives a step-by-step account of the hearings in the Supreme Court of this case that challenged the basic underpinnings of segregation laws. (Rev: BL 7/97; HBG 3/98; SLJ 10/97) [342.73]

9417 Fireside, Harvey, and Sarah B. Fuller. *Brown v. Board of Education: Equal Schooling for All* (6–10). Series: Landmark Supreme Court Cases. 1994, Enslow LB $20.95 (0-89490-469-8). Presents background information, the case itself, and the far-reaching impact it has had. (Rev: BL 11/15/94) [344.73]

9418 Fleming, Maria, ed. *A Place at the Table: Struggles for Equality in America* (7–12). Illus. 2002, Oxford LB $28.00 (0-19-515036-8). Profiles of individuals who have fought for equality since colonial times are interspersed with excerpts from primary sources and photographs. (Rev: BL 2/1/02; HBG 10/02; SLJ 5/02; VOYA 2/02) [323]

9419 Freedman, Estelle B. *No Turning Back: The History of Feminism and the Future of Women*

(8–12). 2002, Ballantine $15.95 (0-345-45054-X). Cultural, economic, educational, and historical information are provided in this overview of the feminist movement around the world. (Rev: BL 3/1/03)

9420 Fremon, David K. *The Jim Crow Laws and Racism* (6–10). Series: In American History. 2000, Enslow LB $20.95 (0-7660-1297-2). This is a history of racism in America from the end of the Civil War to the death of Martin Luther King, Jr., in 1968. (Rev: BL 10/15/2000; HBG 3/01; SLJ 12/00) [973]

9421 Friedan, Betty. *The Feminine Mystique* (10–12). 2001, Norton paper $12.95 (0-393-32257-2). This classic work, first published in 1963, analyzes the roles of women in society since World War II. [305.4]

9422 Frost-Knappman, Elizabeth, and Kathryn Cullen-DuPont. *Women's Rights on Trial: 101 Historic Trials from Anne Hutchinson to the Virginia Military Institute Cadets* (6–12). 1997, Gale $95.00 (0-7876-0384-8). The description of each of these landmark trials defining women's rights includes background information, partial transcripts, courtroom action, and the decision and its significance. (Rev: SLJ 5/97) [346]

9423 Frost-Knappman, Elizabeth, and Kathryn Cullen-DuPont. *Women's Suffrage in America: An Eyewitness History* (9–12). Series: Eyewitness History. 1992, Facts on File $75.00 (0-8160-2309-3). Primary sources including diary and journal entries, speeches, letters, and memoirs offer insights into the women's suffrage movement. (Rev: SLJ 12/92) [324.6]

9424 George, Charles. *Civil Rights: The Struggle for Black Equality* (9–12). Illus. Series: Words That Changed History. 2001, Lucent LB $19.96 (1-56006-799-3). The power of the written and spoken word to influence the outcome of the civil rights struggle is explored in detail in this book, which draws on the works and speeches of key figures including Booker T. Washington, W. E. B. Du Bois, and Malcolm X. (Rev: BL 7/01) [185.61]

9425 Gottfried, Ted. *Homeland Security Versus Constitutional Rights* (8–12). Illus. 2003, Millbrook LB $24.90 (0-7613-2862-9). Gottfried addresses important questions, both historical and contemporary, in the balancing of safety versus civil liberties. (Rev: BL 11/15/03; HBG 4/04; SLJ 12/03; VOYA 2/04) [303.3]

9426 Gottfried, Ted. *Privacy: Individual Rights v. Social Needs* (8–12). 1994, Millbrook LB $25.90 (1-56294-403-7). Discusses debates on privacy in relation to law enforcement, surveillance, abortion, AIDS, and the media. (Rev: BL 9/15/94; SLJ 10/94; VOYA 2/95) [342.73]

9427 Grant, R. G. *The African-American Slave Trade* (6–12). Illus. Series: Lives in Crisis. 2003, Barron's $14.95 (0-7641-5604-7). While focusing on the slave trade to the United States, this book also looks at the international context and at the history of slavery, providing eyewitness accounts. (Rev: BL 10/15/03*; HBG 4/04; SLJ 8/03) [306]

9428 Grapes, Bryan J., ed. *Affirmative Action* (8–12). Series: At Issue. 1999, Greenhaven LB $21.96 (0-7377-0290-7); paper $13.96 (0-7377-0289-3). A wide range of opinions are included about this principle that favors preferential treatment for women and minority groups in employment and education. (Rev: BL 11/15/99) [331.13]

9429 Guernsey, JoAnn B. *Voices of Feminism: Past, Present, and Future* (7–10). Illus. Series: Frontline. 1996, Lerner LB $19.95 (0-8225-2626-3). After a 150-year history of feminism, this account covers the complicated issues and concerns surrounding this subject and discusses past and present leaders in the movement. (Rev: BL 9/15/96; SLJ 7/97; VOYA 4/97) [305.42]

9430 Guinier, Lani, and Susan Sturm. *Who's Qualified?* (10–12). 2001, Beacon paper $12.00 (0-8070-4335-4). This is an examination of the pros and cons of affirmative action, with suggestions on how it should be changed. (Rev: BL 6/1–15/01) [331.13]

9431 Hampton, Henry, and Steve Fayer. *Voices of Freedom: An Oral History of the Civil Rights Movement* (9–12). 1990, Bantam $24.95 (0-553-05734-0). Based on a number of eyewitness accounts, this tells the human side of the civil rights movement. [323.1]

9432 Hendrickson, Paul. *Sons of Mississippi: A Story of Race and Its Legacy* (10–12). Illus. 2003, Knopf $26.95 (0-375-40461-9). A thoughtful look at the civil rights struggle that focuses on the white opposition to African Americans' quest for equality. (Rev: BL 2/15/03) [976.2]

9433 Hinchey, Patricia H. *Student Rights: A Reference Handbook* (9–12). Series: Contemporary Education Issues. 2001, ABC-CLIO $45.00 (1-57607-266-5). A thorough look at student rights, with coverage of such topics as key legislation and Supreme Court decisions. (Rev: BL 10/15/01) [323.4]

9434 Jacobs, Thomas A. *What Are My Rights? 95 Questions and Answers About Teens and the Law* (7–12). 1997, Free Spirit paper $14.95 (1-57542-028-7). Using a question-and-answer format, this topically arranged manual describes in simple terms concerns relating to teens' rights within the family, at school, and on the job. (Rev: BL 4/1/98; SLJ 4/98; VOYA 6/98) [346.7301]

9435 Kowalski, Kathiann M. *Teen Rights: At Home, at School, Online* (6–12). Illus. Series: Issues in Focus. 2000, Enslow LB $19.95 (0-7660-1242-5).

The author lays out teens' rights in areas ranging from school drug testing and Internet use to healthcare and freedom of expression. (Rev: BL 8/00; HBG 9/00; SLJ 8/00; VOYA 2/01) [305.235]

9436 Kranz, Rachel, and Tim Cusick. *Gay Rights* (9–12). Series: Library in a Book. 2000, Facts on File $45.00 (0-8160-4235-7). This is an overview of gay rights in America and the areas where conflict still exists. (Rev: BL 3/1/01; SLJ 5/01) [305.9]

9437 Kuklin, Susan. *Irrepressible Spirit* (7–12). 1996, Putnam $18.95 (0-399-22762-8); paper $9.95 (0-399-23045-9). This moving document profiles, through interviews, 11 activists from around the world and describes each one's struggle for civil rights and social justice. (Rev: BL 5/1/96*; BR 3–4/97; SLJ 4/96; VOYA 2/97) [323]

9438 Landau, Elaine. *Your Legal Rights: From Custody Battles to School Searches, the Headline-Making Cases That Affect Your Life* (6–10). 1995, Walker LB $14.85 (0-8027-8360-0). A review of advances in protection of the legal rights of children and teenagers. (Rev: BL 5/15/95; SLJ 8/95) [346.7301]

9439 Levy, Debbie. *Bigotry* (6–12). 2002, Gale LB $27.45 (1-56006-500-1). Specific examples of racism, anti-Semitism, and homophobia are accompanied by discussion of the incidence of bigotry in America, its history, and the influence of the media. (Rev: BL 2/1/02) [179]

9440 Levy, Debbie. *Civil Liberties* (7–12). Illus. Series: Overview. 1999, Lucent LB $18.96 (1-56006-611-3). This introduction to civil liberties presents the Bill of Rights and covers freedom of speech and assembly, media freedom, religious liberties, and the right to privacy. (Rev: BL 2/1/00; HBG 9/00) [342.73]

9441 *Listen Up: Voices from the Next Feminist Generation.* Rev. ed. (10–12). Ed. by Barbara Findlen. 2001, Seal paper $16.95 (1-58005-054-9). A lively anthology that contains essays by young feminists that cover many subjects, including race, sexual orientation, and maternity. (Rev: BL 8/01) [305.42]

9442 Long, Barbara. *United States v. Virginia: Virginia Military Institute Accepts Women* (7–10). Series: Landmark Supreme Court Cases. 2000, Enslow LB $19.95 (0-7660-1342-1). Virginia Military Institute's battle to continue excluding women cadets is documented here with quotations and excerpts from primary documents. (Rev: HBG 3/01; SLJ 11/00) [344.73]

9443 Lucas, Eileen. *Civil Rights: The Long Struggle* (6–10). Illus. Series: Issues in Focus. 1996, Enslow LB $20.95 (0-89490-729-8). After a discussion of the first 10 amendments to the U.S. Constitution, this account focuses on the civil rights struggles of African Americans. (Rev: BL 9/15/96; BR 5–6/97; SLJ 12/96) [323]

9444 McDonald, Laughlin, and John A. Powell. *The Rights of Racial Minorities* (6–10). Series: ACLU Handbooks for Young Americans. 1998, Penguin paper $9.99 (0-14-037785-9). This handbook traces how the rights of racial minorities have gained legal protection and provides information on current laws. (Rev: BL 5/15/98; SLJ 6/98) [323.4]

9445 McWhorter, Diane. *Carry Me Home: Birmingham, Alabama: The Climactic Battle of the Civil Rights Revolution* (10–12). 2001, Simon & Schuster $35.00 (0-684-80747-5); paper $17.00 (0-7432-1772-1). An exciting account of the people, events, and social background of the struggle for civil rights in Birmingham, Alabama. (Rev: BL 2/15/01) [976.1]

9446 Marable, Manning. *The Great Wells of Democracy: The Meaning of Race in American Life* (10–12). 2003, Basic $26.00 (0-465-04393-3). The history of racism and its enduring role in American life is analyzed in this thought-provoking study. (Rev: BL 12/15/02) [323.1]

9447 Matthews, Jean V. *The Rise of the New Woman: The Women's Movement in America, 1875–1930* (10–12). 2003, Ivan R. Dee $24.95 (1-56663-500-4). A detailed and absorbing overview of the early years of the women's movement, chronicling the changes in women's status that began to emerge in the wake of the Civil War and culminated in the passage of the 19th Amendment. (Rev: BL 3/1/03) [305.42]

9448 Meltzer, Milton. *There Comes a Time: The Struggle for Civil Rights* (7–12). Illus. Series: Landmark Books. 2001, Random LB $18.99 (0-375-90407-7). Slavery, Reconstruction, school desegregation, marches, strikes, and speeches are among the topics that are explored in this book, which follows the civil rights movement through the work and assassination of Dr. King. (Rev: BL 2/1/01; HBG 10/01; SLJ 1/01) [973]

9449 Meltzer, Milton. *They Came in Chains: The Story of the Slave Ships* (6–10). Illus. Series: Great Journeys. 1999, Benchmark LB $21.95 (0-7614-0967-X). Slavery is treated in a global context with material on the horrors of the Middle Passage, and the life of slaves before and after the voyage. (Rev: BL 1/1–15/00; HBG 4/00; SLJ 2/00) [382]

9450 Milios, Rita. *Working Together Against Racism* (7–12). Series: Library of Social Activism. 1995, Rosen LB $16.95 (0-8239-1840-8). A history of civil rights in America and ways to protect citizens from racism. (Rev: BL 4/15/95; SLJ 4/95) [305.8]

9451 Monroe, Judy. *The Susan B. Anthony Women's Voting Rights Trial* (6–10). Series: Headline Court Cases. 2002, Enslow LB $20.95 (0-7660-1759-1). Monroe explores the fight for women's suffrage and the trial of Susan B. Anthony for voting illegally in the 1872 election. (Rev: BL 3/15/03; HBG 3/03; SLJ 12/02) [324.6]

9452 Nash, Carol R. *The Fight for Women's Right to Vote* (7–10). Series: In American History. 1998, Enslow LB $20.95 (0-89490-986-X). The struggle for women's right to vote is told concisely and clearly, with thumbnail sketches of the leading personalities involved. (Rev: BL 8/98; BR 1–2/99; HBG 9/99; SLJ 1/99) [324.6]

9453 Nazer, Mende, and Damien Lewis. *Slave: My True Story* (11–12). 2004, PublicAffairs $25.00 (1-58648-212-2). Mende Nazer, who was captured and sold at a tender age, tells a shocking story of modern-day slavery in Sudan; suitable for mature teens. (Rev: BL 12/1/03*) [305.5]

9454 Oliver, Marilyn Tower. *Gay and Lesbian Rights: A Struggle* (7–12). 1998, Enslow LB $20.95 (0-89490-958-4). After recounting two incidents of gay bashing, the author reviews the history of gay rights from the ancient Greeks to today, with material on discrimination, law, health, and family issues. (Rev: BL 12/1/98; SLJ 2/99; VOYA 10/99) [305.9]

9455 Olson, Lynne. *Freedom's Daughters: The Unsung Heroines of the Civil Rights Movement from 1830 to 1970* (10–12). Illus. 2001, Scribner $30.00 (0-684-85012-5). This volume describes the contribution of the women, black and white, who joined the struggle for civil rights. (Rev: BL 12/15/00) [323]

9456 Patterson, Charles. *The Civil Rights Movement* (6–12). Series: Social Reform Movement. 1995, Facts on File $25.00 (0-8160-2968-7). Chronicles the civil rights movement in the United States, including a timeline, chapter notes, and a reading list. (Rev: BL 11/15/95; SLJ 11/95; VOYA 12/95) [323.1196]

9457 Payne, Charles M. *I've Got the Light of Freedom: The Organizing Tradition and the Mississippi Freedom Struggle* (9–12). 1995, Univ. of California Pr. $45.00 (0-520-08515-9). Community organizing for civil rights, the groundwork laid by the local NAACP, and its impact in the Mississippi Delta. (Rev: BL 4/15/95*) [323.0972]

9458 Peck, Rodney. *Working Together Against Human Rights Violations* (7–12). Series: Library of Social Activism. 1995, Rosen LB $16.95 (0-8239-1778-9). Presents the struggles over a wide range of human rights issues. (Rev: BL 4/15/95; SLJ 4/95) [323]

9459 Pollitt, Katha. *Subject to Debate: Sense and Dissents on Women, Politics, and Culture* (10–12). 2001, Random paper $12.95 (0-679-78343-1). This collection of 80 essays published from 1994 through 2000 deals mainly with the state of feminism and the role that feminism plays in the United States today. (Rev: BL 2/1/01) [814]

9460 Power, Jonathan. *Like Water on Stone: The Story of Amnesty International* (10–12). 2001, Northeastern Univ. Pr. $30.00 (1-55553-487-2). An overview of the 40-year history of Amnesty International with coverage of its work in areas including China, Chile, and Nigeria. (Rev: BL 9/1/01) [323]

9461 Powledge, Fred. *We Shall Overcome: Heroes of the Civil Rights Movement* (7–10). 1993, Scribner $17.00 (0-684-19362-0). A history of the civil rights movement: why it began, the system of segregation that existed with the government's tacit approval, and the movement's milestones and heroes. (Rev: BL 6/1–15/93; VOYA 8/93) [323.1]

9462 Price, Janet R., et al. *The Rights of Students: The Basic ACLU Guide to a Student's Rights* (9–12). 1988, Southern Illinois Univ. Pr. paper $11.95 (0-8093-1423-1). In a question-and-answer format, the civil rights of teenage students are explored. (Rev: BL 5/15/88) [344.73]

9463 Rasmussen, R. Kent. *Farewell to Jim Crow: The Rise and Fall of Segregation in America* (8–12). Series: Library of African American History. 1997, Facts on File $25.00 (0-8160-3248-3). This is a history of segregation in the United States in such areas as housing, education, employment, transportation, and public accommodations, and efforts to end it. (Rev: BR 1–2/98; VOYA 2/98) [973]

9464 Redman, Nina, and Lucille Whalen. *Human Rights: A Reference Handbook.* Second Ed. (9–12). Series: Contemporary World Issues. 1998, ABC-CLIO $45.00 (1-57607-041-7). A one-volume compendium of facts about the historical, religious, philosophical, legal, and political foundations of human rights, the history of international human rights struggles, and material on such pressing concerns as global poverty, the use of land mines, prisons and torture, ethnic cleansing, racism, and the environment. (Rev: BL 3/1/99; VOYA 8/99) [341.4]

9465 Ritchie, Nigel. *The Civil Rights Movement* (6–12). Series: Lives in Crisis. 2003, Barron's $14.95 (0-7641-5602-0). Using a number of well-documented quotations, this account traces the civil rights movement in this country, particularly in the late 20th century. (Rev: BL 10/15/03; HBG 4/04; SLJ 8/03) [331.1196]

9466 Rogers, James T. *The Antislavery Movement* (7–12). Series: Social Reform Movements. 1994, Facts on File $25.00 (0-8160-2907-5). This work traces slavery and its repercussions from 1619 to the present and provides insights into the conflicting interests and positions. (Rev: BL 1/1/95; SLJ 12/94; VOYA 5/95) [973]

9467 Roleff, Tamara L., ed. *Civil Liberties* (8–12). Series: Opposing Viewpoints. 1998, Greenhaven LB $32.45 (1-56510-937-6). This collection of essays explores potential restrictions on freedom of expression, the right to privacy, the separation of church and state, and freedom to use the Internet. (Rev: BL 8/98; SLJ 1/99; VOYA 6/99) [342]

9468 Roleff, Tamara L. *Gay Marriage* (9–12). Series: At Issue. 1997, Greenhaven LB $14.96 (1-56510-693-8); paper $13.96 (1-56510-692-X). Proponents of same-sex marriage believe that homosexuals deserve the same benefits as heterosexuals, but opponents maintain it will undermine the institution of marriage. These and other points of view are presented in this anthology. (Rev: BL 5/1/98; SLJ 7/98) [306.84]

9469 Rubin, Richard. *Confederacy of Silence: A True Tale of the New Old South* (10–12). 2002, Pocket $26.00 (0-671-03666-1). Rubin paints a disturbing portrait of lingering racial prejudice in this memoir of his experiences as a sportswriter for a small Mississippi daily newspaper. (Rev: BL 7/02) [305.8]

9470 Schulz, William F. *In Our Own Best Interest: How Defending Human Rights Benefits All Americans* (10–12). 2001, Beacon $25.00 (0-8070-0226-7). The executive director of Amnesty International (USA) discusses human rights and why their defense is in the best interests of the United States. (Rev: BL 4/1/01; SLJ 5/02) [323]

9471 Schulz, William F. *Tainted Legacy: 9/11 and the Ruin of Human Rights* (10–12). 2003, Thunder's Mouth paper $12.95 (1-56025-489-0). The author, executive director of Amnesty International, asks tough questions about America's suspension of human rights in the wake of September 11, 2001. (Rev: BL 10/15/03) [323]

9472 Shapiro, Joseph P. *No Pity: How the Disability Rights Movement Is Changing America* (9–12). 1993, Times Books $25.00 (0-8129-1964-5). A history of the struggle to overcome negative public perception of the disabled. Discusses the movement's diversity and its aggressive attack on myths and stereotypes through 1992. (Rev: BL 4/15/93) [323.3]

9473 Shein, Lori, ed. *Inequality: Opposing Viewpoints in Social Problems* (9–12). Series: Opposing Viewpoints. 1997, Greenhaven LB $30.96 (1-56510-737-3); paper $21.20 (1-56510-736-5). Leading policymakers, activists, and scientists debate the causes of and solutions to race, gender, age, and class inequality. (Rev: BL 2/15/98; SLJ 4/98) [305]

9474 *Slavery* (10–12). Ed. by Thomas Streissguth. Illus. Series: History Firsthand. 2001, Greenhaven $28.70 (0-7377-0633-3); paper $22.96 (0-7377-0632-5). This overview of slavery uses primary sources to paint a frank and unrelenting account of the institution's massive emotional and physical toll. (Rev: BL 6/1–15/01) [306.3]

9475 *Slavery Today* (6–12). Ed. by Auriana Ojeda. Series: At Issue. 2004, Gale LB $27.45 (0-7377-

1613-4). The problem of slavery today, particularly in some African countries, is explored in this collection of writings. (Rev: BL 2/15/04; SLJ 7/04) [326]

9476 Somerlott, Robert. *The Little Rock School Desegregation Crisis* (6–10). Series: In American History. 2001, Enslow LB $20.95 (0-7660-1298-0). Beginning on September 5, 1957, when nine African American schoolchildren were refused entrance to a Little Rock school, this account looks at the Arkansas school desegregation crisis. (Rev: BL 12/15/01; HBG 3/02; SLJ 9/01) [344.73]

9477 Springer, Jane. *Listen to Us: The World's Working Children* (7–12). Illus. 1997, Douglas & McIntyre $24.95 (0-88899-291-2). This impressive photoessay looks at the exploitation of children around the world in industry, agriculture, the home, the military, and on the street. (Rev: BL 1/1–15/98; SLJ 3/98) [331.3]

9478 Stalcup, Brenda, ed. *The Women's Rights Movement* (9–12). Series: Opposing Viewpoints. 1996, Greenhaven LB $21.96 (1-56510-367-X); paper $16.20 (1-56510-366-1). An extensive collection of documents covering the women's rights movement from colonial times to the present, with emphasis on current controversies. (Rev: BL 6/1–15/96; SLJ 8/96) [973.917]

9479 Stalcup, Brenda, ed. *Women's Suffrage* (8–12). Series: Turning Points in World History. 2000, Greenhaven LB $21.96 (0-7377-0326-1); paper $13.96 (0-7377-0325-3). This collection of essays traces the history of the women's suffrage movement from the declaration of women's rights signed in New York State in 1848 through the impact of the passage of the 19th Amendment on American history. (Rev: BL 5/15/00; SLJ 8/00) [346]

9480 Stearman, Kaye. *Slavery Today* (6–10). Series: Talking Points. 1999, Raintree Steck-Vaughn LB $18.98 (0-8172-5320-3). Examples of modern slavery include child labor, trafficking in people, prostitution, migrant workers who are exploited, and other forms of forced labor. (Rev: BL 12/15/99; HBG 9/00; SLJ 5/00) [326]

9481 Tackach, James. *The Abolition of American Slavery* (7–10). Series: World History. 2002, Gale LB $27.45 (1-59018-002-X). This comprehensive survey of slavery and the abolition movement includes information on key figures and events, with closing information on segregation and the civil rights movement of the 20th century. (Rev: BL 8/02; SLJ 9/02) [973.7]

9482 Thomas, Joyce Carol, ed. *Linda Brown, You Are Not Alone: The Brown v. Board of Education Decision* (6–12). 2003, Hyperion $15.99 (0-7868-0821-7). Well-known children's and YA writers contributed to this collection of fiction, poetry, and memoirs about the important court ruling and its impact on education in the United States. (Rev: BL

12/1/03; HBG 4/04; SLJ 1/04; VOYA 12/03) [344.73]

9483 *Tikvah: Children's Book Creators Reflect on Human Rights* (9–12). Illus. 2001, North-South $19.95 (1-58717-097-3); paper $12.95 (1-58717-098-1). More than 40 illustrators of children's books offer their views — in both words and pictures — in this thoughtful commentary on human rights, including such diverse issues as child labor and abortion. (Rev: BL 2/15/02; HBG 3/02; SLJ 11/01) [758]

9484 Treanor, Nick, ed. *Desegregation* (8–12). Series: Interpreting Primary Documents. 2003, Gale LB $25.96 (0-7377-1302-X); paper $16.96 (0-7377-1308-8). An introduction discussing segregation precedes excerpts from speeches, documents, and other materials by individuals including John F. Kennedy, Martin Luther King Jr., and George Wallace. (Rev: SLJ 5/03) [305.8]

9485 Turner, Chérie. *Everything You Need to Know About the Riot Grrrl Movement: The Feminism of a New Generation* (6–10). Illus. Series: Need to Know Library. 2001, Rosen LB $17.95 (0-8239-3400-4). A look at the movement that evolved from a 1970s aggressive punk attitude to a 1990s emphasis on equality and self-esteem. (Rev: SLJ 12/01) [781.66]

9486 Waldstreicher, David. *The Struggle Against Slavery: A History in Documents* (9–12). Illus. 2002, Oxford $32.95 (0-19-510850-7). This overview of slavery in America draws on primary source documents to chronicle the infamous institution's history from the late 17th century through the end of the Civil War. (Rev: BL 2/15/02; HBG 10/02; SLJ 2/02) [306.3]

9487 Walker, Samuel. *Hate Speech: The History of an American Controversy* (9–12). 1994, Univ. of Nebraska Pr. paper $11.95 (0-8032-9751-3). The first comprehensive history of hate speech and its effects. (Rev: BL 4/15/94) [342.73]

9488 Walter, Lynn. *Women's Rights: A Global View* (10–12). Series: World View of Social Issues. 2000, Greenwood $49.95 (0-313-30890-X). Using case studies from five continents, this book examines the status of women in the world today. [305.4]

9489 Walter, Mildred P. *Mississippi Challenge* (7–12). 1992, Bradbury $18.95 (0-02-792301-0). An in-depth history of the civil rights struggle in Mississippi that tells how ordinary people worked to change the political system. (Rev: BL 11/1/92; SLJ 1/93) [305.896]

9490 Walvin, James. *Slavery and the Slave Trade: A Short Illustrated History* (9–12). Illus. 1983, Univ. Press of Mississippi paper $16.95 (0-87805-181-3). A well-illustrated account that deals with slavery from ancient times through the 19th century. [326]

9491 Watkins, Richard Ross. *Slavery: Bondage Throughout History* (7–12). 2001, Houghton $18.00 (0-395-92289-5). Watkins traces the history of slavery from ancient Babylon through current practices including child prostitution in Southeast Asia. (Rev: BL 2/15/01; HBG 10/01; SLJ 4/01) [306.3]

9492 Wawrose, Susan C. *Griswold v. Connecticut: Contraception and the Right of Privacy* (6–10). Illus. Series: Historic Supreme Court Cases. 1996, Watts LB $25.00 (0-531-11249-7). Many issues involving women's rights, sex, and personal privacy are raised in this discussion of the case against Estelle Griswold, of the Planned Parenthood League in Connecticut, who broke a state law prohibiting distribution of contraceptives. (Rev: BL 7/96; SLJ 9/96; VOYA 10/96) [342.746]

9493 Weatherford, Carole Boston. *The African-American Struggle for Legal Equality* (6–10). Series: In American History. 2000, Enslow LB $20.95 (0-7660-1415-0). From slavery to the present, the account traces the amazing changes that brought African Americans equality before the law. (Rev: BL 10/15/2000; HBG 3/01) [973]

9494 Weatherford, Doris. *A History of the American Suffragist Movement* (10–12). 1998, ABC-CLIO $50.00 (1-57607-065-4). Beginning in 1637, this account traces the long and difficult struggle for women's suffrage that ended with the passing of the 19th Amendment in 1920. (Rev: BR 1–2/99; SLJ 3/99) [324.6]

9495 Webb, Sheyann, and Rachel W. Nelson. *Selma, Lord, Selma: Girlhood Memories of the Civil-Rights Days* (7–12). Illus. 1980, Univ. of Alabama Pr. $17.95 (0-8173-0031-7). Recollections of two girls who, when only ages 8 and 9, participated in the Selma civil rights struggle. (Rev: BL 9/1/87) [323.4]

9496 Weber, Michael. *Causes and Consequences of the African-American Civil Rights Movements* (6–10). Series: Causes and Consequences. 1998, Raintree Steck-Vaughn LB $29.97 (0-8172-4058-6). The author traces the legal and social history of African Americans that led up to the historic 1963 March on Washington; recounts events of the 1950s and 1960s such as the integration of schools, the growing urban tensions, and the rise of the black power movement; and discusses the movement's lasting achievements and current problems. (Rev: SLJ 6/98) [973]

9497 Wepman, Dennis. *The Struggle for Freedom* (7–12). Illus. Series: Library of African American History. 1996, Facts on File $19.95 (0-8160-3270-X). This well-researched work, using many maps and primary sources, traces slavery from ancient Sumerian times and continues through the centuries, exploring the slave trade triangle involving Africa, American, and England, the role of public opinion, slave revolts, working conditions and treatment, the

Underground Railroad, the Civil War, and the revolt of Caribbean slaves led by Toussaint L'Ouverture. (Rev: VOYA 10/96) [973]

9498 Williams, Juan. *Eyes on the Prize: America's Civil Rights Years, 1954–1965* (9–12). 1986, Viking paper $14.95 (0-14-009653-1). Companion to a PBS series, this is a compelling, well-illustrated account of these peak years of civil rights unrest. (Rev: BL 2/15/98) [323.4]

9499 Williams, Juan. *My Soul Looks Back in Wonder: Voices of the Civil Rights Experience* (10–12). Illus. 2004, Sterling $19.95 (1-4027-1415-7). A collection of testimonials from more than 30 individuals (some well-known such as David Dinkins, others not) about the nonviolent struggle for civil rights. (Rev: BL 5/15/04) [323.173]

9500 Williams, Mary, ed. *Human Rights* (9–12). Series: Opposing Viewpoints. 1998, Greenhaven LB $26.20 (1-56510-797-7); paper $20.25 (1-56510-796-9). The rights of women, refugees, child laborers, and political prisoners, the nature of human rights and whether human rights and freedom are culturally relative, and how human rights should be protected are among the issues debated in this anthology of articles and essays. (Rev: BL 5/15/98) [323]

9501 Williams, Mary E., ed. *Civil Rights* (7–12). Series: Examining Issues Through Political Cartoons. 2002, Gale LB $24.95 (0-7377-1100-0); paper $16.20 (0-7377-1099-3). This limited but unusual approach to exploration of the civil rights movement looks at political cartoons in four thematic chapters. (Rev: BR 11–12/02; SLJ 10/02) [323.1]

9502 Williams, Mary E., ed. *Discrimination* (8–12). Series: Opposing Viewpoints. 2002, Gale LB $25.96 (0-7377-1226-0); paper $16.96 (0-7377-1225-2). Williams presents articles and speeches that condemn, defend, and even deny the existence of forms of discrimination including prejudice against women and gays, affirmative action, racial profiling, and reverse discrimination. (Rev: BL 10/1/02; VOYA 2/04) [305]

9503 Williams, Mary E. *The Sexual Revolution* (10–12). Series: New American Social Movements. 2002, Gale LB $32.45 (0-7377-1052-7); paper $21.20 (0-7377-1051-9). From the "free love" movement of the 19th century through the radical changes in sexual mores of the late 20th century, this collection of articles, speeches, and interviews documents America's Sexual Revolution. (Rev: BL 8/02) [306.7]

9504 Wilson, Reginald. *Our Rights: Civil Liberties and the U.S.* (7–12). Illus. 1988, Walker $14.85 (0-8027-6751-6). A book that explains what civil rights are, how we have these freedoms, and how to protect them. (Rev: SLJ 8/88; VOYA 8/88) [323.4]

9505 Winters, Paul A., ed. *The Civil Rights Movement* (8–12). Series: Turning Points in World History. 2000, Greenhaven LB $21.96 (0-7377-0217-6); paper $13.96 (0-7377-0216-8). Essays cover the civil rights struggles of the 1950s and 1960s with material on the leaders, important debates, events, and the continuing struggle. (Rev: BL 2/15/00; SLJ 4/00) [323.1]

9506 Wormser, Richard. *The Rise and Fall of Jim Crow: The African-American Struggle Against Discrimination, 1865–1954* (7–12). Illus. 1999, Watts LB $24.00 (0-531-11443-0). Created as a companion book for the PBS series of the same name, this richly illustrated volume documents harshly racist policies that persisted after the Civil War; gives more depth than Wormser's YA book of the same title published in 1999. (Rev: BL 2/15/00; SLJ 4/00) [305.896073]

9507 Worth, Richard. *Cinqué of the Amistad and the Slave Trade* (6–10). Series: In World History. 2001, Enslow LB $20.95 (0-7660-1460-6). An accessible overview of slave trading from Roman times through the U.S. Civil War, with black-and-white photographs and reproductions and excerpts from source documents. (Rev: HBG 10/01; SLJ 8/01) [326]

9508 Zeinert, Karen. *Free Speech: From Newspapers to Music Lyrics* (7–10). 1995, Enslow LB $20.95 (0-89490-634-8). The censorship battle in the context of various mediums, from a historical perspective. (Rev: BL 4/1/95; SLJ 6/95) [323.44]

Immigration

9509 Ashabranner, Brent. *Our Beckoning Borders: Illegal Immigration to America* (6–10). Illus. 1996, Dutton $15.99 (0-525-65223-X). Individual case studies and good photographs are used to explain the problems of illegal immigration, border patrols, and the involvement of human rights groups. (Rev: BL 4/15/96; BR 11–12/96; SLJ 5/96) [304.8]

9510 Ashabranner, Brent. *Still a Nation of Immigrants* (7–12). 1993, Dutton $15.99 (0-525-65130-6). Looks at the present influx of immigrants and discusses why they come and what they bring with them. (Rev: BL 9/1/93; VOYA 2/94) [325.73]

9511 Barbour, William, ed. *Illegal Immigration* (9–12). Series: Current Controversies. 1994, Greenhaven LB $16.95 (1-56510-072-7); paper $16.20 (1-56510-071-9). An anthology of articles representing a variety of viewpoints regarding the seriousness of the problem of illegal immigration. (Rev: BL 4/15/94; SLJ 3/94) [353.0081]

9512 *Becoming American: Personal Essays by First Generation Immigrant Women* (10–12). Ed. by Meri

Nana-Ama Danquah. 2000, Hyperion $22.95 (0-7868-6589-X). A collection of 24 essays by women from Europe, Latin America, Africa, Asia, and the Caribbean concerning their experiences before and after migrating to the United States. (Rev: BL 2/15/00) [305.48]

9513 Bode, Janet. *The Colors of Freedom: Immigrant Stories* (7–12). 1999, Watts LB $24.00 (0-531-11530-5); paper $9.95 (0-531-15961-2). Using students' writing, artwork, interviews, and poems, the author has collected material on the feelings of young adult immigrants to this country from such areas as Latin America, Europe, and Asia. (Rev: BL 1/1–15/00; SLJ 3/00) [305.8]

9514 Brimelow, Peter. *Alien Nation: Common Sense About Immigration and the American Future* (9–12). 1995, Random $24.00 (0-679-43058-X). A British immigrant probes what he sees as the adverse impact of immigration to the United States and the consequences of current immigration policy. (Rev: BL 3/15/95) [304.8]

9515 Budhos, Marina. *Remix: Conversations with Immigrant Teenagers* (7–12). 1999, Holt $16.95 (0-8050-5113-9). This book contains interviews with 20 older teens from around the world who comment on their experiences as immigrants in the United States and the cultural differences they have encountered. (Rev: BL 9/15/99; HBG 4/00; SLJ 11/99; VOYA 12/99) [341.4]

9516 Caroli, Betty Boyd. *Immigrants Who Returned Home* (6–10). Illus. 1990, Chelsea LB $19.95 (0-87754-864-1). An account of immigrants who found life in the United States less than expected and returned home to their countries. (Rev: BL 4/15/90; SLJ 8/90) [304.8]

9517 Cothran, Helen, ed. *Illegal Immigration* (8–12). Series: Current Controversies. 2001, Greenhaven LB $22.96 (0-7377-0685-6); paper $14.96 (0-7377-0684-8). Cothran presents arguments on both sides of the questions of the treatment and impact of illegal immigrants into the United States. (Rev: SLJ 8/01) [304.873]

9518 Cox, Vic. *The Challenge of Immigration* (7–12). Series: Multicultural Issues. 1995, Enslow LB $20.95 (0-89490-628-3). An introduction to the controversial issues concerning immigration. (Rev: BL 5/1/95; SLJ 5/95) [325.73]

9519 Cozic, Charles P., ed. *Illegal Immigration* (9–12). Series: Opposing Viewpoints. 1997, Greenhaven LB $20.96 (1-56510-514-1); paper $16.20 (1-56510-513-3). Treatment of illegal immigrants, their contributions to the United States, whether illegal immigrants harm the United States, and how the United States should respond to these issues are debated in this collection of essays that replaces the 1990 edition. (Rev: BL 1/1–15/97; BR 5–6/97; SLJ 1/97) [364.6]

9520 *Crossing into America: The New Literature of Immigration* (10–12). Ed. by Louis Mendoza and S. Shankar. 2003, New Pr. $28.95 (1-56584-720-2). This lively anthology of poetry, fiction, essays, and memoirs reflects the hopes and fears of America's new immigrants, who for the last few decades have come mostly from Asia and Latin America. (Rev: BL 3/15/03; SLJ 6/03) [810.8]

9521 Currie, Stephen. *Issues in Immigration* (7–12). Illus. Series: Contemporary Issues. 2000, Lucent LB $19.96 (1-56006-377-7). Questions involving immigration, including bilingual education, are examined from various points of view using quotations from primary sources. (Rev: BL 10/15/00; HBG 3/01; SLJ 12/00) [325.73]

9522 Daniels, Roger. *American Immigration: A Student Companion* (6–12). Series: Oxford Student Companions to American History. 2001, Oxford LB $40.00 (0-19-511316-0). An alphabetically arranged series of articles covering all aspects of immigration to the United States and the various ethnic groups that have made the journey, illustrated with photographs, maps, and reproductions. (Rev: BL 10/15/01; SLJ 6/01) [304.8]

9523 Daniels, Roger. *Coming to America: A History of Immigration and Ethnicity in American Life*. 2nd ed. (10–12). 2002, Perennial paper $17.95 (0-06-050577-X). After a general introduction on immigration, the author discusses various racial and national groups that have migrated to America. [325.73]

9524 Dudley, William, ed. *Illegal Immigration* (7–12). Series: Opposing Viewpoints. 2002, Gale LB $31.20 (0-7377-0911-1); paper $19.95 (0-7377-0910-3). A balanced collection of essays on the topic of illegal arrivals in the United States and the treatment of these immigrants, updated from the 1994 edition. (Rev: BL 4/15/02; SLJ 8/02) [325.73]

9525 Greenberg, Judith E. *Newcomers to America: Stories of Today's Young Immigrants* (7–10). Illus. 1996, Watts LB $23.00 (0-531-11256-X). An overview of the new wave of immigration to this country, followed by excerpts from 14 interviews of recent immigrants who came here as teens. (Rev: BL 6/1–15/96; BR 11–12/96; SLJ 8/96; VOYA 2/97) [304.8]

9526 Hay, Jeff, ed. *Immigration* (7–12). Series: Turning Points in World History. 2001, Greenhaven LB $31.20 (0-7377-0639-2); paper $19.95 (0-7377-0638-4). In a series of engaging essays, the phenomenon of immigration is explored and how shifting populations have changing world history. (Rev: BL 3/15/02) [325]

9527 Hopkinson, Deborah. *Shutting Out the Sky* (5–12). Illus. 2003, Scholastic $17.95 (0-439-37590-8). Five personal stories of young immigrants, striking photographs, and excerpts from primary documents form the backbone of this history of immigration to New York City in the late 19th century. (Rev: BL 11/1/03*; HBG 4/04; SLJ 12/03*; VOYA 6/04) [307.76]

9528 *Immigration* (7–12). Ed. by Tamara L. Roleff. Series: Opposing Viewpoints: World History. 2004, Gale LB $33.70 (0-7377-1701-7). Pros and cons concerning immigration are presented in this collection of opposing viewpoints. (Rev: BL 2/15/04) [325]

9529 Kosof, Anna. *Living in Two Worlds: The Immigrant Children's Experience* (7–12). Illus. 1996, Twenty-First Century LB $23.40 (0-8050-4083-8). After a brief introduction on the history of immigration, this book describes the problems and the reception of present-day teenage immigrants, using many first-person accounts. (Rev: BL 10/1/96; BR 11–12/96; SLJ 10/96; VOYA 2/97) [305.23]

9530 Leinwand, Gerald. *American Immigration: Should the Open Door Be Closed?* (7–12). 1995, Watts paper $24.00 (0-531-13038-X). A historical perspective on the current immigration debate reveals the racism that still underlies the melting-pot argument. (Rev: BL 8/95; VOYA 12/95) [325.73]

9531 Levine, Herbert M. *Immigration* (7–12). Illus. Series: American Issues Debated. 1997, Raintree Steck-Vaughn LB $31.40 (0-8172-4353-4). Questions involving immigration and the economy, the rights of illegal immigrants, and English-only laws are covered from various points of view. (Rev: BL 11/15/97; BR 1–2/98) [304.873]

9532 Meltzer, Milton. *Bound for America: The Story of the European Immigrants* (6–10). Series: Great Journeys. 2001, Benchmark LB $21.95 (0-7614-1227-1). An absorbing examination of the reasons for migration within and from Europe in the 19th and early 20th centuries, and of the hardships these travelers suffered. (Rev: BCCB 3/99; HBG 10/02; SLJ 3/02) [325.73]

9533 Mills, Nicolaus, ed. *Arguing Immigration: The Debate over the Changing Face of America* (9–12). 1994, Simon & Schuster paper $12.00 (0-671-89558-3). Authors such as Toni Morrison discuss immigration, its costs, benefits, and cultural impact. (Rev: BL 9/1/94) [325.73]

9534 Morrow, Robert. *Immigration: Blessing or Burden?* (7–10). Illus. Series: Pro/Con Issues. 1998, Lerner LB $30.35 (0-8225-2613-1). This book examines our changing attitudes toward immigration, how we regard immigration laws, and the controversy over multiculturalism vs. assimilation. (Rev: BL 3/15/98; SLJ 4/98) [304.8]

9535 *Reinventing the Melting Pot: The New Immigrants and What It Means to Be American* (10–12). Ed. by Tamar Jacoby. 2004, Basic $27.50 (0-465-03634-1). In this collection of essays, current trends in American population are examined as well as immigration questions and citizenship concerns. (Rev: BL 2/1/04) [304.8]

9536 Roleff, Tamara L., ed. *Immigration* (8–12). Series: Opposing Viewpoints. 1998, Greenhaven LB $16.20 (1-56510-798-5). Questions concerning restrictions on immigration, the extent of the immigration problem, how to cope with illegal immigrants, and possible reforms in our policies are discussed in this anthology of differing opinions. (Rev: BL 6/1–15/98) [341.4]

9537 Santos, Edward J. *Everything You Need to Know If You and Your Parents Are New Americans* (7–12). Illus. Series: Need to Know Library. 2002, Rosen LB $23.95 (0-8239-3547-7). A useful and attractive guide for immigrant teens that gives practical advice on dealing with various facets of American life and emphasizes the possibility of retaining one's heritage while fitting in to a new culture. (Rev: BL 6/1–15/02; SLJ 4/02; VOYA 2/03) [304.8]

9538 Sawyer, Kem K. *Refugees: Seeking a Safe Haven* (7–12). Series: Multicultural Issues. 1995, Enslow LB $20.95 (0-89490-663-1). This book describes the lives and problems of refugees admitted into this country, with material on why they left their homelands and their reception here. (Rev: BL 6/1–15/95; SLJ 8/95) [362.87]

9539 Stewart, Gail B. *Illegal Immigrants* (9–12). Illus. Series: The Other America. 1997, Lucent LB $17.96 (1-56006-339-4). Four illegal immigrants explain why they are here, describe lives filled with apprehension, work, and fear, and reflect on what they eventually hope to accomplish in America. (Rev: BL 6/1–15/97; BR 11–12/97; SLJ 8/97) [305.9]

9540 Torr, James D., ed. *Primary Sources: Immigrants in America* (6–10). Illus. 2002, Gale LB $27.45 (1-59018-009-7). Excerpts from primary documents are organized in chapters that address the conditions that prompted migrants to leave their homes, the attractions they perceived in America, and the treatment they received on arrival. (Rev: BR 9–10/02; SLJ 9/02) [304.8]

9541 Ungar, Sanford J. *Fresh Blood: The New American Immigrants* (9–12). 1995, Simon & Schuster $24.50 (0-684-80860-9). From the former host of National Public Radio's *All Things Considered* comes this look at the new immigrants — "the illegal aliens" — their relationship to their current communities, and their reception by earlier immigrants. (Rev: BL 10/15/95) [305.8]

9542 Yans-McLaughlin, Virginia, and Marjorie Lightman. *Ellis Island and the Peopling of America: The Official Guide* (10–12). 1997, New Pr. paper $19.95 (1-56584-364-9). This book chronicles the role of Ellis Island in U.S. history and reviews the waves of immigration to this country and past and present immigration policy, using reproductions of letters, visas, editorials and political cartoons, maps, charts and legal documents to bring the facts to life. (Rev: BL 8/97; SLJ 3/98; VOYA 4/98) [973]

Ethnic Groups and Prejudice

General and Miscellaneous

9543 Arana, Marie. *American Chica: Two Worlds, One Childhood* (10–12). 2001, Dial $23.95 (0-385-31962-2). This memoir by the daughter of an American mother and a Peruvian father tells of her feelings about being bilingual, bicultural, and biracial in America. (Rev: BL 4/15/01*; SLJ 11/01) [070]

9544 Barone, Michael. *The New Americans: How the Melting Pot Can Work Again* (10–12). 2001, Regnery $27.95 (0-89526-202-9). The author compares minority groups today with those at the turn of the last century, such as Irish Americans and African Americans, and finds that there is nothing new about multiculturalism. (Rev: BL 6/1–15/01) [305.9]

9545 Barrett, Paul M. *The Good Black: A True Story of Race in America* (10–12). 1999, Plume paper $13.95 (0-452278-59-7). The fascinating story of an African American who makes good, attends Harvard, and joins a law firm only to find continuing evidence of racial discrimination. (Rev: BL 12/1/98*) [305.8]

9546 *CityKids Speak on Prejudice* (7–12). 1995, Random paper $5.99 (0-679-86552-7). Identifies areas in which intolerance is common and cites unexpected examples of discrimination as seen through the eyes of young people. (Rev: BL 5/1/95) [303.3]

9547 Cole, Carolyn Kozo, and Kathy Kobayashi. *Shades of L.A.: Pictures from Ethnic Family Albums* (7–12). 1996, New Pr. paper $20.00 (1-56584-313-4). A collection of photographs of African American, Mexican American, Asian American, and Native American family life in Los Angeles' ethnic and racial neighborhoods prior to 1965. (Rev: BL 8/96; VOYA 2/97) [979.4]

9548 Cruz, Barbara C. *Multiethnic Teens and Cultural Identity: A Hot Issue* (6–10). Series: Hot Issues. 2001, Enslow LB $19.95 (0-7660-1201-8). A concise examination of the challenges facing teens of mixed racial heritage that looks at ethnic diversity during American history and profiles individuals such as Tiger Woods and Halle Berry. (Rev: HBG 10/01; SLJ 7/01) [305.23]

9549 Feagin, Joe R. *Racist America: Roots, Current Realities, and Future Reparations* (10–12). 2000, Routledge $25.00 (0-415-92531-2). This book gives a history of racism in America, particularly as it applies to African Americans, and details how ingrained it is in the American psyche and how radical change will be necessary to change it. (Rev: BL 6/1–15/00) [305.8]

9550 Ferber, Abby L. *White Man Falling: Race, Gender, and White Supremacy* (11–12). 1998, Rowman & Littlefield $24.95 (0-8476-9027-X). Sociologist Ferber dissects the white supremacy movement in America through a thoughtful analysis of the writings and publications of such groups as the National Socialist White People's Party, Ku Klux Klan, and the National Alliance; useful for high school students of history and current events. (Rev: BL 11/15/98) [305.8]

9551 Garg, Samidha, and Jan Hardy. *Racism* (6–10). Illus. Series: Global Issues. 1996, Raintree Steck-Vaughn LB $19.98 (0-8172-4548-0). This study of racism, supplementing statistics and facts with personal experiences, discusses prejudice, immigration, and citizenship, with separate chapters on Europe, South Africa, the United States, and Australia. (Rev: BL 2/1/97) [305.8]

9552 Garza, Hedda. *African Americans and Jewish Americans: A History of Struggle* (8–12). Illus. Series: African American Experience. 1995, Watts paper $24.00 (0-531-11217-9). An overview of the relationship between Jews and African Americans past and present, with material on how relations between these two groups have become strained because of current social developments. (Rev: BL 4/1/96) [973]

9553 Gaskins, Pearl Fuyo, ed. *What Are You? Voices of Mixed-Race Young People* (7–12). 1999, Holt $18.95 (0-8050-5968-7). In essays, interviews, and poetry, 45 mixed-race young people ages 14 to 26 talk about themselves and growing up. (Rev: BL 5/15/99; HB 7–8/99; SLJ 7/99; VOYA 10/99) [973]

9554 Gay, Kathlyn. *I Am Who I Am: Speaking Out About Multiracial Identity* (7–12). 1995, Watts LB $25.00 (0-531-11214-4). A look at what it's like to grow up in a mixed-race environment, including cultural, historical, and political perspectives and opinions from experts. (Rev: BL 6/1–15/95; SLJ 8/95) [305.8]

9555 Gillam, Scott. *Discrimination: Prejudice in Action* (7–12). Series: Multicultural Issues. 1995, Enslow LB $20.95 (0-89490-643-7). This book shows how racial discrimination is still practiced in this country and discusses how it can be combated. (Rev: BL 6/1–15/95; SLJ 9/95) [303.3]

9556 Grearson, Jessie Carroll, and Lauren B. Smith. *Love in a Global Village: A Celebration of Intercultural Families in the Midwest* (10–12). Illus. 2001, Univ. of Iowa Pr. paper $19.95 (0-87745-740-9). This account examines cross-cultural relationships, such as partners from Iran and Lebanon, and from

Germany and Bulgaria. Most of these couples are white but some are black. (Rev: BL 2/15/01) [306.84]

9557 Griffin, John Howard. *Black Like Me*. 2nd ed. (9–12). 1962, Signet paper $6.99 (0-451-19203-6). The true story of a white man who blackened his skin to experience firsthand how it felt to be an African American. [305.8]

9558 Hooks, Bell. *Killing Rage: Ending Racism* (9–12). 1995, Holt $20.00 (0-8050-3782-9). Passionate essays about race and racism written from an African American and feminist point of view. (Rev: BL 9/15/95) [305.8]

9559 *How Race Is Lived in America: Pulling Together, Pulling Apart* (10–12). Illus. 2001, Holt $27.50 (0-8050-6740-X). A collection of columns and responses from the *New York Times* that deal with racial issues and relationships in the United States today, with coverage of political, social, and cultural topics. (Rev: BL 5/1/01) [305.8]

9560 Hurley, Jennifer A., ed. *Racism* (7–12). 1998, Greenhaven LB $32.45 (1-56510-809-4). How prevalent is racism in U.S. society? How does racism affect minorities? Is affirmative action effective? How can racism be combated? These are some of the questions explored in this collection of essays. (Rev: BL 8/98) [305.8]

9561 Immell, Myra H. *Ethnic Violence* (10–12). Series: Contemporary Issues Companion. 2000, Greenhaven LB $31.20 (0-7377-0164-1); paper $19.95 (0-7377-0165-X). Various ethnic groups are highlighted, such as Armenians, Jews, and African Americans, with coverage of ethnic problems in present-day Africa, Asia, and the Balkans. (Rev: SLJ 12/00) [305.8]

9562 Jacobs, Bruce. *Race Manners: Navigating the Minefield Between Black and White Americans* (10–12). 1999, Arcade $22.95 (1-55970-453-5). This book about interracial relations in America today discusses such topics as dating, everyday social life, stereotyping, and ethnic jokes. (Rev: BL 2/15/99; SLJ 5/99) [305.8]

9563 Kassam, Nadya, ed. *Telling It Like It Is: Young Asian Women Talk* (7–12). 1998, Livewire paper $11.95 (0-7043-4941-8). These 22 short, informal essays reveal various attitudes toward sexism and racism as experienced by Hindu and Moslem girls living in Britain whose families are from the Indian subcontinent. (Rev: BL 9/15/98; SLJ 8/98) [305.8914]

9564 Katz, William L. *The Great Migrations: History of Multicultural America* (7–12). Series: History of Multicultural America. 1993, Raintree Steck-Vaughn LB $22.83 (0-8114-6278-1). Shows the impact that women and minorities have had in the formation and development of the United States. (Rev: BL 6/1–15/93; VOYA 10/93) [973]

9565 McKinley, Catherine E. *The Book of Sarahs: A Memoir of Race and Identity* (10–12). 2002, Counterpoint $24.00 (1-58243-259-7). The memoir of a biracial child raised by a white family and her search for the truth about her birth parents. (Rev: BL 10/1/02) [974.4]

9566 Maharidge, Dale. *The Coming White Minority: California's Eruptions and the Nation's Future* (10–12). 1996, Random $25.00 (0-8129-2289-1). The changing racial mix of the American populace is explored through profiles of a Mexican American politician, an African American sheriff, an Asian American student, and a white community activist. (Rev: BL 9/15/96; SLJ 7/97) [325.73]

9567 Major, Clarence. *Come by Here: My Mother's Life* (10–12). 2002, Wiley $24.95 (0-471-41518-9). Poet-novelist Majors reflects on the experiences of his mother — a woman light-skinned enough to move across racial lines, giving her new insights on the nature of racial prejudice. (Rev: BL 5/1/02) [305.896]

9568 Mathis, Deborah. *Yet a Stranger: Why Black Americans Still Don't Feel at Home* (10–12). 2002, Warner $23.95 (0-446-52636-3). A frank look at the evolution of American race relations from the segregation of the past to more subtle — but no less painful — forms of discrimination. (Rev: BL 5/15/02) [305.896]

9569 Myers, Jim. *Afraid of the Dark: What Whites and Blacks Need to Know About Each Other* (10–12). 2000, Lawrence Hill $22.95 (1-55652-342-4). The author describes the different worlds inhabited by black and white Americans, the myths about each race, and offers sensible advice about how they might get together. (Rev: BL 4/1/00) [305.8]

9570 Nash, Gary B. *Forbidden Love: The Secret History of Mixed-Race America* (9–12). 1999, Holt $21.95 (0-8050-4953-3). This book, in many ways a history of racism in the United States, reviews the history of racially mixed people and the fight for tolerance from colonial times to the present. (Rev: BL 5/15/99; HB 7–8/99; SLJ 7/99; VOYA 10/99) [305.868]

9571 *A Nation of Peoples: A Sourcebook on America's Multicultural Heritage* (10–12). Ed. by Elliott Robert Barkan. 1999, Greenwood $110.00 (0-313-29961-7). A group of scholarly essays that covers a number of racial, religious, and ethnic groups. [305.8]

9572 Newman, Gerald, and Eleanor N. Layfield. *Racism: Divided by Color* (7–12). Series: Multicultural Issues. 1995, Enslow LB $20.95 (0-89490-641-0). A well-documented history of color barriers in America and efforts to eradicate them. (Rev: BL 9/15/95; SLJ 12/95; VOYA 2/96) [305.8]

9573 O'Hearn, Claudine Chiawei, ed. *Half and Half: Writers on Growing Up Biracial and Bicultural* (7–12). 1998, Pantheon paper $13.00 (0-375-70011-0). This work contains 18 personal essays by people who live and work in the U.S., but who, because they are biracial and bicultural, are not sure where they belong. (Rev: BL 9/1/98) [306.84]

9574 Pascoe, Elaine. *Racial Prejudice: Why Can't We Overcome?* (7–12). Series: Impact. 1997, Watts paper $24.00 (0-531-11402-3). Explores the causes and effects of racial prejudice through separate chapters on African Americans, Hispanic Americans, Asian Americans, and Native Americans. (Rev: BL 5/15/97) [305.8]

9575 *Race and Ethnicity* (9–12). Ed. by Alma M. Garcia and Richard A. Garcia. Series: Contemporary Issues Companion. 2001, Greenhaven LB $22.96 (0-7377-0464-0); paper $14.96 (0-7377-0463-2). Despite a few essays full of sociology-speak, this collection sheds some light on the problems faced by members of racial and/or ethnic minorities. (Rev: BL 12/15/00) [305.8]

9576 *Race Relations* (9–12). Ed. by Mary E. Williams. Series: Opposing Viewpoints. 2001, Greenhaven LB $27.45 (0-7377-0520-5); paper $17.45 (0-7377-0519-1). The state of American race relations in the early 21st century is assessed in this thought-provoking series of essays, which explore such issues as job discrimination, racial profiling, and diversity training. (Rev: BL 2/1/01; SLJ 4/01) [305.8]

9577 Rekdel, Paisley. *The Night My Mother Met Bruce Lee: Observations on Not Fitting In* (10–12). 2000, Pantheon $22.00 (0-375-40937-8). The author, who is biracial (half-Chinese and half-Norwegian), has written a series of telling, honest essays about the problems of growing up biracial in America. (Rev: BL 9/1/00; VOYA 4/01) [811]

9578 Sharp, Anne Wallace. *The Gypsies* (8–12). Illus. Series: Indigenous Peoples of the World. 2003, Gale $21.96 (1-59018-239-1). The history and culture of the Roma are detailed here, with information on the fate of these groups during World War II and on continuing prejudices. (Rev: BL 4/15/03; SLJ 7/03) [909]

9579 Szumski, Bonnie, ed. *Interracial America* (9–12). Series: Opposing Viewpoints. 1996, Greenhaven LB $21.96 (1-56510-393-9); paper $21.50 (1-56510-392-0). Recent articles representing various points of view are used to explore the current status of race relations in America. (Rev: BL 6/1–15/96; SLJ 7/96) [305.8]

9580 Tatum, Beverly. *Why Are All the Black Kids Sitting Together in the Cafeteria?* (10–12). 1997, HarperCollins $25.00 (0-465-09127-X). Beginning with racial segregation in an integrated school situa-

tion, this book explores race relations and the development of racial identity from many different viewpoints. (Rev: BL 9/1/97; SLJ 3/98) [305.8]

9581 Terkel, Studs. *Race: How Blacks and Whites Think and Feel About the American Obsession* (9–12). 1992, New Pr. paper $15.95 (0-385-46889-X). In this collection of interviews, Terkel explores widely divergent views on the subject of race and how in many ways it continues to polarize Americans. [305.8]

9582 *When Race Becomes Real: Black and White Writers Confront Their Personal Histories* (10–12). Ed. by Bernestine Singley. 2002, Lawrence Hill $26.95 (1-55652-448-X). This collection of thoughtful essays by black and white Americans offers valuable insights into current racial attitudes and their origins. (Rev: BL 6/1–15/02) [305.8]

9583 Williams, Mary, ed. *Interracial America* (6–12). Illus. Series: Opposing Viewpoints. 2001, Greenhaven LB $22.96 (0-7377-0658-9); paper $14.96 (0-7377-0657-0). Essays present various viewpoints on such topics as the advisability of emphasizing ethnic differences, affirmative action, interracial marriage, and transracial adoption. (Rev: BL 7/01) [305.8]

9584 Williams, Mary E. *Issues in Racism* (7–12). Series: Contemporary Issues. 2000, Lucent LB $27.45 (1-56006-478-1). This volume discusses contemporary conditions regarding racism in America and explores such topics as affirmative action, racial profiling, hate crimes, and other issues. (Rev: BL 9/1/00; HBG 3/01) [305.8]

9585 Williams, Mary E. *Minorities* (9–12). Series: Current Controversies. 1998, Greenhaven LB $20.96 (1-56510-681-4); paper $16.20 (1-56510-680-6). A thorough look at discrimination, the present status of race relations, policies that benefit minorities, the changing racial demographics, and other controversial issues of concern to minorities. (Rev: BL 5/1/98) [305.8]

9586 Winstead, Mary. *Back to Mississippi: A Personal Journey Through the Events That Changed America in 1964* (10–12). Illus. 2002, Hyperion $22.95 (0-7868-6796-5). Winstead tells how research into her roots in Mississippi led her to a far broader study of the pivotal role the state, its people, and her own family played in the struggle for civil rights. (Rev: BL 8/02) [976.2]

9587 Winters, Paul A., ed. *Race Relations* (9–12). Series: Opposing Viewpoints. 1996, Greenhaven paper $16.20 (1-56510-356-4). This collection of articles presents a wide range of viewpoints on the state of race relations, affirmative action, the justice system, Black, Asian, and Latino political power-bases, and how race relations can be improved. (Rev: BL 12/15/95; SLJ 1/96; VOYA 6/96) [303.3]

African Americans

9588 Adams, Francis D., and Barry Sanders. *Alienable Rights: The Exclusion of African Americans in a White Man's Land, 1619–2000* (10–12). 2003, HarperCollins $25.95 (0-06-019975-X). A disturbing analysis of the subtle — and not so subtle — ways in which America's white majority has historically suppressed the rights of blacks. (Rev: BL 11/15/03) [305.896]

9589 *African American Frontiers: Slave Narratives and Oral Histories* (9–12). Ed. by Alan B. Govenar. 2000, ABC-CLIO $75.00 (0-87436-867-7). Slave narratives, works from the Federal Writers' Project, and many oral histories are including in this volume that gives an eyewitness perspective on slavery. (Rev: BL 2/15/01; SLJ 5/01) [326]

9590 *African American Humor: The Best Black Comedy from Slavery to Today* (10–12). Ed. by Mel Watkins. 2002, Lawrence Hill $29.95 (1-55652-430-7); paper $18.95 (1-55652-431-5). An entertaining overview of African American humor from the time of slavery through the present, with examples of a wide variety of formats. (Rev: BL 7/02) [817.008]

9591 *African American Quotations* (9–12). 1998, Oryx $65.00 (1-57356-118-5). Interesting to browse through, this compilation of 2,500 quotations from 500 individuals is arranged by such subjects as "Adolescence," "Black Pride," and "Women." (Rev: BR 1–2/99; SLJ 11/98) [080]

9592 Altman, Susan. *The Encyclopedia of African-American Heritage* (6–12). 1997, Facts on File $40.00 (0-8160-3289-0). An alphabetically arranged series of entries that covers African American history from the standpoint of famous people, places, culture, events, and politics. (Rev: BL 3/15/97; BR 1–2/99; SLJ 2/98; VOYA 6/97) [973]

9593 Asante, Molefi K., and Mark T. Mattson. *The African-American Atlas: Black History and Culture — An Illustrated Reference* (9–12). 1998, Macmillan $147.75 (0-02-864984-2). This chronologically arranged atlas introduces African American history by interweaving text about the people and events that influenced the nation's development with maps, charts, reproductions, and photographs. (Rev: BL 4/15/99; SLJ 5/99) [973]

9594 Astor, Gerald. *The Right to Fight: A History of African Americans in the Military* (11–12). Illus. 2001, Da Capo paper $18.50 (0-306-81031-X). This overview of the black experience in the American military focuses largely on the period between the end of World War I and the late 1990s, although it also offers a summary of African American service during the Civil War. (Rev: BL 11/15/98*) [355]

9595 *Autobiography of a People: Three Centuries of African-American History Told by Those Who Lived It* (10–12). Ed. by Herb Boyd. 2000, Doubleday $24.95 (0-385-49278-2). This anthology covers three centuries of African American history by sampling slave narratives, autobiographies, memoirs, and the letters of more than 100 people from Phillis Wheatley to Colin Powell. (Rev: BL 1/1–15/00) [973]

9596 Baldwin, James. *The Fire Next Time* (10–12). 1995, Modern Library $14.95 (0-679-60151-1); paper $9.00 (0-679-74472-X). This prophesy of things to come concerning race relations is based on the author's feelings about Black Muslims and his religious background. [305.8]

9597 Baldwin, James. *Notes of a Native Son*. 3rd ed (10–12). 1990, Beacon paper $13.00 (0-8070-6431-9). A collection of essays about being black in the United States. [305.8]

9598 Ball, Edward. *Slaves in the Family* (10–12). 1998, Farrar $30.00 (0-374-26582-8); Ballantine paper $15.95 (0-345-43105-7). A meticulously researched history of the author's family since their arrival in South Carolina in 1698, tracing their role as slave owners and slave traders, including the author's successful search for several of his distant African American cousins. (Rev: BL 2/15/98; SLJ 6/98) [973]

9599 Banks, William H., Jr. *The Black Muslims* (5–10). Series: African-American Achievers. 1996, Chelsea LB $21.95 (0-7910-2593-4); paper $9.95 (0-7910-2594-2). The story of the founding of the Nation of Islam, its leaders, the Million Man March, and the reign of Louis Farrakhan. (Rev: SLJ 5/97) [323]

9600 *Black Men in Their Own Words* (10–12). Ed. by Patricia Mignon Hinds and Susan L. Taylor. Illus. 2002, Crown $30.00 (0-609-60366-3). Black men in various walks of life share their views on success, family, manhood, and the civil rights movement in this thought-provoking collection of nearly 100 essays. (Rev: BL 2/15/02; SLJ 9/02) [920.71]

9601 Blue, Carroll Parrott. *The Dawn at My Back: Memoir of a Black Texas Upbringing* (10–12). Illus. 2003, Univ. of Texas Pr. $29.95 (0-292-70913-7). Using a variety of primary sources, the author chronicles her life experiences and those of her mother against the backdrop of changes in America's awareness of race issues. (Rev: BL 2/15/03) [791.43]

9602 Boyle, David. *African Americans* (7–10). Series: Coming to America. 2003, Barron's $14.95 (0-7641-5628-4). This account gives an overview of African American history and the many contributions African Americans have made to the economy and culture. (Rev: BL 10/15/03; SLJ 12/03) [973]

9603 Brown, Keith Michael. *Sacred Bond: Black Men and Their Mothers* (11–12). Illus. 1998, Little,

Brown $25.00 (0-316-10556-2). The relationship between mothers and sons, particularly in the context of racial discrimination, is movingly explored in this collection of 35 interviews that also touch on such related pressures as raising biracial children, single motherhood, and dealing with children who have AIDS or are homosexual. (Rev: BL 11/15/98) [306.874]

9604 Buckley, Gail. *American Patriots: The Story of Blacks in the Military, from the Revolution to Desert Storm* (10–12). Illus. 2001, Random $29.95 (0-375-50279-3). For better history students, this is the story of how African American men and women serving in the military have fought for civil and human rights throughout U.S. history. (Rev: BL 5/1/01) [355]

9605 Buckley, Gail. *American Patriots: The Story of Blacks in the Military, from the Revolution to Desert Storm* (7–10). 2003, Crown $15.95 (0-375-82243-7). This book adapted from an adult title describes the segregation, hardships, and triumphs experienced by African Americans in the U.S. military. (Rev: BL 2/15/03; HBG 4/04; SLJ 2/03) [355]

9606 Carrol, Rebecca. *Sugar in the Raw: Voices of Young Black Girls in America* (10–12). 1997, Crown paper $12.00 (0-517-88497-6). This is a collection of 15 monologues by black teenage women about their lives, attitudes, hopes, dreams, frustrations, and experiences. (Rev: BL 12/15/96; BR 5–6/97; SLJ 2/98) [305.8]

9607 Cleaver, Eldridge. *Soul on Ice* (10–12). 1968, McGraw-Hill paper $13.95 (0-385-33379-X). The classic collection of essays for mature readers about a black American and his anger at the state of race relations in the United States. [305.8]

9608 Cole, Harriette, and John Pinderhuges. *Coming Together: Celebrations for African American Families* (4–12). Illus. 2003, Hyperion $22.99 (0-7868-0753-9). Traditions surrounding celebrations including Christmas, Kwanzaa, and naming ceremonies are covered here, with accompanying crafts, menu suggestions, and activities. (Rev: BL 12/15/03; HBG 4/04; VOYA 2/04) [306.8]

9609 Collins, Charles M., and David Cohen, eds. *The African Americans* (9–12). 1993, Viking $45.00 (0-670-84982-0). In choosing African Americans past and present to honor here, the editors selected both famous and ordinary, everyday heroes. Includes photographs and commentary. (Rev: BL 12/15/93) [973]

9610 Cose, Ellis. *The Envy of the World: On Being a Black Man in America* (10–12). 2002, Pocket $22.00 (0-7434-2715-7). In this personalized account, the author explains how people — in particular black men — can deal with racism in the United States. (Rev: BL 12/15/01) [305.38]

9611 Cottman, Michael H. *The Wreck of the Henrietta Marie: An African American's Spiritual Journey to Uncover a Sunken Slave Ship's Past* (10–12). 1999, Harmony $23.00 (0-517-70328-9). The author traces the history of the slave ship *Henrietta Marie* that sank off the Florida keys almost three centuries ago by visiting sites associated with it, including researching its building and its crew in England, visits to the slave port in Senegal, talks with descendants of slaves in Jamaica, and dives undersea at the wreck site. (Rev: BL 2/15/99; SLJ 7/99) [973]

9612 Crowe, Chris. *Getting Away with Murder: The True Story of the Emmett Till Case* (7–12). Illus. 2003, Penguin $18.99 (0-8037-2804-2). A gripping and detailed account of the brutal murder of 14-year-old Emmett Till, an African American boy from Chicago who was visiting relatives in Mississippi in 1954, with discussion of the impact of his death and the ensuing trial on the civil rights movement. (Rev: BL 2/15/03; HB 7–8/03; HBG 10/03; SLJ 5/03*) [364.15]

9613 Davis, Sampson, et al. *The Pact: Three Young Men Make a Promise and Fulfill a Dream* (10–12). 2002, Riverhead $24.95 (1-57322-216-X). Three young African American men from Newark, New Jersey, tell how a youthful pact set them on a path to careers in the medical field. (Rev: BL 5/1/02; SLJ 1/03) [305.896]

9614 De Angelis, Therese. *Louis Farrakhan* (6–10). Series: Black Americans of Achievement. 1998, Chelsea $21.95 (0-7910-4688-5); paper $9.95 (0-7910-4689-3). This book provides information about Farrakhan and explains the evolution of his leadership, but it is more a history of the Nation of Islam movement, with information on African American leaders including Malcolm X, Elijah Muhammad, and Roy Wilkins. (Rev: HBG 3/99; SLJ 2/99) [305.8]

9615 Dent, David J. *In Search of Black America: Discovering the African-American Dream* (10–12). 2000, Simon & Schuster $25.00 (0-684-81072-7). The author explores African American culture in the United States by visiting and describing African American communities, colleges, elite organizations, and the leaders of African American institutions and endeavors. (Rev: BL 2/15/00) [305.86]

9616 Dornfeld, Margaret. *The Turning Tide: From the Desegregation of the Armed Forces to the Montgomery Bus Boycott* (7–10). Series: Milestones in Black American History. 1995, Chelsea LB $21.95 (0-7910-2255-2); paper $9.95 (0-7910-2681-7). This work surveys the period in African American history from 1948 through 1956 and includes Rosa Parks, Ralph Ellison, Charlie Parker, and Adam Clayton Powell, Jr. (Rev: BL 8/95) [973]

9617 Dudley, William, ed. *African Americans* (9–12). Series: Opposing Viewpoints: American History. 1997, Greenhaven LB $21.96 (1-56510-

522-2); paper $16.20 (1-56510-521-4). This anthology of articles documents the history of African Americans from the days of slavery, with coverage of affirmative action, black nationalists, white supremacists, and civil rights movements. (Rev: BL 3/15/97; SLJ 3/97) [973]

9618 Dyson, Michael Eric. *Why I Love Black Women* (10–12). 2003, Basic $23.00 (0-465-01763-0). Dyson praises black women in all walks of life and the important role they have played — and continue to play — in bringing stability to African American families. (Rev: BL 2/1/03) [305]

9619 *Early Black Reformers* (10–12). Ed. by James Tackach. Series: History Firsthand. 2003, Gale LB $32.45 (0-7377-1597-9); paper $21.20 (0-7377-1598-7). This anthology contains the writings and firsthand experiences of African American civil rights advocates before Martin Luther King, Jr. (Rev: BL 6/1–15/03) [973]

9620 Eaton, Susan. *The Other Boston Busing Story* (10–12). 2001, Yale $26.95 (0-300-08765-9). This is a report on the success of busing inner-city black children to white suburban schools since the 1970s and on the personal changes it made in many of the children. (Rev: BL 3/15/01) [379.2]

9621 Ebony, eds. *Ebony Pictorial History of Black America* (7–12). Illus. 1971, JIST $54.95 (set) (0-87485-049-5). These three volumes trace African American history from slavery to today's fight for integration and equality. [305.8]

9622 Ellis, Rex M. *With a Banjo on My Knee: A Musical Journey from Slavery to Freedom* (9–12). 2001, Watts $26.00 (0-531-11747-2). Minstrel shows, jazz, and ragtime are among the musical forms explored in this social history of African Americans. (Rev: BL 1/1–15/02; SLJ 11/01; VOYA 2/02) [787.8]

9623 Feelings, Tom. *The Middle Passage: White Ships Black Cargo* (10–12). 1995, Dial paper $45.00 (0-8037-1804-7). A powerful visual record and concise narrative of the slave trade that describes life in Africa and horrifying details of slave ships. (Rev: BL 10/15/95; SLJ 2/96) [973]

9624 Ferry, Joe. *The History of African-American Civic Organizations* (7–12). Illus. Series: American Mosaic: African-American Contributions. 2003, Chelsea LB $22.95 (0-7910-7270-3). Social, business, and other clubs and groups for African American men, women, and children are explored, with information on membership and rituals. (Rev: BL 10/15/03; HBG 4/04) [36]

9625 Franklin, John Hope. *From Slavery to Freedom: A History of Negro Americans*. 7th ed. (10–12). 1994, McGraw-Hill $34.75 (0-07-021907-9); paper $22.95 (0-685-02834-8). A history that begins with African origins and ends in the 1970s. [305.8]

9626 Freund, David M. P., and Marya Annette McQuirter. *Biographical Supplement and Index* (7–12). Series: Young Oxford History of African Americans. 1997, Oxford $24.00 (0-19-510258-4). In this, the last volume of the fine series, there is an index to the 10-volume set plus brief biographies of key people mentioned in the set. (Rev: BL 9/1/97; BR 11–12/97; VOYA 12/97) [973]

9627 Garrison, Mary. *Slaves Who Dared: The Stories of Ten African-American Heroes* (7–12). Illus. 2002, White Mane LB $19.95 (1-57249-272-4). Historical prints and quotations from original texts lend authenticity to these moving accounts of famous and less-well-known men and women who escaped from slavery. (Rev: BL 9/1/02; HBG 3/03; SLJ 7/02) [973]

9628 Gates, Henry Louis, Jr. *Thirteen Ways of Looking at a Black Man* (10–12). 1997, Random $22.00 (0-679-45713-5). The subject of being a black man in America is explored in a series of articles that deal with various aspects of this subject and uses, as examples, prominent personalities including Colin Powell, Louis Farrakhan, and Wynton Marsalis. (Rev: BL 2/15/97; SLJ 8/97) [973]

9629 Gates, Henry Louis, Jr., and Cornel West. *The African American Century: How Black Americans Have Shaped Our Country* (10–12). Illus. 2000, Free Pr. $30.00 (0-684-86414-2). This book contains profiles of 100 important African Americans of the past century, from W. E. B. Du Bois to Oprah Winfrey, with background historical material. (Rev: BL 9/1/00*) [973]

9630 Genovese, Eugene D. *Roll, Jordan, Roll: The World the Slaves Made* (10–12). 1976, Random paper $18.00 (0-394-71652-3). This is a history of slavery in America that concentrates on the daily life and traditions of slaves. [305.8]

9631 George, Nelson. *Post-Soul Nation: The Explosive, Contradictory, Triumphant, and Tragic 1980s as Experienced by African Americans (Previously Known as Blacks and Before That Negroes)* (10–12). Illus. 2004, Viking $23.95 (0-670-03275-1). Pop culture observer Nelson George offers a thought-provoking portrait of the many ways in which African Americans shaped the popular American culture of the 1980s. (Rev: BL 12/15/03) [973]

9632 Gilbert, Charlene, and Quinn Eli. *Homecoming: The Story of African-American Farmers* (10–12). Illus. 2000, Beacon $35.00 (0-8070-0962-8). Based on a PBS television series, this book traces the relationship between African Americans and property and land ownership from the days of slavery to today. (Rev: BL 11/1/00) [305.5]

9633 Giovanni, Nikki. *Racism 101* (10–12). 1994, Morrow paper $11.00 (0-688-14234-6). A group of essays by Giovannin that explore various aspects of racism in America. (Rev: BL 12/1/93) [814]

9634 Hacker, Andrew. *Two Nations: Black and White, Separate, Hostile, Unequal* (9–12). 1992, Scribner $24.95 (0-684-19148-2). This survey interprets research results on race relations in the United States. (Rev: BL 2/15/92) [305.8]

9635 Halberstam, David. *The Children* (10–12). 1998, Random $29.95 (0-679-41561-0); Fawcett paper $17.95 (0-449-00439-2). This prize-winning reporter profiles the eight courageous students who launched the sit-ins in Nashville, Tennessee, in 1960, outlines the moral and political roots of the civil rights movement and the philosophical divisions that developed, assesses the impact of television coverage of the movement, and traces the eight students' later lives and how their experiences affected them as adults. (Rev: BL 1/1–15/98; SLJ 11/98) [370.19]

9636 Haley, Alex. *Roots* (9–12). 1976, Doubleday $25.00 (0-385-03787-2); paper $7.99 (0-440-17464-3). A thoroughly researched history of a black American's family from Africa to slavery in the United States, ending with the author's own generation. (Rev: BL 9/86) [920]

9637 Hansen, Joyce, and Gary McGowan. *Breaking Ground, Breaking Silence: The Story of New York's African Burial Ground* (8–12). 1998, Holt $19.95 (0-8050-5012-4). The graphic story of the finding, in 1991, of the mid-18th-century African Burial Ground in Manhattan and what it reveals about the lives of slaves in New York. (Rev: BL 5/15/98; HBG 10/98; SLJ 5/98; VOYA 8/98) [974.7]

9638 Harris, Phyllis Y. *From the Soul: Stories of Great Black Parents and the Lives They Gave Us* (9–12). Illus. 2001, Putnam $24.95 (0-399-14706-3). This book contains profiles of 10 African American men and women from various backgrounds and locales who describe their solid family relationships and the strength and love they gained from them. (Rev: BL 9/1/01) [30685]

9639 Haskins, Jim. *Separate but Not Equal: The Dream and the Struggle* (7–10). Illus. 1998, Scholastic paper $15.95 (0-590-45910-4). A history of African Americans' struggle for equality in education beginning from the time of slavery, with coverage of key court cases and incidents and the beliefs of such leaders as W. E. B. Du Bois and Booker T. Washington. (Rev: BL 2/15/98; HBG 9/98; SLJ 2/98; VOYA 10/98) [379.2]

9640 Hauser, Pierre. *Great Ambitions: From the "Separate but Equal" Doctrine to the Birth of the NAACP (1896–1909)* (7–10). Series: Milestones in Black American History. 1995, Chelsea $21.95 (0-7910-2264-1); paper $9.95 (0-7910-2690-6). The history of African Americans at the end of the 19th and beginning of the 20th century, with coverage of such political and cultural pioneers as W. E. B. Du Bois, Charles Chesnutt, Paul Laurence Dunbar, and Scott Joplin. (Rev: BL 2/15/95) [323.1]

9641 Hemphill, Paul. *The Ballad of Little River: A Tale of Race and Restless Youth in the Rural South* (10–12). 2000, Free Pr. $25.00 (0-684-85682-4). For mature readers, this is a graphic account of how racial violence erupted in a small Alabama town in 1997. (Rev: BL 4/15/00) [976.1]

9642 Henry, Christopher. *Forever Free: From the Emancipation Proclamation to the Civil Rights Bill of 1875 (1863–1875)* (7–10). Series: Milestones in Black American History. 1995, Chelsea LB $21.95 (0-7910-2253-6); paper $8.95 (0-7910-2679-5). The history of African Americans during Reconstruction, covering the tearing down of racial barriers and the journey from political impotence to civil power. (Rev: BL 7/95; SLJ 10/95) [323.1]

9643 Hinds, Patricia Mignon, ed. *Essence: 25 Years Celebrating Black Women* (9–12). 1995, Abrams $35.00 (0-8109-3256-3). A celebration of one of the most important publications for African American women, with excellent photography and articles by poets, writers, and scholars. (Rev: BL 11/1/95) [305.48]

9644 Hine, Darlene Clark. *The Path to Equality: From the Scottsboro Case to the Breaking of Baseball's Color Barrier* (7–10). Series: Milestones in Black American History. 1995, Chelsea LB $19.95 (0-7910-2251-X); paper $9.95 (0-7910-2677-9). This section of African American history covers the Great Depression and World War II, and features the accomplishments of individuals including Marian Anderson, Thurgood Marshall, A. Philip Randolph, and Jackie Robinson. (Rev: BL 8/95) [973]

9645 Holliday, Laurel, ed. *Dreaming in Color, Living in Black and White: Our Own Stories of Growing Up Black in America* (8–12). 2000, Pocket paper $4.99 (0-671-04127-4). This is a moving collection of first-person accounts by African Americans who tell of the racism they faced while growing up. (Rev: BL 2/15/00; SLJ 4/00; VOYA 4/00) [305.896]

9646 Hooks, Bell. *Rock My Soul: Black People and Self-Esteem* (11–12). 2003, Atria $23.00 (0-7434-5605-X). This fascinating study, suitable for mature teens, examines the roots of the low self-esteem that blights the lives of so many African Americans. (Rev: BL 1/1–15/03) [306]

9647 Horton, James Oliver, and Lois Horton. *Hard Road to Freedom: The Story of African America* (10–12). Illus. 2001, Rutgers Univ. Pr. $52.00 (0-8135-2850-X); paper $22.00 (0-8135-2851-8). This scholarly but accessible account traces the struggles and contributions of African Americans in America from the days of slavery to the present. (Rev: BL 12/15/00) [973]

9648 Hurmence, Belinda, ed. *Slavery Time When I Was Chillun* (8–12). Illus. 1997, Putnam $9.99 (0-399-23194-3). A disturbing collection of 12 slave narratives that give firsthand accounts of brutality, family separation, and hard labor, as well as some of kindly masters and happy times. (Rev: BL 3/15/98) [975]

9649 Hutchinson, Earl Ofari. *Beyond O.J.: Race, Sex, and Class Lessons for America* (9–12). 1996, Middle Passage $19.95 (1-881032-12-4). A discussion of the implications of the Simpson case regarding race, class, and sex in America. (Rev: BL 12/15/95) [305.8]

9650 Johnson, Paula. *Inner Lives: Voices of African American Women in Prison* (10–12). Illus. 2003, New York Univ. $29.95 (0-8147-4254-8). Best suited for mature teens, this fascinating study examines the lives of African American women in prison, offering interviews with incarcerated black women as well as an overview of the justice system that put them behind bars. (Rev: BL 3/15/03) [365]

9651 Johnson, Venice, ed. *Heart Full of Grace* (10–12). 1995, Simon & Schuster $21.00 (0-684-81428-5). An interesting collection of words of inspiration from African Americans, mostly from the 20th century. (Rev: BL 11/15/95; SLJ 5/96) [808.88]

9652 Jones, Charisse, and Kumea Shorter-Gooden. *Shifting: The Double Lives of Black Women in America* (10–12). 2003, HarperCollins $25.95 (0-06-009054-5). An exploration of African American women's techniques of coping with the challenges of sexism, racism, and false expectations. (Rev: BL 9/15/03) [306.7]

9653 *Keeping the Faith: Stories of Love, Courage, Healing, and Hope from Black America* (10–12). Ed. by Tavis Smiley. 2002, Doubleday $22.95 (0-385-50514-0). A collection of inspiring essays recounting how African Americans have overcome a variety of obstacles. (Rev: BL 11/15/02) [973]

9654 Kimbro, Dennis. *What Keeps Me Standing: Letters from Black Grandmothers on Peace, Hope, and Inspiration* (10–12). 2003, Doubleday $23.95 (0-385-50635-X). This collection of letters, prayers, poems, and scriptures from black grandmothers around the world offers valuable advice for living that will inspire people of all races. (Rev: BL 4/15/03) [305.896]

9655 King, Martin Luther, Jr. *Strength to Love* (10–12). 1985, Fortress paper $16.00 (0-8006-1441-0). A collection of sermons against injustice and racism. [151]

9656 King, Martin Luther, Jr. *A Testament of Hope: The Essential Writings of Martin Luther King, Jr.* (9–12). Ed. by James Melvin Washington. 1986, Harper & Row paper $23.00 (0-06-064691-8). This source contains the most important writing of King arranged by such topics as sermons, essays, and interviews. (Rev: SLJ 8/86) [323.1]

9657 King, Martin Luther, Jr. *Why We Can't Wait* (7–12). 1988, NAL paper $6.95 (0-451-62675-3). A

history of the black civil rights movement up to the struggle in Birmingham, Alabama. [323.4]

9658 King, Martin Luther, Jr. *The Words of Martin Luther King, Jr.* (7–12). Illus. 1983, Newmarket $15.95 (0-937858-28-5). A selection from the writings and speeches of Dr. King that covers a great number of topics. [323.4]

9659 King, Wilma. *Toward the Promised Land: From Uncle Tom's Cabin to the Onset of the Civil War (1851–1861)* (7–10). Series: Milestones in Black American History. 1995, Chelsea paper $9.95 (0-7910-2691-4). This work examines the major trends and personalities in the struggle to end slavery before the Civil War, with material on Frederick Douglass, Sojourner Truth, Harriet Beecher Stowe, and John Brown. (Rev: BL 7/95; SLJ 10/95; VOYA 12/95) [973]

9660 Kleinman, Joseph, and Eileen Kurtis-Kleinman. *Life on an African Slave Ship* (6–10). Series: The Way People Live. 2000, Lucent LB $27.45 (1-56006-653-9). The author uses quotations from primary sources and many illustrations in this portrayal of the terrible conditions endured by slaves bound for America. (Rev: BL 3/1/01; SLJ 5/01) [973.6]

9661 Kotlowitz, Alex. *The Other Side of the River: A Story of Two Towns, a Death, and America's Dilemma* (10–12). 1998, Doubleday $24.95 (0-385-47720-1). Race relations in two small neighboring lake towns in Michigan are explored in the author's investigation of the unsolved 1991 murder of a black teenager who dared to defy racial barriers. (Rev: BL 12/1/97; SLJ 6/98; VOYA 12/98) [305.8]

9662 Latty, Yvonne, and Ron Tarver. *We Were There: A Celebration of African American Veterans from World War II to the War in Iraq* (9–12). Illus. 2004, HarperCollins $23.95 (0-06-054217-9). These short pieces, with photographs of the writers then and now, tell the story of African American combat veterans in wars from World War II to the war in Iraq. (Rev: BL 2/15/04) [355]

9663 Lemann, Nicholas. *The Promised Land: The Great Black Migration and How It Changed America* (9–12). 1991, Knopf $24.95 (0-394-56004-3). Focusing on individual experiences, the author traces the movement of blacks from the rural South to the promise of a new life in the urban North during and after World War I. (Rev: BL 3/1/91*) [973.9]

9664 Lester, Julius. *From Slave Ship to Freedom Road* (5–10). Illus. 1998, Dial $17.99 (0-8037-1893-4). This book combines art, history, and commentary to produce a graphically gripping history of slavery. (Rev: BL 2/15/98; HBG 9/98; SLJ 2/98*) [759.13]

9665 *Let Nobody Turn Us Around: Voices of Resistance, Reform, and Renewal: An African American Anthology* (9–12). Ed. by Manning Marable and

Leith Mullings. 2000, Rowman & Littlefield $35.00 (0-8476-9930-7). This is an excellent collection of primary sources in African American history from slavery and abolition to the present, with valuable introductions for each section. (Rev: BL 2/15/00) [973]

9666 Levine, Ellen. *Freedom's Children: Young Civil Rights Activists Tell Their Own Stories* (6–12). 1993, Avon paper $4.99 (0-380-72114-7). In this collection of oral histories, 30 African Americans who, as children or teenagers, were part of the civil rights struggles in the 1950s–1960s South recall their experiences. (Rev: BL 12/15/92*; SLJ 3/93*) [973]

9667 Lusane, Clarence. *No Easy Victories: Black Americans and the Vote* (8–12). Illus. Series: African-American Experience. 1996, Watts LB $25.00 (0-531-11270-5). This history of African Americans' struggle for the right to vote begins with the Revolutionary War and continues through the Civil War, Reconstruction, the New Deal, and the Voting Rights Acts of 1965, and on to Jesse Jackson's bid for the Democratic nomination for president and the struggles of the early 1990s. (Rev: BL 2/15/97; SLJ 4/97) [323.1]

9668 McKissack, Patricia, and Fredrick McKissack. *Black Hands, White Sails: The Story of African-American Whalers* (6–10). Illus. 1999, Scholastic paper $15.95 (0-590-48313-7). This account of African American involvement in the whaling industry from colonial times through the 19th century also touches on the abolitionist movement, the Underground Railroad, and the Civil War. (Rev: BCCB 11/99; BL 9/1/99; BR 9–10/99; HB 11–12/99; HBG 4/00; VOYA 2/00) [639.2]

9669 Meltzer, Milton. *The Black Americans: A History in Their Own Words, 1619–1983* (7–10). 1984, Crowell paper $10.95 (0-06-446055-X). As told through letters, speeches, articles, and other original sources, this is a history of black people in America. [305.8]

9670 *Mending the World: Stories of Family by Contemporary Black Writers* (10–12). Ed. by Rosemarie Robotham. Illus. 2003, Basic $25.00 (0-465-07062-0). In both fiction and nonfiction, leading black authors paint a picture of happy, well-adjusted African American family life that is often overlooked in the popular media. (Rev: BL 2/1/03) [305.890]

9671 Miller, James, ed. *American Slavery* (6–12). Illus. Series: Complete History Of. 2001, Greenhaven LB $99.00 (0-7377-0424-1). This anthology provides a well-organized and balanced look at slavery in America and includes contributions on a variety of topics by writers including Frederick Douglass and Nat Turner. (Rev: BL 11/1/01; SLJ 8/01) [973.04]

9672 Morrison, Toni. *Remember: The Journey to School Integration* (5–12). 2004, Houghton $18.00 (0-618-39740-X). Through a series of amazing photographs and a text by Morrison, this aspect of the civil rights movement is covered with material on the leaders but mainly on the thoughts and feelings of the young people pictured. (Rev: BL 4/15/04; SLJ 6/04) [379.2]

9673 *My Soul Has Grown Deep: Classics of Early African-American Literature* (9–12). Ed. by John Edgar Wideman. 2001, Running $29.95 (0-7624-1035-3). A large book that contains a generous anthology (many are full-length books) of the works of 11 important 18th- and 19th-century African American writers, among them Booker T. Washington, James Weldon Johnson, and W. E. B. Du Bois. (Rev: BL 9/15/01) [810]

9674 Myers, Walter Dean. *One More River to Cross: An African American Photograph Album* (8–12). 1995, Harcourt $40.00 (0-15-100191-X); paper $18.00 (0-15-202021-7). An oversize volume filled with period photographs that chronicles the history of African Americans from slavery to today. (Rev: SLJ 8/96; VOYA 6/96) [779]

9675 Nash, Sunny. *Bigmama Didn't Shop at Woolworth's* (10–12). 1996, Texas A & M Univ. Pr. $19.95 (0-890-96716-4). A collection of vignettes by an African American woman who remembers growing up in the 1950s in a segregated neighborhood in Bryan, Texas, and the poverty, prejudice, and indignities of the time. (Rev: SLJ 12/96) [323.4]

9676 Okwu, Julian. *Face Forward: Young African American Men in a Critical Age* (10–12). 1997, Chronicle paper $19.95 (0-8118-1215-4). This is a photographic essay that describes the lives and work of 39 African American men who have defied traditional stereotypes and lead interesting, productive lives. (Rev: BL 6/1–15/97; SLJ 2/98; VOYA 10/97) [323.1]

9677 Oliver, Kitty. *Multicolored Memories of a Black Southern Girl* (10–12). Illus. 2001, Univ. Press of Kentucky $25.00 (0-8131-2208-2). The author, an African American who came of age in the 1960s, describes the civil and women's rights movements of the time and her participation in them. (Rev: BL 10/1/01) [975.9]

9678 Peltak, Jennifer. *The History of African-American Colleges and Universities* (7–12). Illus. Series: American Mosaic: African-American Contributions. 2003, Chelsea LB $22.95 (0-7910-7269-X). This volume looks at the history of black colleges and universities, enrollment trends, and the struggle for equality in education. (Rev: BL 10/15/03; HBG 4/04) [378.7]

9679 Potter, Joan, and Constance Claytor. *African-American Firsts* (9–12). 1994, Pinto paper $14.95 (0-9632476-1-1). Celebrates African American contributions to history and culture, from business and government to the theater and visual arts. (Rev: BL 1/15/94; SLJ 8/94) [973]

9680 Raboteau, Albert J. *African-American Religion* (9–12). Series: Religion in American Life. 1999, Oxford $22.00 (0-19-510680-6). The author explores religious freedom as a basic part of American history and society, traces the influence of black churches in America from colonial times to the present, and examines the contributions of varied religious traditions to African American culture and identity, particularly in the struggle against racism. (Rev: BL 9/15/99; SLJ 8/99) [261.1]

9681 *Remembering Jim Crow: African Americans Tell About Life in the Segregated South* (10–12). Ed. by William Chafe et al. Illus. 2001, New Pr. $55.00 (1-56584-697-4). The book and accompanying CD give eyewitness accounts of the brutal segregation policies known as Jim Crowism and of the indignities they involved. (Rev: BL 10/1/01) [305.896]

9682 *Reparations for American Slavery* (6–12). Ed. by James Haley. Series: At Issue. 2004, Gale LB $27.45 (0-7377-1340-2). The arguments for and against the payments or other compensation for the years of slavery to present-day African Americans are the subject of this collection of writings. (Rev: BL 2/15/04) [326]

9683 Robeson, Paul, Jr. *Paul Robeson, Jr. Speaks to America* (9–12). 1993, Rutgers Univ. Pr. $25.00 (0-8135-1985-3). Essays precisely defining the issues at stake in "the struggle between the mosaic and the melting pot" and the nation's angry cultural wars. (Rev: BL 6/1–15/93) [305.8]

9684 Robinson, Randall. *The Debt: What America Owes to Blacks* (10–12). 2000, Dutton $24.95 (0-525-94524-5). In this adult treatise, the author makes a case for affirmative action and increased reparations to African Americans for past injustices. (Rev: BL 1/1–15/00) [305.8]

9685 Rose, Tricia. *Longing to Tell: Black Women Talk About Sexuality and Intimacy* (10–12). 2003, Farrar $25.00 (0-374-19061-5). In first-person accounts, African American women reveal candid information about sexuality, marriage and divorce, AIDS, interracial dating, and sexual abuse; for mature teens. (Rev: BL 5/15/03) [306.7]

9686 *A Small Nation of People: W. E. B. Du Bois and African American Portraits of Progress* (10–12). Illus. 2003, HarperCollins $24.95 (0-06-052342-5). This collection of 150 photographs, originally selected by Du Bois for an exhibit on African American life at the 1900 International Exposition in Paris, offers a valuable look at the lives of black Americans in the late 19th century. (Rev: BL 10/15/03) [305.896]

9687 *Sound the Trumpet! Messages to Empower African American Men* (10–12). Ed. by Darryl D. Sims. 2003, Judson paper $14.00 (0-8170-1437-3). The unique challenges — both social and spiritual — facing African American men are examined in this collection of sermons by such well-known black clergymen as Otis Moss, Ralph West, Jeremiah Wright Jr., and Charles E. Booth. (Rev: BL 2/15/03) [248.8]

9688 Spangenburg, Ray, and Diane Moser. *The African-American Experience* (10–12). Series: American Historic Places. 1996, Facts on File $25.00 (0-8160-3400-1). This book takes readers on a tour of 10 historic sites that have played a significant role in African American history, among them Little Rock Central High School, the African Meeting House in Boston, and the homes of Mary McLeod Bethune, Frederick Douglass, and Harriet Tubman. [917.3]

9689 *These Hands I Know: African-American Writers on Family* (10–12). Ed. by Afaa Michael Weaver. 2002, Sarabande paper $16.95 (1-889330-72-8). A wide-ranging portrait of African American family life is painted in this collection of essays by such well-known writers and poets as Henry Louis Gates, Gwendolyn Brooks, and Alice Walker. (Rev: BL 8/02) [814]

9690 Thomas, Hugh. *The Slave Trade: The Story of the Atlantic Slave Trade, 1440–1870* (10–12). Illus. 1997, Simon & Schuster $37.50 (0-684-81063-8). Every aspect of the slave trade is covered from the early 16th century to its abolition in the early 20th century, with particular attention to the economics and politics of slavery and its worldwide social acceptance and the widespread involvement of governments and people everywhere. (Rev: BL 10/1/97; SLJ 7/98) [326]

9691 Tilove, Jonathan, and Michael Falco. *Along Martin Luther King: Travels on Black America's Main Street* (10–12). Illus. 2003, Random $29.95 (1-4000-6080-X). Essays and photographs document the people and places encountered on cross-country visits to nearly 500 streets named in honor of the civil rights leader. (Rev: BL 11/1/03) [973]

9692 Ugwu-Oju, Dympna. *What Will My Mother Say: A Tribal African Girl Comes of Age in America* (9–12). 1995, Bonus $24.95 (1-56625-042-0). An African American mother born in Nigeria struggles with cultural conflicts while raising her American-born daughter. (Rev: BL 11/1/95) [306]

9693 *Unchained Memories: Readings from Slave Narratives* (10–12). Illus. 2003, Little, Brown $24.95 (0-8212-2842-0). Adapted from the HBO documentary of the same name, this is a collection of first-person accounts of former slaves, gathered during the Depression. (Rev: BL 1/1–15/03) [306.3]

9694 Van Peebles, Mario, et al. *Panther: A Pictorial History of the Black Panthers and the Story Behind the Film* (8–12). 1995, Newmarket paper $16.95 (1-55704-227-6). The first part of this heavily illustrated book recounts the beginnings of the Black Panther Party and its eventual collapse; the second half describes the making of the movie about the party. (Rev: VOYA 2/96) [973]

9695 Weisbrot, Robert. *Marching Toward Freedom* (7–12). Series: Milestones in Black American History. 1994, Chelsea paper $8.95 (0-7910-2682-5). This history covers African American affairs from the founding of the Southern Christian Leadership Conference to the assassination of Malcolm X (1957–1965), with material on Martin Luther King, Jr., James Farmer, Elijah Muhammad, and Malcolm X, among others. (Rev: BL 11/15/94; SLJ 9/94; VOYA 10/94) [973]

9696 White, Deborah Gray. *Too Heavy a Load: Black Women in Defense of Themselves,1894–1994* (11–12). Illus. 1998, Norton $25.95 (0-393-04667-2). History professor Deborah Gray White focuses on conflicting concerns about race, gender, and class in her examination of five organizations formed by African American women. (Rev: BL 11/15/98) [305]

9697 Whittemore, Katharine, and Gerald Marzorati. *Voices in Black and White: Writings on Race in America from Harper's Magazine* (9–12). 1992, Franklin Square LB $21.95 (1-879957-07-8); paper $14.95 (1-879957-06-X). This collection of articles on the American obsession with race includes writings by Mark Twain, William Faulkner, James Baldwin, Shelby Steele, and Jesse Jackson. (Rev: BL 11/15/92) [305.8]

9698 Wiggins, David K., and Patrick B. Miller. *The Unlevel Playing Field: A Documentary History of the African American Experience in Sport* (10–12). Illus. 2003, Univ. of Illinois Pr. $39.95 (0-252-02820-1). Drawing heavily on primary source materials, the authors paint a thoughtful portrait of black Americans' experiences in sports. (Rev: BL 4/15/03) [796]

9699 Williams, Juan, and Quinton Dixie. *This Far by Faith: Stories from the African-American Religious Experience* (10–12). Illus. 2003, Morrow $29.95 (0-06-018863-4). A study of the historical and contemporary importance of religion in the lives of African Americans, with photographs. (Rev: BL 1/1–15/03; VOYA 6/03) [200]

9700 Williams, Lena. *It's the Little Things: The Everyday Interactions That Get Under the Skin of Blacks and Whites* (10–12). 2000, Harcourt $22.00 (0-15-100407-2). The everyday misunderstandings and incivilities that occur between blacks and whites are chronicled in this book about prejudice today. (Rev: BL 9/1/00) [305.8]

9701 Woodson, Jacqueline, ed. *A Way Out of No Way: Writings About Growing Up Black in America* (8–12). Illus. 1996, Holt $15.95 (0-8050-4570-8). A fine collection of prose and poetry, fiction and non-fiction about growing up in America, from some of the best African American writers, among them James Baldwin, Paul Beatty, Jamaica Kincaid, and Langston Hughes. (Rev: BL 2/15/97; BR 11–12/97; SLJ 7/97; VOYA 6/97) [808.898]

9702 Wright, Kai. *Soldiers of Freedom: An Illustrated History of African Americans in the Armed Forces* (10–12). Illus. 2002, Black Dog & Leventhal $19.98 (1-57912-253-1). A well-illustrated presentation of the motivations and contributions of African Americans serving in the country's military. (Rev: BL 9/1/02) [355]

9703 Young, Yolanda. *On Our Way to Beautiful: A Family Memoir* (10–12). 2002, Villard $21.95 (0-375-50493-1). In this inspiring coming-of-age memoir, the African American author tells how being a member of a large, loving family gave her the strength to survive many challenges and tragedies. (Rev: BL 1/1–15/02; SLJ 9/02) [976.3]

Asian Americans

9704 Bandon, Alexandra. *Chinese Americans* (6–12). Series: Footsteps to America. 1994, Silver Burdett LB $13.95 (0-02-768149-1). A look at Chinese people in the United States, from their first large migration in the mid-19th century to the 1990s. (Rev: BL 10/15/94; SLJ 11/94; VOYA 2/95) [973]

9705 Bandon, Alexandra. *Filipino Americans* (6–10). Series: Footsteps to America. 1993, Macmillan LB $13.95 (0-02-768143-2). Examines why Filipino Americans left their homeland and describes their culture, politics, education, religion, and holidays in the United States. (Rev: BL 12/15/93; SLJ 12/93) [973]

9706 Chang, Iris. *The Chinese in America: A Narrative History* (10–12). 2003, Viking $29.95 (0-670-03123-2). Chang chronicles three main waves of Chinese immigrants to America — during the California gold rush, escaping the Communist rise to power in 1949, and the late-20th-century influx triggered by improving U.S.-China relations. (Rev: BL 4/1/03) [304.8]

9707 Chow, Claire S., ed. *Leaving Deep Water: The Lives of Asian American Women at the Crossroads of Two Cultures* (10–12). 1998, Dutton paper $24.95 (0-525-94075-8). In a series of personal narratives, Asian American women describe cultural conflicts, feelings of being different, sexism, and the generation gap. (Rev: BL 3/15/98; SLJ 1/99) [305.8]

9708 Dudley, William, ed. *Asian Americans* (7–12). Series: Opposing Viewpoints: American History.

1997, Greenhaven LB $32.45 (1-56510-524-9). A collection of documents tracing attitudes and policies toward Asian immigrants and Asian American citizens from the 1850s to the present. (Rev: BL 12/15/96) [973]

9709 *Freedomways Reader: Prophets in Their Own Country* (10–12). Ed. by Esther Cooper Jackson and Constance Pohl. Illus. 2000, Westview $28.00 (0-8133-6769-7). Taken chiefly from the pages of the quarterly magazine *Freedomways,* these articles and essays chronicle African American history and culture with contributions from such writers as James Baldwin, Martin Luther King, Jr., W. E. B. Du Bois, Derek Wolcott, and Alice Walker. (Rev: BL 2/15/00) [973]

9710 Galang, M. Evelina. *Her Wild American Self* (10–12). 1996, Coffee House paper $12.95 (1-56689-040-3). In a series of essays, the author tells of her life as a Filipino American woman, her cultural background, and her assimilation into American life. (Rev: SLJ 11/96) [304]

9711 Hoobler, Dorothy, and Thomas Hoobler. *The Chinese American Family Album* (6–10). 1994, Oxford LB $25.00 (0-19-508130-7). The text is excerpted from letters, journals, oral histories, and newspaper accounts of Chinese Americans who describe life in China, their journey to North America, the difficulties they encountered, and the jobs they took. (Rev: BL 4/1/94; SLJ 5/94; VOYA 2/95) [973]

9712 Kessler, Lauren. *Stubborn Twig: Three Generations in the Life of a Japanese American Family* (9–12). 1993, Random $25.00 (0-679-41426-6). Kessler charts the history of a Japanese American family from 1908, when Masuo Yasui and his brothers settled in the Hood River Valley, through World War II and evacuation to internment camps, to the present day. (Rev: BL 11/15/93; SLJ 5/94) [973]

9713 Kim, Elaine H., and Eui-Young Yu. *East to America: Korean American Life Stories* (10–12). 1996, New Pr. $25.00 (1-56584-297-9). Using quotations from 38 interviews, this book presents a good cross-section of Korean American life in all strata of U.S. society. (Rev: SLJ 11/96) [305.895]

9714 Nam, Vickie, ed. *Yell-Oh Girls! Emerging Voices Explore Culture, Identity, and Growing up Asian American* (8–12). Illus. 2001, HarperCollins paper $13.00 (0-06-095944-4). An anthology of fiction and poetry written by Asian American high school and college students, revealing their feelings about topics including heritage, stereotypes, adoption, and interracial dating. (Rev: BL 7/01; SLJ 10/01; VOYA 2/02) [305.235]

9715 Ng, Franklin. *The Taiwanese Americans* (10–12). Series: The New Americans. 1998, Greenwood $39.95 (0-313-29762-2). After an introduc-

tion to Taiwan, this book describes the immigration of Taiwanese to the United States principally after 1965, their reception here, and their present life and contributions. (Rev: SLJ 11/98) [973]

9716 St. Pierre, Stephanie. *Teenage Refugees from Cambodia Speak Out* (7–12). 1995, Rosen LB $16.95 (0-8239-1848-3). Grim stories of the escape from the "killing fields" and powerful testimony to the reality of refugee life. (Rev: BL 5/15/95; SLJ 5/95) [973]

9717 She, Colleen. *Teenage Refugees from China Speak Out* (7–12). Series: In Their Own Voices. 1995, Rosen LB $16.95 (0-8239-1847-5). Interviews with native Chinese teenagers who are now living in the United States. (Rev: BL 6/1–15/95; SLJ 5/95) [305.23]

9718 Springstubb, Tricia. *The Vietnamese Americans* (6–12). Illus. Series: Immigrants in America. 2002, Gale $27.45 (1-56006-964-3). A look at how this ethnic group is faring in America, with stories of individual immigrants adding interest. (Rev: BL 4/1/02; SLJ 6/02) [305.895]

9719 Takaki, Ronald. *Ethnic Islands: The Emergence of Urban Chinese America* (6–10). Series: Asian American Experience. 1994, Chelsea LB $19.95 (0-7910-2180-7). First-person accounts of the Chinese American experience in the 20th century. (Rev: BL 9/15/94; SLJ 9/94) [973]

9720 Takaki, Ronald. *From Exiles to Immigrants: The Refugees from Southeast Asia* (6–10). Series: Asian American Experience. 1995, Chelsea LB $19.95 (0-7910-2185-8). Personal histories of Southeast Asian refugees in the United States. (Rev: BL 8/95; VOYA 12/95) [978]

9721 Takaki, Ronald. *From the Land of Morning Calm: The Koreans in America* (6–10). Series: Asian American Experience. 1994, Chelsea LB $19.95 (0-7910-2181-5). Oral histories and local documents challenge stereotypes that plague Korean Americans. (Rev: BL 9/1/94; SLJ 9/94; VOYA 12/94) [973]

9722 Takaki, Ronald. *In the Heart of Filipino America: Immigrants from the Pacific Isles* (6–10). Series: Asian American Experience. 1994, Chelsea LB $19.95 (0-7910-2187-4). A historic overview of Filipinos in the United States. (Rev: BL 12/15/94; VOYA 4/95) [973]

9723 Takaki, Ronald. *India in the West: South Asians in America* (6–10). Series: Asian American Experience. 1994, Chelsea LB $19.95 (0-7910-2186-6). This overview of the Asian Indian experience in the United States describes how, when, and why South Asians came to this country and the problems they have confronted. (Rev: BL 12/15/94; SLJ 3/95) [970]

9724 Takaki, Ronald T. *Strangers From a Different Shore: A History of Asian Americans.* Rev. ed.

(10–12). 1998, Little, Brown paper $16.95 (0-316-83130-1). Chronicles the diverse experiences of different waves of Asian immigrants to the United States, from early-19th-century Chinese workers on the transcontinental railroad to the late-20th-century arrivals from war-torn Southeast Asia. [305.8]

9725 Wapner, Kenneth. *Teenage Refugees from Vietnam Speak Out* (7–12). Series: In Their Own Voices. 1995, Rosen LB $16.95 (0-8239-1842-4). Interviews with Vietnamese teenagers who are now living in the United States. (Rev: BL 6/1–15/95; SLJ 5/95) [305.23]

9726 Yamaguchi, Yoji. *A Student's Guide to Japanese American Genealogy* (8–12). 1996, Oryx $29.95 (0-89774-979-0). This book describes Japanese immigration to the United States and where the newcomers settled, followed by information on general genealogical research and on researching Japanese Americans' genealogies. (Rev: VOYA 8/96) [973]

9727 Zurlo, Tony. *The Japanese Americans* (6–12). Series: Immigrants in America. 2003, Gale LB $27.45 (1-59018-001-1). From Hawaii's sugar plantations to California's truck farms, this is the story of Japanese Americans and how they fought for full acceptance in America. (Rev: BL 11/15/03) [973]

Hispanic Americans

9728 Anton, Alex, and Roger E. Hernandez. *Cubans in America: A Vibrant History of a People in Exile* (10–12). Illus. 2002, Kensington $30.00 (1-57566-593-X). The centuries-old history of Cuban immigration to the United States — most of it relating to the island's changing political climate — is covered in detail in this fascinating book. (Rev: BL 5/15/02) [305.868]

9729 Bandon, Alexandra. *Mexican Americans* (6–10). Series: Footsteps to America. 1993, Macmillan LB $14.95 (0-02-768142-4). A look at Mexico and the culture of Mexican American immigrants in the United States, with first-person narratives of immigrant experiences. (Rev: BL 12/15/93; SLJ 12/93; VOYA 2/94) [305.868]

9730 Carlson, Lori M., ed. *Barrio Streets Carnival Dreams: Three Generations of Latino Artisty* (9–12). 1996, Holt $15.95 (0-8050-4120-6). In this exploration of Hispanic cultural traditions, three generations of 20th-century American artists of Caribbean, Mexican, and South American ancestry describe their work, the difficulties of assimilation, and their desire to preserve Latino culture. (Rev: BR 1–2/97; SLJ 8/96; VOYA 12/96) [973]

9731 Cerar, K. Melissa. *Teenage Refugees from Nicaragua Speak Out* (7–12). Series: In Their Own Voices. 1995, Rosen LB $16.95 (0-8239-1849-1). The horror of the contra war, after the corrupt rule

of the Somoza family was ended by the Sandinistas, is recalled by Nicaraguan teens who fled their country, leaving their families, to seek refuge in the United States. (Rev: BL 6/1–15/95) [973]

9732 Cockcroft, James D. *The Hispanic Struggle for Social Justice: The Hispanic Experience in the Americas* (8–12). Series: Hispanic Experience in the Americas. 1994, Watts paper $24.00 (0-531-11185-7). After a discussion of the diverse experiences of Mexican Americans, Puerto Ricans, and other Latinos in this country, the author examines their ethnic history and struggles around labor, immigration, civil rights, and women's rights issues. (Rev: BL 2/1/95) [305.868]

9733 Cofer, Judith O., ed. *Riding Low on the Streets of Gold* (6–12). 2003, Arte Publico $14.95 (1-55885-380-4). Latino writers consider issues close to teen hearts in this collection of fiction, poetry, and memoirs. (Rev: BL 12/1/03; SLJ 6/04) [810]

9734 Cofer, Judith O. *The Year of Our Revolution* (9–12). 1998, Arte Publico $16.95 (1-55885-224-7). This collection of stories, poems, and fables explores the experiences of Puerto Rican Americans, focusing in particular on the cultural disconnect between Puerto Rican-born immigrants to the United States and their American-born children. (Rev: BL 7/98; HBG 3/99; VOYA 6/99) [863]

9735 Gay, Kathlyn. *Leaving Cuba: From Operation Pedro Pan to Elian* (6–12). Illus. 2000, Twenty-First Century LB $22.90 (0-7613-1466-0). The plight of young Elian Gonzalez brought attention to Cubans' efforts to escape their oppressive regime and the uncertain welcome they face in the United States. (Rev: BL 3/1/01; HBG 3/01; SLJ 1/01; VOYA 6/01) [362.87]

9736 Gilb, Dagoberte. *Gritos* (10–12). 2003, Grove $23.00 (0-8021-1742-2). New insights into Mexican American life and culture can be found in this very readable collection of essays by Dagoberte Gilb, best known as a short story writer. (Rev: BL 5/15/03) [813]

9737 Gonzalez, Juan. *Harvest of Empire: The History of Latinos in America* (10–12). 2000, Viking $27.95 (0-670-86720-9). For advanced students, this is a history of Latinos in the United States, with material on immigration from the Caribbean, Mexico, Central America, and South America. (Rev: BL 2/15/00) [973]

9738 Gonzalez-Pando, Miguel. *The Cuban Americans* (10–12). Series: The New Americans. 1998, Greenwood $39.95 (0-313-29824-6). Beginning with a history of Cuba including Castro's regime, this book tells why and how Cubans left their homeland and looks at their reception in the U.S. and their current situation. (Rev: BR 11–12/98; SLJ 10/98; VOYA 12/98) [305.868]

9739 *Las Mamis: Favorite Latino Authors Remember Their Mothers* (10–12). Ed. by Esmeralda Santiago and Joie Davidow. Illus. 2000, Knopf $20.00 (0-375-40879-7). In these 14 memoirs, Latin American authors talk about their mothers—some with love, others with guilt, outrage, or humor. (Rev: BL 3/15/00) [306.874]

9740 Martinez, Ruben. *Crossing Over: A Mexican Family on the Migrant Trail* (10–12). Illus. 2001, Holt $25.00 (0-8050-4908-8). Using an extended Mexican family as an example, the author describes Mexican immigrants, legal and otherwise, and the terrors and small victories that their status produces. (Rev: BL 10/15/01; SLJ 6/02) [306.85]

9741 Novas, Himilce. *Everything You Need to Know About Latino History* (9–12). 1994, NAL paper $12.95 (0-452-27100-2). Surveys Latino culture, contributions, and history, including the Spanish-American War and the Mexican War. (Rev: BL 9/15/94) [973]

9742 Olmos, Edward James, et al. *Americanos: Latino Life in the United States* (9–12). 1999, Little, Brown $39.00 (0-316-64914-7); paper $25.00 (0-316-64909-0). Through photographs, essays, poetry, and general commentary in English and Spanish, the life and culture of Hispanic Americans is explored. (Rev: BL 4/1/98) [305.8]

9743 Perez-Brown, Maria. *Mama: Latina Daughters Celebrate Their Mothers* (10–12). Illus. 2003, HarperCollins $27.50 (0-06-008386-7). Inspired by memories of her Puerto Rican-born mother's sacrifices for her children, the author celebrates the lives of other unselfish Latina mothers through the recollections of their daughters. (Rev: BL 5/15/03) [306.874]

9744 Ryskamp, George R., and Peggy Ryskamp. *A Student's Guide to Mexican American Genealogy* (6–10). Series: Oryx Family Tree. 1996, Oryx $24.95 (0-89774-981-2). This book provides an interesting review of Mexican American history as well as an introduction to genealogy and a discussion of nontraditional families. (Rev: SLJ 2/97) [973]

9745 Sonneborn, Liz. *The Cuban Americans* (6–12). Illus. Series: Immigrants in America. 2002, Gale $27.45 (1-56006-902-3). A look at how this ethnic group is faring in America, with stories of individual immigrants adding interest. (Rev: BL 4/1/02) [973]

9746 Sullivan, Charles, ed. *Here Is My Kingdom: Hispanic-American Literature and Art for Young People* (7–12). 1994, Abrams $24.95 (0-8109-3422-1). A collection of Latino prose, poetry, painting, and photography, with profiles of leading figures from Cervantes to singer Gloria Estefan. (Rev: BL 7/94*)

Jewish Americans

9747 Alepher, Joseph, ed. *Encyclopedia of Jewish History: Events and Eras of the Jewish People* (10–12). Illus. 1986, Facts on File $40.00 (0-8160-1220-2). In 100 entries, world Jewish history is detailed with accompanying maps, diagrams, and photographs. (Rev: BL 4/15/86) [909]

9748 Finkelstein, Norman H. *Forged in Freedom: Shaping the Jewish-American Experience* (6–12). Illus. 2002, Jewish Publication Soc. $24.95 (0-8276-0748-2). Text and photographs present an overview of Jews' contributions to the United States, their influence on the culture, and the problems they have faced. (Rev: BL 8/02; HBG 3/03) [973.04]

9749 Frommer, Myrna Katz, and Harvey Frommer. *Growing Up Jewish in America: An Oral History* (9–12). 1995, Harcourt paper $14.35 (0-8032-6900-5). This book resulted from about 100 interviews with Jews who discussed what being a Jew means in contemporary America. [305.8]

9750 Jacoby, Susan. *Half-Jew: A Daughter's Search for Her Family's Buried Past* (10–12). 2000, Scribner $24.00 (0-684-83250-X). The author explores her family's roots and discovers that her father and his siblings all conspired to hide their Jewish backgrounds by converting to Catholicism and marrying Irish Catholics. (Rev: BL 4/1/00) [929]

9751 Schleifer, Jay. *A Student's Guide to Jewish American Genealogy* (7–12). Series: American Family Tree. 1996, Oryx $29.95 (0-89774-977-4). An in-depth survey of Jewish history serves as a framework for realistic genealogical information, with plenty of valuable sources cited. (Rev: SLJ 1/97) [973]

9752 Shamir, Ilana, and Shlomo Shavit, eds. *The Young Reader's Encyclopedia of Jewish History* (5–10). Illus. 1987, Viking $17.95 (0-670-81738-4). From a home for nomadic tribes to the present, this is a history of Israel and the Jewish people in many brief chapters. (Rev: BL 3/15/88; SLJ 2/88) [909]

9753 Stein, Robert. *Jewish Americans* (7–10). Illus. Series: Coming to America. 2003, Barron's $14.95 (0-7641-5626-8). In an absorbing text with compelling illustrations and first-person anecdotes, Stein looks at the reasons for Jewish emigration, the conditions the emigres found when they arrived in the United States, and their contributions to their new country. (Rev: BL 10/15/03*; SLJ 12/03) [973]

9754 Suberman, Stella. *The Jew Store: A Family Memoir* (10–12). 1998, Algonquin $30.95 (1-56512-198-8). Russian immigrant Aaron Bronson moved his family from New York City and opened a store in a tiny Tennessee town in the 1920s. This is the story of the only Jewish family in town as recalled by the youngest member of the family. (Rev: BL 7/98; SLJ 11/98) [305.8]

Native Americans

9755 DeSersa, Esther Black Elk, et al. *Black Elk Lives: Conversations with the Black Elk Family* (10–12). 2000, Univ. of Nebraska Pr. $25.00 (0-8032-3340-X). This book traces the lives and fortunes of the grandchildren and great-grandchildren of the great Lakota wise man Black Elk, who was the subject of the anthropological classic *Black Elk Speaks*. (Rev: BL 11/15/00) [978.004]

9756 Eagle, Adam Fortunate, and Tim Findley. *Heart of the Rock: The Indian Invasion of Alcatraz* (10–12). Illus. 2002, Univ. of Oklahoma Pr. $29.95 (0-8061-3396-1). The 1969 seizure of Alcatraz Island by a small band of Native Americans hoping to call attention to Indian rights is chronicled in this fascinating book. (Rev: BL 3/1/02) [979.4]

9757 Frazier, Ian. *On the Rez* (10–12). 2000, Farrar $25.00 (0-374-22638-5); paper $14.00 (0-312-27859-4). The author describes his experiences and the people he met on the Pine Ridge Reservation in South Dakota. (Rev: BL 11/15/99; SLJ 8/00) [970.004]

9758 *Genocide of the Mind: An Anthology of Native American Writing* (10–12). Ed. by MariJo Moore. 2003, Thunder's Mouth paper $16.95 (1-56025-511-0). This collection of essays by Native American writers, representing more than 25 tribal groups, documents the struggle of native peoples to retain their cultural identity. (Rev: BL 11/1/03) [305.397]

9759 *Here First: Autobiographical Essays by Native American Writers* (10–12). Ed. by Arnold Krupat and Brian Swann. 2000, Random paper $15.95 (0-375-75138-6). Twenty-six contemporary Native American writers describe growing up and finding their identity and culture as Native Americans. (Rev: BL 5/15/00) [810]

9760 Hogan, Linda. *Woman Who Watches over the World: A Native Memoir* (10–12). 2001, Norton $24.95 (0-393-05018-1). As well as a haunting, courageous memoir of an abused Native American girl, this is an indictment of the U.S. government's war on her people. (Rev: BL 5/15/01*) [818]

9761 Nasdijj. *The Blood Runs Like a River Through My Dreams* (10–12). 2000, Houghton $23.00 (0-618-04892-8). The author, who is part Navajo, describes his life, the fate of his people, and the tragic death of his son in this moving and poetic memoir. (Rev: BL 8/00*) [979.1]

9762 Roleff, Tamara L., ed. *Native American Rights* (9–12). Series: Current Controversies. 1997, Greenhaven LB $21.96 (1-56510-685-7); paper $16.20 (1-56510-684-9). This anthology presents a full range of opinions on four controversial issues: Native American culture, resources, sovereignty, and gaming. (Rev: SLJ 3/98) [307.76]

9763 Straub, Deborah G., ed. *Native North American Voices* (6–12). 1997, Gale $55.00 (0-8103-9819-2). This is a collection of important speeches delivered by 20 Native Americans, beginning with one by Joseph Brant in 1794 and ending with the 1944 speech of Ada Deer of the Bureau of Indian Affairs. (Rev: BR 9–10/97; SLJ 11/97) [973]

9764 *Through Indian Eyes: The Untold Story of Native American Peoples* (9–12). 1995, Reader's Digest $40.00 (0-89577-819-X). A heavily-illustrated book that describes the daily experiences, attitudes, and culture of Native Americans. [970.004]

9765 Wright, Ronald. *Stolen Continents: The Americas Through Indian Eyes Since 1492* (9–12). 1992, Houghton paper $16 .00 (0-395-65975-2). A chronicle of the unhappy history of European invasion as seen through the eyes of the Aztecs, Cherokees, Incas, Iroquois, and Mayas. [970.004]

Other Ethnic Groups

9766 Aseel, Maryam Qudrat. *Torn Between Two Cultures: An Afghan-American Woman Speaks Out* (10–12). 2003, Capital $22.95 (1-931868-36-0). Aseel writes engagingly about the impact of current events — most notably the terrorist attacks of 9/11 — on the lives of Muslim Americans in the United States. (Rev: BL 4/15/03) [305.48]

9767 Bandon, Alexandra. *West Indian Americans* (5–10). Series: Footsteps to America. 1994, Silver Burdett LB $13.95 (0-02-768148-3). Describes why some West Indians left their islands to come to the United States, their reception, and their present lifestyles and contributions to their new nation. (Rev: BL 10/15/94; SLJ 12/94) [973]

9768 Brockman, Terra Castiglia. *A Student's Guide to Italian American Genealogy* (7–12). Series: American Family Tree. 1996, Oryx $29.95 (0-89774-973-1). This book, a guide to searching for Italian American ancestors, contains Web sites, computer programs, addresses, and other sources of information. (Rev: SLJ 10/96) [929]

9769 Deignan, Tom. *Irish Americans* (7–10). Illus. Series: Coming to America. 2003, Barron's $14.95 (0-7641-5627-6). An absorbing look at the reasons for Irish emigration, the conditions the emigres found when they arrived in the United States, and their contributions to their new country. (Rev: BL 10/15/03*; SLJ 1/04) [873]

9770 Dezell, Maureen. *Irish America: Coming into Clover* (10–12). Illus. 2001, Doubleday $24.95 (0-385-49595-1). This short book describes the past and present of the Catholic Irish in America and describes their characteristics and accomplishments. (Rev: BL 2/15/01) [305.891]

9771 Franck, Irene M. *The German-American Heritage* (7–12). Illus. 1988, Facts on File $25.00 (0-

8160-1629-1). This book contains not only an account of the progress of Germans in this country but also a brief history of Germany. (Rev: BL 3/15/89; BR 5–6/89) [973]

9772 Halliburton, Warren J. *The West Indian-American Experience* (7–10). 1994, Millbrook LB $23.90 (1-56294-340-5). Tells the story of a Jamaican family's emigration to the United States in the 1980s, the history of the Caribbean, and immigration to the United States. (Rev: BL 4/1/94; SLJ 7/94) [973]

9773 Hossell, Karen Price. *The Irish Americans* (6–12). Series: Immigrants in America. 2003, Gale LB $27.45 (1-56006-752-7). The story of the thousands of Irish people who migrated to America, where they faced discrimination before being assimilated into society and being accepted as true Americans. (Rev: BL 11/15/03) [973]

9774 Johnson, Anne E. *A Student's Guide to British American Genealogy* (7–12). Series: American Family Tree. 1995, Oryx $29.95 (0-89774-982-0). This book gives instructions on how to start a genealogical search, explains English, Scottish, and Welsh history and traditions, and describes names, nobility, clans, and the history of British immigration to America. (Rev: SLJ 4/96) [973]

9775 Katz, William L. *Black Indians: A Hidden Heritage* (7–10). 1986, Macmillan $17.95 (0-689-31196-6). A history of the group that represented a mixture of the Indian and black races and its role in opening up the West. (Rev: BL 6/15/86; SLJ 8/86) [970]

9776 Laurino, Maria. *Were You Always an Italian? Ancestors and Other Icons of Life in Italian America* (10–12). 2000, Norton $23.95 (0-393-04930-2). An interesting, provocative look at Italian Americans, their culture, language, and concerns. (Rev: BL 8/00) [973]

9777 McKenna, Erin. *A Student's Guide to Irish American Genealogy* (7–12). Illus. 1996, Oryx $29.95 (0-89774-976-6). Along with giving practical tips on how to trace Irish ancestors, this book traces Irish history, immigration, Irish culture, and contributions. (Rev: BL 3/1/97; VOYA 4/97) [973]

9778 Moreno, Barry. *Italian Americans* (7–10). Series: Coming to America. 2003, Barron's $14.95 (0-7641-5624-1). This is the story of how and why Italians migrated to this country, their reception, assimilation, and contributions. (Rev: BL 10/15/03; SLJ 1/04) [973]

9779 Naff, Alixa. *The Arab Americans* (6–10). Series: The Immigrant Experience. 1998, Chelsea $21.95 (0-7910-5051-3); paper $9.95 (0-7910-5053-X). After a brief description of Arab culture and homelands, this book describes the cycles of Arab immigration to this country, the reception Arabs received, their new identities and contributions, and famous Arab Americans such as Ralph Nader and Donna Shalala. (Rev: HBG 3/99; SLJ 1/99) [305.8]

9780 Paddock, Lisa, and Carl S. Rollyson. *A Student's Guide to Scandinavian American Genealogy* (7–12). Series: American Family Tree. 1996, Oryx $29.95 (0-89774-978-2). An introduction to the Scandinavian countries, people, and emigration to America, and information on how to research specific nationalities. (Rev: SLJ 10/96) [929]

9781 Ross, Lawrence C. *The Ways of Black Folks: A Year in the Life of a People* (10–12). 2003, Kensington $24.00 (0-7582-0057-9). A fascinating collection of interviews and reports that paint a compelling portrait of the everyday lives of Africans in the Diaspora — in Europe, the Caribbean, and North and South America. (Rev: BL 1/1–15/03) [305.896]

9782 Strazzabosco-Hayn, Gina. *Teenage Refugees from Iran Speak Out* (7–12). 1995, Rosen LB $16.95 (0-8239-1845-9). Iranian teens tell their grim stories as powerful testimony to the reality of refugee life. (Rev: BL 5/15/95; SLJ 5/95) [973]

9783 Tekavec, Valerie. *Teenage Refugees from Haiti Speak Out* (7–12). Series: In Their Own Voices. 1995, Rosen LB $16.95 (0-8239-1844-0). Interviews with native Haitian teenagers who are now living in the United States. (Rev: BL 6/1–15/95; SLJ 6/95) [305.23]

9784 Ueda, Reed, and Sandra Stotsky, eds. *Irish-American Answer Book* (6–10). 1999, Chelsea LB $19.75 (0-7910-4795-4); paper $9.95 (0-7910-4796-2). Using a question-and-answer format, this book examines the history, culture, politics, and religion of Irish Americans from the 1800s to the present. (Rev: VOYA 2/99) [973]

9785 Zamenova, Tatyana. *Teenage Refugees from Russia Speak Out* (7–12). Series: In Their Own Voices. 1995, Rosen LB $16.95 (0-8239-1846-7). Teenage Russian refugees describe their lives under socialism, leaving Russia, and adjusting to life in North America. (Rev: BL 6/1–15/95) [973]

Forms of Dissent

9786 Schultz, Bud, and Ruth Schultz. *The Price of Dissent: Testimonies to Political Repression in America* (10–12). 2001, Univ. of California Pr. paper $24.95 (0-520-22402-7). This is an account of three social movements of the 20th century: the labor, civil rights, and antiwar movements with excerpts from about 100 activists including Paul Robeson, Jr., John Lewis, and Abbie Hoffman. (Rev: BL 11/1/01) [325]

Social Concerns and Problems

General and Miscellaneous

9787 Andryszewski, Tricia. *The Militia Movement in America: Before and After Oklahoma City* (7–12). Illus. 1997, Millbrook LB $24.90 (0-7613-0119-4). This work traces the roots of the anti-government militia movement in the United States from the late 1800s to the present, with coverage of events in Ruby Ridge, Waco, Oklahoma City, and elsewhere. (Rev: BL 2/15/97; BR 9–10/97; SLJ 3/97; VOYA 2/98) [320.4]

9788 Bekoff, Marc, and Carron A. Meaney, eds. *Encyclopedia of Animal Rights and Animal Welfare* (7–12). 1998, Greenwood $67.95 (0-313-29977-3). Signed entries explore different aspects of the animal rights issue, including such topics as hunting, genetic engineering, and laboratory use. (Rev: BL 9/15/98; SLJ 2/99; VOYA 2/99) [179]

9789 Best, Joel. *Damned Lies and Statistics: Untangling Numbers from the Media, Politicians, and Activists* (10–12). 2001, Univ. of California Pr. $19.95 (0-520-21978-3). This book reviews the way statistics are collected and how they can, even in innocent hands, be used to create social problems. (Rev: BL 5/1/01) [001.4]

9790 Cottle, Thomas J. *At Peril: Stories of Injustice* (10–12). 2001, Univ. of Massachusetts Pr. $29.95 (1-55849-278-X). Through a series of true-life stories, the author presents the cases of people who are "at risk" because of health problems, social and economic status, and other factors, and how this often produces injustice. (Rev: BL 2/15/01) [361.1]

9791 Cozic, Charles P., ed. *The Militia Movement* (8–12). Series: At Issue. 1996, Greenhaven LB $26.20 (1-56510-542-7); paper $17.45 (1-56510-541-9). A presentation of a broad spectrum of opinions on the militia movement, from those who say it

is racist, extremist, and potentially violent to advocates who stress the constitutional right to bear arms. (Rev: BL 3/1/97; SLJ 4/97) [322.4]

9792 Cozic, Charles P., and Paul A. Winters, eds. *Gambling* (7–12). Series: Current Controversies. 1995, Greenhaven LB $26.20 (1-56510-235-5); paper $16.20 (1-56510-234-7). A collection of viewpoints on gambling, on why people become addicted, and on its social and economic effects. (Rev: BL 8/95; SLJ 10/95) [363.4]

9793 Davidson, Osha Gray. *Under Fire: The NRA and the Battle for Gun Control* (9–12). 1993, Holt $25.00 (0-8050-1904-9). Focuses on the history, agenda, influence, and status of the powerful National Rifle Association. (Rev: BL 4/1/93*) [363.3]

9794 Desetta, Al, and Sybil Wolin, eds. *The Struggle to Be Strong: True Stories by Teens About Overcoming Tough Times* (6–12). Illus. 2000, Free Spirit paper $14.95 (1-57542-079-1). Teens talk about problems such as addicted and abusive parents, AIDS, drugs and alcohol, school, health, and so forth. (Rev: BR 11–12/00; SLJ 8/00)

9795 Dolan, Edward F., and Margaret M. Scariano. *Guns in the United States* (7–12). 1994, Watts LB $24.00 (0-531-11189-X). Discusses rising gun violence in America, without taking sides in the gun-control debate, to encourage readers to investigate and take a knowledgeable stand on gun control. (Rev: BL 1/15/95; VOYA 5/95) [363.3]

9796 Egendorf, Laura K., ed. *Violence* (6–12). Series: Opposing Viewpoints. 2001, Greenhaven LB $22.96 (0-7377-0660-0); paper $14.96 (0-7377-0659-7). Differing views are offered on a variety of topics ranging from youth violence and contributing factors to gun control, drug abuse, and American culture in general. (Rev: BL 7/01) [303.6]

9797 Emert, Phyllis R. *Top Lawyers and Their Famous Cases* (6–10). Series: Profiles. 1996, Oliver LB $19.95 (1-881508-31-5). Profiles of eight notable lawyers and their outstanding legal cases, from colonial days to the present, including Alexander Hamilton, Morris Dees, Abraham Lincoln, Robert H. Jackson, Joseph Welsh, and Bella Lockwood. (Rev: BR 1–2/97; SLJ 11/96; VOYA 6/97) [920]

9798 Ennew, Judith. *Exploitation of Children* (6–10). Illus. Series: Global Issues. 1996, Raintree Steck-Vaughn LB $19.98 (0-8172-4546-4). This book presents historical material, statistical data, case studies, and differing viewpoints on how children are exploited in many countries of the world. (Rev: BL 2/1/97; VOYA 6/97) [305.23]

9799 Fraser, Laura, et al. *The Animal Rights Handbook: Everyday Ways to Save Animal Lives* (10–12). 1990, Living Planet paper $4.95 (0-9626072-0-7). This guide to animals' rights includes sections on uses of animals, their treatment in various situations, important addresses, and suggestions for change. (Rev: BL 10/1/90; SLJ 4/91) [179.3]

9800 Gay, Kathlyn. *Militias: Armed and Dangerous* (7–12). Illus. Series: Issues in Focus. 1997, Enslow LB $20.95 (0-89490-902-9). A disturbing look at the militia movement in the U.S. and the attraction it holds for such malcontents as survivalists, neo-Nazis, white supremacists, Christian fanatics, and government haters. (Rev: BL 11/15/97; VOYA 2/98) [322.4]

9801 Gay, Kathlyn. *Neo-Nazis: A Growing Threat* (8–12). Illus. Series: In Focus. 1997, Enslow LB $20.95 (0-89490-901-0). After a discussion of eight recent neo-Nazi-related crimes, the author describes the philosophy and goals of this movement, current groups, and how to fight hate crimes. (Rev: BL 9/1/97; BR 11–12/97; SLJ 10/97) [320.53]

9802 Gottfried, Ted. *Deniers of the Holocaust: Who They Are, What They Do, Why They Do It* (6–12). Illus. 2001, Twenty-First Century LB $28.90 (0-7613-1950-6). Gottfried provides ample evidence to dismiss the arguments of those who deny that the Holocaust took place and discusses the racism of white supremacists, the existence of Internet hate sites, and issues of free speech. (Rev: BL 9/1/01; HBG 3/02) [940.53]

9803 Haddock, Patricia. *Teens and Gambling: Who Wins?* (7–12). Illus. Series: Issues in Focus. 1996, Enslow LB $20.95 (0-89490-719-0). The controversial subject of gambling is introduced — its lure, addiction, and problems, particularly as related to teenagers. (Rev: BL 8/96; SLJ 8/96; VOYA 10/96) [363.4]

9804 Hamilton, Neil A. *Militias in America: A Reference Handbook* (9–12). Series: Contemporary World Issues. 1996, ABC-CLIO LB $45.00 (0-

87436-859-6). The history of the militia movement in this country is covered, with material on their philosophies, organization, activities, and motivational focuses such as alienation, paranoia, conspiracy theories, and disenchantment with the government. (Rev: BL 3/1/97; SLJ 3/97; VOYA 6/97) [302.3]

9805 Harnack, Andrew, ed. *Animal Rights* (8–12). Series: Opposing Viewpoints. 1996, Greenhaven LB $17.96 (1-56510-399-8). Topics discussed in this well-balanced anthology cover such questions as: Do animals have rights? Should they be used in experiments? Should animals be used for food and other commodities? Is wildlife protection necessary? and What are the issues that need to be resolved in the animal rights movement? (Rev: SLJ 9/96; VOYA 10/96) [179]

9806 Haughen, David M., ed. *Animal Experimentation* (8–12). Series: At Issue. 1999, Greenhaven LB $21.96 (0-7377-0149-8); paper $13.96 (0-7377-0148-X). A collection of essays by experts that explore various viewpoints concerning animal rights and experimentation on animals. (Rev: BL 11/15/99; SLJ 1/00) [179]

9807 Henderson, Harry. *Gun Control* (9–12). Series: Library in a Book. 2000, Facts on File $45.00 (0-8160-4031-1). A collection of documents that trace the history and issues of gun control from various points of view. (Rev: BL 11/15/00; SLJ 11/00) [363.3]

9808 Hjelmeland, Andy. *Legalized Gambling: Solution or Illusion?* (8–12). Series: Pro/Con Issues. 1998, Lerner LB $30.35 (0-8225-2615-8). After a brief history of gambling since ancient times, this book discusses current legal forms of gambling, including lotteries and casinos, and the attendant topics of controversy. (Rev: HBG 3/99; SLJ 12/98) [795]

9809 Hobbs, Sandy, et al. *Child Labor: A World History Companion* (10–12). 1999, ABC-CLIO (0-87436-956-8). This work gives a world history of child labor and covers contemporary conditions and efforts to prevent abuses. (Rev: BL 3/1/00) [331.3]

9810 Homsher, Deborah. *Women and Guns: Politics and the Culture of Firearms in America* (10–12). 2000, M.E. Sharpe $32.95 (0-7656-0678-X). This contribution to the pro- and anti-gun debate focuses on women and guns throughout American history and how this adds a new dimension to the controversy. (Rev: BL 12/1/00) [363.3]

9811 *Human Nature* (10–12). Ed. by David L. Bender. Series: Opposing Viewpoints. 1999, Greenhaven LB $31.20 (0-7377-0073-4); paper $19.95 (0-7377-0072-6). Human behavior, gender roles, and socialization are covered through a series of differing points of view from such thinkers as Freud, Sartre, Darwin, and Rousseau. [128]

9812 Hurley, Jennifer A. *Animal Rights* (7–12). Series: Opposing Viewpoints Digests. 1998, Greenhaven paper $17.45 (1-56510-868-X). The rights of animals are defined and their place in experimentation and hunting and slaughter for human consumption is explored in this book that presents different attitudes and opinions. (Rev: BL 4/15/99) [179]

9813 Hyde, Margaret O. *Gambling: Winners and Losers* (6–10). 1995, Millbrook LB $23.40 (1-56294-532-7). A timely subject gets rather dry treatment in this book that tells of the history, types, and psychology of gambling, with quotations from many case studies. (Rev: BL 12/15/95; BR 5–6/96; SLJ 3/96) [363.4]

9814 Hyde, Margaret O. *Missing and Murdered Children* (9–12). Illus. 1998, Watts LB $23.60 (0-531-11384-1). Real-life case studies engage the reader's interest in this well-written volume on America's epidemic of missing children, some of whom are victims of kidnapping while others have fled abusive situations or been discarded by uncaring families. (Rev: BL 3/1/98; BR 11–12/98; HBG 9/98; SLJ 3/98) [362.76]

9815 James, Barbara. *Animal Rights* (5–10). Series: Talking Points. 1999, Raintree Steck-Vaughn LB $27.12 (0-8172-5317-3). Various aspects of the animal rights controversy are explored in an objective, straightforward manner. (Rev: BL 8/99; BR 9–10/99) [179.3]

9816 Johnson, John, and Jeff Coplon. *Only Son* (10–12). 2002, Warner $23.95 (0-446-52552-9). African American broadcast journalist Johnson describes his childhood with an abusive father; for mature teens. (Rev: BL 6/1–15/02) [306.87]

9817 Kronenwetter, Michael. *Encyclopedia of Modern American Social Issues* (7–12). 1997, ABC-CLIO LB $65.00 (0-87436-779-4). In alphabetically arranged articles, this book presents well-balanced information on such controversial issues as abortion, child abuse, drug testing, gun control, Head Start, same-sex marriage, Ebonics, and secondhand smoke. (Rev: BR 9–10/98; SLJ 5/98) [306]

9818 Kruschke, Earl R. *Gun Control: A Reference Handbook* (9–12). Series: Contemporary World Issues. 1995, ABC-CLIO LB $48.50 (0-87436-695-X). A culmination of 35 years of research, this handbook presents varied ways of viewing the problem of gun control, citing important historical cases and laws and including a philosophical chronology from Plato to the present. (Rev: BR 9–10/96; SLJ 5/96; VOYA 6/96) [172]

9819 Landau, Elaine. *Land Mines: 100 Million Hidden Killers* (6–12). Series: Issues in Focus. 2000, Enslow LB $20.95 (0-7660-1240-9). This is an overview of where land mines are found, how they got there, and ways in which the danger they present can be overcome. (Rev: BL 9/15/00; HBG 3/01; VOYA 2/01) [363.3]

9820 Lang, Paul. *The English Language Debate: One Nation, One Language?* (7–12). Illus. 1995, Enslow LB $20.95 (0-89490-642-9). A well-documented account that explores such multicultural topics as the English-only movement, bilingual education, and other current political aspects of the teaching, status, and use of English in this country. (Rev: BL 6/1–15/95) [306.4]

9821 Langer, Elinor. *A Hundred Little Hitlers: The Death of a Black Man, the Trial of a White Racist, and the Rise of the Neo-Nazi Movement in America* (10–12). 2003, Holt $26.00 (0-8050-5098-1). In this insightful overview of racial hatred and its consequences, the author focuses on the 1988 murder of an Ethiopian man by three skinheads in Portland, Oregon. (Rev: BL 8/03) [305.8]

9822 *Legalized Gambling* (9–12). Series: Contemporary Issues Companion. 1999, Greenhaven LB $20.96 (1-56510-899-X); paper $12.96 (1-56510-898-1). This work discusses the pros and cons of legalized gambling and the social, economic, and ethical problems involved. [363.4]

9823 Levine, Herbert M. *Animal Rights* (7–12). Illus. Series: American Issues Debated. 1997, Raintree Steck-Vaughn LB $31.40 (0-8172-4350-X). Should animals be banned from use in science? Should hunting be illegal? Should people be ashamed of wearing fur? These and other questions relating to animals are explored from different points of view. (Rev: BL 11/15/97; BR 1–2/98; VOYA 2/98) [179]

9824 Levine, Herbert M. *Gun Control* (7–12). Illus. Series: American Issues Debated. 1997, Raintree Steck-Vaughn LB $31.40 (0-8172-4351-8). The debate on the effectiveness of gun control in reducing crime is presented, along with questions concerning handgun bans, waiting periods, and penalties for illegal gun use. (Rev: BL 11/15/97; BR 1–2/98) [363.3]

9825 Maguire, Stephen, and Bonnie Wren, eds. *Torn by the Issues: An Unbiased Review of the Watershed Issues in American Life* (9–12). 1994, Fithian paper $15.95 (1-56474-093-5). Presents opposing viewpoints surrounding the nation's most contentious social issues, among them abortion, AIDS, animal rights, global warming, homelessness, gun control, and welfare. (Rev: BL 7/94) [306]

9826 Meltzer, Milton. *Cheap Raw Material: How Our Youngest Workers Are Exploited and Abused* (9–12). 1994, Viking paper $15.99 (0-670-83128-X). A survey of the history of child labor that reveals the continuing exploitation of young people in the U.S. workplace. (Rev: BL 3/1/94*; SLJ 7/94) [331.3]

9827 Menhard, Francha Roffe. *School Violence: Deadly Lessons* (8–12). Series: Teen Issues. 2000, Enslow LB $17.95 (0-7660-1358-8). Many acts of violence in schools are described, with material on their causes and possible prevention. (Rev: HBG 3/01; SLJ 9/00) [371.7]

9828 Nisbet, Lee, ed. *The Gun Control Debate: You Decide* (10–12). 1990, Prometheus paper $18.95 (0-87975-618-7). From a variety of sources, this is a collection of 22 essays that explore various aspects of the gun control controversy. (Rev: BL 12/15/90) [363.3]

9829 Ojeda, Auriana, ed. *Technology and Society* (6–12). Series: Opposing Viewpoints. 2002, Gale LB $31.20 (0-7377-0913-8); paper $19.95 (0-7377-0912-X). Technology's contributions to — and negative impact on — society are discussed here, with mention of Internet access, e-mail privacy, biotechnology, government regulation, the divide between rich and poor, and increasing social isolation. (Rev: BL 6/1–15/02; SLJ 6/02) [306.4]

9830 O'Neill, Terry. *Gun Control* (6–12). Illus. Series: Opposing Viewpoints Digests. 2000, Greenhaven LB $21.96 (1-56510-879-5); paper $13.96 (1-56510-878-7). This book explores different questions about gun control and supplies a number of essays that express conflicting viewpoints on each question. (Rev: BL 7/00; SLJ 6/00) [363.3]

9831 *Opposing Viewpoints in Social Issues* (9–12). Ed. by William Dudley. Series: Opposing Viewpoints. 1999, Greenhaven LB $21.96 (0-7377-0123-4); paper $13.96 (0-7377-0122-6). Abortion, the death penalty, gun control, and other important issues in American society are tackled by essayists from both sides. (Rev: BL 3/15/00; SLJ 6/00) [361.1]

9832 Owen, Marna. *Animal Rights: Yes or No?* (6–10). 1993, Lerner LB $30.35 (0-8225-2603-4). A discussion of the various positions on animal rights. (Rev: BL 1/15/94; SLJ 3/94) [179]

9833 Parker, David L., et al. *Stolen Dreams: Portraits of Working Children* (6–12). Illus. 1997, Lerner LB $23.95 (0-8225-2960-2). This compelling photoessay deals with child labor around the world, particularly in the Far East. (Rev: BL 11/1/97; HB 3–4/98; VOYA 2/98) [331.3]

9834 Patterson, Charles. *Animal Rights* (6–10). 1993, Enslow LB $20.95 (0-89490-468-X). A thorough examination of the topic, including a history of animal rights movements. (Rev: BL 10/15/93; SLJ 11/93; VOYA 2/94) [179]

9835 Petley, Julian. *The Media: The Impact on Our Lives* (6–10). Series: 21st Century Debates. 2001, Raintree Steck-Vaughn LB $18.98 (0-7398-3175-5). An absorbing and fact-filled overview of the various forms of media — from newspapers, radio and TV, and film to commercial advertising — and their influence on politics and society. (Rev: SLJ 11/01) [302.23]

9836 Pipher, Mary. *The Middle of Everywhere: The World's Refugees Come to Our Town* (10–12). 2002, Harcourt $25.00 (0-15-100600-8). A very readable overview of newly arrived refugees' struggles to find their place in America, written by a psychologist. (Rev: BL 3/15/02; SLJ 1/03) [305.9]

9837 Pringle, Laurence. *The Animal Rights Controversy* (7–12). Illus. 1989, Harcourt $16.95 (0-15-203559-1). A book about the way animals are abused and misused that covers topics such as factory farming, experimentation, and zoos. (Rev: BL 1/15/90; SLJ 5/90; VOYA 4/90) [197]

9838 Ridgeway, James. *Blood in the Face: The Ku Klux Klan, Aryan Nations, Nazi Skinheads, and the Rise of a New White Culture* (9–12). 1991, Thunder's Mouth $29.95 (1-560250-02-X); paper $19.95 (1-56025-100-X). Analysis of the racist far right and its organized hatred. (Rev: BL 1/15/91) [305.8]

9839 Roleff, Tamara L., ed. *Extremist Groups* (6–12). Series: Opposing Viewpoints. 2001, Greenhaven LB $22.96 (0-7377-0656-2); paper $14.96 (0-7377-0655-4). Contributors give spirited pro and con arguments on topics including religious fundamentalism, white supremacy, animal rights, and socialism. (Rev: BL 9/15/01) [303.48]

9840 Roleff, Tamara L., ed. *Hate Crimes* (6–12). Series: Current Controversies. 2000, Greenhaven LB $22.96 (0-7377-0454-3); paper $14.96 (0-7377-0453-5). After describing what constitutes a hate crime, these essays focus on specific examples, laws, and the threat posed by groups that promote extreme, violent behaviors. (Rev: BL 2/15/01; SLJ 3/01) [364.1]

9841 Roleff, Tamara L. *Hate Groups* (7–12). Series: Opposing Viewpoints Digests. 2001, Greenhaven $19.96 (0-7377-0677-5); paper $12.96 (0-7377-0676-7). A concise and thought-provoking exploration of the problems of group hate and restrictions of free speech. (Rev: BL 1/1–15/02) [364.1]

9842 Roleff, Tamara L., ed. *The Rights of Animals* (6–12). Series: Current Controversies. 1999, Greenhaven LB $20.96 (0-7377-0069-6); paper $12.96 (0-7377-0068-8). This collection of provocative essays discusses such topics as cloning, animal organ transplants, hunting, trapping, and using animals in entertainment and experimentation. (Rev: BL 10/15/99) [179]

9843 Saunders, Carol Silverman. *Straight Talk About Teenage Gambling* (7–12). Series: Straight Talk. 1999, Facts on File $27.45 (0-8160-3718-3). This book details the physical and emotional stakes involved with games of chance and what happens when teens become completely preoccupied with gambling. (Rev: BL 1/1–15/99; BR 9–10/99; SLJ 8/99) [362.2]

9844 Schwartz, Ted. *Kids and Guns: The History, the Present, the Dangers, and the Remedies* (7–12). 1999, Watts LB $23.00 (0-531-11723-5). A look at the issue of kids and guns, the scope of the problem, issues involved in gun ownership, teenage violence and the media, and how to create safe schools. (Rev: BL 7/99; SLJ 9/99) [303.6]

9845 Sherman, Aliza. *Working Together Against Violence Against Women* (6–10). Series: Library of Social Activism. 1996, Rosen LB $16.95 (0-8239-2258-8). An examination of violence against women, including date rape, stranger rape, assault, and domestic violence, and of the actions being taken by both government and private agencies; advice on how teenagers can help themselves, a friend, and their communities is also offered. (Rev: SLJ 2/97; VOYA 6/97) [303.6]

9846 Sherry, Clifford J. *Animal Rights* (7–12). Series: Contemporary World Issues. 1995, ABC-CLIO LB $45.00 (0-87436-733-6). A well-organized volume that introduces the philosophical basis for the animal rights movement, present-day problems, and the pros and cons of using animals in research. (Rev: SLJ 1/96) [346]

9847 *Speaking Out for Animals: True Stories About Real People Who Rescue Animals* (10–12). Ed. by Kim W. Stallwood. Illus. 2001, Booklight paper $18.00 (1-930051-34-4). This account describes the work of such activists as Paul McCartney and how they devote part of their lives to helping animals and promoting animal rights. (Rev: BL 7/01) [179]

9848 Stewart, Gail B. *Militias* (7–12). Illus. Series: Overview. 1997, Lucent LB $27.45 (1-56006-501-X). This book traces the historical development of the militia movement and discusses prominent contemporary militia groups, their purposes, the beliefs and attitudes of their members and leaders, their activities, and why they are flourishing. (Rev: BL 1/1–15/98; HBG 9/98) [322.4]

9849 *Stories That Changed America: Muckrakers of the 20th Century* (10–12). Ed. by Carl Jensen. 2000, Seven Stories $26.95 (1-58322-027-5). This is a collection of important exposés from the past century that includes works by Margaret Sanger, Rachel Carson, I. F. Stone, Edward R. Morrow, Betty Friedan, Malcolm X, Ralph Nader, and Woodward and Bernstein. (Rev: BL 8/00; SLJ 6/01) [070]

9850 Sugarmann, Josh. *NRA: Money, Firepower and Fear* (9–12). 1991, National Press Books $19.95 (0-915765-88-8). An in-depth review of the National Rifle Association and the methods it's used to transform a constitutional right into the social nightmare of unregulated possession of weapons. (Rev: BL 12/1/91) [363.3]

9851 Torr, James D., ed. *Gambling* (7–12). Series: Opposing Viewpoints. 2002, Gale $31.20 (0-7377-0907-3); paper $19.95 (0-7377-0906-5). Essays examine the addictive nature of gambling, the benefits to the Native American tribes that run casinos, sports betting, state lotteries, Internet gambling, and so forth. (Rev: BL 4/15/02) [306.4]

9852 Wand, Kelly, ed. *The Animal Rights Movement* (8–12). Series: American Social Movements. 2002, Gale LB $25.96 (0-7377-1046-2); paper $16.96 (0-7377-1045-4). This collection of essays traces this movement from the advocates of animal welfare of the 18th century through the development of the concept of animal rights of the late-20th century. (Rev: BL 1/1–15/03; SLJ 2/03) [179]

9853 Wekesser, Carol. *Child Welfare: Opposing Viewpoints* (8–12). Series: Opposing Viewpoints. 1998, Greenhaven LB $31.20 (1-56510-679-2); paper $19.95 (1-56510-678-4). All issues that can affect the welfare of children — divorce, economic woes, abuse, and so forth — are discussed from many angles. [362.7]

9854 Williams, Mary E., ed. *Child Labor and Sweatshops* (9–12). Series: At Issue. 1998, Greenhaven LB $20.96 (0-7377-0003-3); paper $12.45 (0-7377-0002-5). This anthology of 17 articles explores the international use of cheap labor, chiefly women and children, and how this terrible exploitation of the most vulnerable can be reduced and perhaps prevented. (Rev: BR 9–10/99; SLJ 6/99) [306]

9855 Williams, Mary E., ed. *Culture Wars* (8–12). Series: Opposing Viewpoints. 2003, Gale LB $33.70 (0-7377-1679-7); paper $22.45 (0-7377-1680-0). These essays explore American cultural values, multiculturalism, popular culture, and the question of a decline in culture from various viewpoints. (Rev: BL 1/1–15/04) [306]

9856 Williams, Mary E., ed. *The White Separatist Movement* (8–12). Series: American Social Movements. 2002, Gale LB $31.20 (0-7377-1054-3); paper $19.95 (0-7377-1053-5). This collection of essays, speeches, book excerpts, and personal observations looks at groups ranging from the Ku Klux Klan to neo-Nazi skinheads and discusses the reasons why people are attracted to such organizations. (Rev: BL 9/15/02) [305.8]

9857 Williams, Mary E., ed. *Working Women* (8–12). Series: Opposing Viewpoints. 1997, Greenhaven LB $26.20 (1-56510-677-6). Differing viewpoints on the impact of women entering the work force, sexual harassment, discrimination, and women in the military are presented in this anthology of articles. (Rev: BL 11/15/97; VOYA 6/98)

9858 Winters, Paul A., ed. *America's Victims* (9–12). Series: Opposing Viewpoints. 1996, Greenhaven LB $20.96 (1-56510-401-3); paper $16.20 (1-56510-400-5). Current selections from books and periodicals explore various points of view on victimhood in America in relation to such areas as the criminal justice system, the civil rights movement, and drug therapy/ recovery programs. (Rev: BL 12/15/96; BR 1–2/97; SLJ 11/96; VOYA 2/97) [306]

9859 Wise, Steven M. *Rattling the Cage: Toward Legal Rights for Animals* (10–12). 2000, Perseus Bks. $25.00 (0-7382-0065-4). A well-reasoned adult book that argues persuasively for the legal rights of animals, particularly apes. (Rev: BL 1/1–15/00) [344]

Environmental Issues

General and Miscellaneous

9860 Amdur, Richard. *The Fragile Earth* (9–12). 1994, Chelsea LB $19.95 (0-7910-1572-6). A discussion, in understandable terms, of the origin of the universe and the interdependence of life. (Rev: BL 5/1/94; VOYA 6/94) [363.7]

9861 *American Environmentalism* (9–12). Ed. by Greg Barton. Illus. Series: American Social Movements. 2002, Gale LB $31.20 (0-7377-1044-6); paper $19.95 (0-7377-1043-8). An excellent historical overview of the American environmental movement, presenting the thoughts of such diverse activists as Ralph Waldo Emerson, Henry David Thoreau, Teddy Roosevelt, and Al Gore. (Rev: BL 9/1/02) [333.7]

9862 Andryszewski, Tricia. *The Environment and the Economy: Planting the Seeds for Tomorrow's Growth* (7–12). 1995, Millbrook LB $24.90 (1-56294-524-6). Traces the emergence of environment-versus-economy issues. (Rev: BL 12/1/95; SLJ 11/95) [363.7]

9863 Barbour, Scott. *The Environment* (6–12). Series: Opposing Viewpoints Digests. 2001, Greenhaven LB $28.70 (1-56510-873-6); paper $14.95 (1-56510-872-8). Teens interested in environmental issues including pollution, ozone, and global warming will find this a useful resource, with a list of organizations and a bibliography. (Rev: BL 2/15/01) [363.7]

9864 Bilger, Burkhard. *Global Warming* (9–12). Series: Earth at Risk. 1991, Chelsea LB $19.95 (0-7910-1575-0). A well-researched book that explains the scientific, political, and social issues relating to global warming. (Rev: BL 4/1/92; SLJ 3/92) [363.73]

9865 Breton, Mary Joy. *Women Pioneers for the Environment* (10–12). 1998, Northeastern Univ. Pr. $37.50 (1-55553-365-5). A collection of biographical profiles, each in a political and social context, of women who have led struggles to combat destruction of the environment over the last 300 years. (Rev: SLJ 5/99) [363.7]

9866 Brower, Michael, and Warren Leon. *The Consumer's Guide to Effective Environmental Choices: Practical Advice from the Union of Concerned Scientists* (9–12). 1999, Three Rivers paper $15.00 (0-609-80281-X). The authors present steps people can take to live more ecologically safe and aware lifestyles. (Rev: BL 4/1/99; SLJ 9/99) [363.7]

9867 Bullard, Robert D., ed. *Unequal Protection: Environmental Justice and Communities of Color* (9–12). 1994, Sierra Club $25.00 (0-87156-450-5). Academics, journalists, activists, and others provide details on environmental racism throughout the United States. (Rev: BL 5/1/94) [363.703]

9868 Caldicott, Helen. *If You Love This Planet: A Plan to Heal the Earth* (9–12). 1992, Norton paper $12.95 (0-393-30835-9). Presents, as a medical metaphor, the diagnosis and tough cure for an ailing planet Earth. (Rev: BL 3/1/92*) [363.7]

9869 Carson, Rachel. *Silent Spring* (10–12). 1994, Houghton $24.95 (0-395-68330-0); paper $14.00 (0-395-68329-7). This is a pioneering publication that alerted America to the use of pesticides and the need for environmental conservation. [363.7]

9870 Chandler, Gary, and Kevin Graham. *Environmental Causes* (5–10). Series: Celebrity Activists. 1997, Twenty-First Century LB $25.90 (0-8050-5232-1). This book discusses how entertainers including Robert Redford, Sting, and Chevy Chase and other celebrities such as Al Gore, Ted Turner, and Jerry Greenfield support environmental causes. (Rev: BR 3–4/98; SLJ 1/98) [363.7]

9871 Christianson, Gale E. *Greenhouse: The 200-Year Story of Global Warming* (10–12). 1999, Walker $25.00 (0-8027-1346-7). The history of global warming is discussed, with material on its causes and effects. (Rev: BL 4/15/99) [363.7]

9872 Collard, Sneed B. *Alien Invaders: The Continuing Threat of Exotic Species* (6–12). Illus. 1996, Watts LB $25.00 (0-531-11298-5). An account that explores the dangers of introducing nonindigenous plants and animals into a new environment. (Rev: BL 11/1/96; BR 3–4/97; SLJ 1/97) [574.5824]

9873 Collins, Carol C., ed. *Our Food, Air and Water: How Safe Are They?* (9–12). Illus. 1985, Facts on File $29.95 (0-87196-967-X). A collection of editorials and cartoons that covers such environmental problems as water pollution and toxic wastes. (Rev: BL 3/15/85) [363.7]

9874 Cothran, Helen, ed. *Energy Alternatives* (6–12). Series: Opposing Viewpoints. 2002, Gale LB $31.20 (0-7377-0905-7); paper $19.95 (0-7377-0904-9). Discussion of the pros and cons of fossil fuels and nuclear power is followed by a look at various alternatives, including solar power, geothermal energy, fuel cells, wind farms, and "biomass" or garbage conversion. (Rev: BL 7/02) [333.79]

9875 Dashefsky, H. Steven. *Environmental Science: High-School Fair Experiments* (7–12). Illus. 1994, TAB paper $12.95 (0-8306-4586-1). Topics covered in this project book suitable for both junior and senior high school students include applied ecology, soil ecosystems, energy, aquatic ecosystems, and environmental problems. (Rev: BL 6/1–15/94) [574.5]

9876 *The Environment* (9–12). Ed. by William Dudley. Series: Opposing Viewpoints. 2001, Greenhaven LB $31.20 (0-7377-0654-6); paper $19.95 (0-7377-0653-8). Environmental problems and protection efforts are explored in this collection of writings that express varying viewpoints. [363.7]

9877 Fisher, Marshall. *The Ozone Layer* (9–12). Series: Earth at Risk. 1991, Chelsea LB $19.95 (0-7910-1576-9). Covers the historical and scientific background and steps that have been taken to counteract the depletion of the ozone layer. (Rev: BL 2/1/92) [363.73]

9878 Fleisher, Paul. *Ecology A to Z* (6–10). 1994, Dillon LB $14.95 (0-87518-561-4). Defines words and phrases relating to ecology and to our interaction with the environment. (Rev: BL 4/1/94; SLJ 5/94; VOYA 6/94) [363.7]

9879 Fridell, Ron. *Global Warming* (6–12). Illus. 2002, Watts LB $24.00 (0-531-11900-9). A detailed look at weather patterns of the past and how they may be used to predict future problems, with discussion of actions we can take to avoid disastrous global warming. (Rev: BL 10/15/02) [363.738]

9880 Gartner, Bob. *Working Together Against the Destruction of the Environment* (7–12). Series: Library of Social Activism. 1995, Rosen LB $16.95 (0-8239-1774-6). Describes efforts to protect the environment, such as recycling, emission laws, and sewage dump restrictions, and provides suggestions for how everyone can help. (Rev: BL 4/15/95) [363.7]

9881 Gay, Kathlyn. *Saving the Environment: Debating the Costs* (8–12). Illus. Series: Impact. 1996, Watts $22.50 (0-531-11263-2). This book explores environmental issues in which there is a conflict between the health of the environment and cost to the economy, such as saving endangered species, and property rights vs. pollution. (Rev: BL 9/1/96; BR 11–12/96; SLJ 10/96; VOYA 10/96) [363.7]

9882 Gelbspan, Ross. *The Heat Is On* (10–12). 1997, Addison-Wesley $23.00 (0-201-13295-8). A sobering, adult look at the coming emergency of global warming caused by mass industrialization. (Rev: BL 5/15/97; SLJ 3/98) [574.5]

9883 *Global Warming* (9–12). Ed. by James Haley. Series: Opposing Viewpoints. 2002, Greenhaven $31.20 (0-7377-0909-X); paper $19.95 (0-7377-0908-1). This collection of documents discusses the meaning of global warming, its extent, and what can be done about it. [363.7]

9884 Gonick, Larry, and Alice Outwater. *The Cartoon Guide to the Environment* (10–12). Illus. 1996, HarperPerennial paper $15.00 (0-06-273274-9). Using cartoons, this sobering account tells how humanity is gradually destroying the earth through heedless misuse of the environment. (Rev: SLJ 9/96) [320.5]

9885 Haddock, Patricia. *Environmental Time Bomb: Our Threatened Planet* (6–12). Series: Issues in Focus. 2000, Enslow LB $20.96 (0-7660-1229-8). Up-to-date information is given on current dangers to our environment. (Rev: BL 9/15/00; HBG 3/01; SLJ 12/00) [363.7]

9886 Lanier-Graham, Susan D. *The Ecology of War: Environmental Impacts of Weaponry and Warfare* (9–12). 1993, Walker $35.95 (0-8027-1262-2). Covers the effects of Agent Orange, Gulf War oil spills and fires, unexploded ammunition in the Pacific, and pollution around military bases. (Rev: BL 5/1/93) [363.73]

9887 Lear, Linda, ed. *Lost Woods: The Discovered Writing of Rachel Carson* (10–12). 1998, Beacon $38.50 (0-8070-8546-4). Previously uncollected or unpublished writings by the great conservationist, covering topics in biology, ecology, and wildlife and wilderness preservation. (Rev: BL 11/1/98; SLJ 3/99) [363.7]

9888 Lynas, Mark. *High Tide: The Truth About Our Climate Crisis* (10–12). 2004, St. Martin's paper $14.00 (0-312-30365-3). This is a shocking exposé of the danger of global warming and of the equally shocking energy policies of the second Bush administration. (Rev: BL 5/15/04) [363.7]

9889 Malaspina, Ann. *Saving the American Wilderness* (8–12). Illus. Series: Overview. 1999, Lucent LB $17.96 (1-56006-505-2). A look at American conservationism and environmentalism and how they have affected the country's land and wildlife. (Rev: BL 11/15/99; HBG 4/00) [333.78]

9890 Netzley, Patricia. *Environmental Groups* (6–10). Illus. Series: Our Endangered Planet. 1997, Lucent LB $27.45 (1-56006-195-2). This objective source introduces conflicting attitudes toward protection of species, lobbying tactics, economic issues, and scientific findings relating to environmental issues. (Rev: SLJ 9/98) [363.7]

9891 Netzley, Patricia. *Issues in the Environment* (7–10). Series: Contemporary Issues. 1997, Lucent LB $27.45 (1-56006-475-7). Proponents and detractors state their cases in this volume that explores methods used to protect the environment, their cost, their effectiveness, and the possible use of other, less drastic alternatives. (Rev: SLJ 4/98) [363.7]

9892 Petrikin, Jonathan S., ed. *Environmental Justice* (8–12). Series: At Issue. 1995, Greenhaven LB

$19.95 (0-56510-264-9). A collection of essays exploring whether the wealthy and powerful are risking the health and living conditions of others while protecting their own resources. (Rev: BL 3/15/95) [363.7]

9893 Philander, S. George. *Is the Temperature Rising? The Uncertain Science of Global Warming* (10–12). 1998, Princeton Univ. Pr. $52.50 (0-691-05775-3); paper $18.95 (0-691-05034-1). The author explores all aspects of the controversy over climate change. (Rev: BL 3/15/98) [551.5]

9894 Pope, Carl, and Paul Rauber. *Strategic Ignorance: Why the Bush Administration Is Recklessly Destroying a Century of Environmental Progress* (10–12). 2004, Sierra Club $24.95 (1-57805-109-6). There is a bold exposé of how the government under President George W. Bush has favored profits over conservation in such actions as rolling back legislation intended to protect American land and its resources. (Rev: BL 5/1/04) [338.973]

9895 Reiss, Bob. *The Coming Storm: Extreme Weather and Our Terrifying Future* (9–12). 2001, Hyperion $24.95 (0-7868-6665-9). This is a scary discussion of the greenhouse effect and how it could produce catastrophic climate changes. (Rev: BL 8/01) [551.6]

9896 Robbins, Ocean, and Sol Solomon. *Choices for Our Future* (7–12). 1994, Book Pub. paper $9.95 (1-57067-002-1). The founders of Youth for Environmental Sanity believe that young people can convince other young people to adopt more ecologically responsible lifestyles. This book explains how we can all help. (Rev: BL 3/15/95) [363.7]

9897 Rosen, Roger, and Patra McSharry, eds. *Planet Earth: Egotists and Ecosystems* (9–12). 1991, Rosen LB $16.95 (0-8239-1334-1); paper $8.95 (0-8239-1335-X). Short stories, articles, and photoessays addressing environmental abuse. (Rev: BL 2/15/92; SLJ 4/92) [809]

9898 Rubin, Charles T. *The Green Crusade: Rethinking the Roots of Environmentalism* (9–12). 1994, Free Pr. $22.95 (0-02-927525-3). A critical examination of utopianism in the environmental movement and the anticapitalist ethics of leading authors in the field. (Rev: BL 2/1/94) [363.7]

9899 Ryan, Bernard. *Protecting the Environment* (7–12). Series: Community Service for Teens. 1998, Ferguson LB $15.95 (0-89434-228-2). After a general introduction on volunteerism, the author describes how teens can become involved in existing conservation projects and begin their own. (Rev: BL 9/15/98; BR 11–12/98; SLJ 2/99; VOYA 8/99) [363.7]

9900 Ryan, John C. *Seven Wonders: Everyday Things for a Healthier Planet* (9–12). 1999, Sierra Club paper $12.95 (1-57805-038-3). Focusing on a handful of everyday items — bicycles, public libraries, ladybugs, condoms, vegetarian foods, clotheslines, and ceiling fans, for example — Ryan explains how each can make a significant difference to the future of the planet. (Rev: SLJ 2/00; VOYA 2/00) [628]

9901 Shaw, Jane. *Global Warming* (7–12). Illus. Series: Critical Thinking About Environmental Issues. 2002, Gale $21.96 (0-7377-1270-8). Readers will find a variety of opinions about the causes and severity of global warming. (Rev: BL 12/15/02) [363.738]

9902 Slobodkin, Larry. *A Citizen's Guide to Ecology* (10–12). 2003, Oxford $40.00 (0-19-516286-2). The author explains in detail what ecology is — and isn't — and makes a strong case for the role of the ecologist in ensuring that our planet remains habitable. (Rev: BL 4/15/03) [577]

9903 Stefoff, Rebecca. *The American Environmental Movement* (7–10). 1995, Facts on File $25.00 (0-8160-3046-4). A study of efforts to preserve the environment from the 15th century to the present, with discussion of prominent figures and events in the movement. (Rev: BL 9/1/95; SLJ 9/95) [363.7]

9904 Stouffer, Marty. *Marty Stouffer's Wild America* (8–12). 1988, Times Books $30.00 (0-8129-1610-7). A wildlife documentary maker discusses his career and the importance of conservation. (Rev: BR 3–4/89; VOYA 4/89) [320.5]

9905 Student Environmental Action Coalition. *The Student Environmental Action Guide: By the Student Environmental Action Coalition (SEAC)* (9–12). 1991, EarthWorks paper $4.95 (1-879682-04-4). A short manual describing opportunities for recycling in the campus environment and including campus success stories that encourage collective student action. (Rev: BL 10/15/91) [363.7]

9906 Turner, Tom. *Sierra Club: 100 Years of Protecting Nature* (9–12). Photos. 1991, Abrams $49.50 (0-8109-3820-0). A commemoration of the Sierra Club's founding that provides a history of the organization, its mission, and its accomplishments. (Rev: BL 11/15/91) [333.9516]

9907 *Welfare Ranching: The Subsidized Destruction of the American West* (10–12). Ed. by George Wuerthner and Mollie Matteson. Illus. 2002, Island Pr. $75.00 (1-55963-942-3); paper $45.00 (1-55963-943-1). Experts in a variety of fields explore the threats facing public lands in the American West, with effective photography. (Rev: BL 9/15/02) [333.74]

9908 Wilcove, David S. *The Condor's Shadow: The Loss and Recovery of Wildlife in America* (9–12). 1999, W. H. Freeman paper $24.95 (0-7167-3115-0). This work discusses the contemporary dangers to wildlife in America, including habitat destruction, pollution, and the introduction of nonnative species. (Rev: BL 3/15/99; SLJ 8/99) [363.7]

9909 Williams, Joy. *Ill Nature: Rants and Reflections on Humanity and Other Animals* (10–12). 2001, Lyons Pr. $22.95 (1-58574-187-6). This is a candid, often scathing group of essays that look at the way mankind is ravaging the environment and destroying wildlife around the world. (Rev: BL 2/15/01; SLJ 8/01) [814]

Pollution

9910 Antonetta, Susanne. *Body Toxic: An Environmental Memoir* (10–12). 2001, Counterpoint $26.00 (1-58243-116-7). The chilling story of a girl who innocently played in a boggy coastal area of New Jersey where DDT was being dumped and the terrible consequences that resulted. (Rev: BL 4/1/01*) [615]

9911 Bang, Molly. *Nobody Particular: One Woman's Fight to Save the Bays* (6–12). Illus. 2001, Holt $18.00 (0-8050-5396-4). Teens will connect to this appealingly presented account about Diane Wilson, who became an environmental activist working to restore the ecology of the bays around her Texas home. (Rev: BCCB 2/01; BL 2/1/01; HB 1–2/01; HBG 10/01; SLJ 1/01; VOYA 4/02) [363.738]

9912 Cozic, Charles P., ed. *Pollution* (9–12). Series: Current Controversies. 1994, Greenhaven LB $26.20 (1-56510-076-X); paper $17.45 (1-56510-075-1). A presentation of differing opinions on how serious pollution is, who is responsible, the effectiveness of recycling and what methods work best, and the role of the Environmental Protection Agency. (Rev: BL 4/15/94) [363.73]

9913 Dolan, Edward F. *Our Poisoned Waters* (7–12). Illus. 1997, Dutton $14.99 (0-525-65220-5). With extensive use of first-person accounts, this book describes the impact that humans have had on the water supply and attempts to conserve and clean our water. The last chapter tells how readers can help the cause. (Rev: BL 3/1/97; BR 11–12/97; SLJ 3/97; VOYA 10/97) [363.739]

9914 Freese, Barbara. *Coal: A Human History* (10–12). 2003, Perseus Bks. $25.00 (0-7382-0400-5). A comprehensive look at the rise and fall of coal as an energy source that also examines the fossil fuel's damaging effects on both the environment and health. (Rev: BL 1/1–15/03; VOYA 12/03) [553.24]

9915 Gay, Kathlyn. *Air Pollution* (7–12). Series: Impact. 1991, Watts paper $24.00 (0-531-13002-9). An examination of the alarming ecological effects and health risks of atmospheric pollution and an outline of combative strategies. (Rev: BL 12/1/91) [363.73]

9916 Hayley, James, ed. *Pollution* (8–12). Series: Current Controversies. 2002, Gale LB $25.96 (0-7377-1188-4); paper $16.96 (0-7377-1187-6). This book features in-depth essays by individuals — environmentalists, politicians, EPA representatives, and others — who present opposing views on the problem of pollution. (Rev: BL 12/15/02) [363.73]

9917 Kidd, J. S., and Renee A. Kidd. *Into Thin Air: The Problem of Atmospheric Pollution* (7–12). Series: Into Thin Air. 1998, Facts on File $25.00 (0-8160-3585-7). This book evaluates how scientists have studied atmospheric chemistry and explores controversial theories on the effects of pollution, acid rain, the greenhouse effect, global warming, and El Niño. (Rev: BL 12/1/98) [363.739]

9918 Nadis, Steve, et al. *Car Trouble* (9–12). Series: Guides to the Environment. 1993, Beacon paper $22.50 (0-8070-8523-5). A book that addresses the impact of automobile pollution on the earth's resources and examines ways to alleviate it. (Rev: BL 1/15/93) [363.73]

9919 Reed, Jennifer Bond. *Love Canal* (6–12). Series: Great Disasters: Reforms and Ramifications. 2002, Chelsea LB $22.95 (0-7910-6742-4). The story of the town that had to be evacuated in the 1970s when hazardous wastes leaked from a disposal site. (Rev: HBG 3/03; SLJ 12/02) [363.738]

9920 Riddle, John. *Bhopal* (6–10). Series: Great Disasters: Reforms and Ramifications. 2002, Chelsea LB $22.95 (0-7910-6741-6). The story of the leak of pesticide gas from a Union Carbide plant that killed more than 3,000 people in India in 1984. (Rev: HBG 3/03; SLJ 12/02; VOYA 12/02) [363.17]

9921 Rock, Maxine. *The Automobile and the Environment* (9–12). Series: Earth at Risk. 1992, Chelsea LB $19.95 (0-7910-1592-0). A description of the pollution and environmental problems caused by automobiles and how it is being addressed. (Rev: BL 12/1/92) [363.73]

9922 Roleff, Tamara L., ed. *Pollution: Disputed Land* (8–12). Series: Opposing Viewpoints. 1999, Greenhaven LB $21.96 (0-7377-0135-8); paper $13.96 (0-7377-0134-X). Some of the questions explored in this anthology of articles are: Is pollution a serious problem? Do chemical pollutants present a health risk? and Is recycling an effective response? (Rev: BL 11/15/99) [363.73]

9923 Tyson, Peter. *Acid Rain* (9–12). Series: Earth at Risk. 1991, Chelsea LB $19.95 (0-7910-1577-7). An objective presentation of the nature, distribution, and dangers of acid rain and prospects for its reduction. (Rev: BL 4/1/92) [363.73]

9924 Wilson, Duff. *Fateful Harvest: The True Story of a Small Town, a Global Industry, and a Toxic Secret* (10–12). 2001, HarperCollins $26.00 (0-06-019369-7). The story of how farmers in a small community in Washington were able to trace their crop failures and sick cattle to hazardous wastes that were being recycled into fertilizer. (Rev: BL 8/01*) [363.19]

Waste Management

9925 Cozic, Charles P., ed. *Garbage and Waste* (7–12). Series: Current Controversies. 1997, Greenhaven LB $32.45 (1-56510-566-4). An anthology of articles about the seriousness of the waste problem, the dangers of toxic waste, the usefulness of recycling, and the extent that government should interfere in this problem. (Rev: BL 7/97; SLJ 10/97) [363.72]

9926 McVicker, Dee. *Easy Recycling Handbook* (9–12). 1994, Grassroots paper $8.95 (0-9638428-5-4). An introduction to recycling methods and waste management, with advice on overcoming limitations posed by time and space. (Rev: BL 3/15/94) [363.7]

9927 Murphy, Pamela, et al. *The Garbage Primer: A Handbook for Citizens* (9–12). 1993, Lyons Pr. paper $12.95 (1-55821-250-7). This describes how society deals with garbage and what people need to know to dispose of it responsibly. Includes a disposal milestone timeline. (Rev: BL 11/15/93) [363.72]

9928 Stefoff, Rebecca. *Recycling* (9–12). Series: Earth at Risk. 1991, Chelsea LB $19.95 (0-7910-1573-4). A wide-ranging overview of the common types of materials recycled, specific recycling procedures, and challenges. (Rev: BL 6/15/91) [363.72]

Population Issues

General and Miscellaneous

9929 Allison, Anthony. *Hear These Voices: Youth at the Edge of the Millennium* (7–12). 1999, Dutton $22.99 (0-525-45353-9). Testimonies from troubled teenagers around the world, such as a 14-year-old Thai girl whose stepfather sold her into prostitution, compose this harrowing anthology of case studies, accompanied by short, follow-up interviews with adults who have tried to help. (Rev: BL 1/1–15/99*; HBG 3/99; SLJ 2/99; VOYA 4/99) [305.235]

9930 Bender, David L. *Global Resources* (8–12). Series: Opposing Viewpoints. 1998, Greenhaven LB $21.96 (1-56510-673-3); paper $18.70 (1-56510-672-5). Differing opinions are offered on the adequacy of Earth's resources in the face of an ever-expanding population. (Rev: SLJ 1/98) [333.7]

9931 Gallant, Roy A. *The Peopling of Planet Earth: Human Population Growth Through the Ages* (7–12). Illus. 1990, Macmillan LB $15.95 (0-02-735772-4). A history of patterns of world population, the present conditions in relation to resources, and the different future we face. (Rev: BL 3/1/90; VOYA 4/90) [304.6]

9932 Hohm, Charles F., ed. *Population* (6–12). Series: Opposing Viewpoints. 2000, Greenhaven LB $21.96 (0-7377-0292-3); paper $13.96 (0-7377-

0291-5). A collection of essays that explore problems with world population, its growth, and its possible control. (Rev: BL 9/15/00) [306]

9933 Howe, Neil, et al. *Millennials Rising: The Next Great Generation* (10–12). Illus. 2000, Random paper $14.00 (0-375-70719-0). A study of the generation born during the Reagan years, and their emerging characteristics, such as a return to conservative family values. (Rev: BL 9/1/00) [305.275]

9934 Roberts, Sam. *Who Are We: A Portrait of America Based on the 1990 Census* (9–12). 1994, Times Books $18.00 (0-8129-2192-5). This analysis of the 1990 census results points out troubling changes in American society, such as increased polarization and economic discrimination. (Rev: BL 2/1/94) [304.6]

9935 *The Third World* (9–12). Ed. by Laura Egendorf. Series: Opposing Viewpoints. 2000, Greenhaven $21.96 (0-7377-0353-9); paper $13.96 (0-7377-0354-7). How to address the problems faced by Third World nations is the focus of this volume. (Rev: BL 6/1–15/00; SLJ 7/00) [909]

9936 Warner, Rachel. *Refugees* (6–10). Illus. Series: Global Issues. 1996, Raintree Steck-Vaughn LB $19.98 (0-8172-4547-2). After a brief history of the refugee problem, current case studies are used to explore this issue and how it is being confronted in today's world. (Rev: BL 3/15/97) [362.87]

9937 Zeaman, John. *Overpopulation* (8–12). 2002, Watts LB $24.00 (0-531-11893-2). Zeaman reviews the causes of the tremendous rise in population in the last century and discusses measures we might take to curtail the negative impact. (Rev: BL 8/02; SLJ 8/02) [363.9]

Aging, Death, and Burial Practices

9938 *Aging in America* (10–12). Ed. by Olivia J. Smith. Series: Reference Shelf. 2000, H.W. Wilson paper $40.00 (0-8242-0984-2). The social, economic, and political aspects of aging in the United States are explored in this collection of essays. [362.6]

9939 Colman, Penny. *Corpses, Coffins, and Crypts: A History of Burial* (7–12). Illus. 1997, Holt $19.95 (0-8050-5066-3). Customs associated with death and burial traditions in various cultures and times are covered in a text enlivened with many photographs. (Rev: BL 11/1/97; HBG 3/98; SLJ 12/97*) [393]

9940 Cozic, Charles P., ed. *An Aging Population* (8–12). Series: Opposing Viewpoints. 1996, Greenhaven LB $26.20 (1-56510-395-5). A collection of documents expressing various points of view on how the aged will affect America in the future, their entitlement programs, quality of life, health care, and society's acceptance of the elderly. (Rev: BL 7/96; BR 1–2/97; SLJ 8/96; VOYA 10/96) [305.26]

9941 Gignoux, Jane Hughes. *Some Folk Say: Stories of Life, Death, and Beyond* (6–12). Illus. 1998, Foulketale $29.95 (0-9667168-0-9). A collection of 38 literary selections on various aspects of death and how people adjust to it, taken from world folklore and such writers as Shakespeare and Walt Whitman. (Rev: BL 2/15/99) [398.27]

Crime, Gangs, and Prisons

9942 Aaseng, Nathan. *Teens and Drunk Driving* (6–12). Illus. Series: Teen Issues. 1999, Lucent LB $18.96 (1-56006-518-4). A straightforward look at the problem of teens who drink and how this impairs their ability to drive, with relevant statistics and information on the law and strategies used to contain this problem. (Rev: BL 3/15/00; HBG 9/00; SLJ 3/00) [363.12]

9943 Anderson, Lloyd C. *Voices from a Southern Prison* (10–12). 2000, Univ. of Georgia Pr. $29.95 (0-8203-2235-0). This book about the U.S. prison system and prison reform tells of a 20-year legal battle by inmates who protested conditions in Kentucky prisons. (Rev: BL 11/15/00) [365]

9944 Armstrong, Joshua, and Anthony Bruno. *The Seekers: Finding Felons and Guiding Men* (10–12). 2000, HarperCollins $24.00 (0-06-019343-3). This book filled with big-city adventures tells the story of a bounty hunter and the team of urban enforcers he founded known as the Seekers. (Rev: BL 6/1–15/00) [363.28]

9945 Axelrod, Alan, and Charles Phillips. *Cops, Crooks, and Criminologists: An International Biographical Dictionary of Law Enforcement* (10–12). 1996, Facts on File $45.00 (0-8160-3016-2). In 600 descriptive entries, this volume features significant figures in the history of crime, criminology, and law enforcement throughout history. (Rev: SLJ 1/97) [364]

9946 Baden, Michael, and Marion Roach. *Dead Reckoning: The New Science of Catching Killers* (10–12). 2001, Simon & Schuster $25.00 (0-684-86758-3). Drawing on actual cases, this is the story of forensic investigations and what happens in a morgue. (Rev: BL 9/1/01; SLJ 12/01) [363.25]

9947 Barbour, Scott. *Teen Violence* (9–12). Series: Opposing Viewpoints Digests. 1999, Greenhaven LB $27.45 (1-56510-865-5); paper $17.45 (1-56510-864-7). Causes, prevention, treatments, and the extent of teen violence are discussed from a variety of points of view. [364.36]

9948 Barbour, Scott, and Karin L. Swisher, eds. *Violence* (9–12). Illus. Series: Opposing Viewpoints. 1996, Greenhaven paper $20.25 (1-56510-354-8). A presentation of different opinions on the causes of violence, policies aimed at reducing it, and various kinds of violence, such as teen and domestic violence. (Rev: BL 4/1/96; SLJ 3/96) [303.6]

9949 Bass, Bill, and Jon Jefferson. *Death's Acre: Inside the Legendary Forensic Lab, the Body Farm Where the Dead Do Tell Tales* (10–12). 2003, Putnam $24.95 (0-399-15134-6). Not for the faint of heart, this is a riveting story of forensic science. (Rev: BL 10/15/03; SLJ 3/04) [614]

9950 Bayer, Linda. *Drugs, Crime, and Criminal Justice* (7–10). Series: Crime, Justice, and Punishment. 2001, Chelsea LB $19.95 (0-7910-4262-6). This book, written by an analyst from the Office of National Drug Control Policy, looks at the relationship between drugs and crime and its impact on our judicial system. (Rev: BL 9/15/01; HBG 3/02) [364]

9951 Beavan, Colin. *Fingerprints: The Origins of Crime Detection and the Murder Case That Launched Forensic Science* (10–12). Illus. 2001, Hyperion $22.95 (0-7868-6607-1). True crime stories involving murder, greed, and intrigue are interwoven with a history of the development of fingerprinting. (Rev: BL 4/1/01; SLJ 10/01) [363.25]

9952 Bedau, Hugo Adam, ed. *The Death Penalty in America: Current Controversies*. Rev. ed. (10–12). Series: Current Controversies. 1997, Oxford $40.00 (0-19-510438-2). The 40 essays in this anthology explore various aspects of the death penalty, its effectiveness, its legality, and disparities in sentencing. (Rev: SLJ 10/97) [364.6]

9953 Bender, David, and Bruno Leone, eds. *Crime and Criminals* (9–12). Series: Opposing Viewpoints. 1995, Greenhaven paper $16.20 (1-56510-177-4). A presentation of opposing viewpoints on the causes and prevention of crime, gun control, and treatment of young offenders. (Rev: BL 4/1/95; VOYA 4/95) [364.973]

9954 Bender, David L. *Guns and Violence* (8–12). Series: Current Controversies. 1999, Greenhaven LB $31.20 (0-7377-0065-3); paper $19.95 (0-7377-0064-5). The pros and cons of gun control and measures to curb violence are among the topics discussed. [363.3]

9955 Black, Andy. *Organized Crime* (7–12). Series: Crime and Detection. 2003, Mason Crest LB $22.95 (1-59084-367-3). Organized crime in the United States and other countries including Russia and Britain is the main focus of this well-illustrated, large-format volume that will appeal to reluctant readers. Also use *Cyber Crime* and *Major Unsolved Crimes* (2003). (Rev: SLJ 10/03) [364.1]

9956 Bode, Janet, and Stanley Mack. *Hard Time* (7–12). Illus. 1996, Delacorte $16.95 (0-385-32186-4). A series of horrifying and heartbreaking case histories about teens, including many who are in prison, who have been either the perpetrators or the victims of excessive violence. (Rev: BL 4/1/96; BR 9–10/96; SLJ 4/96*; VOYA 4/96) [364.3]

9957 Boostrom, Ron, ed. *Enduring Issues in Criminology* (9–12). Series: Opposing Viewpoints. 1995, Greenhaven LB $27.45 (1-56510-256-8); paper $17.45 (1-56510-255-X). A debate on criminology issues through presentation of a question and essays written in response supporting differing viewpoints. (Rev: BL 7/95) [364]

9958 Bosch, Carl. *Schools Under Siege: Guns, Gangs, and Hidden Dangers* (7–12). Illus. Series: Issues in Focus. 1997, Enslow LB $20.95 (0-89490-908-8). This work surveys teenage crime, its history and causes, the juvenile justice system, pertinent Supreme Court decisions, and types of school violence. (Rev: BL 8/97; SLJ 9/97) [363.1]

9959 Bosco, Antoinette. *Choosing Mercy: A Mother of Murder Victims Pleads to End the Death Penalty* (10–12). 2001, Orbis paper $17.00 (1-57075-358-X). A highly personal account by a mother who has had two of her family murdered, this book makes an eloquent plea for an end to capital punishment and for substituting forgiveness. (Rev: BL 3/1/01) [364.66]

9960 Brown, Brooks, and Rob Merritt. *No Easy Answers: The Truth Behind Death at Columbine* (10–12). Illus. 2002, Lantern paper $17.95 (1-59056-031-0). In this chilling memoir, Brooks Brown, a friend of Columbine High School shooters Dylan Klebold and Eric Harris, tells how he escaped the massacre and searches for explanations for the 1999 tragedy. (Rev: BL 10/15/02) [373.788]

9961 Campbell, Andrea. *Forensic Science: Evidence, Clues, and Investigation* (6–12). Illus. Series: Crime, Justice, and Punishment. 2000, Chelsea $19.95 (0-7910-4950-7). An overview of forensic crime investigation with reference to famous cases including the Boston Strangler and Tylenol tampering. (Rev: SLJ 12/99; VOYA 4/00) [363.25]

9962 Cannon, Angie, et al. *23 Days of Terror: The Compelling True Story of the Hunt and Capture of the Beltway Snipers* (10–12). 2003, Pocket paper $6.99 (0-7434-7695-6). A gripping account of the search for the individuals responsible for the string of sniper shootings that had the Washington, D.C., area in a panic for nearly a month in 2002. (Rev: BL 3/1/03) [364.1]

9963 Capote, Truman. *In Cold Blood: A True Account of a Multiple Murder and Its Consequences* (10–12). 1993, Buccaneer $21.95 (1-5684-9152-2); paper $13.00 (0-679-74558-0). The story of a shocking murder case where a family was killed by two psychotic young men. [364.1]

9964 Coppin, Cheryl Branch. *Everything You Need to Know About Healing from Rape Trauma* (7–12). Series: Need to Know Library. 2000, Rosen $25.25 (0-8239-3122-6). Emphasizing that rape is about power not sex and that the victim is blameless, the

author looks in particular at prevention and recovery. (Rev: SLJ 9/00) [362.883]

9965 Cornwell, Patricia. *Portrait of a Killer: Jack the Ripper, Case Closed* (10–12). 2002, Putnam $27.95 (0-399-14932-5). Cornwell takes on one of history's most enduring real-life murder mysteries in her dissection of the Jack the Ripper case. (Rev: BL 12/1/02) [364.1523]

9966 Corwin, Miles. *The Killing Season: A Summer Inside an LAPD Homicide Division* (10–12). 1997, Simon & Schuster $22.50 (0-684-80235-X). A chronicle of seven months in 1994 that the author spent with a supervising detective, Pete Razanskas, and his trainee partner, Marcella Winn, as they work together in Los Angeles' tough South Central area. (Rev: BL 5/1/97; SLJ 1/98) [363.2]

9967 Cothran, Helen, ed. *Sexual Violence* (8–12). Series: Opposing Viewpoints. 2003, Gale LB $32.45 (0-7377-1240-6); paper $21.20 (0-7377-1239-2). Twenty-five essays explore the reasons why people abuse others, the impact on the victims, the different forms of violence, and differing opinions on the extent of this phenomenon. (Rev: BL 6/1–15/03) [364.15]

9968 Cox, Vic. *Guns, Violence, and Teens* (7–12). Illus. Series: Issues in Focus. 1997, Enslow LB $20.95 (0-89490-721-2). Topics covered in this book include the evolution of gun use in America, gun control, teenage violence, and the impact that guns have on teenagers. (Rev: BL 10/15/97; BR 11–12/97; SLJ 1/98; VOYA 2/98) [363.4]

9969 Cozic, Charles P., ed. *America's Prisons* (8–12). Illus. Series: Opposing Viewpoints. 1997, Greenhaven LB $16.20 (1-56510-549-4). A series of articles expressing differing opinions about the effectiveness of America's prisons, their purposes, and alternatives. (Rev: BL 4/15/97; BR 1–2/98) [365]

9970 Cozic, Charles P., ed. *Gangs* (8–12). Series: Opposing Viewpoints. 1995, Greenhaven LB $26.20 (1-56510-363-7); paper $22.45 (1-56510-362-9). A thought-provoking, alarming, and moving discussion of gangs and violence in the United States. (Rev: BL 12/15/95; VOYA 6/96) [364.1]

9971 *Crime and Criminals* (9–12). Ed. by Tamara L. Roleff. Series: Opposing Viewpoints. 1999, Greenhaven LB $21.96 (0-7377-0121-8); paper $13.96 (0-7377-0120-X). Essays cover many issues relating to crime and its prevention, including juvenile crime. (Rev: BL 2/1/00) [364.973]

9972 Day, Nancy. *Violence in Schools: Learning in Fear* (7–12). Illus. Series: Issues in Focus. 1996, Enslow LB $20.95 (0-89490-734-4). Such forms of violence in schools as guns, sexual harassment, gay bashing, and gang fighting are discussed with material on their causes, effects, and the recent formation of student advocacy groups. (Rev: BL 6/1–15/96; SLJ 7/96) [371.5]

9973 De Hahn, Tracee. *Crimes Against Children: Child Abuse and Neglect* (7–12). Series: Crime, Justice, and Punishment. 1999, Chelsea LB $19.95 (0-7910-4253-7). Laws concerning child abuse, the definition of child abuse, and protecting children against abuse are some of the topics covered in this volume. (Rev: HBG 4/00; SLJ 3/00) [362.76]

9974 DeLong, Candice. *Special Agent: My Life on the Front Lines as a Woman in the FBI* (10–12). 2001, Hyperion $23.95 (0-7868-6707-8). The memoir of a woman who spent 20 years with the Federal Bureau of Investigation chasing kidnappers, rapists, serial killers, and terrorists. (Rev: BL 5/15/01) [363.2]

9975 Digges, Deborah. *The Stardust Lounge: Stories from a Boy's Adolescence* (10–12). Illus. 2001, Doubleday $23.95 (0-385-50158-7). The story of a mother who wouldn't give up trying to help her teenage son, who was stealing cars and running with a violent gang. (Rev: BL 5/15/01) [973.9]

9976 *Domestic Violence* (11–12). Ed. by Tamara L. Roleff. Illus. Series: Opposing Viewpoints. 2000, Greenhaven LB $21.96 (0-7377-0346-6); paper $13.96 (0-7377-0345-8). For advanced students, this collection of documents examines factors contributing to domestic abuse, its impact on families, and possible solutions. (Rev: BL 11/15/00; SLJ 9/00) [362.82]

9977 Dulles, Allen. *Great True Spy Stories* (9–12). 1992, Book Sales $7.98 (0-89009-716-X). This is a collection of thrillers about spy capers that really happened.

9978 Duncan, Lois. *Who Killed My Daughter* (10–12). 1994, Dell paper $7.50 (0-440-21342-8). In despair after her college-student daughter was murdered in 1989 and the police came up with no leads, Duncan turned to psychics and a private detective. (Rev: SLJ 8/92) [364]

9979 Egendorf, Laura K., ed. *Gangs* (6–12). Illus. Series: Opposing Viewpoints. 2000, Greenhaven LB $22.96 (0-7377-0510-8); paper $14.96 (0-7377-0509-4). Diverse viewpoints are offered on wide-ranging topics including gang behavior, racist tendencies, girl gangs, and the various laws and efforts to quell gang activities. (Rev: BL 3/1/01; SLJ 4/01) [364.1]

9980 Espejo, Roman, ed. *America's Prisons* (6–12). Series: Opposing Viewpoints. 2001, Gale LB $31.20 (0-7377-0788-7); paper $19.95 (0-7377-0787-9). Balanced essays examine the effectiveness of prisons and the treatment of prison inmates. (Rev: BL 4/1/02) [365]

9981 Essig, Mark. *Edison and the Electric Chair: A Story of Light and Death* (10–12). Illus. 2003, Walker $26.00 (0-8027-1406-4). Essig explores the history of electrocution as a means of capital punishment against the backdrop of the battle between Thomas Edison and George Westinghouse over whether AC (Westinghouse) or DC (Edison) would dominate the newly emerging electric power industry. (Rev: BL 9/15/03) [364.66]

9982 Ferllini, Roxana. *Silent Witness: How Forensic Anthropology Is Used to Solve the World's Toughest Crimes* (10–12). Illus. 2002, Firefly $35.00 (1-55297-625-4); paper $24.95 (1-55297-624-6). A look at the critical role forensic anthropologists play in determining the truth about fatal accidents and crimes; includes graphic descriptions. (Rev: BL 8/02; SLJ 3/03; VOYA 4/03) [363.25]

9983 Fisher, David. *Hard Evidence: How Detectives Inside the FBI's Sci-Crime Lab Have Helped Solve America's Toughest Cases* (9–12). 1995, Simon & Schuster $23.00 (0-671-79369-1). An introduction to the FBI crime laboratory in Washington, D.C. (Rev: BL 3/1/95) [363.2]

9984 Fridell, Ron. *DNA Fingerprinting: The Ultimate Identity* (9–12). Illus. 2001, Watts LB $24.00 (0-531-11858-4). Fridell gives readers a fascinating and thorough introduction to the history of this technology and the ways in which it is used in investigations and courtrooms today. (Rev: BL 7/01; SLJ 9/01; VOYA 6/02) [614]

9985 Fridell, Ron. *Spying: The Modern World of Espionage* (7–12). Illus. 2002, Millbrook LB $21.40 (0-7613-1662-0). What spies do, the technology they use, and the politics of espionage are all covered in this concise volume. (Rev: BL 5/1/02; HBG 10/02; SLJ 4/02; VOYA 12/02) [327.1]

9986 Frost, Helen, ed. *Why Darkness Seems So Light: Young People Speak Out About Violence* (9–12). 1998, Pecan Grove $10.00 (1-877603-58-9). This is a collection of 40 essays by high school students in Allen County, Indiana, who answer the question, "Have you ever been personally affected by violence?" (Rev: VOYA 4/99) [616.85]

9987 Gaines, Ann. *Prisons* (8–12). Series: Crime, Justice, and Punishment. 1998, Chelsea LB $21.95 (0-7910-4315-0). A thought-provoking look inside America's prisons, with background material on the history and philosophy of incarceration and an examination of issues in penology. (Rev: VOYA 4/99) [365]

9988 *Gangs: Stories of Survival from the Streets* (10–12). Ed. by Sean Donohue. Illus. 2002, Thunder's Mouth paper $17.95 (1-56025-425-4). This wide-ranging collection of excerpts from works of fiction and nonfiction offers important insights into gangs and the lives of gang members. (Rev: BL 8/02) [364.1]

9989 Geary, Rick. *The Borden Tragedy: A Memoir of the Infamous Double Murder at Fall River, Mass., 1892* (10–12). 1997, NBM paper $8.95 (1-

56163-189-2). Using a documentary comic-book format, this is an exciting factual presentation of the Borden murders in Fall River, Massachusetts, adapted from the memoirs of someone who was in Fall River at the time of the crime. (Rev: BL 12/1/97; SLJ 3/98) [973.8]

9990 Gerdes, Louise I. *Serial Killers* (11–12). Series: Contemporary Issues Companion. 2000, Greenhaven LB $21.96 (0-7377-0167-6); paper $13.96 (0-7377-0166-8). Articles examine the personalities, motives, methods and victims of serial killers. (Rev: BL 4/1/00) [364.15]

9991 Goodnough, David. *Stalking: A Hot Issue* (7–10). Series: Hot Issues. 2000, Enslow LB $19.95 (0-7660-1364-2). The motivations of stalkers, their strategies, how to deal with stalkers, and the legal actions that can be taken are all examined in this slim volume. (Rev: HBG 3/01; SLJ 12/00) [364.15]

9992 Goodwin, William. *Teen Violence* (7–10). Illus. Series: Overview: Teen Issues. 1997, Lucent LB $27.45 (1-56006-511-7). A clear, in-depth discussion of the scope, causes, and prevention of teen violence; the relationships between the media, gangs, and violence; and the treatment of juvenile offenders in the justice system. (Rev: BL 5/15/98) [364.36]

9993 Grapes, Bryan J., ed. *Prisons* (8–12). Series: Current Controversies. 2000, Greenhaven LB $21.96 (0-7377-0147-1); paper $13.96 (0-7377-0146-3). This collection of sources explores facets of the penal system with material on the effectiveness of incarceration, the treatment of prisoners, privatization questions, and inmate labor. (Rev: BL 3/1/00) [365]

9994 Grapes, Bryan J., ed. *School Violence* (6–12). Series: Contemporary Issues Companion. 2000, Greenhaven LB $21.96 (0-7377-0331-8); paper $13.96 (0-7377-0332-6). Personal stories add to the urgency of the thought-provoking solutions suggested for school violence. (Rev: BL 10/15/00; SLJ 9/00) [371.7]

9995 Grapes, Bryan J., ed. *Violent Children* (8–12). Series: At Issue. 1999, Greenhaven LB $21.96 (0-7377-0159-5); paper $13.96 (0-7377-0158-7). In a series of articles that express many viewpoints, the problem of violent children at home and school is explored. (Rev: BL 11/15/99) [363.4]

9996 Guernsey, JoAnn B. *Youth Violence: An American Epidemic?* (7–10). Series: Frontline. 1996, Lerner LB $19.95 (0-8225-2627-1). Chapters in this book include discussions on violence at home and school, gangs and gang violence, and the influence of such factors as guns, drugs, alcohol, poverty, race, and discrimination. (Rev: SLJ 1/97; VOYA 2/97) [364.3]

9997 *Guns and Crime* (6–12). Ed. by James D. Torr. Series: At Issue. 2004, Gale LB $27.45 (0-7377-

1997-4). The relationship between availability of guns and crime is explored in a series of articles and essays that express different viewpoints. (Rev: BL 2/15/04) [363.4]

9998 Hallinan, Joseph T. *Going Up the River: Travels in a Prison Nation* (10–12). 2001, Random $24.95 (0-375-50263-7). The author describes his visits to prisons, many of them in Texas, and points up the appalling state of prison policies in the United States. (Rev: BL 2/1/01) [365]

9999 Hinojosa, Maria. *Crews: Gang Members Talk to Maria Hinojosa* (9–12). 1995, Harcourt $17.00 (0-15-292873-1); paper $9.00 (0-15-200283-9). A National Public Radio correspondent interviews New York City gang members after a subway stabbing. (Rev: BL 3/15/95; SLJ 4/95*; VOYA 5/95) [302.3]

10000 Hutchinson, Earl Ofari. *The Mugging of Black America* (9–12). 1990, African American Images paper $8.95 (0-913543-21-7). An angry discourse on what defines African Americans as the perpetrators and victims of crime and as the casualties of the criminal justice system. Also offers guidelines for change. (Rev: BL 9/1/91) [305.8]

10001 Innes, Brian. *Forensic Science* (8–12). 2003, Mason Crest LB $22.95 (1-59084-373-8). A well-illustrated exploration of historic and international crime investigations, with a look at evolving techniques and the importance of evidence in court cases. (Rev: SLJ 6/03) [363.25]

10002 Jah, Yusuf, and Sister Shah'Keyah. *Uprising: Crips and Bloods Tell the Story of America's Youth in the Crossfire* (9–12). 1995, Scribner $22.50 (0-684-80460-3). Probing interviews with gang members, who talk about the worthwhile aspects of gang membership and how it can be channeled into peaceful, productive activities. (Rev: BL 11/1/95) [364.1]

10003 *Juvenile Crime* (9–12). Ed. by Auriana Ojeda. Series: Opposing Viewpoints. 2002, Greenhaven LB $31.20 (0-7377-0784-4); paper $19.95 (0-7377-0783-6). Juvenile crime and juvenile violence are examined from a variety of viewpoints in this excellent collection of essays. [364.36]

10004 Kaminer, Wendy. *It's All the Rage: Crime and Culture* (9–12). 1995, Addison-Wesley $22.00 (0-201-62274-2). High-profile cases are used to stimulate discussion of the criminal justice system, cultural mores, and violence. (Rev: BL 4/1/95) [364.1]

10005 Kerrigan, Michael. *The History of Punishment* (7–12). Series: Crime and Detection. 2003, Mason Crest LB $22.95 (1-59084-386-X). A detailed and interesting overview of the kinds of punishments that have been imposed over the centuries on those who fail to adhere to a wide variety of laws and codes of conduct. (Rev: SLJ 12/03) [364.6]

10006 Kersten, Jason. *Journal of the Dead; A Story of Friendship and Murder in the New Mexico Desert* (10–12). Illus. 2003, HarperCollins $24.95 (0-06-018470-1). A gripping, true-crime story of two Boston friends and the death of one at the hands of the other. (Rev: BL 7/03) [364.15]

10007 Khan, Lin Shi, and Tony Perez. *Scottsboro, Alabama: A Story in Linoleum Cuts* (10–12). Ed. by Andrew H. Lee. Illus. 2002, NYU $26.95 (0-8147-5176-8). The story of the Scottsboro Boys — nine African American teens arrested for the alleged rape of two white women — is retold in this series of propaganda posters created in 1935. (Rev: BL 7/02) [345.73]

10008 Kim, Henny H., ed. *Youth Violence* (7–12). 1998, Greenhaven LB $32.45 (1-56510-811-6). This book presents different opinions on the seriousness of youth violence, its causes, how it can be reduced, and punishments for young offenders. (Rev: BL 8/98) [302.3]

10009 King, Rachel. *Don't Kill in Our Names: Families of Murder Victims Speak Out Against the Death Penalty* (11–12). Illus. 2003, Rutgers Univ. Pr. $27.00 (0-8135-3182-9). This fascinating study looks at families of murder victims who continue to oppose the death penalty; for mature teens. (Rev: BL 2/1/03) [364.66]

10010 Kinnear, Karen L. *Gangs: A Reference Handbook* (9–12). 1996, ABC-CLIO LB $45.00 (0-87436-821-9). This book presents an overview of gangs (why people join, racial and ethnic gangs, prevention, etc.) plus a chronology, biographical sketches, documents, and a wide list of sources. (Rev: BR 5–6/97; SLJ 2/97; VOYA 6/97) [302.3]

10011 Kirwin, Barbara. *The Mad, the Bad, and the Innocent: The Criminal Mind on Trial* (10–12). 1997, Little, Brown $23.95 (0-316-49499-2). The author, a New York forensic psychologist who has tested and testified for over 100 defendants who have used the insanity plea, reviews its recent history and criticizes both its misuse and the inadequate way in which the legal system deals with the criminally mentally ill. (Rev: BL 8/97; SLJ 1/98) [363.2]

10012 Klee, Sheila. *Working Together Against School Violence* (6–10). Series: Library of Political Assassinations. 1996, Rosen LB $16.95 (0-8239-2262-6). This guide introduces the increase in school violence and its causes in the context of violence in society, and shows students what they can do to reduce it in their schools. (Rev: SLJ 2/97) [371.5]

10013 Kopka, Deborah L. *School Violence* (7–12). Series: Contemporary World Issues. 1997, ABC-CLIO LB $45.00 (0-87436-861-8). An overview of juvenile violence over the last 30 years, potential risk factors in youth violence, and efforts to curb school violence. (Rev: BR 3–4/98; SLJ 2/98) [371.5]

10014 Landau, Elaine. *Stalking* (7–12). Illus. 1996, Watts LB $25.00 (0-531-11295-0). All kinds of stalking and stalkers, e.g., former husbands, ex-boyfriends, fans, and total strangers, are discussed, with examples from actual case studies. (Rev: BL 2/15/97; SLJ 2/97) [364.1]

10015 Lewis, Brenda Ralph. *Hostage Rescue with the FBI* (6–10). Illus. Series: Rescue and Prevention: Defending Our Nation. 2003, Mason Crest LB $22.95 (1-59084-403-3). Famous hostage situations such as the *Achille Lauro* incident are mentioned in this well-illustrated survey of the process of rescuing hostages, negotiating with their takers, and the use of snipers. Also use *Police Crime Prevention* (2003). (Rev: SLJ 7/03) [364.15]

10016 Lifton, Robert Jay, and Greg Mitchell. *Who Owns Death? Capital Punishment, The American Conscience and the End of Executions* (10–12). 2000, Morrow $25.00 (0-380-97498-3). This book reviews the pros and cons of capital punishment and discusses the psychological and social ramifications of this debate. (Rev: BL 11/15/00) [364.66]

10017 Lock, Joan. *Famous Prisons* (7–12). Series: Crime and Detection. 2003, Mason Crest LB $22.95 (1-59084-380-0). Alcatraz, Sing Sing, San Quentin, and Dartmoor are among the prisons described, with historical and anecdotal information and accounts of famous inmates. (Rev: HBG 4/04; SLJ 12/03) [365]

10018 Margolis, Jeffrey A. *Teen Crime Wave: A Growing Problem* (7–12). Illus. Series: Issues in Focus. 1997, Enslow LB $20.95 (0-89490-910-X). The teenage crime phenomenon is examined, with material on frequency, causes, the juvenile justice system, Supreme Court decisions, and historical background. (Rev: BL 8/97; SLJ 9/97) [364.36]

10019 Marzilli, Alan. *Famous Crimes of the 20th Century* (8–12). Series: Crime, Justice, and Punishment. 2002, Chelsea LB $22.95 (0-7910-6788-2). The author looks at six well-known events — including the assassination of Martin Luther King Jr., the Watergate burglary, and the O. J. Simpson trial — and discusses the social importance of each. (Rev: SLJ 2/03)

10020 Melton, H. Keith. *The Ultimate Spy Book* (10–12). 1996, DK $29.95 (0-7894-0443-5). This book discusses motivations for spying, breaks down the different kinds of spies — couriers, double agents, defectors, saboteurs, moles, etc. — and provides a fascinating description of their equipment, techniques, communications, and weapons. (Rev: SLJ 7/96; VOYA 10/96) [327.12]

10021 Meltzer, Milton. *Crime in America* (6–10). 1990, Morrow $12.95 (0-688-08513-X). Survey of crime, law enforcement, and the justice system, including the strengths and weaknesses of the current judicial structure. (Rev: BL 1/1/91; SLJ 12/90) [364.973]

10022 Morris, Norval, and David J. Rothman, eds. *The Oxford History of the Prison: The Practice of Punishment in Western Society* (9–12). 1995, Oxford $79.95 (0-19-506153-5). A collection of eight historical essays and six articles about prisons. (Rev: BL 12/15/95) [365]

10023 Newman, Katherine S. *Rampage: The Social Roots of School Shootings* (10–12). Illus. 2004, Basic $27.50 (0-465-05103-0). Through 163 interviews, the author investigates the shooting rampages at two schools, one in Kentucky and the other in Arkansas, and draws some interesting conclusions. (Rev: BL 2/1/04) [371.7]

10024 Newton, David E. *Teen Violence: Out of Control* (7–10). Illus. Series: Issues in Focus. 1995, Enslow LB $20.95 (0-89490-506-6). A well-researched account that covers all types of teen violence, the nature-nurture controversy, ways of preventing teen violence, and types of punishment currently being used. (Rev: BL 3/1/96; SLJ 6/96; VOYA 2/96) [364.3]

10025 Oliver, Marilyn Tower. *Prisons: Today's Debate* (7–12). Series: Issues in Focus. 1997, Enslow LB $20.95 (0-89490-906-1). The debate concerning the effectiveness of America's prisons and their purposes is presented clearly, with all sides represented fairly. (Rev: BL 11/15/97; SLJ 12/97) [365]

10026 Orr, Tamra. *Violence in Our Schools: Halls of Hope, Halls of Fear* (6–12). 2003, Watts LB $29.50 (0-531-12268-9). Strategies for avoiding and defusing violence before it erupts are a focus of this volume that traces violent incidents back to the 1920s and looks at topics including bullying, gun control, homeschooling, and current school efforts in these areas. (Rev: BL 1/1–15/04; SLJ 12/03; VOYA 2/04) [371.7]

10027 Owen, David. *Hidden Evidence: 40 True Crimes and How Forensic Science Helped Solve Them* (10–12). Illus. 2000, Firefly paper $24.95 (1-55209-483-9). Using 40 actual crimes as a focus, this book looks at methods of investigation ranging from those used in ancient China to the latest computerized DNA analysis. (Rev: BL 9/1/00; VOYA 2/01) [363.25]

10028 Owen, David. *Police Lab: How Forensic Science Tracks Down and Convicts Criminals* (6–12). Illus. 2002, Firefly $19.95 (1-55297-620-3); paper $9.95 (1-55297-619-X). The nitty-gritty of forensic science is covered here, with information about the

investigations of some well-known crimes and criminals and attention-grabbing photographs, some of them grisly. (Rev: BL 12/15/02; HBG 3/03; SLJ 5/03) [363.25]

10029 Owens, Lois Smith, and Vivian Verdell Gordon. *Think About Prisons and the Criminal Justice System* (6–10). Series: Think. 1991, Walker LB $15.85 (0-8027-8121-7); paper $9.95 (0-8027-7370-2). Basic information on incarceration, crime and its consequences, the criminal justice system, and the basis for laws. (Rev: BL 6/1/92; SLJ 2/92) [364.973]

10030 Pickett, Carroll, and Carlton Stowers. *Within These Walls: Memoirs of a Death House Chaplain* (10–12). Illus. 2002, St. Martin's $24.95 (0-312-28717-8). The experiences of a chaplain who worked on a death row in Texas for 15 years will interest mature teens debating capital punishment. (Rev: BL 5/1/02) [365]

10031 Proulx, Brenda, ed. *The Courage to Change: A Teen Survival Guide* (7–12). Illus. 2002, Second Story paper $16.95 (1-896764-41-X). A thought-provoking compilation of personal stories, poems, and photographs created by teens who participate in Canada's L.O.V.E. (Leave Out ViolencE) program. (Rev: BL 9/1/02; SLJ 7/02; VOYA 8/02) [364.4]

10032 Rabiger, Joanna. *Daily Prison Life* (7–12). Series: Crime and Detection. 2003, Mason Crest LB $22.90 (1-59084-384-3). Readers learn about the daily routine for prisoners in jails across America. (Rev: SLJ 12/03) [365]

10033 Roberts, Anita. *Safe Teen: Powerful Alternatives to Violence* (7–12). 2001, Polestar paper $15.95 (1-896095-99-2). The author offers practical advice for teens looking for peaceful ways to solve potentially dangerous problems. (Rev: BL 12/15/01; SLJ 4/02; VOYA 2/02) [155.5]

10034 Rodriguez, Luis J. *Always Running: A Memoir of La Vida Loca Gang Days in L.A.* (9–12). 1993, Curbstone $19.95 (1-880684-06-3). Frank recollections about the author's membership in a barrio gang in the 1960s and 1970s personalize crime statistics. (Rev: BL 12/15/92*; SLJ 7/93) [364.1]

10035 Roleff, Tamara L., ed. *Guns and Crime* (8–12). Series: At Issue. 1999, Greenhaven LB $21.96 (0-7377-0153-6); paper $13.96 (0-7377-0152-8). Both primary and secondary sources are included in this anthology that explores the relationship between guns and crime and the topic of gun control. (Rev: BL 12/15/99) [363.3]

10036 Roleff, Tamara L., ed. *Police Corruption* (6–12). Series: At Issue. 2003, Gale $20.96 (0-7377-1172-8); paper $13.96 (0-7377-1171-X). This is a thought-provoking exploration of the reasons why corruption can flourish within the law enforcement community. (Rev: BL 4/15/03) [353.4]

10037 Ryan, Patrick J. *Organized Crime* (9–12). Series: Contemporary World Issues. 1995, ABC-CLIO LB $45.00 (0-87436-746-8). Covering 1850 to the present, this work gives a history of organized crime internationally, with material on various criminal organizations and their members. (Rev: BL 11/1/95; BR 9–10/96; SLJ 3/96) [364]

10038 Sadler, A. E., and Scott Barbour, eds. *Juvenile Crime* (6–12). Series: Opposing Viewpoints. 1997, Greenhaven LB $26.20 (1-56510-516-8). Excerpts from books and articles probe different viewpoints on juvenile violence and crime — its causes, frequency, and punishments. (Rev: BL 2/1/97; BR 5–6/97; SLJ 4/97) [364.3]

10039 Salzman, Mark. *True Notebooks* (11–12). 2003, Knopf $24.00 (0-375-41308-1). This illuminating book recounts the author's experiences teaching writing to inmates in a Los Angeles County juvenile offenders facility; recommended for mature teens only. (Rev: BL 8/03*; VOYA 4/04) [365]

10040 *School Shootings* (9–12). Ed. by Laura K. Egendorf. Series: At Issue. 2002, Greenhaven LB $27.45 (0-7377-1276-7); paper $18.70 (0-7377-1275-9). Conservative and liberal points of view are presented on each issue raised concerning school shootings. (Rev: SLJ 8/02) [371.7]

10041 Schroeder, Andreas. *Fakes, Frauds, and Flimflammery: Even More of the World's Most Outrageous Scams* (9–12). 1999, McClelland & Stewart paper $15.95 (0-7710-7954-0). This entertaining work profiles the scams of 16 colorful swindlers, con artists, forgers, and extortionists. (Rev: SLJ 8/99) [364]

10042 Schulman, Arlene. *23rd Precinct: The Job* (10–12). Illus. 2001, Soho Pr. $25.00 (1-56947-237-8). A gritty account of the author's two years riding with the male and female police officers of New York City's 23rd precinct, one of the city's most ethnically diverse, poor, and crime-ridden areas. (Rev: BL 7/01) [363.2]

10043 Silverstein, Herma. *Kids Who Kill* (7–10). Illus. 1997, Twenty-First Century LB $25.90 (0-8050-4369-1). This volume examines the reasons for the escalation in the number of juvenile killers, who they are, why they kill, the environmental factors involved, and how the court system deals with underage criminals. (Rev: BL 12/15/97; SLJ 1/98; VOYA 2/98) [364.14]

10044 Silverstein, Herma. *Threads of Evidence: Using Forensic Science to Solve Crimes* (7–12). 1996, Twenty-First Century LB $26.90 (0-8050-4370-5). A discussion of the new forensic technology now available to criminologists, such as the use of DNA, blood splatters, fibers, and shell casings, and the role this science has played in solving

famous cases. (Rev: BL 12/1/96; SLJ 2/97; VOYA 6/97) [363.2]

10045 Sparks, Beatrice, ed. *Almost Lost: The True Story of an Anonymous Teenager's Life on the Streets* (9–12). 1996, Avon paper $4.99 (0-380-78341-X). This is the story of runaway Sammy, who at 15 was a member of a street gang and who finally returned to his family and began the road to recovery. (Rev: SLJ 7/96; VOYA 10/96) [364.1]

10046 Stewart, Gail B. *Gangs* (8–10). Illus. Series: The Other America. 1997, Lucent LB $27.45 (1-56006-340-8). Four gang members reveal in interviews why they joined, what gang life is like, and problems trying to leave gangs. (Rev: BL 5/15/97; BR 11–12/97; SLJ 3/97; VOYA 4/98) [364.3]

10047 Stewart, Gail B. *Gangs* (7–12). 1998, Greenhaven LB $27.45 (1-56510-751-9); paper $17.45 (1-56510-750-0). Issues discussed in this volume include why gangs attract members, how to control them, and the seriousness of the problem. (Rev: BL 5/15/98; BR 9–10/98; SLJ 6/98) [364.1]

10048 Streissguth, Thomas. *Hoaxers and Hustlers* (7–10). 1994, Oliver LB $19.95 (1-881508-13-7). Chronicles con artists and con games from the 1800s to the present, including pyramid schemes, the "Martian invasion" radio hoax, and Jim and Tammy Faye Bakker's real-estate scam. (Rev: BL 9/1/94; SLJ 7/94) [364.1]

10049 Sullivan, Randall. *LAbyrinth: A Detective Investigates the Murders of Tupac Shakur and Notorious B.I.G., the Implication of Death Row Records' Suge Knight, and the Origins of the Los Angeles Police Scandal* (10–12). Illus. 2002, Grove Atlantic $25.00 (0-87113-838-7). This fascinating and complex true-crime book examines a possible link between the murders of rappers Tupac Shakur and Biggie Smalls and the scandal in the Ramparts Division of the Los Angeles Police Department; for mature teens. (Rev: BL 3/15/02) [364.15]

10050 Torr, James D., ed. *Gun Violence* (6–12). Illus. Series: Opposing Viewpoints. 2001, Greenhaven LB $31.20 (0-7377-0713-5); paper $19.95 (0-7377-0712-7). Twenty-four essays present varied opinions on guns, gun ownership, and gun violence. (Rev: BL 12/1/01) [363.3]

10051 Torr, James D. *Organized Crime* (10–12). Series: Contemporary Issues Companion. 1999, Greenhaven LB $31.20 (1-56510-891-4); paper $19.95 (1-56510-890-6). This book discusses many aspects of organized crime, including the American Mafia, the Mexican drug trade, and organized crime in Russia. [364.1]

10052 *Violence Against Women* (9–12). Ed. by James D. Torr and Karin L. Swisher. Series: Current Controversies. 1998, Greenhaven LB $20.96 (0-7377-0015-7); paper $12.96 (0-7377-0014-9). The many faces of violence against women and its equally diverse causes are thoughtfully examined in this collection of 29 essays that represent a wide spectrum of views. (Rev: BL 3/15/99; BR 5–6/99) [362.88]

10053 Vogel, Jennifer. *Flim-Flam Man* (11–12). 2004, Scribner $23.00 (0-7432-1707-1). The daughter of a criminal on the most-wanted list looks back at a childhood of uncertainty and a rebellious adolescence; for mature teens. (Rev: BL 12/15/03) [304.1]

10054 Volkman, Ernest. *Spies: The Secret Agents Who Changed the Course of History* (9–12). 1994, Wiley $24.95 (0-471-55714-5). Forty-five true spy stories featuring famous and less-familiar moles, defectors, and spy masters. (Rev: BL 1/15/94) [355.3]

10055 *Wall Tappings: An International Anthology of Women's Prison Writings, 200 to the Present* (10–12). Ed. by Judith A. Scheffler. 2003, Feminist Pr. paper $18.95 (1-55861-273-4). This stunning collection gives voice to women in prisons around the world, offering more than 30 chronologically arranged selections, starting with a woman's letters from a Roman prison cell in 203 A.D. (Rev: BL 3/15/03) [365]

10056 Wambaugh, Joseph. *Fire Lover* (10–12). 2002, Morrow $25.95 (0-06-009527-X). In chilling detail, Wambaugh tells the story of California arson investigator John Orr, who in 1998 was convicted of setting 20 fires, including one that claimed the lives of four people. (Rev: BL 4/1/02) [364.16]

10057 Wilkerson, David. *The Cross and the Switchblade* (9–12). 1987, Jove paper $4.99 (0-515-09025-5). A country minister works with the street gangs of New York City. [364.3]

10058 Winters, Paul A., ed. *Crime* (8–12). Series: Current Controversies. 1997, Greenhaven LB $32.45 (1-56510-687-3); paper $21.20 (1-56510-686-5). A collection of articles debating the causes of crime, methods of prevention, whether or not it is increasing, and juvenile crime. (Rev: BL 2/1/98) [364]

10059 Winters, Paul A., ed. *The Death Penalty* (9–12). Series: Opposing Viewpoints. 1997, Greenhaven LB $21.96 (1-56510-510-9); paper $17.45 (1-56510-509-5). Prominent lawyers and writers explore the morality and constitutionality of capital punishment in this new collection of documents that complements the 1991 edition. (Rev: BL 1/1–15/97; BR 5–6/97) [364.6]

10060 Winters, Paul A., ed. *Hate Crimes* (9–12). Series: Current Controversies. 1996, Greenhaven LB $20.96 (1-56510-373-4); paper $16.20 (1-56510-372-6). A collection of articles from 1992–1994 explore such questions as: Are hate crimes a serious

problem? Should hate speech be limited? Are special penalties appropriate? and Are particular groups responsible for these crimes? (Rev: BL 2/1/96; SLJ 6/96) [364.1]

10061 Wormser, Richard. *Juveniles in Trouble* (8–12). 1994, Messner $15.00 (0-671-86775-X). Extensive use of first-person narratives of troubled youths, with hard-hitting facts on important choices kids in trouble need to make. (Rev: BL 5/15/94; SLJ 6/94; VOYA 12/94) [364.3]

10062 Worth, Richard. *Children, Violence, and Murder* (7–10). Series: Crime, Justice, and Punishment. 2001, Chelsea LB $19.95 (0-7910-5154-4). Specific cases of young people who murder are presented, including Columbine High School, in this fascinating account that presents opposing views on the subject. (Rev: BL 6/1–15/01; HBG 10/01; SLJ 7/01) [364]

10063 Wright, Cynthia. *Everything You Need to Know About Dealing with Stalking* (7–12). Series: Need to Know Library. 2000, Rosen LB $17.95 (0-8239-2841-1). What to do if you're being stalked, as well as where to get help. (Rev: HBG 9/00; SLJ 3/00) [362.88]

10064 Wynn, Jennifer. *Inside Rikers: Stories from the World's Largest Penal Colony* (10–12). 2001, St. Martin's $24.95 (0-312-26179-9). The author, who has worked in many programs to help inmates in New York City's Riker's Island prison, tells about the people she has met there and their stories. (Rev: BL 7/01) [365]

10065 Zehr, Howard. *Transcending: Reflections of Crime Victims* (10–12). Illus. 2001, Good Books $29.95 (1-56148-337-0); paper $18.95 (1-56148-333-8). Using a number of first-person accounts, this book explores the rage, despair, and other emotions experienced by crime victims and their families and the need for restorative justice. (Rev: BL 10/1/01) [362.88]

10066 Zeinert, Karen. *Victims of Teen Violence* (7–12). Illus. Series: Issues in Focus. 1996, Enslow LB $20.95 (0-89490-737-9). An exploration of teen violence that focuses on guns, gangs, sexual harassment, and gay bashing, and includes causes, consequences, victims, and solutions. (Rev: BL 6/1–15/96; SLJ 7/96; VOYA 8/96) [362.88]

10067 Ziff, John. *Espionage and Treason* (7–10). Series: Crime, Justice, and Punishment. 1999, Chelsea LB $19.95 (0-7910-4263-4). The Rosenbergs, Aldrich Ames, and Kim Philby are among the 20th-century spies covered in this survey of espionage and the motivations that drive traitors. (Rev: HBG 9/00; SLJ 4/00) [327.12]

10068 Zuckoff, Mitchell, and Dick Lehr. *Judgment Ridge: The True Stories Behind the Dartmouth Murders* (10–12). Illus. 2003, HarperCollins $25.95

(0-06-000844-X). This shattering and dramatic true-crime story chronicles two teenage boys' grisly murder of two Dartmouth College professors and examines the psychological dynamics between the teens that led to disaster. (Rev: BL 9/15/03) [364.15]

Poverty, Homelessness, and Hunger

10069 Albeda, Randy, et al. *The War on the Poor: A Defense Manual* (10–12). Illus. 1996, New Pr. paper $10.95 (1-56581-262-6). This adult book presents alarming facts and statistics about the status of the poor in the United States near the end of the 20th century. (Rev: VOYA 10/96) [339.4]

10070 Balkin, Karen, ed. *Poverty* (8–12). Series: Opposing Viewpoints. 2003, Gale LB $33.70 (0-7377-1697-5); paper $22.45 (0-7377-1698-3). This anthology describes the 36 million Americans living in poverty, debates the seriousness of the problem, and explores how people get out of poverty and how the poor can be helped. (Rev: BL 1/1–15/04) [362.5]

10071 Barbour, Scott, ed. *Hunger* (7–12). Series: Current Controversies. 1995, Greenhaven LB $32.45 (1-56510-239-8). This compilation of articles, essays, and book excerpts written by journalists, scholars, and activists will challenge young people to evaluate the information and develop their own conclusions about world hunger, the extent of the problem, and how it can be reduced. (Rev: BL 8/95; SLJ 10/95) [363.8]

10072 Berck, Judith. *No Place to Be: Voices of Homeless Children* (7–12). 1992, Houghton $17.00 (0-395-53350-3). Honest testimony of homeless young people, with excerpts from their writing, including poetry. (Rev: BL 4/1/92*; SLJ 6/92) [362.7]

10073 Cozic, Charles P., ed. *Welfare Reform* (8–12). Series: At Issue. 1997, Greenhaven LB $26.20 (1-56510-546-X); paper $17.45 (1-56510-545-1). This anthology of different opinions on welfare reform explores such alternatives as workfare, establishment of orphanages, and reliance on private charities. (Rev: BL 1/1–15/97; SLJ 6/97) [361.973]

10074 Cozic, Charles P., and Paul A. Winters, eds. *Welfare* (8–12). Series: Opposing Viewpoints. 1997, Greenhaven LB $32.45 (1-56510-520-6). In this anthology of 35 essays, prominent politicians and writers debate questions about welfare, including its necessity, abuse, and reform. (Rev: BL 12/15/96; BR 5–6/97; SLJ 2/97) [362.5]

10075 De Koster, Katie, ed. *Poverty* (7–12). Series: Opposing Viewpoints. 1994, Greenhaven paper $16.20 (1-56510-065-4). Differing viewpoints are presented on such questions as what causes poverty and why women and minorities suffer from higher rates of poverty than white males. (Rev: BL 1/1/94) [362.5]

10076 Egendorf, Laura K., ed. *Poverty* (8–12). Series: Opposing Viewpoints. 1998, Greenhaven LB $32.45 (1-56510-947-3); paper $21.20 (1-56510-946-5). The seriousness of poverty today, its causes, and how it can be alleviated are covered in this collection of differing opinions on the subject. (Rev: BL 8/98) [362.5]

10077 Ehrenreich, Barbara. *Nickel and Dimed: On (Not) Getting By in Boom-Time America* (10–12). 2001, Holt $23.00 (0-8050-6388-9). This account of America's "working poor" was written by a social critic and Ph.D. who traveled around the United States trying to maintain a decent life while taking low-paying jobs and living in cheap accommodations. (Rev: BL 4/1/01; SLJ 1/02) [305.569]

10078 Erlbach, Arlene. *Everything You Need to Know If Your Family Is on Welfare* (6–10). Series: Need to Know Library. 1997, Rosen LB $25.25 (0-8239-2433-5). This book explains the welfare system and details recipients' rights as well as offering tips on how to cope with being on welfare and the social stigma often associated with it. (Rev: SLJ 4/98) [362.5]

10079 Flood, Nancy Bohac. *Working Together Against World Hunger* (7–12). Series: Library of Social Activism. 1995, Rosen LB $16.95 (0-8239-1773-8). A rundown on world hunger, the conditions that cause it, and ways of becoming active in fighting it. (Rev: BL 4/15/95) [363.8]

10080 Gottfried, Ted. *Homelessness: Whose Problem Is It?* (6–12). Series: Issue and Debate. 1999, Millbrook LB $25.90 (0-7613-0953-5). After reviewing the history of homelessness in the United States, opposing views are presented on the causes of homelessness today, the responsibility of government and the individual, and methods of countering it. (Rev: BL 4/1/99; BR 9–10/99; SLJ 9/99) [305.569]

10081 *Growing Up Poor: A Literary Anthology* (10–12). Ed. by Robert Coles et al. 2001, New Pr. $23.95 (1-56584-623-0). Using sources including William Carlos Williams, Sandra Cisneros, and Langston Hughes, this collection of literary fragments explores the condition of growing up poor and how it changes one, including one's self-image. (Rev: BL 2/15/01; SLJ 6/01; VOYA 6/01) [810.08]

10082 Hombs, Mary Ellen. *Welfare Reform: A Reference Handbook* (9–12). Series: Contemporary World Issues. 1996, ABC-CLIO LB $48.50 (0-87436-844-8). The author traces the history of social welfare programs from their inception in the 1930s to late 20th-century attitudes toward them, examines the effectiveness of state and federal programs, profiles people who have influenced social welfare programs, and furnishes information on forms of assistance, agencies, and resources. (Rev: SLJ 6/97) [353]

10083 *The Homeless* (9–12). Ed. by Jennifer A. Hurley. Series: Opposing Viewpoints. 2002, Greenhaven LB $31.20 (0-7377-0750-X); paper $19.95 (0-7377-0749-6). The causes of homelessness, the living conditions of the homeless, and possible solutions to the problem are discussed in this collection of documents. [362.5]

10084 Johnson, Joan J. *Children of Welfare* (6–10). Illus. 1995, Twenty-First Century LB $23.40 (0-8050-2985-0). A look at the emergence of the welfare system, what it is today, and its impact on young people. (Rev: BL 6/1–15/97; BR 11–12/97; SLJ 6/97) [362.71]

10085 Kowalski, Kathiann M. *Poverty in America: Causes and Issues* (6–12). Series: Issues in Focus. 2003, Enslow LB $20.95 (0-7660-1945-4). An exploration of unequal standards of living in America that looks at differences in levels of poverty and at homelessness, welfare, government efforts to alleviate the problem, and private-sector aid. (Rev: HBG 4/04; SLJ 11/03) [362.5]

10086 Kozol, Jonathan. *Amazing Grace: The Lives of Children and the Conscience of a Nation* (10–12). 1995, Crown paper $14.00 (0-06-097697-7). A telling glimpse into the lives of the people who live in the Mott Haven section of the Bronx, one of the poorest neighborhoods in the nation. (Rev: BL 9/15/95) [362.7]

10087 Kozol, Jonathan. *Rachel and Her Children: Homeless Families in America* (10–12). 1989, Fawcett paper $12.95 (0-449-90339-7). By focusing on a family living in a welfare hotel in New York City, the author explores the pitiful existence of the homeless in America. (Rev: BL 1/1/88; BR 5-6/89; SLJ 3/88; VOYA 10/88) [362.5]

10088 LeBlanc, Adrian Nicole. *Random Family: Love, Drugs, Trouble, and Coming of Age in the Bronx* (10–12). 2003, Scribner $25.00 (0-684-86387-1). The author spent more than a decade chronicling the lives of two Latinas from the Bronx, producing a revealing profile of life among America's urban poor. (Rev: BL 2/15/03) [305.5]

10089 LeVert, Marianne. *The Welfare System* (7–12). 1995, Millbrook LB $25.90 (1-56294-455-X). A look at various issues that form the great welfare debate. (Rev: BL 4/15/95; SLJ 4/95) [361.6]

10090 Parker, Julie. *Everything You Need to Know About Living in a Shelter* (8–12). 1995, Rosen LB $25.25 (0-8239-1874-2). A straightforward account that describes life for teens living in shelters, with material on what they can do to control at least some aspects of their lives. (Rev: SLJ 12/95; VOYA 2/96) [362.5]

10091 Roleff, Tamara L., ed. *Inner-City Poverty* (8–12). Series: Contemporary Issues Companion. 2003, Gale LB $25.96 (0-7377-0841-7); paper $16.96 (0-7377-0840-9). This examination of theories about the causes of urban poverty, the resulting crime and drug use, the impact of the welfare system, and the potential for effective reform provides lots of material for students doing research. (Rev: LMC 4–5/03; SLJ 2/03) [362.5]

10092 S., Tina, and Jamie Pastor Bolnick. *Living at the Edge of the World: A Teenager's Survival in the Tunnels of Grand Central Station* (11–12). 2000, St. Martin's $24.95 (0-312-20047-1). The harrowing story of a girl who spent four years as a homeless drug addict and prostitute living in the tunnels of Grand Central Station. (Rev: BL 9/1/00) [362.74]

10093 Shipler, David K. *The Working Poor: Invisible in America* (10–12). 2004, Knopf $26.00 (0-375-40890-8). Using case studies plus statistics, the author has producing a stirring portrait of people who struggle with low-paying jobs and little social assistance to maintain their lives and their families. (Rev: BL 1/1–15/04) [305.5]

10094 Stavsky, Lois, and I. E. Mozeson. *The Place I Call Home: Faces and Voices of Homeless Teens* (8–12). Illus. 1990, Shapolsky $14.95 (0-944007-81-3). A series of interviews with homeless teens reveals lives of violence, poverty, and drugs. (Rev: BL 11/15/90; SLJ 2/91) [362.7]

10095 Stearman, Kaye. *Homelessness* (5–10). Illus. Series: Talking Points. 1999, Raintree Steck-Vaughn LB $27.12 (0-8172-5312-2). A worldwide view of homelessness, its causes — including eviction, natural disasters, and war — and international efforts to combat it. (Rev: BL 9/1/99; BR 9–10/99; SLJ 8/99) [363.5]

10096 Stewart, Gail B. *Homeless Teens* (8–10). Series: The Other America. 1999, Lucent LB $17.96 (1-56006-398-X). The plight of teens without homes is explored through an overview chapter and a series of interviews with five teens. (Rev: BL 9/15/99; SLJ 8/99) [362.5]

10097 Turner, Sugar, and Tracy Bachrach Ehlers. *Sugar's Life in the Hood: The Story of a Former Welfare Mother* (10–12). 2002, Univ. of Texas Pr. $29.95 (0-292-72102-1). Turner describes how she managed to extricate herself from a web of addiction, prostitution, and welfare to build a better life for herself. (Rev: BL 6/1–15/02) [305.48]

Unemployment

10098 Alpern, Michele. *The Effects of Job Loss on the Family* (6–12). Illus. Series: Focus on Family Matters. 2002, Chelsea LB $19.75 (0-7910-6690-8). Personal teen experiences draw readers into this straightforward account of the financial and emotional upheavals caused by unemployment. (Rev: BL 10/15/02; HBG 3/03) [306.4]

Public Morals

10099 Carnes, Jim. *Us and Them: A History of Intolerance in America* (7–12). Illus. 1996, Oxford $28.00 (0-19-510378-5). Each chapter focuses on an episode of intolerance and prejudice in our history, such as the Cherokee Trail of Tears, the internment of Japanese Americans during World War II, recent race riots in New York City, and the murder of a gay man in Maine. (Rev: BL 6/1–15/96; BR 11–12/96) [305.8]

10100 *Censorship* (9–12). Ed. by Laura K. Egendorf. Series: Current Controversies. 2000, Greenhaven LB $22.96 (0-7377-0450-0); paper $14.96 (0-7377-0449-7). Censorship in all its guises is explored in this series of essays, which examine such specific issues as bans on hate speech, attempts to block access to online pornography, and government regulation of art and popular culture. (Rev: BL 2/15/01; SLJ 3/01) [363.3]

10101 Cothran, Helen, ed. *Pornography* (8–12). Illus. Series: Opposing Viewpoints. 2001, Gale LB $31.20 (0-7377-0761-5); paper $19.95 (0-7377-0760-7). Debating teams will plenty of arguments to defend both sides of questions about the evils of pornography and whether it should be regulated and/or censored. (Rev: SLJ 12/01) [363.4]

10102 Day, Nancy. *Censorship or Freedom of Expression?* (7–12). Series: Pro/Con Issues. 2000, Lerner LB $25.26 (0-8225-2628-X). A look at censorship in areas including schools and the arts and entertainment, with discussion of age appropriateness and use of the Internet. (Rev: HBG 3/01; SLJ 1/01) [363.3]

10103 Dudley, William, ed. *Media Violence* (8–12). Series: Opposing Viewpoints. 1998, Greenhaven LB $32.45 (1-56510-945-7); paper $21.20 (1-56510-944-9). This exploration of violence in television, motion pictures, song lyrics, and other media questions its extent, effects, and proposals to restrict it. (Rev: BL 8/89) [384]

10104 Foerstel, Herbert N. *Banned in the Media: A Reference Guide to Censorship in the Press, Motion Pictures, Broadcasting and the Internet* (9–12). 1998, Greenwood $49.95 (0-313-30245-6). This work begins with a history of censorship in the media, continues with coverage of 28 media-related censorship cases from 1812 to 1997, and ends with six editorial statements from spokespeople including Daniel Schorr and Walter Cronkite. (Rev: BR 1–2/99; SLJ 11/98; VOYA 12/98) [363.3]

10105 *Free Speech* (9–12). Ed. by Scott Barbour. Series: Current Controversies. 1999, Greenhaven LB $21.96 (0-7377-0143-9); paper $13.96 (0-7377-0142-0). A collection of essays on a wide range of topics relating to the issue of free speech. (Rev: BL 12/1/99) [342.73]

10106 Gerdes, Louise I., ed. *Media Violence* (8–12). Series: Opposing Viewpoints. 2003, Gale LB $33.70 (0-7377-2011-5); paper $22.45 (0-7377-2012-3). Violence in television, motion pictures, music lyrics, and other media is explored in this collection of essays with material on how serious the problem is and what, if anything, should be done about it. (Rev: BL 1/1–15/04; SLJ 5/04) [303.6]

10107 Gold, John C. *Board of Education v. Pico (1982)* (6–10). Illus. Series: Supreme Court Decisions. 1994, Twenty-First Century LB $25.90 (0-8050-3660-1). A thorough analysis of the Supreme Court case that began in a Long Island school and involved censoring library materials. (Rev: BL 11/15/94; SLJ 1/95) [344.73]

10108 Gottfried, Ted. *Pornography: Debating the Issues* (9–12). Illus. Series: Issues in Focus. 1997, Enslow LB $19.95 (0-89490-907-X). Supplies historical background on pornography, the complicated social and legal issues that surround it, and the possible connection between violence and sexual exploitation and obscene material. (Rev: BL 4/15/97; BR 11–12/97; SLJ 7/97) [363.4]

10109 Heins, Marjorie. *Not in Front of the Children: "Indecency," Censorship, and the Innocence of Youth* (10–12). Illus. 2001, Farrar $27.00 (0-374-17545-4). After examining the history of child-oriented censorship in the United States, this demanding account looks at modern aspects of the controversy such as filtering TV shows. (Rev: BL 5/15/01) [303.3]

10110 Irons, Peter, ed. *May It Please the Court: Courts, Kids and the Constitution* (10–12). Series: May it Please the Court. 2000, New Pr. $59.95 (1-56584-613-3). This volume, which includes audiotapes, deals with issues involving the constitutional rights of children, such as school prayer, religious clubs, maternity leaves for teachers, teaching evolution, student newspapers, and censorship. (Rev: BL 9/1/00) [344.73]

10111 Kolbert, Kathryn, and Zak Mettger. *Justice Talking: Leading Advocates Debate Today's Most Controversial Issues — Censoring the Web* (10–12). 2001, New Pr. $24.95 (1-56584-715-6). A debate from National Public Radio on Web censorship is reproduced (with an accompanying CD) with relevant original sources. (Rev: BL 12/1/01) [343.7309]

10112 Miller, J. Anthony. *Texas vs. Johnson: The Flag-Burning Case* (6–10). Illus. Series: Landmark Supreme Court Cases. 1997, Enslow LB $20.95 (0-

89490-858-8). The limits of civil disobedience were the subject of this important Supreme Court case. (Rev: BL 7/97; BR 11–12/97) [342.73]

10113 Netzley, Patricia D. *Issues in Censorship* (9–12). Series: Contemporary Issues. 2000, Lucent LB $18.96 (1-56006-609-1). Convincing arguments from all sides of the issue center on actual cases that have called upon the First Amendment. (Rev: BL 6/1–15/00; HBG 9/00; VOYA 4/01) [303.3]

10114 Newton, David E. *Violence and the Media* (9–12). Series: Contemporary World Issues. 1996, ABC-CLIO LB $39.50 (0-87436-843-X). Following an overview of violence in movies, television, music, and video games, there are profiles of key people involved in the debate and excerpts from laws and regulations, court cases, policy statements, research reports, and opinions about TV violence. (Rev: BL 11/15/96; BR 11–12/97; SLJ 12/96) [303.6]

10115 Roleff, Tamara L., ed. *Censorship* (6–12). Series: Opposing Viewpoints. 2001, Gale $31.20 (1-56510-957-0); paper $19.95 (1-56510-956-2). Thoughtful essays address censorship and free speech as they relate to art, pornography, schools, and libraries. (Rev: BL 4/1/02; SLJ 12/01) [363.3]

10116 Stay, Byron L., ed. *Censorship* (8–12). Series: Opposing Viewpoints. 1997, Greenhaven LB $32.45 (1-56510-508-7). This new edition of the 1990 title presents arguments on such controversial areas of the censorship battle as antipornography laws, campus speech codes, and use of the V-chip. (Rev: BL 12/15/96; BR 5–6/97; VOYA 6/97) [363.3]

10117 Steffens, Bradley. *Censorship* (7–10). Illus. 1996, Lucent LB $27.45 (1-56006-166-9). A historical survey that presents the conflict between freedom and censorship, beginning with the Ten Commandments and the Bill of Rights and ending with today's controversy over rock lyrics. (Rev: BL 2/15/96; SLJ 3/96) [363.3]

10118 Torr, James D., ed. *Is Media Violence a Problem?* (6–12). Series: At Issue. 2001, Greenhaven paper $16.20 (0-7377-0802-6). Brief essays look at the kinds of violence found on television and in movies, video games, and rap music, and assess whether this violence engenders further violence. (Rev: BL 1/1–15/02; SLJ 3/02) [302.23]

10119 Torr, James D., ed. *Violence in Film and Television* (6–12). Series: Examining Pop Culture. 2002, Gale $31.20 (0-7377-0865-4); paper $19.95 (0-7377-0864-6). This collection of essays examines the evolution of violence in television, movies, and video games. (Rev: BL 4/1/02; SLJ 3/02) [303.6]

10120 *Violence in the Media* (10–12). Ed. by James D. Torr. Series: Current Controversies. 2001, Greenhaven LB $31.20 (0-7377-0456-X); paper

$19.95 (0-7377-0455-1). A selection of essays and articles that deal with the extent and effects of violence in the media. (Rev: SLJ 3/01) [303.6]

10121 Wekesser, Carol, ed. *Pornography* (8–12). Series: Opposing Viewpoints. 1997, Greenhaven paper $21.20 (1-56510-517-6). What is pornography? Is it harmful? Should it be censored? Can it be controlled on the Internet? These are some of the questions explored in this collection of writings representing different points of view. (Rev: BL 12/15/96; BR 5–6/97; SLJ 2/97) [363.7]

10122 Whitehead, Fred. *Culture Wars* (8–12). Series: Opposing Viewpoints. 1994, Greenhaven LB $26.20 (1-56510-101-4); paper $16.20 (1-56510-100-6). Includes essays by a variety of writers on such cultural topics as intellectual freedom, artistic quality, values, and public morality. (Rev: BL 5/1/94; SLJ 3/94; VOYA 4/94) [306]

Sex Roles

10123 Bender, David, and Bruno Leone, eds. *Male/Female Roles* (9–12). Series: Opposing Viewpoints. 1995, Greenhaven LB $19.95 (1-56510-174-X); paper $14.50 (1-56510-175-8). A discussion of how sex roles are established, whether they have changed for the better, and predictions for the future. (Rev: BL 4/1/95; SLJ 2/95; VOYA 5/95) [305.3]

10124 Bloom, Amy. *Normal: Transsexual CEOs, Crossdressing Cops, and Hermaphrodites with Attitude* (10–12). 2002, Random $23.95 (0-679-45652-X). An eye-opening and perceptive excursion into the world of gender conflict. (Rev: BL 9/1/02) [306.7]

10125 Hanmer, Trudy J. *The Gender Gap in Schools: Girls Losing Out* (7–12). Illus. Series: Issues in Focus. 1996, Enslow LB $20.95 (0-89490-718-2). Sex discrimination at the school level is introduced with an objective presentation of the many facets of this complex question. (Rev: BL 8/96; SLJ 6/96) [376]

10126 Howey, Noelle. *Dress Codes: Of Three Girlhoods — My Mother's, My Father's, and Mine* (11–12). 2002, St. Martin's $24.00 (0-312-26921-8). The impact of her father's transgenderism on the whole family is the focus of this absorbing memoir suitable for mature teens. (Rev: BL 5/15/02; SLJ 8/02) [306.874]

10127 *Male/Female Roles* (9–12). Ed. by Laura K. Egendorf. Series: Opposing Viewpoints. 1999, Greenhaven LB $21.96 (0-7377-0131-5); paper $13.96 (0-7377-0130-7). This book looks at how the sexes relate to each other and addresses the issue of perceptions of oppression. (Rev: BL 1/1–15/00; SLJ 4/00) [305.3]

10128 Stearman, Kaye, and Nikki van der Gaag. *Gender Issues* (6–10). Illus. Series: Global Issues. 1996, Raintree Steck-Vaughn LB $19.98 (0-8172-4545-6). Using historical background material, statistics, and case studies, the various issues involving gender roles and sex discrimination around the world are explored. (Rev: BL 3/15/97; VOYA 6/97) [305.3]

Social Action, Social Change, and Futurism

10129 Ackerman, Peter, and Jack DuVall. *A Force More Powerful: A Century of Nonviolent Conflict* (10–12). Illus. 2000, St. Martin's $29.95 (0-312-22864-3). This companion volume to the PBS television series chronicles many cases of nonviolent action during the 20th century and the resulting social changes in such countries as World War II Denmark, colonial India, the Balkans, Northern Ireland, South Africa, and the United States during the civil rights movement. (Rev: BL 11/15/00) [303.6]

10130 *American Women Activists' Writings: An Anthology, 1637–2001* (10–12). Ed. by Kathryn Cullen-DuPont. 2002, Rowman & Littlefield $35.00 (0-8154-1185-5). Sojourner Truth, Elizabeth Cady Stanton, Elizabeth Blackwell, and Amelia Earhart are among the women whose writings are gathered here. (Rev: BL 3/1/02) [305.4]

10131 Banerjee, Dillon. *So, You Want to Join the Peace Corps . . . What to Know Before You Go* (10–12). Illus. 2000, Ten Speed paper $12.95 (1-58008-097-9). This is a practical guide for those interested in joining the Peace Corps, with material on applications, emotional reactions, training, and concerns about money and health. (Rev: BL 2/15/00; SLJ 7/00) [361.6]

10132 Brooks, Susan M. *Any Girl Can Rule the World* (9–12). 1998, Fairview paper $12.95 (1-57749-068-1). Based on the principle that information and knowledge equals power, this book is a call to action for young women to get involved in social, political, and economic issues, and a guide on how to do so. (Rev: VOYA 4/99) [361.2]

10133 Brownlie, Alison. *Charities — Do They Work?* (6–10). Series: Talking Points. 1999, Raintree Steck-Vaughn LB $18.98 (0-8172-5319-X). In this brief account, the role of charities in American society is explored along with a discussion on their problems and accomplishments. (Rev: BL 12/15/99; HBG 9/00) [361]

10134 Carlson, Richard, and Bruce Goldman. *2020 Visions: Long View of a Changing World* (9–12). 1991, Stanford Alumni Association paper $12.95 (0-916318-44-3). Optimistic futurist speculation that concentrates on the long-term impact of such trends as an aging population, a restructured economy, and a divided society. (Rev: BL 11/1/91) [303.49]

10135 Duper, Linda Leeb. *160 Ways to Help the World: Community Service Projects for Young People* (10–12). 1996, Facts on File LB $25.00 (0-8160-3324-2). A useful resource for teens interested in doing something to help their communities, this guide offers a multitude of practical suggestions. [361.3]

10136 Gaillard, Frye. *If I Were a Carpenter: Twenty Years of Habitat for Humanity* (10–12). 1996, Blair $24.95 (0-89587-148-3). The story of the founding of Habitat for Humanity, its successes and failures in building houses for the poor, and the contributions of such people as Jimmy Carter. (Rev: BL 6/1–15/96; BR 11–12/96; SLJ 10/96) [361.7]

10137 Isler, Claudia. *Volunteering to Help in Your Neighborhood* (6–10). Series: Service Learning. 2000, Children's LB $19.00 (0-516-23374-2); paper $6.95 (0-516-23574-5). For reluctant readers, this volume suggests ways in which teens can help others in their communities. Also use *Volunteering to Help with Animals* (2001). (Rev: SLJ 2/01)

10138 Kronenwetter, Michael. *Protest!* (7–12). Illus. 1996, Twenty-First Century LB $23.40 (0-8050-4103-6). This book describes various forms of protest, from simple actions in everyday life to those aimed at changing social conditions in the U.S. and around the world, providing a historical, sociological, and psychological context. (Rev: BL 1/1–15/97; SLJ 1/97; VOYA 6/97) [303.48]

10139 Kurian, George Thomas, and Graham T. T. Molitor, eds. *The 21st Century* (8–12). 1999, Macmillan $130.00 (0-02-864977-X). This book makes predictions for future developments in such areas as abortion, artificial intelligence, crime, extinction, household appliances, sexual behavior, and utopias. (Rev: BL 4/1/99; SLJ 8/99) [133.3]

10140 Lesko, Wendy Schaetzel. *Youth: The 26% Solution* (7–12). 1998, Information U.S.A. paper $14.95 (1-878346-47-4). A community action handbook for teens prepared by Project 2000 that provides basic, workable advice, based on the premise that the 26 percent of the population of the United States under the age of 18 can make a difference. (Rev: BL 11/1/98; VOYA 12/98) [361.8]

10141 Markley, Oliver W., and Walter R. McCuan, eds. *21st Century Earth* (7–12). Series: Opposing Viewpoints. 1996, Greenhaven LB $26.20 (1-56510-415-3); paper $21.20 (1-56510-414-5). An assortment of forecasts for the near future, including the effects of overpopulation and new technologies. (Rev: BL 4/1/96; SLJ 3/96) [303.49]

10142 Meltzer, Milton. *Who Cares? Millions Do . . . A Book About Altruism* (7–10). 1994, Walker LB $16.85 (0-8027-8325-2). Stories of people who help their fellow beings, both individually and through organizations. (Rev: BL 11/15/94; VOYA 2/95) [171]

10143 Mintzer, Rich. *Helping Hands: How Families Can Reach Out to Their Community* (6–12). Series: Focus on Family Matters. 2002, Chelsea LB $20.75 (0-7910-6952-4). This is a basic introduction to volunteerism with tips on how teens can get involved in activities and projects that complement their interests and abilities. (Rev: BL 1/1–15/03) [361.8]

10144 Perry, Susan K. *Catch the Spirit: Teen Volunteers Tell How They Made a Difference* (7–12). 2000, Watts LB $33.00 (0-531-11883-5); paper $14.95 (0-531-16499-3). Teens discuss their involvement in volunteer work and how the experience made a difference not only in their communities but also in their personal lives. (Rev: SLJ 3/01; VOYA 6/01) [361.3]

10145 Ryan, Bernard. *Caring for Animals* (7–12). 1998, Ferguson LB $15.95 (0-89434-227-4). After a general introduction to volunteerism, this book outlines ways that teens can help care for unwanted and abandoned animals in their neighborhood. (Rev: BL 9/15/98; BR 11–12/98; SLJ 11/98; VOYA 8/99) [361.8]

10146 Ryan, Bernard. *Expanding Education and Literacy* (7–12). Series: Community Service for Teens. 1998, Ferguson LB $15.95 (0-89434-231-2). This book describes literacy and reading programs in the United States and how teens can participate in them. (Rev: BL 9/15/98; BR 11–12/98; SLJ 11/98) [361.3]

10147 Ryan, Bernard. *Helping the Ill, Poor and the Elderly* (7–12). Series: Community Service for Teens. 1998, Ferguson LB $15.95 (0-89434-229-0). Outlines the many ways in which teens can help the less fortunate in their communities both informally and working through service agencies. (Rev: BL 9/15/98; BR 11–12/98; SLJ 11/98) [361.8]

10148 Ryan, Bernard. *Promoting the Arts and Sciences* (7–12). Series: Community Service for Teens. 1998, Ferguson LB $15.95 (0-89434-234-7). This work tells how teens can become involved in local agencies that promote the arts and sciences and how their services can make a difference both to the community and to themselves. (Rev: BL 9/15/98; BR 11–12/98; SLJ 2/99) [361.8]

10149 Ryan, Bernard, Jr. *Participating in Government: Opportunities to Volunteer* (7–12). Series:

Community Service for Teens. 1998, Ferguson LB $15.95 (0-89434-230-4). An upbeat guide that advises teens about how they can volunteer in the areas of government and politics and become involved in their community. Also use *Promoting the Arts and Sciences: Opportunities to Volunteer* (1998). (Rev: BR 11–12/98; SLJ 2/99) [302.14]

10150 Seo, Danny. *Generation React: Activism for Beginners* (7–12). 1997, Ballantine paper $10.95 (0-345-41242-7). This book gives step-by-step directions for starting an activist group, with material on fund raising, protesting and boycotting, lobbying, publicity, and related topics. (Rev: BL 10/1/97; VOYA 2/98) [303.4]

10151 *Volunteerism* (10–12). Ed. by Frank McGuckin. Series: Reference Shelf. 1998, H.W. Wilson paper $25.00 (0-8242-0944-3). These articles by a variety of writers explore various facets of volunteering and how individuals can participate. [361.3]

Social Customs and Holidays

10152 Aiello, Josh, and Matthew Shultz. *A Field Guide to the Urban Hipster* (10–12). Illus. 2003, Broadway paper $12.95 (0-7679-1372-8). A tongue-in-cheek guide to such diverse early-21st-century species as Ravers, Ex-Frats, Urban Moms, and AlternaBoys. (Rev: BL 9/1/03) [305.9]

10153 Bannatyne, Lesley. *A Halloween How-To: Costumes, Parties, Decorations, and Destinations* (9–12). Illus. 2001, Pelican paper $17.95 (1-56554-774-8). After a history of Halloween, this book tells you how to have a great Halloween party, how it is celebrated in various cultures, and how to prepare Halloween food. (Rev: BL 7/01) [394.2]

10154 Breuilly, Elizabeth, and Joanne O'Brien. *Festivals of the World: The Illustrated Guide to Celebrations, Customs, Events and Holidays* (6–12). Illus. 2002, Checkmark $29.95 (0-8160-4481-3). Festivals around the world are organized by religion, with maps, photographs, and interesting sidebar features. (Rev: SLJ 4/03) [394.2]

10155 Coon, Nora E., ed. *It's Your Rite: Girls' Coming-of-Age Stories* (6–12). 2003, Beyond Words paper $9.95 (1-58270-074-5). Young authors from around the world describe practical and ceremonial milestones that mark their coming of age, and the associated worries and joys. (Rev: SLJ 10/03) [305.235]

10156 Dover, Laura D. *The Big Book of Halloween: Creative and Creepy Projects for Revellers of All Ages* (9–12). Illus. 1998, Lark $19.95 (1-57990-

063-1). A variety of Halloween projects from simple to complex are included in this volume, plus historical material about the holiday and Halloween trivia. (Rev: SLJ 10/98) [745.5]

10157 Dresser, Norine. *Multicultural Celebrations: Today's Rules of Etiquette for Life's Special Occasions* (9–12). 1999, Three Rivers paper $14.00 (0-609-80259-3). This book provides practical advice and social dos and don'ts for the customs, rituals, and holidays of various cultures around the world. (Rev: SLJ 9/99) [394.2]

10158 Harris, Jessica. *A Kwanzaa Keepsake: Celebrating the Holiday with New Traditions and Feasts* (9–12). 1995, Simon & Schuster $22.00 (0-684-80045-4). A collection of ethnic recipes for celebrating Kwanzaa, plus an explanation of the seven principles that are the basis of the celebration. (Rev: BL 11/15/95; SLJ 5/96) [394.2]

10159 Karenga, Maulana. *Kwanzaa: A Celebration of Family, Community and Culture, Special Commemorative Edition* (6–12). Illus. 1997, Univ. of Sankore Pr. $24.95 (0-943412-21-8). This complete book on Kwanzaa explains its African and African American origins, devotes a chapter to each of its seven principles, suggests activities, and gives answers to the most frequently asked questions about this holiday. (Rev: SLJ 10/98) [394.2]

10160 McSharry, Patra, and Roger Rosen, eds. *Coca-Cola Culture: Icons of Pop* (10–12). Series: Icarus World Issues. 1994, Rosen LB $16.95 (0-8239-1593-X); paper $8.95 (0-8239-1594-8). Essays and fiction on how America's commercial products have influenced the way other countries perceive us as well as how we see ourselves, using such examples as rock music in China, the TV series *Dallas* in Poland, and the changing portrayal of Native Americans. (Rev: BL 3/1/94) [306.4]

10161 Menard, Valerie. *The Latino Holiday Book: Cinco de Mayo to Dia de los Muertos* (10–12). Illus. 2000, Marlowe paper $15.95 (1-56924-646-7). This book outlines a full year's festivals that have Latino origins, plus ways to celebrate and some recipes. (Rev: BL 10/15/00) [641.5]

10162 Santino, Jack. *All Around the Year: Holidays and Celebrations in American Life* (9–12). 1994, Univ. of Illinois Pr. $24.95 (0-252-02049-9). The effect of holidays on American life. (Rev: BL 4/15/94) [394.269]

10163 Vida, Vendela. *Girls on the Verge: Debutante Dips, Drive-bys, and Other Initiations* (10–12). 1999, St. Martin's $19.95 (0-312-20044-7). A look at the rituals — ranging from the traditional to the bizarre — popular among today's girls and young women. (Rev: VOYA 2/00) [305.242]

Terrorism

10164 Andryszewski, Tricia. *Terrorism in America* (6–10). Illus. Series: Headliners. 2002, Millbrook LB $25.90 (0-7613-2803-3). An overview of attacks against Americans both at home and abroad, with an interesting discussion of the difficulties of protecting civil rights while fighting terrorism. (Rev: BCCB 9/02; BL 8/02; HBG 3/03; SLJ 12/02) [363.3]

10165 Bell, J. Bowyer. *Murder on the Nile: The World Trade Center and Global Terror* (10–12). 2003, Encounter $26.95 (1-893554-63-5). This thought-provoking overview of the rising tide of violence by Islamic fundamentalists focuses on Egypt, where a secular government has met resistance. (Rev: BL 12/15/02) [297]

10166 Bergen, Peter L. *Holy War, Inc.: Inside the Secret World of Osama bin Laden* (10–12). 2001, Free Pr. $26.00 (0-7432-0502-2); paper $14.00 (0-7432-3495-2). This account, which ends in 2001, gives a history of al-Qaeda, profiles its leaders, and describes the life and ideas of Osama bin Laden. (Rev: BL 11/15/01) [958.1]

10167 Bernstein, Richard. *Out of the Blue: The Story of September 11, 2001 from Jihad to Ground Zero* (10–12). Illus. 2002, Holt $26.00 (0-8050-7240-3). In addition to stories of the victims, their families, and rescuers, this volume gives a glimpse into the lives and motivations of the 19 terrorists who carried out the attacks. (Rev: BL 9/1/02; SLJ 1/03) [973.931]

10168 Bull, Chris, and Sam Erman, eds. *At Ground Zero: 25 Stories from Young Reporters Who Where There* (10–12). 2002, Thunder's Mouth paper $15.95 (1-56025-427-0). Young journalists — some of them still in college at the time — offer eyewitness accounts of the devastating terrorist attacks and in the process provide valuable insights into what makes a journalist tick. (Rev: BL 9/1/02) [973.931]

10169 Campbell, Geoffrey. *A Vulnerable America* (7–12). Series: Library of Homeland Security. 2004, Gale LB $27.95 (1-59018-383-5). This book discusses national security, how the government dealt with terrorist attacks in the past, and how 9/11/01 changed intelligence activities. (Rev: BL 4/15/04; SLJ 5/04) [363.3]

10170 Cart, Michael, et al., eds. *911: The Book of Help* (8–12). Illus. 2002, Cricket $17.95 (0-8126-2659-1); paper $9.95 (0-8126-2676-1). A collection of essays, stories, and poems by well-known writers presented in sections titled "Healing," "Searching for History," "Asking Why? Why? Why?," and

"Reacting and Recovering." (Rev: BL 7/02; HB 9–10/02; HBG 3/03; SLJ 9/02*) [818]

10171 Corona, Laurel. *Hunting Down the Terrorists: Declaring War and Policing Global Violations* (7–12). Series: Lucent Library of Homeland Security. 2004, Gale LB $21.96 (1-59018-382-7). This account describes international efforts to hunt down terrorists and the cooperative efforts that are emerging. (Rev: BL 5/15/04; SLJ 4/04) [364.1]

10172 Currie, Stephen. *Terrorists and Terrorist Groups* (6–12). Series: Lucent Terrorism Library. 2002, Gale LB $21.96 (1-59018-207-3). A thorough, well-researched survey of terrorist organizations that looks at their structures, beliefs, tactics, and key figures. (Rev: SLJ 11/02) [973.931]

10173 Dudley, William, ed. *The Attack on America: September 11, 2001* (9–12). Series: At Issue. 2002, Gale LB $24.95 (0-7377-1292-9); paper $16.20 (0-7377-1293-7). The life-altering effects of the September 11, 2001, terrorist attack are explored in a series of excerpts from materials such as op-ed pieces and speeches that present views from across the political spectrum. (Rev: BL 7/02; SLJ 11/02) [973.931]

10174 Esposito, John L. *Unholy War: Terror in the Name of Islam* (10–12). 2002, Oxford $26.00 (0-19-515435-5). The author explains the teachings of Islam and relates them to holy wars, use of violence, and terrorism. (Rev: BL 6/1–15/02) [322.4]

10175 Fink, Mitchell, and Lois Mathias. *Never Forget: An Oral History of September 11, 2001* (10–12). Illus. 2002, HarperCollins $24.95 (0-06-051433-7). First-person accounts describe a variety of unhappy experiences on September 11. (Rev: BL 9/1/02) [974.7]

10176 Gaines, Ann. *Terrorism* (7–12). Series: Crime, Justice, and Punishment. 1998, Chelsea LB $21.95 (0-7910-4596-X). Beginning with the bombing of Pan Am flight 103 over Lockerbie, Scotland, in 1988, this thorough account discusses terrorism around the world and the groups that are responsible. (Rev: BL 12/15/98; SLJ 3/99) [364.1]

10177 Goodman, Robin, and Andrea Henderson Fahnestock. *The Day Our World Changed: Children's Art of 9/11* (7–12). 2002, Abrams $19.95 (0-8109-3544-9). Children's words and art are the main focus of this handsome volume. (Rev: BL 9/15/02) [700]

10178 Gow, Mary. *Attack on America: The Day the Twin Towers Collapsed* (8–12). Illus. Series: American Disasters. 2002, Enslow LB $18.95 (0-7660-2118-1). This dramatic account of the events of September 11, 2001, includes many survivor and eyewitness accounts. (Rev: BL 9/1/02; HBG 3/03; SLJ 1/03) [973.931]

10179 Halberstam, David. *Firehouse* (10–12). 2002, Hyperion $22.95 (1-4013-0005-7). A deeply moving account of how one New York City firehouse came to terms with the devastating loss of 12 of its firemen on September 11, 2001. (Rev: BL 6/1–15/02) [28.9]

10180 Hanson, Victor David. *An Autumn of War: What America Learned from September 11 and the War on Terrorism* (10–12). 2002, Anchor Bks. paper $12.00 (1-4000-3113-3). In this collection of essays, Hanson dissects the tragic events of September 11, 2001, and examines the causes and responses. (Rev: BL 7/02) [808]

10181 Henderson, Harry. *Terrorism* (9–12). Series: Library in a Book. 2001, Facts on File $45.00 (0-8160-4259-4). This book describes terrorist groups, their leaders, counterintelligence efforts, and the attacks of September 11, 2001. (Rev: BL 6/1–15/01; VOYA 2/02) [303.6]

10182 Hendra, Tony, ed. *Brotherhood* (9–12). Illus. 2002, American Express $29.95 (0-916103-73-0). A handsome tribute to the firefighters who gave their lives in the effort to save people from the Twin Towers on September 11, 2001. (Rev: BL 3/1/02) [363.32]

10183 Heyden, William, ed. *September 11, 2001: American Writers Respond* (10–12). 2002, Etruscan paper $19.00 (0-9718228-0-8). This collection of short stories, essays, and poems offers the reactions of more than 120 writers to the terrorist attacks. (Rev: BL 7/02) [818]

10184 Katz, Samuel M. *At Any Cost: National Liberation Terrorism* (7–12). Series: Terrorist Dossiers. 2004, Lerner LB $26.60 (0-8225-0949-0). This is an excellent introduction to the terrorist groups active today whose cause is the liberation of their homelands. (Rev: BL 3/15/04; HBG 4/04; SLJ 3/04; VOYA 4/04) [363.2]

10185 Katz, Samuel M. *Jihad: Islamic Fundamentalist Terrorism* (7–12). Illus. Series: Terrorist Dossiers. 2003, Lerner LB $26.60 (0-8225-4031-2). A look at Middle East-based terrorist groups, their histories, and present-day activities. (Rev: BL 3/15/04; HBG 4/04; SLJ 5/04) [303.6]

10186 Katz, Samuel M. *Raging Within: Ideological Terrorism* (7–12). Series: Terrorist Dossiers. 2004, Lerner LB $26.60 (0-8225-4032-0). This book examines terrorists whose motivation is based on ideologies and religion. (Rev: BL 3/15/04; HBG 4/04; SLJ 5/04) [363.2]

10187 Keeley, Jennifer. *Deterring and Investigating Attack* (7–12). Series: Library of Homeland Security. 2004, Gale LB $27.95 (1-59018-374-6). This volume explores the roles played by both the CIA and FBI in counterterrorism and how various kinds of information are found and used. (Rev: BL 4/15/04) [363.32]

10188 Kreger, Clare, ed. *White Supremacy Groups* (8–12). Series: At Issue. 2003, Gale LB $20.96 (0-7377-1364-X); paper $13.96 (0-7377-1365-8). The White Supremacy movement and the bombing of Oklahoma City are among the topics examined in this book on threats and terrorism. (Rev: BL 2/1/03) [305.8]

10189 Levitas, Mitchel, ed. *A Nation Challenged: A Visual History of 9/11 and Its Aftermath: Young Reader's Edition* (6–12). 2002, Scholastic paper $18.95 (0-439-48803-6). This is a selection of material first published in the *New York Times* that has been chosen as suitable for young readers. (Rev: BL 9/1/02; HBG 10/03; SLJ 9/02*) [973.931]

10190 Longman, Jere. *Among the Heroes: United Flight 93 and the Passengers and Crew Who Fought Back* (10–12). Illus. 2002, HarperCollins $24.95 (0-06-009908-9). The heroism and courage of the passengers and crew of United Flight 93 are celebrated in this riveting story of their resistance against the terrorists. (Rev: BL 9/1/02; SLJ 1/03) [974.7]

10191 Marcovitz, Hal. *Terrorism* (9–12). Series: Great Disasters, Reforms and Ramifications. 2000, Chelsea $21.95 (0-7910-5264-8). The coverage in this volume ends in 2000, but gives background material on such topics as the 1972 Munich Olympics attack, Patty Hearst, and Timothy McVeigh. (Rev: HBG 3/01) [363.3]

10192 Mason, Jeff, ed. *9-11: Emergency Relief* (7–12). Illus. 2002, Alternative Comics paper $14.95 (1-891867-12-1). In this moving collection, some of the world's best comic book artists and writers share with readers their personal reactions to the devastating terrorist attacks of September 11, 2001. (Rev: BL 2/15/02; VOYA 4/02)

10193 Mitch, Frank. *Understanding September 11th: Answering Questions About the Attacks on America* (7–12). Illus. 2002, Viking $16.99 (0-670-03582-3). A thoughtful and thought-provoking, question-and-answer look at terrorism and the forces that can provoke such attacks, with information on Islam and the history of American involvement in the Middle East. (Rev: BL 9/1/02; HBG 3/03; SLJ 9/02; VOYA 12/02) [973.931]

10194 Murphy, Dean E. *September 11: An Oral History* (10–12). Illus. 2002, Doubleday $22.95 (0-385-50768-2). First-person accounts from people working in the World Trade Center and Pentagon, as well as the stories of eyewitnesses and rescue workers paint an unforgettable portrait of the horrors and heroism of September 11. (Rev: BL 9/1/02) [974.7]

10195 Picciotto, Richard, and Daniel Paisner. *Last Man Down: A New York City Fire Chief and the Collapse of the World Trade Center* (10–12). 2002, Berkley $24.95 (0-425-18677-6). A firsthand narrative of experiences during the rescue of people trapped in the World Trade Center on September 11, 2001. (Rev: BL 6/1–15/02) [363.3497]

10196 Rees, David. *Get Your War On* (11–12). Illus. 2002, Soft Skull paper $11.00 (1-887128-76-X). The forthright cynicism of these comic strips exploring the wisdom and conduct of the war on terror is for mature teens only. (Rev: BL 9/15/02) [973.931]

10197 Roleff, Tamara L., ed. *America Under Attack: Primary Sources* (6–12). Illus. Series: Lucent Terrorism Library. 2002, Gale LB $21.96 (1-59018-216-2). Interviews, speeches, articles, and other items relating to the terrorist attacks of September 11, 2001, are collected in a volume that researchers will find useful. (Rev: BL 11/1/02; SLJ 9/02) [973.931]

10198 Sadler, A. E., and Paul A. Winters, eds. *Urban Terrorism* (9–12). Series: Current Controversies. 1996, Greenhaven LB $20.96 (1-56510-411-0); paper $20.25 (1-56510-410-2). Twenty-eight essays explore topics relating to urban terrorism: Should we fear it? Who is responsible for these attacks? Does media coverage encourage terrorism? and Do antiterrorist measures infringe on civil liberties? (Rev: BL 7/96; SLJ 9/96) [363.3]

10199 Schram, Martin. *Avoiding Armageddon: Our Future, Our Choice* (10–12). Illus. 2003, Basic $26.00 (0-465-07255-0). This tie-in to a PBS TV series looks at the threats posed by terrorism and the possible solutions. (Rev: BL 3/15/03)

10200 Stewart, Gail. *America Under Attack: September 11, 2001* (6–12). Series: Lucent Terrorism Library. 2002, Gale LB $21.96 (1-59018-208-1). Accounts of the terrorist attacks of September 11, 2001, include disturbing eyewitness testimonies. (Rev: BL 11/1/02; SLJ 9/02) [973.931]

10201 Stewart, Gail B. *Defending the Borders: The Role of Border and Immigration Control* (7–12). Series: Lucent Library of Homeland Security. 2004, Gale LB $21.96 (1-59018-376-2). This account presents the difficulties in fighting terrorism and other threats while keeping our borders open. (Rev: BL 5/15/04) [364.1]

10202 Streissguth, Thomas. *International Terrorists* (6–10). Illus. Series: Profiles. 1993, Oliver LB $19.95 (1-881508-07-2). This book describes the causes of international terrorism, the responsible organizations, and famous incidents. (Rev: BL 10/15/93; SLJ 1/94; VOYA 2/94) [909.82]

10203 Taylor, Robert. *The History of Terrorism* (6–12). Illus. Series: Lucent Terrorism Library.

2002, Gale LB $21.96 (1-59018-206-5). A chronological look at the history of terrorism around the globe, with discussion of the reasons it has been so widespread and of terrorists' motivation. Also use *Terrorists and Terrorist Groups* (2002). (Rev: BL 11/1/02; SLJ 11/02) [303.6]

10204 Thompson, Marilyn. *The Killer Strain: Anthrax and a Government Exposed* (10–12). Illus. 2003, HarperCollins $25.95 (0-06-052278-X). In her account of the deadly anthrax mailings in the fall of 2001, the author chronicles America's first large-scale exposure to the perils of bioterrorism. (Rev: BL 5/1/03) [363.1]

10205 Torr, James D. *Responding to Attack: Firefighters and Police* (7–12). Series: Lucent Library of Homeland Security. 2004, Gale LB $21.96 (1-59018-375-4). This account chronicles the part that the police and firefighters can play in counteracting a terrorist attack. (Rev: BL 5/15/04) [364.1]

10206 vanden Heuvel, Katrina, ed. *A Just Response: The Nation on Terrorism, Democracy and September 11, 2001* (10–12). 2002, Thunder's Mouth paper $14.95 (1-56025-400-9). In this collection of articles, editorials, and essays, the writers and editors of the *Nation* roundly criticize the Bush administration and the mainstream media for their post-9/11 excesses and sins of omission, respectively. (Rev: BL 4/15/02) [973.931]

Urban and Rural Life

10207 Duany, Andres, et al. *Suburban Nation: The Rise of Sprawl and the Decline of the American Dream* (10–12). Illus. 2000, Farrar $30.00 (0-86547-557-1). The authors survey the rise of suburban sprawl, subdivisions, and shopping malls, contrast them with traditional diverse communities, and offer suggestions for the future. (Rev: BL 3/1/00) [307.76]

10208 Kidder, Tracy. *Home Town* (10–12). 1999, Random $25.95 (0-679-45588-4). A profile of the town of Northampton, Massachusetts, as seen through the eyes of its citizens, particularly a young police officer whose job reveals different aspects of the town, from the plush Northampton of yuppies and Smith College professors to the projects and the seamier sides of life. (Rev: BL 3/1/99; SLJ 8/99) [307.7]

10209 Kozol, Jonathan. *Ordinary Resurrections: Children in the Years of Hope* (10–12). 2000, Crown $25.00 (0-517-70000-X). Social issues are explored through tales told by the children, teachers, and parents involved in the after-school programs of St. Ann's Episcopal Church in the impoverished, racially tense South Bronx. (Rev: BL 3/15/00; SLJ 8/00) [305.23]

10210 Trefil, James. *A Scientist in the City* (9–12). 1994, Doubleday $23.95 (0-385-24797-4). An examination of the technological wonder that is the urban ecosystem, viewed as a natural combination of inanimate structures and living organisms. (Rev: BL 1/1/94; SLJ 9/94) [307.76]

10211 Vergara, Camilo José. *The New American Ghetto* (9–12). 1995, Rutgers Univ. Pr. $49.95 (0-8135-2209-9). Chilean-born Vergara has photographed American ghettos since 1977 and has gathered his work here as a documentation of their geography and ecology. (Rev: BL 12/1/95*) [307.3]

Economics and Business

General and Miscellaneous

10212 Aaseng, Nathan. *You Are the Corporate Executive* (7–10). Illus. Series: Great Decisions. 1997, Oliver LB $19.95 (1-881508-35-8). This book describes the work of a company's CEO and the nature and consequences of the decisions that CEOs have to make. (Rev: BL 6/1–15/97; BR 11–12/97; SLJ 6/97) [658.4]

10213 Brenner, Joel Glenn. *The Emperors of Chocolate: Inside the World of Hershey and Mars* (10–12). 1999, Random $25.95 (0-679-42190-4). Espionage, secrecy, paranoia, personality clashes, dreams, and failures are among the components of this story of the intense rivalry between the Mars and Hershey chocolate empires. (Rev: BL 12/1/98; SLJ 5/99) [338]

10214 Folbre, Nancy, and The Center for Popular Economics. *The New Field Guide to the U.S. Economy: A Compact and Irreverent Guide to Economic Life in America* (9–12). Illus. 1995, New Pr. paper $16.95 (1-56584-153-0). A compact introduction to the U.S. economy and the factors that affect it, presented in a humorous manner through easy-to-read graphs, illustrations, cartoons, and text divided into chapters on workers, women, people of color, health, environment, and the global economy. (Rev: VOYA 12/96) [330.73]

10215 Heilbroner, Robert L., and Lester C. Thurow. *Economics Explained: Everything You Need to Know About How the Economy Works and Where It's Going* (9–12). 1994, Simon & Schuster paper $12.00 (0-671-88422-0). Two well-known economists present a primer on economics and provide an overview of the history of economic thought. (Rev: BL 1/15/94) [330]

10216 Karnes, Frances A., and Suzanne M. Bean. *Girls and Young Women Entrepreneurs: True Stories About Starting and Running a Business Plus How You Can Do It Yourself* (6–10). Illus. 1997, Free Spirit paper $12.95 (1-57542-022-8). This inspirational book introduces dozens of young women ages 9 to 25 who have started business ventures, and provides advice and information for young females who would also like to become entrepreneurs. (Rev: BR 9–10/98; SLJ 6/98) [338]

10217 Katz, Donald. *Just Do It! The Nike Spirit in the Corporate World* (9–12). 1994, Random $23.00 (0-679-43275-2). An examination of all aspects of Nike — its Oregon "campus," its Far East factories, its retailers, the symbiotic relationship between athletes and Nike, its company culture, its successes, and its failures. (Rev: BL 5/1/94; SLJ 11/94) [338.7]

10218 Oleksy, Walter. *Business and Industry* (6–12). Illus. Series: Information Revolution. 1996, Facts on File $25.00 (0-8160-3075-8). This book describes how companies use Powerbook computers, supercomputers, modems, and videophones to distribute information, increase productivity, and make better business decisions. (Rev: BL 2/15/96; BR 9–10/96; VOYA 6/96) [650]

10219 Roleff, Tamara L., ed. *Business Ethics* (9–12). Series: At Issue. 1996, Greenhaven LB $12.95 (1-56510-385-8); paper $11.20 (1-56510-384-X). Excerpts from articles and books explore controversies around inflated CEO salaries, corporate influence buying, and overseas business policies. (Rev: BL 3/15/96) [174]

10220 Savitt, William, and Paula Bottorf. *Global Development* (9–12). Series: Contemporary World Issues. 1995, ABC-CLIO LB $39.50 (0-87436-774-3). This survey of world economic development since World War II contains background information, history, biographical sketches, statistics, organizations, and other resources. (Rev: SLJ 6/96) [330]

10221 Strasser, J. B., and Laurie Becklund. *Swoosh: The Story of Nike and the Men Who Played There* (9–12). 1992, Harcourt $24.95 (0-15-187430-1). This biographical history of the Nike corporation and its key figures describes the company's rise to the top in the athletic-shoe business. (Rev: BL 12/1/91) [338.7]

10222 Waterman, Robert H. *What America Does Right: Learning from Companies That Put People First* (9–12). 1994, Norton $23.00 (0-393-03597-2). Examines the successful operations of companies that recognize, understand, and try to meet their employees' needs. (Rev: BL 2/15/94) [658.5]

Economic Systems and Institutions

General and Miscellaneous

10223 Leone, Bruno, ed. *Capitalism: Opposing Viewpoints*. Rev. ed. (9–12). Illus. Series: Opposing Viewpoints. 1986, Greenhaven paper $16.20 (0-89908-359-5). A collection of primary sources that explore the history of capitalism and its vices and virtues. (Rev: BL 8/86; SLJ 10/86) [330.12]

10224 Leone, Bruno, ed. *Communism: Opposing Viewpoints*. Rev. ed. (9–12). Illus. Series: Opposing Viewpoints. 1986, Greenhaven LB $26.20 (0-89908-385-4); paper $16.20 (0-89908-360-9). This collection of documents explains the concepts involved in communism and enumerates its successes and failures as seen from several viewpoints. (Rev: BL 8/86; SLJ 10/86) [335.43]

10225 O'Neill, Terry, and Karin L. Swisher, eds. *Economics in America* (7–10). Series: Opposing Viewpoints. 1992, Greenhaven paper $16.20 (0-89908-162-2). A look at the state of the U.S. economy, the budget deficit, taxation, the banking system, and the future of labor as of 1990. (Rev: BL 6/15/92) [338.973]

10226 Trahant, LeNora B. *The Success of the Navajo Arts and Crafts Enterprise* (7–10). Illus. Series: Success. 1996, Walker LB $16.85 (0-8027-8337-6). After a brief history of the Navajo Nation, the author describes how the arts and crafts of the Navajos have prospered under a manufacturing and marketing cooperative. (Rev: BL 5/15/96; SLJ 7/96) [381]

Stock Exchanges

10227 Bamford, Janet. *Street Wise: A Guide for Teen Investors* (8–12). 2000, Bloomberg paper $16.95 (1-57660-039-4). In clear prose, the author provides

excellent material for the beginning stock trader or novice with bonds and mutual funds, with fine background material and sage conservative advice. (Rev: BL 10/1/00; SLJ 3/01) [332.6]

10228 Brennan, Kristine. *The Stock Market Crash of 1929* (8–12). Series: Great Disasters: Reforms and Ramifications. 2000, Chelsea LB $19.95 (0-7910-5268-0). This account of the crash and its causes and aftermath looks carefully at the economy of the time and discusses the changes of a similar crash happening today. (Rev: BR 1–2/01; HBG 3/01; SLJ 12/00) [338.5]

10229 Liebowitz, Jay. *Wall Street Wizard: Advice from a Savvy Teen Investor* (6–12). Illus. 2000, Simon $16.00 (0-689-83401-2). This book about Wall Street, the stock market, and investing was written by a 19-year-old money whiz. (Rev: BL 9/1/00; BR 3–4/01; HBG 10/01; SLJ 10/00) [332.65]

Consumerism

10230 Barach, Arnold B. *Famous American Trademarks* (9–12). Illus. 1971, PublicAffairs paper $9.00 (0-8183-0165-1). The origins and history of about 100 trademarks are traced by text and pictures. [341.7]

10231 Klein, David, and Marymae E. Klein. *Getting Unscrewed and Staying That Way: The Sourcebook of Consumer Protection* (9–12). 1993, Holt $25.00 (0-8050-2590-1). Provides addresses and phone numbers for obtaining redress for consumer problems. (Rev: BL 7/93) [381.3]

10232 Lindstrom, Martin, and Patricia B. Seybold. *Brandchild: Insights into the Minds of Today's Global Kids and Their Relationships with Brands* (10–12). Illus. 2003, Kogan Page $39.95 (0-7494-3867-3). The shopping habits and brand-name savvy of "tweens" — children between the ages of 8 and 14 — are explored in depth in this sometimes-surprising report. (Rev: BL 3/1/03) [658.8]

10233 Milios, Rita. *Shopping Savvy* (9–12). Series: Lifeskills Library. 1992, Rosen LB $12.95 (0-8239-1455-0). Basic guidelines for shopping, budgeting, and prioritizing needs. (Rev: BL 2/15/93; SLJ 1/93) [640]

10234 Schlosser, Eric. *Fast Food Nation: The Dark Side of the All-American Meal* (10–12). Illus. 2001, Houghton $25.00 (0-395-97789-4). This book examines the growth of the fast-food phenomenon in America and how it has changed the economy, youth culture, and allied industries. (Rev: BL 1/1–15/01) [394.1]

Employment and Jobs

10235 Atkin, S. Beth, ed. *Voices from the Fields: Children of Migrant Farmworkers Tell Their Stories* (7–12). 1993, Little, Brown $18.95 (0-316-05633-2). Oral histories from nine children. Each interview demonstrates a strong sense of family devotion and provides a reminder that education is the key to escaping the fields. (Rev: BL 5/1/93*; VOYA 2/94) [305.23]

10236 *Sister Circle: Black Women and Work* (10–12). Ed. by Sharon Harley et al. Illus. 2002, Rutgers Univ. Pr. $60.00 (0-8135-3060-1); paper $22.00 (0-8135-3061-X). This collection of essays explores the work experiences of African American women throughout history and the ways in which the work they do affects various aspects of their lives. (Rev: BL 7/02) [331.4]

Labor Unions and Labor Problems

10237 Bendor, David, and Bruno Leone, eds. *Work* (7–12). Illus. Series: Opposing Viewpoints. 1995, Greenhaven LB $32.45 (1-56510-219-3); paper $16.20 (1-56510-218-5). A collection of essays explores problems relating to workers and society such as the education of the workforce, government intervention, and inequality in the workplace. (Rev: BL 7/95; SLJ 8/95) [331]

10238 Featherstone, Liza. *Students Against Sweatshops* (10–12). Illus. 2002, Verso paper $15.00 (1-85984-302-6). Students interested in opposing sweatshop working conditions will find useful information in this slim volume. (Rev: BL 6/1–15/02) [361.2]

10239 Laughlin, Rosemary. *The Pullman Strike of 1894: American Labor Comes of Age* (7–12). 1999, Morgan Reynolds LB $21.95 (1-883846-28-5). An engrossing account of this bitter railroad strike, with good background material on the railroad industry, the planned city of Pullman, the depression of 1893, and the personalities involved, including Eugene Debs. (Rev: BL 7/99; SLJ 8/99; VOYA 4/00) [331.892]

10240 Meltzer, Milton. *Bread and Roses: The Struggle of American Labor* (9–12). 1990, NAL paper $3.95 (0-451-62396-7). A history of how labor organized in America. [331.88]

10241 Stein, R. Conrad. *The Pullman Strike and the Labor Movement in American History* (6–10). Series: In American History. 2001, Enslow LB $20.95 (0-7660-1300-6). This account traces the history of the 1894 strike (one of America's longest) and the parts played by President Grover Cleveland,

George Pullman, Eugene Debs, and social worker Jane Addams. (Rev: BL 8/01; HBG 10/01; SLJ 5/01) [331.892]

Money and Trade

10242 Menhard, Francha Roffe. *Teen Consumer Smarts: Shop, Save, and Steer Clear of Scams* (7–12). Series: Teen Issues. 2002, Enslow LB $17.95 (0-7660-1667-6). A useful guide to money management that recommends regular saving and alerts readers to the dangers of credit cards and fraudulent scams. (Rev: HBG 3/03; SLJ 1/03) [332.024]

10243 Miller, Henri. *Free Trade Versus Protectionism* (9–12). Series: Reference Shelf. 1996, H.W. Wilson paper $45.00 (0-8242-0889-7). This collection of articles offers a variety of viewpoints in the ongoing debate about the benefits of free trade versus protectionism. [382]

Marketing and Advertising

10244 Day, Nancy. *Advertising: Information or Manipulation?* (6–12). Series: Issues in Focus. 1999, Enslow LB $20.95 (0-7660-1106-2). In addition to presenting an introduction to advertising, its history, and its impact on U.S. society, this book questions many advertising practices, provides information on advertising methods and targeting, and offers tips on how to evaluate advertising critically. (Rev: BL 7/99) [659.1]

10245 McMath, Robert. *What Were They Thinking? Marketing Lessons I've Learned from over 80,000 New Products, Innovations, and Idiocies* (10–12). 1998, Times Books $23.00 (0-8129-2950-0). A browsable, easy-to-read book, arranged by subject, that explores the world of marketing, its pitfalls, and its practices. (Rev: SLJ 6/98) [380.1]

10246 Petley, Julian. *Advertising* (7–10). Illus. Series: MediaWise. 2003, Smart Apple LB $28.50 (1-58340-255-1). A good introduction to the world of advertising, with discussion of creative and financial concerns. (Rev: BL 10/15/03; HBG 4/04; SLJ 11/03) [659.1]

10247 Schulberg, Jay. *The Milk Mustache Book: A Behind-the-Scenes Look at America's Favorite Advertising Campaign* (9–12). 1998, Ballantine paper $18.00 (0-345-42729-7). For young readers interested in marketing and advertising, this is the story of the successful "Milk Mustache" campaign, its origins, stars, and aftermath. (Rev: SLJ 3/99) [659.1]

Guidance and Personal Development

Education and Schools

General and Miscellaneous

10248 Banfield, Susan. *The Bakke Case: Quotas in College Admissions* (6–10). Series: Landmark Supreme Court Cases. 1998, Enslow LB $20.95 (0-89490-968-1). The court case that challenged quotas in higher education to correct racial inequality is chronicled in this dramatic account that gives good background information. (Rev: BL 2/15/98; BR 9–10/98; SLJ 6/98) [378]

10249 Borne, Barbara Wood. *100 Research Topic Guides for Students* (10–12). 1996, Greenwood $39.95 (0-313-29552-2). A practical guide to researching topics for reports and presentations, organized in four broad categories: Biography; Science and Technology; Social Issues; and Social Studies. [025.5]

10250 Codell, Esmé Raji. *Educating Esmé: Diary of a Teacher's First Year* (9–12). 1999, Algonquin $28.95 (1-56512-225-9). The journal of a first-time teacher, her year with her 5th-grade class, and her success teaching reading and creative writing. (Rev: BL 3/15/99; SLJ 7/99) [371.1]

10251 Conroy, Pat. *The Water Is Wide* (10–12). 1972, Houghton paper $7.50 (0-553-26893-7). This book deals with a white teacher who goes to an island off the coast of South Carolina to teach a group of poor black children. [371.9]

10252 Corwin, Miles. *And Still We Rise: The Trials and Triumphs of Twelve Gifted Inner-City High School Students* (10–12). 2000, Avon $25.00 (0-380-97650-1). A compelling portrayal of 12 disadvantaged students at Crenshaw High School in Los Angeles and their struggles to gain college admission. (Rev: BL 5/15/00) [371.95]

10253 Cruz, Barbara C. *School Dress Codes: A Pro/Con Issue* (6–10). Series: Hot Pro/Con Issues. 2001, Enslow LB $19.95 (0-7660-1465-7). Cruz presents the case for and against dress codes from the students' and the adults' points of view. (Rev: HBG 3/02; SLJ 7/01) [371.8]

10254 Cruz, Barbara C. *Separate Sexes, Separate Schools* (7–10). Illus. Series: Hot Pro/Con Issues. 2000, Enslow LB $19.95 (0-7660-1366-9). This examination of the issues connected with same-sex schools is well organized and presents differing points of view on this complex topic. (Rev: BCCB 10/00; BL 2/1/01; HBG 3/01; SLJ 12/00; VOYA 6/01) [371.82]

10255 Feldman, Ruth Tenzer. *Don't Whistle in School: The History of America's Public Schools* (6–10). Illus. 2001, Lerner LB $25.26 (0-8225-1745-0). A broad overview of American public education that includes everything from regional differences to education trends and landmark court rulings, with illustrations and photographs. (Rev: BL 11/1/01; HBG 3/02; SLJ 11/01; VOYA 4/02) [370]

10256 Gold, Elizabeth. *Brief Intervals of Horrible Sanity: One Season in a Progressive School* (10–12). 2003, Putnam $24.95 (1-58542-244-4). In this harrowing tale of "alternative education" gone wrong, the author recounts her experiences as a teacher at New York City's School of the New Millennium. (Rev: BL 9/15/03) [373.747]

10257 Greene, Rebecca. *The Teenagers' Guide to School Outside the Box* (8–12). Illus. 2000, Free Spirit paper $15.95 (1-57542-087-2). Many learning opportunities are available to teens, including travel, volunteer work, serving as an intern or apprentice, mentoring, and job shadowing. (Rev: BL 2/15/01; SLJ 3/01; VOYA 4/01) [373.2]

10258 Humes, Edward. *School of Dreams: Making the Grade at a Top American High School* (10–12). 2003, Harcourt $25.00 (0-15-100703-9). Based on his year-long research at one of the top public high schools in Los Angeles, Humes examines the pressure on students to excel. (Rev: BL 9/1/03) [373.794]

10259 Hurwitz, Sue. *High Performance Through Effective Scheduling* (8–12). Illus. Series: Learning-a-Living Library. 1996, Rosen LB $17.95 (0-8239-2204-9). This book discusses the basic skill of scheduling time and how it helps students at school, in extracurricular activities, and on the job. (Rev: BL 8/96; BR 1–2/97; SLJ 12/96; VOYA 2/97) [640]

10260 Johnston, Michael. *In the Deep Heart's Core* (10–12). 2002, Grove $24.00 (0-8021-1721-X). In an account that is both inspiring and depressing, Johnston describes his experiences during a two-year stint with the Teach for America program. (Rev: BL 9/15/02) [373.11]

10261 Kane, Pearl Rock, ed. *The First Year of Teaching: Real-World Stories from America's Teachers* (9–12). 1991, Walker $27.95 (0-8027-1170-7); paper $18.95 (0-8027-7359-1). A collection of the best essays by educators asked to describe the trials and rewards of their first year as teachers. (Rev: BL 10/1/91) [371.1]

10262 Kolbert, Kathryn, and Zak Mettger. *Justice Talking: Leading Advocates Debate Today's Most Controversial Issues — School Vouchers* (10–12). 2001, New Pr. $24.95 (1-56584-716-4). The National Public Radio debate on school vouchers is reprinted, with an accompanying CD and primary sources including three key Supreme Court decisions are included. (Rev: BL 12/1/01) [379.1]

10263 Kopp, Wendy. *One Day, All Children . . . : The Unlikely Triumph of Teach for America and What I Learned Along the Way* (9–12). 2001, PublicAffairs $23.00 (1-891620-92-4). An account of the founding of the Teach for America program, which places college graduates as teachers in poor public schools, and how it has thrived. (Rev: BL 4/1/01) [372.11]

10264 Kozol, Jonathan. *Savage Inequalities: Children in America's Schools* (10–12). 1991, Crown paper $14.00 (0-06-097499-0). In this biting assessment of America's education system toward the end of the 20th century, Kozol found a woeful lack of funding and equipment in predominantly African American schools of inner cities. [371.9]

10265 Llewellyn, Grace. *Real Lives* (9–12). 1993, Lowry House paper $17.00 (0-9629591-3-8). Eleven teens explain why they and their families chose homeschooling over traditional education. (Rev: SLJ 4/1/93) [370]

10266 Marx, Jeff. *How to Win a High School Election* (9–12). 1999, Jeff Marx paper $12.95 (0-9667824-0-2). High school officeholders reveal their strategies for getting elected to student positions. (Rev: BL 9/1/99; SLJ 7/99) [373.159]

10267 Pendleton, Scott. *The Ultimate Guide to Student Contests, Grades 7–12* (6–12). Illus. 1997, Walker paper $15.95 (0-8027-7512-8). This is a guide to various academically oriented contests open to young adults, arranged by such subjects as mathematics and foreign languages. (Rev: BL 8/97) [373.18]

10268 Perrotti, Jeff, and Kim Westheimer. *When the Drama Club Is Not Enough: Lessons from the Safe Schools Program for Gay and Lesbian Students* (10–12). 2001, Beacon $22.00 (0-8070-3130-5). This book offers a guide to people anxious to create a safe climate in schools, particularly for gay and lesbian students. (Rev: BL 8/01) [371.826]

10269 Robb, Daniel. *Crossing the Water: Eighteen Months on an Island Working with Troubled Boys — a Teacher's Memoir* (10–12). 2001, Simon & Schuster $24.00 (0-7432-0238-4). This is the memoir of a teacher who spent 18 months on the Penikese Island School, a floating academy that houses eight troubled teenage boys for six-month terms. (Rev: BL 5/1/01) [362.7]

10270 Rubin, Louis D., Jr., ed. *An Apple for My Teacher: Twelve Authors Tell About Teachers Who Made the Difference* (9–12). Illus. 1987, Algonquin paper $16.95 (0-912697-57-1). In chapters of various lengths, 12 writers discuss their favorite teachers and what made them memorable. (Rev: SLJ 8/87) [371.1]

10271 Sherrow, Victoria. *Challenges in Education* (7–12). Series: Issues for the 90s. 1991, Messner paper $13.95 (0-671-70556-3). An overview of the major questions and concerns facing today's educators. (Rev: BL 11/1/91; SLJ 11/91) [370]

10272 Terkel, Marni, and Susan Neiburg Terkel. *What's an "A" Anyway? How Important Are Grades?* (8–12). Illus. 2001, Watts $24.00 (0-531-11417-1). An examination of the academic grading system, addressing such issues as cheating, grade inflation, unusual grading systems, and whether success in school leads to success in life. (Rev: BL 11/1/01; SLJ 11/01) [371.27]

10273 Williams, Mary E., ed. *Education: Region Under Siege* (8–12). Series: Opposing Viewpoints. 1999, Greenhaven LB $21.95 (0-7377-0125-0); paper $13.96 (0-7377-0124-2). School choice, multicultural education, and educational reforms are three of the topics covered in this collection of different points of view on the subject of education. (Rev: BL 11/15/99) [370]

10274 *Zero Tolerance: Resisting the Drive for Punishment in Our Schools* (10–12). Ed. by William Ayers et al. 2001, Free Pr. paper $17.95 (1-56584-

666-4). This series of articles explores zero tolerance in school discipline and finds that it is not only ineffective but also violates basic civil rights. (Rev: BL 12/15/01) [371.5]

Development of Academic Skills

Study Skills

10275 Frank, Stanley D. *Remember Everything You Read: The Evelyn Wood Seven Day Speed Reading and Learning Program* (9–12). Illus. 1990, Times Books $23.00 (0-8129-1773-1). How to increase one's reading speed and still retain the content. (Rev: BL 4/15/90) [371.3]

10276 Lorayne, Harry. *How to Develop a Super-Power Memory* (10–12). 1974, NAL paper $4.95 (0-451-16149-1). Tips and techniques for increasing one's ability to remember. [371.3]

10277 McCutcheon, Randall J. *Get off My Brain: A Survival Guide for Lazy* Students (*Bored, Frustrated, and Otherwise Sick of School)* (9–12). Illus. 1998, Free Spirit paper $12.95 (1-57542-037-6). This candid, entertaining look at teenage academic life offers advice on how to do better in school, from test-taking strategies and analyzing one's learning skills to brown-nosing teachers and taking advantage of teachers' strengths and weaknesses. (Rev: VOYA 2/99) [371.3]

10278 Maddox, Harry. *How to Study* (10–12). 1983, Fawcett paper $4.50 (0-449-30011-0). Practical tips and strategies are outlined to make studying more effective. [378]

10279 Marks, Lillian S. *Touch Typing Made Simple.* Rev. ed. (8–12). Illus. 1985, Doubleday paper $12.95 (0-385-19426-9). A clear manual that gives information on specialized topics including types of letters, tabulations, and addressing envelopes. Part of a lengthy series. (Rev: BL 2/15/86) [652.3]

10280 Schneider, Zola Dincin, and Phyllis B. Kalb. *Countdown to College: A Student's Guide to Getting the Most Out of High School* (9–12). 1989, College Entrance Examination Board paper $9.95 (0-87447-335-7). A guide for high school students to such topics as time management, academic planning, and extracurricular activities. (Rev: BL 12/1/89; BR 3–4/90; VOYA 2/90) [373]

10281 Simpson, Carolyn. *High Performance Through Organizing Information* (8–12). Illus. Series: Learning-a-Living Library. 1996, Rosen LB $17.95 (0-8239-2207-3). This book discusses the importance of an organized work environment, whether in school, at home, or on the job, and how to create one using filing systems, to-do lists, data sources,

and other strategies. (Rev: BL 8/96; BR 1–2/97; SLJ 8/96; VOYA 2/97) [640]

Tests and Test Taking

10282 *Up Your Score: The Underground Guide to the SAT* (7–12). Ed. by Larry Berger, et al. Illus. 2000, Workman paper $10.95 (0-7611-1988-4). An offbeat guide to taking the SAT, known here as "Slimy and Atrocious Torture." (Rev: VOYA 2/01) [378]

Writing and Speaking Skills

10283 Amberg, Jay, and Mark Larson. *The Creative Writing Handbook* (9–12). 1992, Scott Foresman paper $7.95 (0-673-36013-X). A guide to putting effective words on a page. Does not cover marketing techniques. (Rev: BL 3/1/92) [808.02]

10284 Bauer, Marion Dane. *What's Your Story? A Young Person's Guide to Writing Fiction* (5–10). 1992, Clarion paper $7.95 (0-395-57780-2). An award-winning writer gives advice to young authors, including suggestions for planning, writing, and revising. (Rev: BL 4/15/92; SLJ 6/92*) [808.3]

10285 Block, Francesca L., and Hillary Carlip. *Zine Scene: The Do-It-Yourself Guide to Zines* (8–12). Illus. 1998, Girl Pr. paper $14.95 (0-9659754-3-6). This is a step-by-step guide to producing one's own magazine, from getting started and writing to layout, production, and marketing. (Rev: VOYA 8/99) [808]

10286 Bodart, Joni Richards. *The World's Best Thin Books: What to Read When Your Book Report Is Due Tomorrow* (6–12). 2000, Scarecrow paper $16.95 (1-57886-007-5). For each of the books listed, the author provides background material, themes, characters, and possible book talk or book report ideas. (Rev: BL 1/1–15/00) [028.1]

10287 Brown, Cynthia Stokes. *Like It Was: A Complete Guide to Writing Oral History* (9–12). 1988, Teachers & Writers paper $13.95 (0-915924-12-9). A handbook that tells the reader how to conduct an oral history project, from planning it to the final transcription of the interviews. (Rev: BL 2/1/89; SLJ 6/89) [907]

10288 Clark, Thomas. *Queries and Submissions* (10–12). 1995, Writer's Digest $15.99 (0-89879-660-1). A practical guide to aspiring writers of nonfiction magazine articles with tips on writing effective query letters to editors and how to write dynamically. (Rev: SLJ 1/96) [418]

10289 Craig, Steve. *Sports Writing: A Beginner's Guide* (6–12). Illus. 2002, Discover Writing paper $15.00 (0-9656574-9-3). A fine introduction to writing news and features about sports, to conducting good interviews, and to the training of journalists. (Rev: BL 9/1/02; VOYA 4/03) [070.449]

10290 Detz, Joan. *You Mean I Have to Stand Up and Say Something?* (7–12). 1986, Macmillan LB $13.95 (0-689-31221-0). An entertaining guide to effective speaking and overcoming the fear of facing an audience. (Rev: BCCB 2/87; BL 2/87; SLJ 3/87) [808.5]

10291 Dragisic, Patricia. *How to Write a Letter* (7–12). Series: Speak Out, Write On! 1998, Watts LB $23.00 (0-531-11391-4). A readable, practical guide to writing personal notes, business letters, résumés, applications, memos, e-mail, and other forms of written communication. (Rev: BL 11/15/98; HBG 3/99; SLJ 1/99) [808.6]

10292 Estepa, Andrea, and Philip Kay, eds. *Starting with "I": Personal Essays by Teenagers* (7–12). 1997, Persea paper $13.95 (0-89255-228-X). This is a collection of 35 brief essays written by teenagers about their families, neighborhoods, race, and culture. (Rev: BL 9/15/97; BR 1–2/98; SLJ 10/97; VOYA 10/97) [305.235]

10293 Everhart, Nancy. *How to Write a Term Paper* (7–12). 1995, Watts LB $23.00 (0-531-11200-4). This revised edition of *So You Have to Write a Term Paper* (1987) includes new information on electronic sources and data management by computer. (Rev: BL 6/1–15/95; SLJ 5/95) [808]

10294 Frank, Steven. *The Pen Commandments: A Guide for the Beginning Writer* (9–12). 2003, Pantheon $19.95 (0-375-42228-5). A practical but light-hearted guide to the fundamentals of writing, with many quotations from familiar writers. (Rev: BL 8/03) [808]

10295 Hansen, Randall S., and Katharine Hansen. *Write Your Way to a Higher GPA: How to Dramatically Boost Your GPA Simply by Sharpening Your Writing Skills* (10–12). 1997, Ten Speed paper $11.95 (0-89815-903-2). A guide to virtually any type of writing that might be required in high school or college, as well as where to go for more help at school, in libraries, and online. (Rev: SLJ 1/98) [808]

10296 Harmon, Charles, ed. *Using the Internet, Online Services, and CD-ROMs for Writing Research and Term Papers* (7–12). Illus. Series: NetGuide. 1996, Neal-Schuman paper $32.95 (1-55570-238-4). This book shows all of the steps in writing a report, from selecting and narrowing a topic to collecting information electronically to preparing the final copy. (Rev: BL 4/15/96; SLJ 6/97) [371.2]

10297 Henderson, Kathy. *The Young Writer's Guide to Getting Published: Over 150 Listings of Opportunities for Young Writers.* Rev. ed. (5–12). Illus. 2001, Writer's Digest paper $18.99 (1-58297-057-

2). This guide provides useful tips on identifying the best opportunities for budding writers and relates some young writers' success stories. (Rev: BL 6/1–15/01; SLJ 11/01) [808]

10298 Henry, Thomas. *Better English Made Easy* (10–12). 1985, Warner paper $4.99 (0-446-31190-1). This manual covers such subjects as grammar, spelling, and speech. [420]

10299 James, Elizabeth, and Carol Barkin. *How to Write a Term Paper* (7–12). 1980, Lothrop paper $3.95 (0-688-45025-3). A practical step-by-step approach to report writing that uses many examples. [808]

10300 Janeczko, Paul B., ed. *Seeing the Blue Between: Advice and Inspiration for Young Poets* (7–10). 2002, Candlewick $17.99 (0-7636-0881-5). More than 30 poets who write for young people give advice on writing, reading, and simply enjoying poetry, with selected poems and biographical information. (Rev: BL 3/15/02; HB 7–8/02; HBG 10/02; SLJ 5/02; VOYA 6/02) [811]

10301 Kerr, M. E. *Blood on the Forehead: What I Know About Writing* (6–10). 1998, HarperCollins paper $14.95 (0-06-446207-2). This writer shares where she gets ideas for her stories and books and describes the writing process — which is far from easy, as the title suggests. (Rev: BL 4/1/98; SLJ 5/98; VOYA 6/99) [808.3]

10302 Kowit, Steve. *In the Palm of Your Hand: The Poet's Portable Workshop* (9–12). 1995, Tilbury paper $14.95 (0-88448-149-2). An informal discussion of the technical demands and creative sources of poetry. (Rev: BL 9/1/95) [808.1]

10303 Krementz, Jill. *The Writer's Desk* (10–12). Illus. 1996, Random $35.00 (0-679-45014-9). Fifty-seven prominent writers are captured in stunning photographs and written descriptions of their work habits and techniques. (Rev: SLJ 4/97) [808]

10304 Ledoux, Denis. *Turning Memories into Memoirs: A Handbook for Writing Lifestories* (9–12). 1993, Soleil Pr. paper $19.95 (0-9619373-2-7). A step-by-step handbook that encourages individuals to record their oral histories as a legacy for their families. (Rev: BL 3/15/93) [808.06]

10305 Lester, James D., Sr., and James D. Lester, Jr. *The Research Paper Handbook* (9–12). 1992, Scott Foresman paper $7.95 (0-673-36016-4). A manual with chapters covering topic selection, note taking, outlining, and bibliographies. (Rev: BL 2/15/92) [808.023]

10306 Lewis, Norman. *Thirty Days to Better English* (10–12). 1985, NAL paper $4.95 (0-451-15702-8). One of several fine English handbooks by this author. This one concentrates on grammar and usage. [425]

10307 Lewis, Norman, and Wilfred Funk. *Thirty Days to a More Powerful Vocabulary* (10–12). 1991, Pocket paper $5.99 (0-671-74349-X). This is a proven program for vocabulary building. [413]

10308 Lyon, George Ella. *Where I'm From, Where Poems Come From* (9–12). 1999, Absey & Co. paper $13.95 (1-888842-12-1). Encouragement for beginning poets is interspersed with the author's memories of her childhood and samples of her poetry. (Rev: BL 9/1/99) [811]

10309 Mooney, Bill, and David Holt. *The Storyteller's Guide: Storytellers Share Advice for the Classroom, Boardroom, Showroom, Podium, Pulpit and Central Stage* (9–12). 1996, August House paper $23.95 (0-87483-482-1). Professional storytellers advise young people on every aspect of storytelling, from selecting the right stories to tell to setting up the location and the actual presentation. (Rev: BR 5–6/97; VOYA 6/97) [808.5]

10310 Ochoa, George, and Jeff Osier. *The Writer's Guide to Creating a Science Fiction Universe* (9–12). 1993, Writer's Digest $18.95 (0-89879-536-2). An overview of the sciences to help the sci-fi writer avoid scientific errors. (Rev: BL 3/1/93) [808.3]

10311 Rosen, Lucy. *High Performance Through Communicating Information* (8–12). Illus. Series: Learning-a-Living Library. 1996, Rosen LB $16.95 (0-8239-2201-4). Such communication skills as writing and speaking are discussed, with tips on how to improve them and apply them effectively. (Rev: BL 8/96; BR 1–2/97; SLJ 3/97; VOYA 2/97) [153.6]

10312 Ryan, Margaret. *How to Give a Speech* (7–12). 1995, Watts LB $22.00 (0-531-11199-7). This revision of *So You Have to Give a Speech* (1987) includes new information on electronic sources and data management by computer. (Rev: BL 6/1–15/95; SLJ 6/95) [808.5]

10313 Ryan, Margaret. *How to Write a Poem* (7–12). Illus. 1996, Watts LB $23.00 (0-531-11252-7); paper $7.95 (0-531-15788-1). From the idea to the final product, this helpful guide covers the techniques of writing — along with imagery, form, meter, and other aspects of poetry — and provides tips on entering poetry contests and getting published. (Rev: BL 2/1/97; SLJ 1/97) [808.1]

10314 Safire, William, and Leonard Safir, eds. *Good Advice on Writing: Writers Past and Present on How to Write Well* (9–12). 1992, Simon & Schuster $22.00 (0-671-77005-5). Authors counsel would-be writers. (Rev: BL 9/15/92) [808]

10315 Shipman, Robert Oliver. *A Pun My Word: A Humorously Enlightened Path to English Usage* (9–12). 1991, Littlefield Adams paper $14.95 (0-8226-3011-7). Humorous examples help explain common problems in grammar and word usage. (Rev: BL 7/91) [428]

10316 Sullivan, Helen, and Linda Sernoff. *Research Reports: A Guide for Middle and High School Students* (6–10). 1996, Millbrook LB $24.90 (1-56294-694-3). A well-organized, concise book on writing reports that covers each step from selecting a topic to compiling the final bibliography. (Rev: BR 3–4/97; SLJ 9/96) [372.6]

10317 Vassallo, Wanda. *Speaking with Confidence: A Guide for Public Speakers* (9–12). 1990, Betterway paper $9.95 (1-55870-147-8). For anyone fearful of facing an audience, this is a guide that contains sound, workable advice. (Rev: BL 8/90; SLJ 7/90) [808.5]

10318 Wilber, Jessica. *Totally Private and Personal: Journaling Ideas for Girls and Young Women* (7–12). 1996, Free Spirit paper $9.95 (1-57542-005-8). The author, 14 years old when she wrote this book, offers advice for keeping a journal, including how, why, and what to put in it, with examples from her own journal. (Rev: VOYA 2/97) [808]

10319 Wooldridge, Susan Goldsmith. *Poemcrazy: Freeing Your Life with Words* (6–12). 1996, Clarkson Potter $22.00 (0-517-70370-X); paper $13.00 (0-609-80098-1). The author tries to show young people how to free their minds and spirits to write poetry and shares her own poetic experiences and inspirations as well as those of other poets. (Rev: VOYA 12/97) [811]

10320 Woolley, Persia. *How to Write and Sell Historical Fiction* (10–12). 1997, Writer's Digest $17.99 (0-89879-753-5). This offers pointers on writing historical fiction, techniques to master, and how to sell the final product to publishers and the reading public. (Rev: SLJ 9/97) [372.6]

10321 *The Writer's Digest Guide to Good Writing* (9–12). 1994, Writer's Digest $18.99 (0-89879-640-7). This retrospective anthology organized by decade contains essays providing advice and information for writers, by writers. (Rev: BL 3/15/94) [808.02]

10322 *The Writing Life: Writers on How They Think and Work* (10–12). Ed. by Marie Arana. 2003, PublicAffairs paper $16.00 (1-58648-149-5). Some of America's finest writers discuss the writing process — how they get their ideas and what it takes to turn those ideas into books. (Rev: BL 3/15/03) [810.9]

Academic Guidance

General and Miscellaneous

10323 *Education and College* (9–12). Ed. by William Dudley. Series: Teen Decisions. 2003, Gale LB $31.20 (0-7377-1260-0); paper $19.95 (0-7377-1259-7). This guide for high school students focuses on four key topics: getting a high school diploma, finding the right college, clearing the hurdles to win admission to college, and considering possible alternatives to college study. (Rev: BL 5/1/03) [378.1]

10324 Lieberman, Susan A. *The Real High School Handbook: How to Survive, Thrive, and Prepare for What's Next* (8–12). 1997, Houghton paper $12.00 (0-395-79760-8). A book of tips about prospering in high school and making it enjoyable, with material on topics including grade points, testing, course selection, and getting into a college. (Rev: BL 10/15/97) [373.18]

10325 Llewellyn, Grace. *The Teenage Liberation Handbook: How to Quit School and Get a Real Life and Education* (9–12). 1998, Lowry House paper $19.00 (0-9629591-7-0). This book encourages thoughtful teens to construct their own educational design through independent learning and developing individual ways of satisfying their intellectual curiosity. (Rev: VOYA 12/98) [371.4]

10326 Unger, Harlow G. *But What If I Don't Want to Go to College? A Guide to Success Through Alternative Education* (10–12). 1991, Facts on File LB $22.95 (0-8160-2534-7). Discusses alternate forms of training, job descriptions, résumé and cover-letter writing, job applications, and interviewing techniques. (Rev: BL 1/1/92; SLJ 5/92) [370.11]

10327 Vollstadt, Elizabeth Weiss. *Teen Dropouts* (6–12). Series: Overview: Teen Issues. 2000, Lucent LB $18.96 (1-56006-625-3). The causes, effects, and possible solutions to the problem of teenagers dropping out of school are discussed in this realistic account. (Rev: BL 6/1–15/00; HBG 9/00) [371.2]

Colleges and Universities

10328 Avery, Christopher, et al. *The Early Admissions Game: Joining the Elite* (10–12). 2003, Harvard Univ. Pr. $29.95 (0-674-01055-8). A thorough overview of the early admissions process that includes a section of advice for students. (Rev: VOYA 8/03) [378.1]

10329 Balaban, Mariah, and Jennifer Shields. *Study Away: The Independent Guide to College Abroad* (10–12). Illus. 2003, Anchor Bks. paper $13.95 (1-4000-3189-3). English-language higher education opportunities outside the United States are arranged alphabetically by country. (Rev: BL 9/15/03) [370.116]

10330 Berent, Polly. *Getting Ready for College: Everything You Need to Know Before You Go: From Bike Locks to Laundry Baskets, Financial Aid to Health Care* (11–12). 2003, Random paper $12.95 (0-8129-6896-4). This guide focuses not on what it will take to get into college but rather the practical knowledge needed to survive once there, covering such diverse subjects as homesickness, social life, personal finances, and security. (Rev: BL 6/1–15/03) [379.19]

10331 Carroll, Joan. *The Black College Career Guide* (9–12). 1992, Zulema Enterprises paper $6.95 (1-881223-00-0). Presents information on 104 African American colleges: location, history, enrollment, curriculum, costs, financial aid, and scholarships as of 1991. (Rev: BL 2/15/93) [378.7]

10332 Cochrane, Kerry. *Researching Colleges on the World Wide Web* (10–12). Illus. 1997, Watts paper $16.00 (0-531-11294-2). This book shows how to use the Internet to get information on colleges and how to evaluate it. (Rev: BL 9/1/97; SLJ 1/98; VOYA 8/98) [378.73]

10333 Cohen, Katherine. *Rock Hard Apps: How to Write a Killer College Application* (10–12). 2003, Hyperion paper $16.95 (0-7868-6862-7). Cohen offers solid advice about making a positive impression on college applications. (Rev: BL 6/1–15/03) [37.81]

10334 Cohen, Katherine. *The Truth About Getting In: A Top College Advisor Tells You Everything You Need to Know* (9–12). 2002, Hyperion $21.95 (0-7868-8747-8). A helpful guide to topics including preparation for admissions tests, writing effective essays, and sources of financial aid. (Rev: BL 3/15/02) [378.1]

10335 Davidson, Wilma, and Susan McCloskey. *Writing a Winning College Application Essay* (9–12). 1996, Peterson's paper $9.95 (1-56079-601-4). A step-by-step guide to the process of planning and composing an effective essay, along with numerous samples. [378]

10336 Drewry, Henry N., et al. *Stand and Prosper: Private Black Colleges and Their Students* (10–12). Illus. 2001, Princeton Univ. Pr. $29.95 (0-691-04900-9). An interesting study of the past and present of 45 private black colleges and their hopes for the future. (Rev: BL 10/15/01) [378]

10337 Eberts, Marjorie, and Margaret Gisler. *How to Prepare for College* (9–12). 1990, VGM paper $9.95 (0-8442-6665-5). This account emphasizes such areas as the development of good study, speaking, and writing skills, plus how to define and reach goals. (Rev: BL 3/1/90; BR 5–6/90) [378]

10338 Fives, Theresa. *Getting Through College Without Going Broke* (9–12). Series: Students Helping Students. 2003, Natavi Guides paper $8.95 (1-932204-01-6). This guide offers solid advice to college-bound students about money management and steps they can take to avoid accumulating a mountain of debt. (Rev: BL 4/1/03) [378]

10339 Grant, John, et al. *West Point: The First 200 Years* (10–12). Illus. 2002, Globe Pequot $29.95 (0-7627-1013-6). A look at the history of the U.S. Military Academy, with well-chosen illustrations and discussion of topics including racial integration, female students, and cheating; a companion to a PBS special. (Rev: BL 2/15/02) [355]

10340 Greenfeld, Barbara C., and Robert A. Weinstein. *The Kids' College Almanac: A First Look at College.* 2nd ed. (6–12). 2001, JIST paper $16.95 (1-56370-730-6). College applications, financial aid, identifying the right college, studying, and

enjoying college life to the full are among the topics covered here; includes worksheets. (Rev: VOYA 6/01) [378.1]

10341 *The Harvard Lampoon's Guide to College Admissions: The Comprehensive, Authoritative, and Utterly Useless Source for Where to Go and How to Get In* (10–12). Illus. 2000, Warner paper $12.95 (0-446-67616-0). In the form of a typical new-student guidebook, this is a raucous parody of college admission procedures. (Rev: BL 9/15/00) [378.61]

10342 Hernandez, Michele A. *Acing the College Application: How to Maximize Your Chances for Admission to the College of Your Choice* (10–12). 2002, Ballantine paper $13.95 (0-345-45409-X). This comprehensive guide provides solid advice for the college-bound. (Rev: BL 9/1/02; VOYA 4/03) [378.1]

10343 Jackson, Katherine. *Leaping from Public High to a Top U* (9–12). Series: Students Helping Students. 2003, Natavi Guides paper $6.95 (0-9719392-6-8). Students at some of America's most prestigious universities share their experiences in making the transition from high school and home to the more competitive college setting. (Rev: BL 3/1/03; SLJ 10/03) [378.1]

10344 Kaplan, Ben. *How to Go to College Almost for Free: The Secrets of Winning Scholarship Money.* Rev. ed. (10–12). Illus. 2001, HarperResource paper $22.00 (0-06-093765-3). This book is filled with useful information on merit awards, scholarships, and other forms of tuition remission. (Rev: BL 8/01; VOYA 4/02) [378.3]

10345 Karo, Aaron. *Ruminations on College Life* (11–12). 2002, Simon & Schuster paper $10.00 (0-7434-3293-3). An amusing account of the not-to-be-recommended exploits of a party-loving student. (Rev: BL 8/02) [378.1]

10346 Land, Brad. *Goat* (11–12). 2004, Random $22.95 (1-4000-6093-1). A chilling memoir of experiences with fraternity life. (Rev: BL 12/15/03; SLJ 4/04) [305.235]

10347 Light, Richard J. *Making the Most of College: Students Speak Their Minds* (10–12). 2001, Harvard $24.95 (0-674-00478-7). Though aimed at educators, this volume points out those elements in college life that make it an important experience and makes suggestions on how to help students make the proper choices. (Rev: BL 2/1/01) [378.1]

10348 Lipsky, David. *Absolutely American: Four Years at West Point* (11–12). Illus. 2003, Houghton $25.00 (0-618-09542-X). This portrait of the U.S. Military Academy follows a class through its four years and offers a glimpse of life after graduation; recommended for mature teens. (Rev: BL 7/03) [355]

10349 Lombardo, Allison. *Navigating Your Freshman Year* (9–12). Series: Students Helping Students. 2003, Natavi Guides paper $8.95 (0-9719392-3-3). The straightforward advice offered here, including interviews with students, will help to make readers' freshman year on campus less stressful. (Rev: BL 4/1/03; SLJ 10/03) [387.1]

10350 McGinty, Sarah Myers. *The College Application Essay* (9–12). Illus. 1997, College Board paper $12.95 (0-87447-575-9). A lucid, practical guide to writing effective college application essays, explaining each part of the essay in detail, showing students how to apply the writing skills they've developed during high school, and providing sample essays. (Rev: BL 10/15/97) [378.1]

10351 Mitchell, Joyce Slayton. *Winning the Heart of the College Admissions Dean: An Expert's Advice for Getting into College* (10–12). Illus. 2001, Ten Speed paper $14.95 (1-58008-300-5). College-related topics such as selecting, testing, and applying are covered in this book intended to give students confidence in the college-admission process. (Rev: BL 8/01; SLJ 12/01; VOYA 2/02) [378.1]

10352 Pope, Loren. *Colleges That Change Lives: 40 Schools You Should Know About Even If You're Not a Straight A Student* (10–12). 1996, Penguin paper $11.95 (0-14-023951-0). This book highlights 40 colleges, mostly in the Northeast, South, and Midwest, that select students with a wide range of abilities — not necessarily the top academic achievers. (Rev: SLJ 11/96) [378]

10353 Robbins, Wendy H. *The Portable College Adviser: A Guide for High School Students* (9–12).

1996, Watts LB $25.00 (0-531-11257-8); paper $9.00 (0-531-15790-3). A manual that guides students through preparation for college, including course choices in high school, standardized test preparation, college applications and visits, plus financial aid information. (Rev: BL 7/96; BR 9–10/96; SLJ 8/96; VOYA 10/96) [378.1]

10354 Steinberg, Jacques. *The Gatekeepers: Inside the Admissions Process of a Premier College* (11–12). 2002, Viking $25.95 (0-670-03135-6). This behind-the-scenes look at the admissions policy and process at Wesleyan University offers valuable lessons for college-bound students and their parents. (Rev: BL 8/02; SLJ 5/03) [378.1]

Scholarships and Financial Aid

10355 Kaplan, Ben. *The Scholarship Scouting Report: An Insider's Guide to America's Best Scholarships* (11–12). 2003, HarperResource $21.95 (0-06-093654-1). This accessible guide spotlights more than 100 financial awards programs, providing detailed information about entry requirements, application procedures, and the criteria used in judging applicants. (Rev: BL 1/1–15/03) [378.3]

10356 Minnis, Whitney. *How to Get an Athletic Scholarship: A Student-Athlete's Guide to Collegiate Athletics* (6–12). 1995, ASI paper $12.95 (0-9645153-0-X). Basic information on athletic scholarships and the recruitment process, plus tips on training and academic considerations. (Rev: BL 2/1/96) [796]

Careers and Occupational Guidance

General and Miscellaneous

10357 Baldwin, Louis. *Women of Strength* (9–12). 1996, McFarland paper $28.50 (0-7864-0250-4). This work contains short biographies of 106 women who have succeeded in traditionally male fields like the military, law, social reform, and religion. (Rev: VOYA 8/97) [331.7]

10358 Dwyer, Jack. *The Launch Manual: A Young Person's Introduction to the Principles of World Takeover* (10–12). 1998, Chairman paper $10.95 (0-9658366-5-7). This book describes the mind-set necessary to make sound career choices, including identifying one's strengths and weaknesses and setting goals. (Rev: SLJ 1/99) [650.14]

10359 Figler, Howard. *The Complete Job-Search Handbook: All the Skills You Need to Get Any Job and Have a Good Time Doing It* (9–12). 1995, Holt paper $14.95 (0-8050-0537-4). A practical, confidence-inspiring book that offers sound solutions to many job-hunting problems. (Rev: BL 5/15/88; BR 1–2/89; SLJ 11/88) [371.4]

10360 Jones, Lawrence K. *Job Skills for the 21st Century: A Guide for Students* (9–12). Illus. 1995, Oryx paper $40.75 (0-89774-956-1). This excellent manual on improving job skills and career guidance also shows how to assess one's skills, set realistic goals, and learn new skills. (Rev: BL 2/15/96) [331.7]

10361 Lewis, Sydney. *Help Wanted: Tales from the First Job Front* (10–12). 2001, New Pr. $25.00 (1-56584-369-X). This book consists of 25 interviews with young people about their experiences on entering the work force for the first time, including their hopes, disappointments, and fears. (Rev: BL 2/1/01) [331.3]

10362 McFarland, Rhoda. *The World of Work: The Lifeskills Library* (9–12). Series: Lifeskills Library. 1993, Rosen LB $14.95 (0-8239-1467-4). Takes readers through the process of job hunting, with information on résumés, interviews, applications, general skills, and time management. (Rev: BL 6/1–15/93) [650.14]

10363 McGlothlin, Bruce. *High Performance Through Understanding Systems* (7–10). Series: Learning-a-Living Library. 1996, Rosen LB $17.95 (0-8239-2210-3). Aimed primarily at youths preparing to enter the world of work directly after graduation, this book explains systems ("any combination of elements that operate together and form a whole") in the family, at school, and at work, and tells how individuals can diagnose problems, predict outcomes, and improve the systems. (Rev: SLJ 3/97) [001.6]

10364 Mackall, Dandi. *Self Development Skills* (9–12). Series: Career Skills Library. 1997, Ferguson $14.95 (0-89434-214-2). This title explores behavior, desirable character traits, and habits to develop for the workplace. The seven additional titles in this series each focus on a skill that people looking for a job should be aware of. Three of these titles are: *Teamwork, Communication,* and *Leadership Skills* (all 1998). (Rev: VOYA 8/98) [650.14]

10365 Pedrvola, Cindy, and Debby Hobgood. *How to Get a Job If You Are a Teenager* (9–12). 1998, Alleyside paper $12.95 (0-57950-013-7). Using a question-and-answer format, this book covers all the necessary topics relating to job hunting, from résumés, filling out an application, and preparing for an interview to adjusting to the workplace, time management, and work etiquette. (Rev: BR 9–10/98; SLJ 7/98; VOYA 10/98) [650.14]

10366 Strazzabosco, Jeanne M. *High Performance Through Dealing with Diversity* (8–12). Illus.

Series: Learning-a-Living Library. 1996, Rosen LB $17.95 (0-8239-2202-2). Through applying attitudes of tolerance and positive feelings, this book prepares students to work with diverse populations in a multicultural workplace. (Rev: BL 8/96; BR 1–2/97) [650.1]

Careers

General and Miscellaneous

10367 Alagna, Magdalena. *Life Inside the Air Force Academy* (7–12). Illus. Series: Insider's Look. 2002, Children's $20.00 (0-516-23924-4); paper $6.95 (0-516-24001-3). This look inside the Air Force Academy — which explores the rituals, traditions, and rhythm of daily life at this institution — is intended for reluctant readers and explains the requirements for admittance. Also in this series is *Life Inside the Military Academy* (2002). (Rev: BL 10/15/02) [358.4]

10368 Alagna, Magdalena. *War Correspondents: Life Under Fire* (5–10). Series: Extreme Careers. 2003, Rosen LB $26.50 (0-8239-3798-4). The dangers of wartime assignments are emphasized in this volume that also stresses job requirements that include a good education and broad knowledge of world events. (Rev: BL 9/15/03; SLJ 11/03) [808]

10369 Bowman-Kruhm, Mary. *Careers in Child Care* (7–12). Series: Careers Library. 2000, Rosen LB $18.95 (0-8239-2891-8). A comprehensive, accessible overview of the types of jobs that are available for people who enjoy working with children, with practical guidance on finding employment. (Rev: HBG 10/01; SLJ 3/01)

10370 Brenlove, Milovan S. *Vectors to Spare: The Life of an Air Traffic Controller* (9–12). 1993, Iowa State Univ. Pr. $29.95 (0-8138-0471-X). Conveys the flavor of the job of aerial cop, describing arrogant pilots, boom-lowering supervisors, career politics, and actual crashes and near misses. (Rev: BL 6/1–15/93) [629.136]

10371 *Broadcasting*. 2nd ed. (7–12). Series: Careers in Focus. 2002, Ferguson LB $14.50 (0-89434-440-4). Careers in animation, lighting, reporting, editing, and weather forecasting are just a few of those covered in this concise introduction to the world of broadcasting and its educational requirements, employment outlook, and potential salaries. Also use *Fashion* (2002). (Rev: SLJ 7/01) [384.54]

10372 *The Business of Journalism: Ten Leading Reporters and Editors on the Perils and Pitfalls of the Press* (10–12). Ed. by William Serrin. 2000, New Pr. paper $16.95 (1-56584-581-1). The way modern journalism is conducted is the theme of 10 essays by prominent reporters who also give practi-

cal advice for budding journalists. (Rev: BL 6/1–15/00) [071]

10373 Chmelynski, Carol Ann. *Opportunities in Restaurant Careers* (9–12). 1990, VGM $14.95 (0-8442-8662-1); paper $12.95 (0-8442-8664-8). From fast food to haute cuisine, here is a description of a variety of restaurant-related jobs from beginning level to owning one's own eatery. (Rev: BL 12/1/89; BR 5–6/90) [647]

10374 Donovan, Robert J. *Boxing the Kangaroo: A Reporter's Memoir* (10–12). Illus. 2000, Univ. of Missouri Pr. $24.95 (0-8262-1281-6). This Pulitzer Prize-winning columnist describes the basic elements of a news story and tells how he and other reporters handle these elements in reporting the news and meeting a deadline. (Rev: BL 6/1–15/00) [070]

10375 Duncan, Jane Caryl. *Careers in Veterinary Medicine* (8–12). Illus. 1994, Rosen LB $16.95 (0-8239-1678-2); paper $9.95 (0-8239-1719-3). A veterinarian gives an honest description of her profession and many practical tips. (Rev: BL 9/1/88; SLJ 10/88; VOYA 10/88) [636.089]

10376 Dunlop, Reginald. *Come Fly with Me! Your Nineties Guide to Becoming a Flight Attendant* (9–12). 1993, Maxamillian paper $15.95 (0-9632749-9-6). Gives specifics on increasing the chances of employment in a competitive field. Provides a tutorial for presenting oneself in the best light. (Rev: BL 6/1–15/93) [387.7]

10377 Eberts, Marjorie, and Margaret Gisler. *Careers for Kids at Heart and Others Who Adore Children* (9–12). 1994, VGM $14.95 (0-8442-4110-5); paper $9.95 (0-8442-4111-3). A career guide for those interested in working with children, focusing on jobs in child care, education, recreation, and health. (Rev: BL 8/94; VOYA 12/94) [362.7]

10378 Eberts, Marjorie, and Margaret Gisler. *Careers in Child Care* (9–12). 1994, VGM $17.95 (0-8442-4191-1); paper $13.95 (0-8442-4193-8). Profiles occupations relating to child care, including teaching, sports, recreation, welfare, the arts, and entertainment. (Rev: BL 8/94) [362.7]

10379 Fasulo, Michael, and Jane Kinney. *Careers for Environmental Types* (9–12). 1993, VGM $14.95 (0-8442-4102-4); paper $9.95 (0-8442-4103-2). Outlines the educational preparation necessary for environmental careers. (Rev: BL 5/15/93; VOYA 10/93) [363.7]

10380 Ferguson, J. G. *What Can I Do Now? Preparing for a Career in Journalism* (7–12). 1998, Ferguson $16.95 (0-89434-251-7). This book introduces careers in journalism and related fields, describes the preparation and aptitudes necessary, and suggests how teens can get involved in journalism while still in school. (Rev: SLJ 4/99) [070]

10381 Field, Sally. *Career Opportunities in the Music Industry*. Rev. ed. (10–12). Series: Career Opportunities. 1995, Facts on File $45.00 (0-8160-3047-2). This volume offers realistic information on more than 80 different jobs relating to the music industry, including positions in the record business, radio and television, music retailing and wholesaling, education, publicity, and orchestras. (Rev: SLJ 6/96) [780]

10382 Field, Shelly. *Careers as an Animal Rights Activist* (9–12). 1993, Rosen paper $9.95 (0-8239-1722-3). Concentrates on jobs within animal rights organizations, with lists of organizations and trade associations and a cruelty-free shopping guide. (Rev: BL 5/15/93; SLJ 6/93; VOYA 8/93) [179.4]

10383 Foote-Smith, Elizabeth. *Opportunities in Writing Careers* (9–12). 1988, VGM $14.95 (0-8442-6512-8); paper $11.95 (0-8442-6513-6). Working conditions are described and necessary qualifications are given for a wide variety of jobs requiring writing skills. (Rev: BR 5–6/89; VOYA 4/89) [411]

10384 Girod, Christina. *Aeronautics* (6–12). Series: Careers for the Twenty-First Century. 2002, Gale LB $27.45 (1-56006-894-9). A look at careers as pilots, flight attendants, air traffic controllers, aircraft mechanics, and astronauts. (Rev: BL 10/15/02) [629.13]

10385 Haegele, Katie. *Nature Lovers* (7–12). Series: Cool Careers Without College. 2002, Rosen $30.60 (0-8239-3504-3). Jobs profiled here include Christmas tree farmer, ranch hand, fisherman, park ranger, and river guide, with accompanying information on training, pay, opportunities, and related occupations. (Rev: BL 5/15/02; SLJ 7/02) [331.7]

10386 Hayhurst, Chris. *Cool Careers Without College for Animal Lovers* (7–12). Illus. Series: Cool Careers Without College. 2002, Rosen LB $30.60 (0-8239-3500-0). Veterinary technician, groomer, and pet photographer are some of the options explored in this book that gives information on training and on-the-job activities. (Rev: BL 5/15/02; SLJ 7/02) [636]

10387 Hole, Dorothy. *The Air Force and You* (9–12). Series: Armed Forces. 1993, Macmillan LB $17.95 (0-89686-764-1). This is a concise, interesting guide to careers in the Air Force. (Rev: BL 3/15/94) [358.4]

10388 Hole, Dorothy. *The Army and You* (9–12). Series: Armed Forces. 1993, Silver Burdett $17.95 (0-89686-765-X). Not written as a recruitment text, this volume is an examination of the army as a career. (Rev: BL 3/15/94; SLJ 1/94) [355]

10389 Hole, Dorothy. *The Coast Guard and You* (9–12). Series: Armed Forces. 1993, Macmillan LB $17.95 (0-89686-766-8). A straightforward, factual description of life in the Coast Guard. (Rev: BL 3/15/94; SLJ 1/94) [359.9]

10390 Hole, Dorothy. *The Marines and You* (9–12). Series: Armed Forces. 1993, Macmillan LB $17.95 (0-89686-768-4). The United States Marines offer opportunities for recruits that are explored in this concise guide. (Rev: BL 3/15/94; SLJ 1/94) [359.9]

10391 Hole, Dorothy. *The Navy and You* (9–12). Series: Armed Forces. 1993, Macmillan LB $17.95 (0-89686-767-6). Young people interested in a career in the U.S. Navy will find this concise guide offers practical, honest advice. (Rev: BL 3/15/94) [359]

10392 Kaplan, Andrew. *Careers for Number Lovers* (9–12). Photos. 1991, Millbrook LB $20.90 (1-878841-21-1). Fourteen professionals profile their work, offering personal insights about the joy of working with numbers. (Rev: BL 3/1/91; SLJ 11/91) [510.23]

10393 Kenig, Graciela. *Best Careers for Bilingual Latinos: Market Your Fluency in Spanish to Get Ahead on the Job* (10–12). 1999, VGM paper $14.95 (0-8442-4541-0). This practical, well-researched handbook based on hundreds of interviews with Latino professionals discusses how to market bilingual skills and cope with workplace challenges such as ethnic stereotypes and office politics, and identifies the top fields for bilingual Latinos: health care, financial services, technology, sales and marketing, professional services, and international opportunities. (Rev: SLJ 8/99) [331.6]

10394 Kirkwood, Tim. *The Flight Attendant Career Guide* (9–12). 1993, T K Enterprises paper $14.95 (0-9637301-4-2). Explores the career and lifestyle of a flight attendant, including information helpful for interviewing. (Rev: BL 10/1/93) [387.7]

10395 Krebs, Michelle. *Cars* (9–12). Series: Careers Without College. 1992, Peterson's Guides paper $7.95 (1-56079-221-3). Presents five kinds of jobs relating to cars that may require further education but not a four-year degree. (Rev: BL 2/15/93) [629.2]

10396 Lee, Mary Price. *Opportunities in Animal and Pet Care Careers* (9–12). 1993, VGM $13.95 (0-8442-4079-6); paper $11.95 (0-8442-4081-8). All aspects of these careers are considered. (Rev: BL 3/15/94; VOYA 6/94) [636]

10397 Longshore, Shirley J. *Office* (10–12). Illus. Series: Careers Without College. 1994, Peterson's Guides paper $7.95 (0-56079-353-8). This career guide gives details on various positions in the business office that do not require a college degree. (Rev: BL 9/15/94) [651.3]

10398 Lytle, Elizabeth Stewart. *Careers in Cosmetology* (7–12). 1999, Rosen LB $17.95 (0-8239-

2889-6). A survey of career options in the field of cosmetology, with descriptions of training and qualifications, profiles of cosmetologists, and general advice on job seeking. (Rev: SLJ 4/00) [646.7]

10399 Mackall, Joseph. *Information Management* (9–12). Illus. 1998, Ferguson $14.95 (0-89434-215-0). This title shows teenagers how to collect, organize, and use information as it relates to practical situations on their jobs and careers. Others in this series are: *Organization, Problem-Solving,* and *Learning the Ropes* (all 1998). (Rev: VOYA 8/98) [350.14]

10400 Marriner, Michael, and Nathan Gebhard. *Roadtrip Nation: A Guide to Discovering Your Path in Life* (10–12). Illus. 2003, Ballantine paper $13.95 (0-345-46013-8). The authors recount the cross-country journey they took as college students in an effort to explore the various paths to career success. (Rev: BL 4/15/03; SLJ 7/03) [158]

10401 Martin, Molly, ed. *Hard-Hatted Women: Life on the Job* (10–12). 1997, Seal paper $14.95 (1-878067-91-5). This book contains interviews with 26 women in carpentry, ironwork, mining, truck driving, and other blue-collar work about their jobs, including their experiences with sexism and harassment. (Rev: VOYA 12/97) [331.7]

10402 Mason, Helen. *Great Careers for People Interested in Food* (6–10). Series: Career Connections. 1996, Gale $40.00 (0-7876-0860-2). All kinds of food-related careers are described in this book, along with career-path recommendations, training and experience requirements, and outlooks for the future. (Rev: BR 9–10/96; SLJ 9/96) [355.6]

10403 Mason, Helen. *Great Careers for People Who Like Being Outdoors* (9–12). Series: Career Connections. 1993, Gale $27.75 (0-8103-9390-5). Provides a list of outdoor occupations and a description of the work, profiles various people who hold these jobs, explains job requirements, preparation, and the hiring process, and gives an idea of future prospects. (Rev: BL 3/15/94; SLJ 12/93) [796.5023]

10404 Maynard, Thane. *Working with Wildlife: A Guide to Careers in the Animal World* (6–10). Illus. 1999, Watts LB $26.00 (0-531-11538-0). Many different jobs working with animals are discussed, including training wild animals, working with insects, and being part of a conservation team. (Rev: BCCB 1/00; BL 1/1–15/00; SLJ 3/00) [636]

10405 Miller, Louise. *Careers for Animal Lovers and Other Zoological Types* (9–12). 1991, VGM paper $9.95 (0-8442-8125-5). Information on animal care employment, from pet-sitter to veterinarian. (Rev: BL 6/1/91) [636]

10406 *150 Great Tech Prep Careers* (8–12). 2001, Ferguson paper $29.95 (0-89434-344-0). This book presents "information on 150 careers that can be acquired through on-the-job training, an apprenticeship, a certificate, or an associate degree." [331.7]

10407 Parks, Peggy J. *The News Media* (6–12). Illus. Series: Careers for the Twenty-First Century. 2002, Gale LB $27.45 (1-59018-205-7). A comprehensive look at careers in journalism, with historical information as well as descriptions of the day-to-day requirements and challenges and discussion of the benefits and drawbacks of the profession. (Rev: BL 10/15/02) [070.4]

10408 Pasternak, Ceel, and Linda Thornburg. *Cool Careers for Girls in Air and Space* (6–12). Series: Cool Careers for Girls. 2001, Impact LB $19.95 (1-57023-147-8); paper $12.95 (1-57023-146-X). This account discusses various careers open to women in the aircraft and space industries with information on qualifications, working conditions, and compensation. (Rev: BL 4/15/01; SLJ 4/01) [629]

10409 Pasternak, Ceel, and Linda Thornburg. *Cool Careers for Girls in Food* (5–10). Series: Cool Careers for Girls. 2000, Impact $19.95 (1-57023-127-3); paper $12.95 (1-57023-120-6). The 11 women featured in this book are involved in various aspects of the food industry such as cheese making, baking, wine making, selling health food, and cooking for the military. (Rev: SLJ 2/00) [641]

10410 Pitz, Mary Elizabeth. *Careers in Government* (9–12). 1994, VGM $24.95 (0-8442-4194-6); paper $13.95 (0-8442-4195-4). A guide for those interested in employment in government. Explains the hiring processes for many nonelective occupations and federal jobs. (Rev: BL 8/94) [350]

10411 *Preparing for a Career in the Environment* (9–12). 1998, Ferguson $16.95 (0-89434-249-5). A variety of environmental careers are introduced, with material on aptitude, education, pay, advancement, and employment outlook. (Rev: SLJ 2/99) [331]

10412 *Real Sports Reporting* (10–12). Ed. by Abraham Aamidor. 2003, Indiana Univ. Pr. $49.95 (0-253-34273-2); paper $19.95 (0-253-21616-8). Chapters written by journalists focus on the unique challenges of covering sports and give tips on succeeding in this field. (Rev: BL 9/1/03) [070.4]

10413 Reeves, Diane Lindsey, and Gayle Bryan. *Career Ideas for Kids Who Like Money* (6–10). Illus. Series: Career Ideas. 2001, Facts on File $23.00 (0-8160-4319-1). An attractive introduction to careers such as business manager, e-merchant, entrepreneur, and investment banker, with personal profiles of individuals in the various fields and attractive cartoons. (Rev: BL 7/01; HBG 3/02; SLJ 8/01) [332]

10414 Reeves, Diane Lindsey, and Gayle Bryan. *Career Ideas for Kids Who Like Travel* (6–10). Series: Career Ideas for Kids. 2001, Checkmark

$23.00 (0-8160-4325-6); paper $12.95 (0-8160-4326-4). A number of careers in the travel industry are presented with coverage of qualifications, training, rewards, and working conditions. (Rev: BL 3/15/02; HBG 10/02) [331.7]

10415 Reeves, Diane Lindsey, and Nancy Heubeck. *Career Ideas for Kids Who Like Adventure* (6–10). Series: Career Ideas for Kids. 2001, Facts on File LB $23.00 (0-8160-4321-3). An attractive introduction to careers such as fire fighting, scuba diving, oil rig work, and piloting, with personal profiles of individuals in the various fields and attractive cartoons. (Rev: BL 7/01; HBG 3/02; SLJ 8/01) [331.7]

10416 Reeves, Diane Lindsey, and Nancy Heubeck. *Career Ideas for Kids Who Like Animals and Nature* (6–10). 2000, Facts on File $18.95 (0-8160-4097-4). Careers explored in this volume that includes practical advice plus profiles of workers in these jobs range from veterinarian and animal trainer to arborist and botanist. (Rev: BR 11–12/00; HBG 9/00; SLJ 12/00) [570]

10417 Roberson, Virginia Lee. *Careers in the Graphic Arts* (9–12). 1988, Rosen $10.95 (0-8239-0803-8). Careers involving illustration, paste-up work, layout, art, and design are described with details on job opportunities, qualifications, and working conditions. (Rev: BL 12/15/88; BR 9–10/89; VOYA 6/89) [760]

10418 Rosenberg, Aaron. *Cryptologists: Life Making and Breaking Codes* (5–10). Series: Extreme Careers. 2004, Rosen LB $19.95 (0-8239-3965-0). After some background material on the history of codes, this volume discusses career opportunities as a cryptologist. (Rev: BL 5/15/04) [410]

10419 Ruhlman, Michael. *The Making of a Chef: Mastering Heat at the Culinary Institute of America* (10–12). 1997, Holt $27.50 (0-8050-4674-7). This is an engrossing account of the author's student days at the most prestigious cooking school in the United States, the Culinary Institute of America, with a description of its curriculum and what goes into becoming a master chef. (Rev: SLJ 5/98) [641.5]

10420 Schwager, Tina, and Michele Schuerger. *Cool Women, Hot Jobs — And How You Can Go for It, Too!* (7–12). Illus. 2002, Free Spirit paper $15.95 (1-57542-109-7). Profiles of women who work in a wide variety of jobs — from dolphin training and Egyptology to flying fighter planes and planning weddings — are accompanied by details of the job itself and suggestions for setting and achieving goals. (Rev: BL 6/1–15/02; SLJ 7/02; VOYA 8/02) [650.14]

10421 Seidman, David. *Careers in Journalism* (6–12). Illus. Series: Exploring Careers. 2000, Rosen LB $18.95 (0-8239-3298-2). Print journalism, broadcast journalism, writing, editing, and

design are all covered in this introduction to a widely varied field. (Rev: BL 3/15/01; HBG 10/01; SLJ 2/01) [070.4]

10422 Shenk, Ellen. *Outdoor Careers: Exploring Occupations in Outdoor Fields.* 2nd ed. (10–12). 2000, Stackpole paper $16.95 (0-8117-2873-0). About 60 careers are examined under eight headings including agriculture and food production, biological sciences, engineering, marine careers, recreation, and indoor careers that also involve the outdoors. (Rev: BL 3/1/00) [331.7]

10423 Shorto, Russell. *Careers for Animal Lovers* (9–12). Series: Choices. 1992, Millbrook LB $20.90 (1-56294-160-7). Includes career lists, an index of organizations, and interviews with a zookeeper, snake handler, veterinarian, and pet groomer. (Rev: BL 1/1/92; SLJ 2/92) [636]

10424 Stienstra, Tom, and Robin Schlueter. *Sunshine Jobs: Career Opportunities Working Outdoors* (9–12). 1997, Live Oak $16.95 (0-911781-15-3). This book uses a readable format to describe 103 jobs outdoors, from mountain climbing guide to operator of a canoe rental service. (Rev: VOYA 10/97) [976.5]

10425 *Top 100: The Fastest Growing Careers for the 21st Century.* 3rd ed. (10–12). Ed. by Andrew Morkes, et al. 2001, Ferguson paper $19.95 (0-89434-343-2). The duties, required training, equipment used, and opportunities in a wide range of careers are accompanied by salary ranges and tips for new workers. (Rev: BL 4/1/01; VOYA 8/01) [331.7]

10426 Turner, Chérie. *Adventure Tour Guides: Life on Extreme Outdoor Adventures* (5–10). Series: Extreme Careers. 2003, Rosen LB $26.50 (0-8239-3793-3). A look at the profession of tour guiding on excursions such as white-water rafting and mountain climbing, with material on qualifications and future possibilities. (Rev: BL 9/15/03) [908]

10427 *25 Jobs That Have It All: High Pay, Fast Growth, Most New Jobs* (10–12). Ed. by Andrew Morkes, et al. 2001, Ferguson paper $12.95 (0-89434-327-0). This career guide spotlights the 25 occupational fields that offer the most job openings, highest pay, and fastest growth. (Rev: VOYA 8/01) [331.7]

10428 VGM Career Horizons, eds. *VGM's Careers Encyclopedia.* 4th ed. (9–12). 1997, VGM $39.95 (0-8442-4525-9). A comprehensive report on 200 careers, arranged alphabetically. (Rev: BL 6/1/91) [331.7]

10429 Weiss, Ann E. *The Glass Ceiling: A Look at Women in the Workforce* (8–12). 1999, Twenty-First Century LB $23.90 (0-7613-1365-6). After a brief history of women's place in the world of work, this book focuses on recent changes and new opportunities (and dangers) for women in the workforce. (Rev: BL 6/1–15/99; SLJ 9/99) [331.4]

10430 White, William C., and Donald N. Collins. *Opportunities in Agriculture Careers* (10–12). Illus. 1987, VGM $13.95 (0-8442-6554-3); paper $10.95 (0-8442-6555-1). A guide that covers standard careers plus related ones in transportation, research, and so on. (Rev: BL 6/1/88; BR 5–6/88) [630.203]

10431 Wilson, Wayne. *Careers in Publishing and Communications* (8–12). Series: Latinos at Work. 2001, Mitchell Lane LB $22.95 (1-58415-088-2). This career guide for Latinos explores job opportunities for authors, copy editors, disc jockeys, artists, and agents, and includes personal interviews with successful Hispanic Americans in these fields. (Rev: BL 10/15/01; HBG 3/02) [808]

10432 Zannos, Susan. *Careers in Science and Medicine* (8–12). Series: Latinos at Work. 2001, Mitchell Lane LB $22.95 (1-58415-084-X). Descriptions of careers in these fields are accompanied by information on salary and qualifications as well as profiles of Latino men and women who have found success in a variety of career positions. (Rev: BL 10/15/01; HBG 3/02; SLJ 11/01) [502]

10433 Zannos, Susan. *Latino Entrepreneurs* (8–12). Series: Latinos at Work. 2001, Mitchell Lane LB $22.95 (1-58415-089-0). This book looks at the many possibilities for self-employment for Hispanics with personal interviews of successful Latinos in a variety of fields. (Rev: BL 3/15/02; HBG 10/02; SLJ 3/02) [650.1]

Arts, Entertainment, and Sports

10434 Bartlett, Gillian. *Great Careers for People Interested in Art and Design* (6–10). Series: Career Connections. 1996, Gale $40.00 (0-7876-0863-7). Using case studies of six people who have succeeded in careers relating to art and design, this book discusses opportunities, career-path recommendations, qualifications, and the outlook for the future. (Rev: BR 9–10/96; SLJ 9/96) [746.9]

10435 *Careers in Focus — Sports* (8–12). Series: Careers in Focus. 1998, Ferguson $14.50 (0-89434-247-9). More than 20 careers relating to sports, from golf-course superintendent to professional athlete to stadium vendor, are included in this volume, with information on qualifications, working conditions, salaries, opportunities, rewards, and methods of exploring and entering the field. (Rev: BR 9–10/98; SLJ 8/98) [796]

10436 Flender, Nicole. *People Who Love Movement* (7–12). Series: Cool Careers Without College. 2002, Rosen $30.60 (0-8239-3505-1). Some of the non-college degree careers discussed are dancers, dance and yoga teachers, and fitness instructors in this

book which also covers salaries, and job opportunities. (Rev: BL 5/15/02) [613.7]

10437 Greenspon, Jaq. *Careers for Film Buffs and Other Hollywood Types* (9–12). 1993, VGM $14.95 (0-8442-4100-8); paper $9.95 (0-8442-4101-6). An encyclopedia of job descriptions, covering such departments as production, camera and sound, special effects, grip and electric, makeup and costumes, and more. (Rev: BL 5/15/93) [791.43]

10438 Greenwald, Ted. *Music* (9–12). Series: Careers Without College. 1992, Peterson's Guides paper $7.95 (1-56079-219-1). Presents five types of occupations relating to music that may require further education but not a four-year degree. (Rev: BL 2/15/93) [780]

10439 Hinton, Kerry. *Cool Careers Without College for Music Lovers* (7–12). Illus. Series: Cool Careers Without College. 2002, Rosen LB $30.60 (0-8239-3503-5). Music store clerk, promoter, and instrument repairman are some of the options explored in this book that gives information on training and on-the-job activities. (Rev: BL 5/15/02; SLJ 7/02) [780]

10440 Hopkins, Del, and Margaret Hopkins. *Careers as a Rock Musician* (9–12). 1993, Rosen LB $15.95 (0-8239-1518-2). Emphasizes that a clear understanding of the business side of the profession is vital for success. (Rev: BL 5/15/93; VOYA 10/93) [781.66]

10441 Isenberg, Marc, and Rick Rhoads. *The Real Athletes Guide: How to Succeed in Sports, School, and Life* (9–12). 1998, Athlete Network paper $19.95 (0-9666764-0-8). This overview examines scholarship opportunities in college athletics and tells how to choose the right college, handle the recruitment process, and prepare for a career. (Rev: BL 12/15/98; SLJ 3/99) [378.1]

10442 Jay, Annie, and Luanne Feik. *Stars in Your Eyes . . . Feet on the Ground: A Practical Guide for Teenage Actors (and Their Parents!)* (7–12). Illus. 1999, Theatre Directories paper $16.95 (0-933919-42-5). A young actress gives practical advice on how to break into show business, including information on publicity photographs, auditions, managers, agents, publicity packages, résumés, and casting calls. (Rev: BL 6/1–15/99) [792.02]

10443 Kaplan, Andrew. *Careers for Artistic Types* (9–12). Photos. 1991, Millbrook LB $20.90 (1-878841-20-3). Presents an interesting assortment of artistic careers with information gathered directly from individuals in these occupations. (Rev: BL 3/1/91; SLJ 11/91) [702.3]

10444 Lantz, Francess. *Rock, Rap, and Rad: How to Be a Rock or Rap Star* (6–12). 1992, Avon paper $3.99 (0-380-76793-7). The author takes aspiring rock stars through the basic steps of choosing an instrument, finding other musicians and a place to play, lining up gigs, and on up to the top. (Rev: BL 7/93) [781.66]

10445 Leshay, Jeff. *How to Launch Your Career in TV News* (9–12). 1993, VGM paper $14.95 (0-8442-4138-5). Describes how to get into a career in TV news, from the interviewing process on. Includes interviews with those in the business and information on college programs and scholarships. (Rev: BL 10/1/93) [070]

10446 McDaniels, Pellom. *So, You Want to Be a Pro?* (6–12). Illus. 1999, Addax $14.95 (1-886110-77-8). Atlanta Falcons player McDaniels offers encouragement to would-be professional athletes without encouraging unrealistic expectations. (Rev: BL 11/15/99; SLJ 3/00) [613.7]

10447 Mayfield, Katherine. *Acting A to Z: The Young Person's Guide to a Stage or Screen Career* (6–12). Illus. 1998, Back Stage paper $16.95 (0-8230-8801-4). This slim, eye-catching paperback explores all facets of an acting career, from the general to the practical and the specific, including networking, casting, education, self-esteem, budgeting, résumés, and promotional photographs. (Rev: VOYA 6/99) [792]

10448 Menard, Valerie. *Careers in Sports* (8–12). Series: Latinos at Work. 2001, Mitchell Lane LB $22.95 (1-58415-086-6). This book explores the career possibilities for Hispanic Americans in a variety of sports with several interesting case studies of Latinos who did well in them. (Rev: BL 3/15/02; HBG 10/02) [796]

10449 Mirault, Don. *Dancing . . . for a Living: Where the Jobs Are, What They Pay, What Choreographers Look For, What to Ask* (9–12). 1994, Rafter paper $15.95 (0-9637864-4-X). An experienced professional discusses employment opportunities and gives practical career suggestions for dancers. (Rev: BL 1/15/94) [792.8]

10450 Nagle, Jeanne. *Careers in Coaching* (7–12). Series: Careers Library. 2000, Rosen LB $16.95 (0-8239-2966-3). This guide to how to become a successful coach covers all aspects of the job. (Rev: SLJ 7/00) [796]

10451 Parks, Peggy. *Music* (6–12). Series: Careers for the Twenty-First Century. 2002, Gale LB $27.45 (1-59018-223-5). This book provides a close look at six music-related careers — musician, composer, recording engineer, music therapist, music publicist, and music educator. (Rev: BL 10/15/02) [780]

10452 Pasternak, Ceel, and Linda Thornburg. *Cool Careers for Girls in Sports* (5–10). Series: Cool Careers for Girls. 1999, Impact $19.95 (1-57023-107-9); paper $12.95 (1-57023-104-4). A golf pro, basketball player, ski instructor, sports broadcaster, trainer, sports psychologist, and athletic director are

among the 10 women profiled in this overview of careers for women in sports. (Rev: SLJ 7/99; VOYA 8/99) [796]

10453 Peterson, Linda. *Entertainment* (10–12). Illus. Series: Careers Without College. 1994, Peterson's Guides paper $7.95 (0-56079-352-X). This career guide covers positions in the performing arts and broadcasting. (Rev: BL 9/15/94) [791]

10454 Reeves, Diane Lindsey, and Gayle Bryan. *Career Ideas for Kids Who Like Music and Dance* (6–10). Series: Career Ideas for Kids. 2001, Checkmark $23.00 (0-8160-4323-X); paper $12.95 (0-8160-4324-8). This work presents a number of career opportunities in music and dance with material on training, qualifications, and working conditions. (Rev: BL 3/15/02; HBG 10/02) [790]

10455 Ritzenthaler, Carol L. *Teen Guide to Getting Started in the Arts* (8–12). 2001, Greenwood $39.95 (0-313-31392-X). This is a practical handbook that describes a variety of careers (actor, artist, dancer, writer, and so forth) and the skills required, with useful contact information and advice for parents. (Rev: SLJ 7/02; VOYA 12/02) [700]

10456 Rosenbaum, Jean, and Mary Prine. *Opportunities in Fitness Careers* (9–12). 1991, VGM $14.95 (0-8442-8185-9). Information on educational requirements and income expectations for one of today's fastest-growing industries. (Rev: BL 6/1/91) [613.7]

10457 Salmon, Mark. *Opportunities in Visual Arts Careers* (9–12). 1992, VGM $14.95 (0-8442-4031-1); paper $11.95 (0-8442-4033-8). Discusses working for a company, freelance work, teaching art, and art therapy. (Rev: BL 2/15/93) [702.3]

10458 Sharon, Donna, and Jo Anne Sommers. *Great Careers for People Interested in Travel and Tourism* (6–10). Series: Career Connections. 1996, Gale $40.00 (0-7876-0862-9). Tour director and travel agent are among the jobs discussed in this overview of careers relating to travel and tourism, with information on qualifications, training, and opportunities. (Rev: BR 9–10/96; SLJ 9/96) [658]

10459 Sommers, Michael A. *Wildlife Photographers: Life Through a Lens* (5–10). Series: Extreme Careers. 2003, Rosen LB $26.50 (0-8239-3638-4). A concise explanation of the work of wildlife photographers, the attributes needed, and the training and tenacity required to enter this field. (Rev: BL 9/15/03; SLJ 5/03) [771]

10460 Steele, William Paul. *Stay Home and Star! A Step-by-Step Guide to Starting Your Regional Acting Career* (9–12). 1992, Heinemann paper $13.95 (0-435-08603-0). Practical advice about acting opportunities on the local level, emphasizing a businesslike approach and the basic requirements for success. (Rev: BL 2/1/92) [792]

10461 Torres, John, and Susan Zannos. *Careers in the Music Industry* (8–12). Series: Latinos at Work. 2001, Mitchell Lane LB $22.95 (1-58415-085-8). Along with personal interviews with Hispanics who did well in the music world, there are descriptions of such related careers as singers, songwriters, managers, and agents. (Rev: BL 3/15/02; HBG 10/02) [780]

10462 Weigant, Chris. *Careers as a Disc Jockey* (8–12). Series: Careers. 1997, Rosen LB $16.95 (0-8239-2528-5). This informative book gives many practical tips on how to get started and be successful in radio, with material on making demo tapes, applying for jobs and internships, and working oneself up. There are interviews with eight DJs. Careers in management, sales, technical areas, talk shows, and others are included. (Rev: BR 3–4/98; SLJ 12/97; VOYA 2/98) [384.54]

10463 Wilson, Lee. *Making It in the Music Business: A Business and Legal Guide for Songwriters and Performers* (9–12). 1995, NAL paper $12.95 (0-452-26848-6). A practical handbook of copyright law, trademarks, and other information, by a music attorney. (Rev: BL 4/1/95) [780]

10464 Wilson, Wayne. *Careers in Entertainment* (8–12). Series: Latinos at Work. 2001, Mitchell Lane LB $22.95 (1-58415-083-1). With an emphasis on Hispanic American success stories, this book features careers in film, television, and theater. (Rev: BL 10/15/01; HBG 3/02) [791]

10465 Wormser, Richard. *To the Young Filmmaker: Conversations with Working Filmmakers* (7–12). Series: To the Young . . . 2002, Watts LB $23.00 (0-531-11727-8). Profiles of eight movie industry workers — including a writer, producer, director, and actress — are intended to encourage young people that they too can make films. (Rev: LMC 1/03; SLJ 9/02; VOYA 4/03) [791.43]

Business

10466 Beckett, Kathleen. *Fashion* (9–12). Series: Careers Without College. 1992, Peterson's Guides paper $7.95 (1-56079-220-5). The world of fashion is explored in this career guide that explores occupations that do not require a college degree. (Rev: BL 2/15/93) [687]

10467 Dolber, Roslyn. *Opportunities in Fashion Careers*. 2nd ed. (9–12). 1992, VGM $13.95 (0-8442-4022-2); paper $10.95 (0-8442-4023-0). This career guide surveys the world of the fashion industry and highlights a variety of jobs involved. (Rev: BL 1/1/93) [687]

10468 Giacobello, John. *Careers in the Fashion Industry* (7–12). Series: Exploring Careers. 1999, Rosen LB $17.95 (0-8239-2890-X). This book explains what it takes to get started in a variety of fashion-related careers, and includes tips on writing résumés, interviewing, and so forth. (Rev: SLJ 2/00) [746.9]

10469 Healy, Lisa, ed. *My First Year in Book Publishing: Real-World Stories from America's Book Publishing Professionals* (9–12). 1994, Walker $33.95 (0-8027-1294-0); paper $18.95 (0-8027-7425-3). A guide for those interested in book publishing, including testimony from agents, editors, publicists, and indexers describing their first year of work. (Rev: BL 9/1/94; VOYA 12/94) [070.5]

10470 Mogel, Leonard. *Making It in Advertising: An Insider's Guide to Career Opportunities* (9–12). 1993, Macmillan paper $10.00 (0-02-034552-6). Based on interviews with ad agency professionals, this is an introduction to advertising, describing available positions and the talents needed to succeed. (Rev: BL 4/15/93) [659.1]

10471 Noronha, Shonan F. R. *Careers in Communications* (9–12). 1993, VGM $17.95 (0-8442-4182-2); paper $13.95 (0-8442-4183-0). Information on the fields of journalism, photography, film, radio, multimedia, television and video, advertising, and public relations. (Rev: BL 3/15/94) [384]

10472 Plawin, Paul. *Careers for Travel Buffs and Other Restless Types* (9–12). 1992, VGM $14.95 (0-8442-8109-3); paper $9.95 (0-8442-8127-1). Covers job descriptions, getting into the business, and future prospects of typical travel careers as well as positions that involve less traveling. (Rev: BL 6/1/92; SLJ 3/92) [331.7]

10473 Ring, Gertrude. *Careers in Finance* (9–12). 1993, VGM $17.95 (0-8442-4186-5); paper $13.95 (0-8442-4187-3). A basic guide to careers in the world of finance. (Rev: BL 5/15/93) [332]

10474 Rosenthal, Lawrence. *Exploring Careers in Accounting*. Rev. ed. (9–12). 1993, Rosen LB $16.95 (0-8239-1501-8). Covers types of jobs relating to accounting and training that is required, with appendices of definitions, associations, accounting schools, and other information. (Rev: BL 5/15/93; SLJ 6/93) [657]

10475 Schiff, Kenny. *Opportunities in Desktop Publishing Careers* (9–12). 1993, VGM $14.95 (0-8442-4064-8); paper $11.95 (0-8442-4065-6). Notes the specialized areas where jobs are available and includes interviews with people employed in the field. (Rev: BL 5/15/93; VOYA 10/93) [686.2]

10476 Steinberg, Margery. *Opportunities in Marketing Careers* (9–12). 1993, VGM $14.95 (0-8442-4076-1); paper $12.95 (0-8442-4078-8). Different types of marketing are introduced in this guide, with a rundown on the various occupations associated with each. (Rev: BL 3/15/94) [658.8]

10477 Vogt, Peter. *Career Opportunities in the Fashion Industry* (7–12). 2002, Facts on File $49.50 (0-8160-4616-6). More than 60 jobs in the fashion industry are described with details of daily activities, salary potential, necessary training, and future outlook. (Rev: SLJ 2/03) [746.9]

Construction and Mechanical Trades

10478 Garvey, Lonny D. *Opportunities in the Machine Trades* (9–12). 1994, VGM $14.95 (0-8442-4123-7); paper $10.95 (0-8442-4124-5). The machine trades are introduced, with material on a variety of occupations in each. (Rev: BL 8/94) [671]

10479 Paige, Joy. *Cool Careers Without College for People Who Love to Build Things* (7–12). Series: Cool Careers Without College. 2002, Rosen LB $30.60 (0-8239-3506-X). Twenty careers in construction are outlined with useful information about salary, future prospects, and training. (Rev: BL 1/1–15/03; SLJ 7/02) [690]

10480 Pasternak, Ceel, and Linda Thornburg. *Cool Careers for Girls in Construction* (6–12). Illus. Series: Cool Careers for Girls. 2000, Impact $19.95 (1-57023-135-4); paper $12.95 (1-57023-131-1). From architect to ironworker, this book profiles a number of careers in construction for women, with material on salaries, working conditions, and qualifications needed. (Rev: BL 3/15/00; SLJ 7/00) [624]

Education and Librarianship

10481 Cassedy, Patrice. *Education* (6–12). Series: Careers for the Twenty-First Century. 2002, Gale LB $27.45 (1-56006-898-1). This work explores the duties, training, pay, working conditions, and job outlook for teachers, principals, counselors, and media specialists. (Rev: BL 10/15/02; SLJ 7/03) [371.7]

10482 Edelfelt, Roy A., and Blythe Camenson. *Careers in Education* (9–12). 1992, VGM $17.95 (0-8442-4176-8); paper $13.95 (0-8442-4177-6). This career guide surveys the field of education and profiles various occupations associated with it. (Rev: BL 2/15/93) [370]

10483 Fine, Janet. *Opportunities in Teaching* (10–12). 1984, VGM $13.95 (0-8442-6504-7); paper $10.95 (0-8442-6250-1). Teaching careers at various levels are discussed and questions of suitability explored. [371.7]

10484 Zannos, Susan. *Careers in Education* (8–12). Series: Latinos at Work. 2001, Mitchell Lane LB $22.95 (1-58415-081-5). Descriptions of careers in this field are accompanied by information on salary and qualifications as well as profiles of Latino men and women who have found success in a variety of

career positions. (Rev: BL 10/15/01; HBG 3/02; SLJ 11/01; VOYA 6/02) [370]

Law, Police, and Other Society-Oriented Careers

10485 Bankston, John. *Careers in Community Service* (8–12). Series: Latinos at Work. 2001, Mitchell Lane LB $22.95 (1-58415-082-3). Aimed at Latino youths, this career guide features a multitude of jobs in non-profit agencies, including legal and medical fields, with accompanying stories of success. (Rev: BL 10/15/01; HBG 3/02; SLJ 1/02) [353.001]

10486 Cassedy, Patrice. *Law Enforcement* (6–12). Illus. Series: Careers for the Twenty-First Century. 2002, Gale LB $27.45 (1-56006-899-X). An attractive volume that covers the history of law enforcement and introduces the rewards and challenges of such professions as the police, federal agents, crime scene workers, and probation and correctional officers. (Rev: BL 10/15/02) [363.2]

10487 Croce, Nicholas. *Detectives: Life Investigating Crimes* (5–10). Series: Extreme Careers. 2003, Rosen LB $26.50 (0-8239-3796-8). As well as exploring the exciting side of detective work, this account explains the qualifications and training needed and the techniques that help do this job well. (Rev: BL 9/15/03) [340]

10488 *Fire Fighters: Stories of Survival from the Front Lines of Firefighting* (10–12). Ed. by Clint Willis. Illus. 2002, Thunder's Mouth paper $17.95 (1-56025-402-5). First-person accounts, articles, and book excerpts explore the challenges facing fire fighters in both urban and wilderness settings. (Rev: BL 7/02) [628.9]

10489 Giacobello, John. *Bodyguards: Life Protecting Others* (5–10). Series: Extreme Careers. 2003, Rosen LB $26.50 (0-8239-3795-X). This book explores the duties and responsibilities of a bodyguard and includes information how to stay safe on the job and get ahead in this profession. (Rev: BL 9/15/03; SLJ 11/03) [340]

10490 Hope, Judith Richards. *Pinstripes and Pearls: The Women of the Harvard Law School Class of '64 Who Forged an Old-Girl Network and Paved the Way for Future Generations* (10–12). Illus. 2003, Scribner $26.00 (0-7432-1482-X). A 1964 graduate of Harvard Law School reveals personal and career experiences of 15 classmates who went on to success. (Rev: BL 12/15/02) [340]

10491 Munneke, Gary. *Opportunities in Law Careers* (9–12). 1993, VGM $14.95 (0-8442-4086-9); paper $10.95 (0-8442-4087-7). Various careers connected to the law are discussed, with information on training, opportunities, and aptitude. (Rev: BL 3/15/94; VOYA 6/94) [340]

10492 Murdico, Suzanne J. *Bomb Squad Experts: Life Defusing Explosive Devices* (5–10). Series: Extreme Careers. 2004, Rosen LB $19.95 (0-8239-3968-5). A look at the career opportunities in bomb squads, with material on training, salaries, and working conditions. (Rev: BL 5/15/04) [363]

10493 Pasternak, Ceel, and Linda Thornburg. *Cool Careers for Girls in Law* (6–12). Series: Cool Careers for Girls. 2001, Impact LB $19.95 (1-57023-160-5); paper $12.95 (1-57023-157-5). Ten women who have succeeded in various areas of the legal profession are highlighted, with material on qualifications, salaries, and working conditions. (Rev: BL 4/15/01; SLJ 7/01) [340]

10494 Paul, Caroline. *Fighting Fire* (9–12). 1998, St. Martin's $23.95 (0-312-18581-2); paper $6.99 (0-312-97000-5). A female firefighter, a former journalism student who applied for a firefighter position in order to write about the training and chose to make it her career instead, describes important moments, the courage, bravery, and physical and mental strength needed for the job, and difficulties she faced as a woman firefighter. (Rev: BL 4/15/98; SLJ 10/98) [363]

10495 Schulman, Arlene. *Cop on the Beat: Officer Steven Mayfield in New York City* (7–12). Illus. 2002, Dutton $18.99 (0-525-47064-6); paper $12.99 (0-525-46527-8). The day-to-day professional life of a New York City police officer is accompanied by a brief history of the department and a look at issues including police corruption and violence. (Rev: BL 11/15/02; HBG 3/03; SLJ 12/02; VOYA 12/02) [363.2]

10496 Selden, Annette, ed. *Handbook of Government and Public Service Careers* (9–12). 1993, VGM paper $17.95 (0-8442-4142-3). A reference book presenting basic information about 47 careers that are specific to government or can be found in a government context. (Rev: BL 3/15/94) [353.001]

10497 Sutton, Randy. *True Blue: Police Stories by Those Who Have Lived Them* (10–12). 2004, St. Martin's $23.95 (0-312-32481-2). This collection of 51 moving short pieces of nonfiction gives a behind-the-scenes view of how policemen operate and the emotions they feel. (Rev: BL 1/1–15/04) [363.2]

10498 Taylor, Murry A. *Jumping Fire: A Smokejumper's Memoir of Fighting Wildfire* (10–12). Illus. 2000, Harcourt $26.00 (0-15-100589-3). This inside look at the career of a parachuting smokejumper reads like an adventure story as it supplies graphic details of a gritty profession. (Rev: BL 6/1–15/00) [634.9]

10499 Wade, Linda R. *Careers in Law and Politics* (8–12). Series: Latinos at Work. 2001, Mitchell Lane LB $22.95 (1-58415-080-7). Along with interviews of successful Hispanic Americans in the fields of law and politics, this book describes such careers as lawyer, law professor, judge, police officer, and state representative. (Rev: BL 3/15/02; HBG 10/02; SLJ 3/02) [340]

10500 Wirths, Claudine G. *Choosing a Career in Law Enforcement* (6–10). Series: World of Work. 1996, Rosen LB $17.95 (0-8239-2274-X). Careers in law enforcement, such as police officer, security guard, and private investigator, are explored. (Rev: SLJ 3/97) [363]

Medicine and Health

10501 Asher, Dana. *Epidemiologists: Life Tracking Deadly Diseases* (5–10). Series: Extreme Careers. 2003, Rosen LB $26.50 (0-8239-3633-3). A concise explanation of the work of epidemiologists, the history of this discipline, and the training required to enter this field, with a case study. (Rev: BL 5/15/03; SLJ 5/03) [614.4]

10502 *Careers in Focus — Medical Tech* (8–12). Series: Careers in Focus. 1998, Ferguson $14.50 (0-89434-246-0). More than 20 careers in medical technology are described, covering the nature of the job, educational requirements, rewards, salaries, working conditions, and how to get into the field. (Rev: BR 9–10/98; SLJ 8/98) [610]

10503 Curless, Maura. *Fitness* (9–12). Series: Careers Without College. 1992, Peterson's Guides paper $7.95 (1-56079-223-X). Career opportunities in the fields of physical fitness and health care are explored in this practical guide. (Rev: BL 2/15/93) [613.7]

10504 Edwards, Lois. *Great Careers for People Interested in the Human Body* (9–12). Series: Career Connections. 1993, Gale $21.00 (0-8103-9386-7). Information from representatives of various medical fields, with activities and suggestions to stimulate further investigation. (Rev: BL 3/15/94; SLJ 12/93) [610.69]

10505 Field, Shelly. *Career Opportunities in Health Care*. 2nd ed. (7–12). 2002, Facts on File $49.50 (0-8160-4816-9). Information on 80 or so careers is organized in 16 categories, and includes a job profile, salary outlook, and details of necessary education and skills. (Rev: BL 11/1/02; SLJ 1/03) [610.69]

10506 Frederickson, Keville. *Opportunities in Nursing Careers* (9–12). 1989, VGM paper $10.95 (0-8442-8636-2). This account describes various kinds of nursing careers, the training and personality necessary, and working conditions. (Rev: BR 3–4/90; VOYA 12/89) [610.73]

10507 Gable, Fred B. *Opportunities in Pharmacy Careers*. Rev.ed. (9–12). Illus. 1990, VGM $14.95

(0-8442-8591-9); paper $12.95 (0-8442-8592-7). A variety of pharmaceutical careers are explored with information on suitability, education necessary, and work conditions. (Rev: BL 9/15/90) [615.1]

10508 Gordon, Susan, and Kristin Hohenadel. *Health Care* (9–12). Series: Careers Without College. 1992, Peterson's Guides paper $7.95 (1-56079-222-1). Presents five health-related occupations that may require further education but not a four-year degree. (Rev: BL 2/15/93) [610]

10509 Kacen, Alex. *Opportunities in Paramedical Careers* (9–12). Illus. 1989, VGM $13.95 (0-8442-6506-3); paper $10.95 (0-8442-6507-1). A thorough rundown on the many jobs in the medical field involving technicians and assistants and how to prepare for entrance into these fields. (Rev: BR 5–6/89; VOYA 6/89) [610.69]

10510 Moe, Barbara. *Careers in Sports Medicine* (10–12). Series: Career Resource Library. 2002, Rosen LB $25.25 (0-8239-3538-8). Teens considering a career in sports medicine will find a wealth of information in this guide, which examines fields ranging from aerobics instruction to orthopedic surgery. (Rev: BL 9/1/02; SLJ 8/02) [617.1]

10511 Parks, Peggy. *Medicine* (6–12). Series: Careers for the Twenty-First Century. 2002, Gale LB $27.45 (1-56006-888-4). Such positions as physician, nurse, pharmacist, physical therapist, medical technologist, and emergency medical technician are described with material on working conditions and future possibilities. (Rev: BL 10/15/02; SLJ 9/02) [610.69]

10512 Perry, Michael. *Population 485: Meeting Your Neighbors One Siren at a Time* (10–12). 2002, HarperCollins $24.95 (0-06-019852-4). A volunteer paramedic describes his work in a small Wisconsin town. (Rev: BL 10/15/02) [363.37]

10513 *Preparing for a Career in Nursing* (9–12). Series: What Can I Do Now? 1998, Ferguson $16.95 (0-89434-252-5). This book provides useful information about nursing careers, including a history of the profession, the aptitudes and skills necessary, education, certification, opportunities for advancement, pay, and working conditions. (Rev: SLJ 2/99) [610]

10514 Ramsdell, Melissa, ed. *My First Year As a Doctor: Real-World Stories from America's M.D.'s* (9–12). 1994, Walker $33.95 (0-8027-1290-8); paper $15.95 (0-8027-7418-0). A guide for those interested in becoming doctors, including testimony from professionals describing their first year of working in the field. (Rev: BL 9/1/94; VOYA 4/95) [610.69]

10515 Sacks, Terrence J. *Careers in Medicine* (9–12). Series: VGM Professional Careers. 1992, VGM $16.95 (0-8442-4178-4); paper $12.95 (0-

8442-4179-2). Covers educational expenses, internships, and areas of specialty for physicians. Lists U.S. and Canadian medical schools, organizations, and specialty boards. (Rev: BL 2/15/93) [610.69]

10516 Schafer, R. C. *Opportunities in Chiropractic Health Care Careers* (9–12). 1986, VGM $14.95 (0-8442-6565-9); paper $12.95 (0-8442-6566-7). Schafer gives an overview of the field plus details on training and employment outlook. (Rev: BL 6/1/86; BR 9–10/86) [615.5]

10517 Selden, Annette, ed. *VGM's Handbook of Health Care Careers* (9–12). 1992, VGM paper $12.95 (0-8442-4148-2). A brief survey of a large number of jobs, with information on résumés, cover letters, and interviews. (Rev: BL 2/15/93) [610]

10518 Simpson, Carolyn, and Penelope Hall. *Careers in Medicine* (9–12). 1993, Rosen LB $16.95 (0-8239-1711-8). This description of various types of doctors and specialties includes schooling and licensing procedures and a section on medical ethics. (Rev: BL 3/15/94; SLJ 1/94) [610.69]

10519 Snook, I. Donald. *Opportunities in Hospital Administration Careers* (9–12). 1988, VGM $14.95 (0-8442-6509-8); paper $11.95 (0-8442-6510-1). The types of careers involving hospital administration are described followed by detailed information on education and experience required, job hunting tips, and a typical day at work. (Rev: BR 5–6/89; VOYA 6/89) [362.1]

10520 Snook, I. Donald, and Leo D'Ozraio. *Opportunities in Health and Medical Careers* (10–12). 1990, VGM $14.95 (0-8442-8573-0); paper $12.95 (0-8442-8574-9). This is a fine overview of the many positions available in this expanding field. (Rev: BL 12/15/90) [610]

Science and Engineering

10521 Basta, Nicholas. *Opportunities in Engineering Careers* (9–12). Illus. 1990, VGM $14.95 (0-8442-4591-7). After a general discussion of the field of engineering, this account gives specific information on its branches and the opportunities available. (Rev: BL 6/1/90) [620]

10522 Bortz, Alfred B. *To the Young Scientist: Reflections on Doing and Living Science* (6–12). Series: Venture. 1997, Watts LB $23.00 (0-531-11325-6). The author, five other men, and six women discuss their varied careers in science, why they chose them, and the rewards their professions have given them. (Rev: BL 6/1–15/97; SLJ 6/97; VOYA 4/98) [509]

10523 Burnett, Betty. *Math and Science Wizards* (7–12). Series: Cool Careers Without College. 2002, Rosen $30.60 (0-8239-3502-7). Jobs in medicine and science that do not require college degrees, such as chemical lab workers, miners, and doctors' helpers, are described with information on salaries, duties, training, and future outlooks. (Rev: BL 5/15/02; SLJ 7/02) [520]

10524 Cassedy, Patrice. *Engineering* (6–12). Series: Careers for the Twenty-First Century. 2002, Gale LB $27.45 (1-56006-897-3). Various branches of engineering are introduced with material on education necessary, working conditions, salaries, and the outlook for the future. (Rev: BL 10/15/02) [620]

10525 Cefrey, Holly. *Archaeologists: Life Digging Up Artifacts* (5–10). Series: Extreme Careers. 2004, Rosen LB $19.95 (0-8239-3963-4). This is an introduction to the field of archeology, its problems, its opportunities, and its rewards. (Rev: BL 5/15/04) [930]

10526 Easton, Thomas A. *Careers in Science* (10–12). 1989, VGM $14.95 (0-8442-6123-8); paper $9.95 (0-8442-6124-6). An overview of the jobs available in such areas as the life and physical sciences, mathematics, computers, and related social sciences. [500]

10527 Fisher, Richard V. *Out of the Crater: Chronicles of a Volcanologist* (10–12). Illus. 1999, Princeton Univ. Pr. $24.95 (0-691-00226-6). Fisher's account of his fascination with volcanoes contains much of interest to teens contemplating a career in this field. (Rev: BL 12/1/98) [551.2]

10528 Grant, Lesley. *Great Careers for People Concerned About the Environment* (9–12). Series: Career Connections. 1993, Gale $27.75 (0-8103-9388-3). Profiles various professionals and their educational backgrounds, and includes science-oriented activities aimed at stimulating interest in various environmental fields. (Rev: BL 3/15/94) [363.7]

10529 Hayhurst, Chris. *Arctic Scientists: Life Studying the Arctic* (5–10). Series: Extreme Careers. 2003, Rosen LB $26.50 (0-8239-3794-1). This guide to the life and work of Arctic scientists indicates exciting areas of research such as the plant and animal life and the effects of global warming. (Rev: BL 9/15/03; SLJ 11/03) [500]

10530 Hayhurst, Chris. *Volcanologists: Life Exploring Volcanoes* (5–10). Series: Extreme Careers. 2003, Rosen LB $26.50 (0-8239-3637-6). This career guide explains what is necessary to become a serious student of volcanoes and what to expect when one becomes a volcanologist. (Rev: BL 9/15/03) [551.2]

10531 Murdico, Suzanne J. *Forensic Scientists: Life Investigating Sudden Death* (5–12). Series: Extreme Careers. 2004, Rosen LB $19.95 (0-8239-3966-9). A look at this rapidly growing science and the career opportunities offered. (Rev: BL 5/15/04) [363.2]

10532 Vincent, Victoria. *Great Careers for People Interested in the Past* (6–10). Series: Career Connections. 1996, Gale $40.00 (0-7876-0861-0). Careers in history, paleontology, and anthropology are among the many described in this occupational guide book. (Rev: SLJ 9/96) [930]

10533 *What Can I Do Now? Preparing for a Career in Engineering* (7–12). Series: What Can I Do Now? 1998, Ferguson $16.95 (0-89434-248-7). Following a general introduction to engineering, this book describes jobs in the field, education and skill requirements, and salary ranges, and tells students what they can do now, emphasizing volunteer opportunities and internships. (Rev: SLJ 4/99) [620]

Technical and Industrial Careers

10534 Apel, Melanie Ann. *Careers in Information Technology* (6–12). Illus. Series: Exploring Careers. 2000, Rosen LB $18.95 (0-8239-2892-6). Testimonials from working professionals add to this survey of opportunities in information technology that gives details on skills required and employment outlook. (Rev: BL 3/15/01; HBG 10/01; SLJ 2/01) [004]

10535 Bone, Jan. *Opportunities in Cable Television.* 2nd ed. (9–12). 1992, VGM $14.95 (0-8442-4026-5); paper $10.95 (0-8442-4027-3). This career handbook describes a variety of jobs associated with cable television and gives specifics on working conditions, pay, and education requirements. (Rev: BL 1/1/93) [384.55]

10536 Bonnice, Sherry. *Computer Programmer* (8–12). Series: Careers with Character. 2003, Mason Crest LB $22.95 (1-59084-312-6). An explanation of the job requirements and opportunities of computer programmers is accompanied by discussion of the importance of integrity and ethical behavior. (Rev: LMC 4–5/03; SLJ 2/03) [005.1]

10537 Buell, Tonya. *Web Surfers* (7–12). Series: Cool Careers Without College. 2002, Rosen $30.60 (0-8239-3507-8). This book presents 12 careers for computer buffs with information about salaries, future prospects, and further research possibilities. (Rev: BL 5/15/02; SLJ 7/02; VOYA 2/03) [004.6]

10538 Garcia, Kimberly. *Careers in Technology* (8–12). Series: Latinos at Work. 2001, Mitchell Lane LB $22.95 (1-58415-087-4). An easy-to-read guide to careers in computer technology such as Web designers, programmers, and Internet marketing, with particular emphasis on Hispanic success stories in these fields. (Rev: BL 10/15/01; HBG 3/02; SLJ 1/02) [004.6]

10539 Katz, Jon. *Geeks: How Two Lost Boys Rode the Internet out of Idaho* (10–12). 2000, Villard $22.95 (0-375-50298-X). The true story of two young men who were considered geeks in their hometown in Idaho and how they gained recognition in the computer world in Chicago. (Rev: BL 2/1/00*; SLJ 8/00) [338.7]

10540 Pasternak, Ceel, and Linda Thornburg. *Cool Careers for Girls in Computers* (7–12). Illus. 1999, Impact paper $12.95 (1-57023-103-6). This career book for girls features interviews with 10 women in computer-related fields, including a software engineer, sales executive, online specialist, technology trainer, and network administrator. (Rev: SLJ 4/00; VOYA 8/99) [004.6]

10541 Reed, Maxine K., and Robert M. Reed. *Career Opportunities in Television, Cable, Video, and Multimedia*. 4th ed. (10–12). 1999, Facts on File $49.50 (0-8160-3940-2). More than 100 jobs are profiled in communications, including news writer, camera operator, marketing manager, and webmaster. [384.55]

10542 Scharnberg, Ken. *Opportunities in Trucking Careers* (9–12). 1992, VGM $19.95 (0-8442-8181-6); paper $11.95 (0-8442-8182-4). A thorough discussion of the complexities involved in scheduling and organizing driver, vehicle, client/customer, freight, and destination, as well as salary structures. (Rev: BL 6/1/92) [388.3]

10543 Thornburg, Linda. *Cool Careers for Girls in Cybersecurity and National Safety* (8–11). Series: Cool Careers for Girls. 2004, Impact $21.95 (1-57023-209-1). This volume contains 10 case studies of women who have launched careers dealing with the protection of computer networks and the Internet as well as other high-tech areas. (Rev: BL 3/1/04) [331.7]

10544 White, Katherine. *Oil Rig Workers: Life Drilling for Oil* (5–10). Series: Extreme Careers. 2003, Rosen LB $26.50 (0-8239-3797-6). A look at the lives of oil rig workers and day-to-day activities on a rig. (Rev: BL 9/15/03) [665.5]

Personal Finances

Money-Making Ideas

General and Miscellaneous

10545 Belliston, Larry, and Kurt Hanks. *Extra Cash for Kids* (9–12). 1989, Wolgemuth & Hyatt paper $9.95 (0-943497-70-1). A book that outlines about 100 ways young adults can make money. [650]

10546 Byers, Patricia, et al. *The Kids Money Book: Great Money Making Ideas* (7–10). 1983, Liberty paper $4.95 (0-89709-041-1). A wide variety of jobs are introduced that can be part-time and money-producing. [658.1]

10547 Kravetz, Stacy. *Girl Boss: Running the Show Like the Big Chicks* (7–10). Illus. 1999, Girl Pr. paper $19.95 (0-9659754-2-8). This book gives practical advice and tips for teenage girls who want to start a business of their own. (Rev: VOYA 8/99) [658.1]

10548 Mariotti, Steve. *The Young Entrepreneur's Guide to Starting and Running a Business*. 2d ed. (9–12). 2000, Times Books $15.00 (0-8129-3306-0). An entertaining and informative resource for business-minded teenagers. (Rev: BL 4/1/00) [658.1141]

Baby-sitting

10549 Dayee, Frances S. *Babysitting*. Rev. ed. (9–12). 2000, Watts LB $25.00 (0-531-11745-6); paper $8.95 (0-531-16520-5). A guide to successful babysitting, with material on how to get customers, safety, and how to handle emergencies. (Rev: VOYA 6/01) [649]

10550 Kuch, K. D. *The Babysitter's Handbook* (5–10). Illus. Series: KidBacks. 1997, Random paper $0.99 (0-679-88369-X). This is a fact-filled manual on all aspects of baby-sitting, including feeding and playing with babies, emergency measures, games and songs, and basic first aid. (Rev: SLJ 7/97) [649]

Money Management

10551 Bateman, Katherine R. *The Young Investor: Projects and Activities for Making Your Money Grow* (8–12). Illus. 2001, Chicago Review paper $13.95 (1-55652-396-3). The basics of investing are introduced in a straightforward, reassuring manner, with anecdotes about young investor "Billy Ray Fawns" to hold the reader's interest. (Rev: BL 12/15/01; SLJ 2/02) [332.6]

10552 Bijlefeld, Marjolijn, and Sharon K. Zoumbaris. *Teen Guide to Personal Financial Management* (9–12). 2000, Greenwood $45.00 (0-313-31107-2). This guide to personal finances is directed at teenagers and young adults — a population saddled with increasing debt — and covers such basics as debt management, budgeting, saving, investing, mortgages, and loans. (Rev: BL 12/15/00) [332.024]

10553 Godfrey, Joline. *20 Secrets to Money and Independence: The Dollardiva's Guide to Life* (6–12). 2000, St. Martin's $17.95 (0-312-26279-5). Common-sense advice for women on topics ranging from self-reliance and self-esteem to networking with other women, learning the basics of investing, and staying abreast of financial news. (Rev: BL 9/1/00; VOYA 2/01) [646.7]

10554 Hurwitz, Jane. *High Performance Through Effective Budgeting* (8–12). Illus. Series: Learning-a-Living Library. 1996, Rosen LB $17.95 (0-8239-2203-0). Basic budgeting skills are presented for both personal and on-the-job application. (Rev: BL 8/96; BR 1–2/97; SLJ 10/96; VOYA 2/97) [332.024]

10555 Rendon, Marion, and Rachel Kranz. *Straight Talk About Money* (7–12). Series: Straight Talk. 1992, Facts on File LB $27.45 (0-8160-2612-2). Provides a brief history and description of money and the U.S. economy, followed by suggestions young adults can use when earning and managing money. (Rev: BL 6/15/92) [332.4]

10556 Silver, Don. *The Generation Y Money Book: 99 Smart Ways to Handle Money* (7–12). 2000, Adams-Hall paper $15.95 (0-944708-64-1). Sound advice about money management, credit card use, planning for college, savings, and investment. (Rev: VOYA 6/01) [332.024]

10557 Weiss, Ann E. *Easy Credit* (9–12). 2000, Twenty-First Century LB $22.40 (0-7613-1503-9). In addition to solid advice about using credit wisely and avoiding potential pitfalls, this book provides a history of credit from ancient Mesopotamia through the present. (Rev: BL 9/1/00; HBG 10/01; SLJ 12/00) [332.7]

Health and the Human Body

General and Miscellaneous

10558 Apel, Melanie Ann. *Coping with Stuttering* (6–10). Series: Coping. 2000, Rosen LB $17.95 (0-8239-2970-1). Practical advice for stutterers and for listeners is accompanied by information on celebrities who have conquered this problem. (Rev: SLJ 4/00) [616.85]

10559 The Boston Women's Health Book Collective. *Our Bodies, Ourselves for the New Century: A Book by and for Women* (9–12). 1998, Simon & Schuster paper $24.00 (0-684-84231-9). An updated edition of the classic guide to all aspects of women's health and well-being. [613]

10560 *The Complete Manual of Fitness and Well-Being* (9–12). Illus. 1988, Reader's Digest $34.95 (0-88850-154-4). In addition to exercise and diet, this account covers such topics as human growth, body parts, and health. (Rev: BL 5/1/88; SLJ 6/88) [613]

10561 Costello, Patricia. *Female Fitness Stars of TV and the Movies* (7–12). Series: Legends of Health and Fitness. 2000, Mitchell Lane LB $24.95 (1-58415-050-5). Cher, Goldie Hawn, and Demi Moore are among the actors profiled here as examples of professionals who put fitness high on their list of priorities. (Rev: SLJ 2/01)

10562 Curran, Delores. *Traits of a Healthy Family* (10–12). 1984, Ballantine paper $5.99 (0-345-31750-5). This book reports on a study of 500 families and what keeps them healthy. [610]

10563 Debenedette, Valerie. *Caffeine* (7–10). Series: Drug Library. 1996, Enslow LB $20.95 (0-89490-741-7). A well-documented, well-organized look at caffeine, where it is found, its effects, and its abuse. (Rev: BL 9/15/96; SLJ 9/96) [615]

10564 Gilbert, Richard J. *Caffeine: The Most Popular Stimulant* (8–12). Illus. 1986, Chelsea LB $19.95 (0-87754-756-4). Tea, coffee, and chocolate are covered in this account of what the author calls "the most popular drug in the world." (Rev: BL 7/86) [615]

10565 Hurley, Jennifer A., ed. *Addiction* (6–12). Illus. Series: Opposing Viewpoints. 1999, Greenhaven LB $21.96 (0-7377-0117-X); paper $13.96 (0-7377-0116-1). A collection of essays and opinions that explores various viewpoints on addiction including causes, treatments, and government intervention. (Rev: BL 3/15/00) [362.29]

10566 Isler, Charlotte, and Alwyn T. Cohall. *The Watts Teen Health Dictionary* (7–12). Illus. 1996, Watts LB $24.95 (0-513-11236-5); paper $16.00 (0-531-15792-X). This book in dictionary format contains articles on such subjects as STDs, contraceptives, medications, diseases, eating disorders, breast exams, and immunization. (Rev: BR 11–12/96; VOYA 10/96) [613]

10567 Jukes, Mavis. *The Guy Book: An Owner's Manual* (6–12). Illus. 2002, Crown LB $18.99 (0-679-99028-3); paper $12.95 (0-679-89028-9). Jukes takes an appealing, frank-talking approach to sex, health, and hygiene for young men, covering everything from dating and birth control to choosing clothes and slow dancing. (Rev: BL 1/1–15/02; HBG 10/02; SLJ 3/02; VOYA 6/02) [305.235]

10568 McHugh, Mary. *Special Siblings: Growing Up with Someone with a Disability* (7–12). 1999, Hyperion $23.95 (0-7868-6285-8). This book discusses a variety of physical and mental disabilities and how to cope with these handicaps when they affect a member of your family. (Rev: BL 2/15/99; SLJ 1/00; VOYA 8/99) [616]

10569 O'Neill, Terry. *Biomedical Ethics* (7–12). Series: Opposing Viewpoints Digests. 1998, Greenhaven LB $27.45 (1-56510-875-2); paper $17.45 (1-56510-874-4). This concise overview of biomedical ethics covers topics such as cloning, organ transplants, experiments, and research. (Rev: BL 4/15/99; SLJ 6/99) [575.1]

10570 Powell, Phelan. *Trailblazers of Physical Fitness* (7–12). Series: Legends of Health and Fitness. 2000, Mitchell Lane LB $24.95 (1-58415-024-6). Jack LaLanne and Richard Simmons are among the individuals profiled here as leading proponents of physical fitness. (Rev: SLJ 2/01)

10571 Roche, Lorin. *Meditation Made Easy* (10–12). Illus. 1998, HarperSF paper $16.00 (0-06-251542-X). An excellent introduction to the art of meditation and its wide array of benefits. (Rev: BL 11/15/98) [158]

10572 Roleff, Tamara L., ed. *Biomedical Ethics* (8–12). Series: Opposing Viewpoints. 1998, Greenhaven LB $32.45 (1-56510-793-4); paper $21.20 (1-56510-792-6). An anthology of opinions on ethical considerations relating to cloning, human transplants, modern reproductive techniques, and genetic research. (Rev: BL 6/1–15/98) [573.2]

10573 Sommers, Annie Leah. *Everything You Need to Know About Looking and Feeling Your Best: A Guide for Girls* (6–12). Series: Need to Know Library. 2000, Rosen LB $17.95 (0-8239-3079-3). This book aims to boost girls' self-images as well as their knowledge of health and hygiene. (Rev: HBG 9/00; SLJ 3/00) [613]

10574 Tocci, Salvatore. *High-Tech IDs* (8–12). Illus. 2000, Watts LB $25.00 (0-531-11752-9). This work explores the science of biometrics (using physical or behavioral features to identify a person) with coverage of DNA use, fingerprinting, etc. and problems with the right to privacy. (Rev: BL 4/15/00; SLJ 8/00) [599.9]

10575 Torr, James D., ed. *Health Care: Province Divided* (8–12). Series: Opposing Viewpoints. 1999, Greenhaven LB $21.96 (0-7377-0129-3); paper $13.96 (0-7377-0128-5). The problems of the healthcare system in the United States are presented from a variety of points of view including those of doctors and health policy experts. (Rev: BL 11/15/99; SLJ 2/00) [362.1]

10576 Villarosa, Linda, ed. *Body and Soul: The Black Women's Guide to Physical Health and Emotional Well-Being* (9–12). 1994, HarperPerennial paper $20.00 (0-06-095085-4). Contributors to this straight-from-the-heart guide include black female

scientists, academics, healthcare practitioners, and writers. (Rev: BL 11/15/94*) [613]

Aging and Death

10577 Altman, Linda J. *Death: An Introduction to Medical-Ethical Dilemmas* (6–12). 2000, Enslow LB $19.95 (0-7660-1246-8). Physical, cultural, moral, and psychological issues relating to death are explored in this insightful, informative book. (Rev: BL 6/1–15/00; HBG 9/00; SLJ 8/00) [179.4]

10578 Baird, Robert M., and Stuart E. Rosenbaum, eds. *Euthanasia: The Moral Issues* (10–12). 1989, Prometheus paper $16.95 (0-87975-555-5). In this collection of 19 essays, euthanasia is explained and the various legal and moral questions surrounding it are explored. (Rev: BL 3/1/90) [179.7]

10579 Digiulio, Robert, and Rachel Kranz. *Straight Talk About Death and Dying* (7–12). Series: Straight Talk. 1995, Facts on File $27.45 (0-8160-3078-2). Among the topics covered in this book about death and dying are Kubler-Ross's five psychological stages experienced by the dying and various aspects of mourning. (Rev: BL 9/15/95; SLJ 12/95) [155.9]

10580 Egendorf, Laura K., ed. *Assisted Suicide* (7–12). Series: Current Controversies. 1998, Greenhaven LB $32.45 (1-56510-807-8). An anthology of opinions on topics relating to assisted suicide, including its morality, legal status, and individual rights. (Rev: BL 8/98; SLJ 1/99) [179]

10581 *Euthanasia* (9–12). Ed. by James D. Torr. Series: Opposing Viewpoints. 1999, Greenhaven LB $21.96 (0-7377-0127-7); paper $13.96 (0-7377-0126-9). Thoughtful essays, both pro and con, cover many issues relating to euthanasia. (Rev: BL 2/1/00) [179.7]

10582 *Euthanasia* (9–12). Ed. by James D. Torr. Series: Opposing Viewpoints Digests. 1999, Greenhaven LB $27.45 (1-56510-871-X); paper $17.45 (1-56510-870-1). Opposing viewpoints on euthanasia and its ethical issues are presented in this collection of essays and articles. [179.7]

10583 Fitzgerald, Helen. *The Grieving Teen: A Guide for Teenagers and Their Friends* (9–12). 2000, Simon & Schuster (0-684-86804-0). This book explains the grieving process for teens and gives advice on how to adjust to the death of a friend or family member. [155.9]

10584 Gay, Kathlyn. *The Right to Die: Public Controversy, Private Matter* (7–12). Series: Issue and Debate. 1993, Millbrook LB $24.90 (1-56294-325-

1). Discusses euthanasia and assisted suicide in depth — from Greek times to the present — and includes actual recent cases. (Rev: BL 10/1/93) [179]

10585 Giddens, Sandra, and Owen Giddens. *Coping with Grieving and Loss* (6–10). 2000, Rosen LB $17.95 (0-8239-2894-2). Practical advice about the process of grieving and funerals is accompanied by personal teen stories. (Rev: SLJ 4/00) [155.9]

10586 Gootman, Marilyn E. *When a Friend Dies: A Book for Teens About Grieving and Healing* (8–12). 1994, Free Spirit paper $9.95 (0-915793-66-0). This book is intended to help a teenager who is suffering the loss of a friend or someone else from their generation. (Rev: SLJ 1/00) [155.9]

10587 Grollman, Earl A. *Straight Talk About Death for Teenagers: How to Cope with Losing Someone You Love* (7–12). 1993, Beacon paper $13.00 (0-8070-2501-1). Grollman validates the painful feelings teens experience following the death of a loved one, conveying a sense of the grief as well as the need to get on with life. (Rev: BL 4/1/93; SLJ 6/93; VOYA 8/93) [155.9]

10588 Hawkins, Gail N., ed. *Physician-Assisted Suicide* (6–12). Series: At Issue. 2002, Gale LB $24.95 (0-7377-1056-X); paper $16.20 (0-7377-1044-1). There's plenty of material to spark debate in these essays about the morality, ethics, and possible legalization of physician-assisted suicide. (Rev: BL 6/1–15/02) [174]

10589 Knox, Jean. *Death and Dying* (8–12). Illus. Series: 21st Century Health and Wellness. 2000, Chelsea LB $24.95 (0-7910-5986-3). This comprehensive and detailed volume looks at the variety of rituals that accompany death, at the role of doctors and others in supporting the dying and their families, and at the possibility of an afterlife. (Rev: BL 11/15/00; HBG 10/01; SLJ 2/01) [155.9]

10590 Landau, Elaine. *The Right to Die* (7–12). 1993, Watts LB $24.00 (0-531-13015-0). A balanced, in-depth examination of the controversial issue, including a chapter on the rights of adolescents to refuse medical treatment. (Rev: BL 1/15/94; SLJ 2/94; VOYA 2/94) [174]

10591 Leone, Daniel, ed. *Physician-Assisted Suicide* (8–12). Series: At Issue. 1997, Greenhaven $26.20 (1-56510-019-0); paper $17.45 (1-56510-018-2). Authors represented in this anthology debate whether doctors should be allowed to help terminally ill patients end their lives rather than suffer prolonged pain. (Rev: BL 5/15/98; SLJ 5/98) [179.7]

10592 Medina, John. *The Clock of Ages: Why We Age — How We Age — Winding Back the Clock* (9–12). 1996, Cambridge Univ. Pr. paper $25 .00 (0-521-59456-1). The little-understood process of aging — and the biological factors behind it — are outlined in easy-to-understand language. [612.6]

10593 O'Connor, Nancy. *Letting Go with Love: The Grieving Process* (9–12). 1985, La Mariposa $24.95 (0-9613714-1-2); paper $14.95 (0-9613714-0-4). How to cope with the death of a loved one is the subject of this self-help book. [128]

10594 Roleff, Tamara L. *Teen Suicide* (9–12). Series: At Issue. 2000, Greenhaven LB $24.95 (0-7377-0328-8); paper $17.45 (0-7377-0327-X). The nature of teen suicide is discussed, with material on causes, depression, and the special problems faced by gay teens. [362.28]

10595 Schleifer, Jay. *Everything You Need to Know When Someone You Know Has Been Killed* (6–12). Illus. Series: Need to Know Library. 1998, Rosen LB $25.25 (0-8239-2779-2). This book helps young people deal with sudden death, describes the grieving process, and gives advice concerning the painful issues associated with death. (Rev: BL 10/1/98) [155.9]

10596 Sperekas, Nicole B. *SuicideWise: Taking Steps Against Teen Suicide* (8–12). Series: Teen Issues. 2000, Enslow LB $18.96 (0-7660-1360-X). The causes and prevention of teen suicide are covered, with advice on determining if a friend is in danger of attempting suicide. (Rev: HBG 9/00; VOYA 6/01) [362.28]

10597 *Suicide* (9–12). Ed. by Leslie A. Miller and Paul A. Rose. Series: Current Controversies. 2000, Greenhaven LB $31.20 (0-7377-0318-0); paper $19.95 (0-7377-0317-2). Expressing various points of view, these essays explore the causes of suicide, its prevention, and the right to suicide. [362.28]

10598 Terkel, Studs. *Will the Circle Be Unbroken? Reflections on Death, Rebirth, and Hunger for a Faith* (10–12). 2001, New Pr. $25.95 (1-56584-692-3). The noted author explores the phenomenon of death, how it occurs, and people's reaction to it, in this account that is also a celebration of life. (Rev: BL 8/01*) [128]

10599 Wagner, Heather Lehr. *Dealing with Terminal Illness in the Family* (6–12). Series: Focus on Family Matters. 2002, Chelsea $20.75 (0-7910-6692-4). This account explores the different emotions produced by the terminal illness of a loved one and how to cope with them. (Rev: BL 10/15/02; SLJ 10/02) [618]

10600 Wekesser, Carol, ed. *Euthanasia* (7–12). Series: Opposing Viewpoints. 1995, Greenhaven LB $35.15 (1-56510-244-4). The ethical aspects of euthanasia, whether or not it should be legalized, physician-assisted suicide, and who should make decisions in these matters are addressed from a variety of viewpoints. (Rev: BL 7/95; SLJ 9/95; VOYA 12/95) [179]

10601 West, Michael D. *The Immortal Cell: One Scientist's Daring Quest to Solve the Mystery of Human Aging* (10–12). Illus. 2003, Doubleday $24.95 (0-385-50928-6). West, a proponent of stem-cell research, describes his scientific investigation into the causes of aging. (Rev: BL 9/1/03) [612.6]

10602 Winters, Paul A., ed. *Death and Dying* (8–12). Series: Opposing Viewpoints. 1997, Greenhaven LB $32.45 (1-56510-671-7); paper $21.20 (1-56510-670-9). Topics dealt with in this anthology of articles include the treatment of terminally ill patients, the right to die, how to cope with death, and whether death is the end of life. (Rev: BL 10/15/97; SLJ 2/98) [179]

10603 Wolfelt, Alan D. *Healing a Teen's Grieving Heart: 100 Practical Ideas* (6–12). 2001, Companion Pr. paper $11.95 (1-879651-24-6). Teens who have suffered a loss will find practical reassurance and comfort in the suggestions offered here. (Rev: SLJ 9/01; VOYA 8/01)

10604 Yount, Lisa, ed. *Euthanasia* (6–12). Series: Contemporary Issues. 2002, Gale LB $31.20 (0-7377-0829-8); paper $19.95 (0-7377-0828-X). This volume explores the often controversial positions of those who are for and against euthanasia, presenting statistics and information on the laws both in the United States and abroad. (Rev: BL 5/1/02) [179.7]

10605 Yount, Lisa. *Euthanasia* (6–12). Illus. Series: Overview. 2000, Lucent LB $19.96 (1-56006-697-0). Diverse opinions are presented in this book, allowing readers to formulate their own ideas about this issue. (Rev: BL 1/1–15/01) [179.7]

Alcohol, Drugs, and Smoking

10606 Alagna, Magdalena. *Everything You Need to Know About the Dangers of Binge Drinking* (6–10). Illus. Series: Need to Know Library. 2001, Rosen LB $23.95 (0-8239-3289-3). Warnings about the physical and psychological dangers of alcohol are interwoven with fictional examples. (Rev: BL 5/1/02) [362.292]

10607 Alvergue, Anne. *Ecstasy: The Danger of False Euphoria* (6–10). Illus. Series: Drug Abuse Prevention Library. 1997, Rosen LB $17.95 (0-8239-2506-4). A discussion of how the drug MDMA, known as ecstasy, affects the mind and body. (Rev: SLJ 5/98)

10608 Anderson, M. A. *Tracey: A Mother's Journal of Teenage Addiction* (9–12). 1988, Black Heron paper $7.95 (0-930773-08-X). The harrowing story of one family's fight to save their 14-year-old daughter Tracey from drug addiction. (Rev: VOYA 2/89) [613.8]

10609 Avraham, Regina. *The Downside of Drugs* (8–12). Illus. 1988, Chelsea LB $19.95 (1-55546-232-4). This account covers the effects of such drugs as nicotine, alcohol, narcotics, stimulants, and hallucinogens. (Rev: SLJ 6/88) [613.8]

10610 Avraham, Regina. *Substance Abuse* (8–12). 1988, Chelsea LB $19.95 (1-55546-219-7). This account describes how drugs affect behavior and how addiction is treated. (Rev: BR 1–2/89; VOYA 4/89) [616.86]

10611 Ayer, Eleanor. *Teen Smoking* (6–12). 1998, Lucent LB $27.45 (1-56006-442-0). In spite of warnings, nearly two million teens smoke. This book traces the influences that make them start and gives advice on how to quit. (Rev: BL 1/1–15/99) [362.29]

10612 Banfield, Susan. *Inside Recovery: How the Twelve-Step Program Can Work for You* (7–10). Series: Drug Abuse Prevention Library. 1998, Rosen LB $17.95 (0-8239-2634-6). A look at the 12-steps to recovery and the many problems one can face going through this program, which has been a successful route for many addicts. (Rev: VOYA 2/99) [613.8]

10613 Barbour, Scott, ed. *Alcohol* (8–12). Series: Opposing Viewpoints. 1997, Greenhaven LB $26.20 (1-56510-675-X). Excerpts from books and articles explore questions involving the degree of harm that alcohol causes, treatments for alcoholism, the responsibility of the alcohol industry, and how to reduce alcohol-related problems. (Rev: BL 10/15/97; SLJ 1/98; VOYA 6/98) [613.8]

10614 Barbour, Scott, ed. *Drug Legalization* (6–12). Series: Current Controversies. 2000, Greenhaven LB $21.96 (0-7377-0335-0); paper $13.96 (0-7377-0336-9). In this collection of essays, the drug legalization controversy is examined from various points of view. (Rev: BL 10/15/00) [364.1]

10615 Barter, James. *Hallucinogens* (8–12). Illus. Series: Drug Education Library. 2002, Gale LB $27.45 (1-56006-915-5). This absorbing and comprehensive book explains the effects of hallucinogens on the body, traces their use — in ancient rituals, in medical treatments, and as a recreational drug — and looks at the debates over their legalization. Also in this series is *Marijuana*. (Rev: BL 6/1–15/02; SLJ 6/02) [362.29]

10616 Bayer, Linda. *Strange Visions: Hallucinogen-Related Disorders* (6–10). Illus. Series: Encyclopedia of Psychological Disorders. 2000, Chelsea $27.45 (0-7910-5315-6). Bayer explains how the abuse of certain drugs can produce hallucinations and possible permanent brain damage. (Rev: BL 11/1/00; HBG 9/00) [616.86]

10617 Beal, Eileen. *Ritalin: Its Use and Abuse* (7–10). Series: Drug Abuse Prevention Library.

1999, Rosen LB $17.95 (0-8239-2775-X). This book explores the drug Ritalin, widely used for attention deficit disorder, and presents the controversies surrounding it. (Rev: BL 5/15/99; VOYA 4/00) [616.85]

10618 Benner, Janet. *Smoking Cigarettes: The Unfiltered Truth — Understanding Why and How to Quit* (9–12). 1987, Joelle paper $10.95 (0-942723-12-0). An account that describes the physical effects of smoking on the body and outlines various methods of quitting. (Rev: BL 12/15/87) [613.85]

10619 Berger, Gilda. *Alcoholism and the Family* (8–12). Series: Changing Family. 1993, Watts LB $25.00 (0-531-12548-3). This discussion of alcoholism, presented in question-and-answer format, focuses on its effects on the family and covers causes, prevention, treatment, and recovery. (Rev: BL 1/15/94; SLJ 12/93; VOYA 2/94) [362.29]

10620 Berger, Gilda, and Nancy Levitin. *Crack* (6–12). 1995, Watts LB $24.00 (0-531-11188-1). Emphasizes the dangers of crack to users, the cost to society, and crack's ability to claim innocent victims: crack babies. (Rev: BL 5/1/95) [362.29]

10621 Boyd, George A. *Drugs and Sex* (5–10). Illus. Series: Drug Abuse Prevention Library. 1994, Rosen LB $17.95 (0-8239-1538-7). A careful examination of the hazards of combining drugs and sex, including unsafe sex, pregnancy, AIDS, and other sexually transmitted diseases. (Rev: BL 6/1–15/94; SLJ 5/94) [613.9]

10622 Carroll, Marilyn. *Cocaine and Crack* (9–12). Series: Drug Library. 1994, Enslow LB $19.95 (0-89490-472-8). Everything you need to know about crack and cocaine. (Rev: BL 4/15/95; SLJ 4/95; VOYA 5/95) [616.86]

10623 Claypool, Jane. *Alcohol and You*. 3rd ed. (6–10). Series: Impact Books: Drugs and Alcohol. 1997, Watts LB $23.00 (0-531-11351-5). A readable new edition of a standard, well-respected work on alcohol and teenage drinking problems. (Rev: BR 5–6/98; SLJ 2/98) [613.8]

10624 Clayton, Lawrence. *Tranquilizers* (7–10). Illus. Series: Drug Library. 1997, Enslow LB $20.95 (0-89490-849-9). Information is presented about tranquilizers, their beneficial effects, and the potential consequences of abuse and addiction. (Rev: BL 3/15/97; SLJ 6/97) [615]

10625 Clayton, Lawrence. *Working Together Against Drug Addiction* (6–10). 1996, Rosen LB $16.95 (0-8239-2263-4). In addition to discussing drugs and addiction, this work takes an activist approach by providing ways for teens to locate drug and alcohol counselors and programs and ways they can become involved and make a difference. (Rev: SLJ 5/97) [362]

10626 Connelly, Elizabeth Russell. *Through a Glass Darkly: The Psychological Effects of Marijuana and Hashish* (8–12). Series: Encyclopedia of Psychological Disorders. 1999, Chelsea $27.45 (0-7910-4897-7). After an overview of the history of marijuana and hashish, this volume surveys their medicinal and recreational use, effects of interaction with other drugs, potential disorders from their use, the dangers of addiction, and treatments available. (Rev: VOYA 8/99) [362.29]

10627 Croft, Jennifer. *Drugs and the Legalization Debate* (6–10). Illus. Series: Drug Abuse Prevention Library. 1997, Rosen LB $17.95 (0-8239-2509-9). A well-balanced presentation of the pros and cons of legalizing drugs, along with a discussion of drug abuse and penalties and a brief look at how other countries deal with the issue. (Rev: SLJ 5/98) [362.29]

10628 Croft, Jennifer. *PCP: High Risk on the Streets* (7–10). Series: Drug Abuse Prevention Library. 1998, Rosen LB $17.95 (0-8239-2774-1). This book provides readers with important information about phencyclidine, or angel dust, the behavior it produces, and its dangers. (Rev: BL 11/15/98; BR 1–2/99; SLJ 12/98) [362.29]

10629 *Drugs and Controlled Substances: Information for Students* (10–12). Ed. by Stacey Blachford and Kristine Krapp. 2002, Gale $115.00 (0-7876-6264-X). The composition, history, effects, and uses of common drugs — including addictive, illegal, and abused classes of prescription drugs — are covered in this collection of well-written essays. (Rev: SLJ 6/03) [616.86]

10630 *Drunk Driving* (9–12). Ed. by Louise Gerdes. Series: Contemporary Issues Companion. 2000, Greenhaven LB $31.20 (0-7377-0460-8); paper $19.95 (0-7377-0459-4). A selection of documents that explore the problem of drunk driving in the United States. (Rev: SLJ 4/01) [362.292]

10631 Dudley, William. *Alcohol* (8–12). Series: Teen Decisions. 2000, Greenhaven LB $29.95 (0-7377-0490-X); paper $18.70 (0-7377-0489-6). This primer on alcohol and alcohol abuse for teenagers gives advice to those coping with alcohol-related problems. [362.292]

10632 Dudley, William, ed. *Drugs and Sports* (6–12). Series: At Issue. 2000, Greenhaven LB $17.96 (1-56510-697-0); paper $11.96 (1-56510-696-2). An interesting and thought-provoking exploration of the extensive use of performance-enhancing drugs by amateur and professional athletes. (Rev: BL 4/1/01) [362.29]

10633 Dudman, Martha Tod. *Augusta, Gone* (10–12). 2001, Simon & Schuster $23.00 (0-7432-0409-3). This is a moving account by a mother who lived through the ordeal of trying to reclaim a daughter who had become a drug addict. (Rev: BL 3/1/01) [306.874]

10634 Edwards, Griffith. *Alcohol: The World's Favorite Drug* (10–12). 2002, St. Martin's $23.95 (0-312-28387-3). This is a balanced look at alcohol and its history, regulation, use and abuse, and dangers. (Rev: BL 3/15/02) [641.2]

10635 Egendorf, Laura K., ed. *Teen Alcoholism* (6–12). Series: Contemporary Issues Companion. 2001, Greenhaven LB $22.96 (0-7377-0683-X); paper $14.96 (0-7377-0682-1). Essays explore teen abuse of alcohol, looking at its causes and the effects on the young people themselves and on society as a whole, with contributions from individuals who have close experience with this problem. (Rev: BL 9/1/01) [362.292]

10636 Frey, James. *A Million Little Pieces* (10–12). 2003, Doubleday $22.95 (0-385-50775-5). The author, who as a 23-year-old found himself in the grip of twin addictions to alcohol and crack cocaine, writes inspiringly of his painful struggle to recovery. (Rev: BL 4/15/03; SLJ 8/03) [362.29]

10637 Glowa, John R. *Inhalants: The Toxic Fumes* (9–12). Illus. 1986, Chelsea LB $19.95 (0-87754-758-0). The dangers of using such inhalants as shoe polish are described and places where help can be obtained are given. (Rev: BL 2/15/87) [616.86]

10638 *Go Ask Alice* (9–12). 1971, Avon paper $4.50 (0-380-00523-9). A harrowing account in diary form of a 15-year-old girl's drug addiction and its consequences. [613.8]

10639 Goldish, Meish. *Dangers of Herbal Stimulants* (6–10). Illus. Series: Drug Abuse Prevention Library. 1997, Rosen LB $17.95 (0-8239-2555-2). Teens are enticed to use herbal substances to get high, lose weight, or solve other emotional and physical problems. This book describes the products available, their potential dangers, and the laws that regulate their use. (Rev: SLJ 5/98; VOYA 2/99) [362.29]

10640 Gottfried, Ted. *Should Drugs Be Legalized?* (6–12). Illus. 2000, Twenty-First Century LB $23.90 (0-7613-1314-1). This work features a description of various kinds of drugs, their effects, their harmful aspects, and a discussion of the problems and benefits of legalizing their use. (Rev: BL 4/1/00; HBG 9/00; SLJ 7/00) [362.29]

10641 Grabish, Beatrice R. *Drugs and Your Brain* (6–10). Illus. Series: Drug Abuse Prevention Library. 1998, Rosen paper $6.95 (1-56838-214-6). This book describes how drugs affect the brain and the risks of permanent as well as short-term damage. (Rev: BL 4/15/98; BR 9–10/98; SLJ 6/98) [616.86]

10642 Gwynne, Peter. *Who Uses Drugs?* (7–10). Illus. 1987, Chelsea LB $19.95 (1-55546-223-5). An overview of different kinds of drugs and who uses them. (Rev: BL 5/1/88) [362.2]

10643 Harris, Jonathan. *This Drinking Nation* (7–12). 1994, Four Winds $15.95 (0-02-742744-7). Discusses America's alcohol consumption from 1607 to the present, including information on the Prohibition period of 1920–1933. Also examines teenage drinking and alcoholism. (Rev: BL 7/94; SLJ 9/94; VOYA 10/94) [394.1]

10644 Haughton, Emma. *Alcohol* (7–10). Series: Talking Points. 1999, Raintree Steck-Vaughn LB $27.12 (0-8172-5318-1). A candid look at the use and abuse of alcohol and its physical and emotional effects. (Rev: BL 8/99; BR 9–10/99) [613.8]

10645 Henderson, Elizabeth Connell. *Understanding Addiction* (9–12). Series: Understanding Health and Sickness. 2000, Univ. Press of Mississippi paper $12.00 (1-57806-240-3). This work explores the nature of addition, what causes it, and which are the addictive drugs. (Rev: BL 12/1/00) [362.29]

10646 *Heroin* (9–12). Ed. by Helen Cothran. Series: At Issue. 2000, Greenhaven LB $17.96 (0-7377-0474-8); paper $11.96 (0-7377-0473-X). The sharp rise in heroin addiction — and the toll it has taken on youthful abusers and their families — is explored in harrowing detail in this collection of essays. (Rev: BL 4/1/01) [362.29]

10647 Heyes, Eileen. *Tobacco, USA: The Industry Behind the Smoke* (8–12). Illus. 1999, Twenty-First Century LB $23.90 (0-7613-0974-8). A concise study of the U.S. tobacco industry with material on its history, current farming techniques, government support and regulations, marketing ploys, and the industry's defensive battle against medical facts. (Rev: BL 12/15/99; HBG 4/00; SLJ 1/00) [338.2]

10648 Hodgson, Barbara. *In the Arms of Morpheus: The Tragic History of Morphine, Laudanum, and Patent Medicines* (6–12). Illus. 2001, Firefly $24.95 (1-55297-538-X); paper $14.95 (1-55297-540-1). This thought-provoking survey of opium and its derivatives explores the drugs' history and the countless men and women — celebrated and unknown — who have used and abused them. (Rev: BL 11/15/01; VOYA 4/02) [362.29]

10649 Hoobler, Thomas, and Dorothy Hoobler. *Drugs and Crime* (7–12). Illus. 1987, Chelsea LB $19.95 (1-55546-228-6). An account of how drug traffic is fostered by layers of crime and corruption both international and local. (Rev: BL 3/15/88; SLJ 5/88) [364.2]

10650 Hyde, Margaret O. *Drug Wars* (7–12). 1990, Walker LB $12.85 (0-8027-6901-2). This account discusses the violence and despair that crack cocaine has brought to America and ways in which its production and distribution can be halted. (Rev: SLJ 6/90; VOYA 6/90) [616.86]

10651 Hyde, Margaret O., and John F. Setaro. *Alcohol 101: An Overview for Teens* (5–10). 1999, Twenty-First Century LB $24.90 (0-7613-1274-9). Kinds of alcohol and their effects are described, with material on alcoholism and binge drinking. (Rev: HBG 3/00; SLJ 3/00; VOYA 12/00) [613.8]

10652 Hyde, Margaret O., and John F. Setaro. *Drugs 101: An Overview for Teens* (7–12). 2003, Twenty-First Century LB $25.90 (0-7613-2608-1). This well-researched and accessible introduction to the nature of addiction, illicit drugs, and the harmful results of their use features useful photographs, diagrams, and charts. (Rev: BL 5/15/03; HBG 10/03; SLJ 5/03; VOYA 10/03) [362.29]

10653 Jamiolkowski, Raymond M. *Drugs and Domestic Violence* (7–12). Series: Drug Abuse Prevention Library. 1996, Rosen LB $17.95 (0-8239-2062-3). Domestic violence increases when drugs are used in the home; this volume gives pointers to teens in these situations on how to stay safe. (Rev: SLJ 3/96) [362.2]

10654 Keyishian, Elizabeth. *Everything You Need to Know About Smoking* (6–10). Illus. 1989, Rosen $24.50 (0-8239-1017-2). A look at why people smoke, smoking's effects, and how to quit. (Rev: SLJ 2/90) [613.8]

10655 Klein, Wendy. *Drugs and Denial* (7–10). Series: Drug Abuse Prevention Library. 1998, Rosen LB $17.95 (0-8239-2773-3). This book describes the signs of addiction and the stages of adolescent drug use, helps teens to admit it if they have a drug problem, and provides tips for teens to help people they know who may be in denial. (Rev: BL 11/15/98) [362.29]

10656 Knox, Jean McBee. *Drinking, Driving and Drugs* (7–10). Illus. 1988, Chelsea LB $19.95 (1-55546-231-6). An overview of this national problem with a focus on teenage offenders and victims. (Rev: BL 7/88; BR 1–2/89; SLJ 9/88) [363.1]

10657 Kranz, Rachel. *Straight Talk About Smoking* (6–12). Series: Straight Talk. 1999, Facts on File LB $27.45 (0-8160-3976-3). This no-nonsense account explains why people start smoking, what smoking does to the body, the nature of addiction, and how to give up smoking. (Rev: BL 2/15/00; HBG 4/00; SLJ 3/00) [362.29]

10658 Kuhn, Cynthia, et al. *Buzzed: The Straight Facts About the Most Used and Abused Drugs from Alcohol to Ecstasy* (10–12). 1998, Norton paper $14.95 (0-393-31732-3). A matter-of-fact guide to the effects that various substances — ranging from caffeine to cocaine — have on the body. (Rev: BL 3/1/98) [615]

10659 Kuhn, Cynthia, et al. *Just Say Know: Talking with Kids About Drugs and Alcohol* (10–12). Illus. 2002, Norton paper $14.95 (0-393-32258-0). Teens will also find value in this accessible overview of the types and threats of specific dangerous drugs. (Rev: BL 1/1–15/02) [649]

10660 Landau, Elaine. *Hooked: Talking About Addiction* (5–10). Illus. 1995, Millbrook LB $22.90 (1-56294-469-X). This account defines addiction broadly — from use of alcohol and drugs to various forms of compulsive behavior — and gives suggestions for recovery. (Rev: BL 1/1–15/96; SLJ 1/96) [362.29]

10661 Landau, Elaine. *Teenage Drinking* (7–12). Series: Issues in Focus. 1994, Enslow LB $20.95 (0-89490-575-9). An exploration of the causes and effects of teenage drinking and of prevention measures that have worked. (Rev: BL 11/15/94; SLJ 11/94; VOYA 12/94) [362.29]

10662 Lee, Mary Price, and Richard S. Lee. *Drugs and Codependency* (6–10). Series: Drug Abuse Prevention Library. 1995, Rosen LB $17.95 (0-8239-2065-8). The vulnerability of teens who live in a household where drugs are abused is the focus of this volume. (Rev: BL 9/15/95; SLJ 10/95) [616.869]

10663 Lee, Mary Price, and Richard S. Lee. *Drugs and the Media* (5–10). Illus. Series: Drug Abuse Prevention Library. 1994, Rosen LB $17.95 (0-8239-1537-9). This book shows that the media often unintentionally glamorize drug use and describes how teens can evaluate the media's mixed messages. (Rev: BL 6/1–15/94; SLJ 5/94) [070.4]

10664 Levine, Herbert M. *The Drug Problem* (7–12). Illus. Series: American Issues Debated. 1997, Raintree Steck-Vaughn $31.40 (0-8172-4354-2). The pros and cons of issues relating to drugs are presented fairly, with discussion of the effectiveness of the war on drugs, the concept of decriminalizing drugs, and possible discrimination against minorities in our drug policies. (Rev: BL 11/15/97; BR 1–2/98; VOYA 4/98) [362.2]

10665 Lukas, Scott E. *Steroids* (7–10). Series: Drug Library. 1994, Enslow LB $20.95 (0-89490-471-X). An exploration of the physical, psychological, and legal consequences of using steroids. (Rev: BL 1/1/95; HBG 10/01; SLJ 1/95; VOYA 4/95) [362.29]

10666 McLaughlin, Miriam S., and Sandra P. Hazouri. *Addiction: The "High" That Brings You Down* (7–12). Series: Teen Issues. 1997, Enslow LB $20.95 (0-89490-915-0). This honest, accurate book lists causes of addiction, its characteristics, and the results of compulsive, uncontrolled behavior, with an emphasis on where teen addicts can find help and support at school and in the community. (Rev: SLJ 8/97; VOYA 10/97) [362.29]

10667 McMillan, Daniel. *Teen Smoking: Understanding the Risk* (6–12). Series: Issues in Focus. 1998, Enslow LB $20.95 (0-89490-722-0). An interesting, informative account that discusses nicotine addiction, secondhand smoke, health hazards, smoking prevention, and treatments for people who want to stop. (Rev: VOYA 8/98) [362.2]

10668 Madsen, Christine. *Drinking and Driving* (6–10). Illus. 1989, Watts paper $20.80 (0-531-10799-X). The effects of alcohol are outlined in relation to driving. Material on how society penalizes drunk drivers is also presented. (Rev: SLJ 4/90) [613.8]

10669 *Marijuana* (9–12). Ed. by Louise I. Gerdes. Series: Contemporary Issues Companion. 2002, Gale LB $31.20 (0-7377-0835-2); paper $19.95 (0-7377-0834-4). The controversy over marijuana use is examined in great detail in this balanced book, which addresses such central issues as the drug's harmful effects and possible health benefits and also offers firsthand accounts of "use and abuse." (Rev: BL 2/1/02) [362.29]

10670 Masline, Shelagh Ryan. *Drug Abuse and Teens* (6–12). Illus. Series: Hot Issues. 2000, Enslow LB $19.95 (0-7660-1372-3). A clear, straightforward account that describes different drugs, ways they are abused, and how one can get help for drug problems. (Rev: BL 11/15/00; HBG 3/01) [362.29]

10671 Mass, Wendy. *Teen Drug Abuse* (9–12). Series: Teen Issues. 1998, Lucent LB $27.45 (1-56006-196-0). A look at the reasons why teens abuse drugs, the kinds of drugs they take, and methods of treatment and prevention. [362.29]

10672 Meer, Jeff. *Drugs and Sports* (7–12). Illus. 1987, Chelsea LB $19.95 (1-55546-226-X). An account that explains how various drugs affect an athlete's performance and how this abuse is being viewed by segments of the athletic world. (Rev: BL 11/1/87) [613]

10673 Miller, Maryann. *Drugs and Date Rape* (6–10). Series: Drug Abuse Prevention Library. 1995, Rosen LB $17.95 (0-8239-2064-X). This book shows how drugs can break down important inhibitors, possibly leading to date rape, and how to avoid becoming a victim. (Rev: BL 9/15/95; SLJ 10/95) [362.88]

10674 Miller, Maryann. *Drugs and Gun Violence* (6–10). Series: Drug Abuse Prevention Library. 1995, Rosen LB $17.95 (0-8239-2060-7). This book explores the connection between violent crimes and drug use, with lessons that teens can use for survival. (Rev: BL 9/15/95; SLJ 10/95) [364.2]

10675 Miller, Maryann. *Drugs and Violent Crime* (6–10). Series: Drug Abuse Prevention Library. 1996, Rosen LB $17.95 (0-8239-2282-0). This book

gives general information about drugs and their effects and explores the relationship between drug use and violent crime. (Rev: SLJ 3/97) [362.29]

10676 Mitchell, Hayley R. *Teen Alcoholism* (7–12). Illus. Series: Teen Issues. 1997, Lucent LB $27.45 (1-56006-514-1). This book defines alcoholism and explains its causes, prevention, symptoms, and recovery programs. (Rev: BL 2/1/98) [362.29]

10677 Monroe, Judy. *Antidepressants* (7–10). Series: Drug Library. 1997, Enslow LB $20.95 (0-89490-848-0). Current information is given about these frequently abused drugs, actual case studies are cited, and discussion questions are provided. (Rev: BL 5/15/97) [616.85]

10678 Monroe, Judy. *Nicotine* (7–10). Series: Drug Library. 1995, Enslow LB $20.95 (0-89490-505-8). A concise, easy-to-use look at nicotine, where it is found, its effects, and how to avoid its use. (Rev: BL 7/95; SLJ 9/95) [613.85]

10679 Myers, Arthur. *Drugs and Emotions* (6–10). Series: Drug Abuse Prevention Library. 1996, Rosen LB $17.95 (0-8239-2283-9). This book explains how teens may be attracted to drugs as a way of dealing with feelings of sadness, pain, confusion, and frustration, and how they can become hooked on both legal and illegal drugs. Much of the discussion deals with how to recognize that a problem exists and where to get help. (Rev: SLJ 3/97) [362.29]

10680 Myers, Arthur. *Drugs and Peer Pressure* (6–10). Series: Drug Abuse Prevention Library. 1995, Rosen LB $17.95 (0-8239-2066-6). An exploration of peer pressure as a major reason why teens begin to use drugs, with suggestions for resisting it. (Rev: BL 9/15/95; SLJ 10/95) [362.29]

10681 Newhouse, Eric. *Alcohol: Cradle to Grave* (10–12). 2001, Hazelden $22.95 (1-56838-734-2). This account of alcohol abuse and its impact on society includes interviews with alcoholics trying to cope with their illness. (Rev: BL 8/01) [362.292]

10682 Newman, Gerald, and Eleanor N. Layfield. *PCP* (7–10). Series: Drug Library. 1997, Enslow LB $20.95 (0-89490-852-9). Case studies, discussion questions, and chapter notes are highlights of this informative book on PCP, a frequently abused drug. (Rev: BL 12/15/97; BR 3–4/98; HBG 3/98; SLJ 12/97) [362.2]

10683 Newton, David E. *Drug Testing: An Issue for School, Sports and Work* (6–12). Illus. Series: In Focus. 1999, Enslow LB $20.95 (0-89490-954-1). The question of civil rights vs. drug testing is explored in this volume that presents extreme positions and viewpoints in between. (Rev: BL 4/1/99; BR 5–6/99; SLJ 4/99) [658.3]

10684 Ojeda, Auriana, ed. *Smoking* (8–12). Series: Current Controversies. 2002, Gale LB $31.20 (0-7377-0857-3); paper $19.95 (0-7377-0856-5). A collection of writings that presents both sides of the debates on the controversial aspects of smoking — the provable health risks, the influence of advertising on young smokers, and so forth. (Rev: BL 7/02) [363.4]

10685 Packer, Alex J. *Highs! Over 150 Ways to Feel Really, REALLY Good . . . Without Alcohol or Other Drugs* (6–12). Illus. 2000, Free Spirit paper $14.95 (1-57542-074-0). Grouped into three areas (serenity, physical improvement, and creativity), the author describes 150 ways teenagers can feel good about themselves. (Rev: BL 11/1/00; BR 11–12/00; SLJ 9/00) [158]

10686 Pinsky, Drew. *Cracked: Running Rescue Missions for the Disconnected and Brokenhearted* (11–12). 2003, Regan $24.95 (0-06-009654-3). In harrowing detail, the co-host of radio's popular *Loveline* advice show describes his work with the addicted at a rehabilitation clinic in California. (Rev: BL 8/03) [362.29]

10687 Pringle, Laurence. *Smoking: A Risky Business* (5–10). 1996, Morrow $16.00 (0-688-13039-9). After a history of tobacco, this book describes the dangers of smoking and the advertising strategies used to get people to smoke. (Rev: BL 12/1/96; SLJ 1/97; VOYA 4/97) [362.2]

10688 Robbins, Paul R. *Designer Drugs* (7–12). Series: Drug Library. 1995, Enslow LB $20.95 (0-89490-488-4). An exploration of the growing problem of drugs made by "kitchen chemists." (Rev: BL 5/1/95; SLJ 5/95) [362.29]

10689 Robbins, Paul R. *Hallucinogens* (7–10). Illus. Series: Drug Library. 1996, Enslow LB $20.95 (0-89490-743-3). Drugs that cause auditory and visual hallucinations are described, along with their availability, dangerous effects, and current use. (Rev: BL 6/1–15/96; SLJ 7/96; VOYA 8/96) [362.29]

10690 Roleff, Tamara L., and Mary Williams, eds. *Tobacco and Smoking* (8–12). Series: Opposing Viewpoints. 1998, Greenhaven LB $32.45 (1-56510-803-5); paper $21.20 (1-56510-802-7). This anthology presents different opinions on such topics as the health effects of smoking, the influence of tobacco advertising, government intervention, and possible controls on the tobacco industry. (Rev: BL 6/1–15/98) [613.8]

10691 Santamaria, Peggy. *Drugs and Politics* (6–10). Series: Drug Abuse Prevention Library. 1994, Rosen LB $17.95 (0-8239-1703-7). A discussion of the influence of drugs on politics, such as in Colombia, where the government is involved with and intimidated by powerful drug interests. (Rev: BL 3/15/95; SLJ 3/95) [363.4]

10692 Schleichert, Elizabeth. *Marijuana* (7–10). Illus. Series: Drug Library. 1996, Enslow LB $20.95 (0-89490-740-9). This easy-to-read account discusses the history of marijuana use, its effects, availability, and controversies surrounding it, such as whether it should be made legal. (Rev: BL 6/1–15/96; SLJ 7/96; VOYA 8/96) [362.29]

10693 Schnoll, Sidney. *Getting Help: Treatments for Drug Abuse* (7–12). Illus. 1986, Chelsea LB $19.95 (0-87754-775-0). This book concentrates on the many kinds of treatments available and the agencies involved in supplying this help. (Rev: BL 2/15/87) [362.2]

10694 Sherry, Clifford J. *Drugs and Eating Disorders* (5–10). Illus. Series: Drug Abuse Prevention Library. 1994, Rosen LB $17.95 (0-8239-1540-9). Shows how diet pills and other weight-loss products can lead to drug abuse and, in some cases, addiction. (Rev: BL 6/1–15/94; SLJ 6/94) [616.85]

10695 Sherry, Clifford J. *Inhalants* (5–10). 1994, Rosen LB $17.95 (0-8239-1704-5). A look at inhalants, where they are found, and how they affect the body. (Rev: BL 2/15/95; SLJ 3/95) [362.29]

10696 Shuker, Nancy. *Everything You Need to Know About an Alcoholic Parent.* Rev. ed. (7–12). Illus. 1998, Rosen LB $30.35 (0-8239-2869-1). After a general discussion of alcoholism, Shuker explains how it changes human relationships and how young people can cope with it. (Rev: BL 1/15/90; BR 3–4/90; VOYA 4/90) [362.29]

10697 Silverstein, Alvin, and Virginia Silverstein. *Alcoholism* (7–10). 1975, HarperCollins LB $12.89 (0-397-31648-8). Alcohol use and abuse are introduced, plus alcoholism and the problems it causes. [613.8]

10698 Smith, C. Fraser. *Lenny, Lefty, and the Chancellor: The Len Bias Tragedy and the Search for Reform in Big-Time College Basketball* (9–12). 1992, Bancroft paper $12.95 (0-9631246-0-9). When a college basketball star died of a drug overdose, school officials attempted to avoid a scandal. (Rev: BL 3/15/92; SLJ 8/92) [796.323]

10699 Sonder, Ben. *All About Heroin* (9–12). Illus. 2002, Watts LB $24.00 (0-531-11541-0). An excellent profile of this drug and its users, looking at heroin's properties, how it is made, and the dangers of overdosing and abrupt withdrawal. (Rev: BL 9/15/02; SLJ 7/02) [363.29]

10700 Stewart, Gail B., ed. *Drugs and Sports* (7–10). Series: Opposing Viewpoints Digests. 1998, Greenhaven LB $27.45 (1-56510-749-7); paper $17.45 (1-56510-748-9). Covering topics including the prevention and prevalence of drug use and abuse and the legitimacy of drug testing, this volume explores drugs in both amateur and professional sports. (Rev: BL 8/98) [362.29]

10701 Stewart, Gail B. *Teen Addicts* (7–12). Illus. Series: The Other America. 1999, Lucent LB $18.96 (1-56006-574-5). Four teenage drug addicts of different backgrounds share their stories. (Rev: BL 11/15/99; HBG 9/00) [362.29]

10702 Stewart, Gail B. *Teen Alcoholics* (6–12). Illus. Series: The Other America. 1999, Lucent LB $18.96 (1-56006-606-7). This book focuses on case studies of four teenage alcoholics, how and why they began drinking, and how they are handling their addiction. (Rev: BL 3/15/00; HBG 9/00; SLJ 1/00) [362.292]

10703 Strazzabosco-Hayn, Gina. *Drugs and Sleeping Disorders* (7–12). Series: Drug Abuse Prevention Library. 1996, Rosen LB $17.95 (0-8239-2144-1). An exploration of sleep disorders and potential problems and dangers of using drugs for sleep. (Rev: SLJ 3/96) [362.2]

10704 Swisher, Karin L. *Drug Trafficking* (9–12). Series: Current Controversies. 1991, Greenhaven LB $19.95 (0-89908-576-8); paper $16.20 (0-89908-582-2). The pros and cons of waging a war on drugs, legalizing drugs, and campaigns to stem the flow of drugs into the United States. (Rev: BL 6/15/92; SLJ 5/92) [363.4]

10705 *Teen Smoking* (6–12). Ed. by Hayley Mitchell Haugen. Series: At Issue. 2004, Gale LB $27.45 (0-7377-1971-0). The issues involved in teen smoking, including health and freedom of choice, are explored in this collection of articles, many with different viewpoints. (Rev: BL 2/15/04) [613.85]

10706 Terkel, Susan N. *The Drug Laws: A Time for Change?* (9–12). Illus. 1997, Watts LB $25.00 (0-531-11316-7). A thorough discussion of current drug policies, with attention to arguments for and against legalizing drugs and how this controversy relates to moral, medical, health, economic, and social concerns. (Rev: BL 10/1/97; HBG 3/98) [364.1]

10707 Thompson, Stephen P., ed. *War on Drugs* (7–12). Series: Opposing Viewpoints. 1998, Greenhaven LB $32.45 (1-56510-805-1). In this anthology of various opinions, questions are raised about the techniques used in the war against drugs, the nature of new strategies, and whether some drugs, particularly marijuana, should be legalized under certain conditions. (Rev: BL 7/98) [363.4]

10708 Torr, James D., ed. *Alcoholism* (6–12). Series: Current Controversies. 2000, Greenhaven LB $21.96 (0-7377-0139-0); paper $13.96 (0-7377-0138-2). Various viewpoints on the causes and treatments of alcoholism and on the alcohol industry are voiced in this valuable collection of primary sources. (Rev: BL 4/1/00) [362.292]

10709 Torr, James D., ed. *Drug Abuse* (8–12). Series: Opposing Viewpoints. 1999, Greenhaven LB $32.45 (0-7377-0051-3); paper $21.20 (0-7377-

0050-5). This collection of articles and essays debates such topics as the extent of the nation's drug problem, the effectiveness of various programs, the value of government policies, and the legalization of selected drugs. (Rev: BL 4/15/99) [362.29]

10710 Torr, James D., ed. *Teens and Alcohol* (6–12). Series: Current Controversies. 2001, Gale LB $31.20 (0-7377-0859-X); paper $19.95 (0-7377-0858-1). A thought-provoking collection of essays on alcohol, drunk driving, health, the media, and the law that will be equally useful for report writers and the interested reader. (Rev: BL 5/1/02) [362.292]

10711 Webb, Margot. *Drugs and Gangs* (7–12). Series: Drug Abuse Prevention Library. 1996, Rosen LB $17.95 (0-8239-2059-3). This book describes the connections between gangs and drugs, in both selling and using, and provides teens with tips on how to avoid these dangers. (Rev: SLJ 3/96; VOYA 6/96) [362.29]

10712 Wechsler, Henry, and Bernice Wuethrich. *Dying to Drink: Confronting Binge Drinking on College Campuses* (11–12). 2002, Rodale $24.95 (1-57954-583-1). An in-depth discussion of the problem of binge drinking on America's college campuses and what school administrators are — and aren't — doing about it. (Rev: BL 8/02) [362.292]

10713 Weir, William. *In the Shadow of the Dope Fiend: America's War on Drugs* (9–12). 1995, Shoe String LB $35.00 (0-208-02384-4). A social history of drug use. (Rev: BL 4/1/95; VOYA 12/95) [363.4]

10714 Wekesser, Carol, ed. *Alcoholism* (9–12). Series: Current Controversies. 1994, Greenhaven LB $20.96 (1-56510-074-3); paper $16.20 (1-56510-073-5). An anthology that covers the question of whether alcoholism is a disease, the most effective treatments, the effect of alcohol advertisements, and help for the children of alcoholics. (Rev: BL 4/15/94; SLJ 3/94) [362.29]

10715 Wekesser, Carol, ed. *Chemical Dependency* (8–12). Illus. Series: Opposing Viewpoints. 1997, Greenhaven paper $21.20 (1-56510-551-6). Such topics as the magnitude of chemical dependency, its causes, treatments, and the possible reforming of drug laws are discussed in this collection of articles. (Rev: BL 7/97; BR 1–2/98) [362.29]

10716 Wekesser, Carol, ed. *Smoking* (8–12). Series: At Issue. 1999, Greenhaven LB $21.96 (0-7377-0157-9); paper $13.96 (0-7377-0156-0). From many perspectives including government reports, eyewitness accounts, and scientific journal articles, a wide range of opinions on smoking is explored. (Rev: BL 11/15/99) [362.2]

10717 Wekesser, Carol, ed. *Smoking* (7–12). Series: Current Controversies. 1996, Greenhaven LB $32.45 (1-56510-534-6); paper $21.20 (1-56510-

533-8). This collection of various opinions about smoking covers health risks, the amount of blame that tobacco companies should assume, measures to combat smoking, and the degree to which the government can interfere. (Rev: BL 12/15/96; BR 11–12/97; SLJ 3/97) [362.29]

10718 Wilkinson, Beth. *Drugs and Depression* (6–12). Illus. Series: Drug Abuse Prevention Library. 1994, Rosen LB $30.35 (0-8239-3004-1). Some young people turn to drugs to deal with their depression. This book shows the dangers in this approach and offers positive ways of handling depression and places to get assistance. (Rev: BL 6/1–15/94) [616.86]

10719 Williams, Mary E. *Teen Smoking* (9–12). Series: Contemporary Issues Companion. 2000, Greenhaven LB $31.20 (0-7377-0169-2); paper $19.95 (0-7377-0168-4). Various aspects of teen smoking are discussed, including why teens smoke, the effects of smoking, and cigarette advertising. [362.29]

10720 Winters, Paul A., ed. *Teen Addiction* (7–12). Series: Current Controversies. 1997, Greenhaven LB $32.45 (1-56510-536-2). The causes, effects, prevention, and regulation of teenage drug, tobacco, and alcohol consumption are explored in a series of documents expressing different opinions. (Rev: BL 2/15/97; SLJ 3/97) [362.29]

10721 Woods, Geraldine. *Heroin* (7–10). Series: Drug Library. 1994, Enslow LB $20.95 (0-89490-473-6). A well-researched, clearly written, and carefully sourced book about heroin use and addiction. (Rev: BL 1/1/95; SLJ 1/95; VOYA 4/95) [362.29]

10722 Ziemer, Maryann. *Quaaludes* (7–10). Illus. Series: Drug Library. 1997, Enslow LB $20.95 (0-89490-847-2). The uses and effects of these frequently prescribed drugs are discussed, along with problems of misuse and addiction. (Rev: BL 3/15/97; SLJ 6/97) [613.8]

Bionics and Transplants

10723 Alexander, Brian. *Rapture: How Biotech Became the New Religion* (10–12). 2003, Basic $25.95 (0-7382-0761-6). Alexander investigates the fringes of biotechnology (cryonics and regenerative medicine, for example) and the groups involved, who sport such labels as cryonicists and life extensionists. (Rev: BL 11/15/03) [303.4]

10724 Kittredge, Mary. *Organ Transplants* (8–12). Series: 21st Century Health and Wellness. 1999, Chelsea LB $24.95 (0-7910-5522-1). A history of progress in organ transplants is given, plus material

on the ethical questions involved. (Rev: BL 4/15/00; HBG 9/00; SLJ 6/00) [617.9]

10725 McClellan, Marilyn. *Organ and Tissue Transplants: Medical Miracles and Challenges* (7–12). Series: Issues in Focus. 2003, Enslow LB $20.95 (0-7660-1943-8). The story of a critically injured teen draws readers into this discussion of transplants of organs and tissues and the ethical issues involved. (Rev: HBG 10/03; SLJ 5/03) [617.9]

10726 Murphy, Wendy. *Spare Parts: From Peg Legs to Gene Splices* (6–12). Illus. 2001, Twenty-First Century LB $23.90 (0-7613-1355-9). A history of medical advances that acknowledges the role of war in the development of increasingly advanced designs, with the moving story of one boy's anguish. (Rev: BCCB 3/01; BL 3/15/01; HBG 10/01) [617.9]

10727 Torr, James D., ed. *Organ Transplants* (6–12). Series: At Issue. 2002, Gale $20.96 (0-7377-1162-0); paper $13.96 (0-7377-1161-2). Contributors examine the positive and negative issues relating to transplanting organs. (Rev: BL 1/1–15/03) [174]

Diseases and Illnesses

10728 Aaseng, Nathan. *Multiple Sclerosis* (7–10). Illus. 2000, Watts LB $25.00 (0-531-11531-3). Annette Funicello's experiences with MS draw teens into this study of this neurological disease and its symptoms, diagnosis, and treatment. (Rev: BL 7/00; SLJ 6/00) [616.8]

10729 *AIDS in Developing Countries* (6–12). Ed. by Nancy Harris. Series: At Issue. 2004, Gale LB $27.45 (0-7377-1789-0). Through a series of essays that express different points of view, the AIDS situation in countries in Africa, Asia, and South America is explored. (Rev: BL 2/15/04) [616]

10730 Akers, Charlene. *Obesity* (7–12). Illus. 2000, Lucent $27.45 (1-56006-662-8). A look at obesity and its physiological, psychological, and sociological impact, with assessments of various treatment options. (Rev: HBG 3/01; SLJ 9/00) [616.3]

10731 Altman, Linda J. *Plague and Pestilence: A History of Infectious Disease* (6–12). Illus. Series: Issues in Focus. 1998, Enslow LB $20.95 (0-89490-957-6). A history of plagues and epidemics in world history, from the Black Death and leprosy to AIDS and spinal meningitis. (Rev: BL 3/1/99; HBG 3/99; SLJ 1/99) [614.4]

10732 Ansay, A. Manette. *Limbo* (10–12). 2001, Morrow $25.00 (0-688-17286-5). An inspiring memoir about an excellent music student who is suddenly stricken with a strange illness that eventually cripples her. (Rev: BL 8/01; SLJ 2/02) [813]

10733 Aronson, Virginia. *The Influenza Pandemic of 1918* (7–12). Illus. Series: Great Disasters: Reforms and Ramifications. 2000, Chelsea $21.95 (0-7910-5263-X). This detailed look at the deadly flu of 1918 serves as a reminder that modern travel makes such an event even more likely. (Rev: BL 10/15/00; HBG 3/01; SLJ 11/00; VOYA 2/01) [614.5]

10734 Benowitz, Steven I. *Cancer* (7–12). Series: Diseases and People. 1999, Enslow LB $20.95 (0-7660-1181-X). A discussion of the nature and treatment of various forms of cancer and of possible cures in the future. (Rev: BL 9/15/99; HBG 4/00) [616.994]

10735 Beshore, George. *Sickle Cell Anemia* (7–12). 1994, Watts LB $18.95 (0-531-12510-6). An informative overview that includes a history of the disease, how it is transmitted from parent to child, and the importance of genetic testing. (Rev: BL 1/1/95; SLJ 1/95; VOYA 4/95) [616.1]

10736 Biddle, Wayne. *Field Guide to Germs* (9–12). 1995, Holt $22.50 (0-8050-3531-1). Historical information on the various bacteria and viruses that attack humans, presented in an informal, humorous way. (Rev: BL 8/95; SLJ 1/96) [616]

10737 Biskup, Michael D., and Karin L. Swisher, eds. *AIDS* (7–12). Series: Opposing Viewpoints. 1992, Greenhaven paper $16.20 (0-89908-165-7). The ethical questions surrounding AIDS are discussed, along with the effectiveness of testing and treatment, and the prevention of the disease's spread. (Rev: BL 11/15/92) [362.1]

10738 *The Black Death* (9–12). Ed. by Jordan McMullin. Illus. Series: Great Disasters. 2003, Gale $28.70 (0-7377-1498-0); paper $19.95 (0-7377-1499-9). This volume transports readers back to the middle of the 14th century, when a pandemic of plague swept across Europe leaving millions of dead in its wake. (Rev: BL 11/1/03) [614.5]

10739 Bode, Janet. *Food Fight: A Guide to Eating Disorders for Pre-teens and Their Parents* (5–10). 1997, Simon & Schuster $16.00 (0-689-80272-2). A clearly written account of the physical, psychological, and social aspects of anorexia and bulimia, plus practical suggestions for help. (Rev: BL 6/1–15/97; BR 11–12/97; HB 1–2/97; SLJ 8/97*; VOYA 8/97) [618.92]

10740 Brill, Marlene T. *Tourette Syndrome* (6–12). Illus. Series: Twenty-First Century Medical Library. 2002, Millbrook LB $24.90 (0-7613-2101-2). This volume provides historical and medical information on the disorder named for neurologist Georges Gilles de la Tourette, presenting the stories of three teenagers who suffer from it. (Rev: BL 3/1/02; HBG 10/02; SLJ 4/02) [375]

10741 Broadbent, Patricia, et al. *You Get Past the Tears: A Memoir of Love and Survival* (9–12).

2002, Villard $19.95 (0-679-46314-3). This is the harrowing and inspiring story of an adoptive couple's struggle to keep their AIDS-infected daughter alive. (Rev: BL 2/15/02) [362.1]

10742 Brodman, Michael, et al. *Straight Talk About Sexually Transmitted Diseases* (7–12). Series: Straight Talk. 1993, Facts on File $19.95 (0-8160-2864-8). Discusses the ways sexually transmitted diseases are contracted, symptoms, possible consequences, and treatment. (Rev: BL 3/15/94; SLJ 6/94) [616.95]

10743 Bryan, Jenny. *Eating Disorders* (6–10). Series: Talking Points. 1999, Raintree Steck-Vaughn LB $18.98 (0-8172-5321-1). Statistics and quotations from experts are used in this book that introduces various eating disorders, their causes, and treatments. (Rev: BL 12/15/99; HBG 9/00) [616.85]

10744 Burby, Liza N. *Bulimia Nervosa: The Secret Cycle of Bingeing and Purging* (6–10). Series: Teen Health Library of Eating Disorder Prevention. 1998, Rosen LB $26.50 (0-8239-2762-8). Bulimia is an eating disorder characterized by bingeing and purging. This book describes various eating disorders, then focuses on bulimia, its causes, physical and psychological effects, the roles of peer pressure, media images, family relationships, genetics, and treatment and recovery. (Rev: BR 5–6/99; SLJ 1/99) [616.85]

10745 Burkett, Elinor. *The Gravest Show on Earth: America in the Age of AIDS* (9–12). 1995, Houghton $22.95 (0-395-74537-3). Burkett exposes the profiteering and exploitation of AIDS. (Rev: BL 10/1/95*) [362]

10746 Carson, Mary Kay. *Epilepsy* (7–12). Series: Diseases and People. 1998, Enslow LB $20.95 (0-7660-1049-X). This book describes the causes of epilepsy, gives a history of society's attitude toward epileptics, and describes current treatments and drugs used to control it. (Rev: BL 7/98; BR 1–2/99; SLJ 9/98; VOYA 2/99) [616.8]

10747 Cefrey, Holly. *Coping with Cancer* (6–12). Illus. Series: Coping. 2000, Rosen LB $25.25 (0-8239-2849-7). As well as discussing how cancer develops in various parts of the body, this book gives self-help advice for anyone who is diagnosed with the disease. (Rev: BL 1/1–15/01; SLJ 12/00) [616.99]

10748 Check, William A. *AIDS* (8–12). Illus. Series: Encyclopedia of Health. 1999, Chelsea LB $24.95 (0-7910-4885-3). This updated and revised edition gives a history of the AIDS epidemic, the latest information on breakthrough HIV treatment methods, and advice on how to avoid contracting the disease. (Rev: BL 8/98; SLJ 9/98) [616.9]

10749 Check, William A. *Alzheimer's Disease* (9–12). Illus. 1989, Chelsea LB $19.95 (0-7910-0056-7). A succinct explanation of what Alzheimer's disease is, its possible causes, treatments, and the personal toll it takes on families. (Rev: BL 3/1/89; BR 9–10/89; SLJ 6/89; VOYA 8/89) [618.97]

10750 Chiu, Christina. *Eating Disorder Survivors Tell Their Stories* (7–12). Series: Teen Health Library of Eating Disorder Prevention. 1998, Rosen LB $26.50 (0-8239-2767-9); Hazelden Information & Educational Services paper $6.95 (1-56838-259-6). In candid interviews, survivors of eating disorders share their experiences, treatments, and roads to recovery, and offer advice to other teens who might need help. (Rev: BL 3/1/99; BR 5–6/99; SLJ 1/99; VOYA 4/99) [616.85]

10751 Clarke, Julie M., and Ann Kirby-Payne. *Understanding Weight and Depression* (7–10). Series: Teen Eating Disorder Prevention. 1999, Rosen LB $25.25 (0-8239-2994-9). This book discusses the psychological origins of eating disorders such as anorexia and bulimia and suggests ways to develop a healthy self-image. [616.8]

10752 Cozic, Charles P., and Tamara L. Roleff, eds. *AIDS* (9–12). Series: Opposing Viewpoints. 1997, Greenhaven LB $21.96 (1-56510-667-9); paper $20.25 (1-56510-666-0). The seriousness of the AIDS epidemic, policies on HIV testing, various AIDS treatments, mandatory testing and partner notification, and measures to prevent the spread of AIDS are among the topics debated in this anthology. (Rev: BL 2/15/98; VOYA 6/98) [616.97]

10753 Curran, Christine Perdan. *Sexually Transmitted Diseases* (7–12). 1998, Enslow LB $20.95 (0-7660-1050-3). This work discusses various kinds of sexually transmitted diseases, including those that are bacterial, like syphilis, those that are viral, like HIV, and those that are neither, like scabies and pubic lice. (Rev: BL 12/15/98; VOYA 2/99) [616.95]

10754 Daugirdas, John T. *S.T.D. Sexually Transmitted Diseases, Including HIV/AIDS.* 3rd ed. (8–12). 1992, MedText $14.95 (0-9629279-1-0). This overview simplifies the language and prunes unnecessary medical terminology. (Rev: BL 10/1/92; SLJ 11/92) [616.951]

10755 Decker, Janet M. *Mononucleosis* (9–12). Series: Deadly Diseases and Epidemics. 2004, Chelsea LB $25.95 (0-7910-7700-4). Mononucleosis is explored, with material on the virus involved, and its prevention and treatment. [616.9]

10756 DiSpezio, Michael. *The Science, Spread, and Therapy of HIV Disease: Everything You Need to Know, but Had No Idea Who to Ask* (9–12). 1997, A T L $26.95 (1-882360-20-6); paper $13.95 (1-882360-19-2). This comprehensive book in a question-and-answer format addresses both general and specific topics and gives current information on HIV and AIDS. (Rev: BL 2/15/98; SLJ 5/98; VOYA 6/98) [616.97]

10757 Dominick, Andie. *Needles: A Memoir of Growing Up with Diabetes* (10–12). 1998, Scribner $22.00 (0-684-84232-7). The story of how diabetes affected the life of one family, as told by one of the victims. (Rev: BL 9/1/98; SLJ 5/99; VOYA 2/00) [616]

10758 Donnelly, Karen. *Coping with Lyme Disease* (6–12). Series: Coping. 2001, Rosen LB $18.95 (0-8239-3199-4). This introduction to the symptoms, diagnosis, treatment, and prevention of Lyme disease includes personal stories. (Rev: SLJ 7/01) [616.9]

10759 Drexler, Madeline. *Secret Agents: The Menace of Emerging Infections* (10–12). 2002, National Academy $24.95 (0-309-07638-2). The dangers of diseases that spread from animals and of an unregulated and ill-equipped public health system are examined in thought-provoking fashion. (Rev: BL 2/15/02) [614.4]

10760 Dudley, William, ed. *Epidemics* (8–12). Series: Opposing Viewpoints. 1998, Greenhaven LB $32.45 (1-56510-941-4). Topics covered in this anthology of different points of view include the threat of infectious diseases, the AIDS epidemic, vaccination programs, and the prevention of foodborne illnesses. (Rev: BL 11/15/98) [616.9]

10761 *Eating Disorders* (9–12). Ed. by Jennifer A. Hurley. Series: Opposing Viewpoints. 2001, Greenhaven LB $31.20 (0-7377-0652-X); paper $19.95 (0-7377-0651-1). Varying viewpoints about all kinds of eating disorders are presented in this collection of writings. [616.85]

10762 Edelson, Edward. *Allergies* (7–12). Illus. 1989, Chelsea LB $19.95 (0-7910-0055-9). Various types of allergies are described, including their effects and treatments that have been found to help sufferers. (Rev: BL 9/1/89; BR 11–12/89; SLJ 12/89) [616.97]

10763 Edelson, Edward. *The Immune System* (6–12). Illus. Series: 21st Century Health and Wellness. 2000, Chelsea LB $24.95 (0-7910-5525-6). A revised edition of Edelson's presentation on the immune system and what happens when it fails to function. (Rev: BL 4/15/00; BR 5–6/00; HBG 9/00; SLJ 6/00) [616.07]

10764 Eisenpreis, Bettijane. *Coping with Scoliosis* (7–10). Series: Coping. 1999, Rosen LB $25.25 (0-8239-2557-9). The author explores the physical and emotional issues involved in the diagnosis and treatment of scoliosis, curvature of the spine, using scientific explanations and firsthand accounts. (Rev: SLJ 5/99) [616]

10765 *Epidemic! The World of Infectious Diseases* (10–12). Ed. by Rob DeSalle. 1999, New Pr. paper $19.95 (1-56584-546-3). In brief essays, specialists discuss such topics as methods of infection, key personnel, important case studies, and prevention techniques. (Rev: BL 9/15/99) [614.4]

10766 Epstein, Rachel. *Eating Habits and Disorders* (7–12). Illus. 1990, Chelsea LB $19.95 (0-7910-0048-6). A little history on eating disorders is given, but the major focus of this book is on the kinds of eating disorders and their treatments. (Rev: BL 6/1/90; SLJ 8/90) [616.85]

10767 Farrell, Jeanette. *Invisible Enemies: Stories of Infectious Disease* (7–12). 1997, Farrar $17.00 (0-374-33637-7). This is a dramatic retelling of human reactions to such diseases as malaria, leprosy, tuberculosis, and AIDS, and of the medical breakthroughs associated with each. (Rev: BL 6/1–15/98; SLJ 7/98; VOYA 10/98) [616.909]

10768 Feldman, Douglas A., and Julia Wang Miller. *The AIDS Crisis: A Documentary History* (8–12). Series: Primary Documents in American History and Contemporary Issues. 1998, Greenwood LB $49.95 (0-313-28715-5). Beginning with the first medical report on AIDS in 1981, this is a fine collection of documents relating to the disease and people involved with it. (Rev: BR 1–2/99; VOYA 2/99) [616]

10769 Fine, Judylaine. *Afraid to Ask: A Book About Cancer* (7–12). 1986, Lothrop paper $6.95 (0-688-06196-6). In this straightforward account about the nature, causes, and treatment of cancer, the author tries to minimize the fear and emotion surrounding the topic. (Rev: BL 3/1/86; BR 5–6/86; VOYA 8/86) [616.99]

10770 Finer, Kim Renee. *Tuberculosis* (9–12). Series: Deadly Diseases and Epidemics. 2003, Chelsea (0-7910-7309-2). This work discusses the history of tuberculosis (also known as consumption), as well as its causes, symptoms, and treatment. (Rev: HBG 4/04) [616.9]

10771 Flynn, Tom, and Karen Lound. *AIDS: Examining the Crisis* (7–12). 1995, Lerner LB $19.93 (0-8225-2625-5). An informative explanation in clear language about HIV and AIDS. (Rev: BL 5/1/95; SLJ 6/95) [362.1]

10772 Ford, Michael T. *100 Questions and Answers About AIDS: A Guide for Young People* (8–12). 1992, Macmillan LB $14.95 (0-02-735424-5). Answers to common queries that clarify background, distinguish misinformation, and guide readers toward safer behaviors. (Rev: BL 8/92; SLJ 1/93*) [616.97]

10773 Ford, Michael T. *The Voices of AIDS* (8–12). 1995, Morrow $15.00 (0-688-05322-X). Dedicated to getting the word out about AIDS, told by 12 men and women. (Rev: BL 8/95*; SLJ 11/95) [362.1]

10774 Frankenberger, Elizabeth. *Food and Love: Dealing with Family Attitudes About Weight* (7–12). Series: Teen Health Library of Eating Disorder Prevention. 1998, Rosen LB $26.50 (0-8239-2760-1). This book explores the role the family plays in developing a healthy self-image and affecting a teenager's attitudes toward food. (Rev: BR 5–6/99; VOYA 4/99) [616.85]

10775 Friedlander, Mark P., and Terry M. Phillips. *The Immune System: Your Body's Disease-Fighting Army* (6–10). 1997, Lerner LB $23.93 (0-8225-2858-4). Topics covered in this introduction to the immune system include the makeup of the immune system, how it reacts to invaders, vaccination, nutrition, allergies, disorders of the system, and medicines that help it. (Rev: BL 6/1–15/98) [616.079]

10776 Frissell, Susan, and Paula Harney. *Eating Disorders and Weight Control* (7–10). Illus. 1998, Enslow LB $17.95 (0-89490-919-3). This book covers anorexia, bulimia, binge eating disorders, and weight control issues with material on how to cope with them in a healthy, realistic manner. (Rev: BL 4/15/98; BR 5–6/98; HBG 9/98; SLJ 3/98) [616.85]

10777 Gay, Kathlyn, and Sean McGarrahan. *Epilepsy: The Ultimate Teen Guide* (7–12). Illus. Series: Ultimate Teen Guide. 2003, Scarecrow LB $32.50 (0-8108-4339-0). This informative look at this seizure disease and its impact on typical teen activities (sports, jobs, driving, and so forth) includes the personal experiences of coauthor McGarrahan, who was diagnosed with epilepsy at the age of 16. (Rev: BL 10/15/03; SLJ 10/03) [616]

10778 Gedatus, Gustav Mark. *Mononucleosis* (7–12). Series: Perspectives on Disease and Illness. 1999, Capstone LB $16.95 (0-7368-0283-5). An introduction to this disease, its transmission, and possible treatments. (Rev: SLJ 4/00) [616.9]

10779 Giblin, James Cross. *When Plague Strikes: The Black Death, Smallpox, AIDS* (6–12). 1995, HarperCollins LB $14.89 (0-06-025864-0). A discussion, combining social history, science, and technology, of the great plagues in history. (Rev: BL 10/15/95; SLJ 10/95; VOYA 4/96) [614.4]

10780 Goldsmith, Connie. *Neurological Disorders* (6–10). Illus. Series: Amazing Brain. 2001, Blackbirch LB $21.95 (1-56711-422-9). Conditions such as Alzheimer's, autism, cerebral palsy, and schizophrenia are presented, with information on how the disease affects the brain and on the treatments available now. Also use *Addiction* (2001), which looks at the ways in which chemicals affect the brain and induce dependency. (Rev: BL 10/15/01; HBG 3/02; SLJ 9/01; VOYA 10/01) [616.8]

10781 Gravelle, Karen, and Bertram A. John. *Teenagers Face to Face with Cancer* (7–12). 1986, Messner paper $5.95 (0-671-65975-8). From the accounts of 16 young people ages 13 to 21, one discovers what it is like to live with cancer. (Rev: BL 1/15/87; SLJ 2/87) [618.92]

10782 Greenberg, Alissa. *Asthma* (6–12). Illus. 2000, Watts $25.00 (0-531-11331-0). In this thorough presentation on asthma, readers will learn about the history, treatment, and management of this illness that often attacks people in their youth. (Rev: BL 2/15/01; SLJ 3/01) [616.2]

10783 Harmon, Dan. *Anorexia Nervosa: Starving for Attention* (8–12). Series: Encyclopedia of Psychological Disorders. 1999, Chelsea $27.45 (0-7910-4901-9). Citing many case studies, some of prominent people, this work defines anorexia nervosa, discusses its causes and the physical consequences, and covers the treatments available. (Rev: VOYA 8/99) [616.85]

10784 Harmon, Dan. *Life out of Focus: Alzheimer's Disease and Related Disorders* (7–12). 1999, Chelsea $27.45 (0-7910-4896-9). This title demonstrates the devastating effect of Alzheimer's disease on sufferers and their caregivers, and provides biological and psychological explanations of the symptoms as well as solid data and analysis on research and various treatments. (Rev: BL 8/99) [616.8]

10785 Harris, Jacqueline. *Sickle Cell Disease* (6–10). 2001, Twenty-First Century LB $24.90 (0-7613-1459-8). After introducing three young victims of this disease, the author describes its symptoms and treatment and traces its history. (Rev: BL 9/15/01; HBG 3/02; SLJ 12/01) [616.1]

10786 Hayden, Deborah. *Pox: Genius, Madness, and the Mysteries of Syphilis* (10–12). 2003, Basic $27.50 (0-465-02881-0). A well-researched history of syphilis that offers evidence supporting the claim that Christopher Columbus's crew carried the disease to Europe. (Rev: BL 1/1–15/03) [615.95]

10787 Hoff, Brent H., and Carter Smith. *Mapping Epidemics: A Historical Atlas of Disease* (9–12). Illus. 2000, Watts LB $38.00 (0-531-11713-8). Fascinating information on 32 diseases that have plagued mankind, from leprosy to AIDS, with maps, photographs, and illustrations. (Rev: BL 5/15/00; SLJ 6/00) [614.44]

10788 Hornbacher, Marya. *Wasted: A Memoir of Anorexia and Bulimia* (10–12). 1997, HarperCollins $23.00 (0-06-018739-5). A candid, painful, but hopeful account of a girl who was bulimic as a fourth grader and anorexic at age 15 but whose fortitude and desire to live eventually saved her from death. (Rev: BL 1/1–15/98; SLJ 9/98) [618.92]

10789 Huegel, Kelly. *Young People and Chronic Illness: True Stories, Help, and Hope* (6–12). 1998,

Free Spirit paper $14.95 (1-57542-041-4). After a series of case histories of young people suffering from such chronic illnesses as diabetes and asthma, this book discusses topics including getting support, coping with hospital stays, and planning for the future. (Rev: BL 11/15/98; SLJ 10/98; VOYA 2/99) [618.92]

10790 Hyde, Margaret O., and Elizabeth Forsyth. *AIDS: What Does It Mean to You?* Rev. ed. (6–10). 1995, Walker LB $15.85 (0-8027-8398-8). This book traces the process of infection and the progress of the disease in the body, along with material on its history, treatment, prevention, and worldwide statistics. (Rev: SLJ 3/96; VOYA 4/96) [616.97]

10791 Johannsson, Phillip. *Heart Disease* (7–12). Series: Diseases and People. 1998, Enslow LB $20.95 (0-7660-1051-1). The causes and types of heart disease are described, along with an overview of current treatments and potential future advances. (Rev: BL 7/98) [616.1]

10792 Johnson, Earvin "Magic." *What You Can Do to Avoid AIDS* (9–12). 1992, Times Books paper $3.99 (0-8129-2063-5). Facts, answers to common questions, and interviews comprise this excellent guide to AIDS for teens. (Rev: BL 6/1/92) [616.97]

10793 Jussim, Daniel. *AIDS and HIV: Risky Business* (9–12). Illus. Series: Teen Issues. 1997, Enslow LB $19.95 (0-89490-917-7). A straightforward, carefully researched account that explains AIDS, how it is contracted, how to prevent its spread, and its consequences. (Rev: BL 6/1–15/97; SLJ 8/97; VOYA 6/97) [616.97]

10794 Karlen, Arno. *Man and Microbes* (10–12). 1995, Putnam $24.95 (0-87477-759-3). A history of communicable diseases, including material on plagues that have changed history. This work also has a fine chapter on the AIDS virus and other STDs, and how these diseases are transmitted. (Rev: BL 4/1/95; SLJ 1/96) [616]

10795 Kittredge, Mary. *The Common Cold* (7–12). Illus. Series: 21st Century Health and Wellness. 2000, Chelsea LB $24.95 (0-7910-5985-5). An interesting history of cold cures introduces this overview of the causes, prevention, and treatment of this perennial nuisance. (Rev: BL 11/15/00; HBG 10/01; SLJ 3/01) [616.1]

10796 Kittredge, Mary. *Headaches* (10–12). Series: 21st Century Health and Wellness. 2000, Chelsea LB $24.95 (0-7910-5981-2). Various types of headaches from a slight pressure behind the eyes to intense migraines are discussed, with material on causes and treatments. (Rev: BL 10/15/2000; HBG 10/01) [616.8]

10797 Kittredge, Mary. *Teens with AIDS Speak Out* (8–12). 1992, Messner paper $8.95 (0-671-74543-3). Combines facts and interviews on AIDS and its history, transmission, treatment, and prevention, as well as safer-sex practices and discrimination against people with AIDS. (Rev: BL 6/1/92; SLJ 7/92) [362.1]

10798 Knutson, Roger M. *Fearsome Fauna: A Field Guide to the Creatures That Live in You* (9–12). Illus. 1999, W. H. Freeman paper $9.95 (0-7167-3386-2). A fascinating volume about the various parasites that can invade the human body. (Rev: SLJ 2/00)

10799 Kuffel, Frances. *Passing for Thin: Losing Half My Weight and Finding My Self* (10–12). 2004, Broadway $24.00 (0-7679-1291-8). The author describes how at the age of 42 she took dramatic steps to drop more than half her body weight, only to find she faced another epic struggle to find her identity as a newly thin woman. (Rev: BL 12/1/03; SLJ 3/04) [362.1]

10800 Lamberg, Lynne. *Skin Disorders* (10–12). Series: 21st Century Health and Wellness. 2000, Chelsea LB $24.95 (0-7910-5983-9). Acne, skin cancer, and psoriasis are some of the skin disorders discussed in this account. (Rev: BL 11/15/00; HBG 10/01; SLJ 3/01) [616.5]

10801 Landau, Elaine. *Alzheimer's Disease* (7–12). Illus. Series: Venture: Health and the Human Body. 1996, Watts LB $25.00 (0-531-11268-3). Designed to help young people cope with having an Alzheimer's patient in the family, this book presents several case studies and discusses the cause, nature, and progression of the disease, various treatments, and what family members can do. (Rev: BL 10/15/96; SLJ 8/96) [362.1]

10802 Landau, Elaine. *Parkinson's Disease* (7–12). 1999, Watts LB $20.00 (0-531-11423-6). A well-organized overview that explains the various motor, emotional, and speech symptoms of Parkinson's, with material on the different treatments available and why some are controversial. (Rev: BL 7/99; SLJ 6/99) [616.8]

10803 Landau, Elaine. *Tourette's Syndrome* (6–12). Series: Venture: Health and the Human Body. 1998, Watts LB $20.00 (0-531-11399-X). Tourette's syndrome is a neurological condition involving uncontrollable verbalization and involuntary tics. This book explains its causes and treatments and gives profiles of many people, some of them famous, who are afflicted. (Rev: BL 7/98; BR 11–12/98; SLJ 7/98; VOYA 12/98) [616.8]

10804 Landau, Elaine. *Tuberculosis* (6–10). 1995, Watts LB $20.00 (0-531-12555-6). The author reviews the history and nature of tuberculosis and its treatments, and warns of the danger presented by the rise of new drug-resistant strains today. (Rev: BL 6/1–15/95; SLJ 8/95; VOYA 2/96) [616]

10805 Landau, Elaine. *Why Are They Starving Themselves? Understanding Anorexia Nervosa and Bulimia* (7–10). 1983, Messner paper $5.95 (0-671-49492-9). Case studies are used as a focal point for explaining these eating disorders. [616.8]

10806 Latta, Sara L. *Allergies* (6–10). Series: Diseases and People. 1998, Enslow LB $20.95 (0-7660-1048-1). Using a number of case studies, this book describes the nature of allergies, their symptoms, methods of detection, and treatments. (Rev: BL 7/98) [616.9]

10807 Latta, Sara L. *Food Poisoning and Foodborne Diseases* (7–12). Series: Diseases and People. 1999, Enslow LB $20.95 (0-7660-1183-6). Using case studies and questions and answers, this book describes the causes, effects, and treatments for food poisoning and related illnesses. (Rev: BL 9/15/99; HBG 4/00; SLJ 11/99) [615.9]

10808 Leone, Daniel, ed. *Anorexia* (6–12). Series: At Issue. 2001, Greenhaven LB $22.45 (0-7377-0468-3); paper $14.95 (0-7377-0467-5). Revealing personal accounts provide different perspectives on coping with this condition. (Rev: BL 3/15/01) [616.85]

10809 Leone, Daniel, ed. *The Spread of AIDS* (8–12). Series: At Issue. 1997, Greenhaven paper $17.45 (1-56510-537-0). This anthology of different opinions explores the successes and failures of various educational strategies, healthcare programs, and political policies designed to prevent the spread of AIDS. (Rev: BL 1/1–15/97; SLJ 4/97) [362.1]

10810 Levenkron, Steven. *Treating and Overcoming Anorexia Nervosa* (9–12). 1988, Warner paper $5.99 (0-446-34416-8). Symptoms, causes, stages of development, and therapies connected with anorexia nervosa and bulimia are covered. [616.8]

10811 LeVert, Marianne. *AIDS: A Handbook for the Future* (7–12). Illus. 1996, Millbrook LB $24.90 (1-56294-660-9). This book covers the basic facts about AIDS, its causes, prevention, present treatments, and current research. (Rev: BL 12/15/96; BR 3–4/97; SLJ 11/96; VOYA 6/97) [616.97]

10812 Little, Marjorie. *Diabetes* (7–12). Series: Encyclopedia of Health. 1990, Chelsea LB $19.95 (0-7910-0061-3). A clear, organized account that covers the history of diabetes, its causes, and present-day treatments. (Rev: BL 3/15/91) [616.4]

10813 Little, Marjorie. *Sexually Transmitted Diseases* (10–12). Illus. Series: 21st Century Health and Wellness. 1999, Chelsea LB $24.95 (0-7910-5528-0). This book covers the basics of STDs and sexual health. (Rev: BL 4/1/00; HBG 9/00) [619.95]

10814 McIvor, Kirsten. *Exposure: Victims of Radiation Speak Out* (9–12). 1992, Kodansha paper $12.00 (4-7700-2605-1). Reporters present data on radiation contamination in 15 countries, hoping their effort will help reduce the use of nuclear power for any purpose. (Rev: BL 9/15/92) [363.17]

10815 Majure, Janet. *AIDS* (7–10). 1998, Enslow LB $20.95 (0-7660-1182-8). This informative book describes AIDS, who gets it and how, symptoms, treatment, prevention, and prospects for the future, and touches on related social, economic, and legal issues. (Rev: VOYA 2/99) [616]

10816 Majure, Janet. *Breast Cancer* (7–12). Illus. 2000, Enslow LB $19.95 (0-7660-1312-X). A straightforward look at this disease's diagnosis and treatment, and at its social implications and its incidence around the world. (Rev: HBG 9/00; SLJ 10/00*) [616.99]

10817 Medina, Loreta M., ed. *Bulimia* (6–12). Series: At Risk. 2003, Gale LB $20.96 (0-7377-1164-7); paper $13.96 (0-7377-1163-9). The essays in this book examine issues relating to bulimia, including symptoms, effects, and suggestions for intervention. (Rev: BL 1/1–15/03) [616.85]

10818 Miller, Martha J. *Kidney Disorders* (7–12). Series: Encyclopedia of Health. 1992, Chelsea LB $19.95 (0-7910-0066-4). This book explains the function of the kidneys, how they can malfunction, and treatments that are available, including transplants. (Rev: BL 12/1/92) [616.6]

10819 Moe, Barbara. *Coping with Eating Disorders* (7–10). 1999, Rosen $26.50 (0-8239-2974-4). Actual case histories are used to explain the characteristics of bulimia, anorexia, and compulsive-eating patterns. Practical coping suggestions are also offered. (Rev: BL 7/91; SLJ 11/91) [616.85]

10820 Moe, Barbara. *Coping with PMS* (7–12). Series: Coping. 1998, Rosen LB $25.25 (0-8239-2716-4). Supplemented by personal accounts, this book explains how PMS can be a manageable problem, with material on physiology, diet, lifestyle, attitude, and the relationship between nutrition and PMS control (recipes are included). (Rev: BL 5/15/98; SLJ 5/98) [618.172]

10821 Moe, Barbara. *Coping with Tourette Syndrome and Tic Disorders* (6–10). 2000, Rosen LB $18.95 (0-8239-2976-0). Solid information and many case studies are used in this examination of Tourette's syndrome, tic disorders, and related problems with material on how they affect moods, learning, activities, and sleep. (Rev: BL 7/00) [616.8]

10822 Moe, Barbara. *Everything You Need to Know About Migraines and Other Headaches* (7–12). Series: Need to Know Library. 2000, Rosen LB $17.95 (0-8239-3291-5). An accessible and thorough exploration of the symptoms, treatment, and prevention of migraines and other headaches. (Rev: HBG 10/01; SLJ 4/01) [616.8]

10823 Moe, Barbara. *Inside Eating Disorder Support Groups* (6–10). Series: Teen Health Library of Eating Disorder Prevention. 1998, Rosen LB $26.50 (0-8239-2769-5). After a general discussion of eating disorders and available treatments, this book explains the dynamics of support groups and how they can help teens recover from eating disorders and come to terms with their problems. (Rev: BR 5–6/99; SLJ 1/99) [616.85]

10824 Moehn, Heather. *Everything You Need to Know When Someone You Know Has Leukemia* (5–10). Series: Need to Know Library. 2000, Rosen LB $25.25 (0-8239-3121-8). The basic facts about leukemia are covered with material on its various types and treatments, possible causes, and the emotional aspects of the illness. (Rev: SLJ 9/00) [616.99]

10825 Moehn, Heather. *Understanding Eating Disorder Support Groups* (7–12). Series: Teen Eating Disorder Prevention Library. 2000, Rosen LB $18.95 (0-8239-2992-2). Extensive information on the diagnosis, symptoms, and treatment of eating disorders precedes discussion of the types of support available; case studies appear throughout. (Rev: HBG 10/01; SLJ 2/01)

10826 Murphy, Wendy. *Asthma* (7–12). Series: Millbrook Medical Library. 1998, Millbrook LB $26.90 (0-7613-0364-2). Beginning with the causes of asthma, this book describes what happens during an attack, how the disease is controlled, and various avenues of medical treatment. (Rev: BL 1/1–15/99; HBG 3/99; SLJ 1/99) [616.2]

10827 Murphy, Wendy. *Orphan Diseases: New Hope for Rare Medical Conditions* (7–12). Illus. 2002, Millbrook LB $26.90 (0-7613-1919-0). Autism, cystic fibrosis, and dwarfism are among the conditions discussed, with information on origin, causes, treatment, and how patients cope with the condition. (Rev: BL 10/15/02; HBG 3/03) [362.1]

10828 Nash, Carol R. *AIDS: Choices for Life* (7–12). Illus. Series: Issues in Focus. 1997, Enslow LB $20.95 (0-89490-903-7). This book offers information about AIDS and protease inhibitors, drug cocktails, the AIDS virus, current and future medical concerns, and prevention tactics, plus a history of the disease. (Rev: BL 12/1/97; SLJ 12/97; VOYA 6/98) [616.97]

10829 Neuwirth, Michael, and Kevin Osborn. *The Scoliosis Sourcebook* (10–12). Illus. 2001, NTC paper $16.95 (0-7373-0321-2). This book describes the tests that confirm scoliosis, the symptoms, and the medical and surgical treatments available. (Rev: BL 8/01) [616.7]

10830 Newton, David E., et al. *Sick! Diseases and Disorders, Injuries and Infections* (8–12). 1999, UXL $130.00 (0-7876-3922-2). Arranged alphabetically, this volume covers 140 illnesses, disorders, and injuries with material on symptoms, causes, diagnosis, prevention, and treatment. (Rev: BL 10/1/00) [616]

10831 Nourse, Alan E. *The Virus Invaders* (8–10). 1992, Watts paper $24.00 (0-531-12511-4). Virology is explained in lay terms, including a history of viruses and the prognosis for treatment of killers like malaria and AIDS. (Rev: BL 9/15/92; SLJ 7/92) [616]

10832 O'Brien, Eileen. *Starving to Win: Athletes and Eating Disorders* (6–12). Series: Teen Health Library of Eating Disorder Prevention. 1998, Rosen LB $26.50 (0-8239-2764-4). This book describes the pressures on athletes to gain or lose weight and the temptation, particularly in track, gymnastics, ballet, and wrestling, to resort to dangerous crash diets, fasts, or drugs. The author stresses that health is more important than weight. (Rev: BR 5–6/99; SLJ 2/99) [616.85]

10833 Ouriou, Katie. *Love Ya Like a Sister: A Story of Friendship* (8–12). Ed. by Julie Johnston. 1999, Tundra paper $7.95 (0-88776-454-1). After her death from leukemia when only 16 years old, Katie Ouriou's life and thoughts during her last months were reconstructed from journal entries and e-mail correspondence with her many friends. (Rev: SLJ 5/99; VOYA 6/99) [616.95]

10834 Packer, Kenneth L. *HIV Infection: The Facts You Need to Know* (9–12). Illus. Series: Venture Books. 1998, Watts LB $25.00 (0-531-11333-7). This book provides a clear, concise explanation of HIV and AIDS and teaches young readers to be responsible for their actions and to have compassion for those infected with the virus. (Rev: BL 4/15/98; BR 11–12/98; SLJ 4/98; VOYA 2/99) [616.97]

10835 Peacock, Judith. *Diabetes* (7–12). Series: Perspectives on Disease and Illness. 1999, Capstone LB $16.95 (0-7368-0277-0). An introduction to this disease, its transmission, and possible treatments, with material on how to manage it at home and at school. Also use *Juvenile Arthritis* (1999). (Rev: SLJ 4/00) [616.4]

10836 Pipher, Mary. *Hunger Pains: The Modern Woman's Tragic Quest for Thinness* (7–12). 1997, Ballantine paper $12.00 (0-345-41393-8). This book explains eating disorders, probes into their basic causes, and offers suggestions for help, with separate chapters on bulimia, anorexia, obesity, and diets. (Rev: VOYA 8/97) [616.95]

10837 Potts, Eve, and Marion Morra. *Understanding Your Immune System* (9–12). 1986, Avon paper $3.95 (0-380-89728-8). Using a question-and-answer format, the authors explain the immune system, how it can be strengthened, and what happens when it malfunctions. (Rev: BL 6/1/86) [612]

10838 Powers, Mary C. *Arthritis* (7–12). Series: Encyclopedia of Health. 1992, Chelsea LB $19.95 (0-7910-0057-5). Illustrated with black-and-white pictures, this book describes the causes of arthritis, therapies, and treatments. (Rev: BL 10/1/92) [616.7]

10839 Radetsky, Peter. *The Invisible Invaders: The Story of the Emerging Age of Viruses* (9–12). 1991, Little, Brown $22.95 (0-316-73216-8). What is known about viruses and recent genetic discoveries based on viral research. (Rev: BL 1/1/91) [616.01]

10840 Robbins, Paul R. *Anorexia and Bulimia* (7–12). Series: Diseases and People. 1998, Enslow LB $20.95 (0-7660-1047-3). The history of anorexia, bulimia, and binge eating is given, with material on symptoms, possible causes, prevention, and treatment. (Rev: BL 1/1–15/99; SLJ 1/99) [616.85]

10841 Rocco, Fiammetta. *The Miraculous Fever Tree: Malaria, Medicine, and the Quest for a Cure That Changed the World* (10–12). Illus. 2003, HarperCollins $24.95 (0-06-019951-2). A fascinating overview of the importance of quinine in the treatment of malaria and the politics involved in its eventual acceptance. (Rev: BL 8/03) [016.9]

10842 Rocha, Toni L. *Understanding Recovery from Eating Disorders* (6–10). Series: Teen Eating Disorder Prevention Library. 1999, Rosen $17.95 (0-8239-2884-5). This book offers first-person accounts of survivors of various types of eating disorders and also offers advice for teens who are in recovery programs. (Rev: BL 10/15/99; HBG 9/00; SLJ 7/00) [616.85]

10843 Roleff, Tamara L., ed. *AIDS* (7–12). Illus. Series: Opposing Viewpoints. 2003, Gale LB $33.70 (0-7377-1136-1); paper $22.45 (0-7377-1135-3). Articles address the spread of HIV and the current status of the epidemic, as well as treatment (including recommendations for pregnant women and infants), needle-exchange programs, and partner notification. (Rev: SLJ 11/03) [616.977]

10844 Roth, Geneen. *Feeding the Hungry Heart: The Experience of Compulsive Eating* (10–12). 1983, NAL paper $5.95 (0-451-15825-3). This book explains how one can avoid eating binges by overcoming emotional problems. [615]

10845 Sacker, Ira M., and Marc A. Zimmer. *Dying to Be Thin* (9–12). 1987, Warner paper $14.99 (0-446-38417-8). This account tells about the onset, symptoms, dangers, and treatment of various eating disorders. (Rev: VOYA 12/87) [613.2]

10846 *Sexually Transmitted Diseases* (10–12). Ed. by Bryan J. Grapes. Series: Current Controversies. 2001, Greenhaven LB $31.20 (0-7377-0687-2); paper $19.95 (0-7377-0686-4). Various aspects of sexually transmitted diseases, including prevention and the role of public health agencies, are explored in this collection of essays and articles. [616.95]

10847 Shader, Laurel, and Jon Zonderman. *Mononucleosis and Other Infectious Diseases* (10–12). Series: 21st Century Health and Wellness. 2000, Chelsea $24.95 (0-7910-5520-5). This book covers several infectious diseases but focuses on "mono," a common illness among young people that causes lethargy and weakness. (Rev: BL 4/15/00; SLJ 6/00) [616]

10848 Shmaefsky, Brian. *Syphilis* (9–12). Series: Deadly Diseases and Epidemics. 2003, Chelsea (0-7910-7308-4). This book describes the causes of syphilis and its treatment, as well as its symptoms and its place in modern society. (Rev: HBG 4/04) [616.95]

10849 Shnayerson, Michael, and Mark J. Plotkin. *The Killers Within: The Deadly Rise of Drug-Resistant Bacteria* (10–12). 2002, Little, Brown $24.95 (0-316-71331-7). A chilling look into the future as more and more bacteria develop a resistance to antibiotics. (Rev: BL 9/1/02) [616]

10850 Siegel, Dorothy, and David E. Newton. *Leukemia* (7–12). 1994, Watts LB $20.00 (0-531-12509-2). An introduction to leukemia, emphasizing the advances in research and the cure rate. (Rev: BL 2/15/95; SLJ 1/95; VOYA 4/95) [616.99]

10851 Silverstein, Alvin, et al. *AIDS: An All-About Guide for Young Adults* (6–12). Illus. Series: Issues in Focus. 1999, Enslow LB $19.95 (0-89490-716-6). In addition to discussing the history, diagnosis, treatment, and prevention of AIDS, the authors present interesting sidebar features and profiles of celebrities who have contracted the disease. (Rev: BL 11/15/99; HBG 4/00; SLJ 11/99) [616.97]

10852 Silverstein, Alvin, et al. *Asthma* (7–12). Illus. Series: Diseases and People. 1997, Enslow LB $20.95 (0-89490-712-3). This book discusses the nature, causes, and treatment of asthma and possible cures. (Rev: BL 2/15/97; SLJ 4/97; VOYA 6/97) [616.2]

10853 Silverstein, Alvin, et al. *Chickenpox and Shingles* (6–10). Series: Diseases and People. 1998, Enslow LB $20.95 (0-89490-715-8). The nature and treatment of these two diseases are discussed, supplemented by case studies. (Rev: BL 7/98) [616]

10854 Silverstein, Alvin, et al. *Diabetes* (7–12). Illus. Series: Diseases and People. 1994, Enslow LB $20.95 (0-89490-464-7). An examination of the causes and treatment of diabetes, with material on how to detect it and sources of possible cures. (Rev: BL 10/15/94; SLJ 12/94; VOYA 12/94) [616.4]

10855 Silverstein, Alvin, et al. *Hepatitis* (8–10). Series: Diseases and People. 1994, Enslow $20.95 (0-89490-467-1). The history of hepatitis is given along with material on treatment, prevention, and related ailments. [616.3]

10856 Silverstein, Alvin, et al. *Leukemia* (6–10). Illus. Series: Diseases and People. 2000, Enslow LB $20.95 (0-7660-1310-3). A look at the history, symptoms, diagnosis, treatment, social impact, and future of this disease. (Rev: HBG 10/01; SLJ 9/00) [616.99]

10857 Silverstein, Alvin, et al. *Mononucleosis* (7–10). Series: Diseases and People. 1994, Enslow LB $20.95 (0-89490-466-3). Examines this disease's history, causes, treatment, prevention, and societal response. (Rev: BL 1/15/95; HBG 10/01; SLJ 3/95) [616.9]

10858 Silverstein, Alvin, et al. *Parkinson's Disease* (7–10). Series: Diseases and People. 2001, Enslow LB $20.95 (0-7660-1593-9). Parkinson's disease is described, with information on its causes, symptoms. diagnosis, and treatment. (Rev: HBG 3/03) [616.8]

10859 Silverstein, Alvin, et al. *Rabies* (8–10). Series: Diseases and People. 1994, Enslow LB $20.95 (0-89490-465-5). Various aspects of rabies, including history, diagnosis, treatment, and prevention, are discussed in this account. (Rev: SLJ 7/94) [616.9]

10860 Silverstein, Alvin, et al. *Sickle Cell Anemia* (6–12). Illus. Series: Diseases and People. 1997, Enslow LB $20.95 (0-89490-711-5). A clear, concise description of the causes, effects, and treatment of this condition, with information on why it attacks African Americans in particular. (Rev: BL 2/15/97; SLJ 2/97; VOYA 6/97) [616.1]

10861 Silverstein, Alvin, and Virginia Silverstein. *Allergies* (7–10). Illus. 1977, HarperCollins $13.00 (0-397-31758-1). The types of allergies — such as hay fever and asthma — as well as their causes, effects, and treatments are discussed. [616.97]

10862 Silverstein, Alvin, and Virginia Silverstein. *Measles and Rubella* (6–12). Illus. Series: Diseases and People. 1997, Enslow LB $20.95 (0-89490-714-X). The authors examine the nature of measles and rubella, their treatment, and the possibility of a cure. (Rev: BL 3/1/98; SLJ 5/98) [616.9]

10863 Silverstein, Alvin, and Virginia Silverstein. *Runaway Sugar: All About Diabetes* (7–10). Illus. 1981, HarperCollins LB $12.89 (0-397-31929-0). Among other topics, this book discusses what causes diabetes and how it can be controlled. [616.4]

10864 Silverstein, Alvin, and Virginia B. Silverstein. *Polio* (7–10). Series: Diseases and People. 2001, Enslow LB $20.95 (0-7660-1592-0). The symptoms, causes, prevention, and treatment of polio are discussed, with information on such well-known patients as Franklin D. Roosevelt. (Rev: HBG 3/02) [616.8]

10865 Simpson, Carolyn. *Coping with Sleep Disorders* (7–12). Series: Coping. 1995, Rosen LB

$25.25 (0-8239-2068-2). This book discusses sleeping disorders from snoring to insomnia and offers a wide range of possible solutions. (Rev: SLJ 6/96; VOYA 8/96) [613.7]

10866 Simpson, Carolyn. *Everything You Need to Know About Asthma* (5–10). Illus. Series: Need to Know Library. 1998, Rosen LB $25.25 (0-8239-2567-6). Vital background information is given about the causes and effects, symptoms, and treatments of asthma. (Rev: SLJ 10/98) [616.2]

10867 Smith, Erica. *Anorexia Nervosa: When Food Is the Enemy* (6–10). Series: Teen Health Library of Eating Disorder Prevention. 1998, Rosen LB $26.50 (0-8239-2766-0). The author describes anorexia nervosa and its symptoms and treatment, and discusses what to do if you suspect someone is suffering from the eating disorder. Society's attitudes toward weight and body image and the role of peer pressure, media images, family relationships, and genetics are examined, along with how to deal with these influences. (Rev: BR 5–6/99; SLJ 1/99) [616.85]

10868 Snedden, Robert. *Fighting Infectious Diseases* (6–10). Illus. Series: Microlife. 2000, Heinemann LB $22.79 (1-57572-243-7). The body's immune system and other forms of defense against diseases are discussed in this well-illustrated account. (Rev: BL 9/15/00) [616.8]

10869 Sparks, Beatrice, ed. *It Happened to Nancy* (7–12). 1994, Avon paper $5.99 (0-380-77315-5). In diary format, this is the story of 14-year-old Nancy, who was raped by her boyfriend and infected with the HIV virus. (Rev: BL 6/1–15/94; SLJ 6/94; VOYA 10/94) [362.196]

10870 Stanley, Debbie. *Understanding Anorexia Nervosa* (6–12). Series: Teen Eating Disorder Prevention Library. 1999, Rosen LB $17.95 (0-8239-2877-2). Why people get anorexia, how to get help for it, the dangers of this condition, and some of the myths surrounding it are all covered in this volume. (Rev: HBG 9/00; SLJ 2/00) [616.85]

10871 Stanley, Debbie. *Understanding Bulimia Nervosa* (6–10). Series: Teen Eating Disorder Prevention Library. 1999, Rosen $17.95 (0-8239-2878-0). A look at this eating disorder, in which a person binges and purges, with material on contributing factors and guidance to help recovery. (Rev: BL 10/15/99; HBG 9/00; SLJ 7/00) [616.85]

10872 Stewart, Gail B. *Teens with Cancer* (7–10). Photos by Carl Franzn. Series: The Other America. 2001, Gale LB $27.45 (1-56006-884-1). The first-person stories of four young people with life-threatening cancers reveal the hard realities such teens face. (Rev: SLJ 12/01)

10873 Stewart, Gail B. *Teens with Eating Disorders* (7–12). Illus. Series: The Other America. 2000, Lucent LB $19.96 (1-56006-764-0). Four young adults describe their battles with eating disorders, which become particularly problematic in high school and at college. (Rev: BL 2/1/01) [616.85]

10874 Stone, Tanya L. *Medical Causes* (5–10). Series: Celebrity Activists. 1997, Twenty-First Century LB $25.90 (0-8050-5233-X). The contributions of such celebrity activists as Elizabeth Taylor, Elton John, Paul Newman, Jerry Lewis, and Linda Ellerbee to various medical causes are highlighted, with material on each of their causes. (Rev: BR 3–4/98; SLJ 1/98) [616]

10875 Storad, Conrad J. *Inside AIDS: HIV Attacks the Immune System* (8–12). 1998, Lerner LB $23.93 (0-8225-2857-6). An unusual book about the HIV virus that tells about the cellular structure of the body, its immune system, and how the virus tricks the host cells into replicating it. (Rev: BL 12/15/98; HBG 3/99; SLJ 1/99) [616.97]

10876 Strada, Jennifer L. *Eating Disorders* (6–12). Illus. 2000, Lucent LB $19.96 (1-56006-659-8). Anorexia, bulimia, and binge eating are all described in this easy-to-read text, with discussion of causes, risk factors, treatment, and prevention. (Rev: BL 3/1/01; SLJ 4/01) [616.85]

10877 Thomas, Patricia. *Big Shot: Passion, Politics, and the Struggle for an AIDS Vaccine* (10–12). 2001, PublicAffairs $27.50 (1-891620-88-6). This is the gripping story, for advanced science readers, of the struggle to produce an AIDS vaccine and of the scientific, political, financial, and social problems involved. (Rev: BL 9/15/01) [616.97]

10878 Tierno, Philip M., Jr. *The Secret Life of Germs: Observations and Lessons of a Microbe Hunter* (9–12). 2002, Pocket $25.00 (0-7434-2187-6). An introduction to bacteria and viruses, how they cause diseases, and their impact on today's world. (Rev: BL 12/15/01) [616]

10879 Touchette, Nancy. *The Diabetes Problem Solver: Quick Answers to Your Questions About Treatment and Self-Care* (10–12). 1999, American Diabetes Assn. paper $19.95 (1-58040-009-4). A comprehensive and practical manual that covers prevention and treatment of the various symptoms of diabetes. [616.4]

10880 Trillin, Alice Stewart. *Dear Bruno* (9–12). Illus. 1996, New Pr. $12.00 (1-56584-057-7). Originally intended as a letter to a friend's son who had cancer, this work is filled with love, compassion, and humor in spite of the grim subject. (Rev: VOYA 10/96) [616.99]

10881 Tucker, Jonathan B. *Scourge: The Once and Future Threat of Smallpox* (10–12). 2001, Grove Atlantic $26.00 (0-87113-830-1). A fascinating history of the disease of smallpox, how it was conquered, and how it can be used as a weapon. (Rev: BL 9/1/01) [616.9]

10882 Turkington, Carol A., and Jeffrey S. Dover. *Skin Deep: An A-Z of Skin Disorders, Treatments and Health* (10–12). 1996, Facts on File $45.00 (0-8160-3071-5). Hundreds of topics relating to skin are covered, including the causes, cures, treatments, and symptoms of a wide variety of disorders, with information on current surgeries such as laser therapy and rhinoplasty. (Rev: BR 5–6/96; SLJ 6/96) [616.5]

10883 Veggeberg, Scott. *Lyme Disease* (7–12). 1998, Enslow LB $20.95 (0-7660-1052-X). An overview of the symptoms, diagnosis, treatment, and prevention of Lyme disease. (Rev: BL 7/98; HBG 10/98; SLJ 9/98) [616.7]

10884 Vogel, Carole Garbuny. *Breast Cancer: Questions and Answers for Young Women* (6–12). Illus. 2001, Twenty-First Century LB $25.90 (0-7613-1855-0). Teen readers will find clear answers to both emotional and physiological questions about breasts, breast development, and breast cancer. (Rev: HBG 10/01; SLJ 5/01; VOYA 8/01) [616.99]

10885 Vollstadt, Elizabeth Weiss. *Teen Eating Disorders* (7–12). Series: Teen Issues. 1999, Lucent LB $27.45 (1-56006-516-8). This book defines the various kinds of teenage eating disorders and, using many anecdotes, describes their causes, effects, treatment, and prevention. (Rev: BL 7/99; HBG 4/00; SLJ 8/99) [616.85]

10886 Wade, Mary Dodson. *ALS: Lou Gehrig's Disease* (6–12). Illus. Series: Diseases and People. 2001, Enslow LB $20.95 (0-7660-1594-7). The story of Lou Gehrig's illness introduces this incurable disease and its symptoms, treatment, and the research being conducted in search of a cure. (Rev: BL 1/1–15/02; HBG 10/02; SLJ 2/02) [616.8]

10887 Walker, Pamela. *Understanding the Risk of Diet Drugs* (6–10). Series: Teen Eating Disorder Prevention Library. 2000, Rosen LB $18.95 (0-8239-2991-4). This book examines teen concerns about body image and overall appearance and provides information about eating disorders and weight-loss products. (Rev: BL 2/15/01; SLJ 1/01) [616.85]

10888 Walters, Mark Jerome. *Six Modern Plagues and How We Are Causing Them* (10–12). 2003, Island Pr. $22.00 (1-55963-992-X). This chilling overview of six outbreaks of disease examines the ways in which ill-advised human actions affect the natural environment. (Rev: BL 9/15/03) [614.4]

10889 Weeldreyer, Laura. *Body Blues: Weight and Depression* (6–12). Series: Teen Health Library of Eating Disorder Prevention. 1998, Rosen LB $26.50 (0-8239-2761-X). This book uses case studies of three teenagers who are trying to come to terms with food and their bodies to explore the relationship between weight and depression, and encour-

ages teenagers to learn to accept their bodies rather than aspiring to some media ideal. (Rev: BR 5–6/99; SLJ 2/99) [155.5]

10890 Wilensky, Amy. *The Weight of It: A Story of Two Sisters* (10–12). 2004, Holt $23.00 (0-8050-7312-4). In this memoir of her younger sister's battle with obesity, Wilensky explores how her sister's increasing weight over time became a wedge between them and questions whether she could have been more supportive. (Rev: BL 12/1/03) [362.1]

10891 Willett, Edward. *Alzheimer's Disease* (6–12). Series: Diseases and People. 2002, Enslow LB $20.95 (0-7660-1596-3). As well as discussing the nature, treatment, and possible cures of Alzheimer's disease, this account uses many case studies, including that of President Reagan. (Rev: BL 8/02; HBG 10/02; SLJ 8/02) [616.8]

10892 Willett, Edward. *Hemophilia* (8–10). Series: Diseases and People. 2001, Enslow $20.95 (0-7660-1684-6). This account covers the history, symptoms, treatment, and prevention of hemophilia. (Rev: HBG 3/02; SLJ 12/01) [616.1]

10893 Williams, Mary E., ed. *Terminal Illness* (7–12). Series: Opposing Viewpoints. 2001, Greenhaven LB $22.96 (0-7377-0526-4); paper $18.70 (0-7377-0525-6). Euthanasia, the right to die, pain management, and the legalization of marijuana for the terminally ill are all discussed here, as are the choices of care available. (Rev: BL 5/1/01; SLJ 4/01) [362.1]

10894 Woods, Samuel G. *Everything You Need to Know About Sexually Transmitted Disease* (7–12). Illus. Series: Need to Know Library. 1990, Rosen $12.95 (0-8239-1010-5). Various kinds of venereal diseases are introduced, with their symptoms and treatments. (Rev: SLJ 9/90; VOYA 8/90) [305.4]

10895 Yancey, Diane. *STDs: What You Don't Know Can Hurt You* (6–12). 2002, Millbrook LB $24.90 (0-7613-1957-3). The facts on common sexually transmitted diseases are combined with stories of teenagers with STDs, a section on prevention, and tests to help the reader determine his or her risk of becoming infected. (Rev: BL 4/1/02; HBG 10/02; SLJ 5/02) [616.95]

10896 Yancey, Diane. *Tuberculosis* (7–12). Series: Twenty-First Century Medical Library. 2001, Twenty-First Century LB $24.90 (0-7613-1624-8). Interesting illustrations and case studies draw the reader into this account of the historical and contemporary incidence of this disease. (Rev: HBG 10/01; SLJ 5/01) [616]

10897 Yount, Lisa. *Epidemics* (7–10). Illus. 1999, Lucent LB $18.96 (1-56006-441-2). An interesting overview of epidemics of the past, their causes, and the potential for future epidemics, including ones caused by biological weapons. (Rev: HBG 9/00; SLJ 4/00) [614.4]

Doctors, Hospitals, and Medicine

10898 Adler, Robert E. *Medical Firsts: From Hippocrates to the Human Genome* (9–12). Illus. 2004, Wiley $35.99 (0-471-40175-7). A slender but fact-filled volume about the history of medicine starring such luminaries as Hippocrates, Pasteur, Freud, and Alexander Fleming. (Rev: BL 4/15/04) [610]

10899 Billitteri, Thomas J. *Alternative Medicine* (7–10). Series: Twenty-First Century Medical Library. 2001, Twenty-First Century LB $24.90 (0-7613-0965-9). This overview of alternative therapies such as hypnosis, acupuncture, and homeopathy balances success stories with solid information on the lack of rigorous scientific investigation and of FDA oversight. (Rev: HBG 3/02; SLJ 12/01; VOYA 4/02) [615.5]

10900 Bourdillon, Hilary. *Women As Healers: A History of Women and Medicine* (10–12). Illus. 1989, Cambridge Univ. Pr. paper $13.95 (0-521-31090-3). An account of the roles played by women in the history of western medicine. (Rev: BL 7/89) [610]

10901 Chase, Marilyn. *The Barbary Plague: The Black Death in Victorian San Francisco* (10–12). Illus. 2003, Random $25.95 (0-375-50496-6). A well-researched account of an early-20th-century epidemic of bubonic plague in San Francisco and its political and social ramifications, particularly for the city's Chinese community. (Rev: BL 3/1/03; SLJ 9/03) [362.1]

10902 Edelson, Edward. *Sports Medicine* (8–12). Series: 21st Century Health and Wellness. 1999, Chelsea $24.95 (0-7910-5521-3). This is a close look at sports medicine, its history, and its place in today's world. [617.1]

10903 Fleischman, John. *Phineas Gage: A Gruesome But True Story About Brain Science* (7–10). Illus. 2002, Houghton $16.00 (0-618-05252-6). This riveting story of the amiable man whose personality changed when an iron rod shot through his brain presents lots of information on brain science and medical knowledge in the 19th century. (Rev: BL 3/1/02; HB 5–6/02; HBG 10/02; SLJ 3/02; VOYA 6/02) [362.1]

10904 Friedman, Meyer, and Gerald W. Friedland. *Medicine's 10 Greatest Discoveries* (10–12). 1998, Yale Univ. Pr. $35.00 (0-300-07598-7); paper $14.95 (0-300-08278-9). Arranged chronologically, these 10 discoveries include the circulation of blood, penicillin, and DNA. [610.9]

10905 Giegerich, Steve. *Body of Knowledge: One Semester of Gross Anatomy, the Gateway to Becoming a Doctor* (10–12). 2001, Scribner $24.00 (0-684-86207-7). An account of the human anatomy class in a medical school, the students, the cadaver, and the 14 weeks of learning. (Rev: BL 6/1–15/01) [611]

10906 Glasser, Ronald. *The Light in the Skull: An Odyssey of Medical Discovery* (10–12). 1997, Faber $24.95 (0-571-19916-X). An attention-getting history of medical discoveries and present-day advances in such fields as genetics, the immune system, cancer, microbiology, and evolution, including fascinating tales of the people involved and the influence of politics on medical funding and priorities. (Rev: BL 4/15/97; SLJ 1/98) [610]

10907 Gordon, James S. *Holistic Medicine* (10–12). Series: 21st Century Health and Wellness. 2000, Chelsea LB $24.95 (0-7910-5984-7). Herbal treatments, acupuncture, and meditation are three kinds of holistic medicine that are discussed in this book. (Rev: BL 10/15/2000; HBG 10/01) [615.5]

10908 Hudson, Janice. *Trauma Junkie* (10–12). 2001, Firefly $24.95 (1-55209-503-7); paper $15.95 (1-55209-573-8). The diary of a San Francisco helicopter ambulance nurse includes harrowing moments and some touches of humor. (Rev: BL 5/1/01; SLJ 7/01; VOYA 8/01)

10909 Hyde, Margaret O., and Elizabeth H. Forsyth. *Vaccinations: From Smallpox to Cancer* (6–12). Illus. 2000, Watts LB $20.00 (0-531-11746-4). This fine account traces the history of epidemics from ancient times, explains how diseases attack humans, and how vaccines help the immune system. (Rev: BL 11/15/00) [615]

10910 Judson, Karen. *Medical Ethics: Life and Death Issues* (7–10). 2001, Enslow LB $20.95 (0-7660-1585-8). After defining ethics, Judson presents a balanced overview of the potential positive and negative impacts of medical decisions, and discusses such topics as organ donation and the financial aspects of health care. (Rev: HBG 3/02; SLJ 9/01) [174]

10911 Karam, Jana Abrams. *Into the Breach: A Year of Life and Death with the EMS* (10–12). 2002, St. Martin's $24.95 (0-312-30617-2). Journalist Karam chronicles the drama of a New Jersey inner-city emergency medical service operation. (Rev: BL 11/15/02) [362.18]

10912 Kidd, J. S., and Renee A. Kidd. *Mother Nature's Pharmacy: Potent Medicines from Plants* (7–12). Illus. Series: Science and Society. 1998, Facts on File $25.00 (0-8160-3584-9). An interesting account of the long history of natural plant remedies, the individuals whose discoveries brought plant remedies to public attention, and the expanding role of the government in researching and sanctioning their use, along with information on recent advances. (Rev: BL 10/15/98; SLJ 1/99; VOYA 2/99) [615.32]

10913 Klass, Perri Elizabeth. *A Not Entirely Benign Procedure: Four Years as a Medical Student* (10–12). 1988, NAL paper $4.50 (0-451-15358-8). The process of becoming a doctor as described by a woman who spent four years at Harvard Medical School. (Rev: BL 4/1/87) [610.7]

10914 Kornmehl, Ernest W., et al. *LASIK: A Guide to Laser Vision Correction* (10–12). Illus. 2001, Addicus paper $14.95 (1-886039-54-2). After a survey of the anatomy and physiology of the eye, this book discusses various facets of laser vision correction by LASIK. (Rev: BL 11/1/01) [617.7]

10915 Levy, Debbie. *Medical Ethics* (6–12). Series: Overview. 2001, Lucent LB $27.45 (1-56006-547-8). Such topics as genetic engineering, experimental treatments, assisted suicide, and organ transplants are introduced and their relationship to medical ethics explored. (Rev: BL 9/15/01; SLJ 4/01) [174]

10916 *Medical Ethics* (9–12). Ed. by James D. Torr. Series: Current Controversies. 1999, Greenhaven LB $21.96 (0-7377-0145-5); paper $13.96 (0-7377-0144-7). Essays present both sides of some thorny issues in medicine, such as cloning and euthanasia. (Rev: BL 4/1/00) [172]

10917 Munson, Ronald. *Raising the Dead: Organ Transplants, Ethics, and Society* (10–12). 2002, Oxford $27.50 (0-19-513299-8). Munson tackles many controversial topics in this well-written assessment of the current science and use of organ transplants, which includes some case histories. (Rev: BL 2/1/02) [174]

10918 Murphy, Wendy, and Jack Murphy. *Nuclear Medicine* (7–12). Series: Encyclopedia of Health. 1993, Chelsea LB $19.95 (0-7910-0070-2). This work presents current information on the role played by nuclear research in health care, including radiation treatments. (Rev: BL 12/1/93) [616.07]

10919 Nardo, Don, ed. *Vaccines* (7–10). Illus. Series: Great Medical Discoveries. 2001, Gale LB $27.45 (1-56006-932-5). The history of inoculations (back to ancient China), the discoveries of scientists including Sabine and Salk, and current efforts to find new vaccines are all discussed here. (Rev: BL 3/1/02; SLJ 5/02) [615]

10920 Oleksy, Walter. *Science and Medicine* (6–12). Series: Information Revolution. 1995, Facts on File $25.00 (0-8160-3076-6). A summary of computer technology used in medicine and in science classrooms. (Rev: BL 11/15/95; SLJ 11/95) [502]

10921 Plotkin, Mark J. *Medicine Quest: In Search of Nature's Healing Secrets* (10–12). Illus. 2000,

Viking $22.95 (0-670-86937-6). The author describes the natural medicines derived from bugs, snakes, plants, and bacteria and writes about the many undiscovered medicines that still lie hidden in the natural world. (Rev: BL 3/1/00) [615]

10922 Porter, Roy, ed. *Cambridge Illustrated History of Medicine* (10–12). 1996, Cambridge Univ. Pr. $39.95 (0-521-44211-7). Arranged thematically, this well-illustrated volume presents a concise history of medicine from ancient times to the present, placed in the context of other developments and events of the day. (Rev: BR 3–4/97; SLJ 5/97) [610.9]

10923 Rattenbury, Jeanne. *Understanding Alternative Medicine* (7–10). Illus. 1999, Watts LB $20.00 (0-531-11413-9). An attractive book that supplies information on topics including osteopathy, chiropractic treatments, homeopathy, acupuncture, herbal medicine, and mind–body therapy. (Rev: BL 6/1–15/99; SLJ 7/99) [615]

10924 Viegas, Jennifer. *Stem Cell Research* (6–10). Illus. Series: Library of Future Medicine. 2003, Rosen LB $26.50 (0-8239-3669-4). A look at the composition of cells, the unique qualities of stem cells, and recent scientific discoveries about the use of embryonic stem cells and the growth of new human tissue, with discussion of possible future developments and the accompanying controversies. (Rev: SLJ 6/03) [616.02774]

10925 Yalof, Ina. *Life and Death: The Story of a Hospital* (10–12). 1989, Random $18.95 (0-394-56215-1). Through interviews with 74 various workers at Columbia-Presbyterian Hospital, a profile of life in a big city hospital emerges. (Rev: BL 1/15/89; BR 9–10/89; SLJ 5/89) [362.1]

10926 Yount, Lisa. *Medical Technology* (6–12). Series: Milestones in Discovery and Invention. 1998, Facts on File $25.00 (0-8160-3568-7). An overview of medical inventors, including interesting accounts of the lives and work of such technologists as William Morton, Joseph Lister, Christian Barnard, and Norman Shumway. (Rev: BL 5/15/98; SLJ 6/98) [610.9]

Genetics

10927 Ackerman, Jennifer G. *Chance in the House of Fate: A Natural History of Heredity* (10–12). 2001, Houghton $25.00 (0-618-08287-5). This book explores in exciting prose the world of heredity and genes, chromosomes, antibodies, and pheromones. (Rev: BL 6/1–15/01) [599.93]

10928 Bainbridge, David. *The X in Sex: How the X Chromosome Controls Our Lives* (10–12). Illus.

2003, Harvard $22.95 (0-674-01028-0). The mystery of sex determination and other aspects of genetic science are explored in detail in this readable study of gender selection and the profound effect it has on our lives. (Rev: BL 2/1/03) [611]

10929 *Biotechnology* (10–12). Ed. by Lynn Messina. Series: Reference Shelf. 2000, H.W. Wilson paper $45.00 (0-8242-0985-0). A collection of essays exploring the ethical, social, religious, economic, and political aspects of biotechnology. [660.6]

10930 Boon, Kevin Alexander. *The Human Genome Project: What Does Decoding DNA Mean for Us?* (8–12). Illus. Series: Issues in Focus. 2002, Enslow LB $20.95 (0-7660-1685-4). A discussion of the benefits of and legal and ethical concerns about the Human Genome Project is preceded by information on genes and genetics. (Rev: HBG 3/03; SLJ 11/02) [599.93]

10931 *Cloning* (9–12). Ed. by Bruno J. Leone. Series: At Issue. 2003, Greenhaven LB $27.45 (0-7377-1338-0); paper $18.70 (0-7377-1339-9). The ethics of cloning are explored in this collection of articles that represent a variety of viewpoints. (Rev: SLJ 5/03) [174]

10932 Cohen, Daniel. *Cloning* (7–10). 1998, Millbrook $22.90 (0-7613-0356-1). A balanced examination of the social and ethical concerns raised by the recent cloning of a sheep named Dolly, including the history and scientific background of this area of research and a discussion of genetic engineering. (Rev: SLJ 3/99) [575.1]

10933 Davies, Kevin. *Cracking the Genome: Inside the Race to Unlock Human DNA* (10–12). 2001, Free Pr. $25.00 (0-7432-0479-4). The Human Genome Project is described, with material on its political, economic, and social implications. (Rev: BL 1/1–15/01) [599.93]

10934 Dennis, Carina, and Richard B. Gallagher. *The Human Genome* (10–12). 2001, Nature $32.00 (0-333-97143-4). An illustrated account on the history of the Human Genome Project. [599.93]

10935 Drlica, Karl. *Understanding DNA and Gene Cloning: A Guide for the Curious.* 3rd ed (9–12). 1997, Wiley paper $34.95 (0-471-13774-X). The science and technology underlying today's genetic revolution are explained in easy-to-understand language. [571.6]

10936 DuPrau, Jeanne. *Cloning* (7–12). Illus. 1999, Lucent LB $23.70 (1-56006-583-4). This examination delves into the ethical issues involved in human cloning as well as cloning's use in plants and animals. (Rev: BL 11/15/99; HBG 9/00) [6606]

10937 Edelson, Edward. *Francis Crick and James Watson and the Building Blocks of Life* (9–12). Illus. 1998, Oxford $33.95 (0-19-511451-5). The

exciting story of Watson and Crick and their scientific explorations leading up to the 1953 announcement of the discovery of the molecular structure of DNA. (Rev: BL 6/1–15/98; BR 11–12/98; HBG 3/99; SLJ 8/98) [572.8]

10938 *The Ethics of Human Cloning* (9–12). Ed. by William Dudley. Series: At Issue. 2001, Greenhaven LB $21.20 (0-7377-0472-1); paper $13.70 (0-7377-0471-3). The controversy over human cloning is examined in 11 often quite challenging essays written by experts in the fields of science, law, technology, politics, ethics, and religion. (Rev: BL 2/1/01) [174.25]

10939 Gardner, Robert. *Health Science Projects About Heredity* (7–12). Illus. Series: Science Projects. 2001, Enslow LB $20.95 (0-7660-1438-X). Projects that include tracing an inherited trait and creating a family tree are accompanied by explanatory information and useful charts and diagrams. (Rev: HBG 3/02; SLJ 9/01) [576.5]

10940 *Genetic Engineering* (9–12). Ed. by James D. Torr. Series: Opposing Viewpoints. 2000, Greenhaven LB $31.20 (0-7377-0512-4); paper $19.95 (0-7377-0511-6). The social and ethical issues raised by genetic engineering are examined in essays that express differing viewpoints. (Rev: SLJ 2/01) [174]

10941 Hyde, Margaret O., and John F. Setaro. *Medicine's Brave New World: Bioengineering and the New Genetics* (7–12). Illus. 2001, Millbrook LB $27.90 (0-7613-1706-6). Cloning, stem cell research, and other breakthroughs in genetics are explored in this accessible book that also discusses the ethical issues faced by scientists in this field. (Rev: BL 12/15/01; HBG 10/02; SLJ 12/01; VOYA 2/02) [610]

10942 Kidd, J. S., and Renee A. Kidd. *Life Lines: The Story of the New Genetics* (7–12). Series: Science and Society. 1999, Facts on File $25.00 (0-8160-3586-5). This work explores the history of genetic research, from Mendel's early experiments to recent debates about cloning and genetic engineering. (Rev: BL 12/1/98; BR 9–10/99; SLJ 7/99; VOYA 10/99) [576.5]

10943 Lee, Thomas F. *The Human Genome Project: Cracking the Genetic Code of Life* (9–12). 1991, Plenum $24.50 (0-306-43965-4). Provides background information on DNA and genes, examines the Human Genome Project, and discusses genetic diseases and their possible therapeutic treatment. (Rev: BL 9/15/91) [573.2]

10944 McGee, Glenn. *Beyond Genetics: Putting the Power of DNA to Work in Your Life* (10–12). 2003, Morrow $24.95 (0-06-000800-8). In this thought-provoking look into the not-too-distant future, bioethicist McGee foresees a day when individuals may be able to take charge of their personal genome and ponders the ethical implications. (Rev: BL 10/1/03) [306.4]

10945 Marion, Robert. *Was George Washington Really the Father of Our Country? A Clinical Geneticist Looks at World History* (9–12). 1994, Addison-Wesley $22.95 (0-201-62255-6). An exploration of the impact of genetic abnormalities on world history, including Washington's sterility, Napoleon's growth hormone deficiency, and Lincoln's Marfan's syndrome. (Rev: BL 1/15/94) [909.08]

10946 Marshall, Elizabeth L. *The Human Genome Project: Cracking the Code Within Us* (8–12). Illus. 1996, Watts LB $18.95 (0-531-11299-3). Concepts in genetic research are discussed along with a history of the international Human Genome Project. (Rev: BL 12/1/96; SLJ 8/97) [547.87]

10947 Moore, David S. *The Dependent Gene: The Fallacy of Nature vs. Nurture* (10–12). 2002, W. H. Freeman $27.50 (0-7167-4024-9). This author contends that one of the most dangerous current scientific myths is the belief that genes dictate human characteristics and sets out to show why this belief is wrong. (Rev: BL 12/1/01) [576.5]

10948 Shannon, Thomas A. *Genetic Engineering: A Documentary History* (10–12). Series: Primary Documents in American History and Contemporary Issues. 1999, Greenwood $49.95 (0-313-30457-2). This is a collection of documents that deal with such topics as cloning, ethics, genetically altered food, and the Human Genome Project. [660.6]

10949 Tagliaferro, Linda. *Genetic Engineering: Progress or Peril?* (7–10). Illus. Series: Pro/Con Issues. 1997, Lerner LB $21.27 (0-8225-2620-7). This book presents the complex issues in the controversy over the manipulation of genes, such as the possibility of finding cures for hereditary diseases on the one hand, and on the other, the possibility of abusing it to create a made-to-order human race. (Rev: BL 9/1/97; SLJ 8/97) [575.1]

10950 Wade, Nicholas, ed. *The Science Times Book of Genetics* (10–12). 1999, Lyons Pr. $25.00 (1-55821-765-7). This resource contains some 40 articles on the history and structure of DNA, genetic research, and related ethical concerns, all from the *New York Times*. (Rev: BL 1/1–15/99; SLJ 7/99) [575.1]

10951 Watson, James, and Andrew Berry. *DNA: The Secret of Life* (10–12). Illus. 2003, Knopf $35.00 (0-375-41546-7). A clear explanation of the history of genetics with an interesting discussion of the various controversies, co-written by one of the two scientists who discovered the structure of DNA. (Rev: BL 3/1/03*) [576.5]

10952 Wilcox, Frank H. *DNA: The Thread of Life* (7–10). Illus. 1988, Lerner LB $23.93 (0-8225-

1584-9). The basic DNA structure and functions are explained. (Rev: SLJ 6/88) [574.87]

10953 Winters, Paul A. *Cloning* (8–12). Series: At Issue. 1997, Greenhaven LB $26.20 (1-56510-753-5); paper $17.45 (1-56510-752-7). The successful cloning of a sheep has ignited many ethical questions concerning its application to humans. This controversy is explored in this anthology of various points of view. (Rev: BL 5/15/98; SLJ 1/99; VOYA 8/98) [174.957]

10954 Yount, Lisa. *Biotechnology and Genetic Engineering* (6–12). 2000, Facts on File LB $45.00 (0-8160-4000-1). An excellent resource that gives an overview of genetic engineering plus chapters on scientific achievements, ethnical concerns, court battles, health issues, and scientific problems. (Rev: BL 7/00*) [303.48]

10955 Yount, Lisa, ed. *Cloning* (8–12). Series: Contemporary Issues Companion. 2000, Greenhaven LB $21.96 (0-7377-0330-X); paper $13.96 (0-7377-0329-6). The science and ethics of cloning are covered in this collection of more than 20 articles that cover developments through 1999. (Rev: BL 12/15/00) [571.8]

10956 Yount, Lisa, ed. *Genetic Engineering* (6–12). Series: Current Controversies. 2002, Gale LB $32.45 (0-7377-1124-8); paper $21.20 (0-7377-1123-X). This anthology explores various aspects and attitudes toward this controversial subject, with a good representation of differing viewpoints from known authorities. (Rev: BL 8/02) [575.1]

10957 Yount, Lisa. *Genetics and Genetic Engineering: Milestones in Discovery and Invention* (6–12). Illus. Series: Milestones in Discovery and Invention. 1997, Facts on File $25.00 (0-8160-3566-0). A clear explanation of genetics and its key concepts, with materials on heredity, gene mapping, the structure of DNA, disease-causing genes, and gene therapy. (Rev: BL 12/1/97) [576.5]

Grooming, Personal Appearance, and Dress

10958 Banks, Tyra, and Vanessa T. Bush. *Tyra's Beauty Inside and Out* (10–12). 1998, HarperCollins paper $16.95 (0-06-095210-5). A successful model shares her beauty secrets for skin care, cosmetics, hair, exercise, and fashion. (Rev: SLJ 8/98; VOYA 10/98) [646]

10959 *Body Outlaws: Young Women Write About Body Image and Identity* (10–12). Ed. by Edut Ophira. 2001, Seal $14.95 (1-58005-043-3). This collection of 28 essays chronicles the writers' physical, emotional, and social problems and their paths to self-acceptance. (Rev: BL 1/1–15/02) [155.2]

10960 Bressler, Karen W., and Susan Redstone. *D.I.Y. Beauty* (7–12). Illus. 2000, Penguin paper $5.99 (0-14-130918-0). Beauty experts respond to teen comments on areas including skin care, hair care, and makeup, with an emphasis on safety and interviews with beauty celebrities. (Rev: SLJ 12/00)

10961 Coen, Patricia, and Joe Maxwell. *Beautiful Braids* (9–12). Illus. 1983, Crown paper $4.95 (0-517-55222-1). The techniques and types of hair braiding are introduced in text and pictures. [611]

10962 Dawson, Mildred L. *Beauty Lab: How Science Is Changing the Way We Look* (5–10). 1997, Silver Moon $14.95 (1-881889-84-X). This work on health and hygiene contains chapters on skin, eyes, teeth, fitness, and hair. (Rev: BR 5–6/97; SLJ 3/97) [613.7]

10963 Gay, Kathlyn, and Christine Whittington. *Body Marks: Tattooing, Piercing, and Scarification* (6–12). Illus. 2002, Millbrook LB $29.90 (0-7613-2352-X); paper $14.95 (0-7613-1742-2). A look at the history of body modification around the world, with color photographs and discussion of current trends. (Rev: BL 12/1/02; HBG 3/03; SLJ 10/02) [391.6]

10964 Glicksman, Jane. *The Art of Mehndi* (6–12). Illus. 2000, NTC paper $4.95 (0-7373-0458-8). The practice of drawing on the body with henna is discussed with material on its history and easy do-it-yourself projects. (Rev: BL 10/15/00) [391.6]

10965 Griffin, Karol. *Skin Deep: Tattoos, the Disappearing West, Very Bad Men, and My Deep Love for Them All* (10–12). 2003, Harcourt $24.00 (0-15-100884-1). Best suited for mature teens, this book serves up an embarrassment of riches — one woman's story of how she became a tattoo artist, a history of tattooing and a look at the subculture surrounding the practice, and a fascinating examination of interpersonal relationships. (Rev: BL 8/03*) [391. 6]

10966 Gross, Kim Johnson, and Jeff Stone. *What Should I Wear? Dressing for Occasions* (9–12). Illus. 1998, Knopf $30.00 (0-375-40245-4). Teenagers and young adults agonizing over what to wear for a special event will find useful and informative advice here. (Rev: BL 12/1/98) [391]

10967 Mingay, Marie. *Nail Style: Beautiful Nails for Every Occasion* (10–12). Illus. 2001, Sterling paper $12.95 (0-8069-6669-6). Along with material on good manicure and pedicure, the book gives details on 40 styles of nail art. (Rev: BL 11/15/01) [646.7]

10968 Murray, Maggie Pexton. *Changing Styles in Fashion: Who, What, Why* (10–12). Illus. 1989, Fairchild $46.00 (0-87005-585-2). The world of

high fashion past and present is introduced and several modern couturiers are highlighted. (Rev: BL 4/15/89) [746.92]

10969 Odes, Rebecca, et al. *The Looks Book: A Whole New Approach to Beauty, Body Image, and Style* (7–10). Illus. 2002, Penguin paper $18.00 (0-14-200211-9). Teens looking to learn more about style trends and beauty tips will find ideas in this attractive, colorful book. (Rev: BL 1/1–15/03) [646.7]

10970 Peiss, Kathy. *Hope in a Jar: The Making of America's Beauty Culture* (9–12). 1998, Holt $25.00 (0-8050-5550-9). This is a fascinating look at the history and use of cosmetics in America from colonial days to modern times. (Rev: BL 5/15/98; SLJ 12/98) [391]

10971 Quant, Mary. *Ultimate Makeup and Beauty* (10–12). 1996, DK $24.95 (0-7894-1056-7). An attractive, well-illustrated guide to makeup that uses examples from various ethnic groups as well as different facial shapes. (Rev: SLJ 2/97) [646]

10972 Roach, Martin. *Dr. Martens: The Story of an Icon* (10–12). Illus. 2004, Chrysalis paper $14.95 (1-844110-11-7). Photographs of stars wearing the clunky footwear are accompanied by a discussion of their appearance on the fashion scene and exploration of the social groups that have embraced them. (Rev: BL 12/15/03) [391.4130941]

10973 Silverstein, Alvin, et al. *Overcoming Acne: The How and Why of Healthy Skin Care* (7–12). 1990, Morrow $16.00 (0-688-08344-7). This should be a popular book considering that 90 percent of adolescents suffer from some form of acne and that this account is thorough and balanced. (Rev: BL 4/15/90; SLJ 6/90) [616.5]

10974 Sneddon, Pamela Shires. *Body Image: A Reality Check* (6–10). Series: Issues in Focus. 1999, Enslow LB $20.95 (0-89490-960-6). This book discusses body image and actions, often destructive, that people take to control it, including anorexia, bulimia, steroid use, cosmetic surgery, and body piercing. (Rev: BL 5/1/99; SLJ 7/99) [155.9]

10975 Weiss, Stefanie Iris. *Coping with the Beauty Myth: A Guide for Real Girls* (7–12). Series: Coping. 2002, Rosen LB $26.50 (0-8239-3757-7). Readers are urged to ignore unrealistic images presented in the media and to accept their own attributes and deficiencies as well as those of others. (Rev: SLJ 8/00) [155.5]

10976 Weiss, Stefanie Iris. *Everything You Need to Know About Mehndi, Temporary Tattoos, and Other Temporary Body Art* (8–12). Illus. Series: Need to Know Library. 2000, Rosen LB $17.95 (0-8239-3086-6). This account explores the cultural backgrounds associated with drawing on the body with henna, suggests methods of applying henna, and gives suggestions for patterns. (Rev: BL 7/00) [391.6]

10977 Wilkinson, Beth. *Coping with the Dangers of Tattooing, Body Piercing, and Branding* (9–12). Series: Coping. 1998, Rosen $17.95 (0-8239-2717-2). Tattooing, body piercing, and branding are discussed, including descriptions of the procedures, health risks, care following the procedures, and first-person experiences. The dangers and potential negative consequences are stressed. (Rev: BR 9–10/98; SLJ 4/98; VOYA 8/98) [391]

The Human Body

General and Miscellaneous

10978 Brewer, Sarah, and Naomi Craft. *1001 Facts About the Human Body* (7–12). Illus. Series: Backpack Books. 2002, DK paper $8.95 (0-7894-8451-X). A handy-sized book full of illustrations that gives basic, encyclopedia-style information on the human body. (Rev: BL 3/15/02) [612]

10979 Brynie, Faith. *101 Questions About Your Immune System You Felt Defenseless to Answer . . . Until Now* (7–12). Illus. 2000, Twenty-First Century $27.90 (0-7613-1569-1). A question-and-answer format is used to explain the functioning and vulnerabilities of the immune system. (Rev: BL 6/1–15/00; HBG 9/00; SLJ 9/00; VOYA 4/01) [616.07]

10980 Brynie, Faith. *101 Questions About Your Skin* (7–12). Series: 101 Questions. 1999, Twenty-First Century LB $25.90 (0-7613-1259-5). This comprehensive, well-illustrated look at the composition, care, and diseases of the skin also includes information on tattooing, the effects of the sun, and aging and will attract both report writers and browsers. (Rev: HBG 4/00; SLJ 11/99) [612.7]

10981 *Incredible Voyage: Exploring the Human Body* (9–12). 1998, National Geographic $35.00 (0-7922-7148-3). Interesting text and outstanding photographs trace human growth, anatomy, and physiology through all stages of life, sick or healthy, with information on many of the innovative, developing breakthroughs that are in the news. (Rev: SLJ 2/99) [612]

10982 Kim, Melissa L. *The Endocrine and Reproductive Systems* (5–10). Illus. Series: Human Body Library. 2003, Enslow LB $18.95 (0-7660-2020-7). Kim uses a conversational style to introduce detailed facts about these two body systems, with useful graphics and some practical advice. (Rev: BL 4/15/03; HBG 10/03) [612.4]

10983 Little, Marjorie. *The Endocrine System* (10–12). Series: 21st Century Health and Wellness. 2000, Chelsea LB $24.95 (0-7910-5982-0). This book dis-

cusses all the endocrine glands, with emphasis on the pituitary and the thyroid. (Rev: BL 11/15/00; HBG 10/01) [612]

10984 Llamas, Andreu. *Digestion and Reproduction* (8–12). Illus. Series: Human Body. 1998, Gareth Stevens LB $23.93 (0-8368-2111-4). Using double-page spreads and lavish illustrations, the digestive and reproductive systems are explained. (Rev: BL 12/15/98; HBG 9/99; SLJ 3/99) [612]

10985 Llamas, Andreu. *Respiration and Circulation* (8–12). Illus. Series: Human Body. 1998, Gareth Stevens LB $23.93 (0-8368-2110-6). Double-page spreads and lavish illustrations are used to introduce the human respiration and circulation systems. (Rev: BL 12/15/98; HBG 9/99; SLJ 3/99) [612.1]

10986 *Major Systems of the Body* (9–12). Illus. Series: 21st Century Science. 2002, World Almanac LB $21.95 (0-8368-5007-6). This guide to the systems of the human body offers extensive information about the functioning of the five senses, as well as the nervous, reproductive, respiratory, and other systems. (Rev: BL 12/1/02; SLJ 5/03) [612]

10987 Nilsson, Lennart. *Behold Man: A Photographic Journey of Discovery Inside the Body* (7–12). Illus. 1974, Little, Brown $29.95 (0-316-60751-7). An unusually illustrated book (many photographs represent magnifications of 45,000 times) on the body and its systems. [612]

10988 Orlock, Carol. *Inner Time: The Science of Body Clocks and What Makes Us Tick* (9–12). 1993, Birch Lane $18.95 (1-55972-194-4). A lively overview of the discoveries and science of biological clocks. (Rev: BL 8/93) [574.1882]

10989 *The Structure of the Body* (9–12). Illus. Series: 21st Century Science. 2002, World Almanac LB $21.95 (0-8368-5008-4). This information-packed guide to anatomy focuses first on the cells and progresses to other structural components such as the skin, bones, muscles, and blood. (Rev: BL 12/1/02; SLJ 5/03) [611]

10990 Walker, Pam, and Elaine Wood. *The Immune System* (8–12). Illus. Series: Understanding the Human Body. 2002, Gale LB $21.96 (1-59018-151-4). This is a report-worthy text with useful information about this system in the human body, including some of the diseases relating to it. (Rev: BL 11/1/02; SLJ 2/03) [616.07]

10991 Whitfield, Philip, ed. *The Human Body Explained: A Guide to Understanding the Incredible Living Machine* (9–12). 1995, Holt $56.80 (0-8050-3752-7). A guide to the body, discussing the major organs in terms of day-to-day life and their function in the survival of the species. (Rev: BL 12/1/95) [612]

Brain and Nervous System

10992 August, Paul Nordstrom. *Brain Function* (9–12). Illus. 1987, Chelsea LB $19.95 (0-55546-204-9). An introduction to the nervous system that gives details on the brain and how drugs affect it. (Rev: BL 2/15/88) [612]

10993 Barrett, Susan L. *It's All in Your Head: A Guide to Understanding Your Brain and Boosting Your Brain Power* (6–10). Illus. 1992, Free Spirit paper $10.95 (0-915793-45-8). Covers subjects as diverse as brain anatomy, intelligence, biofeedback, creativity, ESP, and brain scans. (Rev: BL 2/15/93) [153]

10994 Bayer, Linda. *Sleep Disorders* (6–12). Series: Encyclopedia of Psychological Disorders. 2000, Chelsea LB $24.95 (0-7910-5314-8). Insomnia, sleepwalking, and other sleep-related disorders are discussed. (Rev: BL 1/1–15/01; HBG 10/01; SLJ 2/01) [612.8]

10995 Berger, Melvin. *Exploring the Mind and Brain* (7–10). Illus. 1983, HarperCollins LB $12.89 (0-690-04252-3). A book about the functions — both normal and abnormal — of the brain. [612]

10996 Brynie, Faith. *Perception* (6–10). Series: Amazing Brain. 2001, Blackbirch LB $21.95 (1-56711-423-7). An introduction to the brain's role in perception and to disorders that can occur. (Rev: BL 10/15/01; HBG 3/02) [612]

10997 Brynie, Faith. *The Physical Brain* (6–10). Series: Amazing Brain. 2001, Blackbirch $29.94 (1-56711-424-5). Photographs and absorbing text introduce the physical characteristics of the brain. Also use *Neurological Disorders* (2001). (Rev: BL 10/15/01; HBG 3/02; SLJ 9/01; VOYA 10/01) [612.8]

10998 Carter, Rita. *Mapping the Mind* (10–12). 1998, Univ. of California Pr. $45.00 (0-520-21937-6); paper $24.95 (0-520-22461-2). Carter transports readers inside the human brain in this easy-to-understand introduction to brain research, neurobiology, and neurochemistry. (Rev: SLJ 11/99) [612.8]

10999 Edelson, Edward. *Nutrition and the Brain* (10–12). Illus. 1987, Chelsea LB $19.95 (1-55546-210-3). An explanation of how behavior and emotion are influenced by food. (Rev: BL 2/1/88) [612]

11000 Edelson, Edward. *Sleep* (7–10). Series: Encyclopedia of Health. 1991, Chelsea LB $19.95 (0-7910-0092-3). This book discusses the uses of sleep, people's sleeping habits, and sleeping disorders. (Rev: BL 11/15/91) [612.8]

11001 Finger, Stanley. *Minds Behind the Brain: A History of the Pioneers and Their Discoveries* (10–12). Illus. 2000, Oxford $35.00 (0-19-508571-

X). In a readable, well-documented text, the author outlines the contributions and lives of the major figures in the history of brain research. (Rev: BL 2/1/00) [612.8]

11002 Greenfield, Susan A., ed. *The Human Mind Explained: An Owner's Guide to the Mysteries of the Mind* (10–12). 1996, Holt $40.00 (0-8050-4499-X). Using double-page spreads and clear, concise language, this book is a guide to the human brain's composition, areas, functions, processes, and disorders. (Rev: SLJ 5/97) [612]

11003 Hyde, Margaret O., and John F. Setaro. *When the Brain Dies First* (8–12). Illus. 2000, Watts LB $25.00 (0-531-11543-7). This book explores different kinds of brain damage, including skull fractures and Alzheimer's, as well as discussing brain death and giving advice on preventative measures. (Rev: BL 4/15/00; SLJ 7/00) [616.8]

11004 Llamas, Andreu. *The Nervous System* (8–12). Illus. Series: Human Body. 1998, Gareth Stevens LB $23.93 (0-8368-2113-0). The human nervous system is described with double-page spreads and lavish illustrations. (Rev: BL 12/15/98; HBG 9/99; SLJ 3/99) [612.8]

11005 McPhee, Andrew T. *Sleep and Dreams* (7–12). Illus. 2001, Watts LB $25.00 (0-531-11735-9). Normal sleep patterns, sleep deprivation, and sleep disorders (sleep walking and sleep apnea) are discussed along with the nature and symbolism of dreams. (Rev: BL 6/1–15/01; SLJ 8/01) [616.8]

11006 Policoff, Stephen P. *The Dreamer's Companion: A Beginner's Guide to Understanding Dreams and Using Them Creatively* (8–12). Illus. 1997, Chicago Review paper $12.95 (1-55652-280-0). This book covers mastering the art of lucid dreaming, the causes of dreams, how to analyze them, and how to keep a dream journal. (Rev: BL 5/15/98; SLJ 6/98) [154.63]

11007 Ratey, John J., and Albert M. Galaburda. *A User's Guide to the Brain: Perception, Attention, and the Four Theaters of the Brain* (10–12). 2001, Pantheon paper $14.95 (0-375-70107-9). This account introduces the parts of the brain, explains their functions, and gives advice on how to maintain a healthy brain. [612.8]

11008 Restak, Richard. *Brainscapes: An Introduction to What Neuroscience Has Learned About the Structure, Function, and Abilities of the Brain* (9–12). 1995, Hyperion $19.95 (0-7868-6113-4). A neurologist discusses major advances in knowledge about the brain. (Rev: BL 10/1/95) [612.8]

11009 Sekuler, Robert, and Randolph Blake. *Star Trek on the Brain: Alien Minds, Human Minds* (10–12). 1998, W. H. Freeman paper $21.95 (0-7167-3279-3). Episodes and concepts found in *Star Trek* are used to explain the human mind in this up-to-date primer on neurology and the nervous system. (Rev: SLJ 11/98) [616]

11010 Walker, Pam, and Elaine Wood. *The Brain and Nervous System* (8–12). Series: Understanding the Human Body. 2003, Gale LB $21.96 (1-59018-148-4). The roles of the nervous system and the brain in collecting information, processing it, and sending responses to the various parts of the body, are explained in this attractive introduction to this body system. (Rev: BL 3/15/03) [612]

Circulatory System

11011 Avraham, Regina. *Circulatory System* (9–12). Series: 21st Century Health and Wellness. 2000, Chelsea LB $24.95 (0-7910-5519-1). The organs of the circulatory system are described, with a discussion of heart problems and their prevention. [612.1]

11012 Brynie, Faith. *101 Questions About Blood and Circulation: With Answers Straight from the Heart* (6–10). Series: 101 Questions. 2001, Twenty-First Century LB $25.90 (0-7613-1455-5). A clear and comprehensive overview of the circulatory system, how it works, and the importance of proper diet and exercise. (Rev: HBG 10/01; SLJ 4/01) [612.1]

11013 Silverstein, Alvin, and Virginia Silverstein. *Heart Disease: America's #1 Killer*. Rev. ed. (7–10). Illus. 1985, HarperCollins LB $12.89 (0-397-32084-1). After a description of heart diseases, the authors present material on treatments and preventative measures. (Rev: BR 5–6/86; SLJ 1/86) [611]

11014 Silverstein, Alvin, and Virginia Silverstein. *Heartbeats: Your Body, Your Heart* (7–10). Illus. 1983, HarperCollins LB $13.89 (0-397-32038-8). Following a description of the heart and how it works, there are sections on heart disease and research. [612]

Digestive and Excretory Systems

11015 Avraham, Regina. *Digestive System* (9–12). Series: 21st Century Health and Wellness. 2000, Chelsea LB $24.95 (0-7910-5526-4). This book describes the digestive system, the organs involved, and how each functions. [612.3]

11016 Monroe, Judy. *Coping with Ulcers, Heartburn, and Stress-Related Stomach Disorders* (7–12). Series: Coping. 2000, Rosen LB $17.95 (0-8239-2971-X). Fictional case histories convey lots of information about a variety of uncomfortable stomach conditions, stressing the importance of prevention and early treatment. (Rev: SLJ 6/00) [616.3]

11017 Walker, Pam, and Elaine Wood. *The Digestive System* (8–12). Illus. Series: Understanding the Human Body. 2002, Gale LB $21.96 (1-59018-150-

6). This is a report-worthy text with useful information about the digestive system, some of the diseases relating to it, and the ways in which problems are diagnosed. (Rev: BL 11/1/02; SLJ 2/03) [612.3]

Musculoskeletal System

11018 Feinberg, Brian. *The Musculoskeletal System* (7–12). Series: Encyclopedia of Health. 1993, Chelsea LB $19.95 (0-7910-0028-1). An introduction to the muscles and bones in the human body and how they work together to form a single system. (Rev: BL 12/1/93) [612.7]

11019 Gold, Susan Dudley. *The Musculoskeletal System and the Skin* (5–10). Illus. Series: Human Body Library. 2003, Enslow LB $18.95 (0-7660-2023-1). Gold uses a conversational style to introduce detailed facts about the skeletal system, with useful graphics and some practical advice. (Rev: BL 4/15/03; HBG 10/03; SLJ 10/03) [612.7]

11020 Landau, Elaine. *Spinal Cord Injuries* (6–12). Illus. 2001, Enslow LB $20.95 (0-7660-1474-6). Stories of people who have suffered spinal cord injuries, including Gloria Estefan and Christopher Reeve, are interwoven with information on how spinal injuries affect the body and how patients cope. (Rev: BL 2/1/02; HBG 10/02) [617.4]

11021 Llamas, Andreu. *Muscles and Bones* (8–12). Series: Human Body. 1998, Gareth Stevens LB $23.93 (0-8368-2112-2). The musculoskeletal system is introduced in a series of double-page spreads with lavish illustrations. (Rev: BL 12/15/98; HBG 9/99; SLJ 3/99) [612]

11022 Vogel, Steven. *Prime Mover: A Natural History of Muscle* (9–12). Illus. 2002, Norton $25.95 (0-393-02126-2). This lucid account traces how we found out about muscles in both humans and other animals, their makeup, how they work, and how we work them. (Rev: BL 12/15/01) [612.7]

TEETH

11023 Siegel, Dorothy. *Dental Health* (7–12). Series: Encyclopedia of Health. 1994, Chelsea LB $19.95 (0-7910-0014-1). An explanation of what teeth are made of, their uses, diseases, and how to take care of them. (Rev: BL 1/1/94) [617.6]

Respiratory System

11024 Kittredge, Mary. *The Respiratory System* (9–12). Series: 21st Century Health and Wellness. 2000, Chelsea LB $24.95 (0-7910-5524-8). As well as a description of the respiratory system and its components, this book describes such ailments as lung cancer and pneumonia. [612.2]

Senses

11025 Burr, Chandler. *The Emperor of Scent: A Story of Perfume, Obsession, and the Last Mystery of the Senses* (10–12). Illus. 2003, Random $25.95 (0-375-50797-3). By turns amusing and disturbing, this is an absorbing story of how mainstream science frustrated biophysicist Luca Turin's attempts to advance his theory about the science of smell. (Rev: BL 12/1/02*) [612.8]

Hygiene and Physical Fitness

11026 Barbour, Scott, and Karin L. Swisher, eds. *Health and Fitness* (7–12). Series: Opposing Viewpoints. 1996, Greenhaven $26.20 (1-56510-403-X). Using carefully selected articles, this book explores different attitudes and controversies concerning diet, physical fitness, and exercise. (Rev: BL 9/15/96; BR 1–2/97; SLJ 8/96; VOYA 10/96) [613]

11027 Brody, Jane. *Jane Brody's The New York Times Guide to Personal Health* (9–12). Illus. 1982, Random $19.95 (0-686-95972-8); Avon paper $15.00 (0-380-64121-6). A popular introduction to topics relating to health and medicine with emphasis on everyday concerns, prevention, and treatments. [613]

11028 Bull, Deborah C., and Torje Eike. *Totally Fit* (10–12). 1998, DK paper $11.95 (0-7894-2990-X). Though written for adults, this guide to complete fitness through dieting, nutrition, and exercise will appeal to older teens. (Rev: BL 2/15/98; SLJ 7/98) [613]

11029 Christensen, Alice. *The American Yoga Association Beginners' Manual*. Rev. ed. (10–12). Illus. 1987, Simon & Schuster paper $16.00 (0-671-61935-7). A basic manual on the philosophy and practice of yoga with material on 75 postures. (Rev: BL 9/1/87) [613.7]

11030 Feuerstein, Georg, and Stephan Bodian, eds. *Living Yoga: A Comprehensive Guide for Daily Life* (9–12). 1993, Putnam paper $16.95 (0-87477-729-1). Interviews, essays, and articles on yoga's practices and teachings. (Rev: BL 3/15/93) [181.45]

11031 Fitness Magazine, and Karen Andes, eds. *The Complete Book of Fitness: Mind, Body, Spirit* (9–12). 1999, Three Rivers paper $24.95 (0-609-80155-4). A highly readable, oversize book divided into four sections covering all aspects of fitness: strength training, cardiovascular training, diet and nutrition, and wellness. (Rev: SLJ 8/99) [613.7]

11032 Gallagher-Mundy, Chrissie. *The Essential Guide to Stretching* (10–12). 1997, Crown paper $17.00 (0-517-88775-4). A visually attractive guide to stretching: its purpose; warmups; detailed beginning, intermediate, and advanced routines; and stretches for specific personal needs and for particular sports. (Rev: SLJ 11/97) [613.7]

11033 Jenner, Bruce, and Bill Dobbins. *The Athletic Body: A Complete Fitness Guide for Teenagers — Sports, Strength, Health, Agility* (7–12). Illus. 1984, Simon & Schuster $17.95 (0-671-46549-X). A guide to physical fitness through sports, weight training, and good nutrition. [613.7]

11034 Johnson, Marlys. *Understanding Exercise Addiction* (7–12). Series: Teen Eating Disorder Prevention Library. 2000, Rosen LB $17.95 (0-8239-2990-6). This book offers teens the opportunity to assess whether attitudes toward exercise, eating, and the human body are normal. (Rev: SLJ 7/00) [616.86]

11035 Kaminker, Laura. *Exercise Addiction: When Fitness Becomes an Obsession* (6–10). Series: Teen Health Library of Eating Disorder Prevention. 1998, Rosen LB $26.50 (0-8239-2759-8). Some teens become addicted to exercise and exercise too much for the wrong reasons. This book defines the problem, risks, and causes, describes the symptoms, and tells where to get help and support if needed. (Rev: BL 3/1/89; BR 5–6/99; SLJ 1/99) [613.7]

11036 Milan, Albert R. *Breast Self-Examination* (10–12). Illus. 1980, Workman paper $3.50 (0-89480-124-4). A well-illustrated manual on how to conduct a breast examination. [613]

11037 Rosas, Debbie, and Carlos Rosas. *Non-Impact Aerobics: Introducing the NIA Technique* (9–12). Illus. 1988, Avon paper $9.95 (0-380-70522-2). A stress-free exercise system is described in this account with many photographs. (Rev: SLJ 10/88) [613.7]

11038 Self Magazine. *Self's Better Body Book* (9–12). 1998, Clarkson Potter $24.95 (0-609-60319-1). An exercise book with illustrated, step-by-step instructions for young women who want stronger, healthier bodies, also stressing the importance of good nutrition. (Rev: SLJ 11/98) [613.7]

11039 Simon, Nissa. *Good Sports: Plain Talk About Health and Fitness for Teens* (7–10). Illus. 1990, HarperCollins LB $14.89 (0-690-04904-8). This book covers a variety of topics including nutrition, different kinds of exercise, and sports injuries. (Rev: BCCB 12/99; BL 9/15/90) [613]

11040 Sivananda, Swami, and Swami Vishnu de Vananda. *Yoga Mind and Body* (10–12). 1996, DK $24.95 (0-7894-0447-8); paper $15.00 (0-7894-3301-X). Five main principles of yoga, based on "proper living and high thinking," are introduced through words and pictures, with a chapter devoted to each principle, the longest being on proper exercise. The chapter on vegetarianism contains 20 pages of recipes. (Rev: SLJ 7/96) [613.7]

11041 Spilner, Maggie. *Prevention's Complete Book of Walking: Everything You Need to Know to Walk Your Way to Better Health* (10–12). 2000, Rodale paper $14.95 (1-57954-236-0). This book on using walking as a means to fitness gives material on tools, techniques, training programs, workout plans, and treadmills. [613.7]

11042 Stiefer, Sandy. *A Risky Prescription* (7–12). Illus. Series: Sports Issues. 1997, Lerner LB $28.75 (0-8225-3304-9). This book explores the relationship between sports and health, how some sports activities can lead to disabilities, and how performance-enhancing drugs can compromise or even ruin one's health. (Rev: BL 12/1/97; HBG 3/98; SLJ 3/98) [631.7]

11043 Vedral, Joyce L. *Toning for Teens: The 20-Minute Workout That Makes You Look Good and Feel Great!* (7–12). 2002, Warner paper $15.95 (0-446-67815-5). Three sets of dumbbells and a bench or step are the only items required for this daily workout; nutritional and fitness tips are included. (Rev: SLJ 8/02)

Mental Disorders and Emotional Problems

11044 Abeel, Samantha. *My Thirteenth Winter* (7–12). 2003, Scholastic $15.95 (0-439-33904-9). Born with a learning disability, Abeel describes how she coped from kindergarten through college. (Rev: BL 2/15/04; HBG 4/04; SLJ 3/04; VOYA 4/04) [371.92]

11045 Adler, Joe Anne. *Stress: Just Chill Out!* (7–10). 1997, Enslow LB $17.95 (0-89490-918-5). This book identifies three types of stress frequently experienced by teenagers — life transition stress, enduring life stress, and chronic daily stress — with chapters on their causes and treatment. (Rev: SLJ 10/97) [152.4]

11046 *Aquamarine Blue 5: Personal Stories of College Students with Autism* (10–12). Ed. by Dawn Prince-Hughes. 2002, Ohio Univ. $32.95 (0-8040-1053-6); paper $14.95 (0-8040-1054-4). A collection of inspiring personal stories that will give insight to "normal" people. (Rev: BL 11/15/02) [371.94]

11047 Axelrod, Toby. *Working Together Against Teen Suicide* (6–10). Series: Library of Political Assassinations. 1996, Rosen LB $16.95 (0-8239-2261-8). The author examines the reasons for teenage suicide, suggests ways teens can cope with problems, and explains how telephone hotlines,

community agencies, and institutions work to combat teen suicide and how teenagers can help. (Rev: SLJ 5/97) [394]

11048 Barrett, Deirdre. *The Pregnant Man and Other Cases from a Hypnotherapist's Couch* (10–12). 1998, Times Books $23.00 (0-8129-2905-5). Using seven case studies, the author, a hypnotist, shows how hypnotherapy can be helpful when used in conjunction with traditional psychotherapy, and explains why hypnosis will work for some and not others and how people are treated. (Rev: BL 8/98; SLJ 12/98) [154.7]

11049 Bayer, Linda. *Out of Control: Gambling and Other Impulse-Control Disorders* (6–12). Series: Encyclopedia of Psychological Disorders. 2000, Chelsea LB $24.95 (0-7910-5313-X). This account explores the nature, causes, and treatment of such types of compulsive behavior as gambling, kleptomania, pyromania, and hair pulling. (Rev: BL 1/1–15/01; HBG 3/01) [363.4]

11050 Bayer, Linda. *Personality Disorders* (6–12). Illus. Series: Encyclopedia of Psychological Disorders. 2000, Chelsea $27.45 (0-7910-5317-2). Ten types of personality disorders — including paranoid, schizoid, and antisocial — are defined and discussed in this informative account. (Rev: BL 6/1–15/00; HBG 9/00; SLJ 9/00) [616.89]

11051 Bayer, Linda. *Uneasy Lives: Understanding Anxiety Disorders* (8–12). Series: Encyclopedia of Psychological Disorders. 2000, Chelsea LB $27.45 (0-7910-5316-4). Anxiety disorders such as panic attacks, phobias, and obsessive-compulsive disorder are discussed. (Rev: HBG 9/00) [616.85]

11052 Bellenir, Karen, ed. *Mental Health Information for Teens: Health Tips About Mental Health and Mental Illness* (7–12). Series: Teen Health. 2001, Omnigraphics $48.00 (0-7808-0442-2). A comprehensive and easy-to-use overview of topics ranging from self-esteem and physical appearance to abuse, addiction, and specific disorders and phobias, with tips on getting treatment. (Rev: BL 1/1–15/02; SLJ 1/02) [616.89]

11053 Bernstein, Jane. *Loving Rachel: A Family's Journey from Grief* (9–12). 1994, Coyne & Chenoweth paper $15.00 (0-941038-01-7). A mother's story of how she raised her second daughter who was born with learning disorders. (Rev: BL 5/1/88) [362.3]

11054 Bowman-Kruhm, Mary, and Claudine G. Wirths. *Everything You Need to Know About Learning Disabilities* (6–12). Series: Need to Know Library. 1999, Rosen LB $17.95 (0-8239-2956-6). An introduction to learning disabilities and how people cope with them at school and in everyday life, with fictionalized case studies and information on getting help. (Rev: SLJ 1/00; VOYA 4/00) [616.85]

11055 Clarke, Alicia. *Coping with Self-Mutilation: A Helping Book for Teens Who Hurt Themselves* (7–10). Series: Coping. 1999, Rosen LB $25.25 (0-8239-2559-5). This volume defines various forms of self-mutilation, such as cutting and burning, examines the causes and the physiological and psychological effects, and discusses available treatments and self-help measures. (Rev: SLJ 5/99) [362.2]

11056 Cobain, Bev. *When Nothing Matters Anymore: A Survival Guide for Depressed Teens* (7–12). 1998, Free Spirit paper $13.95 (1-57542-036-8). The author, a psychiatric nurse who works with teens, discusses the types, causes, and warning signs of depression, the dangers of addictions and eating disorders, and the relationship between depression and suicide, and provides information on treatment options and suggestions for developing good mental and physical health. (Rev: SLJ 3/99; VOYA 2/99) [155]

11057 Connelly, Elizabeth Russell. *A World Upside Down and Backwards* (9–12). Series: Encyclopedia of Psychological Disorders. 1998, Chelsea $22.95 (0-7910-4894-2). Using brief case studies, this book explores the realities of dyslexia and other learning disorders, with material on the neurological and genetic origins and treatments, as well as examples of how they affect the classroom, family life, and society. Case studies of famous people who have overcome their learning disorder are included. (Rev: BL 4/1/99; SLJ 6/99) [371.91]

11058 Crook, Marion. *Teenagers Talk About Suicide* (7–12). 1988, NC Pr. paper $12.95 (1-55021-013-0). Interviews with 30 Canadian teenagers who have tried suicide are reprinted. (Rev: BR 9–10/88) [362.2]

11059 Davis, Brangien. *What's Real, What's Ideal: Overcoming a Negative Body Image* (7–12). Series: Teen Health Library of Eating Disorder Prevention. 1998, Rosen LB $26.50 (0-8239-2771-7). Because teenager's bodies are changing so quickly, many become confused about an ideal figure. This book describes why teens develop negative body images and offers suggestions for overcoming self-defeating perceptions. (Rev: BR 5–6/99; VOYA 4/99) [305.23]

11060 Demetriades, Helen A. *Bipolar Disorder, Depression, and Other Mood Disorders* (6–12). Series: Diseases and People. 2002, Enslow LB $20.95 (0-7660-1898-9). The causes and nature of unnatural mood swings and states of depression are examined and treatments that are currently available are discussed. (Rev: BL 12/15/02; HBG 3/03) [616.85]

11061 Dinner, Sherry H. *Nothing to Be Ashamed Of: Growing Up with Mental Illness in Your Family* (5–10). 1989, Lothrop LB $12.93 (0-688-08482-6). A psychologist gives good advice to those who live with a mentally ill person. (Rev: BL 6/1/89; BR 11–12/89; SLJ 4/89; VOYA 8/89) [616.89]

11062 Empfield, Maureen, and Nicholas Bakalar. *Understanding Teenage Depression: A Guide to Diagnosis, Treatment, and Management* (10–12). 2001, Holt paper $15.00 (0-8050-6761-2). This succinct resource for both parents and teens offers current information on the diagnosis and treatment of teenage depression, with information on both drug and "talk" therapies. (Rev: BL 8/01) [616.85]

11063 Fynn, Anna. *Mister God, This Is Anna* (10–12). 1985, Ballantine paper $5.99 (0-345-32722-5). The haunting story of the life and death of a London waif. [155.4]

11064 Garland, E. Jane. *Depression Is the Pits, but I'm Getting Better: A Guide for Adolescents* (9–12). 1997, Magination paper $12.95 (1-55798-458-1). This guide explains the nature, causes, and treatment of depression and recounts the experiences of teens who've experienced and overcome this problem. [616.85]

11065 Gilbert, Paul. *Overcoming Depression: A Step-By-Step Approach to Gaining Control over Depression*. 2nd ed. (10–12). 2001, Oxford paper $15.95 (0-19-514311-6). This work explains the causes and effects of depression and offers advice on how to overcome it. [616.85]

11066 Gordon, James S. *Stress Management* (8–12). Illus. Series: 21st Century Health and Wellness. 2000, Chelsea LB $24.95 (0-7910-5987-1). This is a comprehensive and detailed examination of the causes of stress, the negative impact of stress, and ways to reduce stress. (Rev: BL 11/15/00; BR 3–4/01; HBG 10/01; SLJ 2/01) [362]

11067 Grob, Gerald N. *The Mad Among Us: A History of the Care of America's Mentally Ill* (9–12). 1994, Free Pr. $24.95 (0-02-912695-9). An overview of the changing attitudes toward and the treatment of mental illness, showing the 20th-century progression from an asylum-related to a private-office practice. (Rev: BL 2/1/94) [362.2]

11068 Grollman, Earl A., and Max Malikow. *Living When a Young Friend Commits Suicide: Or Even Starts Talking About It* (6–12). 1999, Beacon $24.00 (0-8070-2502-X); paper $12.00 (0-8070-2503-8). Using simple prose and a compassionate attitude, this book examines suicide from many standpoints and gives good advice on the grieving process. (Rev: BL 11/1/99; SLJ 1/00; VOYA 2/00) [368.28]

11069 Gutkind, Lee. *Stuck in Time: The Tragedy of Childhood Mental Illness* (9–12). 1993, Holt $25.00 (0-8050-1469-1). An eye-opening view of a health care system ill-equipped to deal with the problems of mentally ill youth. (Rev: BL 7/93; SLJ 1/94) [616.89]

11070 Harmon, Dan. *Schizophrenia: Losing Touch with Reality* (8–12). Series: Encyclopedia of Psychological Disorders. 2000, Chelsea LB $27.45 (0-7910-4953-1). This author describes the mental condition known as schizophrenia, its symptoms, diagnosis, and treatments. (Rev: SLJ 1/00) [616.89]

11071 Hermes, Patricia. *A Time to Listen: Preventing Youth Suicide* (8–12). 1987, Harcourt $13.95 (0-15-288196-4). Through questions and answers plus many case studies, the author explores many aspects of suicidal behavior and its causes. (Rev: BL 4/1/88; SLJ 3/88; VOYA 6/88) [362.2]

11072 Hurley, Jennifer A., ed. *Mental Health* (7–12). Series: Current Controversies. 1999, Greenhaven LB $32.45 (1-56510-953-8); paper $21.20 (1-56510-952-X). This anthology explores such questions as what constitutes good mental health, what treatments should be used for mentally ill patients, and how society and the legal system should respond to mentally ill people. (Rev: BL 7/99) [616.89]

11073 Hyde, Margaret O., and Elizabeth H. Forsyth. *Depression: What You Need to Know* (6–12). Illus. 2002, Watts $24.00 (0-531-11892-4). Information on celebrities and important figures who have experienced depression add to the details on the history, symptoms, and treatment of the condition. (Rev: BL 10/15/02; SLJ 12/02) [616.85]

11074 Hyman, Bruce M., and Cherry Pedroch. *Obsessive-Compulsive Disorder* (7–10). 2003, Millbrook LB $26.90 (0-7613-2758-4). Profiles of teens with OCD introduce a discussion of the condition that will aid understanding and will be useful for teens experiencing anxieties. (Rev: BL 12/15/03; HBG 4/04; SLJ 1/04; VOYA 2/04) [616.85]

11075 Irwin, Cait. *Conquering the Beast Within: How I Fought Depression and Won . . . And How You Can, Too* (9–12). 1999, Times Books paper $14.00 (0-8129-3247-1). A frank account of a long battle with depression, with solid advice for readers who are suffering from this affliction. (Rev: SLJ 2/00; VOYA 2/00) [616.85]

11076 Kaysen, Susanna. *Girl Interrupted* (10–12). 1994, Vintage paper $12.00 (0-679-74604-8). At the age of 18, the author was hospitalized in psychiatry ward for teens; the brief essays in this book describe with perception and wit her own experiences and those of other patients. (Rev: BL 4/1/93; BR 1/94) [362]

11077 Kent, Deborah. *Snake Pits, Talking Cures, and Magic Bullets: A History of Mental Illness* (6–12). Illus. 2003, Millbrook LB $26.90 (0-7613-2704-5). The madhouses of old, shock treatments,

psychotherapy, psychoanalysis, and today's effective drug therapies are among the topics discussed in this volume. (Rev: BL 5/1/03; HBG 4/04; SLJ 7/03) [616.89]

11078 Kersjes, Mike, and Joe Layden. *A Smile as Big as the Moon: A Teacher, His Class, and Their Unforgettable Journey* (9–12). 2002, St. Martin's $23.95 (0-312-27314-2). A group of kids with emotional and learning problems excel when they are taken to Space Camp in this inspiring book. (Rev: BL 12/15/01) [371.9]

11079 Kingsley, Jason, and Mitchell Levitz. *Count Us In: Growing Up with Down Syndrome* (9–12). 1994, Harcourt $19.95 (0-15-150447-4). The two authors write about their own experiences of living with Down's syndrome, including its effects on their families, marriage, sex, employment, ambitions, and education. (Rev: BL 11/15/93; SLJ 6/94) [362.1]

11080 Kuklin, Susan. *After a Suicide: Young People Speak Up* (7–12). 1994, Putnam $16.95 (0-399-22605-2). Focuses on failed suicide attempts. Also looks at friends and family members who suffer shock, guilt, and loss when suicide succeeds. (Rev: BL 10/15/94; SLJ 12/94; VOYA 2/95) [362.2]

11081 Landau, Elaine. *Autism* (7–12). Illus. 2001, Watts $24.00 (0-531-11780-4). This straightforward look at the history, symptoms, and treatment of autism includes personal stories. (Rev: BL 4/1/02; SLJ 12/01) [616.89]

11082 Leder, Jane. *Dead Serious: A Book for Teenagers About Teenage Suicide* (7–12). 1987, Avon paper $3.50 (0-380-70661-X). This book deals specifically with the symptoms of a suicidal situation and how to cope with the after-effects of the suicide of a relative or friend. (Rev: SLJ 8/87; VOYA 6/87) [179]

11083 Leigh, Vanora. *Mental Illness* (5–10). Series: Talking Points. 1999, Raintree Steck-Vaughn LB $27.12 (0-8172-5311-4). This book defines mental illness, gives examples, and discusses causes, treatments, and how to stay mentally healthy. (Rev: BL 8/99; BR 9–10/99; SLJ 8/99) [362.2]

11084 Levine, Mel. *Keeping a Head in School: A Student's Book About Learning Abilities and Learning Disorders* (8–12). Illus. 1990, Educators Publg. paper $24.75 (0-8388-2069-7). This account deals with all sorts of learning disorders, how they affect the learning process, and how they can be treated. (Rev: BL 6/15/90) [371.9]

11085 Markway, Barbara G., and Gregory P. Markway. *Painfully Shy: Mastering Social Anxiety and Reclaiming Your Life* (10–12). 2001, St. Martin's $23.95 (0-312-26628-6). Millions suffer from social anxiety disorder (extreme shyness), and this book describes the symptoms, causes, and methods for treating this problem. (Rev: BL 4/1/01) [616.85]

11086 Martin, Russell. *Out of Silence: A Journey into Language* (9–12). 1994, Holt $22.50 (0-8050-1998-7). Documents the continuing odyssey of the author's nephew, who was diagnosed as autistic after receiving a routine childhood inoculation. (Rev: BL 3/15/94) [616.8]

11087 Moe, Barbara. *Coping with Mental Illness* (7–10). Series: Coping. 2001, Rosen LB $18.95 (0-8239-3205-2). The diagnosis, symptoms, and treatment of major forms of mental illness are discussed, along with the types of professionals who can help. Also use *Schizophrenia* (2001). (Rev: SLJ 8/01) [616.89]

11088 Moehn, Heather. *Social Anxiety* (7–12). 2001, Rosen LB $25.25 (0-8239-3363-6). A strong fear of social situations often manifests itself during adolescence, and Moehn combines case studies and coping strategies with an overview of the condition itself and a look at treatment alternatives. (Rev: BL 3/1/02; SLJ 5/02) [616.85]

11089 Monroe, Judy. *Phobias: Everything You Wanted to Know, But Were Afraid to Ask* (6–10). Series: Issues in Focus. 1996, Enslow LB $20.95 (0-89490-723-9). This book on phobias contains an "A to Z" list detailing each phobia as well as information on causes, treatments, and where to get help. (Rev: SLJ 6/96; VOYA 8/96) [616.85]

11090 Moragne, Wendy. *Depression* (7–12). Illus. Series: Medical Library. 2001, Twenty-First Century LB $24.90 (0-7613-1774-0). Signs, symptoms, diagnosis, and treatment of depression are introduced clearly and concisely with case histories of seven teenagers. (Rev: BL 5/15/01; HBG 10/01; SLJ 4/01; VOYA 10/01) [616.85]

11091 Paquette, Penny Hutchins, and Cheryl Gerson Tuttle. *Learning Disabilities: The Ultimate Teen Guide* (7–12). Series: It Happened to Me. 2003, Scarecrow LB $32.50 (0-8108-4261-0). Teens suffering from conditions including ADHD and dyslexia will find practical information on these disabilities, success stories, and advice on career and employment choices and strategies. (Rev: SLJ 10/03) [371.9]

11092 Partner, Daniel. *Disorders First Diagnosed in Childhood* (6–12). Series: Encyclopedia of Psychological Disorders. 2000, Chelsea LB $24.95 (0-7910-5312-1). This work discusses the symptoms, causes, and treatments for such disorders as autism and Tourette's syndrome. (Rev: BL 1/1–15/01; HBG 10/01; SLJ 2/01) [616.8]

11093 Pickover, Clifford A. *Strange Brains and Genius: The Secret Lives of Eccentric Scientists and Madmen* (10–12). Illus. 1998, Plenum $28.95 (0-306-45784-9). The author explores the mental disorders of a number of geniuses and talented people, such as Ted Kaczynski, the Unabomber; Francis Galton, world traveler, inventor, and racist; and Nikola Tesla, who was incapable of conversation with anyone wearing pearls. (Rev: SLJ 4/99) [362.2]

11094 Porterfield, Kay M. *Straight Talk About Post-Traumatic Stress Disorder* (10–12). 1995, Facts on File $24.95 (0-8160-3258-0). PTSD (post-traumatic stress disorder) is discussed, with material on its causes, consequences, and ways of dealing with it, and including several case histories. (Rev: VOYA 2/96) [362.2]

11095 Porterfield, Kay Marie. *Straight Talk About Learning Disabilities* (6–12). 1999, Facts on File $27.45 (0-8160-3865-1). Using three fictional case studies, the author discusses various kinds of learning disabilities, their symptoms, methods of diagnosis, and available treatments. (Rev: BL 2/15/00; HBG 4/00; SLJ 2/00; VOYA 4/00) [371.92]

11096 Portner, Jessica. *One in Thirteen: The Silent Epidemic of Teen Suicide* (10–12). 2001, Gryphon House paper $13.00 (1-58904-001-5). As well as exploring the reasons why one in 13 U.S. teens attempts suicide, this account focuses on the case histories of three who succeeded. (Rev: BL 4/1/01; SLJ 8/01) [362.28]

11097 Powell, Mark. *Stress Relief: The Ultimate Teen Guide* (7–12). Series: Ultimate Teen Guide. 2003, Scarecrow LB $32.50 (0-8108-4433-8). Typical causes of teen stress — relationships, homework, money, and so forth — are examined and practical suggestions for dealing with them are spelled out. (Rev: BL 10/15/03; SLJ 7/03; VOYA 4/03) [155.5]

11098 Quinn, Patricia O. *Adolescents and ADD: Gaining the Advantage* (6–12). Illus. 1996, Magination paper $12.95 (0-945354-70-3). As well as citing many case studies, this book on teens and attention deficit disorder provides useful background information plus tips on how to adjust to this condition and how to create a lifestyle that accommodates it. (Rev: BL 1/1–15/96; SLJ 3/96; VOYA 8/96) [371.94]

11099 Roleff, Tamara L., ed. *Suicide* (8–12). Series: Opposing Viewpoints. 1997, Greenhaven LB $32.45 (1-56510-665-2); paper $21.20 (1-56510-664-4). Twenty-four articles express various points of view concerning the ethical and legal aspects of suicide, with special attention to the causes of teen suicide and how it can be prevented. (Rev: BL 11/1/97; BR 11–12/97; SLJ 1/98; VOYA 10/98) [362.28]

11100 Roleff, Tamara L., and Laura K. Egendorf, eds. *Mental Illness* (6–12). Illus. Series: Opposing Viewpoints. 2000, Greenhaven LB $21.96 (0-7377-

0347-4); paper $13.96 (0-7377-0348-2). Differing opinions are offered on a variety of issues relating to mental illness, including diagnosis, treatment, and therapy. (Rev: BL 1/1–15/01) [616.89]

11101 Rosen, Marvin. *The Effects of Stress and Anxiety on the Family* (6–12). Series: Focus on Family Matters. 2002, Chelsea LB $20.75 (0-7910-6950-8). After describing situations that produce stress and anxiety in families, this account outlines effective coping strategies for healthy management of these emotions. (Rev: BL 1/1–15/03; HBG 3/03) [152.4]

11102 Rosen, Marvin. *Understanding Post-Traumatic Stress Disorder* (6–12). Series: Focus on Family Matters. 2003, Chelsea $20.75 (0-7910-6951-6). After a discussion of trauma and situations that cause it in teenagers, this book examines PTSD, its symptoms, and ways in which one can get help. (Rev: BL 10/15/02; SLJ 6/03) [616.89]

11103 Rosenberg, Marsha Sarah. *Coping When a Brother or Sister Is Autistic* (7–12). Series: Coping. 2001, Rosen LB $18.95 (0-8239-3194-3). Siblings of autistic children will find facts about the diagnosis and treatment of the disorder, as well as sympathetic, no-nonsense advice on dealing with the pressures of the situation. (Rev: SLJ 9/01) [618.92]

11104 Sebastian, Richard. *Compulsive Behavior* (7–12). Series: Encyclopedia of Health. 1993, Chelsea LB $19.95 (0-7910-0044-3). This book explores the origins of compulsive behavior, its consequences, and its treatment. (Rev: BL 1/1/93) [616.85]

11105 Sheen, Barbara. *Attention Deficit Disorder* (6–10). Series: Diseases and Disorders. 2001, Lucent LB $19.96 (1-56006-828-0). A comprehensive look at the history, causes, diagnosis, symptoms, and treatment of ADD, with quotations from individuals who suffer from the disorder. (Rev: SLJ 9/01) [616.85]

11106 Shields, Charles. *Mental Illness and Its Effects on School and Work Environments* (6–10). Illus. Series: Encyclopedia of Psychological Disorders. 2000, Chelsea $24.95 (0-7910-5318-0). As well as giving a general introduction to the nature of mental illness, this work discusses how the mentally ill affect American society. (Rev: BL 11/1/00) [616.8]

11107 Silverstein, Alvin. *Depression* (6–10). Illus. Series: Diseases and People. 1997, Enslow LB $20.95 (0-89490-713-1). Topics covered in this appealing examination of depression include types, symptoms, and treatments. An extensive bibliography includes Internet sites. (Rev: BL 2/1/98; SLJ 4/98) [616.85]

11108 Silverstein, Alvin, and Virginia Silverstein. *Epilepsy* (7–10). Illus. 1975, HarperCollins $12.95 (0-397-31615-1). Sweeping aside all the untruths associated with this problem, the authors describe the cause and effect of seizures and their treatment. [616.8]

11109 Simpson, Carolyn, and Dwain Simpson. *Coping with Post-Traumatic Stress Disorder* (7–10). Series: Coping. 1997, Rosen LB $25.25 (0-8239-2080-1). Post-traumatic stress disorder (PTSD) affects people who have experienced natural disasters, rape, war, or other traumatic events. This book explains the causes and primary signs of PTSD and how it affects family and friends, as well as the victim, and provides useful information on treatment. (Rev: SLJ 10/97) [362]

11110 Steele, Ken, and Claire Berman. *The Day the Voices Stopped: A Memoir of Madness and Hope* (10–12). 2001, Basic $25.00 (0-465-08226-2). This is a sad but inspiring story of a schizophrenic who, for 23 years, heard interior voices that dominated his life. (Rev: BL 5/1/01) [616.89]

11111 Stewart, Gail B. *People with Mental Illness* (7–12). Series: The Other America. 2003, Gale LB $21.96 (1-59018-237-5). Personal stories of individuals with different conditions show how they cope with daily life and the impact on the families as well as the patients. (Rev: SLJ 6/03) [616.89]

11112 Stewart, Gail B. *Teen Dropouts* (7–12). Series: The Other America. 1998, Lucent LB $27.45 (1-56006-399-8). Four troubled teenagers — two girls and two boys — tell sad stories about how and why they have become alienated from the mainstream and have withdrawn from life. (Rev: BL 4/15/99; SLJ 4/99) [373.12]

11113 Stewart, Gail B. *Teens and Depression* (6–12). Illus. Series: The Other America. 1997, Lucent LB $27.45 (1-56006-577-X). A discussion of possible causes of teenage clinical depression and how to recognize and treat it as early as possible, supplemented by case studies of four teens and their battles to overcome the condition. (Rev: BL 5/15/98; SLJ 6/98; VOYA 10/98) [616.852700835]

11114 Tocci, Salvatore. *Down Syndrome* (7–12). Illus. 2000, Watts LB $25.00 (0-531-11589-5). This introduces the causes, symptoms, and treatments for the form of mental retardation that bears the name of Dr. John Langdon Down, who identified it in the 1860s. (Rev: BL 5/1/00; SLJ 7/00) [616.85]

11115 Toews, Miriam. *Swing Low* (10–12). 2001, Arcade $23.95 (1-55970-587-6). The memoir by a daughter whose father suffered from manic depression and, without suitable treatment, committed suicide. (Rev: BL 12/15/01) [616.89]

11116 Weaver, Robyn M. *Depression* (9–12). Series: Overview. 1998, Lucent LB $17.96 (1-56006-437-4). The nature and causes of this incapacitating condition are covered, with discussion of various treatments and the stigma that is still often attached to it. (Rev: BL 1/1–15/99; BR 5–6/99) [616.85]

11117 Williams, Julie. *Attention-Deficit / Hyperactivity Disorder* (6–12). Illus. Series: Diseases and People. 2001, Enslow LB $20.95 (0-7660-1598-X). Williams presents the symptoms, diagnosis, and treatment of ADHD, as well as its history, profiles of people who suffer from the condition, research that is being conducted, and the controversies that surround the condition. (Rev: BL 1/1–15/02; HBG 10/02; SLJ 2/02) [618.92]

11118 Williams, Julie. *Pyromania, Kleptomania, and Other Impulse-Control Disorders* (6–12). Series: Diseases and People. 2002, Enslow LB $20.95 (0-7660-1899-7). Various forms of abnormal mental obsessions are discussed with material on causes and treatments. (Rev: BL 12/15/02; HBG 3/03) [616.8]

11119 Wolff, Lisa. *Teen Depression* (6–12). Series: Overview: Teen Issues. 1998, Lucent LB $27.45 (1-56006-519-2). The complexities of teen depression and its causes, symptoms, and treatment are discussed. (Rev: BL 1/1–15/99) [616.85]

11120 Young, Patrick. *Schizophrenia* (9–12). Illus. 1988, Chelsea LB $19.95 (0-7910-0052-4). A look at the origins and treatment of this mysterious disease that sometimes emerges in the late teens. (Rev: BL 7/88; BR 9–10/88) [616.89]

11121 Zeinert, Karen. *Suicide: Tragic Choice* (6–12). Illus. Series: Issues in Focus. 1999, Enslow LB $19.95 (0-7660-1105-4). All aspects of suicide are covered including history, demographic patterns, causes, the grief of survivors, cluster suicide, and assisted suicide. (Rev: BL 12/15/99; HBG 4/00; VOYA 4/00) [362.28]

Nutrition and Diet

11122 Bellenir, Karen, ed. *Diet Information for Teens: Health Tips About Diet and Nutrition, Including Facts About Nutrients, Dietary Guidelines, Breakfasts, School Lunches, Snacks, Party Food, Weight Control, Eating Disorders, and More* (7–12). 2001, Omnigraphics $48.00 (0-7808-0441-4). General nutrition information is amplified by topics of particular interest to teens, such as snacking, school lunches, and eating disorders. (Rev: SLJ 6/01; VOYA 8/01) [613.2]

11123 Bijlefeld, Marjolijn, and Sharon K. Zoumbaris. *Food and You: A Guide to Healthy Habits for Teens* (7–12). 2001, Greenwood $45.00 (0-313-31108-0). A comprehensive guide to healthy eating, weight, and exercise that provides lots of information for report writers. (Rev: SLJ 11/01; VOYA 2/02) [613.7]

11124 Brody, Jane E. *Jane Brody's Nutrition Book: A Lifetime Guide to Good Eating for Better Health and Weight Control* (9–12). 1981, Norton $29.95 (0-393-01429-0). A straightforward calorie-based diet book that stresses sensible eating habits. [613.2]

11125 Craig, Jenny, and Brenda L. Wolfe. *Jenny Craig's What Have You Got to Lose? A Personalized Weight Management Program* (9–12). 1992, Villard $19.50 (0-679-40527-5). Guide to weight-management principles through a program of nutritious foods and regular exercise. (Rev: BL 3/1/92) [613.2]

11126 Dixon, Barbara M., and Josleen Wilson. *Good Health for African-Americans* (9–12). 1994, Crown $26.00 (0-517-59170-7). Nutritionist Dixon places African Americans' health challenges and solutions in historical context and offers advice on lifestyle improvement through a 24-week diet. (Rev: BL 2/15/94) [613]

11127 Drohan, Michele I. *Weight-Loss Programs: Weighing the Risks and Realities* (6–10). Illus. Series: Teen Health Library of Eating Disorder Prevention. 1998, Rosen LB $26.50 (0-8239-2770-9). This book explores weight-loss programs, sheds light on potential dangers, and discusses safe and sensible approaches to weight loss. (Rev: BL 3/1/99; SLJ 1/99) [616.85]

11128 Edelstein, Barbara. *The Woman Doctor's Diet for Teenage Girls* (9–12). 1987, Ballantine paper $5.99 (0-345-34601-7). A cautious approach is recommended in this guide to weight loss for teenage girls. [613.2]

11129 Greene, Bob. *The Get with the Program! Guide to Good Eating* (10–12). 2003, Simon & Schuster $24.00 (0-7432-4310-2). Oprah's trainer offers his suggestions for a sensible and healthy weight-loss eating plan. (Rev: BL 12/1/02) [613.2]

11130 Haas, Robert. *Eat to Win: The Sports Nutrition Bible* (9–12). 1983, NAL paper $5.99 (0-451-15509-2). A sports diet program that gives a 28-day menu program and recipes. [613.2]

11131 *The Human Fuel Handbook: Nutrition for Peak Athletic Performance* (9–12). 1988, Health for Life paper $24.95 (0-944831-17-6). Written primarily for athletes, this is a no-nonsense guide to top performance through proper diet. (Rev: BL 3/1/89) [613.2]

11132 Krizmanic, Judy. *A Teen's Guide to Going Vegetarian* (7–12). 1994, Viking $14.99 (0-670-85114-0); paper $10.99 (0-14-036589-3). Explains the health, ethical, and environmental benefits of switching to a vegetarian diet. Discusses nutrition and provides recipes. (Rev: BL 10/1/94; SLJ 2/95; VOYA 2/95) [613.2]

11133 Lamb, Lawrence E. *The Weighting Game: The Truth About Weight Control* (9–12). Illus. 1988, Lyle Stuart $15.95 (0-8184-0487-6). A practical account of what causes fat accumulation that stresses knowing your own body and learning to live with it. (Rev: BL 1/1/89) [613.2]

11134 Leon, Warren, et al. *Is Our Food Safe? A Consumer's Guide to Healthy Choices* (10–12). Illus. 2002, Crown paper $14.95 (0-609-80782-X). This guide to safe and healthy eating offers practical suggestions for minimizing one's chances of contracting foodborne or food-related illnesses. (Rev: BL 7/02) [613.2]

11135 MacClancy, Jeremy. *Consuming Culture: Why You Eat What You Eat* (9–12). 1993, Holt $23.00 (0-8050-2578-2). A multicultural romp through the history of world cuisine, presenting little-known facts about food taboos, fads, nutritional illogic, food politics, even cannibalism. (Rev: BL 6/1–15/93) [394.1]

11136 Moe, Barbara. *Understanding Negative Body Image* (6–10). Series: Teen Eating Disorder Prevention Library. 1999, Rosen $17.95 (0-8239-2865-9). Our culture stresses body weight and shape, and this book explores the many causes and harmful consequences of a negative body image. (Rev: BL 10/15/99; HBG 9/00; SLJ 1/00; VOYA 2/00) [613.4]

11137 Monroe, Judy. *Understanding Weight-Loss Programs* (6–10). Series: Teen Eating Disorder Prevention Library. 1999, Rosen LB $25.25 (0-8239-2866-7). This book discusses good and bad weight loss programs, how to evaluate them, and how to be on guard for bogus products. (Rev: BL 10/15/99; HBG 9/00; SLJ 1/00) [613.7]

11138 Nardo, Don. *Vitamins and Minerals* (7–12). Series: Encyclopedia of Health. 1994, Chelsea LB $19.95 (0-7910-0032-X). A description of the vitamins and minerals needed by the human body and the importance of each. (Rev: BL 8/94; VOYA 6/94) [613.2]

11139 Navarra, Tova, and Myron A. Lipkowitz. *Encyclopedia of Vitamins, Minerals and Supplements* (10–12). 1996, Facts on File $35.00 (0-8160-3183-5). This reference work contains more than 500 alphabetically arranged entries on vitamins, minerals, and food supplements, with information on their properties, benefits, proper dosage, and effects. (Rev: SLJ 11/96) [641.1]

11140 Nichter, Mimi. *Fat Talk: What Girls and Their Parents Say About Dieting* (9–12). 2000, Harvard Univ. Pr. $25.00 (0-674-00229-6); paper $16.95 (0-674-00681-X). This is a report gathered over a three-year period from more than 200 teenage girls about their attitudes toward appearance, eating habits, and dieting. [613.2]

11141 Parr, Jan. *The Young Vegetarian's Companion* (6–12). Illus. 1996, Watts LB $22.00 (0-531-11277-2). A guide to vegetarianism (with some horrifying descriptions of the meat industry) that stresses health and nutrition and provides a fine directory of further information sources such as films, online sites, and organizations. (Rev: BL 10/15/96; BR 3–4/97; SLJ 12/96; VOYA 6/97) [641.5]

11142 Peavy, Linda, and Ursula Smith. *Food, Nutrition, and You* (7–10). Illus. 1982, Macmillan LB $16.00 (0-684-17461-8). A discussion of digestion, food values, weight, and weight problems. [613.2]

11143 Pierson, Stephanie. *Vegetables Rock! A Complete Guide for Teenage Vegetarians* (7–12). 1999, Bantam paper $13.95 (0-553-37924-0). Animal rights and health issues are touched on in this book that describes philosophical and practical aspects of vegetarianism and provides a guide to good foods and balancing nutritional needs. (Rev: BL 3/1/99) [613.2]

11144 Polunin, Miriam. *Healing Foods: A Practical Guide to Key Foods for Good Health* (10–12). 1997, DK $24.95 (0-7894-1456-2). This is a rundown on the nutritional benefits of a variety of foods that also contains a great deal of food lore, recipes, and examples of 50 foods that promote good health. (Rev: BL 8/97; SLJ 9/97) [641.1]

11145 Reuben, David. *Everything You Always Wanted to Know About Nutrition* (9–12). 1979, Avon paper $4.50 (0-380-44370-8). Through a question-and-answer approach, basic information about foods and the food industry is given. [641.1]

11146 Sherman, Roberta Trattner, and Ron A. Thompson. *Bulimia: A Guide for Family and Friends* (9–12). 1997, Jossey-Bass paper $8.95 (0-7879-0361-2). A valuable resource for bulimia sufferers and their families, this profile of the eating disorder examines its insidious nature and what can be done to treat it. [616.85]

11147 Stare, Frederick J., et al. *Your Guide to Good Nutrition* (9–12). 1991, Prometheus paper $17.95 (0-87975-692-6). Professional, no-nonsense answers to basic questions about nutrition, weight control, dietary supplements, and the claims of the health food industry. (Rev: BL 10/1/91; SLJ 12/91) [613.2]

11148 Tattersall, Clare. *Understanding Food and Your Family* (6–10). Series: Teen Eating Disorder Prevention Library. 1999, Rosen $17.95 (0-8239-2860-8). Using many facts and references to case studies, this book describes family dynamics and how eating patterns are developed within the family structure. (Rev: BL 10/15/99; HBG 9/00; SLJ 11/99; VOYA 2/00) [616.85]

11149 Wann, Marilyn. *Fat! So? Because You Don't Have to Apologize for Your Size* (9–12). 1999, Ten

Speed paper $12.95 (0-89815-995-4). This breezy title filled with facts and humorous anecdotes, aimed largely at oversize women, preaches good health through eating right, exercise, and not worrying about weight. (Rev: SLJ 8/99; VOYA 12/99) [641.1]

11150 Winkler, Kathleen. *Vegetarianism and Teens: A Hot Issue* (9–12). Series: Hot Issues. 2001, Enslow LB $19.95 (0-7660-1375-8). As more teenagers embrace various forms of vegetarianism, this subject has become a source of increased controversy. This account examines varying attitudes and viewpoints. (Rev: BL 9/15/01; HBG 10/01) [613.2]

Physical Disabilities and Problems

11151 Cohen, Leah Hager. *Train Go Sorry: Inside a Deaf World* (9–12). 1994, Houghton paper $14 .00 (0-679-76165-9). This work by the grandchild of deaf immigrants covers many aspects of the world of the deaf. (Rev: BL 2/1/94; SLJ 12/94) [371.9]

11152 Ellison, Brooke, and Jean Ellison. *Miracles Happen: One Mother, One Daughter, One Journey* (9–12). 2002, Hyperion $22.95 (0-7868-6770-1). In alternating chapters, Brooke Ellison, the first quadriplegic to graduate from Harvard, and her mother tell their stories. (Rev: BL 12/15/01) [362.4]

11153 Galli, Richard. *Rescuing Jeffrey* (9–12). 2000, Algonquin $19.95 (1-56512-270-4). A hopeful but harrowing account of a teenager who is paralyzed from the waist down after he hits his head in a swimming accident. (Rev: BL 4/15/00; SLJ 10/00) [362.1]

11154 Gitter, Elisabeth. *The Imprisoned Guest: Samuel Howe and Laura Bridgman, the Original Deaf-Blind Girl* (9–12). Illus. 2001, Farrar $25.00 (0-374-11738-1). Before Helen Keller, the blind and deaf Laura Bridgman was helped to communicate by her teacher Samuel Howe at Boston's Perkins School for the Blind. (Rev: BL 3/15/01) [362.4]

11155 Lutkenhoff, Marlene, and Sonya G. Oppenheimer, eds. *SPINAbilities: A Young Person's Guide to Spina Bifida* (8–12). Illus. 1997, Woodbine paper $16.95 (0-933149-86-7). A collection of essays on spina bifida — the nature of the disability, daily care concerns, and social adjustments. (Rev: BL 2/15/97; SLJ 4/97) [616.8]

11156 Stalcup, Brenda, ed. *The Disabled* (7–12). Series: Current Controversies. 1997, Greenhaven LB $32.45 (1-56510-530-3). This collection of documents explores such questions as the effectiveness of the Americans with Disabilities Act, the degree to which the disabled should be helped, and the advisability of mainstreaming of disabled children. (Rev: BL 2/15/97) [362.4]

11157 Stewart, Gail B. *Teens with Disabilities* (8–12). Photos by Carl Franzén. Series: The Other America. 2000, Lucent LB $19.96 (1-56006-815-9). The personal — and positive — stories of four teens with physical disabilities show how people with these problems can be accommodated in family and social settings. (Rev: SLJ 3/01)

Reproduction and Child Care

11158 *Abortion* (9–12). Ed. by Mary E. Williams. Series: Opposing Viewpoints. 2001, Greenhaven LB $31.20 (0-7377-0778-X); paper $19.95 (0-7377-0777-1). Various aspects of the abortion question are explored in this collection of essays and articles. [363.46]

11159 *The Abortion Controversy* (9–12). Ed. by Lynnette Knapp. Series: Current Controversies. 2001, Greenhaven LB $22.96 (0-7377-0334-2); paper $14.96 (0-7377-0333-4). Both sides of the divisive abortion debate are well represented in this collection of essays that consider not only the morality of abortion but also specific issues including the use of aborted fetuses for medical research. (Rev: BL 3/1/01) [363.46]

11160 Alpern, Michele. *Teen Pregnancy* (6–12). Series: Focus on Family Matters. 2002, Chelsea $20.75 (0-7910-6695-9). This account explores various aspects of teen pregnancy, particularly the way in which it affects the entire family. (Rev: BL 10/15/02; HBG 3/03; SLJ 9/02) [618.2]

11161 Andryszewski, Tricia. *Abortion: Rights, Options, and Choices* (9–12). Illus. Series: Debate. 1996, Millbrook LB $23.90 (1-56294-573-4). This book discusses thoroughly Roe v. Wade and its impact, the moral and medical aspects of abortion, and points of view of groups opposed to or supporting the right to abortion. (Rev: BL 4/15/96; BR 9–10/96; SLJ 5/96; VOYA 10/96) [344.73]

11162 Arnoldi, Katherine. *The Amazing True Story of a Teenage Single Mom* (9–12). 1998, Hyperion $16.00 (0-7868-6420-6). In this autobiography illustrated by the author in comic-book format, an abused child and rape victim copes with becoming a single mother at 17. (Rev: BL 11/15/98; SLJ 1/99; VOYA 2/99) [306.874]

11163 Bode, Janet. *Kids Still Having Kids: Talking About Teen Pregnancy*. Rev. ed. (7–12). 1999, Watts LB $22.50 (0-531-11588-7). Birth control, miscarriage, abortion, adoption, foster care, and parenting are among the topics discussed in this guide that highlights the experiences of individual teens. (Rev: SLJ 10/99) [306.7]

11164 Buckingham, Robert W., and Mary P. Derby. *"I'm Pregnant, Now What Do I Do?"* (10–12). Illus. 1997, Prometheus paper $13.95 (1-57392-117-3). After a brief discussion of the reproductive process, this candid, helpful book discusses the pros and cons of the three alternatives available to pregnant teens — adoption, abortion, or becoming a parent. (Rev: BL 2/15/97) [306.874]

11165 Byers, Ann. *Teens and Pregnancy: A Hot Issue* (6–12). Series: Hot Issues. 2000, Enslow LB $19.95 (0-7660-1365-0). Various aspects of teen pregnancy are discussed, from social factors that put teens at risk to the financial ramifications of single parenthood to ways in which teens can avoid pregnancy. (Rev: HBG 3/01; SLJ 1/01) [306.874]

11166 Caplan, Theresa. *The First Twelve Months of Life: Your Baby's Growth Month by Month* (9–12). 1993, Putnam paper $15.95 (0-399-51804-5). Organized month by month, this book charts the first year of infant development. (Rev: BL 7/93) [613.9]

11167 Coles, Robert. *The Youngest Parents* (8–12). Illus. 1997, Norton $27.50 (0-393-04082-8). The first two-thirds of this adult book consists of interviews by the author, a child psychiatrist, with teenagers who are or about to be parents, and the last part is a moving photoessay featuring many rural, underprivileged teen parents and their children. (Rev: BL 2/1/97; VOYA 6/98) [306.85]

11168 Cozic, Charles P., and Jonathan S. Petrikin, eds. *The Abortion Controversy* (7–12). Series: Current Controversies. 1995, Greenhaven LB $26.20 (1-56510-229-0); paper $16.20 (1-56510-228-2). The morality of abortion and access to it is argued from many points of view. (Rev: BL 3/15/95; SLJ 5/95) [363.4]

11169 Currie, Stephen. *Abortion* (8–12). Illus. Series: Opposing Viewpoints Digests. 2000, Greenhaven $28.70 (0-7377-0229-X); paper $18.70 (0-7377-0228-1). Using primary sources as a foundation, the author presents varied viewpoints on the morality of abortion, laws limiting abortion, and research using aborted fetal tissue. (Rev: SLJ 9/00) [363.46]

11170 Day, Nancy. *Abortion: Debating the Issue* (8–12). Series: Issues in Focus. 1995, Enslow LB $20.95 (0-89490-645-3). A balanced presentation of the subject, with black-and-white photographs, glossary, and extensive notes. (Rev: BL 8/95; SLJ 12/95) [363.4]

11171 *Daycare and Diplomas: Teen Mothers Who Stayed in School* (7–12). Illus. 2001, Fairview paper $9.95 (1-57749-098-3). A group of young women who attend an unusual school that offers childcare relate the difficulties they have experienced in com-

bining parenthood and education. (Rev: BL 5/15/01; VOYA 4/01) [306.874]

11172 Dudley, William. *Pregnancy* (10–12). Series: Teen Decisions. 2001, Greenhaven LB $29.95 (0-7377-0492-6); paper $18.70 (0-7377-0491-8). Teen pregnancy is explored through a series of case studies, with material on adoption, abortion, and parenthood. [362.7]

11173 Durrett, Deanne. *The Abortion Conflict: A Pro/Con Issue* (9–12). Illus. Series: Hot Issues. 2000, Enslow LB $19.95 (0-7660-1193-3). This well-researched account of the continuing American controversy over abortion provides a fairly objective overview and includes the views of both those who stoutly defend a woman's right to terminate an unwanted pregnancy and those adamantly opposed to any form of abortion. (Rev: BL 1/1–15/01; HBG 3/01) [363.46]

11174 Edelson, Paula. *Straight Talk About Teenage Pregnancy* (7–12). Series: Straight Talk. 1998, Facts on File $27.45 (0-8160-3717-5). A frank, non-judgmental discussion on such topics as abstinence, safe sex, abortion, adoption, and teen parenting, to help young people make wise decisions and take responsibility for their actions. (Rev: BL 3/1/99; BR 9–10/99; SLJ 2/99) [306.874]

11175 *The Ethics of Abortion* (10–12). Ed. by Jennifer A. Hurley. Series: At Issue. 2001, Greenhaven LB $17.96 (0-7377-0470-5); paper $11.96 (0-7377-0469-1). The continuing controversy over abortion is examined from a wide variety of viewpoints in this thought-provoking collection of 15 articles. (Rev: BL 3/1/01) [179.7]

11176 Flanagan, Geraldine Lux. *Beginning Life: The Marvelous Journey from Conception to Birth* (10–12). 1996, DK $19.95 (0-7894-0609-8). Using many color photographs and a clear text, this is the story of human life from conception to birth. (Rev: BR 1–2/97; SLJ 5/97; VOYA 2/97) [612]

11177 Fontanel, Beatrice, and Claire D'Harcourt. *Babies: History, Art, and Folklore* (10–12). 1998, Harry N. Abrams $39.95 (0-8109-1244-9). This is a lavishly illustrated history about all aspects of child rearing from ancient to modern times — from teething, hygiene, and nutrition to birth instruments, clothing, and toys — placed in a context of changing theories relating to childbirth and child raising over the centuries. (Rev: SLJ 5/98) [305]

11178 Gay, Kathlyn. *Pregnancy: Private Decisions, Public Debates* (7–12). 1994, Watts LB $22.00 (0-531-11167-9). Discusses topics involving reproductive freedom, including the pro-choice/pro-life debate, reproductive technologies, population growth, and childbirth methods. (Rev: BL 8/94; SLJ 7/94; VOYA 10/94) [363.9]

11179 Gottfried, Ted. *Teen Fathers Today* (8–12). 2001, Twenty-First Century LB $23.90 (0-7613-1901-8). Real-life stories add immediacy to this practical guide to the challenges of becoming a father during the teen years. (Rev: HBG 3/02; SLJ 12/01; VOYA 2/02) [306.874]

11180 Gravelle, Karen, and Leslie Peterson. *Teenage Fathers* (7–12). 1992, Messner paper $5.95 (0-671-72851-2). Thirteen teenage boys describe their situations and feelings when they became fathers, with comments by the authors. (Rev: BL 10/15/92) [306.85]

11181 Hale, Dianne. *Pregnancy and Birth* (10–12). Illus. Series: 21st Century Health and Wellness. 1999, Chelsea LB $24.95 (0-7910-5527-2). This book covers the basics in a straightforward, traditional manner. With an introduction by Dr. C. Everett Koop. (Rev: BL 4/1/00; HBG 9/00; SLJ 11/00) [618.2]

11182 Hales, Dianne. *Pregnancy and Birth* (9–12). Illus. 1989, Chelsea LB $19.95 (0-7910-0040-0). A well-illustrated book that deals with fetal development and methods of childbirth. (Rev: BL 7/89; BR 11–12/89; SLJ 1/90; VOYA 12/89) [618.2]

11183 Heller, Tania. *Pregnant! What Can I Do? A Guide for Teenagers* (6–12). 2002, McFarland $24.95 (0-7864-1169-4). Valuable information about pregnancy, abortion, adoption, prenatal care, and parenting is provided in this thoughtful and reassuring volume. (Rev: SLJ 6/02; VOYA 6/02) [306.874/]

11184 Hughes, Tracy. *Everything You Need to Know About Teen Pregnancy* (7–12). Illus. Series: Need to Know Library. 1988, Rosen $24.50 (0-8239-0810-0). A simple, unbiased introduction to teen pregnancy and the options available. (Rev: SLJ 4/89) [612]

11185 Hurley, Jennifer A. *Teen Pregnancy* (7–10). Illus. Series: Opposing Viewpoints Digests. 2000, Greenhaven LB $22.96 (0-7377-0366-0); paper $14.96 (0-7377-0365-2). The author has effectively summarized the different points of view and stances about teenage pregnancy. (Rev: BL 11/1/00) [306.874]

11186 Iannucci, Lisa. *Birth Defects* (7–12). Illus. 2000, Enslow LB $19.95 (0-7660-1186-0). The stories of two babies with problems introduce this survey of birth defects and their causes, prevention, diagnosis, and treatment, along with discussion of the impact on the mothers. (Rev: HBG 9/00; SLJ 8/00) [616]

11187 Jakobson, Cathryn. *Think About Teenage Pregnancy* (7–12). Illus. 1993, Walker LB $15.85 (0-8027-8128-4); paper $9.95 (0-8027-7372-9). Problems of pregnant teenagers are addressed, with a look at possible options and the social issues involved. (Rev: SLJ 8/88; VOYA 10/88) [612]

11188 Judges, Donald P. *Hard Choices, Lost Voices: How the Abortion Conflict Has Divided America, Distorted Constitutional Rights and Damaged the Courts* (9–12). 1993, Ivan R. Dee $25.00 (1-56663-016-9). A balanced overview of the controversy, concentrating on legal issues, the Supreme Court's role, and the judicial system's seeming ambivalence. (Rev: BL 5/15/93) [363.4]

11189 Keller, Kristin Thoennes. *Parenting an Infant* (8–12). Series: Skills for Teens Who Parent. 2000, Capstone LB $22.60 (0-7368-0702-0). Keller offers straightforward, accessible guidance to teens who are caring for very young children, with quotations from teen parents. Also use *Parenting a Toddler* (2000). (Rev: BR 5–6/01; HBG 10/01; SLJ 7/01) [649]

11190 Kitzinger, Sheila. *The Complete Book of Pregnancy and Childbirth*. Rev. ed. (9–12). Illus. 1989, Knopf $22.50 (0-394-58011-7). A sensitive, thorough account of prenatal development and care and the birth experience. (Rev: BL 12/1/89) [618.2]

11191 Lang, Paul, and Susan S. Lang. *Teen Fathers* (7–12). 1995, Watts LB $25.00 (0-531-11216-0). A fact book not often seen concerning the dilemmas teen fathers face. (Rev: BL 9/1/95; SLJ 12/95) [306.85]

11192 Lerman, Evelyn. *Teen Moms: The Pain and the Promise* (10–12). Illus. 1997, Morning Glory $21.95 (1-885356-24-2); paper $14.95 (1-885356-25-0). Combining good background research and interviews with 50 teens, this resource explores teenage sex, teen pregnancy, and what motherhood means. (Rev: BR 3–4/98; SLJ 1/98) [618.2]

11193 Lindsay, Jeanne W. *Challenge of Toddlers: For Teen Parents — Parenting Your Child from One to Three* (8–12). Illus. Series: Teens Parenting. 1998, Morning Glory $18.95 (1-885356-38-2); paper $12.95 (1-885356-39-0). A practical, updated manual on how to raise toddlers, including information on developmental problems. (Rev: BL 10/15/98; HBG 3/99) [649]

11194 Lindsay, Jeanne W. *Pregnant? Adoption Is an Option: Making an Adoption Plan for a Child* (7–12). Illus. 1996, Morning Glory paper $11.95 (1-885356-08-0). Using quotations from many case studies, this book describes the steps in the adoption process and how to develop an adoption plan. (Rev: BL 12/1/96; SLJ 2/97; VOYA 4/97) [362.7]

11195 Lindsay, Jeanne W. *Your Baby's First Year: A Guide for Teenage Parents* (8–12). Illus. Series: Teens Parenting. 1998, Morning Glory $18.95 (1-885356-32-3); paper $12.95 (1-885356-33-1). This book discusses growth changes that occur in babies from birth to age one and how teenage parents can handle these changes and adjust to them. (Rev: BL 10/15/98; HBG 3/99; SLJ 2/99; VOYA 8/99) [649]

11196 Lindsay, Jeanne W., and Jean Brunelli. *Your Pregnancy and Newborn Journey: A Guide for Pregnant Teens* (8–12). Illus. 1998, Morning Glory $18.95 (1-885356-29-3); paper $12.95 (1-885356-30-7). This guide for teens explains the stages of pregnancy, what healthcare measures should be taken, the process of giving birth, and the special needs of some babies. (Rev: BL 10/15/98; HBG 3/99; SLJ 12/98; VOYA 8/99) [618.2]

11197 Lindsay, Jeanne W., and Sally McCullough. *Discipline from Birth to Three: How Teen Parents Can Prevent and Deal with Discipline Problems with Babies and Toddlers* (8–12). Illus. Series: Teens Parenting. 1998, Morning Glory $18.95 (1-885356-35-8); paper $12.95 (1-885356-36-6). This volume gives practical advice for teen parents on how to handle behavioral problems with young children. (Rev: BL 10/15/98; HBG 3/99) [649.64]

11198 Lindsay, Jeanne Warren. *Teen Dads: Rights, Responsibilities, and Joys*. Rev. ed. (7–12). Illus. 2001, Morning Glory $18.95 (1-885356-67-6); paper $12.95 (1-885356-68-4). Easy-to-read and full of firsthand accounts, this thought-provoking book looks at how teenage fathers view and handle their responsibilities. (Rev: BL 10/15/93; HBG 10/01; SLJ 10/93; VOYA 2/94) [649]

11199 Lowenstein, Felicia. *The Abortion Battle: Looking at Both Sides* (7–12). Illus. Series: Issues in Focus. 1996, Enslow LB $20.95 (0-89490-724-7). After a presentation of the facts, the author analyzes arguments on both sides of the abortion controversy. Appended are a glossary, hotline numbers, and a reading list. (Rev: BL 7/96; BR 9–10/96; SLJ 9/96; VOYA 8/96) [363.4]

11200 Lunneborg, Patricia. *Abortion: A Positive Decision* (9–12). 1992, Bergin & Garvey $19.95 (0-89789-243-7). A look at the pro-choice side of this controversial issue, based on interviews with more than 100 women. (Rev: BL 2/15/92) [363.4]

11201 *Margaret Sanger: Her Life in Her Words* (10–12). Ed. by Miriam Reed. Illus. 2003, Barricade $21.95 (1-56980-255-6); paper $16.95 (1-56980-246-7). Margaret Sanger, a pioneer in the sex education and birth control movement, comes alive in this collection of her writings. (Rev: BL 3/1/03) [363.9]

11202 Marzollo, Jean. *Fathers and Babies: How Babies Grow and What They Need from You from Birth to 18 Months* (9–12). 1993, HarperCollins paper $13.00 (0-06-096908-3). This practical, illustrated guide describes normal chronological development and offers how-to information on such subjects as making simple toys. (Rev: BL 5/1/93) [306.874]

11203 Moe, Barbara. *A Question of Timing: Successful Men Talk About Having Children* (6–12). Illus. Series: Teen Pregnancy Prevention Library. 1997, Rosen LB $23.95 (0-8239-2253-7). Men from a variety of backgrounds talk about why they waited to have children and how they feel about that choice. (Rev: BL 6/1–15/97; BR 9–10/97; VOYA 10/97) [306.874]

11204 Nathanson, Laura Walther. *The Portable Pediatrician for Parents* (9–12). Series: Omnibus. 1994, HarperCollins paper $23.00 (0-06-273176-9). Details what to expect at every stage of infancy and toddlerhood and counsels on broader aspects of child rearing as well. (Rev: BL 2/1/94) [618.92]

11205 Richards, Arlene Kramer, and Irene Willis. *What to Do If You or Someone You Know Is Under 18 and Pregnant* (9–12). Illus. 1983, Lothrop paper $8.95 (0-688-01044-X). A practical guide that covers such topics as abortion, adoption, marriage, sex, and birth control. (Rev: BL 10/15/88) [362.7]

11206 Roleff, Tamara L., ed. *Abortion* (9–12). Series: Opposing Viewpoints. 1997, Greenhaven LB $21.96 (1-56510-506-0); paper $22.00 (1-56510-505-2). This replacement of the 1991 title contains an anthology of writings about abortion that covers morality, ethical concerns, and safety, and also considers justification and whether abortion rights should be restricted. (Rev: BL 1/1–15/97; BR 5–6/97; VOYA 10/97) [363.4]

11207 Romaine, Deborah S. *Roe v. Wade: Abortion and the Supreme Court* (9–12). Series: Famous Trials. 1998, Lucent LB $17.96 (1-56006-274-6). An account of the Supreme Court decision in 1973 that protected a woman's right to abortion. (Rev: BL 8/98; SLJ 9/98) [179]

11208 Sherman, Aliza. *Everything You Need to Know About Placing Your Baby for Adoption* (9–12). Illus. Series: Need to Know. 1997, Rosen LB $17.95 (0-8239-2266-9). This book provides good information on the practical and personal issues involved in deciding whether to place a child for adoption, methods of adoption, and organizations that can help. (Rev: BL 10/15/97; BR 1–2/98; SLJ 2/98) [362.7]

11209 Silverstein, Herma. *Teenage and Pregnant: What You Can Do* (7–12). 1989, Messner paper $5.95 (0-671-65222-2). Options available to pregnant teens are discussed, with related material on such subjects as contraception and care for the expectant mother. (Rev: BL 3/15/89; BR 9–10/89; SLJ 1/89; VOYA 8/89) [306.7]

11210 Simpson, Carolyn. *Coping with an Unplanned Pregnancy* (9–12). Series: Coping. 1996, Rosen LB $17.95 (0-8239-2265-0). This book discusses options available to pregnant teenagers, adjustments that have to be made, and what happens if one decides to become a mother. (Rev: VOYA 8/90) [618.2]

11211 Stewart, Gail B. *Teen Fathers* (7–12). Illus. Series: The Other America. 1998, Lucent LB $27.45 (1-56006-575-3). Using case studies and many photographs, this account reveals the various levels of responsibility assumed by teens when they become fathers. (Rev: BL 4/15/98; SLJ 6/98) [306.874]

11212 Stewart, Gail B. *Teen Parenting* (6–12). Series: Overview: Teen Issues. 2000, Lucent LB $18.96 (1-56006-517-6). This overview discusses the demographics of teen parents, what their lives are like, the implications for their children, and social responses to teen parenting. (Rev: BL 6/1–15/00; HBG 9/00) [649]

11213 Thompson, Stephen P., ed. *Teenage Pregnancy* (9–12). Illus. Series: Opposing Viewpoints. 1997, Greenhaven LB $20.96 (1-56510-562-1); paper $16.20 (1-56510-561-3). Various points of view are expressed in chapters that include: Is teenage pregnancy a serious problem? What factors contribute to teenage pregnancy? How can teenage pregnancy be prevented? and What new initiatives would reduce teenage pregnancy? (Rev: BL 6/1–15/97; BR 1–2/98; SLJ 6/97; VOYA 12/97) [304.6]

11214 Trapani, Margi. *Listen Up: Teenage Mothers Speak Out* (6–12). Illus. Series: Teen Pregnancy Prevention Library. 1997, Rosen LB $23.95 (0-8239-2254-5). Young women speak candidly about why they had children at an early age and the impact this has had on their lives. (Rev: BL 6/1–15/97; BR 9–10/97; SLJ 6/97; VOYA 10/97) [306.874]

11215 Trapani, Margi. *Reality Check: Teenage Fathers Speak Out* (7–10). 1997, Rosen LB $23.95 (0-8239-2255-3). Case studies of teenage fathers who did not plan on becoming parents are discussed in this book that does not shun the hardships of being a teenage parent. (Rev: BL 6/1–15/97; SLJ 6/97; VOYA 10/97) [306.85]

11216 Wekesser, Carol, ed. *Reproductive Technologies* (7–12). Series: Current Controversies. 1996, Greenhaven LB $32.45 (1-56510-377-7). The fact that science has enabled infertile couples to have children has raised a number of ethical and legal concerns. These are explored in this collection of original sources. (Rev: BL 6/1–15/96; SLJ 3/96) [176]

11217 Wilks, Corinne Morgan, ed. *Dear Diary, I'm Pregnant: Teenagers Talk About Their Pregnancy* (7–12). Illus. 1997, Annick paper $9.95 (1-55037-440-0). Ten teenage girls talk about how they got pregnant, what they decided to do, and how the pregnancy has changed their lives. (Rev: BL 2/1/98; BR 11–12/97; SLJ 8/97; VOYA 12/97) [306.874]

11218 *A World of Babies: Imagined Childcare Guides for Seven Societies* (10–12). Ed. by Judy DeLoache and Alma Gottlieb. Illus. 2000, Cambridge Univ. Pr. $49.95 (0-521-66264-8); paper $16.95 (0-521-66475-6). From the Puritans of New England to a Muslim village in Turkey, this book outlines in a fictional/factual format how babies are cared for in seven varied cultures. (Rev: BL 5/1/00) [649.1]

Safety and First Aid

11219 Arnold, Caroline. *Coping with Natural Disasters* (7–10). Illus. 1988, Walker LB $14.85 (0-8027-6717-6). Natural disasters such as earthquakes, hurricanes, and blizzards are discussed, with information on how to react in these emergencies. (Rev: BCCB 6/88; BL 6/15/88; SLJ 6/88; VOYA 10/88) [904]

11220 Auerbach, Paul S. *Medicine for the Outdoors: A Guide to Emergency Medical Procedures and First Aid* (9–12). Illus. 1986, Little, Brown $24.95 (0-316-05928-5); paper $12.95 (0-316-05929-3). A first aid manual for the outdoor person that stresses prevention and safety measures. (Rev: BL 1/15/86) [616.02]

11221 Cothran, Helen. *Teen Pregnancy and Parenting* (10–12). Series: Current Controversies. 2000, Greenhaven LB $31.20 (0-7377-0558-2); paper $19.95 (0-7377-0557-4). A selection of documents on such subjects as premarital sex, welfare dependency, cohabitation, and sex education programs. (Rev: SLJ 7/01) [362.7]

11222 Rosenberg, Stephen N. *The Johnson and Johnson First Aid Book* (9–12). Illus. 1985, Warner paper $16.95 (0-446-38252-3). A spiral-bound handy manual that covers most emergency situations with clear text and line drawings. (Rev: BL 7/85) [616.02]

11223 Wells, Donna K., and Bruce C. Morris. *Live Aware, Not in Fear: The 411 After 9-11 — A Book For Teens* (6–12). 2002, Health Communications paper $9.95 (0-7573-0013-8). The authors offer practical advice for teenagers who want to feel safe again, such as preparing escape routes and keeping a survival kit handy. (Rev: BL 5/15/02; VOYA 6/02) [363.3]

Sex Education and Sexual Identity

11224 Akagi, Cynthia G. *Dear Michael: Sexuality Education for Boys Ages 11–17* (6–10). Illus. 1996, Gylantic $12.95 (1-880197-16-2). Written by a mother to her adolescent son, these letters effectively explore male puberty, the male's role in conception, concerns about dating, and the problems involved in sexual relationships. (Rev: BL 1/1–15/97; VOYA 6/97) [613.9]

11225 Avraham, Regina. *The Reproductive System* (10–12). Series: 21st Century Health and Wellness. 2000, Chelsea LB $24.95 (0-7910-5988-X). After discussing human sexuality, this book describes the reproductive system, with material on such topics as pregnancy and infertility. (Rev: BL 11/15/00; HBG 10/01) [613 9]

11226 Ayer, Eleanor H. *It's Okay to Say No: Choosing Sexual Abstinence* (9–12). Series: Teen Pregnancy Prevention Library. 1997, Rosen LB $23.95 (0-8239-2250-2). While acknowledging the difficulty of making such a choice, Eleanor Ayer makes the case for sexual abstinence, providing a review of such dangers as unwanted pregnancy and infection with a sexually transmitted disease. (Rev: BL 9/1/97; SLJ 1/98) [306.7]

11227 Bell, Ruth. *Changing Bodies, Changing Lives* (9–12). 1998, Times Books paper $23.00 (0-8129-2990-X). A new edition of this ground-breaking, nonjudgmental, explicit book on sex, physical and emotional health, and personal relationships. (Rev: BL 11/1/98) [613.907]

11228 Brimner, Larry Dane. *Being Different: Lambda Youths Speak Out* (9–12). Series: Lesbian and Gay Experience. 1996, Watts LB $24.00 (0-531-11222-5). The author's commentary links the narratives of 15 gay, lesbian, and bisexual young people who tell about their search for sexual identity, coming out, and the pain of being gay in high school, as well as their fears, relationships, hopes, and expectations. (Rev: SLJ 5/96) [305.38]

11229 Brody, Janis. *Your Body: The Girls' Guide* (5–10). 2000, St. Martin's paper $4.99 (0-312-97563-5). This book on puberty and body changes covers such subjects as self-image, menstruation, sexuality, sports participation, nutrition, eating disorders, substance abuse, and counseling. (Rev: SLJ 10/00) [612]

11230 Brynie, Faith. *101 Questions About Sex and Sexuality: With Answers for the Curious, Cautious, and Confused* (6–12). Illus. Series: 101 Questions. 2003, Twenty-First Century LB $27.90 (0-7613-2310-4). Information on abstinence, contraception, sexually transmitted diseases, and other issues of importance to teens is provided in a question-and-answer format with detailed black-and-white illustrations. (Rev: HBG 10/03; SLJ 6/03; VOYA 4/04) [306.7]

11231 Bull, David. *Cool and Celibate? Sex or No Sex* (8–12). 1998, Element Books paper $4.95 (1-901881-17-2). The author argues against teens having sex until they are in stable married relationships. (Rev: SLJ 3/99) [362.29]

11232 Diamond, Shifra N. *Everything You Need to Know About Going to the Gynecologist* (7–12). Series: Need to Know Library. 1999, Rosen LB $25.25 (0-8239-2839-X). This book explains what a gynecologist does, when teenage girls should see one, and how to find one. There is helpful information on menstruation, breast self-examinations, treatments for common reproductive problems, contraception, myths, and what to expect from a pelvic examination. (Rev: SLJ 5/99; VOYA 8/99) [612]

11233 Dobie, Kathy. *The Only Girl in the Car* (11–12). 2003, Dial $23.95 (0-385-31880-4). Suitable for mature teens only, this frank memoir recounts the high price its author had to pay for sexual excesses while still in her early teens. (Rev: BL 3/15/03) [813.6]

11234 Dunbar, Robert E. *Homosexuality* (7–10). Series: Issues in Focus. 1995, Enslow LB $20.95 (0-89490-665-8). An objective introduction to homosexuality that contains some interesting first-person accounts. (Rev: BL 12/15/95; SLJ 6/96; VOYA 2/96) [305.9]

11235 Feldt, Gloria. *Behind Every Choice Is a Story* (9–12). 2003, Univ. of North Texas Pr. $19.95 (1-57441-158-6). Both men and women, including teenagers and teachers, discuss reproductive rights and the value of individual choice. (Rev: BL 3/1/04; VOYA 6/03) [613.9]

11236 Ford, Michael T. *Outspoken: Role Models from the Lesbian and Gay Community* (7–12). 1998, Morrow $16.00 (0-688-14896-4). Six men and five women who represent the gay, lesbian, bisexual, and transgendered community tell about their lives, families, and how they have grown to accept their identity. (Rev: BL 5/1/98; BR 9–10/98; HB 5–6/98; SLJ 6/98; VOYA 8/98) [305.9]

11237 *The Gay Rights Movement* (10–12). Ed. by Jennifer Smith. Series: American Social Movements. 2003, Greenhaven $33.70 (0-7377-1158-2); paper $22.45 (0-7377-1157-4). This clearly written book contains a selection of pro-gay articles by a wide variety of authors. (Rev: SLJ 9/03) [305.9]

11238 Gowen, L. Kris. *Making Sexual Decisions: The Ultimate Teen Guide* (7–12). Illus. Series: It Happened to Me. 2003, Scarecrow $32.50 (0-8108-4647-0). Puberty, safe sex, birth control, and rape are among the topics raised in this volume, which stresses the value of being fully informed about one's options. (Rev: SLJ 11/03) [306.7]

11239 Gravelle, Karen, and Nick Castro. *What's Going on Down There? Answers to Questions Boys Find Hard to Ask* (5–10). 1998, Walker paper $8.95 (0-8027-7540-3). Straightforward information for boys covers such topics as physical changes, sexual intercourse, peer pressure, and pregnancy and birth.

(Rev: BL 11/1/98; BR 5–6/99; HB 1–2/99; HBG 3/99; SLJ 12/98) [613]

11240 Gravelle, Karen, and Jennifer Gravelle. *The Period Book: Everything You Don't Want to Ask (But Need to Know)* (6–10). Illus. 1996, Walker $15.95 (0-8027-8420-8); paper $8.95 (0-8027-7478-4). Presented in an appealing format, this chatty discussion of menstruation gives basic information, with cartoon-style illustrations. (Rev: BL 3/15/96; BR 9–10/96; SLJ 3/96; VOYA 6/96) [618]

11241 Gray, Mary L. *In Your Face: Stories from the Lives of Queer Youth* (9–12). 1999, Haworth $29.95 (0-7890-0076-8); paper $17.95 (1-56023-887-9). This collection of verbatim transcripts of the spoken thoughts of 15 gay, lesbian, and bisexual teens sensitively explores such issues as first sexual encounters and coming out to friends and family. (Rev: BL 6/1–15/99) [305.235]

11242 Gurian, Michael. *Understanding Guys: A Guide for Teenage Girls* (8–10). Illus. Series: Plugged In. 1999, Price Stern Sloan $13.89 (0-8431-7476-5); paper $4.99 (0-8431-7475-7). A practical, often humorous explanation of what boys go through physically, emotionally, and psychologically during puberty, with advice for girls on how to deal with them. (Rev: BR 9–10/99; SLJ 8/99) [612]

11243 Hoch, Dean, and Nancy Hoch. *The Sex Education Dictionary for Today's Teens and Pre-Teens* (7–12). Illus. 1990, Landmark paper $12.95 (0-9624209-0-5). A dictionary of 350 words relating to sex, sexuality, and reproduction all given clear, concise definitions. (Rev: BL 8/90) [306.7]

11244 Hooks, Bell. *All About Love: New Visions* (10–12). 2000, Morrow $22.00 (0-688-16844-2). This adult treatise explores "new ways of thinking about love" with material on the nature of romance and the importance of community. (Rev: BL 1/1–15/00) [306.4]

11245 Huegel, Kelly. *GLBTQ: The Survival Guide for Queer and Questioning Teens* (7–12). Illus. 2003, Free Spirit paper $15.95 (1-57542-126-7). Quotations from teens are interspersed in the practical, common-sense advice for gay, lesbian, bisexual, transgendered, and questioning teens. (Rev: BL 10/1/03; SLJ 12/03; VOYA 12/03) [300.70]

11246 Hyde, Margaret O., and Elizabeth Forsyth. *Know About Gays and Lesbians* (7–12). 1994, Millbrook LB $23.40 (1-56294-298-0). This overview of homosexuality attacks stereotypes, surveys history, examines current controversies, reviews religious responses, and shows how pervasive homophobia still is. (Rev: BL 3/1/94; SLJ 4/94; VOYA 4/94) [305.9]

11247 Kamen, Paula. *Her Way: Young Women Remake the Sexual Revolution* (10–12). 2001, New York Univ. $25.95 (0-8147-4733-7). More than 100 Generation X women candidly reveal their attitudes on such subjects as sexual abstinence, the feminist movement, AIDS, homosexuality, single life, and marriage. (Rev: BL 12/15/00) [306.7]

11248 Lauersen, Niels H., and Eileen Stukane. *You're in Charge: A Teenage Girl's Guide to Sex and Her Body* (8–12). 1993, Ballantine paper $12.00 (0-449-90464-4). An ob/gyn discusses sexual maturation, including pubertal change, sexually transmitted diseases, orgasm, sexual intimacy, condoms, abortion, menstruation, and more. (Rev: BL 5/1/93) [613.9]

11249 Madaras, Lynda, and Area Madaras. *The What's Happening to My Body? Book for Boys: A Growing Up Guide for Parents and Sons*. 3rd ed. (7–12). Illus. 2001, Newmarket $22.95 (1-55704-447-3); paper $12.95 (1-55704-443-0). This new edition of the classic guide has been recast to suit today's children and their earlier puberty. A revised companion workbook is *My Body, My Self for Boys* (2000). (Rev: BL 9/1/01) [613.9]

11250 Madaras, Lynda, and Area Madaras. *The What's Happening to My Body? Book for Girls: A Growing Up Guide for Parents and Daughters*. 3rd ed. (7–12). Illus. 2001, Newmarket $22.95 (1-557044-48-1); paper $12.95 (1-557044-44-9). This new edition of the guide to puberty includes material on such subjects as pregnancy and AIDS. A revised companion workbook is *My Body, My Self for Girls* (2000). (Rev: BL 10/1/01; VOYA 6/89) [612]

11251 Marcus, Eric. *Is It a Choice? Answers to 300 of the Most Frequently Asked Questions About Gays and Lesbians* (9–12). 1993, HarperSF paper $13.00 (0-06-250664-1). A comprehensive primer on homosexuality, answering questions about sex, relationships, discrimination, religion, coming out, AIDS, aging, and many other topics. (Rev: BL 5/1/93) [305.9]

11252 Marcus, Eric. *What If Someone I Know Is Gay? Answers to Questions About Gay and Lesbian People* (7–12). 2000, Price Stern Sloan LB $13.89 (0-8431-7612-1); paper $4.99 (0-8431-7611-3). The author reflects on his own experiences as a gay man, touching on issues including sexuality, relationships, and discrimination. (Rev: BL 3/1/01; HBG 3/01; SLJ 11/00; VOYA 4/01) [306.76]

11253 Marshall, Elizabeth L. *Conquering Infertility: Medical Challenges and Moral Dilemmas* (9–12). Illus. Series: Changing Family. 1997, Watts $25.00 (0-531-11344-2). This book traces the history of modern reproductive medicine, discusses the causes of infertility, presents all of the options currently available to infertile couples, and comments on the controversies surrounding in vitro fertilization. (Rev: BL 12/1/97; BR 5–6/98; SLJ 9/97) [616.6]

715

11254 Mastoon, Adam. *The Shared Heart* (8–12). Illus. 1997, Morrow $24.50 (0-688-14931-6). Through photographs and personal essays, young gays, lesbians, and bisexuals share their memories and the problems of coming out. (Rev: BCCB 3/98; BL 11/15/97; BR 3–4/98; SLJ 2/98*) [305.235]

11255 Montpetit, Charles, ed. *The First Time, vol. 1* (10–12). Series: True Stories. 1996, Orca paper $6.95 (1-55143-037-1). For mature readers, this consists of eight true stories of initial sexual experiences that run the gamut of young love, gay love, sexual abuse, tragic consequences, embarrassment, and bliss. Followed by a second volume that contains eight more vignettes. (Rev: SLJ 8/96; VOYA 10/97) [306.7]

11256 Nilsson, Lennart. *A Child Is Born.* New ed. (9–12). 1990, Delacorte $27.50 (0-385-30237-1). Using both illustrations and text, this is the story of male and female reproductive organs, and the development of a baby from conception to delivery. [612.6]

11257 O'Grady, Kathleen, and Paula Wansbrough, eds. *Sweet Secrets: Telling Stories of Menstruation* (6–10). 1997, Second Story paper $9.95 (0-929005-33-3). Following an interesting review of attitudes and rituals relating to menstruation in various cultures throughout history, the main body of the book recounts 20 anecdotes about young teens and their first periods, interspersed with boxes providing information on topics including tampons, toxic shock syndrome, and breast examinations. (Rev: VOYA 6/98) [530.8]

11258 Ojeda, Auriana, ed. *Homosexuality* (8–12). Series: Opposing Viewpoints. 2003, Gale LB $33.70 (0-7377-1687-8); paper $22.45 (0-7377-1688-6). The essays in this collection debate such topics as the causes of homosexuality, the possibility of changing sexual orientation, and the extent to which gay relationships should be legalized. (Rev: BL 1/1–15/04; SLJ 6/04) [305.9]

11259 Peacock, Judith. *Abstinence: Postponing Sexual Involvement* (7–12). Series: Perspectives on Healthy Sexuality. 2001, LifeMatters LB $22.60 (0-7368-0713-6). This slim volume for reluctant readers defines the concept of abstinence and examines both its benefits and challenges. Also use *Dating and Sex: Defining and Setting Boundaries* (2000). (Rev: HBG 10/01; VOYA 6/01) [306.73]

11260 Peacock, Judith. *Birth Control and Protection: Options for Teens* (7–12). Series: Perspectives on Healthy Sexuality. 2000, Capstone LB $22.60 (0-7368-0715-2). Peacock reviews the reasons for using birth control and explains the various options and the pros and cons of each method. Also recommended in this series is *Dating and Sex: Defining and Setting Boundaries.* (Rev: HBG 10/01; SLJ 4/01) [363.9]

11261 Pogany, Susan Browning. *Sex Smart: 501 Reasons to Hold Off on Sex* (8–12). 1998, Fairview paper $14.95 (1-57749-043-6). The author uses quotations from teenagers, "Dear Abby," and other sources to explore emotional issues involved in making sexual choices and to argue for abstinence. (Rev: VOYA 4/99) [613.9]

11262 Pollack, Rachel, and Cheryl Schwartz. *The Journey Out: A Guide for and About Lesbian, Gay, and Bisexual Teens* (7–12). 1995, Viking $14.99 (0-670-85845-5); Penguin paper $6.99 (0-14-037254-7). An approachable discussion with sections on terms commonly used, the varied character of the gay community, and special concerns of bisexuals; offers support and opportunities for activism. (Rev: BL 12/1/95; BR 9–10/96; SLJ 1/96*; VOYA 4/96) [305.23]

11263 Potash, Marlin S., et al. *Am I Weird or Is This Normal?* (8–12). Illus. 2001, Simon & Schuster paper $13.00 (0-7432-1087-5). A mother and teenage daughter take a question-and-answer look at teen relationships, sex, and other difficult aspects of growing up, with concise and frank information that includes both scientific and slang terms. (Rev: BL 8/01) [305.235]

11264 Reed, Rita. *Growing Up Gay: The Sorrows and Joys of Gay and Lesbian Adolescence* (10–12). 1997, Norton paper $19.95 (0-393-31659-9). This book concentrates on the lives of two teens, one gay and the other lesbian, and their experiences after they came out. (Rev: VOYA 6/98) [305.9]

11265 *Revolutionary Voices: A Multicultural Queer Youth Anthology* (9–12). Ed. by Amy Sonnie. Illus. 2000, Alyson paper $10.95 (1-55583-558-9). This anthology of teen writings reflects the diversity of gay youth culture. (Rev: BL 12/1/00; VOYA 4/01) [305.235]

11266 Rich, Jason R. *Growing Up Gay in America* (10–12). 2002, Franklin Street paper $12.95 (0-9719414-0-8). A comforting book for boys who are gay — or think they might be gay — that addresses sex, religion, family, and the gay community. (Rev: BL 9/1/02)

11267 Roberts, Tara, ed. *Am I the Last Virgin? Ten African-American Reflections on Sex and Love* (10–12). 1997, Simon & Schuster $15.00 (0-689-80449-0); paper $3.99 (0-689-81254-X). A brutally frank collection of 10 essays about sex and sexuality for African American women in their late teens and up. For mature senior high readers. (Rev: BL 2/15/97; SLJ 2/97; VOYA 4/97) [306.7]

11268 Roleff, Tamara L. *Gay Rights* (9–12). Series: Current Controversies. 1997, Greenhaven LB $21.96 (1-56510-532-X); paper $16.20 (1-56510-531-1). This work discusses various points of view on such questions as homosexual marriage, gays in

the military, legal protection, civil rights, child custody problems, and domestic partner benefits. (Rev: BL 4/1/97; SLJ 2/97) [306.76]

11269 Roleff, Tamara L., ed. *Sex Education* (7–12). Series: At Issue. 1999, Greenhaven LB $26.20 (0-7377-0009-2); paper $17.45 (0-7377-0008-4). A collection of essays and opinion on issues relating to teaching about sex, including contraception, sexual abstinence, safe sex, sexual identity, and families with gay parents. (Rev: BL 5/15/99; BR 9–10/99) [613.9]

11270 *Sex* (9–12). Ed. by Mary E. Williams. Series: Opposing Viewpoints. 2000, Greenhaven LB $31.20 (0-7377-0352-0); paper $23.50 (0-7377-0351-2). The essays in this collection present various views on such subjects as contraception, pornography, premarital sex, monogamy, and prostitution. [306.7]

11271 Shaw, Tucker, and Fiona Gibb. *This Book Is About Sex* (8–10). Illus. 2000, Putnam paper $5.99 (0-14-131019-7). A hip presentation on topics including STDs, pregnancy, protection, and more, giving both male and female points of view. (Rev: BL 2/1/01) [613.951]

11272 Shyer, Marlene Fanta, and Christopher Shyer. *Not Like Other Boys: Growing Up Gay: A Mother and Son Look Back* (10–12). 1996, Houghton $21.95 (0-395-70939-3). Told in alternating chapters by a mother and her son, Christopher, this is the story of Chris's life from age 5 until his early adult years, when he told his family that he was gay. (Rev: BL 1/1–15/96; SLJ 10/96) [616.85]

11273 Silver, Diane. *The New Civil War: The Lesbian and Gay Struggle for Civil Rights* (8–12). Series: Lesbian and Gay Experience. 1997, Watts LB $24.00 (0-531-11290-X). As gay and lesbian groups are fighting for equality under the law, conservative and religious groups are opposing it. This book gives an unbiased account of both sides of this question. (Rev: BL 9/15/97; SLJ 11/97) [305.9]

11274 Singer, Bennett L. *Growing Up Gay: An Anthology for Young People* (10–12). 1993, New Pr. paper $9.95 (1-56584-103-4). Gay and lesbian teens uncertain of their identities will find reassurance in this collection of writings by well-known men and women — James Baldwin, Martina Navratilova, and Rita Mae Brown — who've lived through the experience themselves. [808.8]

11275 Solin, Sabrina, and Paula Elbirt. *The Seventeen Guide to Sex and Your Body* (7–10). 1996, Simon & Schuster $17.00 (0-689-80796-1); paper $8.99 (0-689-80795-3). Using a question-and-answer format, this book by the authors of *Seventeen*'s column "Sex and Body" explores common concerns about sex and puberty. (Rev: BL 10/1/96; SLJ 11/96; VOYA 6/97) [613.9]

11276 Stalcup, Brenda, et al., eds. *Human Sexuality* (9–12). Series: Opposing Viewpoints. 1995, Greenhaven LB $21.96 (1-56510-246-0); paper $16.20 (1-56510-245-2). This anthology covers the purposes of sex, gender and sexual orientation, what is considered normal sexually, and society's changing attitudes on this subject. (Rev: BL 9/15/95) [306.7]

11277 Stewart, Gail B. *Gay and Lesbian Youth* (9–12). Illus. Series: The Other America. 1996, Lucent LB $18.96 (1-56006-337-8). Through the painful stories of four gay young people, readers learn the value of friendship, tolerance, and understanding. (Rev: BL 3/1/97; SLJ 6/97; VOYA 8/97) [305.23]

11278 Tone, Andrea. *Devices and Desires: A History of Contraceptives in America* (10–12). Illus. 2001, Hill & Wang $30.00 (0-8090-3817-X). This is a history of contraception—including diaphragms, condoms, and birth-control pills—and attitudes toward it. (Rev: BL 6/1–15/01) [363.9]

11279 White, Joe. *Pure Excitement: A Radical Righteous Approach to Sex, Love, and Dating* (7–12). 1996, Focus on the Family paper $10.99 (1-56179-483-X). Taking a conservative approach, this book, written by a minister and using many conversations with teens, proposes that premarital sex is harmful to young adults. (Rev: VOYA 8/97) [613.9]

Sex Problems (Abuse, Harassment, etc.)

11280 Benedict, Helen. *Safe, Strong, and Streetwise* (8–12). 1987, Little, Brown paper $6.95 (0-87113-100-5). A rape crisis specialist discusses sexual assault, its prevention and treatment. (Rev: BL 1/1/87; BR 1–2/87; SLJ 5/87; VOYA 2/87) [362.7]

11281 Black, Beryl. *Coping with Sexual Harassment* (9–12). Series: Coping. 1987, Rosen LB $17.95 (0-8239-0732-5). Advice for both homosexual and heterosexual males and females on how to handle sexual harassment at school and work. (Rev: BR 11–12/87; SLJ 9/87; VOYA 10/87) [305.4]

11282 Bode, Janet. *Voices of Rape* (9–12). 1998, Watts $25.00 (0-531-11518-6). This updated edition of the 1990 book contains first-person testimonies from victims, a rapist, and corrections officers, plus excerpts from newspaper articles. (Rev: BL 11/1/98; HBG 3/99; SLJ 5/99; VOYA 8/99) [364.15 32 0973]

11283 Chaiet, Donna. *Staying Safe at School* (7–12). Series: Get Prepared Library. 1995, Rosen LB $23.95 (0-8239-1864-5). How to stay alert and protect oneself while at school, plus tips for girls on avoiding violent crimes on or near school campuses. (Rev: BL 11/15/95; BR 1–2/96; SLJ 2/96) [613.6]

11284 Chaiet, Donna. *Staying Safe at Work* (7–12). Series: Get Prepared Library. 1995, Rosen LB $23.95 (0-8239-1867-X). How to stay alert and protect oneself at work, with material for girls on how to create their own space and give clear messages to others. (Rev: BL 11/15/95; BR 1–2/96; SLJ 2/96; VOYA 4/96) [613.6]

11285 Chaiet, Donna. *Staying Safe on Public Transportation* (7–12). Series: Get Prepared Library. 1995, Rosen LB $16.95 (0-8239-1866-1). This book for young women traveling alone on buses, trains, or subways stresses the importance of awareness, verbal and physical self-defense, having a plan, and listening to one's instincts. (Rev: BL 11/15/95; BR 1–2/96; SLJ 2/96; VOYA 4/96) [363.1]

11286 Chaiet, Donna. *Staying Safe on the Streets* (7–12). Series: Get Prepared Library. 1995, Rosen LB $16.95 (0-8239-1865-3). Discusses situations young women should avoid outside the home and protection techniques. (Rev: SLJ 1/96) [613.6]

11287 Chaiet, Donna. *Staying Safe While Shopping* (7–12). Series: Get Prepared Library. 1995, Rosen LB $16.95 (0-8239-1869-6). This book tells girls how to stay alert and protect themselves while shopping. (Rev: BL 11/15/95; BR 1–2/96; SLJ 1/96) [364]

11288 Chaiet, Donna. *Staying Safe While Traveling* (7–12). Series: Get Prepared Library. 1995, Rosen LB $23.95 (0-8239-1868-8). In this book for girls traveling alone, the importance of awareness, how to use verbal and physical self-defense, and listening to one's instincts are stressed and examples are given for handling specific situations. (Rev: BL 11/15/95; BR 1–2/96; SLJ 2/96; VOYA 4/96) [363.1]

11289 Cooney, Judith. *Coping with Sexual Abuse* (9–12). Series: Coping. 1987, Rosen $17.95 (0-8239-0684-1). An explicit report that concentrates on sexual abuse that occurs in the home and how to handle it. (Rev: BL 9/1/87; BR 11–12/87; SLJ 9/87; VOYA 10/87) [362.7]

11290 Cozic, Charles P., and Bruno Leone, eds. *Sexual Values* (9–12). Series: Opposing Viewpoints. 1995, Greenhaven LB $21.96 (1-56510-211-8); paper $14.50 (1-56510-210-X). Debates moral values, how homosexuals should be regarded by society, and sexual values for children. (Rev: BL 4/1/95; SLJ 2/95; VOYA 5/95) [306.7]

11291 *Date Rape* (6–12). Ed. by James Haley. Series: At Issue. 2004, Gale LB $27.45 (0-7377-1569-3). Various controversial issues concerning date rape are explored in this collection of essays and magazine articles. (Rev: BL 2/15/04) [362.88]

11292 *Dating* (9–12). Ed. by Jennifer A. Hurley. Series: Teen Decisions. 2002, Greenhaven LB $31.20 (0-7377-0921-9); paper $19.95 (0-7377-0920-0). Experiences involving dating, breakups, and sex are discussed in this anthology of teen essays. [646.7]

11293 Gerdes, Louise, ed. *Sexual Harassment* (9–12). Series: Current Controversies. 1999, Greenhaven LB $21.96 (0-7377-0067-X); paper $16.20 (0-7377-0066-1). A presentation of a wide range of viewpoints on the depth of the problem of sexual harassment, its causes, how to define it legally, and how it can be reduced. (Rev: BL 9/1/99) [305.3]

11294 Guernsey, JoAnn B. *Sexual Harassment: A Question of Power* (7–12). Series: Frontline. 1995, Lerner LB $19.95 (0-8225-2608-5). The issue of harassment in the workplace, school, and everyday life is discussed. Includes historical background and male perspectives. (Rev: BL 7/95; SLJ 8/95) [305.42]

11295 Hyde, Margaret O., and Elizabeth Forsyth. *The Sexual Abuse of Children and Adolescents* (7–12). Illus. 1997, Millbrook LB $22.40 (0-7613-0058-9). The causes and effects of sexual abuse of children and young adults are covered in this thorough account that also discusses such topics as the history of sexual abuse, Megan's Law, and possible treatments for sex offenders. (Rev: BL 2/15/97; BR 11–12/97; SLJ 3/97; VOYA 8/97) [362.7]

11296 Kinnear, Karen L. *Childhood Sexual Abuse* (9–12). Series: Contemporary World Issues. 1995, ABC-CLIO LB $39.50 (0-87436-691-7). This compendium of information includes material on the nature and frequency of child sexual abuse, federal laws, court decisions, and a directory of organizations and resource materials. (Rev: BR 9–10/96; SLJ 7/96) [305]

11297 Landau, Elaine. *Sexual Harassment* (8–12). 1993, Walker LB $15.85 (0-8027-8266-3). Attempts to establish a sense of what constitutes inappropriate behavior, an issue still not agreed upon in the courts or in American society. (Rev: BL 6/1–15/93) [305.42]

11298 Layman, Nancy S. *Sexual Harassment in American Secondary Schools: A Legal Guide for Administrators, Teachers, and Students* (9–12). 1994, Contemporary Research paper $18.95 (0-935061-52-5). Provides definitions of sexual harassment, examines laws regarding it in secondary schools, and outlines how schools can avoid it or deal with it. (Rev: BL 8/94; VOYA 4/95) [344.73]

11299 Leone, Bruno, ed. *Rape on Campus* (8–12). Series: At Issue. 1995, Greenhaven LB $26.20 (1-56510-296-7); paper $17.45 (1-56510-263-0). This anthology of sources explores the rise in rape cases on campuses and the various definitions of rape. (Rev: BL 3/15/95; SLJ 5/95) [364.1]

11300 Lindquist, Scott. *The Date Rape Prevention Book: The Essential Guide for Girls and Women* (9–12). 2000, Sourcebooks paper $12.95 (1-570-71474-6). As well as a general discussion of this topic, the author presents many practical prevention techniques. (Rev: SLJ 5/00) [362.883]

11301 McFarland, Rhoda. *Working Together Against Sexual Harassment* (7–12). Series: Library of Social Activism. 1996, Rosen LB $16.95 (0-8239-1775-4). Following a review of the history of sexual harassment (of females) and recent scandals, the book emphasizes how teens can combat sexual harassment by responding politically, from fighting for official policies against it at school to organizing chapters of NOW or other organizations. (Rev: SLJ 4/97; VOYA 6/97) [344.73]

11302 McGowan, Keith. *Sexual Harassment* (9–12). Illus. Series: Overview. 1998, Lucent LB $17.96 (1-56006-507-9). The many faces of sexual harassment and its manifestations in the workplace, at school, and in the military are examined in detail in this thoughtful study, which also explores the impact on its victims, both female and male. (Rev: BL 1/1–15/99; BR 5–6/99; SLJ 3/99) [305.3]

11303 Mufson, Susan, and Rachel Kranz. *Straight Talk About Date Rape* (7–12). Series: Straight Talk. 1993, Facts on File $27.45 (0-8160-2863-X). Using examples and analogies, the authors define date rape, tell how it can be avoided, and give suggestions to help date-rape victims. (Rev: BL 9/1/93) [362.88]

11304 Munson, Lulie, and Karen Riskin. *In Their Own Words: A Sexual Abuse Workbook for Teenage Girls* (7–12). 1997, Child Welfare League of America paper $10.95 (0-87868-596-0). This manual (for use in therapy situations) helps girls who have been sexually abused work through their problems and plan for the future. (Rev: VOYA 10/97) [382.88]

11305 Nash, Carol R. *Sexual Harassment: What Teens Should Know* (7–12). Illus. Series: Issues in Focus. 1996, Enslow LB $20.95 (0-89490-735-2). After a general introduction to sexual harassment and its many forms, this account focuses on teens, the ways in which they encounter it, and techniques to fight it. (Rev: BL 7/96; SLJ 10/96; VOYA 8/96) [370.19]

11306 Parrot, Andrea. *Coping with Date Rape and Acquaintance Rape* (9–12). Series: Coping. 1988, Rosen $22.95 (0-8239-0784-8). An examination of types of rape, date rape in particular, and its effects on victims of both sexes. (Rev: BL 10/15/88; SLJ 8/88; VOYA 8/88) [362.8]

11307 *Rape* (10–12). Ed. by Mary E. Williams. Series: Contemporary Issues Companion. 2001, Greenhaven LB $31.20 (0-7377-0554-X); paper $19.95 (0-7377-0553-1). Topics concerning rape, such as causes, the aftermath, and methods of reduction and prevention are included in essays reprinted in this collection. (Rev: SLJ 7/01) [364.1]

11308 Reinert, Dale R. *Sexual Abuse and Incest* (7–12). Series: Teen Issues. 1997, Enslow LB $17.95 (0-89490-916-9). After a general explanation of what constitutes sexual abuse and incest, this work explains how to identify potential abusive situations and what to do about them. (Rev: BL 12/1/97; HBG 3/98; SLJ 12/97; VOYA 6/98) [362.76]

11309 Robson, Ruthann. *Gay Men, Lesbians, and the Law* (9–12). Illus. Series: Contemporary Issues. 1996, Chelsea $24.95 (0-7910-2612-4); paper $16.95 (0-7910-2963-8). After a brief historical background, the author examines the myriad ways in which legal issues affect the everyday lives of gay men and lesbians. (Rev: BL 9/15/96; BR 11–12/96; SLJ 10/96; VOYA 2/97) [346.7301]

11310 Rosen, Marvin. *Dealing with the Effects of Rape and Incest* (6–12). Illus. 2002, Chelsea LB $19.75 (0-7910-6693-2). Teens' personal experiences of sexual abuse draw readers into this straightforward account of the upheavals caused by mistreatment and the various coping strategies recommended for young people. (Rev: BL 10/15/02; SLJ 10/02) [616.85]

11311 *Sexual Harassment: Confrontations and Decisions*. Rev. ed. (9–12). Ed. by Edmund Wall. Series: Contemporary Issues. 2000, Prometheus paper $20.00 (1-57392-830-5). Various aspects of sexual harassment are discussed in this collection of essays, including a thorough examination of the extent of the problem. [305.4]

11312 Shuker-Haines, Frances. *Everything You Need to Know About Date Rape* (7–12). Illus. 1995, Rosen LB $25.25 (0-8239-2882-9). The author explains how date rape occurs and what precautionary measures can be taken. (Rev: BL 1/15/90; VOYA 4/90) [362.88]

11313 Tattersall, Clare. *Date Rape Drugs* (9–12). Series: Drug Abuse Prevention Library. 2000, Rosen LB $23.95 (0-8239-3119-6). After a general discussion of date rape, the author describes what drugs are often used to make the victim defenseless. [362.883]

11314 *Teenage Sexuality* (10–12). Ed. by Tamara L. Roleff. Series: Opposing Viewpoints. 2000, Greenhaven LB $27.95 (0-7377-0524-8); paper $19.95 (0-7377-0523-X). Various aspects of teenage sexuality, such as pregnancy, sex education, and homosexuality, are presented from differing viewpoints. (Rev: SLJ 2/01) [613.9]

11315 Warshaw, Robin. *I Never Called It Rape* (10–12). 1994, HarperCollins paper $13.00 (0-0609-2572-8). Case studies of women who have been raped by friends or acquaintances. (Rev: SLJ 3/89) [364.1]

11316 Wekesser, Carol, et al., eds. *Sexual Harassment* (9–12). Series: Current Controversies. 1992, Greenhaven LB $26.20 (1-56510-021-2); paper $16.20 (1-56510-020-4). Includes arguments about the causes and seriousness of the problem, what constitutes actionable behavior, and the best means to reduce harassment. (Rev: BL 4/15/93; SLJ 5/93) [331.4]

11317 White, Katherine. *Everything You Need to Know About Relationship Violence* (7–12). 2001, Rosen LB $17.95 (0-8239-3398-9). The author offers practical guidance on avoiding dating violence, recognizing risk factors, and assessing the health of a relationship. (Rev: SLJ 12/01) [306.73]

11318 Williams, Mary, ed. *Sexual Violence* (9–12). Illus. Series: Opposing Viewpoints. 1997, Greenhaven LB $21.96 (1-56510-560-5); paper $16.20 (1-56510-559-1). This anthology of articles explores the cause of sexual violence, its consequences, and how it can be prevented. (Rev: BL 7/97; BR 1–2/98; SLJ 7/97) [364.15]

11319 Williams, Mary E., ed. *Date Rape* (10–12). Series: At Issue. 1998, Greenhaven LB $16.96 (1-56510-699-7); paper $12.45 (1-56510-698-9). In this collection of articles, the controversy surrounding rape by an acquaintance is examined. (Rev: BL 4/15/98; SLJ 5/98) [362.883]

11320 Winkler, Kathleen. *Date Rape* (7–12). Illus. Series: Hot Issues. 1999, Enslow LB $21.95 (0-7660-1198-4). Personal stories and easily read data highlight this treatment of the date-rape problem. (Rev: BL 9/15/99; HBG 4/00; VOYA 4/01) [362.883]

11321 Winters, Paul A. *Child Sexual Abuse* (9–12). Series: At Issue. 1997, Greenhaven LB $15.96 (1-56510-689-X); paper $17.25 (1-56510-688-1). A wide range of opinions and information are presented about the causes, effects, and perpetrators of sexual abuse of children. (Rev: BL 5/1/98; SLJ 5/98) [362.760973]

Human Development and Behavior

General and Miscellaneous

11322 Apter, Terri. *The Myth of Maturity: What Teenagers Need from Parents to Become Adults* (10–12). 2001, Norton $24.95 (0-393-04942-6). After interviewing 32 people ages 18 to 32, the author reaches some conclusions about the problems facing this age group after high school. (Rev: BL 5/15/01) [306.874]

11323 Best, Amy. *Prom Night: Youth, Schools, and Popular Culture* (10–12). Illus. 2000, Routledge $75.00 (0-415-92427-8); paper $19.95 (0-415-92428-6). This is an interesting collection of first-person accounts that discuss prom night—the preparations, the event, and the after-prom parties. (Rev: BL 8/00) [394]

11324 Fleischman, Paul, ed. *Cannibal in the Mirror* (5–10). Photos by John Whalen. 2000, Twenty-First Century LB $24.90 (0-7613-0968-3). This thought-provoking book takes 27 quotations that describe barbarous behavior of primitive societies and pairs each with a telling photograph of similar behavior in modern American society. (Rev: BL 4/15/00; HBG 10/00; SLJ 4/00) [150]

11325 Hersch, Patricia. *A Tribe Apart: A Journey into the Heart of American Adolescence* (9–12). 1998, Fawcett (0-449-90767-8). Using many case studies, this book explores the changes that occur in American youth during adolescence and how this affects them and those around them. (Rev: BL 2/15/98) [305.23]

11326 Hirsch, Karen D. *Mind Riot: Coming of Age in Comix* (8–12). 1997, Simon & Schuster paper $9.99 (0-689-80622-1). This is an anthology of comic strips dealing with adolescents — their identity, their sexuality, their feelings, their friendships,

their families, with thumbnail sketches of the artists. (Rev: BL 6/1–15/97; SLJ 8/97) [741.5]

11327 *The Secret Life of Teens: Young People Speak Out About Their Lives* (7–12). Ed. by Gayatri Patnaik and Michelle T Shinseki. 2000, HarperSF paper $12.95 (0-688-17076-5). Teen attitudes about almost everything can be found in this thought-provoking collection of messages posted to Bolt.com, an online forum for teens and young adults. (Rev: VOYA 2/01) [305]

Psychology and Human Behavior

General and Miscellaneous

11328 Acker, Kerry. *Everything You Need to Know About the Goth Scene* (7–12). Illus. 2000, Rosen LB $17.95 (0-8239-3223-0). An informative and reliable guide to the origins, fashions, preferences, and behavior associated with the "Goth" movement. (Rev: BL 12/1/00; SLJ 3/01) [306]

11329 Akeret, Robert U. *Photolanguage: How Photos Reveal the Fascinating Stories of Our Lives and Relationships* (10–12). 2000, Norton $29.95 (0-393-04968-X). Using many black-and-white images of celebrities and others as examples, psychoanalyst Akeret explains how he "reads" photographs to gain understanding of individuals. (Rev: VOYA 2/01) [770]

11330 Allenbaugh, Kay. *Chocolate for a Teen's Dreams: Heartwarming Stories About Making Your Wishes Come True* (8–12). Series: Chocolate. 2003, Fireside paper $12.00 (0-7432-3703-X). A collection of stories by teens and older women about their dreams and desires, and how they came true. (Rev: SLJ 9/03) [305.235]

11331 *Almost Touching the Skies: Women's Coming of Age Stories* (10–12). Ed. by Florence Howe and Jean Casella. 2000, Feminist Pr. $35.00 (1-55861-233-5); paper $15.95 (1-55861-234-3). This collection of fiction and nonfiction written in the past 120 years by 22 authors contains various viewpoints and perspectives on women's coming of age. (Rev: BL 5/1/00; VOYA 8/01) [813]

11332 Alter, Cathy. *Virgin Territory: Stories from the Road to Womanhood* (10–12). 2004, Three Rivers paper $13.95 (1-4000-4781-1). For mature readers, this is a compendium of authentic female voices describing their experiences at various stages in life. (Rev: BL 2/1/04) [305.235]

11333 Broude, Gwen J. *Growing Up: A Cross-Cultural Encyclopedia* (10–12). Series: Encyclopedia of the Human Experience. 1995, ABC-CLIO LB $55.00 (0-87436-767-0). This work on cultural anthropology contrasts nearly 100 practices involving pregnancy, childbirth, and child rearing in about 100 different cultures around the world. The material is presented in alphabetically arranged articles ranging from one to several pages. (Rev: BR 9–10/96; SLJ 8/96) [301]

11334 Carlson, Dale B., and Hannah Carlson. *Where's Your Head? Teenage Psychology* (8–12). Illus. 1998, Bick paper $14.95 (1-884158-19-6). This book explores in readable format the basic elements of psychological thought concerning personality, influences on beliefs and behavior, the stages of adolescence, and mental illness. (Rev: VOYA 8/98) [150]

11335 Espeland, Pamela. *Knowing Me, Knowing You: The I-Sight Way to Understand Yourself and Others* (8–12). 2001, Free Spirit paper $13.95 (1-57542-090-2). Combining psychological theories, self-testing, and interesting sidebar features, this is a look at the reasons why some people immediately appeal to us and others don't. (Rev: SLJ 1/02) [155.2]

11336 Evans, Patricia. *Teen Torment: Overcoming Verbal Abuse at Home and at School* (9–12). 2003, Adams paper $12.95 (1-58062-845-1). Written for teens and their parents and teachers, this valuable guide explores the damage that can be inflicted by verbal abuse and recommends ways to stop this behavior. (Rev: BL 3/15/03) [158.2]

11337 *Fortitude: True Stories of True Grit* (10–12). Ed. by Melinda Teel. Illus. 2000, Red Rock paper $14.95 (0-9669-5737-7). Here are 37 first-person accounts about people who showed unusual inner strength when faced with tremendous obstacles such as racial barriers, disease, and rape. (Rev: BL 9/15/00) [179]

11338 Freud, Sigmund. *The Basic Writings of Sigmund Freud* (10–12). Ed. and trans. by A. A. Brill.

1995, Modern Library $24.95 (0-679-60166-X). This is a reprint of all the major books and articles by Freud, including *The Interpretation of Dreams* and *Totem and Taboo*. [150.19]

11339 Gardner, Robert, and Barbara Gardner Conklin. *Health Science Projects About Psychology* (7–12). Illus. 2002, Enslow LB $20.95 (0-7660-1439-8). Interesting activities that illustrate psychological concepts are extended by suggestions for further investigation. (Rev: HBG 10/02; SLJ 7/02) [150]

11340 Gartner, Bob. *High Performance Through Teamwork* (9–12). Series: Learning-a-Living Library. 1996, Rosen LB $16.95 (0-8239-2209-X). This book shows teens how to work with others and gives advice on how to identify, discuss, and resolve problems as a group. (Rev: BL 9/15/96; BR 1–2/97; SLJ 8/96) [658.3]

11341 Gonzales, Laurence. *Deep Survival: Who Lives, Who Dies, and Why* (10–12). 2003, Norton $24.95 (0-393-05276-1). True stories draw readers into this study of the factors — physiological, psychological, and spiritual — that have helped many to survive close brushes with death. (Rev: BL 9/1/03) [613.6]

11342 Hobson, J. Allan. *Dreaming: An Introduction to the Science of Sleep* (10–12). 2003, Oxford $22.00 (0-19-280304-2). A fascinating exploration of the mysteries of sleep and dreams. (Rev: BL 12/1/02) [154.63]

11343 Jacob, Iris. *My Sisters' Voices: Teenage Girls of Color Speak Out* (7–12). 2002, Holt paper $13.00 (0-8050-6821-X). Teen girls of color describe their feelings, aspirations, and disappointments in prose and poetry. (Rev: BL 3/1/02; SLJ 10/02; VOYA 12/02) [305.235]

11344 Kroeger, Brooke. *Passing: When People Can't Be Who They Are* (10–12). 2003, PublicAffairs $25.00 (1-891620-99-1). This collection of stories of diverse men and women who have adopted false races, sexes, or backgrounds explores the reasons for concealing one's true identity. (Rev: BL 9/1/03) [302]

11345 Maran, Meredith. *Class Dismissed: Senior Year in an American High School* (10–12). 2000, St. Martin's $23.95 (0-312-26568-9). This book chronicles the experiences, concerns, aspirations, and problems faced by three students in their senior year in a California high school. (Rev: BL 10/15/00; SLJ 6/01) [373.794]

11346 Musgrave, Susan, ed. *Nerves Out Loud: Critical Moments in the Lives of Seven Teen Girls* (8–12). 2001, Annick $19.95 (1-55037-693-4); paper $9.95 (1-55037-692-6). Seven adult women look back at events and problems that absorbed them as teenagers. (Rev: BL 10/1/01; HBG 3/02; SLJ 10/01; VOYA 2/02) [305.235]

11347 Nikkah, John. *Our Boys Speak: Adolescent Boys Write About Their Inner Lives* (10–12). 2000, St. Martin's paper $12.95 (0-312-26280-9). This collection of essays, journal entries, letters, stories, and poems by teenagers deals with their feelings, relationships, families, and concerns. (Rev: BL 7/00) [305.2]

11348 O'Halloran, Barbara Collopy. *Creature Comforts: People and Their Security Objects* (6–12). 2002, Houghton $17.00 (0-618-11864-0). First-person accounts, accompanied by photographs, explain why objects such as "blankies" prove invaluable to both children and adults. (Rev: BL 5/1/02; HBG 10/02; SLJ 3/02) [155.4]

11349 Ojeda, Auriana, ed. *Teens at Risk* (8–12). Illus. Series: Opposing Viewpoints. 2003, Gale LB $26.96 (0-7377-1915-X); paper $17.96 (0-7377-1916-8). Questions explored in this anthology involve the factors that put teens at risk, teenage sex and pregnancy, crime and violence, and substance abuse. (Rev: SLJ 11/03) [306]

11350 Pickels, Dwayne E. *Am I Okay? Psychological Testing and What Those Tests Mean* (9–12). Series: Encyclopedia of Psychological Disorders. 1999, Chelsea LB $24.95 (0-7910-5319-9). This work contains a history of psychological testing, the types of tests and areas tested, and how to interpret the results. (Rev: SLJ 1/01; VOYA 6/01) [150]

11351 Quartz, Steven R., and Terrence J. Sejnowski. *Liars, Lovers, and Heroes: What the New Brain Science Reveals About How We Become Who We Are* (10–12). 2002, Morrow $26.95 (0-688-16218-5). "Cultural biology" is the focus of this thought-provoking and accessible exploration of what makes us who we are. (Rev: BL 10/1/02) [612.8]

11352 Ridley, Matt. *Nature via Nurture: Genes, Experience, and What Makes Us Human* (10–12). 2003, HarperCollins $25.95 (0-06-000678-1). A wide-ranging and thought-provoking discussion of the age-old question of nature versus nurture. (Rev: BL 3/15/03) [155.7]

11353 Rue, Nancy N. *Everything you need to know About Abusive Relationships*. Rev. ed. (7–12). Series: Need to Know Library. 1998, Rosen LB $23.95 (0-8239-2832-2). Advice on handling abusive behavior is accompanied by discussion of the kinds of abuse that occur. [362.7]

11354 Salinger, Adrienne. *In My Room: Teenagers in Their Bedrooms* (8–12). 1995, Chronicle paper $16.95 (0-8118-0796-7). A thought-provoking photoessay that explores the thoughts and private domains — the bedrooms — of 40 teenagers, providing a revealing glimpse of the lives of teenagers in the 1990s. (Rev: VOYA 4/96) [612]

11355 Schreibman, Tamar. *Kissing: The Complete Guide* (7–12). 2000, Simon & Schuster paper $3.99 (0-689-83329-6). A breezy look at the history of kissing, different methods of kissing, and kissing games, with quizzes and amusing first-kiss stories. (Rev: SLJ 5/00) [394]

11356 Shaw, Tucker. *Dreams* (6–12). Illus. 2000, Alloy paper $5.99 (0-14-130920-2). An appealing and informative guide that explores different kinds of dreams, looks at some bizarre dreams, and provides tips for tracking and analyzing your own dreams. (Rev: VOYA 2/01) [154.6]

11357 Shehyn, Audrey. *Picture the Girl: Young Women Speak Their Minds* (10–12). Illus. 2000, Hyperion paper $14.95 (0-7868-8567-X). Thirty-five young women ages 14 to 19 voice their opinions and feelings about a variety of subjects from parents and school to self-image and drug abuse. (Rev: BL 8/00) [305.235]

11358 *Teens Write Through It: Essays from Teens Who Have Triumphed over Trouble* (9–12). 1998, Fairview paper $9.95 (1-57749-083-5). A collection of essays written by youngsters ages 12 through 19 about their struggles with anorexia, depression, drug abuse, divorce, sexual assault, death, and other problems. (Rev: SLJ 1/00; VOYA 4/99) [305.2]

11359 Wandberg, Robert. *Peer Mediation: Agreeing on Solutions* (6–12). Series: Life Skills. 2001, Capstone LB $23.95 (0-7368-1023-4). The process of peer mediation and its value in solving problems are explained, with examples, self-assessments, and discussion questions. (Rev: HBG 3/02; SLJ 6/02) [658]

11360 Weill, Sabrina Solin. *We're Not Monsters! Teens Speak Out About Teens in Trouble* (7–12). 2002, HarperCollins LB $15.89 (0-06-029543-0); paper $6.95 (0-380-80703-3). A frank exploration of the stories behind attention-grabbing headlines about teen suicide, school shootings, self-mutilation, and other self-destructive behaviors. (Rev: HBG 3/02; SLJ 2/02; VOYA 2/02) [364.36]

11361 Williams, Angel Kyodo. *Being Black: Zen and the Art of Living with Fearlessness and Grace* (10–12). 2000, Viking $23.95 (0-670-89268-8). This inspirational book, aimed mainly at African Americans, shows how to achieve goals and gain inner peace through meditation, yoga, and other practices of Buddhism. (Rev: BL 9/15/00) [294.3]

11362 Wright, Lawrence. *Twins: Their Remarkable Double Lives and What They Tell Us About Who We Are* (10–12). 1997, Wiley $22.95 (0-471-25220-4). A fascinating book that summarizes 50 years of research on identical twins who were separated at birth yet are found to exhibit similar habits and personalities when reunited as adults. (Rev: BL 2/1/98; SLJ 9/98) [155.4]

Emotions and Emotional Behavior

11363 Alpern, Michele. *Overcoming Feelings of Hatred* (6–12). Series: Focus on Family Matters. 2003, Chelsea $20.75 (0-7910-6953-2). This work explores the social and psychological origins of hatred and show how teens can overcome these feelings, particularly toward other races and ethnicities. (Rev: BL 10/15/02; SLJ 6/03) [616]

11364 Knapp, Caroline. *Appetites: Why Women Want* (10–12). 2003, Counterpoint $24.00 (1-58243-225-2). The unique nature of women's appetites — for food, love, sex, possessions, beauty, and career — is insightfully explored in this fascinating book. (Rev: BL 3/1/03) [362.1]

11365 Latta, Sara. *Dealing with the Loss of a Loved One* (6–12). Series: Focus on Family Matters. 2002, Chelsea LB $20.75 (0-7910-6955-9). This work discusses the many facets of grief and explains how to deal with the behavioral, emotional, and physical changes that may occur after the death of a loved one. (Rev: BL 1/1–15/03; HBG 3/03) [128]

11366 Mosley, Walter. *Workin' on the Chain Gang: Shaking Off the Dead Hand of History* (10–12). 2000, Ballantine $16.95 (0-345-43069-7). The famous adult mystery writer tells how we are still enslaved by the chains of history, economics, self-image, the media, and misuse of technology. (Rev: BL 1/1–15/00*) [305.8]

11367 Muharrar, Aisha. *More than a Label: Why What You Wear and Who You're With Doesn't Define Who You Are* (6–12). Illus. 2002, Free Spirit paper $13.95 (1-57542-110-0). The results of a survey of American youth form the basis of this accessible and lively discussion of the dangers of stereotyping. (Rev: BL 11/1/02; SLJ 12/02; VOYA 12/02) [305.235]

11368 Stefoff, Rebecca. *Friendship and Love* (9–12). Illus. 1989, Chelsea LB $19.95 (0-7910-0039-7). Theories on how friendship and love develop are explained, and ways of coping with these two feelings are explored. (Rev: BL 4/1/89; BR 11–12/89; SLJ 6/89; VOYA 8/89) [177]

Ethics and Moral Behavior

11369 Blumenfeld, Laura. *Revenge: A Story of Hope* (10–12). 2002, Simon & Schuster $25.00 (0-684-85316-7). Using her personal desire to avenge her father's shooting as a starting point, *Washington Post* reporter Blumenfeld set out to investigate the meaning of revenge. (Rev: BL 3/15/02) [179.7]

11370 Canfield, Jack, et al. *Chicken Soup for the Teenage Soul: 101 Stories of Life, Love and Learning* (7–12). 1997, Health Communications paper $12.95 (1-55874-463-0). An inspirational collection of writings, about one third by teenagers, that discuss the problems of growing up. (Rev: BL 10/1/97) [158.1]

11371 Canfield, Jack, and Mark V. Hansen. *Chicken Soup for the Teenage Soul II: 101 More Stories of Life, Love and Learning* (7–12). 1998, Health Communications $24.00 (1-55874-615-3); paper $12.95 (1-55874-616-1). A new collection of personal stories from teens that supply inspiration and guidance. (Rev: BL 11/1/98; HBG 3/99) [158.1]

11372 *Ethics* (10–12). Ed. by Brenda Stalcup. Series: Current Controversies. 2000, Greenhaven LB $21.96 (0-7377-0338-5); paper $13.96 (0-7377-0337-7). Essays and articles, some challenging, probe the nature of — and rationale for — ethical behavior, touching on questions that arise in a variety of different fields, including business, medicine, and education. (Rev: BL 11/1/00) [170]

11373 Hurley, Jennifer A., ed. *American Values* (6–12). Series: Opposing Viewpoints. 2000, Greenhaven LB $21.96 (0-7377-0344-X); paper $13.96 (0-7377-0343-1). Conservative and liberal points of view are expressed in this collection of essays that discuss moral relativism, capitalism, religion, violence, pop culture, and character building. (Rev: BL 9/15/00; SLJ 10/00) [304.6]

11374 Kincher, Jonni. *The First Honest Book About Lies* (7–12). 1992, Free Spirit paper $14.95 (0-915793-43-1). Provides tools to extract "real" information from statistics, advertisements, and so forth, as well as techniques for arguing persuasively. (Rev: BL 3/1/93) [155.9]

11375 Kuklin, Susan. *Speaking Out: Teenagers Take on Sex, Race and Identity* (7–12). 1993, Putnam $8.95 (0-399-22532-3). Students give their views on prejudice, sex, race, and identity. (Rev: BL 8/93; SLJ 7/93) [305.2]

11376 Margulies, Alice. *Compassion* (8–12). Illus. 1990, Rosen LB $15.95 (0-8239-1108-X). A discussion of the different kinds of compassion and how each helps both the individual and society. (Rev: SLJ 6/90) [152.4]

11377 Scully, Matthew. *Dominion: The Power of Man, the Suffering of Animals, and the Call to Mercy* (11–12). 2002, St. Martin's $27.95 (0-312-26147-0). A frank and thought-provoking examination of human behavior toward animals. (Rev: BL 9/15/02) [179]

11378 Simpson, Carolyn. *High Performance Through Negotiation* (8–12). Series: Learning-a-Living Library. 1996, Rosen LB $26.50 (0-8239-2206-5). This book discusses negotiation skills and how students can resolve conflicts in a variety of situations. (Rev: BL 9/15/96; BR 1–2/97; SLJ 10/96; VOYA 2/97) [158]

11379 Sullivan, Evelin. *The Concise Book of Lying* (10–12). 2001, Farrar $25.00 (0-374-12868-5). This is a wonderful overview of how lying has been important in human history, from the Bible to the present day. (Rev: BL 7/01) [177]

11380 *Teens at Risk* (8–12). Ed. by Laura K. Egendorf and Jennifer A. Hurley. Series: Opposing Viewpoints. 1998, Greenhaven LB $32.45 (1-56510-949-X); paper $21.20 (1-56510-948-1). Questions explored in this anthology involve the factors that put teens at risk, teenage crime and violence, prevention of teenage pregnancy, and the roles of government and the media in teenage difficulties. (Rev: BL 9/15/98) [306]

11381 Tivnan, Edward. *The Moral Imagination Confronting the Ethical Issues of Our Day* (9–12). 1995, Simon & Schuster $24.00 (0-671-74708-8). Essays on such controversial topics as suicide, abortion, affirmative action, and capital punishment. (Rev: BL 3/15/95) [170]

11382 Wilker, Josh. *Revenge and Retribution* (10–12). Series: Crime, Justice, and Punishment. 1998, Chelsea LB $48.00 (0-7910-4321-5). The author uses literature, photographs of classical sculptures, reproductions of etchings and paintings, and stills of modern films to illustrate that revenge and retribution have played a role in human relations throughout history. (Rev: BR 1–2/99; SLJ 12/98) [152.4]

Etiquette and Manners

11383 Hoving, Walter. *Tiffany's Table Manners for Teenagers* (7–12). Illus. 1989, Random $17.00 (0-394-82877-1). A practical guide to good table manners. (Rev: BR 9–10/89; SLJ 6/89) [395]

11384 Packer, Alex J. *How Rude! The Teenagers' Guide to Good Manners, Proper Behavior, and Not Grossing People Out* (6–12). Illus. 1997, Free Spirit paper $19.95 (1-57542-024-4). A candid, often humorous guide to good manners for teenagers that stresses common sense and covers situations ranging from inline skating to computer hacking. (Rev: BL 2/1/98; SLJ 2/98; VOYA 6/98) [395.1]

11385 Post, Elizabeth L., and Joan M. Coles. *Emily Post's Teen Etiquette* (7–12). 1995, HarperCollins paper $13.00 (0-06-273337-0). Full of information on good manners and consideration for others. (Rev: BL 10/1/95; VOYA 12/95) [395]

11386 Robert, Henry M. *Robert's Rules of Order* (8–12). 1993, Revell paper $5.99 (0-8007-8610-6). The most authoritative guide to running meetings. [060.4]

Intelligence and Thinking

11387 Galbraith, Judy, and Jim Delisle. *The Gifted Kids' Survival Guide: A Teen Handbook*. Rev. ed. (7–12). Illus. 1996, Free Spirit paper $15.95 (1-57542-003-1). Topics covered in this very useful discussion of gifted children include definitions of giftedness, IQ testing, perfectionism, goal setting, college choices, peers, and suicide. (Rev: SLJ 2/97; VOYA 6/97) [371.95]

11388 Jonsson, Erik. *Inner Navigation: Why We Get Lost and How We Find Our Way* (10–12). Illus. 2002, Scribner $25.00 (0-7432-2206-7). Teens interested in cognitive theory will enjoy this offbeat investigation into the factors that can cause spatial disorientation. (Rev: BL 2/15/02) [153.7]

11389 Pinker, Steven. *How the Mind Works* (9–12). 1997, Norton paper $17.95 (0-393-31848-6). In this informative — and frequently humorous — guide to brain science, psychologist Pinker examines the mysterious workings of the human mind and how it has evolved. [153]

11390 Rue, Nancy N. *Everything You Need to Know About Peer Mediation* (7–12). Illus. Series: Need to Know. 1997, Rosen LB $16.95 (0-8239-2435-1). Through discussion and examples, the author explains the principles of peer mediation and tells how teens can create a peer-mediation program. (Rev: BL 11/15/97; BR 1–2/98; SLJ 2/98) [303.6]

11391 Wartik, Nancy, and La Vonne Carlson-Finnerty. *Memory and Learning* (7–12). Series: Encyclopedia of Health. 1993, Chelsea LB $19.95 (0-7910-0022-2). Explores two operations of the brain and explains how they function and sometimes malfunction. (Rev: BL 3/15/93; VOYA 8/93) [153.1]

Personal Guidance

11392 Allenbaugh, Kay. *Chocolate for a Teen's Heart* (9–12). 2001, Simon & Schuster paper $12.00 (0-7432-1380-7). Fifty-five original stories of first love, heartbreak, friendship, and loss are included in this collection of inspirational tales. (Rev: BL 6/1–15/01) [152.4]

11393 Allenbaugh, Kay. *Chocolate for a Teen's Soul: Life-Changing Stories for Young Women About Growing Wise and Growing Strong* (6–12). 2000, Simon & Schuster $12.00 (0-684-87081-9). Inspiring essays explore a wide array of issues, including first love, disabilities, beauty pageants, friendship, first jobs, and family relations. (Rev: VOYA 4/01) [152.4]

11394 Asgedom, Mawi. *The Code: The Five Secrets of Teen Success* (7–12). 2003, Little, Brown $15.95 (0-316-82633-2); paper $9.99 (0-316-73689-9). Asgedom, a motivational speaker who was a refugee before coming to the United States and later attending Harvard, advises teens on strategies for success. (Rev: HBG 4/04; SLJ 11/03; VOYA 12/03)

11395 Bachel, Beverly K. *What Do You Really Want? How to Set a Goal and Go for It!* (6–12). Illus. 2001, Free Spirit paper $12.95 (1-57542-085-6). Bachel lays out ways to define and achieve goals, supported by quotations from teens who have tried them; reproducible forms are included. (Rev: BL 5/15/01; VOYA 8/01) [153.8]

11396 Bass, Ellen, and Kate Kaufman. *Free Your Mind: The Book for Gay, Lesbian, and Bisexual Youth — and Their Allies* (10–12). 1996, Harper-Perennial paper $15.95 (0-06-095104-4). This practical guide for young gay men, lesbians, and bisexuals offers helpful advice on such topics as coming out to family and friends, building a network with other young gays and lesbians, sex, and establishing healthy relationships. [305.23]

11397 Benson, Peter L., et al. *What Kids Need to Succeed: Proven, Practical Ways to Raise Good Kids* (7–12). 1998, Free Spirit paper $6.95 (1-57542-030-9). This book contains 1,200 ideas for building "assets," such as commitment to learning, positive values, social skills, and positive identity, that have been found to be factors in leading a successful life. (Rev: VOYA 8/99) [305.23]

11398 Benson, Peter L., and Judy Galbraith. *What Teens Need to Succeed: Proven, Practical Ways to Shape Your Own Future* (7–12). Illus. 1998, Free Spirit paper $15.95 (1-57542-027-9). Based on surveys from 350,000 U.S. teens, this book discusses positive "external assets" (families, peers, spiritual support systems, schools) and "internal assets" (honesty, motivation, decision-making skills, resistance skills) that contribute to a successful life. (Rev: SLJ 4/99; VOYA 8/99) [305.23]

11399 Bokram, Karen, and Alexis Sinex, eds. *The Girls' Life Guide to Growing Up* (7–12). 2000, Beyond Words paper $11.95 (1-58270-026-5). A compilation of *Girl's Life* advice on topics from friends and family to school, romance, and self-image. (Rev: SLJ 10/00) [646.7]

11400 Bolden, Tonya, ed. *33 Things Every Girl Should Know: Stories, Songs, Poems and Smart Talk by 33 Extraordinary Women* (6–12). 1998, Crown paper $13.00 (0-517-70936-8). A collection of highly readable pieces by well-known and successful women on the difficult transition from childhood to adulthood. (Rev: BL 5/15/98; BR 11–12/98; HBG 9/98; SLJ 5/98) [810.8092827]

11401 Bridgers, Jay. *Everything You Need to Know About Having an Addictive Personality* (7–12). Series: Need to Know Library. 1998, Rosen LB $25.25 (0-8239-2777-6). The author examines the social, psychological, and biochemical aspects of an

"addictive personality," explains why some people are more susceptible to addiction than others, and offers sound advice on how teens can cope with addiction. (Rev: SLJ 1/99) [157]

11402 Brown, Bobbi, and Annemarie Iverson. *Bobbi Brown Teenage Beauty: Everything You Need to Look Pretty, Natural, Sexy and Awesome* (8–12). 2000, Cliff St. $25.00 (0-06-019636-X). As well as supplying beauty tips, this book stresses the importance of diet and exercise. (Rev: SLJ 12/00) [646.7]

11403 Burke, Delta, and Alexis Lipsitz. *Delta Style* (10–12). 1998, St. Martin's $24.95 (0-312-15454-2); paper $13.99 (0-312-19855-8). The former star of *Designing Women* combines personal anecdotes and reminiscences with beauty tips for large women (like herself), while stressing that a large person has as much unique beauty as a small person and that while looking good is important, the key to happiness is feeling good from within. (Rev: BL 3/15/98; SLJ 9/98) [305.23]

11404 Busby, Cylin. *Getting Dumped . . . and Getting over It* (10–12). 2001, Price Stern Sloan paper $4.99 (0-8431-7679-2). Teen girls suffering through the heartache of a romance gone bad will find reassuring advice and hope for brighter days in this guide that includes quotations from dumpees and helpful quizzes. (Rev: HBG 10/02; SLJ 3/02; VOYA 4/02) [646.7]

11405 Camron, Roxanne. *60 Clues About Guys: A Guide to Feelings, Flirting, and Falling in Like* (6–10). Series: 60 Clues About. 2002, Lunchbox paper $8.95 (0-9678285-5-4). For girls, this is a how-to manual for coping with relationships with the opposite sex, with a personal dating diary at the end. (Rev: SLJ 7/02)

11406 Canfield, Jack, et al., eds. *Chicken Soup for the Christian Teenage Soul: Stories of Faith, Love, Inspiration and Hope* (6–12). 2003, Health Communications paper $12.95 (0-7573-0095-2). Stories, poems, and cartoons of particular relevance to teens are grouped in thematic chapters. (Rev: BL 10/1/03) [242]

11407 Carlson, Richard. *Don't Sweat the Small Stuff for Teens: Simple Ways to Keep Your Cool in Stressful Times* (9–12). 2000, Hyperion paper $11.95 (0-7868-8597-1). Motivational writer Richard Carlson offers solid advice on ways to reduce stress and appreciate life. (Rev: BL 12/1/00) [158.1]

11408 Carter-Scott, Cherie. *If High School Is a Game, Here's How to Break the Rules: A Cutting Edge Guide to Becoming Yourself* (7–12). 2001, Delacorte $12.95 (0-385-32796-X). Topics covered in this guide to teen behavior include substance use and abuse, sexuality, body decorations, and changing family relationships. (Rev: BL 2/15/01; HBG 10/01; SLJ 3/01; VOYA 6/01) [373.238]

11409 Chopra, Deepak. *Fire in the Heart: A Spiritual Guide for Teens* (8–12). 2004, Simon & Schuster $14.95 (0-689-86216-4). In this book of spiritual advice for teens, the author uses the device of having a wise old man named Baba give self-help information. (Rev: BL 5/15/04; SLJ 8/04) [204]

11410 Choron, Sandra, and Harry Choron. *The Book of Lists for Teens* (7–12). 2002, Houghton paper $12.00 (0-618-17907-0). More than 300 lists cover a wide range of topics of interest to teens, such as music videos, sports, eating disorders, substance abuse, and bullying. (Rev: SLJ 1/03; VOYA 4/03) [031.02]

11411 *CityKids Speak on Relationships* (7–12). 1995, Random paper $5.99 (0-679-86553-5). Quick bits on everything from meeting people and falling in love to sexual behavior and harassment. (Rev: BL 5/1/95) [302]

11412 Cohen, Susan, and Daniel Cohen. *Teenage Competition: A Survival Guide* (9–12). 1987, M. Evans $13.95 (0-87131-487-8). A discussion of the constructive and destructive aspects of competition and how teenagers can adjust to them. (Rev: BL 6/1/87; SLJ 8/87) [155.5]

11413 Corriveau, Danielle, ed. *Trail Mix: Stories of Youth Overcoming Adversity* (7–12). Illus. 2001, Corvo Communications $14.95 (0-9702366-0-3). Fourteen teens tell inspiring first-person stories about hard times and the value of spending time in an outdoor program. (Rev: BL 12/1/01; SLJ 1/02) [158.1]

11414 Denson, Al. *I Gotta Know!* (9–12). 1999, Tyndale paper $9.99 (0-8423-3859-4). A Christian evangelist supplies spiritual responses to questions involving drugs and alcohol, peer pressure, rejection, fear of dying, sex, family problems, and other concerns. (Rev: BL 6/1–15/99) [248.8]

11415 Dentemaro, Christine, and Rachel Kranz. *Straight Talk About Student Life* (6–10). Series: Straight Talk. 1993, Facts on File $27.45 (0-8160-2735-8). This book explores problems that students are likely to experience, including communication with teachers and other students, parental pressures, homework, and developing a healthy social life. (Rev: BL 9/1/93) [373.18]

11416 DeVenzio, Dick. *Smart Moves: How to Succeed in School, Sports, Career, and Life* (10–12). 1989, Prometheus paper $17.95 (0-87975-546-6). A compendium of practical advice on such topics as how to do well at school, make and keep friends, and succeed in career goals. (Rev: BR 3–4/90) [155.5]

11417 Devillers, Julia. *GirlWise: How to Be Confident, Capable, Cool, and in Control* (8–12). 2002, Prima paper $12.95 (0-7615-6363-6). Topics covered in this accessible volume of advice from experts range from fashion and diet to car repair and doing laundry. (Rev: SLJ 12/02) [646.7]

11418 Drill, Esther, et al. *Deal with It! A Whole New Approach to Your Body, Brain and Life as a Gurl* (8–12). Illus. 1999, Pocket paper $15.00 (0-671-04157-6). Much of the flavor of the popular Gurl.com site is duplicated in this eye-catching book full of frank information about sex, adolescent development and behavior, and succeeding in life. (Rev: BL 10/1/99) [305.235]

11419 Eagan, Andrea B. *Why Am I So Miserable if These Are the Best Years of My Life?* (9–12). 1976, HarperCollins $12.95 (0-397-31655-0). An updated version of this fine handbook that answers many of the questions adolescents (particularly girls) ask. (Rev: VOYA 8/88) [155.5]

11420 Epstein, Joel. *A Parent's Guide to Sex, Drugs and Flunking Out: Answers to the Questions Your College Student Doesn't Want You to Ask* (10–12). 2001, Hazelden paper $16.00 (1-56838-571-4). Though it is intended for parents, teens can gain from this discussion of such teenage problems as drug and alcohol abuse, selecting the right college, and avoiding depression and other teen maladies. (Rev: BL 8/01) [378.1]

11421 Espeland, Pamela. *Life Lists for Teens: Tips, Steps, Hints, and How-tos for Growing Up, Getting Along, Learning, and Having Fun* (8–12). 2003, Free Spirit paper $11.95 (1-57542-125-9). Lists of suggestions, tips, and resources cover all topics of interest to teens — health, school, homework, safety, bullying, pregnancy, abuse, and so forth. (Rev: LMC 11–12/03; SLJ 5/03; VOYA 6/03) [646.7]

11422 Farro, Rita. *Life Is Not a Dress Size: Rita Farro's Guide to Attitude, Style, and a New You* (10–12). 1996, Chilton paper $16.95 (0-8019-8758-X). This is a practical handbook for large women, with advice on how to dress with style, how to maintain a positive attitude, and how to gain self-esteem and a proper self-image. (Rev: SLJ 5/97) [646]

11423 Folkers, Gladys, and Jeanne Engelmann. *Taking Charge of My Mind and Body: A Girls' Guide to Outsmarting Alcohol, Drugs, Smoking, and Eating Problems* (9–12). 1997, Free Spirit paper $13.95 (1-57542-015-5). Drawing on teens' first-person accounts, this guide offers reassuring advice on a wide variety of subjects, including eating disorders, body image, substance abuse, and physical abuse. (Rev: SLJ 7/97) [613]

11424 Ford, Amanda. *Be True to Yourself: A Daily Guide for Teenage Girls* (6–12). 2001, Conari paper

$15.95 (1-57324-189-X). Drawing on her own experiences, Amanda Ford offers daily inspirational nuggets of wisdom for girls making the difficult passage to womanhood. (Rev: VOYA 6/01) [158.1]

11425 Fox, Annie. *Can You Relate? Real-World Advice for Teens on Guys, Girls, Growing Up, and Getting Along* (6–12). 2000, Free Spirit paper $15.95 (1-57542-066-X). This guidance book tells teens how to form relationships with family, peers, and girl or boy friends, with material on how to understand oneself. (Rev: BL 4/15/00; SLJ 7/00) [305.235]

11426 Goldstein, Mark A., and Myrna Chandler Goldstein. *Boys to Men: Staying Healthy Through the Teen Years* (7–12). 2000, Greenwood $45.00 (0-313-30966-3). This book is divided into three age groups between 12 and 21, and for each there are descriptions of changes that occur and how to adjust to them. (Rev: SLJ 6/01; VOYA 4/01) [613]

11427 Gordon, Sol. *The Teenage Survival Book* (7–12). 1981, Times Books paper $20.00 (0-8129-0972-0). This book discusses the important concerns and worries of adolescents and gives sound practical advice. [155.5]

11428 Grapes, Bryan J., ed. *Interracial Relationships* (8–12). Series: At Issue. 1999, Greenhaven LB $21.96 (0-7377-0152-2); paper $13.96 (0-7377-0154-4). From a variety of perspectives and sources, this book explores the social implications of interracial relationships, including marriage. (Rev: BL 12/15/99; SLJ 7/00) [306.73]

11429 Gray, Heather, and Samantha Phillips. *Real Girl/Real World: Tools for Finding Your True Self* (9–12). Illus. 1998, Seal paper $14.95 (1-58005-005-0). Body image, self-esteem, and sexuality are the focus of this personal guide for teen girls facing the problems of growing up. (Rev: BL 10/1/98; SLJ 3/99; VOYA 2/99) [305.235]

11430 Greene, Bob. *Get with the Program!* Getting Real About Your Weight, Health, and Emotional Well-Being (10–12). Illus. 2002, Simon & Schuster $23.00 (0-7432-2599-6). Oprah's personal trainer has produced an inspirational self-help guide that gives advice on weight, diet, exercise, and changing behavioral patterns. (Rev: BL 12/1/01; SLJ 9/02) [613.7]

11431 Harlan, Judith. *Girl Talk: Staying Strong, Feeling Good, Sticking Together* (6–10). Illus. 1977, Walker $15.95 (0-8027-8640-5); paper $8.95 (0-8027-7524-1). A breezy, lighthearted guide to approaching everyday problems faced by adolescent girls, with practical tips on how to solve them. (Rev: BL 12/1/97; VOYA 2/98) [305.23]

11432 Harper, Suzanne, ed. *Hands On! 33 More Things Every Girl Should Know* (6–12). Illus. 2001, Crown LB $14.99 (0-517-80099-3); paper $12.95

(0-517-80098-5). A variety of people, including authors and a video DJ, give teen girls advice about health, boys, school, and projects. (Rev: BL 2/1/01; HBG 10/01; SLJ 3/01; VOYA 4/01) [158.1]

11433 Harris-Johnson, Debrah. *The African-American Teenagers' Guide to Personal Growth, Health, Safety, Sex and Survival: Living and Learning in the 21st Century* (6–12). 2000, Amber paper $19.95 (0-9655064-4-4). This guide for young African Americans growing up in America today covers such topics as family structure, friendships, sexual orientation, work, and spirituality. (Rev: BL 2/15/00; VOYA 6/02) [646.7]

11434 Keltner, Nancy, ed. *If You Print This, Please Don't Use My Name* (7–12). Illus. 1992, Terra Nova paper $8.95 (0-944176-03-8). Letters from a California advice column for teens on topics ranging from sexuality to school. (Rev: BL 1/1/92; SLJ 7/92) [305.23]

11435 Kimball, Gayle. *The Teen Trip: The Complete Resource Guide* (9–12). 1997, Equality paper $16.95 (0-938795-26-0). Comments by 1,500 teenagers via the Internet are the highlight of this book about the teen experience, from abortion and yeast infection to self-esteem and peer pressure. (Rev: SLJ 6/97) [305.23]

11436 Kirberger, Kimberly. *On Relationships: A Book for Teenagers* (7–12). Series: Teen Love. 1999, Health Communications paper $12.95 (1-55874-734-6). Letters, stories, and poems tackle problems that arise in romantic relationships. (Rev: BL 10/15/99; SLJ 1/00) [306.7]

11437 Kirberger, Kimberly, and Colin Mortensen. *On Friendship: A Book for Teenagers* (6–10). Series: Teen Love. 2000, Health Communications paper $12.95 (1-55874-815-6). This comforting overview of the meaning of friendship features writings by teenagers. (Rev: BL 1/1–15/01; SLJ 4/01) [302.3]

11438 Koehler, Manfred. *Majoring in Life: A Young Adult's Guide to Faith, Friendship, Freedom and Other Stuff That Won't Show on Your Resume* (9–12). 2002, Vine paper $10.99 (1-56955-286-X). Thirty stories offer faith-based counsel for teenagers on such varied topics as sexuality and making sense of the world's tragedies. (Rev: BL 8/02) [248.8]

11439 Kreiner, Anna. *Creating Your Own Support System* (7–10). Series: Need to Know Library. 1996, Rosen LB $25.25 (0-8239-2215-4). An easy-to-read account that teaches how to create a support system of friends, neighbors, relatives, clergy members, and teachers, if support is not available at home. (Rev: SLJ 1/97) [305.23]

11440 Krippayne, Scott. *Hugs for Teens: Stories, Sayings, and Scriptures to Encourage and Inspire* (10–12). Illus. 2001, Howard $11.99 (1-58229-213-

2). Christian teens will find words of inspiration, scriptural passages, and stories that offer guidance for their day-to-day lives in this collection, part of the Hugs series. (Rev: VOYA 12/01)

11441 Landau, Elaine. *Interracial Dating and Marriage* (7–12). 1993, Messner LB $13.98 (0-671-75258-8). Narratives by 10 young adults and five adults relate experiences with and reactions to interracial relationships. (Rev: BL 11/1/93) [306.73]

11442 *Let's Talk About Me! A Girl's Personal, Private, and Portable Instruction Book for Life* (6–10). Illus. 1997, Archway paper $12.00 (0-671-01521-4). A self-help book that discusses problems girls experience growing up, best for use with individuals because of its many fill-in-the-blank quizzes and spaces for diary entries. (Rev: VOYA 2/98) [305.23]

11443 Lindsay, Jeanne W. *Caring, Commitment and Change: How to Build a Relationship That Lasts* (7–12). Series: Teenage Couples. 1995, Morning Glory $15.95 (0-930934-92-X); paper $9.95 (0-930934-93-8). A look at the personal issues involved in marriage. (Rev: BL 4/15/95; SLJ 3/95) [646.7]

11444 Locker, Sari. *Sari Says: The Real Dirt on Everything from Sex to School* (8–12). 2001, HarperCollins paper $11.95 (0-06-447306-6). Teen People online columnist Sari gives frank and friendly advice on everything from braces to sex. (Rev: SLJ 2/02; VOYA 4/02) [305.235]

11445 Lound, Karen. *Girl Power in the Family: A Book About Girls, Their Rights, and Their Voice* (5–10). Series: Girl Power. 2000, Lerner LB $30.35 (0-8225-2692-1). A book that explores the problems of growing up female today with material on gender roles, biases, and relationships. (Rev: HBG 10/00; SLJ 6/00) [303.6]

11446 McCoy, Kathy, and Charles Wibbelsman. *Life Happens* (7–12). 1996, Berkley paper $12.95 (0-399-51987-4). In a concise, practical way, this book covers such teenage crisis-producing situations as death in the family, stress, alcoholism, pregnancy, homosexuality, and the breakup of relationships. (Rev: BL 2/1/96) [616.98]

11447 McCoy, Kathy, and Charles Wibbelsman. *The New Teenage Body Book*. Rev. ed. (7–12). Illus. 1992, Putnam paper $15.95 (0-399-51725-1). This revised edition provides information and advice concerning the use of drugs, alcohol, and cigarettes; how to handle peer pressure; contraceptive methods; and abortion. (Rev: BL 6/15/92; SLJ 5/92) [613]

11448 McCune, Bunny, and Deb Traunstein. *Girls to Women: Sharing Our Stories* (7–10). Illus. 1998, Celestial Arts paper $14.95 (0-89087-881-1). Arranged under thematic chapters that deal with self-esteem, friendships, menstruation, sexuality, and mother–daughter relations, this collection of essays, stories, and poems explores various aspects of being young and female. (Rev: SLJ 4/99) [305.23]

11449 McFarland, Rhoda. *Coping Through Assertiveness* (9–12). 1986, Rosen $12.95 (0-8239-0680-9). The author explains the difference between assertiveness and aggressive behavior and, among other things, how to say "no." (Rev: BL 1/15/87; BR 1–2/87; SLJ 1/87) [158.1]

11450 *More Taste Berries for Teens: A Second Collection of Inspirational Short Stories Encouragement on Life, Love, Friendship and Tough Issues* (6–12). Ed. by Bettie B. Youngs and Jennifer Leig Youngs. Series: Taste Berries for Teens. 2000, Health Communications paper $12.95 (1-55874-813-X). Written almost exclusively by teens, the inspiring stories and essays in this collection touch on such varied issues of teen concern as love and relationships, family relations, friendship, deciding on a career, and getting into college. (Rev: VOYA 2/01)

11451 Morgenstern, Julie, and Jessi Morgenstern-Colon. *Organizing from the Inside Out for Teens: The Foolproof System for Organizing Your Room, Your Time, and Your Life* (7–12). Illus. 2002, Holt paper $15.00 (0-8050-6470-2). Strategies for managing the time, space, and responsibilities of typical teens are presented in this practical manual. (Rev: BL 1/1–15/03) [646.7]

11452 Morgenstern, Mindy. *The Real Rules for Girls* (8–12). Illus. 2000, Girl Pr. $14.95 (0-9659754-5-2). Advice on life, love, friends, and more is presented in an attractive, conversational way. (Rev: SLJ 3/00; VOYA 4/00)

11453 Musgrave, Susan, ed. *You Be Me: Friendship in the Lives of Teen Girls* (7–12). 2002, Annick $18.95 (1-55037-739-6); paper $7.95 (1-55037-738-8). Stories of girls' experiences show the sometimes difficult realities of teenage friendships. (Rev: BL 12/15/02; HBG 3/03; SLJ 1/03; VOYA 12/02) [305.235]

11454 *No Body's Perfect: Stories by Teens About Body Image, Self-Acceptance, and the Search for Identity* (7–12). Ed. by Kimberly Kirberger. 2003, Scholastic paper $12.95 (0-439-42638-3). Mostly written by girls, these stories are intended to help teens grapple with problems of identity and image. (Rev: SLJ 6/03; VOYA 4/03)

11455 Noel, Carol. *Get It? Got It? Good! A Guide for Teenagers* (7–12). Illus. 1996, Serious Business paper $7.95 (0-9649479-0-0). A teen self-help guide that discusses such topics as self-esteem, sex, health, relations with others, goals, and violence. (Rev: BL 6/1–15/96) [361.8]

11456 Nuwer, Hank. *High School Hazing: When Rites Become Wrongs* (8–12). Illus. 2000, Watts LB $25.00 (0-531-11682-4). After a discussion on the rationale behind hazing rituals, this account describes many that have resulted in unnecessary humiliation, physical harm, and even death. (Rev: BL 4/1/00) [373.18]

11457 Packard, Gwen K. *Coping When a Parent Goes Back to Work* (8–12). Series: Coping. 1995, Rosen LB $25.25 (0-8239-1698-7). Gives children whose parents return to work tips on adapting to the new situation. Includes real-life examples. (Rev: BL 7/95) [306.874]

11458 Palmer, Pat, and Melissa Alberti Froehner. *Teen Esteem: A Self-Direction Manual for Young Adults.* 2nd ed. (8–12). 2000, Impact paper $9.95 (1-88623-014-5). This book gives guidance on building self-esteem and positive attitudes to help teens with such common adolescent issues as peer pressure. [155.5]

11459 Parker, Julie. *High Performance Through Leadership* (8–12). Series: Learning-a-Living Library. 1996, Rosen LB $26.50 (0-8239-2205-7). This book discusses the ability to lead and teach others and shows students how they can take the initiative in problem solving and decision making. (Rev: BL 9/15/96; BR 1–2/97; SLJ 12/96) [158]

11460 Paul, Anthea. *Girlosophy: A Soul Survivor Kit* (6–12). Series: Girlosophy. 2001, Allen & Unwin paper $16.95 (1-86508-432-8). This appealing guide aims to help teenage girls achieve their full potential by taking charge of their own destinies. (Rev: SLJ 11/01; VOYA 6/02)

11461 Paul, Anthea. *Girlosophy: The Breakup Survival Kit* (8–12). 2004, Allen & Unwin paper $11.95 (1-74114-077-3). This book, part of a series that gives girls good personal guidance, tells how one can recover from the trauma connected with breakups. (Rev: BL 5/1/04) [646.7]

11462 Pestalozzi, Tina. *Life Skills 101: A Practical Guide to Leaving Home and Living on Your Own* (10–12). 2001, Stonewood paper $14.95 (0-9701334-4-8). This "how-to" book gives advice to teens who are about to go to college or get their first job and move out of the family nest. (Rev: SLJ 7/01) [646.7]

11463 Reeve, Dana. *Care Packages: Letters to Christopher Reeve from Strangers and Other Friends* (6–12). Illus. 1999, Random $20.00 (0-375-50076-6). Christopher Reeve's wife Dana selects words of inspiration and encouragement from the thousands of letters sent to her husband after the accident that left him paralyzed. (Rev: BL 11/1/99; VOYA 6/00) [791.43]

11464 Santamaria, Peggy. *High Performance Through Self-Management* (8–12). Series: Learning-a-Living Library. 1996, Rosen LB $26.50 (0-8239-

2208-1). This volume shows students how to work with others and teaches them to identify, discuss, and resolve problems as a group. (Rev: BL 9/15/96; BR 1–2/97; SLJ 8/96) [640]

11465 Schleifer, Jay. *The Dangers of Hazing* (7–12). Series: Need to Know Library. 1996, Rosen LB $25.25 (0-8239-2217-0). The phenomenon of hazing in high schools and colleges is discussed, with material on how to avoid it, its dangers, and how to report incidents. (Rev: SLJ 1/97) [305.23]

11466 Schwager, Tina, and Michele Schuerger. *Gutsy Girls: Young Women Who Dare* (7–12). Illus. 1999, Free Spirit paper $14.95 (1-57542-059-7). The first part of this book profiles 25 "gutsy" individuals who have tackled a variety of challenges; the second part suggests ways to motivate yourself to achieve more. (Rev: SLJ 11/99; VOYA 2/00) [155.5]

11467 Schwager, Tina, and Michele Schuerger. *The Right Moves: A Girl's Guide to Getting Fit and Feeling Good* (6–12). 1998, Free Spirit paper $15.95 (1-57542-035-X). Topics including self-esteem, diet, and exercise are covered in this upbeat guide for girls that promotes a positive, healthy lifestyle. (Rev: BL 1/1–15/99; BR 5–6/99; SLJ 1/99*; VOYA 8/99) [613.7]

11468 Shaw, Tucker. *"What's That Smell?" (Oh, It's Me): 50 Mortifying Situations and How to Deal* (7–12). Illus. 2003, Penguin paper $7.99 (0-14-250011-9). With a smart, sarcastic tone, this book deals with problems including odors, bodily functions, awkward situations, and legal concerns. (Rev: BL 2/15/03; SLJ 4/03) [646.7]

11469 Shaw, Tucker, and Fiona Gibb. *Any Advice?* (7–12). Illus. 2000, Penguin $5.99 (0-14-130921-0). Compiled from postings to an Internet advice column, this collection of questions and answers covers many topics of concern to today's teens, including sex, family relations, and body image. (Rev: VOYA 12/00)

11470 Shellenberger, Susie, and Greg Johnson. *Cars, Curfews, Parties, and Parents* (9–12). 1995, Bethany paper $7.99 (1-55661-482-9). Written from an openly Christian viewpoint, this is a guide for teens that emphasizes communication with parents, compassion for others, and an attitude of seeking God's will. (Rev: VOYA 6/96) [305.23]

11471 Shellenberger, Susie, and Greg Johnson. *Lockers, Lunch Lines, Chemistry, and Cliques* (9–12). 1995, Bethany paper $7.99 (1-55661-483-7). This faith-based personal guidance book covers topics like time management, organizational skills, building a relationship with God, and keeping healthy. (Rev: SLJ 11/95; VOYA 4/96) [305.23]

11472 Simmons, Rachel. *Odd Girl Speaks Out: Girls Write About Bullies, Cliques, Popularity, and Jealousy* (10–12). 2004, Harcourt paper $13.00 (0-15-602815-8). First-person accounts from teens — victims, perpetrators, and bystanders — are blended with the author's comments on aggression and other typical adolescent problems. (Rev: BL 12/15/03) [305.23]

11473 Steinem, Gloria. *Revolution from Within: A Book of Self-Esteem* (9–12). 1992, Little, Brown paper $14.95 (0-316-81247-1). Drawing on her own personal experiences and those of others, outspoken feminist Gloria Steinem suggests ways in which women can build self-esteem. [155.2]

11474 *Take My Advice: Letters to the Next Generation from People Who Know a Thing or Two* (11–12). Ed. by James L. Harmon. Illus. 2002, Simon & Schuster $18.00 (0-7432-1092-1). Often shocking and subversive, this is frank advice from a wide range of thinkers and artists, suited for mature teens. (Rev: BL 4/15/02)

11475 Taylor, Julie. *The Girls' Guide to Friends* (7–12). 2002, Three Rivers paper $12.00 (0-609-80857-5). A lighthearted look at getting and keeping friends, with quizzes and other entertaining features. (Rev: BL 12/15/02) [158.2]

11476 Taylor, Julie. *The Girls' Guide to Guys: Straight Talk for Teens on Flirting, Dating, Breaking Up, Making Up, and Finding True Love* (7–12). Illus. 2000, Three Rivers $11.00 (0-609-80505-3). Useful and accessible advice, delivered in a conversational manner and interactive format. (Rev: VOYA 6/01) [646.7]

11477 Taylor, Sally. *On My Own: The Ultimate How-to Guide for Young Adults* (11–12). 2002, Silly Goose paper $34.95 (0-9711500-0-1). A comprehensive and practical guide to living independently, covering everything from budgeting and sharing with a roommate to the importance of charity and citizenship. (Rev: BL 1/1–15/03) [646.700842]

11478 Van Buren, Abigail. *The Best of Dear Abby* (10–12). 1989, Andrews & McMeel paper $9.95 (0-8362-6241-7). This is a collection of the best of the advice columns written by this popular counselor. [361.3]

11479 Wesson, Carolyn McLenahan. *Teen Troubles* (7–12). 1988, Walker $17.95 (0-8027-1011-5); paper $11.95 (0-8027-7310-9). A candid, sometimes humorous self-help book on teenage problems and how to face them. (Rev: VOYA 12/88) [155.5]

11480 Weston, Carol. *For Teens Only: Quotes, Notes, and Advice You Can Use* (6–12). 2002, HarperCollins paper $8.99 (0-06-000214-X). More than 500 quotations introduce advice and inspiration

for all areas of teenage life. (Rev: BL 12/1/02; SLJ 2/03; VOYA 2/03) [646.7]

11481 White, Lee, and Mary Ditson. *The Teenage Human Body Operator's Manual* (6–10). Illus. 1999, Northwest Media paper $9.95 (1-892194-01-5). Using an appealing layout and cartoon illustrations, this is an overview of teenagers' physical and psychological needs, touching on hygiene, nutrition, disease, pregnancy and birth control, and mental health. (Rev: SLJ 11/98) [305.23]

11482 Williams, Terrie. *Stay Strong: Simple Life Lessons for Teens* (6–10). 2001, Scholastic $15.95 (0-439-12971-0). Williams offers advice on topics of interest to teens — ethical behavior, manners, money, and relationships — with success stories and quotations from celebrities. (Rev: BL 5/15/01; HBG 10/01; SLJ 6/01; VOYA 6/01) [305.235]

11483 Willis, Teresa Ann. *It's All Good! Daily Affirmations for Teens* (10–12). Illus. 1999, Emp! Emp! Press paper $14.95 (0-9667677-0-5). A daily calendar of quotations and positive, life-affirming messages from celebrities. (Rev: VOYA 2/00)

11484 Winik, Marion. *Rules for the Unruly: Living the Unconventional Life* (10–12). 2001, Simon & Schuster paper $12.00 (0-7432-1603-2). This powerful account tells frank stories of dealing with challenges including drug addiction and unwanted pregnancy. (Rev: BL 3/15/01) [170]

11485 Wirths, Claudine G., and Mary Bowman-Kruhm. *Coping with Confrontations and Encounters with the Police* (7–12). Series: Coping. 1997, Rosen LB $25.25 (0-8239-2431-9). This book gives teens essential and realistic information that will help them deal successfully with police encounters and minimize potential risks. (Rev: SLJ 4/98; VOYA 2/98) [364.3]

11486 Wolfelt, Alan D. *Healing Your Grieving Heart for Teens: 100 Practical Ideas* (6–12). 2001, Companion Pr. paper $11.95 (1-879651-23-8). The author, a teacher and grief counselor, offers 100 practical tips on accepting and dealing with grief and provides tasks that will help teens identify their needs. (Rev: BL 3/15/01; SLJ 9/01; VOYA 8/01)

11487 Youngs, Jennifer Leigh. *Feeling Great, Looking Hot and Loving Yourself: Health, Fitness, and Beauty for Teens* (6–12). Illus. 2000, Health Communications paper $12.95 (1-55874-767-2). Beauty advice delves beneath the skin to address such important issues as self-esteem and goal-setting. (Rev: SLJ 7/00; VOYA 12/00) [613.7]

11488 Zimbardo, Philip G. *Shyness* (10–12). 1990, Addison-Wesley paper $13.00 (0-201-55018-0). What causes shyness and how to relieve this anxiety are explored in this volume. [152.4]

Social Groups

Family and Family Problems

11489 *Adoption* (9–12). Ed. by Helen Cothran. Series: Opposing Viewpoints. 2001, Gale $31.20 (0-7377-0789-5); paper $19.95 (0-7377-0790-9). This collection of thoughtful essays explores a broad range of issues relating to adoption, including adoption by gays and lesbians, transracial adoption, and the thorny question of how to balance an adoptee's right to know his or her parentage with the birth parents' right to privacy. (Rev: BL 2/15/02) [362.73]

11490 Alpern, Michele. *Let's Talk: Sharing Our Thoughts and Feelings During Times of Crisis* (6–12). Series: Focus on Family Matters. 2003, Chelsea $20.75 (0-7910-6954-0). This account examines reactions that accompany times of crisis, such as anxiety and depression, and shows how teens can share their feelings with parents and friends. (Rev: BL 10/15/02) [306.9]

11491 Armitage, Ronda. *Family Violence* (6–10). Series: Talking Points. 1999, Raintree Steck-Vaughn LB $18.98 (0-7398-1371-4). This brief but balanced account explores family violence, its causes, types, and effects. (Rev: BL 12/15/99; HBG 9/00) [362.82]

11492 Beal, Anne C., et al. *The Black Parenting Book: Caring for Our Children in the First Five Years* (10–12). Illus. 1999, Broadway paper $20.00 (0-7679-0196-7). The unique problems facing African American parents are addressed in detail in this book, which is targeted at the adult market but accessible for teens. (Rev: BL 12/1/98) [649]

11493 Block, Joel D., and Susan S. Bartell. *Stepliving for Teens: Getting Along with Stepparents, Parents, and Siblings* (7–12). Series: Plugged In. 2001, Price Stern Sloan LB $13.89 (0-8431-7569-9); paper $4.99 (0-8431-7568-0). This helpful and practical guide to coping with new family members, written by two psychologists, includes advice on communicating effectively. (Rev: BCCB 7–8/01; BR 11–12/01; SLJ 8/01) [306.8]

11494 Bloomfield, Harold H., and Leonard Felder. *Making Peace with Your Parents* (10–12). 1984, Ballantine paper $5.95 (0-345-30904-9). For better readers, this is a manual on how to resolve differences between parents and teenagers. [306.9]

11495 Blue, Rose. *Staying Out of Trouble in a Troubled Family* (7–10). 1998, Twenty-First Century LB $24.90 (0-7613-0365-0). Using eight case studies, this book features family problems that will be familiar to teens, analyses by professionals, and avenues for help. (Rev: BL 2/1/99; HBG 3/99; SLJ 6/99) [362.7]

11496 Bode, Janet. *Truce: Ending the Sibling War* (8–12). 1991, Watts LB $23.00 (0-531-10996-8). Case studies and interviews with teens, followed by professional analyses and potential solutions. (Rev: BL 3/15/91; SLJ 6/91) [155.44]

11497 Bollick, Nancy O'Keefe. *How to Survive Your Parents' Divorce* (7–12). Series: Changing Family. 1994, Watts paper $24.00 (0-531-11054-0). Interviews with teens who have lived through the divorce of their parents, with analysis of their feelings and behaviors. (Rev: BL 1/1/95; SLJ 3/95; VOYA 4/95) [306.89]

11498 Brady, Nelvia M. *This Mother's Daughter* (10–12). 2001, St. Martin's paper $12.95 (0-312-27833-0). This account contains 20 stories gathered from interviews with hundreds of African American mothers and daughters involving such subjects as marriage, abuse, sex, and childbearing. (Rev: BL 4/1/01) [306.874]

11499 Brondino, Jeanne, et al. *Raising Each Other* (7–12). Illus. 1988, Hunter House paper $8.95 (0-89793-044-4). This book, written and illustrated by a high school class, is about parent–teen relationships, problems, and solutions. (Rev: SLJ 1/89; VOYA 4/89) [306.1]

11500 Charlish, Anne. *Divorce* (5–10). Series: Talking Points. 1999, Raintree Steck-Vaughn LB $27.12 (0-8172-5310-6). An overview of the causes of divorce, the legal aspects, and the difficult adjustments that must be made. (Rev: BL 8/99; BR 9–10/99) [306.89]

11501 Cline, Ruth K. J. *Focus on Families* (9–12). 1990, ABC-CLIO LB $39.50 (0-87436-508-2). An account that outlines problems such as single parenting and abuse that often characterize the modern family. (Rev: SLJ 9/90) [306.8]

11502 Davies, Nancy M. *Foster Care* (6–12). 1994, Watts LB $25.00 (0-531-11081-8). Details foster-care laws and operational procedures and explores the varied feelings of children in foster homes, with suggestions for possible alternatives. (Rev: BL 8/94; SLJ 7/94; VOYA 10/94) [362.7]

11503 Desetta, Al, ed. *The Heart Knows Something Different: Teenage Voices from the Foster Care System* (9–12). 1996, Persea $24.95 (0-89255-215-8); paper $13.95 (0-89255-218-2). Divided into four parts, the 57 essays in this book, written by teens who were foster children, tell about individual situations leading to foster-care placement, living in foster homes, self-awareness, and hopes of the future. (Rev: BL 5/15/96; SLJ 6/96; VOYA 8/96) [362.7]

11504 DuPrau, Jeanne. *Adoption: The Facts, Feelings, and Issues of a Double Heritage* (7–12). 1990, Messner LB $12.95 (0-671-69328-X); paper $5.95 (0-671-69329-8). A book that deals primarily with the conflicts and emotional problems relating to adoption and how to get help. (Rev: BL 3/15/90; SLJ 7/90; VOYA 6/90) [362.7]

11505 Evans, Karin. *The Lost Daughters of China: Abandoned Girls, Their Journey to America, and the Search for a Missing Past* (10–12). Illus. 2000, Putnam $23.95 (1-58542-026-3). A compelling story of an American couple who traveled to China to adopt a baby girl and the reason why girl babies are readily available. (Rev: BL 5/15/00) [362.73]

11506 Finneran, Kathleen. *The Tender Land: A Family Love Story* (10–12). 2000, Houghton $24.00 (0-395-98495-5). An older sister and her family come to accept the death of their 15-year-old brother by suicide. (Rev: BL 5/1/00*) [362.28]

11507 Flaming, Allen, and Kate Scowen, eds. *My Crazy Life: How I Survived My Family* (8–12). 2002, Annick paper $9.95 (1-55037-732-9). Ten teen narratives describe how each managed to deal with family problems such as abuse, addiction, AIDS, divorce, and homosexuality. (Rev: BL 9/1/02; HBG 10/02; SLJ 7/02) [306.87]

11508 Ford, Judy, and Amanda Ford. *Between Mother and Daughter: A Teenager and Her Mom Share the Secrets of a Strong Relationship* (6–12). 1999, Conari paper $14.95 (1-57324-164-4). Alternate chapters written by mother and daughter reveal the power of communication. (Rev: BL 8/99; VOYA 2/00) [306.874]

11509 Fraser, Joelle. *The Territory of Men* (11–12). 2002, Villard $22.95 (0-375-50437-0). In this poignant memoir, Fraser relates the lessons she learned from her estranged parents and how these shaped her life and her own relationships. (Rev: BL 7/02) [920]

11510 Gerdes, Louise, ed. *Battered Women* (7–12). Series: Contemporary Issues Companion. 1998, Greenhaven LB $32.45 (1-56510-897-3). Personal narratives of battered women are used in this anthology that investigates patterns of domestic violence and examines legal and other measures that can be used to protect women. (Rev: BL 3/15/99; BR 9–10/99) [362.82]

11511 Ginott, Haim. *Between Parent and Teenager* (9–12). 1982, Avon paper $5.99 (0-380-00820-3). This is a guide to developing good relations between parents and teenagers, plus solid advice about handling the problems of adolescence. [306.9]

11512 Grapes, Bryan J., ed. *Child Abuse* (6–12). Series: Current Controversies. 2001, Greenhaven LB $22.96 (0-7377-0679-1); paper $14.96 (0-7377-0678-3). This collection of essays discusses the extent of child abuse, the underlying factors (substance abuse, poverty, childhood experience, and so forth) that are prevalent in abuse cases, and efforts to end the abuse and to rehabilitate the victims. (Rev: BL 9/1/01; SLJ 11/01) [362.76]

11513 Gravelle, Karen, and Susan Fischer. *Where Are My Birth Parents? A Guide for Teenage Adoptees* (7–12). 1993, Walker LB $15.85 (0-8027-8258-2). Includes firsthand experiences of young people who searched for their birth families with varied success. (Rev: BL 9/1/93; SLJ 7/93; VOYA 10/93) [362.7]

11514 Greenberg, Keith E. *Runaways* (6–10). 1995, Lerner LB $19.93 (0-8225-2557-7). Greenberg uses the personal approach, focusing on the lives of two runaways, to dispel the idea that runaways are "bad" kids. (Rev: BL 10/15/95; SLJ 12/95) [362.7]

11515 Harnack, Andrew. *Adoption* (7–12). Series: Opposing Viewpoints. 1995, Greenhaven LB $26.20 (1-56510-213-4); paper $21.20 (1-56510-212-6). Presents various perspectives on the hot-button issues relating to adoption, with provocative articles from well-known advocates. (Rev: BL 10/15/95; VOYA 6/96) [362.7]

11516 Helmbold, F. Wilbur. *Tracing Your Ancestry* (9–12). 1978, Oxmoor House paper $9.95 (0-8487-0414-2). This is a step-by-step guide to researching one's family history. [929]

11517 Hong, Maria. *Family Abuse: A National Epidemic* (8–12). Illus. Series: Issues in Focus. 1997, Enslow LB $20.95 (0-89490-720-4). This book takes a long, thorough look at this national epidemic that includes spousal and child abuse as well as children terrorizing a family and the abuse of elderly parents. (Rev: BL 12/1/97; SLJ 12/97; VOYA 6/98) [362.82]

11518 Hurley, Jennifer A., ed. *Child Abuse* (8–12). Series: Opposing Viewpoints. 1998, Greenhaven LB $32.45 (1-56510-935-X). Questions explored in this anthology of opinions include the causes of child abuse, false accusations, how the legal system should deal with child molesters, and how child abuse can be reduced. (Rev: BL 9/15/98) [362.7]

11519 Huston, Perdita. *Families as We Are: Conversations from Around the World* (10–12). Illus. 2001, Feminist Pr. $25.95 (1-55861-250-5). Multigenerational families in 11 countries including Thailand, China, Egypt, Brazil, and the United States were asked how changes in such areas as human rights and economics were affecting them. (Rev: BL 7/01) [306.85]

11520 Hyde, Margaret O. *Know About Abuse* (7–12). Series: Know About. 1992, Walker LB $14.85 (0-8027-8177-2). Provides facts on child abuse, reasons, symptoms, examples, and solutions, covering a wide range of abuse, from obvious to subtle. (Rev: BL 11/1/92; SLJ 9/92) [362.7]

11521 Kaminker, Laura. *Everything You Need to Know About Being Adopted* (7–12). Series: Need to Know Library. 1999, Rosen $23.95 (0-8239-2834-9). As well as the legal aspects of adoption, this account explores the problems young people may face when they are adopted. [362.7]

11522 Kempe, C. Henry, and Ray E. Helfer, eds. *The Battered Child.* 4th ed. (10–12). Illus. 1987, National Center for the Prevention of Child Abuse $37.00 (0-318-14670-3). The causes, treatment, and prevention of child abuse are covered in this sympathetic account. [362.7]

11523 Kim, Henny H. *Child Abuse* (6–12). Illus. Series: Opposing Viewpoints Digests. 2000, Greenhaven LB $21.96 (1-56510-867-1); paper $13.96 (1-56510-866-3). Various points of view are reported in this book that discusses the nature of child abuse, its causes, and ways it can be reduced. (Rev: BL 7/00) [362.76]

11524 Kinstlinger-Bruhn, Charlotte. *Everything You Need to Know About Breaking the Cycle of Domestic Violence* (6–10). Series: Need to Know Library. 1997, Rosen LB $25.25 (0-8239-2434-3). This book discusses physical, emotional, and sexual abuse, focusing on dating relationships and parental violence against children, and provides information on warning signs of an abusive relationship, how to seek help, and self-protection. (Rev: SLJ 4/98) [364.3]

11525 Koffinke, Carol. *"Mom, You Don't Understand!": A Mother and Daughter Share Their Views* (9–12). 1993, Deaconess paper $8.95 (0-925190-66-7). A counselor and her daughter, 15, alternately share viewpoints on dating, privacy, and other issues, sometimes with painful honesty. (Rev: BL 6/1–15/93; VOYA 10/93) [306.874]

11526 Kosof, Anna. *Battered Women: Living with the Enemy* (7–12). 1995, Watts LB $25.00 (0-531-11203-9). An attempt to answer the fundamental question "Why don't you just leave?" and a discussion of the development of abusive relationships. (Rev: BL 4/15/95; SLJ 3/95) [362.82]

11527 Lauck, Jennifer. *Blackbird: A Childhood Lost* (10–12). 2000, Pocket $23.95 (0-671-04255-6). For mature readers, this is an account of the hellish childhood of a girl who survived a series of tragedies and cruelties. (Rev: BL 9/15/00*; SLJ 5/01) [979.4]

11528 La Valle, John. *Coping When a Parent Is in Jail* (8–12). Series: Coping. 1995, Rosen LB $18.95 (0-8239-1967-6). Discusses the effects on a child of having a parent in jail and tries to give an idea of what the parent's life in prison is like. (Rev: BL 7/95) [362.7]

11529 Leigh, Sandra. *Two Thousand Minnows: An American Story* (10–12). 2003, Lyons Pr. $24.95 (1-58574-854-4). In this harrowing tale of family dysfunction, physical abuse, and violence, Leigh also explores parents' rights to secrets and children's rights to know the truth; for mature teens. (Rev: BL 5/1/03) [362.82]

11530 Levine, Beth. *Divorce: Young People Caught in the Middle* (7–12). 1995, Enslow LB $20.95 (0-89490-633-X). A straightforward, commonsense manual for teens dealing with divorce. (Rev: BL 3/15/95; SLJ 6/95) [306.89]

11531 Lindsay, Jeanne W. *Coping with Reality: Dealing with Money, In-Laws, Babies and Other Details of Daily Life* (7–12). Series: Teenage Couples. 1995, Morning Glory $15.95 (0-930934-87-3); paper $9.95 (0-930934-86-5). Counsel on the day-to-day aspects of being a part of a couple. (Rev: BL 4/15/95; SLJ 3/95) [306.81]

11532 Lindsay, Jeanne W. *Teenage Couples Expectations and Reality: Teen Views on Living Together, Roles, Work, Jealousy and Partner Abuse* (9–12). Series: Teenage Couples. 1996, Morning Glory $21.95 (0-930934-99-7); paper $14.95 (0-930934-98-9). This book addresses a number of problems teens face when they live together, such as partner abuse, parenting, sharing, and in-laws. (Rev: BR 3–4/97; SLJ 6/96; VOYA 8/96) [649]

11533 Lipper, Joanna. *Growing Up Fast* (10–12). 2003, St. Martin's $25.00 (0-312-42222-9). The lives and interests of six teen mothers are revealed in this volume that draws on taped interviews. (Rev: BL 9/15/03; VOYA 6/04) [306.874]

11534 Lloyd, J. D., ed. *Family Violence* (8–12). Series: Current Controversies. 2000, Greenhaven LB $22.96 (0-7377-0452-7); paper $14.96 (0-7377-0451-9). The 19 selections in this anthology cover various types of family violence, mainly against spouses and children but also directed toward the elderly and gays and lesbians. (Rev: BL 12/1/00) [362.82]

11535 McCue, Margi L. *Domestic Violence* (7–12). Series: Contemporary World Issues. 1995, ABC-CLIO LB $39.50 (0-87436-762-X). This book concentrates on spousal abuse, reactions to the problem, important events, laws and legislation, statistics, and interviews with survivors of violence. (Rev: BR 9–10/96; SLJ 5/96) [362.82]

11536 Mufson, Susan, and Rachel Kranz. *Straight Talk About Child Abuse* (7–12). Series: Straight Talk. 1991, Facts on File $27.45 (0-8160-2376-X). Beginning with a general discussion of child abuse, this book describes the common signs of physical, emotional, and sexual abuse, gives some case studies, and offers some solutions. (Rev: BL 4/1/91; SLJ 3/91) [362.7]

11537 Packer, Alex J. *Bringing Up Parents: The Teenager's Handbook* (8–12). Illus. 1993, Free Spirit paper $15.95 (0-915793-48-2). Discusses in detail the art of coping with parents: building trust, diffusing family power struggles, waging effective verbal battles, developing listening skills, and expressing feelings nonaggressively. (Rev: BL 5/1/93*; VOYA 8/93) [306.874]

11538 Pertman, Adam. *Adoption Nation: How the Adoption Revolution Is Transforming America* (10–12). 2000, Basic $25.00 (0-465-05650-4). This book covers changing attitudes and laws involving adoption in the United States, with material on such topics as adoption by single parents, multiracial families, gays, and older people. (Rev: BL 11/1/00) [362.73]

11539 Plummer, William. *Wishing My Father Well: A Memoir of Fathers, Sons, and Fly-Fishing* (10–12). 2000, Overlook $21.95 (1-58567-031-6). A moving account that explores a father-son relationship by using the father's fishing journals as jumping-off point. (Rev: BL 6/1–15/00) [306.874]

11540 Porterfield, Kay Marie. *Straight Talk About Divorce* (9–12). 1999, Facts on File $27.45 (0-8160-3725-6). This work discusses many aspects of divorce, including legal and financial factors and its effect on young people. [306.89]

11541 Presma, Frances, and Paula Edelson. *Straight Talk About Today's Families* (9–12). 1999, Facts on File $27.45 (0-8160-3905-4). This work discusses different types of families, the challenges of being a part of a family, and ways to deal with family-related problems. [306.8]

11542 Quindlen, Anna. *Siblings* (10–12). 1998, Penguin $24.95 (0-670-87882-0). A series of essays, with photographs, on the subject of life with brothers and sisters. (Rev: BL 11/1/98; SLJ 5/99) [306]

11543 Rebman, Renee C. *Runaway Teens: A Hot Issue* (8–12). Series: Hot Issues. 2001, Enslow $19.95 (0-7660-1640-4). Why teens leave home is covered in this book, which also offers material on what happens to teens on the street and agencies that give them help. (Rev: HBG 10/01) [362.7]

11544 Robinson, Katy. *A Single Square Picture: A Korean Adoptee's Search for Her Roots* (10–12). 2002, Berkley paper $13.95 (0-425-18496-X). Robinson, who was born in Korea but raised by an American family, recounts her search for her birth parents and cultural heritage. (Rev: BL 8/02) [973]

11545 Rofes, Eric, ed. *The Kids' Book of Divorce: By, For and About Kids* (6–10). 1982, Random paper $10.00 (0-394-71018-5). Twenty youngsters from ages 11 to 14 who are children of divorce were asked about their reactions and feelings. [306.8]

11546 Roleff, Tamara L., and Mary E. Williams, eds. *Marriage and Divorce* (8–12). Series: Current Controversies. 1997, Greenhaven LB $32.45 (1-56510-568-0); paper $21.20 (1-56510-567-2). An anthology of 32 articles presenting diverse viewpoints on premarital cohabitation, the effect of divorce on chil-

dren, child custody, and same-sex marriage. (Rev: SLJ 10/97) [306.8]

11547 Rue, Nancy N. *Coping with an Illiterate Parent* (7–12). Series: Coping. 1990, Rosen LB $25.25 (0-8239-1070-9). The causes, problems, and treatment of illiteracy as seen from a teenager's point of view. (Rev: BL 3/1/90; SLJ 10/90) [306]

11548 Ryan, Elizabeth A. *Straight Talk About Parents* (7–12). 1989, Facts on File $27.45 (0-8160-1526-0). A self-help manual to help teens sort out their feelings about parents. (Rev: BL 8/89; BR 11–12/89; SLJ 9/89; VOYA 2/90) [306.8]

11549 Sadler, A. E., ed. *Family Violence* (7–12). Series: Current Controversies. 1996, Greenhaven LB $26.20 (1-56510-371-8); paper $16.20 (1-56510-370-X). An anthology of original sources that explores the prevalence of family violence, its victims and perpetrators, and how this violence can be reduced. (Rev: BL 6/1–15/96; SLJ 4/96) [362.82]

11550 St. Pierre, Stephanie. *Everything You Need to Know When a Parent Is in Jail* (7–12). Illus. Series: Everything You Need to Know. 1994, Rosen $17.95 (0-8239-1526-3). Using many real-life examples, this book gives advice to youngsters who suffer both emotional and financial crises after a parent is sent to prison. (Rev: BL 4/15/94) [362.7]

11551 St. Pierre, Stephanie. *Everything You Need to Know When a Parent Is Out of Work* (6–12). Series: Need to Know Library. 1991, Rosen $12.95 (0-8239-1217-5). Explains how parents can lose their jobs and the effects unemployment can have on a parent's behavior, family routines, and relationships. (Rev: BL 10/1/91) [331.137]

11552 Sander, Joelle. *Before Their Time: Four Generations of Teenage Mothers* (9–12). 1991, Harcourt $19.95 (0-15-111638-5). An oral history of four African American teenage mothers — great-grandmother, grandmother, mother, and daughter — that illustrates a repetitive cycle of poverty, violence, and neglect. (Rev: BL 11/1/91) [306.85]

11553 Sandweiss, Ruth, and Rachel Sandweiss. *Twins* (9–12). Illus. 1998, Running $27.50 (0-7624-0404-3). The unique relationship between twins is explored in this collection of essays and photographs that focuses on 27 sets of twins, among them dancers, athletes, farmers, models, astronauts, identical and fraternal twins, old twins and new twins, twins who married twins, twins separated at birth, and even a set of twin girls who share an undivided torso. (Rev: BL 12/1/98; VOYA 4/99) [618.2]

11554 Shanley, Mary Lyndon. *Making Babies, Making Families: What Matters Most in an Age of Reproductive Technologies, Surrogacy, Adoption, and Same-Sex and Unwed Parents* (10–12). 2001, Beacon $26.00 (0-8070-4408-3). The author explores all kinds of families and related topics such as open adoptions, transracial adoptions, the rights of unwed fathers, and surrogate mothers. (Rev: BL 7/01) [306.85]

11555 Shires-Sneddon, Pamela. *Brothers and Sisters: Born to Bicker?* (6–10). Series: Teen Issues. 1997, Enslow LB $20.95 (0-89490-914-2). This book explores a variety of sibling relationships, how social pressures affect them, and the damaging impact of drugs, alcohol, divorce, death, and abuse. (Rev: BL 4/15/97; BR 9–10/97; VOYA 10/97) [306.875]

11556 Shultz, Margaret A. *Teens with Single Parents: Why Me?* (6–12). Series: Teen Issues. 1997, Enslow LB $20.95 (0-89490-913-4). Using interviews with teens as a focus, this book examines the problems of living with a single parent and makes some suggestions for coping strategies. (Rev: BL 7/97; BR 11–12/97; SLJ 10/97) [306.5]

11557 Simpson, Carolyn. *Everything You Need to Know About Living with a Grandparent or Other Relatives* (8–12). 1995, Rosen LB $25.25 (0-8239-1872-6). This book explores the various situations that may cause teenagers to move in with grandparents, how to adjust, ways to maintain privacy, and the emotions involved on both sides. (Rev: BR 9–10/96; VOYA 2/96) [306]

11558 Smith, Franklin Carter, and Emily Anne Croom. *A Genealogist's Guide to Discovering Your African-American Ancestors: How to Find and Record Your Unique Heritage* (10–12). Illus. 2003, F & W paper $21.99 (1-55870-605-4). This guide offers advice on overcoming the particular challenges that African Americans may face in tracing their ancestry. (Rev: BL 2/15/03) [929.373]

11559 *Split: Stories from a Generation Raised on Divorce* (10–12). Ed. by Ava Chin. 2002, McGraw-Hill paper $14.95 (0-07-139106-1). This collection of essays offers important insights into the lives of children of divorce and what it means to grow up in a broken home. (Rev: BL 8/02) [306.89]

11560 Stewart, Gail B. *Battered Women* (9–12). Illus. Series: The Other America. 1996, Lucent LB $17.96 (1-56006-341-6). Four battered women tell their stories and advise others on how to avoid becoming victims. A section on how the reader can become involved in this social problem is included. (Rev: BL 6/1–15/97; BR 11–12/97; SLJ 8/97) [362.82]

11561 Stewart, Gail B. *Teen Runaways* (9–12). Illus. Series: The Other America. 1996, Lucent LB $17.96 (1-56006-336-X). Four teenage runaways tell about life on the streets, why teens leave home, and ways to help them. (Rev: BL 3/1/97; BR 11–12/97; SLJ 6/97) [362.7]

11562 Stewart, Gail B. *Teens and Divorce* (6–12). Series: Overview: Teen Issues. 2000, Lucent LB

$18.96 (1-56006-656-3). This account concentrates on the effects of divorce on teenagers and coping with such emotions as anger, grief, guilt, and worries about the future. (Rev: BL 6/1–15/00; HBG 9/00) [306.89]

11563 Swisher, Karin L., ed. *Domestic Violence* (8–12). Series: At Issue. 1996, Greenhaven LB $18.70 (1-56510-381-5); paper $17.45 (1-56510-380-7). An anthology of varying viewpoints involving the incidence and seriousness of spousal abuse by both men and women. (Rev: BL 1/1–15/96) [362.82]

11564 Swisher, Karin L., ed. *Single-Parent Families* (8–12). Series: At Issue. 1997, Greenhaven LB $26.20 (1-56510-544-3); paper $17.45 (1-56510-543-5). An anthology that presents different viewpoints about the problems and rewards of being a single parent. (Rev: BL 1/1–15/97; SLJ 7/97) [306.85]

11565 Taylor, Paul, and Diane Taylor. *Coping with a Dysfunctional Family* (7–12). Series: Coping. 1990, Rosen $22.95 (0-8239-1180-2). Through case studies, this account explores family problems that stem from such conditions as abuse, drugs, and neglect. (Rev: BL 11/1/90) [362.82]

11566 Trenka, Jane Jeong. *The Language of Blood* (10–12). 2003, Minnesota Historical Society/Borealis $23.95 (0-87351-466-1). Korean-born Trenka, adopted at a young age by a Minnesota couple, describes her search for her cultural identity. (Rev: BL 9/15/03) [977.6]

11567 *Unrooted Childhoods: Memoirs of Growing Up Global* (10–12). Ed. by Faith Eidse and Nina Sichel. 2004, Nicholas Brealey paper $23.95 (1-85788-338-1). The essays in this collection — all written by men and women who lived the nomadic life as children — will resonate with teens faced with being uprooted. (Rev: BL 12/15/03) [306]

11568 Wagner, Heather Lehr. *The Blending of Foster and Adopted Children into the Family* (6–12). Series: Focus on Family Matters. 2002, Chelsea $20.75 (0-7910-6694-0). Various family structures and situations are described, with material on how to accept, nurture, and embrace these new family constructs. (Rev: BL 10/15/02; HBG 3/03; SLJ 12/02) [606.8]

11569 Wagner, Heather Lehr. *Understanding and Coping with Divorce* (6–12). Series: Focus on Family Matters. 2002, Chelsea $20.75 (0-7910-6691-6). The causes and effects of divorce are discussed, with emphasis on how teens can get through the difficult time when parents divorce. (Rev: BL 10/15/02; HBG 3/03; SLJ 12/02) [306.8]

11570 Weiss, Ann E. *Adoptions Today: Questions and Controversy* (7–12). Illus. 2001, Twenty-First Century LB $24.90 (0-7613-1914-X). This comprehensive and informative overview covers such topics as international adoptions, adoption by unconventional couples, open adoption, and privacy. (Rev: BL 12/15/01; HBG 3/02; VOYA 12/01) [362.73]

11571 Williams, Mary E., ed. *The Family* (8–12). Series: Opposing Viewpoints. 1997, Greenhaven paper $21.20 (1-56510-668-7). An anthology of articles presenting different points of view on the status of the family, divorce, work-related topics, adoption, and the changing values in society that affect the family structure. (Rev: BL 10/15/97; SLJ 12/97) [306.8]

11572 Zanichkowsky, Stephen. *Fourteen: Growing Up Alone in a Crowd* (10–12). 2002, Basic $25.00 (0-465-09400-7). The advantages and disadvantages of growing up in a large family are explored in this matter-of-fact memoir. (Rev: BL 5/1/02) [306.87]

Youth Groups

11573 Cryan, Rosemarie, et al. *A Resource Book for Senior Girl Scouts* (9–12). 1995, Girl Scouts of the USA pap. $10.95 (0-88-441284-9). Details on scouting and its goals and awards are accompanied by information on careers, college admission, health and wellness, and other topics of interest.

11574 Mechling, Jay. *On My Honor: Boy Scouts and the Making of American Youth* (9–12). 2001, Univ. of Chicago Pr. $30.00 (0-226-51704-7). After comparing Scouting in the 1900s with issues of today, the author follows a troop through a summer camp experience and discusses concerns including girls, God, and gays. (Rev: BL 10/1/01) [369.43]

11575 Moore, David L. *Dark Sky, Dark Land: Stories of the Hmong Boy Scouts of Troop 100* (7–10). Illus. 1989, Tessera paper $14.95 (0-9623029-0-2). A collection of stories of hardship and bravery behind Boy Scout Troop 100 in Minneapolis composed of young refugees from war-torn Laos. (Rev: BL 9/15/90) [977.6]

11576 *Out of the Ordinary: Essays on Growing Up with Gay, Lesbian, and Transgender Parents* (10–12). Ed. by Noelle Howey and Ellen Samuels. Illus. 2000, St. Martin's paper $13.95 (0-312-24489-4). These 20 moving memoirs by young people who have been raised by homosexual or gender-altering parents show that parental love and sound values count more than sexual orientation. (Rev: BL 6/1–15/00*) [306.874]

11577 Slayton, Elaine Doremus. *Empowering Teens: A Guide to Developing a Community Based Youth Organization* (10–12). 2000, CROYA $19.95 (0-615-11164-5). This book, a blueprint for good teen programming, is a case study on how one community offered teens a safe place to grow and be a force in the community. (Rev: BL 10/15/00) [362.7]

Physical and Applied Sciences

General and Miscellaneous

11578 Amato, Ivan. *Super Vision: A New View of Nature* (10–12). Illus. 2003, Abrams $40.00 (0-8109-4545-2). From a close-up view of a rose petal's texture to the budding of a deadly virus, this stunning collection of photographs demonstrates scientists' advances in such technologies as spectroscopy; the accompanying text gives technical explanations. (Rev: BL 12/1/03) [502.2]

11579 Amato, Joseph Anthony. *Dust: A History of the Small and the Invisible* (10–12). 2000, Univ. of California Pr. (0-520-21875-2). This is the story of dust, where it comes from, where is goes, and what it does. (Rev: BL 12/1/99) [551.51]

11580 Anton, Ted. *Bold Science: Seven Scientists Who Are Changing Our World* (10–12). 2000, W. H. Freeman $24.95 (0-7167-3512-1). Current scientific research in such areas as extrasolar planets, new forms of energy, theories of immunology, and a new branch of earthly life are discussed in this book on the work of seven contemporary scientists. (Rev: BL 5/15/00) [567.912]

11581 Atkins, Peter. *Galileo's Finger: The Ten Great Ideas of Science* (10–12). Illus. 2003, Oxford $30.00 (0-19-860664-8). In this ambitious attempt to make science understandable, the author focuses on 10 fundamental concepts. (Rev: BL 6/1–15/03) [500]

11582 Berman, Bob. *Strange Universe: The Weird and Wild Science of Everyday Life — on Earth and Beyond* (10–12). 2004, Holt $25.00 (0-8050-7328-0). The author of *Astronomy* magazine's "Strange Universe" column explains the science behind the objects and activities of everyday life. (Rev: BL 12/1/03) [520]

11583 *The Best American Science and Nature Writing, 2003* (10–12). Ed. by Richard Dawkins and Tim Folger. 2003, Houghton $27.50 (0-618-17891-0); paper $13.00 (0-618-17892-9). This 2003 collection reflects the current preoccupation with defense and security concerns but also includes more cheerful pieces such as those celebrating author Rachel Carson and a mother's determination to succeed in the male-dominated field of science. (Rev: BL 10/15/03) [500]

11584 *The Best American Science Writing, 2003* (10–12). Ed. by Oliver Sacks. 2003, HarperCollins $27.50 (0-06-621163-8). Health, astronomy, and the environment are among the topics represented in this collection. (Rev: BL 9/1/03) [500]

11585 Bruno, Leonard C. *Science and Technology Firsts* (6–12). 1997, Gale $95.00 (0-7876-0256-6). More than 4,000 entries chronicle famous "firsts," arranged by branches of science and technology such as agriculture, astronomy, biology, chemistry, communications, and computers. (Rev: BL 8/97; BR 5–6/97; SLJ 5/97) [500]

11586 Bryson, Bill. *A Short History of Nearly Everything* (10–12). 2003, Broadway $26.00 (0-7679-0817-1). Bryson proves his versatility with this easy-to-read introduction to such basic scientific subjects as the atom, cells, light, and the origin of human life. (Rev: BL 4/15/03) [001]

11587 Burke, James. *Circles: 50 Round-Trips Through History, Technology, Science, Culture* (10–12). 2000, Simon & Schuster $25.00 (0-7432-0008-X). A collection of 50 pieces from the pages of *Scientific American* that explore, in a light, amusing manner, a variety of topics relating to science and technology. (Rev: BL 12/1/00; SLJ 7/01) [609]

11588 Calder, Nigel, and John Newell, eds. *On the Frontiers of Science* (9–12). Illus. 1989, Facts on File $35.00 (0-8160-2205-4). A compilation of writings by contemporary scientists about current work being accomplished in many different branches of science. (Rev: BR 5–6/90) [500]

11589 Carlson, Dale. *In and Out of Your Mind: Teen Science: Human Bites* (8–12). 2002, Bick paper $14.95 (1-884158-27-7). Teens with a curious, contemplative nature will find food for thought in this look at the wonders of science, humankind, and the universe that touches on topics including evolution, environmental concerns, and medicine. (Rev: SLJ 9/02) [500]

11590 Cole, K. C. *Mind over Matter: Conversations with the Cosmos* (10–12). 2003, Harcourt $25.00 (0-15-100816-7). In this collection of her *Los Angeles Times* columns, Cole offers her views on a wide variety of science-related topics in reader-friendly prose. (Rev: BL 4/15/03) [500]

11591 Corben, Bert. *The Struggle to Understand: A History of Human Wonder and Discovery* (9–12). 1992, Prometheus $34.95 (0-87975-683-7). How controversial science concepts evolved through history despite opposition. (Rev: BL 2/1/92) [509]

11592 Ehrlich, Robert. *Nine Crazy Ideas in Science: A Few Might Even Be True* (10–12). Illus. 2001, Princeton Univ. Pr. $24.95 (0-691-07001-6). The author discusses and dissects the logic behind nine nutty scientific ideas — such as HIV doesn't cause AIDS, more guns mean less crime, time travel is possible, and there was no "big bang." (Rev: BL 5/1/01) [500]

11593 Enriquez, Juan. *As the Future Catches You: How Genomics and Other Forces Are Changing Your Life, Work, Health and Wealth* (10–12). Illus. 2001, Crown Business $23.00 (0-609-60903-3). A thoughtful book that discusses the current revolution in science and technology and its consequences for business and economics. (Rev: BL 9/1/01) [303.48]

11594 Fisher, Len. *How to Dunk a Doughnut: The Science of Everyday Life* (10–12). Illus. 2003, Arcade $23.95 (1-55970-680-5). Fun and facts abound in this appealing book that explores science's all-pervasive influence on our lives, including such routine tasks as dunking a doughnut or catching a ball. (Rev: BL 10/15/03) [502]

11595 Francis, Raymond L. *The Illustrated Almanac of Science, Technology, and Invention: Day by Day Facts, Figures, and the Fanciful* (6–12). Illus. 1997, Plenum $28.95 (0-306-45633-8). For each day of the year, this almanac cites scientific events that occurred on that date, birth dates of famous scientists, discoveries, interesting technological achievements, or just quirky scientific happenings that made worldwide or even only local headlines. (Rev: BL 12/1/97; SLJ 5/98) [509]

11596 Gardner, Martin. *Did Adam and Eve Have Navels? Discourses on Reflexology, Numerology, Urine Therapy, and Other Dubious Subjects* (9–12). Illus. 2000, Norton $26.95 (0-393-04963-9). This book of 28 short pieces explores and debunks many of the strange beliefs and theories held by people

involving scientific thought. (Rev: BL 9/15/00) [500]

11597 Gould, Stephen Jay. *The Lying Stones of Marrakech: Penultimate Reflections in Natural History* (10–12). Illus. 2000, Crown $25.00 (0-609-60142-3). For sophisticated science students, this collection of essays dwells on such great issues as the origin of fossils, and the fraudulent fossils that are sold to tourists in Marrakesh. (Rev: BL 1/1–15/00) [508]

11598 Gribbin, John. *The Case of the Missing Neutrinos and Other Curious Phenomena of the Universe* (10–12). 1998, Fromm International $22.00 (0-88064-199-1). Teen scientists will enjoy this collection of essays examining a variety of scientific topics, such as the controversy over the age of the earth, solar neutrinos, and black holes. (Rev: BL 12/1/98) [520]

11599 Gribbin, John R., and Mary Gribbin. *Almost Everyone's Guide to Science: The Universe, Life and Everything* (10–12). 1999, Yale Univ. Pr. $30.00 (0-300-08101-4); paper $11.95 (0-300-08460-9). This is a general history of science, with a special focus on biography and theory. (Rev: BL 9/1/99) [500]

11600 Highfield, Roger. *The Science of Harry Potter: How Magic Really Works* (10–12). 2002, Viking $23.95 (0-670-03153-4). An appealing and well-researched look at the science behind some of the magical phenomena found in the Harry Potter books. (Rev: BL 10/15/02) [500]

11601 Holmes, Hannah. *The Secret Life of Dust: From the Cosmos to the Kitchen Counter, the Big Consequences of Little Things* (10–12). 2001, Wiley $22.95 (0-471-37743-0). All kinds of dust are identified and explained, with material on how dust changes our lives. (Rev: BL 6/1–15/01) [515.51]

11602 Horn, Bob, and W. P. Chips. *Dimension-5: Everything You Didn't Know You Didn't Know* (9–12). 1992, Fithian paper $9.95 (1-56474-007-2). Thought-provoking essays, both humorous and serious, on scientific, religious, and philosophical issues. (Rev: BL 2/15/92) [500]

11603 Horvitz, Leslie Alan. *Eureka! Scientific Breakthroughs that Changed the World* (9–12). 2002, Wiley $24.95 (0-471-40276-1). Twelve scientific discoveries and their discoverers are highlighted, such as Einstein and relativity, Fleming and penicillin, Darwin and evolution, and Watson and Crick and the double helix. [509]

11604 Ingram, Jay. *The Barmaid's Brain and Other Strange Tales from Science* (10–12). Illus. 2000, Freeman $23.95 (0-7167-4120-2). This is a collection of popular-science essays that deal with such topics as the nature of laughter, perpetual-motion machines, optical illusions, and the human behavior behind the Salem witch trials. (Rev: BL 10/1/00) [500]

11605 *Inside Out: The Best of National Geographic Diagrams and Cutaways* (6–12). Illus. 1998, National Geographic $25.00 (0-7922-7371-0). A collection of 60 illustrations from the magazine's past 75 years, with drawings, cross sections, and cutaways of such subjects as a prairie dog town, Chernobyl's ruined core, and a beluga whale's sound-producing mechanism. (Rev: BL 10/15/98; SLJ 10/98) [686.2]

11606 Jacob, Francois. *Of Flies, Mice, and Men* (10–12). Trans. by Giselle Weiss. 1999, Harvard $24.00 (0-674-63111-0). Geneticist Jacob relates his own experiences in scientific research and argues that scientists must have the freedom to pursue their theories without government or other oversight. (Rev: BL 12/1/98) [572]

11607 Kurtis, Bill. *New Explorers* (10–12). 1995, WTTW Chicago paper $28.95 (0-9647457-0-4). The frontiers of today's scientific research are divided into four categories — medical advances, great mysteries, amazing creatures, and fragile earth. Topics range from superconductors, endangered species, and care of newborn babies to the history of dinosaurs, pollution, and rain forests. (Rev: SLJ 4/96) [500]

11608 Kuttner, Paul. *Science's Trickiest Questions: 402 Questions That Will Stump, Amuse, and Surprise* (9–12). 1994, Holt paper $10.95 (0-8050-2873-0). Clear, concise answers to unusual questions in science provide entertaining reading. (Rev: BL 4/1/94) [502]

11609 *The Last Word* (9–12). Ed. by Mick O'Hare. Ian. Illus. 1999, Oxford paper $11.95 (0-19-286199-9). Drawn from the pages of Britain's *New Scientist* magazine, this collection of offbeat questions and answers explores such diverse scientific conundrums as why tea made with twice-boiled water tastes worse and why the sky is blue. (Rev: BL 12/1/98) [502]

11610 McGrayne, Sharon Bertsch. *Blue Genes and Polyester Plants: 365 More Surprising Scientific Facts, Breakthroughs and Discoveries* (8–12). 1997, Wiley paper $14.95 (0-471-14575-0). A compendium of strange and unusual facts from various branches of science. [500]

11611 *The Next Fifty Years: Science in the First Half of the Twenty-first Century* (10–12). Ed. by John Brockman. 2002, Random paper $14.00 (0-375-71342-5). Twenty-five essays by scientists offer interesting speculation on the likely direction of scientific research over the next half century. (Rev: BL 3/15/02) [501.12]

11612 Paul, Richard. *A Handbook to the Universe: Explorations of Matter, Energy, Space, and Time for Beginning Scientific Thinkers* (9–12). 1993, Chicago Review paper $14.95 (1-55652-172-3). A straightforward presentation of the principles of physics and astronomy that puts scientists and their work in a historic context. (Rev: BL 1/1/94) [500.2]

11613 Pendergrast, Mark. *Mirror Mirror: A History of the Human Love Affair with Reflection* (10–12). 2003, Basic $27.50 (0-465-05470-6). A useful resource for both science and history students, this well-written overview looks at the varied uses for mirrors through the ages. (Rev: BL 6/1–15/03) [535]

11614 Piel, Gerard. *The Age of Science: What Scientists Learned in the Twentieth Century* (10–12). 2001, Basic $40.00 (0-465-05755-1). Using a clear text and dozens of illustrations, the author has provided an excellent survey of 100 years of science with coverage of such areas as motion, gravitation, light, the anatomy of a cell, evolution, subatomic particles, and the Big Bang. (Rev: BL 10/15/01) [509.04]

11615 Pohl, Frederik. *Chasing Science: Science as Spectator Sport* (10–12). 2000, Tor $23.95 (0-312-86711-5). In this memoir, the famous science fiction author tells of his fascination with science and supplies information on such subjects as space exploration, earthquakes, and tsunamis. (Rev: BL 12/1/00) [500]

11616 Roberts, Royston M. *Serendipity: Accidental Discoveries in Science* (9–12). Illus. 1989, Wiley paper $16.95 (0-471-60203-5). An entertaining collection of anecdotes concerning the unusual circumstances surrounding some scientific discoveries. (Rev: BR 1–2/90; SLJ 11/89) [500]

11617 *Scientific American's Ask the Experts: Intrepid Travels Through the Perplexing and Amazing World of Science* (10–12). 2003, HarperResource paper $14.95 (0-06-052336-0). For science students and trivia fanatics, this is an excellent compilation of facts and figures, arranged in an easy-to-follow question-and-answer format. (Rev: BL 10/1/03) [500]

11618 Siegfried, Tom. *Strange Matters: Undiscovered Ideas at the Frontiers of Space and Time* (10–12). Illus. 2002, National Academy $24.95 (0-309-08407-5). Journalist Siegfried tackles complex scientific concepts and succeeds in making them accessible. (Rev: BL 8/02) [523.1]

11619 Spangenburg, Ray. *The History of Science from 1895 to 1994* (7–12). 1994, Facts on File $25.00 (0-8160-2742-0). Surveys scientific progress, discussing atomic energy, relativity, space exploration, genetics, and the achievements of various scientists spanning 100 years. (Rev: BL 9/1/94; VOYA 10/94) [509]

11620 Spangenburg, Ray, and Diane Moser. *The History of Science from the Ancient Greeks to the Scientific Revolution* (10–12). 1993, Facts on File $25.00 (0-8160-2739-0). This history of scientific discovery starts with the Greeks and ends with the discoveries of the 17th century. (Rev: SLJ 12/93) [509]

11621 Spangenburg, Ray, and Diane Moser. *The History of Science in the Eighteenth Century* (9–12). Series: On the Shoulders of Giants. 1993, Facts on File $19.95 (0-8160-2740-4). This work covers science in the Age of Enlightenment and the Industrial Revolution, and the work of such scientists as Cavendish, Avogado, Franklin, Volta, and Hutton. (Rev: BL 11/1/93) [509]

11622 Spangenburg, Ray, and Diane Moser. *The History of Science in the Nineteenth Century* (10–12). 1994, Facts on File $25.00 (0-8160-2741-2). This valuable account traces the developments in science during the 19th century such as discoveries concerning the atom, evolution, and the elements. [509]

11623 Spangenburg, Ray, and Diane Moser. *Science and Invention* (6–12). Illus. Series: American Historic Places. 1997, Facts on File $25.00 (0-8160-3402-8). Illustrated profiles of eight sites around the country connected with great scientists and inventions, including the homes of Joseph Priestly, Luther Burbank, George Washington Carver, and Rachel Carson as well as Thomas Edison's lab, the Lick Observatory, and the Wright Brothers National Monument. (Rev: BL 12/1/97; BR 5–6/98) [609.73]

11624 Suplee, Curt. *Everyday Science Explained* (10–12). 1996, National Geographic $35.00 (0-7922-3410-3). The wonders of chemistry, physics, and biology, including the human body, are presented in an entertaining yet instructive way with many useful illustrations. (Rev: BL 12/1/96; BR 3–4/97; SLJ 5/97) [500]

11625 Suplee, Curt. *Milestones of Science* (9–12). Illus. 2000, National Geographic $35.00 (0-7922-7906-9). This introductory history of science covers the biggest names — such as Curie, Faraday, Einstein, and Newton — and also the biggest discoveries. (Rev: BL 12/1/00; SLJ 11/00) [509]

11626 Thomas, Lewis. *The Lives of a Cell: Notes of a Biology Watcher* (10–12). 1974, Viking paper

$13.00 (0-14-004743-3). The 29 short essays in this collection deal with a variety of scientific subjects including insect behavior, the cell, and intelligent life in outer space. [570.1]

11627 *Ultimate Visual Dictionary of Science* (6–10). Illus. 1998, DK paper $30.00 (0-7894-3512-8). Though not in dictionary form (as the title suggests), this is a heavily illustrated introduction that presents basic information about physics, chemistry, anatomy, medical science, ecology, earth science, astronomy, electronics, mathematics, and computers. (Rev: BL 12/1/98; SLJ 11/98; VOYA 4/99) [500]

11628 *Why Moths Hate Thomas Edison and Other Inquiries into the Odd Nature of Nature* (9–12). Ed. by Hampton Sides. Illus. 2001, Norton paper $13.95 (0-393-32150-9). This collection of columns from *Outside* magazine covers all sorts of nature questions, such as what causes Arctic mirages and why men have nipples. (Rev: BL 8/01) [508]

11629 *Wildfire* (10–12). Ed. by Alianor True. 2001, Island Pr. $45.00 (1-55963-906-7); paper $17.95 (1-55963-907-5). A collection of stories and legends about fires and their consequences, beginning with Native American folklore and continuing with contributions from Twain, Thoreau, and other great writers. (Rev: BL 7/01) [577.2]

11630 Zimmerman, Barry E., and David J. Zimmerman. *Why Nothing Can Travel Faster Than Light . . . and Other Explorations in Nature's Curiosity Shop* (9–12). 1993, Contemporary paper $14.95 (0-8092-3821-7). Designed to appeal to "scientific illiterates," this book covers the basics of scientific thought, from Newton to quantum mechanics. (Rev: BL 9/15/93) [500]

11631 Zotti, Ed. *Know It All! Everything They Should Have Told You in School but Didn't* (9–12). 1993, Ballantine paper $9.00 (0-345-36232-2). Zotti provides no-nonsense, sometimes amusing, answers to questions about animals, weather, space, time, and many other subjects. (Rev: BL 7/93) [031]

Experiments and Projects

11632 Adams, Richard, and Robert Gardner. *Ideas for Science Projects* (9–12). Illus. Series: Projects for Young Scientists. 1997, Watts $25.00 (0-531-11347-7). A revised edition of the Robert Gardner book that presents more than 100 science projects in astronomy, chemistry, physics, mechanics, psychology, botany, and zoology. (Rev: BL 12/1/97; HBG 3/98; SLJ 12/97) [507]

11633 Adams, Richard, and Robert Gardner. *More Ideas for Science Projects.* Rev. ed. (9–12). Series: Experimental Science. 1998, Watts $25.00 (0-531-11380-9). Using material from many scientific disciplines, including computer science, this revision of the 1989 title offers more than 100 suggestions for projects, most with detailed instructions. (Rev: HBG 3/99; SLJ 1/99) [507]

11634 Bochinski, Julianne Blair. *The Complete Handbook of Science Fair Projects* (7–12). 1996, Wiley $32.50 (0-471-12378-1); paper $14.95 (0-471-12377-3). This revision of the 1991 edition contains 50 experiments (10 of them new) plus material on the international rules for science fairs. (Rev: BL 2/1/96; BR 5–6/96; SLJ 4/96) [507.9]

11635 Bombaugh, Ruth J. *Science Fair Success.* Rev. ed. (8–12). 1999, Enslow LB $20.95 (0-7660-1163-1). This is a general guide to choosing, designing, and completing a successful science project. An appendix lists some prize winners. [507.8]

11636 Brisk, Marion A. *1001 Ideas for Science Projects.* 3rd ed. (8–12). 1999, Macmillan paper $14.95 (0-02-862513-7). A group of interesting science projects in such areas as archaeology, astronomy, space science, and medicine. [507.8]

11637 Brown, Robert J. *333 Science Tricks and Experiments* (7–12). Illus. 1984, McGraw-Hill $15.95 (0-8306-0825-7). Basic scientific principles are demonstrated in experiments and projects. (Rev: BL 4/1/89) [507]

11638 Downie, Neil. *Vacuum Bazookas, Electric Rainbow Jelly, and 27 Other Saturday Science Projects* (9–12). 2001, Princeton Univ. Pr. $39.50 (0-691-00985-6); paper $18.95 (0-691-00986-4). This book outlines several science projects that involve creating strange constructions to prove physical principles behind technology. (Rev: BL 12/1/01) [507.8]

11639 Gardner, Robert. *Science Fair Projects — Planning, Presenting, Succeeding* (8–12). Series: Science Projects. 1999, Enslow LB $20.95 (0-89490-949-5). A general work that gives good advice on choosing and executing a successful science project. [507.8]

11640 Gardner, Robert. *Science Projects About the Science Behind Magic* (6–12). Series: Science Projects. 2000, Enslow LB $19.95 (0-7660-1164-X). Several science projects are outlined that explain the scientific principles behind some magic tricks. (Rev: BL 5/15/00; HBG 9/00; SLJ 7/00) [507]

11641 Iritz, Maxine Haren. *Blue-Ribbon Science Fair Projects* (7–12). 1991, McGraw-Hill paper $9.95 (0-07-157629-0). A variety of science fair projects for the novice are presented, with charts, graphs, photographs, and a chapter on choosing a topic. (Rev: BL 9/15/91) [507.8]

11642 Iritz, Maxine Haren. *Science Fair: Developing a Successful and Fun Project* (8–12). Illus. 1987, TAB $16.95 (0-8306-0936-9); paper $9.95 (0-8306-2936-X). A thorough step-by-step introduction to doing a science project. (Rev: BL 4/15/88) [507]

11643 Krieger, Melanie Jacobs. *How to Excel in Science Competitions.* Rev. ed. (6–10). Series: Science Fair Success. 1999, Enslow LB $19.95 (0-7660-1292-1). Students will find detailed guidance on choosing and conducting a science project, stories of winning projects, and profiles of successful students. (Rev: HBG 4/00; SLJ 4/00) [507.8]

11644 Newton, David E. *Making and Using Scientific Equipment* (9–12). Series: Experimental Science. 1993, Watts LB $25.00 (0-531-11176-8). An explanation of the workings of several pieces of scientific equipment and how to make and use them properly. (Rev: BL 9/1/93; VOYA 2/94) [681]

11645 Newton, David E. *Science/Technology/Society Projects for Young Scientists* (9–12). Series: Projects for Young Scientists. 1991, Watts LB $25.00 (0-531-11047-8). An examination of science and technology issues that relate to everyday life, with suggestions for projects on such topics as population, nutrition, and environmental pollution. (Rev: BL 12/15/91; SLJ 3/92) [507.8]

11646 Rainis, Kenneth G. *Exploring with a Magnifying Glass* (7–12). 1991, Watts LB $25.00 (0-531-12508-4). An introduction to how magnification works and a series of projects exploring photographs, plants, minerals, fabrics, and more. (Rev: BL 1/15/92; SLJ 4/92) [507.8]

11647 Rathjen, Don, et al. *Square Wheels and Other Easy-to-Build, Hands-on Science Activities* (9–12). Illus. Series: Exploratorium Science Snackbook. 2002, Exploratorium paper $19.95 (0-943451-55-8).

Step-by-step instructions are provided for 31 projects that demonstrate basic scientific principles, plus interesting factual tidbits and discussions. (Rev: BL 4/1/02) [507]

11648 Rhatigan, Joe, and Heather Smith. *Sure-to-Win Science Fair Projects* (6–10). Illus. 2001, Sterling $21.95 (1-57990-238-3). Readers will find plenty of science fair ideas complete with planning checklists and other tools. (Rev: BL 12/1/01; SLJ 11/01*) [507]

11649 Rosner, Marc Alan. *Science Fair Success Using the Internet* (8–12). Series: Science Fair Success. 1999, Enslow LB $20.95 (0-7660-1172-0). As well as an explanation of how to use Internet resources, this book explains how the Internet can enhance science projects. [507.8]

11650 Tocci, Salvatore. *How to Do a Science Fair Project* (9–12). Illus. Series: Experimental Science. 1997, Watts $25.00 (0-531-11346-9). This update of a popular title provides step-by-step suggestions for choosing, researching, planning, constructing, displaying, and presenting a science fair project. (Rev: BL 12/1/97; HBG 3/98; SLJ 12/97) [507]

Astronomy and Space Science

General and Miscellaneous

11651 Asimov, Isaac. *Isaac Asimov's Guide to Earth and Space* (9–12). 1991, Random $19.50 (0-679-40437-6). Explains the workings of supernovas, comets, stars, planets, galaxies, and other cosmic phenomena. (Rev: BL 10/15/91) [520]

11652 Barnes-Svarney, Patricia, and Michael R. Porcellino. *Through the Telescope: A Guide for the Amateur Astronomer*. Rev. ed. (10–12). 2000, McGraw-Hill paper $19.95 (0-07-134804-2). As well as describing telescopes, this work shows how to use them to observe the planets, moon, stars, and other objects. [522]

11653 Berman, Bob. *Secrets of the Night Sky: The Most Amazing Things in the Universe You Can See with the Naked Eye* (9–12). 1995, Morrow paper $16.00 (0-06-097687-X). Important concepts in astronomy are revealed in this book that describes a variety of celestial objects. (Rev: BL 2/15/95) [520]

11654 Berry, Richard. *Discover the Stars* (9–12). Illus. 1987, Crown paper $12.95 (0-517-56529-3). A beginner's guide to exploring stars, planets, and the moon with hints on how to use a telescope. (Rev: SLJ 4/88; VOYA 4/88) [523]

11655 Bova, Ben. *Faint Echoes, Distant Stars: The Science and Politics of Finding Life Beyond Earth* (9–12). Illus. 2004, Morrow $25.95 (0-380-97519-X). This book provides a good history of astrobiology or the study of the structure of life in the cosmos as well giving an overview of astronomy and the history of NASA. (Rev: BL 2/15/04) [576.8]

11656 Burnham, Robert, et al. *Advanced Skywatching* (10–12). Series: Nature Company Guides. 1997, Time-Life $29.95 (0-7835-4941-5). This book supplies a wealth of material for dedicated amateur astronomers, including 20 maps of various regions of the sky. (Rev: BR 3–4/98; SLJ 3/98) [523]

11657 Caes, Charles J. *Studies in Starlight: Understanding Our Universe* (10–12). Illus. 1988, TAB paper $12.95 (0-8306-2946-7). A brief history of astronomy plus a discussion of the present status of astrophysics. (Rev: BL 5/15/88) [523.01]

11658 Chown, Marcus. *The Universe Next Door: The Making of Tomorrow's Science* (9–12). 2002, Oxford $26.00 (0-19-514382-5); paper $13.95 (0-19-516884-4). Tough questions in science (Could time run backward? Is there extraterrestrial life?) are discussed in this stimulating book. (Rev: BL 3/1/02*) [523.1]

11659 Croswell, Ken. *The Universe at Midnight: Observations Illuminating the Cosmos* (10–12). 2001, Free Pr. $27.00 (0-684-85931-9). This book explains cosmology for the general reader and discusses the proposition that the universe will expand forever. (Rev: BL 8/01) [523.1]

11660 Dauber, Philip M., and Richard A. Muller. *The Three Big Bangs: Comet Crashes, Exploding Stars, and the Creation of the Universe* (9–12). 1996, Addison-Wesley $25.00 (0-201-40752-3). A description of the three main events that brought life to planet Earth. (Rev: BL 12/1/95) [523.1]

11661 Dickinson, Terence. *NightWatch: A Practical Guide to Viewing the Universe*. Rev. ed. (6–12). Illus. 1998, Firefly $45.00 (1-55209-300-X); paper $29.95 (1-55209-302-6). Exciting text and charts, tables, and full-color photographs make this an excellent handbook for amateur astronomers, with information on the sky, heavenly bodies, kinds of equipment, and how to photograph the universe. (Rev: SLJ 2/99) [523]

11662 Dickinson, Terence. *The Universe and Beyond*. 3rd ed. (9–12). 1999, Firefly paper $29.95 (1-552-

09361-1). Using more than 100 color photographs, such heavenly bodies as comets, planets, black holes, galaxies, and other elements of the universe are introduced. [523.1]

11663 Dickinson, Terence, and Alan Dyer. *The Backyard Astronomer's Guide* (9–12). 1991, Camden House $39.95 (0-921820-11-9). Provides detailed reviews of optical equipment and discusses techniques of observation and astrophotography. (Rev: BL 11/1/91) [520]

11664 Dorminey, Bruce G. *Distant Wanderers: The Search for Planets Beyond the Solar System* (10–12). Illus. 2001, Springer-Verlag $29.95 (0-387-95074-5). This is a enjoyable account concerning the search for planets outside our solar system (more than 60 have already been located) and the complex techniques used in this study. (Rev: BL 12/1/01) [523]

11665 Eicher, David. *The Universe from Your Backyard* (10–12). 1988, Kalmbach $29.95 (0-913135-13-5). Directions are given on how to find almost 700 celestial bodies in this anthology taken from the pages of *Astronomy* magazine. (Rev: BR 5–6/89) [523]

11666 Ekrutt, Joachim W. *Stars and Planets: Identifying Them, Learning About Them, Experiencing Them.* 2nd ed. (9–12). 2000, Barron's paper $13.95 (0-7641-1310-0). This volume gives a month-by-month map of the sky in the Northern and Southern Hemispheres, plus material on the phases of the moon, eclipses, and other general information about celestial objects. [523]

11667 Ferris, Timothy. *Life Beyond Earth* (9–12). Illus. 2001, Simon & Schuster $40.00 (0-684-84937-2). Stunning illustrations are used with a clear text to explore the possibility of life in outer space, perhaps even on one of our nearby planets. (Rev: BL 4/15/01) [576.8]

11668 Ferris, Timothy. *Seeing in the Dark: How Backyard Stargazers Are Probing Deep Space and Guarding Earth from Interplanetary Peril* (10–12). 2002, Simon & Schuster $26.00 (0-684-86579-3). A look at amateur astronomers' contributions to our knowledge and understanding of celestial phenomena, coupled with information on the planets and constellations. (Rev: BL 7/02) [520]

11669 Gorst, Martin. *Measuring Eternity: The Search for the Beginning of Time* (10–12). Illus. 2001, Broadway $23.95 (0-7679-0827-9). This is an entertaining book on how scientists have been able to determine how old the earth and the universe are. (Rev: BL 12/1/01) [529]

11670 Graham-Smith, Francis, and Bernard Lovell. *Pathways to the Universe* (9–12). Illus. 1989, Cambridge Univ. Pr. $38.95 (0-521-32004-6). A readable, well-organized introduction to astronomy that

can be used both for reference and for recreational reading. (Rev: BL 4/15/89; BR 9–10/89) [523]

11671 Gribbin, John. *Hyperspace: Our Final Frontier* (8–12). Illus. 2001, DK $29.95 (0-7894-7838-2). In this lavishly illustrated companion to a BBC/Learning Channel program, Gribbin introduces the basics of astronomy and cosmology and offers his views on such diverse topics as black holes, extraterrestrial life, and the Star of Bethlehem. (Rev: BL 12/1/01; SLJ 12/01; VOYA 2/02)

11672 Halpern, Paul. *The Structure of the Universe* (10–12). 1997, Holt paper $10.95 (0-8050-4029-3). This history of astronomy ends with the current thinking on the organization of the universe and its future. (Rev: SLJ 8/97) [523]

11673 Hoskin, Michael. *The Cambridge Illustrated History of Astronomy* (9–12). 1997, Cambridge Univ. Pr. $40.00 (0-521-41158-0). This beautifully illustrated book chronicles the evolution of astronomy from the celestial observations of early civilizations to the sophisticated science it is today. [520]

11674 Katz, Jonathan I. *The Biggest Bangs* (10–12). Illus. 2002, Oxford $28.00 (0-19-514570-4). The mystery of gamma-ray bursts — an astronomical phenomenon first discovered in the 1960s — is skillfully and understandably unraveled in this book by physicist Katz. (Rev: BL 4/1/02) [522]

11675 Kerrod, Robin. *Hubble: The Mirror on the Universe* (10–12). Illus. 2003, Firefly $35.00 (1-55297-781-1). A collection of stunning images captured by the Hubble Space Telescope. (Rev: BL 12/1/03; VOYA 4/04) [522]

11676 Levy, David H., and Wendee Wallach-Levy. *Cosmic Discoveries: The Wonder of Astronomy* (10–12). Illus. 2001, Prometheus $28.00 (1-57392-931-X). For advanced science students, the 24 pieces in this collection explore various aspects of astronomy, past and present, and the perseverance of astronomers. (Rev: BL 9/15/01) [520]

11677 McAleer, Neil. *The Cosmic Mind-Boggling Book* (9–12). 1982, Warner paper $11.95 (0-446-39046-1). A fascinating collection of unusual facts about the planets, stars, and universe. [523]

11678 Menzel, Donald H., and Jay M. Pasachoff. *A Field Guide to the Stars and Planets.* 2nd ed. (7–12). Illus. 1999, Houghton $9.00 (0-395-93432-X). Photographs, sky maps, charts, and timetables are features of this volume in the Peterson Field Guide series. [523]

11679 Miller, Ron. *Extrasolar Planets* (7–12). Illus. Series: Worlds Beyond. 2002, Millbrook LB $25.90 (0-7613-2354-6). A handsome and accessible overview of the planets in our solar system and elsewhere in the universe that includes historical information, biographies of scientists, basic concepts, and many attention-grabbing illustrations. (Rev: BL 2/15/02; HBG 10/02; SLJ 3/02) [523]

11680 Mitton, Jacqueline, and Stephen P. Maran. *Gems of Hubble* (10–12). 1996, Cambridge Univ. Pr. paper $13.95 (0-521-57100-6). Spectacular color photographs accompany this history of telescopes and detailed coverage on the Hubble Space Telescope and what it has seen. (Rev: SLJ 7/97) [522]

11681 Moore, Patrick. *The New Atlas of the Universe* (7–12). Illus. 1984, Crown $12.99 (0-517-55500-X). A detailed series of maps that introduce our solar system and the universe beyond. [523]

11682 Moore, Patrick. *Stargazing: Astronomy Without a Telescope*. 2nd ed. (9–12). 2001, Cambridge Univ. Pr. $33.00 (0-521-79052-2); paper $19.00 (0-521-79445-5). This guide to the night sky using only the naked eye identifies constellations, planets, comets, and meteors. [523]

11683 Mosley, John. *Stargazing for Beginners: A User-Friendly Guide for Locating and Understanding Constellations, the Sun, the Moon, Eclipses, and More* (10–12). 1998, Lowell House paper $17.00 (1-565-65821-3). Monthly charts are accompanied by advice on choosing the right instruments. [522]

11684 North, John. *The Norton History of Astronomy and Cosmology* (9–12). Series: Norton History of Science. 1994, Norton $35.00 (0-393-03656-1); paper $18.95 (0-393-31193-7). Examines the sciences of astronomy and cosmology from ancient Egypt to the present and their evolution beyond myth and superstition. (Rev: BL 8/94) [520]

11685 Owen, David. *Into Outer Space* (9–12). Illus. 2000, NTC $19.95 (0-7373-0469-3). This well-illustrated album gives views of the International Space Station and artists' conceptions of what bases on the moon and Mars will look like. (Rev: BL 12/1/00) [910]

11686 Panek, Richard. *Seeing and Believing: How the Telescope Opened Our Eyes and Minds to the Heavens* (10–12). 1998, Viking paper $11.94 (0-14-028061-8). Chronicles what humans have learned about the universe through the invention and subsequent refinements of the telescope, from Galileo's early observations to the Hubble space telescope. (Rev: BL 10/1/98) [522]

11687 Parsons, Paul. *The Big Bang: The Birth of Our Universe* (10–12). Illus. 2001, DK $12.95 (0-7894-8161-8). Published as a companion to BBC/Learning Channel programming, this well-illustrated book examines what we know about the origins of the universe. (Rev: SLJ 2/02; VOYA 2/02) [522]

11688 Rasmussen, Richard Michael. *Mysteries of Space* (6–10). Series: Great Mysteries. 1994, Greenhaven LB $22.45 (1-56510-097-2). This introduction to astronomy explores some of the great

unanswered questions about the universe. (Rev: BL 4/15/94) [520]

11689 Raymo, Chet. *An Intimate Look at the Night Sky* (10–12). Illus. 2001, Walker $25.00 (0-8027-1369-6). Though this is not a field guide, the author supplies lots of astronomical information about the heavens, including the stars, planets, and comets, in a personal and engaging manner. (Rev: BL 5/1/01) [520]

11690 Ridpath, Ian. *Stars and Planets* (9–12). Series: Eyewitness Handbooks. 1998, DK $29.95 (0-7894-3560-8); paper $18.95 (0-7894-3521-7). A guide to the stars and the solar system, with advice on stargazing. [520]

11691 Ronan, Colin A. *The Skywatcher's Handbook* (8–12). Illus. 1989, Crown paper $16.00 (0-517-57326-1). An excellent handbook that describes and explains a wide range of phenomena that occur in both the day and night skies. (Rev: BR 3–4/90; VOYA 2/90) [523]

11692 Sagan, Carl. *Cosmos* (9–12). Illus. 1980, Random paper $7.99 (0-345-33135-4). A chronological account of how and what we have learned about our universe. [520]

11693 Savage, Marshall T. *The Millennial Project: Colonizing the Galaxy — in 8 Easy Steps* (9–12). 1993, Empyrean LB $24.95 (0-9633914-8-8); paper $18.95 (0-9633914-9-6). An eight-step program, from colonies in the sea through orbiting colonies. (Rev: BL 1/15/93*) [629.47]

11694 Schaaf, Fred. *Seeing the Sky: 100 Projects, Activities and Explorations in Astronomy* (9–12). Illus. 1990, Wiley paper $18.95 (0-471-51067-X). In addition to many activities, from the simple to the complex, this informative work gives background facts about sky phenomena. (Rev: BL 10/15/90) [523]

11695 *Scientific American: The Amateur Astronomer* (10–12). Ed. by Shawn Carlson. Illus. 2001, Wiley paper $16.95 (0-471-38282-5). This collection of articles on astronomy from *Scientific American* covers such topics as building a telescope, observing the moon, planets, and stars, and the composition and behavior of our sun. (Rev: BL 12/1/00) [520]

11696 *The Scientific American Book of Astronomy* (10–12). 1999, Lyons Pr. $35.00 (1-55821-966-8). This general introduction to astronomy contains chapters on black holes, comets, extraterrestrial life, and the theory of the self-producing universe. (Rev: BL 10/15/99; SLJ 6/00) [520]

11697 *Seeing Stars: The McDonald Observatory and Its Astronomers* (6–10). 1997, Sunbelt Media $16.95 (1-57168-117-5). This is a history of the famous observatory operated by the University of Texas in Austin, with material on the equipment used and the day-to-day operation. (Rev: HBG 9/98; SLJ 5/98) [523]

11698 Shapiro, Robert. *Planetary Dreams: The Quest to Discover Life Beyond Earth* (9–12). 1999, Wiley $27.95 (0-471-17936-1). An engaging look at man's curiosity about this subject, from antiquity to the present day and from many points of view. (Rev: BL 4/99; SLJ 2/00) [576.8]

11699 Snow, Theodore P. *The Cosmic Cycle* (9–12). Illus. 1985, Darwin $14.95 (0-87850-041-3). A fine introduction to astronomy complete with 34 excellent color plates. (Rev: SLJ 3/86) [523]

11700 Steel, Duncan. *Eclipse: The Celestial Phenomenon That Changed the Course of History* (9–12). Illus. 2001, Joseph Henry $24.95 (0-309-07438-X). This work surveys all types of eclipses although the focus is on the solar variety and includes material on famous eclipses. (Rev: BL 10/15/01) [523.78]

11701 Stott, Carole. *New Astronomer* (6–12). Illus. 1999, DK $24.95 (0-7894-4175-6). Charts and illustrations guide newcomers to the night sky, plus advice on basic equipment. (Rev: VOYA 4/00) [520]

11702 Stott, Carole, and Clint Twist. *1001 Facts About Space* (7–12). Illus. Series: Backpack Books. 2002, DK paper $8.95 (0-7894-8450-1). A handy-sized overview full of illustrations that presents useful facts about the universe, galaxies, stars, solar system, and planets as well as pulsars, space history, and stellar classification. (Rev: BL 3/15/02) [590]

11703 Trefil, James S. *Other Worlds: Images of the Cosmos from Earth and Space* (10–12). 1999, National Geographic $35.00 (0-7922-7491-1). This is an illustrated overview of astronomy, cosmology and the nature of the universe beyond our solar system. (Rev: BL 12/1/99) [523.2]

11704 Tyson, Nell De Grasse. *Universe Down to Earth* (9–12). 1994, Columbia Univ. Pr. $33.00 (0-231-07560-X). Translates the fundamental meaning of various scientific models of the cosmos into language comprehensible to the general reader. (Rev: BL 5/1/94) [523.1]

11705 Upgren, Arthur. *The Turtle and the Stars: Observations of an Earthbound Astronomer* (10–12). Illus. 2002, Holt $26.00 (0-8050-7094-X). Browsers and report writers will enjoy Upgren's essays about celestial phenomena and human reactions to the changing skies. (Rev: BL 3/15/02) [520]

11706 Whitfield, Peter. *The Mapping of the Heavens* (9–12). 1995, Pomegranate $35.00 (0-87654-475-8). This album of historical maps moves from Babylonian representations of the zodiac to the mid-19th century and on to scientifically accurate modern maps. (Rev: BL 12/15/95) [525]

11707 Whitney, Charles A. *Whitney's Star Finder: A Field Guide to the Heavens.* Rev. ed. (9–12). Illus. 1985, Random paper $16.95 (0-679-72582-2). A simple guide to stars for use by the amateur without complex equipment. (Rev: BL 1/1/86; SLJ 4/86) [523]

Astronautics and Space Exploration

11708 Ackmann, Martha. *The Mercury 13: The Untold Story of Thirteen American Women and the Dream of Space Flight* (10–12). Illus. 2003, Random $24.95 (0-375-50744-2). The little-told story of 13 women pilots who tried unsuccessfully to become astronauts in the fledgling American space program. (Rev: BL 6/1–15/03; SLJ 11/03) [629.45]

11709 Ackroyd, Peter. *Escape from Earth: Voyages Through Time* (7–10). Illus. Series: Voyages Through Time. 2004, DK $19.99 (0-7566-0171-1). Using many colorful photographs and diagrams, this account traces the past history of space travel and possible future developments. (Rev: BL 5/1/04; SLJ 7/04) [387.8]

11710 Apt, Jay, and Michael Helfert. *Orbit: NASA Astronauts Photograph the Earth* (10–12). 1996, National Geographic $40.00 (0-7922-3714-5). Fascinating details on space travel are included in this book that contains outstanding photographs of Earth from outer space. (Rev: BL 1/1–15/97; SLJ 6/97) [523]

11711 Asimov, Isaac, and Frank White. *Think About Space: Where Have We Been and Where Are We Going?* (7–10). Illus. 1989, Walker LB $14.85 (0-8027-6766-4); paper $5.95 (0-8027-6767-2). A history of space exploration and a discussion of possible future developments. (Rev: BL 10/1/89; BR 5–6/90; SLJ 11/89) [500.5]

11712 Baker, David. *Scientific American Inventions from Outer Space: Everyday Uses for NASA Technology* (10–12). 2000, Random $25.00 (0-375-40979-3). Highlighting such areas as health, medicine, environment, recreation, and computers, this volume discusses the uses made of technology developed by NASA. (Rev: SLJ 10/00) [609]

11713 Benjamin, Marina. *Rocket Dreams: How the Space Age Shaped Our Vision of a World Beyond* (10–12). 2003, Free Pr. $24.00 (0-7432-3343-3). Benjamin explores the radical changes in America's space program that have transformed it from a mission of discovery and exploration to more commercially oriented projects. (Rev: BL 2/15/03) [500.5]

11714 Berry, Adrian. *The Giant Leap: Mankind Heads for the Stars* (10–12). Illus. 2001, Tor $24.95 (0-312-87785-4). The author, who is an advocate of interstellar voyages, writes a "how to" manual on how to travel in space, the conditions out there, and the equipment needed. (Rev: BL 7/01) [629.4]

11715 *Extraterrestrial Life* (10–12). Ed. by Tamara L. Roleff. Series: Contemporary Issues Companion. 2001, Greenhaven LB $31.20 (0-7377-0462-4); paper $19.95 (0-7377-0461-6). A serious study of the possibility of extraterrestrial life as found in a number of articles and scientific essays. [576.8]

11716 Fischer, Daniel. *Mission Jupiter: The Spectacular Journey of the Galileo Space Probe* (10–12). Illus. 2001, Springer-Verlag $32.00 (0-387-98764-9). For advanced science students, this is an account, with pictures, of the successful spacecraft *Galileo*, its mission to Jupiter, and what it found out. (Rev: BL 5/15/01) [629.43]

11717 Koerner, David W., and Simon LeVay. *Here Be Dragons: The Scientific Quest for Extraterrestrial Life* (10–12). Illus. 2000, Oxford $27.50 (0-19-512852-4). A scholarly adult account that explores the origin of life and its possible occurrence outside Earth. (Rev: BL 1/1–15/00) [001.9]

11718 Kraemer, Robert S. *Beyond the Moon: A Golden Age of Planetary Exploration, 1971–1978* (9–12). 2000, Smithsonian $34.95 (1-56098-954-8). This volume traces the space probes launched by NASA, including journeys to Mars, the other planets, and the asteroid belt. [629.43]

11719 Lieurance, Suzanne. *The Space Shuttle Challenger Disaster in American History* (6–10). Series: In American History. 2001, Enslow LB $20.95 (0-7660-1419-3). The story of the tragic destruction of the *Challenger* space shuttle in January, 1986, that killed seven astronauts including teacher Christa McAuliffe. (Rev: BL 8/01; HBG 10/01; SLJ 9/01) [629]

11720 Lovell, Jim, and Jeffrey Kluger. *Lost Moon: The Perilous Voyage of Apollo 13* (9–12). 1994, Houghton $22.95 (0-395-67029-2). Astronaut Lovell chronicles his harrowing, nearly fatal, failed mission to the moon, describing his crew's ingenuity in returning safely to Earth. (Rev: BL 9/15/94) [629.4]

11721 McKay, David W., and Bruce G. Smith. *Space Science Projects for Young Scientists* (7–12). Illus. 1986, Watts paper $24.00 (0-531-10244-0). A series of clearly explained projects that involve possible space environments and forces such as gravity. (Rev: BL 12/15/86; BR 1–2/87; SLJ 12/86) [500.5]

11722 Morton, Oliver. *Mapping Mars: Science, Imagination, and the Birth of a World* (10–12). Illus. 2002, St. Martin's $30.00 (0-312-24551-3). An interesting look at how the physical realities of Mars differ markedly from the images projected by earlier earthbound astronomers. (Rev: BL 7/02) [523.43]

11723 Neal, Valerie, et al. *Spaceflight: A Smithsonian Guide* (9–12). Series: Smithsonian Guide. 1995, Macmillan $38.00 (0-02-860007-X). The history of space flight beginning with Sputnik, with photographs of missions, launches, landings, and designs. (Rev: BL 6/1–15/95) [629.4]

11724 Ordway, Frederick I., III, and Randy Liebermann, eds. *Blueprint for Space: Science Fiction to Science Fact* (9–12). 1992, Smithsonian $60.00 (1-56098-072-9); paper $24.95 (1-56098-073-7). More than 20 contemporary writers spin tales of space travel from the imaginings of ancient people to real-life, present-day missions. (Rev: BL 2/1/92; SLJ 11/92) [629.4]

11725 Pogue, William R. *How Do You Go to the Bathroom in Space?* (7–12). 1991, Tor paper $7.99 (0-8125-1728-8). In a question-and-answer format, the author, who spent 84 days in space, discusses the practical aspects of space travel. (Rev: VOYA 12/85) [629.47]

11726 Reynolds, David West. *Apollo: The Epic Journey to the Moon* (10–12). Illus. 2002, Harcourt $35.00 (0-15-100964-3). This handsome volume provides a comprehensive and highly visual survey of the Apollo space program, from the early visions in the 1950s through the manned missions and the dreams for the future. (Rev: BL 3/1/02) [629.45]

11727 Ride, Sally, and Susan Okie. *To Space and Back* (8–12). Illus. 1986, Lothrop $19.99 (0-688-06159-1); paper $13.95 (0-688-09112-1). A photojourney that begins four hours before launch and ends after landing. (Rev: BL 11/86; BR 11–12/86; SLJ 11/86; VOYA 12/86) [629]

11728 Riva, Peter, and Barbara Hitchcock, comps. *Sightseeing: A Space Panorama* (8–12). Illus. 1985, Knopf $24.95 (0-394-54243-6). A spectacular view of space as pictured in 84 captioned photographs from NASA's archives. (Rev: SLJ 5/86) [629.4]

11729 Sagan, Carl. *Pale Blue Dot: A Vision of the Human Future in Space* (9–12). 1994, Random $35.00 (0-679-43841-6). Examines space exploration and humans' evolutionary urge to explore frontiers and search for their place in the universe. (Rev: BL 10/15/94*) [629]

11730 *Space Exploration* (9–12). Ed. by Christopher Mari. Series: Reference Shelf. 1999, H.W. Wilson paper $50.00 (0-8242-0963-X). A collection of articles that explores past, present, and possible future developments in space exploration, and how knowledge of space has changed human lives. [629]

11731 *Space Shuttle: The First 20 Years* (9–12). Ed. by Tony Reichhardt et al. Illus. 2002, DK $40.00 (0-7894-8425-0). First-person accounts and abundant photographs make this album an engrossing record of space shuttle experiences. (Rev: BL 5/1/02) [387.8]

11732 Spangenburg, Ray, and Diane Moser. *Opening the Space Frontier* (8–12). Illus. 1989, Facts on File $22.95 (0-8160-1848-0). A history of space exploration from the fiction of Jules Verne to the realities of today. (Rev: BR 5–6/90; SLJ 4/90; VOYA 4/90) [500.5]

11733 Taylor, Robert. *Life Aboard the Space Shuttle* (6–10). Series: The Way People Live. 2002, Gale LB $27.45 (1-59018-154-9). How the astronauts live in a space shuttle and their daily chores are covered in this account that uses many primary and secondary quotations. (Rev: BL 7/02) [629.4]

11734 Tribble, Alan C. *A Tribble's Guide to Space: How to Get to Space and What to Do When You Are There* (10–12). Illus. 2000, Princeton Univ. Pr. $24.95 (0-691-05059-7). This is a clear, readable history of space travel with many examples and concrete explanations. (Rev: BL 10/1/00) [500.5]

11735 Voit, Mark. *Hubble Space Telescope: New Views of the Universe* (8–12). 2000, Abrams paper $19.95 (0-8109-2923-6). With an accompanying text, this book includes more than 100 photographs taken by the Hubble Space Telescope. (Rev: SLJ 4/01) [520]

11736 Walsh, Patrick J. *Echoes Among the Stars: A Short History of the U.S. Space Program* (10–12). 2000, M.E. Sharpe $35.95 (0-7656-0537-6). This is a history of manned space flight, from the early successes of the Mercury and Gemini missions to the beginning of the 21st century. [629.4]

11737 Wolfe, Tom. *The Right Stuff* (10–12). 1983, Farrar $30.00 (0-374-25033-2); Bantam paper $7.99 (0-553-27556-9). Profiles of the early astronauts such as Glenn, Schirra, and Shepard. [629.45]

Comets, Meteors, and Asteroids

11738 Bevan, Alex, and John de Laeter. *Meteorites: A Journey Through Space and Time* (10–12). Illus. 2002, Smithsonian $35.95 (1-58834-021-X). Richly illustrated, this overview of meteorites focuses on the information they can reveal about their origins and the history of space. (Rev: BL 5/1/02) [523.5]

11739 Burnham, Robert. *Great Comets* (9–12). 2000, Cambridge Univ. Pr. paper $22.00 (0-521-64600-6). Various comets are identified and described, including Hyakutake in 1996 and Hale-Bopp in 1997. (Rev: BL 12/1/99) [523.6]

11740 Erickson, Jon. *Asteroids, Comets, and Meteorites: Cosmic Invaders of the Earth* (9–12). Series: Living Earth. 2003, Facts on File $55.00 (0-8160-4873-8). This volume explores these invaders from space from the days of the dinosaurs to the present. [551.3]

11741 Hutchinson, Robert, and Andrew Graham, eds. *Meteorites* (9–12). 1994, Sterling paper $12.95 (0-8069-0489-5). Questions and answers about nat-

ural objects that fall from space, with illustrations. (Rev: BL 1/1/94; SLJ 5/94) [523.5]

11742 Levy, David H. *Comets: Creators and Destroyers* (9–12). 1998, Simon & Schuster paper $12.00 (0-684-85255-1). Levy explores the life cycle of a comet and examines theories about comets' potential benefits and dangers. (Rev: BL 5/1/98) [523.6]

11743 Peebles, Curtis. *Asteroids* (10–12). Illus. 2000, Smithsonian $29.95 (1-56098-389-2). As revealed in this book, the study of these small celestial wanderers has led scientists to rethink the structure of the solar system and the history of the earth. (Rev: BL 10/15/00*) [523.44]

11744 Sagan, Carl, and Ann Druyan. *Comet* (9–12). Illus. 1985, Random $27.50 (0-394-54908-2). A richly illustrated book about all kinds of comets, but Halley's in particular. (Rev: BL 10/1/85; BR 11–12/86; VOYA 8/86) [523.6]

11745 Yeomans, Donald. *Comets: A Chronological History of Observation, Science, Myth, and Folklore* (9–12). 1991, Wiley $35.00 (0-471-61011-9). Examines the origins of comets and current scientific theories surrounding them through 1990. (Rev: BL 2/1/91) [523.6]

Earth and the Moon

11746 Dixon, Dougal, and John Adams. *The Future Is Wild: A Natural History of the Future* (6–10). Illus. 2003, Firefly $35.00 (1-55297-724-2); paper $24.95 (1-55297-723-4). Scientists speculate on the future evolution of our planet, envisioning the decline of mankind and the appearance of new species, which are shown in full-color, computer-generated images with detailed habitat. (Rev: SLJ 6/03; VOYA 4/03) [576.8]

11747 Erickson, John. *A History of Life on Earth: Understanding Our Planet's Past* (10–12). Series: Changing Earth. 1995, Facts on File $26.95 (0-8160-3131-2). A chronological study of life on this planet that spans billions of years, describing Earth's origins and its geological and biological history. (Rev: SLJ 5/96; VOYA 2/96) [575]

11748 Erickson, Jon. *Exploring Earth from Space* (8–12). Illus. 1989, TAB paper $15.95 (0-8306-3242-5). Beginning with the history of space exploration, this account also covers how we on Earth profit from the use of space. (Rev: BR 1–2/90) [500.5]

11749 Gallant, Roy A., and Christopher J. Schuberth. *Earth: The Making of a Planet* (7–10). Illus. 1998, Marshall Cavendish $14.95 (0-7614-5012-2). Beginning with the big bang, this book describes the creation of Earth, with material on landforms, seas, the moon, rocks and minerals, and the ocean floor, and speculates about Earth's future. (Rev: BL 7/98; BR 11–12/98; HBG 9/98; SLJ 7/98) [550]

11750 Hockey, Thomas A. *The Book of the Moon* (10–12). Illus. 1986, Prentice Hall $19.95 (0-13-079971-8). Although mainly about the moon, this book also furnishes information on space exploration and astronomy. (Rev: BL 10/15/86) [523.3]

11751 Johnson, Kirk R., and Richard K. Stucky. *Prehistoric Journey* (10–12). 1995, Roberts Rinehart paper $19.95 (1-57098-145-4). A chronology of the evolution of life on Earth from its creation 4.6 billion years ago to the present. (Rev: BR 5–6/96; SLJ 5/96; VOYA 8/97) [575]

11752 Mackenzie, Dana. *The Big Splat; or, How Our Moon Came to Be* (10–12). Illus. 2003, Wiley $24.95 (0-471-15057-6). More than just an exploration of conflicting theories about the moon's origin, this fascinating study also examines the historical evolution of human perceptions of the moon. (Rev: BL 4/15/03) [523.3]

11753 North, Gerald. *Observing the Moon: The Modern Astronomer's Guide* (10–12). Illus. 2000, Cambridge Univ. Pr. $39.95 (0-521-62274-3). For serious science students with an interest in astronomy, this is a detailed work on how to study the moon, equipment needed, types of photography, and so forth. (Rev: BL 7/00) [523.3]

11754 Powell, James Lawrence. *Mysteries of Terra Firma: The Age and Evolution of the Earth* (9–12). Illus. 2001, Free Pr. $25.00 (0-684-87282-X). This book explores Earth's major features — its oceans, continents, and its moon — and explains how we have gathered information about them. (Rev: BL 12/1/01) [551.7]

Stars

11755 Gallant, Roy A. *The Life Stories of Stars* (6–10). Series: Story of Science. 2000, Marshall Cavendish LB $28.50 (0-7614-1152-6). This is a colorful introduction to stars, how they are formed, and how they die. (Rev: BL 12/15/00; HBG 10/01; SLJ 2/01) [523.8]

11756 Kaler, James B. *The Hundred Greatest Stars* (10–12). Illus. 2002, Copernicus $32.50 (0-387-95436-8). This personal selection of the top 100 stars, with a brief description and accompanying image of each, will be useful for reports. (Rev: BL 8/02) [523.8]

11757 Pickover, Clifford A. *The Stars of Heaven* (10–12). Illus. 2001, Oxford $27.50 (0-19-514874-6). The story behind such strange stars as our sun, supergiants, pulsars, neutron stars, black holes, and other stellar bodies. (Rev: BL 12/1/01) [523.8]

11758 Sasaki, Chris. *The Constellations: Stars and Stories* (6–12). Illus. 2003, Sterling $24.95 (0-8069-7635-7). Observing constellations offers an opportunity to connect science and history, and this book provides tips for finding constellations and seeing the patterns that connect to their names. (Rev: BL 2/15/03; HBG 10/03; SLJ 7/03; VOYA 10/03) [523.8]

11759 VanCleave, Janice. *Janice VanCleave's Constellations for Every Kid: Easy Activities That Make Learning Science Fun* (8–12). Illus. 1997, Wiley $32.50 (0-471-15981-6); paper $12.95 (0-471-15979-4). An excellent guide to the heavens, with each chapter presenting a different constellation with concise facts, new concepts, simple activities, and solutions to problems. (Rev: BL 12/1/97; HBG 3/98; SLJ 10/97) [523.8]

Sun and the Solar System

11760 Bone, Neil. *Mars Observer's Guide* (10–12). Illus. 2003, Firefly paper $14.95 (1-55297-802-8). This guide intended for amateur astronomers will also prove invaluable to report writers. (Rev: BL 5/1/03) [523.43]

11761 Cattermole, Peter. *Mars: The Story of the Red Planet* (9–12). 1992, Chapman & Hall paper $59.95 (0-412-44140-3). A detailed, technical look at the scientific study of Mars, filled with photographs, graphs, and charts. (Rev: BL 10/1/92) [523.43]

11762 Cooper, Henry S. F. *The Evening Star: Venus Observed* (9–12). 1993, Farrar $22.00 (0-374-15000-1). An account of the 1989 *Magellan* spacecraft launched to gather data on Venus. (Rev: BL 7/93) [523.4]

11763 Evans, Barry. *The Wrong Way Comet and Other Mysteries of Our Solar System: Essays* (9–12). 1992, TAB $22.95 (0-8306-2679-4); paper $14.95 (0-8306-2670-0). An introduction to mysteries of the solar system in a series of informal essays. (Rev: BL 3/15/92) [523.2]

11764 Gallant, Roy A. *When the Sun Dies* (6–10). 1998, Marshall Cavendish $14.95 (0-7614-5036-X). After discussing the history and structure of the solar system, the author gives a blow-by-blow account of our sun's last 9 billion years and his projections for its likely ending about a billion years from now. (Rev: SLJ 1/99; VOYA 6/99) [523.2]

11765 Golub, Leon, and Jay M. Pasachoff. *Nearest Star: The Surprising Science of Our Sun* (10–12). Illus. 2001, Harvard $29.95 (0-674-00467-1). For better science students, this is a richly illustrated account that explains what we currently know about our sun and how it functions. (Rev: BL 3/1/01) [523.7]

11766 Harrington, Philip S. *Eclipse! The What, Where, When, Why, and How Guide to Watching Solar and Lunar Eclipses* (9–12). 1997, Wiley paper $16.95 (0-471-12795-7). An explanation of lunar and solar eclipses, with advice on how best to view and photograph them. [523.7]

11767 Hartmann, William K. *A Traveler's Guide to Mars* (10–12). Illus. 2003, Workman paper $18.95 (0-7611-2606-6). The history, geography, geology, and topography are covered in detail, with photographs, digital images, and interesting sidebar features. (Rev: BL 8/03; SLJ 12/03) [919.9]

11768 Raeburn, Paul. *Mars: Uncovering the Secrets of the Red Planet* (9–12). 1998, National Geographic $40.00 (0-7922-7373-7). With magnificent illustrations ranging from superpanoramas to technical drawings, this book describes the findings of the Mars Pathfinder expedition and the work of the rover named Sojourner. (Rev: BL 8/98; SLJ 4/99) [523.2]

11769 Ripley, S. Dillon. *Fire of Life: The Smithsonian Book of the Sun* (10–12). Illus. 1981, Norton $24.95 (0-393-80006-7). This book describes what we know about the sun and its effects on the environments of planets including the earth. [523.7]

11770 Sheehan, William, and Stephen James O'Meara. *Mars: The Lure of the Red Planet* (10–12). Illus. 2001, Prometheus $27.00 (1-57392-900-X). From Kepler to today, here is the story of the endless fascination people have had for the planet Mars and what we have found out about it. (Rev: BL 3/15/01) [523.43]

11771 Spangenburg, Ray, and Diane Moser. *Exploring the Reaches of the Solar System* (6–10). Illus. 1990, Facts on File $22.95 (0-8160-1850-2). This is a fine summary of what the space probes have told us about the solar system. For historical information use *Opening the Space Frontier* (1989). (Rev: BL 4/15/90; SLJ 12/90) [639]

11772 Weissman, Paul R., et al. *Encyclopedia of the Solar System* (10–12). 1999, Academic $99.95 (0-12-226805-9). A compact introduction to astronomy, beginning with general information about our solar system and then discussing such topics as satellites, the planets, and the origin of life. (Rev: BL 3/15/99) [523.2]

Universe

11773 Comins, Neil F. *Heavenly Errors: Misconceptions About the Real Nature of the Universe* (10–12). Illus. 2001, Columbia Univ. Pr. $27.95 (0-231-11644-6). Drawing on material he garnered from his college students, the author describes many common scientific misconceptions in astronomy and sets the record straight. (Rev: BL 7/01) [520]

11774 Hawking, Stephen. *A Brief History of Time* (10–12). 1998, Bantam $27.95 (0-553-10953-7); paper $16.95 (0-553-38016-8). This revised edition of Hawking's classic offers an updated overview of what scientists have learned about the natural order of the universe and the questions that remain to be answered. [523.1]

11775 Laidler, Keith J. *The Harmonious Universe: The Beauty and Unity of Scientific Understanding* (10–12). Illus. 2004, Prometheus $28.00 (1-59102-187-1). This overview of material relating to the universe focuses on understanding the atom and discovering facts about mass. (Rev: BL 5/15/04) [500]

11776 McNab, David, and James Younger. *The Planets* (9–12). 1999, Yale Univ. Pr. $35.00 (0-300-08044-1). Illustrated with space-age photographs, this book introduces and compares the planets. (Rev: BL 9/1/99; SLJ 6/00) [523]

11777 Reed, George. *Eyes on the Universe* (6–10). Series: Story of Science. 2000, Marshall Cavendish LB $19.95 (0-7614-1154-2). A clear, attractively presented introduction to the universe and its components. (Rev: BL 12/15/00; HBG 10/01) [523]

11778 Rosen, Joe. *The Capricious Cosmos: Universe Beyond Law* (9–12). 1992, Macmillan $19.95 (0-02-604931-7). A discussion of the nature of science and metaphysics and the impact of modern science on humankind. (Rev: BL 2/15/92) [523.1]

Biological Sciences

General and Miscellaneous

11779 Amos, William H., and Stephen H. Amos. *Atlantic and Gulf Coasts* (9–12). Illus. 1985, Knopf paper $19.95 (0-394-73109-3). This volume describes the habitat thoroughly and then identifies the species that live there. (Rev: BL 7/85; SLJ 9/85) [574.5]

11780 Bakalar, Nicholas. *Where the Germs Are: A Scientific Safari* (10–12). Illus. 2003, Wiley $24.95 (0-471-15589-6). A fascinating exploration of the hidden world of germs, the threats they pose, and the everyday places we are most likely to encounter bad ones. (Rev: BL 2/1/03) [616.014]

11781 Baskin, Yvonne. *A Plague of Rats and Rubber Vines: The Growing Threat of Species Invasion* (10–12). 2002, Island Pr. $25.00 (1-55963-876-1). The costly impact of species invading new territories is examined in this volume that makes a convincing case for regulation of the international movement of animals, plants, and microbes. (Rev: BL 6/1–15/02) [639.9]

11782 Berrill, Michael, and Deborah Berrill. *A Sierra Club Naturalist's Guide to the North Atlantic Coast: Cape Cod to Newfoundland* (10–12). Illus. 1981, Sierra Club paper $16.00 (0-87156-243-X). As well as the general geology and climate of this region, there is extensive coverage on the marine habitats for animal and plant life that these coastlines contain. [574.9]

11783 Birkhead, Tim. *A Brand-New Bird: How Two Amateur Scientists Created the First Genetically Engineered Animal* (10–12). Illus. 2003, Basic $26.00 (0-465-00665-5). Harking back to the early days of genetic engineering, when the practice was known as breeding, the author tells the story of how two Germans — one a scientist and the other a bird breeder — collaborated to produce a red canary. (Rev: BL 10/1/03) [636.6]

11784 Bowler, Peter J. *The Norton History of the Environmental Sciences* (9–12). 1993, Norton $35.00 (0-393-03535-2); paper $17.95 (0-393-31042-6). Historical highlights and development of the environmental sciences. (Rev: BL 7/93) [363.7]

11785 Brooks, Bruce. *The Red Wasteland* (6–10). 1995, Holt $15.95 (0-8050-4495-7). A fine anthology of essays, stories, poems, and book excerpts by some of the best nature writers, who raise themes and questions about crucial issues relating to the environment. (Rev: BL 8/98; BR 1–2/99; HBG 3/99; SLJ 6/98; VOYA 8/98) [808]

11786 Castner, James L. *Layers of Life* (6–12). Illus. Series: Deep in the Amazon. 2001, Marshall Cavendish LB $18.95 (0-7614-1130-5). This volume explores the biodiversity found in each "layer" of the Amazonian rain forest, with color photographs. Also use *Partners and Rivals, River Life,* and *Surviving in the Rain Forest* (all 2001). (Rev: BL 12/15/01; HBG 3/02) [577.34]

11787 Charles, Daniel. *Lords of the Harvest: Biotech, Big Money, and the Future of Food* (10–12). Illus. 2001, Perseus Bks. $26.00 (0-7382-0291-6). After an overview of the genetic revolutions during the 1970s and 1980s, this book discusses genetically engineered plants and both the scientific and business aspects of this development. (Rev: BL 10/1/01) [363.8]

11788 Cook, Charles. *Awakening to Nature: Renewing Your Life by Connecting with the Natural World* (10–12). 2001, NTC paper $14.95 (0-8092-2399-6). As mankind becomes increasingly disconnected with nature, this helpful guide shows how we can bring communion with the nonhuman world back into our lives. (Rev: BL 4/1/01) [508]

11789 Cummins, Ronnie, and Ben Lilliston. *Genetically Engineered Food: A Self-Defense Guide for Consumers* (10–12). 2000, Marlowe paper $13.95 (1-56924-635-1). A discussion of genetically engineered foods and the scientific, political, economic, and health issues they present. (Rev: BL 12/1/01) [363.1]

11790 Dillard, Annie. *Pilgrim at Tinker Creek* (10–12). 1974, Harper & Row paper $13.00 (0-06-095302-0). A wonderful nature study book that records the seasons at Tinker Creek in Virginia. [818]

11791 Duensing, Edward, and A. B. Millmoss. *Backyard and Beyond: A Guide for Discovering the Outdoors* (9–12). 1992, Fulcrum paper $19.95 (1-55591-071-8). Descriptions of various animals, plants, and insects, with tips on how to observe and track them. (Rev: BL 3/15/92) [508.2]

11792 Durrell, Gerald M., and Lee Durrell. *The Amateur Naturalist* (9–12). 1983, Knopf paper $25.00 (0-679-72837-6). This is a guide for the amateur naturalist studying various habitats such as meadows, marshlands, seashores, and, even, one's backyard. (Rev: BCCB 8/84; HB /84) [508]

11793 Ensminger, Peter A. *Life Under the Sun* (10–12). Illus. 2001, Yale $26.95 (0-300-08804-3). This science book about sunlight explains the relationship between Earth's creatures and the Sun. (Rev: BL 3/1/01) [571.4]

11794 Ford, Brian J. *The Secret Language of Life: How Animals and Plants Feel and Communicate* (10–12). Illus. 2000, Fromm $30.00 (0-88064-254-8). This book discusses the sensory behavior of various forms of life from algae to farm animals and birds. (Rev: BL 10/1/00) [578.4]

11795 Foster, Steven, and Roger A. Caras. *A Field Guide to Venomous Animals and Poisonous Plants: North America, North of Mexico* (9–12). 1994, Houghton paper $19.00 (0-395-93608-X). About 90 venomous animals and about 250 plants are described in the field guide. [578.6]

11796 Hoagland, Mahlon, and Bert Dodson. *The Way Life Works* (9–12). 1995, Times Books $35.00 (0-8129-2020-1). A collaboration between Hoagland, a molecular biologist, and Dodson, an artist, emphasizing the unity of life rather than its differences. (Rev: BL 12/1/95) [574]

11797 Jones, Stephen R. *The Last Prairie: A Sandhills Journal* (10–12). 2000, McGraw-Hill $19.95 (0-07-135347-X). A collection of thoughtful, informative essays about life, past and present, in the Sandhills area of Nebraska. (Rev: BL 6/1–15/00) [508]

11798 Lambrecht, Bill. *Dinner at the New Gene Cafe: How Genetic Engineering Is Changing What We Eat, How We Live, and the Global Politics of Food* (10–12). Illus. 2001, St. Martin's $24.95 (0-312-26575-1). An interesting account of how Monsanto's research led to the genetic engineering of plants, and the political and activist battles that have ensued. (Rev: BL 9/1/01) [363 19]

11799 Latourrette, Joe. *The National Wildlife Federation's Wildlife Watcher's Handbook: A Guide to Observing Animals in the Wild* (10–12). Illus. 1997, Holt paper $12.95 (0-8050-4685-2). A practical, informative handbook on how to observe wildlife effectively in habitat regions in the United States and Canada. (Rev: SLJ 4/98) [591]

11800 Lawlor, Elizabeth P. *Discover Nature at Sundown: Things to Know and Things to Do* (9–12). 1995, Stackpole paper $14.95 (0-8117-2527-8). Sensory awareness for nature lovers to track and observe creatures at night. (Rev: BL 2/15/95) [591.5]

11801 Lurquin, Paul. *High Tech Harvest: Understanding Genetically Modified Food Plants* (10–12). Illus. 2002, Westview $25.00 (0-8133-3946-4). Lurquin demystifies the genetic engineering of foods, reminding readers that such manipulation dates back to the earliest agriculture. (Rev: BL 7/02) [631.5]

11802 Marchand, Peter J. *Autumn: A Season of Change* (10–12). Illus. 2000, Univ. Press of New England $50.00 (0-87451-869-5); paper $17.95 (0-87451-870-9). Not just a beautiful work about the season, but an interesting scientific study of how animals and plants change and adjust. (Rev: BL 7/00) [508.3]

11803 Matthews, Anne. *Wild Nights: Nature Returns to the City* (10–12). 2001, Farrar $22.00 (0-86547-560-1). This natural history of New York City and the wildlife it supports could apply to any urban area, and the lessons of conservation and the balance of nature apply everywhere. (Rev: BL 4/1/01) [577.5]

11804 Murray, John A., ed. *American Nature Writing* (9–12). 1994, Sierra Club paper $12.00 (0-87156-479-3). The first of an annual anthology of writings (including poetry) about nature. There are also volumes for 1995, 1996, 1997, 1998, and 1999. (Rev: BL 4/15/94) [810]

11805 Murray, John A., ed. *Nature's New Voices* (9–12). 1992, Fulcrum paper $15.95 (1-55591-117-X). Personal literary observations on natural history by a contemporary generation of nature essayists. (Rev: BL 10/1/92) [508.73]

11806 Nardo, Don, ed. *Cloning* (7–10). Illus. Series: Great Medical Discoveries. 2001, Gale LB $27.45 (1-56006-927-9). The science underlying plant and animal cloning and the controversy over potential human cloning are covered in this balanced and accessible volume. (Rev: BL 3/1/02; SLJ 5/02) [660.6]

11807 O'Brien, Stephen J. *Tears of the Cheetah and Other Tales from the Genetic Frontier* (10–12). 2003, St. Martin's $25.95 (0-312-27286-3). Advanced students will enjoy these stories of research into the genetic makeup of animal species including the lion, panda, and humpback whale. (Rev: BL 9/1/03) [591.3]

11808 Patent, Dorothy Hinshaw. *Biodiversity* (6–10). Illus. 1996, Clarion $18.00 (0-395-68704-7). This book discusses broad topics such as habitats, ecosystems, and important species to show connections in nature. (Rev: BL 12/1/96; SLJ 12/96*) [333.95]

11809 Peck, Robert McCracken. *Land of the Eagle: A Natural History of North America* (9–12). 1991, BBC Books $30.00 (0-671-75596-X). A descriptive celebration of the North American terrain and animal and plant life as experienced by its native peoples and European settlers. (Rev: BL 11/15/91; SLJ 4/92) [508.7]

11810 Quinn, John R. *Wildlife Survivors: The Flora and Fauna of Tomorrow* (9–12). 1994, TAB $21.95 (0-8306-4346-X); paper $12.95 (0-8306-4345-1). A serious study that explores the concept that plants and animals will continue to survive despite the encroachment of human civilization. (Rev: BL 3/1/94) [574.5]

11811 Raham, R. Gary. *Dinosaurs in the Garden: An Evolutionary Guide to Backyard Biology* (6–10). Illus. 1988, Plexus $22.95 (0-937548-10-3). The author uses common creatures to explain how they fit into the scheme of nature and overall patterns of evolution. (Rev: BL 12/1/88) [575]

11812 Rose, Michael R. *Darwin's Spectre: Evolutionary Biology in the Modern World* (10–12). Illus. 1998, Princeton Univ. Pr. $27.95 (0-691-01217-2). A discussion of Darwin's theory of evolution and its widespread influence on such fields as plant and animal breeding and eugenics; useful for biology students. (Rev: BL 12/1/98) [576.8]

11813 Tocci, Salvatore. *Biology Projects for Young Scientists* (9–12). Illus. Series: Projects for Young Scientists. 2000, Watts LB $25.00 (0-531-11703-0); paper $6.95 (0-531-16460-8). This book will be invaluable to students in search of sound biology experiments. (Rev: BL 5/15/00) [570]

11814 Todd, Kim. *Tinkering with Eden: A Natural History of Exotics in America* (10–12). 2001, Norton $27.95 (0-393-04860-8). Todd relates more than a dozen stories of the introduction of non-native species (exotics) to America — such as starlings, pigeons, sparrows, and knapweed — and explains the lasting impact. (Rev: BL 1/1–15/01) [591.6]

11815 Tudge, Colin. *The Variety of Life: The Meaning of Biodiversity* (10–12). Illus. 2000, Oxford $45.00 (0-19-850311-3). For advanced students, the author describes in lucid, interesting terms the mysteries and rationale of scientific classification in biology. (Rev: BL 5/15/00*) [578]

11816 VanCleave, Janice. *Janice VanCleave's A+ Projects in Biology: Winning Experiments for Science Fairs and Extra Credit* (6–10). 1993, Wiley paper $12.95 (0-471-58628-5). Offers a variety of experiments in botany, zoology, and the human body. (Rev: BL 1/15/94; SLJ 11/93) [574]

11817 Widmaier, Eric P. *The Stuff of Life: Profiles of the Molecules That Make Us Tick* (10–12). Illus. 2002, Holt $22.00 (0-8050-7173-3). This guide to biochemistry, written in easy-to-understand language, demystifies the components and fundamentals of life. (Rev: BL 8/02) [572]

Botany

General and Miscellaneous

11818 Bonnet, Robert L., and G. Daniel Keen. *Botany: 49 Science Fair Projects* (6–10). Illus. 1989, TAB $16.95 (0-8306-9277-0). Well-explained projects involving such phenomena as photosynthesis, hydroponics, fungi, and germination. (Rev: BL 1/15/90; BR 1–2/90; VOYA 2/90) [581]

11819 Lincoff, Gary. *The Audubon Society Field Guide to North American Mushrooms* (7–12). Illus. 1981, Knopf $19.95 (0-394-51992-2). More than 700 species are introduced and pictured in color photographs. [589.2]

11820 *Trees and Nonflowering Plants* (10–12). Series: North American Wildlife. 1998, Reader's Digest $17.95 (0-7621-0037-0). Tips on identifying trees by their shape, leaves, bark, flowers, and fruit are accompanied by clear illustrations; also covers nonflowering plants, such as ferns and lichens. [582.16]

11821 Zimmer, Carl. *Parasite Rex: Inside the Bizarre World of Nature's Most Dangerous Creatures* (10–12). 2000, Free Pr. $26.00 (0-684-85638-7). A well-organized survey of such parasites as worms, flukes, and single-celled organisms and the problems they can cause, including river blindness, sleeping sickness, and malaria. (Rev: BL 8/00) [591.7]

Foods, Farms, and Ranches

GENERAL AND MISCELLANEOUS

11822 *Barnyard in Your Backyard: A Beginner's Guide to Raising Chickens, Ducks, Geese, Rabbits, Goats, Sheep, and Cows* (10–12). Ed. by Gail Damerow. Illus. 2002, Storey paper $24.95 (1-58017-456-6). A practical, friendly, and fact-filled guide to the care and feeding of farm animals. (Rev: BL 12/15/02) [636]

11823 Dunn-Georgiou, Elisha. *Everything You Need to Know About Organic Foods* (6–10). Illus. Series: Need to Know Library. 2002, Rosen LB $23.95 (0-8239-3551-5). An examination of the techniques that produce organic foods and the benefits of eating foods that are free of certain additives. (Rev: BL 5/1/02; SLJ 6/02) [641.3]

11824 *Fatal Harvest: The Tragedy of Industrial Agriculture* (10–12). Ed. by Andrew Kimbrell. Illus. 2002, Island Pr. $75.00 (1-55963-940-7); paper $45.00 (1-55963-941-5). Essays document the alarming transformation of farming from its environmentally friendly, small-scale beginnings to the bottom-line-preoccupied big business it is today. (Rev: BL 5/15/02*) [630]

11825 *Food Safety* (9–12). Ed. by Laura Egendorf. Series: At Issue. 2000, Greenhaven LB $24.95 (0-7377-0151-X); paper $16.20 (0-7377-0150-1). Such topics as biotechnology, organic farming, pesticides, and irradiation are covered from differing points of view in the 14 articles reprinted in this volume. (Rev: SLJ 6/00) [363.1]

11826 Goldberg, Jake. *The Disappearing American Farm* (8–12). Illus. 1996, Watts LB $24.00 (0-531-11261-6). After a brief history of farming and the economic aspects of U.S. farm policy, the author discusses the impact of technology and agricultural research on the farm industry, government intervention, and a number of other difficult issues facing farmers and the nation today. (Rev: BL 6/1–15/96; BR 11–12/96; SLJ 6/96; VOYA 10/96) [338.1]

11827 Goldberg, Jake. *Food: The Struggle to Sustain the Human Community* (8–12). Illus. 1999, Watts LB $26.00 (0-531-11411-2). This illustrated volume covers humans' use of food since the beginning of time — including its distribution, production, and politics. (Rev: BL 11/15/99) [641.3]

11828 Goldstein, Myrna Chandler, and Mark A. Goldstein. *Controversies in Food and Nutrition* (9–12). Series: Contemporary Controversies. 2002, Greenwood $45.00 (0-313-31787-9). Such controversial topics as diets, vegetarianism, food irradiation, vitamin supplements, and genetic modification are discussed from differing points of view. (Rev: BL 5/1/03) [641.3]

11829 Hayhurst, Chris. *Everything You Need to Know About Food Additives* (6–10). Illus. Series: Need to Know Library. 2002, Rosen LB $23.95 (0-8239-3548-5). An examination of the kinds of additives used in foods, their benefits and disadvantages, and the alternatives available to people seeking a healthier diet. (Rev: BL 5/1/02) [664]

11830 Haynes, Cynthia. *Raising Turkeys, Ducks, Geese, Pigeons, and Guineas* (10–12). Illus. 1987, TAB $24.95 (0-8306-0803-6). A general guide to the breeding and raising of a variety of poultry species. (Rev: BL 4/1/88) [636.5]

11831 Igoe, Robert S. *Dictionary of Food Ingredients* (10–12). 1989, Van Nostrand paper $39.95 (0-442-31927-4). A dictionary of the approximately 1,000 food ingredients approved by the Food and Drug Administration. [664]

11832 Johnson, Sylvia A. *Potatoes, Tomatoes, Corn, and Beans: How the Foods in America Changed the World* (6–10). Illus. 1997, Simon & Schuster $16.95 (0-689-80141-6). The story of common foods that originated in America is told in this blend of history, botany, culinary arts, and geography. (Rev: BL 4/15/97; BR 11–12/97; SLJ 5/97; VOYA 12/97) [641.6]

11833 Lopez, Ruth. *Chocolate: The Nature of Indulgence* (9–12). Illus. 2002, Abrams $35.00 (0-8109-0403-9). The history — and almost universal appeal — of chocolate is chronicled in readable text and excellent color photographs. (Rev: BL 4/15/02) [641.337]

11834 Lovenheim, Peter. *Portrait of a Burger as a Young Calf: The Story of One Man, Two Cows, and the Feeding of a Nation* (10–12). Illus. 2002, Harmony $23.00 (0-609-60591-7). In this first-person account of farm life, Lovenheim describes raising a group of calves and what he learned about agriculture and both humans and cows in the process. (Rev: BL 6/1–15/02) [636.2]

11835 Millstone, Erik, and Tim Lang. *The Penguin Atlas of Food* (11–12). Illus. 2003, Penguin paper $20.00 (0-14-200224-0). A treasure trove for report writers, this collection of data, maps, and charts offers comprehensive information about the food we eat and eating habits around the world. (Rev: BL 7/03) [664]

11836 Mott, Lawrie, and Karen Snyder. *Pesticide Alert: A Guide to Pesticides in Fruit and Vegetables* (10–12). Illus. 1988, Sierra Club paper $6.95 (0-87156-726-1). A guide to all the pesticides that are used in farming today, their effects, and how to remove them from fruits and vegetables. (Rev: BL 5/1/88; SLJ 7/89) [668]

11837 Patent, Dorothy Hinshaw. *The Vanishing Feast: How Dwindling Genetic Diversity Threatens the World's Food Supply* (6–10). 1994, Harcourt $17.95 (0-15-292867-7). Explains the importance of maintaining plant and animal diversity and describes experiments with genetic engineering and factory farming. (Rev: BL 10/1/94; SLJ 12/94; VOYA 4/95) [338.1]

11838 Satin, Morton. *Food Alert! The Ultimate Sourcebook for Food Safety* (10–12). 1999, Facts on File $38.50 (0-8160-3935-6); paper $14.95 (0-8160-3936-4). This book discusses types of food, food production and processing, and the problems that can arise. (Rev: BL 7/99) [615.9]

11839 Seligson, Susan. *Going with the Grain: A Wandering Bread Lover Takes a Bite out of Life* (10–12). 2002, Simon & Schuster $24.00 (0-7432-0081-0). Seligson surveys the very different methods of bread production around the globe and provides several recipes. (Rev: BL 11/15/02) [800]

11840 Shephard, Sue. *Pickled, Potted and Canned: How the Art and Science of Food Preserving Changed the World* (10–12). Illus. 2001, Simon & Schuster $26.00 (0-7432-1633-4). This history of food preservation covers how to dry, salt, smoke, ferment, pickle, and cure food as well as supplying material on how the ability to preserve food has changed world history. (Rev: BL 9/1/01*; SLJ 4/02) [641.4]

11841 Shulman, Martha Rose. *Foodlover's Atlas of the World* (9–12). 2002, Firefly (1-552-97571-1). Organized geographically, this book gives information of the foods of various regions and countries, including staples, culinary history, specialties, mealtime customs, and some recipes. (Rev: SLJ 7/03) [641.3]

11842 Tannahill, Reay. *Food in History*. Rev. ed. (9–12). 1989, Crown paper $16.00 (0-517-88404-6). From prehistoric times to the present, this is the history of food and how it has changed the course of human development. [641.3]

VEGETABLES

11843 Phillips, Roger, and Martyn Rix. *The Random House Book of Vegetables* (9–12). Series: Random House Garden. 1994, Random paper $25.00 (0-679-75024-X). Reviews the vegetable families and the history of vegetables, and offers advice on cultivation, fertilization, and pest control. (Rev: BL 2/15/94) [635]

11844 Weaver, William Woys. *100 Vegetables and Where They Come From* (9–12). Illus. 2000, Algonquin $18.95 (1-56512-238-0). The author highlights 100 vegetables, describes their characteristics, and tells about the origin of each. (Rev: BL 11/15/00) [635.9]

Forestry and Trees

11845 Brockman, C. Frank. *Trees of North America* (7–12). Illus. 1998, Demco $22.10 (0-606-12005-

X). This handy guide identifies 594 different trees that grow north of Mexico. [582.16]

11846 *Familiar Trees of North America: Eastern Region* (8–12). 1986, Knopf paper $9.00 (0-394-74851-4). As well as pictures and descriptions, this guide supplies historical information, habitats, and uses for 80 trees commonly found in the eastern parts of North America. [582.16]

11847 *Familiar Trees of North America: Western Region* (8–12). 1986, Knopf paper $9.00 (0-394-74852-2). This pocket guide covers 80 trees found commonly in the western United States. [582.16]

11848 Gallant, Roy A. *Earth's Vanishing Forests* (6–10). 1991, Macmillan LB $15.95 (0-02-735774-0). A carefully researched examination of the reasons for the destruction of the planet's forests and the implications of their loss. (Rev: BL 10/1/91; SLJ 5/92) [333.75]

11849 Little, Elbert L. *The Audubon Society Field Guide to North American Trees: Eastern Region* (7–12). Illus. 1980, Knopf $19.95 (0-394-50760-6). This volume describes through text and pictures of leaves, needles, and so on, the trees found east of the Rocky Mountains. [582.16]

11850 Little, Elbert L. *The Audubon Society Field Guide to North American Trees: Western Region* (7–12). Illus. 1980, Knopf $19.95 (0-394-50761-4). Trees west of the Rockies are identified and pictured in photographs and drawings. [582.16]

11851 Martin, Patricia A. Fink. *Woods and Forests* (8–12). Illus. Series: Exploring Ecosystems. 2000, Watts LB $24.00 (0-531-11697-2). Practical projects appear throughout the text, allowing readers to explore the concepts presented. (Rev: SLJ 6/00) [577.3]

11852 Pakenham, Thomas. *Remarkable Trees of the World* (10–12). Illus. 2002, Norton $49.95 (0-393-04911-6). Tall, short, long-lived, revered — trees with "strong personality" are the focus of this absorbing narrative accompanied by eye-catching photographs. (Rev: BL 11/1/02; SLJ 4/03) [582.16]

11853 Petrides, George A. *A Field Guide to Trees and Shrubs* (7–12). Illus. 1973, Houghton paper $19.00 (0-395-35370-X). A total of 646 varieties found in northern United States and southern Canada are described and illustrated. [582.1]

11854 Sutton, Ann, and Myron Sutton. *Eastern Forests* (9–12). Illus. 1985, Knopf paper $19.95 (0-394-73126-3). Although this book chiefly aims to identify species living in eastern forests, it also describes this habitat and their locations. (Rev: BL 7/85; SLJ 9/85) [574.5]

11855 Walker, Laurence C. *Forests: A Naturalist's Guide to Woodland Trees* (9–12). 1997, Univ. of Texas Pr. paper $19.95 (0-292-79112-7). This overview of forest ecology examines many different species of trees and how they are affected by such variables as climate and soil type. [582.16]

11856 Whitney, Stephen. *Western Forests* (9–12). Illus. 1985, Knopf paper $19.95 (0-394-73127-1). A description of each species, color illustrations, and a general introduction to this type of habitat are the highlights of this field guide. (Rev: BL 7/85; SLJ 9/85) [574.5]

Plants and Flowers

11857 Angier, Bradford. *Field Guide to Medicinal Wild Plants* (10–12). Illus. 1978, Stackpole paper $18.95 (0-8117-2076-4). With many color illustrations the author introduces more than 100 wild medicinal plants, many of them originally used by primitive tribes. [581.6]

11858 Attenborough, David. *The Private Life of Plants: A Natural History of Plant Behaviour* (9–12). 1995, Princeton Univ. Pr. $29.95 (0-691-00639-3). This introduction to the behavior of plants covers such topics as feeding, growing, traveling, flowering, surviving, and living together. [581.4]

11859 Buckles, Mary Parker. *The Flowers Around Us: A Photographic Essay on Their Reproductive Structures* (10–12). Illus. 1985, Univ. of Missouri Pr. $29.95 (0-8262-0402-3). Through photographs and text, the author shows the reproductive parts of various flowers and how they function in the production of seeds. (Rev: BL 12/1/85) [582]

11860 Grey-Wilson, Christopher. *Annuals and Biennials* (10–12). Illus. Series: American Horticultural Society Practical Guides. 2000, DK paper $8.95 (0-7894-5066-6). Basic practical information is given, with accompanying color photographs, on a variety of plants, with material on growing requirements, types, and instructions for their care and nurturing. (Rev: BL 2/15/00) [635.9]

11861 Hershey, David R. *Plant Biology Science Projects* (9–12). Series: Best Science Projects for Young Adults. 1995, Wiley paper $12.95 (0-471-04983-2). This book supplies good step-by-step instructions for experiments and projects involving plants. (Rev: SLJ 4/95) [580.7]

11862 Hudler, George W. *Magical Mushrooms, Mischievous Molds* (9–12). 1998, Princeton Univ. Pr. $29.95 (0-691-02873-7). This is a fact-filled, enjoyable history of how fungi have changed history and our lives, from the potato blight in Ireland that caused starvation and mass immigration to the United States to "sick building syndrome," penicillin, athlete's foot, and mushrooms in a salad. (Rev: SLJ 5/99) [589.2]

11863 Kowalchik, Claire, and William H. Hylton, eds. *Rodale's Illustrated Encyclopedia of Herbs* (9–12). Illus. 1987, Rodale $26.95 (0-87857-699-1). In addition to an alphabetically arranged description

of each herb, this lavishly illustrated volume contains background historical material, plus coverage of such subjects as medicinal uses, cooking, and gardening. (Rev: BL 10/15/87) [635]

11864 Musgrave, Toby, and Will Musgrave. *An Empire of Plants: People and Plants that Changed the World* (10–12). 2001, Cassell $29.95 (0-304-35443-5). This work describes the importance of seven plant products in world history: tea, tobacco, sugar, opium, cotton, quinine, and rubber. (Rev: BL 3/15/01) [580]

11865 Niering, William A., and Nancy C. Olmstead. *The Audubon Society Field Guide to North American Wildflowers: Eastern Region* (7–12). Illus. 1979, Knopf $19.00 (0-394-50432-1). From the Rockies to the Atlantic this guide identifies, describes, and pictures the most common wildflowers. [582.13]

11866 Peterson, Roger Tory, and Margaret McKenny. *A Field Guide to Wildflowers of Northeastern and North-Central North America: A Visual Approach Arranged by Color, Form, and Detail* (9–12). 1968, Houghton paper $19.00 (0-395-91172-9). Nearly 1,300 species are discussed and pictured in this invaluable guide. [582.13]

11867 Reader's Digest, eds. *Magic and Medicine of Plants* (9–12). Illus. 1986, Random $28.00 (0-89577-221-3). Information about medicinal plants covers fields ranging from botany and pharmacy to myth and folklore. (Rev: BL 12/86; SLJ 5/87) [581.6]

11868 Richardson, P. Mick. *Flowering Plants: Magic in Bloom* (9–12). Illus. 1986, Chelsea LB $19.95 (0-87754-757-2). The story of plant-derived hallucinogenic substances is given plus information on their effects and their role in world folklore and religion. (Rev: BL 4/15/87) [398]

11869 Silverstein, Alvin, et al. *Plants* (7–10). Series: Kingdoms of Life. 1996, Twenty-First Century LB $25.90 (0-8050-3519-2). The classification system of plants is explained, from simple plants through ferns and on to flowering plants. (Rev: BL 6/1–15/96; SLJ 7/96) [581]

11870 Spellenberg, Richard. *The Audubon Society Field Guide to North American Wildflowers: Western Region* (7–12). Illus. 1979, Knopf $19.00 (0-394-50431-3). A guide to more than 600 wildflowers found from California to Alaska. [582.13]

11871 Spellenberg, Richard. *Familiar Flowers of North America: Eastern Region* (8–12). 1986, Knopf paper $9.00 (0-394-74843-3). Photographs, diagrams, and descriptions are found in this guide to 80 wildflowers found in the eastern regions of North America. Also use *Familiar Flowers of North America: Western Region*. [582.13]

Zoology

General and Miscellaneous

11872 *Animal Experimentation* (9–12). Ed. by Helen Cothran. Illus. Series: Opposing Viewpoints. 2002, Gale LB $31.20 (0-7377-0903-0); paper $19.95 (0-7377-0902-2). Animal rights, justifications for and control of animal experimentation, animal donations for human transplants, and animal cloning are among the topics explored in this balanced volume that looks at both sides of each question. (Rev: BL 7/02; SLJ 5/02) [179]

11873 Bekoff, Marc. *Minding Animals: Awareness, Emotions and Healing* (10–12). Illus. 2002, Oxford $27.50 (0-19-515077-5). Animals' ability to think and feel and humans' responsibility to treat animals with respect are among the topics treated in this very readable volume. (Rev: BL 4/1/02) [591.5]

11874 Dashefsky, H. Steven. *Zoology: 49 Science Fair Projects* (8–12). 1994, TAB paper $11.95 (0-07-015683-2). A step-by-step description of interesting science fair projects. (Rev: BL 1/15/95; SLJ 3/95) [591]

11875 Dashefsky, H. Steven. *Zoology: High School Science Fair Experiments* (7–12). 1995, TAB paper $12.95 (0-07-015687-5). Twenty zoology experiments are presented in the categories of people-related, biocides, animal lives, and animals and the environment. (Rev: BL 6/1–15/95) [591]

11876 Goodall, Jane, and Marc Bekoff. *The Ten Trusts: What We Must Do to Care for the Animals We Love* (10–12). 2002, HarperSF $23.95 (0-06-251757-0). An impassioned plea for compassionate treatment of the earth's animals, with moving stories of animals' intelligence, emotions, and mutually beneficial relationships with humans. (Rev: BL 9/1/02; SLJ 4/03) [333.95]

11877 Greek, C. Ray, and Jean Swingle Greek. *Sacred Cows and Golden Geese: The Human Cost of Experiments on Animals* (10–12). 2000, Continuum $24.95 (0-8264-1226-2). This book opposes experimentation with animals, offering evidence that it is not only cruel but also ineffective. (Rev: BL 5/15/00) [179]

11878 Hecht, Jeff. *Vanishing Life: The Mystery of Mass Extinctions* (7–12). 1993, Scribner LB $15.95 (0-684-19331-0). A study of mass extinctions throughout history and an examination of how geological evidence supports or discredits current theories. (Rev: BL 1/15/94; SLJ 2/94; VOYA 2/94) [575]

11879 *Herd on the Street: Animal Stories from the Wall Street Journal* (10–12). Ed. by Ken Wells. 2003, Free Pr. paper $14.00 (0-7432-5420-1). This delightful collection of more than 50 animal stories from the pages of the *Wall Street Journal* touches on a wide variety of subjects, including a $1.9 million veterinary hospital for hedgehogs and the dangers of canoeing among hippos. (Rev: BL 11/1/03) [590]

11880 Heying, Heather E. *Antipode: Seasons with the Extraordinary Wildlife and Culture of Madagascar* (10–12). Illus. 2002, St. Martin's $25.95 (0-312-28152-8). A field biologist recounts the wonders and misadventures of her wildlife studies on Madagascar. (Rev: BL 6/1–15/02) [508.691]

11881 Lavers, Chris. *Why Elephants Have Big Ears: Understanding Patterns of Life on Earth* (9–12). Illus. 2001, St. Martin's $23.95 (0-312-26902-1). An easy-to-read study that analyzes animal behavior, the rationale behind various habitats, and why animal physiology is either warm- or cold-blooded. (Rev: BL 2/15/01) [590]

11882 McElroy, Susan Chernak. *Animals as Guides for the Soul: Stories of Life-Changing Encounters* (10–12). 1998, Ballantine $23.95 (0-345-42403-4). An exploration of the relationship between animals and humans, using personal anecdotes and stories from readers on such topics as the death of pets, witnessing cruelty to animals, the ethics of using animals in service to humans, and lessons animals can teach, and a discussion of changes in beliefs about the psychology, intelligence, and emotional nature of animals. (Rev: BL 11/1/98; SLJ 3/99) [591]

11883 Martin, Glen. *National Geographic's Guide to Wildlife Watching: 100 of the Best Places in America to See Animals in Their Natural Habitats* (10–12). 1998, National Geographic paper $25.00 (0-7922-7130-0). Beautifully illustrated, this guide profiles 100 prime sites for viewing wildlife, including lists of animals, maps, and visitor information. [591.9]

11884 Mills, Guy, and Martin Harvey. *African Predators* (9–12). Illus. 2001, Smithsonian $39.95 (1-56098-096-6). This handsome book profiles such African predatory animals as cheetahs, lions, leopards, and hyenas. (Rev: BL 12/1/01) [599.7]

11885 Nardi, James B. *The World Beneath Our Feet: A Guide to Life in the Soil* (8–12). Illus. 2003, Oxford LB $35.00 (0-19-513990-9). Creatures that live in the soil (microbes, vertebrates, and invertebrates), soil ecology, and environmental problems such as erosion are the focus of this detailed, well-illustrated study. (Rev: HBG 10/03; SLJ 10/03; VOYA 10/03)

11886 *National Geographic: The Wildlife Photographs* (8–12). Illus. 2001, National Geographic $50.00 (0-7922-6356-1). This collection of photographs explores animal life in five different natural habitats — temperate forests, open country, oceans, tropical forests, and polar regions. (Rev: BL 1/1–15/02) [779]

11887 Petersen, Christine. *Invertebrates* (6–12). Illus. 2002, Watts $24.00 (0-531-12021-X). Covers the lifestyles and adaptations of crustaceans, echinoderms, insects, jellies, mollusks, sponges, and worms in concise, accessible text. (Rev: BL 10/15/02; LMC 1/03; VOYA 8/03) [592]

11888 Petersen, Christine. *Vertebrates* (6–12). Illus. 2002, Watts $24.00 (0-531-12020-1). Covers the lifestyles and adaptations of amphibians, birds, fish, mammals, and reptiles in concise, accessible text. (Rev: BL 10/15/02) [569]

11889 Peterson, Brenda. *Build Me an Ark: A Life with Animals* (10–12). Illus. 2001, Norton $25.95 (0-393-05014-9). This book describes the important role that wild animals have played in the life of the author, particularly in the western states and Hawaii. (Rev: BL 1/1–15/01) [599]

11890 Schwartz, Maxime. *How the Cows Turned Mad* (10–12). Trans. by Edward Schneider. 2003, Univ. of California Pr. $24.95 (0-520-23531-2). This well-researched look at the nature and cause of transmissible spongiform encephalopathies (TSEs), such as Mad Cow Disease, offers a wealth of fascinating information and a clear picture of the research process. (Rev: BL 3/1/03*) [616.8]

11891 Shedd, Warner, and Trudy Nicholson. *Owls Aren't Wise and Bats Aren't Blind: A Naturalist Debunks Our Favorite Fallacies About Wildlife* (9–12). Illus. 2000, Crown $20.00 (0-609-60529-1). The authors discuss the habits and behavior of 30 animals, among them beavers, muskrats, deer, bats, moose, and bears. (Rev: BL 5/15/00; SLJ 10/00) [591.5]

11892 *The Simon and Schuster Encyclopedia of Animals: A Visual Who's Who of the World's Creatures* (7–12). 1998, Simon & Schuster $50.00 (0-684-85237-3). Arranged by broad taxonomic classification, about 2,000 animals are introduced through pictures and information on their appearance, adaptations, habits, and habitats. (Rev: BL 10/15/98; SLJ 2/99) [591]

11893 Stewart, Amy. *The Earth Moved: On the Remarkable Achievements of Earthworms* (10–12). 2004, Algonquin $23.95 (1-56512-337-9). Stewart takes readers on an underground journey to show the world of the earthworm and the important role they play in agriculture and soil ecology. (Rev: BL 10/15/03; SLJ 4/04) [592]

11894 Wolfe, Art. *The Living Wild* (9–12). Illus. 2000, Wildlands $55.00 (0-9675918-0-5). As well as a series of essays about animals, this splendid book contains beautiful photographs showing various creatures in their natural habitats. (Rev: BL 10/15/00) [590]

Amphibians and Reptiles

GENERAL AND MISCELLANEOUS

11895 Allen, Missy, and Michel Peissel. *Dangerous Reptilian Creatures* (9–12). Series: Encyclopedia of Danger. 1993, Chelsea LB $19.95 (0-7910-1789-3). Covers 25 deadly snakes from around the world. (Rev: BL 9/1/93) [597.9]

11896 *Amphibians: The World of Frogs, Toads, Salamanders and Newts* (10–12). Ed. by Robert Hofrichter. Illus. 2000, Firefly $49.95 (1-55209-541-X). Illustrated with beautiful photographs, this collection of essays by 37 scientists introduces the world of amphibians. (Rev: BL 8/00) [597.8]

11897 Behler, John L., and F. W. King. *The Audubon Society Field Guide to North American Reptiles and Amphibians* (9–12). Illus. 1979, Knopf $19.00 (0-394-50824-6). This comprehensive account covers reptiles and amphibians found in continental United States, Canada, and Hawaii. [597.6]

11898 Conant, Roger. *A Field Guide to Reptiles and Amphibians of Eastern and Central North America.* 2nd ed. (9–12). Illus. 1975, Houghton $17.95 (0-395-19979-4); paper $13.95 (0-395-19977-8). Using both photographs and hundreds of maps, 574 species and subspecies are identified and described. A companion volume is *A Field Guide to Western Reptiles and Amphibians* (1985). [597.6]

11899 Conant, Roger, et al. *Peterson First Guides: Reptiles and Amphibians* (9–12). 1992, Houghton paper $5.95 (0-395-62232-8). A useful tool for field observation of amphibians and reptiles with tips for adopting one of these creatures as a pet. [597.9]

11900 Crump, Marty. *Amphibians, Reptiles, and Their Conservation* (6–12). Illus. 2002, Linnet LB $25.00 (0-208-02511-1). After describing these animals and giving the pertinent scientific information, the author describes the challenges to their survival and what can be done to save them. (Rev: BL 12/1/02; HBG 3/03; SLJ 1/03; VOYA 6/03) [597.9]

11901 Fridell, Ron. *Amphibians in Danger: A Worldwide Warning* (7–12). Illus. 1999, Watts LB $23.00 (0-531-11737-5). A wealth of knowledge and lore is presented in this book about the history, place, and role of frogs, toads, and salamanders, along with material on their alarming current death rate and how scientists devise and conduct research. (Rev: BL 6/1–15/99; SLJ 8/99) [597.8]

11902 Gibbons, Whit. *Their Blood Runs Cold: Adventures with Reptiles and Amphibians* (7–12). Illus. 1983, Univ. of Alabama Pr. paper $15.95 (0-8173-0133-X). An informal guide, geographically arranged, to snakes, crocodiles, turtles, salamanders, and toads. [597.6]

11903 Halliday, Tim, and Kraig Adler, eds. *The Encyclopedia of Reptiles and Amphibians* (9–12).

Illus. 1986, Facts on File $29.95 (0-8160-1359-4). A lavishly illustrated book that gives both general information and specific details on each species. (Rev: BL 6/1/86) [597.6]

11904 King, F. Wayne, et al. *Discovery Channel Reptiles and Amphibians: An Explore Your World Handbook* (8–12). 2000, Discovery paper $14.95 (1-56331-839-3). Various reptiles and amphibians are identified in text and pictures, with material on defense mechanisms and habitats, as well as acquiring and caring for these creatures. [597.9]

ALLIGATORS AND CROCODILES

11905 Lockwood, C. C. *The Alligator Book* (9–12). Illus. 2002, Louisiana State $39.95 (0-8071-2828-7). Lavishly illustrated, this is a fascinating profile of the alligator and its interactions with humans. (Rev: BL 9/1/02) [597.98]

11906 Ross, Charles A., ed. *Crocodiles and Alligators* (9–12). Illus. 1989, Facts on File $35.00 (0-8160-2174-0). A richly illustrated volume that tells about the origins, structure, habitats, and behavior of these animals. (Rev: BL 11/1/89) [597.98]

FROGS AND TOADS

11907 Parsons, Harry. *The Nature of Frogs: Amphibians with Attitude* (6–12). Illus. 2001, Douglas & McIntyre $26.95 (1-55054-761-5). Readers will be drawn to the color photographs in this book and then intrigued by the informative text and mentions of these animals' portrayal in stories and legends. (Rev: BL 1/1–15/01; VOYA 6/01) [597.8]

SNAKES AND LIZARDS

11908 Badger, David, and John Netherton. *Lizards: A Natural History of Some Uncommon Creatures — Extraordinary Chameleons, Iguanas, Geckos, and More* (10–12). Illus. 2003, Voyageur $35.00 (0-89658-520-4). The world of lizards is explored in detail in this richly illustrated study, which is supplemented by an extensive bibliography and quotations from historical writings about these fascinating creatures. (Rev: BL 4/15/03) [597.95]

11909 Barth, Kelly L. *Snakes* (7–10). Series: Endangered Animals and Habitats. 2001, Lucent LB $19.96 (1-56006-696-2). This work focuses on the types of snakes that are threatened with extinction and the efforts employed to save them. (Rev: BL 3/15/01) [597.96]

11910 Cherry, Jim. *Loco for Lizards* (7–12). Illus. 2000, Northland paper $7.95 (0-87358-763-4). This eclectic and entertaining overview of these reptiles provides basic scientific information plus a look at their important role in legends and contemporary culture. (Rev: SLJ 2/01) [597.95]

11911 Gaywood, Martin, and Ian Spellerberg. *Snakes* (6–12). Series: WorldLife Library. 1999, Voyageur paper $16.95 (0-89658-449-6). Facts about snakes and their ability to adapt to their environment are accompanied by discussion of their relationship with humans and eye-catching full-color photographs. (Rev: SLJ 4/00) [597.96]

11912 Greene, Harry W. *Snakes: The Evolution of Mystery in Nature* (10–12). 1997, Univ. of California Pr. $45.00 (0-520-20014-4). With unusual photographs and a lucid text, this is a tribute to snakes, their beauty, unique characteristics, history, and place in the environment. (Rev: BL 5/1/97; SLJ 12/97) [597.96]

11913 Mattison, Chris. *The Encyclopedia of Snakes* (10–12). 1995, Facts on File $35.00 (0-8160-3072-3). This book can be used for both browsing and research, because it offers interesting facts about all aspects of reptile life in an attractive text, with many colorful photographs. (Rev: BL 8/95; SLJ 2/96) [597.96]

11914 Mattison, Chris. *Snakes of the World* (9–12). Illus. 1986, Facts on File $29.95 (0-8160-1082-X). A richly illustrated account that covers diet, defense behavior, and the mythology of the snake. (Rev: BL 5/15/86) [597]

11915 Ricciuti, Edward R. *The Snake Almanac: A Fully Illustrated Natural History of Snakes Worldwide* (7–12). Illus. 2001, Lyons Pr. $29.95 (1-58574-178-7). Packed with facts, this is a comprehensive and detailed guide to snakes — their evolution, characteristics, habitats, and so forth — and to snakes' appearances in legends, snake-human relations, conservation efforts, and snakes as pets. (Rev: SLJ 10/01) [597.96]

11916 Rubio, Manny. *Rattlesnake: Portrait of a Predator* (9–12). Illus. 1998, Smithsonian $49.95 (1-56098-808-8). With 250 color photographs and detailed text, this book describes the origin, habitats, physiology, and anatomy of the rattlesnake and chronicles a history of people's different relationships with it, from commercial exploitation to snake-handling religious sects. (Rev: BL 12/1/98; SLJ 4/99) [597.96]

11917 Stafford, Peter J. *Snakes* (9–12). 2000, Smithsonian paper $14.95 (1-560-98997-1). This handbook on all kinds of snakes covers such topics as evolution, anatomy, locomotion, feeding, growth, and reproduction. [597.9]

TORTOISES AND TURTLES

11918 Alderton, David. *Turtles and Tortoises of the World* (9–12). Illus. 1988, Facts on File $29.95 (0-8160-1733-6). This thorough introduction covers such topics as structure, anatomy, reproduction, and origin and distribution. (Rev: BR 5–6/89) [598.92]

763

11919 Hawxhurst, Joan C. *Turtles and Tortoises* (7–10). Series: Endangered Animals and Habitats. 2001, Lucent LB $19.96 (1-56006-731-4). An exploration of the turtles and tortoises that are threatened with extinction, why they are endangered, and methods being used to save them. (Rev: BL 3/15/01) [597.92]

11920 Perrine, Doug. *Sea Turtles of the World* (10–12). Illus. 2003, Voyageur $29.95 (0-89658-555-7). Richly illustrated, this book documents the age-old nesting ritual of female Olive Ridley sea turtles. (Rev: BL 8/03) [597.92]

11921 Ripple, Jeff. *Sea Turtles* (10–12). Series: World Life Library. 1996, Voyageur paper $16.95 (0-89658-315-5). Using more than 50 color photographs, this book introduces the sea turtle and its distribution, behavior, anatomy, history, and characteristics, plus information on current conservation techniques and future trends. (Rev: SLJ 5/97) [597.92]

Animal Behavior

GENERAL AND MISCELLANEOUS

11922 Bruemmer, Fred. *Glimpses of Paradise: The Marvel of Massed Animals* (9–12). Illus. 2002, Firefly $40.00 (1-55297-666-1). This beautiful photoessay explores massive gatherings of certain species of animals, from the well-known to the unfamiliar, with informative text. (Rev: BL 1/1–15/03) [590.222]

11923 Downer, John. *Weird Nature* (10–12). Illus. 2002, Firefly $35.00 (1-55297-587-8); paper $19.95 (1-55297-586-X). This well-illustrated and absorbing companion to the BBC/Discovery Channel television series of the same name looks at mysteries of animal behavior. (Rev: BL 8/02; VOYA 8/02) [508]

11924 Dugatkin, Lee Alan. *Cheating Monkeys and Citizen Bees: The Nature of Cooperation in Animals and Humans* (10–12). 1999, Free Pr. $25.00 (0-684-84341-2). Cooperation as it exists in all forms of animal life, including human life, is the subject of this book. [591.56]

11925 Griffin, Donald R. *Animal Thinking* (10–12). 1984, Harvard Univ. Pr. paper $15.95 (0-674-03713-8). From the lowliest of creatures to communication between chimps, this is a thorough description of what we know about animal intelligence. [591.5]

11926 Halliday, Tim, ed. *Animal Behavior* (9–12). 1994, Univ. of Oklahoma Pr. $19.95 (0-8061-2647-7). A basic book on how animals are born, live, and die. Contains its share of cuddly creatures but does not shy away from portraying (with photographs) their place in the food chain. (Rev: BL 5/1/94) [591.51]

11927 Hauser, Marc D. *Wild Minds: What Animals Really Think* (10–12). 2000, Holt paper $15 .00 (0-8050-5670-X). After a general discussion on how animals view the world, this book covers their mental abilities, communication skills, and sense of morals. (Rev: BL 1/1–15/00) [591.5]

11928 Heinrich, Bernd. *Winter World: The Ingenuity of Animal Survival* (10–12). Illus. 2003, Ecco $24.95 (0-06-019744-7). This fascinating study explores the many ways in which animals survive the bitterly cold months of winter. (Rev: BL 1/1–15/03) [591.4]

11929 Linden, Eugene. *The Octopus and the Orangutan: More True Tales of Animal Intrigue, Intelligence, and Ingenuity* (10–12). 2002, Dutton $23.95 (0-525-94661-6). Anecdotes that provide examples of animal intelligence are both entertaining and informative. (Rev: BL 8/02) [591.5]

11930 Lorenz, Konrad. *On Aggression* (10–12). Trans. by Marjorie Kerr Wilson. 1966, Harcourt paper $13.00 (0-15-668741-0). The author examines aggression in animals and humans and describes both positive and negative aspects of this emotion. [152.4]

11931 McCarthy, Susan. *Becoming a Tiger: How Baby Animals Learn to Live in the Wild* (9–12). 2004, HarperCollins $24.95 (0-06-620924-2). Using a humorous, anecdotal style, the author tells how animals learn and illustrates the ways that they figure out how to live in their world. (Rev: BL 5/1/04) [591.5]

11932 Nichol, John. *Bites and Stings: The World of Venomous Animals* (9–12). Illus. 1989, Facts on File $21.50 (0-8160-2233-X). A guide to animals such as wasps and jellyfish that can cause bodily harm if disturbed, plus information on how to handle such injuries. (Rev: BL 7/89; BR 5–6/90) [591.6]

11933 Page, George. *Inside the Animal Mind: A Groundbreaking Exploration of Animal Intelligence* (9–12). 1999, Doubleday paper $14.95 (0-7679-0559-8). An exploration of animal thinking and behavior, with material on various animal behaviorists. (Rev: BL 11/1/99) [591.5]

11934 Von Kreisler, Kristin. *Beauty in the Beasts: True Stories of Animals Who Choose to Do Good* (10–12). Illus. 2001, Putnam $23.95 (1-58542-093-X). Using all sort of examples from the animal kingdom, the author shows that animals can express emotions that we previously thought could be experienced only by humans. (Rev: BL 5/15/01) [591.5]

11935 Yoerg, Sonja I. *Clever as a Fox: Animal Intelligence and What It Can Teach Us About Ourselves* (10–12). 2001, Bloomsbury $24.95 (1-58234-115-X). This challenging book studies intelligence in a number of animals and describes why different species need different types of intelligence. (Rev: BL 3/1/01) [591.5]

COMMUNICATION

11936 Morton, Eugene S., and Jake Page. *Animal Talk: Science and the Voices of Nature* (9–12). 1992, Random $22.00 (0-394-58337-X). Analysis of the origins and nature of animal communication. (Rev: BL 4/15/92) [591.59]

11937 Rogers, Lesley J., and Gisela Kaplan. *Songs, Roars, and Rituals: Communication in Birds, Mammals, and Other Animals* (10–12). Illus. 2000, Harvard $29.95 (0-674-00058-7). In eight concise chapters, the author covers forms of animal communication, including alarm calls and signals that are used for bluffing purposes. (Rev: BL 9/1/00) [591.59]

HOMES

11938 Farndon, John. *Wildlife Atlas: A Complete Guide to Animals and Their Habitats* (9–12). Illus. 2002, Reader's Digest $29.95 (0-7621-0354-X). This fascinating, well-illustrated overview of animals and where they live identifies eight main habitat types and the unique wildlife species that flourish in each. (Rev: BL 12/1/02) [591.7]

REPRODUCTION AND BABIES

11939 Allport, Susan. *A Natural History of Parenting: From Emperor Penguins to Reluctant Ewes, a Naturalist Looks at Parenting in the Animal World and Ours* (10–12). 1997, Harmony $23.00 (0-517-70799-3). A fascinating look at birth and parenting in a wide variety of birds, fishes, and mammals. (Rev: BL 2/1/97; SLJ 1/98) [591.3]

TRACKS

11940 Murie, Olaus J. *A Field Guide to Animal Tracks*. 2nd ed. (7–12). Illus. 1996, Houghton paper $8.95 (0-395-58297-6). This important volume in the Peterson Field Guide series first appeared in 1954 and now has become a classic in the area of identifying animal tracks and droppings. [591.5]

Animal Species

GENERAL AND MISCELLANEOUS

11941 Alden, Peter. *Peterson First Guide to Mammals of North America* (8–12). Illus. 1988, Houghton paper $5.95 (0-395-91181-8). An uncluttered basic guide to mammal identification with many illustrations and useful background material. (Rev: BL 5/15/87) [599]

11942 Anderson, Sydney, ed. *Simon and Schuster's Guide to Mammals* (9–12). Illus. 1984, Simon & Schuster paper $17.00 (0-671-42805-5). This guide, originally published in Italy, introduces the orders of mammals and highlights 426 species. [599]

11943 Attenborough, David. *The Life of Mammals* (10–12). Illus. 2003, Princeton Univ. Pr. $29.95 (0-691-11324-6). In this richly illustrated companion to the Discovery Channel documentary series of the same name, Attenborough examines in detail the diverse world of mammals. (Rev: BL 4/15/03) [599]

11944 Bramwell, Martyn, and Steve Parker. *Mammals: The Small Plant-Eaters* (6–10). Illus. 1989, Facts on File $19.95 (0-8160-1958-4). An introduction to each animal is given in text and outstanding illustrations. (Rev: VOYA 12/89) [559]

11945 Burt, William Henry. *A Field Guide to the Mammals: North America North of Mexico*. 3rd ed. (7–12). Illus. 1976, Houghton $24.95 (0-395-24082-4); paper $16.95 (0-395-24084-0). An identification guide to 380 species of mammals found in North America. [599]

11946 Davis, Susan E., and Margo DeMello. *Stories Rabbits Tell: A Natural and Cultural History of a Misunderstood Creature* (10–12). Illus. 2003, Lantern paper $20.00 (1-59056-044-2). A lively look at rabbits and their roles in the wild, as pets, and in fantasy and folklore. (Rev: BL 9/1/03) [636.932]

11947 Fenton, M. Brock. *Just Bats* (7–12). Illus. 1983, Univ. of Toronto Pr. paper $15.95 (0-8020-6464-7). An introduction to this frequently misunderstood and very useful flying rodent. [599.4]

11948 Graves, Russell A. *The Prairie Dog: Sentinel of the Plains* (9–12). Illus. 2001, Texas Tech Univ. Pr. $39.95 (0-89672-456-5); paper $19.95 (0-89672-455-7). This beautifully illustrated book transports readers to the world of prairie dogs, exploring their social structure and the important role they once played in the ecosystem of America's Great Plains. (Rev: BL 1/1–15/02) [599.37]

11949 Hodgson, Barbara. *The Rat: A Perverse Miscellany* (10–12). 1997, Ten Speed paper $15.95 (0-89815-926-1). Everything you've wanted to know about rats, including their role throughout history, how different people view them, and how they spread around the world. (Rev: BL 8/97; SLJ 3/98) [599.32]

11950 Lott, Dale F. *American Bison: A Natural History* (10–12). Illus. 2002, Univ. of California Pr. $29.95 (0-520-23338-7). An inviting overview of this American mammal and its difficult history. (Rev: BL 9/15/02) [599.64]

11951 MacDonald, David, ed. *The Encyclopedia of Mammals* (7–12). Illus. 1984, Facts on File $80.00 (0-87196-871-1). Almost 200 animal species are compiled in this volume on living mammals, which is illustrated with both photographs and drawings. [599]

11952 *Mammal* (10–12). Ed. by Don Wilson et al. Illus. 2003, DK $30.00 (0-7894-9972-X). This beautifully illustrated book takes readers on a worldwide tour of mammals and their habitats, with discussion of evolution and classification. (Rev: BL 11/15/03; VOYA 6/04) [599]

11953 Mares, Michael A. *A Desert Calling: Life in a Forbidding Landscape* (10–12). Illus. 2002, Harvard $29.95 (0-674-00747-6). Field biologist Mares transports readers to the deserts of the world to introduce them to the wide array of animal life that flourishes there and to reveal the joys of doing research in the field. (Rev: BL 4/1/02) [599.1754]

11954 North, Sterling. *Rascal: A Memoir of a Better Era* (7–12). Illus. 1963, Dutton $16.99 (0-525-18839-8). Remembrances of growing up in Wisconsin in 1918 and of the joys and problems of owning a pet raccoon. (Rev: BL 9/1/89) [599.74]

11955 Rath, Sara. *The Complete Cow* (10–12). Illus. 1998, Voyageur $29.95 (0-89658-375-9). An eminently readable collection of facts about cows, including a list of the many breeds, how to say "moo" around the globe, and information on the role of cows in religion and legend. (Rev: BL 12/15/98) [636.2]

11956 Rath, Sara. *The Complete Pig: An Entertaining History of Pigs* (9–12). Illus. 2000, Voyageur $29.95 (0-89658-435-6). An entertaining, informative book about pigs, their diversity, history, behavior, and folklore. (Rev: BL 6/1–15/00) [636.4]

11957 Rue, Leonard Lee. *Beavers* (9–12). Illus. 2002, Voyageur paper $16.95 (0-89658-548-4). A beautifully illustrated introduction to the beaver, its amazing building abilities, and its relationship with humans. (Rev: BL 5/1/02) [599.37]

11958 Ryden, Hope. *Lily Pond: Four Years with a Family of Beavers* (10–12). Illus. 1997, Lyons Pr. paper $16.95 (1-55821-455-0). A fascinating account of beaver-watching over a four-year period. (Rev: BL 11/15/89) [599.32]

11959 Tuttle, Merlin D. *America's Neighborhood Bats* (9–12). Illus. 1988, Univ. of Texas Pr. $19.95 (0-292-70403-8); paper $9.95 (0-292-70406-2). A brief account filled with amazing photographs that helps clarify misunderstandings about this very useful animal. (Rev: BL 3/1/89) [599.4]

11960 Whitaker, John O., Jr. *The Audubon Society Field Guide to North American Mammals* (7–12). Illus. 1980, Knopf $19.00 (0-394-50762-2). This excellent guide contains almost 200 pages of color photographs. [599]

APE FAMILY

11961 Dunbar, Robin, and Louise Barrett. *Cousins: Our Primate Relatives* (10–12). Illus. 2001, DK $29.95 (0-7894-7155-8). The origin of primates and their behavior and distribution are discussed group by group. (Rev: BL 6/1–15/01) [599.8]

11962 Fossey, Dian. *Gorillas in the Mist* (9–12). 1983, Houghton paper $14.00 (0-618-08360-X). This account covers 15 years in the author's life when she lived with the mountain gorillas in their natural habitat. (Rev: SLJ 12/83) [599.8]

11963 Gilders, Michelle A. *The Nature of Great Apes: Our Next of Kin* (6–12). Illus. 2001, Douglas & McIntyre $24.95 (1-55054-762-3). The clear information in this book is extended by excellent color photographs that will attract readers and report writers. (Rev: BL 1/1–15/01; VOYA 6/01) [599.88]

11964 Goodall, Jane. *In the Shadow of Man*. Rev. ed. (8–12). 1988, Houghton paper $16.00 (0-395-33145-5). The story of a scientist's observations of chimpanzees at the Gombe Stream Chimpanzee Reserve in Tanzania. (Rev: BR 11–12/88) [599.8]

11965 Jahme, Carole. *Beauty and the Beasts: Woman, Ape and Evolution* (10–12). Illus. 2001, Soho Pr. $25.00 (1-56947-231-9). This is a discussion of women who have contributed to the study of primates, such as Jane Goodall and Dian Fossey. (Rev: BL 6/1–15/01) [599.8]

11966 Levine, Stuart P. *The Orangutan* (7–10). Series: Overview: Endangered Animals and Habitats. 1999, Lucent LB $18.96 (1-56006-560-6). This account introduces the orangutan and its habits with material on why it is endangered and efforts being made to save it. (Rev: BL 12/15/99) [599.8]

11967 Montgomery, Sy. *Walking with the Great Apes: Jane Goodall, Dian Fossey, Biruté Galdikas* (9–12). 1991, Houghton $19.45 (0-395-51597-1). Descriptions of the painstaking research by several scientists in their quest for knowledge about the behavior and habits of the great apes. (Rev: BL 3/15/91*) [599.88]

11968 Preston-Mafham, Rod, and Ken Preston-Mafham. *Primates of the World* (9–12). 1992, Facts on File $32.95 (0-8160-2745-5). A well-illustrated introduction to the lemurs, monkeys, and apes found around the world, their habitats and behavior, and threats to their future. [599.8]

11969 Russon, Anne E. *Orangutans: Wizards of the Rain Forest* (10–12). Illus. 2000, Firefly $29.95 (1-55209-453-7). A well-written, superbly illustrated account of the only great apes found in Asia and of their highly endangered status. (Rev: BL 3/1/00*) [599.883]

11970 Sapolsky, Robert M. *A Primate's Memoir* (10–12). 2001, Scribner $25.00 (0-7432-0247-3). As well as an account of his experiences studying baboons in Kenya for more than 20 years, the author describes the social life and customs of the native people. (Rev: BL 1/1–15/01) [599.8]

11971 Siddle, Sheila, and Doug Cress. *In My Family Tree: A Life with Chimpanzees* (10–12). Illus. 2002, Grove $25.00 (0-8021-1713-9). An engrossing account of how the author and her husband transformed their Zambian farm into the world's largest primate sanctuary. (Rev: BL 5/15/02) [599.885]

11972 Stanford, Craig B. *Significant Others: The Ape-Human Continuum and the Quest for Human Nature* (10–12). 2001, Basic $25.00 (0-465-08171-1). In this study of the relationship between apes and humans, the author maintains that "to understand human nature, you must understand the apes." (Rev: BL 6/1–15/01) [302.5]

11973 Strum, Shirley C. *Almost Human: A Journey into the World of Baboons* (9–12). Illus. 1987, Random $22.50 (0-394-54724-1). A description of the life and habits of the Pumphouse Gang, a group of baboons living in Kenya. (Rev: BL 11/15/87) [599.8]

11974 Swindler, Daris Ray. *Introduction to the Primates* (10–12). 1998, Univ. of Washington Pr. paper $22.00 (0-295-97704-3). Traces the evolutionary history of monkeys and apes and looks at their anatomy, diet and habitat, and behavior. [599.8]

11975 Waal, Frans de. *My Family Album: Thirty Years of Primate Photography* (10–12). Illus. 2003, Univ. of California Pr. $29.95 (0-520-23615-7). De Waal's passion for primates shows in these stunning photographs, which are accompanied by sound scientific details. (Rev: BL 10/1/03) [779]

11976 Weber, Bill, and Amy Vedder. *In the Kingdom of Gorillas: Fragile Species in a Dangerous Land* (9–12). 2001, Simon & Schuster $27.50 (0-7432-0006-3). The story of ongoing field research in Rwanda that began in 1978 when a young American couple began observing gorillas and their habits. (Rev: BL 10/1/01) [599.884]

BEARS

11977 Busch, Robert H. *The Grizzly Almanac* (9–12). Illus. 2001, Lyons Pr. $29.95 (1-58574-143-4). This book reveals all the facts known about grizzlies, their anatomy, habits, habitats, and relations with humans. (Rev: BL 2/1/01) [599.784]

11978 Craighead, Frank C., Jr. *Track of the Grizzly* (10–12). Illus. 1979, Sierra Club paper $16.00 (0-87156-322-3). This introduction to the grizzly bear is the result of a 13-year study in Yellowstone National Park. [599.74]

11979 Craighead, Lance. *Bears of the World* (9–12). Illus. 2001, Voyageur $29.95 (0-89658-503-4). After an overview chapter on the world's bear population, the author devotes separate chapters to eight species, including grizzly, polar, and American black. (Rev: BL 2/1/01; VOYA 10/01) [599.78]

11980 Kilham, Benjamin, and Ed Gray. *Among the Bears: Raising Orphan Cubs in the Wild* (8–12). Illus. 2002, Holt $26.00 (0-8050-6919-4). The author describes his experiences raising two orphaned black bear cubs to adulthood, and the dis-

coveries he made about black bear behavior. (Rev: BL 3/1/02) [599.78]

11981 Lawter, William Clifford. *Smokey Bear 20252: A Biography* (9–12). 1994, Lindsay Smith $26.95 (0-9640017-0-5). Outlines the history of Smokey Bear (a real bear, rescued from a forest fire and sent to the National Zoo), the famous poster, and the uniforms worn by the nation's forest service. (Rev: BL 5/1/94) [363.377]

11982 Montgomery, Sy. *Search for the Golden Moon Bear: Science and Adventure in Pursuit of a New Species* (10–12). Illus. 2002, Simon & Schuster $26.00 (0-7432-0584-7). This riveting account of the author's search for the elusive golden moon bear transports readers into the wilds of Southeast Asia and reveals some harsh truths about the illegal trade in wildlife. (Rev: BL 9/15/02) [599.78]

11983 Ovsyanikov, Nikita. *Polar Bears* (10–12). Illus. Series: World Life Library. 1998, Voyageur paper $16.95 (0-89658-358-9). This absorbing and well-illustrated volume examines in detail the life of polar bears. (Rev: BL 12/15/98) [599.786]

11984 Rosing, Norbert. *The World of the Polar Bear* (10–12). Trans. from German by Tecklenborg Erlag. 1996, Firefly $40.00 (1-55209-068-X). More than half of this book consists of photographs illustrating the behavior and habits of the polar bear and the flora and fauna of the Arctic. (Rev: SLJ 5/97) [599.74]

11985 Schullery, Paul, ed. *Mark of the Bear* (10–12). 1996, Sierra Club $30.00 (0-87156-903-5). Ten naturalists describe their encounters with bears, with more than half the book devoted to full-page, full-color photographs. (Rev: BL 12/1/96; SLJ 1/97) [599.74]

11986 Turbak, Gary. *Grizzly Bears* (6–10). Series: World Life Library. 1997, Voyageur paper $14.95 (0-89658-334-1). High-quality photographs and concise, readable text are used to introduce the grizzly bear's life cycle, origin, habits, anatomy, and future. (Rev: SLJ 10/97) [599.74]

CATS (LIONS, TIGERS, ETC.)

11987 Aaseng, Nathan. *The Cheetah* (7–10). Series: Overview: Endangered Animals and Habitats. 2000, Lucent LB $23.70 (1-56006-680-6). After a description of the cheetah, its habits and environments, there is material on methods employed to save it. (Rev: BL 10/15/2000; HBG 3/01) [599.74]

11988 Aaseng, Nathan. *The Cougar* (7–10). Series: Endangered Animals and Habitats. 2001, Lucent LB $19.96 (1-56006-730-6). This book introduces this large American cat also known as a puma and explains why it is endangered and what efforts are being made to save it. (Rev: BL 3/15/01) [599.73]

11989 Adamson, Joy. *Born Free: A Lioness of Two Worlds* (7–12). 1987, Pantheon $11.95 (0-679-56141-2). First published in 1960, this is an account of a young lioness growing up in captivity in Kenya. [599.74]

11990 Alderton, David. *Wild Cats of the World* (9–12). 1993, Facts on File $32.95 (0-8160-2736-6). This survey of the world's wild cats begins with general material about cats, their anatomy, and habits, etc., followed by a look at specific species. [599.75]

11991 Bertram, Brian. *Lions* (10–12). Illus. Series: World Life Library. 1998, Voyageur paper $16.95 (0-89658-399-6). This absorbing and well-illustrated volume examines in detail the life of lions. (Rev: BL 12/15/98) [599.757]

11992 Bolgiano, Chris. *Mountain Lion: An Unnatural History of Pumas and People* (9–12). 1995, Stackpole $19.95 (0-8117-1044-0). Details the mythological history and the impact of the mountain lion, from its use in Native American tales to its uses in modern advertising. (Rev: BL 8/95) [599.74]

11993 Caputo, Philip. *Ghosts of Tsavo: Stalking the Mystery Lions of East Africa* (10–12). Illus. 2002, National Geographic $27.00 (0-7922-6362-6). Pulitzer Prize-winning novelist Caputo recounts encounters with the big cats and other dangerous wildlife of Kenya's Tsavo region. (Rev: BL 5/1/02) [599.757]

11994 Grace, Eric S., and Art Wolfe. *The Nature of Lions: Social Cats of the Savannas* (9–12). Illus. 2001, Firefly $29.95 (1-55297-542-8). After a discussion of the anatomy, evolution, and general behavior of lions, the author supplies details on the world of the lion. (Rev: BL 12/15/01) [599.757]

11995 Karanth, K. Ullas. *The Way of the Tiger: Natural History and Conservation of the Endangered Big Cat* (9–12). Illus. 2001, Voyageur $29.95 (0-89658-560-3). This nicely illustrated profile provides a wealth of information about these big cats — including their evolution, social life, and the growing threat they face as humans continue to encroach on their habitat. (Rev: BL 1/1–15/02) [599.756]

11996 Levine, Stuart P. *The Tiger* (7–10). Series: Overview: Endangered Animals and Habitats. 1998, Lucent LB $27.45 (1-56006-465-X). This work describes the habits and habitats of the tiger and current efforts to protect it from extinction. (Rev: BL 10/15/98) [599.74]

11997 Malaspina, Ann. *The Jaguar* (7–10). Series: Endangered Animals and Habitats. 2001, Lucent LB $19.96 (1-56006-813-2). An introduction to this large cat that is a native to Central and South America, the reasons why it is endangered, and the methods employed to save it. (Rev: BL 3/15/01) [599.74]

11998 Mangelsen, Thomas D., and Cara Shea Blessley. *Spirit of the Rockies: The Mountain Lions of Jackson Hole* (9–12). Illus. 2000, Images of Nature $19.95 (1-890310-19-0). Beautiful photographs and an interesting text highlight this story of a mother mountain lion and her three cubs during the winter of 1999 in Wyoming. (Rev: BL 5/15/00) [599.75]

11999 National Geographic Society, eds. *The Year of the Tiger* (9–12). 1998, National Geographic $40.00 (0-7922-7377-X). Using more than 100 stunning photographs, this photoessay gives an unprecedented view of the habits, play, and social life of tigers in the wild, with half the book devoted to the tigers of the Bandhavgarh National Park in India, as well as in captivity. (Rev: SLJ 4/99) [599.74]

12000 Savage, Candace. *Wild Cats: Lynx, Bobcats, Mountain Lions* (8–10). 1993, Sierra Club paper $20.00 (0-87156-424-6). These three species of big cats are highlighted through photographs and a text that covers habitats, diet, hunting techniques, and habits. [599.75]

12001 Siedensticker, John. *Tigers* (10–12). Series: World Life Library. 1996, Voyageur paper $19.95 (0-89658-295-7). The distribution, anatomy, behavior, history, and endangered status of the tiger are discussed in this book that contains more than 50 stunning color photographs. (Rev: SLJ 5/97) [599.74]

12002 Sinha, Vivek R. *The Vanishing Tiger* (8–12). Illus. 2004, Trafalgar $29.95 (1-84065-441-4). A wonderful photographic record of an expedition to locate and photograph India's massive Bengal tiger. (Rev: BL 3/1/04) [599.7]

COYOTES, FOXES, AND WOLVES

12003 Askins, Renee. *Shadow Mountain: A Memoir of Wolves, a Woman, and the Wild* (10–12). 2002, Doubleday $24.95 (0-385-48222-1). The founder of the Wolf Fund describes the ultimately successful struggle to return wolves to their original habitat in Yellowstone National Park. (Rev: BL 6/1–15/02) [639.9]

12004 Busch, Robert. *The Wolf Almanac* (9–12). 1995, Lyons Pr. $27.95 (1-55821-351-1). An introduction to wolves, with 100 illustrations. (Rev: BL 5/1/95) [599.74]

12005 Busch, Robert, ed. *Wolf Songs: The Classic Collection of Writing About Wolves* (9–12). 1994, Sierra Club $15.00 (0-87156-411-4). Personal essays about the misunderstood wolf, each arguing that wolves have the right to free existence in nature. (Rev: BL 10/15/94; SLJ 6/95; VOYA 4/95) [599.74]

12006 Dutcher, Jim, et al. *Wolves at Our Door* (9–12). Illus. 2002, Pocket $26.00 (0-7434-0048-8). A captivating story of six years spent photographing a wolf pack and the bonds that developed between humans and animals. (Rev: BL 2/1/02) [599.773]

12007 Hampton, Bruce. *The Great American Wolf* (10–12). 1997, Holt $35.00 (0-8050-3716-0). The author presents information about an organized campaign from the 1890s to eliminate wolves in this country and material on the wolves' habits, habitats, social organization, and food, plus a chapter on Native American wolf lore. (Rev: SLJ 9/97) [599.74]

12008 Landau, Diana. *Wolf: Spirit of the Wild: A Celebration of Wolves in Word and Image* (6–12). Illus. 2000, Sterling $24.95 (0-8069-8717-0). Fiction, poems, and articles about wolves are accompanied by eye-catching color photographs. (Rev: VOYA 12/00) [599.773]

12009 Lawrence, R. D. *In Praise of Wolves* (10–12). 1986, Ballantine paper $5.99 (0-345-34916-4). A book that resulted from the author's many years studying the habits and behavior of wolves. (Rev: VOYA 6/86) [599.74]

12010 Lawrence, R. D. *Secret Go the Wolves* (9–12). 1985, Ballantine paper $5.99 (0-345-33200-8). The story of how Lawrence and his wife raised a pair of wolf pups. [599.7]

12011 Leslie, Robert Franklin. *In the Shadow of a Rainbow* (10–12). 1986, Norton paper $9.95 (0-393-30392-6). The story of an unusual friendship between man and wolf. [599.74]

12012 Lopez, Barry. *Of Wolves and Men* (9–12). 1978, Macmillan paper $18.00 (0-684-16322-5). An account that contrasts the wolf of folklore with the true nature of this caring social creature. [599.74]

12013 Mech, L. David. *The Way of the Wolf* (9–12). 1991, Voyageur $29.95 (0-89658-163-2). Discusses wolves' place in the natural order and their similarity to domesticated dogs, dispels the myth that they attack people, and makes a case for their preservation. (Rev: BL 10/1/91) [599.75]

12014 Rogers, Lesley J., and Gisela Kaplan. *Spirit of the Wild Dog: The World of Wolves, Coyotes, Foxes, Jackals and Dingoes* (10–12). Illus. 2003, Allen & Unwin paper $15.95 (1-86508-673-8). In this fascinating look at wild members of the dog family, the authors examine the characteristics of coyotes, dingoes, foxes, jackals, and wolves and compare them with their domesticated cousins. (Rev: BL 11/1/03) [599.772]

12015 Savage, Candace. *The World of the Wolf* (10–12). 1996, Sierra Club $27.50 (0-87156-899-3). Large color photographs and a simple text introduce the wolf, its habits and behavior, how and where it lives, and its relationship with humankind. (Rev: SLJ 3/97) [599.74]

12016 Steinhart, Peter. *The Company of Wolves* (9–12). 1995, Knopf paper $14 .00 (0-679-74387-1). As well as exploring the habits and behavior of wolves, this volume gives a great deal of information on the relationship between wolves and humans. [599.77]

12017 Thiel, Richard P. *Keepers of the Wolves: The Early Years of Wolf Recovery in Wisconsin* (10–12). Illus. 2001, Univ. of Wisconsin Pr. $50.00 (0-299-17470-0); paper $19.95 (0-299-17474-3). The ecology and behavior of wolves are described as well as a tale of the gray wolf's reclamation of its midwestern range. (Rev: BL 11/15/01) [333.95]

12018 *The Wolves of Minnesota: Howl in the Heartland* (10–12). Ed. by L. David Mech. Illus. 2000, Voyageur $24.95 (0-89658-464-X). Minnesota has a large wolf population, and this book describes their lives and habits and the many attempts made to exterminate them. (Rev: BL 2/1/01) [599.773]

DEER FAMILY

12019 Cox, Daniel, and John Ozoga. *Whitetail Country* (8–12). Illus. 1988, Willow Creek $39.00 (0-932558-43-7). Wonderful photographs complement this account of the life and living habits of the deer. (Rev: BR 3–4/89) [599.73]

12020 Rue, Leonard Lee. *Way of the Whitetail* (9–12). Illus. 2000, Voyageur $35.00 (0-89658-417-8). A readable scientific account with excellent photographs that follows the whitetail deer through the cycle of the seasons. (Rev: BL 9/1/00) [599.65]

ELEPHANTS

12021 Chadwick, Douglas H. *The Fate of the Elephant* (9–12). 1992, Sierra Club $25.00 (0-87156-635-4). A revealing report on the impending extinction of the elephant. (Rev: BL 9/15/92; SLJ 5/93) [599.6]

12022 Denis-Huot, Christine, and Michel Denis-Huot. *The Art of Being an Elephant* (10–12). Illus. 2003, Barnes & Noble $19.95 (0-7607-4300-2). The life of the African elephant is shown in hundreds of color photographs accompanied by facts and discussion of elephant behavior and human and environmental threats. (Rev: BL 12/1/03) [599.07]

12023 Di Silvestro, Roger L. *The African Elephant: Twilight in Eden* (9–12). 1991, Wiley $34.95 (0-471-53207-X). The social behavior of earth's largest land mammal, now endangered because of the ivory trade, and its association with humans from prehistory to the present day. (Rev: BL 10/15/91) [333.95]

12024 Ellis, Gerry. *Wild Orphans* (9–12). Illus. 2002, Welcome $24.95 (0-941807-58-4). In charming detail, author-photographer Ellis shows how eight orphaned baby elephants were lovingly reared at a Kenya wildlife orphanage until they could be returned to the wild. (Rev: BL 7/02) [599.67]

12025 Groning, Karl, and Martin Saller. *Elephants: A Cultural and Natural History* (8–12). 1999, Konemann (3-8290-1752-9). Both the scientific and mythological aspects of elephants are covered, with material on behavior, anatomy, and habitats. (Rev: BL 6/1–15/99; SLJ 5/00) [599.67]

12026 Levine, Stuart P. *The Elephant* (7–10). Illus. Series: Overview: Endangered Animals and Habitats. 1997, Lucent LB $27.45 (1-56006-522-2). After a general introduction to the elephant and its characteristics, evolution, and habitats, the author describes how it has become endangered and current attempts at conservation. (Rev: BL 5/1/98; HBG 9/98) [599.67]

12027 Meredith, Martin. *Elephant Destiny: Biography of an Endangered Species in Africa* (10–12). Illus. 2003, PublicAffairs $24.95 (1-58648-077-4). This is a moving story of the tragic history of human interaction with the African elephant from ancient times through the late 20th century. (Rev: BL 4/1/03) [599.67]

12028 Poole, Joyce. *Elephants* (9–12). Series: World Life Library. 1997, Voyageur paper $14.95 (0-89658-357-0). This slim volume examines the natural history of elephants — both African and Asian — and the growing threat they face as humans invade more of their habitat. [599.67]

12029 Scigliano, Eric. *Love, War, and Circuses: The Age-Old Relationship Between Elephants and Humans* (9–12). 2002, Houghton $24.00 (0-618-01583-3). Scigliano explores the history of human interaction with pachyderms, focusing in particular on Asian elephants, which have long been tamed and trained to perform heavy tasks; suitable for browsing and for reports. (Rev: BL 6/1–15/02) [599.67]

12030 Watson, Lyall. *Elephantoms: Tracking the Elephant* (10–12). Illus. 2002, Norton $25.95 (0-393-05117-X). Personal recollection and natural history are intertwined in this appealing celebration of elephants. (Rev: BL 4/1/02) [599.67]

MARSUPIALS

12031 Malaspina, Ann. *The Koala* (7–10). Series: Endangered Animals and Habitats. 2002, Gale LB $27.45 (1-56006-876-0). That story of this animal that is threatened with extinction is told with material on methods currently employed to save it. (Rev: BL 5/15/02; SLJ 6/02) [599.2]

12032 Phillips, Ken. *Koalas: Australia's Ancient Ones* (9–12). 1994, Prentice Hall $27.50 (0-671-79777-8). A study of Australia's beloved marsupial that chronicles koala rescues and describes the growth of the Koala Hospital. (Rev: BL 10/1/94) [599.2]

PANDAS

12033 Kiefer, Michael. *Chasing the Panda: How an Unlikely Pair of Adventurers Won the Race to Capture the Mythical "White Bear."* (9–12). Illus. 2002, Four Walls Eight Windows $24.95 (1-56858-223-4). This is the little-known story of an American socialite's successful expedition in the 1930s to capture a giant panda; entertaining and useful for reports. (Rev: BL 3/15/02; SLJ 11/02) [599.789]

12034 Presnall, Judith J. *The Giant Panda* (7–10). Illus. Series: Overview: Endangered Animals and Habitats. 1998, Lucent LB $22.45 (1-56006-522-6). A discussion of the giant panda's evolution, habitats, life span, and breeding habits, how it became endangered, and attempts to conserve this dwindling population. (Rev: BL 5/1/98) [599.789]

12035 Schaller, George B. *The Last Panda* (9–12). 1993, Univ. of Chicago Pr. $24.95 (0-226-73628-8). A noted field biologist recounts his experiences researching the giant panda in the wilds of China. (Rev: BL 3/15/93) [599.74]

12036 Zhi, Lu, and George B. Schaller. *Giant Pandas in the Wild: Saving an Endangered Species* (10–12). Illus. 2003, Aperture $35.00 (0-89381-997-2). The life of the giant panda — and the very real threats facing the species — are examined in this photoessay. (Rev: BL 4/15/03) [599.789]

Birds

GENERAL AND MISCELLANEOUS

12037 Adler, Bill. *Impeccable Birdfeeding: How to Discourage Scuffling, Hull-Dropping, Seed-Throwing, Unmentionable Nuisances and Vulgar Chatter at Your Birdfeeder* (9–12). 1992, Chicago Review paper $9.95 (1-55652-157-X). Discusses birdbaths, birdfeeders, and birdhouses, and rates food and bird species on the basis of mess potential. (Rev: BL 10/1/92) [598]

12038 Attenborough, David. *The Life of Birds* (9–12). Illus. 1998, Princeton Univ. Pr. $29.95 (0-691-01633-X). In this book, a companion piece to the PBS series of the same name, Attenborough explores the human fascination with birds and their lives. (Rev: BL 12/1/98) [598.15]

12039 *Birds* (10–12). Series: North American Wildlife. 1998, Reader's Digest paper $16.95 (0-7621-0036-2). More than 300 illustrations and maps ease bird identification, plus discussion of distinguishing traits. [598]

12040 *Book of North American Birds* (9–12). 1990, Random $32.95 (0-89577-351-1). About 600 U.S. and Canadian birds are pictured in color paintings and described in a lucid text. (Rev: BL 9/1/90) [598]

12041 Buff, Sheila. *The Birdfeeder's Handbook: An Orvis Guide* (9–12). 1991, Lyons Pr. paper $10.95

(1-55821-123-3). This manual offers basic information on birdfeeding, birdhouses, and avian behavior, including feeder manners, territories, courtship, breeding, and migration. (Rev: BL 9/1/91) [598]

12042 Bull, John, et al. *Birds of North America, Eastern Region: A Quick Identification Guide to Common Birds* (9–12). Illus. 1985, Macmillan paper $21.95 (0-02-079660-9). A picture guide to 253 species of birds found in the eastern part of Canada and the United States. Also use *Birds of North America, Western Region* (1989). (Rev: BL 8/85) [598]

12043 Burt, William. *Rare and Elusive Birds of North America* (9–12). Illus. 2001, Universe $39.95 (0-7893-0638-7). Illustrated with excellent photographs, this is an account of 20 species of North American birds that are rarely seen. (Rev: BL 11/15/01) [598]

12044 Burton, Robert. *The World of the Hummingbird* (10–12). Illus. 2001, Firefly $40.00 (1-55209-607-6). This account, illustrated with superb photographs reviews the body of knowledge we have amassed about the fascinating hummingbird. (Rev: BL 11/15/01) [598.764]

12045 Cocker, Mark. *Birders: Tales of a Tribe* (10–12). 2002, Grove Atlantic $25.00 (0-87113-844-1). Cocker's memories of a birdwatching youth serve as a backdrop for information on birding in general. (Rev: BL 4/15/02) [598]

12046 Cronin, Edward W. *Getting Started in Bird Watching* (10–12). Illus. 1986, Houghton paper $9.95 (0-395-34397-6). Handy tips and checklists for nine different regions of the United States highlight this beginner's manual. (Rev: BL 6/1/86) [598]

12047 Dunne, Pete. *Pete Dunne on Bird Watching: The How-to, Where-to, and When-to of Birding* (10–12). Illus. 2003, Houghton paper $12.00 (0-395-90686-5). Both veteran and novice bird watchers will find value in this guide, which is loaded with advice on proper equipment and techniques, as well as tips for homeowners who would like to attract birds. (Rev: BL 3/15/03) [598]

12048 Ehrlich, Paul R., et al. *The Birder's Handbook: A Field Guide to the Natural History of North American Birds* (9–12). Illus. 1988, Simon & Schuster paper $18.00 (0-671-65989-8). An extremely comprehensive guide to the 646 birds native to North America. (Rev: BL 10/1/88) [598.297]

12049 Elliott, Lang. *Music of the Birds: A Celebration of Bird Song* (10–12). Illus. 1999, Houghton $35.00 (0-618-00698-2); paper $25.00 (0-618-00697-4). This beautiful book with an accompanying CD and dazzling photographs is a guide to common birds and their songs. (Rev: BL 1/1–15/00) [598.097]

12050 Farrand, John. *How to Identify Birds* (10–12). Illus. 1987, McGraw-Hill paper $17.95 (0-07-019975-2). A noted bird watcher tells how to identify birds by such characteristics as size, habitat, and voice. For more specific information see the author's *Eastern Birds* and *Western Birds* (both 1987). (Rev: BL 11/15/87) [598]

12051 Fuller, Errol. *Dodo: A Brief History* (10–12). Illus. 2003, Universe $22.50 (0-7893-0840-1). A fascinating study of the bird that was found only on the Indian Ocean island of Mauritius. (Rev: BL 3/1/03) [598.65]

12052 Gallagher, Tim. *Parts Unknown: A Naturalist's Journey in Search of Birds and Wild Places* (9–12). Illus. 2001, Lyons Pr. $24.95 (1-58574-275-9). This collection of essays explores various aspects of bird lore with coverage, for example, on the California condor and the habits of sandpipers. (Rev: BL 8/01) [598]

12053 Grimes, William. *My Fine Feathered Friend* (9–12). 2002, Farrar $15.00 (0-86547-632-2). The mysterious appearance of a brightly colored and self-confident chicken in his Queens neighborhood launched the author on a campaign to learn more about the animal. (Rev: BL 3/1/02) [636.5]

12054 Harris, Joan. *One Wing's Gift: Rescuing Alaska's Wild Birds* (7–12). 2002, Alaska Northwest paper $16.95 (0-88240-560-8). The injured birds that are treated in an Alaskan center are celebrated in beautiful, detailed drawings accompanied by sometimes poignant stories. (Rev: SLJ 10/02) [333.95]

12055 Hart-Davis, Duff. *Audubon's Elephant: America's Greatest Naturalist and the Making of "The Birds of America."* (9–12). Illus. 2004, Holt $27.50 (0-8050-7568-2). A handsomely illustrated volume that describes Audubon's years in Edinburgh and London (1826–1838) when he produced his famous *The Birds of America.* (Rev: BL 4/1/04) [598]

12056 Keenan, Philip E. *Birding Across North America: A Naturalist's Observations* (10–12). Illus. 2002, Timber $29.95 (0-88192-528-4). Richly illustrated, this handsome volume offers personal bird-watching experiences and a wealth of valuable advice. (Rev: BL 2/15/02) [598]

12057 Matthiessen, Peter. *The Birds of Heaven: Travels with Cranes* (10–12). Illus. 2001, Farrar $27.00 (0-374-19944-2). The author writes about cranes, his journey in search of all 15 species, 11 of which are on the endangered list, and his contact with scientists who are trying to save them. Illustrations by Robert Bateman. (Rev: BL 9/1/01*; SLJ 6/02) [598.3]

12058 *National Geographic Field Guide to the Birds of North America.* 4th ed, (8–12). 2002, National Geographic $21.95 (0-7922-6877-6). Arranged by family groups, this is an identification guide to more than 800 species of North American birds. [598]

12059 Perrin, Jacques, and Jean-Francois Mongibeaux. *Winged Migration* (10–12). Illus. 2003, Chronicle $50.00 (2-02-061292-5). A companion to the movie of the same name, this attractive volume full of photographs follows birds through their life cycles and migratory journeys. (Rev: BL 11/15/03) [598.156]

12060 Perrins, Christopher M., and Alex L. A. Middleton, eds. *The Encyclopedia of Birds* (9–12). Illus. 1985, Facts on File $45.00 (0-8160-1150-8). This expensive fully illustrated volume gives excellent information on all kinds of birds arranged by their general size. (Rev: BL 8/85) [598]

12061 Peterson, Roger Tory. *A Field Guide to the Birds.* 4th rev. ed. (7–12). Illus. 1980, Houghton $30.00 (0-395-74047-X); paper $18.00 (0-395-26619-X). An exhaustive guide to the birds found east of the Rockies. [598]

12062 Peterson, Roger Tory. *A Field Guide to Western Birds.* 3rd ed. (9–12). Illus. 1990, Houghton $26.00 (0-395-51749-4); paper $17.95 (0-395-51424-X). This book covers the birds found in the Rockies and West plus a section on the Hawaiian Islands. [598]

12063 Peterson, Roger Tory, and Virginia Marie Peterson. *A Field Guide to the Birds of Eastern and Central North America.* 5th ed. (8–12). 2002, Houghton $30.00 (0-395-74047-9). This book identifies birds found east of the Rockies with both verbal and pictorial descriptions. [598]

12064 Rossier, Jay, and Geoff Hansen. *Living with Chickens: Everything You Need to Know to Raise Your Own Backyard Flock* (9–12). Illus. 2002, Lyons Pr. $24.95 (1-58574-452-2). The intricacies of designing coops, roosts, and feeders; hatching eggs; handling eggs; and proper feeding practices are all covered in this attractive guide. (Rev: BL 6/1–15/02) [636.5]

12065 Safina, Carl. *Eye of the Albatross: Visions of Hope and Survival* (9–12). Illus. 2002, Holt $27.50 (0-8050-6228-9). An individual albatross named Amelia is the focus of this fascinating overview of the life cycle of these huge birds, their amazing journeys, and the harm done to them by humans. (Rev: BL 5/1/02*) [598.4]

12066 Sibley, David. *The Sibley Field Guide to Birds of Western North America* (9–12). 2003, Knopf paper $19.95 (0-679-45121-8). This is a reliable, attractive guide to the 703 bird species found west of the Rockies. [598]

12067 Sibley, David. *The Sibley Guide to Birds* (9–12). 2000, Knopf paper $35.00 (0-679-45122-6). Each of 810 species is described in pictures and detailed text, with identification tips. [598]

12068 Stokes, Donald, and Lillian Stokes. *The Bird Feeder Book: An Easy Guide to Attracting, Identify-ing, and Understanding Your Feeder Birds* (8–12). Illus. 1987, Little, Brown paper $12.95 (0-316-81733-3). A manual that describes, with color photographs, 72 backyard birds, plus tips on how to attract and feed them. (Rev: BL 2/1/88) [598]

12069 Stokes, Donald, and Lillian Stokes. *The Complete Birdhouse Book: The Easy Guide to Attracting Nesting Birds* (9–12). Illus. 1990, Little, Brown paper $13.00 (0-316-81714-7). Plans for various birdhouses are given plus instructions on how to build them. (Rev: BL 9/15/90) [598]

12070 Stuart, Chris, and Tilde Stuart. *Birds of Africa: From Seabirds to Seed-Eaters* (10–12). Illus. 2000, MIT $29.95 (0-262-19430-9). A well-illustrated account that offers good basic information about the many species of African birds, their habitats, and their characteristics. (Rev: BL 3/1/00* ; SLJ 11/00) [598]

12071 Thurston, Harry. *The World of the Shorebirds* (10–12). 1996, Sierra Club $27.50 (0-87156-901-9). A variety of shorebirds are introduced in text and large color photographs, with details on their lives, habits, behavior, and relations with people. (Rev: SLJ 3/97) [598]

12072 Toops, Connie. *Hummingbirds: Jewels in Flight* (9–12). 1992, Voyageur $29.95 (0-89658-161-6). The author recounts her trips to observe hummingbirds in the Southwest and along the Gulf Coast and provides information on plants that attract them. (Rev: BL 11/1/92) [598.8]

BEHAVIOR

12073 Dunning, Joan. *Secrets of the Nest: The Family of North American Birds* (9–12). 1994, Houghton $27.50 (0-395-62035-X). The author uses pen-and-ink drawings to illustrate the nesting behavior of robins, hummingbirds, ducks, egrets, the California condor, and other birds. (Rev: BL 3/15/94) [598.256]

12074 Short, Lester L. *The Lives of Birds: The Birds of the World and Their Behavior* (9–12). Series: American Museum of Natural History: Animal Behavior. 1993, Holt $25.00 (0-8050-1952-9). Describes how birds find mates, stake out territories, reproduce, navigate over long distances, what they eat, and why they sing. (Rev: BL 6/1–15/93) [598.2]

12075 Stokes, Donald. *A Guide to the Behavior of Common Birds* (7–12). Illus. 1979, Little, Brown $16.95 (0-316-81722-8); paper $15.00 (0-316-81725-2). The first of three volumes, each of which describes the behavior of 25 different birds. Volume 2 is *A Guide to Bird Behavior: In the Wild and at Your Feeder* (1985); volume 3 is *A Guide to Bird Behavior* (1989). [598]

DUCKS AND GEESE

12076 Lorenz, Konrad, et al. *Here I Am — Where Are You? The Behavior of the Greylag Goose* (9–12). Trans. by Robert D. Martin. 1991, Harcourt $26.95 (0-15-140056-3). Offers intimate observations of the social behavior of the greylag goose and covers decades of scientific inquiry by a pioneering expert on ducks and geese. (Rev: BL 10/15/91) [598]

EAGLES, HAWKS, AND OTHER BIRDS OF PREY

12077 Barghusen, Joan D. *The Bald Eagle* (7–10). Series: Overview: Endangered Animals and Habitats. 1998, Lucent LB $27.45 (1-56006-254-1). An introduction to the structure, habits, and habitats of the bald eagle and a description of the methods employed to save it. (Rev: BL 10/15/98) [598.9]

12078 Barth, Kelly L. *Birds of Prey* (7–10). Series: Overview: Endangered Animals and Habitats. 1999, Lucent LB $18.96 (1-56006-493-5). A well-illustrated account that introduces various birds of prey, explains why they are endangered, and describes methods used to save them. (Rev: BL 12/15/99; HBG 9/00) [598.9]

12079 Clark, William S. *A Field Guide to Hawks: North America* (9–12). Illus. 1987, Houghton $24.95 (0-395-36001-3); paper $16.95 (0-395-44112-9). An extensively illustrated guide to 39 species of hawks. (Rev: BL 10/1/87) [598]

12080 Gessner, David. *Return of the Osprey: A Season of Flight and Wonder* (10–12). Illus. 2001, Algonquin $23.95 (1-56512-254-2). A beautifully written and organized account that covers a season with the ospreys who have returned to Cape Cod after being almost wiped out by the effects of DDT. (Rev: BL 2/1/01*) [598.9]

12081 Heintzelman, Donald S. *Hawks and Owls of Eastern North America* (10–12). Illus. 2004, Rutgers Univ. Pr. $29.95 (0-8135-3350-3). More than 30 species of eagles, hawks, and owls are profiled in this comprehensive guide. (Rev: BL 12/1/03) [598.9]

12082 Houle, Marcy. *The Prairie Keepers: Secrets of the Grasslands* (9–12). 1995, Addison-Wesley $20.00 (0-201-60843-X). A memoir of a field biologist's six-month study of hawks in an Oregon prairie. (Rev: BL 4/1/95*) [598.9]

12083 Savage, Candace. *Peregrine Falcons* (9–12). 1992, Sierra Club $30.00 (0-87156-504-8). A detailed discussion of the tragic effects of pesticide pollution on peregrine falcons. (Rev: BL 11/1/92; SLJ 7/93) [598.9]

12084 Winn, Marie. *Red-Tails in Love: A Wildlife Drama in Central Park* (10–12). 1998, Pantheon $24.00 (0-679-43997-8); paper $13.00 (0-679-75846-1). A true-life adventure involving a group of bird watchers in Central Park and the mating of a pair of red-tail hawks on the 12th-floor facade of a nearby apartment building. (Rev: BL 2/1/98; SLJ 8/98) [598.9]

OWLS

12085 Duncan, James R. *Owls of the World: Their Lives, Behavior and Survival* (10–12). Illus. 2003, Firefly $40.00 (1-55297-845-1). More than 200 species of owls found around the world are introduced, with eye-catching photographs and information about anatomy, behavior, hunting techniques, and nesting practices. (Rev: BL 12/15/03) [598.47]

12086 Sutton, Patricia, and Clay Sutton. *How to Spot an Owl* (9–12). 1994, Chapters paper $14.95 (1-881527-36-0). A good starter book on owling in two sections: "An Introduction to Owling" and "The Owls of North America." (Rev: BL 4/15/94) [598.9]

PENGUINS

12087 Chester, Jonathan. *The World of the Penguin* (10–12). 1996, Sierra Club $27.50 (0-87156-900-0). Readable text and colorful illustrations introduce the penguin's habits, behavior, social life, and methods of survival. (Rev: BL 12/1/96; SLJ 3/97) [598.4]

12088 Kaehler, Wolfgang. *Penguins* (9–12). Illus. 1989, Chronicle $22.95 (0-87701-649-6); paper $12.95 (0-87701-637-2). An inviting glimpse into the varieties of penguins and how and where they live. (Rev: BL 11/1/89) [598.4]

12089 Lanting, Frans. *Penguin* (9–12). Illus. 1999, Taschen $24.99 (3-8228-6519-2). In amazing photographs and a lucid text, this naturalist and photographer describes the penguin and explains the differences in various species. (Rev: BL 2/1/00*) [598.47]

12090 Love, John. *Penguins* (9–12). Series: World Life Library. 1997, Voyageur paper $16.95 (0-89658-339-2). This book uses color photographs to introduce penguins, their anatomy, habits, food, mating rituals, and social life. (Rev: SLJ 1/98) [598]

12091 Naveen, Ron. *Waiting to Fly: Escapades with the Penguins of Antarctica* (10–12). Illus. 1999, Morrow $26.00 (0-688-15894-3). Naturalist Naveen, who has spent many years studying three penguin species in the Antarctic, writes with genuine passion about the region and an obvious love for these birds. (Rev: BL 12/1/98*) [598.47]

12092 Peterson, Roger Tory. *Penguins* (10–12). Illus. 1998, Houghton paper $20.00 (0-395-89897-8). A richly illustrated narrative about the 16 different kinds of penguins and how they live. [598]

773

Environmental Protection and Endangered and Extinct Species

12093 Adams, Douglas, and Mark Carwardine. *Last Chance to See* (10–12). Illus. 1992, Ballantine paper $10.00 (0-345-37198-4). The noted science fiction writer examines the plight of many of the earth's endangered species. (Rev: BL 12/1/90) [591.52]

12094 Askins, Robert A. *Restoring North America's Birds: Lessons from Landscape Ecology* (10–12). Illus. 2000, Yale $30.00 (0-300-07967-2). From a multitude of sources, the author has collected material on nine different habitats and the causes of the disappearance of birds in them. (Rev: BL 2/15/00*) [333.95]

12095 Beach, Patrick. *A Good Forest for Dying: The Tragic Death of a Young Man on the Front Lines of the Environmental Wars* (10–12). 2004, Doubleday $24.95 (0-385-50617-1). The story of the environmental struggle between environmentalists and logging interests over the redwoods in northern California and of the death of one of the protesters. (Rev: BL 3/15/04) [333.72]

12096 *The Biodiversity Crisis: Losing What Counts* (10–12). Ed. by Michael Novacek. Illus. 2000, New Pr. paper $19.95 (1-56584-570-6). A visually attractive book that discusses what species are going extinct, what has caused the extinction of species, and how we can slow the rate of extinction. (Rev: BL 4/1/00) [333.95]

12097 Claggett, Hilary D. *Wildlife Conservation* (10–12). Series: Reference Shelf. 1997, H.W. Wilson paper $40.00 (0-8242-0915-X). Reprinted articles consider the threat to various wildlife species, what is being done to address those threats, and why it's important to save these animals from extinction. [639.9]

12098 Cokinos, Christopher. *Hope Is the Thing with Feathers: A Personal Chronicle of Vanished Birds* (10–12). Illus. 2000, Putnam $24.95 (1-58542-006-9). This book features the stories of six vanished species of birds of North America and how they became extinct. (Rev: BL 2/15/00*) [598.168]

12099 Crawford, Mark. *Habitats and Ecosystems: An Encyclopedia of Endangered America* (10–12). 1999, ABC-CLIO $75.00 (0-87436-997-5). This state-by-state listing covers special natural resources and endangered habitats. (Rev: BL 4/1/00) [578.68]

12100 De Koster, Katie. *Endangered Species* (8–12). Illus. Series: Opposing Viewpoints. 1998, Greenhaven LB $27.45 (1-56510-747-0); paper $17.45 (1-56510-746-2). In some 30 excerpts from such personalities as Al Gore and Edward O. Wilson, this book presents various points of view on issues relating to saving endangered species, including the economics of environment protection, ethical questions, and priorities. (Rev: SLJ 11/98) [591.52]

12101 Dewdney, A. K. *Hungry Hollow: The Story of a Natural Place* (10–12). Illus. 1998, Springer-Verlag $26.00 (0-387-98415-1). This detailed tale of flora and fauna in an area near the author's home in the eastern United States provides an accessible introduction to ecological concepts and concerns. (Rev: BL 12/1/98) [508.74]

12102 Dolin, Eric Jay. *Smithsonian Book of National Wildlife Refuges* (10–12). Illus. 2003, Smithsonian $39.95 (1-58834-117-8). This beautifully illustrated book recounts the National Wildlife Refuge system's history and explores the natural wonders within the more than 530 protected areas. (Rev: BL 4/15/03) [333.95]

12103 Ehrlich, Paul R., and Anne H. Ehrlich. *Extinction* (10–12). 1981, Random $16.95 (0-394-51312-6). A book that explores questions of how and why species become extinct and how each disappearance affects the earth. [560]

12104 Ehrlich, Paul R., et al. *Birds in Jeopardy: The Imperiled and Extinct Birds of the United States and Canada, Including Hawaii and Puerto Rico* (9–12). 1992, Stanford Univ. Pr. paper $22.95 (0-8047-1981-0). Lists the endangered and extinct birds of North America, with information on nesting, food, and breeding. (Rev: BL 2/1/92) [333.95]

12105 *Endangered Species* (8–12). Ed. by Helen Cothran. Series: Opposing Viewpoints. 2000, Greenhaven LB $22.96 (0-7377-0506-X); paper $14.96 (0-7377-0505-1). Differing points of view are expressed concerning endangered species, with material on extinction, property rights, and international cooperation. [578.68]

12106 Erickson, Jon. *Dying Planet: The Extinction of Species* (9–12). 1991, TAB paper $11.95 (0-8306-3615-3). A look at causes of extinction throughout the ages. (Rev: BL 6/1/91) [575]

12107 Flannery, Tim, and Peter Schouten. *A Gap in Nature: Discovering the World's Extinct Animals* (9–12). Illus. 2001, Grove Atlantic $34.95 (0-87113-797-6). In words and illustrations, this book describes the process of extinction and introduces 103 species that have become extinct between 1500 and 1999. (Rev: BL 10/1/01) [591.68]

12108 Goodnough, David. *Endangered Animals of North America: A Hot Issue* (9–12). Series: Hot Issues. 2001, Enslow LB $19.95 (0-7660-1373-1). This work explores the issues involved in saving North American endangered animals, with references to many current practices and controversies. (Rev: BL 9/15/01; HBG 3/02) [591.52]

12109 Grossman, Elizabeth. *Watershed: The Undamming of America* (10–12). 2002, Counterpoint $27.00 (1-58243-108-6). The movement to remove dams and return rivers to their natural courses and ecology is the focus of this interesting study. (Rev: BL 7/02) [333.91]

12110 Grosz, Terry. *Defending Our Wildlife Heritage: The Life and Times of a Special Agent* (9–12). 2001, JIST paper $18.00 (1-55566-316-8). This is a memoir of a former conservation officer and his years defending the nation's natural resources and wildlife. (Rev: BL 11/15/01) [363.28]

12111 Hill, Julia Butterfly. *One Makes the Difference: Inspiring Actions that Change Our World* (10–12). 2002, HarperSF paper $14.95 (0-06-251756-2). An environmental activist offers tips on behaving in a pro-environment manner, gives examples of individual actions that have had good results, and provides lists of facts, organizations, and resources. (Rev: BL 4/1/02) [333.7]

12112 *Life Stories: World-Renowned Scientists Reflect on Their Lives and the Future of Life on Earth* (10–12). Ed. by Heather Newbold. Illus. 2000, Univ. of California Pr. $45.00 (0-520-21114-6); paper $16.95 (0-520-21896-5). Sixteen important scientists write about their lives, share their views on life on earth, and explain their commitment to conservation. (Rev: BL 4/1/00; SLJ 10/00) [363.7]

12113 McClung, Robert M. *Last of the Wild: Vanished and Vanishing Giants of the Animal World* (8–12). Illus. 1997, Shoe String LB $27.50 (0-208-02452-2). Moving from continent to continent, this account gives historical and geographical background material on 60 animal species that have already disappeared or are currently in extreme danger of extinction. (Rev: BL 7/97; HBG 3/98; SLJ 11/97; VOYA 10/97) [591.51]

12114 Mann, Charles C., and Mark L. Plummer. *Noah's Choice: The Future of Endangered Species* (9–12). 1995, Knopf $29.95 (0-679-42002-9). A detailed overview of the biological, economic, and political considerations influencing the Endangered Species Act. (Rev: BL 2/15/95) [574.4]

12115 Nelson, Gaylord, et al. *Beyond Earth Day: Fulfilling the Promise* (10–12). Illus. 2002, Univ. of Wisconsin Pr. $26.95 (0-299-18040-9). The founder of Earth Day and other environmentalists voice their concerns about the continuing toll on our natural resources. (Rev: BL 10/15/02) [333.7]

12116 Pimm, Stuart. *The World According to Pimm: A Scientist Audits the Earth* (10–12). 2001, McGraw-Hill $24.95 (0-07-137490-6). The author, a professor of conservation, has written a clear, uncluttered explanation of our endangered species and our degraded land and water with some projections for the future. (Rev: BL 8/01) [333.7]

12117 Rothman, Hal K. *Saving the Planet: The American Response to the Environment in the Twentieth Century* (10–12). 2000, Ivan R. Dee $24.95 (1-56663-288-9). This lucid, mature account traces the evolution of American environmentalism

with emphasis on its relationship to economics and technology. (Rev: BL 4/1/00) [333.7]

12118 Simmons, Randy. *Endangered Species* (7–12). Illus. Series: Critical Thinking About Environmental Issues. 2002, Gale $21.96 (0-7377-1266-X). Readers will find a variety of opinions about the necessity of protecting endangered species. (Rev: BL 12/15/02; SLJ 6/03) [333.95]

12119 Simon, Noel. *Nature in Danger: Threatened Habitats and Species* (10–12). 1995, Oxford $45.00 (0-19-521152-9); paper $8.95 (0-685-20135-X). This thorough resource covers ecosystems and biomes in geographic regions around the world, including their flora and fauna, physical features, the role humans play there, ecological problems, and possible solutions. (Rev: BL 11/1/95; SLJ 6/96; VOYA 4/96) [363.7]

12120 Stefoff, Rebecca. *Extinction* (9–12). 1991, Chelsea LB $19.95 (0-7910-1578-5). A history of vanished species and how humans have, in some cases, accelerated the process of extinction. (Rev: BL 2/1/92; SLJ 11/91) [333.95]

12121 Tudge, Colin. *Last Animals at the Zoo: How Mass Extinction Can Be Stopped* (9–12). 1992, Island Pr. $30.00 (1-55963-158-9). Explains what zoos have accomplished in the area of conservation breeding. (Rev: BL 3/1/92) [639.9]

12122 Vaitheeswaran, Vijay. *Power to the People: How the Coming Energy Revolution Will Transform an Industry, Change Our Lives, and Maybe Even Save the Planet* (10–12). 2003, Farrar $25.00 (0-374-23675-5). A challenging exploration of the potential for compromise between the energy industry and environmental groups. (Rev: BL 11/1/03) [333.79]

12123 Walker, John Frederick. *A Certain Curve of Horn: The Hundred-Year Quest for the Giant Sable Antelope of Angola* (10–12). 2002, Grove Atlantic $26.00 (0-87113-858-1). The dangers faced by the giant sable antelope, found only in war-torn Angola, are portrayed against a backdrop of social and environmental turmoil. (Rev: BL 9/1/02) [599.64]

12124 Weidensaul, Scott. *The Ghost with Trembling Wings: Science, Wishful Thinking, and the Search for Lost Species* (10–12). Illus. 2002, Farrar $26.00 (0-374-24664-5). Riveting and fact-filled stories of searches for extinct species are accompanied by discussion of the causes of extinction and laws governing human behavior. (Rev: BL 5/1/02) [591.68]

Insects and Arachnids

GENERAL AND MISCELLANEOUS

12125 Berenbaum, May R. *Buzzwords: A Scientist Muses on Sex, Bugs, and Rock 'n' Roll* (10–12). Illus. 2000, Joseph Henry $24.95 (0-309-07081-3); paper $14.95 (0-309-06835-5). This collection of 42 short essays by the author introduces fascinating details about insects—their characteristics, habitats, and behavior. (Rev: BL 8/00) [595.7]

12126 Berger, Cynthia. *Dragonflies* (9–12). Illus. Series: Wild Guides. 2004, Stackpole paper $19.95 (0-8117-2971-0). After an overview of dragonflies and damselflies and an examination of a year in their lives, this well-illustrated book discusses species identification, behavior, anatomy, hunting, and mating. (Rev: BL 2/15/04) [595.7]

12127 Blum, Mark. *Bugs in 3-D* (10–12). Illus. 1998, Chronicle $18.95 (0-8118-1945-0). A stunning 3-D view of insects that uses special photographic plates and a built-in stereoscope attached to the cover of the book. (Rev: SLJ 4/99) [595.7]

12128 Borror, Donald J., and Richard E. White. *A Field Guide to the Insects of America North of Mexico* (9–12). Illus. 1970, Houghton paper $17.00 (0-395-18523-8). In addition to an identification manual, this book explains how to observe insects and how to collect and preserve them. [595.7]

12129 Buchmann, Stephen L., and Gary Paul Nabhan. *The Forgotten Pollinators* (10–12). Illus. 1996, Island Pr. $25.00 (1-55963-352-2). An exploration of how the poisoning of pollinators by herbicides and pesticides threatens the plants that the planet depends upon for survival, and recommendations for how to prevent this. (Rev: BL 7/96; SLJ 4/97) [595.7]

12130 Conniff, Richard. *Spineless Wonders: Strange Tales from the Invertebrate World* (10–12). Illus. 1996, Holt $25.00 (0-8050-4218-0). The fascinating world of invertebrates is introduced with material on such species as flies, leeches, fire ants, giant squids, dragonflies, beetles, worms, mosquitoes, and moths. (Rev: BL 11/1/96; SLJ 4/97) [592]

12131 *Discovery Channel Insects and Spiders: An Explore Your World Handbook* (8–12). 2000, Discovery paper $14.95 (1-56331-841-5). About 160 insects and spiders are identified in text and pictures, with material on their anatomy, behavior, evolution, and the possibility of keeping them as pets. [595.7]

12132 Evans, Arthur V., and Charles L. Bellamy. *An Inordinate Fondness for Beetles* (10–12). 1996, Holt $40.00 (0-8050-3751-9). Amazing photographs and a lucid test are used to explore the world of beetles, their anatomy, history, habits, and uses. (Rev: BL 3/15/97; BR 9–10/97; SLJ 7/97) [595.76]

12133 Evans, Howard Ensign. *The Pleasures of Entomology: Portraits of Insects and the People Who Study Them* (10–12). Illus. 1985, Smithsonian paper $16.95 (0-87474-421-0). An enjoyable personal look at the study of insects plus information on many species and their habits. (Rev: BL 8/85) [595.7]

12134 *Insect Lives: Stories of Mystery and Romance from a Hidden World* (9–12). Ed. by Erich Hoyt and Ted Schultz. 1999, Wiley paper $18.95 (0-674-00952-5). From a variety of authors, beginning with the ancients up to modern writers, and using many illustrations, this volume investigates insects, their habits, and societies. [595.7]

12135 Lowenstein, Frank, and Sheryl Lechner. *Bugs: Insects, Spiders, Centipedes, Millipedes, and Other Closely Related Arthropods* (6–12). 1999, Black Dog & Leventhal $24.98 (1-57912-068-7). Eye-catching photographs are accompanied by solid scientific information. (Rev: SLJ 5/00; VOYA 12/00) [595.7]

12136 Milne, Lorus, and Margery Milne. *The Audubon Society Field Guide to North American Insects and Spiders* (7–12). Illus. 1980, Knopf $19.95 (0-394-50763-0). An extensive use of color photographs makes this a fine guide for identifying insects. [595.7]

12137 O'Toole, Christopher, ed. *The Encyclopedia of Insects* (9–12). Illus. 1986, Facts on File $29.95 (0-8160-1358-6). A large format book with stunning illustrations that gives general information and detailed facts about individual species. (Rev: BL 6/1/86; BR 11–12/86) [595.7]

12138 Purser, Bruce. *Jungle Bugs: Masters of Camouflage and Mimicry* (10–12). Illus. 2003, Firefly $29.95 (1-55297-671-8); paper $19.95 (1-55297-663-7). Beautiful photographs illustrate two strategies of survival for jungle insects. (Rev: BL 8/03) [595.7]

12139 Silsby, Jill. *Dragonflies of the World* (10–12). Illus. 2001, Smithsonian $39.95 (1-56098-959-9). Each of the 29 families of dragonflies and damselflies of the world is discussed separately in this well-illustrated book. (Rev: BL 12/15/01) [595.7]

12140 Spielman, Andrew, and Michael D'Antonio. *Mosquito: A Natural History of Man's Most Persistent and Deadly Foe* (9–12). 2001, Hyperion $29.95 (0-7868-6781-7). This entertaining book tells you everything you wanted to know about mosquitoes, including the fact that there are 2,500 kinds. (Rev: BL 5/15/01) [595.77]

12141 Waldbauer, Gilbert. *Millions of Monarchs, Bunches of Beetles: How Bugs Find Strength in Numbers* (10–12). Illus. 2000, Harvard $24.95 (0-674-00090-0). A fine overview on the behavior of such social insects as monarch butterflies, tent caterpillars, ladybugs, locusts, and corn rootworms. (Rev: BL 3/1/00) [595.7156]

12142 Waldbauer, Gilbert. *What Good Are Bugs? Insects in the Web of Life* (10–12). Illus. 2003, Harvard $29.95 (0-674-01027-2). This fascinating study of insect ecology explores in detail the important role bugs play in maintaining order in the natural world. (Rev: BL 4/15/03) [595.717]

12143 Wangberg, James K. *Do Bees Sneeze? And Other Questions Kids Ask About Insects* (7–10). Illus. 1997, Fulcrum paper $18.95 (1-55591-963-4). Full, interesting answers to more than 200 questions about insects on such subjects as physical characteristics, anatomical features, locomotion, behavior, habitat, and human health and safety. (Rev: BL 1/1–15/98; SLJ 4/98) [595.7]

12144 Wangberg, James K. *Six-Legged Sex: The Erotic Lives of Bugs* (9–12). 2001, Fulcrum paper $17.95 (1-55591-292-3). The sex life of insects is popularized in this whimsical but accurate account of mating behavior in the bug world. (Rev: BL 9/15/01) [595.7]

12145 White, Richard E. *A Field Guide to the Beetles of North America* (9–12). Illus. 1983, Houghton $21.95 (0-395-31808-4); paper $18.00 (0-395-33953-7). An identification guide that also covers such topics as the habits and structure of beetles and how to collect them. [595.7]

12146 Wootton, Anthony. *Insects of the World* (9–12). Illus. 1984, Facts on File $29.95 (0-87196-991-2). This nicely illustrated volume describes how insects evolved, their characteristics, and how to identify them. [595.7]

12147 Young, Allen M. *Small Creatures and Ordinary Places: Essays on Nature* (10–12). Illus. 2000, Univ. of Wisconsin Pr. $50.00 (0-299-16960-X); paper $19.95 (0-299-16964-2). This entertaining science book covers the life cycles of a number of small creatures from the Midwest with an emphasis on insects and their predators. (Rev: BL 11/1/00) [508]

BUTTERFLIES, MOTHS, AND CATERPILLARS

12148 Brock, Jim P., et al. *Butterflies of North America* (10–12). Illus. 2003, Houghton $30.00 (0-618-25400-5); paper $22.00 (0-618-15312-8). This beautifully illustrated field guide to North American butterflies is a must for students and butterfly enthusiasts. (Rev: BL 3/15/03) [595.78]

12149 Halpern, Sue. *Four Wings and a Prayer: Caught in the Mystery of the Monarch Butterfly* (9–12). 2001, Pantheon $23.00 (0-375-40208-X). This account traces the phenomenon of the monarch butterfly's flight to Mexico and the generations of these insects that it takes to make the round trip. (Rev: BL 5/1/01) [595.78]

12150 Majerus, Michael. *Moths* (10–12). Illus. 2002, HarperCollins $60.00 (0-00-220141-0). A thorough and comprehensive survey of the mysterious world of moths. (Rev: BL 11/15/02) [595.78]

12151 Preston-Mafham, Rod, and Ken Preston-Mafham. *Butterflies of the World* (8–12). Illus. 1988, Facts on File $32.95 (0-8160-1601-1). An

attractively illustrated book that introduces butterflies and moths and gives facts about their evolution, structure, types, and life cycles. (Rev: BR 3–4/89) [595.78]

12152 Pyle, Robert Michael. *The Audubon Society Field Guide to North American Butterflies* (7–12). Illus. 1981, Knopf $19.95 (0-394-51914-0). An introduction to more than 600 species of butterflies in about 1,000 color photographs and text. [595.7]

12153 Schappert, Phil. *A World for Butterflies: Their Lives, Behavior and Future* (10–12). Illus. 2000, Firefly $35.00 (1-55209-550-9). This fascinating introduction to these flying insects contains chapters on their diversity, habitats, behavior, conservation, and their cousins, the moths. (Rev: BL 8/00) [595.78]

12154 Taylor, Barbara. *Butterflies and Moths* (9–12). 1996, DK paper $6.95 (0-7894-0605-5). An excellent, richly illustrated field guide that provides basic information about these insects' appearance, behavior, and habitat. [595.7]

SPIDERS AND SCORPIONS

12155 Mason, Adrienne. *The World of the Spider* (10–12). Illus. 1999, Sierra Club $29.95 (1-57805-044-8). This adult account explores in text and beautiful pictures the anatomy, behavior, folklore, and relationship with humans of the spider. (Rev: BL 1/1–15/00) [595.4]

Marine and Freshwater Life

GENERAL AND MISCELLANEOUS

12156 *America's Seashore Wonderlands* (9–12). Illus. 1985, National Geographic $12.95 (0-87044-543-X). Beginning with the northwest coast and ending with New England, this is an illustrated tour of our seashores. (Rev: BL 5/1/86) [574.5]

12157 Banister, Keith, and Andrew Campbell, eds. *The Encyclopedia of Aquatic Life* (9–12). Illus. 1986, Facts on File $45.00 (0-8160-1257-1). Thousands of species are covered in text and illustrations under three headings: fish, aquatic invertebrates, and aquatic mammals. (Rev: BL 2/1/86) [591.92]

12158 Benchley, Peter. *Shark Trouble: True Stories and Lessons About the Sea* (9–12). Illus. 2002, Random $21.95 (0-375-50824-4). Benchley shares stories about his real-life encounters with sharks and other marine creatures, interweaving lots of useful facts and statistics. (Rev: BL 4/15/02) [597.3]

12159 Boschung, Herbert T., Jr., et al. *The Audubon Society Field Guide to North American Fishes, Whales, and Dolphins* (7–12). Illus. 1983, Knopf $19.00 (0-394-53405-0). About 600 marine and freshwater fish and aquatic mammals are identified and described. [597]

12160 Carson, Rachel. *The Edge of the Sea* (10–12). 1955, Houghton paper $14.00 (0-395-28519-4). Shore life of various types is examined by this noted naturalist and writer. [577.7]

12161 Douglass, Jackie Leatherby. *Peterson First Guide to Shells of North America* (7–12). Illus. 1989, Houghton paper $4.95 (0-395-48297-6). This is an abridged edition of the complete field guide that is more accessible and less forbidding than the parent volume. (Rev: BL 6/1/89) [594]

12162 Ellis, Richard. *The Empty Ocean: Plundering the World's Marine Life* (10–12). Illus. 2003, Island Pr. $26.00 (1-55963-974-1). A lively and scathing attack on humans' thoughtless abuse of marine life. (Rev: BL 5/1/03) [307.1]

12163 Ellis, Richard. *Monsters of the Sea* (9–12). 1994, Knopf $35.00 (0-679-40639-5). Examines whales, octopuses, giant squid, sharks, and manatees, once believed to be sea serpents, leviathans, and mermaids. (Rev: BL 11/1/94*) [591.92]

12164 Meinkoth, Norman A. *The Audubon Society Field Guide to North American Seashore Creatures* (7–12). Illus. 1981, Knopf $19.95 (0-394-51993-0). This is a guide to such invertebrates as sponges, corals, urchins, and anemones. [592]

12165 Perrine, Doug. *Sharks and Rays of the World* (8–12). Illus. Series: WorldLife Discovery Guides. 2000, Voyageur $29.95 (0-89658-448-8). Scientific information on sharks and rays and their evolution is accompanied by color photographs, stories of shark attacks, and descriptions of diving to watch these animals. (Rev: SLJ 4/00) [597.3]

12166 Rehder, Harold A. *The Audubon Society Field Guide to North American Seashells* (7–12). Illus. 1981, Knopf $19.95 (0-394-51913-2). Seven hundred of the most common seashells from our coasts are pictured in color photographs and described in the text. [594]

12167 Sammon, Rick. *Rhythm of the Reef: A Day in the Life of the Coral Reef* (10–12). 1995, Voyageur $14.95 (0-89658-311-2). Both browsers and researchers will enjoy this colorfully illustrated journey under the seas to witness the beauty and diversity of life on coral reefs. (Rev: SLJ 6/96) [593.6]

12168 Sargent, William. *Crab Wars: A Tale of Horseshoe Crabs, Bioterrorism, and Human Health* (10–12). 2002, Univ. Press of New England $24.95 (1-58465-168-7). The natural history of the horseshoe crab is lovingly chronicled in this thought-provoking narrative that also explores the threats the species faces from humans. (Rev: BL 12/1/02) [333.95]

12169 Vanstrum, Glenn. *The Saltwater Wilderness* (10–12). Illus. 2003, Oxford $25.00 (0-19-515937-3). A doctor by profession, the Minnesota-born author describes his love affair with the ocean, relat-

ing marine adventures in areas ranging from Alaska to Fiji. (Rev: BL 2/15/03) [508.3162]

12170 Waller, Geoffrey. *SeaLife: A Complete Guide to the Marine Environment* (8–12). 1996, Smithsonian $55.00 (1-56098-633-6). A comprehensive reference to marine biology, including profiles of more than 600 species of marine animals, this guide is written in easy-to-understand language and includes numerous illustrations and maps. [591.7]

CORALS AND JELLYFISH

12171 DuTemple, Lesley A. *Coral Reefs* (9–12). Series: Endangered Animals and Habitats. 2000, Lucent LB $27.45 (1-56006-597-4). A description of the coral reefs of the world, with material on their possible future and how humans affect them. (Rev: HBG 9/00) [577.7]

12172 Love, Rosaleen. *Reefscape: Reflections on the Great Barrier Reef* (10–12). 2001, Joseph Henry $24.95 (0-309-07260-3). General information is given about coral reefs, with in-depth material on the Great Barrier Reef of Australia. [508]

FISHES

12173 Behnke, Robert J., and Joseph R. Tomelleri. *Trout and Salmon of North America* (10–12). Illus. 2002, Free Pr. $40.00 (0-7432-2220-2). A detailed but highly readable guide to the Salmonidae family, which includes such popular fish as the salmon, trout, whitefish, grayling, and char. (Rev: BL 9/15/02) [597.5]

12174 Dipper, Frances. *Extraordinary Fish* (8–12). Illus. 2002, DK $12.95 (0-7894-8268-1). Unusual species such as the mudskipper, sea lamprey, archerfish, leafy seadragon, and spotted trunkfish are featured in this fascinating and well-illustrated study. (Rev: BL 3/1/02; SLJ 5/02) [597]

12175 Eschmeyer, William N., and Earl S. Herald. *A Field Guide to Pacific Coast Fishes* (7–12). Illus. 1983, Houghton $20.00 (0-618-00212-X). In this volume in the Peterson Field Guide series, about 500 fish are described and illustrated. [597]

12176 Filisky, Michael. *Peterson First Guide to Fishes of North America* (7–12). Illus. 1989, Houghton paper $4.95 (0-393-91179-6). This is a concise version of the parent Peterson guide that gives basic material on common fish but with less detail. (Rev: BL 6/1/89) [597]

12177 Page, Lawrence M., and Brooks M. Burr. *A Field Guide to Freshwater Fishes: North America North of Mexico* (9–12). Series: Peterson Field Guides. 1991, Houghton paper $19.00 (0-395-91091-9). This richly illustrated handbook identifies the nearly 800 species of freshwater fishes found in the United States and Canada. [597]

12178 Reebs, Stephan. *Fish Behavior: In the Aquarium and in the Wild* (9–12). Illus. 2001, Cornell $39.95 (0-8014-3915-9); paper $19.95 (0-8014-8772-2). This primer on fish behavior explains how they find food, avoid predators, relate to other fish, mate, and raise young. (Rev: BL 12/1/01) [597.15]

12179 Robins, C. Richard, and G. Carleton Ray. *A Field Guide to Atlantic Coast Fishes of North America* (9–12). Illus. 1986, Houghton paper $17.95 (0-395-39198-9). An excellent field guide that describes almost 1,100 species of fish that are found between the Arctic and the Caribbean. (Rev: BL 6/1/86) [597]

12180 Schweid, Richard. *Consider the Eel* (8–12). Illus. 2002, Univ. of North Carolina Pr. $29.95 (0-8078-2693-6). A fascinating profile of the eel, with information on its history, life cycle, importance as a food product, and appearances in folklore, along with a selection of eel recipes. (Rev: BL 3/15/02) [597]

12181 Weinberg, Samantha. *A Fish Caught in Time: The Search for the Coelacanth* (10–12). Illus. 2000, HarperCollins $24.00 (0-06-019495-2). A scientific study that reads like an adventure novel about the hunt for a mysterious living fossil, the fish known as the coelacanth. (Rev: BL 3/15/00) [597.3]

SHARKS

12182 Capuzzo, Michael. *Close to Shore: The Terrifying Shark Attacks of 1916* (7–12). Illus. 2003, Crown $16.95 (0-375-82231-3). Photographs and newspaper clippings enhance this true story of a shark's brief and dangerous detour into a New Jersey creek in 1916. (Rev: BL 5/15/03; HBG 10/03; SLJ 4/03) [597.3]

12183 Dingerkus, Guido. *The Shark Watchers' Guide* (7–12). Illus. 1989, Messner paper $5.95 (0-671-68815-4). As well as materials on 30 different varieties of sharks, this book tells about shark anatomy, habits, and evolution and gives tips on how to handle a shark attack. (Rev: BL 11/15/85; SLJ 12/85) [597]

12184 Klimley, A. Peter. *The Secret Life of Sharks: A Leading Marine Biologist Reveals the Mysteries of Shark Behavior* (10–12). 2003, Simon & Schuster $25.00 (0-7432-4170-3). Klimley describes his experiences researching sharks and seeks to rehabilitate their bad reputation. (Rev: BL 7/03) [597.3]

12185 Musick, John A., and Beverly McMillan. *The Shark Chronicles: A Scientist Tracks the Consummate Predator* (10–12). Illus. 2002, Holt $26.00 (0-8050-7093-1). A detailed and engaging look at the lives of sharks, covering such diverse subjects as reproduction, hunting and feeding techniques, incidents of attacks on humans, and medical applications for shark-derived products. (Rev: BL 8/02) [597.3]

12186 Pope, Joyce. *1001 Facts About Sharks* (7–12). Series: Backpack Books. 2002, DK paper $8.95 (0-7894-8449-8). More than 550 illustrations and photographs are used to present basic facts about sharks, their anatomy, habits, and varieties. (Rev: BL 3/15/02) [597]

12187 Reader's Digest, eds. *Sharks: Silent Hunters of the Deep* (8–12). Illus. 1987, Reader's Digest $19.95 (0-86438-014-3). This handsomely illustrated account describes the ways of sharks, gives material on famous encounters, and identifies all 344 species. (Rev: BL 5/15/87; BR 11–12/87; SLJ 1/88; VOYA 8/87) [597]

12188 *Shark: Stories of Life and Death from the World's Most Dangerous Waters* (10–12). Ed. by Clint Willis. Illus. 2002, Thunder's Mouth paper $17.95 (1-56025-397-5). Essays, short stories, and excerpts from fiction and nonfiction books discuss sharks and describe a variety of shark experiences. (Rev: BL 6/1–15/02) [597.3]

12189 Springer, Victor G., and Joy P. Gold. *Sharks in Question: The Smithsonian Answer Book* (9–12). Illus. 1989, Smithsonian paper $24.95 (0-87474-877-1). Using a question-and-answer format plus stunning photographs, the authors tell all and explode myths about this sea creature. (Rev: BL 6/1/89; SLJ 8/89) [597]

12190 Stafford-Deitsch, Jeremy. *Shark: A Photographer's Story* (10–12). Illus. 1987, Sierra Club paper $25.00 (0-87156-733-4). After a discussion of shark anatomy and behavior, the author takes you on a well-illustrated global exploration of their haunts. (Rev: BL 11/15/87; BR 3–4/88; VOYA 2/89) [597]

12191 Steel, Rodney. *Sharks of the World* (9–12). Illus. 1985, Facts on File $29.95 (0-8160-1086-2). Straightforward information is given on sharks plus intriguing photographs. (Rev: BL 2/1/86) [597]

12192 Stevens, John D., ed. *Sharks* (9–12). Illus. 1987, Facts on File $35.00 (0-8160-1800-6). An oversize book with stunning photographs on each page and 17 chapters, each written by a shark specialist. (Rev: BL 9/15/87) [591]

WHALES, DOLPHINS, AND OTHER SEA MAMMALS

12193 Baird, Robin W. *Killer Whales of the World: Natural History and Conservation* (9–12). Illus. 2002, Voyageur $29.95 (0-89658-512-3). Information on the killer whale's biology, habitat, sounds, senses, and behavior is complemented by stunning photography and excellent maps. (Rev: BL 1/1–15/03) [599.53]

12194 Bonner, Nigel. *Whales of the World* (9–12). Illus. 1989, Facts on File $29.95 (0-8160-1734-4). A description of various kinds of whales and behavioral patterns, plus a discussion of the possible extinction that many species now face. (Rev: BL 10/1/89; BR 1–2/90) [599.5]

12195 Bright, Michael. *Dolphins* (8–12). Illus. 2002, DK $12.95 (0-7894-8267-3). The anatomy, characteristics, diet, and social behavior of dolphins are covered in this well-illustrated volume; a companion to a series of BBC/Discovery Channel programs. Also use *Killer Whales* (2002). (Rev: BL 3/1/02; SLJ 5/02) [599.93]

12196 Calambokidis, John, and Gretchen Steiger. *Blue Whales* (9–12). Series: World Life Library. 1997, Voyageur paper $16.95 (0-89658-338-4). An oversize book with color photographs and text that explores the evolution, anatomy, and habits of the blue whale and the impact of whaling. (Rev: SLJ 1/98) [599.5]

12197 Clapham, Phil. *Humpback Whales* (10–12). Series: World Life Library. 1996, Voyageur paper $16.95 (0-89658-296-5). Over 50 full-color photographs enhance this introduction to the anatomy, behavior, characteristics, history, and present status of the humpback whale. (Rev: BR 5–6/97; SLJ 5/97) [599.5]

12198 Collet, Anne. *Swimming with Giants: My Encounters with Whales, Dolphins, and Seals* (10–12). Trans. by Gayle Wurst. 2000, Milkweed $22.00 (1-57131-244-7). Scientific facts are combined with a feeling of wonder and awe in this marine biologist's memoir of her encounters with large marine mammals. (Rev: BL 8/00) [599.5]

12199 Darling, Jim. *Gray Whales* (6–12). Series: World Life Library. 1999, Voyageur paper $16.95 (0-89658-447-X). Physiology, behavior, habitat, migration, and relations with humans are all discussed in this volume that contains lots of full-color photographs. (Rev: SLJ 4/00) [599.5]

12200 Ellis, Richard. *The Book of Whales* (9–12). Illus. 1980, Knopf paper $35.00 (0-394-73371-1). A beautifully illustrated book that describes how whales evolved, various species, and their behavior. [599.5]

12201 Ellis, Richard. *Dolphins and Porpoises* (10–12). Illus. 1989, Random paper $35.00 (0-679-72286-6). A detailed account of each of the 43 different species and of the characteristics of each. (Rev: BR 11–12/89; VOYA 2/90) [599.5]

12202 Gardner, Robert. *The Whale Watchers' Guide* (9–12). 1984, Messner paper $5.95 (0-671-49807-X). This guide to an increasingly popular pastime helps one identify 26 different species of whales. [599.5]

12203 Gordon, Jonathan. *Sperm Whales* (10–12). Illus. Series: World Life Library. 1998, Voyageur paper $16.95 (0-89658-398-8). This absorbing and well-illustrated volume examines in detail the life of sperm whales. (Rev: BL 12/15/98) [599.5]

12204 Haley, Delphine, ed. *Marine Mammals of Eastern North Pacific and Arctic Waters.* 2nd ed. (10–12). Illus. 1986, Pacific Search paper $22.95 (0-931397-11-1). Separate articles written by 21 experts are given on each animal. Good illustrations. (Rev: BL 10/1/86) [599.09]

12205 Hand, Douglas. *Gone Whaling: A Search for Orcas in the Northwest Waters* (9–12). 1994, Simon & Schuster $19.50 (0-671-76840-9). The orca, a gentle beast undeservedly known as the "killer whale," is examined in its natural habitat and in captivity. (Rev: BL 7/94) [599.5]

12206 Harrison, Richard, and M. M. Bryden, eds. *Whales, Dolphins and Porpoises* (9–12). Illus. 1988, Facts on File $30.00 (0-8160-1977-0). A handsome oversize volume with lucid text and copious illustrations. (Rev: BL 1/1/89; BR 3–4/89) [599.5]

12207 Hoyt, Erich. *Meeting the Whales: The Equinox Guide to Giants of the Deep* (5–10). Illus. 1991, Camden House paper $9.95 (0-921820-23-2). This guide to 19 whale species describes their origins and habits. Includes a discussion on whale watching and photography. (Rev: BL 8/91) [599.5]

12208 Knudtson, Peter. *Orca: Visions of the Killer Whale* (10–12). 1996, Sierra Club $27.00 (0-87156-906-X). Chapters discuss the history, anatomy, habits, and habitats of orca, the killer whale, but the high point of this volume is its stunning photographs. (Rev: BL 12/1/96; SLJ 6/97) [599.5]

12209 Leatherwood, Stephen, and Randall R. Reeves. *The Sierra Club Handbook of Whales and Dolphins* (9–12). Illus. 1983, Sierra Club paper $18.00 (0-87156-340-1). Through color and black-and-white pictures and an extensive text, 76 species are described. [599.5]

12210 Lord, Nancy. *Beluga Days: Tracking a White Whale's Truths* (10–12). 2004, Counterpoint $25.00 (1-58243-151-5). When the population of the beluga whales began to decline, the author decided to investigate. This account is not only about whales but also about the making of an environmentalist. (Rev: BL 1/1–15/04) [599.5]

12211 Montgomery, Sy. *Journey of the Pink Dolphins: An Amazon Quest* (10–12). Illus. 2000, Simon & Schuster $26.00 (0-684-84558-X). A poetic, intriguing account that introduces and explores the world of the elusive freshwater pink dolphins of the Amazon River. (Rev: BL 2/15/00*) [599.53]

12212 Morton, Alexandra. *Listening to Whales: What the Orcas Have Taught Us* (10–12). Illus. 2002, Ballantine $26.95 (0-345-43794-2). Science and personal experiences are interwoven in this account of researching the killer whale and the animal's communication abilities. (Rev: BL 5/15/02) [599.53]

12213 Norris, Kenneth S. *Dolphin Days: The Life and Times of the Spinner Dolphin* (9–12). 1991,

Norton $21.95 (0-393-02945-X). The author, a researcher, describes a dolphin society, explains the dolphin's language and navigational skills. Includes an unsettling eyewitness report of the deadly disorientation and fear caused by tuna netting. (Rev: BL 9/1/91) [599.5]

12214 Obee, Bruce. *Guardians of the Whales: The Quest to Study Whales in the Wild* (9–12). 1992, Alaska Northwest $34.95 (0-88240-428-8). Profiles the scientists largely responsible for saving whales from near extinction and explains how research on the marine mammals is conducted. (Rev: BL 10/15/92) [599.5]

12215 Owen, Welden. *Whales, Dolphins, and Porpoises.* 2nd ed. (8–12). 1999, Checkmark $39.95 (0-8160-3991-7). Topics discussed include evolution, behavior, intelligence, and communication. [599.5]

12216 Paine, Stefani. *The World of the Arctic Whales: Belugas, Bowheads, Narwhals* (10–12). 1995, Sierra Club $26.00 (0-87156-378-9). Using many photographs, this book describes the diet, mating, birth, life, and death of whales and the impact of humans on their lives throughout history. (Rev: SLJ 3/96; VOYA 6/96) [599.5]

12217 Payne, Roger. *Among Whales* (9–12). 1995, Macmillan $24.00 (0-02-595245-5). An introduction to the anatomy, habits, and characteristics of whales by one of the world's leading marine mammal experts. (Rev: BL 4/15/95*) [599.5]

12218 Peterson, Brenda, and Linda Hogan. *Sightings: The Gray Whales' Mysterious Journey* (10–12). Illus. 2002, National Geographic $26.00 (0-7922-7989-1). In highly readable text, a nature writer and a poet offer their personal perspectives on the gray whale and its amazing migrations. (Rev: BL 8/02) [599.5]

12219 Price-Groff, Claire. *The Manatee* (7–10). Series: Endangered Animals and Habitats. 1999, Lucent LB $27.45 (1-56006-445-5). This well-illustrated book describes this endangered sea mammal and tells about its habits, habitats, and appearance. (Rev: BL 9/15/99; HBG 4/00) [599.53]

12220 Russell, Dick, and Eben Given. *Eye of the Whale: Epic Passage from Baja to Siberia* (10–12). Illus. 2001, Simon & Schuster $30.00 (0-684-86608-0). The story of the gray whale and its migration from the Bering Sea to Baja, California, a distance of 5,000 miles. (Rev: BL 6/1–15/01) [599.5]

12221 Smolker, Rachel. *To Touch a Wild Dolphin* (10–12). 2001, Doubleday $26.00 (0-385-49176-X). This is a delightful report on 15 years of studying the ways of the friendly wild dolphins of Australia's Shark Bay. (Rev: BL 2/15/01; SLJ 8/01) [599.53]

12222 Sullivan, Robert. *A Whale Hunt* (10–12). 2000, Scribner $25.00 (0-684-86433-9). The author spent two years with the Makah Indians on the Olympic Peninsula in Washington while they prepare for and carry out their first whale hunt in 70 years. (Rev: BL 10/1/00) [639.2]

12223 Woog, Adam. *The Whale* (7–10). Series: Endangered Animals and Habitats. 1998, Lucent LB $27.45 (1-56006-460-9). A well-illustrated, fact-filled exploration of the different species of whales and the threats to their survival. (Rev: HBG 9/98) [599.5]

Microscopes, Microbiology, and Biotechnology

12224 De Kruif, Paul. *Microbe Hunters* (10–12). 1996, Harcourt paper $13.00 (0-15-600262-0). This revised edition of De Kruif's classic offers an overview of groundbreaking work in bacteriology by such pioneers as Antonie van Leeuwenhoek, Louis Pasteur, Walter Reed, and Paul Ehrlich, each of whom is profiled. [920]

12225 Margulis, Lynn, and Dorion Sagan. *What Is Life?* (9–12). 1995, Simon & Schuster $40.00 (0-684-81326-2). Explores the multifaceted answer to the question posed by the title. A microscopic complement to Stephen Gould's macroscopic paleobiology in his *Book of Life*. (Rev: BL 9/1/95) [577]

12226 Nachtigall, Werner. *Exploring with the Microscope: A Book of Discovery and Learning* (7–12). Trans. by Elizabeth Reinersmann. 1995, Sterling $19.95 (0-8069-0866-1). A thorough book about microscopes and their uses, with 100 color slides, diagrams, and black-and-white photographs. (Rev: BL 10/1/95; SLJ 11/95) [578]

12227 Rainis, Kenneth G., and George Nassis. *Biotechnology Projects for Young Scientists* (9–12). Series: Projects for Young Scientists. 1998, Watts $25.00 (0-531-11419-8); paper $6.95 (0-531-15913-2). After a discussion of biotechnology and its applications in the areas of food, environment, industry, the courts, and genetic testing, a series of remarkable projects, such as cloning carrots, are presented for the advanced science student. (Rev: BR 1–2/99; SLJ 10/98) [620.8]

12228 Rainis, Kenneth G., and Bruce J. Russell. *Guide to Microlife* (7–12). Illus. 1996, Watts LB $35.00 (0-531-11266-7). A handbook to microscopic animals that describes habitats, the various groups of organisms, and projects. Each entry is accompanied by stunning photographs. (Rev: BL 2/15/97; SLJ 5/97) [576]

12229 Snedden, Robert. *The Benefits of Bacteria* (6–10). Illus. Series: Microlife. 2000, Heinemann LB $22.79 (1-57572-242-9). The beneficial functions of bacteria are discussed in this well-illustrated science book. (Rev: BL 9/15/00; SLJ 12/00) [576]

12230 Snedden, Robert. *Scientists and Discoveries* (6–10). Illus. Series: Microlife. 2000, Heinemann

LB $22.79 (1-57572-244-5). This well-written account traces the development of the microscope and describes some of the discoveries that resulted such as vaccination, bacteriology, germ theory, antibiotics, and DNA. (Rev: BL 9/1/00) [579]

12231 Wolfe, David W. *Tales from the Underground: A Natural History of Subterranean Life* (10–12). Illus. 2001, Perseus Bks. $26.00 (0-7382-0128-6). For better science students, this is an account of a journey underground and of the life found thousands of feet below the surface of the earth. (Rev: BL 6/1–15/01) [578.7]

Pets

GENERAL AND MISCELLANEOUS

12232 Albrecht, Kat. *The Lost Pet Chronicles: Adventures of a K-9 Cop Turned Pet Detective* (8–12). 2004, Bloomsbury $23.95 (1-58234-379-9). This is a memoir of a former police officer who has become a pet detective and a solver of such crimes as dognapping. (Rev: BL 3/1/04) [363.28]

12233 Barrie, Anmarie. *A Step-by-Step Book About Rabbits* (9–12). Illus. 1987, TFH paper $5.95 (0-86622-475-0). After a discussion of types of rabbits, this book tells how to feed and care for them. (Rev: BL 11/15/87) [636.9]

12234 Becker, Marty, and Danelle Morton. *The Healing Power of Pets: Harnessing the Amazing Ability of Pets to Make and Keep People Healthy* (9–12). 2002, Hyperion $22.95 (0-7868-6808-2). A thoughtful and readable study of the unexpected benefits humans can derive from having a pet in their home. (Rev: BL 1/1–15/02) [158]

12235 Birmelin, Immanuel, and Annette Wolter. *The New Parakeet Handbook* (9–12). Illus. 1986, Barron's paper $9.95 (0-8120-2985-2). A manual on selecting and caring for parakeets, also known as budgerigars. (Rev: BL 5/15/86) [636.6]

12236 Burger, Joanna. *The Parrot Who Owns Me: The Story of a Relationship* (9–12). 2001, Villard $23.95 (0-679-46330-5). Burger, an ornithologist, adopted a 35-year-old parrot and the two bonded in an enchanting way. (Rev: BL 4/1/01) [636.6]

12237 Gerstenfeld, Sheldon L. *The Bird Care Book: All You Need to Know to Keep Your Bird Healthy and Happy*. Rev. ed. (8–12). Illus. 1989, Addison-Wesley paper $17.00 (0-201-09559-9). A basic handbook on the choosing, care, and feeding of both pet and wild birds. (Rev: BL 9/15/89) [636.6]

12238 Lantermann, Werner. *The New Parrot Handbook: Everything About Purchase, Acclimation, Care, Diet, Disease, and Behavior of Parrots* (9–12). Illus. 1986, Barron's paper $9.95 (0-8120-3729-4). A complete handbook that covers choosing and caring for a bird with information about species, breeding, and behavior. (Rev: BL 11/1/86) [636.6]

12239 MacPherson, Malcolm. *The Cowboy and His Elephant: The Story of a Remarkable Friendship* (9–12). Illus. 2001, St. Martin's $23.95 (0-312-25209-9). Bob Norris, a cowboy and rancher, adopts an elephant called Amy, and she soon becomes an integral part of the ranch routine. (Rev: BL 4/1/01) [599.67]

12240 *Petspeak: You're Closer Than You Think to a Great Relationship with Your Dog or Cat!* (9–12). Illus. 2000, Rodale $29.95 (1-57954-337-5); paper $16.95 (1-57954-077-5). This huge, attractive book, based on a PBS television series, explains pet behavior and tells how to get along with your cat or dog. (Rev: BL 9/15/00) [636.088]

12241 Raber, David. *Through Cougar's Eyes: Life's Lessons from One Man's Best Friend* (9–12). Illus. 2001, St. Martin's $23.95 (0-312-26918-8). The author bought an 8-week-old cougar cub and this was the beginning of a relationship in which it became his constant companion. (Rev: BL 4/1/01) [636.8]

12242 Simon, Seymour. *Pets in a Jar: Collecting and Caring for Small Wild Animals* (7–10). Illus. 1975, Penguin paper $6.99 (0-14-049186-4). Valuable information is given on caring for such small pets as ants, crickets, crabs, and starfish. [639]

12243 Tarte, Bob. *Enslaved by Ducks: How One Man Went from Head of the Household to Bottom of the Pecking Order* (10–12). 2003, Algonquin $23.95 (1-56512-351-4). In this comic memoir, Tarte tells how his life was changed by the parade of pets taken into his home. (Rev: BL 10/1/03; SLJ 12/03) [636.088]

12244 Taylor, Michael. *Pot Bellied Pigs as a Family Pet* (9–12). 1993, TFH $35.95 (0-86622-081-X). Includes what to feed pot-bellies, how they are related to other swine, and legal restrictions on ownership. (Rev: BL 4/15/93) [636.4]

12245 Vriends, Matthew M. *Pigeons* (7–12). Illus. 1988, Barron's paper $7.95 (0-8120-4044-9). A brief but thorough guide to raising pigeons plus material on their behavior and how to breed them. (Rev: BL 2/1/89) [636.5]

CATS

12246 Altman, Roberta. *The Quintessential Cat* (9–12). 1994, Prentice Hall $27.50 (0-671-85008-3). Includes feline tales, trivia, and tips, specific breeds and their abilities, and cat-loving celebrities such as Robert De Niro. (Rev: BL 10/1/94) [599.74]

12247 Brown, Philip. *Uncle Whiskers* (9–12). Illus. 1980, Warner paper $2.95 (0-446-87108-7). The true story of a remarkable cat that was crippled in an accident. [636.8]

12248 Caras, Roger A. *The Cats of Thistle Hill: A Mostly Peaceable Kingdom* (9–12). 1994, Simon &

Schuster $22.00 (0-671-75462-9). Anecdotes about the personalities and behaviors of the dozens of cats — and countless other animals — that share Caras's home and grounds. (Rev: BL 5/1/94) [636.8]

12249 Denny, D. Michael. *How to Get a Cat to Sit in Your Lap: Confessions of an Unconventional Cat Person* (9–12). 1995, Andiron paper $14.95 (0-9645799-0-1). Based on 30 years of living with cats, the author humorously tells of cat evolution, anatomy, behavior, naming, hunting, eating, and more. (Rev: BL 6/1–15/95) [636.8]

12250 Dibra, Bash, and Elizabeth Randolph. *CatSpeak: How to Learn It, Speak It, and Use It to Have a Happy, Healthy, Well-Mannered Cat* (8–12). Illus. 2001, Putnam $23.95 (0-399-14741-1). Among the topics covered are feline society and behavior, various breeds, how to choose a pet, how cats communicate with you, and behavioral problems. (Rev: BL 9/15/01) [636.8]

12251 Fogle, Bruce. *Know Your Cat: An Owner's Guide to Cat Behavior* (9–12). 1991, DK $24.95 (1-879431-04-1). A veterinarian provides insights into cat behavior, with 350 color photographs. (Rev: BL 1/1/92) [636.8]

12252 Gerstenfeld, Sheldon L. *The Cat Care Book: All You Need to Know to Keep Your Cat Healthy and Happy.* Rev. ed. (8–12). Illus. 1989, Addison-Wesley paper $16.00 (0-201-09569-6). Tips on how to choose a cat and detailed information on taking care of cats as pets. (Rev: BL 9/15/89) [636.8]

12253 Gethers, Peter. *The Cat Who'll Live Forever: The Final Adventures of Norton, the Perfect Cat, and His Imperfect Human* (10–12). 2001, Broadway $22.95 (0-7679-0637-3). For cat lovers, this continuation of *A Cat Abroad* (1993) tells of Norton's further adventures and his death. (Rev: BL 7/01; SLJ 12/01) [818]

12254 Hammond, Sean, and Carolyn Usrey. *How to Raise a Sane and Healthy Cat* (9–12). 1994, Howell Book House $22.95 (0-87605-797-0). Answers questions regarding the many facets of cat care and ownership, including choosing a cat, nutrition, and care of stray cats. (Rev: BL 7/94) [636.8]

12255 Herriot, James. *James Herriot's Cat Stories* (9–12). 1994, St. Martin's $17.95 (0-312-11342-0). A small collection of cat tales, ranging from the informative and scientific to the humorous and poignant. (Rev: BL 7/94) [636.8]

12256 Jordan, William. *A Cat Named Darwin: How a Stray Cat Changed a Man into a Human Being* (10–12). 2002, Houghton $23.00 (0-395-98642-7). A scientist previously unsympathetic to cats recounts his growing affection — and care — for an alley stray. (Rev: BL 11/1/02) [636.8]

12257 McGinnis, Terri. *The Well Cat Book: The Classic Comprehensive Handbook of Cat Care.* 2nd ed. (9–12). 1993, Random $23.00 (0-394-58769-3).

An authoritative guide by a veterinarian, covering feline anatomy, preventive medicine, diagnosis, home care, breeding, reproduction, and choosing a doctor. (Rev: BL 6/1–15/93) [636.808]

12258 Maggitti, Phil. *Owning the Right Cat* (9–12). 1993, Tetra $29.95 (1-56465-111-8). Provides information on feeding, grooming, breeding, showing, laws, history, health care, and genetics, with color photographs and illustrations. (Rev: BL 11/1/93) [636.8]

12259 Morris, Desmond. *Catwatching* (8–12). 1987, Crown $13.00 (0-517-56518-8); paper $8.95 (0-517-88053-9). Using a question-and-answer approach, the author explores many facets of cat behavior. (Rev: BL 4/1/87) [636.8]

12260 Muller, Ulrike. *Long-Haired Cats* (10–12). 1984, Barron's paper $6.95 (0-8120-2803-1). A specialized book on the types of long-haired cats and how to care for them with a special chapter on cat psychology. [636.8]

12261 Pugnetti, Gino. *Simon and Schuster's Guide to Cats* (9–12). 1983, Simon & Schuster paper $14.00 (0-671-49170-9). A guide to the different breeds of cats and how to care for them with additional material on the history of cats and their personality. [636.8]

12262 Steiger, Brad. *Cats Incredible! True Stories of Fantastic Feline Feats* (9–12). 1994, NAL paper $9.95 (0-452-27159-2). An amusing cat miscellany of feline factoids and believe-it-or-not anecdotes. (Rev: BL 3/15/94) [636.8]

12263 Tabor, Roger K. *Understanding Cats: Their History, Nature, and Behavior* (9–12). 1997, Reader's Digest $22.95 (0-89577-916-1). With more than 150 color photographs, this book provides a comprehensive introduction to the world of cats, their domestication, behavior, and care. [636.8]

12264 Taylor, David. *The Ultimate Cat Book* (8–12). 1989, Simon & Schuster $29.95 (0-671-68649-6). The health, behavior, and reproduction of cats are covered in this volume along with material of their origins and breeds. [636.8]

12265 Taylor, David. *You and Your Cat* (9–12). Illus. 1986, Knopf paper $16.95 (0-394-72984-6). Historical and anatomical information is followed by material on each breed and on the care and grooming of your cat. (Rev: BL 7/86; BR 11–12/86) [636.8]

12266 Wilbourn, Carole C. *The Total Cat: Understanding Your Cat's Physical and Emotional Behavior from Kitten to Old Age* (9–12). Illus. 2000, HarperCollins $14.00 (0-380-79051-3). As well as giving information about the care, feeding, and medical needs of cats, this account supplies excellent material on the hows and whys of cat behavior. (Rev: BL 10/1/00) [636.8]

12267 Zistel, Era. *A Gathering of Cats* (9–12). 1993, J. N. Townsend paper $11.95 (1-880158-00-0). Zistel tells the stories of various members of her pride of cats. (Rev: BL 11/1/93) [636.8]

DOGS

12268 American Kennel Club. *The Complete Dog Book.* 19th ed. (7–12). Illus. 1998, Howell Book House $32.95 (0-87605-148-4). The standard manual for dog owners and guide to every AKC-recognized breed. (Rev: BL 6/15/85) [636.7]

12269 Benjamin, Carol Lea. *The Chosen Puppy: How to Select and Raise a Great Puppy from an Animal Shelter* (10–12). Illus. 1990, Howell Book House paper $7.95 (0-87605-417-3). This is an informal guide to selecting and training a dog from an animal shelter; many humorous illustrations. (Rev: BL 9/1/90) [636.7]

12270 Budiansky, Stephen. *The Truth About Dogs: An Inquiry into the Ancestry, Social Conventions, Mental Habits, and Moral Fiber of Canis Familiaris* (9–12). Illus. 2000, Viking $24.95 (0-670-89272-6). A humorous but factual look at dogs and their behavior based on scientific and genetic research. (Rev: BL 9/15/00) [636.7]

12271 Coppinger, Raymond, and Lorna Coppinger. *Dogs: A Startling New Understanding of Canine Origin, Behavior, and Evolution* (9–12). Illus. 2001, Scribner $26.00 (0-684-85530-5). This book about our oldest domestic animal describes its evolution and how and why different breeds came about. (Rev: BL 3/1/01) [636.7]

12272 Coren, Stanley, and Andy Bartlett. *The Pawprints of History: Dogs and the Course of Human Events* (9–12). Illus. 2002, Free Pr. $25.00 (0-7432-2228-8). Appealing to both historians and pet lovers, this fascinating book looks at the complex interrelationship between humans and dogs across roughly 14 millennia. (Rev: BL 3/15/02) [6367]

12273 Delmar, Diana. *The Guilt-Free Dog Owner's Guide: Caring for a Dog When You're Short on Time and Space* (10–12). Illus. 1990, Storey paper $10.95 (0-88266-575-8). A manual on how to keep a dog happy and well trained when you have to be away for hours each day. (Rev: BL 4/1/90) [636.7]

12274 Diller, Steve. *Dogs and Their People: Choosing and Training the Best Dog for You* (9–12). 1998, Hyperion $22.95 (0-7868-6361-7); paper $5.99 (0-7868-5055-8). A dog behavior expert provides useful advice on choosing and then training various breeds of dog. (Rev: BL 3/1/99) [636.7]

12275 Dye, Dan, and Mark Beckloff. *Amazing Gracie: A Dog's Tale* (9–12). 2000, Workman $18.95 (0-7611-1938-X). This amazing story tells how a deaf and partially blind Great Dane inspired her owners to create a chain of specialty dog bakeries. (Rev: BL 10/15/00) [636.73]

12276 Fennell, Jan. *The Dog Listener: Learn How to Communicate with Your Dog for Willing Cooperation* (8–12). 2004, HarperResource paper $16.95 (0-06-008946-6). This comprehensive guide tells how one can peacefully coexist with one's dog and how successful training can be accomplished without violent behavior. (Rev: BL 1/1–15/04) [636.7]

12277 Fogle, Bruce. *ASPCA Complete Dog Care Manual* (9–12). 1993, DK $24.95 (1-56458-168-3). Illustrated information and instructions for novice dog owners on diet, housebreaking, obedience, grooming, and health. (Rev: BL 5/1/93; SLJ 7/93) [636.7]

12278 Fogle, Bruce. *Dog Owner's Manual* (10–12). Illus. 2003, DK paper $25.00 (0-7894-9321-7). This guide covers everything from basic dog anatomy to practical tips about living in harmony with your pet. (Rev: BL 6/1–15/03) [636.7]

12279 Fogle, Bruce, and Patricia Holden White. *New Complete Dog Training Manual* (8–12). 2002, DK $25.00 (0-7894-8398-X). This dog-training book shows how to create routines, implement commands, and break a dog's bad habits. [636.7]

12280 Gerstenfeld, Sheldon L. *The Dog Care Book: All You Need to Know to Keep Your Dog Healthy and Happy.* Rev. ed. (8–12). Illus. 1989, Addison-Wesley paper $17.00 (0-201-09667-6). Tips on selecting a dog plus extensive material on care and feeding. (Rev: BL 9/15/89) [636.7]

12281 Hart, Benjamin, and Lynette Hart. *The Perfect Puppy: How to Choose Your Dog by Its Behavior* (9–12). 1988, Freeman paper $12.95 (0-7167-1829-4). A guide to choosing the right dog that outlines the characteristics of 56 different breeds. (Rev: BR 5–6/88) [599.74]

12282 Herriot, James. *James Herriot's Dog Stories* (9–12). Illus. 1986, St. Martin's $21.95 (0-312-43968-7). The famous veterinarian tells some of his favorite anecdotes about his 50 years working with dogs. (Rev: BL 4/15/86; SLJ 9/86) [636.7]

12283 Kay, William J., and Elizabeth Randolph, eds. *The Complete Book of Dog Health* (9–12). Illus. 1985, Howell Book House paper $15.00 (0-87605-455-6). This is a comprehensive account that covers all topics from diagnosing symptoms to choosing a veterinarian. (Rev: BL 6/1/85) [636.7]

12284 Klever, Ulrich. *The Complete Book of Dog Care: How to Raise a Happy and Healthy Dog* (9–12). Illus. 1989, Barron's paper $12.95 (0-8120-4158-5). The kinds of purebred dogs are profiled, plus information on how to select a dog and how to train and care for it. (Rev: BL 1/15/90) [636.7]

12285 Maggitti, Phil. *Owning the Right Dog* (8–12). 1993, Tetra $29.95 (1-56465-110-X). Provides information on feeding, grooming, breeding, showing, and training, with color illustrations. (Rev: BL 11/1/93) [636.7]

12286 Margolis, Matthew, and Catherine Swan. *The Dog in Your Life* (9–12). 1982, Random paper $16.00 (0-394-71174-2). This book covers selection, care, and training of dogs. [636.7]

12287 Murphy, Claire Rudolf, and Jane G. Haigh. *Gold Rush Dogs* (6–12). Illus. 2001, Alaska Northwest $16.95 (0-88240-534-9). Nine dogs that played important roles in the Yukon are profiled here with many sidebars that provide background historical detail. (Rev: BL 9/1/01; SLJ 9/01) [636.7]

12288 Paulsen, Gary. *My Life in Dog Years* (5–10). Illus. 1998, Delacorte $15.95 (0-385-32570-3). The famous novelist tells about eight wonderful dogs that he has known and loved over the years. (Rev: BCCB 3/98; BL 1/1–15/98; SLJ 3/98; VOYA 4/98) [636.7]

12289 Paulsen, Gary. *Puppies, Dogs, and Blue Northers: Reflections on Being Raised by a Pack of Sled Dogs* (6–10). Illus. 1996, Harcourt $16.00 (0-15-292881-2). In seven short vignettes, Paulsen describes the life of his lead dog, Cookie, and how she raises her pups to race and pull sleds. (Rev: BR 3–4/97; SLJ 11/96; VOYA 2/97) [636.7]

12290 Pinkwater, Daniel. *Uncle Boris in the Yukon and Other Shaggy Dog Stories* (9–12). Illus. 2001, Simon & Schuster $20.00 (0-684-85632-8). A memoir by the author, commentator, and essayist about himself, his family, and the role of dogs in his life. (Rev: BL 11/1/01; VOYA 8/02) [813]

12291 Putney, William W. *Always Faithful: A Memoir of the Marine Dogs of WWII* (9–12). 2001, Free Pr. $25.00 (0-7432-0198-1). This is a story of military animals, World War II, the Marines, and the organization and functions of the U.S. Marine Corps Dog Corps (made up mostly of Doberman Pinschers). (Rev: BL 4/1/01) [940.54]

12292 Scalisi, Danny, and Libby Moses. *When Rover Just Won't Do: Over 2000 Suggestions for Naming Your Puppy* (8–12). 1993, Howell Book House $9.95 (0-87605-691-5). This collection of names for dogs includes more than 2,000 ideas, from Fajita to Rocky and Bullwinkle. (Rev: BL 11/1/93) [636.7]

12293 Schuler, Elizabeth M. *Simon and Schuster's Guide to Dogs* (9–12). Illus. 1980, Simon & Schuster paper $14.00 (0-671-25527-4). A handbook that gives information on 324 breeds. [636.7]

12294 Siegal, Mordecai, and Matthew Margolis. *GRRR! The Complete Guide to Understanding and Preventing Aggressive Behavior* (10–12). Illus. 2000, Little, Brown $23.95 (0-316-79022-2). This introduction to dog behavior and training emphasizes aggressive behavior, its causes, and its cures. (Rev: BL 3/1/00) [636.7]

12295 Smith, Ernie. *Warm Hearts and Cold Noses: A Common Sense Guide to Understanding the Family Dog* (9–12). 1987, Sunstone paper $10.95 (0-86534-109-5). A pet-care manual that covers topics such as feeding, housebreaking, and leash training. (Rev: BR 5–6/88) [636.7]

12296 Taylor, David. *The Ultimate Dog Book* (9–12). Illus. 1990, Simon & Schuster $29.95 (0-671-70988-7). An oversize book that discusses such topics as history, anatomy, breeds, and dog care. (Rev: BL 9/15/90) [636.7]

12297 Taylor, David, and Peter Scott. *You and Your Dog* (9–12). Illus. 1986, Knopf paper $17.00 (0-394-72983-8). Practical suggestions on choosing and caring for your dog are given along with information on history, anatomy, and a description of various breeds. (Rev: BL 7/86; BR 11–12/86; SLJ 9/86; VOYA 8/86) [636.7]

12298 Thomas, Elizabeth Marshall. *The Hidden Life of Dogs* (9–12). 1993, Houghton paper $12.95 (0-671-51700-7). Dog lovers will be captivated by the author's observations about dogs, their behavior, and their needs. [636.7]

12299 Thomas, Elizabeth Marshall, and Jared Taylor Williams. *The Social Lives of Dogs: The Grace of Canine Company* (10–12). Illus. 2000, Simon & Schuster $24.00 (0-684-81026-3). This sequel to the author's *The Hidden Life of Dogs* (1993) continues her story of her pet family and their characteristics, relationships, and behavior. (Rev: BL 6/1–15/00) [636.7]

12300 Vine, Louis L. *The Total Dog Book: The Breeders' and Pet Owners' Complete Guide to Better Dog Care* (9–12). 1988, Warner paper $5.99 (0-446-31483-8). This complete handbook on maintaining healthy dogs stresses prevention of problems. [636.5]

12301 Widmer, Patricia P. *Pat Widmer's Dog Training Book* (9–12). 1980, NAL paper $3.95 (0-451-14468-6). A thorough manual on the care and training of a dog. [636.7]

12302 Woodhouse, Barbara. *Dog Training My Way* (10–12). 1985, Berkley paper $5.99 (0-425-08108-7). This is a print version of the television series on dog training given by the renowned British pet specialist. [636.7]

FISHES

12303 Emmens, Cliff W. *A Step-by-Step Book About Tropical Fish* (8–12). Illus. 1988, TFH paper $5.95 (0-86622-471-8). A brief, brightly illustrated introduction to various types of tropical fish, their care, and housing. (Rev: BL 1/1/89) [639.34]

12304 Harris, Jack C. *A Step-by-Step Book About Goldfish* (9–12). Illus. 1987, TFH $9.95 (0-86622-917-5). Topics covered in this guide include varieties, feeding, and health problems. (Rev: BL 5/1/88) [639.344]

12305 Mills, Dick. *Aquarius Fish* (6–12). Illus. 1996, DK paper $5.00 (0-7894-1074-5). A well-illustrated book that covers all aspects of fish as pets, from selecting healthy fish to maintaining a proper habitat and diet. (Rev: VOYA 4/97) [636.6]

HORSES

12306 Chapple, Judy. *Your Horse: A Step-by-Step Guide to Horse Ownership* (10–12). Illus. 1984, Garden Way paper $16.95 (0-88266-353-4). Starting with how to choose a horse, this guide supplies all kinds of information on caring for and training horses. [636.1]

12307 Edwards, Elwyn Hartley. *The Ultimate Horse Book* (9–12). 1991, Random $34.95 (1-879431-03-3). This illustrated guide introduces more than 80 breeds of horses and ponies, describes their relationship with humans, and discusses equine ownership and care. (Rev: BL 12/1/91) [636.1]

12308 Gray, Peter. *The Organic Horse: The Natural Management of Horses Explained* (10–12). Illus. 2001, David & Charles $29.95 (0-7153-0950-1). In this book on horse care, the author explains the horse's digestive system, how a horse eats, and what constitutes a balanced diet. (Rev: BL 5/1/01) [636.1083]

12309 *The Greatest Horse Stories Ever Told* (9–12). Ed. by Steven D. Price. 2001, Lyons Pr. $24.95 (1-58574-237-6). These 30 short stories, essays, and articles about horses lead to a greater understanding of the bond between horse and rider. (Rev: BL 9/15/01) [636.1]

12310 Kelley, Brent. *The Horse Doctor Is In: A Kentucky Veterinarian's Guide to Horse Health, Care, Disease Prevention and Treatment* (10–12). Illus. 2002, Storey paper $19.95 (1-58017-460-4). Case studies and anecdotes add to the appeal of this accessible and fact-filled guide. (Rev: BL 11/15/02) [636.1]

12311 Midkiff, Mary D. *She Flies Without Wings: How Horses Touch a Woman's Soul* (10–12). 2001, Delacorte $23.95 (0-385-33499-0). The special bond between women and horses is explored in this account that is part natural history and part autobiography. (Rev: BL 3/15/01) [636.1]

12312 Morris, Desmond. *Horsewatching* (10–12). Illus. 1989, Crown $15.00 (0-517-57267-2). Extensive answers are given to questions concerning the anatomy, habits, history, and behavior of the horse. (Rev: BL 5/1/89) [636.1]

12313 Ripart, Jacqueline. *Horses of the World: From the Desert to the Racetrack* (9–12). Trans. by Molly Stevens and Catherine Reep. Illus. 2002, Abrams $39.95 (0-8109-1195-7). Among the breeds covered

in this handsome, well-illustrated volume are Austria's Lipizzans, Argentina's Cimarrones, Irish thoroughbreds, and the wild horses of Southwest Africa's Namib Desert. (Rev: BL 5/15/02) [636.1]

12314 Roberts, Monty. *The Man Who Listens to Horses* (10–12). 1997, Random $23.00 (0-679-45689-9). The story of how the author, a child rodeo star, overcame abuse, rejection, and ridicule to become trainer of Queen Elizabeth II's horses, what he has learned about horses and their ways, and his unique, nonviolent methods of training. (Rev: SLJ 5/98) [636.1]

12315 Rosen, Michael J., ed. *Horse People: Writers and Artists on the Horses They Love* (9–12). Illus. 1998, Artisan $30.00 (1-885183-93-3). A delightful book of essays and artwork by such horse lovers as Dick Francis, Jane Smiley, and Rita Mae Brown, who describe their fascination with these animals and the thrill of working with them. (Rev: SLJ 9/98) [636.1]

12316 Smiley, Jane. *A Year at the Races: Reflections on Horses, Humans, Love, Money, and Luck* (10–12). Illus. 2004, Knopf $22.00 (1-4000-4058-2). The noted novelist chronicles her real experiences with horses particularly after she became a horse owner. (Rev: BL 3/15/04*) [798.4]

12317 Twelveponies, Mary. *There Are No Problem Horses — Only Problem Riders* (10–12). 1982, Houghton paper $14.00 (0-395-33194-3). A book on horsemanship that stresses how horses think and how riders can communicate with them. [636.1]

12318 Vogel, Colin. *The Complete Horse Care Manual* (6–12). 1995, DK $24.95 (0-7894-0170-3). This thorough explanation of caring for a horse covers such topics as housing, feed, disease prevention and treatment, and equipment needed. (Rev: VOYA 4/96) [636.1]

Zoos, Aquariums, and Animal Care

12319 Asma, Stephen T. *Stuffed Animals and Pickled Heads: The Culture and Evolution of Natural History Museums* (10–12). Illus. 2001, Oxford $30.00 (0-19-513050-2). Interviews with natural history museum curators, exhibit designers, and scientists from around the world give insights into the inner workings of these institutions. (Rev: BL 4/15/01) [508]

12320 Axelrod, Herbert R., et al. *Dr. Axelrod's Mini-Atlas of Freshwater Aquarium Fishes* (10–12). Illus. 1987, TFH $35.95 (0-86622-385-1). This large volume not only identifies freshwater aquarium fish but also covers setting up and maintaining an aquarium. (Rev: BL 12/1/87) [639]

12321 Barrie, Anmarie. *A Step-by-Step Book About Our First Aquarium* (9–12). Illus. 1987, TFH paper $5.95 (0-86622-454-8). This introductory guide covers all topics from choosing a tank to maintaining a balanced habitat. (Rev: BL 11/15/87) [639.34]

12322 Glen, Samantha. *Best Friends: The True Story of the World's Most Beloved Animal Sanctuary* (9–12). 2001, Kensington paper $15.00 (1-57566-735-5). This is the heart-warming story of the Best Friends Animal Sanctuary in Angel Canyon, Utah, and how friends pooled their money to buy 3,000 acres of desert scrubland to rescue homeless animals. (Rev: BL 2/15/01) [636]

12323 Hancocks, David. *A Different Nature: The Paradoxical World of Zoos and Their Uncertain Future* (9–12). Illus. 2001, Univ. of California Pr. $35.00 (0-520-21879-5). This is an engrossing history of zoos, a discussion of their role in society, and a plea for naturalistic habitats to ensure the health and happiness of the inmates. (Rev: BL 5/15/01) [590]

12324 McCormack, John. *A Friend of the Flock: Tales of a Country Veterinarian* (10–12). 1997, Crown $23.00 (0-517-70612-1). A funny and sad memoir by the first veterinarian of Chactaw County, Alabama. (Rev: BL 9/15/97; BR 3–4/98; SLJ 1/98) [636]

12325 Mills, Dick. *You and Your Aquarium* (9–12). Illus. 1986, Knopf paper $17.00 (0-394-72985-4). In addition to material on setting up an aquarium, this account features material on fish anatomy, feeding, and breeding. (Rev: BL 7/86; BR 11–12/86; SLJ 11/86) [639.4]

12326 Sandford, Gina. *Aquarium: Owner's Manual* (8–12). 1999, DK paper $17.00 (0-7894-4614-6). As well as creating, stocking, and maintaining a home aquarium, this account covers types of fish and the necessity to safeguard the quality of water. [639.34]

12327 Scanlon, Edward J. *Animal Patients: 50 Years in the Life of an Animal Doctor* (10–12). 2000, Camino paper $14.95 (0-940159-65-1). This is an entertaining, informative look at the life of a big-city veterinarian, his practice, and his patients. (Rev: BL 8/00) [636.089]

12328 Sterba, Gunther, ed. *The Aquarium Encyclopedia* (10–12). Illus. 1983, MIT $45.00 (0-262-19207-1). An alphabetically arranged compendium of information on home aquariums and their upkeep. [639.3]

Chemistry

General and Miscellaneous

12329 Agosta, William C. *Thieves, Deceivers, and Killers: Tales of Chemistry in Nature* (10–12). 2001, Princeton Univ. Pr. $26.95 (0-691-00488-9); paper $16.95 (0-691-09273-7). This book describes how chemical substances are used in nature for communications, defense, and offense, with detail on how they are used as bactericides, repellents, and medicinals. (Rev: BL 11/1/00; SLJ 7/01) [577]

12330 Asimov, Isaac. *A Short History of Chemistry* (9–12). Illus. 1965, Greenwood LB $55.00 (0-313-20769-0). This is a readable account that stresses progress from the 18th century on to the modern age. [540.9]

12331 Ball, Philip. *The Ingredients: A Guided Tour of the Elements* (9–12). 2002, Oxford (0-19-284100-9). An introduction to the elements, how each was discovered, their properties, and uses. (Rev: BL 12/1/02; SLJ 6/03) [546]

12332 Brock, William H. *The Norton History of Chemistry* (9–12). 1993, Norton paper $19.95 (0-393-31043-4). Historical highlights and development of the science of chemistry. (Rev: BL 7/93) [540.9]

12333 Challoner, Jack. *The Visual Dictionary of Chemistry* (6–10). 1996, DK $18.95 (0-7894-0444-3). This beautifully illustrated introduction to chemistry contains material on the structure of atoms and molecules, the periodic table, chemical bonding, chemical reactions, groups of elements, organic chemistry, and chemical analysis. (Rev: BL 11/15/96; BR 3–4/97; SLJ 10/96; VOYA 2/97) [580]

12334 Gardner, Robert. *Science Projects About Chemistry* (6–12). Series: Science Projects. 2001, Enslow LB $20.95 (0-89490-531-7). Gardner conveys the fun of learning in this book about the uses of chemistry and science projects involving chem-

istry. (Rev: BL 3/15/01; HBG 10/01; SLJ 2/95) [540]

12335 Greenberg, Arthur. *A Chemical History Tour: Picturing Chemistry from Alchemy to Modern Molecular Science* (10–12). 2000, Wiley $62.95 (0-471-35408-2). Using all sorts of illustrations and a clear text, this is a history of chemistry from earliest times to today. [540.9]

12336 Hess, Fred C. *Chemistry Made Simple*. Rev. ed. (10–12). Illus. 1984, Doubleday paper $12.95 (0-385-18850-1). An easily understood presentation of the basic concepts and facts in the area of chemistry. One of a large Made Simple series that covers many academic subjects. [540]

12337 Mebane, Robert C., and Thomas R. Rybolt. *Adventures with Atoms and Molecules, Vol. 5: Chemistry Experiments for Young People* (7–10). 1995, Enslow LB $19.95 (0-89490-606-2). A basic user's guide to start young people thinking scientifically, with ideas for science fair projects. (Rev: BL 12/1/95) [540]

12338 Stwertka, Albert. *A Guide to the Elements* (9–12). 1996, Oxford $49.95 (0-19-508083-1). A rundown on each of the elements, with material on symbols, history, uses, and compounds. (Rev: BL 12/1/96; BR 1–2/97; VOYA 6/97) [540]

12339 Stwertka, Albert. *The World of Atoms and Quarks* (7–12). Series: Scientific American Sourcebooks. 1995, Twenty-First Century LB $28.90 (0-8050-3533-8). Using profiles of important scientists, this work traces humankind's quest for an understanding of matter and its building blocks. (Rev: BL 12/1/95; BR 3–4/96; SLJ 2/96) [539.7]

12340 VanCleave, Janice. *Janice VanCleave's A+ Projects in Chemistry: Winning Experiments for Science Fairs and Extra Credit* (6–10). 1993, Wiley $32.50 (0-471-58631-5); paper $12.95 (0-471-58630-7). Thirty experiments that investigate such topics as calories, acids, and electrolytes, among others. (Rev: BL 12/1/95; SLJ 4/94) [930]

Geology and Geography

Earth and Geology

12341 *Earth: The Definitive Visual Guide to Our Planet* (10–12). Ed. by James F. Luhr. Illus. 2003, DK $50.00 (0-7894-9643-7). This richly illustrated and comprehensive guide traces the origins and evolution of the planet in both text and graphics and provides a wealth of information about the atmosphere, tectonic plates and earthquakes, glaciers, all varieties of physical characteristics, and more. (Rev: BL 12/1/03; VOYA 4/04) [550]

12342 Erickson, Jon. *Historical Geology: Understanding Our Planet's Past* (10–12). Series: Living Earth. 2002, Facts on File $55.00 (0-8160-4726-X). After a general introduction to the concepts of geology, there is a series of chapters on each of the geological time periods. [551.7]

12343 Erickson, Jon. *Plate Tectonics: Unraveling the Mysteries of the Earth.* Rev. ed. (10–12). Series: Facts on File Science Library. 2001, Facts on File $55.00 (0-8160-4327-2). Plate tectonic theory is explained, with a look at its importance in evolution and extinction. [551.1]

12344 Erickson, Jon. *Rock Formations and Unusual Geologic Structures: Exploring the Earth's Surface* (9–12). 1993, Facts on File $26.95 (0-8160-2589-4). A detailed explanation of the forces that created the earth's landscape, including the logistics of continental rift and drift. (Rev: BL 5/1/93) [550]

12345 Hartmann, William. *The History of the Earth: An Illustrated Chronicle of an Evolving Planet* (9–12). 1991, Workman $35.00 (1-56305-122-2); paper $19.95 (0-89480-756-0). Illustrated with paintings of often unseen sights, a story of Earth's coming of age. (Rev: BL 11/1/91) [525]

12346 Hehner, Barbara Embury. *Blue Planet* (7–12). Series: Wide World. 1992, Harcourt $17.95 (0-15-200423-8). An examination of the interdependent systems that make up our planet, including plate tectonics, volcanoes, weather, satellites, and the ozone layer. (Rev: BL 11/15/92; SLJ 10/92) [508]

12347 Macdougall, J. D. *A Short History of Planet Earth: Mountains, Mammals, Fire, and Ice* (10–12). Series: Wiley Popular Science. 1996, Wiley $24.95 (0-471-14805-9). Full of charts, graphs, and illustrations, this is a concise introduction to geology. (Rev: SLJ 7/97) [551]

12348 Mathez, Edmond A., and James D. Webster. *The Earth Machine: The Science of a Dynamic Planet* (10–12). Illus. 2004, Columbia Univ. Pr. $39.95 (0-231-12578-X). The story of geology and such phenomena as plate tectonics and how this information has explained such natural wonders as the Grand Canyon, the Alps, and the Hawaiian Islands. (Rev: BL 4/1/04) [550]

12349 Meissner, Rolf. *The Little Book of Planet Earth* (10–12). Illus. 2002, Copernicus $20.00 (0-387-95258-6). A clear and concise natural history of the earth that discusses geology in general along with its many specialties — seismology, mineralogy, and so forth; suitable for advanced students. (Rev: BL 4/15/02) [550]

12350 Officer, Charles, and Jake Page. *Tales of the Earth* (9–12). 1993, Oxford $48.00 (0-19-507785-7). This introduction to earth science presents accounts of natural catastrophes: volcanoes, floods, earthquakes, meteorites and comets, profound climatic change, and mass extinctions. (Rev: BL 5/1/93) [550]

12351 O'Neill, Catherine. *Natural Wonders of North America* (7–12). Illus. 1984, National Geographic LB $12.50 (0-87044-519-7). Excellent color photographs complement the text and maps that describe such natural wonders as tundra regions, volcanoes, glaciers, and the Badlands of South Dakota. [557]

12352 *The Science Times Book of Natural Disasters* (10–12). Ed. by Nicholas Wade. Illus. 2000, Lyons Pr. $25.00 (1-55821-957-9). This collection of columns from the *New York Times* explores, in individual chapters, such phenomena as volcanoes, earthquakes, and cosmic collisions. (Rev: BL 2/15/00) [363.34]

12353 VanCleave, Janice. *Janice VanCleave's A+ Projects in Earth Science: Winning Experiments for Science Fairs and Extra Credit* (5–10). Illus. 1999, Wiley $32.50 (0-471-17769-5); paper $12.95 (0-471-17770-9). Thirty projects varying in complexity are included in this exploration of topography, minerals, atmospheric composition, the ocean floor, and erosion. (Rev: BL 12/1/98; SLJ 6/99) [550]

12354 Walker, Gabrielle. *Snowball Earth: The Story of the Great Global Catastrophe That Spawned Life as We Know It* (10–12). 2003, Crown $24.95 (0-609-60973-4). This absorbing and readable scholarly study looks at the controversial theory — and at the man who supported it — that a super ice age roughly 600 million years contributed to the creation of multicellular life forms. (Rev: BL 1/1–15/03) [551.6]

12355 Ward, Peter D., and Donald Brownlee. *The Life and Death of Planet Earth: How the New Science of Astrobiology Charts the Ultimate Fate of Our World* (10–12). Illus. 2003, Holt $26.00 (0-8050-6781-7). In their bleak vision of the earth's future, the authors forecast a return of the ice ages that will either wipe out human life on the planet or drive it into tiny enclaves near the Equator. (Rev: BL 12/15/02) [525]

Earthquakes and Volcanoes

12356 Bolt, Bruce A. *Earthquakes*. 4th ed. (10–12). 1999, W. H. Freeman $40.05 (0-7167-3396-X). An overview of the history of earthquakes and seismology. [551.2]

12357 Carson, Rob. *Mount St. Helens: The Eruption and Recovery of a Volcano* (9–12). Illus. 1990, Sasquatch paper $19.95 (0-912365-32-3). With excellent photographs, this is the story of the Mount St. Helens eruption, its aftermath, and the condition today. (Rev: BL 6/15/90) [508.79]

12358 Christian, Spencer, and Antonia Felix. *Shake, Rattle and Roll: The World's Most Amazing Natural Forces* (6–10). Series: Spencer Christian's World of Wonders. 1997, Wiley paper $12.95 (0-471-15291-9). This book supplies good information and suitable projects involving earthquakes and volcanoes, with material on topics including plate tectonics, seismic waves, geysers, and hot springs. (Rev: SLJ 6/98) [551.2]

12359 Clarkson, Peter. *Volcanoes* (8–12). Series: World Life Library. 2000, Voyageur paper $16.95 (0-89658-502-6). Illustrated with color photographs

and diagrams, this account gives general information about volcanoes and presents a tour of the world's most famous ones. [551.2]

12360 Erickson, Jon. *Quakes, Eruptions and Other Geologic Cataclysms* (9–12). 1994, Facts on File $26.95 (0-8160-2949-0). Describes the physical mechanisms that cause such geologic cataclysms as earthquakes, volcanoes, landslides, mudflows, and dust storms. (Rev: BL 8/94; SLJ 11/94) [550]

12361 Erickson, Jon. *Volcanoes and Earthquakes* (10–12). Illus. 1988, TAB $22.95 (0-8306-1942-9); paper $15.95 (0-8306-2842-8). In addition to general information on volcanoes and earthquakes the author gives a valuable introduction to plate tectonics and how planets were formed. (Rev: BL 1/1/89) [551.2]

12362 Levy, Matthys, and Mario Salvadori. *Why the Earth Quakes* (9–12). 1995, Norton $25.00 (0-393-03774-6). All about earthquakes and safety precautions. (Rev: BL 9/15/95) [551.2]

12363 Winchester, Simon. *Krakatoa: The Day the World Exploded: August 27, 1883* (10–12). Illus. 2003, HarperCollins $25.95 (0-06-621285-5). This detailed yet absorbing examination of the 1883 explosion of the volcanic island of Krakatoa explores both the local and global impact. (Rev: BL 2/1/03*; SLJ 10/03) [551.21]

Icebergs and Glaciers

12364 Erickson, Jon. *Glacial Geology: How Ice Shapes the Land* (10–12). Series: Changing Earth. 1996, Facts on File $26.95 (0-8160-3355-2). With generous use of photographs and line drawings, this is an exploration of the relationship between glaciers and the land or sea beneath them. (Rev: SLJ 7/96) [551.3]

Physical Geography

General and Miscellaneous

12365 Levinson, David. *Human Environments: A Cross-Cultural Encyclopedia* (10–12). Series: Encyclopedia of the Human Experience. 1995, ABC-CLIO LB $49.50 (0-87436-784-0). This title examines the complex relationships that exists among climate, weather, land forms, and plants, and their interaction with humankind's physical environment. (Rev: SLJ 6/96) [573]

12366 Lisowski, Marylin, and Robert A. Williams. *Wetlands* (7–10). Series: Exploring Ecosystems. 1997, Watts LB $23.00 (0-531-11311-6). Once considered useless places, wetlands are revealed in this book to be areas that provide us with food and water, house a variety of wildlife, act as flood barriers, and provide protection against erosion. (Rev: BL 5/1/97; SLJ 6/97) [574.5]

12367 Moore, Peter D. *Wetlands* (9–12). Series: Ecosystem. 2000, Facts on File $65.00 (0-8160-3930-5). This book examines the flora and fauna of wetlands and how these habitats can be preserved. [577.6]

12368 Niering, William A. *Wetlands* (9–12). Illus. 1985, Knopf paper $19.95 (0-394-73147-6). After identifying and describing the wetlands of North America, this account identifies each species living there. (Rev: BL 7/85; SLJ 9/85) [574.5]

12369 Rezendes, Paul, and Paulette Roy. *Wetlands: The Web of Life* (10–12). 1996, Sierra Club $40.00 (0-87156-851-9); paper $25.00 (0-87156-878-0). A variety of wetland environments such as bottomlands, swamps, mires, mud flats, and wet meadows are examined, showing the diversity of plant and animal life and the wetland systems' critical role in environmental health. (Rev: BL 11/15/96; SLJ 5/97) [574.5]

12370 Taylor, Michael Ray. *Caves: Exploring Hidden Realms* (9–12). Illus. 2001, National Geographic $35.00 (0-7922-7904-2). This visually attractive book discusses the nature and history of caves, the life they support, and spelunkers and their tools, looking at sites in Greenland, the Yucatan, and the United States. (Rev: BL 6/1–15/01) [796.52]

12371 Whitfield, Philip J., and Peter D. Moore. *Biomes and Habitats* (9–12). Series: Macmillan Living Universe. 2002, Macmillan $95.00 (0-02-865633-4). Seventeen habitats are examined in detail, with material on habitat patterns, how they are changing, and the human impact. [577.8]

Deserts

12372 Allaby, Michael. *Deserts* (9–12). Series: Ecosystem. 2001, Facts on File $65.00 (0-8160-3929-1). After a description and history of deserts, the author describes desert people and how they live. (Rev: SLJ 8/01) [577.5]

12373 MacMahon, James A. *Deserts* (9–12). Illus. 1985, Knopf paper $19.95 (0-394-73139-5). This volume not only describes the desert habitat but also, with pictures, describes the various species that live there. (Rev: BL 7/85; SLJ 9/85) [574.5]

Forests and Rain Forests

12374 Allaby, Michael. *Temperate Forests* (10–12). Series: Ecosystem. 1999, Facts on File $65.00 (0-8160-3678-0). Topics covered include the ecology, history, economics, and biology of forests in temperate zones. [577.3]

12375 Cozic, Charles P. *Rainforests* (9–12). Series: At Issue. 1997, Greenhaven paper $17.25 (1-56510-694-6). An anthology of articles and essays by environmentalists, business people, scientists, and journalists presenting different viewpoints on the complex causes of and cures for deforestation of rain forests. (Rev: SLJ 5/98) [574.5]

12376 Johnson, Darv. *The Amazon Rainforest* (7–12). Series: Endangered Animals and Habitats. 1999, Lucent LB $27.45 (1-56006-369-6). After a description of the Amazon rain forest, this book chronicles how it is being destroyed and the efforts being made to save it. [577.3]

12377 Kallen, Stuart A. *Life in the Amazon Rain Forest* (6–10). Series: The Way People Live. 1999, Lucent LB $27.45 (1-56006-387-4). A description of the Amazon rain forest and of the Yanomami people who live there, their traditions, food, shelter, religion, encounters with Europeans, and the continuous threats to their existence. (Rev: HBG 4/00; SLJ 7/99) [574.5]

12378 Lanting, Frans. *Jungles* (9–12). Illus. 2000, Taschen $39.99 (3-8228-6309-2). A beautiful picture book with accompanying essays that introduces the flora and fauna of jungles around the world. (Rev: BL 12/15/00) [578.734]

12379 Lewington, Anna. *Atlas of the Rain Forests* (6–12). 1997, Raintree Steck-Vaughn $22.98 (0-8172-4756-4). Enhanced by maps and photographs, this work contains information on the plant and animal life found in rain forests, the cultures of the people who live in them, and how these environments are changed by economic development. (Rev: BL 5/15/97; SLJ 8/97) [574.5]

12380 McAllister, Ian. *The Great Bear Rain Forest* (9–12). 1998, Sierra Club $40.00 (1-57805-011-1). This magnificently illustrated volume describes the wonders of the west coast of Canada from the U.S. border to the Alaska Panhandle, the home of the coastal grizzly bear and the largest tract of intact temperate rain forest on earth, and makes a powerful case for the need protect it from overdevelopment. (Rev: SLJ 4/99) [971]

12381 Newman, Arnold. *Tropical Rainforest: Our Most Valuable and Endangered Habitat with a Blueprint for Its Survival into the Third Millennium.* Rev. ed. (9–12). 2002, Checkmark $45.00 (0-8160-3973-9). Rain forests around the world are introduced with material on their ecology, threats to their existence, and a plan for their preservation. [577.3]

12382 Oldfield, Sara. *Rainforest* (10–12). Illus. 2003, MIT $29.95 (0-262-15106-5). This clearly written overview of rain forests and the incredible diversity of plant and animal life found there will be especially useful for report writers. (Rev: BL 7/03) [578.734]

12383 Silcock, Lisa, ed. *The Rainforests: A Celebration* (9–12). 1990, Chronicle $35.00 (0-87701-790-5). Rain forest experts describe various aspects of life in this habitat, supplemented by illustrations. (Rev: BL 2/1/91) [508.315]

Ponds, Rivers, and Lakes

12384 Beck, Gregor Gilpin. *Watersheds: A Practical Handbook for Healthy Water* (7–12). Illus. 1999, Firefly $19.95 (1-55037-330-1). This account highlights the importance of water in our lives, with special attention to pollution, flooding, and other environmental problems. (Rev: BL 9/1/99) [333.73]

12385 Lawton, Rebecca. *Reading Water: Lessons from the River* (10–12). 2002, Capital $18.95 (1-931868-09-3). A retired river guide shares the beauty, danger, and excitement of her experiences on the rivers of the West. (Rev: BL 11/1/02) [796.1]

12386 Martin, Patricia A. *Rivers and Streams* (7–12). Illus. 1999, Watts LB $23.00 (0-531-11523-2). This book contains over 30 projects and experiments involving streams, rivers, and the life they support. (Rev: BL 6/1–15/99) [577.6]

12387 Palmer, Tim. *The Snake River: Window to the West* (9–12). 1991, Island Pr. $40.00 (0-933280-59-9). A history of the Snake River is combined with a detailed report on the ecological issues surrounding it. (Rev: BL 8/91) [333.91]

Prairies and Grasslands

12388 Brown, Lauren. *Grasslands* (9–12). Illus. 1985, Knopf paper $19.95 (0-394-73121-2). This volume describes grasslands in the United States and then identifies the species found there. (Rev: BL 7/85; SLJ 9/85) [574.5]

12389 Larrabee, Aimee, and John Altman. *Last Stand of the Tallgrass Prairie* (10–12). Illus. 2001, Friedman $24.95 (1-58663-134-9). Accompanied by more than 150 color photographs, this is a stunning examination of North America's tallgrass ecosystem and how it is endangered. (Rev: BL 6/1–15/01) [577.4]

12390 Martin, Patricia A. Fink. *Prairies, Fields, and Meadows* (8–12). Illus. Series: Exploring Ecosystems. 2003, Scholastic $23.00 (0-531-11859-2). An overview of the geological features and plant and animal life of grasslands, with activities. (Rev: BL 12/1/02) [577.4]

Rocks, Minerals, and Soil

12391 Chesterman, Charles W., and Kurt E. Lowe. *The Audubon Society Field Guide to North American Rocks and Minerals* (7–12). Illus. 1978, Knopf $19.95 (0-394-50269-8). A basic guide that includes color illustrations of nearly 800 rocks and minerals. [549]

12392 Dietrich, R. V., and Reed Wicander. *Minerals, Rocks and Fossils* (9–12). 1983, Wiley paper $9.95 (0-471-89883-X). For the amateur geologist, this is a guide to identifying and collecting rocks, minerals, and fossils. [552]

12393 Erickson, Jon. *An Introduction to Fossils and Minerals: Seeking Clues to the Earth's Past* (9–12). 1992, Facts on File LB $26.95 (0-8160-2587-8). An overview of how rocks, fossils, and minerals have moved naturally over the ages and how they can provide information to the earth's history. (Rev: BL 4/15/92) [560]

12394 Pellant, Christopher, and Roger Phillips. *Rocks, Minerals and Fossils of the World* (9–12). Illus. 1990, Little, Brown paper $25.00 (0-316-69796-6). An identification manual that contains photographs and data in three sections — one each on rocks, minerals, and fossils. (Rev: BL 6/15/90) [552]

12395 Pough, Frederick H. *A Field Guide to Rocks and Minerals*. 4th ed. (7–12). Illus. 1976, Houghton paper $20.00 (0-395-91096-X). This volume in the Peterson Field Guide series gives photographs and identifying information on 270 rocks and minerals. [549]

12396 Vernon, Ron. *Beneath Our Feet: The Rocks of Planet Earth* (10–12). Illus. 2000, Cambridge Univ. Pr. $29.95 (0-521-79030-1). This effectively illustrated volume discusses various kinds of rocks, how they are shaped, rock formations, and how natural forces such as earthquakes and water can change the face of the earth. (Rev: BL 12/1/00) [552]

Mathematics

General and Miscellaneous

12397 Banks, Robert B. *Slicing Pizzas, Racing Turtles, and Further Adventures in Applied Mathematics* (10–12). 1999, Princeton Univ. Pr. $29.95 (0-691-05947-0). A collection of mathematical investigations, some of which are difficult but rewarding. (Rev: BL 9/1/99) [510]

12398 Boyer, Carl B. *A History of Mathematics*. 2nd ed. (10–12). 1989, Wiley $53.95 (0-471-09763-2). This history of mathematics is useful both for the student and the specialist. [510]

12399 Devlin, Keith. *The Language of Mathematics: Making the Invisible Visible* (10–12). Illus. 1998, W. H. Freeman $24.95 (0-7167-3379-X). Advanced high school math students will enjoy this celebration of the intellectual delights of mathematics that focuses on eight specific branches, including arithmetic, calculus, geometry, and topology. (Rev: BL 12/1/98) [610]

12400 Devlin, Keith. *The Millennium Problems: The Seven Greatest Unsolved Mathematical Puzzles of Our Time* (10–12). Illus. 2002, Basic $26.00 (0-465-01729-0). These challenging conundrums will interest advanced math students. (Rev: BL 11/15/02; SLJ 7/03) [510]

12401 Gardner, Robert. *Science Projects About Math* (8–12). Series: Science Projects. 1999, Enslow LB $20.95 (0-89490-950-9). Projects and experiments with mathematics are outlined, involving such subjects as light, time, distance, heights, and velocity. [507.8]

12402 Gardner, Robert. *Science Projects About Methods of Measuring* (6–12). Illus. Series: Science Projects. 2000, Enslow LB $19.95 (0-7660-1169-0). Different kinds of measurements are introduced, their relation to mass, area, volume, and tempera-

ture, and interesting suggestions for science projects in each category. (Rev: BL 4/1/00; HBG 9/00) [530.8]

12403 Guillen, Michael. *Five Equations That Changed the World: The Power and Poetry of Mathematics* (9–12). 1995, Hyperion $22.95 (0-7868-6103-7). A philosophical, biographical, and historical trip through two centuries of changing scientific thought and five scientists who helped shape the future: Newton, Bernoulli, Faraday, Clausius, and Einstein. (Rev: BL 9/1/95) [530.1]

12404 Huff, Darrell. *How to Lie with Statistics* (10–12). Illus. 1954, Norton paper $3.95 (0-393-09426-X). A now-classic account of how numbers can be manipulated to produce desired results. [519.5]

12405 Ifrah, Georges. *The Universal History of Computing: From the Abacus to Quantum Computing* (10–12). Illus. 2000, Wiley $24.95 (0-471-39671-0). From the first grasp of numbers to the possible roles of future computers, this is a history of humankind's ability to manipulate numbers. (Rev: BL 10/15/00) [004]

12406 Jacobs, Harold R. *Mathematics, A Human Endeavor: A Book for Those Who Think They Don't Like the Subject*. 3rd ed. (10–12). 1994, Freeman $79.40 (0-7167-2426-X). An overview of mathematics that delves into its history and many applications. [510]

12407 Kogelman, Stanley, and Barbara R. Heller. *The Only Math Book You'll Ever Need*. Rev. ed. (10–12). 1994, Facts on File $22.95 (0-8160-2767-6). Such daily routines involving math as using credit cards and converting area measurements are discussed in this practical introduction to mathematics. [513]

12408 Kogelman, Stanley, and Joseph Warren. *Mind over Math* (10–12). Illus. 1978, McGraw-Hill paper

$8.95 (0-07-035281-X). Based on the authors' many workshops, this is a course on how to overcome math anxiety. [510]

12409 Krieger, Melanie J. *Means and Probabilities: Using Statistics in Science Projects* (9–12). Illus. Series: Experimental Science. 1996, Watts LB $24.00 (0-531-11225-X). This is an excellent introduction to elementary statistics and statistical methodology and how these principles can be applied in science projects. (Rev: BL 8/96; SLJ 9/96) [001.4]

12410 Lieberthal, Edwin M., and Bernadette Lieberthal. *The Complete Book of Fingermath* (7–12). Illus. 1979, McGraw-Hill $21.96 (0-07-037680-8). How hands and fingers can be turned into primitive computers. [513]

12411 Mankiewicz, Richard. *The Story of Mathematics* (9–12). 2000, Princeton Univ. Pr. $29.95 (0-691-08808-X). Using plenty of illustrations and interesting asides, this is an entertaining history of mathematics. (Rev: BL 4/1/01) [510]

12412 Nahin, Paul J. *When Least Is Best: How Mathematicians Discovered Many Clever Ways to Make Things as Small (or as Large) as Possible* (10–12). Illus. 2004, Princeton Univ. Pr. $29.95 (0-691-07078-4). Nahin explores the varied ways in which mathematicians have dealt with problems of minimization and maximization. (Rev: BL 12/1/03) [511]

12413 Niederman, Derrick, and David Boyum. *What the Numbers Say: A Field Guide to Mastering Our Numerical World* (10–12). 2003, Broadway $24.95 (0-7679-0098-4). An entertaining attempt to demystify and popularize mathematics, this volume recommends that readers regard figures and statistics offered by others with a healthy degree of skepticism. (Rev: BL 5/15/03) [001]

12414 Paulos, John Allen. *Once upon a Number: The Hidden Mathematical Logic of Stories* (11–12). 1998, Basic $20.00 (0-465-05158-8). Avid math students will appreciate this humorous and highly readable examination of the relationship between the stories we tell and mathematical principles. (Rev: BL 11/15/98) [519.5]

12415 Schwartz, David M. *G Is for Googol: A Math Alphabet Book* (6–10). Illus. 1998, Tricycle $15.95 (1-883672-58-9). A humorous romp through mathematical terms and concepts using an alphabetical approach and cartoon illustrations. (Rev: BL 10/15/98; HBG 3/99; SLJ 11/98) [510]

12416 Tobias, Sheila. *Succeed with Math: Every Student's Guide to Conquering Math Anxiety* (10–12). Illus. 1987, College Entrance Examination Board paper $12.95 (0-87447-259-8). A book that helps readers develop problem-solving techniques as well as understand mathematical concepts. (Rev: BL 2/1/88; BR 3–4/88; SLJ 6/88; VOYA 4/88) [510]

12417 Zaslavsky, Claudia. *Fear of Math: How to Get over It and Get On with Your Life* (9–12). 1994, Rutgers Univ. Pr. paper $20.00 (0-8135-2099-1). This book gives many ideas on how to conquer math phobia and enjoy this field of knowledge. (Rev: BL 6/1–15/94) [510.7]

Algebra, Numbers, and Number Systems

12418 Bunch, Bryan. *The Kingdom of Infinite Number: A Field Guide* (10–12). Illus. 2000, W. H. Freeman $23.95 (0-7167-3388-9). For the math-minded, this adult account explores the traits, personalities, and activities of a wide range of numbers from simple ones to logarithms. (Rev: BL 2/15/00) [513]

12419 Clawson, Calvin C. *The Mathematical Traveler: Exploring the Grand History of Numbers* (9–12). 1994, Plenum $25.95 (0-306-44645-6). A mathematical adventure examining the history of numbers as a reflection of the evolution of culture, from the Chinese, Mayans, and Greeks to the modern day. (Rev: BL 5/1/94) [513.2]

12420 Humez, Alexander, et al. *Zero to Lazy Eight: The Romance of Numbers* (9–12). 1993, Simon & Schuster $21.00 (0-671-74282-5). A collection of brain games using prime numbers, square roots, sequences, base-2 arithmetic, and other concepts. (Rev: BL 6/1–15/93) [513.2]

Geometry

12421 Mlodinow, Leonard. *Euclid's Window: The Story of Geometry from Parallel Lines to Hyperspace* (10–12). Illus. 2001, Free Pr. $26.00 (0-684-86523-8). This is a survey of geometry from Euclid to contemporary contributions that is intended for good math students. (Rev: BL 3/1/01) [516]

Mathematical Games and Puzzles

12422 Gardner, Martin. *Aha! Gotcha: Paradoxes to Puzzle and Delight* (7–12). Illus. 1982, W. H. Freeman paper $12.60 (0-7167-1361-6). A book of puzzles from *Scientific American* that involve mathematics and logic. [793.7]

12423 Gardner, Martin. *Hexaflexagons and Other Mathematical Diversions* (10–12). 1988, Univ. of Chicago Pr. paper $13.00 (0-226-28254-6). A collection of brain teasers and mathematical puzzles from the pages of *Scientific American*. (Rev: SLJ 5/89) [793.7]

12424 Gardner, Martin. *Knotted Doughnuts and Other Mathematical Entertainments* (9–12). 1986, W. H. Freeman paper $14.95 (0-7167-1799-9). A collection of puzzles, games, and brainteasers about mathematics with clear instructions and explanations. [793.7]

12425 Gardner, Martin. *Time Travel and Other Mathematical Bewilderments* (10–12). Illus. 1987, W. H. Freeman paper $14.95 (0-7167-1925-8). Another collection of puzzles and explanatory descriptions from *Scientific American*. (Rev: BL 1/15/88) [793.7]

12426 Lobosco, Michael L. *Mental Math Challenges* (5–10). 1999, Sterling $17.95 (1-895569-50-8). The 37 projects in this fascinating collection involve construction of different mathematical applications, models, games, and drawings and are grouped under such headings as "Solitaire Games," "Math in Everyday Life Situations," and "Instant Calculations and Mind Reading." (Rev: SLJ 8/99) [510]

12427 Steinhaus, Hugo. *One Hundred Problems in Elementary Mathematics* (9–12). 1979, Dover paper $7.95 (0-486-23875-X). These are problems that illustrate basic operations in mathematics. [510]

12428 Tahan, Malba. *The Man Who Counted: A Collection of Mathematical Adventures* (9–12). 1993, Norton paper $14.95 (0-393-30934-7). Regales readers with delightful mathematical adventures featuring beautiful princesses, viziers, sultans, and Tahan himself. (Rev: BL 2/15/93*) [793.7]

12429 Vecchione, Glen. *Math Challenges: Puzzles, Tricks and Games* (6–10). Illus. 1997, Sterling $14.95 (0-8069-8114-8). A slim volume that contains a number of mathematical puzzles arranged by subject and followed by the solutions. (Rev: SLJ 10/97) [510]

Meteorology

Storms

12430 Allaby, Michael. *Blizzards* (9–12). Series: Dangerous Weather. 1997, Facts on File $35.00 (0-8160-3518-0). As well as defining blizzards and discussing the climatic conditions that cause them, this volume looks at the areas most susceptible to blizzards, and what can be done to minimize the threat posed by winter hazards. [551.55]

12431 Allaby, Michael. *Hurricanes* (7–12). Series: Dangerous Weather. 1997, Facts on File $35.00 (0-8160-3516-4). An exhaustive introduction to hurricanes covering such topics as conditions that can lead to them, why they are common in particular areas, historic hurricanes, their naming and tracking, and how global climate changes will affect them. (Rev: BR 1–2/98; SLJ 4/98) [551.5]

12432 Allaby, Michael. *Tornadoes* (7–12). Series: Dangerous Weather. 1997, Facts on File $35.00 (0-8160-3517-2). This excellent book on tornadoes describes how they begin, their structure, travel patterns, interiors, historic tornadoes, and when and where tornadoes occur. (Rev: BR 1–2/98; SLJ 4/98) [551.55]

12433 De Hahn, Tracee. *The Blizzard of 1888* (7–12). Series: Great Disasters: Reforms and Ramifications. 2000, Chelsea $21.95 (0-7910-5787-9). Exciting illustrations and eyewitness accounts enhance this exploration of the impact of this famous blizzard and of the changes in infrastructure and services that resulted from it. (Rev: BL 4/15/01; HBG 10/01; SLJ 6/01) [974.7]

12434 Erickson, Jon. *Violent Storms* (10–12). Illus. 1988, TAB $24.95 (0-8306-9042-5); paper $16.95 (0-8306-2942-4). In addition to a description of the nature and causes of storms, the author gives a general introduction to weather and such topics as the

greenhouse effect and acid rain. (Rev: BL 1/1/89; VOYA 4/89) [551.5]

12435 Junger, Sebastian. *The Perfect Storm* (10–12). 1997, Norton $23.95 (0-393-04016-X). This best-selling book re-creates the last few hours of the swordfishing vessel *Andrea Gail* as it heads into "the perfect storm" and tragedy. (Rev: SLJ 11/97) [904]

12436 Larson, Erik. *Isaac's Storm: A Man, a Time, and the Deadliest Hurricane in History* (10–12). 1999, Crown $25.00 (0-609-60233-0). This wide-ranging account of the 1900 hurricane that devastated Galveston, Texas, focuses on the disaster's personal impact on the head of the local office of the fledgling U.S. Weather Bureau. (Rev: BL 6/1–15/99; SLJ 3/00; VOYA 2/00)

12437 Rosenfeld, Jeffrey. *Eye of the Storm: Inside the World's Deadliest Hurricanes, Tornadoes, and Blizzards* (9–12). 1999, Plenum $27.95 (0-306-46014-9). This work covers the causes and nature of hurricanes, tornadoes, and blizzards, with material on the scientists who study them. [551.55]

12438 Sheets, Bob, and Jack Williams. *Hurricane Watch: Forecasting the Deadliest Storms on Earth* (10–12). 2001, Random paper $15.00 (0-375-70390-X). A fascinating account of storm watchers and the most severe storms in history from the time of Columbus through the terrible onslaught on Florida in 1992. (Rev: BL 7/01; SLJ 1/02) [551.55]

12439 *Tornadoes* (9–12). Ed. by Nancy Harris. Illus. Series: Great Disasters. 2003, Gale $28.70 (0-7377-1472-7); paper $19.95 (0-7377-1473-5). This overview of tornadoes engages readers' interest with an eyewitness account of what it's like to live through a twister and includes information on new tracking and prevention technologies. (Rev: BL 11/1/03) [363.34]

12440 Verkaik, Jerrine, and Arjen Verkaik. *Under the Whirlwind: Everything You Need to Know About Tornadoes But Didn't Know Who to Ask* (9–12). Illus. 1997, Whirlwind paper $20.00 (0-9681537-0-4). This book contains a wealth of information about tornadoes, with material on their development and structure, how to survive them, and how to deal with post-tornado trauma. (Rev: SLJ 7/98) [551.5]

Water

12441 Allaby, Michael. *Floods* (8–10). Series: Dangerous Weather. 1998, Facts on File $35.00 (0-8160-3520-2). An overview of floods and flood-related topics such as land development and soil erosion, with graphic information and details of memorable floods of the past. [551.48]

12442 Ball, Philip. *Life's Matrix: A Biography of Water* (10–12). 2000, Farrar paper $18.95 (0-520-23008-6). This book describes the past and present contributions of water to world civilization, and also explains its properties and uses. (Rev: BL 5/15/00) [553.7]

12443 Cossi, Olga. *Water Wars: The Fight to Control and Conserve Nature's Most Precious Resource* (6–12). 1993, Macmillan LB $13.95 (0-02-724595-0). Discusses the sources and uses of fresh water and examines the reasons for drought, water quality problems, and how to conserve water. (Rev: BL 11/1/93; SLJ 2/94; VOYA 4/94) [333.91]

12444 de Villiers, Marq. *Water: The Fate of Our Most Precious Resource* (10–12). 2000, Houghton paper $15 .00 (0-618-12744-5). As well as describing the history, folklore, and politics of water, this account gives details on the worsening water situation worldwide and efforts to avoid an international crisis. [333.91]

12445 Gardner, Robert. *Experimenting with Water* (7–12). Series: Venture. 1993, Watts paper $24.00 (0-531-12549-1). The unusual properties of water are described in these simple experiments and "puzzlers" that provide clear explanations of scientific concepts. (Rev: BL 2/15/94; SLJ 4/94) [546]

12446 Kandel, Robert. *Water from Heaven: The Story of Water from the Big Bang to the Rise of Civilization, and Beyond* (10–12). Illus. 2003, Columbia Univ. Pr. $27.95 (0-231-12244-6). This well-researched study looks at the origins of fresh water, the water cycle, and the formidable threats to the world's fresh water supplies today. (Rev: BL 12/1/02) [551.46]

12447 Ocko, Stephanie. *Water: Almost Enough for Everyone* (5–10). 1995, Atheneum $16.00 (0-689-31797-2). Ocko traces the interconnectedness of the earth's ecosystems and provides ways people can conserve water and care for the environment. (Rev: BL 6/1–15/95; SLJ 6/95; VOYA 12/95) [363.3]

12448 Rothfeder, Jeffrey. *Every Drop for Sale: Our Desperate Battle over Water in a World About to Run Out* (10–12). 2001, Putnam $24.95 (1-58542-114-6). The author maintains that with our record of population growth and misuse, water not oil will become the fluid of scarcity in the 21st century. (Rev: BL 10/15/01) [333.91]

12449 Swanson, Peter. *Water: The Drop of Life* (10–12). Illus. 2001, NorthWord $29.95 (1-55971-782-3). The author and his many contributors — including the Dalai Lama, Jimmy Carter, and Kofi Annan — discuss the importance of water as well as problems with water pollution and water-related diseases. (Rev: BL 11/1/00) [553.7]

Weather

12450 Allaby, Michael. *Droughts* (6–12). Illus. Series: Dangerous Weather. 1997, Facts on File $35.00 (0-8160-3519-9). Topics discussed in this comprehensive volume include how droughts are classified, droughts of the past, the Dust Bowl, irrigation, water storage, saving water, and jet streams and storm tracks. (Rev: BL 12/1/97) [551.55]

12451 Allaby, Michael. *Fog, Smog and Poisoned Rain* (7–12). Series: Dangerous Weather. 2003, Facts on File $35.00 (0-8160-4789-8). Natural sources of pollution such as volcanoes are included in this survey of dangerous weather phenomena. (Rev: SLJ 10/03) [363.739]

12452 Dickinson, Terence. *Exploring the Sky by Day: The Equinox Guide to Weather and the Atmosphere* (7–10). Illus. 1988, Camden House paper $9.95 (0-920656-71-4). A book about weather that explores such subjects as types of clouds and kinds of precipitation. (Rev: BL 3/1/89; SLJ 1/89) [551.6]

12453 Libbrecht, Kenneth, and Patricia Rasmussen. *The Snowflake: Winter's Secret Beauty* (10–12). Illus. 2003, Voyageur $20.00 (0-89658-630-8). Stunning photographs are combined with a clear explanation of the science behind the formation of ice crystals. (Rev: BL 12/1/03) [551.57]

12454 Lockhart, Gary. *The Weather Companion: An Album of Meteorological History, Science, Legend, and Folklore* (9–12). 1988, Wiley paper $17.95 (0-471-62079-3). From ancient myths to modern research, this book covers lore and facts concerning the weather. (Rev: BR 3–4/89; SLJ 6/89) [551.5]

12455 Ludlum, David M. *The American Weather Book* (10–12). 1990, American Meteorological Society paper $20.00 (0-933876-97-1). A collection of facts, myths, and figures all involving the weather. [551.6]

12456 Lynch, John. *The Weather* (10–12). Illus. 2002, Firefly $35.00 (1-55297-640-8); paper $24.95 (1-55297-639-4). A wide array of graphics are used in this lively survey of global weather that is full of disaster stories and other interesting anecdotes. (Rev: BL 12/15/02) [551.6]

12457 Mogil, H. Michael, and Barbara G. Levine. *The Amateur Meteorologist: Explorations and Investigations* (6–10). Illus. Series: Amateur Science. 1993, Watts LB $21.40 (0-531-11045-1). This book shows how to get started in weather observation and forecasting, with projects such as making an anemometer, wind vane, barometer, and rain gauge. (Rev: BL 1/15/94) [551.5]

12458 Nash, J. Madeleine. *El Nino: Unlocking the Secrets of the Master Weather-Maker* (10–12). 2002, Warner $25.95 (0-446-52481-6). Anecdotes of severe weather episodes add to this examination of the El Nino phenomenon, its implications for world weather, and the work of weather researchers. (Rev: BL 2/15/02) [551.6]

12459 Ramsey, Dan. *Weather Forecasting: A Young Meteorologist's Guide* (8–12). Illus. 1990, TAB $19.95 (0-8306-8338-0); paper $10.95 (0-8306-3338-3). A detailed and often technical examination of the techniques of weather forecasting with many tables, charts, and diagrams. (Rev: BL 10/15/90) [551.6]

12460 Stevens, William K. *The Change in the Weather: People, Weather, and the Science of Climate* (10–12). 2000, Delacorte $24.95 (0-385-32012-4). This book explores climatic change through the ages with material on such current topics as greenhouse gases and changes in ocean temperature. (Rev: BL 2/15/00) [551.5]

12461 Upgren, Arthur R., and Jurgen Stock. *Weather: How It Works and Why It Matters* (9–12). 2000, Perseus Bks. paper $18.00 (0-738-20521-4). After describing factors that affect the weather and the causes of seasonal changes, this account discusses current threats such as global warming and ozone depletion. [551.5]

12462 Weart, Spencer. *The Discovery of Global Warming* (10–12). 2003, Harvard $24.95 (0-674-01157-0). Weart chronicles 150 years of research and debate about the causes and the importance — both scientific and political — of global warming. (Rev: BL 8/03) [551.6]

12463 Williams, Jack. *The Weather Book*. 2nd ed. (9–12). 1997, Vintage paper $20.00 (0-679-77665-6). Featuring easy-to-follow color graphics from *USA Today,* this handy guide explores a wide range of weather-related topics, including computer forecasting, basic changes in weather patterns, cold fronts, heat waves, tornadoes, blizzards, hurricanes, and droughts. [551.6]

Oceanography

General and Miscellaneous

12464 Burleigh, Robert, adapt. *The Sea: Exploring Life on an Ocean Planet* (5–12). Photos by Philip Plisson. 2003, Abrams $14.95 (0-8109-4591-6). The power, economic importance, and fragility of the sea are shown in this oversized photoessay with an ecological emphasis. (Rev: HBG 4/04; SLJ 12/03) [551]

12465 Byatt, Andrew, et al. *The Blue Planet: A Natural History of the Oceans* (8–12). Illus. 2002, DK $40.00 (0-7894-8265-7). The oceans, their diverse plant and animal life, and the interaction between water and air are all explored in accessible text and pleasing photographs and graphics; a companion to a BBC/Discovery Channel program. (Rev: BL 3/1/02; VOYA 8/02) [578.77]

12466 Carson, Rachel. *The Sea Around Us* (10–12). 1989, Oxford $30.00 (0-19-506186-1); paper $12.95 (0-19-506997-8). A classic introduction to oceans with material on how they were formed, currents and tides, volcanic islands, and life in the sea. [551.46]

12467 Cramer, Deborah. *Great Waters: An Atlantic Passage* (10–12). Illus. 2001, Norton $27.95 (0-393-02019-3). This is the history and biography of the Atlantic Ocean, its past, present ecosystem, future, and possible death. (Rev: BL 7/01) [551.446]

12468 Day, Trevor. *Oceans* (9–12). Series: Ecosystem. 1999, Facts on File $65.00 (0-8160-3647-0). Topics discussed about oceans include exploration, geography, geology, history, and economic resources. [551.46]

12469 Dudley, William, ed. *Endangered Oceans* (8–12). Series: Opposing Viewpoints. 1999, Greenhaven LB $32.45 (0-7377-0063-7); paper $21.20 (0-7377-0062-9). This anthology of opinions about the spoiling of the oceans debates such topics as the seriousness of the problem, the effectiveness of present practices, international policies, and how to save the whales. (Rev: BL 4/15/99; SLJ 8/99) [574.5]

12470 Ellis, Richard. *Aquagenesis: The Origin and Evolution of Life in the Sea* (10–12). Illus. 2001, Viking $25.95 (0-670-03023-6). This book gives excellent background information on the evolution of life in the sea from single-cell organisms to the present inhabitants. (Rev: BL 10/15/01) [591.77]

12471 Erickson, Jon. *Marine Geology: Undersea Landforms and Life Forms* (10–12). Series: Changing Earth. 1996, Facts on File $26.95 (0-8160-3354-4). This volume covers the entire realm of undersea landscapes and life forms, covering such topics as the seabed, the oceanic crust, undersea mountains and chasms, ocean circulation, and marine biology. (Rev: BL 12/1/95; SLJ 7/96) [551.46]

12472 Erickson, Jon. *The Mysterious Oceans* (9–12). Illus. 1988, TAB paper $15.95 (0-8306-9342-4). After discussing how oceans were formed, the author explores such topics as deep sea life, waves, food resources, and pollution. (Rev: VOYA 2/89) [551.46]

12473 Groves, Don. *The Oceans: A Book of Questions and Answers* (9–12). Illus. 1989, Wiley paper $15.95 (0-471-60712-6). Information is given on the oceans and their exploration in a question-and-answer format. (Rev: BL 4/15/89; BR 11–12/90) [551.46]

12474 Kunzig, Robert. *The Restless Sea: Exploring the World Beneath the Waves* (10–12). 1999, Norton $24.95 (0-393-04562-5). An easily understood history of oceans, from their formation to the present. (Rev: BL 2/15/99) [551.46]

12475 Rice, Tony. *Deep Ocean* (9–12). Series: Natural World. 2000, Smithsonian paper $14.95 (1-

56098-867-3). This book traces the history of oceanography and supplies details on the kinds of life found in oceans. [551.46]

12476 Weber, Michael, and Judith Gradwohl. *The Wealth of Oceans* (9–12). 1995, Norton $25.00 (0-393-03764-9). New discoveries in marine ecology are discussed with regard to the stresses imposed by human societies. (Rev: BL 4/1/95) [333.71]

12477 Wroble, Lisa A. *The Oceans* (7–10). Series: Endangered Animals and Habitats. 1998, Lucent LB $22.45 (1-56006-464-1). A well-illustrated, fact-filled exploration of the oceans as habitats and the environmental dangers that threaten them. (Rev: HBG 9/98) [577.7]

Underwater Exploration and Sea Disasters

12478 Alexander, Caroline. *The Bounty: The True Story of the Mutiny on the Bounty* (9–12). 2003, Viking (0-670-03133-X). This is an excellent and accurate retelling of the mutiny on *HMS Bounty* and its consequences. (Rev: BL 8/03) [996.1]

12479 Ballard, Robert D., and Rick Archbold. *The Discovery of the Titanic* (9–12). Illus. 1987, Warner $35.00 (0-446-51385-7). An account of the complex, often frustrating but eventually successful quest for the wreck of the *Titanic*. (Rev: BL 12/1/87; VOYA 4/88) [622]

12480 Ballard, Robert D., and Will Hively. *The Eternal Darkness: A Personal History of Deep-Sea Exploration* (10–12). Illus. 2000, Princeton Univ. Pr. $29.95 (0-691-02740-4). The discoverer of the *Titanic* presents a scholarly history of deep-sea exploration that includes a review of the work of Beebe, Barton, and Cousteau. (Rev: BL 3/1/00) [551.46]

12481 Callahan, Steven. *Adrift: Seventy-Six Days Lost at Sea* (9–12). Illus. 1986, Ballantine paper $5.95 (0-345-34083-3). The incredible saga of a shipwrecked man who lived for 76 days on a rubber raft in the Atlantic Ocean. (Rev: BL 1/1/86; SLJ 9/86) [910]

12482 Cousteau, Jacques, and Frederic Dumas. *The Silent World* (7–12). Illus. 1987, HarperCollins $19.95 (0-06-010890-8). A description of how the aqualung was developed and how it has opened up the exploration of oceans and their sunken treasures. [551.46]

12483 Cussler, Clive, and Craig Dirgo. *The Sea Hunters* (10–12). 1996, Simon & Schuster $24.00 (0-684-83027-2). This is an account of 12 deep-sea

wrecks, including how and why they happened and attempts to locate them. (Rev: SLJ 3/97) [940.4]

12484 Davie, Michael. *Titanic: The Death and Life of a Legend* (10–12). Illus. 1987, Knopf $19.95 (0-317-58565-7). A re-creation of the sinking of the *Titanic* that highlights the mysteries surrounding it that have not yet been solved. (Rev: BL 6/1/87) [363.1]

12485 Heyer, Paul. *Titanic Legacy: Disaster as Media Event and Myth* (9–12). 1995, Praeger $39.95 (0-275-95352-1). Traces the events surrounding the sinking of the *Titanic,* the heroes and villains, and how the media reported the disaster. (Rev: BL 12/1/95) [363.12]

12486 Hoyt, Erich. *Creatures of the Deep: In Search of the Sea's "Monsters" and the World They Live In* (9–12). Illus. 2001, Firefly $40.00 (1-55209-340-9). After a history of deep-sea research, this book takes the reader on a tour through the underwater zones and gives an introduction to the life at each layer. (Rev: BL 12/1/01; SLJ 2/02) [591]

12487 Kinder, Gary. *Ship of Gold in the Deep Blue Sea: The History and Discovery of America's Richest Shipwreck* (10–12). Illus. 1998, Grove Atlantic $27.50 (0-87113-464-0). An engrossing story of Tommy Thompson, an engineer from Ohio, and his determination to explore and salvage the cargo of the *SS Central America,* a ship that sank in 1857 off the coast of North Carolina. (Rev: BL 6/1–15/98; SLJ 10/98) [910.4]

12488 Lord, Walter. *The Night Lives On* (9–12). 1986, Morrow paper $5.99 (0-380-73203-3). This sequel to *A Night to Remember* continues the story of the *Titanic* based on recent findings. (Rev: SLJ 2/87) [910.4]

12489 Lord, Walter. *A Night to Remember* (7–12). 1956, Bantam paper $6.99 (0-553-27827-4). A brilliant re-creation of the maiden and only voyage of the *Titanic*. (Rev: BL 3/15/98) [910.4]

12490 Marx, Robert F. *The Search for Sunken Treasure* (10–12). 1996, Key Porter paper $19.95 (1-55013-788-3). This is an exciting history of the world's most famous shipwrecks, beginning with the Phoenicians and ancient Greeks up to the more recent *Bismark* and *Edenburgh.* (Rev: SLJ 5/97) [910.4]

12491 Pellegrino, Charles. *Ghosts of the Titanic: An Archaeological Odyssey* (10–12). Illus. 2000, HarperCollins $25.00 (0-688-13955-8). This *Titanic* expert reports on what has been learned concerning the ship and its fate from 12 years of underwater archaeology. (Rev: BL 6/1–15/00; SLJ 12/00) [910]

12492 Ritchie, David. *Shipwrecks: An Encyclopedia of the World's Worst Disasters at Sea* (10–12). 1996, Facts on File $40.00 (0-8160-3163-0). Alphabetically arranged articles chronicle sea disasters, from the sinking of the *Santa Maria* in 1492 to a ferry tragedy in Haiti in 1993. (Rev: SLJ 2/97) [904]

12493 *Titanic: Fortune and Fate* (9–12). 1998, Simon & Schuster $30.00 (0-684-85710-3). Letters, pictures, newspaper articles, and photographs of memorabilia are logically arranged with explanatory captions and minimal text in this catalog of an exhibit that covers background information, life onboard the ship, the sinking itself, and the aftermath, with a detailed list of both passengers and crew that includes age, class, occupation, and whether or not they were lost or saved. (Rev: SLJ 2/99) [910]

12494 Van Dover, Cindy L. *Octopus's Garden* (10–12). 1996, Addison-Wesley $20.00 (0-201-40770-1). This is an autobiographical account of a woman pioneer in the field of oceanography and her experiences piloting the research submersible *Alvin*, where she studied the ocean floor and the sea life that exists there. (Rev: BL 12/15/95; SLJ 9/96) [551.46]

Physics

General and Miscellaneous

12495 Adams, Richard C., and Peter H. Goodwin. *Physics Projects for Young Scientists*. Rev. ed (7–10). Illus. 2000, Watts LB $25.00 (0-531-11667-0); paper $6.95 (0-531-16461-6). After a general discussion of physics, this book presents clear instructions for number of related science activities and projects. (Rev: BL 6/1–15/00) [530]

12496 Al-Khalili, Jim. *Black Holes, Wormholes and Time Machines* (10–12). 1999, Inst. of Physics paper $16.99 (0-7503-0560-6). A clear account of such concepts as relativity, the big bang, black holes, and time. (Rev: BL 10/15/99) [530.1]

12497 Barnett, Lincoln. *The Universe of Dr. Einstein* (8–12). 1980, Amereon $18.95 (0-8488-0146-6). A lucid explanation of Einstein's theory of relativity and how it has changed our ideas of the universe. [530.1]

12498 Berlinski, David. *Newton's Gift: How Sir Isaac Newton Unlocked the System of the World* (10–12). Illus. 2000, Free Pr. $24.00 (0-684-84392-7). In this accessible text, the author explains Newton's theories of gravity and motion and explains their impact on science. (Rev: BL 9/15/00) [530.092]

12499 Bodanis, David. *E = mc²: A Biography of the World's Most Famous Equation* (10–12). 2000, Walker $24.00 (0-8027-1352-1). Everything you wanted to know about Einstein's famous equation of 1905 and its impact on modern science. (Rev: BL 8/00) [530.11]

12500 Bortz, Fred. *Techno Matters: The Materials Behind the Marvels* (7–12). Illus. 2001, Twenty-First Century LB $25.90 (0-7613-1469-5). The author, a physicist, uses plentiful illustrations and clear text to explain different types of matter (electro-matter, poly-matter, super-matter, and so forth) and the kinds of materials that have been produced over the years since the Stone Age. (Rev: BL 4/15/01; HBG 10/01; SLJ 10/01) [620.1]

12501 Brackin, A. J. *Clocks: Chronicling Time* (6–10). Series: Encyclopedia of Discovery and Invention. 1991, Lucent LB $52.44 (1-56006-208-8). A history of the measurement of time and how time devices have changed the world. (Rev: BL 4/15/92) [681.1]

12502 Davies, Paul. *About Time: Einstein's Unfinished Revolution* (9–12). 1995, Simon & Schuster $24.00 (0-671-79964-9). Time warps, black holes, Einstein's theory of relativity, quantum time, and imaginary time are among the topics covered. (Rev: BL 3/1/95) [530.1]

12503 Davies, Paul, and John Gribbin. *The Matter Myth: Dramatic Discoveries That Challenge Our Understanding of Physical Reality* (9–12). 1992, Simon & Schuster paper $13.00 (0-671-72841-5). Astrophysicists reveal recent discoveries that make obsolete the traditional scientific notions of how the world works. (Rev: BL 1/15/92*) [530.2]

12504 Falk, Dan. *Universe on a T-Shirt: The Quest for the Theory of Everything* (10–12). Illus. 2004, Arcade $24.95 (1-55970-707-0). An accessible, sometimes humorous history of physics from the Greeks through Newton and Einstein to today's complex thinking including string theory. (Rev: BL 1/1–15/04) [530.14]

12505 Fleisher, Paul. *Liquids and Gases: Principles of Fluid Mechanics* (6–12). Illus. Series: Secrets of the Universe. 2001, Lerner LB $25.26 (0-8225-2988-2). Archimedes's principle, Pascal's law, and Bernoulli's principle are among the topics covered in this volume adapted from an adult title. (Rev: HBG 3/02; SLJ 12/01) [532]

12506 Fleisher, Paul. *Matter and Energy: Principles of Matter and Thermodynamics* (7–12). Illus. Series:

Secrets of the Universe. 2001, Lerner LB $25.26 (0-8225-2986-6). The periodic tables and the basic principles of thermodynamics and matter are explained in conversational language with clear diagrams and simple experiments. (Rev: BL 8/01; HBG 3/02; SLJ 1/02) [530.11]

12507 Gardner, Robert. *Science Projects About Solids, Liquids, and Gases* (6–12). Series: Science Projects. 2000, Enslow LB $19.95 (0-7660-1168-2). The three states of matter are explored through a series of experiments and projects using material and objects found around the house. (Rev: BL 8/00; HBG 3/01; VOYA 2/01) [507]

12508 Gardner, Robert. *Science Projects About the Physics of Toys and Games* (6–12). Series: Science Projects. 2000, Enslow LB $19.95 (0-7660-1165-8). Ordinary toys and games are used to produce a series of projects that are challenging, educational, and fun. (Rev: BL 8/00; HBG 3/01; VOYA 2/01) [507]

12509 Gardner, Robert, and Eric Kemer. *Science Projects About Temperature and Heat* (6–12). Series: Science Projects. 2001, Enslow LB $20.95 (0-89490-534-1). Using clear instructions and detailed drawings, this book outlines a number of activities involving heat and how it is measured. (Rev: BL 3/15/01; HBG 10/01; SLJ 1/95) [536]

12510 Greene, Brian. *The Fabric of the Cosmos: Space, Time, and the Texture of Reality* (10–12). Illus. 2004, Knopf $28.95 (0-375-41288-3). Using simple imagery to illustrate complicated points, the author explains new conceptions of space and time in this book for better physics students. (Rev: BL 2/15/04*) [523.1]

12511 Hawking, Stephen. *The Universe in a Nutshell* (10–12). Illus. 2001, Bantam $35.00 (0-553-80202-X). For advanced students, this renowned scientist explains the basic laws of physics beginning with a brief history of the concept of relativity. (Rev: BL 12/1/01; SLJ 5/02) [530.12]

12512 Jargodzki, Christopher, and Franklin Potter. *Mad About Physics: Braintwisters, Paradoxes, and Curiosities* (10–12). Illus. 2000, Wiley paper $16.95 (0-471-56961-5). Using a question-and-answer format, this book deals with 397 questions, from the sublime to the ridiculous, about physics. (Rev: BL 11/15/00) [530]

12513 Motz, Lloyd, and Jefferson Hane Weaver. *The Story of Physics* (10–12). Illus. 1989, Plenum $24.50 (0-306-43076-2). A clearly written history of physics that explores such topics as Newton's contributions, optics, relativity, and quantum mechanics. (Rev: BL 5/1/89) [530]

12514 Richards, E. G. *Mapping Time: The Calendar and Its History* (9–12). 1999, Oxford paper $16.95 (0-19-286205-7). After a general introduction to astronomy and time-measuring devices, this account

focuses on calendar systems from prehistory to the present. [529]

12515 Ward, Mark. *Beyond Chaos: The Underlying Theory Behind Life, the Universe and Everything* (11–12). 2002, St. Martin's $24.95 (0-312-27489-0). Ward traces the rise of self-organizing criticality (SOC) as a serious physics discipline and discusses SOC's role in such diverse phenomena as fractals, heartbeats, and DNA. (Rev: BL 7/02) [003.7]

Energy and Motion

General and Miscellaneous

12516 Goodstein, David. *Out of Gas: The End of the Age of Oil* (10–12). Illus. 2004, Norton $21.00 (0-393-05857-3). Goodstein issues a warning about the impending depletion of oil reserves and a plea for accelerated research into energy alternatives. (Rev: BL 12/1/03) [022]

12517 Jacobs, Linda. *Letting Off Steam: The Story of Geothermal Energy* (7–12). Illus. 1989, Carolrhoda LB $21.27 (0-87614-300-1). A lucid account that tells about the sources and the use of geothermal energy. (Rev: BL 9/15/89; SLJ 9/89) [333.8]

12518 Kaufman, Allan. *Exploring Solar Energy: Principles and Projects* (9–12). 1989, Prakken paper $8.95 (0-911168-60-5). An account that explains the three aspects of solar energy and gives eight projects of varying difficulty and sophistication. (Rev: BR 5–6/90) [621.47]

12519 Morgan, Sally. *Alternative Energy Sources* (7–10). Illus. Series: Science at the Edge. 2002, Heinemann LB $27.86 (1-40340-322-8). A discussion of alternatives to fossil fuels and the respective advantages of wind, solar, geothermal, nuclear, and other sources of energy. (Rev: HBG 3/03; SLJ 1/03) [333.79]

12520 Smil, Vaclav. *Energies: An Illustrated Guide to the Biosphere and Civilization* (11–12). Illus. 1998, MIT $25.00 (0-262-19410-4). An information-packed survey of energy sources and the various means humans have used to tap into that power; for advanced science students. (Rev: BL 12/1/98) [531]

12521 Snedden, Robert. *Energy Alternatives* (6–10). Illus. Series: Essential Energy. 2001, Heinemann LB $24.22 (1-57572-441-3). Alternatives to fossil fuels are presented in brief but detailed spreads, with discussion of possible future energy solutions. (Rev: BL 1/1–15/02) [333.79]

Nuclear Energy

12522 Daley, Michael J. *Nuclear Power: Promise or Peril?* (7–12). Illus. Series: Pro/Con Issues. 1997,

Lerner LB $30.35 (0-8225-2611-5). This book examines conflicting opinions about nuclear power, the possibility of nuclear accidents, the demand for energy, and the problems involving storage of nuclear waste. (Rev: BL 11/1/97; SLJ 12/97) [333.792]

12523 Galperin, Anne. *Nuclear Energy/Nuclear Waste* (9–12). 1991, Chelsea LB $19.95 (0-7910-1585-8). The pros and cons of nuclear energy are examined, along with the political and technological problems of radioactive waste disposal. (Rev: BL 2/1/92) [333.792]

12524 Hampton, Wilborn. *Meltdown: A Race Against Nuclear Disaster at Three Mile Island: A Reporter's Story* (7–12). Illus. 2001, Candlewick $19.99 (0-7636-0715-0). Reporter Hampton gives an exciting account of the disaster at Three Mile Island, with details of the development and dangers of nuclear power. (Rev: BL 1/1–15/02; HB 1–2/02; HBG 3/02; SLJ 11/01*; VOYA 2/02) [363.17]

12525 Kidd, J. S., and Renee A. Kidd. *Quarks and Sparks: The Story of Nuclear Power* (7–12). 1999, Facts on File $25.00 (0-8160-3587-3). A history of the development of nuclear power, with good coverage of the nuclear race during World War II and contemporary uses and problems. (Rev: BL 8/99; VOYA 10/99) [621.48]

12526 League of Women Voters Education Fund. *The Nuclear Waste Primer: A Handbook for Citizens* (10–12). 1994, Lyons Pr. paper $10.95 (1-55821-226-4). This concise handbook explains what nuclear wastes are, how they are presently being handled, and how to participate in making decisions involving them. (Rev: BL 12/15/85) [363.7]

12527 *Nuclear and Toxic Waste* (9–12). Ed. by Thomas Streissguth. Series: At Issue. 2001, Greenhaven LB $17.96 (0-7377-0476-4); paper $11.96 (0-7377-0475-6). This selection of primary and secondary documents explores various perspectives on the creation, storage, and disposal of wastes generated by the nuclear and chemical industries. (Rev: BL 8/01) [363.72]

12528 Snedden, Robert. *Nuclear Energy* (6–10). Illus. Series: Essential Energy. 2001, Heinemann LB $24.22 (1-57572-444-8). The process of producing nuclear power is presented in brief but detailed spreads, with discussion of the hazards. (Rev: BL 1/1–15/02) [333.79]

Light, Color, and Laser Science

12529 Billings, Charlene W. *Lasers: The New Technology of Light* (9–12). Series: Science Sourcebooks. 1992, Facts on File LB $19.95 (0-8160-2630-0). A concise overview of lasers, their

development, uses, types, and how they are revolutionizing communications, surgery, industry, scientific research, and other fields with coverage ending in 1991. (Rev: BL 1/15/93) [621.36]

12530 Bova, Ben. *The Story of Light* (10–12). 2001, Sourcebooks $24.95 (1-57071-785-0). This is a wonderful introduction to the world of light, its properties, its physics, its functions, its applications, and its role in astronomy. (Rev: BL 9/1/01) [535]

12531 Nassau, Kurt. *Experimenting with Color* (7–10). Series: Venture Books: Science Experiments and Projects. 1997, Watts LB $25.00 (0-531-11327-2). The general properties of light, the electromagnetic spectrum, color vision, and electron interactions are explored in this book of 17 easily performed experiments and projects. (Rev: SLJ 10/97; VOYA 6/98) [535]

Magnetism and Electricity

12532 Davis, L. J. *Fleet Fire: Thomas Edison and the Pioneers of the Electric Revolution* (10–12). Illus. 2003, Arcade $25.95 (1-55970-655-4). This very readable history of electricity's development includes anecdotes about and digs at pioneers including Benjamin Franklin, Luigi Galvani, Alessandro Volta, and Thomas Edison. (Rev: BL 6/1–15/03) [621.3]

12533 Fara, Patricia. *An Entertainment for Angels: Electricity in the Enlightenment* (10–12). Illus. 2003, Columbia Univ. Pr. $24.95 (0-231-13148-8). Fara tells the story of electricity's discovery, in the process setting the record straight on the importance of Benjamin Franklin's kite-flying exploits. (Rev: BL 11/15/03) [306.4]

12534 Fleisher, Paul. *Waves: Principles of Light, Electricity, and Magnetism* (6–12). Illus. Series: Secrets of the Universe. 2001, Lerner LB $25.26 (0-8225-2987-4). Optics, electric current, and electromagnetism are among the topics covered in this volume adapted from an adult title. (Rev: HBG 3/02; SLJ 12/01) [539.2]

12535 Gardner, Robert. *Science Projects About Electricity and Magnets* (6–12). Series: Science Projects. 2001, Enslow LB $20.95 (0-89490-530-9). A number of interesting projects about electricity and magnets are presented in a clear text with careful drawings and safety tips. (Rev: BL 3/15/01; HBG 10/01; SLJ 1/95) [537]

12536 Stwertka, Albert. *Superconductors: The Irresistible Future* (6–10). Series: Venture. 1991, Watts paper $22.00 (0-531-12526-2). A description of the history, development, and molecular activity of superconducting materials and an explanation of their potential use. (Rev: BL 6/15/91; SLJ 8/91) [621.3]

Nuclear Physics

12537 Cothran, Helen, ed. *Nuclear Security* (6–12). Series: At Issue. 2000, Greenhaven LB $17.96 (0-7377-0478-0); paper $11.96 (0-7377-0477-2). A look at the proliferation of nuclear weapons and the increased danger of accidents that may coincide with the end of the Cold War. (Rev: BL 1/1–15/01) [355.02]

12538 MacKintosh, Ray, et al. *Nucleus: A Trip into the Heart of Matter* (10–12). 2001, Johns Hopkins Univ. Pr. $29.95 (0-8018-6860-2). An illustrated work that introduces nuclear physics, its important concepts, and such topics as radioactivity and the Big Bang theory. [530]

12539 Silverstein, Ken. *The Radioactive Boy Scout: The True Story of a Boy and His Backyard Nuclear Reactor* (10–12). 2004, Random $22.95 (0-375-

50351-X). In a real-life story buttressed by interviews with its key figure, Silverstein recounts how Detroit-area high school student David Hahn almost succeeded in building a breeder nuclear reactor in his backyard shed. (Rev: BL 12/1/03) [621.48]

12540 Taubes, Gary. *Bad Science: The Short Life and Very Hard Times of Cold Fusion* (9–12). 1993, Random $25.00 (0-394-58456-2). Documents the bizarre 1989 episode of two scientists who announced they had created a sustained nuclear-fusion reaction at room temperature and the ensuing scandal. (Rev: BL 5/15/93*) [539.7]

Sound

12541 Gardner, Robert. *Science Projects About Sound* (6–12). Series: Science Projects. 2000, Enslow LB $19.95 (0-7660-1166-6). The experiments contained in the innovative project book explore the properties of sound and how it travels. (Rev: BL 8/00; HBG 3/01) [507]

Technology and Engineering

General Works and Miscellaneous Industries

12542 Aaseng, Nathan. *Twentieth-Century Inventors* (7–10). Series: American Profiles. 1991, Facts on File $25.00 (0-8160-2485-5). Personal profiles of inventors are combined with historical details to explain the events that influenced the development of such items as plastic, rockets, and television. (Rev: BL 11/1/91; SLJ 11/91) [609.2]

12543 Broderick, Damien. *The Spike: How Our Lives Are Being Transformed by Rapidly Advancing Technologies* (10–12). 2001, Tor $24.95 (0-312-87781-1). The author makes predictions about future advances in technology such as artificial intelligence, and how society's adjustments to these advances can be painless. (Rev: BL 2/15/01) [303.48]

12544 Brown, David E. *Inventing Modern America: From the Microwave to the Mouse* (10–12). Illus. 2001, MIT $29.95 (0-262-02508-6). This lively account introduces 35 inventors and their inventions in fields including medicine, consumer products, transportation, energy, computing, and telecommunications. (Rev: BL 12/1/01) [609.73]

12545 Cardwell, Donald. *The Norton History of Technology* (9–12). Series: Norton History of Science. 1994, Norton paper $19.95 (0-393-31192-9). An overview of humankind's technological progress, from simple tools to computers and satellites, focusing on such key areas as transportation, medicine, and energy. (Rev: BL 8/94) [609]

12546 *CDs, Super Glue, and Salsa Series 2: How Everyday Products Are Made* (5–10). 1996, Gale LB $158.40 (0-7876-0870-X). This two-volume set tells how 30 everyday products are made, including air bags, bungee cords, contact lenses, ketchup, pen-

cils, soda bottles, and umbrellas. (Rev: BR 1–2/97; SLJ 8/97) [658.5]

12547 Christianson, David. *Timepieces: Masterpieces of Chronometry* (10–12). Illus. 2003, Firefly $24.95 (1-55297-654-8). Artistry and evolving technology are both traced in this survey of timekeeping devices from the celestial clock to today. (Rev: BL 12/1/02) [681.1]

12548 Cohen, Leah H. *Glass, Paper, Beans: Revelations on the Nature and Value of Ordinary Things* (10–12). 1997, Doubleday $22.95 (0-385-47819-4). Starting with coffee in a glass cup and a newspaper, the author examines glass production, newspaper printing, and coffee manufacturing, and moves on from there to introduce individuals involved in those fields of work and their relationship to technology and the production economy. (Rev: SLJ 11/97) [620]

12549 Coker, Robert. *Roller Coasters: A Thrill Seeker's Guide to the Ultimate Scream Machines* (10–12). Illus. 2002, Friedman $15.98 (1-58663-172-1). A richly illustrated overview of roller coasters past and present. (Rev: BL 8/02; SLJ 8/02) [791]

12550 Dotz, Warren, et al. *Firecrackers: The Art and History* (10–12). Illus. 2000, Ten Speed paper $19.95 (1-58008-150-9). As well as copious illustrations, this attractive book explains in detail the history of firecrackers and their place in present-day American life. (Rev: BL 6/1–15/00; VOYA 4/01) [662]

12551 Dyson, James. *A History of Great Inventions* (9–12). Illus. 2001, Carroll & Graf $35.00 (0-7867-0903-0). Using many illustrations, this is a fine overview of the history of technology and inventions divided into six time periods. (Rev: BL 11/15/01) [609]

12552 Fox, Roy. *Technology* (9–12). 1985, David & Charles $19.95 (0-7134-3710-3). A survey of the

806

developments in technology from the Industrial Revolution to today's frontiers in computers and atomic energy. (Rev: SLJ 11/85) [600]

12553 Friedel, Robert. *Zipper: An Exploration in Novelty* (9–12). Series: Perspectives. 1994, Norton $23.00 (0-393-03599-9). Describes the people who created and manufactured the zipper, and their marketing struggles and patent wars. (Rev: BL 3/15/94) [609]

12554 *How Things Work in Your Home: And What to Do When They Don't* (9–12). Illus. 1985, Holt paper $22.50 (0-8050-0126-3). After a description of how common machines around the house operate, this book tells how to keep them working properly. (Rev: SLJ 9/85) [621.8]

12555 Ierley, Merritt. *Wondrous Contrivances: Technology at the Threshold* (10–12). Illus. 2002, Clarkson Potter $21.00 (0-609-60836-3). The author discusses modern technology and discusses America's original reactions to such developments as the railroad, the telephone, the typewriter, and contrasts these reactions to current ones concerning the computer, television, etc. (Rev: BL 12/1/01) [609]

12556 *Inventors and Discoverers: Changing Our World* (9–12). Illus. 1988, National Geographic $35.00 (0-87044-751-3). A capsule history of modern technology in words and pictures that highlights major inventions from the steam engine to cameras and computers. (Rev: BL 3/15/89) [609]

12557 Levy, Joel. *Really Useful: The Origins of Everyday Things* (9–12). Illus. 2002, Firefly $39.95 (1-55297-623-8); paper $24.95 (1-55297-622-X). A collection of well-researched facts and anecdotes that will appeal to trivia fans. (Rev: BL 1/1–15/03) [608]

12558 Levy, Matthys, and Richard Panchyk. *Engineering the City* (6–12). Illus. 2000, Chicago Review $14.95 (1-55652-419-6). There are many curriculum connections in this book that includes information and activities relating to electricity, garbage, transportation, and other urban infrastructure issues. (Rev: BL 2/15/01) [624]

12559 Lukas, Paul. *Inconspicuous Consumption: An Obsessive Look at the Stuff We Take for Granted, from the Everyday to the Obscure* (10–12). 1997, Crown paper $12.95 (0-517-88668-5). A look at 105 products on the market, some commonplace, others exotic, and how they are manufactured. (Rev: BL 10/15/96; SLJ 9/97) [608]

12560 Macaulay, David, and Neil Ardley. *The New Way Things Work* (6–12). 1998, Houghton $35.00 (0-395-93847-3). With an emphasis on visual cutaways, this revision of a fascinating 1988 introduction to modern machines now includes more material on computers. (Rev: BL 12/1/98; HBG 9/99; SLJ 12/98) [600]

12561 MacFarlane, Alan, and Gerry Martin. *Glass: A World History* (10–12). Illus. 2002, Univ. of Chicago Pr. $27.50 (0-226-50028-4). The history of glassmaking — and its importance in many areas of our lives — is explored in detail in this fascinating study. (Rev: BL 10/15/02) [666]

12562 McKibben, Bill. *Enough: Staying Human in an Engineered Age* (10–12). 2003, Holt $25.00 (0-8050-7096-6). This fascinating study warns of the dangers of uncontrolled technological advances, focusing in particular on such areas as genetic engineering, robotics, and nanotechnology. (Rev: BL 3/1/03) [303.48]

12563 Marsden, Ben. *Watt's Perfect Engine: Steam and the Age of Invention* (10–12). Illus. 2004, Columbia Univ. Pr. $19.50 (0-231-13172-0). The story of the Scotsman James Watt and his contribution to the development of the steam engine. (Rev: BL 3/1/04) [621.1]

12564 Miller, Ron. *The History of Rockets* (6–10). 1999, Watts LB $25.00 (0-531-11430-9). An appealing mix of scientific principles and stories of experiments gone wrong draw readers into this overview of rockets from the earliest days to possible future models. (Rev: SLJ 4/99) [621.43]

12565 Parker, Steve. *The Random House Book of How Things Work* (6–12). 1991, Random $19.99 (0-679-90908-7); paper $18.00 (0-679-80908-2). This well-illustrated book shows how everyday appliances and gadgets work. (Rev: BL 5/15/91; SLJ 7/91) [600]

12566 *The Seventy Wonders of the Modern World: 1,500 Years of Extraordinary Feats of Engineering and Construction* (10–12). Ed. by Neil Parkyn. Illus. 2002, Thames & Hudson $40.00 (0-500-51047-4). Architectural and engineering wonders from around the world are introduced with photographs and technical, historical, and cultural details. (Rev: BL 12/1/02; SLJ 5/03) [720]

12567 Sobey, Ed. *How to Enter and Win an Invention Contest* (6–12). Illus. 1999, Enslow LB $20.95 (0-7660-1173-9). A book that not only describes how to invent a new product but also tells how to enter it in a local or national competition. (Rev: BL 9/1/99) [607.973]

12568 Sutton, Caroline, and Duncan M. Anderson. *How Do They Do That?* (10–12). 1982, Morrow paper $9.95 (0-688-01111-X). An explanation is given for a variety of present-day achievements. [600]

12569 Vare, Ethlie Ann, and Greg Ptacek. *Patently Female: From AZT to TV Dinners, Stories of Women Inventors and Their Breakthrough Ideas* (9–12). Illus. 2001, Wiley $24.95 (0-471-02334-5). An enjoyable survey of women as inventors which includes the women behind Liquid Paper, the windshield wiper, and the first computer language. (Rev: BL 12/1/01) [609]

12570 Vare, Ethlie Ann, and Greg Ptacek. *Women Inventors and Their Discoveries* (6–10). 1993, Oliver LB $19.95 (1-881508-06-4). A review of women who are known in the world of industry and technology for their unusual inventions. (Rev: BL 10/15/93; SLJ 1/94; VOYA 2/94) [609.2]

12571 *Visions of Technology* (11–12). Ed. by Richard Rhodes. Illus. 1999, Simon & Schuster $30.00 (0-684-83903-2). Public ambivalence toward technological advances is explored in detail in this anthology of diverse opinions held during the 20th century. (Rev: BL 12/15/98) [609]

Building and Construction

12572 Bennett, David. *Skyscrapers: Form and Function* (9–12). 1995, Simon & Schuster $35.00 (0-684-80318-6). A look at the functions and interiors of skyscrapers plus an informative history of their evolution. (Rev: BL 10/15/95) [720]

12573 Hawkes, Nigel. *Structures: The Way Things Are Built* (9–12). 1990, Macmillan $39.95 (0-02-549105-9). An illustrated look at some of the marvels of civil engineering throughout the world. (Rev: BL 1/15/91) [624.09]

12574 History Cadbury, Deborah. *Dreams of Iron and Steel: Seven Wonders of the Nineteenth Century, from the Building of the London Sewers to the Panama Canal* (10–12). 2004, HarperCollins $25.95 (0-00-716306-1). Published as a companion to the Learning Channel TV series of the same name, this volume profiles technological achievements including the Hoover Dam, Panama Canal, and transcontinental railroad. (Rev: BL 12/15/03) [909.8]

12575 Korres, Manolis. *The Stones of the Parthenon* (7–12). Trans. by D. Turner. Illus. 2001, Getty paper $14.95 (0-89236-607-9). The construction of the Parthenon is described in text and detailed drawings in this small-format book, which includes notes, a glossary, and a bibliography. (Rev: BL 2/1/01) [622]

12576 Macaulay, David. *Building Big* (7–12). Illus. 2000, Houghton $30.00 (0-395-96331-1). This companion book to a set of videos explains the problems posed by ambitious construction projects such as tunnels, bridges, dams, domes, and skyscrapers. (Rev: BL 12/15/00* ; HB 1–2/01; HBG 3/01; SLJ 11/00; VOYA 4/01) [720]

12577 Macaulay, David. *Underground* (5–10). 1983, Houghton $18.00 (0-395-24739-X); paper $9.95 (0-395-34065-9). An exploration in text and detailed

drawings of the intricate network of systems under city streets. [624]

12578 Tobin, James. *Great Projects: The Epic Story of the Building of America, from the Taming of the Mississippi to the Invention of the Internet* (10–12). Illus. 2001, Free Pr. $40.00 (0-7432-1064-6). Eight great engineering feats, such as the Hoover Dam, and their creators are highlighted in this book about America's greatest construction projects. (Rev: BL 9/1/01) [609.73]

12579 Vandervort, Don. *Home Magazine's How Your House Works* (9–12). 1995, Ballantine paper $14.00 (0-345-40958-2). The basic elements of a house are analyzed, with material on reading plans, basic tools, paints, lumber, and so forth. [643]

12580 Williams, Trevor Illtyd. *A History of Invention: From Stone Axes to Silicon Chips*. Rev. ed. (9–12). 2000, Checkmark $45.00 (0-8160-4072-9). Organized under broad topics such as agriculture, architecture, and machinery, this history of inventions takes into consideration the political, social, and economic conditions of their time. [609]

Clothing, Textiles, and Jewelry

12581 Ruby, Jennifer. *Underwear* (7–12). Series: Costumes in Context. 1996, Batsford $24.95 (0-7134-7663-X). This is a thoughtful, information-filled, illustrated history of underwear from 1066 through the 1990s. (Rev: SLJ 1/97) [646]

Computers, Automation, and the Internet

12582 Bentley, Peter J. *Digital Biology: How Nature Is Transforming Our Technology and Our Lives* (10–12). 2002, Simon & Schuster $24.00 (0-7432-0447-6). Peter J. Bentley tells how digital-age researchers are taking lessons from Mother Nature in order to better create computer-based systems that replicate natural processes. (Rev: BL 1/1–15/02) [570]

12583 Billings, Charlene W. *Supercomputers: Shaping the Future* (7–12). Series: Science Sourcebooks. 1995, Facts on File $25.00 (0-8160-3096-0). A history of the silicon revolution — focusing on the megamachines that are the most powerful computers in the world. (Rev: BL 10/15/95; SLJ 4/96; VOYA 4/96) [004.1]

12584 Bortz, Fred. *Mind Tools: The Science of Artificial Intelligence* (7–12). 1992, Watts LB $25.00 (0-531-12515-7). A concise overview of the controversy surrounding the science of artificial intelligence and new computer technologies, with material on the field's pioneers. (Rev: BL 11/1/92) [006.3]

12585 Brunner, Laurel. *Introducing the Internet* (9–12). Illus. 1997, Totem paper $10.95 (1-874166-84-6). Though now somewhat out of date, this book gives valuable information on the origins of the Internet, introduces Internet language, servers, URLs, and browsers, and discusses the problems we face when we enter the year 2000. (Rev: SLJ 1/98) [004.6]

12586 Burns, Michael. *Digital Fantasy Painting: A Step-by-Step Guide to Creating Visionary Art on Your Computer* (7–12). Illus. 2002, Watson-Guptill paper $24.95 (0-8230-1574-2). Eye-catching illustrations make this an attractive volume for browsing as well as for use as a manual of graphic design. (Rev: SLJ 3/03; VOYA 2/03) [760]

12587 Cate, Fred H. *The Internet and the First Amendment: Schools and Sexually Explicit Expression* (10–12). 1998, Phi Delta Kappa Educ. Foundation paper $12.00 (0-87367-398-0). A discussion of the complex questions surrounding children's access to the Internet and of the legal issues that come into play. (Rev: SLJ 10/98) [342]

12588 *Computers and the Internet* (11–12). Ed. by Judith Galas. Illus. Series: Examining Pop Culture. 2001, Greenhaven LB $31.20 (0-7377-0861-1); paper $19.95 (0-7377-0860-3). The revolutionary impact of computers and the Internet on contemporary culture is examined in thought-provoking detail. (Rev: BL 10/15/01) [306.48]

12589 Cooper, Brian, and Anna Milner, eds. *The Internet: How to Get Connected and Explore the World Wide Web, Exchange News and Email, Download Software, and Communicate On-Line* (10–12). 1996, DK $16.95 (0-7894-1288-8). Though dated, this is a good introduction to the Internet using Windows 95. (Rev: SLJ 4/97; VOYA 6/97) [001.6]

12590 Cothran, Helen, ed. *The Internet* (7–12). Illus. Series: Opposing Viewpoints. 2002, Gale LB $31.20 (0-7377-0780-1); paper $19.95 (0-7377-0779-8). Essays present conflicting opinions on such topics as the value of the Internet as an educational resource, privacy, and the social benefits/disadvantages of the technology. (Rev: SLJ 8/02) [303.48]

12591 Cozic, Charles P., ed. *The Future of the Internet* (9–12). Series: At Issue. 1997, Greenhaven LB $18.70 (1-56510-659-8); paper $15.57 (1-56510-658-X). The popularity of the Internet and computer networks worldwide has led to businesses and governments proposing many changes and regulations. This book presents various viewpoints, both positive and negative, on these issues as well as on such concerns as invasion of privacy, security matters, excessive Internet use as a behavior disorder, and

the impact of the Internet on the quality of life. (Rev: BL 9/1/97; SLJ 12/97) [004.67]

12592 Cozic, Charles P., ed. *The Information Highway* (9–12). 1996, Greenhaven LB $19.95 (1-56510-375-0); paper $16.20 (1-56510-374-2). Although a few years old, this book still provides a good introduction to the Internet and discusses still-timely questions such as filtering sites for children and who should pay for the infrastructure. (Rev: BL 6/1–15/96; SLJ 3/96) [384.3]

12593 Daisey, Mike. *21 Dog Years: Doing Time at Amazon.com* (10–12). 2002, Free Pr. $23.00 (0-7432-2580-5). In entertaining fashion, a self-confessed slacker describes life inside Amazon.com. (Rev: BL 5/1/02) [381]

12594 Dunn, John M. *The Computer Revolution* (7–10). Series: World History. 2002, Gale LB $27.45 (1-56006-848-5). This account, which quotes many original sources, traces the history of the computer and its effects on our economy and society. (Rev: BL 4/15/02; SLJ 4/02) [004.6]

12595 Fritz, Sandy. *Robotics and Artificial Intelligence* (5–10). Illus. Series: Hot Science. 2003, Smart Apple LB $19.95 (1-58340-364-7). After describing robots' contributions in space, in the workplace, in danger spots, and in medicine, Fritz speculates on the future possibilities. (Rev: BL 12/1/03; HBG 4/04; SLJ 4/04) [629.8]

12596 Gates, Bill, et al. *The Road Ahead* (9–12). 1995, Viking (0-670-77289-5). This is a biography of Bill Gates, a history of computers, and a look into the future. [004.6]

12597 Gay, Martin. *The New Information Revolution: A Reference Handbook* (10–12). 1996, ABC-CLIO LB $39.50 (0-87436-847-2). This guidebook to the Information Revolution gives a detailed chronology, definitions of key words, profiles of important figures, and a large bibliography of print and nonprint sources. (Rev: BR 9–10/97; SLJ 5/97) [004]

12598 Godin, Seth. *The Big Red Fez: How to Make Any Web Site Better* (10–12). 2002, Fireside paper $11.00 (0-7432-2790-5). This slim but information-packed volume offers sound and entertaining advice on jazzing up Web sites — mainly for entrepreneurs but full of tips for teens. (Rev: BL 1/1–15/02) [005.7]

12599 Godwin, Mike. *Cyber Rights: Defending Free Speech in the Digital Age* (10–12). 1998, Times Books $27.50 (0-8129-2834-2). This book explores the issue of freedom of expression on the Internet, presenting all sides, and comes out firmly for protecting First Amendment rights and adopting an anti-censorship stance. (Rev: BL 8/98; SLJ 2/99) [004.6]

12600 Goldberg, Matt, ed. *Tripod's Tools for Life: Streetsmart Strategies for Work, Life — and Every-*

thing Else (10–12). 1998, Hyperion paper $16.00 (0-7868-8332-4). After a general introduction to the Internet, its use, and possible problems, this volume gives irreverent but useful information on such topics as job hunting on the Net, health, cooking, and home finding and furnishing. (Rev: SLJ 1/99) [004.6]

12601 Grady, Sean M. *Virtual Reality: Computers Mimic the Physical World* (7–12). Illus. Series: Science Sourcebooks. 1998, Facts on File $25.00 (0-8160-3605-5). This book provides young readers with a working knowledge of virtual reality, how this technology developed, its uses, drawbacks, and the philosophical questions raised by the manufacture of "reality." (Rev: BL 4/15/98; BR 11–12/98; HBG 3/99; SLJ 7/98) [006]

12602 Graham, Ian. *The Internet: The Impact on Our Lives* (6–10). Illus. Series: 21st Century Debates. 2001, Raintree Steck-Vaughn LB $18.98 (0-7398-3173-9). An absorbing and fact-filled overview of the influence of the Internet on politics and society, with material on issues such as censorship, e-business, and e-crime. (Rev: BR 11–12/01; SLJ 11/01; VOYA 10/01) [303.48]

12603 Graham, Ian. *Internet Revolution* (7–10). Illus. Series: Science at the Edge. 2002, Heinemann LB $27.86 (1-40340-325-2). The author traces the history of the Internet, looks at the ways we use it today, and discusses political and privacy issues. (Rev: HBG 3/03; SLJ 1/03) [004.67]

12604 Green, John. *The New Age of Communications* (10–12). 1997, Holt paper $10.95 (0-8050-4027-7). After a general history of communications, this account focuses on what computers will and will not be able to do in the future. (Rev: SLJ 8/97) [004.6]

12605 Henderson, Harry. *Issues in the Information Age* (7–12). Series: Contemporary Issues. 1999, Lucent LB $27.45 (1-56006-365-3). This work examines troubling questions in the new information age involving censorship on the Internet, loss of privacy, parental prerogatives, and human interaction. (Rev: BR 9–10/99; SLJ 7/99) [004.6]

12606 Judson, Karen. *Computer Crime: Phreaks, Spies, and Salami Slicers* (6–10). Illus. Series: Issues in Focus. 2000, Enslow LB $19.95 (0-7660-1243-3). All kinds of cybercrimes are discussed including hacking, viruses, and computer fraud. (Rev: BL 3/15/00; HBG 9/00) [364.16]

12607 Kurzweil, Ray. *The Age of Spiritual Machines: When Computers Exceed Human Intelligence* (10–12). Illus. 1999, Viking $24.95 (0-670-88217-8). Teenage computer enthusiasts will enjoy the author's vision of the radical ways in which computers will transform our lives over the next century. (Rev: BL 12/1/98) [006.3]

12608 Langford, Duncan. *Internet Ethics* (10–12). 2000, St. Martin's $49.95 (0-312-23279-9). Using material from such disciplines as law, philosophy, and security, this book explores such questions as moral wrongdoing when applied to the Internet. (Rev: BL 7/00) [175]

12609 Lawler, Jennifer. *Cyberdanger and Internet Safety: A Hot Issue* (5–10). Series: Hot Issues. 2000, Enslow LB $21.95 (0-7660-1368-5). As well as introducing the Internet, this account explains how people abuse it with hidden identities, threatening or obscene material, loss of privacy, hacking, con tricks, pranks, and hoaxes. (Rev: HBG 3/01; SLJ 1/01; VOYA 4/01) [004.6]

12610 McComb, Gordon. *The Robot Builder's Bonanza: 99 Inexpensive Robotics Projects* (10–12). Illus. 1987, McGraw-Hill paper $17.95 (0-8306-2800-2). For advanced students, an introduction to robotics plus projects involving many practical applications. (Rev: BL 12/1/87) [629.8]

12611 McCormick, Anita Louise. *The Internet: Surfing the Issues* (5–10). Series: Issues in Focus. 1998, Enslow LB $20.95 (0-89490-956-8). A guide to the history, mechanics, and use of the Internet that also covers such topics as surfing, child pornography, hate groups, and censorship. (Rev: BL 10/1/98; SLJ 12/98) [004]

12612 Menhard, Francha Roffe. *Internet Issues: Pirates, Censors, and Cybersquatters* (6–12). Illus. Series: Issues in Focus. 2001, Enslow LB $20.95 (0-7660-1687-0). Menhard's effective overview of problems concerning filtering, copyright, privacy, and piracy uses clear examples, many of which involve young people. (Rev: BL 2/1/02; HBG 10/02; SLJ 2/02) [384.3]

12613 Morris, Dave, and Leo Hartas. *Game Art: The Graphic Art of Computer Games* (6–12). Illus. 2003, Watson-Guptill paper $29.95 (0-8230-2080-0). A highly visual exploration of the design of today's computer games, with thorough explanations of the artistic techniques involved. (Rev: SLJ 10/03; VOYA 10/03) [794]

12614 Moschovitis, Christos J. P., et al. *History of the Internet: A Chronology, 1843 to the Present* (9–12). 1999, ABC-CLIO $65.00 (1-57607-118-9). This is a chronologically arranged history of the Internet from 1843 to 1998. (Rev: BL 8/99; VOYA 2/00) [004.6]

12615 Naughton, John. *A Brief History of the Future: From Radio Days to Internet Years in a Lifetime* (10–12). Illus. 2000, Overlook $26.95 (1-58567-032-4). In this readable narrative, the author traces the history of the Internet and explains its importance in the study of technology. (Rev: BL 7/00; SLJ 6/01) [621.382]

12616 Nuwere, Ejovi, and David Chanoff. *Hacker Cracker: A Journey from the Mean Streets of*

Brooklyn to the Frontiers of Cyberspace (10–12). 2002, Morrow $24.95 (0-06-621079-8). A fascination with computers and hacking transported Nuwere from an impoverished, crime-ridden New York City neighborhood to a successful high-tech career. (Rev: BL 10/1/02; VOYA 6/03) [005.8]

12617 Owen, Trevor, and Ronald Owston. *The Learning Highway: The Student's Guide to the Internet* (9–12). 1997, Key Porter paper $19.95 (1-55013-905-3). This well-written work explains how students can use the Internet to enhance classroom learning, with extensive material on connecting and searching and chapters detailing projects done on the Internet by different schools, plus exercises and programs at the back of the book. (Rev: SLJ 8/98; VOYA 8/98) [004.6]

12618 Peterson, Ivars. *Fatal Defect: Chasing Killer Computer Bugs* (9–12). 1995, Times Books $25.00 (0-8129-2023-6). Peterson, a reporter for *Science News,* describes the work of "bug hunters," software experts who investigate and analyze computer problems. (Rev: BL 6/1–15/95) [005.3]

12619 Reid, T. R. *The Chip: How Two Americans Invented the Microchip and Launched a Revolution.* Rev. ed. (10–12). Illus. 2001, Random paper $13.95 (0-375-75828-3). The book gives a history of electronics and then focuses on the invention of the microchip by rivals Jack Kilby and Robert Noyce. (Rev: BL 9/1/01) [621.381]

12620 Rothman, Kevin F. *Coping with Dangers on the Internet: Staying Safe On-Line* (7–12). Series: Coping. 2001, Rosen LB $18.95 (0-8239-3201-X). Readers will find practical advice on safe use of Web sites, e-mail, chat rooms, newsgroups, and so forth, with a useful list of acronyms and emoticons. (Rev: SLJ 8/01) [025.04]

12621 Ryan, Ken. *Computer Anxiety? Instant Relief!* (9–12). 1991, Castle Mountain paper $9.95 (1-879925-05-2). Using subtle humor, this work attempts to simplify an intimidating subject for novice users, with definitions of computer terms and illustrations of difficult concepts. (Rev: BL 9/1/91) [004]

12622 Smolan, Rick. *One Digital Day: How the Microchip Is Changing Our World* (10–12). Series: Day in the Life. 1998, Digital Day $40.00 (0-8129-3031-2). The lowly microchip is celebrated in this history that reviews its many uses in computers, automobiles, telephones, refrigerators, medicine, and entertainment. (Rev: BL 5/15/98; SLJ 9/98) [004.6]

12623 Sobey, Ed. *How to Build Your Own Prize-Winning Robot* (9–12). Series: Science Fair Success. 2002, Enslow LB $20.95 (0-7660-1627-7). This account furnishes basic information about robotics and supplies instructions for the construction of a personal robot. (Rev: HBG 3/03) [629.8]

12624 Sunstein, Cass. *Republic.com* (10–12). 2001, Princeton Univ. Pr. $19.95 (0-691-07025-3). The author observes the current communications environment and concludes that imposing some regulations on Web sites is necessary and does not infringe on civil rights. (Rev: BL 2/15/01) [303.48]

12625 Thro, Ellen. *Robotics: The Marriage of Computers and Machines* (7–12). Series: Science Sourcebooks. 1993, Facts on File $25.00 (0-8160-2628-9). Presents this complicated subject in interesting, understandable terms, covering artificial intelligence and the use of robots underground, in factories, and in space exploration. (Rev: BL 7/93) [629.8]

12626 Weiss, Ann E. *Virtual Reality: A Door to Cyberspace* (7–12). Illus. 1996, Twenty-First Century LB $26.90 (0-8050-3722-5). This book describes the development of virtual reality and its accomplishments, applications, and uses, as well as the ethical issues surrounding its development. (Rev: BL 5/15/96*; SLJ 7/96; VOYA 10/96) [006]

12627 Wickelgren, Ingrid. *Ramblin' Robots: Building a Breed of Mechanical Beasts* (7–12). Illus. 1996, Watts LB $23.00 (0-531-11301-9). An exciting history of the development of robots with details on current developments. (Rev: BL 11/15/96; SLJ 1/97) [629.8]

12628 Winters, Paul A. *Computers and Society* (7–12). Series: Current Controversies. 1997, Greenhaven LB $32.45 (1-56510-564-8); paper $21.20 (1-56510-563-X). The articles in this anthology discuss the impact of computers on society and education, as well as problems involving privacy and censorship. (Rev: BL 7/97; SLJ 12/97) [303.48]

Electronics

12629 Grob, Bernard. *Basic Electronics.* 6th ed. (10–12). 1988, McGraw-Hill $95.48 (0-07-025119-3). An introduction to the principles of electronics and their applications in radio, television, and other industrial areas. [621.38]

12630 Guzman, Andres. *33 Fun-and-Easy Weekend Electronics Projects* (10–12). Illus. 1987, TAB $14.95 (0-8306-0261-5); paper $8.95 (0-8306-2861-4). Using fairly simple circuitry, this is a good book for the novice electrician. (Rev: BL 4/15/88) [621.381]

12631 Traister, John E., and Robert J. Traister. *Encyclopedic Dictionary of Electronic Terms* (7–12). Illus. 1984, Prentice Hall $18.95 (0-13-276981-6). All of the basic terms in electronics are explained, usually in fairly simple terms. [621.381]

Telecommunications

12632 Coe, Lewis. *The Telegraph: A History of Morse's Invention and Its Predecessors in the United States* (9–12). 1993, McFarland LB $28.50 (0-89950-736-0). This concise history of the telegraph and its uses focuses on its impact on American society. (Rev: BL 3/1/93) [621.383]

12633 McCormick, Anita Louise. *The Invention of the Telegraph and Telephone* (7–10). Series: In American History. 2004, Enslow LB $20.95 (0-7660-1841-5). The story behind these two great inventions and their impact on society are covered in this volume. (Rev: BL 3/15/04) [621]

12634 Webb, Marcus. *Telephones: Words over Wires* (6–10). Series: Encyclopedia of Discovery and Invention. 1992, Lucent LB $52.44 (1-56006-219-3). Covers the history of the telephone — including fax machines, communication satellites, and deregulation of the telephone industry — and looks to the future and the potential impact of such technologies as fiber optics. (Rev: BL 12/15/92) [621]

12635 Winters, Paul A., ed. *The Information Revolution* (8–12). Series: Opposing Viewpoints. 1998, Greenhaven LB $32.45 (1-56510-801-9); paper $28.75 (1-56510-800-0). This anthology of essays explores issues raised by the advances in telecommunication technology via the telephone, television, and computer, and discusses the impact of these advances on society and education. (Rev: BL 6/1–15/98) [384]

Television, Motion Pictures, Radio, and Recording

12636 Alderman, John. *Sonic Boom: Napster, MP3, and the New Pioneers of Music* (10–12). 2001, Perseus Bks. $26.00 (0-7382-0405-6). This work explores digital-compression technologies, such as Napster and MP3, and discusses their impact on the music business. (Rev: BL 9/1/01) [780.285]

12637 Frantz, John P. *Video Cinema: Techniques and Projects for Beginning Filmmakers* (9–12). 1994, Chicago Review paper $14.95 (1-55652-228-2). This excellent handbook for the beginning video camera filmmaker discusses equipment, techniques, direction, and the finished product. (Rev: BL 11/15/94; SLJ 1/95) [791.43]

12638 Gottfried, Ted. *The American Media* (7–12). Illus. Series: Impact. 1997, Watts LB $24.00 (0-531-11315-9). This book provides a look at the history and present-day conditions of the U.S. media — the personalities, major events, the First Amend-

ment and other important issues, and current trends. (Rev: BL 9/1/97; SLJ 6/97) [302.23]

12639 Hahn, Don. *Animation Magic: A Behind-the-Scenes Look At How an Animated Film Is Made.* Millennium ed. (8–12). 2000, Disney $16.99 (0-7868-3261-4). Traditional cell animation is described as it is used in films, together with a step-by-step description of the development of a film. [791.43]

12640 Hampe, Barry. *Making Documentary Films and Reality Videos* (10–12). 1997, Holt paper $17.95 (0-8050-4451-5). A handy, practical manual for aspiring filmmakers on all aspects of film production, from arriving at an idea to distribution of the final product. (Rev: BL 1/1–15/97; SLJ 3/98) [791]

12641 Hampe, Barry. *Making Videos for Money: Planning and Producing Information Videos, Commercials, and Infomercials* (10–12). 1998, Holt paper $17.95 (0-8050-5441-3). From preshooting planning to postproduction promotion, this manual is filled with practical advice on how to make and market videos. (Rev: SLJ 5/99) [791.45]

12642 Hart, Christopher. *How to Draw Animation* (10–12). 1997, Watson-Guptill (0-8230-2365-6). This is a simple, step-by-step guide to cartooning and creating animation. [741.5]

12643 Lewis, Roland. *101 Essential Tips: Video* (6–12). 1995, DK paper $3.95 (0-7894-0183-5). This small-format book gives sound advice on using camcorders for video production and touches on equipment, techniques, composition, lighting, editing, and audio. (Rev: VOYA 6/96) [621]

12644 Oleksy, Walter. *Entertainment* (6–12). Series: Information Revolution. 1996, Facts on File $25.00 (0-8160-3077-4). An exploration of the revolutionary changes in the entertainment industry, including satellite TV broadcasting, digital wide-screen TV, laser disc players, interactive CD-ROMs, and computer movies. (Rev: BL 2/15/96; SLJ 4/96; VOYA 10/96) [621]

12645 Rickett, Richard. *Special Effects: The History and the Technique* (10–12). Illus. 2000, Watson-Guptill $75.00 (0-8230-7733-0). Many of today's movies rely on special effects and this is a history of how they developed, from trick photography to computer-based graphics. (Rev: BL 10/15/00) [791.43]

12646 *Special Effects* (5–10). 1998, DK paper $17.95 (0-7894-2813-X). Using double-page spreads illustrated with many movie stills, this is a dazzling look at how special effects are produced in movies. (Rev: BCCB 9/98; HBG 9/98; SLJ 6/98) [791.43]

12647 Stavros, Michael. *Camcorder Tricks and Special Effects: Over 40 Fun, Easy Tricks Anyone Can Do!* Rev. ed. (8–12). 1999, Amherst Media $17.95 (0-936262-98-2). This book supplies simple instruc-

tions on how to create special effects using a camcorder and a few props. [778.59]

12648 Wachowski, Larry, et al. *The Art of The Matrix* (9–12). Illus. 2001, Newmarket $60.00 (1-55704-405-8). This is a lavish tome that reproduces 600 storyboards and other types of drawings and also gives a fine running commentary on the first film in the Matrix trilogy. (Rev: BL 2/15/01; SLJ 4/01; VOYA 12/01) [791.43]

Transportation

General and Miscellaneous

12649 Davidson, Janet F., and Michael S. Sweeney. *On the Move: Transportation and the American Story* (10–12). Illus. 2003, National Geographic $35.00 (0-7922-5140-7). In addition to exploring the various forms of transportation that have moved Americans and their goods, this well-illustrated volume also looks at the impact on society of improved freedom of movement. (Rev: BL 12/1/03) [388]

Airplanes, Aeronautics, and Ballooning

12650 Blatner, David. *The Flying Book: Everything You've Ever Wondered About Flying on Airplanes* (10–12). Illus. 2003, Walker $22.00 (0-8027-1378-5). This eminently readable book covers not just the science and technology of air travel but also contains fascinating facts about the human side of flight. (Rev: BL 4/1/03) [387.7]

12651 Bryan, C. D. B. *The National Air and Space Museum* (10–12). Illus. 1988, Abrams $75.00 (0-8109-1380-1). A history of aeronautics and the airplane as reflected in the collection of the National Air and Space Museum. (Rev: BL 12/15/88) [629.13]

12652 Crouch, Tom D. *Wings: A History of Aviation, from Kites to the Space Age* (10–12). Illus. 2003, Norton $29.95 (0-393-05767-4). Information on the commercial side of the aviation industry and the importance of military developments make this survey particularly useful for report writers. (Rev: BL 10/15/03) [629.1309]

12653 Crouch, Tom D., and Peter Jakab. *The Wright Brothers and the Invention of the Aerial Age* (10–12). Illus. 2003, National Geographic $35.00 (0-7922-6985-3). This riveting chronicle of the Wright brothers' lives and their lifelong quest for flight is enriched by 100 archival photographs. (Rev: BL 5/1/03) [629.13]

12654 Dalton, Stephen. *The Miracle of Flight.* Rev. ed. (10–12). 1999, Firefly $40.00 (1-55209-378-6). This discussion of flight and how it is accomplished includes sections on insects and birds as well as manned flight. (Rev: BL 12/1/99; SLJ 4/00) [573.7]

12655 Dick, Ron, and Dan Patterson. *Aviation Century: The Early Years* (8–12). Illus. 2003, Boston Mills $39.95 (1-55046-407-8). This volume rich in photographs, the first in a projected three-volume set, covers aviation to the 1930s. (Rev: BL 2/1/04) [629.13]

12656 Friedrich, Belinda. *The Explosion of TWA Flight 800* (8–10). Series: Great Disasters: Reforms and Ramifications. 2001, Chelsea LB $21.95 (0-7910-6325-9). An account of this tragedy over Long Island in 1996, detailing the recovery efforts, the investigation, and the many theories about the cause of the disaster. (Rev: BR 5–6/02; HBG 10/02; SLJ 5/02) [363.12]

12657 Gaffney, Timothy R. *Air Safety: Preventing Future Disasters* (7–12). Illus. Series: Issues in Focus. 1999, Enslow LB $19.95 (0-7660-1108-9). Efforts being made to improve air safety are covered, with information on recent disasters, on why planes crash, and on how the causes of accidents are determined. (Rev: HBG 4/00; SLJ 2/00) [363.12]

12658 Grant, R. G. *Flight: 100 Years of Aviation* (10–12). Illus. 2002, DK $50.00 (0-7894-8910-4). This lavishly illustrated overview of aviation history highlights more than 300 aircraft and describes great achievements in air travel. (Rev: BL 1/1–15/03) [629.13]

12659 Hallion, Richard P. *Taking Flight: Inventing the Aerial Age from Antiquity Through the First World War* (11–12). Illus. 2003, Oxford $35.00 (0-19-516035-5). Aviation authority Hallion traces developments in the human quest for flight from ancient times through the present. (Rev: BL 4/1/03) [629.13]

12660 Lindbergh, Charles A. *The Spirit of St. Louis* (10–12). 1975, Macmillan $60.00 (0-684-14421-2). An autobiographical account first published in 1954 of the first solo transatlantic flight. [629.13]

12661 Lopez, Donald S. *Aviation: A Smithsonian Guide* (9–12). Series: Smithsonian Guide. 1995, Macmillan $38.00 (0-02-860006-1). Looks at the history of aviation, aviation principles, and personalities with two-page, full-color photographs of famous planes. (Rev: BL 6/1–15/95) [629.13]

12662 Nader, Ralph, and Wesley J. Smith. *Collision Course: The Truth About Airline Safety* (9–12). 1993, TAB $21.95 (0-8306-4271-4). Outlines the development of the commercial aviation industry and examines each aspect of the "system" that controls safety measures and regulations. (Rev: BL 7/93) [363.12]

12663 Ramo, Joshua Cooper. *No Visible Horizon: Surviving the World's Most Dangerous Sport* (10–12). 2003, Simon & Schuster $25.00 (0-7432-2950-9). This riveting celebration of aerial acrobatics describes the techniques, introduces some of the masters of the art, and gives a real feeling for the necessary link between man and machine. (Rev: BL 3/15/03) [797.5]

12664 Ryan, Craig. *The Pre-Astronauts: Manned Ballooning on the Threshold of Space* (9–12). 1995, Naval Institute Pr. $32.95 (1-55750-732-5). A chronicle of the achievements of people involved in the dangerous, manned balloon programs after World War II. (Rev: BL 5/1/95) [629.13]

12665 Sullivan, George. *Modern Fighter Planes* (7–12). Series: Military Aircraft. 1991, Facts on File LB $19.95 (0-8160-2352-2). The stories of 11 fighter planes conceived and tested between 1960 and 1990, with black-and-white photographs and a glossary. (Rev: BL 1/15/92; SLJ 3/92) [358.4]

Automobiles and Trucks

12666 Bradsher, Keith. *High and Mighty: SUVs — the World's Most Dangerous Vehicles and How They Got That Way* (10–12). Illus. 2002, PublicAffairs $28.00 (1-58648-123-1). Bradsher provides interesting fodder for discussions about environmental concerns and the popularity of SUVs. (Rev: BL 10/1/02) [629.2]

12667 Italia, Bob. *Great Auto Makers and Their Cars* (6–10). Illus. Series: Profiles. 1993, Oliver LB $19.95 (1-881508-08-0). This is a history of automobiles with coverage of famous cars and biographies of famous engineers and automakers. (Rev: BL 10/15/93; SLJ 11/93) [629.2]

12668 Lukach, Justin. *Pickup Trucks: A History of the Great American Vehicle* (9–12). 1998, Black Dog & Leventhal $24.98 (1-57912-011-3). The history of America's most popular vehicle, the pickup truck, featuring full-color and vintage black-and-white photographs of antique and newer trucks. (Rev: BL 3/1/99; SLJ 9/99) [629.222]

12669 Makower, Joel. *The Green Commuter* (9–12). 1992, National Press Books paper $9.95 (0-915765-95-0). Tips on how to make a car less damaging to the environment, with lists of environmental organizations, government resources, and addresses of major U.S. car manufacturers. (Rev: BL 2/1/92) [363.73]

12670 Schleifer, Jay. *Corvette: America's Sports Car* (6–10). Series: Cool Classics. 1992, Macmillan LB $13.95 (0-89686-697-1). Presents information on styling, engine development, suspension and braking advances, and other technical matters, with color photographs of various Corvette models. Also use *Ferrari*, *Mustang*, and *Porsche* (all 1992). (Rev: BL 10/15/92) [629.222]

12671 Sikorsky, Robert. *From Bumper to Bumper: Robert Sikorsky's Automotive Tips* (9–12). 1991, TAB $16.95 (0-8306-2134-2). Practical advice on automobile maintenance, driving techniques, buying

tips, and motoring information. (Rev: BL 11/1/91) [629.28]

12672 *Speed: Stories of Survival from Behind the Wheel* (10–12). Ed. by Nate Hardcastle. Illus. 2002, Thunder's Mouth paper $17.95 (1-56025-391-6). A wide assortment of highly readable fiction and nonfiction excerpts and essays that capture the excitement of life behind the wheel. (Rev: BL 6/1–15/02) [796.72]

12673 Swan, Tony. *Retro Ride: Advertising Art of the American Automobile* (9–12). 2002, Collectors $39.95 (1-888054-62-X). America's love affair with the car is celebrated in this oversize collection of advertisements from the 1920s to the 1960s. (Rev: BL 9/1/02) [659.1]

12674 Volpe, Ren. *The Lady Mechanic's Total Car Care for the Clueless* (9–12). 1998, Griffin paper $13.95 (0-312-18733-5). A comprehensive guide (useful not just for women) that introduces all aspects of car care, as well as safety tips, advice on handling accidents, and discussions on buying and selling cars. (Rev: BL 7/98; SLJ 1/99) [629.222]

12675 Willson, Quentin. *Cars: A Celebration* (8–12). Illus. 2001, DK $50.00 (0-7894-8155-3). This large-format, well-illustrated volume is a celebration of automobile types and models found around the world in the past few decades. (Rev: BL 9/15/01) [629.222]

12676 Willson, Quentin. *Classic American Cars* (9–12). 1997, DK $29.95 (0-7894-2083-X). Using full-color photographs and clear text, this book features 60 cars, with historical, technical, and design information about each. (Rev: BL 12/1/97; SLJ 7/98) [629.222]

12677 Willson, Quentin. *The Ultimate Classic Car Book* (10–12). 1995, DK $29.95 (0-7894-0159-2). Over 90 classic cars are featured, each with a description and a color photograph, arranged by decade. (Rev: BL 1/1–15/96; SLJ 6/96) [629.2]

Motorcycles

12678 Davidson, Jean. *Jean Davidson's Harley-Davidson Family Album: 100 Years of the World's Greatest Motorcycle in Rare Photos* (9–12). 2003, Voyageur $19.95 (0-89658-629-4). An eye-catching and informative review of the first 100 years of the Harley-Davidson company. (Rev: BL 2/15/03) [629.227]

12679 Davidson, Willie G. *100 Years of Harley-Davidson* (10–12). Illus. 2002, Little, Brown $65.00 (0-8212-2819-6). An affectionate, oversize and highly illustrated overview of an American icon. (Rev: BL 9/1/02) [629.227]

12680 Garson, Paul, et al. *Born to Be Wild: A History of the American Bike and Biker* (10–12). Illus.

2003, Simon & Schuster $26.00 (0-7432-2523-6). This lavishly illustrated celebration of motorcycles and cycling traces the history of the cycle's development and recounts on-the-road experiences of numerous bikers. (Rev: BL 4/15/03) [629.227]

12681 Wilson, Hugo. *Encyclopedia of the Motorcycle* (10–12). 1995, DK $39.95 (0-7894-0150-9). An encyclopedia that pictures more than 1,000 motorcycles and scooters and lists more than 3,000 manufacturers. (Rev: BL 11/15/95; BR 5–6/96; SLJ 2/96) [796.7]

12682 Wilson, Hugo. *Motorcycle Owner's Manual* (10–12). 1997, DK paper $10.00 (0-7894-1615-8). In addition to basic maintenance, this manual covers some more challenging tasks. [629.28]

Railroads

12683 Ambrose, Stephen. *Nothing Like It in the World: The Men Who Built the Transcontinental Railroad, 1863–1869* (10–12). Illus. 2000, Simon & Schuster $28.00 (0-684-84609-8). From the surveyors and engineers to the Chinese and Irish laborers, this is the story of the men who built the transcontinental railroad and of their mighty accomplishment. (Rev: BL 7/00) [385]

12684 Barter, James. *Building the Transcontinental Railroad* (7–10). Series: World History. 2002, Gale LB $27.45 (1-56006-880-9). Using many quotations from primary and secondary sources, this book gives a fine overview of the triumphs and tragedies associated with building the first railroad across the United States. (Rev: BL 4/15/02; SLJ 5/02) [365]

12685 Blumberg, Rhoda. *Full Steam Ahead: The Race to Build a Transcontinental Railroad* (6–12). Illus. 1996, National Geographic $18.95 (0-7922-2715-8). A realistic account that includes stories of the corruption, greed, exploitation, sacrifice, and heroism that went into the building of the first transcontinental railroad. (Rev: BL 6/1–15/96*; SLJ 8/96*) [365]

12686 Murphy, Jim. *Across America on an Emigrant Train* (6–12). 1993, Clarion $18.00 (0-395-63390-7). A cross-country train trip by Robert Louis Stevenson in 1879 is the backdrop for information on the history of railroads. (Rev: BCCB 1/94; BL 12/1/93*; SLJ 12/93*) [625.2]

12687 Warburton, Lois. *Railroads: Bridging the Continents* (6–10). Series: Encyclopedia of Discovery and Invention. 1991, Lucent LB $52.44 (1-56006-216-9). The history of the nation's railroads. (Rev: BL 4/15/92) [385]

Ships and Boats

12688 Archbold, Rick. *Ken Marshall's Art of Titanic* (11–12). Illus. 1998, Hyperion $40.00 (0-7868-

6455-9). The fateful 1912 inaugural voyage of the *Titanic* is faithfully re-created in this collection of Marschall's artwork. (Rev: BL 11/15/98) [759.13]

12689 Butler, Daniel Allen. *Unsinkable: The Full Story of the RMS Titanic* (8–12). 1998, Stackpole $19.95 (0-8117-1814-X). First-person accounts add to the tension of this narrative. (Rev: BL 5/1/98) [910.4]

12690 Geller, Judith B. *Titanic: Women and Children First: Poignant Accounts of Those Caught Up in the World's Worst Maritime Disaster* (11–12). Illus. 1998, Norton $35.00 (0-393-04666-4). The horrors of the sinking of the *Titanic* are brought to life in this collection of firsthand accounts from women and children who were aboard, accompanied by postcards, brochures, and other materials. (Rev: BL 11/15/98) [910]

12691 Jessop, Violet. *Titanic Survivor* (9–12). Illus. 1997, Sheridan House $23.95 (1-57409-035-6). A stewardess tells a compelling story of her voyage on the *Titanic* — and of her subsequent peril on the sistership *Britannic* during World War I. (Rev: BL 3/15/98) [363.12]

12692 Lynch, Don. *Titanic: An Illustrated History* (9–12). Illus. 1992, Hyperion paper $29.95 (0-7868-8147-X). Stunning illustrations and gripping narrative add to the compelling subject matter. (Rev: BL 3/15/98)

12693 Paine, Lincoln P. *Ships of Discovery and Exploration* (9–12). 2000, Houghton paper $17.00 (0-395-98415-7). This work introduces in text and pictures 125 ships that have played important roles in exploration and science. [910.4]

12694 Philbrick, Nathaniel. *Revenge of the Whale: The True Story of the Whaleship Essex* (6–10). Illus. 2002, Putnam $16.99 (0-399-23795-X). This abridged version of *In the Heart of the Sea* (Viking, 2000) relates for a younger audience the amazing story of the sperm whale that sank a ship in 1820 and the survival of a handful of crewmen. (Rev: BCCB 11/02; HB 1–2/03*; HBG 3/03; SLJ 9/02*) [910]

12695 Quinn, Paul J. *Dusk to Dawn: Survivor Accounts of the Last Night on the Titanic* (10–12). Illus. 1999, Fantail $29.95 (0-9655209-9-4). The author re-creates the sinking of the *Titanic* in an hour-by-hour account that uses survivor testimony and archival photographs. (Rev: BL 1/1–15/00) [910.9]

12696 Stillwell, Paul. *Battleship Arizona: An Illustrated History* (9–12). 1991, Naval Institute Pr. $65.00 (0-87021-023-8). The story of Pearl Harbor's most famous "victim." (Rev: BL 1/15/92) [359.3]

12697 Thorpe, Nick. *8 Men and a Duck: An Improbable Voyage by Reed Boat to Easter Island* (10–12). Illus. 2002, Free Pr. $24.00 (0-7432-1928-7). In this offbeat and entertaining survival story, the author relates his experiences as part of an eight-member crew attempting to replicate the voyage of the *Kon-Tiki*. (Rev: BL 4/15/02) [910]

Weapons, Submarines, and the Armed Forces

12698 Caldicott, Helen. *The New Nuclear Danger: George W. Bush's Military-Industrial Complex* (10–12). 2002, New Pr. paper $16.95 (1-56584-740-7). A disturbing overview of the U.S. nuclear weapons program and weapons manufacturers' tireless lobbying for an expansion of a program that, the author argues, would prove largely ineffective against America's terrorist enemies. (Rev: BL 3/15/02) [627.1]

12699 Clancy, Tom. *Submarine: A Guided Tour Inside a Nuclear Warship* (9–12). 1993, Berkley paper $16.00 (0-425-13873-9). An in-depth look at nuclear submarines, including their history, design, weapons, tactics, crew, and scenarios aimed at showing their continued value. (Rev: BL 9/15/93) [623.812]

12700 Clancy, Tom, and John Gresham. *Special Forces: A Guided Tour of U.S. Army Special Forces* (10–12). Illus. 2001, Berkley paper $16.00 (0-425-17268-6). One of several popular military studies, this focuses on the special forces (sometimes known as the Green Berets) and covers recruitment, training, and missions. (Rev: BL 2/1/01) [356]

12701 Cohen, Daniel. *The Manhattan Project* (7–12). 1999, Millbrook LB $24.90 (0-7613-0359-6). This account captures the spies, intrigue, politics, secrecy, and science that became part of the story of the first atomic bomb. (Rev: BL 7/99; SLJ 9/99) [355.8]

12702 Diagram Group. *Weapons: An International Encyclopedia from 5000 B.C. to 2000 A.D.* (9–12). 1991, St. Martin's paper $21.95 (0-312-03950-6). From the clubs of cavemen to nuclear weapons, this account describes them all in pictures and text. [623.4]

12703 Dockery, Kevin. *Navy SEALs: A History of the Early Years* (10–12). Illus. 2001, Berkley $21.95 (0-425-17825-0). This account traces the history of the Navy SEALs from their beginnings in World War II through the roles they played in the Korean and Vietnam Wars. (Rev: BL 8/01) [359.9]

12704 Dudley, William, ed. *Biological Warfare* (8–12). Series: Opposing Viewpoints. 2003, Gale LB $33.70 (0-7377-1671-1); paper $22.45 (0-7377-1672-X). A collection of essays that explore the seriousness of the threat of biological warfare from terrorists using germs as weapons and how the Unit-

ed States and the world should respond. (Rev: BL 1/1–15/04; SLJ 5/04) [356]

12705 Gay, Kathlyn. *Silent Death: The Threat of Biological and Chemical Warfare* (6–12). Illus. 2001, Twenty-First Century LB $24.90 (0-7613-1401-6). Gay presents a thorough and balanced assessment of the threat presented by biological and chemical weapons, compiled before the Iraq war. (Rev: BL 4/1/01; HBG 10/01; SLJ 4/01) [358]

12706 Godson, Susan H. *Serving Proudly: A History of Women in the U.S. Navy* (10–12). Illus. 2001, Naval Institute Pr. $36.95 (1-55750-317-6). This study spans two centuries and covers the role of women in the navy from the front lines to support personnel. (Rev: BL 10/15/01) [359]

12707 Grady, Sean M. *Explosives: Devices of Controlled Destruction* (6–10). Series: Encyclopedia of Discovery and Invention. 1995, Lucent LB $52.44 (1-56006-250-9). A history of explosives and their use in war and peace through the ages. (Rev: BL 4/15/95) [662]

12708 Hurley, Jennifer A., ed. *Weapons of Mass Destruction* (8–12). Series: Opposing Viewpoints. 1999, Greenhaven LB $32.45 (0-7377-0059-9); paper $21.20 (0-7377-0058-0). This collection of writings explores the possibility of a terrorist attack using weapons of mass destruction, domestic and foreign policies concerning these weapons, and ways to defend the country against such attacks. (Rev: BL 4/15/99) [355.02]

12709 Keegan, John. *Intelligence in War: Knowledge of the Enemy from Napoleon to al-Qaeda* (10–12). Illus. 2003, Knopf $30.00 (0-375-40053-2). Keegan examines the role of intelligence in eight historical military engagements. (Rev: BL 10/15/03) [355.3]

12710 Kelly, Jack. *Gunpowder: Alchemy, Bombards, and Pyrotechnics: The History of the Explosive That Changed the World* (10–12). Illus. 2004, Basic $25.00 (0-465-03718-6). From its invention in China a millennium ago to its last use in battle during our Civil War, this is the history of gunpowder. (Rev: BL 4/15/04) [622]

12711 Landau, Elaine. *The New Nuclear Reality* (6–12). Illus. 2000, Twenty-First Century LB $22.90 (0-7613-1555-1). This account chronicles the post-war growth of countries that have nuclear arms including Russia, North Korea, Pakistan, and India. (Rev: BL 7/00; HBG 9/00; SLJ 9/00) [327.1]

12712 Lehman, John. *On Seas of Glory: Heroic Men, Great Ships, and Epic Battles of the American Navy* (9–12). Illus. 2001, Free Pr. $35.00 (0-684-87176-9). This overview of the 200-year history of the U.S. Navy often touches on overlooked individuals and weapons. (Rev: BL 9/1/01) [359]

12713 Levine, Herbert M. *Chemical and Biological Weapons in Our Times* (8–12). Illus. 2000, Watts

LB $25.00 (0-531-11852-5). Levine looks at weapons of mass destruction, and in particular the sarin attack on the Japanese subway, providing a historical perspective to more recent events. (Rev: BL 1/1–15/01) [358]

12714 Light, Michael. *100 Suns: 1945–1962* (10–12). Illus. 2003, Knopf $45.00 (1-4000-4113-9). The awesome power of a nuclear explosion is conveyed in this collection of photographs — both black-and-white and color — of above-ground atom bomb tests. (Rev: BL 10/1/03*) [355.8]

12715 O'Connell, Robert L. *Soul of the Sword: An Illustrated History of Weaponry and Warfare from Prehistory to the Present* (10–12). Illus. 2002, Free Pr. $35.00 (0-684-84407-9). From flint axes to modern weaponry, this is a detailed, accessible, and well illustrated historical overview. (Rev: BL 9/1/02) [355.82]

12716 Parrish, Thomas. *The Submarine* (9–12). 2004, Viking $29.95 (0-670-03313-8). This work gives a lucid, interesting history of the submarine plus an explanation of its crucial role during World War II and the Cold War. (Rev: BL 5/1/04) [359.9]

12717 Rhodes, Richard. *Dark Sun: The Making of the Hydrogen Bomb* (9–12). 1995, Simon & Schuster $32.95 (0-684-80400-X). Examines the history of the hydrogen bomb, from the race to be the first to develop it to the moral implications of its existence and use. (Rev: BL 7/95*) [623.4]

12718 Rice, Earl. *Weapons of War* (6–12). Series: American War Library: The Vietnam War. 2001, Lucent LB $19.96 (1-56006-719-5). The weapons used during the Vietnam War are highlighted in archival photographs and a text that uses many first-hand accounts. (Rev: BL 3/15/01) [959.704]

12719 Richie, Jason. *Weapons: Designing the Tools of War* (5–10). Illus. 2000, Oliver LB $21.95 (1-881508-60-9). Using separate chapters for different categories of weapons — for example, submarines, battleships, and tanks — this is a history of the

development of weaponry from 300 B.C. to today. (Rev: BL 5/1/00; HBG 10/00; SLJ 8/00) [623]

12720 Ruggero, Ed. *Duty First: West Point and the Making of American Leaders* (10–12). Illus. 2001, HarperCollins $27.50 (0-06-019317-4). This account of life at West Point focuses on a single company of about 150 and how they fare during their first year at the military academy. (Rev: BL 2/1/01) [355]

12721 Sherrow, Victoria. *The Making of the Atom Bomb* (7–10). Series: World History. 2000, Lucent LB $18.96 (1-56006-585-0). A review of the development of the bomb, the decision to use the first one, and continuing work on these weapons. (Rev: BL 6/1–15/00; HBG 9/00; SLJ 9/00) [940.54]

12722 Speakman, Jay. *Weapons of War* (6–12). Series: American War Library: The Persian Gulf War. 2000, Lucent LB $19.96 (1-56006-640-0). This heavily illustrated book covers the weapons that were used during the Persian Gulf War of 1991. (Rev: BL 3/1/01) [956.7]

12723 Streissguth, Thomas. *Nuclear Weapons: More Countries, More Threats* (6–12). Series: Issues in Focus. 2000, Enslow LB $20.96 (0-7660-1248-4). An overview of nuclear weapons, who controls the technology to produce them, and the efforts to control this threat to human survival. (Rev: BL 9/15/00; HBG 3/01) [355.02]

12724 VanDeMark, Brian. *Pandora's Keepers: Nine Men and the Atomic Bomb* (10–12). Illus. 2003, Little, Brown $26.95 (0-316-73833-6). In this look back at the dawn of the nuclear age, the author focuses less on the science involved than on the personal interactions between the scientists responsible for its creation. (Rev: BL 6/1–15/03*) [539.7]

12725 Wilcox, Robert K. *Black Aces High: The Story of a Modern Fighter Squadron at War* (10–12). Illus. 2002, St. Martin's $24.95 (0-312-26916-1). An action-packed account of the exploits of the U.S. Navy's Black Aces fighter squadron during the conflict in Kosovo in 1999. (Rev: BL 9/15/02) [949.703]

Recreation and Sports

Crafts, Hobbies, and Pastimes

General and Miscellaneous

12726 Black, Penny. *The Book of Pressed Flowers* (10–12). Illus. 1988, Simon & Schuster $22.00 (0-671-66071-3). A fine craft book on pressing and arranging dried flowers and other plants. (Rev: BL 6/1/88) [745.92]

12727 Bonnell, Jennifer. *D. I. Y. Girl: The Real Girl's Guide to Making Everything from Lip Gloss to Lamps* (7–12). 2003, Penguin paper $12.99 (0-14-250048-8). Cool crafts — gifts, clothes, and decorations — are introduced in a friendly, conversational text with clear instructions and lists of supplies. (Rev: BL 7/03; SLJ 7/03) [745.5]

12728 Brown, Rachel. *The Weaving, Spinning, and Dyeing Book*. Rev. ed. (10–12). Illus. 1983, Knopf paper $40.00 (0-394-71595-0). Various kinds of weaving techniques and patterns are introduced through 50 different projects. [746.1]

12729 *Candle Making Made Easy* (10–12). Ed. by Susan Penny and Martin Penny. Illus. 2000, David & Charles $12.95 (0-7153-0975-7). Easy-to-follow detailed instructions with accompanying illustrations are provided in this attractive book to produce a dozen types of candles. (Rev: BL 6/1–15/00) [745.59]

12730 Cherry, Raymond. *Leathercrafting: Procedures and Projects*. 5th ed. (9–12). Illus. 1979, Glencoe paper $15.00 (0-02-672700-5). A how-to book that explains the basics of leather work with many sample projects. [745.53]

12731 Crane, Anita Louise. *Decorating with Seashells* (9–12). Illus. 2001, Sterling $27.95 (0-8069-3639-8). Using many photographs, this book features projects using seashells, such as picture frames and drawer pulls. (Rev: BL 6/1–15/01) [745.55]

12732 Ellington, Elisabeth, and Jane Freimiller. *A Year of Reading: A Month-by-Month Guide to Classics and Crowd-Pleasers for You and Your Book Group* (10–12). 2002, Sourcebooks paper $12.95 (1-57071-935-7). Five diverse titles are suggested for each month, with discussion questions and related information. (Rev: BL 10/15/02) [011]

12733 Firestein, Cecily Barth. *Making Paper and Fabric Rubbings: Capturing Designs from Brasses, Gravestones, Carved Doors, Coins, and More* (9–12). 1999, Lark $19.95 (1-57990-104-2). This introduction to the hobby of rubbings explains the basics of using pencil and paper, then tells how to create T-shirts, note paper, and framed pictures from the results. (Rev: SLJ 8/99) [760]

12734 Grossman, Andrea. *Designer Scrapbooks with Mrs. Grossman* (9–12). 2004, Sterling $24.95 (1-4027-1058-5). This is a guide on how to turn one's photographs and other memorabilia into an attractive, personal scrapbook. (Rev: BL 5/1/04*) [745.593]

12735 Harris, David. *The Art of Calligraphy: A Practical Guide to the Skills and Techniques* (7–12). Illus. 1995, DK paper $25.00 (1-56458-849-1). After a brief history of the development of Western writing, this beautifully illustrated book shows how to produce intricate lettering and fanciful human figures. (Rev: BR 3–4/96; SLJ 9/95; VOYA 2/96) [741]

12736 Jans, Martin. *Stage Make-Up Techniques* (9–12). 1993, Players paper $24.00 (0-88734-621-9). A primer of basic makeup techniques, including children's makeup, with detailed illustrations of all aspects of the craft. (Rev: BL 11/1/92) [792]

12737 Jennings, Lynette. *Have Fun with Your Room: 28 Cool Projects for Teens* (6–10). 2001, Simon & Schuster paper $12.00 (0-689-82585-4). The author offers a number of affordable ways to decorate bedrooms, with suggestions for walls, windows, headboards, bulletin boards, and so forth. (Rev: SLJ 11/01)

12738 McCormick, Anita Louise. *Shortwave Radio Listening for Beginners* (9–12). 1993, TAB paper $10.60 (0-8306-4135-1). Explains shortwave reception, profiles major broadcasters, summarizes necessary equipment for hobbyists, and includes tables with band frequencies of stations. (Rev: BL 5/15/93) [621.3841]

12739 Maflin, Andrea. *Easy and Elegant Home Decorating: 25 Stylish Projects for Your Home* (10–12). Illus. 1998, Facts on File $24.95 (0-8160-3829-5). Using supplies available at crafts stores, this book outlines many projects like gilding various objects, stenciling, decoupage, printing, and making mosaics. A separate section of templates is included. (Rev: SLJ 9/98) [745]

12740 Marsh, Don. *Calligraphy* (9–12). Series: First Steps. 1996, North Light $18.99 (0-89134-666-X). This introduction to the art of calligraphy offers an easy-to-understand, step-by-step guide to the basic strokes, as well as such simple projects for beginners as invitations and greeting cards. [745.6]

12741 *Nature Craft* (9–12). 1993, North Light paper $16.99 (0-89134-542-6). Projects in basketry, woodworking, flowers, and gardening, based on the British crafts magazine *Creative Hands*. (Rev: BL 11/15/93; SLJ 1/94) [745.5]

12742 Newman, Frederick. *Mouthsounds* (9–12). 1980, Workman paper $6.95 (0-89480-128-7). This is a guide to making all sorts of interesting sounds including tips on how to be a master at whistling. [620.2]

12743 Olson, Beverly, and Judy Lazzara. *Country Flower Drying* (8–12). 1988, Sterling paper $9.95 (0-8069-6746-3). A concise manual on raising and drying flowers plus tips on creating arrangements and other uses of dried flowers. (Rev: BR 11–12/88) [745.92]

12744 Reader's Digest, eds. *Reader's Digest Crafts and Hobbies* (9–12). Illus. 1979, Reader's Digest $27.95 (0-89577-063-6). Information on 37 popular crafts including leatherwork, jewelry making, and bookbinding. [745.5]

12745 Ross, John, et al. *The Complete Printmaker: Techniques, Traditions, Innovations*. Rev. ed. (9–12). Illus. 1989, Free Pr. $49.95 (0-02-927371-4). A thorough introduction to various kinds of printmaking, necessary techniques, and the printmaking business — all well illustrated. (Rev: BL 1/15/90) [760]

12746 Sassoon, Rosemary. *The Practical Guide to Calligraphy* (9–12). 1982, Norton paper $10.95 (0-500-27251-4). A useful guide to calligraphy, from England. [745.6]

12747 Shepherd, Margaret. *Learning Calligraphy: A Book of Lettering, Design and History* (9–12). Illus. 1978, Macmillan paper $15.00 (0-02-015550-6). Basic material on calligraphy is logically presented in this volume that is continued in *Using Calligraphy* (1979). [745.6]

12748 Swinfield, Rosemarie. *Stage Makeup Step-by-Step: The Complete Guide to Basic Makeup, Planning and Designing Makeup, Adding and Reducing Age, Ethnic Makeup, Special Effects, Makeup for Film and Television* (8–12). 1994, Betterway $23.99 (1-558703-90-X). The application of theatrical makeup is covered, plus material on how to create special characters and effects through its use. [792]

12749 *Working with Metal* (10–12). Illus. 1990, Silver Burdett LB $20.60 (0-8094-7388-7). With many illustrations and clear text, this volume covers the basic terms, tools, and practices in metalworking. Part of Time-Life's Home Repair and Improvement series. [684]

Clay Modeling and Ceramics

12750 Cosentino, Peter. *The Encyclopedia of Pottery Techniques* (9–12). Illus. 1990, Running $24.95 (0-89471-892-4). Through many color illustrations, both the finished product and step-by-step instructions on how to create pottery are covered. (Rev: BL 9/15/90) [738]

12751 Kenny, John B. *The Complete Book of Pottery Making*. 2nd ed. (7–12). Illus. 1976, Chilton paper $29.95 (0-8019-5933-0). Easily followed instructions with many photographs outline the steps in making pottery. [738.1]

12752 Nelson, Glenn C. *Ceramics: A Potter's Handbook* (9–12). Illus. 1984, Holt paper $64.00 (0-03-063227-7). A basic how-to guide for both the beginning and experienced potter. [738.1]

12753 Nicholson, Libby, and Yvonne Lau. *Creating with Fimo* (6–10). Illus. Series: Kids Can Crafts. 1999, Kids Can $16.99 (1-55074-310-4); paper $6.99 (1-55074-274-4). Using the nontoxic clay called Fimo (available in crafts stores) and the step-by-step instructions in this book, readers can complete 25 projects suitable for experienced crafters, such as making necklaces, earrings, and pins. (Rev: SLJ 5/99) [738]

Cooking

12754 Amari, Suad. *Cooking the Lebanese Way*. Rev. ed. (5–10). Series: Easy Menu Ethnic Cookbooks. 2003, Lerner LB $25.26 (0-8225-4116-5). Revised to include low-fat and vegetarian foods, this introduction to Lebanese cooking contains about 40 recipes, clearly explained and well-illustrated. (Rev: BL 9/15/02; HBG 3/03) [641.5]

12755 Axcell, Claudia, et al. *Simple Foods for the Pack.* Rev. ed. (10–12). Illus. 1986, Sierra Club paper $9.00 (0-87156-757-1). For the outdoor person, here is a collection of recipes and food suggestions that can be either prepared beforehand or cooked over a campfire. [641.5]

12756 Bacon, Josephine. *Cooking the Israeli Way.* Rev. ed. (5–10). Series: Easy Menu Ethnic Cookbooks. 2002, Lerner LB $25.26 (0-8225-4112-2). After a general introduction to Israel, this book discusses cooking terms and ingredients, and then gives a series of tantalizing recipes with clear instructions. (Rev: BL 7/02; HBG 10/02) [641]

12757 Baggett, Nancy. *The All-American Cookie Book* (9–12). Illus. 2001, Houghton $35.00 (0-395-91537-6). Recipe by recipe, the author traces the history of cookies and how they developed into such amazing varieties. (Rev: BL 10/15/01; SLJ 6/02) [641.8]

12758 Baggett, Nancy. *The International Cookie Cookbook* (9–12). Illus. 1988, Stewart, Tabori & Chang $30.00 (1-55670-041-5). An oversize volume of recipes from around the world, many pictured in lovely color photographs. (Rev: BL 3/15/89) [641.8]

12759 Barnard, Tanya, and Sarah Kramer. *How It All Vegan! Irresistible Recipes for an Animal-Free Diet* (10–12). Illus. 2000, Arsenal Pulp paper $15.95 (1-55152-067-2). The vegan regime, which avoids all animal products, is described, with plenty of nutritious, mouth-watering recipes. (Rev: BL 2/15/00) [641.5]

12760 Bayless, Rick, and Deann Groen Bayless. *Authentic Mexican: Regional Cooking from the Heart of Mexico* (9–12). Illus. 1987, Morrow $28.50 (0-688-04394-1). A thorough guide to genuine Mexican cooking that also features bits of history and information about the country's culture. (Rev: BL 4/15/87) [641]

12761 *Better Homes and Gardens New Cook Book.* 11th ed. (9–12). Illus. 1996, Meredith $25.95 (0-696-20188-7); Bantam paper $7.99 (0-553-57795-6). A fine basic cookbook with easy-to-follow instructions and ample illustrations. (Rev: BL 11/1/89; BR 1–2/90) [641.5]

12762 *Betty Crocker's Great Chicken Recipes* (9–12). 1993, Prentice Hall paper $8.00 (0-671-84689-2). Contains more than 100 recipes, color photographs, food ideas, boxed tips, and practical hints. (Rev: BL 3/1/93) [641.6]

12763 *Betty Crocker's Holiday Baking* (9–12). 1993, Prentice Hall paper $8.00 (0-671-86961-2). More

than 100 simple recipes for the holiday season, including nutritional information for classic and revamped favorites. Color photographs and sidebar tips make directions easy to follow. (Rev: BL 10/1/93) [641.7]

12764 *Betty Crocker's Low-Calorie Cooking* (9–12). 1993, Prentice Hall paper $8.00 (0-671-84690-6). Contains more than 100 recipes, color photographs, food ideas, boxed tips, and practical hints. (Rev: BL 3/1/93) [641.5]

12765 *Betty Crocker's New Choices Cookbook* (9–12). 1993, Prentice Hall paper $25.00 (0-671-86767-9). More than 500 health-conscious recipes are labeled as low calorie, low fat, low cholesterol, low sodium, or high fiber to make eating right easy. (Rev: BL 10/1/93) [641.5]

12766 *Betty Crocker's Quick Dinners: In 30 Minutes or Less* (9–12). 1993, Prentice Hall paper $9.95 (0-671-84692-2). Contains more than 100 recipes, color photographs, food ideas, boxed tips, and practical hints. (Rev: BL 3/1/93) [641.5]

12767 *Betty Crocker's Soups and Stews* (9–12). 1993, Prentice Hall paper $8.00 (0-671-86960-4). More than 100 soups and stews are presented, with color photographs, sidebar explanations and tips, and nutritional information. (Rev: BL 10/1/93) [641.5]

12768 Bisignano, Alphonse. *Cooking the Italian Way.* Rev. ed. (5–10). Series: Easy Menu Ethnic Cookbooks. 2001, Lerner $25.26 (0-8225-4113-0); paper $12.75 (0-8225-4161-0). A revised edition that now includes vegetarian and low-fat recipes as well as an expanded introductory section on the country, the people, and the culture. (Rev: HBG 3/02; SLJ 9/01) [641]

12769 Bladholm, Linda. *Latin and Caribbean Grocery Stores Demystified* (10–12). 2002, Renaissance paper $16.95 (1-58063-212-2). A guide to the culinary delights available in the Latin and Caribbean grocery stores that have become more common around the United States in recent years. (Rev: BL 4/15/02) [641.3]

12770 Branson, Ann, ed. *The Good Housekeeping Illustrated Cookbook.* Rev. ed. (9–12). Illus. 1988, Hearst $27.00 (0-688-08074-X). A fine basic cookbook that contains about 1,500 recipes and many illustrations and drawings. (Rev: BL 1/15/89) [641.5]

12771 Brill, "Wildman" Steve. *The Wild Vegetarian Cookbook* (10–12). Illus. 2002, Harvard Common $29.95 (1-55832-214-0). A selection of appetizing vegetarian recipes that use wild foods such as violets, cow parsnips, and sassafras as key ingredients. (Rev: BL 6/1–15/02) [641.5]

12772 Brody, Lora. *Basic Baking: Everything You Need to Know to Get You Started Plus 101 Luscious Desserts That You Can Make* (10–12). 2000,

HarperCollins $25.00 (0-688-16724-1). This useful cookbook is a fine introduction to baking and a guide to creating cakes, pies, muffins, and more. (Rev: BL 10/15/00) [641.5]

12773 Burros, Marian. *Cooking for Comfort: More Than 100 Wonderful Recipes That Are as Satisfying to Cook as They Are to Eat* (10–12). 2003, Simon & Schuster $24.00 (0-7432-3681-5). An appetizing collection of memorable comfort food recipes. (Rev: BL 5/15/03) [641.5]

12774 Caldicott, Chris, and Carolyn Caldicott. *World Food Cafe: Global Vegetarian Cooking* (10–12). Illus. 1999, Bay $28.00 (1-57959-060-8). For vegetarians and readers looking for international recipes, this adult vegetarian cookbook features recipes collected by the authors while they traveled worldwide for 10 years. (Rev: BL 1/1–15/00) [641.5]

12775 Campbell, Regina. *Regina's International Vegetarian Favorites* (10–12). 2003, Berkley paper $18.95 (0-55788-410-2). Campbell draws on traditional recipes from countries around the world to add new interest to vegetarian cooking. (Rev: BL 9/15/03) [641.5]

12776 Chattman, Lauren. *Mom's Big Book of Baking: 200 Simple, Foolproof Recipes for Delicious Family Treats to Get You Through Every Birthday Party, Class Picnic, Potluck, Bake Sale, Holiday, and No-School Day* (9–12). Illus. 2001, Harvard Common $29.95 (1-55832-192-6); paper $16.95 (1-55832-194-2). Pancakes, muffins, scones, and quiches are among the foods included in this guide to baking. (Rev: BL 10/15/01) [641.8]

12777 Child, Julia. *The Way to Cook* (9–12). 1989, Knopf $65.00 (0-394-53264-3); paper $39.95 (0-679-74765-6). Although this is part recipe book, it is more a guide to cooking methods and useful tips. [641.5]

12778 Chung, Okwha, and Judy Monroe. *Cooking the Korean Way.* Rev. ed. (5–10). Illus. Series: Easy Menu Ethnic Cookbooks. 2003, Lerner LB $25.26 (0-8225-4115-7). Tempting recipes and a brief look at where they come from. (Rev: BL 8/88; HBG 3/03; SLJ 9/88) [641.59519]

12779 Claiborne, Craig. *Craig Claiborne's Kitchen Primer* (9–12). 1972, Knopf $12.95 (0-394-42071-3); paper $10.00 (0-394-71854-2). In this handy manual, the well-known chef explains basic cooking techniques and describes important utensils and their uses. [641.5]

12780 Cornell, Kari. *Holiday Cooking Around the World.* Rev. ed. (5–10). Illus. Series: Easy Menu Ethnic Cookbooks. 2002, Lerner LB $25.26 (0-8225-4128-9); paper $7.95 (0-8225-4159-9). Beginning cooks will appreciate the clear instructions and varied options in this appealing book that includes cultural and social information. (Rev: BL 1/1–15/02; HBG 10/02; SLJ 5/02) [641.5]

12781 Coronado, Rosa. *Cooking the Mexican Way.* Rev. ed. (5–10). Series: Easy Menu Ethnic Cookbooks. 2002, Lerner LB $25.26 (0-8225-4117-3). Recipes organized by type of meal are preceded by a section that covers the geography, culture, and festivals and by information on equipment, ingredients, and eating customs. Other titles in this series include *Cooking the East African Way* and *Cooking the Spanish Way* (both 2001). (Rev: HBG 3/02; SLJ 2/02) [641]

12782 Cox, Beverly, and Martin Jacobs. *Spirit of the Harvest: North American Indian Cooking* (9–12). 1991, Stewart, Tabori & Chang $35.00 (1-55670-186-1). Native American experts have helped the authors with recipes of various North American tribes, adapted for modern kitchens and substituting readily available ingredients when required. (Rev: BL 9/15/91) [641.59]

12783 Cunningham, Marion. *Learning to Cook with Marion Cunningham* (9–12). 1999, Knopf $29.95 (0-375-40118-0). Basic cooking techniques are shown and demonstrated, with 150 simple recipes for the beginning cook. (Rev: BL 5/15/99; SLJ 8/99) [641]

12784 Damerow, Gail. *Ice Cream! The Whole Scoop* (9–12). 1991, Glenbridge $26.95 (0-944435-09-2). This collection of recipes is also a thorough survey of all types of frozen desserts and includes technical information on ingredients, techniques, and special equipment. (Rev: BL 9/1/91) [641.8]

12785 Delmar, Charles. *The Essential Cook* (9–12). Illus. 1989, Hill House $24.95 (0-929694-00-7). An excellent handbook on food preparation that includes such subjects as methods of cooking, equipment needed, and shopping tips. (Rev: BR 11–12/90; SLJ 7/89) [641.5]

12786 Diamond, Marilyn. *The American Vegetarian Cookbook: From the Fit for Life Kitchen* (9–12). 1990, Warner $28.00 (0-446-51561-2). As well as many tempting recipes, this book contains much information on nutrition and health. (Rev: BL 8/90) [641]

12787 Dosier, Susan. *Civil War Cooking: The Union* (6–10). 2000, Blue Earth $22.60 (0-7368-0351-3). Recipes accompany information on the foods eaten at the time, with full-color photographs and reproductions. (Rev: BL 8/00; HBG 9/00; SLJ 9/00) [641.5973]

12788 Farrell-Kingsley, Kathy. *The Complete Vegetarian Handbook: Recipes and Techniques for Preparing Delicious, Healthful Cuisine* (10–12). Illus. 2003, Chronicle paper $19.95 (0-8118-3381-X). In addition to a number of simple but appetizing vegetarian recipes, this book offers a guide to the basic techniques of vegetarian cooking. (Rev: BL 5/15/03) [641.5]

12789 Geiskopf-Hadler, Susann, and Mindy Toomay. *The Complete Vegan Cookbook: Over 200 Tantalizing Recipes, Plus Plenty of Kitchen Wisdom for Beginners and Experienced Cooks* (9–12). 2001, Prima Health (0-7615-2951-9). For both the novice and the seasoned cook, this is a fine collection of vegan recipes. [641.5]

12790 Grant, Amanda. *Fresh and Fast Vegan Pleasures: More Than 140 Delicious, Creative Recipes to Nourish Aspiring and Devoted Vegans* (10–12). 2002, Marlowe paper $14.95 (1-56924-535-4). A collection of tasty and nutritious recipes that can be prepared with a minimum of fuss. (Rev: BL 6/1–15/02) [641.5]

12791 Greenwald, Michelle. *The Magical Melting Pot: The All-Family Cookbook That Celebrates America's Diversity* (7–12). Illus. 2003, Cherry $29.95 (0-9717565-0-3). Chefs from ethnic restaurants around the country contribute favorite recipes and cultural explanations. (Rev: SLJ 11/03)

12792 Gunderson, Mary. *Pioneer Farm Cooking* (6–10). 2000, Blue Earth $22.60 (0-7368-0356-4). Recipes accompany information on the foods eaten at the time, with full-color photographs and reproductions. (Rev: HBG 9/00; SLJ 9/00) [394.1]

12793 Hadamuscin, John. *Special Occasions: Holiday Entertaining All Year Round* (9–12). 1988, Harmony $29.00 (0-517-57005-X). A collection of menus involving notable annual events plus interesting background information on the foods associated with them. (Rev: BL 7/88) [642]

12794 Hall, Dede. *The Starving Students' Vegetarian Cookbook: Over 150 Recipes for Quick, Cheap, and Delicious Meals* (9–12). 2001, Warner paper $11.95 (0-446-67675-6). This book offers vegetarian recipes that provide good food at reasonable prices with minimal fuss and equipment. (Rev: BL 6/1–15/01) [641.5]

12795 Hansen, Barbara. *Mexican Cookery* (9–12). Illus. 1988, Price Stern Sloan paper $14.95 (0-89586-589-0). Easily followed recipes and many illustrations highlight this guide to the food of many different regions of Mexico. [641.5]

12796 Hargittai, Magdolna. *Cooking the Hungarian Way.* Rev. ed. (5–10). Series: Easy Menu Ethnic Cookbooks. 2002, Lerner LB $25.26 (0-8225-4132-7). After an introduction to Hungary and its cuisine, there are about 40 clearly presented recipes from appetizers through desserts. (Rev: BL 9/15/02; HBG 3/03) [641.5]

12797 Harris, Jessica. *The Africa Cookbook: Taste of a Continent* (9–12). Illus. 1998, Simon & Schuster $25.00 (0-684-80275-9). Representative recipes from many African countries are accompanied by information on the cultures and the peoples. (Rev: BL 12/15/98) [641.596]

12798 Harrison, Supenn, and Judy Monroe. *Cooking the Thai Way.* Rev. ed. (5–10). Series: Easy Menu Ethnic Cookbooks. 2002, Lerner LB $25.26 (0-8225-4124-6); paper $7.95 (0-8225-0608-4). The country of Thailand is introduced followed by general information on its foods and several easy-to-follow recipes. (Rev: BL 9/15/02) [641.5]

12799 Herbst, Sharon Tyler. *The Food Lover's Tiptionary* (9–12). 1994, Morrow paper $15.00 (0-688-12146-2). Tips on buying, storing, cooking, preparing, and serving food and drink. (Rev: BL 3/15/94) [641.3]

12800 Hess, Susan. *Bi-Lingual American Cooking / Cocina Americana Bilingue: English and Spanish Family Recipes in Side-by-Side Translations / Ingles y Espanol Recetas de Familias con su Traduccion de Lado a Lado* (10–12). 2002, Meta $19.95 (0-9714051-2-3). Basic traditional North American and Mexican recipes are displayed side by side in both English and Spanish. (Rev: BL 6/1–15/02) [641.5]

12801 Hill, Barbara W. *Cooking the English Way.* Rev. ed. (5–10). Series: Easy Menu Ethnic Cookbooks. 2002, Lerner LB $25.26 (0-8225-4105-X). The land and people of England are briefly introduced followed by material on their favorite dishes and easy-to-follow recipes. (Rev: BL 9/15/02) [641.5]

12802 Kaufman, Cheryl Davidson. *Cooking the Caribbean Way.* Rev. ed. (5–10). Illus. Series: Easy Menu Ethnic Cookbooks. 1988, Lerner LB $25.26 (0-8225-4103-3). A variety of dishes featuring the spices and fresh fruits that come from these islands. (Rev: BL 8/88; SLJ 9/88) [641.59729]

12803 Kirlin, Katherine S., and Thomas Kirlin. *Smithsonian Folklife Cookbook* (9–12). 1991, Smithsonian paper $19.95 (1-56098-089-3). The contributors of these historical recipes, which have been demonstrated at the Smithsonian's Festival of American Folklife, show how they reflect bygone cultural mores and eating habits. (Rev: BL 9/15/91; SLJ 2/92) [641.5973]

12804 Lemlin, Jeanne. *Quick Vegetarian Pleasures* (9–12). 1992, HarperCollins paper $17.00 (0-06-096911-3). Tasty, easy-to-prepare meatless recipes ranging from appetizers to entrees. (Rev: BL 3/1/92) [641.5]

12805 Lemlin, Jeanne. *Vegetarian Pleasures: A Menu Cookbook* (9–12). Illus. 1986, Knopf paper $20.00 (0-394-74302-4). From breakfast to dinner, here is a collection of 250 vegetarian recipes that are simple to prepare. (Rev: BL 5/1/86) [641.5]

12806 Levin, Karen A. *Twenty-Minute Chicken Dishes: Delicious, Easy-to-Prepare Meals Everyone Will Love!* (9–12). 1991, Contemporary paper $12.95 (0-8092-4033-5). This collection of quick, simple chicken dishes includes familiar favorites and ethnic specialties. (Rev: BL 12/1/91) [641.6]

12807 Locricchio, Matthew. *The Cooking of China* (7–12). Series: Superchef. 2002, Marshall Cavendish LB $19.95 (0-7614-1214-X). After a general introduction to cooking principles, this book gives a region-by-region overview of the cuisine of China followed by a variety of authentic recipes. (Rev: BL 3/15/03; HBG 3/03; SLJ 2/03) [641]

12808 Locricchio, Matthew. *The Cooking of France* (7–12). Illus. Series: Superchef. 2002, Marshall Cavendish $19.95 (0-7614-1216-6). Recipes are accompanied by details on technique and equipment and by information about the country's traditions and festivals. Also use *The Cooking of Mexico* (2002). (Rev: BL 12/15/02; HBG 3/03; SLJ 2/03) [641.5944]

12809 Locricchio, Matthew. *The Cooking of Italy* (7–12). Series: Superchef. 2002, Marshall Cavendish LB $19.95 (0-7614-1215-8). The different regional cuisines of Italy are described and a number of traditional recipes clearly outlined and colorfully illustrated. (Rev: BL 3/15/03; HBG 3/03; SLJ 4/03) [641]

12810 McCaffrey, Anne, and John Gregor Betancourt, eds. *Serve It Forth: Cooking with Anne McCaffrey* (9–12). 1996, Warner paper $12.99 (0-446-67161-4). This cookbook features tempting recipes from 80 science fiction and fantasy writers, including Starship Trooper Chili and Night of the Living Meatloaf. (Rev: VOYA 4/97) [641]

12811 Medearis, Angela Shelf. *The African-American Kitchen: Cooking from Our Heritage* (9–12). 1994, Dutton paper $23.95 (0-525-93834-6). Contains more than 250 recipes from Africa, the Caribbean, and the United States for such dishes as Tanzanian baked bananas, pumpkin meat loaf, and baked ham. (Rev: BL 9/15/94) [641.59]

12812 Moll, Lucy. *Vegetarian Times Complete Cookbook* (9–12). 1995, Macmillan paper $29.95 (0-02-621745-7). A former editor of *Vegetarian Times* presents more than 600 recipes in what she hopes will be the standard vegetarian cookbook. Includes nutritional breakdowns for each recipe. (Rev: BL 11/15/95) [641.5]

12813 Montgomery, Bertha Vining, and Constance Nabwire. *Cooking the West African Way*. Rev. ed. (5–10). Series: Easy Menu Ethnic Cookbooks. 2002, Lerner LB $25.26 (0-8225-4163-7). An appealing introduction to West African cuisine, with information on the land, people, and culture, and several low-fat and vegetarian recipes. (Rev: HBG 10/02; SLJ 5/02) [641.5966]

12814 Moore, Marilyn M. *The Wooden Spoon Cookie Book: Favorite Home-Style Recipes from the Wooden Spoon Kitchen* (9–12). 1994, Atlantic Monthly $15.00 (0-87113-601-5). Over 100 recipes for cookies and sweets, from animal crackers to rosy rhubarb squares. (Rev: BL 7/94) [641.8]

12815 Munsen, Sylvia. *Cooking the Norwegian Way*. Rev. ed. (5–10). Series: Easy Menu Ethnic Cookbooks. 2002, Lerner LB $25.26 (0-8225-4118-1). A revised edition of an earlier publication that gives information on the country and culture in addition to a selection of typical recipes. (Rev: BL 7/02; SLJ 9/02) [641.59]

12816 Nguyen, Chi, and Judy Monroe. *Cooking the Vietnamese Way* (5–10). Illus. Series: Easy Menu Ethnic Cookbooks. 1985, Lerner LB $25.26 (0-8225-4125-4). The authors introduce the land and people of Vietnam before giving recipes for regional dishes. (Rev: BL 9/15/85; SLJ 9/85) [641]

12817 Norman, Jill. *The Complete Book of Spices* (9–12). 1991, Viking paper $25.00 (0-670-83437-8). Recipes are divided into three levels of difficulty and explore the world of spices. (Rev: BL 3/1/91) [641.3]

12818 Parnell, Helga. *Cooking the German Way*. Rev. ed. (5–10). Illus. Series: Easy Menu Ethnic Cookbooks. 1988, Lerner LB $25.26 (0-8225-4107-6). Includes such treats as Black Forest torte and apple cake. (Rev: BL 8/88) [641.5943]

12819 Parnell, Helga. *Cooking the South American Way*. Rev. ed. (5–10). Series: Easy Menu Ethnic Cookbooks. 2002, Lerner LB $25.26 (0-8225-4121-1). The continent of South America is introduced followed by about 40 clearly presented recipes from several different countries. (Rev: BL 9/15/02; HBG 3/03) [641.5]

12820 Peters, Colette. *Colette's Cakes: The Art of Cake Decorating* (9–12). 1991, Little, Brown $27.50 (0-316-70205-6). A guide to creative cake design and decorating, not just a cake cookbook, with step-by-step instructions for assembling elaborate baked desserts. (Rev: BL 9/1/91) [641.8]

12821 *Pillsbury Doughboy Family Pleasing Recipes: 170 Recipes for Every Night* (10–12). Illus. 2002, Clarkson Potter $19.95 (0-609-60860-6). This collection of easy-fix recipes uses frozen, processed, or prepared foods as key ingredients. (Rev: BL 4/15/02) [641.5]

12822 Plotkin, Gregory, and Rita Plotkin. *Cooking the Russian Way*. Rev. ed. (5–10). Illus. Series: Easy Menu Ethnic Cookbooks. 2002, Lerner LB $25.26 (0-8225-4120-3). Included along with history and information are such recipes as Russian honey spice cake. (Rev: BL 10/15/86) [641.5947]

12823 Raab, Evelyn. *Clueless in the Kitchen: A Cookbook for Teens and Other Beginners* (8–12). Illus. 1998, Firefly paper $12.95 (1-55209-224-0). Cooking and kitchen basics are explained and recipes for good traditional dishes are given in this beginner's cookbook, with an emphasis on fresh ingredients and a section of suggested menus designed for particular guests or occasions. (Rev: BL 7/98; BR 9–10/98; SLJ 9/98) [641.5]

12824 Raab, Evelyn. *The Clueless Vegetarian: A Cookbook for the Aspiring Vegetarian* (9–12). 2000, Firefly $12.95 (1-55209-497-9). Starting with the belief that the reader knows nothing about vegetarian cooking, this is a beginner's book that defines terms and gives basic recipes. (Rev: BL 9/15/00; VOYA 2/01) [641.5]

12825 Rani. *Feast of India* (9–12). 1991, Contemporary paper $16.95 (0-8092-4095-5). This beginner's guide to Indian cuisine includes recipes for traditional Indian curries, kabobs, pilao, and dals, with modern cooking techniques. (Rev: BL 11/15/91) [641.5954]

12826 Robertson, Robin. *The Vegetarian Meat and Potatoes Cookbook* (10–12). Illus. 2002, Harvard Common $29.95 (1-55832-204-3); paper $16.95 (1-55832-205-1). For vegetarians with carnivore tastes, this is a collection of recipes using satisfying meat substitutes, including eggplant and various types of mushrooms. (Rev: BL 6/1–15/02) [641.5]

12827 Roden, Nadia. *Granita Magic* (10–12). Illus. 2003, Artisan $15.00 (1-57965-223-9). Roden celebrates the universal summertime appeal of the granita — a confection of finely crushed ice blended with such diverse ingredients as fruit, berries, vegetables, alcohol, and spices. (Rev: BL 9/15/03) [641.863]

12828 Rombauer, Irma S., and Marion Rombauer Becker. *Joy of Cooking* (7–12). Illus. 1997, Dutton $18.00 (0-452-27923-2); NAL paper $16.00 (0-452-27915-1). First published in 1931, this has through several editions become one of the standard basic American cookbooks. [641.5]

12829 Rosso, Julee, and Sheila Lukins. *The New Basics Cookbook* (10–12). Illus. 1989, Workman $29.95 (0-89480-392-1); paper $19.95 (0-89480-341-7). A beautifully designed cookbook that contains outstanding basic recipes plus many cooking tips. (Rev: BL 3/1/90) [641.5]

12830 Schloss, Andrew. *Almost from Scratch: 600 Recipes for the New Convenience Cuisine* (10–12). 2003, Simon & Schuster $25.00 (0-7432-2598-8). Prepared foods such as ready-made mayonnaise, curry sauce, and pesto are among the ingredients in these time-saving recipes. (Rev: BL 9/15/03) [641.5]

12831 Schwartz, Joan. *Macaroni and Cheese: 52 Recipes, from Simple to Sublime* (10–12). 2001, Villard paper $15.95 (0-375-75700-7). This book includes enough variations on the basic macaroni and cheese recipe to have a different dish each week for a year. (Rev: BL 10/15/01) [641.8]

12832 See, Anik. *A Taste for Adventure: A Culinary Odyssey Around the World* (10–12). Illus. 2002, Seal paper $14.95 (1-58005-062-X). Recipes accompany See's reflections on her travels and on the insight that food can cast on diverse cultures. (Rev: BL 2/15/02) [394.1]

12833 Segan, Francine. *Shakespeare's Kitchen: Renaissance Recipes for the Contemporary Cook* (10–12). Illus. 2003, Random $35.00 (0-375-50917-8). A food historian introduces readers to the delights of Elizabethan England's cuisine with period recipes updated for today's cooks. (Rev: BL 10/15/03) [641.5945]

12834 Shaw, Maura D., and Synda Altschuler Byrne. *Foods from Mother Earth* (6–10). 1994, Shawangunk Pr. paper $9.95 (1-885482-02-7). A vegetarian cookbook in which most of the recipes can be prepared in three or four easy steps. (Rev: BL 1/15/95; SLJ 2/95) [641.5]

12835 Sokolov, Raymond. *The Cook's Canon: 101 Classic Recipes Everyone Should Know* (10–12). Illus. 2003, HarperCollins $25.95 (0-06-008390-5). A former *New York Times* food editor offers 101 classic dishes he feels should be in the repertoire of every self-respecting cook. (Rev: BL 10/15/03) [641.59]

12836 Villios, Lynne W. *Cooking the Greek Way*. Rev. ed. (5–10). Illus. Series: Easy Menu Ethnic Cookbooks. 2003, Lerner LB $25.26 (0-8225-4131-9). The young cook is introduced to the cuisine of Greece, with a chapter covering utensils and ingredient needs and a glossary of basic cooking terms. Recipes are varied and easy to prepare. (Rev: BL 7/02; SLJ 9/02) [641]

12837 Waldee, Lynne Marie. *Cooking the French Way* (5–10). Illus. 2002, Lerner LB $24.26 (0-8225-4106-8). A nicely illustrated introduction to French recipes including breads and sauces. (Rev: HBG 3/02; SLJ 2/02) [641.5944]

12838 Wayne, Marvin A., and Stephen R. Yarnall. *The New Dr. Cookie Cookbook: Dessert Your Way to Health with More Than 150 Scrumptious Cookies, Cakes, and Treats* (9–12). 1994, Morrow paper $14.00 (0-688-12222-1). Using substitutions and deletions for the health conscious, these two doctors present recipes for more than 150 desserts along with nutritional information such as calorie and fat counts. (Rev: BL 12/15/93) [641.8]

12839 Wedman, Betty. *Quick and Easy Diabetic Menus: More Than 150 Delicious Recipes for Breakfast, Lunch, Dinner, and Snacks* (9–12). 1993, Contemporary paper $14.95 (0-8092-3853-5). These recipes are useful for both diabetics and anyone watching his or her weight. (Rev: BL 7/93) [641.5]

12840 Weiner, Leslie, and Barbara Albright. *Quick Chocolate Fixes: 75 Fast and Easy Recipes for People Who Want Chocolate . . . in a Hurry!* (9–12). 1995, St. Martin's paper $6.95 (0-312-13153-4). Describes 75 quick recipes, all loaded with chocolate, including flourless chocolate cake, gorp clusters, brownie cheese cake, and s'mores ice cream pie. (Rev: BL 7/95) [641.6]

12841 Whitman, Sylvia. *What's Cooking? The History of American Food* (7–10). Illus. 2001, Lerner LB $22.60 (0-8225-1732-9). An absorbing account of how American nutrition and tastes have changed over the years, with discussion of methods of food preparation and preservation, the impact of outside forces such as transportation and war, the use of pesticides, and the advent of fast food. (Rev: BCCB 7–8/01; BL 8/01; HBG 10/01; SLJ 7/01; VOYA 8/01) [394.1]

12842 Woods, Sylvia, and Christopher Styler. *Sylvia's Soul Food: Recipes from Harlem's World-Famous Restaurant* (9–12). 1992, Hearst $18.00 (0-688-10012-0). A Harlem restaurateur and her chef present more than 100 recipes from her kitchen, all representative of African American culture. (Rev: BL 10/15/92) [641.59]

12843 Woodward, Sarah. *The Ottoman Kitchen: Modern Recipes from Turkey, Greece, the Balkans, Lebanon, Syria and Beyond* (10–12). Illus. 2002, Interlink $25.00 (1-56656-412-3). The classic cuisine of the Ottoman Empire is revisited in this collection of recipes adapted for today's cooks. (Rev: BL 4/15/02) [641.595]

12844 Yan, Martin. *Martin Yan's Invitation to Chinese Cooking* (10–12). Illus. 2000, Bay paper $24.95 (1-57959-504-9). A fine introduction to Chinese cooking by a celebrity chef. (Rev: BL 4/15/00) [641.5951]

12845 Yu, Ling. *Cooking the Chinese Way*. Rev. ed. (5–10). Illus. Series: Easy Menu Ethnic Cookbooks. 1982, Lerner LB $25.26 (0-8225-4104-1). From appetizers to desserts, with attractive illustrations. (Rev: HBG 3/02) [641.5]

12846 Zamojska-Hutchins, Danuta. *Cooking the Polish Way*. Rev. ed. (5–10). Illus. Series: Easy Menu Ethnic Cookbooks. 2002, Lerner LB $25.26 (0-8225-4119-X). Simple Polish recipes include traditional dishes such as pierogi. Glossary of terms, plus listing of utensils and ingredients used. (Rev: BL 7/02; HBG 10/02) [641.5]

Costume and Jewelry Making, Dress, and Fashion

12847 Aveline, Erick, and Joyce Chargueraud. *Temporary Tattoos* (6–12). Illus. 2001, Firefly LB $19.95 (1-55209-609-2); paper $9.95 (1-55209-601-7). A book of body art designs that provides plenty of practical tips and guidance on the use of cosmetics. (Rev: BL 11/15/01; HBG 3/02; SLJ 11/01; VOYA 4/02) [391.65]

12848 Busch, Marlies. *Friendship Bands: Braiding, Weaving, Knotting* (6–12). Illus. 1997, Sterling paper $7.95 (0-8069-0309-0). A collection of projects to create bracelets, necklaces, decorations, and hair wraps using basic braiding, knotting, and weaving techniques, plus more complicated projects, all with clear, easy-to-follow instructions. (Rev: BL 5/15/98) [746.4222]

12849 Carnegy, Vicky. *Fashions of a Decade: The 1980s* (7–12). Series: Fashions of a Decade. 1990, Facts on File $25.00 (0-8160-2471-5). This elegantly illustrated volume traces styles and trends in fashion for this decade, linking them to social and political developments. There are volumes in this set for each decade from the 1920s to the 1990s. (Rev: BL 2/15/91; SLJ 5/91) [391]

12850 Coles, Janet, and Robert Budwig. *The Book of Beads* (9–12). Illus. 1990, Simon & Schuster $22.95 (0-671-70525-3). An excellent book with many color illustrations on the kinds and nature of various beads and techniques of beadwork. (Rev: BL 8/90) [745.58]

12851 Crabtree, Caroline, and Pam Stallebrass. *Beadwork: A World Guide* (10–12). Illus. 2002, Rizzoli $50.00 (0-8478-2513-2). An excellent introduction to the art of beadwork, this beautifully illustrated guide explores the roots of the art form in far-flung corners of the globe. (Rev: BL 12/15/02*) [745.582]

12852 Feldman, Elane. *Fashions of a Decade: The 1990s* (7–12). Series: Fashions of a Decade. 1992, Facts on File $25.00 (0-8160-2472-3). This is the last of the eight-volume set that traces fashion trends and styles decade by decade from the 1920s through the 1990s. (Rev: BL 12/15/92) [391]

12853 Hunnisett, Jean. *Period Costume for Stage and Screen: Patterns for Women's Dress, 1500–1800* (9–12). Illus. 1991, Players $50.00 (0-88734-610-3). A discussion of historic costume plus over 20 patterns are given. (Rev: BL 3/1/87) [791.43]

12854 Jackson, Sheila. *Costumes for the Stage: A Complete Handbook for Every Type of Play* (9–12). Illus. 1988, New Amsterdam paper $14.95 (0-941533-36-0). A manual for junior and senior high students on creating costumes for their productions. [792]

12855 Kennett, Frances. *Ethnic Dress* (10–12). 1995, Facts on File $40.00 (0-8160-3136-3). Beautiful photographs and text show contemporary fashions and clothing around the world. (Rev: BL 9/1/95; BR 3–4/96; SLJ 5/96) [355.1]

12856 Kenzle, Linda Fry. *Dazzle: Creating Artistic Jewelry and Distinctive Accessories* (9–12). 1995, Chilton paper $19.95 (0-8019-8638-9). How to create 30 design patterns that customize and personalize outfits. (Rev: BL 10/1/95) [745.594]

12857 LaFerla, Jane. *Make Your Own Great Earrings: Beads, Wire, Polymer Clay, Fabric, Found Objects* (10–12). Illus. 1998, Lark $24.95 (1-57990-031-3); paper $14.95 (1-57990-014-3). Thirty-one artists present 45 different projects for making quality earrings, with simple directions, full-color photographs, and a history of earring making. (Rev: SLJ 10/98) [745.594]

12858 Leuzzi, Linda. *A Matter of Style: Women in the Fashion Industry* (7–12). Illus. Series: Women Then — Women Now. 1996, Watts LB $25.00 (0-531-11303-5). The important part women have played in the fashion industry in such roles as designers, patternmakers, merchandisers, buyers, and models. (Rev: BL 3/15/97; SLJ 2/97) [338.4]

12859 Lister, Margot. *Costume: An Illustrated Survey from Ancient Times to the Twentieth Century* (9–12). Illus. 1968, Plays $35.00 (0-8238-0096-2). A survey of dress from ancient times to 1914 with hints on how to make many of these costumes. [391]

12860 Litherland, Janet, and Sue McAnally. *Broadway Costumes on a Budget: Big Time Ideas for Amateur Producers* (7–12). Illus. 1996, Meriwether paper $15.95 (1-56608-021-5). Information about period costumes is given in this helpful manual with instructions for making costumes for nearly 100 Broadway plays and musicals. (Rev: BL 12/1/96) [792.6]

12861 Morgenthal, Deborah. *The Ultimate T-Shirt Book: Creating Your Own Unique Designs* (10–12). Illus. 1998, Lark paper $14.95 (1-57990-017-8). Providing more than 100 examples, this books offers instructions for six decorative techniques: batik, tie-dying, painting, marbling, stamping, and screen printing. (Rev: SLJ 9/98) [746]

12862 O'Donnol, Shirley Miles. *American Costume, 1915–1970: A Source Book for the Stage Costumer* (9–12). Illus. 1982, Indiana Univ. Pr. $39.95 (0-253-30589-6); paper $19.95 (0-253-20543-3). A nicely illustrated guide to 20th-century fashion that emphasizes women's clothes. [792]

12863 O'Keeffe, Linda. *Shoes: A Celebration of Pumps, Sandals, Slippers and More* (10–12). 1996, Workman paper $12.95 (0-7611-0114-4). Divided by types of shoe, such as sandals and boots, this is an illustrated history of footwear and famous shoe designers, filled with quotations about shoes from celebrities, ordinary people, designers, and historical figures, quips, and historical oddities. (Rev: SLJ 4/97) [646]

12864 Parks, Carol. *Make Your Own Great Vests: 90 Ways to Jazz Up Your Wardrobe* (9–12). 1995, Sterling $27.95 (0-8069-0972-2). A showcase for tailoring unusual vests. (Rev: BL 4/15/95) [646.4]

12865 Peacock, John. *The Chronicle of Western Fashion: From Ancient Times to the Present Day* (9–12). 1991, Abrams $39.95 (0-8109-3953-3). A former BBC costume designer offers a quick review of Western fashion from ancient Egypt to 1980. (Rev: BL 6/1/91) [391]

12866 Rowland-Warne, L. *Costume* (5–10). Series: Eyewitness Books. 1992, Knopf $19.00 (0-679-81680-1). This is a history of dress and fashion with brief, clever text and excellent illustrations. (Rev: BL 8/92; SLJ 2/93) [391]

12867 Schnurnberger, Lynn. *Let There Be Clothes* (9–12). 1991, Workman paper $19.95 (0-89480-833-8). An overview of fashion history from cave dwellers to the present. (Rev: BL 1/15/92; SLJ 12/91) [391]

12868 Taylor, Carol. *Creative Bead Jewelry* (9–12). 1995, Sterling paper $18.95 (0-8069-1306-1). This book, with 70 examples from 38 bead artists, is guaranteed to send one off to the nearest bead emporium. (Rev: BL 11/15/95) [745.594]

12869 Walker, Mark. *Creative Costumes for Any Occasion* (9–12). Illus. 1984, Liberty paper $5.95 (0-89709-138-8). Ideas for 35 different easily made costumes as well as instructions and lists of materials needed. (Rev: BL 3/15/85) [391]

12870 Wilcox, R. Turner. *The Dictionary of Costume* (7–12). Illus. 1969, Macmillan $60.00 (0-684-15150-2). First published in 1969, this book describes in words and drawings more than 3,000 articles of clothing. [391]

12871 Wilcox, R. Turner. *Five Centuries of American Costume* (9–12). Illus. 1963, Macmillan $40.00 (0-684-15161-8). Arranged in chronological order, this is a description of what people wore in America from the Vikings to 1960. [391]

12872 Wilcox, R. Turner. *Folk and Festival Costume of the World* (9–12). Illus. 1965, Macmillan $55.00 (0-684-15379-3). An illustrated survey of folk costumes around the world. [391]

12873 Yarwood, Doreen. *The Encyclopedia of World Costume* (9–12). Illus. 1986, Crown $16.99 (0-517-61943-1). A guide to dress from ancient times to the present in text and more than 2,000 drawings. [391]

Dolls and Other Toys

12874 King, Patricia. *Making Dolls' House Furniture* (9–12). 1993, Sterling paper $15.95 (0-946819-24-6). A how-to guide for using found household objects to create furnishings for every room of an English 19th-century dollhouse. (Rev: BL 5/15/93) [745.5]

12875 McClary, Andrew. *Toys with Nine Lives: A Social History of American Toys* (6–12). Illus. 1997, Linnet LB $35.00 (0-208-02386-0). After a general history of toys and how they have changed in format and manufacture through the centuries, this account gives details on eight kinds of toys, including building blocks, dolls, and marbles. (Rev: BL 2/15/97; BR 9–10/97; SLJ 1/98; VOYA 8/97) [790.1]

12876 Wakefield, David. *How to Make Animated Toys* (9–12). Illus. 1987, Sterling paper $17.95 (0-943822-94-7). A how-to guide to making toys with movable parts such as a hopping kangaroo. (Rev: BL 2/1/87) [745.592]

Drawing and Painting

12877 Albert, Greg, and Rachel Wolf, eds. *Basic Watercolor Techniques* (9–12). 1991, North Light paper $16.99 (0-89134-387-3). An illustrated guide to basic painting methods, materials, and how to paint specific subjects, while also encouraging experimentation. (Rev: BL 10/1/91) [751.42]

12878 Allen, Anne, and Julian Seaman. *Fashion Drawing: The Basic Principles* (9–12). 1993, Trafalgar paper $24.95 (0-7134-7096-8). A large-format paperback that explains techniques in this stylized tradition, with traceable examples of clothing and accessories. (Rev: BL 9/15/93) [746.92]

12879 Bohl, Al. *Guide to Cartooning* (6–12). Illus. 1997, Pelican paper $13.95 (1-56554-177-4). Though actually a textbook, this work is a splendid guide to the history of cartooning as well as a practical guide to all the basics. (Rev: BL 9/15/97) [741.5]

12880 Clark, Roberta C. *How to Paint Living Portraits* (10–12). Illus. 1990, North Light $28.99 (0-89134-326-1). A guide with many illustrations on how to do portraits in various media such as watercolor, oil, and charcoal. (Rev: BL 9/1/90) [751.45]

12881 Clinch, Moira. *The Watercolor Painter's Pocket Palette: Instant, Practical Visual Guidance on Mixing and Matching Watercolors to Suit All Subjects* (9–12). 1991, North Light $17.99 (0-89134-401-2). A guide to mixing watercolors. (Rev: BL 1/1/92) [751.422]

12882 *Complete Guide to Drawing and Painting* (9–12). 1997, Reader's Digest $29.95 (0-89577-956-0). An excellent primer to drawing and painting, covering virtually all media from pencil and charcoal to oils and acrylics. [741.2]

12883 Gerberg, Mort. *Cartooning: The Art and the Business*. Rev. ed. (9–12). Illus. 1989, Morrow paper $15.00 (1-55710-017-9). In addition to basic techniques, this book shows how styles differ within the medium (e.g., comics, children's books) and how to sell the finished product. (Rev: BL 3/15/89) [741.5]

12884 Gordon, Louise. *How to Draw the Human Figure: An Anatomical Approach* (7–10). Illus. 1979, Penguin paper $18.00 (0-14-046477-8). This is both a short course on anatomy and a fine manual on how to draw the human body. [743]

12885 Graves, Douglas R. *Drawing Portraits* (10–12). Illus. 1974, Watson-Guptill paper $14.95 (0-8230-1431-2). An excellent guide to portraiture that covers such topics as posing positions, lighting, and drawing faces and hands. [743]

12886 Hart, Christopher. *Drawing on the Funny Side of the Brain* (7–12). Illus. 1998, Watson-Guptill paper $19.95 (0-8230-1381-2). This book describes how to create single and multipanel comic strips, with tips on joke writing, pacing, framing, color, and dialogue. (Rev: BL 7/98) [741.5]

12887 Hart, Christopher. *How to Draw Comic Book Heroes and Villains* (10–12). Illus. 1995, Watson-Guptill paper $18.95 (0-8230-2245-5). An excellent how-to book for older teens, with numerous sketches to demonstrate how to draw, costume, and equip comic book heroes, heroines, and villains. (Rev: BL 1/1–15/96) [741.5]

12888 Hart, Christopher. *Manga Mania: How to Draw Japanese Comics* (9–12). Illus. 2001, Watson-Guptill paper $19.95 (0-8230-3035-0). Hart looks at the techniques for drawing typical Japanese comic characters and animals, providing examples of published *manga* along with an introduction to the various genres of *manga* and an interview with a *manga* publisher. Also use *Anime Mania: How to Draw Characters for Japanese Animation* (2002). (Rev: BL 7/01; SLJ 7/01) [741.5]

12889 Janson, Klaus. *The DC Comics Guide to Penciling Comics* (7–12). Illus. 2002, Watson-Guptill paper $19.95 (0-8230-1028-7). This practical guide for budding comics creators also contains lots of material for comics fans. (Rev: BL 5/1/02) [741.5]

12890 Johnson, Cathy. *Painting Watercolors* (9–12). 1995, North Light paper $18.99 (0-89134-616-3). A book for beginners. (Rev: BL 9/15/95) [751.42]

12891 Lee, Stan, and John Buscema. *How to Draw Comics the Marvel Way* (9–12). 1984, Simon & Schuster paper $15.00 (0-671-53077-1). Step-by-step instructions are given for drawing cartoons like the Hulk and the Thing. [741.5]

12892 Lloyd, Elizabeth Jane. *Watercolor Still Life* (9–12). Series: DK Art School. 1994, DK $16.95 (1-56458-490-9). Practical advice for beginners and amateurs looking for fresh ideas and inspiration. (Rev: BL 12/15/94; SLJ 4/95) [751.42]

12893 McKenzie, Alan. *How to Draw and Sell Comic Strips for Newspapers and Comic Books* (9–12). Illus. 1987, Writer's Digest $19.95 (0-89134-214-1). In addition to giving detailed instructions with examples on how to draw comics, the author gives a history of comics and tells students how to sell their products. (Rev: SLJ 4/88) [741.5]

12894 Moses, Marcia. *Easy Watercolor: Learn to Express Yourself* (10–12). 2003, Sterling $27.95 (0-8069-9542-4). A step-by-step introduction to painting with watercolors, from tools and materials through the final product. (Rev: BL 12/15/02) [751]

12895 Nice, Claudia. *Creating Textures in Pen and Ink with Watercolor* (9–12). 1995, North Light $27.99 (0-89134-595-7). Instructions for rendering specific objects and materials, with a focus on texture. (Rev: BL 9/15/95) [751.4]

12896 Nicolaides, Kimon. *The Natural Way to Draw: A Working Plan for Art Study* (9–12). Illus. 1990, Houghton paper $15.00 (0-395-53007-5). Using illustrations from both old masters and students, this book demonstrates drawing basics. [741.2]

12897 Okum, David. *Manga Madness* (7–12). Illus. 2004, North Light paper $19.99 (1-58180-534-9). This is an excellent guide for would-be cartoonists and *manga* fans with step-by-step directions on how to produce your own art. (Rev: BL 3/15/04) [741.5]

12898 Petrie, Ferdinand, and John Shaw. *The Big Book of Painting Nature in Watercolor* (9–12). Illus. 1990, Watson-Guptill paper $29.95 (0-8230-0499-6). This book contains 135 separate lessons on techniques of painting subjects from nature using watercolors. (Rev: BL 9/1/90) [751.42]

12899 Sarnoff, Bob. *Cartoons and Comics: Ideas and Techniques* (9–12). Illus. 1988, Davis $20.75 (0-87192-202-9). A basic handbook with plenty of examples to help the novice. (Rev: BL 3/15/89) [741.5]

12900 Seslar, Patrick. *Wildlife Painting Step by Step* (9–12). 1995, North Light $28.99 (0-89134-584-1). A guide to the art of careful observation and meticulous execution as well as a celebration of nature. (Rev: BL 9/15/95) [751.4]

12901 Sheppard, Joseph. *Realistic Figure Drawing* (9–12). 1991, North Light paper $19.99 (0-89134-374-1). A guide to using different materials and approaches to capture figures in rest and in motion. (Rev: BL 5/15/91; SLJ 10/91) [751]

12902 Smith, Ray. *The Artist's Handbook* (10–12). Illus. 1987, Knopf $40.00 (0-394-55585-6). A basic manual and guide to all forms of art techniques from etching to oil painting. (Rev: BL 3/15/88) [760]

12903 Smith, Ray. *Drawing Figures* (9–12). Series: DK Art School. 1994, DK $16.95 (1-56458-666-9). Provides many photographs of materials, examples of techniques, and reproductions of portraits of the very young and the old. (Rev: BL 12/15/94; SLJ 4/95) [743]

12904 Smith, Ray. *How to Draw and Paint What You See* (9–12). Illus. 1984, Knopf paper $0.30 (0-394-72484-4). A comprehensive volume that covers drawing and painting in a variety of media including oil, acrylic, and watercolor. [750]

12905 Tate, Elizabeth. *The North Light Illustrated Book of Painting Techniques* (9–12). Illus. 1986, Writer's Digest $29.99 (0-89134-148-X). An alphabetically arranged guide to over 40 painting techniques explained in both text and illustrations. (Rev: BL 4/1/87; SLJ 3/87) [708]

Gardening

12906 Ackerman, Diane. *Cultivating Delight: A Natural History of My Garden* (10–12). 2001, HarperCollins $25.00 (0-06-019986-5). This delightful book by a well-known naturalist describes the changes in her garden over a year and produces a deep understanding of nature and our place in it. (Rev: BL 9/1/01*) [508]

12907 Beard, Henry, and Roy McKie. *Gardening* (9–12). 1982, Workman paper $6.95 (0-89480-200-3). This is a humorous but instructive guide to this pastime. [635]

12908 *Better Homes and Gardens New Garden Book* (9–12). Illus. 1990, Meredith $29.95 (0-696-00042-3). Forty years after its first edition, this remains one of the best general gardening books available. (Rev: BL 4/1/90) [635]

12909 *Better Homes and Gardens Step-by-Step Garden Basics* (9–12). Illus. 2000, Meredith paper $16.95 (0-696-21030-4). Organized by seasons, this colorful book outlines 50 gardening projects and 100 timesaving and weather-related tips, plus a chapter on gardening basics. (Rev: BL 1/1–15/00) [635]

12910 Bremness, Lesley. *The Complete Book of Herbs: A Practical Guide to Growing and Using Herbs* (9–12). 1988, Viking paper $32.95 (0-670-81894-1). This is a directory of over 100 herbs, their characteristics, and cultivation plus 80 recipes for their use. (Rev: BL 1/1/89) [635.7]

12911 Chiusoli, Alessandro, and Maria Luisa Boriani. *Simon and Schuster's Guide to House Plants* (9–12). Illus. 1987, Simon & Schuster paper $14.00 (0-671-63131-4). This guide gives information on 243 plants and how to care for them. (Rev: BL 5/15/87) [635.9]

12912 Damrosch, Barbara. *The Garden Primer* (9–12). Illus. 1988, Workman paper $16.95 (0-89480-316-6). A multitude of facts and advice on all kinds of plants, including houseplants, with detailed information on about 300 specific varieties. (Rev: BL 11/15/88) [635]

12913 Harding, Deborah C. *The Green Guide to Herb Gardening: Featuring the 10 Most Popular Herbs* (9–12). Illus. 2000, Llewellyn paper $12.95 (1-56718-430-8). Basil, chives, oregano, and parsley are among the 10 herbs featured in this gardening manual that also contains 95 tasty recipes. (Rev: BL 1/1–15/00) [635]

12914 Reader's Digest, eds. *Reader's Digest Guide to Creative Gardening* (9–12). Illus. 1987, Reader's Digest $32.00 (0-276-35223-8). A comprehensive, richly illustrated volume that identifies individual plants and gives their growing requirements. [635]

12915 Rich, Libby. *Odyssey Book of Houseplants* (9–12). Illus. 1990, Plant Odyssey paper $19.95 (0-9625702-0-6). A guide to the characteristics and care of 150 different houseplants. (Rev: BL 3/15/90) [635.965]

12916 Smith, Edward C. *The Vegetable Gardener's Bible: Discover Ed's High-Yield Organic System for Growing Your Best Garden Ever!* (9–12). Illus. 2000, Storey $35.00 (1-58017-213-X); paper $24.95 (1-58017-212-1). Deep-bed gardening is explained in this adult manual that also features growing tips, procedures, soil requirements, organic gardening techniques, and an A–Z list of common vegetables and their characteristics. (Rev: BL 1/1–15/00) [635.2]

12917 Smith, Miranda. *Your Backyard Herb Garden: A Gardener's Guide to Growing over 50 Herbs Plus How to Use Them in Cooking, Crafts, Companion Planting, and More* (9–12). 1997, Rodale $27.95 (0-87596-767-1); paper $16.95 (0-87596-994-1). Both gardeners and cooks will find a useful resource in Miranda Smith's guide to growing and using more than 70 kinds of herbs. [635]

12918 Winckler, Suzanne. *Planting the Seed: A Guide to Gardening* (6–10). Illus. 2002, Lerner LB $25.26 (0-8225-0081-7); paper $7.95 (0-8225-0471-5). This slim volume offers a wide range of gardening guidance, with material on organic gardening, the use of native plants, community gardens, and Native American traditions. (Rev: BL 5/1/02; HBG 10/02; SLJ 8/02) [635]

Home Repair

12919 Time-Life Books, eds. *The Home Workshop* (10–12). Illus. 1989, Silver Burdett LB $23.27 (0-8094-6281-8). A basic guide to setting up and maintaining a practical home workshop. This is part of a 36-volume set from Time-Life Books called the Home Repair and Improvement series that covers all sorts of projects from kitchens and bathrooms to porches and patios. [684]

Magic Tricks and Optical Illusions

12920 Churchill, E. Richard. *Optical Illusion Tricks and Toys* (6–10). Illus. 1989, Sterling $12.95 (0-8069-6868-0). A collection of more than 60 optical illusions and tricks that are both fun to perform and instructive in the principles of optics. (Rev: BL 7/89; SLJ 10/89) [152.1]

12921 Ginn, David. *Clown Magic* (9–12). 1993, Piccadilly paper $20.00 (0-941599-21-3). Advice for new clowns, including skits, gags, magic tricks, and specifics on creating and using surprise-filled props. (Rev: BL 4/15/93) [793.8]

12922 Hay, Henry. *The Amateur Magician's Handbook.* 4th ed. (7–12). 1982, NAL paper $5.99 (0-451-15502-5). Tricks for magicians of all ages, at various levels of difficulty. [793.8]

12923 Kaye, Marvin. *The Stein and Day Handbook of Magic* (9–12). Illus. 1973, Scarborough House paper $8.95 (0-8128-6203-1). Good background material on magic and magicians is given as well as a wide variety of magic tricks. [793.8]

12924 Longe, Bob. *World's Greatest Card Tricks* (9–12). 1996, Sterling paper $5.95 (0-8069-5991-6). In addition to explanations of technique, the author gives tips on deception and conversational gambits. [795.4]

12925 Ogden, Tom. *The Complete Idiot's Guide to Magic Tricks* (8–12). 1999, Alpha $18.95 (0-0286-2707-5). A collection of magic tricks using such material as cards, ropes, coins, and rubber bands. [793.8]

12926 Paulsen, Kathryn. *The Complete Book of Magic and Witchcraft.* Rev. ed. (10–12). 1970, NAL paper $5.95 (0-451-15515-7). A history of magic and witchcraft through the ages. [793.8]

12927 Scarne, John. *Scarne on Card Tricks* (9–12). 1986, NAL paper $5.99 (0-451-15864-4). A description and explanation of 150 card tricks. [795.4]

12928 Severn, Bill. *Bill Severn's Best Magic: 50 Top Tricks to Entertain and Amaze Your Friends on All Occasions* (9–12). 1990, Stackpole paper $14.95 (0-8117-2229-5). Instructions on how to perform over 50 tricks are given so simply that even the beginner can master them. (Rev: BL 3/15/90) [793.8]

Masks and Mask Making

12929 Sivin, Carole. *Maskmaking* (9–12). Illus. 1987, Davis $25.95 (0-87192-178-2). A history of maskmaking plus the techniques and materials needed to create your own. (Rev: BL 3/1/87) [731.75]

12930 Smith, Dick. *Dick Smith's Do-It-Yourself Monster Make-Up Handbook* (9–12). Illus. 1985, Imagine paper $9.95 (0-911137-02-5). An Academy Award-winning makeup artist tells how to create several monster disguises and supplies photographs of the finished products. (Rev: BL 11/1/85) [792.027]

Model Making

12931 Spohn, Terry, ed. *Scale Model Detailing: Projects You Can Do* (9–12). 1995, Kalmbach paper $14.95 (0-89024-209-7). Modelers who have already developed their skills will find this a comprehensive resource for honing them. Includes 20 projects from *FineScale Modeler* magazine. (Rev: BL 9/1/95) [745.5]

Paper Crafts

12932 Ayture-Scheele, Zulal. *Beautiful Origami* (9–12). 1990, Sterling paper $12.95 (0-8069-7382-X). This book includes easy-to-follow instructions for 33 origami projects inspired by plants and animals. [736]

12933 Ayture-Scheele, Zulal. *The Great Origami Book* (9–12). Illus. 1987, Sterling $24.95 (0-8069-6600-9); paper $12.95 (0-8069-6640-8). In easy-to-follow instructions and many illustrations, directions for folding eight basic forms and 40 figures are given. (Rev: BL 11/15/87) [736]

12934 Botermans, Jack. *Paper Capers: An Amazing Array of Games, Puzzles, and Tricks* (9–12). Illus. 1986, Holt paper $16.95 (0-8050-0139-5). A collection of 40 different puzzles that can be made from paper or cardboard. (Rev: BL 12/1/86; SLJ 11/86) [745.54]

12935 Botermans, Jack. *Paper Flight* (9–12). 1984, Holt paper $19.95 (0-8050-0500-5). Simple directions are given on how to build 48 paper airplane models. [629.133]

12936 Fox, Gabrielle. *The Essential Guide to Making Handmade Books* (10–12). Illus. 2000, North Light paper $23.99 (1-58180-019-3). From a simple folded tunnel book to several sewn bindings and a slipcase, this book outlines 11 bookmaking projects with detailed instructions and information on materials and equipment. (Rev: BL 8/00) [686.3]

12937 Jackson, Paul. *The Encyclopedia of Origami and Papercraft* (9–12). 1991, Running $24.95 (1-56138-063-6). Provides technical information and instructions for three-dimensional paper creations from simple folded forms to sculptures using papi-er-mache, paper pulp, and castings. (Rev: BL 12/1/91) [736.98]

12938 Kline, Richard. *The Ultimate Paper Airplane* (9–12). Illus. 1985, Simon & Schuster paper $11.00 (0-671-55551-0). A new concept in airplane design is shown in this paper airplane and seven variations. (Rev: BL 9/1/85) [745.592]

12939 Leland, Nita, and Virginia Lee Williams. *Creative Collage Techniques* (9–12). 1994, North Light $28.99 (0-89134-563-9). Step-by-step instructions for creating collages, with lists of materials that can be used, including fabric, photographs, newspaper, ink, and acrylics. (Rev: BL 10/15/94) [702]

12940 Maurer-Mathison, Diane V., and Jennifer Philippoff. *Paper Art: The Complete Guide to Papercraft Techniques* (9–12). 1997, Watson-Guptill $27.50 (0-8230-3840-8). This truly comprehensive guide to papercraft covers virtually every form of the art, from batik, stamping, stenciling, and embossing to papier-mache, weaving, collage, and sculpture. [745.54]

12941 *Paper Craft* (9–12). 1993, North Light paper $16.99 (0-89134-541-8). Taken from the British crafts publication *Creative Hands,* this explains marbling, making boxes and jewelry, and more, with drawings and photographs. (Rev: BL 11/15/93; SLJ 1/94) [745.54]

12942 Schmidt, Norman. *Fabulous Paper Gliders* (6–12). 1998, Tamos $19.95 (1-895569-21-4). A history of glider development and the basic principles of aerodynamics are given along with patterns and step-by-step instructions for 16 gliders, all but one based on actual craft. (Rev: BL 5/15/98; SLJ 6/98) [745.592]

12943 Stoker, Andrew, and Sasha Williamson. *Fantastic Folds* (10–12). 1997, St. Martin's paper $16.95 (0-312-17095-5). This book on paper crafts for experienced hobbyists contains projects such as creating picture frames, bowls, boxes, and various free-standing forms. (Rev: SLJ 2/98) [745.592]

Photography, Video, and Film Making

12944 Alabiso, Vincent, and Chuck Zoeller, eds. *Flash! The Associated Press Covers the World* (10–12). Illus. 1998, Harry N. Abrams $39.95 (0-8109-1974-5). Arranged under subjects of Leadership, War, Struggle, and Moments, this is an impressive collection of memorable Associated Press news photographs that provide a history of 20th-century events and personalities. (Rev: BL 6/1–15/98; SLJ 8/98; VOYA 12/98) [771]

12945 Fitzharris, Tim. *Wild Bird Photography: National Audubon Society Guide* (10–12). 1996, Firefly paper $19.95 (1-55209-018-3). A complete guide to photographing birds, from choosing equipment, lighting, and closeup techniques to the final product, demonstrated with many excellent photographs. (Rev: SLJ 6/97) [771]

12946 Fitzharris, Tim, and Sierra Club Staff. *Close-Up Photography in Nature* (10–12). 1998, Sierra Club paper $20.00 (0-87156-913-2). Nature photography is covered thoroughly, with discussion of terms, equipment, settings, approaches, subjects, and lastly, digital techniques. (Rev: SLJ 8/98) [771]

12947 Grimm, Tom. *The Basic Book of Photography.* Rev. ed. (9–12). Illus. 1985, NAL paper $15.95 (0-452-26096-5). A complete, well-illustrated guide to modern photography. [770]

12948 Grimm, Tom, et al. *The Basic Darkroom Book.* Rev. ed. (9–12). Illus. 1986, NAL paper $9.95 (0-452-25892-8). A useful manual on techniques and skills involved in successful development of film in the darkroom. (Rev: BL 12/15/86) [770]

12949 Hedgecoe, John. *The Book of Photography: How to See and Take Better Pictures* (10–12). Illus. 1984, Knopf paper $29.95 (0-394-72466-6). An introduction to fine picture taking by a prolific writer in the field who has several other recommended titles in print on photography. [770.2]

12950 Henderson, Kathy. *Market Guide for Young Artists and Photographers* (9–12). 1990, Betterway paper $12.95 (1-55870-176-1). A manual for beginners with information on poster and art competitions as well as art submission policies and hints. (Rev: BL 1/1/91; SLJ 3/91) [706.8]

12951 Joyner, Harry M. *Roll 'em! Action! How to Produce a Motion Picture on a Shoestring Budget* (9–12). 1994, McFarland paper $30.00 (0-89950-860-X). Provides advice on producing and directing film and video projects on a low budget. (Rev: BL 3/15/94) [791.43]

12952 Levy, Edmond. *Making a Winning Short: How to Write, Direct, Edit, and Produce a Short Film* (9–12). 1994, Holt paper $15.95 (0-8050-2680-0). Gives advice and instructions on the creation of short films. (Rev: BL 10/1/94) [791]

12953 *101 Essential Tips: Photography* (9–12). 1996, DK paper $4.95 (0-7894-0174-6). A pocket-size book that covers photography essentials both for the beginner and the expert. (Rev: VOYA 6/96) [771]

12954 Ritchin, Fred. *In Our Own Image: The Coming Revolution in Photography: How Computer Technology Is Changing Our View of the World.* 2nd ed. (10–12). Series: Writers and Artists on Photography. 1999, Aperture $24.95 (0-89381-856-9); paper $16.95 (0-89381-857-7). An introduction to

computer graphics, with emphasis on new technology involving photography. [770]

12955 Rowinski, Jim, and Kate Rowinski. *The L.L. Bean Outdoor Photography Handbook* (9–12). Illus. 1999, Lyons Pr. paper $18.95 (1-55821-879-3). The ins and outs of nature photography are presented in an attractive and inviting format. (Rev: SLJ 2/00)

12956 Schaefer, John P. *Basic Techniques of Photography* (9–12). 1992, Little, Brown $50.00 (0-8212-1801-8); paper $35.00 (0-8212-1882-4). An introduction to photography, with information on techniques, film development, and equipment. (Rev: BL 2/15/92) [771]

12957 *Steven Spielberg: Interviews* (10–12). Ed. by Lester D. Friedman and Brent Notbohm. Series: Conversations with Filmmakers. 2000, Univ. Press of Mississippi $45.00 (1-57806-112-1); paper $18.00 (1-57806-113-X). A collection of interviews in which "the most successful filmmaker in history" discusses his art and technique. (Rev: BL 4/15/00) [791.43]

Sewing and Other Needle Crafts

12958 Colton, Virginia, ed. *Reader's Digest Complete Guide to Needlework* (9–12). Illus. 1979, Reader's Digest $30.00 (0-89577-059-8). From applique to rug making, 10 different needlecrafts are presented. [746.4]

12959 Cream, Penelope, ed. *The Complete Book of Sewing: A Practical Step-by-Step Guide to Sewing Techniques* (9–12). Illus. 1996, DK $39.95 (0-7894-0419-2). A practical guide to sewing, including choosing patterns, selection of fabrics, basic stitches and seams, interfacings, and how to make darts, tucks, and pleats. (Rev: SLJ 10/96) [646.4]

12960 Ellen, Alison. *Hand Knitting: New Directions* (10–12). Illus. 2003, Crowood $45.00 (1-86126-534-4). Best suited for advanced knitters, this guide focuses on technique, covering everything from picking the right equipment to learning complex stitch patterns. (Rev: BL 6/1–15/03) [746.432]

12961 Greenoff, Jane. *The Cross Stitcher's Bible* (10–12). Illus. 2000, David & Charles $27.95 (0-7153-0929-3). This book gives clear explanations for the beginner as well as fresh ideas and new projects for the experienced cross stitcher. (Rev: BL 10/1/00) [746.443]

12962 Ham, Catherine. *Knitting: 20 Simple and Stylish Wearables for Beginners* (10–12). Illus. 2003, Lark paper $14.95 (1-57990-351-7). Ideal for would-be or novice knitters, this richly illustrated introduction is loaded with simply written, step-by-step instructions. (Rev: BL 6/1–15/03) [746.43]

12963 Ham, Catherine. *25 Gorgeous Sweaters for the Brand-New Knitter* (10–12). Illus. 2000, Sterling $24.95 (1-57990-172-7). Intended for the beginner as well as the amateur, this charming book offers practical advice and many ways to be creative. (Rev: BL 2/1/01) [746.43]

12964 *The Handbook of Quilting* (10–12). Ed. by Judy Poulos. Illus. 2001, Sally Millner $29.95 (1-86351-280-2). Featuring 27 very unusual patterns, this is a manual for both beginning and advanced quilters. (Rev: BL 11/1/01) [746.46]

12965 Hiatt, June Hemmons. *The Principles of Knitting: Methods and Techniques of Hand Knitting* (10–12). Illus. 1989, Simon & Schuster $35.00 (0-671-55233-3). A comprehensive overview of all sorts of knitting techniques with many explanatory drawings. (Rev: BL 4/1/89) [746.9]

12966 Kooler, Donna. *Cross-Stitch for the First Time* (9–12). 2000, Sterling $19.95 (0-8069-1963-9). After the basics of cross-stitching are explained, several designs are presented in easy-to-follow formats. (Rev: BL 12/15/00) [746.44]

12967 Ladbury, Ann. *The Sewing Book: A Complete Practical Guide* (9–12). Illus. 1990, Random $14.99 (0-517-00193-4). Everything that a beginner needs to know including how to run a sewing machine and details of dressmaking. (Rev: BL 3/1/86) [646.2]

12968 Ligon, Linda, ed. *Homespun, Handknit: Caps, Socks, Mittens, and Gloves* (10–12). Illus. 1987, Interweave paper $15.00 (0-934026-26-2). Simple enough for the beginner, this includes many styles for various age groups. (Rev: BL 2/15/88) [746.9]

12969 Mably, Brandon. *Brilliant Knits: 25 Contemporary Designs* (10–12). Illus. 2001, Taunton $24.95 (1-56158-511-4). This book features 25 designs for the experienced knitter. (Rev: BL 11/1/01) [746.4]

12970 Margaret, Pat Maixner, and Donna Ingram Slusser. *Watercolor Quilts* (9–12). 1993, That Patchwork Place paper $24.95 (1-56477-031-1). A guide to using color values to achieve striking effects in the creation of quilts suitable for wall hanging. (Rev: BL 1/1/94) [746.3]

12971 Marston, Gwen, and Joe Cunningham. *Quilting with Style: Principles for Great Pattern Design* (9–12). 1993, American Quilter's Society $24.95 (0-89145-814-X). Methods of planning the cable, fan, and feather of a quilt are described, with more than 75 color photographs of traditional quilts and traceable, full-size figures. (Rev: BL 11/1/93) [746.9]

12972 Mumm, Debbie. *Quick Country Quilting: Over 80 Projects Featuring Easy, Timesaving Techniques* (9–12). 1991, Rodale $27.95 (0-87857-984-2). An expert quilter offers 80 sewing projects for the enthusiast who has already mastered some of the basic techniques. (Rev: BL 2/1/92) [746.46]

12973 *Reader's Digest Complete Guide to Sewing.* Rev. ed. (8–12). 1995, Reader's Digest $30.00 (0-88850-247-8). As well as equipment and basic techniques, the manual gives step-by-step instructions for making clothes and home furnishings. [646.2]

12974 *Singer: The Complete Photo Guide to Sewing* (9–12). 1999, Creative Pub. Int. $24.95 (0-86573-173-X). As well as the techniques of sewing, this manual covers such topics as patterns, fabrics, and home decorating. [646.2]

12975 Taylor, Kathleen. *Knit One, Felt Too* (9–12). Illus. 2003, Storey paper $18.95 (1-58017-497-3). Twenty-five projects are described in which, after initial knitting, the product is crafted into a different shape through purposeful shrinking. (Rev: BL 1/1–15/04; SLJ 5/04) [746.48]

12976 *Timesaving Sewing* (9–12). Illus. 1987, Contemporary $16.95 (0-86573-215-9). A fine guide to time-saving techniques from shopping for fabrics to producing dresses, draperies, and placemats. (Rev: BL 1/15/88) [646.2]

12977 Zieman, Nancy, and Robbie Fanning. *The Busy Woman's Sewing Book.* Rev. ed. (9–12). Illus. 1988, Open Chain paper $9.95 (0-932086-03-9). Sewing basics are covered in a time-efficient mode. Well-illustrated. (Rev: BL 5/1/88) [646.2]

Stamp, Coin, and Other Types of Collecting

12978 Green, Paul, and Kit Kiefer. *101 Ways to Make Money in the Trading-Card Market* (9–12). 1994, Bonus paper $8.95 (1-56625-002-1). Advice on investing in, as opposed to collecting, trading cards, including information on identifying undervalued items and when to buy and sell. (Rev: BL 3/15/94) [790.132]

12979 Hobson, Burton. *Coin Collecting for Beginners* (9–12). 1982, Wilshire paper $7.00 (0-87980-022-4). This account supplies solid basic information on how to begin and organize a coin collection. [737]

12980 Mackay, James. *The Guinness Book of Stamps, Facts and Feats* (7–12). Illus. 1989, Guinness $34.95 (0-85112-351-1). All sorts of curiosities about postage stamps such as the most valuable, the largest, and so on. (Rev: BL 4/15/89) [769.56]

12981 Owens, Tom. *Collecting Sports Autographs* (9–12). 1989, Bonus paper $6.95 (0-933893-79-5). A thorough introduction to this hobby that covers topics such as hobby shows, techniques of soliciting, autographing, and organizing collections. (Rev: BL 5/1/89) [929.99]

12982 *Postal Service Guide to U.S. Stamps* (7–12). Illus. 1988, U.S. Postal Service $5.00 (0-9604756-8-0). A well-illustrated history of U.S. postage stamps. [769.56]

12983 *Scott Standard Postage Stamp Catalogue: Countries of the World* (7–12). 1997, Scott paper $35.00 (0-89487-231-1). This is the most comprehensive stamp catalog in print. Volume 1 deals with stamps from the English-speaking world; the other three volumes cover alphabetically the other countries of the world. [769.56]

Woodworking and Carpentry

12984 Blandford, Percy W. *24 Table Saw Projects* (10–12). Illus. 1988, TAB paper $6.95 (0-8306-2964-5). Step-by-step instructions on how to make such items as cabinets and benches. (Rev: BL 5/1/88) [684]

12985 Brann, Donald R. *How to Build Outdoor Projects* (10–12). 1981, Easi-Bild paper $9.95 (0-87733-807-8). Easily followed directions are given to build all sorts of outdoor furniture. [684]

12986 De Cristoforo, R. J. *The Table Saw Book* (10–12). Illus. 1988, TAB paper $16.95 (0-8306-2789-8). An introduction to the table saw, the various types of cuts it can produce, and how to select and use one. (Rev: BL 5/1/88) [684]

12987 Higginbotham, Bill. *Whittling* (9–12). 1982, Sterling paper $11.95 (0-8069-7598-9). An introduction to this folk art is given plus 32 patterns for projects. [684]

12988 Jackson, Albert, et al. *The Complete Manual of Woodworking* (9–12). 1989, Knopf $40.00 (0-394-56488-X); paper $25.00 (0-679-76611-1). Such topics as choosing materials, types of tools, sawing, gluing, and finishing are covered in this fine introduction to woodworking. [684]

12989 Key, Ray. *The Woodturner's Workbook* (9–12). 1993, Batsford $29.95 (0-7134-6667-7). A text for upgrading skills, rather than learning basic techniques, with sections on choosing wood, effects various woods display, and exotic woods. (Rev: BL 9/15/93) [684]

12990 Miller, Wilbur R., et al. *Woodworking* (9–12). Illus. 1978, Glencoe paper $9.33 (0-02-672800-1). A guide that covers basic tools, techniques, and materials in woodworking. [684]

12991 Nelson, John A. *52 Weekend Woodworking Projects* (9–12). 1991, Sterling paper $14.95 (0-8069-8300-0). A collection of short-term projects from the very simple to the intricate, including toys, mirrors, clocks, and furniture. (Rev: BL 11/1/91) [684]

12992 Self, Charles R. *Making Birdhouses and Feeders* (9–12). Illus. 1986, Sterling paper $13.95 (0-8069-6244-5). Over 40 projects are described that even a beginner with few tools can accomplish. (Rev: SLJ 5/86) [684]

12993 Self, Charles R. *Making Fancy Birdhouses and Feeders* (10–12). Illus. 1988, Sterling paper $13.95 (0-8069-6690-4). In addition to specific projects, the author discusses materials, tools, types of joints, and finishing methods. (Rev: BL 5/15/86) [690]

12994 Spielman, Patrick, and Patricia Spielman. *Scroll Saw Puzzle Patterns* (9–12). Illus. 1989, Sterling paper $14.95 (0-8069-6586-X). A total of 80 plans are included for puzzles involving the alphabet, animals, robots, and so on. (Rev: BL 1/15/89) [688.7]

12995 Tangerman, Elmer J. *Complete Guide to Wood Carving* (9–12). Illus. 1985, Sterling paper $17.95 (0-8069-7922-4). This beginner's guide describes the tools and materials needed plus details on how to carve faces, animals, and figures. (Rev: BL 2/15/85; BR 1–2/86) [731.4]

12996 Tangerman, Elmer J. *Whittling and Woodcarving* (9–12). 1936, Dover paper $9.95 (0-486-20965-2). This is a beginner's guide to these ancient crafts. [684]

12997 *Working with Wood* (9–12). Illus. 1979, Silver Burdett LB $20.60 (0-8094-2427-4). Basic woodworking skills, tools, and techniques are introduced in this volume from the Time-Life Home Repair and Improvement series. [694]

Jokes, Puzzles, Riddles, and Word Games

12998 Gleason, Norma. *Cryptograms and Spygrams* (10–12). 1981, Dover paper $5.95 (0-486-24036-3). This is a collection of over 100 puzzles and problems to solve. [793.7]

12999 Moscovich, Ivan. *1000 Playthinks: Puzzles, Paradoxes, Illusions, and Games* (6–12). Illus. 2001, Workman $29.95 (0-7611-1826-8). A compendium of illustrated puzzles, organized by categories and indexed by level of difficulty. (Rev: SLJ 4/02; VOYA 10/03) [793.73]

13000 Phillips, Louis, comp. *The Latin Riddle Book* (10–12). Trans. by Stan Schechter. Illus. 1988, Harmony $9.95 (0-517-56975-2). For Latin students a book of riddles that will keep them guessing. (Rev: SLJ 4/89) [470]

13001 Salny, Abbie, and Burke Lewis Frumkes. *The Mensa Think Smart Book* (9–12). Illus. 1986, HarperCollins paper $10.00 (0-06-091255-3). A collection of word games, puzzles, and quizzes that are mind benders. (Rev: BL 4/1/86) [153]

13002 Sloane, Paul, and Des MacHale. *Challenging Lateral Thinking Puzzles* (9–12). 1993, Sterling paper $6.95 (0-8069-8671-9). More than 90 brainteasers, with clues leading the reader through a "lateral thinking" mode. (Rev: BL 5/1/93) [793.73]

13003 Townsend, Charles Barry. *The Curious Book of Mind-Boggling Teasers, Tricks, Puzzles and Games* (4–12). Illus. 2003, Sterling paper $12.95 (1-4027-0214-0). Classic puzzles, games, and brain teasers are illustrated with Victorian-style drawings and helpful diagrams; solutions are at the back of the book. (Rev: SLJ 11/03)

Mysteries, Curiosities,
and Controversial Subjects

13004 Aaseng, Nathan. *The Bermuda Triangle* (7–10). Series: Mystery Library. 2001, Lucent LB $19.96 (1-56006-769-1). Using a variety of sources, this book explores the past and present of this controversial phenomenon. (Rev: BL 9/15/01) [001.9]

13005 Aaseng, Nathan. *Science Versus Pseudoscience* (7–12). 1994, Watts paper $24.00 (0-531-11182-2). Aaseng explains the difference between true scientific theory and pseudoscience, discussing ESP, near-death experiences, creation science, and cold fusion. (Rev: BL 8/94; SLJ 9/94) [001.7]

13006 Adams, Cecil. *Straight Dope: A Compendium of Human Knowledge* (10–12). 1986, Ballantine paper $6.99 (0-345-33315-2). Answers are provided to niggling questions such as "Why didn't the Incas invent the wheel?" and "Do cats have navels?" [030]

13007 Alexander, Dominic. *Spellbound: From Ancient Gods to Modern Merlins: A Time Tour of Myth and Magic* (8–12). 2002, Reader's Digest $26.95 (0-7621-0379-5). This book traces humankind's fascination with magic from its origins in the ancient Middle East and Egypt through popular notions about witchcraft today. (Rev: SLJ 2/03) [133.4]

13008 Berlitz, Charles. *The Bermuda Triangle* (9–12). Illus. 1987, Avon paper $5.99 (0-380-00465-8). An account that discusses the various mysterious disappearances of planes and ships that have occurred in this stretch of the Atlantic Ocean. [001.9]

13009 Boese, Alex. *The Museum of Hoaxes: A Collection of Pranks, Stunts, Deceptions, and Other Wonderful Stories Contrived for the Public from the Middle Ages to the New Millennium* (10–12). Illus. 2002, Dutton $19.95 (0-525-94678-0). A chronological catalog of outrageous deceptions perpetrated over the past several centuries. (Rev: BL 11/15/02) [001.9]

13010 Bondeson, Jan. *A Cabinet of Medical Curiosities* (10–12). 1997, Cornell Univ. Pr. $35.00 (0-8014-3431-9). A carefully researched series of essays that deal with human curiosities, among them tailed people, a giant, a two-headed boy, and an extremely hairy woman, some exaggerated, some documented, placing them in historical perspective. (Rev: BL 10/15/97; SLJ 4/98) [031.02]

13011 Brier, Bob. *Encyclopedia of Mummies* (10–12). Illus. 1997, Facts on File $35.00 (0-8160-3108-8). A topically arranged history of mummification that occurs both in nature and in various cultures, including such modern examples as John Paul Jones, who was preserved in whiskey, Eva Peron, whose body was infused with wax, and Lenin, whose corpse was chemically treated. (Rev: BL 3/15/98; SLJ 6/98) [001.9]

13012 Bunson, Matthew. *The Vampire Encyclopedia* (9–12). 1993, Crown paper $16.00 (0-517-88100-4). Enough ghoulish lore to satisfy the bloodthirstiest vampire enthusiast. (Rev: SLJ 3/94) [001.9]

13013 Burnam, Tom. *More Misinformation* (9–12). Illus. 1980, HarperCollins $16.95 (0-690-01685-9). An entertaining book that debunks popularly held beliefs. A sequel to *Dictionary of Misinformation* (1975). [001.9]

13014 Cavendish, Richard. *The World of Ghosts and the Supernatural* (9–12). 1994, Facts on File $24.95 (0-8160-3209-2). Describes encounters with the spirit world and other paranormal phenomena, including reports of ghosts haunting the Tower of London. (Rev: BL 8/94; SLJ 6/95) [133.1]

13015 Charpak, Georges, and Henri Broch. *Debunked! ESP, Telekinesis, and Other Pseudoscience* (9–12). Trans. by Bart K. Holland. 2004, Johns Hopkins Univ. Pr. $25.00 (0-8018-7867-5). This is an examination of many kinds of paranormal phenomena, like astrology, by a master debunker. (Rev: BL 4/1/04) [130]

13016 Cohen, Daniel. *The Encyclopedia of Monsters* (9–12). 1990, Dorset $17.95 (0-88029-442-6). A guide to all sorts of monsters, including the vampire, abominable snowman, and giant sea creatures. [398]

13017 Cohen, Daniel. *The Encyclopedia of the Strange* (9–12). Illus. 1985, Avon paper $4.50 (0-380-70268-1). A collection of weird and often bizarre information on such topics as Atlantis, Jack the Ripper, levitation, and King Tut's tomb. (Rev: SLJ 11/85) [001.9]

13018 Craig, Roy. *UFOs: An Insider's View of the Official Quest for Evidence* (9–12). 1995, Univ. of North Texas Pr. paper $19.95 (0-929398-94-7). The controversial investigation of UFOs in the late 1960s is reviewed by a chemist and field investigator who was there. (Rev: BL 10/1/95) [001.9]

13019 Craughwell, Thomas J. *Alligators in the Sewer and 222 Other Urban Legends* (6–12). 1999, Black Dog & Leventhal $8.98 (1-57912-061-X). A comprehensive collection of urban legends, some dating back centuries. (Rev: VOYA 2/00)

13020 Crawford, S., and G. Sullivan. *The Power of Birthdays, Stars and Numbers* (9–12). 1998, Ballantine paper $24.95 (0-345-41819-0). This introduction to astrology not only explains the effects of planets on personality, but also describes each day in the calendar in terms of the zodiac and numerology. (Rev: SLJ 4/99) [133.5]

13021 Crosse, Joanna. *The Element Illustrated Encyclopedia of Mind, Body, Spirit and Earth* (10–12). Illus. 1998, Element Books $24.95 (1-901881-10-5). This volume covers diverse topics like astrology, paranormal phenomena, fortune-telling, numerology, common religions or "belief systems," and health and fitness, organized under four main topics: The Mind, The Body, The Spirit, and The Earth. (Rev: SLJ 8/98) [133]

13022 D'Epiro, Peter, and Mary Desmond Pinkowish. *What Are the Seven Wonders of the World? And 100 Other Great Cultural Lists — Fully Explicated* (9–12). 1998, Doubleday paper $14.95 (0-385-49062-3). A treasure trove of cultural trivia, this almanac-like collection contains lists of numerically organized miscellany ranging from the identities of the Three Furies and Four Horsemen of the Apocalypse to Egypt's 10 plagues and the 14 points of Woodrow Wilson's plan for world peace. (Rev: BL 12/1/98) [031]

13023 Dinsdale, Tim. *Loch Ness Monster.* 4th ed. (9–12). Illus. 1982, Routledge paper $7.95 (0-7100-9022-6). An account of the search for Nessie, the monster that supposedly lives in this picturesque lake in the Scottish Highlands. [001.9]

13024 Drimmer, Frederick. *Incredible People: Five Stories of Extraordinary Lives* (9–12). 1997, Atheneum $16.00 (0-689-31921-5). The five lives retold here are of people who were placed on display as oddities, including a man over 7 feet tall, Siamese twins, an African pygmy, and a child reared in the wilds. (Rev: BL 6/1–15/97; BR 1–2/98; SLJ 5/97; VOYA 8/97) [001.9]

13025 Dugan, Ellen. *Elements of Witchcraft: Natural Magick for Teens* (8–12). 2003, Llewellyn paper $14.94 (1-7387-0393-1). A practicing witch introduces teens to the basics of witchcraft, with tips on proper casting of spells and a discussion of ethical concerns. (Rev: BL 6/1–15/03) [133.4]

13026 Duncan, Lois, and William Rool. *Psychic Connections: A Journey into the Mysterious World of Psi* (6–10). 1995, Delacorte paper $12.95 (0-385-32072-8). After her daughter's murder, Duncan used psychics to learn more about it. Here she joins Psychical Research Foundation project director Rool in a comprehensive look at psychic phenomena. (Rev: BL 6/1–15/95; SLJ 5/95) [133]

13027 Elfman, Eric. *Almanac of Alien Encounters* (6–10). 2001, Random LB $11.99 (0-679-97288-9); paper $4.99 (0-679-87288-4). UFO sightings from the earliest times to the 21st century are the topic of this balanced and thorough survey of encounters worldwide. (Rev: HBG 10/01; SLJ 9/01) [001.942]

13028 Feldman, David. *Why Do Clocks Run Clockwise? And Other Imponderables: Mysteries of Everyday Life* (8–12). 1987, Harper & Row paper $12.95 (0-06-091515-3). Questions about everyday occurrences and objects, like "Why do nurses wear white?" are answered in this book of curiosities. [031.02]

13029 Floyd, E. Randall. *Great American Mysteries* (9–12). 1991, August House paper $9.95 (0-87483-170-9). Thirty-eight well-known mysteries, such as the Salem witchcraft trials, the Lizzie Borden case, the Bermuda Triangle, ghosts, and psychics. (Rev: BL 3/1/91; SLJ 8/91) [001.94]

13030 Fulghum, Hunter S. *Don't Try This at Home: How to Win a Sumo Match, Catch a Great White Shark, Start an Independent Nation and Other Extraordinary Feats (for Ordinary People)* (9–12). Illus. 2002, Broadway paper $12.95 (0-7679-1159-8). This hilarious, offbeat guide provides step-by-step instructions for such daring feats as breaking into Fort Knox and smuggling secret documents. (Rev: BL 9/15/02; VOYA 4/03) [904]

13031 Gardner, Martin. *On the Wild Side: The Big Bang, ESP, the Beast 666, Levitation, Rain Making, Trance-Channeling, Seances and Ghosts, and More* (9–12). 1992, Prometheus $27.95 (0-87975-713-2). A collection of articles that examine, expose, and debunk many offbeat scientific theories, cults, and beliefs. (Rev: BL 2/15/92) [500]

13032 Genge, N. E. *The Book of Shadows: The Unofficial Charmed Companion* (7–12). Illus. 2000, Three Rivers $14.00 (0-609-80652-1). A guide to some of the basic tenets of witchcraft that form the basis for *Charmed,* the popular TV series about teen witches. (Rev: SLJ 2/01; VOYA 6/01)

13033 Goodwin, Simon, and John Gribbin. *XTL: Extraterrestrial Life and How to Find It* (10–12). Illus. 2002, Cassell $29.95 (0-304-35897-5). In this thought-provoking overview of the search for life elsewhere, the authors examine recent research and discoveries. (Rev: BL 6/1–15/02) [523.1]

13034 Gravelle, Karen. *Five Ways to Know About You* (6–12). Illus. 2001, Walker $16.95 (0-8027-8749-5); paper $10.95 (0-8027-7586-1). An excellent introduction to astrology, handwriting analysis, palm reading, numerology, and Chinese horoscopes, with easy-to-follow directions. (Rev: HBG 3/02; SLJ 1/02; VOYA 12/01) [133.3]

13035 Guiley, Rosemary Ellen. *The Encyclopedia of Ghosts and Spirits* (9–12). 1993, Facts on File paper $19.95 (0-8160-2846-X). Comprehensive coverage — 400 entries and many photographs — of the spirit world. (Rev: SLJ 6/93*) [333.1]

13036 Haines, Richard F. *CE-5: 242 Case Files Exposing Alien Contact* (10–12). 1998, Sourcebooks paper $24.95 (1-57071-427-4). Case studies are used to bolster the author's contention that UFOs react to human behavior. (Rev: BL 12/1/98) [001.942]

13037 Harvey, Michael. *The End of the World* (6–10). Series: Great Mysteries: Opposing Viewpoints. 1992, Greenhaven LB $22.45 (0-89908-096-0). A review of many of the dire predictions that foretold the end of the world. (Rev: BL 1/15/93) [001.9]

13038 Hicks, Brian. *Ghost Ship: The Mysterious True Story of the Mary Celeste and Her Missing Crew,* (9–12). Illus. 2004, Ballantine $25.95 (0-345-46391-9). The history of this ghost ship is given in detail and how it was located over one hundred years after its crew disappeared, on a coral reef. (Rev: BL 5/15/04) [910]

13039 Kallen, Stuart A. *Witches* (7–10). Illus. Series: Mystery Library. 2000, Lucent LB $18.96 (1-56006-688-1). A history of witchcraft precedes discussion of the beliefs and rituals of today's Wiccans. (Rev: BL 9/1/00; HBG 3/01; SLJ 9/00) [133.4]

13040 Malone, John. *Predicting the Future: From Jules Verne to Bill Gates* (10–12). 1997, M. Evans $19.95 (0-87131-830-X). This book presents a series of predictions, dates of origin, material about each predictor, and material on whether or not the predictions came true. (Rev: BL 10/1/97; SLJ 5/98) [001.9]

13041 Moseley, James W., and Karl T. Pflock. *Shockingly Close to the Truth: Confessions of a Grave-Robbing Ufologist* (10–12). Illus. 2002, Prometheus $25.00 (1-57392-991-3). The dubious antics of many UFO believers are revealed in this entertaining read. (Rev: BL 2/15/02; SLJ 9/02) [001.942]

13042 Myers, Arthur. *The Ghostly Register* (9–12). Illus. 1986, Contemporary paper $14.95 (0-8092-5081-0). A guide to 64 houses that are reputedly haunted. (Rev: SLJ 3/87) [133.1]

13043 Nerys, Dee. *Fortune-Telling by Playing Cards* (9–12). 1982, Sterling paper $10.95 (0-85030-266-8). How to see into the future through a deck of playing cards. [133.3]

13044 Netzley, Patricia D. *Alien Abductions* (7–10). Series: Mystery Library. 2001, Lucent LB $19.96 (1-56006-767-5). This is a serious examination of claims concerning abductions by aliens with reference to cases that have been reported. (Rev: BL 9/15/01; SLJ 2/01) [001.9]

13045 Netzley, Patricia D. *ESP* (7–10). Series: Mystery Library. 2001, Lucent LB $19.96 (1-56006-770-5). A serious look at the phenomenon known as extrasensory perception, incorporating the latest research on the subject. (Rev: BL 9/15/01; SLJ 5/01) [133]

13046 Netzley, Patricia D. *Haunted Houses* (7–10). Illus. Series: Mystery Library. 2000, Lucent LB $18.96 (1-56006-685-7). A balanced account that examines specific cases of hauntings and discusses such topics as ghosts, poltergeists, seances, and mediums. (Rev: BL 9/1/00; HBG 3/01; SLJ 9/00; VOYA 4/01) [133.1]

13047 Netzley, Patricia D. *Unicorns* (6–10). Illus. Series: Mystery Library. 2000, Lucent LB $19.96 (1-56006-687-3). The unicorn's role in myth and legend is the focus of this interesting, well-illustrated volume. (Rev: SLJ 7/01) [398]

13048 Nickell, Joe. *The Mystery Chronicles: More Real-Life X-Files* (9–12). 2004, Univ. Press of Kentucky $29.95 (0-8131-2318-6). This compilation of 41 reports investigates a number of paranormal phenomena like the Amityville horror. (Rev: BL 3/15/04) [001.94]

13049 Nickell, Joe. *Real-Life X-Files: Investigating the Paranormal* (9–12). Illus. 2001, Univ. Press of Kentucky $27.50 (0-8131-2210-4). With excellent background research, the author debunks such paranormal phenomena as crop circles, stigmata, and spiritualist mediums. (Rev: BL 10/15/01) [133]

13050 Nickell, Joe, and John F. Fischer. *Secrets of the Supernatural: Investigating the World's Occult Mysteries* (9–12). Illus. 1988, Prometheus $28.95 (0-87975-461-3). The scientific investigation of 10 supernatural occurrences. (Rev: BL 9/1/88) [133]

13051 Olmstead, Kathleen. *The Girls' Guide to Tarot* (6–12). 2002, Sterling paper $12.95 (0-8069-

840

8072-9). An introduction to tarot card reading, including the meanings of the cards and how to interpret them, with illustrations. (Rev: BL 11/15/02; SLJ 8/02) [133]

13052 O'Neill, Catherine. *Amazing Mysteries of the World* (7–12). Illus. 1983, National Geographic LB $12.50 (0-87044-502-2). UFOs, Bigfoot, and Easter Island are only three of the many mysteries explored. [001.9]

13053 Pickover, Clifford A. *Dreaming the Future: The Fantastic Story of Prediction* (9–12). 2001, Prometheus $28.00 (1-573-92895-X). This book looks at various forms of fortunetelling, such as tarot cards and the zodiac, and introduces great soothsayers of history, including Nostradamus. (Rev: BL 3/1/01) [133.3]

13054 Rain, Gwinevere. *Spellcraft for Teens: A Magical Guide to Writing and Casting Spells* (10–12). Illus. 2002, Llewellyn paper $12.95 (0-7387-0225-0). Rain, who wrote this when she was 16, offers basic information on Wiccan beliefs and rights; spells, chants, and incantations; advice on safety and how to tell others one is a Wiccan; and resources to find out more. (Rev: VOYA 2/03) [133.4]

13055 Ramsland, Katherine. *Ghost: Investigating the Other Side* (10–12). Illus. 2001, St. Martin's $25.95 (0-312-26164-0). The author, a skeptic, investigated paranormal phenomena and found some that she found inexplicable. (Rev: BL 10/1/01) [133.1]

13056 Randles, Jenny. *UFOs and How to See Them* (9–12). 1993, Sterling paper $14.95 (0-8069-0297-3). This illustrated field guide includes a history of the UFO mystery, identification of objects often mistaken for UFOs, and advice on organizing a sky-watch. (Rev: BL 4/15/93) [001.942]

13057 Reid, Lori. *The Art of Hand Reading* (10–12). 1996, DK $24.95 (0-7894-1060-5). The history, physiology, and how-to of hand reading to learn about a person's health, personality, and background. (Rev: BL 10/15/96; SLJ 3/97; VOYA 8/97) [133.3]

13058 Roberts, Russell. *Vampires* (7–10). Series: Mystery Library. 2001, Lucent LB $19.96 (1-56006-835-3). A research-oriented account that explores the origins of the legends and stories involving vampires. (Rev: BL 9/15/01) [001.9]

13059 Shermer, Michael. *Why People Believe Weird Things: Pseudoscience, Superstition and Other Confusions of Our Time* (10–12). 1997, W. H. Freeman $22.95 (0-7167-3090-1). The author applies scientific reasoning to disprove such phenomena as alien abduction, near-death experiences, and psychics. (Rev: SLJ 3/98) [133]

13060 Shuker, Karl P. N. *Mysteries of Planet Earth: An Encyclopedia of the Inexplicable* (6–12). Illus. 1999, Carlton $22.95 (1-85868-802-7). A well-illus-

trated exploration of unusual — and mostly unexplained — phenomena including the Loch Ness monster, the Shroud of Turin, green polar bears, pea-soup fog, and the dodo bird. (Rev: VOYA 4/00) [001.94]

13061 Skal, David J. *V Is for Vampire: The A–Z Guide to Everything Undead* (8–12). 1996, NAL paper $15.95 (0-452-27173-8). This compendium of information about vampires examines the myths and beliefs surrounding them, the stories behind wooden stakes, zombies, and Dracula lore, and includes lists of vampire movies and novels. (Rev: BL 10/1/95; VOYA 2/97) [001.7]

13062 Snodgrass, Mary Ellen. *Signs of the Zodiac: A Reference Guide to Historical, Mythological, and Cultural Associations* (9–12). 1997, Greenwood $39.95 (0-313-30276-6). An interesting, browsable reference work that describes each zodiac sign, the history of astrology, its influences in art and the sciences, characteristics of each sign, and famous people born under each. (Rev: BR 3–4/98; SLJ 2/98) [133.5]

13063 Strieber, Whitley. *Confirmation: The Hard Evidence of Aliens Among Us* (10–12). Illus. 1998, St. Martin's $23.95 (0-312-18557-X). This book presents the "hard" evidence concerning aliens that should be investigated seriously by scientists, including material on UFO sightings, close encounters, and implants that appear to have been placed in people's bodies. (Rev: BL 3/15/98; SLJ 11/98) [001.9]

13064 Underwood, Peter. *Ghosts and How to See Them* (9–12). 1995, Trafalgar paper $16.95 (1-85470-194-0). Experiencing the paranormal and photographing it. (Rev: BL 2/15/95) [133.1]

13065 Varasdi, J. Allen. *Myth Information* (8–12). 1989, Ballantine paper $5.99 (0-345-35985-2). A fascinating collection of facts that challenge some popular beliefs such as the belief that the American buffalo is really a bison. (Rev: BL 11/1/89) [001.9]

13066 Williams, Mary E., ed. *Paranormal Phenomena* (7–12). Illus. Series: Opposing Viewpoints. 2003, Gale LB $21.96 (0-7377-1238-4); paper $14.96 (0-7377-1237-6). Near-death experiences, eternal life, ghosts, reincarnation, psychic ability, UFOs, and extraterrestrial life are among the subjects explored from all sides in this compilation of essays. (Rev: SLJ 7/03) [133]

13067 Windham, Kathryn Tucker. *Jeffrey Introduces 13 More Southern Ghosts* (7–10). 1978, Univ. of Alabama Pr. paper $13.95 (0-8173-0381-2). A total of 13 ghosts tell their weird stories. [133]

13068 Winters, Paul A. *Paranormal Phenomena* (8–12). Illus. Series: Opposing Viewpoints. 1997, Greenhaven LB $26.20 (1-56510-558-3). This collection of articles explores such controversial topics as UFOs, life after death, and ESP. (Rev: BL 7/97; BR 1–2/98; SLJ 9/97; VOYA 12/97) [133]

13069 Wolf, Leonard. *Dracula: The Connoisseur's Guide* (9–12). Illus. 1997, Broadway paper $16.00 (0-553-06907-1). This book is filled with fascinating vampire lore and discussion of vampire fiction stemming from Bram Stoker's 19th-century novel and the Dracula movies. (Rev: SLJ 6/98) [001.9]

13070 Wyly, Michael J. *Dragons* (7–10). Series: Mystery Library. 2002, Gale LB $27.45 (1-56006-972-4). Numerous illustrations and a clear text are used to explore the phenomenon of dragons, how belief in them began, and why it has persisted to the present. (Rev: BL 7/02) [001.9]

Sports and Games

General and Miscellaneous

13071 Aaseng, Nathan. *The Locker Room Mirror: How Sports Reflect Society* (7–10). 1993, Walker LB $15.85 (0-8027-8218-3). Aaseng argues that problems in professional sports today — cheating, drug abuse, violence, commercialization, discrimination — are reflections of society at large. (Rev: BL 6/1–15/93; SLJ 5/93) [306.4]

13072 Allred, Alexandra Powe. *'Atta Girl! A Celebration of Women in Sports* (9–12). Illus. 2003, Wish $16.95 (1-930546-61-0). This is a history of women in sports with material on those women who fought for equality. (Rev: BL 3/1/04; VOYA 6/03) [796]

13073 Aymar, Brandt. *Men in Sports: Great Sports Stories of All Time From the Greek Olympic Games to the American World Series* (9–12). 1994, Crown paper $25.00 (0-517-88395-3). Arranged alphabetically, this volume contains almost 50 sporting entries that include nonfiction, fiction, and sports reporting. [796]

13074 Barash, David P. *The Great Outdoors* (9–12). 1989, Lyle Stuart $17.95 (0-8184-0496-5). Outdoor pursuits such as horseback riding, backpacking, cross-country skiing, and stargazing are discussed. (Rev: BL 5/1/89) [796.5]

13075 *A Basic Guide to Bobsledding* (6–12). Series: Olympic Guides. 2002, Gareth Stevens LB $22.60 (0-8368-3101-2). Under the editorship of the U.S. Olympic Committee, this is a well-illustrated guide to the sport of bobsledding, the equipment used, and important techniques. (Rev: BL 6/1–15/02; HBG 10/02) [796.9]

13076 Berkow, Ira. *The Minority Quarterback and Other Lives in Sports* (10–12). 2002, Ivan R. Dee $26.00 (1-56663-422-9). This collection of inspiring sports stories spotlights athletes' triumphs over such diverse challenges as racial discrimination, physical disability, and hearing loss. (Rev: BL 2/1/02*) [796]

13077 Berlow, Lawrence H. *Sports Ethics* (7–12). Series: Contemporary World Issues. 1995, ABC-CLIO LB $39.50 (0-87436-769-7). A general introduction to the subject is followed by discussion of questions concerning children in sports, college athletics, the Olympics, racism, women, drug abuse, and media relations. (Rev: BL 8/95; SLJ 1/96) [796]

13078 Borden, Fred, and Jay Elias. *Bowling: Knowledge Is the Key* (9–12). Illus. 1987, Bowling Concepts paper $19.95 (0-9619177-0-9). A straightforward instructional program that is simple to follow and thorough. (Rev: BL 6/15/87) [794.6]

13079 Burgett, Gordon. *Treasure and Scavenger Hunts: How to Plan, Create, and Give Them* (9–12). 1994, Communication Unlimited paper $11.75 (0-910167-25-7). Although this book focuses on adult recreation, it also includes suggestions for teens. (Rev: BL 3/15/94) [796.1]

13080 Ching, Jacqueline. *Adventure Racing* (7–10). Series: Ultra Sports. 2002, Rosen LB $26.50 (0-8239-3555-8). This is a fine introduction to this new, outdoor, multidiscipline sport that involves biking, paddling, and climbing plus survival skills and outdoor savvy. (Rev: BL 9/1/02) [796.5]

13081 Cook, Ann Mariah. *Running North: A Yukon Adventure* (9–12). 1998, Algonquin $21.95 (1-56512-213-5). An exciting story of the Yukon Quest International Sled Dog Race and the Cook family who, with their 32 Siberian huskies, moved from New Hampshire to Alaska to train for the race and participate in it. (Rev: BL 9/1/98; SLJ 1/99) [798.8]

13082 Currie, Stephen. *Issues in Sports* (7–12). Illus. Series: Contemporary Issues. 1997, Lucent LB $27.45 (1-56006-477-3). Issues in sports that are discussed include the use of steroids and other perform-

843

ance-enhancing drugs, drug testing, the commercialization of sports, sky-rocketing salaries, and athletes as role models. (Rev: BL 5/1/98) [306.4830973]

13083 Douglass, Kara. *Becoming an Ironman: First Encounters with the Ultimate Endurance Event* (9–12). 2001, Breakaway $23.00 (1-891369-24-5). This work surveys the history of the Ironman triathlon, which involves swimming, bike riding, and running a marathon in one event. [796]

13084 Dowling, Colette. *The Frailty Myth: Women Approaching Physical Equality* (10–12). 2000, Random $24.95 (0-375-50235-1). Using modern research, the author explodes the myth that men are the stronger sex and makes a plea for greater equality, particularly in sports. (Rev: BL 9/1/00) [305.3]

13085 Egendorf, Laura K., ed. *Sports and Athletes* (7–12). Illus. Series: Opposing Viewpoints. 1999, Greenhaven LB $32.45 (0-7377-0057-2); paper $21.20 (0-7377-0056-4). The 30 essays in this critical anthology cover children in sports, college athletics reform, racial discrimination, gender inequality, and drugs. (Rev: BL 9/15/99) [796]

13086 *ESPN Sports Century* (10–12). Ed. by Michael MacCambridge. 1999, Hyperion $40.00 (0-7868-6471-0). For each decade of the 20th century, a different essayist focuses on a single athlete or athletes who best define that time. [796]

13087 Fair, Erik. *Right Stuff for New Hang Glider Pilots* (9–12). Illus. 1987, Publitec paper $9.95 (0-913581-00-3). A collection of articles by Fair exploring many topics relating to hang gliding. (Rev: BL 4/1/87) [797.5]

13088 Feinberg, Jeremy R. *Reading the Sports Page: A Guide to Understanding Sports Statistics* (7–10). 1992, Macmillan LB $21.00 (0-02-734420-7). Explains how to read baseball, basketball, football, hockey, and tennis statistics in newspaper sports pages. (Rev: BL 1/15/93; SLJ 1/93) [796]

13089 *Fifty Years of Great Writing: Sports Illustrated, 1954–2004* (10–12). Ed. by Rob Fleder. 2003, Sports Illustrated for Kids $25.95 (1-932273-06-9). A collection of excellent sports articles that appeared in America's premier sports magazine. (Rev: BL 11/1/03*) [070.449790]

13090 Finnigan, Dave. *The Joy of Juggling* (9–12). 1993, Jugglebug paper $5.95 (0-9615521-3-1). Describes and provides illustrations for 25 juggling routines, discusses plagiarism of others' acts, and gives performance tips for various audiences. (Rev: BL 12/15/93) [793.8]

13091 Flowers, Pam, and Ann Dixon. *Alone Across the Arctic: One Woman's Epic Journey by Dog Team* (9–12). Illus. 2001, Alaska Northwest $22.95 (0-88240-547-0); paper $15.95 (0-88240-539-X). This Alaska resident and avid dogsledder set out to re-create Norwegian Knud Rasmussen's 1923–1924 expedition from Repulse Bay in Canada to Barrow,

Alaska, a distance of 2,500 miles. (Rev: BL 9/15/01; HBG 3/02; SLJ 11/01*) [919.804]

13092 French, Stephanie Breaux. *The Cheerleading Book* (9–12). 1995, Contemporary paper $15.95 (0-8092-3411-4). Besides a history of cheerleading, this book gives tips on motions, cheering routines, jumps, and warming up drills. [791.6]

13093 Greenberg, Judith E. *Getting into the Game: Women and Sports* (9–12). Series: Women Then — Women Now. 1997, Watts LB $25.00 (0-531-11329-9). From Native American ball games and colonial skating parties to today's tennis, wrestling, road-racing, and gymnastics, this is a history of women's involvement in sports at the amateur, student, and professional levels. (Rev: SLJ 9/97; VOYA 10/97) [796]

13094 Hastings, Penny. *Sports for Her: A Reference Guide for Teenage Girls* (7–12). Illus. 1999, Greenwood $45.00 (0-313-30551-X). The basics of many individual sports are covered, with tips on playing sports in general for the young female athlete. (Rev: SLJ 7/00; VOYA 6/00) [796]

13095 Hinkson, Jim. *Lacrosse Fundamentals* (9–12). 1993, Firefly paper $15.95 (1-895629-11-X). Tips and techniques for stick selection, cradling, grip, catching, passing, offense and defense, shooting, face-offs, and goal-tending. (Rev: BL 11/15/93) [796.34]

13096 Jenkins, Dan, ed. *The Best American Sports Writing, 1995* (9–12). 1995, Houghton paper $12.95 (0-395-70069-8). From short to lengthy essays, this collection has something for nearly every sports fan. (Rev: BL 9/15/95) [796.0973]

13097 Judson, Karen. *Sports and Money: It's a Sell-out!* (7–12). Series: Issues in Focus. 1995, Enslow LB $20.95 (0-89490-622-4). A straightforward presentation that uses first-person accounts concerning the financial side of being in the sports business. (Rev: BL 11/15/95; SLJ 6/96) [796.0619]

13098 Krantz, Les. *Not till the Fat Lady Sings: The Most Dramatic Sports Finishes of All Time* (9–12). Illus. 2003, Triumph $29.95 (1-57243-558-5). The details of 50 dramatic last-minute finishes are accompanied by video footage on DVD. (Rev: BL 11/15/03) [796]

13099 Kuntzleman, Charles T. *The Complete Book of Walking* (10–12). 1989, Pocket paper $5.99 (0-671-70074-X). Tips on how to get the most out of walking are given plus good information on training. [796.4]

13100 Langley, Andrew. *Sports and Politics* (9–12). Series: World Issues. 1990, Rourke LB $25.27 (0-86592-117-2). A look at how politics influence sports. (Rev: BL 1/1/91) [796]

13101 Luby, Thia. *Yoga for Teens: How to Improve Your Fitness, Confidence, Appearance, and Health*

— and Have Fun Doing It (6–12). 2000, Clear Light $14.95 (1-57416-032-X). The benefits of yoga, particularly in the teen years, are presented with eye-catching photographs and clear instructions for achieving the poses. (Rev: SLJ 5/00) [613.7]

13102 McComb, David G. *Sports: An Illustrated History* (8–12). Series: Illustrated Histories. 1998, Oxford $29.95 (0-19-510097-2). From ancient times through the 20th century, this is a history of sports and how they have often interacted with religion, warfare, terrorism, and politics. (Rev: HBG 3/99; SLJ 3/99; VOYA 4/99) [796]

13103 Macy, Sue. *Winning Ways: A Photohistory of American Women in Sports* (7–10). Illus. 1996, Holt $16.95 (0-8050-4147-8). Beginning with the 1880s bicycle craze, this book vividly chronicles the history of women's sports in America. (Rev: BL 6/1–15/96*; SLJ 8/96*; VOYA 10/96) [796]

13104 Malafronte, Victor A. *The Complete Book of Frisbee: The History of the Sport and the First Official Price Guide* (9–12). 1998, American Trends paper $19.95 (0-9663855-2-7). After discussing various flying-disc objects, games associated with them such as quoits, hoops, and skittles, and the history of the frisbee, this book focuses on the modern-day frisbee and related memorabilia, collecting, especially the historical Frisbie pie pan, and a price guide for collectors. (Rev: SLJ 5/99) [796]

13105 Margolis, Jeffrey A. *Violence in Sports* (6–12). Illus. 1999, Enslow LB $20.95 (0-89490-961-4). Using extensive documentation and numerous recent incidents, the author traces the decline in sportsmanship and the effect that violence is having on sports. (Rev: BL 9/1/99; HBG 4/00) [796]

13106 Mizerak, Steve, and Joel Cohen. *Steve Mizerak's Pocket Billiards: Tips and Trick Shots* (10–12). 1982, Contemporary paper $12.95 (0-8092-5779-3). An introduction to billiards and tips on how to build one's skills. Also use: *Inside Pocket Billiards* (1973). [794.7]

13107 Mizerak, Steve, and Michael E. Panozzo. *Steve Mizerak's Complete Book of Pool* (9–12). 1990, Contemporary paper $14.95 (0-8092-4255-9). All facets of the game of pool are covered including rules, history, techniques, drills, and equipment. [794.7]

13108 Nace, Don. *Bowling for Beginners: Simple Steps to Strikes and Spares* (6–12). Photos by Bruce Curtis. 2001, Sterling $19.95 (0-8069-4968-6). Equipment, technique, scoring, competition play, and etiquette are all discussed here, with excellent diagrams and color photographs. (Rev: BL 6/1–15/01; SLJ 7/01) [794.6]

13109 Neil, Randy L., and Elaine Hart. *The All-New Official Cheerleader's Handbook* (9–12). Illus. 1986, Simon & Schuster paper $14.95 (0-671-

61210-7). This guide covers cheerleading from basic movements to complex stunts. [791]

13110 Nelson, Mariah Burton. *The Stronger Women Get, the More Men Love Football: Sexism and the American Culture of Sports* (9–12). 1994, Harcourt $22.95 (0-15-181393-0). A hard-hitting account asserting that women are better athletes than men and capable of competing with men. (Rev: BL 5/15/94) [796]

13111 Orlick, Terry. *Cooperative Sports and Games Book* (9–12). 1996, Kendall Hunt paper $15.00 (0-7872-1928-2). This book describes 100 games that depend on cooperation, rather than competition, for success. [798]

13112 Paulsen, Gary. *Winterdance: The Fine Madness of Running the Iditarod* (9–12). 1994, Harcourt $21.95 (0-15-126227-6). This survival adventure describes the author's experiences running with his dog team in the 1,180-mile Alaskan Iditarod race. (Rev: BL 2/15/94; VOYA 10/94) [798.8]

13113 Paulsen, Gary. *Woodsong* (7–12). Illus. 1990, Bradbury $17.00 (0-02-770221-9). Paulsen describes his experiences with sleds and dogs and his entry into the grueling Iditarod Sled Dog Race in Alaska. (Rev: BL 8/90; SLJ 10/90) [796.5]

13114 Pearl, Bill, and Gary T. Moran. *Getting Stronger: Weight Training for Men and Women* (9–12). Illus. 1986, Random paper $19.95 (0-936070-04-8). A comprehensive account that begins with programs for the novice and continues through high levels and also covers topics like equipment, exercise, and nutrition. (Rev: SLJ 5/87) [796.4]

13115 Pejcic, Bogdan, and Rolf Meyer. *Pocket Billiards: Fundamentals of Technique and Play* (9–12). Trans. by Elisabeth E. Reinersmann. 1994, Sterling paper $4.95 (0-8069-0458-5). An illustrated introduction to the sport of billiards, providing insight into equipment, rules, and playing techniques. (Rev: BL 2/15/94) [794.7]

13116 Peterson, James A., et al. *Strength Training for Women* (9–12). 1995, Human Kinetics paper $16.95 (0-87322-752-2). Weight lifting and training for women is the general theme of this book that includes material on nutrition and overcoming inhibitions. [613.7]

13117 *Points Unknown: A Century of Great Exploration* (10–12). Ed. by David Roberts. 2000, Norton $29.95 (0-393-05000-9). This anthology offers 41 pieces about such sports as mountaineering, trekking, spelunking, and other survival sports, each of which involves an experience that occurred in the 20th century. (Rev: BL 9/15/00) [910.92]

13118 Quirk, Charles F., ed. *Sports and the Law: Major League Cases* (10–12). Series: American Law and Society. 1996, Garland $61.00 (0-8153-0220-7). Fifty essays explore legal cases involving such controversies as the rights and responsibilities of coaches, franchise owners moving their teams from one city to another, and access to locker rooms by female journalists. (Rev: BR 11–12/96; SLJ 10/96) [796]

13119 Savage, Jeff. *A Sure Thing? Sports and Gambling* (7–12). Series: Sports Issues. 1996, Lerner LB $28.75 (0-8225-3303-0). After a brief history of gambling, this book looks at the many forms of gambling available today, from church bingo games to horse racing to Las Vegas casinos, with a focus on the connection between gambling and sports and emphasis on the dangers of gambling addiction. (Rev: BL 7/97; HBG 3/98; SLJ 11/97) [796]

13120 Scheppler, Bill. *The Ironman Triathlon* (7–10). Illus. 2002, Rosen LB $26.50 (0-8239-3556-6). Scheppler provides tips on training body and mind for the challenge of these races that combine running, swimming, and biking. (Rev: BL 9/1/02; VOYA 8/02) [796.42]

13121 Schwartz, Ellen. *I Love Yoga: A Guide for Kids and Teens* (5–12). 2003, Tundra paper $9.95 (0-88776-598-X). Illustrated instructions for 18 basic poses are accompanied by breathing and relaxation exercises, discussion of the benefits of yoga, and a description of the different types of yoga practiced around the world. (Rev: SLJ 12/03; VOYA 10/03) [613.7]

13122 Schwarzenegger, Arnold. *Arnold's Bodybuilding for Men* (10–12). Illus. 1981, Simon & Schuster paper $16.00 (0-671-53163-8). A guide to exercise and weight lifting that stresses a total fitness program. [613.7]

13123 Sherrow, Victoria. *Encyclopedia of Women and Sports* (7–12). 1996, ABC-CLIO LB $75.00 (0-87436-826-X). This alphabetically arranged book on women's involvement in sports from ancient Greece to modern times covers athletes, sports, organizations, and social issues such as discrimination, steroid use, pregnancy, and eating disorders. (Rev: BL 9/1/97; BR 9–10/97; SLJ 8/97) [796]

13124 Smith, Lissa. *Nike Is a Goddess: The History of Women in Sports* (9–12). 1998, Grove Atlantic $24.00 (0-87113-726-7). This is an excellent reference and an interesting read on the history of women in sports. (Rev: BL 9/1/98; SLJ 4/99) [796]

13125 Soden, Garrett. *Falling: How Our Greatest Fear Became Our Greatest Thrill* (10–12). Illus. 2003, Norton $23.95 (0-393-05413-6). A fascinating overview of such gravity-defying pastimes as parachuting and bungee jumping and their growing popularity with people of all ages. (Rev: BL 6/1–15/03) [797.5]

13126 Stark, Peter, and Steven M. Krauzer. *Winter Adventure: A Complete Guide to Winter Sports* (8–12). Series: Trailside Guide. 1995, Norton $17.95 (0-393-31400-6). This is a complete guide to winter sports including sledding, dogsledding, curl-

ing, ice skating, and cross-country skiing with additional material on organizations, safety tips, and information sources. [796.9]

13127 Steiner, Andy. *Girl Power on the Playing Field: A Book About Girls, Their Goals, and Their Struggles* (5–10). Series: Girl Power. 2000, Lerner LB $30.35 (0-8225-2690-5). This book explains women's roles in sports with good personal guidance for young girls on participation and goals. (Rev: HBG 10/00; SLJ 6/00) [796]

13128 Summers, Kit. *Juggling with Finesse* (9–12). Illus. 1987, Finesse Pr. paper $19.95 (0-938981-00-5). Simple instructions, profusely illustrated, on how to juggle a variety of objects. (Rev: BL 10/1/87) [793.8]

13129 Urick, Dave. *Sports Illustrated Lacrosse: Fundamentals for Winning.* Rev. ed. (9–12). Series: Sports Illustrated Winner's Circle. 1991, Sports Illustrated for Kids paper $12.95 (1-56800-071-5). This guide to the fundamentals of lacrosse covers rules game, skills, equipment, and strategy. [796.34]

13130 Weiss, Stefanie Iris. *Everything You Need to Know About Yoga: An Introduction for Teens* (7–12). Series: Need to Know Library. 1999, Rosen LB $17.95 (0-8239-2959-0). Yoga's ability to improve mental, spiritual, and physical health is the main focus of this volume. (Rev: SLJ 5/00) [613.7]

13131 Willker, Joshua D. G. *Everything You Need to Know About the Dangers of Sports Gambling* (5–10). Illus. Series: Need to Know Library. 2000, Rosen LB $25.25 (0-8239-3229-X). This brief, well-written book surveys the world of gambling on sports, its legal and illegal aspects, and how it has ruined the careers of many fine athletes. (Rev: BL 1/1–15/01) [796]

13132 Wirth, Dick. *Ballooning: The Complete Guide to Riding the Winds* (9–12). Illus. 1984, Random paper $12.95 (0-394-72796-7). The parts of the balloon are fully described as well as navigational tips. [797.5]

13133 Woods, Karl Morrow. *The Sports Success Book: The Athlete's Guide to Sports Achievement* (9–12). Illus. 1985, Copperfield $17.95 (0-933857-00-4); paper $12.95 (0-933857-01-2). A guide to becoming a successful athlete from junior high through the Olympics to the pros. (Rev: BL 10/15/85; SLJ 4/86; VOYA 12/85) [796]

13134 Woog, Dan. *Jocks 2* (10–12). 2002, Alyson paper $14.95 (1-55583-726-3). In this follow-up to *Jocks,* veteran soccer coach Dan Woog again explores the unique challenges facing gay athletes and other gay men in the periphery of sports. (Rev: BL 9/1/02) [796]

13135 Woolum, Janet. *Outstanding Women Athletes: Who They Are and How They Influenced Sports in America* (6–12). Illus. 1998, Oryx $65.95 (1-57356-120-7). This update of the 1992 edition on women in sports captures many of the recent advances that women have made, adds 26 new biographies and a new chapter on outstanding teams, and includes a sport-by-sport annotated bibliography and statistics. (Rev: BL 9/1/98; SLJ 11/98; VOYA 12/98) [796]

13136 Young, Perry D. *Lesbians and Gays and Sports* (8–12). Series: Issues in Lesbian and Gay Life. 1995, Chelsea $24.95 (0-7910-2611-6); paper $12.95 (0-7910-2951-4). Looks at homosexuals in sports, with biographies of Kopay, Tilden, King, and Navratilova. (Rev: BL 6/1–15/95) [796]

Automobile Racing

13137 Center, Bill. *Ultimate Stock Car* (7–12). 2000, DK $29.95 (0-7894-5967-1). This history of stock car racing is accompanied by cutaways of engines, team information, and profiles of famous drivers. [796.72]

13138 Gaillard, Frye, and Kyle Petty. *200 M.P.H.: A Sizzling Season in the Petty/NASCAR Dynasty* (9–12). 1993, St. Martin's $19.95 (0-312-09732-8). Petty describes NASCAR racing from the viewpoint of a third-generation driver, emphasizing the camaraderie among drivers, crews, and families. (Rev: BL 10/1/93) [796.72]

13139 Golenbock, Peter. *American Zoom: Stock Car Racing — from the Dirt Tracks to Daytona* (9–12). 1993, Macmillan $23.00 (0-02-544615-0). Presents the history of the sport from the mouths of drivers, mechanics, crew chiefs, and promoters. (Rev: BL 9/15/93*) [796.7]

13140 Hinton, Ed. *Daytona: From the Birth of Speed to the Death of the Man in Black* (9–12). 2001, Warner $29.95 (0-446-52677-0). Combining insightful history with lively biographies, this is the spellbinding story of American stock car racing. (Rev: BL 11/15/01) [796.72]

13141 Latford, Bob. *A Celebration of 50 Years of NASCAR: Half a Century of High-Speed Drama* (9–12). 1999, Carlton $24.95 (1-85868-796-9). A decade-by-decade history of the past 50 years of auto racing, with profiles of top drivers. [796.72]

13142 Menzer, Joe. *The Wildest Ride: A History of NASCAR (or, How a Bunch of Good Ol' Boys Built a Billion-Dollar Industry Out of Wrecking Cars)* (9–12). 2001, Simon & Schuster $24.00 (0-7432-0507-3); paper $14.00 (0-7432-2625-9). A highly entertaining history of NASCAR from the founding France family to the present. (Rev: BL 7/01) [796.72]

13143 Parsons, Benny. *Inside Track: A Photo Documentary of NASCAR Stock Car Racing* (9–12). 1996, Artisan $24.95 (1-885183-59-3). This book examines the National Association of Stock Car

Racing and NASCAR races, traveling stock car shows, the development of super speedways, and the top drivers of yesterday and today. (Rev: VOYA 10/97) [796.7]

13144 Perry, David, and Barry Gifford. *Hot Rod* (9–12). 1997, Chronicle paper $22.95 (0-8118-1593-5). The timeless, unique hot rod culture is captured in 80 sepia photographs of speed racers, drag cars, and souped-up automobiles of all kinds, along with their gearheads, greasers, dollies, and fans — tattoos, beards, shades, cigarettes, and all. (Rev: VOYA 4/98) [629.222]

13145 Taylor, Rich. *Indy: Seventy-Five Years of Racing's Greatest Spectacle* (9–12). 1991, St. Martin's $39.95 (0-312-05447-5). A detailed history of the great car racing event from its beginning in 1911 through its 75th running, with more than 500 photographs. (Rev: BL 5/15/91) [796.7]

Baseball

13146 Adair, Robert Kemp. *The Physics of Baseball.* 2nd ed. (10–12). 1994, HarperPerennial paper $10.00 (0-06-095047-1). A fascinating account that links science to the moves, plays, and maneuvers of baseball. [796.357]

13147 Angell, Roger. *A Pitcher's Story: Innings with David Cone* (9–12). 2001, Warner $24.95 (0-446-52768-8). This excellent book about baseball and pitching follows pitcher David Cone through the year 2000, and the reader learns about his work, his past, and his character. (Rev: BL 4/15/01*) [796.357]

13148 Asinof, Eliot. *Eight Men Out* (9–12). 1981, Holtzman $24.95 (0-941372-00-6); Holt paper $14.00 (0-8050-0346-0). The story of a shameful incident in baseball history when eight Chicago White Sox players in 1919 were bribed into losing the World Series. [796.357]

13149 Baker, Dusty, et al. *You Can Teach Hitting: A Systematic Approach to Hitting for Parents, Coaches and Players* (9–12). 1993, Bittinger paper $24.95 (0-940279-73-8). Presents systematic instruction on hitting a baseball, including drills and situational tips. (Rev: BL 12/1/92*) [796.357]

13150 *The Baseball Anthology: 125 Years of Stories, Poems, Articles, Interviews, Photographs, Drawings, Cartoons, and Other Memorabilia* (8–12). 1994, Abrams $24.98 (0-8109-8151-3). This is both a pictorial and a literary history of baseball, arranged chronologically. [796.357]

13151 *A Basic Guide to Softball* (6–12). Illus. Series: Olympic Guides. 2001, Gareth Stevens LB $22.60 (0-8368-2798-8). This is the U.S. Olympic Committee's guide to the sport that was added to the Games in Atlanta in 1996, with information on the history of the game, rules, and some how-to advice. (Rev: BL 5/1/01; HBG 10/01) [796.357]

13152 Blake, Mike. *Baseball Chronicles: An Oral History of Baseball Through the Decades* (9–12). 1994, Betterway paper $16.95 (1-55870-350-0). Oral histories from 140 former and current major-league players, organized by decade through the early 1990s. (Rev: BL 4/15/94) [796.357]

13153 Buckley, James, and Jim Gigliotti. *Baseball: A Celebration!* (8–12). Illus. 2001, DK $50.00 (0-7894-8018-2). The history and the emotion of the game of baseball are captured in this collection of more than 800 well-captioned photographs. (Rev: BL 11/15/01) [796.357]

13154 Castle, George. *Throwbacks: Old-School Baseball Players of Today's Game* (10–12). Illus. 2003, Brassey's $26.95 (1-57488-453-0). Castle's profiles current players who, he believes, embody the best of the qualities esteemed in baseball players of old. (Rev: BL 7/03) [796.357]

13155 Cockcroft, James D. *Latinos in Béisbol* (9–12). Series: Hispanic Experience in the Americas. 1996, Watts LB $25.00 (0-531-11284-5). This book points out that baseball had its roots in Latin America, where it is still very popular, examines the discrimination against Hispanics in the major leagues throughout the early part of the 20th century and their continued underrepresentation in management and coaching positions today, and cites outstanding Hispanic players. (Rev: SLJ 3/97) [796.357]

13156 Coffey, Michael. *27 Men Out: Baseball's Perfect Games* (8–12). 2004, Atria $25.00 (0-7434-4606-2). In the history of major league baseball, there have been only 14 perfect games in which all of the batters struck out. This is an analysis of each of these games. (Rev: BL 3/1/04*) [796.357]

13157 Collins, Jim. *The Last Best League: One Summer, One Season, One Dream* (9–12). Illus. 2004, Da Capo $24.00 (0-7382-0901-5). The story of the Cape Cod Baseball League, its players, coaches, and local citizens and how they function during the summer. (Rev: BL 4/1/04) [796.357]

13158 Colton, Larry. *Counting Coup: A True Story of Basketball and Honor on the Little Big Horn* (10–12). Illus. 2000, Warner $24.95 (0-446-52683-5). This is an uplifting chronicle of the 15 months Larry Colton, a former pro baseball player, spent on a Crow reservation in Montana observing the Hardin High School girls' basketball team. (Rev: BL 8/00* ; VOYA 8/01) [796.323]

13159 Conan, Neal. *Play by Play: Baseball, Radio, and Life in the Last Chance League* (9–12). 2002, Crown $23.00 (0-609-60871-1). Former NPR reporter Conan recounts his experiences delivering play-by-play commentary for the Aberdeen (Maryland) Arsenal, a fledgling minor league baseball

team in the Atlantic League. (Rev: BL 3/1/02) [796.357]

13160 Dawidoff, Nicholas. *Baseball: A Literary Anthology* (9–12). 2002, Library of America $35.00 (1-931082-09-X). Well-known writers including Damon Runyon, Ring Lardner, James Thurber, and Jacques Barzun are included in this anthology of writings about baseball. (Rev: BL 2/15/02) [810.8]

13161 Dickson, Paul. *The Hidden Language of Baseball: How Signs and Sign Stealing Have Influenced the Course of Our National Pastime* (10–12). Illus. 2003, Walker $22.00 (0-8027-1392-0). A fascinating study of the mysterious world of baseball signs — the signals by which a team's players communicate with each other — and their impact on the game's development. (Rev: BL 5/15/03) [796.357]

13162 Dierker, Larry. *This Ain't Brain Surgery: How to Win the Pennant Without Losing Your Mind* (10–12). 2003, Simon & Schuster $25.00 (0-7432-0400-X). Dierker, who has spent most of his life in Major League Baseball — as a player, commentator, and club manager — offers a fascinating inside look at the workings of the game and at changes in the baseball business over the last few decades. (Rev: BL 6/1–15/03*) [796.357]

13163 Dixon, Phil, and Patrick J. Hannigan. *The Negro Baseball Leagues: A Photographic History* (9–12). 1992, Amereon $34.95 (0-8488-0425-2). Celebrates the defunct Negro Baseball Leagues with anecdotes, newspaper accounts, and hundreds of photographs. (Rev: BL 10/1/92) [796.357]

13164 Eisenhammer, Fred, and Jim Binkley. *Baseball's Most Memorable Trades: Superstars Swapped, All-Stars Copped and Megadeals That Flopped* (8–12). 1997, McFarland paper $28.50 (0-7864-0198-2). The causes and effects of the top 25 baseball trades since the turn of the 20th century are covered. (Rev: VOYA 10/97) [796.323]

13165 Enders, Eric. *100 Years of the World Series* (10–12). Illus. 2003, Barnes & Noble $19.95 (0-7607-4201-4). This richly illustrated volume surveys the first century of the World Series, giving chronological coverage with lively text and plentiful photographs. (Rev: BL 9/1/03*) [790.357]

13166 Fiffer, Steve. *How to Watch Baseball: A Fan's Guide to Savoring the Fine Points of the Game* (9–12). Illus. 1987, Facts on File paper $10.95 (0-8160-2001-9). A guide for spectators on how to enjoy the subtleties of baseball. (Rev: BL 3/15/87) [796.357]

13167 Forker, Dom. *Baseball Brain Teasers* (7–12). 1986, Sterling paper $6.95 (0-8069-6284-4). A baseball trivia book in which baseball situations are described and questions are asked about them. (Rev: BR 11–12/86; SLJ 12/86) [796.357]

13168 Fremon, David K. *The Negro Baseball Leagues* (7–12). Series: American Events. 1994, Silver Burdett paper $7.95 (0-382-24730-2). A history of baseball from the segregated Negro Baseball Leagues' point of view. (Rev: BL 3/15/95) [796.357]

13169 *Game Time: A Baseball Companion* (10–12). Ed. by Roger Angell and Steve Kettmann. 2003, Harcourt $25.00 (0-15-100824-8). Many of these articles about baseball originally appeared in the *New Yorker* magazine. [796.357]

13170 Gilbert, Thomas. *The Soaring Twenties: Babe Ruth and the Home-Run Decade* (7–12). Series: American Game. 1996, Watts LB $24.00 (0-531-11279-9). This book describes an era of spectacular sports stars and business tycoons who "owned" the newly evolving major leagues, widespread graft and game-fixing, beginning with the Black Sox gambling scandal, and the recovery of the game under Babe Ruth and other great players of the 1920s. Coverage is also given to race problems and the Negro Leagues. (Rev: SLJ 1/97) [796.357]

13171 Gould, Stephen Jay. *Triumph and Tragedy in Mudville: A Lifelong Passion for Baseball* (10–12). 2003, Norton $24.95 (0-393-05755-0). This collection of entertaining essays by the late paleontologist and baseball lover explores many sides of America's favorite pastime. (Rev: BL 2/15/03*) [790.357]

13172 Gutman, Dan. *The Way Baseball Works* (9–12). 1996, Simon & Schuster $30.00 (0-684-81606-7). Richly illustrated, this overview of America's national pastime not only dissects the game itself but offers fascinating insights into such topics as the production of balls and gloves, the impact of Astroturf on the game, and the evolution of baseball uniforms. (Rev: BL 7/96) [796.357]

13173 Isaacs, Neil D. *Innocence and Wonder: Baseball Through the Eyes of Batboys* (9–12). 1994, Masters paper $14.95 (1-57028-000-2). Major league batboys from 75 years of baseball history describe their memories of the game and its players. (Rev: BL 9/1/94) [796.357]

13174 James, Bill, and Mary A. Wirth. *The Bill James Historical Baseball Abstract* (9–12). 1988, Random $29.95 (0-394-53713-0); paper $15.95 (0-394-75805-6). This volume provides historical statistics and commentary on baseball. (Rev: BR 11–12/88; SLJ 8/88; VOYA 12/88) [796.357]

13175 Lewis, Michael. *Moneyball: The Art of Winning an Unfair Game* (10–12). 2003, Norton $23.95 (0-393-05765-8). In this fascinating study of Major League Baseball's Oakland Athletics, the author explores the ways in which a smaller team can use its wits to compete with the larger clubs for which money is no object. (Rev: BL 6/1–15/03) [796.357]

13176 Light, Jonathan F. *The Cultural Encyclopedia of Baseball* (7–12). 1997, McFarland LB $75.00 (0-7864-0311-X). This book contains entries on a broad range of baseball topics, such as alcoholism in baseball, baseball in different countries, and the

dumbest players, as well as the standard information including famous players, managers, perfect games and no-hitters, statistics, ballparks, and important games. (Rev: BL 9/1/97; SLJ 2/98) [796.357]

13177 McCarver, Tim, and Danny Peary. *The Perfect Season: Why 1998 Was Baseball's Greatest Year* (10–12). 1999, Villard $19.95 (0-375-50330-7). A look back at that memorable summer's most striking moments. (Rev: BL 5/15/99; SLJ 2/00) [796.357]

13178 McCarver, Tim, and Danny Peary. *Tim McCarver's Baseball for Brain Surgeons and Other Fans: Understanding and Interpreting the Game So You Can Watch It Like a Pro* (10–12). 1998, Villard $23.00 (0-375-50085-5). For the learned baseball fan, this overview looks at the finer aspects of the game, subtle strategies, and complex interpretations. (Rev: SLJ 9/98) [796.357]

13179 McGuire, Mark, and Michael Sean Gormley. *The 100 Greatest Baseball Players of the 20th Century Ranked* (8–12). 2000, McFarland $30.00 (0-7864-0914-2). Using a variety of measuring techniques, the 100 greatest baseball players are ranked by importance. [796.357]

13180 McKissack, Patricia, and Fredrick McKissack. *Black Diamond: The Story of the Negro Baseball Leagues* (6–10). Illus. 1994, Scholastic paper $14.95 (0-590-45809-4). A history of African Americans in baseball and the Negro Baseball Leagues, until Jackie Robinson's entry into the major leagues. (Rev: BL 4/94; VOYA 10/94) [796.357]

13181 Marazzi, Rich, and Len Fiorito. *Aaron to Zuverink* (10–12). 1984, Avon paper $4.50 (0-380-68445-4). More than 1,000 major league players of the 1950s are profiled. [796.357]

13182 Margolies, Jacob. *The Negro Leagues: The Story of Black Baseball* (7–12). Series: African American Experience. 1993, Watts paper $24.00 (0-531-11130-X). The history of African American baseball from the 1880s through the birth of the Negro Leagues in the 1920s and their demise in the 1950s. (Rev: BL 2/15/94; VOYA 6/94) [793.357]

13183 Meyer, Gladys C. *Softball for Girls and Women* (10–12). Illus. 1982, Macmillan paper $11.95 (0-684-18140-1). All facets of softball are explored in this guide geared to the specific needs of women. [796.357]

13184 Miklasz, Bernie, et al. *Celebrating 70: Mark McGwire's Historic Season* (10–12). 1998, Sporting News $29.95 (0-89204-621-X). Readers relive the excitement of the 1998 home-run contest between Mark McGwire and Sammy Sosa in this detailed account. (Rev: BL 12/1/98) [796.357]

13185 Nash, Bruce, and Allan Zullo. *The Baseball Hall of Shame's Warped Record Book* (9–12). 1991, Macmillan paper $9.95 (0-02-029485-9). An amusing collection of unusual baseball "records," such as "longest time trapped in a bathroom during a game" and other weird or embarrassing incidents. (Rev: BL 9/15/91) [796.357]

13186 Ritter, Lawrence. *The Story of Baseball* (6–12). 1999, Morrow $16.95 (0-688-16264-9). This history of baseball from its origins to the McGwire-Sosa race for the record book in 1998 also contains material on elements of the game such as pitching and fielding. (Rev: BL 4/1/99; HBG 10/99; SLJ 4/99; VOYA 10/99) [796.357]

13187 Schenin, Richard. *Field of Screams: The Dark Underside of America's National Pastime* (9–12). 1994, Norton paper $14.95 (0-393-31138-4). A chronologically arranged collection of items from the "underside" of baseball history. (Rev: BL 3/15/94) [796.357]

13188 Schmidt, Mike, and Rob Ellis. *The Mike Schmidt Study: Hitting Theory, Skills and Techniques* (9–12). 1994, McGriff & Bell $22.95 (0-9634609-1-9); paper $18.95 (0-9634609-2-7). Designed to help coaches teach Little Leaguers how to hit, Schmidt explains the three major systems and the mental aspects involved. (Rev: BL 12/15/93) [796.35726]

13189 Skipper, John C. *Umpires: Classic Baseball Stories from the Men Who Made the Calls* (8–12). 1997, McFarland paper $24.95 (0-7864-0364-0). Great, memorable moments in the careers of 19 umpires. (Rev: VOYA 12/97) [796.323]

13190 Smith, Ron. *The Sporting News Selects Baseball's Greatest Players: A Celebration of the 20th Century's Best* (11–12). Illus. 1998, Sporting News $29.95 (0-89204-608-2). A comprehensive look at 20th-century baseball's 100 greatest players, with profiles of such memorable athletes as Ty Cobb, Babe Ruth, Willie Mays, and Bob Gibson, as well as players from the Negro Leagues. (Rev: BL 11/15/98*) [796.37]

13191 Snyder, Brad. *Beyond the Shadow of the Senators: The Untold Story of the Homestead Grays and the Integration of Baseball* (10–12). Illus. 2003, Contemporary $24.95 (0-07-140820-7). A compelling story of an effort to break baseball's color barrier by putting Negro League all-star Buck Leonard on the all-white Washington Senators team. (Rev: BL 2/15/03*) [796.357]

13192 Sports Illustrated. *Home Run Heroes* (9–12). 1998, Simon & Schuster $20.00 (0-684-86357-X). Great photographs and sports writing capture the exciting race in the 1998 major league season to break the home-run records of baseball greats Babe Ruth and Roger Maris. (Rev: SLJ 4/99) [796.357]

13193 Stewart, John. *The Baseball Clinic: Skills and Drills for Better Baseball: A Handbook for Players and Coaches* (6–10). 1999, Burford paper $12.95 (1-58080-073-4). Written by a major league scout,

this book contains useful tips for young baseball players in the areas of pitching, fielding, hitting, base running, and catching. (Rev: SLJ 7/99) [796.357]

13194 Stewart, Mark. *Baseball: A History of the National Pastime* (7–10). Series: Watts History of Sports. 1998, Watts LB $33.50 (0-531-11455-4). A solid overview of the history of baseball, with good coverage of off-the-field aspects including labor-management conflicts and the influence of free agency. (Rev: HBG 9/98; SLJ 7/98) [796.357]

13195 Thorn, John. *Treasures of the Baseball Hall of Fame: The Official Companion to the Collection at Cooperstown* (9–12). 1998, Villard $39.95 (0-375-50143-6). A thrilling history of baseball as reconstructed through some of the exhibits and memorabilia found at the Baseball Hall of Fame in Cooperstown, New York. (Rev: SLJ 1/99) [796.357]

13196 Turner, Frederick. *When the Boys Came Back: Baseball and 1946* (10–12). 1996, Holt $27.50 (0-8050-2645-2). The story of the 1946 baseball season, when many major leaguers returned from the war and the Boston Red Sox and the St. Louis Cardinals played in the World Series. (Rev: BL 6/1–15/96; SLJ 2/97) [796.357]

13197 Ward, Geoffrey, and Ken Burns. *Baseball: An Illustrated History* (9–12). 1994, Knopf $60.00 (0-679-40459-7). A history of the game, published in conjunction with a PBS documentary, with essays, facts, and more than 500 photographs. (Rev: BL 7/94*) [796.357]

13198 Whiting, Robert. *The Meaning of Ichiro: The New Wave from Japan and the Transformation of Our National Pastime* (8–12). Illus. 2004, Warner $25.95 (0-446-53192-8). This collection of essays describes the way baseball is viewed and played in Japan as opposed to the United States and also supplies material on such stars as Ichiro. (Rev: BL 4/15/04) [796.357]

Basketball

13199 Becker, Lisa Liberty. *Net Prospect: The Courting Process of Women's College Basketball Recruiting* (10–12). Illus. 2002, Wish paper $16.95 (1-930546-56-4). Useful information for high school girl basketball players who expect to make the leap to college ball. (Rev: BL 6/1–15/02) [796.323]

13200 Berkow, Ira. *Court Vision: Unexpected Views on the Lure of Basketball* (9–12). 2000, Morrow $24.00 (0-688-16842-6). A number of non-sports-related personalities including Woody Allen, Julia Child, Chris Rock, and Sharon Stone are questioned about what the game of basketball means to them. (Rev: BL 5/15/00) [796.323]

13201 Bird, Larry. *Bird on Basketball: How-to Strategies from the Great Celtics Champion.* Rev. ed. (8–12). Illus. 1988, Addison-Wesley paper $16.00 (0-201-14209-0). The basketball star associated with the Boston Celtics gives advice to young players on basics. [796.32]

13202 Coffey, Wayne. *Winning Sounds Like This: A Season with the Women's Basketball Team at Gallaudet, the World's Only Deaf University* (10–12). 2001, Crown $24.00 (0-609-60765-0). In addition to insights into the camaraderie of a sports team, this book highlights the unique challenges posed for the deaf. (Rev: BL 3/15/02) [796.323]

13203 Feinstein, John. *The Last Amateurs: Playing for Glory and Honor in Division I, Basketball's Least-Known League* (10–12). Illus. 2000, Little, Brown $26.95 (0-316-27701-0). An account by this sports journalist about the 1999–2000 season with basketball's Patriot League, which includes teams from Army, Navy, Lafayette, Holy Cross, and Bucknell — none of which give sports scholarships. (Rev: BL 9/15/00) [796.323]

13204 Frey, Darcy. *The Last Shot: City Streets, Basketball Dreams* (9–12). 1994, Houghton $19.95 (0-395-59770-6). Chronicles a group of teenagers playing for one of the best high school teams in New York City. (Rev: BL 12/1/94) [796.323]

13205 Guffey, Greg. *The Greatest Basketball Story Ever Told: The Milan Miracle, Then and Now* (9–12). 1993, Indiana Univ. Pr. $29.95 (0-253-32688-5); paper $14.95 (0-253-32689-3). The real-life events that inspired the movie *Hoosiers* are explored in this look at the 1954 Milan High School basketball team and changes since then. (Rev: BL 12/1/93) [796.323]

13206 Huet, John. *Soul of the Game: Images and Voices of Street Basketball* (10–12). 1997, Workman $30.00 (0-7611-1028-3). This book chronicles the history of street basketball as played in New York City, highlighting its players — both unsung and famous — and their feats, their lives, and their local tournaments that once drew not only the gifted amateurs but also the pro-basketball stars. (Rev: SLJ 4/98) [796.323]

13207 Jackson, Phil, and Hugh Delehanty. *Scared Hoops: Spiritual Lessons of a Hardwood Warrior* (9–12). 1995, Hyperion $22.95 (0-7868-6206-8). Jackson, former head coach of the Chicago Bulls, offers the coaching philosophy that helped him get his team to pull together spiritually and attain a common goal. (Rev: BL 9/1/95) [796.323]

13208 Jeremiah, Maryalyce. *Basketball: The Woman's Game* (7–12). Illus. 1983, Athletic Inst. paper $5.95 (0-87670-069-5). The fundamentals of basketball as seen through the specific needs of female players. [796.32]

13209 Joravsky, Ben. *Hoop Dreams: A True Story of Hardship and Triumph* (8–12). 1995, Turner paper $13.50 (0-06-097689-6). Based on the movie documentary, this book explores the dream of inner-city kids to play in the NBA. [796.323]

13210 Kaye, Elizabeth. *Ain't No Tomorrow: Kobe, Shaq, and the Making of a Lakers Dynasty* (10–12). 2002, Contemporary $24.95 (0-07-138736-6). The importance of tenacity and focus is highlighted in this chronicle of the Los Angeles Lakers' successful — if occasionally troubled — 2001 campaign to continue as NBA champs. (Rev: BL 5/1/02) [796.32]

13211 Kessler, Lauren. *Full Court Press* (10–12). 1997, Dutton paper $23.95 (0-525-94035-9). The story of the low-rated Oregon Ducks, a university women's basketball team, their heroic coach, Jody Runge, and how they battled their way to the 1994 NCAA tournament, including conflicts and emotional experiences, and their struggles for a share of the university's sports facilities, equipment, and honor they deserved. (Rev: BL 3/15/97; SLJ 2/98) [796.323]

13212 Krzyzewski, Mike, and Donald T. Phillips. *Five-Point Play* (10–12). 2001, Warner $24.95 (0-446-53060-3). The Duke University basketball coach known as Coach K tells the story of the 1999–2000 season. (Rev: BL 11/15/01) [796.323]

13213 Lieberman-Cline, Nancy, and Robin Roberts. *Basketball for Women* (7–12). Illus. 1995, Human Kinetics paper $18.95 (0-87322-610-0). After a brief history of women's basketball, Lieberman-Cline, who has played in college, Olympics, and professional women's basketball, discusses the commitment required of a serious basketball player, how to formulate a plan for skill development, the recruitment process, and other concerns, and devotes seven chapters to more than 100 drill exercises. (Rev: VOYA 6/96) [796.323]

13214 McKissack, Fredrick. *Black Hoops: African-Americans in Basketball* (6–10). 1999, Scholastic paper $15.95 (0-590-48712-4). This work gives a concise history of basketball from the early days to the present, documenting the contributions of black players and teams and placing the development of the sport in a social and historic context. The final chapter presents an overview of African American women's participation in basketball. (Rev: BL 2/15/99; BR 9–10/99; HBG 9/99; SLJ 3/99; VOYA 10/99) [796.32308996073]

13215 Miller, Reggie, and Gene Wojciechowski. *I Love Being the Enemy: A Season on the Court with the NBA's Best Shooter and Sharpest Tongue* (9–12). 1995, Simon & Schuster $23.00 (0-684-81389-0). Miller's diary kept during the 1994–1995 season reveals a side of him not often seen. (Rev: BL 12/1/95) [796.323]

851

13216 Nash, Bruce, and Allan Zullo. *The Basketball Hall of Shame* (9–12). Series: Hall of Shame. 1991, Pocket paper $10.00 (0-671-69414-6). Brief, humorous basketball stories, including battles with referees, strange shots, and weird happenings. (Rev: BL 11/1/91) [796.323]

13217 Pluto, Terry. *Falling from Grace: Can Pro Basketball Be Saved?* (9–12). 1995, Simon & Schuster $22.50 (0-684-80766-1). An examination of a declining sport, with comments from 52 experts bolstering Pluto's assertion that a trash-talking, in-your-face culture of disrespect dominates pro basketball. (Rev: BL 11/15/95) [796.323]

13218 St. Martin, Ted, and Frank Frangie. *The Art of Shooting Baskets: From the Free Throw to the Slam Dunk* (9–12). 1992, Contemporary paper $12.95 (0-8092-4009-2). A well-illustrated, easy-to-follow guide to basketball techniques. [796.323]

13219 Stewart, Mark. *Basketball: A History of Hoops* (6–10). Series: Watts History of Sports. 1999, Watts LB $33.50 (0-531-11492-9). A chronological history of basketball that gives alternating treatment to college and pro games and includes how basketball has been influenced by off-the-court financial and social pressures. (Rev: HBG 9/99; SLJ 8/99) [796.323]

13220 Thomas, Rob. *They Cleared the Lane: The NBA's Black Pioneers* (10–12). Illus. 2002, Univ. of Nebraska Pr. $29.95 (0-8032-4437-1). A historical overview of the integration of professional basketball. (Rev: BL 3/15/02) [796.323]

13221 Vitale, Dick, and Dick Weiss. *Holding Court: Reflections on the Game I Love* (9–12). 1995, Masters $22.95 (1-57028-037-1). College basketball's voice on ESPN and a former coach himself, Vitale reflects on various aspects of the sport, including the intense pressure on coaches to win. (Rev: BL 12/1/95) [796.323]

13222 Weatherspoon, Teresa, et al. *Teresa Weatherspoon's Basketball for Girls* (6–10). 1999, Wiley paper $14.95 (0-471-31784-5). This manual, by the famous basketball star and Olympic gold medalist, gives wonderful, practical information about playing the game and becoming a healthy, happy athlete. (Rev: BL 7/99; SLJ 8/99) [796.323]

13223 Wideman, John Edgar. *Hoop Roots* (10–12). 2001, Houghton $24.00 (0-395-85731-7). This is the story of the African American author's enduring fascination with the game of basketball, first as a young player and later as a spectator. (Rev: BL 9/1/01*) [813]

13224 Wilker, Josh. *The Harlem Globetrotters* (5–10). Series: African-American Achievers. 1996, Chelsea LB $21.95 (0-7910-2585-3); paper $8.95 (0-7910-2586-1). This is a chronologically arranged history of the Harlem Globetrotters, the basketball

team that has been entertaining crowds since 1927. (Rev: SLJ 3/97) [796.357]

13225 Wolff, Alexander. *Big Game, Small World* (9–12). 2002, Warner $24.95 (0-446-52601-0). The author, a writer for *Sports Illustrated,* tells what he learned about basketball's growing influence on his travels to 16 countries and 10 states. (Rev: BL 1/1–15/02*) [796.323]

Bicycling, Motorcycling, etc.

13226 Abt, Samuel. *Tour de France: Three Weeks to Glory* (9–12). 1991, Bicycle $22.95 (0-933201-40-0). Overview of the world's largest, most prestigious bicycle race, its origins, and the sport's leading riders with coverage ending in 1990. (Rev: BL 6/1/91) [796.62]

13227 Ballantine, Richard, and Richard Grant. *Richards' Bicycle Repair Manual* (9–12). 1994, DK paper $9.95 (1-56458-484-4). An illustrated handbook for the home bicycle mechanic, covering routine and preventive maintenance and emergency repairs. (Rev: BL 3/15/94; SLJ 9/94; VOYA 2/95) [629.28]

13228 Bennett, Jim. *The Complete Motorcycle Book* (9–12). 1995, Facts on File $27.95 (0-8160-2899-0). The definitive work on buying, riding, and caring for motorcycles. (Rev: BL 12/15/94; SLJ 6/95) [629.28]

13229 Bicycling Magazine, eds. *Cycling for Women* (9–12). Illus. 1989, Rodale paper $8.95 (0-87857-811-0). General tips for both sexes are interspersed with those specifically aimed at women's abilities and endurance levels. (Rev: BL 3/15/89) [796.6]

13230 Burke, Edmund R., and Ed Pavelka. *The Complete Book of Long-Distance Cycling: Build the Strength, Skills, and Confidence to Ride as Far as You Want* (10–12). Illus. 2000, Rodale paper $19.95 (1-57954-199-2). This well-organized book covers the basics — training, equipment, and safety — plus other topics relating to biking, such as nutrition and bike technology. (Rev: BL 9/1/00) [613.7]

13231 Carmichael, Chris, and Jim Rutberg. *The Ultimate Ride: Get Fit, Get Fast, and Start Winning with the World's Top Cycling Coach* (10–12). Illus. 2003, Putnam $24.95 (0-399-15071-4). Mental preparation and good nutrition are given equal weight with training in this guide that will be useful to cyclists and other athletes. (Rev: BL 7/03) [796.6]

13232 Cotter, Allison. *Cycling* (6–12). Illus. Series: History of Sports. 2002, Gale LB $27.45 (1-59018-071-2). From the invention of the bicycle to today's high-tech mountain and other specialist bikes, Cotter traces cycling's growth and looks at competitive and recreational aspects of the sport. (Rev: BL 9/1/02) [796.6]

13233 Crowther, Nicky. *The Ultimate Mountain Bike Book: The Definitive Illustrated Guide to Bikes, Components, Techniques, Thrills and Trails*. Rev. ed. (7–12). 2002, Firefly paper $24.95 (1-55297-653-X). Beginning and advanced riders will all find material of interest in this revised practical guide full of appealing photographs. (Rev: SLJ 1/03; VOYA 12/02) [796.6]

13234 Gibb, Evelyn McDaniel. *Two Wheels North: Bicycling the West Coast in 1909* (10–12). 2000, Oregon State Univ. $15.95 (0-87071-485-6). The true story of the 1,000 mile, 54-day bicycle trip the author's father took from Santa Rosa, California, to Seattle in 1909. (Rev: BL 11/15/00) [917.904]

13235 King, Dave, and Michael Kaminer. *The Mountain Bike Experience: A Complete Introduction to the Joys of Off-road Riding* (9–12). 1996, Holt paper $16.95 (0-8050-3723-3). Mountain bike enthusiasts and novice bikers will find valuable advice about proper nutrition, conditioning, and biking techniques. [796.6]

13236 LeMond, Greg, and Kent Gordis. *Greg LeMond's Complete Book of Bicycling* (9–12). Illus. 1987, Putnam paper $14.95 (0-399-51594-1). For both the beginner and specialist, this book covers equipment, techniques, and training. (Rev: BL 10/1/87) [796.6]

13237 Oliver, Peter. *Bicycling: Touring and Mountain Bike Basics* (9–12). Series: Trailside Guide. 1995, Norton $17.95 (0-393-31337-9). This mountain bike manual covers topics like equipment, clothing, safety, techniques, maintenance, and organizations. [796.6]

13238 Pavelka, Ed. *Bicycling Magazine's Basic Maintenance and Repair: Simple Techniques to Make Your Bike Ride Better and Last Longer* (8–12). 1999, Rodale paper $9.99 (1-57954-170-4). This book clearly explains how to maintain and repair a bicycle so it remains in tip-top condition. [629.28]

13239 Pavelka, Ed. *Bicycling Magazine's 900 All-Time Best Tips: Top Riders Share Their Secrets to Maximize Fun, Safety, and Performance* (8–12). 2000, Rodale paper $9.95 (1-57954-227-1). This book contains bicycling tips on such subjects as bicycle models, accessories, riding styles, and repair techniques. [796.6]

13240 Turner, Chérie. *Marathon Cycling* (7–10). Series: Ultra Sports. 2002, Rosen LB $26.50 (0-8239-3553-1). Long-distance cycling competitions are described with material on tips and tricks, safety, gear, and racing events. (Rev: BL 9/1/02; SLJ 9/02) [796.6]

13241 Wilson, Hugo. *The Ultimate Harley-Davidson Book* (8–12). 2000, DK $24.95 (0-7894-5165-4). This is a history of the Harley-Davidson motorcycle from 1911 to 1999, with material on its parts and design. [629.227]

13242 Wilson, Hugo. *The Ultimate Motorcycle Book* (9–12). 1993, DK $29.95 (1-56458-303-1). Color photographs of more than 200 bikes illustrate this guide to U.S. and imported motorcycles, their history — including their use in World War II — racing, touring, motocross, and customizing. (Rev: BL 11/1/93) [629.227]

Boxing and Wrestling

13243 Bacho, Peter. *Boxing in Black and White* (7–12). Illus. 1999, Holt $18.95 (0-8050-5779-X). Beginning with a 1926 Filipino boxing champion and ending with Muhammad Ali, this is an interesting study of race relations and the sport of boxing. (Rev: BL 11/1/99; HBG 4/00) [796.83]

13244 DeVito, Basil V. Jr., with Joe Layden. *Wrestlemania: The Official Insider's Story* (6–12). 2001, Regan $49.95 (0-06-039387-4). A well-illustrated behind-the-scenes look at the premier event of the World Wrestling Federation. (Rev: SLJ 8/01; VOYA 10/01)

13245 Douglas, Bobby. *Take It to the Mat* (9–12). 1993, Sigler paper $15.95 (0-9635812-0-1). U.S. Olympic wrestler/coach Douglas presents an introductory guide to competitive wrestling, with photographs of holds and escapes, as well as diet guidelines. (Rev: BL 9/15/93) [796.8]

13246 Greenberg, Keith Elliot. *Pro Wrestling: From Carnivals to Cable TV* (6–12). Illus. 2000, Lerner LB $26.60 (0-8225-3332-4); paper $9.95 (0-8225-9864-7). With both historical and current information, this will please fans of professional wrestling and offer material for reports. (Rev: BL 2/15/01; HBG 3/01; SLJ 2/01; VOYA 2/01) [796.812]

13247 Heenan, Bobby, and Steve Anderson. *Bobby the Brain: Wrestling's Bad Boy Tells All* (10–12). Illus. 2002, Triumph $19.95 (1-57243-465-1). Longtime professional wrestler Bobby "Bobby the Brain" Heenan muses entertaining on his career, his personal life, and the world of wrestling. (Rev: BL 9/1/02) [796.812]

13248 Jarman, Tom, and Reid Hanley. *Wrestling for Beginners* (7–12). Illus. 1983, Contemporary paper $12.95 (0-8092-5656-8). From a history of wrestling, this book moves on to skills, strategies, moves, and holds. [796.8]

Camping, Hiking, Backpacking, and Mountaineering

13249 Banks, Mike. *Mountain Climbing for Beginners* (10–12). Illus. 1978, Scarborough House $8.95 (0-8128-2448-2). This is a guide for those who are interested in basic knowledge of this sport. [796.5]

13250 Berger, Karen. *Hiking and Backpacking: A Complete Guide* (8–12). Series: Trailside Guide. 1995, Norton paper $17.95 (0-393-31334-4). A complete guide to outdoor hiking and backpacking with material on techniques, equipment, safety, camping, and related topics. [796.51]

13251 Bonatti, Walter. *The Mountains of My Life* (10–12). Trans. by Robert Marshall. Illus. 2001, Random paper $14.95 (0-375-75640-X). What mountain climbing has meant to this Italian mountaineer and his part in the conquest of K2, the world's second-highest mountain, in 1954 are the subjects of this adventure-filled memoir. (Rev: BL 2/15/01) [796.5]

13252 Boukreev, Anatoli. *Above the Clouds: The Diaries of a High-Altitude Mountaineer* (9–12). Ed. by Linda Wylie. Illus. 2001, St. Martin's $27.95 (0-312-26970-6). The diary of the mountaineer who disappeared in a Himalayan avalanche in 1997 and his career scaling mountains of peaks 8,000 meters and more. (Rev: BL 10/1/01) [796.52]

13253 Bryson, Bill. *A Walk in the Woods: Rediscovering America on the Appalachian Trail* (10–12). 1998, Broadway $25.00 (0-7679-0251-3). An often hilarious, sometimes moving account of two inept, out-of-condition adventurers and their attempts to hike the Appalachian Trail. (Rev: BL 9/15/98; SLJ 10/98) [796.54]

13254 Child, Greg. *Over the Edge: The True Story of Four American Climbers' Kidnap and Escape in the Mountains of Central Asia* (10–12). Illus. 2002, Villard $24.95 (0-375-50609-8). Four adventurous young American mountaineers ignored State Department warnings about terrorism and found themselves in peril in Kyrgyzstan; suitable for mature teens. (Rev: BL 4/15/02) [796.52]

13255 *Climb: Stories of Survival from Rock, Snow, and Ice* (10–12). Ed. by Clint Willis. 2000, Thunder's Mouth paper $16.95 (1-56025-250-2). This collection of true survival stories explores the phenomenon of risk-taking in outdoor sports like mountain climbing and the motivation behind getting involved in these activities. (Rev: BL 2/15/00) [796.52]

13256 Cook, Charles. *The Essential Guide to Hiking in the United States* (9–12). 1991, Michael Kesend paper $19.95 (0-935576-41-X). Contains information on such hiking essentials as shoes, clothing,

safety, and the best areas for hiking and the trails in each state. (Rev: BL 12/1/91) [996.5]

13257 Curtis, Rick. *The Backpacker's Field Manual: A Comprehensive Guide to Mastering Backcountry Skills* (9–12). 1998, Three Rivers paper $14.95 (0-517-88783-5). This handbook offers solid advice on topics ranging from advance planning and what to pack to picking a campsite, cooking, navigation, safety, wildlife encounters, and first aid. [796.51]

13258 Drury, Bob. *The Rescue Season: A True Story of Heroism on the Edge of the World* (10–12). 2001, Simon & Schuster $25.00 (0-684-86479-7). This is an exciting high-mountain rescue story about three climbers who were stranded on Mount Denali, North America's highest peak. (Rev: BL 12/15/00) [363.34]

13259 *Everest: Summit of Achievement* (10–12). Ed. by the Royal Geographical Society. Illus. 2003, Simon & Schuster $50.00 (0-7432-4386-2). This richly illustrated volume recounts the nine Royal Geographic Society expeditions to Everest that culminated in the successful 1953 ascent by Edmund Hillary and Tenzing Norgay. (Rev: BL 5/1/03; SLJ 9/03) [796.52]

13260 Fletcher, Colin. *The Complete Walker III: The Joys and Techniques of Hiking and Backpacking* (10–12). Illus. 1984, Knopf $22.95 (0-394-51962-0); paper $19.00 (0-394-72264-7). This readable, thorough guide to hiking and backpacking first appeared in 1969 and is in its third edition. [796.5]

13261 Fletcher, David. *Hunted: A True Story of Survival* (10–12). 2002, Carroll & Graf $25.00 (0-7867-0998-7). Fletcher tells how the difficulty factor of his solo ascent of Alaska's Mount Hess was increased exponentially by repeated encounters with an angry grizzly bear. (Rev: BL 5/1/02) [613.6]

13262 Gammelgaard, Lene. *Climbing High: A Woman's Account of Surviving the Everest Tragedy* (10–12). 1999, Seal $25.00 (1-58005-023-9). In this thrilling memoir, Gammelgaard tells the story of her successful 1996 ascent of Mount Everest and how she escaped death in a blizzard that claimed the lives of eight other climbers. (Rev: BL 6/1–15/99; VOYA 2/00) [796.52]

13263 Glowacz, Stefan, and Uli Wiesmeier. *Rocks Around the World* (9–12). Trans. by Martin Boysen. Illus. 1989, Sierra Club $24.95 (0-87156-677-X). The thrilling experiences of Glowacz, an internationally known rock climber, are captured in his text and the impressive photographs of Wiesmeier. (Rev: BL 3/15/89) [796.5]

13264 Grylls, Bear. *The Kid Who Climbed Everest: The Incredible Story of a 23-Year-Old's Summit of Mt. Everest* (10–12). Illus. 2001, Lyons Pr. $24.95 (1-58574-250-3). Despite a serious sports injury that left him paralyzed for months, the author miraculously became the youngest Englishman to climb Mount Everest. (Rev: BL 4/15/01) [796.52]

13265 Hill, Lynn, and Greg Child. *Climbing Free: My Life in the Vertical World* (10–12). Illus. 2002, Norton $24.95 (0-393-04981-7). Hill recounts her lifelong love of sport climbing and her successful conquest of such challenges as Yosemite's El Capitan and Arizona's Granite Mountain. (Rev: BL 3/15/02) [796.52]

13266 Jackson, Monica, and Elizabeth Stark. *Tents in the Clouds: The First Women's Himalayan Expedition* (10–12). Illus. 2000, Seal paper $16.00 (1-58005-033-6). Originally published in 1956, this adventure-filled work tells of the first all-women expedition in 1955 to Jugal Himal, a part of the Himalayas with peaks over 20,000 feet. (Rev: BL 1/1–15/00) [796.52]

13267 Krakauer, Jon. *Eiger Dreams: Ventures Among Men and Mountains* (9–12). 1990, Lyons Pr. $25.00 (1-55821-057-1). The author writes in 12 different short pieces about the dangers and thrills of mountaineering. (Rev: BL 4/1/90; SLJ 8/90) [795.5]

13268 Krakauer, Jon. *Into Thin Air: A Personal Account of the Mt. Everest Disaster* (10–12). 1997, Villard $24.95 (0-679-45752-6). A history of Mount Everest expeditions is intertwined with the disastrous expedition the author was a part of, during which five members were killed by a hurricane-strength blizzard. (Rev: BL 4/1/97; BR 11–12/97; SLJ 11/97) [796.5]

13269 Loughman, Michael. *Learning to Rock Climb* (10–12). Illus. 1981, Sierra Club paper $14.00 (0-87156-281-2). A guide to mountaineering that stresses safety and sound techniques. [796.5]

13270 McManners, Hugh. *The Backpacker's Handbook* (9–12). 1995, DK $14.95 (1-56458-852-1). This how-to book for backpackers includes material on equipment, camping, techniques, and dealing with emergencies. [796.51]

13271 McManners, Hugh. *The Complete Wilderness Training Book* (9–12). 1994, DK $29.95 (1-56458-488-7). Survival techniques for the hardcore survivalist in familiar as well as extreme environments. This British import is more international in scope than American versions. (Rev: BL 5/15/94; VOYA 12/94) [613.6]

13272 Manning, Harvey. *Backpacking One Step at a Time*. Rev. ed. (9–12). Illus. 1986, Random paper $15.00 (0-394-72939-0). In addition to information on equipment and techniques, this book tells how to get the most enjoyment possible out of backpacking. (Rev: SLJ 9/86; VOYA 8/86) [796.5]

13273 Mellor, Don. *American Rock: Region, Rock, and Culture in American Rock Climbing* (9–12). Illus. 2001, Countryman $27.95 (0-88150-428-9). Written by a veteran rock climber and guide, this

book on rock climbing is "not about conquering the mountain, it's about becoming part of the mountain." (Rev: BL 9/1/01) [796,52]

13274 Netzley, Patricia D. *Life of an Everest Expedition* (6–10). Series: The Way People Live. 2001, Lucent LB $19.96 (1-56006-792-6). Using primary source material and black-and-white photographs, this work explores the planning and execution of a climb up Everest. (Rev: BL 6/1–15/01) [796.5]

13275 Norgay, Jamling Tenzing. *Touching My Father's Soul: A Sherpa's Journey to the Top of Everest* (10–12). Illus. 2001, HarperSF $26.00 (0-06-251687-6). This is the story of the exploits, beliefs, and culture of the Sherpa whose father, Tenzing Norgay, accompanied Edmund Hillary on the first ascent of the world's highest mountain. (Rev: BL 4/15/01) [796.52]

13276 Purnell, Karl H. *A Mountain Too Far: A Father's Search for Meaning in the Climbing Death of His Son* (9–12). 2001, New Horizon $24.95 (0-88282-204-7). Torn with grief over the death of his son in a climbing accident, a father takes up mountaineering and accomplishes what his son perished trying to do. (Rev: BL 4/1/01) [796.52]

13277 Randall, Glenn. *The Backpacker's Handbook: An Environmentally Sound Guide* (9–12). 1994, Lyons Pr. paper $14.95 (1-55821-248-5). Tells "how to be comfortable in the wilderness while leaving it untouched for the enjoyment of the next visitor" by providing tips on clothing, packing, safety, and more. (Rev: BL 12/1/93) [796.5]

13278 Riviere, Bill. *The L.L. Bean Guide to the Outdoors* (10–12). Illus. 1981, Random $15.50 (0-394-51928-0). In addition to hiking, camping, and backpacking this general account includes some material on skiing and canoeing. [796.5]

13279 Roberts, David. *Escape from Lucania: An Epic Story of Survival* (10–12). Illus. 2002, Simon & Schuster $23.00 (0-7432-2432-9). A tale of a daring 1937 ascent of Canada's Mount Lucania. (Rev: BL 9/15/02) [796.52]

13280 Salkeld, Audrey. *Kilimanjaro: To the Roof of Africa* (9–12). Illus. 2002, National Geographic $40.00 (0-7922-6466-5). An ascent by five trekkers — two of them teens — serves as the framework for this beautifully illustrated portrait of a mountain and its attractions; published as a companion to writer/mountaineer David Breashear's film of the same name. (Rev: BL 4/15/02) [796.52]

13281 Seaborg, Eric, and Ellen Dudley. *Hiking and Backpacking* (9–12). 1994, Human Kinetics paper $12.95 (0-87322-506-6). An introduction to hiking and backpacking, covering safety gear, safe travel, and the best places to go. (Rev: BL 3/15/94; VOYA 12/94) [796.5]

13282 Venables, Stephen. *To the Top: The Story of Everest* (6–12). 2003, Candlewick $17.99 (0-7636-

2115-3). The mountain itself gets equal treatment in this engaging book that looks at the important aspects of geology, meteorology, politics, and culture as well as the expeditions that have taken place and the role of the Sherpas in making them possible. (Rev: BCCB 6/03; HBG 10/03; SLJ 7/03*; VOYA 6/04)

13283 Viesturs, Ed, and Peter Potterfield. *Himalayan Quest* (10–12). Illus. 2003, National Geographic paper $20.00 (0-7922-6884-9). In this collection of stunning photographs, American-born mountaineering guide Ed Viesturs documents his quest to climb, without bottled oxygen, every Himalayan peak that tops the 8,000-meter mark. (Rev: BL 2/15/03) [796.52]

13284 Waterman, Jonathan. *In the Shadow of Denali: Life and Death on Alaska's Mt. McKinley* (9–12). 1998, Lyons Pr. paper $14.95 (1-55821-726-6). This first-person narrative explores the psychology of climbers who attempt to scale the nation's highest mountain. (Rev: BL 3/1/94) [796.5]

Chess, Checkers, and Other Board and Card Games

13285 De Satnick, Shelly. *Bridge for Everyone: A Step-by-Step Text and Workbook* (10–12). 1982, Avon paper $9.95 (0-380-81083-2). An elementary but excellent introduction to bridge. [795.4]

13286 Frey, Richard. *According to Hoyle* (9–12). 1985, Fawcett paper $5.99 (0-449-21112-6). This handbook supplies instructions, rules, and regulations for over 200 games. [795.4]

13287 Gibson, Walter B. *Hoyle's Modern Encyclopedia of Card Games: Rules of All the Basic Games and Popular Variations* (10–12). Illus. 1974, Dolphin paper $12.95 (0-385-07680-0). The master of "according to Hoyle" fame describes a number of card games including poker and solitaire. [795.4]

13288 Holland, Tim. *Beginning Backgammon* (9–12). 1974, McKay paper $4.95 (0-679-14038-7). An elementary guide for the beginner in this board game that combines chance with skill. [794]

13289 King, Daniel. *Chess* (7–12). 2000, Kingfisher (0-7534-5279-0). A history of chess is given, plus the rules of the game, general background information, and techniques that can be used. [794.1]

13290 Morehead, Albert H., and Geoffrey Mott-Smith, eds. *Hoyle's Rules of Games.* 2nd rev. ed. (9–12). 1983, NAL paper $7.95 (0-452-26049-3). This is a guide on how to play over 200 card and parlor games. [794.4]

13291 Pike, Robert. *Play Winning Checkers: Official American Mensa Game Book* (8–12). 1999, Sterling paper $7.95 (0-8069-3794-7). After a history of the game, this book starts with the basics of checkers and continues through complex strategies. (Rev: SLJ 9/99) [794.2]

13292 Pritchard, D. B. *Begin Chess* (9–12). 1987, NAL paper $2.95 (0-451-14723-5). A fine introduction to this game with clear instructions for the beginner. [794.1]

13293 Redman, Tim, ed. *U.S. Chess Federation's Official Rules of Chess* (10–12). 1987, McKay paper $7.95 (0-679-14154-5). This is the official book of international chess rules and their interpretation. [794.1]

13294 Reinfeld, Fred. *Be a Winner at Chess* (9–12). 1986, Fawcett paper $5.99 (0-449-21257-2). This book presumes a basic knowledge of chess and describes many interesting strategies. Also use by this author: *Beginner's Guide to Winning Chess* (1982), *Chess in a Nutshell* (1989), *The Complete Chessplay* (1982), and *Win at Chess* (1945). [794.1]

13295 Reinfeld, Fred. *How to Win at Checkers* (9–12). 1982, Wilshire paper $7.00 (0-87980-068-2). A guide to this board game and popular pastime. [794]

13296 Sheinwold, Alfred. *101 Best Family Card Games* (5–12). Illus. 1993, Sterling paper $5.95 (0-8069-8635-2). A book filled with games enjoyed by many age groups. (Rev: BL 2/15/93) [795.4]

Fishing and Hunting

13297 Bailey, John. *Ultimate Freshwater Fishing* (10–12). 1998, DK $29.95 (0-7894-2866-0). Full of tips for freshwater fishermen plus eye-catching illustrations and fascinating information about the life cycle and behavior of various species. [799.1]

13298 Capstick, Peter Hathaway. *Sands of Silence* (9–12). 1991, St. Martin's $35.00 (0-312-06459-4). The author muses on life and death in the wild in this story of elephant hunting near the edge of the African Kalahari desert, with an in-depth report on the lives of the region's natives. (Rev: BL 10/15/91) [799.2]

13299 Mason, Bill. *Sports Illustrated Fly Fishing: Learn from a Master.* Rev. ed. (8–12). 1994, Sports Illustrated for Kids paper $14.95 (1-56800-033-2). Equipment and techniques are emphasized in this illustrated introduction to fly fishing. [799.1]

13300 Migdalski, Edward C. *The Inquisitive Angler* (9–12). 1991, Lyons Pr. $27.95 (1-55821-132-2). A serious fishing text, with information on taxonomy, habitat, limnology, and anatomy, designed to improve sports skills. (Rev: BL 12/15/91) [799.1]

13301 Paulsen, Gary. *Father Water, Mother Woods: Essays on Fishing and Hunting in the North Woods* (6–12). 1994, Delacorte $16.95 (0-385-32053-1). Essays reflecting the author's deep love for the wilderness describe his adventures hunting, fishing, canoeing, and camping. (Rev: BL 7/94; SLJ 8/94; VOYA 10/94) [799]

Football

13302 Anastasia, Phil. *Broken Wing, Broken Promise: A Season Inside the Philadelphia Eagles* (9–12). 1993, Camino $18.00 (0-940159-20-1). Reporter Anastasia chronicles the Eagles' 1992 season, including Jerome Brown's death, mistrust of coach Kotite, and the division of team loyalty between two quarterbacks. (Rev: BL 10/1/93) [796.332]

13303 Borowski, Greg. *First and Long: A Black School, a White School and Their Season of Dreams* (9–12). 2004, Badger $25.00 (1-932542-02-7). The story of how a white suburban school and a black Catholic city school joined forces in 2001 to form a joint football team. (Rev: BL 2/15/04) [796.332]

13304 Brown, Scott, and Sam Carchidi. *Miracle in the Making: The Adam Taliaferro Story* (9–12). Illus. 2001, Triumph paper $16.95 (1-57243-422-8). When he was severely injured in a football game and told he would never walk again, Adam Taliaferro and his medical team accomplished a miracle — not only did he walk again, he played football again. (Rev: BL 9/1/01) [362.4]

13305 Grant, Alan. *Return to Glory: Inside Tyrone Willingham's Amazing First Season at Notre Dame* (10–12). Illus. 2003, Little, Brown $24.95 (0-316-60765-7). The story of the college team's reinvigoration under the leadership of Tyrone Willingham, its first African American football coach. (Rev: BL 9/1/03) [796.332]

13306 Harrington, Denis J. *The Pro Football Hall of Fame: Players, Coaches, Team Owners and League Officials, 1963–1991* (9–12). 1991, McFarland LB $35.00 (0-89950-550-3). Thumbnail profiles of football greats, organized by position through 1990. (Rev: BL 1/15/92) [796.332]

13307 McCullough, Bob. *My Greatest Day in Football: The Legends of Football Recount Their Greatest Moments* (8–12). 2001, Thomas Dunne $24.95 (0-312-27211-1); paper $14.95 (0-312-30296-7). Members of the Pro Football Hall of Fame describe their greatest day on the field. (Rev: BL 7/01) [796.332]

13308 Mooney, Chuck. *The Recruiting Survival Guide* (10–12). 1991, 21st Century Pr. paper $9.95 (0-9630239-0-X). A former college ball player explains how recruiters work and the pitfalls and rewards that await the targeted athlete. (Rev: BL 4/15/92) [796.33]

13309 Nash, Bruce, and Allan Zullo. *The Football Hall of Shame* (9–12). 1990, Pocket paper $7.95 (0-671-69413-8). A recent collection that continues to bring into focus some of the low points of the game. (Rev: BL 9/15/90) [796.33]

13310 Parcells, Bill, and Will McDonough. *The Final Season: My Last Year as Head Coach in the NFL* (9–12). Illus. 2000, Morrow $25.00 (0-688-17491-4). This candid diary/memoir tells about the less-than-glorious 1999 football season that Parcells coached the New York Jets. (Rev: BL 9/15/00) [796.332]

13311 Paulson, Carl, and Louis H. Janda. *Rookie on Tour: The Education of a PGA Golfer* (10–12). 1998, Putnam $23.95 (0-399-14378-5). This candid account of the challenges of a PGA tour will appeal to young golfers who wonder about the professional aspects of this sport. (Rev: BL 3/15/98; SLJ 9/98) [796.352]

13312 Peterson, Robert W. *Pigskin: The Early Years of Pro Football* (10–12). 1997, Oxford $48.00 (0-19-507607-9). An absorbing history of professional football from its beginnings in 1889 to the 1958 championship game between the Colts and the Giants. (Rev: BL 11/15/96; SLJ 6/97) [796.48]

13313 Smith, Ron. *Pro Football's Heroes of the Hall* (10–12). Illus. 2003, Sporting News $29.95 (0-89204-712-7). This beautifully illustrated book profiles each of the 217 honorees in the Pro Football Hall of Fame. (Rev: BL 9/1/03) [796.3]

13314 Watterson, John Sayle. *College Football: History, Spectacle, Controversy* (9–12). 2000, Johns Hopkins Univ. Pr. $34.95 (0-8018-6428-3). College football is presented, with an emphasis on its cultural history and its relation to American society. (Rev: BL 9/1/00) [796.332]

13315 Whittingham, Richard. *Rites of Autumn: The Story of College Football* (8–12). Illus. 2001, Simon & Schuster $40.00 (0-7432-2219-9). Using more than 200 photographs, this is an excellent overview of college football — the facts, the players, key games, and the controversies. (Rev: BL 9/1/01) [796.332]

13316 Whittingham, Richard. *What Bears They Were: Chicago Bears Greats Talk About Their Teams, Their Coaches, and the Times of Their Lives* (10–12). Illus. 2002, Triumph $27.95 (1-57243-482-1). A fascinating collection of memories and anecdotes about this famous team, its founder-coach George Halas, and stars, including Dick Butkus and Mike Singletary. (Rev: BL 9/1/02) [796.332]

Golf

13317 Andrisani, John. *The Tiger Woods Way: Secrets of Tiger Woods' Power-Swinging Technique* (10–12). Illus. 1997, Crown $18.00 (0-609-60094-X). This is an in-depth look at the powerful swing of Tiger Woods and, through text and illustrations, provides tips on how readers can develop this technique themselves. (Rev: VOYA 10/97) [796.352]

13318 Anselmo, John, and John Andrisani. *"A-Game" Golf: The Complete Starter Kit for Golfers from Tiger Woods' Amateur Instructor* (9–12). Illus. 2001, Doubleday $25.00 (0-385-49813-6). This book by the man who once taught Tiger Woods gives practical pointers on how to improve one's golf game. (Rev: BL 4/15/01) [796.352]

13319 Barkow, Al. *The Golden Era of Golf: How America Rose to Dominate the Old Scots Game* (9–12). Illus. 2000, St. Martin's $25.95 (0-312-25238-2). The history of American golf, from the first American to win the U.S. Open in 1913 to the arrival of Tiger Woods in the 1990s. (Rev: BL 9/1/00) [796.352]

13320 Callahan, Tom. *In Search of Tiger: A Journey Through Golf with Tiger Woods* (10–12). 2003, Crown $25.00 (0-609-60943-2). Woods's victories in the four "majors" in 1999–2000 are the central focus of this volume that includes comments by other golfing greats. (Rev: BL 1/1–15/03) [796.352]

13321 Campbell, Malcolm. *The Random House International Encyclopedia of Golf: The Definitive Guide to the Game* (9–12). 1991, Random $60.00 (0-394-58893-2). Though somewhat dated, this is a comprehensive reference for golf enthusiasts highlighting courses, equipment, and past tournament winners. (Rev: BL 1/15/92) [796.352]

13322 Campbell, Malcolm. *Ultimate Golf Techniques* (10–12). 1996, DK $34.95 (0-7894-0442-7); paper $14.95 (0-7894-3302-8). Loaded with illustrations, this is an excellent introduction that includes step-by-step guidance on basic swings and plenty of tips from well-known players. [796.352]

13323 *Chasing Tiger: A Tiger Woods Reader* (9–12). Ed. by Glenn Stout. 2002, Da Capo paper $15.00 (0-306-81124-3). This collection of original newspaper and magazine articles chronicles Woods's dazzling career from 1991 to 2001. (Rev: BL 4/15/02) [796.357]

13324 D'Antonio, Michael. *Tin Cup Dreams: A Long Shot Makes It on the PGA Tour* (10–12). 2000, Hyperion $23.95 (0-7868-6497-4). An intriguing account that follows a self-taught Mexican golfer, Esteban Toledo, on his first year on a PGA tour. (Rev: BL 3/1/00) [796.352]

13325 Donegan, Lawrence. *Maybe It Should Have Been a Three Iron: My Years as Caddy for the World's 438th Best Golfer* (9–12). 1998, St. Martin's $21.95 (0-312-18584-7). A caddy's eye view of the sport of golf told with wisdom, candor, and humor. (Rev: BL 5/15/98; SLJ 9/98) [796.352]

13326 Glenn, Rhonda. *The Illustrated History of Women's Golf* (9–12). 1991, Taylor $34.95 (0-87833-743-1). Examines the women's amateur golf circuit from the 1920s through the 1950s, with a complete list of golf records. (Rev: BL 1/1/92) [796.352]

13327 *Golf Rules in Pictures.* Rev. ed. (9–12). 1993, Putnam paper $11.95 (0-399-51799-5). Beautifully illustrated, this easy-to-follow guide to the official rules of golf also covers golfing etiquette and includes a guide to terminology. [796.352]

13328 Grout, Jack. *On the Lesson Tee: Basic Golf Fundamentals* (9–12). 1982, Sterling paper $5.95 (0-87670-064-4). An informal guide to golf basics that is particularly good for the beginner. [796.352]

13329 Hogan, Ben. *Power Golf* (10–12). 1990, Pocket paper $6.50 (0-671-72905-5). Expert advice for people already familiar with the basics of golf. [796.352]

13330 Kaskie, Shirli. *A Woman's Golf Game* (10–12). 1983, Contemporary paper $12.95 (0-8092-5756-4). For both the beginner and the experienced female golfer, this is a fine guide. [796.352]

13331 Lopez, Nancy. *The Complete Golfer* (9–12). Illus. 1989, Contemporary paper $15.95 (0-8092-4711-9). This well-known golf professional gives her tips on the sport for both men and women. (Rev: BR 11–12/89) [796.352]

13332 McDaniel, Pete. *Uneven Lies: The Heroic Story of African-Americans in Golf* (9–12). 2001, American Golfer $50.00 (1-888531-36-3). An attractively illustrated volume that traces the roles played by African Americans in the history of golf, including the story of George Grant who invented the golf tee. (Rev: BL 2/15/01) [796.353]

13333 Nash, Bruce, and Allan Zullo. *The Golf Hall of Shame* (9–12). 1991, Pocket paper $12.00 (0-671-74583-2). Golfing goofs from the caddies to the pros. (Rev: BL 11/15/89) [796.352]

13334 *101 Essential Tips: Golf* (9–12). 1996, DK paper $4.95 (0-7894-0172-X). This book covers such essentials of golf as equipment, club grips, stance, swing control, clothing, and rules. (Rev: VOYA 6/96) [796.352]

13335 Penick, Harvey, and Bud Shrake. *For All Who Love the Game: Lessons and Teachings for Women* (9–12). 1995, Simon & Schuster $19.50 (0-684-80058-6). Goal-directed tips for golf swings. (Rev: BL 4/15/95) [796.352]

13336 Reilly, Rick. *Who's Your Caddy? Looping for the Great, Near Great, and Reprobates of Golf* (10–12). 2003, Doubleday $24.95 (0-385-48885-8). Entertaining new insights into the game of golf can found in sports columnist Reilly's humorous account of his journalistically motivated stint as a caddy. (Rev: BL 5/1/03) [796.352]

13337 Sampson, Curt. *Chasing Tiger* (10–12). 2002, Simon & Schuster $26.00 (0-7432-4212-1). Tiger Woods's championship season in 2001 is seen largely through the eyes of the golfer's rivals. (Rev: BL 6/1–15/02) [796.352]

13338 Stenzel, Kellie. *The Women's Guide to Consistent Golf* (10–12). Illus. 2002, St. Martin's $22.95 (0-312-28230-3). Most of the solid advice found here for intermediate women players will also prove useful for men. (Rev: BL 4/15/02) [796.357]

13339 Whitworth, Kathy, and Rhonda Glenn. *Golf for Women* (9–12). 1990, St. Martin's paper $14.95 (0-312-06984-7). This introductory volume on women's golf covers such topics as fundamentals, grip, stance, equipment, and strategy. [796.352]

Hockey

13340 Atkinson, Jay. *Ice Time: A Tale of Hockey and Hometown Heroes* (9–12). 2001, Crown $23.00 (0-609-60706-5). This memoir explores the author's involvement with hockey, first as a young player and now as a volunteer coach at his old school. (Rev: BL 9/1/01) [796.962]

13341 Baker, Ken. *They Don't Play Hockey in Heaven: A Dream, a Team, and My Comeback Season* (10–12). Illus. 2003, Lyons Pr. $22.95 (1-59228-149-4). The inspiring story of how the author realized his dream of playing professional hockey after being sidelined by surgery for a brain tumor. (Rev: BL 9/1/03) [796.962]

13342 *A Basic Guide to Ice Hockey* (6–12). Series: Olympic Guides. 2002, Gareth Stevens LB $22.60 (0-8368-3103-9). The rules, regulations, and fundamentals of ice hockey are covered in this basic introduction edited by the U.S. Olympic Committee. (Rev: BL 6/1–15/02; HBG 10/02) [796.962]

13343 Dunn, Tricia, et al. *Gold Medal Ice Hockey for Women and Girls* (9–12). 1999, National Book Network $15.95 (1-88628-437-7). This fine book on ice hockey for women includes material on rules, equipment, skills, and the fun of the game. [796.962]

13344 *The Game I'll Never Forget: 100 Hockey Stars' Stories* (10–12). Ed. by Chris McDonnell. Illus. 2002, Firefly paper $24.95 (1-55297-604-1). Excellent for browsing, this is a collection of hockey memories. (Rev: BL 9/15/02) [796.962]

13345 *Hockey Dynasties: Blue Lines and Bloodlines* (10–12). Ed. by Lance Hornby. Illus. 2003, Firefly $40.00 (1-55297-676-9). Action photographs supplement this fascinating study of hockey's first families, including the Bentleys, Espositos, Howes, Hulls, Richards, and Sutters. (Rev: BL 2/1/03) [796.962]

13346 Hubbard, Kevin, and Stan Fischler. *Hockey America: The Ice Game's Past Growth and Bright Future in the U.S.* (8–12). 1998, NTC paper $24.95 (1-57028-196-3). This work traces the history of ice hockey in this country, introduces some key players, and speculates about the sport's future. (Rev: VOYA 10/98) [796.962]

13347 Hunter, Douglas. *A Breed Apart: An Illustrated History of Goaltending* (9–12). Illus. 1995, Triumph $28.95 (1-57243-048-6). A history of goaltending from its earliest years, but mostly after 1943, with portraits of the most renowned goalies. (Rev: BL 10/1/95*) [796.962]

13348 Wolfe, Bernie, and Mitch Henkin. *How to Watch Ice Hockey* (9–12). Illus. 1985, National Pr. paper $9.95 (0-915765-09-8). All of the rules of a hockey match are carefully explained plus a description of each position and the kinds of action one can expect at a typical game. (Rev: BL 12/15/85) [796.96]

Horse Racing and Horsemanship

13349 Best, David Grant. *Portrait of a Racetrack: A Behind the Scenes Look at a Racetrack Community* (9–12). 1992, Best Editions paper $24.95 (0-9634241-0-6). A black-and-white photoessay featuring the horses, jockeys, grooms, and trainers at a Seattle racetrack. (Rev: BL 12/1/92*) [798.4]

13350 Binder, Sibylle Luise, and Gefion Wolf. *Riding for Beginners* (5–10). Trans. from German by Elisabeth E. Reinersmann. 1999, Sterling $21.95 (0-8069-6205-4). A straightforward text, beautiful color photographs and illustrations, and an attractive layout present the English and Western styles of riding and give tips for the novice. (Rev: SLJ 8/99) [798.4]

13351 Edwards, Elwyn Hartley. *The Complete Book of Bits and Bitting* (10–12). Illus. 2001, David & Charles $34.95 (0-7153-0783-5). A specialized, well-illustrated book about the principles and mechanics of the bit used on horses, its types, and its relation to other riding equipment. (Rev: BL 5/1/01) [636.108]

13352 Faurie, Bernadette. *The Horse Riding and Care Handbook* (10–12). Illus. 2000, Lyons Pr. $29.95 (1-58574-058-6). Beginning with an introductory chapter on the evolution of the horse, this is an excellent overview of all phases of horsemanship, including material on equipment and the basic elements of riding. (Rev: BL 5/1/00; SLJ 8/00) [636.1]

13353 Funny Cide Team, and Sally Jenkins. *Funny Cide: How a Horse, a Trainer, a Jockey, and a Bunch of High School Buddies Took on the Sheiks and Bluebloods . . . and Won* (10–12). 2004, Putnam $24.95 (0-399-15179-6). The story of the horse Funny Cide, how he won the Kentucky Derby and Preakness in 2002, and how he is surrounded by a devoted trainer, jockey and owner. (Rev: BL 4/1/04) [798.4]

13354 Hairston, Rachel. *The Essentials of Horsekeeping* (9–12). Illus. 2004, Sterling $24.95 (0-8069-8817-7). This is a primer on how to care for a horse with material on feeding, horse behavior, grooming, health, and therapies. (Rev: BL 4/1/04) [793.2]

13355 Hillenbrand, Laura. *Seabiscuit: An American Legend* (10–12). Illus. 2001, Random $24.95 (0-375-50291-2). This highly acclaimed book, not only tells the rags-to-riches story of this great racehorse but also highlights the lives of those people connected with him. (Rev: BL 1/1–15/01; SLJ 11/01) [798.4]

13356 Nusser, Susan. *In Service to the Horse* (9–12). 2004, Little, Brown $25.95 (0-316-80631-5). A look at the life of overworked and underpaid horse grooms and their contributions to the world of horsemanship. (Rev: BL 4/1/04) [798.2]

13357 Price, Steven D. *Essential Riding: A Realistic Approach to Horsemanship* (10–12). Illus. 2000, Lyons Pr. paper $16.95 (1-58574-002-0). Beginning riders will find excellent practical advice on techniques, equipment, dress, saddles, and so forth. (Rev: BL 9/1/00*) [798.2]

13358 Schramm, Ulrick. *The Undisciplined Horse* (10–12). Illus. 2003, Trafalgar $35.00 (1-57076-251-1). A German veterinarian and horseman explores horse psychology and offers advice on what to do when a horse develops behavioral problems. (Rev: BL 10/15/03) [798.2]

Ice Skating

13359 *A Basic Guide to Figure Skating* (6–12). Series: Olympic Guides. 2002, Gareth Stevens LB $22.60 (0-8368-3102-0). This guide, compiled under the editorship of the U.S. Olympic Committee, is a basic guide to figure skating and its techniques, equipment, and competitions. (Rev: BL 6/1–15/02; HBG 10/02) [796.91]

13360 *A Basic Guide to Speed Skating* (6–12). Series: Olympic Guides. 2002, Gareth Stevens LB

$22.60 (0-8368-3105-5). This easy-to-read guide gives the step-by-step fundamentals of speed skating, more advanced tips, and photographs of speed-skating stars of today. (Rev: BL 6/1–15/02; HBG 10/02) [796.91]

13361 Brennan, Christine. *Inside Edge: A Revealing Journey into the Secret World of Figure Skating* (10–12). 1996, Scribner $22.50 (0-684-80167-1). A hard look at the realities of figure skating by a reporter who covered the sport for the *Washington Post* for 11 years, and including interviews with and profiles of skaters, coaches, parents, and judges. (Rev: BL 1/1–15/96; SLJ 7/96) [796.91]

13362 Foeste, Aaron. *Ice Skating Basics* (6–10). 1999, Sterling $17.95 (0-8069-9517-3). An excellent, well-illustrated introduction to ice skating that enthusiastically describes maneuvers, types of skates, their care and fit, and appropriate clothing. (Rev: SLJ 2/99) [796.91]

13363 Goodwin, Joy. *The Second Mark: Courage, Corruption, and the Battle for Olympic Gold* (9–12). 2004, Simon & Schuster $25.00 (0-7432-4527-X). This is the story of the pairs figure skating competition at the 2002 Olympics and how the scandal it produced changed the lives of the competitors. (Rev: BL 4/15/04) [790.91]

13364 Milton, Steve. *Figure Skating Now: Olympic and World Champions* (9–12). Illus. 2001, Firefly paper $19.95 (1-55297-527-4). Excellent photographs highlight this volume in which there are biographical sketches of international figure-skating champions. (Rev: BL 10/1/01; SLJ 4/02; VOYA 2/02) [796.91]

13365 Sweet, Christopher. *Secrets of Skating* (10–12). 1997, Universe $29.95 (0-7893-0104-0). This book focuses on the life of figure skaters, featuring Oksana Baiul, the Ukrainian gold medalist in the 1994 Olympics. (Rev: SLJ 3/98) [796.911]

13366 Tashman, Patti, et al. *The Essential Figure Skater* (8–12). 2000, Lyons Pr. paper $19.95 (1-55821-993-5). All kinds of topics relating to figure skating are covered, including advice on turns, spins, and jumps. [796.91]

13367 U.S. Figure Skating Association. *The Official Book of Figure Skating* (9–12). 1998, Simon & Schuster $30.00 (0-684-84673-X). This all-inclusive look at figure skating covers its history, past and present champions, skating techniques, fitness advice, tips on creating routines, and the judging system. (Rev: SLJ 3/99) [796.91]

In-Line Skating

13368 Dugard, Martin. *In-Line Skating Made Easy: A Manual for Beginners with Tips for the Experi-*

enced (10–12). 1996, Globe Pequot paper $16.95 (1-56440-903-1). Tips for both the novice and expert are offered, along with information on equipment, competitions, and the dynamics of in-line skating. (Rev: SLJ 6/97) [796.2]

13369 Werner, Doug. *In-Line Skater's Start-Up: A Beginner's Guide to In-Line Skating and Roller Hockey* (6–12). 1995, Tracks paper $9.95 (1-884654-04-5). Using many black-and-white photographs, this book is both a guide to inline skating basics for beginners and an introduction to the growing sport of roller hockey. (Rev: BL 2/1/96) [796.2]

Martial Arts

13370 Konzak, Burt. *Samurai Spirit: Ancient Wisdom for Modern Life* (6–12). 2002, Tundra paper $8.95 (0-88776-611-0). Martial arts are the focus of this combination of traditional tales, historical and cultural information, and advice from the author, a teacher of martial arts. (Rev: SLJ 6/03) [813]

13371 Loren, BK. *The Way of the River: Adventures and Meditations of a Woman Martial Artist* (10–12). 2001, Lyons Pr. $22.95 (1-58574-301-1). The essays in this book describe the author's training in martial arts, the relationship between mind and body in this activity, and the spiritual forces behind martial arts. (Rev: BL 8/01; SLJ 2/02) [796.8]

13372 McFarlane, Stewart. *The Complete Book of T'ai Chi* (10–12). 1997, DK $22.95 (0-7894-1476-7). With numerous, clear illustrations, this book introduces the history of this ancient martial art form, and describes preparatory stretching exercises and its stances and flow of postures. (Rev: SLJ 1/98) [796.8]

13373 Miller, Davis. *The Tao of Bruce Lee: A Martial Arts Memoir* (10–12). 2000, Crown $23.00 (0-609-60477-5). This book combines an autobiography of the author, a biography of pop icon Bruce Lee, and a treatise on the martial arts. (Rev: BL 7/00*) [791.43]

13374 Tegner, Bruce. *Bruce Tegner's Complete Book of Jujitsu* (7–12). Illus. 1978, Thor paper $14.00 (0-87407-027-9). A master in the martial arts introduces this ancient Japanese form of self-defense and gives basic information on stances and routines. [796.8]

13375 Tegner, Bruce. *Bruce Tegner's Complete Book of Self-Defense* (7–12). Illus. 1975, Thor paper $14.00 (0-87407-030-9). A basic primer on ways to defend oneself including hand blows and restraints. [796.8]

13376 Tegner, Bruce. *Karate: Beginner to Black Belt* (7–12). Illus. 1982, Thor paper $14.00 (0-87407-

040-6). Techniques for both the novice and the experienced practitioner are explained in this account that stresses safety and fitness. [796.8]

13377 Tegner, Bruce, and Alice McGrath. *Self-Defense and Assault Prevention for Girls and Women* (7–12). Illus. 1977, Thor paper $10.00 (0-87407-026-0). Various defensive and offensive techniques are introduced in situations where they would be appropriate. [796.8]

13378 Tegner, Bruce, and Alice McGrath. *Solo Forms of Karate, Tai Chi, Aikido and Kung Fu* (9–12). Illus. 1981, Thor paper $10.00 (0-87407-034-1). Routines are described in copious pictures plus text that emphasize exercise and good training. [796.8]

Olympic Games

13379 Bachrach, Susan D. *The Nazi Olympics: Berlin 1936* (6–12). Illus. 2000, Little, Brown $21.95 (0-316-07086-6); paper $14.95 (0-316-07087-4). This is a complete history of the 1936 games, with background material on the Nazi movement in Germany and the growing oppression of Jews. (Rev: BL 2/15/00; HBG 9/00; SLJ 6/00) [796.48]

13380 DK Publishing, eds. *Chronicle of the Olympics, 1896–2000* (9–12). 1998, DK $29.95 (0-7894-2312-X). After a brief discussion of the ancient games, this account traces the history of the Olympics from 1896 in Athens to 1998 in Atlanta, including plans for Nagano in 1998 and Sydney, Australia, in 2000, with photographs capturing the spirit of the games, descriptions of each contest, and charts with statistics. (Rev: BL 2/15/98; SLJ 7/98) [796.4]

13381 Greenspan, Bud. *Frozen in Time: The Greatest Moments at the Winter Olympics* (7–12). 1997, General Publg. $24.95 (1-57544-027-X). The stories of nearly 60 stars of the Winter Olympics are told in two- or three-page accounts, many of them involving personal triumph and courage. (Rev: VOYA 6/98) [796.98]

13382 Guttmann, Allen. *The Olympics, A History of the Modern Games*. 2nd ed. (8–12). Series: Illinois History of Sports. 2002, Univ. of Illinois Pr. $39.95 (0-252-02725-6); paper $16.95 (0-252-07046-1). This is an interesting history of the modern Olympics from Athens in 1896 to Seoul in 1988. with good coverage on social topics. [796.48]

13383 Wallechinsky, David. *The Complete Book of the Winter Olympics* (9–12). 2001, Overlook $25.95 (1-58567-195-9); paper $15.95 (1-58567-185-1). This account provides information and statistics for every one of the winter Olympic games from 1924 on. [796.98]

Running and Jogging

13384 Barrios, Dagny Scott. *Runner's World Complete Guide to Trail Running* (10–12). Illus. 2003, Rodale paper $19.95 (1-57954-466-5). This comprehensive guide to the sport of trail running is loaded with solid information about gear, training, and technique. (Rev: BL 4/1/03) [796.42]

13385 Fixx, James F. *The Complete Book of Running* (10–12). Illus. 1977, Random $25.50 (0-394-41159-5). This book answers all kinds of questions one might have about running. A follow-up is *Jim Fixx's Second Book of Running* (1980). [796.4]

13386 Goldman, Jami, and Andrea Cagan. *Up and Running: The Jami Goldman Story* (10–12). Illus. 2001, Pocket $25.00 (0-7434-2420-4). The inspirational story of the young girl who, after having both legs amputated below the knee, went on to become a motivational speaker and world-class runner. (Rev: BL 9/1/01) [796.42]

13387 Hayhurst, Chris. *Ultra Marathon Running* (7–10). Series: Ultra Sports. 2002, Rosen LB $26.50 (0-8239-3557-4). This work looks at different long running races, the athletes that engage in this sport, and the mind-boggling distances they run. (Rev: BL 9/1/02; SLJ 9/02) [796.4]

13388 Higdon, Hal. *Boston: A Century of Running* (9–12). 1995, Rodale $40.00 (0-87596-283-1). From the senior writer for *Runner's World* and a marathon runner himself, a history of the marathon and information on current runners. (Rev: BL 11/1/95) [796.42]

13389 Johnson, Kirk. *To the Edge: A Man, Death Valley, and the Mystery of Endurance* (9–12). Illus. 2001, Warner $23.95 (0-446-52617-7). This is the story of a newspaper reporter who ran in the Badwater Ultramarathon in Death Valley, a 130-mile ordeal under potentially lethal conditions. (Rev: BL 6/1–15/01) [796.42]

13390 Lear, Chris. *Sub 4:00: Alan Webb and the Quest for the Fastest Mile* (10–12). Illus. 2003, Rodale $22.95 (1-57954-746-X). This is an absorbing account that follows University of Michigan distance runners — led by Alan Webb, high school record holder for the mile — through a complete season. (Rev: BL 8/03) [796.42]

13391 Micheli, Lyle J., and Mark Jenkins. *Healthy Runner's Handbook* (9–12). 1996, Human Kinetics paper $16.95 (0-88011-524-6). In this overview of common running injuries, the authors look at their causes and outline measures that runners can take to prevent them. (Rev: BL 4/1/96) [613.7]

13392 Scott, Dagny. *Runner's World Complete Book of Women's Running: The Best Advice to Get Started, Stay Motivated, Lose Weight, Run Injury Free, Be Safe, and Train for Any Distance* (10–12). Illus. 2000, Rodale $24.95 (1-57954-118-6). Training, racing, proper nutrition, pregnancy, weight loss, and safety are some of the topics covered in this manual suitable for both the beginner and the experienced runner. (Rev: BL 5/1/00) [796.42]

13393 Taylor, Russell. *The Looniness of the Long Distance Runner: An Unfit Londoner's Attempt to Run the New York City Marathon from Scratch* (10–12). 2002, Carlton $22.50 (1-85868-568-5). In hilarious detail, British journalist Taylor tells the story of his foray into the world of marathon running. (Rev: BL 10/1/02) [796]

Sailing, Boating, and Canoeing

13394 Adkins, Jan. *The Craft of Sail* (10–12). 1973, Walker paper $10.95 (0-8027-7214-5). A respected manual on small-boat craftsmanship. [797.1]

13395 Anderson, Scott. *Distant Fires* (8–12). Illus. 1990, Pfeifer-Hamilton paper $14.95 (0-938586-33-5). A journal of a 1,700-mile canoe trip from Minnesota to Canada's Hudson Bay. (Rev: BL 1/15/91; SLJ 4/91) [797.122]

13396 Ashcraft, Tami Oldham, and Susea McGearhart. *Red Sky in Mourning: A True Story of Love, Loss, and Survival at Sea* (10–12). Illus. 2002, Hyperion $23.95 (0-7868-6791-4). In this moving memoir of survival and loss, the author recounts how a storm at sea swept her fiance away, leaving her alone to pilot the damaged craft back to harbor. (Rev: BL 5/1/02) [910.9164]

13397 Caswell, Christopher. *The Illustrated Book of Basic Boating* (9–12). Illus. 1990, Hearst paper $15.00 (0-688-08931-3). A step-by-step guide to power boating, from launching to tying up to a dock. (Rev: BL 7/90) [796.125]

13398 Conner, Dennis, and Michael Levitt. *Learn to Sail* (9–12). 1994, St. Martin's $22.95 (0-312-11020-0). A beginner's guide for the novice sailor. (Rev: BL 5/15/94) [797.1]

13399 Goodman, Di, and Ian Brodie. *Learning to Sail: The Annapolis Sailing School Guide for All Ages* (9–12). 1994, International Marine paper $12.95 (0-07-024014-0). Provides instruction for novices on how to begin recreational sailing, including nautical jargon, safety tips, and helpful drawings. (Rev: BL 7/94) [797.1]

13400 Grant, Gordon. *Canoeing* (9–12). Series: Trailside Guide. 1997, Norton $18.95 (0-393-

31489-8). Both beginners and advanced canoeists will find useful advice in this guide, which covers essential equipment, basic paddling strokes, safety tips, and guidelines for navigating moving water and white water. [797.1]

13401 Hanson, Jonathan. *Essential Sea Kayaking* (10–12). 2000, Lyons Pr. paper $14.95 (1-55821-715-0). As well as discussing how to select and equip a kayak, this guide covers techniques, currents, navigation, and camping. (Rev: SLJ 9/00) [797.1]

13402 Harrison, David. *Canoeing: The Complete Guide to Equipment and Technique* (9–12). 1996, Stackpole paper $15.95 (0-8117-2426-3). An excellent introduction to recreational canoeing, this guide covers all the basics, including canoe types, essential gear, transporting the canoe, basic strokes, and specific techniques for canoeing in quiet, moving, and fast waters. [797.1]

13403 Krauzer, Steven M. *Kayaking: Whitewater and Touring Basics* (9–12). Series: Trailside Guide. 1995, Norton $18.95 (0-393-31336-0). This illustrated guide to kayaking covers equipment, techniques, information sources, and safety tips. [797.1]

13404 Kuhne, Cecil. *Whitewater Rafting: An Introductory Guide* (9–12). 1995, Lyons Pr. paper $16.95 (1-55821-317-1). An introduction to whitewater rafting, including pre-trip checklists and a list of classic whitewater rafting spots. (Rev: BL 2/15/95) [796.1]

13405 Lundy, Derek. *Godforsaken Sea: Racing the World's Most Dangerous Waters* (9–12). 1999, Algonquin $22.95 (1-56512-229-1). This is a gripping account of the Vendee Globe sailing race of 1996–1997, a four-month, single-handed ordeal that involves sailing to Antarctica and back. (Rev: BL 4/15/99; SLJ 9/99) [797.1]

13406 Nichols, Peter. *A Voyage for Madmen* (9–12). Illus. 2001, HarperCollins $26.00 (0-06-019764-1). In 1968, nine men competed in a race to be the first to sail solo nonstop around the world. This is their story. (Rev: BL 4/15/01) [797.14]

13407 Ray, Slim. *The Canoe Handbook: Techniques for Mastering the Sport of Canoeing* (9–12). 1992, Stackpole paper $15.95 (0-8117-3032-8). A handbook covering canoeing fundamentals, including paddling techniques, styles, maneuvers, design, and equipment. (Rev: BL 2/15/92) [797.1]

13408 Riviere, Bill. *The Open Canoe* (9–12). Illus. 1985, Little, Brown paper $12.95 (0-316-74768-8). A fine handbook that is organized by different kinds of canoeing such as recreational and competitive. (Rev: BL 8/85) [797.1]

13409 Stuhaug, Dennis O. *Kayaking Made Easy: A Manual for Beginners, with Tips for the Experienced*. 2nd ed. (10–12). 1998, Globe Pequot paper $17.95 (0-7627-0188-9). This guide covers all the fundamentals of flat-water kayaking, including tips on essential gear, basic kayak design, paddling techniques, and navigation guidance. [797.1]

13410 Swenson, Allan A. *The L.L. Bean Canoeing Handbook* (8–12). 1999, Lyons Pr. paper $18.95 (1-55821-977-3). Equipment, various water conditions, supplies, safety, and trip planning are some of the subjects covered in this guide. [797.1]

13411 Thompson, Luke. *Essential Boating for Teens* (9–12). Series: Outdoor Life. 2000, Children's LB $19.00 (0-516-23352-1); paper $6.99 (0-516-23552-4). As well as the basics of boating, this book describes types of boats, their parts, and also supplies safety tips. (Rev: SLJ 3/01) [797.1]

Skateboarding

13412 Andrejtschitsch, Jan, et al. *Action Skateboarding* (6–12). 1993, Sterling $16.95 (0-8069-8500-3). A handbook that provides a history of skateboarding, reviews equipment, and defines styles and terrains, with tips on tricks and maneuvers. (Rev: BL 6/1–15/93; SLJ 7/93) [795.2]

Skiing and Snowboarding

13413 *A Basic Guide to Skiing and Snowboarding* (6–12). Series: Olympic Guides. 2002, Gareth Stevens LB $22.60 (0-8368-3104-7). In this guide edited by the U.S. Olympic Committee, the sports of skiing and snowboarding are introduced with material on techniques, competitions, and equipment. (Rev: BL 6/1–15/02; HBG 10/02) [796.9]

13414 Bennett, Jeff, and Scott Downey. *The Complete Snowboarder* (9–12). 1994, McGraw-Hill paper $14.95 (0-07-005142-9). Presents tips for prospective snowboarders, with diagrams and illustrations. (Rev: BL 9/15/94) [796.9]

13415 Cazeneuve, Brian. *Cross-Country Skiing: A Complete Guide* (8–12). Series: Trailside Guide. 1995, Norton $17.95 (0-393-31335-2). An illustrated manual that covers equipment, techniques, clothing, safety and other topics relating to cross-country skiing. [796.93]

13416 Fabbro, Mike. *Snowboarding: The Ultimate Freeride* (10–12). Illus. 1996, McClelland & Stewart paper $12.99 (0-7710-3122-X). This is a comprehensive guide to this rising sport, with information on equipment, techniques, competitions, and complex maneuvers. (Rev: SLJ 4/97) [796.9]

13417 Kleh, Cindy. *Snowboarding Skills: The Back-to-Basics Essentials for All Levels* (7–12). Illus. 2002, Annick paper $16.95 (1-55297-626-2). Tips from an expert, with photographs and a glossary, make this a hip title for enthusiasts. (Rev: BL 12/15/02; SLJ 1/03) [796.9]

13418 Masoff, Joy. *Snowboard!* (9–12). Illus. Series: Extreme Sports. 2002, National Geographic paper $8.95 (0-7922-6740-0). An excellent overview of the increasingly popular winter sport of snowboarding, covering equipment, boarding techniques, and training tips. (Rev: BL 3/15/02) [796.93]

13419 Pollack, Pamela. *Ski!* (9–12). Illus. Series: Extreme Sports. 2002, National Geographic paper $8.95 (0-7922-6738-9). Ideal for teens, this is an excellent introduction to the popular sport of skiing, covering such basics as equipment, techniques, and advice on getting in shape for the slopes. (Rev: BL 3/15/02) [796.93]

13420 Richards, Todd, and Eric Blehm. *P3: Parks, Pipes and Powder* (10–12). Illus. 2004, Regan $24.95 (0-06-056040-1). The story of Richards's success as a snowboarder is accompanied by a history of the sport and its recognition as an Olympic event. (Rev: BL 12/1/03) [796.939]

13421 Stiefer, Sandy. *Marathon Skiing* (7–10). Series: Ultra Sports. 2002, Rosen LB $26.50 (0-8239-3554-X). This work describes the sport of marathon skiing — cross-country skiing pushed to its limits. (Rev: BL 9/1/02) [796.95]

13422 Werner, Doug, and Jim Waide. *Snowboarder's Start-Up: A Beginner's Guide to Snowboarding.* Rev. ed. (9–12). Illus. 1999, Tracks paper $9.95 (1-884654-11-8). An appealing introduction to snowboarding, with information on equipment, clothing, and basic techniques. (Rev: BL 12/15/98) [796.9]

Soccer

13423 Bauer, Gerhard. *Soccer Techniques, Tactics and Teamwork* (9–12). 1993, Sterling paper $14.95 (0-8069-8730-8). Basic soccer training and skill development, with color photographs. (Rev: BL 7/93*) [796.344]

13424 Buxton, Ted. *Soccer Skills: For Young Players* (6–12). Illus. 2000, Firefly paper $14.95 (1-55209-329-8). A practical guide to training and technique that will be useful for beginners and advanced players. (Rev: SLJ 10/00; VOYA 12/00) [796.344]

13425 Chyzowych, Walter. *The Official Soccer Book of the United States Soccer Federation* (10–12). 1987, U.S. Soccer Federation paper $7.00 (0-318-16830-8). This manual covers topics such as training, physical fitness, and strategies. [796.334]

13426 Hamm, Mia, and Aaron Heifetz. *Go for the Goal: A Champion's Guide to Winning in Soccer and Life* (9–12). 1999, HarperCollins paper $12.95 (0-06-093159-0). Using anecdotes and pictures, basic soccer skills and techniques are explained. [796.334]

13427 Herbst, Dan. *Sports Illustrated Soccer: The Complete Player* (7–12). Illus. 1988, Sports Illustrated for Kids paper $9.95 (1-56800-038-3). Basic and advanced skills are explained plus a variety of game strategies. [796.334]

13428 Luongo, Albert M. *Soccer Drills: Skill-Builders for Field Control* (9–12). 2000, McFarland paper $24.50 (0-7864-0682-8). This book offers a systematic plan to strengthen one's soccer game from beginning skills to advanced. (Rev: VOYA 6/00) [796.334]

13429 Rosenthal, Gary. *Soccer Skills and Drills* (10–12). 1978, Macmillan LB $14.95 (0-87460-258-0). In addition to a rundown on techniques, this manual includes a glossary and the official rules. [796.334]

13430 Stewart, Mark. *Soccer: An Intimate History of the World's Most Popular Game* (7–10). Series: Watts History of Sports. 1998, Watts LB $33.50 (0-531-11456-2). With clear text and photographs, this book traces the history of soccer in the United States, with interesting material on memorable games, famous players, related off-the-field developments, and a discussion of why soccer is not as popular as other sports in the United States. (Rev: HBG 9/98; SLJ 7/98) [796.334]

13431 Trecker, Jim, and Charles Miers, eds. *Soccer! The Game and the World Cup* (9–12). 1998, Universe paper $27.50 (0-7893-0145-8). A handsomely illustrated paperback on the history of soccer and highlights of World Cup games, with a whole section on women's soccer and women's World Cup games. (Rev: SLJ 1/99) [796.334]

13432 *Women's Soccer: The Game and the World Cup* (7–12). Ed. by Jim Trecker and Charle Miers. 1999, Universe $20.00 (0-7893-0270-5). A richly illustrated and information-packed celebration of women's soccer. (Rev: VOYA 2/00) [796.334]

13433 Woog, Dan. *The Ultimate Soccer Almanac* (6–12). Illus. 1998, Lowell House $12.95 (1-56565-951-1); paper $8.95 (1-56565-891-4). A review of the history of soccer, important players and teams, and rules of the game and how to play it. (Rev: BL 7/98) [796.334]

Surfing, Water Skiing, and Other Water Sports

13434 Brems, Marianne. *The Fit Swimmer: 120 Workouts and Training Tips* (9–12). Illus. 1984, Contemporary paper $12.95 (0-8092-5454-9). For a person who has chosen swimming as a way of keeping fit, this book describes 120 workouts. [797.2]

13435 Counsilman, James E. *The Complete Book of Swimming* (9–12). 1979, Macmillan paper $10.00 (0-689-70583-2). This book for both the novice and the expert gives material on strokes, drills, and advanced techniques. [797.2]

13436 Ecott, Tim. *Neutral Buoyancy: Adventures in a Liquid World* (10–12). Illus. 2001, Grove Atlantic $26.00 (0-87113-794-1). As well as a history of diving from the ancient Greeks on, the author tells of his own adventures underwater exploring reefs and swimming with sharks. (Rev: BL 7/01) [797.2]

13437 Gabbard, Andrea. *Girl in the Curl: A Century of Women in Surfing* (10–12). 2000, Seal paper $29.95 (1-58005-048-4). This eye-catching overview of women surfers spotlights achievements and looks at inequities in the world of professional surfing. (Rev: VOYA 12/01) [797.3]

13438 Grubb, Jake, et al. *The New Sailboard Book* (9–12). Illus. 1990, Norton paper $16.95 (0-393-30682-8). This guide to a fast-growing sport contains information on equipment, basic techniques, and types of competitions. (Rev: BL 5/1/85) [797.124]

13439 Manley, Claudia B. *Ultra Swimming* (7–10). Illus. Series: Ultra Sports. 2002, Rosen LB $26.50 (0-8239-3558-2). An introduction to the history of this demanding new sport that gives tips on improving performance, maintaining safety, and training both body and mind for the challenges. (Rev: BL 9/1/02) [797.2]

13440 Mullen, P. H. *Gold in the Water: The True Story of Ordinary Men and Their Extraordinary Dream of Olympic Glory* (10–12). Illus. 2001, St. Martin's $23.95 (0-312-26595-6). This book chronicles the US swimming team's journey to the 2000 Olympics, from initial dream to the grueling training. (Rev: BL 9/1/01*; VOYA 8/02) [797.2]

13441 *The Perfect Day: 40 Years of Surfer Magazine* (8–12). Ed. by Sam George. 2001, Chronicle $35.00 (0-8118-3117-5). The coverage is international in this collection of articles that spans four decades of Surfer magazine. [797.3]

13442 Werner, Doug. *Surfer's Start-Up: A Beginner's Guide to Surfing*. 2nd ed. (7–12). 1999, Tracks paper $11.95 (1-884654-12-6). A new edition of this standard instructional guide that covers basic instruction, surfing gear, safety, etiquette, and history. (Rev: SLJ 9/99) [797]

Tennis and Other Racquet Games

13443 Allsen, Phillip E., and Alan R. Witbeck. *Racquetball*. 6th ed. (9–12). 1996, W. C. Brown & Benchmark $17.95 (0-697-25627-8). From the simple to the complex, this manual covers the techniques and strategies used in racquetball. [796.34]

13444 Ashe, Arthur, and Alexander McNab. *Arthur Ashe on Tennis: Strokes, Strategy, Traditions, Players, Psychology, and Wisdom* (9–12). 1995, Knopf $20.00 (0-679-43797-5). An instructional guide that also expresses admiration for Ashe the man and his struggle with a heart condition and then with AIDS. (Rev: BL 3/1/95) [796.342]

13445 Boga, Steve. *Badminton* (9–12). 1996, Stackpole paper $10.00 (0-8117-2487-5). Designed for backyard badminton players, this guide explores badminton's history and rules and provides easy-to-follow guidance on such key elements as footwork, racket grip, and strategies for use in singles, doubles, and mixed-doubles play. [796.34]

13446 *International Book of Tennis Drills* (9–12). 1993, Triumph paper $14.95 (1-880141-36-1). The U.S. Professional Tennis Registry presents more than 100 tennis drills, with accompanying diagrams to build basic skills. (Rev: BL 11/15/93) [796.342]

13447 Jennings, Jay, ed. *Tennis and the Meaning of Life: A Literary Anthology of the Game* (9–12). 1995, Breakaway $24.00 (1-55821-378-3). A collection of tennis-related stories and poetry by well-known writers. (Rev: BL 5/15/95) [808.8]

13448 Kittleson, Stan. *Racquetball: Steps to Success* (9–12). 1991, Human Kinetics paper $15.95 (0-88011-440-1). An instructional text for beginning players on mastering 18 basic racquetball skills, each with appropriate drills. (Rev: BL 10/1/91) [796.34]

13449 Lendl, Ivan, and George Mendoza. *Hitting Hot* (9–12). Illus. 1986, Random $14.95 (0-394-55407-8). A 14-day tennis clinic with a specific skill covered on each day. (Rev: BR 5–6/87; VOYA 2/87) [796.342]

13450 MacCurdy, Doug, and Shawn Tully. *Sports Illustrated Tennis: Strokes for Success!* Rev. ed. (8–12). 1994, Sports Illustrated for Kids paper $12.95 (1-56800-006-5). Using many illustrations, this volume covers topics like rules, equipment, techniques, and competitions. [796.342]

13451 *101 Essential Tips: Tennis* (9–12). 1996, DK paper $4.95 (0-7894-0182-7). From equipment to clothing and from strokes to racquet positioning, this book covers the sport of tennis for both the beginner and the expert. (Rev: VOYA 6/96) [796.342]

13452 Schoenfeld, Bruce. *The Match: Althea Gibson and Angela Buxton: How Two Outsiders — One Black, the Other Jewish — Forged a Friendship and Made Sports History* (9–12). Illus. 2004, Amistad $24.95 (0-06-052652-1). This is the story of two doubles partners in tennis, each from opposite cultures, and how they worked together. (Rev: BL 5/15/04) [796.342]

13453 Sherrow, Victoria. *Tennis* (6–12). Series: History of Sports. 2003, Gale LB $21.96 (1-56006-959-7). The origins and evolution of the game are followed by information on recreational and competitive tennis and on outstanding players. (Rev: SLJ 9/03) [796.342]

13454 Turner, Ed, and Woody Clouse. *Winning Racquetball: Skills, Drills, and Strategies* (9–12). 1995, Human Kinetics paper $16.95 (0-87322-721-2). This handbook on racquetball includes drills to

develop recommended shots, strategies, and tips on conditioning. (Rev: BL 12/1/95) [796.34]

13455 Wertheim, L. Jon. *Venus Envy: A Sensational Season Inside the Women's Tour* (9–12). Illus. 2001, HarperCollins $25.00 (0-06-019774-9). A study of the 2000 tour of the women's professional tennis league and of all the people involved, including Venus Williams. (Rev: BL 7/01; VOYA 12/01) [796.342]

Volleyball

13456 Lucas, Jeff. *Pass, Set, Crush: Volleyball Illustrated*. 3rd ed. (9–12). Illus. 1993, Euclid Northwest paper $24.95 (0-9615088-6-8). A guide for players who want to improve their volleyball skills. (Rev: BL 11/15/88) [796.32]

13457 Sherrow, Victoria. *Volleyball* (6–12). Illus. Series: History of Sports. 2002, Gale LB $27.45 (1-56006-961-9). From the invention of volleyball as a second-class version of basketball to today's prominence around the world, Sherrow traces volleyball's growth and looks at competitive and recreational aspects of the sport. (Rev: BL 9/1/02) [796.325]

Author Index

Authors are arranged alphabetically by last name. Authors' and joint authors' names are followed by book titles — which are also arranged alphabetically — and the text entry number. Book titles may refer to those that appear as a main entry or as an internal entry mentioned in the text. Fiction titles are indicated by (F) following the entry number.

Aamodt, Donald. *A Name to Conjure With*, 1626(F)
Aaseng, Nathan. *African-American Athletes*, 6638
Athletes, 6639
The Bermuda Triangle, 13004
Black Inventors, 6506
The Cheetah, 11987
The Cougar, 11988
The Locker Room Mirror, 13071
Multiple Sclerosis, 10728
Paris, 7623
Science Versus Pseudoscience, 13005
Teens and Drunk Driving, 9942
Twentieth-Century Inventors, 12542
The White House, 8969
You Are the Corporate Executive, 10212
You Are the General, 9365
You Are the Juror, 9261
You Are the President, 9223
You Are the President II, 9224
You Are the Senator, 9242
You Are the Supreme Court Justice, 9262
Aaseng, Rolf E. *A Beginner's Guide to Studying the Bible*, 9039
Abani, Chris. *Graceland*, 2476(F)
Abbey, Lynn. *Behind Time*, 1627(F)
Sanctuary, 1628(F)
Unicorn and Dragon, 1629(F)
Abbotson, Susan C. W. *Student Companion to Arthur Miller*, 5496
Abdul-Jabbar, Kareem. *Black Profiles in Courage*, 6147
Kareem, 6692
A Season on the Reservation, 6691
Abeel, Samantha. *My Thirteenth Winter*, 11044
Abell, Sam (jt. author). *The Blue and the Gray*, 8590
Abelove, Joan. *Go and Come Back*, 1556(F)

Saying It Out Loud, 279(F)
Abrahams, Peter. *The Tutor*, 3329(F)
Abrahams, Roger D. *African Folktales*, 5073
Afro-American Folktales, 5120
Abt, Samuel. *Tour de France*, 13226
Abu-Jaber, Diana. *Crescent*, 3859(F)
Acatoz, Sylvio. *Pueblos*, 8416
Accattoli, Luigi. *John Paul II*, 6862
Achebe, Chinua. *Things Fall Apart*, 2477(F)
Acker, Kerry. *Dorothea Lange*, 5759
Everything You Need to Know About the Goth Scene, 11328
Nina Simone, 6122
Ackerman, Diane. *Cultivating Delight*, 12906
Ackerman, Jane. *Louis Pasteur and the Founding of Microbiology*, 6601
Ackerman, Jennifer G. *Chance in the House of Fate*, 10927
Ackerman, Peter. *A Force More Powerful*, 10129
Ackmann, Martha. *The Mercury 13*, 11708
Ackroyd, Peter. *Escape from Earth*, 11709
Aczel, Amir D. *The Riddle of the Compass*, 7387
Adair, Gene. *Alfred Hitchcock*, 6056
Thomas Alva Edison, 6552
Adair, Robert Kemp. *The Physics of Baseball*, 13146
Adams, Ansel. *Ansel Adams*, 7083
The Portfolios of Ansel Adams, 7084
Adams, Cecil. *Straight Dope*, 13006
Adams, Douglas. *The Hitchhiker's Guide to the Galaxy*, 4082(F)
Last Chance to See, 12093
The Long Dark Tea-Time of the Soul, 4083(F)
Mostly Harmless, 4084(F)
The Salmon of Doubt, 4085(F)

Adams, Francis D. *Alienable Rights*, 9588
Adams, John (jt. author). *The Future Is Wild*, 11746
Adams, John Winthrop. *Stars and Stripes Forever*, 8324
Adams, Laurie Schneider. *Italian Renaissance Art*, 7069
Adams, Richard. *Ideas for Science Projects*, 11632
More Ideas for Science Projects, 11633
The Plague Dogs, 1630(F)
Tales from Watership Down, 1631(F)
Watership Down, 1632(F)
Adams, Richard C. *Physics Projects for Young Scientists*, 12495
Adams, Simon. *World War I*, 7604
Adamson, Isaac. *Hokkaido Popsicle*, 3330(F)
Adamson, Joe. *The Bugs Bunny Golden Jubilee*, 7218
Adamson, Joy. *Born Free*, 11989
Adamson, Lydia. *A Cat on Stage Left*, 3331(F)
Adelman, Bob (jt. author). *King*, 6240
Adelson, Alan. *The Diary of Dawid Sierakowiak*, 7624
Adichie, Chimamanda Ngozi. *Purple Hibiscus*, 2478(F)
Adkins, Jan. *The Craft of Sail*, 13394
Adkins, Larry. *Handbook to Life in Ancient Greece*, 7475
Adlard, Charlie (jt. author). *Codeflesh*, 2303(F)
Adler, Bill. *Impeccable Birdfeeding*, 12037
Time Machines, 4086(F)
Adler, C. S. *The Lump in the Middle*, 592(F)
Adler, Jeremy. *Franz Kafka*, 5897
Adler, Joe Anne. *Stress*, 11045

Computer Crimes and Capers, 4114(F)
Devils, 3099(F)
Fantastic Voyage, 4107(F)
Forward the Foundation, 4108(F)
I, Robot, 4109(F)
Isaac Asimov's Guide to Earth and Space, 11651
Nemesis, 4110(F)
Prelude to Foundation, 4111(F)
Robots and Empire, 4112(F)
A Short History of Chemistry, 12330
Tales of the Occult, 3100(F)
Think About Space, 11711
Utopia, 4113(F)
Asinof, Eliot. *Eight Men Out*, 13148
Off-Season, 3340(F)
Asirvatham, Sandy. *The History of Jazz*, 7128
The History of the Blues, 7129
Katharine Graham, 6619
Askins, Renee. *Shadow Mountain*, 12003
Askins, Robert A. *Restoring North America's Birds*, 12094
Asma, Stephen T. *Stuffed Animals and Pickled Heads*, 12319
Asprin, Robert. *Myth Alliances*, 1658(F)
Myth Conception, 1657(F)
No Phule Like an Old Phule, 4116(F)
Phule's Company, 4115(F)
Assiniwi, Bernard. *The Beothuk Saga*, 2394(F)
Aston, Margaret. *Panorama of the Renaissance*, 7522
Astor, Gerald. *The Right to Fight*, 9594
Atangan, Patrick. *The Yellow Jar*, 5080
Atkin, S. Beth. *Voices from the Fields*, 10235
Atkins, Catherine. *Alt Ed*, 892(F)
When Jeff Comes Home, 893(F)
Atkins, Peter. *Galileo's Finger*, 11581
Atkins, Sinclair. *From Stone Age to Conquest*, 8112
Atkinson, Jay. *Ice Time*, 13340
Atkinson, Rick. *In the Company of Soldiers*, 8910
Atlan, Lilane. *The Passersby*, 2997(F)
Atlema, Martha. *A Time to Choose*, 2998(F)
Attebery, Brian (jt. author). *The Norton Book of Science Fiction, 1960–1990*, 4344(F)
Attenborough, David. *The Life of Birds*, 12038
The Life of Mammals, 11943
The Private Life of Plants, 11858
Attie, Alice. *Harlem on the Verge*, 8972

Atwater-Rhodes, Amelia. *Demon in My View*, 3101(F)
Hawksong, 1659(F)
In the Forests of the Night, 3102(F)
Shattered Mirror, 1660(F)
Atwood, Margaret. *Alias Grace*, 2694(F)
Cat's Eye, 1025(F)
The Handmaid's Tale, 4117(F)
Aubert, Rosemary. *Free Reign*, 3341(F)
Auch, Mary Jane. *Ashes of Roses*, 2911(F)
Auchincloss, Louis. *Theodore Roosevelt*, 6364
Woodrow Wilson, 6377
Auden, W. H. *Auden*, 4922
Audley, Anselm. *Heresy*, 1661(F)
Auel, Jean M. *The Mammoth Hunters*, 2386(F)
The Plains of Passage, 2387(F)
Auerbach, Paul S. *Medicine for the Outdoors*, 11220
Auerbach, Susan. *Queen Elizabeth II*, 6835
Augenbraum, Harold. *Growing Up Latino*, 413(F)
August, Paul Nordstrom. *Brain Function*, 10992
Auslander, Joseph. *The Winged Horse*, 5431
Austen, Jane. *Persuasion*, 203(F)
Pride and Prejudice, 204(F)
Austen-Leigh, Joan. *Later Days at Highbury*, 2556(F)
Austin, Hilary Mac (jt. author). *America's Children*, 8403
Ausubel, Nathan. *A Treasury of Jewish Folklore, Stories, Traditions, Legends, Humor, Wisdom and Folk Songs of the Jewish People*, 5054
Aveline, Erick. *Temporary Tattoos*, 12847
Avery, Christopher. *The Early Admissions Game*, 10328
Avi. *Beyond the Western Sea*, 2770(F)
The Man Who Was Poe, 1662(F)
Nothing but the Truth, 1026(F)
Wolf Rider, 3342(F)
Avraham, Regina. *Circulatory System*, 11011
Digestive System, 11015
The Downside of Drugs, 10609
The Reproductive System, 11225
Substance Abuse, 10610
Axcell, Claudia. *Simple Foods for the Pack*, 12755
Axelrod, Alan. *Cops, Crooks, and Criminologists*, 9945
Axelrod, Herbert R. *Dr. Axelrod's Mini-Atlas of Freshwater Aquarium Fishes*, 12320
Axelrod, Toby. *Hans and Sophie Scholl*, 6882

Working Together Against Teen Suicide, 11047
Axelrod-Contrada, Joan. *Women Who Led Nations*, 6759
Ayer, Eleanor. *Berlin*, 7637
A Firestorm Unleashed, 7638
From the Ashes, 7641
Inferno, 7639
Margaret Bourke-White, 5734
Parallel Journeys, 7642
The Survivors, 7640
Teen Smoking, 10611
Ayer, Eleanor H. *It's Okay to Say No*, 11226
Ayers, Harvard. *An Appalachian Tragedy*, 9011
Aymar, Brandt. *Men in Sports*, 13073
Ayral-Clause, Odile. *Camille Claudel*, 5746
Ayres, Alex. *The Wit and Wisdom of Mark Twain*, 5181
Ayres, Katherine. *North by Night*, 2771(F)
Ayture-Scheele, Zulal. *Beautiful Origami*, 12932
The Great Origami Book, 12933
Azuonye, Chukwuma. *Dogon*, 7946
Edo, 7983
Azzarello, Brian. *Batman/Deathblow*, 2297(F)

Babson, Marian. *To Catch a Cat*, 3343(F)
Bach, Richard. *Jonathan Livingston Seagull*, 1663(F)
Bachel, Beverly K. *What Do You Really Want? How to Set a Goal and Go for It!* 11395
Bacho, Peter. *Boxing in Black and White*, 13243
Bachrach, Deborah. *The Charge of the Light Brigade*, 7575
The Crimean War, 7576
The Resistance, 7643
Bachrach, Susan D. *The Nazi Olympics*, 13379
Bacon, Josephine. *Cooking the Israeli Way*, 12756
Bacon, Tony. *The Ultimate Guitar Book*, 7194
Baden, Michael. *Dead Reckoning*, 9946
Badger, David. *Lizards*, 11908
Bagdasarian, Adam. *First French Kiss and Other Traumas*, 1027(F)
Forgotten Fire, 2557(F)
Baggett, Nancy. *The All-American Cookie Book*, 12757
The International Cookie Cookbook, 12758
Bahr, Howard. *The Year of Jubilo*, 2912(F)
Baiev, Khassan. *The Oath*, 6914
Bail, Paul. *John Saul*, 5328
Bailey, Anthony. *Vermeer*, 5796

Bailey, John. *Ultimate Freshwater Fishing*, 13297

Bailey, Ronald H. *Battle for Atlanta*, 8592

The Bloodiest Day, 8593

Forward to Richmond, 8594

Bailey-Williams, Nicole. *A Little Piece of Sky*, 414(F)

Baillargeon, Morgan. *Legends of Our Times*, 8418

Bainbridge, Beryl. *The Birthday Boys*, 7(F)

Bainbridge, David. *The X in Sex*, 10928

Baird, Jon. *Songs from Nowhere Near the Heart*, 281(F)

Baird, Robert M. *Euthanasia*, 10578

Baird, Robin W. *Killer Whales of the World*, 12193

Bakalar, Nicholas. *Where the Germs Are*, 11780

Bakalar, Nicholas (jt. author). *Understanding Teenage Depression*, 11062

Baker, Alan. *The Gladiator*, 7502

The Knight, 7523

Baker, Bob (jt. author). *Burn, Baby! Burn! The Autobiography of Magnificent Montague*, 6095

Baker, Charles (jt. author). *Ancient Egyptians*, 6760

Baker, Charles F. (jt. author). *Ancient Greeks*, 7478

Ancient Romans, 7503

Baker, Christopher P. *Mi Moto Fidel*, 8271

Baker, David. *Scientific American Inventions from Outer Space*, 11712

Baker, Dusty. *You Can Teach Hitting*, 13149

Baker, Jennifer. *Most Likely to Deceive*, 1028(F)

Baker, Julie P. (jt. author). *Till Freedom Cried Out*, 8552

Baker, Kage. *Black Projects, White Knights*, 4118(F)

Mendoza in Hollywood, 1664(F)

Baker, Ken. *They Don't Play Hockey in Heaven*, 13341

Baker, Lindsay. *Till Freedom Cried Out*, 8552

Baker, Patricia. *Fashions of a Decade: The 1940s*, 8331

Fashions of a Decade: The 1950s, 8858

Baker, Paul. *Joker, Joker, Deuce*, 4951

Baker, Rosalie. *Ancient Egyptians*, 6760

Ancient Greeks, 7478

Ancient Romans, 7503

Baker, Russell. *The Norton Book of Light Verse*, 4851

Russell Baker's Book of American Humor, 5201

Baker, William J. *Jesse Owens*, 6732

Balaban, Mariah. *Study Away*, 10329

Balakian, Peter. *Black Dog of Fate*, 8078

Balanchine, George. *101 Stories of the Great Ballets*, 7211

Balasubramanyam, Rajeev. *In Beautiful Disguises*, 2495(F)

Baldacci, David. *Split Second*, 3344(F)

Baldwin, James. *The Fire Next Time*, 9596

Go Tell It on the Mountain, 415(F)

If Beale Street Could Talk, 416(F)

James Baldwin, 9389

Nobody Knows My Name, 5202

Notes of a Native Son, 9597

Baldwin, Louis. *Women of Strength*, 10357

Baldwin, Neil. *Edison*, 6553

Balf, Todd. *The Last River*, 8043

Balkin, Karen. *Poverty*, 10070

Ball, Edward. *Slaves in the Family*, 9598

Ball, Margaret. *Lost in Translation*, 4119(F)

No Earthly Sunne, 1665(F)

The Shadow Gate, 1666(F)

Ball, Pamela. *The Floating City*, 3345(F)

Ball, Philip. *Bright Earth*, 7045

The Ingredients, 12331

Life's Matrix, 12442

Ballance, Alison (jt. author). *South Sea Islands*, 8072

Ballantine, Richard. *Richards' Bicycle Repair Manual*, 13227

Ballard, Allen B. *Where I'm Bound*, 2809(F)

Ballard, J. G. *Empire of the Sun*, 2496(F)

Ballard, John H. *SoulMates*, 2497(F)

Ballard, Robert D. *The Discovery of the Titanic*, 12479

The Eternal Darkness, 12480

Balmer, Randall. *Religion in Twentieth-Century America*, 9043

Balogh, Mary. *Slightly Tempted*, 3866(F)

Bamford, Janet. *Street Wise*, 10227

Bandele, Asha. *Daughter*, 1558(F)

Bandon, Alexandra. *Chinese Americans*, 9704

Filipino Americans, 9705

Mexican Americans, 9729

West Indian Americans, 9767

Banerjee, Dillon. *So, You Want to Join the Peace Corps . . . What to Know Before You Go*, 10131

Banfield, Susan. *The Bakke Case*, 10248

The Fifteenth Amendment, 9202

Inside Recovery, 10612

The Rights of Man, the Reign of Terror, 8091

Bang, Molly. *Nobody Particular*, 9911

Banister, Keith. *The Encyclopedia of Aquatic Life*, 12157

Banks, Iain M. *Inversions*, 4120(F)

Look to Windward, 4121(F)

Banks, Kate. *Walk Softly, Rachel*, 601(F)

Banks, Lynne Reid. *Broken Bridge*, 2558(F)

Melusine, 1667(F)

Banks, Mike. *Mountain Climbing for Beginners*, 13249

Banks, Robert B. *Slicing Pizzas, Racing Turtles, and Further Adventures in Applied Mathematics*, 12397

Banks, Russell. *Rule of the Bone*, 1029(F)

Banks, Tyra. *Tyra's Beauty Inside and Out*, 10958

Banks, William H., Jr. *The Black Muslims*, 9599

Bankston, John. *Careers in Community Service*, 10485

Bannatyne, Lesley. *A Halloween How-To*, 10153

Banner, Stuart. *The Death Penalty*, 9268

Bantock, Nick. *The Artful Dodger*, 5728

Bar-on, Dan. *Legacy of Silence*, 7644

Barach, Arnold B. *Famous American Trademarks*, 10230

Barash, David P. *The Great Outdoors*, 13074

Barber, Benjamin. *The Struggle for Democracy*, 9172

Barbour, Scott. *Alcohol*, 10613

Drug Legalization, 10614

The Environment, 9863

Health and Fitness, 11026

Hunger, 10071

Teen Violence, 9947

Violence, 9948

Barbour, Scott (jt. author). *Juvenile Crime*, 10038

Barbour, William. *Illegal Immigration*, 9511

Barclay, Tessa. *A Lovely Illusion*, 3867(F)

Bard, Mitchell G. *The Holocaust*, 7645, 7646

Barey, Patricia (jt. author). *Simon and Garfunkel*, 6121

Barfoot, Joan. *Critical Injuries*, 1559(F)

Barghusen, Joan D. *The Aztecs*, 8253

The Bald Eagle, 12077

Cults, 9154

Barker, Clive. *Abarat*, 1668(F)

The Thief of Always, 3103(F)

Barkin, Carol (jt. author). *How to Write a Term Paper*, 10299

Barkow, Al. *The Golden Era of Golf*, 13319

Barlowe, Wayne Douglas. *Barlowe's Guide to Extraterrestrials*, 5248

Benduhn, Tea. *Gravel Queen*, 1038(F)

Benedek, Dezso (jt. author). *Ghosts, Vampires, and Werewolves*, 5116

Benedict, Helen. *Safe, Strong, and Streetwise*, 11280

Benet, Stephen Vincent. *The Devil and Daniel Webster*, 1687(F)

Benford, Gregory. *Eater*, 4135(F)
Worlds Vast and Various, 4136(F)

Benjamin, Carol Lea. *The Chosen Puppy*, 12269
The Dog Who Knew Too Much, 3359(F)
This Dog for Hire, 3360(F)

Benjamin, Curt. *The Prince of Dreams*, 1688(F)

Benjamin, David. *The Life and Times of the Last Kid Picked*, 6916

Benjamin, Marina. *Rocket Dreams*, 11713

Benner, Janet. *Smoking Cigarettes*, 10618

Bennett, Cherie. *Love Never Dies*, 1689(F)
Searching for David's Heart, 894(F)
Stranger in the Mirror, 1039(F)

Bennett, David. *Skyscrapers*, 12572

Bennett, James. *Blue Star Rapture*, 4556(F)

Bennett, James W. *Plunking Reggie Jackson*, 1040(F)

Bennett, Jay. *Coverup*, 3361(F)
The Dark Corridor, 3362(F)
The Haunted One, 3363(F)
I Never Said I Love You, 3873(F)
Sing Me a Death Song, 3364(F)
The Skeleton Man, 3365(F)

Bennett, Jeff. *The Complete Snowboarder*, 13414

Bennett, Jim. *The Complete Motorcycle Book*, 13228

Bennett, O. H. *The Colored Garden*, 421(F)

Bennett, William J. *The Country's Founders*, 8518

Benowitz, Steven I. *Cancer*, 10734

Benson, Angela. *Awakening Mercy*, 1041(F)

Benson, Ann. *The Plague Tales*, 1690(F)

Benson, Kathleen (jt. author). *Conjure Times*, 7294

Benson, Peter L. *What Kids Need to Succeed*, 11397
What Teens Need to Succeed, 11398

Benson, Raymond. *Never Dream of Dying*, 3366(F)

Benson, Sonia G. *Korean War: Almanac and Primary Sources*, 7861
Korean War: Biographies, 6761

Bentley, Judith. *Fidel Castro of Cuba*, 6899

Bentley, Peter J. *Digital Biology*, 12582

Bentley, Phyllis. *The Brontës and Their World*, 5820

Berck, Judith. *No Place to Be*, 10072

Berdoll, Linda. *Mr. Darcy Takes a Wife*, 2559(F)

Berenbaum, May R. *Buzzwords*, 12125

Berenbaum, Michael. *The World Must Know*, 7649

Berenson, Laurien. *Watchdog*, 3367(F)

Berent, Polly. *Getting Ready for College*, 10330

Berg, Carol. *Song of the Beast*, 1691(F)

Berg, Elizabeth. *Joy School*, 1042(F)
True to Form, 1043(F)

Bergan, Ronald. *The Coen Brothers*, 7221

Bergen, Peter L. *Holy War, Inc.*, 10168

Berger, Cynthia. *Dragonflies*, 12126

Berger, Gilda. *Alcoholism and the Family*, 10619
Crack, 10620

Berger, Joel (jt. author). *Horn of Darkness*, 7958

Berger, Karen. *Hiking and Backpacking*, 13250

Berger, Lee. *In the Footsteps of Eve*, 7344

Berger, Leslie. *The Grand Jury*, 9269

Berger, Melvin. *Exploring the Mind and Brain*, 10995

Berger, Phil. *Mickey Mantle*, 6673

Berger, Thomas. *Little Big Man*, 2863(F)

Bergreen, Laurence. *Capone*, 6477
Louis Armstrong, 5997

Berkey, John. *Painted Space*, 7031

Berkow, Ira. *Court Vision*, 13200
The Minority Quarterback and Other Lives in Sports, 13076

Berland-Hyatt, Felicia. *Close Calls*, 7650

Berlin, Adam. *Headlock*, 1044(F)

Berlin, Ira. *Remembering Slavery*, 8553

Berlinski, David. *Newton's Gift*, 12498

Berlitz, Charles. *The Bermuda Triangle*, 13008

Berlow, Lawrence H. *Sports Ethics*, 13077

Berman, Avis. *James McNeill Whistler*, 5798

Berman, Bob. *Secrets of the Night Sky*, 11653
Strange Universe, 11582

Berman, Claire (jt. author). *The Day the Voices Stopped*, 11110

Berman, Russell A. *Paul von Hindenburg*, 6853

Bernard, Catherine. *The British Empire and Queen Victoria in World History*, 8114

Bernard, Nancy Stone (jt. author). *Stonehenge*, 7376
Valley of the Kings, 7468

Bernardo, Anilu. *Jumping Off to Freedom*, 9(F)
Loves Me, Loves Me Not, 3874(F)

Berndt, Jeff (jt. author). *Vogelein*, 2320(F)

Berne, Suzanne. *A Crime in the Neighborhood*, 608(F)

Bernhardt, William. *Naked Justice*, 3368(F)

Bernotas, Bob. *Jim Thorpe*, 6736
Sitting Bull, 6452

Bernstein, Carl. *All the President's Men*, 8860

Bernstein, Carl (jt. author). *The Final Days*, 8906

Bernstein, Jane. *Loving Rachel*, 11053

Bernstein, Jeremy. *Albert Einstein and the Frontiers of Physics*, 6556

Bernstein, Mark. *World War II on the Air*, 8829

Bernstein, Richard. *Out of the Blue*, 10169

Bernstein, Richard B. *The Congress*, 9243
The Presidency, 9225
The Supreme Court, 9270

Berra, Yogi. *Yogi*, 6663

Berrill, Deborah (jt. author). *A Sierra Club Naturalist's Guide to the North Atlantic Coast*, 11782

Berrill, Michael. *A Sierra Club Naturalist's Guide to the North Atlantic Coast*, 11782

Berry, Adrian. *The Giant Leap*, 11714

Berry, Andrew (jt. author). *DNA*, 10951

Berry, F. Clifton. *United States Army at War*, 8913

Berry, Jack. *West African Folktales*, 5074

Berry, James. *Ajeemah and His Son*, 2695(F)
A Thief in the Village and Other Stories, 609(F)

Berry, James R. *Everywhere Faces Everywhere*, 5046

Berry, Liz. *The China Garden*, 1692(F)

Berry, Michael. *Georgia O'Keeffe*, 5774

Berry, Richard. *Discover the Stars*, 11654

Berson, Robin Kadison. *Young Heroes in World History*, 6906

Bert, Deb (jt. author). *Play it Again!* 4786

Bert, Norman A. *Play it Again!* 4786

Berthrong, John H. *Confucianism*, 9045

Bertram, Brian. *Lions*, 11991

Bertrand, Diane Gonzales. *Lessons of the Game*, 3875(F)

Sweet Fifteen, 422(F)

Trino's Time, 1045(F)

Beshore, George. *Sickle Cell Anemia*, 10735

Best, Amy. *Prom Night*, 11323

Best, David Grant. *Portrait of a Racetrack*, 13349

Best, Joel. *Damned Lies and Statistics*, 9789

Betancourt, John Gregor (jt. author). *Serve It Forth*, 12810

Bettelheim, Bruno. *The Uses of Enchantment*, 5055

Bettmann, Otto L. *Johann Sebastian Bach As His World Knew Him*, 5978

Bevan, Alex. *Meteorites*, 11738

Beye, Charles Rowan. *Odysseus*, 2416(F)

Beyer, Rick. *The Greatest Stories Never Told*, 7391

Bickman, Connie. *Tribe of Women*, 9378

Bicycling Magazine. *Cycling for Women*, 13229

Biddle, Wayne. *Field Guide to Germs*, 10736

Biel, Timothy L. *Life in the North During the Civil War*, 8598

Bierhorst, John. *The Mythology of North America*, 5123

Native American Stories, 5124

The Way of the Earth, 5125

The White Deer and Other Stories Told by the Lenape, 5126

Biesele, Megan. *San*, 7953

Bigler, Philip. *Washington in Focus*, 8973

Bijlefeld, Marjolijn. *Food and You*, 11123

Teen Guide to Personal Financial Management, 10552

Bilger, Burkhard. *Global Warming*, 9864

Billings, Charlene W. *Lasers*, 12529

Supercomputers, 12583

Billitteri, Thomas J. *Alternative Medicine*, 10899

The Gault Case, 9271

Billout, Guy. *Something's Not Quite Right*, 7032

Binchy, Maeve. *Evening Class*, 284(F)

The Glass Lake, 3876(F)

Binder, Sibylle Luise. *Riding for Beginners*, 13350

Binkley, Jim (jt. author). *Baseball's Most Memorable Trades*, 13164

Binstock, R. C. *Tree of Heaven*, 2498(F)

Biracree, Tom. *Althea Gibson*, 6724

Grandma Moses, 5773

Wilma Rudolph, 6735

Bird, Christiane. *Neither East Nor West*, 8213

Bird, Jessica. *Leaping Hearts*, 285(F)

Bird, Larry. *Bird on Basketball*, 13201

Birkhead, Tim. *A Brand-New Bird*, 11783

Birmelin, Immanuel. *The New Parakeet Handbook*, 12235

Birstein, Ann. *What I Saw at the Fair*, 5815

Bishop, Debbie. *Black Tide*, 2300(F)

Bishop, Jack. *Ralph Ellison*, 5854

Bishop, Morris. *The Middle Ages*, 7524

Bishop, Rudine Sims. *Presenting Walter Dean Myers*, 5331

Bisignano, Alphonse. *Cooking the Italian Way*, 12768

Biskup, Michael D. *AIDS*, 10737

Criminal Justice, 9272

Bisson, Terry. *Nat Turner*, 6273

The Pickup Artist, 1693(F)

Talking Man, 1694(F)

Bittner, Rosanne. *Into the Wilderness*, 2737(F)

Bitton-Jackson, Livia. *I Have Lived a Thousand Years*, 7651

My Bridges of Hope, 6917

Bizot, Francois. *The Gate*, 7862

Bjornlund, Britta. *The Cold War*, 7863

Bjornlund, Lydia. *The Iroquois*, 8421

The U.S. Constitution, 9204

Black, Andy. *Organized Crime*, 9955

Black, Baxter. *Horseshoes, Cowsocks and Duckfeet*, 5184

Black, Beryl. *Coping with Sexual Harassment*, 11281

Black, Christine M. *The Pursuit of the Presidency*, 9226

Black, Eric. *Bosnia*, 8079

Northern Ireland, 8115

Black, Holly. *Tithe*, 1695(F)

Black, Johnny. *Jimi Hendrix*, 6053

Black, Jonah. *The Black Book (Diary of a Teenage Stud)*, 1046(F)

Black, Penny. *The Book of Pressed Flowers*, 12726

Black, Veronica. *A Vow of Adoration*, 3369(F)

Black Elk. *Black Elk Speaks*, 6468

Blackburn, Simon. *Think*, 9023

Blackman, Cally. *The 20s and 30s*, 8783

Blackwell, Lawana. *The Maiden of Mayfair*, 2560(F)

Blackwood, Gary L. *Life in a Medieval Castle*, 7525

Bladholm, Linda. *Latin and Caribbean Grocery Stores Demystified*, 12769

Blainey, Geoffrey. *A Short History of the World*, 7392

Blair, Clifford. *The Guns of Sacred Heart*, 2864(F)

Blair, Sheila (jt. author). *Islam*, 9127

Blair, Walter. *Tall Tale America*, 5137

Blake, John. *Children of the Movement*, 9391

Blake, Michael. *Airman Mortensen*, 3877(F)

The Holy Road, 2865(F)

Blake, Mike. *Baseball Chronicles*, 13152

Blake, Randolph (jt. author). *Star Trek on the Brain*, 11009

Blakely, Mike. *Summer of Pearls*, 3370(F)

Blanco, Jodee. *Please Stop Laughing at Me . . . One Woman's Inspirational Journey*, 6919

Blandford, Percy W. *24 Table Saw Projects*, 12984

Blanning, T. C. W. *The Oxford Illustrated History of Modern Europe*, 8074

Blatner, David. *The Flying Book*, 12650

Blauer, Ettagale. *South Africa*, 7954

Bledsoe, Jerry. *The Angel Doll*, 610(F)

Blehm, Eric (jt. author). *P3*, 13420

Bles, Mark. *Child at War*, 7652

Blessley, Cara Shea (jt. author). *Spirit of the Rockies*, 11998

Bligh, William. *Mutiny on Board HMS Bounty*, 8064

Blinn, William. *Brian's Song*, 4787

Blisson, Terry. *Pirates of the Universe*, 4139(F)

Block, Barbara. *Blowing Smoke*, 3371(F)

Block, Francesca L. *Baby Be-Bop*, 1047(F)

Cherokee Bat and the Goat Guys, 1048(F)

Dangerous Angels, 1696(F)

Echo, 1049(F)

Girl Goddess #9, 1050(F)

The Hanged Man, 611(F)

I Was a Teenage Fairy, 1697(F)

Missing Angel Juan, 1698(F)

The Rose and the Beast, 5056

Violet and Claire, 1051(F)

Wasteland, 1052(F)

Weetzie Bat, 1053(F)

Witch Baby, 612(F)

Zine Scene, 10285

Block, Gay. *Rescuers*, 7653

Block, Ira (jt. author). *Saving America's Treasures*, 8415

Block, Joel D. *Stepliving for Teens*, 11493

Blom, Margaret Howard. *Charlotte Brontë*, 5264

Blood-Patterson, Peter. *Rise Up Singing*, 7202

Bloom, Amy. *Normal*, 10124

Bloom, Harold. *American Women Fiction Writers 1900–1960*, 5684

Anton Chekhov, 5432

Black American Poets and Dramatists of the Harlem Renaissance, 5685

Black American Prose Writers of the Harlem Renaissance, 4611(F)

Black American Women Fiction Writers, 5686

Black American Women Poets and Dramatists, 5687

Carson McCullers, 5332

Charlotte Brontë's Jane Eyre, 5265

The Crucible, 5501

Ernest Hemingway's The Sun Also Rises, 5333

Eudora Welty, 5334

Fyodor Dostoevsky's Crime and Punishment, 5313

Gwendolyn Brooks, 5502

Hamlet, 5461

Harper Lee's To Kill a Mockingbird, 5335 ·

How to Read and Why, 5242

Invisible Man, 5336

Lord of the Flies, 5266

Major Modern Black American Writers, 5688

Maya Angelou, 5337

Maya Angelou's I Know Why the Caged Bird Sings, 5338

Native American Women Writers, 5689

Poets of World War I, 4854

Shakespeare, 5462

Sophocles' Oedipus Plays, 5433

William Shakespeare's A Midsummer Night's Dream, 5463

Bloom, Jonathan. *Islam*, 9127

Bloom, Susan P. (jt. author). *Presenting Avi*, 5811

Bloomfield, Harold H. *Making Peace with Your Parents*, 11494

Bloor, Edward. *Crusader*, 1561(F)

Tangerine, 1054(F)

Blount, Roy. *Robert E. Lee*, 6416

Blow, Richard. *American Son*, 6329

Blue, Adrianne. *Martina*, 6725

Blue, Carroll Parrott. *The Dawn at My Back*, 9601

Blue, Rose. *Barbara Jordan*, 6411

Monica Seles, 6727

Staying Out of Trouble in a Troubled Family, 11495

Whoopi Goldberg, 6049

Blum, David. *Quintet*, 5690

Blum, Joshua. *The United States of Poetry*, 4953

Blum, Mark. *Bugs in 3-D*, 12127

Blumberg, Arnold. *The History of Israel*, 8195

Blumberg, Rhoda. *Full Steam Ahead*, 12685

Blume, Judy. *Forever . . .*, 1055(F)

Places I Never Meant to Be, 4612(F)

Summer Sisters, 1056(F)

Tiger Eyes, 1057(F)

Blumenfeld, Laura. *Revenge*, 11369

Blumenthal, Karen. *Six Days in October*, 8784

Bly, Stephen. *The Senator's Other Daughter*, 3878(F)

Bo, Ben. *Skullcrack*, 4557(F)

Boas, Jacob. *We Are Witnesses*, 7654

Bober, Natalie S. *Abigail Adams*, 6279

Countdown to Independence, 8519

Bobrick, Benson. *Testament*, 8601

Bochinski, Julianne Blair. *The Complete Handbook of Science Fair Projects*, 11634

Bodanis, David. $E = mc2$, 12499

Bodart, Joni Richards. *The World's Best Thin Books*, 10286

Boddy, Janice (jt. author). *Aman*, 7917

Bode, Janet. *The Colors of Freedom*, 9513

Food Fight, 10739

Hard Time, 9956

Kids Still Having Kids, 11163

Truce, 11496

Voices of Rape, 11282

Bodian, Stephan (jt. author). *Living Yoga*, 11030

Bodnarchuk, Kari. *Rwanda*, 7918

Bodnarchuk, Karl J. *Kurdistan*, 8214

Boekkhoff, P. M. (jt. author). *Leonardo da Vinci*, 5750

Boerst, William J. *Galileo Galilei and the Science of Motion*, 6571

Isaac Newton, 6596

Boese, Alex. *The Museum of Hoaxes*, 13009

Boettcher, Thomas D. *Vietnam*, 8914

Boffa, Alessandro. *You're an Animal, Viskovitz*, 3260(F)

Boga, Steve. *Badminton*, 13445

Bogues, Tyrone "Muggsy". *In the Land of the Giants*, 6693

Bohannon, Lisa Frederiksen. *Women's Rights and Nothing Less*, 6261

Bohl, Al. *Guide to Cartooning*, 12879

Boisclaire, Yvonne. *In the Shadow of the Rising Sun*, 7655

Bokram, Karen. *The Girls' Life Guide to Growing Up*, 11399

Bolaane, Maitseo. *Batswana*, 7955

Bolden, Tonya. *Rites of Passage*, 423(F)

33 Things Every Girl Should Know, 11400

Wake Up Our Souls, 7087

Bolgiano, Chris. *Mountain Lion*, 11992

Boller, Paul F. *Presidential Inaugurations*, 9227

Bollick, Nancy O'Keefe. *How to Survive Your Parents' Divorce*, 11497

Bolnick, Jamie Pastor (jt. author). *Living at the Edge of the World*, 10092

Bolt, Bruce A. *Earthquakes*, 12356

Bolt, Robert. *A Man for All Seasons*, 4767

Bombaugh, Ruth J. *Science Fair Success*, 11635

Bombeck, Erma. *At Wit's End*, 5185

Family, 5186

Bonafoux, Pascal. *Van Gogh*, 5791

Bonatti, Walter. *The Mountains of My Life*, 13251

Bond, Fred G. *Flatboating on the Yellowstone, 1877*, 8422

Bond, Nancy. *The Love of Friends*, 1058(F)

Bondeson, Jan. *A Cabinet of Medical Curiosities*, 13010

Bone, Howard. *Side Show*, 7283

Bone, Ian. *The Song of an Innocent Bystander*, 3372(F)

Bone, Jan. *Opportunities in Cable Television*, 10535

Bone, Neil. *Mars Observer's Guide*, 11760

Bonnell, Jennifer. *D. I. Y. Girl*, 12727

Bonner, Cindy. *Lily*, 2866(F)

Bonner, John Tyler. *Lives of a Biologist*, 6540

Bonner, Nigel. *Whales of the World*, 12194

Bonnet, Robert L. *Botany*, 11818

Bonnice, Sherry. *Computer Programmer*, 10536

Bono, Chastity. *The End of Innocence*, 6920

Bonosky, Phillip. *A Bird in Her Hair and Other Stories*, 613(F)

Bontemps, Arna. *Great Slave Narratives*, 6153

Bonvillain, Nancy. *Black Hawk*, 6384

Native American Religion, 8423

Boock, Paula. *Dare Truth or Promise*, 1059(F)

Book, Rick. *Necking With Louise*, 1060(F)

Booker, Cedella Marley. *Bob Marley, My Son*, 6086

Booker, Christopher C. *African-Americans and the Presidency*, 9392

Boon, Kevin Alexander. *The Human Genome Project*, 10930

Boorstin, Daniel J. *An American Primer*, 8333

The Americans: The Colonial Experience, 8497

The Americans: The Democratic Experience, 8334

The Americans: The National Experience, 8554

The Seekers, 9024

Boostrom, Ron. *Enduring Issues in Criminology*, 9957

Boot, Adrian. *Bob Marley*, 6087

Brokaw, Tom. *An Album of Memories*, 8337
The Greatest Generation, 8338
A Long Way from Home, 6007
Brondino, Jeanne. *Raising Each Other*, 11499
Bronner, Stephen Eric. *Albert Camus*, 5826
Brontë, Charlotte. *Emma Brown*, 2564(F)
Jane Eyre, 205(F), 5267(F)
Brontë, Emily. *Wuthering Heights*, 206(F)
Brooke, Peggy. *Jake's Orphan*, 2956(F)
Brooks, Bruce. *All That Remains*, 4613(F)
Dolores, 287(F)
Midnight Hour Encores, 620(F)
The Red Wasteland, 11785
What Hearts, 621(F)
Brooks, Geraldine. *Foreign Correspondence*, 6923
Brooks, Gwendolyn. *In Montgomery*, 4954
Brooks, Kevin. *Kissing the Rain*, 1069(F)
Lucas, 3384(F)
Martyn Pig, 622(F)
Brooks, Martha. *Being with Henry*, 1070(F)
Bone Dance, 1071(F)
Traveling On into the Light, 1072(F)
True Confessions of a Heartless Girl, 1073(F)
Two Moons in August, 3881(F)
Brooks, Polly Schoyer. *Cleopatra*, 6776
Brooks, Susan M. *Any Girl Can Rule the World*, 10132
Brooks, Terry. *The Druid of Shannara*, 1723(F)
The Elf Queen of Shannara, 1724(F)
First King of Shannara, 1725(F)
Jarka Ruus, 1726(F)
A Knight of the Word, 1727(F)
Morgawr, 1728(F)
Running with the Demon, 1729(F)
The Scions of Shannara, 1730(F)
The Talismans of Shannara, 1731(F)
The Tangle Box, 1732(F)
The Voyage of the Jerle Shannara: Antrax, 1733(F)
The Voyage of the Jerle Shannara: Ilse Witch, 1734(F)
The Wishsong of Shannara, 1735(F)
Wizard at Large, 4160(F)
Brotherton, Mike. *Star Dragon*, 4161(F)
Broude, Gwen J. *Growing Up*, 11333
Brouwer, Sigmund. *Evening Star*, 2869(F)

Brower, Michael. *The Consumer's Guide to Effective Environmental Choices*, 9866
Brown, Bobbi. *Bobbi Brown Teenage Beauty*, 11402
Brown, Brooks. *No Easy Answers*, 9960
Brown, Claude. *Manchild in the Promised Land*, 5822
Brown, Cynthia Stokes. *Like It Was*, 10287
Brown, Dale. *Tiger in a Lion's Den*, 6694
Brown, David E. *Inventing Modern America*, 12544
Brown, Dee. *The American West*, 8697
Bury My Heart at Wounded Knee, 8424
Wondrous Times on the Frontier, 8698
Brown, Dee Alexander. *The Way to Bright Star*, 2812(F)
Brown, Don. *Our Time on the River*, 3076(F)
Brown, Elaine. *The Condemnation of Little B*, 9273
Brown, Gene. *Duke Ellington*, 6038
Brown, Irene Bennett. *The Long Road Turning*, 2870(F)
Reap the South Wind, 2871(F)
Brown, Joanne. *Presenting Kathryn Lasky*, 5905
Brown, John Gregory. *The Wrecked, Blessed Body of Shelton LaFleur*, 424(F)
Brown, John Russell. *The Oxford Illustrated History of Theatre*, 7284
Brown, Jordan. *Elizabeth Blackwell*, 6538
Brown, Keith Michael. *Sacred Bond*, 9603
Brown, Kevin. *Romare Bearden*, 5729
Brown, Larry. *Billy Ray's Farm*, 5209
Joe, 1074(F)
Brown, Lauren. *Grasslands*, 12388
Brown, Linda Beatrice. *Crossing over Jordon*, 425(F)
Brown, Mary. *Pigs Don't Fly*, 1736(F)
The Unlikely Ones, 1737(F)
Brown, Molly. *Invitation to a Funeral*, 2565(F)
Brown, Pam (jt. author). *Martin Luther King Jr.*, 6244
Brown, Philip. *Uncle Whiskers*, 12247
Brown, Rachel. *The Weaving, Spinning, and Dyeing Book*, 12728
Brown, Rita Mae. *Catch as Cat Can*, 3385(F)
Murder on the Prowl, 3386(F)
Brown, Robert J. *333 Science Tricks and Experiments*, 11637

Brown, Rosellen. *Half a Heart*, 623(F)
Brown, Sam. *The Trail to Honk Ballard's Bones*, 14(F)
Brown, Sandra. *Hello, Darkness*, 3387(F)
Brown, Scott. *Miracle in the Making*, 13304
Brown, Simon. *Inheritance*, 1738(F)
Brown, Sneaky Pie (jt. author). *Catch as Cat Can*, 3385(F)
Murder on the Prowl, 3386(F)
Brown, Tom, Jr. *The Way of the Scout*, 5626
Brown, Warren. *Colin Powell*, 6444
Robert E. Lee, 6417
Brown, Wesley. *Imagining America*, 426(F)
Browne, N. M. *Basilisk*, 1739(F)
Warriors of Alavna, 1740(F)
Brownlee, Donald (jt. author). *The Life and Death of Planet Earth*, 12355
Brownlie, Alison. *Charities — Do They Work?* 10133
Brownrigg, Sylvia. *Pages for You*, 3882(F)
Brownstone, David M. (jt. author). *Across Asia by Land*, 7998
Brubaker, Ed. *Crooked Little Town*, 2302(F)
Brubaker, Paul. *The Cuban Missile Crisis in American History*, 7864
Bruccoli, Matthew Joseph (jt. author). *Literary Masters: F. Scott Fitzgerald*, 5329
Bruchac, Joseph. *Bowman's Store*, 5823
The Girl Who Married the Moon, 5128
Lasting Echoes, 8425
The Native American Sweat Lodge, 8426
Our Stories Remember, 5127
Pocahontas, 2738(F)
Sacajawea, 2732(F)
Turtle Meat and Other Stories, 2716(F)
The Winter People, 2739(F)
Bruck, Edith. *Who Loves You Like This*, 6924
Bruder, Gerry. *Heroes of the Horizon*, 8995
Bruemmer, Fred. *Glimpses of Paradise*, 11922
Brugman, Alyssa. *Walking Naked*, 1075(F)
Brunelli, Jean (jt. author). *Your Pregnancy and Newborn Journey*, 11196
Bruni, Frank. *Ambling into History*, 6288
Brunner, Laurel. *Introducing the Internet*, 12585
Bruno, Anthony (jt. author). *The Seekers*, 9944

Carvell, Marlene. *Who Will Tell My Brother?* 1563(F)

Carver, Jeffrey A. *Eternity's End*, 4181(F)

A Neptune Crossing, 4182(F)

Carver, Raymond. *American Short Story Masterpieces*, 4618(F)

Carwardine, Mark (jt. author). *Last Chance to See*, 12093

Cary, Eve. *The Rights of Students*, 9397

Cary, Lorene. *Black Ice*, 6928

Case, John. *The Genesis Code*, 3399(F)

Case, Robert. *Japan*, 8036

Caselberg, Jay. *Wyrmhole*, 4183(F)

Caseley, Judith. *Losing Louisa*, 632(F)

Casey, Joe. *Codeflesh*, 2303(F)

Cassady, Marsh. *Great Scenes from Minority Playwrights*, 4788

The Theatre and You, 7286

Cassedy, Patrice. *Education*, 10481

Engineering, 10524

Law Enforcement, 10486

Understanding Flowers for Algernon, 5346

Castaldo, Meg. *The Foreigner*, 3400(F)

Castaneda, Omar S. *Among the Volcanoes*, 1564(F)

Castelli, Alfredo. *The Snowman*, 19(F)

Castillo, Ana. *My Daughter, My Son, the Eagle, the Dove*, 8254

Castle, George. *Throwbacks*, 13154

Castner, James L. *Layers of Life*, 11786

Native Peoples, 8282

Caston, Rodney (jt. author). *Megatokyo*, 2316(F)

Castro, Adam-Troy. *Spider-Man*, 4184(F)

Castro, Fidel. *My Early Years*, 6900

Castro, Nick (jt. author). *What's Going on Down There?* 11239

Caswell, Christopher. *The Illustrated Book of Basic Boating*, 13397

Catalano, Grace. *Meet the Stars of Dawson's Creek*, 7263

Cate, Fred H. *The Internet and the First Amendment*, 12587

Cather, Willa. *Death Comes for the Archbishop*, 241(F)

My Antonia, 242(F)

Willa Cather: Early Novels and Stories, 243(F)

Willa Cather: Later Novels, 244(F)

Willa Cather: Stories, Poems, and Other Writings, 245(F)

Cattermole, Peter. *Mars*, 11761

Catton, Bruce. *The Civil War*, 8607

Reflections on the Civil War, 8608

A Stillness at Appomattox, 8609

This Hallowed Ground, 8610

Caudill, Edward. *The Scopes Trial*, 8788

Cavanaugh, Jack. *While Mortals Sleep*, 3002(F)

Cavelos, Jeanne. *The Science of Star Wars*, 7224

The Science of The X-Files, 7264

Cavendish, Richard. *The World of Ghosts and the Supernatural*, 13014

Caws, Mary Ann. *Virginia Woolf*, 5968

Cayleff, Susan E. *Babe*, 6755

Babe Didrikson, 6756

Cazeneuve, Brian. *Cross-Country Skiing*, 13415

Cefrey, Holly. *Archaeologists*, 10525

Coping with Cancer, 10747

Celsi, Teresa. *Ralph Nader*, 6430

Center, Bill. *Ultimate Stock Car*, 13137

The Center for Popular Economics (jt. author). *The New Field Guide to the U.S. Economy*, 10214

Century, Douglas. *Toni Morrison*, 5912

Ceram, C. W. *Gods, Graves, and Scholars*, 7370

Cerar, K. Melissa. *Teenage Refugees from Nicaragua Speak Out*, 9731

Cerf, Bennett. *Famous Ghost Stories*, 3115(F)

Thirty Famous One-Act Plays, 4742

24 Favorite One-Act Plays, 4743

Cerf, Christopher (jt. author). *The Gulf War Reader*, 8947

Cha, Dia (jt. author). *Folk Stories of the Hmong*, 5085

Chabon, Michael. *Summerland*, 1755(F)

Chacham, Remit. *Breaking Ranks*, 8197

Chadwick, Douglas H. *The Fate of the Elephant*, 12021

Chaiet, Donna. *Staying Safe at School*, 11283

Staying Safe at Work, 11284

Staying Safe on Public Transportation, 11285

Staying Safe on the Streets, 11286

Staying Safe While Shopping, 11287

Staying Safe While Traveling, 11288

Chaikin, Linda. *Swords and Scimitars*, 2443(F)

Chalberg, John C. *Isolationism*, 9174

Chalfant, William Y. *Dangerous Passage*, 8555

Chalker, Jack L. *Midnight at the Well of Souls*, 1756(F)

Challoner, Jack. *The Visual Dictionary of Chemistry*, 12333

Chamberlain, Diane. *The Courage Tree*, 3401(F)

Kiss River, 3402(F)

Chamberlin, Ann. *The Merlin of the Oak Wood*, 1757(F)

Chambers, Aidan. *NIK*, 1093(F)

Postcards from No Man's Land, 1094(F)

Chambers, Veronica. *The Harlem Renaissance*, 8789

When Did You Stop Loving Me, 633(F)

Chan, Gillian. *A Foreign Field*, 3003(F)

Glory Days and Other Stories, 1095(F)

Golden Girl and Other Stories, 1096(F)

Chance, Megan. *Susanna Morrow*, 2774(F)

Chandler, Elizabeth. *Dark Secrets*, 3403(F)

Chandler, Gary. *Environmental Causes*, 9870

Chang, Iris. *The Chinese in America*, 9706

Chanoff, David (jt. author). *Hacker Cracker*, 12616

Chapple, Judy. *Your Horse*, 12306

Charbonneau, Eileen. *Honor to the Hills*, 2775(F)

Rachel LeMoyne, 2872(F)

Chargueraud, Joyce (jt. author). *Temporary Tattoos*, 12847

Charles, Daniel. *Lords of the Harvest*, 11787

Charlish, Anne. *Divorce*, 11500

Charnas, Suzy McKee. *The Kingdom of Kevin Malone*, 1758(F)

Charpak, Georges. *Debunked! ESP, Telekinesis, and Other Pseudoscience*, 13015

Charters, Ann (jt. author). *The Portable Jack Kerouac*, 4656

Chase, Marilyn. *The Barbary Plague*, 10901

Chase-Riboud, Barbara. *The President's Daughter*, 2776(F)

Chasteen, John Charles. *Born in Blood and Fire*, 8283

Chatters, James C. *Ancient Encounters*, 7345

Chattman, Lauren. *Mom's Big Book of Baking*, 12776

Chaucer, Geoffrey. *The Portable Chaucer*, 5435

Chazin, Suzanne. *Flashover*, 3404(F)

Chbosky, Stephen. *The Perks of Being a Wallflower*, 1097(F)

Che, Sunny. *Forever Alien*, 6929

Cheaney, J. B. *The Playmaker*, 2567(F)

The True Prince, 2568(F)

Check, William A. *AIDS*, 10748

Alzheimer's Disease, 10749

Chedid, Andree. *The Multiple Child*, 1098(F)

Chekhov, Anton Pavlovich. *Anton Chekhov's Plays — Backgrounds, Criticism*, 5436

Coulter, Catherine. *Hemlock Bay*, 3445(F)

Lord of Falcon Ridge, 2444(F)

Riptide, 3446(F)

Counsilman, James E. *The Complete Book of Swimming*, 13435

Counts, Wilma. *Rules of Marriage*, 3893(F)

Courgeon, Rémi (jt. author). *Montezuma and the Aztecs*, 8259

Courlander, Harold. *Treasury of African Folklore*, 5075

Coursen, Herbert R. *Macbeth*, 5465

Cousteau, Jacques. *The Silent World*, 12482

Coville, Bruce. *Half-Human*, 1780(F)

Coville, Bruce (jt. author). *Armageddon Summer*, 159(F)

Covington, Dennis. *Lasso the Moon*, 1568(F)

Lizard, 906(F)

Cowell, Stephanie. *Marrying Mozart*, 2578(F)

Cowie, Peter. *World Cinema*, 7225

Cowley, Robert. *The Reader's Companion to Military History*, 7395

Cox, Beverly. *Spirit of the Harvest*, 12782

Cox, Brenda S. *Who Talks Funny? A Book About Languages for Kids*, 5542

Cox, Clinton. *Fiery Vision*, 6202

Cox, Daniel. *Whitetail Country*, 12019

Cox, Elizabeth. *Night Talk*, 1125(F)

Cox, Michael. *The Oxford Book of English Ghost Stories*, 3118(F)

Cox, Ted. *The Temptations*, 6132

Cox, Vic. *The Challenge of Immigration*, 9518

Guns, Violence, and Teens, 9968

Coyle, Harold. *Look Away*, 2815(F)

Coyne, Tom. *A Gentleman's Game*, 4561(F)

Cozic, Charles P. *The Abortion Controversy*, 11168

An Aging Population, 9940

AIDS, 10752

America's Prisons, 9969

The Future of the Internet, 12591

Gambling, 9792

Gangs, 9970

Garbage and Waste, 9925

Illegal Immigration, 9519

The Information Highway, 12592

The Militia Movement, 9791

Nationalism and Ethnic Conflict, 9177

Politicians and Ethics, 9348

Pollution, 9912

Rainforests, 12375

Sexual Values, 11290

U.S. Policy Toward China, 8006

Welfare, 10074

Welfare Reform, 10073

Crabtree, Caroline. *Beadwork*, 12851

Craddock, Curtis. *Sparrow's Flight*, 1781(F)

Craft, Naomi (jt. author). *1001 Facts About the Human Body*, 10978

Craig, Jenny. *Jenny Craig's What Have You Got to Lose? A Personalized Weight Management Program*, 11125

Craig, Roy. *UFOs*, 13018

Craig, Steve. *Sports Writing*, 10289

Craighead, Frank C., Jr. *Track of the Grizzly*, 11978

Craighead, Lance. *Bears of the World*, 11979

Cramer, Carol. *Thomas Edison*, 6554

Cramer, Deborah. *Great Waters*, 12467

Cramer, Kathryn (jt. author). *The Hard SF Renaissance*, 4292(F)

Cramer, Richard Ben. *Joe DiMaggio*, 6664

Crane, Anita Louise. *Decorating with Seashells*, 12731

Crane, Cynthia A. *Divided Lives*, 7670

Crane, Kathleen. *Sea Legs*, 6543

Crane, Milton. *50 Great American Short Stories*, 4623(F)

Crane, Stephen. *The Complete Poems of Stephen Crane*, 5504

The Red Badge of Courage, 247(F)

Craughwell, Thomas J. *Alligators in the Sewer and 222 Other Urban Legends*, 13019

Craven, Margaret. *I Heard the Owl Call My Name*, 300(F)

Walk Gently This Good Earth, 3006(F)

Craven, Wayne. *American Art*, 7017

Crawford, Mark. *Habitats and Ecosystems*, 12099

Crawford, S. *The Power of Birthdays, Stars and Numbers*, 13020

Cray, Jordan. *Gemini 7*, 3119(F)

Cream, Penelope. *The Complete Book of Sewing*, 12959

Creamer, Robert W. *Babe*, 6685

Creed, Alexander. *Uganda*, 7922

Creeden, Sharon. *Fair Is Fair*, 5058

Cress, Doug (jt. author). *In My Family Tree*, 11971

Cresswell, Helen. *Mystery Stories*, 3447(F)

Crew, Gary. *Angel's Gate*, 3448(F)

Crew, Linda. *Brides of Eden*, 301(F)

Crichton, Michael. *Airframe*, 3449(F)

The Andromeda Strain, 4212(F)

The Great Train Robbery, 2579(F)

Jurassic Park, 4213(F)

Prey, 3450(F)

Sphere, 4214(F)

The Terminal Man, 4215(F)

Timeline, 1782(F)

Crider, Bill. *Murder Takes a Break*, 3451(F)

A Romantic Way to Die, 3452(F)

Crimp, Susan. *The Many Lives of Elton John*, 6068

Crisp, George. *Miles Davis*, 6026

Crispin, A. C. *The Paradise Snare*, 1783(F)

Voices of Chaos, 1784(F)

Crispino, Enrica. *Van Gogh*, 5792

Crist-Evans, Craig. *Amaryllis*, 3078(F)

Criswell, Millie. *Mad About Mia*, 3894(F)

Croce, Nicholas. *Detectives*, 10487

Croft, Jennifer. *Drugs and the Legalization Debate*, 10627

PCP, 10628

Crompton, Anne E. *Gawain and Lady Green*, 2580(F)

Merlin's Harp, 1785(F)

Crompton, Samuel Willard. *Pakistan*, 8025

Cronin, A. J. *The Citadel*, 1126(F)

The Keys of the Kingdom, 1127(F)

Cronin, Edward W. *Getting Started in Bird Watching*, 12046

Cronkite, Walter. *A Reporter's Life*, 6023

Cronon, E. David. *Black Moses*, 6223

Crook, Marion. *Teenagers Talk About Suicide*, 11058

Croom, Emily Anne (jt. author). *A Genealogist's Guide to Discovering Your African-American Ancestors*, 11558

Cropper, William H. *Great Physicists*, 6511

Crosby, Jay (jt. author). *Our National Archive*, 8339

Cross, Amanda. *The Collected Stories of Amanda Cross*, 3453(F)

Honest Doubt, 3454(F)

Cross, Charles R. *Heavier than Heaven*, 6018

Cross, Gillian. *Phoning a Dead Man*, 3455(F)

Tightrope, 1128(F)

Crosse, Joanna. *The Element Illustrated Encyclopedia of Mind, Body, Spirit and Earth*, 13021

Croswell, Ken. *The Universe at Midnight*, 11659

Crouch, Tom D. *Wings*, 12652

The Wright Brothers and the Invention of the Aerial Age, 12653

Crowe, Carole. *Waiting for Dolphins*, 1129(F)

Crowe, Chris. *Getting Away with Murder*, 9612

Mississippi Trial, 1955, 2983(F)

Presenting Mildred D. Taylor, 5348

Crowther, Nicky. *The Ultimate Mountain Bike Book*, 13233

Crump, Donald J. *Exploring America's Scenic Highways*, 8344

Giants from the Past, 7346

Crump, Marty. *Amphibians, Reptiles, and Their Conservation*, 11900

DeVos, Elisabeth. *The Seraphim Rising*, 1812(F)

De Vries, Anke. *Bruises*, 1139(F)

Dewdney, A. K. *Hungry Hollow*, 12101

Dewey, Jennifer Owlings. *Borderlands*, 913(F)

DeWitt, Howard A. *The Beatles*, 6004

Dezell, Maureen. *Irish America*, 9770

Dhanjal, Beryl. *Sikhism*, 9053

D'Harcourt, Claire (jt. author). *Babies*, 11177

Diagram Group. *Weapons*, 12702

Diamond, Arthur. *Malcolm X*, 6249

Diamond, Diana. *The Babysitter*, 3480(F)

Diamond, Marilyn. *The American Vegetarian Cookbook*, 12786

Diamond, Maxine. *Matt Damon*, 6025

Diamond, Shifra N. *Everything You Need to Know About Going to the Gynecologist*, 11232

Diamonstein, Barbaralee. *Singular Voices*, 6155

Diaz del Castillo, Bernal. *Cortez and the Conquest of Mexico by the Spaniards in 1521*, 8255

Dibra, Bash. *CatSpeak*, 12250

Di Cagno, Gabriella. *Michelangelo*, 5767

Dick, Philip K. *Do Androids Dream of Electric Sheep*, 4225(F)

Dick, Ron. *Aviation Century*, 12655

Dickens, Charles. *A Christmas Carol*, 212(F), 213(F)

David Copperfield, 214(F)

Great Expectations, 215(F)

Martin Chuzzlewit, 216(F)

The Mystery of Edwin Drood, 217(F)

Oliver Twist, 218(F)

A Tale of Two Cities, 219(F)

Dickerson, James L. *Dixie Chicks*, 6034

Dickinson, Emily. *The Complete Poems of Emily Dickinson*, 4961

Final Harvest, 5506

New Poems of Emily Dickinson, 4962

The Selected Poems of Emily Dickinson, 4963

Dickinson, Patti. *Hollywood the Hard Way*, 34(F)

Dickinson, Peter. *AK*, 2479(F)

A Bone from a Dry Sea, 2390(F)

Eva, 4226(F)

Po's Story, 2391(F)

The Ropemaker, 1813(F)

Shadow of a Hero, 2582(F)

Dickinson, Peter (jt. author). *Water*, 4668(F)

Dickinson, Terence. *The Backyard Astronomer's Guide*, 11663

Exploring the Sky by Day, 12452

NightWatch, 11661

The Universe and Beyond, 11662

Dicks, Brian. *Brazil*, 8284

Dickson, Gordon R. *The Dragon and the Fair Maid of Kent*, 1814(F)

The Dragon and the Gnarly King, 1815(F)

The Dragon, the Earl, and the Troll, 1816(F)

Dickson, Paul. *The Hidden Language of Baseball*, 13161

Dierker, Larry. *This Ain't Brain Surgery*, 13162

Dietrich, R. V. *Minerals, Rocks and Fossils*, 12392

Dietrich, William. *Hadrian's Wall*, 2583(F)

Dietz, William C. *Death Day*, 4227(F)

Rebel Agent, 4228(F)

Diezeno, Patricia. *Why Me? The Story of Jenny*, 914(F)

Digeronimo, Theresa Foy (jt. author). *Dropping In with Andy Mac*, 6745

Digges, Deborah. *The Stardust Lounge*, 9975

Diggs, Anita D. *A Meeting in the Ladies Room*, 3481(F)

Digiulio, Robert. *Straight Talk About Death and Dying*, 10579

Dillard, Annie. *Pilgrim at Tinker Creek*, 11790

Diller, Steve. *Dogs and Their People*, 12274

Dillon, Diane (jt. author). *Enchantress from the Stars*, 4242(F)

Dillon, Katherine V. (jt. author). *Amelia*, 5644

Rain of Ruin, 7700

Dimartino, Nick. *Seattle Ghost Story*, 3123(F)

Diner, Hasia. *Her Works Praise Her*, 9146

Dines, Carol. *Talk to Me*, 1140(F)

Dinesen, Isak. *Out of Africa and Shadows on the Grass*, 5848

Dingerkus, Guido. *The Shark Watchers' Guide*, 12183

Dingus, Lowell (jt. author). *Walking on Eggs*, 7313

Dini, Paul. *The Batman Adventures*, 2307(F)

Dinner, Sherry H. *Nothing to Be Ashamed Of*, 11061

Dinsdale, Tim. *Loch Ness Monster*, 13023

Diouf, Sylviane A. *Growing Up in Slavery*, 8523

Dipper, Frances. *Extraordinary Fish*, 12174

Dirgo, Craig (jt. author). *The Sea Hunters*, 12483

Disher, Gary. *The Divine Wind*, 3008(F)

Di Silvestro, Roger L. *The African Elephant*, 12023

DiSpezio, Michael. *The Science, Spread, and Therapy of HIV Disease*, 10756

Ditson, Mary (jt. author). *The Teenage Human Body Operator's Manual*, 11481

Divakaruni, Chitra Banerjee. *The Unknown Errors of Our Lives*, 439(F)

The Vine of Desire, 1141(F)

Dixie, Quinton (jt. author). *This Far by Faith*, 9699

Dixon, Ann (jt. author). *Alone Across the Arctic*, 13091

Dixon, Barbara M. *Good Health for African-Americans*, 11126

Dixon, Chuck. *Way of the Rat*, 2308(F)

Dixon, Dougal. *The Future Is Wild*, 11746

Dixon, Larry (jt. author). *The Silver Gryphon*, 1997(F)

Dixon, Phil. *The Negro Baseball Leagues*, 13163

DK Publishing. *Chronicle of the Olympics, 1896–2000*, 13380

Dobbins, Bill (jt. author). *The Athletic Body*, 11033

Dobbs, Michael. *Saboteurs*, 8834

Dobie, Kathy. *The Only Girl in the Car*, 11233

Dockery, Kevin. *Navy SEALs*, 12703

Doctorow, Cory. *Down and Out in the Magic Kingdom*, 1817(F)

Eastern Standard Tribe, 4229(F)

Doctorow, E. L. *Ragtime*, 2916(F)

Dodge, Hazel (jt. author). *The Ancient City*, 7446

Dodson, Bert (jt. author). *The Way Life Works*, 11796

Doherty, Berlie. *Dear Nobody*, 1142(F)

Holly Starcross, 660(F)

Doherty, Craig A. *Arnold Schwarzenegger*, 6118

Doherty, Craig A. (jt. author). *King Richard the Lionhearted and the Crusades*, 7531

Doherty, Katherine M. *King Richard the Lionhearted and the Crusades*, 7531

Doherty, Katherine M. (jt. author). *Arnold Schwarzenegger*, 6118

Doherty, Kieran. *Ranchers, Homesteaders, and Traders*, 5616

Doherty, Paul. *The Mysterious Death of Tutankhamun*, 7457

Doherty, Robert. *Area 51*, 1818(F)

Dokey, Cameron. *Hindenburg, 1937*, 3903(F)

The Storyteller's Daughter, 5082(F)

Dolan, Edward. *America in the Korean War*, 7867

Dolan, Edward F. *Beyond the Frontier*, 8703
Guns in the United States, 9795
Our Poisoned Waters, 9913
Shaping U.S. Foreign Policy, 9245
Your Privacy, 9401
Dolan, Sean. *Magic Johnson*, 6698
Michael Jordan, 6699
Pursuing the Dream, 8865
Dolber, Roslyn. *Opportunities in Fashion Careers*, 10467
Dolin, Eric Jay. *Smithsonian Book of National Wildlife Refuges*, 12102
Dolnick, Edward. *Down the Great Unknown*, 8967
Dominic, Catherine C. *Shakespeare's Characters for Students*, 4769
Dominick, Andie. *Needles*, 10757
Dommermuth-Costa, Carol. *Indira Gandhi*, 6793
Donald, David Herbert. *Lincoln*, 6335
Donaldson, Stephen R. *Lord Foul's Bane*, 1819(F)
Donegan, Lawrence. *Maybe It Should Have Been a Three Iron*, 13325
Donnelly, Adelaide (jt. author). *Sorrow Mountain*, 6985
Donnelly, Jennifer. *A Northern Light*, 2917(F)
The Tea Rose, 2584(F)
Donnelly, Karen. *Coping with Lyme Disease*, 10758
Donofrio, Beverly. *Riding in Cars with Boys*, 6936
Donoghue, Emma. *Kissing the Witch*, 1820(F)
Donovan, Robert J. *Boxing the Kangaroo*, 10374
Doody, Margaret Anne. *The Annotated Anne of Green Gables*, 661(F)
Doohan, James. *The Independent Command*, 4230(F)
Doran, Colleen. *A Distant Soil*, 2309(F)
Dore, Anita. *The Premier Book of Major Poets*, 4858
Dorminey, Bruce G. *Distant Wanderers*, 11664
Dornberg, John. *Central and Eastern Europe*, 8076
Western Europe, 8077
Dornfeld, Margaret. *The Turning Tide*, 9616
Dorris, Michael. *A Yellow Raft in Blue Water*, 440(F)
Dorson, Richard M. *Folktales Told Around the World*, 5061
Dosier, Susan. *Civil War Cooking*, 12787
Doss, James D. *Grandmother Spider*, 3482(F)
White Shell Woman, 3483(F)
Doster, Stephen. *Lord Baltimore*, 304(F)

Dotz, Warren. *Firecrackers*, 12550
Doughty, Anne. *The Woman from Kerry*, 2585(F)
Doughty, Louise. *An English Murder*, 3484(F)
Fires in the Dark, 3009(F)
Douglas, Bobby. *Take It to the Mat*, 13245
Douglas, Ed (jt. author). *Regions of the Heart*, 6744
Douglass, Frederick. *Autobiographies*, 6210
Escape from Slavery, 6211
The Life and Times of Frederick Douglass, 6212
Narrative of the Life of Frederick Douglass, an American Slave, 6213
Douglass, Jackie Leatherby. *Peterson First Guide to Shells of North America*, 12161
Douglass, Kara. *Becoming an Ironman*, 13083
Douglass, Sara. *Beyond the Hanging Wall*, 1821(F)
God's Concubine, 1822(F)
Threshold, 1823(F)
The Wayfarer Redemption, 1824(F)
Dove, Rita. *The Darker Face of the Earth*, 4789
Mother Love, 4964
Selected Poems, 4965
Dover, Jeffrey S. (jt. author). *Skin Deep*, 10882
Dover, Laura D. *The Big Book of Halloween*, 10156
Dow, Unity. *Far and Beyon'*, 2480(F)
Dowling, Colette. *The Frailty Myth*, 13084
Downer, John. *Weird Nature*, 11923
Downes, Belinda. *Silent Night*, 7204
Downey, Scott (jt. author). *The Complete Snowboarder*, 13414
Downie, Neil. *Vacuum Bazookas, Electric Rainbow Jelly, and 27 Other Saturday Science Projects*, 11638
Downing, Taylor (jt. author). *Cold War*, 7872
Doyle, Arthur Conan. *The Adventures of Sherlock Holmes*, 220(F)
The Best Supernatural Tales of Arthur Conan Doyle, 3124(F)
The Complete Sherlock Holmes, 221(F)
The Hound of the Baskervilles, 222(F)
Sherlock Holmes, 223(F)
The Sign of Four, 224(F)
A Study in Scarlet, 225(F)
Tales of Terror and Mystery, 226(F)
The White Company, 2447(F)
Doyle, Debra. *Requiem for Boone*, 4231(F)

Doyle, Malachy. *Georgie*, 916(F)
Doyle, Paul A. *Pearl S. Buck*, 5358
Doyon, Stephanie. *Leaving Home*, 35(F)
Taking Chances, 305(F)
Dozois, Gardner. *Isaac Asimov's Moons*, 4234(F)
The Year's Best Science Fiction: Eleventh Annual Collection, 4232(F)
The Year's Best Science Fiction: Fifteenth Annual Collection, 4233(F)
D'Ozraio, Leo (jt. author). *Opportunities in Health and Medical Careers*, 10520
Dragisic, Patricia. *How to Write a Letter*, 10291
Dragonwagon, Crescent. *To Take a Dare*, 1143(F)
Drake, David. *Lt. Leary, Commanding*, 4235(F)
Mistress of the Catacombs, 1826(F)
Drake, David (jt. author). *Fortune's Stroke*, 1852(F)
Dramer, Kim. *Native Americans and Black Americans*, 8436
Draper, Allison Stark. *The Assassination of Malcolm X*, 8866
Draper, Sharon M. *The Battle of Jericho*, 306(F)
Darkness Before Dawn, 307(F)
Double Dutch, 308(F)
Forged by Fire, 662(F)
Romiette and Julio, 1144(F)
Tears of a Tiger, 917(F)
Drechsler, Debbie. *Summer of Love*, 2310(F)
Dressen, Sarah. *The Truth About Forever*, 663(F)
Dresser, Norine. *Multicultural Celebrations*, 10157
Drew, Eileen. *The Ivory Crocodile*, 2481(F)
Drewry, Henry N. *Stand and Prosper*, 10336
Drexler, Madeline. *Secret Agents*, 10759
Drez, Ronald J. *Twenty-Five Yards of War*, 7677
Drill, Esther. *Deal with It!* 11418
Drimmer, Frederick. *Incredible People*, 13024
Drlica, Karl. *Understanding DNA and Gene Cloning*, 10935
Drohan, Michele I. *Weight-Loss Programs*, 11127
Drucker, Malka. *Jacob's Rescue*, 3010(F)
Drucker, Malka (jt. author). *Rescuers*, 7653
Druckman, Nancy. *American Flags*, 8346
Druett, Joan. *She Captains*, 5617
Drury, Bob. *The Rescue Season*, 13258

Druyan, Ann (jt. author). *Comet*, 11744

Dry, Richard. *Leaving*, 441(F)

D'Souza, Dinesh. *What's So Great About America*, 9379

Duane, Diane. *The Book of Night with Moon*, 1827(F)

Doctor's Orders, 4236(F)

A Wizard Alone, 1828(F)

Duany, Andres. *Suburban Nation*, 10207

Dubis, Michael. *The Hangman*, 3011(F)

Dubois, Daniel (jt. author). *Indian Signs and Signals*, 8440

DuBois, Michelle (jt. author). *The Complete Jacob Lawrence*, 7102

Du Bois, W. E. B. *The Autobiography of W. E. B. Du Bois*, 6217

The Oxford W. E. B. Du Bois Reader, 9402

Ducker, Bruce. *Bloodlines*, 3485(F)

Duckett, Alfred A. (jt. author). *I Never Had It Made*, 6682

Ducornet, Rikki. *Gazelle*, 1145(F)

Dudley, Ellen (jt. author). *Hiking and Backpacking*, 13281

Dudley, Mark E. *Gideon v. Wainwright (1963)*, 9283

United States v. Nixon (1974), 9284

Dudley, William. *African Americans*, 9617

Alcohol, 10631

The American Revolution, 8524

American Slavery, 8559

America's Future, 8868

Asian Americans, 9708

The Bill of Rights, 9205

Biological Warfare, 12704

The Civil Rights Movement, 9403

The Creation of the Constitution, 9206

Drugs and Sports, 10632

Endangered Oceans, 12469

Epidemics, 10760

Genocide, 9178

The Great Depression, 8792

Illegal Immigration, 9524

The Industrial Revolution, 8347

Iraq, 8920

Japanese American Internment Camps, 8835

Media Violence, 10103

The Middle East, 8186

Native Americans, 8437

The 1960s, 8348, 8867

Opposing Viewpoints in American History, Vol. 1, 8349

Opposing Viewpoints in American History, Vol. 2, 8350

Pregnancy, 11172

Religion in America, 9054

The Vietnam War, 8919

World War I, 7608

World War II, 7678

Dudman, Martha Tod. *Augusta, Gone*, 10633

Duensing, Edward. *Backyard and Beyond*, 11791

Duffy, Carol Ann. *Stopping for Death*, 4859

Duffy, James P. *Czars*, 8153

Dufresne, John. *Deep in the Shade of Paradise*, 3904(F)

Dufty, William (jt. author). *Lady Sings the Blues*, 6058

Dugain, Marc. *The Officer's Ward*, 2993(F)

Dugan, Ellen. *Elements of Witchcraft*, 13025

Dugard, Martin. *Farther than Any Man*, 5632

In-Line Skating Made Easy, 13368

Into Africa, 7923

Dugatkin, Lee Alan. *Cheating Monkeys and Citizen Bees*, 11924

Duiker, William J. *Ho Chi Minh*, 6801

Dukthas, Ann. *In the Time of the Poisoned Queen*, 2586(F)

Dulles, Allen. *Great True Spy Stories*, 9977(F)

Dumas, Alexandre. *The Count of Monte Cristo*, 187(F)

The Man in the Iron Mask, 188(F)

The Three Musketeers, 189(F)

Dumas, Firoozeh. *Funny in Farsi*, 6937

Dumas, Frederic (jt. author). *The Silent World*, 12482

Du Maurier, Daphne. *Echoes from the Macabre*, 3126(F)

Jamaica Inn, 2587(F)

My Cousin Rachel, 2588(F)

Rebecca, 3486(F)

Dunant, Sarah. *Fatlands*, 3487(F)

Dunbar, Paul Laurence. *The Complete Poems of Paul Laurence Dunbar*, 4966

In His Own Voice, 4967

Dunbar, Robert E. *Homosexuality*, 11234

Dunbar, Robin. *Cousins*, 11961

Duncan, Dave. *Impossible Odds*, 1829(F)

Sky of Swords, 1830(F)

Duncan, David. *The Stricken Field*, 1831(F)

Duncan, David Ewing. *Hernando de Soto*, 5639

Duncan, Dayton. *Lewis and Clark*, 8490

People of the West, 8704

Duncan, James R. *Owls of the World*, 12085

Duncan, Jane Caryl. *Careers in Veterinary Medicine*, 10375

Duncan, Lois. *Daughters of Eve*, 3488(F)

Don't Look Behind You, 3489(F)

Down a Dark Hall, 3490(F)

I Know What You Did Last Summer, 3491(F)

Killing Mr. Griffin, 3492(F)

Locked in Time, 3127(F)

Night Terrors, 3128(F)

Psychic Connections, 13026

Stranger with My Face, 3129(F)

Summer of Fear, 3130(F)

The Third Eye, 3493(F)

Trapped! 1146(F)

The Twisted Window, 3494(F)

Who Killed My Daughter, 9978

Dunlay, Thomas W. *Kit Carson and the Indians*, 6478

Dunlop, Reginald. *Come Fly with Me! Your Nineties Guide to Becoming a Flight Attendant*, 10376

Dunn, Charles. *Everyday Life in Traditional Japan*, 8037

Dunn, Hilda. *The Hanged Man*, 3495(F)

Dunn, John M. *The Computer Revolution*, 12594

Dunn, Susan (jt. author). *George Washington*, 6370

Dunn, Tricia. *Gold Medal Ice Hockey for Women and Girls*, 13343

Dunn, Wendy (jt. author). *Famous Hispanic Americans*, 6177

Dunn-Georgiou, Elisha. *Everything You Need to Know About Organic Foods*, 11823

Dunne, Pete. *Pete Dunne on Bird Watching*, 12047

Dunnigan, James. *Dirty Little Secrets of the Vietnam War*, 8921

Dunnigan, James F. *Victory at Sea*, 7679

Dunning, Joan. *Secrets of the Nest*, 12073

Dunning, John. *The Bookman's Wake*, 3496(F)

Duper, Linda Leeb. *160 Ways to Help the World*, 10135

DuPrau, Jeanne. *Adoption*, 11504

Cloning, 10936

Durant, Alan. *Vampire and Werewolf Stories*, 3131(F)

Durant, Ariel (jt. author). *The Age of Louis XIV*, 8094

Durant, William James. *The Age of Faith*, 7532

The Age of Louis XIV, 8094

The Reformation, 7533

The Renaissance, 7534

The Story of Philosophy, 9026

Durbin, William. *The Journal of Otto Peltonen*, 2918(F)

Durden, Robert F. *Carter G. Woodson*, 5967

Durham, Michael S. *The Mid-Atlantic States*, 8976

Durrell, Gerald M. *The Amateur Naturalist*, 11792

Durrell, Lee (jt. author). *The Amateur Naturalist*, 11792

Durrett, Deanne. *The Abortion Conflict*, 11173

Healers, 8438

Unsung Heroes of World War II, 7680

Durschmied, Erik. *Blood of Revolution,* 7401

Duskis, Neil (jt. author). *Barlowe's Guide to Fantasy,* 5249(F)

Dutcher, Jim. *Wolves at Our Door,* 12006

DuTemple, Lesley A. *Coral Reefs,* 12171

DuVall, Jack (jt. author). *A Force More Powerful,* 10129

Duvall, Jill D. *Congressional Committees,* 9246

Dvorkin, David. *The Captain's Honor,* 4237(F)
Timetrap, 4238(F)

Dwyer, Frank. *Henry VIII,* 6852
James I, 6860

Dwyer, Jack. *The Launch Manual,* 10358

Dwyer, William L. *In the Hands of the People,* 9285

Dybek, Stuart. *I Sailed with Magellan,* 1147(F)

Dye, Dan. *Amazing Gracie,* 12275

Dyer, Alan (jt. author). *The Backyard Astronomer's Guide,* 11663

Dyer, Daniel. *Jack London,* 5906

Dygard, Thomas J. *Backfield Package,* 4570(F)
The Rebounder, 4571(F)
The Rookie Arrives, 4572(F)
Running Wild, 4573(F)
Second Stringer, 4574(F)

Dyson, James. *A History of Great Inventions,* 12551

Dyson, Michael Eric. *Holler if You Hear Me,* 6120
I May Not Get There with You, 6237
Why I Love Black Women, 9618

Eagan, Andrea B. *Why Am I So Miserable if These Are the Best Years of My Life?* 11419

Eagle, Adam Fortunate. *Heart of the Rock,* 9756

Eagle, Kathleen. *Once Upon a Wedding,* 3905(F)
You Never Can Tell, 442(F)

Eagleton, Terry. *The Truth About the Irish,* 8120

Earhart, Amelia. *The Fun of It,* 5643

Earle, Robert. *The Way Home,* 664(F)

Earley, Tony. *Jim the Boy,* 2957(F)

Earls, Irene. *Young Musicians in World History,* 5696

Early, Gerald. *One Nation Under a Groove,* 7281

Easton, Kelly. *The Life History of a Star,* 3079(F)

Easton, Thomas A. *Careers in Science,* 10526

Eaton, Susan. *The Other Boston Busing Story,* 9620

Ebert, Roger. *The Future of the Movies,* 7226

Eberts, Marjorie. *Careers for Kids at Heart and Others Who Adore Children,* 10377
Careers in Child Care, 10378
How to Prepare for College, 10337

Ebony. *Ebony Pictorial History of Black America,* 9621

Ebrey, Patricia Buckley. *The Cambridge Illustrated History of China,* 8007

Echlin, Kim. *Inanna,* 5148

Echo-Hawk, Roger C. *Battlefields and Burial Grounds,* 7372

Echo-Hawk, Walter R. (jt. author). *Battlefields and Burial Grounds,* 7372

Ecott, Tim. *Neutral Buoyancy,* 13436

Eddings, David. *The Belgariad,* 1832(F)
Guardians of the West, 1833(F)

Edelfelt, Roy A. *Careers in Education,* 10482

Edelson, Edward. *Allergies,* 10762
Francis Crick and James Watson and the Building Blocks of Life, 10937
Gregor Mendel, 6590
The Immune System, 10763
Nutrition and the Brain, 10999
Sleep, 11000
Sports Medicine, 10902

Edelson, Paula. *Straight Talk About Teenage Pregnancy,* 11174

Edelson, Paula (jt. author). *Straight Talk About Today's Families,* 11541

Edelstein, Barbara. *The Woman Doctor's Diet for Teenage Girls,* 11128

Edey, Maitland Armstrong (jt. author). *Lucy,* 7352

Edgerton, Leslie H. *Monday's Meal,* 3132(F)

Edgerton, Robert B. *The Troubled Heart of Africa,* 7924

Edgerton, Teresa. *The Queen's Necklace,* 1834(F)

Edghill, India. *Queenmaker,* 2399(F)

Edghill, Rosemary. *Paying the Piper at the Gates of Dawn,* 4628(F)

Edghill, Rosemary (jt. author). *Mad Maudlin,* 1998(F)

Edinger, Ray. *Fury Beach,* 8304

Edmonds, Walter D. *Tales My Father Never Told,* 5852

Edvardson, Cordelia. *Burned Child Seeks the Fire,* 7681

Edwards, David H. *The World Don't Owe Me Nothing,* 6037

Edwards, Elwyn Hartley. *The Complete Book of Bits and Bitting,* 13351
The Ultimate Horse Book, 12307

Edwards, Grace. *If I Should Die,* 3497(F)

Edwards, Grace F. *A Toast Before Dying,* 3498(F)

Edwards, Griffith. *Alcohol,* 10634

Edwards, Judith. *Jamestown,* 8499
Lewis and Clark's Journey of Discovery, 5653
The Lindbergh Baby Kidnapping, 8793
Nat Turner's Slave Rebellion, 6274

Edwards, Lois. *Great Careers for People Interested in the Human Body,* 10504

Effinger, George Alec. *Budayeen Nights,* 4239(F)

Egan, Jennifer. *Look at Me,* 918(F)

Egendorf, Laura K. *Assisted Suicide,* 10580
The Death Penalty, 9286
Gangs, 9979
Human Rights, 9404
Poverty, 10076
Sports and Athletes, 13085
Teen Alcoholism, 10635
Violence, 9796

Egendorf, Laura K. (jt. author). *Mental Illness,* 11100

Eggers, Dave. *A Heartbreaking Work of Staggering Genius,* 5853

Ehlers, Tracy Bachrach (jt. author). *Sugar's Life in the Hood,* 10097

Ehlert, Willis J. *America's Heritage,* 8351

Ehrenfeld, Norbert. *You're the Jury,* 9287

Ehrenreich, Barbara. *Nickel and Dimed,* 10077

Ehrlich, Anne H. (jt. author). *Extinction,* 12103

Ehrlich, Eugene. *Les Bons Mots,* 5543

Ehrlich, Gretel. *John Muir,* 6593

Ehrlich, Paul R. *The Birder's Handbook,* 12048
Birds in Jeopardy, 12104
Extinction, 12103

Ehrlich, Robert. *Nine Crazy Ideas in Science,* 11592

Ehrlich, Scott. *Paul Robeson,* 6111

Eichengreen, Lucille. *From Ashes to Life,* 6831

Eicher, David. *The Universe from Your Backyard,* 11665

Eichhoefer, Gerald W. *Enduring Issues in Philosophy,* 9027

Eickhoff, Randy Lee. *Bowie,* 2877(F)

Eidson, Tom. *All God's Children,* 2919(F)

Eike, Torje (jt. author). *Totally Fit,* 11028

Eire, Carlos. *Waiting for Snow in Havana,* 6938

Eisen, Adrienne. *Making Scenes,* 1148(F)

Eisenhammer, Fred. *Baseball's Most Memorable Trades,* 13164

Foner, Eric. *Who Owns History? Rethinking the Past in a Changing World*, 7407

Fontanel, Beatrice. *Babies*, 11177

Foon, Dennis. *Double or Nothing*, 1165(F)

Foote-Smith, Elizabeth. *Opportunities in Writing Careers*, 10383

Forbes, Esther. *Paul Revere and the World He Lived In*, 6447

Forbes, Kathryn. *Mama's Bank Account*, 673(F)

Forbes, Tracy. *My Enchanted Enemy*, 1853(F)

Ford, Amanda. *Be True to Yourself*, 11424

Ford, Amanda (jt. author). *Between Mother and Daughter*, 11508

Ford, Brian J. *The Secret Language of Life*, 11794

Ford, G. M. *Cast in Stone*, 3508(F)

Ford, Judy. *Between Mother and Daughter*, 11508

Ford, Michael Curtis. *The Last King*, 2423(F)

Ford, Michael T. *100 Questions and Answers About AIDS*, 10772

Outspoken, 11236

The Voices of AIDS, 10773

Ford, Michael Thomas. *Paths of Faith*, 9058

Forest, Heather. *Wisdom Tales from Around the World*, 5063

Forester, C. S. *The African Queen*, 38(F)

Mr. Midshipman Hornblower, 2593(F)

Forker, Dom. *Baseball Brain Teasers*, 13167

Forman, Jack Jacob. *Presenting Paul Zindel*, 5977

Forman, Werner (jt. author). *The Eskimos*, 8302

Forrest, Elizabeth. *Killjoy*, 3135(F)

Forrester, Sandra. *My Home Is over Jordan*, 2925(F)

Forstchen, William R. *Down to the Sea*, 4257(F)

We Look Like Men of War, 2820(F)

Forster, E. M. *A Room with a View*, 2594(F)

Forsyth, Elizabeth (jt. author). *AIDS*, 10790

Know About Gays and Lesbians, 11246

The Sexual Abuse of Children and Adolescents, 11295

Forsyth, Elizabeth H. (jt. author). *Depression*, 11073

Vaccinations, 10909

Forsyth, Frederick. *Avenger*, 3509(F)

The Day of the Jackal, 39(F)

The Devil's Alternative, 40(F)

The Dogs of War, 41(F)

The Fist of God, 42(F)

The Odessa File, 43(F)

Forte, Maurizio. *Virtual Archaeology*, 7373

Fortey, Richard. *Trilobite! Eyewitness to Evolution*, 7321

Forward, Robert L. *Dragon's Egg*, 4258(F)

Foss, Clive. *Fidel Castro*, 6901

Foss, Joe. *Top Guns*, 5618

Fossey, Dian. *Gorillas in the Mist*, 11962

Foster, Alan Dean. *The Deluge Drivers*, 4259(F)

Drowning World, 4260(F)

The Hand of Dinotopia, 4261(F)

Jed the Dead, 4262(F)

Kingdoms of Light, 1854(F)

Quozl, 4263(F)

Reunion, 4264(F)

Spellsinger, 1855(F)

Splinter of the Mind's Eye, 4265(F)

A Triumph of Souls, 1856(F)

Foster, John. *Let's Celebrate*, 4861

Foster, Leila M. *Kuwait*, 8217

Foster, Lynn V. *A Brief History of Central America*, 8244

A Brief History of Mexico, 8257

Foster, Robert. *The Complete Guide to Middle-Earth*, 5270

Foster, Sharon Ewell. *Riding Through Shadows*, 448(F)

Foster, Steven. *A Field Guide to Venomous Animals and Poisonous Plants*, 11795

Fountain, John W. *True Vine*, 6941

Fountain, Nigel. *WWII*, 7688

Fox, Annie. *Can You Relate? Real-World Advice for Teens on Guys, Girls, Growing Up, and Getting Along*, 11425

Fox, Carol. *In Times of War*, 4633(F)

Fox, Gabrielle. *The Essential Guide to Making Handmade Books*, 12936

Fox, Karen. *The Chain Reaction*, 6513

Fox, Laurie. *The Lost Girls*, 1166(F)

Fox, Paula. *Borrowed Finery*, 5860

The Eagle Kite, 674(F)

The Moonlight Man, 675(F)

Fox, Roy. *Technology*, 12552

Fradin, Dennis B. *Bound for the North Star*, 8560

Ida B. Wells, 6276

My Family Shall Be Free! The Life of Peter Still, 7003

Fradin, Judith B. (jt. author). *Ida B. Wells*, 6276

Fradkin, Philip L. *Wildest Alaska*, 8997

Frady, Marshall. *Martin Luther King, Jr.*, 6238

Fralon, Jose-Alain. *A Good Man in Evil Times*, 7594

Frame, Ronald. *The Lantern Bearers*, 1167(F)

France, Peter. *An Encyclopedia of Bible Animals*, 9059

Francia, Luis H. *Eye of the Fish*, 8066

Francis, Dick. *Bolt*, 3510(F)

Come to Grief, 3511(F)

The Edge, 3512(F)

Shattered, 3513(F)

To the Hilt, 3514(F)

Whip Hand, 3515(F)

Wild Horses, 3516(F)

Francis, Raymond L. *The Illustrated Almanac of Science, Technology, and Invention*, 11595

Franck, Irene M. *Across Asia by Land*, 7998

The German-American Heritage, 9771

Franco, Betsy. *Things I Have to Tell You*, 1168(F)

You Hear Me? Poems and Writings by Teenage Boys, 4970

Frangie, Frank (jt. author). *The Art of Shooting Baskets*, 13218

Frank, Anne. *Anne Frank's Tales from the Secret Annex*, 3014

The Diary of a Young Girl, 6843

The Diary of a Young Girl: The Definitive Edition, 6844

The Diary of Anne Frank, 6845

Frank, E. R. *America*, 926(F)

Friction, 1169(F)

Life Is Funny, 1170(F)

Frank, Hillary. *Better Than Running at Night*, 313(F)

Frank, Lucy. *Will You Be My Brussels Sprout?* 3915(F)

Frank, Stanley D. *Remember Everything You Read*, 10275

Frank, Steven. *The Pen Commandments*, 10294

Frankel, David. *Masterpieces*, 7035

Frankel, Lory (jt. author). *Henri Matisse*, 5766

Frankenberger, Elizabeth. *Food and Love*, 10774

Frankl, Ron. *Bruce Springsteen*, 6128

Charlie Parker, 6100

Duke Ellington, 6040

Miles Davis, 6027

Franklin, Benjamin. *The Autobiography of Benjamin Franklin*, 6403

Franklin, John Hope. *Black Leaders of the Twentieth Century*, 6156

From Slavery to Freedom, 9625

Frankowski, Leo. *The Fata Morgana*, 1857(F)

Frantz, Donald. *Beauty and the Beast*, 7291

Frantz, John P. *Video Cinema*, 12637

Fraser, Antonia. *Marie Antoinette*, 6867

Fraser, Joelle. *The Territory of Men*, 11509

Fraser, Laura. *The Animal Rights Handbook*, 9799

Fraustino, Lisa R. *Ash*, 927(F)

Dirty Laundry, 676(F)

Soul Searching, 4634(F)

Frayn, Michael. *Spies*, 3015(F)

Frazer, James George. *The Golden Bough*, 5150

Frazier, Charles. *Cold Mountain*, 2821(F)

Frazier, Ian. *On the Rez*, 9757

Fredericks, Mariah. *The True Meaning of Cleavage*, 1171(F)

Frederickson, Keville. *Opportunities in Nursing Careers*, 10506

Fredriksson, Marianne. *Hanna's Daughters*, 677(F)

Freeberg, Ernest. *The Education of Laura Bridgman*, 6475

Freedman, Benedict. *Mrs. Mike*, 44(F)

Freedman, Estelle B. *No Turning Back*, 9419

Freedman, Nancy (jt. author). *Mrs. Mike*, 44(F)

Freedman, Russell. *Babe Didrikson Zaharias*, 6757

Buffalo Hunt, 8706

In Defense of Liberty, 9208

The Life and Death of Crazy Horse, 6395

The Wright Brothers, 6606

Freedman, Suzanne. *Clay v. United States*, 8924

Freehling, William W. *The South vs. the South*, 8631

Freeman, Charles. *Crisis in Rwanda*, 7925

The Rise of the Nazis, 7689

Freeman, John W. *The Metropolitan Opera Stories of the Great Operas*, 7187

Freeman, Joseph. *Job*, 7690

Freer, Dave. *Rats, Bats and Vats*, 4266(F)

Freese, Barbara. *Coal*, 9914

Freimiller, Jane (jt. author). *A Year of Reading*, 12732

Fremon, Celeste. *Father Greg and the Homeboys*, 6921

Fremon, David K. *The Alaska Purchase in American History*, 8755

The Great Depression, 8794

The Holocaust Heroes, 7691

Japanese-American Internment in American History, 8836

The Jim Crow Laws and Racism, 9420

The Negro Baseball Leagues, 13168

The Watergate Scandal in American History, 8872

French, Howard W. *A Continent for the Taking*, 7900

French, Stephanie Breaux. *The Cheerleading Book*, 13092

Freud, Sigmund. *The Basic Writings of Sigmund Freud*, 11338

Freund, David M. P. *Biographical Supplement and Index*, 9626

Freund, Diane. *Four Corners*, 678(F)

Frey, Darcy. *The Last Shot*, 13204

Frey, James. *A Million Little Pieces*, 10636

Frey, Jennifer (jt. author). *Chamique Holdsclaw*, 6697

Frey, Richard. *According to Hoyle*, 13286

Freymann-Weyr, Garret. *The Kings Are Already Here*, 314(F)

My Heartbeat, 1172(F)

When I Was Older, 315(F)

Fridell, Ron. *Amphibians in Danger*, 11901

DNA Fingerprinting, 9984

Global Warming, 9879

Solving Crimes, 6514

Spying, 9985

Friedan, Betty. *The Feminine Mystique*, 9421

Friedel, Robert. *Zipper*, 12553

Friedland, Gerald W. (jt. author). *Medicine's 10 Greatest Discoveries*, 10904

Friedlander, Mark P. *The Immune System*, 10775

Friedman, C. S. *Crown of Shadows*, 1858(F)

Friedman, Carl. *Nightfather*, 3016(F)

Friedman, Ina R. *Flying Against the Wind*, 6887

Friedman, Kinky. *God Bless John Wayne*, 3517(F)

Friedman, Meyer. *Medicine's 10 Greatest Discoveries*, 10904

Friedman, Norman. *Desert Victory*, 8925

Friedrich, Belinda. *The Explosion of TWA Flight 800*, 12656

Friel, Maeve. *Charlie's Story*, 1173(F)

Friesen, Gayle. *Losing Forever*, 679(F)

Frissell, Susan. *Eating Disorders and Weight Control*, 10776

Fritz, April Young. *Waiting to Disappear*, 680(F)

Fritz, Jean. *China Homecoming*, 5861

Homesick, My Own Story, 5862

Stonewall, 6409

Fritz, Sandy. *Robotics and Artificial Intelligence*, 12595

Froehner, Melissa Alberti (jt. author). *Teen Esteem*, 11458

Froese, Deborah. *Out of the Fire*, 1174(F)

Frome, Keith (jt. author). *The Columbia Book of Civil War Poetry*, 5005

Fromm, Pete. *As Cool as I Am*, 681(F)

How All This Started, 1175(F)

Frommer, Harvey (jt. author). *Growing Up Jewish in America*, 9749

Frommer, Myrna Katz. *Growing Up Jewish in America*, 9749

Fronval, George. *Indian Signs and Signals*, 8440

Frost, Helen. *Keesha's House*, 1176(F)

Why Darkness Seems So Light, 9986

Frost, Robert. *Collected Poems, Prose, and Plays*, 4971

Frost-Knappman, Elizabeth. *Women's Rights on Trial*, 9422

Women's Suffrage in America, 9423

Frumkes, Burke Lewis (jt. author). *The Mensa Think Smart Book*, 13001

Fry, Annette R. *The Orphan Trains*, 8756

Fry, Stephen. *Making History*, 1859(F)

Fuchs, Arved. *In Shackleton's Wake*, 8305

Fuchs, Thomas. *The Hitler Fact Book*, 6854

Fugard, Athol. *"Master Harold" — and the Boys*, 4782

Fulbrook, Mary. *A Concise History of Germany*, 8106

Fulghum, Hunter S. *Don't Try This at Home*, 13030

Fulghum, Robert. *All I Really Need to Know I Learned in Kindergarten*, 9028

Fuller, Alexandra. *Don't Let's Go to the Dogs Tonight*, 7960

Scribbling the Cat, 7961

Fuller, Cheri. *When Teens Pray*, 9060

Fuller, Errol. *Dodo*, 12051

Fuller, Jamie. *The Diary of Emily Dickinson*, 2926(F)

Fuller, Kimberly. *Home*, 4267(F)

Fuller, Sarah B. (jt. author). *Brown v. Board of Education*, 9417

Fulton, John. *Retribution*, 1177(F)

Funderburk, Robert. *Winter of Grace*, 3518(F)

Funk, Wilfred (jt. author). *Thirty Days to a More Powerful Vocabulary*, 10307

Funke, Cornelia. *Inkheart*, 1860(F)

Funny Cide Team. *Funny Cide*, 13353

Fuqua, Jonathon Scott. *The Reappearance of Sam Webber*, 682(F)

Furbee, Mary,. *Mohandas Gandhi*, 6795

Furbee, Mary R. *Anne Bailey*, 6467

Furbee, Mike (jt. author). *Mohandas Gandhi*, 6795

Furey, Joan A. (jt. author). *Visions of War, Dreams of Peace*, 8952

Furey, Maggie. *Heart of Myrial*, 1861(F)

Furgurson, Ernest B. *Ashes of Glory*, 8632

Chancellorsville 1863, 8633

Furia, Philip. *The Poets of Tin Pan Alley*, 7143

Furlong, Monica. *Juniper*, 1862(F)

Goodwin, Doris Kearns. *Lyndon Johnson and the American Dream*, 6316
No Ordinary Time, 8837
Goodwin, Joy. *The Second Mark*, 13363
Goodwin, Peter H. (jt. author). *Physics Projects for Young Scientists*, 12495
Goodwin, Simon. *XTL*, 13033
Goodwin, William. *Pakistan*, 8026
Teen Violence, 9992
Goolrick, William K. *Rebels Resurgent*, 8641
Goonan, Kathleen Ann. *Crescent City Rhapsody*, 4277(F)
Gootman, Marilyn E. *When a Friend Dies*, 10586
Gordimer, Nadine. *Crimes of Conscience*, 2484(F)
My Son's Story, 1573(F)
Selected Stories, 1574(F)
Gordis, Kent (jt. author). *Greg LeMond's Complete Book of Bicycling*, 13236
Gordon, James S. *Holistic Medicine*, 10907
Stress Management, 11066
Gordon, Jonathan. *Sperm Whales*, 12203
Gordon, Katharine. *The Long Love*, 3923(F)
The Palace Garden, 2513(F)
Gordon, Lawrence. *User Friendly*, 1880(F)
Gordon, Lesley J. *General George E. Pickett in Life and Legend*, 6441
Gordon, Linda (jt. author). *America's Working Women*, 8332
Gordon, Louise. *How to Draw the Human Figure*, 12884
Gordon, Lyndall. *Charlotte Brontë*, 5819
Gordon, Mary. *Joan of Arc*, 6861
Gordon, Matthew. *Islam*, 9130
Islam: Origins, Practices, Holy Texts, Sacred Persons, Sacred Places, 9131
Gordon, Robert. *Can't Be Satisfied*, 6138
Deborah Butterfield, 7093
Gordon, Ruth. *Peeling the Onion*, 4866
Pierced by a Ray of Sun, 4867
Under All Silences, 4868
Gordon, Sheila. *Waiting for the Rain*, 455(F)
Gordon, Sol. *The Teenage Survival Book*, 11427
Gordon, Susan. *Health Care*, 10508
Gordon, Vivian Verdell (jt. author). *Think About Prisons and the Criminal Justice System*, 10029
Gordon-Reed, Annette (jt. author). *Vernon Can Read!* 6232
Gore, Ariel. *Atlas of the Human Heart*, 5867

Gorkin, Michael. *Three Mothers, Three Daughters*, 8200
Gormley, Michael Sean (jt. author). *The 100 Greatest Baseball Players of the 20th Century Ranked*, 13179
Gorn, Elliott J. *Mother Jones*, 6230
Gorog, Judith. *Please Do Not Touch*, 3143(F)
When Nobody's Home, 3144(F)
Gorrell, Gena K. *Catching Fire*, 9256
North Star to Freedom, 8562
Gorst, Martin. *Measuring Eternity*, 11669
Gottesfeld, Jeff (jt. author). *Stranger in the Mirror*, 1039(F)
Gottfried, Ted. *Alexander Fleming*, 6565
The American Media, 12638
Capital Punishment, 9291
Children of the Slaughter, 7702
The Death Penalty, 9292
Deniers of the Holocaust, 9802
Displaced Persons, 7703
Georges Clemenceau, 6830
Homeland Security Versus Constitutional Rights, 9425
Homelessness, 10080
James Baldwin, 5812
Martyrs to Madness, 7704
Nazi Germany, 7705
Police Under Fire, 9293
Pornography, 10108
Privacy, 9426
The Road to Communism, 8155
Should Drugs Be Legalized? 10640
Teen Fathers Today, 11179
Gottlieb, Eli. *The Boy Who Went Away*, 686(F)
Goulart, Ron. *Comic Book Culture*, 5585
Groucho Marx, 3539(F)
Gould, Lewis L. *American First Ladies*, 6158
Gould, Stephen Jay. *The Lying Stones of Marrakech*, 11597
Triumph and Tragedy in Mudville, 13171
Gould, Steven. *Blind Waves*, 4278(F)
Wild Side, 4279(F)
Gourley, Catherine. *Beryl Markham*, 5668
Good Girl Work, 8758
Gourse, Leslie. *Aretha Franklin, Lady Soul*, 6044
Blowing on the Changes, 7147
Deep Down in Music, 7148
Dizzy Gillespie and the Birth of Bebop, 6047
Fancy Fretwork, 5698
Mahalia Jackson, 6064
Striders to Beboppers and Beyond, 7149
Swingers and Crooners, 5699
Govignon, Brigitte. *The Beginner's Guide to Art*, 7036

Gow, Mary. *Attack on America*, 10179
Gowdy, Barbara. *The Romantic*, 323(F)
Gowen, L. Kris. *Making Sexual Decisions*, 11238
Gowing, Lawrence. *Biographical Dictionary of Artists*, 5700
Grabish, Beatrice R. *Drugs and Your Brain*, 10641
Grace, C. L. *The Merchant of Death*, 3540(F)
Grace, Eric S. *The Nature of Lions*, 11994
Grace, Fran. *Carry A. Nation*, 6432
Gracen, Jorie B. *Paul McCartney*, 6082
Gradwohl, Judith (jt. author). *The Wealth of Oceans*, 12476
Grady, Sean M. *Explosives*, 12707
Virtual Reality, 12601
Graff, Henry. *Grover Cleveland*, 6293
Graff, Henry F. *The Presidents*, 9231
Grafton, Sue. *G Is for Gumshoe*, 3541(F)
M Is for Malice, 3542(F)
P Is for Peril, 3543(F)
Gragg, Rod. *The Civil War Quiz and Fact Book*, 8642
Graham, Andrew (jt. author). *Meteorites*, 11741
Graham, Ian. *The Internet*, 12602
Internet Revolution, 12603
Graham, Kevin. *Ralph Nader*, 6431
Graham, Kevin (jt. author). *Environmental Causes*, 9870
Graham, Kristen. *The Great Monologues from the Women's Project*, 4798
Graham, Robin Lee. *Dove*, 5648
Graham, Rosemary. *My Not-So-Terrible Time at the Hippie Hotel*, 687(F)
Graham-Smith, Francis. *Pathways to the Universe*, 11670
Granfield, Linda. *I Remember Korea*, 8928
Gransden, K. W. *Virgil, the Aeneid*, 5441
Grant, Alan. *Dragon*, 1881(F)
Return to Glory, 13305
Grant, Amanda. *Fresh and Fast Vegan Pleasures*, 12790
Grant, Charles. *Riders in the Sky*, 1882(F)
Grant, Cynthia D. *The Cannibals*, 1193(F)
Mary Wolf, 688(F)
The White Horse, 929(F)
Grant, Donna (jt. author). *Far from the Tree*, 652(F)
Tryin' to Sleep in the Bed You Made, 438(F)
Grant, Douglas. *Classic American Short Stories*, 4639(F)
Grant, Gordon. *Canoeing*, 13400

Grey, Amelia. *A Dash of Scandal*, 3925(F)

Grey, Zane. *The Last Trail*, 2882(F)
Riders of the Purple Sage, 2883(F)
The Wolf Tracker and Other Animal Tales, 171(F)

Grey-Wilson, Christopher. *Annuals and Biennials*, 11860

Gribbin, John. *The Case of the Missing Neutrinos and Other Curious Phenomena of the Universe*, 11598
Hyperspace, 11671

Gribbin, John (jt. author). *The Matter Myth*, 12503
XTL, 13033

Gribbin, John R. *Almost Everyone's Guide to Science*, 11599

Gribbin, Mary (jt. author). *Almost Everyone's Guide to Science*, 11599

Grieve, James. *They're Only Human*, 1197(F)

Griffin, Donald R. *Animal Thinking*, 11925

Griffin, Farah Jasmine. *If You Can't Be Free, Be a Mystery*, 6057

Griffin, John Howard. *Black Like Me*, 9557

Griffin, Justin. *The Holy Grail*, 9107

Griffin, Karol. *Skin Deep*, 10965

Griffler, Keith P. *Front Line of Freedom*, 8564

Griggs, Winnie. *Whatever It Takes*, 3926(F)

Grima, Tony. *Not the Only One*, 1198(F)

Grimes, Martha. *Biting the Moon*, 49(F)
Hotel Paradise, 1199(F)

Grimes, Nikki. *Bronx Masquerade*, 1200(F)
Jazmin's Notebook, 456(F)

Grimes, William. *My Fine Feathered Friend*, 12053

Grimm, Tom. *The Basic Book of Photography*, 12947
The Basic Darkroom Book, 12948

Grimm Brothers. *The Complete Grimms' Fairy Tales*, 5105

Grimsley, Jim. *The Ordinary*, 1887(F)

Grinde, Donald A., Jr. (jt. author). *Encyclopedia of Native American Biography*, 8446

Grindle, Lucretia. *The Nightspinners*, 3548(F)

Grisham, John. *The Client*, 3549(F)
A Painted House, 1201(F)
The Pelican Brief, 3550(F)
The Street Lawyer, 3551(F)

Gritzner, Jeffrey A. *Afghanistan*, 8048

Grob, Bernard. *Basic Electronics*, 12629

Grob, Gerald N. *The Mad Among Us*, 11067

Grohs-Martin, Silvia. *Silvie*, 7710

Grollman, Earl A. *Living When a Young Friend Commits Suicide*, 11068
Straight Talk About Death for Teenagers, 10587

Groning, Karl. *Elephants*, 12025

Grooms, Anthony. *Bombingham*, 457(F)

Gross, Andrew (jt. author). *The Jester*, 2458(F)

Gross, Ernie. *The American Years*, 8361

Gross, Gwendolen. *Getting Out*, 689(F)

Gross, Kim Johnson. *What Should I Wear?* 10966

Grossman, Andrea. *Designer Scrapbooks with Mrs. Grossman*, 12734

Grossman, David. *Death as a Way of Life*, 8201
Someone to Run With, 3927(F)

Grossman, Elizabeth. *Watershed*, 12109

Grosvenor, Edwin S. *Alexander Graham Bell*, 6536

Grosz, Terry. *Defending Our Wildlife Heritage*, 12110

Grote, David. *Staging the Musical*, 7292

Grout, Jack. *On the Lesson Tee*, 13328

Grove, Andrew S. *Swimming Across*, 6622

Grove, Vicki. *Rimwalkers*, 1888(F)

Groves, Don. *The Oceans*, 12473

Grubb, Jake. *The New Sailboard Book*, 13438

Gruen, Sara. *Riding Lessons*, 690(F)

Gruhn, George. *Acoustic Guitars and Other Fretted Instruments*, 7197

Gruhzit-Hoyt, Olga. *They Also Served*, 7711

Grunwald, Lisa. *New Year's Eve*, 691(F)

Gruver, Edward. *Koufax*, 6670

Grylls, Bear. *The Kid Who Climbed Everest*, 13264

Guelzo, Allen C. *Lincoln's Emancipation Proclamation*, 8643

Guernsey, Alfred H. *Harper's Pictorial History of the Civil War*, 8644

Guernsey, JoAnn B. *Sexual Harassment*, 11294
Voices of Feminism, 9429
Youth Violence, 9996

Guerrilla Girls Staff. *The Guerrilla Girls' Bedside Companion to the History of Western Art*, 7051

Guest, Judith. *Errands*, 692(F)
Ordinary People, 693(F)

Guffey, Greg. *The Greatest Basketball Story Ever Told*, 13205

Guiley, Rosemary Ellen. *The Encyclopedia of Ghosts and Spirits*, 13035

Guillaume, Geri. *Hearts of Steel*, 3928(F)

Guillen, Michael. *Five Equations That Changed the World*, 12403

Guinier, Lani. *Who's Qualified?* 9430

Gunderson, Mary. *Pioneer Farm Cooking*, 12792

Gunesekera, Romesh. *Reef*, 2514(F)

Gunn, Robin Jones. *I Promise*, 3929(F)

Gunther, John. *Death Be Not Proud*, 6949

Guralnick, Peter. *Careless Love*, 6104
Last Train to Memphis, 6105

Gurian, Michael. *Understanding Guys*, 11242

Gurley-Highgate, Hilda. *Sapphire's Grave*, 460(F)

Gurr, Andrew. *Rebuilding Shakespeare's Globe*, 5469

Gutcheon, Beth. *More than You Know*, 3930(F)

Guterman, Jimmy. *The Worst Rock and Roll Records of All Time*, 7152

Guterson, David. *Our Lady of the Forest*, 324(F)
Snow Falling on Cedars, 2985(F)

Guthrie, Woody. *Bound for Glory*, 5981

Gutkind, Lee. *Stuck in Time*, 11069

Gutman, Bill. *Grant Hill*, 6696
Sammy Sosa, 6687
Teammates, 6641

Gutman, Dan. *The Way Baseball Works*, 13172

Guttmann, Allen. *The Olympics, A History of the Modern Games*, 13382

Guttridge, Leonard. *Ghosts of Cape Sabine*, 8306

Guy, David. *Football Dreams*, 4579(F)

Guy, Rosa. *The Disappearance*, 3552(F)
The Music of Summer, 461(F)
My Love, My Love, or the Peasant Girl, 931(F)

Guzman, Andres. *33 Fun-and-Easy Weekend Electronics Projects*, 12630

Gwynne, Peter. *Who Uses Drugs?* 10642

Haas, Carol. *Engel v. Vitale*, 9295

Haas, Jessie. *Hoofprints*, 5511
Skipping School, 1202(F)

Haas, Robert. *Eat to Win*, 11130

Habila, Helon. *Waiting for an Angel*, 2485(F)

Hachemi, Chekeba (jt. author). *My Forbidden Face*, 8054

Hacker, Andrew. *Two Nations*, 9634

Hadamuscin, John. *Special Occasions*, 12793

Hadden, Gerry. *Teenage Refugees from Guatemala Speak Out*, 8246

Teenage Refugees from Mexico Speak Out, 8258

Haddix, Margaret P. *Don't You Dare Read This, Mrs. Dunphrey*, 694(F)

Just Ella, 1203(F)

Takeoffs and Landings, 695(F)

Turnabout, 4283(F)

Haddock, Patricia. *Environmental Time Bomb*, 9885

Teens and Gambling, 9803

Haegele, Katie. *Nature Lovers*, 10385

Hagedorn, Ann. *Beyond the River*, 8565

Hager, Jenny (jt. author). *An Appalachian Tragedy*, 9011

Hager, Tom. *Linus Pauling and the Chemistry of Life*, 6603

Haggard, H. Rider. *King Solomon's Mines*, 50(F)

Hague, Nora. *Letters from an Age of Reason*, 2825(F)

Hahn, Don. *Animation Magic*, 12639

Hahn, Mary D. *Look for Me by Moonlight*, 3146(F)

The Wind Blows Backward, 3931(F)

Haigh, Jane G. (jt. author). *Gold Rush Dogs*, 12287

Gold Rush Women, 5620

Haines, Lise. *In My Sister's Country*, 696(F)

Haines, Richard F. *CE-5*, 13036

Haines, Tim. *Walking with Dinosaurs*, 7323

Walking with Prehistoric Beasts, 7324

Hainey, Michael. *Blue*, 7096

Hairston, Rachel. *The Essentials of Horsekeeping*, 13354

Haizlip, Shirley Taylor. *The Sweeter the Juice*, 6950

Hakim, Joy. *Freedom*, 8362

Halaby, Laila. *West of the Jordan*, 1575(F)

Halam, Ann. *Dr. Franklin's Island*, 4284(F)

Taylor Five, 2515(F)

Halasa, Malu. *Mary McLeod Bethune*, 6201

Halberstam, David. *The Children*, 9635

Firehouse, 10180

The Teammates, 6642

Halbrook, David (jt. author). *In Search of the Lost Mountains of Noah*, 9050

Haldeman, Joe. *Forever Peace*, 4285(F)

Tool of the Trade, 51(F)

Hale, Deborah. *Carpetbagger's Wife*, 2929(F)

Hale, Dianne. *Pregnancy and Birth*, 11181

Hale, Gena. *Paradise Island*, 3932(F)

Hale, Janet Campbell. *The Owl's Song*, 462(F)

Hale, Shannon. *The Goose Girl*, 5064(F)

Hales, Dianne. *Pregnancy and Birth*, 11182

Haley, Alex. *Mama Flora's Family*, 463(F)

Roots, 9636

Haley, Alex (jt. author). *The Autobiography of Malcolm X*, 6251

Haley, Delphine. *Marine Mammals of Eastern North Pacific and Arctic Waters*, 12204

Hall, Barbara. *Dixie Storms*, 697(F)

Hall, Dede. *The Starving Students' Vegetarian Cookbook*, 12794

Hall, Eleanor J. *Ancient Chinese Dynasties*, 7448

Life Among the Samurai, 8038

Hall, James N. (jt. author). *The Bounty Trilogy*, 121(F)

Hall, Jonathan. *Mark McGwire*, 6672

Hall, Linda. *An Anthology of Poetry by Women*, 4870

Hall, Lynn. *Flying Changes*, 698(F)

If Winter Comes, 1576(F)

A Killing Freeze, 3553(F)

Ride a Dark Horse, 3554(F)

Where Have All the Tigers Gone? 1204(F)

Hall, Penelope (jt. author). *Careers in Medicine*, 10518

Hall, Rachel Howzell. *A Quiet Storm*, 932(F)

Hallam, Elizabeth. *The British Inheritance*, 8122

Halliburton, Warren J. *Historic Speeches of African Americans*, 5214

The West Indian-American Experience, 9772

Halliday, John. *Shooting Monarchs*, 933(F)

Halliday, Tim. *Animal Behavior*, 11926

The Encyclopedia of Reptiles and Amphibians, 11903

Hallinan, Joseph T. *Going Up the River*, 9998

Halline, Allan G. *Six Modern American Plays*, 4800

Hallion, Richard P. *Taking Flight*, 12659

Hallissy, Margaret. *A Companion to Chaucer's Canterbury Tales*, 5271

Hallowell, Janis. *The Annunciation of Francesca Dunn*, 934(F)

Halo, Thea. *Not Even My Name*, 6951

Halperin, James L. *The First Immortal*, 4286(F)

Halperin, Michael (jt. author). *Jacob's Rescue*, 3010(F)

Halpern, Charna. *Truth in Comedy*, 7293

Halpern, Paul. *The Structure of the Universe*, 11672

Halpern, Sue. *The Book of Hard Things*, 1205(F)

Four Wings and a Prayer, 12149

Ham, Catherine. *Knitting*, 12962

25 Gorgeous Sweaters for the Brand-New Knitter, 12963

Hambly, Barbara. *Ishmael*, 4287(F)

Knight of the Demon Queen, 1889(F)

Sisters of the Night, 3148(F)

The Time of the Dark, 1890(F)

Traveling with the Dead, 3147(F)

Hambly, Barbara (jt. author). *Magic Time*, 4554(F)

Hamilton, Dorothy. *Mythology*, 5152

Hamilton, Edith. *The Greek Way*, 7480

The Roman Way, 7506

Hamilton, Jane. *Disobedience*, 699(F)

Hamilton, Janet. *Lise Meitner*, 6589

Hamilton, Julia. *Other People's Rules*, 464(F)

Hamilton, Leni. *Clara Barton*, 6382

Hamilton, Martha. *How and Why Stories*, 5065

Hamilton, Neil A. *Militias in America*, 9804

Hamilton, Peter F. *Pandora's Star*, 4288(F)

Hamilton, Rick (jt. author). *A Midsummer Night's Dream*, 5477

Romeo and Juliet, 5478

The Taming of the Shrew, 5479

Hamilton, Virginia. *Anthony Burns*, 6203

Junius over Far, 700(F)

Justice and Her Brothers, 1891(F)

M.C. Higgins, the Great, 701(F)

Sweet Whispers, Brother Rush, 3149(F)

A White Romance, 465(F)

Hamlett, Christina. *Humorous Plays for Teen-Agers*, 4801

Hamlyn, Robin. *William Blake*, 5731

Hamm, Mia. *Go for the Goal*, 13426

Hammel, Bob (jt. author). *Knight*, 6702

Hammond, Sean. *How to Raise a Sane and Healthy Cat*, 12254

Hammond, Wayne G. *J.R.R. Tolkien*, 5944

Hampe, Barry. *Making Documentary Films and Reality Videos*, 12640

Making Videos for Money, 12641

Hampton, Bruce. *The Great American Wolf*, 12007

Karam, Jana Abrams. *Into the Breach*, 10911

Karanth, K. Ullas. *The Way of the Tiger*, 11995

Karapalides, Harry J. *Dates of the American Revolution*, 8532

Karas, Phyllis. *The Hate Crime*, 3601(F)

Karbo, Karen (jt. author). *Big Girl in the Middle*, 6747

Karenga, Maulana. *Kwanzaa*, 10159

Karlen, Arno. *Man and Microbes*, 10794

Karlin, Wayne. *The Other Side of Heaven*, 3082(F)

Karnes, Frances A. *Girls and Young Women Entrepreneurs*, 10216

Karnow, Stanley. *Vietnam*, 8050

Karo, Aaron. *Ruminations on College Life*, 10345

Karr, Kathleen. *Gilbert and Sullivan Set Me Free*, 338(F)

Karson, Jill. *Cults*, 9157
Readings on A Separate Peace, 5378
Readings on Of Mice and Men, 5379
Readings on The Pearl, 5380

Kaschula, Russel. *Xhosa*, 7967

Kasdan, Lawrence. *Return of the Jedi*, 7235

Kasdan, Lawrence (jt. author). *The Empire Strikes Back*, 7222

Kashina, Anna. *The Princess of Dhagabad*, 1954(F)

Kashner, Sam. *When I Was Cool*, 6964

Kaskie, Shirli. *A Woman's Golf Game*, 13330

Kassam, Nadya. *Telling It Like It Is*, 9563

Kastner, Janet. *More Than an Average Guy*, 6986

Kata, Elizabeth. *A Patch of Blue*, 946(F)

Katcher, Philip. *The Civil War Source Book*, 8651

Katovsky, Bill. *Embedded*, 5588

Katz, Donald. *Just Do It! The Nike Spirit in the Corporate World*, 10217

Katz, Jane B. *We Rode the Wind*, 8455

Katz, Jon. *Geeks*, 10539

Katz, Jonathan I. *The Biggest Bangs*, 11674

Katz, Joseph (jt. author). *The Great Trials of the Twenties*, 9294

Katz, Samuel M. *At Any Cost*, 10184
Jerusalem or Death, 8202
Jihad, 10185
Raging Within, 10186

Katz, Welwyn W. *Whalesinger*, 174(F)

Katz, William L. *Black Indians*, 9775
Black Legacy, 8979
Black Pioneers, 8712

Breaking the Chains, 8571

Exploration to the War of 1812, 1492–1814, 8374

The Great Migrations, 9564

Kaufman, Alan S. *The Worst Baseball Pitchers of All Time*, 6645

Kaufman, Allan. *Exploring Solar Energy*, 12518

Kaufman, Bel. *Up the Down Staircase*, 3282(F)

Kaufman, Cheryl Davidson. *Cooking the Caribbean Way*, 12802

Kaufman, J. B. (jt. author). *Walt in Wonderland*, 7242

Kaufman, James C. (jt. author). *The Worst Baseball Pitchers of All Time*, 6645

Kaufman, Kate (jt. author). *Free Your Mind*, 11396

Kaufman, Moises. *The Laramie Project*, 5517

Kaufman, Murray S. *Reefs and Rain Forests*, 8051

Kay, Guy Gavriel. *The Last Light of the Sun*, 1955(F)

Kay, Philip (jt. author). *Starting with "I,"* 10292

Kay, Susan. *Phantom*, 3957(F)

Kay, William J. *The Complete Book of Dog Health*, 12283

Kaye, Elizabeth. *Ain't No Tomorrow*, 13210

Kaye, Harvey J. *Thomas Paine*, 6435

Kaye, Marilyn. *Amy, Number Seven*, 4323(F)

Kaye, Marvin. *The Stein and Day Handbook of Magic*, 12923

Kaye, Tony. *Lyndon B. Johnson*, 6317

Kaysen, Susanna. *Girl Interrupted*, 11076

Keating, H. R. F. *Breaking and Entering*, 2524(F)

Keatman, Martin (jt. author). *King Arthur*, 5112

Keats, John. *Poems*, 4936

Keay, John. *The Great Arc*, 8027
India, 8028

Keegan, John. *An Illustrated History of the First World War*, 7614
Intelligence in War, 12709
The Second World War, 7733
War and Our World, 9182

Keeley, Jennifer. *Deterring and Investigating Attack*, 10187
Life in the Hitler Youth, 7734
Understanding I Am the Cheese, 5381
The Yearling, 5382

Keely, Jennifer. *Rap Music*, 7161

Keen, G. Daniel (jt. author). *Botany*, 11818

Keenan, Philip E. *Birding Across North America*, 12056

Keene, Ann T. *Willa Cather*, 5828

Kehret, Peg. *Encore! More Winning Monologs for Young Actors*, 4750
Night of Fear, 80(F)

Keiler, Allan. *Marian Anderson*, 5994

Keillor, Garrison. *Lake Wobegon Summer 1956*, 1249(F)
Leaving Home, 5188

Keith, Lois. *A Different Life*, 947(F)

Keizer, Garret. *God of Beer*, 1585(F)

Kelleher, Victor. *Del-Del*, 3160(F)

Keller, Annan. *Marian Anderson*, 5995

Keller, Beverly. *The Amazon Papers*, 3283(F)

Keller, Helen. *The Story of My Life*, 6489

Keller, Kristin Thoennes. *Parenting an Infant*, 11189

Kellerman, Faye. *The Forgotten*, 3602(F)
Stalker, 3603(F)

Kelley, Brent. *The Horse Doctor Is In*, 12310

Kelley, William. *The Sweet Summer*, 484(F)

Kellogg, Marjorie. *The Book of Water*, 1956(F)
Tell Me That You Love Me, Junie Moon, 1250(F)

Kelly, Clara Olink. *The Flamboya Tree*, 7735

Kelly, Jack. *Gunpowder*, 12710

Kelly, Martin. *Parents Book of Baby Names*, 5549

Kelly, Mary Anne. *Foxglove*, 3604(F)

Kelly, Mary D. (jt. author). *Dream's End*, 8652

Kelly, Michael. *Bill Clinton*, 6295

Kelly, Orr. *Dream's End*, 8652

Kelly, Richard. *Lewis Carroll*, 5276

Kelsey, Harry. *Sir Francis Drake*, 5641

Keltner, Nancy. *If You Print This, Please Don't Use My Name*, 11434

Kemal, Yasher. *Memed, My Hawk*, 1586(F)

Kemelman, Harry. *The Day the Rabbi Resigned*, 3605(F)

Kemer, Eric (jt. author). *Science Projects About Temperature and Heat*, 12509

Kemp, Kenny. *I Hated Heaven*, 1957(F)

Kemp, Kristen. *Jewel: Pieces of a Dream*, 6067

Kempe, C. Henry. *The Battered Child*, 11522

Kemprecos, Paul (jt. author). *Fire Ice*, 33(F)

Kenan, Randall. *James Baldwin*, 5813

Keneally, Thomas. *Abraham Lincoln*, 6338

King, Emily. *A Century of Movie Posters*, 7237

King, F. W. (jt. author). *The Audubon Society Field Guide to North American Reptiles and Amphibians*, 11897

King, F. Wayne. *Discovery Channel Reptiles and Amphibians*, 11904

King, Gabriel. *The Golden Cat*, 1965(F)

The Wild Road, 1966(F)

King, John. *Conflict in the Middle East*, 8188

The Gulf War, 7876

King, Laurie R. *The Beekeeper's Apprentice*, 3609(F)

A Darker Place, 3610(F)

A Monstrous Regiment of Women, 3611(F)

The Moor, 3612(F)

King, Martin Luther, Jr. *The Autobiography of Martin Luther King, Jr.*, 6241

Strength to Love, 9655

A Testament of Hope, 9656

Why We Can't Wait, 9657

The Words of Martin Luther King, Jr., 9658

King, Michael R. *Who Killed King Tut? Using Modern Forensics to Solve a 3,300-Year-Old Mystery*, 7461

King, Patricia. *Making Dolls' House Furniture*, 12874

King, Perry Scott. *Jefferson Davis*, 6400

King, Rachel. *Don't Kill in Our Names*, 10009

King, Stephen. *Black House*, 3177(F)

Carrie, 3162(F)

Christine, 3163(F)

Cujo, 3164(F)

The Dead Zone, 3165(F)

Different Seasons, 3166(F)

The Drawing of the Three, 1967(F)

Dreamcatcher, 3167(F)

Everything's Eventual, 3168(F)

The Eyes of the Dragon, 1968(F)

Firestarter, 3169(F)

Four Past Midnight, 3170(F)

The Girl Who Loved Tom Gordon, 82(F)

The Green Mile, 3613(F)

The Gunslinger, 1969(F)

Night Shift, 3171(F)

Nightmares and Dreamscapes, 3172(F)

On Writing, 5901

Pet Sematary, 3173(F)

The Shining, 3174(F)

Skeleton Crew, 3175(F)

Song of Susannah, 1970(F)

The Stand, 3176(F)

The Waste Lands, 1971(F)

King, Susan. *The Sword Maiden*, 2615(F)

King, Tabitha. *One on One*, 3958(F)

King, Wilma. *Toward the Promised Land*, 9659

King-Smith, Dick. *Chewing the Cud*, 5899

King-Smith, Richard. *Godhanger*, 1972(F)

Kingsbury, Karen. *A Treasury of Miracles for Teens*, 9067

Kingsland, Rosemary. *The Secret Life of a Schoolgirl*, 6965

Kingsley, Jason. *Count Us In*, 11079

Kingsolver, Barbara. *The Bean Trees*, 1264(F)

High Tide in Tucson, 5220

The Poisonwood Bible, 2487(F)

Kinnear, Karen L. *Childhood Sexual Abuse*, 11296

Gangs, 10010

Kinney, Jane (jt. author). *Careers for Environmental Types*, 10379

Kinsella, Sophie. *Shopaholic Ties the Knot*, 3284(F)

Kinsella, W. P. *Shoeless Joe*, 4582(F)

Kinsolving, William. *Mister Christian*, 83(F)

Kinstlinger-Bruhn, Charlotte. *Everything You Need to Know About Breaking the Cycle of Domestic Violence*, 11524

Kipling, Rudyard. *Captains Courageous*, 229(F)

Gunga Din, 4937

Kim, 230(F)

Kipling's Fantasy, 1973(F)

The Portable Kipling, 231(F)

Kipnis, Claude. *The Mime Book*, 7295

Kirberger, Kimberly. *On Friendship*, 11437

On Relationships, 11436

Kirby, John T. *Classical Greek Civilization, 800–323 B.C.E.*, 7482

Kirby-Payne, Ann (jt. author). *Understanding Weight and Depression*, 10751

Kirkland, Martha. *An Inconvenient Heir*, 3959(F)

The Secret Diary, 3960(F)

Kirkpatrick, Jane. *All Together in One Place*, 2887(F)

Kirkwood, Burton. *The History of Mexico*, 8261

Kirkwood, Gwen. *The Laird of Lochandee*, 3961(F)

Kirkwood, Tim. *The Flight Attendant Career Guide*, 10394

Kirlin, Katherine S. *Smithsonian Folklife Cookbook*, 12803

Kirlin, Thomas (jt. author). *Smithsonian Folklife Cookbook*, 12803

Kirshenbaum, Binnie. *An Almost Perfect Moment*, 1265(F)

Kirtley, Karen (jt. author). *Alma Rose*, 7770

Kirwin, Barbara. *The Mad, the Bad, and the Innocent*, 10011

Kitchen, Martin. *The Cambridge Illustrated History of Germany*, 8108

Kittleson, Stan. *Racquetball*, 13448

Kittredge, Mary. *The Common Cold*, 10795

Headaches, 10796

Jane Addams, 6465

Organ Transplants, 10724

The Respiratory System, 11024

Teens with AIDS Speak Out, 10797

Kitzinger, Sheila. *The Complete Book of Pregnancy and Childbirth*, 11190

Kizilos, Peter. *Quebec*, 8239

Tibet, 8052

Kjelle, Marylou Morano. *Hitler's Henchmen*, 6765

Klasky, Mindy. *The Glasswright's Progress*, 1974(F)

Klasky, Mindy L. *The Glasswrights' Test*, 1975(F)

Klass, David. *California Blue*, 175(F)

Danger Zone, 4583(F)

Home of the Braves, 1266(F)

Klass, Perri Elizabeth. *A Not Entirely Benign Procedure*, 10913

Klass, Sheila S. *Next Stop*, 1267(F)

Rhino, 951(F)

Klause, Annette Curtis. *Blood and Chocolate*, 3178(F)

The Silver Kiss, 3179(F)

Klaveness, Jan O'Donnell. *Ghost Island*, 84(F)

Klee, Sheila. *Working Together Against School Violence*, 10012

Kleh, Cindy. *Snowboarding Skills*, 13417

Klein, David. *Getting Unscrewed and Staying That Way*, 10231

Klein, Gerda Weissmann. *The Hours After*, 7737

Klein, Kurt (jt. author). *The Hours After*, 7737

Klein, Marymae E. (jt. author). *Getting Unscrewed and Staying That Way*, 10231

Klein, Norma. *Breaking Up*, 736(F)

Family Secrets, 1268(F)

Going Backwards, 737(F)

It's OK If You Don't Love Me, 738(F)

Sunshine, 952(F)

Klein, Robin. *Tearaways*, 3180(F)

Klein, Wendy. *Drugs and Denial*, 10655

Kleinman, Joseph. *Life on an African Slave Ship*, 9660

Klever, Ulrich. *The Complete Book of Dog Care*, 12284

Kliment, Bud. *Billie Holiday*, 6059

Count Basie, 6002

Klimley, A. Peter. *The Secret Life of Sharks*, 12184

Kline, Lisa Williams. *Eleanor Hill*, 2931(F)

Madaras, Lynda. *The What's Happening to My Body? Book for Boys*, 11249
The What's Happening to My Body? Book for Girls, 11250
Maddox, Brenda. *Rosalind Franklin*, 6568
Maddox, Harry. *How to Study*, 10278
Maddox, Robert James. *Weapons for Victory*, 7759
Madison, Bob. *American Horror Writers*, 5709
Mado, Michio. *The Animals*, 5050
Madsen, Christine. *Drinking and Driving*, 10668
Maflin, Andrea. *Easy and Elegant Home Decorating*, 12739
Magee, Bryan. *The Story of Philosophy*, 9030
Maggitti, Phil. *Owning the Right Cat*, 12258
Owning the Right Dog, 12285
Magida, Arthur J. *How to Be a Perfect Stranger*, 9073
Magistrale, Tony. *Student Companion to Edgar Allan Poe*, 5386
Magorian, Michelle. *Not a Swan*, 3988(F)
Maguire, Gregory. *Oasis*, 1326(F)
Maguire, Stephen. *Torn by the Issues*, 9825
Mah, Adeline Yen. *Chinese Cinderella*, 6975
Maharidge, Dale. *The Coming White Minority*, 9566
Yosemite, 9003
Mahfouz, Naguib. *Akhenaten*, 2406(F)
Mahon, K. L. *Just One Tear*, 1327(F)
Mahone-Lonesome, Robyn. *Charles Drew*, 6551
Mahy, Margaret. *Alchemy*, 2066(F)
The Catalogue of the Universe, 1328(F)
The Changeover, 2067(F)
Don't Read This! 3200(F)
Memory, 966(F)
The Other Side of Silence, 1329(F)
24 Hours, 103(F)
Majerus, Michael. *Moths*, 12150
Major, Clarence. *Calling the Wind*, 508(F)
Come by Here, 9567
The Garden Thrives, 5004
Major, Devorah. *Brown Glass Windows*, 509(F)
Major, Marcus. *A Family Affair*, 1330(F)
Majure, Janet. *AIDS*, 10815
Breast Cancer, 10816
Makiya, Kanan. *The Rock*, 2627(F)
Makower, Joel. *The Green Commuter*, 12669
Makris, Kathryn. *A Different Way*, 1331(F)
Malafronte, Victor A. *The Complete Book of Frisbee*, 13104

Malamud, Bernard. *The Assistant*, 511(F)
The Fixer, 2628(F)
Malaspina, Ann. *The Jaguar*, 11997
The Koala, 12031
Saving the American Wilderness, 9889
Malcolm X. *The Autobiography of Malcolm X*, 6251
Malikow, Max (jt. author). *Living When a Young Friend Commits Suicide*, 11068
Mallory, James (jt. author). *The Outstretched Shadow*, 2001(F)
Mallory, Tess. *Highland Fling*, 3989(F)
Malloy, Brian. *The Year of Ice*, 1332(F)
Malone, Caroline. *Stonehenge*, 7376
Malone, John. *The Civil War Quiz Book*, 8661
Predicting the Future, 13040
Malone, John Williams. *It Doesn't Take a Rocket Scientist*, 6520
Malone, Michael. *Red Clay, Blue Cadillac*, 3662(F)
Maltz, Leora. *The Founding of America*, 8536
Man, John. *Atlas of the Year 1000*, 7551
Manaugh, Sara. *Judges and Sentencing*, 9316
Mancall, Peter C. *American Eras*, 8719
Manchester, William. *One Brief Shining Moment*, 6323
Mandela, Nelson. *Mandela*, 6784
Mandell, Sherri Lederman. *Writers of the Holocaust*, 5710
Manes, Stephen. *Comedy High*, 3294(F)
Mangelsen, Thomas D. *Spirit of the Rockies*, 11998
Manicka, Rani. *The Rice Mother*, 2531(F)
Manji, Irshad. *The Trouble with Islam*, 9135
Mankiewicz, Richard. *The Story of Mathematics*, 12411
Manley, Claudia B. *Ultra Swimming*, 13439
Manley, Frank. *The Cockfighter*, 770(F)
Manley, Joan B. *She Flew No Flags*, 3040(F)
Mann, Charles C. *Noah's Choice*, 12114
Mann, Gruinder Singh. *Buddhists, Hindus, and Sikhs in America*, 9074
Mann, Kenny. *Kongo Ndongo*, 7989
Monomotapa, Zulu, Basuto, 7969
Oyo, Benin, Ashanti, 7990
Manning, Harvey. *Backpacking One Step at a Time*, 13272
Manning, Jo. *The Sicilian Amulet*, 3990(F)

Manning, Sarra. *Guitar Girl*, 352(F)
Mannis, William (jt. author). *Cowgirls*, 8705
Mansbach, Adam. *Shackling Water*, 353(F)
Many, Paul. *My Life, Take Two*, 1333(F)
These Are the Rules, 3295(F)
Walk Away Home, 1334(F)
Manz, Bruno. *A Mind in Prison*, 7760
Maples, Jack. *Reconstructed Yankee*, 2833(F)
Marable, Manning. *The Great Wells of Democracy*, 9446
W. E. B. Du Bois, 6218
Maran, Meredith. *Class Dismissed*, 11345
Maran, Stephen P. (jt. author). *Gems of Hubble*, 11680
Marani, Pietro C. *Leonardo da Vinci*, 7076
Maraniss, David. *First in His Class*, 6296
Marazzi, Rich. *Aaron to Zuverink*, 13181
Marberry, Craig. *The Spirit of Harlem*, 8983
Marcellas, Diana. *Mother Ocean, Daughter Sea*, 2069(F)
Marchand, Peter J. *Autumn*, 11802
Marchetta, Melina. *Looking for Alibrandi*, 2532(F)
Marco, John. *The Saints of the Sword*, 2070(F)
Marcovitz, Hal. *Jordan*, 8223
Terrorism, 10191
Marcus, Eric. *Is It a Choice? Answers to 300 of the Most Frequently Asked Questions About Gays and Lesbians*, 11251
What If Someone I Know Is Gay? Answers to Questions About Gay and Lesbian People, 11252
Mares, Michael A. *A Desert Calling*, 11953
Margaret, Pat Maixner. *Watercolor Quilts*, 12970
Margolies, Jacob. *The Negro Leagues*, 13182
Margolin, Phillip. *Sleeping Beauty*, 3663(F)
Margolis, Jeffrey A. *Teen Crime Wave*, 10018
Violence in Sports, 13105
Margolis, Matthew. *The Dog in Your Life*, 12286
Margolis, Matthew (jt. author). *GRRR! The Complete Guide to Understanding and Preventing Aggressive Behavior*, 12294
Margulies, Alice. *Compassion*, 11376
Margulies, Edward. *Bad Movies We Love*, 7240
Margulis, Lynn. *What Is Life?* 12225

Miller, Edwin Haviland. *Salem Is My Dwelling Place*, 5876

Miller, Frances A. *The Truth Trap*, 118(F)

Miller, Frank. *Batman*, 2337(F)

Miller, Henri. *Free Trade Versus Protectionism*, 10243

Miller, J. Anthony. *Texas vs. Johnson*, 10112

Miller, James. *American Slavery*, 9671

Miller, James Andrew (jt. author). *Live from New York*, 7277

Miller, Julia Wang (jt. author). *The AIDS Crisis*, 10768

Miller, Karen E. Quinones. *I'm Telling*, 972(F)
Satin Doll, 518(F)

Miller, Keith. *The Book of Flying*, 2082(F)

Miller, Lee. *From the Heart*, 8463
Roanoke, 8507

Miller, Linda Lael. *Courting Susannah*, 2938(F)
The Last Chance Cafe, 3676(F)

Miller, Louise. *Careers for Animal Lovers and Other Zoological Types*, 10405

Miller, Martha J. *Kidney Disorders*, 10818

Miller, Mary Beth. *Aimee*, 973(F)

Miller, Maryann. *Drugs and Date Rape*, 10673
Drugs and Gun Violence, 10674
Drugs and Violent Crime, 10675

Miller, Montana (jt. author). *Circus Dreams*, 7290

Miller, Nathan. *War at Sea*, 7765

Miller, Patrick B. (jt. author). *The Unlevel Playing Field*, 9698

Miller, Reggie. *I Love Being the Enemy*, 13215

Miller, Ron. *Extrasolar Planets*, 11679
The History of Rockets, 12564
The History of Science Fiction, 5254

Miller, Walter M., Jr. *A Canticle for Leibowitz*, 4391(F)

Miller, Wilbur R. *Woodworking*, 12990

Miller-Lachmann, Lyn. *Hiding Places*, 1355(F)

Millett, Larry. *Sherlock Holmes and the Secret Alliance*, 2939(F)

Millmoss, A. B. (jt. author). *Backyard and Beyond*, 11791

Mills, Cliff. *Virginia Woolf*, 5969

Mills, Dick. *Aquarius Fish*, 12305
You and Your Aquarium, 12325

Mills, Guy. *African Predators*, 11884

Mills, Judie. *Robert Kennedy*, 6330

Mills, Kay. *From Pocahontas to Power Suits*, 8380

Mills, Nicolaus. *Arguing Immigration*, 9533

Mills, Randy. *Unexpected Journey*, 8940

Mills, Roxanne (jt. author). *Unexpected Journey*, 8940

Millstone, Erik. *The Penguin Atlas of Food*, 11835

Milne, Lorus. *The Audubon Society Field Guide to North American Insects and Spiders*, 12136

Milne, Margery (jt. author). *The Audubon Society Field Guide to North American Insects and Spiders*, 12136

Milner, Anna (jt. author). *The Internet*, 12589

Milner, Richard. *Charles Darwin*, 6549

Milstein, Janet. *The Ultimate Audition Book for Teens*, 5450

Milton, John. *The Portable Milton*, 5451

Milton, Steve. *Figure Skating Now*, 13364

Min, Anchee. *Empress Orchid*, 2533(F)
Red Azalea, 6806
Wild Ginger, 2534(F)

Minchin, Adele. *The Beat Goes On*, 974(F)

Mindich, David T. Z. *Just the Facts*, 5593

Mingay, Marie. *Nail Style*, 10967

Minks, Benton (jt. author). *The Revolutionary War*, 8537

Minks, Louise. *The Revolutionary War*, 8537

Minnis, Whitney. *How to Get an Athletic Scholarship*, 10356

Minter, J. *The Insiders*, 356(F)

Mintzer, Rich. *Helping Hands*, 10143

Mirault, Don. *Dancing . . . for a Living*, 10449

Mirriam-Goldberg, Caryn. *Write Where You Are*, 5561

Mitch, Frank. *Understanding September 11th*, 10192

Mitcham, Samuel W., Jr. *Rommel's Greatest Victory*, 7766

Mitchard, Jacquelyn. *The Most Wanted*, 781(F)
A Theory of Relativity, 782(F)

Mitchell, Greg (jt. author). *Who Owns Death? Capital Punishment, The American Conscience and the End of Executions*, 10016

Mitchell, Hayley R. *The Death Penalty*, 9317, 9318
Readings on a Doll's House, 5452
Readings on Wuthering Heights, 5278
Teen Alcoholism, 10676

Mitchell, Joseph B. *Decisive Battles of the American Revolution*, 8538

Mitchell, Joyce Slayton. *Winning the Heart of the College Admissions Dean*, 10351

Mitchell, Kathryn. *Proud and Angry Dust*, 519(F)

Mitchell, Margaret. *Gone with the Wind*, 2835(F)

Mitchell, Sara. *Trial of the Innocent*, 3677(F)

Mitchell, Sharon. *Near Perfect*, 4001(F)

Mitchell, Stephen. *Jesus*, 9111

Mitchell, W. I. T. *The Last Dinosaur Book*, 7332

Mitton, Jacqueline. *Gems of Hubble*, 11680

Mixon, Laura J. *Burning the Ice*, 4392(F)

Mizerak, Steve. *Steve Mizerak's Complete Book of Pool*, 13107
Steve Mizerak's Pocket Billiards, 13106

Mizuno, Ryo. *Record of Lodoss War*, 2338(F)

Mlodinow, Leonard. *Euclid's Window*, 12421

Moats, David. *Civil Wars*, 9319

Mochizuki, Ken. *Beacon Hill Boys*, 520(F)

Modesitt, L. E. *Chaos Balance*, 4393(F)
Legacies, 2083(F)
Magi'i of Cyador, 2084(F)
The Octagonal Raven, 4394(F)
Scion of Cyador, 2085(F)
The Shadow Sorceress, 2086(F)
Wellspring of Chaos, 2087(F)

Modesitt, L. E., Jr. *The Death of Chaos*, 4395(F)
The Soprano Sorceress, 2088(F)

Modley, Rudolf. *Handbook of Pictorial Symbols*, 5538

Moe, Barbara. *Careers in Sports Medicine*, 10510
Coping with Eating Disorders, 10819
Coping with Mental Illness, 11087
Coping with PMS, 10820
Coping with Tourette Syndrome and Tic Disorders, 10821
Everything You Need to Know About Migraines and Other Headaches, 10822
Inside Eating Disorder Support Groups, 10823
A Question of Timing, 11203
Understanding Negative Body Image, 11136

Moe, Jörgen (jt. author). *Norwegian Folk Tales*, 5097

Moehn, Heather. *Everything You Need to Know When Someone You Know Has Leukemia*, 10824
Social Anxiety, 11088
Understanding Eating Disorder Support Groups, 10825

Moeller, Christopher. *Faith Conquers*, 2339(F)

Moeyaert, Bart. *Bare Hands*, 1356(F) *Hornet's Nest*, 357(F)

Mogel, Leonard. *Making It in Advertising*, 10470

Mogil, H. Michael. *The Amateur Meteorologist*, 12457

Mohan, Kim. *Amazing Stories*, 4396(F)

Molitor, Graham T. T. (jt. author). *The 21st Century*, 10139

Moll, Lucy. *Vegetarian Times Complete Cookbook*, 12812

Molotsky, Irvin. *The Flag, the Poet and the Song*, 8574

Monaghan, Tom. *The Slave Trade*, 7580

Monath, Norman. *How to Play Popular Piano in Ten Easy Lessons*, 7198

Monfredo, Miriam G. *The Stalking Horse*, 2789(F)

Monfredo, Miriam Grace. *Must the Maiden Die*, 3678(F) *Sisters of Cain*, 2836(F)

Mongibeaux, Jean-Francois (jt. author). *Winged Migration*, 12059

Monk, Linda R. *The Words We Live By*, 9214

Monroe, Judy. *Antidepressants*, 10677

Coping with Ulcers, Heartburn, and Stress-Related Stomach Disorders, 11016

Nicotine, 10678

Phobias, 11089

The Sacco and Vanzetti Controversial Murder Trial, 9320

The Susan B. Anthony Women's Voting Rights Trial, 9451

Understanding Weight-Loss Programs, 11137

Monroe, Judy (jt. author). *Cooking the Korean Way*, 12778 *Cooking the Thai Way*, 12798 *Cooking the Vietnamese Way*, 12816

Monroe, Mary Alice. *Skyward*, 358(F)

Monsarrat, Nicholas. *The Cruel Sea*, 3048(F)

Monseau, Virginia R. *Presenting Ouida Sebestyen*, 5927

Montague, Magnificent. *Burn, Baby! Burn! The Autobiography of Magnificent Montague*, 6095

Montgomery, Bertha Vining. *Cooking the West African Way*, 12813

Montgomery, Sy. *Journey of the Pink Dolphins*, 12211

Search for the Golden Moon Bear, 11982

Walking with the Great Apes, 11967

Montpetit, Charles. *The First Time, vol. 1*, 11255

Montville, Leigh. *At the Altar of Speed*, 6656

Moody, Anne. *Coming of Age in Mississippi*, 6977

Moody, Bill. *The Sound of the Trumpet*, 3679(F)

Moon, Elizabeth. *Against the Odds*, 2089(F)

Remnant Population, 4397(F)

The Speed of Dark, 975(F)

Moon, Marliss. *By Starlight*, 4002(F)

Moon, Russell. *Witch Boy*, 3208(F)

Mooney, Bill. *The Storyteller's Guide*, 10309

Mooney, Chuck. *The Recruiting Survival Guide*, 13308

Moorcock, Michael. *The Dreamthief's Daughter*, 2090(F)

Moore, Alan. *Alan Moore's America's Best Comics. 2004*, 2340(F) *Promethea*, 2091(F)

Moore, Barbara (jt. author). *The Nine-Ton Cat*, 9260

Moore, Christopher. *Lamb*, 3297(F)

Moore, David L. *Dark Sky, Dark Land*, 11575

Moore, David S. *The Dependent Gene*, 10947

Moore, Deborah (jt. author). *Cityscapes*, 8985

Moore, Ishbel. *Daughter*, 783(F)

Moore, James A. *Fireworks*, 4398(F)

Moore, Joseph Thomas. *Pride Against Prejudice*, 6666

Moore, Margaret. *Gwyneth and the Thief*, 4003(F)

Moore, Marilyn M. *The Wooden Spoon Cookie Book*, 12814

Moore, Michael Scott. *Too Much of Nothing*, 3209(F)

Moore, Patrick. *The New Atlas of the Universe*, 11681 *Stargazing*, 11682

Moore, Peter. *Blind Sighted*, 1357(F)

Moore, Peter D. *Wetlands*, 12367

Moore, Peter D. (jt. author). *Biomes and Habitats*, 12371

Moore, Richard. *Boneyard, v.2*, 2341

Moore, Robert. *A Time to Die*, 8164

Moore, Robin. *The Bread Sister of Sinking Creek*, 2896(F)

The Man with the Silver Oar, 2749(F)

Moore, Terry. *Strangers in Paradise*, 359(F)

Moore, Yvette. *Freedom Songs*, 521(F)

Mora, Pat. *My Own True Name*, 5011

Moragne, Wendy. *Depression*, 11090

Moran, Gary T. (jt. author). *Getting Stronger*, 13114

Moran, Richard. *Executioner's Current*, 9321

Moreau, C. X. *Promise of Glory*, 2837(F)

Morehead, Albert H. *Hoyle's Rules of Games*, 13290

Morell, Virginia. *Ancestral Passions*, 6584

Morell, Virginia (jt. author). *Wildlife Wars*, 7931

Morella, Joseph. *Simon and Garfunkel*, 6121

Moreno, Barry. *Italian Americans*, 9778

Morey, Eileen. *Readings on The Scarlet Letter*, 5388

Morey, Janet Nomura. *Famous Hispanic Americans*, 6177

Morey, Walt. *Death Walk*, 119(F)

Morgan, David. *Knowing the Score*, 7243

Morgan, David Lee. *LeBron James*, 6703

Morgan, Edmund S. *Benjamin Franklin*, 6406

Morgan, Kenneth O. *The Oxford Illustrated History of Britain*, 8134

Morgan, Peggy. *Buddhism*, 9079

Morgan, Robert. *Brave Enemies*, 2761(F)

This Rock, 784(F)

Morgan, Sally. *Alternative Energy Sources*, 12519

Morgan, Ted. *Wilderness at Dawn*, 8232

Morgenstern, Julie. *Organizing from the Inside Out for Teens*, 11451

Morgenstern, Mindy. *The Real Rules for Girls*, 11452

Morgenstern, Susie. *Three Days Off*, 1358(F)

Morgenstern-Colon, Jessi (jt. author). *Organizing from the Inside Out for Teens*, 11451

Morgenthal, Deborah. *The Ultimate T-Shirt Book*, 12861

Mori, Kyoko. *One Bird*, 785(F)

Shizuko's Daughter, 1359(F)

Moriarty, Jaclyn. *Feeling Sorry for Celia*, 360(F)

Moriarty, Laura. *The Center of Everything*, 1360(F)

Morin, Isobel V. *Impeaching the President*, 9234

Our Changing Constitution, 9215

Politics, American Style, 9350

Women of the U.S. Congress, 6178

Women Who Reformed Politics, 6179

Moring, Marcel. *The Dream Room*, 786(F)

Morra, Marion (jt. author). *Understanding Your Immune System*, 10837

Morrell, David. *Fireflies*, 787(F)

Morrell, Virginia. *Blue Nile*, 7905

Morressy, John. *The Juggler*, 2454(F)

Morrill, John. *The Oxford Illustrated History of Tudor and Stuart Britain*, 8135

Morris, Bruce C. (jt. author). *Live Aware, Not in Fear*, 11223

Morris, Dave. *Game Art*, 12613

Morris, Deborah. *Teens 911*, 361(F)

Morris, Desmond. *Catwatching*, 12259

Horsewatching, 12312

Morris, Gilbert. *Heart of a Lion*, 2408(F)

Morris, Gilbert (jt. author). *Toward the Sunrising*, 2940(F)

Morris, Jan. *Lincoln*, 6342

Morris, Jeannie. *Brian Piccolo*, 6714

Morris, Jim. *The Oldest Rookie*, 6679

Morris, Lynn. *Toward the Sunrising*, 2940(F)

Morris, Michael. *Slow Way Home*, 788(F)

Morris, Norval. *The Oxford History of the Prison*, 10022

Morris, Richard. *The Big Questions*, 9031

Morris, Richard B. *Basic Documents in American History*, 8382

Morris, Rod. *South Sea Islands*, 8072

Morris, Willie. *Taps*, 1361(F)

Morris, Winifred. *Liar*, 1362(F)

Morrison, Grant. *Deus ex Machina*, 5594

Morrison, Toni. *Beloved*, 2941(F)

The Bluest Eye, 522(F)

Remember, 9672

Morrissey, Donna. *Kit's Law*, 2706(F)

Morrow, James. *Nebula Awards 26*, 4399(F)

Nebula Awards 27, 4400(F)

Morrow, Lance. *Evil*, 9032

Morrow, Robert. *Immigration*, 9534

Morse, Tim. *Classic Rock Stories*, 7166

Mortensen, Colin (jt. author). *On Friendship*, 11437

Mortimer, Sean (jt. author). *Hawk*, 6748

Mortman, Doris. *Before and Again*, 3680(F)

Morton, Alexandra. *Listening to Whales*, 12212

Morton, Danelle (jt. author). *The Healing Power of Pets*, 12234

Morton, Eugene S. *Animal Talk*, 11936

Morton, Laura (jt. author). *The Truth Is —*, 6043

Morton, Oliver. *Mapping Mars*, 11722

Morvan, Jean David. *Wake*, 2342(F)

Morwood, Peter. *Star Trek*, 4401(F)

Moschovitis, Christos J. P. *History of the Internet*, 12614

Moscovich, Ivan. *1000 Playthinks*, 12999

Moseley, James W. *Shockingly Close to the Truth*, 13041

Moseley, Michael Edward. *The Incas and Their Ancestors*, 8292

Moser, Barry. *Great Ghost Stories*, 3210(F)

Moser, Diane. *Political and Social Movements*, 8383

Moser, Diane (jt. author). *The African-American Experience*, 9688

Eleanor Roosevelt, 6358

Exploring the Reaches of the Solar System, 11771

The History of Science from the Ancient Greeks to the Scientific Revolution, 11620

The History of Science in the Eighteenth Century, 11621

The History of Science in the Nineteenth Century, 11622

Opening the Space Frontier, 11732

Science and Invention, 11623

Moser, Kit (jt. author). *The Crime of Genocide*, 9196

Moses, Libby (jt. author). *When Rover Just Won't Do*, 12292

Moses, Marcia. *Easy Watercolor*, 12894

Mosher, Howard Frank. *The True Account*, 2897(F)

Mosier, Elizabeth. *My Life as a Girl*, 1363(F)

Mosiman, Billie Sue. *Malachi's Moon*, 3211(F)

Mosley, John. *Stargazing for Beginners*, 11683

Mosley, Walter. *Bad Boy Brawly Brown*, 3681(F)

Workin' on the Chain Gang, 11366

Moss, Leonard. *Arthur Miller*, 5520

Moss, Nathaniel. *Ron Kovic*, 6494

Mott, Lawrie. *Pesticide Alert*, 11836

Mott-Smith, Geoffrey (jt. author). *Hoyle's Rules of Games*, 13290

Motz, Lloyd. *The Story of Physics*, 12513

Mowat, Farley. *Woman in the Mists*, 6566

Mowry, Jess. *Babylon Boyz*, 976(F)

Way Past Cool, 523(F)

Moynahan, Brian. *Rasputin*, 6878

Moynahan, Molly. *Stone Garden*, 1364(F)

Mozeson, I. E. *Jerusalem Mosaic*, 8205

Mozeson, I. E. (jt. author). *The Place I Call Home*, 10094

Mrazek, Robert. *Unholy Fire*, 2838(F)

Mrazek, Robert J. *Stonewall's Gold*, 2839(F)

Muckenhoupt, Margaret. *Sigmund Freud*, 6569

Mueller, Melinda. *What the Ice Gets*, 5521

Mufson, Susan. *Straight Talk About Child Abuse*, 11536

Straight Talk About Date Rape, 11303

Muharrar, Aisha. *More than a Label*, 11367

Muhlberger, Richard. *What Makes a Raphael a Raphael?* 7078

What Makes a Rembrandt a Rembrandt? 7079

Mukherjee, Bharati. *Desirable Daughters*, 362(F)

Mullane, Deirdre. *Crossing the Danger Water*, 524

Mullen, P. H. *Gold in the Water*, 13440

Muller, Karin. *Along the Inca Road*, 8293

Muller, Marcia. *Point Deception*, 3682(F)

While Other People Sleep, 3683(F)

Muller, Melissa. *Anne Frank*, 6847

Muller, Richard A. (jt. author). *The Three Big Bangs*, 11660

Muller, Ulrike. *Long-Haired Cats*, 12260

Mumm, Debbie. *Quick Country Quilting*, 12972

Munker, Dona (jt. author). *Daughter of Persia*, 6792

Munneke, Gary. *Opportunities in Law Careers*, 10491

Munsen, Sylvia. *Cooking the Norwegian Way*, 12815

Munson, Lulie. *In Their Own Words*, 11304

Munson, Ronald. *Raising the Dead*, 10917

Murdico, Suzanne J. *Bomb Squad Experts*, 10492

Forensic Scientists, 10531

Murguia, Alejandro. *This War Called Love*, 525(F)

Murie, Olaus J. *A Field Guide to Animal Tracks*, 11940

Murowchick, Robert E. *China*, 8017

Murphey, Cecil (jt. author). *I Choose to Stay*, 7007

With Byrd at the Bottom of the World, 8321

Murphy, Claire R. *Gold Rush Women*, 5620

Murphy, Claire Rudolf. *Daughters of the Desert*, 9080

Free Radical, 1365(F)

Gold Rush Dogs, 12287

Murphy, Dallas. *Rounding the Horn*, 8294

Murphy, Dean E. *September 11*, 10193

Murphy, Donald J. *World War I*, 7616

Murphy, Jack (jt. author). *Nuclear Medicine*, 10918

Murphy, Jim. *Across America on an Emigrant Train*, 12686

An American Plague, 8539

Packer, Alex J. *Bringing Up Parents*, 11537

Highs! Over 150 Ways to Feel Really, REALLY Good . . . Without Alcohol or Other Drugs, 10685

How Rude! The Teenagers' Guide to Good Manners, Proper Behavior, and Not Grossing People Out, 11384

Packer, Ann. *The Dive from Clausen's Pier*, 984(F)

Packer, Kenneth L. *HIV Infection*, 10834

Packer, ZZ. *Drinking Coffee Elsewhere*, 4685(F)

Paddock, Jennifer. *A Secret Word*, 1389(F)

Paddock, Lisa. *Facts About the Supreme Court of the United States*, 9323

A Student's Guide to Scandinavian American Genealogy, 9780

Padian, Kevin (jt. author). *Encyclopedia of Dinosaurs*, 7317

Padover, Saul Kussiel. *The Living U.S. Constitution*, 9216

Page, George. *Inside the Animal Mind*, 11933

Page, Jake. *In the Hands of the Great Spirit*, 8467

Page, Jake (jt. author). *Animal Talk*, 11936

A Fabulous Kingdom, 8315

Tales of the Earth, 12350

Page, Lawrence M. *A Field Guide to Freshwater Fishes*, 12177

Paige, Joy. *Cool Careers Without College for People Who Love to Build Things*, 10479

Paine, Lauran. *Riders of the Trojan Horse*, 2899(F)

Paine, Lincoln P. *Ships of Discovery and Exploration*, 12693

Paine, Stefani. *The World of the Arctic Whales*, 12216

Paine, Thomas. *Rights of Man and Common Sense*, 5227

Pais, Abraham. *The Genius of Science*, 6524

Paisner, Daniel (jt. author). *Last Man Down*, 10195

Pakenham, Thomas. *Remarkable Trees of the World*, 11852

Paldiel, Mordecai. *Saving the Jews*, 7780

Paley, Grace. *Begin Again*, 5016

Palmer, Alan. *The Decline and Fall of the Ottoman Empire*, 7500

Palmer, Catherine. *A Victorian Rose*, 4009(F)

Palmer, Chris (jt. author). *Wide Open*, 6746

Palmer, Douglas. *Fossils*, 7335

Palmer, Kris E. *Constitutional Amendments, 1789 to the Present*, 9217

Palmer, Michael. *Fatal*, 3707(F)

The Patient, 3708(F)

Palmer, Pat. *Teen Esteem*, 11458

Palmer, Tim. *The Snake River*, 12387

Palmer, William J. *The Dons and Mr. Dickens*, 3709(F)

Palmiotti, Jimmy. *The Conduit*, 2345(F)

Panchyk, Richard (jt. author). *Engineering the City*, 12558

Panek, Richard. *Seeing and Believing*, 11686

Panozzo, Michael E. (jt. author). *Steve Mizerak's Complete Book of Pool*, 13107

Pantoja, Antonia. *Memoir of a Visionary*, 6254

Paolicelli, Paul. *Dances with Luigi*, 8148

Paolini, Christopher. *Eragon*, 2124(F)

Pappano, Marilyn. *Heaven on Earth*, 3710(F)

Pappas, Peter (jt. author). *Russia*, 8165

Paquette, Penny Hutchins. *Learning Disabilities*, 11091

Parcells, Bill. *The Final Season*, 13310

Pare, Michael A. *Sports Stars: Series 2*, 6647

Sports Stars: Series 3, 6648

Sports Stars: Series 4, 6649

Paretsky, Sara. *Guardian Angel*, 3711(F)

Pargeter, Edith. *The Heaven Tree Trilogy*, 2457(F)

Parini, Jay. *The Columbia Anthology of American Poetry*, 5017

John Steinbeck, 5934

Paris, Erna. *The End of Days*, 8184

Parish, Peter (jt. author). *The Divided Union*, 8596

Parker, Daniel. *April*, 4420(F)

Parker, David L. *Stolen Dreams*, 9833

Parker, Geoffrey (jt. author). *The Reader's Companion to Military History*, 7395

Parker, Julie. *Everything You Need to Know About Living in a Shelter*, 10090

High Performance Through Leadership, 11459

Parker, Linda Busby. *Seven Laureis*, 538(F)

Parker, Steve. *The Practical Paleontologist*, 7336

The Random House Book of How Things Work, 12565

Parker, Steve (jt. author). *Mammals*, 11944

Parker, Thomas. *Day by Day*, 7878

Parkman, Francis. *The Oregon Trail*, 8722

Parks, Adele. *Larger Than Life*, 3302(F)

Parks, Carol. *Make Your Own Great Vests*, 12864

Parks, Gordon. *Half Past Autumn*, 5776

The Learning Tree, 539(F)

Parks, Peggy. *Medicine*, 10511

Music, 10451

Parks, Peggy J. *The News Media*, 10407

Parks, Rosa. *Rosa Parks*, 6258

Parnell, Helga. *Cooking the German Way*, 12818

Cooking the South American Way, 12819

Parr, Delia. *Home to Trinity*, 800(F)

Parr, Jan. *The Young Vegetarian's Companion*, 11141

Parra, Nancy J. *Loving Lana*, 4010(F)

A Wanted Man, 4011(F)

Parrinder, Geoffrey. *World Religions from Ancient History to the Present*, 9083

Parrish, Thomas. *The Submarine*, 12716

Parrot, Andrea. *Coping with Date Rape and Acquaintance Rape*, 11306

Parry, Richard. *Trial by Ice*, 8316

Parsons, Benny. *Inside Track*, 13143

Parsons, Harry. *The Nature of Frogs*, 11907

Parsons, Paul. *The Big Bang*, 11687

Partner, Daniel. *Disorders First Diagnosed in Childhood*, 11092

The House of Representatives, 9251

Partridge, Elizabeth. *Restless Spirit*, 5761

This Land Was Made for You and Me, 5983

Partridge, Elizabeth (jt. author). *Dorothea Lange — a Visual Life*, 5760

Pasachoff, Jay M. (jt. author). *A Field Guide to the Stars and Planets*, 11678

Nearest Star, 11765

Pasachoff, Naomi. *Frances Perkins*, 6439

Links in the Chain, 6768

Marie Curie and the Science of Radioactivity, 6544

Niels Bohr, 6539

Pascal, Francine. *Can't Stay Away*, 4012(F)

Twisted, 3712(F)

Pascal, Janet B. *Arthur Conan Doyle*, 5849

Paschall, Rod. *Witness to War*, 8942

Pascoe, Elaine. *Mexico and the United States*, 8263

The Pacific Rim, 7999

Racial Prejudice, 9574

Pasternak, Boris Leonidovich. *Doctor Zhivago*, 2642(F)

Pasternak, Ceel. *Cool Careers for Girls in Air and Space*, 10408

Phillips, Samantha (jt. author). *Real Girl/Real World*, 11429

Phillips, Susan Elizabeth. *Breathing Room*, 4015(F)

Phillips, Terry M. (jt. author). *The Immune System*, 10775

Phy, Allene Stuart. *Presenting Norma Klein*, 5903

Picciotto, Richard. *Last Man Down*, 10195

Pickels, Dwayne E. *Am I Okay? Psychological Testing and What Those Tests Mean*, 11350

Pickens, Andrea. *The Banished Bride*, 4016(F)

Pickett, Carroll. *Within These Walls*, 10030

Pickover, Clifford A. *Dreaming the Future*, 13053
The Stars of Heaven, 11757
Strange Brains and Genius, 11093

Picoult, Jodi. *My Sister's Keeper*, 808(F)
Plain Truth, 3721(F)

Pieczenik, Steve (jt. author). *Virtual Vandals*, 4192(F)

Piel, Gerard. *The Age of Science*, 11614

Pierce, Christina (jt. author). *Africa*, 7914

Pierce, Meredith Ann. *The Darkangel*, 3217(F)
Treasure at the Heart of the Tanglewood, 2130(F)
Waters Luminous and Deep, 2131(F)

Pierce, Tamora. *Cold Fire*, 2132(F)
The Realms of the Gods, 2133(F)
Trickster's Choice, 2134(F)
Wild Magic, 2135(F)

Piercy, Marge. *The Third Child*, 1406(F)

Pierre, DBC. *Vernon God Little*, 1604(F)

Pierson, Stephanie. *Vegetables Rock!* 11143

Pietrusza, David. *The Battle of Waterloo*, 7582
The Roaring '20s, 8814

Pijoan, Teresa. *White Wolf Woman*, 5132

Pike, Christopher. *Bury Me Deep*, 3218(F)
Chain Letter, 3722(F)
Gimme a Kiss, 3723(F)
Last Act, 3724(F)
Last Vampire, 3219(F)
Scavenger Hunt, 3220(F)
Slumber Party, 3725(F)
Spellbound, 3726(F)

Pike, Robert. *Play Winning Checkers*, 13291

Pilcher, Robin. *A Risk Worth Taking*, 809(F)

Pilcher, Rosamunde. *Winter Solstice*, 810(F)

Pile, Robert B. *Top Entrepreneurs and Their Business*, 6525
Women Business Leaders, 6526

Pilobolus. *Twisted Yoga*, 7215

Pimm, Stuart. *The World According to Pimm*, 12116

Pinderhuges, John (jt. author). *Coming Together*, 9608

Pines, T. *Thirteen*, 3221(F)

Pini, Richard (jt. author). *ElfQuest*, 2347(F)

Pini, Wendy. *ElfQuest*, 2347(F)

Pinker, Steven. *How the Mind Works*, 11389

Pinkney, Andrea D. *Raven in a Dove House*, 1407(F)

Pinkowish, Mary Desmond (jt. author). *What Are the Seven Wonders of the World? And 100 Other Great Cultural Lists — Fully Explicated*, 13022

Pinkwater, Daniel. *The Education of Robert Nifkin*, 3307(F)
Uncle Boris in the Yukon and Other Shaggy Dog Stories, 12290

Pinsker, Ann (jt. author). *Understanding The Catcher in the Rye*, 5393

Pinsker, Sanford. *Understanding The Catcher in the Rye*, 5393

Pinsky, Drew. *Cracked*, 10686

Pious, Richard M. *The Presidency of the United States*, 9236

Pipes, Richard. *Communism*, 9163
A Concise History of the Russian Revolution, 8166

Pipher, Mary. *Hunger Pains*, 10836
The Middle of Everywhere, 9836

Pirsig, Robert M. *Zen and the Art of Motorcycle Maintenance*, 9034

Pisano, Dominic A. *Charles Lindbergh and the Spirit of St. Louis*, 5663

Pitz, Mary Elizabeth. *Careers in Government*, 10410

Placide, Jaira. *Fresh Girl*, 540(F)

Plain, Belva. *Eden Burning*, 4017(F)

Plath, Sylvia. *The Bell Jar*, 986(F)
The Collected Poems, 5018

Platt, Kin. *Crocker*, 1408(F)

Platt, Randall B. *The Cornerstone*, 1409(F)

Platt, Randall Beth. *The Likes of Me*, 1410(F)

Plawin, Paul. *Careers for Travel Buffs and Other Restless Types*, 10472

Plimpton, George. *Ernest Shackleton*, 5680

Plitt, Jane R. *Martha Matilda Harper and the American Dream*, 6624

Plotkin, Gregory. *Cooking the Russian Way*, 12822

Plotkin, Mark J. *Medicine Quest*, 10921

Plotkin, Mark J. (jt. author). *The Killers Within*, 10849

Plotkin, Rita (jt. author). *Cooking the Russian Way*, 12822

Plum-Ucci, Carol. *The Body of Christopher Creed*, 3727(F)
The She, 3728(F)
What Happened to Lani Garver, 1411(F)

Plumb, J. H. (jt. author). *The American Heritage Book of the Revolution*, 8533

Plummer, Louise. *The Unlikely Romance of Kate Bjorkman*, 4018(F)

Plummer, Mark L. (jt. author). *Noah's Choice*, 12114

Plummer, William. *Wishing My Father Well*, 11539

Pluto, Terry. *Falling from Grace*, 13217

Plympton, Bill. *Hair High*, 7246

Pockell, Leslie. *The 13 Best Horror Stories of All Time*, 3222(F)

Poe, Edgar Allan. *The Collected Tales and Poems of Edgar Allan Poe*, 261
Complete Poems, 5019
The Complete Tales and Poems of Edgar Allan Poe, 262(F)
The Fall of the House of Usher and Other Tales, 263(F)
The Pit and the Pendulum and Other Stories, 3223(F)
Tales of Edgar Allan Poe, 264(F)

Poe, Elizabeth Ann. *Presenting Barbara Wersba*, 5954

Pogany, Susan Browning. *Sex Smart*, 11261

Pogrund, Benjamin. *Nelson Mandela*, 6785

Pogue, William R. *How Do You Go to the Bathroom in Space?* 11725

Pohl, Frederik. *Chasing Science*, 11615
Land's End, 4425(F)
Midas World, 4424(F)

Pohl, John M. D. *The Legend of Lord Eight Deer*, 5121

Pohl, Peter. *I Miss You, I Miss You!* 811(F)

Polakow, Amy. *Daisy Bates*, 6200

Polesetsky, Matthew (jt. author). *Women in the Military*, 9376

Policoff, Stephen P. *The Dreamer's Companion*, 11006

Pollack, Pamela. *Ski!* 13419

Pollack, Rachel. *The Journey Out*, 11262

Pollitt, Katha. *Subject to Debate*, 9459

Polo, Marco. *The Travels of Marco Polo*, 5674

Polunin, Miriam. *Healing Foods*, 11144

Pomerance, Bernard. *The Elephant Man*, 5455

Prince, Maggie. *The House on Hound Hill*, 2145(F)

Prine, Mary (jt. author). *Opportunities in Fitness Careers*, 10456

Pringer, Nancy. *Toughing It*, 817(F)

Pringle, Heather. *The Mummy Congress*, 7379

Pringle, Laurence. *The Animal Rights Controversy*, 9837
Smoking, 10687

Pritchard, D. B. *Begin Chess*, 13292

Pritchett, V. S. *The Oxford Book of Short Stories*, 4693(F)

Probosz, Kathlyn S. *Martha Graham*, 6050

Prochnau, William. *Once Upon a Distant War*, 8943

Proctor, Pam (jt. author). *Love, Miracles, and Animal Healing*, 6996
Song of Saigon, 6995

Pronzini, Bill. *A Wasteland of Strangers*, 3734(F)

Prose, Francine. *After*, 1605(F)

Prosser, Robert. *France*, 8101

Protopopescu, Orel (jt. author). *A Thousand Peaks*, 5049

Proulx, Annie. *That Old Ace in the Hole*, 375(F)

Proulx, Brenda. *The Courage to Change*, 10031

Prowell, Sandra West. *The Killing of Monday Brown*, 3735(F)
When Wallflowers Die, 3736(F)

Prue, Sally. *The Devil's Toenail*, 2146(F)

Pruett, Lynn. *Ruby River*, 376(F)

Psihoyos, Louie. *Hunting Dinosaurs*, 7337

Ptacek, Greg (jt. author). *Patently Female*, 12569
Women Inventors and Their Discoveries, 12570

Pugnetti, Gino. *Simon and Schuster's Guide to Cats*, 12261

Pullman, Philip. *The Amber Spyglass*, 2147(F)
The Broken Bridge, 546(F)
Detective Stories, 3737(F)
The Golden Compass, 2148(F)
The Ruby in the Smoke, 2646(F)
The Subtle Knife, 2149(F)
The Tiger in the Well, 129(F)
The Tin Princess, 2150(F)

Purnell, Karl H. *A Mountain Too Far*, 13276

Purser, Ann. *Murder on Monday*, 3738(F)

Purser, Bruce. *Jungle Bugs*, 12138

Purvis, Thomas L. *Colonial America to 1763*, 8509
Revolutionary America, 1763–1800, 8542

Putin, Vladimir. *First Person*, 6877

Putney, William W. *Always Faithful*, 12291

Puzo, Mario. *The Godfather*, 130(F)

Pyle, Howard. *Merry Adventures of Robin Hood*, 5113
The Story of King Arthur and His Knights, 5114
The Story of Sir Launcelot and His Companions, 5115

Pyle, Robert Michael. *The Audubon Society Field Guide to North American Butterflies*, 12152

Pyne, Stephen J. *How the Canyon Became Grand*, 9020

Quaife, Milo Milton. *Kit Carson's Autobiography*, 6479

Qualey, Marsha. *Close to a Killer*, 3739(F)
Come in from the Cold, 3089(F)
One Night, 377(F)
Revolutions of the Heart, 548(F)
Thin Ice, 3740(F)
Too Big a Storm, 2989(F)

Quant, Mary. *Ultimate Makeup and Beauty*, 10971

Quarles, Heather. *A Door Near Here*, 818(F)

Quartz, Steven R. *Liars, Lovers, and Heroes*, 11351

Quick, Amanda. *I Thee Wed*, 3741(F)

Quindlen, Anna. *Black and Blue*, 819(F)
Object Lessons, 820(F)
Siblings, 11542

Quinn, Daniel. *After Dachau*, 2152(F)

Quinn, John R. *Wildlife Survivors*, 11810

Quinn, Patricia O. *Adolescents and ADD*, 11098

Quinn, Paul J. *Dusk to Dawn*, 12695

Quinn, Susan. *Marie Curie*, 6545

Quintana, Anton. *The Baboon King*, 2491(F)

Quirk, Charles F. *Sports and the Law*, 13118

Raab, Evelyn. *Clueless in the Kitchen*, 12823
The Clueless Vegetarian, 12824

Rabagliati, Michel. *Paul Has a Summer Job*, 2351(F)

Rabb, M. E. *The Chocolate Lover*, 3742(F)

Raber, David. *Through Cougar's Eyes*, 12241

Rabiger, Joanna. *Daily Prison Life*, 10032

Rabinovici, Schoschana. *Thanks to My Mother*, 7784

Rabkin, Eric S. *Fantastic Worlds*, 2153(F)

Raboteau, Albert J. *African-American Religion*, 9680

Radetsky, Peter. *The Invisible Invaders*, 10839

Radzinsky, Edvard. *Stalin*, 6883

Raeburn, Michael. *The Chronicle of the Opera*, 7191

Raeburn, Paul. *Mars*, 11768

Ragaza, Angelo. *Lives of Notable Asian Americans*, 6527

Raham, R. Gary. *Dinosaurs in the Garden*, 11811

Rain, Gwinevere. *Spellcraft for Teens*, 13054

Rainey, Richard. *The Monster Factory*, 5256

Rainis, Kenneth G. *Biotechnology Projects for Young Scientists*, 12227
Exploring with a Magnifying Glass, 11646
Guide to Microlife, 12228

Raleigh, Michael. *The Blue Moon Circus*, 378(F)

Rambach, Peggy. *Fighting Gravity*, 1416(F)

Ramen, Fred. *The Rights of the Accused*, 9330

Ramo, Joshua Cooper. *No Visible Horizon*, 12663

Ramos, Jorge. *No Borders*, 6989

Ramsay, Eileen. *Never Call It Loving*, 4021(F)

Ramsdell, Melissa. *My First Year As a Doctor*, 10514

Ramsey, Dan. *Weather Forecasting*, 12459

Ramsland, Katherine. *Ghost*, 13055

Ramthun, Bonnie. *Earthquake Games*, 3743(F)

Rana, Indi. *The Roller Birds of Rampur*, 549(F)

Rand, Ayn. *Anthem*, 1606(F)
Atlas Shrugged, 1607(F)
The Fountainhead, 379(F)

Randall, Glenn. *The Backpacker's Handbook*, 13277

Randall, Marta. *John F. Kennedy*, 6325

Randle, Kevin D. *Operation Roswell*, 4428(F)

Randle, Kristen D. *Breaking Rank*, 4022(F)
Slumming, 380(F)

Randles, Jenny. *UFOs and How to See Them*, 13056

Randolph, Elizabeth (jt. author). *CatSpeak*, 12250
The Complete Book of Dog Health, 12283

Random House. *Mary Stuart's Scotland*, 6868
Muhammad Ali, 6708

Rani. *Feast of India*, 12825

Rankin, Ian. *A Good Hanging*, 3744(F)

Raphael, Ray. *A People's History of the American Revolution*, 8543

Rapp, Adam. *The Buffalo Tree*, 1417(F)
The Copper Elephant, 2154(F)
Little Chicago, 987(F)

Robinson, Elisabeth. *The True and Outstanding Adventures of the Hunt Sisters*, 828(F)

Robinson, Francis. *The Cambridge Illustrated History of the Islamic World*, 9139

Robinson, George. *Essential Judaism*, 9151

Robinson, Jackie. *I Never Had It Made*, 6682

Robinson, Katy. *A Single Square Picture*, 11544

Robinson, Lynda S. *Eater of Souls*, 3757(F)

Murder at the Feast of Rejoicing, 3758(F)

Slayer of Gods, 2412(F)

Robinson, Peter. *In a Dry Season*, 3759(F)

Playing with Fire, 3760(F)

Robinson, Randall. *The Debt*, 9684

Robinson, Ray. *Iron Horse*, 6667

Matty, 6677

Robinson, Spider. *The Free Lunch*, 2164(F)

God Is an Iron and Other Stories, 4436(F)

Robison, Mary. *Tell Me*, 4695(F)

Robson, Lucia St. Clair. *The Tokaido Road*, 2539(F)

Robson, Ruthann. *Gay Men, Lesbians, and the Law*, 11309

Rocco, Fiammetta. *The Miraculous Fever Tree*, 10841

Rocha, Toni L. *Understanding Recovery from Eating Disorders*, 10842

Roche, Lorin. *Meditation Made Easy*, 10571

Rochelle, Warren. *The Wild Boy*, 2165(F)

Rochlin, Harriet. *On Her Way Home*, 2902(F)

Rochman, Hazel. *Bearing Witness*, 7796

Leaving Home, 132(F)

Somehow Tenderness Survives, 1608(F)

Rock, Howard B. *Cityscapes*, 8985

Rock, Maxine. *The Automobile and the Environment*, 9921

Roden, Nadia. *Granita Magic*, 12827

Rodi, Rob. *Crossovers*, 2352(F)

Rodionoff, Hans. *Lovecraft*, 2353(F)

Rodowsky, Colby. *Lucy Peale*, 4037(F)

Remembering Mog, 1430(F)

Rodriguez, K. S. *Will Smith*, 6124

Rodriguez, Luis. *The Republic of East L.A*, 4696(F)

Rodriguez, Luis J. *Always Running*, 10034

Rofes, Eric. *The Kids' Book of Divorce*, 11545

Rogasky, Barbara. *Smoke and Ashes*, 7797

Rogers, Dale Evans. *Angel Unaware*, 6939

Rogers, James T. *The Antislavery Movement*, 9466

The Secret War, 7798

Woodrow Wilson, 6378

Rogers, Lesley J. *Songs, Roars, and Rituals*, 11937

Spirit of the Wild Dog, 12014

Rogers, Mark E. *Samurai Cat Goes to the Movies*, 2166(F)

Rohr, Janelle. *Science and Religion*, 9086

Roiphe, Anne. *To Rabbit, with Love and Squalor*, 5405

Roiphe, Katie. *Still She Haunts Me*, 2650(F)

Rold, Marlys. *Heart of a Tiger*, 133(F)

Roleff, Tamara L. *Abortion*, 11206

AIDS, 10843

America Under Attack, 10197

The Atom Bomb, 7799

Biomedical Ethics, 10572

Business Ethics, 10219

Censorship, 10115

Civil Liberties, 9467

Extremist Groups, 9839

Gay Marriage, 9468

Gay Rights, 11268

Guns and Crime, 10035

Hate Crimes, 9840

Hate Groups, 9841

Immigration, 9536

Inner-City Poverty, 10091

The Legal System, 9332

Marriage and Divorce, 11546

Mental Illness, 11100

Native American Rights, 9762

Police Brutality, 9333

Police Corruption, 10036

Pollution, 9922

The Rights of Animals, 9842

Satanism, 9158

Sex Education, 11269

Suicide, 11099

Teen Suicide, 10594

Tobacco and Smoking, 10690

War, 9193

Roleff, Tamara L. (jt. author). *AIDS*, 10752

Rolling Stone. *Neil Young*, 6143

Rollins, Charlemae Hill. *Christmas Gif'*, 9114

Rollins, James. *Amazonia*, 3761(F)

Ice Hunt, 3762(F)

Rollyson, Carl S. *Teenage Refugees from Eastern Europe Speak Out*, 8088

Rollyson, Carl S. (jt. author). *A Student's Guide to Scandinavian American Genealogy*, 9780

Romain, Joseph. *The Mystery of the Wagner Whacker*, 4591(F)

Romaine, Deborah S. *Roe v. Wade*, 11207

Roman, Joseph. *King Philip*, 6440

Rombauer, Irma S. *Joy of Cooking*, 12828

Romei, Francesca. *Leonardo da Vinci*, 5752

The Story of Sculpture, 7061

Rommelmann, Nancy (jt. author). *The Real Real World*, 7265

Ronan, Colin A. *The Skywatcher's Handbook*, 11691

Rool, William (jt. author). *Psychic Connections*, 13026

Rooney, Andrew A. *A Few Minutes with Andy Rooney*, 5194

Not That You Asked . . ., 5195

Roos, Stephen. *Confessions of a Wayward Preppie*, 1431(F)

Roosevelt, Elliott. *Murder and the First Lady*, 3763(F)

Murder at the Palace, 3764(F)

Murder in the Oval Office, 3765(F)

The White House Pantry Murder, 3766(F)

Roosevelt, Theodore. *The Rough Riders*, 8765

Rosaforte, Tim. *Raising the Bar*, 6752

Tiger Woods, 6753

Rosas, Carlos (jt. author). *Non-Impact Aerobics*, 11037

Rosas, Debbie. *Non-Impact Aerobics*, 11037

Rose, David. *Regions of the Heart*, 6744

Rose, Joel. *New York Sawed in Half*, 8580

Rose, Michael R. *Darwin's Spectre*, 11812

Rose, Norman. *Churchill*, 6828

Rose, Phyllis. *The Norton Book of Women's Lives*, 6910

Rose, Tricia. *Black Noise*, 7172

Longing to Tell, 9685

Roseman, Janet Lynn. *Dance Masters*, 7216

Rosen, Joe. *The Capricious Cosmos*, 11778

Rosen, Lucy. *High Performance Through Communicating Information*, 10311

Rosen, Marvin. *Dealing with the Effects of Rape and Incest*, 11310

The Effects of Stress and Anxiety on the Family, 11101

Understanding Post-Traumatic Stress Disorder, 11102

Rosen, Michael. *Shakespeare's Romeo and Juliet*, 4772

Rosen, Michael J. *Horse People*, 12315

Rosen, Roger. *Border Crossings*, 383(F)

Coming of Age, 1432(F)

East-West, 5230

On Heroes and the Heroic, 4698(F)

Planet Earth, 9897

Teenage Soldiers, Adult Wars, 4697(F)

Rosen, Roger (jt. author). *Coca-Cola Culture,* 10160

Rosenbaum, Jean. *Opportunities in Fitness Careers,* 10456

Rosenbaum, Stuart E. (jt. author). *Euthanasia,* 10578

Rosenberg, Aaron. *Cryptologists,* 10418

Rosenberg, Joel. *Not Quite Scaramouche,* 2167(F)

Not Really the Prisoner of Zenda, 2168(F)

Rosenberg, Liz. *Earth-Shattering Poems,* 4903

Heart and Soul, 1433(F)

The Invisible Ladder, 5020

Light-Gathering Poems, 4904

Roots and Flowers, 4905

17, 1434(F)

Rosenberg, Marsha Sarah. *Coping When a Brother or Sister Is Autistic,* 11103

Rosenberg, Stephen N. *The Johnson and Johnson First Aid Book,* 11222

Rosenblum, Joseph. *Shakespeare,* 5484

Rosenburg, John. *First in Peace,* 6374

First in War, 2768(F)

Rosenfeld, Jeffrey. *Eye of the Storm,* 12437

Rosenfeld, Lucinda. *What She Saw In . . .,* 3311(F)

Rosenfeld, Stephanie. *Massachusetts, California, Timbuktu,* 829(F)

Rosenthal, Gary. *Soccer Skills and Drills,* 13429

Rosenthal, Lawrence. *Exploring Careers in Accounting,* 10474

Rosenthal, Lucy. *Great American Love Stories,* 4038(F)

Rosing, Norbert. *The World of the Polar Bear,* 11984

Rosner, Marc Alan. *Science Fair Success Using the Internet,* 11649

Ross, Alex. *Mythology,* 7103

Ross, Anne. *Druids, Gods and Heroes of Celtic Mythology,* 5154

Ross, Bill D. *Iwo Jima,* 7800

Ross, Charles A. *Crocodiles and Alligators,* 11906

Ross, Deborah J. (jt. author). *The Fall of Neskaya,* 1714(F)

Ross, Gayle (jt. author). *The Girl Who Married the Moon,* 5128

Ross, John. *The Complete Printmaker,* 12745

Ross, Lawrence C. *The Ways of Black Folks,* 9781

Ross, Leonard Q. *The Education of H*Y*M*A*N K*A*P*L*A*N,* 3312(F)

Ross, Mark C. *Dangerous Beauty,* 7938

Ross, Mary Jane (jt. author). *In the Company of Men,* 6973

Ross, Michael Elsohn. *Salvador Dali and the Surrealists,* 5749

Ross, Stewart. *The Arab-Israeli Conflict,* 8206

Causes and Consequences of the Great Depression, 8817

Causes and Consequences of World War I, 7618

The Rise of Japan and the Pacific Rim, 8041

The United Nations, 9167

World War II, 7801

Ross, Val. *The Road to There,* 7307

Rossier, Jay. *Living with Chickens,* 12064

Rossner, Judith. *Emmeline,* 2799(F)

Rosso, Julee. *The New Basics Cookbook,* 12829

Rostkowski, Margaret I. *The Best of Friends,* 3090(F)

Moon Dancer, 4039(F)

Roth, Arlen. *Arlen Roth's Complete Acoustic Guitar,* 7199

Roth, Geneen. *Feeding the Hungry Heart,* 10844

Roth, Philip. *Goodbye, Columbus, and Five Short Stories,* 4699(F)

Rothenberg, Jerome. *Poems for the Millennium,* 4906

Rothfarb, Ed. *In the Land of Taj Mahal,* 8032

Rothfeder, Jeffrey. *Every Drop for Sale,* 12448

Rothman, David J. (jt. author). *The Oxford History of the Prison,* 10022

Rothman, Hal K. *Saving the Planet,* 12117

Rothman, Kevin F. *Coping with Dangers on the Internet,* 12620

Rothschild, Mary Logan. *Doing What the Day Brought,* 8730

Rottman, S. L. *Rough Waters,* 1435(F)

Shadow of a Doubt, 830(F)

Stetson, 1436(F)

Roubickova, Eva M. *We're Alive and Life Goes On,* 7802

Rougeau, Remy. *All We Know of Heaven,* 384(F)

Roukes, Nicholas. *Humor in Art,* 7062

Rovin, Jeff. *Aliens, Robots, and Spaceships,* 5258

Rowell, Trevor. *The Scramble for Africa,* 7910

Rowh, Mark. *W. E. B. DuBois,* 6219

Rowinski, Jim. *The L.L. Bean Outdoor Photography Handbook,* 12955

Rowinski, Kate (jt. author). *The L.L. Bean Outdoor Photography Handbook,* 12955

Rowland, Mark (jt. author). *The Jazz Musician,* 7174

Rowland, Mary Canaga. *As Long As Life,* 6993

Rowland-Warne, L. *Costume,* 12866

Rowley, Hazel. *Richard Wright,* 5972

Rowling, J. K. *Harry Potter and the Order of the Phoenix,* 2169(F)

Rowse, A. L. *Shakespeare the Man,* 5930

Roy, Arundhati. *War Talk,* 9194

Roy, Paulette (jt. author). *Wetlands,* 12369

Royal, Kxao (jt. author). *San,* 7953

Royal, Lauren. *Amber,* 2651(F)

Violet, 4040(F)

Rozan, S. J. *Concourse,* 3767(F)

Winter and Night, 3768(F)

Rozema, Vicki. *Voices from the Trail of Tears,* 8473

Rubel, David (jt. author). *The Story of America,* 8410

Rubenstein, Gillian. *Galax-Arena,* 4437(F)

Rubin, Charles T. *The Green Crusade,* 9898

Rubin, Louis D., Jr. *An Apple for My Teacher,* 10270

Rubin, Richard. *Confederacy of Silence,* 9469

Rubin, Robert Alden. *Poetry Out Loud,* 4907

Rubin, Susan G. *Fireflies in the Dark,* 7803

Frank Lloyd Wright, 5800

Rubin, Susan Goldman. *Margaret Bourke-White,* 5736

Searching for Anne Frank, 7804

Rubinstein, Danny. *The Mystery of Arafat,* 6788

Rubio, Manny. *Rattlesnake,* 11916

Ruby, Jennifer. *Underwear,* 12581

Ruby, Lois. *Skin Deep,* 1609(F)

Rucker, Rudy. *Frek and the Elixir,* 4438(F)

Ruckman, Ivy. *The Hunger Scream,* 989(F)

Rue, Leonard Lee. *Beavers,* 11957

Way of the Whitetail, 12020

Rue, Nancy N. *Coping with an Illiterate Parent,* 11547

Everything you need to know About Abusive Relationships, 11353

Everything You Need to Know About Peer Mediation, 11390

Ruff, Matt. *Set This House in Order,* 990(F)

Ruggero, Ed. *Duty First,* 12720

Ruhlman, Michael. *The Making of a Chef,* 10419

Rummel, Jack. *Langston Hughes,* 5887

Mexico, 8264

Muhammad Ali, 6710

Robert Oppenheimer, 6600

Rusch, Kristine Kathryn. *Stories for an Enchanted Afternoon*, 4439(F)

Rushby, Kevin. *Hunting Pirate Heaven*, 7431

Rushford, Patricia H. *Betrayed*, 3769(F)
Dying to Win, 3770(F)
Stranded, 3771(F)

Rushton, Julian. *Classical Music*, 7122

Russell, Barbara T. *The Taker's Stone*, 2170(F)

Russell, Bertrand. *A History of Western Philosophy*, 9035

Russell, Bruce J. (jt. author). *Guide to Microlife*, 12228

Russell, Colin A. *Michael Faraday*, 6563

Russell, Dick. *Eye of the Whale*, 12220

Russell, Eric Frank. *Entities*, 4440(F)

Russell, Jeffrey B. *A History of Witchcraft*, 7432

Russell, Kirk. *Shell Games*, 3772(F)

Russell, P. Craig (jt. author). *Murder Mysteries*, 2315(F)

Russell, Sharon A. *Revisiting Stephen King*, 5406
Stephen King, 5407

Russell, Tony. *The Blues*, 7173

Russon, Anne E. *Orangutans*, 11969

Rutberg, Becky. *Mary Lincoln's Dressmaker*, 6493

Rutberg, Jim (jt. author). *The Ultimate Ride*, 13231

Ruth, Maria Mudd. *The Mississippi River*, 8391
The Pacific Coast, 9005

Rutherford, Edward. *London*, 2652(F)

Ryan, Alan. *Haunting Women*, 3231(F)
The Reader's Companion to Alaska, 9006

Ryan, Bernard. *Caring for Animals*, 10145
Expanding Education and Literacy, 10146
Helping the Ill, Poor and the Elderly, 10147
Promoting the Arts and Sciences, 10148
Protecting the Environment, 9899
Serving with Police, Fire, and EMS, 9258

Ryan, Bernard, Jr. *Participating in Government*, 10149

Ryan, Cornelius. *The Last Battle*, 7805

Ryan, Craig. *The Pre-Astronauts*, 12664

Ryan, Elizabeth A. *Straight Talk About Parents*, 11548

Ryan, John C. *Seven Wonders*, 9900

Ryan, Ken. *Computer Anxiety? Instant Relief!* 12621

Ryan, Margaret. *How to Give a Speech*, 10312
How to Write a Poem, 10313

Ryan, Mary. *The Song of the Tide*, 831(F)

Ryan, Mary C. *Who Says I Can't?* 3313(F)

Ryan, Mary E. *Alias*, 3773(F)

Ryan, Patrick J. *Organized Crime*, 10037

Ryan, Sarah. *Empress of the World*, 1437(F)

Rybczynski, Witold. *The Look of Architecture*, 7020

Rybolt, Thomas R. (jt. author). *Adventures with Atoms and Molecules, Vol. 5*, 12337

Rydell, Robert W. *Fair America*, 8392

Ryden, Hope. *Lily Pond*, 11958

Rydjord, John. *Indian Place-Names*, 8964

Rylant, Cynthia. *I Had Seen Castles*, 3060(F)
Soda Jerk, 5021
Something Permanent, 5022

Ryskamp, George R. *A Student's Guide to Mexican American Genealogy*, 9744

Ryskamp, Peggy (jt. author). *A Student's Guide to Mexican American Genealogy*, 9744

S., Tina. *Living at the Edge of the World*, 10092

Saberhagen, Fred. *Ariadne's Web*, 2171(F)
The Arms of Hercules, 2172(F)
Berserker Prime, 4441(F)
God of the Golden Fleece, 2173(F)
Gods of Fire and Thunder, 2174(F)
A Sharpness on the Neck, 3232(F)

Sabin, E. Rose. *A Perilous Power*, 2175(F)
A School for Sorcery, 2176(F)

Sacco, Joe. *Safe Area Gorazde*, 2354(F)

Sachs, Marilyn. *Baby Sister*, 832(F)
Thunderbird, 4041(F)

Sacker, Ira M. *Dying to Be Thin*, 10845

Sacks, David. *Encyclopedia of the Ancient Greek World*, 7495

Sacks, Oliver. *Uncle Tungsten*, 6604

Sacks, Terrence J. *Careers in Medicine*, 10515

Sadeh, Pinhas. *Jewish Folktales*, 5067

Sadler, A. E. *Family Violence*, 11549
Juvenile Crime, 10038
Urban Terrorism, 10198

Saenger, Diana,. *Life as a POW*, 7883

Safina, Carl. *Eye of the Albatross*, 12065

Safir, Leonard (jt. author). *Good Advice on Writing*, 10314

Safire, William. *Good Advice on Writing*, 10314

Sagan, Carl. *Comet*, 11744
Cosmos, 11692
Pale Blue Dot, 11729

Sagan, Dorion (jt. author). *What Is Life?* 12225

Sagan, Nick. *Idlewild*, 4442(F)

St. Antoine, Sara. *Stories from Where We Live*, 9014

Saint-Exupery, Antoine de. *The Little Prince*, 2177(F)

St. George, Judith. *Crazy Horse*, 6398

St. James, Renwick (jt. author). *Voyage of the Basset*, 1765(F)

St. Martin, Ted. *The Art of Shooting Baskets*, 13218

St. Pierre, Stephanie. *Everything You Need to Know When a Parent Is in Jail*, 11550
Everything You Need to Know When a Parent Is Out of Work, 11551
Teenage Refugees from Cambodia Speak Out, 9716

Salas, Osvaldo. *Fidel's Cuba*, 8276

Salas, Roberto (jt. author). *Fidel's Cuba*, 8276

Saldana, Rene. *Finding Our Way*, 4701(F)

Saldana, Rene, Jr. *The Jumping Tree*, 553(F)

Saldinger, Anne Green. *Life in a Nazi Concentration Camp*, 7806

Salinger, Adrienne. *In My Room*, 11354

Salinger, J. D. *The Catcher in the Rye*, 1438(F)
Franny and Zooey, 833(F)
Nine Stories, 4702(F)

Salinger, Margaretta. *Masterpieces of American Painting in the Metropolitan Museum of Art*, 7104

Salisbury, Gay. *The Cruelest Miles*, 9007

Salisbury, Graham. *Blue Skin of the Sea*, 4703(F)
Island Boyz, 4704(F)
Shark Bait, 134(F)

Salisbury, Harrison E. *Heroes of My Time*, 5614
Tiananmen Diary, 8019

Salisbury, Harrison Evans. *The 900 Days*, 7807

Salisbury, Laney (jt. author). *The Cruelest Miles*, 9007

Salisbury, Mark. *Planet of the Apes*, 7248

Salkeld, Audrey. *Kilimanjaro*, 13280

Sallah, Tijan M. *Wolof*, 7996

Saller, Martin (jt. author). *Elephants*, 12025

Salmon, Mark. *Opportunities in Visual Arts Careers*, 10457

Setaro, John F. (jt. author). *Alcohol 101*, 10651

Drugs 101, 10652

Medicine's Brave New World, 10941

When the Brain Dies First, 11003

Seto, Andy. *Crouching Tiger, Hidden Dragon*, 2356(F)

Sevastiades, Patra M. (jt. author). *Coming of Age*, 1432(F)

On Heroes and the Heroic, 4698(F)

Severance, John B. *Braving the Fire*, 2848(F)

Einstein, 6559

Thomas Jefferson; Architect of Democracy, 6313

Severin, Tim. *In Search of Robinson Crusoe*, 5297

Severn, Bill. *Bill Severn's Best Magic*, 12928

Seybold, Patricia B. (jt. author). *Brandchild*, 10232

Seymour, Tres. *The Revelation of Saint Bruce*, 1442(F)

Shaara, Jeff. *Gods and Generals*, 2849(F)

Shaara, Michael. *The Killer Angels*, 2850(F)

Shabazz, Ilyasah. *Growing Up X*, 6997

Shachtman, Tom (jt. author). *25 to Life*, 6456

Shader, Laurel. *Mononucleosis and Other Infectious Diseases*, 10847

Shaffer, Peter. *Amadeus*, 4824

Shah, Saira. *The Storyteller's Daughter*, 8059

Shah'Keyah, Sister (jt. author). *Uprising*, 10002

Shakespeare, William. *The Complete Works of William Shakespeare*, 4773

The Essential Shakespeare, 4940

A Midsummer Night's Dream, 4774

Poems, 5485

Romeo and Juliet, 4775

The Sonnets, 5486

Shales, Tom. *Live from New York*, 7277

Shamir, Ilana. *The Young Reader's Encyclopedia of Jewish History*, 9752

Shamsie, Kamila. *Kartography*, 1612(F)

Shange, Ntozake. *For Colored Girls Who Have Considered Suicide/When The Rainbow Is Enuf*, 5526

Shanley, Mary Lyndon. *Making Babies, Making Families*, 11554

Shannon, David. *The Great Depression*, 8818

Shannon, Thomas A. *Genetic Engineering*, 10948

Shanower, Eric. *A Thousand Ships, Volume 1*, 2357

Shapiro, Joseph P. *No Pity*, 9472

Shapiro, Miles. *Maya Angelou*, 5808

Shapiro, Robert. *Planetary Dreams*, 11698

Sharer, Robert J. *Daily Life in Maya Civilization*, 8251

Sharkey, Joe (jt. author). *Lady Gold*, 3335(F)

Sharon, Donna. *Great Careers for People Interested in Travel and Tourism*, 10458

Sharp, Anne Wallace. *The Gypsies*, 9578

Sharp, Ken (jt. author). *Kiss*, 7162

Sharrar, Jack (jt. author). *Great Monologues for Young Actors*, 4758

Great Scenes for Young Actors from the Stage, 4759

Multicultural Monologues for Young Actors, 4760

Multicultural Scenes for Young Actors, 4761

Short Plays for Young Actors, 4762

Shatner, William. *Beyond the Stars*, 4456(F)

Shavit, Shlomo (jt. author). *The Young Reader's Encyclopedia of Jewish History*, 9752

Shaw, Jane. *Global Warming*, 9901

Shaw, John (jt. author). *The Big Book of Painting Nature in Watercolor*, 12898

Shaw, Maura D. *Foods from Mother Earth*, 12834

Shaw, Tucker. *Any Advice?* 11469

Dreams, 11356

Flavor of the Week, 3315(F)

Peace, 9195

This Book Is About Sex, 11271

"What's That Smell?" (Oh, It's Me), 11468

Shawcross, William. *Queen and Country*, 6838

Shay, Kathryn. *Promises to Keep*, 4044(F)

Trust in Me, 1443(F)

She, Colleen. *Teenage Refugees from China Speak Out*, 9717

Shea, Daniel M. (jt. author). *New Party Politics*, 9353

Shea, Suzanne Strempek. *Around Again*, 4045(F)

Shea, William L. *Pea Ridge*, 8677

Sheafer, Silvia A. *Aretha Franklin*, 6045

Women in America's Wars, 8395

Shearman, Deirde. *David Lloyd George*, 6866

Shedd, Warner. *Owls Aren't Wise and Bats Aren't Blind*, 11891

Sheehan, Jacqueline. *Truth*, 6268(F)

Sheehan, Sean. *Great African Kingdoms*, 7913

Guatemala, 8252

Lebanon, 8225

Rome, 7520

Sheehan, William. *Mars*, 11770

Sheen, Barbara. *Attention Deficit Disorder*, 11105

Sheets, Bob. *Hurricane Watch*, 12438

Sheffield, Charles. *The Amazing Dr. Darwin*, 3787(F)

Cold As Ice, 4457(F)

The Ganymede Club, 2189(F)

Godspeed, 4458(F)

The Lady Vanishes and Other Oddities of Nature, 4459(F)

Putting Up Roots, 4460(F)

Resurgence, 4461(F)

The Spheres of Heaven, 4462(F)

Shehadeh, Raja. *When the Birds Stopped Singing*, 8208

Shehyn, Audrey. *Picture the Girl*, 11357

Shein, Lori. *Inequality*, 9473

Sheinwold, Alfred. *101 Best Family Card Games*, 13296

Sheldon, Dyan. *The Boy of My Dreams*, 4046(F)

My Perfect Life, 3316(F)

Planet Janet, 1444(F)

Sheldon, Richard N. *Dag Hammarskjold*, 6851

Shellenberger, Susie. *Cars, Curfews, Parties, and Parents*, 11470

Lockers, Lunch Lines, Chemistry, and Cliques, 11471

Shelley, Mary. *Frankenstein*, 4463(F)

Shengold, Nina. *The Actor's Book of Contemporary Stage Monologues*, 4757

Shenk, Ellen. *Outdoor Careers*, 10422

Shenkman, Richard. *Presidential Ambition*, 9239

Shepard, Jim. *Project X*, 1445(F)

Shepard, Karen. *An Empire of Women*, 846(F)

Shepard, Leslie. *The Dracula Book of Great Horror Stories*, 3236(F)

Shepard, Richard. *The Paper's Papers*, 5606

Shepard, Sam. *Great Dream of Heaven*, 4708(F)

Shephard, Sue. *Pickled, Potted and Canned*, 11840

Shepherd, Esther. *Paul Bunyan*, 5144

Shepherd, Margaret. *Learning Calligraphy*, 12747

Sheppard, Joseph. *Realistic Figure Drawing*, 12901

Sheppard, Mary C. *Seven for a Secret*, 1446(F)

Sher, Ira. *Gentlemen of Space*, 2190(F)

Sherbaniuk, Richard. *The Fifth Horseman*, 3788(F)

Sherman, Aliza. *Everything You Need to Know About Placing Your Baby for Adoption*, 11208

Working Together Against Violence Against Women, 9845

Sokolov, Raymond. *The Cook's Canon*, 12835

Sole, Linda. *Bridget*, 4051(F)
Kathy, 2663(F)
The Rose Arch, 2664(F)

Solin, Sabrina. *The Seventeen Guide to Sex and Your Body*, 11275

Solomon, Charles. *The Disney That Never Was*, 7255

Solomon, Robert C. *A Short History of Philosophy*, 9036

Solomon, Sol (jt. author). *Choices for Our Future*, 9896

Solomon, Susan. *The Coldest March*, 8320

Solomon, Susan (jt. author). *Romeo and Juliet*, 4770

Solow, Herbert F. *Inside Star Trek*, 7278

Solwitz, Sharon. *Bloody Mary*, 386(F)

Solzhenitsyn, Alexander. *One Day in the Life of Ivan Denisovich*, 1614(F)

Somerlott, Robert. *The Little Rock School Desegregation Crisis*, 9476
The Spanish-American War, 8768

Somerset, Anne. *Elizabeth I*, 6833

Sommers, Annie Leah. *Everything You Need to Know About Looking and Feeling Your Best*, 10573

Sommers, Jo Anne (jt. author). *Great Careers for People Interested in Travel and Tourism*, 10458

Sommers, Michael A. *Wildlife Photographers*, 10459

Sommerville, Donald. *Revolutionary and Napoleonic Wars*, 7585

Somtow, S. P. *The Vampire's Beautiful Daughter*, 3319(F)

Sonder, Ben. *All About Heroin*, 10699
Evolutionism and Creationism, 7363

Sondheim, Stephen. *Into the Woods*, 7192

Sone, Monica. *Nisei Daughter*, 7001

Sones, Sonya. *One of Those Hideous Books Where the Mother Dies*, 853(F)
What My Mother Doesn't Know, 1457(F)

Sonneborn, Liz. *The American West*, 8399
The Cuban Americans, 9745
Will Rogers, 6115

Sonnenfeld, Kelly. *Memories of Clason Point*, 8819

Sonnenfeld, Sandi. *This Is How I Speak*, 7217

Sontag, Susan (jt. author). *Women*, 7101

Soocher, Stan. *They Fought the Law*, 7176

Soto, Gary. *The Afterlife*, 3241(F)

Buried Onions, 1458(F)
The Effects of Knut Hamsun on a Fresno Boy, 5232
A Fire in My Hands, 5025
Jesse, 565(F)
Jessie de la Cruz, 6208
A Natural Man, 5026
Nerdlandia, 4834
New and Selected Poems, 5027

Souad. *Burned Alive*, 8209

Souhami, Diana. *Selkirk's Island*, 5678

Soukhanov, Anne H. *Watch Word*, 5555

Soukhanov, Anne H. (jt. author). *Speaking Freely*, 5545

South, Coleman. *Jordan*, 8226

Southern, Eileen. *The Music of Black Americans*, 7123

Southgate, Martha. *The Fall of Rome*, 566(F)

Spalding, John D. *A Pilgrim's Digress*, 9037

Spangenburg, Ray. *The African-American Experience*, 9688
The Crime of Genocide, 9196
Eleanor Roosevelt, 6358
Exploring the Reaches of the Solar System, 11771
The History of Science from 1895 to 1994, 11619
The History of Science from the Ancient Greeks to the Scientific Revolution, 11620
The History of Science in the Eighteenth Century, 11621
The History of Science in the Nineteenth Century, 11622
Opening the Space Frontier, 11732
Science and Invention, 11623

Spangenburg, Ray (jt. author). *Political and Social Movements*, 8383

Spariosu, Mihai I. *Ghosts, Vampires, and Werewolves*, 5116

Spark, Muriel. *The Prime of Miss Jean Brodie*, 1459(F)

Sparks, Beatrice. *Almost Lost*, 10045
It Happened to Nancy, 10869

Sparks, Nicholas. *A Bend in the Road*, 4052(F)
The Guardian, 4053(F)
The Wedding, 4054(F)

Spaulding, John (jt. author). *Civil War Recipes*, 8681

Spaulding, Lily May. *Civil War Recipes*, 8681

Speakman, Jay. *Weapons of War*, 12722

Speare, Elizabeth G. *The Bronze Bow*, 2413(F)

Specht, Robert. *Tisha*, 6959

Spellenberg, Richard. *The Audubon Society Field Guide to North American Wildflowers*, 11870
Familiar Flowers of North America, 11871

Spellerberg, Ian (jt. author). *Snakes*, 11911

Spencer, Lauren. *The Assassination of John F. Kennedy*, 6326

Spencer, Lloyd. *Introducing the Enlightenment*, 7586

Spencer, William. *Iraq*, 8227
Islam Fundamentalism in the Modern World, 9140
The United States and Iran, 8228

Spencer, William Browning. *Zod Wallop*, 2204(F)

Sperekas, Nicole B. *SuicideWise*, 10596

Spiegelman, Art. *Maus*, 7825

Spielman, Andrew. *Mosquito*, 12140

Spielman, Patricia (jt. author). *Scroll Saw Puzzle Patterns*, 12994

Spielman, Patrick. *Scroll Saw Puzzle Patterns*, 12994

Spilling, Michael. *Estonia*, 8169
Georgia, 8170

Spilner, Maggie. *Prevention's Complete Book of Walking*, 11041

Spinelli, Angelo M. *Life Behind Barbed Wire*, 7826

Spinelli, Jerry. *Jason and Marceline*, 1460(F)
Milkweed, 3062(F)

Spink, Kathryn. *Mother Teresa*, 6813

Spinner, Stephanie. *Quiver*, 5175(F)

Spitz, Marc. *How Soon Is Never?* 387(F)

Spitzer, Robert J. *The Right to Bear Arms*, 9220

Spohn, Terry. *Scale Model Detailing*, 12931

Sports Illustrated. *Home Run Heroes*, 13192

Spoto, Donald. *Jacqueline Bouvier Kennedy Onassis*, 6354
Reluctant Saint, 6841

Sprague, Stuart Seely. *His Promised Land*, 6255

Sprigg, June. *Simple Gifts*, 9115

Springer, Jane. *Listen to Us*, 9477

Springer, Nancy. *I Am Mordred*, 2466(F)
I Am Morgan le Fay, 2467(F)
Secret Star, 1461(F)

Springer, Victor G. *Sharks in Question*, 12189

Springstubb, Tricia. *The Vietnamese Americans*, 9718

Sprinkle, Patricia. *The Remember Box*, 567(F)

Spruill, Steven. *Daughter of Darkness*, 3242(F)

Squires, Susan. *No More Lies*, 3797(F)

Stabenow, Dana. *A Cold-Blooded Business*, 3798(F)
A Fine and Bitter Snow, 3799(F)
A Grave Denied, 3800(F)
Red Planet Run, 4482(F)

Stableford, Brian. *Dark Ararat*, 4483(F)

Stoppard, Tom. *Rosencrantz and Guildenstern Are Dead*, 4776

Storad, Conrad J. *Inside AIDS*, 10875

Storr, Robert. *Art 21*, 7108

Stotsky, Sandra (jt. author). *Irish-American Answer Book*, 9784

Stott, Carole. *New Astronomer*, 11701

1001 Facts About Space, 11702

Stouffer, Marty. *Marty Stouffer's Wild America*, 9904

Stout, Glenn (jt. author). *DiMaggio*, 6665

Stovall, TaRessa. *The Buffalo Soldiers*, 8740

Stover, Leon. *Robert A. Heinlein*, 5412

Stover, Lois T. *Presenting Phyllis Reynolds Naylor*, 5413

Stowe, Harriet Beecher. *The Oxford Harriet Beecher Stowe Reader*, 5031

Uncle Tom's Cabin, 265(F)

Stowers, Carlton (jt. author). *Within These Walls*, 10030

Strachey, Lytton. *Queen Victoria*, 6892

Strada, Jennifer L. *Eating Disorders*, 10876

Strahinich, Helen. *The Holocaust*, 7832

Straight, Susan. *Highwire Moon*, 571(F)

Stranger, Joyce. *A Cherished Freedom*, 2668(F)

Strangis, Joel. *Lewis Hayden and the War Against Slavery*, 6227

Strasser, J. B. *Swoosh*, 10221

Strasser, Todd. *Can't Get There from Here*, 1466(F)

Girl Gives Birth to Own Prom Date, 3320(F)

Give a Boy a Gun, 1617(F)

How I Changed My Life, 1467(F)

How I Spent My Last Night on Earth, 4061(F)

Strathern, Paul. *Einstein and Relativity*, 6560

Stratton, Allan. *Leslie's Journal*, 995(F)

Stratton, Joanne L. *Pioneer Women*, 8741

Straub, Cindie. *Mime*, 7303

Straub, Deborah G. *Hispanic American Voices*, 6186

Native North American Voices, 9763

Straub, Matthew (jt. author). *Mime*, 7303

Straub, Peter. *Lost Boy Lost Girl*, 3805(F)

Straub, Peter (jt. author). *Black House*, 3177(F)

Strauss, Victoria. *Guardian of the Hills*, 2213(F)

Strazzabosco, Jeanne M. *High Performance Through Dealing with Diversity*, 10366

Strazzabosco-Hayn, Gina. *Drugs and Sleeping Disorders*, 10703

Teenage Refugees from Iran Speak Out, 9782

Street, James, Jr. *The Struggle for Tennessee*, 8685

Streissguth, Thomas. *The Attack on Pearl Harbor*, 8848

Charismatic Cult Leaders, 9161

The Comanche, 8478

Hoaxers and Hustlers, 10048

International Terrorists, 10203

Legendary Labor Leaders, 6187

Life Among the Vikings, 8181

Life in Ancient Egypt, 7471

Life in Communist Russia, 8171

Nuclear Weapons, 12723

Raoul Wallenberg, 6894

The Rise of the Soviet Union, 8172

Utopian Visionaries, 8401

Wounded Knee, 1890, 8479

Streitmatter, Rodger. *Voices of Revolution*, 5608

Stremlow, Mary V. *Coping with Sexism in the Military*, 9374

Strickland, Michael R. *African-American Poets*, 5719

My Own Song, 5032

Strickler, Jim. *Russia of the Tsars*, 8173

Strieber, Whitley. *Confirmation*, 13063

The Wild, 2214(F)

Stroff, Stephen M. *Discovering Great Jazz*, 7177

Strong, Beret E. (jt. author). *Pacific Island Legends*, 5090

Stroud, Jonathan. *The Amulet of Samarkand*, 2215(F)

Strouthes, Daniel P. *Law and Politics*, 7437

Strum, Shirley C. *Almost Human*, 11973

Strunk, William. *The Elements of Style*, 5556

Stuart, Chris. *Birds of Africa*, 12070

Stuart, Tilde (jt. author). *Birds of Africa*, 12070

Stuart-Clark, Christopher (jt. author). *The Oxford Book of Christmas Poems*, 4872

Stucky, Richard K. (jt. author). *Prehistoric Journey*, 11751

Student Environmental Action Coalition. *The Student Environmental Action Guide*, 9905

Stuhaug, Dennis O. *Kayaking Made Easy*, 13409

Stukane, Eileen (jt. author). *You're in Charge*, 11248

Stuprich, Michael. *Horror*, 5261

Sturgis, Alexander. *Understanding Paintings*, 7041

Sturm, James. *The Golem's Mighty Swing*, 2360

Sturm, Susan (jt. author). *Who's Qualified?* 9430

Stux, Erica. *Eight Who Made a Difference*, 5720

Stwertka, Albert. *A Guide to the Elements*, 12338

Superconductors, 12536

The World of Atoms and Quarks, 12339

Styler, Christopher (jt. author). *Sylvia's Soul Food*, 12842

Styron, William. *The Confessions of Nat Turner*, 2804(F)

Sophie's Choice, 1618(F)

Suberman, Stella. *The Jew Store*, 9754

When It Was Our War, 7004

Sugarmann, Josh. *NRA*, 9850

Sullivan, Caroline. *Bye Bye Baby*, 7178

Sullivan, Charles. *Here Is My Kingdom*, 9746

Imaginary Animals, 4914

Imaginary Gardens, 5033

Sullivan, Evelin. *The Concise Book of Lying*, 11379

Sullivan, G. (jt. author). *The Power of Birthdays, Stars and Numbers*, 13020

Sullivan, George. *Mathew Brady*, 5738

Modern Fighter Planes, 12665

Quarterbacks! 6653

Strange but True Stories of World War II, 7833

Sullivan, Helen. *Research Reports*, 10316

Sullivan, Mark. *Our Times*, 8402

Sullivan, Mary. *Ship Sooner*, 1468(F)

Sullivan, Mary Rose (jt. author). *Crime Classics*, 3392(F)

Sullivan, Otha Richard. *African American Women Scientists and Inventors*, 6528

Sullivan, Paul. *Legend of the North*, 184(F)

The Unforgiving Land, 140(F)

Sullivan, Randall. *LAbyrinth*, 10049

Sullivan, Robert. *A Whale Hunt*, 12222

Sultan, Faye. *Over the Line*, 996(F)

Summer, Lauralee. *Learning Joy from Dogs Without Collars*, 7005

Summers, Kit. *Juggling with Finesse*, 13128

Summers, Rowena. *September Morning*, 4062(F)

Sumner, M. C. *Night Terrors*, 3806(F)

Sumner, Melanie. *The School of Beauty and Charm*, 1469(F)

Sundel, Al. *Christopher Columbus and the Age of Exploration in World History*, 5631

Title Index

This index contains both main entry and internal titles cited in the entries. References are to entry numbers, not page numbers. All fiction titles are indicated by (F), following the entry number.

Subject/Grade Level Index

All entries are listed by subject and then according to grade level suitability (see the key at the foot of pages for grade level designations). Subjects are arranged alphabetically and subject heads may be subdivided into nonfiction (e.g., "Trucks") and fiction (e.g. "Trucks — Fiction"). References to entries are by entry number, not page number.

A

Aaron, Hank
JS: 6658 S: 6660 S–Adult: 6659

Abandoned children — Fiction
JS: 776, 1477

Abdul-Jabbar, Kareem
S: 6692 S–Adult: 6691

Abeel, Samantha
JS: 11044

Abelard and Heloise — Fiction
JS: 2465

Abernathy, Ralph
JS: 6196

Abolitionists
See also Slavery
JS: 8558, 9384, 9466, 9481, 9659
S–Adult: 8556, 8565

Abolitionists — Biography
JS: 6202, 6209, 6215–16, 8585
S: 6170, 6212–14, 6226, 6269, 9609
S–Adult: 6210

Abolitionists — Fiction
S–Adult: 6268

Aborigines (Australia) — Folklore
JS: 5091

Abortion
JS: 9304, 9336, 9338, 11168–70, 11199
S: 9831, 11158–59, 11161, 11164,
11173, 11188, 11200, 11206–7
S–Adult: 9307, 11175

Abortion — Fiction
JS: 1158, 1277, 1551

Absalom, Absalom! **— Criticism**
S: 5338

Abusive relationships
JS: 11353

Academic guidance
JS: 10324 S: 10277 S–Adult: 11420

Academy Award (motion pictures) — History
S: 7230

Academy of Motion Picture Arts and Sciences
JS: 7245

Accidents — Fiction
JS: 118, 1174, 3491 S: 3722
S–Adult: 330, 371

Accounting — Careers
S: 10474

Acid rain
See also Ecology and environment — Problems
S: 9923

Acne
JS: 10973

Acting
JS: 4752, 4755, 4799, 7296, 7301
S: 7293

Acting — Biography
JS: 6021, 6024–25, 6030, 6032, 6046,
6049, 6062, 6071, 6093–94, 6096, 6109,
6111, 6118, 6123–26, 6137 S: 5991,
6022, 6072, 6074, 6097, 6112–13, 6115
S–Adult: 5726, 5726, 6102, 6110

Acting — Careers
JS: 10447 S: 10460

Acting — Fiction
JS: 501, 1494 S: 3716

Activism
See also Social action
JS: 10150 S–Adult: 9786

Activism — Fiction
JS: 400 S–Adult: 2713

Activism — History
S–Adult: 8876

Adams, Abigail
JS: 6279–80

Adams, Ansel
JS: 5727 S: 7084

Adams, John
JS: 6281 S–Adult: 6282

Adams, John — Fiction
JS: 2762

Adams, John Quincy
S–Adult: 6283

Adams, John Quincy — Fiction
S: 2795

Adams, Samuel
S: 6379

Adamson, Joy
JS: 6775

Adaptation (biology)
S: 11810

Addams, Jane
JS: 6464–65

Addictions
See also Alcoholism; Drugs and drug
abuse; Smoking
JS: 10565, 10666, 10780, 11401
S: 10645 S–Adult: 10636, 10686

Addictive personality
JS: 11401

Adirondacks — Fiction
S: 78

Adolescence
See also Coming of age; Puberty
JS: 4642, 11334, 11354, 11458
S: 11325, 11419, 11511
S–Adult: 519, 1308, 1511, 6956, 9975,
11323, 11345

Adolescence — Boys
JS: 11242, 11426 S–Adult: 11347

Adolescence — Comic strips
JS: 11326

Adolescence — Fiction
JS: 447, 1302, 1476, 1554, 3264
S: 278, 398, 1213, 1333, 1410, 4717
S–Adult: 415, 448, 563, 633, 860,
1031, 1167, 1246, 1249, 1352, 1421,
1465, 2502, 2697, 2706, 3290

Adolescence — Girls
JS: 1168 S–Adult: 11357

Adolescence — Humor
S–Adult: 5192

Adolescence — Plays
S–Adult: 4815

Adolescence — Women
S–Adult: 11331

Adoption
See also Foster care; Stepfamilies
JS: 11194, 11504, 11513, 11515,
11521, 11568, 11570 S: 11164, 11208,
11489 S–Adult: 11505, 11538, 11544,
11566

Adoption — Fiction
JS: 719, 729, 753, 1108 S: 623, 889
S–Adult: 365, 593, 782

Adventure and adventurers
JS: 8296, 8491 S: 5627, 8287, 8492,
8965 S–Adult: 5615, 6946, 7403,
8301, 8313, 8577, 8967, 11341, 12697

**Adventure and adventurers —
Biography**
JS: 5630–31, 5633–34, 5640, 5642,
5648–49, 5653, 5667, 5679
S: 5628–29, 5636, 5638–39, 5651–52,
5664, 5666, 5674, 5678, 9000
S–Adult: 5632, 5637, 5665, 5671,
5680, 6154, 7923

**Adventure and adventurers —
Fiction**
See also Mystery stories — Fiction;
Sea stories — Fiction; Survival —
Fiction
J: 125, 2362 JS: 1–2, 4, 6, 10, 17–18,
25–27, 30, 35–36, 44, 46–47, 52, 55, 62,
67, 69–73, 80, 84, 90–91, 106–7,
109–10, 113, 118–19, 122–23, 127, 129,
132, 134, 136–37, 140, 142, 147–48,
151–53, 157, 159–60, 174, 189,
198–200, 211, 229, 235, 259, 266–67,
275, 604, 942, 1394, 1435, 1621, 2231,
2276, 2369, 2391, 2397, 2440, 2454,
2473, 2501, 2515, 2535, 2552, 2612,
2625, 2646, 2648, 2701, 2709, 2720,
2749, 2770, 2772, 2888–90, 2900, 3476,
3582–83, 3864, 4431 JS–Adult: 2311
S: 3, 5, 7, 7–8, 15, 19–24, 29, 31–32,
37–43, 45, 49–51, 54, 56, 58–61, 68,
75–76, 78–79, 81–83, 85–86, 88–89,
92–93, 95–100, 102–3, 105, 111,
114–15, 121, 128, 139, 143, 145–46,
149–50, 154, 158, 161, 163, 230, 258,
2153, 2333, 2418–19, 2443, 2572, 2579,
2587, 2593, 2596, 2608–10, 2622, 2745,
2778, 2812, 2839, 2864, 2868, 2955,
3080, 3276, 3337–38, 3417, 3424,
3437–38, 3449, 3457–58, 3510, 3518,
3524, 3531, 3538, 3615, 3626, 3739,
3943–44, 4139, 7965, 8240, 12478
S–Adult: 13, 16, 28, 33, 53, 77, 120,
133, 135, 156, 207, 272, 2288, 2303,
2312, 2364, 2458, 2527, 2603, 2614,
2651, 2666, 2707, 2736, 2782, 2843,
2874, 3334, 3366, 3431, 3439, 3485,
3495, 3507, 3547, 3594, 3618, 3629,
3708, 3762, 3788, 3932, 4483, 7403,
7426, 7905, 7997, 8043, 8056, 8073,

8241, 8293–94, 8305, 8314, 8967, 8994,
9181, 13038, 13091, 13258, 13406

**Adventure and adventurers —
Women**
S–Adult: 5617

Adventure racing
JS: 13080

The Adventures of Huckleberry Finn
— Criticism
S: 5353, 5371, 5408

The Adventures of Tom Sawyer —
Criticism
S: 5354

Advertising
JS: 10244, 10246, 11374 S: 10247

Advertising — Biography
JS: 6626

Advertising — Careers
S: 10470–71

Advertising — History
S–Adult: 7237, 12673

Aeneid — Criticism
S–Adult: 5444

Aerialists — Biography
S: 6136

Aerobics
S: 11037

Aeronautics
See also Airplanes; Aviation
S–Adult: 12663

Aeronautics — Careers
JS: 10384

Aeronautics — History
S: 12651, 12661

Aeronautics — Safety
S: 12662

Aerosmith (rock group)
S: 5990

Affirmative action
See also Social action
JS: 9428, 9560, 9583, 10248
S–Adult: 9399, 9430, 9684, 10252

Afghanistan
JS: 8046, 8048 S: 8055
S–Adult: 7860, 8044, 8053, 8058–59,
8061, 8913

Afghanistan — Biography
S–Adult: 6913, 8054

Afghanistan — Fiction
S–Adult: 2521

**Afghanistan — Women —
Biography**
S: 7015

Africa
See also specific countries and
regions, e.g., Ethiopia; West Africa
JS: 7901, 7914, 7964, 7977 S: 4614,
7891, 7896, 7909, 9636
S–Adult: 6999, 7897, 7900, 7903–4

Africa — Animals
JS: 11964, 11989 JS–Adult: 7981
S: 11973, 12023 S–Adult: 7893,
7940, 7966, 11884, 12123

Africa — Art
S: 7068

Africa — Atlases
S: 7906

Africa — Biography
JS: 6771, 6775 S–Adult: 5848

Africa — Biology
S–Adult: 7893

Africa — Birds
S–Adult: 12070

Africa — Cookbooks
J: 12813 S–Adult: 12797

Africa — Exploration
S–Adult: 7923

Africa — Fiction
JS: 418, 1024, 1588, 2468, 2479, 2483,
2486, 2488, 2491, 4252 S: 38, 41, 50,
139, 2480–81, 2484, 2487

Africa — Folklore
JS: 5073, 5076–77 S: 5074–75
S–Adult: 5078

Africa — Geography
JS–Adult: 7908, 7916
S–Adult: 7893, 7907

Africa — History
J: 7913 JS: 7902, 7915, 7969,
7989–90 S: 7766, 7894–95, 7899,
7910–11, 7951 S–Adult: 7898

Africa — Hunting
S: 13298

Africa — Peoples
See also specific peoples, e.g., Zulu
(African people)
JS: 7892, 7921, 7926–27, 7929–30,
7932–37, 7943–46, 7950, 7953, 7955,
7963, 7967, 7972–76, 7979, 7982–83,
7987–88, 7991, 7993–94, 7996

Africa — Poetry
S: 5048

Africa — Prehistoric art
S–Adult: 7067

Africa — Religion
JS: 9070 S: 9092

Africa — Slavery
S–Adult: 7912

Africa — Wildlife
S–Adult: 7931, 7938

Africa — Women
S–Adult: 7980

African Americans
See also Civil rights; Civil War
(U.S.); Kwanzaa; Slavery; and
names of individuals, e.g.,
Robinson, Jackie
J: 9599 JS: 4637, 5975, 9392, 9493,
9552, 9612, 9624, 9627, 9645, 9678,
9682 S: 5364, 6153, 9596, 9617, 9623,
9628, 9634, 9649, 9651, 9661, 9675,

JS = Junior High/Senior High;   S = Senior High;   S–Adult = Senior High/Adult

1094

JS = Junior High/Senior High;   S = Senior High;   S–Adult = Senior High/Adult

African Americans — Sex education
S: 11267

African Americans — Teenagers
S: 9606

African Americans — Television
JS: 7270

African Americans — Tennis
JS: 6723

African Americans — War veterans
S: 8951

African Americans — Women
S: 5499, 9643, 10576 **S–Adult:** 9618,
9650, 9652, 9685, 9696, 10236

**African Burial Ground (New York
City)**
JS: 9637

African Canadians — Fiction
S: 836 **S–Adult:** 491

African kingdoms — History
See also specific kingdoms, e.g., Zulu
(African kingdom)
J: 7913

Africans
S–Adult: 9781

Aggression
S–Adult: 11930

Agikuyu (African people)
JS: 7930

Aging
See also Death; Elderly persons;
Euthanasia
JS: 9940 **S:** 9938, 10592
S–Adult: 10601

Agriculture
JS: 9930

Agriculture — Careers
S: 10430

Agriculture — History
See also Farms and farm life
JS: 11827 **S–Adult:** 11824

AIDS
See also HIV (virus)
JS: 10729, 10737, 10748, 10760,
10768, 10771–73, 10779, 10790, 10797,
10809, 10811, 10815, 10828, 10843,
10851, 10869, 10875 **S:** 10745, 10752,
10756, 10792–93, 10834
S–Adult: 6979, 10741, 10877

AIDS — Biography
JS: 6698, 6908

AIDS — Fiction
JS: 674, 812, 1590, 2380 **S:** 1256
S–Adult: 717

Air Force One
JS: 9232

Air Force (U.S.) — Careers
JS: 10367 **S:** 10387

Air Force (U.S.) — Fiction
S–Adult: 484

Air Force (U.S.) — History
S: 8840

Air pollution
See also Ecology and environment —
Problems; Pollution
JS: 9915, 12451 **S:** 9918, 9921

Air traffic controllers — Careers
S: 10370

Airplane crashes
S: 8297

Airplane crashes — Fiction
JS: 26

Airplane pilots — Alaska
S: 8995

Airplane pilots — Biography
S: 5618, 6473

Airplane pilots — Fiction
S: 115

Airplane pilots — Women
JS: 5619

Airplanes
See also Aviation; Military airplanes
JS: 9232 **S:** 12654

Airplanes — Accidents
JS: 12656

Airplanes — Armed forces
JS: 12665

Airplanes — Biography
JS: 5643, 5657–58, 5660–62, 5668,
6607 **S:** 5644, 5646, 5656, 5669
S–Adult: 5645, 5659, 5663

Airplanes — Careers
JS: 10408

Airplanes — Fiction
S: 3083

Airplanes — History
JS: 6606 **JS–Adult:** 12655 **S:** 7657,
12660–61

Airplanes — Paper
S: 12938

Airplanes — Safety
JS: 12657 **S:** 12662

Airplanes (model)
S: 12935

Akamba (African people)
JS: 7944

al-Qaeda
S: 10166

al-Qaeda — Biography
JS: 6789

Alabama
S–Adult: 9641

Alabama — Fiction
JS: 1302 **S–Adult:** 538

Alamo, Battle of the
S–Adult: 8579

Alamo (TX)
S: 8572

Alamo (TX) — Fiction
S: 2877 **S–Adult:** 2779

Alaska
JS: 8993, 12054, 13113 **S:** 6959, 8995,
9000, 9006, 13081 **S–Adult:** 8997,
8999, 9009

Alaska — Fiction
JS: 70, 73, 119, 1454 **S:** 1599
S–Adult: 53, 1246, 2392, 3791,
3799–800

Alaska — History
JS: 5620, 8755 **S–Adult:** 8989, 9007

Alaska — Islands
S–Adult: 8994

Alaska — Poetry
S: 5053

Alaska Gold Rush
See Gold Rush (Alaska and Yukon)

Alaska Purchase
JS: 8755

Alaska Purchase — Biography
JS: 6451

Albanians — Fiction
J: 2632

Albany, A. J.
S–Adult: 6911

Albany (NY) — Fiction
S: 2962

Albatrosses
S–Adult: 12065

Albinos — Fiction
JS: 956, 1344

Albright, Madeleine
JS: 6380–81

Alcatraz Island
JS: 8990 **S–Adult:** 9756

Alchemy — Fiction
JS: 2070

Alcohol
J: 10651 **JS:** 10613, 10623, 10625,
10641, 10643–44, 10656, 10668, 10676,
10685, 10702, 10720 **S:** 10630
S–Adult: 10634, 10712

Alcohol — Fiction
JS: 1585 **S:** 1212, 4066

Alcohol — Teenagers
JS: 10661

Alcoholism
See also Drugs and drug abuse
J: 10651 **JS:** 10606, 10612–13, 10619,
10631, 10635, 10643, 10661, 10676,
10696–97, 10702, 10708, 10710
S: 10714 **S–Adult:** 10681, 11529

Alcoholism — Fiction
JS: 512, 605, 675, 817–18, 1156, 1320,
1392, 1436 **S:** 530, 867, 1074

Alcott, Louisa May
S–Adult: 5803

Aleuts — Fiction
JS: 3027

Alexander, Donnell
S–Adult: 6912

Alexander, Sally Hobart
JS: 6466

Alexander the Great
S: 7498

Alexander the Great — Fiction
S: 2414

Alexandria (Egypt)
JS: 7464

Alfred the Great — Fiction
S–Adult: 1960

Algonquin Indians — History
JS: 8451

Ali, Muhammad
JS: 6707–8, 6710–11, 8924 **S:** 6706
S–Adult: 6709

Alice in Wonderland **— Fiction**
S–Adult: 2650

Alien abductions
JS: 13044

Aliens
See Extraterrestrial life; Illegal aliens;
Immigration (U.S.)

All Quiet on the Western Front **—**
Criticism
S: 5321

Allen, Woody
S: 5991

Allende, Isabel
S–Adult: 5804

Allergies
JS: 10762, 10806, 10861

Alligators and crocodiles
S: 11906, 11906 **S–Adult:** 11905

Almanacs
S: 13022

Alomar, Roberto
JS: 6661

Alonso, Alicia
JS: 5992

Alou, Moises
JS: 6662

Alphabet
S: 5552

Alphabets — History
JS: 5548

Alternative energy
JS: 9874, 12519, 12521
S–Adult: 12516

Alternative medicine
JS: 10899, 10923

Alvarez, Julia
S: 5805

Alzheimer's disease
JS: 10784, 10801, 10891 **S:** 10749

Alzheimer's disease — Fiction
JS: 80, 783 **S:** 737, 966

Amazing Stories **(periodical)**
S: 4404

Amazon.com
S–Adult: 12593

Amazon jungle — Fiction
S: 3

Amazon rain forest
JS: 12376

Amazon River
JS: 8282, 11786, 12377 **S:** 8287–88
S–Adult: 12211

Amazons (mythology)
S–Adult: 7497

Amelia Earhart
JS: 5643

American-Cuban Relations
See Cuban-American relations

American culture
JS: 9855

American English
S: 5545

**American literature — History and
criticism**
S: 5325, 5352, 5414–15

American Revolution
See Revolutionary War (U.S.)

American Sign Language
See also Sign language
S–Adult: 5536

Ameru (African people)
JS: 7943

Amish
JS: 9120 **S:** 9118 **S–Adult:** 9105

Amish — Fiction
JS: 1061 **S–Adult:** 498, 3525, 3721

Amish — Women
S: 9118

Amistad **mutiny**
JS: 8588 **S:** 2795, 7219

Amnesia — Fiction
JS: 1034, 3106 **S:** 49, 98, 3939, 4472

Amnesty International
S–Adult: 9460

Amphibians
See also specific animal names, e.g.,
Frogs and toads
JS: 11900–2, 11904 **S:** 11897–99,
11903 **S–Adult:** 11896

Amputations — Fiction
JS: 1008

Amsterdam — History
JS: 7812

Anasazi Indians
S: 8471

Anastasia (Romanov)
S: 6879

Anatomy
See Human body

Ancient civilizations
S–Adult: 7453

Ancient Greece — Plays
S: 5454

Ancient history
JS: 7443, 7449, 7473, 7494
S: 7377–78, 7452, 7479, 7483

Ancient history — Wars
JS: 7444

Ancient world — Art
JS: 7060

Anderson, Marian
JS: 5993, 5995 **S:** 5994

Andersonville Prison — Fiction
JS: 2846 **S–Adult:** 2832

Angel dust (drug)
See also Drugs and drug abuse
JS: 10628

Angelou, Maya
JS: 5807–8 **S:** 5200, 5389, 5806

Angelou, Maya — Criticism
JS: 5337 **S:** 5535 **S–Adult:** 5336

Angels
JS: 9081

Anglo Saxons — Fiction
JS: 2471

Angola
JS: 7934, 7973, 7979 **S–Adult:** 7970

Animal Farm **— Criticism**
S: 5291, 5298

Animal rights
JS: 9842 **S–Adult:** 11876

Animal welfare
S–Adult: 11377

Animals
See also Amphibians; Endangered
animals; Endangered species;
Fables; Farms and farm life;
Invertebrates; Marine animals; Pets;
Prehistoric animals; Ranches and
ranch life; Wildlife conservation;
Zoos; as a subdivision under
country or continent names; e.g.,
Africa — Animals; and individual
animal species; or as part of a
specific biome, e.g., Rain forests
JS: 11892 **JS–Adult:** 6063, 11886
S: 11882 **S–Adult:** 11879–80, 11889,
11894

Animals — Art
S: 12900

Animals — Babies
S: 11939

Animals — Behavior
S: 11924, 11926, 11933
S–Adult: 6992, 11794, 11873, 11876,
11881, 11891, 11922–23, 11928–30,
11934

Animals — Bible
S: 9059

Animals — Care
S–Adult: 12322

JS = Junior High/Senior High;   S = Senior High;   S–Adult = Senior High/Adult

Animals — Care — Careers
JS: 10404 S: 10382, 10396, 10405, 10423

Animals — Care — Volunteerism
JS: 10145

Animals — Communication
S: 11936, 12329 S–Adult: 11937

Animals — Emotions
S–Adult: 11934

Animals — English language
S: 5541

Animals — Experimentation
JS: 9806 S: 11872 S–Adult: 11877

Animals — Extinct
JS: 11878 S: 12103

Animals — Fiction
S: 171, 177, 258, 2125 S–Adult: 690

Animals — Folklore
JS: 5132

Animals — Habitats
S–Adult: 11881, 11883, 11938, 11953

Animals — Intelligence
S: 11925, 11927, 11933
S–Adult: 11931, 11935

Animals — Learning
S–Adult: 11931

Animals — Poetry
J: 5050

Animals — Poisonous
S: 11932, 11932

Animals — Predators
S–Adult: 11884

Animals — Reproduction
S: 11939

Animals — Rights
J: 9815 JS: 9788, 9805–6, 9812, 9823, 9832, 9834, 9837, 9846, 9852 S: 9799, 11872 S–Adult: 9847, 9859, 11377

Animals — Rights — Fiction
S: 1197

Animals — South America
JS: 11786

Animals — Tracks
JS: 11940 S–Adult: 6992

Animals — Venomous
S–Adult: 11795

Animation (motion pictures)
JS: 7099, 12639 S: 7220, 7227, 7238, 7242, 7255–56, 12642 S–Adult: 7246

Anorexia nervosa
See also Eating disorders
JS: 10776, 10783, 10805, 10808, 10819, 10836, 10840, 10867, 10870
S: 10788, 10810

Anorexia nervosa — Fiction
JS: 940, 989, 1527 S: 957, 997, 2997, 3746

Ansary, Tamim
S–Adult: 6913

Antarctic
See also Arctic; Polar regions
JS: 8300 S: 8307, 8317
S–Adult: 8301, 8305, 8320, 12091

Antarctic — Biography
S–Adult: 5637

Antarctic — Exploration
S–Adult: 5680, 8299, 8311

Antarctic — Fiction
JS: 3634

Antarctic — Poetry
S–Adult: 5521

Antelopes
S–Adult: 12123

Anthologies
JS: 4633 S–Adult: 4471, 4690, 4855, 4967, 5203, 5207–8, 5213, 5218, 7980, 9010, 9199, 9520, 11583–84

Anthony, Susan B.
JS: 6198–99, 9451 S: 6197

Anthropology
JS: 7362, 8282 S: 7356, 7359
S–Adult: 7344–45, 7348, 7352

Anthropology — Biography
JS: 6587 S: 6584

Anthropology — Careers
JS: 10532

Anthropology — Fiction
JS: 1556

Anti-Semitism
S: 9754 S–Adult: 9750

Anti-Semitism — Fiction
JS: 559, 2641, 2654, 3036, 3601
S: 1413, 3018

Anti-Semitism — History
JS: 7626

Antidepressants (drugs)
JS: 10677

Antietam, Battle of
JS: 8668

Antietam, Battle of — Fiction
S–Adult: 2837, 2844

Antigone — Criticism
S: 5455

Antiwar movements — History
S–Adult: 9786

Antony, Mark — Fiction
S: 2436

Anxiety
JS: 11088

Anxiety disorders
JS: 11051

Apache Indians
JS: 8417, 8421 S: 6407

Apache Indians — Biography
S: 6393 S–Adult: 6498

Apache Indians — Fiction
JS: 2720 S: 2862

Apalachee Indians — Fiction
S–Adult: 2743

Apartheid — Biography
J: 6785 JS: 6781, 6783 S: 6780

Apartheid — Fiction
JS: 455, 4675 S: 1573, 1601, 2484
S–Adult: 2492

Apartheid — South Africa
JS: 6782 S–Adult: 7962

Apes
See also individual species, e.g., Gorillas
JS: 11963 S: 11967
S–Adult: 11961, 11965, 11975

Apes — Behavior
S–Adult: 11972

Apes — Fiction
JS: 4140

Apollo (space expedition)
S: 11720 S–Adult: 11726

Appalachia
S–Adult: 8330

Appalachia — Fiction
JS: 701, 1461, 2937 S: 4716

Appalachian Mountains — Pollution
S: 9011

Appalachian Trail
S: 13253

Aqualung
JS: 12482

Aquariums
JS: 12326 S: 12320–21, 12325, 12328

Aquatic animals
S: 12157, 12204

Arab Americans
JS: 9779

Arab Americans — Fiction
S–Adult: 1575

Arab-Israeli relations
See also Israeli-Arab relations
JS: 8188, 8205–6

Arab-Israeli relations — Fiction
JS: 2558

Arabia — History
S–Adult: 7615

Arabian Nights
JS: 2400

Arabian Nights — Fiction
JS: 5082

Arabs
JS: 7950

Arabs — Biography
JS: 6787 S: 6788

Arabs — Fiction
S–Adult: 1575

Arabs — History
JS: 8192

JS = Junior High/Senior High;   S = Senior High;   S–Adult = Senior High/Adult

Arafat, Yasir
JS: 6787 **S:** 6788

Arapaho Indians — Fiction
S: 3433

Archaeology
JS: 7372, 7375, 7381–83, 7385, 8235
S: 5191, 7370–71, 7373, 7377–78,
7384, 7476, 8292 **S–Adult:** 7345,
7379–80, 7463, 8230

Archaeology — Biography
S: 6584

Archaeology — Careers
J: 10525

Archaeology — Egypt
S–Adult: 7374

Archaeology — Fiction
JS: 36 **S:** 3717 **S–Adult:** 3527–28,
3719, 7386

Archimedes — Fiction
S: 2420

Architecture
See also Building and construction
JS: 12576 **S:** 7021 **S–Adult:** 7020,
7027, 12566

Architecture — Biography
JS: 5745, 5772, 5799 **S:** 5800

Architecture — Fiction
S–Adult: 379

Architecture — History
JS: 7510 **S:** 7022–23, 7026, 7446
S–Adult: 7019

Arctic
See also Antarctic; North Pole; Polar
regions
JS: 8322 **S:** 8312, 8318, 11984
S–Adult: 8308–9, 8316, 8323, 13091

Arctic — Biography
S–Adult: 5671

Arctic — Careers
J: 10529

Arctic — Discovery and exploration
S: 8315 **S–Adult:** 8303–4, 8306, 8314

Arctic — Fiction
S: 3798

Arden, Elizabeth
JS: 6608

Aristide, Jean-Bertrand — Fiction
JS: 2712

Arizona — Fiction
S: 2269, 2905

Arizona — History
S: 9016

Arizona (battleship)
S: 12696

Arkansas — Fiction
JS: 2968 **S–Adult:** 1201

Armed forces — History
S: 7395

Armed forces (U.S.)
See also specific branches, e.g., Air
Force (U.S.)
JS: 9365 **S:** 9375, 9886
S–Adult: 9368

**Armed forces (U.S.) — African
Americans**
JS: 9605 **S–Adult:** 9604, 9662

Armed forces (U.S.) — Biography
JS: 6444, 6446, 7777 **S:** 6445, 6476
S–Adult: 6483

Armed forces (U.S.) — Careers
S: 10387–91

Armed forces (U.S.) — Women
JS: 9374, 9377 **S:** 9376

Armenia — Genocide — Fiction
JS: 2557

Armenia — History
S: 8078

Arms control
See also Gun control
S: 9220

Armstrong, Lance
JS: 6740–41 **S–Adult:** 6738–39

Armstrong, Louis
JS: 5999 **S:** 5996, 5998
S–Adult: 5997

Armstrong, Neil
S–Adult: 5624

Army (U.S.)
See also Armed forces (U.S.)
JS: 9370 **S:** 8917 **S–Adult:** 8913,
12720

Army (U.S.) — Biography
JS: 6449 **S:** 6425

Army (U.S.) — Careers
S: 10388

Army (U.S.) — Special Forces
S–Adult: 12700

Arnold, Benedict — Fiction
JS: 2763

Arson — Fiction
JS: 80, 3530 **S:** 1017, 3169, 3853

Art
See also Art appreciation; Drawing
and painting; Museums; and as a
subdivision under other subjects,
e.g., Animals — Art; and names of
individuals, e.g., Van Gogh,
Vincent
J: 4869 **JS:** 4856, 5033, 7032,
7036–37, 7089, 7095, 8981, 12586
S: 5101, 5111 **S–Adult:** 7039, 7057,
7094, 7447

Art — African Americans
JS: 7087 **S:** 5730

Art — American
S: 7104 **S–Adult:** 7085

Art — Biography
J: 7078–79 **JS:** 5704, 5729, 5733,
5744, 5747, 5750–52, 5754–57, 5763,
5767–68, 5770–71, 5773–75, 5777,
5779–82, 5784–85, 5791–93, 5795,
5798, 5801, 7070 **JS–Adult:** 5928
S: 5683, 5693, 5700, 5718, 5739–43,
5749, 5783, 5794, 5796–97
S–Adult: 5728, 5731, 5753, 5764–65,
5769, 5778, 5802, 7074, 7102

Art — Careers
JS: 10434 **S:** 10443, 10457

Art — Contemporary
S–Adult: 7108

Art — Dictionaries
S: 7042

Art — Egypt
S–Adult: 7459

Art — Fiction
JS: 1557, 2562 **S:** 1087, 2570, 2667,
3437 **S–Adult:** 3867

Art — Galleries
J: 9260 **S:** 7035

Art — History
JS: 7030, 7033, 7055, 7060, 7070,
7072–73, 7075, 7077, 7081 **S:** 5693,
5766, 7016–17, 7034–35, 7041,
7046–48, 7050–51, 7058, 7062, 7104,
7528 **S–Adult:** 7029, 7044–45, 7049,
7054, 7056, 7065, 7069, 7071, 7076,
7085–86, 7109–11

Art — United States
S–Adult: 7106, 7108

Art — World War II
S–Adult: 7097

Art appreciation
J: 7078 **JS:** 7030, 7095 **S:** 7034, 7066
S–Adult: 7029

Art deco
S: 7018

Art Institute of Chicago
S–Adult: 7065

Arthritis
JS: 10835, 10838

Arthur, Chester A.
S: 6284

Arthur, King
JS: 5114–15, 5119 **S:** 5102, 5108,
5112

Arthur, King — Fiction
JS: 1916, 2188, 2264, 2466–67, 2470,
2475, 5110 **S:** 1711, 1786, 1931, 2010,
2132, 2213, 2262–63, 2580, 2635, 2685,
2689 **S–Adult:** 1802, 2220, 2250,
2452, 2633, 3271

Arthur, King — Plays
JS: 4812

Artificial intelligence
JS: 12584 **S–Adult:** 12607

Artists — American
S: 7100

Arts — Careers
JS: 10455

Ashanti (African kingdom)
JS: 7990

Ashe, Arthur
JS: 6722–23

Asia
See also specific countries, e.g., China
JS: 5230 S–Adult: 7997

Asia — Economy
JS: 7999

Asia — Folklore
S: 5085 S–Adult: 5083

Asia — History
JS: 6798, 7998

Asia — Mythology
S–Adult: 5083

Asian Americans
J: 8846 JS: 5230, 9008, 9704–5, 9708, 9711, 9714, 9716–17, 9719–23, 9723, 9725 S: 9707 S–Adult: 9724

Asian Americans — Biography
See also specific groups, e.g., Chinese Americans
JS: 5692, 5941, 6527, 6530 S–Adult: 6015

Asian Americans — Fiction
JS: 428, 495, 589, 2509 S: 476, 493, 573, 3087

Asian Americans — History
S: 9712

Assassinations
JS: 8861–62, 8866, 8896

Assassinations — Fiction
S: 39, 3338

Assertiveness
S: 11449

Asteroids
S: 11740 S–Adult: 11743

Asthma
J: 10866 JS: 10782, 10826, 10852

Astrobiology
S–Adult: 11655

Astrology
JS: 13034 S: 13020, 13062 S–Adult: 11659, 13015

Astronauts
JS: 11727 S: 11737 S–Adult: 11708, 11731

Astronauts — Biography
JS: 5622, 5650, 5676 S–Adult: 5624, 5635

Astronomy
JS: 11661, 11671, 11678–79, 11681, 11688, 11691, 11697, 11701–2, 11735 S: 11612, 11651, 11654, 11656–58, 11662–63, 11665–66, 11670, 11673, 11677, 11682, 11684, 11690, 11692, 11696, 11699, 11703–4, 11706–7, 11772, 11778 S–Adult: 11653, 11655, 11664, 11668, 11674, 11676, 11683, 11689, 11695, 11705, 11760, 11773

Astronomy — Biography
JS: 6571, 6574 S: 6582 S–Adult: 6573

Astronomy — Experiments and projects
JS: 11759 S: 11694

Astronomy — History
S: 11672

Astrophysics
S: 11657

Atalanta (Greek mythology)
JS: 5175

Ataturk, Kemal
JS: 6817

Athletes — Biography
See also specific sports, e.g., Tennis — Biography; and names of athletes, e.g., Williams, Venus and Serena
JS: 6638, 6756–58

Athletes — Women
JS: 6643

Atlanta (GA) — Fiction
JS: 798 S–Adult: 2986

Atlanta (GA) — History
S: 8692

Atlantic Coast
S: 11779, 11782

Atlantic Ocean
S–Adult: 12467

Atlases
See also Maps and globes
JS: 7305

Atmosphere
JS: 12452

Atmosphere — Problems
JS: 9917

Atomic bomb
JS: 7701, 7706, 7761, 7799, 12701, 12721 S: 7700, 7754, 7759, 7858 S–Adult: 7719, 8898, 12714

Atomic bomb — Biography
JS: 6564, 6588 S: 6809

Atomic bomb — Fiction
JS: 1619

Atomic bomb — History
JS: 6600, 7758, 7814 S–Adult: 12724

Atomic structure
JS: 12339

Attention deficit disorder
See also Learning disabilities
JS: 11098, 11105, 11117

Audubon, John James
S–Adult: 12055

Aurora borealis
See Northern lights

Austen, Jane
S: 5809 S–Adult: 5810

Austen, Jane — Criticism
S: 5266–67, 5303, 5305, 5308

Austen, Jane — Fiction
S: 3352 S–Adult: 2554

Australia
S: 6816, 8063, 8069 S–Adult: 8073

Australia — Animals
S: 12032

Australia — Biography
S: 6052

Australia — Dolphins
S–Adult: 12221

Australia — Fiction
JS: 94, 104, 106–10, 160, 345, 360, 708, 967, 1103, 1312, 2516, 2518, 2532, 3160, 3196, 3268, 3288, 3448, 3648, 3666 S: 105, 867, 1213, 2528, 3008, 3372, 3397, 3472, 4622 S–Adult: 824, 2527, 2529, 3811, 3852

Australia — Folklore
JS: 5090

Austria — Fiction
JS: 3051

Austrian Americans — Biography
JS: 6118

Authors
JS: 5975 S: 10303 S–Adult: 5562, 5565

Authors — African American
See African Americans — Authors

Authors — Biography
J: 5719, 5921, 5926 JS: 5290, 5692, 5702–3, 5709, 5711–12, 5808, 5811–12, 5814, 5824, 5828–30, 5833–34, 5836, 5838–40, 5843, 5847, 5849, 5851, 5858–59, 5864, 5866, 5869, 5871–73, 5877, 5879–81, 5884–87, 5891–92, 5894, 5898–900, 5902, 5906–8, 5911–15, 5917, 5919, 5922, 5925, 5927, 5932, 5935–38, 5940–41, 5945–46, 5952, 5954, 5960, 5962, 5967, 5971, 5974, 6206, 12686 JS–Adult: 5928, 5949 S: 5376, 5684, 5689, 5722, 5805, 5809, 5813, 5817–18, 5820, 5823, 5826, 5831, 5841, 5850, 5852, 5854, 5863, 5876, 5878, 5883, 5895, 5904–5, 5909, 5920, 5929, 5933–34, 5939, 5943–44, 5947–48, 5950, 5953, 5955, 5963, 5969, 6926 S–Adult: 5688, 5695, 5697, 5707, 5714, 5731, 5803–4, 5810, 5819, 5827, 5832, 5835, 5837, 5844–45, 5848, 5853, 5857, 5860, 5874, 5882, 5888–90, 5897, 5901, 5910, 5923, 5930–31, 5942, 5951, 5959, 5966, 5968, 5972

Authors — Criticism
JS: 5374

Authors — Fiction
S–Adult: 2650, 3642

Authors — Hispanic American
JS: 5716

Authors — Memoirs
S–Adult: 5815

Authors — Native Americans
S–Adult: 9759

Authors — Science fiction
S: 5398

JS = Junior High/Senior High;   S = Senior High;   S–Adult = Senior High/Adult

Authors — Women
See Women — Authors

Autism
JS: 11081, 11092, 11103 **S:** 11086
S–Adult: 11046

Autism — Fiction
S–Adult: 975

Autobiography — Criticism
S: 5241

Autograph collecting
S: 12981

Automation
See also Computers; Robots
JS: 12627

Automobile accidents — Fiction
JS: 624, 983, 1310, 1484

Automobile driving
S: 12671

Automobile driving — Fiction
JS: 1113

Automobile industry — Careers
S: 10395

Automobile racing
JS: 13137 **S:** 13138–39, 13141–43,
13145 **S–Adult:** 6656, 12672

Automobile racing — Fiction
JS: 4555

Automobile racing — History
S–Adult: 13140

Automobiles
JS: 12670 **S:** 12669, 12671, 13144
S–Adult: 12666, 12672

Automobiles — Biography
JS: 6615

Automobiles — Design
JS–Adult: 12675

Automobiles — Fiction
S: 3163

Automobiles — History
JS: 12667 **S:** 12676–77
S–Adult: 12673

Automobiles — Maintenance and repair
S: 12671, 12674

Automobiles — Pollution
S: 9918, 9921

Autumn
S–Adult: 11802

Avant-garde movement
S: 7016

Avi (author)
JS: 5811

Aviation
See also Airplanes
S–Adult: 12650, 12653

Aviation — Biography
S–Adult: 6546

Aviation — History
S–Adult: 12652, 12658–59

Avignon — Fiction
S–Adult: 2442

Aztecs
See also Mexico — History
J: 8260 **JS:** 8253, 8256, 8259, 8262
S: 5636, 8255, 8265, 8268
S–Adult: 8269

Aztecs — Fiction
JS: 2703 **S–Adult:** 2698

Aztecs — Poetry
JS: 8254

B

Babbage, Charles
S–Adult: 6534

Babies
S–Adult: 11256

Babies — Fiction
J: 1077 **S:** 3889

Baboons
S: 11973 **S–Adult:** 11970

Baboons — Fiction
JS: 2491

Baby boom (post World War II)
JS: 8884

Baby-sitting
J: 10550 **S:** 10549

Baby-sitting — Fiction
JS: 850, 1397, 3144 **S–Adult:** 350,
1311, 3998, 4000

Babylon 5 (television series)
JS: 4221, 7267

Bach, Johann Sebastian
S: 5978

Backgammon
S: 13288

Backpacking
JS–Adult: 13250 **S:** 13260, 13272,
13277, 13281 **S–Adult:** 13270

Backpacking — Fiction
S–Adult: 2508

Bacteria
See also Germs
JS: 12229 **S:** 10736, 10794, 10878
S–Adult: 10849, 11780

Bacteriology
S–Adult: 12224

Bacteriology — Biography
JS: 6565 **S–Adult:** 12224

Badminton
S: 13445

Baha'i (religion)
JS: 4848, 9061

Bahamas — Fiction
JS: 3694

Bahrain
JS: 8219

Baiev, Khassan
S–Adult: 6914

Bailey, Anne
JS: 6467

Baiul, Oksana
S: 13365

Baking — Cookbooks
S–Adult: 12772, 12776

Balakian, Peter
S: 8078

Balanchine, George
S–Adult: 6000

Bald eagles
See also Birds of prey; Eagles
JS: 12077

Baldwin, James
JS: 5812 **S:** 5813 **S–Adult:** 9389

Balkans
JS: 8083 **S:** 8081 **S–Adult:** 8085

Ballet
JS: 7211

Ballet — Biography
JS: 5992, 6048 **S–Adult:** 6000

Ballet — Fiction
JS: 314, 472, 943, 4026
S–Adult: 3947

Balloons and ballooning
S: 13132

Balloons and ballooning — History
S: 12664

Ballroom dancing — Fiction
JS: 3467

Bands (music) — Fiction
JS: 280 **S–Adult:** 281

Banjo
S: 7197

Banks and banking — Biography
JS: 6628

Banneker, Benjamin
JS: 6535

Bantock, Nick
S–Adult: 5728

Barnum, P. T.
JS: 6144 **S:** 6145–46

Barnum, P. T. — Fiction
S–Adult: 2946

Barrow, Clyde
S–Adult: 6185

Barton, Clara
J: 6382 **S–Adult:** 6383

Baseball
JS: 13151, 13164, 13167, 13176,
13179, 13186, 13189, 13193
JS–Adult: 13153, 13156 **S:** 13146,
13149, 13160, 13166, 13169, 13172,
13177–78, 13181, 13183, 13185,
13187–88, 13192 **S–Adult:** 6671,
13147, 13154, 13157–59, 13161–62,
13171, 13175, 13184

JS = Junior High/Senior High;   S = Senior High;   S–Adult = Senior High/Adult

Baseball — Biography
J: 6683 **JS:** 6640, 6642, 6658, 6661–62, 6668, 6672, 6675, 6681, 6684, 6687–88 **JS–Adult:** 6678, 6682 **S:** 6645, 6660, 6663–67, 6674, 6676–77, 6680, 6686, 6690 **S–Adult:** 6659, 6669–70, 6673, 6679, 6685, 6689

Baseball — Fiction
JS: 373, 733, 1365, 1871, 4559, 4562, 4566, 4569, 4572, 4587, 4590–91, 4598–600 **S:** 1533, 4593 **S–Adult:** 638, 1175, 4582

Baseball — Graphic novels
S–Adult: 2360

Baseball — History
JS: 13168, 13170, 13180, 13182, 13194 **JS–Adult:** 13150 **S:** 13148, 13152, 13155, 13163, 13172–73, 13195–97 **S–Adult:** 13165, 13190–91

Baseball — Japan
JS–Adult: 13198

Baseball — Statistics
S: 13174

Basie, Count
JS: 6001

Basketball
J: 13224 **JS:** 13201 **JS–Adult:** 13209 **S:** 6644, 13204–7, 13211–12, 13215–18, 13221 **S–Adult:** 5835, 13200, 13203, 13223, 13225

Basketball — Biography
JS: 6388, 6641, 6646, 6696–700, 6703–4 **S:** 6387, 6692–95 **S–Adult:** 6691, 6701–2, 6705

Basketball — Drugs
S: 10698

Basketball — Fiction
JS: 293, 528, 1100, 2344, 4556, 4567–68, 4571, 4583, 4585, 4594–95 **S:** 907, 1418, 3958, 4032, 4589

Basketball — History
JS: 13214, 13219 **S–Adult:** 13220

Basketball — Poetry
JS: 4982

Basketball — Women
JS: 13208, 13213, 13222 **S–Adult:** 13199, 13202

Bass (musical instrument)
JS: 7148

Basuto (African kingdom)
JS: 7969

Batboys
S: 13173

Bates, Daisy
JS: 6200

Bath (England) — Fiction
S–Adult: 3646

Bats (animal)
JS: 11947 **S:** 11959

Batswana (African people)
JS: 7955

Battles (military)
See also specific battles, e.g., Bull Run, battle of
S: 7399, 7420, 8538, 8665

Baughman, Michael
S: 8420

Bawden, Nina
JS: 5814

Bay City Rollers
S–Adult: 7178

Beaches
See Seashores

Beads and beadwork
S: 12850, 12868 **S–Adult:** 12851

Bearden, Romare
JS: 5729 **S:** 5730

Bears
See also specific kinds, e.g., Grizzly bears
JS: 11986 **JS–Adult:** 11980 **S:** 11978, 11981, 11985 **S–Adult:** 11977, 11979, 11982, 13261

Bears — Fiction
JS: 168, 173 **S:** 145, 507

Beat Generation
S–Adult: 6964

Beat Generation — Fiction
S: 948

Beatles (musical group)
JS: 6079, 6081 **S:** 6003–4, 6080 **S–Adult:** 6002, 6051

Beatles (musical group) — Biography
S: 6082

Beauty
JS: 10969, 10975

Beauty and the Beast **(musical)**
S: 7291

Beauty care
See also Grooming
S: 10958

Beauty contests — Fiction
JS: 3281

Beavers
S: 11958 **S–Adult:** 11957

Bees — Fiction
JS: 2007

Beetles
S: 12132, 12145

Behavior
J: 11324 **JS:** 11348 **S:** 11449 **S–Adult:** 9811

Behavior — Fiction
JS: 892

Behavioral problems — Children
JS: 11197

Behavioral problems — Young adults
S–Adult: 11322

Beiderbecke, Bix
JS: 6006 **S:** 6005

Beirut — Fiction
S–Adult: 2681

Belgian Congo — Fiction
S: 2487

Belgium — Biography
S: 7652

Bell, Alexander Graham
JS: 6537 **S:** 6536

Bell, Margaret.
S–Adult: 6915

Belleau Wood, Battle of
JS: 7617

Belli, Gioconda
S–Adult: 8243

Beloved **(motion picture)**
S: 7258

Beluga whales
S–Adult: 12210

Bengal tigers
JS–Adult: 12002

Benin (African kingdom)
JS: 7990

Benjamin, David
S–Adult: 6916

Beothuk (people) — Fiction
S–Adult: 2394

Beowulf
S–Adult: 4924

Beowulf **— Criticism**
S: 5309

Beowulf **— Fiction**
S: 1870

Berbers
JS: 7950

Berland-Hyatt, Felicia
S: 7650

Berlin — Fiction
S–Adult: 3993

Berlin — History
JS: 7637 **S:** 7785 **S–Adult:** 7683, 7805

Berlin Wall
JS: 8107

Bermuda — Fiction
S: 161

Bermuda Triangle
JS: 13004 **S:** 13008

Bernstein, Leonard
JS: 5979

Berra, Yogi
S: 6663

JS = Junior High/Senior High;   S = Senior High;   S–Adult = Senior High/Adult

JS = Junior High/Senior High;   S = Senior High;   S–Adult = Senior High/Adult

Bits (horses)
S: 13351

Bitton-Jackson, Livia
JS: 6917

Black Americans
See African Americans

Black authors — Fiction
JS: 423

Black Boy — Criticism
JS: 5361 S: 5390

Black Death
S–Adult: 7527

Black Elk (Native American)
S–Adult: 6468

Black Hawk (Sac chief)
S: 6384

Black Hawk War
S: 6384

Black magic — Fiction
S: 1680

Black Muslims — Biography
JS: 6249, 6251–52 S: 6250, 6253

Black Panthers (political organization)
JS: 8875, 9694

Blackfoot Indians
JS: 8477

Blackfoot Indians — Fiction
S: 2727

Blacks — Fiction
JS: 546, 2712 S: 419, 2484

Blacks — Great Britain
S: 6922

Blacks — History
S: 7911

Blackwell, Elizabeth
JS: 6538

Blake, William
S–Adult: 5731

Blanco, Jodee
S–Adult: 6919

Blessings
See Prayers

Blind
S–Adult: 11154

Blind — Biography
JS: 6014, 6141, 6466 S: 6475, 6495, 6804 S–Adult: 5682, 6488

Blind — Fiction
JS: 91, 1549, 1943 S: 946, 1357

Blish, Captain William
S–Adult: 5625

Blizzard of 1888
JS: 12433

Blizzards
S: 12430, 12437

Blizzards — Fiction
JS: 364

Blue (color)
J: 7096

Blue Nile
S–Adult: 7905

Blue whales
See also Whales
S: 12196

Blues (music)
JS: 7129 S: 7117, 7170
S–Adult: 7173, 7183

Blues (music) — Biography
S–Adult: 6070, 6138

Blume, Judy — Criticism
S: 5426

Bly, Nellie
JS: 5694 S: 6469–70

Board of Education *v.* Pico
JS: 10107

Boarding schools — Fiction
S–Adult: 1288

Boats and boating
See Sailing and boating; Ships and boats

Bobsledding
JS: 13075

Body decoration
JS: 10963, 12847

Body image
JS: 11136 S: 10959

Body painting
JS: 10976

Body piercing
JS: 10974 S: 10977

Bodybuilding
S: 13114

Bodybuilding — Biography
JS: 6118

Bodybuilding — Fiction
JS: 3962

Bodyguards — Careers
J: 10489

Bogues, Tyrone "Muggsy"
S: 6693

Bohr, Niels
JS: 6539

Bolivar, Simon
JS: 6897

Bomb squads — Careers
J: 10492

Bonaparte, Napoleon
JS: 6875 S–Adult: 6874

Bones
JS: 11021

Bonner, John Tyler
S–Adult: 6540

Bonney, William
JS: 6471

Bono, Chastity
S–Adult: 6920

Book illustration
S–Adult: 7110–11

Book making
See also Publishing
S–Adult: 12936

Book making — History
S: 5568 S–Adult: 5564

Book reports
JS: 10286

Book talks
JS: 10286

Books and reading
S–Adult: 12732

Books and reading — Fiction
S: 3496

Boomerangs
S: 8069

Boone, Daniel
JS: 6385–86

Borden, Lizzie
S: 9989

Borneo
S–Adult: 8051, 8070

Borneo — Fiction
JS: 2499, 2515

Bosch, Hieronymus
S: 5732

Bosnia
JS: 8083 S: 8079

Bosnia — Biography
S: 6837

Bosnia — Graphic novels
S: 2354

Bosnia — History
S: 6837

Boston (MA) — Fiction
S: 2942

Boston (MA) — Schools
S–Adult: 9620

Boston Massacre — Fiction
JS: 2762

Boston Red Sox (baseball team) — Biography
JS: 6642

Boston Tea Party
JS: 8529

Botany — Biography
S–Adult: 6591

Botany — Experiments and projects
JS: 11818

Botswana
JS: 7953, 7955, 7979 S–Adult: 7966

Botswana — Fiction
S: 2480

Bounty hunters
S–Adult: 9944

Bounty (ship)
S: 12478

JS = Junior High/Senior High;   S = Senior High;   S–Adult = Senior High/Adult

Bourgeois, Louise
JS: 5733

Bourke-White, Margaret
JS: 5734–37 S: 7088

Bowie, James — Fiction
S: 2877

Bowling
JS: 13108 S: 13078

Boxing
JS: 13243

Boxing — Biography
JS: 6707–8, 6710–11, 6713 S: 6652, 6706, 6712 S–Adult: 6709

Boxing — Fiction
JS: 500–1, 503, 4558, 4602 S: 502
S–Adult: 484

Boy Scouts
See also Scouts and scouting
JS: 11575 S–Adult: 11574

Boyfriends — Fiction
JS: 3308

Boyle, Father Greg
S: 6921

Boys — Adolescence
See also Coming of age
S–Adult: 11347

Boys — Fiction
JS: 1496, 4704

Boys Choir of Harlem
S: 7115

Bradbury, Ray — Criticism
S: 5384

Bradley, Bill
JS: 6388 S: 6387

Bradley, Guy
S–Adult: 6472

Brady, Mathew
JS: 5738 S: 8638

Bragg, Janet Harmon
S: 6473

Bragg, Rick
S: 5816

Brain and nervous system
JS: 10780, 10903, 10993, 10993,
10995–97, 11003–4, 11004, 11010,
11010 S: 10992, 10999, 11002,
11007–8, 11008–9, 11009, 11389
S–Adult: 10998, 11001

Brain damage
JS: 11003

Braithwaite, E. R.
S: 6922

Branding
S: 10977

Brandywine school (artists)
S–Adult: 7110

Brant, Joseph
S: 8420

Braque, Georges
S: 5739

Brave New World — Criticism
S: 5283

Bray, Rosemary
S: 5817

Brazil
JS: 8280, 8284, 12377 S: 8288

Brazile, Donna L.
S–Adult: 6474

Bread
S–Adult: 11839

Breast cancer
JS: 10816, 10884

Breast cancer — Fiction
S: 806

Breslin, Rosemary
S: 5818

Bridge (game)
S: 13285

Bridgers, Sue Ellen — Criticism
S: 5367

Bridgman, Laura
S: 6475 S–Adult: 11154

Britain, Battle of
See also World War II
JS: 7788

British Columbia
S: 12380

British Empire
JS: 8127

Broadcasting — Biography
JS: 6140, 6633 S: 6023, 6083
S–Adult: 6007, 6129

Broadcasting — Careers
JS: 10371

Brokaw, Tom
S–Adult: 6007

Brontë, Charlotte
S: 5264 S–Adult: 5819

Brontë, Charlotte — Criticism
See also Brontë family
JS: 5265 S: 5281

Brontë, Emily — Criticism
See also Brontë family
S: 5285

Brontë, Emily — Fiction
S: 3952

Brontë family
S: 5820

Brontë family — Criticism
JS: 5290

Bronx (NY)
S–Adult: 10086

Bronx (NY) — Biography
S–Adult: 8980

Brooklyn (NY) — Fiction
JS: 1170 S: 542, 1618, 2951

Brooks, Garth
JS: 6008

Brooks, Geraldine
S: 6923

Brooks, Gwendolyn
JS: 5821 S–Adult: 4954

Brooks, Gwendolyn — Criticism
S: 5502

Brother-sister relationships
S–Adult: 1112

Brothers and sisters
JS: 11555 S–Adult: 1175

Brothers and sisters — Fiction
JS: 296, 1039, 1172, 1430, 3076, 3660
S: 1555 S–Adult: 702, 709, 762, 784,
808, 894, 932, 1030, 2974

Brown, Claude
S: 5822

Brown, Dale
S: 6694

Brown, Jesse Leroy
S: 6476

Brown, John
JS: 6202, 8558, 8585

Brown, John — Fiction
JS: 2798

Brown, Tom, Jr.
S: 5626

Brown v. Board of Education
JS: 9482 S–Adult: 9341

Browning, Robert
JS: 4932

Bruchac, Joseph
S: 5823

Bryan, William Jennings
JS: 8812, 9296

Buck, Pearl S.
JS: 5824

Buck, Pearl S. — Criticism
S: 5358

Buddha
S–Adult: 6790

Buddhism
JS: 9064, 9074, 9078–79, 9085, 9096
S: 9089 S–Adult: 6790, 7013, 11361

Buddhism — Fiction
S: 2519

Budgets and budgeting
JS: 10554 S: 10233

Buffalo Soldiers
JS: 8740

Buffy the Vampire Slayer — Fiction
S–Adult: 3155

Buffy the Vampire Slayer (television series)
JS–Adult: 7275

Bugs Bunny cartoons
S: 7218

Building and construction
See also Architecture; and types of
buildings, e.g., Skyscrapers

JS = Junior High/Senior High;   S = Senior High;   S–Adult = Senior High/Adult

JS: 12576 **S:** 12573, 12578
S–Adult: 12566, 12574, 12579

**Building and construction —
Careers**
JS: 10479–80

Bulgaria
JS: 8086

Bulimia
See also Eating disorders
JS: 10744, 10776, 10805, 10817,
10819, 10836, 10840, 10871 **S:** 10788,
11146

Bull Run, Battle of
JS: 8630

Bull Run, Battle of — Fiction
JS: 2818

Bull Run, Second Battle of
JS: 8675

Bullies
S–Adult: 11472

Bullies — Fiction
JS: 1173, 1272, 1343, 1486, 4563
S: 492, 682 **S–Adult:** 1011

Bunche, Ralph
JS: 6390 **S:** 6391 **S–Adult:** 6389

Burch, Jennings Michael
S: 6925

Burial customs
JS: 9939

Buried treasure
JS: 8119

Buried treasure — Fiction
S: 128

Burnett, Carol
S: 6009

Burns, Anthony
JS: 6203

Burr, Aaron — Fiction
S–Adult: 2790

Bush, George H. W.
JS: 6285–87

Bush, George W.
JS: 6289, 9238 **S:** 9359
S–Adult: 6288

Business ethics
S: 10219

Butterflies and moths
See also specific breeds, e.g.,
Monarch butterflies
JS: 12151–52 **S–Adult:** 7351,
12148–50, 12153–54

Butterflies and moths — Fiction
JS: 175

Buxton, Angela
S: 13452

Byrd Antarctic Expedition
S: 8321

Byron, Lord
S: 5825

Byzantine Empire
S: 7555

Byzantium — Fiction
S–Adult: 1855

C

Cable television
JS: 6634

Cable television — Careers
S: 10535

Caddying (golf)
S: 13325

Caesar, Julius
JS: 6818–19, 7512

Caffeine
JS: 10563–64

Cahill, Tim
S: 5627

Cahuilla Indians — Fiction
JS: 1932

Cake decorating
S: 12820

Calder, Alexander
S: 5740

Calendars
See also Time
S: 12514

Calendars — Fiction
S: 2658

California — Fiction
JS: 116, 174, 1294, 2807, 2890 **S:** 79,
183, 462, 554, 1616, 2885, 3182, 3426,
3682, 3846 **S–Adult:** 851, 2953

California — History
JS: 7206, 8998

California — Poetry
S: 5026

California Gold Rush
See Gold Rush (California)

California Trail
JS: 8707

***The Call of the Wild* — Criticism**
S: 5355

Calligraphy
JS: 12735 **S:** 12740, 12746–47

Calvin, John
JS: 6820

Cambodia
S–Adult: 7862

Cambodian Americans
JS: 9716

Camcorders
JS: 12643, 12647

Cameroon
JS: 7921, 7991

Campaign financing (politics)
S: 9347

Camps and camping
JS: 13301 **S–Adult:** 13257

Camps and camping — Fiction
JS: 17, 321, 747, 1301, 1409, 1471,
3695, 3804, 4039 **S:** 2351
S–Adult: 77

Camus, Albert
S: 5826

Canada
JS: 8234 **S–Adult:** 8241, 13279

Canada — Biography
JS: 6731 **S:** 5909 **S–Adult:** 5665

Canada — Fiction
J: 2702 **JS:** 44, 55, 69, 84, 168, 184,
300, 332, 454, 732, 870, 1060, 1420,
1613, 2739, 3060, 3281, 3881 **S:** 75,
744, 936, 1071, 1073, 1513, 2694, 2700,
3847 **S–Adult:** 491, 709, 745, 2394

Canada — History
JS: 2796, 8237, 8239 **S:** 8242, 8512

Cancer
JS: 6949, 10734, 10747, 10769, 10781,
10872 **S:** 6988, 10880

Cancer — Fiction
JS: 279, 481, 635, 943, 958, 1411,
1548, 3982–83 **S:** 644, 787, 952
S–Adult: 1235

***Candide* — Criticism**
S: 5323

Candle making
S–Adult: 12729

Canoes and canoeing
JS: 13395, 13410 **S:** 13400, 13402,
13407–8

Canoes and canoeing — Fiction
S: 68

***Canterbury Tales* — Criticism**
S: 5277, 5287

Cantwell, Mary
S: 6926

**Canyonlands National Park —
Fiction**
JS: 71

Cape Cod Baseball League
S–Adult: 13157

Cape Cod (MA)
S–Adult: 12080

Cape Cod (MA) — Fiction
JS: 592 **S:** 962, 3427
S–Adult: 1923, 2928

Cape Horn — History
S–Adult: 8294

Capital punishment
See Death penalty

Capitalism
S: 10223

Capone, Al
S: 6477

JS = Junior High/Senior High; S = Senior High; S–Adult = Senior High/Adult

Card collecting
S: 12978

Card games
JS: 13296 S: 13286–87, 13290

Card tricks
See also Tricks
S: 12924, 12927

Careers
See also Vocational guidance; and
specific fields, e.g., Economics and
business — Careers
J: 10368, 10409, 10426, 10452, 10459,
10487, 10489, 10501, 10529–30, 10544
JS: 10246, 10369, 10371, 10375,
10380, 10384–86, 10398, 10402, 10404,
10406–8, 10413–16, 10420–21,
10431–36, 10439, 10442, 10444,
10447–48, 10450–51, 10454–55, 10458,
10461–62, 10464–65, 10477, 10479–81,
10484–86, 10493, 10495, 10499–500,
10502, 10505, 10511, 10522–24,
10532–34, 10537–38, 10540, 10546
S: 10373, 10383, 10417, 10424, 10483,
10506–7, 10509, 10516, 10519–21,
10526 S–Adult: 10361

Careers — Hispanic Americans
S: 10393

Careers — Motion pictures
JS: 7234

Careers — Science
S–Adult: 12319

Careers — Sports
JS: 10446

Careers — Sports medicine
S: 10510

Careers — Women
S: 10357, 10401

Carey, Mariah
J: 6010 JS: 6011

Caribbean Islands
JS: 8270

Caribbean Islands — Cookbooks
J: 12802 S–Adult: 12769

Caribbean Islands — Fiction
JS: 609 S: 700, 931, 1262

Caribbean Sea — Fiction
S–Adult: 2707

Carlos the Jackal
S–Adult: 6898

Carnegie, Andrew
JS: 6609 S–Adult: 6610

Carols
See Christmas — Songs and carols

Carpentry
S: 12989, 12991 S–Adult: 12988

Carroll, Jim
S–Adult: 6927

Carroll, Lewis
S–Adult: 5827

Carroll, Lewis — Criticism
S: 5282

Carroll, Lewis — Fiction
S–Adult: 2650

Cars
See Automobiles

Carson, Kit
S: 6478–79

Carson, Rachel
JS: 6541

Carter, Eddie
S–Adult: 6480

Carter, Jennifer
S: 5628

Carter, Jimmy
JS: 6292 S: 6291 S–Adult: 6290,
9100

Carter, Rubin "Hurricane"
S: 6712

Carthage
JS: 7516

Cartoonists
S: 5758 S–Adult: 5581

Cartoonists — Biography
JS: 5788 S–Adult: 5787

Cartoons
JS: 7092, 7099, 12879, 12886, 12897
S: 7220, 12883, 12888, 12891, 12899
S–Adult: 5581, 5585

Carver, George Washington
S–Adult: 6542

Cary, Elizabeth
JS: 6821

Cary, Lorene
S: 6928

Cash, Johnny
S–Adult: 6012

Cassatt, Mary
S: 5741

Castles
See also Middle Ages
J: 7541 JS: 7025, 7525, 7545 S: 7540

Castles — Fiction
JS: 3261

Castro, Fidel
JS: 6899 S: 6902 S–Adult: 6900–1,
8276

Catalpa (ship)
S–Adult: 7587

Catastrophes — Fiction
S: 4496

The Catcher in the Rye — Criticism
JS: 5359, 5399

Cathedrals
See also Middle Ages
JS: 7024

Cather, Willa
JS: 5828–29

Catherine the Great
JS: 6823 S–Adult: 6822

Catholicism
S: 4780 S–Adult: 9104, 9108

Catholicism — Biography
JS: 6821 S–Adult: 6860

Catholicism — Fiction
S–Adult: 1487

Catholicism — History
JS: 7565 S–Adult: 9109

Cats
See also Big cats
JS: 12252 JS–Adult: 12250, 12264
S: 12246–49, 12251, 12253–55,
12257–58, 12260–62, 12265, 12267
S–Adult: 7442, 12240, 12256, 12263,
12266

Cats — Behavior
JS: 12259

Cats — Fiction
JS: 1202, 1683, 2219 S: 166, 1940,
1971–72, 2099, 2118, 2168, 3380, 3685,
4416 S–Adult: 1678, 2098, 3343,
3504, 3686

Cats — Folklore
S: 5060

Cats — Poetry
S: 4930

Cattle
S–Adult: 11955

Catwoman — Fiction
S–Adult: 2302

Cavalho, Solomon
JS: 8709

Cavalry (U.S.) — History
S–Adult: 8765

Caves
S–Adult: 12370

Caves — Fiction
S: 143

Caving
S–Adult: 6961

Celts
JS: 7411

Celts — Fiction
S: 1806 S–Adult: 2410

Celts — Mythology
JS: 5149, 5154

Censorship
JS: 9508, 10102, 10107, 10115–17,
10121 S: 9212, 10100, 10104–5, 10113

Censorship — Children
S–Adult: 10109

Censorship — Fiction
JS: 1184, 1578, 1596, 1603

Censorship — Internet
S: 12599 S–Adult: 10111, 10111

Central African Republic
JS: 7921

Central America — Fiction
S: 1595

Central America — History
S: 8244, 8265 S–Adult: 8269

Central Intelligence Agency (U.S.)
JS: 9184, 9244

Cerebral palsy
S: 6986

Cerebral palsy — Fiction
JS: 970, 1007

Cezanne, Paul
S: 5742

Chaco Canyon
JS: 7385

Chad
JS: 7892

Chagall, Marc
JS: 5744 S: 5743

Challenger (space shuttle)
JS: 11719

Chambers, Whittaker
JS: 9263

Chancellorsville, Battle of
JS: 8611 S: 8633 S–Adult: 8674

Chaplin, Charlie
JS: 6013

Charge of the Light Brigade
JS: 7575

Charities
JS: 10133

Charities — Fiction
S–Adult: 405

Charlemagne
JS: 6824, 7566

Charles, Ray
JS: 6014

Charles II, King of England — Fiction
S: 2565

Charleston, Siege of
JS: 8612

Chaucer, Geoffrey — Criticism
S: 5277, 5437

Chavez, Cesar
JS: 6204–5

Che, Sunny
S–Adult: 6929

Cheating — Fiction
JS: 1284, 3395 S: 493

Chechnya — Memoirs
S–Adult: 6914

Checkers
JS: 13291 S: 13295

Cheerleading
S: 13109 S–Adult: 13092

Cheerleading — Fiction
S: 3726

Cheetahs
JS: 11987

Chekhov, Anton — Criticism
S: 5240, 5432 S–Adult: 5438

Chemical dependency
See also Drugs and drug abuse
JS: 10715

Chemical weapons
JS: 12705, 12713

Chemistry
JS: 12339 S: 12336, 12338

Chemistry — Biography
S: 6603

Chemistry — Dictionaries
JS: 12333

Chemistry — Experiments and projects
JS: 12334, 12337, 12340

Chemistry — History
S: 12330, 12332, 12335

Cherokee Indians
JS: 8445, 8459

Cherokee Indians — Biography
S: 6424, 6450

Cherokee Indians — Fiction
S: 1264, 2718 S–Adult: 2719

Cherokee Indians — History
JS: 8476 S–Adult: 8441, 8473

Chesnutt, Charles
JS: 5830

Chess
JS: 13289 S: 13292–94

Chess — Fiction
JS: 314

Cheyenne Indians
JS: 8469

Cheyenne Indians — Fiction
S: 2725

Cheyenne Indians — History
S: 8475

Chicago (IL) — Fiction
JS: 2932 S: 586, 2949, 3307
S–Adult: 432, 1037, 1147

Chicago (IL) — History
JS: 8754 S: 6477

Chicago Seven
JS: 8856

Chicanos — Poetry
S: 5026

Chickamauga, Battle of
JS: 8613

Chicken pox
JS: 10853

Chickens
S–Adult: 12053, 12064

Chief Joseph (Nez Perce Indian)
JS: 6392, 8422

Child, Lydia Maria
JS: 6206

Child abuse
See also Child sexual abuse; Physical abuse
JS: 9798, 9929, 9973, 11512, 11517–18, 11520, 11523, 11536
S: 9814, 11063, 11296, 11321, 11522
S–Adult: 9816

Child abuse — Fiction
JS: 122, 293, 654, 798, 816, 871, 876, 908, 941, 1208, 1482, 1498 S: 939, 1512, 2688 S–Adult: 972

Child care
JS: 9853, 11180, 11189, 11191, 11193, 11195, 11198, 11531 S: 11166, 11202, 11204 S–Adult: 11218

Child care — Careers
JS: 10369 S: 10377–78

Child care — History
S: 11177

Child labor
JS: 8758, 9798, 9833 S: 9809, 9826, 9854

Child labor — Biography
JS: 6805 S–Adult: 6230

Child labor — History
JS: 8752

Child sexual abuse
S: 11296, 11321

Child sexual abuse — Fiction
See also Child abuse; Sexual abuse
S–Adult: 752

Childbirth
See also Birth
S: 11182, 11190

Childbirth — Poetry
S: 4911

Childhood
JS: 4642

Childhood — History
S–Adult: 8715

Children — Courts
S–Adult: 10110

Children — Diseases and illnesses
JS: 11092

Children — Exploitation
JS: 9477, 9798

Children — Fiction
JS: 30

Children — Middle Ages
S–Adult: 7556

Children — Poetry
JS: 4938, 4988 S: 4911

Children — Rights
JS: 9267, 9397, 9438, 9477

Children — United States
JS: 8411

Children — United States — History
S–Adult: 8403, 8791

Children — Violence
JS: 9995

JS = Junior High/Senior High;   S = Senior High;   S–Adult = Senior High/Adult

Children — War
S–Adult: 9192

Children — World War II
S: 7671

Children's literature — Biography
JS: 5711, 5834, 5960

Children's literature — Criticism
S: 5250

Children's literature — History and criticism
S: 5426 S–Adult: 5394

Children's rights
See Children — Rights

Chile — Biography
JS: 5917

Chimpanzees
JS: 6576, 11964 S–Adult: 11971

China
JS: 5861, 6803, 8003, 8009 S: 8004, 8012, 8019–20 S–Adult: 8002, 8015

China — Animals
S: 12035

China — Baby adoption
S–Adult: 11505

China — Biography
JS: 5824, 6814–15 S: 6806
S–Adult: 6943, 7014

China — Cookbooks
J: 12845 JS: 12807

China — Fiction
JS: 1374, 1584, 1677, 2334, 2398, 2500, 2536, 2552–53 S: 24, 2498, 2526
S–Adult: 2502, 2523, 2533–34, 2542, 2550

China — Folklore
JS: 5089 S: 5087

China — History
JS: 7448, 7567, 8001, 8010–11
S: 5862, 6806, 8007–8, 8016–17
S–Adult: 8005, 8013, 8018

China — Memoirs
S–Adult: 6934, 6978

China — Poetry
JS: 5049

China — Women
S–Adult: 8021

China-Japan War — Fiction
S: 2498

China-U.S. relations
See U.S.-China relations

Chinese Americans
See also Asian Americans
JS: 9704, 9711, 9717, 9719
S–Adult: 9706, 10901

Chinese Americans — Biography
JS: 5940, 6975

Chinese Americans — Fiction
JS: 532, 590, 1374, 2924, 4732
S: 492–93, 534, 573, 886, 2914
S–Adult: 572

Chinese Americans — Poetry
S: 4863

Chinese Canadians — Biography
S–Adult: 6931

Chippewa Indians — Fiction
JS: 548, 1092

Chiropractic — Careers
S: 10516

Chisholm Trail
JS: 8731

Chivalry, Age of
S: 5117

Cho, Margaret
S–Adult: 6015

Chocolate
S: 12840 S–Adult: 11833

Chocolate — Manufacture
S: 10213

Choctaw Indians — Fiction
S: 2872

Choctaw Indians — Folklore
JS: 5133

Choirs (music)
S: 7115

Chong, Gordon H.
JS: 5745

Choquette, Sonia
S–Adult: 6930

Choreography
S: 7214

Choreography — Biography
JS: 6050 S: 6031 S–Adult: 7216

Choy, Wayson
S–Adult: 6931

Christian life — Fiction
JS: 1242

Christian Science
JS: 9122

Christianity
JS: 9111, 9119 S: 9063, 9097, 9110, 9112, 11414, 11438, 11440
S–Adult: 9057, 9099

Christianity — Biography
JS: 6820

Christianity — Fiction
JS: 981, 1131, 2413 S: 852, 3002, 3055 S–Adult: 1897

Christianity — History
JS: 8456

Christianity — Orthodox
JS: 9103

Christie, Agatha
S: 5831

Christie, Agatha — Criticism
S: 5294, 5311

Christmas
J: 9114 S: 9110, 9117, 9121
S–Adult: 4616, 9100

Christmas — Carols
See Christmas — Songs and carols

Christmas — Fiction
J: 252, 4687 JS: 212–13, 1115, 1309
S: 610, 4638 S–Adult: 1338, 4677, 4734

Christmas — Greece
J: 9101

Christmas — Plays
JS: 4749

Christmas — Poetry
JS: 4872

Christmas — Songs and carols
JS: 7204 S–Adult: 7203

Christmas — Wales
S: 4942

A Christmas Carol — Criticism
S: 5280

The Chronicles of Narnia — Criticism
S: 5263

Church and state — United States
See also Freedom of religion
JS: 9266, 9295 S: 9209

Churchill, Sir Winston
S: 6825 S–Adult: 8842

Cicero
S–Adult: 6826

Cinque, Joseph — Fiction
S: 2795

Circulatory system
See also Heart
JS: 10985, 11012 S: 11011

Circuses
JS: 7290 S–Adult: 7283

Circuses — Biography
JS: 6144 S: 6136, 6145–46

Circuses — Fiction
JS: 956, 1635 S: 100 S–Adult: 378, 1441, 1469, 3244

Cities and city life
See also names of specific cities, e.g., Boston (MA)
J: 12577 S: 10208, 10210–11
S–Adult: 10207

Cities and city life — Fiction
JS: 4724

Cities and city life — Nature study
S–Adult: 11803

Civil disobedience
JS: 10112

Civil engineering
JS: 12558

Civil liberties
JS: 9425

Civil rights
See also names of civil rights leaders, e.g., King, Martin Luther, Jr.; and specific civil rights, e.g., Human rights; Women's rights

JS = Junior High/Senior High; S = Senior High; S–Adult = Senior High/Adult

1109

JS = Junior High/Senior High;   S = Senior High;   S–Adult = Senior High/Adult

Coast Guard (U.S.) — Careers
S: 10389

Cobain, Kurt
S–Adult: 6018

Cocaine
See also Drugs and drug abuse
JS: 10620, 10650 S: 10622

Cochise (Apache chief)
S: 6393

Cock fighting — Fiction
S: 770

Codes and ciphers
JS: 5539 S: 5553

Codes and ciphers — Careers
J: 10418

Cody, Buffalo Bill
S: 6394

Coelacanth
S–Adult: 12181

Coen, Joel and Ethan
S–Adult: 7221

Coffee
S: 12548

Cohn, Marthe
S–Adult: 7669

Coin collecting
S: 12979

Cold (disease)
JS: 10795

Cold fusion
S: 12540

Cold War
JS: 7863, 7869, 8167, 8905
S–Adult: 7872

Cold War — Documents
S: 7885

Cold War — Fiction
S–Adult: 348, 875, 3398

Coleridge, Samuel Taylor
JS: 4926

Collage
S: 12939

Collecting and collections
S: 12979

College application essay
S: 10350

College life — Fiction
S: 1102

College studies — Fiction
S–Adult: 3882

Colleges and universities
S: 10323, 10331, 10337–38, 10343, 10349 S–Adult: 10329, 10345–46, 10712

Colleges and universities — Academic guidance
S: 10353 S–Adult: 10347

Colleges and universities — Admissions
JS: 10248, 10340 S: 10328, 10334–35, 10342, 10350–53 S–Adult: 10333, 10354

Colleges and universities — Admissions — Humor and satire
S–Adult: 10341

Colleges and universities — African American
S–Adult: 10336

Colleges and universities — Fiction
JS: 959, 1101, 1350, 3389 S: 313, 1479, 3322 S–Adult: 392, 552, 1260, 1404, 1416, 4005, 5103

Colleges and universities — Financial aid
S–Adult: 10344, 10355

Colleges and universities — World Wide Web
S: 10332

Colombia — Fiction
JS: 2701

Colombia — History
JS: 8281

Colonial period (U.S.)
J: 8513 JS: 8506, 8510 S: 8500, 8507, 8509, 8512 S–Adult: 8497, 8504

Colonial period (U.S.) — Biography
JS: 6221, 6404–5 S: 6403
S–Adult: 6406

Colonial period (U.S.) — Documents
S: 8498

Colonial period (U.S.) — Fiction
JS: 2740–41, 2746, 2748, 2750–54, 2756, 2762, 2769 S: 250, 2717–18, 2744–45, 2755 S–Adult: 2743, 2747

Colonial period (U.S.) — History
JS: 8505, 8514–15 S: 8501–3

Colonial period (U.S.) — Speeches
JS: 8536

The Color Purple — Criticism
S: 5329

Colorado
S: 8965

Colorado — Fiction
JS: 1435, 3267, 3656 S–Adult: 2886, 3743

Colorado River
S–Adult: 8967

Colors
S–Adult: 7447

Colors — Fiction
S–Adult: 2506

Coltrane, John
JS: 6019–20

Columbus, Christopher
JS: 5630–31 S: 5629

Columbus, Christopher — Fiction
S: 4176

Comanche Indians
JS: 8462, 8478 S: 8555

Comanche Indians — Biography
S: 6438

Comanche Indians — Fiction
JS: 2895

Comedians
S: 7236

Comedians — Biography
JS: 6021, 6049, 6091, 6096, 6133
S: 5991, 6009, 6022, 6115
S–Adult: 6015

Comedy — Fiction
S–Adult: 551

Comets
S: 11739–40, 11744–45
S–Adult: 11742

Comets — Fiction
S: 4202, 4527

Comic books
JS: 2307, 5570, 5573, 5580, 10192, 12889 S: 5578, 7825, 12887–88, 12893
S–Adult: 282, 2267, 2341, 5172, 5566, 5576, 5583, 5589–90, 5594, 5609, 6236, 7103, 7410

Comic books — Biography
S: 5718

Comic books — Fiction
JS: 3478 S: 2374 S–Adult: 2094, 2337

Comic books — History
S–Adult: 5585, 5612

Comic strips
JS: 5601, 11326 S–Adult: 5581, 5586

Comic strips — Fiction
S–Adult: 2297

Coming of age
See also Adolescence; Puberty
JS: 10155 S: 3838 S–Adult: 10163

Coming of age — Biography
S–Adult: 5855

Coming of age — Fiction
JS: 427, 1179, 1324, 1495, 4714
S: 541, 1241, 3649 S–Adult: 304, 341, 386, 431, 488, 594, 681, 827, 955, 1029–30, 1035, 1145, 1147, 1149, 1166, 1187, 1205, 1224, 1229, 1248, 1265, 1287–88, 1292, 1311, 1330, 1338, 1360, 1380, 1388, 1396, 1399, 1412, 1468, 1470, 1489, 1499, 1539, 1593, 2306, 2310, 2367, 2505, 2540, 2626, 2662, 4278, 4641

Commandos
S: 9375

Commercial art
S: 12878 S–Adult: 7091

Communication
JS: 5546, 10311 S: 12604

Communications — Careers
S: 10471, 10541

JS = Junior High/Senior High; S = Senior High; S–Adult = Senior High/Adult

Communism
JS: 6423, 8107, 8155, 8905, 8908, 9263
S: 8160, 10224

Communism — Biography
JS: 6886

Communism — China
S: 8014

Communism — Fiction
S–Adult: 875

Communism — History
JS: 8171

Community service
S: 10135

Compasses
S–Adult: 7387

Compassion
JS: 11376

Competition
S: 11412

Composers — Biography
JS: 5986–88 S: 5978, 5985, 5989, 7229

Composers — Motion pictures
S–Adult: 7243

Compulsive behavior
See also Mental disorders
JS: 11049, 11104

Compulsive eating
See Eating disorders

Computer graphics
JS: 12586, 12613 S: 12954

Computers
See also specific topics, e.g., Internet; World Wide Web
J: 12609, 12611 JS: 5567, 10218, 12583–84, 12601, 12625, 12628
S: 5595, 12585, 12588–89, 12591–92, 12596–97, 12600, 12604, 12608, 12614, 12617, 12621–22 S–Adult: 12405, 12582, 12607, 12615, 12619

Computers — Biography
JS: 6522, 6616, 6621 S–Adult: 6622, 12616

Computers — Careers
JS: 10534, 10536–38, 10540, 10543
S–Adult: 10539

Computers — Censorship
S–Adult: 10111

Computers — Crime
JS: 12606

Computers — Fiction
JS: 3416 S: 2050, 4114, 4175, 4200, 4216, 4280, 4357 S–Adult: 3774–75

Computers — History
JS: 6522, 12594 S–Adult: 6534

Computers — Medicine
JS: 10920

Computers — Report writing
JS: 10296

Computers — Social issues
JS: 12605

Computers — Software
S: 12618

Computers — Women
JS: 10543

Con games
See also Crime and criminals
JS: 10048

Concentration camps
See Holocaust

Conduct of life
JS: 11330

Conduct of life — Fiction
S–Adult: 3209

Cone, David
S–Adult: 13147

Conflict management
JS: 11359

Confucianism
S: 9045

Congo
JS: 7921, 7934 S–Adult: 7924

Congress
S–Adult: 9250

Congress (U.S.)
See also Government (U.S.); Senate (U.S.)
JS: 9243, 9253 S: 9246

Congress (U.S.) — Biography
JS: 6178, 6388, 6411–12, 6422–23
S: 6387, 6413, 6459

Congressional committees
S: 9246

Conquerors — Biography
JS: 6769

Conquistadors
S–Adult: 8269

Conquistadors — Fiction
JS: 2733

Conrad, Joseph — Criticism
S: 5302, 5304

Conroy, Pat
S–Adult: 5835

Conroy, Pat — Criticism
S: 5341

Conservation
See also Ecology and environment; Pollution
J: 9870 JS: 9881, 9890–91, 9904
S: 9868, 9884, 9887 S–Adult: 9894, 9909, 11788, 11803, 12095, 12110, 12389

Conservation — Biography
JS: 6508, 6541, 6594, 6775 S: 9865
S–Adult: 6593, 6595

Conservation — History
JS: 9889

Constellations
See also Stars
JS: 11758–59

Constitution (U.S.)
See also Government (U.S.)
JS: 8371, 9204, 9207, 9210–11
S: 8520, 8541, 9203, 9205–6, 9209, 9212, 9337 S–Adult: 9214, 9216, 9221

Constitution (U.S.) — Amendments
JS: 9202, 9213, 9219, 9222 S: 9215, 9217

Constitutional Convention, 1787
S: 8520

Construction
See Building and construction

Consumer credit
S: 10557

Consumer protection
S: 10231

Consumer protection — Biography
JS: 6429–31

Consumerism
S: 10231 S–Adult: 10232

Consumerism — Fiction
JS: 393

Contests
JS: 10267

Contraception
S–Adult: 11278

Conway, Eustace
S–Adult: 6932

Conway, Jill Ker
S: 6816

Cook, Captain James
JS: 5633–34 S–Adult: 5632

Cook, Frederick
JS: 8322 ·

Cookbooks
JS: 11132, 12791, 12823, 12828, 12834
S: 8716, 10158, 11841, 12755, 12758, 12761–67, 12770, 12782–86, 12789, 12793, 12803–6, 12810–12, 12814, 12817, 12820, 12825, 12829, 12838–40, 12842 S–Adult: 12757, 12769, 12772–73, 12776–77, 12788, 12800, 12821, 12827, 12830–31, 12833, 12835, 12843

Cookbooks — Africa
S–Adult: 12797

Cookbooks — China
S–Adult: 12844

Cookbooks — Civil War (U.S.)
JS: 12787 S: 8681

Cookbooks — Ethnic
J: 12754, 12756, 12768, 12778, 12780–81, 12796, 12798, 12801–2, 12813, 12815–16, 12818–19, 12822, 12836–37, 12845–46 JS: 12807, 12809
S: 12760, 12795 S–Adult: 12832, 12844

Cookbooks — France
JS: 12808

Cookbooks — Frontier life (U.S.)
JS: 12792

JS = Junior High/Senior High; S = Senior High; S–Adult = Senior High/Adult

Cookbooks — Hispanic Americans
S–Adult: 10161

Cookbooks — Vegan
S–Adult: 12759

Cookbooks — Vegetarian
S–Adult: 12771, 12774–75, 12790,
12794, 12824, 12826

Cookies
S: 12814, 12838 S–Adult: 12757

Cooking
See also Cookbooks
S: 12779, 12799, 12817, 12917
S–Adult: 12777

Cooking — Biography
S: 6990

Cooking — Careers
S: 10419

Cooking — Fiction
JS: 3924

Cooking — History
JS: 12841 S: 8716

Coolidge, Calvin
JS: 6298

Cooper, Cynthia
S: 6695

Cooper, Gordon
S–Adult: 5635

Cooperation
S: 11924

Copts
JS: 7950

Coral reefs
S: 12167, 12171–72

Cormier, Robert — Criticism
JS: 5381 S: 5343

Cornwall — Fiction
S–Adult: 3984

Corporations
JS: 9349 S: 10222

Corporations — Executives
JS: 10212

Corporations — Power
JS: 9349

Cortes, Hernando
JS: 8256, 8262 S: 5636

Corvette (automobile)
JS: 12670

Cosby, Bill
JS: 6021 S: 6022

Cosmetics
S: 10971

Cosmetics — Biography
J: 6635 S: 6580

Cosmetics — Careers
JS: 10398

Cosmetics — History
S: 10970

Cosmology
JS: 11671 S: 11703
S–Adult: 11655, 11659

Costumes — Folk
S: 12872

Costumes — History
S: 12853, 12859, 12871, 12873

Costumes and costume making
See also Clothing and dress
JS: 12860, 12870 S: 12854, 12862,
12869, 12873

Cougars
JS: 11988 S: 11992, 11998
S–Adult: 12241

Counterterrorism
See also Homeland security;
Terrorism
JS: 10187

Country music
S: 7141

Country music — Biography
JS: 6008 S: 7139 S–Adult: 6012,
6034, 6139

Country music — History
S: 7169

Courage
S–Adult: 11337

Courage — Fiction
JS: 3792

Courlander, Harold
JS: 5836

Courtroom trials
JS: 8558, 9261, 9263–64, 9271,
9282–84, 9290, 9295–96, 9301–4, 9309,
9313, 9315, 9320, 9325–27, 9331, 9336,
9338–39, 9342, 9409, 9416, 9482,
10107, 10112 S: 9312
S–Adult: 10006

Courts — Vermont
S–Adult: 9319

Courts (U.S.)
See also Jury system; Supreme Court
(U.S.)
JS: 9269, 9277, 9310, 9315, 9332, 9422
S: 9272, 9287

Courts (U.S.) — History
S–Adult: 9294

Cowboys
S: 8700, 8733

Cowboys — Fiction
JS: 137 S: 34, 2898

Cowboys — History
JS: 8720, 8736 S–Adult: 8236, 8418

Cowgirls
S–Adult: 8705

Cows
See Cattle

Coyotes
S–Adult: 12014

Crack (drug)
See also Cocaine; Drugs and drug
abuse
JS: 10620, 10650 S: 10622

Crafts
See also specific crafts, e.g., Paper
crafts
JS: 12727, 12737 S: 9117, 12739,
12741, 12744, 12861

Crafts — Seashells
S–Adult: 12731

Crane, Kathleen
S–Adult: 6543

Crane, Stephen
S–Adult: 5837

Crane, Stephen — Criticism
S: 5342, 5372, 5420

Cranes (birds)
S–Adult: 12057

Crazy Horse
JS: 6395–96, 6398 S: 6397

Crean, Tom
S–Adult: 5637

Creation — Mythology
JS: 5072 S: 5155

Creationism
JS: 7363, 7366 S–Adult: 9052

Crichton, Michael — Criticism
S: 5422

Crick, Francis
S: 10937

Crime and criminals
JS: 6514, 9274, 9311, 9315, 9322,
9344, 9950, 9955–56, 9970, 9997,
10018–19, 10021, 10029, 10035–36,
10038, 10048, 10058, 10061–63, 10649,
10675, 12606 S: 9953, 9957, 9963,
9966, 9971, 9983, 9989–90,
9999–10000, 10002, 10004, 10011,
10022, 10037, 10041, 10051, 10057,
10060 S–Adult: 5924, 8561, 9944,
9951, 9962, 9965, 9988, 10006, 10027,
10042, 10049, 10053, 10055–56, 10064,
10068

Crime and criminals — Biography
JS: 6504 S: 6477 S–Adult: 6185

Crime and criminals — Fiction
JS: 849, 933, 3537, 4558 S: 130, 390,
882, 900, 1314, 1383, 3581
S–Adult: 1604, 2964, 3509, 3559

Crime and criminals — History
S: 9945

Crime and criminals — Juvenile
JS: 9310

Crime and criminals — Victims
S–Adult: 10065

***Crime and Punishment* — Criticism**
S: 5313, 5319

Crime laboratories
S–Adult: 10027

Crimean War
JS: 7575–76

JS = Junior High/Senior High;   S = Senior High;   S–Adult = Senior High/Adult

1113

Criminal justice
JS: 9277, 9310–11, 9330, 10021, 10029
S: 9272, 9335, 9343, 9957, 10000, 10004, 10022 S–Adult: 9273, 9650, 10007

Criminals
See Crime and criminals

Crocodiles
See Alligators and crocodiles

Cromwell, Oliver
JS: 8130

Cronkite, Walter
S: 6023

Cross-country skiing
JS: 13415, 13421

Cross culturalism
See Interculturalism; Multiculturalism

Cross-stitching
S: 12966 S–Adult: 12961

Crow Indians
S–Adult: 13158

The Crucible — Criticism
S: 5501, 5530

Crusades
JS: 7531, 7560 S: 7562, 7564
S–Adult: 7546

Crusades — Fiction
JS: 2438, 2441, 2469 S: 2443
S–Adult: 2589, 2619

Crutcher, Chris
JS: 5838–39

Cryptograms and cryptography
See Codes and ciphers

Cryptology — Careers
J: 10418

Cub Scouts
See Scouts and scouting

Cuba
JS: 6899, 8277 S: 8275
S–Adult: 8271, 8274, 8276

Cuba — Biography
JS: 5992, 6899, 6903–4 S: 6902
S–Adult: 6669, 6900–1, 6938

Cuba — Fiction
JS: 9 S: 92 S–Adult: 741, 2697

Cuba — History
S: 9738

Cuban-American relations
S: 8275

Cuban Americans
See also Hispanic Americans
JS: 9735, 9745 S: 9738
S–Adult: 9728

Cuban Americans — Fiction
JS: 536, 3874 S: 316 S–Adult: 515, 741

Cuban Missile Crisis
JS: 7864, 8871

Cults
JS: 9154, 9156, 9158, 9161–62
S: 9157, 9159 S–Adult: 9160

Cults — Fiction
JS: 159, 301, 317, 1560 S: 1134, 3610

Cults — History
JS: 9155

Cultural anthropology
S: 11333

Cultural Revolution (China)
JS: 6803 S–Adult: 8018

Cultural Revolution (China) — Fiction
S–Adult: 2502, 2542

Cultural values
JS: 10122 S: 8900

Culture
JS: 9855

Curie, Marie
JS: 6544 S–Adult: 6545

Curiosities
JS: 13005, 13037, 13052, 13060, 13065
JS–Adult: 13028 S: 13010, 13013, 13017, 13021, 13024, 13029, 13031
S–Adult: 7389, 13048

Curiosities — Science
S–Adult: 11596

Curtis, Edward S.
JS: 5748 S–Adult: 8433

Curtiss, Glenn
S–Adult: 6546

Custer, George Armstrong
JS: 6398 S: 8474, 8485, 8746
S–Adult: 6399

Custer, George Armstrong — Fiction
S–Adult: 2863

Cycling
See Bicycles

Cyrano de Bergerac (play) — Criticism
S: 5439

Czech Republic
JS: 8090

Czechoslovakia
S–Adult: 875 S–Adult: 7647, 7840

D

D-Day (1944)
JS: 8847 S–Adult: 7647, 7840

d'Aboville, Gerard
S: 5638

Da Chen
S–Adult: 6934

Dahl, Roald
JS: 5840 S: 5841

Dalai Lama
JS: 6791

Dali, Salvador
S: 5749

Daman, Hortense
S: 7652

Damon, Matt
JS: 6024–25

Damselflies
S–Adult: 12126, 12139

Dance
JS: 7212, 7215 S: 7214
S–Adult: 7216–17

Dance — Biography
JS: 6050

Dance — Careers
JS: 10436, 10454 S: 10449

Dance — Fiction
JS: 1546, 2544

D'Angelo, Pascal
JS: 5842

Dante Alighieri — Criticism
S: 5433

Dante Alighieri — Fiction
S–Adult: 2605

Danziger, Paula
JS: 5843

Darling, Grace — Fiction
S: 2680

Darrow, Clarence
JS: 8812, 9296

Darwin, Charles
JS: 6550 S: 6547–48, 7364
S–Adult: 6549, 7347

Datcher, Michael
S–Adult: 6207

Date rape
See also Rape
JS: 9845, 10673, 11291, 11299, 11303, 11312, 11320 S: 11300, 11306, 11315, 11319

Date rape — Drugs
S: 11313

Date rape — Fiction
JS: 971

Dating (social)
JS: 11259–60, 11405, 11443, 11476
S: 11292

Dating (social) — Fiction
JS: 1457, 3901

Dating (social) — Violence
See also Date rape
JS: 995, 999, 11317

Dave Matthews Band
JS: 7140

Da Vinci, Leonardo
JS: 5750–52 S–Adult: 5753, 7076

Davis, Donald
S: 6481

JS = Junior High/Senior High;   S = Senior High;   S–Adult = Senior High/Adult

Davis, Jefferson
JS: 6400

Davis, Miles
JS: 6027 S: 6026, 6029
S–Adult: 6028, 7167

Dawson's Creek (television series)
JS: 7263

Day, Dorothy
JS: 6401

DDT
S–Adult: 9910

Deafness and the deaf
S–Adult: 11151, 13202

Deafness and the deaf — Biography
S: 7011 S–Adult: 6488, 6966

Deafness and the deaf — Fiction
JS: 2451 S: 992

Dean, James
JS: 6030

Death
JS: 5233, 6949, 9939, 9941, 10577,
10579, 10584–87, 10589–90, 10595,
10599–600, 10602, 10833, 10893,
11365 S: 6939, 6972, 10581, 10583,
10593 S–Adult: 7430, 8056, 10598,
13276

Death — Fiction
J: 766, 1327 JS: 298, 300, 303, 334,
347, 599, 601, 622, 624, 628, 635, 654,
671, 718, 751, 755, 763, 774, 814, 817,
848, 858, 876, 904, 917, 942–43, 1057,
1062, 1080, 1113, 1129, 1162, 1188,
1202, 1286, 1296, 1310, 1315, 1326,
1370, 1400, 1405, 1407, 1430, 1485,
1505, 1518, 1536, 1538, 1542, 1545–46,
1548, 1932, 2561, 3151, 3506, 3696,
3723, 3865, 3881, 3983, 4613 S: 644,
655, 663, 691–93, 744, 787, 811, 952,
1071, 1106, 1212, 1230, 1337, 1351,
1356, 1516, 1553, 1804, 3872, 3900
S–Adult: 309, 598, 607, 782, 865,
1019, 1219, 1282, 1317–18, 1364, 1534,
1558, 1937, 2318, 3705, 4056

Death — Poetry
JS: 4859

Death of a Salesman — Criticism
S: 5528

Death penalty
JS: 9279, 9286, 9291–92, 9301–2,
9317–18, 9334 S: 9275, 9275–76,
9276, 9280, 9280, 9831, 9952, 10059,
10059 S–Adult: 9268, 9281, 9281,
9321, 9959, 9959, 9981, 10009, 10016,
10016, 10030

Death Valley
S–Adult: 13389

Deer
JS: 12019 S–Adult: 12020

Deer — Fiction
JS: 1768

De Ferrari, Gabriella
S: 6935

Degas, Edgar
JS: 5754

De La Cruz, Jessie
JS: 6208

de la Rocque, Marguerite — Fiction
JS: 48

Delaware Indians — Folklore
JS: 5126 S: 8461

Demeter (mythology) — Poetry
S: 4964

De Mille, Agnes
S: 6031

Democracy
JS: 9201 S: 9172

Denali National Park
S: 9000 S–Adult: 9009

Denmark — Fiction
JS: 3038, 3059 S–Adult: 2676

Denmark — Folklore
See also Scandinavia — Folklore
S: 5095

Denmark — History
JS: 7751

Dental care
See also Teeth
JS: 11023

Denver — Fiction
S: 2907

Depression, Great
JS: 8784–85, 8790, 8792, 8794, 8798,
8800, 8806, 8809–11, 8813, 8817, 8819,
8825, 9644 S: 8778, 8780, 8786, 8818,
8820–23 S–Adult: 6962, 7086, 8337,
8791, 8795, 8807–8, 8826

Depression, Great — Biography
S: 6980

Depression, Great — Fiction
JS: 516, 2516, 2710, 2960, 2972–73,
2975, 3306 S: 539, 838, 2962, 2969,
2977–78, 3006 S–Adult: 2957–58,
2964, 2974

Depression, Great — Poetry
JS: 5022

Depression, Great — Speeches
JS: 8796

Depression (mental state)
See also Mental disorders
JS: 10718, 10751, 10889, 11056,
11060, 11073, 11090, 11107, 11113,
11119 S: 11064–65, 11075, 11116
S–Adult: 11062, 11115

Depression (mental state) — Fiction
JS: 347, 917, 960, 1015, 3091 S: 944
S–Adult: 833

Deserts
S: 12372–73 S–Adult: 7898, 11953

Deserts — Fiction
JS: 1615

Design
See Clothing and dress; Fashion
design

Designer drugs
See also Drugs and drug abuse
JS: 10688

Desktop publishing
JS: 5567

Desktop publishing — Careers
S: 10475

de Soto, Hernando
JS: 5640 S: 5639

Desserts
S: 12784, 12814, 12820, 12838, 12840

Detectives — Fiction
See also Mystery stories — Fiction
JS: 3737 S: 3463 S–Adult: 3373,
3418, 3434, 3602, 3627, 3689, 3713,
3812, 4169

Developing countries
S: 7592

Devers, Gail
JS: 6728

Diabetes
JS: 10812, 10835, 10854, 10863
S: 10757 S–Adult: 10879

Diabetes — Cookbooks
S: 12839

Diabetes — Fiction
JS: 937

Diamonds
S: 8240 S–Adult: 7984

Diaries
JS: 8909 S: 9188 S–Adult: 6927,
7217, 7808

Diaries — Fiction
J: 1327, 2702 JS: 870, 1444, 2805,
2996, 3263–65 S: 1102, 3324
S–Adult: 2662, 4013

Diary of a Young Girl — Criticism
S: 5316

DiCaprio, Leonardo
JS: 6032

Dickens, Charles
JS: 212 S–Adult: 5844–45

Dickens, Charles — Criticism
S: 5278–80, 5288–89, 5301

Dickens, Charles — Fiction
S–Adult: 3709

Dickinson, Emily
JS: 5847 S: 4814 S–Adult: 5846

Dickinson, Emily — Criticism
S: 5508, 5515

Dickinson, Emily — Fiction
S: 1153, 2926

Dictionaries
JS: 12870 S: 5559

Die, right to
See Right to die

Diets and dieting
See also Eating disorders

JS = Junior High/Senior High;   S = Senior High;   S–Adult = Senior High/Adult

1115

Drawing and painting
See also Art; Crafts
JS: 7090, 12879, 12884, 12889
S: 12877, 12880–83, 12885, 12887–88, 12890, 12892–93, 12895–96, 12898–905 **S–Adult:** 12894

Dreams and dreaming
JS: 11005–6, 11356 **S–Adult:** 11342

Dreams and dreaming — Fiction
JS: 1228, 2499 **S:** 4350

Dred Scott Case
JS: 8568 **S:** 8573

Dress
See Clothing and dress; Fashion design

Dress codes
JS: 10253

Dressmaking
See also Clothing and dress; Fashion design
S: 12967

Drew, Charles
JS: 6551

Drinking and driving
See also Alcohol
JS: 9942, 10656, 10668 **S:** 10630

Drinking and driving — Fiction
JS: 917, 1188

Dropouts
JS: 10327

Drought
J: 12447 **JS:** 12450

Drought — Fiction
JS: 2710–11

Drowning — Fiction
JS: 3363

Drug testing
JS: 9328, 10683

Drug trade
JS: 10691 **S:** 6940, 10704, 10713

Drugs and drug abuse
See also specific drugs, e.g., Cocaine
J: 10621, 10663, 10694–95 **JS:** 9950, 10607, 10609–10, 10612, 10614, 10616–17, 10619–20, 10625, 10627–28, 10632, 10639–42, 10648–50, 10652–53, 10655, 10661–62, 10664–66, 10670, 10672–75, 10677, 10679–80, 10682–83, 10685, 10688–89, 10691–93, 10700–1, 10703, 10707, 10709, 10711, 10715, 10718, 10720–21 **S:** 10608, 10622, 10629, 10637–38, 10645, 10671, 10698, 10704, 10706, 10713–14, 10992, 11313, 11484, 11868 **S–Adult:** 10092, 10097, 10633, 10658–59, 10921

Drugs and drug abuse — Fiction
JS: 65–66, 233, 377, 429, 528, 903, 969, 1135, 1425, 1613 **S:** 21, 898, 929, 979, 1367, 3794, 3798 **S–Adult:** 734, 851, 1316, 1577, 1589, 3927

**Drugs and drug abuse —
Legalization**
JS: 10614, 10627, 10640 **S:** 10706

Drugs and drug abuse — Memoirs
S–Adult: 6927

Drugs and drug abuse — Sports
JS: 10632, 10683

Druids — Fiction
S–Adult: 2679

Drunk driving
See Drinking and driving

Du Bois, W. E. B.
JS: 6219 **S:** 6217–18 **S–Adult:** 9402

Du Bois, W. E. B. — Criticism
S: 5247

Ducks and geese
S: 12076, 12076

Ducks and geese — Fiction
JS: 170

Dumas, Firoozeh
S–Adult: 6937

Dunbar, Paul Laurence
JS: 5851 **S–Adult:** 4967

Dunkerque, Battle of
JS: 170

Dust
S: 11579 **S–Adult:** 11601

Dust Bowl
JS: 8806 **S–Adult:** 8826

Dvorak, Antonin
JS: 5980

Dylan, Bob
JS: 6036 **S–Adult:** 6035

Dyslexia
See also Learning disabilities
S: 11057

E

E-mail — Fiction
JS: 1473

Eagles
See also Birds of prey
JS: 12077 **S–Adult:** 12081

Earhart, Amelia
S: 5644, 5646 **S–Adult:** 5645

Earhart, Amelia — Fiction
S: 115

Earnhardt, Dale
S–Adult: 6656

Earring making
See also Jewelry making
S: 12857

Earth
See also Geology
JS: 11748–49, 12346 **S:** 9860, 11710, 11747, 11751, 12345, 12347
S–Adult: 11669, 11754

Earth — Disasters
S–Adult: 12352

Earth — Geology
S–Adult: 12341

Earth — History
S: 12342

Earth science
S: 12350, 12364 **S–Adult:** 12341, 12355

Earth science — Experiments and projects
J: 12353 **JS:** 7408

Earthquakes
JS: 8996, 12358 **S:** 12356, 12360–62 **S–Adult:** 9001

Earthquakes — Fiction
S: 56

Earthworms
S–Adult: 11893

East Hampton (N.Y.) — Fiction
S–Adult: 3625

East Timor
JS: 8071

Easter Island
S: 8067

Eastern Europe
JS: 8082, 8088 **S:** 8076, 8084

Eastman, George
JS: 6611–12

Eating disorders
See also specific disorders, e.g., Bulimia
J: 10694, 10739 **JS:** 10743–44, 10750–51, 10766, 10774, 10776, 10783, 10805, 10819, 10825, 10832, 10836, 10842, 10867, 10870, 10873, 10876, 10885, 10887, 10889, 10974 **S:** 10761, 10810, 10844–45

Eating disorders — Fiction
S: 957, 997 **S–Adult:** 1148, 3964

Eating disorders — Support groups
JS: 10823

Eccentricity — Fiction
S–Adult: 304

Eclipses
S: 11766 **S–Adult:** 11700

Ecology — North America
S–Adult: 8230

Ecology and environment
See also Conservation; Pollution
JS: 8391, 8992, 9005, 9878, 9880–81, 9881, 9892, 9903, 11848 **S:** 9861, 9887, 9906, 12329, 12365, 12383, 12387 **S–Adult:** 9012, 9894, 9902, 10888, 11781, 12101, 12111, 12117, 12142, 12162

**Ecology and environment —
Biography**
JS: 6508 **S:** 9865 **S–Adult:** 6472, 6593, 6595, 7010

**Ecology and environment —
Careers**
JS: 6518 **S:** 10379, 10411, 10528

JS = Junior High/Senior High; S = Senior High; S–Adult = Senior High/Adult

**Ecology and environment —
Experiments and projects**
JS: 9875, 9875

Ecology and environment — Fiction
JS: 858, 1571 **S:** 1645, 4266
S–Adult: 375, 1582, 1600, 3772, 3799

**Ecology and environment —
Problems**
See also Conservation; Ecology and
environment; Pollution; and
specific problems, e.g., Acid rain
J: 9870 **JS:** 9862, 9872, 9878, 9880,
9885, 9890–92, 9896, 9899, 9903, 9915,
9917, 11785, 12100 **S:** 9860, 9864,
9866–68, 9873, 9876–77, 9882, 9884,
9886–87, 9897–98, 9905–6, 9908, 9918,
9921, 9923, 9927, 11784, 11810, 12099,
12119, 12367 **S–Adult:** 9869, 9888,
9907, 9909–10, 9924, 12095, 12112,
12116, 12210, 12389, 12448

**Ecology and environment —
Protection**
JS: 9863, 9911 **S:** 9912
S–Adult: 12110, 12115, 12117

Economic forecasting
S: 10134

Economics and business
See also Capitalism; Money-making
ideas
JS: 9349, 10218, 10225 **S:** 10214–15,
10222, 10245, 10548 **S–Adult:** 11593

**Economics and business —
Biography**
J: 8737 **JS:** 6507, 6515, 6525–26,
6609, 6612, 6619, 6633
S–Adult: 6610, 6624, 6636–37

Economics and business — Careers
JS: 10212 **S:** 10473

**Economics and business —
International**
S: 10220

Ecstasy (drug)
See also Drugs and drug abuse
JS: 10607

Ecuador
JS: 8296

Eddy, Mary Baker
JS: 9122

Eden, Garden of — Fiction
S: 1634

Edison, Thomas Alva
JS: 6552, 6554 **S:** 6553
S–Adult: 6555

Edmonds, Walter D.
S: 5852

Education
See also Colleges and universities;
Schools; Teachers
JS: 10257, 10272–73 **S–Adult:** 7007,
10256, 10260

Education — African Americans
JS: 9639

Education — Biography
JS: 5692, 6191

Education — Careers
JS: 10481, 10484 **S:** 10482

Education (U.S.)
JS: 10255, 10271 **S:** 10261, 10264

Educational guidance
S: 10325

Edwards, Bruce
S–Adult: 6742

Edwards, Honeyboy
S: 6037

Eels
JS–Adult: 12180

Efficiency experts — Biography
JS–Adult: 6157

Eggers, Dave
S–Adult: 5853

Egypt
See also Valley of the Kings (Egypt)
JS: 8193 **S–Adult:** 10165

Egypt — Biography
JS: 6760, 6776, 6778–79
S–Adult: 6777, 6786

Egypt — Fiction
S: 2402–3, 2414, 2436, 3406, 3437,
3717, 3757–58 **S–Adult:** 2404, 2406,
2412, 2482, 3718–19

Egypt — History
See also Pyramids
J: 7467 **JS:** 6760, 6776, 7450, 7460,
7462, 7465–66, 7468–69, 7471–74
JS–Adult: 8194 **S:** 7454–56, 7470
S–Adult: 6786, 7374, 7459, 7461,
7463

Egypt — Mythology
JS: 5174

Egypt — Poetry
S–Adult: 5430

Eichengreen, Lucille
S: 6828

Eichmann, Adolf
J: 7625 **JS:** 7659

Eiffel Tower
JS: 8097

Eighteenth century
JS: 8354, 8354

Einstein, Albert
JS: 6559, 6561, 12497 **S:** 6556, 6560
S–Adult: 6557–58, 12499

Eire, Carlos
S–Adult: 6938

Eisenhower, Dwight D.
JS: 6300, 6302 **S:** 7635
S–Adult: 6299, 6301, 8842

El Niño (weather)
S–Adult: 12458

El Salvador — Fiction
JS: 1620

Elderly persons
See also Aging; Death; Euthanasia
JS: 9940

Elderly persons — Fiction
JS: 1371, 1947 **S:** 966

Eleanor of Aquitaine
S: 6829

Elections
JS: 9226, 9358, 9360, 9364 **S:** 9347,
9355 **S–Adult:** 9353, 9357, 9362

Elections — 2000
S–Adult: 9357

Elections — Fiction
JS: 3289

Elections — Schools
S: 10266

Elections (U.S.) — Fiction
JS: 394

Electric chair
S–Adult: 9321

Electricity
JS: 12534, 12536 **S–Adult:** 9981,
12532–33

**Electricity — Experiments and
projects**
JS: 12535

Electronics
See also Lasers; Telecommunications
JS: 12631 **S:** 12629–30
S–Adult: 12619

Elements
S: 12331, 12338

Elephants
JS: 12025–26 **S:** 12023, 12028
S–Adult: 12022, 12024, 12027,
12029–30, 12239

Elephants — Fiction
JS: 165

Eliot, George — Criticism
S: 5275

Elizabeth I, Queen of England
JS: 6830, 8128 **S:** 6831–32

**Elizabeth I, Queen of England —
Fiction**
S: 2601

Elizabeth II, Queen
JS: 6833 **JS–Adult:** 6836
S–Adult: 6834–35

Elizabethan England
JS: 8133 **S:** 5442, 7537, 8135
S–Adult: 5472, 5483, 5930, 8132

Elizabethan England — Biography
S: 5929

Elizabethan England — Fiction
JS: 2567, 2602 **S–Adult:** 2566, 2590,
2598, 2614, 2674

Ellington, Duke
JS: 6038, 6040–41 **S:** 6039

Ellis Island
S: 9542

Ellison, Ralph
S: 5854

JS = Junior High/Senior High;   S = Senior High;   S–Adult = Senior High/Adult

JS = Junior High/Senior High; S = Senior High; S–Adult = Senior High/Adult

JS = Junior High/Senior High;   S = Senior High;   S–Adult = Senior High/Adult

Falcons
See also Peregrine falcons
S: 12083

Falcons — Fiction
S: 936

Fame — Fiction
JS: 393

Family abuse
See Family problems

Family life
See also Single parents
JS: 11148 **S:** 6481, 10562, 11333, 11541–42 **S–Adult:** 11218, 11519, 11554, 11572, 11576

Family life — African American
JS: 4649 **S–Adult:** 9689

Family life — Fiction
J: 766 **JS:** 147, 294, 312, 334, 360, 422, 471, 481, 495, 512, 553, 604, 618, 653, 661, 670, 673, 695, 701, 732, 747, 802–3, 835, 847, 862, 945, 1032, 1045, 1049, 1054, 1060, 1215, 1242, 1286, 1302, 1476, 1519, 1523, 1531, 1541, 1893, 2097, 2753, 2956, 2979, 3317, 3621, 4567 **JS–Adult:** 617
S: 409–10, 534, 580, 610, 616, 629, 631, 639, 700, 707, 727, 838, 841, 886, 889, 988, 1218, 1497, 2381, 2581, 2919, 2927, 2952, 3086, 4017, 5186, 9675
S–Adult: 283, 327, 348, 441, 490, 567, 600, 607, 645, 657, 666, 689, 720, 745, 771, 779, 786, 792, 799–801, 815, 824, 826, 840, 846, 854, 857, 1043, 1249, 1354, 2546, 2781, 2816, 2892, 3657, 3948, 9638, 9739, 12290

Family life — Memoirs
S–Adult: 6933

Family life — Poetry
JS: 5045 **S:** 4905

Family life — Problems
S–Adult: 761

Family planning
JS: 11203

Family problems
See also specific problems, e.g.,
Divorce
JS: 647, 9929, 10599, 10696, 11082, 11490–91, 11493, 11495–96, 11499, 11504, 11507, 11510, 11513–15, 11517, 11526, 11528, 11531, 11534–35, 11537, 11548–51, 11555, 11557, 11562–63, 11565, 11568, 11571 **S:** 6925, 6980, 10757, 11470, 11494, 11501, 11511, 11525, 11541, 11552 **S–Adult:** 571, 5875, 6974, 6982–83, 6999, 9739, 10633, 11506, 11509, 11527, 11529, 11539

Family problems — Fiction
J: 615 **JS:** 62, 117, 180, 279, 298, 308, 315, 370, 388, 420, 430, 453, 514, 532, 546, 577, 601–3, 605, 612, 619–22, 625, 628, 632, 636, 642, 646, 648–51, 654, 659–60, 662, 669, 671–72, 674–75, 680, 688, 694, 697–98, 704, 706, 708, 716, 719, 729, 731, 739, 742, 746, 749–51, 753, 755, 757, 763, 765, 772–77, 785,

789–91, 794, 796, 798, 804–5, 807, 812–14, 817–18, 830, 832, 837, 843, 848–49, 853, 858, 861, 863, 866, 870–71, 873–74, 876, 878, 881, 885, 887–88, 899, 980, 1004, 1009, 1023, 1066, 1080–81, 1084, 1122, 1133, 1176, 1202, 1220, 1299, 1312, 1321, 1324, 1326, 1334, 1344, 1363, 1371, 1385, 1387, 1420, 1424, 1436, 1444, 1454, 1463, 1500, 1521, 1603, 1908, 2516, 2532, 2930, 2968, 2971, 2973, 2988, 2998, 3078–79, 3160, 3320, 3377, 3389, 3666, 3740, 3756, 3773, 3839, 3901, 4557, 4580, 4584, 4586, 11556 **S:** 181, 240, 254, 316, 340, 402, 463, 479, 530, 558, 595, 608, 611, 614, 626–27, 630, 637, 640–41, 643–44, 663, 668, 676–77, 682–83, 686, 691–93, 710, 725, 728, 730, 735, 737–38, 740, 743–44, 754, 767–70, 780–81, 819–20, 823, 836, 859, 864, 867, 872, 879, 882–83, 1033, 1098, 1194, 1217, 1268, 1304, 1375, 1410, 1491, 1572, 1580, 2361, 2487, 2490, 2525, 2948, 3844, 3876, 3975, 4014, 4063, 4070 **S–Adult:** 391, 396, 448, 464, 593, 597–98, 606, 633, 638, 652, 658, 664–65, 678, 681, 690, 696, 699, 702–3, 705, 712–13, 717, 726, 734, 748, 759–60, 778, 782, 788, 793, 808–10, 821, 825, 827–29, 831, 833–34, 839, 842, 845, 851, 860, 865, 868–69, 875, 877, 880, 884, 890, 909, 924, 1019, 1035, 1089, 1145, 1148, 1178, 1261, 1276, 1282, 1330, 1332, 1360, 1406, 1455–56, 1600, 2478, 2541, 2706, 2902, 2987, 2990, 2999, 3430, 3594, 3996, 4056–57

Family problems — Plays
S: 4793, 4829

Family violence
See Domestic violence; Family problems

Fantasy — Criticism
S: 5263, 5284

Fantasy — Fiction
See also Fables; Folklore; Mythology; Science fiction; Supernatural; Time travel — Fiction
J: 1942, 1949, 2362, 2370 **JS:** 104, 108, 110, 208, 213, 237–38, 270, 896, 1080, 1633, 1635, 1660–61, 1663, 1668–69, 1672–77, 1683–85, 1690, 1693, 1696, 1698–700, 1702–3, 1718, 1729, 1740–41, 1744, 1750, 1759, 1768–69, 1773, 1778–79, 1781, 1785, 1788–90, 1792–94, 1816, 1818, 1832, 1839–40, 1847, 1849, 1852, 1857, 1863, 1865, 1871, 1883, 1886, 1896, 1898–900, 1908, 1916, 1919–20, 1925–26, 1929, 1932, 1934–36, 1939, 1943–46, 1950, 1952, 1957–58, 1978, 1980, 2000, 2007, 2011–12, 2014, 2017, 2019, 2021, 2031, 2033–35, 2039, 2042, 2061, 2064–65, 2069–71, 2082, 2096–97, 2104–5, 2107–8, 2113–14, 2116, 2127, 2130–31, 2133–38, 2140, 2142, 2147–52, 2162, 2171–72, 2178–79, 2188, 2193–95, 2197, 2200, 2210–11, 2216, 2218–19, 2224–26, 2229, 2231, 2240–41, 2243, 2245–47, 2252, 2261, 2264–65, 2272–73, 2276,

2278–80, 2282–83, 2286–87, 2291, 2295–96, 2320, 2325, 2338, 2346, 2352, 2372, 2454, 2561, 3050, 3104, 3136–37, 3225, 4007, 4591, 4626, 4654, 4668, 5109–10 **JS–Adult:** 1864, 2340
S: 163, 190, 683, 1626, 1630–32, 1634, 1637, 1639, 1641, 1643–49, 1651–55, 1657–58, 1664, 1666–67, 1679–82, 1687–88, 1691, 1695, 1697, 1701, 1704–13, 1722, 1724–26, 1728, 1730–33, 1736–38, 1746, 1748, 1751–54, 1757, 1762, 1765–67, 1770, 1772, 1780, 1786, 1791, 1797, 1803–4, 1806–7, 1814, 1817, 1820–21, 1824, 1831, 1835, 1837, 1841, 1848, 1858, 1861–62, 1866, 1870, 1875, 1879, 1882, 1887, 1895, 1907, 1917–18, 1931, 1933, 1940, 1953–55, 1962–63, 1965, 1967–68, 1971–75, 1977, 1979, 1982, 1986, 1990–91, 1994–97, 2001–2, 2008–10, 2018, 2022, 2024–26, 2028, 2036–38, 2040–41, 2043–45, 2050, 2055, 2059–60, 2062, 2074, 2080, 2083, 2091, 2099–100, 2110–11, 2115, 2117–18, 2120–21, 2123, 2125, 2132, 2139, 2143, 2153, 2155–58, 2160, 2163, 2168, 2181, 2184, 2186–87, 2189, 2191, 2198, 2203, 2205, 2207–8, 2213, 2217, 2227–28, 2232, 2239, 2242, 2244, 2249, 2254, 2257, 2260, 2262–63, 2266, 2269, 2271, 2274, 2277, 2281, 2285, 2289–90, 2292, 2304, 2347, 2417, 3122, 3685, 4403, 4407–8, 4447, 4524, 4547
S–Adult: 1627–29, 1636, 1638, 1640, 1642, 1650, 1656, 1659, 1662, 1665, 1670–71, 1678, 1686, 1689, 1692, 1694, 1714–17, 1719–21, 1723, 1727, 1734–35, 1739, 1742–43, 1745, 1747, 1749, 1755–56, 1758, 1760–61, 1763–64, 1771, 1774–77, 1782, 1787, 1795–96, 1799–802, 1805, 1808–13, 1815, 1819, 1822–23, 1826–30, 1833–34, 1836, 1838, 1842–46, 1850–51, 1853–56, 1859–60, 1867–69, 1872–74, 1876–78, 1880–81, 1884–85, 1888–92, 1894, 1897, 1901–6, 1909–12, 1914–15, 1921–24, 1927–28, 1930, 1937–38, 1941, 1951, 1956, 1959–61, 1966, 1969–70, 1976, 1981, 1983–85, 1987–89, 1992–93, 1998–99, 2003–6, 2013, 2015–16, 2020, 2023, 2027, 2029–30, 2032, 2046–49, 2051–54, 2056–58, 2066–68, 2072–73, 2075–79, 2081, 2084–90, 2092–95, 2098, 2101–2, 2106, 2109, 2112, 2119, 2122, 2126, 2128, 2141, 2144–46, 2154, 2159, 2161, 2164–67, 2169–70, 2173–77, 2180, 2182–83, 2185, 2190, 2192, 2196, 2199, 2201–2, 2204, 2206, 2209, 2212, 2214–15, 2220–22, 2230, 2233–38, 2248, 2250–51, 2253, 2255–56, 2258–59, 2268, 2270, 2275, 2284, 2288, 2345, 2355, 2365, 2416, 3108, 3142, 3177, 3233, 3271, 3479, 3902, 3955, 4027, 4582, 4605, 4625, 4627–28, 4669, 4734, 7094

Fantasy — History and criticism
JS: 5249, 5387 **S:** 5252–53, 5274, 5397–98 **S–Adult:** 5262

Fantasy — Poetry
S–Adult: 1801

JS = Junior High/Senior High;   S = Senior High;   S–Adult = Senior High/Adult

Faraday, Michael
JS: 6563 **S:** 6562

A Farewell to Arms — **Criticism**
S: 5427

Farm animals
See also specific animals, e.g., Cattle
S–Adult: 11822, 11834

Farman Farmaian, Sattareh
S: 6792

Farms and farm life
JS: 11826 **S–Adult:** 11834

Farms and farm life — Biography
JS: 6204–5

Farms and farm life — Fiction
JS: 1313, 1362, 1390, 1893, 1920, 4600
S: 614, 1132, 1528, 2904, 2952
S–Adult: 1522, 2668

Farnsworth, Philo
S–Adult: 6613–14

Farrakhan, Louis
JS: 6220, 9614

Fascism
S–Adult: 7757

Fascism — Biography
JS: 6871 **S:** 6872 **S–Adult:** 6873

Fashion
JS: 10969 **S:** 10966 **S–Adult:** 10972

Fashion — Careers
JS: 10371

Fashion — History
J: 12866 **JS:** 8331, 8802, 8858, 12849, 12852 **S:** 12865, 12867

Fashion design
See also Clothing and dress
S: 12878

Fashion design — Biography
S: 6623, 6926

Fashion design — Careers
JS: 10468

Fashion design — History
J: 8379, 8783, 8889, 8893, 8895

Fashion industry
JS: 12858

Fashion industry — Careers
JS: 10434, 10477 **S:** 10466–67

Fast food industry
S–Adult: 10234

Father-daughter relationships
S–Adult: 760

Father-son relationships
S: 9034 **S–Adult:** 77, 415, 1011, 11539

Father-son relationships — Fiction
JS: 849 **S:** 864

Fathers
JS: 11180, 11191 **S:** 11202

Fathers — Fiction
JS: 1032, 2645

Faulkner, William — Criticism
S: 5338, 5360, 5417

Federal Bureau of Investigation (U.S.)
JS: 9248 **S:** 9983 **S–Adult:** 9974

Federal Bureau of Investigation (U.S.) — Fiction
S: 3823

Feig, Paul
S–Adult: 5855

Fellows, Warren
S: 6940

Female circumcision — Fiction
JS: 1567, 2486

Feminism
JS: 9390, 9429, 9485 **S:** 9411, 9421
S–Adult: 9406, 9441, 9459

Feminism — Biography
JS: 6264–65

Feminism — History
JS: 9419 **S:** 9412

Feral children — Fiction
JS: 1562

Fermi, Enrico
JS: 6564

Ferrell *v.* Dallas
JS: 9339

Festivals
JS: 10154

Feudalism
See also Middle Ages
JS: 7545

Feuds — History
S: 7402

Fiction — Criticism
S: 5266–67, 5269–70, 5272, 5314, 5340, 5405, 5514

Fiction — History and criticism
S–Adult: 5404

Fiction — Writing
See also Writing — Fiction
J: 10284 **S:** 10283, 10310, 10314, 10321

Fifteenth century
S: 7568

Fighter pilots — Biography
S: 5618

Figure skating
See Ice skating

Filar, Marian
S–Adult: 7684

Filipino Americans
JS: 9705, 9722 **S:** 9710

Filipino Americans — Short stories
S: 459

Filipovic, Zlata
S: 6837

Film making — Fiction
S: 1333

Finance — Careers
S: 10473

Finances (personal)
JS: 10546, 10553, 10556 **S:** 10338, 10552, 10557

Finger nails
S–Adult: 10967

Fingerprinting
S–Adult: 9951

Finnish Americans — Fiction
JS: 2918

Fire Island — Fiction
S: 3556

Firecrackers
S–Adult: 12550

Firefighters
JS: 10205 **S:** 9255 **S–Adult:** 10179, 10195, 10488, 10498

Firefighters — Careers
S: 10494

Firefighters — History
JS: 9256 **S–Adult:** 10182

Firefighters — Women
S: 10494

Fires — Fiction
JS: 25 **S:** 3853

Fires — History
JS: 8753 **S:** 9255 **S–Adult:** 11629

First aid
See Safety

First aid manuals
S: 11220, 11222

First Amendment
S: 10113 **S–Adult:** 12587

First Ladies (U.S.)
S–Adult: 8408

First Ladies (U.S.) — Biography
See Presidents (U.S.) — Wives — Biography

First Ladies (U.S.) — Fiction
S: 3763–66

Fish
See also different kinds of fish, e.g., Sharks
JS: 12159, 12175–76, 12303, 12326
JS–Adult: 12174 **S:** 12157, 12177, 12179, 12304, 12320–21, 12325, 12328
S–Adult: 12173, 12178, 12181, 13297

Fish — Pets
JS: 12305

Fisher, Antwone Quenton
S: 5856

Fishing
JS: 13301 **JS–Adult:** 13299
S: 13300 **S–Adult:** 8978, 11539, 13297

Fishing — Fiction
JS: 70 **S:** 54

Fitness
See also Physical fitness

S–Adult: 11129

Fitzgerald, F. Scott
JS: 5858 **S–Adult:** 5857

Fitzgerald, F. Scott — Criticism
S: 5326, 5333, 5351, 5356

Flag burning
JS: 10112

Flags — History
S: 8324

Flags (U.S.)
JS: 8346 **S:** 8324, 8394
S–Adult: 8393, 8574

Fleischman, Sid
JS: 5859

Fleming, Alexander
JS: 6565

Fleming, Edward
S–Adult: 6483

Flight
S: 12654

Flight attendants — Careers
S: 10376, 10394

Flipper, Henry O.
S: 5647

Floods
JS: 12441

Florida — Fiction
JS: 179, 805, 2851, 3318 **S:** 477, 3098,
3845 **S–Adult:** 2743

Flowers
JS–Adult: 11871 **S:** 11859, 11868
S–Adult: 11866

Flowers — Dried
JS: 12743

Flowers — Pressed
S: 12726

Flowers for Algernon **— Criticism**
JS: 5346

Fluid mechanics
JS: 12505

Fly fishing
JS–Adult: 13299

Flying — Fiction
S–Adult: 4682

Fog
JS: 12451

Folk art
S: 12987

Folk art — Biography
JS: 5757

Folk music
See also Folk songs
S–Adult: 7125, 7205

Folk songs
See also Songs

Folk songs — African American
J: 9114 **S–Adult:** 7205

Folk songs (U.S.)
JS: 7202, 7208 **S:** 7209

Folk tales
See Folklore

Folklore
See also Mythology; and specific
countries and regions, e.g.,
Germany — Folklore; and specific
topics, e.g., Animals — Folklore
JS: 5090, 5114, 5121, 5133 **S:** 5061,
5066 **S–Adult:** 5071, 5080, 5086

Folklore — Africa
S–Adult: 5078

Folklore — African American
S: 5120 **S–Adult:** 5890

Folklore — Anthologies
J: 5065 **JS:** 5057, 5073, 5139
S: 4610, 4672, 5058, 5060, 5062–63,
5069, 5075, 5081, 5093, 5100, 5105–6,
5129

Folklore — Asia
S–Adult: 5083

Folklore — Biography
JS: 5836

Folklore — Hispanic
S–Adult: 5147

Folklore — History and criticism
S–Adult: 5262

Folklore — Jews
S: 5118

Folklore — Mesopotamia
JS–Adult: 5148

Folklore — Plays
S: 4754

Folklore — South America
S–Adult: 5147

Folklore (U.S.)
JS: 5144 **S:** 4716, 5137–38, 5143,
5145 **S–Adult:** 5141, 5141

Folklore (U.S.) — Plays
JS: 4816

Food
JS: 11142, 11827 **S:** 11144, 11147,
11789, 11825, 11828, 11831, 11838
S–Adult: 11134, 11835, 12832

Food — Additives
JS: 11829

Food — Careers
J: 10409

Food — Genetics
JS: 11837

Food — History
JS: 11832, 12841 **S:** 11135

Food — Women
J: 10409

Food poisoning
JS: 10807 **S–Adult:** 11134

Food processing
S: 11838

Food production
S: 11825, 11838

Food service
S–Adult: 10234

Food service — Careers
JS: 10402

Food supply
S–Adult: 11134

Foods — Atlases
S: 11841

Foods — History
S–Adult: 11842

Foods — Preservation
S–Adult: 11840

Football
J: 6653 **JS:** 13307 **JS–Adult:** 13315
S: 4787, 13302, 13308, 13314
S–Adult: 13303, 13305, 13310, 13313,
13316

Football — Biography
J: 6653 **JS:** 6715 **S:** 6716, 6736
S–Adult: 6714, 13304

Football — Colleges and universities
S: 13314

Football — Fiction
JS: 374, 496, 4560, 4564, 4569–70,
4573–74, 4586 **S:** 1033, 4579
S–Adult: 4581

Football — History
S: 13306, 13309, 13312

Ford, Henry
JS: 6615

Forensic sciences
JS: 9961, 10001, 10028, 10044
S: 10011 **S–Adult:** 9946, 9949, 9982,
10027

Forensic sciences — Biography
JS: 6514

Forensic sciences — Careers
JS: 10531

Forest fires
S: 11981 **S–Adult:** 8961

Forest rangers — Fiction
S–Adult: 3349

Forest scouts — Biography
S: 5626

Forests and forestry
See also Rain forests
JS: 11848, 11851 **S:** 8368, 11854–56,
11981, 12374, 12381, 12383

Forests and forestry — Fiction
JS: 1344

Forests and forestry — Pollution
S: 9011

Forgiveness — Fiction
JS: 364

Fort Sumter
JS: 8618

Fortune telling
See also Hand readings; Predictions
JS: 13051 **S:** 13043, 13053

JS = Junior High/Senior High;   S = Senior High;   S–Adult = Senior High/Adult

1124

Fungi
See also specific fungi, e.g.,
Mushrooms
S: 11862

Funny Cide (horse)
S–Adult: 13353

Fur trade
JS: 8237

Furman v. Georgia
JS: 9301–2

Futurism
JS: 10141 **S:** 10134 **S–Adult:** 5217,
12355, 12543

Futurism — Fiction
JS: 4150 **S:** 4245

G

Gabon — Animals
JS–Adult: 7981

Gaines, Ernest — Criticism
S: 5344

Galapagos Islands
JS: 8279, 8289

**Galapagos Islands Biosphere
Reserve**
JS: 8289

Galdikas, Birute
S: 11967

Galileo
JS: 6571–72, 6574 **S:** 4780
S–Adult: 6573

Galileo (spacecraft)
S–Adult: 11716

Gallagher, Hugh
S: 6484

Gallic Wars
JS: 7512

Gambling
JS: 9792, 9803, 9808, 9813, 9843,
9851, 11049, 13119 **S:** 9822
S–Adult: 6967

Gambling — Fiction
JS: 1165, 1207 **S–Adult:** 1044

Gambling — Sports
J: 13131

Game hunters — Fiction
S: 139

Games
See also Picture puzzles; Puzzles;
Sports; and specific games, e.g.,
Chess
JS: 13296 **S:** 13079, 13111

Games — Experiments and projects
JS: 12508

Gamma-ray bursts
S–Adult: 11674

Gandhi, Indira
JS: 6793

Gandhi, Mahatma
JS: 6795, 6797 **S:** 6794
S–Adult: 6796

Gangs
JS: 9970, 9979, 10046–47, 10711
S: 9999, 10002, 10010, 10034, 10045,
10057 **S–Adult:** 9975, 9988

Gangs — Biography
S: 6921

Gangs — Fiction
JS: 63–64, 91, 331, 587, 1024, 1128,
1144, 4022 **S:** 523, 1314

Gantos, Jack
JS: 5864

Gao, Anhua
S–Adult: 6943

Garbage
JS: 9925 **S:** 9926–28

Garcia Marquez, Gabriel
S–Adult: 5865

Gardens and gardening
JS: 12918 **S:** 12907–8, 12912,
12914–15, 12917 **S–Adult:** 11860,
12906, 12909, 12913, 12916

Garfunkel, Art
S: 6121

Garibaldi, Giuseppi
JS: 6848

Garner, Eleanor
JS: 6944

Garrett, Pat — Fiction
S: 2879

Garvey, Marcus
JS: 6222, 6224–25 **S–Adult:** 6223

Gases
JS: 12505

Gates, Bill
JS: 6616 **S:** 12596

Gauguin, Paul
JS: 5756

Gay men and lesbians
See also Homosexuality
JS: 4609, 11234, 11236, 11246,
11246, 11254, 11262 **S:** 11228, 11251,
11251, 11264, 11268, 11277, 11277,
11396

Gay men and lesbians — Biography
JS: 5829 **S:** 5813, 5963, 6043, 6073

Gay men and lesbians — Civil rights
JS: 11273, 11273 **S:** 9436, 11309,
11309

Gay men and lesbians — Fiction
JS: 585, 674, 1059, 1184, 1285, 1403,
1485, 1529, 3067 **S:** 340, 1033, 1038,
1183, 1198, 1280, 1464, 1825, 4589
S–Adult: 600

Gay men and lesbians — Marriage
S: 9468, 9468 **S–Adult:** 9319, 9319

Gay men and lesbians — Plays
S–Adult: 5517

Gay rights
JS: 9387, 9454 **S:** 9436, 9468, 11237,
11268

Gay youth
JS: 4609, 11234, 11254, 11262
S: 1253, 11228, 11241, 11264–65

Gay youth — Biography
S: 11272

Gay youth — Fiction
JS: 1047, 1184, 1238, 1259, 1490, 4563
S: 886, 1099, 1198, 1474, 1507, 1528

Gay youths — Schools
S–Adult: 10268

Gaza Strip (Israel)
JS: 8210

Gbaya (African people)
JS: 7921

Geese
See Ducks and geese

Gehrig, Lou
S: 6667

Geisha — Fiction
S: 2512

Gender bias
S–Adult: 13084

Gender roles
See also Sex roles
JS: 10128

Gene therapy
See Genetic engineering

Genealogy
JS: 9744, 9768, 9774, 9780 **S:** 11516
S–Adult: 11558

Genealogy — Irish
JS: 9777

Genealogy — Japanese Americans
JS: 9726

Genetic engineering
See also Clones and cloning
JS: 10932, 10941–42, 10949, 10954,
10956–57 **S:** 10940, 10948, 10950
S–Adult: 11783, 11798, 12562

Genetic engineering — Fiction
S: 3838, 4214

Genetic engineering — Foods
S–Adult: 11801

Genetically altered food
S: 11789

Genetics
JS: 10572, 10930, 10932, 10936,
10939, 10942, 10946, 10949, 10952,
10957, 11837 **S:** 7368, 10931,
10933–35, 10937, 10943, 10945, 10948,
10950, 11789 **S–Adult:** 10927–28,
10944, 10947, 10951, 11351, 11807

Genetics — Biography
JS: 6585 **S–Adult:** 6568

Genetics — Fiction
S–Adult: 3650

Genetics — Plants
S–Adult: 11787

JS = Junior High/Senior High;   S = Senior High;   S–Adult = Senior High/Adult

JS = Junior High/Senior High;   S = Senior High;   S–Adult = Senior High/Adult

Gore, Ariel
S–Adult: 5867

Gorillas
See also Apes
S: 6566 S–Adult: 11962, 11976

Gospel music
S–Adult: 7121

Gospel music — Biography
JS: 6064–65

Goth (social movement)
JS: 11328

Government (U.S.)
JS: 9201, 9211, 9233, 9242, 9345, 9363
S: 9200, 9247, 9356, 9361
S–Adult: 10206

Government (U.S.) — Biography
JS: 6330

Government (U.S.) — Careers
S: 10410, 10496

Graham, Billy
JS: 6485

Graham, Katharine
JS: 6619–20

Graham, Martha
JS: 6050 S: 7214

Graham, Robin Lee
JS: 5648

Grail
See Holy Grail

Grammar
S: 5556, 10298, 10306, 10315

Grand Canyon
S–Adult: 9020

Grand Canyon — Fiction
JS: 72 S: 68

Grand Central Station (NY)
S–Adult: 10092

Grandfathers — Fiction
JS: 1247, 2562

Grandmothers — Fiction
JS: 532, 659, 1047, 3306

Grandmothers — Poetry
JS: 4977

Grandparents
JS: 11557

Grandparents — Fiction
S: 700, 737

Grant, Ulysses S.
JS: 6303 S: 6184, 6304

Grape growing — Fiction
S–Adult: 657

The Grapes of Wrath — Criticism
S: 5428

Graphic art
S–Adult: 7091

Graphic art — Careers
S: 10417

Graphic art — Fiction
S–Adult: 1260

Graphic novels
J: 2362 JS: 248, 2295–96, 2298,
2300–1, 2308, 2313, 2320, 2325, 2328,
2334–35, 2338, 2343–44, 2346, 2352,
2356, 2369, 2372, 2376–77, 2380, 2382,
2384–85 JS–Adult: 2299, 2311, 2332,
2340, 5600 S: 260, 2304, 2309, 2316,
2321, 2327, 2331, 2333, 2336, 2342,
2347–49, 2354, 2358–59, 2361, 2368,
2371, 2381 S–Adult: 194, 2293–94,
2297, 2302–3, 2305–6, 2310, 2312,
2314–15, 2318–19, 2322–24, 2326,
2329–30, 2339, 2345, 2350, 2353, 2355,
2363–67, 2373, 2375, 2378–79, 2383,
3239, 6499

Grasslands
JS: 2390 S: 12082, 12388
S–Adult: 12389

Grateful Dead (musical group)
S–Adult: 7156

Gravity
JS: 6597 S–Adult: 12498

Gray, Amy
S–Adult: 6947

Great Barrier Reef (Australia)
S: 12172

Great Britain
See also England; Northern Ireland;
Scotland; Wales
JS: 8116

Great Britain — Biography
JS: 6833, 6864, 6888
JS–Adult: 6836 S: 6825, 6889–90
S–Adult: 6834–35, 6892

Great Britain — Documents
S: 8122

Great Britain — Fiction
JS: 2471, 2675 S: 2444, 3532
S–Adult: 2655

Great Britain — History
JS: 6891, 8114, 8127 S: 6825, 7418,
8122, 8134–35 S–Adult: 8126

Great Britain — Theater
S: 7304

Great Depression
See Depression, Great

Great Expectations — Criticism
S: 5278–79

Great Famine
S: 7547

The Great Gatsby — Criticism
S: 5333, 5356

The Great Gatsby — Fiction
S: 1275

Great Lakes
S–Adult: 8960

Great Sioux War
S: 8472

Greece — Ancient
See also Greece — History
S: 7479, 7483

Greece — Architecture
S: 7446

Greece — Biography
S: 7478

Greece — Christmas
J: 9101

Greece — Cookbooks
J: 12836

Greece — Fiction
JS: 2421, 2429, 3022, 3887 S: 2420,
2424, 2433, 3046 S–Adult: 2416,
2611

Greece — History
See also Greece — Ancient
J: 7481 JS: 7445, 7477, 7484–91,
7493–94, 7499 S: 7475–76, 7482,
7492, 7495–96 S–Adult: 7480, 7497

Greece — Literature
S: 4877–78, 5245 S–Adult: 7480

Greece — Mythology
See also Mythology — Classical;
Mythology — Greece
J: 5158 JS: 5152, 5156, 5159–67,
5177–78 S: 2357, 5157, 5168, 5170,
5173

Greece — Plays
S–Adult: 4785

Greece — Poetry
S–Adult: 4945

Greece — Sports
J: 7451

Greece — Theater
S: 5457

Greely expedition (Arctic)
S–Adult: 8306

Greenberg, Alvin
S–Adult: 6948

Greenhouse effect
S: 9864 S–Adult: 9895

Greenland
S: 6749

Greenland — Fiction
JS: 2639 S: 32

Grey whales
S–Adult: 12220

Grief
JS: 10586, 11486

Grief — Fiction
JS: 332, 343, 718, 1001, 1034 S: 1236

Grimke, Angelina
S: 6226

Grizzly bears
See also Bears
JS: 11986 S: 8965, 11978
S–Adult: 11977

Grooming
See also Cosmetics
J: 10962 JS: 11487 S: 10958, 11422

Grooms — Horses
S–Adult: 13356

JS = Junior High/Senior High;   S = Senior High;   S–Adult = Senior High/Adult

Grove, Andrew
JS: 6621 S–Adult: 6622

Growing up
See also Adolescence; Coming of
age; Personal problems — Fiction
JS: 11346 S–Adult: 5207

Growing up — Fiction
JS: 122, 287, 302, 360, 1027, 1040,
1046, 1049, 1084, 1200, 1239, 1334,
1531, 2930, 3079 S–Adult: 396

Growing up — Poetry
JS: 4996

Grylls, Bear
S–Adult: 13264

Guam — Fiction
JS: 721

Guatemala
JS: 8246, 8252

Guatemala — Biography
JS: 6905

Guatemala — Fiction
JS: 1564, 2705

Guevara, Che
JS: 6903

Guidance
S–Adult: 11420

Guilt — Fiction
S–Adult: 309, 1535

Guitars
JS: 7196 S: 7194, 7197, 7199

Guitars — Biography
JS: 6054 S–Adult: 6053, 6116

Gulf Coast (U.S.)
JS: 9014 S: 11779

Gulf War
See Persian Gulf War

Gulf Wars
S–Adult: 8913

Gulliver's Travels — Criticism
S: 5312

Gun control
See also Arms control
JS: 9795, 9824, 9830, 9844, 9968,
9997, 10035 S: 9220, 9793, 9807,
9818, 9828, 9831, 9850, 9953
S–Adult: 9810

Gunpowder — History
S–Adult: 12710

Guns
JS: 9954, 10035, 10050, 10674

Guns — Fiction
JS: 1315, 1407, 1617

Guns — Schools
JS: 9968

Guns — Women
S–Adult: 9810

Gunther, John
JS: 6949

Guthrie, Woody
JS: 5982–84 S: 5981

Guy, Rosa
S: 5868

Gymnastics — Biography
S: 6717

Gynecology
JS: 11232

Gypsies
JS: 9578

Gypsies — Fiction
S–Adult: 3009

Gypsies — History
S–Adult: 3007

H

Habitat for Humanity
S: 10136

Habitats
S: 12371

Hadrian's Wall — Fiction
S–Adult: 2583

Hahn, David
S–Adult: 12539

Haiku
JS: 4880

Hair
S: 10961

Haiti
JS: 8278

Haiti — Fiction
JS: 1621, 2712 S: 2696

Haitian Americans
JS: 9783

Haitian Americans — Biography
S–Adult: 6266

Haitian Americans — Fiction
JS: 540

Haizlip, Shirley Taylor
S: 6950

Haley, Alex
JS: 5869

Hall, Glenn
S–Adult: 6718

Halley's Comet
S: 11744

Halloween
See also Holidays
S: 10156 S–Adult: 10153

Halloween — Fiction
JS: 1702

Hallucinogenic drugs
See also Drugs and drug abuse
JS: 10615–16, 10689 S: 11868

Halo, Thea
S–Adult: 6951

***Hamlet* (play)**
S–Adult: 2676

***Hamlet* (play) — Criticism**
JS: 5474 S: 5475 S–Adult: 5461

***Hamlet* (play) — Fiction**
S: 3911

Hammarskjold, Dag
JS: 6849

Hand reading
See also Fortune telling
S: 13057

Handicaps
See Mental handicaps; Physical
disabilities; and specific types of
handicaps, e.g., Dyslexia

Hang gliding
S: 13087

Hankins, Anthony M.
S: 6623

Hannam, Charles
S: 6952

Hannibal
JS: 7516

Hansberry, Lorraine
JS: 5871–73 S: 5870

Hanukkah
See also Jewish holy days

Hanukkah — Fiction
JS: 561

Harding, Warren G.
S–Adult: 6305

Hardy, Thomas — Criticism
S: 5269, 5307

Hares
See Rabbits

Hargreaves, Alison
S–Adult: 6744

Harlem Globetrotters
J: 13224

Harlem (NY)
JS: 8984 JS–Adult: 8972 S: 5822,
5868 S–Adult: 5215, 8983

Harlem (NY) — Fiction
JS: 456, 516, 526, 529 S: 502
S–Adult: 3497

Harlem Renaissance
JS: 5894, 8787, 8789, 8801, 8803, 8805
S: 8799 S–Adult: 4611, 4661

Harlem Renaissance — Biography
JS: 5891–92 S–Adult: 5685

Harley-Davidson motorcycles
JS: 13241

Harper, Martha Matilda
S–Adult: 6624

Harper's Ferry Raid — Fiction
JS: 2798

Harriot, Thomas
JS: 6577

Harrison, George
S–Adult: 6051

JS = Junior High/Senior High; S = Senior High; S–Adult = Senior High/Adult

Harrison, Jim
S–Adult: 5874

Harrison, John
S: 6578

Harrison, Kathryn
S–Adult: 5875

Harvest festivals
See Thanksgiving Day

Hashish
See also Drugs and drug abuse
JS: 10626

Hastings, Battle of
S–Adult: 8125

Hate groups and hate crimes
JS: 9801–2, 9840–41, 9856, 10188, 10188 S: 9487, 9838, 10060
S–Adult: 9821

**Hate groups and hate crimes —
Fiction**
JS: 1592, 1609 S–Adult: 3843

Hatfield-McCoy feud
JS: 2945

Haunted houses
JS: 13046 S: 13042

Haunted houses — Fiction
S: 3158

Hautzig, Esther
JS: 6953

Hawaii — Fiction
JS: 134, 4704 S: 725 S–Adult: 3345

Hawaii — History
JS: 9008

Hawking, Stephen
JS: 6581 S: 6580 S–Adult: 6579

Hawkins, Dwight
JS: 6713

Hawks
See also Birds of prey
S: 12079, 12082, 12084
S–Adult: 12081

Hawks — Fiction
JS: 837

Hawthorne, Nathaniel
S: 5415, 5876

Hawthorne, Nathaniel — Criticism
S: 5327, 5373, 5392, 5403

Hayden, Lewis
JS: 6227

Hayes, Rutherford B.
S–Adult: 6306

Haymarket Square Riot
JS: 8754

Hazardous wastes
S–Adult: 9924

Hazing — Schools
JS: 11456, 11465

Headaches
JS: 10822 S: 10796

Health and health care
See also Exercise; Hygiene
J: 10962 JS: 10566, 10573, 10575,
10762, 11026, 11042, 11123, 11447,
11467–68 S: 10560, 10562, 10576,
11027, 11144

Health and health care — Careers
JS: 10502, 10505, 10511 S: 10456,
10503–4, 10508, 10515, 10517,
10519–20

Health and health care — Women
S–Adult: 10559

Hearing
See Deafness and the deaf

Hearst, William Randolph
JS: 6625

Heart
See also Circulatory system
JS: 11013–14 S: 11011

Heart disease
JS: 10791, 11013–14

Heart of Darkness — Criticism
S: 5302

Heat — Experiments and projects
JS: 12509

Heaven — Fiction
S: 1963

Heavy Metal (music)
S–Adult: 7136, 7162

Hecht, Thomas T.
S: 7717

Heenan, Bobby
S–Adult: 13247

Height, Dorothy
S–Adult: 6228

Heinlein, Robert A. — Criticism
S: 5412

Helfgott, David
S: 6052

Helicopter pilots — Biography
S–Adult: 6483

Hemingway, Ernest
JS: 5877, 5879–80 S: 5878

Hemingway, Ernest — Criticism
S: 5331, 5350, 5421, 5425, 5427

Hemophilia
JS: 10892

Hendrix, Jimi
JS: 6054 S–Adult: 6053

Henna decorations
JS: 10964

Henna painting
JS: 10976

Henrietta Marie (slave ship)
S: 9611

Henry, Marguerite
JS: 5881

**Henry II, King of England —
Fiction**
S–Adult: 2461

Henry VIII, King of England
JS: 6850

**Henry VIII, King of England —
Fiction**
S–Adult: 2005

Henson, Jim
S: 6055 S–Adult: 7098

Henson, Matthew
JS: 5649

Hepatitis
JS: 10855

Herbert, Frank
S–Adult: 5882

Herbs
JS: 10639 S: 11863, 12910, 12917
S–Adult: 12913

Hercules — Fiction
S–Adult: 2174

Heredity
S–Adult: 10927

Heredity — Biography
S–Adult: 6591

Herero (African people)
JS: 7979

Hernandez, Orlando "El Duque"
S–Adult: 6669

Heroes and heroism — Biography
S: 5614 S–Adult: 6154

Heroes and heroism — Fiction
JS: 361, 3660, 4698

Heroin
See also Drugs and drug abuse
JS: 10721 S: 10646, 10699

Herriot, James
JS: 6954 S: 6955

Hershey Company
S: 10213

Herzl, Theodor
JS: 6799

Hesse, Hermann — Criticism
S: 5314

Hickam, Homer
S–Adult: 6956–57

Higa, Tomiko
S: 6958

High schools
JS: 11408 S: 10280
S–Adult: 10258, 11345

High schools — Biography
S: 7008

High schools — Fiction
JS: 294, 307, 322, 344, 789, 892, 935,
1272, 1486, 3109 S: 1275, 1304, 1377,
4565 S–Adult: 1224, 1316, 1502

High schools — Handbooks
JS: 10324

Highwaymen — Fiction
S–Adult: 2651

JS = Junior High/Senior High;   S = Senior High;   S–Adult = Senior High/Adult

1129

Highways
S: 8344

Hiking
See also Walking
JS–Adult: 13250 S: 13253, 13256,
13260, 13271, 13277, 13281
S–Adult: 13257

Hill, Grant
JS: 6696

Hill, Lynn
S–Adult: 13265

Hillesum, Etty
S: 7721

Himalayas
S: 8000 S–Adult: 13266

Himalayas — Fiction
JS: 4

Hindenburg, Paul von
JS: 6851

Hindenburg (dirigible)
JS: 3903

Hindu-Muslim relations — Fiction
S–Adult: 2545

Hinduism
JS: 9074 S: 9093

Hindus — Fiction
S–Adult: 362

Hingis, Martina
JS: 6654

Hinton, S. E.
JS: 5368

Hinton, S. E. — Criticism
S: 5349

Hip-hop — Biography
S–Adult: 6120

Hip-hop — Music
JS: 7163

Hip-hop — Poetry
JS: 4947 S: 4951

Hip-hop — Women
S–Adult: 7155

Hirohito (emperor of Japan)
S: 6800

Hiroshima
JS: 7706, 7761, 7814 S: 6809, 7700,
7754, 7759, 7858 S–Adult: 7719

Hispanic Americans
See also specific groups, e.g.,
Mexican Americans
JS: 9729, 9731–32, 9744 S: 9738,
9742, 10034 S–Adult: 9739–40, 9743

Hispanic Americans — Art
JS: 7089 S: 9730

Hispanic Americans — Baseball
S: 13155

Hispanic Americans — Biography
J: 6114, 6119 JS: 5702, 6090, 6134,
6177, 6186, 6204–5, 6208, 6482, 6523,
6640, 6662, 6688, 6715, 9746 S: 5805,
6503 S–Adult: 6410

Hispanic Americans — Careers
JS: 10431–33, 10448, 10461, 10464,
10484–85, 10499, 10538 S: 10393

Hispanic Americans — Cookbooks
S–Adult: 10161

Hispanic Americans — Essays
S–Adult: 5232

Hispanic Americans — Fiction
J: 480 JS: 422, 433, 470–71, 514, 577,
711, 1045, 1458, 1490, 1568, 1620,
3874, 4722, 9733 S: 406, 409–10, 413,
434, 505, 550, 565 S–Adult: 396, 411,
432, 437, 504, 515, 525, 563, 1880,
4677, 4710

Hispanic Americans — Folklore
S: 5122

Hispanic Americans — History
S: 9741 S–Adult: 9737

Hispanic Americans — Holidays
S–Adult: 10161

Hispanic Americans — Literature
JS: 9746 S–Adult: 469

Hispanic Americans — Memoirs
JS: 9733

Hispanic Americans — Plays
JS: 4834

Hispanic Americans — Poetry
JS: 4955, 5011, 9733 S: 550
S–Adult: 4987, 5027

Hiss, Alger
JS: 9263

Historic sites
S: 8381

History
See also under specific countries and
continents, e.g., Africa — History;
and wars and historical eras, e.g.,
Colonial period (U.S.), Fifteenth
century
S: 7420, 7439, 7574 S–Adult: 6762,
7389, 7405

History — Ancient
See Ancient history

History — Methodology
S: 7413 S–Adult: 7407

History — Women
S–Adult: 7417

Hit-and-run accidents — Fiction
JS: 3693 S: 3722

Hitchcock, Alfred
JS: 6056

Hitler, Adolf
JS: 6853, 6856, 7689, 7741, 8110
S: 6852, 6855 S–Adult: 6854, 6857,
7805, 7817

Hitler, Adolf — Death
S–Adult: 7683

Hitler, Adolf — Fiction
S: 154, 1862

Hitler Youth
JS: 7720, 7734

HIV (virus)
See also AIDS
JS: 10748, 10790, 10875 S: 10752,
10756, 10793, 10834

HIV (virus) — Fiction
JS: 974

Ho Chi Minh
S: 6801

Hoaxes
S–Adult: 8580, 13009

Hobbes, Anne
S: 6959

Hockey
See Ice hockey

Hodgkin's Disease — Biography
JS: 6720

Holdsclaw, Chamique
JS: 6697

Holiday, Billie
JS: 6059 S: 6060 S–Adult: 6057–58

Holidays
See also specific ethnic groups, e.g.,
African Americans — Holidays;
and specific holidays, e.g.,
Christmas
JS: 10154 S: 10157, 10162

Holidays — Cookbooks
S: 12763, 12793

Holidays — Hispanic Americans
S–Adult: 10161

Holidays — Poetry
JS: 4861

Holistic medicine
S: 10907

Hollywood — Fiction
S: 1701 S–Adult: 2984

Holmes, Sherlock — Fiction
S: 3555

Holocaust
J: 6884, 7625, 7627, 7630, 7709, 7803,
7843 JS: 3014, 7626, 7628–29, 7631,
7638–39, 7641–42, 7645–46, 7651,
7654, 7656, 7659, 7685, 7691, 7694,
7702–5, 7707–8, 7712, 7738, 7743–44,
7747, 7751, 7755, 7763, 7769, 7784,
7796–97, 7802, 7806, 7813, 7816,
7820–22, 7832, 7842, 7889, 9178, 9180,
9802 S: 6772, 7624, 7640, 7643–44,
7649, 7653, 7673, 7693, 7721, 7723,
7725, 7740, 7742, 7746, 7750, 7752,
7764, 7772–73, 7779, 7781, 7790–91,
7815, 7825, 7837, 7847
S–Adult: 7594, 7648, 7670, 7682,
7686–87, 7696–97, 7710, 7737, 7745,
7770, 7780, 7795, 7808, 7830, 7838,
7848, 7850–51

Holocaust — Biography
JS: 6763, 6840–44, 6846, 6881,
6894–95, 6917, 6991, 7731 S: 5710,
6828, 6845, 6880, 6924, 6945, 6952,
7650, 7681, 7690, 7717, 7776
S–Adult: 6847, 6893, 6942, 7684

JS = Junior High/Senior High;   S = Senior High;   S–Adult = Senior High/Adult

Holocaust — Fiction
JS: 1122, 2328, 2641, 3004, 3010, 3031, 3036, 3038, 3041–42, 3044, 3050, 3052–54, 3058, 3062, 3068–70, 3074, 3869, 7662, 7796 **S:** 2281, 2997, 3011, 3016, 3033, 3035, 3045–46, 3056, 3066 **S–Adult:** 339, 3009, 3025, 3061

Holocaust — Gypsies
S–Adult: 3007

Holocaust — Italy
S–Adult: 7757

Holocaust — Museums
S: 8988

Holocaust — Plays
JS: 4797

Holocaust — Poetry
JS: 7796 **S:** 4908

Holocaust — Resources
JS: 7819

Holocaust Museum (Washington, DC)
S: 7649, 8988

Holy Grail
S–Adult: 9107

Holy Grail — Fiction
S: 1655

Holy Roman Empire
JS: 7566

Home schooling
S–Adult: 10265

Homeland security
JS: 10169, 10187

Homeland Security, Department of
JS: 9249

Homeless people
See also Poverty
J: 10095 **JS:** 10080, 10090, 10094 **S:** 10083, 10087 **S–Adult:** 10092

Homeless people — Children
JS: 10072

Homeless people — Fiction
JS: 688, 1070, 1466, 1557 **S:** 3551

Homeless people — Teenagers
JS: 10072, 10096

Homer — Criticism
S: 5320

Homesteading
See Frontier life (U.S.)

Homophobia
JS: 9439, 11246

Homophobia — Plays
S–Adult: 5517

Homosexuality
See also Gay men and lesbians; Gay youth
JS: 4609, 11234, 11236, 11245–46, 11252, 11254, 11258, 11262 **S:** 1253, 11237, 11251, 11266, 11268, 11272, 11274, 11277, 11309, 11396 **S–Adult:** 10268

Homosexuality — Family life
S–Adult: 11576

Homosexuality — Fiction
JS: 381, 585, 674, 1047, 1091, 1155, 1172, 1206, 1221, 1259, 1271, 1285, 1372, 1403, 1411, 1490, 1500, 3067, 4563 **S:** 1053, 1099, 1183, 1198, 1280, 1378, 1437, 1439, 1450, 1464, 1475, 1507, 1528, 3291, 3976, 4032 **S–Adult:** 396, 545, 1167, 1332, 1456, 1511, 1537, 1539, 3882

Homosexuality — Marriage
S: 9468

Homosexuality — Memoirs
S–Adult: 6920

Honesty — Fiction
JS: 1066, 1536

Hong Kong
JS: 8022

Hong Kong — Fiction
S: 3536

Hooks, Bell
S: 5883

Hope — Fiction
JS: 998, 4648

Hopi Indians — Fiction
JS: 3656

Horror — Poetry
S–Adult: 1801

Horror stories — Fiction
See also Mystery stories — Fiction; Supernatural
JS: 233, 264, 3093, 3096, 3104–5, 3117, 3119, 3128, 3134, 3143–44, 3146, 3154, 3157, 3159–60, 3179–80, 3221, 3226, 3237–38, 3246–47, 3251, 3257–58, 3275, 5116 **S:** 234, 236, 260, 263, 1918, 2359, 3097–98, 3122, 3126, 3132, 3135, 3145, 3147, 3150, 3161–64, 3166, 3168, 3171–74, 3182–83, 3186, 3188–89, 3191–93, 3198, 3203, 3215, 3217, 3220, 3229–32, 3234, 3236, 3253, 3440–41 **S–Adult:** 194, 1799–801, 2293, 2353, 2375, 2378, 3103, 3108, 3110–11, 3113, 3116, 3125, 3138, 3140–41, 3156, 3167, 3170, 3175, 3177, 3185, 3187, 3194, 3201–2, 3204–6, 3222, 3227, 3233, 3235, 3239, 3244, 3252, 3618, 4627, 4669, 4706

Horror stories — Folklore
JS: 5139

Horror stories — History and criticism
JS: 5256, 5261 **S:** 5324, 5406

Horse racing
S: 13349 **S–Adult:** 12316, 13353, 13355

Horse racing — Fiction
JS: 180 **S:** 3512, 3515 **S–Adult:** 779, 3513, 4592

Horseback riding
J: 13350 **S:** 12317, 13351 **S–Adult:** 12316, 13352, 13354, 13357

Horses
JS: 12318 **S:** 12306–7, 12312, 12314–15, 12317 **S–Adult:** 7093, 12308–11, 12313, 12316, 13354, 13358

Horses — Fiction
JS: 67, 94, 178–80, 2042, 2764, 2889, 2972, 3554 **S:** 169, 181, 183, 1710, 2704 **S–Adult:** 176, 285

Horses — Grooming
S–Adult: 13356

Horses — Poetry
JS: 5511

Horses — Training
S: 12314 **S–Adult:** 13352

Horseshoe crabs
S–Adult: 12168

Hospitals
S: 10925

Hospitals — Careers
S: 10519

Hospitals — Fiction
JS: 1550

Hostages
JS: 10015

Hot rods
S: 13144

Hotels — Fiction
S: 1547

Houdini, Harry
S: 6061

House of Representatives (U.S.)
See also Congress (U.S.); Government (U.S.)
JS: 9251 **S:** 9247

Houseplants
S: 12911, 12915

Houses
See also Building and construction
S–Adult: 12579

Houston (TX) — Fiction
JS: 1521

Howard, Ron
JS: 6062

Howe, Samuel
S–Adult: 11154

Hubble, Edwin
S: 6582

Hubble space telescope
JS: 11735 **S:** 11680 **S–Adult:** 11675

Hughes, Langston
JS: 5884–87 **S:** 5363 **S–Adult:** 4991

Hughes, Langston — Criticism
S: 5518

Human behavior
S: 11924

Human body
See also specific parts and systems of the human body, e.g., Circulatory system

JS: 10974, 10978, 10987, 12884
S: 10981, 10986, 10988–89, 10989, 10991, 11036 **S–Adult:** 10905

Human development and behavior
See also Personal guidance; Psychology
JS: 10995, 11334 **S–Adult:** 11366

Human Genome Project
JS: 10946 **S:** 10933–34, 10943

Human rights
See also Civil rights
J: 7630 **JS:** 6171, 9383, 9400, 9418, 9458 **S:** 9464, 9473, 9483, 9500
S–Adult: 9460, 9470–71

Humanitarians — Biography
JS: 6894 **S–Adult:** 6893

Hummingbirds
S: 12072 **S–Adult:** 12044

Humor and satire
See also Wit and humor
S: 5201, 13030, 13253
S–Adult: 5182, 5193, 5592, 5853, 9590, 10341

Humor and satire — Art
S: 7062

Humor and satire — Fiction
JS: 266, 268, 632, 1124, 1138, 1193, 1225, 1300–1, 1386, 1482, 1549, 3180, 3259, 3261, 3264–65, 3267–70, 3274–75, 3277–81, 3283, 3286, 3288–89, 3292–95, 3298, 3300, 3303, 3305–6, 3309–10, 3313, 3315, 3317–20, 3325, 3327–28, 3912, 3992 **S:** 346, 727, 1048, 1305, 1982, 2168, 2223, 3262, 3272, 3276, 3282, 3285, 3287, 3291, 3307, 3312, 3314, 3321–24, 3326, 3566, 3626, 3630, 3741, 4083, 5190, 5201 **S–Adult:** 350, 600, 1604, 1659, 1749, 1937, 1989, 2146, 2897, 3260, 3266, 3271, 3273, 3284, 3290, 3296–97, 3299, 3301–2, 3304, 3311, 3330, 3333, 3521, 3921, 3971, 3995, 3998–99, 4075, 4116, 4422, 5237, 12290

Humor and satire — Literature
S: 5393

Humor and satire — Quotations
S: 5196

Humorous poetry
See Poetry — Humorous

Humpback whales
S: 12197

Hundred Years' War — Fiction
S–Adult: 2577

Hungary — Biography
JS: 6998

Hungary — Cookbooks
J: 12796

Hungary — Fiction
JS: 3004 **S:** 3035

Hungary — History
JS: 7712

Hunger
See also Poverty

JS: 10071, 10079

Hunter, Clementine
JS: 5757

Hunter-Gault, Charlayne
S: 6486

Hunters and hunting
JS: 13301 **S:** 13298

Hunters and hunting — Fiction
JS: 942

Huntley, Paula
S–Adult: 6960

Hurd, Barbara
S–Adult: 6961

Hurricanes
See also Storms
JS: 12431 **S:** 12437 **S–Adult:** 12436

Hurricanes — Fiction
JS: 36 **S–Adult:** 12438

Hurston, Zora Neale
JS: 5891–92, 5894 **S:** 5893
S–Adult: 5888–90

Hurston, Zora Neale — Criticism
S–Adult: 5365

Hussein, Saddam
JS: 6802, 8945

Hussein, Saddam — Fiction
S: 42

Huxley, Aldous — Criticism
S: 5283

Hydrogen bomb
S: 12717

Hygiene
See also Health care
J: 10962 **JS:** 10573, 11481

Hynes, Samuel
S–Adult: 6962

Hypnotherapy
S: 11048 **S:** 5389

I

***I Know Why the Caged Bird Sings* — Criticism**
JS: 5337 **S:** 5389

Ibo (African people)
S: 7992

Ibsen, Henrik — Criticism
S: 5453

Ice Age — Fiction
S–Adult: 2389

Ice Ages
JS: 7346 **S–Adult:** 7340, 12354

Ice cream
S: 12784

Ice hockey
JS: 13342, 13342, 13346 **S:** 13348
S–Adult: 13340–41, 13344–45

Ice hockey — Biography
JS: 6720 **S–Adult:** 6718

Ice hockey — Fiction
JS: 4578, 4584 **S:** 4577

Ice hockey — History
S: 13347

Ice hockey — Women
S: 13343

Ice skating
JS: 13359, 13359–60, 13362, 13366, 13366 **S:** 13361, 13361, 13365, 13367, 13367 **S–Adult:** 13363, 13363–64

Ice skating — Biography
JS: 6719, 6719, 6721 **S–Adult:** 13364

Ice skating — Fiction
JS: 294

Iceland
S: 6749

Ichiro (baseball player)
JS–Adult: 13198

Idaho
S: 8968

Iditarod Sled Dog Race
S: 13112

Igbo (African people)
JS: 7993

***Iliad* — Adaptations**
JS: 5177

***Iliad* — Criticism**
S: 5320

Illegal aliens
JS: 9509, 9524 **S:** 9511, 9539, 9541

Illegal aliens — Fiction
JS: 1395, 1568, 1620

Illinois — Fiction
JS: 2930

Illiteracy
JS: 11547

Illiteracy — Fiction
JS: 308

Illness
See Diseases and illness

Illustrations
S–Adult: 7038

Illustrations — Birds
S–Adult: 12055

Illustrators — Biography
S–Adult: 5728

Imaginary languages
JS: 7223

Immigration
JS: 9521, 9526, 9528, 9532 **S:** 9523

Immigration — Fiction
JS: 454, 1024, 2770, 3063 **S:** 216
S–Adult: 560

Immigration (U.S.)
See also Ethnic groups
JS: 7928, 8033, 8204, 8246, 8258, 9509–10, 9513, 9515–16, 9518, 9522,

9524–25, 9527, 9529–31, 9534,
9536–38, 9540, 9564, 9718, 9720, 9727,
9745, 9753, 9769, 9772–73 **S:** 8232,
9511, 9514, 9533, 9539, 9541–42, 9715
S–Adult: 9512, 9520, 9535

Immigration (U.S.) — Fiction
JS: 52, 470, 540, 746, 2536, 2911,
3040, 4732 **S:** 426, 1624, 2660

Immigration (U.S.) — History
S–Adult: 9706

Immigration (U.S.) — Illegal
See also Illegal aliens
JS: 9517 **S:** 9519

Immune system
JS: 10763, 10775, 10868, 10909,
10979, 10990

Immunology
S: 10837

Impeachment
JS: 9234

Imperialism
JS: 7434

Impressionism (art)
JS: 7081 **S:** 5766, 7066
S–Adult: 7071

Improvisation (theater)
JS: 7285 **S:** 7293, 7298

Inaugurations
JS: 9241

Inca Trail
S–Adult: 8293

Incas
J: 8298 **JS:** 8295 **S:** 8285, 8291–92

Incest
See also Family problems; Sexual
abuse
JS: 11308, 11310

Incest — Fiction
S: 611, 641, 1052

Inchon, Invasion of (Korean War)
JS: 7880 **S–Adult:** 8918

Indentured servants — Fiction
JS: 2762

India
JS: 8023, 8033 **S:** 8031
S–Adult: 8030

India — Biography
JS: 6793, 6795, 6797 **S–Adult:** 6796

India — Cookbooks
S: 12825

India — Fiction
JS: 454, 2501, 2544 **S:** 230, 1611,
2497, 2507, 2519 **S–Adult:** 439, 1141,
2494–95, 2505, 2508, 2513, 2524, 2545,
3923, 3987

India — Folklore
JS: 5084 **S:** 5081

India — History
JS: 8034 **S:** 6794, 8024, 8028, 8032
S–Adult: 8027

India — Poetry
JS: 4937

Indian Americans — Fiction
S: 474 **S–Adult:** 439, 488

Indian British — Fiction
JS: 549

Indiana — Fiction
S: 3463

**Indianapolis Speedway Race —
History**
S: 13145

Indians
S: 6950

**Indians of Central America —
Dance**
S: 7213

**Indians of Central America —
Fiction**
JS: 1564

Indians of North America
See Native Americans and specific
groups, e.g., Cherokee Indians

Indians of North America — Fiction
JS: 1564

Indians of South America
JS: 8296 **S:** 8288, 8291

**Indians of South America —
Folklore**
JS: 5151

**Indians of South America —
History**
S: 8430, 8450

Indigenous peoples
S–Adult: 7348

Individualism — Fiction
S: 1606–7

Indonesia — Fiction
S–Adult: 2547

Industrial Revolution
JS: 7577, 8758

**Industrial Revolution — United
States**
S: 8347

Industry — Biography
JS: 6608, 6617 **S–Adult:** 6618

Industry — History
JS: 6609 **S:** 8347

Infanticide — Fiction
S–Adult: 3810

Infertility
S: 11253

Influenza — Fiction
S: 4379

Influenza epidemic (1918)
JS: 10733 **S–Adult:** 8782

Information handling
JS: 10281

Information Revolution
JS: 12635 **S:** 12597

Inhalants
J: 10695 **S:** 10637

Injuries
JS: 10830

Inline skating
JS: 13369 **S:** 13368

Inner cities
JS: 10091 **S:** 10211

Insanity — Fiction
S: 4216

Insanity defense
JS: 9344 **S:** 10011

Insects
See also names of specific insects,
e.g., Butterflies and moths
JS: 12131, 12135–36, 12143
S: 12127–30, 12133–34, 12137, 12146
S–Adult: 12125, 12138, 12142, 12147

Insects — Reproduction
S: 12144

Insects — Societies
S–Adult: 12141

Insomnia
JS: 10994

Intel Corporation — Biography
JS: 6621 **S–Adult:** 6622

Intelligence
See also Human development and
behavior
JS: 11387 **S:** 11389 **S–Adult:** 11388

Intelligence service
JS: 9184

Interculturalism
S–Adult: 9556

International crime
JS: 9176

International relations
JS: 9173, 9175, 9193 **S:** 7418, 9174,
9183, 9185

Internet
See also World Wide Web
J: 12609, 12611 **JS:** 11649, 12590,
12602–3, 12612, 12620 **S:** 10332,
12585, 12588–89, 12591–92, 12597,
12599–600, 12608, 12617
S–Adult: 12587, 12615

Internet — Censorship
JS: 12605

Internet — Ethics
S: 12608

Internet — Fiction
JS: 1386 **S:** 3581

Internet — History
S: 12614

Internet — Regulation
S–Adult: 12624

Internment camps
S: 8845

Interpersonal relations
JS: 11335 **S–Adult:** 11366

JS = Junior High/Senior High;   S = Senior High;   S–Adult = Senior High/Adult

Italy — Plays
S: 4784

Iwo Jima, Battle of
JS: 7658, 7680 S: 7800

J

Jack the Ripper
S–Adult: 9965

Jackson, Andrew
JS: 6307–8 S: 8484, 8578

Jackson, Andrew — Fiction
S: 2794, 2803

Jackson, Jesse
JS: 6229

Jackson, Mahalia
JS: 6064–65

Jackson, Michael
S: 6066

Jackson, Stonewall
JS: 6409

Jacobs, Harriet A. — Fiction
JS: 2787

Jacobs, Lionel and Barron
J: 8737

Jacobsen, Ruth
JS: 7731

Jaguars
JS: 11997

Jaguars — Fiction
JS: 2711

Jamaica — Biography
S: 6087–88 S–Adult: 6086

Jamaica — Fiction
JS: 609 S–Adult: 2695

Jamaica — Music
JS: 7153

Jamaica — Poetry
JS: 5046

Jamaican Americans
JS: 9772

James I, King of England
JS: 6858

Jamestown (VA) — Fiction
JS: 2738

Jamestown (VA) — History
JS: 8499

Jane Eyre **— Criticism**
JS: 5265 S: 5281

Japan
JS: 8035–36, 8039–42

Japan — Biography
S: 6800 S–Adult: 6929, 6984

Japan — Fiction
JS: 1542, 1793–94, 1934, 2517, 2520, 2535, 2551 S: 1359, 2371, 2512, 2530,

2539 S–Adult: 2504, 2506, 2538, 3330

Japan — Folklore
S: 5088 S–Adult: 5080

Japan — History
JS: 7761, 8038 S: 6800, 8037

Japan — World War II
S: 7818

Japanese — Biography
JS–Adult: 6678

Japanese Americans
See also Asian Americans
J: 8846 JS: 8827, 8830, 8836, 8851, 8853–54, 9726–27 S: 7829, 8828, 8841, 8845

Japanese Americans — Biography
JS: 6721 S: 5950, 7001, 9712

Japanese Americans — Fiction
JS: 478, 483, 517, 535 S: 520, 579, 725, 4589 S–Adult: 723, 1000, 2985

Japanese Americans — History
J: 8846 JS: 8832, 8835, 8838, 8844 S: 8833

Jaramillo, Mari-Luci
S–Adult: 6410

Java — Fiction
S–Adult: 2546

Jazz
JS: 7128, 7147–48 S: 7132–33, 7164, 7174, 7177 S–Adult: 7165, 7167, 7179

Jazz — Biography
JS: 5698, 5721, 5999, 6001, 6006, 6019–20, 6027, 6038, 6040–41, 6047, 6100, 7149 S: 5996, 5998, 6005, 6026, 6029, 6039, 6089 S–Adult: 5997, 6028

Jazz — History
JS: 7138 S: 7146 S–Adult: 7159, 7175, 7181

Jefferson, Thomas
JS: 6311–14 S: 6310 S–Adult: 6309

Jefferson, Thomas — Fiction
JS: 2767 S: 2776

Jemison, Mae
JS: 5650

Jennings, Cedric
S: 6963

Jerusalem
JS: 8205

Jerusalem — Fiction
S–Adult: 2619, 2627, 2673

Jesus Christ — Fiction
S: 202 S–Adult: 3297

Jewel (singer)
JS: 6067

Jewelry — Fiction
S: 209

Jewelry making
See also Earring making
JS: 12848 S: 12850, 12856–57, 12868

Jewett, Sarah Orne
S: 5895

Jewish Americans
JS: 8819, 9748, 9751, 9753 S: 9754
S–Adult: 9749–50

Jewish Americans — Biography
J: 8737

Jewish Americans — Fiction
JS: 3043 S–Adult: 1265

Jewish holy days
See also specific holy days, e.g., Hanukkah
S: 9145, 9152

Jewish holy days — Fiction
JS: 561

Jewish humor
S: 5054

Jews
JS: 9153, 9552 S–Adult: 9749

Jews — Biography
JS: 6917 S: 6772 S–Adult: 7004, 7770

Jews — Fiction
JS: 1379, 1588, 2405, 2407, 2411, 2413, 2630, 2654, 3010, 3022, 3031, 3036–37, 3041–44, 3050–52, 3058, 3063, 3068, 3869 S: 541–42, 930, 1414, 1618, 2997, 3033, 3035, 3046, 3312 S–Adult: 391, 399, 511, 1085, 2442, 2628, 2631, 2677, 4604, 4712

Jews — Folklore
S: 5054, 5067, 5118

Jews — History
See also Holocaust; Immigration (U.S.); Israeli-Arab relations; World War II
J: 6884, 7709, 7803, 7843, 9752
JS: 7626, 7628, 7638–39, 7641–42, 7646, 7651, 7662, 7691, 7707, 7743–44, 7751, 7769, 7813, 7816, 7819–20, 7842, 7889, 9751 S: 2597, 6952, 7433, 7640, 7673, 7725, 7740, 7750, 7752, 7773, 7815, 7847, 8184, 9148, 9150, 9747
S–Adult: 7409, 7648, 7682, 7686–87, 7696–97, 7710, 7745, 7780, 7795, 7851, 7859, 9144

Jews — Musicals
S: 4835

Jews — Plays
S: 4793, 4829

Jiang, Ji-li
JS: 6803

Jim Crow laws
JS: 9420

Jim Crowism
JS: 9506 S–Adult: 8386, 9681

Joan of Arc
JS: 8100 S–Adult: 6859

Joan of Arc — Fiction
JS: 2446 S: 2596 S–Adult: 1758, 2615

JS = Junior High/Senior High;   S = Senior High;   S–Adult = Senior High/Adult

Job hunting
See also Occupational guidance;
Vocational guidance
JS: 10546 **S:** 10359, 10365, 10508

Jobs — Fiction
JS: 3692

Jogging
See Running and jogging

John, Elton
S: 6068–69

John Paul II, Pope
S: 6861 **S–Adult:** 6860

Johnny Tremain **— Criticism**
JS: 5424

Johnson, James Weldon
S: 5896

Johnson, Lyndon B.
JS: 6315, 6317, 6319 **S:** 6318
S–Adult: 6316

Johnson, Magic
JS: 6698

Johnson, Robert
S–Adult: 6070

Jokes and riddles
S: 13000

Jones, Caroline
JS: 6626

Jones, Dr. Bobby
S–Adult: 6487

Jones, James Earl
JS: 6071 **S:** 6072

Jones, Mother
JS: 6231, 8752 **S–Adult:** 6230

Joplin, Scott
JS: 5986–87 **S:** 5985

Jordan
J: 8226 **JS:** 8223 **S–Adult:** 8221

Jordan, Barbara
JS: 6411–12 **S:** 6413

Jordan, Michael
JS: 6641, 6699–700 **S–Adult:** 6701

Jordan, Vernon E.
S–Adult: 6232

Joseph (Bible) — Fiction
S: 2402–3

Joseph (Nez Perce chief)
S: 6415 **S–Adult:** 6414

Journal keeping
JS: 10318 **S:** 10304

Journalism
JS: 5577, 5579, 5582 **S:** 5595
S–Adult: 5588, 5591, 5593, 5596–98,
5604–5, 8927, 9849, 10168, 10374,
11879, 13089

Journalism — African Americans
JS: 5603

Journalism — Biography
JS: 5599, 5694, 5715, 5724, 6183,
6620, 6625, 6630 **S:** 5816, 6469–70,
6486, 6629, 6631 **S–Adult:** 8912

Journalism — Careers
J: 10368 **JS:** 10380, 10407, 10421
S–Adult: 6989, 10372, 10412

Journalism — Fiction
JS: 866, 1594 **S:** 1481

Journalism — News reporting
S–Adult: 5602

Journalism — Tabloid
JS: 5577, 5579

Journalism — Women
JS: 6619 **S:** 6469

Journals
See also Diaries

Journals — Fiction
JS: 2918

Joyce, James — Criticism
S: 5300

Joyner-Kersee, Jackie
JS: 6729

Judaism
See also Jews; Jews — History;
Religion
JS: 9147, 9153 **S:** 9145, 9148,
9151–52 **S–Adult:** 9144, 9146, 9149

Judaism — Biography
S: 6768

Judaism — Fiction
JS: 2411

Judge, Oney — Fiction
JS: 2766

Judges
JS: 9316

Judges — Biography
S–Adult: 6456

Judicial system
JS: 9316

Juggling
S: 13090, 13128

Jujitsu
JS: 13374

Julius Caesar **(play) — Criticism**
JS: 5468 **S:** 5476

Jungles
See also Rain forests
S–Adult: 12378

Jungles — Fiction
S: 15 **S–Adult:** 133

Jupiter (planet)
S–Adult: 11716

Jury system
JS: 9261, 9269 **S:** 9287
S–Adult: 9285

Justice
JS: 9274

Justice — Folklore
S: 5058

Juvenile delinquency
JS: 10061–62 **S–Adult:** 9975, 10039

Juvenile delinquency — Fiction
JS: 63–66, 126, 715, 1505

Juvenile delinquency — Schools
S–Adult: 10269

Juvenile violence
See Teenagers — Violence; Violence

K

K2 (mountain)
S–Adult: 13251

Kafka, Franz
S–Adult: 5897

Kane, Bob
S: 5758

Kansas — Fiction
S–Adult: 2870, 2923

Kansas — History
JS: 8589 **S:** 8741, 8964

Karate
See also Martial arts
JS: 13376

Kashmir
S–Adult: 8029

Kashner, Sam
S–Adult: 6964

Kayaks and kayaking
JS: 8993 **S:** 13401 **S–Adult:** 8043,
13403, 13409

Kaysen, Susanna
S–Adult: 11076

Kazakhstan
JS: 8150

Keller, Helen
JS: 6490–91 **JS–Adult:** 6489
S–Adult: 6488

Kelly, Clara Olink
S–Adult: 7735

Kennedy, Jacqueline
See Onassis, Jacqueline Kennedy

Kennedy, John F.
JS: 6321, 6324–28 **S:** 6322–23, 8880

Kennedy, John F. — Assassination
S–Adult: 9237

Kennedy, John F., Jr.
S–Adult: 6329

Kennedy, Robert F.
JS: 6330, 8862 **S–Adult:** 6331–32

**Kennedy Center (Washington, DC)
— Fiction**
S: 3824

Kennedy family
JS: 6320

Kentucky — Fiction
JS: 2945

Kenya
JS: 7919–20, 7926–27, 7929–30, 7943–45 S–Adult: 7931, 11970, 11993

Kenya — Biography
JS: 6968 S–Adult: 7942

Kerr, M. E.
JS: 10301

Kerr, M. E. — Criticism
JS: 5898

Kesey, Ken — Criticism
S: 5377

Key, Francis Scott
S–Adult: 8574

Kibbutz life — Fiction
JS: 2558, 2629

Kidd, Captain
S–Adult: 7394

Kidnapping
S: 9814

Kidnapping — Fiction
JS: 113, 299, 649, 777, 1405, 2061, 3377, 3492, 3494, 3552, 3585, 3828, 4479 S: 402, 893, 3623, 3783
S–Adult: 3339

Kidney diseases
JS: 10818

Kidney failure — Fiction
JS: 964

Kiley, Deborah Scaling
S: 5651

Killer whales
S: 12205, 12208 S–Adult: 12212

King, Coretta Scott
JS: 6234 S: 6233

King, Dexter
S–Adult: 6235

King, Martin Luther, Jr.
J: 6244 JS: 6239, 6243, 6247, 8861, 9658 S: 6233, 6242, 6245–46, 6502
S–Adult: 6235–38, 6240–41

King, Stephen
JS: 5900, 5902 S–Adult: 5901

King, Stephen — Criticism
S: 5402, 5405–6, 5423, 5429

King Arthur
See Arthur, King

King Philip's War
S: 6440

King-Smith, Dick
JS: 5899

Kingsland, Rosemary
S–Adult: 6965

Kingsley, Anna Madgigine Jai
S–Adult: 6492

Kiowa Indians — Fiction
S: 2726

Kissing
JS: 11355

Kleckley, Elizabeth
JS: 6493

Klein, Norma
S: 5903

Knight, Bobby
S–Adult: 6702

Knights
See also Middle Ages
J: 7541 JS: 7530 S: 7539
S–Adult: 7523

Knights — Fiction
JS: 2438 S: 2266, 2447
S–Adult: 2589

Knitting
S: 12965, 12968 S–Adult: 12960, 12962–63, 12969, 12975

Knossos (palace)
JS: 7381

Knowles, John — Criticism
S: 5378

Koalas
JS: 12031 S: 12032

Kongo (African people)
JS: 7934

Kongo Ndongo (African kingdom)
JS: 7989

Koontz, Dean
S: 5904

Koran — Women
JS: 9080

Kordi, Gobar
S: 6804

Korea — Biography
S–Adult: 6929

Korea — Fiction
See also North Korea; Korean War
JS: 2503, 2551, 3077 S: 5, 2525
S–Adult: 2541

Korean Americans
JS: 9721 S: 9713

Korean Americans — Fiction
JS: 495–96, 1101 S: 530, 3087
S–Adult: 487

Korean War
JS: 7861, 7867, 7873, 7884, 8928
S: 8929, 8942 S–Adult: 5047, 8940, 8949

Korean War — Battles
JS: 7880

Korean War — Biography
JS: 6761

Korean War — Fiction
JS: 3077 S: 3083

Korman, Marvin
S–Adult: 8980

Kosovo
S–Adult: 6960, 12725

Kosovo War — Fiction
J: 2632

Koufax, Sandy
S–Adult: 6670

Kovic, Ron
JS: 6494 S: 8932

Kraft, Chris
S–Adult: 6583

Ku Klux Klan — Fiction
JS: 2961

Kung fu — Fiction
JS: 2398

Kurdistan
JS: 8214 S: 8224

Kurds — Fiction
JS: 489

Kursk
S–Adult: 8164

Kuusisto, Stephen
S: 6495

Kuwait
See also Persian Gulf War
J: 8217 JS: 8219 S: 8925

Kwan, Michael David
S–Adult: 8015

Kwan, Michelle
JS: 6719

Kwanzaa
JS: 10159 S: 10158

Kyrgyzstan
JS: 8150 S–Adult: 13254

L

Labor camps — Fiction
S: 1614

Labor movements — Biography
JS: 6231 S–Adult: 6230

Labor movements — Fiction
JS: 2950

Labor problems
JS: 8754, 10241

Labor problems — Fiction
JS: 557

Labor unions
JS: 10237

Labor unions — Biography
JS: 6187

Labor unions — History
JS: 10239, 10241 S: 10240
S–Adult: 9786

Laborit, Emmanuelle
S–Adult: 6966

Lacrosse
S: 13095, 13129

Lakes (U.S.)
See Great Lakes

Lakota Indians
JS: 8479 S: 8468 S–Adult: 9755

JS = Junior High/Senior High;   S = Senior High;   S–Adult = Senior High/Adult

Landmines
JS: 9819

Landmines — Fiction
JS: 1570

lang, k. d.
S: 6073

Lange, Dorothea
JS: 5761 S: 5759 S–Adult: 5760

Language
See also Dictionaries
JS: 5542 S: 5541, 5550
S–Adult: 5554, 5558

Large women
S: 11403

Las Vegas — Biography
JS: 6504

Las Vegas — Fiction
S–Adult: 1044

Laser vision correction
S–Adult: 10914

Lasers
S: 12529 S–Adult: 10914

LASIK
S–Adult: 10914

Lasky, Kathryn
S: 5905

Latifah, Queen
S: 6074

Latimer, Lewis
JS: 6627

Latin
S: 13000

Latin America
See Caribbean Islands; Central
America; South America; national
and ethnic groups, e.g., Hispanic
Americans; and specific countries,
e.g., Mexico

Latin America — Cookbooks
S–Adult: 12769

Latin America — History
S–Adult: 8283

Latin Americans
See Hispanic Americans

Law
See also Legal system
JS: 9267, 9277, 9322, 9332, 9340,
10005 S: 7437 S–Adult: 7176

Law — Careers
JS: 10493, 10499 S: 10491

Law — United States
S: 9288

Law enforcement
See also Police
JS: 10021

Law enforcement — Careers
J: 10487 JS: 10486, 10500

Law enforcement — History
S: 9945

Law school — Women
S–Adult: 10490

Lawrence, Jacob
S–Adult: 7102

Lawyers
JS: 9297

Lawyers — Biography
JS: 6195, 9797

Lawyers — Fiction
S: 3551 S–Adult: 2943

Lawyers — Women
S: 9289, 9298

Leach, Terry
S–Adult: 6671

Leadership
JS: 11459

Leakey, Louis
S: 6584

Leap year — Fiction
JS: 355

Learning
See also Psychology
JS: 11391

Learning disabilities
See also specific disabilities, e.g.,
Attention deficit disorder; Dyslexia
JS: 11054, 11084, 11091, 11095
S: 11053, 11057 S–Adult: 11078

Learning disabilities — Biography
JS: 11044

Learning disabilities — Fiction
JS: 1405

Leather work
S: 12730

Lebanese Americans — Biography
JS: 6429

Lebanon
J: 8225

Lebanon — Cookbooks
J: 12754

Lebanon — Fiction
S: 1098

LeBron, James
JS: 6703

Led Zeppelin
S–Adult: 7142

Lederer, Katy
S–Adult: 6967

Lee, Bruce
J: 6076 JS: 6075 S–Adult: 13373

Lee, Harper — Criticism
S: 5334, 5395

Lee, Robert E.
JS: 6417 S: 6184, 6418–19
S–Adult: 6416

Lee, Spike
JS: 6077–78

Legal system
See also Law; Law enforcement

JS: 9332 S: 9288

Lekuton, Joseph Lemasolai
JS: 6968

Lemieux, Mario
JS: 6720

Lenape Indians — Fiction
S: 3557

Lenin, Vladimir Ilich
JS: 6862–63

Leningrad — History
JS: 7713 S–Adult: 7807

Leningrad, Siege of
JS: 7713

Lennon, John
JS: 6079, 6081 S: 6080

Leonowens, Anna
JS: 6969

Leprosy — Fiction
JS: 2638

Lerner, Betsy
S–Adult: 6970

Lerner, Gerda
S–Adult: 6971

Lesbians
See Gay men and lesbians;
Homosexuality

Letter writing
JS: 10291

Letters
S: 9188 S–Adult: 7854, 8791, 8934

Letters — Fiction
JS: 3065 S–Adult: 138

Leukemia
J: 10824 JS: 10833, 10850, 10856
S: 6972

Leukemia — Biography
S: 6809

Leukemia — Fiction
JS: 942 S: 922 S–Adult: 808

Lewin, Ted
JS: 5762

Lewis, Carl
JS: 6730

Lewis, Edmonia
JS: 5763

Lewis, John
S: 6248

Lewis, Meriwether
JS: 5653 S: 5652

Lewis and Clark Expedition
JS: 5653 JS–Adult: 8494 S: 5652,
5654–55, 8490 S–Adult: 8489, 8495

**Lewis and Clark Expedition —
Fiction**
JS: 2732 S: 2731, 2735
S–Adult: 2734, 2736, 2897

Libby Prison — Fiction
S: 2823

JS = Junior High/Senior High;   S = Senior High;   S–Adult = Senior High/Adult

M

Lungs
See Respiratory system

Lyme disease
JS: 10758, 10883

Lymphoma — Fiction
JS: 943

Lyric authors
S: 7143

Macaroni — Cookbooks
S–Adult: 12831

MacArthur, Douglas
JS: 6421

Macbeth — Criticism
S: 5467, 5479, 5487

Macbeth — Fiction
S–Adult: 2161

McCaffrey, Anne
JS: 5908

McCain, John
JS: 6422

McCall, Bruce
S: 5909

McCandless, Chris
S: 9000

McCarthy, Joseph
JS: 6423, 8863, 8908

McCartney, Paul
S: 6082

McClintock, Barbara
JS: 6585

McCullers, Carson — Criticism
S–Adult: 5330

MacDonald, Andy
JS: 6745

Mace, Nancy
JS: 6973

McGrath, Jeremy
S–Adult: 6746

McGwire, Mark
JS: 6672

Machiavelli, Niccolo
S: 9025

Machines and machinery
JS: 12560 **S:** 12554

**Machines and machinery —
Careers**
S: 10478

McKay, Jim
S: 6083

Mackenzie, Alexander
S–Adult: 5665

McKinley, Catherine E.
S–Adult: 9565

McKinley, William
S–Adult: 6347

McKoy, Millie and Christine
S–Adult: 6084

McLain, Paula
S–Adult: 6974

McNeill, Robert
S–Adult: 6499

Mad cow disease
S–Adult: 11890

Mad (magazine)
S–Adult: 5592

Madagascar
JS: 7963

Madagascar — Animals
S–Adult: 11880

Madison, James
S–Adult: 6348

Madonna (singer)
JS: 6085

Mafia
S: 10051

Mafia — Fiction
S: 130 **S–Adult:** 3751

Magazines
JS: 5584, 10285 **S–Adult:** 5574

Magellan, Ferdinand
JS: 5667 **S:** 5666

Magellan (space expedition)
S: 11762

Magic and magicians
JS: 5273, 12922, 12925, 13025
S: 12921, 12923, 12928
S–Adult: 11600

Magic and magicians — Biography
JS: 5725 **S:** 6061

**Magic and magicians —
Experiments and projects**
JS: 11640

Magic and magicians — Fiction
JS: 2011, 2017, 2070, 3225 **S:** 1626,
1658, 1731, 1953, 2257, 3803, 3872

Magic and magicians — History
JS: 13007 **S:** 12926

Magic tricks
See Magic and magicians

Magnetism
JS: 12534

**Magnetism — Experiments and
projects**
JS: 12535

**Magnifying glasses — Experiments
and projects**
JS: 11646

Mah, Adeline Yen
JS: 6975

Maine
S–Adult: 8978

Maine — Fiction
JS: 2947 **S:** 2952

Makah Indians
S–Adult: 12222

Makeup
See also Cosmetics
S: 10971

Makeup (stage)
JS–Adult: 12748 **S:** 12736, 12930

Malawi
JS: 7932

Malaysia — Fiction
S–Adult: 2531

Malcolm X
JS: 6249, 6251–52, 6259, 8866
S: 6250, 6253 **S–Adult:** 6260, 6997

Mali
JS: 7946, 7991 **S–Adult:** 7948

Mammals
See also specific mammals, e.g.,
Bears
JS: 11941, 11944–45, 11951, 11960
S: 11942 **S–Adult:** 11943, 11952

Mammals — Extinct
JS: 7346

Mammoths
S–Adult: 7316, 7340

Manassas, Battle of
JS: 8630

Manatees
JS: 12219

Mandela, Nelson
J: 6785 **JS:** 6781–83 **S:** 6780
S–Adult: 6784

Mandelbaum, Jack
J: 7843

Manet, Edouard
S–Adult: 5764

Manga
JS: 12897

Manhattan — Fiction
S: 398

Manhattan Project
JS: 12701

Manhattan Project — Fiction
JS: 3075

Manias
JS: 11118

Manic depression
S–Adult: 11115

Manitoba — Fiction
JS: 1525

Mankiller, Wilma
S: 6424

Manners
See Etiquette

Mantle, Mickey
S: 6674 **S–Adult:** 6673

JS = Junior High/Senior High;   S = Senior High;   S–Adult = Senior High/Adult

JS = Junior High/Senior High;   S = Senior High;   S–Adult = Senior High/Adult

Matter (physics) — Experiments and projects
JS: 12507

Mauretania **(ship)**
S–Adult: 3333

Mayan Indians
JS: 8247, 8251 S: 8249, 8265

Mayan Indians — Fiction
JS: 1564, 2711

Mayer, Maria Goeppert
JS: 6586

Mazer, Norma Fox — Criticism
S: 5400

Mbundu (African people)
JS: 7973

Mbuti (African people)
JS: 7933

Mead, Margaret
JS: 6587

Measles
JS: 10862

Measures and measurement — Experiments and projects
JS: 12402

Medea **(play) — Criticism**
S: 5456

Media
See Mass media

Mediation
JS: 11390

Medical care
See also Health care
S–Adult: 10512, 10911

Medical ethics
See also Ethics and ethical behavior
JS: 10910, 10915 S: 10578, 10916

Medical school
S–Adult: 10905

Medical technology
JS: 10926

Medici, Lorenzo de
JS: 6869

Medicinal plants
S: 11857, 11867 S–Adult: 10921

Medicine
See also Diseases and illness; Doctors
J: 10874 JS: 10726, 10918, 10924, 10926 S: 10900, 11027
S–Adult: 10921

Medicine — Biography
S–Adult: 6599

Medicine — Careers
JS: 10432, 10523 S: 10510, 10514–15, 10517–18, 10520 S–Adult: 9613

Medicine — Computers
JS: 10920

Medicine — Fiction
JS: 2675 S–Adult: 3645, 3707

Medicine — History
JS: 8438, 10903, 10912 S: 7470, 10906, 10922 S–Adult: 10841, 10898, 10904

Medicine — Sports
JS: 10902

Medieval times
See Middle Ages

Meditation
S–Adult: 10571

Mediterranean — Cookbooks
S–Adult: 12843

Mediterranean Sea — Fiction
S: 40

Mehndi
JS: 10964, 10976

Meitner, Lise
JS: 6588–89

Melville, Herman
S–Adult: 5910

Melville, Herman — Criticism
S: 5419

Memoirs
JS: 4621, 11346 S: 4888, 5856, 6072, 6924, 6940, 7008, 7717, 7776, 12691
S–Adult: 4707, 5695, 5804, 5815, 5832, 5835, 5855, 5865, 5867, 5874–75, 5918, 5924, 5942, 6092, 6095, 6129, 6228, 6235, 6254, 6456, 6543, 6599, 6738, 6743, 6746, 6911, 6913, 6915–16, 6919–20, 6933, 6937–38, 6941, 6947–48, 6961–62, 6964–65, 6967, 6970–71, 6974, 6978–79, 6982–83, 6987, 6989, 6992, 6994–95, 6997, 6999–7000, 7004–7, 7010, 7012, 7217, 7684, 7729, 7735, 7809, 7830, 7841, 7904, 8029, 8054, 8243, 8918, 8978, 8980, 9405, 9565, 9586, 9601, 9703, 9816, 9960, 10053, 10126, 10269, 10346, 10741, 10799, 10890, 10965, 11233, 11509, 11544, 11566, 11971, 12045, 12256, 12290, 12385, 13265, 13396

Memory
JS: 11391 S: 10276

Mendel, Gregor
JS: 6590 S–Adult: 6591

Mendes, Aristides de Sousa
S–Adult: 7594

Mennonites — Fiction
JS: 1061

Menstruation
See also Puberty
JS: 11240, 11257

Menstruation — Fiction
JS: 915

Mental disorders
See also Mental illness; and specific disorders, e.g., Compulsive behavior
JS: 11106 S: 11057

Mental disorders — Fiction
S–Adult: 924

Mental handicaps
See also Depression (mental state); Dyslexia; Epilepsy; Learning disabilities
JS: 10568 S: 11053, 11067, 11069, 11086

Mental handicaps — Fiction
JS: 1016 S: 950

Mental health
JS: 11052, 11072

Mental illness
See also Mental disorders; and specific disorders, e.g., Compulsive behavior
J: 11061, 11083 JS: 9344, 11050, 11055, 11060, 11070, 11072, 11077, 11087, 11100, 11104, 11106, 11111, 11118 S: 11048, 11093, 11120
S–Adult: 11076, 11110

Mental illness — Biography
S: 6052

Mental illness — Children
S: 11069

Mental illness — Fiction
JS: 619, 680, 757, 896, 916, 945, 967, 978, 980, 982, 993, 1013, 1079, 1366, 3494 S: 686, 911, 927, 930, 1002, 3850
S–Adult: 328, 901, 932, 949, 986, 990

Mental illness — History
S: 11067

Mental illness — Teenagers
S: 11069

Mental problems
See Mental disorders

Mental retardation
S: 11079

Mental retardation — Fiction
JS: 2935, 3149

The Merchant of Venice **— Criticism**
S: 5489

Meridian **— Criticism**
S: 5329

Merina (African people)
JS: 7963

Merlin — Fiction
JS: 1673

Mermaids and mermen — Fiction
JS: 2432

Mermaids and mermen — Folklore
JS: 5070

Mesopotamia — Folklore
JS–Adult: 5148

Metalwork
S: 12749

Meteorites
S: 11741 S–Adult: 11738

Meteorology
See also Weather

Meteorology — Experiments and projects
JS: 12457

JS = Junior High/Senior High; S = Senior High; S–Adult = Senior High/Adult

Meteors
S: 11740

Methadone
See Drugs and drug abuse

Mexican-American War
S: 8555

Mexican Americans
See also Hispanic Americans
JS: 9729, 9744 S: 10034
S–Adult: 9736, 9740

Mexican Americans — Biography
JS: 6433, 6715

Mexican Americans — Fiction
J: 480 JS: 52, 422, 427, 553, 577, 711,
1239, 1490, 2807, 3621, 3669, 4694,
4701, 4722 S: 406, 505, 550, 554, 565,
1194 S–Adult: 389, 431

Mexican Americans — Folklore
S: 5122

**Mexican War (1846–1848) —
Fiction**
JS: 2807

Mexico
JS: 8258, 8264 S: 8257
S–Adult: 8267

Mexico — Art
JS: 5785

Mexico — Biography
JS: 5775

Mexico — Cookbooks
J: 12781 S: 12760, 12795

Mexico — Fiction
JS: 470, 1392, 2703, 2708 S: 655, 855,
1218, 2704 S–Adult: 445, 2698–99

Mexico — Folklore
JS: 5121, 5146

Mexico — History
See also Aztecs
J: 8260 JS: 8259, 8262, 8266
S: 8255, 8261, 8265 S–Adult: 8269

Mexico-U.S. relations
JS: 8263

Michelangelo
JS: 5767–68, 7080 S–Adult: 5769

Michigan
S: 9661

Microbes
JS: 11885 S: 10794

Microbiology
See Microscopes and microbiology

Microchips
S: 12622 S–Adult: 12619

Microscopes and microbiology
JS: 6601, 12226, 12228, 12230, 12230
S: 12225 S–Adult: 12231

**Microscopes and microbiology —
Biography**
JS: 6602

Microsoft — Biography
JS: 6616

Middle Ages
See also Castles; Cathedrals;
Feudalism
J: 7541 JS: 7024–25, 7525, 7529–30,
7543, 7545, 7548, 7560–61, 7566, 8136
S: 5102, 7535, 7540, 7542, 7544, 7547,
7553–54, 7562, 7564, 7569, 7571–72
S–Adult: 7523–24, 7527, 7532, 7551,
7556, 7573

Middle Ages — Art
JS: 7073

Middle Ages — Biography
JS: 6824 S: 6829

Middle Ages — Documents
JS: 7549

Middle Ages — Fiction
JS: 1865, 2437–38, 2440, 2445, 2448,
2451, 2454, 2456, 2462, 2466, 2468–69,
2473, 2636 S: 1783, 1821, 2443–44,
2450, 2453, 2457, 2459–60, 3540, 3720
S–Adult: 1819, 2442, 2449, 2455,
2458, 2461, 2463–64, 2474, 2563, 2573,
2577, 2589, 3784, 3965, 3968, 4002

Middle Ages — Poetry
S: 4923

Middle Ages — Wars
JS: 7552

Middle class — Fiction
S: 255

Middle East
See also specific countries, e.g., Israel
JS: 8186, 8188–89 S: 8191

Middle East — Biography
JS: 6774, 6787, 6802 S: 6788

Middle East — Cookbooks
S–Adult: 12843

Middle East — Fiction
S: 735 S–Adult: 3061

Middle East — Folklore
S–Adult: 5086

Middle East — History
S–Adult: 8190

Middle East — Poetry
J: 4889 JS: 5052

Middle East — Women
JS: 8187

A Midsummer Night's Dream —
Criticism
JS: 5480 S: 5465, 5493

Midwest (U.S.)
See specific states, e.g., Indiana

Midwest (U.S.) — Animal life
S–Adult: 12147

Midwest (U.S.) — Biography
S: 5953

Midwest (U.S.) — Essays
S: 5231

Midwest (U.S.) — Fiction
JS: 274, 1394 S: 242, 256, 539, 616,
2880

Midwives — Fiction
JS: 2445 S–Adult: 2965

Migrant workers
JS: 10235 S–Adult: 571, 9740

Migrant workers — Fiction
J: 480 JS: 618, 1239, 1313 S: 2978

Mijikenda (African people)
JS: 7945

Mikkelsen, Einar
S–Adult: 5671

Military Academy (West Point)
See also Army (U.S.)
S–Adult: 10339, 10348

**Military Academy (West Point) —
Fiction**
S: 493

Military airplanes
JS: 12665

Military history
S: 7395 S–Adult: 9594, 12709

Military policy
JS: 9365

Militia movement (U.S.)
See also Neo-Nazis
JS: 9787, 9791, 9800, 9848 S: 9804

Militia movement (U.S.) — Fiction
JS: 117, 147

Milk — Advertising
S: 10247

Millay, Edna St. Vincent
JS: 5911

Miller, Arthur — Criticism
S: 5496, 5501, 5520, 5527–28, 5530

Miller, Davis
S–Adult: 13373

Miller, Frank
S–Adult: 5583

Miller, Reggie
S: 13215

Miller, Shannon
S: 6717

Mime
JS: 7295, 7303 S: 7282

Min, Anchee
S: 6806

Mind control — Fiction
S: 23

Minerals
See Rocks and minerals

Minerals (food supplement)
S: 11139

Mines and mining — Fiction
JS: 2918

Mines and mining — History
S–Adult: 8238

Minik
JS: 6976

Minnesota
J: 5921

Minnesota — Fiction
JS: 1390, 2918 S–Adult: 2939

Minnesota — Wolves
S–Adult: 12018

Minorities
See also Ethnic groups
S: 9585

Miracles
S: 9063

Miracles — Fiction
S–Adult: 336

Miranda rights
JS: 9290, 9331, 9342 S: 9305

Miranda v. Arizona
JS: 9342

Miró, Joan
JS: 5770

Mirrors
S–Adult: 11613

Miss America — Biography
S: 7011

Missiles — Fiction
S: 4199

Missing children — Fiction
JS: 292, 706, 2710

Missionaries — Biography
S: 5664

Missionaries — Fiction
JS: 2488 S: 1127, 1440, 2487
S–Adult: 241

Missions — California
JS: 8998

Mississippi
JS: 9414, 9489 S–Adult: 10260

Mississippi — Fiction
JS: 2976 S: 479 S–Adult: 1361,
2912, 2920

Mississippi — History
S–Adult: 857

Mississippi Natchez Trace Parkway
S–Adult: 3351

Mississippi River
JS: 8391 S: 5198

Mississippi River — Fiction
JS: 266, 2211 S: 2868, 2921, 3381

Missouri (state) — Fiction
S: 1512 S–Adult: 2959

Mithradates, King of Pontus —
Fiction
S–Adult: 2423

Model making
S: 12931

Modeling (fashion) — Fiction
S: 1368 S–Adult: 918

Modern art
S–Adult: 7043

Modern history
JS: 7868

Mohammed
JS: 6807

Mohawk Indians — Fiction
JS: 2742

Mohawk Indians — History
S: 8420

Monarch butterflies
S–Adult: 12149

Monasteries — Fiction
S: 3720 S–Adult: 384

Monet, Claude
JS: 5771

Money
JS: 10555

Money-making ideas
JS: 10227, 10547 S: 10545

Money management
JS: 10227, 10551, 10555 S: 10338,
10552

Mongolia — History
JS: 6798, 7567

Mongols
JS: 6811

Monks — Fiction
S–Adult: 384, 2589

Monologues
JS: 4744, 4790, 4836 S: 4735–39,
4750–51, 4757–58, 4760, 4798, 4805,
5451, 7254

Monomatapa (African kingdom)
JS: 7969

Mononucleosis
JS: 10778, 10857 S: 10755, 10847

Monroe, James
JS: 6349

Monroe, Marilyn
JS: 6093–94

Monsters
S: 12930, 13016, 13023

Monsters — Fiction
See also Fantasy; Folklore;
Mythology; Supernatural
S: 1870, 1918

Monsters — Mythology
JS: 5153

Montague, Magnificent
S–Adult: 6095

Montana
S: 8968

Montana — Fiction
S: 141, 507, 3736

Montenegro
S–Adult: 8080

Montezuma
JS: 8259

Months
See Calendars

Monuments — Preservation
S–Adult: 7388

Moody, Anne
S: 6977

Moon
S: 11720, 11750 S–Adult: 11752–54

Moon — Fiction
JS: 4525 S: 3457, 4241, 4307
S–Adult: 3520

Morals, public
See also Ethics and ethical behavior
JS: 10122, 11373 S: 11290, 11381

More, Sir Thomas — Plays
S: 4767

Morgan, J. P.
JS: 6628

Morgan, Julia
JS: 5772

Morgan, Sir Henry
JS: 5672

Mormons
S–Adult: 9098

Mormons — Biography
S–Adult: 6505

Mormons — Fiction
JS: 380 S: 225

Morocco
S–Adult: 7947, 7949

Morris, Jim
S–Adult: 6679

Morrison, Toni
JS: 5912–14

Morse, Samuel F. B.
S–Adult: 6592

Moscow
JS: 8151, 8157

Moscow — Fiction
S: 3597

Moses, Grandma
JS: 5773

Moses (Bible) — Fiction
S–Adult: 2415

Mosquitos
S–Adult: 12140

Mossi (African people)
JS: 7987–88

Mother-daughter relationships
JS: 11508 S: 629, 663
S–Adult: 793, 11498

Mother-daughter relationships —
Fiction
JS: 400 S: 767 S–Adult: 684, 703,
741, 856

Mother-daughter relationships —
Folklore
S–Adult: 5071

Mother-daughter relationships —
Poetry
JS: 4915

Mother Goose — Parodies
S: 5008

JS = Junior High/Senior High;   S = Senior High;   S–Adult = Senior High/Adult

Mother of Invention (music group)
S–Adult: 7157

Mother-son relationships
S–Adult: 9975

Motherhood
See also Parenting; Parents
S: 5229, 11192

Motherhood — Fiction
S: 781, 795

Motherhood — Poetry
S: 4862

Moths
See Butterflies and moths

Motion (physics)
JS: 6596 S–Adult: 12498

Motion pictures
See also Animation (motion pictures)
JS: 7231, 7233–34, 7247–48, 7270,
9694, 10119, 12644 S: 5991, 7218–19,
7224, 7226–28, 7250, 7254, 7258,
12951–52 S–Adult: 7249

Motion pictures — Awards
JS: 7245

Motion pictures — Biography
J: 6076, 6114 JS: 5701, 6013, 6056,
6075, 6077–78, 6127, 6133 S: 6033,
6130, 6503

Motion pictures — Careers
JS: 7247, 10465 S: 10437

Motion pictures — Composers
S–Adult: 7243

Motion pictures — Fiction
JS: 3277 S–Adult: 325

Motion pictures — History
JS: 7241, 7253 S: 7220, 7230, 7236,
7240, 7242, 7244, 7251, 7255
S–Adult: 7237

Motion pictures — Musicals
S: 7229

Motion pictures — Production
S: 7225, 12640 S–Adult: 7221, 12957

Motion pictures — Science fiction
JS: 7252

Motion pictures — Scripts
JS: 7222, 7235 S: 7239

Motion pictures — Special effects
J: 12646 S–Adult: 12645, 12648

Motocross — Biography
S–Adult: 6746

Motorcycles
JS: 13241 S: 12681–82, 13228, 13242
S–Adult: 12678–80

Motown (recording company)
S: 7281

Mount Denali
S–Adult: 13258

Mount Everest
JS: 5673, 13274, 13282 S: 13268
S–Adult: 13259, 13262, 13264, 13275

Mount Everest — Fiction
S: 19

Mount Kilimanjaro
S–Adult: 13280

Mount McKinley
S: 13284 S–Adult: 9009

Mount Rushmore National Park
JS: 8963 S–Adult: 8962

Mount St. Helens
S: 12357

Mountain and rock climbing
JS: 13274, 13282 S: 13249, 13263,
13267–69, 13269, 13273, 13273, 13284
S–Adult: 6744, 8070, 13251–52,
13254–55, 13258–59, 13261–62, 13264,
13266, 13275–76, 13279–80, 13283

**Mountain and rock climbing —
Biography**
JS: 5673 S–Adult: 5682, 13265

**Mountain and rock climbing —
Fiction**
S: 19

**Mountain and rock climbing —
Women**
S–Adult: 13266

Mountain bikes
JS: 13233 S: 13235 S–Adult: 13237

Mountain life — Fiction
JS: 1014

Mountain lions
S: 11992, 11998

Mountain States (U.S.)
See specific states, e.g., Colorado

Mountaineering
See Mountain and rock climbing

Movies
See Motion pictures

Moving
S–Adult: 11567

Moving — Fiction
JS: 805, 1524 S: 1042, 1342

**Mozart, Wolfgang Amadeus —
Fiction**
S–Adult: 2578

**Mozart, Wolfgang Amadeus —
Plays**
S: 4824

Mrs. Dalloway — **Criticism**
S–Adult: 5292

Muckraking
S–Adult: 9849

Mughal Empire
S: 8032

Muhammad
See Mohammed

Muir, John
JS: 6594 S–Adult: 6593, 6595

Multiculturalism
JS: 9554, 9564, 9583, 10366 S: 9570
S–Adult: 9544, 9556

Multiculturalism — Fiction
JS: 451

Multiple sclerosis
JS: 10728

Mummies
S: 13011 S–Adult: 7379, 7430

Mummies — Fiction
S–Adult: 2253

Municipal engineering
JS: 12558

Muppets
S: 6055 S–Adult: 7098

Murder
S: 9990 S–Adult: 9978, 10068

Murder — Fiction
JS: 596, 749, 796, 1121, 2983, 3241,
3336 S: 1068, 2980 S–Adult: 328,
354, 752, 844, 2584, 2986, 3624, 3653,
3822

Murphy, Eddie
JS: 6096

Murrow, Edward R.
JS: 8829

Musculoskeletal system
J: 11019 JS: 11018, 11018, 11018,
11021 S–Adult: 11022

Museums — Natural history
S–Adult: 12319

Museums (U.S.)
J: 9260 S: 8975, 8988

Mushrooms
JS: 11819

Musial, Stan
S: 6680

Music
See also Christmas — Songs and
carols; Composers — Biography;
Folk songs; Musical instruments;
Opera; Rock music; Songs; specific
instruments, e.g., Guitars; and as a
subdivision under country names,
e.g., Jamaica — Music
S–Adult: 7116

Music — African American
S: 7123

Music — Biography
JS: 5696, 5698, 5721, 5979–80,
5982–84, 5999 S: 5978, 5981, 6037
S–Adult: 5690, 6018, 6116, 7145

Music — Careers
JS: 10439, 10444, 10451, 10454, 10461
S: 10381, 10438, 10440, 10463

Music — Fiction
JS: 928, 1190 S: 352, 1513, 1533
S–Adult: 353, 2578, 3981

Music — History
JS: 7120, 7153 S: 7124
S–Adult: 7122, 7125

Music — Manuals
JS–Adult: 7112

JS = Junior High/Senior High;   S = Senior High;   S–Adult = Senior High/Adult

Music — Poetry
JS: 4883, 5032

Music — Teenage
S–Adult: 7131

Music appreciation
S: 7164

Musical instruments
See also Wind instruments; specific
instruments, e.g., Guitars
JS: 7195

Musicals
See also Motion pictures — Musicals
S: 7188–90, 7192, 7291–92

Muslim Americans
S–Adult: 9766

Muslims
See Islam

Mussolini, Benito
JS: 6871 S: 6870, 6872
S–Adult: 6873

Mutes and mutism — Fiction
S–Adult: 1796

Mutiny
S: 8064 S–Adult: 5625

Myers, Walter Dean
JS: 5915–16

Myers, Walter Dean — Criticism
S: 5328

Mystery stories — Criticism
S: 5396

Mystery stories — Fiction
See also Detectives — Fiction
JS: 118, 205, 220–21, 223, 274–75,
291–92, 297, 318, 321, 370, 732, 751,
1243, 1329, 1663, 2520, 2568, 3106,
3114, 3137, 3214, 3223, 3226, 3248,
3342, 3361–65, 3370, 3384, 3389,
3394–96, 3403, 3416, 3421, 3447–48,
3467, 3476, 3478, 3488–92, 3494, 3503,
3505–6, 3529–30, 3545, 3552–54, 3558,
3571, 3582–83, 3593, 3596, 3601,
3606–8, 3621, 3634–36, 3641, 3648,
3648, 3656, 3666, 3669, 3678, 3691–99,
3701–2, 3712, 3723–25, 3727–28, 3733,
3737, 3740, 3742, 3745, 3755–56,
3769–71, 3773, 3801–2, 3804, 3806–7,
3813, 3820, 3836–37, 3839–40, 3858,
3969 S: 8, 114, 209–10, 217, 222,
224–26, 346, 1199, 2099, 2331, 2422,
2459, 2586, 2601, 2694, 2726, 2836,
2876, 2942, 3331–32, 3335, 3337–38,
3341, 3346, 3348, 3350, 3352, 3354–56,
3358–60, 3367–69, 3372, 3376,
3379–82, 3386–89, 3391, 3393, 3397, 3399,
3405–15, 3417, 3419, 3422, 3424–28,
3433, 3435–38, 3440–44, 3451, 3453,
3456, 3468, 3470–72, 3486–87, 3496,
3498–500, 3502, 3508, 3510–12,
3514–19, 3523, 3526, 3531–33, 3536,
3538–42, 3546, 3549–51, 3555–57,
3564, 3566, 3568–70, 3572–75,
3577–80, 3586–89, 3595, 3597–98,
3604–5, 3610–13, 3615, 3620, 3622–23,
3631–32, 3637–38, 3643, 3651–52,
3655, 3659, 3661, 3668, 3670–71, 3675,
3677, 3679, 3682–83, 3685, 3690, 3700,

3703–4, 3706, 3710–11, 3714–17, 3720,
3722, 3726, 3729, 3731–32, 3734–36,
3739, 3741, 3746–47, 3753–54,
3757–59, 3763–66, 3776–77, 3779,
3781–83, 3785, 3789, 3794, 3798, 3803,
3817–18, 3823–24, 3826–27, 3830,
3832–34, 3838, 3841, 3844–50,
3853–55, 3957, 4089, 4290, 4318, 4356,
4454, 4517, 4615 S–Adult: 53, 156,
272, 362, 464, 801, 1187, 1539, 1877,
2095, 2098, 2345, 2412, 2434, 2463–64,
2524, 2566, 2573, 2590, 2598–99,
2617–18, 2643, 2687, 2801, 2939, 2946,
3111, 3155, 3329–30, 3333, 3339–40,
3343, 3345, 3347, 3349, 3351, 3353,
3357, 3366, 3371, 3373–75, 3378, 3383,
3385, 3387–88, 3390, 3392, 3400–2,
3404, 3418, 3420, 3423, 3429, 3432,
3434, 3439, 3445–46, 3450, 3452, 3454,
3459–62, 3464–66, 3469, 3473–75,
3477, 3479–84, 3495, 3497, 3501, 3504,
3513, 3520–22, 3525, 3527–28,
3534–35, 3543–44, 3547–48, 3560–63,
3565, 3576, 3584, 3590, 3592,
3599–600, 3602–3, 3609, 3614,
3616–17, 3619, 3624–25, 3627–28,
3640, 3642, 3644, 3646–47, 3650, 3654,
3657–58, 3662–65, 3667, 3672–74,
3676, 3680–81, 3684, 3686–89, 3707,
3709, 3713, 3718–19, 3721, 3730, 3738,
3743–44, 3748–52, 3760–62, 3767–68,
3772, 3774–75, 3778, 3780, 3784,
3786–87, 3791, 3793, 3795–97,
3799–800, 3805, 3808–12, 3814–16,
3819, 3821, 3825, 3829, 3831, 3842,
3851–52, 3856–57, 3868, 3927,
3945–46, 3999, 4033, 4035, 4049, 4169,
4179, 4387, 4706, 8561

Mystery stories — Poetry
JS: 4983

Mythology
See also Folklore; and specific
mythological beings, e.g., Amazons
(mythology); as subdivision under
other subjects, e.g., Monsters —
Mythology; and as subdivision of
specific countries, e.g., Greece —
Mythology
JS: 1900, 5072, 5149, 5152–54, 5156,
5174 S: 2425, 5157, 5171
S–Adult: 5150, 8190

Mythology — Asia
S–Adult: 5083

Mythology — Classical
See also specific countries, e.g. ,
Greece — Mythology
JS: 2124, 5159, 5164, 5166–67
S: 2357, 5168, 5176

Mythology — Fiction
JS: 2429, 2431 S–Adult: 2173–75

Mythology — General
S: 1766, 5155

Mythology — Greece
See also Mythology — Classical;
Greece — Mythology
J: 5158 JS: 2124, 2432, 5169, 5177
S: 2433, 5170, 5173 S–Adult: 5172

Mythology — Greece — Poetry
S–Adult: 4864

Mythology — Rome
See also Mythology — Classical;
Rome — Mythology
JS: 5179–31

N

Nader, Ralph
JS: 6429–31

Nagasaki
JS: 7706 S: 7858

Nail art
S–Adult: 10967

Names
S: 5549

Namibia
JS: 7953, 7979 S: 7958

Namibia — Fiction
JS: 418

Namu, Yang Erche
S–Adult: 6978

Napoleon
See Bonaparte, Napoleon

Napoleonic Wars
JS: 7582 S: 8103

Napoleonic Wars — Fiction
S–Adult: 2575

Napster
S–Adult: 12636

Narcotics
See Drugs and drug abuse

Narrangansett Indians — Fiction
S–Adult: 2860

NASA
S: 11712, 11718 S–Adult: 11655

NASCAR
S: 13142–43

NASCAR — Biography
S–Adult: 6656–57

NASCAR — History
S: 13141

Nashville (TN)
S: 9635

Nation, Carry
S: 6432

Nation of Islam
J: 9599 JS: 9614

Nation of Islam — Biography
JS: 6220 S–Adult: 6709

**National Air and Space Museum
(U.S.)**
S: 12651

***National Geographic* (magazine)**
S: 7428

**National Museum of American Art
(U.S.)**
S: 7100

JS = Junior High/Senior High;   S = Senior High;   S–Adult = Senior High/Adult

National parks (U.S.)
See also specific national parks, e.g.,
Yellowstone National Park
S: 7429, 8355 **S–Adult:** 11883

National parks (U.S.) — Art
S: 7083

National Public Radio — Stories
S–Adult: 5219

National Rifle Association
S: 9793, 9850

National Storytelling Festival
S: 4610, 4672

National Trust
S–Adult: 8415

Nationalism
S: 9177, 9186

Native Americans
See also Inuit; and specific Indian
tribes, e.g., Sioux Indians
J: 8431 **JS:** 8417, 8421–22, 8442,
8448, 8452, 8469, 8478 **S:** 8439, 8466,
8468, 8482–83, 9757, 9762
S–Adult: 6691, 8433, 9755–56, 9758,
9761, 9764, 12222, 13158

Native Americans — Armed forces
JS: 7680

Native Americans — Art
S–Adult: 8495

Native Americans — Authors
S–Adult: 9759

Native Americans — Biography
JS: 5704, 5763, 6164, 6278, 6392,
6395–96, 6398, 6453, 6458, 6639, 6731,
8455 **S:** 5677, 5689, 5823, 5965, 6384,
6393, 6397, 6407, 6415, 6424, 6438,
6440, 6442–43, 6450, 6452, 6454, 6457,
6736, 6950 **S–Adult:** 6455, 6468,
6497–98, 9760

Native Americans — Burial grounds
JS: 7372

**Native Americans —
Communication**
S: 8440

Native Americans — Cookbooks
S: 12782

Native Americans — Crafts
JS: 5704

Native Americans — Dance
S: 7213

Native Americans — Fiction
J: 569 **JS:** 67, 123, 173, 246, 300, 475,
500–1, 537, 548, 1088, 1092, 1519,
1563, 1932, 2216, 2720, 2722–23, 2728,
2733, 2746, 2797, 2859, 2889, 2895,
3745, 4039, 4722 **S:** 407, 440, 462,
467, 578, 1071, 2186, 2715–18,
2724–27, 2730, 2862, 2872, 3433,
3572–73, 3735, 3817–18, 4676
S–Adult: 176, 408, 435, 442, 564, 570,
2185, 2719, 2729, 2743, 2863, 2865,
2874, 3375, 3432, 3482–83, 3527–28,
3628, 3793, 3978

Native Americans — Folklore
JS: 5123–26, 5131–32, 5134–35
S: 2716, 5128–29, 8426, 8461
S–Adult: 5127, 5130, 5136

Native Americans — History
J: 7354 **JS:** 5748, 8231, 8419, 8425,
8427–28, 8436, 8438, 8445, 8447, 8451,
8453–54, 8457–60, 8465, 8476, 8479,
8481, 8487, 8493, 8706, 9763, 9775
S: 7213, 8416, 8420, 8424, 8426, 8430,
8432, 8437, 8443, 8446, 8449–50, 8463,
8466, 8471–72, 8474–75, 8480,
8484–86, 8488, 8555, 9765
S–Adult: 6399, 8418, 8429, 8434–35,
8444, 8464, 8467, 8470, 9760

Native Americans — Place names
S: 8964, 8964

Native Americans — Poetry
J: 5041 **JS:** 4952 **S:** 4676
S–Adult: 5015, 5136

Native Americans — Religion
JS: 8423, 8456, 9075

Native Americans — Sports
S: 6737

Native Americans — Women
S: 8488 **S–Adult:** 408

Native Son **— Criticism**
S: 5391

Natural disasters
JS: 11219 **S–Adult:** 12352, 12363

Natural history
See also Nature study
JS: 9904 **S:** 11809 **S–Adult:** 7424

Natural history — Essays
S: 11602, 11804–5

Natural history — New England
S: 11782

Natural history — United States
S: 11779

Natural history museums
S–Adult: 12319

Naturalists — Biography
JS: 6518, 6567, 6575–76

Nature
See also Biology; Natural history;
Nature study
JS: 8981 **S–Adult:** 11578, 12582

Nature — Careers
JS: 10385

Nature — Chemicals
S: 12329

Nature — Crafts
S: 12741

Nature — Photography
S: 12955

Nature — Poetry
JS: 5028

Nature study
JS: 8971, 11785 **S:** 11791, 11800
S–Adult: 5236, 11788, 11790, 11792,
11797, 11803, 11889, 12906

Nature study — Africa
S–Adult: 7966

Nature study — Biography
JS: 6594

Nava, Julian
JS: 6433

**Navajo Arts and Crafts Enterprise
(NACE)**
JS: 10226

Navajo Indians
JS: 7732, 10226 **S–Adult:** 9761

Navajo Indians — Fiction
JS: 67, 2721, 3545, 3820 **S:** 467, 2724,
3572–73, 3575, 3577, 3818
S–Adult: 3576, 3816, 3819

Navajo Indians — Poetry
JS: 4952

Naval Academy (U.S.)
JS: 9367 **S:** 9369, 9372

Navigation
S–Adult: 7387, 11388

Navratilova, Martina
S: 6725

Navy SEALs
S–Adult: 12703

Navy (U.S.)
See also Armed forces (U.S.)
JS: 9367 **S:** 7726 **S–Adult:** 12703

Navy (U.S.) — African Americans
S: 9373

Navy (U.S.) — Biography
JS: 6500

Navy (U.S.) — Careers
S: 10391

Navy (U.S.) — Fiction
S–Adult: 2843, 3937

Navy (U.S.) — History
S: 8646 **S–Adult:** 12712

Navy (U.S.) — Women
S–Adult: 12706

Navy (U.S.) — World War II
S: 7765

**Naylor, Phyllis Reynolds —
Criticism**
S: 5413

Nazi Germany
S: 7742, 8111

Nazi Germany — Army
JS: 8105

Nazi Germany — Biography
S: 7718 **S–Adult:** 6854

Nazi Germany — Fiction
S: 3002

Nazis and Nazism
See also Germany — History;
Holocaust; Nazi Germany; World
War II
JS: 7689, 7705, 7734, 13379 **S:** 6855
S–Adult: 7760

JS = Junior High/Senior High;   S = Senior High;   S–Adult = Senior High/Adult

Nazis and Nazism — Fiction
S: 43, 95

Ndebele (African people)
JS: 7976

Nebraska
S–Adult: 11797

Needlecrafts
See also Knitting; Sewing
S: 12958, 12970–72 S–Adult: 12961

Negotiation skills
JS: 11378

Negro League baseball
JS: 13168, 13180, 13182 S: 13163

Neo-Nazis
See also Militia movement (U.S.)
JS: 9801 S: 9838

Neo-Nazis — Fiction
JS: 1609, 3050

Nepal — Fiction
S–Adult: 2549

Neptune (planet) — Fiction
S: 4183

Neruda, Pablo
JS: 5917 S–Adult: 5051

Nervous system
See Brain and nervous system

Netherlands — Art
S: 5732

Netherlands — Biography
JS: 6991 S: 5796

Netherlands — Fiction
JS: 1139, 2648, 2998, 7728, 7842
S: 2570

Netherlands — History
JS: 7694

Neurology
S: 11009

Nevada — Fiction
JS: 2966

New Deal
JS: 8792, 8810–11, 8824
S–Adult: 8807, 8826

New England
See also specific states, e.g.,
Massachusetts
S: 11782

New England — Fiction
JS: 1257, 2935 S: 1002, 1688, 3427

New England — Plays
S: 4839

New Guinea
S: 8065

New Guinea — Fiction
JS: 18 S: 1572 S–Adult: 2511

New Hampshire — Fiction
S–Adult: 690

New Jersey — Fiction
S–Adult: 4027

New Jersey — History
JS: 12182 S–Adult: 8976

New Mexico
S–Adult: 9019

New Mexico — Fiction
JS–Adult: 617 S–Adult: 241, 411,
834

New Mexico — History
S: 9016

New Orleans — Poetry
S–Adult: 5034

New York — Fiction
S–Adult: 1492, 2584

New York City
JS–Adult: 8972 S–Adult: 10042,
10209, 11803

New York City — Fiction
JS: 326, 429, 526, 529, 584, 891, 1355,
1438, 1466, 2971 S: 130, 3360, 3732
S–Adult: 289, 437, 518, 2785, 2801,
2915, 2946, 3266, 3271, 3767

New York City — History
JS: 8803, 8979, 8982, 9527, 9637
JS–Adult: 8985 S–Adult: 8561,
8580, 8974

New York City — Plays
S: 4825

New York City — Police
S–Adult: 9254

New York City — Subway system
JS: 8982

New York Jets (football team)
S–Adult: 13310

New York State
JS: 8981

New York State — Fiction
JS: 253, 2775, 2805, 2910 S: 78, 2917
S–Adult: 1522, 2916

New York State — History
S–Adult: 8976

New York Times
S: 5606, 6629 S–Adult: 8663

New Zealand — Fiction
JS: 62, 1059, 1312, 2510, 2522,
3529–30 S: 103, 556, 1474
S–Adult: 2548

New Zealand — Folklore
JS: 5092

Newfoundland — Fiction
S: 1446 S–Adult: 2394, 2706

Newspapers
JS: 5582 S: 5606

Newspapers — Fiction
JS: 1594 S–Adult: 289, 1509, 3750

Newspapers — History
JS: 5603 S–Adult: 5608

Newton, Sir Isaac
JS: 6596–97 S–Adult: 6598, 12498

Newts
S–Adult: 11896

Nez Perce Indians
JS: 8422 S: 6415

Nez Perce Indians — Biography
JS: 6392 S–Adult: 6414

Ngoni (African people)
JS: 7932

Nicaragua — Biography
S–Adult: 8243

Nicaragua — Fiction
S: 1595

Nicaraguan Americans
JS: 9731

Nicholas II (Emperor of Russia)
S–Adult: 8162

Nicotine
See also Smoking; Tobacco industry
JS: 10678

Niger
JS: 7892

Nigeria
JS: 7982–83, 7986, 7991, 7993
S: 7992

Nigeria — Fiction
S: 419 S–Adult: 2476–78, 2485

Nigeria — History
S–Adult: 7985

Night (book) — Criticism
S: 5318

Nightmares — Fiction
JS: 3505, 3801

Nike (firm)
S: 10217, 10221

Nile River
S–Adult: 7905

Nimoy, Leonard
S: 6097

1930s — Fiction
S–Adult: 2965

1950s — Memoirs
S–Adult: 6916

1960s
S–Adult: 4690

1970s — Fiction
S–Adult: 2981

Nineteenth century
S–Adult: 7589

Nineteenth century — Science
S–Adult: 11622

Nixon, Richard M.
JS: 6350, 6353, 8872, 8878, 9284
S: 6352, 8860, 8906 S–Adult: 6351

Noah's Ark
S–Adult: 9050

Nobel Prize
S: 7404

Nobel Prize winners — Biography
JS: 6512, 6585–86

JS = Junior High/Senior High;   S = Senior High;   S–Adult = Senior High/Adult

Nonconformists — Biography
S–Adult: 6149

Nonviolence
S–Adult: 10129

Norgay, Jamling Tenzing
S–Adult: 13275

Norling, Donna Scott
S: 6980

Norman Britain — Fiction
S–Adult: 1827

Normandy invasion
S–Adult: 7846

North America — Biology
S: 11809

North America — Birds
S: 12073

North America — Ecology
S–Adult: 8230

North America — Exploration
JS: 8491

North America — Geography
JS: 12351

North Carolina — Biography
S: 6481

North Carolina — Fiction
JS: 521, 2931 S: 1132, 2936, 2948, 3272 S–Adult: 2957

North Dakota
S: 8968

North Dakota — Fiction
JS: 2956

North Korea
JS: 8057

North Pole
See also Arctic; Polar regions
JS: 8322

Northampton (MA)
S: 10208

Northeast Indians
JS: 8452

Northern Ireland
JS: 8115, 9180 S: 8124

Northern Ireland — Fiction
JS: 55 S–Adult: 2626

Northern lights
S–Adult: 8309

Northwest Passage
S–Adult: 8304, 8323

Northwest Passage — Exploration
S–Adult: 8303

Northwest Territories
S: 8240

Northwest (U.S.) — Native Americans
JS: 8419, 8448

Norway — Cookbooks
J: 12815

Norway — Fiction
JS: 2638

Norway — Folklore
See Scandinavia — Folklore

Norwegian Americans — Fiction
JS: 673 S: 2904

Nova Scotia — Fiction
JS: 675 S–Adult: 1104

Nubia (African empire) — History
JS: 7450

Nuclear accidents
JS: 12524 S: 10814

Nuclear accidents — Fiction
S: 40

Nuclear energy
JS: 12522, 12524–25, 12528 S: 12523

Nuclear holocaust — Fiction
JS: 2211

Nuclear medicine
JS: 10918

Nuclear physics
JS: 12339 S: 12538, 12540
S–Adult: 12539

Nuclear physics — Biography
JS: 6513, 6588–89

Nuclear war — Fiction
JS: 116, 1209, 1576, 1602, 4419

Nuclear waste
S: 12523, 12526–27

Nuclear waste — Fiction
JS: 3634

Nuclear weapons
JS: 7814, 9175, 12537, 12708, 12711, 12723 S: 7700, 7759, 7858, 12717
S–Adult: 12698

Numbers
See also Mathematics; Statistics
S: 12420 S–Adult: 12418

Numbers — History
S: 12419 S–Adult: 12405

Nunez, Tommy
JS: 6704

Nupe (African people)
JS: 7987

Nuremberg trials
J: 7625 JS: 7792 S: 7775

Nursery rhymes
JS: 7092

Nurses
S: 10908

Nurses — Fiction
JS: 3091

Nursing — Careers
S: 10506, 10513

Nutrition
JS: 11033, 11039, 11123, 11142
S: 10560, 10999, 11028, 11031, 11130–31, 11144–45, 11147, 11149
S–Adult: 11124, 11129

Nuwere, Ejovi
S–Adult: 12616

Nye, Naomi Shihab
S: 6981–99

O

Oakley, Annie
S: 6098–99

Obesity
See also Weight problems
JS: 10730 S–Adult: 10799, 10890

Obesity — Fiction
JS: 908, 928, 1301, 1839 S: 1384, 1464

Observatories
JS: 11697

Obsessive-compulsive disorder
JS: 11074

Obsessive-compulsive disorder — Fiction
JS: 935, 938

Occupational guidance
See also Vocational guidance
S: 10326, 10358, 10360, 10362, 10364–65, 10392, 10399, 10428, 10507, 10521 S–Adult: 10361

Occupations and work
See Careers; and specific occupations, e.g., Aeronautics — Careers

Ocean floor — Fiction
S: 4429

Oceanography
See also Marine biology; Marine life; Underwater exploration
JS: 12482 S: 12468, 12471–73, 12475, 12494 S–Adult: 12466, 12470, 12480, 12486

Oceanography — Biography
S–Adult: 5621, 6543

Oceans
See also Marine animals, etc; Oceanography; Seashores; and specific oceans, e.g., Atlantic Ocean
JS: 12464, 12469, 12477
JS–Adult: 12465 S: 12468, 12471, 12474–76, 13008 S–Adult: 12467, 12486

Ochs, Adolph S.
S: 6629

O'Connor, Larry
S–Adult: 6982

O'Connor, Sandra Day
JS: 6434

Odysseus
J: 5158

Odysseus — Fiction
S–Adult: 2416

Odyssey — Criticism
S: 5320

Odyssey — Fiction
S: 5171

Odyssey (mythology) — Fiction
S: 2425

Oedipus plays
S: 4789

Oedipus plays — Criticism
S: 5434

Oertelt, Henry A.
S: 7776

Of Mice and Men — Criticism
S: 5379

Office occupations — Careers
S: 10397

Ofri, Danielle
S–Adult: 6599

Ohno, Apolo Anton
JS: 6721

Oil
S–Adult: 12516

Oil industry — Biography
S: 6632

Oil rigs — Careers
J: 10544

Oil spills
See Ecology and environment —
Problems

Ojibwa Indians — Fiction
JS: 548, 1092

O'Keeffe, Georgia
JS: 5774

Okinawa, Battle of
S: 7748

Oklahoma — Fiction
JS: 2995 S: 1290 S–Adult: 575

Oklahoma — History
S: 8552

Oklahoma City bombing (1995)
JS: 10188

The Old Man and the Sea —
Criticism
S: 5421

Olympic Games
JS: 13381 S: 13380
S–Adult: 13363, 13440

Olympic Games — Biography
JS: 6734

Olympic Games — History
JS: 13379, 13382

Olympic Games (Winter) — History
S: 13383

Onassis, Jacqueline Kennedy
S: 6354

One Flew Over the Cuckoo's Nest —
Criticism
S: 5377

O'Neal, Shaquille
S–Adult: 6705

O'Neill, Eugene — Criticism
S: 5529

Opera
JS: 7186 S: 7185, 7187
S–Adult: 7191

Opera — Biography
S: 6101

Opera — Fiction
S: 3789

Operation Desert Storm — Fiction
S–Adult: 3088

Oppenheimer, Robert
JS: 6600

Optical illusions
JS: 12920

Oral history
S: 7413, 10287, 10304

Orangutans
JS: 11966 S–Adult: 11969

Oregon Trail
JS: 8738 S: 8722

Oregon Trail — Fiction
S–Adult: 2887

Organ transplants
JS: 10569, 10724–25, 10727
S–Adult: 10917

Organ transplants — Fiction
S–Adult: 894

Organic foods
JS: 11823

Origami
S: 12933, 12937 S–Adult: 12932

Orozco, Jose
JS: 5775

Orphan Train
JS: 8756

Orphans — Fiction
JS: 612, 843, 2162, 2956 S: 3087
S–Adult: 2541, 3594

Orpheus (mythology)
S: 5173

Orr, Gregory
S–Adult: 5918

Ortlip, Carol A.
S–Adult: 6983

Orwell, George
JS: 5919

Orwell, George — Criticism
S: 5272, 5291, 5298

Osborn, Shane
JS: 6500

Oscars (motion picture awards)
JS: 7245

Ospreys
S–Adult: 12080

Othello — Criticism
S: 5477

Ototake, Hirotada
S–Adult: 6984

Ottoman Empire — Biography
JS: 6885

Our Town (play) — Criticism
S: 5523

Out-of-body experiences — Fiction
S: 3354

Outdoor cooking
S: 12755

Outdoor life
See also specific activities, e.g.,
Backpacking
J: 5921 JS: 13080, 13113 S: 11220,
13074, 13271–72, 13278

Outdoor life — Careers
JS: 10385, 10416 S: 10403
S–Adult: 10422

Outer Banks — Fiction
S–Adult: 3402

The Outsiders (novel) — Criticism
JS: 5368

Owen, Wilfred
JS: 4854

Owens, Jesse
JS: 6733–34 S: 6732

Owls
S: 12086 S–Adult: 12081, 12085

Oxford — Fiction
S: 3611

Oxford English Dictionary
S: 5559

Oxymorons
J: 5540

Oyo (African kingdom)
JS: 7990

Oz books — Fiction
S–Adult: 3462

Ozarks — Fiction
JS: 3256 S: 4716

Ozone layer
S: 9877, 12461

P

Pachen, Ani
S–Adult: 6985

Pacific Coast (U.S.)
JS: 9005

Pacific Islands
S–Adult: 8072

Pacific Islands — Folklore
JS: 5090

Pacific Northwest
JS: 8992

Pacific Northwest — Fiction
JS: 1344 S: 3847 S–Adult: 324

JS = Junior High/Senior High;   S = Senior High;   S–Adult = Senior High/Adult

JS = Junior High/Senior High;   S = Senior High;   S–Adult = Senior High/Adult

JS = Junior High/Senior High;   S = Senior High;   S–Adult = Senior High/Adult

Philippines — Fiction
S–Adult: 2540, 3028

Philosophy
JS: 9029, 9038 S: 9023, 9025,
9027–28, 9034 S–Adult: 9021, 9024,
9030–31, 9033, 9036–37, 11352

Philosophy — History
S–Adult: 9026, 9035

Phish (rock band)
S–Adult: 7145

Phobias
JS: 11051, 11089

Phobias — Fiction
S–Adult: 3296

Photography
See also Photojournalism; and
specific individuals; e.g. Adams,
Ansel
JS: 5503 S: 7083–84, 7088, 8369,
8778, 8892, 12944–50, 12953,
12955–56 S–Adult: 7101, 7107, 8005,
8051, 8327, 8915, 9386, 13283

Photography — Biography
JS: 5705–6, 5717, 5727, 5734–38,
5748, 5761, 5776, 6611–12 S: 5759
S–Adult: 5760, 5789

Photography — Careers
J: 10459 S–Adult: 5587

Photography — Computers
S: 12954

Photography — Fiction
JS: 319, 3870 S–Adult: 846

Photography — History
JS: 6611, 7063–64 S: 7059
S–Adult: 7052–53

Photography — Native Americans
S–Adult: 8433

Photography — Poetry
JS: 4986

Photography — United States
S–Adult: 7105

Photojournalism — Biography
JS: 5786

Physical abuse
See also Child abuse
JS: 11510, 11524, 11526
S–Adult: 1150

Physical abuse — Fiction
JS: 822, 1139, 1228 S: 768, 819, 867,
1010

Physical disabilities
See also Blind; Cerebral palsy;
Deafness and the deaf; Physical
disabilities; Obesity; etc.
JS: 10568, 11156–57
S–Adult: 11151–54, 13304, 13386

Physical disabilities — Biography
JS: 5747, 6363, 6466, 6490–91, 6494
JS–Adult: 6489 S: 6475, 6484, 6495,
6580 S–Adult: 6984

Physical disabilities — Civil rights
S: 9472

Physical disabilities — Fiction
JS: 293, 698, 953, 958, 960, 970, 983,
994, 1007–8, 1018, 1405, 4562 S: 145,
169, 424, 947, 992 S–Adult: 1623,
3617, 3968

Physical disfigurements — Fiction
JS: 908, 951 S: 906

Physical fitness
See also Exercise
JS: 10561, 10570, 11026, 11033, 11043
S: 11028, 11031, 11038, 11041, 13434

Physical fitness — Careers
JS: 10436 S: 10456, 10503

Physical geography
S: 12365

Physical handicaps
See Physical disabilities, and specific
handicaps, e.g., Deafness and the
deaf

Physical problems — Fiction
JS: 1138 S: 962, 984

Physician-assisted suicide
See also Suicide
JS: 10580, 10588, 10591

Physics
JS: 12500, 12506 S: 11612, 11778,
12502–3, 12513, 12538, 12540
S–Adult: 11774–75, 12498, 12510–12,
12515

Physics — Biography
JS: 6539, 6559, 6571, 6581, 6586, 6600
S: 6556, 6580 S–Adult: 6511, 6524,
6557–58, 6579

**Physics — Experiments and
projects**
JS: 12495

Physics — History
S–Adult: 12504

Pianists — Biography
JS: 7149 S: 6052

Pianists — Fiction
JS: 1190

Piano
S: 7198

Picasso, Pablo
JS: 5777, 5779–80 S–Adult: 5778

Piccolo, Brian
S–Adult: 6714

Pickett, George Edward
S–Adult: 6441

Picture puzzles
JS: 7032

Pigeons
JS: 12245

Pigs
S: 12244 S–Adult: 11956

Pilots
See Airplane pilots

Pioneer life (U.S.)
See Frontier life (U.S.)

Pippen, Scottie
JS: 6641

Pirates
JS: 5623, 7396, 7415 S–Adult: 7394,
7431, 7865

Pirates — Biography
JS: 5672

Pirates — Fiction
JS: 131, 153, 235, 2625, 2709 S: 150
S–Adult: 2657, 2707, 3431

Pirsig, Robert M.
S: 9034

Pisa (Italy)
JS: 8144

Pitchers (baseball) — Biography
S: 6645

Place names
S: 8964

The Plague — **Criticism**
JS: 5315

Plagues
JS: 10731, 10779

Plagues — Fiction
S: 1691, 2044, 4213

Plagues — History
S: 10738

Plains (U.S.)
See specific states, e.g., Nebraska

Planets
See also Solar system; and specific
planets, e.g., Mars
JS: 11678–79 S: 11769, 11772, 11776
S–Adult: 11664

Planets — Fiction
S: 4098–99, 4244, 4370–71, 4374,
4377, 4409

Plantation life (U.S.) — History
JS: 8557 S: 9013

Plants
JS: 11869 S: 11857, 11867
S–Adult: 11820, 11858, 11860

Plants — Experiments and projects
S–Adult: 11861

Plants — Fiction
S: 2009, 4546

Plants — Genetic engineering
S–Adult: 11787, 11798

Plants — History
S: 11864

Plants — Medicinal
JS: 10912

Plants — Poisonous
S–Adult: 11795

Plants — South America
JS: 11786

Plastic surgery — Fiction
JS: 951

Plate tectonics
S: 12343–44 S–Adult: 12348

JS = Junior High/Senior High; S = Senior High; S–Adult = Senior High/Adult

1153

Plath, Sylvia
S–Adult: 4934

Plays
See also Shakespeare, William; Theater
JS: 4745, 4834 S: 4780–81, 4944, 7297 S–Adult: 4729, 4820

Plays — African American
S: 4821, 4844

Plays — American
JS: 4762, 4786, 4790, 4794–95, 4803, 4807, 4809, 4812, 4816, 4826, 4837 S: 4747, 4789, 4793, 4796, 4800, 4804, 4806, 4810–11, 4813, 4817–18, 4823, 4825, 4827–28, 4830, 4832, 4835, 4839, 4841–43, 4846–47 S–Adult: 4792, 4815, 4819, 4822, 4838, 4840, 4845, 5498, 5513, 5517

Plays — Anthologies
JS: 4749, 4753, 4756, 4765, 4801, 4833 S: 4741–42, 4763, 4767, 4787, 4808, 4831

Plays — Caribbean
JS: 4766

Plays — Criticism
S: 5240, 5464, 5496, 5500, 5532

Plays — Elizabethan
S: 5442

Plays — English
S: 4747, 4768, 4773–75, 4778, 4824 S–Adult: 4776, 4929, 5458

Plays — European
S–Adult: 5448–49

Plays — Folktales
S: 4754

Plays — History and criticism
S: 5529 S–Adult: 5472

Plays — Holocaust
JS: 4797

Plays — Humorous
S: 5180

Plays — Irish
S–Adult: 4779

Plays — Latin American
JS: 4766

Plays — Multicultural
S: 4788

Plays — Norwegian
S: 5447

Plays — One-act
J: 4748 JS: 4791

Plays — Production
JS: 4794, 7296, 12860 S: 4743

Plays — Scenes
JS: 4799 S: 4746, 4759, 4761, 4764, 4802 S–Adult: 4740

Plays — Spain
JS: 4766

Plays — Women
S: 4814

Playwrights — Fiction
JS: 1549

Plessy *v.* Ferguson
JS: 9416

Poaching
S: 12021

Pocahontas
JS: 8499 S: 6442–43

Pocahontas — Fiction
JS: 2738

Poe, Edgar Allan
JS: 5922 S: 261

Poe, Edgar Allan — Criticism
S: 5339, 5383, 5388, 5418

Poe, Edgar Allan — Fiction
S–Adult: 2801, 2946

Poetry
See also Epic poetry; as subdivision of other subjects, e.g., Animals — Poetry; and as subdivision of countries or ethnic groups, e.g., England — Poetry
J: 4889 JS: 46, 318, 589, 4854, 4882, 4910, 4915–17, 4920, 4926, 4932, 4993, 4996, 5007, 5011, 5025, 5029, 5036, 5039–40, 5049, 5459 S: 245, 2926, 4614, 4885, 4888, 4905, 4909, 4940, 4944, 4998, 5024, 5026, 5486 S–Adult: 4729, 4855, 4874–75, 4912, 4934, 4949, 4954, 4958–59, 4963, 4968, 4975, 4978, 4985, 4991, 5000, 5014–15, 5030, 5047, 5051, 5228, 5445, 9199, 9520

Poetry — African American
JS: 4956 S: 4980, 5004, 5510, 5512 S–Adult: 510, 5010, 5038, 5519

Poetry — American
JS: 4947, 4952, 4955, 4977, 4984, 4990, 5002, 5019–20, 5022, 5028, 5035, 5044 S: 4858, 4951, 4953, 4957, 4960–61, 4964–65, 4974, 4976, 4979, 4981, 5003, 5005, 5012–13, 5018, 5053, 5507 S–Adult: 4962, 4971, 5017, 5043, 5504, 5506

Poetry — American — History and criticism
S: 5515

Poetry — Animals
JS: 4914

Poetry — Anthologies
J: 5042 JS: 4856, 4866–67, 4883–84, 4887, 4890–93, 4903–4, 4921, 4966, 4986, 4989, 4992, 4995, 5009, 5021, 5033 S: 4849, 4851–52, 4860, 4862, 4870–71, 4879, 4897, 4901, 4906, 4908, 4919, 4946, 5001, 5048, 5507 S–Adult: 4865, 4898, 4900, 4907, 5430, 5435, 5443

Poetry — Art
J: 4869

Poetry — Aztecs
JS: 8254

Poetry — Biography
JS: 5821, 5842, 5866, 5917, 5961–62, 5976 S: 5825, 5863, 5970 S–Adult: 5846, 5918, 5956, 6542

Poetry — Boys
JS: 4970

Poetry — British
S: 5970

Poetry — Children authors
JS: 5503

Poetry — Collections
S: 4897 S–Adult: 4853, 5016

Poetry — Contemporary
JS: 4881

Poetry — Criticism
S: 4901, 5433, 5497, 5502, 5518, 5525, 5533

Poetry — England
JS: 4925, 4937–38 S: 4858, 4923, 4927, 4930–31, 4935, 5446 S–Adult: 4922, 4929, 4936, 4941, 4943, 5452

Poetry — Fiction
JS: 1200 S–Adult: 2611

Poetry — Greece
S: 4877–78 S–Adult: 4945

Poetry — Handbooks
JS: 5441 S: 4894, 5436, 5450, 10302

Poetry — Hispanic Americans
S–Adult: 5027

Poetry — History and criticism
S: 4857, 5431

Poetry — Holidays
JS: 4861

Poetry — Horses
JS: 5511

Poetry — Humorous
JS: 4928 S: 4851, 5006, 5012–13

Poetry — Ireland
S: 4933

Poetry — Italy
S–Adult: 5440

Poetry — Japan
J: 5050

Poetry — Jewish
S: 4908

Poetry — Love
JS: 4868, 4969

Poetry — Memoirs
S–Adult: 6927

Poetry — Modern
JS: 4881, 4890 S: 4879

Poetry — Mythology
S–Adult: 4864

Poetry — Rome
S: 4918 S–Adult: 4945

Poetry — Shakespeare, William
S–Adult: 5485

JS = Junior High/Senior High;   S = Senior High;   S–Adult = Senior High/Adult

Poetry — Teenage authors
JS: 4970, 4972 S: 4899

Poetry — Teenagers
J: 4994 JS: 4850 S: 4873

Poetry — United States
JS: 5522 S–Adult: 4973, 5023

Poetry — Wales
S: 4939, 4942

Poetry — Women
JS: 4895 S: 4886

Poetry — Writing
JS: 4850, 10300, 10313 S: 10308

Pohl, Frederik — Criticism
S: 5347

Poland
JS: 8087

Poland — Biography
S: 6772

Poland — Cookbooks
J: 12846

Poland — Fiction
JS: 2641, 3010, 3052 S: 2281
S–Adult: 2999, 3025

Poland — History
JS: 7743 S: 7624, 7690, 7825

Polar bears
S: 11984 S–Adult: 11983

Polar regions
See also Antarctic; Arctic
S: 8321

Polar regions — Exploration
S–Adult: 8310

Polaris Expedition
S–Adult: 8308, 8316

Police
See also Law enforcement
JS: 9293, 10205 S–Adult: 5014,
10042

Police — Brutality
JS: 9265, 9278, 9293 S: 9333
S–Adult: 9329

Police — Careers
JS: 10495 S–Adult: 9254, 10497

Police — Corruption
JS: 10036

Police questioning
JS: 9331, 11485

Police questioning — Fiction
JS: 1121

Polio
JS: 10864

Polio — Biography
S: 6484

Polio — Fiction
S: 610 S–Adult: 912

Polio vaccine — Biography
JS: 6605

Political parties
S–Adult: 9353

Political parties (U.S.) — History
JS: 9350

Political science
S: 9025

Politics
JS: 9346, 9349, 9354, 9363 S: 7437,
9200, 9347, 9356, 9361, 10243
S–Adult: 9353, 9357, 9379

Politics — African Americans
JS: 9667

Politics — Biography
JS: 6439, 6750, 6770 S–Adult: 6474

Politics — Careers
JS: 10499

Politics — Ethics
JS: 9348

Politics — Fiction
JS: 3289, 3691 S: 3754
S–Adult: 3954

Politics — Scandals
JS: 9351

Politics — Women
JS: 6172

Polk, James K.
S–Adult: 6355

Pollination
S: 12129

Pollution
See also Ecology and environment;
and specific types of pollution, e.g.,
Water pollution
JS: 9885, 9896, 9911, 9913, 9915–16,
9919–20, 9922 S: 9011, 9866–68,
9873, 9876, 9886, 9897–98, 9905, 9908,
9912, 9918, 9921, 12527
S–Adult: 9869, 9910, 9914, 9924,
12116

Pollution — Fiction
S: 2026

Polo, Marco
S: 5674

Pony Express
JS: 8718, 8728, 8751

Pony Express — Fiction
J: 2891

Pool (game)
S–Adult: 13107

Pool (game) — Fiction
S–Adult: 1261

Pop music
See Popular music

Popes — Biography
S: 6861 S–Adult: 6860

Popular culture
JS: 8869 S: 7332, 9171, 10160, 12588
S–Adult: 8398, 9631

Popular music
See also specific types of music, e.g.,
Rock music
S: 7143, 7151 S–Adult: 7125, 7131,
7135, 7150, 7176

Popular music — Fiction
S–Adult: 281, 369

Population
JS: 9931–32, 9937 S: 9934

Population — Characteristics
S–Adult: 9933

Population problems
JS: 8884, 9932, 11178 S: 9566

Pornography
JS: 10101, 10121 S: 10100, 10108

Porpoises
JS: 12215 S: 12201, 12206

*A Portrait of the Artist as a Young
Man* — Criticism
S: 5300

Portrait painting
S: 12880, 12885

Post, Mary Titus
JS: 8527

Post-traumatic stress disorder
JS: 11102, 11109 S: 11094

Posters — Motion pictures
S: 7259

Posters — Science fiction films
S: 7259

Postmodernism — Criticism
S: 5255

Pot-bellied pigs
S: 12244

Potter, Harry
JS: 5273 S–Adult: 11600

Pottery
JS: 12751 S: 12750, 12752

Poultry
S: 11830

Poverty
See also Homeless people; Hunger
J: 10095 JS: 8412, 10070–71,
10074–76, 10078, 10080, 10085, 10089,
10091 S: 8131, 10069, 10082
S–Adult: 8267, 9362, 10077, 10081,
10086, 10088, 10093, 10209

Poverty — Fiction
JS: 331, 404, 456, 537, 557, 618, 650,
669–70, 688, 885, 885, 887, 1387, 1566,
1583, 2516, 2574 S: 976, 1616, 1622,
2497, 2688, 2792, 2951, 2977
S–Adult: 1537

Powell, Colin
JS: 6444, 6446 S: 6445

Powell, John Wesley
S–Adult: 8967

Power boats
S: 13397

Powhatan Indians — Biography
S: 6442

Prague
S: 2597

Prairie dogs
S–Adult: 11948

JS = Junior High/Senior High; S = Senior High; S–Adult = Senior High/Adult

Prairies
See Grasslands

Prayers
See also Schools — Prayer
S: 9060

Prayers — Africa
S: 9092

Predictions
See also Fortune telling
JS: 10139, 13037 **S:** 8868, 13040, 13053, 13053

Pregnancy
JS: 11160, 11178, 11184–85, 11187, 11194, 11203, 11209, 11217 **S:** 11164, 11172, 11181–82, 11190, 11205, 11210, 11213, 11221, 11484

Pregnancy — Fiction
J: 1077 **JS:** 625, 1152, 1277, 1376, 1472 **S:** 416, 977, 1217, 1401, 3188, 3291 **S–Adult:** 1233, 3302

Pregnancy — Teenage
JS: 11163 **S:** 11226

Prehistoric animals
See also Dinosaurs; Mammoths
JS: 7333 **S:** 7324

Prehistoric art — Africa
S–Adult: 7067

Prehistoric life
See also Paleontology
JS: 7360, 8231 **S–Adult:** 7340

Prehistoric life — Fiction
JS: 2390–91 **S:** 2189, 2386–87
S–Adult: 2221, 2388–89, 2392, 7386

Prejudice
See also Discrimination; Racism
JS: 9439, 9546, 9551, 9555, 9572, 9574, 9583, 10099 **S:** 9579–80, 9587, 9661, 9675 **S–Adult:** 9549, 9559, 9610, 9700, 9750

Prejudice — Fiction
JS: 318, 381, 397, 436, 453, 472, 483, 496, 517, 521, 537, 548, 559, 574, 590, 1483, 1588, 1592, 1750, 2924, 2995, 4080 **S:** 582, 836, 2371
S–Adult: 249, 1111

Premenstrual syndrome
JS: 10820

Premice, Josephine
S–Adult: 6102

Presidency (U.S.)
JS: 9233, 9358 **S–Adult:** 9228

Presidents (U.S.)
JS: 6298, 6337, 9224–26, 9240, 9392
S: 9231, 9236, 9239 **S–Adult:** 9228

Presidents (U.S.) — Biography
See also individual presidents, e.g.,
Bush, George W.
JS: 6281, 6285–87, 6289, 6292, 6295, 6300, 6302–3, 6307–8, 6311–15, 6317, 6319, 6321, 6324–28, 6334, 6341, 6344, 6349–50, 6353, 6357, 6360, 6363, 6365–66, 6369, 6373–74, 6376, 6378
S: 6151, 6174, 6284, 6291, 6294, 6296–97, 6304, 6310, 6318, 6322–23,

6333, 6335, 6339, 6343, 6345, 6352, 6356, 6361, 6367–68, 6372, 6375, 8906
S–Adult: 6175, 6181, 6282–83, 6288, 6290, 6293, 6299, 6301, 6305–6, 6309, 6316, 6336, 6338, 6342, 6346–48, 6351, 6355, 6362, 6364, 6370–71, 6377, 8890

Presidents (U.S.) — Elections
JS: 9238, 9363 **S:** 9355–56, 9359, 9361

Presidents (U.S.) — Families
S: 6151

Presidents (U.S.) — Fiction
JS: 881

Presidents (U.S.) — History
JS: 9223

Presidents (U.S.) — Impeachment
JS: 9229–30, 9234

Presidents (U.S.) — Inaugurations
S–Adult: 9227

Presidents (U.S.) — Mothers — Biography
S: 6150

Presidents (U.S.) — Speeches
JS: 9241 **S:** 6340

Presidents (U.S.) — Wives
S–Adult: 8408

Presidents (U.S.) — Wives — Biography
JS: 6176, 6279–80, 6358–59 **S:** 6158, 6354

Presidents (U.S.) — Wives — Fiction
S: 2803

Presley, Elvis
JS: 6103, 6108 **S:** 6104, 6106
S–Adult: 6105, 6107

Presley, Elvis — Fiction
JS: 512 **S–Adult:** 288, 856

Press, freedom of the
See Freedom of the press

Press, role in social change
S–Adult: 5608

Price, Michelle
S: 6988

Pride and Prejudice
S–Adult: 4004

Pride and Prejudice — Criticism
S: 5305, 5308

Priests — Fiction
S–Adult: 3547

Prieto, Jorgé
JS: 6715

Primates
S: 11968 **S–Adult:** 11974

Primitive peoples
S: 7359

Prince Edward Island — Fiction
JS: 661

Princes — Fiction
JS: 377

Princesses — Fiction
JS: 2475, 2690, 3263, 3265, 5064

Printing
See also Books and reading
JS: 5567

Printing — History
S: 5568

Printmaking
S: 12745

Prison reform
S–Adult: 9943

Prisoners of war
S: 7661

Prisoners of war — World War II
S–Adult: 7826

Prisons
JS: 9969, 9980, 9987, 9993, 10017, 10025, 10029, 10032, 11528, 11550
S: 6940, 10022 **S–Adult:** 7949, 9998, 10039, 10055, 10064

Prisons — Fiction
JS: 187, 338, 790, 1154, 2518, 2613, 2708 **S:** 1216, 1383, 1417, 1599, 2289, 3000 **S–Adult:** 320, 714

Privacy rights
JS: 9401, 9426 **S:** 9381

Private detectives — Biography
S–Adult: 6947

Private schools — Fiction
JS: 1117, 1431, 3490, 3606
S: 1269–70, 1459, 3974

Pro Football Hall of Fame
S: 13306

Prohibition (U.S.)
JS: 8804, 9213

Prohibition (U.S.) — Fiction
JS: 2975

Prohibitionism — Biography
S: 6432

Proms (high school)
S–Adult: 11323

Prophecies
See Predictions

Prophets (Bible)
JS: 9076

Prostitution
S–Adult: 10097

Prostitution — Fiction
JS: 891, 1395

Protestantism
JS: 9113

Protests and demonstrations
JS: 10138

Proverbs (Bible)
JS: 9049

Psychiatrists — Fiction
JS: 3505 **S–Adult:** 1112

Psychic abilities
S: 13059

JS = Junior High/Senior High;   S = Senior High;   S–Adult = Senior High/Adult

Psychic abilities — Biography
S–Adult: 6930

Psychic abilities — Fiction
JS: 291–92

Psychoanalysis
JS: 6570 S: 6569, 11338

Psychological testing
S: 11350

Psychology
See also Human development and
behavior
JS: 11334, 11339 S: 11329, 11338
S–Adult: 11352

Puberty
See also Adolescence; Menstruation
J: 11229 S: 11325 S–Adult: 11331

Puberty — Boys
J: 11239 JS: 11242, 11249

Puberty — Girls
JS: 11249–50

Public service — Careers
JS: 10485

Public speaking
JS: 10290 S: 10317

Publishing
See also Book making
JS: 5584

Publishing — Biography
JS: 6625 S–Adult: 6329

Publishing — Careers
S: 10469, 10475

Publishing — Fiction
S: 3589 S–Adult: 3481

Pueblo Indians
JS: 5135, 8487 S: 8416

Pueblo Indians — Fiction
JS: 2733 S: 2730

Pueblo Indians — Legends
JS: 5134

Puerto Ricans
S: 9734

Puerto Ricans — Biography
JS: 6090 S: 6503 S–Adult: 6254

Puerto Ricans — Fiction
JS: 433, 871 S: 434

Puerto Rico
JS: 8272–73

Pulitzer, Joseph
JS: 6630

Pulitzer, Joseph, II
S: 6631

Pullman strike (1894)
JS: 10239, 10241

Puma
See Cougars

Punic Wars
JS: 7511, 7516

Punishment
JS: 10005

Puns
S: 10315

Puppeteers — Biography
S: 6055

Puppets and marionettes
S–Adult: 7098

Puppets and marionettes — Fiction
JS: 3104

Puritans — Fiction
JS: 2746, 2750

Putin, Vladimir
S–Adult: 6877

Puzzles
See also Games; Mathematics —
Puzzles
JS: 12999, 13003 S: 12934, 12998,
13001–2

Pyramids
See also Egypt — History
JS: 7460, 7473 S–Adult: 7458

Q

Quaaludes (drugs)
See also Drugs and drug abuse
JS: 10722

Quadriplegics
S–Adult: 11152

Quakers
JS: 9123

Quakers — Fiction
S: 2855, 2919

Quapaw Indians — Fiction
JS: 2216

Quebec (province)
JS: 8239

Quebec (province) — Fiction
S: 836

Quilts and quilting
S: 12970–72 S–Adult: 12964

Quilts and quilting — Fiction
JS: 2753 S: 3671

Quinceanera (coming-of-age ritual) — Fiction
JS: 536

Quotations
J: 5563 JS: 11480

Quotations — African Americans
S: 9591, 9651 S–Adult: 11946

R

Rabbits
S: 12233 S–Adult: 11946

Rabbits — Fiction
JS: 1633 S: 4270

Rabies
JS: 10859

Rabies — Fiction
JS: 2966

Rabin, Yitzhak
S: 6808

Raccoons
JS: 11954

Race relations
S: 9396, 9557–58, 9562, 9575–76,
9581, 9596, 9634, 9683
S–Adult: 9568, 9582, 9588, 9691,
9696, 9700, 13303

Race relations — Fiction
JS: 2982 S–Adult: 545

Racial profiling
S–Adult: 9299

Racially mixed people
JS: 9548, 9553, 9573 S: 9570
S–Adult: 9577

Racially mixed people — Biography
S–Adult: 9565

Racially mixed people — Fiction
JS: 420, 739, 797, 812 S: 558, 623,
1241 S–Adult: 491

Racing cars
See Automobile racing

Racism
See also Discrimination; Prejudice;
Segregation (U.S.)
JS: 7769, 9170, 9311, 9416, 9450,
9546, 9551, 9555, 9560, 9572, 9583–84,
9645, 10188, 11363, 11375, 13243
S: 9455, 9558, 9562, 9576, 9579, 9587,
9634, 9649, 9661, 9683, 9697, 9838
S–Adult: 5202, 9329, 9341, 9388,
9405, 9410, 9432, 9446, 9469, 9545,
9549–50, 9559, 9567, 9569, 9610, 9633,
9641, 9656, 9681, 9700

Racism — Biography
S: 6950

Racism — Fiction
JS: 436, 453, 483, 495, 512, 585, 590,
1122, 1313, 1578, 2509, 2814, 2842,
2954, 2961, 2970, 2976, 2983 S: 265,
468, 522, 556, 565, 579, 1449, 2484
S–Adult: 249, 382, 446, 490, 531, 567,
588, 2958, 3979

Racism — Poetry
S: 4960

Racquetball
S: 13443, 13448

Racquetball — Technique
S: 13454

Radiation
See also Nuclear energy
S: 10814

Radicalism
JS: 9839 S–Adult: 9352

Radio
S: 12738

JS = Junior High/Senior High; S = Senior High; S–Adult = Senior High/Adult

Radio — Careers
JS: 10462

Radio — Fiction
JS: 377

Radio — History
JS: 8829 S: 7269

Radioactive materials
See also Nuclear energy
JS: 9175

Rafting
S: 13404

Railroads and trains — Fiction
S: 2579, 2794, 2955, 3412, 3512

Railroads and trains — History
JS: 8770, 10239, 12684–87
S–Adult: 12683

Rain forests
See also Forests and forestry
JS: 8282, 8992, 11786, 11848,
12376–77, 12379 S: 8288, 12375,
12381, 12383 S–Adult: 8051, 12378,
12382

Rain forests — Canada
S: 12380

Rain forests — Fiction
JS: 708 S–Adult: 3761

Rainmaking — Fiction
S: 79

A Raisin in the Sun — Criticism
JS: 5516

Raleigh, Sir Walter
JS: 5675, 8511

Ramos, Jorge
S–Adult: 6989

Ranches and ranch life — Fiction
JS: 475, 715 S: 183 S–Adult: 748,
792, 3862, 3891

Rap music
JS: 7161, 7163 S: 7154, 7172
S–Adult: 10049

Rap music — Biography
S–Adult: 6042

Rap music — Careers
JS: 10444

Rap music — Fiction
JS: 535

Rape
See also Date rape
JS: 9964, 11280, 11291, 11299, 11303,
11310, 11312, 11320 S: 11282,
11306–7, 11315, 11319

Rape — Fiction
JS: 494, 914, 971, 1003, 1021–22,
1397, 1519, 4037 S: 1082, 1099, 1298,
1624 S–Adult: 1597

Raphael (painter)
J: 7078

Rasputin
S: 6878

Rats
S: 11949

Rattlesnakes
S: 11916

Rawlings, Marjorie Kinnan
JS: 5382 S–Adult: 5923

Ray, James Earl
S: 6502

Rays
JS: 12165

Reading
S: 10275 S–Adult: 5242

Reading — Fiction
JS: 4150

Reagan, Ronald
JS: 6357, 8883 S: 6356

The Real World (television series)
S: 7265

Realism — Literature
S: 5409

Reality shows — Television
JS: 7274

Ream, Vinnie — Fiction
JS: 2847

Recipes
See Cookbooks

**Reconstruction to World War I
(U.S.)**
See also United States (1865–1914)
— History
JS: 8760, 8769, 9642 S–Adult: 2912

**Reconstruction to World War I
(U.S.) — Fiction**
JS: 268, 2910, 2925 S: 2868, 2909,
2933, 2940

Reconstruction (U.S.)
JS: 8595, 8759, 8774 S–Adult: 8766

Reconstruction (U.S.) — Fiction
S–Adult: 2833, 2929

Recorders (music)
S: 7201

Recycling
See also Waste recycling
S: 9905, 9926, 9928

The Red Badge of Courage —
Criticism
S: 5366, 5372

Red Cross — Biography
J: 6382 S–Adult: 6383

The Red Pony — Criticism
S: 5416

Red Shirt, Delphine
S: 8468

Redwoods (trees)
S–Adult: 12095

Reece, Gabrielle
S: 6747

Reefs
S–Adult: 8051

Reeve, Christopher
JS: 6109, 11463 S–Adult: 6110

Reformation
S: 7570 S–Adult: 7533

Refugees
JS: 7703, 8246, 8258, 9187, 9538,
9720, 9936, 11575 S–Adult: 9836

Refugees — Fiction
JS: 489, 1620–21, 1625, 2551, 3077
S: 3994

Refugees — Teenage
JS: 9716–17, 9725, 9731, 9782–83,
9785

Reggae music
S–Adult: 7130

Reggae music — Biography
S: 6087–88 S–Adult: 6086

Reggae music — History
JS: 7153

Reichl, Ruth
S: 6990

Reid, Jan
S–Adult: 5924

Reincarnation — Fiction
JS: 3641 S–Adult: 2154

Reiss, Johanna
JS: 6991

Relatives — Fiction
JS: 697, 1271

Relativity (physics)
JS: 12497 S: 6560, 12496, 12502
S–Adult: 12499, 12511

Relativity (physics) — Biography
S–Adult: 6558

Religion
See also Prayers; and specific
religions, e.g., Christianity
JS: 9040, 9043, 9048, 9051, 9053–54,
9056, 9058, 9066–67, 9074, 9079, 9088,
9090–91, 9111, 9119 S: 9022, 9039,
9046, 9060, 9063, 9068, 9071, 9086,
9094–95 S–Adult: 8626, 9024, 9055,
9065, 9069, 9082, 9087, 9699

Religion — Africa
JS: 9070 S: 9092

Religion — African Americans
S: 9680

Religion — Biography
JS: 6485, 6820

Religion — Comparative
JS: 9048 S–Adult: 9073

Religion — Cults
S: 9157

Religion — Fiction
JS: 366, 388, 1226, 1258, 1603, 4634,
4713 S: 1093, 1414, 1440
S–Adult: 310, 324, 336, 376, 513, 788,
934, 1178, 1443, 2967

Religion — History
JS: 9047 S: 9077, 9083
S–Adult: 5150

Religion — Stories
JS: 9072

JS = Junior High/Senior High;   S = Senior High;   S–Adult = Senior High/Adult

Religion — United States
JS: 9047 S: 9077 S–Adult: 9073

Religious liberty
See Freedom of religion

Remarque, Erich Maria
S: 5321

Remarriage — Fiction
S: 1268

Rembrandt van Rijn
J: 7079 JS: 5781–82 S: 5783

Renaissance
JS: 7070, 7559 S: 7522, 7528, 7536, 7538, 7557–58 S–Adult: 7534

Renaissance — Art
JS: 7072, 7075, 7077 S: 7048
S–Adult: 7069

Renaissance — Biography
JS: 5750–52, 6572, 6869
S–Adult: 5753

Renaissance — Fiction
S: 2658

Renaissance — Wars
JS: 7526

Renoir, Pierre Auguste
JS: 5784

Report writing
JS: 10293, 10296, 10316 S: 10305

Reporters
See Journalism

Reproduction
See also Sex education
S: 11176

Reproduction — Human
JS: 10572, 11216 S–Adult: 11256

Reproductive rights
S–Adult: 11235

Reproductive system
J: 10982 JS: 10984 S: 11225

Reptiles
See also specific reptiles, e.g., Alligators and crocodiles
JS: 11900, 11902, 11904 S: 11895, 11897–99, 11903

Research — Guides
S: 10249

Resistance movement (World War II)
JS: 7822

Respiratory system
JS: 10985 S: 11024

Restaurants — Careers
S: 10373

Restorative justice
S–Adult: 10065

Resurrection — Fiction
S: 4255

Revenge
S: 11382 S–Adult: 11369

Revenge — Fiction
JS: 905

Revere, Paul
S–Adult: 6447

Revere, Paul — Fiction
JS: 2765

Revolution, French
See French Revolution

Revolutionary period (U.S.)
See also Revolutionary War (U.S.)
JS: 8354, 8516, 8518–19, 8529
S: 8520, 8534 S–Adult: 8542

Revolutionary period (U.S.) — African Americans
S–Adult: 8548

Revolutionary period (U.S.) — Biography
JS: 6192, 6279–81, 6404–5 S: 6379, 6402–3 S–Adult: 6182, 6406, 6447, 8525

Revolutionary period (U.S.) — Fiction
JS: 2763, 2768

Revolutionary period (U.S.) — Speeches
JS: 8536

Revolutionary period (U.S.) — Women
S–Adult: 6182

Revolutionary War (U.S.)
See also Revolutionary period (U.S.)
JS: 7585, 8354, 8522, 8527, 8531–32, 8535, 8537, 8540, 8544, 8551 S: 8517, 8524, 8533, 8538, 8547
S–Adult: 8528, 8543, 8549

Revolutionary War (U.S.) — Battles
S–Adult: 8550

Revolutionary War (U.S.) — Biography
JS: 6349, 6386, 6435, 6437, 6467
S: 6436

Revolutionary War (U.S.) — Fiction
J: 2758 JS: 2760, 2764–65 S: 2759
S–Adult: 2761

Revolutionary War (U.S.) — Weapons
JS: 8546

Revolutionary War (U.S.) — Women
JS: 8545

Revolutions
S–Adult: 7401

Rezendes, Paul
S–Adult: 6992

Rhinoceroses
S: 7958

Rhode Island — Biography
S: 6277

Rhode Island — Fiction
S–Adult: 657

Rhodesia — Civil war
S–Adult: 7961

Rice, Condoleezza
JS: 6448

Richard I, King of England
JS: 7531

Richard III, King of England — Fiction
S–Adult: 3814

Richards, Todd
S–Adult: 13420

Richmond (VA) — History
S: 8632

Riddles
See Jokes and riddles

Ride, Sally
JS: 5676

Rift Valley (Africa)
S–Adult: 7907

Right to die
See also Euthanasia; Suicide
JS: 10584, 10590, 10600

Rikers Island (prison)
S–Adult: 10064

Rio de Janeiro — Fiction
JS: 331

Riot Grrrl movement
JS: 9485

Ritalin (drug)
See also Drugs and drug abuse
JS: 10617

Rivera, Diego
JS: 5785

Rivers
S: 8287 S–Adult: 7997, 12109, 12385

Rivers — Experiments and projects
JS: 12386

Rivers — Fiction
S: 2921

Roanoke Colony
JS: 6577, 8505, 8511 S: 8507

Robbers and robbery — Fiction
JS: 1081

Roberts, Monty
S: 12314

Robeson, Paul
JS: 6111 S: 6112–13

Robin Hood
S: 5107

Robin Hood — Fiction
JS: 2439–40, 2472 S–Adult: 2474

Robinson, Jackie
J: 6683 JS: 6684 JS–Adult: 6682

Robinson, Katy
S–Adult: 11544

Robinson Crusoe
S–Adult: 5296

Robotics
JS: 12625 S: 12623 S–Adult: 7279, 12562

Robots
J: 12595 JS: 12625, 12627 S: 12610

JS = Junior High/Senior High;   S = Senior High;   S–Adult = Senior High/Adult

Robots — Experiments and projects
S: 12623

Robots — Fiction
JS: 4322 S: 4109, 4112–13, 4427

Rock and roll
S–Adult: 7157

Rock and roll — Biography
S–Adult: 7178

Rock and Roll Hall of Fame
JS: 7180

Rock carvings — Fiction
JS: 4039

Rock climbing
See Mountain and rock climbing

Rock music
JS: 7127, 7140, 7160, 7180, 8877
S: 7134, 7152, 7158, 7166, 7168, 7184,
7193 S–Adult: 7142, 7144, 7171,
7182

Rock music — Biography
JS: 6054, 6079, 6081, 6085, 6103,
6108, 6128, 6134, 6141 S: 5990,
6003–4, 6016–17, 6043, 6066, 6068–69,
6080, 6106, 6142–43 S–Adult: 6002,
6018, 6051, 6053, 6105, 6107

Rock music — Careers
JS: 10444 S: 10440

Rock music — Fiction
JS: 814, 3278 S: 1048, 1251, 3849
S–Adult: 387, 1035, 1589

Rock music — Women
S: 7119, 7137

Rockefeller, John D.
S: 6632

Rockets
JS: 12564

Rockport (ME) — Fiction
JS: 1463

Rocks and minerals
See also Geology
JS: 11138, 12391, 12395 S: 12392–94
S–Adult: 12396

Rodeos — Fiction
JS: 1155, 2972

Rodriguez, Robert
J: 6114

Roe v. Wade
JS: 9304, 9336, 9338 S: 11207
S–Adult: 9307

Rogers, Will
S: 6115

Roller coasters
S–Adult: 12549

Roller hockey
JS: 13369

Rolling Stone (magazine)
S: 5611

Rolling Stones (musical group)
S: 7184

Roman Empire
See also Italy — History; Rome —
History
J: 7520 JS: 7507, 7511–14, 7516–17,
7521 S: 7504–5, 7509

Roman Empire — Architecture
JS: 8147 S: 7446

Roman Empire — Biography
JS: 6818–19 S: 7503, 7519

**Roman Empire — Building and
construction**
JS: 8147

Roman Empire — Fiction
JS: 2435 S: 197, 202, 2417–19, 2422,
3468 S–Adult: 2653

Roman Empire — Literature
S: 5245

Romance — Fiction
See also Love — Fiction
JS: 44, 315, 367, 592, 732, 736, 858,
861, 919, 963, 1014, 1059, 1078, 1100,
1123, 1136, 1144, 1211, 1244, 1247,
1254–55, 1323, 1328, 1336, 1347, 1347,
1363, 1366, 1425, 1429, 1467, 1526,
1550–51, 1557, 1579, 1609, 1693,
1778–79, 2069, 2261, 2395, 2465, 2489,
2644, 2775, 2783, 2867, 2884, 2910,
2945, 3003, 3269, 3283, 3292, 3309,
3313, 3315, 3807, 3864–65, 3869–70,
3874–75, 3881, 3887–88, 3892, 3896,
3896–97, 3899, 3903, 3912–13, 3915,
3918–20, 3924, 3931, 3933–34, 3934,
3940–41, 3949, 3953, 3956, 3962, 3969,
3982–83, 3992, 4003, 4007, 4012, 4018,
4020, 4022, 4026, 4037, 4039, 4041,
4046–47, 4055, 4061, 4068, 4073–74,
4077, 4079–80, 4468, 4733, 5271
S: 74, 141, 204, 206, 254, 313, 461,
581, 852, 922, 931, 1055, 1065, 1183,
1210, 1268, 1305, 1348, 1357, 1377,
1413, 1423, 1528, 1555, 1996, 2062,
2351, 2424, 2444, 2453, 2460, 2498,
2507, 2556, 2604, 2609–10, 2635, 2660,
2696, 2724, 2778, 2786, 2858, 2866,
2882, 2898, 2906, 2909, 2921, 2994,
3230, 3262, 3567, 3580, 3677, 3710,
3747, 3844, 3850, 3860–61, 3872–73,
3876–77, 3889, 3900, 3906, 3939,
3942–44, 3952, 3957–58, 3963,
3974–75, 3975–76, 3988, 3994, 4006,
4014, 4017, 4032, 4034, 4038, 4038,
4058, 4063, 4066, 4069–71, 4076, 4081
S–Adult: 13, 133, 203, 285, 323, 358,
369, 401, 442, 684, 689, 779, 831, 834,
1041, 1416, 1612, 1717, 1856, 1892,
1985, 2072, 2164–65, 2199, 2442, 2449,
2513, 2527, 2559–60, 2584, 2595, 2600,
2603, 2615–16, 2651, 2656–57,
2663–64, 2672, 2678, 2737, 2782, 2785,
2825, 2827, 2915, 2928–29, 2934, 2938,
2953, 2959, 2963, 2990, 3005, 3254,
3302, 3311, 3344, 3383, 3387, 3402,
3430–31, 3459–60, 3479, 3534, 3600,
3619, 3644, 3647, 3672–73, 3676, 3680,
3752, 3856, 3859, 3862–63, 3866–68,
3871, 3878–80, 3882–86, 3890–91,
3893–95, 3898, 3902, 3904–5, 3907–10,
3914, 3916–17, 3921–23, 3925–28,
3930, 3932, 3935–38, 3945–48,
3950–51, 3954–55, 3959–61, 3964–68,

3970–73, 3977–81, 3984–87, 3989–91,
3993, 3995–4002, 4004–5, 4008–11,
4013, 4015–16, 4019, 4021, 4023–25,
4027–31, 4033, 4035–36, 4040,
4042–45, 4048–54, 4056–57, 4059–60,
4062, 4064–65, 4067, 4072, 4075, 4078,
4163

Romance — Poetry
JS: 5037

Romania
S: 8089

Romania — Biography
S–Adult: 7009

Romania — Fiction
JS: 5116

Romanov family (Russia)
S–Adult: 8162

Romanticism — Literature
S: 5370

Rome — Biography
S–Adult: 6826

Rome — Fiction
S–Adult: 1901, 2423, 2426–27, 2434,
2583, 3469, 3780

Rome — History
See also Roman Empire
J: 7520 JS: 7445, 7507, 7510,
7513–15 S: 8145 S–Adult: 7502,
7506, 7508

Rome — Literature
S–Adult: 186, 5444, 7506

Rome — Mythology
See also Mythology — Classical
JS: 5179 S: 5168

Rome — Poetry
S–Adult: 4945

Rome — Sports
J: 7451

Rome — Women
JS: 7518

Romeo and Juliet (play)
S: 4770

Romeo and Juliet (play) — Criticism
JS: 5481, 5494 S: 5478

Romeo and Juliet (play) — Retelling
JS: 4772

Rommel, General Erwin
S: 7766

Roosevelt, Eleanor
JS: 6358–59 S: 8837

Roosevelt, Eleanor — Fiction
S: 3763–66

Roosevelt, Franklin D.
JS: 6360, 6363, 8824 S: 6361, 8837
S–Adult: 6362

Roosevelt, Theodore
S–Adult: 6364, 8765

Rose, Alma
S–Adult: 7770

JS = Junior High/Senior High;   S = Senior High;   S–Adult = Senior High/Adult

JS = Junior High/Senior High;   S = Senior High;   S–Adult = Senior High/Adult

4149, 4151, 4154, 4156, 4160, 4162, 4164, 4166, 4170–73, 4175–76, 4178, 4181, 4183, 4188, 4190–91, 4195, 4198–203, 4206, 4211, 4213–16, 4224, 4230, 4237–38, 4241, 4243–45, 4248, 4254–56, 4259–60, 4265–66, 4269–70, 4280–81, 4285, 4287, 4290, 4293–95, 4299–302, 4304–5, 4307, 4313–14, 4316–17, 4321, 4325–27, 4330–31, 4336–37, 4340, 4350, 4353–57, 4359, 4361, 4363, 4369–75, 4377–79, 4382, 4385–86, 4388, 4391, 4398, 4401, 4404–5, 4407–9, 4411, 4416, 4418, 4427, 4429, 4435, 4447–49, 4454, 4460–61, 4463, 4470, 4472, 4475, 4485, 4493, 4496, 4500, 4502, 4507, 4513–14, 4516–17, 4520, 4524, 4526–27, 4529, 4535–36, 4538, 4540, 4546–47, 4550–51, 4647 **S–Adult:** 1650, 2284, 2294, 2314, 2339, 3790, 4088, 4090–91, 4095, 4102–4, 4116, 4118, 4120–26, 4128–30, 4133, 4135–38, 4143–45, 4147–48, 4155, 4157–59, 4161, 4163, 4167–69, 4174, 4177, 4179, 4182, 4184, 4186–87, 4189, 4196, 4204–5, 4207–8, 4210, 4212, 4218–20, 4222–23, 4227, 4229, 4231–36, 4239–40, 4242, 4246–47, 4251, 4257–58, 4261–64, 4267, 4271, 4273, 4276, 4278–79, 4283–84, 4286, 4288–89, 4296–98, 4315, 4319–20, 4323–24, 4333–35, 4338–39, 4341–43, 4352, 4360, 4362, 4365–68, 4376, 4380–81, 4383–84, 4387, 4389–90, 4392–95, 4397, 4399–400, 4402, 4406, 4410, 4412, 4417, 4421–23, 4428, 4430, 4432–33, 4436–39, 4441–45, 4450–53, 4455–59, 4462, 4464–65, 4467, 4469, 4471, 4473–74, 4476, 4483–84, 4486, 4488–92, 4494, 4497–99, 4501, 4505–6, 4508–9, 4511–12, 4515, 4518–19, 4521–23, 4532–34, 4537, 4539, 4541–45, 4548–49, 4552–54, 4605, 4625, 4627–28, 4669, 4734, 7094

Science fiction — Biography
JS: 5908 **S–Adult:** 5882

Science fiction — Criticism
S: 5384

Science fiction — Films
JS: 7252 **S:** 7259

Science fiction — History and criticism
JS: 5254, 5257–58 **S:** 4475, 5248, 5251, 5259, 5398

Science fiction — Illustration
S: 7031

Science fiction — Writing
S: 10310

Science projects
See Science — Experiments and projects

Scientific expeditions
S–Adult: 7423

Scientific research — Fiction
S: 1631

Scientists — Women
S–Adult: 11965

Scoliosis
JS: 10764 **S–Adult:** 10829

Scooters
S: 12681

Scopes Trial
See also Evolution
JS: 8812, 9296 **S–Adult:** 8788

Scorsese, Martin
S: 7226

Scotland
See also Great Britain
S: 13023

Scotland — Biography
JS: 6858, 6868 **S:** 6867

Scotland — Fiction
JS: 2612–13, 2690, 3660 **S:** 37, 1058, 1459, 2572, 2669, 2691, 3355
S–Adult: 1167, 2161, 2615–16, 2656, 2665, 3744, 3961, 4023

Scotland — History
S–Adult: 8138

Scott, Dred
JS: 8568

Scott, Robert F.
S–Adult: 8320

Scott, Robert F. — Fiction
S: 7

Scott, Tony
JS: 6748

Scottish Americans
JS: 9774

Scottsboro Trial (AL)
S: 9306

Scouts and scouting
JS: 11575

Scrapbooks
S–Adult: 12734

Scuba diving — Fiction
JS: 36, 3218

Sculpture
S–Adult: 7093

Sculpture — Biography
JS: 5733 **S:** 5740 **S–Adult:** 5746

Sculpture — Fiction
JS: 2847

Sculpture — History
JS: 7040, 7061

Sea disasters
See also Shipwrecks
S: 12435, 12492–93 **S–Adult:** 12491

Sea mammals
S: 12204 **S–Adult:** 12198

Sea stories
See also Adventure and adventurers — Fiction
JS: 1420, 4668 **S:** 163, 7965, 12478
S–Adult: 5617, 5625, 7426, 8068, 8343, 8576, 8997, 13038

Sea stories — Fiction
JS: 9, 144, 229, 259, 1621 **S:** 83, 101, 121, 161, 3048 **S–Adult:** 2666, 2679, 2782, 2843

Sea turtles
S: 11921

Sea voyages
S: 7414

Seabiscuit (horse)
S–Adult: 13355

Seafarers — Biography
S–Adult: 5641

Seafarers — Women
S–Adult: 5617

Seafaring — Fiction
S: 2593

Seals
S–Adult: 12198

SEALs (navy)
S–Adult: 12703

Seances — Fiction
JS: 3698

Search warrants
JS: 9326

Seashells
JS: 12161, 12166

Seashells — Crafts
S–Adult: 12731

Seashores
JS: 12164 **S:** 12156 **S–Adult:** 12160

Seattle (WA) — Fiction
JS: 862, 2979 **S:** 4673
S–Adult: 2938

Sebestyen, Ouida
JS: 5927

Second City (theatric group)
S–Adult: 7299

Secretary of Defense (U.S.) — Biography
JS: 9252

Secretary of State (U.S.) — Biography
JS: 6380–81, 6451, 9245, 9252

Secularism (U.S.) — History
S–Adult: 8370

Segregation
JS: 9420, 9672 **S–Adult:** 8386

Segregation — Fiction
S: 2980 **S–Adult:** 457, 506

Segregation — History
S: 8840

Segregation (U.S.)
See also Prejudice; Racism
JS: 9416–17, 9482, 9484, 9506
S: 9635 **S–Adult:** 9681

Segregation (U.S.) — History
JS: 9463, 9476 **S–Adult:** 9386

Seismology
S: 12356

JS = Junior High/Senior High;   S = Senior High;   S–Adult = Senior High/Adult

Selena
J: 6119

Seles, Monica
JS: 6727

Self-defense
JS: 13375, 13377

Self-esteem
See also Personal guidance
JS: 11059, 11458, 11487 **S:** 11473
S–Adult: 9646

Self-esteem — Fiction
JS: 1321

Self-esteem — Women
S: 11422

Self-image
JS: 10975

Self-image — Fiction
JS: 1243, 1541 **S:** 522

Self-mutilation
JS: 11055

Self-mutilation — Fiction
JS: 961

Self-realization — Fiction
S: 1682

Selkirk, Alexander
S: 5678

Senate (U.S.)
See also Congress (U.S.);
Government (U.S.)
JS: 9242 **S:** 9247

Senegal
JS: 7996

Senses
See also specific senses, e.g., Smell
(sense)
JS: 10996

A Separate Peace — **Criticism**
S: 5378

September 11, 2001
See also Terrorism; World Trade
Center
JS: 4836, 10170, 10177–78, 10189,
10193, 10197, 10200 **S:** 10173, 10181
S–Adult: 4820, 5203, 9471, 10167–68,
10175, 10179–80, 10182–83, 10190,
10194–95, 10206

September 11, 2001 — Fiction
S–Adult: 1593

Sequoyah (Cherokee chief)
S: 6450

Serbo-Croatians — Fiction
S: 2659

Serengeti Plain (Tanzania)
S–Adult: 7940

Sermons
S: 9655

Sesame Street **(television series)**
S: 7260

Seuss, Dr.
JS–Adult: 5928

Seward, William
JS: 6451

Sewing
See also Needlecrafts
JS–Adult: 12973 **S:** 12959,
12966–67, 12970–72, 12974, 12976–77

Sex — Fiction
JS: 1494, 3888, 3934 **S:** 1055, 1241,
1283, 1348, 4663 **S–Adult:** 681

Sex education
See also Reproduction
J: 10621, 11239 **JS:** 10567, 11174,
11184, 11224, 11230–32, 11238, 11243,
11248, 11250, 11260–61, 11263, 11269,
11271, 11275, 11279, 11411, 11481
S: 11225–27, 11253, 11270, 11276,
11306, 11429 **S–Adult:** 11235, 11256,
11278

Sex education — African Americans
S: 11267

Sex roles
See also Gender roles
S: 10123, 10127 **S–Adult:** 10124,
10928

Sex roles — Fiction
JS: 1339 **S:** 2543 **S–Adult:** 921

Sex roles — Poetry
JS: 4892

Sexism
See also Sexual discrimination;
Sexual harassment
JS: 9374, 11294, 11297 **S:** 9298,
10401, 13110

Sexual abuse
See also Child sexual abuse
JS: 11280, 11295, 11304, 11308, 11310
S: 11289

Sexual abuse — Fiction
JS: 662, 685, 733, 739, 965, 1014,
1426, 1462 **S:** 740, 907, 926, 987,
1197, 1528 **S–Adult:** 348

Sexual abuse — Poetry
JS: 5036

Sexual assault
See Date rape; Rape

Sexual behavior
JS: 11259, 11375 **S:** 9503, 11226,
11255 **S–Adult:** 9685, 10124, 10126,
11233

Sexual discrimination
See also Sexism; Sexual harassment
JS: 10125, 10128 **S:** 13110

Sexual ethics
S: 11290

Sexual harassment
See also Sexism; Sexual
discrimination
JS: 11294, 11297, 11301, 11305
S: 11281, 11293, 11298, 11302, 11311,
11316

Sexual harassment — Fiction
JS: 1349, 1478 **S–Adult:** 4005

Sexual problems
S: 11314

Sexual violence
See also Date rape; Rape
JS: 9967 **S:** 10052, 11318

Sexuality
S: 11255

Sexually transmitted diseases
JS: 10742, 10753–54, 10894–95
S: 10813, 10846, 11226

Shabazz, Betty
JS: 6259 **S–Adult:** 6260, 6997

Shabazz, Ilyasah
S–Adult: 6997

Shackleton, Sir Ernest
JS: 5679, 8300 **S:** 8307
S–Adult: 5521, 5680, 8299, 8305

Shakers (religion)
JS: 9124 **S:** 9115–16

Shakespeare, William
JS: 5460, 5474, 5494 **S:** 4770, 5929
S–Adult: 5472, 5930–31, 8132

Shakespeare, William —
Adaptations
JS: 5470

Shakespeare, William — Collected
works
S: 4773

Shakespeare, William — Criticism
JS: 4771, 5468, 5480–82 **S:** 5464–66,
5473, 5475–78, 5486–89, 5491–93,
5495 **S–Adult:** 5461–62, 5483–84

Shakespeare, William — Fiction
JS: 2567, 2602 **S–Adult:** 1938,
2598–99, 2674

Shakespeare, William — History
and criticism
S–Adult: 5469

Shakespeare, William — Plays
S: 4769, 5467, 5479

Shakespeare, William — Plays —
Criticism
S: 5463

Shakespeare, William — Plays —
Fiction
S: 3911

Shakespeare, William — Poetry
S: 4940 **S–Adult:** 5485

Shakespeare, William — Sonnets —
Criticism
S: 5490

Shakespeare, William — Theater
S: 5471

Shakur, Tupac
S–Adult: 6120

Sharks
JS: 12165, 12182–83, 12186–87
S: 12189–92 **S–Adult:** 12158,
12184–85, 12188

Sharks — Fiction
JS: 18 **JS–Adult:** 162

JS = Junior High/Senior High;   S = Senior High;   S–Adult = Senior High/Adult

1164

6121–22, 6135 **S–Adult:** 6035, 6057–58, 6105, 6107

Singers and singing — Fiction
JS: 802

Single parents
JS: 11209, 11556, 11564

Single parents — Fiction
JS: 404, 885 **S–Adult:** 6936

Single-sex schools
JS: 10254

Sioux Indians
S: 8472, 8485, 9757

Sioux Indians — Biography
S: 6397, 6454

Sioux Indians — Fiction
S: 543 **S–Adult:** 544

Sistine Chapel
JS: 7080

Sitting Bull
JS: 6453 **S:** 6452, 6454
S–Adult: 6455

Sixteenth century
S: 7568

Skateboarding
JS: 13412

Skateboarding — Biography
JS: 6745, 6748

Skateboarding — Fiction
JS: 4576

Skating
See Ice skating

Skeletal system
See Musculoskeletal system

Skeletons
JS: 11021

Skiing — Biography
S: 6749

Skill development
S: 10360

Skin
JS: 10980

Skin care
JS: 10973, 10980 **S:** 10882

Skin disorders
S: 10800, 10882

Skinheads — Fiction
S: 3958

Skis and skiing
JS: 13413, 13415, 13421 **S:** 13419

Skyscrapers — History
S: 12572

Slang
S: 5541

Slaughter, Carolyn
S–Adult: 6999

Slave narratives — Criticism
S: 5246

Slave trade
JS: 7580, 9427, 9660

Slavery
See also related topics, e.g., African Americans — History; Underground Railroad
J: 8562, 9664 **JS:** 2796, 6270, 6274, 7579, 8508, 8557, 8559, 8568, 8581, 8583, 8586–89, 8605, 8688, 9219, 9384, 9400, 9449, 9466, 9475, 9480–81, 9491, 9497, 9507, 9648, 9659–60 **S:** 6153, 6170, 6255, 7583, 7894, 8552–53, 8571, 8573, 8584, 9490, 9589, 9598, 9611, 9623, 9625, 9630, 9690
S–Adult: 2780, 9453

Slavery — Africa
S–Adult: 7912

Slavery — Biography
JS: 6188, 6203, 6221, 6273, 6493

Slavery — Fiction
JS: 131, 2709, 2754, 2767, 2769, 2771, 2773, 2775, 2787, 2793, 2802, 2841, 2851, 2954 **S:** 265, 449, 497, 2777, 2791, 2795, 2822, 2834, 2936, 5031
S–Adult: 421, 2695, 2804, 2829, 2941, 6268

Slavery — History
JS: 8397 **S–Adult:** 7581

Slavery — Poetry
JS: 4997

Slavery — Reparations
JS: 9682

Slavery (U.S.)
JS: 8560, 9427, 9627, 9671 **S:** 9474
S–Adult: 8556, 8564, 9693

Slavery (U.S.) — Biography
JS: 7003 **S–Adult:** 6492

Slavery (U.S.) — Fiction
JS: 2766, 2800, 2846 **S–Adult:** 2788

Slavery (U.S.) — History
JS: 8523 **S:** 9486 **S–Adult:** 8567, 8766

Sled dogs
See also Iditarod Sled Dog Race
JS: 12289

Sled dogs — Racing
JS: 13113 **S:** 13081, 13112

Sleep
JS: 11000, 11005–6 **S–Adult:** 11342

Sleep disorders
JS: 10865, 10994

Sleeping Beauty (fairy tale) — Adaptations
S: 2281

Sleepwalking
JS: 10994

Slovakia — Fiction
JS: 3069

Slugs — Fiction
JS: 4277

Slums
S: 10211 **S–Adult:** 10086

Slums — Fiction
JS: 473

Smallpox
JS: 10779 **S–Adult:** 10881

Smell (sense)
S–Adult: 11025

Smith, Captain John
JS: 8499

Smith, Joseph
S–Adult: 6505

Smith, Will
JS: 6123–26

Smithsonian Institution (Washington, DC)
S: 8975

Smoke jumpers
S–Adult: 10498

Smokey Bear
S: 11981

Smoking
See also Nicotine; Tobacco industry
J: 10687 **JS:** 10611, 10654, 10657, 10667, 10678, 10684, 10690, 10705, 10716–17, 10720 **S:** 10618, 10719

Snake River — Ecology
S: 12387

Snakes
See also individual species, e.g., Rattlesnakes
JS: 11909, 11911, 11915 **S:** 11895, 11912–14, 11916–17

Sneden, Robert Knox
S–Adult: 7106

Snow
S–Adult: 12453

Snowboarding
JS: 13413, 13417 **S:** 13414, 13416, 13418, 13422 **S–Adult:** 13420

Snyder, Leslie Crocker
S–Adult: 6456

Soccer
JS: 13424, 13427, 13432–33 **S:** 13423, 13425–26, 13428–29

Soccer — Fiction
JS: 1054, 1266, 4596 **S:** 1283

Soccer — History
JS: 13430 **S:** 13431

Social action
See also Activism; Affirmative action; Volunteerism
JS: 10079, 10140, 10142 **S:** 10132
S–Adult: 9847, 10129, 11577

Social action — History
S–Adult: 7393, 8876

Social anxiety disorder
S–Adult: 11085

Social change
JS: 10150 **S–Adult:** 5608

Social concerns and conflicts
JS: 9817 **S:** 9825 **S–Adult:** 9811, 11357

JS = Junior High/Senior High;   S = Senior High;   S–Adult = Senior High/Adult

Social concerns and conflicts —
Women
S–Adult: 11247

Social customs
S: 10157

Social groups
See also Scouts and scouting; and
ethnic groups, e.g., Hispanic
Americans
S–Adult: 10152

Social issues
S–Adult: 11519

Social problems
See also specific problems, e.g.,
Poverty
JS: 9437 S: 9831, 9858
S–Adult: 9790, 10110, 10209, 11322

Social problems — Fiction
S–Adult: 2594

Social problems — Statistics
S–Adult: 9789

Social problems — Teenagers
S–Adult: 11577

Social work — Biography
JS: 6401, 6464–65

Society
JS: 9829

Sociology
S: 11333

Sociology — Modern
S–Adult: 9933

Socrates
S: 7492

Soffee, Anne Thomas
S–Adult: 7000

Soffel, Katherine — Fiction
JS: 297

Softball
See also Baseball
S: 13183

Soil ecology
JS: 11885

Sojourner **(Mars rover)**
S: 11768

Solar eclipses
S–Adult: 11700

Solar energy
S: 12518

Solar system
See also Astronomy; Comets;
Extraterrestrial life; Moon; Planets;
Space exploration; Stars; Sun
JS: 11764, 11771 S: 11763, 11772

Somalia
JS: 7928 S: 7917

Sone, Monica
S: 7001

Songbooks
JS: 7202

Songs
See also Folk music
J: 9114 JS: 7206–7

Songs — Christmas
S–Adult: 7203

Songs — History
S–Adult: 7210

Songwriting
S: 7113–14

Sonnets
S–Adult: 5443

Sophocles — Criticism
S: 5434, 5455, 5457

Sosa, Sammy
JS: 6687–88

Sound — Experiments and projects
JS: 12541

The Sound and the Fury —
Criticism
S: 5338

Sound effects
S: 12742

Soups
S: 12767

South — Memoirs
S–Adult: 6933

South Africa
J: 7954 JS: 7953, 7956, 7959, 7967,
7971–72, 7974–77 S: 7965
S–Adult: 7957

South Africa — Animals
S–Adult: 7968

South Africa — Biography
J: 6785 JS: 6781–83 S: 6780
S–Adult: 6784

South Africa — Fiction
JS: 157, 298, 455, 1608, 4675
S: 1573–74, 1601, 2484, 2490
S–Adult: 2492

South Africa — History
S: 7978 S–Adult: 6784, 7952, 7962

South Africa — National Parks
S–Adult: 7968

South Africa — Plays
S–Adult: 4782

South America
See also individual countries, e.g.,
Brazil
S: 8290 S–Adult: 6946

South America — Biography
JS: 6897

South America — Cookbooks
J: 12819

South America — Fiction
S: 190

South America — Geography
S–Adult: 8293

South America — History
JS: 8295 S–Adult: 8283, 8294

South America — Mythology
JS: 5151

South Carolina
S: 9013 S–Adult: 10251

South Carolina — Fiction
S–Adult: 567

South Carolina — History
S–Adult: 8680

South Dakota
JS: 8963 S: 8468

South Dakota — Fiction
S–Adult: 792

South Korea — Cookbooks
J: 12778

South Pole
See also Antarctic; Polar regions
S: 8321 S–Adult: 8320

South Pole — Fiction
S: 7

South (U.S.)
See also specific states, e.g., Texas
JS: 8785 S: 6977

South (U.S.) — Civil War
S: 8685

South (U.S.) — Fiction
JS: 179, 494, 574, 2813, 2856 S: 265,
2854, 2913, 3199, 4671
S–Adult: 2781

South (U.S.) — History
S: 8650, 8666 S–Adult: 8864

Southeast Asia
S–Adult: 11982

Southeast Indians
JS: 8442

Southwest (U.S.)
See also specific states, e.g., New
Mexico
JS: 7385, 9017 S: 8439, 8572

Southwest (U.S.) — Biography
S: 5647

Southwest (U.S.) — Fiction
S: 406, 3572, 3818

Southwest (U.S.) — History
JS: 9018 S: 8471, 9016

Southwest (U.S.) — Native
Americans
JS: 8453

Soviet Union
See also Russia and other separate
states, e.g., Ukraine
JS: 8156, 8158, 8167, 8172 S: 8160,
8166, 8179

Soviet Union — Biography
JS: 6862–63 S–Adult: 6883

Soviet Union — Fiction
S: 1587, 1614

Soviet Union — History
JS: 8155 S–Adult: 8163

Space
S–Adult: 12510

JS = Junior High/Senior High;   S = Senior High;   S–Adult = Senior High/Adult

Space and time
See also Time
S: 12502 **S–Adult:** 11774

Space colonies
S: 11693

Space colonies — Fiction
S: 4110

Space exploration
See also Astronauts; Extraterrestrial
life; Planets; Space colonies, etc.
JS: 11688, 11709, 11711, 11725,
11727–28, 11732, 11748, 11771
S: 11693, 11698, 11710, 11712, 11715,
11718, 11720, 11723–24, 11729–30,
11736–37, 11750, 11761–62, 11778
S–Adult: 11667, 11685, 11713, 11716,
11734

Space exploration — Biography
S–Adult: 5624, 6583

Space exploration — Careers
JS: 10408

**Space exploration — Experiments
and projects**
JS: 11721

Space exploration — Fiction
JS: 4197 **S–Adult:** 4145

Space flights
S: 11736

Space shuttles
JS: 11719, 11733 **S–Adult:** 11731

Space stations — Fiction
S: 4355 **S–Adult:** 4288

Space technology
S: 11712

Space travel
See also Space exploration
S–Adult: 11714, 11734

Space travel — Fiction
JS: 4308–10, 4312

Spacecraft
See specific spacecraft, e.g., *Galileo*
(spacecraft)

Spacecraft — Fiction
S: 4191, 4201, 4215

Spain — Biography
S: 5636

Spain — Fiction
JS: 2469 **S:** 2604 **S–Adult:** 2288

Spain — History
JS: 8183, 8235 **S:** 8184

Spanish-American War
JS: 8764, 8768, 8773 **S–Adult:** 8757,
8765

Spanish-American War — Fiction
S–Adult: 2934

Spanish Armada
JS: 7550, 8183

Spanish Harlem (New York City)
JS–Adult: 8972

Spanish Inquisition
JS: 7565, 8185, 8185 **S:** 8184

Spanish language
JS: 5547

Spanish language — Poetry
JS: 4988

Spanish Main
JS: 8235

Speaking skills
JS: 10311–12

Special effects (motion pictures)
S–Adult: 12645

Special interest groups (U.S.)
JS: 9345

Speech, freedom of
See Freedom of speech

Speeches
JS: 5214, 5223, 7869, 9240 **S:** 5221,
8404, 9424 **S–Adult:** 5218

Speed (methamphetamine)
See Drugs and drug abuse

Speed skating
JS: 13360

Spelling
S–Adult: 5557

Spelling bees — Fiction
JS: 471

Spices
S: 12817

Spider-Man — Fiction
JS: 367

Spiders
JS: 12131, 12135–36 **S–Adult:** 12155

Spiders — Fiction
S: 5079

Spielberg, Steven
JS: 6127 **S:** 7226 **S–Adult:** 12957

Spies and spying
JS: 9184, 9985, 10067 **S:** 9183, 9977,
10020 **S–Adult:** 9191

Spies and spying — Biography
S–Adult: 7669

Spies and spying — Fiction
JS: 136, 2763 **S:** 20–21, 37, 42–43, 51,
100, 2811, 3147, 3456, 3523, 3568–69,
3626, 3630 **S–Adult:** 28, 2600, 3334,
3507, 3509, 3629, 3639

Spies and spying — History
JS: 7798 **S:** 10054 **S–Adult:** 7698

Spina bifida
JS: 11155

Spinal cord
JS: 11020

Spiritual healing — Fiction
JS: 295

Sports
See also Games; and specific sports,
e.g., Baseball
JS: 6651, 11039, 13085 **S:** 13096,
13111, 13124, 13133, 13185
S–Adult: 9698, 13076, 13089, 13098,
13117

Sports — Biography
See also under specific sports, e.g.,
Baseball — Biography
JS: 6639, 6647–49, 6655 **S:** 13152
S–Adult: 6650

Sports — Careers
J: 10452 **JS:** 10435, 10446, 10448,
10450 **S:** 10441, 10510

Sports — Colleges and universities
S: 10441, 13308

Sports — Diet
JS: 10832

Sports — Drugs
JS: 10672, 10700, 11042, 13071

Sports — Economic aspects
JS: 13071, 13097 **S:** 10217, 10221

Sports — Equipment and supplies
S: 10217, 10221

Sports — Fiction
JS: 302, 1040, 1130, 1301, 1495, 3249,
4563 **S–Adult:** 3645

Sports — Gambling
J: 13131

Sports — Gay men and lesbians
JS: 13136, 13136 **S–Adult:** 13134

Sports — General
S–Adult: 13073

Sports — Girls
JS: 13094

Sports — History
J: 7451 **JS:** 7515, 13102

Sports — Injuries
JS: 11042

Sports — Journalism
S: 13096

Sports — Legal aspects
JS: 13077 **S:** 13118

Sports — Medicine
JS: 10902

Sports — Nutrition
S: 11130

Sports — Poetry
JS: 4995

Sports — Politics
S: 13100

Sports — Problems
JS: 10832, 13071, 13077, 13082
S: 13118

Sports — Scholarships
JS: 10356

Sports — Sexism
S: 13110

Sports — Statistics
JS: 13088

Sports — Twentieth century
S: 13086

Sports — Violence
JS: 13071, 13105

JS = Junior High/Senior High; S = Senior High; S–Adult = Senior High/Adult

Sports — Winter
See also invididual sports e.g. Skis and skiing
JS–Adult: 13126, 13126

Sports — Women
J: 13127 **JS:** 6643, 6756–58, 13103, 13123 **S:** 13093, 13124
S–Adult: 13072

Sports stories — Fiction
JS: 4558 **S–Adult:** 435, 4561, 4581

Springsteen, Bruce
JS: 6128

Spying
See Spies and spying

Sri Lanka
JS: 8062

Sri Lanka — Fiction
S: 2514 **S–Adult:** 1582

Stalin, Joseph
S–Adult: 6883, 8163

Stalking
JS: 9991, 10014, 10063

Stamp collecting
JS: 12983

Stamps
JS: 12980

Stamps — History
JS: 12982

Stanley, Sir Henry Morton
S–Adult: 7923

Stanton, Elizabeth Cady
JS: 6261–63

Star-Spangled Banner
S–Adult: 8574

***Star Trek* (TV and motion picture series)**
JS: 7268 **S:** 6097, 7271, 7278

***Star Wars* (TV and motion picture series)**
JS: 4487, 7222–23, 7233, 7235, 7257
S: 1784, 7224, 7232, 7250

Stars
See also Constellations
JS: 11678, 11755, 11758–59 **S:** 11654, 11707 **S–Adult:** 11756–57

Stars — Fiction
S: 4265

Staten Island (NY) — Fiction
S: 3578

States (U.S.) — Capitals
JS: 8351

States (U.S.) — Rights
JS: 9257

Statistics
JS: 11374 **S:** 12404, 12409
S–Adult: 9789

Steam engines — History
S–Adult: 12563

Steichen, Edward
S–Adult: 7107

Steinbeck, John
JS: 5935–36 **S:** 5414, 5934

Steinbeck, John — Criticism
S: 5340, 5379–80, 5416, 5428

Steinem, Gloria
JS: 6264–65 **S:** 11473

Stem cells
JS: 10924

Stepbrothers — Fiction
JS: 1386

Stepfamilies
See also Adoption
JS: 11493

Stepfamilies — Fiction
JS: 84, 299, 621, 660, 733, 2845, 3146

Stepfathers — Fiction
J: 615

Stepparents — Fiction
JS: 3756

Stereotype (psychology)
JS: 11367

Steroids
JS: 10665

Stevenson, Robert Louis
JS: 12686

Stevenson, Robert Louis — Criticism
S: 5295

Stewart, Bridgett
JS: 7002

Stewart, Martha
JS: 6633

Stewart, Shelley
S–Adult: 6129

Stewart, Tony
S–Adult: 6657

Still, Peter
JS: 7003

Stine, R. L. — Criticism
S: 5375

Stock car racing
JS: 13137

Stock markets
JS: 10229

Stock markets — Crash of 1929
See also Depression, Great
JS: 8784, 8790, 10228 **S–Adult:** 8795

Stoker, Bram
JS: 5937

Stone, Oliver
S: 6130

Stone Age
See Prehistoric life

Stonehenge
JS: 7376

Stonehenge — Fiction
S–Adult: 2388, 2393

Storms
See also Weather; and specific types of storms, e.g., Hurricanes
S: 12434–35 **S–Adult:** 9895

Storms — History
S–Adult: 12438

Storytelling
S: 10309 **S–Adult:** 5127

Storytelling — Fiction
JS: 1477, 2400

Stowe, Harriet Beecher
JS: 5938 **S:** 5939

Streams
See Rivers

Stress (mental state)
JS: 11045, 11066, 11097, 11101
S: 11094, 11407

Stretching
S: 11032

Stuart England
S: 8135

Student resistance — History
S–Adult: 7393

Student rights
JS: 9327, 9409 **S:** 9433

Study skills
JS: 10281, 10299 **S:** 10275, 10277–78, 10280, 10337

Stuttering
JS: 10558

Stuttering — Fiction
JS: 1635

Suberman, Stella
S–Adult: 7004

Submarines
S: 12699 **S–Adult:** 8164, 12716

Suburban life
S: 5189 **S–Adult:** 10207

Subways
J: 12577

Subways — Fiction
JS: 1371

Sudan
JS: 7892, 7929 **S–Adult:** 9453

Suez Canal
JS: 8193

Suffrage and suffragists — Biography
See Women's rights

Sugihara, Chiune
J: 6884

Suicide
See also Physician-assisted suicide; Right to die
JS: 10584, 10596, 11047, 11058, 11068, 11071, 11080, 11082, 11099, 11121 **S:** 10594, 10597
S–Adult: 11096, 11115, 11506

JS = Junior High/Senior High;   S = Senior High;   S–Adult = Senior High/Adult

JS = Junior High/Senior High;   S = Senior High;   S–Adult = Senior High/Adult

JS = Junior High/Senior High;   S = Senior High;   S–Adult = Senior High/Adult

Television — Talk shows
S–Adult: 7266

Temperature — Experiments and
projects
JS: 12509

Temptations (musical group)
JS: 6132

Tender Is the Night — Criticism
S: 5333

Tennessee
S: 9754

Tennessee — Fiction
JS: 1018, 2096

Tennis
JS: 13453 JS–Adult: 13450
S: 13444, 13446–47, 13449, 13451–52
S–Adult: 13455

Tennis — Biography
JS: 6654, 6722–24, 6726–27 S: 6725,
6755

Tennis — Fiction
JS: 667, 4588, 4601 S: 1278

Teresa, Mother
S: 6813 S–Adult: 6812

Terezin (concentration camp)
J: 7803

Term papers
S: 10295

Terrorism
See also Counterterrorism; Homeland
security; September 11, 2001;
specific terrorist organizations, e.g.,
al-Qaeda
JS: 8202, 9195, 9244, 9425, 9787,
10164, 10169–72, 10176–78, 10184–88,
10192–93, 10197, 10200–2, 10205,
11223, 12705 S: 10166, 10173–74,
10181, 10191, 10198 S–Adult: 7027,
7860, 9128, 10165, 10196, 10199,
10206, 13254

Terrorism — Biography
JS: 6789 S–Adult: 6898

Terrorism — Fiction
JS: 27, 30 S: 12, 22, 32, 60, 3510,
3524, 3536 S–Adult: 1582, 3591,
3788, 3835

Terrorism — History
JS: 10203

Terrorism — Palestine
JS: 8202

Tess of the d'Urbervilles — Criticism
S: 5307

Tet Offensive
See also Vietnam War
JS: 7881

Texas — Fiction
JS: 142, 1331, 1395, 3370 S: 452,
1194, 3326, 3700 S–Adult: 375, 519,
784, 1175, 1421, 1465, 2779

Texas — History
S: 8572, 8820 S–Adult: 8579, 12436

Texas *v.* Johnson
JS: 10112

Thailand
JS: 6969

Thailand — Cookbooks
J: 12798

Thailand — Fiction
JS: 1579

Thanksgiving Day
S–Adult: 4616

Theater
See also Acting; Plays
S: 5451, 7286, 7292, 7297

Theater — Biography
JS: 5723

Theater — Careers
S: 7286

Theater — Elizabethan
JS: 7287, 8143

Theater — Fiction
JS: 1467, 3724 S: 906
S–Adult: 1248

Theater — History
JS: 7294 S: 7284, 7304
S–Adult: 5472, 7289

Thebes — History
JS–Adult: 8194

Thermodynamics
JS: 12506

Third World
S: 9935

Thirteenth century
S: 7574

Thomas-EL, Salome
S–Adult: 7007

Thoreau, Henry David
S: 5943

Thoreau, Henry David — Criticism
S: 5243

Thorpe, Jim
S: 6736–37

The Three Stooges
JS: 6133

Thrillers — Fiction
See Adventure and adventurers —
Fiction; Mystery stories — Fiction

Thurmond, Strom
S: 6459

Tiananmen Square (Beijing)
S: 8019

Tibet
JS: 8052, 8060 S: 8000
S–Adult: 8043, 8056

Tibet — Biography
JS: 6791 S–Adult: 6985

Tidal waves — Fiction
JS: 18

Tigers
JS: 11996 JS–Adult: 12002
S: 11999, 12001 S–Adult: 11995

Till, Emmett
JS: 9612

Time
See also Calendars; Space and time
S: 12496, 12502 S–Adult: 12510

Time — Measurement
S: 12514

Time and clocks
See Clocks and watches

Time management
JS: 10259

Time travel — Fiction
JS: 270, 1778–79, 1789–90, 1908,
1913, 2021, 2082, 2148, 2162, 2245,
3044, 3050, 3074, 3336, 3892, 4358,
4425, 4431, 4530 JS–Adult: 4415
S: 1783, 1806, 1820, 1862, 2223, 4086,
4146, 4176, 4250, 4295, 4304–5
S–Adult: 1795, 1853, 1869, 1892,
2109, 2215, 3465, 3902, 3989, 4289,
4491

Tinker *v.* Des Moines
JS: 9409

Titanic (motion picture)
JS: 7231

Titanic (ship)
JS: 12489 JS–Adult: 12689
S: 5628, 12479, 12484–85, 12493,
12692 S–Adult: 12488, 12491, 12690,
12695

Titanic (ship) — Art
S–Adult: 12688

Titanic (ship) — Biography
S: 12691

Titanic (ship) — Fiction
JS: 372, 3941 S: 31, 3785
S–Adult: 2268

Tito, Josip Broz
JS: 6886

To Kill a Mockingbird — Criticism
S: 5334, 5395

Toads
See Frogs and toads

Tobacco
See Smoking

Tobacco industry
See also Smoking
JS: 10647, 10657

Tokyo
JS: 8039

Tokyo — Fiction
S–Adult: 3812

Tokyo — History
JS: 7771

Tolkien, J. R. R.
S: 5944

Tolkien, J. R. R. — Art
S–Adult: 7038

Tolkien, J. R. R. — Criticism
S: 5284, 5310 S–Adult: 5276, 5297

Tomboys
S: 4667

Tooth decay
See Teeth

Topaa Indians — Fiction
S–Adult: 7386

Tornadoes
See also Storms
JS: 12432 S: 12437, 12439–40

Tornadoes — Fiction
JS: 1036

Toronto (ON) — Fiction
JS: 1322

Tortoises
JS: 11919

Tour de France (bicycle race)
S: 13226

Tour guides — Careers
J: 10426

Tourette's syndrome
JS: 10740, 10803, 10821, 11092

Tourism — Careers
JS: 10458

Toussaint, Pierre
S–Adult: 6266

Tower of Pisa
JS: 8144

Toxic waste
S: 12527

Toy making
S: 12876

Toys — Experiments and projects
JS: 12508

Toys — History
JS: 12875

Track and field
See also Running and jogging
S–Adult: 13390

Track and field — Biography
JS: 6728–30, 6733–35 S: 6732, 6736–37

Track and field — Fiction
JS: 175, 1484, 4580 S: 1236, 1346

Trade
S: 10243

Trade — History
S–Adult: 7416

Trademarks
S: 10230

Trail of Tears
JS: 8445 S: 8484, 8486
S–Adult: 8441

Trains
See Railroads and trains

Tramps (U.S.)
JS: 8412

Tranquilizing drugs
See also Drugs and drug abuse
JS: 10624

Transplants
See Organ transplants

Transportation
See specific types of transportation, e.g., Automobiles

Transportation (U.S.) — History
S–Adult: 12649

Trappist monasteries — Fiction
S–Adult: 384

Travel
S–Adult: 12832

Travel — Careers
JS: 10414, 10458 S: 10472

Travel — Fiction
JS: 305

Travel guides
S: 7425

Traveling carnivals
S–Adult: 7283

Travels
See Voyages and travels

Treasure — Fiction
S: 2839

Treasure hunts
S: 13079

Treasure Island — Fiction
S–Adult: 207

Trees
JS: 11845, 11849–50, 11853
JS–Adult: 11846 S: 12383
S–Adult: 11820, 11852

Trees — Experiments and projects
JS: 11851

Trees — United States
JS–Adult: 11847

Trenka, Jane Jeong
S–Adult: 11566

Trials
See also Courts (U.S.)
JS: 8754, 8856, 9324, 9328, 9414–15, 9442, 9451, 9492, 9612, 10019 S: 7421

Trials — Fiction
JS: 970, 2748, 2751 S: 193, 363, 468, 3415 S–Adult: 2492, 2985, 3822

Trials — Plays
S: 4810

Triangle Shirtwaist Factory fire
JS: 8753

Triangle Shirtwaist Factory fire — Fiction
JS: 2911

Triathlons
JS: 13120

Triathlons — Fiction
JS: 4563

Triathlons — Ironman
S: 13083

Tricks
See also Card tricks; Magic and magicians
JS: 12920, 12925

Trilobites
S–Adult: 7321

Tristan and Iseult — Fiction
S–Adult: 2634

Trivia
S: 13022 S–Adult: 13006

Trojan War
JS: 5177

Trojan War — Fiction
See also Iliad
JS: 2430 S: 1707 S–Adult: 2428

Tropical fish
JS: 12303

Tropical forests
See Rain forests

Troy (Turkey)
S: 2357

Trucking — Careers
S: 10542

Trucks
S: 12668

Trujillo, Rafael — Fiction
S: 2693

Truman, Harry S
JS: 6365–66 S: 6367–68

Truth, Sojourner
JS: 6267 S: 6269

Truth, Sojourner — Fiction
S–Adult: 6268

Tuberculosis
JS: 10804, 10896 S: 10770

Tuberculosis — Fiction
JS: 919

Tubman, Harriet
JS: 6270 S–Adult: 6271–72

Tubman, Harriet — Poetry
JS: 4997

Tubu (African people)
JS: 7892

Tum, Rigoberta Menchu
JS: 6905

Turkana (African people)
JS: 7929

Turkey
S: 7500 S–Adult: 6951

Turkey — Biography
JS: 6817

Turkey — Fiction
JS: 2557 S: 1586 S–Adult: 2611, 3788

U

United States — Government
See Government (U.S.)

United States — Historic sites
S: 8388

United States — History
See also specific periods and events,
e.g., Colonial period (U.S.); Civil
War (U.S.)
JS: 6166, 8328, 8333, 8349–50, 8354,
8357, 8361, 8363, 8365, 8371, 8374,
8383, 8395, 8411, 8493, 9224
JS–Adult: 8366 **S:** 7418, 8329,
8339–40, 8345, 8347, 8352–53, 8360,
8364, 8367, 8369, 8378, 8381, 8384,
8388–89, 8402, 8492 **S–Adult:** 7105,
8326, 8336, 8362, 8373, 8396, 8409–10,
8415, 8554, 12712

**United States — History —
Documents**
JS–Adult: 8376 **S:** 8325
S–Adult: 8382

United States — History — Modern
JS: 8857, 8871, 8877, 8891, 8902, 8908
S: 8779, 8868, 8882, 8892, 9663
S–Adult: 8334

United States — History — Women
S–Adult: 8385

United States — Immigration
See Immigration (U.S.)

United States — Intelligence service
S: 9183

United States — Monuments
S: 8381

United States — People
S–Adult: 8894

United States — Photography
S–Adult: 7105

United States — Pioneer life
See Frontier life (U.S.)

United States — Poetry
S: 4953 **S–Adult:** 4959

United States — Politics
JS: 9224

United States — Politics — Fiction
S: 1598

United States — Presidents
See Presidents (U.S.)

United States — Revolutionary War
See Revolutionary War (U.S.)

United States — Twentieth century
S: 8390

United States — Wars
See also specific wars, e.g., World
War II
S–Adult: 8335

United States — Women
JS: 8363 **S–Adult:** 8341, 8377

**United States (1776–1876) —
History**
See also specific topics, e.g., Civil
War (U.S.)
JS: 8375

United States (1789–1861) — Fiction
JS: 2807

**United States (1789–1861) —
History**
JS: 8583

**United States (1800–1860) —
History**
JS: 8719

United States (1815–1861) — Fiction
JS: 2770

United States (1828–1860) — Fiction
S: 2789

United States (1865–1914) — Fiction
S: 2913, 2949

**United States (1865–1914) —
History**
See also Reconstruction to World
War I (U.S.)
JS: 8761

United States (1900s) — History
JS: 8762, 8772

United States (1910s) — History
JS: 8405

**United States (1915–1945) —
History**
JS: 8781, 8814

United States (1920s) — Fiction
S: 2922

United States (1920s) — History
JS: 8413–14, 8802 **S:** 8815–16
S–Adult: 9294

United States (1940s) — History
J: 8406 **JS:** 8331, 8358

United States (1980s) — History
JS: 8869, 8883, 8903

United States (1990s) — Fiction
JS: 2931

United States (1990s) — History
JS: 8887

United States Army
See Army (U.S.)

United States Coast Guard
See Coast Guard (U.S.) — Careers

United States-China relations
JS: 8006

United States-Israel relations
See Israel-U.S. relations

United States Marine Corps
See Marine Corps (U.S.)

United States-Mexico relations
See Mexico-U.S. relations

United States (1930s) — History
JS: 8797

United States (1950s)
S: 8901

United States (1950s) — Fiction
JS: 2983

United States (1950s) — History
JS: 8858, 8869, 8886, 8888, 8897

United States (1960s) — Fiction
JS: 2991 **S:** 2989

United States (1960s) — History
JS: 8348, 8857, 8869, 8881, 8885
S: 7878, 8867, 8882, 8892, 8904, 8948
S–Adult: 8870, 8876, 8907

United States (1970s) — History
JS: 8899

United States-Soviet Union relations
S: 7885

United States *v.* Nixon
JS: 9284

Universe
JS: 11681, 11777 **S:** 11660, 11662,
11684, 11687, 11703–4, 12496
S–Adult: 11669, 11774–75

Universities and colleges
See Colleges and universities

Unmarried mothers — Fiction
S: 2948

Unsolved crimes
S–Adult: 8561

Urban legends
JS: 13019

Urban life
JS: 12558

Uruguay
JS: 8286

Uruguay — Fiction
S: 12

USS *Indianapolis*
JS: 7768 **S–Adult:** 7828

USSR
See Soviet Union

Utah — Fiction
JS: 3090

Ute Indians — Fiction
JS: 173 **S–Adult:** 3482

Utopias
JS: 8401

Utopias — Fiction
S: 4435

Uzbekistan
JS: 8150

V

V-E Day, 1945
S: 7695

Vacations — Fiction
JS: 2031, 3887

Vaccines
JS: 10909, 10919

Valens, Ritchie
JS: 6134

Valley of the Kings (Egypt)
JS: 7468 **JS–Adult:** 8194

JS = Junior High/Senior High;   S = Senior High;   S–Adult = Senior High/Adult

Vampires
JS: 13058, 13061 S: 13012, 13069
S–Adult: 3108

Vampires — Biography
S–Adult: 7009

Vampires — Fiction
J: 3131 JS: 385, 937, 1661, 3096,
3101–2, 3146, 3179, 3247, 3571
S: 236, 2277, 3147–48, 3193, 3195,
3217, 3229, 3232, 3240, 3242, 3499
S–Adult: 3125, 3152–53, 3211, 3219,
3224, 3252, 3254

Van Beek, Cato Bontjes
JS: 6887

Vancouver (Canada) — Fiction
S–Adult: 3985

Van Gogh, Vincent
JS: 5791–93, 5795 S: 5794

Van Gogh, Vincent — Fiction
S: 2667

Vegans
S–Adult: 12759

Vegans — Fiction
S: 1102

Vegetables
S: 11843 S–Adult: 11844, 12916

Vegetarian cooking
JS: 11132, 12834 S: 12786, 12789,
12804–5, 12812 S–Adult: 12759,
12774, 12788, 12794, 12824

Vegetarianism
JS: 11132, 11141, 11143 S: 11150

Velmans, Loet
S–Adult: 7841

Vendee Globe (sailing race)
S: 13405

Venice — Fiction
JS: 2637, 2645 S–Adult: 2004

Venice — History
JS: 5988

Ventriloquism
JS: 7300

Ventura, Jesse
JS: 6750

Venus (planet)
S: 11762

Verbal abuse
S: 11336

Vermeer, Johannes
S: 5796

Vermeer, Johannes — Fiction
S: 2570

Vermont
JS: 8971

Vermont — Fiction
JS: 1257, 1267, 3258

Versailles, Palace of
JS: 8092

Vertebrates
JS: 11885, 11888

Vests
S: 12864

Veterinarians
S: 12282, 12324 S–Adult: 12327

Veterinarians — Biography
JS: 6954 S: 6955, 6996

Veterinarians — Careers
JS: 10375

Veterinarians — Fiction
S: 2123

Vice Presidents (U.S.) — Biography
S: 6194

Vicksburg, Siege of
JS: 8689

Victims' rights
JS: 9407

Victoria, Queen of England
JS: 6888, 6891, 8114, 8137
S: 6889–90 S–Adult: 6892

Victorian Age
JS: 8137 S: 5306, 7578, 8118, 8139

Victorian Age — Fiction
JS: 129 S: 2569 S–Adult: 2560,
2617, 2687, 3709

Victorian Age — Literature
S: 5270

Video recordings
S: 12641

Video games — Fiction
S: 1561

Video recordings
JS: 12643 S: 12637, 12951

Vienna — Fiction
S: 3716

Vietnam
JS: 8045 S: 8049–50 S–Adult: 8047

Vietnam — Biography
S: 6801 S–Adult: 6995

Vietnam — Cookbooks
J: 12816

Vietnam — Fiction
JS: 2509 S–Adult: 2537

Vietnam War
J: 7886 JS: 7866, 7871, 7874, 7879,
7881–83, 7888, 7890, 8348, 8924, 8931,
8935–36, 8958, 12718 S: 8050, 8911,
8914, 8916, 8919, 8922–23, 8930, 8932,
8938–39, 8943, 8946, 8951, 8953–55,
8957 S–Adult: 6499, 8912, 8915,
8921, 8933–34, 8937, 8944, 8956

Vietnam War — Art
S: 8941

Vietnam War — Biography
JS: 6422, 6494

Vietnam War — Fiction
JS: 1023, 3078–79, 3081, 3090–92
S: 872, 1337, 3080, 3082, 3084–86,
3089

Vietnam War — Protests
JS: 8926

Vietnam War — Women
S: 8952

Vietnamese Americans
See also Asian Americans
JS: 9718, 9725

Vietnamese Americans — Biography
S–Adult: 6995

Vietnamese Americans — Fiction
JS: 453 S: 452

Vikings
JS: 8180–81 S–Adult: 8182

Vikings — Fiction
JS: 2395–97 S: 1933, 2444, 2671
S–Adult: 2401

Violence
See also Teenagers — Violence
JS: 8281, 9796, 9845, 9954, 9958,
9970, 9994–96, 10008, 10024, 10031,
10033, 10050, 10062, 10066, 10103,
10653, 10675, 11491, 11510, 11524,
11535, 11549, 11563, 13105 S: 9948,
9986, 9999, 10003, 11318, 11560
S–Adult: 5000, 10023

Violence — Fiction
JS: 650, 796, 1164, 1191, 1244, 3384
S: 3633 S–Adult: 909, 1445, 1559

Violence — Mass media
See Mass media — Violence

Violinists — Biography
S–Adult: 7770

Virginia — Biography
JS: 6501

Virginia — Fiction
JS: 2741 S–Adult: 446

Virtual reality
JS: 12601, 12626

Virtual reality — Fiction
S: 2050, 3633

Viruses
JS: 10831 S: 10736, 10839, 10878

Viruses (computers)
S: 12618

Vision
S–Adult: 7039

Vitamins
JS: 11138 S: 11139

Vivaldi, Antonio
JS: 5988

Vizzini, Ned
S: 7008

Vlad III, Prince of Wallachia
S–Adult: 7009

Von Trapp family
S: 6135

Vocabulary
S: 10307

Vocational education
S: 10326

JS = Junior High/Senior High; S = Senior High; S–Adult = Senior High/Adult

Vocational guidance
See also Careers; Occupational guidance
JS: 10366–67 **S:** 10323, 10358–59, 10362, 10376–79, 10382, 10387–92, 10394–96, 10403, 10405, 10410, 10423, 10425, 10427–28, 10430, 10437–38, 10440, 10443, 10445, 10449, 10456–57, 10460, 10463, 10466–67, 10469–76, 10478, 10482–83, 10491, 10496, 10503–4, 10506, 10508–9, 10514–20, 10526, 10528, 10535, 10542
S–Adult: 10400

Voigt, Cynthia — Criticism
S: 5401

Volcanoes
JS: 12358–59 **S:** 12357, 12360–61
S–Adult: 12363

Volcanoes — Careers
J: 10530

Volcanoes — Fiction
JS: 18, 199, 2279

Volleyball
JS: 13457 **S:** 13456

Volleyball — Biography
S: 6747

Volleyball — Fiction
JS: 1493

Voltaire — Criticism
S: 5323

Volunteerism
See also Social action
JS: 9258, 9899, 10137, 10140, 10142–49 **S:** 10132, 10136, 10151
S–Adult: 10131, 10263

Volunteerism — Fiction
JS: 395, 1590, 2489

Vonnegut, Kurt
S–Adult: 5951

Voting rights — African Americans
JS: 9202, 9667

Voting rights — Biography
S: 6462

Voting rights — Women
See also Women's rights
JS: 6262, 9451–52, 9479 **S:** 9494

Voyages and travels
JS: 5226 **S:** 5674 **S–Adult:** 7419, 7442

Voyages and travels — Women
S–Adult: 7441

W

Wa Wamwere, Koigi
S–Adult: 7942

Wakeman, Sarah Rosetta
S: 8606

Wales
See also Great Britain

S: 4942

Wales — Biography
JS: 5840

Wales — Fiction
JS: 546 **S:** 2460, 2621
S–Adult: 2668, 2679, 3650

Wales — History
S: 7540

Wales — Plays
S–Adult: 4777

Walker, Alice
JS: 5952

Walker, Alice — Criticism

S: 5329

Walker, Madam C. J.
J: 6635 **S–Adult:** 6636–37

Walking
See also Hiking
S: 11041, 13099

Wall Street
JS: 10229

Wall Street — Fiction
S–Adult: 320

Wallenberg, Raoul
JS: 6894 **S–Adult:** 6893

Wallenda, Delilah
S: 6136

Walton, Jenny
S: 5953

Wamesit Indians — Fiction
JS: 2746

War
See also specific battles and wars, e.g., Alamo, Battle of the; World War II
JS: 8357, 9178, 9180, 9193 **S:** 7427, 9171 **S–Adult:** 9181–82, 9194, 9199, 12725

War — Children
JS: 9190 **S–Adult:** 9192

War — Essays
JS: 5222

War — Fiction
J: 2632 **JS:** 108, 2988, 3328, 4606, 4633 **S:** 23, 3056 **S–Adult:** 1610, 1623, 2540, 2681, 3088, 3509

War — History
JS: 7444, 7465, 7585, 7590 **S:** 7420, 8367

War — Memoirs
JS: 4633 **S:** 9188

War — North America
S: 7422

War — Photographs
S–Adult: 5587

War — Poetry
JS: 4633, 4896, 4902 **S:** 4913

War — South and Central America
S: 7422

War crimes
JS: 9170 **S:** 9197

War games — Fiction
S: 81

War of 1812
JS: 8563, 8566, 8575 **S:** 8578
S–Adult: 8569, 8574

War of 1812 — Fiction
JS: 2797 **S:** 2778

Warfare
JS: 12705

Warhol, Andy
S: 5797

Warner Brothers cartoons
S: 7220

Warren, Earl
JS: 6460–61

Wars of the Roses
S–Adult: 8141

Wars of the Roses — Fiction
JS: 232 **S–Adult:** 2595

Warsaw Ghetto
JS: 7743 **S–Adult:** 7852

Warships — Fiction
S: 101

Washington, Booker T.
JS: 6275

Washington, Denzel
JS: 6137

Washington, George
JS: 6369, 6373–74, 6376, 8535
S: 6372, 6375 **S–Adult:** 6370–71

Washington, George — Fiction
JS: 2768 **S:** 2745

Washington (DC)
S: 8973, 8987

Washington (DC) — Fiction
JS: 2808, 2944 **S:** 3670, 3823–24, 3826–27

Washington Monument (DC)
JS–Adult: 8970

Washington (state)
S–Adult: 12222

Washington (state) — Fiction
S: 1410 **S–Adult:** 2985

Waste recycling
See also Recycling
JS: 9925

Watches
See Clocks and watches

Water
See also Water pollution
J: 12447 **JS:** 12384, 12443 **S:** 12442, 12444 **S–Adult:** 12448–49

Water — Experiments and projects
JS: 12445

Water — Fiction
JS: 2134

Water birds
See Ducks and geese

Water cycle
S–Adult: 12446

Water pollution
See also Ecology and environment —
Problems; Pollution
JS: 9913, 12443 **S:** 12444
S–Adult: 12449

Water pollution — Fiction
S–Adult: 2713

Water sports
See specific sports, e.g., Surfing

Water supply
S–Adult: 12446

Watercolor painting
S: 12877, 12881, 12890, 12892, 12895,
12898

Watercolors
JS: 7033

Watergate affair
JS: 8872, 8878, 9284 **S:** 8860, 8873,
8906

Waterloo, Battle of
JS: 7582 **S:** 8103

Waters, Muddy
S–Adult: 6138

Watson, James
S: 10937 **S–Adult:** 10951

Watson, Paul
S–Adult: 7010

Watt, James
S–Adult: 12563

Wayne, "Mad" Anthony — Fiction
JS: 2764

Weapons
JS: 12704, 12722 **S:** 12702

Weapons — Fiction
S: 4516

Weapons — History
J: 12719 **JS:** 7465, 8546, 12707
S–Adult: 12715

Weapons — World War II
JS: 7845

Weapons of mass destruction
JS: 12708

Weather
See also Climate; Storms; and
specific types of weather, e.g.,
Tornadoes
JS: 12452 **S:** 12434, 12454–55, 12461,
12463 **S–Adult:** 12456, 12460

**Weather — Experiments and
projects**
JS: 12457

Weather — Forecasting
JS: 12459 **S:** 12463

Weaving
S: 12728

Webb, Matthew
S–Adult: 5681

Webber, Andrew Lloyd
S: 5989

Weddings — Fiction
JS: 3929 **S–Adult:** 3284

Weight control
See also Diets and dieting
JS: 10887 **S:** 11133

Weight lifting
S: 13114, 13122

Weight lifting — Women
S–Adult: 13116

Weight-loss programs
JS: 11127, 11137

Weight problems
See also Eating disorders; Obesity
JS: 11127, 11136–37, 11142, 11148
S: 11422 **S–Adult:** 6970

Weight problems — Fiction
JS: 959, 1012, 1196, 1321, 1467

Weight training — Women
S–Adult: 13116

Welfare
JS: 10075, 10089 **S–Adult:** 10097

Welfare — Fiction
JS: 1591

Welfare (U.S.)
See also Poverty
JS: 10073–74, 10078, 10084 **S:** 10082

Welhenmayer, Erik
S–Adult: 5682

Wells, David
S–Adult: 6689

Wells, Ida B.
J: 6276 **JS:** 5694

Welsh Americans
JS: 9774

Welty, Eudora — Criticism
S: 5332

Werewolves — Fiction
J: 3131 **S:** 3178, 3253
S–Adult: 3184

Wersba, Barbara
JS: 5954

West Africa
JS: 7988

West Africa — Folklore
JS: 5076

West Bank (Israel)
JS: 8210

West Indian Americans
J: 9767

West Indian Americans — Fiction
S: 486

West Indians — Emigration
JS: 9772

West Indies
See Caribbean Islands

West Point (military academy)
S–Adult: 12720

West (U.S.)
See also individual states, e.g.,
California
JS: 8708, 8728, 8743, 11850 **S:** 4646,
8702, 8733 **S–Adult:** 5184, 9004,
12385

West (U.S.) — Art
S–Adult: 7109

West (U.S.) — Biography
JS: 8747

West (U.S.) — Birds
S: 12062

West (U.S.) — Fiction
JS: 10, 475, 2900 **S:** 11, 14, 87, 102,
141, 2869, 2873, 2883, 2908, 3276,
4646 **S–Adult:** 2863, 4603

West (U.S.) — History
See also Frontier life (U.S.)
J: 8704 **JS:** 8399, 8703, 8729, 8750,
9775 **S:** 8424, 8665, 8697–99, 8713,
8725, 8730, 8748–49 **S–Adult:** 8717

West (U.S.) — Poetry
JS: 5035

West Virginia
S–Adult: 6956–57

West Virginia — Fiction
JS: 2945 **S–Adult:** 2963, 2965

Western music
See Country music

Westerns — Fiction
JS: 10, 137, 2867, 3745 **S:** 2866, 2875,
2899 **S–Adult:** 4064

Wetlands
JS: 12366 **S:** 12367–69

Whales
J: 12207 **JS:** 12159, 12199, 12215,
12223 **S:** 12194, 12196–97, 12200,
12202, 12205–6, 12208–9, 12214,
12216–17 **S–Adult:** 12193, 12198,
12203, 12210, 12218, 12220

Whales — Fiction
JS: 174

Whaling
JS: 12694 **S–Adult:** 12222

Whaling — Fiction
JS: 248

Whaling — History
JS: 8233, 9668 **S–Adult:** 8576

Wharton, Edith
S: 5955

Wharton, Edith — Criticism
S: 5410

Wheatley, Phillis
JS: 5958 **S:** 5957 **S–Adult:** 5956

Wheatley, Phillis — Fiction
JS: 2752

Whedon, Joss
S–Adult: 5959

JS = Junior High/Senior High;   S = Senior High;   S–Adult = Senior High/Adult

Wheelchairs — Fiction
JS: 3455

Whistler, James McNeill
JS: 5798

Whistling
S: 12742

White, E. B.
JS: 5960

White House press secretary — History
S: 9235

White House (U.S.)
JS: 8969 S–Adult: 8986

White House (U.S.) — Fiction
S: 3826

White House (U.S.) — History
S: 8977

White-water rafting
S: 13404

White-water rafting — Fiction
JS: 1435

Whitestone, Heather
S: 7011

Whitetail deer
S–Adult: 12020

Whitman, Walt
JS: 5044, 5961–62

Whitman, Walt — Criticism
S: 5525, 5533–34

Whitman, Walt — Poetry
JS: 5002

Whittling
S: 12987, 12996

The Who (musical group)
S: 7193

Wiccans — Fiction
S–Adult: 3748

Wiesel, Elie
S: 5318

Wiesenthal, Simon
JS: 6895

Wild West shows
JS: 7288

Wild West shows — Biography
S: 6098–99

Wilde, Oscar
S: 5963

Wilder, Laura Ingalls
S: 5964

Wilder, Thornton — Criticism
S: 5357, 5523

Wilderness areas — Fiction
S–Adult: 689

Wildflowers
JS: 11865, 11865, 11870
JS–Adult: 11871 S–Adult: 11866

Wildlife — Careers
JS: 10404

Wildlife — Observation
S: 11799

Wildlife conservation
S: 12028, 12097 S–Adult: 7931, 12102

Wildlife conservation — Fiction
S: 1580

Wildlife photography — Careers
J: 10459

Wilkes-Barre (PA) — Fiction
JS: 2740

William the Conqueror
S–Adult: 8125

Williams, Aeneas
S: 6716

Williams, Hank
S–Adult: 6139

Williams, Philip Lee
S–Adult: 7012

Williams, Roger
S: 6277

Williams, Ted
S: 6690

Williams, Tennessee — Criticism
S: 5531–32

Williams, Venus and Serena
JS: 6654

Williams, William Carlos
JS: 5522

Willis, Jan
S–Adult: 7013

Wilson, August — Criticism
S: 5500

Wilson, Woodrow
JS: 6378 S–Adult: 6377

Wind instruments
See also Musical instruments
JS: 7147

Winfrey, Oprah
JS: 6140

Winnemucca, Sarah
S: 5965

Winston, Keith
JS: 7849

Winter sports
See invididual sports e.g. Skis and skiing

Wisconsin
S–Adult: 8961

Wisconsin — Fiction
JS: 548

Wishes — Fiction
S: 3900

Wit and humor
See also Humor and satire
S: 5180–81, 5185, 5187–89, 5191, 5194–95, 5198–99 S–Adult: 5192–93, 5197, 5592

Wit and humor — Fiction
S: 5186

Wit and humor — Poetry
S: 5012–13

Witchcraft
JS: 8514, 13025, 13032, 13039
S: 8501, 13054

Witchcraft — Fiction
JS: 1832, 1832, 1865, 2019, 2071, 2142, 2240–41, 2272–73, 2278, 2728, 2748, 2750–51, 3101, 3130, 3245, 5109
S: 1738, 1887, 2062, 2257, 3186, 3191
S–Adult: 3208

Witchcraft — Folklore
JS: 5146

Witchcraft — History
JS: 13007 S: 7432, 12926

Witchcraft — Plays
S: 4817

Witchcraft trials — Salem
JS: 8510, 8514 S: 8496, 8501, 8503

Witchcraft trials — Salem — Fiction
JS: 2748, 2751 S–Adult: 2774

Wolff, Tobias
S–Adult: 5966

Wollstonecraft, Mary
JS: 6896

Wolof (African people)
JS: 7996

Wolves
JS: 12008 S: 12004–5, 12007, 12009–13, 12015 S–Adult: 12003, 12006, 12014, 12016–18

Wolves — Fiction
JS: 164, 184, 1769 S: 2217
S–Adult: 2095

Women
See also Feminism; and subdivisions of other topics, e.g., Frontier life (U.S.) — Women
JS: 9378 S: 4614, 5229
S–Adult: 7980, 8211, 9087, 9146, 10055, 11332

Women — Abuse
JS: 11526 S: 10052

Women — Activists
JS: 6171

Women — Armed services
S–Adult: 7839

Women — Artists
JS: 5720 S: 7051

Women — Authors
JS: 5260, 5694, 5724, 5814, 5828, 5828–29, 5834, 5834, 5843, 5843, 5861, 5891, 5891–92, 5892, 5912, 5912, 5927, 5927, 5938, 5938 S: 5376, 5806, 5820, 5862, 5868, 5870, 5893, 5895, 5895, 5903, 5939, 5939, 5955, 5955, 5957, 5964–65 S–Adult: 5686

JS = Junior High/Senior High;   S = Senior High;   S–Adult = Senior High/Adult

1179

Women — Aviators
JS: 5643, 5668 **S:** 5644, 5646, 5669
S–Adult: 5645

Women — Biography
J: 6509 **JS:** 5650, 5676, 5717, 5724,
5733–37, 5763, 5772–74, 5807–8, 5814,
5821, 5824, 5828–29, 5833–34, 5847,
5871–73, 5881, 5894, 5898, 5908, 5911,
5914, 5925, 5932, 5940–41, 5952, 5954,
6044–45, 6048–50, 6059, 6064–65,
6140, 6160, 6167, 6171, 6178–79, 6200,
6206, 6231, 6257–59, 6261–65, 6267,
6270, 6279–80, 6358–59, 6411–12,
6439, 6448, 6463–67, 6490–91, 6493,
6528, 6533, 6567, 6575, 6585–86, 6589,
6608, 6626, 6643, 6756–59, 6764,
6775–76, 6778–79, 6793, 6821, 6823,
6830, 6833 **JS–Adult:** 6489, 6836
S: 2776, 5613, 5684, 5689, 5691, 5741,
5805, 5809, 5817–18, 5820, 5883, 5905,
5933, 5950, 5953, 5965, 6060, 6098–99,
6122, 6226, 6413, 6462, 6469–70, 6503,
6566, 6816, 6831–32, 6910, 6939
S–Adult: 5686, 5746, 5803–4, 5810,
5815, 5819, 5832, 5846, 5848, 5875,
5888–89, 5956, 6057–58, 6102, 6182,
6230, 6254, 6256, 6260, 6272, 6456,
6545, 6568, 6599, 6777, 6822, 6835

Women — Business
J: 6635 **JS:** 6526, 10216
S–Adult: 6624

Women — Careers
J: 10452 **JS:** 10408, 10420, 10429,
10480, 10493, 10540 **S–Adult:** 10490

Women — Fashion industry
JS: 12858

**Women — Federal Bureau of
Investigation**
S–Adult: 9974

Women — Fiction
JS: 4617 **S:** 4117 **S–Adult:** 460

Women — Government
JS: 6767

Women — Healthand health care
S–Adult: 10559

Women — History
JS: 6148, 8363, 8365, 8522, 8582,
8735, 8739, 8767, 8831 **S:** 5613, 8332,
8342, 8378, 8380, 8628, 8730
S–Adult: 7412, 7417, 8341, 8343,
9108

Women — Horses
S–Adult: 12311

Women — Journalists
JS: 5715

Women — Law
S: 9289, 9298

Women — Literature
JS: 5260

Women — Mathematicians
JS: 6510

Women — Medicine
S: 10900, 10913

Women — Middle East
JS: 8187

Women — Military careers
JS: 9374 **S:** 7711, 8952, 9376

Women — Music
S: 7137, 7168

Women — Photographers
JS: 5705

Women — Photographs
S–Adult: 7101

Women — Pioneers
S: 8741

Women — Poetry
JS: 4895 **S:** 4979

Women — Poets
S: 4870, 4876, 4964–65, 5018, 5048

Women — Politicians
JS: 6172, 6179, 6190, 6767, 6770, 9394

Women — Scientists
JS: 6510, 6512, 6519, 6529, 6532,
6541, 6544

Women — Sea stories
S–Adult: 8343

Women — Self-defense
JS: 13377

Women — Sex roles
S: 4667

Women — Social attitudes
S–Adult: 11247

Women — Sports
J: 13127 **JS:** 13103, 13123, 13135,
13135, 13208, 13213, 13222, 13432
S: 6747, 13093, 13124, 13183, 13211,
13229, 13326, 13330–31, 13437
S–Adult: 13084

Women — War
JS: 8395, 9377 **S:** 8852

Women — Workers
JS: 9857, 10429 **S:** 8332, 10357,
10401

Women (U.S.)
S–Adult: 8377, 8385

Women's rights
See also Civil rights; Voting rights —
Women
JS: 5216, 6171, 8767, 9390, 9422,
9429, 9451–52, 9479 **S:** 9289,
9411–12, 9478, 9488, 9494
S–Adult: 8044, 8061, 8209, 8221,
9406, 9441, 9447, 10130

Women's rights — Biography
J: 6276 **JS:** 6162, 6198–99, 6261–63,
6463, 6896, 6973 **S:** 6197, 6226, 6462
S–Adult: 8054, 9677

Women's rights — Fiction
J: 2702 **S:** 2569

Women's suffrage
S: 9423

Wonder, Stevie
JS: 6141

Woodcarving
S: 12995–96

Woodhull, Victoria
JS: 6463 **S:** 6462

Woods, Tiger
JS: 6754 **S:** 6751–53, 13317
S–Adult: 13320, 13323, 13337

Woodson, Carter G.
JS: 5967

Woodwork and woodworking
S: 12984–86, 12989–94, 12997
S–Adult: 12988

Woolf, Virginia
S: 5969 **S–Adult:** 5292, 5968

Word games and puzzles
See Games; Puzzles

Words
S: 5541 **S–Adult:** 5558

Wordsworth, William
JS: 4926 **S:** 5970

Workers and laboring classes
JS: 10237 **S–Adult:** 10238, 10361

Working mothers
JS: 11457

Workshops
S: 12919

World history
JS: 7391, 7598 **S:** 7390, 7421, 7438,
7568, 7588 **S–Adult:** 7387, 7392,
7410, 7423, 7440, 7447, 7551, 7589

World history — Controversies
JS: 7436

World history — Disasters
S: 7398

World history — Feuds
S: 7402

World history — Foods
S: 11841

World history — Monuments
S–Adult: 7388

World history — Plants
S: 11864

World history — Women
S–Adult: 7412

World history (1000s)
S: 7571

World history (1100s)
S: 7535

World history (1300s)
S: 7569

World history (1400s)
S: 7538

World history (1500s)
S: 7537

World history (1600s)
S: 7563

World history (1700s)
S: 7584

JS = Junior High/Senior High;   S = Senior High;   S–Adult = Senior High/Adult

World history (1800s)
S: 7578

World history (Middle Ages)
S: 7554

World Monuments Watch
S–Adult: 7388

World Trade Center
See also September 11, 2001
S–Adult: 7027, 10182

World War I
JS: 7604–8, 7616, 7618, 8405, 8413, 8775–77 S: 7603, 7609, 7613–14, 7619
S–Adult: 7610–12, 7615, 7620–22

World War I — Battles
JS: 7617

World War I — Fiction
JS: 2992, 2995–96, 3530 S: 196, 2994, 3939, 4507 S–Adult: 2576, 2663, 2993

World War I — Poetry
JS: 4854

World War II
See also specific topics, e.g., Holocaust
J: 6884, 7709, 7803, 7843, 8406
JS: 5790, 7623, 7628–29, 7631, 7634, 7636–39, 7641–42, 7651, 7654, 7658–60, 7662, 7674–76, 7678, 7680, 7685, 7688, 7691–92, 7694, 7701, 7704–7, 7712–14, 7720, 7722, 7727–28, 7730, 7732, 7734, 7738–39, 7741, 7743–44, 7747, 7751, 7755–56, 7763, 7767–68, 7771, 7784, 7787, 7789, 7792–94, 7798, 7801–2, 7804, 7806, 7810, 7812–14, 7820, 7827, 7832–36, 7844–45, 7849, 7856–57, 7889, 8105, 8358, 8827, 8830, 8832, 8835–36, 8838–39, 8843–44, 8847–48, 8851, 8853–54, 9180, 9644, 12721
JS–Adult: 7753 S: 3011, 6870, 7624, 7632–33, 7635, 7640, 7643–44, 7649, 7653, 7655, 7657, 7661, 7665–66, 7671, 7673, 7677, 7693, 7695, 7700, 7715–16, 7718, 7721, 7723, 7725–26, 7736, 7740, 7742, 7748–50, 7752, 7754, 7759, 7764–66, 7772–73, 7775, 7778–79, 7781–83, 7785–86, 7790–91, 7800, 7815, 7818, 7829, 7831, 7837, 7847, 7855, 7858, 8111, 8828, 8833, 8837, 8840–41, 8845, 8850, 8852, 12696
S–Adult: 7004, 7594, 7647–48, 7663–64, 7667–68, 7670, 7672, 7679, 7682–83, 7686–87, 7696–99, 7710, 7719, 7724, 7729, 7733, 7737, 7745, 7757, 7760, 7762, 7774, 7795, 7805, 7807, 7809, 7817, 7823–24, 7826, 7828, 7839, 7841, 7846, 7850–51, 7853–54, 7859, 7870, 8070, 8337, 8834, 8842, 8849, 12291

World War II — Art
S–Adult: 7097

World War II — Battles
JS: 7788

World War II — Biography
J: 6766 JS: 6421, 6763, 6765, 6853, 6856, 6882, 6887, 6944, 6953, 6991, 7777 S: 5950, 6825, 6828, 6852, 6945,

7650, 7652, 7681, 7690
S–Adult: 6480, 6604, 6857, 6942, 7811, 8855

World War II — Fiction
JS: 170, 835, 1252, 2328, 2503, 2510, 2551, 2641, 2998, 3001, 3003–4, 3010, 3020, 3022, 3026–27, 3029, 3031, 3034, 3037, 3040–43, 3051–52, 3054, 3057–60, 3063–65, 3067–69, 3073, 3075 JS–Adult: 617 S: 20, 57–59, 101, 1094, 2997, 3000, 3006, 3008, 3018, 3023–24, 3030, 3033, 3035, 3046, 3048, 3055–56, 3066, 3071–72, 3759, 3988 S–Adult: 562, 2236, 2496, 2531, 2974, 2999, 3005, 3012–13, 3015, 3017, 3019, 3021, 3025, 3028, 3032, 3039, 3047, 3049, 3061, 3522

World War II — Memoirs
S: 6958 S–Adult: 7735

World War II — Poetry
S: 4908

World War II — Radio coverage
JS: 8829

World War II — Women
JS: 8831 S: 7711 S–Adult: 7669

World Wide Web
JS: 12620 S: 10332, 12589
S–Adult: 12598

World Wide Web — Regulation
S–Adult: 12624, 12624

World's Fairs — History
JS: 8392

World's Fairs — United States
JS: 8392

Wounded Knee, Battle of
JS: 8479

Wrestling
JS: 13244, 13246, 13248 S: 13245
S–Adult: 6743

Wrestling — Biography
JS: 5762, 6750 S–Adult: 13247

Wrestling — Fiction
S: 4597

Wright, Frank Lloyd
JS: 5799 S: 5800

Wright, Richard
JS: 5971, 5973–75 S–Adult: 5972

Wright, Richard — Criticism
JS: 5361 S: 5364, 5390–91

Wright, Wilbur and Orville
JS: 6606–7 S–Adult: 12653

Writers
See Authors

Writing
See also Writing — Skills
J: 10284 JS: 5260, 5712, 5916, 10285, 10293, 10300–1, 10316, 10318
S: 5552, 5561, 10283, 10288, 10295, 10302–4, 10310, 10314, 10321
S–Adult: 5202, 5562, 5565, 5572, 10294, 10322

Writing — Careers
JS: 10289, 10431 S: 10383

Writing — Fiction
JS: 443, 3325 S: 1076
S–Adult: 1532

Writing — Handbooks
JS: 5560, 10297 S: 5556
S–Adult: 5569

Writing — Historical fiction
S: 10320

Writing — History
JS: 5548

Writing — Poetry
JS: 10313, 10319

Writing — Skills
JS: 10289, 10299 S: 5561
S–Adult: 5569, 5572, 5901

Writing — Study skills
JS: 10311

Writing schools — Fiction
S: 1076

***Wuthering Heights* — Criticism**
S: 5285

Wyeth, Andrew
JS: 5801 S–Adult: 5802

Wyeth, N. C.
S–Adult: 7110

Wyoming
S: 8968

Wyoming — Fiction
J: 2891 S: 1580, 2898

X

***X-Files* (television series)**
JS: 7264

Xhosa (African people)
JS: 7967

Y

Yana Indians — Fiction
JS: 3745

Yanomami (people)
JS: 12377

***The Yearling* (novel) — Criticism**
JS: 5382

Yeats, William Butler
JS: 4926, 5976 S: 4944

Yellow fever
JS: 8539

Yellow fever — Fiction
JS: 2757

Yellowstone National Park
S: 8966, 9015, 11978 S–Adult: 12003

JS = Junior High/Senior High; S = Senior High; S–Adult = Senior High/Adult

**Yellowstone National Park —
Fiction**
S–Adult: 138

Yemen
S–Adult: 8222

Yep, Laurence — Criticism
JS: 5374

Ying, Hong
S–Adult: 7014

Yoga
JS: 13101, 13121, 13130 S: 11029–30,
11040

Yoruba (African People)
JS: 7982

Yosemite National Park (CA)
S: 9003

Young, Neil
S: 6142–43

Young, Yolanda
S–Adult: 9703

Young adult literature — Biography
JS: 5843, 5927

Young adult literature — Criticism
JS: 5345, 5898 S: 5343, 5349, 5868,
5903, 5977

**Young adult literature — History
and criticism**
S: 5362, 5367, 5401, 5407, 5413

Yugoslavia — Biography
JS: 6886

Yugoslavia — Fiction
S: 2659

Yukon — History
JS: 5620

**Yukon Quest International Sled Dog
Race**
S: 13081–58 S: 6755

Z

Zaharias, Babe Didrikson
JS: 6756–58 S: 6755

Zaire
JS: 7921, 7933–34, 7937

Zama, Battle of
JS: 7511

Zamora, Pedro
JS: 2380

Zappa, Frank
S–Adult: 7157

Zedong, Mao
JS: 6814–15

Zen Buddhism
S–Adult: 11361

Zero tolerance
S–Adult: 10274

Zimbabwe
S–Adult: 7960–61

Zimbabwe — Fiction
JS: 4252

Zindel, Paul
S: 5977

Zippers
S: 12553

Zitkala-Sa (Red Bird)
JS: 6278

Zoo animals
S: 12121

Zoology
JS: 11892

Zoology — Careers
JS: 10416

**Zoology — Experiments and
projects**
JS: 11875

Zoos
S–Adult: 12323

Zoroastrianism
JS: 9062

Zoya
S: 7015

Zulu (African kingdom)
JS: 7969

Zulu (African people)
JS: 7972

JS = Junior High/Senior High;   S = Senior High;   S–Adult = Senior High/Adult

1182